In This Issue

The IRS Mission

Provide America's taxpayers top quality service by helping them understand and meet their tax responsibilities and by applying the tax law with integrity and fairness to all.

Introduction

The Internal Revenue Bulletin is the authoritative instrument of the Commissioner of Internal Revenue for announcing official rulings and procedures of the Internal Revenue Service and for publishing Treasury Decisions, Executive Orders, Tax Conventions, legislation, court decisions, and other items of general interest. It is published weekly and may be obtained from the Superintendent of Documents on a subscription basis. Bulletin contents are consolidated semiannually into Cumulative Bulletins, which are sold on a single-copy basis.

It is the policy of the Service to publish in the Bulletin all substantive rulings necessary to promote a uniform application of the tax laws, including all rulings that supersede, revoke, modify, or amend any of those previously published in the Bulletin. All published rulings apply retroactively unless otherwise indicated. Procedures relating solely to matters of internal management are not published; however, statements of internal practices and procedures that affect the rights and duties of taxpayers are published.

Revenue rulings represent the conclusions of the Service on the application of the law to the pivotal facts stated in the revenue ruling. In those based on positions taken in rulings to taxpayers or technical advice to Service field offices, identifying details and information of a confidential nature are deleted to prevent unwarranted invasions of privacy and to comply with statutory requirements.

Rulings and procedures reported in the Bulletin do not have the force and effect of Treasury Department Regulations, but they may be used as precedents. Unpublished rulings will not be relied on, used, or cited as precedents by Service personnel in the disposition of other cases. In applying published rulings and procedures, the effect of subsequent legislation, regulations, court decisions, rulings, and procedures must be considered, and Service personnel and others concerned are cautioned against reaching the same conclusions in other cases unless the facts and circumstances are substantially the same.

The Cumulative Bulletin (C.B.) is composed of reprints of the weekly Internal Revenue Bulletins (I.R.B.s) issued during the year, bound together to form the C.B. Volume 1 contains I.R.B. issues 1 through 26 and Volume 2 contains I.R.B. issues 27 through 52. Public laws relating to taxes are published in Volume 3 of the C.B. If needed, additional volumes are published and labeled consecutively.

The C.B. also includes the following items:

- Numerical Finding List.
- Finding List of Current Actions on Previously Published Items.
- Code Sections Affected by Current Actions. This list is organized by code section and identifies the actions that impact the code section.
- Cumulative List of Actions on Decisions (if applicable).
- Cumulative Lists of Disbarments and Suspensions (if applicable).
- Index.

For sale by the Superintendent of Documents, U.S. Government Printing Office, Washington, DC 20402.

For sale by the Superintendent of Documents, U.S. Government Printing Office
Internet: bookstore.gpo.gov Phone: toll free (866) 512-1800; DC area (202) 512-1800
Fax: (202) 512-2104 Mail: Stop IDCC, Washington, DC 20402-0001

ISBN 978-0-16-082006-9

Definition of Terms

Revenue rulings and revenue procedures (hereinafter referred to as "rulings") that have an effect on previous rulings use the following defined terms to describe the effect:

Amplified describes a situation where no change is being made in a prior published position, but the prior position is being extended to apply to a variation of the fact situation set forth therein. Thus, if an earlier ruling held that a principle applied to A, and the new ruling holds that the same principle also applies to B, the earlier ruling is amplified. (Compare with *modified*, below).

Clarified is used in those instances where the language in a prior ruling is being made clear because the language has caused, or may cause, some confusion. It is not used where a position in a prior ruling is being changed.

Distinguished describes a situation where a ruling mentions a previously published ruling and points out an essential difference between them.

Modified is used where the substance of a previously published position is being changed. Thus, if a prior ruling held that a principle applied to A but not to B, and the new ruling holds that it applies to both A and B, the prior ruling is modified because it corrects a published position. (Compare with *amplified* and *clarified*, above).

Obsoleted describes a previously published ruling that is not considered determinative with respect to future transactions. This term is most commonly used in a ruling that lists previously published rulings that are obsoleted because of changes in laws or regulations. A ruling may also be obsoleted because the substance has been included in regulations subsequently adopted.

Revoked describes situations where the position in the previously published ruling is not correct and the correct position is being stated in a new ruling.

Superseded describes a situation where the new ruling does nothing more than restate the substance and situation of a previously published ruling (or rulings). Thus, the term is used to republish under the 1986 Code and regulations the same position published under the 1939 Code and regulations. The term is also used when it is desired to republish in a single ruling a series of situations, names, etc., that were previously published over a period of time in separate rulings. If the new ruling does more than restate the substance of a prior ruling, a combination of terms is used. For example, *modified* and *superseded* describes a situation where the substance of a previously published ruling is being changed in part and is continued without change in part and it is desired to restate the valid portion of the previously published ruling in a new ruling that is self contained. In this case, the previously published ruling is first modified and then, as modified, is superseded.

Supplemented is used in situations in which a list, such as a list of the names of countries, is published in a ruling and that list is expanded by adding further names in subsequent rulings. After the original ruling has been supplemented several times, a new ruling may be published that includes the list in the original ruling and the additions, and supersedes all prior rulings in the series.

Suspended is used in rare situations to show that the previous published rulings will not be applied pending some future action such as the issuance of new or amended regulations, the outcome of cases in litigation, or the outcome of a Service study.

Abbreviations

The following abbreviations in current use and formerly used will appear in material published in the Bulletin.

A—Individual.
Acq.—Acquiescence.
B—Individual.
BE—Beneficiary.
BK—Bank.
B.T.A.—Board of Tax Appeals.
C—Individual.
C.B.—Cumulative Bulletin.
CFR—Code of Federal Regulations.
CI—City.
COOP—Cooperative.
Ct.D.—Court Decision.
CY—County.
D—Decedent.
DC—Dummy Corporation.
DE—Donee.
Del. Order—Delegation Order.
DISC—Domestic International Sales Corporation.
DR—Donor.
E—Estate.
EE—Employee.
E.O.—Executive Order.
ER—Employer.
ERISA—Employee Retirement Income Security Act.
EX—Executor.
F—Fiduciary.
FC—Foreign Country.
FICA—Federal Insurance Contributions Act.
FISC—Foreign International Sales Company.
FPH—Foreign Personal Holding Company.
F.R.—Federal Register.
FUTA—Federal Unemployment Tax Act.
FX—Foreign corporation.
G.C.M.—Chief Counsel's Memorandum.
GE—Grantee.
GP—General Partner.
GR—Grantor.
IC—Insurance Company.
I.R.B.—Internal Revenue Bulletin.
LE—Lessee.
LP—Limited Partner.
LR—Lessor.
M—Minor.
Nonacq.—Nonacquiescence.
O—Organization.
P—Parent Corporation.
PHC—Personal Holding Company.
PO—Possession of the U.S.
PR—Partner.
PRS—Partnership.
PTE—Prohibited Transaction Exemption.
Pub. L.—Public Law.
REIT—Real Estate Investment Trust.
Rev. Proc.—Revenue Procedure.
Rev. Rul.—Revenue Ruling.
S—Subsidiary.
S.P.R.—Statement of Procedural Rules.
Stat.—Statutes at Large.
T—Target Corporation.
T.C.—Tax Court.
T.D. —Treasury Decision.
TFE—Transferee.
TFR—Transferor.
T.I.R.—Technical Information Release.
TP—Taxpayer.
TR—Trust.
TT—Trustee.
U.S.C.—United States Code.
X—Corporation.
Y—Corporation.
Z —Corporation.

Numerical Finding List

Revenue Procedures— Continued:

Revenue Rulings:

Tax Conventions:

Treasury Decisions:

Finding List of Current Actions on Previously Published Items

Announcements:

2006-45
Updated and superseded by
Ann. 2007-47, *1260*

Notices:

2002-45
Modified by
Notice 2007-22, *670*

2005-1
Obsoleted in part by
T.D. 9321, *1123*

2005-29
Modified and superseded by
Notice 2007-4, *260*

2005-86
Modified by
Notice 2007-22, *670*

2005-98
Modified and superseded by
Notice 2007-26, *870*

2006-2
Modified and superseded by
Notice 2007-4, *260*

2006-4
Superseded in part by
T.D. 9321, *1123*

2006-13
Obsoleted by
T.D. 9315, *891*

2006-24
Clarified, modified, amplified, and superseded by
Notice 2007-52, *1456*

2006-25
Clarified, modified, amplified, and superseded by
Notice 2007-53, *1474*

2006-50
Amplified, clarified, and modified by
Notice 2007-11, *405*

2006-64
Superseded for taxable years on or after
January 1, 2008 by
T.D. 9321, *1123*

2006-77
Clarified, modified, and amplified by
Notice 2007-36, *1000*

2006-85
Amplified by
Notice 2007-48, *1428*

Notices— Continued:

2006-87
Modified and supplemented by
Notice 2007-25, *760*

2007-19
Amended and supplemented by
Notice 2007-31, *971*

Proposed Regulations:

REG-208270-86
Corrected by
Ann. 2007-4, *518*

REG-121509-00
Corrected by
Ann. 2007-17, *597*

REG-139059-02
Corrected by
Ann. 2007-36, *953*
Ann. 2007-37, *954*

REG-113365-04
Corrected by
Ann. 2007-35, *949*

REG-144859-04
Corrected by
Ann. 2007-54, *1383*

REG-141901-05
Corrected by
Ann. 2007-7, *377*

REG-142270-05
Corrected by
Ann. 2007-2, *263*

REG-125632-06
Corrected by
Ann. 2007-26, *682*

REG-127819-06
Corrected by
Ann. 2007-5, *376*

REG-136806-06
Corrected by
Ann. 2007-6, *376*
Hearing cancelled by
Ann. 2007-19, *521*

REG-156779-06
Corrected by
Ann. 2007-53, *1383*

Revenue Procedures:

86-46
Modified by
Notice 2007-44, *1320*

98-20
Superseded by
Rev. Proc. 2007-12, *354*

Revenue Procedures— Continued:

2000-38
Modified by
Rev. Proc. 2007-16, *358*

2000-42
Obsoleted in part by
T.D. 9315, *891*

2000-50
Modified by
Rev. Proc. 2007-16, *358*

2001-31
Superseded by
Rev. Proc. 2007-29, *1004*

2001-42
Modified and amplified by
Rev. Proc. 2007-19, *515*

2002-9
Modified and amplified by
Rev. Proc. 2007-14, *357*
Rev. Proc. 2007-33, *1289*
Modified by
Rev. Proc. 2007-16, *358*

2003-35
Superseded by
Rev. Proc. 2007-32, *1322*

2003-69
Modified and superseded by
Rev. Proc. 2007-38, *1442*

2004-11
Superseded by
Rev. Proc. 2007-16, *358*

2004-65
Modified and superseded by
Rev. Proc. 2007-20, *517*

2005-12
Superseded by
Rev. Proc. 2007-17, *368*

2005-51
Amplified by
Rev. Proc. 2007-25, *761*

2005-60
Superseded by
Rev. Proc. 2007-40, *1488*

2005-69
Superseded by
Rev. Proc. 2007-15, *300*

2005-74
Superseded by
Rev. Proc. 2007-24, *692*

2006-1
Superseded by
Rev. Proc. 2007-1, *1*

Revenue Procedures— Continued:

2006-2
Superseded by
Rev. Proc. 2007-2, *88*

2006-3
Superseded by
Rev. Proc. 2007-3, *108*

2006-4
Superseded by
Rev. Proc. 2007-4, *118*

2006-5
Superseded by
Rev. Proc. 2007-5, *161*

2006-6
Superseded by
Rev. Proc. 2007-6, *189*

2006-7
Superseded by
Rev. Proc. 2007-7, *227*

2006-8
Superseded by
Rev. Proc. 2007-8, *230*

2006-17
Obsoleted in part by
Rev. Proc. 2007-26, *814*

2006-20
Obsoleted in part by
Rev. Proc. 2007-31, *1225*

2006-35
Modified by
Rev. Proc. 2007-22, *675*

2006-53
Section 3.24(1) modified and superseded by
Rev. Proc. 2007-36, *1335*

2007-3
Amplified by
Rev. Proc. 2007-39, *1446*

Revenue Rulings:

54-19
Obsoleted in part by
Rev. Rul. 2007-14, *747*

55-132
Obsoleted by
Rev. Rul. 2007-14, *747*

56-462
Obsoleted by
Rev. Rul. 2007-14, *747*

56-518
Obsoleted by
Rev. Rul. 2007-14, *747*

Revenue Rulings— Continued:

57-505
Obsoleted by
Rev. Rul. 2007-14, *747*

58-370
Obsoleted by
Rev. Rul. 2007-14, *747*

58-500
Obsoleted by
Rev. Rul. 2007-14, *747*

69-141
Modified by
Notice 2007-22, *670*

69-212
Obsoleted by
Rev. Rul. 2007-14, *747*

69-587
Revoked by
Rev. Rul. 2007-12, *685*

71-477
Obsoleted by
Rev. Rul. 2007-14, *747*

74-245
Obsoleted by
Rev. Rul. 2007-35, *1317*

75-161
Obsoleted by
Rev. Rul. 2007-8, *469*

76-188
Obsoleted by
Rev. Rul. 2007-8, *469*

78-330
Modified by
Rev. Rul. 2007-8, *469*

81-18
Distinguished by
Rev. Rul. 2007-32, *1278*

81-225
Clarified and amplified by
Rev. Rul. 2007-7, *468*

82-45
Obsoleted by
Rev. Rul. 2007-35, *1317*

92-19
Supplemented in part by
Rev. Rul. 2007-10, *660*

96-51
Amplified by
Rev. Rul. 2007-12, *685*

2002-41
Modified by
Notice 2007-22, *670*

Revenue Rulings— Continued:

2003-43
Modified by
Notice 2007-2, *254*

2003-92
Clarified and amplified by
Rev. Rul. 2007-7, *468*

2003-102
Modified by
Notice 2007-22, *670*

2003-109
Superseded by
Rev. Rul. 2007–28, *1039*

2005-24
Modified by
Notice 2007-22, *670*

2005-76
Supplemented and superseded by
Rev. Rul. 2007-4, *351*

2006-36
Modified by
Notice 2007-22, *670*

Treasury Decisions:

9263
Corrected by
Ann. 2007-22, *631*

9276
Corrected by
Ann. 2007-20, *599*
Ann. 2007-21, *630*

9278
Corrected by
Ann. 2007-9, *417*
Ann. 2007-10, *464*

9286
Corrected by
Ann. 2007-8, *416*

9298
Corrected by
Ann. 2007-32, *734*

9303
Corrected by
Ann. 2007-25, *682*

9313
Corrected by
Ann. 2007-48, *1274*

9315
Corrected by
Ann. 2007-49, *1300*

Treasury Decisions— Continued:

9319

Corrected by

Ann. 2007-57, *1418*
Ann. 2007-58, *1448*

9322

Corrected by

Ann. 2007-50, *1337*

Code Sections Affected by Current Actions

Cumulative List of Actions on Decisions

It is the policy of the Internal Revenue Service to announce at an early date whether it will follow the holdings in certain cases. An Action on Decision is the document making such an announcement. An Action on Decision will be issued at the discretion of the Service only on unappealed issues decided adverse to the government. Generally, an Action on Decision is issued where its guidance would be helpful to Service personnel working with the same or similar issues. Unlike a Treasury Regulation or a Revenue Ruling, an Action on Decision is not an affirmative statement of Service position. It is not intended to serve as public guidance and may not be cited as precedent.

Actions on Decisions shall be relied upon within the Service only as conclusions applying the law to the facts in the particular case at the time the Action on Decision was issued. Caution should be exercised in extending the recommendation of the Action on Decision to similar cases where the facts are different. Moreover, the recommendation in the Action on Decision may be superseded by new legislation, regulations, rulings, cases, or Actions on Decisions.

Prior to 1991, the Service published acquiescence or nonacquiescence only in certain regular Tax Court opinions. The Service has expanded its acquiescence program to include other civil tax cases where guidance is determined to be helpful. Accordingly, the Service now may acquiesce or nonacquiesce in the holdings of memorandum Tax Court opinions, as well as those of the United States District Courts, Claims Court, and Circuit Courts of Appeal. Regardless of the court deciding the case, the recommendation of any Action on Decision will be published in the Internal Revenue Bulletin.

The recommendation in every Action on Decision will be summarized as acquiescence, acquiescence in result only, or nonacquiescence. Both "acquiescence" and "acquiescence in result only" mean that the Service accepts the holding of the court in a case and that the Service will follow it in disposing of cases with the same controlling facts. However, "acquiescence" indicates neither approval nor disapproval of the reasons assigned by the court for its conclusions; whereas, "acquiescence in result only" indicates disagreement or concern with some or all of those reasons. "Nonacquiescence" signifies that, although no further review was sought, the Service does not agree with the holding of the court and, generally, will not follow the decision in disposing of cases involving other taxpayers. In reference to an opinion of a circuit court of appeals, a "nonacquiescence" indicates that the Service will not follow the holding on a nationwide basis. However, the Service will recognize the precedential impact of the opinion on cases arising within the venue of the deciding circuit.

The Actions on Decisions published in the weekly Internal Revenue Bulletins are consolidated semiannually in the Cumulative Bulletins.

The Commissioner does NOT ACQUIESCE in the following decision:

North Dakota State University v. United States,[1]
255 F.3d 599 (8th Cir. 2001),
nonacq., 2001–2 C.B. xv

Moore v. Commissioner,[2]
T.C. Memo. 2006–171,
T.C. Docket No. 11634–05L

[1] Nonacquiescence relating to whether early retirement payments that the taxpayer made to tenured faculty members are wages subject to Federal Insurance Contributions Act ("FICA") taxes. The litigating position in the Action on Decision dated December 31, 2001, is modified and replaced. The Service's nonacquiescence in the Eighth Circuit's decision remains unchanged.

[2] Nonacquiescence relating to whether prohibited *ex parte* communications during a collection due process hearing before the Office of Appeals may be remedied by sharing the content of the communications with the taxpayer and allowing the taxpayer an opportunity to respond.

Announcement of Disciplinary Actions Involving Attorneys, Certified Public Accountants, Enrolled Agents, and Enrolled Actuaries — Suspensions, Censures, Disbarments, and Resignations

Under Title 31, Code of Federal Regulations, Part 10, attorneys, certified public accountants, enrolled agents, and enrolled actuaries may not accept assistance from, or assist, any person who is under disbarment or suspension from practice before the Internal Revenue Service if the assistance relates to a matter constituting practice before the Internal Revenue Service and may not knowingly aid or abet another person to practice before the Internal Revenue Service during a period of suspension, disbarment, or ineligibility of such other person.

To enable attorneys, certified public accountants, enrolled agents, and enrolled actuaries to identify persons to whom these restrictions apply, the Director, Office of Professional Responsibility, will announce in the Internal Revenue Bulletin their names, their city and state, their professional designation, the effective date of disciplinary action, and the period of suspension. This announcement will appear in the weekly Bulletin at the earliest practicable date after such action and will continue to appear in the weekly Bulletins for five successive weeks.

Consent Suspensions From Practice Before the Internal Revenue Service

Under Title 31, Code of Federal Regulations, Part 10, an attorney, certified public accountant, enrolled agent, or enrolled actuary, in order to avoid the institution or conclusion of a proceeding for his or her disbarment or suspension from practice before the Internal Revenue Service, may offer his or her consent to suspension from such practice. The Director, Office of Professional Responsibility, in his discretion, may suspend an attorney, certified public accountant, enrolled agent, or enrolled actuary in accordance with the consent offered.

The following individuals have been placed under consent suspension from practice before the Internal Revenue Service:

Name	Address	Designation	Date of Suspension
Hankinson, Eugene M.	Somerset, PA	CPA	Indefinite from November 15, 2006
Canzano, Richard M.	Winchester, MA	Attorney	Indefinite from November 20, 2006
Sims, Jr., Lionel	Houston, TX	CPA	Indefinite from November 20, 2006
Wendekier, Raymond J.	Patton, PA	Attorney	Indefinite from November 21, 2006
Golden, Larry	Hinesville, GA	CPA	Indefinite from November 28, 2006
Lane, David B.	Hanover, MA	Attorney	Indefinite from November 28, 2006
Brown, Arthur I.	Miami, FL	CPA	Indefinite from December 1, 2006

Name	Address	Designation	Date of Suspension
Frisk, Daniel J.	Fargo, ND	Attorney	Indefinite from December 1, 2006
Small, Kenneth A.	McMurray, PA	CPA	Indefinite from December 1, 2006
Vazquez, Sonya M.	Port Orchard, WA	CPA	Indefinite from December 1, 2006
Swistak, Anthony	Adams, MA	Enrolled Agent	Indefinite from December 6, 2006
Lenahan, Jr., Robert J.	Elizabeth, NJ	Attorney	Indefinite from December 11, 2006
Hayes, Richard A.	Havervill, MA	Attorney	Indefinite from December 14, 2006
Scheller, Stephen M.	Coppell, TX	CPA	Indefinite from December 15, 2006
Wilson, James M.	Berlin, NJ	CPA	Indefinite from December 15, 2006
Franzese, Joseph P.	Winthrop, MA	Attorney	Indefinite from December 18, 2006
Black, Charles C.	Marietta, GA	Attorney	Indefinite from January 1, 2007
Enright, III, Robert A.	Naples, FL	Attorney	Indefinite from January 1, 2007
Fromovitz, Norman M.	Brooklyn, NY	CPA	Indefinite from January 1, 2007
Saylor, Mary A.	Iowa City, IA	Enrolled Agent	Indefinite from January 1, 2007
Seeherman, Alan	Wynnewood, PA	CPA	Indefinite from January 1, 2007
Beistel, Theodore L.	Canton, OH	CPA	Indefinite from January 3, 2007

Name	Address	Designation	Date of Suspension
Myers, Robert J.	Fairport Harbor, OH	CPA	Indefinite from January 9, 2007
Burrus, Robert V.	Valparaiso, IN	CPA	Indefinite from January 22, 2007
Patterson, Douglas W.	Newburgh, IN	Attorney	Indefinite from January 31, 2007
Lang, Jeffrey H.	Fishers, IN	CPA	Indefinite from January 22, 2007
Chickering, David	Vermillion, SD	CPA	February 5, 2007 to November 4, 2007
Moss, Steve E.	Henderson, NC	CPA	Indefinite from February 5, 2007
Hazlip, Kevin	Orange Park, FL	Enrolled Agent	Indefinite from February 10, 2007
Adelson, Robert A.	Newton, MA	Attorney	Indefinite from February 15, 2007
Boyer, Daniel D.	North Judson, IN	CPA	Indefinite from February 15, 2007
LaRusso, Anthony J.	North Caldwell, NJ	Attorney	Indefinite from February 15, 2007
Martin, Spencer R.	Lancaster, PA	CPA	Indefinite from February 15, 2007
Hursh, Stephanie S.	Brush Prairie, WA	Enrolled Agent	Indefinite from February 20, 2007
Guidera, George C.	Weston, CT	Attorney	Indefinite from February 26, 2007
Ruth, Christopher A.	Cypress, CA	CPA	Indefinite from February 27, 2007
Elias, Lenard S.	El Cajon, CA	Enrolled Agent	Indefinite from March 1, 2007
Ikeji, Chuck	Orlando, FL	CPA	Indefinite from March 1, 2007

Name	Address	Designation	Date of Suspension
Lewis, Craig S.	Savannah, GA	CPA	Indefinite from March 1, 2007
Sloan, Eric R.	Brighton, MI	CPA	Indefinite from March 1, 2007
Gostomski, Michael	Stamford, CT	CPA	Indefinite from March 5, 2007
Hafer, Charles J.	Hamburg, PA	Enrolled Agent	Indefinite from March 5, 2007
Jones, Phillip G.	Andalusia, AL	Enrolled Agent	Indefinite from March 7, 2007
Agashiwala, Mahesh J.	New York, NY	CPA	Indefinite from March 22, 2007
Berndgen, Michael	Plantation, FL	CPA	Indefinite from April 1, 2007
Grahn, Charles R.	Indianapolis, IN	Attorney	Indefinite from April 1, 2007
Shaw, G. Joyce	Hebron, KY	Enrolled Agent	Indefinite from April 1, 2007
Pikaart, Jr., Edward H.	N. Branford, CT	CPA	Indefinite from April 10, 2007
Kelley, Richard S.	Beverly, MA	Attorney	Indefinite from May 1, 2007
Crabtree, Michael L.	San Dimas, CA	Enrolled Agent	Indefinite from May 15, 2007
Hausmann, Mark D.	Troy, NY	Attorney	Indefinite from May 15, 2007

Expedited Suspensions From Practice Before the Internal Revenue Service

Under Title 31, Code of Federal Regulations, Part 10, the Director, Office of Professional Responsibility, is authorized to immediately suspend from practice before the Internal Revenue Service any practitioner who, within five years from the date the expedited proceeding is instituted (1) has had a license to practice as an attorney, certified public accountant, or actuary suspended or revoked for cause or (2) has been convicted of certain crimes.

The following individuals have been placed under suspension from practice before the Internal Revenue Service by virtue of the expedited proceeding provisions:

Name	Address	Designation	Date of Suspension
Hatchett, William M.	Pontiac, MI	Attorney	Indefinite from November 13, 2006
Jacobs, Mark L.	Jackson Heights, NY	Attorney	Indefinite from November 21, 2006
Sylver, Peter T.	E. Longmeadow, MA	Attorney	Indefinite from November 21, 2006
Portlock, David R.	Pensacola, FL	Enrolled Agent	Indefinite from November 27, 2006
Ascher, Michael P.	North Port, FL	Attorney	Indefinite from November 28, 2006
Barrett, Norman W.	Dover, DE	CPA	Indefinite from November 28, 2006
Burd, Gene	Houston, TX	Attorney	Indefinite from November 28, 2006
Caceres, Carlos H.	Silver Spring, MD	Attorney	Indefinite from November 28, 2006
Carrabotta, Peter S.	Niles, IL	Attorney	Indefinite from November 28, 2006
Davis, Carleton W.	St. Louis, MO	Attorney	Indefinite from November 28, 2006
Frasier, Roland B.	Rancho Santa Fe, CA	Attorney	Indefinite from November 28, 2006
Hubbard, Edward	Chicago, IL	Attorney	Indefinite from November 28, 2006

Name	Address	Designation	Date of Suspension
Hynes, Richard W.	Brookline, MA	Attorney	Indefinite from November 28, 2006
Johnson, Barbara C.	Andover, MA	Attorney	Indefinite from November 28, 2006
Konas, Theodore V.	Lancaster, PA	CPA	Indefinite from November 28, 2006
Korson, Daniel M.	Muskegon, MI	CPA	Indefinite from November 28, 2006
Lee, III, Norman J.	Collegeville, PA	Attorney	Indefinite from November 28, 2006
Loiben, Alan A.	Skokie, IL	Attorney	Indefinite from November 28, 2006
McGarry, Thomas H.	Denver, CO	Attorney	Indefinite from November 28, 2006
Roberts, Quinton D.	Elkridge, MD	Attorney	Indefinite from November 28, 2006
Schofield, Peter L.	Spencer, MA	Attorney	Indefinite from November 28, 2006
Shultz, Ryan K.	Mitchell, NE	Attorney	Indefinite from November 28, 2006
Stenger, Jeanne P.	Temecula, CA	Attorney	Indefinite from November 28, 2006
Wood, Gary K.	Edina, MN	Attorney	Indefinite from November 28, 2006
Bakare, Adigun S.	Laurel, MD	Attorney	Indefinite from December 6, 2006
Biagini, Marc J.	Downers Grove, IL	Attorney	Indefinite from December 6, 2006
Birchall, Richard G.	Brewster, MA	Attorney	Indefinite from December 6, 2006

Name	Address	Designation	Date of Suspension
Brown, Edward E.	Indianapolis, IN	Attorney	Indefinite from December 6, 2006
Cunningham, Jr., Shirley A.	Ft. Lauderdale, FL	Attorney	Indefinite from December 6, 2006
Docherty, Scott R.	Branson West, MO	Attorney	Indefinite from December 6, 2006
Dressler, Peter P.	West Chicago, IL	Attorney	Indefinite from December 6, 2006
Henry, William J.	Irvington, NJ	Attorney	Indefinite from December 6, 2006
Hubbard, Cynthia A.	Geneva, IL	Attorney	Indefinite from December 6, 2006
Jackson, Jr., Donald H.	Hanover, MA	Attorney	Indefinite from December 6, 2006
Katz, Norman H.	Owings Mills, MD	Attorney	Indefinite from December 6, 2006
Lakin, Leonard S.	Wellesley Hills, MA	Attorney	Indefinite from December 6, 2006
McGreevy, Jacqueline K.	Carbondale, CO	Attorney	Indefinite from December 6, 2006
Zepp, Dale D.	Ferguson, MO	Attorney	Indefinite from December 6, 2006
Triplett, Austin H.	Homewood, IL	Attorney	Indefinite from December 11, 2006
Murphy, Patrick W.	Honolulu, HI	Attorney	Indefinite from December 11, 2006
Cronin, Jr., Edward M.	Cambridge, MA	Attorney	Indefinite from December 11, 2006
Christof, Kevin F.	Santa Monica, CA	Attorney	Indefinite from December 21, 2006
Heath, Kenneth J.	Canaan, VT	CPA	Indefinite from December 21, 2006

Name	Address	Designation	Date of Suspension
Madigan, Brian C.	Binghamton, NY	Attorney	Indefinite from December 21, 2006
Malloy, Terry P.	Tulsa, OK	Attorney	Indefinite from December 21, 2006
Baynes, Robert M.	Indianapolis, IN	CPA	Indefinite from December 27, 2006
Ceresa, Richard A.	Woodbridge, CA	CPA	Indefinite from December 27, 2006
Crews, Richard A.	Henderson, CO	Attorney	Indefinite from December 27, 2006
Menkveld, Paul G.	Tucson, AZ	Attorney	Indefinite from December 27, 2006
Worischeck, Joseph H.	Tempe, AZ	Attorney	Indefinite from December 27, 2006
Brown, Kirk P.	Pueblo, CO	Attorney	Indefinite from December 28, 2006
Dowling, Stanley W.	Scotts Valley, CA	CPA	Indefinite from December 28, 2006
Simmons, Henry L.	Greensboro, NC	CPA	Indefinite from December 28, 2006
Steele, Regina D.	San Diego, CA	Attorney	Indefinite from December 29, 2006
Craig, III, William A.	Austin, TX	Attorney	Indefinite from January 1, 2007
Acker, Thomas R.	Hollis Center, ME	Attorney	Indefinite from January 8, 2007
Baxter, Laura M.	Monee, IL	CPA	Indefinite from January 8, 2007
Herald, Sally J.	Cold Spring, KY	Attorney	Indefinite from January 8, 2007
Klapheke, II, William T.	Bowling Green, KY	Attorney	Indefinite from January 8, 2007

Name	Address	Designation	Date of Suspension
McCarthy, Charles C.	Encino, CA	Attorney	Indefinite from January 8, 2007
Bolling, Darius C.	Chicago, IL	CPA	Indefinite from January 10, 2007
Breitlauch, Linda	Saylorsburg, PA	Attorney	Indefinite from January 10, 2007
Coddington, Paul F.	Concord, NH	Attorney	Indefinite from January 10, 2007
Davis, Jr., William E.	Pinehurst, TX	CPA	Indefinite from January 10, 2007
Esola, Louis A.	Greensburg, PA	CPA	Indefinite from January 10, 2007
Finch, Judith A.	Walnut Creek, CA	Attorney	Indefinite from January 10, 2007
Jeing, Thomas C.	San Francisco, CA	Attorney	Indefinite from January 10, 2007
Ledbetter, Dean D.	Pelham, AL	CPA	Indefinite from January 10, 2007
McDiarmid, Katherine B.	Greensboro, NC	Attorney	Indefinite from January 10, 2007
Mills, George P.	Oceanside, CA	Attorney	Indefinite from January 10, 2007
Rather, James L.	Irvine, CA	Attorney	Indefinite from January 10, 2007
Rivera, Eduardo M.	Torrance, CA	Attorney	Indefinite from January 10, 2007
Stepovich, Michael A.	Fairbanks, AK	Attorney	Indefinite from January 10, 2007
Ulbrich, David L.	Woodland Hills, CA	CPA	Indefinite from January 10, 2007
Swanson, Todd-Ellis	Greenville, SC	CPA	Indefinite from January 20, 2007

Name	Address	Designation	Date of Suspension
Rubin, Deborah L.	Delray Beach, FL	Attorney	Indefinite from January 26, 2007
Wood, Brent E.	Cary, NC	Attorney	Indefinite from January 26, 2007
Currin, Samuel T.	Raleigh, NC	Attorney	Indefinite from February 7, 2007
Lupo, Robert N.	Weston, MA	Attorney	Indefinite from February 20, 2007
Taggart, Lawrence W.	El Cajon, CA	Attorney	Indefinite from March 7, 2007
Fife, III, James H.	Schererville, IN	Attorney	Indefinite from March 8, 2007
Katsis, Kevin G.	Riverside, IL	Attorney	Indefinite from March 8, 2007
O'Driscoll, Dennis M.	Quincy, MA	Attorney	Indefinite from March 8, 2007
Siever, Beth F.	Austin, TX	Attorney	Indefinite from March 8, 2007
Wheatley-Clark, Sheila R.	Houston, TX	CPA	Indefinite from March 8, 2007

Suspensions From Practice Before the Internal Revenue Service After Notice and an Opportunity for a Proceeding

Under Title 31, Code of Federal Regulations, Part 10, after notice and an opportunity for a proceeding before an administrative law judge, the following individuals have been placed under suspension from practice before the Internal Revenue Service:

Name	Address	Designation	Effective Date
Redmond, Debra	Gifford, PA	Enrolled Agent	Indefinite from March 5, 2007

Disbarments From Practice Before the Internal Revenue Service After Notice and an Opportunity for a Proceeding

Under Title 31, Code of Federal Regulations, Part 10, after notice and an opportunity for a proceeding before an administrative law judge, the following individuals have been disbarred from practice before the Internal Revenue Service:

Name	Address	Designation	Effective Date
Brookstein, Gary	Huntingdon Valley, PA	CPA	December 15, 2006
James T. Jubb	Baltimore, MD	CPA	December 15, 2006

Censure Issued by Consent

Under Title 31, Code of Federal Regulations, Part 10, in lieu of a proceeding being instituted or continued, an attorney, certified public accountant, enrolled agent, or enrolled actuary, may offer his or her consent to the issuance of a censure. Censure is a public reprimand.

The following individuals have consented to the issuance of a Censure:

Name	Address	Designation	Date of Censure
Zucker, Robert W.	Boca Raton, FL	CPA	November 14, 2006
Montgomery, David E.	Pleasanton, CA	Enrolled Agent	November 15, 2006
Higgins, James M.	S. Boston, MA	Attorney	December 1, 2006
Pennington, Debra L.	Lees Summit, MO	Enrolled Agent	January 29, 2007
Goodwin, Steven C.	Concord, MA	Attorney	February 2, 2007
Francis, Andrew W.E.	Houston, TX	CPA	February 21, 2007
Griffin, Richard M.	Duluth, GA	CPA	February 28, 2007

Resignations of Enrolled Agents

Under Title 31, Code of Federal Regulations, Part 10, an enrolled agent, in order to avoid the institution or conclusion of a proceeding for his or her disbarment or suspension from practice before the Internal Revenue Service, may offer his or her resignation as an enrolled agent. The Director, Office of Professional Responsibility, in his discretion, may accept the offered resignation.

The Director, Office of Professional Responsibility, has accepted offers of resignation as an enrolled agent from the following individuals:

Name	Address	Date of Resignation
Filipski, Kenneth M.	Bakersfield, CA	April 16, 2007

Part III. Administrative, Procedural, and Miscellaneous

26 CFR 601.201: Rulings and determination letters.

Rev. Proc. 2007–1

TABLE OF CONTENTS

SECTION 1. WHAT IS THE PURPOSE OF THIS REVENUE PROCEDURE?

This revenue procedure explains how the Service provides advice to taxpayers on issues under the jurisdiction of the Associate Chief Counsel (Corporate), the Associate Chief Counsel (Financial Institutions and Products), the Associate Chief Counsel (Income Tax and Accounting), the Associate Chief Counsel (International), the Associate Chief Counsel (Passthroughs and Special Industries), the Associate Chief Counsel (Procedure and Administration), and the Division Counsel/Associate Chief Counsel (Tax Exempt and Government Entities). It explains the forms of advice and the manner in which advice is requested by taxpayers and provided by the Service. A sample format of a request for a letter ruling is provided in Appendix B. *See* section 4 of this revenue procedure for issues outside the scope of this revenue procedure.

Description of terms used in this revenue procedure

.01 For purposes of this revenue procedure—

(1) the term "Service" includes the Internal Revenue Service, the four operating divisions of the Internal Revenue Service that are responsible for meeting the needs of the taxpayers they serve, and the Associate offices. The four operating divisions are:

(a) Large and Mid-Size Business Division (LMSB), which generally serves corporations, including S corporations, and partnerships, with assets in excess of $10 million;

(b) Small Business/Self-Employed Division (SB/SE), which generally serves corporations, including S corporations, and partnerships, with assets less than or equal to $10 million; estates and trusts; individuals filing an individual federal income tax return with accompanying Schedule C (*Profit or Loss From Business (Sole Proprietorship)*), Schedule E (*Supplemental Income and Loss*), Schedule F (*Profit or Loss From Farming*), Form 2106, *Employee Business Expenses*, or Form 2106–EZ, *Unreimbursed Employee Business Expenses*; and individuals with international tax returns;

(c) Wage and Investment Division (W&I), which generally serves individuals with wage and investment income only (and with no international tax returns) filing an individual federal income tax return without accompanying Schedule C, E, or F, or Form 2106 or Form 2106–EZ; and

(d) Tax Exempt and Government Entities Division (TE/GE), which serves three distinct taxpayer segments: employee plans, exempt organizations, and government entities.

(2) the term "Associate office" refers to the Office of Associate Chief Counsel (Corporate), the Office of Associate Chief Counsel (Financial Institutions and Products), the Office of Associate Chief Counsel (Income Tax and Accounting), the Office of Associate Chief Counsel (International), the Office of Associate Chief Counsel (Passthroughs and Special Industries), the Office of Associate Chief Counsel (Procedure and Administration), or the Office of Division Counsel/Associate Chief Counsel (Tax Exempt and Government Entities), as appropriate.

(3) the term "Director" refers to the Director, Field Operations, LMSB; the Area Director, Field Examination, SB/SE; Chief, Estate & Gift Tax Operations, SB/SE; Chief, Employment Tax Operations, SB/SE; Chief, Excise Tax Operations, SB/SE; or the Director, Compliance, W&I; the Deputy Commissioner, International, LMSB; the Director, Employee Plans Examinations; the Director, Exempt Organizations Examinations; the Director, Federal, State & Local Governments; the Director, Tax Exempt Bonds; or the Director, Indian Tribal Governments, as appropriate.

(4) the term "field office" refers to the respective offices of the Directors, as appropriate.

(5) the term "taxpayer" includes all persons subject to any provision of the Internal Revenue Code (including issuers of § 103 obligations) and, when appropriate, their representatives.

Updated annually

.02 This revenue procedure is updated annually as the first revenue procedure of the year, but may be modified or amplified during the year.

SECTION 2. WHAT IS THE FORM IN WHICH THE SERVICE PROVIDES ADVICE TO TAXPAYERS?

The Service provides advice in the form of letter rulings, closing agreements, determination letters, information letters, and oral advice.

Letter ruling

.01 A "letter ruling" is a written determination issued to a taxpayer by an Associate office in response to a written inquiry from an individual or an organization about its status for tax purposes or the tax effects of its acts or transactions, prior to the filing of returns or reports that are required by the revenue laws. A letter ruling interprets and applies the tax laws to the taxpayer's specific set of facts and is given when appropriate in the interest of sound tax administration. A letter ruling includes the written permission or denial of permission by an Associate office to a request for a change in a taxpayer's accounting method or accounting period. Once issued, a letter ruling may be revoked or modified for any number of reasons, as explained in section 11 (section 9.19 for a change in accounting method letter ruling) of this revenue procedure, unless it is accompanied by a "closing agreement."

Closing agreement

.02 A "closing agreement" is a final agreement between the Service and a taxpayer on a specific issue or liability. It is entered into under the authority in § 7121 and is final unless fraud, malfeasance, or misrepresentation of a material fact can be shown.

A taxpayer may request a closing agreement with the letter ruling, or in lieu of a letter ruling, with respect to a transaction that would be eligible for a letter ruling. In such situations, the Associate Chief Counsel with subject matter jurisdiction signs the closing agreement on behalf of the Service.

A closing agreement may be entered into when it is advantageous to have the matter permanently and conclusively closed or when a taxpayer can show that there are good reasons for an agreement and that making the agreement will not prejudice the interests of the Government. In appropriate cases, a taxpayer may be asked to enter into a closing agreement as a condition for the issuance of a letter ruling.

If, in a single case, a closing agreement is requested for each person or entity in a class of taxpayers, separate agreements are entered into only if the class consists of 25 or fewer taxpayers. If the issue and holding are identical for the class and there are more than 25 taxpayers in the class, a "mass closing agreement" will be entered into with the taxpayer who is authorized by the others to represent the class.

Determination letter

.03 A "determination letter" is a written determination issued by a Director that applies the principles and precedents previously announced by the Service to a specific set of facts. It is issued only when a determination can be made based on clearly established rules in a statute, a tax treaty, the regulations, a conclusion in a revenue ruling, or an opinion or court decision that represents the position of the Service.

Information letter

.04 An "information letter" is a statement issued either by an Associate office or by a Director. It calls attention to a well-established interpretation or principle of tax law (including a tax treaty) without applying it to a specific set of facts. An information letter may be issued if the taxpayer's inquiry indicates a need for general information or if the taxpayer's request does not meet the requirements of this revenue procedure and the Service thinks that general information will help the taxpayer. An information letter is advisory only and has no binding effect on the Service. If the Associate office issues an information letter in response to a request for a letter ruling that does not meet the requirements of this revenue procedure, the information letter is not a substitute for a letter ruling. The taxpayer should provide a daytime telephone number with the taxpayer's request for an information letter.

Information letters that are issued by the Associate offices to members of the public are made available to the public. Information letters that are issued by the field offices are not made available to the public.

Because information letters do not constitute written determinations as defined in § 6110, they are not subject to public inspection under § 6110. The Service makes the information letters available to the public under the Freedom of Information Act ("FOIA"). Before any information letter is made available to the public, an Associate office will delete any name, address, and other identifying information as appropriate under the FOIA (for example, FOIA personal privacy exemption of 5 U.S.C. § 552(b)(6) and tax details exempt pursuant to § 6103, as incorporated into FOIA by 5 U.S.C. § 552(b)(3)).

The following documents also will not be available for public inspection as part of this process:

(1) transmittal letters in which the Service furnishes publications or other publicly available material to taxpayers, without any significant legal discussion;

(2) responses to taxpayer or third party contacts that are inquiries with respect to a pending request for: a letter ruling, technical advice memorandum, or Chief Counsel Advice (which are subject to public inspection under § 6110 after their issuance); and

(3) responses to taxpayer or third party communications with respect to any investigation, audit, litigation, or other enforcement action.

Oral Advice

.05

(1) No oral rulings and no written rulings in response to oral requests.

The Service does not orally issue letter rulings or determination letters, nor does it issue letter rulings or determination letters in response to oral requests from taxpayers. Service employees ordinarily will discuss with taxpayers or their representatives inquiries regarding whether the Service will rule on particular issues and questions relating to procedural matters about submitting requests for letter rulings or determination letters for a particular case.

(2) Discussion possible on substantive issues.

At the discretion of the Service and as time permits, substantive issues also may be discussed. Such a discussion will not be binding on the Service in general or on the Office of Chief Counsel in particular and cannot be relied upon as a basis for obtaining retroactive relief under the provisions of § 7805(b).

Substantive tax issues involving the taxpayer that are under examination, in Appeals, or in litigation will not be discussed by Service employees not directly involved in the examination, appeal, or litigation of the issues unless the discussion is coordinated with those Service employees who are directly involved in the examination, appeal, or litigation of the issues. The taxpayer or the taxpayer's representative ordinarily will be asked whether the oral request for advice or information relates to a matter pending before another office of the Service or before a federal court.

If a tax issue is not under examination, in appeals, or in litigation, the tax issue may be discussed even though the issue is affected by a nontax issue pending in litigation.

A taxpayer may seek oral technical guidance from a taxpayer service representative in a field office or Service Center when preparing a return or report. Oral guidance is advisory only, and the Service is not bound to recognize it, for example, in the examination of the taxpayer's return.

The Service does not respond to letters seeking to confirm the substance of oral discussions and the absence of a response to such a letter is not a confirmation.

SECTION 3. ON WHAT ISSUES MAY TAXPAYERS REQUEST WRITTEN ADVICE UNDER THIS PROCEDURE?

Taxpayers may request letter rulings, information letters, and closing agreements under this revenue procedure on issues within the jurisdiction of the Associate offices. Taxpayers uncertain as to whether an Associate has jurisdiction with regard to a specific factual situation may call the telephone number for the Associate office listed in section 10.07(1) of this revenue procedure.

Taxpayers also may request determination letters from the Director in the appropriate operating division on subjects that relate to the Code sections under the jurisdiction of the respective Associate offices. *See* section 12.08 of this revenue procedure for information on where to send the requests for determination letters.

Issues under the jurisdiction of the Associate Chief Counsel (Corporate)

.01 Issues under the jurisdiction of the Associate Chief Counsel (Corporate) include those that involve consolidated returns, corporate acquisitions, reorganizations, liquidations, redemptions, spinoffs, transfers to controlled corporations, distributions to shareholders, corporate bankruptcies, the effect of certain ownership changes on net operating loss carryovers and other tax attributes, debt vs. equity determinations, allocation of income and deductions among taxpayers, acquisitions made to evade or avoid income tax, and certain earnings and profits questions.

Issues under the jurisdiction of the Associate Chief Counsel (Financial Institutions and Products)

.02 Issues under the jurisdiction of the Associate Chief Counsel (Financial Institutions and Products) include those that involve income taxes and accounting method changes of banks, savings and loan associations, real estate investment trusts (REITs), regulated investment companies (RICs), real estate mortgage investment conduits (REMICs), insurance companies and products, and financial products.

Issues under the jurisdiction of the Associate Chief Counsel (Income Tax and Accounting)

.03 Issues under the jurisdiction of the Associate Chief Counsel (Income Tax and Accounting) include those that involve recognition and timing of income and deductions of individuals and corporations, sales and exchanges, capital gains and losses, installment sales, equipment leasing, long-term contracts, inventories, the alternative minimum tax, net operating losses generally, including accounting method changes for these issues, and accounting periods.

Issues under the jurisdiction of the Associate Chief Counsel (International)

.04 Issues under the jurisdiction of the Associate Chief Counsel (International) include the tax treatment of nonresident aliens and foreign corporations, withholding of tax on nonresident aliens and foreign corporations, foreign tax credit, determination of sources of income, income from sources without the United States, subpart F questions, domestic international sales corporations (DISCs), foreign sales corporations (FSCs), exclusions under § 114 for extraterritorial income (ETI) pursuant to § 941(a)(5)(A), international boycott determinations, treatment of certain passive foreign investment companies, income affected by treaty, and other matters relating to the activities of non-U.S. persons within the United States or U.S.-related persons outside the United States, and accounting method changes.

For the procedures to obtain advance pricing agreements under § 482, *see* Rev. Proc. 2004–40, 2004–2 C.B. 50.

For competent authority procedures related to bilateral and multilateral advance pricing agreements, *see* Rev. Proc. 2006–54, 2006–49 I.R.B. 1035.

Issues under the jurisdiction of the Associate Chief Counsel (Passthroughs and Special Industries)

.05 Issues under the jurisdiction of the Associate Chief Counsel (Passthroughs and Special Industries) include those that involve income taxes of S corporations (except accounting periods and methods) and certain noncorporate taxpayers (including partnerships, common trust funds, and trusts), entity classification, estate, gift, generation-skipping transfer, and certain excise taxes, amortization, depreciation, depletion, and other engineering issues, accounting method changes for depreciation and amortization, cooperative housing corporations, farmers' cooperatives (under § 521), the low-income housing, disabled access, and qualified electric vehicle credits, research and experimental expenditures, shipowners' protection and indemnity associations (under § 526), and certain homeowners associations (under § 528).

Issues under the jurisdiction of the Associate Chief Counsel (Procedure and Administration)

.06 Issues under the jurisdiction of the Associate Chief Counsel (Procedure and Administration) include those that involve federal tax procedure and administration, disclosure and privacy law, reporting and paying taxes, assessing and collecting taxes (including interest and penalties), abating, crediting, or refunding overassessments or overpayments of tax, and filing information returns.

Issues under the jurisdiction of the Division Counsel/Associate Chief Counsel (Tax Exempt and Government Entities)

.07 Issues under the jurisdiction of the Division Counsel/Associate Chief Counsel (Tax Exempt and Government Entities) include those that involve income tax and other tax aspects of executive compensation and employee benefit programs, including accounting method changes for these issues (other than those within the jurisdiction of the Commissioner, Tax Exempt and Government Entities Division), section 457 arrangements, employment taxes, taxes on self-employment income, tax-exempt obligations, mortgage credit certificates, qualified zone academy bonds (QZABS), and federal, state, local, and Indian tribal governments.

SECTION 4. ON WHAT ISSUES MUST WRITTEN ADVICE BE REQUESTED UNDER DIFFERENT PROCEDURES?

Alcohol, tobacco, and firearms taxes

.01 The procedures for obtaining letter rulings, etc., that apply to federal alcohol, tobacco, and firearms taxes under subtitle E of the Code are under the jurisdiction of the Alcohol and Tobacco Tax and Trade Bureau of the Department of the Treasury.

Employee plans and exempt organizations

.02 The procedures for obtaining letter rulings, determination letters, etc., on employee plans and exempt organizations are under the jurisdiction of the Commissioner, Tax Exempt and Government Entities Division. *See* Rev. Proc. 2007–4, this Bulletin. *See also* Rev. Proc. 2007–6, this Bulletin, for the procedures for issuing determination letters on the qualified status of pension, profit-sharing, stock bonus, annuity, and employee stock ownership plans under

§§ 401, 403(a), 409, and 4975(e)(7), and the status for exemption of any related trusts or custodial accounts under § 501(a).

For the user fee requirements applicable to requests for letter rulings, determination letters, etc., under the jurisdiction of the Commissioner, Tax Exempt and Government Entities Division, *see* Rev. Proc. 2007–8, this Bulletin.

SECTION 5. UNDER WHAT CIRCUMSTANCES DO THE ASSOCIATE OFFICES ISSUE LETTER RULINGS?

In income and gift tax matters

.01 In income and gift tax matters, an Associate office generally issues a letter ruling on a proposed transaction or on a completed transaction if the letter ruling request is submitted before the return is filed for the year in which the transaction is completed.

Special relief for late S corporation and related elections

.02 In lieu of requesting a letter ruling under this revenue procedure, a taxpayer may obtain relief for certain late S corporation and related elections by following the procedures in Rev. Proc. 2004–49, 2004–2 C.B. 210; Rev. Proc. 2004–48, 2004–2 C.B. 172; Rev. Proc. 2003–43, 2003–1 C.B. 998, or Rev. Proc. 97–48, 1997–2 C.B. 521. These procedures, which are in lieu of the letter ruling process, do not require payment of any user fee. *See* section 4.04 of Rev. Proc. 2004–49, section 3.01 of Rev. Proc. 2004–48, section 3.01 of Rev. Proc. 2003–43, section 3 of Rev. Proc. 97–48, and section 15.03(3) of this revenue procedure.

A § 301.9100 request for extension of time for making an election or for other relief

.03 An Associate office will consider a request for an extension of time for making an election or other application for relief under § 301.9100–3 of the Regulations on Procedure and Administration, even if submitted after the return covering the issue presented in the § 301.9100 request has been filed, an examination of the return has begun, or the issues in the return are being considered by Appeals or a federal court. A § 301.9100 request is a letter ruling request. Therefore, the § 301.9100 request should be submitted pursuant to this revenue procedure. An election made pursuant to § 301.9100–2 for an automatic extension of time is not a letter ruling request and does not require payment of any user fee. *See* § 301.9100–2(d) and section 15.03(1) of this revenue procedure.

(1) Format of request. A § 301.9100 request (other than an election made pursuant to § 301.9100–2) must be in the general form of, and meet the general requirements for, a letter ruling request. These requirements are given in section 7 of this revenue procedure. In addition, a § 301.9100 request must include the information required by § 301.9100–3(e).

(2) Period of limitations. The running of any applicable period of limitations is not suspended for the period during which a § 301.9100 request has been filed. *See* § 301.9100–3(d)(2). If the period of limitation on assessment under § 6501(a) for the taxable year in which an election should have been made or any taxable year that would have been affected by the election had it been timely made will expire before receipt of a § 301.9100 letter ruling, the Associate office ordinarily will not issue a § 301.9100 ruling. *See* § 301.9100–3(c)(1)(ii). If, however, the taxpayer secures consent to extend the period of limitations on assessment under § 6501(c)(4), the Associate office may issue the letter ruling. Note that the filing of a claim for refund under § 6511 does not extend the period of limitation on assessment. If § 301.9100 relief is granted, the Associate office may require the taxpayer to consent to an extension of the period of limitation on assessment. *See* § 301.9100–3(d)(2).

(3) Taxpayer must notify the Associate office if examination of its return begins while the request is pending. If the Service starts an examination of the taxpayer's return for the taxable year in which an election should have been made or any taxable year that would have been affected by the election had it been timely made while a § 301.9100 request is pending, the taxpayer must notify the Associate office. This notification must include the name and telephone number of the examining agent. *See* § 301.9100–3(e)(4)(i) and section 7.04(1)(b) of this revenue procedure.

(4) Associate office will notify examination agents, appeals officer, or government counsel of a § 301.9100 request if the taxpayer's return is being examined by a field office or is being considered by Appeals or a federal court. If the taxpayer's return for the taxable year in which an election should have been made or any taxable year that would have been affected by the election had it been timely made is being examined by a field office or considered by Appeals or a federal court, the Associate office will notify the appropriate examining agent, appeals officer, or government counsel that a § 301.9100 request has been submitted to the Associate office. The examining officer, appeals officer, or government counsel is not authorized to deny consideration of a § 301.9100 request. The letter ruling will be mailed to the taxpayer and a copy will be sent to the appropriate Service official in the operating division that has examination jurisdiction of the taxpayer's tax return, appeals officer, or government counsel.

(5) Relief for late initial classification election. In lieu of requesting a letter ruling under § 301.9100–1 through § 301.9100–3 and this revenue procedure, an entity newly formed under local law may apply for late classification election relief under Rev. Proc. 2002–59, 2002–2 C.B. 615. Requests for such relief are not subject to user fees. *See* section 3 of Rev. Proc. 2002–59 and section 15.03(2) of this revenue procedure.

Determinations under § 999(d) of the Internal Revenue Code

.04 As provided in Rev. Proc. 77–9, 1977–1 C.B. 542, the Associate Chief Counsel (International) issues determinations under § 999(d) that may deny certain benefits of the foreign tax credit, deferral of earnings of foreign subsidiaries and domestic international sales corporations (DISCs) to a person, if that person, is a member of a controlled group (within the meaning of § 993(a)(3)) that includes the person, or a foreign corporation of which a member of the controlled group is a United States shareholder, agrees to participate in, or cooperate with, an international boycott. The same principles shall apply with respect to exclusions under § 114 for exterritorial income (ETI) pursuant to § 941(a)(5)(A). Requests for determinations under Rev. Proc. 77–9 are letter ruling requests and, therefore, should be submitted to the Associate office pursuant to this revenue procedure.

In matters involving § 367

.05 Unless the issue is covered by section 6 of this revenue procedure, the Associate Chief Counsel (International) may issue a letter ruling under § 367 even if the taxpayer does not request a letter ruling as to the characterization of the transaction under the reorganization provisions of the Code. The Associate office will determine the § 367 consequences of a transaction based on the taxpayer's characterization of the transaction but will indicate in the letter ruling that it expresses no opinion as to the characterization of the transaction under the reorganization. The Associate office may decline to issue a § 367 ruling in situations in which the taxpayer inappropriately characterizes the transaction under the reorganization provisions.

In estate tax matters

.06 In general, the Associate Chief Counsel (Passthroughs and Special Industries) issues letter rulings on transactions affecting the estate tax on the prospective estate of a living person. The Associate office will not issue letter rulings for prospective estates on computations of tax, actuarial factors, and factual matters. With respect to the transactions affecting the estate tax of the decedent's estate, generally, the Associate office issues letter rulings before the decedent's estate tax return is filed.

If the taxpayer is requesting a letter ruling regarding a decedent's estate tax and the estate tax return is due to be filed before the letter ruling is expected to be issued, the taxpayer should obtain an extension of time for filing the return and should notify the Associate office branch considering the letter ruling request that an extension has been obtained.

If the return is filed before the letter ruling is received from the Associate office, the taxpayer must disclose on the return that a letter ruling has been requested, attach a copy of the pending letter ruling request to the return, and notify the Associate office that the return has been filed. *See* section 7.04 of this revenue procedure. The Associate office will make every effort to issue the letter ruling within 3 months of the date the return was filed.

If the taxpayer requests a letter ruling after the return is filed, but before the return is examined, the taxpayer must notify the field office having jurisdiction over the return, that a letter ruling has been requested, attach a copy of the pending letter ruling request, and notify the Associate office that a return has been filed. *See* section 7.04 of this revenue procedure. The Associate office will make every effort to issue the letter ruling within 3 months of the date the return has been filed.

If the letter ruling cannot be issued within that 3-month period, the Associate office will notify the field office having jurisdiction over the return, who may, by memorandum to the Associate office, grant an additional period for the issuance of the letter ruling.

In matters involving additional estate tax under § 2032A(c)

.07 In matters involving additional estate tax under § 2032A(c), the Associate Chief Counsel (Passthroughs and Special Industries) issues letter rulings on proposed transactions and on completed transactions that occurred before the return is filed.

In matters involving qualified domestic trusts under § 2056A

.08 In matters involving qualified domestic trusts under § 2056A, the Associate Chief Counsel (Passthroughs and Special Industries) issues letter rulings on proposed transactions and on completed transactions that occurred before the return is filed.

In generation-skipping transfer tax matters

.09 In general, the Associate Chief Counsel (Passthroughs and Special Industries) issues letter rulings on proposed transactions that affect the generation-skipping transfer tax and on completed transactions that occurred before the return is filed. In the case of a generation-skipping trust or trust equivalent, letter rulings are issued either before or after the trust or trust equivalent has been established.

In employment and excise tax matters

.10 In employment and excise tax matters, the Associate offices issue letter rulings on proposed transactions and on completed transactions either before or after the return is filed for those transactions.

Requests regarding employment status (employer/employee relationship) from federal agencies and instrumentalities should be submitted directly to the Associate Chief Counsel (Tax Exempt and Government Entities). Requests regarding employment status from other taxpayers must first be submitted to the appropriate Service office listed on the current Form SS–8 (Rev. June 2003). *See* section 12.04 of this revenue procedure. Generally, the employer is the taxpayer and requests the letter ruling. If the worker asks for the letter ruling, both the worker and the employer are considered to be the taxpayer and both are entitled to the letter ruling.

In administrative provisions matters

.11 The Associate Chief Counsel (Procedure and Administration) issues letter rulings on matters arising under the Code and related statutes and regulations that involve—

(1) the time, place, manner, and procedures for reporting and paying taxes; or

(2) the filing of information returns.

In Indian tribal government matters

.12 Pursuant to Rev. Proc. 84–37, 1984–1 C.B. 513, as modified by Rev. Proc. 86–17, 1986–1 C.B. 550, and Rev. Proc. 2007–1, this revenue procedure, the Office of Division Counsel/Associate Chief Counsel (Tax Exempt and Government Entities) issues determinations recognizing a tribal entity as an Indian tribal government within the meaning of § 7701(a)(40) or as a political subdivision of an Indian tribal government under § 7871(d) if it determines, after consultation with the Secretary of the Interior, that the entity satisfies the statutory definition of an Indian tribal government or has been delegated governmental functions of an Indian tribal government. Requests for determinations under Rev. Proc. 84–37 are letter ruling requests, and, therefore, should be submitted to the Office of Division Counsel/Associate Chief Counsel (Tax Exempt and Government Entities) pursuant to this revenue procedure.

(1) Definition of Indian tribal government. The term "Indian tribal government" is defined under § 7701(a)(40) to mean the governing body of any tribe, band, community, village or group of Indians, or (if applicable) Alaska Natives, that is determined by the Secretary of the Treasury, after consultation with the Secretary of the Interior, to exercise governmental functions. Section 7871(d) provides that, for purposes of § 7871, a subdivision of an Indian tribal government shall be treated as a political subdivision of a state if the Secretary of the

Treasury determines, after consultation with the Secretary of the Interior, that the subdivision has been delegated the right to exercise one or more of the substantial governmental functions of the Indian tribal government.

(2) Inclusion in list of tribal governments. Rev. Proc. 2002–64, 2002–2 C.B. 717, provides a list of Indian tribal governments that are treated similarly to states for certain federal tax purposes. Rev. Proc. 84–36, 1984–1 C.B. 510, as modified by Rev. Proc. 86–17, provides a list of political subdivisions of Indian tribal governments that are treated as political subdivisions of states for certain federal tax purposes. Under Rev. Proc. 84–37, tribal governments or subdivisions recognized under § 7701(a)(40) or § 7871(d) will be included in the list of recognized tribal government entities in revised versions of Rev. Proc. 2002–64 or Rev. Proc. 84–36.

On constructive sales price under § 4216(b) or § 4218(c)

.13 The Associate Chief Counsel (Passthroughs and Special Industries) will issue letter rulings in all cases on the determination of a constructive sales price under § 4216(b) or § 4218(c) and in all other cases on prospective transactions if the law or regulations require a determination of the effect of a proposed transaction for tax purposes.

May be issued before the issuance of a regulation or other published guidance

.14 Unless the issue is covered by section 6 of this revenue procedure, Rev. Proc. 2007–3, this Bulletin, or Rev. Proc. 2007–7, this Bulletin, a letter ruling may be issued before the issuance of a temporary or final regulation or other published guidance that interprets the provisions of any act.

In such situations, an Associate office may issue letter rulings under the following conditions:

(1) Answer is clear or is reasonably certain. If the letter ruling request presents an issue for which the answer seems clear by applying the statute to the facts or for which the answer seems reasonably certain but not entirely free from doubt.

(2) Answer is not reasonably certain. If the letter ruling request presents an issue for which the answer does not seem reasonably certain, the Associate office may issue the letter ruling, using its best efforts to arrive at a determination, if it is in the best interests of tax administration. *But see* section 6.09 of this revenue procedure.

SECTION 6. UNDER WHAT CIRCUMSTANCES DOES THE SERVICE NOT ISSUE LETTER RULINGS OR DETERMINATION LETTERS?

Ordinarily not if the request involves an issue under examination, or consideration, or in litigation

.01 The Service ordinarily does not issue a letter ruling or a determination letter if, at the time of the request the identical issue is involved in the taxpayer's return for an earlier period and that issue—

(1) is being examined by a field office;

(2) is being considered by Appeals;

(3) is pending in litigation in a case involving the taxpayer or a related taxpayer;

(4) has been examined by a field office or considered by Appeals and the statutory period of limitations on assessment or on filing a claim for refund or credit of tax has not expired; or

(5) has been examined by a field office or considered by Appeals and a closing agreement covering the issue or liability has not been entered into by a field office or by Appeals.

If a return dealing with an issue for a particular year is filed while a request for a letter ruling on that issue is pending, an Associate office will issue the letter ruling unless it is notified by the taxpayer or otherwise learns that an examination of that issue or the identical issue on an earlier year's return has been started by a field office. *See* section 7.04 of this revenue procedure. In income and gift tax matters, even if an examination has begun, an Associate office ordinarily will issue the letter ruling if the field office agrees, by memorandum, to the issuance of the letter ruling.

Ordinarily not in certain areas because of factual nature of the problem

.02 The Service ordinarily does not issue letter rulings or determination letters in certain areas because of the factual nature of the problem involved or because of other reasons. Rev. Proc. 2007–3, this Bulletin, and Rev. Proc. 2007–7, this Bulletin, provide a list of these areas. This list is not all-inclusive because the Service may decline to issue a letter ruling or a determination letter when appropriate in the interest of sound tax administration or on other grounds whenever warranted by the facts or circumstances of a particular case.

Instead of issuing a letter ruling or determination letter, the Service may, when it is considered appropriate and in the best interests of the Service and after consulting with the taxpayer to determine if taxpayer wishes to pay the user fee listed under section (A)(6) of Appendix A to this revenue procedure, issue an information letter calling attention to well-established principles of tax law.

Ordinarily not on part of an integrated transaction

.03 An Associate office ordinarily will not issue a letter ruling on only part of an integrated transaction. If a part of a transaction falls under a no-rule area, a letter ruling on other parts of the transaction may be issued. Before preparing the letter ruling request, a taxpayer should call a branch having jurisdiction for the matters on which the taxpayer is seeking a letter ruling to discuss whether the Associate office will issue a letter ruling on part of the transaction.

Ordinarily not on which of two entities is a common law employer

.04 The Service does not ordinarily issue a letter ruling or a determination letter on which of two entities, under common law rules applicable in determining the employer-employee relationship, is the employer, when one entity is treating the worker as an employee.

Generally not to business associations or groups

.05 The Service does not issue letter rulings or determination letters to business, trade, or industrial associations or to similar groups concerning the application of the tax laws to members of the group. But groups and associations may submit suggestions of generic issues that could be appropriately addressed in revenue rulings. *See* Rev. Proc. 89–14, 1989–1 C.B. 814, which states the objectives of, and standards for, the publication of revenue rulings and revenue procedures in the Internal Revenue Bulletin.

The Service may issue letter rulings or determination letters to groups or associations on their own tax status or liability if the request meets the requirements of this revenue procedure.

Generally not where the request does not address the tax status, liability, or reporting obligations of the requester

.06 The Service generally does not issue letter rulings or determination letters regarding the tax consequences of a transaction for taxpayers who are not directly involved in the request if the requested letter ruling or determination letter would not address the tax status, liability, or reporting obligations of the requester. For example, a taxpayer may not request a letter ruling relating to the tax consequences of a transaction to a customer or client, if the tax status, liability or reporting obligations of the taxpayer would not be addressed in the ruling, because the customer or client is not directly involved in the letter ruling request. The tax liability of each shareholder is, however, directly involved in a letter ruling on the reorganization of a corporation. Accordingly, a corporate taxpayer could request a letter ruling that solely addressed the tax consequences to its shareholders of a proposed reorganization.

Revenue Procedure 96–16, 1996–1 C.B. 630, sets forth rules for letter ruling requests involving state and local government obligations.

Generally not to foreign governments

.07 The Service does not issue letter rulings or determination letters to foreign governments or their political subdivisions about the U.S. tax effects of their laws. The Associate offices also do not issue letter rulings on the effect of a tax treaty on the tax laws of a treaty country for purposes of determining the tax of the treaty country. *See* section 13.02 of Rev. Proc. 2006–54, 2006–49 I.R.B. 1035. Treaty partners can continue to address matters such as these under the provisions of the applicable tax treaty. In addition, the Associate offices may issue letter rulings to foreign governments or their political subdivisions on their own tax status or liability under U.S. law if the request meets the requirements of this revenue procedure.

Ordinarily not on federal tax consequences of proposed legislation

.08 The Associate offices ordinarily do not issue letter rulings on a matter involving the federal tax consequences of any proposed federal, state, local, municipal, or foreign legislation. The Office of Division Counsel/Associate Chief Counsel (Tax Exempt and Government Entities) may issue letter rulings regarding the effect of proposed state, local, or municipal legislation upon an eligible deferred compensation plan under § 457(b) provided that the letter ruling request relating to the plan complies with the other requirements of this revenue procedure. The Associate offices also may provide general information in response to an inquiry.

Not before issuance of a regulation or other published guidance

.09 Generally, the Service will not issue a letter ruling or a determination letter if the request presents an issue that cannot be readily resolved before a regulation or any other published guidance is issued. When the Service has closed a regulation project or any other published guidance project that might have answered the issue or decides not to open a regulation project or any other published guidance project, the Associate offices may consider all letter ruling requests unless the issue is covered by section 6 of this revenue procedure, Rev. Proc. 2007–3, this Bulletin, or Rev. Proc. 2007–7, this Bulletin.

Not on frivolous issues

.10 The Service will not issue a letter ruling or a determination letter on frivolous issues. A "frivolous issue" is one without basis in fact or law, or that espouses a position which has been held by the courts to be frivolous or groundless. Examples of frivolous or groundless issues include, but are not limited to:

(1) frivolous "constitutional" claims, such as claims that the requirement to file tax returns and pay taxes constitutes an unreasonable search barred by the Fourth Amendment; violates Fifth and Fourteenth Amendment protections of due process; violates Thirteenth Amendment protections against involuntary servitude; or is unenforceable because the Sixteenth Amendment does not authorize nonapportioned direct taxes or because it was never ratified;

(2) claims that income taxes are voluntary, that the term "income" is not defined in the Internal Revenue Code, or that preparation and filing of income tax returns violates the Paperwork Reduction Act;

(3) claims that tax may be imposed only on coins minted under a gold or silver standard or that receipt of Federal Reserve Notes does not cause an accretion to wealth;

(4) claims that a person is not taxable on income because he or she falls within a class entitled to "reparation claims" or an extra-statutory class of individuals exempt from tax, *e.g.*, "free-born" individuals;

(5) claims that a taxpayer can refuse to pay taxes on the basis of opposition to certain governmental expenditures;

(6) claims that taxes apply only to federal employees; only to residents of Puerto Rico, Guam, the U.S. Virgin Islands, the District of Columbia, or "federal enclaves"; or that sections 861 through 865 or any other provision of the Code imposes taxes on U.S. citizens and residents only on income derived from foreign based activities;

(7) claims that wages or personal service income are not "income," are "nontaxable receipts," or are a "nontaxable exchange for labor;"

(8) claims that income tax withholding by an employer on wages is optional; or

(9) other claims that the courts have characterized as frivolous or groundless.

No "comfort" letter rulings

.11 Except as otherwise provided in Rev. Proc. 2007–3, this Bulletin, (*e.g.*, under section 3.01(33), where the Associate office already is ruling on a significant issue in the same transaction), a letter ruling will not be issued with respect to an issue that is clearly and adequately addressed by statute, regulations, decisions of a court, revenue rulings, revenue procedures, notices, or other authority published in the Internal Revenue Bulletin. The Associate office may in its discretion determine to issue a letter ruling on such an issue if the Associate office is otherwise issuing a ruling to the taxpayer on another issue arising in the same transaction.

Not on alternative plans or hypothetical situations

.12 The Service will not issue a letter ruling or a determination letter on alternative plans of proposed transactions or on hypothetical situations.

Not on property conversion after return filed

.13 An Associate office will not issue a letter ruling on the replacement of involuntarily converted property, whether or not the property has been replaced, if the taxpayer has already filed a return for the taxable year in which the property was converted. A Director may issue a determination letter in this case. *See* section 12.01 of this revenue procedure.

Circumstances under which determination letters are not issued by a Director

.14 A Director will not issue a determination letter if—

(1) it appears that the taxpayer has directed a similar inquiry to an Associate office;

(2) the same issue, involving the same taxpayer or a related taxpayer, is pending in a case in litigation or before Appeals;

(3) the request involves an industry-wide problem;

(4) the specific employment tax question at issue in the request has been, or is being, considered by the Central Office of the Social Security Administration or the Railroad Retirement Board for the same taxpayer or a related taxpayer; or

(5) the request is for a determination of constructive sales price under § 4216(b) or § 4218(c), which deal with special provisions applicable to the manufacturers excise tax. The Associate Chief Counsel (Passthroughs and Special Industries) will, in certain circumstances, issue letter rulings in this area. *See* section 5.13 of this revenue procedure.

SECTION 7. WHAT ARE THE GENERAL INSTRUCTIONS FOR REQUESTING LETTER RULINGS AND DETERMINATION LETTERS?

This section explains the general instructions for requesting letter rulings and determination letters. *See* section 9 of this revenue procedure for the specific and additional procedures for requesting a change in accounting method.

Requests for letter rulings, closing agreements, and determination letters require the payment of the applicable user fee listed in Appendix A of this revenue procedure. Certain changes in accounting methods under the automatic change request procedures (*see* section 9.01(1) of this revenue procedure) and certain changes in accounting periods made under automatic change request procedures do not require payment of a user fee (*see* Appendix E of this revenue procedure). For additional user fee requirements, *see* section 15 of this revenue procedure.

Specific and additional instructions also apply to requests for letter rulings and determination letters on certain matters. Those matters are listed in Appendix E of this revenue procedure followed by a reference (usually to another revenue procedure) where more information can be obtained.

Certain information required in all requests

.01

Facts

(1) Complete statement of facts and other information. Each request for a letter ruling or a determination letter must contain a complete statement of all facts relating to the transaction. These facts include—

(a) names, addresses, telephone numbers, and taxpayer identification numbers of all interested parties (the term "all interested parties" does not mean all shareholders of a widely held corporation requesting a letter ruling relating to a reorganization or all employees where a large number may be involved);

(b) the annual accounting period, and the overall method of accounting (cash or accrual) for maintaining the accounting books and filing the federal income tax return, of all interested parties;

(c) a description of the taxpayer's business operations;

(d) a complete statement of the business reasons for the transaction; and

(e) a detailed description of the transaction.

Documents and foreign laws

(2) Copies of all contracts, wills, deeds, agreements, instruments, other documents, and foreign laws.

(a) Documents. True copies of all contracts, wills, deeds, agreements, instruments, trust documents, proposed disclaimers, and other documents pertinent to the transaction must be submitted with the request.

If the request concerns a corporate distribution, reorganization, or similar transaction, the corporate balance sheet and profit and loss statement should also be submitted. If the request relates to a prospective transaction, the most recent balance sheet and profit and loss statement should be submitted.

If any document, including any balance sheet and profit and loss statement, is in a language other than English, the taxpayer must also submit a certified English translation of the document, along with a true copy of the document. For guidelines on the acceptability of such documents, *see* paragraph (c) of this section 7.01(2).

Each document, other than the request, should be labeled and attached to the request in alphabetical sequence. Original documents, such as contracts, wills, etc., should not be submitted because they become part of the Service's file and will not be returned.

(b) Foreign laws. The taxpayer must submit with the request a copy of the relevant parts of all foreign laws, including statutes, regulations, administrative pronouncements, and any other relevant legal authority. The documents submitted must be in the official language of the country involved and must be copied from an official publication of the foreign government or another widely available, generally accepted publication. If English is not the official language of the country involved, the taxpayer must also submit a copy of an English language version of the relevant parts of all foreign laws. This translation must be: (i) from an official publication of the foreign government or another widely available, generally accepted publication; or (ii) a certified English translation submitted in accordance with paragraph (c) of this section 7.01(2).

The taxpayer must identify the title and date of publication, including updates, of any widely available, generally accepted publication that the taxpayer (or the taxpayer's qualified translator) uses as a source for the relevant parts of the foreign law.

(c) Standards for acceptability of submissions of documents in a language other than English and certified English translations of laws in a language other than English. The taxpayer must submit with the request an accurate and complete certified English translation of the relevant parts of all contracts, wills, deeds, agreements, instruments, trust documents, proposed disclaimers, or other documents, which are in a language other than English. If the taxpayer chooses to submit certified English translations of foreign laws, those translations must be based on an official publication of the foreign government or another widely available, generally accepted publication. In either case, the translation must be that of a qualified translator and must be attested to by the translator. The attestation must contain: (i) a statement that the translation submitted is a true and accurate translation of the foreign language document or law; (ii) a statement as to the attestant's qualifications as a translator and as to that attestant's qualifications and knowledge regarding tax matters or foreign law if the law is not a tax law; and (iii) the attestant's name and address.

Analysis of material facts

(3) Analysis of material facts. The request must be accompanied by an analysis of facts and their bearing on the issue or issues. If documents attached to a request contain material facts, they must be included in the taxpayer's analysis of facts in the request rather than merely incorporated by reference.

Same issue in an earlier return

(4) Statement regarding whether same issue is in an earlier return. The request must state whether, to the best of the knowledge of both the taxpayer and the taxpayer's representatives, any return of the taxpayer (or any return of a related taxpayer within the meaning of § 267 or of a member of an affiliated group of which the taxpayer is also a member within the meaning of § 1504) that would be affected by the requested letter ruling or determination letter is under examination, before Appeals, or before a federal court.

Same or similar issue previously submitted or currently pending

(5) Statement regarding whether same or similar issue was previously ruled on or requested, or is currently pending. The request must state whether, to the best of the knowledge of both the taxpayer and the taxpayer's representatives—

(a) the Service previously ruled on the same or a similar issue for the taxpayer (or a related taxpayer within the meaning of § 267 or a member of an affiliated group of which the taxpayer is also a member within the meaning of § 1504 (related taxpayer)) or a predecessor;

(b) the taxpayer, a related taxpayer, a predecessor, or any representatives previously submitted a request (including an application for change in accounting method) involving the same or a similar issue to the Service but no letter ruling or determination letter was issued;

(c) the taxpayer, a related taxpayer, or a predecessor previously submitted a request (including an application for change in accounting method) involving the same or a similar issue that is currently pending with the Service; or

(d) at the same time as this request, the taxpayer or a related taxpayer is presently submitting another request (including an application for change in accounting method) involving the same or a similar issue to the Service.

If the statement is affirmative for (a), (b), (c), or (d) of this section 7.01(5), the statement must give the date the request was submitted, the date the request was withdrawn or ruled on, if applicable, and other details of the Service's consideration of the issue.

Interpretation of a substantive provision of an income or estate tax treaty

(6) Statement regarding interpretation of a substantive provision of an income or estate tax treaty. If the request involves the interpretation of a substantive provision of an income or estate tax treaty, the request must state whether—

(a) the tax authority of the treaty jurisdiction has issued a ruling on the same or similar issue for the taxpayer, a related taxpayer (within the meaning of § 267 or a member of an affiliated group of which the taxpayer is also a member within the meaning of § 1504 (related taxpayer)), or any predecessor;

(b) the same or similar issue for the taxpayer, a related taxpayer, or any predecessor is being examined, or has been settled, by the tax authority of the treaty jurisdiction or is otherwise the subject of a closing agreement in that jurisdiction; and

(c) the same or similar issue for the taxpayer, a related taxpayer, or any predecessor is being considered by the competent authority of the treaty jurisdiction.

Letter from Bureau of Indian Affairs relating to Indian tribal government

(7) Letter from Bureau of Indian Affairs relating to a letter ruling request for recognition of Indian tribal government status or status as a political subdivision of an Indian tribal government. To facilitate prompt action on a letter ruling request for recognition of Indian tribal government status or status as a political subdivision of an Indian tribal government, the taxpayer must submit with the letter ruling request a letter from the Department of the Interior, Bureau of Indian Affairs ("BIA"), verifying that the tribe is recognized by BIA as an Indian tribe and that the tribal government exercises governmental functions or that the political subdivision of the Indian tribal government has been delegated substantial governmental functions. A letter ruling request that does not contain this letter from BIA cannot be resolved until the Service obtains a letter from BIA regarding the tribe's status.

The taxpayer should send a request to verify tribal status to the following address:

Branch of Tribal Government & Alaska
Division of Indian Affairs
Office of the Solicitor, Room 6456
U. S. Department of the Interior
1849 C Street, NW
Washington, DC 20240

Statement of authorities supporting taxpayer's views

(8) Statement of supporting authorities. If the taxpayer advocates a particular conclusion, an explanation of the grounds for that conclusion and the relevant authorities to support it must be included. Even if not advocating a particular tax treatment of a proposed transaction, the taxpayer must still furnish views on the tax results of the proposed transaction and a statement of relevant authorities to support those views.

In all events, the request must include a statement of whether the law in connection with the request is uncertain and whether the issue is adequately addressed by relevant authorities.

Statement of authorities contrary to taxpayer's views

(9) Statement of contrary authorities. In order to avoid inevitable delay in the ruling process, contrary authorities should be brought to the attention of the Service at the earliest possible opportunity. If there are significant contrary authorities, it is usually helpful to discuss them in a presubmission conference prior to submitting the ruling request. See section 10.07 of this revenue procedure as to presubmission conferences. The taxpayer is strongly encouraged to inform the Service about, and discuss the implications of, any authority believed to be contrary to the position advanced, such as legislation, tax treaties, court decisions, regulations, notices, revenue rulings, revenue procedures, or announcements. If the taxpayer determines that there are no contrary authorities, a statement in the request to this effect would be helpful. If the taxpayer does not furnish either contrary authorities or a statement that none exists, the Service in complex cases or those presenting difficult or novel issues may request submission of contrary authorities or a statement that none exists. Failure to comply with this request may result in the Service's refusal to issue a letter ruling or determination letter.

Identifying and discussing contrary authorities will generally enable Service personnel to understand the issue and relevant authorities more quickly. When Service personnel receive the request, they will have before them the taxpayer's thinking on the effect and applicability of contrary authorities. This information should make research easier and lead to earlier action by the Service. If the taxpayer does not disclose and distinguish significant contrary authorities, the Service may need to request additional information, which will delay action on the request.

Statement identifying pending legislation

(10) Statement identifying pending legislation. At the time of filing the request, the taxpayer must identify any pending legislation that may affect the proposed transaction. In addition, if legislation is introduced after the request is filed but before a letter ruling or determination letter is issued, the taxpayer must notify the Service.

Deletion statement required by § 6110

(11) Statement identifying information to be deleted from copy of letter ruling or determination letter for public inspection. The text of letter rulings and determination letters is open to public inspection under § 6110. The Service makes deletions from the text before it is made available for inspection. To help the Service make the deletions required by § 6110(c), a request for a letter ruling or determination letter must be accompanied by a statement indicating the deletions desired ("deletion statement"). If the deletion statement is not submitted with the request, a Service representative will tell the taxpayer that the request will be closed if the Service does not receive the deletion statement within 21 calendar days. *See* section 8.05 of this revenue procedure.

(a) Format of deletion statement. A taxpayer who wants only names, addresses, and identifying numbers to be deleted should state this in the deletion statement. If the taxpayer wants more information deleted, the deletion statement must be accompanied by a copy of the request and supporting documents on which the taxpayer should bracket the material to be deleted. The deletion statement must include the statutory basis under § 6110(c) for each proposed deletion.

If the taxpayer decides to ask for additional deletions before the letter ruling or determination letter is issued, additional deletion statements may be submitted.

(b) Location of deletion statement. The deletion statement must not appear in the request, but instead must be made in a separate document and placed on top of the request for a letter ruling or determination letter.

(c) Signature. The deletion statement must be signed and dated by the taxpayer or the taxpayer's authorized representative. A stamped signature or faxed signature is not permitted.

(d) Additional information. The taxpayer should follow the same procedures of this section 7.01(11) to propose deletions from any additional information submitted after the initial request. An additional deletion statement is not required with each submission of additional information if the taxpayer's initial deletion statement requests that only names, addresses, and identifying numbers are to be deleted and the taxpayer wants only the same information deleted from the additional information.

(e) Taxpayer may protest deletions not made. After receiving from the Service the notice under § 6110(f)(1) of intention to disclose the letter ruling or determination letter (including a copy of the version proposed to be open to public inspection and notation of third-party communications under § 6110(d)), the taxpayer may protest the disclosure of certain information in the letter ruling or determination letter. The taxpayer must send a written statement to the Service office indicated on the notice of intention to disclose, within 20 calendar days of the date the notice of intention to disclose is mailed to the taxpayer. The statement must identify those deletions that the Service has not made and that the taxpayer believes should have been made. The taxpayer must also submit a copy of the version of the letter ruling or determination letter and bracket the deletions proposed that have not been made by the Service. Generally, the Service will not consider deleting any material that the taxpayer did not propose to be deleted before the letter ruling or determination letter was issued.

Within 20 calendar days after the Service receives the response to the notice under § 6110(f)(1), the Service will mail to the taxpayer its final administrative conclusion regarding the deletions to be made. The taxpayer does not have the right to a conference to resolve any disagreements concerning material to be deleted from the text of the letter ruling or determination letter. These matters may be taken up at any conference that is otherwise scheduled regarding the request.

(f) Taxpayer may request delay of public inspection. After receiving the notice under § 6110(f)(1) of intention to disclose, but within 60 calendar days after the date of notice, the taxpayer may send a written request for delay of public inspection under either § 6110(g)(3) or (4). The request for delay must be sent to the Service office indicated on the notice of intention to disclose. A request for delay under § 6110(g)(3) must contain the date on which it is expected that the underlying transaction will be completed. The request for delay under § 6110(g)(4) must contain a statement from which the Commissioner of Internal Revenue ("Commissioner") may determine whether there are good reasons for the delay.

Signature on request

(12) Signature by taxpayer or authorized representative. The request for a letter ruling or determination letter must be signed and dated by the taxpayer or the taxpayer's authorized representative. A stamped signature or faxed signature is not permitted.

Authorized representatives

(13) (a) Authorized representatives. To sign the request or to appear before the Service in connection with the request, the taxpayer's authorized representative (for rules on who may practice before the Service, *see* Treasury Department Circular No. 230, 31 C.F.R. part 10, July 26, 2002) must be:

Attorney

(1) An attorney who is a member in good standing of the bar of the highest court of any state, possession, territory, commonwealth, or the District of Columbia and who is not currently under suspension or disbarment from practice before the Service. He or she must file a written declaration with the Service showing current qualification as an attorney and current authorization to represent the taxpayer;

Certified public accountant

(2) A certified public accountant who is duly qualified to practice in any state, possession, territory, commonwealth, or the District of Columbia and who is not currently under suspension or disbarment from practice before the Service. He or she must file a written declaration with the Service showing current qualification as a certified public accountant and current authorization to represent the taxpayer;

Enrolled agent

(3) An enrolled agent who is a person, other than an attorney or certified public accountant, who is currently enrolled to practice before the Service and who is not currently under suspension or disbarment from practice before the Service. He or she must file a written declaration with the Service showing current enrollment and authorization to represent the taxpayer. The enrollment number must be included in the declaration;

Enrolled actuary

(4) An enrolled actuary who is a person, other than an attorney or certified public accountant, who is currently enrolled as an actuary by the Joint Board for the Enrollment of Actuaries pursuant to 29 U.S.C. § 1242 and who is not currently under suspension or disbarment from practice before the Service. He or she must file a written declaration with the Service showing current qualification as an enrolled actuary and current authorization to represent the taxpayer. Practice before the Service as an enrolled actuary is limited to representation with respect to issues involving §§ 401, 403(a), 404, 412, 413, 414, 419, 419A, 420, 4971, 4972, 4976, 4980, 6057, 6058, 6059, 6652(e), 6652(f), 6692, and 7805(b); former § 405; and 29 U.S.C. § 1083; or

A person with a "Letter of Authorization"

(5) Any other person, including a foreign representative, who has received a "Letter of Authorization" from the Director of the Office of Professional Responsibility under section 10.7(d) of Treasury Department Circular No. 230. A person may make a written request for a "Letter of Authorization" to: Office of Professional Responsibility, SE:OPR, Internal Revenue Service, 1111 Constitution Ave., NW, Washington, DC 20224. Section 10.7(d) of Circular No. 230 authorizes the Commissioner to allow an individual who is not otherwise eligible to practice before the Service to represent another person in a particular matter.

Representative authorized based on relationship to taxpayer

(b) A regular full-time employee representing his or her employer; a general partner representing his or her partnership; a *bona fide* officer representing his or her corporation, association, or organized group; a regular full-time employee representing a trust, receivership, guardianship, or estate; or an individual representing an immediate family member may sign the request or appear before the Service in connection with the request.

Return preparer

(c) A return preparer who is not described in 13(a) and 13(b) of this section may not sign the request, or appear before the Service, or represent a taxpayer in connection with a letter ruling or a determination letter. *See* section 10.7(c) of Treasury Department Circular No. 230.

Foreign representative

(d) A foreign representative, other than a person referred to in 13(a) and 13(b) of this section, is not authorized to practice before the Service within the United States and, therefore, must withdraw from representing a taxpayer in a request for a letter ruling or a determination letter. In this situation, the nonresident alien or foreign entity must submit the request for a letter ruling or a determination letter on the individual's or the entity's own behalf or through a person referred to in (13)(a) and (b) of this section.

Power of attorney and declaration of representative

(14) Power of attorney and declaration of representative. It is preferred that Form 2848, *Power of Attorney and Declaration of Representative*, be used to provide the representative's authority (Part I of Form 2848, *Power of Attorney*) and the representative's qualification (Part II of Form 2848, *Declaration of Representative*). The name of the person signing Part I of Form 2848 should also be typed or printed on this form. A stamped signature is not permitted. An original, a copy, or a facsimile transmission (fax) of the power of attorney is acceptable so long as its authenticity is not reasonably disputed. For additional information regarding the power of attorney form, *see* section 7.02(2) of this revenue procedure.

The taxpayer's authorized representative, whether or not enrolled, must comply with Treasury Department Circular No. 230, which provides the rules for practice before the Service. In situations where the Service believes that the taxpayer's representative is not in compliance with Circular 230, the Service will bring the matter to the attention of the Office of Professional Responsibility.

Penalties of perjury statement

(15) Penalties of perjury statement.

(a) Format of penalties of perjury statement. A request for a letter ruling or determination letter and any change in the request submitted at a later time must be accompanied by the following declaration: **"Under penalties of perjury, I declare that I have examined [Insert, as appropriate: this request or this modification to the request], including accompanying documents, and, to the best of my knowledge and belief, [Insert, as appropriate: the request or the modification] contains all the relevant facts relating to the request, and such facts are true, correct, and complete."**

See section 8.05(4) of this revenue procedure for the penalties of perjury statement applicable for submissions of additional information.

(b) Signature by taxpayer. The declaration must be signed and dated by the taxpayer, not the taxpayer's representative. A stamped signature or faxed signature is not permitted.

The person who signs for a corporate taxpayer must be an officer of the corporate taxpayer who has personal knowledge of the facts and whose duties are not limited to obtaining a letter ruling or determination letter from the Service. If the corporate taxpayer is a member of an affiliated group filing consolidated returns, a penalties of perjury statement must also be signed and submitted by an officer of the common parent of the group.

The person signing for a trust, a state law partnership, or a limited liability company must be, respectively, a trustee, general partner, or member-manager who has personal knowledge of the facts.

Number of copies of request to be submitted

(16) Number of copies of request to be submitted. Generally, a taxpayer needs to submit the original and one copy of the request for a letter ruling or determination letter. If more than one issue is presented in the letter ruling request, the taxpayer is encouraged to submit additional copies of the request.

Further, the original and two copies of the request for a letter ruling or determination letter are required if—

(a) the taxpayer is requesting separate letter rulings or determination letters on different issues as explained later under section 7.02(1) of this revenue procedure; or

(b) the taxpayer is requesting deletions other than names, addresses, and identifying numbers, as explained in section 7.01(11)(a) of this revenue procedure (one copy is the request for the letter ruling or determination letter and the second copy is the deleted version of such request); or

(c) a closing agreement (as defined in section 2.02 of this revenue procedure) is being requested on the issue presented.

Sample format for a letter ruling request

(17) Sample format for a letter ruling request. To assist a taxpayer or the taxpayer's representative in preparing a letter ruling request, a sample format for a letter ruling request is provided in Appendix B of this revenue procedure. This format is not required to be used by the taxpayer or the taxpayer's representative.

Checklist

(18) Checklist for letter ruling requests. An Associate office will be able to respond more quickly to a taxpayer's letter ruling request if the request is carefully prepared and complete. The checklist in Appendix C of this revenue procedure is designed to assist taxpayers in preparing a request by reminding them of the essential information and documents to be furnished with the request. The checklist in Appendix C must be completed to the extent required by the instructions in the checklist, signed and dated by the taxpayer or the taxpayer's representative, and placed on top of the letter ruling request. If the checklist in Appendix C is not received, a branch representative will ask the taxpayer or the taxpayer's representative to submit the checklist; this may delay action on the letter ruling request.

For letter ruling requests on certain matters, specific checklists supplement the checklist in Appendix C. These checklists are listed in section 1 of Appendix E of this revenue procedure and must also be completed and placed on top of the letter ruling request along with the checklist in Appendix C.

Copies of the checklist in Appendix C can be obtained by calling (202) 622–7560 (not a toll-free call) or a copy can be obtained from this revenue procedure in Internal Revenue Bulletin 2007–1 on the IRS web site at *www.irs.gov* by accessing the Newsroom link, and then the IRS Guidance link, to obtain Internal Revenue Bulletin 2007–1. A photocopy of this checklist may be used.

Additional procedural information required with request

.02

Multiple issues

(1) To request separate letter rulings for multiple issues in a single situation. If more than one issue is presented in a request for a letter ruling, the Associate office generally will issue a single letter ruling covering all the issues. If the taxpayer requests separate letter rulings on any of the issues (because, for example, one letter ruling is needed sooner than another), the Associate office usually will comply with the request unless it is not feasible or not in the best interests of the Associate office to do so. A taxpayer who wants separate letter rulings on multiple issues should make this clear in the request and submit the original and two copies of the request.

In issuing each letter ruling, the Associate office will state that it has issued separate letter rulings or that requests for other letter rulings are pending.

Power of attorney used to indicate recipient of a copy or copies of a letter ruling or a determination letter

(2) Power of attorney used to indicate recipient or recipients of a copy or copies of a letter ruling or a determination letter. Once the Service signs the letter ruling or determination letter, it will send the original to the taxpayer. The Service will not send the original letter ruling or determination letter to the taxpayer's representative. The Service may send copies of the letter ruling or determination letter to the taxpayer's representative, but in no case to more than two representatives.

Unless otherwise indicated by the taxpayer on the Form 2848, the Service will send a copy of the letter ruling or determination letter to the first representative listed on the Form 2848. If the taxpayer appoints more than one representative on the Form 2848 and checks the Box (a) on Line 7, an additional copy will be sent to the second representative listed on the Form 2848. The Service will not send a copy of the letter ruling or determination letter to any representative if the taxpayer checks the Box (b) on Line 7 on the Form 2848 indicating that notices or written communications from the Service should not be sent to the taxpayer's representative.

It is preferred that the taxpayers use the Form 2848, *Power of Attorney and Declaration of Representative*, to appoint representatives. If a taxpayer does not use Form 2848 to appoint a representative, a copy of the letter ruling or determination letter will be mailed to the first representative listed on the power of attorney, unless the taxpayer indicates that an additional copy of the letter ruling or determination letter should be mailed to a second representative, or that no copies of the letter ruling or determination letter should be mailed to the taxpayer's representative.

"Two-Part" letter ruling requests

(3) To request a particular conclusion on a proposed transaction. A taxpayer who is requesting a particular conclusion on a proposed transaction may make the request for a letter ruling in two parts. This type of request is referred to as a "two-part" letter ruling request. The first part must include the complete statement of facts and related documents described in section 7.01 of this revenue procedure. The second part must include a summary statement of the facts the taxpayer believes to be controlling in reaching the conclusion requested.

If the Associate office accepts the taxpayer's statement of controlling facts, it will base its letter ruling on these facts. Ordinarily, this statement will be incorporated into the letter ruling. The Associate office reserves the right to rule on the basis of a more complete statement of the facts and to seek more information in developing the facts and restating them.

A taxpayer who chooses this two-part procedure has all the rights and responsibilities provided in this revenue procedure.

Taxpayers may not use the two-part procedure if it is inconsistent with other procedures, such as those dealing with requests for permission to change accounting methods or periods, applications for recognition of exempt status under § 521, or rulings on employment tax status.

After the Associate office has resolved the issues presented by a letter ruling request, the Associate office representative may request that the taxpayer submit a proposed draft of the letter ruling to expedite the issuance of the ruling. *See* section 8.07 of this revenue procedure.

Expedited handling

(4) To request expedited handling. The Service ordinarily processes requests for letter rulings and determination letters in order of the date received. Expedited handling means that a request is processed ahead of the regular order. Expedited handling is granted only in rare and unusual cases, both out of fairness to other taxpayers and because the Service seeks to process all requests as expeditiously as possible and to give appropriate deference to normal business exigencies in all cases not involving expedited handling. Notwithstanding the previous sentence, expedited handling may be available for certain transactions intended to qualify as reorganizations described in § 368 or distributions described in § 355, as provided below.

A taxpayer who has a compelling need to have a request processed ahead of the regular order may request expedited handling. This request must explain in detail the need for expedited handling. The request must be made in writing, preferably in a separate letter with, or soon after filing, the request for the letter ruling or determination letter. If the request is not made in a separate letter, then the letter in which the letter ruling or determination letter request is made should say, at the top of the first page: **"Expedited Handling Is Requested. See page _____ of this letter."**

A request for expedited handling will not be forwarded to a branch for action until the check for the user fee is received.

Whether a request for expedited handling will be granted is within the Service's discretion. The Service may grant the request when a factor outside a taxpayer's control creates a real business need to obtain a letter ruling or determination letter before a certain time in order to avoid serious business consequences. Examples include situations in which a court or governmental agency has imposed a specific deadline for the completion of a transaction, or a transaction must be completed expeditiously to avoid an imminent business emergency (such as the hostile takeover of a corporate taxpayer), provided that the taxpayer can demonstrate that the deadline or business emergency, and the need for expedited handling, resulted from circumstances that could not reasonably have been anticipated or controlled by the taxpayer. To qualify for expedited handling in such situations, the taxpayer must also demonstrate that the taxpayer submitted the request as promptly as possible after becoming aware of the deadline or emergency. The extent to which the letter ruling or determination letter complies with all of the applicable requirements of this revenue procedure, and fully and clearly presents the issues, is a factor in determining whether expedited treatment will be granted. When the Service agrees to process a request out of order, it cannot give assurance that any letter ruling or determination letter will be processed by the time requested.

The scheduling of a closing date for a transaction or a meeting of the board of directors or shareholders of a corporation, without regard for the time it may take to obtain a letter ruling or determination letter, will not be considered a sufficient reason to process a request ahead of its regular order. Also, the possible effect of fluctuation in the market price of stocks on a transaction will not be considered a sufficient reason to process a request out of order.

Because most requests for letter rulings and determination letters cannot be processed ahead of the regular order, the Service urges all taxpayers to submit their requests well in advance of the contemplated transaction. In addition, to facilitate prompt action on letter ruling requests, taxpayers are encouraged to ensure that their initial submissions comply with all of the requirements of this revenue procedure (including the requirements of other applicable guidelines set forth in Appendix E of this revenue procedure), to prepare "two-part" requests described in section 7.02(3) of this revenue procedure when possible, and to provide any additional information requested by the Service promptly.

EXPEDITED LETTER RULING PROCESS FOR REORGANIZATIONS AND FOR DISTRIBUTIONS UNDER SECTION 355: If a taxpayer requests a letter ruling on whether a transaction constitutes a reorganization under § 368 or a distribution under § 355 and asks for expedited handling pursuant to this provision, the Service will grant expedited handling. If expedited handling is granted, the Service will endeavor to complete and issue the letter ruling subject to Section 3.01(33) of Rev. Proc. 2007–3 within ten weeks after receiving the ruling request. If the transaction involves an issue or issues not entirely within the jurisdiction of the Associate Chief Counsel (Corporate), the letter ruling request will be processed in the usual manner, unless each Associate Chief Counsel having jurisdiction over an issue in the transaction agrees to process the letter ruling request on an expedited basis.

To initiate this process, the taxpayer must (i) state at the top of the first page of the request letter: "Expedited Handling is Requested" and (ii) provide the Associate Chief Counsel (Corporate) with a copy of the request letter by facsimile transmission (fax), without attachments, when the formal request is submitted. The fax copy should be sent to (202) 622–7707, Attn: CC:CORP (Expedite); and shortly after the fax is sent receipt should be confirmed by calling the telephone number for the office of the Associate Chief Counsel (Corporate) that is in section 10.07(1)(a) of this revenue procedure. In due course, the taxpayer must also provide the Associate Chief Counsel (Corporate) with a draft ruling letter setting forth the relevant facts, applicable representations, and requested rulings in a manner consistent with the format used by the Associate Chief Counsel (Corporate) in similar cases. See section 7.02(3) of this revenue procedure. In addition, the taxpayer must ensure that the formal submission of its letter ruling request complies with all of the requirements of this revenue procedure (including the requirements of other applicable guidelines set forth in Appendix E of this revenue procedure). See section 8.05(1) of this revenue procedure for a modified requirement regarding the submission of additional information. If the taxpayer does not satisfy the requirements of this paragraph, the letter ruling request will not be processed on an expedited basis, but instead will be processed in the usual manner. **For further information regarding this EXPEDITED LETTER RULING PROCESS FOR REORGANIZATIONS AND FOR DISTRIBUTIONS UNDER SECTION 355, call the telephone number provided in section 10.07(1)(a) of this revenue procedure for pre-submission conferences with the Office of Associate Chief Counsel (Corporate).**

Facsimile transmission (fax) to taxpayer or taxpayer's authorized representative of any document related to the letter ruling request

(5) Taxpayer requests to receive any document related to the letter ruling request by facsimile transmission (fax). If the taxpayer requests, the Associate office may fax a copy of any document related to the letter ruling request to the taxpayer or the taxpayer's authorized representative (for example, a request for additional information or the letter ruling).

A request to fax a copy of any document related to the letter ruling request to the taxpayer or the taxpayer's authorized representative must be made in writing, either as part of the original letter ruling request or prior to the mailing, or with respect to the letter ruling prior to the signing, of the document. The request must contain the fax number of the taxpayer or the taxpayer's authorized representative to whom the document is to be faxed.

A document other than the letter ruling will be faxed by a branch representative. The letter ruling may be faxed by either a branch representative or the Disclosure and Litigation Support Branch of the Legal Processing Division (CC:PA:LPD:DLS). For purposes of § 301.6110–2(h), a letter ruling is not issued until the ruling is mailed.

Requesting a conference

(6) To request a conference. A taxpayer who wants to have a conference on the issues involved should indicate this in writing when, or soon after, filing the request. *See also* sections 10.01, 10.02, and 11.11(2) of this revenue procedure.

Address to send the request

.03

Original letter ruling requests must be sent to the appropriate Associate office. The package should be marked: RULING REQUEST SUBMISSION.

(1) Requests for letter rulings should be sent to the following address:

Internal Revenue Service
Attn: CC:PA:LPD:DRU
P.O. Box 7604
Ben Franklin Station
Washington, DC 20044

If a private delivery service is used, the address is:

Internal Revenue Service
Attn: CC:PA:LPD:DRU, Room 5336
1111 Constitution Ave., NW
Washington, DC 20224

(2) Requests for letter rulings may also be hand delivered between the hours of 8:00 a.m. and 4:00 p.m. to the courier's desk at the loading dock (behind the 12th Street security station) of 1111 Constitution Avenue, NW, Washington, DC. A receipt will be given at the courier's desk. The package should be addressed to:

Courier's Desk
Internal Revenue Service
Attn: CC:PA:LPD:DRU, Room 5336
1111 Constitution Ave., NW
Washington, DC 20224

(3) Requests for letter rulings must not be submitted by fax. (But see section 7.02(4), above, regarding submissions of an initial fax in certain situations where expedited handling is requested.)

Pending letter ruling requests

.04

(1) Circumstances under which the taxpayer must notify the Associate office. The taxpayer must notify the Associate office if, after the letter ruling request is filed but before a letter ruling is issued, the taxpayer knows that—

(a) an examination of the issue or the identical issue on an earlier year's return has been started by a field office;

(b) in the case of a § 301.9100 request, an examination of the return for the taxable year in which an election should have been made or any taxable year that would have been affected by the election had it been timely made, has been started by a field office. *See* § 301.9100–3(e)(4)(i) and section 5.03(3) of this revenue procedure;

(c) legislation that may affect the transaction has been introduced. *See* section 7.01(10) of this revenue procedure; or

(d) another letter ruling request (including an application for change in accounting method) has been submitted by the taxpayer (or a related party within the meaning of § 267 or a member of an affiliated group of which the taxpayer is also a member within the meaning of § 1504) involving the same or similar issue that is currently pending with the Service.

(2) Taxpayer must notify the Associate office if a return is filed and must attach the request to the return. If the taxpayer files a return before a letter ruling is received from the Associate office concerning an issue in the return, the taxpayer must notify the Associate office that the return has been filed. The taxpayer must also attach a copy of the letter ruling request to the return to alert the field office and thereby avoid premature field action on the issue. Alternatively, taxpayers filing their returns electronically may satisfy this requirement by attaching a statement to their return that provides the date of the letter ruling request and control number of the letter ruling.

If, under the limited circumstances permitted in section 5 of this revenue procedure, the taxpayer requests a letter ruling after the return is filed, but before the return is examined, the taxpayer must notify the Associate office that the return has been filed. The taxpayer must also notify the field office having jurisdiction over the return and attach a copy of the letter ruling request to the notification to alert the field office and thereby avoid premature field action on the issue.

This section 7.04 also applies to pending requests for a closing agreement on a transaction for which a letter ruling is not requested or issued.

For purposes of this section 7.04, the term "return" includes the original return, amended return, and claim for refund.

When to attach letter ruling to return

.05 A taxpayer who receives a letter ruling before filing a return about any transaction that is relevant to the return being filed must attach a copy of the letter ruling to the return when it is filed. Alternatively, taxpayers filing their returns electronically may satisfy this requirement by attaching a statement to their return that provides the date and control number of the letter ruling.

For purposes of this section 7.05, the term "return" includes the original return, amended return, and claim for refund.

How to check on status of request

.06 The taxpayer or the taxpayer's authorized representative may obtain information regarding the status of a request by calling the person whose name and telephone number are shown on the acknowledgment of receipt of the request or the appropriate branch representative who contacts the taxpayer as explained in section 8.02 of this revenue procedure.

Request may be withdrawn or Associate office may decline to issue letter ruling

.07

(1) In general. A taxpayer may withdraw a request for a letter ruling or determination letter at any time before the letter ruling or determination letter is signed by the Service. Correspondence and exhibits related to a request that is withdrawn or related to a letter ruling request for which an Associate office declines to issue a letter ruling will not be returned to the taxpayer. *See* section 7.01(2) of this revenue procedure. In appropriate cases, an Associate office may publish its conclusions in a revenue ruling or revenue procedure.

(2) Notification of appropriate Service official.

(a) Letter ruling requests. If a taxpayer withdraws a letter ruling request or if the Associate office declines to issue a letter ruling, the Associate office generally will notify, by memorandum, the appropriate Service official in the operating division that has examination jurisdiction of the taxpayer's tax return and may give its views on the issues in the request to the Service official to consider in any later examination of the return. This section 7.07(2)(a) generally does not apply if the taxpayer withdraws the letter ruling request and submits a written statement that the transaction has been, or is being, abandoned and if the Associate office has not already formed an adverse opinion. *See*, in appropriate cases, section 7.07(1) above.

(b) Notification of Service official may constitute Chief Counsel Advice. If the memorandum to the Service official referred to in paragraph (a) of this section 7.07(2) provides more than the fact that the request was withdrawn and the Associate office was tentatively adverse, or that the Associate office declines to issue a letter ruling, the memorandum may constitute Chief Counsel Advice, as defined in § 6110(i)(1), subject to disclosure under § 6110.

(3) Refund of user fee. Ordinarily, the user fee will not be returned for a letter ruling request that is withdrawn. If the Associate office declines to issue a letter ruling on all of the issues in the request, the user fee will be returned. If the Associate office issues a letter ruling on some, but not all, of the issues, the user fee will not be returned. *See* section 15.10 of this revenue procedure for additional information regarding the refund of user fees.

SECTION 8. HOW DO THE ASSOCIATE OFFICES HANDLE LETTER RULING REQUESTS?

The Associate offices will issue letter rulings on the matters and under the circumstances explained in sections 3 and 5 of this revenue procedure and in the manner explained in this section and section 11 of this revenue procedure. *See* section 9 of this revenue procedure for procedures for change in accounting method requests.

Docket, Records, and User Fee Branch receives, initially controls and refers the request to the appropriate Associate office

.01 All requests for letter rulings will be received and initially controlled by the Docket, Records, and User Fee Branch of the Legal Processing Division of the Associate Chief Counsel (Procedure and Administration) (CC:PA:LPD:DRU). That office will process the incoming documents and the user fee, and will forward the file to the appropriate Associate office for assignment to a branch that has jurisdiction over the specific issue involved in the request.

Branch representative of the Associate office contacts taxpayer within 21 days

.02 Within 21 calendar days after a letter ruling request has been received in the branch of the Associate office that has jurisdiction over the issue, a representative of the branch will discuss the procedural issues in the letter ruling request with the taxpayer or, if the request includes a properly executed power of attorney, with the authorized representative unless the power of attorney provides otherwise. If the case is complex or a number of issues are involved, it may not be possible for the branch representative to discuss the substantive issues during this initial contact. When possible, for each issue within the branch's jurisdiction, the branch representative will tell the taxpayer—

(1) whether the branch representative will recommend that the Associate office rule as the taxpayer requested, rule adversely on the matter, or not rule;

(2) whether the taxpayer should submit additional information to enable the Associate office to rule on the matter;

(3) whether the letter ruling complies with all of the provisions of this revenue procedure, and if not, which requirements have not been met; or

(4) whether, because of the nature of the transaction or the issue presented, a tentative conclusion on the issue cannot be reached.

If the letter ruling request involves matters within the jurisdiction of more than one branch or Associate office, a representative of the branch that received the original request will tell the taxpayer within the initial 21 days—

(1) that the matters within the jurisdiction of another branch or Associate office have been referred to that branch or Associate office for consideration, and the date the referral was made, and

(2) that a representative of that branch or Associate office will contact the taxpayer within 21 calendar days after receiving the referral to discuss informally the procedural and, to the extent possible, the substantive issues in the request.

This section 8.02 applies to all matters except for cases involving a request for change in accounting method or accounting period and cases within the jurisdiction of the Associate Chief Counsel (Financial Institutions and Products) concerning insurance issues requiring actuarial computations.

Determines if transaction can be modified to obtain favorable letter ruling

.03 If less than a fully favorable letter ruling is indicated, the branch representative will tell the taxpayer whether minor changes in the transaction or adherence to certain published positions would bring about a favorable ruling. The branch representative may also tell the taxpayer the facts that must be furnished in a document to comply with Service requirements. The branch representative will not suggest precise changes that would materially alter the form of the proposed transaction or materially alter a taxpayer's proposed accounting period.

If, at the end of this discussion, the branch representative determines that a meeting in the Associate office would be more helpful to develop or exchange information, a meeting will be offered and an early meeting date arranged. When offered, this meeting is in addition to the taxpayer's conference of right that is described in section 10.02 of this revenue procedure.

Is not bound by informal opinion expressed

.04 The Service will not be bound by the informal opinion expressed by the branch representative or any other Service representative, and such an opinion cannot be relied upon as a basis for obtaining retroactive relief under the provisions of § 7805(b).

Additional information

.05

Must be submitted within 21 calendar days

(1) Additional information must be submitted within 21 days. If the request lacks essential information, which may include additional information needed to satisfy the procedural requirements of this revenue procedure as well as substantive changes to transactions or documents needed from the taxpayer, the branch representative will tell the taxpayer during the initial contact, or subsequent contacts, that the request will be closed if the Associate office does not receive the information within 21 calendar days from the date of the request for additional information, unless an extension of time is granted. To facilitate prompt action on letter ruling requests, taxpayers are encouraged to request that the Associate office request additional information by fax. *See* section 7.02(5) of this revenue procedure.

Material facts furnished to the Associate office by telephone or fax, or orally at a conference, must be promptly confirmed by letter to the Associate office. This confirmation and any additional information requested by the Associate office that is not part of the information requested during the initial contact must be furnished within 21 calendar days from the date the Associate office makes the request.

The Service will not endeavor to process a ruling request on the expedited basis for requests regarding reorganizations and distributions under section 355 provided by section 7.02(4) of this revenue procedure, unless the branch representative in Associate Chief Counsel (Corporate) receives all requested additional information within 10 calendar days from the date of the request for such additional information, unless an extension of time is granted. If the information is not provided within 10 calendar days (with any extension) but is provided within 21 calendar days (with any extension), the letter ruling request will cease to be processed on an expedited basis and instead will be processed in the usual manner.

Extension of reply period if justified and approved

(2) Extension of reply period. An extension of the 21-day period for providing additional information will be granted only if justified in writing by the taxpayer and approved by the branch reviewer. A request for extension should be submitted before the end of the 21-day period. If unusual circumstances close to the end of the 21-day period make a written request impractical, the taxpayer should notify the Associate office within the 21-day period that there is a problem and that the written request for extension will be coming soon. The taxpayer will be told promptly of the approval or denial of the requested extension. If the extension request is denied, there is no right of appeal.

Letter ruling request closed if the taxpayer does not submit additional information

(3) Letter ruling request closed if the taxpayer does not submit additional information. If the taxpayer does not submit the information requested during the initial contact, or subsequent contacts, within the time provided, the letter ruling request will be closed and the taxpayer will be notified in writing. **If the information is received after the request is closed, the request will be reopened and treated as a new request as of the date the information is received. The taxpayer must pay another user fee before the case can be reopened.**

Penalties of perjury statement for additional information

(4) Penalties of perjury statement. Additional information submitted to the Service must be accompanied by the following declaration: **"Under penalties of perjury, I declare that I have examined this information, including accompanying documents, and, to the best of my knowledge and belief, the information contains all the relevant facts relating to**

the request for the information, and such facts are true, correct, and complete." This declaration must be signed in accordance with the requirements in section 7.01(15)(b) of this revenue procedure.

Faxing request and additional information

(5) Faxing request and additional information. To facilitate prompt action on letter ruling requests, taxpayers are encouraged to request that the Associate office request additional information by fax. *See* section 7.02(5) of this revenue procedure. Taxpayers also are encouraged to submit additional information by fax as soon as the information is available. The Associate office representative who requests additional information can provide a telephone number to which the information can be faxed. The original of the faxed material and a signed perjury statement must be mailed or delivered to the Associate office.

Address to send additional information

(6) Address to send additional information.

(a) If a private delivery service is not used, the additional information should be sent to:

Internal Revenue Service
ADDITIONAL INFORMATION
Attn: [Name, office symbols, and
room number of the Associate office
representative who requested
the information]
P. O. Box 7604
Ben Franklin Station
Washington, DC 20044

For cases involving a request for change in accounting method or period under the jurisdiction of the Associate Chief Counsel (Income Tax and Accounting), or a § 301.9100 request for an extension of time on a request for change in accounting method or period, the additional information should be sent to:

Internal Revenue Service
ADDITIONAL INFORMATION
Attn: [Name, office symbols, and
room number of the Associate office
representative who requested
the information]
P. O. Box 14095
Ben Franklin Station
Washington, DC 20044

(b) If a private delivery service is used, the additional information for all cases should be sent to:

Internal Revenue Service
ADDITIONAL INFORMATION
Attn: [Name, office symbols, and
room number of the Associate office
representative who requested
the information]
1111 Constitution Ave., NW
Washington, DC 20224

Identifying information included in additional information

(7) Identifying information. For all cases, the additional information should include the name, office symbols, and room number of the Associate office representative who requested the information, and the taxpayer's name and the case control number, which the Associate office representative can provide.

Number of copies of additional information to be submitted

(8) Number of copies. Generally, a taxpayer needs only to submit one copy of the additional information, although in appropriate cases, the Associate office may request additional copies of the information.

Near the completion of the ruling process, advises the taxpayer of conclusions and, if the Associate office will rule adversely, offer the taxpayer the opportunity to withdraw the letter ruling request

.06 Generally, after the conference of right as discussed in section 10 of this revenue procedure is held but before the letter ruling is issued, the branch representative will orally inform the taxpayer or the taxpayer's representative of the Associate office's conclusions. If the Associate office is going to rule adversely, the taxpayer will be offered the opportunity to withdraw the letter ruling request. Unless an extension is granted, if the taxpayer or the taxpayer's representative does not notify the branch representative of a decision to withdraw the ruling request within 10 days of the notification, the adverse letter ruling will be issued. The user fee will not be refunded for a letter ruling request that is withdrawn. *See* section 15.10(1)(a) of this revenue procedure.

May request draft of proposed letter ruling near the completion of the ruling process

.07 To accelerate the issuance of letter rulings, in appropriate cases near the completion of the ruling process, the Associate office representative may request that the taxpayer or the taxpayer's representative submit a proposed draft of the letter ruling on the basis of discussions of the issues. The taxpayer is not required to prepare a draft letter ruling to receive a letter ruling.

The format of the submission should be discussed with the Associate office representative who requests the draft letter ruling. The representative usually can provide a sample format of a letter ruling and will discuss the facts, analysis, and letter ruling language to be included.

Taxpayer may also submit draft on a computer disk

In addition to a typed draft, taxpayers are encouraged to submit this draft on a computer disk in Microsoft Word to the Associate office. The typed draft will become part of the permanent files of the Associate office, and the computer disk will not be returned. The proposed letter ruling (both typed draft and computer disk) should be sent to the same address as any additional information and contain in the transmittal the information that should be included with any additional information (for example, a penalties of perjury statement is required). *See* section 8.05(4) of this revenue procedure.

Issues separate letter rulings for substantially identical letter rulings and generally issues a single letter ruling for related § 301.9100 letter

.08

(1) Substantially identical letter rulings. For letter ruling requests qualifying for the user fee provided in paragraph (A)(5)(a) of Appendix A of this revenue procedure for substantially identical letter rulings, a separate letter ruling generally will be issued for each entity with a common member or sponsor, or for each member of a common entity.

(2) Related § 301.9100 letter rulings. For a § 301.9100 letter ruling request for an extension of time to file Form 3115 requesting an identical accounting method change for multiple separate and distinct trades or businesses (including a qualified subchapter S subsidiary or a single-member limited liability company of a taxpayer, multiple members of a consolidated group, or multiple eligible CFCs qualifying under section 15.07(4) for the user fee provided in paragraph (A)(5)(d) of Appendix A of this revenue procedure, the Associate office generally will issue a single letter on behalf of all separate and distinct trades or businesses of the taxpayer, all members of the consolidated group, or all eligible CFCs that are the subject of the request.

Sends a copy of the letter ruling to appropriate Service official

.09 The Associate office will send a copy of the letter ruling, whether favorable or adverse, to the appropriate Service official in the operating division that has examination jurisdiction of the taxpayer's tax return.

SECTION 9. WHAT ARE THE SPECIFIC AND ADDITIONAL PROCEDURES FOR A REQUEST FOR A CHANGE IN ACCOUNTING METHOD FROM THE ASSOCIATE OFFICES?

This section provides the specific and additional procedures applicable to a request for a change in accounting method.

A request for a change in accounting method is a specialized type of request for a letter ruling. *See* section 2.01 of this revenue procedure.

Automatic and advance consent change in accounting method requests

.01

Automatic change in accounting method

(1) Procedures for requesting an automatic change in accounting method. Certain changes in accounting methods may be made under automatic change request procedures. A change in accounting method provided in an automatic change request procedure must be made using that automatic change request procedure if the taxpayer requesting the change is within the scope of the automatic change request procedure and the change is an automatic change for the requested year of the change. The Commissioner's consent to an otherwise qualifying automatic change in accounting method is granted only if the taxpayer timely complies with the applicable automatic change request procedures. *But see* section 9.19 of this revenue procedure concerning review by an Associate office and a field office.

See section 9.22 of this revenue procedure for a list of automatic change request procedures. *See also* section 9.23 of this revenue procedure for a list of sections, in addition to this section 9, and Appendices of this revenue procedure that apply to a request for an accounting method change. No user fee is required for a change made under an automatic change request procedure.

Advance consent change in accounting method

(2) Advance consent letter ruling requests. If a change in accounting method may not be made under an automatic change request procedure, the taxpayer may request an advance consent letter ruling by filing a current Form 3115, *Application for Change in Accounting Method*, under Rev. Proc. 97–27, 1997–1 C.B. 680, as modified and amplified by Rev. Proc. 2002–19, 2002–1 C.B. 696, and amplified and clarified by Rev. Proc. 2002–54, 2002–2 C.B. 432 (or successors); and this revenue procedure (see section 9.23 for a list of the sections and Appendices of this revenue procedure in addition to this section 9 that apply to a request for an accounting method change). A Form 3115 filed under Rev. Proc. 97–27 and this revenue procedure is hereinafter referred to as an "advance consent Form 3115." A taxpayer filing an advance consent Form 3115 must submit the required user fee with the completed Form 3115. *See* section 15 and Appendix A of this revenue procedure for information about user fees.

Ordinarily only one change in accounting method on a Form 3115 and a separate Form 3115 for each taxpayer and for each separate and distinct trade or business

.02

Ordinarily, a taxpayer may request only one change in accounting method on a Form 3115. If the taxpayer wants to request a change in accounting method for more than one unrelated item or submethod of accounting, the taxpayer must submit a separate Form 3115 for each unrelated item or submethod, except in certain situations in which the Service specifically permits certain unrelated changes to be included on a single Form 3115 (for example, *see* section 5.05 in the Appendix of Rev. Proc. 2002–9, 2002–1 C.B. 327, or its successor).

Further, a separate Form 3115 (and, therefore, a separate user fee pursuant to section 15 and Appendix A of this revenue procedure) must be submitted for each taxpayer and each separate trade or business of a taxpayer, including a qualified S subsidiary (QSUB) or a single-member limited liability company (single member LLC), requesting a change in accounting method, except as specifically permitted or required in guidance published by the Service. *See*, for example, section 15.07(4) of this revenue procedure.

Information required with a Form 3115

.03

Facts and other information

(1) Facts and other information requested on Form 3115 and in applicable revenue procedures. In general, a taxpayer requesting a change in accounting method must file a Form 3115, unless the procedures applicable to the specific type of change in accounting method do not require a Form 3115 to be submitted.

To be eligible for approval of the requested accounting method change, the taxpayer must provide all information requested on the Form 3115 and in its instructions and in either Rev. Proc. 97–27, 1997–1 C.B. 680, as modified and amplified by Rev. Proc. 2002–19, 2002–1 C.B. 696, and amplified and clarified by Rev. Proc. 2002–54, 2002–2 C.B. 432 (or successors) or the applicable automatic change request procedure. In addition, the taxpayer must provide all information requested in the applicable sections of this revenue procedure, including a detailed and complete description of the item being changed, the taxpayer's present and proposed method for the item being changed, information regarding whether the taxpayer is under examination, or before Appeals or a federal court, and a summary of the computation of the § 481(a) adjustment and an explanation of the methodology used to determine the adjustment.

For an advance consent Form 3115, the taxpayer must also include a full explanation of the legal basis and relevant authorities supporting the proposed method, a detailed and complete description of the facts and explanation of how the law applies to the taxpayer's situation, whether the law in connection with the request is uncertain or inadequately addresses the issue, statement of the applicant's reasons for the proposed change, and copies of all documents related to the proposed change.

The applicant must provide the requested information to be eligible for approval of the requested accounting method change. The taxpayer may be required to provide information specific to the requested accounting method change, such as an attached statement. The taxpayer must provide all information relevant to the requested accounting method change, even if not specifically requested by the Form 3115.

See also sections 7.01(1) and 7.01(8) of this revenue procedure.

Statement of authorities contrary to taxpayer's views

(2) Statement of contrary authorities. For an advance consent Form 3115, the taxpayer is encouraged to inform the Associate office about, and discuss the implications of, any authority believed to be contrary to the proposed change in accounting method, such as legislation, court decisions, regulations, notices, revenue rulings, revenue procedures, or announcements.

If the taxpayer does not furnish either contrary authorities or a statement that none exists, the Associate office may request submission of contrary authorities or a statement that none exists. Failure to comply with this request may result in the Associate office's refusal to issue a change in accounting method letter ruling.

Documents

(3) Copies of all contracts, agreements, and other documents. True copies of all contracts, agreements, and other documents pertinent to the requested change in accounting method must be submitted with an advance consent Form 3115. Original documents should not be submitted because they become part of the Associate office's file and will not be returned.

Analysis of material facts

(4) Analysis of material facts. When submitting any document with a Form 3115 or in a supplemental letter, the taxpayer must explain and provide an analysis of all material facts in the document (rather than merely incorporating the document by reference). The analysis of the facts must include their bearing on the requested change in accounting method, specifying the provisions that apply.

Same issue in an earlier return

(5) Information regarding whether same issue is in an earlier return. A Form 3115 must state whether, to the best of the knowledge of both the taxpayer and the taxpayer's representatives, any return of the taxpayer (or any return of a current or former consolidated group in which the taxpayer is or was a member) in which the taxpayer used the accounting method being changed is under examination, before Appeals, or before a federal court. *See* Rev. Proc. 97–27 and Rev. Proc. 2002–9, both as modified and amplified by Rev. Proc. 2002–19.

Issue previously submitted or currently pending

(6) Statement regarding prior requests for a change in accounting method and other pending requests.

(a) Other requests for a change in accounting method within the past five years. A Form 3115 must state, to the best of the knowledge of both the taxpayer and the taxpayer's representatives, whether the taxpayer (or a related taxpayer within the meaning of § 267 or a member of a current or former affiliated group of which the taxpayer is or was a member within the meaning of § 1504) or a predecessor requested or made within the past five years (including the year of the requested change), or is currently filing, any request for a change in accounting method.

If the statement is affirmative, for each separate and distinct trade or business, give a description of each request and the year of change and whether consent was obtained. If any application was withdrawn, not perfected, or denied, or if a Consent Agreement was sent to the taxpayer but was not signed and returned to the Associate office, or if the change was not made in the requested year of change, give an explanation.

(b) Any other pending request(s). A Form 3115 must state, to the best of the knowledge of both the taxpayer and the taxpayer's representatives, whether the taxpayer (or a related taxpayer within the meaning of § 267 or a member of a current or former affiliated group of which the taxpayer is or was a member within the meaning of § 1504) or a predecessor currently have pending (including any concurrently filed request) any request for a private letter ruling, a change in accounting method, or a technical advice.

If the statement is affirmative, for each request, give the name(s) of the taxpayer, identification number(s), the type of request (private letter ruling, request for change in accounting method, or request for technical advice), and the specific issues in the request.

Statement identifying pending legislation

(7) Statement identifying pending legislation. At the time the taxpayer files an advance consent Form 3115, the taxpayer must identify any pending legislation that may affect the proposed change in accounting method. In addition, if legislation is introduced after the request is filed but before a change in accounting method letter ruling is issued, the taxpayer must so notify the Associate office.

Authorized representatives

(8) Authorized representatives. To appear before the Service in connection with a request for a change in accounting method, the taxpayer's authorized representative must be an attorney, a certified public accountant, an enrolled agent, an enrolled actuary, a person with a "Letter of Authorization," an employee, general partner, *bona fide* officer, administrator, trustee, etc., as described in section 7.01(13) of this revenue procedure.

Power of attorney and declaration of representative

(9) Power of attorney and declaration of representative. Any authorized representative, whether or not enrolled to practice, must comply with Treasury Department Circular No. 230, which provides the rules for practice before the Service, and the conference and practice requirements of the Statement of Procedural Rules, which provide the rules for representing a taxpayer before the Service. *See* section 7.01(14) of this revenue procedure. It is preferred that Form 2848, *Power of Attorney and Declaration of Representative*, be used to provide the representative's authority.

Penalties of perjury statement

(10) Penalties of perjury statement.

(a) Format of penalties of perjury statement. A Form 3115, and any change to a Form 3115 submitted at a later time, must be accompanied by the following declaration: **"Under penalties of perjury, I declare that I have examined this application, including accompanying schedules and statements, and to the best of my knowledge and belief, the application contains all the relevant facts relating to the application, and it is true, correct, and complete."**

See section 9.08(3) of this revenue procedure for the penalties of perjury statement required for submissions of additional information.

(b) Signature by taxpayer. A Form 3115 must be signed by, or on behalf of, the taxpayer requesting the change by an individual with authority to bind the taxpayer in such matters. For example, an officer must sign on behalf of a corporation, a general partner on behalf of a state law partnership, a member-manager on behalf of a limited liability company, a trustee on behalf of a trust, or an individual taxpayer on behalf of a sole proprietorship. If the taxpayer is a member of a consolidated group, a Form 3115 should be submitted on behalf of the taxpayer by the common parent and must be signed by a duly authorized officer of the common parent.

Refer to the signature requirements set forth in the instructions for the current Form 3115 regarding those who are to sign. *See also* section 8.08 of Rev. Proc. 97–27 and section 6.02(5) of Rev. Proc. 2002–9. A stamped signature or faxed signature is not permitted.

(c) Signature by preparer. Declaration of preparer (other than the taxpayer) is based on all information of which the preparer has any knowledge.

Additional procedural information required in certain circumstances

.04

Recipients of original and copy of correspondence

(1) Recipients of original and copy of change in accounting method correspondence. The Service will send the signed original of the change in accounting method letter ruling and other related correspondence to the taxpayer, and copies to the taxpayer's representative, if instructed on Form 2848. *See* section 7.02(2) of this revenue procedure for how to designate alternative routing of the copies of the letter ruling and other correspondence.

Expedited handling

(2) To request expedited handling. The Associate offices ordinarily process advance consent Forms 3115 in order of the date received. A taxpayer who has a compelling need to have an advance consent Form 3115 processed on an expedited basis, may request expedited handling. *See* section 7.02(4) of this revenue procedure for procedures.

Facsimile transmission (fax) of any document to the taxpayer or taxpayer's authorized representative

(3) To receive the change in accounting method letter ruling or any other correspondence related to a Form 3115 by facsimile transmission (fax). If the taxpayer wants a copy of the change in accounting method letter ruling or any other correspondence related to a Form 3115, such as a request for additional information, faxed to the taxpayer or the taxpayer's authorized representative, the taxpayer must submit a written request to fax the letter ruling or related correspondence, preferably as part of the Form 3115. The request may be submitted at a later date, but must be received prior to the mailing of correspondence other than the letter ruling and prior to the signing of the change in accounting method letter ruling.

The request to have correspondence relating to the Form 3115 faxed to the taxpayer or taxpayer's authorized representative must contain the fax number of the taxpayer or the taxpayer's authorized representative to whom the correspondence is to be faxed.

A document other than the change in accounting method letter ruling will be faxed by a branch representative. The change in accounting method letter ruling may be faxed by either a branch representative or the Disclosure and Litigation Support Branch of the Legal Processing Division of the Office of Associate Chief Counsel (Procedure and Administration) (CC:PA:LPD:DLS).

For purposes of § 301.6110–2(h), a change in accounting method letter ruling is not issued until the change in accounting method letter ruling is mailed.

Requesting a conference

(4) To request a conference. The taxpayer must complete the appropriate line on the Form 3115 to request a conference of right, or request a conference in a later written communication, if an adverse response is contemplated by the Associate office. *See* section 8.10 of Rev. Proc. 97–27, section 10.03 of Rev. Proc. 2002–9, and sections 10.01, 10.02 of this revenue procedure.

Associate office address for Forms 3115

.05 Associate office address to send Forms 3115. Submit the original Form 3115, in the case of an advance consent Form 3115, or the national office copy of the Form 3115, in the case of an automatic change request, as follows:

(a) Associate office mailing address if private delivery service is not used. If a private delivery service is not used, a taxpayer, other than an exempt organization, must send the original completed Form 3115 and the required user fee (in the case of an advance consent Form 3115) or the national office copy of the completed Form 3115 (in the case of an automatic change request) to:

Internal Revenue Service
Attn: [insert either "CC:PA:LPD:DRU"
for an advance consent Form 3115 or
"CC:ITA — Automatic Ruling Branch"
for an automatic change request]
P.O. Box 7604
Benjamin Franklin Station
Washington, DC 20044

An exempt organization must send the original completed Form 3115 and the required user fee (in the case of an advance consent Form 3115) or the national office copy of the completed Form 3115 (in the case of an automatic change Form 3115) to:

Internal Revenue Service
Tax Exempt & Government Entities
Attn: TEGE:EO
P.O. Box 27720
McPherson Station
Washington, DC 20038

See Rev. Proc. 2007–8, this Bulletin, for the applicable user fee for exempt organization Forms 3115.

(b) Mailing address if private delivery service is used. If a private delivery service is used, a taxpayer, other than an exempt organization, must send the original completed Form 3115 and the required user fee (in the case of an advance consent Form 3115) or the national office copy of the completed Form 3115 (in the case of an automatic change request) to:

Internal Revenue Service
Attn: [insert either "CC:PA:LPD:DRU" for an
advance consent Form 3115 or
"CC:ITA—Automatic Rulings Branch" for an
automatic change request]
Room 5336
1111 Constitution Ave., NW
Washington, DC 20224

If a private delivery service is used, an exempt organization must send the original completed Form 3115 and the required user fee (in the case of an advance consent Form 3115) or the national office copy of the completed Form 3115 (in the case of an automatic change request) to:

Internal Revenue Service
Tax Exempt & Government Entities
Attn: TEGE:EO
1750 Pennsylvania Ave., NW
Washington, DC 20038

See Rev. Proc. 2007–8, this Bulletin, for the applicable user fee for exempt organization Forms 3115.

(c) Address if hand-delivered to the IRS Courier's desk. For taxpayers other than an exempt organization, the original completed Form 3115 and the required user fee (in the case of an advance consent Form 3115) or the national office copy of the completed Form 3115 (in the case of an automatic change request), may be hand delivered between the hours of 8:00 a.m. and 4:00 p.m. to the courier's desk at the loading dock (located behind the 12th

Street security station) of 1111 Constitution Ave., NW, Washington, DC. A receipt will be given at the courier's desk. The package should be addressed to:

Courier's Desk
Internal Revenue Service
Attn: CC:PA:LPD:DRU, Room 5336
1111 Constitution Ave., NW
Washington, DC 20224

A Form 3115 must not be submitted by fax

.06 A completed Form 3115 must not be submitted by fax.

Controls Form 3115 and refers it to the appropriate Associate office

.07 An advance consent Form 3115 is received and controlled by the Docket, Records, and User Fee Branch, Legal Processing Division of the Associate Chief Counsel (Procedure and Administration) (CC:PA:LPD:DRU) if the required user fee is submitted with the Form 3115. Once controlled, the Form 3115 is forwarded to the appropriate Associate office for assignment and processing.

Additional information

.08

Incomplete Form 3115

(1) Incomplete Form 3115.

(a) Advance consent Form 3115 — 21-day rule. In general, for an advance consent Form 3115, additional information requested by the Associate office and additional information furnished to the Associate office by telephone or fax must be furnished in writing within 21 calendar days from the date of the information request. The Associate office may impose a shorter reply period for a request for additional information made after an initial request. *See* section 10.06 of this revenue procedure for the 21-day rule for submitting information after any conference.

(b) Automatic change request — 30-day rule. In general, for an automatic change in accounting method request, additional information requested by the Associate office, and additional information furnished to the Associate office by telephone or fax, must be furnished in writing within 30 calendar days from the date of the information request. The Associate office may impose a shorter reply period for a request for additional information made after an initial request. *See* section 10.06 of this revenue procedure for the 21-day rule for submitting information after any conference with the Associate office.

Extension of reply period

(2) Request for extension of reply period.

(a) Advance consent Form 3115. For an advance consent Form 3115, an additional period, not to exceed 15 days, to furnish information may be granted to a taxpayer. Any request for an extension of time must be made in writing and submitted before the end of the original 21-day period. If unusual circumstances close to the end of the 21-day period make a written request impractical, the taxpayer should notify the Associate office within the 21-day period that there is a problem and that the written request for extension will be coming soon. An extension of the 21-day period will be granted only if approved by a branch reviewer. An extension of the 21-day period ordinarily will not be granted to furnish information requested on Form 3115. The taxpayer will be told promptly, and later in writing, of the approval or denial of the requested extension. If the extension request is denied, there is no right of appeal.

(b) Automatic change request. For an automatic change in accounting method request, an additional period, not to exceed 30 days, to furnish information may be granted to a taxpayer. Any request for an extension of time must be made in writing and submitted before the end of the original 30-day period. If unusual circumstances close to the end of the 30-day period make a written request impractical, the taxpayer should notify the Associate office within the 30-day period that there is a problem and that the written request for extension will be coming soon. An extension of the 30-day period will be granted only if approved by a branch reviewer. An extension of the 30-day period ordinarily will not be granted to furnish information requested on Form 3115. The taxpayer will be told promptly, and later in writing, of the approval or denial of the requested extension. If the extension request is denied, there is no right of appeal.

Penalties of perjury statement for additional information

(3) Penalties of perjury statement. Additional information submitted to the Associate office must be accompanied by the following declaration: **"Under penalties of perjury, I declare that I have examined this information, including accompanying documents, and, to the best of my knowledge and belief, the information contains all the relevant facts relating to the request for the information, and such facts are true, correct, and complete."** This declaration must be signed in accordance with the requirements in section 9.03(10)(b) of this revenue procedure.

Identifying information included in additional information

(4) Identifying information. The additional information should also include the name, office symbols, and room number of the Associate office representative who requested the information, and the taxpayer's name and the case control number, which the Associate office representative can provide.

Faxing information request and additional information

(5) Faxing information request and additional information. To facilitate prompt action on a change in accounting method ruling request, taxpayers are encouraged to request that the Associate office request additional information by fax. *See* section 9.04(3) of this revenue procedure.

Taxpayers also are encouraged to submit additional information by fax as soon as the information is available. The Associate office representative who requests additional information can provide a telephone number to which the information can be faxed. A copy of the requested information and an original signed penalties of perjury statement also must be mailed or delivered to the Associate office.

Address to send additional information

(6) Address to send additional information.

(a) Address if private delivery service not used. For a request for change in accounting method under the jurisdiction of the Associate Chief Counsel (Income Tax and Accounting), if a private delivery service is not used, the additional information should be sent to:

Internal Revenue Service
ADDITIONAL INFORMATION
Attn: [Name, office symbols, and
room number of the Associate office
representative who requested
the information]
P.O. Box 14095
Ben Franklin Station
Washington, DC 20044

For a request for change in accounting method for an exempt organization, if a private delivery service is not used, the additional information should be sent to:

Internal Revenue Service
Tax Exempt & Governmental Entities
P.O. Box 27720
McPherson Station
Washington, DC 20038

For any other request for change in accounting method, if a private delivery service is not used, the additional information should be sent to:

Internal Revenue Service
ADDITIONAL INFORMATION
Attn: [Name, office symbols, and
room number of the Associate office
representative who requested
the information]
P.O. Box 7604
Ben Franklin Station
Washington, DC 20044

(b) Address if private delivery service is used.

For a request for a change in accounting method for other than an exempt organization, if a private delivery service is used, the additional information should be sent to:

Internal Revenue Service
ADDITIONAL INFORMATION
Attn: [Name, office symbols, and
room number of the Associate office
representative who requested
the information]
1111 Constitution Ave., NW
Washington, DC 20224

For a request for change in accounting method for an exempt organization, if a private delivery service is used the additional information should be sent to:

Internal Revenue Service
Tax Exempt & Governmental Entities
1750 Pennsylvania Ave., NW
Washington, DC 20038

Failure to timely submit additional information

(7) If taxpayer does not timely submit additional information.

(a) Advance consent Form 3115. In the case of an advance consent Form 3115, if the required information is not furnished to the Associate office within the reply period, the Form 3115 will not be processed and the case will be closed. The taxpayer or authorized representative will be so notified in writing.

(b) Automatic change request. In the case of an automatic change in accounting method request, if the required information is not furnished to the Associate office within the reply period, the request does not qualify for the automatic consent procedure. In such a case, the Associate office will notify the taxpayer that consent to make the change in accounting method is not granted.

(c) Submitting the additional information at a later date. If the taxpayer wants to submit the additional information at a later date, the taxpayer must submit it with a new completed Form 3115 (and user fee, if applicable) for a year of change for which such new Form 3115 is timely filed under the applicable change in accounting method procedure.

Circumstances in which the taxpayer must notify the Associate office

.09

For an advance consent Form 3115, the taxpayer must promptly notify the Associate office if, after the Form 3115 is filed but before a change in accounting method letter ruling is issued, the taxpayer knows that—

(1) an examination of the present or proposed accounting method has been started by a field office;

(2) an examination of the proposed year of change has been started by a field office;

(3) legislation that may affect the change in accounting method has been introduced, *see* section 9.03(7) of this revenue procedure; or

(4) another letter ruling request (including another Form 3115) has been submitted by the taxpayer (or a related party within the meaning of § 267 or a member of an affiliated group of which the taxpayer is a member within the meaning of §1504).

Determines if proposed accounting method can be modified to obtain favorable letter ruling

.10 If a less than fully favorable change in accounting method letter ruling is indicated, the branch representative will tell the taxpayer whether minor changes in the proposed accounting method would bring about a favorable ruling. The branch representative will not suggest precise changes that materially alter a taxpayer's proposed accounting.

Near the completion of processing the Form 3115, advises the taxpayer if the Associate office will rule adversely and offers the taxpayer the opportunity to withdraw Form 3115

.11 Generally, after the conference of right is held (or offered, in the event no conference is held) and before issuing any change in accounting method letter ruling that is adverse to the requested change in accounting method, the taxpayer will be offered the opportunity to withdraw the Form 3115. *See* section 9.12 of this revenue procedure. Unless an extension is granted, if the taxpayer or the taxpayer's representative does not notify the branch representative of a decision to withdraw the Form 3115 within 10 days of the notification, the adverse change in accounting method letter ruling will be issued. Ordinarily, the user fee (in the case of an advance consent Form 3115) will not be refunded for a Form 3115 that is withdrawn.

Advance consent Form 3115 may be withdrawn or Associate office may decline to issue a change in accounting method letter ruling

.12

(1) In general. A taxpayer may withdraw an advance consent Form 3115 at any time before the change in accounting method letter ruling is signed by the Associate office. The Form 3115, correspondence, and any documents relating to the Form 3115 that is withdrawn or for which the Associate office declines to issue a letter ruling will not be returned to the taxpayer. *See* section 9.03(3) of this revenue procedure. In appropriate cases, the Service may publish its conclusions in a revenue ruling or revenue procedure.

(2) Notification of appropriate Service official. If a taxpayer withdraws or the Associate office declines to grant (for any reason) a request to change from or to an improper accounting method, the Associate office will notify, in writing, the appropriate Service official in the operating division that has examination jurisdiction of the taxpayer's tax return and the Change in Method of Accounting Technical Advisor, and may give its views on the issues in the request to the Service official to consider in any later examination of the return.

If the memorandum to the Service official provides more than the fact that the request was withdrawn and the Associate office was tentatively adverse, or that the Associate office declines to grant a change in accounting method, the memorandum may constitute Chief Counsel Advice, as defined in § 6110(i)(1), subject to disclosure under § 6110.

(3) Refund of user fee. Ordinarily, the user fee will not be returned for an advance consent Form 3115 that is withdrawn. *See* section 15.10 of this revenue procedure for information regarding refunds of user fees.

How to check status of a pending Form 3115

.13 The taxpayer or the taxpayer's authorized representative may obtain information regarding the status of an advance consent Form 3115 by calling the person whose name and telephone number are shown on the acknowledgement of receipt of the Form 3115.

Is not bound by informal opinion expressed

.14 The Service will not be bound by any informal opinion expressed by the branch representative or any other Service representative, and such an opinion cannot be relied upon as a basis for obtaining retroactive relief under the provisions of § 7805(b).

Single letter ruling issued to a taxpayer or consolidated group for qualifying identical change in accounting method

.15 For an advance consent Form 3115 qualifying under section 15.07(4) for the user fee provided in paragraph (A)(5)(b) of Appendix A of this revenue procedure for identical accounting method changes, the Associate office generally will issue a single letter ruling on behalf of all affected separate and distinct trades or businesses of a taxpayer, all affected members of the consolidated group, or all eligible and affected CFCs.

Letter ruling ordinarily not issued for one of two or more interrelated items or submethods

.16 If two or more items or submethods of accounting are interrelated, the Associate office ordinarily will not issue a letter ruling on a change in accounting method involving only one of the items or submethods.

Consent Agreement

.17 Ordinarily, for an advance consent Form 3115, the Commissioner's permission to change a taxpayer's accounting method is set forth in a letter ruling (original and a Consent Agreement copy). If the taxpayer agrees to the terms and conditions contained in the change in accounting method letter ruling, the taxpayer must sign and date the Consent Agreement copy of the letter ruling in the appropriate space. The Consent Agreement copy must not be signed by the taxpayer's representative. The signed copy of the letter ruling will constitute an agreement (Consent Agreement) within the meaning of § 1.481–4(b) of the regulations. The signed Consent Agreement copy of the letter ruling must be returned to the Associate office within 45 days. In addition, a photocopy of the signed Consent Agreement copy of the letter ruling must be attached to the taxpayer's income tax return for the year of change. *See* section 8.11 of Rev. Proc. 97–27. If the taxpayer has filed its income tax return for the year of change before the ruling has been received and the Consent Agreement has been signed and returned, the photocopy of the signed Consent Agreement copy of the letter ruling should be attached to the amended return for the year of change that the taxpayer files to implement the change in accounting method.

A taxpayer must secure the consent of the Commissioner before changing a method of accounting for federal income tax purposes. Treas. Reg. section 1.446–1(e)(2)(i). For an advance consent accounting method change, a taxpayer has secured the consent of the Commissioner when it timely signs and returns the Consent Agreement copy of the letter ruling from the Associate office granting permission to make the accounting method change. A taxpayer that timely files an advance consent accounting method change request and takes the change into account in its federal income tax return for the year of change (and any subsequent tax year) prior to receiving the letter ruling granting permission for the requested change, may nevertheless rely on the letter ruling received from the Associate office after it is received, as provided in section 9.19 of this revenue procedure. If, however, the requested change is modified or is withdrawn, denied, or similarly closed without the Associate office having granted consent, taxpayers are not relieved of any interest, penalties, or other adjustments resulting from the improper implementation of the change.

A copy of the change in accounting method letter ruling is sent to appropriate Service official

.18 The Associate office will send a copy of each change in accounting method letter ruling, whether favorable or adverse, to the appropriate Service official in the operating division that has examination jurisdiction of the taxpayer's tax return.

Consent to change an accounting method may be relied on subject to limitations

.19 A taxpayer may rely on a change in accounting method letter ruling received from the Associate office, subject to certain conditions and limitations. *See* sections 9, 10, and 11 of Rev. Proc. 97–27, as modified and amplified by Rev. Proc. 2002–19.

A qualifying taxpayer complying timely with an automatic change request procedure may rely on the consent of the Commissioner as provided in the automatic change request procedure to change the taxpayer's accounting method, subject to certain conditions and limitations. *See*, in general, sections 6.01, 7 and 8 of Rev. Proc. 2002–9, as modified and amplified by Rev. Proc. 2002–19. An Associate office may review a Form 3115 filed under an automatic change request procedure and will notify the taxpayer if additional information is needed or if consent is not granted to the taxpayer for the requested change. *See* section 10 of Rev. Proc. 2002–9. Further, the field office that has jurisdiction over the taxpayer's return may review the Form 3115. *See* section 9 of Rev. Proc. 2002–9.

Change in accounting method letter ruling will not apply to another taxpayer

.20 A taxpayer may not rely on a change in accounting method letter ruling issued to another taxpayer. *See* § 6110(k)(3).

Associate office discretion to permit requested change in accounting method

.21 The Associate office reserves the right to decline to process any advance consent Form 3115 in situations in which it would not be in the best interest of sound tax administration to permit the requested change. In this regard, the Associate office will consider whether the change in method of accounting would clearly and directly frustrate compliance efforts of the Service in administering the income tax laws. *See* section 8.01 of Rev. Proc. 97–27.

List of automatic change in accounting method request procedures

.22 For procedures regarding requests for an automatic change in accounting method, refer to the following published automatic change request procedures. The Commissioner's consent to an otherwise qualifying automatic change in accounting method is granted only if the taxpayer complies timely with the applicable automatic change request procedure.

The automatic change request procedures for obtaining a change in accounting method include:

(1) Rev. Proc. 2002–9, 2002–1 C.B. 327, as modified and clarified by Announcement 2002–17, 2002–1 C.B. 561, as modified and amplified by Rev. Proc. 2002–19, 2002–1 C.B. 696, as amplified, clarified and modified by Rev. Proc. 2002–54, 2002–2 C.B. 432, and as modified by Rev. Proc. 2003–45, 2003–2 C.B. 11, which, for most (but not all) types of changes provided therein, requires a completed Form 3115. Rev. Proc. 2002–9 applies to the accounting method changes described in the Appendix of Rev. Proc. 2002–9 involving §§ 56, 61, 77, 162, 166, 167, 168, 171, 174, 179B, 181, 197, 263, 263A, 267, 404, 446, 448, 451, 454, 455, 458, 460, 461, 471, 472, 475, 585, 832, 846, 861, 985, 1272, 1273, 1278, 1281, 1286, 1400I, 1400L, 1400N, and former § 168.

(2) The following automatic change request procedures modify and amplify Rev. Proc. 2002–9 in that they add the following changes to the list of accounting method changes listed in the Appendix of Rev. Proc. 2002–9 or require certain automatic changes to be made using the provisions of Rev. Proc. 2002–9:

Rev. Rul. 2004–62, 2004–1 C.B. 1072 (section 162 — post-establishment fertilization of established timber stands);

Notice 2006–47, 2006–20 I.R.B. 892 (section 167(g) — for property subject to the income forecast method and placed in service by the taxpayer after October 22, 2004, an election either to include in the adjusted basis of the property participations and residuals expected to be paid before the end of the tenth taxable year following the placed-in-service year of the property, or to exclude participations and residuals from the adjusted basis of the property and deduct the participations and residuals in the taxable year in which paid);

Rev. Proc. 2002–27, 2002–1 C.B. 802 (section 168 — depreciation of original and replacement tires of certain vehicles);

Rev. Rul. 2003–54, 2003–1 C.B. 982 (section 168 — depreciation of gas pump canopies);

Rev. Rul. 2003–81, 2003–2 C.B. 126 (section 168 — depreciation of utility assets);

Rev. Proc. 2003–63, 2003–2 C.B. 304 (section 168 — depreciation of cable TV fiber optics);

Regs. § 1.168(i)–1(l)(2)(ii) (change in general asset account treatment due to a change in the use of MACRS property);

Regs. § 1.168(i)–4(g)(2) (change in method of accounting for depreciation due to a change in the use of MACRS property);

Regs. § 1.168(i)–6T(k)(2) (for a like-kind exchange or involuntary conversion of MACRS property for which the time of disposition, the time of replacement, or both, occurred on or before February 27, 2004, change in method of accounting for depreciation for relinquished MACRS property and replacement MACRS property);

Rev. Proc. 2004–11, 2004–1 C.B. 311, (or its successor) (sections 56(a)(1), 56(g)(4)(A), 167, 168, 197, 1400I, and 1400L — revised sections 2.01 and 2.02 and 2B of the Appendix and added section 2.05 to the Appendix of Rev. Proc. 2002–9);

Rev. Proc. 2006–43, 2006–45 I.R.B. 849 (sections 168(k) and 1400L(b) — change in method of accounting to comply with the final regulations under § 1.168(k)–1 or § 1.1400L(b)–1);

Notice 2006–47, 2006–20 I.R.B. 892 (section 179B — election by a small business refiner to deduct 75 percent of qualified capital costs paid or incurred after December 31, 2002, in taxable years ending after that date);

Notice 2006–47, 2006–20 I.R.B. 892 (section 181 — for any qualified film or television production for which the taxpayer begins principal photography after October 22, 2004, but first paid or incurred costs of the production before October 23, 2004, election to treat the costs of the production as an expense);

Rev. Proc. 2005–9, 2005–1 C.B. 303, as modified by Rev. Proc. 2005–17, 2005–1 C.B. 797 (section 263 — amounts paid or incurred to acquire or create intangibles or to facilitate an acquisition of a trade or business, change in the capital structure of a business entity, and certain other transactions, for a taxpayer's second taxable year ending on or after December 31, 2003);

Rev. Rul. 2002–9, 2002–1 C.B. 614 (section 263A — impact fees incurred in connection with construction of a new residential rental building);

Rev. Rul. 2004–18, 2004–1 C.B. 509 (section 263A — environmental remediation costs);

Rev. Rul. 2005–42, 2005–2 C.B. 67 (section 263A — allocation of environmental remediation costs to production);

Regs. § 1.263A–1T(k)(1) (section 263A — change in method of accounting for mixed service costs to comply with the temporary regulations);

Regs. § 1.263A–2T(e)(1) (section 263A — change in method of accounting for additional section 263A costs to comply with the temporary regulations); Rev. Proc. 2004–11, 2004–1 C.B. 311, (or its successor) (sections 56(a)(1), 56(g)(4)(A), 167, 168, 197, 1400I, and 1400L, and former section 168 – replaced sections 2.01 and 2.02 and 2B of the Appendix of Rev. Proc. 2002–9 and added section 2.05 to the Appendix of Rev. Proc 2002–9);

Regs. § 1.280F–6(f)(2)(iv) (for certain qualified nonpersonal use vehicles placed in service before July 7, 2003, exclusion from limits on depreciation applicable to passenger automobiles);

Rev. Rul. 2002–46, 2002–2 C.B. 117, as modified by Rev. Rul. 2002–73, 2002–2 C.B. 805 (section 404 — grace period contributions);

Rev. Proc. 2002–28, 2002–1 C.B. 815 (section 446 — certain small businesses who seek to change to the cash method and/or to a method of accounting for inventoriable items as materials and supplies that are not incidental);

Rev. Proc. 2004–30, 2004–1 C.B. 950 (section 446 — inducement fees received in connection with becoming holders of noneconomic residual interests in Real Estate Mortgage Investment Conduits);

Rev. Proc. 2004–32, 2004–1 C.B. 988 (section 446 — credit card annual fees);

Rev. Proc. 2004–36, 2004–1 C.B. 1063 (section 446 — safe harbor method of accounting for film producers' treatment of certain creative property costs);

Rev. Proc. 2002–36, 2002–1 C.B. 993 (section 451 — certain taxpayers who purchase vehicles subject to leases who seek to change to the capital cost reduction (CCR) method);

Rev. Rul. 2003–3, 2003–1 C.B. 252 (section 451 — accrual method taxpayer with state or local income or franchise tax refund);

Rev. Proc. 2004–34, 2004–1 C.B. 991 (section 451 — certain advance payments);

Rev. Proc. 2005–35, 2005–2 C.B. 76 (section 451 — up-front network upgrade payments made to utilities);

Rev. Proc. 2002–17, 2002–1 C.B. 676 (section 472 — certain automobile dealers seeking to change to the replacement cost method for vehicle parts inventory);

Rev. Proc. 2003–20, 2003–1 C.B. 445 (section 471 — valuation of remanufactured motor vehicle core parts);

Rev. Proc. 2006–14, 2006–4 I.R.B. 350 (sections 471, 472, and 481 — change in method of accounting to adopt safe harbor method of accounting for heavy equipment parts inventory)

Rev. Proc. 2002–46, 2002–2 C.B. 105 (section 832 — certain insurance companies seeking to change to safe harbor method for premium acquisition expenses);

Rev. Proc. 2004–41, 2004–2 C.B. 90 (section 832 — insurance companies' incentive payments to health care providers);

Rev. Proc. 2002–74, 2002–2 C.B. 980 (section 846 — insurance companies other than life insurance companies computing discounted unpaid losses);

Rev. Proc. 2004–33, 2004–1 C.B. 989 (section 1272 — credit card late fees);

Rev. Proc. 2005–47, 2005–2 C.B. 269 (section 1273 — credit card cash advance fees);

Rev. Proc. 2006–16, 2006–9 I.R.B. 539 (section 1400I — election of commercial revitalization deduction for a qualified revitalization building that is placed in service by the taxpayer after December 31, 2001, in the area of a renewal community that was expanded by the U.S. Department of Housing and Urban Development and for which the taxpayer receives a retroactive commercial revitalization expenditure allocation);

Rev. Proc. 2005–43, 2005–2 C.B. 107 (section 1400L(c) — retroactive election to use the 5-year recovery period (or 9-year recovery period, if applicable) for qualified New York Liberty Zone leasehold improvement property placed in service after September 10, 2001, during the 2000, 2001, 2002, 2003, or 2004 taxable year); and

Notice 2006–77, 2006–40 I.R.B. 590 (section 1400N(d) — to claim the Gulf Opportunity (GO) Zone additional first year depreciation deduction for qualified GO Zone property that is placed in service by the taxpayer on or after August 28, 2005, during the taxable year beginning in 2004 or 2005, and is in a class of property for which the taxpayer did not claim the GO Zone additional first year depreciation deduction).

(3) The following automatic change request procedures, which require a completed Form 3115, provide both the type of accounting method change that may be made automatically and the procedures under which such change must be made:

Regs. § 1.166–2(d)(3) (bank conformity for bad debts);

Regs. § 1.448–1 (to an overall accrual method for the taxpayer's first taxable year it is subject to Code section 448);

Regs. § 1.448–2T and Notice 88–51 (nonaccrual experience method);

Regs. § 1.458–1 and –2 (exclusion for certain returned magazines, paperbacks, or records);

Rev. Proc. 97–43, 1997–2 C.B. 494 (section 475 — electing out of certain exemptions from securities dealer status); and

Rev. Proc. 91–51, 1991–2 C.B. 779 (section 1286 — certain taxpayers under examination that sell mortgages and retain rights to service the mortgages).

(4) The following automatic change request procedures, which do not require a completed Form 3115, provide the type of accounting method change that may be made automatically and also provide the procedures under which such change must be made:

Notice 96–30, 1996–1 C.B. 378 (section 446 — change to comply with Statement of Financial Accounting Standards No. 116);

Rev. Proc. 92–29, 1992–1 C.B. 748 (section 461 — change in real estate developer's method for including costs of common improvements in the basis of property sold);

Rev. Proc. 98–58, 1998–2 C.B. 710 (certain taxpayers seeking to change to the installment method of accounting under § 453 for alternative minimum tax purposes for certain deferred payment sales contracts relating to property used or produced in the trade or business of farming);

Regs. § 1.472–2 (taxpayers changing to the last-in, first-out (LIFO) inventory method);

Code § 585(c) and Regs. §§ 1.585–6 and 1.585–7 (large bank changing from the reserve method of section 585); and

Rev. Proc. 92–67, 1992–2 C.B. 429 (election under § 1278(b) to include market discount in income currently or election under § 1276(b) to use constant interest rate to determine accrued market discount).

(5) *See* Appendix E for the list of revenue procedures for automatic changes in accounting period.

Other sections of this revenue procedure that are applicable to a Form 3115

.23 In addition to this section 9, the following sections of this revenue procedure are applicable to Forms 3115:

1 (purpose of Rev. Proc. 2007–1);

2.01 (definition of "letter ruling");

2.02 (definition of "closing agreement");

2.05 (oral guidance);

3.01 (issues under the jurisdiction of the Associate Chief Counsel (Corporate));

3.02 (issues under the jurisdiction of the Associate Chief Counsel (Financial Institutions and Products));

3.03 (issues under the jurisdiction of the Associate Chief Counsel (Income Tax and Accounting));

3.04 (issues under the jurisdiction of the Associate Chief Counsel (International));

3.05 (issues under the jurisdiction of the Associate Chief Counsel (Passthroughs and Special Industries))

3.07 (issues under the jurisdiction of the Associate Chief Counsel (Tax Exempt and Governmental Entities));

6.02 (letter rulings ordinarily not issued in certain areas because of the factual nature of the problem);

6.05 (letter rulings generally not issued to business associations or groups);

6.06 (letter rulings generally not issued where the request does not address the tax status, liability, or reporting obligations of the requester);

6.08 (letter rulings ordinarily not issued on federal tax consequences of proposed legislation);

6.10 (letter rulings not issued on frivolous issues);

6.12 (letter rulings not issued on alternative plans or hypothetical situation);

7.01(1) (statement of facts and other information);

7.01(8) (statement of supporting authorities);

7.01(13) (authorized representatives);

7.01(14) (power of attorney and declaration of representative);

7.02(2) (power of attorney used to indicate recipient of a copy or copies of a letter ruling or a determination letter);

7.02(4) (expedited handling);

7.04(2) (notify Associate office if a return, amended return, or claim for refund is filed while request is pending and attach request to the return);

7.05 (attach letter ruling to the return, amended return or claim for refund);

10 (scheduling conferences);

15 (user fees);

16 (significant changes to Rev. Proc. 2006–1);

17 (effect of Rev. Proc. 2007–1 on other documents);

18 (effective date of this revenue procedure);

Appendix A (schedule of user fees); and

Appendix E (revenue procedures and notices regarding letter ruling requests relating to specific Code sections and subject matters).

SECTION 10. HOW ARE CONFERENCES FOR LETTER RULINGS SCHEDULED?

Schedules a conference if requested by taxpayer

.01 A taxpayer may request a conference regarding a letter ruling request. Normally, a conference is scheduled only when the Associate office considers it to be helpful in deciding the case or when an adverse decision is indicated. If conferences are being arranged for more than one request for a letter ruling involving the same taxpayer, they will be scheduled so as to cause the least inconvenience to the taxpayer. As stated in sections 7.02(6) and 9.04(4) of this revenue procedure, a taxpayer who wants to have a conference on the issue or issues involved should indicate this in writing when, or soon after, filing the request.

If a conference has been requested, the taxpayer or the taxpayer's representative will be notified by telephone, if possible, of the time and place of the conference, which must then be held within 21 calendar days after this contact. Instructions for requesting an extension of the 21-day period and notifying the taxpayer or the taxpayer's representative of the Associate office's approval or denial of the request for extension are the same as those explained in section 8.05(2) (section 9.08(2)(a) for a change in accounting method request) of this revenue procedure regarding providing additional information.

Permits taxpayer one conference of right

.02 A taxpayer is entitled, as a matter of right, to only one conference in the Associate office, except as explained under section 10.05 of this revenue procedure. This conference is normally held at the branch level and is attended by a person who has the authority to sign the letter ruling in his or her own name or for the branch chief.

When more than one branch has taken an adverse position on an issue in a letter ruling request or when the position ultimately adopted by one branch will affect that adopted by another, a representative from each branch with the authority to sign in his or her own name or for the branch chief will attend the conference. If more than one subject is to be discussed at the conference, the discussion will constitute a conference on each subject.

To have a thorough and informed discussion of the issues, the conference usually will be held after the branch has had an opportunity to study the case. At the request of the taxpayer, the conference of right may be held earlier.

No taxpayer has a right to appeal the action of a branch to an Associate Chief Counsel or to any other official of the Service. *But see* section 10.05 of this revenue procedure for situations in which the Associate office may offer additional conferences.

In employment tax matters, only the party entitled to the letter ruling is entitled to a conference. *See* section 5.10 of this revenue procedure.

Disallows verbatim recording of conferences

.03 Because conference procedures are informal, no tape, stenographic, or other verbatim recording of a conference may be made by any party

Makes tentative recommendations on substantive issues

.04 The senior Associate office representative present at the conference ensures that the taxpayer has the opportunity to present views on all the issues in question. An Associate office representative explains the Associate office's tentative decision on the substantive issues and the reasons for that decision. If the taxpayer asks the Associate office to limit the retroactive effect of any letter ruling or limit the revocation or modification of a prior letter ruling, an Associate office representative will discuss the recommendation concerning this issue and the reasons for the recommendation. The Associate office representatives will not make a commitment regarding the conclusion that the Associate office will finally adopt.

May offer additional conferences

.05 The Associate office will offer the taxpayer an additional conference if, after the conference of right, an adverse holding is proposed, but on a new issue, or on the same issue but on different grounds from those discussed at the first conference. There is no right to another conference when a proposed holding is reversed at a higher level with a result less favorable to the taxpayer, if the grounds or arguments on which the reversal is based were discussed at the conference of right.

The limit on the number of conferences to which a taxpayer is entitled does not prevent the Associate office from offering additional conferences, including conferences with an official higher than the branch level, if the Associate office decides they are needed. These conferences are not offered as a matter of course simply because the branch has reached an adverse decision. In general, conferences with higher level officials are offered only if the Associate office determines that the case presents significant issues of tax policy or tax administration and that the consideration of these issues would be enhanced by additional conferences with the taxpayer.

Requires written confirmation of information presented at conference

.06 The taxpayer should furnish to the Associate office any additional data, reasoning, precedents, etc., that were proposed by the taxpayer and discussed at the conference but not previously or adequately presented in writing. The taxpayer must furnish the additional information within 21 calendar days from the date of the conference. If the additional information is not received within that time, a letter ruling will be issued on the basis of the information on hand or, if appropriate, no ruling will be issued. *See* section 8.05 of this revenue procedure for instructions on submission of additional information for a letter ruling request other than a change in accounting method request. *See* section 9.08 of this revenue procedure for instructions on submitting additional information for a change in accounting method request.

May schedule a pre-submission conference

.07 Sometimes it will be advantageous to both the Associate office and the taxpayer to hold a conference before the taxpayer submits the letter ruling request to discuss substantive or procedural issues relating to a proposed transaction. These conferences are held only if the identity of the taxpayer is provided to the Associate office, only if the taxpayer actually intends to make a request, only if the request involves a matter on which a letter ruling is ordinarily issued, and only at the discretion of the Associate office and as time permits. For example, a pre-submission conference will not be held on an income tax issue if, at the time the pre-submission conference is requested, the identical issue is involved in the taxpayer's return for an earlier period and that issue is being examined by a field office. *See* section 6.01(1) of this revenue procedure. A letter ruling request submitted following a pre-submission conference will not necessarily be assigned to the branch that held the pre-submission conference. Also, when a letter ruling request is not submitted following a pre-submission conference, the Associate office may notify, by memorandum, the appropriate Service official in the operating division that has examination jurisdiction of the taxpayer's tax return and may give its views on the issues raised during the pre-submission conference. This memorandum may constitute Chief Counsel Advice, as defined in § 6110(i), subject to disclosure under § 6110.

(1) Taxpayer may request a pre-submission conference in writing or by telephone. A taxpayer or the taxpayer's representative may request a pre-submission conference in writing or by telephone. If the taxpayer's representative is requesting the pre-submission conference, a power of attorney is required. It is preferred that Form 2848, *Power of Attorney and Declaration of Representative*, be used to provide the representative's authority. If multiple taxpayers and/or their authorized representatives will attend or participate in the pre-submission conference, cross powers of attorney (or tax information authorizations) are required. If the taxpayer's representative is requesting the pre-submission conference by telephone, the Associate office's representative (see list of phone numbers below) will provide the fax number to send the power of attorney prior to scheduling the pre-submission conference.

The request should identify the taxpayer and include a brief explanation of the primary issue so that an assignment to the appropriate branch can be made. If submitted in writing, the request should also identify the Associate office expected to have jurisdiction over the request for a letter ruling. A written request for a pre-submission conference should be sent to the appropriate address listed in section 7.03 of this revenue procedure.

To request a pre-submission conference by telephone, call:

(a) (202) 622–7700 (not a toll-free call) for matters under the jurisdiction of the Office of Associate Chief Counsel (Corporate);

(b) (202) 622–3900 (not a toll-free call) for matters under the jurisdiction of the Office of Associate Chief Counsel (Financial Institutions and Products);

(c) (202) 622–4800 (not a toll-free call) for matters under the jurisdiction of the Office of Associate Chief Counsel (Income Tax and Accounting);

(d) (202) 622–3800 (not a toll-free call) for matters under the jurisdiction of the Office of Associate Chief Counsel (International);

(e) (202) 622–3000 (not a toll-free call) for matters under the jurisdiction of the Office of Associate Chief Counsel (Passthroughs and Special Industries);

(f) (202) 622–3400 (not a toll-free call) for matters under the jurisdiction of the Office of Associate Chief Counsel (Procedure and Administration); or

(g) (202) 622–6000 (not a toll-free call) for matters under the jurisdiction of the Office of Division Counsel/Associate Chief Counsel (Tax Exempt and Government Entities).

(2) **Pre-submission conferences held in person or by telephone.** Depending on the circumstances, pre-submission conferences may be held in person at the Associate office or may be conducted by telephone.

(3) Certain information required to be submitted to the Associate office prior to the pre-submission conference. Generally, the taxpayer will be asked to provide, at least three business days before the scheduled pre-submission conference, a statement of whether the issue is an issue on which a letter ruling is ordinarily issued, a draft of the letter ruling request or other detailed written statement of the proposed transaction, issue, and legal analysis. If the taxpayer's authorized representative will attend or participate in the pre-submission conference, a power of attorney is required.

(4) Discussion of substantive issues is not binding on the Service. Any discussion of substantive issues at a pre-submission conference is advisory only, is not binding on the Service in general or on the Office of Chief Counsel in particular, and cannot be relied upon as a basis for obtaining retroactive relief under the provisions of § 7805(b).

May schedule a conference to be held by telephone

.08 Depending on the circumstances, conferences, including conferences of right and pre-submission conferences, may be held by telephone. This may occur, for example, when a taxpayer wants a conference of right but believes that the issue involved does not warrant incurring the expense of traveling to Washington, DC, or if it is believed that scheduling an in person conference of right will substantially delay the ruling process. If a taxpayer makes such a request, the branch reviewer will decide if it is appropriate in the particular case to hold a conference by telephone. If the request is approved, the taxpayer will be advised when to call the Associate office representatives (not a toll-free call).

SECTION 11. WHAT EFFECT WILL A LETTER RULING HAVE?

May be relied on subject to limitations

.01 A taxpayer ordinarily may rely on a letter ruling received from the Associate office subject to the conditions and limitations described in this section.

Will not apply to another taxpayer

.02 A taxpayer may not rely on a letter ruling issued to another taxpayer. *See* § 6110(k)(3).

Will be used by a field office in examining the taxpayer's return

.03 When determining a taxpayer's liability, the field office must ascertain whether—

(1) the conclusions stated in the letter ruling are properly reflected in the return;

(2) the representations upon which the letter ruling was based reflected an accurate statement of the controlling facts;

(3) the transaction was carried out substantially as proposed; and

(4) there has been any change in the law that applies to the period during which the transaction or continuing series of transactions were consummated.

If, when determining the liability, the field office finds that a letter ruling should be revoked or modified, the findings and recommendations of the field office will be forwarded through the appropriate Director to the Associate office for consideration before further action is taken by the field office. Otherwise, the letter ruling is to be applied by the field office in the determination of the taxpayer's liability. Appropriate coordination with the Associate office must be undertaken if any field office having jurisdiction over a return or other matter proposes to reach a conclusion contrary to a letter ruling previously issued to the taxpayer.

May be revoked or modified if found to be in error or there has been a change in law

.04 Unless it was part of a closing agreement as described in section 2.02 of this revenue procedure, a letter ruling found to be in error or not in accord with the current views of the Service may be revoked or modified. If a letter ruling is revoked or modified, the revocation or modification applies to all years open under the period of limitations unless the Service uses its discretionary authority under § 7805(b) to limit the retroactive effect of the revocation or modification.

A letter ruling may be revoked or modified by —

(1) a letter giving notice of revocation or modification to the taxpayer to whom the letter ruling was issued;

(2) the enactment of legislation or ratification of a tax treaty;

(3) a decision of the United States Supreme Court;

(4) the issuance of temporary or final regulations; or

(5) the issuance of a revenue ruling, revenue procedure, notice, or other statement published in the Internal Revenue Bulletin.

Consistent with these provisions, if a letter ruling relates to a continuing action or a series of actions, it ordinarily will be applied until any one of the events described above occurs or until it is specifically withdrawn.

Publication of a notice of proposed rulemaking will not affect the application of any letter ruling issued under this revenue procedure.

Where a letter ruling is revoked or modified by a letter to the taxpayer, the letter will state whether the revocation or modification is retroactive. Where a letter ruling is revoked or modified by the issuance of final or temporary regulations or by the publication of a revenue ruling, revenue procedure, notice or other statement in the Internal Revenue Bulletin, the document may contain a statement as to its retroactive effect on letter rulings.

Letter ruling revoked or modified based on material change in facts applied retroactively

.05 An Associate office will revoke or modify a letter ruling and apply the revocation retroactively to the taxpayer for whom the letter ruling was issued or to a taxpayer whose tax liability was directly involved in the letter ruling if—

(1) there has been a misstatement or omission of controlling facts; or

(2) the facts at the time of the transaction are materially different from the controlling facts on which the letter ruling was based; or

(3) if the transaction involves a continuing action or series of actions, the controlling facts change during the course of the transaction.

Not otherwise generally revoked or modified retroactively

.06 Where the revocation or modification of a letter ruling is for reasons other than a change in facts as described in section 11.05 of this revenue procedure, it will generally not be applied retroactively to the taxpayer for whom the letter ruling was issued or to a taxpayer whose tax liability was directly involved in the letter ruling provided that—

(1) there has been no change in the applicable law;

(2) the letter ruling was originally issued for a proposed transaction; and

(3) the taxpayer directly involved in the letter ruling acted in good faith in relying on the letter ruling, and revoking or modifying the letter ruling retroactively would be to the taxpayer's detriment. For example, the tax liability of each shareholder is directly involved in a letter ruling on the reorganization of a corporation. The shareholders' reliance on the letter ruling may, depending on all facts and circumstances, be in good faith. The tax liability of a member of an industry, however, is not directly involved in a letter ruling issued to another member of the same industry and, therefore, a nonretroactive revocation or modification of a letter ruling to one member of an industry will not extend to other members of the industry who have not received letter rulings. By the same reasoning, a tax practitioner may not extend to one client the nonretroactive application of a revocation or modification of a letter ruling previously issued to another client.

If a letter ruling is revoked or modified by a letter with retroactive effect, the letter will, except in fraud cases, state the grounds on which the letter ruling is being revoked or modified and explain the reasons why it is being revoked or modified retroactively.

Retroactive effect of revocation or modification applied to a particular transaction

.07 A letter ruling issued on a particular transaction represents a holding of the Service on that transaction only. It will not apply to a similar transaction in the same year or any other year. And, except in unusual circumstances, the application of that letter ruling to the transaction will not be affected by the later issuance of regulations (either temporary or final) if conditions (1) through (3) in section 11.06 of this revenue procedure are met.

If a letter ruling on a transaction is later found to be in error or no longer in accord with the position of the Service, it will not protect a similar transaction of the taxpayer in the same year or later year.

Retroactive effect of revocation or modification applied to a continuing action or series of actions

.08 If a letter ruling is issued covering a continuing action or series of actions and the letter ruling is later found to be in error or no longer in accord with the position of the Service, the appropriate Associate Chief Counsel or Division Counsel/Associate Chief Counsel ordinarily will limit the retroactive effect of the revocation or modification to a date that is not earlier than that on which the letter ruling is revoked or modified. For example, the retroactive effect of the revocation or modification of a letter ruling covering a continuing action or series of actions ordinarily would be limited in the following situations when the letter ruling is in error or no longer in accord with the position of the Service:

(1) A taxpayer received a letter ruling that certain payments are excludable from gross income for federal income tax purposes. The taxpayer ordinarily would be protected only for the payment received after the letter ruling was issued and before the revocation or modification of the letter ruling.

(2) A taxpayer rendered a service or provided a facility that is subject to the excise tax on services or facilities and, in relying on a letter ruling received, did not pass the tax on to the user of the service or the facility.

(3) An employer incurred liability under the Federal Insurance Contributions Act but, in relying on a letter ruling received, neither collected the employee tax nor paid the employee and employer taxes under the Federal Insurance Contributions Act. The retroactive effect would be limited for both the employer and employee tax. The limitation would be conditioned on the employer furnishing wage data, as may be required by § 31.6011(a)–1 of the Employment Tax Regulations.

Generally not retroactively revoked or modified if related to sale or lease subject to excise tax

.09 A letter ruling holding that the sale or lease of a particular article is subject to the manufacturer's excise tax or the retailer's excise tax may not retroactively revoke or modify an earlier letter ruling holding that the sale or lease of such an article was not taxable if the taxpayer to whom the letter ruling was issued, in relying on the earlier letter ruling, gave up possession or ownership of the article without passing the tax on to the customer. (Section 1108(b), Revenue Act of 1926.)

May be retroactively revoked or modified when transaction is entered into before the issuance of the letter ruling

.10 A taxpayer is not protected against retroactive revocation or modification of a letter ruling involving a transaction completed before the issuance of the letter ruling or involving a continuing action or series of actions occurring before the issuance of the letter ruling because the taxpayer did not enter into the transaction relying on a letter ruling.

Taxpayer may request that retroactivity be limited

.11 Under § 7805(b), the Service may prescribe any extent to which a revocation or modification of a letter ruling will be applied without retroactive effect.

A taxpayer to whom a letter ruling has been issued may request that the appropriate Associate Chief Counsel limit the retroactive effect of any revocation or modification of the letter ruling.

Format of request

(1) Request for relief under § 7805(b) must be made in required format.

A request to limit the retroactive effect of the revocation or modification of a letter ruling must be in the general form of, and meet the general requirements for, a letter ruling request. These requirements are given in section 7 of this revenue procedure. Specifically, the request must also—

(a) state that it is being made under § 7805(b);

(b) state the relief sought;

(c) explain the reasons and arguments in support of the relief requested (including a discussion of section 11.05 of this revenue procedure and the three items listed in section 11.06 of this revenue procedure and any other factors as they relate to the taxpayer's particular situation); and

(d) include any documents bearing on the request.

A request that the Service limit the retroactive effect of a revocation or modification of a letter ruling may be made in the form of a separate request for a letter ruling when, for example, a revenue ruling has the effect of modifying or revoking a letter ruling previously issued to the taxpayer or when the Service notifies the taxpayer of a change in position that will have the effect of revoking or modifying the letter ruling.

When notice is given by the field office during an examination of the taxpayer's return or by Appeals, during consideration of the taxpayer's return before Appeals, a request to limit retroactive effect must be made in the form of a request for technical advice as explained in section 14.02 of Rev. Proc. 2007–2, this Bulletin.

When germane to a pending letter ruling request, a request to limit the retroactive effect of a revocation or modification of a letter ruling may be made as part of the request for the letter ruling, either initially or at any time before the letter ruling is issued. When a letter ruling that concerns a continuing transaction is revoked or modified by, for example, a subsequent revenue ruling, a request to limit retroactive effect must be made before the examination of the return that contains the transaction that is the subject of the letter ruling request.

Request for conference

(2) Taxpayer may request a conference on application of § 7805(b).

A taxpayer who requests the application of § 7805(b) in a separate letter ruling request has the right to a conference in the Associate office as explained in sections 10.02, 10.04, and 10.05 of this revenue procedure. If the request is made initially as part of a pending letter ruling request or is made before the conference of right is held on the substantive issues, the § 7805(b) issue will be discussed at the taxpayer's one conference of right as explained in section 10.02 of this revenue procedure. If the request for the application of § 7805(b) relief is made as part of a pending letter ruling request after a conference has been held on the substantive issue and the Associate office determines that there is justification for having delayed the request, the taxpayer is entitled to one conference of right concerning the application of § 7805(b), with the conference limited to discussion of this issue only.

SECTION 12. UNDER WHAT CIRCUMSTANCES DO DIRECTORS ISSUE DETERMINATION LETTERS?

Directors issue determination letters only if the question presented is specifically answered by a statute, tax treaty, or regulations, a conclusion stated in a revenue ruling, or an opinion or court decision that represents the position of the Service.

Under no circumstances will a Director issue a determination letter unless it is clearly shown that the request concerns a return that has been filed or is required to be filed and over which the Director has, or will have, examination jurisdiction.

A determination letter does not include assistance provided by the U.S. competent authority pursuant to the mutual agreement procedure in tax treaties as set forth in Rev. Proc. 2006–54, 2006–49 I.R.B. 1035.

In income and gift tax matters

.01 In income and gift tax matters, Directors issue determination letters in response to taxpayers' written requests on completed transactions that affect returns over which they have examination jurisdiction. A determination letter usually is not issued for a question concerning a return to be filed by the taxpayer if the same question is involved in a return already filed.

Normally, Directors do not issue determination letters on the tax consequences of proposed transactions. A Director may issue a determination letter on the replacement, even though not yet made, of involuntarily converted property under § 1033, if the taxpayer has filed an income tax return for the year in which the property was involuntarily converted.

In estate tax matters

.02 In estate tax matters, Directors issue determination letters in response to written requests affecting the estate tax returns over which they have examination jurisdiction. They do not issue determination letters on matters concerning the application of the estate tax to the prospective estate of a living person.

In generation-skipping transfer tax matters

.03 In generation-skipping transfer tax matters, Directors issue determination letters in response to written requests affecting the generation-skipping transfer tax returns over which they have examination jurisdiction. They do not issue determination letters on matters concerning the application of the generation-skipping transfer tax before the distribution or termination takes place.

In employment and excise tax matters

.04 In employment and excise tax matters, Directors issue determination letters in response to taxpayers' written requests on completed transactions over which they have examination jurisdiction. *See also* section 5.10 of this revenue procedure.

Requests concerning income, estate, or gift tax returns

.05 A request received by a Director on a question concerning an income, estate, or gift tax return already filed generally will be considered in connection with the examination of the return. If a response is made to the request before the return is examined, it will be considered a tentative finding in any later examination of that return.

Attach a copy of determination letter to taxpayer's return

.06 A taxpayer who, before filing a return, receives a determination letter about any transaction that has been consummated and that is relevant to the return being filed should attach a copy of the determination letter to the return when it is filed.

Review of determination letters

.07 Determination letters issued under sections 12.01 through 12.04 of this revenue procedure are not reviewed by the Associate offices before they are issued. If a taxpayer believes that a determination letter of this type is in error, the taxpayer may ask the Director to reconsider the matter or to request technical advice from an Associate office as explained in Rev. Proc. 2007–2, this Bulletin.

Addresses to send determination letter requests

.08 (a) For taxpayers under the jurisdiction of LMSB, send a request for a determination letter to the following address:

Internal Revenue Service
Attn: Manager, Office of Pre-Filing and Technical Services
Large and Mid-Size Business Division
SE:LM:PFT:PFTS
Mint Building, 3rd Floor
1111 Constitution Ave., NW
Washington, DC 20224

(b) SB/SE and W&I taxpayers should send requests for determination letters to the appropriate SB/SE office listed in Appendix D.

(c) For a determination letter under the jurisdiction of the Commissioner, Tax Exempt and Government Entities Division, *see* Rev. Proc. 2007–4, this Bulletin.

(d) For fees required with determination letter requests, *see* section 15 and Appendix A of this revenue procedure.

SECTION 13. WHAT EFFECT WILL A DETERMINATION LETTER HAVE?

Has same effect as a letter ruling

.01 A determination letter issued by a Director has the same effect as a letter ruling issued to a taxpayer under section 11 of this revenue procedure.

If a field office proposes to reach a conclusion contrary to that expressed in a determination letter, that office need not refer the matter to the Associate office as is required for a letter ruling found to be in error. The field office must, however, refer the matter to the Associate office through the appropriate Director, if it desires to have the revocation or modification of the determination letter limited under § 7805(b).

Taxpayer may request that retroactive effect of revocation or modification be limited

.02 Under § 7805(b), the Service may prescribe the extent to which a revocation or modification of a determination letter will be applied without retroactive effect. A Director does not have authority under § 7805(b) to limit the revocation or modification of the determination letter. Therefore, if the field office proposes to revoke or modify a determination letter, the taxpayer may request limitation of the retroactive effect of the revocation or modification by asking the Director that issued the determination letter to seek technical advice from the Associate office. *See* section 14.02 of Rev. Proc. 2007–2, this Bulletin.

Format of request

(1) Request for relief under § 7805(b) must be made in required format.

A taxpayer's request to limit the retroactive effect of the revocation or modification of the determination letter must be in the form of, and meet the general requirements for, a technical advice request. *See* section 14.02 of Rev. Proc. 2007–2, this Bulletin. The request must also—

(a) state that it is being made under § 7805(b);

(b) state the relief sought;

(c) explain the reasons and arguments in support of the relief sought (including a discussion of section 11.05 of this revenue procedure and the three items listed in section 11.06 of this revenue procedure and any other factors as they relate to the taxpayer's particular situation); and

(d) include any documents bearing on the request.

Request for conference

(2) Taxpayer may request a conference on application of § 7805(b).

When technical advice is requested regarding the application of § 7805(b), the taxpayer has the right to a conference with the Associate office to the same extent as does any taxpayer who is the subject of a technical advice request. *See* section 14.04 of Rev. Proc. 2007–2, this Bulletin.

SECTION 14. UNDER WHAT CIRCUMSTANCES ARE MATTERS REFERRED BETWEEN A DIRECTOR AND AN ASSOCIATE OFFICE?

Requests for determination letters

.01 Requests for determination letters received by a Director with respect to which it may not issue a determination letter, under the provisions of this revenue procedure, will be forwarded to an Associate office for reply. The field office will notify the taxpayer that the matter has been referred.

Directors will also refer to an Associate office any request for a determination letter that in their judgment should have the attention of the Associate office.

No-rule areas

.02 If the request involves an issue on which the Service will not issue a letter ruling or determination letter, the request will not be forwarded to an Associate office. The Director will notify the taxpayer that the Service will not issue a letter ruling or a determination letter on the issue. *See* section 6 of this revenue procedure for a description of no-rule areas.

Requests for letter rulings

.03 Requests for a letter ruling received by an Associate office that, under section 6 of this revenue procedure, may not be acted upon by the Associate office may, in the office's discretion, be forwarded to the field office that has examination jurisdiction over the taxpayer's return. The taxpayer will be notified of this action. If the request is on an issue or in an area of the type discussed in section 6 of this revenue procedure and the Service decides not to issue a letter ruling or a determination letter, the Associate office will notify the taxpayer and will then forward the request to the appropriate field office for association with the related return.

Letter ruling request mistakenly sent to a Director

.04 A request for a letter ruling mistakenly sent to a Director will be returned by the Director to the taxpayer so that the taxpayer can send it to an Associate office.

SECTION 15. WHAT ARE THE USER FEE REQUIREMENTS FOR REQUESTS FOR LETTER RULINGS AND DETERMINATION LETTERS?

Legislation authorizing user fees

.01 Section 7528 of the Internal Revenue Code provides that the Secretary of the Treasury or delegate (the "Secretary") shall establish a program requiring the payment of user fees for requests to the Service for letter rulings, opinion letters, determination letters, and similar requests. The fees apply to requests made through September 30, 2014. The fees charged under the program are to: (1) vary according to categories or subcategories established by the Secretary; (2) be determined after taking into account the average time for, and difficulty of, complying with requests in each category and subcategory; and (3) be payable in advance. The Secretary is to provide for exemptions and reduced fees under the program as the Secretary determines to be appropriate, but the average fee applicable to each category must not be less than the amount specified in § 7528.

Requests to which a user fee applies

.02 In general, user fees apply to all requests for—

(1) letter rulings (including advance consent Forms 3115), determination letters, information letters and advance pricing agreements;

(2) closing agreements described in paragraph (A)(3)(d) of Appendix A of this revenue procedure and pre-filing agreements described in Rev. Proc. 2005–12, 2005–1 C.B. 311 or its successor;

(3) renewal of advance pricing agreements; and

(4) reconsideration of letter rulings or determination letters.

Requests to which a user fee applies must be accompanied by the appropriate fee as determined from the fee schedule provided in Appendix A of this revenue procedure. The fee may be refunded as provided in section 15.10 of this revenue procedure.

Requests to which a user fee does not apply

.03 User fees do not apply to—

(1) elections made pursuant to § 301.9100–2, pertaining to automatic extensions of time (*see* section 5.03 of this revenue procedure);

(2) late initial classification elections made pursuant to Rev. Proc. 2002–59 (see section 5.03(5) of this revenue procedure);

(3) late S corporation and related elections made pursuant to Rev. Proc. 2004–49, Rev. Proc. 2004–48, Rev. Proc. 2003–43 or Rev. Proc. 97–48 (*see* section 5.02 of this revenue procedure); or

(4) requests for a change in accounting period or accounting method permitted to be made by a published automatic change revenue procedure (*see* section 9.01(1) of this revenue procedure).

Exemptions from the user fee requirements

.04 The user fee requirements do not apply to—

(1) departments, agencies, or instrumentalities of the United States if they certify that they are seeking a letter ruling or determination letter on behalf of a program or activity funded by federal appropriations. The fact that a user fee is not charged does not have any bearing on whether an applicant is treated as an agency or instrumentality of the United States for purposes of any provision of the Code; or

(2) requests as to whether a worker is an employee for federal employment taxes and income tax withholding purposes (Subtitle C of the Code) submitted on Form SS–8, *Determination of Worker Status for Purposes of Federal Employment Taxes and Income Tax Withholding*, or its equivalent.

Fee schedule

.05 The schedule of user fees is provided in Appendix A of this revenue procedure. For the user fee requirements applicable to—

(1) requests for advance pricing agreements or renewals of advance pricing agreements, *see* section 4.12 of Rev. Proc. 2004–40, 2004–2 C.B. 50; or 5.14 of Rev. Proc. 96–53, 1996–2 C.B. at 379; or

(2) requests for letter rulings, determination letters, etc., under the jurisdiction of the Commissioner, Tax Exempt and Government Entities Division, *see* Rev. Proc. 2007–8, this Bulletin.

Applicable user fee for a request involving multiple offices, fee categories, issues, transactions, or entities

.06

(1) Requests involving several offices. If a request dealing with only one transaction involves more than one of the offices within the Service (for example, one issue is under the jurisdiction of the Associate Chief Counsel (Passthroughs and Special Industries) and another issue is under the jurisdiction of the Commissioner, Tax Exempt and Government Entities Division), only one fee applies, namely the highest fee that otherwise would apply to each of the offices involved. *See* Rev. Proc. 2007–8, this Bulletin for the user fees applicable to issues under the jurisdiction of the Commissioner, Tax Exempt and Government Entities Division.

(2) Requests involving several fee categories. If a request dealing with only one transaction involves more than one fee category, only one fee applies, namely the highest fee that otherwise would apply to each of the categories involved.

(3) Requests involving several issues. If a request dealing with only one transaction involves several issues, a request for a change in accounting method dealing with only one item or submethod of accounting involves several issues, or a request for a change in accounting period dealing with only one item involves several issues, the request is treated as one request. Therefore, only one fee applies, namely the fee that applies to the particular category or subcategory involved. The addition of a new issue relating to the same transaction, item, or submethod will not result in an additional fee, unless the issue places the transaction, item, or submethod in a higher fee category.

(4) Requests involving several unrelated transactions. If a request involves several unrelated transactions, a request for a change in accounting method involves several unrelated items or submethods of accounting, or a request for a change in accounting period involves several unrelated items, each transaction or item is treated as a separate request. As a result, a separate fee will apply for each unrelated transaction, item, or submethod. An additional fee will apply if the request is changed by the addition of an unrelated transaction, item, or submethod not contained in the initial request. An example of a request involving unrelated transactions is a request involving relief under § 301.9100–3 and the underlying issue.

(5) Requests involving several entities. Each entity involved in a transaction (for example, a reorganization) that desires a separate letter ruling in its own name must pay a separate fee regardless of whether the transaction or transactions may be viewed as related. *But see* section 15.07 of this revenue procedure.

Applicable user fee for requests for substantially identical letter rulings or identical accounting method changes

.07

(1) In general. The user fees provided in paragraph (A)(5) of Appendix A of this revenue procedure apply to the situations described in sections 15.07(2) and 15.07(4) of this revenue procedure. To assist in the processing of these user fee requests, all letter ruling requests submitted under this section 15.07 should—

(a) Except for advance consent Forms 3115, type or print at the top of the letter ruling request: "REQUEST FOR USER FEE UNDER SECTION 15.07 OF REV. PROC. 2007–1";

(b) List on the first page of the submission all taxpayers and entities, and separate and distinct trades or businesses, including qualified subchapter S subsidiaries (QSUBs) or single member limited liability companies (single member LLCs), requesting a letter ruling (including the taxpayer identification number, and the amount of user fee submitted, for each taxpayer, entity, or separate and distinct trade or business); and

(c) Submit one check to cover all user fees.

If the Service determines that the letter ruling requests do not qualify for the user fee provided in paragraph (A)(5) of Appendix A of this revenue procedure, the Service will request the proper fee. *See* section 15.09 of this revenue procedure.

(2) Substantially identical letter rulings. The user fee provided in paragraph (A)(5)(a) of Appendix A of this revenue procedure applies to a taxpayer that requests substantially identical letter rulings (including accounting period, accounting method, and earnings and profits requests other than those submitted on Forms 1128, 2553, 3115, and 5452) for either multiple entities with a common member or sponsor, or multiple members of a common entity. To qualify for this user fee, all information and underlying documents must be substantially identical and all letter ruling requests must be submitted at the same time. In addition, the letter ruling requests must—

(a) State that the letter ruling requests, and all information and underlying documents, are substantially identical; and

(b) Specifically identify the extent to which the letter ruling requests, information, and underlying documents are not identical.

(3) Substantially identical plans under section 25(c)(2)(B). The user fee provided in paragraph (A)(5)(b) of Appendix A of this revenue procedure shall apply to a taxpayer that submits substantially identical plans for administering the 95-percent requirement of section 143(d)(1) following the submission and approval of an initial plan for administering the requirement. The request for subsequent approvals of substantially identical plans must: (1) state that a prior plan was submitted and approved and include a copy of the prior plan and approval; (2) state that the subsequent plan is substantially identical to the approved plan; and (3) describe any differences between the approved plans and the subsequent plan.

(4) Identical accounting method changes and related § 301.9100 letter rulings. The following situations are eligible for the user fees provided in paragraphs (A)(5)(b) and (d) of Appendix A of this revenue procedure:

(i) A taxpayer requests an identical accounting method change on a single Form 3115, or an extension of time to file Form 3115 under § 301.9100–3 for the identical accounting method change, for two or more separate and distinct trades or businesses (for purposes of § 1.446–1(d)) of that taxpayer, including QSUBs and single member LLCs;

(ii) A common parent requests the identical accounting method change on a single Form 3115, or an extension of time to file Form 3115 under § 301.9100–3 for the identical accounting method change, on behalf of two or more members of the consolidated group;

(iii) A common parent requests the identical accounting method change on a single Form 3115, or an extension of time to file Form 3115 under § 301.9100–3 for the identical accounting method change, on behalf of two or more controlled foreign corporations (CFCs) that do not engage in a trade or business within the United States where all controlling U.S. shareholders of the CFCs are members of the consolidated group; or

(iv) A taxpayer requests an identical accounting method change on a single Form 3115, or an extension of time to file Form 3115 under § 301.9100–3 for the identical accounting method change, on behalf of two or more CFCs that do not engage in a trade or business within the United States for which the taxpayer is the sole controlling U.S. shareholder of the CFCs.

To qualify as an identical accounting method change the multiple separate and distinct trades or businesses of a taxpayer, including QSUBs and single member LLCs, the multiple members of a consolidated group, or the multiple eligible CFCs must request to change from an identical present method of accounting to an identical proposed method of accounting. All aspects of the requested accounting method change, including the present and proposed methods, the underlying facts and the authority for the request, must be identical, except for the § 481(a) adjustments for the year of change. If the Associate office determines that the requested accounting method changes are not identical, additional user fees will be required before any letter ruling is issued.

The taxpayer or common parent must, for each separate and distinct trade or business (including a QSUB or single-member LLC) member of a consolidated group, or eligible CFC for which the accounting method change is being requested, attach to the Form 3115 a schedule providing the name, employer identification number (where applicable), and § 481(a) adjustment for the year of change. If the request is on behalf of eligible CFCs, the taxpayer or common parent must attach a statement that "[a]ll controlling U.S. shareholders (as defined in § 1.964–1(c)(5)) of all the CFCs to which the request relates are members of the common parent's consolidated group" or that "[t]he taxpayer filing the request is the sole controlling U.S. shareholder (as defined in § 1.964–1(c)(5)) of the CFCs to which the request relates," as applicable.

In the case of a § 301.9100 request for an extension of time to file a Form 3115 requesting an identical accounting method change for multiple separate and distinct trades or businesses of a taxpayer (including QSUBs or single-member LLCs) multiple members of the consolidated group or multiple eligible CFCs, the taxpayer or common parent must submit the information required in the preceding paragraph in addition to the information required by section 5.03 of this revenue procedure.

Method of payment

.08 Each request to the Service for a letter ruling, determination letter, information letter, advance pricing agreement, closing agreement described in paragraph (A)(3)(d) of Appendix A of this revenue procedure, or reconsideration of a letter ruling or determination letter must be accompanied by a check or money order in U.S. dollars, payable to the Internal Revenue Service, in the appropriate amount. (The user fee check or money order should not be attached to the Form 2553, *Election by a Small Business Corporation*, when it is filed at the Service Center. If on the Form 2553 an electing S corporation requests a ruling to use a fiscal year under section 6.03 of Rev. Proc. 2002–39, 2002–1 C.B. 1046, the Service Center will forward the request to the Associate office. When the Associate office receives the Form 2553 from the Service Center, it will notify the taxpayer that the fee is due.) Taxpayers should not send cash.

Effect of nonpayment or payment of incorrect amount

.09 If a request is not accompanied by a properly completed check or money order or is accompanied by a check or money order for less than the correct amount, the respective office within the Service that is responsible for issuing the letter ruling, determination letter, information letter, advance pricing agreement, closing agreement, or reconsideration of a letter ruling or determination letter generally will exercise discretion in deciding whether to return immediately the request. If a request is not immediately returned, the taxpayer will be contacted and given a reasonable amount of time to submit the proper fee. If the proper fee is not received within a reasonable amount of time, the entire request will then be returned. The Service will usually defer substantive consideration of a request until proper payment has been received. The return of a request to the taxpayer may adversely affect substantive rights if the request is not perfected and resubmitted to the Service within 30 days of the date of the cover letter returning the request.

If a request is accompanied by a check or money order for more than the correct amount, the request will be accepted and the amount of the excess payment will be returned to the taxpayer.

Refunds of user fee

.10 In general, the user fee will not be refunded unless the Service declines to rule on all issues for which a ruling is requested.

(1) The following situations are examples of situations in which the user fee will not be refunded:

(a) The request for a letter ruling, determination letter, etc., is withdrawn at any time subsequent to its receipt by the Service, unless the only reason for withdrawal is that the Service has advised the taxpayer that a higher user fee than was sent with the request is applicable and the taxpayer is unwilling to pay the higher fee.

(b) The request is procedurally deficient, although accompanied by the proper fee or an overpayment, and is not timely perfected. When there is a failure to perfect timely the request, the case will be considered closed and the failure to perfect will be treated as a withdrawal for purposes of this revenue procedure. *See* section 8.05(3) of this revenue procedure.

(c) The Associate office notifies the taxpayer that the Associate office will not issue the letter ruling and has closed the case as a result of the taxpayer's failure to submit timely the additional information requested by the Associate office. The failure to submit the additional information will be treated as a withdrawal for purposes of this revenue procedure. *See* section 8.05(3) of this revenue procedure (section 9.08(7) for a request for a change in accounting method).

(d) A letter ruling, determination letter, etc., is revoked in whole or in part at the initiative of the Service. The fee paid at the time the original letter ruling, determination letter, etc., was requested will not be refunded.

(e) The request contains several issues, and the Service rules on some, but not all, of the issues. The highest fee applicable to the issues on which the Service rules will not be refunded.

(f) The taxpayer asserts that a letter ruling the taxpayer received covering a single issue is erroneous or not responsive (other than an issue on which the Associate office has declined to rule) and requests reconsideration. The Associate office, upon reconsideration, does not agree that the letter ruling is erroneous or is not responsive. The fee accompanying the request for reconsideration will not be refunded.

(g) The situation is the same as described in paragraph (f) of this section 15.10(1) except that the letter ruling covered several unrelated transactions. The Associate office, upon reconsideration, does not agree with the taxpayer that the letter ruling is erroneous or is not responsive for all of the transactions, but does agree that it is erroneous as to one transaction. The fee accompanying the request for reconsideration will not be refunded except to the extent applicable to the transaction for which the Associate office agrees the letter ruling was in error.

(h) The request is for a supplemental letter ruling, determination letter, etc., concerning a change in facts (whether significant or not) relating to the transaction on which the Service ruled.

(i) The request is for reconsideration of an adverse or partially adverse letter ruling or a final adverse determination letter, and the taxpayer submits arguments and authorities not submitted before the original letter ruling or determination letter was issued.

(2) The following situations are examples of situations in which the user fee will be refunded:

(a) In a situation to which section 15.10(1)(i) of this revenue procedure does not apply, the taxpayer asserts that a letter ruling the taxpayer received covering a single issue is erroneous or is not responsive (other than an issue on which the Associate office declined to rule) and requests reconsideration. The Associate office agrees, upon reconsideration, that the letter ruling is erroneous or is not responsive. The fee accompanying the taxpayer's request for reconsideration will be refunded.

(b) In a situation to which section 15.10(1)(i) of this revenue procedure does not apply, the taxpayer requests a supplemental letter ruling, determination letter, etc., to correct a mistake that the Service agrees it made in the original letter ruling, determination letter, etc., such as a mistake in the statement of facts or in the citation of a Code section. Once the Service agrees that it made a mistake, the fee accompanying the request for the supplemental letter ruling, determination letter, etc., will be refunded.

(c) The taxpayer requests and is granted relief under § 7805(b) in connection with the revocation in whole or in part, of a previously issued letter ruling, determination letter, etc. The fee accompanying the request for relief will be refunded.

(d) In a situation to which section 15.10(1)(e) of this revenue procedure applies, the taxpayer requests reconsideration of the Service's decision not to rule on an issue. Once the Service agrees to rule on the issue, the fee accompanying the request for reconsideration will be refunded.

(e) The letter ruling is not issued and taking into account all the facts and circumstances, including the Service's resources devoted to the request, the responsible Associate Chief Counsel in his or her sole discretion decides a refund is appropriate.

Request for reconsideration of user fee

.11 A taxpayer that believes the user fee charged by the Service for its request for a letter ruling, determination letter, advance pricing agreement, or closing agreement is either inapplicable or incorrect and wishes to receive a refund of all or part of the amount paid (*see* section 15.10 of this revenue procedure) may request reconsideration and, if desired, the opportunity for an oral discussion by sending a letter to the Service at the appropriate address given in section 7.03 in this revenue procedure. Both the incoming envelope and the letter requesting such reconsideration should be prominently marked "USER FEE RECONSIDERATION REQUEST." No user fee is required for these requests. The request should be marked for the attention of:

If the matter involves primarily:	*Mark for the attention of:*
Associate Chief Counsel (Corporate) letter ruling requests	Associate Chief Counsel (Corporate)
Associate Chief Counsel (Financial Institutions and Products) letter ruling requests	Associate Chief Counsel (Financial Institutions and Products)
Associate Chief Counsel (Income Tax and Accounting) letter ruling requests	Associate Chief Counsel (Income Tax and Accounting)
Associate Chief Counsel (International) letter ruling and advance pricing agreement requests	Associate Chief Counsel (International)
Associate Chief Counsel (Passthroughs and Special Industries) letter ruling requests	Associate Chief Counsel (Passthroughs and Special Industries)
Associate Chief Counsel (Procedure and Administration) letter ruling requests	Associate Chief Counsel (Procedure and Administration)

If the matter involves primarily:	*Mark for the attention of:*
Division Counsel/Associate Chief Counsel (Tax Exempt and Government Entities) letter ruling requests	Assistant Chief Counsel ( ) (Complete by using whichever of the following designations applies: (Employee Benefits) or (Employment Tax/Exempt Organizations/Government Entities)
Determination letter requests submitted pursuant to this revenue procedure by taxpayers under the jurisdiction of LMSB	Manager, Office of Pre-Filing and Technical Services
Determination letter requests submitted pursuant to this revenue procedure by taxpayers under the jurisdiction of SB/SE, W&I	The appropriate SB/SE official listed in Appendix D
Determination letter requests submitted pursuant to this revenue procedure by taxpayers under the jurisdiction of TE/GE	Director, Employee Plans Examinations Director, Exempt Organizations Examinations Director, Federal, State & Local Governments Director, Tax Exempt Bonds Director, Indian Tribal Governments (Add name of field office handling the request)

SECTION 16. WHAT SIGNIFICANT CHANGES HAVE BEEN MADE TO REV. PROC. 2006–1?

.01 Section 9.17 was revised to clarify the procedure for requesting consent for a change in accounting method.

SECTION 17. WHAT IS THE EFFECT OF THIS REVENUE PROCEDURE ON OTHER DOCUMENTS?

Rev. Proc. 2006–1, 2006–1 C.B. 1 is superseded.

SECTION 18. WHAT IS THE EFFECTIVE DATE OF THIS REVENUE PROCEDURE?

This revenue procedure is effective January 2, 2007.

SECTION 19. PAPERWORK REDUCTION ACT

The collections of information contained in this revenue procedure have been reviewed and approved by the Office of Management and Budget in accordance with the Paperwork Reduction Act (44 U.S.C. § 3507) under control number 1545–1522.

An agency may not conduct or sponsor, and a person is not required to respond to, a collection of information unless the collection of information displays a valid control number.

The collections of information in this revenue procedure are in sections 5.06, 7.01, 7.02, 7.03, 7.04, 7.05, 7.07, 8.02. 8.05, 8.07, 10.01, 10.06, 10.07, 11.11, 12.06, 13.02, 15.02, 15.07, 15.08, 15.09, 15.11, paragraph (B)(1) of Appendix A, Appendix C, and Appendix E (subject matter—rate orders; regulatory agency; normalization). This information is required to evaluate and process the request for a letter ruling or determination letter. In addition, this information will be used to help the Service delete certain information from the text of the letter ruling or determination letter before it is made available for public inspection, as required by § 6110. The collections of information are required to obtain a letter ruling or determination letter. The likely respondents are business or other for-profit institutions.

The estimated total annual reporting and/or recordkeeping burden is 305,140 hours.

The estimated annual burden per respondent/recordkeeper varies from 1 to 200 hours, depending on individual circumstances, with an estimated average burden of 80.3 hours. The estimated number of respondents and/or recordkeepers is 3,800.

The estimated annual frequency of responses is on occasion.

Books or records relating to a collection of information must be retained as long as their contents may become material in the administration of any internal revenue law. Generally, tax returns and tax return information are confidential, as required by § 6103.

DRAFTING INFORMATION

The principal author of this revenue procedure is Matthew Howard of the Office of Associate Chief Counsel (Procedure and Administration). For further information regarding this revenue procedure for matters under the jurisdiction of—

(1) the Associate Chief Counsel (Corporate), contact Richard Todd at (202) 622–7700 (not a toll-free call),

(2) the Associate Chief Counsel (Financial Institutions and Products), contact Arturo Estrada at (202) 622–3900 (not a toll-free call),

(3) the Associate Chief Counsel (Income Tax and Accounting), contact Brenda Wilson at (202) 622–4800 (not a toll-free call),

(4) the Associate Chief Counsel (Passthroughs and Special Industries), contact Stephanie Bland at (202) 622–7830 (not a toll-free call),

(5) the Associate Chief Counsel (Procedure and Administration), contact George Bowden or Henry Schneiderman at (202) 622–3400 (not a toll-free call),

(6) the Division Counsel/Associate Chief Counsel (Tax Exempt and Government Entities), contact Calder Robertson at (202) 622–6000 (not a toll-free call), or

(7) the Associate Chief Counsel (International), contact Willard Yates at (202) 622–3164 (not a toll-free call).

For further information regarding user fees, contact the Docket, Records, and User Fee Branch at (202) 622–7560 (not a toll-free call).

INDEX

References are to sections in Rev. Proc. 2007–1

INDEX

References are to sections in Rev. Proc. 2007–1

INDEX
References are to sections in Rev. Proc. 2007–1

APPENDIX A

SCHEDULE OF USER FEES

NOTE: Checks or money orders must be in U.S. dollars.

(A) *FEE SCHEDULE*

CATEGORY	*USER FEE*
(1) User fee for a request for a determination letter from a Director. The user fee for each determination letter request governed by Rev. Proc. 2007–1, this revenue procedure.	$275
(2) User fee for a request for an advance pricing agreement or a renewal of an advance pricing agreement.	*See* section 4.12 of Rev. Proc. 2006–9, 2006–2 I.R.B. 278
(3) User fee for a request for a letter ruling or closing agreement. Except for the user fees for advance pricing agreements and renewals, the reduced fees provided in paragraph (A)(4) of this appendix, the user fees provided in paragraph (A)(5) of this appendix, and the exemptions provided in section 15.04 of Rev. Proc. 2007–1, this revenue procedure, the user fee for each request for a letter ruling or closing agreement under the jurisdiction of the Associate Chief Counsel (Corporate), the Associate Chief Counsel (Financial Institutions and Products), the Associate Chief Counsel (Income Tax and Accounting), the Associate Chief Counsel (International), the Associate Chief Counsel (Passthroughs and Special Industries), the Associate Chief Counsel (Procedure and Administration), or the Division Counsel/Associate Chief Counsel (Tax Exempt and Government Entities) is as follows:	
(a) Accounting periods	
(i) Form 1128 (except as provided in paragraph (A)(4)(a) or (b) of this appendix)	$1,500
(ii) Requests made on Part II of Form 2553 to use a fiscal year based on a business purpose (except as provided in paragraph (A)(4)(a) or (b) of this appendix)	$1,500
(iii) Letter ruling requests for extensions of time to file Form 1128, Form 8716, or Part II of Form 2553 under § 301.9100–3 (except as provided in paragraph (A)(4)(a) or (b) of this appendix)	$1,500
(b) Changes in Accounting Methods	
(i) Form 3115 (except as provided in paragraph (A)(4)(a) or (b), or (5)(b) of this appendix)	$2,500
(ii) Letter ruling requests for extensions of time to file Form 3115 under § 301.9100–3 (except as provided in paragraph (A)(4)(a) or (b), or (5)(c) of this appendix)	$2,500
NOTE: No user fee is required if the change in accounting period or accounting method is permitted to be made pursuant to a published automatic change request procedure. *See* section 9.22 and Appendix E of Rev. Proc. 2007–1, this revenue procedure, for the list of automatic change request procedures published and/or in effect as of December 31, 2006.	
(c) All other letter ruling requests (which includes accounting period and accounting method requests other than those properly submitted on Form 1128, Part II of Form 2553, or Form 3115) (except as provided in paragraph (A)(4)(a) or (b), or (5)(a) of this appendix)	$10,000

CATEGORY	USER FEE
(d) Requests for closing agreements on a proposed transaction or on a completed transaction before a return for the transaction has been filed in which a letter ruling on that transaction is not requested or issued (except as provided in paragraph (A)(4)(a) or (b) of this appendix)	$10,000
NOTE: A taxpayer that receives relief under § 301.9100–3 (for example, an extension of time to file Form 3115) will be charged a separate user fee for the letter ruling request on the underlying issue (for example, the accounting period or accounting method application).	
(4) Reduced user fee for a request for a letter ruling or closing agreement. A reduced user fee is provided in the following situations if the person provides the certification described in paragraph (B)(1) of this appendix:	
(a) Request involves a personal or business tax issue from a person with gross income (as determined under paragraphs (B)(2) and (4) of this appendix) of less than $250,000	$625
(b) Request involves a personal or business-related tax issue (for example, including home-office expenses, residential rental property issues) from a person with gross income (as determined under paragraphs (B)(3) and (4) of this appendix) of less than $1 million and more than $250,000.	$2,500
(5) User fee for substantially identical letter ruling requests, identical accounting method changes, or plans from issuing authorities under section 25(c)(2)(B). If the requirements of section 15.07 of Rev. Proc. 2007–1, this revenue procedure, are satisfied, the user fee for the following situations is as follows:	
(a) Substantially identical letter rulings requested	
Situations in which a taxpayer requests substantially identical letter rulings for multiple entities with a common member or sponsor, or for multiple members of a common entity, or for two or more identical trusts or for multiple beneficiaries of a trust or a trust divided into identical subtrusts or for husband and wife making split gifts, for each additional letter ruling request after the $7,000 fee or reduced fee, as applicable, has been paid for the first letter ruling request	$700
NOTE: Each entity or member that is entitled to the user fee under paragraph (A)(5)(a) of this appendix, that receives relief under § 301.9100–3 (for example, an extension of time to file an election) will be charged a separate user fee for the letter ruling request on the underlying issue.	
(b) Identical accounting method change requested on a single Form 3115	
Situations in which a common parent requests the identical accounting method change on a single Form 3115 on behalf of two or more members of a consolidated group or two or more eligible CFCs (see section 15.07(4)), or in which a taxpayer requests the identical accounting method change on a single Form 3115 for two or more eligible CFCs (see section 15.07(4)) or two or more separate and distinct trades or businesses, including qualified subchapter S subsidiaries (QSUBs) and single-member limited liability companies (single-member LLCs) (*see* § 1.446–1(d) for what constitutes a separate and distinct trade or business), for each additional member of the group, eligible CFC, or separate and distinct trade or business of the taxpayer seeking the identical accounting method change on the same Form 3115 after the $1,500 fee or $625 reduced fee, as applicable, has been paid for the first member of the group, eligible CFC, or separate and distinct trade or business.	$150
(c) Substantially identical plans under section 25(c)(2)(B)	$700

CATEGORY		USER FEE
	Situations where an issuing authority under section 25 submits substantially identical plans for administering the 95-percent requirement of section 143(d)(1) following the submission of an initial plan that was approved.	
(d)	Extension of time requested to file Form 3115 for an identical accounting method change	
	Situations in which a common parent requests an extension of time under § 301.9100–3 to file a single Form 3115 for the identical accounting method change on behalf of two or more members of a consolidated group or two or more eligible CFCs (see section 15.07(4)), or in which a taxpayer requests an extension of time under § 301.9100–3 to file a single Form 3115 for the identical accounting method change for two or more eligible CFCs (see section 15.07(4)) or two or more separate and distinct trades or businesses, including QSUBs and single-member LLCs (*see* § 1.446–1(d) for what constitutes a separate and distinct trade or business), for each additional member of the group, eligible CFC or separate and distinct trade or business of the taxpayer seeking the identical accounting method change on the same Form 3115 after the $1,500 fee or $625 reduced fee as applicable, has been paid for the first member of the group, eligible CFC, or separate and distinct trade or business.	$75
	NOTE: When an extension of time to file Form 3115 is granted under § 301.9100–3 for multiple members of a consolidated group, eligible CFCs, or separate and distinct trades or businesses of a taxpayer, including QSUBs and single-member LLCs, a separate user fee will be charged for the accounting method change application, Form 3115.	
(6) User fee for information letter requests.		$2,000
(7) User fee for pre-filing agreements		$50,000

(B) *PROCEDURAL MATTERS*

(1) Required certification. A person seeking a reduced user fee under paragraph (A)(4) of this appendix must provide the following certification in order to obtain the reduced user fee:

(a) If a person is seeking a reduced user fee under paragraph (A)(4)(a) of this appendix, the person must certify in the request that his, her, or its gross income, as defined under paragraphs (B)(2) and (4) of this appendix, is less than $250,000 for the last full (12 months) taxable year ending before the date the request is filed.

(b) If a person is seeking a reduced user fee under paragraph (A)(4)(b) of this appendix, the person must certify in the request that his, her, or its gross income, as defined under paragraphs (B)(3) and (4) of this appendix, is less than $1 million and more than $250,000 for the last full (12 months) taxable year ending before the date the request is filed.

The certification must be attached as part of the ruling request.

(2) Gross income for a request involving a personal tax issue. For purposes of the reduced user fees provided in paragraphs (A)(4)(a) and (b) of this appendix of—

(a) U.S. citizens and resident alien individuals, domestic trusts, and domestic estates, "gross income" is equal to "total income" as reported on their last federal income tax return (as amended) filed for a full (12 months) taxable year ending before the date the request is filed, plus any interest income not subject to tax under § 103 (interest on state and local bonds) for that period. "Total income" is a line item on federal tax returns. For example, if the 2004 Form 1040, *U.S. Individual Income Tax Return*, is the most recent 12-month taxable year return filed by a U.S. citizen, "total income" on the Form 1040 is the amount entered on line 22.

In the case of a request for a letter ruling or closing agreement from a domestic estate or trust that, at the time the request is filed, has not filed a federal income tax return for a full taxable year, the reduced user fee in paragraph (A)(4)(a) of this appendix will apply if the decedent's or (in the case of an individual grantor) the grantor's total income as reported on the last federal income tax return filed for a full taxable year ending before the date of death or the date of the transfer, taking into account any additions required to be made to total income described in this paragraph (B)(2)(a), is less than $250,000. In this case, the executor or administrator of the decedent's estate or the grantor must provide the certification required under paragraph (B)(1) of this appendix.

(b) Nonresident alien individuals, foreign trusts, and foreign estates "gross income" is equal to "total effectively connected income" as reported on their last federal income tax return (as amended) filed for a full (12 months) taxable year ending before the date the request is filed, plus any income for the period from United States or foreign sources that is not taxable by the United States, whether by reason of § 103, an income tax treaty, § 871(h) (regarding portfolio interest), or otherwise, plus the total amount of any fixed or determinable annual or periodical income from United States sources, the United States tax liability for which is satisfied by withholding at the source. "Total effectively connected income" is a line item on federal tax returns. For example, if the 2004 Form 1040NR, *U.S. Nonresident Alien Income Tax Return*, is the most recent 12-month taxable year return filed by a nonresident alien individual, "total effectively connected income" on the Form 1040NR is the amount entered on line 23.

In the case of a request for a letter ruling or closing agreement from a foreign estate or trust that, at the time the request is filed, has not filed a federal income tax return for a full taxable year, the reduced user fee in paragraph (A)(4)(a) of this appendix will apply if the decedent's or (in the case of an individual grantor) the grantor's total income or total effectively connected income, as relevant, as reported on the last federal income tax return filed for a full taxable year ending before the date of death or the date of the transfer, taking into account any additions required to be made to total income or total effectively connected income described respectively in paragraph (B)(2)(a) of this appendix or in this paragraph (B)(2)(b), is less than $250,000. In this case, the executor or administrator of the decedent's estate or the grantor must provide the certification required under paragraph (B)(1) of this appendix.

(3) Gross income for a request involving a business-related tax issue. For purposes of the reduced user fees provided in paragraphs (A)(4)(a) and (b) of this appendix of—

(a) U.S. citizens and resident alien individuals, domestic trusts, and domestic estates, "gross income" is equal to gross income as defined under paragraph (B)(2)(a) of this appendix, plus "cost of goods sold" as reported on the same federal income tax return.

(b) Nonresident alien individuals, foreign trusts, and foreign estates, "gross income" is equal to gross income as defined under paragraph (B)(2)(b) of this appendix, plus "cost of goods sold" as reported on the same federal income tax return.

(c) Domestic partnerships and corporations, "gross income" is equal to "total income" as reported on their last federal income tax return (as amended) filed for a full (12 months) taxable year ending before the date the request is filed, plus "cost of goods sold" as reported on the same federal income tax return, plus any interest income not subject to tax under § 103 (interest on state and local bonds) for that period. If a domestic partnership or corporation is not subject to tax, "total income" and "cost of goods sold" are the amounts that the domestic partnership or corporation would have reported on the federal income tax return if the domestic partnership or corporation were subject to tax.

"Cost of goods sold" and "total income" are line items on federal tax returns. For example, if the 2004 Form 1065, *U.S. Return of Partnership Income*, is the most recent 12-month taxable year return filed by a domestic partnership, "cost of goods sold" and "total income" on the Form 1065 are the amounts entered on lines 2 and 8, respectively, and if the 2004 Form 1120, *U.S. Corporation Income Tax Return*, is the most recent 12-month taxable year return filed by a domestic corporation, "cost of goods sold" and "total income" on the Form 1120 are the amounts entered on lines 2 and 11, respectively.

If, at the time the request is filed, a domestic partnership or corporation subject to tax has not filed a federal income tax return for a full taxable year, the reduced user fee in paragraph (A)(4)(b) of this appendix will apply if, in the aggregate, the partners' or the shareholders' gross income (as defined in paragraph (B)(3)(a), (b), (c), or (d) of this appendix, as applicable) is less than $1 million for the last full (12 months) taxable year ending before the date the request is filed. In this case, the partners or the shareholders must provide the certification required under paragraph (B)(1) of this appendix.

(d) Organizations exempt from income tax under "Subchapter F-Exempt Organizations" of the Code, "gross income" is equal to the amount of gross receipts for the last full (12 months) taxable year ending before the date the request for a letter ruling or closing agreement is filed.

(e) Gross income of state, local, and Indian tribal government entities, "gross income" is equal to the annual operating revenue of the government requesting the ruling for its last fiscal year ending before the date of the ruling request. The annual operating revenue is to be determined at the government level and not at the level of the government entity or agency making the request.

(4) Special rules for determining gross income. For purposes of paragraphs (B)(2) and (3) of this appendix, the following rules apply for determining gross income.

(a) Gross income of individuals, trusts, and estates.

(1) In the case of a request from a married individual, the gross incomes (as defined in paragraph (B)(2) or (3) of this appendix, as applicable) of the applicant and the applicant's spouse must be combined. This rule does not apply to an individual who: (1) is legally separated from his or her spouse and (2) the spouse does not file a joint income tax return with his or her spouse; and

(2) If there are two or more applicants filing the request, the gross incomes (as defined in paragraph (B)(2) or (3) of this appendix, as applicable) of the applicants must be combined.

(b) Gross income of domestic partnerships and corporations.

(1) In the case of a request from a domestic corporation, the gross income (as defined in paragraph (B)(3) of this appendix) of (i) all members of the applicant's controlled group (as defined in § 1563(a)), and (ii) any related taxpayer that is involved in the transaction on which the letter ruling or closing agreement is requested, must be combined; and

(2) In the case of a request from a domestic partnership, the gross income (as defined in paragraph (B)(3) of this appendix) of (i) the partnership, and (ii) any partner who owns, directly or indirectly, 50 percent or more of the capital interest or profits interest in the partnership, must be combined.

(c) Gross income of exempt organizations. If there are two or more organizations exempt from income tax under Subchapter F filing the request, the gross receipts (as defined in paragraph (B)(3)(d) of this appendix) of the applicants must be combined.

APPENDIX B

SAMPLE FORMAT FOR A LETTER RULING REQUEST

INSTRUCTIONS

To assist you in preparing a letter ruling request, the Service is providing this sample format. You are not required to use this sample format. If your request is not identical or similar to the sample format, the different format will not defer consideration of your request.

(Insert the date of request)

Internal Revenue Service
Insert either: Associate Chief Counsel (Insert one of the following: Corporate, Financial Institutions and Products, Income Tax and Accounting, International, Passthroughs and Special Industries, or Procedure and Administration) *or* Division Counsel/Associate Chief Counsel (Tax Exempt and Government Entities)
Attn: CC:PA:LPD:DRU
P.O. Box 7604
Ben Franklin Station
Washington, DC 20044

Dear Sir or Madam:

(Insert the name of the taxpayer) requests a ruling on the proper treatment of *(insert the subject matter of the letter ruling request)* under section *(insert the number)* of the Internal Revenue Code..

[If the taxpayer is requesting expedited handling, a statement to that effect must be attached to, or contained in, the letter ruling request. The statement must explain the need for expedited handling. *See* section 7.02(4) of Rev. Proc. 2007–1, 2007–1 I.R.B. 1. Hereafter, all references are to Rev. Proc. 2007–1 unless otherwise noted.]

A. STATEMENT OF FACTS

1. Taxpayer Information

[Provide the statements required by sections 7.01(1)(a) and (b).]

2. Description of Taxpayer's Business Operations

[Provide the statement required by section 7.01(1)(c).]

3. Facts Relating to Transaction

[The ruling request must contain a complete statement of the facts relating to the transaction that is the subject of the letter ruling request. This statement must include a detailed description of the transaction, including material facts in any accompanying documents, and the business reasons for the transaction. *See* sections 7.01(1)(d), 7.01(1)(e), and 7.01(2).]

B. RULING REQUESTED

[The ruling request should contain a concise statement of the ruling requested by the taxpayer. It is preferred that the language of the requested ruling be exactly the same as that the taxpayer wishes to receive.]

C. STATEMENT OF LAW

[The ruling request must contain a statement of the law in support of the taxpayer's views or conclusion and identify any pending legislation that may affect the proposed transaction. The taxpayer also is strongly encouraged to identify and discuss any authorities believed to be contrary to the position advanced in the ruling request. *See* sections 7.01(6), 7.01(8), 7.01(9), and 7.01(10).]

D. ANALYSIS

[The ruling request must contain a discussion of the facts and an analysis of the law. The taxpayer also is strongly encouraged to identify and discuss any authorities believed to be contrary to the position advanced in the ruling request. *See* sections 7.01(3), 7.01(6), 7.01(8), 7.01(9), and 7.01(10).]

E. CONCLUSION

[The ruling request should contain a statement of the taxpayer's conclusion on the ruling requested.]

F. PROCEDURAL MATTERS

1. Revenue Procedure 2007–1 Statements

   a. [Provide the statement required by section 7.01(4) regarding whether the same issue in the letter ruling request is in an earlier return of the taxpayer or in a return for any year of a related taxpayer.]

   b. [Provide the statement required by section 7.01(5)(a) regarding whether the Service previously ruled on the same or similar issue for the taxpayer, a related taxpayer, or a predecessor. Please further note that if a reduced user fee is being submitted, a certification of eligibility for the reduced fee must be included with the ruling request.]

   c. [Provide the statement required by section 7.01(5)(b) regarding whether the taxpayer, a related taxpayer, a predecessor, or any representatives previously submitted a request (including an application for change in accounting method) involving the same or similar issue but withdrew the request before a letter ruling or determination letter was issued.]

   d. [Provide the statement required by section 7.01(5)(c) regarding whether the taxpayer, a related taxpayer, or a predecessor previously submitted a request (including an application for change in accounting method) involving the same or a similar issue that is currently pending with the Service.]

   e. [Provide the statement required by section 7.01(5)(d) regarding whether, at the same time as this request, the taxpayer or a related taxpayer is presently submitting another request (including an application for change in accounting method) involving the same or similar issue to the Service.]

   f. [If the letter ruling request involves the interpretation of a substantive provision of an income or estate tax treaty, provide the statement required by section 7.01(6) regarding whether the tax authority of the treaty jurisdiction has issued a ruling on the same or similar issue for the taxpayer, a related taxpayer, or a predecessor; whether the same or similar issue is being examined, or has been settled, by the tax authority of the treaty jurisdiction or is otherwise the subject of a closing agreement in that jurisdiction; and whether the same or similar issue is being considered by the competent authority of the treaty jurisdiction.]

   g. [Provide the statement required by section 7.01(8) regarding whether the law in connection with the letter ruling request is uncertain and whether the issue is adequately addressed by relevant authorities.]

   h. [If the taxpayer determines that there are no contrary authorities, a statement to that effect would be helpful. *See* section 7.01(9).]

   i. [If the taxpayer wants to have a conference on the issues involved in the letter ruling request, the ruling request should contain a statement to that effect. *See* section 7.02(6).]

   j. [If the taxpayer is requesting a copy of any document related to the letter ruling request to be sent by facsimile (fax) transmission, the ruling request should contain a statement to that effect. *See* section 7.02(5).]

   k. [If the taxpayer is requesting separate letter rulings on multiple issues, the letter ruling request should contain a statement to that effect. *See* section 7.02(1).]

   l. [If the taxpayer is seeking to obtain the user fee provided in paragraph (A)(5)(a) of Appendix A for substantially identical letter rulings, the letter ruling request must contain the statements required by section 15.07.]

2. Administrative

   a. [The ruling request should state: "The deletion statement and checklist required by Rev. Proc. 2007–1 are enclosed." *See* sections 7.01(11) and 7.01(18).]

   b. [The ruling request should state: "The required user fee of $ (*Insert the amount of the fee*) is enclosed." Please note that the check or money order must be in U.S. dollars and made payable to the Internal Revenue Service. *See* section 15 and Appendix A.]

   c. [If the taxpayer's authorized representative is to sign the letter ruling request or is to appear before the Service in connection with the request, the ruling request should state: "A Power of Attorney is enclosed." *See* sections 7.01(13), 7.01(14), and 7.02(2).]

Sincerely yours,

(*Insert the name of the taxpayer or the taxpayer's authorized representative*)

By:

Signature Date

Typed or printed name of
person signing request

DECLARATION: [See section 7.01(15).]

Under penalties of perjury, I declare that I have examined this request, including accompanying documents, and, to the best of my knowledge and belief, the request contains all the relevant facts relating to the request, and such facts are true, correct, and complete.

(*Insert the name of the taxpayer*)

By:

____

Signature Title Date

(*must be signed by taxpayer, not by taxpayer's representative, see section 7.01(15)(b) of this revenue procedure*)

Typed or printed name of
person signing declaration

[If the taxpayer is a corporation that is a member of an affiliated group filing consolidated returns, the above declaration must also be signed and dated by an officer of the common parent of the group. *See* section 7.01(15).]

APPENDIX C

CHECKLIST
IS YOUR LETTER RULING REQUEST COMPLETE?

INSTRUCTIONS

The Service will be able to respond more quickly to your letter ruling request if it is carefully prepared and complete. To ensure that your request is in order, use this checklist. Complete the four items of information requested before the checklist. Answer each question by circling "Yes," "No," or "N/A." When a question contains a place for a page number, insert the page number (or numbers) of the request that gives the information called for by a yes answer to a question. **Sign and date the checklist (as taxpayer or authorized representative) and place it on top of your request.**

If you are an authorized representative submitting a request for a taxpayer, you must include a completed checklist with the request, or the request will either be returned to you or substantive consideration of it will be deferred until a completed checklist is submitted. **If you are a taxpayer preparing your own request without professional assistance, an incomplete checklist will not either cause the return of your request or defer substantive consideration of your request.** You should still complete as much of the checklist as possible and submit it with your request.

TAXPAYER'S NAME ______________________

TAXPAYER'S I.D. NO. ______________________

ATTORNEY/P.O.A. ______________________

PRIMARY CODE SECTION ______________________

CIRCLE ONE	ITEM
Yes No	1. Does your request involve an issue under the jurisdiction of the Associate Chief Counsel (Corporate), the Associate Chief Counsel (Financial Institutions and Products), the Associate Chief Counsel (Income Tax and Accounting), the Associate Chief Counsel (International), the Associate Chief Counsel (Passthroughs and Special Industries), the Associate Chief Counsel (Procedure and Administration), or the Division Counsel/Associate Chief Counsel (Tax Exempt and Government Entities)? *See* section 3 of Rev. Proc. 2007–1, 2007–1 I.R.B. 1. For issues under the jurisdiction of other offices, *see* section 4 of Rev. Proc. 2007–1. (Hereafter, all references are to Rev. Proc. 2007–1 unless otherwise noted.)
Yes No	2. Have you read Rev. Proc. 2007–3, 2007–1 I.R.B. 108, and Rev. Proc. 2007–7, 2007–1 I.R.B. 227, to see if part or all of the request involves a matter on which letter rulings are not issued or are ordinarily not issued?
Yes No N/A	3. If your request involves a matter on which letter rulings are not ordinarily issued, have you given compelling reasons to justify the issuance of a letter ruling? Before preparing your request, you may want to call the branch in the Office of Associate Chief Counsel (Corporate), the Office of Associate Chief Counsel (Financial Institutions and Products), the Office of Associate Chief Counsel (Income Tax and Accounting), the Office of Associate Chief Counsel (International), the Office of Associate Chief Counsel (Passthroughs and Special Industries), the Office of Associate Chief Counsel (Procedure and Administration), or the Office of Division Counsel/Associate Chief Counsel (Tax Exempt and Government Entities) responsible for substantive interpretations of the principal Internal Revenue Code section on which you are seeking a letter ruling to discuss the likelihood of an exception. For matters under the jurisdiction of—

(a) the Office of Associate Chief Counsel (Corporate), the Office of Associate Chief Counsel (Financial Institutions and Products), the Office of Associate Chief Counsel (Income Tax and Accounting), the Office of Associate Chief Counsel (Passthroughs and Special Industries), or the Office of Division Counsel/Associate Chief Counsel (Tax Exempt and Government Entities), the Office of the Associate Chief Counsel (Procedure and Administration), the appropriate branch to call may be obtained by calling (202) 622–7560 (not a toll-free call);

(b) the Office of the Associate Chief Counsel (International), the appropriate branch to call may be obtained by calling (202) 622–3800 (not a toll-free call).

Yes No N/A Page _____	4. If the request deals with a completed transaction, have you filed the return for the year in which the transaction was completed? *See* section 5.01.
Yes No	5. Are you requesting the letter ruling on a hypothetical situation or question? *See* section 6.12.
Yes No	6. Are you requesting the letter ruling on alternative plans of a proposed transaction? *See* section 6.12.
Yes No	7. Are you requesting the letter ruling for only part of an integrated transaction? *See* sections 6.03.
Yes No	8. Are you requesting the letter ruling for a business, trade, industrial association, or similar group concerning the application of tax law to its members? *See* section 6.05.
Yes No	9. Are you requesting the letter ruling for a foreign government or its political subdivision? *See* section 6.07.
Yes No Pages _____	10. Have you included a complete statement of all the facts relevant to the transaction? *See* section 7.01(1).
Yes No N/A	11. Have you submitted with the request true copies of all wills, deeds, and other documents relevant to the transaction, and labeled and attached them in alphabetical sequence? *See* section 7.01(2).
Yes No N/A	12. Have you submitted with the request a copy of all applicable foreign laws, and certified English translations of documents that are in a language other than English or of foreign laws in cases where English is not the official language of the foreign country involved? *See* section 7.01(2).
Yes No Page _____	13. Have you included an analysis of facts and their bearing on the issues? Have you included, rather than merely incorporated by reference, all material facts from the documents in the request? *See* section 7.01(3).
Yes No Page _____	14. Have you included the required statement regarding whether the same issue in the letter ruling request is in an earlier return of the taxpayer or in a return for any year of a related taxpayer? *See* section 7.01(4).
Yes No Page _____	15. Have you included the required statement regarding whether the Service previously ruled on the same or similar issue for the taxpayer, a related taxpayer, or a predecessor? *See* section 7.01(5)(a).
Yes No Page _____	16. Have you included the required statement regarding whether the taxpayer, a related taxpayer, a predecessor, or any representatives previously submitted a request (including an application for change in accounting method) involving the same or similar issue but withdrew the request before the letter ruling or determination letter was issued? *See* section 7.01(5)(b).

Yes No Page ____	17. Have you included the required statement regarding whether the taxpayer, a related taxpayer, or a predecessor previously submitted a request (including an application for change in accounting method) involving the same or similar issue that is currently pending with the Service? *See* section 7.01(5)(c).
Yes No Page ____	18. Have you included the required statement regarding whether, at the same time as this request, the taxpayer or a related taxpayer is presently submitting another request (including an application for change in accounting method) involving the same or similar issue to the Service? *See* section 7.01(5)(d).
Yes No N/A Page ____	19. If your request involves the interpretation of a substantive provision of an income or estate tax treaty, have you included the required statement regarding whether the tax authority of the treaty jurisdiction has issued a ruling on the same or similar issue for the taxpayer, a related taxpayer, or a predecessor; whether the same or similar issue is being examined, or has been settled, by the tax authority of the treaty jurisdiction or is otherwise the subject of a closing agreement in that jurisdiction; and whether the same or similar issue is being considered by the competent authority of the treaty jurisdiction? *See* section 7.01(6).
Yes No N/A Page ____	20. If your request is for recognition of Indian tribal government status or status as a political subdivision of an Indian tribal government, does your request contain a letter from the Bureau of Indian Affairs regarding the tribe's status? *See* section 7.01(7), which states that taxpayers are encouraged to submit this letter with the request and provides the address for the Bureau of Indian Affairs.
Yes No Pages ____	21. Have you included the required statement of relevant authorities in support of your views? *See* section 7.01(8).
Yes No Page ____	22. Have you included the required statement regarding whether the law in connection with the request is uncertain and whether the issue is adequately addressed by relevant authorities? *See* section 7.01(8).
Yes No Pages ____	23. Does your request discuss the implications of any legislation, tax treaties, court decisions, regulations, notices, revenue rulings, or revenue procedures that you determined to be contrary to the position advanced? *See* section 7.01(9), which states that taxpayers are encouraged to inform the Service of such authorities.
Yes No N/A Page ____	24. If you determined that there are no contrary authorities, have you included a statement to this effect in your request? *See* section 7.01(9).
Yes No N/A Page ____	25. Have you included in your request a statement identifying any pending legislation that may affect the proposed transaction? *See* section 7.01(10).
Yes No	26. Is the request accompanied by the deletion statement required by § 6110? *See* section 7.01(11).
Yes No Page ____	27. Have you (or your authorized representative) signed and dated the request? *See* section 7.01(12).
Yes No N/A	28. If the request is signed by your representative or if your representative will appear before the Service in connection with the request, is the request accompanied by a properly prepared and signed power of attorney with the signatory's name typed or printed? *See* section 7.01(14).
Yes No Page ____	29. Have you included, signed, and dated the penalties of perjury statement in the format required by section 7.01(15)?

Yes No N/A — 30. Are you submitting your request in duplicate if necessary? *See* section 7.01(16).

Yes No N/A
Pages ____ — 31. If you are requesting separate letter rulings on different issues involving one factual situation, have you included a statement to that effect in each request? *See* section 7.02(1).

Yes No N/A — 32. If you want copies of the letter ruling sent to a representative, does the power of attorney contain a statement to that effect? *See* section 7.02(2).

Yes No N/A — 33. If you do not want a copy of the letter ruling to be sent to any representative, does the power of attorney contain a statement to that effect? *See* section 7.02(2).

Yes No N/A — 34. If you are making a two-part letter ruling request, have you included a summary statement of the facts you believe to be controlling? *See* section 7.02(3).

Yes No N/A
Page ____ — 35. If you want your letter ruling request to be processed ahead of the regular order or by a specific date, have you requested expedited handling in the manner required by section 7.02(4) and stated a compelling need for such action in the request? But, a request dealing solely with a section 368 reorganization or a section 355 distribution may receive expedited treatment without stating a compelling need. Section 7.02(4) of this revenue procedure.

Yes No N/A
Page ____ — 36. If you are requesting a copy of any document related to the letter ruling request to be sent by facsimile (fax) transmission, have you included a statement to that effect? *See* section 7.02(5).

Yes No N/A
Page ____ — 37. If you want to have a conference on the issues involved in the request, have you included a request for conference in the letter ruling request? *See* section 7.02(6).

Yes No — 38. Have you included the correct user fee with the request and is your check or money order in U.S. dollars and payable to the Internal Revenue Service? *See* section 15 and Appendix A to determine the correct amount.

Yes No N/A
Page ____ — 39. If your request involves a personal tax issue and you qualify for the reduced user fee when gross income is less than $250,000, have you included the required certification? *See* paragraphs (A)(4)(a) and (B)(1) of Appendix A.

Yes No N/A
Page ____ — 40. If your request involves a business-related tax issue and you qualify for the reduced user fee when gross income is less than $1 million, have you included the required certification? *See* paragraphs (A)(4)(b) and (B)(1) of Appendix A.

Yes No N/A
Page ____ — 41. If you qualify for the user fee for substantially identical letter rulings, have you included the required information? *See* section 15.07(2) and paragraph (A)(5)(a) of Appendix A.

Yes No N/A
Page ____ — 42. If you qualify for the user fee for a § 301.9100 request to extend the time for filing an identical accounting method change on a single Form 3115, have you included the required information? *See* section 15.07(4) and paragraph (A)(5)(d) of Appendix A.

Yes No N/A — 43. If your request is covered by any of the checklists, guideline revenue procedures, notices, safe harbor revenue procedures, or other special requirements listed in Appendix E, have you complied with all of the requirements of the applicable revenue procedure or notice?

Rev. Proc. List other applicable revenue procedures or notices, including checklists, used or relied upon in the preparation of this letter ruling request (Cumulative Bulletin or Internal Revenue Bulletin citation not required).

_____

_____

_____

Yes No N/A
Page _____

44. If you are requesting relief under § 7805(b) (regarding retroactive effect), have you complied with all of the requirements in section 11.11?

Yes No

45. Have you addressed your request to the attention of the Associate Chief Counsel (Corporate), the Associate Chief Counsel (Financial Institutions and Products), the Associate Chief Counsel (Income Tax and Accounting), the Associate Chief Counsel (International), the Associate Chief Counsel (Passthroughs and Special Industries), the Associate Chief Counsel (Procedure and Administration), or the Division Counsel/Associate Chief Counsel (Tax Exempt and Government Entities), as appropriate? The mailing address is:

Internal Revenue Service
Attn: CC:PA:LPD:DRU
P. O. Box 7604
Ben Franklin Station
Washington, DC 20044

If a private delivery service is used, the address is:

Internal Revenue Service
Attn: CC:PA:LPD:DRU, Room 5336
1111 Constitution Ave., NW
Washington, DC 20224

The package should be marked: RULING REQUEST SUBMISSION. Improperly addressed requests may be delayed (sometimes for over a week) in reaching CC:PA:LPD:DRU for initial processing.

____

Signature Title or Authority Date

Typed or printed name of person signing checklist

APPENDIX D

LIST OF SMALL BUSINESS/SELF-EMPLOYED OPERATING DIVISION (SB/SE) OFFICES FOR REQUESTING DETERMINATION LETTERS

Requests for determination letters under Rev. Proc. 2007–1, this revenue procedure, from SB/SE and W&I taxpayers, should be sent to the appropriate SB/SE office listed below based upon the type of tax involved. Both the request and the envelope in which it is sent should be marked "DETERMINATION LETTER REQUEST."

INCOME TAX

Requests for determination letters regarding income tax (including requests from international taxpayers) should be sent to:

Office of the Director, Technical Services
Internal Revenue Service
Attn: SE:S:E:TS
Mail Stop 5000
24000 Avila Road
Laguna Niguel, CA 92677

ESTATE AND GIFT TAXES

Requests for determination letters regarding estate and gift tax should be sent to:

Chief, Estate & Gift Tax Operations
Internal Revenue Service
SE:S:SP:E&G
1222 Spruce Street
M/S 1022STL
St. Louis, MO 63103–2839

EMPLOYMENT TAXES

Requests for determination letters regarding employment tax (except for requests for determination of worker status, which should be sent to the appropriate office listed in the instructions to Form SS–8) should be sent to:

Chief, Employment Tax Operations
Internal Revenue Service
Attn: SE:S:SP:ET
5000 Ellin Road
Room C9–202
Lanham, MD 20706

EXCISE TAXES

Requests for determination letters regarding excise taxes should be sent to:

Chief, Excise Tax Operations
Internal Revenue Service
Attn: SE:S:SP:EX
5000 Ellin Road
Room C9–207
Lanham, MD 20706

APPENDIX E

CHECKLISTS, GUIDELINE REVENUE PROCEDURES, NOTICES, SAFE HARBOR REVENUE PROCEDURES, AND AUTOMATIC CHANGE REVENUE PROCEDURES

Specific revenue procedures and notices supplement the general instructions for requests explained in section 7 of this revenue procedure and apply to requests for letter rulings or determination letters regarding the Code sections and matters listed in this section.

Checklists, guideline revenue procedures, and notices

.01 For requests relating to the following Code sections and subject matters, refer to the following checklists, guideline revenue procedures, and notices.

CODE OR REGULATION SECTION	*REVENUE PROCEDURE AND NOTICE*
103, 141–150, 7478, and 7871 Issuance of state or local obligations	Rev. Proc. 96–16, 1996–1 C.B. 630 (for a reviewable ruling under § 7478 and a nonreviewable ruling); Rev. Proc. 88–31, 1988–1 C.B. 832 (for approval of areas of chronic economic distress); and Rev. Proc. 82–26, 1982–1 C.B. 476 (for "on behalf of" and similar issuers). For approval of areas of chronic economic distress, Rev. Proc. 88–31 explains how this request for approval must be submitted to the Assistant Secretary for Housing/Federal Housing Commissioner of the Department of Housing and Urban Development.
1.166–2(d)(3) Uniform express determination letter for making election	Rev. Proc. 92–84, 1992–2 C.B. 489.
Subchapter C—(Corporate Distributions and Adjustments	Rev. Proc. 77–37, 1977–2 C.B. 568, as modified by Rev. Proc. 89–30, 1989–1 C.B. 895, and as amplified by Rev. Proc. 77–41, 1977–2 C.B. 574, Rev. Proc. 83–81, 1983–2 C.B. 598 (*see also* Rev. Proc. 2007–3, this Bulletin), Rev. Proc. 84–42, 1984–1 C.B. 521 (superseded as to no-rule areas by Rev. Proc. 2007–3, this Bulletin), Rev. Proc. 86–42, 1986–2 C.B. 722, and Rev. Proc. 89–50, 1989–2 C.B. 631. *But see* section 3.01 of Rev. Proc. 2007–3, this Bulletin, (corporate distributions, transfers, and reorganizations under §§ 332, 351, 368(a)(1)(A), 368(a)(1)(B), 368(a)(1)(C), 368(a)(1)(E), 368(a)(1)(F), and 1036), which describes certain corporate transactions where the Service will not issue letter rulings or determination letters.
301 Nonapplicability on sales of stock of employer to defined contribution plan	Rev. Proc. 87–22, 1987–1 C.B. 718.
302, 311 Checklist questionnaire	Rev. Proc. 86–18, 1986–1 C.B. 551; and Rev. Proc. 77–41, 1977–2 C.B. 574.
302(b)(4) Checklist questionnaire	Rev. Proc. 81–42, 1981–2 C.B. 611.
311 Checklist questionnaire	Rev. Proc. 86–16, 1986–1 C.B. 546.
332 Checklist questionnaire	Rev. Proc. 90–52, 1990–2 C.B. 626. *But see* section 3.01 of Rev. Proc. 2007–3, this Bulletin, which describes certain corporate transactions where the Service will not issue letter rulings or determination letters.
338 Extension of time to make elections	Rev. Proc. 2003–33, 2003–1 C.B. 803, provides guidance as to how an automatic extension of time under § 301.9100–3 of the Regulations on Procedure and Administration may be obtained to file elections under § 338. This revenue procedure also informs taxpayers who do not qualify for the automatic extension, of the information necessary to obtain a letter ruling.

351 Checklist questionnaire	Rev. Proc. 83–59, 1983–2 C.B. 575. *But see* section 3.01 of Rev. Proc. 2007–3, this Bulletin, which describes certain transfers to controlled corporations where the Service will not issue letter rulings or determination letters.
355 Checklist questionnaire	Rev. Proc. 96–30, 1996–1 C.B. 696, as modified and amplified by Rev. Proc. 2003–48, 2003–2 C.B. 86.
368(a)(1)(E) Checklist questionnaire	Rev. Proc. 81–60, 1981–2 C.B. 680. *But see* section 3.01 of Rev. Proc. 2007–3, this Bulletin, which describes circumstances under which the Service will not issue letter rulings or determination letters as to whether a transaction constitutes a corporate recapitalization within the meaning of § 368(a)(1)(E) (or a transaction that also qualifies under § 1036).
461(h) Alternative method for the inclusion of common improvement costs in basis	Rev. Proc. 92–29, 1992–1 C.B. 748.
482 Advance pricing agreements	Rev. Proc. 96–53, 1996–2 C.B. 375, as modified by Notice 98–65, 1998–2 C.B. 803, and amplified by Rev. Proc. 2006–54, 2006–49 I.R.B. 1035.
521 Appeal procedure with regard to adverse determination letters and revocation or modification of exemption letter rulings and determination letters	Rev. Proc. 90–27, 1990–1 C.B. 514.
1.817–5(a)(2) Issuer of a variable contract requesting relief	Rev. Proc. 92–25, 1992–1 C.B. 741.
877, 2107, and 2501(a)(3) Individuals who lose U.S. citizenship or cease to be taxed as long-term U.S. residents with a principal purpose to avoid U.S. taxes	Notice 97–19, 1997–1 C.B. 394, as modified by Notice 98–34, 1998–2 C.B. 29.
1362(b)(5) and 1362(f) Relief for late S corporation and related elections under certain circumstances	Rev. Proc. 2004–49, 2004–2 C.B. 210; Rev. Proc. 2003–43, 2003–1 C.B. 998; Rev. Proc. 97–48, 1997–2 C.B. 521.
1362(b)(5) and 301.7701–3 Automatic extensions of time for late S corporation election and late corporate entity classification	Rev. Proc. 2004–48, 2004–2 C.B. 172.

1.1502–13(e)(3) Consent to treat intercompany transactions on a separate entity basis and revocation of this consent	Rev. Proc. 97–49, 1997–2 C.B. 523.
1.1502–76(a)(1) Consent to file a consolidated return where member(s) of the affiliated group use a 52–53 week taxable year	Rev. Proc. 89–56, 1989–2 C.B. 643.
1504(a)(3)(A) and (B) Waiver of application of § 1504(a)(3)(A) for certain corporations	Rev. Proc. 2002–32, 2002–1 C.B. 959.
1552 Consent to elect or change method of allocating affiliated group's consolidated federal income tax liability	Rev. Proc. 90–39, 1990–2 C.B. 365, as clarified by Rev. Proc. 90–39A, 1990–2 C.B. 367.
2642 Allocations of generation-skipping transfer tax exemption	Rev. Proc. 2004–46, 2004–2 C.B. 142, provides an alternative method for requesting relief to make a late allocation of the generation-skipping transfer tax exemption. This revenue procedure also informs taxpayers who are denied relief or who are outside the scope of the revenue procedure of the information necessary for obtaining a letter ruling.
2652(a)(3) Reverse qualified terminable interest property elections	Rev. Proc. 2004–47, 2004–1, C.B. 169, provides an alternative method for certain taxpayers to obtain an extension of time to make a late reverse qualified terminable interest property election under § 2652(a)(3). This revenue procedure also informs taxpayers who are denied relief or who are outside the scope of the revenue procedure of the information necessary to obtain a letter ruling.
4980B Failure to satisfy continuation coverage requirements of group health plans	Rev. Proc. 87–28, 1987–1 C.B. 770 (treating references to former § 162(k) as if they were references to § 4980B).
7701 Relief for a late initial classification election for a newly formed entity	Rev. Proc. 2002–59, 2002–2 C.B. 615.
7701(a)(40) and 7871(d) Indian tribal governments and subdivision of Indian tribal governments	Rev. Proc. 84–37, 1984–1 C.B. 513, as modified by Rev. Proc. 86–17, 1986–1 C.B. 550, and Rev. Proc. 2007–1, this revenue procedure, (provides guidelines for obtaining letter rulings recognizing Indian tribal government or tribal government subdivision status; also provides for inclusion in list of recognized tribal governments in revised versions of Rev. Proc. 2002–64, 2002–2 C.B. 717, or in list of recognized subdivisions of Indian tribal governments in revised versions of Rev. Proc. 84–36, 1984–1 C.B. 510, as modified and made permanent by Rev. Proc. 86–17).

301.7701–2(a) Classification of undivided fractional interests in rental real estate	Rev. Proc. 2002–22, 2002–1 C.B. 733 (specifies the conditions under which the Service will consider a letter ruling request that an undivided fractional interest in rental real property (other than a mineral property as defined in § 614) is not an interest in a business entity).
301.7701–3 Automatic extensions of time for late S corporation election and late corporate entity classification	Rev. Proc. 2004–48, 2004–2 C.B. 172.
301.9100–3 Extension of time to make entity classification election	Rev. Proc. 2002–59, 2002–2 C.B. 615.
7702 Closing agreement for failed life insurance contracts	Notice 99–48, 1999–2 C.B. 429; Rev. Rul. 91–17, 1991–1 C.B. 190.
7702A Relief for inadvertent non-egregious failure to comply with modified endowment contract rules	Rev. Proc. 2001–42, 2001–2 C.B. 212.
7704(g) Revocation of election	Notice 98–3, 1998–1 C.B. 333.

SUBJECT MATTERS	*REVENUE PROCEDURE*
Accounting periods; changes in period	Rev. Proc. 2002–39, 2002–1 C.B. 1046, as clarified and modified by Notice 2002–72, 2002–2 C.B. 843, and as modified by Rev. Proc. 2003–34, 2003–1 C.B. 856; and Rev. Proc. 2007–1, this revenue procedure, for which sections 1, 2.01, 2.02, 2.05, 3.03, 5.02, 6.03, 6.05, 6.07, 6.11, 7.01(1), 7.01(2), 7.01(3), 7.01(4), 7.01(5), 7.01(6), 7.01(8), 7.01(9), 7.01(10), 7.01(13), 7.01(14), 7.01(15), 7.02(2), 7.02(4), 7.02(5), 7.02(6), 7.03, 7.04, 7.05, 7.07, 8.01, 8.03, 8.04, 8.05, 8.06, 10, 11, 15, 17, 18, Appendix A, and Appendix E are applicable.
Classification of liquidating trusts	Rev. Proc. 82–58, 1982–2 C.B. 847, as modified and amplified by Rev. Proc. 94–45, 1994–2 C.B. 684, and as amplified by Rev. Proc. 91–15, 1991–1 C.B. 484 (checklist questionnaire), as modified and amplified by Rev. Proc. 94–45.
Earnings and profits determinations	Rev. Proc. 75–17, 1975–1 C.B. 677; Rev. Proc. 2007–1, this revenue procedure, sections 2.05, 3.03, 7, 8, and 10.05; and Rev. Proc. 2007–3, this Bulletin, section 3.01.
Estate, gift, and generation-skipping transfer tax issues	Rev. Proc. 91–14, 1991–1 C.B. 482 (checklist questionnaire).
Deferred intercompany transactions; election not to defer gain or loss	Rev. Proc. 97–49, 1997–2 C.B. 523.
Leveraged leasing	Rev. Proc. 2001–28, 2001–1 C.B. 1156, and Rev. Proc. 2001–29, 2001–1 C.B. 1160.

Rate orders; regulatory agency; normalization	A letter ruling request that involves a question of whether a rate order that is proposed or issued by a regulatory agency will meet the normalization requirements of § 168(f)(2) (pre-Tax Reform Act of 1986, § 168(e)(3)) and former §§ 46(f) and 167(l) ordinarily will not be considered unless the taxpayer states in the letter ruling request whether— (1) the regulatory authority responsible for establishing or approving the taxpayer's rates has reviewed the request and believes that the request is adequate and complete; and (2) the taxpayer will permit the regulatory authority to participate in any Associate office conference concerning the request. If the taxpayer or the regulatory authority informs a consumer advocate of the request for a letter ruling and the advocate wishes to communicate with the Service regarding the request, any such communication should be sent to: Internal Revenue Service, Associate Chief Counsel (Procedure & Administration), Attn: CC:PA:LPD:DRU, P.O. Box 7604, Ben Franklin Station, Washington, DC 20044 (or, if a private delivery service is used: Internal Revenue Service, Associate Chief Counsel (Procedure & Administration), Attn: CC:PA:LPD:DRU, Room 5336, 1111 Constitution Ave., NW, Washington, DC 20224). These communications will be treated as third party contacts for purposes of § 6110.
Unfunded deferred compensation	Rev. Proc. 71–19, 1971–1 C.B. 698, as amplified by Rev. Proc. 92–65, 1992–2 C.B. 428. *See* Rev. Proc. 92–64, 1992–2 C.B. 422, as modified by Notice 2000–56, 2000–2 C.B. 393, for the model trust for use in Rabbi Trust Arrangements.

Safe harbor revenue procedures

.02 For requests relating to the following Code sections and subject matters, refer to the following safe harbor revenue procedures.

CODE OR REGULATION SECTION	*REVENUE PROCEDURE*
103 and 141–150 Issuance of state or local obligations	Rev. Proc. 93–17, 1993–1 C.B. 507 (change of use of proceeds); Rev. Proc. 97–13, 1997–1 C.B. 632, as modified by Rev. Proc. 2001–39, 2001–2 C.B. 38 (management contracts); and Rev. Proc. 97–14, 1997–1 C.B. 634 (research agreements).
61 Utility Cost Recovery Securitization Transactions	Rev. Proc. 2005–62, 2005–2 C.B. 507.
162 Restaurant Small Wares Costs	Rev. Proc. 2002–12, 2002–1 C.B. 374.
165 Casualty and theft losses from hurricanes	Rev. Proc. 2006–32, 2006–28 I.R.B. 61.
168 Depreciation of original and replacement tires for certain vehicles	Rev. Proc. 2002–27, 2002–1 C.B. 802.
168 Depreciation of fiber optic node and trunk line of a cable television distribution system	Rev. Proc. 2003–63, 2003–2 C.B. 304.

280B Certain structural modifications to a building not treated as a demolition	Rev. Proc. 95–27, 1995–1 C.B. 704.
446 Film producer's treatment of certain creative property costs	Rev. Proc. 2004–36, 2004–1 C.B. 1063.
451 Up-front network upgrade payments made to utilities	Rev. Proc. 2005–35, 2005–2 C.B. 76.
471 Estimating inventory shrinkage	Rev. Proc. 98–29, 1998–1 C.B. 857.
471 Valuation of remanufactured cores	Rev. Proc. 2003–20, 2003–1 C.B. 445.
584(a) Qualification of a proposed common trust fund plan	Rev. Proc. 92–51, 1992–1 C.B. 988.
642(c)(5) Qualification of trusts as pooled income funds	Rev. Proc. 88–53, 1988–2 C.B. 712.
664 Charitable remainder trusts	Rev. Proc. 2005–24, 2005–1 C.B. 909.
664(d)(1) Qualification of trusts as charitable remainder annuity trusts	Rev. Proc. 2003–53, 2003–2 C.B. 230; Rev. Proc. 2003–54, 2003–2 C.B. 236; Rev. Proc. 2003–55, 2003–2 C.B. 242; Rev. Proc. 2003–56, 2003–2 C.B. 249; Rev. Proc. 2003–57, 2003–2 C.B. 257; Rev. Proc. 2003–58, 2003–2 C.B. 262; Rev. Proc. 2003–59, 2003–2 C.B. 268; Rev. Proc. 2003–60, 2003–2 C.B. 274.
664(d)(2) and (3) Qualification of trusts as charitable remainder unitrusts	Rev. Proc. 2005–52, 2005–2 C.B. 326; Rev. Proc. 2005–53, 2005–2 C.B. 339; Rev. Proc. 2005–54, 2005–2 C.B. 353; Rev. Proc. 2005–55, 2005–2 C.B. 367; Rev. Proc. 2005–56, 2005–2 C.B. 383; Rev. Proc. 2005–57, 2005–2 C.B. 392; Rev. Proc. 2005–58, 2005–2 C.B. 402; Rev. Proc. 2005–59, 2005–2 C.B. 412.
856(c) Certain loans treated as real estate assets	Rev. Proc. 2003–65, 2003–2 C.B. 336.
860H Transfers of ownership interests in Financial Asset Securitization Investment Trusts	Rev. Proc. 2001–12, 2001–1 C.B. 335.
1031(a) Qualification as a qualified exchange accommodation arrangement	Rev. Proc. 2000–37, 2000–2 C.B. 308.

1286 Determination of reasonable compensation under mortgage servicing contracts	Rev. Proc. 91–50, 1991–2 C.B. 778.
1362(f) Automatic inadvertent termination relief to certain corporations	Rev. Proc. 2003–43, 2003–1 C.B. 998.
2056A Qualified Domestic Trust	Rev. Proc. 96–54, 1996–2 C.B. 386.
2702(a)(3)(A) and 25.2702–5(c) Qualified Personal Residence Trust	Rev. Proc. 2003–42, 2003–1 C.B. 993.
4051(a)(2) Imposition of tax on heavy trucks and trailers sold at retail	Rev. Proc. 2005–19, 2005–1 C.B. 832.
1.7704–2(d) New business activity of existing partnership is closely related to pre-existing business	Rev. Proc. 92–101, 1992–2 C.B. 579.

SUBJECT MATTERS	*REVENUE PROCEDURE*
Certain rent-to-own contracts treated as leases	Rev. Proc. 95–38, 1995–2 C.B. 397.

Automatic change in accounting period revenue procedures

.03 For requests for an automatic change in accounting period, refer to the following automatic change revenue procedures published and/or in effect as of December 31, 2006:

Rev. Proc. 2002–37, 2002–1 C.B. 1030, as clarified and modified by Notice 2002–72, 2002–2 C.B. 843, and as modified by Rev. Proc. 2003–34, 2003–1 C.B. 856 (certain corporations); Rev. Proc. 2002–38, 2002–2 C.B. 1037, as clarified and modified by Notice 2002–72, 2002–2 C.B. 843 (certain partnerships, S corporations, electing S corporations, or personal service corporations); and Rev. Proc. 2003–62, 2003–2 C.B. 299 (individual seeking a calendar year); and as clarified, modified, amplified, and superseded by Rev. Proc. 2006–45, 2006–45 I.R.B. 851 (corporations) and Rev. Proc. 2006–46, 2006–45 I.R.B. 859 (partnership and Subchapter S corporations) for changes in annual accounting periods for which the first effective year ends after October 17, 2006.

The Commissioner's consent to an otherwise qualifying automatic change in accounting period is granted only if the taxpayer timely complies with the applicable automatic change revenue procedure.

Rev. Proc. 2007–1, 2007–1 I.R.B. 1.

26 CFR 601.105: *Examination of returns and claims for refund, credit or abatement; determination of correct tax liability.*

Rev. Proc. 2007–2

TABLE OF CONTENTS

SECTION 1. PURPOSE AND AUTHORITY

Description of purpose

.01 Technical advice. This revenue procedure explains when and how the Associate Chief Counsel (Corporate), the Associate Chief Counsel (Financial Institutions and Products), the Associate Chief Counsel (Income Tax and Accounting), the Associate Chief Counsel (International), the Associate Chief Counsel (Passthroughs and Special Industries), the Associate Chief Counsel (Procedure and Administration), and the Division Counsel/Associate Chief Counsel (Tax Exempt and Government Entities) issue technical advice memoranda (TAMs) to a director or an appeals area director. It also explains the rights that a taxpayer has when a field office requests a TAM regarding a tax matter. Rev. Proc. 2006–2 superseded.

Updated annually

.02 This revenue procedure is updated annually as the second revenue procedure of the year, but may be modified during the year.

Delegation authority

.03 The provisions of this revenue procedure apply if the authority normally exercised by the director has been properly delegated to another official.

SECTION 2. DEFINITIONS

Operating division

.01 The term "operating division" means the (1) Large and Mid-Size Business Division (LMSB); (2) the Small Business/Self-Employed Division (SB/SE); (3) the Wage and Investment Division (W&I); (4) the Tax Exempt and Government Entities Division (TE/GE).

Director

.02 The term "director" means (1) the Director, Field Operations (LMSB) for the taxpayer's industry; (2) a Territory Manager, Field Compliance (SB/SE); (3) the Director, Compliance (W&I); (4) the Director, International (LMSB); (5) the Director, Employee Plans Examinations; (6) the Director, Exempt Organizations Examinations; (7) the Director, Federal, State & Local Governments; (8) the Director, Tax Exempt Bonds; (9) the Director, Indian Tribal Governments; (10) the Appeals Area Director; (11) any official to whom the authority normally exercised by a director has properly been delegated.

Territory manager

.03 The term "territory manager" means (1) a territory manager (LMSB); (2) a territory manager, examination (SB/SE); (3) a territory manager, specialty (SB/SE); (4) the Director, Compliance (W&I); (5) the Employee Plans Examinations Area manager; (6) the Exempt Organizations Examinations Area manager; (7) the Employee Plans Determinations manager; (8) the Exempt Organizations Determinations manager; (9) the group manager, Federal, State &

Local Governments; (10) the manager, field operations, Tax Exempt Bonds; or (11) the group manager, Indian Tribal Governments.

Appeals officer

.04 The term "Appeals officer" means the appeals officer assigned to the taxpayer's case and includes an Appeals Team Case Leader.

Taxpayer

.05 The term "taxpayer" means any person subject to any provision of the Internal Revenue Code, including an issuer of obligations the interest on which is excluded from gross income under § 103, and their representatives.

Associate office

.06 The term "Associate office" means (1) the Office of Associate Chief Counsel (Corporate); (2) the Office of Associate Chief Counsel (Financial Institutions and Products); (3) the Office of Associate Chief Counsel (Income Tax and Accounting); (4) the Office of Associate Chief Counsel (International); (5) the Office of Associate Chief Counsel (Passthroughs and Special Industries); (6) the Office of Associate Chief Counsel (Procedure and Administration); or (7) the Office of Division Counsel/Associate Chief Counsel (Tax Exempt and Government Entities).

Field office

.07 The term "field office" means personnel in any examination or Appeals office.

Field counsel

.08 The term "field counsel" means any attorney assigned to the Division Counsel for an operating division who is not a member of Division Counsel Headquarters.

SECTION 3. THE NATURE OF TECHNICAL ADVICE

When advice furnished

.01 Technical advice is advice furnished by an Associate office in a memorandum that responds to any request, submitted under this revenue procedure, for assistance on any technical or procedural question that develops during any proceeding before the IRS. The field office may request a TAM when the application of the law to the facts involved is unclear. The question must be on the interpretation and proper application of tax laws, tax treaties, regulations, revenue rulings, notices, or other precedents to a specific set of facts that concerns the treatment of an item in a year under examination or appeal. A TAM may not be requested for prospective or hypothetical transactions. Proceedings include: (1) the examination of a taxpayer's return; (2) the consideration of a taxpayer's claim for credit or refund; (3) any matter under examination or in Appeals pertaining to tax-exempt bonds, tax credit bonds, or mortgage credit certificates; and (4) any other matter involving a specific taxpayer under the jurisdiction of a director. Technical advice does not include any oral legal advice or any written legal advice furnished to the field office that is not submitted and processed under this revenue procedure.

TAM may be requested even if previous TAM on same matter was issued

.02 A director may raise an issue in any tax period, even if a TAM was requested and furnished for the same or similar issue for another tax period. The field office may also request a TAM on an issue even if Appeals disposed of the same or similar issue for another tax period of the same taxpayer.

Taxpayer Participation

.03 Taxpayers will be afforded an opportunity to participate in the TAM process. Taxpayer participation is preferred but not required in order to process a request for technical advice. A taxpayer's failure to participate in stages that are identified as "material", however, will constitute waiver of the right to the conference described in Section 9.

Under no circumstances will a taxpayer be treated as having waived its right to see the issued TAM or to have waived its rights regarding disclosure and deletions described in Section 10.

SECTION 4. TYPES OF ISSUES NOT SUBJECT TO THIS PROCEDURE

Alcohol, tobacco, and firearms taxes

.01 The procedures for obtaining technical advice specifically applicable to federal alcohol, tobacco, and firearms taxes under subtitle E of the Code are currently under the jurisdiction of the Alcohol and Tobacco Tax and Trade Bureau of the Treasury Department.

Tax exempt and government entities

.02 The procedures for requesting technical advice on issues under the jurisdiction of the Commissioner, Tax Exempt and Government Entities Division, are found in *Rev. Proc. 2007–5*, this Bulletin. The procedures under Rev. Proc. 2007–2, however, must be followed to request technical advice on issues pertaining to tax-exempt bonds, Indian tribal governments, federal, state, or local governments, mortgage credit certificates, and deferred compensation plans under § 457.

Farmers' cooperatives

.03 Even though the Associate Chief Counsel (Passthroughs and Special Industries) has jurisdiction over issues arising under § 521, the procedures under Rev. Proc. 2007–5 of this Bulletin and Rev. Proc. 90–27, 1990–1 C.B. 514, must be followed.

Issues under § 301.9100

.04 A request for an extension of time for making an election or other application for relief under § 301.9100–3 of the Procedure and Administration Regulations is not submitted as a request for technical advice. Instead, the request is submitted as a request for a letter ruling, even if submitted after the examination of the taxpayer's return has begun or after the issues in the return are being considered in Appeals or a federal court. Therefore, a request under § 301.9100 should be submitted under Rev. Proc. 2007–1 (this Bulletin), and the payment of the applicable user fee is determined under Appendix A of Rev. Proc. 2007–1.

Frivolous issues

.05 Associate offices will not issue a TAM on frivolous issues. The field office will deny a taxpayer's request for a TAM if it involves frivolous issues. For purposes of this revenue procedure, a "frivolous issue" is one without basis in fact or law or one espousing a position held by revenue ruling, case law, or any court to be frivolous or groundless. Examples of frivolous or groundless issues may be found in IRS publications (including but not limited to Section 6.10 of Rev. Proc. 2007–1 and I.R.M. Section 4.10.12.1.1) or guidance and are described on the IRS website at *www.irs.gov/pub/irs-utl/friv_tax.pdf*

Issues in a docketed case

.06 A field office may not request technical advice on an issue if the same issue of the same taxpayer (or of a related taxpayer within the meaning of § 267 or a member of an affiliated group of which the taxpayer is also a member within the meaning of § 1504) is in a docketed case for any taxable year. If a case is docketed for an estate tax issue of a taxpayer while a request for technical advice on the same issue of the same taxpayer is pending, the Associate office may issue the TAM only if the appropriate Appeals officer and field counsel agree, by memorandum, to the issuance of the TAM.

Collection issues

.07 The Associate Chief Counsel (Procedure and Administration) does not provide technical advice on matters arising under the Internal Revenue Code and related statutes and regulations that involve the collection of taxes (including interest and penalties). With respect to such matters, the Associate Chief Counsel (Procedure and Administration) may issue alternate forms of advice.

SECTION 5. INITIATING A REQUEST FOR TECHNICAL ADVICE

Initiating a request for technical advice

.01 Because technical advice is issued to assist field offices, it is the field office that determines whether to request it. In determining whether to request technical advice, the field office should consider whether other forms of guidance, *e.g.*, published guidance, generic advice, or some other form of advice, would be more appropriate. Before requesting technical advice, however, the field office must request assistance and a recommendation from field counsel. If the field office disagrees with that recommendation, the field office must seek reconciliation with field counsel through their respective supervisors. Any request for technical advice must be approved in writing by the director.

Taxpayer may request technical advice

.02 While a case is under the jurisdiction of a director, a taxpayer may request that an issue be referred to the Associate office for technical advice. The request may be oral or written and should be directed to the field office. If the field office decides that a taxpayer's request for referral of an issue to the Associate office for a TAM is unwarranted, the field office will notify the taxpayer. A taxpayer's request for referral of an issue for technical advice will not be denied merely because the Associate office has already provided legal advice other than a TAM to the field office on the matter.

Appeal of field office denial of TAM request

.03 The taxpayer may appeal the decision by submitting to the field office, within 30 calendar days after notification that the request was denied, a written statement of the reasons why the matter should be referred to the Associate office. The statement should include a description of all pertinent facts (including any facts in dispute); a statement of the issue that the taxpayer would like to have addressed; a discussion of any relevant statutory or administrative provision, tax treaties, case law, or other authority; and an explanation of the taxpayer's position and the need for technical advice. Any extensions of the 30-day period must be requested in writing and must be approved by the director or, for LMSB, the territory manager. Decisions by the director or LMSB territory manager are final and may not be appealed.

Upon receipt, the field office will refer the taxpayer's written statement, along with the field office's statement of why the issue should not be referred to the Associate office for technical advice, to the director or, for LMSB, the territory manager, for decision. The director or LMSB territory manager will determine whether the issue should be referred for technical advice on the basis of the statements of the field office and the taxpayer. No conference will be held with the taxpayer or the taxpayer's representative. If the director or LMSB territory manager determines that a TAM is not warranted, the taxpayer will be informed in writing of the proposed denial of the request and the reasons for the denial (unless doing so would prejudice the Government's best interests).

The director or LMSB territory manager's decision may be reviewed but not appealed

.04 The taxpayer may not appeal the decision of the director or LMSB territory manager not to request a TAM. If the taxpayer does not agree with the proposed denial, all data on the issue for which a TAM has been sought, including the taxpayer's written request and statements, will be submitted for review to the director, LMSB; Examination Area Director, SB/SE; the Director, Compliance, W&I; the Director, Federal, State & Local Governments; the Director, Tax Exempt Bonds; the Director, Indian Tribal Governments or Appeals Director, Tax Policy and Procedure (Exam). Review of the proposed denial will be based solely on the written record; no conference will be held with the taxpayer or the taxpayer's representative. The person responsible for review may consult with the Associate office, if necessary, and will notify the field office whether the proposed denial of the taxpayer's request is approved or denied within 45 days of receiving all information. The field office will then notify the taxpayer. While the matter is being reviewed, the field office will suspend any final decision on the issue (except when the delay would prejudice the Government's interests). If the TAM has been denied because the issue is frivolous as described in 4.05 above, this review process is not available.

SECTION 6. PRE-SUBMISSION CONFERENCES

Purpose

.01 A pre-submission conference helps the field office, field counsel, the taxpayer, and the Associate office agree on the appropriate scope of the request for technical advice and the factual information and documents that must be included in the request. A pre-submission conference is not an alternative procedure for addressing the merits of the substantive positions advanced by the field office or by the taxpayer. During the pre-submission conference, the parties should discuss the framing of the issues and the background information and documents that should be included in the formal submission of the request for technical advice.

Pre-submission conferences are mandatory

.02 Pre-submission conferences include the taxpayer and representatives from the field office, field counsel, and the Associate office. These conferences are mandatory because they promote expeditious processing of requests for technical advice. If a request for technical advice is submitted without first holding a pre-submission conference, the Associate office will return the request for advice. Requests for technical advice can proceed even if a taxpayer declines to participate in a pre-submission conference.

Actions before a pre-submission conference

.03 Before requesting a pre-submission conference, the field office and the taxpayer must exchange proposed statements of the pertinent facts and issues. The proposed statements should include any facts in dispute, the issues that the parties intend to discuss, any legal analysis and supporting authorities, and any background documents that the parties believe would facilitate the Associate office's understanding of the issues to be discussed during the conference. Prior to the scheduled pre-submission conference, the field office and the taxpayer must submit to the Associate office their respective statements of pertinent facts and issues. The legal analysis provided in the parties' statements should be sufficient to enable the Associate office to become reasonably informed about the subject matter. The field office or the taxpayer must ensure that the Associate office receives a copy of any required power of attorney, preferably on Form 2848, *Power of Attorney and Declaration of Representative* (Rev. March 2004). The assigned branch of the Associate office must receive the pre-submission materials at least 10 business days before the conference is held.

Initiating a pre-submission conference

.04 A request for a pre-submission conference must be submitted in writing by the field office, with the assistance of field counsel. The request should identify the Associate office expected to have jurisdiction over the request for a TAM and should include a brief explanation of the primary issue so that an assignment to the appropriate branch of an Associate can be made. If the request is submitted by Appeals, field counsel assignments will be subject to the *ex parte* rules set forth in section 1001(a)(4) of the Internal Revenue Service Restructuring and Reform Act of 1998, Pub. L. No. 105–206, and Rev. Proc. 2000–43, 2000–2 C.B. 404. If the request involves an issue under the office of the Director, ATAT Examination, SB/SE, an issue under the office of the Director, OTSA, LMSB, or an industry issue under the Office of Pre-Filing and Technical Guidance, LMSB, then the field office and field counsel should coordinate with the technical advisor and field counsel contact. If the request is from Appeals and involves a coordinated issue or emerging issue under the Appeals Technical Guidance or Appeals Coordinated Issue (ACI) Program, the Appeals officer must coordinate with the Appeals Technical Guidance Coordinator/Specialist.

Manner of transmitting pre-submission materials

.05 To obtain the protection of taxpayer information offered by the Chief Counsel Intranet firewall, the pre-submission materials must be electronically transmitted by field counsel to the Technical Services Support Branch (TSS4510). TSS4510 will ensure delivery of the pre-submission materials to the appropriate Associate office. The TSS4510 email box cannot accept encrypted mail.

If documents are not electronically available, or if documents cannot reasonably be transmitted electronically, the request may be sent by fax to TSS4510 at 202–622–4817. If the documents are sent by fax, the director must also confirm the request in writing. Email or fax may be used to confirm the request. The Associate office will confirm receipt of the fax within one business day after receipt by the Associate office. Copies of the taxpayer's statement of deletions, penalties of perjury statement, and Form 2848, *Power of Attorney and Declaration of Representative* (Rev. March 2004) should be transmitted by fax to the Associate office attorney assigned to the case.

The field office should send the original of the materials sent by fax, and any supporting materials, to the Associate office attorney assigned to the case by express mail or private delivery service in order to avoid any delays in regular mail.

Scheduling the pre-submission conference

.06 After the materials have been received, the branch of the Associate office responsible for conducting the pre-submission conference will contact the taxpayer, the field office, and field counsel to arrange a mutually convenient time for the parties to participate in the conference. The conference generally should be held within 15, but not more than 30, calendar days after the field office is contacted.

Pre-submission Conferences may be conducted in person

.07 Although pre-submission conferences are generally conducted by telephone, the parties may also choose to conduct the conference in person.

Pre-submission conference may not be taped

.08 No tape, stenographic, or other verbatim recording of a conference may be made by any party.

Discussion of substantive issues is not binding on the Service

.09 Any discussion of substantive issues at a pre-submission conference is advisory only, is not binding on the Service or on the Office of Chief Counsel, and cannot be relied upon as a basis for obtaining retroactive relief under the provisions of § 7805(b).

New issues may be raised at pre-submission conference

.10 During the pre-submission conference, the Office of Chief Counsel may raise new issues in addition to those submitted by the field office and the taxpayer.

SECTION 7. SUBMITTING THE REQUEST FOR TECHNICAL ADVICE

Memorandum of issues, facts, law, and arguments; submission of relevant foreign laws and documents in a language other than English; statement regarding interpretation of an income or estate tax treaty; deletions statement

.01 Every request for technical advice must include a memorandum that describes the facts, issues, applicable law, and arguments supporting the taxpayer's position on the issues and the field office's position on the issues. The field office will prepare this statement with the assistance of field counsel. The memorandum must include a statement of all the facts and the issues. If the taxpayer and the field office disagree about ultimate findings of fact or about the relevance of facts, all of the facts should be included with an explanation that highlights the areas of disagreement. The memorandum must include an explanation of the taxpayer's position. This explanation must include a discussion of any relevant statutory provisions, tax treaties, court decisions, regulations, revenue rulings, revenue procedures, notices, and any other authority supporting the taxpayer's position. The memorandum must also include a similar explanation of the field office's position. Both the field office and the taxpayer should comment on any existing or pending legislation, tax treaties, regulations, revenue rulings, revenue procedures, or court decisions contrary to their respective positions. If either party determines that there are no authorities contrary to its position, that statement should be noted in the memorandum.

Transaction involving multiple taxpayers

.02 If the subject matter of the request involves a transaction among multiple taxpayers, the Associate office may issue a single TAM, but only if each taxpayer agrees to participate in the process.

Foreign laws and documents

.03 If applicable, the request for technical advice must include a copy of the relevant parts of all foreign laws, including statutes, regulations, administrative pronouncements, and any other relevant legal authority. This copy must be in the official language of the country involved and must be produced from an official publication of the foreign government or another widely available, generally accepted publication. If English is not the official language of the country involved, the submission must also include a copy of an English translation of the relevant parts of all foreign laws. The translation must be from an official publication of the foreign government or another widely available, generally accepted publication or from a certified English translation submitted in accordance with Section 7.03(2) of this revenue procedure. The taxpayer or the field office must identify the title and date of publication, including updates, of any widely available, generally accepted publication used by the taxpayer or its qualified translator as a source for the relevant parts of the foreign law. The taxpayer and the field office must inform the Associate office of the implications of any authority believed to interpret the foreign law, such as pending legislation, treaties, court decisions, notices, and administrative decisions.

(1) If the interpretation of a foreign law or foreign document is a material fact, the Associate office, at its discretion, may refuse to issue a TAM. This section applies whether or not the field office and the taxpayer dispute the interpretation of a foreign law or foreign document. The interpretation of a foreign law or foreign document means making a judgment about the import or effect of the foreign law or document that goes beyond its plain meaning.

(2) If applicable, a request for technical advice must include an accurate and complete certified English translation of the relevant parts of all contracts, wills, deeds, agreements, instruments, trust documents, proposed disclaimers, or other documents in a language other than English. If the taxpayer or the field office chooses to submit certified English translations of foreign laws, those translations must be based on an official publication of the foreign government or another widely available, generally accepted publication. In either case, the translation must be that of a qualified translator and must be attested to by the translator. The attestation must contain: (1) the attestant's name and address; (2) a statement that the translation submitted is a true and accurate translation of the foreign language document or law; and (3) a statement about the attestant's qualifications as a translator and that attestant's qualifications and knowledge regarding tax matters or any foreign law translated if the law is not a tax law.

(3) A request for technical advice involving the interpretation of a substantive provision of an income or estate tax treaty must include a written statement addressing whether: (1) the tax authority of the treaty jurisdiction has issued a ruling on the same or similar issue for the taxpayer, a related taxpayer (within the meaning of § 267 or a member of an affiliated group of which the taxpayer is also a member within the meaning of § 1504 (related taxpayer)), or any predecessor; (2) the same or similar issue for the taxpayer, a related taxpayer, or any predecessor is being examined, or has been settled, by the tax authority of the treaty jurisdiction or is otherwise the subject of a closing agreement in that jurisdiction; and (3) the same or similar issue for the taxpayer, a related taxpayer, or any predecessor is being considered by the competent authority of the treaty jurisdiction.

Statement recommending information to be deleted from public inspection

.04 Every request for technical advice must include a statement of proposed deletions from public inspection. The text of TAMs are open to public inspection under § 6110(a). The Service deletes certain information from the text before it is made available to the public in order to protect the privacy of taxpayers. To help the Service make the necessary deletions, the taxpayer must provide a statement indicating the deletions desired. A taxpayer who wants only names, addresses, and identifying numbers deleted should state this in the deletion statement. A taxpayer who wants more information deleted must provide a copy of the TAM request and supporting documents on which the taxpayer has placed brackets around the material to be deleted plus a statement indicating the statutory basis under § 6110(c) for each proposed deletion. The deletion statement must not appear in the memorandum described in Section 7.01 of this revenue procedure. Instead, the deletion statement must be made in a separate document that is signed and dated by the taxpayer or the taxpayer's authorized representative. A stamped signature or faxed signature is not permitted. If the deletion statement is not submitted, the taxpayer will be notified and advised by the field office that the statement is required. If the deletion statement is not received within 10 calendar days after the notification, the field office will use its best effort to provide the Associate office with an appropriate deletion statement. The taxpayer should follow this same process to propose deletions from any additional information submitted after the initial request for a TAM. An additional deletion statement is not required with each submission of additional information if the taxpayer's initial deletion statement requests that only names, addresses, and identifying numbers are to be deleted and the taxpayer wants only the same information deleted from the additional information.

Preparation of the memorandum; resolution of disagreements

.05 The field office prepares the memorandum described in Section 7.01 of this revenue procedure with the assistance of field counsel and sends it to the taxpayer by mail or fax transmission. The taxpayer then will have 5 calendar days from the date of mailing or fax transmission to respond by providing a written statement specifying any disagreement on the facts and issues. A taxpayer who needs more than 5 calendar days must submit a written request for an extension of time, subject to the approval of the director. The director shall make a determination on the request for extension as soon as reasonably possible. The request for extension shall be considered denied unless the director informs the taxpayer otherwise. The decision of the director on whether to approve an extension, and the length of any extension granted, is final and may not be appealed. After the taxpayer's response has been received by the field office, the parties will have 10 calendar days to resolve remaining disagreements. If all disagreements about the statement of facts and issues are resolved, then the field office will prepare a single statement of those agreed facts and issues. If disagreements continue, both the taxpayer's set of facts and issues and the field's sets of facts and issues will be forwarded to the Associate office. The field office, with the assistance of field counsel, will prepare a memorandum for the Associate office highlighting the material factual differences, and provide a copy to the taxpayer. This memorandum will be forwarded with the initial request for technical advice. The taxpayer's statement of facts and issues must be accompanied by the following declaration: "Under penalties of perjury, I declare that I have examined this information, including accompanying documents, and, to the best of my knowledge and belief, the information contains all the relevant facts relating to the request for technical advice, and such facts are true, correct, and complete." This declaration must be signed in accordance with the requirements in section 7.01(15)(b) of Rev. Proc. 2007–1. The field office must submit this declaration with the initial request for technical advice. If no agreement is reached regarding the facts, the Associate office may rely on the facts presented by the field office.

The field office will offer the taxpayer an opportunity to participate in the development of the TAM. If the taxpayer participates in the process, the field office will continue to offer the taxpayer the opportunity to participate. If the taxpayer does not participate in a material stage of the process after being offered an opportunity, the Associate office will nonetheless process the request, and the taxpayer will have waived the right to participate in the development and issuance of the TAM, including the right to the conference described in section 9.

Under no circumstances will a taxpayer be treated as having waived its right to see the issued TAM or to have waived its rights regarding disclosure and deletions described in Section 10.

A taxpayer's failure to participate in the development of the memorandum will be considered a failure to participate in a material stage of the TAM process and result in a waiver of the right to the conference discussed in Section 9.

Transmittal Form 4463, *Request for Technical Advice*

.06 The field counsel, with whom the TAM request was coordinated, must use Form 4463, *Request for Technical Advice*, for submitting a request for a TAM through TSS4510 to the Associate office. While the field office is responsible for preparing Form 4463, field counsel must submit the Form 4463 for a TAM request to the TSS4510 email address. To the extent feasible, the accompanying documents should also be submitted to the TSS4510 email address, followed by hard copy upon the request of the assigned branch of the Associate office.

All supporting and additional documents

.07 Field counsel should send additional or supporting documents that are not available in electronic form by fax to TSS4510 at 202–622–4817 or by express mail or private delivery service to the following address to avoid any delays in regular mail:

Internal Revenue Service
Attn: CC:PA:LPD:TSS, Room 5329
1111 Constitution Avenue, NW
Washington, DC 20224

Whenever possible, all documents should contain the case number and name of the Associate office attorney assigned to the pre-submission conference for the TAM request.

The field office must indicate on the Form 4463 the proper mailing address of the director to whom the Associate office should mail a copy of its reply to the TAM request under Section 10.06 of this revenue procedure.

Number of copies of request to be submitted

.08 The field office must submit three paper copies of the request for a TAM to the address in Section 7.07 of this revenue procedure, one paper copy to the Division Counsel of the operating division that has jurisdiction of the taxpayer's tax return, and if the request is from an Appeals office, one paper copy to the Appeals Director, Technical Services.

Power of attorney

.09 Any authorized representative, as described in section 7.01(13) of Rev. Proc. 2007–1, whether or not enrolled to practice, must comply with Treasury Department Circular No. 230 (31 C.F.R. part 10 (2002)) and with the conference and practice requirements of the Statement of Procedural Rules (26 C.F.R. §§ 601.501–601.509 (2002)). Form 2848, *Power of Attorney and Declaration of Representative* (Rev. March 2004), should be used. An original, a copy, or a fax transmission of the power of attorney is acceptable if its authenticity is not reasonably disputed.

Service not barred from issuing 30-day letter while a TAM request is pending.

.10 After consultation with Appeals, the Service may send the taxpayer a letter (Letter 950 (DO) or other letter from the 950 series, also known as a 30-day letter) notifying the taxpayer of the right to appeal the proposed changes within 30 days, while a request for technical advice is pending.

SECTION 8. INITIAL PROCESSING OF THE REQUEST FOR TECHNICAL ADVICE BY THE ASSOCIATE OFFICE

Assignment and initial review by Associate office attorney

.01 After a request for technical advice has been received by the appropriate Associate office, it will be assigned to an Associate office attorney within a branch. The Associate office attorney determines whether the request meets all procedural requirements of sections 4, 5, 6, and 7 of this revenue procedure and whether it raises issues that are appropriately addressed in a TAM.

Other forms of guidance

.02 If the assigned reviewer in the Associate office determines that guidance other than a TAM should be provided, the reviewer will immediately notify the Associate Chief Counsel. This other form of guidance may be published guidance, generic advice, or case-specific advice. Although the reviewer should make this determination as soon as possible, it may be made at any time during the processing of the request for advice. To make this determination, the reviewer should consider whether the issue has a broad application to similarly situated taxpayers or an industry and whether resolution of the issue is important to a clear understanding of the tax laws. The Associate Chief Counsel, after consultation with Division Counsel Headquarters and the Operating Division, will decide whether to issue the TAM or issue guidance in another form. The Associate Chief Counsel may decide to issue the TAM as well as another type of guidance, if doing so would promote sound tax administration.

Initial acknowledgment and processing

.03 Upon receipt of a request for technical advice, the Associate office attorney who has been assigned as the primary attorney on the request should immediately contact the field office. The purpose of this contact is only to acknowledge receipt of the request. Unless otherwise indicated, all references in this section to the Associate office or Associate office attorney are to the Associate office and attorney with primary responsibility for the TAM request.

Deficiencies in request leading to return

.04 Within 7 calendar days after assignment, the Associate office attorney will contact the field office and field counsel to discuss any deficiencies in the request and will work with the field office and field counsel to correct them. If they cannot be corrected within 7 calendar days, the request will be closed and returned to the field office. The request may be resubmitted when the deficiencies are corrected.

If only minor procedural deficiencies exist, the Associate office attorney will request the additional information without returning the case. If substantial additional information is required to resolve an issue or if major procedural problems cannot be resolved, the Associate office attorney will inform the field office and field counsel that the request for technical advice will be returned. If a request is returned, the field office should promptly notify the taxpayer of that decision and the reasons for the decision.

Initial discussion

.05 The Associate office attorney should contact the field office within 21 calendar days of receipt to discuss the procedural and substantive issues in the request. The Associate office attorney should also inform the field office about any matters referred to another Associate office or branch for assistance and provide points of contact for the other Associate offices or branches.

If additional information requested

.06 If additional information is needed, the Associate office attorney will obtain that information from the taxpayer, the director, or the Appeals Area Director in the most expeditious manner possible. Any additional information requested from the taxpayer by the Associate office must be submitted by letter with a penalties of perjury statement that conforms with the penalties of perjury statement set forth in Section 7.05 of this revenue procedure within 10 calendar days after the request for information is made. To facilitate prompt action, the Service and taxpayers are encouraged to use fax or email to exchange information whenever feasible. A taxpayer's failure to submit the additional information requested will be considered failure to participate in a material stage of the TAM process and result in a waiver of the right to the conference discussed in Section 9.

Taxpayer request for extension of time to submit additional information

.07 A taxpayer's request for an extension of time to submit additional information must be made in writing and received by the Associate office within the 10-day period. It must provide compelling facts and circumstances to justify an extension. Only the Associate Chief Counsel of the primary office to which the case is assigned may determine whether to grant or deny the request for an extension. Except in rare and unusual circumstances, the Associate office will not agree to an extension of more than 10 calendar days beyond the end of the 10-day period. There is no right to appeal the denial of a request for an extension.

Where to send additional information

.08 Any additional information submitted by the taxpayer should be sent to the attention of the assigned Associate office attorney. Generally, only the original of the additional information is necessary. In appropriate cases, however, the Associate office may request additional copies of the information. The taxpayer must also send a copy of the additional information to the director for comment. Any comments by the director must be furnished within an agreed period of time to the Associate office with primary responsibility for the TAM request. If the director does not have any comments, he or she must notify the Associate office attorney promptly. When the director receives a copy of the additional information from the taxpayer, the director must provide field counsel with a copy.

Tentative conclusions

.09 The Associate office attorney will inform the field office and field counsel when all necessary substantive and procedural information has been received. If possible, the Associate office attorney will provide a tentative conclusion. If no tentative conclusion has been reached, the Associate office is encouraged to discuss the underlying complexities with the field office and field counsel. Because the Associate office attorney's tentative conclusion may change during the preparation and review of the TAM, the tentative conclusion should not be considered final. If the tentative conclusion is changed, the Associate office attorney will inform the field office and field counsel. Neither the Associate office, the field office, nor the field counsel should discuss the tentative conclusion and its underlying rationale with the taxpayer or the taxpayer's representative until the Associate office is ready to issue a TAM that agrees with the taxpayer's position or is ready to hold an adverse conference. To afford taxpayers an appropriate opportunity to prepare and present their position at an adverse conference, however, the taxpayer or the taxpayer's representative shall be told (by the Associate office attorney) the tentative conclusion when scheduling the adverse conference. Field counsel should be notified and given the opportunity to participate in the notification to the taxpayer of the tentative conclusions and scheduling of the adverse conference.

SECTION 9. TAXPAYER CONFERENCES

Notification of conference

.01 If the Associate office proposes to issue a TAM that will be adverse to the taxpayer, and if the taxpayer has not waived its right to a conference, the taxpayer will be informed of the time and place of the conference.

Scheduling conference

.02 The conference for a TAM must be held within 10 calendar days after the taxpayer is informed that an adverse TAM is proposed. The Associate office will notify the field office and field counsel of the scheduled conference and will offer the field office and field counsel the opportunity to participate in the conference.

Taxpayers may request extensions

.03 Only an Associate Chief Counsel may approve an extension of the 10-day period for holding a conference. Although extensions will be granted in appropriate circumstances in the discretion of the Associate Chief Counsel, taxpayers should not expect extensions to be routinely granted. The taxpayer must submit a request for an extension in writing to the Associate Chief Counsel of the primary office to which the case is assigned, and must immediately notify the field office and field counsel of the request. The request must contain a detailed justification for the extension and must be submitted sufficiently before the end of the 10-day period to allow the Associate Chief Counsel to consider, and either approve or deny, the request before the end of the 10-day period. If unusual circumstances near the end of the 10-day period make a timely written request impractical, the taxpayer may orally inform the assigned Associate office attorney or reviewer before the end of the 10-day period about the need for an extension and then promptly submit the written request. The Associate office attorney will inform the taxpayer by telephone of the approval or denial of a requested extension. There is no right to appeal the denial of a request for extension.

One conference of right

.04 In general, a taxpayer who has not waived the right to a conference is entitled by right to only one conference with the Associate office. The conference is normally held at the branch level. A person who has authority to sign the transmittal memorandum in his or her own name, or on behalf of the branch chief, will participate. When more than one branch of an Associate office has taken an adverse position on issues in the request or when the position ultimately adopted by one branch will affect another branch's determination, a representative from each branch with authority to sign in his or her own name, or for the branch chief, will participate in the conference. The conference is the conference of right for each subject discussed.

Additional conferences may be offered

.05 After the conference of right, the Service will offer the taxpayer an additional conference of right only if an adverse holding is proposed on a new issue or on the same issue but on grounds different from those discussed at the first conference. If a tentative position is reversed at a higher level with a result less favorable to the taxpayer, the taxpayer has no right to another conference if the grounds or arguments on which the reversal is based were discussed at the conference of right. The limitation on the number of conferences to which a taxpayer is entitled does not prevent the Associate office from inviting a taxpayer to participate in additional conferences if that office determines that additional conferences would be useful. These additional conferences are not offered routinely following an adverse decision.

Additional information submitted after the conference

.06 In order to ensure that the conference of right is productive, the taxpayer should make a reasonable effort to supply all information, documents, and arguments in writing well before the conference. Sometimes, however, it becomes apparent that new information may be helpful in resolving issues discussed at the conference. If the Associate office and the taxpayer agree that such information would be helpful, all such materials must be submitted and received within 10 calendar days after the conference. Any extension of the 10-day period must be requested by the taxpayer in writing and must be approved by the Associate Chief Counsel. Extensions will not be routinely granted. Taxpayers have no right to submit additional materials after the conference, and are discouraged from providing additional copies or versions of materials already submitted. If the additional information is not received from the taxpayer within 10 calendar days plus any extensions granted by an Associate Chief Counsel, the TAM will be issued on the basis of the existing record.

The taxpayer must also send a copy of the additional information to the director for comment. The director must provide a copy to the field counsel assigned to the request for technical advice. If the additional information has a significant impact on the facts in the request, the Associate office will ask the director for comments. The director will respond within the agreed period of time. If the director has no comments, he or she must notify the Associate office attorney promptly.

Normally conducted in person

.07 Conferences under this section are generally conducted in person, but may be conducted by telephone.

Service makes only tentative recommendations

.08 At the conclusion of the conference, no commitment will be made about the conclusion that the Service will finally adopt for any issue, including the outcome of a request for relief under § 7805(b).

Conference may not be taped

.09 No tape, stenographic, or other verbatim recording of a conference may be made by any party.

SECTION 10. PREPARATION OF THE TECHNICAL ADVICE

Reply consists of two parts

.01 The Associate office prepares replies to requests for technical advice in two parts. Each part identifies the taxpayer by name, address, identification number, and year or years involved. The first part of the reply is a transmittal memorandum (Form M–6000). If the transmittal memorandum provides information not in the TAM, or the case is returned for further development, the transmittal memorandum may be Chief Counsel Advice, as defined in § 6110(i)(1), subject to public inspection under § 6110. The second part is the TAM, which contains: (1) a statement of the issues; (2) the conclusions of the Associate office; (3) a statement of the facts pertinent to the issues; (4) a statement of the pertinent law, tax treaties, regulations, revenue rulings, and other precedents published in the Internal Revenue Bulletin, and court decisions; and (5) a discussion of the rationale supporting the conclusions reached by the Associate office. The conclusions give direct answers, whenever possible, to the specific issues raised by the field office. The Associate office is not bound by the issues as submitted by the taxpayer or by the field office and may reframe the issues to be answered in a TAM after consultation with the field office and field counsel. The discussion of the issues in a TAM will be in sufficient detail so that the field or Appeals officials will understand the reasoning underlying the conclusion.

Status of a request

.02 The taxpayer or the taxpayer's authorized representative may obtain information on the status of the request by contacting the field office that requested the advice. The Associate office attorney or reviewer assigned to the TAM request will give frequent status updates to the field office and field counsel.

Section 6110

.03 Accompanying the TAM is a notice under § 6110(f)(1) of intention to disclose a TAM, including a copy of the version proposed to be open to public inspection and notations of third party communications under § 6110(d). Before issuing a TAM, the Associate office will inform the taxpayer orally or in writing of the material likely to appear in the TAM that the taxpayer proposed for deletion but that the Service has determined should not be deleted. If so informed, the taxpayer may submit within 10 calendar days any further information or arguments supporting the taxpayer's proposed deletions. The Service attempts to resolve all disagreements about proposed deletions before the Associate office issues a TAM. The taxpayer does not have the right to a conference to resolve any disagreements about material to be deleted from the text of the TAM.

Opportunity for field counsel review

.04 The Associate office attorney will inform the field counsel of the Associate office's final conclusions before the TAM is issued. The field counsel will be offered a reasonable opportunity to review and informally discuss these conclusions before the TAM is issued.

Copy of preliminary TAM to field office and field counsel

.05 After the field counsel is given a reasonable opportunity to review the Associate office's final conclusions but before the TAM is issued, the Associate Office attorney will provide a draft of the proposed final version of the TAM to the field office and field counsel. If the field office or field counsel disagrees with the proposed final conclusions, normal reconciliation and reconsideration procedures will be followed to resolve the differing views

Routing of reply

.06 A TAM is generally addressed to the field office that requested it. A copy of the reply to a request from LMSB should be mailed simultaneously to the appropriate Industry Director. A reply to a request from Appeals should be addressed to the appropriate field office, through the Appeals Director, Technical Services, C:AP.

Copy of final TAM to field counsel and Division Counsel

.07 The Associate office will provide a copy of the reply to the request for technical advice (the final TAM) to the individual field counsel attorney who assisted the field office in submitting the request and to that attorney's Associate Area Counsel. The Associate office also will provide a copy of the final TAM to the Division Counsel for the operating division from which the request was initiated or that has jurisdiction over the particular matter in the TAM. The reply may be transmitted electronically if it is in .pdf format, or may be sent by mail or fax transmission.

Reconsideration

.08 The director may formally request reconsideration. Before formally requesting reconsideration, the director must consult with field counsel. Requests for reconsideration must describe with specificity the errors in the analysis and conclusions. Requests should focus on points that the TAM overlooked or misconstrued rather than simply re-argue points raised in the initial request. The Associate office will give priority consideration to the request and should act on the request as expeditiously as possible. The Associate office may request further submissions from the field or the taxpayer, but the parties should otherwise make no additional submissions. If a request for reconsideration fails to follow the procedures set forth in this section of this revenue procedure, or the request fails to raise issues or arguments different from those asserted in the initial request for technical advice, the Associate office may return the request for reconsideration without ruling on the request for reconsideration. The taxpayer is not entitled to be informed that a request for reconsideration is being considered.

Discussing contents with the taxpayer

.09 The Associate office will not discuss the specific contents of the TAM with the taxpayer until after the field office has given a copy of the TAM to the taxpayer.

TAM takes effect when taxpayer receives a copy

.10 After a TAM is sent to the director, the director gives the taxpayer a copy of the issued TAM, the notice of intention to disclose under § 6110 (f)(1), and a copy of the version proposed to be open to public inspection, which includes notations of third party communications under § 6110. If a request for technical advice pertains to more than one taxpayer, the director will provide each pertinent taxpayer with a copy of the TAM and will notify the Associate office when this occurs. The requirement to give a taxpayer a copy of the TAM does not apply to a TAM involving civil fraud or a criminal investigation, relating to a civil fraud or criminal investigation, or involving a jeopardy or termination assessment.

Taxpayer may protest deletions not made

.11 Generally, the Associate office considers only the deletion of material that the taxpayer has proposed for deletion or other deletions as required under § 6110(c) before the TAM is sent to the director. After receiving the notice under § 6110(f)(1) of intention to disclose the TAM, the taxpayer may protest the disclosure of certain information in it by submitting a written statement within 20 calendar days which identifies those deletions not made by the Service that the taxpayer believes should have been made. The taxpayer must also submit a copy of the version of the TAM proposed to be open to public inspection with brackets around the deletions proposed by the taxpayer that have not been made by the Associate office plus a statement indicating the statutory basis under § 6110 for each proposed deletion. Within 20 calendar days after it receives the taxpayer's response to the notice under § 6110(f)(1), the Associate office must mail to the taxpayer its final administrative conclusion about the deletions to be made.

Public inspection of § 6104 applications for exemption and letter rulings issued to certain exempt organizations

.12 The public inspection provisions of § 6110, including taxpayer notification and deletion processes, do not apply to any document to which § 6104 applies.

Public inspection in civil fraud or criminal investigation cases

.13 The provisions of this section about referring issues upon the taxpayer's request, telling the taxpayer about the referral of issues, giving the taxpayer a copy of the arguments submitted, submitting proposed deletions, granting conferences in the Associate office, or providing a copy of the TAM to the taxpayer do not apply to a TAM described in § 6110(g)(5)(A) that involves any matter that is the subject of a civil fraud or criminal investigation, is otherwise closely related to a civil fraud or criminal investigation, or involves a jeopardy or termination assessment. In these cases, a copy of the TAM may be given to the taxpayer only after all proceedings in the investigations or assessments are complete, but before the Commissioner mails the notice of intention to disclose the TAM under § 6110(f)(1). The taxpayer may then provide the statement of proposed deletions to the Associate office.

SECTION 11. WITHDRAWAL OF REQUESTS FOR TECHNICAL ADVICE

Taxpayer notified

.01 Once a request for a TAM has been sent to the Associate office, only a director may withdraw the request, but this must be done before the responding transmittal memorandum for the TAM is signed. To withdraw the request, the director must first notify the taxpayer of the intent to withdraw unless: (1) the period of limitations on assessment is about to expire and the taxpayer has declined to give written consent to extend the period or (2) the notification would be prejudicial to the best interests of the Government. If the taxpayer does not agree that the request should be withdrawn and wishes to request review of the decision, the procedures in Section 5.04 of this revenue procedure for review must be followed.

Acknowledgment of withdrawal

.02 Acknowledgment of the withdrawal of a request submitted by a director or Appeals should be sent to the appropriate director or Appeals office, through the Appeals Director, Technical Services, C:AP.

Associate office may decide not to issue a TAM

.03 If the Associate office determines that a TAM should not be issued, it may return the TAM unanswered. This determination must be made on the basis of sound tax administration and must be approved by the Associate Chief Counsel. The decision not to issue a TAM should be an infrequent occurrence and should be made only after consultation with field counsel and the requesting field office. If field counsel disagrees with this determination, they may request reconsideration through existing reconciliation procedures.

Associate office may provide views

.04 If a request for technical advice is withdrawn or an Associate office decides not to issue a TAM, the Associate office may address the substantive issues through published guidance, such as a regulation or revenue ruling, by some other form of legal advice, or through generic advice. The decision to address the issues through these other forms of guidance will be based on the general standards for issuing those types of guidance.

SECTION 12. USE OF THE TECHNICAL ADVICE

Generally applies advice in processing the taxpayer's case

After a TAM is issued, the director must process the taxpayer's case on the basis of the conclusions in the TAM. Specifically, if a TAM provides conclusions involving a § 103 obligation and the issuer of this obligation, the director must apply the conclusions to the issuer and any holder of the obligation, unless the holder also initiates a request for a TAM on the same issue addressed in the TAM involving the issuer, and the Associate office issues a TAM involving that issue and that holder. The Appeals Area Director may settle the issue under its existing settlement authority.

SECTION 13. RETROACTIVITY AND RELIANCE

Usually applies retroactively

.01 The holdings in a TAM are applied retroactively, whether they are initial holdings or they are later holdings that modify or revoke holdings in a prior TAM. The Associate Chief Counsel with jurisdiction over the TAM, however, may exercise the discretionary authority under § 7805(b) to limit the retroactive effect of any holding. This authority is exercised in rare and unusual circumstances.

Revocation or modification of an earlier letter ruling or TAM

.02 Generally, a TAM revoking or modifying a letter ruling or an earlier TAM will not be applied retroactively if: (1) the applicable law has not changed; (2) the taxpayer directly involved in the letter ruling or earlier TAM relied in good faith on it; and (3) revoking or modifying the letter ruling or earlier TAM would be detrimental to the taxpayer. The new TAM will be applied retroactively to the taxpayer whose tax liability was directly involved in the letter ruling or TAM if: (1) controlling facts have been misstated or omitted or (2) the facts at the time of the transaction are materially different from the controlling facts on which the letter ruling or earlier TAM was based. If a letter ruling or a TAM is modified or revoked with retroactive effect, the notice to the taxpayer, except in fraud cases, should set forth the grounds on which the modification or revocation is being made and the reason why the modification or revocation is being applied retroactively.

Continuing action or series of actions

.03 If a TAM relates to a continuing action or a series of actions, it is generally applied until it is withdrawn or until the conclusion is modified or revoked by a final decision in favor of the taxpayer with respect to the issue addressed by the TAM, the enactment of legislation, the ratification of a tax treaty, a decision of the United States Supreme Court, or the issuance of temporary regulations, final regulations, a revenue ruling, or other statement published in the Internal Revenue Bulletin. Publication of a notice of proposed rulemaking does not affect the application of a TAM. If a new holding in a TAM is less favorable to the taxpayer than the holding in an earlier TAM, the new holding is generally not applied to the period when the taxpayer relied on the earlier holding. It will be applied to that period, however, if material facts on which the earlier TAM was based have changed.

Other taxpayers

.04 Under § 6110(k)(3), a taxpayer may not rely on a TAM issued by the Service for another taxpayer. In addition, retroactive or non-retroactive treatment to one member of an industry directly involved in a letter ruling or TAM does not extend to another member of that same industry, and retroactive or non-retroactive treatment to one client of a tax practitioner does not extend to another client of that same practitioner.

SECTION 14. HOW MAY RETROACTIVE EFFECT BE LIMITED?

Requests for relief under § 7805(b).

.01 A taxpayer for whom a TAM was issued or for whom a TAM request is pending may request that the appropriate Associate Chief Counsel limit the retroactive effect of any holding in the TAM or of any subsequent modification or revocation of the TAM. For a pending request for technical advice, the taxpayer should make the request for relief under § 7805(b) as part of the initial request for advice. The Associate office will consider a request for relief under § 7805(b) made at a later time if there is justification for having delayed the request.

Form of request for relief — In general

.02 During the course of an examination of a taxpayer's return by the director or during consideration of the taxpayer's return by the Appeals Area Director, a taxpayer's request to limit retroactivity must be made in the form of a request for a TAM. This includes recommendations by the director that an earlier letter ruling or TAM be modified or revoked. The request must meet the general requirements of a request for technical advice. It must also: (1) state that it is being made under § 7805(b); (2) state the relief sought; (3) explain the reasons and arguments in support of the relief sought; and (4) include any documents bearing on the request. The taxpayer's request must be submitted to the director, who should then forward the request to the Associate office for consideration.

Form of request for relief — continuing transaction before examination of return

.03 A request for relief under § 7805(b) must be made in the form of a request for a letter ruling if (1) a TAM addressing a continuing transaction is modified or revoked by later published guidance and (2) the request for relief is submitted before an examination has begun covering those years for which relief is sought. The requirements for a letter ruling request are given in Rev. Proc. 2007–1 (this Bulletin).

Taxpayer's right to a conference

.04 When a request for a TAM concerns only the application of § 7805(b), the taxpayer has the right to a conference with the Associate office in accordance with the provisions of Section 9 of this revenue procedure. If the request for application of § 7805(b) is included in the request for a TAM on the substantive issues or is made before the conference of right on the substantive issues, the § 7805(b) issues will be discussed at the taxpayer's one conference of right. If the request for the application of § 7805(b) is made as part of a pending TAM request after a conference has been held on the substantive issues and the Service determines that there is justification for having delayed the request, then the taxpayer will have the right to one conference of right concerning the application of § 7805(b), with the conference limited to discussion of this issue only.

Reconsideration of request for relief under § 7805(b)

.05 When a TAM grants a taxpayer relief under § 7805(b), the director may not request reconsideration of the § 7805(b) issue unless the director determines there has been a misstatement or omission of controlling facts by the taxpayer in its request for § 7805(b) relief.

SECTION 15. SIGNIFICANT CHANGES MADE TO REV. PROC. 2006–2

Overview

.01 In 2006, the Office of Chief Counsel adopted certain changes to the process by which it provides legal advice to IRS operating divisions and to Appeals. Some of these changes affect the TAM process and are intended to improve the timeliness and usefulness of TAMs. This revenue procedure incorporates these changes, the most significant of which are listed in paragraphs .02 through .06 below. The Office of Chief Counsel will evaluate the effect these changes have on the TAM process and, if necessary, further modify these procedures in the future to ensure that the process results in the provision of timely and accurate legal advice and operates in a manner that is fair to taxpayers.

Request regarding same taxpayer or transaction

.02 With respect to the same taxpayer or the same transaction, when the issue is under the jurisdiction of Appeals and the applicability of more than one kind of federal tax is dependent upon the resolution of that issue, a director may now request technical advice on the applicability of any of the taxes involved. A case remains under the jurisdiction of the director even though Appeals has the identical issue under consideration for another taxpayer (not related within the meaning of § 267 or a member of an affiliated group of which the taxpayer is not also a member within the meaning of § 1504) in a different transaction.

Request when issue pending in Appeals

.03 A Director may request technical advice even though the issue is pending in Appeals for the same taxpayer.

Taxpayer participation

.04 Taxpayers are strongly encouraged to consistently and timely participate in the TAM process from the very beginning. A failure to participate in stages of the TAM process identified as "material" will constitute a waiver of rights to a taxpayer conference regarding a proposed adverse ruling.

Additional information requested from taxpayer

.05 Additional information requested from the taxpayer must be submitted to the Associate office within 10 calendar days after the request for information is made.

Elimination of TEAM procedures

.06 TEAM procedures have been eliminated.

SECTION 16. EFFECT ON OTHER DOCUMENTS

.01 Rev. Proc. 2006–2, 2006–1 I.R.B. 89, is superseded.

SECTION 17. EFFECTIVE DATE

This revenue procedure is effective January 2, 2007.

DRAFTING INFORMATION

The principal author of this revenue procedure is Rosy Lor of the Office of Associate Chief Counsel (Procedure & Administration). For further information regarding this revenue procedure for matters under the jurisdiction of:

(1) the Associate Chief Counsel (Corporate), contact Richard Todd at (202) 622–7700 (not a toll-free call);

(2) the Associate Chief Counsel (Financial Institutions and Products), contact Arturo Estrada at (202) 622–3900 (not a toll-free call);

(3) the Associate Chief Counsel (Income Tax and Accounting), contact Arlene Blume at (202) 622–4800 (not a toll-free call);

(4) the Associate Chief Counsel (Passthroughs and Special Industries), contact Stephanie Bland at (202) 622–3110 (not a toll-free call);

(5) the Associate Chief Counsel (Procedure and Administration), contact George Bowden or Henry Schneiderman at (202) 622–3400 (not a toll-free call);

(6) the Division Counsel/Associate Chief Counsel (Tax Exempt and Government Entities), contact Calder Robertson at (202) 622–6000 (not a toll-free call);

(7) the Associate Chief Counsel (International), contact Bill Yates at 202 622–3164 (not a toll-free call);

(8) the Commissioner (Large and Mid-Size Business Division), contact Shirley S. Lee at (202) 283–8417 (not a toll-free call);

(9) the Commissioner (Small Business/Self-Employed Division), contact Ronald E. Hartman at (856) 414–6447 (not a toll-free call);

(10) the Commissioner (Wage and Investment Division), contact Geoffrey Gerbore at (631) 447–4428 (not a toll-free call); or

(11) the Chief Appeals, contact Sandy Cohen at (202) 435–5617 (not a toll-free call).

INDEX

References are to sections in Rev. Proc. 2007–2

Rev. Proc. 2007–3

SECTION 1. PURPOSE AND NATURE OF CHANGES

.01 The purpose of this revenue procedure is to update Rev. Proc. 2006–3, 2006–1 C.B. 122, by providing a revised list of those areas of the Internal Revenue Code under the jurisdiction of the Associate Chief Counsel (Corporate), the Associate Chief Counsel (Financial Institutions and Products), the Associate Chief Counsel (Income Tax and Accounting), the Associate Chief Counsel (Passthroughs and Special Industries), the Associate Chief Counsel (Procedure and Administration), and the Division Counsel/Associate Chief Counsel (Tax Exempt and Government Entities) relating to issues on which the Internal Revenue Service will not issue letter rulings or determination letters. For a list of areas under the jurisdiction of the Associate Chief Counsel (International) relating to international issues on which the Service will not issue letter rulings or determination letters, see Rev. Proc. 2007–7, this Bulletin. For a list of areas under the jurisdiction of the Commissioner, Tax Exempt and Government Entities Division relating to issues, plans or plan amendments on which the Service will not issue letter rulings and determination letters, see, respectively, section 8 of Rev. Proc. 2007–4 (this Bulletin) and section 3.02 of Rev. Proc. 2007–6 (this Bulletin).

.02 Changes.

(1) New section 3.01(58) (Section 2601.—Tax Imposed. Exceptions: Retention of Trust's Generation-Skipping Transfer Tax Exempt Status in the Case of Modifications, Etc.) has been added.

(2) New section 3.01(65) (Section 7704.—Certain Publicly Traded Partnerships Treated as Corporations) has been added.

(3) New section 5.03 (Sections 162 and 1502.—Trade or Business Expenses; Consolidated Returns) has been added.

(4) New section 5.04 (Sections 302 and 304.—Certain Redemptions) has been added.

(5) New section 5.05 (Sections 351, 358 and 362(a).—Transfers to Corporation Controlled by Transferors; Basis to Distributees; Basis to Corporations) has been added.

(6) Old Section 5.10 (Sections 3121, 3306, and 3401.—Definitions; Employment Taxes) has been deleted.

(7) Section 6.07 (Sections 1502, 1504, and 1552.—Regulations; Definitions; Earnings and Profits) updated with cites to Rev. Proc. 2006–21, 2006–24 I.R.B. 1050.

SECTION 2. BACKGROUND AND SCOPE OF APPLICATION

.01 Background.

Whenever appropriate in the interest of sound tax administration, it is the policy of the Service to answer inquiries of individuals and organizations regarding their status for tax purposes and the tax effects of their acts or transactions, prior to the filing of returns or reports that are required by the revenue laws.

There are, however, certain areas in which, because of the inherently factual nature of the problems involved, or for other reasons, the Service will not issue rulings or determination letters. These areas are set forth in four sections of this revenue procedure. Section 3 reflects those areas in which rulings and determinations will not be issued. Section 4 sets forth those areas in which they will not ordinarily be issued. "Not ordinarily" means that unique and compelling reasons must be demonstrated to justify the issuance of a ruling or determination letter. Those sections reflect a number of specific questions and problems as well as general areas. Section 5 lists specific areas for which the Service is temporarily not issuing rulings and determinations because those matters are under study. Finally, section 6 of this revenue procedure lists specific areas where the Service will not ordinarily issue rulings because the Service has provided automatic approval procedures for these matters.

See Rev. Proc. 2007–1 (this Bulletin) particularly section 6 captioned "Under What Circumstances Does The Service Not Issue Letter Rulings Or Determination Letters?" for general instructions and other situations in which the Service will not or ordinarily will not issue letter rulings or determination letters.

With respect to the items listed, revenue rulings or revenue procedures may be published in the Internal Revenue Bulletin from time to time to provide general guidelines regarding the position of the Service.

Additions or deletions to this revenue procedure as well as restatements of items listed will be made by modification of this revenue procedure. Changes will be published as they occur throughout the year and will be incorporated annually in a new revenue procedure published as the third revenue procedure of the year. These lists should not be considered all-inclusive. Decisions not to rule on individual cases (as contrasted with those that present significant pattern issues) are not reported in this revenue procedure and will not be added to subsequent revisions.

.02 Scope of Application.

This revenue procedure does not preclude the submission of requests for technical advice to the National Office from other offices of the Service.

.03 No-Rule Issues Part of Larger Transactions.

If it is impossible for the Service to determine the tax consequences of a larger transaction without knowing the resolution of an issue on which the Service will not issue rulings and determinations under this revenue procedure involving a part of the transaction or a related transaction, the taxpayer must state in the request to the best of the taxpayer's knowledge and belief the tax consequences of the no-rule issue. The Service's ruling or determination letter will state that the Service did not consider, and no opinion is expressed upon, that issue. In appropriate cases the Service may decline to issue rulings or determinations on such larger transactions due to the relevance of the no-rule issue, despite the taxpayer's representation.

SECTION 3. AREAS IN WHICH RULINGS OR DETERMINATION LETTERS WILL NOT BE ISSUED

.01 Specific questions and problems.

(1) Section 61.—Gross Income Defined.—Whether amounts voluntarily deferred by a taxpayer under a deferred-compensation plan maintained by an organization described in § 501 (other than a plan maintained by an eligible employer

pursuant to the provisions of § 457) are currently includible in the taxpayer's gross income.

(2) Section 61.—Gross Income Defined. —Whether a split dollar life insurance arrangement is "materially modified" within the meaning of § 1.61–22(j)(2) of the Income Tax Regulations. (Also §§ 83, 301, 1401, 2501, 3121, 3231, 3306, 3401, and 7872.)

(3) Sections 61, 451, and 1001.—Gross Income Defined; General Rule for Taxable Year of Inclusion; Determination of Amount and Recognition of Gain or Loss.—Whether, under authorization by an appropriate State agency to recover certain costs pursuant to State specified cost recovery legislations, any investor-owned utility company realizes income upon: (i) the creation of an intangible property right; (ii) the transfer of that intangible property right; or (iii) the securitization of the intangible property right.

(4) Section 79.—Group-Term Life Insurance Purchased for Employees.—Whether a group insurance plan for 10 or more employees qualifies as group-term insurance, if the amount of insurance is not computed under a formula that would meet the requirements of § 1.79–1(c)(2)(ii) of the regulations if the group consisted of fewer than 10 employees.

(5) Section 83.—Property Transferred in Connection with Performance of Services.—Whether a restriction constitutes a substantial risk of forfeiture, if the employee is a controlling shareholder. Also, whether a transfer has occurred, if the amount paid for the property involves a nonrecourse obligation.

(6) Section 83.—Property Transferred in Connection with Performance of Services.—Which corporation is entitled to the deduction under § 83(h) in cases where a corporation undergoes a corporate division if the facts are not similar to those described in Rev. Rul. 2002–1, 2002–1 C.B. 268.

(7) Section 101.—Certain Death Benefits.—Whether there has been a transfer for value for purposes of § 101(a) in situations involving a grantor and a trust when (i) substantially all of the trust corpus consists or will consist of insurance policies on the life of the grantor or the grantor's spouse, (ii) the trustee or any other person has a power to apply the trust's income or corpus to the payment of premiums on policies of insurance on the life of the grantor or the grantor's spouse, (iii) the trustee or any other person has a power to use the trust's assets to make loans to the grantor's estate or to purchase assets from the grantor's estate, and (iv) there is a right or power in any person that would cause the grantor to be treated as the owner of all or a portion of the trust under §§ 673 to 677.

(8) Sections 101, 761, and 7701.—Definitions.—Whether, in connection with the transfer of a life insurance policy to an unincorporated organization, (i) the organization will be treated as a partnership under §§ 761 and 7701, or (ii) the transfer of the life insurance policy to the organization will be exempt from the transfer for value rules of § 101, when substantially all of the organization's assets consists or will consist of life insurance policies on the lives of the members.

(9) Section 105(h).—Amount Paid to Highly Compensated Individuals Under Discriminatory Self-Insured Medical Expense Reimbursement Plan.—Whether a self-insured medical reimbursement plan satisfies the requirements of § 105(h) for a plan year.

(10) Section 107.—Rental Value of Parsonages.—Whether amounts distributed to a retired minister from a pension or annuity plan should be excludible from the minister's gross income as a parsonage allowance under § 107.

(11) Section 107.—Rental Value of Parsonages.—Whether an individual is a "minister of the gospel" for Federal tax purposes. (Also §§ 1402(a)(8), (c)(4), and (e), 3121(b)(8)(A), and 3401(a)(9).)

(12) Section 115.—Income of States, Municipalities, Etc.—The results of transactions pursuant to a plan or arrangement created by State statute a primary objective of which is to enable participants to pay for the costs of a post-secondary education for themselves or a designated beneficiary, including: (i) whether the plan or arrangement, itself, is an entity separate from a State and, if so, how the plan or arrangement is treated for Federal tax purposes; and (ii) whether any contract under the plan or arrangement is a debt instrument and, if so, how interest or original issue discount attributable to the contract is treated for Federal tax purposes. (Also §§ 61, 163, 1275, 2501, and 7701.)

(13) Section 115.—Income of States, Municipalities, Etc.—Whether the income of membership organizations established by States exclusively to reimburse members for losses arising from workmen's compensation claims is excluded from gross income under § 115.

(14) Section 117.—Qualified Scholarships.—Whether an employer-related scholarship or fellowship grant is excludible from the employee's gross income, if there is no intermediary private foundation distributing the grants, as there was in Rev. Proc. 76–47, 1976–2 C.B. 670.

(15) Section 119.—Meals or Lodging Furnished for the Convenience of the Employer.—Whether the value of meals or lodging is excludible from gross income by an employee who is a controlling shareholder of the employer.

(16) Section 121.—Exclusion of Gain from Sale of Principal Residence.—Whether property qualifies as the taxpayer's principal residence.

(17) Section 125.—Cafeteria Plans.—Whether amounts used to provide group-term life insurance under § 79, accident and health benefits under §§ 105 and 106, and dependent care assistance programs under § 129 are includible in the gross income of participants and considered "wages" for purposes of §§ 3401, 3121, and 3306 when the benefits are offered through a cafeteria plan.

(18) Section 162.—Trade or Business Expenses.—Whether compensation is reasonable in amount.

(19) Section 163.—Interest.—The income tax consequences of transactions involving "shared appreciation mortgage" (SAM) loans in which a taxpayer, borrowing money to purchase real property, pays a fixed rate of interest on the mortgage loan below the prevailing market rate and will also pay the lender a percentage of the appreciation in value of the real property upon termination of the mortgage. This applies to all SAM arrangements where the loan proceeds are used for commercial or business activities, or where used to finance a personal residence, if the facts

are not similar to those described in Rev. Rul. 83–51, 1983–1 C.B. 48. (Also §§ 61, 451, 461, 856, 1001, and 7701.)

(20) Section 170.—Charitable, Etc., Contributions and Gifts.—Whether a taxpayer who advances funds to a charitable organization and receives therefor a promissory note may deduct as contributions, in one taxable year or in each of several years, amounts forgiven by the taxpayer in each of several years by endorsement on the note.

(21) Section 213.—Medical, Dental, Etc., Expenses.—Whether a capital expenditure for an item that is ordinarily used for personal, living, or family purposes, such as a swimming pool, has as its primary purpose the medical care of the taxpayer or the taxpayer's spouse or dependent, or is related directly to such medical care.

(22) Section 264(b).—Certain Amounts Paid in Connection with Insurance Contracts.—Whether "substantially all" the premiums of a contract of insurance are paid within a period of 4 years from the date on which the contract is purchased. Also, whether an amount deposited is in payment of a "substantial number" of future premiums on such a contract.

(23) Section 264(c)(1).—Certain Amounts Paid in Connection with Insurance Contracts.—Whether § 264(c)(1) applies.

(24) Section 269.—Acquisitions Made to Evade or Avoid Income Tax.—Whether an acquisition is within the meaning of § 269.

(25) Section 274.—Disallowance of Certain Entertainment, Etc., Expenses.—Whether a taxpayer who is traveling away from home on business may, in lieu of substantiating the actual cost of meals, deduct a fixed per-day amount for meal expenses that differs from the amount authorized by the revenue procedure providing optional rules for substantiating the amount of travel expenses for the period in which the expense was paid or incurred.

(26) Section 302.—Distributions in Redemption of Stock.—Whether § 302(b) applies when the consideration given in redemption by a corporation consists entirely or partly of its notes payable, and the shareholder's stock is held in escrow or as security for payment of the notes with the possibility that the stock may or will be returned to the shareholder in the future, upon the happening of specific defaults by the corporation.

(27) Section 302.—Distributions in Redemption of Stock.—Whether § 302(b) applies when the consideration given in redemption by a corporation in exchange for a shareholder's stock consists entirely or partly of the corporation's promise to pay an amount based on, or contingent on, future earnings of the corporation, when the promise to pay is contingent on working capital being maintained at a certain level, or any other similar contingency.

(28) Section 302.—Distributions in Redemption of Stock.—Whether § 302(b) applies to a redemption of stock, if after the redemption the distributing corporation uses property that is owned by the shareholder from whom the stock is redeemed and the payments by the corporation for the use of the property are dependent upon the corporation's future earnings or are subordinate to the claims of the corporation's general creditors. Payments for the use of property will not be considered to be dependent upon future earnings merely because they are based on a fixed percentage of receipts or sales.

(29) Section 302.—Distributions in Redemption of Stock.—Whether the acquisition or disposition of stock described in § 302(c)(2)(B) has, or does not have, as one of its principal purposes the avoidance of Federal income taxes within the meaning of that section, unless the facts and circumstances are materially identical to those set forth in Rev. Rul. 85–19, 1985–1 C.B. 94; Rev. Rul. 79–67, 1979–1 C.B. 128; Rev. Rul. 77–293, 1977–2 C.B. 91; Rev. Rul. 57–387, 1957–2 C.B. 225; Rev. Rul. 56–584, 1956–2 C.B. 179; or Rev. Rul. 56–556, 1956–2 C.B. 177.

(30) Section 302(b)(4) and (e).—Redemption from Noncorporate Shareholder in Partial Liquidation; Partial Liquidation Defined.—The amount of working capital attributable to a business or portion of a business terminated that may be distributed in partial liquidation.

(31) Section 312.—Effect on Earnings and Profits.—The determination of the amount of earnings and profits of a corporation.

(32) Sections 331, 453, and 1239.—The Tax Effects of Installment Sales of Property Between Entities with Common Ownership.—The tax effects of a transaction in which there is a transfer of property by a corporation to a partnership or other noncorporate entity (or the transfer of stock to such entity followed by a liquidation of the corporation) when more than a nominal amount of the stock of such corporation and the capital or beneficial interests in the purchasing entity (that is, more than 20 percent in value) is owned by the same persons, and the consideration to be received by the selling corporation or the selling shareholders includes an installment obligation of the purchasing entity.

(33) Sections 332, 351, 368(a)(1)(A), (B), (C), (E) and (F), and 1036.—Complete Liquidations of Subsidiaries; Transfer to Corporation Controlled by Transferor; Definitions Relating to Corporate Reorganizations; and Stock for Stock of Same Corporation.—Whether a transaction qualifies under § 332, § 351 or § 1036 for nonrecognition treatment, or whether it constitutes a corporate reorganization within the meaning of § 368(a)(1)(A) (including a transaction that qualifies under § 368(a)(1)(A) by reason of § 368(a)(2)(D) or § 368(a)(2)(E)), § 368(a)(1)(B), § 368(a)(1)(C), § 368(a)(1)(E) or § 368(a)(1)(F), and whether various consequences (such as nonrecognition and basis) result from the application of that section, unless the Service determines that there is a significant issue that must be resolved in order to decide those matters. If the Service determines that there is a significant issue, and to the extent the transaction is not described in another no-rule section, the Service will rule on the entire transaction, and not just the significant issue. Notwithstanding the preceding paragraph, the Service will rule on the application of § 351 to a controlled corporation when the transaction is undertaken prior to the distribution of the stock of the controlled corporation in a transaction qualifying under § 355.

SIGNIFICANT ISSUE: A significant issue is an issue of law that meets the three following tests: (1) the issue is not clearly and adequately addressed by a statute, regulation, decision of a court, tax treaty, revenue ruling, revenue procedure, notice, or other authority published in the Internal

Revenue Bulletin; (2) the resolution of the issue is not essentially free from doubt; and (3) the issue is legally significant and germane to determining the major tax consequences of the transaction. An issue of law will be considered not clearly and adequately addressed by the authorities above, and its resolution will not be essentially free from doubt when, because of concern over a legal issue (as opposed to a factual issue), taxpayer's counsel is unable to render an unqualified opinion on what the tax consequences of the transaction will be.

OBTAINING A RULING: To obtain a ruling on a transaction involving a significant issue, the taxpayer must in its ruling request explain the significance of the issue, set forth the authorities most closely related to the issue, and explain why the issue is not resolved by these authorities.

(34) Section 351.—See section 3.01(33), above.

(35) Section 358.—Basis to Distributees.—The acceptability of an estimation procedure or the acceptability of a specific sampling procedure to determine the basis of stock acquired by an acquiring corporation in a reorganization described in § 368(a)(1)(B).

(36) Section 368.—See section 3.01(33), above.

(37) Section 424.—Substitution or Assumption of Incentive Stock Options.—Whether the substitution of a new Incentive Stock Option ("ISO") for an old ISO, or the assumption of an old ISO, by an employer by reason of a corporate transaction constitutes a modification which results in the issuance of a new option by reason of failing to satisfy the spread test requirement of § 424(a)(1) or the ratio test requirement of § 1.425–1(a)(4). The Service will continue to rule on the issue of whether the new ISO or the assumption of the old ISO gives the employee additional benefits not present under the old option within the meaning of § 424(a)(2).

(38) Section 451.—See section 3.01(3), above.

(39) Section 451.—General Rule for Taxable Year of Inclusion.—The tax consequences of a non-qualified unfunded deferred-compensation arrangement with respect to a controlling shareholder-employee eligible to participate in the arrangement.

(40) Section 451.—General Rule for Taxable Year of Inclusion.—The tax consequences of unfunded deferred-compensation arrangements where the arrangements fail to meet the requirements of Rev. Proc. 92–65, 1992–2 C.B. 428; and Rev. Proc. 71–19, 1971–1 C.B. 698.

(41) Sections 451 and 457.—General Rule for Taxable Year of Inclusion; Deferred Compensation Plans of State and Local Governments and Tax-Exempt Organizations.—The tax consequences to unidentified independent contractors in nonqualified unfunded deferred-compensation plans. This applies to plans established under § 451 by employers in the private sector and to plans of State and local governments and tax-exempt organizations under § 457. However, a ruling with respect to a specific independent contractor's participation in such a plan may be issued.

(42) Section 453.—See section 3.01(32), above.

(43) Section 457.—See section 3.01(41), above.

(44) Section 641.—Imposition of Tax.—Whether the period of administration or settlement of an estate or a trust (other than a trust described in § 664) is reasonable or unduly prolonged.

(45) Section 642(c).—Deduction for Amounts Paid or Permanently Set Aside for a Charitable Purpose.—Allowance of an unlimited deduction for amounts set aside by a trust or estate for charitable purposes when there is a possibility that the corpus of the trust or estate may be invaded.

(46) Section 664.—Charitable Remainder Trusts.—Whether the settlement of a charitable remainder trust upon the termination of the noncharitable interest is made within a reasonable period of time.

(47) Section 671.—Trust Income, Deductions, and Credits Attributable to Grantors and Others as Substantial Owners.—Whether the grantor will be considered the owner of any portion of a trust when (i) substantially all of the trust corpus consists or will consist of insurance policies on the life of the grantor or the grantor's spouse, (ii) the trustee or any other person has a power to apply the trust's income or corpus to the payment of premiums on policies of insurance on the life of the grantor or the grantor's spouse, (iii) the trustee or any other person has a power to use the trust's assets to make loans to the grantor's estate or to purchase assets from the grantor's estate, and (iv) there is a right or power in any person that would cause the grantor to be treated as the owner of all or a portion of the trust under §§ 673 to 677.

(48) Section 704(e).—Family Partnerships.—Matters relating to the validity of a family partnership when capital is not a material income producing factor.

(49) Section 761.—See section 3.01(8), above.

(50) Section 856.—Definition of Real Estate Investment Trust.—Whether a corporation whose stock is "paired" with or "stapled" to stock of another corporation will qualify as a real estate investment trust under § 856, if the activities of the corporations are integrated.

(51) Section 1001.—See section 3.01(3), above.

(52) Section 1036.—See section 3.01(33), above.

(53) Section 1221.—Capital Asset Defined.—Whether specialty stock allocated to an investment account by a registered specialist on a national securities exchange is a capital asset.

(54) Section 1239.—See section 3.01(32), above.

(55) Section 1551.—Disallowance of the Benefits of the Graduated Corporate Rates and Accumulated Earnings Credit.—Whether a transfer is within § 1551.

(56) Section 2031.—Definition of Gross Estate.—Actuarial factors for valuing interests in the prospective gross estate of a living person.

(57) Section 2512.—Valuation of Gifts.—Actuarial factors for valuing prospective or hypothetical gifts of a donor.

(58) Section 2601.—Tax Imposed. Exceptions: Retention of Trust's Generation-Skipping Transfer Tax Exempt Status in the Case of Modifications, Etc.—Whether a trust exempt from generation-skipping transfer (GST) tax under § 26.2601–1(b)(1), (2), or (3) of the Generation-Skipping Transfer Tax Regulations will retain its GST exempt status when

there is a modification of a trust, change in the administration of a trust, or a distribution from a trust in a factual scenario that is similar to a factual scenario set forth in one or more of the examples contained in § 26.2601–1(b)(4)(i)(E).

(59) Sections 3121, 3306, and 3401.—Definitions.—For purposes of determining prospective employment status, whether an individual will be an employee or an independent contractor. A ruling with regard to prior employment status may be issued.

(60) Sections 3121, 3306, and 3401.—Definitions; Employment Taxes.—Who is the employer of an "employee-owner" as defined in § 269A(b)(2).

(61) Sections 3121, 3306, and 3401.—Definitions.—For purposes of determining employment classification pursuant to the filing of Form SS–8, *Determination of Worker Status for Purposes of Federal Employment Taxes and Income Tax Withholding*, whether a worker is a *bona fide* partner and, therefore, not an employee of the business is at issue.

(62) Section 4980B.—Failure to Satisfy Continuation Coverage Requirements of Group Health Plans.—Whether an action is "gross misconduct" within the meaning of § 4980B(f)(3)(B). (*See* section 3.05 of Rev. Proc. 87–28, 1987–1 C.B. 770, 771.)

(63) Section 7701.—Definitions.—The classification of an instrument that has certain voting and liquidation rights in an issuing corporation but whose dividend rights are determined by reference to the earnings of a segregated portion of the issuing corporation's assets, including assets held by a subsidiary.

(64) Section 7701.—See section 3.01(8), above.

(65) Section 7704.—Certain Publicly Traded Partnerships Treated as Corporations.—Whether interests in a partnership that are not traded on an established securities market (within the meaning of § 7704(b) and § 1.7704–1(b)) are readily tradable on a secondary market or the substantial equivalent thereof under § 1.7704–1(c)(1) of the Procedure and Administration Regulations.

.02 General Areas.

(1) The results of transactions that lack a *bona fide* business purpose or have as their principal purpose the reduction of Federal taxes.

(2) A matter upon which a court decision adverse to the Government has been handed down and the question of following the decision or litigating further has not yet been resolved.

(3) A matter involving alternate plans of proposed transactions or involving hypothetical situations.

(4) Whether under Subtitle F (Procedure and Administration) reasonable cause, due diligence, good faith, clear and convincing evidence, or other similar terms that require a factual determination exist.

(5) Whether a proposed transaction would subject the taxpayer to a criminal penalty.

(6) A request that does not comply with the provisions of Rev. Proc. 2007–1 (this Bulletin).

(7) Whether, under the common law rules applicable in determining the employer-employee relationship, a professional staffing corporation (loan-out corporation) or the subscriber is the employer of individuals, if:

(i) the loan-out corporation hires employees of the subscriber and assigns the employees back to the subscriber, or

(ii) the loan-out corporation assigns individuals to subscribers for more than a temporary period (1 year or longer).

(8) Questions that the Service determines, in its discretion, should not be answered in the general interests of tax administration.

(9) Any frivolous issue, as that term is defined in section 6.10 of Rev. Proc. 2007–1 (this Bulletin).

SECTION 4. AREAS IN WHICH RULINGS OR DETERMINATION LETTERS WILL NOT ORDINARILY BE ISSUED

.01 Specific questions and problems.

(1) Sections 38, 39, 46, and 48.—General Business Credit; Carryback and Carryforward of Unused Credits; Amount of Credit; Energy Credit; Reforestation Credit.—Application of these sections where the formal ownership of property is in a party other than the taxpayer, except when title is held merely as security.

(2) Section 61.—Gross Income Defined.—Determination as to who is the true owner of property in cases involving the sale of securities, or participation interests therein, where the purchaser has the contractual right to cause the securities, or participation interests therein, to be purchased by either the seller or a third party.

(3) Sections 61 and 163.—Gross Income Defined; Interest.—Determinations as to who is the true owner of property or the true borrower of money in cases in which the formal ownership of the property, or the liability for the indebtedness, is in another party.

(4) Sections 83 and 451.—Property Transferred in Connection with Performance of Services; General Rule for Taxable Year of Inclusion.—When compensation is realized by a person who, in connection with the performance of services, is granted a nonstatutory option without a readily ascertainable fair market value to purchase stock at a price that is less than the fair market value of the stock on the date the option is granted.

(5) Section 103.—Interest on State and Local Bonds.—Whether the interest on State or local bonds will be excludible from gross income under § 103(a), if the proceeds of issues of bonds (other than advance refunding issues) are placed in escrow or otherwise not expended for a governmental purpose for an extended period of time even though the proceeds are invested at a yield that will not exceed the yield on the State or local bonds prior to their expenditure.

(6) Section 103.—Interest on State and Local Bonds.—Whether a State or local governmental obligation that does not meet the criteria of section 5 of Rev. Proc. 89–5, 1989–1 C.B. 774, is an "arbitrage bond" within the meaning of former § 103(c)(2) solely by reason of the investment of the bond proceeds in acquired nonpurpose obligations at a materially higher yield more than 3 years after issuance of the bonds or 5 years after issuance of the bonds in the case of construction issues described in former § 1.103–13(a)(2)(ii)(E) or § 1.148–2(e)(2)(ii).

(7) Sections 104(a)(2) and 3121.—Compensation for Injuries or Sickness; Definitions.—Whether an allocation of the amount of a settlement award (including a lump sum award) between back pay, compensatory damages, punitive damages, etc., is a proper allocation for Federal tax purposes.

(8) Section 141.—Private Activity Bond; Qualified Bond.—Whether State or local bonds will meet the "private business use test" and the "private security or payment test" under § 141(b)(1) and (2) in situations in which the proceeds are used to finance certain output facilities and, pursuant to a contract to take, or take or pay for, a nongovernmental person purchases 30 percent or more of the actual output of the facility but 10 percent or less of the: (i) subparagraph (5) output of the facility as defined in § 1.103–7(b)(5)(ii)(b) (issued under former § 103(b)), or (ii) available output of the facility as defined in § 1.141–7(b)(1). In similar situations, the Service will not ordinarily issue rulings or determination letters concerning questions arising under paragraphs (3), (4), and (5) of § 141(b).

(9) Sections 142 and 144.—Exempt Facility Bond; Qualified Small Issue Bond.—Whether an issue of private activity bonds meets the requirements of § 142 or § 144(a), if the sum of—

(i) the portion of the proceeds used to finance a facility in which an owner (or related person) or a lessee (or a related person) is a user of the facility both after the bonds are issued and at any time before the bonds were issued, and

(ii) the portion used to pay issuance costs and non-qualified costs equals more than 5 percent of the net proceeds, as defined in § 150(a)(3).

(10) Section 148.—Arbitrage.—Whether amounts received as proceeds from the sale of municipal bond financed property and pledged to the payment of debt service or pledged as collateral for the municipal bond issue are sinking fund proceeds within the meaning of former § 1.103–13(g) (issued under former § 103(c)) or replaced proceeds described in § 148(a)(2) (or former § 103(c)(2)(B)).

(11) Sections 162 and 262.—Trade or Business Expenses; Personal, Living, and Family Expenses.—Whether expenses are nondeductible commuting expenses, except for situations governed by Rev. Rul. 99–7, 1999–1 C.B. 361.

(12) Section 163.—See section 4.01(3), above.

(13) Section 167.—Depreciation.

(i) Useful lives of assets.

(ii) Depreciation rates.

(iii) Salvage value of assets.

(14) Sections 167 and 168.—Depreciation; Accelerated Cost Recovery System.—Application of those sections where the formal ownership of property is in a party other than the taxpayer except when title is held merely as security.

(15) Section 170.—Charitable, Etc., Contributions and Gifts.—Whether a transfer to a pooled income fund described in § 642(c)(5) qualifies for a charitable contribution deduction under § 170(f)(2)(A).

(16) Section 170(c).—Charitable, Etc., Contributions and Gifts.—Whether a taxpayer who transfers property to a charitable organization and thereafter leases back all or a portion of the transferred property may deduct the fair market value of the property transferred and leased back as a charitable contribution.

(17) Section 170.—Charitable, Etc., Contributions and Gifts.—Whether a transfer to a charitable remainder trust described in § 664 that provides for annuity or unitrust payments for one or two measuring lives qualifies for a charitable deduction under § 170(f)(2)(A).

(18) Section 216.—Deduction of Taxes, Interest, and Business Depreciation by Cooperative Housing Corporation Tenant-Stockholder.—If a cooperative housing corporation (CHC), as defined in § 216(b)(1), transfers an interest in real property to a corporation (not a CHC) in exchange for stock or securities of the transferee corporation, which engages in commercial activity with respect to the real property interest transferred, whether (i) the income of the transferee corporation derived from the commercial activity, and (ii) any cash or property (attributable to the real property interest transferred) distributed by the transferee corporation to the CHC will be considered as gross income of the CHC for the purpose of determining whether 80 percent or more of the gross income of the CHC is derived from tenant-stockholders within the meaning of § 216(b)(1)(D).

(19) Section 262.—See section 4.01(11), above.

(20) Section 265(a)(2).—Expenses and Interest Relating to Tax-Exempt Income.—Whether indebtedness is incurred or continued to purchase or carry obligations the interest on which is wholly exempt from the taxes imposed by subtitle A.

(21) Section 302.—Distributions in Redemption of Stock.—The tax effect of the redemption of stock for notes, when the payments on the notes are to be made over a period in excess of 15 years from the date of issuance of such notes.

(22) Section 302(b)(4) and (e).—Redemption from Noncorporate Shareholder in Partial Liquidation; Partial Liquidation Defined.—Whether a distribution will qualify as a distribution in partial liquidation under § 302(b)(4) and (e)(1)(A), unless it results in a 20 percent or greater reduction in (i) gross revenue, (ii) net fair market value of assets, and (iii) employees. (Partial liquidations that qualify as § 302(e)(2) business terminations are not subject to this provision.)

(23) Sections 302(b)(4) and (e), 331, 332, and 346(a).—Effects on Recipients of Distributions in Corporate Liquidations.—The tax effect of the liquidation of a corporation preceded or followed by the transfer of all or a part of the business assets to another corporation (1) that is the alter ego of the liquidating corporation, and (2) which, directly or indirectly, is owned more than 20 percent in value by persons holding directly or indirectly more than 20 percent in value of the liquidating corporation's stock. For purposes of this section, ownership will be determined by application of the constructive ownership rules of § 318(a) as modified by § 304(c)(3).

(24) Section 306.—Dispositions of Certain Stock.—Whether the distribution or disposition or redemption of "section 306 stock" in a closely held corporation is in pursuance of a plan having as one of its principal purposes the avoidance of

Federal income taxes within the meaning of § 306(b)(4).

(25) Sections 331 and 332.—See section 4.01(23), above.

(26) Sections 331 and 346(a).—Gain or Loss to Shareholders in Corporate Liquidations.—The tax effect of the liquidation of a corporation by a series of distributions, when the distributions in liquidation are to be made over a period in excess of 3 years from the adoption of the plan of liquidation.

(27) Section 346(a).—See sections 4.01(23) and (26), above.

(28) Section 351.—Transfer to Corporation Controlled by Transferor.—Whether § 351 applies to the transfer of an interest in real property by a cooperative housing corporation (as described in § 216(b)(1)) to a corporation in exchange for stock or securities of the transferee corporation, if the transferee engages in commercial activity with respect to the real property interest transferred.

(29) Section 355.—Distribution of Stock and Securities of a Controlled Corporation.—Whether the active business requirement of § 355(b) is met when, within the 5-year period described in § 355(b)(2)(B), a distributing corporation acquired control of a controlled corporation as a result of the distributing corporation transferring cash or other liquid or inactive assets to the controlled corporation in a transaction in which gain or loss was not recognized as a result of the transfer meeting the requirements of § 351(a) or § 368(a)(1)(D).

(30) Section 441(i).—Taxable Year of Personal Service Corporations.—Whether the principal activity of the taxpayer during the testing period for the taxable year is the performance of personal services within the meaning of § 1.441–3(c)(1)(iii).

(31) Section 448(d)(2)(A).—Limitation on Use of Cash Method of Accounting; Qualified Personal Service Corporation.—Whether 95 percent or more of the time spent by employees of the corporation, serving in their capacity as such, is devoted to the performance of services within the meaning of § 1.448–1T(e)(4)(i).

(32) Section 451.—General Rule for Taxable Year of Inclusion.—The tax consequences of a nonqualified deferred compensation arrangement using a grantor trust where the trust fails to meet the requirements of Rev. Proc. 92–64, 1992–2 C.B. 422.

(33) Section 451.—See section 4.01(4), above.

(34) Section 451.—General Rule for Taxable Year of Inclusion.—The income tax consequences as a result of being a beneficiary of a trust that an Indian tribe (as defined in 25 U.S.C. § 2703(5)) establishes to receive and invest *per capita* payments for its members who are minors or legal incompetents under the Indian Gaming Regulatory Act (25 U.S.C. §§ 2701–2721), if the trust meets the requirements of section 5.02 of Rev. Proc. 2003–14, 2003–1 C.B. 319.

(35) Section 584.—Common Trust Funds.—Whether a common trust fund plan meets the requirements of § 584. (For § 584 plan drafting guidance, see Rev. Proc. 92–51, 1992–1 C.B. 988.)

(36) Section 642.—Special Rules for Credits and Deductions; Pooled Income Fund.—Whether a pooled income fund satisfies the requirements described in § 642(c)(5).

(37) Section 664.—Charitable Remainder Trusts.—Whether a charitable remainder trust that provides for annuity or unitrust payments for one or two measuring lives or for annuity or unitrust payments for a term of years satisfies the requirements described in § 664.

(38) Section 664.—Charitable Remainder Trusts.—Whether a trust that will calculate the unitrust amount under § 664(d)(3) qualifies as a § 664 charitable remainder trust when a grantor, a trustee, a beneficiary, or a person related or subordinate to a grantor, a trustee, or a beneficiary can control the timing of the trust's receipt of trust income from a partnership or a deferred annuity contract to take advantage of the difference between trust income under § 643(b) and income for Federal income tax purposes for the benefit of the unitrust recipient.

(39) Sections 671 to 679.—Grantors and Others Treated as Substantial Owners.—In a nonqualified, unfunded deferred compensation arrangement described in Rev. Proc. 92–64, the tax consequences of the use of a trust, other than the model trust described in that revenue procedure.

(40) Sections 671 to 679.—Grantors and Others Treated as Substantial Owners.—Whether an Indian tribe (as defined in 25 U.S.C. § 2703(5)) that establishes a trust to receive and invest *per capita* payments for its members who are minors or legal incompetents under the Indian Gaming Regulatory Act (25 U.S.C. §§ 2701–2721) is the grantor and owner of the trust, if the trust meets the requirements of section 5.02 of Rev. Proc. 2003–14, 2003–1 C.B. 319.

(41) Section 1362.—Election; Revocation; Termination.—All situations in which the Service has provided an automatic approval procedure or administrative procedure for an S corporation to obtain relief for late S corporation, qualified subchapter S subsidiary, qualified subchapter S trust, or electing small business trust elections. See Rev. Proc. 2003–43, 2003–1 C.B. 998; Rev. Proc. 2004–48, 2004–2 C.B. 172; and Rev. Proc. 2004–49, 2004–2 C.B. 210. (For instructions on how to seek this relief, see the preceding revenue procedures.)

(42) Section 1502.—Regulations.—Whether a parent cooperative housing corporation (as defined in § 216(b)(1)) will be permitted to file a consolidated income tax return with its transferee subsidiary, if the transferee engages in commercial activity with respect to the real property interest transferred to it by the parent.

(43) Section 2055.—Transfers for Public, Charitable, and Religious Uses.—Whether a transfer to a pooled income fund described in § 642(c)(5) qualifies for a charitable deduction under § 2055(e)(2)(A).

(44) Section 2055.—Transfers for Public, Charitable, and Religious Uses.—Whether a transfer to a charitable remainder trust described in § 664 that provides for annuity or unitrust payments for one or two measuring lives or a term of years qualifies for a charitable deduction under § 2055(e)(2)(A).

(45) Section 2503.—Taxable Gifts.—Whether the transfer of property to a trust will be a gift of a present interest in property when (i) the trust corpus consists or will consist substantially of insurance policies on the life of the grantor or the grantor's spouse, (ii) the

trustee or any other person has a power to apply the trust's income or corpus to the payment of premiums on policies of insurance on the life of the grantor or the grantor's spouse, (iii) the trustee or any other person has a power to use the trust's assets to make loans to the grantor's estate or to purchase assets from the grantor's estate, (iv) the trust beneficiaries have the power to withdraw, on demand, any additional transfers made to the trust, and (v) there is a right or power in any person that would cause the grantor to be treated as the owner of all or a portion of the trust under §§ 673 to 677.

(46) Section 2514.—Powers of Appointment.—If the beneficiaries of a trust permit a power of withdrawal to lapse, whether § 2514(e) will be applicable to each beneficiary in regard to the power when (i) the trust corpus consists or will consist substantially of insurance policies on the life of the grantor or the grantor's spouse, (ii) the trustee or any other person has a power to apply the trust's income or corpus to the payment of premiums on policies of insurance on the life of the grantor or the grantor's spouse, (iii) the trustee or any other person has a power to use the trust's assets to make loans to the grantor's estate or to purchase assets from the grantor's estate, (iv) the trust beneficiaries have the power to withdraw, on demand, any additional transfers made to the trust, and (v) there is a right or power in any person that would cause the grantor to be treated as the owner of all or a portion of the trust under §§ 673 to 677.

(47) Section 2522.—Charitable and Similar Gifts.—Whether a transfer to a pooled income fund described in § 642(c)(5) qualifies for a charitable deduction under § 2522(c)(2)(A).

(48) Section 2522.—Charitable and Similar Gifts.—Whether a transfer to a charitable remainder trust described in § 664 that provides for annuity or unitrust payments for one or two measuring lives or a term of years qualifies for a charitable deduction under § 2522(c)(2)(A).

(49) Section 2601.—Tax Imposed.—Whether a trust that is excepted from the application of the generation-skipping transfer tax because it was irrevocable on September 25, 1985, will lose its excepted status if the situs of the trust is changed from the United States to a situs outside of the United States.

(50) Section 2702.—Special Valuation Rules in Case of Transfers of Interests in Trusts.—Whether annuity interests are qualified annuity interests under § 2702 if the amount of the annuity payable annually is more than 50 percent of the initial net fair market value of the property transferred to the trust, or if the value of the remainder interest is less than 10 percent of the initial net fair market value of the property transferred to the trust. For purposes of the 10 percent test, the value of the remainder interest is the present value determined under § 7520 of the right to receive the trust corpus at the expiration of the term of the trust. The possibility that the grantor may die prior to the expiration of the specified term is not taken into account, nor is the value of any reversion retained by the grantor or the grantor's estate.

(51) Section 2702.—Special Valuation Rules in Case of Transfers of Interests in Trusts.—Whether a trust with one term holder satisfies the requirements of § 2702(a)(3)(A) and § 25.2702–5(c) to be a qualified personal residence trust.

(52) Section 3121.—Definitions.—Determinations as to which of two entities, under common law rules applicable in determining the employer-employee relationship, is the employer, when one entity is treating the worker as an employee.

(53) Section 3121.—See section 4.01(7), above.

.02 General areas.

(1) Any matter in which the determination requested is primarily one of fact, *e.g.*, market value of property, or whether an interest in a corporation is to be treated as stock or indebtedness.

(2) Situations where the requested ruling deals with only part of an integrated transaction. Generally, a letter ruling will not be issued on only part of an integrated transaction. If, however, a part of a transaction falls under a no-rule area, a letter ruling on other parts of the transaction may be issued. Before preparing the letter ruling request, a taxpayer should call the Office of the Associate Chief Counsel having jurisdiction for the matters on which the taxpayer is seeking a letter ruling to discuss whether a letter ruling will be issued on part of the transaction. To determine which division has jurisdiction over a particular issue see section 3 of Rev. Proc. 2007–1 (this Bulletin). For a list of telephone numbers for the different divisions see section 10.07 of Rev. Proc. 2007–1.

(3) Situations where two or more items or sub-methods of accounting are interrelated. If two or more items or sub-methods of accounting are interrelated, ordinarily a letter ruling will not be issued on a change in accounting method involving only one of the items or sub-methods.

(4) The tax effect of any transaction to be consummated at some indefinite future time.

(5) Any matter dealing with the question of whether property is held primarily for sale to customers in the ordinary course of a trade or business.

(6) The tax effect of a transaction if any part of the transaction is involved in litigation among the parties affected by the transaction, except for transactions involving bankruptcy reorganizations.

(7) (a) Situations where the taxpayer or a related party is domiciled or organized in a foreign jurisdiction with which the United States does not have an effective mechanism for obtaining tax information with respect to civil tax examinations and criminal tax investigations, which would preclude the Service from obtaining information located in such jurisdiction that is relevant to the analysis or examination of the tax issues involved in the ruling request.

(b) The provisions of subsection (a) above shall not apply if the taxpayer or affected related party (i) consents to the disclosure of all relevant information requested by the Service in processing the ruling request or in the course of an examination in order to verify the accuracy of the representations made and to otherwise analyze or examine the tax issues involved in the ruling request, and (ii) waives all claims to protection of bank or commercial secrecy laws in the foreign jurisdiction with respect to the information requested by the Service. In the event the taxpayer's or related party's consent to disclose relevant information or to waive protection of bank or commercial secrecy is determined by the Service to be ineffective or of no force and effect, then the Service may retroactively rescind any ruling rendered in reliance on such consent.

(8) A matter involving the Federal tax consequences of any proposed Federal, State, local, municipal, or foreign legislation. The Service may provide general information in response to an inquiry. However, the Office of Division Counsel/Associate Chief Counsel (Tax Exempt and Government Entities) may issue letter rulings regarding the effect of proposed State, local, or municipal legislation upon an eligible deferred compensation plan under § 457(b) provided that the letter ruling request relating to the plan complies with the other requirements of Rev. Proc. 2007–1.

(9) Except as otherwise provided in this revenue procedure (*e.g.*, under section 3.01(33), where the Service already is ruling on a significant issue in the same transaction), a letter ruling will not ordinarily be issued with respect to an issue that is clearly and adequately addressed by statute, regulations, decisions of a court, revenue rulings, revenue procedures, notices, or other authority published in the Internal Revenue Bulletin. However, the Service may in its discretion determine to issue a ruling on such an issue if the Service otherwise is issuing a ruling on another issue arising in the same transaction.

SECTION 5. AREAS UNDER STUDY IN WHICH RULINGS OR DETERMINATION LETTERS WILL NOT BE ISSUED UNTIL THE SERVICE RESOLVES THE ISSUE THROUGH PUBLICATION OF A REVENUE RULING, REVENUE PROCEDURE, REGULATIONS OR OTHERWISE

.01 Section 62(c).—Reimbursement Arrangements.—Whether amounts related to a salary reduction and paid under a purported reimbursement or other expense allowance arrangement will be treated as paid under an "accountable plan" in accordance with § 1.62–2(c)(2).

.02 Sections 101 and 7702.—Certain Death Benefits; Life Insurance Contract Defined.—Whether amounts received under an arrangement that is not regulated as an insurance company may be treated as received under a "life insurance contract" within the meaning of §§ 101(a) and 7702.

.03 Sections 162 and 1502.—Trade or Business Expenses; Consolidated Returns.—Treatment of manufacturer incentive payments under the intercompany transaction regulations of § 1.1502–13. *See* T.D. 9261, 2006–21 I.R.B. 919.

.04 Sections 302 and 304.—Certain Redemptions.—Treatment of basis in a § 302 and/or a § 304 redemption. See Announcement 2006–30, 2006–19 I.R.B. 879.

.05 Sections 351, 358 and 362(a).—Transfers to Corporation Controlled by Transferors; Basis to Distributees; Basis to Corporations.—The issues described as being under study in Rev. Rul. 2006–2, 2006–2 I.R.B. 261.

.06 Section 409A.—Inclusion in Gross Income of Deferred Compensation Under Nonqualified Deferred Compensation Plans.—Rulings on the tax consequences of arrangements described in § 409A, including rulings as to whether an arrangement is an arrangement described in § 409A, will not be issued until this subsection of this revenue procedure is revised.

.07 Section 451.—General Rule for Taxable Year of Inclusion.—The income tax consequences as a result of being a beneficiary of a trust that an Indian tribe (as defined in 25 U.S.C. § 2703(5)) establishes to receive and invest *per capita* payments for its members (regardless of whether they are minors or legal incompetents) under the Indian Gaming Regulatory Act (25 U.S.C. §§ 2701–2721) if the trust does not meet the requirements of section 5.02 of Rev. Proc. 2003–14, 2003–1 C.B. 319.

.08 Sections 671 to 679.—Grantors and Others Treated as Substantial Owners.—Whether an Indian tribe (as defined in 25 U.S.C. § 2703(5)) that establishes a trust to receive and invest *per capita* payments for its members (regardless of whether they are minors or legal incompetents) under the Indian Gaming Regulatory Act (25 U.S.C. §§ 2701–2721) is the grantor and owner of the trust if the trust does not meet the requirements of section 5.02 of Rev. Proc. 2003–14, 2003–1 C.B. 319.

.09 Section 1361.—Definition of a Small Business Corporation.—Whether a State law limited partnership electing under § 301.7701–3 to be classified as an association taxable as a corporation has more than one class of stock for purposes of § 1361(b)(1)(D). The Service will treat any request for a ruling on whether a State law limited partnership is eligible to elect S corporation status as a request for a ruling on whether the partnership complies with § 1361(b)(1)(D).

.10 Section 2036.—Transfers with Retained Life Estate.—Whether the corpus of a trust will be included in a grantor's estate when the trustee of the trust is a private trust company owned partially or entirely by members of the grantor's family.

.11 Section 2038.—Revocable Transfers.—Whether the corpus of a trust will be included in a grantor's estate when the trustee of the trust is a private trust company owned partially or entirely by members of the grantor's family.

.12 Section 2041.—Powers of Appointment.—Whether the corpus of a trust will be included in an individual's estate when the trustee of the trust is a private trust company owned partially or entirely by members of the individual's family.

.13 Section 6050P.—Returns Relating to the Cancellation of Indebtedness by Certain Entities.—Whether amounts reduced pursuant to the terms of a debt instrument are reportable under § 6050P and the regulations.

.14 Section 7702.—See section 5.02, above.

SECTION 6. AREAS COVERED BY AUTOMATIC APPROVAL PROCEDURES IN WHICH RULINGS WILL NOT ORDINARILY BE ISSUED

.01 Section 338.—Certain Stock Purchases Treated as Asset Acquisitions.—All requests for an extension of time under § 301.9100–3 within which to make an election under § 338(g) or (h)(10) where the Service has provided an administrative procedure to seek an extension. See Rev. Proc. 2003–33, 2003–1 C.B. 803 (extension automatically granted to certain persons required to file Form 8023 to make a valid section 338 election that have not filed Form 8023 by its due date).

.02 Section 442.—Change of Annual Accounting Period.—All requests for change in annual accounting period where the Service has provided an automatic change procedure for obtaining a change in annual accounting period. *See* Rev. Proc. 2002–39, 2002–1 C.B. 1046 (general procedures for prior approval), as clarified and modified by Notice 2002–72, 2002–2 C.B. 843, and modified by Rev. Proc. 2003–34, 2003–1 C.B. 856, and Rev. Proc. 2003–79, 2003–2 C.B. 1036; Rev. Proc. 2002–37, 2002–1 C.B. 1030 (certain corporations), as clarified and modified by Notice 2002–72 and modified by Rev. Proc. 2003–34; Rev. Proc. 2002–38, 2002–1 C.B. 1037 (partnership, S corporation, or personal service corporation seeking a natural business year or an ownership taxable year), as clarified and modified by Notice 2002–72 and modified by Rev. Proc. 2003–79; and Rev. Proc. 2003–62, 2003–2 C.B. 299 (individual seeking a calendar year).

.03 Section 446.—General Rule for Methods of Accounting.—Except as otherwise specifically provided in applicable procedures published in the Internal Revenue Bulletin, all requests for change in method of accounting where the Service has provided an automatic change request procedure for obtaining a change in method of accounting. See the automatic change request procedures listed in section 9.22 of Rev. Proc. 2007–1 (this Bulletin).

.04 Section 461.—General Rule for Taxable Year of Deduction.—All requests for making or revoking an election under § 461 where the Service has provided an administrative procedure for making or revoking an election under § 461. *See* Rev. Proc. 92–29, 1992–1 C.B. 748 (dealing with the use of an alternative method for including in basis the estimated cost of certain common improvements in a real estate development).

.05 Section 704(c).—Contributed Property.—Requests from Qualified Master Feeder Structures, as described in section 4.02 of Rev. Proc. 2001–36, 2001–1 C.B. 1326, for permission to aggregate built-in gains and losses from contributed qualified financial assets for purposes of making § 704(c) and reverse § 704(c) allocations.

.06 Section 1362.—Election; Revocation; Termination.—All situations in which an S corporation qualifies for automatic late S corporation relief under Rev. Proc. 97–48, 1997–2 C.B. 521.

.07 Sections 1502, 1504, and 1552.—Regulations; Definitions; Earnings and Profits.—All requests for waivers or consents on consolidated return issues where the Service has provided an administrative procedure for obtaining waivers or consents on consolidated return issues. *See* Rev. Proc. 2002–32, 2002–1 C.B. 959, as modified by Rev. Proc. 2006–21, 2006–24 I.R.B. 1050 (certain corporations seeking reconsolidation within the 5-year period specified in § 1504(a)(3)(A)); Rev. Proc. 90–39, 1990–2 C.B. 365, as modified by Rev. Proc. 2006–21, 2006–24 I.R.B. 1050, and as clarified by Rev. Proc. 90–39A, 1990–2 C.B. 367 (certain affiliated groups of corporations seeking, for earnings and profits determinations, to make an election or a change in their method of allocating the group's consolidated Federal income tax liability); and Rev. Proc. 89–56, 1989–2 C.B. 643, as modified by Rev. Proc. 2006–21, 2006–24 I.R.B. 1050 (certain affiliated groups of corporations seeking to file a consolidated return where member(s) of the group use a 52–53 week taxable year).

SECTION 7. EFFECT ON OTHER REVENUE PROCEDURES

Rev. Proc. 2006–3, 2006–1 C.B. 122, is superseded.

SECTION 8. EFFECTIVE DATE

This revenue procedure is effective January 2, 2007.

SECTION 9. PAPERWORK REDUCTION ACT

The collections of information contained in this revenue procedure have been reviewed and approved by the Office of Management and Budget in accordance with the Paperwork Reduction Act (44 U.S.C. § 3507) under control number 1545–1522.

An agency may not conduct or sponsor, and a person is not required to respond to, a collection of information unless the collection of information displays a valid control number.

The collections of information in this revenue procedure are in sections 2.03, 3.01(33), 3.02(1) and (3), and 4.02(7)(b).

This information is required to evaluate whether the request for a letter ruling or determination letter is not covered by the provisions of this revenue procedure. The collections of information are required to obtain a letter ruling or determination letter. The likely respondents are business or other for-profit institutions.

The estimated total annual reporting and/or recording burden is 90 hours.

The estimated annual burden per respondent/recordkeeper varies from 15 minutes to 3 hours, depending on individual circumstances, with an estimated average burden of 2 hours. The estimated number of respondents and/or recordkeepers is 45.

The estimated annual frequency of responses is on occasion.

Books or records relating to a collection of information must be retained as long as their contents may become material in the administration of any internal revenue law. Generally, tax returns and tax return information are confidential, as required by § 6103.

DRAFTING INFORMATION

The principal author of this revenue procedure is Michael Danbury of the Office of the Associate Chief Counsel (Corporate). For further information about this revenue procedure, please contact Mr. Danbury at (202) 622–7550 (not a toll-free call), or call the division contacts listed in section 10.07 of Rev. Proc. 2007–1 (this Bulletin). To determine which division has jurisdiction over a particular issue see section 3 of Rev. Proc. 2007–1.

Rev. Proc. 2007–4

TABLE OF CONTENTS

SECTION 1. WHAT IS THE PURPOSE OF THIS REVENUE PROCEDURE?

This revenue procedure explains how the Internal Revenue Service gives guidance to taxpayers on issues under the jurisdiction of the Commissioner, Tax Exempt and Government Entities Division. It explains the kinds of guidance and the manner in which guidance is requested by taxpayers and provided by the Service. A sample format of a request for a letter ruling is provided in Appendix A.

SECTION 2. WHAT CHANGES HAVE BEEN MADE TO REV. PROC. 2006–4?

.01 This revenue procedure is a general update of Rev. Proc. 2006–4, 2006–1 I.R.B. 132, which contains the Service's general procedures for employee plans and exempt organizations letter ruling requests. Most of the changes to Rev. Proc. 2006–4 involve minor revisions, such as updating citations to other revenue procedures.

.02 The Service has determined that letter rulings will not be issued with respect to individual cases under § 414(d), pending the issuance of general guidance that is currently being developed in coordination with the Department of Labor and the Pension Benefit Guaranty Corporation. Accordingly, section 6.02(1) is revised to delete the reference to § 414(d) and section 8.12 is revised to clarify that EP Technical will no longer issue governmental plan rulings under § 414(d), including rulings involving plans of Indian tribal governments.

.03 Additional no rule areas for EO Technical are added as section 6.14 and 6.16.

.04 An additional no rule area for EP Technical and EO Technical is added as section 6.15.

.05 Section 7.04(2) is clarified with respect to the non-issuance of determination letters by EO Determinations on completed transactions.

SECTION 3. IN WHAT FORM IS GUIDANCE PROVIDED BY THE COMMISSIONER, TAX EXEMPT AND GOVERNMENT ENTITIES DIVISION?

In general

.01 The Service provides guidance in the form of letter rulings, closing agreements, compliance statements, determination letters, opinion letters, advisory letters, information letters, revenue rulings, and oral advice.

Letter ruling

.02 A "letter ruling" is a written statement issued to a taxpayer by the Service's Employee Plans Technical office or Exempt Organizations Technical office that interprets and applies the tax laws or any nontax laws applicable to employee benefit plans and exempt organizations to the taxpayer's specific set of facts. Once issued, a letter ruling may be revoked or modified for any number of reasons, as explained in section 13 of this revenue procedure, unless it is accompanied by a "closing agreement."

Closing agreement

.03 A closing agreement is a final agreement between the Service and a taxpayer on a specific issue or liability. It is entered into under the authority in § 7121 and is final unless fraud, malfeasance, or misrepresentation of a material fact can be shown.

A closing agreement prepared in an office under the responsibility of the Commissioner, TE/GE, may be based on a ruling that has been signed by the Commissioner, TE/GE, or the Commissioner, TE/GE's, delegate that says that a closing agreement will be entered into on the basis of the ruling letter.

A closing agreement may be entered into when it is advantageous to have the matter permanently and conclusively closed, or when a taxpayer can show that there are good reasons for an agreement and that making the agreement will not prejudice the interests of the Government. In appropriate cases, taxpayers may be asked to enter into a closing agreement as a condition to the issuance of a letter ruling.

If, in a single case, a closing agreement is requested for each person in a class of taxpayers, separate agreements are entered into only if the class consists of 25 or fewer taxpayers. However, if the issue and holding are identical for the class and there are more than 25 taxpayers in the class, a "mass closing agreement" will be entered into with the taxpayer who is authorized by the others to represent the class.

In appropriate cases, a closing agreement may be made with sponsors of master and prototype plans.

A closing agreement may also be entered into with respect to retirement plan failures corrected under the Audit Closing Agreement Program of the Employee Plans Compliance Resolution System (EPCRS), as set forth in Rev. Proc. 2006–27, 2006–22 I.R.B. 945.

Determination letter

.04 A "determination letter" is a written statement issued by the Manager, EP Determinations, or the Manager, EO Determinations that applies the principles and precedents previously announced to a specific set of facts. It is issued only when a determination can be made based on clearly established rules in the statute, a tax treaty, or the regulations, or based on a conclusion in a revenue ruling, opinion, or court decision published in the Internal Revenue Bulletin that specifically answers the questions presented.

The Manager, EP Determinations, issues determination letters involving §§ 401, 403(a), 409, and 4975(e)(7) as provided in Rev. Proc. 2007–6, page 189, this Bulletin.

Opinion letter

.05 An "opinion letter" is a written statement issued by Employee Plans Rulings and Agreements to a sponsor as to the acceptability (for purposes of §§ 401 and 501(a)) of the form of a master or prototype plan and any related trust or custodial account under §§ 401, 403(a), and 501(a), or as to the conformance of a prototype trust, custodial account, or individual annuity with the requirements of § 408(a), (b), or (k), as applicable. *See* Rev. Proc. 2005–16, 2005–1 C.B. 674. *See also* Rev. Proc. 91–44, 1991–2 C.B. 733, and Rev. Proc. 92–38, 1992–1 C.B. 859.

Information letter

.06 An "information letter" is a statement issued either by the Director, Employee Plans Rulings and Agreements or the Director, Exempt Organizations Rulings and Agreements. It calls attention to a well-established interpretation or principle of tax law (including a tax treaty) without applying it to a specific set of facts. To the extent resources permit, an information letter may be issued if the taxpayer's inquiry indicates a need for general information or if the taxpayer's request does not meet the requirements of this revenue procedure and the Service thinks general information will help the taxpayer. The taxpayer should provide a daytime telephone number with the taxpayer's request for an information letter. Requests for information letters should be sent to the address stated in section 9.04(2) of this revenue procedure. The requirements of section 9.02 of this revenue procedure are not applicable to information letters. An information letter is advisory only and has no binding effect on the Service.

Revenue ruling

.07 A "revenue ruling" is an interpretation by the Service that has been published in the Internal Revenue Bulletin. It is the conclusion of the Service on how the law is applied to a specific set of facts. Revenue rulings are published for the information and guidance of taxpayers, Service personnel, and other interested parties.

Because each revenue ruling represents the conclusion of the Service regarding the application of law to the entire statement of facts involved, taxpayers, Service personnel, and other concerned parties are cautioned against reaching the same conclusion in other cases unless the facts and circumstances are substantially the same. They should consider the effect of subsequent legislation, regulations, court decisions, revenue rulings, notices, and announcements. *See* Rev. Proc. 89–14, 1989–1 C.B. 814, which states the objectives of and standards for the publication of revenue rulings and revenue procedures in the Internal Revenue Bulletin.

Oral guidance

.08

(1) No oral rulings and no written rulings in response to oral requests.

The Service does not orally issue letter rulings or determination letters, nor does it issue letter rulings or determination letters in response to oral requests from taxpayers. However, Service employees ordinarily will discuss with taxpayers or their representatives inquiries regarding whether the Service will rule on particular issues and questions relating to procedural matters about submitting requests for letter rulings, determination letters, and requests for recognition of exempt status for a particular organization.

(2) Discussion possible on substantive issues.

At the discretion of the Service, and as time permits, substantive issues may also be discussed. However, such a discussion will not be binding on the Service, and cannot be relied on as a basis for obtaining retroactive relief under the provisions of § 7805(b).

Substantive tax issues involving the taxpayer that are under examination, in appeals, or in litigation will not be discussed by Service employees not directly involved in the examination, appeal, or litigation of the issues unless the discussion is coordinated with those Service employees who are directly involved in the examination, appeal, or litigation of the issues. The taxpayer or the taxpayer's representative ordinarily will be asked whether the oral request for guidance or information relates to a matter pending before another office of the Service.

If a tax issue is not under examination, in appeals, or in litigation, the tax issue may be discussed even though the issue is affected by a nontax issue pending in litigation.

A taxpayer may seek oral technical guidance from a taxpayer service representative in TE/GE Customer Account Services when preparing a return or report. Oral guidance is advisory only, and the Service is not bound to recognize it, for example, in the examination of the taxpayer's return.

The Service does not respond to letters seeking to confirm the substance of oral discussions, and the absence of a response to such a letter is not confirmation of the substance of the letter.

Nonbank trustee requests

.09 In order to receive approval to act as a nonbank custodian of plans qualified under § 401(a) or accounts described in § 403(b)(7), and as a nonbank trustee or nonbank custodian for individual retirement arrangements (IRAs) established under § 408(a), (b), or (h), or for a Coverdell educational savings account established under § 530 or an Archer medical savings account established under § 220, or a Health Savings Account under § 223, a written application must be filed that demonstrates how the applicant complies with the requirements of § 1.408–2(e)(2) through (5) of the Income Tax Regulations.

The Service must have clear and convincing proof in its files that the requirements of the regulations are met. If there is a requirement that the applicant feels is not applicable, the application must provide clear and convincing proof that such requirement is not germane to the manner in which the applicant will administer any trust or custodial account. *See* § 1.408–2(e)(6).

The completed application should be sent to:

Internal Revenue Service
Commissioner, TE/GE
Attention: SE:T:EP:RA
P.O. Box 27063
McPherson Station
Washington, DC 20038

Section 6.01(6) of Rev. Proc. 2007–8, page 230, this Bulletin, imposes a user's fee for anyone applying for approval to become a nonbank trustee or custodian.

Compliance Statement

.10 A compliance statement is a binding written agreement between the Service and a taxpayer with respect to certain retirement plan failures identified by a taxpayer in a voluntary submission under the Voluntary Correction Program of the EPCRS (see Rev. Proc. 2006–27). The compliance statement addresses the failures identified in the VCP submission, the terms of correction, including any revision of administrative procedures, and the time period within which proposed corrections must be implemented. A compliance statement is conditioned on (i) there being no misstatement or omission of material facts in connection with the submission, and (ii) the implementation of the specific corrections and satisfaction of any other conditions in the compliance statement.

SECTION 4. ON WHAT ISSUES MAY TAXPAYERS REQUEST WRITTEN GUIDANCE UNDER THIS PROCEDURE?

Taxpayers may request letter rulings, information letters and closing agreements on issues within the jurisdiction of the Commissioner, Tax Exempt and Government Entities Division under this revenue procedure. The Service issues letter rulings to answer written inquiries of individuals and organizations about their status for tax purposes and the tax effects of their acts or transactions when appropriate in the interest of sound tax administration.

Taxpayers also may request determination letters that relate to Code sections under the jurisdiction of the Commissioner, Tax Exempt and Government Entities Division. *See* Rev. Proc. 2007–6, this Bulletin.

SECTION 5. ON WHAT ISSUES MUST WRITTEN GUIDANCE BE REQUESTED UNDER DIFFERENT PROCEDURES?

Determination letters

.01 The procedures for obtaining determination letters involving §§ 401, 403(a), 409, and 4975(e)(7), and the status for exemption of any related trusts or custodial accounts under § 501(a) are contained in Rev. Proc. 2007–6, this Bulletin.

Master and prototype plans and volume submitter plans

.02 The procedures for obtaining opinion letters for master and prototype plans and any related trusts or custodial accounts under §§ 401(a), 403(a) and 501(a) and advisory letters for volume submitter plans are contained in Rev. Proc. 2005–16. The procedures for obtaining opinion letters for prototype trusts, custodial accounts or annuities under § 408(a) or (b) are contained in Rev. Proc. 87–50, as modified by Rev. Proc. 92–38 and Rev. Proc. 2002–10, 2002–1 C.B. 401. The procedures for obtaining opinion letters for prototype trusts under § 408(k) are contained in Rev. Proc. 87–50, as modified by Rev. Proc. 91–44 (as modified by Rev. Proc. 2007–8) and Rev. Proc. 2002–10. The procedures for obtaining opinion letters for SIMPLE IRAs under § 408(p) are contained in Rev. Proc. 97–29, 1997–1 C.B. 698. The procedures for obtaining opinion letters for Roth IRAs under § 408A are contained in Rev. Proc. 98–59, 1998–2 C.B. 727.

Closing agreement program for defined contribution plans that purchased GICs or GACs

.03 Rev. Proc. 95–52, 1995–1 C.B. 439, restates and extends for an indefinite period the closing agreement program for defined contribution plans that purchased guaranteed investment contracts (GICs) or group annuity contracts (GACs) from troubled life insurance companies.

Employee Plans Compliance Resolution System

.04 The procedures for obtaining compliance statements, etc., for certain failures of plans qualified under § 401(a), § 403(b) plans, SEPs and § 457 plans under the Employee Plans Compliance Resolution System (EPCRS) are contained in Rev. Proc. 2006–27.

Chief Counsel

.05 The procedures for obtaining rulings, closing agreements, and information letters on issues within the jurisdiction of the Chief Counsel are contained in Rev. Proc. 2007–1, page 1, this Bulletin, including tax issues involving interpreting or applying the federal tax laws and income tax treaties relating to international transactions.

Alcohol, tobacco, and firearms taxes

.06 The procedures for obtaining letter rulings, etc., that apply to federal alcohol, tobacco, and firearms taxes under subtitle E of the Internal Revenue Code are under the jurisdiction of the Alcohol and Tobacco Tax and Trade Bureau within the Treasury Department.

SECTION 6. UNDER WHAT CIRCUMSTANCES DOES TE/GE ISSUE LETTER RULINGS?

In exempt organizations matters

.01 In exempt organizations matters, the Exempt Organizations Technical Office issues letter rulings on proposed transactions and on completed transactions if the request is submitted before the return is filed for the year in which the transaction that is the subject of the request was completed. Exempt Organizations Technical issues letter rulings involving:

(1) Organizations exempt from tax under § 501, including private foundations;

(2) Organizations described in § 170(b)(1)(A) (except clause (v));

(3) Political organizations described in § 527;

(4) Qualified tuition programs described in § 529 other than state run programs;

(5) Trusts described in § 4947(a);

(6) Other matters including issues under §§ 501 through 514, 4911, 4912, 4940 through 4948, 4955, 4958, 4976, 6033, 6104, 6113, and 6115.

In employee plans matters

.02 In employee plans matters, the Employee Plans Technical Office issues letter rulings on proposed transactions and on completed transactions either before or after the return is filed. Employee Plans Technical issues letter rulings involving:

(1) §§ 72, 101(d), 219, 381(c)(11), 402, 403(b), 404, 408, 408A, 412, 414(e), 419, 419A, 511 through 514, 4971, 4972, 4973, 4974, 4978, 4979, and 4980;

(2) Waiver of the minimum funding standard (*See* Rev. Proc. 2004–15, 2004–1 C.B. 490), and changes in funding methods and actuarial assumptions under § 412(c)(5);

(3) Waiver of the liquidity shortfall (as that term is defined in § 412(m)(5)) excise tax under § 4971(f)(4);

(4) Waiver under § 4980F(c)(4) of all or part of the excise tax imposed for failure to satisfy the notice requirements described in § 4980F(e);

(5) Whether a plan amendment is reasonable and provides for only *de minimis* increases in plan liabilities in accordance with §§ 401(a)(33) and 412(f)(2)(A) of the Code (*See* Rev. Proc. 79–62, 1979–2 C.B. 576);

(6) A change in the plan year of an employee retirement plan and the trust year of a tax-exempt employees' trust (*See* Rev. Proc. 87–27, 1987–1 C.B. 769);

(7) The tax consequences of prohibited transactions under §§ 503 and 4975;

(8) Whether individual retirement accounts established by employers or associations of employees meet the requirements of § 408(c). (*See* Rev. Proc. 87–50, as modified by Rev. Proc. 91–44 (as modified by Rev. Proc. 2007–8) and Rev. Proc. 92–38);

(9) With respect to employee stock ownership plans and tax credit employee stock ownership plans, §§ 409(l), 409(m), and 4975(d)(3). Other subsections of §§ 409 and 4975(e)(7) involve qualification issues within the jurisdiction of EP Determinations.

(10) Where the Commissioner, Tax Exempt and Government Entities Division has authority to grant extensions of certain periods of time within which the taxpayer must perform certain transactions (for example, the 90-day period for reinvesting in employer securities under § 1.46–8(e)(10) of the regulations), the taxpayer's request for an extension of such time period must be postmarked (or received, if hand delivered to the headquarters office) no later than the expiration of the original time period. Thus, for example, a request for an extension of the 90-day period under § 1.46–8(e)(10) must be made before the expiration of this period. However, see section 6.04 below with respect to elections under § 301.9100–1 of the Procedure and Administration Regulations.

In qualifications matters

.03 The Employee Plans Technical office ordinarily will not issue letter rulings on matters involving a plan's qualified status under §§ 401 through 420 and § 4975(e)(7). These matters are generally handled by the Employee Plans Determinations program as provided in Rev. Proc. 2007–6, this Bulletin, Rev. Proc. 93–10 and Rev. Proc. 93–12. Although the Employee Plans Technical office will not ordinarily issue rulings on matters involving plan qualification, a ruling may be issued where, (1) the taxpayer has demonstrated to the Service's satisfaction that the qualification issue involved is unique and requires immediate guidance, (2) as a practical matter, it is not likely that such issue will be addressed through the determination letter process, and (3) the Service determines that it is in the interest of good tax administration to provide guidance to the taxpayer with respect to such qualification issue.

Request for extension of time for making an election or for other relief under § 301.9100–1 of the Procedure and Administration Regulations

.04 Employee Plans Technical or Exempt Organizations Technical will consider a request for an extension of time for making an election or other application for relief under § 301.9100–1 of the Procedure and Administration Regulations even if submitted after the return covering the issue presented in the § 301.9100–1 request has been filed and even if submitted after an examination of the return has begun or after the issues in the return are being considered by an appeals office or a federal court. In such a case, EP or EO Technical will notify the Director, EP or EO Examinations.

Except for those requests pertaining to applications for recognition of exemption, § 301.9100–1 requests, even those submitted after the examination of the taxpayer's return has begun, are letter ruling requests and therefore should be submitted pursuant to this revenue procedure, and require payment of the applicable user fee, referenced in section 9.02(14) of this revenue procedure. In addition, the taxpayer must include the information required by § 301.9100–3(e).

However, an election made pursuant to § 301.9100–2 is not a letter ruling and does not require payment of any user fee. *See* § 301.9100–2(d). Such an election pertains to an automatic extension of time under § 301.9100–1.

Issuance of a letter ruling before the issuance of a regulation or other published guidance

.05 Unless the issue is covered by section 8 of this procedure, a letter ruling may be issued before the issuance of a temporary or final regulation or other published guidance that interprets the provisions of any act under the following conditions:

(1) Answer is clear or is reasonably certain. If the letter ruling request presents an issue for which the answer seems clear by applying the statute to the facts or for which the answer seems reasonably certain but not entirely free from doubt, a letter ruling will be issued.

(2) Answer is not reasonably certain. The Service will consider all letter ruling requests and use its best efforts to issue a letter ruling even if the answer does not seem reasonably certain where the issuance of a letter ruling is in the best interest of tax administration.

(3) Issue cannot be readily resolved before a regulation or any other published guidance is issued. A letter ruling will not be issued if the letter ruling request presents an issue that cannot be readily resolved before a regulation or any other published guidance is issued.

Issues in prior return

.06 The Service ordinarily does not issue rulings if, at the time the ruling is requested, the identical issue is involved in the taxpayer's return for an earlier period, and that issue—

(1) is being examined by the Director, EP or EO Examinations,

(2) is being considered by an appeals office,

(3) is pending in litigation in a case involving the taxpayer or related taxpayer, or

(4) has been examined by the Director, EP or EO Examinations or considered by an appeals office, and the statutory period of limitation has not expired for either assessment or filing a claim for a refund or a closing agreement covering the issue of liability has not been entered into by the Director, EP or EO Rulings and Agreements or by an appeals office.

If a return dealing with an issue for a particular year is filed while a request for a ruling on that issue is pending, EP or EO Technical will issue the ruling unless it is notified by the taxpayer that an examination of that issue or the identical issue on an earlier year's return has been started by the Director, EP or EO Examinations. *See* section 9.05. However, even if an examination has begun, EP or EO Technical ordinarily will issue the letter ruling if the Director, EP or EO Examinations agrees, by memorandum, to permit the ruling to be issued.

Generally not to business associations or groups

.07 EP or EO Technical does not issue letter rulings to business, trade, or industrial associations or to similar groups concerning the application of the tax laws to members of the group. But groups and associations may submit suggestions of generic issues that would be appropriately addressed in revenue rulings. *See* Rev. Proc. 89–14, which states objectives of, and standards for, the publication of revenue rulings and revenue procedures in the Internal Revenue Bulletin.

EP or EO Technical, however, may issue letter rulings to groups or associations on their own tax status or liability if the request meets the requirements of this revenue procedure.

Generally not to foreign governments

.08 EP or EO Technical does not issue letter rulings to foreign governments or their political subdivisions about the U.S. tax effects of their laws. However, EP or EO Technical may issue letter rulings to foreign governments or their political subdivisions on their own tax status or liability under U.S. law if the request meets the requirements of this revenue procedure.

Generally not on federal tax consequences of proposed legislation

.09 EP or EO Technical does not issue letter rulings on a matter involving the federal tax consequences of any proposed federal, state, local, municipal, or foreign legislation. EP or EO Technical, however, may provide general information in response to an inquiry.

Not on certain matters under § 53.4958–6 of the Foundation and Similar Excise Taxes Regulations

.10 EO Technical does not issue letter rulings as to whether a compensation or property transaction satisfies the rebuttable presumption that the transaction is not an excess benefit transaction as described in § 53.4958–6 of the Foundation and Similar Excise Taxes Regulations.

Not on stock options

.11 EP Technical does not issue letter rulings on the income tax (including unrelated business income tax) or excise tax consequences of the contribution of stock options to, or their subsequent exercise from, plans described in Part I of Subchapter D of Subtitle A of the Code.

Generally not on EO joint venture with a for-profit organization

.12 With the exception of when the issue is present in an initial application for recognition of exemption, EO Technical does not issue letter rulings as to whether a joint venture with a for-profit organization affects an organization's exempt status or results in unrelated business income.

Not on qualification of state run programs under § 529

.13 EO Technical will not issue letter rulings as to whether a state run tuition program qualifies under § 529.

Not on UBIT issues involving certain investments of a charitable lead trust

.14 EO Technical will not issue letter rulings pertaining to unrelated business income tax issues arising when charitable lead trust assets are invested with charitable organizations.

Not on issues under § 4965

.15 The Service will not issue letter rulings under § 4965, as added by section 516 of the Tax Increase Prevention and Reconciliation Act of 2005, before the issuance of temporary or final regulations or other published guidance that interprets the provision.

Not on issues under §§ 4966 and 4967

.16 EO Technical will not issue letter rulings under § 4966 or § 4967, as added by section 1231 of the Pension Protection Act of 2006, before the issuance of temporary or final regulations or other published guidance that interprets these provisions.

SECTION 7. UNDER WHAT CIRCUMSTANCES DOES EP OR EO DETERMINATIONS ISSUE DETERMINATION LETTERS?

Circumstances under which determination letters are issued

.01 Employee Plans or Exempt Organizations Determinations issues determination letters only if the question presented is specifically answered by a statute, tax treaty, or regulation, or by a conclusion stated in a revenue ruling, opinion, or court decision published in the Internal Revenue Bulletin.

In general

.02 In employee plans and exempt organizations matters, the EP or EO Determinations office issues determination letters in response to taxpayers' written requests on completed transactions. However, see section 13.08 of this revenue procedure. A determination letter usually is not issued for a question concerning a return to be filed by the taxpayer if the same question is involved in a return under examination.

In situations involving continuing transactions, such as whether an ongoing activity is an unrelated trade or business, EP or EO Technical would issue a ruling covering future tax periods and periods for which a return had not yet been filed.

EP or EO Determinations does not issue determination letters on the tax consequences of proposed transactions, except as provided in sections 7.03 and 7.04 below.

Under no circumstances will EP or EO Determinations issue a determination letter unless it is clearly shown that the request concerns a return that has been filed or is required to be filed.

In employee plans matters

.03 In employee plans matters, the Employee Plans Determinations office issues determination letters on the qualified status of employee plans under §§ 401, 403(a), 409 and 4975(e)(7), and the exempt status of any related trust under § 501. *See* Rev. Proc. 2007–6, this Bulletin, Rev. Proc. 93–10 and Rev. Proc. 93–12.

In exempt organizations matters

.04 In exempt organizations matters, the Exempt Organizations Determinations office issues determination letters involving:

(1) Initial qualification for exempt status of organizations described in §§ 501 and 521 to the extent provided in Rev. Proc. 90–27, 1990–1 C.B. 514, as modified by Rev. Proc. 2007–8;

(2) Updated exempt status letter to reflect changes to an organization's name or address, or to replace a lost exempt status letter, but not to approve or disapprove any completed transaction or the effect of changes in activities on exempt status, except in the situations specifically listed in paragraphs (3) through (12) below;

(3) Classification of private foundation status as provided in Rev. Proc. 76–34, 1976–2 C.B. 656;

(4) Reclassification of private foundation status, including update of private foundation status at the end of an organization's advance ruling period;

(5) Recognition of unusual grants to certain organizations under §§ 170(b)(1)(A)(vi) and 509(a)(2);

(6) Requests for relief under § 301.9100–1 of the Procedure and Administration Regulations in connection with applications for recognition of exemption;

(7) Advance approval of terminations under § 507(b)(1)(B);

(8) Whether certain organizations qualify as exempt operating foundations described in § 4940(d);

(9) Advance approval of certain set-asides described in § 4942(g)(2);

(10) Advance approval under § 4945 of organizations' grant making procedures;

(11) Advance approval of voter registration activities described in § 4945(f); and

(12) Whether an organization is exempt from filing annual information returns under § 6033 as provided in Rev. Procs. 83–23, 1983–1 C.B. 687, 95–48, 1995–2 C.B. 418, and 96–10, 1996–1 C.B. 577.

Circumstances under which determination letters are not issued

.05 EP or EO Determinations will not issue a determination letter in response to any request if—

(1) it appears that the taxpayer has directed a similar inquiry to EP or EO Technical;

(2) the same issue involving the same taxpayer or a related taxpayer is pending in a case in litigation or before an appeals office;

(3) the determination letter is requested by an industry, trade association, or similar group on behalf of individual taxpayers within the group (other than subordinate organizations covered by a group exemption letter); or

(4) the request involves an industry-wide problem.

Requests involving returns already filed

.06 A request received by the Service on a question concerning a return that is under examination, will be, in general, considered in connection with the examination of the return. If a response is made to the request before the return is examined, it will be considered a tentative finding in any later examination of that return.

Attach a copy of determination letter to taxpayer's return

.07 A taxpayer who, before filing a return, receives a determination letter about any transaction that has been consummated and that is relevant to the return being filed should attach a copy of the determination letter to the return when it is filed.

Review of determination letters

.08 Determination letters issued under sections 7.02 through 7.04 of this revenue procedure are not reviewed by EP or EO Technical before they are issued. If a taxpayer believes that a determination letter of this type is in error, the taxpayer may ask EP or EO Determinations to reconsider the matter or to request technical advice from EP or EO Technical as explained in Rev. Proc. 2007–5, page 161, this Bulletin.

(1) In employee plans matters, the procedures for review of determination letters relating to the qualification of employee plans involving §§ 401 and 403(a) are provided in Rev. Proc. 2007–6, Rev. Proc. 93–10 and Rev. Proc. 93–12.

(2) In exempt organizations matters, the procedures for the review of determination letters relating to the exemption from federal income tax of certain organizations under §§ 501 and 521 are provided in Rev. Proc. 90–27, as modified by Rev. Proc. 2007–8.

SECTION 8. UNDER WHAT CIRCUMSTANCES DOES THE SERVICE HAVE DISCRETION TO ISSUE LETTER RULINGS AND DETERMINATION LETTERS?

Ordinarily not in certain areas because of factual nature of the problem

.01 The Service ordinarily will not issue a letter ruling or determination letter in certain areas because of the factual nature of the problem involved or because of other reasons. The Service may decline to issue a letter ruling or a determination letter when appropriate in the interest of sound tax administration or on other grounds whenever warranted by the facts or circumstances of a particular case.

No "comfort" letter rulings

.02 No letter ruling will be issued with respect to an issue that is clearly and adequately addressed by statute, regulations, decision of a court of appropriate jurisdiction, revenue ruling, revenue procedure, notice or other authority published in the Internal Revenue Bulletin. Instead of issuing a letter ruling, the Service may, when it is considered appropriate and in the best interests of the Service, issue an information letter calling attention to well-established principles of tax law.

Not on alternative plans or hypothetical situations

.03 A letter ruling or a determination letter will not be issued on alternative plans of proposed transactions or on hypothetical situations.

Ordinarily not on part of an integrated transaction

.04 The Service ordinarily will not issue a letter ruling on only part of an integrated transaction. If, however, a part of a transaction falls under a no-rule area, a letter ruling on other parts of the transaction may be issued. Before preparing the letter ruling request, a taxpayer should call the office having jurisdiction for the matters on which the taxpayer is seeking a letter ruling to discuss whether the Service will issue a letter ruling on part of the transaction.

Not on partial terminations of employee plans

.05 The Service will not issue a letter ruling on the partial termination of an employee plan. Determination letters involving the partial termination of an employee plan may be issued.

Law requires ruling letter

.06 The Service will issue rulings on prospective or future transactions if the law or regulations require a determination of the effect of a proposed transaction for tax purposes.

Issues under consideration by PBGC or DOL

.07 A letter ruling or determination letter relating to an issue that is being considered by the Pension Benefit Guaranty Corporation (PBGC) or the Department of Labor (DOL), and involves the same taxpayer, shall be issued at the discretion of the Service.

Cafeteria plans

.08 The Service does not issue letter rulings or determination letters on whether a cafeteria plan satisfies the requirements of § 125. *See also* Rev. Proc. 2007–3, also in this Bulletin, for areas under the jurisdiction of the Division Counsel/Associate Chief Counsel (Tax Exempt and Government Entities) involving cafeteria plans in which advance rulings or determination letters will not be issued.

Determination letters

.09 *See* section 3.02 of Rev. Proc. 2007–6 for employee plans matters on which determination letters will not be issued.

Domicile in a foreign jurisdiction

.10

(1) The Service is ordinarily unwilling to rule in situations where a taxpayer or a related party is domiciled or organized in a foreign jurisdiction with which the United States does not have an effective mechanism for obtaining tax information with respect to civil tax examinations and criminal investigations, which would preclude the Service from obtaining information located in such jurisdiction that is relevant to the analysis or examination of the tax issues involved in the ruling request.

(2) The provisions of subsection 8.10(1) above shall not apply if the taxpayer or affected related party (a) consents to the disclosure of all relevant information requested by the Service in processing the ruling request or in the course of an examination to verify the accuracy of the representations made and to otherwise analyze or examine the tax issues involved in the

ruling request, and (b) waives all claims to protection of bank and commercial secrecy laws in the foreign jurisdiction with respect to the information requested by the Service. In the event the taxpayer's or related party's consent to disclose relevant information or to waive protection of bank or commercial secrecy is determined by the Service to be ineffective or of no force and effect, then the Service may retroactively rescind any ruling rendered in reliance on such consent.

Employee Stock Ownership Plans

.11

(1) The Service does not issue a letter ruling on whether or not the renewal, extension or refinancing of an exempt loan satisfies the requirements of § 4975(d)(3) of the Internal Revenue Code.

(2) The Service does not issue a letter ruling on whether the pre-payment of ESOP loans satisfies the requirements of § 4975(d)(3) other than with respect to plan termination.

Governmental Plans

.12 The Service does not issue a letter ruling on whether or not a plan is a governmental plan under § 414(d).

SECTION 9. WHAT ARE THE GENERAL INSTRUCTIONS FOR REQUESTING LETTER RULINGS AND DETERMINATION LETTERS?

In general

.01 This section explains the general instructions for requesting letter rulings and determination letters on all matters. Requests for letter rulings and determination letters require the payment of the applicable user fee discussed in section 9.02(14) of this revenue procedure.

Specific and additional instructions also apply to requests for letter rulings and determination letters on certain matters. Those matters are listed in section 10 of this revenue procedure followed by a reference (usually to another revenue procedure) where more information can be obtained.

Certain information required in all requests

.02

Facts

(1) Complete statement of facts and other information. Each request for a letter ruling or a determination letter must contain a complete statement of all facts relating to the transaction. These facts include—

(a) names, addresses, telephone numbers, and taxpayer identification numbers of all interested parties. (The term "all interested parties" does not mean all shareholders of a widely held corporation requesting a letter ruling relating to a reorganization, or all employees where a large number may be involved.);

(b) a complete statement of the business reasons for the transaction; and

(c) a detailed description of the transaction.

The Service will usually not rule on only one step of a larger integrated transaction. *See* section 8.04 of this revenue procedure. However, if such a letter ruling is requested, the facts, circumstances, true copies of relevant documents, etc., relating to the entire transaction must be submitted.

Documents

(2) Copies of all contracts, wills, deeds, agreements, instruments, plan documents, and other documents. True copies of all contracts, wills, deeds, agreements, instruments, plan documents, trust documents, proposed disclaimers, and other documents pertinent to the transaction must be submitted with the request.

Each document, other than the request, should be labelled alphabetically and attached to the request in alphabetical order. Original documents, such as contracts, wills, etc., should not be submitted because they become part of the Service's file and will not be returned.

Analysis of material facts

(3) Analysis of material facts. All material facts in documents must be included rather than merely incorporated by reference, in the taxpayer's initial request or in supplemental letters. These facts must be accompanied by an analysis of their bearing on the issue or issues, specifying the provisions that apply.

Same issue in an earlier return

(4) Statement regarding whether same issue is in an earlier return. The request must state whether, to the best of the knowledge of both the taxpayer and the taxpayer's representatives, the same issue is in an earlier return of the taxpayer (or in a return for any year of a related taxpayer within the meaning of § 267, or of a member of an affiliated group of which the taxpayer is also a member within the meaning of § 1504).

If the statement is affirmative, it must specify whether the issue—

(a) is being examined by the Service;

(b) has been examined and if so, whether or not the statutory period of limitations has expired for either assessing tax or filing a claim for refund or credit of tax;

(c) has been examined and if so, whether or not a closing agreement covering the issue or liability has been entered into by the Service;

(d) is being considered by an appeals office in connection with a return from an earlier period;

(e) has been considered by an appeals office in connection with a return from an earlier period and if so, whether or not the statutory period of limitations has expired for either assessing tax or filing a claim for refund or credit of tax;

(f) has been considered by an appeals office in connection with a return from an earlier period and whether or not a closing agreement covering the issue or liability has been entered into by an appeals office;

(g) is pending in litigation in a case involving the taxpayer or a related taxpayer; or

(h) in employee plans matters, is being considered by the Pension Benefit Guaranty Corporation or the Department of Labor.

Same or similar issue previously submitted or currently pending

(5) Statement regarding whether same or similar issue was previously ruled on or requested, or is currently pending. The request must also state whether, to the best of the knowledge of both the taxpayer and the taxpayer's representatives—

(a) the Service previously ruled on the same or similar issue for the taxpayer (or a related taxpayer within the meaning of § 267, or a member of an affiliated group of which the taxpayer is also a member within the meaning of § 1504) or a predecessor;

(b) the taxpayer, a related taxpayer, a predecessor, or any representatives previously submitted the same or similar issue to the Service but withdrew the request before a letter ruling or determination letter was issued;

(c) the taxpayer, a related taxpayer, or a predecessor previously submitted a request involving the same or a similar issue that is currently pending with the Service; or

(d) at the same time as this request, the taxpayer or a related taxpayer is presently submitting another request involving the same or a similar issue to the Service.

If the statement is affirmative for (a), (b), (c), or (d) of this section 9.02(5), the statement must give the date the request was submitted, the date the request was withdrawn or ruled on, if applicable, and other details of the Service's consideration of the issue.

Statement of authorities supporting taxpayer's views

(6) Statement of supporting authorities. If the taxpayer advocates a particular conclusion, an explanation of the grounds for that conclusion and the relevant authorities to support it must also be included. Even if not advocating a particular tax treatment of a proposed transaction, the taxpayer must still furnish views on the tax results of the proposed transaction and a statement of relevant authorities to support those views.

In all events, the request must include a statement of whether the law in connection with the request is uncertain and whether the issue is adequately addressed by relevant authorities.

Statement of authorities contrary to taxpayer's views

(7) Statement of contrary authorities. The taxpayer is also encouraged to inform the Service about, and discuss the implications of, any authority believed to be contrary to the position advanced, such as legislation (or pending legislation), tax treaties, court decisions, regulations, revenue rulings, revenue procedures, notices or announcements. If the taxpayer determines that there are no contrary authorities, a statement in the request to this effect would be helpful. If the taxpayer does not furnish either contrary authorities or a statement that none exists, the Service in complex cases or those presenting difficult or novel issues may request submission of contrary authorities or a statement that none exists. Failure to comply with this request may result in the Service's refusal to issue a letter ruling or determination letter.

Identifying and discussing contrary authorities will generally enable Service personnel to understand the issue and relevant authorities more quickly. When Service personnel receive the request, they will have before them the taxpayer's thinking on the effect and applicability of contrary authorities. This information should make research easier and lead to earlier action by the Service. If the taxpayer does not disclose and distinguish significant contrary authorities, the Service may need to request additional information, which will delay action on the request.

Statement identifying pending legislation

(8) Statement identifying pending legislation. At the time of filing the request, the taxpayer must identify any pending legislation that may affect the proposed transaction. In addition, if applicable legislation is introduced after the request is filed but before a letter ruling or determination letter is issued, the taxpayer must notify the Service.

Deletions statement required by § 6110

(9) Statement identifying information to be deleted from copy of letter ruling or determination letter for public inspection. The text of certain letter rulings and determination letters is open to public inspection under § 6110. The Service makes deletions from the text before it is made available for inspection. To help the Service make the deletions required by § 6110(c), a request for a letter ruling or determination letter must be accompanied by a statement indicating the deletions desired ("deletions statement"). If the deletions statement is not submitted with the request, a Service representative will tell the taxpayer that the request will be closed if the Service does not receive the deletions statement within 30 calendar days. *See* section 11.03 of this revenue procedure.

(a) Format of deletions statement. A taxpayer who wants only names, addresses, and identifying numbers to be deleted should state this in the deletions statement. If the taxpayer wants more information deleted, the deletions statement must be accompanied by a copy of the request and supporting documents on which the taxpayer should bracket the material to be deleted. The deletions statement must indicate the statutory basis under § 6110(c) for each proposed deletion.

If the taxpayer decides to ask for additional deletions before the letter ruling or determination letter is issued, additional deletions statements may be submitted.

(b) Location of deletions statement. The deletions statement must not appear in the request, but instead must be made in a separate document and placed on top of the request for a letter ruling or determination letter.

(c) Signature. The deletions statement must be signed and dated by the taxpayer or the taxpayer's authorized representative. A stamped or faxed signature is not permitted.

(d) Additional information. The taxpayer should follow the same procedures above to propose deletions from any additional information submitted after the initial request. An additional deletions statement, however, is not required with each submission of additional information if the taxpayer's initial deletions statement requests that only names, addresses, and identifying numbers are to be deleted and the taxpayer wants only the same information deleted from the additional information.

(e) Taxpayer may protest deletions not made. After receiving from the Service the notice under § 6110(f)(1) of intention to disclose the letter ruling or determination letter (including a copy of the version proposed to be open to public inspection and notation of third-party communications under § 6110(d)), the taxpayer may protest the disclosure of certain information in the letter ruling or determination letter. The taxpayer must send a written statement within 20 calendar days to the Service office indicated on the notice of intention to disclose. The statement must identify those deletions that the Service has not made and that the taxpayer believes should have been made. The taxpayer must also submit a copy of the version of the letter ruling or determination letter and bracket the deletions proposed that have not been made by the Service. Generally, the Service will not consider deleting any material that the taxpayer did not propose to be deleted before the letter ruling or determination letter was issued.

Within 20 calendar days after the Service receives the response to the notice under § 6110(f)(1), the Service will mail to the taxpayer its final administrative conclusion regarding the deletions to be made. The taxpayer does not have the right to a conference to resolve any disagreements concerning material to be deleted from the text of the letter ruling or determination letter. However, these matters may be taken up at any conference that is otherwise scheduled regarding the request.

(f) Taxpayer may request delay of public inspection. After receiving the notice under § 6110(f)(1) of intention to disclose, but within 60 calendar days after the date of notice, the taxpayer may send a request for delay of public inspection under either § 6110(g)(3) or (4). The request for delay must be sent to the Service office indicated on the notice of intention to disclose. A request for delay under § 6110(g)(3) must contain the date on which it is expected that the underlying transaction will be completed. The request for delay under § 6110(g)(4) must contain a statement from which the Commissioner of Internal Revenue may determine that there are good reasons for the delay.

Section 6110(l)(1) states that § 6110 disclosure provisions do not apply to any matter to which § 6104 applies. Therefore, letter rulings, determination letters, technical advice memoranda, and related background file documents dealing with the following matters (covered by § 6104) are not subject to § 6110 disclosure provisions—

(i) An approved application for exemption under § 501(a) as an organization described in § 501(c) or (d), or notice of status as a political organization under § 527, together with any papers submitted in support of such application or notice;

(ii) An application for exemption under § 501(a) with respect to the qualification of a pension, profit-sharing or stock bonus plan, or an individual retirement account described in § 408 or § 408A, whether the plan or account has more than 25 or less than 26 participants, or any application for exemption under § 501(a) by an organization forming part of such a plan or an account;

(iii) Any document issued by the Internal Revenue Service in which the qualification or exempt status of a plan or account is granted, denied, or revoked or the portion of any document in which technical advice with respect thereto is given;

(iv) Any application filed and any document issued by the Internal Revenue Service with respect to the qualification or status of EP master and prototype plans; and

(v) The portion of any document issued by the Internal Revenue Service with respect to the qualification or exempt status of a plan or account of a proposed transaction by such plan, or account.

Signature on request

(10) Signature by taxpayer or authorized representative. The request for a letter ruling or determination letter must be signed and dated by the taxpayer or the taxpayer's authorized representative. Neither a stamped signature nor a faxed signature is permitted.

Authorized representatives

(11) Authorized representatives. To sign the request or to appear before the Service in connection with the request, the representative must be:

Attorney

(a) An attorney who is a member in good standing of the bar of the highest court of any state, possession, territory, commonwealth, or the District of Columbia and who is not currently under suspension or disbarment from practice before the Service. He or she must file a written declaration with the Service showing current qualification as an attorney and current authorization to represent the taxpayer;

Certified public accountant

(b) A certified public accountant who is qualified to practice in any state, possession, territory, commonwealth, or the District of Columbia and who is not currently under suspension or disbarment from practice before the Service. He or she must file a written declaration with the Service showing current qualification as a certified public accountant and current authorization to represent the taxpayer;

Enrolled agent

(c) An enrolled agent who is a person, other than an attorney or certified public accountant, that is currently enrolled to practice before the Service and is not currently under suspension or disbarment from practice before the Service, including a person enrolled to practice only for employee plans matters. He or she must file a written declaration with the Service showing current enrollment and authorization to represent the taxpayer. Either the enrollment number or the expiration date of the enrollment card must be included in the declaration. For the rules on who may practice before the Service, see Treasury Department Circular No. 230;

Enrolled actuary

(d) An enrolled actuary who is a person enrolled as an actuary by the Joint Board for the Enrollment of Actuaries pursuant to 29 U.S.C. 1242 and qualified to practice in any state, possession, territory, commonwealth, or the District of Columbia and who is not currently under suspension or disbarment from practice before the Service. He or she must file a written declaration with the Service showing current qualification as an enrolled actuary and current authorization to represent the taxpayer. Practice as an enrolled actuary is limited to representation with respect to issues involving the following statutory provisions: §§ 401, 403(a), 404, 412, 413, 414, 4971, 6057, 6058, 6059, 6652(d), 6652(e), 6692, 7805(b), and 29 U.S.C. 1083;

A person with a "Letter of Authorization"

(e) Any other person, including a foreign representative who has received a "Letter of Authorization" from the Director, Office of Professional Responsibility under section 10.7(d) of Treasury Department Circular No. 230. A person may make a written request for a "Letter of Authorization" to: Office of Director, Office of Professional Responsibility, Internal Revenue Service, 1111 Constitution Avenue, N.W., Washington, DC 20224. Section 10.7(d) of Circular No. 230 authorizes the Commissioner to allow an individual who is not otherwise eligible to practice before the Service to represent another person in a particular matter. For additional information, see section 9.02(12) below.

Employee, general partner, *bona fide* officer, administrator, trustee, etc.

(f) The above requirements do not apply to a regular full-time employee representing his or her employer, to a general partner representing his or her partnership, to a *bona fide* officer representing his or her corporation, association, or organized group, to a trustee, receiver, guardian, personal representative, administrator, or executor representing a trust, receivership, guardianship, or estate, or to an individual representing his or her immediate family. A preparer of a return (other than a person referred to in paragraph (a), (b), (c), (d) or (e) of this section 9.02(11)) who is not a full-time employee, general partner, a *bona fide* officer, an administrator, trustee, etc., or an individual representing his or her immediate family may not represent a taxpayer in connection with a letter ruling, determination letter or a technical advice request. *See* section 10.7(c) of Treasury Department Circular No. 230.

Foreign representative

(g) A foreign representative (other than a person referred to in paragraph (a), (b), (c), (d) or (e) of this section 9.02(11)) is not authorized to practice before the Service and, therefore, must withdraw from representing a taxpayer in a request for a letter ruling or a determination letter. In this situation, the nonresident alien or foreign entity must submit the request for a letter ruling or a determination letter on the individual's or entity's own behalf or through a person referred to in paragraph (a), (b), (c), (d) or (e) of this section 9.02(11).

Power of attorney and declaration of representative

(12) Power of attorney and declaration of representative. Any authorized representative, whether or not enrolled to practice, must also comply with the conference and practice requirements of the Statement of Procedural Rules (26 C.F.R. § 601.501–601.509 (2005)), which provide the rules for representing a taxpayer before the Service. In addition, an unenrolled preparer must file a Form 8821 (Rev. April 2004), Tax Information Authorization, for certain limited employee plans matters.

Form 2848 (Rev. March 2004), *Power of Attorney and Declaration of Representative*, must be used to provide the representative's authorization (Part I of Form 2848, *Power of Attorney*) and the representative's qualification (Part II of Form 2848, *Declaration of Representative*). The name of the person signing Part I of Form 2848 should also be typed or printed on this form. A stamped signature is not permitted. An original, a copy, or a facsimile transmission (fax) of the power of attorney is acceptable so long as its authenticity is not reasonably disputed. For additional information regarding the power of attorney form, see section 9.03(2) of this revenue procedure.

For the requirement regarding compliance with Treasury Department Circular No. 230, see section 9.09 of this revenue procedure.

Penalties of perjury statement

(13) Penalties of perjury statement.

(a) Format of penalties of perjury statement. A request for a letter ruling or determination letter and any change in the request submitted at a later time must be accompanied by the following declaration: **"Under penalties of perjury, I declare that I have examined this request, or this modification to the request, including accompanying documents, and, to the best of my knowledge and belief, the request or the modification contains all the relevant facts relating to the request, and such facts are true, correct, and complete."** See section 11.04 of this revenue procedure for the penalties of perjury statement applicable for submissions of additional information.

(b) Signature by taxpayer. The declaration must be signed and dated by the taxpayer, not the taxpayer's representative. Neither a stamped signature nor a faxed signature is permitted.

The person who signs for a corporate taxpayer must be an officer of the corporate taxpayer who has personal knowledge of the facts, and whose duties are not limited to obtaining a letter ruling or determination letter from the Service. If the corporate taxpayer is a member of an affiliated group filing consolidated returns, a penalties of perjury statement must also be signed and submitted by an officer of the common parent of the group.

The person signing for a trust, a state law partnership, or a limited liability company must be, respectively, a trustee, general partner, or member-manager who has personal knowledge of the facts.

Applicable user fee

(14) Applicable user fee. Section 7528 of the Code, as added by section 202 of the Temporary Assistance for Needy Families Block Grant Program and extended by section 690 of the American Jobs Creation Act of 2004 requires taxpayers to pay user fees for requests for rulings, opinion letters, determination letters, and similar requests. Rev. Proc. 2007–8, page 230, this Bulletin, contains the schedule of fees for each type of request under the jurisdiction of the Commissioner, Tax Exempt and Government Entities Division and provides guidance for administering the user fee requirements. If two or more taxpayers are parties to a transaction and each requests a letter ruling, each taxpayer must satisfy the rules herein and additional user fees may apply.

Number of copies of request to be submitted

(15) Number of copies of request to be submitted. Generally a taxpayer needs only to submit one copy of the request for a letter ruling or determination letter. If, however, more than one issue is presented in the letter ruling request, the taxpayer is encouraged to submit additional copies of the request.

Further, two copies of the request for a letter ruling or determination letter are required if—

(a) the taxpayer is requesting separate letter rulings or determination letters on different issues as explained later under section 9.03(1) of this revenue procedure;

(b) the taxpayer is requesting deletions other than names, addresses, and identifying numbers, as explained in section 9.02(9) of this revenue procedure. (One copy is the request for the letter ruling or determination letter and the second copy is the deleted version of such request.); or

(c) a closing agreement (as defined in section 3.03 of this revenue procedure) is being requested on the issue presented.

Sample of a letter ruling request

(16) Sample format for a letter ruling request. To assist a taxpayer or the taxpayer's representative in preparing a letter ruling request, a sample format for a letter ruling request is provided in Appendix A. This format is not required to be used by the taxpayer or the taxpayer's representative. If the letter ruling request is not identical or similar to the format in Appendix A, the different format will neither defer consideration of the letter ruling request nor be cause for returning the request to the taxpayer or taxpayer's representative.

Checklist

(17) Checklist for letter ruling requests. The Service will be able to respond more quickly to a taxpayer's letter ruling request if it is carefully prepared and complete. The checklist in Appendix B of this revenue procedure is designed to assist taxpayers in preparing a request by reminding them of the essential information and documents to be furnished with the request. The checklist in Appendix B must be completed to the extent required by the instructions in the checklist, signed and dated by the taxpayer or the taxpayer's representative, and placed on top of the letter ruling request. If the checklist in Appendix B is not received, a group representative will ask the taxpayer or the taxpayer's representative to submit the checklist, which may delay action on the letter ruling request. A photocopy of this checklist may be used.

Additional information required in certain circumstances

.03

Multiple issues

(1) To request separate letter rulings for multiple issues in a single situation. If more than one issue is presented in a request for a letter ruling, the Service generally will issue a single ruling letter covering all the issues. However, if the taxpayer requests separate letter rulings on any of the issues (because, for example, one letter ruling is needed sooner than another), the Service will usually comply with the request unless it is not feasible or not in the best interests of the Service to do so. A taxpayer who wants separate letter rulings on multiple issues should make this clear in the request and submit two copies of the request. Additional checklists are solely for the specific issues designated.

In issuing each letter ruling, the Service will state that it has issued separate letter rulings or that requests for other letter rulings are pending.

Power of attorney

(2) Recipient of original of letter ruling or determination letter. The Service will send the original of the letter ruling or determination letter to the taxpayer and a copy of the letter ruling or determination letter to the taxpayer's representative. In this case, the letter ruling or determination letter is addressed to the taxpayer. A Form 2848, *Power of Attorney and Declaration of Representative* (Rev. March 2004), must be used to provide the representative's authorization except in certain employee plans matters. *See* section 9.02(12) of this revenue procedure.

Copies of letter ruling or determination letter sent to multiple representatives

(a) To have copies sent to multiple representatives. When a taxpayer has more than one representative, the Service will send the copy of the letter ruling or determination letter to the first representative named on the most recent power of attorney. If the taxpayer wants an additional copy of the letter ruling or determination letter sent to the second representative listed in the power of attorney, the taxpayer must check the appropriate box on Form 2848. If this form is not used, the taxpayer must state in the power of attorney that a copy of the letter ruling or determination letter is to be sent to the second representative listed in the power of attorney. Copies of the letter ruling or determination letter, however, will be sent to no more than two representatives.

Copy of letter ruling or determination letter sent to taxpayer's representative

(b) To have copy sent to taxpayer's representative.

A copy of the letter ruling or determination letter will be sent to the taxpayer's representative.

If the taxpayer wants a copy of the letter ruling or determination letter sent to the taxpayer's second representative, the taxpayer must check the appropriate box on Form 2848.

No copy of letter ruling or determination letter sent to taxpayer's representative

(c) To have no copy sent to taxpayer's representative. If a taxpayer does not want a copy of the letter ruling or determination letter sent to any representative, the taxpayer must check the appropriate box on Form 2848.

Expedited handling

(3) To request expedited handling. The Service ordinarily processes requests for letter rulings and determination letters in order of the date received. Expedited handling means that a request is processed ahead of the regular order. Expedited handling is granted only in rare and unusual cases, both out of fairness to other taxpayers and because the Service seeks to process all requests as expeditiously as possible and to give appropriate deference to normal business exigencies in all cases not involving expedited handling.

A taxpayer who has a compelling need to have a request processed ahead of the regular order may request expedited handling. This request must explain in detail the need for expedited handling. The request must be made in writing, preferably in a separate letter with, or soon after filing, the request for the letter ruling or determination letter. If the request is not made in a separate letter, then the letter in which the letter ruling or determination letter request is made should say, at the top of the first page: **"Expedited Handling Is Requested. See page ___ of this letter."**

A request for expedited handling will not be forwarded to the appropriate group for action until the check or money order for the user fee in the correct amount is received.

Whether the request will be granted is within the Service's discretion. The Service may grant a request when a factor outside a taxpayer's control creates a real business need to obtain a letter ruling or determination letter before a certain time in order to avoid serious business consequences. Examples include situations in which a court or governmental agency has imposed a specific deadline for the completion of a transaction, or a transaction must be completed expeditiously to avoid an imminent business emergency (such as the hostile takeover of a corporate taxpayer), provided that the taxpayer can demonstrate that the deadline or business emergency, and the need for expedited handling, resulted from circumstances that could not reasonably have been anticipated or controlled by the taxpayer. To qualify for expedited handling in such situations, the taxpayer must also demonstrate that the taxpayer submitted the request as promptly as possible after becoming aware of the deadline or emergency. The extent to which the letter ruling or determination letter complies with all of the applicable requirements of this revenue procedure, and fully and clearly presents the issues, is a factor in determining whether expedited treatment will be granted. When the Service agrees to process a request out of order, it cannot give assurance that any letter ruling or determination letter will be processed by the time requested. The scheduling of a closing date for a transaction or a meeting of the board of directors or shareholders of a corporation, without regard for the time it may take to obtain a letter ruling or determination letter, will not be considered a sufficient reason to process a request ahead of its regular order. Also, the possible effect of fluctuation in the market price of stocks on a transaction will not be considered a sufficient reason to process a request out of order.

Because most requests for letter rulings and determination letters cannot be processed ahead of their regular order, the Service urges all taxpayers to submit their requests well in advance of the contemplated transaction. In addition, in order to facilitate prompt action on letter ruling requests taxpayers are encouraged to ensure that their initial submissions comply with all of the requirements of this revenue procedure (including the requirements of other applicable guidelines set forth in section 10 of this revenue procedure), and to provide any additional information requested by the Service promptly.

Facsimile transmission (fax)

(4) To receive a letter ruling or submit a request for a letter ruling by facsimile transmission (fax).

(a) To receive a letter ruling by fax. A letter ruling ordinarily is not sent by fax. However, if the taxpayer requests, a copy of a letter ruling may be faxed to the taxpayer or the taxpayer's authorized representative. A letter ruling, however, is not issued until the ruling is mailed. *See* § 301.6110–2(h).

A request to fax a copy of the letter ruling to the taxpayer or the taxpayer's authorized representative must be made in writing, either as part of the original letter ruling request or prior to the approval of the letter ruling. The request must contain the fax number of the taxpayer or the taxpayer's authorized representative to whom the letter ruling is to be faxed.

In addition, because of the nature of a fax transmission, a statement containing a waiver of any disclosure violations resulting from the fax transmission must accompany the request. Nevertheless, the Service will take certain precautions to protect confidential information. For example, the Service will use a cover sheet that identifies the intended recipient of the fax and the number of pages transmitted. The cover sheet, if possible, will not identify the specific taxpayer by name, and it will be the first page covering the letter ruling being faxed.

(b) To submit a request for a letter ruling by fax. Original letter ruling requests sent by fax are discouraged because such requests must be treated in the same manner as requests by letter. For example, the faxed letter ruling request will not be forwarded to the applicable office for action until the check for the user fee is received.

Requesting a conference

(5) To request a conference. A taxpayer who wants to have a conference on the issues involved should indicate this in writing when, or soon after, filing the request. *See also* sections 12.01, 12.02, and 13.09(2) of this revenue procedure.

Address to send the request

.04

Requests for letter rulings

(1) Requests for letter rulings should be sent to the following offices (as appropriate):

Internal Revenue Service
Attention: EP Letter Rulings
P.O. Box 27063
McPherson Station
Washington, DC 20038

Internal Revenue Service
Attention: EO Letter Rulings
P.O. Box 27720
McPherson Station
Washington, DC 20038

Hand delivered requests must be marked RULING REQUEST SUBMISSION. The delivery should be made between the hours of 8:30 a.m. and 4:00 p.m.; where a receipt will be given:

Courier's Desk
Internal Revenue Service
Attention: SE:T:EP:RA or SE:T:EO:RA
1111 Constitution Avenue, NW – PE
Washington, DC 20224

Requests for information letters

(2) Requests for information letters on either employee plans matters or exempt organizations matters should be sent to Employee Plans or Exempt Organizations (as appropriate):

Internal Revenue Service
Commissioner, TE/GE
Attention: SE:T:EP:RA or SE:T:EO:RA
1111 Constitution Avenue, NW – PE
Washington, DC 20224

Requests for determination letters

(3) Requests for determination letters should be sent to:

Internal Revenue Service
P.O. Box 192
Covington, KY 41012–0192

For fees required with determination letter requests, see section 6 of Rev. Proc. 2007–8.

Pending letter ruling requests

.05

(1) Circumstances under which the taxpayer must notify EP or EO Technical. The taxpayer must notify EP or EO Technical if, after the letter ruling request is filed but before a letter ruling is issued, the taxpayer knows that—

(a) an examination of the issue or the identical issue on an earlier year's return has been started by an EP or EO Examinations office;

(b) in employee plans matters, the issue is being considered by the Pension Benefit Guaranty Corporation or the Department of Labor; or

(c) legislation that may affect the transaction has been introduced (*see* section 9.02(8) of this revenue procedure).

(2) Taxpayer must notify EP or EO Technical if return is filed and must attach request to return. If the taxpayer files a return before a letter ruling is received from EP or EO Technical concerning the issue, the taxpayer must notify EP or EO Technical that the return has been filed. The taxpayer must also attach a copy of the letter ruling request to the return to alert the EP or EO Examinations office and thereby avoid premature EP or EO Examinations office action on the issue.

When to attach letter ruling to return

.06 A taxpayer who receives a letter ruling before filing a return about any transaction that is relevant to the return being filed must attach a copy of the letter ruling to the return when it is filed.

How to check on status of request

.07 The taxpayer or the taxpayer's authorized representative may obtain information regarding the status of a request by calling the person whose name and telephone number are shown on the acknowledgement of receipt of the request.

Request may be withdrawn or EP or EO Technical may decline to issue letter ruling

.08

(1) In general. A taxpayer may withdraw a request for a letter ruling or determination letter at any time before the letter ruling or determination letter is signed by the Service. Correspondence and exhibits related to a request that is withdrawn or related to a letter ruling request for which the Service declines to issue a letter ruling will not be returned to the taxpayer. *See* section 9.02(2) of this revenue procedure. In appropriate cases, the Service may publish its conclusions in a revenue ruling or revenue procedure.

A request for a letter ruling will not be suspended in EP or EO Technical at the request of a taxpayer.

(2) Notification of Director, EP or EO Examinations. If a taxpayer withdraws a request for a letter ruling or if EP or EO Technical declines to issue a letter ruling, EP or EO Technical will notify the Director, EP or EO Examinations and may give its views on the issues in the request to the Director, EP or EO Examinations to consider in any later examination of the return.

(3) Refunds of user fee. The user fee will not be returned for a letter ruling request that is withdrawn. If the Service declines to issue a letter ruling on all of the issues in the request, the user fee will be returned. If the Service, however, issues a letter ruling on some, but not all, of the issues, the user fee will not be returned. *See* section 10 of Rev. Proc. 2007–8 for additional information regarding refunds of user fees.

Compliance with Treasury Department Circular No. 230

.09 The taxpayer's authorized representative, whether or not enrolled, must comply with Treasury Department Circular No. 230, which provides the rules for practice before the Service. In those situations when EP or EO Technical believes that the taxpayer's representative is not in compliance with Circular No. 230, EP or EO Technical will bring the matter to the attention of the Director, Office of Professional Responsibility.

For the requirement regarding compliance with the conference and practice requirements, see section 9.02(12) of this revenue procedure.

SECTION 10. WHAT SPECIFIC, ADDITIONAL PROCEDURES APPLY TO CERTAIN REQUESTS?

In general

.01 Specific revenue procedures supplement the general instructions for requests explained in section 9 of this revenue procedure and apply to requests for letter rulings or determination letters regarding the Code sections and matters listed in this section.

Exempt Organizations

.02 If the request is for the qualification of an organization for exemption from federal income tax under § 501 or 521, see Rev. Proc. 72–5, 1972–1 C.B. 709, regarding religious and apostolic organizations; Rev. Proc. 80–27, 1980–1 C.B. 677, concerning group exemptions; and Rev. Proc. 90–27, 1990–1 C.B. 514 (as modified by Rev. Proc. 2007–8), regarding applications for recognition of exemption.

Employee Plans

.03

(1) For requests to obtain approval for a retroactive amendment described in § 412(c)(8) of the Code and section 302(c)(8) of the Employee Retirement Income Security Act of 1974 (ERISA) that reduces accrued benefits, see Rev. Proc. 94–42, 1994–1 C.B. 717.

(2) For requests for a waiver of the minimum funding standard, see Rev. Proc. 2004–15.

(3) For requests for a waiver of the 100 percent tax imposed under § 4971(b) of the Code on a pension plan that fails to meet the minimum funding standards of § 412, see Rev. Proc. 81–44, 1981–2 C.B. 618.

(4) For requests for a determination that a plan amendment is reasonable and provides for only *de minimis* increases in plan liabilities in accordance with §§ 401(a)(33) and 412(f)(2)(A), see Rev. Proc. 79–62, 1979–2 C.B. 576.

(5) For requests to obtain approval for an extension of an amortization period of any unfunded liability in accordance with § 412(e), see Rev. Proc. 2004–44, 2004–2 C.B. 134.

(6) For requests by administrators or sponsors of a defined benefit plan to obtain approval for a change in funding method, see Rev. Proc. 2000–41, 2000–2 C.B. 371.

(7) For requests for the return to the employer of certain nondeductible contributions, see Rev. Proc. 90–49, 1990–2 C.B. 620 (as modified by Rev. Proc. 2007–8).

(8) For requests for determination letters for plans under §§ 401, 403(a), 409, and 4975(e)(7), and for the exempt status of any related trust under § 501, see Rev. Proc. 2007–6, Rev. Proc. 93–10 and Rev. Proc. 93–12.

SECTION 11. HOW DOES EP OR EO TECHNICAL HANDLE LETTER RULING REQUESTS?

In general

.01 The Service will issue letter rulings on the matters and under the circumstances explained in sections 4 and 6 of this revenue procedure and in the manner explained in this section and section 13 of this revenue procedure.

Is not bound by informal opinion expressed

.02 The Service will not be bound by the informal opinion expressed by the group representative or any other authorized Service representative under this procedure, and such an opinion cannot be relied upon as a basis for obtaining retroactive relief under the provisions of § 7805(b).

Tells taxpayer if request lacks essential information during initial contact

.03 If a request for a letter ruling or determination letter does not comply with all the provisions of this revenue procedure, the request will be acknowledged and the Service representative will tell the taxpayer during the initial contact which requirements have not been met.

Information must be submitted within 30 calendar days

If the request lacks essential information, which may include additional information needed to satisfy the procedural requirements of this revenue procedure, as well as substantive changes to transactions or documents needed from the taxpayer, the Service representative will tell the taxpayer during the initial contact that the request will be closed if the Service does not receive the information within 30 calendar days unless an extension of time is granted. *See* section 11.04 of this revenue procedure for information on extension of time and instructions on submissions of additional information.

Letter ruling request mistakenly sent to EP or EO Determinations Processing

A request for a letter ruling sent to EP/EO Determinations Processing that does not comply with the provisions of this revenue procedure will be returned by EP/EO Determinations Processing so that the taxpayer can make corrections before sending it to EP or EO Technical.

Requires prompt submission of additional information requested after initial contact

.04 Material facts furnished to the Service by telephone or fax, or orally at a conference, must be promptly confirmed by letter to the Service. This confirmation and any additional information requested by the Service that is not part of the information requested during the initial contact must be furnished within 21 calendar days to be considered part of the request.

Additional information submitted to the Service must be accompanied by the following declaration: **"Under penalties of perjury, I declare that I have examined this information, including accompanying documents, and, to the best of my knowledge and belief, the information contains all the relevant facts relating to the request for the information, and such facts are true, correct, and complete."** This declaration must be signed in accordance with the requirements in section 9.02(13)(b) of this revenue procedure. A taxpayer who submits additional factual information on several occasions may provide one declaration subsequent to all submissions that refers to all submissions.

Encourage use of fax

(1) To facilitate prompt action on letter ruling requests, taxpayers are encouraged to submit additional information by fax as soon as the information is available. The Service representative who requests additional information can provide a telephone number to which the information can be faxed. A copy of this information and a signed perjury statement, however, must be mailed or delivered to the Service.

Address to send additional information

(2) Additional information should be sent to the same address as the original letter ruling request. *See* section 9.04. However, the additional information should include the name, office symbols, and room number of the Service representative who requested the information and the taxpayer's name and the case control number (which the Service representative can provide).

Number of copies of additional information to be submitted

(3) Generally, a taxpayer needs only to submit one copy of the additional information. However, in appropriate cases, the Service may request additional copies of the information.

30-day or 21-day period may be extended if justified and approved

(4) An extension of the 30-day period under section 11.03 or the 21-day period under section 11.04, will be granted only if justified in writing by the taxpayer and approved by the manager of the group to which the case is assigned. A request for extension should be submitted before

the end of the 30-day or 21-day period. If unusual circumstances close to the end of the 30-day or 21-day period make a written request impractical, the taxpayer should notify the Service within the 30-day or 21-day period that there is a problem and that the written request for extension will be coming soon. The taxpayer will be told promptly, and later in writing, of the approval or denial of the requested extension. If the extension request is denied, there is no right of appeal.

If taxpayer does not submit additional information

(5) If the taxpayer does not follow the instructions for submitting additional information or requesting an extension within the time provided, a letter ruling will be issued on the basis of the information on hand, or, if appropriate, no letter ruling will be issued. When the Service decides not to issue a letter ruling because essential information is lacking, the case will be closed and the taxpayer notified in writing. If the Service receives the information after the letter ruling request is closed, the request may be reopened and treated as a new request. However, the taxpayer must pay another user fee before the case can be reopened.

Near the completion of the ruling process, advises taxpayer of conclusions and, if the Service will rule adversely, offers the taxpayer the opportunity to withdraw the letter ruling request

.05 Generally, after the conference of right is held before the letter ruling is issued, the Service representative will inform the taxpayer or the taxpayer's authorized representative of the Service's final conclusions. If the Service is going to rule adversely, the taxpayer will be offered the opportunity to withdraw the letter ruling request. If the taxpayer or the taxpayer's representative does not promptly notify the Service representative of a decision to withdraw the ruling request, the adverse letter will be issued. The user fee will not be refunded for a letter ruling request that is withdrawn. *See* section 10 of Rev. Proc. 2007–8.

May request draft of proposed letter ruling near the completion of the ruling process

.06 To accelerate issuance of letter rulings, in appropriate cases near the completion of the ruling process, the Service representative may request that the taxpayer or the taxpayer's representative submit a proposed draft of the letter ruling on the basis of discussions of the issues. The taxpayer, however, is not required to prepare a draft letter ruling in order to receive a letter ruling.

The format of the submission should be discussed with the Service representative who requests the draft letter ruling. The representative usually can provide a sample format of a letter ruling and will discuss the facts, analysis, and letter ruling language to be included.

Taxpayer may also submit draft on a word processing disk

In addition to a typed draft, taxpayers are encouraged to submit this draft on a disk in Rich Text Format. The typed draft will become part of the permanent files of the Service, and the word processing disk will not be returned. If the Service representative requesting the draft letter ruling cannot answer specific questions about the format of the word processing disk, the questions can be directed to Frances Sloan at (202) 283–9626 (Employee Plans), or Ted Lieber at (202) 283–8999 (Exempt Organizations) (not toll-free calls).

The proposed letter ruling (both typed draft and word processing disk) should be sent to the same address as any additional information and contain in the transmittal the information that should be included with any additional information (for example, a penalties of perjury statement is required). *See* section 11.04 of this revenue procedure.

SECTION 12. HOW ARE CONFERENCES SCHEDULED?

Schedules a conference if requested by taxpayer

.01 A taxpayer may request a conference regarding a letter ruling request. Normally, a conference is scheduled only when the Service considers it to be helpful in deciding the case or when an adverse decision is indicated. If conferences are being arranged for more than one request for a letter ruling involving the same taxpayer, they will be scheduled so as to cause the least inconvenience to the taxpayer. As stated in section 9.03(5) of this revenue procedure, a taxpayer who wants to have a conference on the issue or issues involved should indicate this in writing when, or soon after, filing the request.

If a conference has been requested, the taxpayer will be notified by telephone, if possible, of the time and place of the conference, which must then be held within 21 calendar days after this contact. Instructions for requesting an extension of the 21-day period and notifying the taxpayer or the taxpayer's representative of the Service's approval or denial of the request for extension are the same as those explained in section 11.04 of this revenue procedure regarding providing additional information.

Permits taxpayer one conference of right

.02 A taxpayer is entitled, as a matter of right, to only one conference, except as explained under section 12.05 of this revenue procedure. This conference normally will be held at the group level and will be attended by a person who, at the time of the conference, has the authority to sign the ruling letter in his or her own name or for the group manager.

When more than one group has taken an adverse position on an issue in a letter ruling request, or when the position ultimately adopted by one group will affect that adopted by another, a representative from each group with the authority to sign in his or her own name or for the group manager will attend the conference. If more than one subject is to be discussed at the conference, the discussion will constitute a conference on each subject.

To have a thorough and informed discussion of the issues, the conference usually will be held after the group has had an opportunity to study the case. However, at the request of the taxpayer, the conference of right may be held earlier.

No taxpayer has a right to appeal the action of a group to any other official of the Service. But see section 12.05 of this revenue procedure for situations in which the Service may offer additional conferences.

Disallows verbatim recording of conferences

.03 Because conference procedures are informal, no tape, stenographic, or other verbatim recording of a conference may be made by any party.

Makes tentative recommendations on substantive issues

.04 The senior Service representative present at the conference ensures that the taxpayer has the opportunity to present views on all the issues in question. A Service representative explains the Service's tentative decision on the substantive issues and the reasons for that decision. If the taxpayer asks the Service to limit the retroactive effect of any letter ruling or limit the revocation or modification of a prior letter ruling, a Service representative will discuss the recommendation concerning this issue and the reasons for the recommendation. The Service representatives will not make a commitment regarding the conclusion that the Service will finally adopt.

May offer additional conferences

.05 The Service will offer the taxpayer an additional conference if, after the conference of right, an adverse holding is proposed, but on a new issue, or on the same issue but on different grounds from those discussed at the first conference. There is no right to another conference when a proposed holding is reversed at a higher level with a result less favorable to the taxpayer, if the grounds or arguments on which the reversal is based were discussed at the conference of right.

The limit on the number of conferences to which a taxpayer is entitled does not prevent the Service from offering additional conferences, including conferences with an official higher than the group level, if the Service decides they are needed. Such conferences are not offered as a matter of course simply because the group has reached an adverse decision. In general, conferences with higher level officials are offered only if the Service determines that the case presents significant issues of tax policy or tax administration and that the consideration of these issues would be enhanced by additional conferences with the taxpayer.

Requires written confirmation of information presented at conference

.06 The taxpayer should furnish to the Service any additional data, reasoning, precedents, etc., that were proposed by the taxpayer and discussed at the conference but not previously or adequately presented in writing. The taxpayer must furnish the additional information within 21 calendar days from the date of the conference. *See* section 11.04 of this revenue procedure for instructions on submission of additional information. If the additional information is not received within that time, a ruling will be issued on the basis of the information on hand or, if appropriate, no ruling will be issued.

Procedures for requesting an extension of the 21-day period and notifying the taxpayer or the taxpayer's representative of the Service's approval or denial of the requested extension are the same as those stated in section 11.04 of this revenue procedure regarding submitting additional information.

May schedule a pre-submission conference

.07 Sometimes it will be advantageous to both the Service and the taxpayer to hold a conference before the taxpayer submits the letter ruling request to discuss substantive or procedural issues relating to a proposed transaction. These conferences are held only if the identity of the taxpayer is provided to the Service, only if the taxpayer actually intends to make a request, only if the request involves a matter on which a letter ruling is ordinarily issued, and only at the discretion of the Service and as time permits. For example, a pre-submission conference will not be held on an income tax issue if, at the time the pre-submission conference is requested, the identical issue is involved in the taxpayer's return for an earlier period and that issue is being examined. *See* section 6 of this revenue procedure. Generally, the taxpayer will be asked to provide before the pre-submission conference a statement of whether the issue is an issue on which a letter ruling is ordinarily issued and a draft of the letter ruling request or other detailed written statement of the proposed transaction, issue, and legal analysis. If the taxpayer's representative will attend the pre-submission conference, a power of attorney form is required. A Form 2848, *Power of Attorney and Declaration of Representative*, must be used to provide the representative's authorization.

Any discussion of substantive issues at a pre-submission conference is advisory only, is not binding on the Service, and cannot be relied upon as a basis for obtaining retroactive relief under the provisions of § 7805(b). A letter ruling request submitted following a pre-submission conference will not necessarily be assigned to the group that held the pre-submission conference.

Under limited circumstances, may schedule a conference to be held by telephone

.08 A taxpayer may request that their conference of right be held by telephone. This request may occur, for example, when a taxpayer wants a conference of right but believes that the issue involved does not warrant incurring the expense of traveling to Washington, DC. If a taxpayer makes such a request, the group manager will decide if it is appropriate in the particular case to hold the conference of right by telephone. If the request is approved by the group manager, the taxpayer will be advised when to call the Service representatives (not a toll-free call).

SECTION 13. WHAT EFFECT WILL A LETTER RULING HAVE?

May be relied on subject to limitations

.01 A taxpayer ordinarily may rely on a letter ruling received from the Service subject to the conditions and limitations described in this section.

Will not apply to another taxpayer

.02 A taxpayer may not rely on a letter ruling issued to another taxpayer. *See* § 6110(k)(3).

Will be used by the Director, EP or EO Examinations in examining the taxpayer's return

.03 When determining a taxpayer's liability, the Director, EP or EO Examinations must ascertain whether—

(1) the conclusions stated in the letter ruling are properly reflected in the return;

(2) the representations upon which the letter ruling was based reflected an accurate statement of the material facts;

(3) the transaction was carried out substantially as proposed; and

(4) there has been any change in the law that applies to the period during which the transaction or continuing series of transactions were consummated.

If, when determining the liability, the Director, EP Examinations finds that a letter ruling should be revoked or modified, unless a waiver is obtained from EP Technical, the findings and recommendations of the Director, EP Examinations will be forwarded to EP Technical for consideration before further action is taken by the Director, EP Examinations. Such a referral to EP Technical will be treated as a request for technical advice and the procedures of Rev. Proc. 2007–5 will be followed. Otherwise, the letter ruling is to be applied by the Director, EP

Examinations in determining the taxpayer's liability. Appropriate coordination with EP Technical will be undertaken if any field official having jurisdiction over a return or other matter proposes to reach a conclusion contrary to a letter ruling previously issued to the taxpayer.

In certain exempt organizations cases, section 4.04 of Rev. Proc. 2007–5 provides that a request for a TAM is mandatory.

May be revoked or modified if found to be in error

.04 Unless it was part of a closing agreement as described in section 3.03 of this revenue procedure, a letter ruling found to be in error or not in accord with the current views of the Service may be revoked or modified. If a letter ruling is revoked or modified, the revocation or modification applies to all years open under the statute of limitations unless the Service uses its discretionary authority under § 7805(b) to limit the retroactive effect of the revocation or modification.

A letter ruling may be revoked or modified due to—

(1) a notice to the taxpayer to whom the letter ruling was issued;

(2) the enactment of legislation or ratification of a tax treaty;

(3) a decision of the United States Supreme Court;

(4) the issuance of temporary or final regulations; or

(5) the issuance of a revenue ruling, revenue procedure, notice, or other statement published in the Internal Revenue Bulletin.

Consistent with these provisions, if a letter ruling relates to a continuing action or a series of actions, it ordinarily will be applied until any one of the events described above occurs or until it is specifically withdrawn.

Publication of a notice of proposed rulemaking will not affect the application of any letter ruling issued under this revenue procedure.

Not generally revoked or modified retroactively

.05 Except in rare or unusual circumstances, the revocation or modification of a letter ruling will not be applied retroactively to the taxpayer for whom the letter ruling was issued or to a taxpayer whose tax liability was directly involved in the letter ruling provided that—

(1) there has been no misstatement or omission of material facts;

(2) the facts at the time of the transaction are not materially different from the facts on which the letter ruling was based;

(3) there has been no change in the applicable law;

(4) the letter ruling was originally issued for a proposed transaction; and

(5) the taxpayer directly involved in the letter ruling acted in good faith in relying on the letter ruling, and revoking or modifying the letter ruling retroactively would be to the taxpayer's detriment. For example, the tax liability of each employee covered by a ruling relating to a qualified plan of an employer is directly involved in such ruling. However, the tax liability of a member of an industry is not directly involved in a letter ruling issued to another member and, therefore, the holding in a revocation or modification of a letter ruling to one member of an industry may be retroactively applied to other members of the industry. By the same reasoning, a tax practitioner may not extend to one client the non-retroactive application of a revocation or modification of a letter ruling previously issued to another client.

If a letter ruling is revoked or modified by letter with retroactive effect, the letter will, except in fraud cases, state the grounds on which the letter ruling is being revoked or modified and explain the reasons why it is being revoked or modified retroactively.

Retroactive effect of revocation or modification applied only to a particular transaction

.06 A letter ruling issued on a particular transaction represents a holding of the Service on that transaction only. It will not apply to a similar transaction in the same year or any other year. And, except in unusual circumstances, the application of that letter ruling to the transaction will not be affected by the later issuance of regulations (either temporary or final), if conditions (1) through (5) in section 13.05 of this revenue procedure are met.

However, if a letter ruling on a transaction is later found to be in error or no longer in accord with the position of the Service, it will not protect a similar transaction of the taxpayer in the same year or later year.

Retroactive effect of revocation or modification applied to a continuing action or series of actions

.07 If a letter ruling is issued covering a continuing action or series of actions and the letter ruling is later found to be in error or no longer in accord with the position of the Service, the Commissioner, Tax Exempt and Government Entities Division, ordinarily will limit the retroactive effect of the revocation or modification to a date that is not earlier than that on which the letter ruling is revoked or modified.

May be retroactively revoked or modified when transaction is completed without reliance on the letter ruling

.08 A taxpayer is not protected against retroactive revocation or modification of a letter ruling involving a completed transaction other than those described in section 13.07 of this revenue procedure, because the taxpayer did not enter into the transaction relying on a letter ruling.

Taxpayer may request that retroactivity be limited

.09 Under § 7805(b), the Service may prescribe any extent to which a revocation or modification of a letter ruling or determination letter will be applied without retroactive effect.

A taxpayer to whom a letter ruling or determination letter has been issued may request that the Commissioner, Tax Exempt and Government Entities Division, limit the retroactive effect of any revocation or modification of the letter ruling or determination letter.

Format of request

(1) Request for relief under § 7805(b) must be made in required format.

A request to limit the retroactive effect of the revocation or modification of a letter ruling must be in the general form of, and meet the general requirements for, a letter ruling request. These requirements are given in section 9 of this revenue procedure. Specifically, the request must also—

(a) state that it is being made under § 7805(b);

(b) state the relief sought;

(c) explain the reasons and arguments in support of the relief requested (including a discussion of the five items listed in section 13.05 of this revenue procedure and any other factors as they relate to the taxpayer's particular situation); and

(d) include any documents bearing on the request. A request that the Service limit the retroactive effect of a revocation or modification of a letter ruling may be made in the form of a separate request for a letter ruling when, for example, a revenue ruling has the effect of revoking or modifying a letter ruling previously issued to the taxpayer, or when the Service notifies the taxpayer of a change in position that will have the effect of revoking or modifying the letter ruling. However, when notice is given by the Director, EP or EO Examinations during an examination of the taxpayer's return or by the Appeals Area Director, Area 4, or the Appeals Area Director, LMSB, during consideration of the taxpayer's return before an appeals office, a request to limit retroactive effect must be made in the form of a request for technical advice as explained in section 19 of Rev. Proc. 2007–5.

When germane to a pending letter ruling request, a request to limit the retroactive effect of a revocation or modification of a letter ruling may be made as part of the request for the letter ruling, either initially or at any time before the letter ruling is issued. When a letter ruling that concerns a continuing transaction is revoked or modified by, for example, a subsequent revenue ruling, a request to limit retroactive effect must be made before the examination of the return that contains the transaction that is the subject of the letter ruling request.

Consideration of relief under § 7805(b) will be included as one of the taxpayer's steps in exhausting administrative remedies only if the taxpayer has requested such relief in the manner described in this revenue procedure. If the taxpayer does not complete the applicable steps, the taxpayer will not have exhausted the taxpayer's administrative remedies as required by § 7428(b)(2) and § 7476(b)(3) and will, thus, be precluded from seeking a declaratory judgment under § 7428 or § 7476. Where the taxpayer has requested § 7805(b) relief, the taxpayer's administrative remedies will not be considered exhausted until the Service has had a reasonable time to act upon the request.

Request for conference

(2) Taxpayer may request a conference on application of § 7805(b).

A taxpayer who requests the application of § 7805(b) in a separate letter ruling request has the right to a conference in EP or EO Technical as explained in sections 12.01, 12.02, 12.03, 12.04 and 12.05 of this revenue procedure. If the request is made initially as part of a pending letter ruling request or is made before the conference of right is held on the substantive issues, the § 7805(b) issue will be discussed at the taxpayer's one conference of right as explained in section 12.02 of this revenue procedure. If the request for the application of § 7805(b) relief is made as part of a pending letter ruling request after a conference has been held on the substantive issue and the Service determines that there is justification for having delayed the request, the taxpayer is entitled to one conference of right concerning the application of § 7805(b), with the conference limited to discussion of this issue only.

SECTION 14. WHAT EFFECT WILL A DETERMINATION LETTER HAVE?

Has same effect as a letter ruling

.01 A determination letter issued by EP or EO Determinations has the same effect as a letter ruling issued to a taxpayer under section 13 of this revenue procedure.

If the Director, EP or EO Examinations proposes to reach a conclusion contrary to that expressed in a determination letter, he or she need not refer the matter to EP or EO Technical. However, the Director, EP or EO Examinations must refer the matter to EP or EO Technical if the Director, EP or EO Examinations desires to have the revocation or modification of the determination letter limited under § 7805(b).

Taxpayer may request that retroactive effect of revocation or modification be limited

.02 The Director, EP or EO Examinations does not have authority under § 7805(b) to limit the revocation or modification of the determination letter. Therefore, if the Director, EP or EO Examinations proposes to revoke or modify a determination letter, the taxpayer may request limitation of the retroactive effect of the revocation or modification by asking EP or EO Determinations to seek technical advice from EP or EO Technical. *See* section 19 of Rev. Proc. 2007–5.

Format of request

(1) Request for relief under § 7805(b) must be made in required format.

A taxpayer's request to limit the retroactive effect of the revocation or modification of the determination letter must be in the form of, and meet the general requirements for, a technical advice request. *See* section 18.06 of Rev. Proc. 2007–5. The request must also—

(a) state that it is being made under § 7805(b);

(b) state the relief sought;

(c) explain the reasons and arguments in support of the relief sought (including a discussion of the five items listed in section 13.05 of this revenue procedure and any other factors as they relate to the taxpayer's particular situation); and

(d) include any documents bearing on the request.

Request for conference

(2) Taxpayer may request a conference on application of § 7805(b).

When technical advice is requested regarding the application of § 7805(b), the taxpayer has the right to a conference in EP or EO Technical to the same extent as does any taxpayer who is the subject of a technical advice request. *See* section 11 of Rev. Proc. 2007–5.

Exhaustion of administrative remedies

(3) Taxpayer steps in exhausting administrative remedies.

Consideration of relief under § 7805(b) will be included as one of the taxpayer's steps in exhausting administrative remedies only if the taxpayer has requested such relief in the manner described in this revenue procedure. If the taxpayer does not complete the applicable steps, the taxpayer will not have exhausted the taxpayer's administrative remedies as required by § 7428(b)(2) and § 7476(b)(3) and will, thus, be precluded from seeking a declaratory judgment under § 7428 or § 7476. Where the taxpayer has requested § 7805(b) relief, the taxpayer's administrative remedies will not be considered exhausted until the Service has had a reasonable time to act upon the request.

SECTION 15. UNDER WHAT CIRCUMSTANCES ARE MATTERS REFERRED BETWEEN DETERMINATIONS AND TECHNICAL?

Requests for determination letters

.01 Requests for determination letters received by EP or EO Determinations that, under the provisions of this revenue procedure, may not be issued by EP or EO Determinations, will be forwarded to EP or EO Technical for reply. EP or EO Determinations will notify the taxpayer that the matter has been referred.

EP or EO Determinations will also refer to EP or EO Technical any request for a determination letter that in its judgment should have the attention of EP or EO Technical.

No-rule areas

.02 If the request involves an issue on which the Service will not issue a letter ruling or determination letter, the request will not be forwarded to EP or EO Technical. EP or EO Determinations will notify the taxpayer that the Service will not issue a letter ruling or a determination letter on the issue. See section 8 of this revenue procedure for a description of no-rule areas.

Requests for letter rulings

.03 Requests for letter rulings received by EP or EO Technical that, under section 6 of this revenue procedure, may not be acted upon by EP or EO Technical will be forwarded to the Director, EP or EO Examinations. The taxpayer will be notified of this action. If the request is on an issue or in an area of the type discussed in section 8 of this revenue procedure, and the Service decides not to issue a letter ruling or an information letter, EP or EO Technical will notify the taxpayer and will then forward the request to the Director, EP or EO Examinations for association with the related return.

SECTION 16. WHAT ARE THE GENERAL PROCEDURES APPLICABLE TO INFORMATION LETTERS ISSUED BY THE HEADQUARTERS OFFICE?

Will be made available to the public

.01 Information letters that are issued by the headquarters office to members of the public will be made available to the public. These documents provide general statements of well-defined law without applying them to a specific set of facts. See section 3.06 of this revenue procedure. Information letters that are issued by the field, however, will not be made available to the public.

The following documents also will not be available for public inspection as part of this process:

(1) letters that merely transmit Service publications or other publicly available material, without significant legal discussion;

(2) responses to taxpayer or third party contacts that are inquiries with respect to a pending request for a letter ruling, technical advice memorandum, or Chief Counsel Advice (whose public inspection is subject to § 6110); and

(3) responses to taxpayer or third party communications with respect to any investigation, audit, litigation, or other enforcement action.

Deletions made under the Freedom of Information Act

.02 Before any information letter is made available to the public, the headquarters office will delete any name, address, and other identifying information as appropriate under the Freedom of Information Act ("FOIA") (for example, FOIA personal privacy exemption of 5 U.S.C. § 552(b)(6) and tax details exempt pursuant to § 6103, as incorporated into FOIA by 5 U.S.C. § 552(b)(3). Because information letters do not constitute written determinations (including Chief Counsel Advice) as defined in § 6110, these documents are not subject to public inspection under § 6110.

Effect of information letters

.03 Information letters are advisory only and have no binding effect on the Service. See section 3.06 of this revenue procedure. If the headquarters office issues an information letter in response to a request for a letter ruling that does not meet the requirements of this revenue procedure, the information letter is not a substitute for a letter ruling.

SECTION 17. WHAT IS THE EFFECT OF THIS REVENUE PROCEDURE ON OTHER DOCUMENTS?

Rev. Proc. 2006–4 is superseded.

SECTION 18. EFFECTIVE DATE

This revenue procedure is effective January 2, 2007.

SECTION 19. PAPERWORK REDUCTION ACT

The collections of information contained in this revenue procedure have been reviewed and approved by the Office of Management and Budget in accordance with the Paperwork Reduction Act (44 U.S.C. § 3507) under control number 1545–1520.

An agency may not conduct or sponsor, and a person is not required to respond to, a collection of information unless the collection of information displays a valid OMB control number.

The collections of information in this revenue procedure are in sections 7.07, 9.02, 9.03, 9.04, 9.05, 9.06, 10.02, 10.03, 11.03, 11.04(1)–(5), 11.06, 12.01, 12.06, 12.07, 13.09(1), 14.02(1), and in Appendices B, C, D and E. This information is required to evaluate and process the request for a letter ruling or determination letter. In addition, this information will be used to help the Service delete certain information from the text of the letter ruling or determination letter before it is made available for public inspection, as required by § 6110. The collections of information are required to obtain a letter ruling or determination letter. The likely respondents are businesses or other for-profit institutions.

The estimated total annual reporting and/or recordkeeping burden is 12,650 hours.

The estimated annual burden per respondent/recordkeeper varies from 15 minutes to 16 hours, depending on individual circumstances and the type of request involved, with an estimated average burden of 6.01 hours. The estimated number of respondents and/or recordkeepers is 2,103.

The estimated annual frequency of responses is one request per applicant, except that a taxpayer requesting a letter ruling may also request a presubmission conference.

Books or records relating to a collection of information must be retained as long as their contents may become material in the administration of any internal revenue law. Generally, tax returns and tax return information are confidential, as required by § 6103.

DRAFTING INFORMATION

The principal author of this revenue procedure is Ingrid Grinde of the Employee Plans, Tax Exempt and Government Entities Division. For further information regarding how this revenue procedure applies to employee plans matters, contact the Employee Plans Customer Assistance Service at 877–829–5500 (a toll-free call). Ms. Grinde's telephone number is (202) 283–9888 (not a toll-free call). For exempt organization matters, please contact Mr. Ted Lieber at (202) 283–8999 or Mr. Wayne Hardesty (202) 283–8976 (not toll-free calls).

INDEX

APPENDIX A

SAMPLE FORMAT FOR A LETTER RULING REQUEST

(Insert the date of request)

Internal Revenue Service
Commissioner, TE/GE
Attention: SE:T:EP:RA
P.O. Box 27063
McPherson Station
Washington, DC 20038

Dear Sir or Madam:

(Insert the name of the taxpayer) (the "Taxpayer") requests a ruling on the proper treatment of *(insert the subject matter of the letter ruling request)* under § *(insert the number)* of the Internal Revenue Code.

[*If the taxpayer is requesting expedited handling, the letter ruling request must contain a statement to that effect. This statement must explain the need for expeditious handling. See section 9.03(3).*]

A. STATEMENT OF FACTS

1. Taxpayer Information

[Provide the statements required by sections 9.02(1)(a), (b), and (c) of Rev. Proc. 2007–4, 2007–1 I.R.B. 118. (Hereafter, all references are to Rev. Proc. 2007–4 unless otherwise noted.)]

For example, a taxpayer that maintains a qualified employee retirement plan and files an annual Form 5500 series of returns may include the following statement to satisfy sections 9.02(1)(a), (b), and (c):

The Taxpayer is a construction company with principal offices located at 100 Whatever Drive, Wherever, Maryland 12345, and its telephone number is (123) 456–7890. The Taxpayer's federal employer identification number is 00–1234567. The Taxpayer uses the Form 5500 series of returns on a calendar year basis to report its qualified employee retirement plan and trust.

2. Detailed Description of the Transaction.

[The ruling request must contain a complete statement of the facts relating to the transaction that is the subject of the letter ruling request. This statement must include a detailed description of the transaction, including material facts in any accompanying documents, and the business reasons for the transaction. See sections 9.02(1)(b), 9.02(1)(c), and 9.02(2).]

B. RULING REQUESTED

[The ruling request should contain a concise statement of the ruling requested by the taxpayer.]

C. STATEMENT OF LAW

[The ruling request must contain a statement of the law in support of the taxpayer's views or conclusion, including any authorities believed to be contrary to the position advanced in the ruling request. This statement must also identify any pending legislation that may affect the proposed transaction. See sections 9.02(6), 9.02(7), and 9.02(8).]

D. ANALYSIS

[The ruling request must contain a discussion of the facts and an analysis of the law. See sections 9.02(3), 9.02(6), 9.02(7), and 9.02(8).]

E. CONCLUSION

[The ruling request should contain a statement of the taxpayer's conclusion on the ruling requested.]

F. PROCEDURAL MATTERS

1. Rev. Proc. 2007–4 statements

a. [The statement required by section 9.02(4).]

b. [The statement required by section 9.02(5).]

c. [The statement required by section 9.02(6) regarding whether the law in connection with the letter ruling request is uncertain and whether the issue is adequately addressed by relevant authorities.]

d. [The statement required by section 9.02(7) when the taxpayer determines that there are no contrary authorities.]

e. [If the taxpayer wants to have a conference on the issues involved in the letter ruling request, the ruling request should contain a statement to that effect. See section 9.03(5).]

f. [If the taxpayer is requesting the letter ruling to be issued by fax, the ruling request should contain a statement to that effect. This statement must also contain a waiver of any disclosure violations resulting from the fax transmission. See section 9.03(4).]

g. [If the taxpayer is requesting separate letter rulings on multiple issues, the letter ruling request should contain a statement to that effect. See section 9.03(1).]

2. Administrative

a. A Power of Attorney is enclosed. [See sections 9.02(12) and 9.03(2).]

b. The deletions statement and checklist required by Rev. Proc. 2007–4 are enclosed. [See sections 9.02(9) and 9.02(17).]

c. The required user fee is enclosed. [See section 9.02(14).]

Very truly yours,

(*Insert the name of the taxpayer or the taxpayer's authorized representative*)

By:

_______________ _____

Signature Date

Typed or printed name
of person signing request

DECLARATION: [See section 9.02(13).]

Under penalties of perjury, I declare that I have examined this request, including accompanying documents, and to the best of my knowledge and belief, the request contains all the relevant facts relating to the request and such facts are true, correct, and complete.

(*Insert the name of the taxpayer*)

By:

____

Signature Title Date

Typed or printed name of
person signing declaration

APPENDIX B

CHECKLIST
IS YOUR RULING REQUEST COMPLETE?

INSTRUCTIONS

The Service will be able to respond more quickly to your letter ruling request if it is carefully prepared and complete. To ensure that your request is in order, use this checklist. Complete the four items of information requested before the checklist. Answer each question by circling "Yes," "No," or "N/A." When a question contains a place for a page number, insert the page number (or numbers) of the request that gives the information called for by a yes answer to a question. **Sign and date the checklist (as taxpayer or authorized representative) and place it on top of your request.**

If you are an authorized representative submitting a request for a taxpayer, you must include a completed checklist with the request, or the request will either be returned to you or substantive consideration of it will be deferred until a completed checklist is submitted. **If you are a taxpayer preparing your own request without professional assistance, an incomplete checklist will not be cause for returning your request or deferring substantive consideration of the request.** However, you should still complete as much of the checklist as possible and submit it with your request.

TAXPAYER'S NAME ______________________________

TAXPAYER'S I.D. No. ______________________________

ATTORNEY/P.O.A. ______________________________

PRIMARY CODE SECTION ______________________________

CIRCLE ONE	ITEM
Yes No N/A	1. Does your request involve an issue under the jurisdiction of the Commissioner, Tax Exempt and Government Entities Division? See section 5 of Rev. Proc. 2007–4, 2007–1 I.R.B. 118, for issues under the jurisdiction of other offices. (Hereafter, all references are to Rev. Proc. 2007–4 unless otherwise noted.)
Yes No N/A	2. If your request involves a matter on which letter rulings are not ordinarily issued, have you given compelling reasons to justify the issuance of a private letter ruling? Before preparing your request, you may want to call the office responsible for substantive interpretations of the principal Internal Revenue Code section on which you are seeking a letter ruling to discuss the likelihood of an exception. The appropriate office to call for this information may be obtained by calling (202) 283–9660 (Employee Plans matters), or (202) 283–2300 (Exempt Organizations matters) (not toll-free calls).
Yes No N/A Page ____	3. If the request involves an employee plans qualification matter under § 401(a), § 409, or § 4975(e)(7), have you demonstrated that the request satisfies the three criteria in section 6.03 for a headquarters office ruling?
Yes No N/A Page ____	4. If the request deals with a completed transaction, have you filed the return for the year in which the transaction was completed? See sections 6.01 and 6.02.
Yes No	5. Are you requesting a letter ruling on a hypothetical situation or question? See section 8.03.
Yes No	6. Are you requesting a letter ruling on alternative plans of a proposed transaction? See section 8.03.
Yes No	7. Are you requesting the letter ruling for only part of an integrated transaction? See section 8.04.
Yes No	8. Have you submitted another letter ruling request for the transaction covered by this request?
Yes No	9. Are you requesting the letter ruling for a business, trade, industrial association, or similar group concerning the application of tax law to its members? See section 6.07.

Yes No Pages ____	10. Have you included a complete statement of all the facts relevant to the transaction? See section 9.02(1).
Yes No N/A	11. Have you submitted with the request true copies of all wills, deeds, plan documents, and other documents relevant to the transaction, and labeled and attached them in alphabetical sequence? See section 9.02(2).
Yes No Page ____	12. Have you included, rather than merely by reference, all material facts from the documents in the request? Are they accompanied by an analysis of their bearing on the issues that specifies the document provisions that apply? See section 9.02(3).
Yes No Page ____	13. Have you included the required statement regarding whether the same issue in the letter ruling request is in an earlier return of the taxpayer or in a return for any year of a related taxpayer? See section 9.02(4).
Yes No Page ____	14. Have you included the required statement regarding whether the Service previously ruled on the same or similar issue for the taxpayer, a related taxpayer, or a predecessor? See section 9.02(5).
Yes No Page ____	15. Have you included the required statement regarding whether the taxpayer, a related taxpayer, a predecessor, or any representatives previously submitted the same or similar issue but withdrew it before the letter ruling was issued? See section 9.02(5).
Yes No Page ____	16. Have you included the required statement regarding whether the law in connection with the request is uncertain and whether the issue is adequately addressed by relevant authorities? See section 9.02(6).
Yes No Pages ____	17. Have you included the required statement of relevant authorities in support of your views? See section 9.02(6).
Yes No N/A Pages ____	18. Does your request discuss the implications of any legislation, tax treaties, court decisions, regulations, notices, revenue rulings, or revenue procedures you determined to be contrary to the position advanced? See section 9.02(7), which states that taxpayers are encouraged to inform the Service of such authorities.
Yes No N/A Page ____	19. If you determined that there are no contrary authorities, have you included a statement to this effect in your request? See section 9.02(7).
Yes No N/A Page ____	20. Have you included in your request a statement identifying any pending legislation that may affect the proposed transaction? See section 9.02(8).
Yes No	21. Is the request accompanied by the deletions statement required by § 6110? See section 9.02(9).
Yes No N/A Page ____	22. Have you (or your authorized representative) signed and dated the request? See section 9.02(10).
Yes No N/A	23. If the request is signed by your representative, or if your representative will appear before the Service in connection with the request, is the request accompanied by a properly prepared and signed power of attorney with the signatory's name typed or printed? See section 9.02(12).
Yes No N/A Page ____	24. Have you included, signed and dated, the penalties of perjury statement in the form required by section 9.02(13)?
Yes No N/A	25. Have you included the correct user fee with the request and made your check or money order payable to the United States Treasury? See section 9.02(14) and Rev. Proc. 2007–8, page 230, this Bulletin, for the correct amount and additional information on user fees.
Yes No N/A	26. Are you submitting your request in duplicate if necessary? See section 9.02(15).
Yes No N/A Pages ____	27. If you are requesting separate letter rulings on different issues involving one factual situation, have you included a statement to that effect in each request? See section 9.03(1).
Yes No N/A	28. If you do not want a copy of the letter ruling to be sent to any representative, does the power of attorney contain a statement to that effect? See section 9.03(2).
Yes No N/A Page ____	29. If you have more than one representative, have you designated whether the second representative listed on the power of attorney is to receive a copy of the letter ruling? See section 9.03(2).

Yes No N/A Page ____	30. If you want your letter ruling request to be processed ahead of the regular order or by a specific date, have you requested expedited handling in the form required by section 9.03(3) and stated a compelling need for such action in the request?
Yes No N/A Page ____	31. If you are requesting that a copy of the letter ruling be issued by facsimile (fax) transmission, have you included a statement containing a waiver of any disclosure violations resulting from the fax transmission? See section 9.03(4).
Yes No N/A Page ____	32. If you want to have a conference on the issues involved in the request, have you included a request for conference in the ruling request? See section 9.03(5).
Yes No N/A	33. If your request is covered by any of the guideline revenue procedures or other special requirements listed in section 10 of Rev. Proc. 2007–4, have you complied with all of the requirements of the applicable revenue procedure?
Yes No N/A Page ____	34. If you are requesting relief under § 7805(b) (regarding retroactive effect), have you complied with all of the requirements in section 13.09?
Yes No N/A	35. Have you addressed your request to the appropriate office listed in section 9.04? Improperly addressed requests may be delayed (sometimes for over a week) in reaching the appropriate office for initial processing.

______________________	______________________	__________
Signature	Title or authority	Date

____

Typed or printed name of
person signing checklist

APPENDIX C

Additional Checklist for Roth IRA Recharacterization Ruling Requests

In order to assist EP Technical in processing a ruling request involving a Roth IRA recharacterization, in addition to the items in Appendix B, please check the following list.

Yes No N/A Page ____	1. Did you include the name(s) of trustee and/or custodian of the traditional individual retirement account (IRA) (generally, a financial institution)?
Yes No N/A Page ____	2. Is each IRA identification number present?
Yes No N/A Page ____	3. If the ruling request involves Roth conversions both of a husband and wife, is the necessary information with respect to each IRA of each party present? Note: as long as husband and wife file a joint federal Form 1040, the Service can issue one ruling covering both parties. Furthermore, if a joint federal income tax return has been filed for the year or years in question, the Service only requires one user fee even if both husband and wife had failed conversions.
Yes No N/A Page ____	4. If there was one or more attempted conversions, are the applicable dates on which the attempted IRA conversion(s) occurred included?
Yes No N/A Page ____	5. If the reason that a conversion failed is that the taxpayer or related taxpayers relied upon advice of a tax professional such as a CPA, an attorney, or an enrolled actuary, is the name and occupation of that adviser included?
Yes No N/A Page ____	6. Is certification that the taxpayer or taxpayers timely filed the relevant federal tax return(s) present?
Yes No N/A Page ____	7. Is there a short statement of facts with respect to the conversion? For example, if the ruling request involves a conversion attempted in 1998, there should be a statement of the facts that includes a representation of why the due date(s) found in Announcement 99–57 and Announcement 99–104 were not met.
Yes No N/A Page ____	8. If the taxpayer recharacterized his/her Roth IRA to a traditional IRA prior to submitting a request for § 9100 relief, are the date(s) of the recharacterization(s), name(s) of trustees and/or custodians, and the identification numbers of the traditional IRA(s) present?
Yes No N/A Page ____	9. Does the request include the type of contribution (*i.e.*, regular or conversion) and amount of the contribution being recharacterized?

APPENDIX D

Additional Checklist for Government Pick-Up Plan Ruling Requests

In order to assist EP Technical in processing a ruling request involving government pick-up plans, in addition to thc items in Appendix B please check the following list.

Yes No N/A Page ____	1. Is the plan qualified under § 401(a) of the Code? (Evidence of qualification or representation that the plan is qualified.)
Yes No N/A Page ____	2. Is the organization that established the plan a State or political subdivision thereof, or any agency or instrumentality of the foregoing? An example of this would be a representation that the organization that has established the plan is a political subdivision or municipality of the State.
Yes No N/A Page ____	3. Is there specific information regarding who are the eligible participants?
Yes No N/A Page ____	4. Are the contributions that are the subject of the ruling request mandatory employee contributions? These contributions must be for a specified dollar amount or a specific percentage of the participant's compensation and the dollar amount or percentage of compensation cannot be subject to change.
Yes No N/A Page ____	5. Does the plan provide that the participants do not have the election to opt in and/or out of the plan?
Yes No N/A Page ____	6. Are copies of the enacting legislation providing that the contributions although designated as employee contributions are being paid by the employer in lieu of contributions by the employee included?
Yes No N/A Page ____	7. Are copies of the specific enabling authorization that provides the employee must not have the option of choosing to receive the contributed amounts directly instead of having them paid by the employer to the plan included? For example, a resolution, ordinance, plan provision, or collective bargaining agreement could specify this information.

APPENDIX E

Additional Checklist for Church Plan Ruling Requests

In order to assist EP Technical in processing a church plan ruling request, in addition to the items in Appendix B, please check the following list.

Yes No N/A Page ____	1. Is there specific information showing that the submission is on behalf of a plan established by a named church or convention or association of churches? The information must show how the sponsoring organization is controlled by, or associated with, the named church or convention or association of churches. For example, the sponsoring organization might be listed in the church's official directory of related organizations whose mission is to further the objectives of the church. In order to be considered associated with a church or convention or association of churches, the organization must share common religious bonds and convictions with that church or convention or association of churches.
Yes No N/A Page ____	2. Is there specific information showing that the organization that has established the plan is a tax-exempt organization as described in § 501 of the Code?
Yes No N/A Page ____	3. Is there representation that the plan for which the ruling is being requested is qualified under § 401(a) of the Code or meets the requirements of § 403(b) of the Code?
Yes No N/A Page ____	4. Does the ruling clearly state who are the eligible participants and the name of the employer of these eligible participants?
Yes No N/A Page ____	5. Is there a representation that none of the eligible participants are or can be considered employed in connection with one or more unrelated trades or businesses within the meaning of § 513 of the Code?
Yes No N/A Page ____	6. Is there a representation that all of the eligible participants are or will be employed by the named church or convention or association of churches, and will not include employees of for-profit entities? An example of an eligible employee includes a duly ordained, commissioned, or licensed minister of a church in the exercise of his or her ministry.
Yes No N/A Page ____	7. Is there specific information showing an existing plan committee whose principal purpose or function is the administration or funding of the plan. This committee must be controlled by or associated with the named church or convention or association of churches?
Yes No N/A Page ____	8. Is the composition of the committee stated?

Rev. Proc. 2007–5

TABLE OF CONTENTS

SECTION 1. WHAT IS THE PURPOSE OF THIS REVENUE PROCEDURE?

.01 This revenue procedure explains when and how Employee Plans Technical or Exempt Organizations Technical issue technical advice memoranda (TAMs) to an Employee Plans (EP) Examinations Area manager, an Exempt Organizations (EO) Examinations Area manager, an Employee Plans (EP) Determinations manager, an Exempt Organizations (EO) Determinations manager, or an Appeals Area Director, Area 4, in the employee plans areas (including actuarial matters) and exempt organizations areas. It also explains the rights a taxpayer has when an EP or EO Examinations Area manager, an EP or EO Determinations manager, or the Appeals Area Director, Area 4, requests a TAM regarding a tax matter. Similarly, this revenue procedure may be used by another Operating Division of the Service involved in an examination where EP Technical does not have audit jurisdiction but has interpretive jurisdiction as enumerated in section 6.02 of Rev. Proc. 2007–4, page 118 of this Bulletin.

.02 Although taxpayer participation during all stages of the process is preferred, it is not required in order to request technical advice.

SECTION 2. WHAT SIGNIFICANT CHANGES HAVE BEEN MADE TO REV. PROC. 2006–5?

.01 This revenue procedure is a general update of Rev. Proc. 2006–5, 2006–1 I.R.B. 174, which contains the general procedures for technical advice requests for matters within the jurisdiction of the Commissioner, Tax Exempt and Government Entities Division.

.02 Section 4.04 pertaining to mandatory technical advice is modified to reflect the enactment of the Pension Protection Act of 2006 on August 17, 2006, and a related change is made by the deletion of section 4.05.

.03 The routing procedures for incoming TAM requests by Appeals described in section 10.05 are altered.

.04 In numerous places throughout this revenue procedure, the references to technical expedited advice memorandums (TEAMs) have been deleted.

SECTION 3. WHAT IS THE DEFINITION OF TECHNICAL ADVICE?

"Technical advice" means advice or guidance in the form of a memorandum furnished by the Employee Plans Technical or Exempt Organizations Technical office, (hereinafter referred to as "EP or EO Technical"), upon the request of an EP or EO Examinations Area manager, an EP or EO Determinations manager or the Appeals Area Director, Area 4, submitted in accordance with the provisions of this revenue procedure in response to any technical or procedural question that develops during any proceeding on the interpretation and proper application of tax law, tax treaties, regulations, revenue rulings, notices or other precedents published by the headquarters office to a specific set of facts. (The references in this revenue procedure to the Appeals Area Director, Area 4, or an appeals office include, when appropriate, an Appeals Area Director, LMSB, a Deputy Appeals Area Director, LMSB, a Deputy Appeals Area Director, Area 4, an Appeals Team Manager and include in employee plans matters another Operating Division of the Service described in the last sentence of section 1.01 above.) Such proceedings include (1) the examination of a taxpayer's return, (2) consideration of a taxpayer's claim for refund or credit, (3) a taxpayer's request for a determination letter, (4) any other matter involving a specific taxpayer under the jurisdiction of EP or EO Examinations, EP or EO Determinations, or an appeals office or (5) processing and considering nondocketed cases of a taxpayer in an appeals office. However, they do not include cases in which the issue in the case is in a docketed case for any year.

For purposes of TAMs, the term "taxpayer" includes all persons subject to any provision of the Internal Revenue Code (including tax-exempt entities such as governmental units which issue municipal bonds within the meaning of § 103), and when appropriate, their representatives. However, the instructions and the provisions of this revenue procedure do not apply to requests for TAMs involving any matter pertaining to tax-exempt bonds or to § 457 plans maintained by state or local governments or tax-exempt organizations or to mortgage credit certificates. Instead, in those instances the procedures under Rev. Proc. 2007–2, page 88, this Bulletin, must be followed.

TAMs help Service personnel resolve complex issues and help establish and maintain consistent holdings throughout the Internal Revenue Service. An EP or EO Examinations, an EP or EO Determinations or an appeals office may raise an issue in any tax period, even though technical advice may have been requested and furnished for the same or similar issue for another tax period.

Technical advice does not include oral or written legal advice furnished to the EP or EO Examinations or the EP or EO Determinations or the appeals office, other than advice furnished pursuant to this revenue procedure. In accordance with section 12.01 of this revenue procedure, a taxpayer's request for referral of an issue to the headquarters office for technical advice will not be denied merely because EP or EO Technical has already provided legal advice, other than advice furnished pursuant to this revenue procedure, to the EP or EO Examinations or the EP or EO Determinations or the appeals office on the matter.

Although taxpayer participation during all stages of the process is preferred, generally, it is not required in order to request a TAM.

SECTION 4. ON WHAT ISSUES MAY OR MUST TAMs BE REQUESTED UNDER THIS PROCEDURE?

Issues under the jurisdiction of the Commissioner, Tax Exempt and Government Entities Division

.01 Generally, the instructions of this revenue procedure apply to requests for TAMs on any issue under the jurisdiction of the Commissioner, Tax Exempt and Government Entities Division.

Farmers' cooperatives

.02 If an EP or EO Examinations, an EP or EO Determinations, an appeals office or a taxpayer requests technical advice on a determination letter under § 521 of the Code, the procedures under this revenue procedure, Rev. Proc. 90–27, 1990–1 C.B. 514, as well as § 601.201(n) of the Statement of Procedural Rules (26 CFR § 601.201(n) (2006)), must be followed.

Basis for requesting TAMs

.03 Requests for TAMs are encouraged on any technical or procedural questions arising in connection with any case of the type described in section 3 at any stage of the proceedings in an EP or EO Examinations, an EP or EO Determinations or an appeals office case that cannot be resolved on the basis of law, regulations, or a clearly applicable revenue ruling or other published precedent.

Areas of mandatory technical advice

.04 Requests for § 7805(b) relief are mandatory TAMs with respect to all exempt organizations and employee plans matters.

Regarding exempt organizations matters, EO Examinations, EO Determinations and appeals offices are required to request a TAM on their exempt organization cases concerning qualification for exemption or foundation status for which there is no published precedent or for which there is reason to believe that non-uniformity exists. (Exemption application cases handled in EO Technical in accordance with Rev. Procs. 72–5, 80–27, or 90–27 are not covered by this provision.) A request for a TAM is not required if the Director, EO Examinations proposes to revoke or modify (1) a letter ruling found to be in error or not in accord with the current views of the Service, or (2) a letter recognizing tax-exempt status issued by the headquarters office.

Regarding employee plans matters, a request for a TAM is required in cases concerning (1) proposed adverse or proposed revocation letters on collectively-bargained plans, (2) plans for which the Service is proposing to issue a revocation letter because of certain fiduciary actions that violate the exclusive benefit rule of § 401(a) of the Code and are subject to Part 4 of Subtitle B of Title I of the Employee Retirement Income Security Act of 1974, Pub. L. No. 93–406, 1974–3 C.B. 1, 43, or (3) amendments to defined contribution plans pursuant to Rev. Proc. 2004–15, 2004–1 C.B. 490, in connection with a waiver of the minimum funding standard and a request for a determination letter (see section 15 of Rev. Proc. 2007–6, page 189, this Bulletin, and section 3.04 of Rev. Proc. 2004–15).

SECTION 5. ON WHAT ISSUES MUST TAMS BE REQUESTED UNDER DIFFERENT PROCEDURES?

Matters (other than farmers' cooperatives) under the jurisdiction of the Associate Chief Counsel (Corporate), the Associate Chief Counsel (Financial Institutions & Products),the Associate Chief Counsel (Income Tax & Accounting), the Associate Chief Counsel (International) the Associate Chief Counsel (Passthroughs & Special Industries), the Division Counsel/Associate Chief Counsel (TE/GE), and the Associate Chief Counsel (Procedure & Administration)

.01 All procedures for obtaining TAMs on issues (other than farmers' cooperatives) under the interpretive jurisdiction of the Associate Chief Counsel (Corporate), the Associate Chief Counsel (Financial Institutions & Products), the Associate Chief Counsel (Income Tax & Accounting), the Associate Chief Counsel (International), the Associate Chief Counsel (Passthroughs & Special Industries), or the Division Counsel/Associate Chief Counsel (TE/GE), and on certain issues under the jurisdiction of the Associate Chief Counsel (Procedure & Administration), including any matter pertaining to (1) tax-exempt bonds or mortgage credit certificates, (2) deferred compensation plans under § 457, (3) § 526 of the Code (shipowners' protection and indemnity associations), (4) § 528 (certain homeowners' associations), (5) Indian tribal governments, (6) federal, state or local governments, and (7) issues involving the interpretation or application of the federal income tax laws and income tax treaties relating to international transactions are contained in Rev. Proc. 2007–2.

Alcohol, tobacco, and firearms taxes

.02 The procedures for obtaining a TAM specifically applicable to federal alcohol, tobacco, and firearms taxes under subtitle E of the Code are currently under the jurisdiction of the Alcohol and Tobacco Tax and Trade Bureau within the Treasury Department.

Excise taxes

.03 A TAM regarding excise taxes (other than excise taxes imposed under Chapters 41, 42 and 43 of the Code), and employment taxes that employee plans and exempt organizations are subject to, is set forth in Rev. Proc. 2007–2.

SECTION 6. MAY TAM UNDER § 301.9100–1 BE REQUESTED DURING THE COURSE OF AN EXAMINATION?

A § 301.9100–1 request is a letter ruling request

.01 Except with regard to exemption application matters involving §§ 505(c) and 508, a request for an extension of time for making an election or other application for relief under § 301.9100–1 of the Procedure and Administration Regulations is not a request for a TAM; instead, the request is submitted as a letter ruling request even if the request is submitted after the examination of the taxpayer's return has begun or after the issues in the return are being considered by an appeals office or a federal court. Therefore, a § 301.9100–1 request should be submitted pursuant to Rev. Proc. 2007–4, page 118, this Bulletin (including the payment of the applicable user fee listed in section 6 of Rev. Proc. 2007–8).

Statute of limitations

.02 The running of any applicable period of limitations is not suspended for the period during which a § 301.9100–1 request has been filed. *See* § 301.9100–3(d)(2). If the period of limitations on an assessment under § 6501(a) for the taxable year in which an election should have been made, or any taxable year that would have been affected by the election had it been timely made, will expire before receipt of a § 301.9100–1 letter ruling, the Service ordinarily will not issue a § 301.9100–1 ruling. *See* § 301.9100–3(c)(1)(ii). Therefore, the taxpayer must secure a consent under § 6501(c)(4) to extend the period of limitations on assessment. Note that the filing of a protective claim for refund under § 6511 does not extend the period of limitations on assessment. If § 301.9100–1 relief is granted, the Service may require the taxpayer to consent to an extension of the period of limitations for assessment. *See* § 301.9100–3(d)(2).

Address to send a § 301.9100–1 request

.03 Requests made under § 301.9100–1, pursuant to Rev. Proc. 2007–4, together with the appropriate user fee, must be submitted to the Internal Revenue Service by the taxpayer and addressed as follows:

Requests involving employee plans matters:

Internal Revenue Service
Commissioner, Tax Exempt and Government Entities
Attn: SE:T:EP:RA
P. O. Box 27063
McPherson Station
Washington, DC 20038

Requests involving exempt organization matters:

Internal Revenue Service
Commissioner, Tax Exempt and Government Entities
Attn: SE:T:EO:RA
P. O. Box 27720
McPherson Station
Washington, DC 20038

A § 301.9100–1 request may also be hand delivered between the hours of 8:30 a.m. and 4:00 p.m. where a receipt will be given at the Courier's Desk. In each instance, the package should be marked RULING REQUEST SUBMISSION. *See* Rev. Proc. 2007–8 for the appropriate user fee. Deliver to:

Courier's Desk
Internal Revenue Service
Attn: SE:T:EP:RA or SE:T:EO:RA
1111 Constitution Avenue, NW – PE
Washington, DC 20224

If return is being examined or considered by an appeals office or a federal court, the taxpayer must notify EP or EO Technical who will notify the EP or EO Examinations Area manager, Appeals Area Director, Area 4, or government counsel

.04 If the taxpayer's return for the taxable year in which an election should have been made or any taxable year that would have been affected by the election had it been timely made is being examined by EP or EO Examinations or the issues in the return are being considered by an appeals office or a federal court, the taxpayer must notify EP or EO Technical. *See* § 301.9100–3(e)(4)(i) and section 6.04 of Rev. Proc. 2007–4. EP or EO Technical will notify the appropriate EP or EO Examinations Area manager or Appeals Area Director, Area 4, or government counsel considering the return that a request for § 301.9100–1 relief has been submitted. The EP or EO specialist, appeals officer or government counsel is not authorized to deny consideration of a request for § 301.9100–1 relief. The letter ruling will be mailed to the taxpayer and a copy will be sent to the appropriate EP or EO Examinations Area manager, or Appeals Area Director, Area 4, or government counsel.

SECTION 7. WHO IS RESPONSIBLE FOR REQUESTING TAMs?

EP or EO Examinations Area manager or EP or EO Determinations manager or Appeals Area Director, Area 4, determines whether to request the advice

.01 The EP or EO Examinations Area manager, the EP or EO Determinations manager or the Appeals Area Director, Area 4, determines whether to request a TAM on an issue. Each request must be submitted through proper channels and signed by a person who is authorized to sign for the EP or EO Examinations Area manager, the EP or EO Determinations manager or the Appeals Area Director, Area 4. The mandatory technical advice described in section 4.04(3) of this revenue procedure, for cases concerning amendments to defined contribution plans in connection with a waiver of the minimum funding standard and a request for a determination letter, is treated as if it had been a request for technical advice submitted by the EP Determinations manager. *See* section 15 of Rev. Proc. 2007–6 and section 3.04 of Rev. Proc. 2004–15 for the procedural rules applicable to this particular mandatory technical advice.

Taxpayer may ask that issue be referred for TAM

.02 While a case is under the jurisdiction of EP or EO Examinations, EP or EO Determinations, or the Appeals Area Director, Area 4, a taxpayer may request that an issue be referred to the EP or EO Technical office for a TAM.

SECTION 8. WHEN SHOULD A TAM BE REQUESTED?

Uniformity of position lacking

.01 A TAM should be requested when there is a lack of uniformity regarding the disposition of an issue or when an issue is unusual or complex enough to warrant consideration by EP or EO Technical.

When can a TAM be requested

.02 Generally, except as provided in section 1.01, the provisions of this revenue procedure apply only to a case under the jurisdiction of EP or EO Examinations, EP or EO Determinations or the Appeals Area Director, Area 4. A TAM may also be requested on issues considered in a prior appeals disposition, not based on mutual concessions for the same tax period of the same taxpayer, if the appeals office that had the case concurs in the request.

(1) EP or EO Examinations or EP or EO Determinations may not request a TAM on an issue if an appeals office is currently considering an identical issue of the same taxpayer (or of a related taxpayer within the meaning of § 267 or an affiliated group of which the taxpayer is also a member within the meaning of § 1504).

(2) A case remains under the jurisdiction of EP or EO Examinations or EP or EO Determinations even though an appeals office has the identical issue under consideration in the case of another taxpayer (not related within the meaning of § 267 or § 1504) in an entirely different transaction. With respect to the same taxpayer or the same transaction, when the issue is under the jurisdiction of an appeals office, and the applicability of more than one kind of federal tax is dependent upon the resolution of that issue, EP or EO Examinations or EP or EO Determinations may not request a TAM on the applicability of any of the taxes involved.

(3) EP or EO Examinations or EP or EO Determinations or an Appeals Area Director, Area 4, also may not request a TAM on an issue if the same issue of the same taxpayer (or of a related taxpayer within the meaning of § 267 or a member of an affiliated group of which the taxpayer is also a member within the meaning of § 1504) is in a docketed case for the same taxpayer (or for a related taxpayer or a member of an affiliated group of which the taxpayer is also a member) for any taxable year.

At the earliest possible stage

.03 Once an issue is identified, all requests for a TAM should be made at the earliest possible stage in the proceeding. The fact that the issue is raised late in the examination, determination or appeals process should not influence, however, EP or EO Examinations', EP or EO Determinations' or the Appeals Area Director, Area 4's, decision to request a TAM.

SECTION 9. HOW ARE PRE-SUBMISSION CONFERENCES SCHEDULED?

Pre-submission conference generally is permitted when a request for TAM is likely and all parties agree to request the conference

.01 In an effort to promote expeditious processing of requests for a TAM, EP or EO Technical generally will discuss the issue(s) with the EP or EO Examinations or the EP or EO Determinations or the appeals office and the taxpayer prior to the time any request for technical advice is formally submitted to EP or EO Technical. In all cases, other than mandatory TAMs which are described in section 4.04, a pre-submission conference is mandatory.

A request for a pre-submission conference should be made, however, only after the EP or EO Examinations or the EP or EO Determinations or the appeals office determines that it will likely request a TAM.

If the request for a TAM will involve more than one function, representatives from each function involved must participate in the pre-submission conference.

Purpose of pre-submission conference

.02 A pre-submission conference is intended to facilitate agreement between the parties as to the appropriate scope of the request for a TAM or any collateral issues that either should or should not be included in the request for a TAM, and any other substantive or procedural considerations that will allow EP or EO Technical to provide the parties with a TAM as expeditiously as possible.

A pre-submission conference is not intended to create an alternate procedure for determining the merits of the substantive positions advocated by the EP or EO Examinations or the EP or EO Determinations or the appeals office or by the taxpayer. Rather, the conference is intended only to facilitate the overall process.

Request for pre-submission conference must be submitted in writing by the EP or EO Examinations or the EP or EO Determinations or the appeals office

.03 A request for a pre-submission conference must be submitted in writing by the EP or EO Examinations or the EP or EO Determinations or the appeals office. The request should identify the office expected to have jurisdiction over the request for a TAM. The request should include a brief explanation of the primary issue so that an assignment to the appropriate group can be made.

Group will contact the EP or EO Examinations or the EP or EO Determinations or the appeals office to arrange the pre-submission conference

.04 Within 5 working days after it receives the request, the group assigned responsibility for conducting the pre-submission conference will contact the EP or EO Examinations or the EP or EO Determinations or the appeals office to arrange a mutually convenient time for the parties to meet (generally by telephone) in the EP or EO Technical office. The conference generally should be held within 30 calendar days after the EP or EO Examinations or the EP or EO Determinations or the appeals office is contacted. The EP or EO Examinations or the EP or EO Determinations or the appeals office will be responsible for coordinating with the taxpayer as well as with any other Service personnel whose attendance the EP or EO Examinations or the EP or EO Determinations or the appeals office believes would be appropriate.

Pre-submission conference generally held by telephone

.05 Generally, pre-submission conferences for TAMs are held by telephone with EP or EO Technical unless the parties specifically request that the conference be held in person.

Certain information required to be submitted to EP or EO Technical prior to the pre-submission conference

.06 At least 10 working days before the scheduled pre-submission conference, the EP or EO Examinations or the EP or EO Determinations or the appeals office and the taxpayer should submit to EP or EO Technical a statement of the pertinent facts (including any facts in dispute), a statement of the issues that the parties would like to discuss, and any legal analysis, authorities, or background documents that the parties believe would facilitate EP or EO Technical's understanding of the issues to be discussed at the conference. The legal analysis provided for the pre-submission conference need not be as fully developed as the analysis that ultimately will accompany the request for a TAM, but it should allow EP or EO Technical to become reasonably informed regarding the subject matter of the conference prior to the meeting. The EP or EO Examinations or the EP or EO Determinations or the appeals office or the taxpayer should ensure that the EP or EO Technical office receives a copy of any required power of attorney, on Form 2848, *Power of Attorney and Declaration of Representative.*

Manner of submitting pre-submission materials

.07 The pre-submission materials must be submitted electronically. In order to obtain the protection of taxpayer information offered by the Service's Intranet "firewall," the pre-submission materials must be electronically transmitted by the Service office assigned to the request.

To the extent that supporting materials cannot be submitted electronically, such materials should be sent by fax or by express mail or private delivery service to the tax law specialist or actuary in Headquarters assigned to the request. In such cases, the appropriate provisions of section 10.05 should be followed.

Pre-submission conference may not be taped

.08 Because pre-submission conference procedures are informal, no tape, stenographic, or other verbatim recording of a conference may be made by any party.

Discussion of substantive issues is not binding on the Service

.09 Any discussion of substantive issues at a pre-submission conference is advisory only, is not binding on the Service, and cannot be relied upon as a basis for obtaining retroactive relief under the provisions of § 7805(b).

SECTION 10. WHAT MUST BE INCLUDED IN THE REQUEST FOR A TAM?

Statement of issues, facts, law, and arguments

.01 Whether initiated by the taxpayer or by an EP or EO Examinations or an EP or EO Determinations or an appeals office, a request for a TAM must include the facts and the issues for which the TAM is requested, and a written statement that clearly sets forth the applicable law and the arguments in support of both the Service's and the taxpayer's positions on the issue or issues.

Taxpayer must submit statement if the taxpayer initiates request for a TAM

(1) If the taxpayer initiates the request for a TAM, the taxpayer must submit to the EP or EO specialist or appeals office, at the time the taxpayer initiates the request, a written statement—

(a) stating the facts and the issues;

(b) explaining the taxpayer's position;

(c) discussing any relevant statutory provisions, tax treaties, court decisions, regulations, revenue rulings, revenue procedures, notices, or any other authority supporting the taxpayer's position; and

(d) stating the reasons for requesting technical advice.

If the EP or EO specialist or the appeals office determines that a TAM will be requested, the taxpayer's statement will be forwarded to EP or EO Technical with the request for the TAM.

Taxpayer is encouraged to submit statement if Service initiates request for a TAM

(2) If the request for a TAM is initiated by an EP or EO Examinations office or by an EP or EO Determinations office or by an appeals office, the taxpayer is encouraged to submit the written statement described in section 10.01(1) of this revenue procedure. If the taxpayer's statement is received after the request for the TAM has been forwarded to EP or EO Technical, the statement will be forwarded to EP or EO Technical for association with the TAM.

Statement of authorities contrary to taxpayer's position

(3) Whether the request for a TAM is initiated by the taxpayer or by an EP or EO Examinations office or by an EP or EO Determinations office or by an appeals office, the taxpayer is encouraged to comment on any legislation, tax treaties, regulations, revenue rulings, revenue procedures, or court decisions contrary to the taxpayer's position. If the taxpayer determines that there are no contrary authorities, a statement to this effect would be helpful. If the taxpayer does not furnish either contrary authorities or a statement that none exists, the Service, in complex cases or those presenting difficult or novel issues, may request submission of contrary authorities or a statement that none exists.

General provisions of §§ 6104 and 6110

.02 Generally, § 6104(a)(1)(B) provides that an application filed with respect to: (1) the qualification of a pension, profit-sharing, or stock bonus plan under § 401(a) or § 403(a) or an individual retirement arrangement under § 408(a) or § 408(b) will be open to public inspection pursuant to regulations as will (2) any application filed for an exemption from tax under § 501(a) of an organization forming part of a plan or account described above. Generally, § 6110(a) provides that except as provided otherwise, written determinations (defined in § 6110(b)(1) as rulings, determination letters, technical advice memorandums and Chief Counsel advice) and any related background file document will be open to public inspection pursuant to regulations.

Application of § 6104

.03 The requirements for submitting statements and other materials or proposed deletions in TAMs before public inspection is allowed do not apply to requests for any documents to the extent § 6104 applies.

Statement identifying information to be deleted from public inspection

.04 The text of a TAM subject to § 6110(a) may be open to public inspection. The Service deletes certain information from the text before it is made available for inspection. To help the Service make the deletions required by § 6110(c), the taxpayer must provide a statement indicating the deletions desired ("deletions statement"). If the taxpayer does not submit the deletions statement, the Service will follow the procedures in section 11.06 of this revenue procedure.

A taxpayer who wants only names, addresses, and identifying numbers deleted should state this in the deletions statement. If the taxpayer wants more information deleted, the deletions statement must be accompanied by a copy of the TAM request and supporting documents on which the taxpayer should bracket the material to be deleted. The deletions statement must indicate the statutory basis, under § 6110(c) for each proposed deletion.

The taxpayer may submit additional deletions statements before the TAM is issued.

The deletions statement must not appear in the request for a TAM but, instead, must be made in a separate document.

The deletions statement must be signed and dated by the taxpayer or the taxpayer's authorized representative. A stamped signature or a faxed signature is not permitted.

The taxpayer should follow these same procedures to propose deletions from any additional information submitted after the initial request for a TAM. An additional deletions statement, however, is not required with each submission of additional information if the taxpayer's initial deletions statement requests that only names, addresses, and identifying numbers are to be deleted and the taxpayer wants the same information deleted from the additional information.

Transmittal Form 5565, Request for Technical Advice — EP/EO

.05 The EP or EO Examinations or the EP or EO Determinations or the appeals office (including another Operating Division of the Service involved in an examination where EP Technical does not have audit jurisdiction but has interpretive jurisdiction as enumerated in section 6.02 of Rev. Proc. 2007–4) should use Form 5565, *Request for Technical Advice — EP/EO*, for transmitting a request for technical advice to EP or EO Technical.

The appropriate office of the Service must submit electronically, the Form 5565 for a TAM request to *David.W.Welty@irs.gov* for EP matters and *Theodore.R.Lieber@irs.gov* for EO matters. To the extent feasible, the accompanying documents should be submitted to the same e-mail address (followed by a hard copy if requested by the assigned group). *See* section 9.07 for additional information.

The applicable office should submit additional documents that are not available in electronic form by fax to 202–283–9654 for EP matters and 202–283–8858 for EO matters or by express mail or private delivery service to the address below.

Whenever possible, all documents should contain the case number and name of the tax law specialist or actuary assigned to the pre-submission conference for the TAM request. Documents that are being sent in hardcopy should be sent on the business day before the day that the request for a TAM is submitted via e-mail, so as not to delay the process. It is anticipated that most, if not all, such documents will be identified during the pre-submission conference.

The field and the taxpayer are encouraged to provide electronic versions of a proposed TAM containing the taxpayer's deletions and legends for EP Technical's or EO Technical's use.

Address to send requests from EP or EO Examinations or EP or EO Determinations offices or another Operating Division

Employee Plans

Internal Revenue Service
Attn: SE:T:EP:RA
1111 Constitution Ave., NW – PE
Washington, DC 20224

Exempt Organizations

Internal Revenue Service
Attn: SE:T:EO:RA
1111 Constitution Ave., NW – PE
Washington, DC 20224

If a request is from an Appeals office and is within EP/EO's jurisdiction, the field office must send the request for a TAM to one of the above offices with a copy of the request to the Appeals Director, Technical Services at the address below.

Internal Revenue Service
Director, Technical Services
Attn: C:AP
Franklin Court Building
1099 14th Street, NW
Washington, DC 20005

Power of attorney

.06 Any authorized representative, as described in section 9.02 of Rev. Proc. 2007–4, whether or not enrolled to practice, must comply with Treasury Department Circular No. 230, as revised, and with the conference and practice requirements of the Statement of Procedural Rules (26 CFR part 601). A Form 2848, *Power of Attorney and Declaration of Representative*, must be used with regard to requests for a TAM under this revenue procedure. An original, a copy or a fax transmission of the power of attorney is acceptable so long as its authenticity is not reasonably disputed.

SECTION 11. HOW ARE REQUESTS HANDLED?

Taxpayer notified

.01 Regardless of whether the taxpayer or the Service initiates the request for a TAM, the EP or EO Examinations or the EP or EO Determinations or the appeals office: (1) will notify the taxpayer that the TAM is being requested; and (2) at or before the time the request is submitted to EP or EO Technical, will give to the taxpayer a copy of the arguments that are being provided to EP or EO Technical in support of its position.

If the EP or EO specialist or appeals office initiates the request for a TAM, he or she will give to the taxpayer a copy of the statement of the pertinent facts and the issues proposed for submission to EP or EO Technical.

This section 11.01 does not apply to a TAM described in section 11.07 of this revenue procedure.

Consider whether published guidance is appropriate

.02 Whenever the assigned reviewer suspects that general guidance should be published regarding the issue presented, the reviewer will notify the Manager, Technical who in turn will notify the Manager, Technical Guidance and Quality Assurance. The Manager, Technical Guidance and Quality Assurance will then determine if the issue meets publication standards. In general, except where policy issues and concerns regarding proper administration of the tax laws require otherwise, the TAM will be issued in advance of published guidance.

Conference offered

.03 When notifying the taxpayer that technical advice is being requested, the EP or EO specialist or appeals office will also tell the taxpayer about the right to a conference in EP or EO Technical if an adverse decision is indicated and will ask the taxpayer whether such a conference is desired.

If the taxpayer disagrees with the Service's statement of facts

.04 If the EP or EO specialist or appeals office initiates the request for a TAM, the taxpayer has 10 calendar days after receiving the statement of facts and specific issues to submit to that specialist or office a written statement specifying any disagreement on the facts and issues. A taxpayer who needs more than 10 calendar days must justify, in writing, the request for an extension of time. The extension is subject to the approval of the EP or EO Examinations Area manager or the EP or EO Determinations manager or the Appeals Area Director, Area 4.

After receiving the taxpayer's statement of the areas of disagreement, every effort should be made to reach agreement on the facts and the specific points at issue before the matter is referred to EP or EO Technical. If an agreement cannot be reached, the EP or EO Examinations or the EP or EO Determinations or the appeals office will notify the taxpayer in writing. Within 10 calendar days after receiving the written notice, the taxpayer may submit a statement of the taxpayer's understanding of the facts and the specific points at issue. A taxpayer who needs more than 10 calendar days to prepare the statement of understanding must justify, in writing, the request for an extension of time. The extension is subject to the approval of the EP or EO Examinations Area manager or the EP or EO Determinations manager or the Appeals Area Director, Area 4. Both the statements of the taxpayer and the EP or EO Examinations or EP or

EO Determinations or appeals office will be forwarded to EP or EO Technical with the request for a TAM.

When EP or EO Examinations or EP or EO Determinations or the Appeals Area Director, Area 4, and the taxpayer cannot agree on the material facts and the request for a TAM does not involve the issue of whether a letter ruling or determination letter should be modified or revoked, EP or EO Technical, at its discretion, may refuse to provide technical advice. If EP or EO Technical chooses to issue the TAM, it will base its advice on the facts provided by the EP or EO Examinations or EP or EO Determinations or appeals office.

If a request for a TAM involves the issue of whether a letter ruling or determination letter should be modified or revoked, EP or EO Technical will issue the TAM.

If the Service disagrees with the taxpayer's statement of facts

.05 If the taxpayer initiates the action to request a TAM, and the taxpayer's statement of the facts and issues is not wholly acceptable to the EP or EO Examinations or the EP or EO Determinations or the appeals office, the Service will notify the taxpayer in writing of the areas of disagreement. The taxpayer has 10 calendar days after receiving the written notice to reply to it. A taxpayer who needs more than 10 calendar days must justify in writing the request for an extension of time. The extension is subject to the approval of the EP or EO Examinations Area manager, or the EP or EO Determinations manager or the Appeals Area Director, Area 4.

If an agreement cannot be reached, both the statements of the taxpayer and the EP or EO Examinations or EP or EO Determinations or appeals office will be forwarded to EP or EO Technical with the request for a TAM. When the disagreement involves material facts essential to the preliminary assessment of the case, the EP or EO Examinations Area manager, the EP or EO Determinations manager or the Appeals Area Director, Area 4, may refuse to refer a taxpayer initiated request for the TAM to EP or EO Technical.

If EP or EO Examinations or EP or EO Determinations or the Appeals Area Director, Area 4, submits a case involving a disagreement of material facts, EP or EO Technical, at its discretion, may refuse to provide the TAM. If EP or EO Technical chooses to issue the TAM, it will base its advice on the facts provided by the EP or EO Examinations or the EP or EO Determinations or the appeals office.

If the taxpayer has not submitted the required deletions statement

.06 When the EP or EO Examinations or the EP or EO Determinations or the appeals office initiates the request for a TAM, the taxpayer has 10 calendar days after receiving the statement of facts and issues to be submitted to EP or EO Technical to provide the deletions statement required under § 6110 if public inspection is permitted pursuant to § 6110 (*see* section 10.05 of this revenue procedure). In such a case, if the taxpayer does not submit the deletions statement, the EP or EO Examinations or the EP or EO Determinations or the appeals office, will tell the taxpayer that the statement is required.

When the taxpayer initiates the request for a TAM and does not submit with the request a deletions statement as required by § 6110, the EP or EO Examinations or the EP or EO Determinations or the Appeals Area Director, Area 4, will ask the taxpayer to submit the statement. If EP or EO Examinations or EP or EO Determinations or the Appeals Area Director, Area 4, does not receive the deletions statement within 10 calendar days after asking the taxpayer for it, EP or EO Examinations or EP or EO Determinations or the Appeals Area Director, Area 4, may decline to submit the request for the TAM.

However, if EP or EO Examinations or EP or EO Determinations or the Appeals Area Director, Area 4, decides to request a TAM, whether initiated by the EP or EO Examinations or the EP or EO Determinations or the appeals office or by the taxpayer, in a case in which the taxpayer has not submitted the deletions statement, EP or EO Technical will make those deletions that the Commissioner of Internal Revenue determines are required by § 6110(c).

Criminal or civil fraud cases

.07 The provisions of this section (about referring issues upon the taxpayer's request, obtaining the taxpayer's statement of the areas of disagreement, telling the taxpayer about the referral of issues, giving the taxpayer a copy of the arguments submitted, submitting proposed deletions, and granting conferences in EP or EO Technical) do not apply to a TAM described in § 6110(g)(5)(A) that involves a matter that is the subject of or is otherwise closely related to a criminal or civil fraud investigation, or a jeopardy or termination assessment.

In these cases, a copy of the TAM is given to the taxpayer after all proceedings in the investigations or assessments are complete, but before the Service mails the notice of intention to disclose the TAM under § 6110(f)(1). The taxpayer may then provide the statement of proposed deletions to EP or EO Technical.

SECTION 12. HOW DOES A TAXPAYER APPEAL AN EP OR EO MANAGER'S OR AN APPEALS AREA DIRECTOR'S DECISION NOT TO SEEK TECHNICAL ADVICE?

Taxpayer notified of decision not to seek a TAM

.01 If the EP or EO specialist's or the appeal's referral of an issue to EP or EO Technical for a TAM is not warranted, the EP or EO specialist or the appeals office will tell the taxpayer. A taxpayer's request for such a referral will not be denied merely because EP or EO Technical provided legal advice, other than advice furnished pursuant to this revenue procedure, to the EP or EO Examinations or EP or EO Determinations or appeals office on the matter.

Taxpayer may request review of decision not to seek a TAM

.02 The taxpayer may request review of the decision of the EP or EO specialist or the appeals office not to request a TAM in all instances. To do so, the taxpayer must submit to that specialist or office, within 10 calendar days after being told of the decision, a written statement of the facts, law, and arguments on the issue and the reasons why the taxpayer believes the matter should be referred to EP or EO Technical for a TAM. A taxpayer who needs more than 10 calendar days must justify in writing the request for an extension of time. The extension is subject to the approval of the EP or EO Examinations Area manager or the EP or EO Determinations manager or the appropriate appeals office.

EP or EO Examinations Area manager or EP or EO Determinations manager or Appeals Area Director, Area 4, determines whether technical advice will be sought

.03 The EP or EO specialist or the appeals office submits the taxpayer's statement through proper channels to the EP or EO Examinations Area manager or the EP or EO Determinations manager or the Appeals Area Director, Area 4, along with the EP or EO specialist's or the appeals office's statement of why the issue should not be referred to EP or EO Technical. The manager or chief determines, on the basis of the statements, whether a TAM will be requested.

If the manager or chief determines that a TAM is not warranted and proposes to deny the request, the taxpayer is told in writing about the determination. In the letter to the taxpayer, the manager or chief states the reasons for the proposed denial (except in unusual situations when doing so would be prejudicial to the best interests of the Government). The taxpayer has 10 calendar days after receiving the letter to notify the manager or chief of agreement or disagreement with the proposed denial.

Manager or area director's decision may be reviewed but not appealed

.04 The taxpayer may not appeal the decision of the EP or EO Examinations Area manager or the EP or EO Determinations manager or the Appeals Area Director, Area 4, not to request a TAM from EP or EO Technical. However, if the taxpayer does not agree with the proposed denial, all data on the issue for which the TAM has been sought, including the taxpayer's written request and statements, will be submitted to the Commissioner, Tax Exempt and Government Entities Division or the Director, Appeals, Technical Services as appropriate.

The Commissioner, Tax Exempt and Government Entities Operating Division through the Director, Employee Plans, or the Director, Exempt Organizations or, if appropriate, the Chief, Appeals will review the proposed denial solely on the basis of the written record, and no conference will be held with the taxpayer or the taxpayer's representative. The appropriate Director or Chief or his or her representative may consult with EP or EO Technical and the Office of Chief Counsel, if necessary, and will notify the EP or EO Examinations or the EP or EO Determinations or the appeals office within 45 calendar days of receiving all the data regarding the request for a TAM whether the proposed denial is approved or disapproved. The EP or EO Examinations or the EP or EO Determinations or appeals office will then notify the taxpayer.

While the matter is being reviewed, the EP or EO Examinations office or the EP or EO Determinations office or the appeals office suspends action on the issue (except when the delay would prejudice the Government's interest).

The provisions of this revenue procedure regarding review of the proposed denial of a request for a TAM continue to be applicable in those situations in which the authority normally exercised by the EP or EO Examinations Area manager, the EP or EO Determinations manager, or the Appeals Area Director, Area 4, has been delegated to another official.

SECTION 13. HOW ARE REQUESTS FOR TAMS WITHDRAWN?

Taxpayer notified

.01 Once a request for a TAM has been sent to EP or EO Technical, only an EP or EO Examinations Area manager, an EP or EO Determinations manager or the Appeals Area Director, Area 4, may withdraw that request for the TAM. He or she may ask to withdraw a request at any time before the responding transmittal memorandum transmitting the TAM is signed.

The EP or EO Examinations Area manager, the EP or EO Determinations manager or the Appeals Area Director, Area 4, as appropriate, must notify the taxpayer in writing of an intent to withdraw the request for the TAM except—

(1) when the period of limitations on assessment is about to expire and the taxpayer has declined to sign a consent to extend the period, or

(2) when such notification would be prejudicial to the best interests of the Government.

If the taxpayer does not agree that the request for a TAM should be withdrawn, the procedures in section 12 of this revenue procedure must be followed.

EP or EO Technical may provide views

.02 When a request for a TAM is withdrawn, EP or EO Technical may send its views to the EP or EO Examinations office or the EP or EO Determinations office or the Appeals Area Director, Area 4, when acknowledging the withdrawal request. In an appeals case, acknowledgment of the withdrawal request should be sent to the appropriate appeals office, through the Director, Technical Services, C:AP. In appropriate cases, the subject matter may be published as a revenue ruling or as a revenue procedure.

SECTION 14. HOW ARE CONFERENCES SCHEDULED?

If requested, offered to the taxpayer when adverse TAM proposed

.01 If, after the TAM is analyzed, it appears that a TAM adverse to the taxpayer will be given, and if a conference has been requested, the taxpayer will be informed, by telephone if possible, of the time and place of the conference.

Timeline

.02 The conference for a TAM must be held within 21 calendar days after the taxpayer is contacted.

If conferences are being arranged for more than one request for a TAM for the same taxpayer, they will be scheduled to cause the least inconvenience to the taxpayer. If considered appropriate, EP or EO Technical will notify the EP or EO specialist or the appeals office of the scheduled conference and will offer the EP or EO specialist or the appeals officer the opportunity to attend the conference. The Commissioner, Tax Exempt and Government Entities Division, the Chief, Appeals, the EP or EO Examinations Area manager, the EP or EO Determinations manager, or the Appeals Area Director, Area 4, may designate other Service representatives to participate in the conference in lieu of, or in addition to, the EP or EO specialist or the appeals officer.

21-day period may be extended if justified and approved

.03 An extension of the 21-day period will be granted only if the taxpayer justifies it in writing, and the group manager (or his or her delegate) of the office to which the case is assigned approves it. No extension will be granted without the approval of the group manager (or his or her delegate). The taxpayer (or an authorized representative) must notify the EP Specialist or the EO Specialist or the appeals office of the request for an extension. Except in rare and unusual circumstances, EP or EO Technical will not agree to an extension of more than 10 working days beyond the end of the 21-day period.

The taxpayer's request for an extension must be submitted before the end of the 21-day period, and should be submitted sufficiently before the end of this period to allow EP or EO Technical to consider, and either approve or deny, the request before the end of the 21-day period. If unusual circumstances near the end of the period make a timely written request impractical, the taxpayer (or an authorized representative) should orally inform the assigned tax law specialist or actuary before the end of the period about the problem and about the forthcoming written request for an extension. The written request for an extension must be submitted to EP or EO Technical promptly after the oral request. The taxpayer will be told promptly (and later in writing) of the approval or denial of the requested extension.

Denial of extension cannot be appealed

.04 There is no right to appeal the denial of a request for an extension of a TAM. If EP or EO Technical is not advised of problems with meeting the 21-day period, or if the written request is not sent promptly after EP or EO Technical is notified of problems with meeting the 21-day period, the TAM will be processed on the basis of the existing record.

Entitled to one conference of right

.05 A taxpayer is entitled by right to only one conference in EP or EO Technical except as provided in section 14.09 of this revenue procedure. This conference is normally held at the group level in EP Technical or EO Technical, whichever is appropriate. It is attended by a person who has authority to sign the transmittal memorandum discussed in section 16.13 on behalf of the group manager.

When more than one group has taken an adverse position on an issue in the request, or when the position ultimately adopted by one group will affect another group's determination, a representative from each group with authority to sign for the group manager will attend the conference. If more than one subject is discussed at the conference, the discussion constitutes the conference of right for each subject discussed.

To have a thorough and informed discussion of the issues, the conference usually is held after the group has had an opportunity to study the case. However, the taxpayer may request that the conference of right be held earlier in the consideration of the case than the Service would ordinarily designate.

The taxpayer has no right to appeal the action of a group to any other Service official. But see section 14.09 for situations in which the Service may offer additional conferences.

Conference may not be taped

.06 Because conference procedures are informal, no tape, stenographic, or other verbatim recording of a conference may be made by any party.

Conference may be delayed to address a request for relief under § 7805(b)

.07 In the event of a tentative adverse determination, the taxpayer may request in writing a delay of the conference so that the taxpayer can prepare and submit a brief requesting relief under § 7805(b) (discussed in section 19 of this revenue procedure). The group manager (or his or her delegate) of the office to which the case is assigned will determine whether to grant or deny the request for delaying the conference. If such request is granted, the Service will schedule a conference on the tentatively adverse position and the § 7805(b) relief request within 10 days of receiving the taxpayer's § 7805(b) request. *See* section 19.06 of this revenue procedure for the conference procedures if the § 7805(b) request is made after the conference on the substantive issues has been held.

Service makes tentative recommendations

.08 The senior Service representative at the conference ensures that the taxpayer has full opportunity to present views on all the issues in question. The Service representatives explain the tentative decision on the substantive issues.

If the taxpayer requests relief under § 7805(b) (regarding limitation of retroactive effect), the Service representatives will discuss the tentative recommendation concerning the request for relief and the reason(s) for the tentative recommendation.

No commitment will be made as to the conclusion that the Service will finally adopt regarding any issue, including the outcome of the § 7805(b) request for relief.

Additional conferences may be offered

.09 The Service will offer the taxpayer an additional conference if, after the conference of right, an adverse holding is proposed on a new issue or on the same issue but on grounds different from those discussed at the first conference.

When a proposed holding is reversed at a higher level with a result less favorable to the taxpayer, the taxpayer has no right to another conference if the grounds or arguments on which the reversal is based were discussed at the conference of right.

The limitation on the number of conferences to which a taxpayer is entitled does not prevent EP or EO Technical from inviting a taxpayer to attend additional conferences, including conferences with an official higher than the group level, if EP or EO Technical personnel think they are necessary. Such conferences are not offered as a matter of course simply because the group has reached an adverse decision. In general, conferences with higher level officials are offered only if the Service determines that the case presents significant issues of tax policy or tax administration and that the consideration of these issues would be enhanced by additional conferences with the taxpayer.

In accordance with section 14.02 of this revenue procedure, the EP or EO specialist or the appeals office may be offered the opportunity to participate in any additional taxpayer's conference, including a conference with an official higher than the group level. Section 14.02 of this revenue procedure also provides that other Service representatives are allowed to participate in the conference.

Additional information submitted after the conference

.10 After the conference, the taxpayer must furnish to EP or EO Technical, whichever is applicable, any additional data, lines of reasoning, precedents, etc., that the taxpayer proposed and discussed at the conference but did not previously or adequately present in writing. This additional information must be submitted by letter with a penalties of perjury statement in the form described in section 16.10 of this revenue procedure.

The taxpayer must also send a copy of the additional information to the EP or EO Examinations office or the EP or EO Determinations office or the Appeals Area Director, Area 4, for comment. Any comments on additional information by Service personnel must be furnished promptly to the appropriate group in EP or EO Technical. If the EP or EO Examinations office or the EP or EO Determinations office or the Appeals Area Director, Area 4, does not have any comments, he or she must notify the group representative promptly.

If the additional information has a significant impact on the facts in the request for a TAM, EP or EO Technical will ask EP or EO Examinations or EP or EO Determinations or the Appeals Area Director, Area 4, for comments on the facts contained in the additional information submitted. The EP or EO Examinations office or the EP or EO Determinations office or the Appeals Area Director, Area 4, will give the additional information prompt attention.

If the additional information is not received from the taxpayer within 21 calendar days, the TAM will be issued on the basis of the existing record.

An extension of the 21-day period for TAMs may be granted only if the taxpayer justifies it in writing, and the group manager (or his or her delegate) of the office to which the case is assigned approves the extension. Such extension will not be routinely granted. The procedures for requesting an extension of the 21-day period and notifying the taxpayer of the Service's decision are the same as those in sections 14.03 and 14.04 of this revenue procedure.

Normally held by telephone

.11 The conference will be conducted by telephone, unless the taxpayer or the field requests that the conference be held in person. The taxpayer will be advised when to call the Service representatives (not a toll-free call). In no event will the conference be delayed to provide an in-person conference rather than a telephone conference.

In accordance with section 14.02 of this revenue procedure, the EP or EO specialist or appeals office will be offered the opportunity to participate in the telephone conference. Section 14.02 of this revenue procedure also provides that other Service representatives are allowed to participate in the conference.

SECTION 15. HOW IS STATUS OF REQUEST OBTAINED?

Taxpayer or taxpayer's representative may request status from EP or EO Examinations or EP or EO Determinations or appeals office

.01 The taxpayer or the taxpayer's representative may obtain information on the status of the request for a TAM by contacting the EP or EO Examinations office or the EP or EO Determinations office or the appeals office that requested the TAM. *See* section 16.08 of this revenue procedure concerning the time for discussing the tentative conclusion with the taxpayer's representative. *See* section 17.03 of this revenue procedure regarding discussions of the contents of the TAM with the taxpayer or the taxpayer's representative.

EP or EO Technical will give status updates to the EP or EO Examinations or EP or EO Determinations or Appeals Area Director, Area 4

.02 The group representative or manager to whom the TAM request is assigned will give status updates on the request once a month to the EP or EO Examination Area manager or the EP or EO Determinations manager or the Appeals Area Director, Area 4. In addition, an EP or EO Examinations Area manager or an EP or EO Determinations manager or an Appeals Area Director, Area 4, may get current information on the status of the request for a TAM by calling the person whose name and telephone number are shown on acknowledgment of receipt of the request for the TAM.

See section 16.09 of this revenue procedure about discussing the final conclusions with the EP or EO Examinations office or the EP or EO Determinations office or the appeals office. Further, the EP or EO Examinations office or the EP or EO Determinations office or the Appeals Area Director, Area 4, will be notified at the time the TAM is mailed.

SECTION 16. HOW DOES EP OR EO TECHNICAL PREPARE THE TAM?

Delegates authority to group managers

.01 The authority to issue a TAM on issues under the jurisdiction of the Commissioner, Tax Exempt and Government Entities Operating Division has largely been delegated to the managers of the Employee Plans Rulings & Agreements Technical and Actuarial groups, and the Technical Guidance and Quality Assurance group (collectively referred to as "EP Technical"); and of the Exempt Organizations Rulings & Agreements Technical groups and the Technical Guidance and Quality Assurance group (collectively referred to as "EO Technical").

Determines whether request has been properly made

.02 A request for a TAM generally is given priority and processed expeditiously. As soon as the request for a TAM is assigned, the technical employee analyzes the file to see whether it meets all of the requirements of sections 7, 8, and 10 of this revenue procedure.

However, if the request does not comply with the requirements of section 10.04 of this revenue procedure relating to the deletions statement, the Service will follow the procedure in section 11.06 of this revenue procedure.

Contacts the EP or EO Examinations or EP or EO Determinations or appeals office to discuss issues

.03 Upon receipt of a request for a TAM, a representative of the group assigned the TAM will telephone the EP or EO Examinations office or the EP or EO Determinations office or the appeals office to acknowledge receipt of the TAM and to establish a point of contact. Within 21 calendar days from the receipt of a TAM, the tax law specialist or actuary should contact the EP or EO specialist or appeals office to discuss the procedural and substantive issues in the request that come within the group's jurisdiction.

Informs the EP or EO Examinations or EP or EO Determinations or appeals office if any matters in the request have been referred to another group or office

.04 If the technical advice request concerns matters within the jurisdiction of more than one group or office, a representative of the group that received the original technical advice request generally informs the EP or EO Examinations office or the EP or EO Determinations office or the appeals office within 21 calendar days of receiving the request that—

(1) the matters within the jurisdiction of another group or office have been referred to the other group or office for consideration, and

(2) a representative of the other group or office will contact the EP or EO Examinations office or the EP or EO Determinations office or the appeals office about the referral of the technical advice request within 21 calendar days after receiving it in accordance with section 16.03 above.

Informs the EP or EO Examinations or EP or EO Determinations or appeals office if additional information is needed

.05 The group representative will inform the EP or EO Examinations office or the EP or EO Determinations office or the appeals office that the case is being returned if substantial additional information is required to resolve an issue. Cases also should be returned for additional information when significant unresolved factual variances exist between the statement of facts submitted by the EP or EO Examinations office or the EP or EO Determinations office or the appeals office and the taxpayer. They should also be returned if major procedural problems cannot be resolved by telephone. The EP or EO Examinations office or the EP or EO Determinations office or the appeals office should promptly notify the taxpayer of the decision to return the case for further factual development or other reasons.

If only minor procedural deficiencies exist, the group will request the additional information in the most expeditious manner without returning the case.

Informs the EP or EO Examinations or EP or EO Determinations or appeals office of the tentative conclusion

.06 If all necessary information has been provided, the group representative informs the EP or EO Examinations office or the EP or EO Determinations office or the appeals office within 21 calendar days after receiving the information for a TAM of his or her tentative conclusion.

If a tentative conclusion has not been reached, gives date estimated for tentative conclusion

.07 If a tentative conclusion has not been reached because of the complexity of the issue, the group representative informs the EP or EO Examinations office or the EP or EO Determinations office or the appeals office of the estimated date the tentative conclusion will be made.

Advises the EP or EO Examinations or EP or EO Determinations or appeals office that preliminary conclusion not final

.08 Because the group representative's tentative conclusion may change during the preparation and review of the TAM, the tentative conclusion should not be considered final. Therefore, neither the group representative nor the EP or EO Examinations office or the EP or EO Determinations or the appeals office should advise the taxpayer or the taxpayer's representative of the tentative conclusion before the scheduling of the adverse conference or between the scheduling and the commencement of the adverse conference.

Advises the EP or EO Examinations or EP or EO Determinations or appeals office of final conclusions

.09 In all cases, the group representative should inform the EP or EO specialist or appeals office of EP or EO Technical's final conclusions. The EP or EO specialist or the appeals office should be offered the opportunity to discuss the issues and EP or EO Technical's final conclusions before the TAM is issued.

If needed, requests additional information

.10 If, following the initial contact referenced in section 16.03 of this revenue procedure, it is determined, after discussion with the appropriate group manager or reviewer, that additional information is needed, a group representative will obtain the additional information from the taxpayer, the EP or EO Examinations office or the EP or EO Determinations office or the Appeals Area Director, Area 4, in the most expeditious manner possible. Any additional information requested from the taxpayer by EP or EO Technical must be submitted by letter, accompanied by a penalties of perjury statement, within 21 calendar days after the request for information is made.

Request for additional information by fax

(1) To facilitate prompt action on TAM requests, the Service may request any additional information from the taxpayer by fax.

A request to fax a copy of additional information to the taxpayer or the taxpayer's authorized representative must be made in writing, either as part of the original TAM request or prior to the mailing of the request for additional information. The request to fax additional information must contain the fax number of the taxpayer or the taxpayer's authorized representative to and from whom the document is to be faxed.

Because of the unsecured nature of a fax transmission, the Service will take certain precautions to protect confidential information. For example, the Service will use a cover sheet that identifies the intended recipient of the fax and the number of pages transmitted, that does not identify the taxpayer by name or tax identifying number and that contains a statement prohibiting unauthorized disclosure of the document if a recipient of the faxed document is not the intended recipient of the fax. Also, for example, the cover sheet should be faxed in an order in which it will become the first page covering the faxed document.

Penalties of perjury statement

(2) Additional information submitted to EP or EO Technical must be accompanied by the following declaration: **"Under penalties of perjury, I declare that I have examined this information, including accompanying documents, and, to the best of my knowledge and belief, the information contains all the relevant facts relating to the request for the information and such facts are true, correct, and complete."** This declaration must be signed and dated by the taxpayer, not the taxpayer's representative. A stamped signature or a faxed signature is not permitted.

(3) A written request for an extension of time to submit additional information must be received by EP or EO Technical within the 21-day period, giving compelling facts and circumstances to justify the proposed extension. The group manager (or his or her delegate) of the office to which the case is assigned will determine whether to grant or deny the request for an extension. Except in rare and unusual circumstances, EP or EO Technical will not agree to an extension of more than 10 working days beyond the end of the 21-day period. There is no right to appeal the denial of a request for an extension.

(4) If EP or EO Technical does not receive the additional information within 21 calendar days, plus any extensions granted by the appropriate group manager (or his or her delegate), EP or EO Technical will process the TAM based on the existing record.

Requests taxpayer to send additional information to the EP or EO Technical and a copy to the EP or EO Examinations or EP or EO Determinations or Appeals Area Director, Area 4

.11 Whether or not requested by the Service, any additional information submitted by the taxpayer should be sent to the headquarters office. Generally, the taxpayer needs only to submit the original of the additional information to EP or EO Technical. However, in appropriate cases, EP or EO Technical may request additional copies of the information.

Also, the taxpayer must send a copy to either the EP or EO Examinations office or the EP or EO Determinations office or the Appeals Area Director, Area 4, for comment. Any comments must be furnished promptly to the appropriate group in EP or EO Technical. If the EP or EO Examinations office or the EP or EO Determinations office or the Appeals Area Director, Area 4, does not have any comments, he or she must notify the group representative promptly.

Informs the taxpayer when requested deletions will not be made

.12 Generally, before replying to the request for a TAM, EP or EO Technical informs the taxpayer orally or in writing of the material likely to appear in the TAM that the taxpayer proposed be deleted but that the Service has determined should not be deleted.

If so informed, the taxpayer may submit within 10 calendar days any further information or other arguments supporting the taxpayer's proposed deletions.

The Service will attempt to resolve all disagreements about proposed deletions before EP or EO Technical replies to the request for a TAM. However, the taxpayer does not have the right to a conference to resolve any disagreements about material to be deleted from the text of the TAM. These matters, however, may be considered at any conference otherwise scheduled for the request.

Prepares reply in two parts

.13 EP or EO Technical's reply to a TAM request is in two parts. Each part identifies the taxpayer by name, address, identification number, and year or years involved.

The first part of the reply is a transmittal memorandum. In unusual cases, it is a way of giving the EP or EO Examinations office or the EP or EO Determinations office or the appeals office administrative or other information that under the nondisclosure statutes or for other reasons may not be discussed with the taxpayer.

The second part is the TAM, which contains—

(1) a statement of the issues;

(2) a statement of the facts pertinent to the issues;

(3) a statement of the pertinent law, tax treaties, regulations, revenue rulings, and other precedents published in the Internal Revenue Bulletin, and court decisions;

(4) a discussion of the rationale underlying the conclusions reached by EP or EO Technical; and

(5) the conclusions of EP or EO Technical.

The conclusions give direct answers, whenever possible, to the specific issues raised by the EP or EO Examinations office or the EP or EO Determinations office or the appeals office. However, EP or EO Technical is not bound by the precise statement of the issues as submitted by the taxpayer or by the EP or EO Examinations office or the EP or EO Determinations office or the appeals office and may reframe the issues to be answered in the TAM. The discussion in the TAM of the issues will be in sufficient detail so that the EP or EO Examinations or EP or EO Determinations or appeals officials will understand the reasoning underlying the conclusion.

Accompanying a TAM subject to § 6110, is a notice under § 6110(f)(1) of intention to disclose the TAM (including a copy of the version proposed to be open to public inspection and notations of third party communications under § 6110(d)).

Routes replies to appropriate office

.14 Replies to requests for TAMs from EO Examinations Area managers and EO Determinations managers are addressed to:

Internal Revenue Service
Attn: EO Mandatory Review
MC 4920 DAL
1100 Commerce Street
Dallas, TX 75242

The EO Mandatory Review Staff will ensure that copies are forwarded to the EO Examinations Area manager or the EO Determinations manager.

Replies to requests for TAMs from EP Examinations Area managers as well as replies to all requests for TAMs from other Operating Divisions of the Service involved in an examination where EP Technical does not have audit jurisdiction but has interpretive jurisdiction as enumerated in section 6.02 of Rev. Proc. 2007–4, are addressed to:

Internal Revenue Service
Attn: EP Special Review – Room 1550
SE:T:EP:E:PR:SR:Technical Advice Coordinator
P. O. Box 13163
Baltimore, MD 21203

The EP Special Review Staff will ensure that copies are forwarded to the applicable manager.

Replies to requests for TAMs from EP Determinations managers, are addressed to:

Internal Revenue Service
Attn: EP Determinations Quality Assurance
P.O. Box 2508
Cincinnati, OH 45201

Replies to requests for TAMs from the Appeals Area Director, Area 4, are routed to the appropriate appeals office through Technical Services, C:AP.

SECTION 17. HOW DOES AN EP OR EO EXAMINATIONS OR EP OR EO DETERMINATIONS OR AN APPEALS OFFICE USE THE TAMs?

Generally applies advice in processing the taxpayer's case

.01 The EP or EO Examinations Area manager or the EP or EO Determinations manager or the Appeals Area Director, Area 4, must process the taxpayer's case on the basis of the conclusions in the TAM unless—

(1) the EP or EO Examinations Area manager or the EP or EO Determinations manager or the Appeals Area Director, Area 4, decides that the conclusions reached by EP or EO Technical in a TAM should be reconsidered (the reconsideration process may include a conference held with the EP or EO specialist or appeals office that requested the TAM and the tax law specialist or actuary who drafted the TAM), or

(2) the Appeals Area Director, Area 4, in the case of a TAM unfavorable to the taxpayer, decides to settle the issue in the usual manner under existing authority.

Subject to a request for reconsideration of the conclusions in a TAM, EP or EO Examinations or EP or EO Determinations must follow the conclusions in a TAM as to all issues and the Appeals Area Director, Area 4, must follow the conclusions in a TAM on issues of an organization's/plan's status or qualification. Thus, if the TAM received by EP or EO Examinations or EP or EO Determinations concerns an organization's/plan's status or qualification, the organization/plan has no appeal to the appeals office on those specific issues.

Reconsideration

.02 The EP or EO Examinations office or the EP or EO Determinations office or the Appeals Area Director, Area 4, has 30 calendar days after receipt of a TAM to either formally request reconsideration or give the adopted TAM to the taxpayer. Requests for TAM reconsideration must describe with specificity the errors in the TAM analysis and conclusions. Requests for reconsideration should not reargue points raised in the initial request, but should instead focus on points that the TAM overlooked or misconstrued in the arguments by the EP or EO Examinations office or the EP or EO Determinations office or the Appeals Area Director, Area 4, in support of their request. The Headquarters office may request further submissions from the field or the taxpayer, but the parties should make no additional submissions in the absence of such a request.

If the field does not request reconsideration of a TAM, the TAM will take effect when the field provides a copy of the adopted TAM to the taxpayer, or at the end of the 30-day period following the issuance of the TAM to the field.

Discussion with the taxpayer

.03 EP or EO Technical will not discuss the contents of the TAM with the taxpayer or the taxpayer's representative until the taxpayer has been given a copy by the EP or EO Examinations office or the EP or EO Determinations office or the appeals office.

Gives copy to the taxpayer

.04 The EP or EO Examinations office or the EP or EO Determinations office or the Appeals Area Director, Area 4, only after adopting the TAM, gives the taxpayer (1) a copy of the TAM described in section 16.13, and (2) the notice under § 6110(f)(1) of intention to disclose the TAM (including a copy of the version proposed to be open to public inspection and notations of third party communications under § 6110(d)).

This requirement does not apply to a TAM involving a criminal or civil fraud investigation, or a jeopardy or termination assessment, as described in section 11.07 of this revenue procedure, or documents to which § 6104 (document open to public inspection) applies as described in section 10.03.

Taxpayer may protest deletions not made

.05 After receiving the notice under § 6110(f)(1) of intention to disclose the TAM, the taxpayer may protest the disclosure of certain information in it. The taxpayer must submit a written statement within 20 calendar days identifying those deletions not made by the Service that the taxpayer believes should have been made. The taxpayer must also submit a copy of the version of the TAM proposed to be open to public inspection with brackets around deletions proposed by the taxpayer that have not been made by EP or EO Technical.

Generally, EP or EO Technical considers only the deletion of material that the taxpayer has proposed be deleted or other deletions as required under § 6110(c) before the EP or EO Technical reply is sent to the EP or EO Examinations office or the EP or EO Determinations office or the Appeals Area Director, Area 4. Within 20 calendar days after it receives the taxpayer's response to the notice under § 6110(f)(1), EP or EO Technical must mail the taxpayer its final administrative conclusion about the deletions to be made.

When no copy is given to the taxpayer

.06 If EP or EO Technical tells the EP or EO Examinations office or the EP or EO Determinations office or the Appeals Area Director, Area 4, that a copy of the TAM should not be given to the taxpayer and the taxpayer requests a copy, the EP or EO Examinations office or the EP or EO Determinations office or the Appeals Area Director, Area 4, will tell the taxpayer that no copy will be given.

SECTION 18. WHAT IS THE EFFECT OF A TAM?

Applies only to the taxpayer for whom TAM was requested

.01 A taxpayer may not rely on a TAM issued by the Service for another taxpayer.

Usually applies retroactively

.02 Except when stated otherwise, a holding in a TAM is applied retroactively, unless the Commissioner, Tax Exempt and Government Entities Division exercises discretionary authority under § 7805(b) to limit the retroactive effect of the holding. Section 18.06 below lists the criteria necessary for granting § 7805(b) relief, and section 18 of this revenue procedure describes the effect of § 7805(b) relief.

Generally applied retroactively to modify or revoke prior TAM

.03 A holding that modifies or revokes a holding in a prior TAM is applied retroactively, with one exception. If the new holding is less favorable to the taxpayer than the earlier one, it generally is not applied to the period when the taxpayer relied on the prior holding in situations involving continuing transactions.

Applies to continuing action or series of actions until specifically withdrawn, modified or revoked

.04 If a TAM relates to a continuing action or a series of actions, ordinarily it is applied until specifically withdrawn or until the conclusion is modified or revoked by enactment of legislation, ratification of a tax treaty, a decision of the United States Supreme Court, or the issuance of regulations (temporary or final), a revenue ruling, or other statement published in the Internal Revenue Bulletin. Publication of a notice of proposed rulemaking does not affect the application of a TAM.

Applies to continuing action or series of actions until material facts change

.05 A taxpayer is not protected against retroactive modification or revocation of a TAM involving a continuing action or a series of actions occurring after the material facts on which the TAM is based have changed.

Does not apply retroactively under certain conditions

.06 Generally, a TAM that modifies or revokes a letter ruling or another TAM or a determination letter is not applied retroactively either to the taxpayer to whom or for whom the letter ruling or TAM or determination letter was originally issued, or to a taxpayer whose tax liability was directly involved in such letter ruling or TAM or determination letter if —

(1) there has been no misstatement or omission of material facts;

(2) the facts at the time of the transaction are not materially different from the facts on which the letter ruling or TAM or determination letter was based;

(3) there has been no change in the applicable law;

(4) in the case of a letter ruling, it was originally issued on a prospective or proposed transaction; and

(5) the taxpayer directly involved in the letter ruling or TAM or determination letter acted in good faith in relying on the letter ruling or TAM or determination letter, and the retroactive modification or revocation would be to the taxpayer's detriment. For example, the tax liability of each employee covered by a letter ruling or TAM or determination letter relating to a pension plan of an employer is directly involved in the letter ruling or TAM or determination letter. However, the tax liability of members of an industry is not directly involved in a letter ruling or TAM or determination letter issued to one of the members, and the holding in a modification or revocation of a letter ruling or TAM or determination letter to one member of an industry may be retroactively applied to other members of the industry. By the same reasoning, a tax practitioner may not obtain the nonretroactive application to one client of a modification or revocation of a letter ruling or TAM or determination letter previously issued to another client.

When a letter ruling or determination letter to a taxpayer or a TAM involving a taxpayer is modified or revoked with retroactive effect, the notice to the taxpayer, except in fraud cases, sets forth the grounds on which the modification or revocation is being made and the reason why the modification or revocation is being applied retroactively.

In order for a TAM that modifies or revokes a letter ruling or another TAM or a determination letter not to be applied retroactively either to the taxpayer to whom or for whom the letter ruling, TAM or determination letter was originally issued, or to a taxpayer whose tax liability was directly involved in such letter ruling, TAM or determination letter, such taxpayer generally must request relief under § 7805(b) in the manner described in section 19 below.

SECTION 19. HOW MAY RETROACTIVE EFFECT BE LIMITED?

Commissioner has discretionary authority under § 7805(b)

.01 Under § 7805(b) the Commissioner or the Commissioner's delegate has the discretion to prescribe the extent, if any, to which a TAM will be applied without retroactive effect.

Taxpayer may request Commissioner to exercise authority

.02 A taxpayer who has received a TAM or for whom a TAM request is pending may request that the Commissioner, Tax Exempt and Government Entities Division, the Commissioner of Internal Revenue's delegate, exercise the discretionary authority under § 7805(b) to limit the retroactive effect of any holding stated in the TAM, which may still be pending, which must have been issued, or to limit the retroactive effect of any subsequent modification or revocation of a TAM.

Form of request to limit retroactivity—before an examination

.03 When a TAM that concerns a continuing transaction is modified or revoked by, for example, a subsequent revenue ruling or final regulations, a request to limit the retroactive effect of the modification or revocation of the TAM must be made in the form of a request for a letter ruling if submitted before examination of the return that contains the transaction that is the subject of the request for the letter ruling. *See* Rev. Proc. 2007–4.

Form of request to limit retroactivity—during course of an examination

.04 When, during the course of an examination of a taxpayer's return by EP or EO Examinations or consideration by the Appeals Area Director, Area 4, a taxpayer is informed that EP or EO Examinations or the Appeals Area Director, Area 4, recommends that a TAM be modified or revoked, a request to limit the retroactive application of the modification or revocation of the TAM must itself be made in the form of a request for a TAM. *See* sections 7, 8 and 10 of this revenue procedure and sections 19.07 and 19.08 below.

The taxpayer must also submit a statement that the request is being made pursuant to § 7805(b). This statement must also indicate the relief requested and give the reasons and arguments in support of the relief requested. It must also be accompanied by any documents bearing on the request. The explanation should discuss the five items listed in section 18.06 of this revenue procedure as they relate to the taxpayer's situation.

The taxpayer's request, including the statement that the request is being made pursuant to § 7805(b), must be forwarded by EP or EO Examinations or the Appeals Area Director, Area 4, to EP or EO Technical for consideration.

Form of request to limit retroactivity—technical advice that does not modify or revoke prior memorandum

.05 A request to limit the retroactive effect of a holding in a TAM that does not modify or revoke a TAM may be made as part of that TAM request, either initially, or at any time before the TAM is issued by EP or EO Technical. In such a case, the taxpayer must also submit a statement in support of the application of § 7805(b), as described in section 19.04 above.

Taxpayer's right to a conference

.06 When a request for a TAM concerns only the application of § 7805(b), the taxpayer has the right to a conference in EP or EO Technical in accordance with the provisions of section 14 of this revenue procedure.

If the request for application of § 7805(b) is included in the request for a TAM on the substantive issues or is made before the conference of right on the substantive issues, the § 7805(b) issues will be discussed at the taxpayer's one conference of right.

If the request for the application of § 7805(b) is made as part of a pending TAM request after a conference has been held on the substantive issues, and the Service determines that there is justification for having delayed the request, then the taxpayer will have the right to one conference of right concerning the application of § 7805(b), with the conference limited to discussion of this issue.

Exhaustion of administrative remedies — employee plans determination letter requests

.07 Where the applicant has requested EP Determinations to seek a TAM on the applicability of § 7805(b) relief to a qualification issue under § 401(a) pursuant to a determination letter request, the applicant's administrative remedies will not be considered exhausted until EP Technical has a reasonable time to act on the request for a TAM. (*See* section ***20*** of Rev. Proc. 2007–6.)

Exhaustion of administrative remedies — exempt organization matters

.08 Where a TAM has been requested pursuant to an exempt organization's request for § 7805(b) relief from the retroactive application of an adverse determination within the meaning of § 7428(a)(1), the exempt organization's administrative remedies will not be considered exhausted, within the meaning of § 7428(b)(2), until EO Technical has a reasonable time to act on the request for a TAM.

SECTION 20. WHAT IS THE EFFECT OF THIS REVENUE PROCEDURE ON OTHER DOCUMENTS?

Rev. Proc. 2006–5 is superseded.

SECTION 21. EFFECTIVE DATE

This revenue procedure is effective January 2, 2007.

SECTION 22. PAPERWORK REDUCTION ACT

The collections of information contained in this revenue procedure have been reviewed and approved by the Office of Management and Budget in accordance with the Paperwork Reduction Act (44 U.S.C. § 3507) under control number 1545–1520.

An agency may not conduct or sponsor, and a person is not required to respond to, a collection of information unless the collection of information displays a valid OMB control number.

The collections of information in this revenue procedure are in sections 6.03, 9, 10.01, 10.05, 11.04, 11.05, 11.06, 12.02, 12.03, 13.01, 14.03, 14.10, 16.10, 16.12, 17.05, 19.03, 19.04, and 19.05. This information is required to evaluate and process the request for a TAM. In addition, this information will be used to help the Service delete certain information from the text of the TAM before it is made available for public inspection, as required by § 6110. The collections of information are required to obtain a TAM. The likely respondents are businesses or other for-profit institutions and not-for-profit institutions.

The estimated total annual reporting and/or recordkeeping burden is 1,950 hours.

The estimated annual burden per respondent/recordkeeper varies from 4 hours to 60 hours, depending on individual circumstances, with an estimated average of 19.5 hours. The estimated number of respondents and/or recordkeepers is 100.

The estimated annual frequency of responses is one request per applicant.

Books or records relating to a collection of information must be retained as long as their contents may become material in the administration of any internal revenue law. Generally, tax returns and tax return information are confidential, as required by § 6103.

DRAFTING INFORMATION

The principal author of this revenue procedure is Michael Rubin of the Employee Plans, Tax Exempt and Government Entities Division. For further information regarding how this revenue procedure applies to employee plans matters, please contact the Employee Plans Customer Assistance Service at 877–829–5500 (a toll-free number) between the hours of 8:30 am and 4:30 pm Eastern time, Monday through Friday. In the alternative, please contact Mr. Rubin at (202) 283–9888 (not a toll-free number). For exempt organizations matters, please contact Mr. Theodore Lieber at (202) 283–8999 or Mr. Wayne Hardesty at (202) 283–8976 (not toll-free numbers).

INDEX

References are to sections in Rev. Proc. 2007–5

INDEX

References are to sections in Rev. Proc. 2007–5

Rev. Proc. 2007–6

TABLE OF CONTENTS

SECTION 1. WHAT IS THE PURPOSE OF THIS REVENUE PROCEDURE?

Purpose of revenue procedure

.01 This revenue procedure sets forth the procedures of the various offices of the Internal Revenue Service for issuing determination letters on the qualified status of pension, profit-sharing, stock bonus, annuity, and employee stock ownership plans (ESOPs) under §§ 401, 403(a), 409 and 4975(e)(7) of the Internal Revenue Code of 1986, and the status for exemption of any related trusts or custodial accounts under § 501(a). Also see Rev. Proc. 2005–66, 2005–2 C.B. 509, which contains a description of the determination letter program, including when to submit a request for a determination letter within the 5-year and 6-year staggered remedial amendment cycles, that apply to individually designed and pre-approved plans.

Organization of revenue procedure

.02 Part I of this revenue procedure contains instructions for requesting determination letters for various types of plans and transactions. Part II contains procedures for providing notice to interested parties and for interested parties to comment on determination letter requests. Part III contains procedures concerning the processing of determination letter requests and describes the effect of a determination letter.

SECTION 2. WHAT CHANGES HAVE BEEN MADE TO THIS PROCEDURE?

In general

.01 This revenue procedure is a general update of Rev. Proc. 2006–6, 2006–1 I.R.B 204, which contains the Service's general procedures for employee plans determination letter requests.

Other changes

.02 In addition to minor revisions, such as updating references, the following changes have been made:

(1) Section 2.03 is revised to reference the 2006 Cumulative List, Notice 2007–3, 2007–2 I.R.B. (January 8, 2007).

(2) Section 3.03 is revised to reference the first submission period for Cycle B individually designed plans and multiple employer plans.

(3) Section 6.04 is revised to include Employee Plans Compliance Resolution System documentation when requesting a determination letter.

(4) Section 6.19 is revised to change the pre-notification contact for authorized representatives submitting determination applications for 30 or more on-cycle plans.

(5) Section 7.02 is revised to reference the first submission period for Cycle B individually designed plans and multiple employer plans.

(6) Section 7.03 is revised to clarify the language regarding the inclusion of copies of plan amendments with determination letter applications.

(7) Section 7.04 is revised to add language from section 15.04 of Rev. Proc. 2005–66 regarding plan restatements.

(8) Section 12.01 is revised to include Form 8905, *Certification of Intent To Adopt a Pre-Approved Plan*.

(9) Section 12.07 is added to include that a plan that terminates prior to the end of an on-cyle submission period does not have to be restated.

Other guidance

.03 Other guidance affecting this revenue procedure:

Rev. Proc. 2005–16, 2005–1 C.B. 674, describes the procedures for the "pre-approval" of plans under the master and prototype (M&P) program and the volume submitter (VS) program. Rev. Proc. 2005–66, 2005–2 C.B. 509, describes a new system of remedial amendment cycles that applies to pre-approved plans and individually designed plans, and the deadlines to submit applications for opinion, advisory and determination letters. The Service issues a Cumulative List every year identifying changes affecting plan qualification requirements to be used by plans whose remedial amendment cycle begins in the month of February following the publication of the Cumulative List. The 2004 Cumulative List is contained in Notice 2004–84, 2004–2 C.B. 1030, the 2005 Cumulative List is contained in Notice 2005–101, 2005–2 C.B. 1219, and the 2006 Cumulative List is contained in Notice 2007–3, 2007–2 I.R.B. (January 8, 2007).

PART I. PROCEDURES FOR DETERMINATION LETTER REQUESTS

SECTION 3. ON WHAT ISSUES MAY TAXPAYERS REQUEST WRITTEN GUIDANCE UNDER THIS PROCEDURE?

Types of requests

.01 Determination letters may be requested on completed and proposed transactions as set forth in the table below:

		TYPE OF REQUEST	FORMS	REV. PROC. SECTION
1.	**Initial Qualification, etc.**			
	a.	Individually-Designed Plans (including collectively bargained plans)	5300, Schedule Q (optional)	7
	b.	ESOPs	5300, 5309 Schedule Q (optional)	7
	c.	Adoptions of Master & Prototype Plans	5307, Schedule Q (optional)	9
	d.	Adoptions of Volume Submitter Planss	5307, Schedule Q (optional)	9
	e.	Multiple Employer Plans	5300, Schedule Q (optional)	10
	f.	Group Trusts	Cover letter	13
2.	**Minor Amendments**		6406	11
3.	**Termination**			
	a.	In general	5310, 6088 Schedule Q (optional)	12
	b.	Multiemployer plan covered by PBGC insurance	5300, 6088, Schedule Q (optional)	12
Note: Form 5310–A, *Notice of Plan Merger, Consolidation, Spinoff, or Transfer of Plan Assets or Liabilities; Notice of Qualified Separate Lines of Business*, generally must be filed not less than 30 days before the merger, consolidation or transfer of assets and liabilities. The filing of Form 5310–A will not result in the issuance of a determination letter.				
4.	**Special Procedures**			
	a.	Affiliated Service Group Status (§ 414(m)), Leased Employees (§ 414(n))	5300, Schedule Q (optional)	14
	b.	Minimum Funding Waiver	5300, Schedule Q (optional)	15
	c.	Section 401(h) Determination Letters	5300, Schedule Q (optional)	16
	d.	Section 420 Determination Letters Including Other Matters Under § 401(a)	5300, Schedule Q (optional), Cover letter, Checklist	16
	e.	Section 420 Determination Letters Excluding Other Matters Under § 401(a)	Cover letter, Checklist	16

Areas in which determination letters will not be issued

.02 Determination letters issued in accordance with this revenue procedure do not include determinations on the following issues within the jurisdiction of the Commissioner, TE/GE:

(1) Issues involving §§ 72, 79, 105, 125, 127, 129, 402, 403 (other than 403(a)), 404, 409(l), 409(m), 412, 457, 511 through 515, and 4975 (other than 4975(e)(7)), unless these determination letters are authorized under section 7 of Rev. Proc. 2007–4, page 118, this Bulletin.

(2) Plans or plan amendments for which automatic approval is granted pursuant to section 19.01 of Rev. Proc. 2005–16.

(3) Plan amendments described below (these amendments will, to the extent provided, be deemed not to alter the qualified status of a plan under § 401(a)).

(a) An amendment solely to permit a trust forming part of a plan to participate in a pooled fund arrangement described in Rev. Rul. 81–100, 1981–1 C.B. 326, as clarified and modified by Rev. Rul. 2004–67, 2004–2 C.B. 28;

(b) An amendment that merely adjusts the maximum limitations under § 415 to reflect annual cost-of-living increases under § 415(d), other than an amendment that adds an automatic cost-of-living adjustment provision to the plan; and

(c) An amendment solely to include language pursuant to § 403(c)(2) of Title I of the Employee Retirement Income Security Act of 1974 (ERISA) concerning the reversion of employer contributions made as a result of mistake of fact.

(4) This section applies to determination letter requests with respect to plans that combine an ESOP (as defined in § 4975(e)(7) of the Code) with retiree medical benefit features described in § 401(h) (HSOPs).

(a) In general, determination letters will not be issued with respect to plans that combine an ESOP with an HSOP with respect to:

(i) whether the requirements of § 4975(e)(7) are satisfied;

(ii) whether the requirements of § 401(h) are satisfied; or

(iii) whether the combination of an ESOP with an HSOP in a plan adversely affects its qualification under § 401(a).

(b) A plan is considered to combine an ESOP with an HSOP if it contains ESOP provisions and § 401(h) provisions.

(c) However, an arrangement will not be considered covered by section 3.02(4) of this revenue procedure if, under the provisions of the plan, the following conditions are satisfied:

(i) No individual accounts are maintained in the § 401(h) account (except as required by § 401(h)(6));

(ii) No employer securities are held in the § 401(h) account;

(iii) The § 401(h) account does not contain the proceeds (directly or otherwise) of an exempt loan as defined in § 54.4975–7(b)(1)(iii) of the Pension Excise Tax Regulations; and

(iv) The amount of actual contributions to provide § 401(h) benefits (when added to actual contributions for life insurance protection under the plan) does not exceed 25 percent of the sum of: (1) the amount of cash contributions actually allocated to participants' accounts in the plan and (2) the amount of cash contributions used to repay principal with respect to the exempt loan, both determined on an aggregate basis since the inception of the § 401(h) arrangement.

EGTRRA

.03 On February 1, 2007, the Service will begin to accept applications for determination letters for some individually designed plans (depending on their cycle)and multiple employer plans that take into account the qualification requirements of the Code as amended by EGTRRA, and other items identified on the 2006 Cumulative List in Notice 2007–3. This opening of the determination letter program for the initial remedial amendment cycle (*i.e.*, EGTRRA remedial amendment period) is for individually designed plans and multiple employer plans that fall within Cycle B, and the submission period for Cycle B plans ends on January 31, 2008. The cycles commence in different years for different plans within a staggered five-year period, so not all individually designed plans will have the same cycle or submission period. Further, the submission periods for pre-approved defined contribution and defined benefit plans are different than those that apply to individually designed plans. *See* Rev. Proc. 2005–16 and Rev. Proc. 2005–66 for details.

SECTION 4. ON WHAT ISSUES MUST WRITTEN GUIDANCE BE REQUESTED UNDER DIFFERENT PROCEDURES?

TE/GE

.01 Other procedures for obtaining rulings, determination letters, opinion letters, etc., on matters within the jurisdiction of the Commissioner, TE/GE are contained in the following revenue procedures:

(1) Employee Plans Technical (EP Technical) letter rulings, information letters, etc.: *See* Rev. Proc. 2007–4, page 118, this Bulletin.

(2) M&P and VS plans: *See* Notice 2001–42, 2001–2 C.B. 70, Notice 2001–57, 2001–2 C.B. 279, Rev. Proc. 2001–55, 2001–2 C.B. 552, Rev. Proc. 2002–29, 2002–1 C.B. 1176 (as modified by Rev. Proc. 2003–10, 2003–1 C.B. 259), Rev. Proc. 2002–73, 2002–2 C.B. 932, Rev. Proc. 2003–72, 2003–2 C.B. 578, Rev. Proc. 2004–25, 2004–1 C.B. 791, Notice 2004–84, 2004–2 C.B. 1030, Rev. Proc. 2005–16, and Rev. Proc. 2005–66.

(3) Technical advice requests: *See* Rev. Proc. 2007–5, page 161, this Bulletin.

Chief Counsel's revenue procedure

.02 For the procedures for obtaining letter rulings, determination letters, etc., on matters within the jurisdiction of the Division Counsel/Associate Chief Counsel (Tax Exempt and Government Entities), or within the jurisdiction of other offices of Chief Counsel, see Rev. Proc. 2007–1, page 1, this Bulletin.

SECTION 5. WHAT IS THE GENERAL SCOPE OF A DETERMINATION LETTER?

Scope of this section

.01 This section delineates, generally, the scope of an employee plan determination letter. It identifies certain qualification requirements, relating to nondiscrimination, that are considered by the Service in its review of a plan only at the election of the applicant. This section also identifies certain qualification requirements that are not considered by the Service in its review of a plan and with respect to which determination letters do not provide reliance. This section applies to all determination letters other than letters issued in response to an application filed on Form 6406, *Short Form Application for Determination for Minor Amendment of Employee Benefit Plan*, letters relating to the qualified status of group trusts; and certain letters relating solely to the requirements of § 420, regarding the transfer of assets in a defined benefit plan to a health benefit account described in § 401(h). For additional information pertaining to the scope of reliance on a determination letter, see sections 8, 9 and 21 of this revenue procedure, and section 19 of Rev. Proc. 2005–16.

Scope of determination letters

.02 In general, employee plans are reviewed by the Service for compliance with the form requirements (that is, those plan provisions that are required as a condition of qualification under § 401(a)). In addition, as described below, certain nondiscrimination requirements are considered if the applicant specifically requests that they be considered. For terminating plans, the requirements are those that apply as of the date of termination. See Rev. Proc. 2005–66 for further details on the scope of the Service's review of determination letter applications.

Nondiscrimination in amount requirement

.03 Unless the applicant elects otherwise, a plan will not be reviewed for, and a determination letter may not be relied on with respect to, whether a plan satisfies one of the safe harbors or the general test for nondiscrimination in amount of contributions or benefits requirements under § 1.401(a)(4)–1(b)(2) of the Income Tax Regulations.

Minimum coverage and § 401(a)(26) participation requirements

.04 Unless the applicant elects otherwise, a plan will not be reviewed for, and a determination letter may not be relied on with respect to, the minimum coverage requirements of § 410(b). If the applicant demonstrates that the plan satisfies the coverage requirements of § 410(b), the determination letter may also be relied on with respect to the participation requirements of § 401(a)(26).

Nondiscriminatory current availability requirement

.05 If the applicant demonstrates that the plan satisfies the coverage requirements of § 410(b), the determination letter may also be relied on as to whether the plan satisfies the nondiscriminatory current availability requirements of § 1.401(a)(4)–4(b) with respect to those benefits, rights, and features that are currently available (within the meaning of § 1.401(a)(4)–4(b)(2)) to all employees in the plan's coverage group. The plan's coverage group consists of those employees who are treated as currently benefiting under the plan (within the meaning of § 1.410(b)–3(a)) for purposes of demonstrating that the plan satisfies the minimum coverage requirements of § 410(b). Applications will not be reviewed as to, and determination letters may not be relied on with respect to, whether the plan satisfies the requirements of § 1.401(a)(4)–4(b) with respect to any benefit, right, or feature other than the ones described above, except those that are specified by the applicant and for which the applicant has provided information relevant to the determination.

Other nondiscrimination requirements

.06 An applicant may also ask that the review of its plan consider certain other nondiscrimination requirements which are described in Schedule Q (Form 5300), such as whether a definition of compensation satisfies § 414(s).

Reliance conditioned on retention of information

.07 A favorable determination letter may be relied on with respect to whether a plan satisfies a coverage or nondiscrimination requirement only if the application, demonstrations and other information submitted to the Service in support of a favorable determination is retained by the applicant.

Effective availability requirement

.08 In no event will any plan be reviewed to determine, and a determination letter may not be relied on with respect to, whether any benefit, right, or feature under the plan satisfies the effective availability requirement of § 1.401(a)(4)–4(c).

Other limits on scope of determination letter

.09 Determination letters may generally be relied on with respect to whether the timing of a plan amendment (or series of amendments) satisfies the nondiscrimination requirements of § 1.401(a)(4)–5(a) of the regulations, unless the plan amendment is part of a pattern of amendments that significantly discriminates in favor of highly compensated employees. A favorable determination letter does not provide reliance for purposes of § 404 and § 412 with respect to whether an interest rate (or any other actuarial assumption) is reasonable. Furthermore, a favorable determination letter will not constitute a determination with respect to the use of the substantiation guidelines contained in Rev. Proc. 93–42, 1993–2 C.B. 540, *e.g.*, a determination letter will not consider whether data submitted with an application is substantiation quality. Lastly, a favorable determination letter will not constitute a determination with respect to whether any requirements of § 414(r), relating to whether an employer is operating qualified separate lines of business, are satisfied. However, if an employer is relying on § 414(r) to satisfy the minimum coverage or § 401(a)(26) participation requirements, and the applicant so requests, a determination letter will take into account whether the plan satisfies the nondiscriminatory classification test of § 410(b)(5)(B). In this case, if the requirements of § 410(b) or § 401(a)(26) are to be applied on an employer-wide basis under the special rules for employer-wide plans, a determination letter will take into account whether the requirements of the applicable special rule set forth in § 1.414(r)–1(c)(2)(ii) or § 1.414(r)–1(c)(3)(ii) are met.

Publication 794

.10 Publication 794, *Favorable Determination Letter*, contains other information regarding the scope of a determination letter, including the requirement that all information submitted with the application be retained as a condition of reliance. In addition, the specific terms of each letter may further define its scope and the extent to which it may be relied upon.

SECTION 6. WHAT IS THE GENERAL PROCEDURE FOR REQUESTING DETERMINATION LETTERS?

Scope

.01 This section contains procedures that are generally applicable to all determination letter requests. Additional procedures for specific requests are contained in sections 7 through 16.

Qualified trusteed plans

.02 A trust created or organized in the United States and forming part of a pension, profit-sharing, stock bonus or annuity plan of an employer for the exclusive benefit of its employees or their beneficiaries that meets the requirements of § 401 is a qualified trust and is exempt from federal income tax under § 501(a) unless the exemption is denied under § 502, relating to feeder organizations, or § 503, relating to prohibited transactions, if, in the latter case, the plan is one described in § 503(a)(1)(B).

Qualified nontrusteed annuity plans

.03 A nontrusteed annuity plan that meets the applicable requirements of § 401 and other additional requirements as provided under § 403(a) and § 404(a)(2), (relating to deductions of employer contributions for the purchase of retirement annuities), qualifies for the special tax treatment under § 404(a)(2), and the other sections of the Code, if the additional provisions of such other sections are also met.

Complete information required

.04 An applicant requesting a determination letter must file the material required by this revenue procedure with the Employee Plans Determinations manager (EP Determinations) at the address in section 6.17. The filing of the application, when accompanied by all information and documents required by this revenue procedure, will generally serve to provide the Service with the information required to make the requested determination. However, in making the determination, the Service may require the submission of additional information. Information submitted to the Service in connection with an application for determination may be subject to public inspection to the extent provided by § 6104. The applicant should include Employee Plans Compliance Resolution System documentation, if any, (*e.g.*, closing agreement or compliance statement) with the determination letter application.

Complete copy of plan and trust instrument required

.05 Except in the case of applications involving master and prototype plans filed on Form 5307, minor amendments described in section 11, or determination letters for volume submitter plans under section 9.02(2)(d), a complete copy of the plan and trust instrument is required to be included with the determination letter application. The determination letter application must include a copy of the signed and dated timely good faith EGTRRA amendments and other plan amendments (even if these amendments are dated earlier than a previous determination letter issued with respect to the plan) to show that the conditions for eligibility for the EGTRRA remedial amendment period as set forth in Notice 2001–42 are satisfied. See sections 7.03 and 7.04 for what must be included with applications involving plan amendments that are not minor amendments.

Section 9 of Rev. Proc. 2007–4 applies

.06 Section 9 of Rev. Proc. 2007–4 is generally applicable to requests for determination letters under this revenue procedure.

Separate application for each single § 414(l) plan

.07 A separate application is required for each single plan within the meaning of § 414(l). This requirement does not pertain to applications regarding the qualified status of group trusts.

Coverage and nondiscrimination requirements

.08 An applicant may request that the plan be reviewed to determine that the ratio percentage test of § 410(b)(1) is satisfied or that the plan satisfies one of the design-based safe harbors under § 401(a)(4) by completing the appropriate elective lines on Form 5300 or Form 5307. Schedule Q (Form 5300) may be filed with the application, other than an application filed on Form 6406, to request consideration of the general test under § 401(a)(4), the average benefit test of § 410(b)(2), or any of the other requirements described on Schedule Q. The applicant must include with the application form the material and demonstrations called for in the instructions to Form 5300 or Form 5307, and, if applicable, Schedule Q.

Prior letters

.09 If the plan has received a favorable determination letter in the past, the application must include a copy of the latest determination letter, if available. If the letter is not available, an explanation must be included with the application, and the employer must include a copy of the prior plan or adoption agreement, including the opinion or advisory letter, if applicable.

User fees

.10 The appropriate user fee, if applicable, must be paid according to the procedures of Rev. Proc. 2007–8, page 230, this Bulletin. Form 8717, *User Fee for Employee Plan Determination Letter Request*, must accompany each determination letter request. If the criteria for the user fee exemption are met in accordance with Notice 2003–49, 2003–2 C.B. 294, the certification on Form 8717 must be signed. Stamped signatures are not acceptable.

Interested party notification and comment

.11 Before filing an application, the applicant requesting a determination letter must satisfy the requirements of section 3001(a) of ERISA, and § 7476(b)(2) of the Code and the regulations thereunder, which provide that an applicant requesting a determination letter on the qualified status of certain retirement plans must notify interested parties of such application. The general rules of the Service with respect to notifying interested parties of requests for determination letters relating to the qualification of plans involving §§ 401 and 403(a) are set out below in sections 17 and 18 of this revenue procedure.

Contrary authority must be distinguished

.12 If the application for determination involves an issue where contrary authorities exist, failure to disclose or distinguish such significant contrary authorities may result in requests for additional information, which will delay action on the application.

Employer/employee relationship

.13 The Service ordinarily does not make determinations regarding the existence of an employer-employee relationship as part of its determination on the qualification of a plan, but relies on the applicant's representations or assumptions, stated or implicit, regarding the existence of such a relationship. The Service will, however, make a determination regarding the existence of an employer-employee relationship when so requested by the applicant. In such cases, the application with respect to the qualification of the plan should be filed in accordance with the provisions of this revenue procedure, contain the information and documents in the instructions to the application, and be accompanied by a completed Form SS–8, *Determination of Worker Status for Purposes of Federal Employment Taxes and Income Tax Withholding*, and any information and copies of documents the organization deems appropriate to establish its status. The Service may, in addition, require further information that it considers necessary to determine the employment status of the individuals involved or the qualification of the plan. After the employer-employee relationships have been determined, EP Determinations may issue a determination letter as to the qualification of the plan.

Incomplete applications returned

.14 If an applicant requesting a determination letter does not comply with all the required provisions of this revenue procedure, EP Determinations, in its discretion, may return the application and point out to the applicant those provisions which have not been met. The failure to provide information required by an application, including any supplemental information required by the instructions for the application, may result in the application being returned to the applicant as incomplete. The request may also be returned pursuant to Rev. Proc. 2007–8 if the correct user fee is not attached. If such a request is returned to the applicant, the 270-day period described in § 7476(b)(3) will not begin to run until such time as the provisions of this section have been satisfied.

Effect of failure to disclose material fact

.15 The Service may determine, based on the application form, the extent of review of the plan document. A failure to disclose a material fact or misrepresentation of a material fact on the application may adversely affect the reliance that would otherwise be obtained through issuance by the Service of a favorable determination letter. Similarly, failure to accurately provide any of the information called for on any form required by this revenue procedure may result in no reliance.

Data requirements

.16 The applicant is responsible for the accuracy of any factual representations and conclusions contained in the application. In some circumstances, applicants may not be able to use precise data in preparing demonstrations or schedules that may be required to be submitted with the application. Therefore, the use of estimated data in these demonstrations and schedules is not prohibited. In addition, the data used may be for a prior plan year, provided the following conditions are satisfied: (1) the data is the most recent data available, (2) there is no misstatement or omission of material fact with respect to such prior year's data, (3) there has been no material change in the facts (including a change in the benefits provided under the plan and employee demographics) since such prior plan year, (4) the same data is used throughout the application, (5) the data is relevant to the operational effect of the plan provisions that are under review, and (6) the applicant clearly discloses that prior year's data is being submitted with the application. The use of estimated or prior year's data is not a misrepresentation of material fact. A determination letter that is based on estimated or prior year's data, however, may not be relied upon to the extent that such data does not satisfy the substantiation guidelines in Rev. Proc. 93–42. Regardless of whether the data is actual or estimated, or whether it is for the current or a prior year, data that is presented in a determination letter application must reflect any changes in the law that are considered by the Service in its determination of the plan's qualified status.

Where to file requests

.17 Requests for determination letters are to be addressed to EP Determinations at the following address:

Internal Revenue Service
P.O. Box 192
Covington, KY 41012–0192

Requests shipped by Express Mail or a delivery service should be sent to:

Internal Revenue Service
201 West Rivercenter Blvd.
Attn: Extracting Stop 312
Covington, KY 41011

Determination letter applications will not be accepted via fax.

Submission of related plans

.18 If applications for two or more plans of the same employer are submitted together, each application should include a cover letter that identifies the name of the employer and the plan numbers and employer identification numbers of all the related plans submitted together.

Submission of 30 or more on-cycle applications by authorized representative

.19 An authorized representative who will be submitting determination letter applications for 30 or more on-cycle plans at one time should pre-notify the Service of the submissions so that the Service can endeavor to ensure that the applications will be reviewed in one area. The pre-notification should be e-mailed to *David.J.Nelson@irs.gov* and should include the following information: the firm name, the names of the authorized representative(s) submitting the plans, the name and phone number of the contact person, the approximate number of submissions, and the expected date(s) of the submissions. Upon receipt of the e-mail, the representative will be contacted and assigned a number that must be entered in green ink at the upper left hand corner of the applications. For further discussion, see the Spring/Summer 2002 edition of the Employee Plans Newsletter available at *www.irs.gov*/retirement.

Withdrawal of requests

.20 The applicant's request for a determination letter may be withdrawn by a written request at any time prior to the issuance of a final adverse determination letter. If an appeal to a proposed adverse determination letter is filed, a request for a determination letter may be withdrawn at any time prior to the forwarding of the proposed adverse action to the Chief, Appeals Office. In the case of a withdrawal, the Service will not issue a determination of any type. A failure to issue a determination letter as a result of a withdrawal will not be considered a failure of the Secretary or his delegate to make a determination within the meaning of § 7476. However, the Service may consider the information submitted in connection with the withdrawn request in a subsequent examination. Generally, the user fee will not be refunded if the application is withdrawn.

Right to status conference

.21 An applicant for a determination letter has the right to a have a conference with the EP Determinations Manager concerning the status of the application if the application has been pending at least 270 days. The status conference may be by phone or in person, as mutually agreed upon. During the conference, any issues relevant to the processing of the application may be addressed, but the conference will not involve substantive discussion of technical issues. No tape, stenographic, or other verbatim recording of a status conference may be made by any party. Subsequent status conferences may also be requested if at least 90 days have passed since the last preceding status conference.

How to request status conference

.22 A request for a status conference with the EP Determinations Manager is to be made in writing and is to be sent to the specialist assigned to review the application or, if the applicant does not know who is reviewing the application, to the EP Determinations Manager at the address in section 6.17. If, pursuant to section 15, the application for a determination letter has been submitted to Employee Plans Technical (EP Technical) together with a request for a waiver of minimum funding, the request for a status conference should be sent to the address in section 15.03. In this case, the right to a status conference will be with the EP Technical Manager or designee.

SECTION 7. INITIAL QUALIFICATION, ETC.

Scope

.01 This section contains the procedures for requesting determination letters for individually-designed defined contribution and defined benefit plans including employee stock ownership plans in the following circumstances:

(1) Initial qualification.

(2) Amendment (other than minor amendments described in section 11 below for which Form 6406 is appropriate).

(3) Restatement of plan.

(4) Qualification of a plan in the event of a partial termination.

(5) Change in scope of determination letter. This means that the applicant has previously received a favorable determination letter for the plan and now wishes to modify the scope of the letter, for example, by requesting the Service to review the plan for certain nondiscrimination requirements that were not within the scope of the earlier letter.

(6) Other circumstances (excluding plan termination) such as a change in the demographics of the employer or a change in the method of testing the plan that was used in a demonstration submitted in support of an earlier application.

Forms

.02 A determination letter request for the items listed in section 7.01 is made by filing the appropriate form according to the instructions to the form and any prevailing revenue procedures, notices, and announcements. In addition, all determination letter submissions must be submitted timely under the procedures set forth in Rev. Proc. 2005–66. The timing of the submission period for any particular individually designed plan within staggered remedial amendment cycles will depend on the plan's particular cycle. The first submission period for Cycle B individually designed plans and multiple employer plans will begin February 1, 2007 and will end on January 31, 2008. *See* Rev. Proc. 2005–66 for details.

(1) Form 5300, *Application for Determination for Employee Benefit Plan*, must be filed to request a determination letter for individually designed plans, including collectively bargained plans.

(2) Form 5309, *Application for Determination of Employee Stock Ownership Plan*, must be filed as an attachment with a Form 5300, in order to request a determination whether the plan is an ESOP under § 409 or § 4975(e)(7).

(3) Schedule Q, (Form 5300), *Elective Determination Requests*, may be filed as an attachment with Form 5300.

Application must include copy of plan and amendments

.03 Because a plan amendment, other than a minor amendment described in section 11, may affect other portions of a plan so as to cause plan disqualification, a determination letter issued on such an amendment to a plan will express an opinion on the entire plan, as amended. Therefore, the determination letter application must include a copy of the plan and trust instrument plus all plan amendments made to the date of the application. The application must also include a statement explaining how any amendments made since the last determination letter affect the plan or any other plan maintained by the employer. In addition, the applicant must send the Service any amendments that are adopted and/or proposed after the date of the determination letter application and before the Service issues the determination letter. The applicant must submit a cover letter that references the date that the pending application was submitted, the identity of the employer and the plan, and any other helpful identifying information. The amendments must be attached to the letter. Send the cover letter and the attachments to: Internal Revenue Service, TE/GE Correspondence Unit, P.O. Box 2508, Room 4024, Cincinnati, Ohio 45201. Although all such amendments must be provided to the Service, it is possible that the determination letter may not provide reliance for all of these amendments. *See* Rev. Proc. 2005–66 for the scope of the Service's review with respect to a particular determination letter application.

The Service will not consider amendments that predate a prior determination letter as part of a current determination letter application. Amendments that predate a prior determination letter are amendments that were adopted and/or proposed prior to the date a previous favorable determination letter was issued but that were not submitted as a part of that earlier determination letter application. If that amended language is part of the current restated plan document, that language may be considered in the current determination letter application, provided that Rev. Proc. 2005–66 is met regarding the scope of the Service's review. In any event, the new determination letter will not provide reliance for the period prior to the effective date of that new letter.

Restatements may be required

.04 In general, individually designed plans must be restated when they are submitted for determination letter applications for the initial remedial amendment cycle (that is, EGTRRA remedial amendment period) and subsequent remedial amendment cycles. For this purpose, submission of a working copy of the plan in a restated format will suffice.

A restated plan is required to be submitted if four or more amendments (excluding amendments making only non-substantive changes) have been made since the last restated plan was submitted. In addition, the Service may require restatement of a plan or submission of a working copy of the plan in a restated format when considered necessary. Where a working copy is submitted with executed amendments integrated into the working copy, all such amendments must also be separately submitted. For example, restatement may be required when there have been major changes in law. A restated plan or a working copy of the plan in a restated format must be submitted for a plan that has not previously received a determination letter that takes into account all requirements of EGTRRA.

Controlled groups, etc.

.05 For a controlled group of corporations as defined in § 414(b), trades or businesses under common control as defined in § 414(c), an affiliated service group within the meaning of § 414(m), and entities utilizing the services of leased employees within the meaning of § 414(n), the coverage items on the application forms referred to in this revenue procedure must be completed as though the controlled group, commonly controlled trades or businesses, affiliated service group, etc., constitutes a single entity. Leased employees within the meaning of § 414(n) must be included as employees of the recipient entity (except in the case of a safe-harbor plan described in § 414(n)(5)). See sections 9 through 11 of Rev. Proc. 2005–66 for a discussion of the five-year remedial amendment cycle that applies in certain special circumstances, including the cycle that applies to plans maintained by multiple members of a controlled group and to plans maintained by employers that are members of an affiliated service group under § 414(m).

SECTION 8. EMPLOYER RELIANCE ON M&P AND VOLUME SUBMITTER PLANS

Scope

.01 The conditions under which, and the extent to which, adopting employers of M&P and volume submitter plans may rely on favorable opinion or advisory letters without having to request individual determination letters are set forth in section 19 of Rev. Proc. 2005–16. Rev. Proc. 2005–16 describes the requirements that apply to M&P and volume submitter plans and the procedures for requesting opinion letters and advisory letters on M&P and volume submitter plans. Section 9 of this revenue procedure describes the procedures for requesting determination letters on M&P and volume submitter plans for adopting employers who need to obtain a determination letter in order to have reliance or who otherwise wish to obtain a determination letter, for example to expand the scope of reliance.

Reliance equivalent to determination letter

.02 If an employer can rely on a favorable opinion or advisory letter pursuant to section 19 of Rev. Proc. 2005–16, the opinion or advisory letter shall be equivalent to a favorable determination letter. For example, the favorable opinion or advisory letter shall be treated as a favorable determination letter for purposes of section 21 of this revenue procedure, regarding the effect of a determination letter, and section 5.01(4) of Rev. Proc. 2006–27, 2006–22 I.R.B. 945, regarding the definition of "favorable letter" for purposes of the Employee Plans Compliance Resolution System.

SECTION 9. DETERMINATION LETTER FILING PROCEDURES FOR M&P AND VOLUME SUBMITTER PLANS

Scope

.01 This section contains procedures for requesting determination letters for adopting employers of volume submitter plans and M&P plans.

Determination letter for adoption of volume submitter plan

.02 With respect to determination letters for adopting employers of volume submitter plans:

(1) A request for a determination letter for an employer's adoption of an approved volume submitter plan must be sent to the address provided in section 6.17.

(2) The request for a determination letter must include the following:

(a) Form 5307, *Application for Determination for Adopters of Master or Prototype or Volume Submitter Plans* (Schedule Q is optional);

(b) Form 2848, *Power of Attorney and Declaration of Representative*, or other written authorization allowing the volume submitter practitioner to act as a representative of the employer with respect to the request for a determination letter;

(c) A copy of the advisory letter for the practitioner's volume submitter specimen plan;

(d) A copy of the plan and trust instrument or, if the employer has made no changes to the specimen plan and trust other than completing options permitted under the adoption agreement, a copy of the completed adoption agreement;

(e) A written representation made by the volume submitter practitioner which:

(i) states whether the plan and trust instrument are word-for-word identical to the approved specimen plan;

(ii) if the plan and trust are not word-for-word identical to the approved specimen plan, explains how the plan and trust instrument differ from the approved specimen plan, describing the location, nature and effect of each deviation from the language of the approved specimen plan; and

(iii) if the latest advisory letter for the approved specimen plan does not consider all the changes made by GUST, states that the plan satisfies all requirements of GUST, including those first effective in plan years beginning after December 31, 1998, and identifies those deviations from the language of the approved specimen plan that are intended to satisfy specific GUST requirements;

(f) A copy of the plan's latest favorable determination letter, if applicable; and

(g) Any other information or material that may be required by the Service.

(3) Deviations from the language of the approved specimen plan will be evaluated based on the extent and complexities of the changes. If the changes are determined not to be compatible with the volume submitter program, the Service may require the applicant to file Form 5300 and pay the higher user fee.

(4) An employer will not be treated as having adopted a volume submitter plan if the employer has signed or otherwise adopted the plan prior to the date on the volume submitter specimen plan's advisory letter. In this case, the determination letter application for the employer's plan may not be filed on Form 5307 and will not be eligible for a reduced user fee. A determination letter application for a volume submitter plan must be based on the approved volume submitter specimen plan with any applicable modifications.

(5) In addition, the practitioner will be able to file determination letter requests on behalf of employers adopting substantially similar plans who need a determination letter to have reliance or who otherwise desire a determination letter.

Determination letter for adoption of M&P plan

.03 Form 5307 must be filed to request a determination letter for the adoption of an M&P plan by an adopting employer. Schedule Q may be filed as an attachment to Form 5307.

Required information

.04 The determination letter request must include the following:

(1) An adoption agreement showing which elections the employer is making with respect to the elective provisions contained in the plan;

(2) A copy of the plan's most recent opinion letter; and

(3) In the case of a determination letter request for an M&P plan that uses a separate trust or custodial account, a copy of the employer's trust or custodial account document.

Amended plan is treated as an individually-designed plan

.05 Except to the extent provided in section 5.02 and 19.03 of Rev. Proc. 2005–16, an employer that amends any provision of an M&P plan or its adoption agreement (other than to choose among the options offered by the sponsor if the plan permits or contemplates such options), or an employer that chooses to discontinue participation in such a plan as amended by its sponsor and does not substitute another approved plan referred to in this section is considered to have adopted an individually-designed plan. The requirements stated in this revenue procedure relating to the issuance of determination letters for individually-designed plans will then apply to such plan. Also see section 19.01 of Rev. Proc. 2005–66.

Requests made prior to the issuance of opinion letter

.06 An application submitted by an employer with respect to an M&P plan will be treated as an application for an individually-designed plan if it is executed prior to the time the M&P plan is approved. Also see sections 5.11 and 19.03 of Rev. Proc. 2005–16 regarding the requirement that adopting employers sign new adoption agreements when M&P plans are restated.

EGTRRA

.07 In accordance with Part IV of Rev. Proc. 2005–66, adopting employers of M&P plans and volume submitter plans have a six-year remedial amendment cycle. The Service's announced deadline for an adopting employer to adopt the approved M&P or volume submitter plan will be the end of the plan's remedial amendment cycle with respect to all disqualifying provisions for which the remedial amendment period would otherwise end during the cycle. An adopting employer of a M&P plan or a volume submitter plan who must obtain a determination letter for reliance under EGTRRA or who desires a determination letter for additional reliance under EGTRRA must not submit such determination letter application until the Service's announced deadline for employers to adopt a pre-approved plan and, if necessary, file a determination letter application, as described in Part IV of Rev. Proc. 2005–66. See section 17 of Rev. Proc. 2005–66 for the eligibility requirements that must be satisfied in order to be considered an adopting employer of a M&P plan or a volume submitter plan and thus eligible for the six-year remedial amendment cycle.

SECTION 10. MULTIPLE EMPLOYER PLANS

Scope

.01 This section contains procedures for applications filed with respect to plans described in § 413(c). A plan is not described in § 413(c) if all the employers maintaining the plan are members of the same controlled group or affiliated service group under § 414(b), (c) or (m).

Option to file for the plan only or for both the plan and employers maintaining the plan

.02 A determination letter applicant for a multiple employer plan can request either (1) a letter for the plan in the name of the controlling member or (2) a letter for the plan and a letter for each employer maintaining the plan with respect to whom a separate Form 5300 is filed.

(1) An applicant requesting a letter for the plan submits one Form 5300 application for the plan in the name of the controlling member, omitting the optional minimum coverage questions and Schedule Q and either including or omitting the design-based safe harbor questions. The user fee for a single employer plan will apply. An employer maintaining a multiple employer plan can rely on a favorable determination letter issued for the plan without having to request its own determination letter except with respect to the requirements of §§ 401(a)(4), 401(a)(26), 401(l), 410(b) and 414(s), and, if the employer maintains or has ever maintained another plan, §§ 415 and 416.

(2) An applicant requesting a letter for the plan and an employer must submit the filing required in (1) above as well as a separate Form 5300 application, completed through line 8, and, if applicable, a completed adoption agreement, for each employer requesting a separate letter. Each employer may elect to respond to the Form 5300 questions regarding minimum coverage and design-based safe harbors and to file Schedule Q to request a determination on the average benefit test, the general test or any other nondiscrimination requirement addressed by the Schedule Q. The user fee for the application will be determined under the user fee schedules for multiple employer plans in section 6.07 of Rev. Proc. 2007–8, treating the entire application as a general test or average benefit test application if any employer requests a determination on either of these tests.

(3) Rules similar to the rules in section 19 of Rev. Proc. 2005–16 also apply in the case of an employer maintaining a multiple employer plan. See also Rev. Proc. 2005–66, including section 10.

Where to file

.03 The complete application, including all Forms 5300 (and, if applicable, adoption agreements) for employers maintaining the plan who request separate letters must be filed as one package submission with EP Determinations. The application is to be sent to the address in section 6.17.

Determination letter sent to each employer who files Form 5300

.04 The Service will mail a determination letter to each employer maintaining the plan for whom a separate Form 5300 has been filed.

Addition of employers

.05 An employer may continue to rely on a favorable determination letter after another employer commences participation in the plan, regardless of whether the first employer's reliance is based on its own letter or the letter issued for the plan and regardless of whether an application for a determination letter for the new employer is filed. An application for a determination letter that takes into account the addition of such other employer should include a completed Form 5300 for the plan in the name of the controlling member on the Form 5300 filed pursuant to section 10.02 above, and a supplemental Form 5300 and optional Schedule Q (and, if applicable, adoption agreement) for each new employer who desires a separate determination letter. The Service will send the determination letter only to the applicant and the new employers. However, a new employer that joins a multiple employer plan after the existing multiple employer plan was timely submitted in Cycle B (the applicable cycle as described in section 10 of Rev. Proc. 2005–66), will be subject to the rules under Rev. Proc. 2005–66, including the off-cycle filing rules under section 14 of that revenue procedure.

SECTION 11. MINOR AMENDMENT OF PREVIOUSLY APPROVED PLAN

Scope

.01 This section contains procedures for requesting determination letters on the effect of a minor plan amendment.

Form 6406

.02 Form 6406, *Short Form Application for Determination for Minor Amendment of Employee Benefit Plan*, may be filed to request a determination letter on a minor plan amendment. This form may be used for minor amendments of individually-designed plans (including volume submitter plans, multiemployer plans and multiple employer plans) or permitted changes to adoption agreement elections in master or prototype plans, provided the changes constitute minor amendments. The Service may also designate other specific amendments that may be submitted using Form 6406.

Additional information

.03 All applications must be accompanied by a copy of the new amendments, a statement as to how the amendments affect or change the plan or any other plan maintained by the employer, and a copy of the latest determination letter. In the case of a master or prototype or volume submitter plan, a copy of the opinion or advisory letter should also be included. A copy of the plan or trust instrument should not be filed with the Form 6406.

Minor amendment procedures may not be used for complex amendments or EGTRRA letter

.04 Since determination letters issued on minor amendments express an opinion only as to whether the amendments, in and of themselves, affect the qualification of employee plans under § 401 or 403(a), the minor amendment procedures cannot be used for complex amendments that may affect other portions of the plan so as to cause plan disqualification. Thus, the minor amendment procedures may not be used for an amendment to add a § 401(k) or an ESOP provision to a plan, or to restate a plan. The minor amendment procedures also may not be used to obtain a determination letter on plan amendments involving plan mergers or consolidations, transfers of assets or liabilities, or plan terminations (including partial terminations). In addition, the minor amendment procedures may not be used for an amendment that involves a significant change to plan benefits or coverage. The minor amendment procedures may not be used to obtain a EGTRRA determination letter.

EP Determinations has discretion to determine whether use of minor amendment procedures is appropriate

.05 EP Determinations has discretion to determine whether a plan amendment may be submitted as a minor plan amendment and may request additional information, including the filing of a Form 5300 series application if it determines that the application and the attachments filed under the minor amendment procedures do not contain sufficient information, or that the Form 6406 is inappropriate. In addition, it is expected that this Form 6406 will be discontinued at a date to be announced by the Service in the future, due to its decreased utility under the new programs for pre-approved and individually designed plans, as described in Rev. Proc. 2005–16 and Rev. Proc. 2005–66.

SECTION 12. TERMINATION OR DISCONTINUANCE OF CONTRIBUTIONS; NOTICE OF MERGERS, CONSOLIDATIONS, ETC.

Scope

.01 This section contains procedures for requesting determination letters involving plan termination or discontinuance of contributions. This section also contains procedures regarding required notice of merger, consolidation, or transfer of assets or liabilities.

Forms

.02 Required forms.

(1) Form 5310, *Application for Determination for Terminating Plan*, is filed by plans other than multiemployer plans covered by the insurance program of the Pension Benefit Guaranty Corporation (PBGC).

(2) Form 5300, *Application for Determination of Employee Benefit Plan*, is filed in the case of a multiemployer plan covered by PBGC insurance.

(3) Schedule Q, *Elective Determination Requests*, may be filed as an attachment to Form 5310 or Form 5300.

(4) Form 6088, *Distributable Benefits From Employee Pension Benefit Plans*, is also required of a sponsor or plan administrator of a defined benefit plan or an underfunded defined contribution plan who files only an application for a determination letter regarding plan termination. For collectively bargained plans, a Form 6088 is required only if the plan benefits employees who are not collectively bargained employees within the meaning of § 1.410(b)–6(d). A separate Form 6088 is required for each employer employing such employees.

(5) Form 5310–A, *Notice of Plan Merger or Consolidation, Spinoff, or Transfer of Plan Assets or Liabilities — Notice of Qualified Separate Lines of Business*, if required, generally must be filed not later than 30 days before merger, consolidation or transfer of assets and liabilities. The filing of Form 5310–A will not result in the issuance of a determination letter.

(6) Form 8905, *Certification of Intent To Adopt a Pre-approved Plan*, filed before the end of the employer's 5-year remedial cycle as determined under Part III of Rev. Proc. 2005–66.

Supplemental information

.03 The application for a determination letter involving plan termination must also include any supplemental information or schedules required by the forms or form instructions. For example, the application must include copies of all records of actions taken to terminate the plan (such as a resolution of the board of directors) and a schedule providing certain information regarding employees who separated from vesting service with less than 100% vesting.

Required demonstration of nondiscrimination requirements

.04 An applicant requesting a determination letter upon termination may not decline to elect that the plan be reviewed for the minimum coverage requirements or the nondiscrimination in amount requirement, as otherwise permitted, unless the following conditions are satisfied:

(1) With respect to the coverage requirements, in the year of termination the plan must use the average benefit test and the plan must have received a prior favorable determination letter that considered whether the plan satisfied the requirements of the test;

(2) With respect to the nondiscrimination in amount requirement, in the year of termination the plan must use either a nondesign-based safe harbor or the general test for nondiscrimination in amount and the plan must have received a prior favorable determination letter that considered whether the plan satisfied the requirements of either a nondesign-based safe harbor or the general test;

(3) The favorable determination letter was issued during the immediately preceding three plan years; and

(4) There has been no material change in the facts (including benefits provided under the plan and employee demographics) or law upon which the determination was based.

If these conditions are satisfied, but the prior determination letter does not state that the average benefit test, general test or nondesign-based safe harbor (as applicable) was considered, the applicant must include a copy of the prior submission in order to decline to have the test or safe harbor considered in the review of the application for determination on plan termination.

Compliance with Title IV of ERISA

.05 In the case of plans subject to Title IV of ERISA, a favorable determination letter issued in connection with a plan's termination is conditioned on approval that the termination is a valid termination under Title IV of ERISA. Notification by PBGC that a plan may not be terminated will be treated as a material change of fact.

Termination prior to time for amending for change in law

.06 A plan that terminates after the effective date of a change in law, but prior to the date that amendments are otherwise required, must be amended to comply with the applicable provisions of law from the date on which such provisions become effective with respect to the plan. Because such a terminated plan would no longer be in existence by the required amendment date and therefore could not be amended on that date, such plan must be amended in connection with the plan termination to comply with those provisions of law that become effective with respect to the plan on or before the date of plan termination. (Such amendments include any amendments made after the date of plan termination that were required in order to obtain a favorable determination letter.) In addition, annuity contracts distributed from such terminated plans also must meet all the applicable provisions of any change in law. See also section 8 of Rev. Proc. 2005–66.

Termination prior to end of the on-cycle submission period

.07 A plan that terminates prior to the end of the on-cycle submission period does not have to be restated. However, see .06 above.

SECTION 13. GROUP TRUSTS

Scope

.01 This section provides special procedures for requesting a determination letter on the qualified status of a group trust under Rev. Rul. 81–100, as clarified and modified by Rev. Rul 2004–67.

Required information

.02 A request for a determination letter on the status of a group trust as described in Rev. Rul. 81–100 is made by submitting a written request demonstrating how the group trust satisfies the five criteria listed in Rev. Rul. 81–100, together with the trust instrument and related documents. Rev. Rul. 2004–67 extends the ability to participate in group trusts to eligible governmental plans under § 457(b) and clarifies the ability of certain individual retirement accounts under § 408 to participate. The revenue ruling provides model language, one for group trusts that have received favorable determination letters and the other for trusts that have received letter rulings.

SECTION 14. AFFILIATED SERVICE GROUPS; LEASED EMPLOYEES

Scope

.01 This section provides procedures for determination letter requests on affiliated service group status under § 414(m), and the effect of leased employees on a plan's qualified status.

Types of requests under § 414(m) and § 414(n)

.02 In accordance with section 7.01, an employer that is subject to § 414(m) or (n) may request a determination letter under the following circumstances: (1) with respect to the initial qualification of its plan, (2) on a plan amendment, and (3) in certain circumstances, even though the plan has not been amended (for example, where there has been a change in membership in the affiliated service group or where the employer did not previously have reliance).

Employer must request the determination under § 414(m) or § 414(n)

.03 Generally, a determination letter will cover § 414(m) or § 414(n) only if the employer requests such determination, and submits with the determination letter application the information specified in section 14.09 or section 14.10 below.

Forms

.04 Form 5300 (with Schedule Q optional) is submitted for a request on affiliated service group status or leased employee status. Form 5307 cannot be used for this purpose.

Employer is responsible for determining status under § 414(m) and § 414(n)

.05 An employer is responsible for determining at any particular time whether it is a member of an affiliated service group and, if so, whether its plan(s) continues to meet the requirements of § 401(a) after the effective date of § 414(m), including § 414(m)(5). An employer or plan administrator is also responsible for taking action relative to the employer's qualified plan if that employer becomes, or ceases to be, a member of an affiliated service group. An employer that is the recipient of services of leased employees within the meaning of § 414(n) is also responsible for determining at any particular time whether a leased employee is deemed to be an employee of the recipient for qualified plan purposes.

Omission of material fact

.06 Failure to properly indicate that there is or may be an affiliated service group and to provide the information specified in section 14.09 of this revenue procedure, or failure to properly indicate that an employer is utilizing the services of leased employees and to provide the information specified in section 14.10, is an omission of a material fact. The failure of the employer to follow the procedures in this section will result in the employer being unable to rely on any favorable determination letter concerning the effect of § 414(m) or § 414(n) on the qualified status of the plan.

Service will indicate whether § 414(m) or § 414(n) was considered

.07 If the Service considers whether the plan of an employer satisfies the requirements of § 414(m) or § 414(n), the determination letter issued to the employer will state that questions arising under § 414(m) or § 414(n) have been considered, and that the plan satisfies qualification requirements relating to that section. Absent such a statement pertaining to § 414(m) or § 414(n), a determination letter does not apply to any qualification issue arising by reason of such provisions.

M&P plans

.08 An employer that has adopted an M&P plan (including a standardized plan) and wants a determination as to the effect of § 414(m) or § 414(n) on the qualified status of its plan must attach the information required by section 14.09 or section 14.10 of this revenue procedure to Form 5300 and submit the information, Form 5300, and any other materials necessary to make a determination.

Required information for § 414(m) determination

.09 A determination letter issued with respect to a plan's qualification under § 401(a), 403(a), or 4975(e)(7) will be a determination as to the effect of § 414(m) upon the plan's qualified status only if the application includes:

(1) A description of the nature of the business of the employer, specifically whether it is a service organization or an organization whose principal business is the performance of management functions for another organization, including the reasons therefor;

(2) The identification of other members (or possible members) of the affiliated service group;

(3) A description of the business of each member (or possible member) of the affiliated service group, describing the type of organization (corporation, partnership, etc.) and indicating whether the member is a service organization or an organization whose principal business is the performance of management functions for the other group member(s);

(4) The ownership interests between the employer and the members (or possible members) of the affiliated service group (including ownership interests as described in § 414(m)(2)(B)(ii) or § 414(m)(6)(B));

(5) A description of services performed for the employer by the members (or possible members) of the affiliated service group, or vice versa (including the percentage of each member's (or possible member's) gross receipts and service receipts provided by such services, if available, and data as to whether such services are a significant portion of the member's business) and whether, as of December 13, 1980, it was not unusual for the services to be performed by employees of organizations in that service field in the United States;

(6) A description of how the employer and the members (or possible members) of the affiliated service group associate in performing services for other parties;

(7) In the case of a management organization under § 414(m)(5):

(a) A description of the management functions, if any, performed by the employer for the member(s) (or possible member(s)) of the affiliated service group, or received by the employer from any other members (or possible members) of the group (including data explaining whether the management functions are performed on a regular and continuous basis) and whether or not it is unusual for such management functions to be performed by employees of organizations in the employer's business field in the United States;

(b) If management functions are performed by the employer for the member (or possible members) of the affiliated service group, a description of what part of the employer's business constitutes the performance of management functions for the member (or possible member) of the group (including the percentage of gross receipts derived from management activities as compared to the gross receipts from other activities);

(8) A brief description of any other plan(s) maintained by the members (or possible members) of the affiliated service group, if such other plan(s) is designated as a unit for qualification purposes with the plan for which a determination letter has been requested;

(9) A description of how the plan(s) satisfies the coverage requirements of § 410(b) if the members (or possible members) of the affiliated service group are considered part of an affiliated service group with the employer;

(10) A copy of any ruling issued by the headquarters office on whether the employer is an affiliated service group; a copy of any prior determination letter that considered the effect of § 414(m) on the qualified status of the employer's plan; and, if known, a copy of any such ruling or determination letter issued to any other member (or possible member) of the same affiliated service group, accompanied by a statement as to whether the facts upon which the ruling or determination letter was based have changed.

Required information for § 414(n) determination

.10 Unless the plan provides that all leased employees within the meaning of § 414(n)(2) are treated as common law employees for all purposes under the plan, a determination letter issued with respect to the plan's qualification under § 401(a), 403(a), or 4975(e)(7) will be a determination as to the effect of § 414(n) upon the plan's qualified status only if the application includes:

(1) A description of the nature of the business of the recipient organization;

(2) A copy of the relevant leasing agreement(s);

(3) A description of the function of all leased employees within the trade or business of the recipient organization (including data as to whether all leased employees are performing services on a substantially full-time basis);

(4) A description of facts and circumstances relevant to a determination of whether such leased employees' services are performed under primary direction or control by the recipient organization (including whether the leased employees are required to comply with instructions of the recipient about when, where, and how to perform the services, whether the services must be performed by particular persons, whether the leased employees are subject to the supervision of the recipient, and whether the leased employees must perform services in the order or sequence set by the recipient); and

(5) If the recipient organization is relying on any qualified plan(s) maintained by the employee leasing organization for purposes of qualification of the recipient organization's plan, a description of such plan(s) (including a description of the contributions or benefits provided for all leased employees which are attributable to services performed for the recipient organization, plan eligibility, and vesting).

SECTION 15. WAIVER OF MINIMUM FUNDING

Scope

.01 This section provides procedures with respect to defined contribution plans for requesting a waiver of the minimum funding standard account and requesting a determination letter on any plan amendment required for the waiver.

Applicability of Rev. Proc. 2004–15

.02 The procedures in Rev. Proc. 2004–15, 2004–1 C.B. 490, apply to the request for a waiver of the minimum funding requirement. Section 2 of that revenue procedure contains the procedures for obtaining waivers of the minimum funding standards in the instance of defined benefit plans. In order to provide maximum flexibility in requesting a waiver for a defined contribution pension plan, section 3 of the revenue procedure contains three alternative methods as described more fully in Rev. Proc. 2004–15.

Waiver request submitted to EP Technical

.03 The first two alternatives involve (1) a waiver ruling only, without submission of a plan amendment, and (2) a waiver ruling only, with submission of a plan amendment. Under these first two procedures, requests for waivers must be submitted to:

Employee Plans
Internal Revenue Service
Commissioner, TE/GE
Attention: SE:T:EP:RA
P. O. Box 27063
McPherson Station
Washington, DC 20038

In both cases, the applicant must satisfy the requirements of section 2 of Rev. Proc. 2004–15, other than the parts applicable only to defined benefit plans.

If a plan amendment is not submitted or is not already part of a plan, the Service will supply an amendment which will, if adopted, satisfy section 3 of Rev. Rul. 78–223, 1978–1 C.B. 125. The waiver will be conditioned upon the plan being amended by adoption of that amendment, within a reasonable period of time, and will contain a caveat stating that the ruling is not a ruling as to the effect the plan provision may have on the qualified status of the plan. The applicant may request reconsideration within 60 days of the date of the letter if the amendment is inappropriate, by submitting a letter to the above address.

If the request for the waiver is submitted along with a plan amendment, the plan provisions necessary to satisfy section 3 of Rev. Rul. 78–223 must be included. All waivers issued pursuant to this alternative will contain a caveat indicating that the ruling is not a ruling as to the effect any plan provision may have on the qualified status of the plan.

Waiver and determination letter request submitted to EP Technical

.04 The third alternative is a request for a waiver ruling and a determination letter request. Both requests must be submitted by the applicant to EP Technical where it will be treated as if it had been submitted as a request for technical advice from the Determinations Manager. The request must:

(1) satisfy all the procedural requirements of 3.03 of Rev. Proc. 2004–15;

(2) include a completed Form 5300 and all necessary documents, plan amendments and information required by the Form 5300 and Rev. Proc. 2004–15 for approval;

(3) indicate which Area Office has audit jurisdiction over the return; and

(4) submit the user fee for both requests to EP Technical.

In addition, the procedures for notice and comment by interested parties, contained in sections 17, 18 and 19 of this revenue procedure, and the notice and comment procedures provided in section 2.02 of Rev. Proc. 2004–15 must be satisfied. Comments will be forwarded to the Determinations Office that is considering the determination letter request for the plan amendments.

Handling of the request

.05 The waiver request described in section 15.04 above will be handled by EP Technical as follows:

(1) The waiver request and supporting documents will be forwarded to EP Technical, SE:T:EP:RA:T, which will treat the request as a technical advice on the qualification issue with respect to the plan provisions necessary to satisfy section 3 of Rev. Rul. 78–223.

(2) The appropriate Determinations Office will be notified of the request. In order not to delay the processing of the request, all materials relating to the determination letter request

will be forwarded by EP Technical to the Determinations Manager for consideration while the technical advice request is completed.

(3) EP Technical will consider both issues. If a waiver is to be granted and if EP Technical believes that qualification of the plan is not adversely affected by the plan amendment, the mandatory technical advice memorandum will be issued to the Determinations Manager. The Determinations Manager must decide within 10 working days from the date of the technical advice memorandum either to furnish the applicant with the technical advice memorandum and with a favorable advance determination letter, or to ask for reconsideration of the technical advice memorandum. This request must be in writing. An initial written notice of intent to make this request may be submitted within 10 working days of the date of the technical advice memorandum and followed by a written request within 30 working days from the date of such written notice. If the Determinations Manager does not ask for reconsideration of the technical advice memorandum within 10 working days, EP Technical will issue the waiver ruling. This ruling will not contain the caveat described in section 3.02 of Rev. Proc. 2004–15.

When waiver request should be submitted

.06 In the case of a plan other than a multiemployer plan, all waiver requests must be submitted to the Service no later than the 15th day of the third month following the close of the plan year for which the waiver is requested. The Service may not extend this statutory deadline. A request for a waiver with respect to a multiemployer plan generally must be submitted no later than the close of the plan year following the plan year for which the waiver is requested.

In seeking a waiver with respect to a plan year that has not yet ended, the applicant may have difficulty in furnishing sufficient current evidence in support of the request. For this reason it is generally advisable that such advance request be submitted no earlier than 180 days prior to the end of the plan year for which the waiver is requested.

SECTION 16. SECTION 401(h) AND § 420 DETERMINATION LETTERS

Scope

.01 This section provides procedures for requesting determination letters (i) with respect to whether the requirements of § 401(h) are satisfied in a plan with retiree medical benefit features and (ii) on plan language that permits, pursuant to § 420, the transfer of assets in a defined benefit plan to a health benefit account described in § 401(h).

Required information for § 401(h) determination

.02 EP Determinations will issue a determination letter that considers whether the requirements of § 401(h) are satisfied in a plan with retiree medical benefit features only if the plan sponsor's application includes, in addition to the application forms and any other material required by this revenue procedure, a cover letter that requests consideration of § 401(h). The cover letter must specifically state that consideration is being requested with regard to § 401(h) in addition to other matters under § 401(a) and must specifically state the location of plan provisions that satisfy the requirements of § 401(h). Part I of the checklist in the Appendix of this revenue procedure may be used to identify the location of relevant plan provisions. Form 6406 may not be used to request a determination letter that considers § 401(h).

Required information for § 420 determination

.03 EP Determinations will consider the qualified status of certain plan language designed to comply with § 420 only if the plan sponsor requests such consideration in a cover letter. The cover letter must specifically state (i) whether consideration is being requested only with regard to § 420, or (ii) whether consideration is being requested with regard to § 420 in addition to other matters under § 401(a). (If consideration of other matters under § 401(a) is being requested, the application forms and other material required by this revenue procedure must also be submitted. Form 6406 may not be used for this purpose.) The cover letter must specifically state the location of plan provisions that satisfy each of the following requirements. Parts I and II of the checklist in the Appendix of this revenue procedure may be used to identify the location of relevant plan provisions.

(1) The plan must include a health benefits account as described in § 401(h).

(2) The plan must provide that transfers shall be limited to transfers of "excess assets" as defined in § 420(e)(2).

(3) The plan must provide that only one transfer may be made in a taxable year. However, for purposes of determining whether the rule in the preceding sentence is met, a plan may provide that a transfer will not be taken into account if it is a transfer that:

(a) Is made after the close of the taxable year preceding the employer's first taxable year beginning after December 31, 1990, and before the earlier of (i) the due date (including extensions) for the filing of the return of tax for such preceding year, or (ii) the date such return is filed; and

(b) Does not exceed the expenditures of the employer for qualified current retiree health liabilities for such preceding taxable year.

(4) The plan must provide that the amount transferred shall not exceed the amount which is reasonably estimated to be the amount the employer will pay out (whether directly or through reimbursement) of the health benefit account during the taxable year of the transfer for "qualified current retiree health liabilities," as defined in § 420(e)(1).

(5) The plan must provide that no transfer will be made after December 31, 2013.

(6) The plan must provide that any assets transferred, and any income allocable to such assets, shall be used only to pay qualified current retiree health liabilities for the taxable year of transfer.

(7) The plan must provide that any amounts transferred to a health benefits account (and income attributable to such amounts) which are not used to pay qualified current retiree health liabilities shall be transferred back to the defined benefit portion of the plan.

(8) The plan must provide that the amounts paid out of a health benefits account will be treated as paid first out of transferred assets and income attributable to those assets.

(9) The plan must provide that the accrued pension benefits for participants and beneficiaries must become nonforfeitable as if the plan had terminated immediately prior to the transfer (or in the case of a participant who separated during the 1-year period ending on the date of transfer immediately before such separation). In the case of a transfer described in § 420(b)(4) that relates to a prior year, the plan must provide that the accrued benefit of a participant who separated from service during the taxable year to which such transfer relates will be recomputed and treated as nonforfeitable immediately before such separation.

(10) The plan must provide that a transfer will be permitted only if each group health plan or arrangement under which health benefits are provided contains provisions satisfying § 420(c)(3). The plan must define "applicable employer cost", "cost maintenance period", and "benefit maintenance period", as applicable, consistent with § 420(c)(3), as amended. If applicable, the provisions of the plan must also reflect the transition rule in § 535(c)(2) of the Tax Relief Extension Act of 1999 (TREA '99). The plan may provide that § 420(c)(3) is satisfied separately with respect to individuals eligible for benefits under Title XVIII of the Social Security Act at any time during the taxable year and with respect to individuals not so eligible.

(11) The plan must provide that transferred assets cannot be used for key employees (as defined in § 416(i)(1)).

PART II. INTERESTED PARTY NOTICE AND COMMENT

SECTION 17. WHAT RIGHTS TO NOTICE AND COMMENT DO INTERESTED PARTIES HAVE?

Rights of interested parties

.01 Persons who qualify as interested parties under § 1.7476–1(b), have the following rights:

(1) To receive notice, in accordance with section 18 below, that an application for an advance determination will be filed regarding the qualification of plans described in §§ 401, 403(a), 409 and/or 4975(e)(7);

(2) To submit written comments with respect to the qualification of such plans to the Service;

(3) To request the Department of Labor to submit a comment to the Service on behalf of the interested parties; and

(4) To submit written comments to the Service on matters with respect to which the Department of Labor was requested to comment but declined.

Comments by interested parties

.02 Comments submitted by interested parties must be received by EP Determinations by the 45th day after the day on which the application for determination is received by EP Determinations. (However, see sections 17.03 and 17.04 for filing deadlines where the Department of Labor has been requested to comment.) Such comments must be in writing, signed by the interested parties or by an authorized representative of such parties (as provided in section 9.02(11) of Rev. Proc. 2007–4), addressed to EP Determinations at the address in section 6.17, and contain the following information:

(1) The names of the interested parties making the comments;

(2) The name and taxpayer identification number of the applicant for a determination;

(3) The name of the plan, the plan identification number, and the name of the plan administrator;

(4) Whether the parties submitting the comment are:

(a) Employees eligible to participate under the plan,

(b) Employees with accrued benefits under the plan, or former employees with vested benefits under the plan,

(c) Beneficiaries of deceased former employees who are eligible to receive or are currently receiving benefits under the plan,

(d) Employees not eligible to participate under the plan.

(5) The specific matters raised by the interested parties on the question of whether the plan meets the requirements for qualification involving §§ 401 and 403(a), and how such matters relate to the interests of the parties making the comment; and

(6) The address of the interested party submitting the comment (or if a comment is submitted jointly by more than one party, the name and address of a designated representative) to which all correspondence, including a notice of the Service's final determination with respect to qualification, should be sent. (The address designated for notice by the Service will also be used by the Department of Labor in communicating with the parties submitting a request for comment.) The designated representative may be one of the interested parties submitting the comment or an authorized representative. If two or more interested parties submit a single comment and one person is not designated in the comment as the representative for receipt of correspondence, a notice of determination mailed to any interested party who submitted the

comment shall be notice to all the interested parties who submitted the comment for purposes of § 7476(b)(5) of the Code.

Requests for DOL to submit comments

.03 A request to the Department of Labor to submit to EP Determinations a comment pursuant to section 3001(b)(2) of ERISA must be made in accordance with the following procedures.

(1) The request must be received by the Department of Labor by the 25th day after the day the application for determination is received by EP Determinations. However, if the parties requesting the Department to submit a comment wish to preserve the right to comment to EP Determinations in the event the Department declines to comment, the request must be received by the Department by the 15th day after the day the application for determination is received by EP Determinations.

(2) The request to the Department of Labor to submit a comment to EP Determinations must:

(a) Be in writing;

(b) Be signed as provided in section 17.02 above;

(c) Contain the names of the interested parties requesting the Department to comment and the address of the interested party or designated representative to whom all correspondence with respect to the request should be sent. See also section 17.02(6) above;

(d) Contain the information prescribed in section 17.02(2), (3), (4), (5) and (6) above;

(e) Indicate that the application was or will be submitted to EP Determinations at the address in section 6.17;

(f) Contain a statement of the specific matters upon which the Department's comment is sought, as well as how such matters relate to the interested parties making the request; and

(g) Be addressed as follows:

Deputy Assistant Secretary
Employee Benefits Security Administration
U.S. Department of Labor
200 Constitution Avenue, NW
Washington, DC 20210
Attention: 3001 Comment Request

Right to comment if DOL declines to comment

.04 If a request described in 17.03 is made and the Department of Labor notifies the interested parties making the request that it declines to comment on a matter concerning qualification of the plan which was raised in the request, the parties submitting the request may still submit a comment to EP Determinations on such matter. The comment must be received by the later of the 45th day after the day the application for determination is received by EP Determinations or the 15th day after the day on which notification is given by the Department that it declines to submit a comment on such matter. (See section 17.07 for the date of notification.) In no event may the comment be received later than the 60th day after the day the application for determination was received. Such a comment must comply with the requirements of section 17.02 and include a statement that the comment is being submitted on matters raised in a request to the Department upon which the Department declined to comment.

Confidentiality of comments

.05 For rules regarding the confidentiality of contents of written comments submitted by interested parties to the Service pursuant to section 17.02 or 17.04, see § 601.201(o)(5) of the Statement of Procedural Rules.

Availability of comments

.06 For rules regarding the availability to the applicant of copies of all comments on the application submitted pursuant to section 17.01(1), (2), (3) and (4) of this revenue procedure, see § 601.201(o)(5) of the Statement of Procedural Rules.

When comments are deemed made

.07 An application for an advance determination, a comment to EP Determinations, or a request to the Department of Labor shall be deemed made when it is received by EP Determinations, or the Department. Notification by the Department that it declines to comment shall be deemed given when it is received by the interested party or designated representative. The notice described in section 18.01 below shall be deemed given when it is posted or sent to the person in the manner described in § 1.7476–2. In the case of an application, comment, request, notification, or notice that is sent by mail or a private delivery service that has been designated under § 7502(f), the date as of which it shall be deemed received will be determined under § 7502. However, if such an application, comment, request, notification, or notice is not received within a reasonable period from the date determined under § 7502, the immediately preceding sentence shall not apply.

SECTION 18. WHAT ARE THE GENERAL RULES FOR NOTICE TO INTERESTED PARTIES?

Notice to interested parties

.01 Notice that an application for an advance determination regarding the qualification of a plan that is described in §§ 401, 403(a), 409 and 4975(e)(7) and that is subject to § 410 is to be made must be given to all interested parties in the manner prescribed in § 1.7476–2(c) and in accordance with the requirements of this section. A notice to interested parties is deemed to be provided in a manner that satisfies § 1.7476–2(c) if the notice is delivered using an electronic medium under a system that satisfies the requirements of § 1.402(f)–1 Q&A–5.

Time when notice must be given

.02 Notice must be given not less than 10 days nor more than 24 days prior to the day the application for a determination is made. If, however, an application is returned to the applicant for failure to adequately satisfy the notification requirements with respect to a particular group or class of interested parties, the applicant need not cause notice to be given to those groups or classes of interested parties with respect to which the notice requirement was already satisfied merely because, as a result of the resubmission of the application, the time limitations of this subsection would not be met.

Content of notice

.03 The notice referred to in section 18.01 shall contain the following information:

(1) A brief description identifying the class or classes of interested parties to whom the notice is addressed (*e.g.*, all present employees of the employer, all present employees eligible to participate);

(2) The name of the plan, the plan identification number, and the name of the plan administrator;

(3) The name and taxpayer identification number of the applicant for a determination;

(4) That an application for a determination as to the qualified status of the plan is to be made to the Service at the address in section 6.17, and stating whether the application relates to an initial qualification, a plan amendment, termination, or a partial termination;

(5) A description of the class of employees eligible to participate under the plan;

(6) Whether or not the Service has issued a previous determination as to the qualified status of the plan;

(7) A statement that any person to whom the notice is addressed is entitled to submit, or request the Department of Labor to submit, to EP Determinations, a comment on the question of whether the plan meets the requirements of § 401 or 403(a); that two or more such persons may join in a single comment or request; and that if such persons request the Department of Labor to submit a comment and the Department of Labor declines to do so with respect to one or more

matters raised in the request, the persons may still submit a comment to EP Determinations with respect to the matters on which the Department declines to comment. The Pension Benefit Guaranty Corporation (PBGC) may also submit comments. In every instance where there is either a final adverse termination or a distress termination, the Service formally notifies the PBGC for comments;

(8) The specific dates by which a comment to EP Determinations or a request to the Department of Labor must be received in order to preserve the right of comment (see section 17 above);

(9) The number of interested parties needed in order for the Department of Labor to comment; and

(10) Except to the extent that the additional informational material required to be made available by sections 18.05 through 18.09 are included in the notice, a description of a reasonable procedure whereby such additional informational material will be available to interested parties (see section 18.04). (Examples of notices setting forth the above information, in a case in which the additional information required by sections 18.05 through 18.09 will be made available at places accessible to the interested parties, are set forth in the Exhibit attached to this revenue procedure.)

Procedures for making information available to interested parties

.04 The procedure referred to in section 18.03(10), whereby the additional informational material required by sections 18.05 through 18.09 will (to the extent not included in the notice) be made available to interested parties, may consist of making such material available for inspection and copying by interested parties at a place or places reasonably accessible to such parties, or supplying such material by using a method of delivery or a combination thereof that is reasonably calculated to ensure that all interested parties will have access to the materials, provided such procedure is immediately available to all interested parties, is designed to supply them with such additional informational material in time for them to pursue their rights within the time period prescribed, and is available until the earlier of: 1) the filing of a pleading commencing a declaratory judgment action under § 7476 with respect to the qualification of the plan; or 2) the 92nd day after the day the notice of final determination is mailed to the applicant. Reasonable charges to interested parties for copying and/or mailing such additional informational material are permissible.

Information to be available to interested parties

.05 Unless provided in the notice, or unless section 18.06 applies, there shall be made available to interested parties under a procedure described in section 18.04:

(1) An updated copy of the plan and the related trust agreement (if any); and

(2) The application for determination.

Special rules if there are less than 26 participants

.06 If there would be less than 26 participants in the plan, as described in the application (including, as participants, former employees with vested benefits under the plan, beneficiaries of deceased former employees currently receiving benefits under the plan, and employees who would be eligible to participate upon making mandatory employee contributions, if any), then in lieu of making the materials described in section 18.05 available to interested parties who are not participants (as described above), there may be made available to such interested parties a document containing the following information:

(1) A description of the plan's requirements respecting eligibility for participation and benefits and the plan's benefit formula;

(2) A description of the provisions providing for nonforfeitable benefits;

(3) A description of the circumstances which may result in ineligibility, or denial or loss of benefits;

(4) A description of the source of financing of the plan and the identity of any organization through which benefits are provided;

(5) A description of any optional forms of benefits described in § 411(d)(6) which have been reduced or eliminated by plan amendment; and

(6) Any coverage schedule or other demonstration submitted with the application to show that the plan meets the requirements of §§ 401(a)(4) and 410(b).

However, once an interested party or designated representative receives a notice of final determination, the applicant must, upon request, make available to such interested party (whether or not the plan has less than 26 participants) an updated copy of the plan and related trust agreement (if any) and the application for determination.

Information described in § 6104(a)(1)(D) should not be included

.07 Information of the type described in § 6104(a)(1)(D) should not be included in the application, plan, or related trust agreement submitted to the Service. Accordingly, such information should not be included in any of the material required by section 18.05 or 18.06 to be available to interested parties.

Availability of additional information to interested parties

.08 Unless provided in the notice, there shall be made available to interested parties under a procedure described in section 18.04, any additional document dealing with the application which is submitted by or for the applicant to the Service, or furnished by the Service to the applicant; provided, however, if there would be less than 26 participants in the plan as described in the application (including, as participants, former employees with vested benefits under the plan, beneficiaries of deceased former employees currently receiving benefits under the plan, and employees who would be eligible to participate upon making mandatory employee contributions, if any), such additional documents need not be made available to interested parties who are not participants (as described above) until they, or their designated representative, receive a notice of final determination. The applicant may also withhold from such inspection and copying information described in § 6104(a)(1)(C) and (D) which may be contained in such additional documents.

Availability of notice to interested parties

.09 Unless provided in the notice, there shall be made available to all interested parties under a procedure described in section 18.04 the material described in sections 17.02 through 17.07 above.

PART III. PROCESSING DETERMINATION LETTER REQUESTS

SECTION 19. HOW DOES THE SERVICE HANDLE DETERMINATION LETTER REQUESTS?

Oral advice

.01 Oral advice.

(1) The Service does not issue determination letters on oral requests. However, personnel in EP Determinations ordinarily will discuss with taxpayers or their representatives inquiries regarding: substantive tax issues; whether the Service will issue a determination letter on particular issues; and questions relating to procedural matters about submitting determination letter requests. Any discussion of substantive issues will be at the discretion of the Service on a time available basis, will not be binding on the Service, and cannot be relied upon as a basis of obtaining retroactive relief under the provisions of § 7805(b). A taxpayer may seek oral technical assistance from a taxpayer service representative when preparing a return or report, under established procedures. Oral advice is advisory only, and the Service is not bound to recognize it in the examination of the taxpayer's return.

(2) The advice or assistance furnished, whether requested by personal appearance, telephone, or correspondence will be limited to general procedures, or will direct the inquirer to source material, such as pertinent Code provisions, regulations, revenue procedures, and revenue rulings that may aid the inquirer in resolving the question or problem.

Conferences

.02 EP Determinations may grant a conference upon written request from a taxpayer or his representative, provided the request shows that a substantive plan, amendment, etc., has been developed for submission to the Service, but that special problems or issues are involved, and EP Determinations concludes that a conference would be warranted in the interest of facilitating review and determination when the plan, etc., is formally submitted. See section 6.21 and 6.22 regarding the right to a status conference on applications pending for at least 270 days.

Determination letter based solely on administrative record

.03 Administrative Record

(1) In the case of a request for a determination letter, the determination of EP Determinations or the appeals office on the qualification or non-qualification of the retirement plan shall be based solely upon the facts contained in the administrative record. The administrative record shall consist of the following:

(a) The request for determination, the retirement plan and any related trust instruments, and any written modifications or amendments made by the applicant during the proceedings within the Service;

(b) All other documents submitted to the Service by, or on behalf of, the applicant with respect to the request for determination;

(c) All written correspondence between the Service and the applicant with respect to the request for determination and any other documents issued to the applicant from the Service;

(d) All written comments submitted to the Service pursuant to sections 17.01(2), (3), and (4) above, and all correspondence relating to comments submitted between the Service and persons (including PBGC and the Department of Labor) submitting comments pursuant to sections 17.01(2), (3), and (4) above; and

(e) In any case in which the Service makes an investigation regarding the facts as represented or alleged by the applicant in the request for determination or in comments submitted pursuant to sections 17.01(2), (3), and (4) above, a copy of the official report of such investigation.

(2) The administrative record shall be closed upon the earlier of the following events:

(a) The date of mailing of a notice of final determination by the Service with respect to the application for determination; or

(b) The filing of a petition with the United States Tax Court seeking a declaratory judgment with respect to the retirement plan.

(3) Any oral representation or modification of the facts as represented or alleged in the application for determination or in a comment filed by an interested party, which is not reduced to writing shall not become a part of the administrative record and shall not be taken into account in the determination of the qualified status of the retirement plan by EP Determinations or the appeals office.

Notice of final determination

.04 In the case of final determination, the notice of final determination:

(1) Shall be the letter issued by EP Determinations or the appeals office which states that the applicant's plan satisfies the qualification requirements of the Code. The favorable determination letter will be sent by certified or registered mail where either an interested party, the Department of Labor, or the PBGC has commented on the application for determination.

(2) Shall be the letter issued, by certified or registered mail, by EP Determinations or the appeals office subsequent to a letter of proposed determination, stating that the applicant's plan fails to satisfy the qualification requirements of the Code.

Issuance of the notice of final determination

.05 EP Determinations or the appeals office will send the notice of final determination to the applicant, to the interested parties who have previously submitted comments on the application to the Service (or to the persons designated by them to receive such notice), to the Department of Labor in the case of a comment submitted by the Department, and to PBGC if it has filed a comment.

SECTION 20. EXHAUSTION OF ADMINISTRATIVE REMEDIES

In general

.01 For purposes of § 7476(b)(3), a petitioner shall be deemed to have exhausted the administrative remedies available within the Service upon the completion of the steps described in sections 20.02, 20.03, 20.04, or 20.05 subject, however, to sections 20.06 and 20.07. If applicants, interested parties, or the PBGC do not complete the applicable steps described below, they will not have exhausted their respective available administrative remedies as required by § 7476(b)(3) and will, thus, be precluded from seeking declaratory judgment under § 7476 except to the extent that section 20.05 or 20.08 applies.

Steps for exhausting administrative remedies

.02 In the case of an applicant, with respect to any matter relating to the qualification of a plan, the steps referred to in section 20.01 are:

(1) Filing a completed application with EP Determinations pursuant to this revenue procedure;

(2) Complying with the requirements pertaining to notice to interested parties as set forth in this revenue procedure and § 1.7476–2 of the regulations; and,

(3) Appealing to the appropriate appeals office pursuant to paragraph 601.201(o)(6) of the Statement of Procedural Rules, in the event a notice of proposed adverse determination is issued by EP Determinations.

Applicant's request for § 7805(b) relief

.03 Consideration of relief under § 7805(b) will be included as one of the applicant's steps in exhausting administrative remedies only if the applicant requests EP Determinations to seek technical advice from EP Technical on the applicability of such relief. The applicant's request must be made in writing according to the procedures for requesting technical advice (*see* section 19 of Rev. Proc. 2007–5).

Interested parties

.04 In the case of an interested party or the PBGC, the steps referred to in section 20.01 are, with respect to any matter relating to the qualification of the plan, submitting to EP Determinations a comment raising such matter in accordance with section 17.01(2) above, or requesting the Department of Labor to submit to EP Determinations a comment with respect to such matter in accordance with section 17.01(3) and, if the Department of Labor declines to comment, submitting the comment in accordance with section 17.01(4) above, so that it may be considered by the Service through the administrative process.

Deemed exhaustion of administrative remedies

.05 An applicant, an interested party, or the PBGC shall in no event be deemed to have exhausted administrative remedies prior to the earlier of:

(1) The completion of those steps applicable to each as set forth in sections 20.01, 20.02, 20.03 or 20.04, which constitute their administrative remedies; or,

(2) The expiration of the 270-day period described in § 7476(b)(3), which period shall be extended in a case where there has not been a completion of all the steps referred to in section 20.02 and the Service has proceeded with due diligence in processing the application for determination.

Service must act on appeal

.06 The step described in section 20.02(3) will not be considered completed until the Service has had a reasonable time to act upon the appeal.

Service must act on § 7805(b) request

.07 Where the applicant has requested EP Determinations to seek technical advice on the applicability of § 7805(b) relief, the applicant's administrative remedies will not be considered exhausted until EP Technical has had a reasonable time to act upon the request for technical advice.

Effect of technical advice request

.08 The step described in section 20.02(3) will not be available or necessary with respect to any issue on which technical advice has been obtained from EP Technical.

SECTION 21. WHAT EFFECT WILL AN EMPLOYEE PLAN DETERMINATION LETTER HAVE?

Scope of reliance on determination letter

.01 A determination letter issued pursuant to this revenue procedure contains only the opinion of the Service as to the qualification of the particular plan involving the provisions of §§ 401 and 403(a) and the status of a related trust, if any, under § 501(a). Such a determination letter is based on the facts and demonstrations presented to the Service in connection with the application for the determination letter and may not be relied upon after a change in material fact or the effective date of a change in law, except as provided. The Service may determine, based on the application form, the extent of review of the plan document. Failure to disclose a material fact or misrepresentation of a material fact may adversely affect the reliance that would otherwise be obtained through the issuance by the Service of a favorable determination letter. Similarly, failure to accurately provide any of the information called for on any form required by this revenue procedure may result in no reliance. Applicants are advised to retain copies of all demonstrations and supporting data submitted with their applications. Failure to do so may limit the scope of reliance.

Effect of determination letter on minor plan amendment

.02 Determination letters issued on minor amendments to plans and trusts under this revenue procedure will merely express an opinion whether the amendment, in and of itself, affects the existing status of the plan's qualification and the exempt status of the related trust. In no event should such a determination letter be construed as an opinion on the qualification of the plan as a whole and the exempt status of the related trust as a whole.

Sections 13 and 14 of Rev. Proc. 2007–4 applicable

.03 Except as otherwise provided in this section, determination letters referred to in sections 21.01 and 21.02 are governed, generally, by the provisions of sections 13 and 14 of Rev. Proc. 2007–4.

Effect of subsequent publication of revenue ruling, etc.

.04 The prior qualification of a plan as adopted by an employer will not be considered to be adversely affected by the publication of a revenue ruling, a revenue procedure, or an administrative pronouncement within the meaning of § 1.6661–3(b)(2) of the regulations where:

(1) Thc plan was the subject of a favorable determination letter and the request for that letter contained no misstatement or omission of material facts;

(2) The facts subsequently developed are not materially different from the facts on which the determination letter was based;

(3) There has been no change in the applicable law; and

(4) The employer that established the plan acted in good faith in reliance on the determination letter.

However, all such plans must be amended to comply with the published guidance for subsequent years, in accordance with the rules set forth in Rev. Proc. 2005–66. See, in particular, Part II of that revenue procedure.

Determination letter does not apply to taxability issues

.05 While a favorable determination letter may serve as a basis for determining deductions for employer contributions thereunder, it is not to be taken as an indication that contributions are necessarily deductible as made. This latter determination can be made only upon an examination of the employer's tax return, in accordance with the limitations, and subject to the conditions of, § 404.

SECTION 22. EFFECT ON OTHER REVENUE PROCEDURES

Rev. Proc. 2006–6 is superseded.

SECTION 23. EFFECTIVE DATE

This revenue procedure is effective January 2, 2007.

SECTION 24. PAPERWORK REDUCTION ACT

The collections of information contained in this revenue procedure have been reviewed and approved by the Office of Management and Budget in accordance with the Paperwork Reduction Act (44 U.S.C. 3507) under control number 1545–1520.

An agency may not conduct or sponsor, and a person is not required to respond to, a collection of information unless the collection of information displays a valid OMB control number.

The collections of information in this revenue procedure are in sections 6.16, 6.18, 6.19, 6.20, 7.04, 13, 14, 15, 16, 19.02, and 21.04. This information is required to determine plan qualification. This information will be used to determine whether a plan is entitled to favorable tax treatment. The collections of information are mandatory. The likely respondents are businesses or other for-profit institutions.

The estimated total annual reporting and/or recordkeeping burden is 163,186 hours.

The estimated annual burden per respondent/recordkeeper varies from 1 hour to 40 hours, depending on individual circumstances, with an estimated average of 2.02 hours. The estimated number of respondents and/or recordkeepers is 80,763.

The estimated annual frequency of responses (used for reporting requirements only) is once every three years.

Books or records relating to a collection of information must be retained as long as their contents may become material in the administration of any internal revenue law. Generally tax returns and tax return information are confidential, as required by 26 U.S.C. 6103.

DRAFTING INFORMATION

The principal author of this revenue procedure is Angelique V. Carrington of the Employee Plans, Tax Exempt and Government Entities Division. For further information regarding this revenue procedure, please contact the Employee Plans' taxpayer assistance telephone service at 1–877–829–5500 (a toll-free number), between the hours of 8:30 a.m. and 4:30 p.m. Eastern Time, Monday through Friday. Ms. Carrington may be reached at 1–202–283–9888 (not a toll-free number).

EXHIBIT: SAMPLE NOTICE TO INTERESTED PARTIES

The Exhibit set forth below, may be used to satisfy the requirements of section 18 of this revenue procedure.

EXHIBIT: SAMPLE NOTICE TO INTERESTED PARTIES

1. Notice To: ______________________ [describe class or classes of interested parties]

An application is to be made to the Internal Revenue Service for an advance determination on the qualification of the following employee pension benefit plan:

2. ______________________

(name of plan)

3. ______________________

(plan number)

4. ______________________

(name and address of applicant)

5. ______________________

(applicant EIN)

6. ______________________

(name and address of plan administrator)

7. The application will be filed on ______________ for an advance determination as to whether the plan meets the qualification requirements of § 401 or 403(a) of the Internal Revenue Code of 1986, with respect to the plan's ______________________ [initial qualification, amendment, termination, or partial termination]. The application will be filed with:

EP Determinations
Internal Revenue Service
P.O. Box 192
Covington, KY 41012–0192

8. The employees eligible to participate under the plan are:

9. The Internal Revenue Service ______________ [has/has not] previously issued a determination letter with respect to the qualification of this plan.

RIGHTS OF INTERESTED PARTIES

10. You have the right to submit to EP Determinations, at the above address, either individually or jointly with other interested parties, your comments as to whether this plan meets the qualification requirements of the Internal Revenue Code.

You may instead, individually or jointly with other interested parties, request the Department of Labor to submit, on your behalf, comments to EP Determinations regarding qualification of the plan. If the Department declines to comment on all or some of the matters you raise, you may, individually, or jointly if your request was made to the Department jointly, submit your comments on these matters directly to EP Determinations.

REQUESTS FOR COMMENTS BY THE DEPARTMENT OF LABOR

11. The Department of Labor may not comment on behalf of interested parties unless requested to do so by the lesser of 10 employees or 10 percent of the employees who qualify as interested parties. The number of persons needed for the Department to comment with respect to this plan is ____________________. If you request the Department to comment, your request must be in writing and must specify the matters upon which comments are requested, and must also include:

(1) the information contained in items 2 through 5 of this Notice; and

(2) the number of persons needed for the Department to comment.

A request to the Department to comment should be addressed as follows:

Deputy Assistant Secretary
Employee Benefits Security Administration
ATTN: 3001 Comment Request
U.S. Department of Labor
200 Constitution Avenue, NW
Washington, DC 20210

COMMENTS TO THE INTERNAL REVENUE SERVICE

12. Comments submitted by you to EP Determinations must be in writing and received by it by ____________________. However, if there are matters that you request the Department of Labor to comment upon on your behalf, and the Department declines, you may submit comments on these matters to EP Determinations to be received by it within 15 days from the time the Department notifies you that it will not comment on a particular matter, or by ____________________, whichever is later, but not after ____________________. A request to the Department to comment on your behalf must be received by it by ____________________ if you wish to preserve your right to comment on a matter upon which the Department declines to comment, or by ____________________ if you wish to waive that right.

ADDITIONAL INFORMATION

13. Detailed instructions regarding the requirements for notification of interested parties may be found in sections 17 and 18 of Rev. Proc. 2007–6. Additional information concerning this application (including, where applicable, an updated copy of the plan and related trust; the application for determination; any additional documents dealing with the application that have submitted to the Service; and copies of section 17 of Rev. Proc. 2007–6 are available at ____________________ during the hours of ____________________ for inspection and copying. (There is a nominal charge for copying and/or mailing.)

APPENDIX

Checklist As part of a § 401(h) or § 420 determination letter request described in section 16 of this revenue procedure the following checklist may be completed and attached to the determination letter request. If the request relates to § 401(h) but not to § 420, complete Part I only. If the request relates to § 420, complete Parts I and II.

PART I

		CIRCLE	*SECTION*
1.	Does the Plan contain a medical benefits account within the meaning of § 401(h) of the Code? If the medical benefits account is a new provision, items "a" through "h" should be completed.	Yes No	
a.	Does the medical benefits account specify the medical benefits that will be available and contain provisions for determining the amount that will be paid?	Yes No	_____
b.	Does the medical benefits account specify who will benefit?	Yes No	_____
c.	Does the medical benefits account indicate that such benefits, when added to any life insurance protection in the Plan, will be subordinate to retirement benefits? (This requirement will not be satisfied unless the amount of actual contributions to provide § 401(h) benefits (when added to actual contributions for life insurance protection under the Plan) does not exceed 25 percent of the total actual contributions to the Plan (other than contributions to fund past service credits), determined on an aggregate basis since the inception of the § 401(h) arrangement.)	Yes No	_____
d.	Does the medical benefits account maintain separate accounts with respect to contributions to key employees (as defined in § 416(i)(1) of the Code) to fund such benefits?	Yes No	_____
e.	Does the medical benefits account state that amounts contributed must be reasonable and ascertainable?	Yes No	_____
f.	Does the medical benefits account provide for the impossibility of diversion prior to satisfaction of liabilities (other than item "7" below)?	Yes No	_____
g.	Does the medical benefits account provide for reversion upon satisfaction of all liabilities (other than item "7" below)?	Yes No	_____
h.	Does the medical benefits account provide that forfeitures must be applied as soon as possible to reduce employer contributions to fund the medical benefits?	Yes No	_____

PART II

2.	Does the Plan limit transfers to "Excess Assets" as defined in § 420(e)(2) of the Code?	Yes No	_____

3. Does the Plan provide that only one transfer may be made in a taxable year (except with regard to transfers relating to prior years pursuant to § 420(b)(4) of the Code)? Yes No ____

4. Does the Plan provide that the amount transferred shall not exceed the amount reasonably estimated to be paid for qualified current retiree health liabilities? Yes No ____

5. Does the Plan provide that no transfer will be made after December 31, 2013? Yes No ____

6. Does the Plan provide that transferred assets and income attributable to such assets shall be used only to pay qualified current retiree health liabilities for the taxable year of transfer? Yes No ____

7. Does the Plan provide that any amounts transferred (plus income) that are not used to pay qualified current retiree health liabilities shall be transferred back to the defined benefit portion of the Plan? Yes No ____

8. Does the Plan provide that amounts paid out of a health benefits account will be treated as paid first out of transferred assets and income attributable to those assets? Yes No ____

9. Does the Plan provide that participants' accrued benefits become nonforfeitable on a termination basis (i) immediately prior to transfer, or (ii) in the case of a participant who separated within 1 year before the transfer, immediately before such separation? Yes No ____

10. In the case of transfers described in § 420(b)(4) of the Code relating to 1990, does the Plan provide that benefits will be recomputed and become nonforfeitable for participants who separated from service in such prior year as described in § 420(c)(2)? Yes No ____

11. Does the Plan provide that transfers will be permitted only if each group health plan or arrangement contains provisions satisfying § 420(c)(3) of the Code, as amended? Yes No ____

12. Does the Plan define "applicable employer cost", "cost maintenance period" and" benefit maintenance period", as needed, consistently with § 420(c)(3) of the Code, as amended? Yes No ____

13. Do the Plan's provisions reflect the transition rule in section 535(c)(2) of TREA '99, if applicable? Yes No ____

14. Does the Plan provide that transferred assets cannot be used for key employees? Yes No ____

---

26 CFR 601.201: Rulings and determination letters.

Rev. Proc. 2007–7

SECTION 1. PURPOSE AND NATURE OF CHANGES

.01 This revenue procedure updates Rev. Proc. 2006–7, 2006–1 C.B. 242, by providing a current list of those areas of the Internal Revenue Code under the jurisdiction of the Associate Chief Counsel (International) relating to matters on which the Internal Revenue Service will not issue letter rulings or determination letters.

.02 Change

(1) Section 4.01(29) dealing with the determination under section 7874 of whether, after the acquisition of the entity, the expanded affiliated group has substantial business activities in the foreign country in which, or under the law of which, the acquiring foreign entity is created or organized, when compared to the total business activities of the expanded affiliated group, has been added.

SECTION 2. BACKGROUND AND SCOPE OF APPLICATION

.01 Background

In the interest of sound tax administration, the Service answers inquiries from individuals and organizations regarding their status for tax purposes and the tax effects of their acts or transactions before the filing of returns or reports that are required by the Internal Revenue Code. There are, however, areas where the Service will not issue letter rulings or determination letters, either because the issues are inherently factual or for other reasons. These areas are set forth in sections 3 and 4 of this revenue procedure.

Section 3 lists areas in which letter rulings and determination letters will not be issued under any circumstances.

Section 4 lists areas in which they will not ordinarily be issued; in these areas, unique and compelling reasons may justify issuing a letter ruling or determination letter. A taxpayer who plans to request a letter ruling or determination letter in an area described in Section 4 should contact (by telephone or in writing) the Office of Associate Chief Counsel (International) (hereinafter "the Office") prior to making such request and discuss with the Office the unique and compelling reasons that the taxpayer believes justify issuing such letter ruling or determination letter. While not required, a written submission is encouraged since it will enable Office personnel to arrive more quickly at an understanding of the unique facts of each case. A taxpayer who contacts the Office by telephone may be requested to provide a written submission. The Service may provide a general information letter in response to inquiries in areas on either list.

These lists are not all-inclusive. Future revenue procedures may add or delete items. The Service may also decline to rule on an individual case for reasons peculiar to that case, and such decision will not be announced in the Internal Revenue Bulletin.

.02 Scope of Application

This revenue procedure does not preclude the submission of requests for technical advice to the Office from other offices of the Service.

SECTION 3. AREAS IN WHICH RULING OR DETERMINATION LETTERS WILL NOT BE ISSUED

.01 Specific Questions and Problems

(1) Section 861.—Income from Sources Within the United States.—A method for determining the source of a pension payment to a nonresident alien individual from a trust under a defined benefit plan that is qualified under § 401(a) if the proposed method is inconsistent with §§ 4.01, 4.02, and 4.03 of Rev. Proc. 2004–37, 2004–1 C.B. 1099.

(2) Section 862.—Income from Sources Without the United States.—A method for determining the source of a pension payment to a nonresident alien individual from a trust under a defined benefit plan that is qualified under § 401(a) if the proposed method is inconsistent with §§ 4.01, 4.02, and 4.03 of Rev. Proc. 2004–37, 2004–1 C.B. 1099.

(3) Section 871(g).—Special Rules for Original Issue Discount.—Whether a debt instrument having original issue discount within the meaning of § 1273 is not an original issue discount obligation within the meaning of § 871(g)(1)(B)(i) when the instrument is payable 183 days or less from the date of original issue (without regard to the period held by the taxpayer).

(4) Section 894.—Income Affected by Treaty.—Whether a person that is a resident of a foreign country and derives income from the United States is entitled to benefits under the United States income tax treaty with that foreign country pursuant to the limitation on benefits article. However, the Service may rule regarding the legal interpretation of a particular provision within the relevant limitation on benefits article.

(5) Section 954.—Foreign Base Company Income.—The effective rate of tax that a foreign country will impose on income.

(6) Section 1503(d).—Dual Consolidated Loss.—Whether the conditions under the regulations for excepting a net operating loss of a dual resident corporation from the definition of a dual consolidated loss, or for rebutting the presumption that an event constitutes a triggering event for purposes of § 1.1503–2(g)(2)(iii)(B), are satisfied.

(7) Section 7701(b).—Definition of Resident Alien and Nonresident Alien.—Whether an alien individual is a nonresident of the United States, including whether the individual has met the requirements of the substantial presence test or exceptions to the substantial presence test. However, the Service may rule regarding the legal interpretation of a particular provision of § 7701(b) or the regulations thereunder.

.02 General Areas.

(1) The prospective application of the estate tax to the property or the estate of a living person, except that rulings may be issued on any international issues in a ruling request accepted pursuant to § 5.06 of Rev. Proc. 2007–1.

(2) Whether reasonable cause exists under Subtitle F (Procedure and Administration) of the Code.

(3) Whether a proposed transaction would subject a taxpayer to criminal penalties.

(4) Any area where the ruling request does not comply with the requirements of Rev. Proc. 2007–1.

(5) Any area where the same issue is the subject of the taxpayer's pending request

for competent authority assistance under a United States tax treaty.

(6) A "comfort" ruling will not be issued with respect to an issue that is clearly and adequately addressed by statute, regulations, decisions of a court, tax treaties, revenue rulings, or revenue procedures absent extraordinary circumstances (*e.g.*, a request for a ruling required by a governmental regulatory authority in order to effectuate the transaction.)

(7) Any frivolous issue, as that term is defined in § 6.10 of Rev. Proc. 2007–1.

SECTION 4. AREAS IN WHICH RULING OR DETERMINATION LETTERS WILL NOT ORDINARILY BE ISSUED

.01 Specific Questions and Problems

(1) Section 367(a).—Transfers of Property from the United States.—Whether an oil or gas working interest is transferred from the United States for use in the active conduct of a trade or business for purposes of § 367(a)(3); and whether any other property is so transferred, where the determination requires extensive factual inquiry.

(2) Section 367(b).—Other Transfers.—Whether a foreign corporation is considered a corporation for purposes of any nonrecognition provision listed in § 367(b), and related issues, unless the ruling request presents a significant legal issue or subchapter C rulings are requested in the context of reorganizations or liquidations involving foreign corporations.

(3) Section 864.—Definitions and Special Rules.—Whether a taxpayer is engaged in a trade or business within the United States, and whether income is effectively connected with the conduct of a trade or business within the United States; whether an instrument is a security as defined in § 1.864–2(c)(2); whether a taxpayer effects transactions in the United States in stocks or securities under § 1.864–2(c)(2); whether an instrument or item is a commodity as defined in § 1.864–2(d)(3); and for purposes of § 1.864–2(d)(1) and (2), whether a commodity is of a kind customarily dealt in on an organized commodity exchange, and whether a transaction is of a kind customarily consummated at such place.

(4) Section 871.—Tax on Nonresident Alien Individuals.—Whether the income earned on contracts that do not qualify as annuities or life insurance contracts because of the limitations imposed by § 72(s) and § 7702(a) is portfolio interest as defined in § 871(h).

(5) Section 881.—Tax on Income of Foreign Corporations Not Connected with United States Business.—Whether the income earned on contracts that do not qualify as annuities or life insurance contracts because of the limitations imposed by § 72(s) and § 7702(a) is portfolio interest as defined in § 881(c).

(6) Section 892.—Income of Foreign Governments and of International Organizations.—Whether income derived by foreign governments and international organizations from sources within the United States is excluded from gross income and exempt from taxation and any underlying issue related to that determination.

(7) Section 893.—Compensation of Employees of Foreign Governments and International Organizations.—Whether wages, fees, or salary of an employee of a foreign government or of an international organization received as compensation for official services to such government or international organization is excluded from gross income and exempt from taxation and any underlying issue related to that determination.

(8) Section 894.—Income Affected by Treaty.—Whether the income received by an individual in respect of services rendered to a foreign government or a political subdivision or a local authority thereof is exempt from federal income tax or withholding under any of the United States income tax treaties which contain provisions applicable to such individuals.

(9) Section 894.—Income Affected by Treaty.—Whether a taxpayer has a permanent establishment in the United States for purposes of any United States income tax treaty and whether income is attributable to a permanent establishment in the United States.

(10) Section 894.—Income Affected by Treaty.—Whether certain persons will be considered liable to tax under the laws of a foreign country for purposes of determining if such persons are residents within the meaning of any United States income tax treaty. But see Rev. Rul. 2000–59, 2000–2 C.B. 593.

(11) Section 894.—Income Affected by Treaty.—Whether the income received by a nonresident alien student or trainee for services performed for a university or other educational institution is exempt from federal income tax or withholding under any of the United States income tax treaties which contain provisions applicable to such nonresident alien students or trainees.

(12) Section 894.—Income Affected by Treaty.—Whether the income received by a nonresident alien performing research or teaching as personal services for a university, hospital or other research institution is exempt from federal income tax or withholding under any of the United States income tax treaties which contain provisions applicable to such nonresident alien teachers or researchers.

(13) Section 894.—Income Affected by Treaty.—Whether a foreign recipient of payments made by a United States person is ineligible to receive the benefits of a United States tax treaty under the principles of Rev. Rul. 89–110, 1989–2 C.B. 275.

(14) Section 894.—Income Affected by Treaty.—Whether a recipient of payments is or has been a resident of a country for purposes of any United States tax treaty. Pursuant to § 1.884–5(f), however, the Service may rule whether a corporation representing that it is a resident of a country is a qualified resident thereof for purposes of § 884.

(15) Section 894.—Income Affected by Treaty.—Whether an entity is treated as fiscally transparent by a foreign jurisdiction for purposes of § 894(c) and the regulations thereunder.

(16) Section 901.—Taxes of Foreign Countries and of Possessions of United States.—Whether a foreign levy meets the requirements of a creditable tax under § 901.

(17) Section 901.—Taxes of Foreign Countries and of Possessions of United States.—Whether a person claiming a credit has established, based on all of the relevant facts and circumstances, the amount (if any) paid by a dual capacity taxpayer under a qualifying levy that is not paid in exchange for a specific economic benefit. See § 1.901–2A(c)(2).

(18) Section 903.—Credit for Taxes in Lieu of Income, Etc., Taxes.—Whether a foreign levy meets the requirements of a creditable tax under § 903.

(19) Sections 927(a) (Repealed), 936(h)(5), 943(a) (Repealed), 954(d), 993(c).—Manufactured Product.—Whether a product is manufactured or produced for purposes of § 927(a) (Repealed), § 936(h)(5), § 943(a) (Repealed), § 954(d), and § 993(c).

(20) Section 936.—Puerto Rico and Possession Tax Credit.—What constitutes a substantial line of business.

(21) Section 956.—Investment of Earnings in United States Property.—Whether a pledge of the stock of a controlled foreign corporation is an indirect pledge of the assets of that corporation. See § 1.956–2(c)(2).

(22) Section 985.—Functional Currency.—Whether a currency is the functional currency of a qualified business unit.

(23) Section 989(a).—Qualified Business Unit.—Whether a unit of the taxpayer's trade or business is a qualified business unit.

(24) Section 1058.—Transfers of Securities under Certain Agreements.—Whether the amount of any payment described in § 1058(b)(2) or the amount of any other payment made in connection with a transfer of securities described in § 1058 is from sources within or without the United States; the character of such amounts; and whether the amounts constitute a particular kind of income for purposes of any United States income tax treaty.

(25) Section 1503(d).—Dual Consolidated Loss.—Whether an event presumptively constitutes a triggering event for purposes of § 1.1503–2(g)(2)(iii)(A)(1)–(7), apart from possible rebuttal of the presumption under § 1.1503–2(g)(2)(iii)(B). See § 3.01(6), Rev. Proc. 2007–7.

(26) Section 2501.—Imposition of Tax.—Whether a partnership interest is intangible property for purposes of § 2501(a)(2) (dealing with transfers of intangible property by a nonresident not a citizen of the United States).

(27) Section 7701.—Definitions.—Whether an estate or trust is a foreign estate or trust for federal income tax purposes.

(28) Section 7701.—Definitions.—Whether an intermediate entity is a conduit entity under § 1.881–3(a)(4); whether a transaction is a financing transaction under § 1.881–3(a)(ii); whether the participation of an intermediate entity in a financing arrangement is pursuant to a tax avoidance plan under § 1.881–3(b); whether an intermediate entity performs significant financing activities under § 1.881–3(b)(3)(ii); whether an unrelated intermediate entity would not have participated in a financing arrangement on substantially the same terms under § 1.881–3(c).

(29) Section 7874.—Expatriated Entities and their Foreign Parents.—Whether, after the acquisition, the expanded affiliated group has substantial business activities in the foreign country in which, or under the law of which, the acquiring foreign entity is created or organized, when compared to the total business activities of the expanded affiliated group.

.02 General Areas

(1) Whether a taxpayer has a business purpose for a transaction or arrangement.

(2) Whether a taxpayer uses a correct North American Industry Classification System (NAICS) code or Standard Industrial Classification (SIC) code.

(3) Any transaction or series of transactions that is designed to achieve a different tax consequence or classification under U.S. tax law (including tax treaties) and the tax law of a foreign country, where the results of that different tax consequence or classification are inconsistent with the purposes of U.S. tax law (including tax treaties).

(4)(a) Situations where a taxpayer or a related party is domiciled or organized in a foreign jurisdiction with which the United States does not have an effective mechanism for obtaining tax information with respect to civil tax examinations and criminal tax investigations, which would preclude the Service from obtaining information located in such jurisdiction that is relevant to the analysis or examination of the tax issues involved in the ruling request.

(b) The provisions of subsection 4.02(4)(a) above shall not apply if the taxpayer or affected related party (i) consents to the disclosure of all relevant information requested by the Service in processing the ruling request or in the course of an examination to verify the accuracy of the representations made and to otherwise analyze or examine the tax issues involved in the ruling request, and (ii) waives all claims to protection of bank or commercial secrecy laws in the foreign jurisdiction with respect to the information requested by the Service. In the event the taxpayer's or related party's consent to disclose relevant information or to waive protection of bank or commercial secrecy is determined by the Service to be ineffective or of no force and effect, then the Service may retroactively rescind any ruling rendered in reliance on such consent.

(5) The federal tax consequences of proposed federal, state, local, municipal, or foreign legislation.

(6)(a) Situations involving the interpretation of foreign law or foreign documents. The interpretation of a foreign law or foreign document means making a judgment about the import or effect of the foreign law or document that goes beyond its plain meaning.

(b) The Service, at its discretion, may consider rulings that involve the interpretation of foreign laws or foreign documents. In these cases, the Service may request information in addition to that listed in §§ 7.01(2)(b) and (c) of Revenue Procedure 2007–1, including a discussion of the implications of any authority believed to interpret the foreign law or foreign document, such as pending legislation, treaties, court decisions, notices or administrative decisions.

SECTION 5. EFFECT ON OTHER REVENUE PROCEDURE

Rev. Proc. 2006–7 is superseded.

SECTION 6. EFFECTIVE DATE

This revenue procedure is effective January 2, 2007.

SECTION 7. DRAFTING INFORMATION

This revenue procedure was compiled by Willard W. Yates of the Office of Associate Chief Counsel (International). For further information about this revenue procedure, please contact Mr. Yates at (202) 622–3164 (not a toll-free number).

Rev. Proc. 2007–8

TABLE OF CONTENTS

SECTION 1. PURPOSE

This revenue procedure provides guidance for complying with the user fee program of the Internal Revenue Service as it pertains to requests for letter rulings, determination letters, etc., on matters under the jurisdiction of the Commissioner, Tax Exempt and Government Entities Division; and requests for administrative scrutiny determinations under Rev. Proc. 93–41, 1993–2 C.B. 536.

SECTION 2. CHANGES

.01 *In general.* This revenue procedure is a general update of Rev. Proc. 2006–8, 2006–1 I.R.B. 245.

.02 Section 6.10 is revised to reflect section 507 termination cases now being handled by EO Determinations.

.03 Section 10.01 is revised to include determination letters.

.04 Section 10.02(1)(b) is clarified as to when a refund of user fees will not be issued.

SECTION 3. BACKGROUND

.01 *Legislation authorizing user fees.* Section 7528 was added to the Code by section 202 of the Temporary Assistance for Needy Families Block Grant Program, Pub. L. No. 108–89, and was extended to September 30, 2014, by section 690 of the American Jobs Creation Act of 2004, Pub. L. No.108–357. Section 7528 of the Code directs the Secretary of the Treasury or delegate (the "Secretary") to establish a program requiring the payment of user fees for requests to the Service for letter rulings, opinion letters, determination letters, and similar requests. The fees charged under the program (1) are to vary according to categories or subcategories established by the Secretary; (2) are to be determined after taking into account the average time for, and difficulty of, complying with requests in each category and subcategory; and (3) are payable in advance. Section 7528(b)(3) directs the Secretary to provide for exemptions and reduced fees under the program as the Secretary determines to be appropriate, but the average fee applicable to each category may not be less than the amount specified in § 7528.

.02 *Related revenue procedures.* The various revenue procedures that require payment of a user fee, or an administrative scrutiny determination user fee are described in the appendix to this revenue procedure.

SECTION 4. SCOPE

.01 *Requests to which user fees apply.* In general, user fees apply to all requests for letter rulings, opinion letters, determination letters, and advisory letters submitted by or on behalf of taxpayers, sponsoring organizations or other entities as described in this revenue procedure. Further, administrative scrutiny determination user fees, described in Rev. Proc. 93–41, are collected through the user fee program described in this revenue procedure. Requests to which a user fee or an administrative scrutiny determination user fee is applicable must be accompanied by the appropriate fee as determined from the fee schedule set forth in section 6 of this revenue procedure. The fee may be refunded in limited circumstances as set forth in section 10.

.02 *Requests and other actions that do not require the payment of a user fee.* Actions which do not require the payment of a user fee include the following:

(1) Requests for information letters as defined in Rev. Proc. 2007–4, page 118, this Bulletin.

(2) Elections pertaining to automatic extensions of time under § 301.9100–1 of the Procedure and Administration regulations.

(3) Use of forms which are not to be filed with the Service. For example, no user fee is required in connection with the use of Form 5305, *Traditional Individual Retirement Trust Account*, or Form 5305–A, *Traditional Individual Retirement Custodial Account*, in order to adopt an individual retirement account under § 408(a).

(4) In general, plan amendments whereby sponsors amend their plans by adopting, word-for-word, the model language contained in a revenue procedure which states that the amendment should not be submitted to the Service and that the Service will not issue new opinion, advisory, ruling or determination letters for plans that are amended solely to add the model language.

(5) Change in accounting period or accounting method permitted by a published revenue procedure that permits an automatic change without prior approval of the Commissioner.

(6) *Compliance and Correction Fees.* Compliance fees and compliance correction fees under the Employee Plans Compliance Resolution System are not described in this procedure because they are compliance fees or compliance correction fees and not user fees. For further guidance, please see Rev. Proc. 2006–27, 2006–22 I.R.B. 945.

.03 *Exemptions from the user fee requirements.* The following exemptions apply to the user fee requirements. These are the only exemptions that apply.

(1) Departments, agencies, or instrumentalities of the United States that certify that they are seeking a letter ruling, determination letter, opinion letter or similar letter on behalf of a program or activity funded by federal appropriations. The fact that a user fee is not charged has no bearing on whether an applicant is treated as an agency or instrumentality of the United States for purposes of any provision of the Code except for § 7528.

(2) Requests as to whether a worker is an employee for federal employment taxes and federal income tax withholding purposes (chapters 21, 22, 23, and 24 of sub-

title C of the Code) submitted on Form SS–8, *Determination of Worker Status for Purposes of Federal Employment Taxes and Income Tax Withholding*, or its equivalent. Such a request may be submitted in connection with an application for a determination on the qualification of a plan when it is necessary to determine whether an employer-employee relationship exists. See section 6.13 of Rev. Proc. 2007–6, page 189, this Bulletin. In that case, although no user fee applies to the request submitted on Form SS–8, the applicable user fee must be paid in connection with the application for determination on the plan's qualification.

SECTION 5. DEFINITIONS

The following terms used in this revenue procedure are defined in the pertinent revenue procedures referred to below, which are described in the appendix:

Administrative scrutiny determination	Rev. Proc. 93–41
Adoption agreement	Rev. Proc. 2005–16
Advisory letter	Rev. Procs. 2005–16, 2007–6
Basic plan document	Rev. Proc. 2005–16
Determination letter	Rev. Procs. 90–27, 2007–4
Dual-purpose IRA	Rev. Proc. 98–59
Group exemption letter	Rev. Proc. 80–27
Information letter	Rev. Proc. 2007–4
Letter ruling	Rev. Proc. 2007–4
Mass submitter	Rev. Procs. 87–50, 2005–16
Mass submitter plan	Rev. Proc. 2005–16
Master plan	Rev. Proc. 2005–16
Minor modification	Rev. Procs. 87–50, 2005–16
Opinion letter	Rev. Procs. 2005–16, 2007–4
Prototype plan	Rev. Proc. 2005–16
Roth IRA	Rev. Proc. 98–59
SIMPLE IRA	Rev. Proc. 97–29
SIMPLE IRA Plan	Rev. Proc. 97–29
Plan Sponsor	Rev. Proc. 2005–16
Sponsoring organization	Rev. Procs. 87–50, Rev. Proc. 2005–16
Staggered Remedial Amendment Period	Rev. Proc. 2005–66
Volume submitter lead specimen plan	Rev. Proc. 2005–16
Volume submitter plan	Rev. Proc. 2005–16
Volume submitter specimen plan	Rev. Proc. 2005–16
Word-for-word identical adoption	Rev. Procs. 87–50, 2005–16

SECTION 6. FEE SCHEDULE

The amount of the user fee payable with respect to each category or subcategory of submission is as set forth in the following schedule.

CATEGORY	
EMPLOYEE PLANS USER FEES	
.01 *Letter ruling requests.*	
(1) Computation of exclusion for annuitant under § 72	$380
(2) Change in plan year (Form 5308)	$380
(3) Certain waivers of 60-day rollover period	
(a) Rollover less than $50,000	$500
(b) Rollover equal to or greater than $50,000 and less than $100,000	$1,500
(c) Rollover equal to or greater than $100,000	$3,000
Note: No user fee is required if the requested change is permitted to be made pursuant to the procedure for automatic approval set forth in Rev. Proc. 87–27, 1987–1 C.B. 769. In such a case, Form 5308 should not be submitted to the Service.	
(4) Change in funding method	$2,800
(5) Letter ruling under Rev. Proc. 90–49, 1990–2 C.B. 620	$2,800
(6) Approval to become a nonbank trustee (see §1.408–2(e) of the Income Tax Regulations)	$14,500
(7) Letter ruling involving the determination of the account limit under § 419A(c)	$14,500
(8) Waiver of minimum funding standard or excise tax (§ 412(d), 4971(b) or 4971(f))	
(a) Waiver of $1,000,000 or more	$13,000
(b) Waiver of less than $1,000,000	$6,100
(9) Individually designed simplified employee pension (SEP)	$9,000
(10) All other letter rulings	$9,000
.02 *Requests for certain administrative exemptions.*	
Requests for administrative exemptions for participant-directed transactions that are in compliance with the regulations under § 404(c) of the Employee Retirement Income Security Act of 1974 (ERISA) but may result in prohibited transactions under § 4975	$2,570
.03 *Administrative scrutiny determinations with respect to separate lines of business.*	
(1) For the first separate line of business for which a determination is requested	$4,915
(2) For each additional separate line of business for which a determination is requested	$1,580

.04 *Opinion letters on prototype individual retirement accounts and/or annuities, simplified employee pensions, SIMPLE IRAs, SIMPLE IRA Plans, and Roth IRAs.*

(1) Mass submission of a prototype IRA, SEP, SIMPLE IRA, SIMPLE IRA Plan, or Roth IRA, per plan document, new or amended	$3,000
(2) Sponsoring organization's nonmass submission of prototype IRA, SEP, SIMPLE IRA, SIMPLE IRA Plan, or Roth IRA, per plan document	$3,000
(3) Sponsoring organization's word-for-word identical adoption of mass submitter's prototype IRA, SEP, SIMPLE IRA, SIMPLE IRA Plan, or Roth IRA, per plan document or an amendment thereof	$200

Note: If a mass submitter submits, in any 12-month period ending January 31, more than 300 applications on behalf of word-for-word adopters of prototype IRAs with respect to a particular plan document, only the first 300 such applications will be subject to the fee; no fee will apply to those in excess of the first 300 such applications submitted within the 12-month period.

(4) Sponsoring organization's word-for-word identical adoption of mass submitter's prototype dual-purpose IRA, per plan document or an amendment thereof	$200

Note: If a mass submitter submits, in any 12-month period ending January 31, more than 300 applications on behalf of word-for-word adopters of prototype dual-purpose IRAs with respect to a particular plan document, only the first 300 such applications will be subject to the fee; no fee will apply to those in excess of the first 300 such applications submitted within the 12-month period.

(5) Sponsoring organization's minor modification of mass submitter's prototype IRA, SEP, SIMPLE IRA, SIMPLE IRA Plan, or Roth IRA, per plan document	$750
(6) Sponsoring organization's minor modification of mass submitter's prototype dual-purpose IRA, per plan document	$750
(7) Opinion letters on dual-purpose (combined traditional and Roth) IRAs:	
(a) Mass submission of a prototype dual-purpose IRA, per plan document, new or amended	$4,500
(b) Sponsoring organization's nonmass submission of prototype dual-purpose IRA, per plan document	$4,500

.05 *Opinion letters on master and prototype plans.*

(1) Mass submitter M & P plan, per basic plan document, new or amended, with one adoption agreement	$9,000
(2) Nonmass submission (new or amended) by M & P sponsor, per adoption agreement	$9,000
(3) Mass submitter M & P plan, per each additional adoption agreement	$650
(4) Sponsor's minor modification of M & P mass submitter's plan document, per adoption agreement	$650
(5) M & P mass submitter's request for an advisory letter with respect to the addition of optional provisions following issuance of a favorable opinion letter (see section 12.031(c) of Rev. Proc. 2005–16), per basic plan document (regardless of the number of adoption agreements)	$650

(6) M & P mass submitter's addition of new adoption agreements after the basic plan document and associated adoption agreements have been approved, per adoption agreement	$650
Note 1: Mass submitters that are sponsors in their own right are liable for this fee.	
Note 2: If a mass submitter submits, in any 12-month period ending January 31, more than 300 applications on behalf of word-for-word adopters with respect to a particular adoption agreement, only the first 300 such applications will be subject to the fee; no fee will apply to those in excess of the first 300 such applications submitted within the 12-month period.	
(7) Sponsor's word-for-word identical adoption of M & P mass submitter's basic plan document (or an amendment thereof), per adoption agreement	$200
(8) Assumption of sponsorship of an approved M & P plan, without any amendment to the plan document, by a new entity, as evidenced by a change of employer identification number	$200
(9) Mass submitter or sponsor per trust document in excess of 10	$650
.06 *Advisory letters on volume submitter plans.*	
(1) Volume submitter specimen plans	$9,000
(2) Volume submitter lead specimen plan	$9,000
(3) Volume submitter specimen plan that is word-for-word identical to a lead specimen plan	$200
.07 *Determination letters*	
(1) If the plan is intended to satisfy a design-based or nondesign-based safe harbor, or if the applicant is not electing to receive a determination with respect to any of the general tests, and the applicant is not electing to receive a determination with respect to the average benefit test:	
(a) Form 5300 *(Application for Determination for Employee Benefit Plan)*	$1,000
(b) Form 5310 *(Application for Determination for Terminating Plan)*	$1,000
(c) Form 5307 *(Application for Determination for Adopters of Master or Prototype or Volume Submitter Plans)*	$300
(d) Form 6406 *(Short Form Application for Determination for Minor Amendment of Employee Benefit Plan)*	$300
(e) Multiple employer plans (Form 5300):	
(i) 2 to 10 Forms 5300	$1,500
(ii) 11 to 99 Forms 5300	$1,500
(iii) 100 to 499 Forms 5300	$10,000
(iv) Over 499 Forms 5300	$10,000
Note: In the case of a multiple employer plan that is adopted by other employers after the initial submission, the fee would be the same as in paragraph (1) above.	
(f) Multiple employer plans (Form 5310):	
(i) 2 to 10 employers	$1,500
(ii) 11 to 99 employers	$1,500

(iii) 100 to 499 employers	$10,000
(iv) Over 499 employers	$10,000
(2) If the applicant is electing to receive a determination with respect to the average benefit test and/or any of the general tests:	
(a) Form 5300 *(Application for Determination for Employee Benefit Plan)*	$1,800
(b) Form 5310 *(Application for Determination for Terminating Plan)*	$1,800
(c) Form 5307 *(Application for Determination for Adopters of Master or Prototype or Volume Submitter Plans)*	$1,000
(d) Multiple employer plans (Form 5300):	
(i) 2 to 10 Forms 5300	$2,300
(ii) 11 to 99 Forms 5300	$2,300
(iii) 100 to 499 Forms 5300	$15,000
(iv) Over 499 Forms 5300	$15,000
Note: In the case of a multiple employer plan that is adopted by other employers after the initial submission, the fee would be the same as in paragraph (2) above.	
(e) Multiple employer plans (Form 5310):	
(i) 2 to 10 employers	$2,300
(ii) 11 to 99 employers	$2,300
(iii) 100 to 499 employers	$15,000
(iv) Over 499 employers	$15,000
(3) Group trusts contemplated by Rev. Rul. 81–100, 1981–1 C.B. 326, and Rev. Rul. 2004–67, 2004–2 C.B. 28.	$750

EXEMPT ORGANIZATIONS USER FEES

.08 *Letter rulings.*

(1) Applications with respect to change in accounting period (Form 1128)	$350
Note: No user fee is charged if the procedure described in Rev. Proc. 85–58, 1985–2 C.B. 740, is used by timely filing the appropriate information return, or if the procedure described in Rev. Proc. 76–10, 1976–1 C.B. 548, for organizations with group exemptions is followed.	
(2) Applications with respect to change in accounting method (Form 3115)	$275
Note: No user fee is charged if the method described in Rev. Proc. 2002–9, 2002–1 C.B. 327, is used. Taxpayers complying timely with Rev. Proc. 2002–9 will be deemed to have obtained the consent of the Commissioner of Internal Revenue to change their method of accounting.	
(3) Request for approval of a qualified subsidiary related to a § 501(c)(25) organization.	$900
(4) All other letter rulings	$8,700

.09 *Determination letters and requests for group exemption letters*

(1) Initial application for exemption under § 501 or § 521 from organizations (other than pension, profit-sharing, and stock bonus plans described in § 401) that have had annual gross receipts averaging not more than $10,000 during the preceding four years, or new organizations that anticipate gross receipts averaging not more than $10,000 during their first four years	$300
Note: Organizations seeking this reduced fee must sign a certification with their application that the receipts are or will be not more than the indicated amounts.	
(2) Initial application for exempt status from organizations otherwise described in paragraph (1) of this section 6.09 whose actual or anticipated gross receipts exceed the $10,000 average annually	$750
Note: If an organization that is already recognized as exempt under § 501(c) seeks reclassification under another subparagraph of § 501(c), a new user fee will be charged whether or not a new application is required. An additional fee applies to organizations that seek recognition of exemption under § 501(c)(4) (unless requested at the time of the § 501(c)(3) application) for a period for which they do not qualify for exemption under § 501(c)(3) because their application was filed late and they do not qualify for relief under § 301.9100–1.	
(3) Group exemption letters	$900
Note: An additional fee under (1) or (2) above is required when a central organization submits an initial application for exemption with its request for a group exemption letter.	
(4) Canadian registered charities	none
In accordance with the income tax treaty between the United States and Canada, Canadian registered charities are automatically recognized as exempt under § 501(c)(3) without filing an application for exemption. For details, see Notice 99–47, 1999–2 C.B. 391. Therefore, no user fee is required when a Canadian registered charity submits all or part of a Form 1023 or other written request to be listed in Publication 78, or for a determination on its private foundation status.	

.10 *Summary of exempt organization fees*

This table summarizes the various types of exempt organization issues, indicates the office of jurisdiction for each type, and lists the applicable user fee. Reduced fees may be applicable in certain instances.

ISSUE	TECHNICAL OFFICE	USER FEE
Accounting method changes		$275
Accounting period changes		$350
Qualified subsidiaries of § 501(c)(25) organizations		$900
Section 514(b)(3) Neighborhood Land Use Rule		None
Section 4943(c)(7) extensions of disposal period		$8,700

ISSUE	DETERMINATIONS OFFICE	USER FEE
Application for recognition of exemption		$750
Reduced fee described in section 6.09(1)		$300
Advance ruling period inquiries		None
Confirmation of exemption (to replace lost exempt status letter, and to reflect name and address changes)		Nonc
Reclassification of private foundation status		None
Regulations § 301.9100 relief in connection with applications for recognition of exemption		None
Section 507 terminations – advance ruling under § 507(b)(1)(B) and notice under § 507(a)(1) or 507(b)(1)(B)		None
Section 4940(d) exempt operating foundation status		None
Section 4942(g)(2) set asides – advance approval		None
Section 4945 advance approval of organization's grant making procedures		None
Section 4945(f) advance approval of voter registration activities		None
Section 6033 annual information return filing requirements		None
Unusual grants to certain organizations under §§ 170(b)(1)(A)(vi) and 509(a)(2)		None

SECTION 7. MAILING ADDRESS FOR REQUESTING LETTER RULINGS, DETERMINATION LETTERS, ETC.

.01 *Matters handled by EP or EO Technical.* Requests should be mailed to the appropriate address set forth in this section 7.01.

(1) *Employee plans letter rulings under Rev. Procs. 79–62, 87–50, 90–49, 94–42, 2000–41, 2004–15, 2004–44 or 2007–4:*

Internal Revenue Service
Attention: EP Letter Rulings
P.O. Box 27063
McPherson Station
Washington, DC 20038

(2) *Employee plans opinion letters under Rev. Procs. 87–50, 97–29, and 98–59:*

Internal Revenue Service
Attention: EP Opinion Letter
P.O. Box 27063
McPherson Station
Washington, DC 20038

(3) *Employee plans administrative scrutiny determinations under Rev. Proc. 93–41:*

Internal Revenue Service
Attention: Administrative Scrutiny
P.O. Box 27063
McPherson Station
Washington, DC 20038

(4) *Exempt organizations letter rulings:*

Internal Revenue Service
Attention: EO Letter Rulings
P.O. Box 27720
McPherson Station
Washington, DC 20038

Note: Hand delivered requests must be marked RULING REQUEST SUBMISSION. The delivery should be made:

To the following address between the hours of 8:30 a.m. and 4:00 p.m.; where a receipt will be given:

Courier's Desk
Internal Revenue Service
Attention: SE:T:EP [or SE:T:EO]
1111 Constitution Avenue, NW — PE
Washington, DC 20224

.02 *Matters handled by EP or EO Determinations Office.* The following types of requests and applications are handled by the EP or EO Determinations Office and should be sent to thc Internal Revenue Service Center in Covington, Kentucky, at the address shown below: requests for determination letters on the qualified status of employee plans under §§ 401, 403(a), or 409, and the exempt status of any related trust under § 501; applications for recognition of tax exemption on Form 1023, Form 1024 and Form 1028; and other applications for recognition of qualification or exemption. The address is:

Internal Revenue Service
P.O. Box 192
Covington, KY 41012–0192

The following types of requests and applications are handled by the EP Determinations Office and should be sent to the Internal Revenue Service at the address shown below: requests for opinion letters and for volume submitter advisory letters on the form of employee plans under § 401 or 403(a) and the exempt status of any related trust under § 501. The address is:

Internal Revenue Service
P.O. Box 2508
Rm. 5106
Cincinnati, OH 45201

Applications shipped by Express Mail or a delivery service should be sent to:

Internal Revenue Service
201 West Rivercenter Blvd.
Attn: Extracting Stop 312
Covington, KY 41011

SECTION 8. REQUESTS INVOLVING MULTIPLE OFFICES, FEE CATEGORIES, ISSUES, TRANSACTIONS, OR ENTITIES

.01 *Requests involving several offices.* If a request dealing with only one transaction involves more than one of the offices within Headquarters (for example, one issue is under the jurisdiction of the Associate Chief Counsel (Income Tax & Accounting) and another issue is under the jurisdiction of the Commissioner, Tax Exempt and Government Entities Division), only one fee applies, namely the highest fee that otherwise would apply to each of the offices involved. See Rev. Proc. 2007–1, this Bulletin, for the user fees applicable to issues under the jurisdiction of the Associate Chief Counsel (Corporate), the Associate Chief Counsel (Financial Institutions & Products), the Associate Chief Counsel (Income Tax & Accounting), the Associate Chief Counsel (Passthroughs & Special Industries), the Associate Chief Counsel (Procedure and Administration), the Associate Chief Counsel (International) or the Division Counsel/Associate Chief Counsel (Tax Exempt and Government Entities).

.02 *Requests involving several fee categories.* If a request dealing with only one transaction involves more than one fee category, only one fee applies, namely the highest fee that otherwise would apply to each of the categories involved.

.03 *Requests involving several issues.* If a request dealing with only one transaction involves several issues, or a request for a change in accounting method dealing with only one item or sub-method of accounting involves several issues, or a request for a change in accounting period dealing with only one item involves several issues, the request is treated as one request. Therefore, only one fee applies, namely the fee that applies to the particular category or subcategory involved. The addition of a new issue relating to the same transaction will not result in an additional fee, unless the issue places the transaction in a higher fee category.

.04 *Requests involving several unrelated transactions.* If a request involves several unrelated transactions, or a request for a change in accounting method involves several unrelated items or sub-methods of accounting, or a request for a change in accounting period involves several unrelated items, each transaction or item is treated as a separate request. As a result, a separate fee will apply for each unrelated transaction or item. An additional fee will apply if the request is changed by the addition of an unrelated transaction or item not contained in the initial submission.

.05 *Requests for separate letter rulings for several entities.* Each entity involved in a transaction (for example, an exempt hospital reorganization) that desires a separate letter ruling in its own name must pay a separate fee regardless of whether the transaction or transactions may be viewed as related.

SECTION 9. PAYMENT OF FEE

.01 *Method of payment.* Each request to the Service for a letter ruling, determination letter, opinion letter, etc., must be accompanied by a check or money order, payable to the United States Treasury, in the appropriate amount. Taxpayers should not send cash.

.02 *Transmittal forms.* Form 8717, *User Fee for Employee Plan Determination, Opinion, and Advisory Letter Request*, and Form 8718, *User Fee for Exempt Organization Determination Letter Request*, are intended to be used as attachments to certain determination letter, opinion letter and advisory letter applications. Space is reserved for the attachment of the applicable user fee check or money order. No similar form has been designed to be used in connection with requests for letter rulings or administrative scrutiny determinations.

.03 *Effect of nonpayment or payment of incorrect amount.* It will be the general practice of the Service that:

(1) The respective offices within the Service that are responsible for issuing letter rulings, determination letters, etc., will exercise discretion in deciding whether to immediately return submissions that are not accompanied by a properly completed check or money order or that are accompanied by a check or money order for less than the correct amount. In those instances where the submission is not immediately returned, the requester will be contacted and given a reasonable amount of time to submit the proper fee. If the proper fee is not received within a reasonable amount of time, the entire submission will then be returned. However, the respective offices of the Service, in their discretion, may defer substantive consideration of a submission until proper payment has been received.

(2) An application for a determination letter will not be returned merely because Form 8717 or Form 8718 was not attached.

(3) The return of a submission to the requester may adversely affect substantive rights if the submission is not perfected and resubmitted to the Service within 30 days of the date of the cover letter returning the submission. Examples of this are: (a) where an application for a determination letter is submitted prior to the expiration of the remedial amendment period under § 401(b) and is returned because no user fee was attached, the submission will be timely if it is resubmitted by the expiration of the remedial amendment period or, if later, within 30 days after the application was returned; and (b) where an application for exemption under § 501(c)(3) is submitted before expiration of the period provided by § 1.508–1(a)(2) and is re-

turned because no user fee was attached, the submission will be timely if it is resubmitted before expiration of the period provided by § 1.508–1(a)(2) or within 30 days, whichever is later.

(4) If a check or money order is for more than the correct amount, the submission will be accepted and the amount of the excess payment will be returned to the requester.

SECTION 10. REFUNDS

.01 *General rule.* In general, the fee will not be refunded unless the Service declines to rule or make a determination on all issues for which a ruling or determination letter is requested. In the case of a request for a letter ruling, if the case has been closed by the Service because essential information has not been submitted timely, the request may be reopened and treated as a new request, but the taxpayer must pay another user fee before the case can be reopened. *See*, section 11.04(5) of Rev. Proc. 2007–4, page 118, this Bulletin.

.02 *Examples.*

(1) The following are examples of situations in which the fee will not be refunded:

(a) The request for a letter ruling, determination letter, etc., is withdrawn at any time subsequent to its receipt by the Service, unless the only reason for withdrawal is that the Service has advised the requester that a higher user fee than was sent with the request is applicable and the requester is unwilling to pay the higher fee. For example, no fee will be refunded where the taxpayer has been advised that a proposed adverse ruling is contemplated and subsequently withdraws its submission.

(b) The request is procedurally deficient, although accompanied by the proper fee, if it is not timely perfected by the requester. When there is a failure to timely perfect the request, the case will be considered closed and the failure to perfect will be treated as a withdrawal for purposes of this revenue procedure. An exemption application that is not substantially complete is considered a procedurally deficient request for a letter ruling or a determination letter on exempt status.

(c) A letter ruling, determination letter, etc., is revoked in whole or in part at the initiative of the Service. The fee paid at the time the original letter ruling, determination letter, etc., was requested will not be refunded.

(d) The request contains several issues and the Service rules on some, but not all, of the issues. The highest fee applicable to the issues on which the Service rules will not be refunded.

(e) The taxpayer asserts that a letter ruling the taxpayer received covering a single issue is erroneous or not responsive (other than an issue on which the Service has declined to rule) and requests reconsideration. The Service, upon reconsideration, does not agree that the letter ruling is erroneous or is not responsive. The fee accompanying the request for reconsideration will not be refunded.

(f) The situation is the same as described in subparagraph (e) of this section 10.02(1) except that the letter ruling covered several unrelated transactions. The Service, upon reconsideration, does not agree with the taxpayer that the letter ruling is erroneous or is not responsive for all of the transactions, but does agree that it is erroneous as to one transaction. The fee accompanying the request for reconsideration will not be refunded except to the extent applicable to the transaction for which the Service agrees the letter ruling was in error.

(g) The request is for a supplemental letter ruling, determination letter, etc., concerning a change in facts (whether significant or not) relating to the transaction ruled on.

(h) The request is for reconsideration of an adverse or partially adverse letter ruling or a final adverse determination letter, and the taxpayer submits arguments and authorities not submitted before the original letter ruling or determination letter was issued.

(2) The following are examples of situations in which the fee will be refunded:

(a) In a situation to which section 10.02(1)(h) of this revenue procedure does not apply, the taxpayer asserts that a letter ruling the taxpayer received covering a single issue is erroneous or is not responsive (other than an issue on which the Service declined to rule) and requests reconsideration. The Service agrees, upon reconsideration, that the letter ruling is erroneous or is not responsive. The fee accompanying the taxpayer's request for reconsideration will be refunded.

(b) In a situation to which section 10.02(1)(h) of this revenue procedure does not apply, the requester requests a supplemental letter ruling, determination letter, etc., to correct a mistake that the Service agrees it made in the original letter ruling, determination letter, etc., such as a mistake in the statement of facts or in the citation of a Code section. Once the Service agrees that it made a mistake, the fee accompanying the request for the supplemental letter ruling, determination letter, etc., will be refunded.

(c) The taxpayer requests and is granted relief under § 7805(b) in connection with the revocation in whole or in part, of a previously issued letter ruling, determination letter, etc. The fee accompanying the request for relief will be refunded.

(d) In a situation to which section 10.02(1)(d) of this revenue procedure applied, the taxpayer requests reconsideration of the Service's decision not to rule on an issue. Once the Service agrees to rule on the issue, the fee accompanying the request for reconsideration will be refunded.

SECTION 11. REQUEST FOR RECONSIDERATION OF USER FEE

A taxpayer that believes the user fee charged by the Service for its request for a letter ruling, determination letter, etc., is either not applicable or incorrect and wishes to receive a refund of all or part of the amount paid (see section 10 of this revenue procedure) may request reconsideration and, if desired, the opportunity for an oral discussion by sending a letter to the Internal Revenue Service at the applicable Post Office Box or other address given in section 7. Both the incoming envelope and the letter requesting such reconsideration should be prominently marked "USER FEE RECONSIDERATION REQUEST." No user fee is required for these requests. The request should be marked for the attention of:

If the matter involves primarily:	*Mark for the attention of:*
Employee plans letter ruling requests and all other employee plans matters handled by EP Technical	Employee Plans Technical
Exempt organizations letter ruling requests	Exempt Organizations Technical
Employee plans determination letter requests and opinion letter and advisory letter requests pursuant to Rev. Proc. 2005–16	Manager, EP Determinations Quality Assurance
Exempt organizations determination letter requests	Manager, EO Determinations Quality Assurance

SECTION 12. EFFECT ON OTHER DOCUMENTS

Rev. Proc. 2006–8 is superseded.

SECTION 13. EFFECTIVE DATE

This revenue procedure is effective January 2, 2007.

SECTION 14. PAPERWORK REDUCTION ACT

The collections of information contained in this revenue procedure have been reviewed and approved by the Office of Management and Budget in accordance with the Paperwork Reduction Act (44 U.S.C. 3507) under control number 1545–1520.

An agency may not conduct or sponsor, and a person is not required to respond to, a collection of information unless the collection of information displays a valid OMB control number.

The collections of information in this revenue procedure are in section 6.09. This information is required to substantiate that a taxpayer or an exempt organization seeking to pay a reduced user fee with respect to a request for a determination letter is entitled to pay the reduced fee; to identify the user fee category and corresponding fee required to be paid with respect to determination letter requests; to request reconsideration of the user fee charged by the Service and, in connection with such a request, to indicate whether an oral discussion is desired. This information will be used to enable the Service to determine whether the taxpayer or exempt organization is entitled to pay a reduced user fee, to ascertain whether reconsideration of the user fee is being requested and, if it is being requested, whether an oral discussion is requested. The collections of information are voluntary, to obtain a benefit. The likely respondents are individuals, businesses or other for-profit institutions, nonprofit institutions, and small businesses or organizations.

The estimated total annual reporting and/or recordkeeping burden is 300 hours.

The estimated annual burden per respondent/recordkeeper varies from one hour to ten hours, depending on individual circumstances, with an estimated average of three hours. The estimated number of respondents and/or recordkeepers is 90 (requests for reduced fees) and 10 (requests for reconsideration of fee).

The estimated annual frequency of responses is on occasion.

Books or records relating to a collection of information must be retained as long as their contents may become material in the administration of any internal revenue law. Generally tax returns and tax return information are confidential, as required by 26 U.S.C. 6103.

DRAFTING INFORMATION

The principal author of this revenue procedure is Michael Rubin of the Employee Plans, Tax Exempt and Government Entities Division. For further information regarding employee plans matters in this revenue procedure, please contact the Employee Plans' taxpayer assistance telephone service 877–829–5500 (a toll-free number) between the hours of 8:30 a.m. and 4:30 p.m., Eastern time, Monday through Friday. For employee plans matters, please contact Mr. Rubin at (202) 283–9888 (not a toll-free number). For exempt organization matters, please contact Mr. Ted Lieber at (202) 283–8999 or Mr. Wayne Hardesty at (202) 283–8976 (not toll-free numbers).

APPENDIX

Following is a list of revenue procedures requiring payment of a user fee or an administrative scrutiny determination user fee.

A. *Procedures applicable to both Employee Plans and Exempt Organizations*

Rev. Proc. 2007–4, this Bulletin, provides procedures for issuing letter rulings, information letters, etc., on matters relating to matters under the jurisdiction of the Commissioner, Tax Exempt and Government Entities Division.

B. *Procedures applicable to Employee Plans matters other than actuarial matters*

Rev. Proc. 75–26, 1975–1 C.B. 722, sets forth the general procedures of the Internal Revenue Service for the processing of applications for exemption under § 4975(c)(2) of the Code.

Rev. Proc. 87–50, 1987–2 C.B. 647, as modified by Rev. Proc. 91–44, Rev. Proc. 92–38, and Rev. Proc. 2002–10, 2002–1 C.B. 401, sets forth the procedures of the Service relating to the issuance of rulings and opinion letters with respect to the establishment of individual retirement accounts and annuities (IRAs) under § 408, the entitlement to exemption of related trusts or custodial accounts under § 408(e), and the acceptability of the form of prototype simplified employee pension (SEP) agreements under §§ 408(k) and 415.

Rev. Proc. 92–24, 1992–1 C.B. 739, provides procedures for requesting determination letters on the effect on a plan's qualified status under § 401(a) of the Code of plan language that permits, pursuant to § 420, the transfer of assets in a defined benefit plan to a health benefits account described in § 401(h).

Rev. Proc. 92–38, 1992–1 C.B. 859, provides notice that individual retirement arrangement trusts, custodial account agreements, and annuity contracts must be amended to provide for the required distribution rules in § 408(a)(6) or (b)(3). In addition, Rev. Proc. 92–38 modifies the guidance in Rev. Proc. 87–50 with regard to opinion letters issued to sponsoring organizations, including mass submitters and sponsors of prototype IRAs.

Rev. Proc. 93–41, 1993–2 C.B. 536, sets forth the procedures of the Service relating to the issuance of an administrative scrutiny determination as to whether a separate line of business satisfies the requirement of administrative scrutiny within the meaning of § 1.414(r)–6.

Rev. Proc. 97–29, 1997–1 C.B. 698, describes model amendments for SIMPLE IRAs; guidance to drafters of prototype SIMPLE IRAs on obtaining opinion letters; permissive amendments to sponsors of nonSIMPLE IRAs; the opening of a prototype program for SIMPLE IRA Plans; and transitional relief for users of SIMPLE IRAs and SIMPLE IRA Plans that have not been approved by the Service.

Rev. Proc. 98–59, 1998–2 C.B. 727, provides guidance on obtaining opinion letters to drafters of prototype Roth IRAs, and provides transitional relief for users of Roth IRAs that have not been approved by the Internal Revenue Service.

Rev. Proc. 2003–16, 2003–1 C.B. 359, sets forth guidelines for the implementation of the provision for a waiver of the 60-day rollover period described in section 644 of EGTRRA.

Rev. Proc. 2005–16, 2005–1 C.B. 674, revises and combines the Service's master and prototype (M&P) and volume submitter program into a unified program for the pre-approval of pension, profit-sharing and annuity plans.

Rev. Proc. 2005–66, 2005–2 C.B. 509, describes the Service's procedure for issuing determination letters pursuant to § 401(a) of the Code under a staggered remedial amendment system.

Rev. Proc. 2007–6, this Bulletin, provides procedures for issuing determination letters on the qualified status of employee plans under §§ 401(a), 403(a), 409, and 4975(e)(7).

C. *Procedures applicable to Employee Plans actuarial matters*

Rev. Proc. 79–62, 1979–2 C.B. 576, outlines the procedure by which a plan sponsor or administrator may request a determination that a plan amendment is reasonable and provides for only *de minimis* increases in plan liabilities in accordance with § 412(f)(2)(A) of the Code and § 304(b)(2)(A) of ERISA.

Rev. Proc. 90–49, 1990–2 C.B. 620, modifies and replaces Rev. Proc. 89–35, 1989–1 C.B. 917, in order to extend the effective date to contributions made for plan years beginning after December 31, 1989, to change the deadline for requesting rulings under the revenue procedure, to revise the information requirements for a ruling request made under the revenue procedure, to furnish a worksheet for actuarial computations, and to provide a special rule under which certain_ *de minimis* nondeductible employer contributions to a qualified defined benefit plan may be returned to the taxpayer without a formal ruling or disallowance from the Service.

Rev. Proc. 94–42, 1994–1 C.B. 717, sets forth a procedure for obtaining approval of an amendment to a qualified plan that, under § 412(c)(8), reduces the accrued benefits of plan participants.

Rev. Proc. 2000–41, 2000–2, C.B. 371, sets forth the procedure by which a plan administrator or plan sponsor may obtain approval of the Secretary of the Treasury for a change in funding method as provided by § 412(c)(5) of the Code and section 302(c)(5) of ERISA.

Rev. Proc. 2004–15, 2004–1 C.B. 490, sets forth procedures for requesting waivers of the minimum funding standard described in § 412(d) and the issuance of such waivers by the office of the Director, Employee Plans, Tax Exempt and Government Entities Division.

Rev. Proc. 2004–44, 2004–2 C.B. 134, outlines the procedure by which a plan administrator or plan sponsor may request and obtain approval for an extension of an amortization period in accordance with § 412(e) of the Code and section 304(a) of ERISA.

D. *Procedures applicable to Exempt Organizations matters only*

Rev. Proc. 80–27, 1980–1 C.B. 677, as modified by Rev. Proc. 96–40, 1996–2 C.B. 301, provides procedures under which recognition of exemption from federal income tax under § 501(c) may be obtained on a group basis for subordinate organizations affiliated with and under the general supervision or control of a central organization. This procedure relieves each of the subordinates covered by a group exemption letter from filing its own application for recognition of exemption.

Rev. Proc. 90–27, 1990–1 C.B. 514, sets forth revised procedures with regard to applications for recognition of exemption from federal income tax under §§ 501 and 521.

Part IV. Items of General Interest

Cumulative List of Announcements Relating to Section 7428(c) Validation of Certain Contributions Made During Pendency of Declaratory Judgment Proceedings from January 1, 2006 through December 31, 2006

Announcement 2007–1

The following is a cumulative listing of names of organizations that are presently challenging, under section 7428 of the Internal Revenue Code, the revocation of their status as organizations entitled to receive deductible contributions in declaratory judgment suits in the Tax Court, the United States District Court for the District of Columbia, or the United States Court of Federal Claims. The purpose of this announcement is to inform potential donors to these organizations of the protection under 7428(c) for certain contributions made during the litigation period.

Protection under section 7428(c) of the Code begins on the date that the notice of revocation is published in the Internal Revenue Bulletin and ends on the date on which a court first determines that an organization is not described in section 170(c)(2), as more particularly set forth in section 7428(c)(1). In the case of individual contributors, the maximum amount of contributions protected during this period is limited to $1,000.00, with a husband and wife being treated as one contributor. This protection is not extended to any individual who was responsible, in whole or in part, for the acts or omissions of the organization that were the basis for the revocation. This protection also applies (but without limitation as to amount) to organizations described in section 170(c)(2) which are exempt from tax under section 501(a). If the organization ultimately prevails in its declaratory judgment suit, deductibility of contributions would be subject to the normal limitations set forth under section 170.

I. The organizations listed below continue to be involved in pending declaratory judgment suits under section 7428 of the Code, challenging revocation of their status as eligible donees under section 170(c)(2). Protection under section 7428(c) begins on the date indicated.

Michael and Laura Gallop Family Foundation (June 28, 2004)	Agoura Hills, CA
Rameses School of San Antonio, Texas (January 30, 2005)	San Antonio, TX

II. The organization listed below is no longer described in section 170(c)(2) and is not recognized as exempt under section 501(c)(3) of the Code.

South Community Association	Middletown, OH

III. The organizations listed below continue to be described in section 170(c)(2) and are recognized as exempt under section 501(c)(3) of the Code.

Fountainview at College Road, Inc.	Monsey, NY
Northern Manor Multicare, Inc.	Monsey, NY
Northern Metropolitan Foundation for Healthcare, Inc.	Monsey, NY
Northern Metropolitan, Inc.	Monsey, NY
Northern Riverview, Inc.	Monsey, NY
Northern Services Group, Inc.	Monsey, NY

Part I. Rulings and Decisions Under the Internal Revenue Code of 1986

Section 61.—Gross Income Defined

26 CFR 1.61–21(e): Vehicle cents-per-mile valuation.

A revenue procedure provides maximum vehicle values for which the special valuation rules of regulations sections 1.61–21(d) and (e) may be used. See Rev. Proc. 2007-11, page 261.

Section 63.—Taxable Income Defined

26 CFR 1.9300–1T: Reduction in taxable income for housing Hurricane Katrina displaced individuals.

T.D. 9301

DEPARTMENT OF THE TREASURY Internal Revenue Service 26 CFR Part 1

Reduction in Taxable Income for Housing Hurricane Katrina Displaced Individuals

AGENCY: Internal Revenue Service (IRS), Treasury.

ACTION: Temporary regulations.

SUMMARY: This document contains temporary regulations relating to the reduction in taxable income under section 302 of the Katrina Emergency Tax Relief Act of 2005. The regulations affect taxpayers who provide housing in their principal residences to individuals displaced by Hurricane Katrina. The text of the temporary regulations also serves as the text of the proposed regulations (REG–152043–05) set forth in the notice of proposed rulemaking on this subject in this issue of the Bulletin.

DATES: *Effective Date:* These regulations are effective December 11, 2006.

Applicability Date: For date of applicability, see §1.9300–1T(g).

FOR FURTHER INFORMATION CONTACT: Marnette M. Myers, 202–622–4920 (not a toll-free number).

SUPPLEMENTARY INFORMATION:

Background

This document contains amendments to the Income Tax Regulations (26 CFR Part 1) relating to the reduction in taxable income for housing provided to displaced individuals under section 302 of the Katrina Emergency Tax Relief Act of 2005 (Pub. L. No. 109–73, 119 Stat. 2016) (KETRA).

For taxable years beginning in 2005 and 2006, a taxpayer may reduce taxable income by $500 for each Hurricane Katrina displaced individual to whom the taxpayer provides free housing in the taxpayer's principal residence for a period of 60 consecutive days that ends in the taxable year. No reduction is allowed if the taxpayer receives rent or other compensation from any source for providing the housing.

A taxpayer may not claim a reduction in taxable income with respect to the same Hurricane Katrina displaced individual in more than one taxable year and must include the Hurricane Katrina displaced individual's tax identification number on the taxpayer's return. Generally, the total reduction for all taxable years is $2,000.

A Hurricane Katrina displaced individual is defined as a natural person who was displaced from a principal place of abode that, on August 28, 2005, was in the Hurricane Katrina core disaster area. A Hurricane Katrina displaced individual also is defined as an individual whose principal place of abode was located in the Hurricane Katrina disaster area, but outside the core disaster area, if the abode was damaged by Hurricane Katrina or the individual was evacuated from the abode because of Hurricane Katrina. A Hurricane Katrina displaced individual may not be the taxpayer's spouse or dependent.

Under section 2(1) of KETRA, the Hurricane Katrina disaster area is the area with respect to which a major disaster by reason of Hurricane Katrina has been declared by the President before September 14, 2005, under section 401 of the Robert T. Stafford Disaster Relief and Emergency Assistance Act (42 U.S.C. 5170) (Stafford Act). For purposes of relief provided under KETRA, this area comprises the states of Louisiana, Mississippi, Alabama, and Florida. Under section 2(2) of KETRA, the Hurricane Katrina core disaster area is the portion of the Hurricane Katrina disaster area determined by the President to warrant individual or individual and public assistance from the federal government under the Stafford Act. See Appendix to Notice 2005–73, 2005–2 C.B. 723, (Oct. 17, 2005) (listing parishes and counties designated for assistance under the Stafford Act).

Explanation of Provisions

Provision of Housing

The temporary regulations provide that a taxpayer is considered to provide housing if the housing is provided either in, or on the site of, the taxpayer's principal residence. In addition, the taxpayer must be an owner or lessee of the residence to be treated as providing housing to a Hurricane Katrina displaced individual. The term *principal residence* has the same meaning as in section 121 and the regulations thereunder. Amounts in connection with the provision of housing (for which the taxpayer may not be reimbursed or compensated) include rent and utilities. Amounts for telephone calls, food, clothing and transportation are not amounts in connection with the provision of housing for this purpose.

Limitations on Amount of Reduction

The temporary regulations provide that the $2,000 aggregate limit on the reduction in taxable income applies to unmarried individuals and married taxpayers filing a joint tax return. Married taxpayers who file separate returns may reduce taxable income by $1,000 each for all taxable years.

The temporary regulations clarify that a taxpayer may reduce taxable income with respect to a specific Hurricane Katrina displaced individual in 2005 or 2006, but not both years. Additionally, the temporary regulations provide that a Hurricane Katrina displaced individual may be taken into account by only one taxpayer occupying the same principal residence.

Effective Date

The temporary regulations apply to taxable years beginning after December 31, 2004, and before January 1, 2007, and ending on or after December 11, 2006, which is the date the temporary regulations were filed with the **Federal Register**. Taxpayers may rely on the temporary regulations with respect to taxable years ending before the filing date, but may not rely on the absence of regulations for taxable years ending before the filing date for a result contrary to that under the temporary regulations.

Special Analyses

It has been determined that this Treasury decision is not a significant regulatory action as defined in Executive Order 12866. Therefore, a regulatory assessment is not required. It also has been determined that section 553(b) of the Administrative Procedure Act (5 U.S.C. chapter 5) does not apply to these regulations. Please refer to the cross-referenced notice of proposed rulemaking published elsewhere in this issue of the Bulletin for applicability of the Regulatory Flexibility Act (5 U.S.C. chapter 6). Pursuant to section 7805(f) of the Code, these temporary regulations will be submitted to the Chief Counsel for Advocacy of the Small Business Administration for comment on their impact on small business.

Drafting Information

The principal author of these regulations is Marnette M. Myers of the Office of the Associate Chief Counsel (Income Tax and Accounting). However, other personnel from the IRS and Treasury Department participated in their development.

* * * * *

Adoption of Amendments to the Regulations

Accordingly, 26 CFR part 1 is amended as follows:

PART 1—INCOME TAXES

Paragraph 1. The authority citation for part 1 continues to read, in part, as follows:

Authority: 26 U.S.C. 7805 * * *

Section 1.9300–1T also issued under 26 U.S.C. 6001. * * *

Par. 2. Section 1.9300–1T is added to read as follows:

§1.9300–1T Reduction in taxable income for housing Hurricane Katrina displaced individuals.

(a) *In general.* For a taxable year beginning in 2005 or 2006, a taxpayer who is a natural person may reduce taxable income by $500 for each Hurricane Katrina displaced individual (as defined in paragraph (e)(1) of this section) to whom the taxpayer provides housing free of charge in, or on the site of, the taxpayer's principal residence for a period of 60 consecutive days ending in the taxable year. A taxpayer may not claim the reduction in taxable income unless the taxpayer includes the taxpayer identification number of the Hurricane Katrina displaced individual on the taxpayer's income tax return.

(b) *Provision of housing*—(1) *Principal residence.* For purposes of this section, the term *principal residence* has the same meaning as in section 121 and the regulations thereunder. See §1.121–1(b)(1) and (b)(2).

(2) *Legal interest required.* A taxpayer is treated as providing housing for purposes of this section only if the taxpayer is an owner or lessee (including a co-owner or co-lessee) of the residence.

(3) *Compensation for providing housing*—(i) *In general.* No reduction in taxable income is allowed under this section to a taxpayer who receives rent or any other amount from any source in connection with the provision of housing.

(ii) *Amounts in connection with the provision of housing.* For purposes of this section, amounts in connection with the provision of housing include (but are not limited to) amounts for rent and utilities. Amounts for telephone calls, food, clothing, and transportation are examples of amounts not in connection with the provision of housing.

(c) *Limitations*—(1) *Dollar limitation*—(i) *In general.* The reduction under paragraph (a) of this section may not exceed the maximum dollar limitation reduced by the amount of the reduction under this section for all prior taxable years. The maximum dollar limitation is—

(A) $2,000 in the case of an unmarried individual;

(B) $2,000 in the case of a husband and wife who file a joint income tax return; and

(C) $1,000 in the case of a married individual who files a separate income tax return.

(ii) *Married individuals with separate principal residences.* The limitations in paragraphs (c)(1)(i)(B) and (c)(1)(i)(C) of this section apply without regard to whether the married individuals occupy the same principal residence. A person is treated as married for purposes of this section if the individual is treated as married under section 7703.

(2) *Spouse or dependent of the taxpayer.* No reduction is allowed for a Hurricane Katrina displaced individual who is the spouse or dependent of the taxpayer.

(3) *Individual taken into account only once.* A taxpayer may not reduce taxable income under paragraph (a) of this section with respect to a Hurricane Katrina displaced individual who was taken into account by the taxpayer for any prior taxable year.

(4) *Taxpayers occupying the same principal residence.* A Hurricane Katrina displaced individual may be taken into account by only one taxpayer occupying the same principal residence for all taxable years.

(d) *Substantiation.* A taxpayer claiming a reduction under this section must prepare and maintain records sufficient to show entitlement to the reduction as provided in Form 8914 *(Exemption Amount for Taxpayers Housing Individuals Displaced by Hurricane Katrina)* or other forms, instructions, publications or guidance published by the IRS.

(e) *Definitions.* The following definitions apply for purposes of this section.

(1) *Hurricane Katrina displaced individual.* The term *Hurricane Katrina displaced individual* means any natural person if the following requirements are met—

(i) The person's principal place of abode on August 28, 2005, was in the Hurricane Katrina disaster area (as defined in paragraph (e)(2) of this section);

(ii) The person was displaced from that abode; and

(iii) If the abode was located outside the Hurricane Katrina core disaster area (as defined in paragraph (e)(3) of this section)—

(A) The abode was damaged by Hurricane Katrina; or

(B) The person was evacuated from that abode by reason of Hurricane Katrina.

(2) *Hurricane Katrina disaster area.* The term *Hurricane Katrina disaster area* means the states of Alabama, Florida, Louisiana, and Mississippi.

(3) *Hurricane Katrina core disaster area.* The term *Hurricane Katrina core disaster area* means the portion of the Hurricane Katrina disaster area designated by the President to warrant individual or individual and public assistance from the federal government under the Robert T. Stafford Disaster Relief and Emergency Assistance Act (42 U.S.C. 5170).

(f) *Examples.* The provisions of this section are illustrated by the following examples in which each Hurricane Katrina displaced individual, who is not a dependent or spouse of the taxpayer, is provided housing (within the meaning of paragraph (b) of this section) in, or on the site of, the taxpayer's principal residence for a period of at least 60 consecutive days ending in the applicable taxable year. The examples are as follows:

Example 1. Taxpayer A provides housing to N, a Hurricane Katrina displaced individual, from September 1, 2005, until March 10, 2006. Under paragraphs (a) and (c)(3) of this section, A may reduce taxable income by $500 on A's 2005 income tax return or A's 2006 income tax return, but not both, with respect to N.

Example 2. The facts are the same as in *Example 1* except that A and B, A's unmarried roommate and co-lessee, provide housing to N. Under paragraphs (a) and (c)(4) of this section, either A or B, but not both, may reduce taxable income by $500 for 2005 with respect to N. If either A or B reduces taxable income for 2005 with respect to N, neither A nor B may reduce taxable income with respect to N for 2006.

Example 3. Unmarried roommates and co-lessees C and D provide housing to eight Hurricane Katrina displaced individuals during 2005. Under paragraphs (a) and (c)(1)(i)(A) of this section, C and D each may reduce taxable income by $2,000 on their 2005 income tax returns.

Example 4. (i) H and W are married to each other and provide housing to a Hurricane Katrina displaced individual, O, in 2005. H and W file their 2005 income tax return married filing jointly. Under paragraphs (a) and (c)(4) of this section, H and W may reduce taxable income by $500 on their 2005 income tax return with respect to O.

(ii) In 2006, H and W provide housing to O and to another Hurricane Katrina displaced individual, P. H and W file their 2006 income tax return married filing separately. Because H and W reduced their 2005 taxable income with respect to O, under paragraph (c)(3) of this section, neither H nor W may reduce taxable income on their 2006 income tax return with respect to O. Under paragraphs (a) and (c)(4) of this section, either H or W, but not both, may reduce taxable income by $500 on his or her 2006 income tax return with respect to P.

(g) *Effective date.* This section applies for taxable years beginning after December 31, 2004, and before January 1, 2007, and ending on or after December 11, 2006.

Linda M. Kroening,
Acting Deputy Commissioner for Services and Enforcement.

Approved December 1, 2006.

Eric Solomon,
Acting Deputy Assistant Secretary of the Treasury (Tax Policy).

(Filed by the Office of the Federal Register on December 11, 2006, 8:45 a.m., and published in the issue of the Federal Register for December 12, 2006, 71 F.R. 74467)

Section 280F.—Limitation on Depreciation for Luxury Automobiles; Limitation Where Certain Property Used for Personal Purposes

A revenue procedure provides maximum vehicle values for which the special valuation rules of regulations sections 1.61–21(d) and (e) may be used. See Rev. Proc. 2007-11, page 261.

Section 6011.—General Requirement of Return, Statement, or List

26 CFR 1.556–2: Adjustments to taxable income.

T.D. 9300

DEPARTMENT OF THE TREASURY Internal Revenue Service 26 CFR Parts 1, 301 and 602

Guidance Necessary to Facilitate Business Electronic Filing

AGENCY: Internal Revenue Service (IRS), Treasury.

ACTION: Final regulations and removal of temporary regulations.

SUMMARY: This document contains final regulations designed to eliminate regulatory impediments to the electronic filing of certain income tax returns and other forms. These regulations affect business taxpayers who file income tax returns electronically. This document also makes conforming changes to certain current regulations.

DATES: *Effective Date:* These regulations are effective on December 8, 2006.

Applicability Date: These regulations apply with respect to taxable years beginning after December 31, 2002. The applicability of §§1.170A–11T, 1.556–2T, 1.565–1T, 1.936–7T, 1.1017–1T, 1.1368–1T, 1.1377–1T, 1.1502–21T(b)(3)(i) and (b)(3)(ii)(B), 1.1502–75T, 1.1503–2T, 1.6038B–1T(b)(1)(ii) and 301.7701–3T will expire on December 8, 2006.

FOR FURTHER INFORMATION CONTACT: Nathan Rosen, (202) 622–4910 (not a toll-free number).

SUPPLEMENTARY INFORMATION:

Paperwork Reduction Act

The collection of information contained in these regulations has been reviewed and approved by the Office of Management and Budget in accordance with the Paperwork Reduction Act of 1995 (44 U.S.C. 3507(d)) under control number 1545–1868. The collection of information in these final regulations is in §1.170A–11(b)(2). The information required in §1.170A–11(b)(2) concerning the date on which a corporation's board of directors authorizes a certain type of charitable contribution assists the IRS in determining the deductibility of such contributions. Responses to this collection of information are mandatory.

An agency may not conduct or sponsor, and a person is not required to respond to, a collection of information unless the collection of information displays a valid control number assigned by the Office of Management and Budget.

The estimated annual burden per respondent is .25 hours.

Comments concerning the accuracy of this burden estimate and suggestions for reducing this burden should be sent to the **Internal Revenue Service**,

Attn: IRS Reports, Clearance Officer, SE:W:CAR:MP:T:T:SP, Washington, DC 20224, and to the **Office of Management and Budget**, Attn: Desk Officer for the Department of the Treasury, Office of Information and Regulatory Affairs, Washington, DC 20503.

Books and records relating to a collection of information must be retained as long as their contents may become material in the administration of any internal revenue law. Generally, tax returns and tax return information are confidential, as required by 26 U.S.C. 6103.

Background

This document contains amendments to 26 CFR part 1 and 26 CFR part 301 designed to eliminate regulatory impediments to the electronic submission of tax returns and other forms filed by corporations, partnerships, other business entities, and their owners.

In 1998, Congress enacted the Internal Revenue Service Restructuring and Reform Act of 1998 (RRA 1998), Pub. L. No. 105–206 (112 Stat. 685) (1998). RRA 1998 states a Congressional policy to promote the paperless filing of Federal tax returns. Section 2001(a) of RRA 1998 set a goal for the IRS to have at least 80 percent of all Federal tax and information returns filed electronically by 2007. Section 2001(b) of RRA 1998 requires the IRS to establish a 10-year strategic plan to eliminate barriers to electronic filing.

Finalization of December 2003 Regulations Facilitating Electronic Filing

On December 19, 2003, the IRS and Treasury published in the **Federal Register** (T.D. 9100, 2004–1 C.B. 297 [68 FR 70701]) temporary and final regulations modifying the regulations under sections 170, 556, 565, 936, 1017, 1368, 1377, 1502, 1503, 6038B and 7701 of the Internal Revenue Code. In the same issue of the **Federal Register**, the IRS and Treasury published a notice of proposed rulemaking (REG–116664–01, 2004–1 C.B. 319 [68 FR 70747]) proposing to amend regulations under the code sections noted in the previous sentence. The temporary, final, and proposed regulations published on December 19, 2003, are collectively referred to as the December 2003 Regulations.

The December 2003 Regulations generally affect taxpayers who must file any of the following forms: Form 926, "*Return by a U.S. Transferor of Property to a Foreign Corporation*"; Form 972, "*Consent of Shareholder To Include Specific Amount in Gross Income*"; Form 973, "*Corporation Claim for Deduction for Consent Dividends*"; Form 982, "*Reduction of Tax Attributes Due to Discharge of Indebtedness (and Section 1082 Basis Adjustment)*"; Form 1120, "*U.S. Corporation Income Tax Return*"; Form 1120S, "*U.S. Income Tax Return for an S Corporation*"; Form 1122, "*Authorization and Consent of Subsidiary Corporation To Be Included in a Consolidated Income Tax Return*"; Form 5471, "*Information Return of U.S. Persons With Respect To Certain Foreign Corporations*"; Form 5712–A, "*Election and Verification of the Cost Sharing or Profit Split Method Under Section 936(h)(5)*"; and Form 8832, "*Entity Classification Election.*"

Prior to the changes adopted by the December 2003 Regulations, certain regulations under the code sections cited above impeded electronic filing of returns. Some of these regulations, for example, impeded electronic filing by requiring taxpayers to include third-party signatures on their tax returns or by requiring taxpayers to attach documents or statements generated by a third party. Other regulations required a taxpayer to sign an IRS form and file it as an attachment to the taxpayer's income tax return. To address certain situations in which regulations required taxpayers to attach documents or statements to their tax returns, for example, the December 2003 Regulations allowed taxpayers to retain such items in their books and records. Taxpayers would be obligated, of course, to make the items available for inspection by the IRS.

The IRS received no comments responding to the December 2003 Regulations, and no public hearing regarding the proposed regulations was requested or held. Accordingly, the temporary and proposed regulations are adopted with no substantive change by this Treasury decision, and the corresponding temporary regulations are removed. These final regulations make certain non-substantive changes to the December 2003 Regulations as described below.

Section 556 was repealed by the American Jobs Creation Act, Pub. L. No. 108–357 (118 Stat. 1418), effective for taxable years of foreign corporations beginning after December 31, 2004, and effective for taxable years of United States shareholders with or within which such taxable years of foreign corporations end. The provision in the December 2003 Regulations eliminating an electronic filing impediment under section 556 applied to tax years ending before the repeal of section 556. Therefore, these final regulations amend section 1.556–2 of the Income Tax Regulations despite the repeal of section 556 itself.

These final regulations remove certain portions of section 1.1502–21T and place such language in sections 1.1502–21(b)(3)(i) and (b)(3)(ii)(B), so as to eliminate impediments to the electronic filing of Form 1120. Other portions of that temporary regulation, however, predate the December 2003 Regulations or relate to matters other than electronic filing, and this document does not revise those portions.

The regulations as finalized by this Treasury decision clarify that references in the following regulations to tax return due dates include extensions of such due dates: See 1.565–1(b)(3), 1.936–7(b), Q. & A. 1, 1.1368–1(f)(5)(iii) and (g)(2)(iii) and 1.1503–2(g)(2)(i) and (iv)(B)(3)(*iii*).

January 2006 Final Regulations Facilitating Electronic Filing

On January 23, 2006, the IRS and Treasury released final regulations (T.D. 9243, 2006–8 I.R.B. 475 [71 FR 4276]) (the January 2006 Final Regulations) which, among other things, removed an impediment to electronic filing of Form 926. In the December 2003 Regulations, the IRS and Treasury had previously amended both sections 1.6038B–1(b)(1)(i) and 1.6038B–1(b)(1)(ii) of the Income Tax Regulations to eliminate an impediment to electronic filing of Form 926. The January 2006 Final Regulations amended section 1.6038B–1(b)(1)(i) and removed temporary regulations section 1.6038B–1T(b)(1)(i). Therefore, because the amendment in the December 2003 Regulations to 1.6038B–1T(b)(1)(i) has already been adopted in final regulations, these final regulations amend 1.6038B–1(b)(1)(ii) and remove 1.6038B–1T(b)(1)(ii), but do not address section 1.6038B–1(b)(1)(i).

May 2006 Regulations Facilitating Electronic Filing

On May 26, 2006, the IRS and Treasury Department released final and temporary regulations (T.D. 9264, 2006–26 I.R.B. 1150 [71 FR 30591]) (the May 2006 Regulations), which contained numerous temporary regulations amending or replacing final regulations. Some of these final regulations had required taxpayers to provide detailed information about a transaction. In other cases, the scope of various reporting requirements was not clear. The May 2006 Regulations simplified, clarified or, in some cases, eliminated these reporting burdens.

The May 2006 Regulations also eliminated regulatory impediments to the electronic filing of certain statements that taxpayers are required to include on or with their Federal income tax returns. In some cases, this impediment was removed by deleting the requirement that the taxpayer sign such statement. In other cases, where the taxpayer and a third party were both required to sign such statement, this impediment was removed by requiring each party to indicate on such statement that it had entered into an agreement with the other party addressing the substantive matters covered by the final regulations. Requiring such a statement from the parties in place of the dual signatures eliminates an e-file impediment, but to protect the Service's interests, the May 2006 regulations require each party to keep either the original or a copy of the underlying agreement in its records.

Special Analyses

It has been determined that this Treasury decision is not a significant regulatory action as defined in Executive Order 12866. Therefore, a regulatory assessment is not required. It also has been determined that section 553(b) of the Administrative Procedure Act (5 U.S.C. chapter 5) does not apply to these regulations. It is hereby certified that the collection of information in these regulations will not have a significant economic impact on a substantial number of small entities. This certification is based on the fact that the collection of information in these regulations involves an insignificant expenditure of time by taxpayers, as noted above under the heading "Paperwork Reduction Act." Accordingly, a Regulatory Flexibility Analysis under the Regulatory Flexibility Act (5 U.S.C. chapter 6) is not required. Pursuant to section 7805(f) of the Code, the December 2003 Regulations and the December 2003 notice of proposed rulemaking were submitted to the Chief Counsel for Advocacy of the Small Business Administration for comment on their impact on small business.

Drafting Information

The principal author of these regulations is Nathan Rosen, Office of Associate Chief Counsel (Procedure and Administration), Administrative Provisions and Judicial Practice Division.

* * * * *

Adoption of Amendments to the Regulations

Accordingly, 26 CFR parts 1, 301 and 602 is amended as follows:

PART 1—INCOME TAXES

Paragraph 1. The authority citation for part 1 continues to read, in part, as follows:

Authority: 26 U.S.C. 7805 * * *

Par. 2. Section 1.170A–11 is amended by revising paragraph (b)(2) to read as follows:

§1.170A–11 Limitation on, and carryover of, contributions by corporations.

* * * * *

(b) * * *

(2) The election must be made at the time the return for the taxable year is filed, by reporting the contribution on the return. There shall be attached to the return when filed a written declaration stating that the resolution authorizing the contribution was adopted by the board of directors during the taxable year. For taxable years beginning before January 1, 2003, the declaration shall be verified by a statement signed by an officer authorized to sign the return that it is made under penalties of perjury, and there shall also be attached to the return when filed a copy of the resolution of the board of directors authorizing the contribution. For taxable years beginning after December 31, 2002, the declaration must also include the date of the resolution, the declaration shall be verified by signing the return, and a copy of the resolution of the board of directors authorizing the contribution is a record that the taxpayer must retain and keep available for inspection in the manner required by §1.6001–1(e).

* * * * *

§1.170A–11T [Removed]

Par. 3. Section 1.170A–11T is removed.

Par. 4. Section 1.556–2 is amended by revising paragraph (e)(2)(vii) and adding paragraph (e)(3) to read as follows:

§1.556–2 Adjustments to taxable income.

* * * * *

(e) * * *

(2) * * *

(vii) In the case of a return for a taxable year beginning before January 1, 2003, a copy of the contract, lease, or rental agreement;

* * * * *

(3) If the statement described in §1.556–2(e)(2) is attached to a taxpayer's income tax return for a taxable year beginning after December 31, 2002, a copy of the applicable contract, lease or rental agreement is not required to be submitted with the return, but must be retained by the taxpayer and kept available for inspection in the manner required by §1.6001–1(e).

* * * * *

§1.556–2T [Removed]

Par. 5. Section 1.556–2T is removed.

Par. 6. Section 1.565–1 is amended by revising paragraph (b)(3) to read as follows:

§1.565–1 General rule.

* * * * *

(b) * * *

(3) A consent may be filed at any time not later than the due date (including extensions) of the corporation's income tax return for the taxable year for which the dividends paid deduction is claimed. With such return, and not later than the due

date (including extensions) thereof, the corporation must file Forms 972 for each consenting shareholder, and a return on Form 973 showing by classes the stock outstanding on the first and last days of the taxable year, the dividend rights of such stock, distributions made during the taxable year to shareholders, and giving all the other information required by the form. For taxable years beginning before January 1, 2003, the Form 973 filed with the corporation's income tax return shall contain or be verified by a written declaration that is made under the penalties of perjury and the Forms 972 filed with the return must be duly executed by the consenting shareholders. For taxable years beginning after December 31, 2002, the Form 973 filed with the corporation's income tax return shall be verified by signing the return and the Forms 972 filed with the return must be duly executed by the consenting shareholders or, if unsigned, must contain the same information as the duly executed originals. If the corporation submits unsigned Forms 972 with its return for a taxable year beginning after December 31, 2002, the duly executed originals are records that the corporation must retain and keep available for inspection in the manner required by §1.6001–1(e).

* * * * *

§1.565–1T [Removed]

Par. 7. Section 1.565–1T is removed.

Par. 8. Section 1.936–7 is amended by revising paragraph (b), Q. & A. 1, to read as follows:

§1.936–7 Manner of making election under section 936(h)(5); special election for export sales; revocation of election under section 936(a).

* * * * *

(b) *Manner of making election.*

Q. 1: How does a possessions corporation make an election to use the cost sharing method or profit split method?

A. 1: A possessions corporation makes an election to use the cost sharing or profit split method by filing Form 5712–A *("Election and Verification of the Cost Sharing or Profit Split Method Under Section 936(h)(5)")* and attaching it to its tax return. Form 5712–A must be filed on or before the due date (including extensions) of the tax return of the possessions corporation for its first taxable year beginning after December 31, 1982. The electing corporation must set forth on the form the name and the taxpayer identification number or address of all members of the affiliated group (including foreign affiliates not required to file a U.S. tax return). All members of the affiliated group must consent to the election. For elections filed with respect to taxable years beginning before January 1, 2003, an authorized officer of the electing corporation must sign the statement of election and must declare that he has received a signed statement of consent from an authorized officer, director, or other appropriate official of each member of the affiliated group. Elections filed for taxable years beginning after December 31, 2002, must incorporate a declaration by the electing corporation that it has received a signed consent from an authorized officer, director, or other appropriate official of each member of the affiliated group and will be verified by signing the return. The election is not valid for a taxable year unless all affiliates consent. A failure to obtain an affiliate's written consent will not invalidate the election out if the possessions corporation made a good faith effort to obtain all the necessary consents or the failure to obtain the missing consent was inadvertent. Subsequently created or acquired affiliates are bound by the election. If an election out is revoked under section 936(h)(5)(F)(iii), a new election out with respect to that product area cannot be made without the consent of the Commissioner. The possessions corporation shall file an amended Form 5712–A with its timely filed (including extensions) income tax return to reflect any changes in the names or number of the members of the affiliated group for any taxable year after the first taxable year to which the election out applies. By consenting to the election out, all affiliates agree to provide information necessary to compute the cost sharing payment under the cost sharing method or combined taxable income under the profit split method, and failure to provide such information shall be treated as a request to revoke the election out under section 936(h)(5)(F)(iii).

* * * * *

§1.936–7T [Removed]

Par. 9. Section 1.936–7T is removed.

Par. 10. Section 1.1017–1 is amended by revising paragraph (g)(2)(iii)(B) to read as follows:

§1.1017–1 Basis reductions following a discharge of indebtedness.

* * * * *

(g) * * *

(2) * * *

(iii) * * *

(B) *Taxpayer's requirement.* For taxable years beginning before January 1, 2003, statements described in §1.1017–1(g)(2)(iii)(A) must be attached to a taxpayer's timely filed (including extensions) Federal income tax return for the taxable year in which the taxpayer has COD income that is excluded from gross income under section 108(a). For taxable years beginning after December 31, 2002, taxpayers must retain the statements and keep them available for inspection in the manner required by §1.6001–1(e), but are not required to attach the statements to their returns.

* * * * *

§1.1017–1T [Removed]

Par. 11. Section 1.1017–1T is removed.

Par. 12. Section 1.1368–1 is amended by revising paragraphs (f)(5)(iii) and (g)(2)(iii) to read as follows:

§1.1368–1 Distributions by S corporations.

* * * * *

(f) * * *

(5) * * *

(iii) *Corporate statement regarding elections.* A corporation makes an election for a taxable year under §1.1368–1(f) by attaching a statement to a timely filed (including extensions) original or amended return required to be filed under section 6037 for that taxable year. In the statement, the corporation must identify the election it is making under §1.1368–1(f) and must state that each shareholder consents to the election. In the case of elections for taxable years beginning before January 1, 2003, an officer of the corporation must sign under penalties of perjury the statement on behalf of the corporation. In the case of elections for taxable years beginning after December 31, 2002, the statement described in this paragraph (f)(5)(iii) shall be verified by signing the return. A statement of election to make a deemed dividend under §1.1368–1(f) must include the amount of the deemed dividend that is distributed to each shareholder.

* * * * *

(g) * * *

(2) * * *

(iii) *Time and manner of making election.* A corporation makes an election under §1.1368–1(g)(2)(i) for a taxable year by attaching a statement to a timely filed (including extensions) original or amended return required to be filed under section 6037 for a taxable year (without regard to the election under §1.1368–1(g)(2)(i)). In the statement, the corporation must state that it is electing for the taxable year under §1.1368–1(g)(2)(i) to treat the taxable year as if it consisted of separate taxable years. The corporation also must set forth facts in the statement relating to the qualifying disposition (*e.g.*, sale, gift, stock issuance, or redemption), and state that each shareholder who held stock in the corporation during the taxable year (without regard to the election under §1.1368–1(g)(2)(i)) consents to this election. For purposes of this election, a shareholder of the corporation for the taxable year is a shareholder as described in section 1362(a)(2). A single election statement may be filed for all elections made under §1.1368–1(g)(2)(i) for the taxable year. An election made under §1.1368–1(g)(2)(i) is irrevocable. In the case of elections for taxable years beginning before January 1, 2003, the statement through which a corporation makes an election under §1.1368–1(g)(2)(i) must be signed by an officer of the corporation under penalties of perjury. In the case of elections for taxable years beginning after December 31, 2002, the statement described in the preceding sentence shall be verified by signing the return.

* * * * *

§1.1368–1T [Removed]

Par. 13. Section 1.1368–1T is removed.

Par. 14. Section 1.1377–1 is amended by revising paragraph (b)(5)(i)(C) to read as follows:

§1.1377–1 Pro rata share .

* * * * *

(b) * * *

(5) * * *

(i) * * *

(C) The signature on behalf of the S corporation of an authorized officer of the corporation under penalties of perjury, except that for taxable years beginning after December 31, 2002, the election statement described in §1.1377–1(b)(5)(i) of this section shall be verified, and the requirement of this paragraph (b)(5)(i)(C) is satisfied, by the signature on the Form 1120S filed by the S corporation.

* * * * *

§1.1377–1T [Removed]

Par. 15. Section 1.1377–1T is removed.

Par. 16. Section 1.1502–21 is amended by revising paragraphs (b)(3)(i) and (b)(3)(ii)(B) to read as follows:

§1.1502–21 Net operating losses.

* * * * *

(b)

* * *

(3) *Special rules*—(i) *Election to relinquish carryback.* A group may make an irrevocable election under section 172(b)(3) to relinquish the entire carryback period with respect to a CNOL for any consolidated return year. Except as provided in §1.1502–21(b)(3)(ii)(B), the election may not be made separately for any member (whether or not it remains a member), and must be made in a separate statement entitled "THIS IS AN ELECTION UNDER §1.1502–21(b)(3)(i) TO WAIVE THE ENTIRE CARRYBACK PERIOD PURSUANT TO SECTION 172(b)(3) FOR THE [insert consolidated return year] CNOLs OF THE CONSOLIDATED GROUP OF WHICH [insert name and employer identification number of common parent] IS THE COMMON PARENT." The statement must be filed with the group's income tax return for the consolidated return year in which the loss arises. If the consolidated return year in which the loss arises begins before January 1, 2003, the statement making the election must be signed by the common parent. If the consolidated return year in which the loss arises begins after December 31, 2002, the election may be made in an unsigned statement.

(ii) * * *

(B) *Acquisition of member from another consolidated group.* If one or more members of a consolidated group becomes a member of another consolidated group, the acquiring group may make an irrevocable election to relinquish, with respect to all consolidated net operating losses attributable to the member, the portion of the carryback period for which the corporation was a member of another group, provided that any other corporation joining the acquiring group that was affiliated with the member immediately before it joined the acquiring group is also included in the waiver. This election is not a yearly election and applies to all losses that would otherwise be subject to a carryback to a former group under section 172. The election must be made in a separate statement entitled "THIS IS AN ELECTION UNDER §1.1502–21(b)(3)(ii)(B)(*2*) TO WAIVE THE PRE-[insert first taxable year for which the member (or members) was not a member of another group] CARRYBACK PERIOD FOR THE CNOLs attributable to [insert names and employer identification number of members]." The statement must be filed with the acquiring consolidated group's original income tax return for the year the corporation (or corporations) became a member. If the year in which the corporation (or corporations) became a member begins before January 1, 2003, the statement must be signed by the common parent and each of the members to which it applies. If the year in which the corporation (or corporations) became a member begins after December 31, 2002, the election may be made in an unsigned statement.

* * * * *

Par. 17. Section 1.1502–21T is amended by revising paragraphs (a) through (b)(3)(ii)(B) to read as follows:

§1.1502–21T Net operating losses (Temporary).

(a) through (b)(3)(ii)(B) [Reserved]. For further guidance, see §1.1502–21(a) through (b)(3)(ii)(B).

* * * * *

Par. 18. Section 1.1502–75 is amended by revising paragraph (h)(2) to read as follows:

§1.1502–75 Filing of consolidated returns.

* * * * *

(h) * * *

(2) *Filing of Form 1122 for first year.* If, under the provisions of paragraph (a)(1) of this section, a group wishes to file a consolidated return for a taxable year, then a Form 1122 ("*Authorization and Consent of Subsidiary Corporation To Be Included in a Consolidated Income Tax Return*") must be executed by each subsidiary. For taxable years beginning before January 1, 2003, the executed Forms 1122 must be attached to the consolidated return for the taxable year. For taxable years beginning after December 31, 2002, the group must attach either executed Forms 1122 or unsigned copies of the completed Forms 1122 to the consolidated return. If the group submits unsigned Forms 1122 with its return, it must retain the signed originals in its records in the manner required by §1.6001–1(e). Form 1122 is not required for a taxable year if a consolidated return was filed (or was required to be filed) by the group for the immediately preceding taxable year.

* * * * *

§1.1502–75T [Removed]

Par. 19. Section 1.1502–75T is removed.

Par. 20. Section 1.1503–2 is amended by revising paragraphs (g)(2)(i), (g)(2)(iv)(B)(*3*)(*iii*) and (g)(2)(vi)(B) to read as follows:

§1.1503–2 Dual consolidated loss.

* * * * *

(g) * * *

(2) * * *

(i) *In general.* Paragraph (b) of this section shall not apply to a dual consolidated loss if the consolidated group, unaffiliated dual resident corporation, or unaffiliated domestic owner elects to be bound by the provisions of this paragraph (g)(2). In order to elect relief under this paragraph (g)(2), the consolidated group, unaffiliated dual resident corporation, or unaffiliated domestic owner must attach to its timely filed (including extensions) U.S. income tax return for the taxable year in which the dual consolidated loss is incurred an agreement described in paragraph (g)(2)(i)(A) of this section. The agreement must be signed under penalties of perjury by the person who signs the return. For taxable years beginning after December 31, 2002, the agreement attached to the income tax return of the consolidated group, unaffiliated dual resident corporation or unaffiliated domestic owner pursuant to the preceding sentence may be an unsigned copy. If an unsigned copy is attached to the return, the consolidated group, unaffiliated dual resident corporation, or unaffiliated domestic owner must retain the original in its records in the manner specified by §1.6001–1(e). The agreement must include the following items, in paragraphs labeled to correspond with the items set forth in paragraph (g)(2)(i)(A) through (F) of this section.

(A) A statement that the document submitted is an election and an agreement under the provisions of paragraph (g)(2) of this section.

(B) The name, address, identifying number, and place and date of incorporation of the dual resident corporation, and the country or countries that tax the dual resident corporation on its worldwide income or on a residence basis, or, in the case of a separate unit, identification of the separate unit, including the name under which it conducts business, its principal activity, and the country in which its principal place of business is located.

(C) An agreement by the consolidated group, unaffiliated dual resident corporation, or unaffiliated domestic owner to comply with all of the provisions of §1.1503–2(g)(2)(iii)–(vii).

(D) A statement of the amount of the dual consolidated loss covered by the agreement.

(E) A certification that no portion of the dual resident corporation's or separate unit's losses, expenses, or deductions taken into account in computing the dual consolidated loss has been, or will be, used to offset the income of any other person under the income tax laws of a foreign country.

(F) A certification that arrangements have been made to ensure that no portion of the dual consolidated loss will be used to offset the income of another person under the laws of a foreign country and that the consolidated group, unaffiliated dual resident corporation, or unaffiliated domestic owner will be informed of any such foreign use of any portion of the dual consolidated loss.

* * * * *

(iv) * * *

(B) * * *

(*3*) * * *

(*iii*) The unaffiliated domestic corporation or new consolidated group must file, with its timely filed (including extensions) income tax return for the taxable year in which the event described in paragraph (g)(2)(iv)(B)(*1*) or (*2*) of this section occurs, an agreement described in paragraph (g)(2)(i) of this section (new (g)(2)(i) agreement), whereby it assumes the same obligations with respect to the dual consolidated loss as the corporation or consolidated group that filed the original (g)(2)(i) agreement with respect to that loss. The new (g)(2)(i) agreement must be signed under penalties of perjury by the person who signs the return and must include a reference to this paragraph (g)(2)(iv)(B)(*3*)(*iii*). For taxable years beginning after December 31, 2002, the agreement attached to the return pursuant to the preceding sentence may be an unsigned copy. If an unsigned copy is attached to the return, the corporation or consolidated group must retain the original in its records in the manner specified by §1.6001–1(e).

* * * * *

(vi) * * *

(B) *Annual certification.* Except as provided in §1.1503–2(g)(2)(vi)(C), until and unless Form 1120 or the Schedules thereto contain questions pertaining to dual consolidated losses, the consolidated group, unaffiliated dual resident corporation, or unaffiliated domestic owner must file with its income tax return for each of the 15 taxable years following the taxable year in which the dual consolidated loss is incurred a certification that the losses, expenses, or deductions that make up the dual consolidated loss have not been used to offset the income of another person under the tax laws of a foreign country. For taxable years beginning before January 1, 2003, the annual certification must be signed under penalties of perjury by a person authorized to sign the agreement described in §1.1503–2(g)(2)(i). For taxable years beginning after December 31, 2002, the certification is verified by signing the return with which the certification is filed. The certification for a taxable year must identify the dual consolidated loss to which it pertains by setting forth the taxpayer's year in which the loss was incurred and the amount of such loss. In addition, the certification must warrant that arrangements have been made to ensure that the loss will not be used to offset the income of another person under the laws of a foreign country and that the taxpayer will be informed of any such foreign use of any portion of the loss. If dual consolidated losses of more than one taxable year are subject to the rules of this paragraph (g)(2)(vi)(B), the certifications for those years may be combined in a single document but each dual consolidated loss must be separately identified.

* * * * *

§1.1503–2T [Removed]

Par. 21. Section 1.1503–2T is removed.

Par. 22. Section 1.6038B–1 is amended by revising paragraph (b)(1)(ii) to read as follows:

§1.6038B–1 Reporting of certain transfers to foreign corporations.

* * * * *

(b) * * *

(1) * * *

(ii) *Reporting by corporate transferor.* For transfers by corporations in taxable years beginning before January 1, 2003, Form 926 must be signed by an authorized officer of the corporation if the transferor is not a member of an affiliated group under section 1504(a)(1) that files a consolidated Federal income tax return and by an authorized officer of the common parent corporation if the transferor is a member of such an affiliated group. For transfers by corporations in taxable years beginning after December 31, 2002, Form 926 shall be verified by signing the income tax return to which the form is attached.

* * * * *

Par. 23. Section 1.6038B–1T is amended by revising paragraphs (a) through (b)(3) to read as follows:

§1.6038B–1T Reporting of certain transactions to foreign corporations (Temporary).

(a) through (b)(3) [Reserved]. For further guidance, see §1.6038B–1(a) through (b)(3).

* * * * *

PART 301 — PROCEDURE AND ADMINISTRATION

Par. 24. The authority citation for part 301 continues to read, in part, as follows:

Authority: 26 U.S.C. 7805 * * *

Par. 25. Section 301.7701–3 is amended by revising paragraph (c)(1)(ii) to read as follows:

§301.7701–3 Classification of certain business entities.

* * * * *

(c) * * * (1) * * *

(ii) *Further notification of elections.* An eligible entity required to file a Federal tax or information return for the taxable year for which an election is made under §301.7701–3(c)(1)(i) must attach a copy of its Form 8832 to its Federal tax or information return for that year. If the entity is not required to file a return for that year, a copy of its Form 8832 (*"Entity Classification Election"*) must be attached to the Federal income tax or information return of any direct or indirect owner of the entity for the taxable year of the owner that includes the date on which the election was effective. An indirect owner of the entity does not have to attach a copy of the Form 8832 to its return if an entity in which it has an interest is already filing a copy of the Form 8832 with its return. If an entity, or one of its direct or indirect owners, fails to attach a copy of a Form 8832 to its return as directed in this section, an otherwise valid election under §301.7701–3(c)(1)(i) will not be invalidated, but the non-filing party may be subject to penalties, including any applicable penalties if the Federal tax or information returns are inconsistent with the entity's election under §301.7701–3(c)(1)(i). In the case of returns for taxable years beginning after December 31, 2002, the copy of Form 8832 attached to a return pursuant to this paragraph (c)(1)(ii) is not required to be a signed copy.

* * * * *

§301.7701–3T [Removed]

Par. 26. Section 301.7701–3T is removed.

PART 602—OMB CONTROL NUMBERS UNDER THE PAPERWORK REDUCTION ACT

Par. 27. The authority citation for part 602 continues to read as follows:

Authority: 26 U.S.C. 7805.

Par. 28. In §602.101, paragraph (b) is amended by removing the entry for "1.170A–11T" and revising the entry for "1.170A–11" to read as follows:

§602.101 OMB Control numbers

* * * * *

(b) * * *

CFR part or section where identified and described	Current OMB control No.
* * * * *	
1.170A–11	1545–0123 1545–0074 1545–1868
* * * * *	

Linda M. Kroening,
Acting Deputy Commissioner for Services and Enforcement.

Approved November 29, 2006.

Eric Solomon,
Acting Deputy Assistant Secretary of the Treasury (Tax Policy).

(Filed by the Office of the Federal Register on December 7, 2006, 8:45 a.m., and published in the issue of the Federal Register for December 8, 2006, 71 F.R. 71040)

Part III. Administrative, Procedural, and Miscellaneous

T.D. 9281 Effective Date

Notice 2007–1

On August 17, 2006, the Treasury Department and the IRS published temporary and proposed income tax regulations T.D. 9281, 2006–39 I.R.B. 517 [71 FR 47443] under §1.882–5 regarding the determination of the interest expense allocable to effectively connected income of foreign corporations engaged, or treated as engaged in a trade or business within the United States, and under §1.884–1(e)(3) regarding the determination of branch profits tax under a liability reduction election. The temporary and proposed regulations revised final regulations under §1.882–5 issued in T.D. 8658, 1996–1 C.B. 161 [61 FR 15891] and under §1.884–1 issued in T.D. 8432, 1992–2 C.B. 157 [57 FR 41644].

The temporary regulations provided in T.D. 9281 are effective for the first tax year end for which a foreign corporate taxpayer's original tax return due date (including extensions) is after August 17, 2006. Accordingly, for calendar-year taxpayers, the applicability date for T.D. 9281 is the tax year ended December 31, 2005, for which an original tax return due date (including extensions) was September 15, 2006. The temporary regulations provide a one-time, additional period for taxpayers whose original tax return due date (including extensions) is after August 17, 2006, and not later than December 31, 2006, to adopt the tax return elections covered by the temporary regulations on an amended income tax return within 180 days after the original allowable extended due date (whether or not the taxpayer timely filed its tax return by the original due date (without regard to extensions)).

This notice permits foreign corporations engaged, or treated as engaged in a trade or business within the United States whose tax year end is on or after September 30, 2005, and whose original tax return due date (including extensions) was on or after June 15, 2006, and on or before August 17, 2006, to elect to apply the provisions of T.D. 9281 for such earlier tax return filing period. Such taxpayers may adopt the rules provided in T.D. 9281, including the one-time amended return elections of §§1.882–5T(a)(7)(iii), 1.882–5T(d)(5)(ii)(B) and 1.884–1T (e)(3)(iv), and the mandatory conforming election in §1.882–5(b)(2)(ii)(A)(2) for such year only if the rules are adopted in their entirety on an amended return filed within 180 days of December 18, 2006. Accordingly, a taxpayer may not file an amended return for the tax period provided in this notice to adopt the annual published LIBOR rate election of §1.882–5T(d)(5)(ii)(B) and also remain on the 93-percent fixed ratio election and branch profits tax rules that were amended by the temporary rules in T.D. 9281. This notice does not change any of the temporary and proposed rules provided in T.D. 9281 other than allowing eligible taxpayers to elect to apply such rules to the earlier tax return filing period provided in this notice within 180 days of December 18, 2006.

The principal author of this notice is Gregory A. Spring of the Office of Associate Chief Counsel (International). For further information regarding this notice, contact Gregory A. Spring or Paul S. Epstein at (202) 622–3870 (not a toll-free call).

Amounts Received Under Accident and Health Plans

Notice 2007–2

PURPOSE

This notice provides transition relief with respect to the use of debit cards for medical expense reimbursements at certain merchants with non-health care related merchant category codes. It also addresses the use of debit cards for medical expense reimbursements at stores with the Drug Stores and Pharmacies merchant category code.

BACKGROUND

Rev. Rul. 2003–43, 2003–1 C.B. 935, sets forth rules for determining whether employer-provided medical expense reimbursements made through debit cards and other electronic media (debit cards) are excludable from gross income under §105(b) of the Internal Revenue Code. Situation 1 of the ruling describes an employer who sponsors both a health flexible spending arrangement (health FSA) and a health reimbursement arrangement (HRA). In conjunction with the health FSA and HRA, the employer permits electronic reimbursement of medical expenses through the use of debit cards. Under the arrangement, the cardholder's use of the card is limited to merchants and service providers with specific merchant category codes related to health care. The ruling states that, "the card's use is limited to physicians, pharmacies, dentists, vision care offices, hospitals, and other medical care providers." Thus, the use of the card at other than these merchants or service providers would be rejected.

Situation 1 of Rev. Rul. 2003–43 also sets forth rules for substantiation of medical expenses and provides that debit card charges other than matched copayments, recurring expenses and real-time substantiation are treated as conditional pending confirmation of the charges through additional third-party information. If the debit card charges are subsequently identified as not qualifying for medical reimbursement, the employer must follow certain correction procedures with respect to the improper payments. The after-the-fact substantiation and correction procedures described in Situation 1 of Rev. Rul. 2003–43 are sometimes referred to as "pay and chase." The ruling holds that employer-provided medical expense reimbursements made through the cards, as described in Situation 1, are excludable from gross income under § 105(b).

Notice 2006–69, 2006–31 I.R.B. 107, describes an inventory information approval system that may be used by merchants with non-health care related merchant category codes for substantiating employees' claimed medical expenses. It has been determined that transition relief is warranted for a limited period, in order for these non-health care merchants to implement the inventory information approval system.

TRANSITION RELIEF

All supermarkets, grocery stores, discount stores, and wholesale clubs that do not have a merchant category code related to health care will nevertheless be deemed to be an "other medical care provider" within the meaning of Situation 1 of Rev. Rul. 2003–43 with respect to debit card transactions occurring on or before December 31, 2007. In addition, mail order vendors and web-based vendors that sell prescription drugs will also be deemed to be an "other medical care provider" with respect to debit card transactions occurring on or before December 31, 2007. As required in Rev. Rul. 2003–43, employers must substantiate all debit card charges incurred during the relief period and follow the correction procedures in Rev. Rul. 2003–43 with respect to any unsubstantiated payment. After December 31, 2007, health FSA or HRA debit cards may not be used at any store, vendor or merchant that does not have health care related merchant category codes unless the store, vendor or merchant has implemented an inventory information approval system as described in Notice 2006–69.

STORES WITH DRUG STORES AND PHARMACIES MERCHANT CATEGORY CODE

Under Rev. Rul. 2003–43, health FSA and HRA debit cards may be used at stores with the merchant category code for Drug Stores and Pharmacies. However, many stores with this code also sell a significant number of items which do not qualify as medical expenses under § 213(d). In order to curtail the ability to purchase non-medical items with such debit cards, as well as to provide a level playing field, the IRS and Treasury have determined that it is appropriate to require similar substantiation rules for all stores that sell a significant number of items which do not qualify as medical expenses under § 213(d).

Accordingly, after December 31, 2008, health FSA and HRA debit cards may not be used at stores with the Drug Stores and Pharmacies merchant category code unless (1) the store participates in the inventory information approval system as described in Notice 2006–69, or (2) on a store location by store location basis, 90 percent of the store's gross receipts during the prior taxable year consisted of items which qualify as expenses for medical care under § 213(d) (including nonprescription medications as described in Rev. Rul. 2003–102, 2003–2 C.B. 559).

EFFECT ON OTHER DOCUMENTS

Rev. Rul. 2003–43, 2003–1 C.B. 935, is modified.

DRAFTING INFORMATION

The principal author of this notice is Stephanie L. Caden of the Office of Division Counsel/Associate Chief Counsel (Tax Exempt and Government Entities). For further information regarding this notice, contact Ms. Caden at (202) 622–6080 (not a toll-free call).

2006 Cumulative List of Changes in Plan Qualification Requirements

Notice 2007–3

I. PURPOSE

This notice contains the 2006 Cumulative List of Changes in Plan Qualification Requirements (2006 Cumulative List) described in section 4 of Rev. Proc. 2005–66, 2005–2 C.B. 509. The 2006 Cumulative List is to be used primarily by (1) plan sponsors of individually designed plans (that is, single employer individually designed defined contribution plans, including employee stock ownership plans (ESOPs), and single employer individually designed defined benefit plans) and plan sponsors of multiple employer plans that fall in Cycle B and (2) plan sponsors and practitioners in drafting defined benefit pre-approved plans (that is, defined benefit plans that are master and prototype (M&P) or volume submitter (VS) plans) for their first submission under the initial remedial amendment cycle under Rev. Proc. 2005–66. An individually designed plan is in Cycle B if the last digit of the employer identification number is 2 or 7. Multiple employer plans are also in Cycle B, pursuant to section 10.03 of Rev. Proc. 2005–66.

The list of changes in section V of this notice does not extend the deadline by which a plan must be amended to comply with any statutory, regulatory, or guidance changes. The general deadline for timely adoption of an interim or discretionary amendment can be found in section 5.05 of Rev. Proc. 2005–66. Section III of Notice 2005–95, 2005–2 C.B. 1172, provides that the general timing rules to adopt a plan amendment described in section 5.05 of Rev. Proc. 2005–66 do not apply if a statutory provision or guidance issued by the Service provides an earlier or later date than the deadline set forth in Rev. Proc. 2005–66.

II. BACKGROUND

Rev. Proc. 2005–66 sets forth procedures for issuing opinion, advisory, and determination letters and establishes the five-year remedial amendment cycle for individually designed plans and the six-year remedial amendment cycle for pre-approved plans. In addition, section 5.05 of Rev. Proc. 2005–66 provides the deadline for timely adoption of an interim amendment or discretionary amendment. Notice 2005–95 clarifies the interaction of the Rev. Proc. 2005–66 amendment timing deadlines for qualified plans with the deadlines set forth in statutory provisions or guidance issued by the Service.

Under section 4 of Rev. Proc. 2005–66, the Internal Revenue Service intends to annually publish a Cumulative List to identify statutory, regulatory and guidance changes that must be taken into account in submissions by plan sponsors to the Service for opinion, advisory and determination letters whose remedial amendment period begins on February 1st following issuance of the Cumulative List.

In Notice 2005–101, 2005–2 C.B. 1219, the Service published the 2005 Cumulative List of Changes in Plan Qualification Requirements (2005 Cumulative List). The 2005 Cumulative List is used primarily by plan sponsors of individually designed plans that fall in Cycle A that must be submitted to the Service for review by January 31, 2007. Thus, the 2005 Cumulative List set forth those plan qualification requirements that applied to individually designed defined contribution plans, including ESOPs, and individually designed defined benefit plans. Plan qualification requirements included statutory changes and guidance that became effective after December 31, 2001. The Service stated that plan language for guidance issued after December 13, 2005 would not be reviewed, unless it was on the 2005 Cumulative List.

In Notice 2004–84, 2004–2 C.B. 1030, the Service published the 2004 Cumulative List of Changes in Plan Qualification Requirements (2004 Cumulative List). The 2004 Cumulative List was used primarily by plan sponsors and practitioners in drafting defined contribution pre-approved plans (that is, defined contribution plans that are master and prototype or volume submitter plans) that were required to be submitted to the Service for review by January 31, 2006. Thus, the 2004 Cumulative List set forth only those plan qualification requirements that applied to defined contribution pre-approved plans. Plan qualification requirements included statutory changes and guidance that became effective after December 31, 2001 and any relevant qualification requirements not contained in the 2004 Cumulative List. The Service also stated that plan language for guidance issued after December 14, 2004 would not be reviewed, unless it was on the 2004 Cumulative List.

III. APPLICATION OF 2006 CUMULATIVE LIST

This notice is being issued in conjunction with the determination letter program for individually designed plans and multiple employer plans eligible for Cycle B and the opinion and advisory letter programs for M&P and VS defined benefit pre-approved plans. In Rev. Proc. 2005–66, the Service announced the opening of the initial five-year remedial amendment cycle. In accordance with Rev. Proc. 2005–66, the Service will start accepting determination letter applications for Cycle B individually designed plans (*i.e.*, the last digit of the plan sponsor's employer identification number is 2 or 7) and multiple employer plans beginning on February 1, 2007. The 12-month submission period for Cycle B individually designed plans and multiple employer plans will end January 31, 2008. In addition, the Service will start accepting opinion and advisory letter applications for defined benefit pre-approved plans beginning on February 1, 2007. The 12-month submission period for non-mass submitter sponsors and practitioners, word-for-word identical adopters, and M&P minor modifier placeholder applications will end January 31, 2008. The 9-month submission period for mass-submitters and national sponsors will end October 31, 2007, as provided in section 18.02 of Rev. Proc. 2005–66.

The 2006 Cumulative List, set forth in sections V and VI of this notice, informs plan sponsors of issues the Service has specifically identified for review in determining whether an individually designed plan, multiple employer plan or defined benefit pre-approved plan has been properly updated. Specifically, the 2006 Cumulative List reflects law changes under the Economic Growth and Tax Relief Reconciliation Act of 2001 (EGTRRA), Pub. L. 107–16 (with technical corrections made by the Job Creation and Worker Assistance Act of 2002 (JCWAA), Pub. L. 104–147), the Pension Funding Equity Act of 2004 (PFEA), Pub. L. 108–218, the American Jobs Creation Act of 2004 (AJCA), Pub. L. 108–357, the Gulf Opportunity Zone Act of 2005 (GOZA), Pub. L. 109–135, and certain law changes under the Pension Protection Act of 2006 (PPA '06), Pub. L. 109–280, described below. In order to be qualified, a plan must comply with all relevant qualification requirements, not just those on the 2006 Cumulative List. The following items on the 2006 Cumulative List include guidance that has not yet been published: 2, 8, 11, 18, 25, 28, 29, 30, 31, 32, and 33.

Except for the items listed in section V and the items listed in section VI (to the extent provided in section IV) of this notice, the Service will not consider in its review of any opinion, advisory or determination letter application, for the submission period that begins February 1, 2007, any:

1. guidance published after December 14, 2006;
2. statutes enacted after December 14, 2006;
3. qualification requirements first effective in 2008 or later; or
4. statutory provisions that are first effective in 2007, for which there is no guidance identified in this notice.

Terminating plans must include all law changes in effect at the time of termination. See section 8 of Rev. Proc. 2005–66 regarding plan termination.

IV. SPECIAL RULES FOR THE PENSION PROTECTION ACT OF 2006

Under section 1107 of PPA '06, a plan amendment made pursuant to any amendment made by PPA '06 generally may be retroactively effective, if, in addition to meeting the other applicable requirements, the amendment is made on or before the last day of the first plan year beginning on or after January 1, 2009 (January 1, 2011 in the case of a governmental plan). Section VI of the notice includes certain PPA '06 law changes effective in 2006 and 2007.

Master and prototype plan sponsors and VS practitioners are required to include applicable PPA '06 provisions listed in section VI of this notice in plan documents submitted with their opinion and advisory letter applications for pre-approved defined benefit plans. The Service will consider PPA '06 in issuing opinion and advisory letters, and such letters may be relied on with respect to PPA '06, but only for the PPA '06 provisions listed in section VI of this notice under items 27, 28, 31, 32, and 33.

Individually designed plans and multiple employer plans can be amended, at the option of plan sponsors, to include the applicable PPA '06 provisions listed in section VI of this notice. Individually designed plans and multiple employer plans must identify which PPA '06 provisions the plan has been amended to include and the plan provision that reflects the PPA '06 provision when submitting the determination letter application. However, the Service will not consider PPA '06 in issuing determination letters for individually designed plans and multiple employer plans, and such letters cannot be relied on with respect to any plan provision identified as reflecting PPA '06, regardless of whether the plan has been amended to reflect PPA '06 provisions.

Terminating plans must include the applicable PPA '06 provisions that are in effect at the time of termination.

V. 2006 CUMULATIVE LIST OF CHANGES IN PLAN QUALIFICATION REQUIREMENTS

The following list consists of statutory provisions and associated guidance which reflect changes to plan qualification requirements. Miscellaneous guidance is also provided. The Service has identified below plan qualification requirements which were not on the 2005 Cumulative List as "(New)". Thus, the 2006 Cumulative List contains those plan qualification requirements listed in the 2004 and 2005 Cumulative Lists as well as additional 2006 plan qualification requirements.

1. 72(p): Section 1.72(p)–1 of the Income Tax Regulations relating to plan loans was published on December 3, 2002 (67 Fed. Reg. 71821). (2004 C. L.).

2. 401(a): Final Regulations under § 401(a) of the Code regarding permissible normal retirement ages will be published soon. (New).

3. 401(a)(4):

   - Amendments to § 1.401(a)(4)–8 of the Regulations relating to new comparability plans were published on June 29, 2001 (66 Fed. Reg. 34535). (2004 C. L.).
     - Rev. Rul. 2001–30, 2001–2 C.B. 46. (2004 C. L.).
   - Amendments to § 1.401(a)(4)–9 of the Regulations relating to new comparability plans were published on June 29, 2001 (66 Fed. Reg. 34535). (2005 C. L.).
     - Rev. Rul. 2004–21, 2004–1 C.B. 544. (2005 C. L.).

4. 401(a)(9):

   - Sections 1.401(a)(9)–1 through –9 of the Regulations were published on April 17, 2002 and June 15, 2004 (67 Fed. Reg. 18988 and 69 Fed. Reg. 33288). (2004 C. L.).

5. 401(a)(17): Section 401(a)(17) of the Code was amended by § 611(c) of EGTRRA to increase the compensation limit to $200,000. (2004 C. L.).

   - Notice 2001–56, 2001–2 C.B. 277. (2004 C. L.).

6. 401(a)(31):

   - Section 401(a)(31) was amended by § 643(b) of EGTRRA to allow employees' after-tax contributions to be rolled over under certain circumstances. (2004 C. L.).
   - Section 401(a)(31)(B) was amended by § 657(a) of EGTRRA (as amended by § 411(t) of JCWAA) to provide for the automatic rollover of certain mandatory distributions. The effective date is March 28, 2005. (2004 C. L.).
     - Notice 2005–5, 2005–1 C.B. 337. (2004 C. L.).

   - Sections 641, 642 and 643 of EGTRRA (as amended by § 411(q) of JCWAA) amended the definition of eligible retirement plan in § 402 to include a § 403(b) annuity contract and eligible governmental § 457(b) plan. (2004 C. L.).
   - Section 636(b) of EGTRRA modified the definition of eligible rollover distribution to exclude hardship distributions. (2004 C. L.).

7. 401(k) & 401(m):

   - Section 401(k)(2) and § 401(k)(10) of the Code were amended by § 646(a)(1) of EGTRRA to permit distributions of elective deferrals from a § 401(k) plan upon severance from employment. (2004 C. L.).
     - Notice 2002–4, 2002–1 C.B. 298. (2004 C. L.).
   - Section 636(a) of EGTRRA directed the Secretary of the Treasury to revise the regulations relating to safe harbor hardship distributions of elective deferrals from § 401(k) plans so that the time the employee is prohibited from making elective and employee contributions is reduced from one year to six months after a hardship distribution. (2004 C. L.).
     - Notice 2001–56. (2004 C. L.).
     - Notice 2002–4. (2004 C. L.).
   - Section 401(k)(11) of the Code was amended by § 611(f) of EGTRRA to increase the maximum amount of qualified salary reduction contributions that can be made to SIMPLE 401(k) plans. (2004 C. L.).
   - Section 402(g) of the Code was amended by § 611(d) of EGTRRA to increase the applicable dollar amount. (2004 C. L.).
   - Section 401(m)(9) of the Code was amended by § 666 of EGTRRA to eliminate the multiple use test. (2004 C. L.).
   - Final Regulations under § 401(k) and § 401(m) of the Code were published on December 29, 2004 (69 Fed. Reg 78144). (2004 C. L.).

8. 402A: Section 402A of the Code was added by § 617 of EGTRRA to offer optional treatment of elective deferrals as designated Roth contributions to defined contribution plans, effective for taxable years beginning after December 31, 2005. (2004 C. L.).

   - Final Regulations under § 401(k) and § 401(m) of the Code relating to designated Roth contributions were published on January 3, 2006 (71 Fed. Reg. 6). (2005 C. L.).
     - Notice 2006–44, 2006–20 I.R.B. 889, provides a sample amendment for Roth § 401(k) plans. (New).
   - Final Regulations under § 402A will be issued soon.[1] (New).

9. 404:

   - Section 404(k)(2)(A) of the Code was amended by § 662(a) of EGTRRA (as amended by § 411(w) of JCWAA) to allow ESOP dividends to be reinvested without the loss of dividend deductions. (2005 C. L.).
     - Notice 2002–2, 2002–1 C.B. 285, provides guidance with respect to the changes made to § 404(k) of the Code and on the effective date of § 409(p) of the Code. (2005 C. L.).

[1] Proposed Regulations under § 402A were published on January 26, 2006 (71 Fed. Reg. 4320). (2005 C. L.).

10. 408(q): Section 408(q) of the Code was added by § 602 of EGTRRA (as amended by § 411(i) of JCWAA) to allow for deemed individual retirement accounts (IRAs) in an eligible retirement plan. (2004 C. L.).

    - Section 1.408(q)–1 of the Regulations was published on July 22, 2004 (69 Fed. Reg. 43735). (2004 C. L.).

11. 409: Section 409(p) of the Code was added by § 656 of EGTRRA relating to restrictions on the allocation of employer securities in an ESOP maintained by an S corporation. (2005 C. L.).

    - Section 1.409(p)–1T of the Regulations was published on July 21, 2003 (68 Fed. Reg. 42970). (2005 C. L.).
    - Section 1.409(p)–1T of the Regulations was published on December 17, 2004 (69 Fed. Reg. 75455). (2005 C. L.).
    - Rev. Proc. 2003–23, 2003–1 C.B. 599, as modified and superseded by Rev. Proc. 2004–14, 2004–1 C.B. 489, allows a direct rollover from an ESOP maintained by an S corporation to an individual retirement plan (IRA). (2005 C. L.).
    - Rev. Rul. 2003–6, 2003–1 C.B. 286, provides guidance with respect to whether an ESOP maintained by an S corporation is eligible for the delayed effective date of § 409(p) under § 656(d)(2) of EGTRRA. (2005 C. L.).
    - Rev. Rul. 2004–4, 2004–1 C.B. 414, provides guidance relating to synthetic equity owned by a disqualified person in a nonallocation year of an ESOP maintained by an S corporation. (2005 C. L.).
    - Final Regulations will be published soon that provide guidance concerning requirements under § 409(p) for ESOPs holding stock of S corporations. (New).

12. 410(b): Final Regulations were published on July 21, 2006 (71 Fed. Reg. 41357) permitting some employees of tax-exempt organizations to be excluded when determining whether a § 401(k) plan meets the § 410(b) minimum coverage requirements. (New).

13. 411(a):

    - Section 411(a) of the Code was amended by § 633 of EGTRRA (as amended by § 411(o) of JCWAA) to provide for faster vesting of matching contributions. (2004 C. L.).
    - Rev. Rul. 2003–65, 2003–1 C.B. 1035. (2005 C. L.).
    - Amendments to § 1.411(d)–3 of the Final Regulations were published on August 9, 2006 (71 Fed. Reg. 45379) with respect to the interaction between the anti-cutback rules of § 411(d)(6) and the nonforfeitability requirements of § 411(a). (New).

14. 411(a)(11): Section 411(a)(11)(D) of the Code was added by § 648(a) of EGTRRA (as amended by § 411(r) of JCWAA) to allow amounts attributable to rollover contributions to be disregarded in determining the value of an account balance for involuntary distributions. (2004 C. L.).

15. 411(d)(6):

    - *Central Laborers' Pension Fund v. Heinz*, 124 S.Ct. 2230 (2004). (2005 C. L.).
        - Rev. Proc. 2005–23, 2005–1 C.B. 991, as modified by Rev. Proc. 2005–76, 2005–2 C.B. 1139. (2005 C. L.).
        - Amendments to § 1.411(d)–3 of the Final Regulations were published on August 9, 2006 (71 Fed. Reg. 45379) with respect to the interaction between the anti-cutback rules of § 411(d)(6) and the nonforfeitability requirements of § 411(a). (New).
    - Section 645(b)(3) of EGTRRA directed the Secretary of the Treasury to issue regulations under § 411(d)(6)(B). (2005 C. L.).
        - Section 1.411(d)–3 of the Regulations was published on August 12, 2005 (70 Fed. Reg. 47109). (2005 C. L.).
        - Amendments to § 1.411(d)–3 of the Final Regulations were published on August 9, 2006 (71 Fed. Reg. 45379) with respect to a utilization test. (New).
    - Section 411(d)(6)(D) and § 411(d)(6)(E) of the Code were added by § 645 of EGTRRA to permit the elimination of certain optional forms of benefit under certain conditions. (2005 C. L.).
        - Section 1.411(d)–4, Q&A–2(e) of the Regulations was published on January 25, 2005 (70 Fed. Reg. 3475) to implement § 411(d)(6)(E). (2005 C. L.).

16. 412:

    - Rev. Rul. 2004–20, 2004–1 C.B. 546, provides guidance with respect to whether a qualified pension plan can be a § 412(i) plan if the plan holds life insurance contracts and annuity contracts for benefits at normal retirement age in excess of a participant's benefits at normal retirement age under the plan. (2005 C. L.).
    - Notice 2004–59, 2004–2 C.B. 447, provides guidance with respect to restrictions placed on plan amendments following an employer's election of an alternative deficit reduction contribution. (2005 C. L.).

17. 414(v): Section 414(v) of the Code was added by § 631 of EGTRRA (as amended by § 411(o) of JCWAA) to allow for catch-up contributions for individuals age 50 or older. (2004 C. L.).

    - Regulations under § 414(v) were published on July 8, 2003 (68 Fed. Reg. 40510). (2004 C. L.).
        - Notice 2002–4. (2004 C. L.).

18. 415:

    - Section 415(b) of the Code was amended by § 611 of EGTRRA to increase the dollar limit and change the age when the limit is reduced or increased. (2005 C. L.).
        - Rev. Rul. 2001–51, 2001–2 C.B. 427. (2004 C. L.).

- Section 415(b)(2)(E)(ii) of the Code was amended by § 101(b)(4) of PFEA to fix the percentage at 5.5%. (2005 C. L.).
  - Notice 2004–78, 2004–2 C.B. 879, provides the actuarial assumptions that must be used for distributions with annuity starting dates occurring during the plans years beginning in 2004 and 2005. (2005 C. L.).
- Section 415(c) of the Code was amended by §§ 611(b) and 632 of EGTRRA (as amended by § 411(p) of JCWAA) to increase the maximum annual additions permitted to the lesser of $40,000 or 100% of compensation. (2004 C. L.).
  - Rev. Rul. 2001–51, 2001–2 C.B. 427. (2004 C. L.).
- Rev. Rul. 2002–27, 2002–1 C.B. 925, provided that "compensation" within the meaning of § 415(c) could in certain situations include "deemed § 125 compensation". (2004 C. L.).
- Final Regulations under § 415 with respect to pre-PPA '06 law will be published soon.[2] (New).
  - See section VI of this notice for PPA '06 provisions related to § 415 that will be reflected in the § 415 Final Regulations. (New).

19. 416: Section 416 of the Code was amended by § 613 of EGTRRA (as amended by § 411(k) of JCWAA) to make several changes to the top-heavy rules. (2004 C. L.).

- Section 416(g)(4)(H) of the Code was added by § 613(d) of EGTRRA to provide certain safe harbor § 401(k) plans and § 401(m) plans an exemption from the top-heavy rules. (2004 C. L.).
  - Rev. Rul. 2004–13, 2004–1 C.B. 485. (2004 C. L.).
- Section 416(c)(1)(C) of the Code was amended by § 613(e) of EGTRRA (as amended by § 411(k)(1) of JCWAA) to provide when a frozen defined benefit plan is exempt from the minimum benefit requirements. (2005 C. L.).

20. 417:

- Section 1.417(e)–1 of the Regulations was published on July 16, 2003 (68 Fed. Reg. 41906) relating to retroactive annuity starting date. (2005 C. L.).
- Final Regulations under § 417(a)(3) were published on March 24, 2006 (71 Fed. Reg. 14798) regarding the disclosure of the relative value of optional forms of benefit. (New).

21. 4975:

- Section 4975 of the Code was amended by § 612 of EGTRRA to allow plan loans for Subchapter S shareholder-employees. (2004 C. L.).
- Section 4975(f) of the Code was amended by § 240 of AJCA to allow an S corporation distribution on allocated shares to pay off an exempt loan as long as equal amounts are allocated to participant accounts. (2005 C. L.).

22. Hurricane Relief:

- Katrina Emergency Tax Relief Act of 2005, P.L. 109–73. (2005 C. L.).
  - Notice 2005–92, 2005–2 C.B. 1165. (2005 C. L.).
- Announcement 2005–70, 2005–2 C.B. 682. (2005 C. L.).
- Gulf Opportunity Zone Act of 2005, P.L. 109–135, added § 1400M and § 1400Q to the Code to provide certain tax benefits to those areas affected by Hurricanes Katrina, Wilma, and Rita. (New).

23. Miscellaneous:

- Rev. Rul. 2001–62, 2001–2 C.B. 632, provides guidance with respect to the mortality table under § 415(b)(2)(E)(v) of the Code and the applicable mortality table under § 417(e)(3)(A)(ii)(I) of the Code. (2005 C. L.).
- Rev. Rul. 2002–42, 2002–1 C.B. 76, provides guidance with respect to a situation where a money purchase pension plan is merged or converted into a profit sharing plan. (2004 C. L.).
- Rev. Proc. 2002–21, 2002–1 C.B. 911, provides guidance with respect to defined contribution retirement plans maintained by professional employer organizations. (2004 C. L.).
- Rev. Proc. 2003–86, 2003–2 C.B. 1211, amplifies Rev. Proc. 2002–21 relating to relief provided for certain defined contribution plans maintained by professional employer organizations. (2004 C. L.).
- Rev. Rul. 2003–11, 2003–1 C.B. 285, provides guidance with respect to satisfying the nondiscrimination rules under § 401(a)(4) of the Code and the minimum coverage requirements under § 410(b) of the Code when applying the increased compensation limit to former employees. (2005 C. L.).
- Rev. Rul. 2004–10, 2004–1 C.B. 484, provides guidance with respect to charging administrative expenses to former and current employees. (2004 C. L.).
- Rev. Rul. 2004–12, 2004–1 C.B. 478, provides guidance with respect to the distribution restrictions applicable to rollover contributions. (2004 C. L.).
- Rev. Rul. 2005–55, 2005–2 C.B. 284, provides guidance with respect to medical reimbursement accounts under a profit sharing plan. (2005 C. L.).
- Section 1.401(a)–21 of the Final Regulations were published on October 20, 2006 (71 Fed. Reg. 61877) setting forth standards for the use of an electronic medium to applicable notices to recipients or to make participant elections. (New).

The following guidance contains sample or model amendments: Notice 2001–57, 2001–1 C.B. 279 (miscellaneous EGTRRA amendments); Rev. Rul.

[2] Section 1.415(c)–2(e) of the Proposed Regulations under § 415 was published on May 31, 2005 (70 Fed. Reg. 31214). (2004 C. L.).

2001–62, 2001–2 C.B. 632 (applicable mortality table); Rev. Proc. 2002–29, 2002–2 C.B. 1176 (required minimum distribution amendments); Rev. Proc. 2003–13, 2003–1 C.B. 317 (required language for deemed IRAs); Notice 2005–5 (automatic rollover); and Notice 2006–44, 2006–20 I.R.B. 889 (Roth section 401(k) plans).

VI. PENSION PROTECTION ACT OF 2006 PROVISIONS

The following is a list of PPA '06 provisions effective in 2007 or earlier. See section IV of this notice for rules that apply to the PPA '06 provisions identified below:

24. 401(a)(35): PPA '06 § 901(a)(1) added § 401(a)(35) requiring that defined contribution plans provide employees with the freedom to divest publicly traded securities. (New).
    - Notice 2006–107, 2006–51 I.R.B. 1114 (December 18, 2006). (New).
25. 401(k): PPA '06 § 826 modified the rules relating to distributions from a § 401(k) plan on account of a participant's hardship to permit the plan to treat a participant's beneficiary under the plan the same as the participant's spouse or dependent. (New).
    - Guidance regarding PPA '06 § 826 will be issued soon. (New).
26. 401(k)(2)(B)(i)(V): PPA '06 § 827 permits reservists called to active duty after September 11, 2001 and before 2008 to take in-service distributions from a § 401(k) plan. (New).
27. 402(c)(2)(A): PPA '06 § 822(a) amended § 402(c)(2)(A) to permit nontaxable distributions from a qualified plan to be directly rolled over tax-free to either another qualified plan or a § 403(b) plan if the separate accounting requirements are met. (New).
28. 402(c)(11): PPA '06 § 829(a)(1) added § 402(c)(11) to allow non-spouse beneficiaries to roll over distributions from a qualified plan to an individual retirement plan. (New).
    - Guidance regarding § 402(c)(11) will be issued soon. (New).
29. 411: PPA '06 § 701 provides rules for cash balance plans and other hybrid defined benefit plans. (New).
    - Guidance will be issued regarding cash balance plans and other hybrid defined benefit plans soon. (New).
30. 411(a): Section 411(a) of the Code was amended by § 904 of PPA '06 to provide for faster vesting of employer nonelective contributions. (New).
    - Guidance regarding § 411(a), as amended by § 904 of PPA '06, will be issued soon. (New).
31. 415(b)(2)(E)(ii): Section 415(b)(2)(E)(ii) of the Code was amended by § 303 of PPA '06 regarding the interest rate assumption for applying benefit limitations to lump sum distributions. (New).
    - Guidance regarding § 415(b)(2)(E)(ii), as amended by PPA '06, will be included in the § 415 Final Regulations, to be issued soon. (New).
32. 415(b)(11): PPA '06 § 867(a) removed the 100% of compensation limitation for a church plan participant if the participant has never been a highly compensated employee of the church. (New).
    - Guidance regarding § 415(b)(11), as added by PPA '06, will be included in the § 415 Final Regulations, to be issued soon. (New).
33. PPA '06 § 1102(a) provides that notice required to be provided under §§ 402(f), 411(a)(11), or 417 may be provided as much as 180 days before the annuity starting date. Section 1102(b) of PPA '06 provides that the notice under § 411(a)(11) also include a description of the consequences of failing to defer receipt of a distribution. (New).
    - Guidance regarding PPA '06 § 1102 will be issued soon. (New).

DRAFTING INFORMATION

The principal author of this notice is Angelique V. Carrington of the Employee Plans, Tax Exempt and Government Entities Division. For further information regarding this notice, please contact the Employee Plans' taxpayer assistance telephone service at 1–877–829–5500 (a toll-free number) between the hours of 8:30 a.m. and 4:30 p.m. Eastern Time, Monday through Friday. Ms. Carrington may be reached at (202) 283–9888 (not a toll-free number).

Transition Relief for Certain Partnerships and Other Pass-Thru Entities Under § 470

Notice 2007–4

PURPOSE

This notice extends by one year the transition relief in Notice 2006–2, 2006–2 I.R.B. 278, and Notice 2005–29, 2005–1 C.B. 796, provided previously to partnerships and other pass-thru entities that are treated under § 470 of the Internal Revenue Code as holding tax-exempt use property solely as a result of the application of § 168(h)(6).

BACKGROUND

Section 848 of the American Jobs Creation Act of 2004, Pub. L. No. 108–357, 118 Stat. 1418, 1602 (AJCA), enacted on October 22, 2004, added § 470, which imposes new limitations on the deductibility of losses relating to tax-exempt use property. Under § 470(c)(2), "tax-exempt use property" has the meaning provided under § 168(h) (with certain modifications). Under § 168(h)(6), if any property that is not otherwise "tax-exempt use property" under § 168(h) is owned by a partnership that has both a tax-exempt entity and a person who is not a tax-exempt entity as partners, and any allocation to the tax-exempt entity of partnership items is not a qualified allocation, an amount equal to the tax-exempt entity's proportionate share of the property generally is treated as tax-exempt use property. Section 168(h)(6)(E) provides that, for purposes of determining whether property is tax-exempt use property, rules similar to those applicable to partnerships apply to other pass-thru entities. Section 849(a) of the AJCA provides that § 470 generally applies to leases entered into after March 12, 2004. Section 403(ff) of the Gulf Opportunity Zone Act of 2005, Pub. L. No. 109–135, 119 Stat. 2632, amended § 849(a) of the AJCA to provide that, in the case of property treated as tax-exempt use property solely by reason of § 168(h)(6), § 470 applies to property acquired after March 12, 2004.

Notice 2006–2 and Notice 2005–29 provide transition relief to partnerships and other pass-thru entities that are treated by § 470 as holding tax-exempt use property as a result of the application of § 168(h)(6). Specifically, Notice 2006–2 and Notice 2005–29 provide that, in the case of partnerships and pass-thru entities described in § 168(h)(6)(E), for taxable years that begin before January 1, 2006, and January 1, 2005, respectively, the Internal Revenue Service will not apply § 470 to disallow losses associated with property that is treated as tax-exempt use property solely as a result of the application of § 168(h)(6). Notice 2006–2 was issued subsequent to the receipt by the Treasury Department of a letter from the Chairmen and Ranking Members of both the Senate Finance Committee and House Ways and Means Committee requesting that the Treasury Department consider extending the transition relief provided in Notice 2005–29 for taxable years beginning before January 1, 2006.

On September 29, 2006, the Tax Technical Corrections Act of 2006 was introduced in Congress. This legislation addresses, among other things, the application of § 470 to partnerships and other pass-thru entities with tax-exempt use property as a result of § 168(h)(6). See H.R. 6264, 109th Cong. 2nd Sess. § 6(e) (2006) and S. 4026, 109th Cong. 2nd Sess. § 6(e) (2006). The Chairmen of the Senate Finance Committee and House Ways and Means Committee solicited comments regarding the legislation. As of the date of this notice, no congressional action has been taken on the legislation.

If enacted in its current form, the legislation will be effective retroactively, in the case of property treated as tax-exempt use property solely by reason of § 168(h)(6), to property acquired after March 12, 2004. However, the DESCRIPTION OF THE TAX TECHNICAL CORRECTIONS ACT OF 2006, as prepared by the Staff of the Joint Committee on Taxation (October 2, 2006, JCX–48–06), provides that it is not intended that the effective date of the legislation supersede the rules set forth in Notice 2006–2 and Notice 2005–29, with respect to the application of § 470 in the case of partnerships and other pass-thru entities, for taxable years of these entities beginning in 2005 and 2004, respectively. The Service will continue to apply the rules set forth in Notice 2005–29 and Notice 2006–2. Additionally, in the case of partnerships and pass-thru entities described in § 168(h)(6)(E), for taxable years beginning before January 1, 2007, the Service will not apply § 470 to disallow losses associated with property that is treated as tax-exempt use property solely as a result of the application of § 168(h)(6).

EXTENSION OF TRANSITION RELIEF

In the case of partnerships and other pass-thru entities described in § 168(h)(6)(E), for taxable years that begin before January 1, 2007, the Service will not apply § 470 to disallow losses associated with property that is treated as tax-exempt use property solely as a result of the application of § 168(h)(6). Abusive transactions involving partnerships and other pass-thru entities remain subject to challenge by the Service under other provisions of the tax law.

EFFECT ON OTHER DOCUMENTS

Notice 2006–2 and Notice 2005–29 are modified and superseded.

DRAFTING INFORMATION

For further information regarding this notice, contact John Aramburu of the Office of the Associate Chief Counsel (Income Tax & Accounting) at (202) 622–4960 (not a toll-free call).

---

26 CFR 1.61–21: Taxation of fringe benefits.
(Also Internal Revenue Code §§ 61, 280F.)

Rev. Proc. 2007–11

SECTION 1. PURPOSE

.01 This revenue procedure provides: (1) the maximum value of employer-provided vehicles first made available to employees for personal use in calendar year 2007 for which the vehicle cents-per-mile valuation rule provided under section 1.61–21(e) of the Income Tax Regulations may be applicable is $15,100 for a passenger automobile and $16,100 for a truck or van; (2) the maximum value of employer-provided vehicles first made available to employees for personal use in calendar year 2007 for which the fleet-average valuation rule provided under section 1.61–21(d) of the regulations may be applicable is $20,100 for a passenger automobile and $21,100 for a truck or van.

SECTION 2. BACKGROUND

.01 If an employer provides an employee with a vehicle that is available to the employee for personal use, the value of the personal use must generally be included in the employee's income and wages. Internal Revenue Code § 61; Treas. Reg. § 1.61–21.

.02 For employer-provided passenger automobiles (including trucks and vans) made available to employees for personal use that meet the requirements of section 1.61–21(e)(1) of the regulations, generally the value of the personal use may be determined under the vehicle cents-per-mile valuation rule of section 1.61–21(e). However, regulations section 1.61–21(e)(1)(iii)(A) provides that for a passenger automobile first made available after 1988 to any employee of the employer for personal use, the value of the personal use may not be determined under the vehicle cents-per-mile valuation rule for a calendar year if the fair market value of the passenger automobile (determined pursuant to regulations section 1.61–21(d)(5)(i) through (iv)) on the first date the passenger automobile is made available to the employee exceeds a specified dollar limit.

.03 For employer-provided vehicles available to employees for personal use for an entire year, generally the value of the personal use may be determined under the automobile lease valuation rule of section 1.61–21(d) of the regulations. Under this valuation rule, the value of the personal use is the Annual Lease Value. Provided the requirements of regulations section 1.61–21(d)(5)(v) are met, an employer with a fleet of 20 or more automobiles may use a fleet-average value for purposes of calculating the Annual Lease Values of the automobiles in the employer's fleet. The fleet-average value is the average of the fair market values of all the automobiles in the fleet. However, section 1.61–21(d)(5)(v)(D) of the regulations provides that for an automobile first made available after 1988 to an employee of the employer for personal use, the value of the personal use may not be determined under the fleet-average valuation rule for a calendar year if the fair market value of the automobile (determined pursuant to regulations section 1.61–21(d)(5)(i) through (v)) on the first date the passenger automobile is made available to the employee exceeds a specified dollar limit.

.04 The maximum passenger automobile values for applying the vehicle cents-per-mile and the fleet-average value rules reflect the automobile price inflation adjustment of Code section 280F(d)(7). The method of calculating this price inflation amount for automobiles other than trucks and vans uses the "new car" component of the Consumer Price Index (CPI) "automobile component". When calculating this price inflation adjustment for trucks and vans, the "new trucks" component of the CPI is used. This results in somewhat higher maximum values for trucks and vans. This change reflects the higher rate of price inflation that trucks and vans have been subject to since 1988, and is consistent with the change announced in Rev. Proc. 2003–75, 2003–2 C.B. 1018, for purposes of calculating depreciation deductions. See also Rev. Proc. 2004–20, 2004–1 C.B. 642, Rev. Proc. 2005–13, 2005–1 C.B. 759, and Rev. Proc. 2006–18, 2006–12 I.R.B. 645. For purposes of this revenue procedure, the term "trucks and vans" refers to passenger automobiles that are built on a truck chassis, including minivans and sport utility vehicles (SUVs) that are built on a truck chassis.

SECTION 3. PROCEDURE

.01 Maximum Automobile Value for Using the Cents-per-mile Valuation Rule. An employer providing a passenger automobile for the first time in calendar year 2007 for the personal use of any employee may determine the value of the personal use by using the vehicle cents-per-mile valuation rule in section 1.61–21(e) of the regulations if its fair market value on the date it is first made available does not exceed $15,100 for a passenger automobile other than a tuck or van, or $16,100 for a truck or van. If the fair market value of the passenger automobile exceeds this amount, the employer may determine the value of the personal use under the general valuation rules of regulations section 1.61–21(b) or under the special valuation rules of section 1.61–21(d) (Automobile lease valuation) or section 1.61–21(f) (Commuting valuation) if the applicable requirements are met. See Rev. Proc. 2005–48, 2005–2 C.B. 271, for guidance on determining the maximum value of passenger automobiles first made available during calendar year 2005, and Rev. Proc. 2006–15, 2006–5 I.R.B. 387, for guidance on determining the maximum value of passenger automobiles first made available during calendar year 2006.

.02 Maximum Automobile Value for Using the Fleet-Average Valuation Rule. An employer with a fleet of 20 or more automobiles providing an automobile for the first time in calendar year 2007 for the personal use of any employee for an entire year may determine the value of the personal use by using the fleet-average valuation rule in regulations section 1.61–21(d)(5)(v) to calculate the Annual Lease Values of the automobiles in the fleet. The fleet-average valuation rule may not be used to determine the Annual Lease Value of any automobile if its fair market value on the date it is first made available exceeds $20,100 for a passenger automobile other than a truck or van, or $21,100 for a truck or van. If all other applicable requirements are met, an employer with a fleet of 20 or more vehicles consisting of passenger automobiles other than trucks or vans as well as trucks and vans may use the fleet-average valuation rule as long as none of the vehicles exceed their respective maximum allowable values. If the fair market value of any passenger automobile in the fleet exceeds these amounts, the employer may determine the value of the personal use under regulations section 1.61–21(f) (Commuting valuation) or the general valuation rules of section 1.61–21(b) or may determine the Annual Lease Value of such automobile separately under the automobile lease valuation rule of section 1.61–21(d)(2) if the applicable requirements are met.

SECTION 4. EFFECTIVE DATE

This revenue procedure applies to employer-provided passenger automobiles first made available to employees for personal use in calendar year 2007.

SECTION 5. DRAFTING INFORMATION

The principal author of this revenue procedure is Don M. Parkinson of the Office of the Division Counsel/Associate Chief Counsel (Tax Exempt & Government Entities). For further information regarding the maximum automobile value for applying the valuation rules of regulations section 1.61–21(e)(1)(iii)(A) (the vehicle cents-per-mile valuation rule), and section 1.61–21(d)(5)(v)(D) (the fleet average valuation rule), contact Don M. Parkinson at (202) 622–6040 (not a toll-free call).

Part IV. Items of General Interest

Notice of Proposed Rulemaking by Cross-Reference to Temporary Regulations

Reduction in Taxable Income for Housing Hurricane Katrina Displaced Individuals

REG–152043–05

AGENCY: Internal Revenue Service (IRS), Treasury.

ACTION: Notice of proposed rulemaking by cross-reference to temporary regulations.

SUMMARY: In this issue of the Bulletin, the IRS is issuing temporary regulations (T.D. 9301) relating to the reduction in taxable income under section 302 of the Katrina Emergency Tax Relief Act of 2005. The regulations affect taxpayers that provide housing in their principal residences to individuals displaced by Hurricane Katrina. The text of those regulations also serves as the text of these proposed regulations.

DATES: Written or electronic comments must be received by March 12, 2007.

ADDRESSES: Send submissions to: CC:PA:LPD:RU (REG–152043–05), Internal Revenue Service, POB 7604, Ben Franklin Station, Washington, DC 20044. Submissions may be hand-delivered Monday through Friday between the hours of 8 a.m. and 4 p.m. to CC:PA:LPD:PR (REG–152043–05), Courier's Desk, Internal Revenue Service, 1111 Constitution Avenue, NW, Washington, DC. Alternatively, taxpayers may submit comments electronically via the IRS Internet site at *www.irs.gov/regs* or the Federal eRulemaking Portal at *http://www.regulations.gov* (IRS REG–152043–05).

FOR FURTHER INFORMATION CONTACT: Concerning the proposed regulations, Marnette M. Myers, (202) 622–4920 (not a toll-free number); concerning submission of comments and/or to request a public hearing, Richard Hurst at *Richard.A.Hurst@irscounsel.treas.gov*.

SUPPLEMENTARY INFORMATION:

Background

Temporary regulations in this issue of the Bulletin amend the Income Tax Regulations (26 CFR part 1). The text of those regulations also serves as the text of these proposed regulations. The preamble to the temporary regulations explains the amendments.

Special Analyses

It has been determined that this notice of proposed rulemaking is not a significant regulatory action as defined in Executive Order 12866. Therefore, a regulatory assessment is not required. It also has been determined that section 553(b) of the Administrative Procedure Act (5 U.S.C. chapter 5) does not apply to these regulations, and, because the regulations do not impose a collection of information on small entities, the Regulatory Flexibility Act (5 U.S.C. chapter 6) does not apply. Pursuant to section 7805(f) of the Code, this notice of proposed rulemaking will be submitted to the Chief Counsel for Advocacy of the Small Business Administration for comment on its impact on small business.

Comments and Requests for a Public Hearing

Before these proposed regulations are adopted as final regulations, consideration will be given to any written comments (a signed original and eight (8) copies) or electronic comments that are submitted timely to the IRS. The IRS and Treasury Department specifically request comments on the clarity of the proposed rule and how it may be made easier to understand. All comments will be available for public inspection and copying. A public hearing will be scheduled if requested in writing by any person that timely submits written comments. If a public hearing is scheduled, notice of the date, time and place for the public hearing will be published in the **Federal Register**.

Drafting Information

The principal author of these regulations is Marnette M. Myers of the Office of Associate Chief Counsel (Income Tax & Accounting). However, other personnel from the IRS and Treasury Department participated in their development.

* * * * *

Proposed Amendments to the Regulations

Accordingly, 26 CFR part 1 is proposed to be amended as follows:

PART 1—INCOME TAXES

Paragraph 1. The authority citation for part 1 continues to read, in part, as follows:

Authority: 26 U.S.C. 7805 * * *

Par. 2. Section 1.9300–1 is added to read as follows:

[The text of proposed §1.9300–1 is the same as the text of §1.9300–1T published elsewhere in this issue of the Bulletin.]

Linda M. Kroening,
Acting Deputy Commissioner for Services and Enforcement.

(Filed by the Office of the Federal Register for December 11, 2006, 8:45 a.m., and published in the issue of the Federal Register for December 12, 2006, 71 F.R. 74482)

Railroad Track Maintenance Credit; Hearing Cancellation

Announcement 2007–2

AGENCY: Internal Revenue Service (IRS), Treasury.

ACTION: Cancellation of notice of public hearing on proposed rulemaking by cross-reference to temporary regulations.

SUMMARY: This document cancels a public hearing on proposed regulations (REG–142270–05, 2006–43 I.R.B. 791) by cross-reference to temporary regulations relating to the railroad track maintenance credit determined for qualified railroad track maintenance expenditures paid or incurred by a Class II or Class III railroad and other eligible taxpayers during the taxable year.

DATES: The public hearing, originally scheduled for January 9, 2007 at 10 a.m. is cancelled.

FOR FURTHER INFORMATION CONTACT: Kelly Banks of the Publications and Regulations Branch, Legal Processing Division, Associate Chief Counsel (Procedure and Administration) at (202) 622–0392 (not a toll-free number).

SUPPLEMENTARY INFORMATION: A notice of proposed rulemaking by cross-reference to temporary regulations and notice of public hearing that appeared in the **Federal Register** on Friday, September 8, 2006 (71 FR 53053), announced that a public hearing was scheduled for January 9, 2006, at 10 a.m. in the IRS Auditorium, New Carrollton Federal Building, 5000 Ellin Road, Lanham, MD 20706. The subject of the public hearing is under section 45G of the Internal Revenue Code.

The public comment period expired on December 7, 2006. The notice of proposed rulemaking by cross-reference to temporary regulations and notice of public hearing instructed those interested in testifying at the public hearing to submit an outline of the topics to be addressed. As of Monday, December 11, 2006, no one has requested to speak. Therefore, the public hearing scheduled for January 9, 2007, is cancelled.

LaNita Van Dyke,
Branch Chief, Publications and Regulations Branch, Legal Processing Division, Associate Chief Counsel (Procedure and Administration).

(Filed by the Office of the Federal Register on December 26, 2006, 8:45 a.m., and published in the issue of the Federal Register for December 27, 2006, 71 F.R. 77654)

Part I. Rulings and Decisions Under the Internal Revenue Code of 1986

Section 42.—Low-Income Housing Credit

The adjusted applicable federal short-term, mid-term, and long-term rates are set forth for the month of January 2007. See Rev. Rul. 2007-2, page 266.

Section 280G.—Golden Parachute Payments

Federal short-term, mid-term, and long-term rates are set forth for the month of January 2007. See Rev. Rul. 2007-2, page 266.

Section 382.—Limitation on Net Operating Loss Carryforwards and Certain Built-In Losses Following Ownership Change

The adjusted applicable federal long-term rate is set forth for the month of January 2007. See Rev. Rul. 2007-2, page 266.

Section 412.—Minimum Funding Standards

The adjusted applicable federal short-term, mid-term, and long-term rates are set forth for the month of January 2007. See Rev. Rul. 2007-2, page 266.

Section 451.—General Rule for Taxable Year of Inclusion

26 CFR 1.451–1: Taxable year of inclusion.
(Also: §§ 61, 446.)

Credit card nonsufficient funds (NSF) fee. This ruling provides that a credit card nonsufficient funds (NSF) fee as described in the ruling is not interest for federal income tax purposes. Also, this ruling holds that a credit card NSF fee is includible in income by the issuer of the credit card when the NSF Event, as defined therein, occurs.

Rev. Rul. 2007–1

ISSUES

(1) If a credit card issuer becomes entitled to a fee if it refuses to honor a credit card convenience check that, if honored, would leave the cardholder over the cardholder's credit limit, is the fee interest income for federal income tax purposes?

(2) When is the credit card fee that is described in Issue (1) includible in gross income by the card issuer?

FACTS

X, a taxpayer that uses an overall accrual method of accounting for federal income tax purposes, issues a credit card to *A*. The credit card allows *A* to access a revolving line of credit to make purchases of goods and services and to obtain cash advances, including cash advances obtained through *A*'s use of a convenience check made available through A's credit card account (an "account check").

There is a written agreement between *X* and *A* that sets forth the terms and conditions governing *A*'s use of the credit card (the "Cardholder Agreement"). Under the terms and conditions of the Cardholder Agreement, *X* is not required to honor one of *A*'s account checks if, when the account check is presented to *X* for payment, either *A* is overdrawn on *A*'s line of credit or payment of the check would cause *A* to become overdrawn. Under the agreement *X* is entitled to impose a $25 fee (the "Credit Card NSF Fee") on *A* if an account check is presented to *X* that, if honored, would leave *A* overdrawn and *X* does not in fact honor the check (the "NSF Event").

A writes an account check and uses it to make a payment to a third party. *X* does not honor *A*'s account check when the third party presents it for payment because *A* would be overdrawn on *A*'s line of credit if *X* honored the account check at that time. *X* is therefore entitled to impose a $25 Credit Card NSF Fee on *A* in accordance with the terms of *X*'s Cardholder Agreement with *A*.

LAW AND ANALYSIS

For federal income tax purposes, interest is an amount that is paid in compensation for the use or forbearance of money. *Deputy v. DuPont*, 308 U.S. 488 (1940); *Old Colony Railroad Co. v. Commissioner*, 284 U.S. 552 (1932). Neither the label used for the fee nor a taxpayer's treatment of the fee for financial or regulatory reporting purposes is determinative of the proper federal income tax characterization of that fee. *See Thor Power Tool Co. v. Commissioner*, 439 U.S. 522, 542–43 (1979); Rev. Rul. 72–315, 1972–1 C.B. 49.

When *X* determines that it will not honor *A*'s account check that the third party has presented for payment because *A* would be overdrawn on *A*'s line of credit, *X* is denying *A* the use of *X*'s funds. Thus, the $25 Credit Card NSF Fee does not compensate *X* for the use or forbearance of money, and it is not interest income for federal income tax purposes.

Under § 451(a) of the Internal Revenue Code, the amount of any item of gross income is includible in gross income for the taxable year in which it is received by the taxpayer, unless that amount is to be properly accounted for in a different period under the method of accounting used by the taxpayer in computing taxable income.

Under § 1.451–1(a) of the Income Tax Regulations, income is includible in gross income by a taxpayer that uses an accrual method of accounting when all events have occurred that fix the taxpayer's right to receive that income and the amount of that income can be determined with reasonable accuracy. *See also* § 1.446–1(c)(1)(ii)(A). Generally, all the events that fix the right to receive income occur either when the required performance takes place, when payment is due, or when payment is made, whichever occurs first (the "All Events Test"). *See, e.g.*, Rev. Rul. 2004–52, 2004–1 C.B. 973 (addressing credit card issuers' treatment of credit card annual fees).

X is required to include the Credit Card NSF Fee in gross income under section 451 when the NSF Event occurs because the NSF Event fixes *X*'s right to receive the income and the amount can be determined with reasonable accuracy. Thus, the All Events Test is satisfied when the NSF Event occurs.

A change in the treatment of Credit Card NSF fees to comply with this revenue ruling is a change in method of accounting within the meaning of §§ 446 and 481 and the regulations issued thereunder. Accordingly, a taxpayer wishing to change its treatment of Credit Card NSF fees to comply with this revenue ruling must obtain the consent of the Commissioner under § 446(e) and § 1.446–1(e)(2)(i) by following the procedures in Rev. Proc. 97–27, 1997–1 C.B. 680 (or its successor).

HOLDINGS

(1) The Credit Card NSF Fee is not interest for federal income tax purposes.

(2) The Credit Card NSF Fee is includible in gross income for federal income tax purposes when the NSF Event occurs.

DRAFTING INFORMATION

The principal authors of this revenue ruling are Jonathan Silver and Tina Jannotta of the Office of Associate Chief Counsel (Financial Institutions & Products). For further information regarding this revenue ruling, contact the principal authors at (202) 622 3930 (not a toll-free call).

Section 467.—Certain Payments for the Use of Property or Services

The adjusted applicable federal short-term, mid-term, and long-term rates are set forth for the month of January 2007. See Rev. Rul. 2007-2, page 266.

Section 468.—Special Rules for Mining and Solid Waste Reclamation and Closing Costs

The adjusted applicable federal short-term, mid-term, and long-term rates are set forth for the month of January 2007. See Rev. Rul. 2007-2, page 266.

Section 482.—Allocation of Income and Deductions Among Taxpayers

Federal short-term, mid-term, and long-term rates are set forth for the month of January 2007. See Rev. Rul. 2007-2, page 266.

Section 483.—Interest on Certain Deferred Payments

The adjusted applicable federal short-term, mid-term, and long-term rates are set forth for the month of January 2007. See Rev. Rul. 2007-2, page 266.

Section 642.—Special Rules for Credits and Deductions

Federal short-term, mid-term, and long-term rates are set forth for the month of January 2007. See Rev. Rul. 2007-2, page 266.

Section 807.—Rules for Certain Reserves

The adjusted applicable federal short-term, mid-term, and long-term rates are set forth for the month of January 2007. See Rev. Rul. 2007-2, page 266.

Section 832.—Insurance Company Taxable Income

26 CFR 1.832–4: Gross income.

The salvage discount factors are set forth for 2006. These factors must be used to compute discounted estimated salvage recoverable for purposes of section 832 of the Code. See Rev. Proc. 2007-10, page 289.

Section 846.—Discounted Unpaid Losses Defined

The adjusted applicable federal short-term, mid-term, and long-term rates are set forth for the month of January 2007. See Rev. Rul. 2007-2, page 266.

26 CFR 1.846–1: Application of discount factors.

The loss payment patterns and discount factors are set forth for the 2006 accident year. These factors will be used for computing discounted unpaid losses under section 846 of the Code. See Rev. Proc. 2007-9, page 278.

26 CFR 1.846–1: Application of discount factors.

The salvage discount factors are set forth for 2006. These factors must be used to compute discounted estimated salvage recoverable for purposes of section 832 of the Code. See Rev. Proc. 2007-10, page 289.

Section 1274.—Determination of Issue Price in the Case of Certain Debt Instruments Issued for Property

(Also Sections 42, 280G, 382, 412, 467, 468, 482, 483, 642, 807, 846, 1288, 7520, 7872.)

Federal rates; adjusted federal rates; adjusted federal long-term rate and the long-term exempt rate. For purposes of sections 382, 642, 1274, 1288, and other sections of the Code, tables set forth the rates for January 2007.

Rev. Rul. 2007–2

This revenue ruling provides various prescribed rates for federal income tax purposes for January 2007 (the current month). Table 1 contains the short-term, mid-term, and long-term applicable federal rates (AFR) for the current month for purposes of section 1274(d) of the Internal Revenue Code. Table 2 contains the short-term, mid-term, and long-term adjusted applicable federal rates (adjusted AFR) for the current month for purposes of section 1288(b). Table 3 sets forth the adjusted federal long-term rate and the long-term tax-exempt rate described in section 382(f). Table 4 contains the appropriate percentages for determining the low-income housing credit described in section 42(b)(2) for buildings placed in service during the current month. Table 5 contains the federal rate for determining the present value of an annuity, an interest for life or for a term of years, or a remainder or a reversionary interest for purposes of section 7520. Finally, Table 6 contains the deemed rate of return for transfers made during calendar year 2007 to pooled income funds described in section 642(c)(5) that have been in existence for less than 3 taxable years immediately preceding the taxable year in which the transfer was made.

REV. RUL. 2007–2 TABLE 1

Applicable Federal Rates (AFR) for January 2007

Period for Compounding

	Annual	*Semiannual*	*Quarterly*	*Monthly*
Short-term				
AFR	4.88%	4.82%	4.79%	4.77%
110% AFR	5.37%	5.30%	5.27%	5.24%
120% AFR	5.86%	5.78%	5.74%	5.71%
130% AFR	6.37%	6.27%	6.22%	6.19%
Mid-term				
AFR	4.58%	4.53%	4.50%	4.49%
110% AFR	5.04%	4.98%	4.95%	4.93%
120% AFR	5.51%	5.44%	5.40%	5.38%
130% AFR	5.98%	5.89%	5.85%	5.82%
150% AFR	6.92%	6.80%	6.74%	6.71%
175% AFR	8.09%	7.93%	7.85%	7.80%
Long-term				
AFR	4.73%	4.68%	4.65%	4.64%
110% AFR	5.22%	5.15%	5.12%	5.10%
120% AFR	5.70%	5.62%	5.58%	5.56%
130% AFR	6.17%	6.08%	6.03%	6.00%

REV. RUL. 2007–2 TABLE 2

Adjusted AFR for January 2007

Period for Compounding

	Annual	*Semiannual*	*Quarterly*	*Monthly*
Short-term adjusted AFR	3.39%	3.36%	3.35%	3.34%
Mid-term adjusted AFR	3.54%	3.51%	3.49%	3.48%
Long-term adjusted AFR	4.03%	3.99%	3.97%	3.96%

REV. RUL. 2007–2 TABLE 3

Rates Under Section 382 for January 2007

Adjusted federal long-term rate for the current month	4.03%
Long-term tax-exempt rate for ownership changes during the current month (the highest of the adjusted federal long-term rates for the current month and the prior two months.)	4.15%

REV. RUL. 2007–2 TABLE 4

Appropriate Percentages Under Section 42(b)(2) for January 2007

Appropriate percentage for the 70% present value low-income housing credit	8.08%
Appropriate percentage for the 30% present value low-income housing credit	3.46%

REV. RUL. 2007–2 TABLE 5	
Rate Under Section 7520 for January 2007	
Applicable federal rate for determining the present value of an annuity, an interest for life or a term of years, or a remainder or reversionary interest	5.6%

REV. RUL. 2007–2 TABLE 6	
Deemed Rate for Transfers to New Pooled Income Funds During 2007	
Deemed rate of return for transfers during 2007 to pooled income funds that have been in existence for less than 3 taxable years	4.8%

Section 1288.—Treatment of Original Issue Discount on Tax-Exempt Obligations

The adjusted applicable federal short-term, mid-term, and long-term rates are set forth for the month of January 2007. See Rev. Rul. 2007-2, page 266.

Section 7520.—Valuation Tables

The adjusted applicable federal short-term, mid-term, and long-term rates are set forth for the month of January 2007. See Rev. Rul. 2007-2, page 266.

Section 7872.—Treatment of Loans With Below-Market Interest Rates

The adjusted applicable federal short-term, mid-term, and long-term rates are set forth for the month of January 2007. See Rev. Rul. 2007-2, page 266.

Part III. Administrative, Procedural, and Miscellaneous

This Notice Clarifies and Modifies Certain Provisions of the Temporary and Proposed Regulations Under Section 482 of the Code Relating to Controlled Services Transactions, and Section 6662 of the Code Relating to Transfer Pricing Documentation Penalties

Notice 2007–5

SECTION 1. PURPOSE

On August 4, 2006, the Treasury Department and the IRS published T.D. 9278, 2006–34 I.R.B. 256, containing temporary and proposed regulations that address controlled services under section 482 (71 Fed. Reg. 44466). This notice makes several clarifications concerning provisions in the temporary and proposed regulations, primarily relating to the services cost method. In addition, this notice makes certain modifications to the effective date of the temporary regulations.

SECTION 2. BACKGROUND

The temporary and proposed regulations provided for a new transfer pricing method applicable to certain controlled services transactions, the services cost method (SCM). Under specified circumstances, the SCM allows the arm's length charge for a controlled services transaction to be determined by reference to total services costs, without a markup. Two categories of covered services are potentially eligible for this method, specified covered services and low margin covered services, both defined in Temp. Treas. Reg. § 1.482–9T(b)(4). To demonstrate that a particular controlled service qualifies for the SCM, the taxpayer must reasonably conclude, in its business judgment, that the service does not contribute significantly to key competitive advantages, core capabilities, or fundamental risks of success or failure in one or more trades or businesses of the renderer, the recipient, or both. Temp. Treas. Reg. § 1.482–9T(b)(2) (business judgment rule). Specified covered services are those controlled services that the Commissioner identifies by means of a revenue procedure. Low-margin covered services are controlled services transactions for which the arm's length mark-up, determined by reference to comparable uncontrolled transactions, equals 7% or less.

The Treasury Department and the IRS issued a proposed revenue procedure that identified specified covered services. *See* Announcement 2006–50, 2006–34 I.R.B. 321 (August 21, 2006). That proposed revenue procedure identified forty-eight activities or groups of activities that constitute specified covered services. Contemporaneously with the issuance of this notice, the IRS intends to issue a final revenue procedure on this topic before December 31, 2006. The revenue procedure may be further updated, as appropriate, including in connection with the conclusion of the one-year transition period provided by this notice and in the course of finalization of the temporary regulations in response to comments.

The temporary and proposed regulations also added a provision in Temp. Treas. Reg. § 1.482–9T(b)(5) concerning shared services arrangements (SSAs). Provided that the taxpayer satisfies the conditions for use of an SSA, which includes reasonably concluding that the SSA utilizes the most reliable measure of the participants' respective shares of the reasonably anticipated benefits from the covered services, the IRS will not make an adjustment to the taxpayer's allocation. An SSA must be structured such that: (1) it includes two or more participants; (2) each participant reasonably anticipates a benefit from one or more covered services specified in the SSA; and (3) each covered service confers a benefit on at least one participant in the SSA. *See* Temp. Treas. Reg. § 1.482–9T(b)(5). Services eligible to be included in an SSA are limited to services that qualify for the SCM. Temp. Treas. Reg. § 1.482–9T(b)(5)(i).

The temporary and proposed regulations are generally effective for taxable years that begin after December 31, 2006. Temp. Treas. Reg. § 1.482–9T(n). A taxpayer may elect to apply the temporary regulations to open tax years that begin after September 10, 2003.

SECTION 3. CLARIFICATIONS, PARTIAL MODIFICATION OF EFFECTIVE DATE

Numerous public comments were submitted concerning both Announcement 2006–50 and the temporary and proposed regulations. In response to these comments, this notice describes modifications to the list of specified covered services, as adopted in the final revenue procedure. The notice also modifies the effective date of the temporary regulations in several respects, as described below. Lastly, the notice makes several clarifications concerning the intended application of the regulations, as described below. These clarifications will be considered during the process of finalizing the temporary regulations. In the interim, and pending the issuance of final regulations under Treas. Reg. § 1.482–9, and other related provisions, taxpayers may rely on the guidance contained in this notice.

§ 3.01 Partial Modification of Effective Date — SCM Provisions

The temporary and proposed regulations are effective for tax years beginning after December 31, 2006 (with retroactive application for tax years beginning after September 10, 2003, at the election of the taxpayer). *See* Temp. Treas. Reg. § 1.482–9T(n). Several commentators requested that the effective date of the entire regulations be moved back one year, which in their view would provide taxpayers sufficient time to modify accounting systems and to take other steps, including preparation of contractual agreements and other transfer pricing documentation, deemed necessary to comply fully with the temporary regulations.

In response to these comments, this notice partially modifies the effective date of Temp. Treas. Reg. § 1.482–9T(b) of the temporary regulations. Subject to the exceptions described below, the effective date of the temporary regulations, as they pertain to the identification of controlled services eligible to be priced at cost, is moved back one year. The temporary regulations will thus apply to taxable years after December 31, 2007, for all provisions related to the SCM in Temp. Treas. Reg.

§ 1.482–9T(b). The only SCM provision that has immediate effect, *i.e.*, for taxable years beginning after December 31, 2006, is the business judgment rule in Temp. Treas. Reg. § 1.482–9T(b)(2).

The net effect of this modification is that, for taxable years with beginning dates from January 1, 2007 to December 31, 2007, taxpayers may apply the existing regulations in Treas. Reg. § 1.482–2(b) for purposes of identifying controlled services that are eligible to be priced on a cost basis, without a markup. For such taxable years, services that are priced on a cost basis must be "non-integral" within the meaning of existing Treas. Reg. § 1.482–2(b)(7), and they must also satisfy the SCM business judgment test in Temp. Treas. Reg. § 1.482–9T(b)(2). Other SCM related provisions, including the documentation provision in Temp. Treas. Reg. § 1.482–9T(b)(3)(i) and the excluded transactions in Temp. Treas. Reg. § 1.482–9T(b)(3)(ii), are inapplicable to transactions during this one-year period. Consequently, in this context, the existing documentation standards applicable to controlled services will apply to transactions during this one-year period. Alternatively, for tax years beginning between January 1, 2007 and December 31, 2007, taxpayers may elect to apply the SCM as set forth in Temp. Treas. Reg. § 1.482–9T(b), without taking into account any of the modifications described above.

The provisions of Temp. Treas. Reg. § 1.482–9T(b) will be effective in all respects for taxable years beginning after December 31, 2007.

§ 3.02 Services Cost Method Applies Only at Option of Taxpayer

Several commentators requested confirmation that application of the SCM was a matter within the control of the taxpayer, assuming that the underlying transactions qualified for the SCM. Commentators observed that the temporary regulations could be interpreted as *requiring* a taxpayer to apply the SCM, if all the conditions for that method were satisfied. In the view of commentators, this would conflict with the ability of a taxpayer to apply the best method rule, including by applying a transfer pricing method other than the SCM.

This notice confirms that under the temporary regulations the SCM is elective by taxpayers. A statement in its books and records evidencing the taxpayer's intent to apply the SCM is required as a necessary condition to applicability of the SCM. Temp. Treas. Reg. § 1.482–9T(b)(3)(i) (second sentence). This notice also confirms that there is no requirement for a taxpayer to attach such statement to its tax return, as typically is the case with elections that are to be flagged to the IRS' attention.

§ 3.03 Listing of Specified Covered Services in Announcement 2006–50

Several commentators contended that the proposed list of specified covered services in Announcement 2006–50 was too narrow to be of practical use. Some commentators suggested that the list should refer to departments or to accounting classifications, rather than to specific activities or groups of activities. One commentator suggested that all activities in particular departments should be identified as eligible for the SCM. Other commentators supported the general approach taken in Announcement 2006–50, but suggested that the list include certain additional activities, so as to describe the back office in a more comprehensive manner.

The SCM is intended to provide a practical and administrable means of identifying low-margin services that may be evaluated by reference to total services cost without a markup. The SSA provision affords taxpayers the flexibility to analyze specified covered services and low margin covered services that produce benefits to multiple recipients, under a joint-benefit approach. Flexible grouping rules are adopted for purposes of the SCM and the SSA provisions. Temp. Treas. Reg. § 1.482–9T(b)(4) (first sentence parenthetical) and (b)(5)(iii)(B). In the view of the Treasury Department and the IRS, these provisions afford flexibility to analyze covered services in a way that does not impose inappropriate compliance burdens. Accordingly, the Treasury Department and the IRS decline to adopt a departmental approach to identification of specified covered services eligible for the SCM.

In response to public comments, however, the Treasury Department and the IRS have concluded that certain modifications to the list of specified covered services in Announcement 2006–50 are appropriate. Several further categories will be added, and further activities will be specified within the categories. In addition, the individual categories of specified covered services will also include "other similar activities." This reflects the conclusion of the Treasury Department and the IRS that the list of specified covered services should be structured and interpreted in a practical, common-sense manner. The changes described in this paragraph are reflected in Rev. Proc. 2007–13, which is published contemporaneously with this notice.

§ 3.04 Business Judgment Rule

In finalizing the regulations, the Treasury Department and the IRS will incorporate provisions consistent with the following interpretations of the business judgment rule.

(1) Applies by Reference to Controlled Group

In evaluating whether a controlled services transaction qualifies for the SCM, the temporary regulations provide that the business judgment rule should be applied by reference to "one or more trades or businesses *of the renderer, recipient, or both*." Temp. Treas. Reg. § 1.482–9T(b)(2) (emphasis added). Commentators observed that this rule may yield incorrect results in some cases, for example, where a dedicated services subsidiary performs primarily low margin covered services or specified covered services, and few other activities. The activities performed by such an entity would potentially be ineligible for the SCM under the business judgment rule, because they would constitute the entity's core capability.

This notice provides that taxpayers are to apply the business judgment rule by reference to one or more trades or businesses of the *controlled group*, as defined in Treas. Reg. § 1.482–1(i)(6), instead of "the renderer, recipient, or both," as stated in Temp. Treas. Reg. § 1.482–9T(b)(2).

(2) Evaluates Contributions to Operating Profit

This notice provides that the business judgment rule in Temp. Treas. Reg. § 1.482–9T(b)(2) should take into account whether a particular activity contributes to the operating profit of one or more controlled parties, as that term is defined in Treas. Reg. § 1.482–5(d)(3). For example, the activities performed by a corporate tax department should not be disqualified from the SCM, given that these activities primarily affect foreign income taxes (as defined in § 1.901–2(a)) and domestic income taxes, which are not classified as operating expenses. *See* Treas. Reg. § 1.482–5(d)(3).

(3) Taxpayer's Reasonable Business Judgment

Several commentators expressed concern over how the business judgment rule would be administered. They raised questions concerning how to evidence the necessary business judgment, for example, whether an executive's representation must be preferred to the tax director's. Commentators also requested that statements from the preamble to the temporary regulations be incorporated in final regulations.

The Treasury Department and the IRS reiterate that the temporary regulations already incorporate a high threshold for application of the business judgment rule to exclude services otherwise eligible for the SCM. The exclusion is inapplicable so long as the taxpayer reasonably concludes in its business judgment that the covered services do not contribute significantly to key competitive advantages, core capabilities, or fundamental risks of success or failure in one or more trades or businesses of the controlled group.

The test is satisfied by a reasonable exercise of the taxpayer's business judgment, not a reasonable exercise of the IRS's judgment in examining the taxpayer. In the view of the Treasury Department and the IRS, the gloss in the preamble to the temporary regulations, such as that this is a business judgment preeminently within the business person's own expertise, flows directly from the regulations' specification that the matter lies in the taxpayer's reasonable business judgment. The evidence necessary to establish the taxpayer's reasonable business judgment is determined under all the facts and circumstances. No source, executive or otherwise, is generally more probative than another.

§ 3.05 Shared Services Concept Applicable to non-SCM Services

In general, commentators supported the SSA provision as a useful mechanism for allocation of costs from shared or centralized services. Commentators called into question, however, the need to restrict SSAs to covered services eligible to be analyzed under the SCM. In the view of the commentators, extending the SSA concept to all controlled services would produce accurate results and would also be consistent with the OECD *Transfer Pricing Guidelines for Multinational Enterprises and Tax Administrations*, in particular, the provisions pertaining to cost contribution arrangements.

This notice confirms that taxpayers may also make allocations of arm's length charges for services ineligible for the SCM that yield a benefit to multiple members of a controlled group. In such a case, however, the flexible rules under the SCM for establishing the joint benefits and selecting the allocation key are inapplicable. Instead, the more robust analysis under the general transfer pricing rules applies for purposes of determining the appropriate arm's length charges, benefits, allocation keys, etc.

§ 3.06 Documentation Provisions

This notice clarifies that the documentation for services analyzed under the SCM, described in Temp. Treas. § 1.482–9T(b)(3)(i) (adequate books and records) need not be generated contemporaneously with the filing of the income tax return.

In addition, for tax years beginning after December 31, 2006, and on or before December 31, 2007, the written contract specified by Temp. Treas. Reg. § 1.482–9T(i)(2) need not be entered into prior to, or contemporaneous with the start of the activity or group of activities. Instead, the written contract need only be prepared prior to, or contemporaneous with the filing of the income tax return.

§ 3.07 Penalty Relief for Certain Controlled Services Transactions

During a one-year transition period, the Treasury Department and the IRS intend that taxpayers' reasonable efforts to comply with the temporary regulations, as modified by this notice, will avoid the imposition of penalties for controlled services transactions, except for those evaluated under Treas. Reg. § 1.482–2(b), as modified by section 3.01 of this notice.

Accordingly, this notice provides that penalties, including but not limited to penalties within the meaning of section 6662(e) and (h) of the Code, will not apply to controlled services transactions (except for those evaluated under Treas. Reg. § 1.482–2(b)(3), as modified by section 3.01 of this notice), for taxable years beginning after December 31, 2006 and on or before December 31, 2007, provided that the taxpayer makes reasonable efforts to comply with documentation provisions in I.R.C. § 6001 and Treas. Reg. § 1.6662–6(d)(2)(iii).

In determining whether a taxpayer's efforts are reasonable, the Service will take into consideration that a taxpayer may not yet have all of its intercompany agreements in place and may be implementing changes to its accounting systems during this one-year transition period. If, however, the taxpayer fails to provide the Service with any transfer pricing documentation in connection with its controlled services transactions within the applicable time period, such actions will be deemed unreasonable.

This relief from penalties is intended to provide a reasonable transition period during which taxpayers may analyze the temporary and proposed regulations, execute any required contractual agreements, and prepare transfer pricing documentation for transactions subject to the regulations. This clarification does not limit the ability of the Commissioner to make section 482 allocations with respect to charges for services transactions that take place during this period or to apply penalties to controlled services transactions that are evaluated under Treas. Reg. § 1.482–2(b), as modified by section 3.01 of this notice.

SECTION 4. REQUEST FOR COMMENTS

The Treasury Department and the IRS request further comments from interested persons on the rules announced in this notice. In addition, the revenue procedure issued contemporaneously with this notice is intended to be an evolving list of services that are eligible for the SCM. The Treasury Department and the IRS contemplate issuing updates as appropriate, including a further revision of the revenue procedure to coincide with the end of the one-year transition period and in response to comments received on the temporary regulations. Comments are solicited on the categories and listed activities in the revenue procedure, possible additions, and other revisions. For example, comments are solicited whether warehousing and other functions that support distribution should be eligible for the SCM in light of Temp. Treas. Reg. § 1.482–9T(b)(3)(ii)(E) (reselling, distribution ineligible for SCM).

Written comments may be submitted to CC:INTL:6 (Notice 2007–5), room 4607, Internal Revenue Service, P.O. Box 7604, Ben Franklin Station, Washington, DC 20224. Submissions may be hand delivered Monday through Friday between the hours of 8 a.m. and 5 p.m. to: CC:INTL:6 (Notice 2007–5) Courier's desk, Internal Revenue Service, 1111 Constitution Avenue, NW, Washington, DC 20224. Alternatively, taxpayers may submit comments electronically via the following e-mail address: *Notice.Comments@irscounsel.treas.gov*. Please include "Notice 2007–5" in the subject line of any electronic communications.

SECTION 5. DRAFTING INFORMATION

The principal authors of this notice are Thomas A. Vidano and Carol B. Tan of the Office of Associate Chief Counsel (International). For further information regarding this notice, contact Thomas A. Vidano or Carol B. Tan at (202) 622–5265 (not a toll-free call).

Cash Balance and Other Hybrid Defined Benefit Pension Plans

Notice 2007–6

I. PURPOSE

This notice announces that the Service is beginning to process determination letter and examination cases in which an application for a determination letter or a plan under examination involves an amendment to change a traditional defined benefit plan into a cash balance plan and provides related guidance. This notice also provides transitional guidance on the requirements of §§ 411(a)(13) and 411(b)(5) of the Internal Revenue Code (Code), as added by section 701(b) of the Pension Protection Act of 2006, Public Law 109–280 (PPA '06), which was enacted on August 17, 2006. This guidance generally relates to cash balance plans and other hybrid defined benefit pension plans and to amendments that convert defined benefit pension plans to hybrid defined benefit pension plans. This notice also requests comments on certain issues raised by §§ 411(a)(13) and 411(b)(5).

II. BACKGROUND

A defined benefit pension plan generally must satisfy the minimum vesting standards of § 411(a) and the accrual requirements of § 411(b) in order to be qualified under § 401(a). Both sections have been modified by section 701(b) of PPA '06, which added §§ 411(a)(13) and 411(b)(5) to the Code.

Section 411(a)(13)(A) provides that a plan described in § 411(a)(13)(C) is not treated as failing to meet either (i) the requirements of § 411(a)(2) (subject to a special vesting rule in § 411(a)(13)(B) with respect to benefits derived from employer contributions), or (ii) the requirements of § 411(c) or § 417(e) with respect to benefits derived from employer contributions, solely because the present value of the accrued benefit (or any portion thereof) of any participant is, under the terms of the plan, equal to the amount expressed as the balance in a hypothetical account or as an accumulated percentage of the participant's final average compensation.

A plan is described in § 411(a)(13)(C)(i) if the plan is a defined benefit plan under which the accrued benefit (or any portion thereof) of a participant is calculated as the balance of a hypothetical account maintained for the participant or as an accumulated percentage of the participant's final average compensation. Under § 411(a)(13)(C)(ii), the Secretary is to issue regulations that treat any defined benefit plan (or any portion of such a plan) that has an effect similar to a plan described in § 411(a)(13)(C)(i) as if it were described in § 411(a)(13)(C)(i). For purposes of this notice, a plan described either in § 411(a)(13)(C)(i) or in regulations or other guidance issued pursuant to § 411(a)(13)(C)(ii) is referred to as a *statutory hybrid plan*.

Section 411(b)(1)(H)(i) provides that a defined benefit plan fails to comply with § 411(b) if, under the plan, an employee's benefit accrual is ceased, or the employee's rate of benefit accrual is reduced, because of the attainment of any age. Section 411(b)(5)(A), as added by section 701(b)(1) of PPA '06, generally provides that a plan will not be treated as failing to meet the requirements of § 411(b)(1)(H)(i) if a participant's benefit accrued to date, as determined as of any date under the terms of the plan, would be equal to or greater than that of any similarly situated, younger individual who is or could be a participant. For purposes of this notice, a participant's benefit accrued to date is referred to as the participant's *accumulated benefit*. Under § 411(b)(5)(A)(iv), for purposes of the safe harbor standard of § 411(b)(5)(A), a participant's accumulated benefit may, under the terms of the plan, be expressed as an annuity payable at normal retirement age, the balance of a hypothetical account, or the current value of the accumulated percentage of the employee's final average compensation.

Section 411(b)(5)(B) imposes several requirements on a statutory hybrid plan as a condition of satisfying § 411(b)(1)(H). First, § 411(b)(5)(B)(i) provides that a statutory hybrid plan is treated as failing to meet the requirements of § 411(b)(1)(H) if the terms of the plan provide for an interest credit (or an equivalent amount) for any plan year at a rate that is greater than a market rate of return. Second, § 411(b)(5)(B)(ii) and (iii) contain minimum benefit rules that apply if, after June 29, 2005, an amendment is adopted that converts a defined benefit plan to a statutory hybrid plan. For purposes of this notice, such an amendment is referred to as a *conversion amendment*. Third, § 411(b)(5)(B)(vi) provides a special rule for projecting variable interest crediting rates in the case of a terminating statutory hybrid plan. In addition, § 411(a)(13)(B) requires a statutory hybrid plan to provide that an employee who has completed at least 3 years of service has a nonforfeitable right to 100 percent of the employee's accrued benefit derived from employer contributions.

Section 411(b)(5)(E) provides that a plan is not treated as failing to meet the requirements of § 411(b)(1)(H) solely because the plan provides for indexing of accrued benefits under the plan. Under § 411(b)(5)(E)(iii), indexing means, in connection with an accrued benefit, the periodic adjustment of the accrued benefit by means of the application of a recognized investment index or methodology.

Section 701(a) of PPA '06 added provisions to the Employee Retirement Income Security Act of 1974, Public Law 93–406 (ERISA) that are parallel to the above described sections of the Code that were added by section 701(b) of PPA '06. The guidance provided in this notice with respect to the Code also applies for purposes of the parallel amendments to ERISA made by PPA '06.[1]

Section 701(c) of PPA '06 added provisions to the Age Discrimination in Employment Act of 1967, Public Law 90–202 (ADEA), that are parallel to § 411(b)(5) of the Code. Executive Order 12067 requires all Federal departments and agencies to advise and offer to consult with the Equal Employment Opportunity Commission (EEOC) during the development of any proposed rules, regulations, policies, procedures or orders concerning equal employment opportunity. Treasury and the Service have consulted with the EEOC prior to the issuance of this notice.

The amendments made by section 701 of PPA '06 are generally effective for periods beginning on or after June 29, 2005. There are a number of special effective date rules, some of which are described in this notice. Section 701(d) of PPA '06 provides that nothing in the amendments made by section 701 should be construed to create an inference concerning the treatment of statutory hybrid plans or conversions of plans into such plans under § 411(b)(1)(H), or concerning the determination of whether a statutory hybrid plan fails to meet the requirements of § 411(a)(2), 411(c), or 417(e) as in effect before such amendments solely because the present value of the accrued benefit (or any portion thereof) of any participant is equal to the amount expressed as the balance in a hypothetical account or as an accumulated percentage of the participant's final average compensation.

Section 702 of PPA '06 requires the Secretary to prescribe regulations for the application of the provisions of section 701 of PPA '06 in cases where the conversion of a plan to a statutory hybrid plan is made with respect to a group of employees who become employees by reason of a merger, acquisition, or similar transaction.

Proposed regulations (EE–184–86, 1988–1 C.B. 881) under §§ 411(b)(1)(H) and 411(b)(2) were published by Treasury and the Service in the Federal Register on April 11, 1988 (53 F.R. 11876), as part of a package of regulations that also included proposed regulations under §§ 410(a), 411(a)(2), 411(a)(8), and 411(c) (relating to the maximum age for participation, vesting, normal retirement age, and actuarial adjustments after normal retirement age, respectively).[2]

Notice 96–8, 1996–1 C.B. 359, described the application of §§ 411 and 417(e), prior to the enactment of PPA '06, to a single-sum distribution under a cash balance plan where interest credits under the plan are frontloaded (*i.e.*, where future interest credits to an employee's hypothetical account balance are not conditioned upon future service and thus accrue at the same time that the benefits attributable to a hypothetical allocation to the account accrue). Under the analysis set forth in Notice 96–8, in order to comply with §§ 411(a) and 417(e) in calculating the amount of a single-sum distribution under a cash balance plan, the balance of an employee's hypothetical account must be projected to normal retirement age and converted to an annuity under the terms of the plan, and then the employee must be paid at least the present value of the projected annuity, determined in accordance with § 417(e). Under that analysis, where a cash balance plan provides frontloaded interest credits using an interest rate that is higher than the § 417(e) applicable interest rate, payment of a single-sum distribution equal to the current hypothetical account balance as a complete distribution of the employee's accrued benefit may result in a violation of § 417(e) or a forfeiture in violation of § 411(a). In addition, Notice 96–8 proposed a safe harbor that provided that, if frontloaded interest credits are provided under a plan at a rate no greater than the sum of identified standard indices and associated margins, no violation of § 411(a) or 417(e) would result if the employee's entire accrued benefit is distributed in the form of a single-sum distribution equal to the employee's hypothetical account balance, provided the plan uses appropriate annuity conversion factors.

On September 15, 1999, the Service's Director, Employee Plans, issued a field directive requiring that open determination letter applications and examination cases that involved the conversion of a defined benefit plan formula into a benefit formula commonly known as a cash balance formula be submitted for technical advice with respect to the conversion's effect on the qualified status of the plan (referred to in this notice as the *1999 Field Directive*). The 1999 Field Directive identified as a cash balance formula a benefit formula in a defined benefit plan by whatever name (*e.g.*, personal account plan, pension equity plan, life cycle plan, cash account plan, etc.) that, rather than expressing the accrued benefit as a life annuity commencing at normal retirement age, defines benefits for each employee by reference to a single-sum distribution amount. In Announcement 2003–1, 2003–1 C.B. 281, the Service announced that the cases that were the subject of the 1999 Field Directive would not be processed pending issuance of regulations addressing age discrimination.

III. TRANSITIONAL GUIDANCE

This part III provides transitional guidance with respect to rules in §§ 411(a)(13) and 411(b)(5) that relate to statutory hybrid plans and the conversion of a defined benefit plan into a statutory hybrid plan.

[1] Under section 101 of Reorganization Plan No. 4 of 1978 (43 F.R. 47713), the Secretary has interpretive jurisdiction over the subject matter addressed by this notice for purposes of ERISA.

[2] On December 11, 2002, Treasury and the Service issued proposed regulations (REG–209500–86; REG–164464–02, 2003–1 C.B. 262) regarding the age discrimination requirements of § 411(b)(1)(H) that specifically addressed cash balance plans as part of a package of regulations that also addressed § 401(a)(4) nondiscrimination cross-testing rules applicable to cash balance plans (67 F.R. 76123). The 2002 proposal was intended to replace the 1988 proposal. In Announcement 2003–22, 2003–1 C.B. 847, Treasury and the Service announced the withdrawal of the 2002 proposed regulations under § 401(a)(4), and in Announcement 2004–57, 2004–2 C.B. 15, Treasury and the Service announced the withdrawal of the 2002 proposed regulations relating to age discrimination.

The transitional guidance provided in this part III applies pending the issuance of further guidance.

A. *Section 411(a)(13)(C): Definition of statutory hybrid plan.*

1. *In general.* A statutory hybrid plan described in § 411(a)(13)(C)(i) and (ii) is a plan that is either a lump sum based plan or a plan that has a similar effect to a lump sum based plan. For purposes of this notice, the term *lump sum based plan* means a defined benefit plan under the terms of which the accumulated benefit of a participant is expressed as the balance of a hypothetical account maintained for the participant or as the current value of the accumulated percentage of the participant's final average compensation, and includes a plan under which the accrued benefit under the terms of the plan is calculated as the actuarial equivalent of such a hypothetical account balance or accumulated percentage. Whether a plan is a lump sum based plan is determined based on how the accumulated benefit of a participant is expressed under the terms of the plan, and does not depend on whether the plan provides for an optional form of benefit in the form of a lump sum payment.

2. *Similar effect to a lump sum based plan.*

(i) *Treated as having a similar effect.* Except as provided below in part IIIA(2)(ii) of this notice, a plan that is not a lump sum based plan is treated as having a similar effect to a lump sum based plan if the plan provides that a participant's accrued benefit (payable at normal retirement age) is expressed as a benefit that includes automatic periodic increases through normal retirement age that results in the payment of a larger amount at normal retirement age to a similarly situated participant who is younger. This includes a plan that provides for indexing of accrued benefits within the meaning of § 411(b)(5)(E)(iii), such as a plan that expresses the accrued benefit as an indexed annuity.

(ii) *Not treated as having a similar effect.*

(I) *Plan with post-retirement adjustment.* A plan described in § 411(b)(5)(E) that solely provides for post-retirement adjustment of the amounts payable to a participant is not treated as having a similar effect to a lump sum based plan.

(II) *Variable annuity plan.* A variable annuity plan is not treated as having a similar effect to a lump sum based plan if it has an assumed interest rate used for purposes of adjustment of amounts payable to a participant that is at least five percent. For this purpose, a variable annuity plan includes any plan which provides that the amount payable is periodically adjusted by reference to the difference between the rate of return of plan assets (or specified market indices) and the assumed interest rate.

B. *Section 411(a)(13): Special rules for the application of §§ 411(a)(2), 411(c), and 417(e).*

1. *In general.* Section 411(a)(13)(A) provides special rules with respect to §§ 411(a)(2), 411(c), and 417(e) for benefits expressed as the balance of a hypothetical account maintained for a participant or as the current value of the accumulated percentage of a participant's final average compensation under a lump sum based plan. Specifically, with respect to such benefits, a lump sum based plan is not treated as failing to meet the requirements of § 411(a)(2), or the requirements of §§ 411(c) and 417(e) with respect to such benefits derived from employer contributions, solely because the present value of such benefits of any participant is, under the terms of the plan, equal to the amount expressed as the balance in the hypothetical account or as the accumulated percentage of the participant's final average compensation. Section 411(a)(13)(A) does not apply to benefits under a statutory hybrid plan that are expressed neither as the balance of a hypothetical account maintained for a participant nor as the current value of the accumulated percentage of a participant's final average compensation.

2. *Effective date.* Section 411(a)(13)(A) is effective for distributions made after August 17, 2006. The Service expects to issue regulations shortly interpreting the effective date of § 411(a)(13)(A).

3. *Section 411(d)(6) relief.* In the case of a lump sum based plan that provides for a single-sum distribution to a participant that exceeds the participant's hypothetical account balance or accumulated percentage of final average compensation, the plan may be amended to eliminate the excess for distributions made after August 17, 2006, under the rules of section 1107 of PPA '06. Because such an amendment is made pursuant to section 701 of PPA '06, section 1107 of PPA '06 applies to the amendment if the amendment satisfies the requirements specified in section 1107. Thus, if the amendment is adopted on or before the last day of the first plan year beginning on or after January 1, 2009 (January 1, 2011, for a governmental plan), and the plan is operated as if such amendment were in effect as of the first date the amendment is effective, then the amendment does not violate section 411(d)(6) with respect to distributions made after the later of August 17, 2006, or the effective date of the amendment.

4. *Section 4980F.* Pursuant to this notice, in the case of an amendment described in section B(3) of this part III, a notice required under § 4980F (and the parallel provision at section 204(h) of ERISA) must be provided at least 30 days before the date the amendment is first effective. Thus, if an amendment described in section B(3) of this part III that significantly reduces the rate of future benefit accrual for purposes of § 4980F is adopted retroactively (*i.e.*, is adopted after the effective date of the amendment) as an amendment under the rules of section 1107 of PPA '06, then the notice required under § 4980F must be provided at least 30 days before the earliest date on which the plan is operated in accordance with the amendment.

5. *Vesting.* See § 411(a)(13)(B) for a special 3-year vesting schedule for statutory hybrid plans.

C. *Section 411(b)(5)(A)(iv): Scope of rule.* In applying the age discrimination test set forth in § 411(b)(5)(A)(i), a lump sum based plan may under § 411(b)(5)(A)(iv) determine the accumulated benefit of a participant as the balance of a hypothetical account or the current value of the accumulated percentage of the employee's final average compensation even if the plan defines the participant's accrued benefit as an annuity at normal retirement age that is actuarially equivalent to such balance or value.

D. *Section 411(b)(5)(B)(i): Market rate of return.*

1. *Future guidance on market rate of return.* During 2007, Treasury and the Service expect to issue guidance that addresses the market rate of return rules at § 411(b)(5)(B)(i), including the special rule regarding preservation of capital under § 411(b)(5)(B)(i)(II) and the minimum

rate of return rules in the second sentence of § 411(b)(5)(B)(i)(I). The guidance is also expected to address the extent to which § 411(d)(6) relief provided under section 1107 of PPA '06 applies to an amendment to a statutory hybrid plan that changes the plan's interest crediting rate where such amendment is adopted after August 17, 2006.

2. *Safe harbor.* Pending further guidance, a market rate of return for purposes of § 411(b)(5)(B)(i) includes the rate of interest on long-term investment grade corporate bonds (as described in § 412(b)(5)(B)(ii)(II) prior to amendment by PPA '06 for plan years beginning prior to January 1, 2008, and the third segment rate described in § 430(h)(2)(C)(iii) for subsequent plan years) or the rate of interest on 30-year Treasury securities (as described in § 417(e)(3) prior to amendment by PPA '06). In addition, a market rate of return for purposes of § 411(b)(5)(B)(i) includes the sum of any of the standard indices and the associated margin for that index as described in part IV of Notice 96–8.

3. *Certain plan termination requirements.* See § 411(b)(5)(B)(vi) for required plan terms related to termination of a statutory hybrid plan.

E. *Section 411(b)(5)(B)(ii) — (iv): Special rules for conversion amendments.*

1. *In general.* Section 411(b)(5)(B)(ii) provides that if a conversion amendment is adopted with respect to a plan after June 29, 2005, the plan is treated as failing to meet the requirements of § 411(b)(1)(H) unless the requirements of § 411(b)(5)(B)(iii) are met with respect to each individual who was a participant in the plan immediately before the adoption of the conversion amendment.

2. *Requirements of § 411(b)(5)(B)(iii).* Subject to § 411(b)(5)(B)(iv), § 411(b)(5)(B)(iii) is satisfied with respect to any participant if the accrued benefit of the participant under the terms of the plan as in effect after the conversion amendment is not less than the sum of—

(i) the participant's accrued benefit for years of service before the effective date of the conversion amendment, determined under the terms of the plan as in effect before the amendment, and

(ii) the participant's accrued benefit for years of service after the effective date of the amendment, determined under the terms of the plan as in effect after the amendment.

3. *Requirements of § 411(b)(5)(B)(iv).* Under § 411(b)(5)(B)(iv), a plan must credit the accumulation account or similar account for purposes of the accrued benefit described in part IIIE(2)(ii) of this notice with the amount of any early retirement benefit or retirement-type subsidy for the plan year in which the participant retires if, as of such time, the participant has met the age, years of service, and other requirements under the plan for entitlement to such benefit or subsidy. For this purpose, the date on which a participant retires means the annuity starting date for the participant's benefit.

4. *Effective date.* Section 411(b)(5)(B)(ii) applies to a conversion amendment that is adopted after, and takes effect after, June 29, 2005. See section 701(e)(5) of PPA '06 for a special election with respect to § 411(b)(5)(B)(ii).

F. *Safe harbor for conversions related to mergers and acquisitions.*

1. *Future guidance on conversions related to mergers and acquisitions.* In accordance with section 702 of PPA '06, the Service expects to issue regulations not later than August 17, 2007, regarding an amendment to convert a defined benefit plan into a hybrid defined benefit plan with respect to a group of employees who become employees by reason of a merger, acquisition, or similar transaction.

2. *Safe harbor.* Pending further guidance, a plan amendment described in part IIIE that is also described in part IIIF(1) of this notice is not treated as failing to meet the requirements of § 411(b)(1)(H) if the benefit of each participant under the plan as amended is not less than the sum of:

(A) the participant's section 411(d)(6) protected benefit (as defined in § 1.411(d)–3(g)(14)) with respect to service before the effective date of the conversion amendment, determined under the terms of the plan as in effect before the amendment, and

(B) the participant's section 411(d)(6) protected benefit with respect to service on and after the effective date of the conversion amendment, determined under the terms of the plan as in effect after the amendment.

For purposes of this paragraph F(2), the benefits under clause (A) and the benefits under clause (B) of this paragraph F(2) must each be determined in the same manner as if they were provided under separate plans that are independent of each other (*e.g.*, without any benefit offsets).

IV. DETERMINATION LETTERS

In light of the enactment of section 701 of PPA '06, the Service is no longer applying the 1999 Field Directive and Announcement 2003–1 and is beginning to process the determination letters and examination cases that were the subject of such field directive and announcement (referred to as *moratorium plans* in this notice). This part IV describes certain rules that will be applied for purposes of processing moratorium plans. Qualification requirements that are not described in this part IV (*e.g.*, the backloading rules of § 411(b)(1)(A), (B), and (C)) continue to apply.

A. *Age discrimination.*

1. *In general.* Except as provided in part IVA(2) of this notice, a moratorium plan will be reviewed as to whether accruals under the plan that relate to service performed by the participant after the conversion violate § 411(b)(1)(H). For this purpose, a moratorium plan will not be treated as failing to satisfy the requirements of § 411(b)(1)(H) merely because a moratorium plan that is frontloaded provides that interest credits through normal retirement age are accrued in the year of the related hypothetical allocation.

2. *Pre-6/30/05 conversions.* For purposes of processing a determination letter application for a moratorium plan, the plan will not be reviewed as to whether the conversion of the plan satisfies the requirements of § 411(b)(1)(H) if the amendment that results in the conversion was adopted prior to June 30, 2005. Therefore, determination letters issued to moratorium plans will not consider, and may not be relied on with respect to, whether such a conversion satisfies the requirements of § 411(b)(1)(H), as in effect prior to the addition of § 411(b)(5) by PPA '06, including the effect of any wearaway.

3. *Post-6/29/05 conversions.* In the case of a moratorium plan that involves a conversion of the plan to a statutory hybrid plan pursuant to an amendment that is adopted after June 29, 2005, the conversion must satisfy the requirements of

§ 411(b)(5)(B)(ii) (described in part IIIE of this notice).

B. *Distributions before August 18, 2006.* The Service expects to issue regulations interpreting the effective date of § 411(a)(13)(A) (described in part IIIB(2) of this notice). Until this guidance is issued, the Service will not process a moratorium plan that does not satisfy the requirements of Notice 96–8 with respect to distributions made before August 18, 2006.

C. *Terminating plans.* Under Title IV of ERISA, a standard termination may only occur if, when the final distribution of assets occurs, the plan is sufficient for benefit liabilities determined as of the termination date. *See* § 4041(b)(1)(D) of ERISA; 29 C.F.R. § 4041.8(a). The Pension Benefit Guaranty Corporation (PBGC) has informed the Service that, for purposes of Title IV of ERISA, a terminating plan with a termination date that is prior to August 18, 2006, cannot apply § 411(a)(13)(A) in determining its benefit liabilities with respect to any distributions made by the terminating plan.

V. COMMENTS REQUESTED AND FUTURE REGULATIONS

Treasury and the Service expect to issue regulations with respect to the transitional guidance provided in this notice and the issues described in part IIIB(2) of this notice. These initial regulations may address some additional issues, but will not address all of the outstanding issues relating to §§ 411(a)(13) and 411(b)(5).

Comments are requested on the following additional issues. These comments will be considered in conjunction with the comments received in response to the initial regulations in developing additional guidance.

- Identification of when two or more amendments, or the coordination of two or more defined benefit plans, have the effect of a conversion into a statutory hybrid plan.
- The definition of market rate of return for purposes of § 411(b)(5)(B)(i), including the following related issues:
  - The impact of the minimum rate of return rules in the second sentence of § 411(b)(5)(B)(i)(I) on the definition of market rate of return.
  - The impact of the preservation of capital rule in § 411(b)(5)(B)(i)(II) on the definition of market rate of return.
  - The application of § 411(d)(6) to an amendment to the interest crediting rate specified in a statutory hybrid plan, and the circumstances under which the § 411(d)(6) relief provided under section 1107 of PPA '06 should apply to such an amendment.
- Application of the special rules for hybrid plans in the case of a plan in which only certain participants' accrued benefits, or only a portion of a participant's accrued benefit, is determined by reference to a hypothetical account balance or an accumulated percentage of final average compensation, including plans in which the benefit payable under one plan is offset by the benefit provided under another plan.
- The application of qualification requirements other than §§ 411(b)(1)(H) and 417(e) to a defined benefit plan under which the accrued benefit is calculated as an accumulated percentage of the participant's final average compensation (commonly referred to as a pension equity plan or PEP), including the treatment of interest credited with respect to terminated vested participants.
- The definition of a recognized index or methodology for purposes of § 411(b)(5)(E) and whether there are any types of indexed plans that should not be treated as statutory hybrid plans other than those described in part IIIA(2)(i) above.

Written comments should be submitted by April 16, 2007. Send submissions to CC:PA:LPD:DRU (Notice 2007–6), Room 5203, Internal Revenue Service, POB 7604 Ben Franklin Station, Washington, D.C. 20044. Comments may be hand delivered to CC:PA:LPD:DRU (Notice 2007–6), Room 5203, Internal Revenue Service, 1111 Constitution Avenue, NW, Washington, DC. Alternatively, comments may be submitted via the Internet at *notice.comments@irscounsel.treas.gov* (Notice 2007–6). All comments will be available for public inspection.

VI. DRAFTING INFORMATION

The principal authors of this notice are Kathleen J. Herrmann of the Employee Plans, Tax Exempt and Government Entities Division and Christopher A. Crouch, Lauson C. Green, and Linda S. F. Marshall of the Office of the Division Counsel/Associate Chief Counsel (Tax Exempt and Government Entities). For further information regarding this notice, contact Ms. Herrmann at (202) 283–9888 and Mr. Crouch, Mr. Green, and Ms. Marshall at (202) 622–6090 (not toll-free numbers).

In-Service Benefits Permitted to be Provided at Age 62 by a Pension Plan

Notice 2007–8

I. PURPOSE

The Treasury Department and the Internal Revenue Service are considering proposing guidance under § 401(a)(36) of the Internal Revenue Code, as added by section 905 of the Pension Protection Act of 2006, Public Law 109–280, 120 Stat. 780 (PPA '06). This notice requests comments on issues presented by § 401(a)(36) of the Code with respect to defined benefit plans.

II. BACKGROUND

In-service distributions from a pension plan

Section 401(a) provides rules for qualified pension plans, profit-sharing plans, and stock bonus plans. Section 1.401–1(a)(2) of the Income Tax Regulations provides that a qualified pension plan (*i.e.*, a qualified defined benefit plan or money purchase pension plan) is a definite written program and arrangement that is communicated to employees and that is established and maintained by an employer to provide for the livelihood of the employees or their beneficiaries after the retirement of such employees through the payment of benefits. Under § 1.401–1(b)(1)(i), a qualified pension plan must be established and maintained by an employer primarily to provide systematically for the payment of definitely determinable benefits for employees over a period of years, usually for life, after retirement. Following the enactment of the Employee Retirement Income Security Act of 1974 (ERISA), Public Law 93–406 (88 Stat. 829), the regulations under § 401(a) were modified to provide that § 1.401–1(b)(1)(i) continues to apply, except as otherwise provided. *See* § 1.401(a)–1(b)(1)(i). Accordingly, a qualified pension plan is generally not permitted to pay benefits before retirement. *See also* Rev. Rul. 56–693, 1956–2 C.B. 282, as modified by Rev. Rul. 60–323, 1960–2 C.B. 148.

A notice of proposed rulemaking (REG–114726–04, 2004–2 C.B. 857) under § 401(a) was published in the **Federal Register** (69 FR 65108) (the proposed regulations) on November 10, 2004. The proposed regulations would permit a qualified pension plan to make in-service distributions to a participant before normal retirement age under a *bona fide* phased retirement program. In addition, the proposed regulations would modify § 1.401(a)–1(b)(1) by permitting a qualified pension plan to make in-service distributions to a participant upon the participant's attainment of normal retirement age and by clarifying that a plan's normal retirement age cannot be set so low as to be a subterfuge for avoiding the requirements of § 401(a). On March 14, 2005, the IRS held a public hearing on the proposed regulations. Written comments responding to the proposed rulemaking were also received.

Section 401(a)(36), as added by section 905(b) of PPA '06, provides that, for plan years beginning after December 31, 2006, a pension plan does not fail to qualify under § 401(a) solely because the plan provides that a distribution may be made to an employee who has attained age 62 and who has not separated from employment at the time of the distribution.

Application of § 411(a) and (b) to defined benefit plans

Section 401(a)(7) provides that a plan must satisfy the requirements of § 411.[1] Section 411(a) provides that a qualified plan must provide that an employee's right to his or her normal retirement benefit is nonforfeitable upon the attainment of normal retirement age, and also provides vesting requirements with respect to an employee's accrued benefit. For purposes of a defined benefit plan, § 411(a)(7) generally defines the term "accrued benefit" as an employee's accrued benefit determined under the plan and expressed in the form of an annual benefit commencing at normal retirement age. Under § 411(a)(9), the term "normal retirement benefit" is defined as the greater of the early retirement benefit under the plan or the benefit under the plan commencing at normal retirement age.

Under § 411(a), a defined benefit plan must satisfy one of the three anti-backloading rules described §§ 411(b)(1)(A), 411(b)(1)(B), and 411(b)(1)(C). These anti-backloading rules govern the minimum rate at which a participant's accrued benefit accrues. These rules are designed to ensure that the minimum vesting rules of § 411(a) are not circumvented through a plan formula under which accruals are inappropriately deferred. In addition, under § 411(b)(1)(G), a defined benefit plan is not permitted to reduce a participant's accrued benefit on account of any increase in the participant's age or service, and under § 411(b)(1)(H), a defined benefit plan is not permitted to cease a participant's benefit accrual, or reduce the rate of an employee's benefit accrual, because of the attainment of any age.

Section 411(d)(6) protections

Most of the § 411 requirements outlined above protect a participant's accrued benefit. Section 411(d)(6)(A) generally provides that a plan is treated as not satisfying the requirements of § 411 if the accrued benefit of a participant is decreased by a plan amendment. In addition, § 411(d)(6)(B) provides that a plan amendment that has the effect of eliminating or reducing an early retirement benefit or a retirement-type subsidy, or eliminating an optional form of benefit, with respect to benefits attributable to service before the amendment is treated as impermissibly reducing accrued benefits.

Sections 1.411(d)–3 and 1.411(d)–4 provide rules relating to § 411(d)(6) protected benefits. Section 1.411(d)–3(g) distinguishes among the types of benefits protected under § 411(d)(6). A § 411(d)(6) protected early retirement benefit is defined as the right to commence distribution of a retirement-type benefit at a particular date after severance from employment with the employer and before normal retirement age. Generally, under these regulations, a § 411(d)(6) protected retirement-type subsidy, such as a subsidized early retirement benefit and a subsidized qualified joint and survivor annuity, is the excess of the actuarial present value of a retirement-type benefit over the actuarial present value of the accrued benefit commencing at normal retirement age or at the actual commencement date. A plan provision that permits a participant to receive an in-service distribution is an optional form of benefit that is protected under § 411(d)(6), but is not an early retirement benefit. *See* §§ 1.411(d)–3(g)(6) and 1.411(d)–4, Q&A–1(a)(3), Q&A–1(b)(1), and Q&A–2(a)(1).

III. COMMENTS REQUESTED

The Treasury Department and the Internal Revenue Service are considering issuing guidance with respect to § 401(a)(36). Comments are requested on the guidance that should be issued. In particular, comments on the following specific issues related to § 401(a)(36) and defined benefit plans are requested:

- Should in-service distribution of a benefit to a participant who has attained age 62 but who has not attained normal retirement age be limited to no greater than the benefit to which the participant would be entitled at normal retirement age, reduced in accordance with reasonable actuarial assumptions (*e.g.*, should only unsubsidized benefits be permitted pursuant to § 401(a)(36))?

[1] Under § 411(e), certain plans are treated as meeting the requirements of § 411 if such plans meet the vesting requirements resulting from the application of §§ 401(a)(4) and 401(a)(7) as in effect on September 1, 1974.

- If subsidized benefits are permitted to be distributed to a participant who has attained age 62 but is still in-service and has not yet attained normal retirement age, how should the subsidized benefits be characterized for purposes of § 411?
  - For example, should the subsidized benefits be treated as a subsidized early retirement benefit despite the fact that the participant has not yet separated from employment?
  - If the subsidized benefits are not treated as a subsidized early retirement benefit, should the subsidized benefits be treated as a part of the participant's accrued benefit, or is there some other characterization of the subsidized benefits for purposes of § 411?
  - Whether final regulations permitting in-service distributions under a *bona fide* phased retirement program should be issued, in light of the ability of plans to permit in-service distributions after age 62 pursuant to § 401(a)(36)?

Written comments should be submitted by April 16, 2007. Send submissions to CC:PA:LPD:DRU (Notice 2007–8), Room 5203, Internal Revenue Service, POB 7604, Ben Franklin Station, Washington, D.C. 20044. Comments may be hand delivered between the hours of 8 a.m. and 5 p.m., Monday through Friday, to Courier's Desk, Internal Revenue Service, Attn: CC:PA:LPD:DRU (Notice 2007–8), 1111 Constitution Avenue, NW, Washington, D.C. Alternatively, comments may be submitted via the Internet at *notice.comments@irscounsel.treas.gov* (Notice 2007–8). All comments will be available for public inspection.

DRAFTING INFORMATION

The principal drafter of this notice is Kathleen Herrmann of the Employee Plans, Tax Exempt and Government Entities Division. For further information regarding this notice, please contact the Employee Plans' taxpayer assistance telephone service at 1–877–829–5500 (a toll-free number) between the hours of 8:30 a.m. and 4:30 p.m. Eastern Time, Monday through Friday. Ms. Herrmann may be reached at (202) 283–9888 (not a toll-free number).

---

26 CFR 601.201: Rulings and determination letters. (Also Part I, Sections 846; 1.846–1.)

Rev. Proc. 2007–9

SECTION 1. PURPOSE

This revenue procedure prescribes the loss payment patterns and discount factors for the 2006 accident year. These factors will be used for computing discounted unpaid losses under § 846 of the Internal Revenue Code. *See* Rev. Proc. 2003–17, 2003–1 C.B. 427, for background concerning the loss payment patterns and application of the discount factors.

SEC. 2. SCOPE

This revenue procedure applies to any taxpayer that is required to discount its unpaid losses under § 846 for a line of business using discount factors published by the Secretary.

SEC. 3. TABLES OF DISCOUNT FACTORS

.01 The following tables present separately for each line of business the discount factors under § 846 for accident year 2006. All the discount factors presented in this section were determined using the applicable interest rate under § 846(c) for 2006, which is 3.98 percent, and by assuming all loss payments occur in the middle of the calendar year.

.02 If the groupings of individual lines of business on the annual statement change, taxpayers must discount the unpaid losses on the affected lines of business in accordance with the discounting patterns that would have applied to those unpaid losses based on their classification on the 2000 annual statement. *See* Rev. Proc. 2003–17, 2003–1 C.B. 427, section 2, for additional background on discounting under section 846 and the use of the Secretary's tables.

.03 Section V of Notice 88–100, 1988–2 C.B. 439, sets forth a composite method for computing discounted unpaid losses for accident years that are not separately reported on the annual statement. The tables separately provide discount factors for taxpayers who elect to use the composite method of section V of Notice 88–100. *See* Rev. Proc. 2002–74, 2002–2 C.B. 980.

.04 Section 2.03(4) of Rev. Proc 2003–17 requested comments as to whether a methodology should be adopted to smooth the raw payment data and thus produce a more stable pattern of discount factors. This issue will be addressed in the new determination year, which is 2007. Accordingly, taxpayers may still submit comments that should include a reference to **Rev. Proc. 2007–9** on this issue to the following address:

CC:PA:LPD:PR (**Rev. Proc. 2007–9**), room 5203, Internal Revenue Service, POB 7604, Ben Franklin Station, Washington, DC 20044. Comments may be hand delivered between the hours of 8 a.m. and 4 p.m. to CC:PA:LPD (**Rev. Proc. 2007–9**), Courier's Desk, Internal Revenue Service, 1111 Constitution Avenue, NW, Washington, DC 20224. Alternatively, e-mail comments to *Notice.Comments@irscounsel.treas.gov*. All comments will be available for public inspection and copying.

.05 Tables.

Tables of Factors to be Used to Discount Unpaid Losses Incurred in Accident Year 2006

(Interest rate: 3.98 percent)

Accident and Health (Other Than Disability Income or Credit Disability Insurance)

Taxpayers that do not use the composite method of Notice 88–100 should use 98.0675 percent to discount unpaid losses incurred in this line of business in the 2006 accident year and that are outstanding at the end of the 2006 and later taxable years.

Taxpayers that use the composite method of Notice 88–100 should use 98.0675 percent to discount all unpaid losses in this line of business that are outstanding at the end of the 2006 taxable year.

Auto Physical Damage

Tax Year	Estimated Cumulative Losses Paid (%)	Estimated Losses Paid Each Year (%)	Unpaid Losses at Year End (%)	Discounted Unpaid Losses at Year End (%)	Discount Factors (%)
2006	89.6468	89.6468	10.3532	10.1356	97.8981
2007	99.6845	10.0377	0.3155	0.3035	96.1907

Taxpayers that do not use the composite method of Notice 88–100 should use the following factor to discount unpaid losses incurred in this line of business in the 2006 accident year and that are outstanding at the end of the tax year shown.

2008 and later years		0.1578	0.1578	0.1547	98.0675

Taxpayers that use the composite method of Notice 88–100 should use 98.0675 percent to discount unpaid losses incurred in this line of business in 2006 and prior years and that are outstanding at the end of the 2008 taxable year.

Commercial Auto/Truck Liability/Medical

Tax Year	Estimated Cumulative Losses Paid (%)	Estimated Losses Paid Each Year (%)	Unpaid Losses at Year End (%)	Discounted Unpaid Losses at Year End (%)	Discount Factors (%)
2006	28.8244	28.8244	71.1756	65.9439	92.6497
2007	54.9871	26.1626	45.0129	41.8903	93.0628
2008	72.8039	17.8168	27.1961	25.3896	93.3575
2009	85.0572	12.2533	14.9428	13.9054	93.0572
2010	91.6276	6.5704	8.3724	7.7589	92.6725
2011	94.9514	3.3239	5.0486	4.6784	92.6676
2012	97.0453	2.0938	2.9547	2.7295	92.3768
2013	98.1574	1.1121	1.8426	1.7041	92.4822
2014	98.7370	0.5796	1.2630	1.1809	93.4978
2015	99.1070	0.3700	0.8930	0.8506	95.2504

Commercial Auto/Truck Liability/Medical

Taxpayers that do not use the composite method of Notice 88–100 should use the following factors to discount unpaid losses incurred in this line of business in the 2006 accident year and that are outstanding at the end of the tax year shown.

2016	0.3700	0.5230	0.5072	96.9692
2017 and later years	0.3700	0.1530	0.1501	98.0675

Taxpayers that use the composite method of Notice 88–100 should use 97.1689 percent to discount unpaid losses incurred in this line of business in 2006 and prior years and that are outstanding at the end of the 2016 taxable year.

Composite

Tax Year	Estimated Cumulative Losses Paid (%)	Estimated Losses Paid Each Year (%)	Unpaid Losses at Year End (%)	Discounted Unpaid Losses at Year End (%)	Discount Factors (%)
2006	40.9985	40.9985	59.0015	53.7593	91.1153
2007	65.8439	24.8454	34.1561	30.5639	89.4832
2008	77.5023	11.6583	22.4977	19.8923	88.4193
2009	84.6221	7.1198	15.3779	13.4239	87.2935
2010	90.2455	5.6234	9.7545	8.2239	84.3094
2011	92.2780	2.0325	7.7220	6.4788	83.8997
2012	94.3974	2.1195	5.6026	4.5754	81.6658
2013	95.2526	0.8552	4.7474	3.8854	81.8439
2014	96.2792	1.0266	3.7208	2.9933	80.4470
2015	96.4323	0.1531	3.5677	2.9562	82.8624

Taxpayers that do not use the composite method of Notice 88–100 should use the following factors to discount unpaid losses incurred in this line of business in the 2006 accident year and that are outstanding at the end of the tax year shown.

2016	0.1531	3.4145	2.9177	85.4512
2017	0.1531	3.2614	2.8777	88.2363
2018	0.1531	3.1083	2.8361	91.2444
2019	0.1531	2.9551	2.7928	94.5083
2020 and later years	0.1531	2.8020	2.7478	98.0675

Taxpayers that use the composite method of Notice 88–100 should use 88.1508 percent to discount unpaid losses incurred in this line of business in 2006 and prior years and that are outstanding at the end of the 2016 taxable year.

Fidelity/Surety

Tax Year	Estimated Cumulative Losses Paid (%)	Estimated Losses Paid Each Year (%)	Unpaid Losses at Year End (%)	Discounted Unpaid Losses at Year End (%)	Discount Factors (%)
2006	38.3328	38.3328	61.6672	58.1879	94.3581
2007	58.8485	20.5156	41.1515	39.5839	96.1907

Taxpayers that do not use the composite method of Notice 88–100 should use the following factor to discount unpaid losses incurred in this line of business in the 2006 accident year and that are outstanding at the end of the tax year shown.

2008 and later years	20.5758	20.5758	20.1781	98.0675

Taxpayers that use the composite method of Notice 88–100 should use 98.0675 percent to discount unpaid losses incurred in this line of business in 2006 and prior years and that are outstanding at the end of the 2008 taxable year.

Financial Guaranty/Mortgage Guaranty

Tax Year	Estimated Cumulative Losses Paid (%)	Estimated Losses Paid Each Year (%)	Unpaid Losses at Year End (%)	Discounted Unpaid Losses at Year End (%)	Discount Factors (%)
2006	4.0723	4.0723	95.9277	90.7812	94.6350
2007	40.7639	36.6916	59.2361	56.9796	96.1907

Taxpayers that do not use the composite method of Notice 88–100 should use the following factor to discount unpaid losses incurred in this line of business in the 2006 accident year and that are outstanding at the end of the tax year shown.

Tax Year	Estimated Cumulative Losses Paid (%)	Estimated Losses Paid Each Year (%)	Unpaid Losses at Year End (%)	Discounted Unpaid Losses at Year End (%)	Discount Factors (%)
2008 and later years		29.6180	29.6180	29.0457	98.0675

Taxpayers that use the composite method of Notice 88–100 should use 98.0675 percent to discount unpaid losses incurred in this line of business in 2006 and prior years and that are outstanding at the end of the 2008 taxable year.

International (Composite)

Tax Year	Estimated Cumulative Losses Paid (%)	Estimated Losses Paid Each Year (%)	Unpaid Losses at Year End (%)	Discounted Unpaid Losses at Year End (%)	Discount Factors (%)
2006	40.9985	40.9985	59.0015	53.7593	91.1153
2007	65.8439	24.8454	34.1561	30.5639	89.4832
2008	77.5023	11.6583	22.4977	19.8923	88.4193
2009	84.6221	7.1198	15.3779	13.4239	87.2935
2010	90.2455	5.6234	9.7545	8.2239	84.3094
2011	92.2780	2.0325	7.7220	6.4788	83.8997
2012	94.3974	2.1195	5.6026	4.5754	81.6658
2013	95.2526	0.8552	4.7474	3.8854	81.8439
2014	96.2792	1.0266	3.7208	2.9933	80.4470
2015	96.4323	0.1531	3.5677	2.9562	82.8624

Taxpayers that do not use the composite method of Notice 88–100 should use the following factors to discount unpaid losses incurred in this line of business in the 2006 accident year and that are outstanding at the end of the tax year shown.

Tax Year	Estimated Cumulative Losses Paid (%)	Estimated Losses Paid Each Year (%)	Unpaid Losses at Year End (%)	Discounted Unpaid Losses at Year End (%)	Discount Factors (%)
2016		0.1531	3.4145	2.9177	85.4512
2017		0.1531	3.2614	2.8777	88.2363
2018		0.1531	3.1083	2.8361	91.2444
2019		0.1531	2.9551	2.7928	94.5083
2020 and later years		0.1531	2.8020	2.7478	98.0675

Taxpayers that use the composite method of Notice 88–100 should use 88.1508 percent to discount unpaid losses incurred in this line of business in 2006 and prior years and that are outstanding at the end of the 2016 taxable year.

Medical Malpractice — Claims-Made

Tax Year	Estimated Cumulative Losses Paid (%)	Estimated Losses Paid Each Year (%)	Unpaid Losses at Year End (%)	Discounted Unpaid Losses at Year End (%)	Discount Factors (%)
2006	7.3447	7.3447	92.6553	83.4596	90.0754
2007	29.0191	21.6744	70.9809	64.6798	91.1228
2008	53.3108	24.2917	46.6892	42.4836	90.9925
2009	69.1517	15.8409	30.8483	28.0215	90.8363
2010	82.0981	12.9464	17.9019	15.9352	89.0139
2011	86.3995	4.3014	13.6005	12.1832	89.5793
2012	89.7111	3.3116	10.2889	9.2913	90.3038
2013	92.4688	2.7577	7.5312	6.8490	90.9420
2014	94.5163	2.0475	5.4837	5.0337	91.7950
2015	95.7635	1.2471	4.2365	3.9624	93.5285

Taxpayers that do not use the composite method of Notice 88–100 should use the following factors to discount unpaid losses incurred in this line of business in the 2006 accident year and that are outstanding at the end of the tax year shown.

Tax Year	Estimated Cumulative Losses Paid (%)	Estimated Losses Paid Each Year (%)	Unpaid Losses at Year End (%)	Discounted Unpaid Losses at Year End (%)	Discount Factors (%)
2016		1.2471	2.9894	2.8483	95.2819
2017		1.2471	1.7422	1.6900	97.0008
2018 and later years		1.2471	0.4951	0.4855	98.0675

Taxpayers that use the composite method of Notice 88–100 should use 95.9709 percent to discount unpaid losses incurred in this line of business in 2006 and prior years and that are outstanding at the end of the 2016 taxable year.

Medical Malpractice — Occurrence

Tax Year	Estimated Cumulative Losses Paid (%)	Estimated Losses Paid Each Year (%)	Unpaid Losses at Year End (%)	Discounted Unpaid Losses at Year End (%)	Discount Factors (%)
2006	0.8316	0.8316	99.1684	84.5630	85.2721
2007	7.4573	6.6257	92.5427	81.1723	87.7134
2008	23.5575	16.1002	76.4425	67.9856	88.9369
2009	41.0062	17.4487	58.9938	52.8989	89.6685
2010	55.5832	14.5770	44.4168	40.1400	90.3712
2011	68.9413	13.3581	31.0587	28.1163	90.5261
2012	78.2095	9.2682	21.7905	19.7844	90.7937
2013	82.8727	4.6632	17.1273	15.8167	92.3480
2014	86.3178	3.4451	13.6822	12.9332	94.5260
2015	91.0834	4.7656	8.9166	8.5884	96.3200

Taxpayers that do not use the composite method of Notice 88–100 should use the following factor to discount unpaid losses incurred in this line of business in the 2006 accident year and that are outstanding at the end of the tax year shown.

Tax Year	Estimated Cumulative Losses Paid (%)	Estimated Losses Paid Each Year (%)	Unpaid Losses at Year End (%)	Discounted Unpaid Losses at Year End (%)	Discount Factors (%)
2016 and later years		4.7656	4.1510	4.0708	98.0675

Taxpayers that use the composite method of Notice 88–100 should use 98.0675 percent to discount unpaid losses incurred in this line of business in 2006 and prior years and that are outstanding at the end of the 2016 taxable year.

Miscellaneous Casualty

Tax Year	Estimated Cumulative Losses Paid (%)	Estimated Losses Paid Each Year (%)	Unpaid Losses at Year End (%)	Discounted Unpaid Losses at Year End (%)	Discount Factors (%)
2006	79.7790	79.7790	20.2210	19.5491	96.6770
2007	94.9417	15.1627	5.0583	4.8656	96.1907

Taxpayers that do not use the composite method of Notice 88–100 should use the following factor to discount unpaid losses incurred in this line of business in the 2006 accident year and that are outstanding at the end of the tax year shown.

2008 and later years		2.5292	2.5292	2.4803	98.0675

Taxpayers that use the composite method of Notice 88–100 should use 98.0675 percent to discount unpaid losses incurred in this line of business in 2006 and prior years and that are outstanding at the end of the 2008 taxable year.

Multiple Peril Lines
(Homeowners/Farmowners, Commercial Multiple Peril, and Special Liability (Ocean Marine, Aircraft (All Perils), Boiler and Machinery))

Tax Year	Estimated Cumulative Losses Paid (%)	Estimated Losses Paid Each Year (%)	Unpaid Losses at Year End (%)	Discounted Unpaid Losses at Year End (%)	Discount Factors (%)
2006	59.7445	59.7445	40.2555	37.4341	92.9914
2007	81.0347	21.2902	18.9653	17.2142	90.7672
2008	87.3325	6.2978	12.6675	11.4775	90.6059
2009	91.0659	3.7334	8.9341	8.1273	90.9698
2010	95.1781	4.1122	4.8219	4.2575	88.2964
2011	95.7605	0.5824	4.2395	3.8331	90.4149
2012	97.0539	1.2933	2.9461	2.6668	90.5202
2013	97.6441	0.5903	2.3559	2.1711	92.1567
2014	98.7037	1.0596	1.2963	1.1770	90.8007
2015	98.6217	-0.0821	1.3783	1.3076	94.8644

Taxpayers that do not use the composite method of Notice 88–100 should use the following factors to discount unpaid losses incurred in this line of business in the 2006 accident year and that are outstanding at the end of the tax year shown.

2016		0.5226	0.8558	0.8267	96.6061
2017 and later years		0.5226	0.3332	0.3267	98.0675

Taxpayers that use the composite method of Notice 88–100 should use 96.9550 percent to discount unpaid losses incurred in this line of business in 2006 and prior years and that are outstanding at the end of the 2016 taxable year.

Other (Including Credit)

Tax Year	Estimated Cumulative Losses Paid (%)	Estimated Losses Paid Each Year (%)	Unpaid Losses at Year End (%)	Discounted Unpaid Losses at Year End (%)	Discount Factors (%)
2006	69.1729	69.1729	30.8271	29.7431	96.4837
2007	91.2168	22.0439	8.7832	8.4487	96.1907

Taxpayers that do not use the composite method of Notice 88–100 should use the following factor to discount unpaid losses incurred in this line of business in the 2006 accident year and that are outstanding at the end of the tax year shown.

2008 and later years		4.3916	4.3916	4.3068	98.0675

Taxpayers that use the composite method of Notice 88–100 should use 98.0675 percent to discount unpaid losses incurred in this line of business in 2006 and prior years and that are outstanding at the end of the 2008 taxable year.

Other Liability — Claims-Made

Tax Year	Estimated Cumulative Losses Paid (%)	Estimated Losses Paid Each Year (%)	Unpaid Losses at Year End (%)	Discounted Unpaid Losses at Year End (%)	Discount Factors (%)
2006	14.9618	14.9618	85.0382	75.3352	88.5898
2007	36.2113	21.2494	63.7887	56.6653	88.8328
2008	54.2876	18.0763	45.7124	40.4881	88.5713
2009	64.2163	9.9288	35.7837	31.9751	89.3567
2010	73.2732	9.0569	26.7268	24.0123	89.8438
2011	80.5748	7.3016	19.4252	17.5225	90.2054
2012	87.6200	7.0452	12.3800	11.0359	89.1433
2013	89.9155	2.2955	10.0845	9.1344	90.5790
2014	93.3946	3.4791	6.6054	5.9503	90.0827
2015	94.6170	1.2223	5.3830	4.9407	91.7827

Taxpayers that do not use the composite method of Notice 88–100 should use the following factors to discount unpaid losses incurred in this line of business in the 2006 accident year and that are outstanding at the end of the tax year shown.

2016		1.2223	4.1607	3.8909	93.5158
2017		1.2223	2.9383	2.7993	95.2689
2018		1.2223	1.7160	1.6643	96.9877
2019 and later years		1.2223	0.4936	0.4841	98.0675

Taxpayers that use the composite method of Notice 88–100 should use 94.6440 percent to discount unpaid losses incurred in this line of business in 2006 and prior years and that are outstanding at the end of the 2016 taxable year.

Other Liability — Occurrence

Tax Year	Estimated Cumulative Losses Paid (%)	Estimated Losses Paid Each Year (%)	Unpaid Losses at Year End (%)	Discounted Unpaid Losses at Year End (%)	Discount Factors (%)
2006	19.1133	19.1133	80.8867	69.7012	86.1714
2007	36.4434	17.3301	63.5566	54.8037	86.2281
2008	52.1648	15.7215	47.8352	40.9536	85.6140
2009	63.2383	11.0734	36.7617	31.2919	85.1209
2010	72.0780	8.8397	27.9220	23.5235	84.2469
2011	75.9021	3.8241	24.0979	20.5602	85.3195
2012	82.9305	7.0284	17.0695	14.2116	83.2573
2013	85.1441	2.2136	14.8559	12.5200	84.2763
2014	89.3006	4.1565	10.6994	8.7799	82.0597
2015	89.9898	0.6892	10.0102	8.4266	84.1796

Taxpayers that do not use the composite method of Notice 88–100 should use the following factors to discount unpaid losses incurred in this line of business in the 2006 accident year and that are outstanding at the end of the tax year shown.

2016		0.6892	9.3210	8.0591	86.4622
2017		0.6892	8.6318	7.6771	88.9398
2018		0.6892	7.9426	7.2798	91.6560
2019		0.6892	7.2533	6.8668	94.6705
2020 and later years		0.6892	6.5641	6.4373	98.0675

Taxpayers that use the composite method of Notice 88–100 should use 90.4497 percent to discount unpaid losses incurred in this line of business in 2006 and prior years and that are outstanding at the end of the 2016 taxable year.

Private Passenger Auto Liability/Medical

Tax Year	Estimated Cumulative Losses Paid (%)	Estimated Losses Paid Each Year (%)	Unpaid Losses at Year End (%)	Discounted Unpaid Losses at Year End (%)	Discount Factors (%)
2006	43.1926	43.1926	56.8074	53.5261	94.2237
2007	72.2008	29.0082	27.7992	26.0766	93.8032
2008	84.5632	12.3625	15.4368	14.5083	93.9856
2009	91.9316	7.3684	8.0684	7.5722	93.8501
2010	95.8729	3.9413	4.1271	3.8546	93.3975
2011	97.7804	1.9075	2.2196	2.0629	92.9415
2012	98.7957	1.0153	1.2043	1.1098	92.1473
2013	99.2491	0.4535	0.7509	0.6915	92.0971
2014	99.5195	0.2703	0.4805	0.4434	92.2703
2015	99.6353	0.1159	0.3647	0.3429	94.0275

Taxpayers that do not use the composite method of Notice 88–100 should use the following factors to discount unpaid losses incurred in this line of business in the 2006 accident year and that are outstanding at the end of the tax year shown.

2016		0.1159	0.2488	0.2384	95.8137
2017		0.1159	0.1330	0.1297	97.5849
2018 and later years		0.1159	0.0171	0.0168	98.0675

Taxpayers that use the composite method of Notice 88–100 should use 96.3943 percent to discount unpaid losses incurred in this line of business in 2006 and prior years and that are outstanding at the end of the 2016 taxable year.

Products Liability — Claims-Made

Tax Year	Estimated Cumulative Losses Paid (%)	Estimated Losses Paid Each Year (%)	Unpaid Losses at Year End (%)	Discounted Unpaid Losses at Year End (%)	Discount Factors (%)
2006	6.5804	6.5804	93.4196	80.2960	85.9520
2007	26.7183	20.1379	73.2817	62.9570	85.9110
2008	43.1834	16.4652	56.8166	48.6731	85.6671
2009	43.9209	0.7375	56.0791	49.8583	88.9071
2010	54.3806	10.4597	45.6194	41.1768	90.2617
2011	78.3630	23.9824	21.6370	18.3607	84.8579
2012	82.8643	4.5013	17.1357	14.5014	84.6271
2013	68.2184	-14.6459	31.7816	30.0132	94.4355
2014	79.1582	10.9399	20.8418	20.0522	96.2118
2015	89.6963	10.5381	10.3037	10.1045	98.0675

Taxpayers that do not use the composite method of Notice 88–100 should use the following factor to discount unpaid losses incurred in this line of business in the 2006 accident year and that are outstanding at the end of the tax year shown.

2016 and later years	98.0675

Taxpayers that use the composite method of Notice 88–100 should use 98.0675 percent to discount unpaid losses incurred in this line of business in 2006 and prior years and that are outstanding at the end of the 2016 taxable year.

Products Liability — Occurrence

Tax Year	Estimated Cumulative Losses Paid (%)	Estimated Losses Paid Each Year (%)	Unpaid Losses at Year End (%)	Discounted Unpaid Losses at Year End (%)	Discount Factors (%)
2006	9.4198	9.4198	90.5802	76.5659	84.5283
2007	20.5845	11.1647	79.4155	68.2285	85.9133
2008	36.7807	16.1962	63.2193	54.4286	86.0950
2009	55.5974	18.8167	44.4026	37.4074	84.2460
2010	66.6238	11.0263	33.3762	27.6526	82.8511
2011	77.2636	10.6399	22.7364	17.9036	78.7443
2012	79.1888	1.9251	20.8112	16.6531	80.0197
2013	83.6816	4.4928	16.3184	12.7345	78.0378
2014	85.5507	1.8691	14.4493	11.3354	78.4496
2015	85.7291	0.1784	14.2709	11.6047	81.3169

Taxpayers that do not use the composite method of Notice 88–100 should use the following factors to discount unpaid losses incurred in this line of business in the 2006 accident year and that are outstanding at the end of the tax year shown.

2016	0.1784	14.0925	11.8846	84.3329
2017	0.1784	13.9141	12.1757	87.5062
2018	0.1784	13.7357	12.4784	90.8463
2019	0.1784	13.5573	12.7931	94.3632
2020 and later years	0.1784	13.3789	13.1204	98.0675

Taxpayers that use the composite method of Notice 88–100 should use 89.8177 percent to discount unpaid losses incurred in this line of business in 2006 and prior years and that are outstanding at the end of the 2016 taxable year.

Reinsurance A (Nonproportional Assumed Property)

Tax Year	Estimated Cumulative Losses Paid (%)	Estimated Losses Paid Each Year (%)	Unpaid Losses at Year End (%)	Discounted Unpaid Losses at Year End (%)	Discount Factors (%)
2006	25.0571	25.0571	74.9429	69.5252	92.7708
2007	52.0402	26.9831	47.9598	44.7775	93.3645
2008	82.4709	30.4307	17.5291	15.5292	88.5910
2009	85.6387	3.1678	14.3613	12.9170	89.9434
2010	92.7228	7.0840	7.2772	6.2075	85.3001
2011	91.8604	-0.8624	8.1396	7.3339	90.1015
2012	96.5016	4.6412	3.4984	2.8932	82.6989
2013	96.1872	-0.3143	3.8128	3.3288	87.3078
2014	97.6206	1.4333	2.3794	1.9998	84.0432
2015	97.8419	0.2214	2.1581	1.8536	85.8925

Taxpayers that do not use the composite method of Notice 88–100 should use the following factors to discount unpaid losses incurred in this line of business in the 2006 accident year and that are outstanding at the end of the tax year shown.

Tax Year		Estimated Losses Paid Each Year (%)	Unpaid Losses at Year End (%)	Discounted Unpaid Losses at Year End (%)	Discount Factors (%)
2016		0.2214	1.9367	1.7017	87.8641
2017		0.2214	1.7154	1.5437	89.9920
2018		0.2214	1.4940	1.3794	92.3296
2019		0.2214	1.2727	1.2086	94.9667
2020 and later years		0.2214	1.0513	1.0310	98.0675

Taxpayers that use the composite method of Notice 88–100 should use 90.9754 percent to discount unpaid losses incurred in this line of business in 2006 and prior years and that are outstanding at the end of the 2016 taxable year.

Reinsurance B (Nonproportional Assumed Liability)

Tax Year	Estimated Cumulative Losses Paid (%)	Estimated Losses Paid Each Year (%)	Unpaid Losses at Year End (%)	Discounted Unpaid Losses at Year End (%)	Discount Factors (%)
2006	8.9223	8.9223	91.0777	76.3687	83.8500
2007	27.3618	18.4395	72.6382	60.6053	83.4344
2008	44.5758	17.2140	55.4242	45.4641	82.0294
2009	53.8781	9.3023	46.1219	37.7880	81.9307
2010	60.8896	7.0115	39.1104	32.1422	82.1834
2011	69.7327	8.8430	30.2673	24.4042	80.6288
2012	76.6292	6.8965	23.3708	18.3431	78.4871
2013	79.4030	2.7738	20.5970	16.2447	78.8690
2014	83.8936	4.4906	16.1064	12.3121	76.4422
2015	80.1707	-3.7229	19.8293	16.5983	83.7063

Taxpayers that do not use the composite method of Notice 88–100 should use the following factors to discount unpaid losses incurred in this line of business in the 2006 accident year and that are outstanding at the end of the tax year shown.

Reinsurance B (Nonproportional Assumed Liability)

2016	1.1805	18.6487	16.0552	86.0925
2017	1.1805	17.4682	15.4904	88.6775
2018	1.1805	16.2877	14.9031	91.4992
2019	1.1805	15.1072	14.2924	94.6071
2020 and later years	1.1805	13.9266	13.6575	98.0675

Taxpayers that use the composite method of Notice 88–100 should use 90.3273 percent to discount unpaid losses incurred in this line of business in 2006 and prior years and that are outstanding at the end of the 2016 taxable year.

Reinsurance C (Nonproportional Assumed Financial Lines)

Tax Year	Estimated Cumulative Losses Paid (%)	Estimated Losses Paid Each Year (%)	Unpaid Losses at Year End (%)	Discounted Unpaid Losses at Year End (%)	Discount Factors (%)
2006	17.1195	17.1195	82.8805	74.5159	89.9077
2007	46.6590	29.5395	53.3410	47.3601	88.7874
2008	67.7135	21.0545	32.2865	27.7757	86.0287
2009	78.1379	10.4244	21.8621	18.2513	83.4837
2010	89.7346	11.5967	10.2654	7.1524	69.6754
2011	92.1268	2.3921	7.8732	4.9978	63.4788
2012	89.7323	-2.3945	10.2677	7.6384	74.3925
2013	90.0460	0.3137	9.9540	7.6225	76.5774
2014	94.8867	4.8407	5.1133	2.9898	58.4711
2015	86.7041	-8.1827	13.2959	11.4527	86.1367

Taxpayers that do not use the composite method of Notice 88–100 should use the following factors to discount unpaid losses incurred in this line of business in the 2006 accident year and that are outstanding at the end of the tax year shown.

2016	1.4277	11.8683	10.4527	88.0727
2017	1.4277	10.4406	9.4129	90.1568
2018	1.4277	9.0129	8.3317	92.4421
2019	1.4277	7.5852	7.2075	95.0203
2020 and later years	1.4277	6.1575	6.0385	98.0675

Taxpayers that use the composite method of Notice 88–100 should use 91.0632 percent to discount unpaid losses incurred in this line of business in 2006 and prior years and that are outstanding at the end of the 2016 taxable year.

Special Property
(Fire, Allied Lines, Inland Marine, Earthquake, Glass, Burglary and Theft)

Tax Year	Estimated Cumulative Losses Paid (%)	Estimated Losses Paid Each Year (%)	Unpaid Losses at Year End (%)	Discounted Unpaid Losses at Year End (%)	Discount Factors (%)
2006	62.9320	62.9320	37.0680	35.7122	96.3422
2007	88.4950	25.5631	11.5050	11.0667	96.1907

Taxpayers that do not use the composite method of Notice 88–100 should use the following factor to discount unpaid losses incurred in this line of business in the 2006 accident year and that are outstanding at the end of the tax year shown.

Special Property
(Fire, Allied Lines, Inland Marine, Earthquake, Glass, Burglary and Theft)

2008 and later years	5.7525	5.7525	5.6413	98.0675

Taxpayers that use the composite method of Notice 88–100 should use 98.0675 percent to discount unpaid losses incurred in this line of business in 2006 and prior years and that are outstanding at the end of the 2008 taxable year.

Workers' Compensation

Tax Year	Estimated Cumulative Losses Paid (%)	Estimated Losses Paid Each Year (%)	Unpaid Losses at Year End (%)	Discounted Unpaid Losses at Year End (%)	Discount Factors (%)
2006	28.2489	28.2489	71.7511	64.2325	89.5214
2007	57.8739	29.6249	42.1261	36.5803	86.8351
2008	71.2999	13.4260	28.7001	24.3455	84.8274
2009	77.7584	6.4585	22.2416	18.7287	84.2059
2010	81.9301	4.1717	18.0699	15.2202	84.2298
2011	83.7739	1.8437	16.2261	13.9459	85.9472
2012	86.5350	2.7611	13.4650	11.6854	86.7836
2013	88.4367	1.9017	11.5633	10.2113	88.3080
2014	89.5926	1.1559	10.4074	9.4390	90.6955
2015	91.6441	2.0515	8.3559	7.7228	92.4232

Taxpayers that do not use the composite method of Notice 88–100 should use the following factors to discount unpaid losses incurred in this line of business in the 2006 accident year and that are outstanding at the end of the tax year shown.

2016		2.0515	6.3045	5.9383	94.1919
2017		2.0515	4.2530	4.0828	95.9970
2018		2.0515	2.2016	2.1534	97.8116
2019 and later years		2.0515	0.1501	0.1472	98.0675

Taxpayers that use the composite method of Notice 88–100 should use 95.2214 percent to discount unpaid losses incurred in this line of business in 2006 and prior years and that are outstanding at the end of the 2016 taxable year.

DRAFTING INFORMATION

The principal author of this revenue procedure is Katherine A. Hossofsky of the Office of Associate Chief Counsel (Financial Institutions & Products). For further information regarding this revenue procedure, contact Ms. Hossofsky at (202) 622–8435 (not a toll-free call).

---

26 CFR 601.201: Rulings and determination letters. (Also Part I, Sections 832, 846; 1.832–4, 1.846–1.)

Rev. Proc. 2007–10

SECTION 1. PURPOSE

This revenue procedure prescribes the salvage discount factors for the 2006 accident year. These factors must be used to compute discounted estimated salvage recoverable under § 832 of the Internal Revenue Code.

SEC. 2. BACKGROUND

Section 832(b)(5)(A) requires that all estimated salvage recoverable (including that which cannot be treated as an asset for state accounting purposes) be taken into account in computing the deduction for losses incurred. Under § 832(b)(5)(A), paid losses are to be reduced by salvage and reinsurance recovered during the taxable year. This amount is adjusted to reflect changes in discounted unpaid losses on nonlife insurance contracts and in unpaid losses on life insurance contracts. An adjustment is then made to reflect any changes in discounted estimated salvage recoverable and in reinsurance recoverable.

Pursuant to § 832(b), the amount of estimated salvage is determined on a discounted basis in accordance with procedures established by the Secretary.

SEC. 3. SCOPE

This revenue procedure applies to any taxpayer that is required to discount estimated salvage recoverable under § 832.

SEC. 4. APPLICATION

.01 The following tables present separately for each line of business the discount factors under § 832 for the 2006 accident year. All the discount factors presented in this section were determined using the applicable interest rate under § 846(c) for 2006, which is 3.98 percent, and by assuming all estimated salvage is recovered in the middle of each calendar year. *See*

Rev. Proc. 2003–18, 2003–1 C.B. 439, for background regarding the tables.

.02 These tables must be used by taxpayers irrespective of whether they elected to discount unpaid losses using their own historical experience under § 846.

.03 Section V of Notice 88–100, 1988–2 C.B. 439, provides a composite discount factor to be used in determining the discounted unpaid losses for accident years that are not separately reported on the NAIC Annual Statement. The tables separately provide discount factors for taxpayers who elect to use the composite method. Rev. Proc. 2002–74, 2002–2 C.B. 980, clarifies that for certain insurance companies subject to tax under § 831 the composite method for discounting unpaid losses set forth in Notice 88–100, section V, 1988–2 C.B. 439, is permitted but not required. This revenue procedure further provides alternative methods for computing discounted unpaid losses that are permitted for insurance companies not using the composite method, and sets forth a procedure for insurance companies to obtain automatic consent of the Commissioner to change to one of the methods described in Rev. Proc. 2002–74.

.04 Tables.

Tables of Factors to be Used to Discount Salvage Recoverable With Respect to Losses Incurred in Accident Year 2006

(Interest rate: 3.98 percent)

Accident and Health (Other Than Disability Income or Credit Disability Insurance)

Taxpayers that do not use the composite method of Notice 88–100 should use 98.0675 percent to discount salvage recoverable with respect to losses incurred in this line of business in the 2006 accident year as of the end of the 2006 and later taxable years.

Taxpayers that use the composite method of Notice 88–100 should use 98.0675 percent to discount all salvage recoverable in this line of business as of the end of the 2006 taxable year.

Auto Physical Damage

Tax Year	Discount Factors (%)
2006	97.1334
2007	96.1907

Taxpayers that do not use the composite method of Notice 88–100 should use the following factor to discount salvage recoverable as of the end of the tax year shown with respect to losses incurred in this line of business in the 2006 accident year.

2008 and later years	98.0675

Taxpayers that use the composite method of Notice 88–100 should use 98.0675 percent to discount salvage recoverable as of the end of the 2008 taxable year with respect to losses incurred in this line of business in 2006 and prior years.

Commercial Auto/Truck Liability/Medical

Tax Year	Discount Factors (%)
2006	92.1380
2007	91.8882
2008	91.6949
2009	92.1286
2010	92.5860
2011	92.1065
2012	93.1945
2013	94.1358
2014	94.3956
2015	96.2168

Commercial Auto/Truck Liability/Medical

Taxpayers that do not use the composite method of Notice 88–100 should use the following factor to discount salvage recoverable as of the end of the tax year shown with respect to losses incurred in this line of business in the 2006 accident year.

2016 and later years	98.0675

Taxpayers that use the composite method of Notice 88–100 should use 98.0675 percent to discount salvage recoverable as of the end of the 2016 taxable year with respect to losses incurred in this line of business in 2006 and prior years.

Composite

Tax Year	Discount Factors (%)
2006	92.0337
2007	90.8802
2008	90.4072
2009	89.8712
2010	88.8367
2011	88.9101
2012	88.6960
2013	88.6734
2014	88.8118
2015	90.4886

Taxpayers that do not use the composite method of Notice 88–100 should use the following factors to discount salvage recoverable as of the end of the tax year shown with respect to losses incurred in this line of business in the 2006 accident year.

2016	92.2048
2017	93.9577
2018	95.7372
2019	97.4944
2020 and later years	98.0675

Composite

Taxpayers that use the composite method of Notice 88–100 should use 93.6350 percent to discount salvage recoverable as of the end of the 2016 taxable year with respect to losses incurred in this line of business in 2006 and prior years.

Fidelity/Surety

Tax Year	Discount Factors (%)
2006	94.2975
2007	96.1907

Taxpayers that do not use the composite method of Notice 88–100 should use the following factor to discount salvage recoverable as of the end of the tax year shown with respect to losses incurred in this line of business in the 2006 accident year.

2008 and later years	98.0675

Taxpayers that use the composite method of Notice 88–100 should use 98.0675 percent to discount salvage recoverable as of the end of the 2008 taxable year with respect to losses incurred in this line of business in 2006 and prior years.

Financial Guaranty/Mortgage Guaranty

Tax Year	Discount Factors (%)
2006	95.5547
2007	96.1907

Financial Guaranty/Mortgage Guaranty

Taxpayers that do not use the composite method of Notice 88–100 should use the following factor to discount salvage recoverable as of the end of the tax year shown with respect to losses incurred in this line of business in the 2006 accident year.

2008 and later years	98.0675

Taxpayers that use the composite method of Notice 88–100 should use 98.0675 percent to discount salvage recoverable as of the end of the 2008 taxable year with respect to losses incurred in this line of business in 2006 and prior years.

International (Composite)

Tax Year	Discount Factors (%)
2006	92.0337
2007	90.8802
2008	90.4072
2009	89.8712
2010	88.8367
2011	88.9101
2012	88.6960
2013	88.6734
2014	88.8118
2015	90.4886

Taxpayers that do not use the composite method of Notice 88–100 should use the following factors to discount salvage recoverable as of the end of the tax year shown with respect to losses incurred in this line of business in the 2006 accident year.

International (Composite)

2016	92.2048
2017	93.9577
2018	95.7372
2019	97.4944
2020 and later years	98.0675

Taxpayers that use the composite method of Notice 88–100 should use 93.6350 percent to discount salvage recoverable as of the end of the 2016 taxable year with respect to losses incurred in this line of business in 2006 and prior years.

Medical Malpractice — Claims-Made

Tax Year	Discount Factors (%)
2006	87.6804
2007	83.3538
2008	87.7437
2009	85.5621
2010	86.5072
2011	81.4476
2012	90.5680
2013	93.2658
2014	96.4532
2015	98.0675

Taxpayers that do not use the composite method of Notice 88–100 should use the following factor to discount salvage recoverable as of the end of the tax year shown with respect to losses incurred in this line of business in the 2006 accident year.

2016 and later years	98.0675

Taxpayers that use the composite method of Notice 88–100 should use 98.0675 percent to discount salvage recoverable as of the end of the 2016 taxable year with respect to losses incurred in this line of business in 2006 and prior years.

Medical Malpractice — Occurrence

Tax Year	Discount Factors (%)
2006	83.9442
2007	85.0591
2008	88.4295
2009	89.8198
2010	78.2945
2011	87.5838
2012	92.3237
2013	95.1299
2014	96.7311
2015	98.0675

Taxpayers that do not use the composite method of Notice 88–100 should use the following factor to discount salvage recoverable as of the end of the tax year shown with respect to losses incurred in this line of business in the 2006 accident year.

2016 and later years	98.0675

Taxpayers that use the composite method of Notice 88–100 should use 98.0675 percent to discount salvage recoverable as of the end of the 2016 taxable year with respect to losses incurred in this line of business in 2006 and prior years.

Miscellaneous Casualty

Tax Year	Discount Factors (%)
2006	96.6963
2007	96.1907

Taxpayers that do not use the composite method of Notice 88–100 should use the following factor to discount salvage recoverable as of the end of the tax year shown with respect to losses incurred in this line of business in the 2006 accident year.

Miscellaneous Casualty

2008 and later years	98.0675

Taxpayers that use the composite method of Notice 88–100 should use 98.0675 percent to discount salvage recoverable as of the end of the 2008 taxable year with respect to losses incurred in this line of business in 2006 and prior years.

Multiple Peril Lines (Homeowners/Farmowners, Commercial Multiple Peril, and Special Liability (Ocean Marine, Aircraft (All Perils), Boiler and Machinery))

Tax Year	Discount Factors (%)
2006	92.9300
2007	91.3642
2008	92.0510
2009	91.7902
2010	91.4227
2011	92.5705
2012	92.6261
2013	92.8131
2014	94.2424
2015	96.0540

Taxpayers that do not use the composite method of Notice 88–100 should use the following factors to discount salvage recoverable as of the end of the tax year shown with respect to losses incurred in this line of business in the 2006 accident year.

2016	97.8851
2017 and later years	98.0675

Taxpayers that use the composite method of Notice 88–100 should use 97.8836 percent to discount salvage recoverable as of the end of the 2016 taxable year with respect to losses incurred in this line of business in 2006 and prior years.

Other (Including Credit)

Tax Year	Discount Factors (%)
2006	96.8727
2007	96.1907

Taxpayers that do not use the composite method of Notice 88–100 should use the following factor to discount salvage recoverable as of the end of the tax year shown with respect to losses incurred in this line of business in the 2006 accident year.

2008 and later years	98.0675

Taxpayers that use the composite method of Notice 88–100 should use 98.0675 percent to discount salvage recoverable as of the end of the 2008 taxable year with respect to losses incurred in this line of business in 2006 and prior years.

Other Liability — Claims-Made

Tax Year	Discount Factors (%)
2006	91.5341
2007	82.9787
2008	70.3678
2009	89.1316
2010	85.8677
2011	85.2144
2012	90.8949
2013	94.0739
2014	91.1910
2015	92.9193

Taxpayers that do not use the composite method of Notice 88–100 should use the following factors to discount salvage recoverable as of the end of the tax year shown with respect to losses incurred in this line of business in the 2006 accident year.

Other Liability — Claims-Made

2016	94.6785
2017	96.4455
2018 and later years	98.0675

Taxpayers that use the composite method of Notice 88–100 should use 95.5684 percent to discount salvage recoverable as of the end of the 2016 taxable year with respect to losses incurred in this line of business in 2006 and prior years.

Other Liability — Occurrence

Tax Year	Discount Factors (%)
2006	86.8418
2007	88.1391
2008	89.1356
2009	86.1576
2010	89.3069
2011	91.5372
2012	91.8852
2013	93.7371
2014	94.9176
2015	96.6537

Taxpayers that do not use the composite method of Noticc 88–100 should use the following factor to discount salvage recoverable as of the end of the tax year shown with respect to losses incurred in this line of business in the 2006 accident year.

2016 and later years	98.0675

Taxpayers that use the composite method of Notice 88–100 should use 98.0675 percent to discount salvage recoverable as of the end of the 2016 taxable year with respect to losses incurred in this line of business in 2006 and prior years.

Private Passenger Auto Liability/Medical

Tax Year	Discount Factors (%)
2006	94.7409
2007	94.5642
2008	94.3153
2009	93.5866
2010	93.3908
2011	92.4796
2012	92.4373
2013	92.5029
2014	93.5781
2015	95.3333

Taxpayers that do not use the composite method of Notice 88–100 should use the following factors to discount salvage recoverable as of the end of the tax year shown with respect to losses incurred in this line of business in the 2006 accident year.

2016	97.0529
2017 and later years	98.0675

Taxpayers that use the composite method of Notice 88–100 should use 97.2228 percent to discount salvage recoverable as of the end of the 2016 taxable year with respect to losses incurred in this line of business in 2006 and prior years.

Products Liability — Claims-Made

Tax Year	Discount Factors (%)
2006	88.1034
2007	88.1497
2008	89.6228
2009	21.8302
2010	82.4271
2011	88.1330
2012	92.1902
2013	95.8876
2014	37.3999
2015	96.2692

Taxpayers that do not use the composite method of Notice 88–100 should use the following factor to discount salvage recoverable as of the end of the tax year shown with respect to losses incurred in this line of business in the 2006 accident year.

2016 and later years	98.0675

Taxpayers that use the composite method of Notice 88–100 should use 98.0675 percent to discount salvage recoverable as of the end of the 2016 taxable year with respect to losses incurred in this line of business in 2006 and prior years.

Products Liability — Occurrence

Tax Year	Discount Factors (%)
2006	83.0564
2007	85.4302
2008	86.0203
2009	88.3994
2010	86.1113
2011	89.2324
2012	91.9553
2013	92.5997
2014	87.8074
2015	89.4589

Products Liability — Occurrence

Taxpayers that do not use the composite method of Notice 88–100 should use the following factors to discount salvage recoverable as of the end of the tax year shown with respect to losses incurred in this line of business in the 2006 accident year.

2016	91.1499
2017	92.8787
2018	94.6400
2019	96.4133
2020 and later years	98.0675

Taxpayers that use the composite method of Notice 88–100 should use 92.7786 percent to discount salvage recoverable as of the end of the 2016 taxable year with respect to losses incurred in this line of business in 2006 and prior years.

Reinsurance A (Nonproportional Assumed Property)

Tax Year	Discount Factors (%)
2006	87.5637
2007	85.0097
2008	88.6909
2009	92.0150
2010	92.5920
2011	94.1411
2012	95.7082
2013	96.8174
2014	97.3356
2015	98.0675

Taxpayers that do not use the composite method of Notice 88–100 should use the following factor to discount salvage recoverable as of the end of the tax year shown with respect to losses incurred in this line of business in the 2006 accident year.

2016 and later years	98.0675

Reinsurance A (Nonproportional Assumed Property)

Taxpayers that use the composite method of Notice 88–100 should use 98.0675 percent to discount salvage recoverable as of the end of the 2016 taxable year with respect to losses incurred in this line of business in 2006 and prior years.

Reinsurance B (Nonproportional Assumed Liability)

Tax Year	Discount Factors (%)
2006	86.9992
2007	84.9315
2008	87.8351
2009	85.8777
2010	79.6478
2011	82.8774
2012	82.3201
2013	84.3658
2014	79.9064
2015	86.6394

Taxpayers that do not use the composite method of Notice 88–100 should use the following factors to discount salvage recoverable as of the end of the tax year shown with respect to losses incurred in this line of business in the 2006 accident year.

2016	88.5090
2017	90.5090
2018	92.6892
2019	95.1430
2020 and later years	98.0675

Taxpayers that use the composite method of Notice 88–100 should use 91.2561 percent to discount salvage recoverable as of the end of the 2016 taxable year with respect to losses incurred in this line of business in 2006 and prior years.

Reinsurance C (Nonproportional Assumed Financial Lines)

Tax Year	Discount Factors (%)
2006	86.8509
2007	87.5301
2008	90.6247
2009	88.3441
2010	91.1866
2011	85.1209
2012	87.9777
2013	94.0073
2014	95.2074
2015	96.9266

Taxpayers that do not use the composite method of Notice 88–100 should use the following factor to discount salvage recoverable as of the end of the tax year shown with respect to losses incurred in this line of business in the 2006 accident year.

2016 and later years	98.0675

Taxpayers that use the composite method of Notice 88–100 should use 98.0675 percent to discount salvage recoverable as of the end of the 2016 taxable year with respect to losses incurred in this line of business in 2006 and prior years.

Special Property (Fire, Allied Lines, Inland Marine, Earthquake, Glass, Burglary and Theft)

Tax Year	Discount Factors (%)
2006	94.6724
2007	96.1907

Special Property (Fire, Allied Lines, Inland Marine, Earthquake, Glass, Burglary and Theft)

Taxpayers that do not use the composite method of Notice 88–100 should use the following factor to discount salvage recoverable as of the end of the tax year shown with respect to losses incurred in this line of business in the 2006 accident year.

2008 and later years	98.0675

Taxpayers that use the composite method of Notice 88–100 should use 98.0675 percent to discount salvage recoverable as of the end of the 2008 taxable year with respect to losses incurred in this line of business in 2006 and prior years.

Workers' Compensation

Tax Year	Discount Factors (%)
2006	87.6219
2007	88.7710
2008	89.1706
2009	89.1058
2010	88.5191
2011	89.2639
2012	89.0972
2013	89.2683
2014	90.0193
2015	91.7175

Taxpayers that do not use the composite method of Notice 88–100 should use the following factors to discount salvage recoverable as of the end of the tax year shown with respect to losses incurred in this line of business in the 2006 accident year.

2016	93.4488
2017	95.2002
2018	96.9195
2019 and later years	98.0675

Workers' Compensation

Taxpayers that use the composite method of Notice 88–100 should use 94.5920 percent to discount salvage recoverable as of the end of the 2016 taxable year with respect to losses incurred in this line of business in 2006 and prior years.

DRAFTING INFORMATION

The principal author of this revenue procedure is Katherine A. Hossofsky of the Office of the Associate Chief Counsel (Financial Institutions & Products). For further information regarding this revenue procedure, contact Ms. Hossofsky at (202) 622–8435 (not a toll-free call).

---

26 CFR 601.105: Examination of returns and claims for refund, credit, or abatement; determination of correct tax liability.
(Also: Part I, §§ 482; 1.482–9T.)

Rev. Proc. 2007–13

SECTION 1. PURPOSE

This revenue procedure identifies specified covered services within the meaning of Temp. Treas. Reg. § 1.482–9T(b)(4)(i). The activities identified in this revenue procedure are support services common among taxpayers in a variety of industry sectors, and generally do not involve a significant arm's length markup on total services costs. Services identified in this revenue procedure must meet the other conditions set forth in Temp. Treas. Reg. § 1.482–9T(b) to be evaluated under the services cost method.

SECTION 2. BACKGROUND

The section 482 regulations provide pricing methods for transactions between controlled parties, including transactions involving services. The existing regulations for transactions involving services were issued in 1968. Section 1.482–2(b) of the existing regulations provides a "cost safe harbor" that permits certain "non-integral" services to be priced at cost. In 2003, the Treasury Department and IRS issued proposed regulations that set forth a simplified cost based method (SCBM) intended to preserve some benefits of the current Treas. Reg. § 1.482–2(b) cost safe harbor. A number of commentators noted that SCBM called for quantitative judgments that business people are not qualified to make by themselves. As a practical matter, taxpayers would be required to devote significant compliance resources to enlist outside consultants or otherwise to develop support for those judgments.

In 2006, the Treasury Department and the IRS issued temporary regulations that eliminated the SCBM and replaced it with the services cost method (SCM), as set forth in Temp. Treas. Reg. § 1.482–9T(b). The Treasury Department and IRS recognized that because the section 482 services regulations potentially affect a large volume of intragroup back office services that are common across many industries, it is in the interest of sound tax administration to minimize the compliance burden of such services, which would typically bear low arm's length markups.

The SCM evaluates whether the price for covered services, as defined, is arm's length by reference to the total services costs with no markup. Section 1.482–9T(b)(4) of the temporary regulations provides for two categories of covered services eligible for the SCM. The first category is described in Temp. Treas. Reg. § 1.482–9T(b)(4)(i) and consists of specified covered services that will be identified in this revenue procedure. These specified covered services are so identified because they constitute support services of a type common across industry sectors that generally do not involve a significant arm's length markup on total services costs. A second category of services described in Temp. Treas. Reg. § 1.482–9T(b)(4)(ii), low margin covered services, has a median comparable arm's length markup on total services costs of less than or equal to 7 percent. The second category is not addressed in this revenue procedure.

The Internal Revenue Service identified forty-eight activities that constitute specified covered services in a proposed revenue procedure included in Announcement 2006–50, 2006–34 I.R.B. 321, which was published in the Internal Revenue Bulletin on August 21, 2006. A number of public comments were received with respect to the SCM in general and Announcement 2006–50.

Notice 2007–5, issued contemporaneously with this Revenue Procedure, contains clarifications concerning several provisions related to the SCM. In addition, the notice partially modifies the effective date of the temporary regulations. Subject to the exceptions described below, the effective date of the temporary regulations, insofar as they pertain to the identification of controlled services eligible to be priced at cost, is moved back one year. The provisions related to the SCM in Temp. Treas. Reg. § 1.482–9T(b) will thus apply to taxable years beginning after December 31, 2007. The only SCM provision that has immediate effect, *i.e.*, for taxable years beginning after December 31, 2006, is the business judgment rule in Temp. Treas. Reg. § 1.482–9T(b)(2).

The net effect of this modification is that, for taxable years with beginning dates from January 1, 2007 to December 31, 2007, taxpayers may apply the existing regulations in Treas. Reg. § 1.482–2(b) for purposes of identifying controlled services that are eligible to be priced on a cost basis, without a markup. For such taxable years, any services priced at cost must be "non-integral" within the meaning of existing Treas. Reg. § 1.482–2(b)(7), and they must also satisfy the SCM business judgment test in Temp. Treas. Reg. § 1.482–9T(b)(2).

Alternatively, for tax years beginning between January 1, 2007 and December 31, 2007, taxpayers may elect to apply the SCM as set forth in Temp. Treas. Reg. § 1.482–9T(b), without taking into account any of the modifications described in the previous two paragraphs.

A number of commentators stated that the list of specified covered services in Announcement 2006–50 was too narrow. In response to comments, this revenue procedure significantly broadens the existing categories and adds a number of new activities to the list of specified covered services. In addition, a provision covering "other similar activities" has been added to each category of activities.

SECTION 3. SCOPE

The following categories of services are eligible for treatment as specified covered services under Temp. Treas. Reg. § 1.482–9T(b)(4)(i):

Payroll:

1. Compiling and posting employee time and other information needed to calculate periodic compensation to employees. Computing employees' time worked, production, and commissions. Computing and posting wages and deductions to appropriate accounting records. Preparing paychecks, travel reimbursement and expense reimbursement.

2. Preparing payroll tax forms (such as the preparation of Forms 940, 941 and W–2 in order to comply with U.S. requirements or similar requirements under another country's laws).

3. Administering garnishment and other wage withholding orders.

4. Other activities similar to those specified in paragraphs (1) through (3).

Premiums for Unemployment, Disability and Workers Compensation:

5. Processing employees' unemployment insurance premiums, disability premiums and workers compensation premiums.

6. Other activities similar to those specified in paragraph (5).

Accounts Receivable:

7. Compiling, analyzing and recording current credit data and other financial information regarding individuals or firms (including preparing reports with this information for use in decisionmaking).

8. Compiling and recording billing, accounting and other numerical data for billing purposes. Preparing billing invoices for services rendered or for delivery or shipment of goods.

9. Locating and notifying customer(s) of delinquent accounts by mail (either electronic or otherwise) or telephone to solicit payment. Receiving payment from customers and posting payment to customer accounts. If customer fails to respond, preparing statements to credit department, initiating repossession proceedings or service disconnection. Keeping records of collection activities and status of accounts.

10. Other activities similar to those specified in paragraphs (7) through (9).

Accounts Payable:

11. Compiling information and records to draw up purchase orders for procurement of materials and services.

12. Making payment to vendors and posting payment to status of accounts.

13. Other activities similar to those specified in paragraphs (11) and (12).

General Administrative:

14. Performing clerical and administrative functions such as drafting correspondence, scheduling appointments, and organizing and maintaining paper and electronic files.

15. Performing data entry through use of a keyboard or scanning device, including verifying data and preparing materials for printing.

16. Using a word processor/computer or typewriter to generate (without substantial modification) letters, reports, forms, or other material from another person's rough draft, corrected copy, or voice recording.

17. Performing duties relating to office management systems and procedures, such as answering telephones, bookkeeping, typing, word processing, office machine operation, and filing.

18. Operating any of the following office machines: photocopying, scanning and facsimile machines.

19. Providing interoffice service/document delivery, including mailroom services, document management, and graphics, video, and website preparation.

20. Other activities similar to those specified in paragraphs (14) through (19).

Corporate and Public Relations:

21. Planning and executing a public relations program or corporate communication policy, including the distribution of internal and external corporate communications, but not to include specific advertising and/or marketing of a product or service.

22. Other activities similar to those specified in paragraph (21).

Meeting Coordination and Travel Planning:

23. Coordinating activities of staff and convention personnel to make arrangements for group meetings and conventions.

24. Negotiating airline, rental car, and hotel contracts.

25. Assisting in travel arrangements, including providing a system for reservations and ticket purchases.

26. Managing motor pool and fleet.

27. Other activities similar to those specified in paragraphs (23) through (26).

Accounting and Auditing:

28. Gathering and reviewing information in accounting records for use in preparing financial statements.

29. Computing, classifying, and recording numerical data to maintain accurate and complete financial records, performing any combination of calculating, posting, and verifying duties to obtain primary financial data for use in maintaining accounting records, checking the accuracy of figures, calculations, and postings pertaining to business transactions recorded by other workers; and calculating investment performance and net asset values of investments.

30. Consolidating legal entity financial results per country for use in statutory financial statements and tax returns and consolidating worldwide results by business area for use in management accounting.

31. Developing a company-wide accounting manual that prescribes accounting policies and methods to be used and providing related advice.

32. Performing operational and financial internal audits.

33. Preparing government census and related forms required by a service recipient's home country.

34. Preparing reports required by escheat laws required by a service recipient's home country.

35. Completing import/export documentation and arranging for customs payment.

36. Overseeing audits by customs authorities.

37. Other activities similar to those specified in paragraphs (28) through (36).

Tax:

38. Processing tax payments according to prescribed laws and regulations.

39. Gathering information from accounting records and including that information in the preparation of income, property, sales/use, VAT, excise and other tax returns.

40. Overseeing audits conducted by tax authorities.

41. Providing tax advice to businesses to ensure compliance with tax laws, including access to electronic research and tax compliance software.

42. Reviewing local country tax provisions for purposes of inclusion in the consolidated world-wide provision and preparation of the world-wide tax provision.

43. Negotiating advance pricing agreements and other local incentives that benefit the consolidated organization.

44. Other activities similar to those specified in paragraphs (38) through (43).

Health, Safety, Environmental and Regulatory Affairs:

45. Developing company health, safety, and environment standards, monitoring compliance with such standards, and training affected personnel.

46. Gathering information and preparing documentation relating to eligibility for or compliance with laws and regulations governing contracts, licenses and permits.

47. Gathering information, verifying data and preparing documentation relating to compliance with laws and regulations governing financial and securities institutions and financial and real estate transactions. Examining and verifying correctness of, or establishing authenticity of records.

48. Providing security services (*e.g.*, executive protection or global headquarters security).

49. Providing common health risk management systems development, clinical services, industrial hygiene, alcohol and drug testing services (laboratory analyses done by third parties), and advice to business management on health issues.

50. Providing guidance and support operations, integrity management support implementation, coaching, and conducting operations integrity management assessments, development and implementation of safety behavior based programs, and incident reporting and accident investigations.

51. Providing strategies, resources, and training for effective crisis preparedness and response.

52. Other activities similar to those specified in paragraphs (45) through (51).

Budgeting:

53. Compiling data for use by cost estimators in determining cost projections and in preparing budget estimates, including verifying information for completeness, accuracy, and conformance with internal procedures and regulations.

54. Compiling data to prepare budget and accounting reports for management.

55. Other activities similar to those specified in paragraphs (53) and (54).

Treasury Activities:

56. Establishing bank accounts and lock boxes for use by controlled parties, including overdraft facilities and lines of credit.

57. Providing staff and facilities to hedge currency exposures that arise from operations in the normal course of business. This paragraph does not apply to banks (including investment banks), insurance companies, investment companies, similar entities that provide financial services to the public, and investment funds (including hedge and private equity funds).

58. Coordinating investment activities in connection with short-term management of cash generated from operations in the normal course of business. This paragraph does not apply to related-party factoring activities, or to banks (including investment banks), insurance companies, investment companies, similar entities that provide financial services to the public, and investment funds (including hedge and private equity funds).

59. Other activities that are ancillary to the activities specified in paragraphs (56) through (58).

Statistical Assistance:

60. Compiling data for use in statistical studies.

61. Other activities similar to those specified in paragraph (60).

Staffing and Recruiting:

62. Providing staffing support that includes creating job announcements, determining eligibility, evaluating qualifications of candidates, conducting background checks on final candidates, verifying references, developing performance evaluation procedures and forms, and conducting exit interviews for departed employees.

63. Coordinating with temporary employment agencies, applicants, and management throughout the recruiting process.

64. Providing information to applicants regarding open positions, the application and recruiting process, and employment policies.

65. Providing administrative support that includes sourcing and processing resumes, arranging interview schedules for open positions, preparing offer letters, and entering new employee information into the human resource system.

66. Establishing and maintaining employee files relating to payroll, performance and other personnel issues.

67. Assisting with new employee orientations and paperwork.

68. Implementing recruiting plan and locating potential candidates by working with professional search firms, colleges, universities and professional associations. Organizing and attending job fairs and other recruitment events.

69. Developing recruiting and marketing materials and assisting in developing and maintaining content for recruiting website.

70. Analyzing recruiting data and review all job analysis, promotion and placement products.

71. Posting job opening advertisements in appropriate markets through publications, journals and other media.

72. Managing company-wide job postings and employee referral program.

73. Administering a compensation policy, including grading and determining salary ranges for positions.

74. Other activities similar to those specified in paragraphs (62) through (73).

Training and Employee Development:

75. Assisting in training of personnel including assessing development and training needs, creating and conducting internal development and training programs and communicating training opportunities to personnel.

76. Arranging for management training on employment law compliance, employer liability avoidance, interviewing, hiring, terminations, promotions, performance reviews, safety, and sexual harassment.

77. Developing and implementing plans regarding career-development and succession.

78. Developing and implementing a job evaluation process including procedures and forms.

79. Other activities similar to those specified in paragraphs (75) through (78).

Benefits:

80. Developing and implementing employee compensation and benefits including healthcare, life insurance, 401(k), pension, worker's compensation, unemployment, dental, profit sharing, employee incentive compensation, and employee assistance programs.

81. Providing benchmarking studies for compensation and other benefit programs.

82. Providing guidance and direction to employees regarding elections for benefits, applications for benefits and receipt of benefits (including providing assistance to employees in completing all necessary forms).

83. Arranging annual benefit enrollment meetings and employee benefit seminars.

84. Processing employee benefits inquiries and complaints, and reconciling billing issues.

85. Coordinating with hospitals, physicians, insurers, employees, and beneficiaries to facilitate proper and complete utilization of benefits for all employees.

86. Other activities similar to those specified in paragraphs (80) through (85).

Information and Technology (IT) Services:

87. Supporting company-wide computer systems including those used in connection with operations, accounting, manufacturing, customer service, human resources, payroll, and email.

88. Formulating guidelines with respect to the use of IT systems.

89. Maintaining and repairing IT systems.

90. Providing telecommunications facilities.

91. Providing technical assistance and training to users of computer systems and other information technology devices. Answering questions or resolving technical problems relating to computer systems and other information technology devices in person, via telephone or from remote location. Providing assistance concerning the use of computer hardware and software, including printing, installation, word processing, electronic mail, and operating systems, as well as disaster recovery back-up services.

92. Maintaining and testing existing computer databases (including implementing security measures to safeguard computer databases), but not to include analyzing user needs or developing hardware or software solutions (such as systems integration, website design, writing computer programs, modifying general applications software, or recommending the purchase of commercially available hardware or software).

93. Supporting an organization's existing local area network (LAN), wide area network (WAN), and Internet system or a segment of a network system, regular maintenance of network hardware and software, monitoring network to ensure network availability to all system users and performing necessary maintenance to support network availability, supervising other network support and client server specialists (including implementing network security measures), but not to include analyzing user needs or developing hardware or software solutions (such as systems integration, website design, writing computer programs, modifying general applications software, or recommending commercially available software).

94. Other activities similar to those specified in paragraphs (87) through (93).

Legal Services:

95. General legal services performed on behalf of the taxpayer by in-house legal counsel, including but not limited to, drafting, negotiating and review of contracts or agreements, legal documents, and opinions, representation and advocacy before courts, administrative agencies, arbitrators, legislatures, or other bodies, preparing advice in respect of structuring and reorganization, acquisition, and divestment transactions, and maintaining corporate books and records. Support and administrative functions associated with the above activities (legal research, secretarial, filing and document retrieval, etc.).

96. Other activities similar to those specified in paragraph (95).

Insurance Claims Management:

97. Securing insurance coverage for general, product, and worker's compensation liability, property loss, business interruption, and other business risks.

98. Coordinating with third party insurers, with respect to insurance policies, including preparing claims for submission to such third party insurers.

99. Other activities similar to those specified in paragraphs (97) and (98).

Purchasing:

100. Planning and executing procurement of services and material pursuant to company standard for support functions.

101. Other activities similar to those specified in paragraph (100).

SECTION 4. APPLICATION

The services cost method (SCM) as set forth in Temp. Treas. Reg. § 1.482–9T(b) evaluates whether the price for covered services, as defined, is arm's length by reference to the total services costs with no markup. Two categories of covered services are eligible for the SCM. The first category, specified covered services, is described in Temp. Treas. Reg. § 1.482–9T(b)(i) and is limited to services that are described in this revenue procedure. The second category, low margin covered services, is not described in this revenue procedure.

SECTION 5. EFFECTIVE DATE

This revenue procedure is generally effective for taxable years beginning after December 31, 2007. Taxpayers may elect to apply retroactively the provisions of Section 1.482–9T of the temporary regulations to certain taxable years. See Temp. Treas. Reg. §1.482–9T(n)(1). In the case of a valid election, this revenue procedure would also apply to the taxable years subject to such an election.

SECTION 6. REQUEST FOR COMMENTS

The Treasury Department and the IRS request further comments from interested persons on the listing contained in this revenue procedure. The revenue procedure is intended to be an evolving list of services that are eligible for the SCM. The Treasury Department and the IRS contemplate issuing updates as appropriate, including a further revision of the revenue procedure to coincide with the end of the one-year transition period and in response to comments received on the temporary regulations. Comments are solicited on the categories and listed activities in the revenue procedure, possible additions, and other revisions. For example, comments are solicited whether warehousing and other functions that support distribution should be eligible for the SCM in light of Temp. Treas. Reg. §1.482–9T(b)(3)(ii)(E) (reselling, distribution ineligible for SCM).

Written comments may be submitted to CC:INTL:Br6 (Rev. Proc. 2007–13), room 4607, Internal Revenue Service, P.O. Box 7604, Ben Franklin Station, Washington, DC 20224. Submissions may be hand delivered Monday through Friday between the hours of 8 a.m. and 5 p.m. to: CC:INTL:Br6 (Rev. Proc. 2007–13) Courier's desk, Internal Revenue Service, 1111 Constitution Avenue, NW, Washington, DC 20224. Alternatively, taxpayers may submit comments electronically via the following e-mail address: *Notice.Comments@irscounsel.treas.gov*. Please include "Rev. Proc. 2007–13" in the subject line of any electronic communications.

SECTION 7. DRAFTING INFORMATION

The principal authors of this revenue procedure are Thomas A. Vidano and Carol B. Tan of the Office of Associate Chief Counsel (International). For further information regarding this revenue procedure, contact Thomas A. Vidano or Carol B. Tan at (202) 435–5265 (not a toll-free call).

Note. This revenue procedure will be reproduced as the next revision of IRS Publication 1179, General Rules and Specifications for Substitute Forms 1096, 1098, 1099, 5498, W-2G, and 1042-S.

26 CFR 601.602: Forms and instructions.
(Also Part 1, Sections 220, 408, 408A, 529, 530(h), 1441, 6041, 6041A, 6042, 6043, 6044, 6045, 6047, 6049, 6050A, 6050B, 6050D, 6050E, 6050H, 6050J, 6050N, 6050P, 6050Q, 6050R, 6050S, 1.408–5, 1.408–7, 1.408A–7, 1.1441–1 through 1.1441–5, 1.6041–1, 7.6041–1, 1.6042–2, 1.6042–4, 1.6044–2, 1.6044–5, 1.6045–1, 5f.6045–1, 1.6045–2, 1.6045–4, 1.6047–1, 1.6049–4, 1.6049–6, 1.6049–7, 1.6050A–1, 1.6050B–1, 1.6050D–1, 1.6050E–1, 1.6050H–1, 1.6050H–2, 1.6050J–1T, 1.6050N–1, 1.6050P–1.)

Rev. Proc. 2007–15

TABLE OF CONTENTS

Part 1 General Information

Part 1
General Information

Section 1.1 — Overview of Revenue Procedure 2007–15

1.1.1 Purpose

The purpose of this revenue procedure is to set forth the 2006 requirements for:

- Using official Internal Revenue Service (IRS) forms to file information returns with the IRS,
- Preparing acceptable substitutes of the official IRS forms to file information returns with the IRS, and
- Using official or acceptable substitute forms to furnish information to recipients.

1.1.2 Which Forms Are Covered?

This revenue procedure contains specifications for these information returns:

Form	Title
1096	Annual Summary and Transmittal of U.S. Information Returns
1098	Mortgage Interest Statement
1098-C	Contributions of Motor Vehicles, Boats, and Airplanes
1098-E	Student Loan Interest Statement

Form	Title
1098-T	Tuition Statement
1099-A	Acquisition or Abandonment of Secured Property
1099-B	Proceeds From Broker and Barter Exchange Transactions
1099-C	Cancellation of Debt
1099-CAP	Changes in Corporate Control and Capital Structure
1099-DIV	Dividends and Distributions
1099-G	Certain Government Payments
1099-H	Health Coverage Tax Credit (HCTC) Advance Payments
1099-INT	Interest Income
1099-LTC	Long-Term Care and Accelerated Death Benefits
1099-MISC	Miscellaneous Income
1099-OID	Original Issue Discount
1099-PATR	Taxable Distributions Received From Cooperatives
1099-Q	Payments From Qualified Education Programs (Under Sections 529 and 530)
1099-R	Distributions From Pensions, Annuities, Retirement or Profit-Sharing Plans, IRAs, Insurance Contracts, etc.
1099-S	Proceeds From Real Estate Transactions
1099-SA	Distributions From an HSA, Archer MSA, or Medicare Advantage MSA
5498	IRA Contribution Information
5498-ESA	Coverdell ESA Contribution Information
5498-SA	HSA, Archer MSA, or Medicare Advantage MSA Information
W-2G	Certain Gambling Winnings
1042-S	Foreign Person's U.S. Source Income Subject to Withholding

1.1.3 Scope

For purposes of this revenue procedure, a substitute form or statement is one that is not printed by the IRS. For a substitute form or statement to be acceptable to the IRS, it must conform to the official form or the specifications outlined in this revenue procedure. Do not submit any substitute forms or statements listed above to the IRS for approval. Privately printed forms may not state, "This is an IRS approved form."

Filers making payments to certain recipients during a calendar year are required by the Internal Revenue Code (the Code) to file information returns with the IRS for these payments. These filers must also provide this information to their recipients. In some cases, this also applies to payments received. See *Part 4* for specifications that apply to recipient statements (generally Copy B).

In general, section 6011 of the Code contains requirements for filers of information returns. A filer must file information returns on magnetic media, through electronic media, or on paper. A filer who is required to file 250 or more information returns of any one type during a calendar year must file those returns by magnetic media or electronic media.

Although not required, small volume filers (fewer than 250 returns during a calendar year) may file the forms on magnetic media or electronically. See the legal requirements for filing information returns (and providing a copy to a payee) in the 2006 General Instructions for Forms 1099, 1098, 5498, and W-2G and the 2006 Instructions for Form 1042-S. In addition, see

Revenue Procedure 2006–33 published as Publication 1220, *Specifications for Filing Forms 1098, 1099, 5498, and W-2G Electronically or Magnetically.*

1.1.4 For More Information

The IRS prints and provides the forms on which various payments must be reported. Alternatively, filers may prepare substitute copies of these IRS forms and use such forms to report payments to the IRS.

- For copies of the official forms and instructions, call our toll-free number at 1–800–TAX–FORM (1–800–829–3676).
- The IRS operates a central call site to answer questions related to information returns, penalties, and backup withholding. The hours of operation are Monday through Friday from 8:30 a.m. to 4:30 p.m., Eastern time. For your convenience, you may call the toll-free number, 1–866–455–7438. You may still use the original telephone number, 304–263–8700 (not toll-free). For TTY/TDD equipment, call 304–267–3367 (not toll-free). The call site can also be reached by email at *mccirp@irs.gov*.
- For other tax information related to business returns or accounts, call 1–800–829–4933. If you have access to TTY/TDD equipment, call 1–800–829–4059 to ask tax account questions or to order forms and publications.

1.1.5 What's New

The following changes have been made to this year's Revenue Procedure:

- Form W-2G: The American Jobs Creation Act of 2004 Section 419 (P.L. 108–357) exempted certain types of pari-mutuel winnings from withholding and reporting after October 22, 2004. See Foreign Persons in the W-2 instructions for these exemptions relating to live dog racing and horse racing.
- Form 1098-C: New boxes 6a, 6b, and 6c have been added to comply with the new reporting requirements added by the Gulf Opportunity Zone Act of 2005. New box 7 has been added to Form 1098-C to allow this form to be used as the contemporaneous written acknowledgment under section 170(f)(8) for a qualified vehicle with a claimed value of at least $250 but not more than $500.
- Form 1098-T: Box 3 has been revised to alert students that institutions have changed their reporting method as required under new Revenue Procedure 2005–50 which is available on page 272 of Internal Revenue Bulletin 2005–32 at *www.irs.gov/pub/irs-irbs/irb05–32.pdf*.
- Form 1099-INT: Amendments to section 6049 have added two new items of reportable interest income. Section 1303 of the Energy Tax Incentives Act of 2005 added new section 54 that allows for a credit to holders of clean renewable energy bonds. The Gulf Opportunity Act of 2005 added new section 1400N that allows a credit to holders of Gulf bonds. Both new items are treated as interest income as required by new section 6049(d)(8) and are reported on Form 1099-INT, Interest income. Section 502 of the Tax Increase Prevention and Reconciliation Act of 2006 amended section 6049(d) and now requires the reporting of certain tax-exempt interest. New boxes will be required to meet this new reporting requirement.
- Form 1099-R: The title of box 5 has been revised to include the addition of the reporting of the basis of distributions from designated Roth accounts. The untitled box to the left of box 10 has been reserved for the reporting of the first year of the 5-year period that is one of the conditions for a qualified designated Roth account distribution. Please note that the following changes have been made to the Specific Instructions for Form 1099-R. Box 2a Taxable Amount: The reporting instructions have been changed for distributions under section 408(d)(5). The Designated Roth account distributions: Section 402, which was added by the Economic Growth and Tax Reconciliation Act of 2001, provides that a participant in a section 401(k) plan or a section 403(b) salary reduction agreement that includes a Roth contribution program may elect to make designated Roth contributions to the plan or program in lieu of elective deferrals. As a result of these changes, a new distribution code has been added to report these distributions, Code B-Designated Roth distribution.
- Form 5498: The following changes have been made to the Specific Instructions for Form 5498. Instructions for the reporting of an account closure have added to the discussion of

an IRA revocation. A caution has been added to remind filers that Form 5498 is required to be filed even after required minimum distributions or other payments have started. Section 2 of the Heroes Earned Retirement Opportunities (HERO) Act of 2006 amended section 219(f) and allows combat pay that is excluded under section 112 to be included in compensation for determining the amounts that may be contributed to both traditional and Roth IRAs. These rules will be applied retroactively to allow contributions for tax years 2004 and 2005. For the special reporting rules, see page R–13 of the 1099-R instructions.

Section 1.2 — General Requirements for Acceptable Substitute Forms 1096, 1098, 1099, 5498, W-2G, and 1042-S

1.2.1 Introduction

Paper substitutes for Form 1096 and Copy A of Forms 1098, 1099, 5498, W-2G, and 1042-S that totally conform to the specifications listed in this revenue procedure may be privately printed and filed as returns with the IRS. The reference to the Department of the Treasury — Internal Revenue Service should be included on all such forms.

If you are uncertain of any specification and want it clarified, you may submit a letter citing the specification, stating your understanding and interpretation of the specification, and enclosing an example of the form (if appropriate) to:

Internal Revenue Service
Attn: Substitute Forms Program
SE:W:CAR:MP:T:T:SP
1111 Constitution Ave., NW
Room 6406
Washington, DC 20224

Note. Allow at least 30 days for the IRS to respond.

You may also contact the Substitute Forms Program via e-mail at **taxforms@irs.gov*. Please enter "Substitute Forms" on the Subject Line.

Forms 1096, 1098, 1099, 5498, W-2G, and 1042-S are subject to annual review and possible change. Therefore, filers are cautioned against overstocking supplies of privately printed substitutes. The specifications contained in this revenue procedure apply to 2006 forms only.

1.2.2 Copy A Specifications

Proposed substitutes of Copy A must be an exact replica of the official IRS form with respect to layout and content. Proposed substitutes for Copy A that do not conform to the specifications in this revenue procedure are not acceptable. Further, if you file such forms with the IRS, you may be subject to a penalty for failure to file a correct information return under section 6721 of the Code. Generally, the penalty is $50 for each return where such failure occurs (up to $250,000). No IRS office is authorized to allow deviations from this revenue procedure.

Caution: Overuse of proportional fonts may cause you to be subject to penalties and delays in processing.

1.2.3 Copy B and Copy C Specifications

Copies B and Copies C of the following forms must contain the information in *Part 4* to be considered a "statement" or "official form" under the applicable provisions of the Code. The format of this information is at the discretion of the filer with the exception of the location of the tax year, form number, form name, and the information for composite Form 1099 statements as outlined under *Section 4.2.*

Copy B, of the forms below, are for the following recipients.

Form	Recipient
1098	For Payer
1098-C	For Donor
1098-E; 1099-A	For Borrower
1098-T	For Student
1099-C	For Debtor
1099-CAP	For Shareholder
1099-LTC	For Policyholder
1099-R; W-2G	Indicates that these forms may require Copy B to be attached to the federal income tax return.
1099-S	For Transferor
All other Forms 1099; 1042-S	For Recipient
5498; 5498-SA	For Participant
5498-ESA	For Beneficiary

Copy C of the following forms are:

Form	Recipient
1098-C	For Donor's Records
1099-CAP	For Corporation
1099-LTC	For Insured
1099-R	For Recipient's Records
All other Forms 1099	See *Section 4.4.2*
5498-ESA	For Trustee
W-2G	For Winner's Records

Note. On Copy C, Form 1099-LTC, you may reverse the locations of the policyholder's and the insured's name, street address, city, state, and ZIP code for easier mailing.

Section 1.3 — Definitions

1.3.1 Form Recipient

Form recipient means the person to whom you are required by law to furnish a copy of the official form or information statement. The form recipient may be referred to by different names on various Forms 1099 and related forms ("payer," "borrower," "student," "debtor," "policyholder," "insured," "transferor," "recipient," "participant," "donor," or, in the case of Form W-2G, the "winner"). See *Section 1.2.3,* earlier.

1.3.2 Filer

Filer means the person or organization required by law to file a form listed in *Section 1.1.2* with the IRS. As outlined earlier, a filer may be a payer, creditor, recipient of mortgage or student loan interest payments, educational institution, broker, barter exchange, person reporting real estate transactions, trustee or issuer of any individual retirement arrangement or medical savings account, lender who acquires an interest in secured property or who has reason to know that the property has been abandoned, or certain donees of motor vehicles, boats, and airplanes.

1.3.3 Substitute Form

Substitute form means a paper substitute of Copy A of an official form listed in *Section 1.1.2* that totally conforms to the provisions in this revenue procedure.

1.3.4 Substitute Form Recipient Statement

Substitute form recipient statement means a paper statement of the information reported on a form listed in *Section 1.1.2.* This statement must be furnished to a person (form recipient), as defined under the applicable provisions of the Code and the applicable regulations.

1.3.5 Composite Substitute Statement

Composite substitute statement means one in which two or more required statements (for example, Forms 1099-INT and 1099-DIV) are furnished to the recipient on one document. However, each statement must be designated separately and must contain all the requisite Form 1099 information except as provided under *Section 4.2.* A composite statement may not be filed with the IRS.

Part 2
Specifications for Substitute Forms 1096 and Copies A of Forms 1098, 1099, and 5498 (All Filed with the IRS)

Section 2.1 — Specifications

2.1.1 General Requirements

Form identifying numbers (for example, 9191 for Form 1099-DIV) must be printed in non-reflective black carbon-based ink in print positions 15 through 19 using an OCR A font. The check boxes to the right of the form identifying numbers must be 10-point boxes. The "VOID" checkbox is in print position 25. The "CORRECTED" check box is in position 33. Measurements are made from the left edge of the paper, not including the perforated strip. See *Exhibits E* and *N.*

The substitute form must be an exact replica of the official IRS form with respect to layout and content. To determine the correct form measurements, see *Exhibits A* through *Z* at the end of this publication.

Hot wax and cold carbon spots are not permitted on any of the internal form plies. These spots are permitted on the back of a mailer top envelope ply.

Use of chemical transfer paper for Copy A is acceptable.

The Government Printing Office (GPO) symbol must be deleted.

2.1.2 Color and Paper Quality

Color and paper quality for Copy A (cut sheets and continuous pinfeed forms) as specified by JCP Code 0–25, dated November 29, 1978, must be white 100% bleached chemical wood, optical character recognition (OCR) bond produced in accordance with the following specifications.

Note. Reclaimed fiber in any percentage is permitted provided the requirements of this standard are met.

- Acidity: Ph value, average, not less than. 4.5
- Basis Weight: 17 x 22-500 cut sheets 18-20
- Metric equivalent–g/m^2 75

  A tolerance of ±5 pct. is allowed.

- Stiffness: Average, each direction, not less than-milligrams 50
- Tearing strength: Average, each direction, not less than-grams 40
- Opacity: Average, not less than-percent 82
- Thickness: Average-inch 0.0038
- Metric equivalent-mm.. 0.097

  A tolerance of +0.0005 inch (0.0127 mm) is allowed. Paper cannot vary more than 0.0004 inch (0.0102 mm) from one edge to the other.
- Porosity: Average, not less than-seconds 10
- Finish (smoothness): Average, each side-seconds..................... 20-55
- For information only, the Sheffield equivalent-units.................. 170-100
- Dirt: Average, each side, not to exceed-parts per million 8

2.1.3 Chemical Transfer Paper

Chemical transfer paper is permitted for Copy A only if the following standards are met:

- Only chemically backed paper is acceptable for Copy A. Front and back chemically treated paper cannot be processed properly by machine.
- Carbon-coated forms are not permitted.
- Chemically transferred images must be black.

All copies must be clearly legible. Hot wax and cold carbon spots are not permitted for Copy A. Interleaved carbon should be black and must be of good quality to assure legibility on all copies and to avoid smudging. Fading must be minimized to assure legibility.

2.1.4 Printing

All print on Copy A of Forms 1098, 1099, 5498, and the print on Form 1096 above the statement, "Return this entire page to the Internal Revenue Service. Photocopies are not acceptable." must be in Flint J–6983 red OCR dropout ink or an exact match. However, the four-digit form identifying number must be in nonreflective carbon-based black ink in OCR A font.

The shaded areas of any substitute form should generally correspond to the format of the official form.

The printing for the Form 1096 statement and the following text may be in any shade or tone of black ink. Black ink should only appear on the lower part of the reverse side of Form 1096, where it will not bleed through and interfere with scanning.

Note. The instructions on the front and back of Form 1096, which include filing addresses, must be printed.

Separation between fields must be 0.1 inch.

Except for Form 1099-R and 1099-MISC, the numbered captions are printed as solid with no shaded background.

Other printing requirements are discussed below.

2.1.5 OCR Specifications

The contractor must initiate or have a quality control program to assure OCR ink density. Readings will be made when printed on approved 20 lb. white OCR bond with a reflectance of not less than 80%. Black ink must not have a reflectance greater than 15%. These readings are based on requirements of the "Scan-Optics Series 9000" Optical Scanner using Flint J–6983 red OCR dropout ink or an exact match.

The following testers and ranges are acceptable:

- *MacBeth PCM-II.* The tested Print Contrast Signal (PCS) values when using the MacBeth PCM-II tester on the "C" scale must range from .01 minimum to .06 maximum.
- *Kidder 082A.* The tested PCS values when using the Kidder 082A tester on the Infra Red (IR) scale must range from .12 minimum to .21 maximum. White calibration disc must be 100%. Sensitivity must be set at one (1).
- *Alternative testers.* Alternative testers must be approved by the Government so that tested PCS values can be established. You may obtain approval by writing to the following address:

  Commissioner of Internal Revenue
  Attn: SE:W:CAR:MP:P:B:T
  Business Publishing – Tax Products
  1111 Constitution Ave., NW
  Washington, DC 20224

2.1.6 Typography

Type must be substantially identical in size and shape to the official form. All rules are either 1/2-point or 3/4-point. Rules must be identical to those on the official IRS form.

Note. The form identifying number must be nonreflective carbon-based black ink in OCR A font.

2.1.7 Dimensions

Generally, three Forms 1098, 1099, or 5498 (Copy A) are contained on a single page, 8 inches wide (without any snap-stubs and/or pinfeed holes) by 11 inches deep.

Exceptions. Forms 1098-C, 1099-B, 1099-DIV, 1099-MISC, 1099-R, and 1042-S contain two documents per page.

There is a .33 inch top margin from the top of the corrected box, and a .25 inch right margin. There is a 1/32 (0.0313) inch tolerance for the right margin. If the right and top margins are properly aligned, the left margin for all forms will be correct. All margins must be free of print. See *Exhibits A* through *Z* in this publication for the correct form measurements.

These measurements are constant for all Forms 1098, 1099, and 5498. These measurements are shown only once in this publication, on Form 1098 (Exhibit B). Exceptions to these measurements are shown on the rest of the exhibits.

The depth of the individual trim size of each form on a page must be 3 2/3 inches, the same depth as the official form.

Exceptions. The depth of Forms 1098-C, 1099-B, 1099-DIV, 1099-MISC, 1099-R, and 1042-S is 5 1/2 inches.

2.1.8 Perforation

Copy A (three per page; two per page for Forms 1098-C, 1099-B, 1099-DIV, 1099-MISC, 1099-R, and 1042-S) of privately printed continuous substitute forms must be perforated at each 11" page depth. No perforations are allowed between the 3 2/3" forms (5 1/2" for Forms 1098-C, 1099-B, 1099-DIV, 1099-MISC, or 1099-R) on a single copy page of Copy A.

The words "Do Not Cut or Separate Forms on This Page" must be printed in red dropout ink (as required by form specifications) between the three forms (two for Forms 1098-C, 1099-B, 1099-DIV, 1099-MISC, or 1099-R).

Note. Perforations are required between all the other individual copies (Copies B and C, and Copies 1 and 2 for Forms 1099-R and 1099-MISC, and Copy D for Forms 1098-C, 1099-LTC and 1099-R) in the set.

2.1.9 What To Include

You must include the OMB Number on Copies A and Form 1096 in the same location as on the official form.

The words "For Privacy Act and Paperwork Reduction Act Notice, see the 2006 General Instructions for Forms 1099, 1098, 5498, and W-2G" must be printed on Copy A; "For more information and the Privacy Act and Paperwork Reduction Act Notice, see the 2006 General Instructions for Forms 1099, 1098, 5498, and W-2G" must be printed on Form 1096.

A postal indicia may be used if it meets the following criteria:

- It is printed in the OCR ink color prescribed for the form, and
- No part of the indicia is within one print position of the scannable area.

The printer's symbol (GPO) must not be printed on substitute Copy A. Instead, the employer identification number (EIN) of the forms printer must be entered in the bottom margin on the face of each individual form of Copy A, or on the bottom margin on the back of each Form 1096.

The Catalog Number (Cat. No.) shown on the 2006 forms is used for IRS distribution purposes and need not be printed on any substitute forms.

The form must not contain the statement "IRS approved" or any similar statement.

Section 2.2 — Instructions for Preparing Paper Forms That Will Be Filed with the IRS

2.2.1 Recipient Information

The form recipient's name, street address, city, state, ZIP code, and telephone number (if required) should be typed or machine printed in black ink in the same format as shown on the official IRS form. The city, state, and ZIP code must be on the same line.

The following rules apply to the form recipient's name(s):

- The name of the appropriate form recipient must be shown on the first or second name line in the area provided for the form recipient's name.
- No descriptive information or other name may precede the form recipient's name.
- Only one form recipient's name may appear on the first name line of the form.
- If the multiple recipients' names are required on the form, enter on the first name line the recipient name that corresponds to the recipient taxpayer identification number (TIN) shown on the form. Place the other form recipients' names on the second name line (only 2 name lines are allowable).

Because certain states require that trust accounts be provided in a different format, generally filers should provide information returns reflecting payments to trust accounts with the:

- Trust's employer identification number (EIN) in the recipient's TIN area,
- Trust's name on the recipient's first name line, and
- Name of the trustee on the recipient's second name line.

Although handwritten forms will be accepted, the IRS prefers that filers type or machine print data entries. Also, filers should insert data in the middle of blocks well separated from other printing and guidelines, and take measures to guarantee clear, dark black, sharp images. Carbon copies and photocopies are not acceptable.

2.2.2 Account Number Box

Use the account number box on all Forms 1098, 1099, 5498, and W-2G for an account number designation when required by the official IRS form. The account number is required if you have multiple accounts for a recipient for whom you are filing more than one information return of the same type. Additionally, the IRS encourages you to include the recipients' account number on paper forms if your system of records uses the account number rather than the name or TIN for identification purposes. Also, the IRS will include the account number in future notices to you about backup withholding. If you use window envelopes and a reduced rate to mail statements to recipients, be sure the account number does not appear in the window. Otherwise, the Postal Service may not accept them for mailing.

Exception. Form 1098-T can have third party provider information.

2.2.3 Specifications and Restrictions

Machine-printed forms should be printed using a 6 lines/inch option, and should be printed in 10 pitch pica (10 print positions per inch) or 12 pitch elite (12 print positions per inch). Proportional spaced fonts are unacceptable.

Substitute forms prepared in continuous or strip form must be burst and stripped to conform to the size specified for a single sheet before they are filed with the IRS. The size specified does not include pin feed holes. Pin feed holes must not be present on forms filed with the IRS.

Do not:

- Use a felt tip marker. The machine used to "read" paper forms generally cannot read this ink type.
- Use dollar signs ($), ampersands (&), asterisks (*), commas (,), or other special characters in the numbered money boxes.
  Exception. Use decimal points to indicate dollars and cents (for example, 2000.00 is acceptable).
- Use apostrophes ('), asteriks (*), or other special characters on the payee name line.
- Fold Forms 1096, 1098, 1099, or 5498 mailed to the IRS. Mail these forms flat in an appropriately sized envelope or box. Folded documents cannot be readily moved through the machine used in IRS processing.
- Staple Forms 1096 to the transmitted returns. Any staple holes near the return code number may impair the IRS's ability to machine scan the type of documents.
- Type other information on Copy A.
- Cut or separate the individual forms on the sheet of forms of Copy A (except Forms W-2G).

2.2.4 Where To File

Mail completed paper forms to the IRS service center shown in the Instructions for Form 1096 and in the 2006 General Instructions for Forms 1099, 1098, 5498, and W-2G. Specific information needed to complete the forms mentioned in this revenue procedure are given in the specific form instructions. A chart is included in the 2006 General Instructions for Forms 1099, 1098, 5498, and W-2G giving a quick guide to which form must be filed to report a particular payment.

Part 3
Specifications for Substitute Form W-2G (Filed with the IRS)

Section 3.1 — General

3.1.1 Purpose

The following specifications give the format requirements for substitute Form W-2G (Copy A only), which is filed with the IRS.

A filer may use a substitute Form W-2G to file with the IRS (referred to as "substitute Copy A"). The substitute form must be an exact replica of the official form with respect to layout and content.

Section 3.2 — Specifications for Copy A of Form W-2G

3.2.1 Substitute Form W-2G (Copy A)

You must follow these specifications when printing substitute Copy A of the Form W-2G.

Item	Substitute Form W-2G (Copy A)
Paper Color and Quality	Paper for Copy A must be white chemical wood bond, or equivalent, 20 pound (basis 17 x 22-500), plus or minus 5 percent. The paper must consist substantially of bleached chemical wood pulp. It must be free from unbleached or ground wood pulp or post-consumer recycled paper. It also must be suitably sized to accept ink without feathering.
Ink Color and Quality	All printing must be in a high quality non gloss black ink.
Typography	The type must be substantially identical in size and shape to the official form. All rules on the document are either 1/2 point (.007 inch), 1 point (0.015 inch), or 3 point (0.045). Vertical rules must be parallel to the left edge of the document, horizontal rules to the top edge.
Dimensions	The official form is 8 inches wide x 3 2/3 inches deep, exclusive of a 2/3 inch snap stub on the left side of the form. Any substitute Copy A must be the same dimensions. The snap feature is not required on substitutes. All margins must be free of print. The top and right margins must be 1/4 inch plus or minus .0313. If the top and right margins are properly aligned, the left margin for all forms will be correct. If the substitute forms are in continuous or strip form, they must be burst and stripped to conform to the size specified for a single form.
Hot Wax and Cold Carbon Spots	Hot wax and cold carbon spots are not permitted on any of the internal form plies. These spots are permitted on the back of a mailer top envelope ply. Interleaved carbons, if used, should be black and of good quality to avoid smudging.
Printer's Symbol	The Government Printing Office (GPO) symbol must not be printed on substitute Forms W-2G. Instead, the employer identification number (EIN) of the forms printer must be printed in the bottom margin on the face of each individual Copy A on a sheet. The form must not contain the statement "IRS approved" or any similar statement.
Catalog Number	The Catalog Number (Cat. No.) shown on Form W-2G is used for IRS distribution purposes and need not be printed on any substitute forms.

Part 4
Substitute Statements to Form Recipients and Form Recipient Copies

Section 4.1 — Specifications

4.1.1 Introduction

If you do not use the official IRS form to furnish statements to recipients, you must furnish an acceptable substitute statement. To be acceptable, your substitute statement must comply with the rules in this section. If you are furnishing a substitute form, see Regulations sections 1.6042–4, 1.6044–5, 1.6049–6, and 1.6050N–1 to determine how the following statements must be provided to recipients for most Forms 1099-DIV and 1099-INT, all Forms 1099-OID and 1099-PATR, and Form 1099-MISC or 1099-S for royalties. Generally, information returns may be furnished electronically with the consent of the recipient. See Section 4.5.1.

Note. A trustee of a grantor-type trust may choose to file Forms 1099 and furnish a statement to the grantor under Regulations sections 1.671–4(b)(2)(iii) and (b)(3)(ii). The statement required by those regulations is not subject to the requirements outlined in this section.

4.1.2 Substitute Statements to Recipients for Certain Forms 1099-INT and 1099-DIV, and for Forms 1099-OID and 1099-PATR

The rules in this section apply to Form 1099-INT (except for interest reportable under section 6041), 1099-DIV (except for section 404(k) dividends), 1099-OID, and 1099-PATR only. You may furnish form recipients with Copy B of the official Form 1099 or a substitute Form 1099 (form recipient statement) if it contains the same language as the official IRS form (such as aggregate amounts paid to the form recipient, any backup withholding, the name, address, and TIN of the person making the return, and any other information required by the official form). Except for state income tax withholding information, information not required by the official form should not be included on the substitute form.

You may enter a total of the individual accounts listed on the form only if they have been paid by the same payer. For example, if you are listing interest paid on several accounts by one financial institution on Form 1099-INT, you may also enter the total interest amount. You may also enter a date next to the corrected box if that box is checked.

A substitute form recipient statement for Forms 1099-INT, 1099-DIV, 1099-OID, or 1099-PATR must comply with the following requirements:

(1) Box captions and numbers that are applicable must be clearly identified, using the same wording and numbering as on the official form.
Note. For Form 1099-INT, if box 3 is not on your substitute form, you may drop "not included in box 3" from the box 1 caption.

(2) The form recipient statement (Copy B) must contain all applicable form recipient instructions provided on the front and back of the official IRS form. You may provide those instructions on a separate sheet of paper.

(3) The form recipient statement must contain the following in bold and conspicuous type:
This is important tax information and is being furnished to the Internal Revenue Service. If you are required to file a return, a negligence penalty or other sanction may be imposed on you if this income is taxable and the IRS determines that it has not been reported.

(4) The box caption **"Federal income tax withheld"** must be in boldface type on the form recipient statement.

(5) The form recipient statement must contain the Office of Management and Budget (OMB) number as shown on the official IRS form. See *Part 5.*

(6) The form recipient statement must contain the tax year (for example, 2006), form number (for example, Form 1099-INT), and form name (for example, Interest Income) of the official IRS Form 1099. This information must be displayed prominently together in one area of the statement. For example, the tax year, form number, and form name could be shown in the upper right part of the statement. Each copy must be appropriately labeled (such as Copy B, For Recipient). See *Section 4.4* for applicable labels and arrangement of assembly of forms.
Note. Do not include the words "Substitute for" or "In lieu of" on the form recipient statement.

(7) Layout and format of the form is at the discretion of the filer. However, the IRS encourages the use of boxes so that the statement has the appearance of a form and can be easily distinguished from other non-tax statements.

(8) Each recipient statement of Forms 1099-DIV, 1099-INT, 1099-OID, and 1099-PATR must include the direct access telephone number of an individual who can answer questions about the statement. Include that telephone number conspicuously anywhere on the recipient statement.

(9) Until new regulations are issued, the IRS will not assess penalties for use of a logo (for example, the name of the payer in any typeface, font, or style, and/or a symbolic icon) or slogan on a recipient statement if the logo or slogan is used by the payer in the ordinary course

of its trade or business. In addition, use of the logo or slogan must not make it less likely for a reasonable payee to recognize the importance of the statement for tax reporting purposes.

(10) A mutual fund family may state separately on one document (for example, one piece of paper) the dividend income earned by a recipient from each fund within the family of funds as required by Form 1099-DIV. However, each fund and its earnings must be stated separately. The form must contain an instruction to the recipient that each fund's dividends and name, not the name of the mutual fund family, must be reported on the recipient's tax return. The form cannot contain an aggregate total of all funds. In addition, a mutual fund family may furnish a single statement (as a single filer) for Forms 1099-INT, 1099-DIV, and 1099-OID information. Each fund and its earnings must be stated separately. The form must contain an instruction to the recipient that each fund's earnings and name, not the name of the mutual fund family, must be reported on the recipient's tax return. The form cannot contain an aggregate total of all funds.

4.1.3 Substitute Statements to Recipients for Certain Forms 1098, 1099, 5498, and W-2G

Statements to form recipients for Forms 1098, 1098-C, 1098-E, 1098-T, 1099-A, 1099-B, 1099-C, 1099-CAP, 1099-G, 1099-H, 1099-LTC, 1099-MISC, 1099-Q, 1099-R, 1099-S, 1099-SA, 5498, 5498-ESA, 5498-SA, W-2G, 1099-DIV (only for section 404(k) dividends reportable under section 6047), and 1099-INT (only for interest of $600 or more made in the course of a trade or business reportable under section 6041) can be copies of the official forms or an acceptable substitute.

Caution. The IRS does not require a donee to use Form 1098-C as the written acknowledgment for contributions of motor vehicles, boats, and airplanes. However, if you choose to use copies of Form 1098-C or an acceptable substitute as the written acknowledgment, then you must follow the requirements of this section 4.1.3.

To be acceptable, a substitute form recipient statement must meet the following requirements.

(1) The tax year, form number, and form name must be the same as the official form and must be displayed prominently together in one area on the statement. For example, they may be shown in the upper right part of the statement.

(2) The filer's and the form recipient's identifying information required on the official IRS form must be included.

(3) Each substitute recipient statement for Forms W-2G, 1098, 1098-C, 1098-E, 1098-T, 1099-A, 1099-B, 1099-CAP, 1099-DIV, 1099-G (excluding state and local income tax refunds), 1099-H, 1099-INT, 1099-LTC, 1099-MISC (excluding fishing boat proceeds), 1099-OID, 1099-PATR, 1099-Q, and 1099-S must include the direct access telephone number of an individual who can answer questions about the statement. Include the telephone number conspicuously anywhere on the recipient statement. Although not required, payers reporting on Forms 1099-C, 1099-R, 1099-SA, 5498, 5498-ESA, and 5498-SA are encouraged to furnish telephone numbers.

(4) All applicable money amounts and information, including box numbers, required to be reported to the form recipient must be titled on the form recipient statement in substantially the same manner as those on the official IRS form. The box caption "Federal income tax withheld" must be in boldface type on the form recipient statement.

Exception. If you are reporting a payment as "Other income" in box 3 of Form 1099-MISC, you may substitute appropriate language for the box title. For example, for payments of accrued wages and leave to a beneficiary of a deceased employee, you might change the title of box 3 to "Beneficiary payments" or something similar.

Note. You cannot make this change on Copy A.

Note. If federal income tax is withheld and shown on Form 1099-R or W-2G, Copy B and Copy C must be furnished to the recipient. If federal income tax is not withheld, only Copy C of Form 1099-R and W-2G must be furnished. However, for Form 1099-R, instructions similar to those on the back of the official Copy B and Copy C of Form 1099-R must be furnished to the recipient. For convenience, you may choose to provide both Copies B and C of Form 1099-R to the recipient.

(5) You must provide appropriate instructions to the form recipient similar to those on the official IRS form, to aid in the proper reporting on the form recipient's income tax return. For payments reported on Forms 1099-B, and 1099-CAP, the requirement to include instructions substantially similar to those on the official IRS form may be satisfied by providing form recipients with a single set of instructions for all Forms 1099-B and 1099-CAP statements required to be furnished in a calendar year.

(6) If you use carbonless sets to produce recipient statements, the quality of each copy in the set must meet the following standards:

- All copies must be clearly legible,
- All copies must be able to be photocopied, and
- Fading must not diminish legibility and the ability to photocopy.

In general, black chemical transfer inks are preferred, but other colors are permitted if the above standards are met. Hot wax and cold carbon spots are not permitted on any of the internal form plies. The back of a mailer top envelope ply may contain these spots.

(7) A mutual fund family may state separately on one document (for example, one piece of paper) the Form 1099-B information for a recipient from each fund as required by Form 1099-B. However, the gross proceeds, etc., from each transaction within a fund must be stated separately. The form must contain an instruction to the recipient that each fund's (not the mutual fund family's) name and amount must be reported on the recipient's tax return. The form cannot contain an aggregate total of all funds.

(8) You may use a Uniform Settlement Statement (under the Real Estate Settlement Procedures Act of 1974 (RESPA)) for Form 1099-S. The Uniform Settlement Statement is acceptable as the written statement to the transferor if you include the legend for Form 1099-S in *Section 4.3.2* and indicate which information on the Uniform Settlement Statement is being reported to the IRS on Form 1099-S.

(9) For reporting state income tax withholding and state payments, you may add an additional box(es) to recipient copies as appropriate.

Note. You cannot make this change on Copy A.

(10) On Copy C of Form 1099-LTC, you may reverse the location of the policyholder's and the insured's name, street address, city, state, and ZIP code for easier mailing.

(11) If an institution insurer uses a third party service provider to file Form 1098-T, then in addition to the institution or insurers name, address, and telephone number, the same information may be included for the third party service provider in the space provided on the form.

(12) Logos are permitted on substitute recipient statements for the forms listed in this section *(Section 4.1.3).*

Section 4.2 — Composite Statements

4.2.1 Composite Substitute Statements for Certain Forms 1099-INT, 1099-DIV, 1099-MISC, and 1099-S, and for Forms 1099-OID and 1099-PATR

A composite form recipient statement is permitted for reportable payments of interest, dividends, original issue discount, patronage dividends, and royalties (Forms 1099-INT (except for interest reportable under section 6041), 1099-DIV (except for section 404(k) dividends), 1099-MISC or 1099-S (for royalties only), 1099-OID, or 1099-PATR) when one payer is reporting more than one of these payments during a calendar year to the same form recipient. Generally, do not include any other Form 1099 information (for example, 1098 or 1099-A) on a composite statement with the information required on the forms listed in the preceding sentence.

Exception. A filer may include Form 1099-B information on a composite form with the forms listed above.

Although the composite form recipient statement may be on one sheet, the format of the composite form recipient statement must satisfy the following requirements in addition to the requirements listed earlier in *Section 4.1.2.*

- All information pertaining to a particular type of payment must be located and blocked together on the form and separate from any information covering other types of payments

included on the form. For example, if you are reporting interest and dividends, the Form 1099-INT information must be presented separately from the Form 1099-DIV information.
- The composite form recipient statement must prominently display the tax year, form number, and form name of the official IRS form together in one area at the beginning of each appropriate block of information.
- Any information required by the official IRS forms that would otherwise be repeated in each information block is required to be listed only once in the first information block on the composite form. For example, there is no requirement to report the name of the filer in each information block. This rule does not apply to any money amounts (for example, federal income tax withheld) or to any other information that applies to money amounts.
- A composite statement is an acceptable substitute only if the type of payment and the recipient's tax obligation with respect to the payment are as clear as if each required statement were furnished separately on an official form.

4.2.2 Composite Substitute Statements to Recipients for Forms Specified in Section 4.1.3

A composite form recipient statement for the forms specified in *Section 4.1.3* is permitted when one filer is reporting more than one type of payment during a calendar year to the same form recipient. A composite statement is not allowed for a combination of forms listed in *Section 4.1.3* and forms listed in *Section 4.1.2.*

Exceptions:

- Substitute payments in lieu of dividends reported in Box 8 of Form 1099-MISC may be reported on a composite substitute statement with Form 1099-DIV.
- Form 1099-B information may be reported on a composite form with the forms specified in *Section 4.1.2* as described in *Section 4.2.1.*
- Forms 1099-A and 1099-C transactions, if related, may be combined on Form 1099-C.
- Royalties reported on Form 1099-MISC or 1099-S may be reported on a composite form only with the forms specified in Section 4.1.2.

Although the composite form recipient statement may be on one sheet, the format of the composite form recipient statement must satisfy the requirements listed in *Section 4.2.1* as well as the requirements in *Section 4.1.3.* A composite statement of Forms 1098 and 1099-INT (for interest reportable under section 6049) is not allowed.

Section 4.3 — Required Legends

4.3.1 Required Legends for Forms 1098

Form 1098 recipient statements (Copy B) must contain the following legends:

- Form 1098—

(1) "The information in boxes 1, 2, and 3 is important tax information and is being furnished to the Internal Revenue Service. If you are required to file a return, a negligence penalty or other sanction may be imposed on you if the IRS determines that an underpayment of tax results because you overstated a deduction for this mortgage interest or for these points or because you did not report this refund of interest on your return."

(2) "**Caution.** The amount shown may not be fully deductible by you. Limits based on the loan amount and the cost and value of the secured property may apply. Also, you may only deduct interest to the extent it was incurred by you, actually paid by you, and not reimbursed by another person."

- Form 1098-C:

  Copy B — "In order to take a deduction of more than $500 for this for contribution, you must attach this copy to your federal tax return."

  Copy C — "This information is being furnished to the Internal Revenue Service unless box 7 is checked."

- Form 1098-E — "This is important tax information and is being furnished to the Internal Revenue Service. If you are required to file a return, a negligence penalty or other sanction may be imposed on you if the IRS determines that an underpayment of tax results because you overstated a deduction for student loan interest."

- Form 1098-T — "This is important tax information and is being furnished to the Internal Revenue Service."

4.3.2 Required Legends for Forms 1099 and W-2G

- Forms 1099-A, 1099-C, and 1099-CAP:

  Copy B — "This is important tax information and is being furnished to the Internal Revenue Service. If you are required to file a return, a negligence penalty or other sanction may be imposed on you if taxable income results from this transaction and the IRS determines that it has not been reported."
- Forms 1099-B, 1099-DIV, 1099-G, 1099-INT, 1099-MISC, 1099-OID, 1099-PATR, and 1099-Q:

  Copy B — "This is important tax information and is being furnished to the Internal Revenue Service. If you are required to file a return, a negligence penalty or other sanction may be imposed on you if this income is taxable and the IRS determines that it has not been reported."
- Forms 1099-H:

  Copy B — "This is important tax information and is being furnished to the Internal Revenue Service."
- Form 1099-LTC:

  Copy B — "This is important tax information and is being furnished to the Internal Revenue Service. If you are required to file a return, a negligence penalty or other sanction may be imposed on you if this item is required to be reported and the IRS determines that it has not been reported."

  Copy C — "Copy C is provided to you for information only. Only the policyholder is required to report this information on a tax return."
- Form 1099-R:

  Copy B — "Report this income on your federal tax return. If this form shows federal income tax withheld in box 4, attach this copy to your return."

  Copy C — "This information is being furnished to the Internal Revenue Service."
- Form 1099-S:

  Copy B — "This is important tax information and is being furnished to the Internal Revenue Service. If you are required to file a return, a negligence penalty or other sanction may be imposed on you if this item is required to be reported and the IRS determines that it has not been reported."
- Form 1099-SA:

  Copy B — "This information is being furnished to the Internal Revenue Service."
- Form W-2G:

  Copy B — "This information is being furnished to the Internal Revenue Service. Report this income on your federal tax return. If this form shows federal income tax withheld in box 2, attach this copy to your return."

  Copy C — "This is important tax information and is being furnished to the Internal Revenue Service. If you are required to file a return, a negligence penalty or other sanction may be imposed on you if this income is taxable and the IRS determines that it has not been reported."

4.3.3 Required Legends for Forms 5498

Form 5498 recipient statements (Copy B) must contain the following legends:

- Form 5498 — "This information is being furnished to the Internal Revenue Service."

  Note. If you do not furnish another statement to the participant because no contributions were made for the year, the statement of the fair market value and any required minimum distribution, of the account must contain this legend and a designation of which information is being furnished to the IRS.

- Form 5498-ESA — "The information in boxes 1 and 2 is being furnished to the Internal Revenue Service."
- Form 5498-SA — "The information in boxes 1 through 6 is being furnished to the Internal Revenue Service."

Section 4.4 — Miscellaneous Instructions for Copies B, C, D, 1, and 2

4.4.1 Copies

Copies B, C, and in some cases, D, 1, and 2 are included in the official assembly for the convenience of the filer. You are not legally required to include all these copies with the privately printed substitute forms. Furnishing Copies B and, in some cases, C will satisfy the legal requirement to provide statements of information to form recipients.

Note. If an amount of federal income tax withheld is shown on Form 1099-R or W-2G, Copy B (to be attached to the tax return) and Copy C must be furnished to the recipient. Copy D (Forms 1099-R and W-2G) may be used for filer records. Only Copy A should be filed with the IRS.

4.4.2 Arrangement of Assembly

Copy A ("For Internal Revenue Service Center") of all forms must be on top. The rest of the assembly must be arranged, from top to bottom, as follows.

- Form 1098 — Copy B "For Payer"; Copy C "For Recipient."
- Form 1098-C — Copy B "For Donor"; Copy C "For Donor's Records"; Copy D "For Donee."
- Form 1098-E — Copy B "For Borrower"; Copy C "For Recipient."
- Form 1098-T — Copy B "For Student"; Copy C "For Filer."
- Form 1099-A — Copy B "For Borrower"; Copy C "For Lender."
- Forms 1099-B, 1099-DIV, 1099-G, 1099-H, 1099-INT, 1099-OID, 1099-PATR, 1099-Q, and 1099-SA — Copy B "For Recipient"; Copy C "For Payer."
- Form 1099-C — Copy B "For Debtor"; Copy C "For Creditor."
- Form 1099-CAP — Copy B "For Shareholder"; Copy C "For Corporation."
- Form 1099-LTC — Copy B "For Policyholder"; Copy C "For Insured"; and Copy D "For Payer."
- Form 1099-MISC — Copy 1 "For State Tax Department"; Copy B "For Recipient"; Copy 2 "To be filed with recipient's state income tax return, when required"; and Copy C "For Payer."
- Form 1099-R — Copy 1 "For State, City, or Local Tax Department"; Copy B "Report this income on your federal tax return. If this form shows federal income tax withheld in box 4, attach this copy to your return"; Copy C "For Recipient's Records"; Copy 2 "File this copy with your state, city, or local income tax return, when required"; Copy D "For Payer."
- Form 1099-S — Copy B "For Transferor"; Copy C "For Filer."
- Form 5498 — Copy B "For Participant"; Copy C "For Trustee or Issuer."
- Form 5498-ESA — Copy B "For Beneficiary"; Copy C "For Trustee."
- Form 5498-SA — Copy B "For Participant"; Copy C "For Trustee."
- Form W-2G — Copy 1 "For State Tax Department"; Copy B "Report this income on your federal tax return. If this form shows federal income tax withheld in box 2, attach this copy to your return"; Copy C "For Winner's Records"; Copy 2 "Attach this copy to your state income tax return, if required."; Copy D "For Payer."

4.4.3 Perforations

Perforations are required between forms on all copies except Copy A to make separating the forms easier. (Copy A of Form W-2G may be perforated.)

Section 4.5 — Electronic Delivery of Form 1099 and Form 5498 Payee Statements

4.5.1 Electronic Recipient Statements

If you are required to furnish a written statement (Copy B or an acceptable substitute) to a recipient, then you may furnish the statement electronically instead of on paper. This includes furnishing the statement to recipients of Forms 1098, 1098-E, 1098-T, 1099-A, B, C, CAP, DIV, H, INT, G, LTC, MISC, OID, PATR, Q, R, S, SA, 5498, 5498-ESA, and 5498-SA. It also includes Form W-2G (except for horse and dog racing, jai alai, sweepstakes, wagering pools, and lotteries).

Note. Until further guidance is issued, you can not furnish Form 1098-C electronically.

If you meet the requirements listed below, you are treated as furnishing the statement timely.

Consent

The recipient must consent in the affirmative and not have withdrawn the consent before the statement is furnished. The consent by the recipient must be made electronically in a way that shows that he or she can access the statement in the electronic format in which it will be furnished.

You must notify the recipient of any hardware or software changes prior to furnishing the statement. A new consent to receive the statement electronically is required after the new hardware or software is put into service.

Prior to furnishing the statements electronically, you must provide the recipient a statement with the following statements prominently displayed:

- If the recipient does not consent to receive the statement electronically, a paper copy will be provided.
- The scope and duration of the consent. For example, whether the consent applies to every year the statement is furnished or only for the January 31 immediately following the date of the consent.
- How to obtain a paper copy after giving consent.
- How to withdraw the consent. The consent may be withdrawn at any time by furnishing the withdrawal in writing (electronically or on paper) to the person whose name appears on the statement. Confirmation of the withdrawal also will be in writing (electronically or on paper).
- Notice of termination. The notice must state under what conditions the statements will no longer be furnished to the recipient.
- Procedures to update the recipient's information.
- A description of the hardware and software required to access, print and retain a statement, and a date the statement will no longer be available on the website.

Format, Posting, and Notification

Additionally, you must:

- Ensure the electronic format contains all the required information and complies with the guidelines in this document.
- Post, on or before the January 31 due date, the applicable statement on a website accessible to the recipient through October 15 of that year.
- Inform the recipient, electronically or by mail, of the posting and how to access and print the statement.

For more information, see Regulations section 31.6051–1. For electronic furnishing of Forms 1098-E and 1098-T, see Regulations section 1.6050S–2. For electronic furnishing of Forms 1099-R, 1099-SA, 1099-Q, 5498, 5498-ESA, and 5498-SA, see Notice 2004–10, 2004–6 I.R.B. 433.

Part 5
Additional Instructions for Substitute Forms 1098, 1099, 5498, W-2G, and 1042-S

Section 5.1 — Paper Substitutes for Form 1042-S

5.1.1 Paper Substitutes

Paper substitutes of Copy A for Form 1042-S, *Foreign Person's U.S. Source Income Subject to Withholding*, that totally conform to the specifications contained in this procedure may be privately printed without prior approval from the Internal Revenue Service. Proposed substitutes not conforming to these specifications must be submitted for consideration.

Note. Copies B, C, D, and E of Form 1042-S may contain multiple income entries for the same recipient, that is multiple rows of the top boxes 1-8 of the form.

5.1.2 Time Frame For Submission of Form 1042-S

The request should be submitted by November 15 of the year prior to the year the form is to be used. This is to allow the Service adequate time to respond and the submitter adequate time to make any corrections. These requests should contain a copy of the proposed form, the need for the specific deviation(s), and the number of information returns to be printed.

5.1.3 Revisions

Form 1042-S is subject to annual review and possible change. Withholding agents and form suppliers are cautioned against overstocking supplies of the privately printed substitutes.

5.1.4 Obtaining Copies

Copies of the official form for the reporting year may be obtained from most Service offices. The Service provides only cut sheets (no carbon interleaves) of these forms. Continuous fanfold/pin-fed forms are not provided.

5.1.5 Instructions For Withholding Agents

Instructions for withholding agents:

- Only original copies may be filed with the Service. Carbon copies and reproductions are not acceptable.
- The term "Recipient's U.S. TIN" for an individual means the social security number (SSN) or IRS individual taxpayer identification number (ITIN), consisting of nine digits separated by hyphens as follows: 000–00–0000. For all other recipients, the term means employer identification number (EIN) or qualified intermediary employer identification number (QI-EIN). The QI-EIN designation includes a withholding foreign partnership employer identification number (WP-EIN) and a withholding foreign trust employer identification number (WT-EIN). The EIN and QI-EIN consist of nine digits separated by a hyphen as follows: 00–0000000. The taxpayer identification number (TIN) must be in one of these formats.
- Withholding agents are requested to type or machine print whenever possible, provide quality data entries on the forms (that is, use black ribbon and insert data in the middle of blocks well separated from other printing and guidelines), and take other measures to guarantee a clear, sharp image. Withholding agents are not required, however, to acquire special equipment solely for the purpose of preparing these forms.
- The "VOID," "CORRECTED," and "PRO-RATA BASIS REPORTING" boxes must be printed at the top center of the form under the title and checked, if applicable.
- Substitute forms prepared in continuous or strip form must be burst and stripped to conform to the size specified for a single form before they are filed with the Service. The dimensions are found below. Computer cards are acceptable provided they meet all requirements regarding layout, content, and size.

5.1.6 Substitute Form 1042-S Format Requirements

Property	Substitute Form 1042-S Format Requirements
Printing	Privately printed substitute Forms 1042-S must be exact replicas of the official forms with respect to layout and content. Only the dimensions of the substitute form may differ. The Government Printing Office (GPO) symbol must be deleted. The exact dimensions are found below.
Box Entries	Only one item of income may be represented on the copy submitted to the Service (Copy A). Multiple income items may be shown on copies provided to recipients or retained by withholding agent. All boxes appearing on the official form must be present on the substitute form, with appropriate captions.
Color and Quality of Ink	All printing must be in high quality non-gloss black ink. Bar codes should be free from picks and voids.
Typography	Type must be substantially identical in size and shape to corresponding type on the official form. All rules on the document are either 1 point (0.015") or 3 point (0.045"). Vertical rules must be parallel to the left edge of the document; horizontal rules must be parallel to the top edge.
Carbons	Carbonized forms or "spot carbons" are not permissible. Interleaved carbons, if used, must be of good quality to preclude smudging and should be black.
Assembly	If all five parts are present, the parts of the assembly shall be arranged from top to bottom as follows: Copy A (Original) "for Internal Revenue Service," Copies B, C, and D "for Recipient," and Copy E "for Withholding Agent."
Color Quality of Paper	• Paper for Copy A must be white chemical wood bond, or equivalent, 20 pound (basis 17 x 22–500), plus or minus 5 percent; or offset book paper, 50 pound (basis 25 x 38–500). No optical brighteners may be added to the pulp or paper during manufacture. The paper must consist of principally bleach chemical wood pulp or recycled printed paper. It also must be suitably sized to accept ink without feathering. • Copies B, C, D (for Recipient), and E (For Withholding Agent) are provided in the official assembly solely for the convenience of the withholding agent. Withholding agents may choose the format, design, color, and quality of the paper used for these copies.

Property	Substitute Form 1042-S Format Requirements
Dimensions	• The official form is 8 inches wide x 5 1/2 inches deep, exclusive of a 1/2 inch snap stub on the left side of the form. The snap feature is not required on substitutes. • The width of a substitute Copy A must be a minimum of 7 inches and a maximum of 8 inches, although adherence to the size of the official form is preferred. If the width of substitute Copy A is reduced from that of the official form, the width of each field on the substitute form must be reduced proportionately. The left margin must be 1/2 inch and free of all printing other than that shown on the official form. • The depth of a substitute Copy A must be a minimum of 5 1/6 inches and a maximum of 5 1/2 inches.
Other Copies	Copies B, C, and D must be furnished for the convenience of payees who must send a copy of the form with other federal and state returns they file. Copy E may be used as a withholding agent's record/copy.

Section 5.2 — OMB Requirements for All Forms in This Revenue Procedure

5.2.1 OMB Requirements

The Paperwork Reduction Act (the Act) of 1995 (Public Law 104–13) requires that:

- OMB approves all IRS tax forms that are subject to the Act. Each IRS form contains (in or near the upper right corner) the OMB approval number, if any. (The official OMB numbers may be found on the official IRS printed forms and are also shown on the forms in the exhibits in *Part 6*.)
- Each IRS form (or its instructions) states:

(1) Why the IRS needs the information,
(2) How it will be used, and
(3) Whether or not the information is required to be furnished to the IRS.

This information must be provided to any users of official or substitute IRS forms or instructions.

5.2.2 Substitute Form Requirements

The OMB requirements for substitute IRS forms are:

- Any substitute form or substitute statement to a recipient must show the OMB number as it appears on the official IRS form.
- For Copy A, the OMB number must appear exactly as shown on the official IRS form.
- For any copy other than Copy A, the OMB number must use one of the following formats.

(1) OMB No. XXXX-XXXX (preferred) or
(2) OMB # XXXX-XXXX (acceptable).

5.2.3 Required Explanation to Users

All substitute forms (Copy A only) must state "For Privacy Act and Paperwork Reduction Act Notice, see the 2006 General Instructions for Forms 1099, 1098, 5498, and W-2G." (or "For Privacy Act and Paperwork Reduction Act Notice, see separate instructions." for Copy A of Form 1042-S).

If no instructions are provided to users of your forms, you must furnish them with the exact text of the Privacy Act and Paperwork Reduction Act Notice.

Section 5.3 — Reproducible Copies of Forms

5.3.1 Introduction

You can order official IRS forms and publications 24 hours a day, 7 days a week, by calling 1–800–TAX–FORM (1–800–829–3676). Other ways to get federal tax material include:

- The Internet.
- CD-ROM.
- GPO Superintendent of Documents Bookstores.

Note. Several IRS forms are provided electronically on the IRS home page and on the Federal Tax Forms CD-ROM, but Copy A of Forms 1096, the 1098 series, 1099 series, and 5498 series cannot be used for filing with the IRS when printed from a conventional printer. These forms contain drop-out ink requirements as described in Part 2 of this publication.

5.3.2 Internet

You can download tax materials from the Internet by visiting the IRS web site at *www.irs.gov*.

5.3.3 IRS Federal Tax Forms CD-ROM

The IRS also offers an alternative to downloading electronic files and provides current and prior-year access to tax forms and instructions through its *Federal Tax Forms CD-ROM*. The CD, Pub. 1796, *Federal Tax Products on CD-ROM*, will be available for the upcoming filing season. You may buy the CD-ROM on the Internet at *www.irs.gov/cdorders* or by calling 1–877–CDFORMS (1–877–233–6767).

5.3.4 GPO Supt. of Documents Bookstores

The Government Printing Office (GPO) Superintendent of Documents Bookstores also sell individual copies of tax forms, instructions, and publications.

Section 5.4 — Effect on Other Revenue Procedures

5.4.1 Other Revenue Procedures

Revenue Procedure 2005–69, 2005–2 C.B. 864, which provides rules and specifications for private printing of 2005 substitute forms and statements to recipients, is superseded.

Part 6
Exhibits

Section 6.1 — Exhibits of Forms in the Revenue Procedure

6.1.1 Purpose

Exhibits A through Z illustrate some of the specifications that were discussed earlier in this revenue procedure. The dimensions apply to the actual size forms, but the exhibits have been reduced in size.

Generally, the illustrated dimensions apply to all like forms. For example, Exhibit B shows 11.00” from the top edge to the bottom edge of Form 1098 and .85” between the bottom rule of the top form and the top rule of the second form on the page. These dimensions apply to all forms that are printed three to a page.

6.1.2 Guidelines

Keep in mind the following guidelines when printing substitute forms.

- Closely follow the specifications to avoid delays in processing the forms.
- Always use the specifications as outlined in this revenue procedure and illustrated in the exhibits.
- Do not add the text line "Do Not Cut or Separate Forms on This Page" to the bottom form. This will cause inconsistency with the specifications.

Exhibit A

Do Not Staple 6969

.50"

Form **1096**
Department of the Treasury
Internal Revenue Service

Annual Summary and Transmittal of U.S. Information Returns

OMB No. 1545-0108

2006

FILER'S name

Street address (including room or suite number)

City, state, and ZIP code

1.33" 2.25" 7.30" 4.50"

Name of person to contact	Telephone number ( )
Email address	Fax number ( )

For Official Use Only

.35" .25"

1 Employer identification number	2 Social security number	3 Total number of forms	4 Federal income tax withheld	5 Total amount reported with this Form 1096
1.40"	1.40"	1.20"	$ 1.40"	$ 1.90"

Enter an "X" in only one box below to indicate the type of form being filed. If this is your **final return**, enter an "X" here . . . ▶ ☐

W-2G 32	1098 81	1098-C 78	1098-E 84	1098-T 83	1099-A 80	1099-B 79	1099-C 85	1099-CAP 73	1099-DIV 91	1099-G 86	1099-H 71	1099-INT 92	1099-LTC 93
☐	☐	☐	☐	☐	☐	☐	☐	☐	☐	☐	☐	☐	☐
1099-MISC 95	1099-OID 96	1099-PATR 97	1099-Q 31	1099-R 98	1099-S 75	1099-SA 94	5498 28	5498-ESA 72	5498-SA 27				
☐	☐	☐	☐	☐	☐	☐	☐	☐	☐				

Return this entire page to the Internal Revenue Service. Photocopies are not acceptable.

Under penalties of perjury, I declare that I have examined this return and accompanying documents, and, to the best of my knowledge and belief, they are true, correct, and complete.

8.00"

Signature ▶ **Title ▶** **Date ▶**

11.0"

Instructions

Purpose of form. Use this form to transmit paper Forms 1099, 1098, 5498, and W-2G to the Internal Revenue Service. Do not use Form 1096 to transmit electronically or magnetically. For magnetic media, see Form 4804, Transmittal of Information Returns Reported Magnetically; for electronic submissions, see Pub. 1220, Specifications for Filing Forms 1098, 1099, 5498, and W-2G Electronically or Magnetically.

Who must file. The name, address, and TIN of the filer on this form must be the same as those you enter in the upper left area of Forms 1099, 1098, 5498, or W-2G. A filer includes a payer; a recipient of mortgage interest payments (including points) or student loan interest; an educational institution; a broker; a barter exchange; a creditor; a person reporting real estate transactions; a trustee or issuer of any individual retirement arrangement, a Coverdell ESA, an HSA, an Archer MSA (including a Medicare Advantage MSA); certain corporations; certain donees of motor vehicles, boats, and airplanes; and a lender who acquires an interest in secured property or who has reason to know that the property has been abandoned.

Preaddressed Form 1096. If you received a preaddressed Form 1096 from the IRS with Package 1099, use it to transmit paper Forms 1099, 1098, 5498, and W-2G to the Internal Revenue Service. If any of the preprinted information is incorrect, make corrections on the form.

If you are not using a preaddressed form, enter the filer's name, address (including room, suite, or other unit number), and TIN in the spaces provided on the form.

When to file. File Form 1096 as follows.

- With Forms 1099, 1098, or W-2G, file by February 28, 2007.
- With Forms 5498, 5498-ESA, or 5498-SA, file by May 31, 2007.

Where To File

Except for Form 1098-C, send all information returns filed on paper with Form 1096 to the following:

If your principal business, office or agency, or legal residence in the case of an individual, is located in	Use the following Internal Revenue Service Center address
Alabama, Arizona, Arkansas, Connecticut, Delaware, Florida, Georgia, Kentucky, Louisiana, Maine, Massachusetts, Mississippi, New Hampshire, New Jersey, New Mexico, New York, North Carolina, Ohio, Pennsylvania, Rhode Island, Texas, Vermont, Virginia, West Virginia	Austin, TX 73301
Alaska, California, Colorado, District of Columbia, Hawaii, Idaho, Illinois, Indiana, Iowa, Kansas, Maryland, Michigan, Minnesota, Missouri, Montana, Nebraska, Nevada, North Dakota, Oklahoma, Oregon, South Carolina, South Dakota, Tennessee, Utah, Washington, Wisconsin, Wyoming	Kansas City, MO 64999

For more information and the Privacy Act and Paperwork Reduction Act Notice, see the 2006 General Instructions for Forms 1099, 1098, 5498, and W-2G. Cat. No. 14400O Form **1096** (Rev. 7-2006)

Exhibit B

.65" .33" .50" 4.70"

8181 VOID CORRECTED

RECIPIENT'S/LENDER'S name, address, and telephone number			OMB No. 1545-0901 **2006** Form **1098**	**Mortgage Interest Statement**
RECIPIENT'S federal identification no.	PAYER'S social security number	1 Mortgage interest received from payer(s)/borrower(s) $		**Copy A** **For Internal Revenue Service Center** File with Form 1096. For Privacy Act and Paperwork Reduction Act Notice, see the **2006 General Instructions for Forms 1099, 1098, 5498, and W-2G.**
PAYER'S/BORROWER'S name		2 Points paid on purchase of principal residence $		
Street address (including apt. no.)		3 Refund of overpaid interest $		
City, state, and ZIP code		4		
Account number (see instructions)				

3.33" 1.70" 2.80" .25" 3.40" 2.83"

Form **1098** Cat. No. 14402K Department of the Treasury - Internal Revenue Service

Do Not Cut or Separate Forms on This Page — Do Not Cut or Separate Forms on This Page

7.30" 8.00" .85"

8181 VOID CORRECTED

RECIPIENT'S/LENDER'S name, address, and telephone number			OMB No. 1545-0901 **2006** Form **1098**	**Mortgage Interest Statement**
RECIPIENT'S federal identification no.	PAYER'S social security number	1 Mortgage interest received from payer(s)/borrower(s) $		**Copy A** **For Internal Revenue Service Center** File with Form 1096. For Privacy Act and Paperwork Reduction Act Notice, see the **2006 General Instructions for Forms 1099, 1098, 5498, and W-2G.**
PAYER'S/BORROWER'S name		2 Points paid on purchase of principal residence $		
Street address (including apt. no.)		3 Refund of overpaid interest $		
City, state, and ZIP code		4		
Account number (see instructions)				

Form **1098** Cat. No. 14402K Department of the Treasury - Internal Revenue Service

Do Not Cut or Separate Forms on This Page — Do Not Cut or Separate Forms on This Page

11.00"

8181 VOID CORRECTED

RECIPIENT'S/LENDER'S name, address, and telephone number			OMB No. 1545-0901 **2006** Form **1098**	**Mortgage Interest Statement**
RECIPIENT'S federal identification no.	PAYER'S social security number	1 Mortgage interest received from payer(s)/borrower(s) $		**Copy A** **For Internal Revenue Service Center** File with Form 1096. For Privacy Act and Paperwork Reduction Act Notice, see the **2006 General Instructions for Forms 1099, 1098, 5498, and W-2G.**
PAYER'S/BORROWER'S name		2 Points paid on purchase of principal residence $		
Street address (including apt. no.)		3 Refund of overpaid interest $		
City, state, and ZIP code		4		
Account number (see instructions)				

Form **1098** Cat. No. 14402K Department of the Treasury - Internal Revenue Service

Exhibit C

7878 ☐ CORRECTED

DONEE'S name, street address, city, state, ZIP code, and telephone no.

1 Date of contribution

OMB No. 1545-1959

2006

Form **1098-C**

Contributions of Motor Vehicles, Boats, and Airplanes

2 Make, model, and year of vehicle

2.80"

DONEE'S federal identification number

DONOR'S identification number

3.40"

3 Vehicle or other identification number

DONOR'S name

4a ☐ Donee certifies that vehicle was sold in arm's length transaction to unrelated party

Street address (including apt. no.)

4b Date of sale

City, state, and ZIP code

4c Gross proceeds from sale (see instructions)

$

Copy A

For Internal Revenue Service Center

File with Form 1096.

For Privacy Act and Paperwork Reduction Act Notice, see the **2006 General Instructions for Forms 1099, 1098, 5498, and W-2G.**

5a ☐ Donee certifies that vehicle will not be transferred for money, other property, or services before completion of material improvements or significant intervening use

5b ☐ Donee certifies that vehicle is to be transferred to a needy individual for significantly below fair market value in furtherance of donee's charitable purpose

7.16"

5c Donee certifies the following detailed description of material improvements or significant intervening use and duration of use

6a Did you provide goods or services in exchange for the vehicle? . . . . ▶ Yes ☐ No ☐

6b Value of goods and services provided in exchange for the vehicle

$

6c Describe the goods and services, if any, that were provided. If this box is checked, donee certifies that the goods and services consisted solely of intangible religious benefits . . . . ▶ ☐

7 Under the law, the donor may not claim a deduction of more than $500 for this vehicle if this box is checked . . . . . ▶ ☐

Form **1098-C** Cat. No. 39732R Department of the Treasury - Internal Revenue Service

Exhibit D

8484 ☐ VOID ☐ CORRECTED

RECIPIENT'S/LENDER'S name, address, and telephone number		OMB No. 1545-1576 2006 Form 1098-E	Student Loan Interest Statement
RECIPIENT'S federal identification no.	BORROWER'S social security number	1 Student loan interest received by lender $ 2.80"	Copy A For Internal Revenue Service Center File with Form 1096. For Privacy Act and Paperwork Reduction Act Notice, see the 2006 General Instructions for Forms 1099, 1098, 5498, and W-2G.
BORROWER'S name 3.40"			
Street address (including apt. no.)			
City, state, and ZIP code 2.83"			
Account number (see instructions)		2 Check if box 1 includes loan origination fees and/or capitalized interest . . . . ☐	

Form **1098-E** Cat. No. 25088U Department of the Treasury - Internal Revenue Service

Do Not Cut or Separate Forms on This Page — Do Not Cut or Separate Forms on This Page

8484 ☐ VOID ☐ CORRECTED

RECIPIENT'S/LENDER'S name, address, and telephone number		OMB No. 1545-1576 2006 Form 1098-E	Student Loan Interest Statement
RECIPIENT'S federal identification no.	BORROWER'S social security number	1 Student loan interest received by lender $	Copy A For Internal Revenue Service Center File with Form 1096. For Privacy Act and Paperwork Reduction Act Notice, see the 2006 General Instructions for Forms 1099, 1098, 5498, and W-2G.
BORROWER'S name			
Street address (including apt. no.)			
City, state, and ZIP code			
Account number (see instructions)		2 Check if box 1 includes loan origination fees and/or capitalized interest . . . . ☐	

Form **1098-E** Cat. No. 25088U Department of the Treasury - Internal Revenue Service

Do Not Cut or Separate Forms on This Page — Do Not Cut or Separate Forms on This Page

8484 ☐ VOID ☐ CORRECTED

RECIPIENT'S/LENDER'S name, address, and telephone number		OMB No. 1545-1576 2006 Form 1098-E	Student Loan Interest Statement
RECIPIENT'S federal identification no.	BORROWER'S social security number	1 Student loan interest received by lender $	Copy A For Internal Revenue Service Center File with Form 1096. For Privacy Act and Paperwork Reduction Act Notice, see the 2006 General Instructions for Forms 1099, 1098, 5498, and W-2G.
BORROWER'S name			
Street address (including apt. no.)			
City, state, and ZIP code			
Account number (see instructions)		2 Check if box 1 includes loan origination fees and/or capitalized interest . . . . ☐	

Form **1098-E** Cat. No. 25088U Department of the Treasury - Internal Revenue Service

Exhibit E

.33"

8383 VOID CORRECTED 6.25"

FILER'S name, street address, city, state, ZIP code, and telephone number		1 Payments received for qualified tuition and related expenses $ 2 Amounts billed for qualified tuition and related expenses $	OMB No. 1545-1574 2006 Form 1098-T	Tuition Statement
FILER'S federal identification no.	STUDENT'S social security number	3 Check if you have changed your reporting method for 2006 ☐		Copy A For Internal Revenue Service Center .25" File with Form 1096. For Privacy Act and Paperwork Reduction Act Notice, see the 2006 General Instructions for Forms 1099, 1098, 5498, and W-2G.
STUDENT'S name 3.40"		4 Adjustments made for a prior year $	5 Scholarships or grants $ 1.40"	
Street address (including apt. no.) City, state, and ZIP code		6 Adjustments to scholarships or grants for a prior year $	7 Check this box if the amount in box 1 or 2 includes amounts for an academic period beginning January - March 2007 ► ☐ 2.80"	
Service Provider/Acct. No. (see instr.)	8 Check if at least half-time student ☐	9 Check if a graduate student . . . ☐	10 Ins. contract reimb./refund $	

Form **1098-T** Cat. No. 25087J Department of the Treasury - Internal Revenue Service

Do Not Cut or Separate Forms on This Page — Do Not Cut or Separate Forms on This Page

8383 VOID CORRECTED

FILER'S name, street address, city, state, ZIP code, and telephone number		1 Payments received for qualified tuition and related expenses $ 2 Amounts billed for qualified tuition and related expenses $	OMB No. 1545-1574 2006 Form 1098-T	Tuition Statement
FILER'S federal identification no.	STUDENT'S social security number	3 Check if you have changed your reporting method for 2006 ☐		Copy A For Internal Revenue Service Center File with Form 1096. For Privacy Act and Paperwork Reduction Act Notice, see the 2006 General Instructions for Forms 1099, 1098, 5498, and W-2G.
STUDENT'S name		4 Adjustments made for a prior year $	5 Scholarships or grants $	
Street address (including apt. no.) City, state, and ZIP code		6 Adjustments to scholarships or grants for a prior year $	7 Check this box if the amount in box 1 or 2 includes amounts for an academic period beginning January - March 2007 ► ☐	
Service Provider/Acct. No. (see instr.)	8 Check if at least half-time student ☐	9 Check if a graduate student . . . ☐	10 Ins. contract reimb./refund $	

Form **1098-T** Cat. No. 25087J Department of the Treasury - Internal Revenue Service

Do Not Cut or Separate Forms on This Page — Do Not Cut or Separate Forms on This Page

8383 VOID CORRECTED

FILER'S name, street address, city, state, ZIP code, and telephone number		1 Payments received for qualified tuition and related expenses $ 2 Amounts billed for qualified tuition and related expenses $	OMB No. 1545-1574 2006 Form 1098-T	Tuition Statement
FILER'S federal identification no.	STUDENT'S social security number	3 Check if you have changed your reporting method for 2006 ☐		Copy A For Internal Revenue Service Center File with Form 1096. For Privacy Act and Paperwork Reduction Act Notice, see the 2006 General Instructions for Forms 1099, 1098, 5498, and W-2G.
STUDENT'S name		4 Adjustments made for a prior year $	5 Scholarships or grants $	
Street address (including apt. no.) City, state, and ZIP code		6 Adjustments to scholarships or grants for a prior year $	7 Check this box if the amount in box 1 or 2 includes amounts for an academic period beginning January - March 2007 ► ☐	
Service Provider/Acct. No. (see instr.)	8 Check if at least half-time student ☐	9 Check if a graduate student . . . ☐	10 Ins. contract reimb./refund $	

Form **1098-T** Cat. No. 25087J Department of the Treasury - Internal Revenue Service

Exhibit F

8080 ☐ VOID ☐ CORRECTED

LENDER'S name, street address, city, state, ZIP code, and telephone no.			OMB No. 1545-0877 2006 Form 1099-A	Acquisition or Abandonment of Secured Property
LENDER'S federal identification number	BORROWER'S identification number	1 Date of lender's acquisition or knowledge of abandonment	2 Balance of principal outstanding $	Copy A For Internal Revenue Service Center
BORROWER'S name		3	4 Fair market value of property $	File with Form 1096.
Street address (including apt. no.)		5 Was borrower personally liable for repayment of the debt? ☐ Yes ☐ No		For Privacy Act and Paperwork Reduction Act Notice, see the **2006 General Instructions for Forms 1099, 1098, 5498, and W-2G.**
City, state, and ZIP code		6 Description of property		
Account number (see instructions)				

1.40" 1.40" 1.80"

Form **1099-A** Cat. No. 14412G Department of the Treasury - Internal Revenue Service

Do Not Cut or Separate Forms on This Page — Do Not Cut or Separate Forms on This Page

8080 ☐ VOID ☐ CORRECTED

LENDER'S name, street address, city, state, ZIP code, and telephone no.			OMB No. 1545-0877 2006 Form 1099-A	Acquisition or Abandonment of Secured Property
LENDER'S federal identification number	BORROWER'S identification number	1 Date of lender's acquisition or knowledge of abandonment	2 Balance of principal outstanding $	Copy A For Internal Revenue Service Center
BORROWER'S name		3	4 Fair market value of property $	File with Form 1096.
Street address (including apt. no.)		5 Was borrower personally liable for repayment of the debt? ☐ Yes ☐ No		For Privacy Act and Paperwork Reduction Act Notice, see the **2006 General Instructions for Forms 1099, 1098, 5498, and W-2G.**
City, state, and ZIP code		6 Description of property		
Account number (see instructions)				

Form **1099-A** Cat. No. 14412G Department of the Treasury - Internal Revenue Service

Do Not Cut or Separate Forms on This Page — Do Not Cut or Separate Forms on This Page

8080 ☐ VOID ☐ CORRECTED

LENDER'S name, street address, city, state, ZIP code, and telephone no.			OMB No. 1545-0877 2006 Form 1099-A	Acquisition or Abandonment of Secured Property
LENDER'S federal identification number	BORROWER'S identification number	1 Date of lender's acquisition or knowledge of abandonment	2 Balance of principal outstanding $	Copy A For Internal Revenue Service Center
BORROWER'S name		3	4 Fair market value of property $	File with Form 1096.
Street address (including apt. no.)		5 Was borrower personally liable for repayment of the debt? ☐ Yes ☐ No		For Privacy Act and Paperwork Reduction Act Notice, see the **2006 General Instructions for Forms 1099, 1098, 5498, and W-2G.**
City, state, and ZIP code		6 Description of property		
Account number (see instructions)				

Form **1099-A** Cat. No. 14412G Department of the Treasury - Internal Revenue Service

Exhibit G

7979 ☐ VOID ☐ CORRECTED

PAYER'S name, street address, city, state, ZIP code, and telephone no.		1a Date of sale or exchange	OMB No. 1545-0715	Proceeds From Broker and Barter Exchange Transactions
		1b CUSIP no.	2006 Form 1099-B	
		2 Stocks, bonds, etc. $	Reported to IRS ☐ Gross proceeds 1.90" ☐ Gross proceeds less commissions and option premiums	
PAYER'S federal identification number	RECIPIENT'S identification number	3 Bartering $ 3.90"	4 Federal income tax withheld $	Copy A For Internal Revenue Service Center
RECIPIENT'S name		5 No. of shares exchanged 1.40"	6 Classes of stock exchanged 1.40"	File with Form 1096.
Street address (including apt. no.)		7 Description		For Privacy Act and Paperwork Reduction Act Notice, see the 2006 General Instructions for Forms 1099, 1098, 5498, and W-2G.
City, state, and ZIP code		8 Profit or (loss) realized in 2006 $	9 Unrealized profit or (loss) on open contracts—12/31/2005 $	
CORPORATION'S name		10 Unrealized profit or (loss) on open contracts–12/31/2006 $	11 Aggregate profit or (loss) $	
Account number (see instructions) 2.80"	2nd TIN not. ☐	12 Check the box if recipient cannot take a loss on their tax return based on the amount in box 2 . . . . ☐ 4.15"		

Form **1099-B** .60" Cat. No. 14411V Department of the Treasury - Internal Revenue Service

7979 ☐ VOID ☐ CORRECTED

PAYER'S name, street address, city, state, ZIP code, and telephone no.		1a Date of sale or exchange	OMB No. 1545-0715	Proceeds From Broker and Barter Exchange Transactions
		1b CUSIP no.	2006 Form 1099-B	
		2 Stocks, bonds, etc. $	Reported to IRS ☐ Gross proceeds ☐ Gross proceeds less commissions and option premiums	
PAYER'S federal identification number	RECIPIENT'S identification number	3 Bartering $	4 Federal income tax withheld $	Copy A For Internal Revenue Service Center
RECIPIENT'S name		5 No. of shares exchanged	6 Classes of stock exchanged	File with Form 1096.
Street address (including apt. no.)		7 Description		For Privacy Act and Paperwork Reduction Act Notice, see the 2006 General Instructions for Forms 1099, 1098, 5498, and W-2G.
City, state, and ZIP code		8 Profit or (loss) realized in 2006 $	9 Unrealized profit or (loss) on open contracts—12/31/2005 $	
CORPORATION'S name		10 Unrealized profit or (loss) on open contracts–12/31/2006 $	11 Aggregate profit or (loss) $	
Account number (see instructions)	2nd TIN not. ☐	12 Check the box if recipient cannot take a loss on their tax return based on the amount in box 2 . . . . ☐		

Form **1099-B** Cat. No. 14411V Department of the Treasury - Internal Revenue Service

Exhibit H

8585 ☐ VOID ☐ CORRECTED

CREDITOR'S name, street address, city, state, and ZIP code			OMB No. 1545-1424 2006 Form 1099-C	Cancellation of Debt
CREDITOR'S federal identification number	DEBTOR'S identification number	1 Date canceled 1.40"	2 Amount of debt canceled $ 1.40"	**Copy A For Internal Revenue Service Center** File with Form 1096. For Privacy Act and Paperwork Reduction Act Notice, see the **2006 General Instructions for Forms 1099, 1098, 5498, and W-2G.** 1.35"
DEBTOR'S name 3.40"		3 Interest if included in box 2 $	4	
Street address (including apt. no.)		5 Debt description		
City, state, and ZIP code				
Account number (see instructions)		6 Check for bankruptcy ☐	7 Fair market value of property $	

Form **1099-C** Cat. No. 26280W Department of the Treasury - Internal Revenue Service

Do Not Cut or Separate Forms on This Page — Do Not Cut or Separate Forms on This Page

8585 ☐ VOID ☐ CORRECTED

CREDITOR'S name, street address, city, state, and ZIP code			OMB No. 1545-1424 2006 Form 1099-C	Cancellation of Debt
CREDITOR'S federal identification number	DEBTOR'S identification number	1 Date canceled	2 Amount of debt canceled $	**Copy A For Internal Revenue Service Center** File with Form 1096. For Privacy Act and Paperwork Reduction Act Notice, see the **2006 General Instructions for Forms 1099, 1098, 5498, and W-2G.**
DEBTOR'S name		3 Interest if included in box 2 $	4	
Street address (including apt. no.)		5 Debt description		
City, state, and ZIP code				
Account number (see instructions)		6 Check for bankruptcy ☐	7 Fair market value of property $	

Form **1099-C** Cat. No. 26280W Department of the Treasury - Internal Revenue Service

Do Not Cut or Separate Forms on This Page — Do Not Cut or Separate Forms on This Page

8585 ☐ VOID ☐ CORRECTED

CREDITOR'S name, street address, city, state, and ZIP code			OMB No. 1545-1424 2006 Form 1099-C	Cancellation of Debt
CREDITOR'S federal identification number	DEBTOR'S identification number	1 Date canceled	2 Amount of debt canceled $	**Copy A For Internal Revenue Service Center** File with Form 1096. For Privacy Act and Paperwork Reduction Act Notice, see the **2006 General Instructions for Forms 1099, 1098, 5498, and W-2G.**
DEBTOR'S name		3 Interest if included in box 2 $	4	
Street address (including apt. no.)		5 Debt description		
City, state, and ZIP code				
Account number (see instructions)		6 Check for bankruptcy ☐	7 Fair market value of property $	

Form **1099-C** Cat. No. 26280W Department of the Treasury - Internal Revenue Service

Exhibit I

7373 ☐ VOID ☐ CORRECTED

CORPORATION'S name, street address, city, state, ZIP code, and telephone no.	1 Date of sale or exchange	OMB No. 1545-1814 **2006** Form **1099-CAP**	**Changes in Corporate Control and Capital Structure**
	2 Aggregate amount received $ ←1.40"→		
	3 No. of shares exchanged	4 Classes of stock exchanged ←1.40"→	←1.35"→
CORPORATION'S federal identification no. | SHAREHOLDER'S identification no.			**Copy A For Internal Revenue Service Center** File with Form 1096. For Privacy Act and Paperwork Reduction Act Notice, see the **2006 General Instructions for Forms 1099, 1098, 5498, and W-2G.**
SHAREHOLDER'S name			
Street address (including apt. no.)	5		
City, state, and ZIP code ←3.4"→			
Account number (see instructions)	6 Check the box if this shareholder cannot claim a loss based on the amount in box 2 . . . . . . ☐		

Form **1099-CAP** Cat. No. 35115M Department of the Treasury - Internal Revenue Service

Do Not Cut or Separate Forms on This Page — Do Not Cut or Separate Forms on This Page

7373 ☐ VOID ☐ CORRECTED

CORPORATION'S name, street address, city, state, ZIP code, and telephone no.	1 Date of sale or exchange	OMB No. 1545-1814 **2006** Form **1099-CAP**	**Changes in Corporate Control and Capital Structure**
	2 Aggregate amount received $		
	3 No. of shares exchanged	4 Classes of stock exchanged	
CORPORATION'S federal identification no. | SHAREHOLDER'S identification no.			**Copy A For Internal Revenue Service Center** File with Form 1096. For Privacy Act and Paperwork Reduction Act Notice, see the **2006 General Instructions for Forms 1099, 1098, 5498, and W-2G.**
SHAREHOLDER'S name			
Street address (including apt. no.)	5		
City, state, and ZIP code			
Account number (see instructions)	6 Check the box if this shareholder cannot claim a loss based on the amount in box 2 . . . . . . ☐		

Form **1099-CAP** Cat. No. 35115M Department of the Treasury - Internal Revenue Service

Do Not Cut or Separate Forms on This Page — Do Not Cut or Separate Forms on This Page

7373 ☐ VOID ☐ CORRECTED

CORPORATION'S name, street address, city, state, ZIP code, and telephone no.	1 Date of sale or exchange	OMB No. 1545-1814 **2006** Form **1099-CAP**	**Changes in Corporate Control and Capital Structure**
	2 Aggregate amount received $		
	3 No. of shares exchanged	4 Classes of stock exchanged	
CORPORATION'S federal identification no. | SHAREHOLDER'S identification no.			**Copy A For Internal Revenue Service Center** File with Form 1096. For Privacy Act and Paperwork Reduction Act Notice, see the **2006 General Instructions for Forms 1099, 1098, 5498, and W-2G.**
SHAREHOLDER'S name			
Street address (including apt. no.)	5		
City, state, and ZIP code			
Account number (see instructions)	6 Check the box if this shareholder cannot claim a loss based on the amount in box 2 . . . . . . ☐		

Form **1099-CAP** Cat. No. 35115M Department of the Treasury - Internal Revenue Service

Exhibit J

9191 ☐ VOID ☐ CORRECTED

PAYER'S name, street address, city, state, ZIP code, and telephone no.		1a Total ordinary dividends $	OMB No. 1545-0110	Dividends and Distributions
		1b Qualified dividends 1.40" $	2006 Form 1099-DIV	
		2a Total capital gain distr. $	2b Unrecap. Sec. 1250 gain $	Copy A For Internal Revenue Service Center File with Form 1096.
PAYER'S federal identification number	RECIPIENT'S identification number			
RECIPIENT'S name		2c Section 1202 gain $	2d Collectibles (28%) gain $	For Privacy Act and Paperwork Reduction Act Notice, see the **2006 General Instructions for Forms 1099, 1098, 5498, and W-2G.**
		3 Nondividend distributions $	4 Federal income tax withheld $	
Street address (including apt. no.)			5 Investment expenses $	
City, state, and ZIP code		6 Foreign tax paid $	7 Foreign country or U.S. possession	
Account number (see instructions) 2.80"	2nd TIN not. ☐	8 Cash liquidation distributions 4.50" $	9 Noncash liquidation distributions $	

Form **1099-DIV** Cat. No. 14415N Department of the Treasury - Internal Revenue Service

Do Not Cut or Separate Forms on This Page — Do Not Cut or Separate Forms on This Page

9191 ☐ VOID ☐ CORRECTED

PAYER'S name, street address, city, state, ZIP code, and telephone no.		1a Total ordinary dividends $	OMB No. 1545-0110	Dividends and Distributions
		1b Qualified dividends $	2006 Form 1099-DIV	
		2a Total capital gain distr. $	2b Unrecap. Sec. 1250 gain $	Copy A For Internal Revenue Service Center File with Form 1096.
PAYER'S federal identification number	RECIPIENT'S identification number			
RECIPIENT'S name		2c Section 1202 gain $	2d Collectibles (28%) gain $	For Privacy Act and Paperwork Reduction Act Notice, see the **2006 General Instructions for Forms 1099, 1098, 5498, and W-2G.**
		3 Nondividend distributions $	4 Federal income tax withheld $	
Street address (including apt. no.)			5 Investment expenses $	
City, state, and ZIP code		6 Foreign tax paid $	7 Foreign country or U.S. possession	
Account number (see instructions)	2nd TIN not. ☐	8 Cash liquidation distributions $	9 Noncash liquidation distributions $	

Form **1099-DIV** Cat. No. 14415N Department of the Treasury - Internal Revenue Service

Exhibit K

8686 ☐ VOID ☐ CORRECTED

PAYER'S name, street address, city, state, ZIP code, and telephone no.		1 Unemployment compensation ←1.40"→ $ 2 State or local income tax refunds, credits, or offsets $	OMB No. 1545-0120 **2006** Form **1099-G**	**Certain Government Payments**
PAYER'S federal identification number	RECIPIENT'S identification number	3 Box 2 amount is for tax year	4 Federal income tax withheld $	←1.10"→ **Copy A For Internal Revenue Service Center**
RECIPIENT'S name		5 ATAA payments $	6 Taxable grants $	**File with Form 1096.**
Street address (including apt. no.)		7 Agriculture payments $	8 Check if box 2 is trade or business income ► ☐	For Privacy Act and Paperwork Reduction Act Notice, see the **2006 General Instructions for Forms 1099, 1098, 5498, and W-2G.**
City, state, and ZIP code				
Account number (see instructions)				

Form **1099-G** Cat. No. 14438M Department of the Treasury - Internal Revenue Service

Do Not Cut or Separate Forms on This Page — Do Not Cut or Separate Forms on This Page

8686 ☐ VOID ☐ CORRECTED

PAYER'S name, street address, city, state, ZIP code, and telephone no.		1 Unemployment compensation $ 2 State or local income tax refunds, credits, or offsets $	OMB No. 1545-0120 **2006** Form **1099-G**	**Certain Government Payments**
PAYER'S federal identification number	RECIPIENT'S identification number	3 Box 2 amount is for tax year	4 Federal income tax withheld $	**Copy A For Internal Revenue Service Center**
RECIPIENT'S name		5 ATAA payments $	6 Taxable grants $	**File with Form 1096.**
Street address (including apt. no.)		7 Agriculture payments $	8 Check if box 2 is trade or business income ► ☐	For Privacy Act and Paperwork Reduction Act Notice, see the **2006 General Instructions for Forms 1099, 1098, 5498, and W-2G.**
City, state, and ZIP code				
Account number (see instructions)				

Form **1099-G** Cat. No. 14438M Department of the Treasury - Internal Revenue Service

Do Not Cut or Separate Forms on This Page — Do Not Cut or Separate Forms on This Page

8686 ☐ VOID ☐ CORRECTED

PAYER'S name, street address, city, state, ZIP code, and telephone no.		1 Unemployment compensation $ 2 State or local income tax refunds, credits, or offsets $	OMB No. 1545-0120 **2006** Form **1099-G**	**Certain Government Payments**
PAYER'S federal identification number	RECIPIENT'S identification number	3 Box 2 amount is for tax year	4 Federal income tax withheld $	**Copy A For Internal Revenue Service Center**
RECIPIENT'S name		5 ATAA payments $	6 Taxable grants $	**File with Form 1096.**
Street address (including apt. no.)		7 Agriculture payments $	8 Check if box 2 is trade or business income ► ☐	For Privacy Act and Paperwork Reduction Act Notice, see the **2006 General Instructions for Forms 1099, 1098, 5498, and W-2G.**
City, state, and ZIP code				
Account number (see instructions)				

Form **1099-G** Cat. No. 14438M Department of the Treasury - Internal Revenue Service

Exhibit L

7171 ☐ VOID ☐ CORRECTED

ISSUER'S/PROVIDER'S name, street address, city, state, ZIP code, and telephone no.		1 Amount of HCTC advance payments $	OMB No. 1545-1813 **2006** Form **1099-H**	**Health Coverage Tax Credit (HCTC) Advance Payments**
		2 No. of mos. HCTC advance payments received		
ISSUER'S/PROVIDER'S federal identification no.	RECIPIENT'S identification number	3 Jan. $	9 July ←1.40"→ $	**Copy A For Internal Revenue Service Center**
RECIPIENT'S name		4 Feb. $	10 Aug. $	**File with Form 1096.**
←3.40"→		5 Mar. $	11 Sept. $	For Privacy Act and Paperwork Reduction Act Notice, see the **2006 General Instructions for Forms 1099, 1098, 5498, and W-2G.**
Street address (including apt. no.)		6 Apr. ←1.40"→ $	12 Oct. $	
City, state, and ZIP code		7 May $	13 Nov. $	
		8 June $	14 Dec. $	

Form **1099-H** Cat. No. 34912D Department of the Treasury - Internal Revenue Service

Do Not Cut or Separate Forms on This Page — Do Not Cut or Separate Forms on This Page

7171 ☐ VOID ☐ CORRECTED

ISSUER'S/PROVIDER'S name, street address, city, state, ZIP code, and telephone no.		1 Amount of HCTC advance payments $	OMB No. 1545-1813 **2006** Form **1099-H**	**Health Coverage Tax Credit (HCTC) Advance Payments**
		2 No. of mos. HCTC advance payments received		
ISSUER'S/PROVIDER'S federal identification no.	RECIPIENT'S identification number	3 Jan. $	9 July $	**Copy A For Internal Revenue Service Center**
RECIPIENT'S name		4 Feb. $	10 Aug. $	**File with Form 1096.**
		5 Mar. $	11 Sept. $	For Privacy Act and Paperwork Reduction Act Notice, see the **2006 General Instructions for Forms 1099, 1098, 5498, and W-2G.**
Street address (including apt. no.)		6 Apr. $	12 Oct. $	
City, state, and ZIP code		7 May $	13 Nov. $	
		8 June $	14 Dec. $	

Form **1099-H** Cat. No. 34912D Department of the Treasury - Internal Revenue Service

Do Not Cut or Separate Forms on This Page — Do Not Cut or Separate Forms on This Page

7171 ☐ VOID ☐ CORRECTED

ISSUER'S/PROVIDER'S name, street address, city, state, ZIP code, and telephone no.		1 Amount of HCTC advance payments $	OMB No. 1545-1813 **2006** Form **1099-H**	**Health Coverage Tax Credit (HCTC) Advance Payments**
		2 No. of mos. HCTC advance payments received		
ISSUER'S/PROVIDER'S federal identification no.	RECIPIENT'S identification number	3 Jan. $	9 July $	**Copy A For Internal Revenue Service Center**
RECIPIENT'S name		4 Feb. $	10 Aug. $	**File with Form 1096.**
		5 Mar. $	11 Sept. $	For Privacy Act and Paperwork Reduction Act Notice, see the **2006 General Instructions for Forms 1099, 1098, 5498, and W-2G.**
Street address (including apt. no.)		6 Apr. $	12 Oct. $	
City, state, and ZIP code		7 May $	13 Nov. $	
		8 June $	14 Dec. $	

Form **1099-H** Cat. No. 34912D Department of the Treasury - Internal Revenue Service

Exhibit M

9292 ☐ VOID ☐ CORRECTED

PAYER'S name, street address, city, state, ZIP code, and telephone no.

Payer's RTN (optional)

OMB No. 1545-0112

1 Interest income $

2006 **Interest Income**

2 Early withdrawal penalty $

Form **1099-INT**

PAYER'S federal identification number | RECIPIENT'S identification number

3 Interest on U.S. Savings Bonds and Treas. obligations $

Copy A For Internal Revenue Service Center

File with Form 1096.

For Privacy Act and Paperwork Reduction Act Notice, see the **2006 General Instructions for Forms 1099, 1098, 5498, and W-2G.**

RECIPIENT'S name

4 Federal income tax withheld 1.40" $

5 Investment expenses $

Street address (including apt. no.)

6 Foreign tax paid $

7 Foreign country or U.S. possession

City, state, and ZIP code

8 Tax-exempt interest $

9 Specified private activity bond interest $ 4.15"

Account number (see instructions) 2.80"

2nd TIN not. ☐ .60"

Form **1099-INT** Cat. No. 14410K Department of the Treasury - Internal Revenue Service

Do Not Cut or Separate Forms on This Page — Do Not Cut or Separate Forms on This Page

9292 ☐ VOID ☐ CORRECTED

PAYER'S name, street address, city, state, ZIP code, and telephone no.

Payer's RTN (optional)

OMB No. 1545-0112

1 Interest income $

2006 **Interest Income**

2 Early withdrawal penalty $

Form **1099-INT**

PAYER'S federal identification number | RECIPIENT'S identification number

3 Interest on U.S. Savings Bonds and Treas. obligations $

Copy A For Internal Revenue Service Center

File with Form 1096.

For Privacy Act and Paperwork Reduction Act Notice, see the **2006 General Instructions for Forms 1099, 1098, 5498, and W-2G.**

RECIPIENT'S name

4 Federal income tax withheld $

5 Investment expenses $

Street address (including apt. no.)

6 Foreign tax paid $

7 Foreign country or U.S. possession

City, state, and ZIP code

8 Tax-exempt interest $

9 Specified private activity bond interest $

Account number (see instructions)

2nd TIN not. ☐

Form **1099-INT** Cat. No. 14410K Department of the Treasury - Internal Revenue Service

Do Not Cut or Separate Forms on This Page — Do Not Cut or Separate Forms on This Page

9292 ☐ VOID ☐ CORRECTED

PAYER'S name, street address, city, state, ZIP code, and telephone no.

Payer's RTN (optional)

OMB No. 1545-0112

1 Interest income $

2006 **Interest Income**

2 Early withdrawal penalty $

Form **1099-INT**

PAYER'S federal identification number | RECIPIENT'S identification number

3 Interest on U.S. Savings Bonds and Treas. obligations $

Copy A For Internal Revenue Service Center

File with Form 1096.

For Privacy Act and Paperwork Reduction Act Notice, see the **2006 General Instructions for Forms 1099, 1098, 5498, and W-2G.**

RECIPIENT'S name

4 Federal income tax withheld $

5 Investment expenses $

Street address (including apt. no.)

6 Foreign tax paid $

7 Foreign country or U.S. possession

City, state, and ZIP code

8 Tax-exempt interest $

9 Specified private activity bond interest $

Account number (see instructions)

2nd TIN not. ☐

Form **1099-INT** Cat. No. 14410K Department of the Treasury - Internal Revenue Service

Exhibit N

9393 ◄ VOID ☐ CORRECTED ☐ 4.50" ►

PAYER'S name, street address, city, state, ZIP code, and telephone no.	1 Gross long-term care benefits paid $ 2 Accelerated death benefits paid $	OMB No. 1545-1519 **2006** Form **1099-LTC**	**Long-Term Care and Accelerated Death Benefits**
PAYER'S federal identification number / POLICYHOLDER'S identification number	3 Check one: ☐ Per diem ☐ Reimbursed amount	INSURED'S social security no. ◄ 1.40" ►	**Copy A For Internal Revenue Service Center**
POLICYHOLDER'S name ◄ 3.40" ►	INSURED'S name		**File with Form 1096.**
Street address (including apt. no.)	Street address (including apt. no.) ◄ 2.80" ►		For Privacy Act and Paperwork Reduction Act Notice, see the **2006 General Instructions for Forms 1099, 1098, 5498, and W-2G.**
City, state, and ZIP code	City, state, and ZIP code		
Account number (see instructions) / 4 Qualified contract ☐ (optional)	5 Check, if applicable: (optional) ☐ Chronically ill ☐ Terminally ill	Date certified	

Form **1099-LTC** Cat. No. 23021Z Department of the Treasury - Internal Revenue Service

Do Not Cut or Separate Forms on This Page — Do Not Cut or Separate Forms on This Page

9393 ☐ VOID ☐ CORRECTED

PAYER'S name, street address, city, state, ZIP code, and telephone no.	1 Gross long-term care benefits paid $ 2 Accelerated death benefits paid $	OMB No. 1545-1519 **2006** Form **1099-LTC**	**Long-Term Care and Accelerated Death Benefits**
PAYER'S federal identification number / POLICYHOLDER'S identification number	3 Check one: ☐ Per diem ☐ Reimbursed amount	INSURED'S social security no.	**Copy A For Internal Revenue Service Center**
POLICYHOLDER'S name	INSURED'S name		**File with Form 1096.**
Street address (including apt. no.)	Street address (including apt. no.)		For Privacy Act and Paperwork Reduction Act Notice, see the **2006 General Instructions for Forms 1099, 1098, 5498, and W-2G.**
City, state, and ZIP code	City, state, and ZIP code		
Account number (see instructions) / 4 Qualified contract ☐ (optional)	5 Check, if applicable: (optional) ☐ Chronically ill ☐ Terminally ill	Date certified	

Form **1099-LTC** Cat. No. 23021Z Department of the Treasury - Internal Revenue Service

Do Not Cut or Separate Forms on This Page — Do Not Cut or Separate Forms on This Page

9393 ☐ VOID ☐ CORRECTED

PAYER'S name, street address, city, state, ZIP code, and telephone no.	1 Gross long-term care benefits paid $ 2 Accelerated death benefits paid $	OMB No. 1545-1519 **2006** Form **1099-LTC**	**Long-Term Care and Accelerated Death Benefits**
PAYER'S federal identification number / POLICYHOLDER'S identification number	3 Check one: ☐ Per diem ☐ Reimbursed amount	INSURED'S social security no.	**Copy A For Internal Revenue Service Center**
POLICYHOLDER'S name	INSURED'S name		**File with Form 1096.**
Street address (including apt. no.)	Street address (including apt. no.)		For Privacy Act and Paperwork Reduction Act Notice, see the **2006 General Instructions for Forms 1099, 1098, 5498, and W-2G.**
City, state, and ZIP code	City, state, and ZIP code		
Account number (see instructions) / 4 Qualified contract ☐ (optional)	5 Check, if applicable: (optional) ☐ Chronically ill ☐ Terminally ill	Date certified	

Form **1099-LTC** Cat. No. 23021Z Department of the Treasury - Internal Revenue Service

Exhibit O

.3125 .50" 5.50" 4.50" 1.40" .25" 3.40"

9595 ☐ VOID ☐ CORRECTED

PAYER'S name, street address, city, state, ZIP code, and telephone no.	1 Rents $ 2 Royalties $	OMB No. 1545-0115 **2006** Form **1099-MISC**	**Miscellaneous Income**
	3 Other income $	4 Federal income tax withheld $	**Copy A For Internal Revenue Service Center** **File with Form 1096.**
PAYER'S federal identification number / RECIPIENT'S identification number	5 Fishing boat proceeds $	6 Medical and health care payments $	
RECIPIENT'S name	7 Nonemployee compensation $	8 Substitute payments in lieu of dividends or interest $	For Privacy Act and Paperwork Reduction Act Notice, see the **2006 General Instructions for Forms 1099, 1098, 5498, and W-2G.**
Street address (including apt. no.)	9 Payer made direct sales of $5,000 or more of consumer products to a buyer (recipient) for resale ▶ ☐	10 Crop insurance proceeds $	
City, state, and ZIP code	11	12	
Account number (see instructions) / 2nd TIN not. ☐	13 Excess golden parachute payments $	14 Gross proceeds paid to an attorney $	
15a Section 409A deferrals $ / 15b Section 409A income $	16 State tax withheld $ $	17 State/Payer's state no.	18 State income $ $

Form **1099-MISC** Cat. No. 14425J Department of the Treasury - Internal Revenue Service

Do Not Cut or Separate Forms on This Page — Do Not Cut or Separate Forms on This Page

1.00" .45"

9595 ☐ VOID ☐ CORRECTED

PAYER'S name, street address, city, state, ZIP code, and telephone no.	1 Rents $ 2 Royalties $	OMB No. 1545-0115 **2006** Form **1099-MISC**	**Miscellaneous Income**
	3 Other income $	4 Federal income tax withheld $	**Copy A For Internal Revenue Service Center** **File with Form 1096.**
PAYER'S federal identification number / RECIPIENT'S identification number	5 Fishing boat proceeds $	6 Medical and health care payments $	
RECIPIENT'S name	7 Nonemployee compensation $	8 Substitute payments in lieu of dividends or interest $	For Privacy Act and Paperwork Reduction Act Notice, see the **2006 General Instructions for Forms 1099, 1098, 5498, and W-2G.**
Street address (including apt. no.)	9 Payer made direct sales of $5,000 or more of consumer products to a buyer (recipient) for resale ▶ ☐	10 Crop insurance proceeds $	
City, state, and ZIP code	11	12	
Account number (see instructions) / 2nd TIN not. ☐	13 Excess golden parachute payments $	14 Gross proceeds paid to an attorney $	
15a Section 409A deferrals $ / 15b Section 409A income $	16 State tax withheld $ $	17 State/Payer's state no.	18 State income $ $

Form **1099-MISC** Cat. No. 14425J Department of the Treasury - Internal Revenue Service

Exhibit P

9696 ☐ VOID ☐ CORRECTED

PAYER'S name, street address, city, state, ZIP code, and telephone no.	1 Original issue discount for 2006 ◄— 1.40" —► $ 2 Other periodic interest $	OMB No. 1545-0117 **2006** Form **1099-OID**	**Original Issue Discount**
PAYER'S federal identification number / RECIPIENT'S identification number	3 Early withdrawal penalty $	4 Federal income tax withheld $	**Copy A For Internal Revenue Service Center**
RECIPIENT'S name	5 Description		**File with Form 1096.**
Street address (including apt. no.)	6 Original issue discount on U.S. Treasury obligations $		For Privacy Act and Paperwork Reduction Act Notice, see the **2006 General Instructions for Forms 1099, 1098, 5498, and W-2G.**
City, state, and ZIP code	7 Investment expenses $		
Account number (see instructions) ◄— 2.80" —► / 2nd TIN not. ☐	◄— 4.15" —►		

Form **1099-OID** Cat. No. 14421R Department of the Treasury - Internal Revenue Service

Do Not Cut or Separate Forms on This Page — Do Not Cut or Separate Forms on This Page

9696 ☐ VOID ☐ CORRECTED

PAYER'S name, street address, city, state, ZIP code, and telephone no.	1 Original issue discount for 2006 $ 2 Other periodic interest $	OMB No. 1545-0117 **2006** Form **1099-OID**	**Original Issue Discount**
PAYER'S federal identification number / RECIPIENT'S identification number	3 Early withdrawal penalty $	4 Federal income tax withheld $	**Copy A For Internal Revenue Service Center**
RECIPIENT'S name	5 Description		**File with Form 1096.**
Street address (including apt. no.)	6 Original issue discount on U.S. Treasury obligations $		For Privacy Act and Paperwork Reduction Act Notice, see the **2006 General Instructions for Forms 1099, 1098, 5498, and W-2G.**
City, state, and ZIP code	7 Investment expenses $		
Account number (see instructions) / 2nd TIN not. ☐			

Form **1099-OID** Cat. No. 14421R Department of the Treasury - Internal Revenue Service

Do Not Cut or Separate Forms on This Page — Do Not Cut or Separate Forms on This Page

9696 ☐ VOID ☐ CORRECTED

PAYER'S name, street address, city, state, ZIP code, and telephone no.	1 Original issue discount for 2006 $ 2 Other periodic interest $	OMB No. 1545-0117 **2006** Form **1099-OID**	**Original Issue Discount**
PAYER'S federal identification number / RECIPIENT'S identification number	3 Early withdrawal penalty $	4 Federal income tax withheld $	**Copy A For Internal Revenue Service Center**
RECIPIENT'S name	5 Description		**File with Form 1096.**
Street address (including apt. no.)	6 Original issue discount on U.S. Treasury obligations $		For Privacy Act and Paperwork Reduction Act Notice, see the **2006 General Instructions for Forms 1099, 1098, 5498, and W-2G.**
City, state, and ZIP code	7 Investment expenses $		
Account number (see instructions) / 2nd TIN not. ☐			

Form **1099-OID** Cat. No. 14421R Department of the Treasury - Internal Revenue Service

Exhibit Q

9797 ☐ VOID ☐ CORRECTED

PAYER'S name, street address, city, state, ZIP code, and telephone no.			1 Patronage dividends $ ← 1.40" →	OMB No. 1545-0118	Taxable Distributions Received From Cooperatives
			2 Nonpatronage distributions $	**2006**	
			3 Per-unit retain allocations $	Form **1099-PATR**	
PAYER'S federal identification number	RECIPIENT'S identification number		4 Federal income tax withheld $		**Copy A For Internal Revenue Service Center** File with Form 1096. For Privacy Act and Paperwork Reduction Act Notice, see the **2006 General Instructions for Forms 1099, 1098, 5498, and W-2G.**
RECIPIENT'S name			5 Redemption of nonqualified notices and retain allocations $	6 Domestic production activities deduction $	
Street address (including apt. no.)				7 Investment credit $	
City, state, and ZIP code			8 Work opportunity credit $	9 Patron's AMT adjustment $	
Account number (see instructions) ← 2.80" →		2nd TIN not. ☐	10 Other credits and deductions $ ← 4.15" →		

Form **1099-PATR** Cat. No. 14435F Department of the Treasury - Internal Revenue Service

Do Not Cut or Separate Forms on This Page — Do Not Cut or Separate Forms on This Page

9797 ☐ VOID ☐ CORRECTED

PAYER'S name, street address, city, state, ZIP code, and telephone no.			1 Patronage dividends $	OMB No. 1545-0118	Taxable Distributions Received From Cooperatives
			2 Nonpatronage distributions $	**2006**	
			3 Per-unit retain allocations $	Form **1099-PATR**	
PAYER'S federal identification number	RECIPIENT'S identification number		4 Federal income tax withheld $		**Copy A For Internal Revenue Service Center** File with Form 1096. For Privacy Act and Paperwork Reduction Act Notice, see the **2006 General Instructions for Forms 1099, 1098, 5498, and W-2G.**
RECIPIENT'S name			5 Redemption of nonqualified notices and retain allocations $	6 Domestic production activities deduction $	
Street address (including apt. no.)				7 Investment credit $	
City, state, and ZIP code			8 Work opportunity credit $	9 Patron's AMT adjustment $	
Account number (see instructions)		2nd TIN not. ☐	10 Other credits and deductions $		

Form **1099-PATR** Cat. No. 14435F Department of the Treasury - Internal Revenue Service

Do Not Cut or Separate Forms on This Page — Do Not Cut or Separate Forms on This Page

9797 ☐ VOID ☐ CORRECTED

PAYER'S name, street address, city, state, ZIP code, and telephone no.			1 Patronage dividends $	OMB No. 1545-0118	Taxable Distributions Received From Cooperatives
			2 Nonpatronage distributions $	**2006**	
			3 Per-unit retain allocations $	Form **1099-PATR**	
PAYER'S federal identification number	RECIPIENT'S identification number		4 Federal income tax withheld $		**Copy A For Internal Revenue Service Center** File with Form 1096. For Privacy Act and Paperwork Reduction Act Notice, see the **2006 General Instructions for Forms 1099, 1098, 5498, and W-2G.**
RECIPIENT'S name			5 Redemption of nonqualified notices and retain allocations $	6 Domestic production activities deduction $	
Street address (including apt. no.)				7 Investment credit $	
City, state, and ZIP code			8 Work opportunity credit $	9 Patron's AMT adjustment $	
Account number (see instructions)		2nd TIN not. ☐	10 Other credits and deductions $		

Form **1099-PATR** Cat. No. 14435F Department of the Treasury - Internal Revenue Service

Exhibit R

4.5"

3131 ☐ VOID ☐ CORRECTED

PAYER'S/TRUSTEE'S name, street address, city, state, ZIP code, and telephone number

2.83"

3.4"

1 Gross distribution

1.4"

$

2 Earnings

$

OMB No. 1545-1760

2006

Form 1099-Q

Payments From Qualified Education Programs (Under Sections 529 and 530)

PAYER'S/TRUSTEE'S federal identification no.

RECIPIENT'S social security number

3 Basis

$

4 Trustee-to-trustee transfer ☐

1.4"

Copy A

For

Internal Revenue Service Center

File with Form 1096.

For Privacy Act and Paperwork Reduction Act Notice, see the **2006 General Instructions for Forms 1099, 1098, 5498, and W-2G.**

RECIPIENT'S name

5 Check one:

• Qualified tuition program—

Private ☐ **or** State ☐

• Coverdell ESA ☐

6 Check if the recipient is not the designated beneficiary ☐

3.25"

Street address (including apt. no.)

City, state, and ZIP code

Account number (see instructions)

Form **1099-Q** Cat. No. 32223J Department of the Treasury - Internal Revenue Service

Do Not Cut or Separate Forms on This Page — Do Not Cut or Separate Forms on This Page

3131 ☐ VOID ☐ CORRECTED

PAYER'S/TRUSTEE'S name, street address, city, state, ZIP code, and telephone number

1 Gross distribution

$

2 Earnings

$

OMB No. 1545-1760

2006

Form 1099-Q

Payments From Qualified Education Programs (Under Sections 529 and 530)

PAYER'S/TRUSTEE'S federal identification no.

RECIPIENT'S social security number

3 Basis

$

4 Trustee-to-trustee transfer ☐

Copy A

For

Internal Revenue Service Center

File with Form 1096.

For Privacy Act and Paperwork Reduction Act Notice, see the **2006 General Instructions for Forms 1099, 1098, 5498, and W-2G.**

RECIPIENT'S name

5 Check one:

• Qualified tuition program—

Private ☐ **or** State ☐

• Coverdell ESA ☐

6 Check if the recipient is not the designated beneficiary ☐

Street address (including apt. no.)

City, state, and ZIP code

Account number (see instructions)

Form **1099-Q** Cat. No. 32223J Department of the Treasury - Internal Revenue Service

Do Not Cut or Separate Forms on This Page — Do Not Cut or Separate Forms on This Page

3131 ☐ VOID ☐ CORRECTED

PAYER'S/TRUSTEE'S name, street address, city, state, ZIP code, and telephone number

1 Gross distribution

$

2 Earnings

$

OMB No. 1545-1760

2006

Form 1099-Q

Payments From Qualified Education Programs (Under Sections 529 and 530)

PAYER'S/TRUSTEE'S federal identification no.

RECIPIENT'S social security number

3 Basis

$

4 Trustee-to-trustee transfer ☐

Copy A

For

Internal Revenue Service Center

File with Form 1096.

For Privacy Act and Paperwork Reduction Act Notice, see the **2006 General Instructions for Forms 1099, 1098, 5498, and W-2G.**

RECIPIENT'S name

5 Check one:

• Qualified tuition program—

Private ☐ **or** State ☐

• Coverdell ESA ☐

6 Check if the recipient is not the designated beneficiary ☐

Street address (including apt. no.)

City, state, and ZIP code

Account number (see instructions)

Form **1099-Q** Cat. No. 32223J Department of the Treasury - Internal Revenue Service

Exhibit S

.3125   .50"   5.50"   4.50"

9898   VOID   CORRECTED

PAYER'S name, street address, city, state, and ZIP code		1 Gross distribution (1.40") $	OMB No. 1545-0119 **2006** Form **1099-R**	**Distributions From Pensions, Annuities, Retirement or Profit-Sharing Plans, IRAs, Insurance Contracts, etc.**
		2a Taxable amount $		
		2b Taxable amount not determined ☐ (2.65")	Total distribution ☐	(1.25") **Copy A For Internal Revenue Service Center**
PAYER'S federal identification number	RECIPIENT'S identification number	3 Capital gain (included in box 2a) $	4 Federal income tax withheld $	**File with Form 1096.** (.25")
RECIPIENT'S name		5 Employee contributions /Designated Roth contributions or insurance premiums $ (.40")	6 Net unrealized appreciation in employer's securities $	For Privacy Act and Paperwork Reduction Act Notice, see the **2006 General Instructions for Forms 1099, 1098, 5498, and W-2G.**
Street address (including apt. no.)		7 Distribution code(s) (1.00") / IRA/ SEP/ SIMPLE ☐	8 Other (1.00") $ (2.50") / (.40") %	
City, state, and ZIP code		9a Your percentage of total distribution %	9b Total employee contributions $	
	1st year of desig. Roth contrib.	10 State tax withheld $ $	11 State/Payer's state no.	12 State distribution (1.10") $ $
Account number (see instructions)		13 Local tax withheld $ $	14 Name of locality	15 Local distribution $ $

Form **1099-R**   Cat. No. 14436Q   Department of the Treasury — Internal Revenue Service

Do Not Cut or Separate Forms on This Page — Do Not Cut or Separate Forms on This Page

1.00"   .45"

9898   VOID   CORRECTED

PAYER'S name, street address, city, state, and ZIP code		1 Gross distribution $	OMB No. 1545-0119 **2006** Form **1099-R**	**Distributions From Pensions, Annuities, Retirement or Profit-Sharing Plans, IRAs, Insurance Contracts, etc.**
		2a Taxable amount $		
		2b Taxable amount not determined ☐	Total distribution ☐	**Copy A For Internal Revenue Service Center**
PAYER'S federal identification number	RECIPIENT'S identification number	3 Capital gain (included in box 2a) $	4 Federal income tax withheld $	**File with Form 1096.**
RECIPIENT'S name		5 Employee contributions /Designated Roth contributions or insurance premiums $	6 Net unrealized appreciation in employer's securities $	For Privacy Act and Paperwork Reduction Act Notice, see the **2006 General Instructions for Forms 1099, 1098, 5498, and W-2G.**
Street address (including apt. no.)		7 Distribution code(s) / IRA/ SEP/ SIMPLE ☐	8 Other $ / %	
City, state, and ZIP code		9a Your percentage of total distribution %	9b Total employee contributions $	
	1st year of desig. Roth contrib.	10 State tax withheld $ $	11 State/Payer's state no.	12 State distribution $ $
Account number (see instructions)		13 Local tax withheld $ $	14 Name of locality	15 Local distribution $ $

Form **1099-R**   Cat. No. 14436Q   Department of the Treasury — Internal Revenue Service

Exhibit T

7575 ☐ VOID ☐ CORRECTED

FILER'S name, street address, city, state, ZIP code, and telephone no.	1 Date of closing ◄—1.40"—► 2 Gross proceeds $	OMB No. 1545-0997 **2006** Form **1099-S**	**Proceeds From Real Estate Transactions**
FILER'S federal identification number ◄—1.70"—► / TRANSFEROR'S identification number ◄—1.70"—►	3 Address or legal description (including city, state, and ZIP code) ◄—2.80"—►		◄—1.10"—► **Copy A For Internal Revenue Service Center** File with Form 1096. For Privacy Act and Paperwork Reduction Act Notice, see the **2006 General Instructions for Forms 1099, 1098, 5498, and W-2G.**
TRANSFEROR'S name			
Street address (including apt. no.)			
City, state, and ZIP code	4 Check here if the transferor received or will receive property or services as part of the consideration. ► ☐		
Account or escrow number (see instructions)	5 Buyer's part of real estate tax $		

Form **1099-S** Cat. No. 64292E Department of the Treasury - Internal Revenue Service

Do Not Cut or Separate Forms on This Page — Do Not Cut or Separate Forms on This Page

7575 ☐ VOID ☐ CORRECTED

FILER'S name, street address, city, state, ZIP code, and telephone no.	1 Date of closing 2 Gross proceeds $	OMB No. 1545-0997 **2006** Form **1099-S**	**Proceeds From Real Estate Transactions**
FILER'S federal identification number / TRANSFEROR'S identification number	3 Address or legal description (including city, state, and ZIP code)		**Copy A For Internal Revenue Service Center** File with Form 1096. For Privacy Act and Paperwork Reduction Act Notice, see the **2006 General Instructions for Forms 1099, 1098, 5498, and W-2G.**
TRANSFEROR'S name			
Street address (including apt. no.)			
City, state, and ZIP code	4 Check here if the transferor received or will receive property or services as part of the consideration. ► ☐		
Account or escrow number (see instructions)	5 Buyer's part of real estate tax $		

Form **1099-S** Cat. No. 64292E Department of the Treasury - Internal Revenue Service

Do Not Cut or Separate Forms on This Page — Do Not Cut or Separate Forms on This Page

7575 ☐ VOID ☐ CORRECTED

FILER'S name, street address, city, state, ZIP code, and telephone no.	1 Date of closing 2 Gross proceeds $	OMB No. 1545-0997 **2006** Form **1099-S**	**Proceeds From Real Estate Transactions**
FILER'S federal identification number / TRANSFEROR'S identification number	3 Address or legal description (including city, state, and ZIP code)		**Copy A For Internal Revenue Service Center** File with Form 1096. For Privacy Act and Paperwork Reduction Act Notice, see the **2006 General Instructions for Forms 1099, 1098, 5498, and W-2G.**
TRANSFEROR'S name			
Street address (including apt. no.)			
City, state, and ZIP code	4 Check here if the transferor received or will receive property or services as part of the consideration. ► ☐		
Account or escrow number (see instructions)	5 Buyer's part of real estate tax $		

Form **1099-S** Cat. No. 64292E Department of the Treasury - Internal Revenue Service

Exhibit U

9494 ☐ VOID ☐ CORRECTED

TRUSTEE'S/PAYER'S name, street address, city, state, and ZIP code			OMB No. 1545-1517 2006 Form 1099-SA	**Distributions From an HSA, Archer MSA, or Medicare Advantage MSA**
PAYER'S federal identification number	RECIPIENT'S identification number	1 Gross distribution $	2 Earnings on excess cont. $	**Copy A For Internal Revenue Service Center**
RECIPIENT'S name		3 Distribution code	4 FMV on date of death $	**File with Form 1096.**
Street address (including apt. no.)		5 HSA ☐ Archer MSA ☐ MA MSA ☐		For Privacy Act and Paperwork Reduction Act Notice, see the **2006 General Instructions for Forms 1099, 1098, 5498, and W-2G.**
City, state, and ZIP code				
Account number (see instructions)				

Form **1099-SA** Cat. No. 38471D Department of the Treasury - Internal Revenue Service

Do Not Cut or Separate Forms on This Page — Do Not Cut or Separate Forms on This Page

9494 ☐ VOID ☐ CORRECTED

TRUSTEE'S/PAYER'S name, street address, city, state, and ZIP code			OMB No. 1545-1517 2006 Form 1099-SA	**Distributions From an HSA, Archer MSA, or Medicare Advantage MSA**
PAYER'S federal identification number	RECIPIENT'S identification number	1 Gross distribution $	2 Earnings on excess cont. $	**Copy A For Internal Revenue Service Center**
RECIPIENT'S name		3 Distribution code	4 FMV on date of death $	**File with Form 1096.**
Street address (including apt. no.)		5 HSA ☐ Archer MSA ☐ MA MSA ☐		For Privacy Act and Paperwork Reduction Act Notice, see the **2006 General Instructions for Forms 1099, 1098, 5498, and W-2G.**
City, state, and ZIP code				
Account number (see instructions)				

Form **1099-SA** Cat. No. 38471D Department of the Treasury - Internal Revenue Service

Do Not Cut or Separate Forms on This Page — Do Not Cut or Separate Forms on This Page

9494 ☐ VOID ☐ CORRECTED

TRUSTEE'S/PAYER'S name, street address, city, state, and ZIP code			OMB No. 1545-1517 2006 Form 1099-SA	**Distributions From an HSA, Archer MSA, or Medicare Advantage MSA**
PAYER'S federal identification number	RECIPIENT'S identification number	1 Gross distribution $	2 Earnings on excess cont. $	**Copy A For Internal Revenue Service Center**
RECIPIENT'S name		3 Distribution code	4 FMV on date of death $	**File with Form 1096.**
Street address (including apt. no.)		5 HSA ☐ Archer MSA ☐ MA MSA ☐		For Privacy Act and Paperwork Reduction Act Notice, see the **2000 General Instructions for Forms 1099, 1098, 5498, and W-2G.**
City, state, and ZIP code				
Account number (see instructions)				

Form **1099-SA** Cat. No. 38471D Department of the Treasury - Internal Revenue Service

Exhibit V

2828 ☐ VOID ☐ CORRECTED

TRUSTEE'S or ISSUER'S name, street address, city, state, and ZIP code		1 IRA contributions (other than amounts in boxes 2–4 and 8–10) $	OMB No. 1545-0747	IRA Contribution Information
		2 Rollover contributions ◄— 1.40" —► $	2006 Form 5498	
TRUSTEE'S or ISSUER'S federal identification no.	PARTICIPANT'S social security number	3 Roth IRA conversion amount $	4 Recharacterized contributions $	Copy A For Internal Revenue Service Center File with Form 1096.
PARTICIPANT'S name		5 Fair market value of account $	6 Life insurance cost included in box 1 $	For Privacy Act and Paperwork Reduction Act Notice, see the 2006 General Instructions for Forms 1099, 1098, 5498, and W-2G.
Street address (including apt. no.)		7 IRA ☐ SEP ☐	SIMPLE ☐ Roth IRA ☐	
City, state, and ZIP code		8 SEP contributions ◄$— 1.40" —►	9 SIMPLE contributions ◄$— 1.40" —►	
Account number (see instructions)		10 Roth IRA contributions $	11 Check if RMD for 2007 ☐	

Form 5498 Cat. No. 50010C Department of the Treasury - Internal Revenue Service

Do Not Cut or Separate Forms on This Page — Do Not Cut or Separate Forms on This Page

2828 ☐ VOID ☐ CORRECTED

TRUSTEE'S or ISSUER'S name, street address, city, state, and ZIP code		1 IRA contributions (other than amounts in boxes 2–4 and 8–10) $	OMB No. 1545-0747	IRA Contribution Information
		2 Rollover contributions $	2006 Form 5498	
TRUSTEE'S or ISSUER'S federal identification no.	PARTICIPANT'S social security number	3 Roth IRA conversion amount $	4 Recharacterized contributions $	Copy A For Internal Revenue Service Center File with Form 1096.
PARTICIPANT'S name		5 Fair market value of account $	6 Life insurance cost included in box 1 $	For Privacy Act and Paperwork Reduction Act Notice, see the 2006 General Instructions for Forms 1099, 1098, 5498, and W-2G.
Street address (including apt. no.)		7 IRA ☐ SEP ☐	SIMPLE ☐ Roth IRA ☐	
City, state, and ZIP code		8 SEP contributions $	9 SIMPLE contributions $	
Account number (see instructions)		10 Roth IRA contributions $	11 Check if RMD for 2007 ☐	

Form 5498 Cat. No. 50010C Department of the Treasury - Internal Revenue Service

Do Not Cut or Separate Forms on This Page — Do Not Cut or Separate Forms on This Page

2828 ☐ VOID ☐ CORRECTED

TRUSTEE'S or ISSUER'S name, street address, city, state, and ZIP code		1 IRA contributions (other than amounts in boxes 2–4 and 8–10) $	OMB No. 1545-0747	IRA Contribution Information
		2 Rollover contributions $	2006 Form 5498	
TRUSTEE'S or ISSUER'S federal identification no.	PARTICIPANT'S social security number	3 Roth IRA conversion amount $	4 Recharacterized contributions $	Copy A For Internal Revenue Service Center File with Form 1096.
PARTICIPANT'S name		5 Fair market value of account $	6 Life insurance cost included in box 1 $	For Privacy Act and Paperwork Reduction Act Notice, see the 2006 General Instructions for Forms 1099, 1098, 5498, and W-2G.
Street address (including apt. no.)		7 IRA ☐ SEP ☐	SIMPLE ☐ Roth IRA ☐	
City, state, and ZIP code		8 SEP contributions $	9 SIMPLE contributions $	
Account number (see instructions)		10 Roth IRA contributions $	11 Check if RMD for 2007 ☐	

Form 5498 Cat. No. 50010C Department of the Treasury - Internal Revenue Service

Exhibit W

7272 ☐ VOID ☐ CORRECTED

TRUSTEE'S or ISSUER'S name, street address, city, state, and ZIP code ← 3.40" →	1 Coverdell ESA contributions $ 2 Rollover contributions $	OMB No. 1545-1815 2006 Form 5498-ESA	Coverdell ESA Contribution Information
TRUSTEE'S/ISSUER'S federal identification no. / BENEFICIARY'S social security number			Copy A For Internal Revenue Service Center File with Form 1096. For Privacy Act and Paperwork Reduction Act Notice, see the **2006 General Instructions for Forms 1099, 1098, 5498, and W-2G.**
BENEFICIARY'S name		← 1.40" →	
Street address (including apt. no.)			
City, state, and ZIP code			
Account number (see instructions)			

.45"

Form **5498-ESA** Cat. No. 34011J Department of the Treasury - Internal Revenue Service

Do Not Cut or Separate Forms on This Page — Do Not Cut or Separate Forms on This Page

7272 ☐ VOID ☐ CORRECTED

TRUSTEE'S or ISSUER'S name, street address, city, state, and ZIP code	1 Coverdell ESA contributions $ 2 Rollover contributions $	OMB No. 1545-1815 2006 Form 5498-ESA	Coverdell ESA Contribution Information
TRUSTEE'S/ISSUER'S federal identification no. / BENEFICIARY'S social security number			Copy A For Internal Revenue Service Center File with Form 1096. For Privacy Act and Paperwork Reduction Act Notice, see the **2006 General Instructions for Forms 1099, 1098, 5498, and W-2G.**
BENEFICIARY'S name			
Street address (including apt. no.)			
City, state, and ZIP code			
Account number (see instructions)			

Form **5498-ESA** Cat. No. 34011J Department of the Treasury - Internal Revenue Service

Do Not Cut or Separate Forms on This Page — Do Not Cut or Separate Forms on This Page

7272 ☐ VOID ☐ CORRECTED

TRUSTEE'S or ISSUER'S name, street address, city, state, and ZIP code	1 Coverdell ESA contributions $ 2 Rollover contributions $	OMB No. 1545-1815 2006 Form 5498-ESA	Coverdell ESA Contribution Information
TRUSTEE'S/ISSUER'S federal identification no. / BENEFICIARY'S social security number			Copy A For Internal Revenue Service Center File with Form 1096. For Privacy Act and Paperwork Reduction Act Notice, see the **2006 General Instructions for Forms 1099, 1098, 5498, and W-2G.**
BENEFICIARY'S name			
Street address (including apt. no.)			
City, state, and ZIP code			
Account number (see instructions)			

Form **5498-ESA** Cat. No. 34011J Department of the Treasury - Internal Revenue Service

Exhibit X

2727 ☐ VOID ☐ CORRECTED

TRUSTEE'S name, street address, city, state, and ZIP code		1 Employee or self-employed person's Archer MSA contributions made in 2006 and 2007 for 2006 $	OMB No. 1545-1518 **2006** Form **5498-SA**	**HSA, Archer MSA, or Medicare Advantage MSA Information**
		2 Total contributions made in 2006 $		
TRUSTEE'S federal identification number	PARTICIPANT'S social security number	3 Total HSA or Archer MSA contributions made in 2007 for 2006 $		**Copy A For Internal Revenue Service Center** File with Form 1096. For Privacy Act and Paperwork Reduction Act Notice, see the **2006 General Instructions for Forms 1099, 1098, 5498, and W-2G.**
PARTICIPANT'S name		4 Rollover contributions $	5 Fair market value of HSA, Archer MSA, or MA MSA $	
Street address (including apt. no.)		6 HSA ☐ Archer MSA ☐ MA MSA ☐		
City, state, and ZIP code				
Account number (see instructions)				

Form **5498-SA** Cat. No. 38467V Department of the Treasury - Internal Revenue Service

Do Not Cut or Separate Forms on This Page — Do Not Cut or Separate Forms on This Page

2727 ☐ VOID ☐ CORRECTED

TRUSTEE'S name, street address, city, state, and ZIP code		1 Employee or self-employed person's Archer MSA contributions made in 2006 and 2007 for 2006 $	OMB No. 1545-1518 **2006** Form **5498-SA**	**HSA, Archer MSA, or Medicare Advantage MSA Information**
		2 Total contributions made in 2006 $		
TRUSTEE'S federal identification number	PARTICIPANT'S social security number	3 Total HSA or Archer MSA contributions made in 2007 for 2006 $		**Copy A For Internal Revenue Service Center** File with Form 1096. For Privacy Act and Paperwork Reduction Act Notice, see the **2006 General Instructions for Forms 1099, 1098, 5498, and W-2G.**
PARTICIPANT'S name		4 Rollover contributions $	5 Fair market value of HSA, Archer MSA, or MA MSA $	
Street address (including apt. no.)		6 HSA ☐ Archer MSA ☐ MA MSA ☐		
City, state, and ZIP code				
Account number (see instructions)				

Form **5498-SA** Cat. No. 38467V Department of the Treasury - Internal Revenue Service

Do Not Cut or Separate Forms on This Page — Do Not Cut or Separate Forms on This Page

2727 ☐ VOID ☐ CORRECTED

TRUSTEE'S name, street address, city, state, and ZIP code		1 Employee or self-employed person's Archer MSA contributions made in 2006 and 2007 for 2006 $	OMB No. 1545-1518 **2006** Form **5498-SA**	**HSA, Archer MSA, or Medicare Advantage MSA Information**
		2 Total contributions made in 2006 $		
TRUSTEE'S federal identification number	PARTICIPANT'S social security number	3 Total HSA or Archer MSA contributions made in 2007 for 2006 $		**Copy A For Internal Revenue Service Center** File with Form 1096. For Privacy Act and Paperwork Reduction Act Notice, see the **2006 General Instructions for Forms 1099, 1098, 5498, and W-2G.**
PARTICIPANT'S name		4 Rollover contributions $	5 Fair market value of HSA, Archer MSA, or MA MSA $	
Street address (including apt. no.)		6 HSA ☐ Archer MSA ☐ MA MSA ☐		
City, state, and ZIP code				
Account number (see instructions)				

Form **5498-SA** Cat. No. 38467V Department of the Treasury - Internal Revenue Service

Exhibit Y

3232 ☐ CORRECTED

PAYER'S name Street address 3.00" City, state, and ZIP code Federal identification number Telephone number	1 Gross winnings 1.45"	2 Federal income tax withheld 1.45"	OMB No. 1545-0238 2006 **Form W-2G** **Certain Gambling Winnings**
	3 Type of wager	4 Date won	
	5 Transaction	6 Race	
	7 Winnings from identical wagers	8 Cashier	1.40"
WINNER'S name 2.85" Street address (including apt. no.) City, state, and ZIP code	9 Winner's taxpayer identification no.	10 Window	For Privacy Act and Paperwork Reduction Act Notice, see the **2006 General Instructions for Forms 1099, 1098, 5498, and W-2G.**
	11 First I.D.	12 Second I.D.	
	13 State/Payer's state identification no.	14 State income tax withheld	**File with Form 1096.**

Under penalties of perjury, I declare that, to the best of my knowledge and belief, the name, address, and taxpayer identification number that I have furnished correctly identify me as the recipient of this payment and any payments from identical wagers, and that no other person is entitled to any part of these payments.

Signature ► **Date ►**

Copy A For Internal Revenue Service Center

Form **W-2G** Cat. No. 10138V Department of the Treasury - Internal Revenue Service

3232 ☐ CORRECTED

PAYER'S name Street address City, state, and ZIP code Federal identification number Telephone number	1 Gross winnings	2 Federal income tax withheld	OMB No. 1545-0238 2006 **Form W-2G** **Certain Gambling Winnings**
	3 Type of wager	4 Date won	
	5 Transaction	6 Race	
	7 Winnings from identical wagers	8 Cashier	
WINNER'S name Street address (including apt. no.) City, state, and ZIP code	9 Winner's taxpayer identification no.	10 Window	For Privacy Act and Paperwork Reduction Act Notice, see the **2006 General Instructions for Forms 1099, 1098, 5498, and W-2G.**
	11 First I.D.	12 Second I.D.	
	13 State/Payer's state identification no.	14 State income tax withheld	**File with Form 1096.**

Under penalties of perjury, I declare that, to the best of my knowledge and belief, the name, address, and taxpayer identification number that I have furnished correctly identify me as the recipient of this payment and any payments from identical wagers, and that no other person is entitled to any part of these payments.

Signature ► **Date ►**

Copy A For Internal Revenue Service Center

Form **W-2G** Cat. No. 10138V Department of the Treasury - Internal Revenue Service

3232 ☐ CORRECTED

PAYER'S name Street address City, state, and ZIP code Federal identification number Telephone number	1 Gross winnings	2 Federal income tax withheld	OMB No. 1545-0238 2006 **Form W-2G** **Certain Gambling Winnings**
	3 Type of wager	4 Date won	
	5 Transaction	6 Race	
	7 Winnings from identical wagers	8 Cashier	
WINNER'S name Street address (including apt. no.) City, state, and ZIP code	9 Winner's taxpayer identification no.	10 Window	For Privacy Act and Paperwork Reduction Act Notice, see the **2006 General Instructions for Forms 1099, 1098, 5498, and W-2G.**
	11 First I.D.	12 Second I.D.	
	13 State/Payer's state identification no.	14 State income tax withheld	**File with Form 1096.**

Under penalties of perjury, I declare that, to the best of my knowledge and belief, the name, address, and taxpayer identification number that I have furnished correctly identify me as the recipient of this payment and any payments from identical wagers, and that no other person is entitled to any part of these payments.

Signature ► **Date ►**

Copy A For Internal Revenue Service Center

Form **W-2G** Cat. No. 10138V Department of the Treasury - Internal Revenue Service

Exhibit Z

5.50"

Form **1042-S**
Department of the Treasury
Internal Revenue Service

Foreign Person's U.S. Source Income Subject to Withholding

2006

OMB No. 1545-0096

Copy A for Internal Revenue Service

☐ **AMENDED** ☐ **PRO-RATA BASIS REPORTING**

1 Income code	2 Gross income	3 Withholding allowances	4 Net income	5 Tax rate	6 Exemption code	7 U.S. Federal tax withheld	8 Amount repaid to recipient

9 Withholding agent's EIN ▶ ☐ EIN ☐ QI-EIN

10a WITHHOLDING AGENT'S name — Check here if nominee ☐

10b Address (number and street)

10c Additional address line (room or suite no.)

10d City or town, province or state, and country

10e ZIP code or foreign postal code

11 Recipient's account number (optional)

12 Recipient code

13a RECIPIENT'S name

13b Address (number and street)

13c Additional address line (room or suite no.)

.375"

13d City or town, province or state, and country

13e ZIP code or foreign postal code

14 Recipient's U.S. TIN, if any ▶ ☐ SSN or ITIN ☐ EIN ☐ QI-EIN

15 Recipient's country of residence for tax purposes

16 Country code

17 NONQUALIFIED INTERMEDIARY'S (NQI's)/ FLOW-THROUGH ENTITY'S name

18 Country code

19a NQI's/Flow-through entity's address (number and street)

19b Additional address line (room or suite no.)

19c City or town, province or state, and country

19d ZIP code or foreign postal code

20 NQI's/Flow-through entity's TIN, if any ▶

21 PAYER'S name and TIN (if different from withholding agent's)

22 State income tax withheld

23 Payer's state tax no.

24 Name of state

7.25"

For Privacy Act and Paperwork Reduction Act Notice, see page 15 of the separate instructions. Cat. No. 11386R Form **1042-S** (2006)

8.00"

Form **1042-S**
Department of the Treasury
Internal Revenue Service

Foreign Person's U.S. Source Income Subject to Withholding

2006

OMB No. 1545-0096

Copy A for Internal Revenue Service

☐ **AMENDED** ☐ **PRO-RATA BASIS REPORTING**

1 Income code	2 Gross income	3 Withholding allowances	4 Net income	5 Tax rate	6 Exemption code	7 U.S. Federal tax withheld	8 Amount repaid to recipient

9 Withholding agent's EIN ▶ ☐ EIN ☐ QI-EIN

10a WITHHOLDING AGENT'S name — Check here if nominee ☐

10b Address (number and street)

10c Additional address line (room or suite no.)

10d City or town, province or state, and country

10e ZIP code or foreign postal code

11 Recipient's account number (optional)

12 Recipient code

13a RECIPIENT'S name

13b Address (number and street)

13c Additional address line (room or suite no.)

13d City or town, province or state, and country

13e ZIP code or foreign postal code

14 Recipient's U.S. TIN, if any ▶ ☐ SSN or ITIN ☐ EIN ☐ QI-EIN

15 Recipient's country of residence for tax purposes

16 Country code

17 NONQUALIFIED INTERMEDIARY'S (NQI's)/ FLOW-THROUGH ENTITY'S name

18 Country code

19a NQI's/Flow-through entity's address (number and street)

19b Additional address line (room or suite no.)

19c City or town, province or state, and country

19d ZIP code or foreign postal code

20 NQI's/Flow-through entity's TIN, if any ▶

21 PAYER'S name and TIN (if different from withholding agent's)

22 State income tax withheld

23 Payer's state tax no.

24 Name of state

For Privacy Act and Paperwork Reduction Act Notice, see page 15 of the separate instructions. Cat. No. 11386R Form **1042-S** (2006)

Part I. Rulings and Decisions Under the Internal Revenue Code of 1986

Section 446.—General Rule for Methods of Accounting

This revenue procedure provides procedures by which a taxpayer may obtain automatic consent to change its method of accounting for services or insurance under section 461 to comply with Rev. Rul. 2007-3, page 350, this Bulletin. See Rev. Proc. 2007-14, page 357.

---

26 CFR 1.446–1: General rule for methods of accounting.

May a taxpayer change its method of accounting under § 446(e) of the Internal Revenue Code for depreciable or amortizable property after its disposition? See Rev. Proc. 2007-16, page 358.

Section 461.—General Rule for Taxable Year of Deduction

This revenue procedure provides procedures by which a taxpayer may obtain automatic consent to change its method of accounting for services or insurance under section 461 to comply with Rev. Rul. 2007-3, page 350, this Bulletin. See Rev. Proc. 2007-14, page 357.

---

26 CFR 1.461–1: General rule for taxable year of deduction.
(Also §§ 1.461–4, 1.461–5.)

Executory contract liabilities. This ruling provides guidance on when a taxpayer using an accrual method of accounting incurs a liability for services or insurance under section 461 of the Code.

Rev. Rul. 2007–3

ISSUES

(1) Under § 461 of the Internal Revenue Code, when does a taxpayer using an accrual method of accounting incur a liability for services?

(2) Under § 461, when does a taxpayer using an accrual method of accounting incur a liability for insurance?

FACTS

X is a corporation that uses an accrual method of accounting and files its federal income tax returns on a calendar year basis.

Situation 1. On December 15, 2006, *X* executes a contract with *Y* for the provision of services. The contract provides for services to begin on January 15, 2007, and end on January 31, 2007. Under the terms of the contract, payment for the services is due to *Y* on January 15, 2007, and *X* pays *Y* for the services on January 15, 2007. *X* uses the recurring item exception under § 1.461–5.

Situation 2. On December 15, 2006, *X* executes a contract with *W*, an insurance company regulated under state law, for the provision of insurance. The insurance contract covers the period from January 15, 2007, through December 31, 2007. Under the terms of the contract, payment of the insurance premium is due to *W* on January 15, 2007, and *X* pays the premium to *W* on January 15, 2007. *X* uses the recurring item exception under § 1.461–5.

LAW

Section 461(a) provides that the amount of any deduction or credit must be taken for the taxable year that is the proper taxable year under the method of accounting used by the taxpayer in computing taxable income.

Section 1.461–1(a)(2)(i) of the Income Tax Regulations provides that, under an accrual method of accounting, a liability is incurred, and is generally taken into account for federal income tax purposes, in the taxable year in which (1) all the events have occurred that establish the fact of the liability, (2) the amount of the liability can be determined with reasonable accuracy, and (3) economic performance has occurred with respect to the liability (the "all events test"). *See also* § 1.446–1(c)(1)(ii)(A).

The first prong of the all events test requires that all the events have occurred that establish the fact of the liability. Therefore, it is fundamental to the all events test that although expenses may be deductible before they become due and payable, liability first must be firmly established. *United States v. General Dynamics Corp.*, 481 U.S. 239, 243–4 (1987).

Generally, under § 1.461–1(a)(2), all the events have occurred that establish the fact of the liability when (1) the event fixing the liability, whether that be the required performance or other event, occurs, or (2) payment therefore is due, whichever happens earliest. Rev. Rul. 80–230, 1980–2 C.B. 169; Rev. Rul. 79–410, 1979–2 C.B. 213, *amplified by* Rev Rul. 2003–90, 2003–2 C.B. 353. The terms of a contract are relevant in determining the events that establish the fact of a taxpayer's liability. *See, e.g., Decision, Inc. v. Commissioner*, 47 T.C. 58 (1966), *acq.*, 1967–2 C.B. 2.

Section 461(h) and § 1.461–4 provide that, for purposes of determining whether an accrual basis taxpayer can treat the amount of any liability as incurred, the all events test is not treated as met any earlier than the taxable year in which economic performance occurs with respect to the liability.

Section 1.461–4(d)(2) provides that if a liability of a taxpayer arises out of the providing of services or property to the taxpayer by another person, economic performance occurs as the services or property is provided.

Section 1.461–4(g)(5) provides that if a liability of a taxpayer arises out of the provision to the taxpayer of insurance, economic performance occurs as payment is made to the person to which the liability is owed.

Section 1.461–5(b)(1) provides a recurring item exception to the general rule of economic performance. Under the recurring item exception, a liability is treated as incurred for a taxable year if: (i) at the end of the taxable year, all events have occurred that establish the fact of the liability and the amount can be determined with reasonable accuracy; (ii) economic performance occurs on or before the earlier of (a) the date that the taxpayer files a return (including extensions) for the taxable year, or (b) the 15th day of the ninth calendar month after the close of the taxable year; (iii) the liability is recurring in nature; and (iv) either the amount of the liability is not material or accrual of the liability in the taxable year results in better matching of the liability against the income to which it relates than would result from accrual of the liability in the taxable year in which economic performance occurs.

ANALYSIS

Situation 1. In *Situation 1*, the first event that occurs to establish the fact of *X*'s liability for services is that payment is due under the contract on January 15, 2007. *See* Rev. Rul. 80–230; Rev. Rul. 79–410. Thus, for purposes of § 461, the fact of the liability is established on January 15, 2007. At that time, the amount can be determined with reasonable accuracy. Economic performance with respect to the liability occurs as the services are provided, from January 15, 2007, through January 31, 2007. *See* § 1.461–4(d)(2). Therefore, *X* incurs a liability for services in 2007.

The fact of the liability is not established in 2006, even though *X* executed the service contract on December 15, 2006. It is well established that an accrual basis obligor is not permitted to deduct an expense stemming from a bilateral contractual arrangement, that is, mutual promises, prior to the performance of the contracted for services by the obligee. Rev. Rul. 80–182, 1980–2 C.B. 167, citing *Levin v. Commissioner*, 21 T.C. 996 (1954), *aff'd*, 219 F.2d 588 (3d Cir. 1955) (an agreement for services to be performed in the next year did not establish the fact of the taxpayer's liability but was simply an agreement under which a liability would be incurred in the future) and *Amalgamated Housing Corp. v. Commissioner*, 37 B.T.A. 817 (1938), *aff'd per curium*, 108 F.2d 1010 (2d Cir. 1940) (an agreement to renovate property in the future did not establish the fact of the taxpayer's liability; the accrual was for services in renovating, not the duty to renovate). Thus, the mere execution of the contract by *X* in 2006 is not sufficient, by itself, to establish the fact of the liability. Further, the recurring item exception does not apply because the fact of the liability is not established in 2006.

Situation 2. In *Situation 2*, the first event that occurs to establish the fact of *X*'s liability for insurance is that the premium is due under the contract. *See* Rev. Rul. 80–230; Rev. Rul. 79–410. Thus, for purposes of § 461, the fact of the liability is established on January 15, 2007. At that time, the amount can be determined with reasonable accuracy. Economic performance with respect to the liability occurs as payment is made, on January 15, 2007. *See* § 1.461–4(g)(5). Therefore, *X* incurs a liability for insurance in 2007.

The fact of the liability is not established in 2006, even though *X* executed the insurance contract on December 15, 2006. *See* Rev. Rul. 80–182. Although federal or state regulations may impose certain legal obligations on taxpayers, those obligations, without more, do not necessarily establish the fact of a taxpayer's liability under § 461. *See Chrysler Corp. v. Commissioner*, 436 F.3d 644 (6th Cir. 2006) (statutory obligation related to warranty obligation was not sufficient to establish the fact of the taxpayer's liability to provide warranty services). Further, the recurring item exception does not apply because the fact of the liability is not established in 2006.

HOLDINGS

(1) Under § 461, all the events have occurred that establish the fact of the liability for services provided to the taxpayer when (1) the event fixing the liability, whether that be the required performance or other event, occurs, or (2) payment is due, whichever happens earliest. The mere execution of a contract, without more, does not establish the fact of a taxpayer's liability for services.

(2) Under § 461, all the events have occurred that establish the fact of the liability for insurance when (1) the event fixing the liability, whether that be the required performance or other event, occurs, or (2) payment is due, whichever happens earliest. The mere execution of a contract, without more, does not establish the fact of a taxpayer's liability for insurance.

APPLICATION

A change in the treatment of liabilities for services or insurance to comply with this revenue ruling is a change in method of accounting within the meaning of §§ 446 and 481 and the regulations issued thereunder. Accordingly, a taxpayer that wants to change its treatment of liabilities for services or insurance to comply with this revenue ruling must obtain the consent of the Commissioner under § 446(e) and § 1.446–1(e)(2)(i) by following the procedures in Rev. Proc. 2007–14, page 357, this Bulletin.

DRAFTING INFORMATION

The principal author of this revenue ruling is Leta A. Ayres of the Office of Associate Chief Counsel (Income Tax & Accounting). For further information regarding this revenue ruling, contact Ms. Ayres at (202) 622–5020 (not a toll-free call).

Section 481.—Adjustments Required by Changes in Method of Accounting

This revenue procedure provides procedures by which a taxpayer may obtain automatic consent to change its method of accounting for services or insurance under section 461 to comply with Rev. Rul. 2007-3, page 350, this Bulletin. See Rev. Proc. 2007-14, page 357.

Section 1016.—Adjustments to Basis

26 CFR 1.1016–3: Exhaustion, wear and tear, obsolescence, amortization, and depletion for periods since February 28, 1913.

Does the allowed or allowable rule under § 1016(a)(2) of the Internal Revenue Code permanently affect a taxpayer's lifetime income for purposes of determining whether a change in depreciation or amortization is a change in method of accounting? See Rev. Proc. 2007-16, page 358.

Section 1274A.—Special Rules for Certain Transactions Where Stated Principal Amount Does Not Exceed $2,800,000

26 CFR 1.1274A–1: Special rules for certain transactions where stated principal amount does not exceed $2,800,000.
(Also §§ 483, 1274, 7872.)

Section 1274A – Inflation adjusted numbers for 2007. This ruling provides the dollar amounts, increased by the 2007 inflation adjustment, for section 1274A of the Code. Rev. Rul. 2005–76 supplemented and superseded.

Rev. Rul. 2007–4

This revenue ruling provides the dollar amounts, increased by the 2007 inflation adjustment, for § 1274A of the Internal Revenue Code. This ruling also provides that the Internal Revenue Service will no longer publish the inflation adjustment under § 7872(g)(2) because of amendments made to § 7872 by the Tax Increase Prevention and Reconciliation Act of 2005 (TIPRA), Pub. L. No. 109–222, 120 Stat. 345, and the Tax Relief and Health Care Act of 2006, Pub. L. No. 109–432, 120 Stat. 2922.

BACKGROUND

In general, §§ 483 and 1274 determine the principal amount of a debt instrument given in consideration for the sale or exchange of nonpublicly traded property. In addition, any interest on a debt instrument subject to § 1274 is taken into account under the original issue discount provisions of the Code. Section 1274A, however, modifies the rules under §§ 483 and 1274 for certain types of debt instruments.

In the case of a "qualified debt instrument," the discount rate used for purposes of §§ 483 and 1274 may not exceed 9 percent, compounded semiannually. Section 1274A(b) defines a qualified debt instrument as any debt instrument given in consideration for the sale or exchange of property (other than new § 38 property within the meaning of § 48(b), as in effect on the day before the date of enactment of the Revenue Reconciliation Act of 1990) if the stated principal amount of the instrument does not exceed the amount specified in § 1274A(b). For debt instruments arising out of sales or exchanges before January 1, 1990, this amount is $2,800,000.

In the case of a "cash method debt instrument," as defined in § 1274A(c), the borrower and lender may elect to use the cash receipts and disbursements method of accounting. In particular, for any cash method debt instrument, § 1274 does not apply, and interest on the instrument is accounted for by both the borrower and the lender under the cash method of accounting. A cash method debt instrument is a qualified debt instrument that meets the following additional requirements: (A) In the case of instruments arising out of sales or exchanges before January 1, 1990, the stated principal amount does not exceed $2,000,000; (B) the lender does not use an accrual method of accounting and is not a dealer with respect to the property sold or exchanged; (C) § 1274 would have applied to the debt instrument but for an election under § 1274A(c); and (D) an election under § 1274A(c) is jointly made with respect to the debt instrument by the borrower and lender. Section 1.1274A–1(c)(1) of the Income Tax Regulations provides rules concerning the time for, and manner of, making this election.

Section 1274A(d)(2) provides that, for any debt instrument arising out of a sale or exchange during any calendar year after 1989, the dollar amounts stated in § 1274A(b) and § 1274A(c)(2)(A) are increased by the inflation adjustment for the calendar year. Any increase due to the inflation adjustment is rounded to the nearest multiple of $100 (or, if the increase is a multiple of $50 and not of $100, the increase is increased to the nearest multiple of $100). The inflation adjustment for any calendar year is the percentage (if any) by which the CPI for the preceding calendar year exceeds the CPI for calendar year 1988. Section 1274A(d)(2)(B) defines the CPI for any calendar year as the average of the Consumer Price Index as of the close of the 12-month period ending on September 30 of that calendar year.

INFLATION-ADJUSTED AMOUNTS UNDER § 1274A

For debt instruments arising out of sales or exchanges after December 31, 1989, the inflation-adjusted amounts under § 1274A are shown in Table 1.

Rev. Rul. 2007–4 Table 1

Inflation-Adjusted Amounts Under § 1274A

Calendar Year of Sale or Exchange	*1274A(b) Amount (qualified debt instrument)*	*1274A(c)(2)(A) Amount (cash method debt instrument)*
1990	$2,933,200	$2,095,100
1991	$3,079,600	$2,199,700
1992	$3,234,900	$2,310,600
1993	$3,332,400	$2,380,300
1994	$3,433,500	$2,452,500
1995	$3,523,600	$2,516,900
1996	$3,622,500	$2,587,500
1997	$3,723,800	$2,659,900
1998	$3,823,100	$2,730,800
1999	$3,885,500	$2,775,400
2000	$3,960,100	$2,828,700
2001	$4,085,900	$2,918,500
2002	$4,217,500	$3,012,500
2003	$4,280,800	$3,057,700
2004	$4,381,300	$3,129,500

Rev. Rul. 2007–4 Table 1

Inflation-Adjusted Amounts Under § 1274A – Continued

Calendar Year of Sale or Exchange	*1274A(b) Amount (qualified debt instrument)*	*1274A(c)(2)(A) Amount (cash method debt instrument)*
2005	$4,483,000	$3,202,100
2006	$4,630,300	$3,307,400
2007	$4,800,800	$3,429,100

Note: These inflation adjustments were computed using the All-Urban, Consumer Price Index, 1982–1984 base, published by the Bureau of Labor Statistics.

INFLATION-ADJUSTED AMOUNTS UNDER § 7872(g)(2)

The Service will no longer publish the inflation adjustment under § 7872(g)(2), regarding the amount that a taxpayer may lend to a qualifying continuing care facility without incurring imputed interest, because of amendments made to § 7872 by TIPRA and the Tax Relief and Health Care Act of 2006.

Section 7872(g)(2) provides an exception for certain below-market loans to qualified continuing care facilities only to the extent that the aggregate outstanding amount of any loan to which § 7872(g)(1) applies (determined without regard to § 7872(g)(2)), when added to the aggregate outstanding amount of all other previous loans between the lender (or the lender's spouse) and any qualified continuing care facility to which § 7872(g)(1) applies, does not exceed $90,000. Section 7872(g)(5) generally provides that, for loans made during any calendar year after 1986 to which § 7872(g)(1) applies, the $90,000 limit specified in § 7872(g)(2) is increased by an inflation adjustment.

Section 7872(g)(6) generally suspends the application of § 7872(g) for any calendar year to which § 7872(h), as amended by TIPRA, applies. Section 7872(h) generally provides that § 7872 shall not apply for any calendar year to any below-market loan owed by a facility which on the last day of such year is a qualified continuing care facility, if such loan was made pursuant to a continuing care contract and if the lender (or the lender's spouse) attains age 62 before the close of such year. Section 7872(h)(4) provided that paragraph (h) shall not apply for any calendar year after 2010. Section 425 of the Tax Relief and Health Care Act of 2006 amended § 7872(h) by striking subsection (4), making the § 7872(h) exception for loans to qualified continuing care facilities permanent.

EFFECT ON OTHER DOCUMENTS

Rev. Rul. 2005–76, 2005–2 C.B. 1072, is supplemented and superseded.

DRAFTING INFORMATION

The author of this revenue ruling is Richard C. LaFalce of the Office of the Associate Chief Counsel (Financial Institutions and Products). For further information regarding this revenue ruling, please contact Mr. LaFalce at (202) 622–3930 (not a toll-free call).

Part III. Administrative, Procedural, and Miscellaneous

Classification of Certain Foreign Entities

Notice 2007–10

This notice announces that Treasury and the Internal Revenue Service (IRS) will amend § 301.7701–2(b)(8) of the Procedure and Administration Regulations to add the Bulgarian aktsionerno druzhestvo entity to the list of entities that are always treated as corporations under section 7701 of the Internal Revenue Code (Code).

BACKGROUND

The IRS and Treasury issued final regulations concerning the classification of business entities under section 7701 of the Code on December 18, 1996 (check-the-box regulations). See generally, T.D. 8697, 1997–1 C.B. 215 [61 FR 66584] and §§ 301.7701–1 through 3. Under the check-the-box regulations, a business entity generally can elect its classification for federal tax purposes. However, § 301.7701–2(b)(8) provides a list of certain foreign business entities that are always classified as corporations for federal tax purposes (the *per se* corporation list).

On December 16, 2005, the IRS and Treasury published regulations (T.D. 9235, 2006–4 I.R.B. 338 [70 FR 74658]) under section 7701 of the Code adding certain foreign business entities to the *per se* list of corporations. These regulations were in response to the adoption by the Council of the European Union of a Council Regulation (2157/2001 2001 O.J. (L 294)) (the EU Regulation) that recognized a new business entity, the European public limited liability company (Societas Europaea or SE).

The SE is a public limited liability company. The EU Regulation provides general rules that govern the formation and operation of an SE, and supplements those rules for specified issues and issues it does not otherwise address by reference to the laws with respect to public limited liability companies for the country in which the SE has its registered office. An SE must have a registered office in one of the Member States of the European Economic Area (which includes all Member States of the European Union plus Norway, Iceland, and Liechtenstein). For further background see T.D. 9197, 2005–1 C.B. 985 [70 FR 19697] and Notice 2004–68, 2004–2 C.B. 706.

As of January 1, 2007, Bulgaria will become a member of the European Union. Accordingly, an SE will be eligible to have its registered office in Bulgaria and those SEs with a registered office in Bulgaria will, to a certain extent, be subject to the laws of the public limited liability company in Bulgaria. As a result, and consistent with T.D. 9235, it is appropriate for the IRS and Treasury to add the public limited liability company for Bulgaria to the *per se* list.

DISCUSSION

The IRS and Treasury will issue temporary and proposed regulations that will modify § 301.7701–2 to include the Bulgarian aktsionerno druzhestvo on the *per se* corporation list. This entity has been identified as the public limited liability company in Bulgaria.

EFFECTIVE DATE

The temporary and proposed regulations to be issued adding the Bulgarian aktsionerno druzhestvo to § 301.7701–2(b)(8) generally will apply to such entities formed on or after January 1, 2007. However, they shall also apply to an entity formed before such date upon a 50 percent or greater change of ownership subsequent to such date.

The principal author of this notice is Ronald M. Gootzeit of the Office of Associate Chief Counsel (International). For further information regarding this notice, contact Ronald M. Gootzeit at (202) 622–3860 (not a toll-free call).

---

26 CFR 601.602: Tax forms and instructions.
26 CFR 1.6045–4: Information reporting on real estate transactions with dates of closing on or after January 1, 1991.

Rev. Proc. 2007–12

SECTION 1. PURPOSE

This revenue procedure supersedes Rev. Proc. 98–20, 98–1 C.B. 549, and sets forth the acceptable form of the written assurances (certification) that a real estate reporting person must obtain from the seller of a principal residence to except the sale or exchange of such principal residence from the information reporting requirements for real estate transactions under § 6045(e)(5) of the Internal Revenue Code (Code). This revenue procedure incorporates amendments to section 121 of the Code made by section 840 of the American Jobs Creation Act of 2004, Pub. L. No. 108–357, 118 Stat. 1418 (October 22, 2004) (AJCA), as amended by section 403(ee) of the Gulf Opportunity Zone Act of 2005, Pub. L. No. 109–135, 119 Stat. 2631 (December 21, 2005) (the GO Zone Act).

SECTION 2. BACKGROUND

.01 Section 6045(e) and § 1.6045–4 of the Income Tax Regulations generally require a real estate reporting person (as defined in § 6045(e)(2) and § 1.6045–4(e)) to file an information return regarding a real estate transaction and to furnish a payee statement to the seller regarding that transaction. The information return and statement must include the name, address, and taxpayer identification number (TIN) of the seller, and the gross proceeds of the real estate transaction. This information is reported on Form 1099–S, *Proceeds From Real Estate Transactions*.

.02 Section 312 of the Taxpayer Relief Act of 1997 (TRA 1997), Pub. L. No. 105–34, 111 Stat. 788 (August 5, 1997), as amended by the Internal Revenue Service Restructuring and Reform Act of 1998, Pub. L. No. 105–206, 112 Stat. 805 (July 22, 1998), effective for sales or exchanges after May 6, 1997, amended § 6045(e) by adding a new paragraph (5), which excepts a sale or exchange of a principal residence from the § 6045(e) information reporting requirements if the seller provides the real estate reporting person with a certification setting forth certain written assurances, including an assurance that the residence is the seller's principal residence (within the meaning of § 121) and an assurance that the full amount of the gain on the sale or exchange of the principal residence is excludable from gross income under § 121.

.03 Section 312 of TRA 1997 also amended § 121 to provide new rules for the exclusion of gain on certain sales or exchanges of a principal residence. Section 121, as amended, provides that a taxpayer may exclude from gross income up to $250,000 of gain on the sale or exchange of a principal residence if certain conditions are met. In certain circumstances, a married individual filing a joint return for the taxable year of the sale or exchange may exclude from gross income up to $500,000 of gain. This exclusion also applies to the sale or exchange of stock held by a tenant-stockholder in a cooperative housing corporation (as defined in § 216) and may apply to the sale or exchange of a remainder interest in a principal residence if the taxpayer so elects. *See* Code §§ 121(d)(4) and (d)(8).

.04 Section 840 of the AJCA, as amended by the GO Zone Act, amended § 121 to provide that the exclusion for gain on the sale or exchange of a principal residence does not apply if the principal residence was acquired by the taxpayer in a like-kind exchange in which any gain was not recognized under § 1031(a) or (b) within the prior five years.

SECTION 3. SCOPE

This revenue procedure applies to the information reporting requirements under § 6045(e) for a sale or exchange of a principal residence.

SECTION 4. SELLER CERTIFICATION

.01 To be excepted from the information reporting requirements in § 6045(e) on the sale or exchange of a principal residence (including stock in a cooperative housing corporation), the real estate reporting person must obtain from the seller a written certification, signed by the seller under penalties of perjury, that assurances (1) through (6) set forth in section 4.02 of this revenue procedure are true (or, in the case of assurance (6), not applicable). For purposes of this certification, the term "seller" includes each owner of the residence that is sold or exchanged. Thus, if a residence has more than one owner, a real estate reporting person must either obtain a certification from each owner (whether married or not) or file an information return and furnish a payee statement for any owner that does not make the certification.

.02 The assurances are:

(1) The seller owned and used the residence as the seller's principal residence for periods aggregating 2 years or more during the 5-year period ending on the date of the sale or exchange of the residence.

(2) The seller has not sold or exchanged another principal residence during the 2-year period ending on the date of the sale or exchange of the residence.

(3) No portion of the residence has been used for business or rental purposes after May 6, 1997, by the seller (or by the seller's spouse or former spouse, if the seller was married at any time after May 6, 1997).

(4) At least one of the following three statements applies:

The sale or exchange is of the entire residence for $250,000 or less.

OR

The seller is married, the sale or exchange is of the entire residence for $500,000 or less, and the gain on the sale or exchange of the entire residence is $250,000 or less.

OR

The seller is married, the sale or exchange is of the entire residence for $500,000 or less, and (a) the seller intends to file a joint return for the year of the sale or exchange, (b) the seller's spouse also used the residence as his or her principal residence for periods aggregating 2 years or more during the 5-year period ending on the date of the sale or exchange of the residence, and (c) the seller's spouse also has not sold or exchanged another principal residence during the 2-year period ending on the date of the sale or exchange of the residence.

(5) During the 5-year period ending on the date of the sale or exchange of the residence, the seller did not acquire the residence in an exchange to which section 1031 applied.

(6) In cases where the seller's basis in the residence is determined by reference to the basis in the hands of a person who acquired the residence in an exchange to which section 1031 applied, the exchange to which section 1031 applied occurred more than 5 years prior to the date of the seller's sale or exchange of the residence.

SECTION 5. FORMAT FOR MAKING SELLER CERTIFICATION

A sample certification form that may be used by a real estate reporting person to obtain the applicable assurances from the seller is provided in the Appendix of this revenue procedure. Use of this sample certification form is not required. The requirements of the certification under § 6045(e)(5) will be met if the content and wording of a written certification provide the same information as required by section 4 of this revenue procedure.

SECTION 6. OBTAINING AND RETAINING SELLER CERTIFICATION

The real estate reporting person may obtain a certification at any time on or before January 31 of the year following the year of the sale or exchange of the residence. The certification must be retained by the real estate reporting person for 4 years after the year of the sale or exchange of the residence to which the certification applies.

SECTION 7. PENALTIES

A real estate reporting person who relies on a certification made in compliance with this revenue procedure will not be liable for the penalties under § 6721 for failure to file an information return, or under § 6722 for failure to furnish a payee statement to the seller, unless the real estate reporting person has actual knowledge that any assurance is incorrect.

SECTION 8. EFFECT ON OTHER DOCUMENTS (when applicable)

Rev. Proc. 98–20 is superseded.

SECTION 9. EFFECTIVE DATE

This revenue procedure is effective for sales or exchanges of a principal residence occurring after January 22, 2007.

SECTION 10. PAPERWORK REDUCTION ACT

The collections of information contained in this revenue procedure have been reviewed and approved by the Office of Management and Budget in accordance with the Paperwork Reduction Act (44 U.S.C. 3507) under control number 1545–1592.

An agency may not conduct or sponsor, and a person is not required to respond to, a collection of information unless the collection of information displays a valid OMB control number.

The collection of information in this revenue procedure is in section 4 and 5 of this revenue procedure. This information is required to exempt a real estate reporting person from the requirement to file an information return and furnish a payee statement reporting the sale or exchange of a principal residence. The likely respondents are individual taxpayers who sell or exchange a principal residence and real estate businesses.

The estimated total annual reporting burden for respondents is 383,000 hours.

The estimated burden per respondent is 10 minutes. The estimated number of respondents is 2,300,000. The frequency of responses is on occasion.

The estimated total annual burden for recordkeepers is 37,500 hours.

The estimated annual burden per recordkeeper is 25 minutes. The estimated number of recordkeepers is 90,000.

Books or records relating to a collection of information must be retained as long as their content may become material in the administration of any internal revenue law. Generally, tax returns and return information are confidential, as required by 26 U.S.C. 6103.

SECTION 11. DRAFTING INFORMATION

The principal author of this revenue procedure is Timothy S. Sheppard of the Office of Associate Chief Counsel (Procedure & Administration). For further information regarding this revenue procedure, contact Mr. Sheppard at (202) 622–4910 (not a toll-free call).

APPENDIX

CERTIFICATION FOR NO INFORMATION REPORTING ON THE SALE OR EXCHANGE OF A PRINCIPAL RESIDENCE

This form may be completed by the seller of a principal residence. This information is necessary to determine whether the sale or exchange should be reported to the seller, and to the Internal Revenue Service on Form 1099–S, *Proceeds From Real Estate Transactions*. If the seller properly completes Parts I and III, and makes a "true" response to assurances (1) through (6) in Part II (or a "not applicable" response to assurance (6)), no information reporting to the seller or to the Service will be required for that seller. The term "seller" includes each owner of the residence that is sold or exchanged. Thus, if a residence has more than one owner, a real estate reporting person must either obtain a certification from each owner (whether married or not) or file an information return and furnish a payee statement for any owner that does not make the certification.

Part I. Seller Information

1. Name ________________________________

2. Address or legal description (including city, state, and ZIP code) of residence being sold or exchanged ________________________________

____

____

3. Taxpayer Identification Number (TIN) ____________________

Part II. Seller Assurances

Check "true" or "false" for assurances (1) through (5), and "true", "false", or "not applicable" for assurance (6).

True	False	
[ ]	[ ]	(1) I owned and used the residence as my principal residence for periods aggregating 2 years or more during the 5-year period ending on the date of the sale or exchange of the residence.
[ ]	[ ]	(2) I have not sold or exchanged another principal residence during the 2-year period ending on the date of the sale or exchange of the residence.
[ ]	[ ]	(3) I (or my spouse or former spouse, if I was married at any time during the period beginning after May 6, 1997, and ending today) have not used any portion of the residence for business or rental purposes after May 6, 1997.

True	False	N/A	
[ ]	[ ]		(4) At least one of the following three statements applies:
			The sale or exchange is of the entire residence for $250,000 or less.
			OR
			I am married, the sale or exchange is of the entire residence for $500,000 or less, and the gain on the sale or exchange of the entire residence is $250,000 or less.
			OR
			I am married, the sale or exchange is of the entire residence for $500,000 or less, and (a) I intend to file a joint return for the year of the sale or exchange, (b) my spouse also used the residence as his or her principal residence for periods aggregating 2 years or more during the 5-year period ending on the date of the sale or exchange of the residence, and (c) my spouse also has not sold or exchanged another principal residence during the 2-year period ending on the date of the sale or exchange of the principal residence.
[ ]	[ ]		(5) During the 5-year period ending on the date of the sale or exchange of the residence, I did not acquire the residence in an exchange to which section 1031 of the Internal Revenue Code applied.
[ ]	[ ]	[ ]	(6) If my basis in the residence is determined by reference to the basis in the hands of a person who acquired the residence in an exchange to which section 1031 of the Internal Revenue Code applied, the exchange to which section 1031 applied occurred more than 5 years prior to the date I sold or exchanged the residence.

Part III. Seller Certification

Under penalties of perjury, I certify that all the above information is true as of the end of the day of the sale or exchange.

______________________________ ______________________

Signature of Seller Date

---

26 CFR 601.204: Changes in accounting periods and in methods of accounting.
(Also Part I, §§ 446, 461, 481; 1.446–1.)

Rev. Proc. 2007–14

SECTION 1. PURPOSE

This revenue procedure provides procedures by which a taxpayer may obtain the automatic consent of the Commissioner under § 446(e) of the Internal Revenue Code to change its method of accounting for liabilities for services or insurance to comply with Rev. Rul. 2007–3, page 350, this Bulletin.

SECTION 2. BACKGROUND

.01 In Rev. Rul. 2007–3, the Internal Revenue Service addressed the issue of when a taxpayer using an accrual method of accounting incurs a liability for services or insurance under § 461. The ruling holds that a liability for services or insurance is not fixed by the mere execution of a contract for the future provision of services or insurance. Instead, all the events have occurred that establish the fact of the liability when (1) the event fixing the liability, whether that be the required performance or other event, occurs, or (2) payment is due, whichever happens earliest.

.02 Under § 446(e) and § 1.446–1(e)(2)(i) of the Income Tax Regulations, a taxpayer generally must secure the consent of the Commissioner before changing a method of accounting for federal income tax purposes. To obtain the Commissioner's consent to a change in method, § 1.446–1(e)(3)(i) generally requires a taxpayer to file Form 3115, *Application for Change in Accounting Method*, during the taxable year in which the taxpayer wants to make the proposed change. Section 1.446–1(e)(3)(ii) authorizes the Commissioner to prescribe administrative procedures that provide the terms and conditions necessary for a taxpayer to obtain consent to change a method of accounting. The terms and conditions the Commissioner may prescribe include whether the change is to be made with a § 481(a) adjustment, and if so, the § 481(a) adjustment period, or on a cut-off basis.

.03 Rev. Proc. 2002–9, 2002–1 C.B. 327 (as modified and clarified by Announcement 2002–17, 2002–1 C.B. 561, modified and amplified by Rev. Proc. 2002–19, 2002–1 C.B. 696, and amplified, clarified and modified by Rev. Proc. 2002–54, 2002–2 C.B. 432), provides procedures under § 446(e) and § 1.446–1(e) for obtaining the automatic consent of the Commissioner to change certain methods of accounting for federal income tax purposes. Specifically, Rev. Proc. 2002–9 applies to a taxpayer requesting the Commissioner's consent to change to a method of accounting described in the APPENDIX of that revenue procedure. Rev. Proc. 2002–9 is the exclusive procedure for a taxpayer within its scope to obtain the Commissioner's consent. See Rev. Proc. 2002–9, sections 1 and 4.01.

SECTION 3. SCOPE

This revenue procedure applies to any taxpayer that is currently treating the mere execution of a contract for services or insurance as establishing the fact of the liability under § 461 and wants to change its method of accounting for liabilities for services or insurance to comply with Rev. Rul. 2007–3.

SECTION 4. APPLICATION

.01 *In General.* A change in the treatment of liabilities for services or insurance to comply with Rev. Rul. 2007–3 is a change in method of accounting within the meaning of §§ 446 and 481 and the regulations issued thereunder. Accordingly, a taxpayer within the scope of this revenue procedure that wants to change its treatment of liabilities for services or insurance to comply with Rev. Rul. 2007–3 must obtain the consent of the Commissioner under § 446(e) and § 1.446–1(e)(3).

.02 *Automatic Change.* A taxpayer within the scope of this revenue procedure that wants to change its method of accounting for liabilities for services or insurance must obtain the consent of the Commissioner by following the automatic consent procedures in Rev. Proc. 2002–9 (or its successor). For purposes of section 6.02(4)(a) of Rev. Proc. 2002–9, the taxpayer must include on line 1a of the Form 3115 the designated automatic accounting method change number 106.

SECTION 5. EFFECT ON OTHER DOCUMENTS

Rev. Proc. 2002–9 is modified and amplified to include in the APPENDIX the automatic change provided in this revenue procedure.

SECTION 6. EFFECTIVE DATE

This revenue procedure is effective for taxable years ending on or after December 31, 2006.

DRAFTING INFORMATION

The principal author of this revenue procedure is Leta A. Ayres of the Office of Associate Chief Counsel (Income Tax & Accounting). For further information regarding this revenue procedure, contact Ms. Ayres at (202) 622–5020 (not a toll-free call).

---

26 CFR 601.204: Changes in accounting periods and in methods of accounting.
(Also: Part I, §§ 446, 1016; 1.446–1, 1.1016–3.)

Rev. Proc. 2007–16

SECTION 1. PURPOSE

This revenue procedure provides an automatic consent procedure allowing a taxpayer to make a change in method of accounting under § 446(e) of the Internal Revenue Code for depreciable or amortizable property (hereinafter referred to collectively as "depreciable property") after its disposition. This revenue procedure also waives the application of the two-year rule set forth in Rev. Rul. 90–38, 1990–1 C.B. 57, for certain changes in depreciation or amortization (hereinafter referred to collectively as "depreciation"). This revenue procedure clarifies, modifies, amplifies, and supersedes Rev. Proc. 2004–11, 2004–1 C.B. 311. This revenue procedure also modifies Rev. Proc. 2002–9, 2002–1 C.B. 327 (as modified and clarified by Announcement 2002–17, 2002–1 C.B. 561, modified and amplified by Rev. Proc. 2002–19, 2002–1 C.B. 696, and amplified, clarified, and modified by Rev. Proc. 2002–54, 2002–2 C.B. 432), and other revenue procedures to conform with § 1.446–1(e)(2)(ii)(*d*) of the Income Tax Regulations.

SECTION 2. BACKGROUND AND CHANGES

.01 Section 446(e) and § 1.446–1(e) provide that, except as otherwise provided, a taxpayer must secure the consent of the Commissioner of Internal Revenue before changing a method of accounting for federal income tax purposes. Section 1.446–1(e)(3)(ii) authorizes the Commissioner to prescribe administrative procedures setting forth the limitations, terms, and conditions deemed necessary to permit a taxpayer to obtain consent to change a method of accounting.

.02 On January 20, 2004, the Internal Revenue Service published Rev. Proc. 2004–11, which provided an automatic consent procedure allowing a taxpayer to make a change in method of accounting under § 446(e) for depreciable property after its disposition. Rev. Proc. 2004–11 also waived the application of the two-year rule set forth in Rev. Rul. 90–38 for certain changes in depreciation. In addition, Rev. Proc. 2004–11 modified Rev. Proc. 2002–9 and other revenue procedures to conform with § 1.446–1T(e)(2)(ii)(*d*) of the temporary Income Tax Regulations.

.03 Concurrent with the issuance of this revenue procedure, §§ 1.446–1(e)(2)(ii)(*d*) and 1.1016–3(h) have been promulgated. Section 1.446–1(e)(2)(ii)(*d*) identifies the changes in depreciation that are (and are not) considered a change in method of accounting. Section 1.1016–3(h) provides that for purposes of determining whether a change in depreciation is a change in method of accounting under § 446(e), the "allowed or allowable" rule under § 1016(a)(2) will not be considered to permanently affect a taxpayer's lifetime income.

.04 In general, if a taxpayer uses an impermissible method of accounting in two or more consecutively filed federal tax returns the taxpayer has adopted a method of accounting. *See* Rev. Rul. 90–38. The Service and Treasury Department recognize that with respect to changes in depreciation this two-year rule may increase administrative and compliance costs because many taxpayers changing from an impermissible to permissible method of accounting for depreciation used the impermissible method for depreciable properties placed in service in the taxable year immediately preceding the year of change. Accordingly, in the interest of sound tax administration, the Service and Treasury have decided to waive the two-year rule in Rev. Rul. 90–38 for a change in depreciation to which § 1.446–1(e)(2)(ii)(*d*) applies.

.05 If depreciable property is transferred in a transaction in which the transferee is treated as the transferor for purposes of computing the depreciation allowance for the property with respect to so much of the basis in the hands of the transferee as does not exceed the adjusted depreciable basis in the hands of the transferor (for example, in transactions subject to § 168(i)(7) or § 381(c)(6)), the transferee may file a Form 3115, *Application for Change in Accounting Method*, to change from an impermissible method of accounting adopted by the transferor for that portion of the basis of the property to a permissible method of accounting for depreciation for the same portion of the basis of the property, provided the impermissible method of accounting for that portion of the basis of the property has not been changed by the transferor (through filing, for example, a Form 3115 or an amended return) or by the Service upon examination of the transferor's tax returns. In this case, the § 481 adjustment will include any necessary adjustments since the property's placed-in-service date by the transferor.

.06 The significant changes to Rev. Proc. 2004–11 include:

(1) The application of section 3 is extended to allow a taxpayer to file a Form 3115 with an original federal tax return for the taxable year in which the depreciable property is disposed of by the taxpayer that claimed less than the depreciation allowable for that property.

(2) A new section 4.01 is added, clarifying that a change from an impermissible method of determining depreciation for depreciable property in two or more consecutively filed federal tax returns is a change in method of accounting under § 446(e) and § 1.446–1(e).

(3) A new section 6.03 is added, extending the application of section 3 of this revenue procedure to dispositions of depreciable property occurring in taxable years ending before December 30, 2003.

.07 The significant changes to Rev. Proc. 2002–9 include:

(1) Section 2.01 of the APPENDIX of Rev. Proc. 2002–9 is changed to clarify that section 2.01 of this APPENDIX does not apply to any property for which a taxpayer is revoking a timely valid election or making a late election under § 179, or to any change in method of accounting involving a change from capitalizing and depreciation the cost or other basis of any property to deducting the cost or other basis as an expense.

(2) Section 2B of the APPENDIX of Rev. Proc. 2002–9 is changed to remove section 2B.03, which provided that the change under section 2B does not apply to a change in useful life under the method described in section 5.01(2) or 6.01(2) of Rev. Proc. 2000–50.

SECTION 3. METHOD CHANGE PROCEDURE FOR DISPOSED DEPRECIABLE OR AMORTIZABLE PROPERTY

.01 *Scope.*

(1) *Applicability.* Except as provided in section 3.01(2) of this revenue procedure, section 3 of this revenue procedure applies to a taxpayer that is changing from an impermissible method of accounting for depreciation to a permissible method of accounting for depreciation for any item of depreciable property subject to §§ 167, 168, 197, 1400I, 1400L(c), to former § 168, or to any additional first year depreciation deduction provision of the Internal Revenue Code (for example, § 168(k), § 1400L(b), or § 1400N(d)):

(a) that has been disposed of by the taxpayer during the year of change (as defined in section 3.02(3)(b) of this revenue procedure); and

(b) for which the taxpayer did not take into account any depreciation allowance, or did take into account some depreciation but less than the depreciation allowable (hereinafter, both are referred to as "claimed less than the depreciation allowable"), in the year of change (as defined in section 3.02(3)(b) of this revenue procedure) or any prior taxable year.

(2) *Inapplicability.* Section 3 of this revenue procedure does not apply to:

(a) any property to which § 1016(a)(3) (regarding property held by a tax-exempt organization) applies;

(b) any property for which a taxpayer is revoking a timely valid depreciation election, or making a late depreciation election, under the Code or regulations thereunder, or under other guidance published in the Internal Revenue Bulletin (including under § 13261(g)(2) or (3) of the Revenue Reconciliation Act of 1993, 1993–3 C.B. 1, 128 (relating to amortizable § 197 intangibles));

(c) any property for which the taxpayer deducted the cost or other basis of the property as an expense; or

(d) any property disposed of by the taxpayer in a transaction to which a nonrecognition section of the Code applies (for example, § 1031, transactions subject to § 168(i)(7)(B)(i)). However, this section 3.01(2)(d) does not apply to property disposed of by the taxpayer in a § 1031 or § 1033 transaction if the taxpayer elects under § 1.168(i)–6T(i) and (j) to treat the entire basis (that is, both the exchanged and excess basis (as defined in § 1.168(i)–6T(b)(7) and (8), respectively)) of the replacement MACRS property (as defined in § 1.168(i)–6T(b)(1)) as property placed in service by the taxpayer at the time of replacement and treat the adjusted depreciable basis of the relinquished MACRS property (as defined in § 1.168(i)–6T(b)(2)) as being disposed of by the taxpayer at the time of disposition.

.02 *Change in method of accounting.*

(1) *Change made on original return for year of change.* On its timely filed (including extensions) original federal tax return for the year of change (as defined in section 3.02(3)(b) of this revenue procedure), a taxpayer within the scope of section 3 of this revenue procedure may change from an impermissible method of accounting for depreciation to a permissible method of accounting for depreciation for any item of depreciable property within the scope of section 3 of this revenue procedure, provided the taxpayer files the original Form 3115 in accordance with section 6.02(3) of Rev. Proc. 2002–9 (or its successor).

(2) *Change made on an amended return for year of change.* On an amended federal tax return for the year of change (as defined in section 3.02(3)(b) of this revenue procedure), a taxpayer within the scope of section 3 of this revenue procedure may change from an impermissible method of accounting for depreciation to a permissible method of accounting for depreciation for any item of depreciable property within the scope of section 3 of this revenue procedure, provided:

(a) the taxpayer files the original Form 3115 in accordance with section 3.02(3)(c) of this revenue procedure prior to the expiration of the period of limitation for assessment under § 6501(a) for the taxable year in which the item of depreciable or amortizable property was disposed of by the taxpayer; and

(b) the taxpayer files an amended federal tax return for the year of change (as defined in section 3.02(3)(b) of this revenue procedure) that includes the adjustments to taxable income and any collateral adjustments to taxable income or tax liability (for example, adjustments to the amount or character of the gain or loss of the disposed depreciable or amortizable property) resulting from the change in method of accounting for depreciation made by the taxpayer under this section 3.

(3) *Application Procedures.* A taxpayer making a change in method of accounting under section 3 of this revenue procedure must follow the automatic change in method of accounting provisions in Rev. Proc. 2002–9 (or its successor), with the following modifications:

(a) The scope limitations in section 4.02 of Rev. Proc. 2002–9 do not apply. If the taxpayer is under examination, before an appeals office, or before a federal court at the time that a copy of the Form 3115 is filed with the national office, the taxpayer must provide a copy of the Form 3115 to the examining agent, appeals officer, or counsel for the government, as appropriate, at the time the copy of the Form 3115 is filed with the national office. The Form 3115 must contain the name(s) and telephone number(s) of the examining agent, appeals officer, or counsel for the government, as appropriate.

(b) The year of change is the taxable year in which the item of depreciable property was disposed of by the taxpayer.

(c) If section 3.02(2) of this revenue procedure applies to the taxpayer, section 6.02(3)(a) of Rev. Proc. 2002–9 is modified to require the original of the Form 3115 to be attached to the taxpayer's timely filed amended federal tax return for the year of change and a copy (with signature) of the Form 3115 to be filed with the national office no later than when the original Form 3115 is filed with the amended federal tax return for the year of change.

(d) For purposes of section 6.02(4)(a) of Rev. Proc. 2002–9, the taxpayer should include on line 1a of the Form 3115 (revised December 2003) the designated automatic accounting method change number for the change in method of accounting for depreciation made under this section 3. This number for this method change is 107.

.03 *Taxpayer or property outside scope.* If a taxpayer is precluded from using section 3 of this revenue procedure because the taxpayer or the item of depreciable property is outside the scope of section 3 of this revenue procedure (for example, the item of depreciable property was not disposed of by the taxpayer), any change in method of accounting for depreciation must be made in accordance with the requirements of Rev. Proc. 97–27, 1997–1 C.B. 680 (or its successor), or Rev. Proc. 2002–9 (or its successor), as applicable.

SECTION 4. WAIVER OF TWO-YEAR RULE IN REV. RUL. 90–38

.01 *In general.* If a taxpayer uses an impermissible method of determining depreciation for a depreciable property, the taxpayer adopts that method of accounting for the property when the taxpayer treats the property in the same way in determining gross income or deductions in two or more consecutively filed federal tax returns. Accordingly, the taxpayer changing from that impermissible method of accounting must file a Form 3115 in accordance with the requirements of § 1.446–1(e)(3)(i) and, as applicable, Rev. Proc. 97–27 or Rev. Proc. 2002–9. *See* Rev. Rul. 90–38.

.02 *Waiver of two-year rule.* Notwithstanding Rev. Rul. 90–38, a taxpayer may file a Form 3115 under Rev. Proc. 97–27 or Rev. Proc. 2002 9, as applicable, to change from an impermissible method of accounting for depreciation to a permissible method of accounting for depreciation under § 1.446–1(e)(2)(ii)(*d*) for any depreciable property subject to § 1.446–1(e)(2)(ii)(*d*) and placed in service by the taxpayer in the taxable year immediately preceding the year of change (as defined in section 5.02(2) of Rev. Proc. 97–27 or section 5.02 of Rev. Proc. 2002–9, as applicable) (hereinafter, this property is referred to as "1-year depreciable property"), provided the additional term and condition in section 4.03 of this revenue procedure is satisfied. Alternatively, the taxpayer may make the change from the impermissible depreciation method to the permissible depreciation method for the 1-year depreciable property by filing an amended federal tax return for the placed-in-service year prior to the date the taxpayer files its federal tax return for the taxable year succeeding the placed-in-service year.

.03 *Additional term and condition for filing a Form 3115.* In addition to the terms and conditions provided in Rev. Proc. 97–27 or Rev. Proc. 2002–9, as applicable, the § 481 adjustment reported on a Form 3115 that is filed by a taxpayer in accordance with section 4.02 of this revenue procedure to make a change in method of accounting for depreciation under § 1.446–1(e)(2)(ii)(*d*) for any 1-year depreciable property, must include the amount of any adjustment attributable to all property (including the 1-year depreciable property) subject to the Form 3115.

SECTION 5. EFFECT ON OTHER DOCUMENTS

.01 Rev. Proc. 2004–11 is clarified, modified, amplified, and superseded.

.02 The heading for section 2 of the APPENDIX of Rev. Proc. 2002–9 is modified to read as follows: "SECTION 2. DEPRECIATION OR AMORTIZATION (§ 56(a)(1), 56(g)(4)(A), 167, 168, 197, 1400I, 1400L, OR 1400N(d), OR FORMER § 168)".

.03 Rev. Proc. 2002–9 (as modified by Rev. Proc. 2004–11) is modified by deleting sections 2.01, 2.02, 2B, and 2.05 of the APPENDIX and replacing them with the text in, respectively, sections 1, 2, 3, and 4 of the APPENDIX of this revenue procedure.

.04 Section 6.03 of Rev. Proc. 2000–38, 2000–2 C.B. 310, 313, is modified by deleting "*See* § 1.446–1(e)(2)(ii)(*b*)." and replacing it with "*See* § 1.446–1(e)(2)(ii)(*d*)(*3*)(*i*)."

.05 Section 8.01 of Rev. Proc. 2000–50, 2000–2 C.B. 601, is modified to read as follows: "A change in a taxpayer's treatment of costs paid or incurred to develop, purchase, lease, or license computer software to a method described in section 5, 6, or 7 of this revenue procedure is a change in method of accounting to which §§ 446 and 481 apply. Further, a change in useful life under the method described in section 6.01(2) of this revenue procedure is a change in method of accounting to which §§ 446 and 481 apply. Additionally, if a taxpayer is currently treating costs paid or incurred to develop computer software under section 5.01(2) of this revenue procedure in accordance with the rules provided in § 167(f)(1) and the regulations thereunder but is not currently using a useful life of 36 months, a change in useful life to 36 months is a change in method of accounting to which §§ 446 and 481 apply. *See* § 1.446–1(e)(2)(ii)(*d*)(*3*)(*i*).

SECTION 6. EFFECTIVE DATE

.01 *In general.* Except as provided in sections 6.02, 6.03, and 6.04 of this revenue procedure, this revenue procedure is effective for a Form 3115 filed for taxable years ending on or after December 26, 2006.

.02 *Transition rule for previously filed Forms 3115 for automatic consent.*

(1) For a taxable year ending on or after December 26, 2006, a taxpayer may make a change in method of accounting previously authorized in section 2.01, 2.02, or 2B of the APPENDIX of Rev. Proc. 2002–9 in effect on the date on which the Form 3115 was filed with the national office by the taxpayer (*see* Rev. Proc. 2004–11) if:

(a) before December 26, 2006, the taxpayer filed a completed Form 3115 with the national office to make that change in method of accounting; and

(b) the taxpayer makes that change in method of accounting in compliance with all the applicable provisions of Rev. Proc. 2002–9 for the requested year of change (as defined in section 5.02 of Rev. Proc. 2002–9) on that Form 3115.

(2) If a taxpayer filed a Form 3115 with the national office to make a change in method of accounting previously authorized in section 2.01, 2.02, or 2B of the APPENDIX of Rev. Proc. 2002–9 in effect on the date on which the Form 3115 was filed with the national office by the taxpayer for a year of change for which this revenue procedure is effective (see section 6.01 of this revenue procedure) and the taxpayer's original federal tax return for that year of change was not filed before December 26, 2006, the taxpayer may make the change in method of accounting authorized under section 2.01, 2.02, or 2B, as applicable, of the APPENDIX of Rev. Proc. 2002–9 as revised by this revenue procedure. However, the Service will process the Form 3115 in accordance with the section of the APPENDIX of Rev. Proc. 2002–9 in effect on the date on which the Form 3115 was filed with the national office by the taxpayer unless on or before the due date (including extensions) of the taxpayer's federal tax return for the requested year of change (as defined in section 5.02 of Rev. Proc. 2002–9) on that Form 3115, the taxpayer completes a new Form 3115 to make the change under section 2.01, 2.02, or 2B, as applicable, of the APPENDIX of Rev. Proc. 2002–9 as revised by this revenue procedure and files this newly completed Form 3115 in duplicate in accordance with section 6.02(3)(a) of Rev. Proc. 2002–9. Additionally, the newly completed Form 3115 must include the statement: "Section [*insert, as appropriate: 2.01, 2.02, or 2B*] of the APPENDIX of Rev. Proc. 2002–9 as revised by Rev. Proc. 2007–16." This statement must be legibly printed or typed on the appropriate line on, or at the top of page 1 of, the Form 3115.

.03 *Application of section 3.* Section 3 of this revenue procedure is effective for a Form 3115 filed on or after December 26, 2006.

.04 *Changes made to Rev. Proc. 2000–50.* The changes made in section 5.06 of this revenue procedure to section 8.01 of Rev. Proc. 2000–50 are effective for a Form 3115 filed for the taxable years ending on or after December 26, 2006, except that:

(1) the change made to section 8.01 of Rev. Proc. 2000–50 providing that a change in useful life under the method described in section 6.01(2) of Rev. Proc. 2000–50 is a change in method of accounting is effective for property placed in service by the taxpayer in a taxable year ending on or after December 30, 2003; and

(2) the change made to section 8.01 of Rev. Proc. 2000–50 providing that a change in useful life to 36 months made by a taxpayer that is currently treating costs paid or incurred to develop computer software under section 5.01(2) of Rev. Proc. 2000–50 in accordance with the rules provided in § 167(f)(1) and the regulations thereunder but is not currently using a useful life of 36 months is a change in method of accounting is effective for property placed in service by the taxpayer in a taxable year ending on or after December 30, 2003.

SECTION 7. DRAFTING INFORMATION

The principal author of this revenue procedure is Douglas H. Kim of the Office of Associate Chief Counsel (Passthroughs & Special Industries). For further information regarding this revenue procedure, contact Mr. Kim at (202) 622–3110 (not a toll-free call).

APPENDIX

SECTION 1. Section 2.01 of the APPENDIX of Rev. Proc 2002–9 is deleted and replaced with the following:

".01 *Impermissible to permissible method of accounting for depreciation or amortization.*

(1) *Description of change and scope.*

(a) *Applicability.* This change applies to a taxpayer that wants to change from an impermissible to a permissible method of accounting for depreciation or amortization (depreciation) for any item of depreciable or amortizable property:

(i) for which the taxpayer used the impermissible method of accounting in at least the two taxable years immediately preceding the year of change (but see section 2.01(1)(b) of this APPENDIX for property placed in service in the taxable year immediately preceding the year of change);

(ii) for which the taxpayer is making a change in method of accounting under § 1.446–1(e)(2)(ii)(*d*);

(iii) for which depreciation is determined under § 56(a)(1), § 56(g)(4)(A), § 167, § 168, § 197, § 1400I, or § 1400L(c), under § 168 prior to its amendment in 1986 (former § 168), or under any additional first year depreciation deduction provision of the Internal Revenue Code (for example, § 168(k), § 1400L(b), or § 1400N(d)); and

(iv) that is owned by the taxpayer at the beginning of the year of change (but see section 2.05 of this APPENDIX for property disposed of before the year of change).

(b) *Taxpayer has not adopted a method of accounting for the item of property.* If a taxpayer does not satisfy section 2.01(1)(a)(i) of this APPENDIX for an item of depreciable or amortizable property because this item of property is placed in service by the taxpayer in the taxable year immediately preceding the year of change ("1-year depreciable property"), the taxpayer may change from the impermissible method of determining depreciation to the permissible method of determining depreciation for the 1-year depreciable property by filing a Form 3115 for this change, provided the § 481 adjustment reported on the Form 3115 includes the amount of any adjustment that is attributable to all property (including the 1-year depreciable property) subject to the Form 3115. Alternatively, the taxpayer may change from the impermissible method of determining depreciation to the permissible method of determining depreciation for a 1-year depreciable property by filing an amended federal tax return for the property's placed-in-service year prior to the date the taxpayer files its federal tax return for the taxable year succeeding the placed-in-service year.

(c) *Certain scope limitations inapplicable.* The scope limitations in sections 4.02(7) and 4.02(8) of this revenue procedure are not applicable to this change.

(d) *Inapplicability.* This change does not apply to:

(i) any property to which § 1016(a)(3) (regarding property held by a tax-exempt organization) applies;

(ii) any taxpayer that is subject to § 263A and that is required to capitalize the costs with respect to which the taxpayer wants to change its method of accounting under section 2.01 of this APPENDIX, if the taxpayer is not capitalizing the costs as required;

(iii) any property for which a taxpayer is making a change in depreciation under § 1.446–1(e)(2)(ii)(*d*)(*2*)(*vi*) or (*vii*);

(iv) any property subject to § 167(g) (regarding property depreciated under the income forecast method);

(v) any § 1250 property that a taxpayer is reclassifying to an asset class of Rev. Proc. 87–56, 1987–2 C.B. 674, or Rev. Proc. 83–35, 1983–1 C.B. 745, as appropriate, that does not explicitly include § 1250 property (for example, asset class 57.0, Distributive Trades and Services);

(vi) any property for which a taxpayer is revoking a timely valid election, or making a late election, under § 167, § 168, § 179, § 1400I, § 1400L(c), former § 168, § 13261(g)(2) or (3) of the Revenue Reconciliation Act of 1993 (1993 Act), 1993–3 C.B. 1, 128 (relating to amortizable § 197 intangibles), or any additional first year depreciation deduction provision of the Internal Revenue Code (for example, § 168(k), § 1400L(b), or § 1400N(d)). A taxpayer may request consent to revoke or make the election by submitting a request for a letter ruling under Rev. Proc. 2006–1, 2006–1 I.R.B. 1 (or any successor). However, if a taxpayer is revoking or making an election under § 179, see §179(c) and § 1.179–5. *See* § 1.446–1(e)(2)(ii)(*d*)(*3*)(*iii*);

(vii) any property for which depreciation is determined under § 56(g)(4)(A) or § 167 (other than under § 168, § 1400I, § 1400L(c), former § 168, or any additional first year depreciation deduction provision of the Code (for example, § 168(k), § 1400L(b), or § 1400N(d))) and a taxpayer is changing the useful life of the property. A change in the useful life of property is corrected by adjustments in the applicable taxable year provided under § 1.446–1(e)(2)(ii)(*d*)(*5*)(*iv*). However, this section 2.01(1)(d)(vii) of this APPENDIX does not apply if the taxpayer is changing to or from a useful life, recovery period, or amortization period that is specifically assigned by the Internal Revenue Code (for example, § 167(f)(1), § 168(c)), the regulations thereunder, or other guidance published in the Internal Revenue Bulletin and, therefore, this change is a change in method of accounting (unless section 2.01(1)(d)(xv) of this APPENDIX applies). *See* § 1.446–1(e)(2)(ii)(*d*)(*3*)(*i*);

(viii) any depreciable property for which the use changes in the hands of the same taxpayer. *See* § 1.446–1(e)(2)(ii)(*d*)(*3*)(*ii*);

(ix) any property for which depreciation is determined in accordance with § 1.167(a)–11 (regarding the Class Life Asset Depreciation Range System (ADR));

(x) any change in method of accounting involving a change from deducting the cost or other basis of any property as an expense to capitalizing and depreciating the cost or other basis, or *vice versa*;

(xi) any change in method of accounting involving a change from one permissible method of accounting for the property to another permissible method of accounting for the property. For example:

(A) a change from the straight-line method of depreciation to the income forecast method of depreciating for videocassettes. *See* Rev. Rul. 89–62, 1989–1 C.B. 78; or

(B) a change from charging the depreciation reserve with costs of removal and crediting the depreciation reserve with salvage proceeds to deducting costs of removal as an expense (provided the costs of removal are not required to be capitalized under any provision of the Code, such as, § 263(a)) and including salvage proceeds in taxable income (see section 2.02 of this APPENDIX for making this change for property for which depreciation is determined under § 167);

(xii) any change in method of accounting involving both a change from treating the cost or other basis of the property as nondepreciable or nonamortizable property to treating the cost or other basis of the property as depreciable or amortizable property and the adoption of a method of accounting for depreciation requiring an election under § 167, § 168, § 1400I, § 1400L(c), former § 168, § 13261(g)(2) or (3) of the 1993 Act, or any additional first year depreciation deduction provision of the Code (for example, a change in the treatment of the space consumed in landfills placed in service in 1990 from nondepreciable to depreciable property (assuming section 2.01(1)(d)(xiii) of the APPENDIX does not apply) and the making of an election under § 168(f)(1) to depreciate this property under the unit of production method of depreciation under § 167);

(xiii) any change in method of accounting for any item of income or deduction other than depreciation, even if the change results in a change in computing depreciation under § 1.446–1(e)(2)(ii)(*d*)(*2*)(*i*), (*ii*), (*iii*), (*iv*), (*v*), (*vi*), (*vii*), or (*viii*). For example, a change in method of accounting involving:

(A) a change in inventory costs (for example, when property is reclassified from inventory property to depreciable property, or *vice versa*) (but see section 3.02 of this APPENDIX for making a change from inventory property to depreciable property for unrecoverable line pack gas or unrecoverable cushion gas); or

(B) a change in the character of a transaction from sale to lease, or *vice versa* (but see section 2.03 of this APPENDIX for making this change);

(xiv) a change from determining depreciation under § 168 to determining depreciation under former § 168 for any property subject to the transition rules in § 203(b) or 204(a) of the Tax Reform Act of 1986, 1986–3 (Vol. 1) C.B. 1, 60–80;

(xv) any change in the placed-in-service date of a depreciable or amortizable property. This change is corrected by adjustments in the applicable taxable year provided under § 1.446–1(e)(2)(ii)(*d*)(*5*)(*v*); or

(xvi) any property for which the rehabilitation credit under § 47 was claimed and that a taxpayer is reclassifying to 3-year property, 5-year property, 7-year property, 10-year property, 15-year property, 20-year property, or water utility property (other than real property with a class life of more than 12.5 years).

(2) *Additional requirements.* A taxpayer also must comply with the following:

(a) *Permissible method of accounting for depreciation.* A taxpayer must change to a permissible method of accounting for depreciation for the item of depreciable or amortizable property. The permissible method of accounting is the same method that determines the depreciation allowable for the item of property (as provided in section 2.01(5) of this APPENDIX).

(b) *Statements required.* A taxpayer must provide the following statements, if applicable, and attach them to the completed application:

(i) a detailed description of the former and new methods of accounting. A general description of these methods of accounting is unacceptable (for example, MACRS to MACRS, erroneous method to proper method, claiming less than the depreciation allowable to claiming the depreciation allowable);

(ii) to the extent not provided elsewhere on the application, a statement describing the taxpayer's business or income-producing activities. Also, if the taxpayer has more than one business or income-producing activity, a statement describing the taxpayer's business or income-producing activity in which the item of property at issue is primarily used by the taxpayer;

(iii) to the extent not provided elsewhere on the application, a statement of the facts and law supporting the new method of accounting, new classification of the item of property, and new asset class in, as appropriate, Rev. Proc. 87–56 or Rev. Proc. 83–35. If the taxpayer is the owner and lessor of the item of property at issue, the statement of the facts and law supporting the new asset class also must describe the business or income-producing activity in which that item of property is primarily used by the lessee;

(iv) to the extent not provided elsewhere on the application, a statement identifying the year in which the item of property was placed in service;

(v) if any item of property is public utility property within the meaning of § 168(i)(10) or former § 167(l)(3)(A), as applicable, a statement providing that the taxpayer agrees to the following additional terms and conditions:

(A) a normalization method of accounting (within the meaning of former § 167(l)(3)(G), former § 168(e)(3)(B), or § 168(i)(9), as applicable) will be used for the public utility property subject to the application;

(B) as of the beginning of the year of change, the taxpayer will adjust its deferred tax reserve account or similar reserve account in the taxpayer's regulatory books of account by the amount of the deferral of federal income tax liability associated with the § 481(a) adjustment applicable to the public utility property subject to the application; and

(C) within 30 calendar days of filing the federal income tax return for the year of change, the taxpayer will provide a copy of the completed application to any regulatory body having jurisdiction over the public utility property subject to the application;

(vi) if the taxpayer is changing the classification of an item of § 1250 property placed in service after August 19, 1996, to a retail motor fuels outlet under § 168(e)(3)(E)(iii), a statement containing the following representation: "For purposes of § 168(e)(3)(E)(iii) of the Internal Revenue Code, the taxpayer represents that (A) 50 percent or more of the gross revenue generated from the item of § 1250 property is from the sale of petroleum products (not including gross revenue from related services, such as the labor cost of oil changes and gross revenue from the sale of nonpetroleum products such as tires and oil filters), (B) 50 percent or more of the floor space in the item of property is devoted to the sale of petroleum products (not including floor space devoted to related services, such as oil changes and floor space devoted to nonpetroleum products such as tires and oil filters), or (C) the time of § 1250 property is 1,400 square feet or less."; and

(vii) if the taxpayer is changing the classification of an item of property from § 1250 property to § 1245 property under § 168 or former § 168, a statement of the facts and law supporting the new § 1245 property classification, and a statement containing the following representation: "Each item of depreciable property that is the subject of the application filed under section 2.01 of the APPENDIX of Rev. Proc. 2002–9 for the year of change beginning [*Insert the date*], and that is reclassified from [*Insert, as appropriate: nonresidential real property, residential rental property, qualified leasehold improvement property, qualified restaurant property, 19-year real property, 18-year real property, or 15-year real property*] to an asset class of [*Insert, as appropriate, either: Rev. Proc. 87–56, 1987–2 C.B. 674, or Rev. Proc. 83–35, 1983–1 C.B. 745*] that does not explicitly include § 1250 property, is § 1245 property for depreciation purposes."

(3) *Section 481(a) adjustment.* Because the adjusted basis of the property is changed as a result of a method change made under section 2.01 of this APPENDIX (*see* section 2.01(4) of this APPENDIX), items are duplicated or omitted. Accordingly, this change is made with a § 481(a) adjustment. This adjustment may result in either a negative § 481(a) adjustment (a decrease in taxable income) or

a positive § 481(a) adjustment (an increase in taxable income) and may be a different amount for regular tax, alternative minimum tax, and adjusted current earnings purposes. This § 481(a) adjustment equals the difference between the total amount of depreciation taken into account in computing taxable income for the property under the taxpayer's former method of accounting (including the amount attributable to any property described in section 2.01(1)(b) of this APPENDIX that is included in the taxpayer's Form 3115), and the total amount of depreciation allowable for the property under the taxpayer's new method of accounting (as determined under section 2.01(5) of this APPENDIX, and including the amount attributable to any property described in section 2.01(1)(b) of this APPENDIX that is included in the taxpayer's Form 3115), for open and closed years prior to the year of change. However, the amount of the § 481(a) adjustment must be adjusted to account for the proper amount of the depreciation allowable that is required to be capitalized under any provision of the Code (for example, § 263A) at the beginning of the year of change.

(4) *Basis adjustment.* As of the beginning of the year of change, the basis of depreciable property to which section 2.01 of this APPENDIX applies must reflect the reductions required by § 1016(a)(2) for the depreciation allowable for the property (as determined under section 2.01(5) of this APPENDIX).

(5) *Meaning of depreciation allowable.*

(a) *In general.* Section 2.01(5) of this APPENDIX provides the amount of the depreciation allowable determined under § 56(a)(1), § 56(g)(4)(A), § 167, § 168, § 197, § 1400I, or § 1400L(c), or former § 168. This amount, however, may be limited by other provisions of the Code (for example, § 280F).

(b) *Section 56(a)(1) property.* The depreciation allowable for any taxable year for property for which depreciation is determined under § 56(a)(1) is determined by using the depreciation method, recovery period, and convention provided for under § 56(a)(1) that applies for the property's placed-in-service date.

(c) *Section 56(g)(4)(A) property.* The depreciation allowable for any taxable year for property for which depreciation is determined under § 56(g)(4)(A) is determined by using the depreciation method, recovery period or useful life, as applicable, and convention provided for under § 56(g)(4)(A) that applies for the property's placed-in-service date.

(d) *Section 167 property.* Generally, for any taxable year, the depreciation allowable for property for which depreciation is determined under § 167, is determined either:

(i) under the depreciation method adopted by a taxpayer for the property; or

(ii) if that depreciation method does not result in a reasonable allowance for depreciation or a taxpayer has not adopted a depreciation method for the property, under the straight-line depreciation method.

For determining the estimated useful life and salvage value of the property, see § 1.167(a)–1(b) and (c), respectively.

The depreciation allowable for any taxable year for property subject to § 167(f) (regarding certain property excluded from § 197) is determined by using the depreciation method and useful life prescribed in § 167(f). If computer software is depreciated under § 167(f)(1) and is qualified property (as defined in § 168(k)(2) and § 1.168(k)–1 of the Income Tax Regulations), 50-percent bonus depreciation property (as defined in § 168(k)(4) and § 1.168(k)–1), qualified New York Liberty Zone (Liberty Zone) property (as defined in § 1400L(b)(2) and § 1.1400L(b)–1), or qualified Gulf Opportunity Zone (GO Zone) property (as defined in sections 2.02 and 2.03 of Notice 2006–77, 2006–40 I.R.B. 590), the depreciation allowable for that computer software under § 167(f)(1) is also determined by taking into account the additional first year depreciation deduction provided by § 168(k), § 1400L(b), or § 1400N(d), as applicable, unless the taxpayer made a timely valid election not to deduct any additional first year depreciation for the computer software.

(e) *Section 168 property.* The depreciation allowable for any taxable year for property for which depreciation is determined under § 168, is determined as follows:

(i) by using either:

(A) the general depreciation system in § 168(a); or

(B) the alternative depreciation system in § 168(g) if the property is required to be depreciated under the alternative depreciation system pursuant to § 168(g)(1) or other provisions of the Code (for example, property described in § 263A(e)(2)(A) or § 280F(b)(1)). Property required to be depreciated under the alternative depreciation system pursuant to § 168(g)(1) includes property in a class (as set out in § 168(e)) for which the taxpayer made a timely valid election under § 168(g)(7); and

(ii) if the property is qualified property, 50-percent bonus depreciation property, Liberty Zone property, or GO Zone property, by taking into account the additional first year depreciation deduction provided by § 168(k), § 1400L(b), or § 1400N(d), as applicable, unless the taxpayer made a timely valid election not to deduct the additional first year depreciation (or made a deemed election not to deduct the additional first year depreciation; for further guidance, see Rev. Proc. 2002–33, 2002–1 C.B. 963, Rev. Proc. 2003–50, 2003–2 C.B. 119, or Notice 2006–77) for the class of property (as defined in § 1.168(k)–1(e)(2), § 1.1400L(b)–1(e)(2), or section 4.02 of Notice 2006–77, as applicable) in which that property is included.

(f) *Section 197 property.* The depreciation allowable for any taxable year for an amortizable § 197 intangible (including any property for which a timely election under § 13261(g)(2) of the 1993 Act was made) is determined in accordance with § 1.197–2(f).

(g) *Former § 168 property.* The depreciation allowable for any taxable year for property subject to former § 168 is determined by using either:

(i) the accelerated method of cost recovery applicable to the property (for example, for 5-year property, the recovery method under former § 168(b)(1)); or

(ii) the straight-line method applicable to the property if the property is required to be depreciated under the straight-line method (for example, property described in former § 168(f)(12) or former § 280F(b)(2)) or if the taxpayer elected to determine the depreciation allowance under the optional straight-line percentage (for example, the straight-line method in former § 168(b)(3)).

(h) *Qualified revitalization building*. The depreciation allowable for any taxable year for any qualified revitalization building (as defined in § 1400I(b)(1)) for which the taxpayer has made a timely valid election under § 1400I(a) is determined as follows:

(i) if the taxpayer elected to deduct one-half of any qualified revitalization expenditures (as defined in § 1400I(b)(2)) chargeable to a capital account with respect to the qualified revitalization building for the taxable year in which the building is placed in service by the taxpayer, the depreciation allowable for the property's placed-in-service year is equal to one-half of the qualified revitalization expenditures for the property and the depreciation allowable for the remaining recovery period of the property is determined using the general depreciation system of § 168(a) or the alternative depreciation system of § 168(g), as applicable; or

(ii) if the taxpayer elected to amortize all of the qualified revitalization expenditures chargeable to a capital account with respect to the qualified revitalization building ratably over the 120-month period beginning with the month in which the building is placed in service, the depreciation allowable is determined in accordance with this election.

(i) *Qualified New York Liberty Zone leasehold improvement property*. The depreciation allowable for any taxable year for qualified New York Liberty Zone leasehold improvement property (as defined in § 1400L(c)(2)) is determined by using the depreciation method and recovery period prescribed in § 1400L(c) unless the taxpayer made a timely valid election under § 1400L(c) not to use that recovery period."

SECTION 2. Section 2.02 of the APPENDIX of Rev. Proc. 2002–9 is deleted and replaced with the following:

".02 *Permissible to permissible method of accounting for depreciation*.

(1) *Description of change*. This change applies to a taxpayer that wants to change from a permissible method of accounting for depreciation under § 56(g)(4)(A)(iv) or § 167 to another permissible method of accounting for depreciation under § 56(g)(4)(A)(iv) or § 167. Pursuant to § 1.167(a)–7(a) and (c), a taxpayer may account for depreciable property either by treating each individual asset as an account or by combining two or more assets in a single account and, for each account, depreciation allowances are computed separately.

(2) *Scope*.

(a) *Applicability*. This change applies to any taxpayer wanting to make a change in method of accounting for depreciation specified in section 2.02(3) of this APPENDIX for the property in an account:

(i) for which the present and proposed methods of accounting for depreciation specified in section 2.02(3) of this APPENDIX are permissible methods for the property under § 56(g)(4)(A)(iv) or § 167; and

(ii) that is owned by the taxpayer at the beginning of the year of change.

(b) *Certain scope limitations inapplicable*. The scope limitations in sections 4.02(7) and 4.02(8) of this revenue procedure are not applicable to this change.

(c) *Inapplicability*. This change does not apply to:

(i) any taxpayer that is subject to § 263A and that is required to capitalize the costs with respect to which the taxpayer wants to change its method of accounting under section 2.02 of this APPENDIX, if the taxpayer is not capitalizing the costs as required;

(ii) any property to which § 1016(a)(3) (regarding property held by a tax-exempt organization) applies;

(iii) any property described in § 167(f) (regarding certain property excluded from § 197);

(iv) any property subject to § 167(g) (regarding property depreciated under the income forecast method);

(v) any property for which depreciation is determined under § 56(a)(1), § 56(g)(4)(A)(i), (ii), (iii), or (v), § 168, § 1400I, § 1400L(c), § 168 prior to its amendment in 1986 (former § 168), or any additional first year depreciation deduction provision of the Internal Revenue Code (for example, § 168(k), § 1400L(b), or § 1400N(d));

(vi) any property that the taxpayer elected under § 168(f)(1) or former § 168(e)(2) to exclude from the application of, respectively, § 168 or former § 168;

(vii) any property for which depreciation is determined in accordance with § 1.167(a)–11 (regarding the Class Life Asset Depreciation Range System (ADR));

(viii) any depreciable property for which the taxpayer is changing the depreciation method pursuant to § 1.167(e)–1(b) of the Income Tax Regulations (change from declining-balance method to straight-line method), § 1.167(e)–1(c) (certain changes for § 1245 property), or § 1.167(e)–1(d) (certain changes for § 1250 property). These changes must be made prospectively and are not permitted under the cited regulations for property for which the depreciation is determined under § 168, § 1400I, § 1400L, or former § 168; or

(ix) any distributor commissions (as defined by section 2 of Rev. Proc. 2000–38, 2000–2 C.B. 310) for which the taxpayer is changing the useful life under the distribution fee period method or the useful life method (both described in Rev. Proc. 2000–38). A change in this useful life is corrected by adjustments in the applicable taxable year provided under § 1.446–1(e)(2)(ii)(*d*)(*5*)(*iv*).

(3) *Changes covered*. Section 2.02 of this APPENDIX only applies to the following changes in methods of accounting for depreciation:

(a) a change from the straight-line method to the sum-of-the-years-digits method, the sinking fund method, the unit-of-production method, or the declining-balance method using any proper percentage of the straight-line rate;

(b) a change from the declining-balance method using any percentage of the straight-line rate to the sum-of-the-years-digits method, the sinking fund method, or the declining-balance method using a different proper percentage of the straight-line rate;

(c) a change from the sum-of-the-years-digits method to the sinking fund method, the declining-balance method using any proper percentage of the straight-line rate, or the straight-line method;

(d) a change from the unit-of-production method to the straight-line method;

(e) a change from the sinking fund method to the straight-line method, the unit-of-production method, the sum-of-the-years-digits method, or the declining-balance method using any proper percentage of the straight-line rate;

(f) a change in the interest factor used in connection with a compound interest method or sinking fund method;

(g) a change in averaging convention as set forth in § 1.167(a)–10(b). However, as specifically provided in § 1.167(a)–10(b), in any taxable year in which an averaging convention substantially distorts the depreciation allowance for the taxable year, it may not be used (*see* Rev. Rul. 73–202, 1973–1 C.B. 81);

(h) a change from charging the depreciation reserve with costs of removal and crediting the depreciation reserve with salvage proceeds to deducting costs of removal as an expense and including salvage proceeds in taxable income as set forth in § 1.167(a)–8(e)(2). *See* Rev. Rul. 74–455, 1974–2 C.B. 63. This change, however, may be made under this revenue procedure only if:

(i) the change is applied to all items in the account for which the change is being made; and

(ii) the removal costs are not required to be capitalized under any provision of the Code (for example, § 263(a), 263A, or 280B);

(i) a change from crediting the depreciation reserve with the salvage proceeds realized on normal retirement sales to computing and recognizing gains and losses on the sales (*see* Rev. Rul. 70–165, 1970–1 C.B. 43);

(j) a change from crediting ordinary income (including the combination method of crediting the lesser of estimated salvage value or actual salvage proceeds to the depreciation reserve, with any excess of salvage proceeds over estimated salvage value credited to ordinary income) with the salvage proceeds realized on normal retirement sales, to computing and recognizing gains and losses on the sales (*see* Rev. Rul. 70–166, 1970–1 C.B. 44);

(k) a change from item accounting for specific assets to multiple asset accounting (pooling) for the same assets, or *vice versa*;

(l) a change from one type of multiple asset accounting (pooling) for specific assets to a different type of multiple asset accounting (pooling) for the same assets;

(m) a change from one method described in Rev. Proc. 2000–38 for amortizing distributor commissions (as defined by section 2 of Rev. Proc. 2000–38, 2000–2 C.B. 310) to another method described in Rev. Proc. 2000–38 for amortizing distributor commissions; or

(n) a change from pooling to a single asset, or *vice versa*, for distributor commissions (as defined by section 2 of Rev. Proc. 2000–38, 2000–2 C.B. 310) for which the taxpayer is using the distribution fee period method or the useful life method (both described in Rev. Proc. 2000–38).

(4) *Additional requirements.* A taxpayer also must comply with the following:

(a) *Basis for depreciation.* At the beginning of the year of change, the basis for depreciation of property to which this change applies is the adjusted basis of the property as provided in § 1011 at the end of the taxable year immediately preceding the year of change (determined under the taxpayer's present method of accounting for depreciation). If applicable under the taxpayer's proposed method of accounting for depreciation, this adjusted basis is reduced by the estimated salvage value of the property (for example, a change to the straight-line method).

(b) *Rate of depreciation.* The rate of depreciation for property changed to:

(i) the straight-line or the sum-of-the-years-digits method of depreciation must be based on the remaining useful life of the property as of the beginning of the year of change; or

(ii) the declining-balance method of depreciation must be based on the useful life of the property measured from the placed-in-service date, and not the expected remaining life from the date the change becomes effective.

(c) *Regulatory requirements.* For changes in method of depreciation to the sum-of-the-years-digits or declining-balance method, the property must meet the requirements of § 1.167(b)–0 or 1.167(c)–1, as appropriate.

(d) *Public utility property.* If any item of property is public utility property within the meaning of former § 167(l)(3)(A), the taxpayer must attach to the application a statement providing that the taxpayer agrees to the following additional terms and conditions:

(i) a normalization method of accounting within the meaning of former § 167(l)(3)(G) will be used for the public utility property subject to the application; and

(ii) within 30 calendar days of filing the federal income tax return for the year of change, the taxpayer will provide a copy of the completed application to any regulatory body having jurisdiction over the public utility property subject to the application.

(5) *Section 481(a) adjustment.* Because the adjusted basis of the property is not changed as a result of a method change made under section 2.02 of this APPENDIX, no items are being duplicated or omitted. Accordingly, no § 481(a) adjustment is required or necessary."

SECTION 3. Section 2B of the APPENDIX of Rev. Proc. 2002–9 is deleted and replaced with the following:

"SECTION 2B. COMPUTER SOFTWARE EXPENDITURES (§§ 162, 167, AND 197)

.01 *Description of change.* This change applies to a taxpayer that wants to change its method of accounting for the costs of computer software to a method described in Rev. Proc. 2000–50, 2000–2 C.B. 601, as modified by Rev. Proc. 2007–16, 2007–4 I.R.B. 358. Section 5 of Rev. Proc. 2000–50 describes the methods applicable to the costs of developing computer software. Section 6 of Rev. Proc. 2000–50 describes the method applicable to the costs of acquired computer software. Section 7 of Rev. Proc. 2000–50 describes the method applicable to leased or licensed computer software. If a taxpayer treats the costs of computer software in accordance with the applicable method described in Rev. Proc. 2000–50, the Service will not disturb the taxpayer's treatment of its costs of computer software.

.02 *Scope.* This change applies to all costs of computer software as defined in section 2 of Rev. Proc. 2000–50. However, this change does not apply to any computer software that is subject to amortization as an "amortizable section 197 intangible" as defined in § 197(c) and the regulations thereunder, or to costs that a taxpayer has treated as research and experimentation expenditures under § 174.

.03 *Statement required.* If a taxpayer is changing to the method described in section 5.01(2) of Rev. Proc. 2000–50, the taxpayer must attach to the application a statement providing the information required in section 8.02(2) of Rev. Proc. 2000–50.

SECTION 4. Section 2.05 of the APPENDIX of Rev. Proc. 2002–9 is added to read as follows:

".05 *Impermissible to permissible method of accounting for depreciation or amortization for disposed depreciable or amortizable property.*

(1) *Description of change.* This change applies to a taxpayer that wants to make the change in method of accounting for depreciation or amortization (depreciation) provided under section 3 of Rev. Proc. 2007–16, 2007–4 I.R.B. 358, for an item of depreciable or amortizable property that has been disposed of by the taxpayer. Section 3 of Rev. Proc. 2007–16 allows a taxpayer to make a change in method of accounting for depreciation for the disposed property if the taxpayer used an impermissible method of accounting for depreciation for the property under which the taxpayer did not take into account any depreciation allowance, or did take into account some depreciation but less than the depreciation allowable, in the year of change (as defined in section 2.05(4) of this APPENDIX) or any prior taxable year.

(2) *Scope.*

(a) *Applicability.* Except as provided in section 2.05(2)(b) of this APPENDIX, section 2.05 of this APPENDIX applies to a taxpayer that is changing from an impermissible method of accounting for depreciation to a permissible method of accounting for depreciation for any item of depreciable or amortizable property subject to §§ 167, 168, 197, 1400I, or 1400L(c), to former § 168, or to any additional first year depreciation deduction provision of the Internal Revenue Code (for example, § 168(k), § 1400L(b), or § 1400N(d)):

(i) that has been disposed of by the taxpayer during the year of change (as defined in section 2.05(4) of this APPENDIX); and

(ii) for which the taxpayer did not take into account any depreciation allowance, or did take into account some depreciation but less than the depreciation allowable (hereinafter, both are referred to as "claimed less than the depreciation allowable"), in the year of change (as defined in section 2.05(4) of this APPENDIX) or any prior taxable year.

(b) *Inapplicability.* Section 2.05 of this APPENDIX does not apply to:

(i) any property to which § 1016(a)(3) (regarding property held by a tax-exempt organization) applies;

(ii) any property for which a taxpayer is revoking a timely valid depreciation election, or making a late depreciation election, under the Code or regulations thereunder, or under other guidance published in the Internal Revenue Bulletin (including under § 13261(g)(2) or (3) of the Revenue Reconciliation Act of 1993, 1993–3 C.B. 1, 128 (relating to amortizable § 197 intangibles));

(iii) any property for which the taxpayer deducted the cost or other basis of the property as an expense; or

(iv) any property disposed of by the taxpayer in a transaction to which a nonrecognition section of the Code applies (for example, § 1031, transactions subject to § 168(i)(7)(B)(i)). However, this section 2.05(2)(b)(iv) does not apply to property disposed of by the taxpayer in a § 1031 or § 1033 transaction if the taxpayer elects under § 1.168(i)–6T(i) and (j) to treat the entire basis (that is, both the exchanged and excess basis (as defined in § 1.168(i)–6T(b)(7) and (8), respectively)) of the replacement MACRS property (as defined in § 1.168(i)–6T(b)(1)) as property placed in service by the taxpayer at the time of replacement and treat the adjusted depreciable basis of the relinquished MACRS property (as defined in § 1.168(i)–6T(b)(2)) as being disposed of by the taxpayer at the time of disposition.

(3) *Manner of making the change.*

(a) *Change made on an original return for year of change.* This change may be made on a taxpayer's timely filed (including extensions) original federal tax return for the year of change (as defined in section 2.05(4) of this APPENDIX), provided the taxpayer files the original Form 3115 in accordance with section 6.02(3) of this revenue procedure.

(b) *Change made on an amended return for year of change.* This change may also be made on an amended federal tax return for the year of change (as defined in section 2.05(4) of this APPENDIX), provided:

(i) the taxpayer files the original Form 3115 with the taxpayer's amended federal tax return for the year of change (as defined in section 2.05(4) of this APPENDIX) prior to the expiration of the period of limitation for assessment under § 6501(a) for the taxable year in which the item of depreciable or amortizable property was disposed of by the taxpayer; and

(ii) the taxpayer's amended federal tax return for the year of change (as defined in section 2.05(4) of this APPENDIX) includes the adjustments to taxable income and any collateral adjustments to taxable income or tax liability (for example, adjustments to the amount or character of the gain or loss of the disposed depreciable or amortizable property) resulting from the change in method of accounting for depreciation made by the taxpayer under section 2.05 of this APPENDIX.

(4) *Year of change.* The year of change for this change is the taxable year in which the item of depreciable or amortizable property was disposed of by the taxpayer.

(5) *Scope limitations inapplicable.* The scope limitations in section 4.02 of this revenue procedure do not apply. If the taxpayer is under examination, before an appeals office, or before a federal court at the time that a copy of the Form 3115 is filed with the national office, the taxpayer must provide a copy of the Form 3115 to the examining agent, appeals officer, or counsel for the government, as appropriate, at the time the copy of the Form 3115 is filed with the national office. The Form 3115 must contain the name(s) and telephone number(s) of the examining agent, appeals officer, or counsel for the government, as appropriate.

(6) *Filing requirements.* Notwithstanding section 6.02(3)(a) of this revenue procedure, a taxpayer making this change in accordance with section 2.05(3)(b) of this APPENDIX must attach the original Form 3115 to the taxpayer's timely filed amended federal tax return for the year of change and must file the required copy (with signature) of the Form 3115 with the national office no later than when the original Form 3115 is filed with the amended federal tax return for the year of change. If a taxpayer is making this change in accordance with section 2.05(3)(a) of this APPENDIX, the filing requirements in section 6.02(3)(a) of this revenue procedure apply.

(7) *Section 481(a) adjustment period.* A taxpayer must take the § 481(a) adjustment into account in the year of change."

---

26 CFR 601.202: Closing agreements.
(Also Part I, §§ 446, 482, 7121; 1.446–1, 301.7121–1.)

Rev. Proc. 2007–17

TABLE OF CONTENTS

SECTION 1. PURPOSE

.01 This revenue procedure permits a taxpayer under the jurisdiction of the Large and Mid-Size Business Division to request that the Service examine specific issues relating to tax returns before those returns are filed. This revenue procedure supersedes Rev. Proc. 2005–12, 2005–1 C.B. 311. This revenue procedure provides the framework within which a taxpayer and the Service may work together in a cooperative environment to resolve, after examination, issues accepted into the program. If the taxpayer and the Service are able to resolve the examined issues before the returns that they affect are filed, this revenue procedure authorizes the taxpayer and the Service to memorialize their agreement by executing an LMSB Pre-Filing Agreement (PFA).

.02 This revenue procedure outlines the procedures for resolving issues through pre-filing examinations. Taxpayers and the Service often resolve issues more effectively and efficiently through a pre-filing examination than a post-filing examination, because the taxpayer and the Service have more timely access to the records and personnel that are relevant to the issues. A pre-filing examination also provides the taxpayer with certainty regarding the examined issue at an earlier point in time than a post-filing examination. These procedures benefit both taxpayers and the Service by improving the quality of tax compliance while reducing costs, burdens, and delays. Unlike letter rulings and other forms of written advice provided by the Offices of the Associates Chief Counsel (see Rev. Proc. 2006–1, 2006–1 I.R.B. 1), a PFA does not determine the tax treatment of prospective or future transactions or events, but only of completed transactions or events whose tax treatment has not yet been reported on a return.

SECTION 2. BACKGROUND

.01 In Rev. Proc. 2001–22, 2001–1 C.B. 745, the Service provided procedures for LMSB taxpayers to request an examination and resolve specific issues relating to returns that were neither due (taking into account any extensions of time to file) nor filed.

.02 Because Rev. Proc. 2001–22 limited the eligible years for the PFA program to current or prior taxable years for which returns were neither due nor filed, taxpayers and the Service could not resolve issues for multiple future taxable years or issues regarding appropriate methodologies for determining tax consequences that would affect future taxable years.

.03 In Rev. Proc. 2005–12, the Service expanded the scope of the PFA program by allowing taxpayers and the Service to address certain issues over a limited number of future taxable years. In addition, the Service revised the domestic and international issues eligible for the PFA program. Section 12 of Rev. Proc. 2005–12 provided that that revenue procedure would remain in effect until December 31, 2006, unless sooner revoked, modified, or superseded.

.04 The Service has determined to renew the PFA program as described in Rev. Proc. 2005–12 with minimal changes. This revenue procedure largely continues the existing PFA program, clarifying procedures for processing a PFA request and updating the user fee requirements for a PFA. The objective of the PFA program remains to resolve, before returns are filed, issues that are likely to be disputed in post-filing audits.

SECTION 3. SCOPE

.01 *Eligible taxpayers.* This revenue procedure applies to taxpayers under the jurisdiction of LMSB that desire to resolve through a PFA issues that otherwise may be the subject of a post-filing examination.

.02 *Eligible taxable years.*

(1) *Current, past, and future taxable years.* An eligible taxpayer may request a PFA for the current taxable year, any prior taxable year for which the original return is not yet due (taking into account any extensions of time to file) and is not yet filed and, except in the case of a PFA provided under section 3.09(2), for a limited number of future taxable years.

(2) *Agreements for future taxable years.* Agreements for future taxable years are limited to four taxable years beyond the current taxable year.

.03 *Eligible issues generally.*

(1) *Factual issues and well-established law.* The Service will consider entering into a PFA on any issue that requires either a determination of facts or the application of well-established legal principles to known facts.

(2) *Issues that involve a methodology.* The Service also will, in general, consider entering into a PFA regarding a methodology used by a taxpayer to determine the appropriate amount of an item of income, allowance, deduction, or credit.

(3) *Issues under the jurisdiction of other Service divisions.* The Service will consider entering into a PFA on an issue under the jurisdiction of an operating division of the Service other than LMSB, but only with the concurrence of that operating division.

.04 *Relationship of eligible issues to eligible taxable years.* An issue also must relate to an eligible taxable year or years in order to be an eligible issue.

.05 *Eligible domestic and eligible international issues require coordination and consultation with Associate Chief Counsel.* There is no list of eligible domestic and international issues. Any domestic or international issue that requires either a determination of facts or application of well-established legal principles to known facts and that is not excluded under section 3.08 or section 3.09 of this revenue procedure is *likely* suitable for a PFA.

The Service may, in its sole discretion, refuse to address an issue in a PFA based on considerations of sound tax administration. Before any decision is made to proceed with the taxpayer's request for a PFA, the Service must coordinate and consult with the Associate Chief Counsel having subject matter jurisdiction over any issue proposed to be determined by a PFA. As part of this coordination and consultation, the Associate Chief Counsel may consider whether the issue is more appropriately resolved by a letter ruling or other form of written advice from the Offices of the Associates Chief Counsel, as described in Rev. Proc. 2006–1, 2006–1 I.R.B. 1, or its successors, and whether the issue is currently one with respect to which the Service will never, or will not ordinarily, issue a letter ruling. See Rev. Proc. 2006–3, 2006–1 I.R.B. 122, Rev. Proc. 2006–7, 2006–1 I.R.B. 242, and their successors.

.06 *Eligible international issues requiring Associate Chief Counsel (International) concurrence in execution.* This subsection lists specific international issues that are *likely* suitable for a PFA, but also require that the Associate Chief Counsel (International) concur with the acceptance of the issue into the PFA Program and execution of the PFA. Even though an issue in a particular case appears on this list, the Service may, in its sole discretion, refuse to address that issue based on considerations of sound tax administration. The eligible issues are:

(1) whether a unit of the taxpayer's trade or business is a qualified business unit within the meaning of section 989(a) and the regulations promulgated under that section;

(2) whether the taxpayer is engaged in a trade or business within the United States (excluding questions under section 864(b)(2));

(3) the amount of gross income that is effectively connected with the conduct by the taxpayer of a trade or business within the United States;

(4) factual determinations concerning the extent to which, under section 882(c), deductions are connected with income that is effectively connected with the taxpayer's conduct of a trade or business within the United States; and

(5) whether the taxpayer has a permanent establishment in the United States for purposes of a bilateral income tax convention to which the United States is a party and, if so, what profits are attributable to that permanent establishment.

.07 *Special provisions for requests on international issues.* The provisions of this section apply, in addition to the generally applicable provisions of this revenue procedure, to any request for a PFA on an issue having international implications.

(1) A PFA and any factual information contained in the background files is subject to exchange of information under income tax treaties or tax information exchange agreements in accordance with the terms of such treaties and agreements (including terms regarding relevancy, confidentiality, and the protection of trade secrets). In cases where the exchange of information would be discretionary, information may be exchanged to the extent consistent with sound tax administration and the practices of the relevant foreign competent authority.

(2) To minimize taxpayer and governmental uncertainty and administrative cost, taxpayers who seek a PFA on an

international issue are encouraged to seek competent authority consideration under the mutual agreement procedure of any applicable United States income tax convention. This consideration will be given after the PFA is concluded, and the PFA may be modified to reflect the outcome of the mutual agreement procedure.

(3) A taxpayer may request a PFA for an international issue that is the subject of a previously submitted request for competent authority assistance. The consideration of this competent authority request will not be suspended during the PFA process. If the taxpayer requests a PFA and the previously submitted request for competent authority assistance is ongoing, if appropriate, the taxpayer also should make a request for the Accelerated Competent Authority Procedure of Rev. Proc. 2002–52, 2002–2 C.B. 242.

.08 *Excluded issues*. The Service will not enter into a PFA on the following types of issues:

(1) Transfer pricing issues. *See* Rev. Proc. 2004–40, 2004–2 C.B. 50 (Advance Pricing Agreement program);

(2) Except as provided in section 3.09(2) of this revenue procedure, issues involving a change in accounting method. *See* Treas. Reg. § 1.446–1(e). This includes issues that are or have been the subject of a request by or with respect to the taxpayer for consent to change a method of accounting under procedures such as Rev. Proc. 97–27, 1997–1 C.B. 680 (as modified and amplified by Rev. Proc. 2002–19, 2002–1 C.B. 696, and as amplified and clarified by Rev. Proc. 2002–54, 2002–2 C.B. 432), or its predecessor or successor, or of an application filed under automatic consent procedures such as Rev. Proc. 2002–9, 2002–1 C.B. 327 (as modified and clarified by Announcement 2002–17, 2002–1 C.B. 561, as modified and amplified by Rev. Proc. 2002–19, and as amplified, clarified, and modified by Rev. Proc. 2002–54), or its predecessor or successor. This also includes issues for which a change in accounting method is necessary to resolve the issue. A taxpayer must obtain consent to make an accounting method change by using applicable administrative procedures. See generally Rev. Proc. 97–27 and Rev. Proc. 2002–9, or their successors;

(3) Issues involving the annual accounting period. See Treas. Reg. § 1.442–1. This includes issues that are or have been the subject of a request by or with respect to the taxpayer for permission to adopt, change, or retain an annual accounting period under procedures such as Rev. Proc. 2002–39, 2002–1 C.B. 1046, (as clarified and modified by Notice 2002–72, 2002–2 C.B. 843, and as modified by Rev. Proc. 2003–34, 2003–1 C.B. 856), or an application filed under automatic procedures such as Rev. Proc. 2002–37, 2002–1 C.B. 1030, and Rev. Proc. 2002–38, 2002–1 C.B. 1037, or their predecessors or successors. This also includes issues for which a ruling regarding an annual accounting period is necessary to resolve the issue;

(4) Issues of reasonable cause, due diligence, good faith, clear and convincing evidence, or any other similar standard under Subtitle F (Procedure and Administration) of the Internal Revenue Code;

(5) Issues involving the applicability of any penalty or criminal sanction;

(6) Issues that are, or will be, the subject of a pending or proposed request for a determination letter, technical advice memorandum, or letter ruling issued to or regarding the taxpayer;

(7) Issues for which the taxpayer proposes a resolution that is contrary to a private letter ruling, determination letter, technical advice memorandum, or closing agreement previously issued to or regarding the taxpayer;

(8) Issues for which the taxpayer proposes a resolution that is contrary to a position proposed by the Service in response to a request for a private letter ruling or determination letter that was withdrawn by the taxpayer;

(9) Issues that are the subject of pending litigation between the Service and the taxpayer for an earlier taxable year;

(10) Issues designated for litigation for an earlier taxable year of the taxpayer by the Office of Chief Counsel;

(11) Issues that involve a tax shelter described in section 6662(d)(2)(C)(ii);

(12) Issues that require the Service to determine whether the taxpayer, rather than another entity, is the common law employer; and

(13) Issues relating to transactions that have not yet occurred, regardless of whether the issue otherwise would qualify as one on which the Service will issue letter rulings or other forms of written guidance as described in Rev. Proc. 2006–1, 2006–1 I.R.B. 1, and successor revenue procedures.

.09 *Methods of accounting*.

(1) Except as provided in section 3.09(2) of this revenue procedure, the Service will not enter into a PFA for issues relating to a change in method of accounting. In applying the law to the facts, or establishing the facts, a change in the overall plan of accounting for gross income or deductions from the treatment of such items in prior taxable years, or a change in the treatment of any item that involves the proper time for the inclusion of an item or the taking of an item as a deduction from the treatment of such item in prior taxable years generally may be a change in method of accounting. A PFA may not be used to change a taxpayer's method of accounting.

(2) If the Service has issued a letter ruling granting consent to a change in method of accounting under Rev. Proc. 97–27, or its successor, a taxpayer may request and the Service may enter into a PFA with respect to the approved change in method of accounting. In such case, a PFA may include determinations described in section 11 of Rev. Proc. 97–27 or a similar provision of its successor. Thus, for example, a taxpayer may request and the Service may enter into a PFA with respect to the amount of the section 481(a) adjustment and the implementation of the change in method of accounting in accordance with the terms and conditions of the consent agreement and Rev. Proc. 97–27. A PFA under this provision may only apply to the taxable year of change and may not apply to any other taxable years, except that a determination of the amount of the section 481(a) adjustment under section 11.01(2) of Rev. Proc. 97–27, or a successor, shall apply to any other taxable year for which such amount is taken into account (*i.e.*, any spread period). A PFA under this provision may not be entered into with respect to a change in method of accounting requested pursuant to automatic consent procedures, such as Rev. Proc. 2002–9.

.10 *Definition of taxpayer*. For purposes of section 3 of this revenue procedure, any reference to the taxpayer also includes a related taxpayer and any predecessor of the taxpayer or a related taxpayer.

A related taxpayer is one related within the meaning of section 267 or a member of an affiliated group within the meaning of section 1504 that includes the taxpayer. A predecessor is an entity for whose tax liability the taxpayer or a related taxpayer is or was primarily or secondarily liable.

SECTION 4. REQUESTING A PRE-FILING AGREEMENT

.01 *Required information.* A request for a PFA must contain the following information:

(1) Names, addresses, telephone numbers, and taxpayer identification numbers of all interested parties;

(2) The name, title, address and telephone number of a person to contact. If the person to contact is an authorized representative of the taxpayer, a properly executed Form 2848, *Power of Attorney and Declaration of Representative*, must accompany the request;

(3) The annual accounting period and the overall method of accounting (for example, cash receipts and disbursements or accrual) for maintaining the accounting books and filing the federal income tax returns of all interested parties;

(4) The location of the taxpayer's tax staff and records;

(5) A brief description of the taxpayer's business operations, including the principal business activity code used by the taxpayer on its last filed return;

(6) The taxable year(s) for which the PFA is sought, the last date on which the taxpayer may file (with extensions) a timely return for that year (or for the first of those taxable years), and, if earlier, the date on which the taxpayer intends to file that return; and

(7) The dollar amount of assets reflected on the most recently filed return.

.02 *Specific descriptions of issues.* A request for a PFA should also contain a separate written statement for each proposed issue that concisely:

(1) Describes the issue;

(2) Summarizes all the facts that are relevant and material to the issue and, in the case of agreements for future taxable years, any related factual assumptions that may be appropriate (see section 7.02(2), below);

(3) States whether the issue involves an item or transaction in which two or more persons may take contrary positions (a "whipsaw" issue);

(4) Summarizes all relevant legal authorities, including citations to specific sections of the Internal Revenue Code, Income Tax Regulations, case law, tax treaties, and other authorities, and discusses why the issue is an eligible issue, as defined in section 3 of this revenue procedure;

(5) Summarizes and discusses the implications of any known authorities that may be potentially contrary to the position advanced, such as legislation (or pending legislation), court decisions, regulations, revenue rulings, revenue procedures, notices (including notices of proposed rulemaking), or announcements;

(6) Discusses whether and how the PFA will affect taxable years before or after the taxable year for which the PFA is sought;

(7) Describes any proposed methodology to be used;

(8) Discusses whether the issue qualifies for mutual agreement procedure consideration under any United States income tax treaty, specifies the treaty, and states whether the taxpayer previously applied or will apply for competent authority assistance with respect to the issue for the year or years in question or any prior year;

(9) States whether the taxpayer has, for the current taxable year or any prior taxable year, requested a private letter ruling (including a request for consent to a change in method of accounting or a request to adopt, change, or retain an annual accounting period), determination letter, or technical advice on the issue;

(10) Discusses whether the issue can reasonably be resolved by the earliest date on which the taxpayer intends to file any relevant return; and

(11) Describes the availability, organization, and location of the records and other information that substantiate the taxpayer's proposed position on the issue.

.03 *Perjury statement.* A request for a PFA, and any supplemental submissions (including additional documents), must include a declaration, signed by a person currently authorized to sign the taxpayer's federal income tax return, in the following form:

> Under penalties of perjury, I declare that I have examined this request, including accompanying documents, and to the best of my knowledge and belief, the facts presented in support of the request for the Pre-Filing Agreement are true, correct, and complete.

.04 *Agreement regarding examination or inspection of records.* The request for a PFA also must contain a statement by the taxpayer in the following form:

> The taxpayer agrees that the review of records and information under the PFA procedures does not constitute an inspection within the meaning of section 7605(b) and will not preclude or impede (under section 7605(b) or any administrative provisions adopted by the Service) the Service from later examining any return or inspecting any records. The taxpayer further agrees that procedural restrictions, such as providing notice under section 7605(b), do not apply to actions taken under the PFA procedures.

.05 *Signature.* The request for a PFA must be signed by the taxpayer or a representative properly authorized by the taxpayer in an accompanying Form 2848, *Power of Attorney and Declaration of Representative*.

.06 *Where to submit request.* (1) In the case of a taxpayer whose return for any taxable year is currently under examination by LMSB, a request for a PFA should be submitted to the LMSB Team Manager in charge of the examination; or

(2) In the case of a taxpayer who has no returns under examination for any taxable year, a request for a PFA should be sent by any of the following methods:

(a) mail to the following address:

Internal Revenue Service
Attn: LMSB:PFT:PFS
PFA Program Manager
Mint Building
1111 Constitution Avenue, NW
Washington, DC 20224;

(b) facsimile transmission to the attention of the PFA Program Manager at (202) 283–8406 (not a toll-free call); or

(c) electronic transmission to *pfa.info@irs.gov*.

SECTION 5. SELECTING TAXPAYERS FOR THE PFA PROGRAM

.01 *Jurisdiction of LMSB Industry Director and coordination and consultation with the Associate Chief Counsel.* The LMSB Industry Director having jurisdiction over the taxpayer, after coordination and consultation with the Associate Chief Counsel having subject matter jurisdiction over any issue proposed to be determined by a PFA, will decide whether to accept the taxpayer's request for a PFA. (For purposes of this revenue procedure, the term "LMSB Industry Director" includes a duly authorized designee of an LMSB Industry Director.) The decision regarding the acceptance of any PFA involving an international issue also will require the concurrence of the Deputy Commissioner, International (LMSB). In general, the Associate Chief Counsel will respond within 10 business days to a request for coordination and consultation to proceed with the PFA.

.02 *Criteria for selection.* The criteria for selecting taxpayers to participate in the PFA program include, but are not limited to:

(1) Whether the specific issue presented by the taxpayer's facts is an eligible issue under section 3 of this revenue procedure and is otherwise suitable for the PFA program;

(2) The direct or indirect impact of a PFA upon other years, issues, taxpayers, or related cases;

(3) Whether Service resources are available;

(4) Whether the taxpayer is willing and able to dedicate sufficient resources to the PFA process;

(5) Whether the PFA is likely to result in two or more persons taking contrary positions on an item or transaction (a "whipsaw" issue);

(6) The time remaining until the due date and expected filing date, if earlier than the due date, of the earliest return to which the PFA relates; and

(7) The overall probability of completing the process and entering into a PFA by the proposed date for filing the earliest return to which the PFA relates.

Early submission of a request will facilitate completion of a PFA before any associated returns become due. As a result, early requests are more likely to be selected for the PFA program and the Service urges taxpayers to submit PFA requests as early as possible.

.03 *Notification.* A representative of LMSB will contact the taxpayer within 15 business days of actual receipt of the taxpayer's request for a PFA to acknowledge that the Service has received the request. After a PFA request is received, a representative of LMSB will inform the taxpayer in writing whether the request has been selected for the PFA program and the issues the Service will consider.

.04 *Requests not accepted.* A taxpayer may not appeal the Service's decision not to accept a request for a PFA. A taxpayer not selected for the PFA program remains eligible for other early issue resolution procedures, including the Accelerated Issue Resolution (AIR) program (see Rev. Proc. 94–67, 1994–2 C.B. 800).

SECTION 6. PROCESSING A REQUEST FOR A PFA

.01 *Planning.* If the Service accepts the taxpayer's request for a PFA, a representative of LMSB will contact the taxpayer and schedule an orientation meeting with the taxpayer and examination personnel to discuss the PFA process and explain the roles and responsibilities of each participant. Immediately after the orientation meeting, the taxpayer and the Service should meet to formulate a plan and timeline that will result in a thorough development of the facts and a successful resolution of the issues before any associated returns are due. During the planning phase and throughout the PFA process, the taxpayer must provide information requested by the Service and assist the Service in the timely and efficient resolution of the examined issues. If, at any time after a request for a PFA has been accepted, the facts that are relevant and material to the request for a PFA significantly change or, in the case of proposed agreements for future taxable years, any factual assumptions that may be appropriate significantly change, the taxpayer must promptly inform the Service through the examination team assigned to the PFA.

.02 *Continuing coordination.* After a request for a PFA has been accepted, the LMSB Industry Director having jurisdiction over the PFA request will, through the examination team and local counsel assigned to the PFA, coordinate and consult with the Associate Chief Counsel having subject matter jurisdiction over the issue proposed to be determined by the PFA to ensure that that issue remains suitable for a PFA. The LMSB Industry Director will, through the examination team and local counsel assigned to the PFA, inform the Associate Chief Counsel if, at any time after a request for a PFA has been accepted, the facts that are relevant and material to the issue significantly change or, in the case of agreements for future taxable years, any factual assumptions that may be appropriate significantly change.

.03 *Drafting.* After the development of the facts and issues, the Team Manager will meet informally with the taxpayer to determine whether the parties agree on a PFA. If the parties reach agreement, the taxpayer will work with the Service to prepare the initial draft of the PFA. The PFA will be prepared by the taxpayer and the audit team with assistance, as necessary, from the PFA Program Manager, the Office of Chief Counsel, or other Service personnel. Except as provided in section 3.06, the Associate Chief Counsel having subject matter jurisdiction over the issue in the PFA need not execute or give final approval to the proposed PFA; however, upon execution of the PFA, the PFA Program Manager will immediately forward a copy of the PFA to the office of that Associate Chief Counsel.

.04 *Return filing requirements.* The Service's acceptance of a taxpayer's request for a PFA does not suspend or waive the normal filing requirements for any tax returns that may be affected by the proposed PFA.

.05 *TEFRA taxpayers.* If the procedures set forth in sections 6221 through 6233 apply to the taxpayer requesting the PFA and the issue determined by the PFA is a partnership item as defined in section 6231, the PFA process will be terminated for that issue if no agreement is reached with all partners by the date that is 30 business days before the due date for the partnership return (taking into account any extensions of time to file that may be in effect).

.06 *Execution prior to filing.* If a PFA is executed before a return is filed, the taxpayer must report the issues determined by the PFA according to the terms and conditions of the PFA. A copy of the PFA must be attached to the return.

.07 *Execution after filing.* If the Service and the taxpayer do not reach agreement on an issue before the taxpayer files an associated return, the Service and the taxpayer may still attempt to resolve the issue and enter into a PFA. If the filed return is inconsistent with the terms and conditions of the contemplated PFA, the taxpayer must agree to file an amended return consistent with those terms and conditions. A post-filing PFA should state whether the taxpayer is required to file an amended return. It should further state that the Service may assess additional tax due, if any, if an amended return is not filed. The taxpayer must attach a copy of the PFA to any amended return.

SECTION 7. NATURE AND EFFECT OF A PFA

.01 *Criteria for issuance.* An authorized Service official may execute a PFA if that official determines that:

(1) Entering into the PFA is consistent with the goals of the PFA program;

(2) The resolution of issues in the PFA reflects well-settled legal principles and correctly applies those principles to the facts established by the examination team;

(3) The issues determined by the PFA are eligible issues under section 3 of this revenue procedure;

(4) Any methodology approved for use by a taxpayer to determine the appropriate amount of an item of income, allowance, deduction, or credit has a documented factual basis; and

(5) There is an advantage in having the issues permanently and conclusively resolved for the taxable years covered by the PFA, or the taxpayer shows good and sufficient reasons for desiring a PFA and the United States will suffer no disadvantage if the agreement is executed.

.02 *Form and content.*

(1) A PFA that makes determinations for the current taxable year (and any prior taxable year for which a return is not yet due) is a closing agreement under section 7121. The form and content of this type of PFA must comply with Rev. Proc. 68–16, 1968–1 C.B. 770.

(2) A PFA that makes a determination for one or more future taxable years as well as for the current taxable year (and any prior taxable year for which a return is not yet due) is a non-statutory agreement. Although not a closing agreement under section 7121, this type of PFA is a binding contract between the Service and a taxpayer. It is subject to any legislative enactment that is applicable to the taxable years to which the PFA relates. There is no prescribed format for such an agreement. The parties to a non-statutory agreement may, by mutual consent (and, if applicable, the further mutual agreement between the United States and any treaty partner that has entered into a mutual agreement that is a basis for the PFA), modify or terminate the agreement. A taxpayer who wants to modify or terminate a non-statutory agreement should submit a request to the office that originally processed the taxpayer's request for a PFA. The parties to a non-statutory agreement also may condition its determinations on the continuing validity of certain stated assumptions. A "stated assumption" is any fact (whether or not within the control of the taxpayer) related to the taxpayer, a third party, an industry, or business and economic conditions whose continued existence is material to the determinations of the PFA. A stated assumption might include, for example, a particular mode of conducting business operations. If a stated assumption is no longer valid, a non-statutory agreement conditioned on such stated assumption will terminate as of the first day of the taxable year in which the stated assumption is no longer valid.

(3) A PFA concerning international issues will not be subject to the special limitation of section 7.05, *Effect of Agreements or Judicial Determinations on Competent Authority Proceedings*, of Rev. Proc. 2002–52, 2002–2 C.B. 242, which sets forth the effect of a closing agreement on the procedure for competent authority consideration under the mutual agreement procedure of United States income tax conventions.

.03 *Methods and periods of accounting.*

(1) A PFA does not constitute the consent of the Commissioner under section 446(e) to any change in method of accounting or the approval under section 442 of any adoption, change, or retention of an annual accounting period by the taxpayer.

(2) A PFA does not constitute a final determination regarding the adoption, change, or retention of an annual accounting period by the taxpayer,

(3) A PFA does not constitute a final determination regarding the methods of accounting of the taxpayer for any taxable year, except to the extent authorized by section 3.09(2).

(4) A PFA authorized under section 3.09(2) must include the following agreement:

> Nothing in this agreement precludes the taxpayer from requesting, or the Service from requiring, a change in the taxpayer's method of accounting for years after the year of change.

SECTION 8. WITHDRAWAL

.01 At any time prior to the execution of the PFA, either the taxpayer or the Service may withdraw from consideration all or part of the request for a PFA. The withdrawal must be in writing and signed by the party initiating the withdrawal, *i.e.*, the taxpayer or his authorized representative or the Industry Director, Director Field Operations, or the Director Field Specialists.

.02 Notwithstanding the withdrawal by either the taxpayer or the Service of any or all the issues that are the subject of the request for a PFA, the taxpayer's agreement under section 4.04 of this revenue procedure will remain in effect.

SECTION 9. NO PFA EXECUTED

.01 *Post-filing procedures.* If the Service and the taxpayer do not agree upon and execute a PFA that resolves an issue, either before or after the filing of the return to which the PFA relates, and the Service subsequently disagrees with the taxpayer's treatment of the issue on the return, the taxpayer and the Service may continue their efforts to reach an agreement using post-filing procedures, such as the Accelerated Issue Resolution (AIR) procedures under Rev. Proc. 94–67, 1994–2 C.B. 800. This continuation of the process does not require a new application.

.02 *Administrative appeals.* If the Service and the taxpayer are unable to resolve an issue by a PFA or an AIR agreement, the taxpayer may pursue an administrative appeal either by requesting an early referral to Appeals under the procedures set forth in Rev. Proc. 99–28, 1999–2 C.B. 109, or by protesting any proposed deficiency related to the issue.

SECTION 10. USER FEE

.01 *Taxpayers subject to fees.* Taxpayers are subject to a user fee only if they are selected to participate in the PFA program.

.02 *Amount of fee.* The user fee for taxpayers selected to participate in the PFA program is $50,000. A fee will be assessed for each separate and distinct issue. The orientation meeting or the first substantive meeting with the taxpayer to discuss the PFA issues will not take place until after the fee is received.

.03 *Time and method of payment.* Payment of the user fee must be made within 15 business days of notification that the issues have been selected for the PFA program. Payment must be made by check or money order payable to the Internal Revenue Service and submitted to the address indicated in section 4.06 of this revenue procedure.

.04 *Withdrawal.* Notwithstanding the withdrawal by either the taxpayer or the Service of any or all of the issues in the request for a PFA after acceptance of the request, the user fee paid by the taxpayer generally will not be refundable. A refund or waiver of the user fee will not be entertained unless a hardship has occurred (for example, a disaster loss) or if other circumstances beyond the control of the taxpayer exist. The Industry Director has discretion in granting a request for a refund of a user fee based on considerations of sound tax administration.

SECTION 11. DISCLOSURE

PFAs are agreements described in section 6103(b)(2)(D). A PFA and the information generated or received by the Service during the PFA process constitute confidential return information. As required by the Conference Report to H.R. 4577, The Community Renewal Tax Relief Act of 2000 (Pub. L. 106–554), H.R. Conf. Rep. No. 1033, 106th Cong., 2d Sess. 1033 (2000), the Service will, consistent with the restrictions of section 6103, continue to publish annual reports summarizing the operation of the PFA program. PFAs are not written determinations under section 6110 and, accordingly, are exempt from disclosure to the public under the Freedom of Information Act.

SECTION 12. EFFECTIVE DATE AND DURATION OF PROCEDURE

This revenue procedure is effective on December 26, 2006. This revenue procedure will remain in effect until December 31, 2008, unless sooner revoked, modified, or superseded. A request for a PFA that has been accepted into the program under section 5 of this revenue procedure will remain subject to the provisions of this revenue procedure, notwithstanding the preceding sentence.

SECTION 13. EFFECT ON OTHER DOCUMENTS

Rev. Proc. 2005–12, 2005–1 C.B. 311, is superseded.

SECTION 14. RECORD-KEEPING REQUIREMENTS

.01 No aspect of the PFA process will affect the record-keeping requirements imposed by any section of the Internal Revenue Code.

.02 The taxpayer must maintain a copy of the PFA supporting documents and books of account and records to enable the Service to ensure the taxpayer's compliance with the PFA. These records may be specified in the PFA itself or in separate agreements.

SECTION 15. PAPERWORK REDUCTION ACT

The collection of information contained in this revenue procedure has been reviewed and approved by the Office of Management and Budget in accordance with the Paperwork Reduction Act of 1995 (44 U.S.C. 3507) under the control number 1545–1684.

An agency may not conduct or sponsor, and a person is not required to respond to, a collection of information unless it displays a valid OMB control number. The collections of information in this revenue procedure are in sections 4, 6, and 14. The information collected under section 4 is required to provide the Service with the information necessary to determine which taxpayers should be included in the PFA program. The information collected under section 6 will be used to resolve the taxpayer's issue and to support any PFA entered into between the taxpayer and the Service. The record-keeping requirements under section 14 will be used for tax administration. The collections of information under sections 4 and 6 are voluntary. Once a PFA is entered into, the record-keeping requirements under section 14 are mandatory. The likely respondents are businesses or other for-profit institutions.

The estimated total annual reporting and/or record-keeping burden is 13,134 hours.

The estimated annual burden per respondent varies from 5 hours to 1,092 hours, depending on whether a taxpayer applying to the PFA program is accepted into the program. The estimated annual burden per respondent for taxpayers who apply to the PFA program and are accepted is 1,092 hours. The estimated annual burden per respondent for taxpayers who apply to the PFA program and are not accepted is 5 hours. The estimated number of taxpayers who apply to the PFA program and are accepted is 12. The estimated number of taxpayers who apply to the PFA program and are not accepted is 6. The estimated total number of applicants and/or recordkeepers is 18.

The estimated annual frequency of responses is on occasion.

Books or records relating to a collection of information must be retained so long as their contents may become material in the administration of any internal revenue law. Generally, tax returns and tax return information are confidential, as required by 26 U.S.C. 6103.

SECTION 16. DRAFTING INFORMATION

The principal author of this revenue procedure is Stuart Spielman of the Office of Associate Chief Counsel (Procedure & Administration). For further information about this revenue procedure, contact Melanie Perrin, Senior Program Analyst, LMSB Office of Pre-Filing and Technical Guidance, at (202) 283–8408 (voice) (not a toll-free call), (202) 283–8406 (fax) (not a toll-free call).

Part IV. Items of General Interest

Deletions From Cumulative List of Organizations Contributions to Which are Deductible Under Section 170 of the Code

Announcement 2007–3

The names of organizations that no longer qualify as organizations described in section 170(c)(2) of the Internal Revenue Code of 1986 are listed below.

Generally, the Service will not disallow deductions for contributions made to a listed organization on or before the date of announcement in the Internal Revenue Bulletin that an organization no longer qualifies. However, the Service is not precluded from disallowing a deduction for any contributions made after an organization ceases to qualify under section 170(c)(2) if the organization has not timely filed a suit for declaratory judgment under section 7428 and if the contributor (1) had knowledge of the revocation of the ruling or determination letter, (2) was aware that such revocation was imminent, or (3) was in part responsible for or was aware of the activities or omissions of the organization that brought about this revocation.

If on the other hand a suit for declaratory judgment has been timely filed, contributions from individuals and organizations described in section 170(c)(2) that are otherwise allowable will continue to be deductible. Protection under section 7428(c) would begin on January 22, 2007, and would end on the date the court first determines that the organization is not described in section 170(c)(2) as more particularly set forth in section 7428(c)(1). For individual contributors, the maximum deduction protected is $1,000, with a husband and wife treated as one contributor. This benefit is not extended to any individual, in whole or in part, for the acts or omissions of the organization that were the basis for revocation.

Corporate Responsibility Capital
Partners, Inc.
Washington, DC

HR–57 Center for the Advancement
and Preservation of Jazz and Blues
Washington, DC

National Association of
Credit Counseling, Inc.
Ft. Myers, FL

Personal Credit Assistance, Inc.
Sacramento, CA

TIPRA Amendments to Section 199

Announcement 2007–5

AGENCY: Internal Revenue Service (IRS), Treasury.

ACTION: Change of location of public hearing.

SUMMARY: On October 19, 2006, on page 61692 of the **Federal Register** (71 FR 61692), a notice of proposed rulemaking by cross-reference to temporary regulations and notice of public hearing (REG–127819–06, 2006–48 I.R.B. 1013) announced that a public hearing concerning the application of section 199, which provides a deduction for income attributable to domestic production activities will be held February 5, 2007 in the auditorium of the New Carrollton Federal Building, 5000 Ellin Road, Lanham, MD 20706. The location of the public hearing has changed.

ADDRESSES: The public hearing will be held in the IRS Auditorium, Internal Revenue Building, 1111 Constitution Avenue, NW, Washington, DC.

FOR FURTHER INFORMATION CONTACT: Concerning submissions of comments, the hearing, and/or to be placed on the building access list to attend the hearing, Kelly Banks, (202) 622–0392 (not a toll-free number).

LaNita Van Dyke,
Branch Chief,
Publications and Regulations,
Legal Processing Division,
Associate Chief Counsel
(Procedure and Administration).

(Filed by the Office of the Federal Register on December 22, 2006, 8:45 a.m., and published in the issue of the Federal Register for December 26, 2006, 71 F.R. 77353)

Treatment of Payments in Lieu of Taxes Under Section 141

Announcement 2007–6

AGENCY: Internal Revenue Service (IRS), Treasury.

ACTION: Change of location of public hearing.

SUMMARY: On October 19, 2006, on page 61693 of the **Federal Register** (71 FR 61693), a notice of proposed rulemaking and notice of public hearing (REG–136806–06, 2006–47 I.R.B. 950) announced that a public hearing concerning applying the private security or payment test for State and local governmental issuers of tax-exempt bonds will be held February 13, 2007 in the auditorium of the New Carrollton Federal Building, 5000 Ellin Road, Lanham, MD 20706. The location of the public hearing has changed.

ADDRESSES: The public hearing will be held in the IRS Auditorium, Internal Revenue Building, 1111 Constitution Avenue, NW, Washington, DC.

FOR FURTHER INFORMATION CONTACT: Concerning submissions of comments, the hearing, and/or to be placed on the building access list to attend the hearing, Kelly Banks, (202) 622–0392 (not a toll-free number).

LaNita Van Dyke,
Branch Chief,
Publications and Regulations,
Legal Processing Division,
Associate Chief Counsel
(Procedure and Administration).

(Filed by the Office of the Federal Register on December 22, 2006, 8:45 a.m., and published in the issue of the Federal Register for December 26, 2006, 71 F.R. 77352)

Exchanges of Property for an Annuity

Announcement 2007–7

AGENCY: Internal Revenue Service (IRS), Treasury.

ACTION: Change of location of public hearing.

SUMMARY: On October 18, 2006, on page 61693 of the **Federal Register** (71 FR 61441), a notice of proposed rulemaking and notice of public hearing (REG–141901–05, 2006–47 I.R.B. 947) announced that a public hearing concerning guidance on the taxation of the exchange of property for an annuity contract will be held February 16, 2007 in the auditorium of the New Carrollton Federal Building, 5000 Ellin Road, Lanham, MD 20706. The location of the public hearing has changed.

ADDRESSES: The public hearing will be held in the IRS Auditorium, Internal Revenue Building, 1111 Constitution Avenue, NW, Washington, DC.

FOR FURTHER INFORMATION CONTACT: Concerning submissions of comments, the hearing, and/or to be placed on the building access list to attend the hearing, Kelly Banks, (202) 622–0392 (not a toll-free number).

LaNita Van Dyke,
Branch Chief,
Publications and Regulations,
Legal Processing Division,
Associate Chief Counsel
(Procedure and Administration).

(Filed by the Office of the Federal Register on December 26, 2006, 8:45 a.m., and published in the issue of the Federal Register for December 27, 2006, 71 F.R. 77653)

Part I. Rulings and Decisions Under the Internal Revenue Code of 1986

Section 42.—Low-Income Housing Credit

Low-income housing credit; satisfactory bond; "bond factor" amounts for the period January through March 2007. This ruling provides the monthly bond factor amounts to be used by taxpayers who dispose of qualified low-income buildings or interests therein during the period January through March 2007.

Rev. Rul. 2007–5

In Rev. Rul. 90–60, 1990–2 C.B. 3, the Internal Revenue Service provided guidance to taxpayers concerning the general methodology used by the Treasury Department in computing the bond factor amounts used in calculating the amount of bond considered satisfactory by the Secretary under § 42(j)(6) of the Internal Revenue Code. It further announced that the Secretary would publish in the Internal Revenue Bulletin a table of bond factor amounts for dispositions occurring during each calendar month.

Rev. Proc. 99–11, 1999–1 C.B. 275, established a collateral program as an alternative to providing a surety bond for taxpayers to avoid or defer recapture of the low-income housing tax credits under § 42(j)(6). Under this program, taxpayers may establish a Treasury Direct Account and pledge certain United States Treasury securities to the Internal Revenue Service as security.

This revenue ruling provides in Table 1 the bond factor amounts for calculating the amount of bond considered satisfactory under § 42(j)(6) or the amount of United States Treasury securities to pledge in a Treasury Direct Account under Rev. Proc. 99–11 for dispositions of qualified low-income buildings or interests therein during the period January through March 2007.

Table 1
Rev. Rul. 2007–5
Monthly Bond Factor Amounts for Dispositions Expressed
As a Percentage of Total Credits

	Calendar Year Building Placed in Service or, if Section 42(f)(1) Election Was Made, the Succeeding Calendar Year										
Month of Disposition	1993	1994	1995	1996	1997	1998	1999	2000	2001	2002	2003
Jan '07	17.39	32.44	45.52	56.97	66.95	69.23	71.86	74.74	78.09	81.82	85.82
Feb '07	17.39	32.44	45.52	56.97	66.95	69.08	71.70	74.56	77.89	81.60	85.57
Mar '07	17.39	32.44	45.52	56.97	66.95	68.92	71.53	74.39	77.71	81.40	85.33

Table 1 (cont'd)
Rev. Rul. 2007–5
Monthly Bond Factor Amounts for Dispositions Expressed
As a Percentage of Total Credits

	Calendar Year Building Placed in Service or, if Section 42(f)(1) Election Was Made, the Succeeding Calendar Year										
Month of Disposition	2004	2005	2006	2007							
Jan '07	89.79	93.41	96.70	97.21							
Feb '07	89.50	93.07	96.27	97.21							
Mar '07	89.22	92.75	95.89	97.21							

For a list of bond factor amounts applicable to dispositions occurring during other calendar years, see: Rev. Rul. 98–3, 1998–1 C.B. 248; Rev. Rul. 2001–2, 2001–1 C.B. 255; Rev. Rul. 2001–53, 2001–2 C.B. 488; Rev. Rul. 2002–72, 2002–2 C.B. 759; Rev. Rul. 2003–117, 2003–2 C.B. 1051; Rev. Rul. 2004–100, 2004–2 C.B. 718; Rev. Rul. 2005–67, 2005–2 C.B. 771; and Rev. Rul. 2006–51, 2006–41 I.R.B. 632.

DRAFTING INFORMATION

The principal author of this revenue ruling is David McDonnell of the Office of Associate Chief Counsel (Passthroughs and Special Industries). For further information regarding this revenue ruling, contact Mr. McDonnell at (202) 622–3040 (not a toll-free call).

Section 368.—Definitions Relating to Corporate Reorganizations

26 CFR 1.368–2: Definition of terms.

T.D. 9303

DEPARTMENT OF THE TREASURY
Internal Revenue Service
26 CFR Part 1

Corporate Reorganizations; Distributions Under Sections 368(a)(1)(D) and 354(b)(1)(B)

AGENCY: Internal Revenue Service (IRS), Treasury.

ACTION: Final and temporary regulations.

SUMMARY: This document contains temporary regulations under section 368 of the Internal Revenue Code of 1986 (Code). The temporary regulations provide guidance regarding the qualification of certain transactions as reorganizations described in section 368(a)(1)(D) where no stock and/or securities of the acquiring corporation is issued and distributed in the transaction. These regulations affect corporations engaging in such transactions and their shareholders. The text of the temporary regulations also serves as the text of the proposed regulations (REG–125632–06) set forth in the notice of proposed rulemaking on this subject in this issue of the Bulletin.

DATES: *Effective Date:* These regulations are effective on December 19, 2006.

Applicability Date: For dates of applicability, see §1.368–2T(l)(4)(i).

FOR FURTHER INFORMATION CONTACT: Bruce A. Decker at (202) 622–7550 (not a toll-free number).

SUPPLEMENTARY INFORMATION:

Background

The IRS and Treasury Department have received requests for immediate guidance regarding whether certain acquisitive transactions can qualify as reorganizations described in section 368(a)(1)(D) where no stock of the transferee corporation is issued and distributed in the transaction. Currently, the IRS and Treasury Department are undertaking a broad study of issues related to acquisitive section 368(a)(1)(D) reorganizations. In the interest of efficient tax administration, the IRS and Treasury Department are issuing these temporary regulations to provide the requested certainty for taxpayers regarding these acquisitive transactions pending the broader study of issues. Although these rules also are being proposed in this issue of the Bulletin, the IRS and Treasury Department contemplate that the proposed rules may change upon completion of this broader study and the comments received.

The Code provides general nonrecognition treatment for reorganizations specifically described in section 368(a). Section 368(a)(1)(D) describes as a reorganization a transfer by a corporation (transferor corporation) of all or a part of its assets to another corporation (transferee corporation) if, immediately after the transfer, the transferor corporation or one or more of its shareholders (including persons who were shareholders immediately before the transfer), or any combination thereof, is in control of the transferee corporation; but only if stock or securities of the controlled corporation are distributed in pursuance of a plan of reorganization in a transaction that qualifies under section 354, 355, or 356.

Section 354(a)(1) provides that no gain or loss shall be recognized if stock or securities in a corporation a party to a reorganization are, in pursuance of the plan of reorganization, exchanged solely for stock or securities in such corporation or in another corporation a party to the reorganization. Section 354(b)(1)(B) provides that section 354(a)(1) shall not apply to an exchange in pursuance of a plan of reorganization described in section 368(a)(1)(D) unless the transferee corporation acquires substantially all of the assets of the transferor corporation, and the stock, securities, and other properties received by such transferor corporation, as well as the other properties of such transferor corporation, are distributed in pursuance of the plan of reorganization.

Further, section 356 provides that if section 354 or 355 would apply to an exchange but for the fact that the property received in the exchange consists not only of property permitted by section 354 or 355 without the recognition of gain or loss but also of other property or money, then the gain, if any, to the recipient shall be recognized, but not in excess of the amount of money and fair market value of such other property. Accordingly, in the case of an acquisitive transaction, there can only be a distribution to which section 354 or 356 applies where the target shareholder(s) receive at least some property permitted to be received by section 354.

Notwithstanding the requirement in section 368(a)(1)(D) that "stock or securities of the corporation to which the assets are transferred are distributed in a transaction which qualifies under section 354, 355, or 356", the IRS and the courts have not required the actual issuance and distribution of stock and/or securities of the transferee corporation in circumstances where the same person or persons own all the stock of the transferor corporation and the transferee corporation. In such circumstances, the IRS and the courts have viewed an issuance of stock to be a "meaningless gesture" not mandated by sections 368(a)(1)(D) and 354(b).

In Revenue Ruling 70–240, 1970–1 C.B. 81 (see §601.601(d)(2) of this chapter), B owned all of the stock of both corporation X and corporation Y. X sold its operating assets to Y for $34x dollars, which represented the fair market value of X's assets. X had $33x of other assets, consisting generally of cash, accounts receivables, and investments in stocks and bonds, so that the assets sold by X to Y constituted approximately 51% of X's total assets. Following the sale to Y, X paid its debts, which amounted to $38x, and then liquidated, distributing $29x to B, while Y continued to conduct the business formerly operated by X. The IRS concluded that "although no actual shares of the stock of Y were distributed to B as a result of the transaction, B is treated as having received Y stock since he already owned all the stock of Y." Accordingly, the IRS held that the sale of the operating assets by X to Y, followed by the liquidation and distribution of X's assets to B, resulted in a reorganization under section 368(a)(1)(D) and a distribution under section 356(a), despite the absence of an actual issuance and distribution of Y stock.

When considering a similar transaction between two corporations owned in identical proportions by a husband and wife, the Tax Court concluded that there was in substance an exchange of stock which meets the requirements of section 354 and 356, and stated, "[t]he issuance of further stock would have been a meaningless gesture, and we cannot conclude that the statute requires such a vain act." *James Armour, Inc. v. Commissioner*, 43 T.C. 295, 307 (1964). See also *Wilson v. Commissioner*, 46 T.C. 334 (1966). The IRS has also applied this meaningless gesture doctrine to circumstances where the transferor corporation and the transferee corporation are wholly owned by a single party directly or indirectly through subsidiaries, or as a result of family attribution pursuant to section 318(a)(1).

However, the application of this meaningless gesture doctrine has generally been limited to situations in which there is identical shareholder identity and proportionality of interest in the transferor corporation and the transferee corporation. For example, in *Warsaw Photographic Associates, Inc. v. Commissioner*, 84 T.C. 21 (1985), there was no issuance of stock by the transferee corporation to the transferor corporation, and the stock ownership in the two corporations was not identical. On the basis of these facts, the Tax Court concluded that the distribution of stock would not be a mere formality and refused to apply the meaningless gesture doctrine. Accordingly, the transaction failed to qualify as a section 368(a)(1)(D) reorganization because there was no distribution of stock of the transferee corporation under sections 368(a)(1)(D) and 354(b)(1)(B).

Explanation of Provisions

These temporary regulations provide guidance regarding the circumstances in which the distribution requirement under sections 368(a)(1)(D) and 354(b)(1)(B) is deemed satisfied despite the fact that no stock and/or securities are actually issued in a transaction otherwise described in section 368(a)(1)(D). In cases where the same person or persons own, directly or indirectly, all of the stock of the transferor and transferee corporations in identical proportions, these temporary regulations provide that the distribution requirement under sections 368(a)(1)(D) and 354(b)(1)(B) will be treated as satisfied even though no stock is actually issued in the transaction. For purposes of determining whether the same person or persons own all of the stock of the transferor and transferee corporations in identical proportions, these temporary regulations provide that an individual and all members of his family that have a relationship described in section 318(a)(1) will be treated as one individual.

The temporary regulations also provide that the distribution requirement under sections 368(a)(1)(D) and 354(b)(1)(B) will be treated as satisfied in the absence of any issuance of stock and/or securities where there is a *de minimis* variation in shareholder identity or proportionality of ownership in the transferor and transferee corporations. Further, stock described in section 1504(a)(4) is disregarded for purposes of determining whether the same person or persons own all of the stock of the transferor and transferee corporations in identical proportions.

Under these temporary regulations, in each case where it is determined that the same person or persons own all of the stock of the transferor and transferee corporations in identical proportions, a nominal share of stock of the transferee corporation will be deemed issued in addition to the actual consideration exchanged in the transaction. The nominal share of stock in the transferee corporation will then be deemed distributed by the transferor corporation to its shareholders and, in appropriate circumstances, further transferred to the extent necessary to reflect the actual ownership of the transferor and transferee corporations.

These temporary regulations are being issued in response to requests for immediate guidance regarding whether transactions otherwise described in section 368(a)(1)(D) qualify as reorganizations where no stock and/or securities of the transferee corporation are actually issued in the transaction. The IRS and Treasury Department currently are undertaking a broad study of issues related to acquisitive reorganizations, including issues addressed by these temporary regulations. The IRS and Treasury Department are issuing these temporary regulations in order to provide certainty for taxpayers while these issues are under study.

The IRS and Treasury Department believe that these temporary regulations are a reasonable interpretation of section 368(a)(1)(D) and section 354(b)(1)(B) given the history of those provisions and the manner in which they have previously been interpreted by the courts and the IRS. However, no inference should be drawn from these temporary regulations regarding the law prior to the effective date of these temporary regulations. In this issue of the Bulletin, the IRS and Treasury Department are requesting comments on several issues relating to acquisitive reorganizations described in section 368(a)(1)(D).

In addition, the IRS and Treasury Department note that these temporary regulations do not expressly implement Prop. Reg. §1.368–1(f)(4) (FR 70, 11903–11912), which provides that there must be an exchange of net value except in the case of a transaction that would otherwise qualify as a reorganization described in section 368(a)(1)(D), provided that the fair market value of the property transferred to the acquiring corporation by the target corporation exceeds the amount of liabilities of the target corporation immediately before the exchange (including any liabilities cancelled, extinguished, or assumed in connection with the exchange), and the fair market value of the assets of the acquiring corporation equals or exceeds the amount of its liabilities immediately after the exchange. The solvency requirement remains the IRS's and Treasury Department's proposal but the IRS and Treasury Department continue to consider whether this solvency requirement should be applied to the transactions described in these temporary regulations.

Special Analyses

It has been determined that this Treasury decision is not a significant regulatory action as defined in Executive Order 12866. Therefore, a regulatory assessment is not required. It also has been determined that section 553(b) of the Administrative Procedure Act (5 U.S.C. chapter 5) does not apply to these regulations. For the applicability of the Regulatory Flexibility Act, please refer to the cross-reference notice of proposed rulemaking published elsewhere in this Bulletin. Pursuant to section 7805(f) of the Internal Revenue Code, these regulations were submitted to the Chief Counsel for Advocacy of the Small Business Administration for comment on their impact on small business.

Drafting Information

The principal author of these regulations is Bruce A. Decker of the Office of the Associate Chief Counsel (Corporate).

* * * * *

Amendments to the Regulations

Accordingly, 26 CFR part 1 is amended as follows:

PART 1—INCOME TAXES

Paragraph 1. The authority citation for part 1 continues to read as follows:

Authority: 26 U.S.C. 7805 * * *

Par. 2. Section 1.368–2 is amended by revising paragraph (l) to read as follows:

§1.368–2 Definition of terms.

* * * * *

(l) [Reserved]. For further guidance, see §1.368–2T(l).

Par. 3. Section 1.368–2T is added to read as follows:

§1.368–2T Definition of terms (temporary).

(a) through (k) [Reserved]. For further guidance, see §1.368–2(a) through (k).

(l) *Certain transactions treated as reorganizations described in section 368(a)(1)(D)*—(1) *General rule.* In order to qualify as a reorganization under section 368(a)(1)(D), a corporation (transferor corporation) must transfer all or part of its assets to another corporation (transferee corporation) and immediately after the transfer the transferor corporation, or one or more of its shareholders (including persons who were shareholders immediately before the transfer), or any combination thereof, must be in control of the transferee corporation; but only if, in pursuance of the plan, stock or securities of the transferee are distributed in a transaction which qualifies under section 354, 355, or 356.

(2) *Distribution requirement*—(i) *In general.* For purposes of paragraph (l)(1) of this section, a transaction otherwise described in section 368(a)(1)(D) will be treated as satisfying the requirements of sections 368(a)(1)(D) and 354(b)(1)(B) notwithstanding that there is no actual issuance of stock and/or securities of the transferee corporation if the same person or persons own, directly or indirectly, all of the stock of the transferor and transferee corporations in identical proportions. In such cases, the transferee corporation will be deemed to issue a nominal share of stock to the transferor corporation in addition to the actual consideration exchanged for the transferor corporation's assets. The nominal share of stock in the transferee corporation will then be deemed distributed by the transferor corporation to its shareholders and, where appropriate, further transferred through chains of ownership to the extent necessary to reflect the actual ownership of the transferor and transferee corporations.

(ii) *Attribution.* For purposes of paragraph (l)(2)(i) of this section, ownership of stock will be determined by applying the principles of section 318(a)(2) without regard to the 50 percent limitation in section 318(a)(2)(C). In addition, an individual and all members of his family described in section 318(a)(1) shall be treated as one individual.

(iii) *De minimis variations in ownership and certain stock not taken into account.* For purposes of paragraph (l)(2)(i) of this section, the same person or persons will be treated as owning, directly or indirectly, all of the stock of the transferor and transferee corporations in identical proportions notwithstanding the fact that there is a *de minimis* variation in shareholder identity or proportionality of ownership. Additionally, for purposes of paragraph (l)(2)(i) of this section, stock described in section 1504(a)(4) is not taken into account.

(3) *Examples.* The following examples illustrate the principles of paragraph (l) of this section. For purposes of these examples, each of A, B, C, and D is an individual, T is the acquired corporation, S is the acquiring corporation, P is the parent corporation, and each of S1, S2, S3, and S4 is a direct or indirect subsidiary of P. Further, all of the requirements of section 368(a)(1)(D) other than the requirement that stock or securities be distributed in a transaction to which section 354 or 356 applies are satisfied. The examples are as follows:

Example 1. A owns all the stock of T and S. The T stock has a fair market value of $100x. T sells all of its assets to S in exchange for $100x of cash and immediately liquidates. Because there is complete shareholder identity and proportionality of ownership in T and S, under paragraph (l)(2)(i) of this section, the requirements of sections 368(a)(1)(D) and 354(b)(1)(B) are treated as satisfied notwithstanding the fact that no S stock is issued. Pursuant to paragraph (l)(2)(i) of this section, S will be deemed to issue a nominal share of S stock to T in addition to the $100x of cash actually exchanged for the T assets, and T will be deemed to distribute all such consideration to A. The transaction qualifies as a reorganization described in section 368(a)(1)(D).

Example 2. The facts are the same as in *Example 1* except that C, A's son, owns all of the stock of S. Under paragraph (l)(2)(ii) of this section, A and C are treated as one individual. Accordingly, there is complete shareholder identity and proportionality of ownership in T and S. Therefore, under paragraph (l)(2)(i) of this section, the requirements of sections 368(a)(1)(D) and 354(b)(1)(B) are treated as satisfied notwithstanding the fact that no S stock is issued. Pursuant to paragraph (l)(2)(i) of this section, S will be deemed to issue a nominal share of S stock to T in addition to the $100x of cash actually exchanged for the T assets, and T will be deemed to distribute all such consideration to A. A will be deemed to transfer the nominal share of S stock to C. The transaction qualifies as a reorganization described in section 368(a)(1)(D).

Example 3. P owns all of the stock of S1 and S2. S1 owns all of the stock of S3, which owns all of the stock of T. S2 owns all of the stock of S4, which owns all of the stock of S. The T stock has a fair market value of $70x. T sells all of its assets to S in exchange for $70x of cash and immediately liquidates. Under paragraph (l)(2)(ii) of this section, there is indirect, complete shareholder identity and proportionality of ownership in T and S. Accordingly, the requirements of sections 368(a)(1)(D) and 354(b)(1)(B) are treated as satisfied notwithstanding the fact that no S stock is issued. Pursuant to paragraph (l)(2)(i) of this section, S will be deemed to issue a nominal share of S stock to T in addition to the $70x of cash actually exchanged for the T assets, and T will be deemed to distribute all such consideration to S3. S3 will be deemed to distribute the nominal share of S stock to S1, which, in turn, will be deemed to distribute the nominal share of S stock to P. P will be deemed to transfer the nominal share of S stock to S2, which, in turn, will be deemed to transfer such share of S stock to S4. The transaction qualifies as a reorganization described in section 368(a)(1)(D).

Example 4. A, B, and C own 34%, 33%, and 33%, respectively, of the stock of T. The T stock has a fair market value of $100x. A, B, and C each own 33% of the stock of S. D owns the remaining 1% of the stock of S. T sells all of its assets to S in exchange for $100x of cash and immediately liquidates. For purposes of determining whether the distribution requirement of sections 368(a)(1)(D) and 354(b)(1)(B) is met, under paragraph (l)(2)(iii) of this section, D's ownership of a *de minimis* amount of stock of S is disregarded and the transaction is treated as if there is complete shareholder identity and proportionality of ownership in T and S. Because there is complete shareholder identity and proportionality of ownership in T and S, under paragraph (l)(2)(i) of this section, the requirements of sections 368(a)(1)(D) and 354(b)(1)(B) are treated as satisfied notwithstanding the fact that no S stock is issued. Pursuant to paragraph (l)(2)(i) of this section, S will be deemed to issue a nominal share of S stock to T in addition to the $100x of cash actually exchanged for the T assets, T will be deemed to distribute all such consideration to A, B, and C, and the nominal S stock will be deemed transferred among the S shareholders to the extent necessary to reflect their actual ownership of S. The transaction qualifies as a reorganization described in section 368(a)(1)(D).

Example 5. The facts are the same as in *Example 4* except that A, B, and C own 34%, 33%, and 33%, respectively, of the common stock of T and S. D owns preferred stock in S described in section 1504(a)(4). For purposes of determining whether the distribution requirement of sections 368(a)(1)(D) and 354(b)(1)(B) is met, under paragraph (l)(2)(iii) of this section, D's ownership of S stock described in section 1504(a)(4) is ignored and the transaction is treated as if there is complete shareholder identity and proportionality of ownership in T and S. Because there is complete shareholder identity and proportionality of ownership in T and S, under paragraph (l)(2)(i) of this section, the requirements of sections 368(a)(1)(D) and 354(b)(1)(B) are treated as satisfied notwithstanding the fact that no S stock is issued. Pursuant to paragraph (l)(2)(i) of this section, S will be deemed to issue a nominal share of S stock to T in addition to the $100x of cash actually exchanged for the T assets, and T will be deemed to distribute all such consideration to A, B, and C. The transaction qualifies as a reorganization described in section 368(a)(1)(D).

Example 6. A and B each own 50% of the stock of T. The T stock has a fair market value of $100x. B and C own 90% and 10%, respectively, of the stock of S. T sells all of its assets to S in exchange for $100x of cash and immediately liquidates. Because complete shareholder identity and proportionality of ownership in T and S does not exist, paragraph (l)(2)(i) of this section does not apply. The requirements of sections 368(a)(1)(D) and 354(b)(1)(B) are not satisfied, and the transaction does not qualify as a reorganization described in section 368(a)(1)(D).

(4) *Effective date.* (i) *In general.* This section applies to transactions occurring on or after March 19, 2007, except that they do not apply to any transaction occurring pursuant to a written agreement which is binding before December 19, 2006, and at all times thereafter. A taxpayer may apply the provisions of these temporary regulations to transactions occurring before March 19, 2007. However, the transferor corporation, the transferee corporation, any direct or indirect transferee of transferred basis property from either of the foregoing, and any shareholder of the transferor or transferee corporation may not apply the provisions of these temporary regulations unless all such taxpayers apply the provisions of the temporary regulations.

(ii) *Expiration.* This section expires on or before December 18, 2009.

Mark E. Matthews,
Deputy Commissioner for Services and Enforcement.

Approved December 6, 2006.

Eric Solomon,
Acting Deputy Assistant Secretary of the Treasury (Tax Policy).

(Filed by the Office of the Federal Register on December 18, 2006, 8:45 a.m., and published in the issue of the Federal Register for December 19, 2006, 71 F.R. 75879)

Section 409.—Qualifications for Tax Credit Employee Stock Ownership Plans

26 CFR 1.409(p)–1: Prohibited allocation of securities in an S corporation.

T.D. 9302

DEPARTMENT OF THE TREASURY
Internal Revenue Service
26 CFR Part 1

Prohibited Allocations of Securities in an S Corporation

AGENCY: Internal Revenue Service (IRS), Treasury.

ACTION: Final regulations.

SUMMARY: This document contains final regulations that provide guidance concerning requirements under section 409(p) of the Internal Revenue Code for employee stock ownership plans (ESOPs) holding stock of Subchapter S corporations. These final regulations generally affect plan sponsors of, and participants in, ESOPs holding stock of Subchapter S corporations.

DATES: *Effective Date:* These regulations are effective December 20, 2006.

Applicability Dates: These regulations are generally applicable with respect to plan years beginning on or after January 1, 2006. See the Effective Date section of the preamble for specific information.

FOR FURTHER INFORMATION CONTACT: John T. Ricotta or Veronica A. Rouse at (202) 622–6090 (not a toll-free number).

SUPPLEMENTARY INFORMATION:

Background

This document contains final regulations (26 CFR Part 1) under section 409(p) of the Internal Revenue Code (Code).

Section 409(p)(1) requires an ESOP holding employer securities consisting of stock in an S corporation to provide that, during an allocation year, no portion of the assets of the plan attributable to, or allocable in lieu of, the employer securities may accrue (or be allocated directly or indirectly under any plan of the employer meeting the requirements of section 401(a)) for the benefit of any disqualified person. Section 409(p)(3)(A) provides that a nonallocation year includes any plan year during which the ownership of the S corporation is so concentrated among disqualified persons that they own or are deemed to own at least 50 percent of its shares. Section 409(p)(4) provides, in general, that a disqualified person is any person whose deemed-owned ESOP shares (allocated ESOP shares and proportion of suspense account shares) are at least 10 percent of the number of deemed-owned shares of S corporation stock held by an ESOP or for whom the aggregate number of shares owned by such person and the members of such person's family is at least 20 percent of deemed-owned ESOP shares. Under section 409(p)(5), the determination of whether a person is a disqualified person and whether a plan year is a nonallocation year is also made separately taking into account synthetic equity if such treatment results in treating the person as a disqualified person or the year as a nonallocation year.

Temporary regulations (T.D. 9081, 2003–2 C.B. 420) under section 409(p) were issued on July 21, 2003, (68 FR 42970). The text of those temporary regulations also served as the text of a notice of proposed rulemaking (REG–129709–03,

2003–2 C.B. 506) published at 68 FR 43058. The 2003 regulations provided guidance on identifying disqualified persons, determining whether an ESOP has a nonallocation year, and defining synthetic equity under section 409(p)(5), and reserved some issues, including the definition of a prohibited allocation, the tax effect of a prohibited allocation, and certain issues relating to the definition of synthetic equity.

A public hearing on the 2003 regulations was held on November 17, 2003. New temporary regulations under section 409(p) (T.D. 9164, 2005–1 C.B. 320) were published in the **Federal Register** on December 17, 2004, (69 FR 75455). The new temporary regulations (2004 temporary regulations) addressed certain issues raised in the comments, as well as addressing the topics reserved in the 2003 temporary regulations. The text of the 2004 temporary regulations also served as the text for a notice of proposed rulemaking (REG–129709–03, 2005–1 C.B. 351) published at 69 FR 75492.

A public hearing on the 2004 proposed regulations was held on April 20, 2005. After consideration of the comments received, these final regulations adopt the provisions of the proposed regulations with certain modifications discussed in this preamble.

Explanation of Provisions

Definition of Prohibited Allocation

These regulations retain the rule of the 2004 temporary regulations concerning prohibited allocations under which there is an impermissible accrual to the extent employer securities consisting of stock in an S corporation are held under the ESOP for the benefit of a disqualified person during a nonallocation year. Thus, in the event of a nonallocation year, S corporation shares held in a disqualified person's account and all other ESOP assets attributable to S corporation stock, including distributions, sales proceeds, and earnings, are treated as an impermissible accrual whether attributable to contributions in the current year or a prior year. A commentator questioned whether the definition of prohibited allocation in the 2004 temporary regulations should include account balances of disqualified persons from prior years. The rule of the 2004 temporary regulations has been retained because it is consistent with the intent of the statute, and the IRS and Treasury Department believe it is necessary to prevent the concentration of ownership interests that section 409(p) was intended to prevent.

A commentator also questioned the treatment of proceeds from the sale of stock previously allocated to a disqualified person's account under the 2004 temporary regulations. The commentator expressed concern that treating the sales proceeds as an impermissible accrual when the original allocation of stock is already a prohibited allocation is a double penalty. The final regulations do not change this rule in the 2004 temporary regulations. An allocation of sales proceeds from stock held for the benefit of a disqualified person back into the account of the disqualified person is as valuable an accrual for the disqualified person as an investment in employer stock. This treatment is also consistent with the prohibition in section 409(p)(1) with respect to amounts that are "allocable in lieu of" employer stock.

Effect of a Prohibited Allocation

These regulations retain the rule of the 2004 regulations that if there is a prohibited allocation during a nonallocation year, the ESOP fails to satisfy the requirements of section 4975(e)(7) and ceases to be an ESOP. As a result, the exemption from the excise tax on prohibited transactions for loans to leveraged ESOPs contained in section 4975(d)(3) would cease to apply to any loan (with the result that the employer would owe an excise tax with respect to the previously exempt loan). These regulations clarify that an additional result would be the plan's failure to satisfy the qualification requirements under section 401(a) for not operating the plan in accordance with its terms to reflect section 409(p). Other consequences include imposition of an excise tax on the S corporation under section 4979A. An example has been added to these final regulations to illustrate the impact of these rules on an S corporation ESOP.

These regulations include the rule from the 2004 regulations under which a prohibited allocation is a deemed distribution that is not an eligible rollover distribution. These regulations also add that same rule to the list of distributions that are not eligible rollover distributions in the regulations under section 402(c) (at §1.402(c)–2 of the Treasury Regulations). As a result, under recently proposed regulations relating to designated Roth contributions under section 402A, a deemed distribution as a result of a section 409(p) prohibited allocation with respect to a designated Roth account would not constitute a qualified distribution for purposes of section 402A. See proposed §1.402A–1, A–11, at 71 FR 4320 (January 26, 2006).

Prevention of Nonallocation Year

The preamble to the 2004 regulations described methods that a plan might use to prevent the occurrence of a nonallocation year, including (1) a reduction of synthetic equity (for example, through cancellation or distribution), (2) a sale of the S corporation securities held in the participant's ESOP account before a nonallocation year occurs so that the account is not invested in S corporation stock, or (3) a transfer of the S corporation securities held for the participant under the ESOP into a separate portion of the plan that is not an ESOP or to another qualified plan of the employer that is not an ESOP.

Any methods of preventing a nonallocation year must satisfy applicable legal and qualification requirements, including the nondiscrimination requirements of section 401(a)(4) (including the rules at §1.401(a)(4)–4 relating to benefits, rights and features), and implementation of these methods must be completed before a nonallocation year occurs. These regulations retain the special rule provided in the 2004 regulations for applying the nondiscrimination requirements under section 401(a)(4) for a plan that uses the transfer method. Thus, these regulations provide that, if a transfer is made from an ESOP to a separate portion of the plan (or to another qualified plan of the employer) that is not an ESOP in order to prevent a nonallocation year, then both the ESOP and the plan that is not an ESOP will not fail to satisfy the requirements of §1.401(a)(4)–4 merely because of the transfer. Similarly, these regulations provide that, subsequent to the transfer, the plan will not fail to satisfy the requirements of §1.401(a)(4)–4 merely because of the benefits, rights, and features with respect to the transferred benefits if those benefits, rights, and features would satisfy the requirements of §1.401(a)(4)–4 if the mandatory disaggregation rule for ESOPs at §1.410(b)–7(c)(2) did not apply. These regulations clarify that any such transfers must be effectuated by an affirmative action taken no later than the date of the transfer, and all subsequent actions (including benefit statements) must be consistent with the transfer having occurred on that date. Further, in order to use the transfer method to prevent a nonallocation year, the plan must provide for the transfer of the stock to the non-ESOP portion of the plan.

A commentator described another method of preventing a nonallocation year under which stock of a participant is exchanged for cash or other assets, which are already in the accounts of other participants in order to change the stock holdings among participants before a nonallocation year occurs, but which does not change the overall stock holding of the ESOP trust. This method has been referred to as reshuffling. The commentator requested that relief from the nondiscriminatory availability requirements be extended to this method.

Absent a special rule for applying the nondiscrimination requirements of section 401(a)(4), it will be difficult for a plan to prevent a nonallocation year through reshuffling without violating section 401(a)(4). The right of each participant to have or not have a particular investment in his or her account (either as a participant-directed investment or as a trustee-directed investment) is a plan right or feature that is subject to the current and effective availability requirements of §1.401(a)(4)–4. Accordingly, if assets in the accounts of one or more non-highly compensated employees (NHCEs) are mandatorily exchanged, then, in the absence of other relevant factors, the plan would generally be expected to fail to satisfy the nondiscriminatory availability requirements of §1.401(a)(4)–4.

The IRS and Treasury Department do not believe that it would be appropriate to provide a special rule that would materially weaken the standard for nondiscriminatory availability of participant rights to a particular investment under the plan. By contrast, the special nondiscrimination rules for stock transferred out of the ESOP do not change the rights of NHCEs to any particular investment in the plan as a whole, but simply allow the transfer and allow the rights of participants whose stock is transferred out of the ESOP to be taken into account in determining whether the rights of participants whose stock remains in the ESOP satisfy the nondiscriminatory availability requirements of §1.401(a)(4)–4.

An S corporation may be able to achieve the same result as reshuffling by reducing contributions for HCEs who are or may become disqualified persons, by providing additional benefits to NHCEs who are not disqualified persons, by expanding coverage to include all employees, or by diversifying out of employer stock for HCEs who are or may become disqualified persons and who are qualified participants within the meaning of section 401(a)(28)(B)(iii) (that is, by mandating diversification using one of the diversification options that are offered to all qualified participants, for which there is an existing special nondiscrimination rule at §1.401(a)(4)–4(d)(6)). Thus, in addition to plan transfers, any of these actions may help prevent the concentration of deemed-owned ESOP shares that section 409(p) prohibits, without the nondiscrimination problems otherwise associated with reshuffling. Of course, any transfer or other method used to ensure compliance with section 409(p) must also satisfy any other legal requirements that may apply, including section 407(b)(2) of the Employee Retirement Income Security Act of 1974 (ERISA) (88 Stat. 829) Public Law 93–406 (which, in relevant part, generally prohibits a plan from investing more than 10 percent of elective deferral accounts in employer stock, unless the plan is an ESOP, the investment is at the direction of the participant, or another exception applies).

Treatment of Family Members as Disqualified Persons

The 2004 regulations included a number of attribution rules, which these regulations retain, including the application of the section 318 attribution rules to ownership of synthetic equity in determining who is a disqualified person. Section 409(p) contains references to the section 318 rules in certain cases, such as in determining a nonallocation year, but commentators pointed out that the section 318 rules did not apply for purposes of the disqualified person definition, which was not reflected in an example. Another commentator pointed out that the rules for determining whether family members are disqualified persons varies according to the individual being tested. For example, the technical language of section 409(p)(4)(D) treats parents-in-law as members of a married child's family when testing whether a child is a disqualified person, but not as members of the same family as the child's parents when testing whether the child's parents are disqualified persons. In response to comments, the regulations have been modified to clarify these rules, including revisions in the examples to illustrate the application of the rules to specific factual patterns.

Determination of Number of Shares of Non-Stock-Based Synthetic Equity

These regulations retain the rules from both the 2003 and the 2004 regulations regarding calculation of the number of shares of synthetic equity that are not determined by reference to shares of stock of the S corporation. These regulations provide that the person who is entitled to the synthetic equity is treated as owning a number of shares of stock in the S corporation equal to the present value of the synthetic equity (with such value determined without regard to any lapse restriction as defined under the section 83 regulations) divided by the fair market value of a share of the S corporation's stock as of the same date. These regulations also retain the special rule under the 2004 regulations that permits the ESOP to provide, on a reasonable and consistent basis for all persons, for the number of synthetic equity shares treated as owned on a determination date to remain constant for up to a 3-year period from that date (triennial method). This rule addresses concerns raised in comments to the 2003 regulations regarding the volatility of the number of shares of synthetic equity where that calculation is based on the value of an S corporation share.

A commentator questioned whether the triennial method of the 2004 regulations should be expanded to permit a more flexible triennial period that allows for the acceleration or delay of the triennial determination date. The commentator argued that, since the triennial method's purpose is to eliminate the risk attributable to volatility of the present value of the nonqualified deferred compensation stock and the risk attributable to the fair market value of company stock, the inability to delay or accelerate the date, automatically and daily if necessary, weakens the purpose of the method.

These regulations include changes in the triennial methodology to permit the ability, during the 3-year period, to accelerate a determination date prospectively in the event of a change in the plan year or any merger, consolidation, or transfer of ESOP assets under section 414(l). However, a determination date may not be changed retroactively and the change must be effectuated by a plan amendment adopted before the new determination date.[1]

A commentator also requested clarification regarding how shares of synthetic equity are calculated with respect to nonqualified deferred compensation. Specifically, the commentator wanted to know what discount rate should be used to calculate the present value of nonqualified deferred compensation, and how to determine the number of equivalent shares for a split-dollar life insurance arrangement. These regulations do not mandate a specific discount rate for calculating the present value of nonqualified deferred compensation or a specific method for determining the equivalent number of shares for a split dollar arrangement. However, any assumptions used for such purposes must be reasonable.

Finally, a commentator asked whether an individual S corporation shareholder's right of first refusal to acquire S corporation stock from an ESOP for its fair market value is considered synthetic equity. The regulations have been revised to clarify that the right of first refusal to acquire stock held by an ESOP is not treated as a right to acquire stock of an S corporation under these regulations if the right to acquire stock would not be taken into account under §1.1361–1(l)(2)(iii)(A) in determining whether an S corporation has a second class of stock and the price at which the stock is acquired under the right of first refusal is not less than the price determined for purposes of the put right required by section 409(h). See §54.4975–11(d)(5) of the Excise Tax Regulations. Of course, any right of first refusal must comply with the requirements of §54.4975–7(b)(9) of the Excise Tax Regulations. In addition, these regulations give the Commissioner the authority to treat a right of first refusal as synthetic equity if the Commissioner determines, based on the facts and circumstances, that the right to acquire stock held by the ESOP constitutes an avoidance or evasion of section 409(p).

Effective Dates

These regulations generally are applicable for plan years beginning on or after January 1, 2006. However, these regulations retain, by cross reference, the 2004 regulations for plan years beginning before January 1, 2006.

Special Analyses

It has been determined that this Treasury decision is not a significant regulatory action as defined in Executive Order 12866. Therefore, a regulatory assessment is not required. It also has been determined that section 553(b) of the Administrative Procedure Act (5 U.S.C. chapter 5) does not apply to these regulations, and because the regulation does not impose a collection of information requirement upon small entities, the Regulatory Flexibility Act (5 U.S.C. chapter 6) does not apply. Pursuant to section 7805(f) of the Internal Revenue Code, the temporary and proposed regulations preceding these final regulations were submitted to the Chief Counsel for Advocacy of the Small Business Administration for comment on its impact on small business.

Drafting Information

The principal authors of these regulations are John T. Ricotta and Veronica A. Rouse of the Office of the Division Counsel/Associate Chief Counsel (Tax Exempt and Government Entities); however, other personnel from the IRS and Treasury participated in their development.

* * * * *

Adoption of Amendments to the Regulations

Accordingly, 26 CFR part 1 is amended as follows:

PART 1—INCOME TAXES

Paragraph 1. The authority citation for part 1 is amended by adding an entry to read, in part, as follows:

Authority: 26 U.S.C. 7805 * * *

Section 1.409(p)–1 is also issued under 26 U.S.C. 409(p)(7). * * *

Par. 2. Section 1.402(c)–2, A–4, is revised by redesignating paragraph (g) as (h) and adding a new paragraph (g) to read as follows:

§1.402(c)–2 Eligible rollover distributions; questions and answers.

* * * * *

A–4. * * *

(g) Prohibited allocations that are treated as deemed distributions pursuant to section 409(p). * * *

Par. 3. Section 1.409(p)–1 is added to read as follows:

§1.409(p)–1 Prohibited allocation of securities in an S corporation.

(a) *Organization of this section and definition*—(1) *Organization of this section.* Section 409(p) applies if a nonallocation year occurs in an ESOP that holds shares of stock of an S corporation that are employer securities. Paragraph (b) of this section sets forth the general rule under section 409(p)(1) and (2) prohibiting any accrual or allocation to a disqualified person in a nonallocation year. Paragraph (c) of this section sets forth rules under section 409(p)(3), (5), and (7) for determining whether a year is a nonallocation year, generally based on whether disqualified persons own at least 50 percent of the shares of the S corporation, either taking into account only the outstanding shares of the S corporation (including shares held by the

[1] As indicated in Notice 2005–95, 2005–2 C.B. 1172, dated December 19, 2005, the general deadline for discretionary amendments in Rev. Proc. 2005–66, 2005–2 C.B. 509, does not apply if a statute or regulation specifically provides an earlier deadline. These regulations provide such an earlier deadline.

ESOP) or taking into account both the outstanding shares and synthetic equity of the S corporation. Paragraphs (d), (e), and (f) of this section contain definitions of disqualified person under section 409(p)(4) and (5), deemed-owned ESOP shares under section 409(p)(4)(C), and synthetic equity under section 409(p)(6)(C). Paragraph (g) of this section contains a standard for determining when the principal purpose of the ownership structure of an S corporation constitutes an avoidance or evasion of section 409(p).

(2) *Definitions*. The following definitions apply for purposes of section 409(p) and this section, as well as for purposes of section 4979A, which imposes an excise tax on certain events.

(i) *Deemed-owned ESOP shares* has the meaning set forth in paragraph (e) of this section.

(ii) *Disqualified person* has the meaning set forth in paragraph (d) of this section.

(iii) *Employer* has the meaning set forth in §1.410(b)–9.

(iv) *Employer securities* means employer securities within the meaning of section 409(l).

(v) *ESOP* means an employee stock ownership plan within the meaning of section 4975(e)(7).

(vi) *Prohibited allocation* has the meaning set forth in paragraph (b)(2) of this section.

(vii) *S corporation* means S corporation within the meaning of section 1361.

(viii) *Synthetic equity* has the meaning set forth in paragraph (f) of this section.

(b) *Prohibited allocation in a nonallocation year*—(1) *General rule*. Section 409(p)(1) provides that an ESOP holding employer securities consisting of stock in an S corporation must provide that no portion of the assets of the plan attributable to (or allocable in lieu of) such employer securities may, during a nonallocation year, accrue under the ESOP, or be allocated directly or indirectly under any plan of the employer (including the ESOP) meeting the requirements of section 401(a), for the benefit of any disqualified person.

(2) *Additional rules*—(i) *Prohibited allocation definition*. For purposes of section 409(p) and this section, a *prohibited allocation* means an impermissible accrual or an impermissible allocation. Whether there is impermissible accrual is determined under paragraph (b)(2)(ii) of this section and whether there is an impermissible allocation is determined under paragraph (b)(2)(iii) of this section. The amount of the prohibited allocation is equal to the sum of the amount of the impermissible accrual plus the amount of the impermissible allocation.

(ii) *Impermissible accrual*. There is an impermissible accrual to the extent that employer securities consisting of stock in an S corporation owned by the ESOP and any assets attributable thereto are held under the ESOP for the benefit of a disqualified person during a nonallocation year. For this purpose, assets attributable to stock in an S corporation owned by an ESOP include any distributions, within the meaning of section 1368, made on S corporation stock held in a disqualified person's account in the ESOP (including earnings thereon), plus any proceeds from the sale of S corporation securities held for a disqualified person's account in the ESOP (including any earnings thereon). Thus, in the event of a nonallocation year, all S corporation shares and all other ESOP assets attributable to S corporation stock, including distributions, sales proceeds, and earnings on either distributions or proceeds, held for the account of such disqualified person in the ESOP during that year are an impermissible accrual for the benefit of that person, whether attributable to contributions in the current year or in prior years.

(iii) *Impermissible allocation*. An impermissible allocation occurs during a nonallocation year to the extent that a contribution or other annual addition (within the meaning of section 415(c)(2)) is made with respect to the account of a disqualified person, or the disqualified person otherwise accrues additional benefits, directly or indirectly under the ESOP or any other plan of the employer qualified under section 401(a) (including a release and allocation of assets from a suspense account, as described at §54.4975–11(c) and (d) of this chapter) that, for the nonallocation year, would have been added to the account of the disqualified person under the ESOP and invested in employer securities consisting of stock in an S corporation owned by the ESOP but for a provision in the ESOP that precludes such addition to the account of the disqualified person, and investment in employer securities during a nonallocation year.

(iv) *Effects of prohibited allocation*—(A) *Deemed distribution*. If a plan year is a nonallocation year, the amount of any prohibited allocation in the account of a disqualified person as of the first day of the plan year, as determined under this paragraph (b)(2), is treated as distributed from the ESOP (or other plan of the employer) to the disqualified person on the first day of the plan year. In the case of an impermissible accrual or impermissible allocation that is not in the account of the disqualified person as of the first day of the plan year, the amount of the prohibited allocation, as determined under this paragraph (b)(2), is treated as distributed on the date of the prohibited allocation. Thus, the fair market value of assets in the disqualified person's account that constitutes an impermissible accrual or allocation is included in gross income (to the extent in excess of any investment in the contract allocable to such amount) and is subject to any additional income tax that applies under section 72(t). A deemed distribution under this paragraph (b)(2)(iv)(A) is not an actual distribution from the ESOP. Thus, the amount of the prohibited allocation is not an eligible rollover distribution under section 402(c). However, for purposes of applying sections 72 and 402 with respect to any subsequent distribution from the ESOP, the amount that the disqualified person previously took into account as income as a result of the deemed distribution is treated as investment in the contract.

(B) *Other effects*. If there is a prohibited allocation, then the plan fails to satisfy the requirements of section 4975(e)(7) and ceases to be an ESOP. In such a case, the exemption from the excise tax on prohibited transactions for loans to leveraged ESOPs contained in section 4975(d)(3) would cease to apply to any loan (with the result that the employer would owe an excise tax with respect to the previously exempt loan). As a result of these failures, the plan would lose the prohibited transaction exemption for loans to an ESOP under section 4975(d)(3) of the Code and section 408(b)(3) of Title I of the Employee Retirement Income Security Act of 1974, as amended (ERISA). Finally, a plan that does not operate in accordance with its terms to reflect section 409(p) fails to satisfy the qualification requirements of section 401(a), which would cause the corporation's S election to terminate under section 1362. See also section 4979A(a) which imposes an excise tax in certain events, including a prohibited allocation under section 409(p).

(C) *Example.* The rules of this paragraph (b)(2)(iv) are illustrated by the following example:

Example. (i) *Facts.* Corporation M, an S corporation under section 1361, establishes Plan P as an ESOP in 2006, with a calendar plan year. Plan P is a qualified plan that includes terms providing that a prohibited allocation will not occur during a nonallocation year in accordance with section 409(p). On December 31, 2006, all of the 1,000 outstanding shares of stock of Corporation M, with a fair market value of $30 per share, are contributed to Plan P and allocated among accounts established within Plan P for the benefit of Corporation M's three employees, individuals A, B, and C, based on their compensation for 2006. As a result, on December 31, 2006, participant A's account includes 800 of the shares ($24,000); participant B's account includes 140 of the shares ($4,200); and participant C's account includes the remaining 60 shares ($1,800). The plan year 2006 is a nonallocation year, participants A and B are disqualified persons on December 31, 2006, and a prohibited allocation occurs for A and B on December 31, 2006.

(ii) *Conclusion.* On December 31, 2006, participants A and B each have a deemed distribution as a result of the prohibited allocation, resulting in income of $24,000 for participant A and $4,200 for participant B. Corporation M owes an excise tax under section 4979A, based on an amount involved of $28,200. Plan P ceases to be an ESOP on the date of the prohibited allocation (December 31, 2006) and also fails to satisfy the qualification requirements of section 401(a) on that date due to the failure to comply with the provisions requiring compliance with section 409(p). As a result of having an ineligible shareholder under section 1361(b)(1)(B), Corporation M ceases to be an S corporation under section 1361 on December 31, 2006.

(v) *Prevention of prohibited allocation*—(A) *Transfer of account to non-ESOP.* An ESOP may prevent a nonallocation year or a prohibited allocation during a nonallocation year by providing for assets (including S corporation securities) allocated to the account of a disqualified person (or a person reasonably expected to become a disqualified person absent a transfer described in this paragraph (b)(2)(v)(A)) to be transferred into a separate portion of the plan that is not an ESOP, as described in §54.4975–11(a)(5) of this chapter, or to another plan of the employer that satisfies the requirements of section 401(a) and that is not an ESOP. Any such transfer must be effectuated by an affirmative action taken no later than the date of the transfer, and all subsequent actions (including benefit statements) generally must be consistent with the transfer having occurred on that date. In the event of such a transfer involving S corporation securities, the recipient plan is subject to tax on unrelated business taxable income under section 512.

(B) *Relief from nondiscrimination requirement.* Pursuant to this paragraph (b)(2)(v)(B), if a transfer described in paragraph (b)(2)(v)(A) of this section is made from an ESOP to a separate portion of the plan or to another qualified plan of the employer that is not an ESOP, then both the ESOP and the plan or portion of a plan that is not an ESOP do not fail to satisfy the requirements of §1.401(a)(4)–4 merely because of the transfer. Further, subsequent to the transfer, that plan will not fail to satisfy the requirements of §1.401(a)(4)–4 merely because of the benefits, rights, and features with respect to the transferred benefits if those benefits, rights, and features would satisfy the requirements of §1.401(a)(4)–4 if the mandatory disaggregation rule for ESOPs at §1.410(b)–7(c)(2) did not apply.

(c) *Nonallocation year.* A year is a nonallocation year if it is described in the general definition in paragraph (c)(1) of this section or if the special rule of paragraph (c)(3) of this section applies.

(1) *General definition.* For purposes of section 409(p) and this section, a *nonallocation year* means a plan year of an ESOP during which, at any time, the ESOP holds any employer securities that are shares of an S corporation and either—

(i) Disqualified persons own at least 50 percent of the number of outstanding shares of stock in the S corporation (including deemed owned ESOP shares); or

(ii) Disqualified persons own at least 50 percent of the sum of:

(A) The outstanding shares of stock in the S corporation (including deemed-owned ESOP shares); and

(B) The shares of synthetic equity in the S corporation owned by disqualified persons.

(2) *Attribution rules.* For purposes of this paragraph (c), the rules of section 318(a) apply to determine ownership of shares in the S corporation (including deemed-owned ESOP shares) and synthetic equity. However, for this purpose, section 318(a)(4) (relating to options to acquire stock) is disregarded and, in applying section 318(a)(1), the members of an individual's family include members of the individual's family under paragraph (d)(2) of this section. In addition, an individual is treated as owning deemed-owned ESOP shares of that individual notwithstanding the employee trust exception in section 318(a)(2)(B)(i). If the attribution rules in paragraph (f)(1) of this section apply, then the rules of paragraph (f)(1) of this section are applied before (and in addition to) the rules of this paragraph (c)(2).

(3) *Special rule for avoidance or evasion.* (i) Any ownership structure described in paragraph (g)(3) of this section results in a nonallocation year. In addition, each individual referred to in paragraph (g)(3) of this section is treated as a disqualified person and the individual's interest in the separate entity described in paragraph (g)(3) of this section is treated as synthetic equity.

(ii) Pursuant to section 409(p)(7)(B), the Commissioner, in revenue rulings, notices, and other guidance published in the Internal Revenue Bulletin (see §601.601(d)(2)(ii)(*b*) of this chapter), may provide that a nonallocation year occurs in any case in which the principal purpose of the ownership structure of an S corporation constitutes an avoidance or evasion of section 409(p). For any year that is a nonallocation year under this paragraph (c)(3), the Commissioner may treat any person as a disqualified person. See paragraph (g) of this section for guidance regarding when the principal purpose of an ownership structure of an S corporation involving synthetic equity constitutes an avoidance or evasion of section 409(p).

(4) *Special rule for certain stock rights.* (i) For purposes of paragraph (c)(1) of this section, a person is treated as owning stock if the person has an exercisable right to acquire the stock, the stock is both issued and outstanding, and the stock is held by persons other than the ESOP, the S corporation, or a related entity (as defined in paragraph (f)(3) of this section).

(ii) This paragraph (c)(4) applies only if treating persons as owning the shares described in paragraph (c)(4)(i) of this section results in a nonallocation year. This paragraph (c)(4) does not apply to a right to acquire stock of an S corporation held by a shareholder that is subject to Federal income tax that, under

§1.1361–1(l)(2)(iii)(A) or (l)(4)(iii)(C), would not be taken into account in determining if an S corporation has a second class of stock, provided that a principal purpose of the right is not the avoidance or evasion of section 409(p). Under the last sentence of paragraph (f)(2)(i) of this section, this paragraph (c)(4)(ii) does not apply for purposes of determining ownership of deemed-owned ESOP shares or whether an interest constitutes synthetic equity.

(5) *Application with respect to shares treated as owned by more than one person.* For purposes of applying paragraph (c)(1) of this section, if, by application of the rules of paragraph (c)(2), (c)(4), or (f)(1) of this section, any share is treated as owned by more than one person, then that share is counted as a single share and that share is treated as owned by disqualified persons if any of the owners is a disqualified person.

(6) *Effect of nonallocation year.* See paragraph (b) of this section for a prohibition applicable during a nonallocation year. See also section 4979A for an excise tax applicable in certain cases, including section 4979A(a)(3) and (4) which applies during a nonallocation year (whether or not there is a prohibited allocation during the year).

(d) *Disqualified persons.* A person is a disqualified person if the person is described in paragraph (d)(1), (d)(2), or (d)(3) of this section.

(1) *General definition.* For purposes of section 409(p) and this section, a *disqualified person* means any person for whom—

(i) The number of such person's deemed-owned ESOP shares of the S corporation is at least 10 percent of the number of the deemed-owned ESOP shares of the S corporation;

(ii) The aggregate number of such person's deemed-owned ESOP shares and synthetic equity shares of the S corporation is at least 10 percent of the sum of—

(A) The total number of deemed-owned ESOP shares of the S corporation; and

(B) The person's synthetic equity shares of the S corporation;

(iii) The aggregate number of the S corporation's deemed-owned ESOP shares of such person and of the members of such person's family is at least 20 percent of the number of deemed-owned ESOP shares of the S corporation; or

(iv) The aggregate number of the S corporation's deemed-owned ESOP shares and synthetic equity shares of such person and of the members of such person's family is at least 20 percent of the sum of—

(A) The total number of deemed-owned ESOP shares of the S corporation; and

(B) The synthetic equity shares of the S corporation owned by such person and the members of such person's family.

(2) *Treatment of family members; definition*—(i) *Rule.* Each member of the family of any person who is a disqualified person under paragraph (d)(1)(iii) or (iv) of this section and who owns any deemed-owned ESOP shares or synthetic equity shares is a disqualified person.

(ii) *General definition.* For purposes of section 409(p) and this section, *member of the family* means, with respect to an individual—

(A) The spouse of the individual;

(B) An ancestor or lineal descendant of the individual or the individual's spouse;

(C) A brother or sister of the individual or of the individual's spouse and any lineal descendant of the brother or sister; and

(D) The spouse of any individual described in paragraph (d)(2)(ii)(B) or (C) of this section.

(iii) *Spouse.* A spouse of an individual who is legally separated from such individual under a decree of divorce or separate maintenance is not treated as such individual's spouse under paragraph (d)(2)(ii) of this section.

(3) *Special rule for certain nonallocation years.* See paragraph (c)(3) of this section (relating to avoidance or evasion of section 409(p)) for special rules under which certain persons are treated as disqualified persons.

(4) *Example.* The rules of this paragraph (d) are illustrated by the following examples:

Example 1. (i) *Facts.* An S corporation has 800 outstanding shares, of which 100 are owned by individual O and 700 are held in an employee stock ownership plan (ESOP) during 2006, including 200 shares held in the ESOP account of O, 65 shares held in the ESOP account of participant P, 65 shares held in the ESOP account of participant Q who is P's spouse, and 14 shares held in the ESOP account of R, who is the daughter of P and Q. There are no unallocated suspense account shares in the ESOP. The S corporation has no synthetic equity.

(ii) *Conclusion.* Under paragraph (d)(1)(i) of this section, O is a disqualified person during 2006 because O's account in the ESOP holds at least 10% of the shares owned by the ESOP (200 is 28.6% of 700). During 2006, neither P, Q, nor R is a disqualified person under paragraph (d)(1)(i) of this section, because each of their accounts holds less than 10% of the shares owned by the ESOP. However, each of P, Q, and R is a disqualified person under paragraph (d)(1)(iii) of this section because P and members of P's family own at least 20% of the deemed-owned ESOP shares (144 (the sum of 65, 65 and 14) is 20.6% of 700). As a result, disqualified persons own at least 50% of the outstanding shares of the S corporation during 2006 (O's 100 directly owned shares, O's 200 deemed-owned shares, P's 65 deemed-owned shares, Q's 65 deemed-owned shares, and R's 14 deemed-owned shares are 55.5% of 800).

Example 2. (i) *Facts.* An S corporation has shares that are owned by an ESOP and various individuals. Individuals S and T are married and have a son, U. Individuals V and W are married and have a daughter, X. Individuals U and X are married. Individual V has a brother Y. Their percentages of the deemed-owned ESOP shares of the S corporation are as follows: T has 6%; U has 7%; and V has 8%. Neither S, W, X, nor Y has any deemed-owned ESOP shares and the S corporation has no synthetic equity. However, individual S and individual Y each own directly a number of shares of the outstanding shares of the S corporation.

(ii) *Conclusion.* In this example, individual U is a disqualified person under paragraph (d)(1) of this section (because U's family consists of S, T, U, V, W, and X, and, in the aggregate, those persons own more than 20% of the deemed-owned ESOP shares) and individual X is also a disqualified person under paragraph (d)(1) of this section (because X's family consists of S, T, U, V, W, and X, and, in the aggregate, those persons own more than 20% of the deemed-owned ESOP shares). Further, individuals T and V are each a disqualified person under paragraph (d)(2) of this section because each is a member of a family that includes one or more disqualified persons and each has deemed-owned ESOP shares. However, individuals S, W, and Y are not disqualified persons under this paragraph (d). For example, S does not own more than 10% of the deemed-owned ESOP shares, and S's family, which consists of S, T, U, and X, owns, in the aggregate, only 13% of the deemed-owned ESOP shares (X's parents are not members of S's family because the family members of a person do not include the parents-in-law of the person's descendants). Further, note that, for purposes of determining whether the ESOP has a nonallocation year under paragraph (c) of this section, the shares directly owned by S and Y would be taken into account as shares owned by disqualified persons under the attribution rules in paragraph (c)(2) of this section.

(e) *Deemed-owned ESOP shares.* For purposes of section 409(p) and this section, a person is treated as owning his or her deemed-owned ESOP shares. Deemed-owned ESOP shares owned by a person mean, with respect to any person—

(1) Any shares of stock in the S corporation constituting employer securities that are allocated to such person's account under the ESOP; and

(2) Such person's share of the stock in the S corporation that is held by the ESOP but is not allocated to the account of any participant or beneficiary (with such person's share to be determined in the same proportion as the shares released and allocated from a suspense account, as described at §54.4975–11(c) and (d) of the Excise Tax Regulations, under the ESOP for the most recently ended plan year for which there were shares released and allocated from a suspense account, or if there has been no such prior release and allocation from a suspense account, then determined in proportion to a reasonable estimate of the shares that would be released and allocated in the first year of a loan repayment).

(f) *Synthetic equity and rights to acquire stock of the S corporation*—(1) *Ownership of synthetic equity*. For purposes of section 409(p) and this section, synthetic equity means the rights described in paragraph (f)(2) of this section. Synthetic equity is treated as owned by the person that has any of the rights specified in paragraph (f)(2) of the section. In addition, the attribution rules as set forth in paragraph (c)(2) of this section apply for purposes of attributing ownership of synthetic equity.

(2) *Synthetic equity*—(i) *Rights to acquire stock of the S corporation*—(A) *General rule*. Synthetic equity includes any stock option, warrant, restricted stock, deferred issuance stock right, stock appreciation right payable in stock, or similar interest or right that gives the holder the right to acquire or receive stock of the S corporation in the future. Rights to acquire stock in an S corporation with respect to stock that is, at all times during the period when such rights are effective, both issued and outstanding, and held by a person other than the ESOP, the S corporation, or a related entity are not synthetic equity but only if that person is subject to federal income taxes. (See also paragraph (c)(4) of this section.)

(B) *Exception for certain rights of first refusal*. A right of first refusal to acquire stock held by an ESOP is not treated as a right to acquire stock of an S corporation under this paragraph if the right to acquire stock would not be taken into account under §1.1361–1(l)(2)(iii)(A) in determining if an S corporation has a second class of stock and the price at which the stock is acquired under the right of first refusal is not less than the price determined under section 409(h). See §54.4975–11(d)(5) of the Excise Tax Regulations. The right of first refusal must also comply with the requirements of §54.4975–7(b)(9) of the Excise Tax Regulations. This paragraph (f)(2)(i)(B) does not apply if, based on the facts and circumstances, the Commissioner finds that the right to acquire stock held by the ESOP constitutes an avoidance or an evasion of section 409(p). See also section 408(d) of ERISA, under which the exemption provided by section 408(e) of ERISA (and the related exemption at section 4975(d)(13) of the Code) does not apply to an owner-employee, including an employee or officer of an S corporation who is a 5 percent owner.

(ii) *Special rule for certain stock rights*. Synthetic equity also includes a right to a future payment (payable in cash or any other form other than stock of the S corporation) from an S corporation that is based on the value of the stock of the S corporation, such as appreciation in such value. Thus, for example, synthetic equity includes a stock appreciation right with respect to stock of an S corporation that is payable in cash or a phantom stock unit with respect to stock of an S corporation that is payable in cash.

(iii) *Rights to acquire interests in or assets of an S corporation or a related entity*. Synthetic equity includes a right to acquire stock or other similar interests in a related entity to the extent of the S corporation's ownership. Synthetic equity also includes a right to acquire assets of an S corporation or a related entity other than either rights to acquire goods, services, or property at fair market value in the ordinary course of business or fringe benefits excluded from gross income under section 132.

(iv) *Special rule for nonqualified deferred compensation*. (A) Synthetic equity also includes any of the following with respect to an S corporation or a related entity: any remuneration to which section 404(a)(5) applies; remuneration for which a deduction would be permitted under section 404(a)(5) if separate accounts were maintained; any right to receive property, as defined in §1.83–3(e) of the Income Tax Regulations (including a payment to a trust described in section 402(b) or to an annuity described in section 403(c)) in a future year for the performance of services; any transfer of property in connection with the performance of services to which section 83 applies to the extent that the property is not substantially vested within the meaning of §1.83–3(i) by the end of the plan year in which transferred; and a split-dollar life insurance arrangement under §1.61–22(b) entered into in connection with the performance of services (other than one under which, at all times, the only economic benefit that will be provided under the arrangement is current life insurance protection as described in §1.61–22(d)(3)). Synthetic equity also includes any other remuneration for services under a plan, method, or arrangement deferring the receipt of compensation to a date that is after the 15th day of the 3rd calendar month after the end of the entity's taxable year in which the related services are rendered. However, synthetic equity does not include benefits under a plan that is an eligible retirement plan within the meaning of section 402(c)(8)(B).

(B) For purposes of applying paragraph (f)(2)(iv)(A) of this section with respect to an ESOP, synthetic equity does not include any interest described in such paragraph (f)(2)(iv)(A) of this section to the extent that—

(*1*) The interest is nonqualified deferred compensation (within the meaning of section 3121(v)(2)) that was outstanding on December 17, 2004;

(*2*) The interest is an amount that was taken into account (within the meaning of §31.3121(v)(2)–1(d) of this chapter) prior to January 1, 2005, for purposes of taxation under chapter 21 of the Internal Revenue Code (or income attributable thereto); and

(*3*) The interest was held before the first date on which the ESOP acquires any employer securities.

(v) *No overlap among shares of deemed-owned ESOP shares or synthetic equity*. Synthetic equity under this paragraph (f)(2) does not include shares that are deemed-owned ESOP shares (or any rights with respect to deemed-owned ESOP shares to the extent such rights are specifically provided under section 409(h)). In addition, synthetic equity under a specific subparagraph of this paragraph (f)(2) does not include anything that is synthetic equity under a preceding provision of paragraph (f)(2)(i), (ii), (iii), or (iv) of this section.

(3) *Related entity*. For purposes of this paragraph (f), *related entity* means any en-

tity in which the S corporation holds an interest and which is a partnership, a trust, an eligible entity that is disregarded as an entity that is separate from its owner under §301.7701–3 of this chapter, or a qualified subchapter S subsidiary under section 1361(b)(3).

(4) *Number of synthetic shares*—(i) *Synthetic equity determined by reference to S corporation shares.* In the case of synthetic equity that is determined by reference to shares of stock of the S corporation, the person who is entitled to the synthetic equity is treated as owning the number of shares of stock deliverable pursuant to such synthetic equity. In the case of synthetic equity that is determined by reference to shares of stock of the S corporation, but for which payment is made in cash or other property (besides stock of the S corporation), the number of shares of synthetic equity treated as owned is equal to the number of shares of stock having a fair market value equal to the cash or other property (disregarding lapse restrictions as described in §1.83–3(i)). Where such synthetic equity is a right to purchase or receive S corporation shares, the corresponding number of shares of synthetic equity is determined without regard to lapse restrictions as described in §1.83–3(i) or to any amount required to be paid in exchange for the shares. Thus, for example, if a corporation grants an employee of an S corporation an option to purchase 100 shares of the corporation's stock, exercisable in the future only after the satisfaction of certain performance conditions, the employee is the deemed owner of 100 synthetic equity shares of the corporation as of the date the option is granted. If the same employee were granted 100 shares of restricted S corporation stock (or restricted stock units), subject to forfeiture until the satisfaction of performance or service conditions, the employee would likewise be the deemed owner of 100 synthetic equity shares from the grant date. However, if the same employee were granted a stock appreciation right with regard to 100 shares of S corporation stock (whether payable in stock or in cash), the number of synthetic equity shares the employee is deemed to own equals the number of shares having a value equal to the appreciation at the time of measurement (determined without regard to lapse restrictions).

(ii) *Synthetic equity determined by reference to shares in a related entity.* In the case of synthetic equity that is determined by reference to shares of stock (or similar interests) in a related entity, the person who is entitled to the synthetic equity is treated as owning shares of stock of the S corporation with the same aggregate value as the number of shares of stock (or similar interests) of the related entity (with such value determined without regard to any lapse restriction as defined at §1.83–3(i)).

(iii) *Other synthetic equity*—(A) *General rule.* In the case of any synthetic equity to which neither paragraph (f)(4)(i) of this section nor paragraph (f)(4)(ii) of this section apply, the person who is entitled to the synthetic equity is treated as owning on any date a number of shares of stock in the S corporation equal to the present value (on that date) of the synthetic equity (with such value determined without regard to any lapse restriction as defined at §1.83–3(i)) divided by the fair market value of a share of the S corporation's stock as of that date.

(B) *Use of annual or more frequent determination dates.* A year is a nonallocation year if the thresholds in paragraph (c) of this section are met at any time during that year. However, for purposes of this paragraph (f)(4)(iii), an ESOP may provide that the number of shares of S corporation stock treated as owned by a person who is entitled to synthetic equity to which this paragraph (f)(4)(iii) applies is determined annually (or more frequently), as of the first day of the ESOP's plan year or as of any other reasonable determination date or dates during a plan year. If the ESOP so provides, the number of shares of synthetic equity to which this paragraph (f)(4)(iii) applies that are treated as owned by that person for any period from a given determination date through the date immediately preceding the next following determination date is the number of shares treated as owned on the given determination date.

(C) *Use of triennial recalculations.* (*1*) Although an ESOP must have a determination date that is no less frequent than annually, if the terms of the ESOP so provide, then the number of shares of synthetic equity with respect to grants of synthetic equity to which this paragraph (f)(4)(iii) applies may be fixed for a specified period from a determination date identified under the ESOP through the day before a determination date that is not later than the third anniversary of the identified determination date. Thus, the ESOP must provide for the number of shares of synthetic equity to which this paragraph (f)(4)(iii) applies to be re-determined not less frequently than every three years, based on the S corporation share value on a determination date that is not later than the third anniversary of the identified determination date and the aggregate present value of the synthetic equity to which this paragraph (f)(4)(iii) applies (including all grants made during the three-year period) on that determination date.

(*2*) However, additional accruals, allocations, or grants (to which this paragraph (f)(4)(iii) applies) that are made during such three-year period are taken into account on each determination date during that period, based on the number of synthetic equity shares resulting from the additional accrual, allocation, or grant (determined as of the determination date on or next following the date of the accrual, allocation, or grant). See *Example 3* of paragraph (h) of this section for an example illustrating this paragraph (f)(4)(iii)(C).

(*3*) If, as permitted under this paragraph (f)(4)(iii)(C), an ESOP provides for the number of shares of synthetic equity to be fixed for a specified period from a determination date to a subsequent determination date, then that subsequent determination date can be changed to a new determination date, subject to the following conditions:

(*i*) The change in the subsequent determination date must be effectuated through a plan amendment adopted before the new determination date;

(*ii*) The new determination date must be earlier than the prior determination date (that is, the new determination date must be earlier than the determination date applicable in the absence of the plan amendment);

(*iii*) The conditions in paragraph (f)(4)(iii)(C)(*2*) of this section must be satisfied measured from the new determination date; and

(*iv*) Except to the extent permitted by the Commissioner in revenue rulings, notices, or other guidance published in the Internal Revenue Bulletin (see §601.601(d)(2)(ii)(b) of this chapter), the change must be adopted in connection with either a change in the plan year of the ESOP or a merger, consolidation, or transfer of plan assets of the ESOP under section 414(l) (and the new determination date must be consistent with that plan year change or section 414(l) event).

(*4*) *Conditions for application of rules.* This paragraph (f)(4)(iii)(C) only applies with respect to grants of synthetic equity to which this paragraph (f)(4)(iii) applies. In addition, paragraph (f)(4)(iii)(C) of this section applies only if the fair market value of a share of the S corporation securities on any determination date is not unrepresentative of the value of the S corporation securities throughout the rest of the plan year and only if the terms of the ESOP include provisions conforming to paragraph (f)(4)(iii)(C)(*1*) of this section which are consistently used by the ESOP for all persons. In addition, paragraph (f)(4)(iii)(C)(*1*) of this section applies only if the terms of the ESOP include provisions conforming to paragraphs (f)(4)(iii)(C)(*1*) of this section which are consistently used by the ESOP for all persons.

(iv) *Adjustment of number of synthetic equity shares where ESOP owns less than 100 Percent of S corporation.* The number of synthetic shares otherwise determined under this paragraph (f)(4) is decreased ratably to the extent that shares of the S corporation are owned by a person who is not an ESOP and who is subject to Federal income taxes. For example, if an S corporation has 200 outstanding shares, of which individual A owns 50 shares and the ESOP owns the other 150 shares, and individual B would be treated under this paragraph (f)(4) as owning 100 synthetic equity shares of the S corporation but for this paragraph (f)(4)(iv), then, under the rule of this paragraph (f)(4)(iv), the number of synthetic shares treated as owned by B under this paragraph (f)(4) is decreased from 100 to 75 (because the ESOP only owns 75 percent of the outstanding stock of the S corporation, rather than 100 percent).

(v) *Special rule for shares with greater voting power than ESOP shares.* Notwithstanding any other provision of this paragraph (f)(4), if a synthetic equity right includes (directly or indirectly) a right to purchase or receive shares of S corporation stock that have per-share voting rights greater than the per-share voting rights of one or more shares of S corporation stock held by the ESOP, then the number of shares of deemed owned synthetic equity attributable to such right is not less than the number of shares that would have the same voting rights if the shares had the same per-share voting rights as shares held by the ESOP with the least voting rights. For example, if shares of S corporation stock held by the ESOP have one voting right per share, then an individual who holds an option to purchase one share with 100 voting rights is treated as owning 100 shares of synthetic equity.

(g) *Avoidance or evasion of section 409(p) involving synthetic equity*—(1) *General rule.* Paragraph (g)(2) of this section sets forth a standard for determining whether the principal purpose of the ownership structure of an S corporation involving synthetic equity constitutes an avoidance or evasion of section 409(p). Paragraph (g)(3) of this section identifies certain specific ownership structures that constitute an avoidance or evasion of section 409(p). See also paragraph (c)(3) of this section for a rule under which the ownership structures in paragraph (g)(3) of this section result in a nonallocation year for purposes of section 409(p).

(2) *Standard for determining when there is an avoidance or evasion of section 409(p) involving synthetic equity.* For purposes of section 409(p) and this section, whether the principal purpose of the ownership structure of an S corporation involving synthetic equity constitutes an avoidance or evasion of section 409(p) is determined by taking into account all the surrounding facts and circumstances, including all features of the ownership of the S corporation's outstanding stock and related obligations (including synthetic equity), any shareholders who are taxable entities, and the cash distributions made to shareholders, to determine whether, to the extent of the ESOP's stock ownership, the ESOP receives the economic benefits of ownership in the S corporation that occur during the period that stock of the S corporation is owned by the ESOP. Among the factors indicating that the ESOP receives those economic benefits include shareholder voting rights, the right to receive distributions made to shareholders, and the right to benefit from the profits earned by the S corporation, including the extent to which actual distributions of profits are made from the S corporation to the ESOP and the extent to which the ESOP's ownership interest in undistributed profits and future profits is subject to dilution as a result of synthetic equity. For example, the ESOP's ownership interest is not subject to dilution if the total amount of synthetic equity is a relatively small portion of the total number of shares and deemed-owned shares of the S corporation.

(3) *Specific transactions that constitute an avoidance or evasion of section 409(p) involving segregated profits.* Taking into account the standard in paragraph (g)(2) of this section, the principal purpose of the ownership structure of an S corporation constitutes an avoidance or evasion of section 409(p) in any case in which—

(i) The profits of the S corporation generated by the business activities of a specific individual or individuals are not provided to the ESOP, but are instead substantially accumulated and held for the benefit of the individual or individuals on a tax-deferred basis within an entity related to the S corporation, such as a partnership, trust, or corporation (such as in a subsidiary that is a disregarded entity), or any other method that has the same effect of segregating profits for the benefit of such individual or individuals (such as nonqualified deferred compensation described in paragraph (f)(2)(iv) of this section);

(ii) The individual or individuals for whom profits are segregated have rights to acquire 50 percent or more of those profits directly or indirectly (for example, by purchase of the subsidiary); and

(iii) A nonallocation year would occur if this section were separately applied with respect to either the separate entity or whatever method has the effect of segregating profits of the individual or individuals, treating such entity as a separate S corporation owned by an ESOP (or in the case of any other method of segregation of profits by treating those profits as the only assets of a separate S corporation owned by an ESOP).

(h) *Examples.* The rules of this section are illustrated by the following examples:

Example 1. Relating to determination of disqualified persons and nonallocation year if there is no synthetic equity. (i) *Facts.* Corporation X is a calendar year S corporation that maintains an ESOP. X has a single class of common stock, of which there are a total of 1,200 shares outstanding. X has no synthetic equity. In 2006, individual A, who is not an employee of X (and is not related to any employee of X), owns 100 shares directly, B, who is an employee of *X*, owns 100 shares directly, and the remaining 1,000 shares are owned by an ESOP maintained by X for its employees. The ESOP's 1,000 shares are allocated to the accounts of individuals who are employees of X (none of whom are related), as set forth in columns 1 and 2 in the following table:

1 Shareholders	2 Deemed-Owned ESOP Shares (total of 1,000)	3 Percentage Deemed-Owned ESOP Shares	4 Disqualified Person
B	330	33%	Yes
C	145	14.5%	Yes
D	75	7.5%	No
E	30	3%	No
F	20	2%	No
Other participants	400 (none exceed 10 shares)	1% or less	No

(ii) *Conclusion with respect to disqualified persons.* As shown in column 4 in the table contained in paragraph (i) of *Example 1*, individuals B and C are disqualified persons for 2006 under paragraph (d)(1) of this section because each owns at least 10% of X's deemed-owned ESOP shares. However, the synthetic equity shares owned by any person do not affect the calculation for any other person's ownership of shares.

(iii) *Conclusion with respect to nonallocation year.* 2006 is not a nonallocation year under section 409(p) because disqualified persons do not own at least 50% of X's outstanding shares (the 100 shares owned directly by B, B's 330 deemed-owned ESOP shares, plus C's 145 deemed-owned ESOP shares equal only 47.9% of the 1,200 outstanding shares of X).

Example 2. Relating to determination of disqualified persons and nonallocation year if there is synthetic equity. (i) *Facts.* The facts are the same as in *Example 1*, except that, as shown in column 4 of the table in this *Example 2*, individuals E and F have options to acquire 110 and 130 shares, respectively, of the common stock of X from X:

1 Shareholder	2 Deemed-Owned ESOP Shares (total of 1,000)	3 Percentage Deemed-Owned ESOP Shares	4 Options (240)	5 Shareholder Percentage of Deemed-Owned ESOP plus Synthetic Equity Shares	6 Disqualified Person
B	330	33%			Yes (col. 3)
C	145	14.5%			Yes (col. 3)
D	75	7.5%			No
E	30	3%	110	11.1% ([30+ 91.7] divided by 1,091.7)	Yes (col. 5)
F	20	2%	130	11.6% ([20 +108.3] divided by 1,108.3)	Yes (col. 5)
Other participants	400 (none exceeds 10 shares)	1% or less			No

(ii) *Conclusion with respect to disqualified persons.* Individual E's synthetic equity shares are counted in determining whether E is a disqualified person for 2006, and individual F's synthetic equity shares are counted in determining whether F is a disqualified person for 2006. Applying the rule of paragraph (f)(4)(iv) of this section, E's option to acquire 110 shares of the S corporation converts under paragraph (f)(4)(iv) of this section, into 91.7 shares of synthetic equity (110 times the ratio of the 1,000 deemed-owned ESOP shares to the sum of the 1,000 deemed-owned ESOP shares plus the 200 shares held outside the ESOP by A and B). Similarly, F's option to acquire 130 shares of the S corporation converts into 108.3 shares of synthetic equity (130 times the ratio of the 1,000 deemed-owned ESOP shares to the sum of the 1,000 deemed-owned ESOP shares plus the 200 shares held outside the ESOP by A and B). However, the synthetic equity shares owned by any person do not affect the calculation for any other person's ownership of shares. Accordingly, as shown in column 6 in the table contained in paragraph (i) of *Example 2*, individuals B, C, E, and F are disqualified persons for 2006.

(iii) *Conclusion with respect to nonallocation year.* The 100 shares owned directly by B, B's 330 deemed-owned ESOP shares, C's 145 deemed-owned ESOP shares, E's 30 deemed-owned ESOP shares, E's 91.7 synthetic equity shares, F's 20 deemed-owned ESOP shares, plus F's 108.3 synthetic equity shares total 825, which equals 58.9% of 1,400, which is the sum of the 1,200 outstanding shares of X and the 200 shares of synthetic equity shares of X held by disqualified persons. Thus, 2006 is a nonallocation year for X's ESOP under section 409(p) because disqualified persons own at least 50% of the total shares of outstanding stock of X and the total synthetic equity shares of X held by disqualified persons. In addition, independent of the preceding conclusion, 2006 would be a nonallocation year because disqualified persons own at least 50% of X's outstanding shares because the 100 shares owned directly by B, B's 330 deemed-owned ESOP shares, C's 145 deemed-owned ESOP shares, E's 30 deemed-owned ESOP shares, plus F's 20 deemed-owned ESOP shares equal 52.1% of the 1,200 outstanding shares of X.

Example 3. Relating to determination of number of shares of synthetic equity. (i) *Facts.* Corporation Y is a calendar year S corporation that maintains an ESOP. Y has a single class of common stock, of which there are a total of 1,000 shares outstanding, all of which are owned by the ESOP. Y has no synthetic equity, except for four grants of nonqualified deferred compensation that are made to an individual during the period from 2005 through 2011, as set forth in column 2 in the following table. The ESOP provides for the rules in paragraph (f)(4)(iii) of this section to determine the number of shares of synthetic equity owned by that individual with a determination date of January 1 and the triennial rule redetermining value, as shown in columns 4 and 5:

1 Determination Date	2 Present Value of Nonqualified Deferred Compensation on Determination Date	3 Share Value on Determination Date	4 New Shares of Synthetic Equity on Determination Date	5 Aggregate Number of Synthetic Equity Shares on Determination Date
January 1, 2005	A grant is made on January 1, 2005, with a present value of $1,000. An additional grant of nonqualified deferred compensation with a present value of $775 is made on March 1, 2005.	$10 per share	100	100
January 1, 2006	An additional grant is made on December 31, 2005, which has a present value of $800 on January 1, 2006. The March 1, 2005, grant has a present value on January 1, 2006, of $800.	$8 per share	200	300
January 1, 2007	No new grants made.	$12 per share		300
January 1, 2008	An additional grant is made on December 31, 2007, which has a present value of $3,000 on January 1, 2008. The grants made during 2005 through 2007 have an aggregate present value on January 1, 2008, of $3,750.	$15 per share	200	450
January 1, 2009	No new grants are made.	$11 per share		450
January 1, 2010	No new grants are made.	$22 per share		450
January 1, 2011	No new grants are made. The grants made during 2005 through 2008 have an aggregate present value on January 1, 2011, of $7,600.	$20 per share		380

(ii) *Conclusion.* The grant made on January 1, 2005, is treated as 100 shares until the determination date in 2008. The grant made on March 1, 2005, is not taken into account until the 2006 determination date and its present value on that date, along with the then present value of the grant made on December 31, 2005, is treated as a number of shares that are based on the $8 per share value on the 2006 determination date, with the resulting number of shares continuing to apply until the determination date in 2008. On the January 1, 2008, determination date, the grant made on the preceding day is taken into account at its present value of $3,000 on January 1, 2008 and the $15 per share value on that date with the resulting number of shares (200) continuing to apply until the next determination date. In addition, on the January 1, 2008, determination date, the number of shares determined under other grants made between January 1, 2005 and December 31, 2007, must be revalued. Accordingly, the aggregate value of all nonqualified deferred compensation granted during that period is determined to be $3750 on January 1, 2008, and the corresponding number of shares of synthetic equity based on the $15 per share value is determined to be 250 shares on the 2008 determination date, with the resulting aggregate number of shares (450) continuing to apply until the determination date in 2011. On the January 1, 2011, determination date, the aggregate value of all nonqualified deferred compensation is determined to be $7,600 and the corresponding number of shares of synthetic equity based on the $20 per share value on the 2011 determination date is determined to be 380 shares (with the resulting number of shares continuing to apply until the day before the determination date in 2014, assuming no further grants are made).

(i) *Effective dates*—(1) *Statutory effective date.* (i) Except as otherwise provided in paragraph (i)(1)(ii) of this section, section 409(p) applies for plan years ending after March 14, 2001.

(ii) If an ESOP holding stock in an S corporation was established on or before March 14, 2001, and the election under section 1362(a) with respect to that S corporation was in effect on March 14, 2001, section 409(p) applies for plan years beginning on or after January 1, 2005.

(2) *Regulatory effective date.* This section applies for plan years beginning on or after January 1, 2006. For plan years beginning before January 1, 2006, §1.409(p)–1T (as it appeared in the April 1, 2005, edition of 26 CFR part 1) applies.

Mark E. Matthews,
Deputy Commissioner for Services and Enforcement.

Approved November 30, 2006.

Eric Solomon,
Acting Deputy Assistant Secretary of the Treasury (Tax Policy).

(Filed by the Office of the Federal Register on December 19, 2006, 8:45 a.m., and published in the issue of the Federal Register for December 20, 2006, 71 F.R. 76134)

Section 472.—Last-in, First-out Inventories

26 CFR 1.472–1: Last-in, first-out inventories.

LIFO; price indexes; department stores. The November 2006 Bureau of Labor Statistics price indexes are accepted for use by department stores employing the retail inventory and last-in, first-out inventory methods for valuing inventories for tax years ended on, or with reference to, November 30, 2006.

Rev. Rul. 2007–6

The following Department Store Inventory Price Indexes for November 2006 were issued by the Bureau of Labor Statistics (BLS). The indexes are accepted by the Internal Revenue Service, under § 1.472–1(k) of the Income Tax Regulations and Rev. Proc. 86–46, 1986–2 C.B. 739, for appropriate application to inventories of department stores employing the retail inventory and last-in, first-out inventory methods for tax years ended on, or with reference to, November 30, 2006.

The Department Store Inventory Price Indexes are prepared on a national basis and include (a) 23 major groups of departments, (b) three special combinations of the major groups — soft goods, durable goods, and miscellaneous goods, and (c) a store total, which covers all departments, including some not listed separately, except for the following: candy, food, liquor, tobacco, and contract departments.

BUREAU OF LABOR STATISTICS, DEPARTMENT STORE
INVENTORY PRICE INDEXES BY DEPARTMENT GROUPS
(January 1941 = 100, unless otherwise noted)

Groups	Nov. 2005	Nov. 2006	Percent Change from Nov. 2005 to Nov. 2006[1]
1. Piece Goods	480.6	471.2	-2.0
2. Domestics and Draperies	508.2	478.1	-5.9
3. Women's and Children's Shoes	684.7	678.1	-1.0
4. Men's Shoes	868.9	894.2	2.9
5. Infants' Wear	564.1	573.3	1.6
6. Women's Underwear	548.8	560.2	2.1
7. Women's Hosiery	339.8	346.5	2.0
8. Women's and Girls' Accessories	582.1	542.0	-6.9
9. Women's Outerwear and Girls' Wear	368.3	373.5	1.4
10. Men's Clothing	542.1	529.6	-2.3
11. Men's Furnishings	574.9	574.9	0.0
12. Boys' Clothing and Furnishings	403.5	411.3	1.9
13. Jewelry	861.4	893.3	3.7
14. Notions	803.1	817.9	1.8
15. Toilet Articles and Drugs	1001.0	1005.1	0.4
16. Furniture and Bedding	596.7	596.9	0.0
17. Floor Coverings	612.3	623.2	1.8
18. Housewares	701.9	689.7	-1.7
19. Major Appliances	204.3	208.9	2.3
20. Radio and Television	38.1	34.4	-9.7
21. Recreation and Education[2]	77.6	76.7	-1.2
22. Home Improvements[2]	137.2	141.3	3.0
23. Automotive Accessories[2]	116.5	122.2	4.9
Groups 1–15: Soft Goods	561.0	561.9	0.2
Groups 16–20: Durable Goods	376.2	371.2	-1.3
Groups 21–23: Misc. Goods[2]	93.1	94.2	1.2
Store Total[3]	495.4	495.3	0.0

[1]Absence of a minus sign before the percentage change in this column signifies a price increase.

[2]Indexes on a January 1986 = 100 base.

[3]The store total index covers all departments, including some not listed separately, except for the following: candy, food, liquor, tobacco, and contract departments.

DRAFTING INFORMATION

The principal author of this revenue ruling is John Roman Faron of the Office of Associate Chief Counsel (Income Tax and Accounting). For further information regarding this revenue ruling, contact Mr. Faron at (202) 622–8142 (not a toll-free call).

Part III. Administrative, Procedural, and Miscellaneous

Miscellaneous Pension Protection Act Changes

Notice 2007–7

I. PURPOSE

This notice provides guidance in the form of questions and answers with respect to certain provisions of the Pension Protection Act of 2006, P.L. 109–280 ("PPA '06"), that are effective in 2007 or earlier. The sections of PPA '06 addressed in this notice, which are primarily related to distributions, are § 303 (relating to interest rate assumptions for lump sum distributions), § 826 (relating to hardship distributions), § 828 (relating to early distributions to public safety employees), § 829 (relating to rollovers for nonspouse beneficiaries), § 845 (relating to distributions to pay for accident or health insurance for public safety officers), § 904 (relating to vesting of nonelective contributions), § 1102 (relating to the notice and consent period for distributions), and § 1201 (relating to distributions from IRAs to charitable organizations).

II. SECTION 303 OF PPA '06

Section 415(b) of the Code provides limitations on annual benefits under a defined benefit plan. Under § 415(b)(2)(B), if a benefit is payable in a form other than a straight life annuity, the benefit is adjusted to an actuarially equivalent straight life annuity for purposes of determining whether the limitations of § 415(b) have been satisfied. Section 415(b)(2)(E) provides limitations on the actuarial assumptions that can be used in making the adjustment under § 415(b)(2)(B). Prior to the enactment of PPA '06, for purposes of adjusting a benefit payable in a form that is subject to the minimum present value requirements of § 417(e)(3), § 415(b)(2)(E)(ii) provided that the interest rate assumption must not be less than the greater of the applicable interest rate as defined in § 417(e)(3) or the rate specified in the plan. However, § 101(b)(4) of the Pension Funding Equity Act of 2004, P.L. 108–218, amended § 415(b)(2)(E)(ii) to provide that, for plan years beginning in 2004 and 2005, 5.5% must be used in lieu of the applicable interest rate (as defined in § 417(e)(3)) for purposes of adjusting the benefit.

Section 303(a) of PPA '06 amended § 415(b)(2)(E)(ii) to provide that the interest rate assumption for purposes of adjusting a benefit payable in a form that is subject to the minimum present value requirements of § 417(e)(3) must not be less than the greatest of (i) 5.5%, (ii) the rate that provides a benefit of not more than 105% of the benefit that would be provided if the applicable interest rate (as defined in § 417(e)(3)) were the interest rate assumption, or (iii) the rate specified under the plan.

Q–1. What is the effective date of the changes made to § 415 of the Code by § 303(a) of PPA '06?

A–1. The changes to § 415 of the Code made by § 303(a) of PPA '06 apply to distributions made in plan years beginning after December 31, 2005. However, the changes do not apply to a plan with a termination date that is on or before August 17, 2006, the date of enactment of PPA '06.

Q–2. May a plan be amended retroactively to comply with the requirements of § 303(a) of PPA '06 without violating the anti-cutback rules provided in § 411(d)(6) of the Code?

A–2. Yes. Under § 1107 of PPA '06, a plan does not violate the anti-cutback rules of § 411(d)(6) of the Code if it is amended retroactively to comply with § 303(a) of PPA '06, provided the amendment is adopted on or before the last day of the first plan year beginning on or after January 1, 2009 (2011 in the case of a governmental plan), and the plan is operated as if such amendment were in effect as of the first date the amendment is effective.

Q–3. If a plan made a distribution in a plan year beginning in 2006 that satisfied the limitations of § 415(b) prior to the enactment of PPA '06 but which is in excess of the limitations of § 415(b) taking into account the amendments to § 415 made by § 303(a) of PPA '06 (a "§ 303 excess distribution"), does the distribution violate the requirements of § 415(b)?

A–3. Yes. However, three methods are available for correcting a § 303 excess distribution. First, Q&A–4 of this notice sets forth a special correction method that is available for a § 303 excess distribution made prior to September 1, 2006, provided that the correction is completed by March 15, 2007. Second, if correction is completed by December 31, 2007 (even if the § 303 excess distribution occurs after September 1, 2006), a plan may correct a § 303 excess distribution by using the correction method for a § 415(b) excess distribution described in the Employee Plans Compliance Resolution System ("EPCRS") (see section 2.04(1) in Appendix B in Rev. Proc. 2006–27, 2006–22 I.R.B. 945) even if the plan does not meet the requirements specified in Rev. Proc. 2006–27, including the special requirements for self correction under Part IV of Rev. Proc. 2006–27. Finally, a plan that meets the requirements of Rev. Proc. 2006–27 may correct § 303 excess distributions by using the correction method for § 415(b) excess distributions under EPCRS even after December 31, 2007. A plan that is amended retroactively to comply with § 303(a) of PPA '06 will not fail to satisfy the requirement in § 1107(b)(2)(A) of PPA '06 (that the plan be operated in accordance with the terms of the amendment) merely because it made a § 303 excess distribution, provided the § 303 excess distribution is corrected using one of these three correction methods.

Q–4. What special correction method is available to correct a § 303 excess distribution made prior to September 1, 2006?

A–4. A special correction method is available for a § 303 excess distribution made prior to September 1, 2006, provided the correction is completed by March 15, 2007. Under the special correction method, a plan may use the EPCRS correction method for a § 415(b) excess distribution (as described in section 2.04(1) in Appendix B in Rev. Proc. 2006–27, even if the plan does not otherwise meet the requirements of Rev. Proc. 2006–27, including the special requirements for self correction) with the following modifications. The excess amount (*i.e.*, the amount by which the distribution actually made exceeds the distribution permitted using the interest assumption specified in § 415(b) as amended by PPA '06) is not required to be returned to the plan (as otherwise required under the EPCRS correction method). Instead, a plan must issue two Forms 1099–R (*Distributions From Pensions, Annuities, Retirement or Profit-Sharing Plans, IRAs*, Insurance Contracts, etc.) to a participant who has received a § 303 excess distribution. The first Form 1099–R should include only the amount that would have been distributed had the benefit payable been adjusted using the interest assumptions specified in § 415(b) as amended by PPA '06. The second Form 1099–R should include only the excess amount that was distributed, and should include code "E" in box 7 to identify the amount as an excess distribution. As provided in the EPCRS correction, this excess amount is not an eligible rollover distribution, and therefore must be included in gross income in the year distributed from the plan.

III. SECTION 826 OF PPA '06

An employee's elective contributions under a cash or deferred arrangement can only be distributed upon the occurrence of certain events, one of which is the employee's hardship. A distribution is made on account of hardship only if the distribution both is made on account of an immediate and heavy financial need of the employee and is necessary to satisfy the financial need. A distribution made for any of the expenses listed in Regulation § 1.401(k)–1(d)(3)(iii)(B) is deemed to be on account of an immediate and heavy financial need of the employee. Several of these listed expenses can be expenses of the employee's spouse or dependents.

Section 826 of PPA '06 directs the Secretary of the Treasury to modify the rules relating to distributions from § 401(k), § 403(b), § 409A, and § 457(b) plans on account of a participant's hardship or unforeseeable financial emergency to permit such plans to treat a participant's beneficiary under the plan the same as the participant's spouse or dependent in determining whether the participant has incurred a hardship or unforeseeable financial emergency.

Q–5. What changes are being made pursuant to § 826 of PPA '06 in the rules relating to hardship distributions from § 401(k) plans and § 403(b) plans and relating to distributions on account of an unforeseeable financial emergency from a plan described in § 457(b) or § 409A?

A–5. (a) *Hardship distributions from § 401(k) plans and § 403(b) plans*. A § 401(k) plan that permits hardship distributions of elective contributions to a participant only for expenses described in § 1.401(k)–1(d)(3)(iii)(B) may, beginning August 17, 2006, permit distributions for expenses described in § 1.401(k)–1(d)(3)(iii)(B)(*1*), (*3*), or (*5*) (relating to medical, tuition, and funeral expenses, respectively) for a primary beneficiary under the plan. For this purpose, a "primary beneficiary under the plan" is an individual who is named as a beneficiary under the plan and has an unconditional right to all or a portion of the participant's account balance under the plan upon the death of the participant. A plan that adopts these expanded hardship provisions must still satisfy all the other requirements applicable to hardship distributions, such as the requirement that the distribution be necessary to satisfy the financial need. These rules also apply to § 403(b) plans.

(b) *Distributions on account of an unforeseeable financial emergency from a plan described in § 457(b) or § 409A*. In applying § 457(d)(1)(A)(iii), § 1.457–6(c)(2)(i), § 409A(a)(2)(A)(vi), and Proposed Regulation § 1.409A–3(g)(3)(i), a plan described in § 457(b) or § 409A may treat a participant's beneficiary under the plan the same as the participant's spouse or dependent in determining whether the participant has incurred an unforeseeable financial emergency. This will be reflected in the upcoming final regulations under § 409A.

IV. SECTION 828 OF PPA '06

Section 72(t)(1) of the Code provides for a 10% additional tax on an early distribution from a qualified retirement plan (as defined in § 4974(c)), unless the early distribution qualifies for one of the exceptions listed in § 72(t)(2). For example, § 72(t)(2)(A)(v) provides an exception to the 10% additional tax for distributions made to an employee who separates from service after attainment of age 55. Under § 72(t)(3)(A), § 72(t)(2)(A)(v) does not apply to individual retirement plans.

Section 828 of PPA '06 amended § 72 of the Code by adding § 72(t)(10), which provides that in the case of a distribution to a qualified public safety employee from a governmental defined benefit plan, § 72(t)(2)(A)(v) is applied by substituting age 50 for age 55. Thus, the 10% additional tax on early distributions under § 72(t)(1) does not apply to a distribution from a governmental defined benefit plan made to a qualified public safety employee who separates from service after attainment of age 50. This exception to the 10% additional tax applies to distributions made after August 17, 2006 (the date of enactment of PPA '06).

Q–6. Who is a qualified public safety employee?

A–6. For purposes of § 72(t)(10), the term "qualified public safety employee" means an employee of a State or of a political subdivision of a State (such as a county or city) whose principal duties include services requiring specialized training in the area of police protection, firefighting services, or emergency medical services for any area within the jurisdiction of the State or the political subdivision of the State.

Q–7. How does a qualified public safety employee qualify for the exception to the 10% additional tax under § 72(t)(10)?

A–7. In order to qualify for the exception to the 10% additional tax under § 72(t)(10), a qualified public safety employee (i) must have received the distribution from a governmental defined benefit plan after separating from service with the employer maintaining the plan and (ii) the separation from service must have occurred during or after the calendar year in which the qualified public safety employee attained age 50. For example, a qualified public safety employee who separated from service on June 30, 2006, and attained age 50 on December 12, 2006, is eligible for the exception under § 72(t)(10) with respect to distributions made after August 17, 2006.

Q–8. What are the consequences if, before August 18, 2006, a qualified public safety employee began receiving substantially equal periodic payments that qualify for the exception to the 10% additional tax described in § 72(t)(2)(A)(iv) and then modified the periodic payments after August 17, 2006?

A–8. If the payments satisfy the requirements in Q&A–7 of this notice, payments received by the qualified public safety employee after August 17, 2006, would qualify for the exception to the 10% additional tax under § 72(t)(10). However, if the modification would result in the imposition of the recapture tax under the rules of § 72(t)(4), then the recapture tax applies to the payments made before August 18, 2006.

Q–9. Does the exception to the 10% additional tax under § 72(t)(10) apply if the qualified public safety employee rolls over distributions from a governmental defined benefit plan into an IRA or a defined contribution plan and subsequently takes an early distribution from the IRA or defined contribution plan?

A–9. No. The exception to the 10% additional tax under § 72(t)(10) applies only to amounts distributed from a governmental defined benefit plan and does not apply to distributions from a defined contribution plan or an individual retirement plan.

Q–10. How does a payer report distributions that qualify for the exception to the 10% additional tax under § 72(t)(10) on Form 1099–R?

A–10. A payer is permitted to use distribution code 2 (early distribution, exception applies) in box 7 of Form 1099–R. However, a payer is also permitted to use distribution code 1 (early distribution, no known exception) in box 7 of Form 1099–R, if the payer does not know whether the exception under § 72(t)(10) applies. For further information on reporting, see Instructions for Forms 1099–R and 5498.

V. SECTION 829 OF PPA '06

Under § 402(c)(11) of the Code, which was added by § 829 of PPA '06, if a direct trustee-to-trustee transfer of any portion of a distribution from an eligible retirement plan is made to an individual retirement plan described in § 408(a) or (b) (an "IRA") that is established for the purpose of receiving the distribution on behalf of a designated beneficiary who is a nonspouse beneficiary, the transfer is treated as a direct rollover of an eligible rollover distribution for purposes of § 402(c). The IRA of the nonspouse beneficiary is treated as an inherited IRA within the meaning of § 408(d)(3)(C). Section 402(c)(11) applies to distributions made after December 31, 2006.

Q–11. Can a qualified plan described in § 401(a) offer a direct rollover of a distribution to a nonspouse beneficiary?

A–11. Yes. Under § 402(c)(11), a qualified plan described in § 401(a) can offer a direct rollover of a distribution to a nonspouse beneficiary who is a designated beneficiary within the meaning of § 401(a)(9)(E), provided that the distributed amount satisfies all the requirements to be an eligible rollover distribution other than the requirement that the distribution be made to the participant or the participant's spouse. (See § 1.401(a)(9)–4 for rules regarding designated beneficiaries.) The direct rollover must be made to an IRA established on behalf of the designated beneficiary that will be treated as an inherited IRA pursuant to the provisions of § 402(c)(11). If a nonspouse beneficiary elects a direct rollover, the amount directly rolled over is not includible in gross income in the year of the distribution. See § 1.401(a)(31)–1, Q&A–3 and–4, for procedures for making a direct rollover.

Q–12. Can other types of plans offer a direct rollover of a distribution to a nonspouse beneficiary?

A–12. Yes. Section 402(c)(11) also applies to annuity plans described in § 403(a) or (b) and to eligible governmental plans under § 457(b).

Q–13. How must the IRA be established and titled?

A–13. The IRA must be established in a manner that identifies it as an IRA with respect to a deceased individual and also identifies the deceased individual and the beneficiary, for example, "Tom Smith as beneficiary of John Smith."

Q–14. Is a plan required to offer a direct rollover of a distribution to a nonspouse beneficiary pursuant to § 402(c)(11)?

A–14. No. A plan is not required to offer a direct rollover of a distribution to a nonspouse beneficiary. If a plan does offer direct rollovers to nonspouse beneficiaries of some, but not all, participants, such rollovers must be offered on a nondiscriminatory basis because the opportunity to make a direct rollover is a benefit, right, or feature that is subject to § 401(a)(4). In the case of distributions from a terminated defined contribution plan pursuant to 29 C.F.R. § 2550.404a–3(d)(1)(ii), the plan will be considered to offer direct rollovers pursuant to § 402(c)(11) with respect to such distributions without regard to plan terms.

Q–15. For what purposes is the direct rollover of a distribution by a nonspouse beneficiary treated as a rollover of an eligible rollover distribution?

A–15. Section 402(c)(11) provides that a direct rollover of a distribution by a nonspouse beneficiary is a rollover of an eligible rollover distribution only for purposes of § 402(c). Accordingly, the distribution is not subject to the direct rollover requirements of § 401(a)(31), the notice requirements of § 402(f), or the mandatory withholding requirements of § 3405(c). If an amount distributed from a plan is received by a nonspouse beneficiary, the distribution is not eligible for rollover.

Q–16. If the named beneficiary of a decedent is a trust, is a plan permitted to make a direct rollover to an IRA established with the trust as beneficiary?

A–16. Yes. A plan may make a direct rollover to an IRA on behalf of a trust where the trust is the named beneficiary of a decedent, provided the beneficiaries of the trust meet the requirements to be designated beneficiaries within the meaning of § 401(a)(9)(E). The IRA must be established in accordance with the rules in Q&A–13 of this notice, with the trust identified as the beneficiary. In such a case, the beneficiaries of the trust are treated as having been designated as beneficiaries of the decedent for purposes of determining the distribution period under § 401(a)(9), if the trust meets the requirements set forth in § 1.401(a)(9)–4, Q&A–5, with respect to the IRA.

Q–17. How is the required minimum distribution (an amount not eligible for rollover) determined with respect to a nonspouse beneficiary if the employee dies before his or her required beginning date within the meaning of § 401(a)(9)(C)?

A–17. (a) *General rule.* If the employee dies before his or her required beginning date, the required minimum distributions for purposes of determining the amount eligible for rollover with respect to a nonspouse beneficiary are determined under either the 5-year rule described in § 401(a)(9)(B)(ii) or the life expectancy rule described in § 401(a)(9)(B)(iii). See Q&A–4 of § 1.401(a)(9)–3 to determine which rule applies to a particular designated beneficiary. Under either rule, no amount is a required minimum distribution for the year in which the employee dies. The rule in Q&A–7(b) of § 1.402(c)–2 (relating to distributions before an employee has attained age 70½) does not apply to nonspouse beneficiaries.

(b) *Five-year rule.* Under the 5-year rule described in § 401(a)(9)(B)(ii), no amount is required to be distributed until the fifth calendar year following the year of the employee's death. In that year, the entire amount to which the beneficiary is entitled under the plan must be distributed. Thus, if the 5-year rule applies with respect to a nonspouse beneficiary who is a designated beneficiary within the meaning of § 401(a)(9)(E), for the first 4 years after the year the employee dies, no amount payable to the beneficiary is ineligible for direct rollover as a required minimum distribution. Accordingly, the beneficiary is permitted to directly roll over the beneficiary's entire benefit until the end of the fourth year (but, as described in Q&A–19 of this notice, the 5-year rule must also apply to the IRA to which the rollover contribution is made). On or after January 1 of the fifth year following the year in which the employee died, no amount payable to the beneficiary is eligible for rollover.

(c) *Life expectancy rule.* (1) *General rule.* If the life expectancy rule described in § 401(a)(9)(B)(iii) applies, in the year following the year of death and each subsequent year, there is a required minimum distribution. See Q&A–5(c)(1) of § 1.401(a)(9)–5 to determine the applicable distribution period for the nonspouse beneficiary. The amount not eligible for rollover includes all undistributed required minimum distributions for the year in which the direct rollover occurs and any prior year (even if the excise tax under § 4974 has been paid with respect to the failure in the prior years). See the last sentence of § 1.402(c)–2, Q&A–7(a).

(2) *Special rule.* If, under paragraph (b) or (c) of Q&A–4 of § 1.401(a)(9)–3, the 5-year rule applies, the nonspouse designated beneficiary may determine the required minimum distribution under the plan using the life expectancy rule in the case of a distribution made prior to the end of the year following the year of death. However, in order to use this rule, the required minimum distributions under the IRA to which the direct rollover is made must be determined under the life expectancy rule using the same designated beneficiary.

Q–18. How is the required minimum distribution with respect to a nonspouse beneficiary determined if the employee dies on or after his or her required beginning date?

A–18. If an employee dies on or after his or her required beginning date, within the meaning of § 401(a)(9)(C), for the year of the employee's death, the required minimum distribution not eligible for rollover is the same as the amount that would have applied if the employee were still alive and elected the direct rollover. For the year after the year of the employee's death and subsequent years, see Q&A–5 of § 1.401(a)(9)–5 to determine the applicable distribution period to use in calculating the required minimum distribution. As in the case of death before the employee's required beginning date, the amount not eligible for rollover includes all undistributed required minimum distributions for the year in which the direct rollover occurs and any prior year, including years before the employee's death.

Q–19. After a direct rollover by a nonspouse designated beneficiary, how is the required minimum distribution determined with respect to the IRA to which the rollover contribution is made?

A–19. Under § 402(c)(11), an IRA established to receive a direct rollover on behalf of a nonspouse designated beneficiary is treated as an inherited IRA within the meaning of § 408(d)(3)(C). The required minimum distribution requirements set forth in § 401(a)(9)(B) and the regulations thereunder apply to the inherited IRA. The rules for determining the required minimum distributions under the plan with respect to the nonspouse beneficiary also apply under the IRA. Thus, if the employee dies before his or her required beginning date and the 5-year rule in § 401(a)(9)(B)(ii) applied to the nonspouse designated beneficiary under the plan making the direct rollover, the 5-year rule applies for purposes of determining required minimum distributions under the IRA. If the life expectancy rule applied to the nonspouse designated beneficiary under the plan, the required minimum distribution under the IRA must be determined using the same applicable distribution period as would have been used under the plan if the direct rollover had not occurred. Similarly, if the employee dies on or after his or her required beginning date, the required minimum distribution under the IRA for any year after the year of death must be determined using the same applicable distribution period as would have been used under the plan if the direct rollover had not occurred.

VI. SECTION 845 OF PPA '06

Code § 402(l), which was added by § 845(a) of PPA '06, provides for an exclusion from gross income for distributions from certain retirement plans (referred to in this notice as "Eligible Government Plans") used to pay qualified health insurance premiums of an eligible retired public safety officer. The exclusion applies with respect to an eligible retired public safety officer who elects to have qualified health insurance premiums deducted from amounts distributed from an Eligible Government Plan and paid directly to the insurer. Qualified health insurance premiums include premiums for accident and health insurance or qualified long-term care insurance contracts for the eligible retired public safety officer and his or her spouse and dependents. The distribution is excluded from gross income to the extent that the aggregate amount of the distributions does not exceed the amount used to pay the qualified health insurance premiums of the eligible retired public safety officer and his or her spouse and dependents. An "Eligible Government Plan" is a governmental plan described in § 414(d) that is either: a § 401(a), § 403(a), or § 403(b) plan; or an eligible governmental plan under § 457(b). Section 402(l) applies to distributions in taxable years beginning after December 31, 2006.

Q–20. Who is an eligible retired public safety officer for purposes of the exclusion under § 402(l)?

A–20. An employee is an eligible retired public safety officer for purposes of the exclusion under § 402(l) only if the employee is an individual who separated from service, either by reason of disability or after attainment of normal retirement age, as a public safety officer with the employer who maintains the Eligible Government Plan from which the distributions to pay qualified health insurance premiums are made. Thus, a public safety officer who retires before attainment of normal retirement age is not an eligible retired public safety officer unless the public safety officer retires by reason of disability. The terms of the Eligible Government Plan from which the participant will be receiving the distributions apply in determining whether a public safety officer has separated from service by reason of disability or after attainment of normal retirement age.

Q–21. Who is a public safety officer?

A–21. For purposes of § 402(l), the term "public safety officer" means an individual serving a public agency in an official capacity, with or without compensation, as a law enforcement officer, a firefighter, a chaplain, or as a member of a rescue squad or ambulance crew. See § 1204(9)(A) of the Omnibus Crime Control and Safe Streets Act of 1968 (42 U.S.C. 3796b(9)(A)).

Q–22. Under what circumstances are the provisions of § 402(l) available for eligible retired public safety officers?

A–22. The favorable tax treatment under § 402(l) is available only when an eligible retired public safety officer elects to have an amount subtracted from his or her distributions from an Eligible Government Plan and such amount is used to pay qualified health insurance premiums. The employer sponsoring the Eligible Government Plan is not required to offer such an election.

Q–23. Can the accident or health plan receiving the payments of qualified health insurance premiums be a self-insured plan?

A–23. No. The accident or health plan must be an accident or health insurance plan. Thus, the plan must be providing insurance issued by an insurance company regulated by a State (including a managed care organization that is treated as issuing insurance).

Q–24. Will an eligible retired public safety officer be entitled to favorable tax treatment under § 402(l) with respect to benefits attributable to service other than as a public safety officer?

A–24. Yes. Benefits attributable to service other than as a public safety officer are eligible for favorable tax treatment under § 402(l), as long as the individual separates from service as a public safety officer, by reason of disability or after attainment of normal retirement age, with the employer maintaining the Eligible Government Plan.

Q–25. If an eligible retired public safety officer dies, are amounts subtracted from distributions made to the decedent's surviving spouse or dependents eligible for favorable tax treatment under § 402(l)?

A–25. No. Section 402(l) provides that the distribution is not includible in the gross income of an employee who is an eligible retired public safety officer. Thus, the exclusion would not extend to amounts subtracted from distributions to other distributees.

Q–26. Is an eligible retired public safety officer limited in the amount that the officer can exclude from gross income for distributions from an Eligible Government Plan used to pay qualified health insurance premiums?

A–26. Yes. The aggregate amount that is permitted to be excluded, with respect to any taxable year, from an eligible retired public safety officer's gross income by reason of § 402(l) is limited to $3,000. For purposes of applying this $3,000 limitation, distributions with respect to the eligible retired public safety officer that are used to pay for qualified health insurance premiums from all Eligible Government Plans are aggregated.

Q–27. Are amounts used to pay qualified health insurance premiums that are excluded from gross income under § 402(l) taken into account for purposes of determining the itemized deduction for medical care expenses under § 213?

A–27. No. Amounts used to pay qualified health insurance premiums that are excluded from gross income under § 402(l) are not taken into account in determining the itemized deduction for medical care expenses under § 213.

VII. SECTION 904 OF PPA '06

Prior to the effective date of PPA '06 § 904, a defined contribution plan satisfied the minimum vesting requirements of Code § 411(a) with respect to employer nonelective contributions if it maintained a 5-year vesting schedule or a 3 to 7 year vesting schedule. Section 904 of PPA '06 amended the minimum vesting requirements to require faster vesting of employer nonelective contributions to a defined contribution plan. Under Code § 411(a)(2)(B) as amended by § 904 of PPA '06, a defined contribution plan satisfies the minimum vesting requirements with respect to employer nonelective contributions if it has a 3-year vesting schedule or a 2 to 6 year vesting schedule. Code § 411(a)(2)(B) as amended by § 904 of PPA '06 generally applies to contributions for plan years beginning after December 31, 2006.

Q–28. If a plan amendment changes the plan's vesting schedule to satisfy Code § 411(a)(2)(B) as amended by § 904 of PPA '06, is the plan amendment required to satisfy § 411(a)(10)?

A–28. Yes. A plan amendment that changes the vesting schedule must satisfy Code § 411(a)(10). Although § 411(a)(10)(B) would require a participant with at least 3 years of service to elect to have the nonforfeitable percentage of his accrued benefit determined without regard to the amendment, the plan must ensure that any such election satisfies the vesting requirements of § 411(a)(2)(B), as amended by § 904 of PPA '06. Thus, such a participant must be provided, at all times, a vesting percentage that is no less than the minimum under a vesting schedule that satisfies § 904 and the vesting percentage determined under the plan without regard to the amendment. Under Temporary Regulation § 1.411(a)–8T, no election need be provided for any participant whose nonforfeitable percentage under the plan, as amended, at any time cannot be less than such percentage determined without regard to such amendment.

Q–29. Can a plan have separate vesting schedules for employer nonelective contributions that are and are not subject to Code § 411(a)(2)(B), as amended by § 904 of PPA '06?

A–29. Yes. A plan can have a vesting schedule for employer nonelective contributions for plan years beginning after December 31, 2006, and another vesting schedule for other employer nonelective contributions under the plan, provided that the plan separately accounts for the contributions made under the vesting schedule in effect prior to the first day of the first plan year beginning after December 31, 2006, and the vesting schedule for employer nonelective contributions for plan years beginning after December 31, 2006, satisfies Code § 411(a)(2)(B), as amended by § 904 of PPA '06.

Q–30. If a plan maintains a bifurcated vesting schedule, how is it determined whether a contribution is for a plan year beginning before January 1, 2007?

A–30. A contribution is for a plan year that begins before January 1, 2007, if it is allocated under the terms of the plan as of a date in that plan year and is not subject to any conditions that have not been satisfied by the end of that plan year. This applies even if the contribution is not made until the next plan year. Thus, for example, if a plan with a calendar-year plan year makes a contribution as of December 31, 2006, based on compensation and service in 2006, and the contribution is not contingent on the occurrence of an event after 2006, then the contribution is treated as made for the 2006 plan year and is not subject to Code § 411(a)(2)(B), as amended by § 904 of PPA '06, even if it is not contributed until 2007. Forfeitures and ESOP allocations from a suspense account are treated in the same manner for this purpose.

VIII. SECTION 1102 OF PPA '06

Section 1102 of PPA '06 makes certain changes to the notice requirements related to distributions. Section 1102(a) provides that a notice required to be provided under § 402(f), § 411(a)(11), or § 417 may be provided to a participant as much as 180 days before the annuity starting date. Section 1102(b) directs the Secretary to modify the regulations under § 411(a)(11) of the Code and § 205 of ERISA to provide that the description of a participant's right to defer a distribution must also include a description of the consequences of failing to defer receipt of a distribution. The modifications made by § 1102 apply to years beginning after December 31, 2006. However, § 1102(b)(2)(B) provides that a plan will not be treated as failing to meet the new requirements under § 1102(b) if the plan administrator makes a reasonable attempt to comply with the new requirements under that section during the period that is within 90 days of the issuance of regulations required by § 1102(b).

Q–31. How does the effective date of § 1102 operate?

A–31. The provisions of § 1102 apply to plan years that begin after December 31, 2006. This means that the new rules relating to the content of the notices apply only to notices issued in those plan years, without regard to the annuity starting date for the distributions. Similarly, the 180-day period for distributing notices applies to notices distributed in a plan year that begins after December 31, 2006. This change to the 180-day period also modifies the definition of the maximum QJSA explanation period under § 1.411(d)–3(g), which is used in applying the timing rules for the effective date of a plan amendment under the rules of § 1.411(d)–3(c) and (f) in the case of an amendment that is adopted in a plan year that begins after December 31, 2006.

Q–32. Is a plan required to revise the notice under § 411 pursuant to the modifications made by § 1102(b) before the regulations are amended to reflect the requirement?

A–32. Yes. A plan administrator is required to revise the notice under § 411 to reflect the modifications to the requirements made by § 1102(b) for notices provided in plan years beginning after December 31, 2006. However, pursuant to § 1102(b)(2)(B) of PPA '06, a plan will not be treated as failing to meet the new requirements under § 1102(b) if the plan administrator makes a reasonable attempt to comply with the new requirements under that section in the case of a notice that is provided prior to the 90th day after the issuance of regulations reflecting the modifications required by § 1102(b).

Q–33. Is there a safe harbor available to a plan administrator that would be considered a reasonable attempt to comply with the requirement in § 1102(b)(1) that a description of a participant's right to defer receipt of a distribution include a description of the consequences of failing to defer?

A–33. Yes. A description that is written in a manner reasonably calculated to be understood by the average participant and that includes the following information is a reasonable attempt to comply with the requirements of § 1102(b)(2)(B): (a) in the case of a defined benefit plan, a description of how much larger benefits will be if the commencement of distributions is deferred; (b) in the case of a defined contribution plan, a description indicating the investment options available under the plan (including fees) that will be available if distributions are deferred; and (c) the portion of the summary plan description that contains any special rules that might materially affect a participant's decision to defer. For purposes of clause (a), a plan administrator can use a description that includes the financial effect of deferring distributions, as described in § 1.417(a)(3)–1(d)(2)(i), based solely on the normal form of benefit.

IX. SECTION 1201 OF PPA '06

Section 1201(a) of PPA '06 adds § 408(d)(8) to the Code, which is applicable to distributions made in taxable years 2006 and 2007. Under § 408(d)(8), generally, if a distribution from an IRA owned by an individual after the individual has attained age 70½ is made directly by the trustee to certain organizations described in § 170(b)(1)(A), the distribution is excluded from gross income. The exclusion is only available to the extent that the distribution would otherwise have been includible in gross income, and § 408(d)(8)(D) provides a special rule for determining the amount that would otherwise be includible in gross income. In addition, the exclusion applies only if the contribution would otherwise qualify for a charitable contribution deduction under § 170 (without regard to the percentage limitations of § 170(b)). A distribution that is eligible for this exclusion is called a qualified charitable distribution.

Q–34. Is there an overall limit on the amount that may be excluded from gross income for qualified charitable distributions that are made in a year?

A–34. Yes. The income exclusion for qualified charitable distributions only applies to the extent that the aggregate amount of qualified charitable distributions made during any taxable year with respect to an IRA owner does not exceed $100,000. Thus, if an IRA owner maintains multiple IRAs in a taxable year, and qualified charitable distributions are made from more than one of these IRAs, the maximum total amount that may be excluded for that year by the IRA owner is $100,000. For married individuals filing a joint return, the limit is $100,000 per individual IRA owner.

Q–35. Is the exclusion for qualified charitable distributions available for a distribution made to any organization eligible to receive charitable contributions that are deductible by the donor for income tax purposes?

A–35. No. Qualified charitable distributions may be made to an organization described in § 170(b)(1)(A), other than supporting organizations described in

§ 509(a)(3) or donor advised funds that are described in § 4966(d)(2).

Q–36. Is the exclusion for qualified charitable distributions available for distributions from any type of IRA?

A–36. Generally, the exclusion for qualified charitable distributions is available for distributions from any type of IRA (including a Roth IRA described in § 408A and a deemed IRA described in § 408(q)) that is neither an ongoing SEP IRA described in § 408(k) nor an ongoing SIMPLE IRA described in § 408(p). For this purpose, a SEP IRA or a SIMPLE IRA is treated as ongoing if it is maintained under an employer arrangement under which an employer contribution is made for the plan year ending with or within the IRA owner's taxable year in which the charitable contributions would be made.

Q–37. Is the exclusion for qualified charitable distributions available for distributions from an IRA maintained for a beneficiary if the beneficiary has attained age 70½ before the distribution is made?

A–37. Yes. The exclusion from gross income for qualified charitable distributions is available for distributions from an IRA maintained for the benefit of a beneficiary after the death of the IRA owner if the beneficiary has attained age 70½ before the distribution is made.

Q–38. If a 2006 distribution satisfies all the requirements under § 408(d)(8), but it was made before August 17, 2006 (the date PPA '06 was enacted), is the amount distributed excludable as a qualified charitable distribution?

A–38. Yes. Section 408(d)(8) is applicable to distributions made at any time in 2006. Thus, a distribution made in 2006 that satisfies the requirements under § 408(d)(8) is a qualified charitable distribution even if it was made before August 17, 2006.

Q–39. Is the amount of a qualified charitable distribution deductible as a charitable contribution under § 170?

A–39. No. For purposes of determining the amount of charitable contributions that may be deducted under § 170, qualified charitable distributions which are excluded from income under § 408(d)(8) are not taken into account. However, qualified charitable distributions must still satisfy the requirements to be deductible charitable contributions under § 170 (other than the percentage limits of § 170(b)), including the substantiation requirements under § 170(f)(8).

Q–40. Is a qualified charitable distribution subject to withholding under § 3405?

A–40. No. A qualified charitable distribution is not subject to withholding under § 3405 because an IRA owner that requests such a distribution is deemed to have elected out of withholding under § 3405(a)(2). For purposes of determining whether a distribution requested by an IRA satisfies the requirements under § 408(d)(8), the IRA trustee, custodian, or issuer may rely upon reasonable representations made by the IRA owner.

Q–41. Is a check from an IRA made payable to a charitable organization described in § 408(d)(8) and delivered by the IRA owner to the charitable organization a direct payment to such organization?

A–41. Yes. If a check from an IRA is made payable to a charitable organization described in § 408(d)(8) and delivered by the IRA owner to the charitable organization, the payment to the charitable organization will be considered a direct payment by the IRA trustee to the charitable organization for purposes of § 408(d)(8)(B)(i).

Q–42. Will a qualified charitable distribution be taken into account in determining whether the required minimum distribution requirements of §§ 408(a)(6), 408(b)(3), and 408A(c)(5) have been satisfied?

A–42. Yes. The amount distributed in a qualified charitable distribution is an amount distributed from the IRA for purposes of §§ 408(a)(6), 408(b)(3), and 408A(c)(5).

Q–43. What are the tax consequences of a direct payment of an amount from an IRA to a charity where the transaction is intended to satisfy the requirements of § 408(d)(8) but fails to do so?

A–43. If an amount intended to be a qualified charitable distribution is paid to a charitable organization but fails to satisfy the requirements of § 408(d)(8), the amount paid is treated as (1) a distribution from the IRA to the IRA owner that is includible in gross income under the rules of § 408 or § 408A, as applicable; and (2) a contribution from the IRA owner to the charitable organization that is subject to the rules under § 170 (including the percentage limits of § 170(b)).

Q–44. Will a distribution made directly by the trustee to a § 170(b)(1)(A) organization (as permitted by § 408(d)(8)(B)(i)) be treated as a receipt by the IRA owner under § 4975(d)(9)?

A–44. Yes. The Department of Labor, which has interpretive jurisdiction with respect to § 4975(d), has advised Treasury and the IRS that a distribution made by an IRA trustee directly to a § 170(b)(1)(A) organization (as permitted by § 408(d)(8)(B)(i)) will be treated as a receipt by the IRA owner under § 4975(d)(9), and thus would not constitute a prohibited transaction. This would be true even if the individual for whose benefit the IRA is maintained had an outstanding pledge to the receiving charitable organization.

DRAFTING INFORMATION

The principal author of this notice is Angelique V. Carrington of the Employee Plans, Tax Exempt and Government Entities Division. For further information regarding this notice, please contact the Employee Plans taxpayer assistance telephone service at (877) 829–5500 (a toll-free number) between the hours of 8:30 am and 4:30 pm Eastern Time, Monday through Friday. Ms. Carrington may be reached at (202) 283–9888 (not a toll-free number).

Look-thru Rule for Related Controlled Foreign Corporations

Notice 2007–9

SECTION 1. OVERVIEW

This notice provides guidance under section 954(c)(6) of the Internal Revenue Code (Code) enacted by the Tax Increase Prevention and Reconciliation Act of 2005 and amended by the Tax Relief and Health Care Act of 2006. In general, and subject to certain limitations, section 954(c)(6) provides that dividends, interest, rents, and royalties received or accrued by one controlled foreign corporation (CFC) from another CFC which is a related person shall not be treated as foreign personal holding company income to the extent attributable or properly allocable to income of the related person which is neither subpart F income nor income treated as effectively connected with the conduct of a trade or business in the United States (ECI). The provisions of section 954(c)(6) apply to taxable years of foreign corporations beginning after December 31, 2005, and before January 1, 2009, and to taxable years of United States shareholders with or within which such taxable years of the foreign corporations end.

The Internal Revenue Service (IRS) and the Treasury Department intend to issue additional guidance concerning section 954(c)(6). The IRS and the Treasury Department expect to issue regulations that incorporate the guidance provided in this notice and in any subsequent guidance.

SECTION 2. BACKGROUND

Section 951(a)(1) provides that if a foreign corporation is a CFC for an uninterrupted period of 30 days or more during any taxable year, every person who is a United States shareholder of such corporation and who owns stock in such corporation on the last day, in such year, on which such corporation is a CFC shall include in its gross income, for its taxable year in which or with which such taxable year of the corporation ends, its *pro rata* share of the corporation's subpart F income for such year.

Section 957(a) defines a CFC as any foreign corporation if more than 50 percent of the total combined voting power of all classes of stock of such corporation entitled to vote, or more than 50 percent of the total value of the stock of such corporation, is owned (within the meaning of section 958(a)), or is considered as owned by applying the rules of ownership of section 958(b), by United States shareholders on any day during the taxable year of such corporation. Section 951(b) defines a United States shareholder as a United States person who owns (within the meaning of section 958(a)), or is considered as owning by applying the rules of ownership of section 958(b), 10 percent or more of the total combined voting power of all classes of stock entitled to vote of such foreign corporation.

Section 952(a)(2) provides that subpart F income includes foreign base company income (FBCI). Subject to certain exceptions, section 954(a)(1) provides that FBCI includes foreign personal holding company income (FPHCI) for the taxable year. Section 954(c)(1)(A) provides that FPHCI includes dividends, interest, royalties, rents, and annuities. Section 954(c) also provides special rules and exceptions to the definition of FPHCI (*e.g.*, sections 954(c)(2) and (3)).

Section 103(b) of the Tax Increase Prevention and Reconciliation Act of 2005 (TIPRA) (P.L. 109–222), enacted on May 17, 2006, added section 954(c)(6) to the Code. Section 426(a) of Division A of the Tax Relief and Health Care Act of 2006 (P.L. 109–432), enacted on December 20, 2006, made technical corrections to section 954(c)(6).

Section 954(c)(6)(A) provides that for purposes of section 954(c), dividends, interest, rents, and royalties received or accrued from a CFC which is a related person shall not be treated as FPHCI to the extent attributable or properly allocable (determined under rules similar to the rules of subparagraphs (C) and (D) of section 904(d)(3)) to income of the related person which is neither subpart F income nor ECI (section 954(c)(6) exception). For this purpose, interest includes factoring income which is treated as income equivalent to interest for purposes of section 954(c)(1)(E). Section 954(c)(6)(A) also provides that the Secretary shall prescribe such regulations as may be necessary or appropriate to carry out the provision, including regulations to prevent the abuse of the purposes of the provision.

Section 954(c)(6)(B) provides that subparagraph (A) applies to taxable years of foreign corporations beginning after December 31, 2005, and before January 1, 2009, and to taxable years of United States shareholders with or within which such taxable years of the foreign corporations end.

For purposes of section 954(c)(6), a related person has the meaning provided in section 954(d)(3) and Treas. Reg. § 1.954–1(f). The CFCs must be related persons only at the time the particular dividend, interest, rent, or royalty in question is received or accrued. The section 954(c)(6) exception is not elective, and so applies to all covered transactions.

SECTION 3. DIVIDENDS

For purposes of section 954(c)(6), the term "dividend" has the meaning provided in section 316(a), including any amount treated as a section 301(c)(1) distribution as a result of a redemption described in either section 302 or section 304. That term also includes gains treated as dividends pursuant to sections 964(e) and 356(a)(2).

If a CFC is an exchanging shareholder and includes in income as a deemed dividend the all earnings and profits amount pursuant to Treas. Reg. § 1.367(b)–3(b)(3)(i), such inclusion is not eligible for the section 954(c)(6) exception.

With respect to the types of dividends above that are eligible for the section 954(c)(6) exception, the earnings and profits of the distributing CFC need not be accumulated during a period when it was a CFC, or during a period when the CFC receiving the dividend was a related person. The key requirement in this regard is that the relevant CFCs are related persons at the time the dividend is received.

Dividends are not eligible for the section 954(c)(6) exception to the extent they are distributed out of earnings and profits that are attributable to subpart F income or income that is (or is treated as) ECI. Because of the way the subpart F rules operate, distributions of earnings from a CFC to a related CFC typically will not be attributable to subpart F income for purposes of the section 954(c)(6) exception. Such a distribution will be attributable either to earnings and profits which are, or have been, included in a United States shareholder's gross income under section 951(a) (*i.e.*, previously taxed income) or, to the extent the distributions are attributable to earnings and profits that are not PTI, to income that is not subpart F income. Dividends that are attributable to income that is (or is treated as) ECI are not eligible for the section 954(c)(6) exception.

SECTION 4. PARTNERSHIPS

If interest is received or accrued from a partnership with one or more partners that are CFCs, such interest will be treated as received or accrued from a CFC for purposes of section 954(c)(6) to the extent that such CFC partner would be treated as the payor of the interest under Treas. Reg. § 1.954–2(b)(4)(i)(B). Similarly, if rents or royalties are received or accrued from a partnership with one or more partners that are CFCs, such rents or royalties will be treated as received or accrued from a CFC for purposes of section 954(c)(6) to the extent that such CFC partner would be treated as the payor of the rents or royalties under Treas. Reg. § 1.954–2(b)(5)(i)(B).

If dividends, interest, rents, or royalties are received by a partnership with one or more partners that are CFCs, such amounts will be treated as received or accrued by a CFC for purposes of section 954(c)(6) to the extent provided under Treas. Reg. §§ 1.702–1(a)(8)(ii), 1.952–1(g), and 1.954–1(g), as applicable.

SECTION 5. ALLOCATION AND ATTRIBUTION RULES FOR INTEREST

This section applies for purposes of determining the extent to which interest is attributable or properly allocable to income of the related person which is neither subpart F income nor ECI.

(a) *Interest properly allocable or apportionable to non-subpart F income*

Interest is not eligible for the section 954(c)(6) exception to the extent the deduction for the interest payment is allocated and apportioned under section 954(b)(5) and Treas. Reg. § 1.954–1(a)(4) and (c) to reduce the related CFC payor's adjusted gross FBCI (as defined in Treas. Reg. § 1.954–1(a)(3)), adjusted gross insurance income (as defined in Treas. Reg. § 1.954–1(a)(6)), or any other category of income included in subpart F income under section 952(a).

In general, interest that is allocated and apportioned to income that is not subpart F income is eligible for the section 954(c)(6) exception (subject to the rules below for ECI), even if interest deductions exceed the gross income of the related CFC payor in the year paid or accrued. However, interest is not eligible for the section 954(c)(6) exception to the extent interest deductions create (or increase) a deficit which under section 952(c) may reduce the subpart F income of the related CFC payor or another CFC.

(b) *Interest properly allocable or apportionable to non-ECI*

Interest is not eligible for the section 954(c)(6) exception to the extent the deduction for the interest payment is allocated and apportioned under section 882(c) and Treas. Reg. § 1.882–5, to gross income of the related CFC payor that is (or is treated as) ECI, or as expressly provided by or pursuant to a U.S. income tax treaty or accompanying documents (such as an exchange of notes), is allocated and apportioned to gross income of the related CFC payor that is attributable to a U.S. permanent establishment.

This paragraph applies if, in a single taxable year, the related CFC payor incurs both interest expense that, but for the application of section 5(b) of this notice, is eligible for the section 954(c)(6) exception (section 954(c)(6) interest expense), and other interest expense. In such a case, the amount of interest expense that is treated as allocated and apportioned to gross income of the related CFC payor that is (or is treated as) ECI, or under an applicable treaty, that is allocated and apportioned to gross income of the related CFC payor that is attributable to a U.S. permanent establishment, is the related CFC payor's interest expense for the taxable year multiplied by a fraction equal to the amount of section 954(c)(6) interest expense over the related CFC payor's total interest expense incurred during the taxable year.

Interest is not eligible for the section 954(c)(6) exception to the extent interest deductions create (or increase) a net operating loss carryover that is effectively connected with the conduct of a trade or business within the United States (or that is attributable to a permanent establishment, in the context of an applicable U.S. income tax treaty).

SECTION 6. ALLOCATION AND ATTRIBUTION RULES FOR RENTS AND ROYALTIES

This section applies for purposes of determining the extent to which rents and royalties are attributable or properly allocable to income of the related person which is neither subpart F income nor ECI.

(a) *Rents and royalties properly allocable or apportionable to non-subpart F income*

Rents and royalties are not eligible for the section 954(c)(6) exception to the extent the deductions for the rent or royalty payments are allocated and apportioned under section 954(b)(5) and Treas. Reg. § 1.954–1(a)(4) and (c) to reduce the related CFC payor's adjusted gross FBCI (as defined in Treas. Reg. § 1.954–1(a)(3)), adjusted gross insurance income (as defined in Treas. Reg. § 1.954–1(a)(6)), or any other category of income included in subpart F income under section 952(a).

In general, rents and royalties that are allocated and apportioned to income that is not subpart F income are eligible for the section 954(c)(6) exception (subject to the rules below for ECI), even if deductions for such amounts exceed the gross income of the related CFC payor in the year paid or accrued. However, rents and royalties are not eligible for the section 954(c)(6) exception to the extent deductions for such amounts create (or increase) a deficit which under section 952(c) may reduce the subpart F income of the related CFC payor or another CFC.

(b) *Rents and royalties properly allocable or apportionable to non-ECI*

Rents and royalties are not eligible for the section 954(c)(6) exception to the extent the deductions for the rent or royalty payments are allocated and apportioned under section 882(c) and Treas. Reg. § 1.861–8, to gross income of the related CFC payor that is (or is treated as) ECI.

Rents and royalties are not eligible for the section 954(c)(6) exception to the extent deductions for such amounts create (or increase) a net operating loss carryover that is effectively connected with the conduct of a trade or business within the United States.

SECTION 7. ANTI-ABUSE RULES

(a) *Overview*

In addition to the general grant of regulatory authority, section 954(c)(6)(A) specifically grants the Secretary the authority to prescribe regulations to prevent the abuse of the purposes of section 954(c)(6). The transactions described below are abusive of the purposes of section 954(c)(6). However, the IRS and the Treasury Department do not intend this to be an exclusive list of abusive transactions and expect to provide further anti-abuse rules in subsequent guidance. For example, the IRS and the Treasury Department are considering a rule similar to the one described in section 7(d) of this notice for principal purpose domestic partnerships.

(b) *Amounts that reduce the U.S. income tax base, including factoring income*

Transactions abuse the purposes of section 954(c)(6) if they reduce income from the U.S. income tax base by having the net effect of creating a deduction of a payment, accrual, or loss of a person subject to U.S. tax without a corresponding inclusion in the subpart F income of the CFC recipient, where such inclusion would have resulted in the absence of section 954(c)(6).

For purposes of section 954(c)(6), interest includes factoring income which is treated as income equivalent to interest for purposes of section 954(c)(1)(E) and interest described in section 864(d) (collectively, factoring income). However, certain factoring income is not eligible for the section 954(c)(6) exception. Any factoring income derived from a transaction which has the net effect of creating a deduction of a payment, accrual, or loss of a person subject to U.S. tax without a corresponding inclusion in the subpart F income of the CFC recipient, where such inclusion would have resulted in the absence of section 954(c)(6), is not eligible for the section 954(c)(6) exception. The following example illustrates the application of this paragraph:

Example. (i) *Facts.* USP, a domestic corporation, owns 100% of the stock of CFC1 and CFC2. USP sells inventory to CFC1 in exchange for receivables. USP sells the CFC1 receivables to CFC2 at a discount, and CFC2 generates income on the collection of the CFC1 receivables.

(ii) *Analysis.* The income earned by CFC2 on the collection of receivables is related person factoring income as defined in section 864(d) and, therefore, is treated as interest income received on a loan from CFC2 to CFC1. However, because CFC2 acquired the CFC1 receivables from USP at a discount, resulting in a current loss for USP, such interest income is not eligible for the section 954(c)(6) exception.

(c) *Avoidance of section 956*

If a dividend reduces or eliminates the applicable earnings of a CFC, within the meaning of section 956(b)(1), such that it reduces a U.S. shareholder's inclusion pursuant to section 951(a)(1)(B), the dividend is not eligible for the section 954(c)(6) exception. See also Treas. Reg. § 1.956–1T(b)(4). The following example illustrates the application of this paragraph:

Example. (i) *Facts.* USP, a domestic corporation, owns 100% of the stock of CFC1 which, in turn, owns 100% of the stock of CFC2. At the beginning of Year 1, at a time when the stock of CFC2 has a value of $300 and CFC2 has zero applicable earnings (within the meaning of section 956(b)(1)), CFC2 loans $100 to USP in exchange for a note. During Year 1, CFC2 generates $100 of non-subpart F earnings and profits. Shortly before the end of Year 1, CFC2 distributes $100 to CFC1 that results in a $100 dividend to CFC1 and, as a result, CFC2 takes the position that it's applicable earnings under section 956(b)(1) are reduced from $100 to $0.

(ii) *Analysis.* The USP note held by CFC2 is United States property (within the meaning of section 956(c)(1)(C)), and CFC2 generated $100 of earnings and profits during Year 1. As a result, USP would have an income inclusion of $100 pursuant to section 951(a)(1)(B), but for the applicable earnings limitation under section 956(b)(1). However, as a result of the Year 1 dividend CFC2 paid to CFC1, CFC2 does not have any applicable earnings and USP, therefore, would not have a section 951(a)(1)(B) inclusion. Thus, the dividend income of CFC1 is not eligible for the section 954(c)(6) exception.

(d) *Use of options or similar interests*

When the use of options or similar interests causes a foreign corporation to become a CFC payor, and a principal purpose for the use of the options or similar interests is to qualify dividends, interest, rents, or royalties paid by the foreign corporation for the section 954(c)(6) exception, the dividends, interest, rents, or royalties received or accrued from such foreign corporation will not be treated as being received or accrued from a CFC payor and, therefore, will not be eligible for the section 954(c)(6) exception. For purposes of this paragraph, an interest that is similar to an option includes, but is not limited to, a warrant, a convertible debt instrument, an instrument other than debt that is convertible into stock, a put, a stock interest subject to risk of forfeiture, and a contract to acquire or sell stock.

(e) *Change of character of income through the use of a conduit entity*

When a transaction changes the character of the underlying income, is effected through the use of a conduit entity, and a principal purpose for the use of the conduit entity is to qualify the underlying income for the section 954(c)(6) exception, the dividends, interest, rents, or royalties received or accrued will not be treated as being received or accrued from a related CFC and, therefore, will not be eligible for the section 954(c)(6) exception. The following example illustrates the application of this paragraph:

Example. (i) *Facts.* USP, a domestic corporation, owns 100% of the stock of CFC1, a country Y corporation, and CFC2, a country Z corporation. FC, a country Z corporation, is not a CFC, but is a related person under section 954(d)(3). In year 1, FC leases property from CFC1 for $100. USP causes the rental payment to be made through CFC2. Thus, CFC2 receives a payment from FC that is excluded from FPHCI under section 954(c)(3)(A)(i). CFC2 then makes a payment to CFC1, in satisfaction of the rent owed by FC, which is intended to qualify for the section 954(c)(6) exception. A principal purpose for the involvement of CFC2 in the transaction is to qualify the rental payment from FC to CFC1 as eligible for the section 954(c)(6) exception.

(ii) *Analysis.* If the rental payment had been made directly from FC to CFC1, it would have been included as FPHCI under section 954(c)(1)(A). By causing the payment to be made through CFC2, USP sought to convert the character of the income from FPHCI to income excluded from FPHCI. However, because a principal purpose of including CFC2 in the transaction as a conduit entity was to avoid inclusion of the rental payment from FC to CFC1 as FPHCI, the payment from CFC2 to CFC1 will be treated as being made from FC to CFC1. Therefore, the payment is not eligible for the section 954(c)(6) exception.

SECTION 8. EFFECTIVE DATE

Sections 3, 4, 5, 6, 7(b) and 7(c) of this notice are effective for taxable years of foreign corporations beginning after December 31, 2005. Sections 7(d) and 7(e) of this notice are effective for taxable years of foreign corporations beginning after December 31, 2006.

SECTION 9. DRAFTING INFORMATION

The principal author of this notice is Paul J. Carlino of the Office of Associate Chief Counsel (International). For further information regarding this notice, contact Mr. Carlino at (202) 622–3840 (not a toll-free call).

Request for Comments

Comments may be submitted to CC:PA:LPD:PR (Notice 2007–9), Room 5203, Internal Revenue Service, PO Box 7604, Washington, DC 20044. Submissions may also be hand-delivered Monday through Friday between the hours of 8 a.m. and 4 p.m. to the Courier's Desk at

1111 Constitution Avenue, NW, Washington, DC 20224, Attn: CC:PA:LPD:PR (Notice 2007–9) Room 5203. Submissions may also be sent electronically via the internet to the following email address: *Notice.comments@irscounsel.treas.gov*. Include the notice number (Notice 2007–9) in the subject line.

Communications Excise Tax; Toll Telephone Service

Notice 2007–11

SECTION 1. PURPOSE

This notice amplifies, clarifies, and modifies Notice 2006–50, 2006–25 I.R.B. 1141. That notice provides that the tax imposed by § 4251 of the Internal Revenue Code (relating to communications excise tax) does not apply to amounts paid for long distance service and bundled service (collectively, nontaxable service) and also provides that taxpayers may request a credit or refund of tax on nontaxable service that was billed to the taxpayer after February 28, 2003, and before August 1, 2006, only on their 2006 federal income tax returns. This notice—

(a) Provides the conditions under which individual taxpayers may use the standard amounts announced in IR–2006–137 (August 31, 2006) on their 2006 federal income tax returns to request a credit or refund of the excise tax paid on nontaxable service;

(b) Provides guidance regarding the Business and Nonprofit Estimation Method, announced in IR–2006–179 (November 16, 2006);

(c) Answers questions that have been raised since the issuance of Notice 2006–50; and

(d) Modifies the requirement for claims filed on or before May 25, 2006.

SECTION 2. BACKGROUND

For the statutory background of the tax imposed by § 4251, see section 2 of Notice 2006–50. When used in this notice, *local-only service*, *long distance service*, and *nontaxable service* have the meaning given to the terms in section 3 of Notice 2006–50. *Bundled service* has the meaning given to the term by section 5 of this notice.

SECTION 3. STANDARD AMOUNT

(a) *Conditions to allowance of standard amount*. A request for credit or refund of the standard amount, instead of the actual amount of federal communications excise tax paid for nontaxable service, may be made on a 2006 Form 1040 Series, *U.S. Individual Income Tax Return*, if any person filing the return, or any dependent listed on the return—

(1) Paid for any nontaxable service (other than for a prepaid telephone card or prepaid cellular telephone) that was billed to the taxpayer after February 28, 2003, and before August 1, 2006;

(2) Paid all federal communications excise taxes billed by their telecommunications provider after February 28, 2003, and before August 1, 2006;

(3) Has not received a credit or refund of these taxes from the telecommunications provider;

(4) Has not requested a credit or refund from the telecommunications provider or, if so requested, has withdrawn any such request; and

(5) Did not file any other claim or request for credit or refund with the IRS for the federal communications excise tax for a period after February 28, 2003.

(b) *Calculating standard amounts*—(1) *In general*—(i) *2006 Form 1040 Series (other than EZ)*. To determine the standard amount, taxpayers must first determine the number of exemptions for which they are entitled on their 2006 Form 1040 Series federal income tax return (other than the 2006 Form 1040 EZ). The Instructions to the 2006 Form 1040 Series federal income tax return and Publication 501, *Exemptions, Standard Deduction, and Filing Information*, provide guidance on determining the correct number of exemptions. Once the individual determines the number of exemptions, the individual can select the appropriate standard amount based upon the number of those exemptions. Individuals should refer to the 2006 federal income tax return instructions to ensure that the standard amount is entered on the appropriate part of the return.

(ii) *2006 Form 1040 EZ*. On line 5, a taxpayer that checks the box for "you" is treated as having one exemption. A taxpayer that checks the boxes for "you" and "spouse" is treated as having two exemptions.

(2) *Amounts*—(i) For each 2006 Form 1040 Series federal income tax return filed showing one exemption for purposes of determining the standard amount, the standard amount allowed on that return is $30.

(ii) For each 2006 Form 1040 Series federal income tax return filed showing two exemptions for purposes of determining the standard amount, the standard amount allowed on that return is $40.

(iii) For each 2006 Form 1040 Series federal income tax return filed showing three exemptions for purposes of determining the standard amount, the standard amount allowed on that return is $50.

(iv) For each 2006 Form 1040 Series federal income tax return filed showing four or more exemptions for purposes of determining the standard amount, the standard amount allowed on that return is $60.

(c) *Interest*. The standard amount represents both the overpayment of the federal communications excise tax paid on nontaxable service and the interest on that overpayment.

(d) *Actual Amounts*. To request a credit or refund for the actual amount of federal communications excise tax paid, taxpayers must complete Form 8913, *Credit for Federal Telephone Excise Tax Paid*, and attach that form to their 2006 Form 1040 Series federal income tax return.

(e) *Examples*. The following examples illustrate the application of this section.

Example 1. A, an individual, files a joint return with Z, A's spouse. A meets the conditions to allowance described in paragraph (a) of this section. A used the 2006 federal income tax return instructions to determine that their correct number of exemptions is two. A may request the credit or refund of the federal communications excise tax under § 4251 for $40.

Example 2. B, an individual, used the 2006 federal income tax return instructions to determine that she had one exemption. B further used her telephone bills for the period March 1, 2003, through July 31, 2006, to determine that the total amount paid for federal communications excise tax under § 4251 for nontaxable service to all telecommunications providers was $45. Completing Form 8913 and attaching it to her 2006 Form 1040 Series federal income tax return, B may request a credit or refund of $45, the actual amount she paid in federal communications excise tax on nontaxable service under § 4251. As an alternative, B may request a credit or refund of the standard amount of $30 without having to complete Form 8913.

SECTION 4. DISTINCTION BETWEEN LOCAL-ONLY SERVICE AND BUNDLED SERVICE

(a) *Technology for transmitting telephone call.* The method for sending or receiving a call, such as on a landline telephone, wireless (cellular) telephone or some other method, does not affect whether a service is local-only or bundled.

(b) *Combined local exchanges.* If two or more telecommunications providers combine their resources to expand the geographic area that each treats as "local" service and each bills its customers for that service as local-only service, then that service is local-only service.

(c) *Billing method.* Section 3(a) of Notice 2006–50 and section 5 of this notice provide that bundled service is local and long distance service provided under a plan that does not separately state the charge for the local telephone service. Thus, if local and long distance service is billed to a customer on a single bill but the telecommunications company separately states the amount paid for local-only service and the amount paid for long distance service, the amount paid for local-only service is subject to federal communications excise tax.

(d) *Examples.* The following examples illustrate the application of this section.

Example 1. Customer A purchases telecommunications service from B, a telecommunications provider. Such service includes both local-only service and long distance service. B's bill to A states $X for telecommunications service. The bill does not separately state a charge for either local-only service or long distance service. Since the bill does not separately state the charge for local-only service, the service is a bundled service. Thus, the entire amount of A's telecommunications service is bundled service and thus nontaxable service.

Example 2. Customer C purchases telecommunications service from D, a telecommunications provider. Such service includes both local-only service and long distance service. D's bill to C states $X amount for telecommunications service. The bill further states $Y amount for local-only service and $Z amount for long distance service. Since the charges for local-only service and long distance service are separately stated, the service is not bundled service. Accordingly, only the amounts charged for long distance service are for nontaxable service; tax is imposed on the amounts paid for the local-only service.

SECTION 5. CLARIFICATION OF DEFINITION OF BUNDLED SERVICE

(a) *Present definition.* Section 3(a) of Notice 2006–50 defines bundled service as local and long distance service provided under a plan that does not separately state the charge for the local telephone service. Bundled service includes, for example, Voice over Internet Protocol service, prepaid telephone cards, and plans that provide both local and long distance service for either a flat monthly fee or a charge that varies with the elapsed transmission time for which the service is used. Telecommunications companies provide bundled service for both landline and wireless (cellular) service.

(b) *Reason for clarification.* The example in the second sentence of the definition of bundled service incorrectly assumes that all Voice over Internet Protocol (VoIP) service would provide both local and long distance service and that the charges for the two services would not be separately stated. As noted in section 4(a) of this notice, the method of transmitting a call is not a factor in determining whether a service is local-only or bundled. Accordingly, a VoIP service that provides local-only service is treated as local-only service.

(c) *Revised definition.* Accordingly, the definition of bundled service is clarified to read as follows:

> Bundled service is local and long distance service provided under a plan that does not separately state the charge for the local telephone service. Bundled service includes plans that provide both local and long distance service for either a flat monthly fee or a charge that varies with the elapsed transmission time for which the service is used. Telecommunications companies provide bundled service for both landline and wireless (cellular) service. If Voice over Internet Protocol service provides both local and long distance service and the charges are not separately stated, such service is bundled service.

SECTION 6. PREPAID TELEPHONE CARDS (PTC)

(a) *In general*—(1) *Prepaid telephone cards.* Section 4251(d) and § 49.4251–4 of the Facilities and Services Excise Taxes Regulations provide rules for prepaid telephone cards (PTC). Section 49.4251–4(b) defines PTC as a card or similar arrangement that permits its holder to obtain a fixed amount of communications services by means of a code (such as a personal identification number (PIN)) or other access device provided by the carrier and to pay for those services in advance. The amount paid for PTCs is determined under the rules of §§ 4251(d)(1) and (2) and § 49.4251–4(c). Under this notice, the PTC will be treated as nontaxable service unless a PTC expressly states it is for local-only service.

(2) *Other cards.* This section does not address cards that permit the holder to purchase various services in addition to telecommunications services. Such services include, but are not limited to, ring tone downloads, music downloads, text messaging, picture messaging, web browsing, game downloads, or screen saver downloads.

(b) *Application of the tax*—(1) *Definitions.* Section 49.4251–4(b) provides that—

(i) *Carrier* means a telecommunications carrier as defined in 47 U.S.C. 153.

(ii) *Holder* means a person that purchases other than for resale.

(iii) *Transferee* means the first person that is not a carrier to whom a PTC is transferred by a carrier.

(2) *Imposition, liability, and collection.* Section 4251(d) provides that the § 4251 tax is imposed on the transfer of a PTC to a transferee; § 49.4251–4(d)(1) provides that the person liable for the tax is the transferee and that the person responsible for collecting the tax generally is the carrier transferring the PTC to the transferee. Section 49.4251–4(d)(1) further provides that if a holder purchases a PTC from a transferee reseller, the amount the holder pays for the PTC is not treated as an amount paid for communications services and thus tax is not imposed on that payment.

(c) *Person eligible to request credit or refund.* The transferee is the person liable for the tax paid on a PTC and thus generally is the person eligible to request a credit or refund of the tax it paid. The carrier is eligible to request a credit or refund only if it meets the conditions of section 5(d)(4) of Notice 2006–50. The holder is not liable for the tax and thus cannot request a credit or refund.

SECTION 7. PREPAID CELLULAR TELEPHONES

(a) *In general*—(1) *Prepaid cellular telephones.* Certain telecommunications providers offer wireless (cellular) telecommunications service on a prepaid service basis (prepaid telephones) whereby a customer purchases the cellular telephone with a set number of minutes available for telecommunications. When the customer exhausts the number of minutes on the prepaid telephone, the customer may purchase additional minutes. The customer does not enter into a contract with the telecommunications provider; there are no service charges after the additional purchase and no monthly bills. Under this notice, the prepaid telephone will be treated as nontaxable service unless the terms of the prepaid telephone service expressly state it is for local-only service.

(2) *Other prepaid cellular telephones.* This section does not address arrangements that permit the holder to purchase various services in addition to telecommunications services. Such services include, but are not limited to, ring tone downloads, music downloads, text messaging, picture messaging, web browsing, game downloads, or screen saver downloads.

(b) *Application of the tax.* Rules similar to the rules for PTCs, as described in section 6 of this notice, apply to prepaid telephones. Thus, the person liable for tax is the person (transferee) that buys the prepaid telephone from the telecommunications provider (carrier) and the carrier is responsible for collecting the tax. Any holder of a prepaid telephone (that is, a person that buys the prepaid telephone other than for resale) is not liable for tax.

(c) *Person eligible to request credit or refund.* The transferee is the person liable for the tax paid on a prepaid telephone and thus generally is the person eligible to request a credit or refund of the tax it paid. The carrier is eligible to request a credit or refund only if it meets the conditions of section 5(d)(4) of Notice 2006–50. The holder is not liable for the tax and thus cannot request a credit or refund.

SECTION 8. CHARGES IN CONNECTION WITH LOCAL-ONLY SERVICE

(a) *Background.* Section 3(b) of Notice 2006–50 defines local-only service as including certain services and facilities provided in connection with local telephone service, even though these services may also be used in connection with long distance service. As examples, the notice cites to Rev. Rul. 72–537, 1972–2 C.B. 574 (telephone amplifier), Rev. Rul. 73–171, 1973–1 C.B. 445 (automatic call distributing equipment), and Rev. Rul. 73–269, 1973–1 C.B. 444 (special telephone).

(b) *Subscriber line charges.* In addition to the examples in paragraph (a) of this section, amounts paid for subscriber line charges, which are described in Rev. Rul. 87–108, 1987–2 C.B. 260, are also amounts paid for local telephone service. This charge may appear on a bill as "Federal Access Charge," "Customer or Subscriber Line Charge," or "Interstate Access Charge."

(c) *Universal service fees*—(1) *Background.* All telecommunications companies that provide interstate and international telecommunications service contribute to the federal Universal Service Fund (USF). Their contributions support four Universal Service programs established and overseen by the Federal Communications Commission (FCC). Some telecommunications companies recover their contribution to the USF directly from their customers by billing them for this charge. The FCC does not require companies to pass on these costs to their customers. Each company makes a business decision about whether and how to recover USF costs. A company that separately states this charge on a bill may call it a "Federal Universal Service Fee" or "Universal Connectivity Fee."

(2) *Application.* Because telecommunications providers charge the USF to their customers in connection with their customers' long distance service, amounts paid for separately stated USF amounts are not amounts paid for local-only service.

SECTION 9. PERSON TO MAKE REQUEST IF TAXPAYER IS NO LONGER IN BUSINESS OR DECEASED

Neither Notice 2006–50 nor this notice create any special rules regarding the person to request a credit or refund of tax for a taxpayer that no longer exists or is deceased. The same rules that apply to requests for credits or refunds of other federal taxes also apply to similar requests of the tax imposed under § 4251. These rules depend upon the facts and circumstances relating to the reasons that the taxpayer no longer exists. The Form 8913 Instructions and Publication 559, *Survivors, Executors, and Administrators*, provide general guidance for taxpayers regarding deceased taxpayers.

SECTION 10. EFFECT OF NOTICE 2006–50 ON STATE AND LOCAL TELECOMMUNICATIONS TAXES

Neither Notice 2006–50 nor this notice affect the ability of state or local governments to impose or collect telecommunication taxes under the respective statutes of those governments.

SECTION 11. NO OBLIGATION OF TELECOMMUNICATIONS PROVIDERS TO SUPPLY RECORDS TO CUSTOMERS

The IRS has been asked to require telecommunications providers to supply their customers with those customers' telecommunications bills for periods after February 28, 2003, and before August 1, 2006. Neither Notice 2006–50 nor this notice requires telecommunications providers to supply billing records to their customers.

SECTION 12. BUSINESS AND NONPROFIT ESTIMATION METHOD

(a) *In general.* This section provides rules for the Business and Nonprofit Estimation Method (EM) that eligible entities may use to determine the amount of their credit or refund for nontaxable service. Eligible entities may, but are not required to, use the EM instead of the actual amount of federal communications excise tax they paid on nontaxable service to calculate the amount of their credit or refund.

(b) *Definitions*. The following definitions apply to this section.

(1) *Eligible entity* means—

(i) Any—

(A) Business entity (including a corporation or partnership);

(B) Trust or estate;

(C) Tax-exempt organization; and

(D) Individual owner of rental property and any self-employed individual (including an independent contractor, sole proprietor, or farmer) but only if the individual (including a married couple filing a joint return) reports gross rental and business income totaling more than $25,000 on his or her 2006 federal income tax return;

(ii) That was in operation during any time from March 1, 2003 through July 31, 2006; and

(iii) That received and paid for telecommunications service that was reflected on bills dated in April 2006 and September 2006.

(2) *Total telephone expenses* means all amounts paid to every telecommunications provider used by the eligible entity for telephone service that were billed after February 28, 2003, and before August 1, 2006. These amounts include, but are not limited to, amounts paid for long distance service, local-only service, bundled service, 900 number service, universal service fees, federal, state, and local taxes. If an eligible entity is billed for telephone and non-telephone services on one bill each month and does not separately track non-telephone services in its books and records, the entire amount of that bill is included in total telephone expenses. An eligible entity may determine the amount of its total telephone expenses by examining its books and records, including, for example, its general ledger, check register, and canceled checks.

(3) *Employee* means any person working for the taxpayer full or part time as reported on the eligible entity's Form 941, *Employer's Quarterly Federal Tax Return*, for the 2nd quarter of 2006, other than any person employed as a household employee, in a non-pay status, on a pension, or an active member of the Armed Forces.

(c) *Using the EM to determine the amount of the credit or refund*—(1) *Determining the federal excise tax as a percentage of the telephone bill*—(i) First, determine the amount of federal communications excise tax on all telephone bills dated in April 2006 and all telephone bills dated in September 2006. The amount is generally separately stated on the bill as "FET" or "federal tax".

(ii) Next, for all the April telephone bills and all the September telephone bills, divide the amount of federal communications excise tax included on the bills by the total telephone expenses on the bills. The resulting amounts are the April and September percentages, respectively.

(iii) Next, subtract the September percentage from the April percentage. For purposes of this notice, this amount is the federal excise tax percentage (FETP).

(2) *Capping the FETP*—(i) Determine the number of employees.

(ii) For taxpayers with 250 or fewer employees, the FETP is capped at 2 percent.

(iii) For taxpayers with more than 250 employees, the FETP is capped at 1 percent.

(d) *Calculating the amount of the credit or refund*—(1) *Records kept on a monthly basis*. If the entity has maintained its telephone expense records on a monthly basis, multiply the FETP amount by the taxpayer's monthly total telephone expenses for each month of the 41 month period from March 2003 through July 2006. The product of this calculation is the taxpayer's credit or refund amount.

(2) *Records kept on an annual basis*. If the entity has maintained its telephone expense records on an annual basis rather than a monthly basis, prorate its annual amount equally to each month of that year. Thus, for example, a taxpayer maintaining annual telephone expense records for 2003 would divide its total telephone expenses by 12. Next, the taxpayer would use that monthly amount to complete the calculations for the credit or refund amount for 2003.

(e) *Actual Amounts*. Use of the EM is optional. Taxpayers may use the actual amounts paid for federal communications excise tax for nontaxable service to determine the amount of their credit or refund.

(f) *Examples*. The following examples illustrate the application of this section.

Example 1—(i) *Facts*. Business A has 250 employees. A's April 2006 telephone bill is $1,700, including federal communications excise tax of $47.60. A's September 2006 telephone bill is $1,600, including federal communications excise tax of $24.00. A's total telephone expenses, for which it does not have monthly records, are as follows:

2003 — $10,800.00
2004 — $16,000.00
2005 — $20,000.00
2006 — $20,571.37.

(ii) *Determining the April and September percentages*. A's April percentage is 2.8 percent (47.60 ÷ 1,700). A's September percentage is 1.5 percent (24 ÷ 1,600).

(iii) *Determining the FETP*. The difference between A's April percentage and September percentage is 1.3 percent (2.8 - 1.5). Thus, the FETP is 1.3 percent.

(iv) *Capping the FETP*. Because A's number of employees does not exceed 250, A's FETP is not capped at 1 percent.

(v) *Prorating*. Because A did not maintain its total telephone expense records by month, it prorates those amounts equally to each month within the March 2003 — July 2006 period for each particular year. For 2003, A divides its total telephone expense of $10,800 by 12 and multiplies that result by 10 (the number of months between March and December). ([10,800 ÷ 12] x 10 = 9,000.) For 2006, A divides its total telephone expense of $20,571.37 by 12 and multiplies that result by 7 (the number of months between January and July). ([20,571.37 ÷ 12] x 7 = 12,000.)

(vi) *Calculating the amount of the credit or refund*. Using the EM, the amount of A's credit or refund is calculated as follows:

2003: $9,000 x .013 = $117 (117÷10 = 11.7) Monthly amount $11.70

2004: $16,000 x .013 = $208 (208÷12 = 17.33) Monthly amount $17.33

2005: $20,000 x .013 = $260 (260÷12 = 21.67) Monthly amount $21.67

2006: $12,000 x .013 = $156 (156÷7 = 22.29) Monthly amount $22.29

(vii) *Reporting the credit or refund amounts on Form 8913*—(A) Because the credit or refund period does not align with the calendar quarters, Form 8913 requires taxpayers to report the credit or refund amounts in 13 three-month intervals and one two-month interval. Thus, A would report credit or refund amounts on Form 8913 as follows:

March, April, May 2003 — $35.10 (11.70 x 3 = 35.10)

June, July, August 2003 — $35.10 (11.70 x 3 = 35.10)

September, October, November 2003 — $35.10 (11.70 x 3 = 35.10)

December 2003, January, February 2004 — $46.36 (11.70 + [17.33 x 2] = 46.36)

March, April, May 2004 — $51.99 (17.33 x 3 = 51.99)

June, July, August 2004 — $51.99 (17.33 x 3 = 51.99)

September, October, November 2004 — $51.99 (17.33 x 3 = 51.99)

December 2004, January, February 2005 — $60.67 (17.33 + [21.67 x 2] = 60.67)

March, April, May 2005 — $65.01 (21.67 x 3 = 65.01)

June, July, August 2005 — $65.01 (21.67 x 3 = 65.01)

September, October, November 2005 — $65.01 (21.67 x 3 = 65.01)

December 2005, January, February 2006 — $66.25 (21.67 + [22.29 x 2] = 66.25)

March, April, May 2006 — $66.87 (22.29 x 3 = 66.87)

June, July 2006 — $44.58 (22.29 x 2 = 44.58)

(B) After determining the amount of credit or refund using the EM, A reports the amounts on Form 8913, and attaches the Form 8913 to A's 2006 federal income tax return.

Example 2. The same facts as *Example 1* except that A has 500 employees. A's FETP is capped at 1 percent. Thus, A must make the same calculation as in *Example 1* to determine the proper amount of A's credit or refund of federal communications excise tax using the FETP of 1 percent, rather than 1.3 percent.

SECTION 13. FORM 1040EZ–T, REQUEST FOR REFUND OF FEDERAL TELEPHONE EXCISE TAX

Individuals who do not have to file a federal income tax return and who meet the conditions for requesting a refund of the federal communications excise tax may file Form 1040EZ–T to request the refund. Individuals requesting a refund of actual amounts of federal communications excise tax paid must complete Form 8913 and attach that form to the Form 1040EZ–T.

SECTION 14. MODIFICATION OF PROVISION REGARDING REQUESTS FOR CREDIT OR REFUND

(a) *Present requirement.* Section 5(g) of Notice 2006–50 provides as follows:

> *Requests that do not follow the provisions of this notice.* Requests that do not follow the provisions of this notice (whether filed before or after its publication)—
>
> (1) Will not be processed to the extent they relate to the tax paid on nontaxable service that was billed after February 28, 2003; and
>
> (2) Will be processed normally to the extent they relate to the tax paid on nontaxable service that was billed before March 1, 2003.

(b) *Reason for modification.* Many of the pending refund claims that were filed on or before May 25, 2006, include refund claims for nontaxable service that was billed before March 1, 2003, and after February 28, 2003. In the interest of sound tax administration and efficiency, the IRS will process all claims for credit or refund that were filed on or before May 25, 2006.

(c) *Revised requirement.* Accordingly, section 5(g) of Notice 2006–50 is modified to read as follows:

> (1) Requests that do not follow the provisions of Notice 2006–50 and that were filed on or before May 25, 2006, will be processed normally.
>
> (2) Requests that were filed on or after May 26, 2006, and do not follow the provisions of Notice 2006–50, will not be processed to the extent they relate to the tax paid on nontaxable service that was billed after February 28, 2003.

SECTION 15. EFFECT ON OTHER DOCUMENTS

Notice 2006–50 is amplified, clarified, and modified.

SECTION 16. DRAFTING INFORMATION

The principal author of this notice is Barbara B. Franklin of the Office of the Associate Chief Counsel (Passthroughs and Special Industries). For further information regarding this notice, contact 202–622–3130 (not a toll-free number).

Weighted Average Interest Rates Update

Notice 2007–12

This notice provides guidance as to the corporate bond weighted average interest rate and the permissible range of interest rates specified under § 412(b)(5)(B)(ii)(II) of the Internal Revenue Code. In addition, it provides guidance as to the interest rate on 30-year Treasury securities under § 417(e)(3)(A)(ii)(II).

CORPORATE BOND WEIGHTED AVERAGE INTEREST RATE

Sections 412(b)(5)(B)(ii) and 412(l)(7)(C)(i), as amended by the Pension Funding Equity Act of 2004 and by the Pension Protection Act of 2006, provide that the interest rates used to calculate current liability and to determine the required contribution under § 412(l) for plan years beginning in 2004 through 2007 must be within a permissible range based on the weighted average of the rates of interest on amounts invested conservatively in long term investment grade corporate bonds during the 4-year period ending on the last day before the beginning of the plan year.

Notice 2004–34, 2004–1 C.B. 848, provides guidelines for determining the corporate bond weighted average interest rate and the resulting permissible range of interest rates used to calculate current liability. That notice establishes that the corporate bond weighted average is based on the monthly composite corporate bond rate derived from designated corporate bond indices. The methodology for determining the monthly composite corporate bond rate as set forth in Notice 2004–34 continues to apply in determining that rate. See Notice 2006–75, 2006–36 I.R.B. 366.

The composite corporate bond rate for December 2006 is 5.75 percent. Pursuant to Notice 2004–34, the Service has determined this rate as the average of the monthly yields for the included corporate bond indices for that month.

The following corporate bond weighted average interest rate was determined for plan years beginning in the month shown below.

For Plan Years Beginning in: Month	Year	Corporate Bond Weighted Average	90% to 100% Permissible Range
January	2007	5.78	5.21 to 5.78

30-YEAR TREASURY SECURITIES INTEREST RATE

Section 417(e)(3)(A)(ii)(II) defines the applicable interest rate, which must be used for purposes of determining the minimum present value of a participant's benefit under § 417(e)(1) and (2), as the annual rate of interest on 30-year Treasury securities for the month before the date of distribution or such other time as the Secretary may by regulations prescribe. Section 1.417(e)–1(d)(3) of the Income Tax Regulations provides that the applicable interest rate for a month is the annual interest rate on 30-year Treasury securities as specified by the Commissioner for that month in revenue rulings, notices or other guidance published in the Internal Revenue Bulletin.

The rate of interest on 30-year Treasury securities for December 2006 is 4.68 percent. The Service has determined this rate as the monthly average of the daily determination of yield on the 30-year Treasury bond maturing in February 2036.

Drafting Information

The principal authors of this notice are Paul Stern and Tony Montanaro of the Employee Plans, Tax Exempt and Government Entities Division. For further information regarding this notice, please contact the Employee Plans' taxpayer assistance telephone service at 877–829–5500 (a toll-free number), between the hours of 8:30 a.m. and 4:30 p.m. Eastern time, Monday through Friday. Mr. Stern may be reached at 202–283–9703. Mr. Montanaro may be reached at 202–283–9714. The telephone numbers in the preceding sentences are not toll-free.

Modification of the Substantial Assistance Rules

Notice 2007–13

SECTION 1. OVERVIEW

This notice announces that the Treasury Department and the Internal Revenue Service (the IRS) will amend Treas. Reg. § 1.954–4(b)(1)(iv) and (b)(2)(ii) and the examples thereunder, which provide that substantial assistance rendered by a related person or persons to a controlled foreign corporation ("CFC") is included within the definition of foreign base company services income under section 954(e) of the Internal Revenue Code (Code). These amended regulations will limit the types of activities that constitute substantial assistance to certain assistance rendered, directly or indirectly, by a United States person or persons (as the term is defined in section 957(c) of the Code) to a related CFC. Until regulations reflecting these changes are issued, taxpayers may rely on this notice.

In addition, in light of the repeal of the foreign base company shipping income rules under subpart F, this notice confirms that income that previously was foreign base company shipping income will continue to be foreign base company income to the extent that it is within the definition of a remaining category of foreign base company income. This notice also clarifies that Treas. Reg. § 1.954–6, which provides rules addressing foreign base company shipping income, is effective only for purposes of applying the rules for the withdrawal of previously excluded subpart F income from qualified investments under section 955.

SECTION 2. SUBSTANTIAL ASSISTANCE RULES

A. BACKGROUND

Under section 951(a)(1)(A)(i) of the Code, a United States shareholder of a CFC includes in gross income each year its *pro rata* share of the CFC's subpart F income for the taxable year of the CFC which ends with or within such taxable year of the shareholder. Section 952(a)(2) defines the term "subpart F income" to mean, in part, foreign base company income (as defined under section 954).

Section 954(a)(3) of the Code defines "foreign base company income" to include "foreign base company services income" for the taxable year. Section 954(e)(1) defines "foreign base company services income" for purposes of section 954(a)(3) to mean income derived in connection with the performance of services which are performed (1) for, or on behalf of, any related person and (2) outside the country under the laws of which the CFC is created or organized. The statute does not explicitly provide for substantial assistance rules under section 954(e). Those rules are promulgated under the Secretary's authority under section 7805(a) to issue regulations interpreting the term "for, or on behalf of, any related person" under section 954(a)(3).

Treas. Reg. § 1.954–4(b)(1)(iv) defines "services which are performed for, or on behalf of, a related person" to include substantial assistance contributing to the performance of services by a CFC that has been furnished by a related person or persons. Treas. Reg. § 1.954–4(b)(2)(ii) sets forth the rules for the application of the substantial assistance test. Treas. Reg. § 1.954–4(b)(2)(ii)(a) states, in general, that assistance "shall include, but shall not be limited to, direction, supervision, services, know-how, financial assistance (other than contributions to capital), and equipment, material, or supplies." Treas. Reg. § 1.954–4(b)(2)(ii)(b) and (c) then provide separate tests depending on whether the assistance provided by the related person or persons is in the form of (1) direction, supervision, services or know-how, or (2) financial assistance, equipment, material or supplies.

Treas. Reg. § 1.954–4(b)(2)(ii)(b) provides that assistance in the form of direction, supervision, services or know-how may be substantial under either a subjective or an objective test. Under the subjective test, assistance in the form of direction, supervision, services or know-how will be considered substantial if the assistance provides the CFC with skills which are a principal element in producing the income from the performance of such services by such CFC (the principal element test). For example, a CFC enters into a contract with an unrelated person to drill an oil well. The technical and supervisory personnel who oversee the drilling of the well are employees of M, a person related to CFC. In such an instance, the services performed by CFC for the unrelated party are considered foreign base company services because the services performed by M substantially assist CFC in the performance of the contract and the services performed by M are a principal element in producing the income from the performance of the drilling contract. *Cf.* Treas. Reg. § 1.954–4(b)(3), Ex. 2.

Alternatively, under the objective test, assistance in the form of direction, supervision, services or know-how may be substantial if the cost to the CFC of the assistance furnished by persons related to the CFC equals 50 percent or more of the total cost to the CFC of performing the services performed by such CFC (the cost test). For these purposes, costs are determined after taking into account adjustments (if any) made under section 482. *See* Treas. Reg. § 1.954–4(b)(2)(ii)(b).

Treas. Reg. § 1.954–4(b)(2)(ii)(c) states, in general, that financial assistance, equipment, material, or supplies furnished by a person related to the CFC shall be considered assistance only in the amount, after taking into account adjustments (if any) made under section 482, by which the consideration actually paid by the CFC to the related person for the purchase or use of such item is less than the arm's length charge for such purchase or use. The total of all such amounts from all related persons is compared with the profits derived by the CFC from the performance of the services to determine whether the related party's contributions qualify as substantial assistance.

Treas. Reg. § 1.954–4(b)(2)(ii)(d) expands on the tests in Treas. Reg. § 1.954–4(b)(2)(ii)(b) and (c) by providing that, even if assistance furnished by a related person or persons to a CFC is not considered substantial under paragraphs (b) or (c) in isolation, it may nevertheless constitute substantial assistance when taken together or in combination with other assistance furnished by a related person or persons to the CFC. Treas. Reg. § 1.954–4(b)(2)(ii)(e) provides that, in applying Treas. Reg. § 1.954–4(b)(2)(ii)(b) and (d), assistance in the form of direction, supervision, services, or know-how shall not be taken into account, unless the assistance so furnished assists the CFC directly in the performance of the services performed. Treas. Reg. § 1.954–4(b)(3) sets forth examples, including examples addressing the application of the substantial assistance test.

B. DISCUSSION

The substantial assistance rules were published as final regulations in 1968 (T.D. 6981, 1968–2 C.B. 314). The purpose of the substantial assistance rules is to treat as foreign base company services income, income received by a CFC from rendering services to an unrelated person where in rendering those services a related person substantially contributes to the CFC's performance of such services in a manner that suggests that the CFC, rather than the related party, entered into the contract to obtain a lower rate of tax on the service income. Since the regulations were published in 1968, there has been a substantial expansion in the reach of the global economy, particularly in the provision of global services. As a result, many of the U.S. multinationals that provide services outside of the United States currently have globally integrated businesses with support capabilities for unrelated customer projects in different geographic locations, largely based on factors such as expertise and cost efficiencies.

For example, a CFC may contract with an unrelated person to provide installation and subsequent repair services. A related CFC, however, is the foreign corporation that provides the repair services. Although the foreign related CFC that is providing the support services will continue to have foreign base company services income to the extent that it performs those services outside of its country of incorporation, it does not seem appropriate in the current global economy to continue to treat the profits of the CFC contracting to furnish services to the unrelated person as foreign base company services income because of the support services provided by a related foreign person. If the substantial assistance regulations are not amended to deal with these types of businesses structures, the regulations may cause taxpayers to change the way they do business or structure their operations in light of the substantial assistance rules, even if such a structure would be less efficient from a business perspective by, for example, requiring a taxpayer to duplicate a full service infrastructure in each country.

The Treasury Department and the IRS, however, remain concerned about the ability of related United States persons to shift profits offshore to CFCs organized in low tax jurisdictions in cases where the related United States person or persons provides so much assistance to the CFC that the CFC cannot be said to be providing services on its own account and thus acting as an independent entity. Accordingly, the Treasury Department and the IRS will re vise the regulations to eliminate the substantial assistance rules, except in certain limited instances in which a United States person or persons provide sufficient assistance directly or indirectly to a related CFC.

C. PROPOSED GUIDANCE

The Treasury Department and the IRS will amend Treas. Reg. § 1.954–4(b)(1)(iv) and (b)(2)(ii) and the examples thereunder. Treas. Reg. § 1.954–4(b)(1)(iv) as amended will provide that services performed by a CFC in a case where substantial assistance by a related United States person or persons (as the term is defined in section 957(c) of the Code) contributes to the performance of such service will constitute "services which are performed for, or on behalf of, a related person." Treas. Reg. § 1.954–4(b)(2)(ii) as amended will provide that "substantial assistance" consists of assistance furnished (directly or indirectly) by a related United States person or persons to the CFC if the assistance satisfies an objective cost test. The subjective "principal element" test will no longer apply to determine substantial assistance. For purposes of the objective cost test, the definition of the term "assistance" will include, but will not be limited to, direction, supervision, services, know-how, financial assistance (other than contributions to capital), and equipment, material, or supplies provided directly or indirectly by a related United States person to a CFC.

The cost test will be satisfied if the cost to the CFC of the assistance furnished by the related United States person or persons equals or exceeds 80 percent of the total cost to the CFC of performing the services. The term "cost" will be determined after taking into account adjustments, if any, made under section 482 of the Code. Taxpayers may apply the cost test either by demonstrating that the assistance provided, directly or indirectly, by related United States persons is below the 80 percent cost threshold, or, alternatively, by demonstrating that the cost of the services provided by the CFC itself, and/or by a related CFC, is more than 20 percent of the total cost to the CFC of performing the services. For this purpose, services provided by a CFC itself are not assistance provided "indirectly" by a related United States person (or persons). However, employees, officers, or directors of the CFC who are concurrently employees, officers, or directors of a related United States person during a taxable year of the CFC will be considered employees, officers or directors solely of the related United States person for such taxable year for purposes of this notice.

The examples under Treas. Reg. § 1.954–4(b)(2)(ii) will be amended to reflect the amendments to the regulations. The application of the proposed cost test is illustrated by the following examples.

Example 1: USP, a U.S. corporation, wholly owns CFC1 and CFC2, each a foreign corporation. CFC1 enters into a contract with FP, an unrelated foreign person, to design a bridge for FP in Country Y, a foreign country that is not CFC1's country of organization. CFC1 incurs a total of $100x of costs to design the bridge for FP. USP performs supervisory services in Country Y for CFC1 with respect to the contract for which CFC1 pays USP a fee. CFC1 directly performs services related to the performance of that contract that cost CFC1 $15x. CFC2 performs centralized support services related to the performance of that contract in Country X, its country of organization, for which CFC1 pays CFC2 $10x. CFC1 is not treated as receiving substantial assistance in the performance of that contract because more than 20% of the cost of that contract is attributable to services furnished directly by CFC1 or a related CFC (CFC2).

Example 2: USP, a U.S. corporation, wholly owns CFC1 and CFC2, each a foreign corporation. CFC2 enters into a contract with FP, an unrelated person, to design a bridge in Country Y, a foreign country that is not CFC2's country of organization. With respect to the contract with FP, USP performs services in Country Y for CFC1 in the form of design and technical services for which CFC1 pays USP $85x. CFC1 contracts with CFC2 to provide those services and others to CFC2 for $90x. CFC2 uses those services together with services it performs itself that cost CFC2 $10x to design the bridge for FP. Pursuant to the cost test, USP provides substantial assistance to CFC2 in the performance of its contract for FP because USP indirectly furnishes assistance to CFC2 (through CFC1) that exceeds 80 percent of the total cost to CFC2 for performing the contract.

Example 3: USP, a U.S. corporation, wholly owns CFC1 and CFC2, each a foreign corporation. CFC2 enters into a contract with FP, an unrelated person, to design a bridge in Country Y, a foreign country that is not CFC2's country of organization. With respect to the contract with FP, USP performs services in Country Y for CFC1 in the form of design and technical services for which CFC1 pays USP $60x. CFC1 contracts with CFC2 to provide those services and others to CFC2 for $70x. CFC2 uses those services together with services it performs itself that cost CFC2 $30x to design the bridge for FP. CFC2 is not treated as receiving substantial assistance in the performance of that contract because more than 20% of the cost of that contract is attributable to services furnished directly by CFC2.

D. EFFECTIVE DATE

Regulations to be issued incorporating the guidance set forth in this notice will apply to taxable years of foreign corporations beginning on or after January 1, 2007 and to taxable years of United States shareholders in which or with which such taxable years of the foreign corporations end. Until such regulations are issued, taxpayers may rely on this notice.

SECTION 3. FOREIGN BASE COMPANY SHIPPING RULES

Section 415 of the American Jobs Creations Act ("AJCA") repealed sections 954(a)(4) and 954(f) of the Code, (the foreign base company shipping rules). It also made conforming amendments by repealing sections 954(b)(6) and (b)(7) and striking a reference to foreign base company shipping income in section 954(b)(5). These changes are effective for taxable years of foreign corporations beginning after December 31, 2004, and taxable years of U.S. shareholders in which or with which such taxable years of the foreign corporations end. Further, section 415 of the AJCA enacted a special safe harbor for certain leasing activities under section 954(c)(2)(A). The special safe harbor rule has been addressed in a separate published guidance project. *See* Notice 2006–48, 2006–21 I.R.B. 922.

As a result of, and as of the effective date of, the repeal of the foreign base company shipping income rules, Treas. Reg. § 1.954–1(e)(4)(i)(A), which provides that income that qualifies as foreign base company shipping income will not be considered insurance income or income in any other category of foreign base company income, is obsolete and Treas. Reg. § 1.954–6, which prescribes rules for determining foreign base company shipping income, is only effective for purposes of applying the rules for the withdrawal of previously excluded subpart F income from qualified investments under section 955. Accordingly, Treas. Reg. § 1.954–6 will be amended to include new applicability language.

Moreover, the repeal of sections 954(a)(4) and 954(f) of the Code was only intended to eliminate the separate category of foreign base company shipping income. It was not intended to exclude income from subpart F that would otherwise qualify under another category of foreign base company income. Income that might have been described in sections 954(a)(4) and 956(f) before the AJCA still must be tested under the remaining categories of foreign base company income. Consequently, this notice confirms that income described in section 954(f) as it existed before its repeal will continue to constitute subpart F income to the extent that it falls within another category of foreign base company income.

SECTION 4. REQUEST FOR COMMENTS

The Treasury Department and the IRS request comments on the new substantial assistance rules proposed in this notice. Comments are requested on whether the new rules are appropriately targeted and whether any modifications to the rules should be made before they are promulgated as regulations. In particular, comments are requested on whether the proposed cost test is appropriate for certain industries, and if not, how the rules could be modified or supplemented to properly address those industries while still addressing the Treasury Department's and the IRS' concerns about shifting profits offshore to CFCs organized in low tax jurisdictions. In addition, the Treasury Department and the IRS understand that taxpayers are also concerned with the special rule concerning a guaranty of performance contained in Treas. Reg. § 1.954–4(b)(2)(i). The Treasury Department and the IRS are reviewing this rule, particularly in light of Treas. Reg. § 1.482–9T, and request comments on whether changes to this rule are warranted and, if so, how it should be modified.

Written comments on the issues addressed in this notice may be submitted to the Office of Associate Chief Counsel International, Attention: Notice 2007–13, room 4710, CC:INTL:BR2, Internal Revenue Service, 1111 Constitution Avenue, NW, Washington, DC 20224. Alternatively, taxpayers may submit comments electronically to *Notice.Comments@m1.irscounsel.treas.gov*.

Comments will be available for public inspection and copying.

SECTION 5. DRAFTING INFORMATION

The principal author of this notice is Ethan Atticks of the Office of Associate Chief Counsel (International). For further information regarding this notice, contact Ethan Atticks at (202) 622–3840 (not a toll-free call).

---

26 CFR 601.601: Rules and regulations.
(Also Part 1, § 1397E.)

Rev. Proc. 2007–18

SECTION 1. PURPOSE

Pursuant to § 1397E(e)(2) of the Internal Revenue Code, this revenue procedure sets forth the maximum face amount of Qualified Zone Academy Bonds ("Bond" or "Bonds") that may be issued for each State for each of the calendar years 2006 and 2007. For this purpose, "State" includes the District of Columbia and the possessions of the United States.

SECTION 2. BACKGROUND

.01 Section 226 of the Taxpayer Relief Act of 1997, Pub. L. 105–34, 111 Stat. 821 (1997), added § 1397E to the Internal Revenue Code to provide a credit to holders of Bonds under certain circumstances so that the Bonds generally can be issued without discount or interest. Ninety-five percent of Bond proceeds are to be used for qualified purposes, as defined by § 1397E(d)(5), with respect to a qualified zone academy, as defined by § 1397E(d)(4).

.02 Section 1397E(e)(1), as amended by § 107 of the Tax Relief and Health Care Act of 2006, Pub. L. 109–432, 120 Stat. 2922 (2006), provides that the national Bond limitation is $400 million for each of the years 1998, 1999, 2000, 2001, 2002, 2003, 2004, 2005, 2006, and 2007. This amount is to be allocated among the States by the Secretary on the basis of their respective populations below the poverty level (as defined by the Office of Management and Budget) and is to be further allocated by each State to qualified zone academies within the State.

.03 Section 1397E(e)(4), as amended by § 509 of the Tax Relief Extension Act of 1999, Pub. L. 106–170, 113 Stat. 1860 (1999), provides that any carryforward of a limitation amount may be carried forward only to the first 2 years (3 years for carryforwards from 1998 or 1999) following the unused limitation year. For this purpose, a limitation amount shall be treated as used on a first-in, first-out basis.

.04 Rev. Proc. 98–9, 1998–1 C.B. 341; Rev. Proc. 98–57, 1998–2 C.B. 682; Rev. Proc. 2000–10, 2000–1 C.B. 287; Rev. Proc. 2001–14, 2001–1 C.B. 343; Rev. Proc. 2002–25, 2002–1 C.B. 800; Rev. Proc. 2002–72, 2002–2 C.B. 931; Rev. Proc. 2004–61, 2004–2 C.B. 707; and Rev. Proc. 2004–72, 2004–2 C.B. 1033, allocated among the States the national limitation for 1998, 1999, 2000, 2001, 2002, 2003, 2004, and 2005, respectively.

SECTION 3. NATIONAL QUALIFIED ZONE ACADEMY BOND LIMITATION FOR 2006 AND 2007

The national limitation for Bonds for each of the calendar years 2006 and 2007 is $400 million. This amount is allocated among the States as follows:

STATE	MAXIMUM FACE AMOUNT OF BONDS THAT MAY BE ISSUED FOR EACH OF THE CALENDAR YEARS 2006 AND 2007 (thousands of dollars)
Alabama	7,698
Alaska	677
Arizona	9,412
Arkansas	3,921
California	48,404
Colorado	5,440
Connecticut	3,346
Delaware	801
District of Columbia	1,180
Florida	20,271
Georgia	13,322
Hawaii	1,129
Idaho	1,468
Illinois	14,790
Indiana	7,944
Iowa	3,356
Kansas	3,459
Kentucky	6,148
Louisiana	7,677
Maine	1,704
Maryland	5,563
Massachusetts	6,579
Michigan	12,275
Minnesota	4,229
Mississippi	5,861

STATE	MAXIMUM FACE AMOUNT OF BONDS THAT MAY BE ISSUED FOR EACH OF THE CALENDAR YEARS 2006 AND 2007 (thousands of dollars)
Missouri	6,764
Montana	1,314
Nebraska	1,714
Nevada	2,669
New Hampshire	749
New Jersey	6,076
New Mexico	3,562
New York	28,328
North Carolina	11,444
North Dakota	718
Ohio	14,287
Oklahoma	5,573
Oregon	4,475
Pennsylvania	14,082
Rhode Island	1,304
South Carolina	6,425
South Dakota	924
Tennessee	8,950
Texas	37,781
Utah	2,381
Vermont	482
Virginia	7,020
Washington	6,528
West Virginia	2,833
Wisconsin	5,676
Wyoming	554
American Samoa	363
Guam	397
Northern Marianas	380
Puerto Rico	19,230
Virgin Islands	363
Total	$400,000

SECTION 4. EFFECTIVE DATE

This revenue procedure is effective for Bonds issued pursuant to the national limitation for calendar year 2006 on or after January 1, 2006, and Bonds issued pursuant to the national limitation for calendar year 2007 on or after January 1, 2007.

SECTION 5. DRAFTING INFORMATION

The principal author of this revenue procedure is David White of the Office of Division Counsel/Associate Chief Counsel (Tax Exempt & Government Entities). For further information regarding this revenue procedure, contact Mr. White at (202) 622–3980 (not a toll-free call).

Part IV. Items of General Interest

Notice of Proposed Rulemaking by Cross-Reference to Temporary Regulations

Corporate Reorganizations; Distributions Under Sections 368(a)(1)(D) and 354(b)(1)(B)

REG–125632–06

AGENCY: Internal Revenue Service (IRS), Treasury.

ACTION: Notice of proposed rulemaking by cross-reference to temporary regulations.

SUMMARY: In this issue of the Bulletin, the IRS is issuing temporary regulations (T.D. 9303) that provide guidance regarding the qualification of certain transactions as reorganizations described in section 368(a)(1)(D) where no stock and/or securities of the acquiring corporation is issued and distributed in the transaction. These regulations affect corporations engaging in such transactions and their shareholders. The text of those regulations also serves as the text of these proposed regulations.

DATES: Written or electronic comments and requests for a public hearing must be received by March 19, 2007.

ADDRESSES: Send submissions to: CC:PA:LPD:PR (REG–125632–06), Internal Revenue Service, PO Box 7604, Ben Franklin Station, Washington, DC 20044. Submissions may be hand delivered to CC:PA:LPD:PR (REG–147144–06), Courier Desk, Internal Revenue Service, Crystal Mall 4, 1901 South Bell Street, Arlington, Virginia, or sent electronically, via the IRS Internet site at *www.irs.gov/regs* or via the Federal eRulemaking Portal at *www.regulations.gov* (IRS REG–125632–06).

FOR FURTHER INFORMATION CONTACT: Concerning the proposed regulations, Bruce A. Decker, (202) 622–7550; concerning submission of comments, requests for a public hearing, and/or a publication and regulations specialist, Treena Garrett, (202) 622–7180.

SUPPLEMENTARY INFORMATION:

Background

Temporary regulations in this issue of the Bulletin amend 26 CFR part 1. The temporary regulations provide guidance on circumstances where the distribution of stock and/or securities under section 354(b)(1)(B) will be deemed satisfied in the absence of an actual issuance of stock and/or securities pursuant to a reorganization described in section 368(a)(1)(D). The text of those regulations also serves as the text of these proposed regulations. The preamble to the temporary regulations explains the amendments.

Explanation of Provisions

These temporary regulations provide guidance regarding the circumstances in which the distribution requirement under sections 368(a)(1)(D) and 354(b)(1)(B) is deemed satisfied despite the fact that no stock and/or securities are actually issued in a transaction otherwise described in section 368(a)(1)(D). These regulations will affect certain cash sales of assets between two corporations that have the same direct or indirect shareholders or a *de minimis* variation in shareholder identity and proportionality.

Special Analyses

It has been determined that this notice of proposed rulemaking is not a significant regulatory action as defined in Executive Order 12866. Therefore, a regulatory assessment is not required. It also has been determined that section 553(b) of the Administrative Procedure Act (5 U.S.C. chapter 5) does not apply to these regulations, and because the regulation does not impose a collection of information on small entities, the Regulatory Flexibility Act (5 U.S.C. chapter 6) does not apply. Pursuant to section 7805(f) of the Internal Revenue Code, this notice of proposed rulemaking will be submitted to the Chief Counsel for Advocacy of the Small Business Administration for comment on its impact on small business.

Comments and Requests for a Public Hearing

Before these proposed regulations are adopted as final regulations, consideration will be given to any written (a signed original and eight (8) copies) or electronic comments that are submitted timely to the IRS. The IRS and Treasury Department request comments on the clarity of the proposed rules and how they can be made easier to understand. The IRS and Treasury Department request comments on several issues relating to acquisitive reorganizations described in section 368(a)(1)(D). Specifically, the IRS and Treasury Department request comments on whether the meaningless gesture doctrine is inconsistent with the distribution requirement in sections 368(a)(1)(D) and 354(b)(1)(B), especially in situations in which the cash consideration received equals the full fair market value of the property transferred such that there is no missing consideration for which the nominal share of stock deemed received and distributed could substitute. The IRS and Treasury Department also request comments on the extent, if any, to which the continuity of interest requirement should apply to a reorganization described in section 368(a)(1)(D). The IRS and Treasury Department request comments on whether these temporary regulations should apply when the parties to the reorganization are members of a consolidated group. Finally, the IRS and Treasury Department request comments on the continued vitality of various liquidation-reincorporation authorities after the enactment of the Tax Reform Act of 1986, Public Law 99–514 (100 Stat. 2085 (1986)). All comments will be available for public inspection and copying. A public hearing will be scheduled if requested in writing by any person that timely submits written comments. If a public hearing is scheduled, notice of the date, time, and place for the public hearing will be published in the **Federal Register**.

Drafting Information

The principal author of these regulations is Bruce A. Decker, Office of Associate Chief Counsel (Corporate).

* * * * *

Proposed Amendments to the Regulations

Accordingly, 26 CFR part 1 is proposed to be amended as follows:

PART 1—INCOME TAXES

Paragraph 1. The authority citation for part 1 continues to read as follows:

Authority: 26 U.S.C. 7805 * * *

Par. 2. Section 1.368–2 is amended by revising paragraph (l) to read as follows:

§1.368–2 Definition of terms.

* * * * *

(l) [The text of this proposed amendment to §1.368–2(l) is the same as the text of §1.368–2T(l)(1) through (l)(4)(i) published elsewhere in this issue of the Bulletin.

Mark E. Matthews,
Deputy Commissioner for Services and Enforcement.

(Filed by the Office of the Federal Register on December 18, 2006, 8:45 a.m., and published in the issue of the Federal Register for December 18, 2006, 71 F.R. 75898)

Railroad Track Maintenance Credit; Correction

Announcement 2007–8

AGENCY: Internal Revenue Service (IRS), Treasury.

ACTION: Correction to temporary regulations.

SUMMARY: This document contains corrections to temporary regulations (T.D. 9286, 2006–43 I.R.B. 750) that were published in the **Federal Register** on Friday, September 8, 2006 (71 FR 53009) providing rules for claiming the railroad track maintenance credit under section 45G of the Internal Revenue Code for qualified railroad track maintenance expenditures paid or incurred by a Class II railroad or Class III railroad and other eligible taxpayers during the taxable year.

DATES: This correction is effective September 8, 2006.

FOR FURTHER INFORMATION CONTACT: Winston H. Douglas, (202) 622–3110 (not a toll-free number).

SUPPLEMENTARY INFORMATION:

Background

The correction notice that is the subject of this document is under section 45G of the Internal Revenue Code.

Need for Correction

As published, temporary regulations (T.D. 9286) contain errors that may prove to be misleading and are in need of clarification.

Correction of Publication

Accordingly, the publication of the temporary regulations (T.D. 9286), which was the subject of FR Doc. E6–14858, is corrected as follows:

1. On page 53010, column 1, in the preamble, under the paragraph heading "*General Overview*", first and second lines from the bottom of the second paragraph, the language "assigned to such person by such a railroad." is corrected to read "assigned to such person by a Class II railroad or a Class III railroad.".

2. On page 53010, column 2, in the preamble, under the paragraph heading "*Scope*", first paragraph of the column, last line of the paragraph, the language "of controlled groups under section 45G." is corrected to read "of controlled groups under section 45G with respect to the RTMC.".

3. On page 53010, column 2, in the preamble, under the paragraph heading "*Eligible Taxpayer*", fourth line of the first paragraph, the language "defined in the temporary regulations as:" is corrected to read "defined as:".

4. On page 53010, column 2, in the preamble, under the paragraph heading "*Eligible Taxpayer*", third line from the bottom of the first paragraph, the language "railroad track assigned to the person for" is corrected to read "railroad track assigned to the taxpayer for".

5. On page 53010, column 2, in the preamble, under the paragraph heading "*Eligible Taxpayer*", second through the sixth line from the bottom of the second paragraph, the language "Price Index)). 49 CFR part 1201, subpart A, §1–1(a). In general, Class III railroads have annual carrier operating revenues of $20 million or less after applying the railroad revenue deflator formula. 49" is corrected to read "Price Index)). See 49 CFR part 1201, subpart A, §1–1(a). In general, Class III railroads have annual carrier operating revenues of $20 million or less after applying the railroad revenue deflator formula. See 49".

6. On page 53010, column 3, in the preamble, under the paragraph heading "*Eligible Taxpayer*", second paragraph of the column, tenth to seventeenth lines, the language "services are the transport of freight by rail, the loading and unloading of freight transported by rail, locomotive leasing or rental, and maintenance of a railroad's right-of-way (including vegetation control). Examples of services that are not railroad-related services are general business services," is corrected to read "services include the transport of freight by rail, the loading and unloading of freight transported by rail, locomotive leasing or rental, and maintenance of a railroad's right-of-way (including vegetation control). Examples of services that are not railroad-related services include general business services,".

7. On page 53011, column 1, in the preamble, under the paragraph heading "*Determination of QRTME Paid or Incurred*", second paragraph, third and fourth lines, the language "to a taxpayer using an accrual method of accounting. In this case, paid or" is corrected to read "to taxpayers using an accrual method of accounting. For such taxpayers, paid or".

8. On page 53011, column 1, in the preamble, under the paragraph heading "*Determination of QRTME Paid or Incurred*", second paragraph, fifteenth to twentieth lines, the language "any such expenditures. The temporary regulations provide that reimbursements may consist of amounts paid either directly or indirectly to the taxpayer. Examples of indirect reimbursements are discounted freight shipping rates," is corrected to read "any expenditures that would otherwise qualify as QRTME. The temporary regulations provide that reimbursements may consist of amounts paid either directly or indirectly to the taxpayer. Examples of indirect reimbursements include discounted freight shipping rates,".

9. On page 53011, column 1, in the preamble, under the paragraph heading "*Determination of QRTME Paid or Incurred*", third paragraph, first line, the language

"If an eligible taxpayer (assignee) pays" is corrected to read "The IRS and Treasury believe that the statute is intended to allow suppliers and shippers to claim the credit for providing the funding for the QRTME performed on railroad track owned by, or leased to, a Class II railroad or Class III railroad. However, the suppliers and shippers may not have the necessary expertise to perform the repairs and improvements. The IRS and Treasury believe that these eligible taxpayers should be able to claim the credit for providing the funding to the extent that the Class II railroads and Class III railroads use such funding to perform the repairs and improvements to the track. Therefore, if an eligible taxpayer (assignee) pays".

10. On page 53011, column 1, in the preamble, under the paragraph heading "*Determination of QRTME Paid or Incurred*", third paragraph, fifth line from the bottom of the column, the language "paragraph, this QRTME would be" is corrected to read "paragraph, QRTME would be".

11. On page 53011, column 2, in the preamble, under the paragraph heading "*Assignment of Railroad Track Miles*", first paragraph, first through fifth lines, the language "For purposes of section 45G, the temporary regulations provide that an assignment of a mile of railroad track is not a legal transfer of title, but merely a designation. This designation must be" is corrected to read "The temporary regulations provide that an assignment of a mile of railroad track is not a legal transfer of title, but merely a designation made solely for purposes of section 45G. This designation must be".

12. On page 53011, column 2, in the preamble, under the paragraph heading "*Assignment of Railroad Track Miles*", second paragraph, fifth line, the language "track. Thus, if a Class II railroad or Class" is corrected to read "track. If a Class II railroad or Class".

13. On page 53011, column 2, in the preamble, under the paragraph heading "*Assignment of Railroad Track Miles*", fourth paragraph, second line, the language "that a taxpayer must file Form 8900," is corrected to read "that a taxpayer file Form 8900,".

14. On page 53011, column 3, in the preamble, last paragraph of the column, first line, the language "The temporary regulations also" is corrected to read "The temporary regulations".

15. On page 53012, column 1, in the preamble, first paragraph of the column, first line, the language "assignment is properly reported." is corrected to read "assignment is reported.".

16. On page 53012, column 1, in the preamble, under the paragraph heading "*Special Rules*", first paragraph, second through fourth lines from the bottom of the paragraph, the language "structure (railroad track, roadbed, bridges, and related track structures) and intangible assets to which the" is corrected to read "structure and intangible assets to which the".

17. On page 53012, column 1, in the preamble, under the paragraph heading "*Special Rules*", second paragraph, sixth line, the language "of the RTMC allowable. This reduction" is corrected to read "of the RTMC allowable. The basis reduction".

18. On page 53012, column 1, in the preamble, under the paragraph heading "*Special Rules*", third paragraph, first line, the language "The temporary regulations also" is corrected to read "The temporary regulations do not".

19. On page 53012, column 2, in the preamble, under the paragraph heading "*Special Rules*", first paragraph of the column, fourth line to the last of the paragraph, the language "legislative history does not refer to, any exception to this rule. Accordingly, pursuant to section 61 and the regulations under section 61, the owner of the tangible assets (for example, railroad track and roadbed) with respect to which the QRTME is paid or incurred by another person that does not have a depreciable interest in those assets has gross income in the amount of that QRTME. However, the application of section 61 to QRTME paid or incurred with respect to eligible railroad track that is leased by a Class II railroad or Class III railroad raises a question as to under what circumstances the owner or lessee should recognize gross income with respect to QRTME. The IRS and Treasury Department request comments on this issue." is replaced to read "legislative history does not refer to, any exception to this rule for an owner of tangible assets (for example, railroad track and roadbed) for the value of the repairs or improvements to such assets with respect to which QRTME is paid or incurred by another person that does not have a depreciable interest in such assets."

LaNita Van Dyke,
Chief, Publications and Regulations Branch,
Legal Processing Division,
Associate Chief Counsel
(Procedure and Administration).

(Filed by the Office of the Federal Register on December 7, 2006, 8:45 a.m., and published in the issue of the Federal Register for December 8, 2006, 71 F.R. 71045)

Treatment of Services Under Section 482; Allocation of Income and Deductions From Intangibles; Stewardship Expense; Correction

Announcement 2007–9

AGENCY: Internal Revenue Service (IRS), Treasury.

ACTION: Correcting amendments.

SUMMARY: This document contains corrections to final and temporary regulations (T.D. 9278, 2006–34 I.R.B. 256) that was published in the **Federal Register** on Friday, August 4, 2006 (71 FR 44466) regarding the treatment of controlled services transactions under section 482 and the allocation of income from intangibles, in particular with respect to contributions by a controlled party to the value of an intangible owned by another controlled party. This document also contains corrections to final and temporary regulations that modify the regulations under section 861 concerning stewardship expenses to be consistent with the changes made to the regulations under section 482.

EFFECTIVE DATE: The amendments are effective on January 1, 2007.

FOR FURTHER INFORMATION CONTACT: Thomas A. Vidano, (202) 435–5265, or Carol B. Tan (202) 435–5159, for matters relating to section 482, and David F. Bergkuist, (202) 622–3850, for matters relating to stewardship expenses (not toll-free numbers).

SUPPLEMENTARY INFORMATION:

Background

The final and temporary regulations that are the subject of these corrections are under sections 482 and 861 of the Internal Revenue Code.

Need for Correction

As published, the final and temporary regulations (T.D. 9278) contains errors that may prove to be misleading and are in need of clarification.

* * * * *

Correction of Publication

Accordingly, 26 CFR part 1 is corrected by making the following correcting amendments:

PART 1—INCOME TAXES

Paragraph 1. The authority citation for part 1 continues to read in part as follows:

Authority: 26 U.S.C. 7805 * * *

Par. 2. Section 1.482–0T is amended by removing the entries for paragraphs (i)(1) through (i)(10), (j)(1), (j)(2) and (j)(3) from §1.482–1T.

Par. 3. Section 1.482–1 is amended by revising paragraph (i) introductory text to read as follows:

§1.482–1 Allocation of income and deductions among taxpayers.

* * * * *

(i) [Reserved]. For further guidance, see §1.482–1T(i) introductory text.

* * * * *

Par. 4. Section 1.482–1T is amended as follows:

1. Paragraphs (i)(1) through (i)(10) are added and reserved.

2. Paragraphs (j)(1) through (j)(5) are amended by adding "§" before the language "1.482–1(j)(1)".

The addition reads as follows:

§1.482–1T Allocation of income and deductions among taxpayers (temporary).

* * * * *

(i)(1) through (i)(10) [Reserved]. For further guidance, see §1.482–1(i)(1) through (i)(10).

* * * * *

Par. 5. Section 1.482–8T is amended by revising paragraph (b) *Example 12.* (iv), second sentence to read as follows:

§1.482–8T Example of the best method rule (temporary).

* * * * *

(b) * * *

Example 12. (i) * * *

(iv) * * * USP contributed the long-term endorsement contracts with professional athletes. * * *

* * * * *

Par. 6. Section 1.482–9T is amended as follows:

1. Paragraph (b)(6), *Example 22.* (vi), introductory text is revised.

2. Paragraph (g)(2), *Example 2.* (iv), fifth sentence is revised.

3. Paragraph (i)(2) is revised.

4. Paragraph (i)(5), *Example 1.* (iii), first sentence is revised.

5. Paragraph (i)(5), *Example 3.* (ii), first sentence is revised.

6. Paragraph (l)(5), *Example 20.* (i), second sentence is revised.

7. Paragraph (m)(5), *Example 1.* (ii), fourth sentence is revised.

The revisions read as follows:

§1.482–9T Methods to determine taxable income in connection with a controlled services transaction (temporary).

* * * * *

(b) * * *

(6) * * *

Example 22. (i) * * *

(vi) In contrast, if aggregated services AB were allocated by reference to the total U.S. dollar value of sales to uncontrolled parties (trade sales) by each company, the following results would obtain:

* * * * *

(g) * * *

(2) * * *

Example 2. * * *

(iv) * * * In the bid on the Country 2 contract for Level 1 waste remediation, Company B proposes to use a multidisciplinary team of specialists from Company A and Company B. * * *

* * * * *

(i) * * *

(2) * * * For purposes of this paragraph (i), an arrangement will be treated as a contingent-payment arrangement if it meets all of the requirements in paragraph (i)(2)(i) of this section and is consistent with the economic substance and conduct requirement in paragraph (i)(2)(ii) of this section.

* * * * *

(5) * * *

Example 1. (i) * * *

(iii) The years under examination are years 6 through 9. ***

* * * * *

Example 3. (i) * * *

(ii) The years under examination are years 6 through 9. * * *

* * * * *

(l) * * *

(5) * * *

Example 20. (i) * * * Y, a Country B corporation, is a distribution and marketing company that also performs clinical trials for X in Country B. * * *

* * * * *

(m) * * *

(5) * * *

Example 1. (i) * * *

(ii) * * * The comparable profits method may provide the most reliable measure of an arm's length result if uncontrolled parties are identified that perform similar, combined functions of maintaining and providing spare parts for similar equipment. * * *

* * * * *

Par. 7. Section 1.861–8T is amended as follows:

1. Paragraph (b)(3) is revised.

2. Paragraph (g), paragraph (i) following *Example 30.* (i)(C) is redesignated as paragraph (ii) and the paragraph designation for *Example 30.* (i)(C) is removed.

3. Paragraph (h)(1), first three sentences are revised.

4. Paragraph (h)(3) is revised.

The revisions read as follows:

§1.861–8T Computation of taxable income from sources within the United States and from other sources and activities (temporary).

* * * * *

(b) * * *

(3) *Supportive functions.* Deductions which are supportive in nature (such as overhead, general and administrative, and supervisory expenses) may relate to other deductions which can more readily be allocated to gross income. In such instance, such supportive deductions may be allocated and apportioned along with the deductions to which they relate. On the other hand, it would be equally acceptable to attribute supportive deductions on

some reasonable basis directly to activities or property which generate, have generated or could reasonably be expected to generate gross income. This would ordinarily be accomplished by allocating the supportive expenses to all gross income or to another broad class of gross income and apportioning the expenses in accordance with paragraph (c)(1) of this section. For this purpose, reasonable departmental overhead rates may be utilized. For examples of the application of the principles of this paragraph (b)(3) to expenses other than expenses attributable to stewardship activities, see *Examples 19* through *21* of paragraph (g) of this section. See paragraph (e)(4)(ii) of this section for the allocation and apportionment of deductions attributable to stewardship expenses. However, supportive deductions that are described in §1.861–14T(e)(3) shall be allocated and apportioned in accordance with the rules of §1.861–14T and shall not be allocated and apportioned by reference only to the gross income of a single member of an affiliated group of corporations as defined in §1.861–14T(d).

* * * * *

(h) * * * (1) * * * In general, the rules of this section, as well as the rules of §§1.861–9T, 1.861–10T, 1.861–11T, 1.861–12T, and 1.861–14T apply for taxable years beginning after December 31, 1986, except for paragraphs (a)(5)(ii), (b)(3), (e)(4), (f)(4)(i), and paragraph (g) *Example 17*, *Example 18*, and *Example 30* of this section, which are generally applicable for taxable years beginning after December 31, 2006. Also, see §§1.861–8(e)(12)(iv) and 1.861–14(e)(6) for rules concerning the allocation and apportionment of deductions for charitable contributions. In the case of corporate taxpayers, transition rules set forth in §1.861–13T provide for the gradual phase-in of certain provisions of this and the foregoing sections. * * *

(3) *Expiration date*. The applicability of the paragraphs (a)(5)(ii), (b)(3), (e)(4), (f)(4)(i), and paragraph (g) *Example 17*, *Example 18*, and *Example 30* of this section, expires on or before July 31, 2009.

Par. 8. Section 1.6662–6T is amended by revising paragraph (d)(2)(ii)(B), first sentence to read as follows:

§1.6662–6T Transactions between parties described in section 482 and net section 482 transfer price adjustments (temporary).

* * * * *

(d)(2)(ii)(B) A taxpayer's selection of the services cost method for certain services, described in §1.482–9T(b), and its application of that method to a controlled services transaction will be considered reasonable for purposes of the specified method requirement only if the taxpayer reasonably allocated and apportioned costs in accordance with §1.482–9T(k), reasonably concluded that the controlled services transaction meets the conditions of §1.482–9T(b)(3), and reasonably concluded that the controlled services transaction is not described in §1.482–9T(b)(2). * * *

* * * * *

Cynthia Grigsby,
Senior Federal Register Liaison Officer,
Legal Processing Division,
Associate Chief Counsel
(Procedure and Administration).

(Filed by the Office of the Federal Register on December 21, 2006, 8:45 a.m., and published in the issue of the Federal Register for December 22, 2006, 71 F.R. 76902)

Part I. Rulings and Decisions Under the Internal Revenue Code of 1986

Section 42.—Low-Income Housing Credit

The adjusted applicable federal short-term, mid-term, and long-term rates are set forth for the month of February 2007. See Rev. Rul. 2007-9, page 422.

Section 280G.—Golden Parachute Payments

Federal short-term, mid-term, and long-term rates are set forth for the month of February 2007. See Rev. Rul. 2007-9, page 422.

Section 300 (31 USC 9701).—Installment Agreement Fee

300.1: Installment agreement fee.

T.D. 9306

DEPARTMENT OF THE TREASURY
Internal Revenue Service
26 CFR Part 300

User Fees for Processing Installment Agreements

AGENCY: Internal Revenue Service (IRS), Treasury.

ACTION: Final regulations.

SUMMARY: This document contains amendments to the regulations relating to user fees for installment agreements. The amendments update the fees to reflect the actual costs of the services provided and create an exception to the increased fee for entering into installment agreements for low-income taxpayers. The amendments affect taxpayers who wish to pay their liabilities through installment agreements.

DATES: *Effective Date:* These regulations are effective on **December 28, 2006.**

Applicability Date: These regulations apply to installment agreements entered into, restructured, or reinstated on or after January 1, 2007.

FOR FURTHER INFORMATION CONTACT: Concerning cost methodology, Eva Williams, 202–435–5514; concerning the regulations, William Beard, 202–622–3620 (not toll-free numbers).

SUPPLEMENTARY INFORMATION:

Background

This document contains amendments to 26 CFR part 300. On August 30, 2006, a notice of proposed rulemaking (REG–148576–05, 2006–40 I.R.B. 627) relating to the user fees charged for processing installment agreements was published in the **Federal Register** (71 FR 51538). The charging of user fees implements the Independent Offices Appropriations Act (IOAA), which is codified at 31 U.S.C. 9701. The notice of proposed rulemaking proposed an increase in the amount of the user fees to reflect the full cost of the service provided, as directed by OMB Circular A–25, 58 FR 38142 (July 15, 1993) (the OMB Circular).

The notice of proposed rulemaking proposed to increase the fee under §300.1 for entering into an installment agreement from $43 to $105 and to increase the fee under §300.2 for restructuring an installment agreement from $24 to $45. The notice of proposed rulemaking also proposed an exception to the full-cost requirement in cases where the taxpayer chooses to pay by way of a direct debit from the taxpayer's bank account. The OMB Circular allows the Office of Management and Budget to grant a waiver of the full cost requirement and, pursuant to such a waiver, the proposed fee for entering into a direct-debit agreement was $52 to encourage this type of payment.

No public hearing on the notice of proposed rulemaking was held because no one requested to speak. Eight comments were received. After consideration of all the comments, this Treasury decision adopts the proposed regulations with the following change: the fee for entering into an installment agreement will remain $43 for low-income taxpayers, that is, taxpayers whose incomes fall at or below 250% of the dollar criteria established by the poverty guidelines updated annually in the **Federal Register** by the U.S. Department of Health and Human Services or such other measure as the Secretary may adopt. The IRS sought and received an additional waiver from OMB to charge less than full cost to low-income taxpayers.

Summary of Comments and Explanation of Revisions

Of the eight comments on the proposed regulations, five stated that the increased fees would have an adverse impact on low-income taxpayers. Other commentators stated that many low-income taxpayers do not have bank accounts and cannot take advantage of the reduced fee for direct-debit installment agreements. To accommodate these concerns, the final regulations except low-income taxpayers from the increase of the fee for entering into an installment agreement. Therefore the fee for entering into an installment agreement remains $43 for low-income taxpayers, that is, taxpayers whose income fall at or below 250% of the dollar poverty criteria established by the U.S. Department of Health and Human Services. The exception does not apply to the fee for restructuring or reinstating an installment agreement.

Other commentators recommended that the installment agreement user fee be reduced for any taxpayer who requests an agreement on-line (over the internet). Under the IOAA, user fees should be fair and based on the costs to the government, the value of the service to the recipient, and the public policy or interest served. No exception was created for installment agreements requested on-line because the benefit of the installment agreement program to the taxpayer does not change depending on how the installment agreement is requested, the convenience of on-line requests provides ample incentive for this type of application for taxpayers who have internet access, and taxpayers who do not have internet access could not take advantage of the lower fee. The IRS intends to consider a cost methodology for installment agreement user fees that reflects cost differences attributable to various types of installment agreements, as well as whether additional exceptions to full cost are warranted.

Special Analyses

It has been determined that this notice of rulemaking is not a significant regulatory action as defined in Executive Order 12866. Therefore, a regulatory assessment is not required. It is hereby certified that these regulations will not have a significant economic impact on a substantial number of small entities. Accordingly, a regulatory flexibility analysis is not required. This certification is based on the information that follows. The economic impact of these regulations on any small entity would result from the entity being required to pay a fee prescribed by these regulations in order to obtain a particular service. The dollar amount of the fee is not, however, substantial enough to have a significant economic impact on any entity subject to the fee. Pursuant to section 7805(f) of the Internal Revenue Code, the notice of proposed rulemaking preceding this regulation was submitted to the Chief Counsel for Advocacy of the Small Business Administration for comment on its impact on small business.

Although the Administrative Procedures Act prescribes a thirty-day waiting period between the date of publication in the **Federal Register** and the applicability date, this regulation is being made applicable after a shorter period under the authority provided by section 7805(b)(1)(B).

Drafting Information

The principal author of these regulations is William Beard, Office of Associate Chief Counsel (Procedure and Administration), Collection, Bankruptcy and Summonses Division.

* * * * *

Adoption of Amendments to the Regulations

Accordingly, 26 CFR part 300 is amended as follows:

PART 300—USER FEES

Paragraph 1. The authority citation for part 300 continues to read as follows:

Authority: 31 U.S.C. 9701.

Par. 2. Section 300.0 is amended by revising paragraph (c) to read as follows:

§300.0 User fees; in general.

* * * * *

(c) *Effective date*. This part 300 is applicable March 16, 1995, except that the user fee for processing offers in compromise is applicable November 1, 2003; the user fee for the special enrollment examination, enrollment, and renewal of enrollment for enrolled agents is applicable November 6, 2006; the user fee for entering into installment agreements on or after January 1, 2007, is applicable January 1, 2007; and the user fee for restructuring or reinstatement of an installment agreement on or after January 1, 2007, is applicable January 1, 2007.

Par. 3. Section 300.1 is amended by revising paragraph (b) to read as follows:

§300.1 Installment agreement fee.

* * * * *

(b) *Fee*. The fee for entering into an installment agreement before January 1, 2007, is $43. The fee for entering into an installment agreement on or after January 1, 2007, is $105, except that:

(1) The fee is $52 when the taxpayer pays by way of a direct debit from the taxpayer's bank account; and

(2) Notwithstanding the method of payment, the fee is $43 if the taxpayer is a low-income taxpayer, that is, an individual who falls at or below 250% of the dollar criteria established by the poverty guidelines updated annually in the **Federal Register** by the U.S. Department of Health and Human Services under authority of section 673(2) of the Omnibus Budget Reconciliation Act of 1981 (95 Stat. 357, 511), or such other measure that is adopted by the Secretary.

* * * * *

Par. 4. Section 300.2 is amended by revising paragraph (b) to read as follows:

§300.2 Restructuring or reinstatement of installment agreement fee.

* * * * *

(b) *Fee*. The fee for restructuring or reinstating an installment agreement before January 1, 2007, is $24. The fee for restructuring or reinstating an installment agreement on or after January 1, 2007, is $45.

* * * * *

Kevin M. Brown,
Acting Deputy Commissioner for Services and Enforcement.

Approved December 21, 2006.

Eric Solomon,
Assistant Secretary of the Treasury (Tax Policy).

(Filed by the Office of the Federal Register on December 27, 2006, 8:45 a.m., and published in the issue of the Federal Register for December 28, 2006, 71 F.R. 78074)

Section 382.—Limitation on Net Operating Loss Carryforwards and Certain Built-In Losses Following Ownership Change

The adjusted applicable federal long-term rate is set forth for the month of February 2007. See Rev. Rul. 2007-9, page 422.

Section 412.—Minimum Funding Standards

The adjusted applicable federal short-term, mid-term, and long-term rates are set forth for the month of February 2007. See Rev. Rul. 2007-9, page 422.

Section 467.—Certain Payments for the Use of Property or Services

The adjusted applicable federal short-term, mid-term, and long-term rates are set forth for the month of February 2007. See Rev. Rul. 2007-9, page 422.

Section 468.—Special Rules for Mining and Solid Waste Reclamation and Closing Costs

The adjusted applicable federal short-term, mid-term, and long-term rates are set forth for the month of February 2007. See Rev. Rul. 2007-9, page 422.

Section 482.—Allocation of Income and Deductions Among Taxpayers

Federal short-term, mid-term, and long-term rates are set forth for the month of February 2007. See Rev. Rul. 2007-9, page 422.

Section 483.—Interest on Certain Deferred Payments

The adjusted applicable federal short-term, mid-term, and long-term rates are set forth for the month of February 2007. See Rev. Rul. 2007-9, page 422.

Section 642.—Special Rules for Credits and Deductions

Federal short-term, mid-term, and long-term rates are set forth for the month of February 2007. See Rev. Rul. 2007-9, page 422.

Section 807.—Rules for Certain Reserves

The adjusted applicable federal short-term, mid-term, and long-term rates are set forth for the month of February 2007. See Rev. Rul. 2007-9, page 422.

Section 846.—Discounted Unpaid Losses Defined

The adjusted applicable federal short-term, mid-term, and long-term rates are set forth for the month of February 2007. See Rev. Rul. 2007-9, page 422.

Section 1274.—Determination of Issue Price in the Case of Certain Debt Instruments Issued for Property

(Also Sections 42, 280G, 382, 412, 467, 468, 482, 483, 642, 807, 846, 1288, 7520, 7872.)

Federal rates; adjusted federal rates; adjusted federal long-term rate and the long-term exempt rate. For purposes of sections 382, 642, 1274, 1288, and other sections of the Code, tables set forth the rates for February 2007.

Rev. Rul. 2007–9

This revenue ruling provides various prescribed rates for federal income tax purposes for February 2007 (the current month). Table 1 contains the short-term, mid-term, and long term applicable federal rates (AFR) for the current month for purposes of section 1274(d) of the Internal Revenue Code. Table 2 contains the short-term, mid-term, and long-term adjusted applicable federal rates (adjusted AFR) for the current month for purposes of section 1288(b). Table 3 sets forth the adjusted federal long-term rate and the long-term tax-exempt rate described in section 382(f). Table 4 contains the appropriate percentages for determining the low-income housing credit described in section 42(b)(2) for buildings placed in service during the current month. Finally, Table 5 contains the federal rate for determining the present value of an annuity, an interest for life or for a term of years, or a remainder or a reversionary interest for purposes of section 7520.

REV. RUL. 2007–9 TABLE 1

Applicable Federal Rates (AFR) for February 2007

	Period for Compounding			
	Annual	*Semiannual*	*Quarterly*	*Monthly*
Short-term				
AFR	4.93%	4.87%	4.84%	4.82%
110% AFR	5.43%	5.36%	5.32%	5.30%
120% AFR	5.93%	5.84%	5.80%	5.77%
130% AFR	6.43%	6.33%	6.28%	6.25%
Mid-term				
AFR	4.69%	4.64%	4.61%	4.60%
110% AFR	5.17%	5.10%	5.07%	5.05%
120% AFR	5.65%	5.57%	5.53%	5.51%
130% AFR	6.12%	6.03%	5.99%	5.96%
150% AFR	7.08%	6.96%	6.90%	6.86%
175% AFR	8.28%	8.12%	8.04%	7.99%
Long-term				
AFR	4.86%	4.80%	4.77%	4.75%
110% AFR	5.35%	5.28%	5.25%	5.22%
120% AFR	5.84%	5.76%	5.72%	5.69%
130% AFR	6.34%	6.24%	6.19%	6.16%

REV. RUL. 2007–9 TABLE 2 Adjusted AFR for February 2007 *Period for Compounding*				
	Annual	*Semiannual*	*Quarterly*	*Monthly*
Short-term adjusted AFR	3.46%	3.43%	3.42%	3.41%
Mid-term adjusted AFR	3.58%	3.55%	3.53%	3.52%
Long-term adjusted AFR	4.07%	4.03%	4.01%	4.00%

REV. RUL. 2007–9 TABLE 3 Rates Under Section 382 for February 2007	
Adjusted federal long-term rate for the current month	4.07%
Long-term tax-exempt rate for ownership changes during the current month (the highest of the adjusted federal long-term rates for the current month and the prior two months.)	4.14%

REV. RUL. 2007–9 TABLE 4 Appropriate Percentages Under Section 42(b)(2) for February 2007	
Appropriate percentage for the 70% present value low-income housing credit	8.11%
Appropriate percentage for the 30% present value low-income housing credit	3.48%

REV. RUL. 2007–9 TABLE 5 Rate Under Section 7520 for February 2007	
Applicable federal rate for determining the present value of an annuity, an interest for life or a term of years, or a remainder or reversionary interest	5.6%

Section 1288.—Treatment of Original Issue Discount on Tax-Exempt Obligations

The adjusted applicable federal short-term, mid-term, and long-term rates are set forth for the month of February 2007. See Rev. Rul. 2007-9, page 422.

Section 1561.—Limitations on Certain Multiple Tax Benefits in the Case of Certain Controlled Corporations

26 CFR 1.1561–1T: General rules regarding certain tax benefits available to the component members of a controlled group of corporations (temporary).

T.D. 9304

DEPARTMENT OF THE TREASURY
Internal Revenue Service
26 CFR Parts 1 and 5

Guidance Necessary to Facilitate Business Electronic Filing Under Section 1561

AGENCY: Internal Revenue Service (IRS), Treasury.

ACTION: Final and temporary regulations.

SUMMARY: This document contains temporary regulations that affect component members of controlled groups of corporations and consolidated groups filing life-nonlife Federal income tax returns. They provide guidance regarding the apportionment of tax benefit items and the amount and type of information these members are required to submit with their returns. The text of the temporary regulations also serves as the text of the proposed regulations (REG–161919–05) set forth in the notice of proposed rulemaking on this subject in this issue of the Bulletin.

DATES: *Effective Date:* These regulations are effective on December 22, 2006.

Applicability Date: For dates of applicability, see §§1.1502–43T(e)(1), 1.1502–47T(t)(1), 1.1561–1T(d)(1), 1.1561–2T(f)(1), 1.1561–3T(d)(1) and 1.1563–1T(e)(1). The applicability of these regulations will expire on December 21, 2009.

FOR FURTHER INFORMATION CONTACT: Grid Glyer, (202) 622–7930 (not a toll-free number).

SUPPLEMENTARY INFORMATION:

Background

Section 1561(a) provides that the *component members* of a *controlled group of corporations* (as those terms are defined in section 1563) are limited to using the amounts of certain tax benefit items described therein in the same manner as if they were one corporation. Although section 1561(a) provides that these amounts shall generally be divided equally among those members, it also provides that if those members consent to adopt an apportionment plan, then, except as provided below, they will be permitted to allocate these amounts among themselves unequally. Section 1.1561–3(b) provides the procedural format by which those members may adopt an apportionment plan.

On May 26, 2006, the IRS and Treasury Department released temporary regulations (T.D. 9264, 2006–26 I.R.B. 1150), which, among other things, eliminated regulatory impediments to the electronic filing (e-filing) of many statements that corporate taxpayers were previously required to include on or with their Federal income tax returns. As noted in section 2.C. of the preamble to those regulations, §1.1561–3(b) presents an impediment to the e-filing of that information which each member of a controlled group is required to provide with its Federal income tax return when it makes the consent provided therein. These temporary regulations remove that impediment and also clarify the amount and type of information that each member of such group is required to submit with its return, whether or not the group chooses to apportion unequally the specified tax benefit items among its members. Thus, these regulations require each member of such group to provide the requisite information, whether or not it consents to adopt an apportionment plan, on a form (*i.e.*, Schedule O or any successor to that form) to be filed with each member's Federal income tax return for each taxable year for which it is a component member of a controlled group.

Explanation of Provisions

1. *Revision of the regulations under section 1561.*

The IRS and Treasury Department are publishing temporary regulations under section 1561 for several reasons. First, the current regulations are outdated in that they refer to tax benefit items that are no longer listed in section 1561(a). Except as provided below, to minimize this issue in the future, the temporary regulations refer generically to the tax benefit items listed in section 1561(a) rather than refer specifically to those items by listing and describing each one.

Second, the current regulations do not provide guidance to taxpayers regarding how to allocate the amounts of the section 1561(a) tax benefit items among the component members of a controlled group of corporations which have an apportionment plan in effect. As a result, the IRS often can not determine whether taxpayers have correctly allocated these items. Thus, the temporary regulations refer to a new form (*i.e.*, Schedule O or any successor to that form) on which such members will provide information about these items.

Except as provided below, each component member of a controlled group must file this form every year with its Federal income tax return whether or not: (1) an apportionment plan is in effect, or (2) any change is made to the group's apportionment of its section 1561(a) tax benefit items from the previous year. However, whenever one or more of the component members of a controlled group of corporations are also members of a consolidated group, the parent of such consolidated group shall file one form on behalf of all of its members. That form shall contain all the information required for each such member.

Finally, §1.1561–3(b) presents an impediment to e-filing where such members have consented to the adoption of an apportionment plan. That section requires each member of a controlled group to attach to its return, for each year following the adoption of the plan, a copy of its signed consent to such plan. As explained in T.D. 9264, that signature requirement presents an impediment to e-filing. These temporary regulations eliminate this impediment and provide that the form will be the mechanism by which such member adopts (and also amend or terminate) such plan. Thus, each member of the group (that is not a member of a consolidated group) will file this form to consent to adopt a plan, even if it is a wholly-owned subsidiary of the group. *Compare* §1.1561–3(b)(2)(i) (a wholly-owned subsidiary of a controlled group was not required to consent to adopt a plan because it was deemed to consent if all the component members of that group that are not wholly owned subsidiaries consent). Thus, these temporary regulations eliminate the deemed consent provision of §1.1561–3(b)(2)(i).

2. *Regulation authorizing the component members of a controlled group to apportion the accumulated earnings credit unequally if they have an apportionment plan in effect.*

Section 1561(a) provides that the component members of a controlled group of corporations must divide the amount of the accumulated earnings credit (the credit) equally unless the Secretary prescribes regulations permitting an unequal allocation of that amount. However, §1.1561–2(c) requires that they divide that amount equally. The IRS and Treasury Department have concluded that they no longer will require such members to divide that amount equally. Therefore, these temporary regulations now provide that the component members of a controlled group may choose to allocate the amount of that credit unequally among themselves if they have an apportionment plan in effect.

3. *Revisions to §1.1563–1.*

A. *Reformatting the regulation.*

For the sake of consistency, the IRS and Treasury Department are reformatting §1.1563–1 to conform it to current formatting conventions. It is not intended that any such reformatting constitute a substantive change. Moreover, the changes described in this paragraph of the preamble are only limited to formatting. Thus, for example, except for the changes described below, no examples in §1.1563–1 have been updated to reflect current law. Such changes are beyond the scope of this project and will be addressed in a separate regulation project.

B. *Updating the definition of a brother-sister controlled group.*

Section 900 of the American Jobs Creation Act of 2004, Pub. L. 108–357, 118 Stat. 1418 (the 2004 amendment), revised the definition of a brother-sister controlled group in section 1563(a)(2). Prior to this 2004 amendment, commonly owned corporations qualified as a brother-sister controlled group if five or fewer persons who are individuals, estates, or trusts own (within the meaning of section 1563(d)(2)) stock possessing: (A) at least 80 percent of the total combined voting power of all classes of stock entitled to vote or at least 80 percent of the total value of shares of all classes of stock of each corporation (the 80 percent requirement) and (B) more than 50 percent of the total combined voting power of all classes of stock entitled to vote or more than 50 percent of the total value of shares of all classes of stock of each corporation, taking into account the stock ownership of each such person only to the extent such stock ownership is identical with respect to each such corporation (the more-than-50 percent requirement).

The 2004 amendment eliminated the 80 percent requirement from the section 1563(a)(2) definition of a brother-sister controlled group. As a result, for purposes of section 1561, corporations are component members of a brother-sister controlled group if just the more-than-50 percent requirement is satisfied. However, for all other provisions of law that incorporate the section 1563(a) definition of a brother-sister controlled group, both the more-than-50 percent requirement and the 80 percent requirement must be satisfied in order to qualify as a brother-sister controlled group. *See* section 1563(f)(5). Therefore, these temporary regulations reflect this change.

These temporary regulations apply to tax years beginning on or after the date they are published in the **Federal Register**. However, the above described 2004 amendment to section 1563(a)(2) is effective for tax years beginning after October 22, 2004.

C. *Clarifying that an S corporation is treated as an excluded member of a controlled group under current law.*

Section 1.1561–1(c)(1) provides that, for purposes of sections 1561 and 1563, the term *corporation* includes an electing small business corporation and refers to §1.1563–1(b)(2)(ii)(*c*) for the treatment of such a corporation as an excluded member of a controlled group of corporations. Specifically, §1.1563–1(b)(2)(ii)(*c*) provides that only an electing small business corporation which is not subject to the tax imposed by section 1378 will be treated as an excluded member.

Section 1378, as in effect when §1.1563–1(b)(2)(ii)(*c*) was published (old section 1378), taxed the income of an electing small business corporation if its income exceeded a certain threshold. That income was taxed at the lower of the rate determined under section 1201(a) or section 11. Thus, when such corporation was subject to tax under section 11, it was appropriate to treat such corporation as a component member of a controlled group for purposes of allocating its section 11 tax benefit amount.

Old section 1378 was ultimately repealed as part of the Tax Reform Act of 1986 (Pub. L. 99–514, 100 Stat. 2085). Thus, §1.1563–1(b)(2)(ii)(*c*) became obsolete.

Under current law, an S corporation (the successor to an electing small business corporation) is generally subject to tax at the entity level under only two provisions: (1) section 1374, which imposes tax on certain recognized built-in gain, and (2) section 1375, which imposes tax on passive investment income under certain circumstances. However, in both cases, the amount of tax imposed on an S corporation is computed by applying the highest rate of tax specified in section 11(b). *See* sections 1374(b)(1) and 1375(a). Thus, under either of these provisions, no portion of any of the lower tax bracket amounts of section 11(b) could be allocated to such a corporation.

In other instances, an S corporation is partially liable for taxes that were imposed on the income of its predecessor C corporation that it must now recapture. *See, e.g.*, sections 167(g), 460(b), 1363(d) and 1371(d)(2). However, these recapture taxes are not being imposed on an S corporation's own income.

Since an S corporation is not *currently* subject to any tax to which either the tax bracket amounts of section 11(b) apply, or any other tax benefit item to which section 1561(a) applies, it is appropriate to treat that corporation as an excluded member of a controlled group.

These temporary regulations clarify that only to the extent that a particular tax (and thus a particular tax benefit item to which section 1561(a)) applies to an S corporation is that type of corporation treated as a component member of the group. This general reference to a tax that applies to an S corporation is intended to avoid the issue in §1.1563–1(b)(2)(ii)(*c*) of referring to a particular Code section that later became obsolete (*i.e.*, old section 1378).

D. *Clarifying that the life insurance company provisions do not apply to the controlled group rules where that type of company is a member (whether eligible or ineligible) of a life-nonlife affiliated group for the consolidated return year for which a section 1504(c)(2) election is effective.*

The current regulations under section 1563 describe the treatment of life insurance companies under the controlled group rules. Section 1.1563–1(a)(5) provides that two or more life insurance companies that are members of a controlled group are treated as a distinct controlled group of corporations composed only of life insurance companies. Section 1.1563–1(b)(2)(ii)(*e*) defines a life insurance company as an excluded member unless that type of company is a member of a separate life insurance company controlled group described in §1.1563–1(a)(5).

Section 1504(c)(2) provides that if an affiliated group includes any domestic life insurance companies that would otherwise not be treated as includible members of the group, then, except as provided therein, the common parent of such group may elect (pursuant to regulations prescribed by the Secretary) to treat all such companies as includible corporations. Paragraph (f)(6) of §1.1502–47 implements section 1504(c)(2) as it relates to section 1563.

These temporary regulations provide that if one or more life insurance companies are members (whether eligible or ineligible) of an affiliated group for the consolidated return year for which a section 1504(c)(2) election is effective, then those members are not treated as either excluded members of the controlled group or as members of a separate life insurance controlled group. *See* §1.1502–47(f)(6). Rather, any eligible members are treated as members of the consolidated group, and any ineligible members are treated, along with the eligible and includible members of the consolidated group, as members of a life-nonlife controlled group.

These temporary regulations apply to tax years beginning on or after the date they are published in the **Federal Register**. However, paragraph (f)(6) of §1.1502–47 applies to tax years of consolidated groups beginning on or after January 1, 1982. *See* T.D. 7877, 1983–1 C.B. 207.

4. *Revisions to two consolidated return regulations.*

A. *§1.1502–43.*

Section 1.1502–43 provides rules for calculating the consolidated accumulated earnings tax. Section 1.1502–43(d) is currently reserved. These temporary regulations clarify that if the consolidated group is part of a controlled group then section 1561 applies in determining the amount of that credit.

These temporary regulations apply to consolidated return years for which a return is due (without extensions) after the date it is published in the **Federal Register**. However, pursuant to the Tax Reform Act of 1969, Pub. L. 91–172, 78 Stat. 116, the accumulated earnings credit became a full tax benefit item under section 1561(a) for tax years beginning after December 31, 1974.

B. *§1.1502–47.*

Section 1.1502–47 provides rules for a life-nonlife consolidated group to calculate its consolidated taxable income. Paragraph (s) of §1.1502–47 requires a consolidated group to provide a notation on the face of its return identifying it as a life-nonlife return. This requirement presents an impediment to e-filing. These temporary regulations remove the impediment by deleting the requirement to provide that notation.

5. *Deleting obsolete regulations.*

As part of this Treasury decision, the IRS and Treasury Department are deleting numerous obsolete regulations. This effort is part of an ongoing process to remove those types of regulations from the Code of Federal Regulations (the CFR). Therefore, the following regulations are deleted from the CFR: §§1.342–1, 1.371–1 through 1.371–2, 1.372–1, 1.374–1 through 1.374–4, 1.1018–1, 1.1562–0 through 1.1562–7, 1.1564–1 and 5.1561–1.

Special Analyses

It has been determined that this Treasury decision is not a significant regulatory action as defined in Executive Order 12866. Therefore, a regulatory assessment is not required. It has also been determined that section 553(b) of the Administrative Procedure Act (5 U.S.C. chapter 5) does not apply to these regulations. For the applicability of the Regulatory Flexibility Act (5 U.S.C. chapter 6), refer to the Special Analyses section of the preamble to the cross-reference notice of proposed rulemaking published in this issue of the Bulletin. Pursuant to section 7805(f) of the Code, these temporary regulations will be submitted to the Chief Counsel for Advocacy of the Small Business Administration for comment on their impact on small business.

Drafting Information

The principal author of these regulations is Grid Glyer, Office of Associate Chief Counsel (Corporate). However, other personnel from the IRS and Treasury Department participated in their development.

* * * * *

Adoption of Amendments to the Regulations

Accordingly, 26 CFR parts 1 and 5 are amended as follows:

PART 1—INCOME TAXES

Paragraph 1. The authority citation for part 1 is amended by adding entries in numerical order to read, in part, as follows:

Authority: 26 U.S.C. 7805 * * *

Section 1.1502–43T also issued under 26 U.S.C. 1502. * * *

Section 1.1561–2T also issued under 26 U.S.C. 1561. * * *

§1.108–1 [Removed]

Par. 2. Section 1.108–1 is removed and reserved.

§1.342–1 [Removed]

Par. 3. Section 1.342–1 is removed.

§1.371–1 [Removed]

Par. 4. Section 1.371–1 is removed.

§1.371–2 [Removed]

Par. 5. Section 1.371–2 is removed.

§1.372–1 [Removed]

Par. 6. Section 1.372–1 is removed.

§1.374–1 [Removed]

Par. 7. Section 1.374–1 is removed.

§1.374–2 [Removed]

Par. 8. Section 1.374–2 is removed.

§1.374–3 [Removed]

Par. 9. Section 1.374–3 is removed.

§1.374–4 [Removed]

Par. 10. Section 1.374–4 is removed.

§1.924(a)–1T [Amended]

Par. 10A. For each entry in the "Location" column of the following table, remove the language in the "Remove" column and add the language in the "Add" column in its place:

Location	Remove	Add
The fifth sentence of §1.924(a)–1T(j)(2)(i)	a statement	completing the form (*i.e.*, Schedule O or any successor to that form)
The fifth sentence of §1.924(a)–1T(j)(2)(i)	§1.1561–3(b)	§1.1561–3T
The sixth sentence of §1.924(a)–1T(j)(2)(i)	§1.1561–3(c)	§1.1561–3T(a)

§1.1018–1 [Removed]

Par. 11. Section 1.1018–1 is removed.

Par. 12. Section 1.1502–43 is amended by revising paragraph (d) and adding paragraph (e) to read as follows:

§1.1502–43 Consolidated accumulated earnings tax.

* * * * *

(d) [Reserved]. For further guidance, see §1.1502–43T(d).

(e) [Reserved]. For further guidance, see §1.1502–43T(e)(1).

Par. 13. Section 1.1502–43T is added to read as follows:

§1.1502–43T Consolidated accumulated earnings tax (temporary).

(a) through (c) [Reserved]. For further guidance, see §1.1502–43(a) through (c).

(d) *Consolidated accumulated earnings credit*— (1) *In general.* [Reserved]

(2) *Special rule if consolidated group part of controlled group.* If a consolidated group is treated as a component member of a controlled group, or if each member of a consolidated group is treated as a component member of a controlled group, see section 1561 for determining the portion of the accumulated earnings credit to be allocated to such group or to such members.

(e) *Effective date*— (1) *Applicability date.* This section applies to any consolidated Federal income tax return due (without extensions) after December 22, 2006. However, a consolidated group may apply this section to any consolidated Federal income tax return filed on or after December 22, 2006.

(2) *Expiration date.* The applicability of this section will expire on December 21, 2009.

Par. 14. Section 1.1502–47 is amended by revising paragraph (s) and adding paragraph (t) to read as follows:

§1.1502–47 Consolidated returns by life-nonlife groups.

* * * * *

(s) [Reserved]. For further guidance, see §1.1502–47T(s).

(t) [Reserved]. For further guidance, see §1.1502–47T(t)(1).

Par. 15. Section 1.1502–47T is amended by revising paragraph (s) and adding paragraph (t) to read as follows:

§1.1502–47T Consolidated returns by life-nonlife groups (temporary).

* * * * *

(s) *Filing requirements.* Nonlife consolidated taxable income or loss under paragraph (h) of §1.1502–47 shall be determined on a separate Form 1120 or 1120–PC, and consolidated partial LICTI under paragraph (j) of §1.1502–47 shall be determined on a separate Form 1120–L. The consolidated return shall be made on a separate Form 1120, 1120–PC, or 1120–L filed by the common parent (if the group includes a life company), which shows the set-offs under paragraphs (g), (m), and (n) of §1.1502–47 and clearly indicates on the face of the return that it is a life-nonlife consolidated return (if the group includes a life company). See also §1.1502–75(j), relating to statements and schedules for subsidiaries.

(t) *Effective date*— (1) *Applicability date.* Paragraph (s) of this section applies to any consolidated Federal income tax return due (without extensions) after December 22, 2006. However, a consolidated group may apply paragraph (s) of this section to any consolidated Federal income tax return filed on or after December 22, 2006.

(2) *Expiration date.* The applicability of paragraph (s) of this section will expire on December 21, 2009.

Par. 16. Section 1.1502–90 is amended by:

1. Removing and reserving the entry for §1.1502–95(e)(8).

2. Removing and reserving the entry for §1.1502–95(f).

3. Reserving an entry for §1.1502–95(g).

4. Adding entries for §1.1502–95T.

The additions read as follows:

§1.1502–90 Table of contents.

* * * * *

§1.1502–95 Rules on ceasing to be a member of a consolidated group (or loss subgroup).

* * * * *

(g) [Reserved]

§1.1502–95T Rules on ceasing to be a member of a consolidated group (or loss subgroup) (temporary).

(a) through (e)(7) [Reserved]

(e)(8) Reporting requirements.

(i) Common Parent.

(ii) Former Member.

(iii) Exception.

(f) Filing the election to apportion the section 382 limitation and net unrealized built-in gain.

(1) Form of the election to apportion.

(i) Statement.

(ii) Agreement.

(2) Signing the agreement.

(3) Filing of the election.

(i) Filing by the common parent.

(ii) Filing by the former member.

(4) Revocation of election.

(g) Effective date.

(1) Applicability date.

(2) Expiration date.

§1.1561–0 [Removed]

Par. 17. Section 1.1561–0 is removed.

§1.1561–1 [Removed]

Par. 18. Section 1.1561–1 is removed.

Par. 19. Section 1.1561–1T is added to read as follows:

§1.1561–1T General rules regarding certain tax benefits available to the component members of a controlled group of corporations (temporary).

(a) *In general.* (1) Part II (section 1561 and following) of subchapter B of chapter 6 of the Internal Revenue Code (part II) provides rules to limit the amounts of certain specified tax benefit items of component members of a controlled group of corporations on a December 31, for their taxable years which include such December 31. The component members of such a group shall be limited for purposes of subtitle A of the Code to the amounts of certain items, set forth in section 1561(a), as if they were one corporation. Certain other tax items also set forth in section 1561(a) (*e.g.*, the additional tax imposed by section 11(b)(1) and the section 55(d)(3) phase out of the alternative minimum tax exemption amount) will be determined by combining the taxable income of all such members and then allocating the amount of such items among such members.

(2) For certain definitions (including the definition of a *controlled group of corporations* and a *component member*) and special rules for purposes of this part II, see section 1563.

(b) *Special rules.* (1) For purposes of this part II, the term *corporation* includes a small business corporation (as defined in section 1361). However, for the treatment of such a corporation as an *excluded member* of a controlled group of corporations see §1.1563–1(b)(2)(ii)(C).

(2) In the case of corporations electing a 52–53-week taxable year under section 441(f)(1), the provisions of this part II shall be applied in accordance with the special rule of section 441(f)(2)(A). See §1.441–2.

(c) *Tax avoidance.* The provisions of this part II do not delimit or abrogate any principle of law established by judicial decision, or any existing provisions of the Code, such as sections 269, 482, and 1551, which have the effect of preventing the avoidance or evasion of income taxes.

(d) *Effective date*— (1) *Applicability date.* This section applies to any taxable year beginning on or after December 22, 2006. However, taxpayers may apply this section to any Federal income tax return filed on or after December 22, 2006.

(2) *Expiration date.* The applicability of this section will expire on December 21, 2009.

Par. 20. Section 1.1561–2 is amended by removing and reserving paragraphs (a) and (b), revising paragraph (c), removing and reserving paragraph (d) and adding paragraph (f) to read as follows:

§1.1561–2 Determination of amount of tax benefits.

* * * * *

(c) [Reserved]. For further guidance, see §1.1561–2T(c).

* * * * *

(f) [Reserved]. For further guidance, see §1.1561–2T(f)(1).

Par. 21. Section 1.1561–2T is added to read as follows:

§1.1561–2T Determination of amount of tax benefits (temporary).

(a) through (b) [Reserved]

(c) *Accumulated earnings credit.* The component members of a controlled group of corporations may allocate the amount of the accumulated earnings credit unequally if they have an apportionment plan in effect.

(d) [Reserved]

(e) [Reserved]. For further guidance, see §1.1561–2(e).

(f) *Effective date*— (1) *Applicability date.* This section applies to any taxable year beginning on or after December 22, 2006. However, taxpayers may apply this section to any Federal income tax return filed on or after December 22, 2006.

(2) *Expiration date.* The applicability of this section will expire on December 21, 2009.

§1.1561–3 [Removed]

Par. 22. Section 1.1561–3 is removed.

Par. 23. Section 1.1561–3T is added to read as follows:

§1.1561–3T Allocation of the section 1561(a) tax items (temporary).

(a) *Filing of form*— (1) *In general.* For each taxable year that a corporation is a component member of the same controlled group of corporations on a December 31, for its taxable year that includes such December 31, such corporation and all other component members of such group must each file the required form (*i.e.*, Schedule O or any successor to that form) with each Federal income tax return. Each such corporation must file that form with its return whether or not—

(i) An apportionment plan is in effect; or

(ii) Any change is made in the group's apportionment of its section 1561(a) tax benefit items from the previous year.

(2) *Exception for component members that are members of a consolidated group.* If one or more of the component members of a controlled group of corporations are also members of a consolidated group, the parent of such consolidated group shall file only one form on behalf of all of such members. Such form shall contain the information required for each such member.

(b) *No apportionment plan in effect.* If the component members of a controlled group of corporations do not have an apportionment plan in effect, the amounts of the section 1561(a) items must be divided equally among all such members. For purposes of the preceding sentence, if any component members of a controlled group of corporations are also members of a consolidated group, such members will each be treated as a separate component member of the controlled group.

(c) *Apportionment plan in effect*— (1) *Adoption of plan.* The component members of a controlled group of corporations consent to the adoption (or amendment) of an apportionment plan by checking the box to that effect on such form. For purposes of this paragraph (c)—

(i) An apportionment plan that is adopted (including a plan that has been amended) continues in effect until it is terminated;

(ii) A consolidated group is treated as one component member of such group; and

(iii) The members must allocate the amounts of the section 1561(a) items between or among themselves as described in the plan.

(2) *Limitation on adopting a plan*— (i) *Sufficient statute of limitations period.* The members may only adopt or amend such a plan if there is at least one year re-

maining in the statutory period (including any extensions thereof) for the assessment of a deficiency against every member the tax liability of which would be increased by the adoption of such a plan.

(ii) *Insufficient statute of limitations period.* If any member cannot satisfy the requirement of paragraph (c)(2)(i) of this section, the members may not adopt or amend such a plan unless the member not satisfying such requirement has entered into an agreement with the Internal Revenue Service to extend the statute of limitations for the limited purpose of assessing any deficiency against such member attributable to the adoption of such a plan.

(3) *Termination of plan.* An apportionment plan that is in effect for the component members of a controlled group with respect to a particular December 31 is terminated with respect to a succeeding December 31 if—

(i) Each member of such group consents to the termination of such a plan for such succeeding December 31 by checking the box to that effect on its form;

(ii) The controlled group ceases to remain in existence (within the meaning of section 1563(a)) during the calendar year ending on such succeeding December 31;

(iii) Any corporation which was a component member of such group on the particular December 31 is not a component member of such group on such succeeding December 31; or

(iv) Any corporation which was not a component member of such group on the particular December 31 is a component member of such group on such succeeding December 31.

(d) *Effective date*— (1) *Applicability date.* This section applies to any taxable year beginning on or after December 22, 2006. However, taxpayers may apply this section to any Federal income tax return filed on or after December 22, 2006.

(2) *Expiration date.* The applicability of this section will expire on December 21, 2009.

§1.1562–0 [Removed]

Par. 24. Section 1.1562–0 is removed.

§1.1562–1 [Removed]

Par. 25. Section 1.1562–1 is removed.

§1.1562–2 [Removed]

Par. 26. Section 1.1562–2 is removed.

§1.1562–3 [Removed]

Par. 27. Section 1.1562–3 is removed.

§1.1562–4 [Removed]

Par. 28. Section 1.1562–4 is removed.

§1.1562–5 [Removed]

Par. 29. Section 1.1562–5 is removed.

§1.1562–6 [Removed]

Par. 30. Section 1.1562–6 is removed.

§1.1562–7 [Removed]

Par. 31. Section 1.1562–7 is removed.

§1.1563–1 [Removed]

Par. 32. Section 1.1563–1 is removed.

Par. 33. Section 1.1563–1T is amended by revising paragraphs (a), (b), (c)(1), (c)(2)(iv), (d) and (e) to read as follows:

§1.1563–1T Definition of controlled group of corporations and component members (temporary).

(a) *Controlled group of corporations*— (1) *In general.* For purposes of sections 1561 through 1563, the term *controlled group of corporations* means any group of corporations which is either a *parent-subsidiary controlled group* (as defined in paragraph (a)(2) of this section), a *brother-sister controlled group* (as defined in paragraph (a)(3)(i) of this section), a *combined group* (as defined in paragraph (a)(4) of this section), or a *life insurance controlled group* (as defined in paragraph (a)(5) of this section). For the exclusion of certain stock for purposes of applying the definitions contained in this paragraph, see section 1563(c) and §1.1563–2.

(2) *Parent-subsidiary controlled group.* (i) The term *parent-subsidiary controlled group* means one or more chains of corporations connected through stock ownership with a common parent corporation if—

(A) Stock possessing at least 80 percent of the total combined voting power of all classes of stock entitled to vote or at least 80 percent of the total value of shares of all classes of stock of each of the corporations, except the common parent corporation, is owned (directly and with the application of §1.1563–3(b)(1), relating to options) by one or more of the other corporations; and

(B) The common parent corporation owns (directly and with the application of §1.1563–3(b)(1), relating to options) stock possessing at least 80 percent of the total combined voting power of all classes of stock entitled to vote or at least 80 percent of the total value of shares of all classes of stock of at least one of the other corporations, excluding, in computing such voting power or value, stock owned directly by such other corporations.

(ii) The definition of a parent-subsidiary controlled group of corporations may be illustrated by the following examples:

Example 1. P Corporation owns stock possessing 80 percent of the total combined voting power of all classes of stock entitled to vote of S Corporation. P is the common parent of a parent-subsidiary controlled group consisting of member corporations P and S.

Example 2. Assume the same facts as in *Example 1.* Assume further that S owns stock possessing 80 percent of the total value of shares of all classes of stock of T Corporation. P is the common parent of a parent-subsidiary controlled group consisting of member corporations P, S, and T. The result would be the same if P, rather than S, owned the T stock.

Example 3. L Corporation owns 80 percent of the only class of stock of M Corporation and M, in turn, owns 40 percent of the only class of stock of O Corporation. L also owns 80 percent of the only class of stock of N Corporation and N, in turn, owns 40 percent of the only class of stock of O. L is the common parent of a parent-subsidiary controlled group consisting of member corporations L, M, N, and O.

Example 4. X Corporation owns 75 percent of the only class of stock of Y and Z Corporations; Y owns all the remaining stock of Z; and Z owns all the remaining stock of Y. Since intercompany stockholdings are excluded (that is, are not treated as outstanding) for purposes of determining whether X owns stock possessing at least 80 percent of the voting power or value of at least one of the other corporations, X is treated as the owner of stock possessing 100 percent of the voting power and value of Y and of Z for purposes of paragraph (a)(2)(i)(B) of this section. Also, stock possessing 100 percent of the voting power and value of Y and Z is owned by the other corporations in the group within the meaning of paragraph (a)(2)(i)(A) of this section. (X and Y together own stock possessing 100 percent of the voting power and value of Z, and X and Z together own stock possessing 100 percent of the voting power and value of Y.) Therefore, X is the common parent of a parent-subsidiary controlled group of corporations consisting of member corporations X, Y, and Z.

(3) *Brother-sister controlled group*—(i) *In general.* The term *brother-sister controlled group* means two or more corporations if the same five or fewer persons who are individuals, estates, or trusts own (directly and with the application of the rules contained in §1.1563–3(b)) stock possessing more than 50 percent of the total combined voting power of all classes of stock entitled to vote or more than 50 percent of the total value of shares of all classes of stock of each corporation, taking into account the stock ownership of each such person only to the extent such stock ownership is identical with respect to each such corporation.

(ii) *Additional stock ownership requirement for purposes of certain other provisions of law.* For purposes of any provision of law (other than sections 1561 through 1563) that incorporates the section 1563(a) definition of a controlled group, the term *brother-sister controlled group* means two or more corporations if the same five or fewer persons who are individuals, estates, or trusts own (directly and with the application of the rules contained in §1.1563–3(b)) stock possessing—

(A) At least 80 percent of the total combined voting power of all classes of stock entitled to vote or at least 80 percent of the total value of shares of all classes of stock of each corporation (the 80 percent requirement);

(B) More than 50 percent of the total combined voting power of all classes of stock entitled to vote or more than 50 percent of the total value of shares of all classes of stock of each corporation, taking into account the stock ownership of each such person only to the extent such stock ownership is identical with respect to each such corporation (the more-than-50 percent identical ownership requirement); and

(C) The five or fewer persons whose stock ownership is considered for purposes of the 80 percent requirement must be the same persons whose stock ownership is considered for purposes of the more-than-50 percent identical ownership requirement.

(iii) *Examples.* The principles of paragraph (a)(3)(ii) of this section may be illustrated by the following examples:

Example 1. (i) The outstanding stock of corporations P, Q, R, S, and T, which have only one class of stock outstanding is owned by the following unrelated individuals:

Individuals	CORPORATIONS					
	P	Q	R	S	T	Identical ownership
A	55%	51%	55%	55%	55%	51%
B	45%	49%				(45% in P & Q)
C			45%			
D				45%		
E					45%	
Total	100%	100%	100%	100%	100%	

(ii) Corporations P and Q are members of a brother-sister controlled group of corporations. Although the more-than-50 percent identical ownership requirement is met for all 5 corporations, corporations R, S, and T are not members because at least 80 percent of the stock of each of those corporations is not owned by the same 5 or fewer persons whose stock ownership is considered for purposes of the more-than-50 percent identical ownership requirement.

Example 2. (i) The outstanding stock of corporations U and V, which have only one class of stock outstanding, is owned by the following unrelated individuals:

Individuals	Corporations	
	U	V
A	12%	12%
B	12%	12%
C	12%	12%
D	12%	12%
E	13%	13%
F	13%	13%
G	13%	13%
H	13%	13%
Total	100%	100%

(ii) Any group of five of the shareholders will own more than 50 percent of the stock in each corporation, in identical holdings. However, U and V are not members of a brother-sister controlled group because at least 80 percent of the stock of each corporation is not owned by the same five or fewer persons.

Example 3. (i) Corporation X and Y each have two classes of stock outstanding, voting common and non-voting common. (None of this stock is excluded from the definition of stock under section 1563(c).) Unrelated individuals A and B own the following percentages of the class of stock entitled to vote (voting) and of the total value of shares of all classes of stock (value) in each of corporations X and Y:

Individuals	Corporations X	Corporations Y
A	100% voting, 60% value.	75% voting, 60% value.
B	0% voting, 10% value.	25% voting, 10% value.

(ii) No other shareholder of X owns (or is considered to own) any stock in Y. X and Y are a brother-sister controlled group of corporations. The group meets the more-than-50 percent identical ownership requirement because A and B own more than 50 percent of the total value of shares of all classes of stock of X and Y in identical holdings. (The group also meets the more-than-50 percent identical ownership requirement because of A's voting stock ownership.) The group meets the 80 percent requirement because A and B own at least 80 percent of the total combined voting power of all classes of stock entitled to vote.

Example 4. Assume the same facts as in *Example 3* except that the value of the stock owned by A and B is not more than 50 percent of the total value of shares of all classes of stock of each corporation in identical holdings. X and Y are not a brother-sister controlled group of corporations. The group meets the more-than-50 percent identical ownership requirement because A owns more than 50 percent of the total combined voting power of the voting stock of each corporation. For purposes of the 80 percent requirement, B's voting stock in Y cannot be combined with A's voting stock in Y since B, who does not own any voting stock in X, is not a person whose ownership is considered for purposes of the more-than-50 percent identical ownership requirement. Because no other shareholder owns stock in both X and Y, these other shareholders' stock ownership is not counted towards meeting either the more-than-50 percent identical ownership requirement or the 80 percent ownership requirement.

(iv) *Special rule if prior law applies.* Paragraph (a)(3)(ii) of this section, as amended by T.D. 8179, 1988–1 C.B. 122, applies to taxable years ending on or after December 31, 1970. See, however, the transitional rule in paragraph (d) of this section.

(4) *Combined group.* (i) The term *combined group* means any group of three or more corporations if—

(A) Each such corporation is a member of either a parent-subsidiary controlled group of corporations or a brother-sister controlled group of corporations; and

(B) At least one of such corporations is the common parent of a parent-subsidiary controlled group and also is a member of a brother-sister controlled group.

(ii) The definition of a combined group of corporations may be illustrated by the following examples:

Example 1. Smith, an individual, owns stock possessing 80 percent of the total combined voting power of all classes of the stock of corporations X and Y. Y, in turn, owns stock possessing 80 percent of the total combined voting power of all classes of the stock of corporation Z. X, Y, and Z are members of the same combined group since—

(i) X, Y, and Z are each members of either a parent-subsidiary or brother-sister controlled group of corporations; and

(ii) Y is the common parent of a parent-subsidiary controlled group of corporations consisting of Y and Z, and also is a member of a brother-sister controlled group of corporations consisting of X and Y.

Example 2. Assume the same facts as in *Example 1*, and further assume that corporation X owns 80 percent of the total value of shares of all classes of stock of corporation T. X, Y, Z, and T are members of the same combined group.

(5) *Life insurance controlled group.* (i) The term *life insurance controlled group* means two or more life insurance companies each of which is a member of a controlled group of corporations described in paragraph (a)(2), (a)(3)(i), or (a)(4) of this section and to which §1.1502–47(f)(6) does not apply. Such insurance companies shall be treated as a controlled group of corporations separate from any other corporations which are members of a controlled group described in such paragraph (a)(2), (a)(3)(i), or (a)(4). For purposes of this section, the common parent of the controlled group described in paragraph (a)(2) of this section shall be referred to as the common parent of the life insurance controlled group.

(ii) The following examples illustrate the definition of a life insurance controlled group. In these examples, L indicates a life company, another letter indicates a non-life company and each corporation uses the calendar year as its taxable year.

Example 1. Since January 1, 1999, corporation P has owned all the stock of corporations L_1 and Y, and L_1 has owned all the stock of corporation X. On January 1, 2005, Y acquired all of the stock of corporation L_2. Since L_1 and L_2 are members of a parent-subsidiary controlled group of corporations, such companies are treated as members of a life insurance controlled group separate from the parent-subsidiary controlled group consisting of P, X and Y. For purposes of this section, P is referred to as the common parent of the life insurance controlled group even though P is not a member of such group.

Example 2. The facts are the same as in *Example 1*, except that, beginning with the 2005 tax year, the P affiliated group elected to file a consolidated return and P made a section 1504(c)(2) election. Pursuant to paragraph (a)(5)(i) of this section, L_1 and L_2 are not members of a separate life insurance controlled group. Instead, P, X, Y, L_1 and L_2 constitute one controlled group. *See* §1.1502–47(f)(6).

(6) *Voting power of stock.* For purposes of this section, and §§1.1563–2 and 1.1563–3, in determining whether the stock owned by a person (or persons) possesses a certain percentage of the total combined voting power of all classes of stock entitled to vote of a corporation, consideration will be given to all the facts and circumstances of each case. A share of stock will generally be considered as possessing the voting power accorded to such share by the corporate charter, by-laws, or share certificate. On the other hand, if there is any agreement, whether express or implied, that a shareholder will not vote his stock in a corporation, the formal voting rights possessed by his stock may be disregarded in determining the percentage of the total combined voting power possessed by the stock owned by other shareholders in the corporation, if the result is that the corporation becomes a component member of a controlled group of corporations. Moreover, if a shareholder agrees to vote his stock in a corporation in the manner specified by another shareholder in the corporation, the voting rights possessed by the stock owned by the first shareholder may be considered to be possessed by the stock owned by such other shareholder if the result is that the corporation becomes a component member of a controlled group of corporations.

(b) *Component members*— (1) *In general.* For purposes of sections 1561 through 1563, a corporation is a component member of a controlled group of corporations on a December 31 (and with respect to the taxable year which includes such December 31) if such corporation—

(i) Is a member of such controlled group on such December 31 and is not treated as an excluded member under paragraph (b)(2) of this section; or

(ii) Is not a member of such controlled group on such December 31 but is treated as an additional member under paragraph (b)(3) of this section.

(2) *Excluded members.* (i) A corporation, which is a member of a controlled group of corporations on the December 31 included within its taxable year, but was a member of such group for less than one-half of the number of days in such taxable year which precede such December 31, shall be treated as an excluded member of such group on such December 31.

(ii) A corporation which is a member of a controlled group of corporations on any December 31 shall be treated as an excluded member of such group on such date if, for its taxable year including such date, such corporation is—

(A) Exempt from taxation under section 501(a) (except a corporation which is subject to tax on its unrelated business taxable income under section 511) or 521 for such taxable year;

(B) A foreign corporation not subject to taxation under section 882(a) for the taxable year;

(C) An S corporation (as defined in section 1361) for purposes of any tax benefit item described in section 1561(a) to which it is not subject;

(D) A franchised corporation (as defined in section 1563(f)(4) and §1.1563–4); or

(E) An insurance company subject to taxation under section 801, unless such insurance company (without regard to this paragraph (b)(2)(ii)(E)) is a component member of a life insurance controlled group described in paragraph (a)(5)(i) of this section or unless §1.1502–47(f)(6) applies (which treats a life insurance company, for which a section 1504(c)(2) election is effective, as a member (whether eligible or ineligible) of a life-nonlife affiliated group).

(3) *Additional members.* A corporation shall be treated as an additional member of a controlled group of corporations on the December 31 included within its taxable year if it—

(i) Is not a member of such group on such December 31;

(ii) Is not described, with respect to such taxable year, in paragraph (b)(2)(ii)(A), (B), (C), (D), or (E) of this section; and

(iii) Was a member of such group for one-half (or more) of the number of days in such taxable year which precede such December 31.

(4) *Examples.* The provisions of this paragraph may be illustrated by the following examples:

Example 1. Brown, an individual, owns all of the stock of corporations W and X on each day of 1964. W and X each uses the calendar year as its taxable year. On January 1, 1964, Brown also owns all the stock of corporation Y (a fiscal year corporation with a taxable year beginning on July 1, 1964, and ending on June 30, 1965), which stock he sells on October 15, 1964. On December 1, 1964, Brown purchases all the stock of corporation Z (a fiscal year corporation with a taxable year beginning on September 1, 1964, and ending on August 31, 1965). On December 31, 1964, W, X, and Z are members of the same controlled group. However, the component members of the group on such December 31 are W, X, and Y. Under paragraph (b)(2)(i) of this section, Z is treated as an excluded member of the group on December 31, 1964, since Z was a member of the group for less than one-half of the number of days (29 out of 121 days) during the period beginning on September 1, 1964 (the first day of its taxable year) and ending on December 30, 1964. Under paragraph (b)(3) of this section, Y is treated as an additional member of the group on December 31, 1964, since Y was a member of the group for at least one-half of the number of days (107 out of 183 days) during the period beginning on July 1, 1964 (the first day of its taxable year) and ending on December 30, 1964.

Example 2. On January 1, 1964, corporation P owns all the stock of corporation S, which in turn owns all the stock of corporation S–1. On November 1, 1964, P purchases all of the stock of corporation X from the public and sells all of the stock of S to the public. Corporation X owns all the stock of corporation Y during 1964. P, S, S–1, X, and Y file their returns on the basis of the calendar year. On December 31, 1964, P, X, and Y are members of a parent-subsidiary controlled group of corporations; also, corporations S and S–1 are members of a different parent-subsidiary controlled group on such date. However, since X and Y have been members of the parent-subsidiary controlled group of which P is the common parent for less than one-half the number of days during the period January 1 through December 30, 1964, they are not component members of such group on such date. On the other hand, X and Y have been members of a parent-subsidiary controlled group of which X is the common parent for at least one-half the number of days during the period January 1 through December 30, 1964, and therefore they are component members of such group on December 31, 1964. Also since S and S–1 were members of the parent-subsidiary controlled group of which P is the common parent for at least one-half the number of days in the taxable years of each such corporation during the period January 1 through December 30, 1964, P, S, and S–1 are component members of such group on December 31, 1964.

Example 3. Throughout 1964, corporation M owns all the stock of corporation F which, in turn, owns all the stock of corporations L–1, L–2, X, and Y. M is a domestic mutual insurance company subject to taxation under section 821, F is a foreign corporation not engaged in a trade or business within the United States, L–1 and L–2 are domestic life insurance companies subject to taxation under section 802, and X and Y are domestic corporations subject to tax under section 11 of the Code. Each corporation uses the calendar year as its taxable year. On December 31, 1964, M, F, L–1, L–2, X, and Y are members of a parent-subsidiary controlled group of corporations. However, under paragraph (b)(2)(ii) of this section, M, F, L–1, and L–2 are treated as excluded members of the group on December 31, 1964. Thus, on December 31, 1964, the component members of the parent-subsidiary controlled group of which M is the common parent include only X and Y. Furthermore, since paragraph (b)(2)(ii)(E) of this section does not result in L–1 and L–2 being treated as excluded members of a life insurance controlled group, L–1 and L–2 are component members of a life insurance controlled group on December 31, 1964.

(5) *Application of constructive ownership rules.* For purposes of paragraphs (b)(2)(i) and (3) of this section, it is necessary to determine whether a corporation was a member of a controlled group of corporations for one-half (or more) of the number of days in its taxable year which precede the December 31 falling within such taxable year. Therefore, the constructive ownership rules contained in §1.1563–3(b) (to the extent applicable in making such determination) must be applied on a day-by-day basis. For example, if P Corporation owns all the stock of X Corporation on each day of 1964, and on December 30, 1964, acquires an option to purchase all the stock of Y Corporation (a calendar-year taxpayer which has been in existence on each day of 1964), the application of §1.1563–3(b)(1) on a day-by-day basis results in Y being a member of the brother-sister controlled group on only one day of Y's 1964 year which precedes December 31, 1964. Accordingly, since Y is not a member of such group for one-half or more of the number of days in its 1964 year preceding December 31, 1964, Y is treated as an excluded member of such group on December 31, 1964.

(c) *Overlapping groups*— (1) *In general.* If on a December 31 a corporation is a component member of a controlled group of corporations by reason of ownership of stock possessing at least 80 percent of the total value of shares of all classes of stock of the corporation, and if on such December 31 such corporation is also a component member of another controlled group of corporations by reason of ownership of other stock (that is, stock not used to satisfy the at-least-80 percent total value test) possessing at least 80 percent of the total combined voting power of all classes of stock of the corporation entitled to vote, then such corporation shall be treated as a component member only of the controlled group of which it is a component member by reason of the ownership of at least 80 percent of the total value of its shares.

(2) *Brother-sister controlled groups.*

* * * * *

(iv) The provisions of this paragraph (c)(2) may be illustrated by the following examples (in which it is assumed that all the individuals are unrelated):

Example 1. (i) On each day of 1970 all the outstanding stock of corporations M, N, and P is held in the following manner:

Individuals	Corporations M	N	P
A	55%	40%	5%
B	40%	20%	40%
C	5%	40%	55%

(ii) Since the more-than-50 percent identical ownership requirement of section 1563(a)(2) is met with respect to corporations M and N and with respect to corporations N and P, but not with respect to corporations M, N, and P, corporation N would, without the application of this paragraph (c)(2), be a component member on December 31, 1970, of overlapping groups consisting of M and N and of N and P. If N does not file an election in accordance with paragraph (c)(2)(i) of this section, the Internal Revenue Service will determine the group in which N is to be included.

Example 2. (i) On each day of 1970, all the outstanding stock of corporations S, T, W, X, and Z is held in the following manner:

Individuals	Corporations S	T	W	X	Z
D	52	52	52	52	52
E	40	2	2	2	2
F	2	40	2	2	2
G	2	2	40	2	2
H	2	2	2	40	2
I	2	2	2	2	40

(ii) On December 31, 1970, the more-than-50 percent identical ownership requirement of section 1563(a)(2) may be met with regard to any combination of the corporations but all five corporations cannot be included as component members of a single controlled group because the inclusion of all the corporations in a single group would be dependent upon taking into account the stock ownership of more than five persons. Therefore, if the corporations do not file a statement in accordance with paragraph (c)(2)(ii) of this section, the Internal Revenue Service will determine the group in which each corporation is to be included. The corporations or the Internal Revenue Service, as the case may be, may designate that three corporations be included in one group and two corporations in another, or that any four corporations be included in one group and that the remaining corporation not be included in any group.

(d) *Transitional rules*— (1) *In general.* Treasury decision 8179 amended paragraph (a)(3)(ii) of this section to revise the definition of a brother-sister controlled group of corporations. In general, those amendments are effective for taxable years ending on or after December 31, 1970.

(2) *Limited nonretroactivity.* (i) Under the authority of section 7805(b), the Internal Revenue Service will treat an old group as a brother-sister controlled group corporations for purposes of applying sections 401, 404(a), 408(k), 409A, 410, 411, 412, 414, 415, and 4971 of the Code and sections 202, 203, 204, and 302 of the Employment Retirement Income Security Act of 1974 (ERISA) in a plan year or taxable year beginning before March 2, 1988, to the extent necessary to prevent an adverse effect on any old member (or any other corporation), or on any plan or other entity described in such sections (including plans, etc., of corporations not part of such old group), that would result solely from the retroactive effect of the amendment to this section by T.D. 8179. An adverse effect includes the disqualification of a plan or the disallowance of a deduction or credit for a contribution to a plan. The Internal Revenue Service, however, will not treat an old member as a member of an old group to the extent that such treatment will have an adverse effect on that old member.

(ii) Section 7805(b) will not be applied pursuant to paragraph (d)(2)(i) of this section to treat an old member of an old group as a member of a brother-sister controlled group to prevent an adverse effect for a taxable year if, for that taxable year, that old member treats or has treated itself as not being a member of that old group for purposes of sections 401, 404(a), 408(k), 409A, 410, 411, 412, 414, 415, and 4971 of the Code and sections 202, 203, 204, and 302 and Title IV of ERISA for such taxable year (such as by filing, with respect to such taxable year, a return, amended return, or claim for credit or refund in which the amount of any deduction, credit, limitation, or tax due is determined by treating itself as not being a member of the old group for purposes of those sections). However, the fact that one or more (but not all) of the old members do not qualify for section 7805(b) treatment because of the preceding sentence will not preclude that old member (or members) from being treated as a member of the old group under paragraph (d)(2)(i) of this section in order to prevent the disallowance of a deduction or credit of another old member (or other corporation) or to prevent the disqualification of, or other adverse effect on, another old member's plan (or other entity) described in the sections of the Code and ERISA enumerated in such paragraph.

(3) *Election of general nonretroactivity.* In the case of a taxable year ending on or after December 31, 1970, and before March 2, 1988, an old group will be treated as a brother-sister controlled group of corporations for all purposes of the Code for such taxable year if—

(i) Each old member files a statement consenting to such treatment for such taxable year with the District Director having audit jurisdiction over its return within six months after March 2, 1988; and

(ii) No old member—

(A) Files or has filed, with respect to such taxable year, a return, amended return, or claim for credit or refund in which the amount of any deduction, credit, limitation, or tax due is determined by treating any old member as not a member of the old group; or

(B) Treats the employees of all members of the old group as not being employed by a single employer for purposes of sections 401, 404(a), 408(k), 409A, 410, 411, 412, 414, 415, and 4971 of the Code and sections 202, 203, 204, and 302 of ERISA for such taxable year.

(4) *Definitions.* For purposes of this paragraph (d)—

(i) An *old group* is a brother-sister controlled group of corporations, determined by applying paragraph (a)(3)(ii) of this section as in effect before the amendments made by Treasury decision 8179, that is not a brother-sister controlled group of corporations, determined by applying paragraph (a)(3)(ii) of this section as amended by such Treasury decision; and

(ii) An *old member* is any corporation that is a member of an old group.

(5) *Election to choose between membership in more than one controlled group.* If—

(i) An old member has filed an election under paragraph (c)(2) of this section to be treated as a component member of an old group for a December 31 before March 2, 1988; and

(ii) That corporation would (without regard to such paragraph) be a component member of more than one brother-sister controlled group (not including an old group) on the December 31, that corporation may make an election under that paragraph by filing an amended return on or before September 2, 1988. This paragraph (d)(5) does not apply to a corporation that is treated as a member of an old group under paragraph (d)(3) of this section.

(6) *Refunds.* See section 6511(a) for period of limitation on filing claims for credit or refund.

(e) *Effective date*— (1) *Applicability date.* Paragraphs (a), (b), (c)(1), (c)(2)(iv) and (d) of this section apply to taxable years beginning on or after December 22, 2006. However, taxpayers may apply these paragraphs to any Federal income tax return filed on or after December 22, 2006. Paragraphs (c)(2)(i) through (iii) of this section apply to any original Federal income tax return (including any amended return filed on or before the due date (including extensions) of such original return) timely filed on or after May 30, 2006.

(2) *Expiration date.* The applicability of paragraphs (a), (b), (c)(1), (c)(2)(iv) and (d) of this section will expire on December 21, 2009. The applicability of paragraphs (c)(2)(i) through (iii) of this section will expire on May 26, 2009.

§1.1563–3 [Amended]

Par. 34. In §1.1563–3, at the end of paragraph (d)(3) Example 3, add the phrase "for purposes of paragraph (a)(3)(ii) of §1.1563–1T".

§1.1564–1 [Removed]

Par. 35. Section 1.1564–1 is removed.

PART 5—TEMPORARY INCOME TAX REGULATIONS UNDER THE REVENUE ACT OF 1978

Par. 36. The authority citation for part 5 continues to read as follows:

Authority: 26 U.S.C. 7805.

§5.1561–1 [Removed]

Par. 37. Section 5.1561–1 is removed.

Mark E. Matthews,
Deputy Commissioner for Services and Enforcement.

Approved December 12, 2006.

Eric Solomon,
Acting Deputy Assistant Secretary of the Treasury (Tax Policy).

(Filed by the Office of the Federal Register on December 21, 2006, 8:45 a.m., and published in the issue of the Federal Register for December 22, 2006, 71 F.R. 76904)

Section 7520.—Valuation Tables

The adjusted applicable federal short-term, mid-term, and long-term rates are set forth for the month of February 2007. See Rev. Rul. 2007-9, page 422.

Section 7872.—Treatment of Loans With Below-Market Interest Rates

The adjusted applicable federal short-term, mid-term, and long-term rates are set forth for the month of February 2007. See Rev. Rul. 2007-9, page 422.

Section 9802.—Prohibiting Discrimination Against Individual Participants and Beneficiaries Based on Health Status

26 CFR 54.9802–1: Prohibiting discrimination against participants and beneficiaries based on a health factor.

T.D. 9298

DEPARTMENT OF THE TREASURY
Internal Revenue Service
26 CFR Part 54

DEPARTMENT OF LABOR
Employee Benefits Security Administration
29 CFR Part 2590

DEPARTMENT OF HEALTH AND HUMAN SERVICES
Centers for Medicare & Medicaid Services
45 CFR Part 146

Final Rules for Nondiscrimination and Wellness Programs in Health Coverage in the Group Market

AGENCIES: Internal Revenue Service, Department of the Treasury; Employee Benefits Security Administration, Department of Labor; Centers for Medicare & Medicaid Services, Department of Health and Human Services.

ACTION: Final rules.

SUMMARY: This document contains final rules governing the provisions prohibiting discrimination based on a health factor for group health plans and issuers of health insurance coverage offered in connection with a group health plan. The rules contained in this document implement changes made to the Internal Revenue Code of 1986 (Code), the Employee Retirement Income Security Act of 1974 (ERISA), and the Public Health Service Act (PHS Act) enacted as part of the Health Insurance Portability and Accountability Act of 1996 (HIPAA).

DATES: *Effective date:* These final regulations are effective February 12, 2006.

Applicability dates: These final regulations apply for plan years beginning on or after July 1, 2007.

FOR FURTHER INFORMATION CONTACT: Russ Weinheimer, Internal Revenue Service, Department of the Treasury, at (202) 622–6080; Amy Turner or Elena Lynett, Employee Benefits Security Administration, Department of Labor, at (202) 693–8335; or Karen Levin or Adam Shaw, Centers for Medicare & Medicaid Services, Department of Health and Human Services, at (877) 267–2323 extension 65445 and 61091, respectively.

CUSTOMER SERVICE INFORMATION: Individuals interested in obtaining copies of Department of Labor publications concerning health care laws may request copies by calling the Department of Labor (DOL), Employee Benefits Security Administration (EBSA) Toll-Free Hotline at 1–866–444–EBSA (3272) or may request a copy of the Department of Health and Human Services (HHS), Centers for Medicare & Medicaid Services (CMS) publication entitled "Protecting Your Health Insurance Coverage" by calling 1–800–633–4227. These regulations as well as other information on HIPAA's nondiscrimination rules and other health care laws are also available on the Department of Labor's website (*http://www.dol.gov/ebsa*), including the interactive web pages Health Elaws.

SUPPLEMENTARY INFORMATION:

I. Background

The Health Insurance Portability and Accountability Act of 1996 (HIPAA), Public Law 104–191 (110 Stat. 1936), was enacted on August 21, 1996. HIPAA amended the Internal Revenue Code of 1986 (Code), the Employee Retirement Income Security Act of 1974 (ERISA), and the Public Health Service Act (PHS Act) to provide for, among other things, improved portability and continuity of health coverage. HIPAA added section 9802 of the Code, section 702 of ERISA, and section 2702 of the PHS Act, which prohibit discrimination in health coverage based on a health factor. Interim final rules implementing the HIPAA provisions were published in the **Federal Register** on April 8, 1997 (T.D. 8716, 1997–1 C.B. 225 [62 FR 16894]) (1997 interim rules). On December 29, 1997, the Department of Labor, the Department of Health and Human Services, and the Department of the Treasury (the Departments) published a clarification of the April 1997 interim rules as they relate to individuals who were denied coverage before the effective date of HIPAA on the basis of any health factor (62 FR 67689).

On January 8, 2001, the Departments published interim final regulations (2001 interim rules) on many issues under the HIPAA nondiscrimination provisions (T.D. 8931, 2001–1 C.B. 542 [66 FR 1378]) and proposed regulations on wellness programs under those nondiscrimination provisions (REG–114084–00, 2001–1 C.B. 633 [66 FR 1421]). These regulations being published today in the **Federal Register** finalize both the 2001 interim rules and the proposed rules.

II. Overview of the Regulations

Section 9802 of the Code, section 702 of ERISA, and section 2702 of the PHS Act (the HIPAA nondiscrimination provisions) establish rules generally prohibiting group health plans and group health insurance issuers from discriminating against individual participants or beneficiaries based on any health factor of such participants or beneficiaries. The 2001 interim rules —

- Explained the application of these provisions to benefits;
- Clarified the relationship between the HIPAA nondiscrimination provisions and the HIPAA preexisting condition exclusion limitations;
- Explained the application of these provisions to premiums;
- Described similarly situated individuals;
- Explained the application of these provisions to actively-at-work and nonconfinement clauses; and
- Clarified that more favorable treatment of individuals with medical needs generally is permitted.

In general, these final regulations do not change the 2001 interim rules or the proposed rules on wellness programs. However, these regulations do not republish the expired transitional rules regarding individuals who were denied coverage based on a health factor prior to the applicability date of the 2001 interim rules. (These regulations do republish, and slightly modify, the special transitional rule for self-funded nonfederal governmental plans that had denied any individual coverage due to the plan's election to opt out of the nondiscrimination requirements under 45 CFR 146.180, in cases where the plan sponsor subsequently chooses to bring the plan into compliance with those requirements). These regulations clarify how the source-of-injury rules apply to the timing of a diagnosis of a medical condition and add an example to illustrate how the benefits rules apply to the carryover feature of health reimbursement arrangements (HRAs). For wellness programs, the final regulations clarify some ambiguities in the proposed rules, make some changes in terminology and organization, and add a description of wellness programs not required to satisfy additional standards.

Application to Benefits

Under the 2001 interim rules and these regulations, a plan or issuer is not required to provide coverage for any particular benefit to any group of similarly situated individuals. However, benefits provided must be uniformly available to all similarly situated individuals. Likewise, any restriction on a benefit or benefits must apply uniformly to all similarly situated individuals and must not be directed at individual participants or beneficiaries based on any health factor of the participants or beneficiaries (determined based on all the relevant facts and circumstances).

With respect to these benefit rules, the Departments received many inquiries about HRAs and one comment about nondiscrimination requirements under other laws. Under HRAs, employees are reimbursed for medical expenses up to a maximum amount for a period, based on the employer's contribution to the plan. These plans may or may not be funded. Another common feature is that the plans typically allow amounts remaining available at the end of the period to be used to reimburse medical expenses in later periods. Because the maximum reimbursement available under a plan to an employee in any single period may vary based on the claims experience of the employee, concerns have arisen about the application of the HIPAA nondiscrimination rules to these plans.

To address these concerns, these final regulations include an example under which the carryforward of unused employer-provided medical care reimbursement amounts to later years does not violate the HIPAA nondiscrimination requirements, even though the maximum reimbursement amount for a year varies among employees within the same group of similarly situated individuals based on prior claims experience. In the example, an employer sponsors a group health plan under which medical care expenses are reimbursed up to an annual maximum amount. The maximum reimbursement amount with respect to an employee for a year is a uniform amount multiplied by the number of years the employee has participated in the plan, reduced by the total reimbursements for prior years. Because employees who have participated in the plan for the same length of time are eligible for the same total benefit over that length of time, the example concludes that the arrangement does not violate the HIPAA nondiscrimination requirements.

The Equal Employment Opportunity Commission (EEOC) asked the Departments to clarify that certain plan practices or provisions permitted under the benefits paragraphs of the 2001 interim rules may violate the Americans with Disabilities Act of 1990 (ADA) or Title VII of the Civil Rights Act of 1964 (Title VII). Specifically, the 2001 interim rules allow plans to exclude or limit benefits for certain types of conditions or treatments. The EEOC commented that, if such a benefit limit were applied to AIDS, it would be a disability-based distinction that violates the ADA (unless it is permitted under section 501(c) of the ADA). In addition, the EEOC commented that an exclusion from coverage of prescription contraceptives, but not of other preventive treatments, would violate Title VII because prescription contraceptives are used exclusively by women.

Paragraph (h) of the 2001 interim rules and these final regulations is entitled "No effect on other laws." This section clarifies that compliance with the nondiscrimination rules is not determinative of compliance with any other provision of ERISA, or any other State or Federal law, including the ADA. Moreover, in paragraph (b) of the 2001 interim rules and these final regulations, the general rule governing the application of the nondiscrimination rules to benefits clarifies that whether any plan provision or practice with respect to benefits complies with these rules does not affect whether the provision or practice is permitted under any other provision of the Code, ERISA, or the PHS Act, the Americans with Disabilities Act, or any other law, whether State or Federal.

Many other laws may regulate plans and issuers in their provision of benefits to participants and beneficiaries. These laws include the ADA, Title VII, the Family and Medical Leave Act, ERISA's fiduciary provisions, and State law. The Departments have not attempted to summarize the requirements of those laws in the HIPAA nondiscrimination rules. Instead, these rules clarify the application of the HIPAA nondiscrimination rules to group health plans, which may permit certain practices that other laws prohibit. Nonetheless, to avoid misleading plans and issuers as to the permissibility of any plan provision under other laws, the Departments included, in both paragraph (h) and paragraph (b) of the regulations, references to the potential applicability of other laws. Employers, plans, issuers, and other service providers should consider the applicability of these laws to their coverage and contact legal counsel or other government agencies such as the EEOC and State insurance departments if they have questions under those laws.

Source-of-Injury Exclusions

Some plans and issuers, while generally providing coverage for the treatment of an injury, deny benefits if the injury arose from a specified cause or activity. These kinds of exclusions are known as source-of-injury exclusions. Under the 2001 interim rules, if a plan or issuer provides benefits for a particular injury, it may not deny benefits otherwise provided for treatment of the injury due to the fact that the injury results from a medical condition or an act of domestic violence. Two examples in the 2001 interim rules illustrate the application of this rule, to injuries resulting from an attempted suicide due to depression and to injuries resulting from bungee jumping.

These final regulations retain the provisions in the 2001 interim rules and add a clarification. Some people have inquired if a suicide exclusion can apply if an individual had not been diagnosed with a medical condition such as depression before the suicide attempt. These final regulations clarify that benefits may not be denied for injuries resulting from a medical condition even if the medical condition was not diagnosed before the injury.

Some comments expressed concern that the discussion of the source-of-injury rule in the 2001 interim rules might be used to support the use of vague language to identify plan benefit exclusions, especially to identify source-of-injury exclusions. Requirements for plan benefit descriptions are generally outside of the scope of these regulations. Nonetheless, Department of Labor regulations at 29 CFR 2520.102–2(b) provide, "The format of the summary plan description must not have the effect of misleading, misinforming or failing to inform participants and beneficiaries. Any description of exception, limitations, reductions, and other restrictions of plan benefits shall not be minimized, rendered obscure or otherwise made to appear unimportant … The advantages and disadvantages of the plan shall be presented without either exaggerating the benefits or minimizing the limitations." State laws governing group insurance or nonfederal governmental plans may provide additional protections.

The Departments received thousands of comments protesting that the source-of-injury provisions in the 2001 interim rules would generally permit plans or issuers to exclude benefits for the treatment of injuries sustained in the activities listed in the conference report to HIPAA (motorcycling, snowmobiling, all-terrain vehicle riding, horseback riding, skiing, and other similar activities). Many comments requested that the source-of-injury rule be amended to provide that a source-of-injury exclusion could not apply if the injury resulted from (in addition to an act of domestic violence or a medical condition) participation in legal recreational activities such as those listed in the conference report. Some comments expressed the concern that the rule in the 2001 interim rules would cause plans and issuers to begin excluding benefits for treatment of injuries sustained in these kinds of activities.

One comment generally supported the position in the 2001 interim rules. That comment expressed the belief that Congress intended with this issue, as with many other issues, to continue its longstanding deference to the States on the regulation of benefit design under health insurance. The comment also noted that the source-of-injury rule in the 2001 interim rules would not change the practice of plans or issuers with regard to the activities listed in the conference report and that the practice of plans and issuers in this regard would continue to be governed, as they had been before HIPAA, by market conditions and the States.

The Departments have not added the list of activities from the conference report to the source-of-injury rule in the final regulations. The statute itself is unclear about how benefits in general are affected by the nondiscrimination requirements and is silent with respect to source-of-injury exclusions in particular. The legislative history provides that the inclusion of evidence of insurability in the list of health factors is intended to ensure, among other things, that individuals are not excluded from health care coverage due to their participation in the activities listed in the conference report. This language is unclear because the term "health care coverage" could mean only eligibility to enroll for coverage under the plan, so that people who participate in the activities listed in the conference report could not be kept out of the plan but could be denied benefits for injuries sustained in those activities. Alternatively, it could mean eligibility both to enroll for coverage and for benefits, so that people who participate in those activities could not be kept out of the plan or denied benefits for injuries sustained in those activities. Without any indication in the statute and without a clear indication in the legislative history about this issue, and in light of the overall scheme of the statute, the Departments have made no changes to the regulations.

Moreover, to the extent not prohibited by State law, plans and issuers have been free to impose source-of-injury exclusions since before HIPAA. There is no reason to believe that plans and issuers will begin to impose source-of-injury exclusions with respect to the conference report activities merely because such exclusions are not prohibited under the 2001 interim rules and these final regulations.

Relationship of Prohibition on Nonconfinement Clauses to State Extension-of-Benefits Laws

Questions have arisen about the relationship of the prohibition on nonconfinement clauses in the 2001 interim rules to State extension-of-benefits laws. Plan provisions that deny an individual benefits based on the individual's confinement to a hospital or other health care institution at the time coverage would otherwise become effective are often called nonconfinement clauses. The 2001 interim rules prohibit such nonconfinement clauses. At the same time, many States require issuers to provide benefits beyond the date on which coverage under the policy would otherwise have ended to individuals who continue to be hospitalized beyond that date. Example 2 in the 2001 interim rules illustrated that a current issuer cannot impose a nonconfinement clause that restricts benefits for an individual based on whether that individual is entitled to continued benefits from a prior issuer pursuant to a State law requirement. The final sentence in Example 2 provided that HIPAA does not affect the prior issuer's obligation under State law and does not affect any State law governing coordination of benefits.

Under the laws of some States, a prior issuer has the obligation to provide health benefits to an individual confined to a hospital beyond the nominal end of the policy only if the hospitalization is not covered by a succeeding issuer. Because HIPAA requires a succeeding issuer to provide benefits that it would otherwise provide if not for the nonconfinement clause, in such a case State law would not require the prior issuer to provide benefits for a confinement beyond the nominal end of the policy. In this context, the statement in the final sentence of Example 2 — that HIPAA does not affect the prior issuer's obligation under State law — could be read to conflict with the text of the rule and the main point of Example 2 that the succeeding issuer must cover the confinement.

There has been some dispute about how this potential ambiguity should be resolved. One interpretation is that the succeeding issuer can never impose a nonconfinement clause, and if this has the effect under State law of not requiring the prior issuer to provide benefits beyond the nominal end of the policy, then the prior issuer is not obligated to provide the extended benefits. This interpretation is consistent with the text of the nonconfinement rule and the main point of Example 2, though it could be read to conflict with the last sentence in Example 2.

Another interpretation proposed by some is that, consistent with the last sentence of Example 2, the obligation of a prior issuer is never affected by the HIPAA prohibition against nonconfinement clauses. Under this interpretation, if a State law conditions a prior issuer's obligation on there being no succeeding issuer with the obligation, then in order to leave the prior issuer's obligation unaffected under State law, the succeeding issuer could apply a nonconfinement clause and the HIPAA prohibition would not apply. This interpretation elevates a minor clarification at the end of an example to supersede not only the main point of the example but also the express text of the rule the example illustrates. This proposed interpretation is clearly contrary to the intent of the 2001 interim rules.

To avoid other interpretations, these final rules have replaced the final sentence of Example 2 in the 2001 interim rules with three sentences. The new language clarifies that: State law cannot change the succeeding issuer's obligation under HIPAA; a prior issuer may also have an obligation; and in a case in which a succeeding issuer has an obligation under HIPAA and a prior issuer has an obligation under State law to provide benefits for a confinement, any State laws designed to prevent more than 100 percent reimbursement, such as State coordination-of-benefits laws, continue to apply. Thus, under HIPAA a succeeding issuer cannot deny benefits to an individual on the basis of a nonconfinement clause. If this requirement under HIPAA has the effect under State law of removing a prior issuer's obligation to provide benefits, then the prior issuer is not obligated to provide benefits for the confinement. If under State law this requirement under HIPAA has the effect of obligating both the prior issuer and the succeeding issuer to provide benefits, then any State coordination-of-benefits law that is used to determine the order of payment and to prevent more than 100 percent reimbursement continues to apply.

Actively-at-Work Rules and Employer Leave Policies

The final regulations make no changes to the 2001 interim rules relating to actively-at-work provisions. Actively-at-work clauses are generally prohibited, unless individuals who are absent from work due to any health factor are treated, for purposes of health coverage, as if they are actively at work. Nonetheless, a plan or issuer may distinguish between groups of similarly situated individuals (provided the distinction is not directed at individual participants or beneficiaries based on a health factor). Examples in the regulations illustrate that a plan or issuer may condition coverage on an individual's meeting the plan's requirement of working full-time (such as a minimum of 250 hours in a three-month period or 30 hours per week).

Several members of the regulated community have asked the Departments to clarify the applicability of the actively-at-work rules to various plan provisions that require an individual to perform a minimum amount of service per week in order to be eligible for coverage. It is the Departments' experience that much of the complexity in applying these rules derives from the myriad variations in the operation of employers' leave policies. The Departments believe that the 2001 interim rules provide adequate principles for applying the actively-at-work provisions to different types of eligibility provisions. In order to comply with these rules, a plan or issuer should apply the plan's service requirements consistently to all similarly situated employees eligible for coverage under the plan without regard to whether an employee is seeking eligibility to enroll in the plan or continued eligibility to remain in the plan. Accordingly, if a plan imposes a 30-hour-per-week requirement and treats employees on paid leave (including sick leave and vacation leave) who are already in the plan as if they are actively-at-work, the plan generally is required to credit time on paid leave towards satisfying the 30-hour-per-week requirement for employees seeking enrollment in the plan. Similarly, if a plan allowed employees to continue eligibility under the plan while on paid leave and for an additional period of 30 days while on unpaid leave, the plan is generally required to credit these same periods for employees seeking enrollment in the plan.[1] To help ensure consistency in application, plans and issuers may wish to clarify, in writing, how employees on various types of leave are treated for purposes of interpreting a service requirement. Without clear plan rules, plans and issuers might slip into inconsistent applications of their rules, which could lead to violations of the actively-at-work provisions.

Wellness Programs

The HIPAA nondiscrimination provisions do not prevent a plan or issuer from establishing discounts or rebates or modifying otherwise applicable copayments or deductibles in return for adherence to programs of health promotion and disease prevention. The 1997 interim rules refer to these programs as "*bona fide* wellness programs." In the preamble to the 1997 interim rules, the Departments invited comments on whether additional guidance was needed concerning, among other things, the permissible standards for determining *bona fide* wellness programs. The Departments also stated their intent to issue further regulations on the nondiscrimination requirements and that in no event would the Departments take any enforcement action against a plan or issuer that had sought to comply in good faith with section 9802 of the Code, section 702 of ERISA, and section 2702 of the PHS Act before the publication of additional guidance. The preambles to the 2001 interim final and proposed rules noted that the period for nonenforcement in cases of good faith compliance with the HIPAA nondiscrimination provisions generally ended on the applicability date of those regulations but continued with respect to wellness programs until the issuance of further guidance. Accordingly, the nonenforcement policy of the Departments ends upon the applicability date of these final regulations for cases in which a plan or issuer fails to comply with the regulations but complies in good faith with an otherwise reasonable interpretation of the statute.

The HIPAA nondiscrimination provisions generally prohibit a plan or issuer from charging similarly situated individuals different premiums or contributions based on a health factor. These final regulations also generally prohibit a plan or issuer from requiring similarly situated individuals to satisfy differing deductible, copayment, or other cost-sharing requirements. However, the HIPAA nondiscrimination provisions do not prevent a plan or issuer from establishing premium discounts or rebates or modifying otherwise applicable copayments or deductibles in return for adherence to programs of health promotion and disease prevention. Thus, there is an exception to the general rule prohibiting discrimination based on a health factor if the reward, such as a premium discount or waiver of a cost-sharing requirement, is based on participation in a program of health promotion or disease prevention.

Both the 1997 interim rules and the 2001 proposed regulations refer to programs of health promotion and disease prevention allowed under this exception as "*bona fide* wellness programs." These regulations generally adopt the provisions in the 2001 proposed rules. However, as more fully explained below, the final regulations no longer use the term "*bona fide*" in connection with wellness programs, add a description of wellness programs that do not have to satisfy additional requirements in order to comply with the nondiscrimination requirements, reorganize the four requirements from the proposed rules into five requirements, provide that the reward for a wellness program — coupled with the reward for other wellness programs with respect to the plan that require satisfaction

[1] These nondiscrimination rules do not address the applicability of the Family and Medical Leave Act to employers or group health coverage.

of a standard related to a health factor — must not exceed 20% of the total cost of coverage under the plan, and add examples and make other changes to more accurately describe how the requirements apply.

The term "wellness program". Comments suggested that the use of the term "*bona fide*" with respect to wellness programs was confusing because, under the proposed rules, some wellness programs that are not "*bona fide*" within the narrow meaning of that term in the proposed rules nonetheless satisfy the HIPAA nondiscrimination requirements. To address this concern, these final regulations do not use the term "*bona fide* wellness program." Instead the final regulations treat all programs of health promotion or disease prevention as wellness programs and specify which of those wellness programs must satisfy additional standards to comply with the nondiscrimination requirements.

Programs not subject to additional standards. The preamble to the 2001 proposed rules described a number of wellness programs that comply with the HIPAA nondiscrimination requirements without having to satisfy any additional standards. However, the text of the regulation did not make such a distinction. The Departments have received many comments and inquiries about whether programs like those described in the 2001 preamble would have to satisfy the additional standards in the proposed rules. As a result, a paragraph has been added to the final regulations defining and illustrating programs that comply with the nondiscrimination requirements without having to satisfy any additional standards (assuming participation in the program is made available to all similarly situated individuals). Such programs are those under which none of the conditions for obtaining a reward is based on an individual satisfying a standard related to a health factor or under which no reward is offered. The final regulations include the following list to illustrate the wide range of programs that would not have to satisfy any additional standards to comply with the nondiscrimination requirements:

- A program that reimburses all or part of the cost for memberships in a fitness center.

- A diagnostic testing program that provides a reward for participation and does not base any part of the reward on outcomes.

- A program that encourages preventive care through the waiver of the copayment or deductible requirement under a group health plan for the costs of, for example, prenatal care or well-baby visits.

- A program that reimburses employees for the costs of smoking cessation programs without regard to whether the employee quits smoking.

- A program that provides a reward to employees for attending a monthly health education seminar.

Only programs under which any of the conditions for obtaining a reward is based on an individual satisfying a standard related to a health factor must meet the five additional requirements described in paragraph (f)(2) of these regulations in order to comply with the nondiscrimination requirements.

Limit on the reward. As under the proposed rules, the total reward that may be given to an individual under the plan for all wellness programs is limited. A reward can be in the form of a discount or rebate of a premium or contribution, a waiver of all or part of a cost-sharing mechanism (such as deductibles, copayments, or coinsurance), the absence of a surcharge, or the value of a benefit that would otherwise not be provided under the plan. Under the proposed rule, the reward for the wellness program, coupled with the reward for other wellness programs with respect to the plan that require satisfaction of a standard related to a health factor, must not exceed a specified percentage of the cost of employee-only coverage under the plan. The cost of employee-only coverage is determined based on the total amount of employer and employee contributions for the benefit package under which the employee is receiving coverage.

Comments indicated that in some circumstances dependents are permitted to participate in the wellness program in addition to the employee and that in those circumstances the reward should be higher to reflect dependent participation in the program. These final regulations provide that if, in addition to employees, any class of dependents (such as spouses or spouses and dependent children) may participate in the wellness program, the limit on the reward is based on the cost of the coverage category in which the employee and any dependents are enrolled.

The proposed regulations specified three alternative percentages: 10, 15, and 20. The final regulations provide that the amount of the reward may not exceed 20 percent of the cost of coverage. The proposed regulations solicited comments on the appropriate percentage. The percentage limit is designed to avoid a reward or penalty being so large as to have the effect of denying coverage or creating too heavy a financial penalty on individuals who do not satisfy an initial wellness program standard that is related to a health factor. Comments from one employer and two national insurance industry associations requested that the level of the percentage for rewards should provide plans and issuers maximum flexibility for designing wellness programs. Comments suggested that plans and issuers have a greater opportunity to encourage healthy behaviors through programs of health promotion and disease prevention if they are allowed flexibility in designing such programs. The 20 percent limit on the size of the reward in the final regulations allows plans and issuers to maintain flexibility in their ability to design wellness programs, while avoiding rewards or penalties so large as to deny coverage or create too heavy a financial penalty on individuals who do not satisfy an initial wellness program standard that is related to a health factor.

Reasonably-designed and at-least-once-per-year requirements. In the 2001 proposed rules, the second of four requirements was that the program must be reasonably designed to promote good health or prevent disease. The regulations also provided that a program did not meet this standard unless it gave individuals eligible for the program the opportunity to qualify for the reward at least once per year.

One comment suggested a safe harbor under which a wellness program that allows individuals to qualify at least once a year for the reward under the program would satisfy the "reasonably designed" standard without regard to other attributes of the program. The Departments have not adopted this suggestion. The "reasonably designed" standard is a broad standard. A wide range of factors could affect the reasonableness of the design of a wellness program, not just the frequency with which a participant could qualify for the reward. For example, a program might not be reasonably designed to promote good health or prevent disease if it imposed, as a condition to obtaining the reward, an overly burdensome time commitment or a requirement to engage in illegal behavior. The once-per-year requirement was included in the proposed rules merely as a bright-line standard for determining the minimum frequency that is consistent with a reasonable design for promoting good health or preventing disease. Thus, this second requirement of the proposed rules has been divided into two requirements in the final rules (the second and the third requirements). This division was made to emphasize that a program that must satisfy the additional standards in order to comply with the nondiscrimination requirements must allow eligible individuals to qualify for the reward at least once per year and must also be otherwise reasonably designed to promote health or prevent disease.

Comments also expressed other concerns about the "reasonably designed" requirement. While acknowledging that this standard provides significant flexibility, these comments were concerned that this flexible approach might also require substantial resources in evaluating all the facts and circumstances of a proposed program to determine whether it was reasonable in its design.

The "reasonably designed" requirement is intended to be an easy standard to satisfy. To make this clear, the final regulations have added language providing that if a program has a reasonable chance of improving the health of participants and it is not overly burdensome, is not a subterfuge for discriminating based on a health factor, and is not highly suspect in the method chosen to promote health or prevent disease, it satisfies this standard. There does not need to be a scientific record that the method promotes wellness to satisfy this standard. The standard is intended to allow experimentation in diverse ways of promoting wellness. For example, a plan or issuer could satisfy this standard by providing rewards to individuals who participated in a course of aromatherapy. The requirement of reasonableness in this standard prohibits bizarre, extreme, or illegal requirements in a wellness program.

One comment requested that the final regulations set forth one or more safe harbors that would demonstrate compliance with the "reasonably designed" standard. The examples in the proposed and final regulations present a range of wellness programs that are well within the borders of what is considered reasonably designed to promote health or prevent disease. The examples serve as safe harbors, so that a plan or issuer could adopt a program identical to one described as satisfying the wellness program requirements in the examples and be assured of satisfying the requirements in the regulations. Wellness programs similar to the examples also would satisfy the "reasonably designed" requirement. The Departments, though, do not want plans or issuers to feel constrained by the relatively narrow range of programs described by the examples but want plans and issuers to feel free to consider innovative programs for motivating individuals to make efforts to improve their health.

Reasonable alternative standard. Under the 2001 proposed rules and these final regulations, a wellness program that provides a reward requiring satisfaction of a standard related to a health factor must provide a reasonable alternative standard for obtaining the reward for certain individuals. This alternative standard must be available for individuals for whom, for that period, it is unreasonably difficult due to a medical condition to satisfy the otherwise applicable standard, or for whom, for that period, it is medically inadvisable to attempt to satisfy the otherwise applicable standard. A program does not need to establish the specific reasonable alternative standard before the program commences. It is sufficient to determine a reasonable alternative standard once a participant informs the plan that it is unreasonably difficult for the participant due to a medical condition to satisfy the general standard (or that it is medically inadvisable for the participant to attempt to achieve the general standard) under the program.

Some comments suggested that the requirement to devise and offer such a reasonable alternative standard potentially creates a significant burden on plans and issuers. Comments also suggested that the Departments should define a "safe harbor" for what constitutes a reasonable alternative standard, and that plans and issuers should be permitted to establish a single alternative standard, rather than having to tailor a standard for each individual for whom a reasonable alternative standard must be offered.

The Departments understand that, in devising wellness programs, plans and issuers strive to improve the health of participating individuals in a way that is not administratively burdensome or expensive. Under the proposed and final rules, it is permissible for a plan or issuer to devise a reasonable alternative standard by lowering the threshold of the existing health-factor-related standard, substituting a different standard, or waiving the standard. (For the alternative standard to be reasonable, the individual must be able to satisfy it without regard to any health factor.) To address the concern regarding the potential burden of this requirement, the final regulations explicitly provide that a plan or issuer can waive the health-factor-related standard for all individuals for whom a reasonable alternative standard must be offered. Additionally, the final regulations include an example demonstrating that a reasonable alternative standard could include following the recommendations of an individual's physician regarding the health factor at issue. Thus, a plan or issuer need not assume the burden of designing a discrete alternative standard for each individual for whom an alternative standard must be offered. An example also illustrates that if an *alternative* standard is health-factor-related (*i.e.*, walking three days a week for 20 minutes a day), the wellness program must provide an additional alternative standard (*i.e.*, following the individual's physician's recommendations regarding the health factor at issue) to the appropriate individuals.

The 2001 proposed rules included an example illustrating a smoking cessation program. Comments expressed concern that, under the proposed regulations, individuals addicted to nicotine who comply with a reasonable alternative standard year after year would always be entitled to the reward even if they did not quit using tobacco. Comments questioned whether this result is consistent with the goal of promoting wellness. The final regulations retain the example from the proposed rules. Comments noted that overcoming an addiction sometimes requires a cycle of failure and renewed effort. For those individuals for whom it remains unreasonably difficult due to an addiction, a reasonable alternative standard must continue to be offered. Plans and issuers can accommodate this health factor by continuing to offer the same or a new reasonable alternative standard. For example, a plan or issuer using a smoking cessation class might use different classes from year to year or might change from using a class to providing nicotine replacement therapy. These final regulations provide an additional example of a reasonable alternative standard of viewing, over a period of 12 months, a 12-hour video series on health problems associated with tobacco use.

Concern has been expressed that individuals might claim that it would be unreasonably difficult or medically inadvisable to meet the wellness program standard, when in fact the individual could meet the standard. The final rules clarify that plans may seek verification, such as a statement from a physician, that a health factor makes it unreasonably difficult or medically inadvisable for an individual to meet a standard.

Disclosure requirements. The fifth requirement for a wellness program that provides a reward requiring satisfaction of a standard related to a health factor is that all plan materials describing the terms of the program must disclose the availability of a reasonable alternative standard. This requirement is unchanged from the proposed rules. The 2001 proposed rules and these final regulations include the same model language that can be used to satisfy this requirement; examples also illustrate substantially similar language that would satisfy the requirement.

The final regulations retain the two clarifications of this requirement. First, plan materials are not required to describe specific reasonable alternative standards. It is sufficient to disclose that some reasonable alternative standard will be made available. Second, any plan materials that describe the general standard would also have to disclose the availability of a reasonable alternative standard. However, if the program is merely mentioned (and does not describe the general standard), disclosure of the availability of a reasonable alternative standard is not required.

Special Rule for Self-Funded Nonfederal Governmental Plans Exempted Under 45 CFR 146.180

The sponsor of a self-funded nonfederal governmental plan may elect under section 2721(b)(2) of the PHS Act and 45 CFR 146.180 to exempt its group health plan from the nondiscrimination requirements of section 2702 of the PHS Act and 45 CFR 146.121. Under the interim final nondiscrimination rules, if the plan sponsor subsequently chooses to bring the plan into compliance with the nondiscrimination requirements, the plan must provide notice to that effect to individuals who were denied enrollment based on one or more health factors, and afford those individuals an opportunity, that continues for at least 30 days, to enroll in the plan. (An individual is considered to have been denied coverage if he or she failed to apply for coverage because, given an exemption election under 45 CFR 146.180, it was reasonable to believe that an application for coverage would have been denied based on a health factor). The notice must specify the effective date of compliance, and inform the individual regarding any enrollment restrictions that may apply under the terms of the plan once the plan comes into compliance. The plan may not treat the individual as a late enrollee or a special enrollee. These final regulations retain this transitional rule, and state that the plan must permit coverage to be effective as of the first day of plan coverage for which an exemption election under 45 CFR 146.180 (with regard to the nondiscrimination requirements) is no longer in effect. (These final regulations delete the reference giving the plan the option of having the coverage start July 1, 2001, because that option implicated the expired transitional rules regarding individuals who were denied coverage based on a health factor prior to the applicability of the 2001 interim rules. As previously stated, those transitional rules have not been republished in these final regulations.) Additionally, the examples illustrating how the special rule for nonfederal governmental plans operates have been revised slightly.

Applicability Date

These regulations apply for plan years beginning on or after July 1, 2007. Until the applicability date for this regulation, plans and issuers are required to comply with the corresponding sections of the regulations previously published in the **Federal Register** (66 FR 1378) and other applicable regulations.

III. Economic Impact and Paperwork Burden

Summary — Department of Labor and Department of Health and Human Services

HIPAA's nondiscrimination provisions generally prohibit group health plans and group health insurance issuers from discriminating against individuals in eligibility or premiums on the basis of health factors. The Departments have crafted these regulations to secure the protections from discrimination as intended by Congress in as economically efficient a manner as possible, and believe that the economic benefits of the regulations justify their costs.

The primary economic benefits associated with securing HIPAA's nondiscrimination provisions derive from increased access to affordable group health plan coverage for individuals with health problems. Increased access benefits both newly-covered individuals and society at large. It fosters expanded health coverage, timelier and more complete medical care, better health outcomes, and improved productivity and quality of life. This is especially true for the individuals most affected by HIPAA's nondiscrimination provisions — those with adverse health conditions. Denied health coverage, individuals in poorer health are more likely to suffer economic hardship, to forego badly needed care for financial reasons, and to suffer adverse health outcomes as a result. For them, gaining health coverage is more likely to mean gaining economic security, receiving timely, quality care, and living healthier, more productive lives. Similarly, participation by these individuals in wellness programs fosters better health outcomes, increases productivity and quality of life, and has the same outcome in terms of overall gains in economic security. The wellness provisions of these regulations will result in fewer instances in which wellness programs shift costs to high-risk individuals, and more instances in which these individuals succeed at improving health habits and health.

Additional economic benefits derive directly from the improved clarity provided by the regulations. The regulations will reduce uncertainty and costly disputes and promote confidence in health benefits' value, thereby improving labor market efficiency and fostering the establishment and continuation of group health plans and their wellness program provisions.

The Departments estimate that the dollar value of the expanded coverage attributable to HIPAA's nondiscrimination provisions is approximately $850 million annually. The Departments believe that the cost of HIPAA's nondiscrimination provisions is borne by covered workers. Costs can be shifted to workers through increases in employee premium shares or reductions (or smaller increases) in pay or other components of compensation, by increases in deductibles or other cost sharing, or by reducing the richness of health benefits. Whereas the benefits of the nondiscrimination provisions are concentrated in a relatively small population, the costs are distributed broadly across plans and enrollees.

The proposed rules on wellness programs impose certain requirements on wellness programs providing rewards that would otherwise discriminate based on a health factor in order to ensure that the exception for wellness programs does not eviscerate the general rule contained in HIPAA's nondiscrimination provisions. Costs associated with the wellness program provisions are justified by the benefits received by those individuals now able, through alternative standards, to participate in such programs. Because the new provisions limit rewards for wellness programs that require an individual to satisfy a standard related to a health factor to 20 percent of the cost of single coverage (with additional provisions related to rewards that apply also to classes of dependents), some rewards will be reduced and this reduction might compel some individuals to decline coverage. The number of individuals affected, however, is thought to be small. Moreover, the Departments estimate that the cost of the reduction in rewards that would exceed the limit will amount to only $6 million. Establishing reasonable alternative standards, which should increase coverage for those now eligible for discounts as well as their participation in programs designed to promote health or prevent disease, is expected to cost between $2 million to $9 million. The total costs should therefore fall within a range between $8 million and $15 million annually.

New economic costs may be also incurred in connection with the wellness provisions if reductions in rewards result in the reduction of wellness programs' effectiveness, but this effect is expected to be very small. Other new economic costs may be incurred by plan sponsors to make available reasonable alternative standards where required. The Departments are unable to estimate these costs due to the variety of options available to plan sponsors for bringing wellness programs into compliance with these rules.

Executive Order 12866 — Department of Labor and Department of Health and Human Services

Under Executive Order 12866, the Departments must determine whether a regulatory action is "significant" and therefore subject to the requirements of the Executive Order and subject to review by the Office of Management and Budget (OMB). Under section 3(f), the order defines a "significant regulatory action" as an action that is likely to result in a rule (1) having an annual effect on the economy of $100 million or more, or adversely and materially affecting a sector of the economy, productivity, competition, jobs, the environment, public health or safety, or State, local or tribal governments or communities (also referred to as "economically significant"); (2) creating serious inconsistency or otherwise interfering with an action taken or planned by another agency; (3) materially altering the budgetary impacts of entitlement grants, user fees, or loan programs or the rights and obligations of recipients thereof; or (4) raising novel legal or policy issues arising out of legal mandates, the President's priorities, or the principles set forth in the Executive Order.

Pursuant to the terms of the Executive Order, this action is "economically significant" and subject to OMB review under Section 3(f) of the Executive Order. Consistent with the Executive Order, the Departments have assessed the costs and benefits of this regulatory action. The Departments performed a comprehensive, unified analysis to estimate the costs and benefits attributable to the final regulations for purposes of compliance with the Executive Order 12866, the Regulatory Flexibility Act, and the Paperwork Reduction Act. The Departments' analyses and underlying assumptions are detailed below. The Departments believe that the benefits of the final regulations justify their costs.

Regulatory Flexibility Act — Department of Labor and Department of Health and Human Services

The Regulatory Flexibility Act (5 U.S.C. 601 *et seq.*) (RFA) imposes certain requirements with respect to federal rules that are subject to the notice and comment requirements of section 553(b) of the Administrative Procedure Act (5 U.S.C. 551 *et seq.*) and likely to have a significant economic impact on a substantial number of small entities. Unless an agency certifies that a final rule will not have a significant economic impact on a substantial number of small entities, section 604 of the RFA requires that the agency present a final regulatory flexibility analysis (FRFA) at the time of the publication of the notice of final rulemaking describing the impact of the rule on small entities. Small entities include small businesses, organizations, and governmental jurisdictions.

Because the 2001 interim rules were issued as final rules and not as a notice of proposed rulemaking, the RFA did not apply and the Departments were not required to either certify that the rule would not have a significant impact on a substantial number of small entities or conduct a regulatory flexibility analysis. The Departments nonetheless crafted those regulations in careful consideration of effects on small entities, and conducted an analysis of the likely impact of the rules on small entities. This analysis was detailed in the preamble to the interim final rule.

The Departments also conducted an initial regulatory flexibility analysis in connection with the proposed regulations on wellness programs and present here a FRFA with respect to the final regulations on wellness programs pursuant to section 604 of the RFA. For purposes of their unified FRFA, the Departments adhered to EBSA's proposed definition of small entities. The Departments consider a small entity to be an employee benefit plan with fewer than 100 participants. The basis of this definition is found in section 104(a)(2) of ERISA, which permits the Secretary of Labor to prescribe simplified annual reports for pension plans that cover fewer than 100 participants. The Departments believe that assessing the impact of this final rule on small plans is an appropriate substitute for evaluating the effect on small entities as that term is defined in the RFA. This definition of small entity differs, however, from the definition of small business based on standards promulgated by the Small Business Administration (13 CFR 121.201) pursuant to the Small Business Act (15 U.S.C. 631 *et seq.*). Because of this difference, the Departments requested comments on the appropriateness of this size standard for evaluating the impact of the proposed regulations on small entities. No comments were received.

The Departments estimate that 35,000 plans with fewer than 100 participants vary employee premium contributions or cost-sharing across similarly situated individuals based on health factors.[2] While this represents just one percent of all small plans, the Departments believe that because of the large number of plans, this may constitute a substantial number of small entities. The Departments also note that at least some premium rewards may be large. Premium discounts associated with wellness programs are believed to range as high as $920 per affected participant per year. Therefore, the Departments believe that the impact of this regulation on at least some small entities may be significant.

Under these final regulations on wellness programs, such programs are not subject to additional requirements if none of the conditions for obtaining a reward is based on an individual satisfying a standard that is related to a health factor (or if a wellness program does not provide a reward).

Where a condition for obtaining a reward is based on an individual satisfying a standard related to a health factor, the wellness program will not violate the nondiscrimination provisions if additional requirements are met. The first requirement limits the maximum allowable reward or total of rewards to a maximum of 20 percent of the cost of employee-only coverage under the plan (with additional provisions related to rewards that apply also to classes of dependents). The magnitude of the limit is intended to offer plans maximum flexibility while avoiding the effect of denying coverage or creating an excessive financial penalty for individuals who cannot satisfy the initial standard based on a health factor.

The Departments estimate that 4,000 small plans and 22,000 small plan participants will be affected by this limit.[3] These plans can comply with this requirement by reducing the discount to the regulated maximum. This will result in an increase in premiums (or decrease in cost-sharing) by about $1.3 million on aggregate for those participants receiving qualified premium discounts.[4] This constitutes an ongoing, annual cost of $338 on average per affected plan. The regulation does not limit small plans' flexibility to shift this cost to all participants in the form of small premium increases or benefit cuts.

The second requirement provides that wellness programs must be reasonably designed to promote health or prevent disease. Comments received by the Departments and available literature on employee wellness programs suggest that existing wellness programs generally satisfy this requirement. The requirement therefore is not expected to compel small plans to modify existing wellness programs.

The third requirement is that the program give individuals eligible for the program the opportunity to qualify for the reward at least once per year. This provision was included within the terms of the requirements for reasonable design in the proposed regulations. The Departments did not anticipate that a cost would arise from the requirements related to reasonable design when taken together, but requested comments on their assumptions. Because no comments were received, the Departments have not attributed a cost to this provision of the final rule.

The fourth requirement provides that rewards under wellness programs must be available to all similarly situated individuals. Rewards are not available to similarly situated individuals unless a program allows a reasonable alternative standard or waiver of the applicable standard, if it is unreasonably difficult due to a medical condition or medically inadvisable to attempt to satisfy the otherwise applicable standard. The Departments believe that some small plans' wellness programs do not currently satisfy this requirement and will have to be modified.

The Departments estimate that 3,000 small plans' wellness programs include initial standards that may be unreasonably difficult due to a medical condition or medically inadvisable for some participants to meet.[5] These plans are estimated to include 4,000 participants for whom the standard is in fact unreasonably difficult due to a medical condition or medically inadvisable to meet.[6] Satisfaction of alternative standards by these participants will result in cost increases for plans as these individuals qualify for discounts or avoid surcharges. If all of these participants request and then satisfy an alternative standard, the cost would amount to about

[2] Based on tabulations of the 2003 Medical Expenditure Panel Survey Insurance Component (MEPS-IC) and 1997 Survey of Government Finances (SGF), the Departments estimate that roughly 2.4 million small health plans exist. Of these, 1.2 percent of these plans are believed to vary premiums (as suggested in a 1993 study by the Robert Woods Johnson Foundation) while .5 percent are thought to vary benefits (as suggested in, *Spec Summary. United States Salaried Managed Health/Health Promotion Initiatives, 2003–2004*, Hewitt Associates, July, 2003.). Assuming that half of those that vary premiums also vary benefits, the Departments conclude that 1.5 percent of all small plans are potentially affected by the statute.

[3] Simulations run by the Departments suggest that 10.7 percent of all plans exceed the capped premium discount. For the purposes of this analysis, it was assumed that the affected plans were proportionally distributed between large and small plans. However, it is likely that larger plans would have more generous welfare programs and therefore, this estimate is likely an upper bound.

[4] Estimate is based on the 2003–04 Hewitt Study and various measures of the general health of the labor force suggest that roughly 30 percent of health plan participants will not qualify for the discount. While plans exceeding the capped discount could meet the statutes requirements by transferring the excess amount, on average $57, to the non-qualifying participants, given current trends in the health insurance industry, it is considered more likely that plans would instead lower the amount of the discount given to the 70 percent of participants that qualify. This transfer would roughly total $1.3 million dollars

[5] The 2003–04 Hewitt Survey finds that 9 percent of its respondents require participants to achieve a certain health standard to be eligible for discounts. Based on assumptions about the general health of the labor force, approximately 2.3 percent of health plan participants may and 1.5 percent will find these standards difficult to achieve.

[6] Many small plans are very small, having fewer than 10 participants. Hence, many small plans will include no participant for whom either of these standards apply.

$2 million annually. If one-half request alternative standards and one-half of those meet them, the cost would be $0.5 million.[7]

In addition to the costs associated with new participants qualifying for discounts through alternative standards, small plans may also incur new economic costs by simply providing alternative standards. However, plans can satisfy this requirement by providing inexpensive alternative standards and have the flexibility to select whatever reasonable alternative standard is most desirable or cost effective. Plans not wishing to provide alternative standards also have the option of eliminating health status-based variation in employee premiums or waiving standards for individuals for whom the program standard is unreasonably difficult due to a medical condition or medically inadvisable to meet. The Departments expect that the economic cost to provide alternatives combined with the associated cost of granting discounts or waiving surcharges will not exceed the cost associated with granting discounts or waiving surcharges for all participants who qualify for an alternative. Those costs are estimated here at $0.5 million to $2 million, or about $160 to $650 per affected plan. Plans have the flexibility to pass back some or all of this cost to all participants in the form of small premium increases or benefit cuts.

The fifth requirement provides that plan materials describing wellness program standards disclose the availability of reasonable alternative standards. This requirement will affect the approximately 4,000 small plans that condition rewards on satisfaction of a standard. These plans will incur economic costs to revise affected plan materials. The estimated 1,000 to 4,000 small plan participants who will succeed at satisfying these alternative standards will benefit from these disclosures. The disclosures need not specify what alternatives are available unless the plan describes the initial standard in writing and the regulation provides sample language that can be used to satisfy this requirement. Legal requirements other than this regulation generally require plans and issuers to maintain accurate materials describing plans. Plans and issuers generally update such materials on a regular basis as part of their normal business practices. This requirement is expected to represent a negligible fraction of the ongoing, normal cost of updating plans' materials. This analysis therefore attributes no cost to this requirement.

Paperwork Reduction Act — Department of Labor and Department of the Treasury

The 2001 interim rules included an information collection request (ICR) related to the notice of the opportunity to enroll in a plan where coverage had been denied based on a health factor before the effective date of HIPAA. That ICR was approved under OMB control numbers 1210–0120 and 1545–1728, and was subsequently withdrawn from OMB inventory because the notice, if applicable, was to have been provided only once.

The proposed regulations on wellness programs did not include an information collection request. Like the proposed regulations, the final regulations include a requirement that, if a plan's wellness program requires individuals to meet a standard related to a health factor in order to qualify for a reward and if the plan materials describe this standard, the materials must also disclose the availability of a reasonable alternative standard. If plan materials merely mention that a program is available, the disclosure relating to alternatives is not required. The regulations include samples of disclosures that could be used to satisfy the requirements of the final regulations.

In concluding that the proposed rules did not include an information collection request, the Departments reasoned that much of the information required was likely already provided as a result of state and local mandates or the usual business practices of group health plans and group health insurance issuers in connection with the offer and promotion of health care coverage. In addition, the sample disclosures would enable group health plans to make any modifications necessary with minimal effort.

Finally, although neither the proposed or final regulations include a new information collection request, the regulations might have been interpreted to require a revision to an existing collection of information. Administrators of group health plans covered under Title I of ERISA are generally required to make certain disclosures about the terms of a plan and material changes in terms through a Summary Plan Description (SPD) or Summary of Material Modifications (SMM) pursuant to sections 101(a) and 102(a) of ERISA and related regulations. The ICR related to the SPD and SMM is currently approved under OMB control number 1210–0039. While these materials may in some cases require revisions to comply with the final regulations, the associated burden is expected to be negligible, and is in fact already accounted for in connection with the SPD and SMM ICR by a burden estimation methodology that anticipates ongoing revisions. Therefore, any change to the existing information collection request arising from these final regulations is not substantive or material. Accordingly, no application for approval of a revision to the existing ICR has been made to OMB in connection with these final regulations.

Paperwork Reduction Act — Department of Health and Human Services

Collection of Information Requirements

Under the Paperwork Reduction Act of 1995, we are required to provide notice in the **Federal Register** and solicit public comment before a collection of information requirement is submitted to the Office of Management and Budget (OMB) for review and approval. In order to fairly evaluate whether an information collection should be approved by OMB, section 3506(c)(2)(A) of the Paperwork Reduction Act of 1995 requires that we solicit comment on the following issues:

- The need for the information collection and its usefulness in carrying out the proper functions of our agency.
- The accuracy of our estimate of the information collection burden.
- The quality, utility, and clarity of the information to be collected.
- Recommendations to minimize the information collection burden on the

[7] Simulations run by the Departments find that the average premium discount for all health plans after the cap is enforced will be approximately $450 dollars. This average is then applied to the upper and lower bounds of those able to pass the alternative standards in small health plans in order to determine the upper and lower bound of the transfer cost.

affected public, including automated techniques.

Department regulations in 45 CFR 146.121(i)(4) require that if coverage has been denied to any individual because the sponsor of a self-funded nonfederal governmental plan has elected under 45 CFR Part 146 to exempt the plan from the requirements of this section, and the plan sponsor subsequently chooses to bring the plan into compliance, the plan must: notify the individual that the plan will be coming into compliance; afford the individual an opportunity to enroll that continues for at least 30 days, specify the effective date of compliance; and inform the individual regarding any enrollment restrictions that may apply once the plan is in compliance.

The burden associated with this requirement was approved by The Office of Management and Budget (OMB) under OMB control number 0938–0827, with a current expiration date of April 30, 2009.

In addition, CMS–2078–P, published in the **Federal Register** on January 8, 2001 (66 FR 1421) describes the *bona fide* wellness programs and specifies their criteria. Section 146.121(f)(1)(iv) further stipulates that the plan or issuer disclose in all plan materials describing the terms of the program the availability of a reasonable alternative standard to qualify for the reward under a wellness program. However, in plan materials that merely mention that a program is available, without describing its terms, the disclosure is not required.

The burden associated with this requirement was approved by OMB control number 0938–0819, with a current expiration date of April 30, 2009.

Special Analyses — Department of the Treasury

Notwithstanding the determinations of the Departments of Labor and of Health and Human Services, for purposes of the Department of the Treasury it has been determined that this Treasury decision is not a significant regulatory action. Therefore, a regulatory assessment is not required. It has also been determined that section 553(b) of the Administrative Procedure Act (5 U.S.C. chapter 5) does not apply to these regulations, and, because these regulations do not impose a collection of information on small entities, a Regulatory Flexibility Analysis under the Regulatory Flexibility Act (5 U.S.C. chapter 6) is not required. Pursuant to section 7805(f) of the Code, the notice of proposed rulemaking preceding these regulations was submitted to the Small Business Administration for comment on its impact on small business.

Congressional Review Act

These final regulations are subject to the Congressional Review Act provisions of the Small Business Regulatory Enforcement Fairness Act of 1996 (5 U.S.C. 801 *et seq.*) and have been transmitted to Congress and the Comptroller General for review. These regulations, however, constitute a "major rule," as that term is defined in 5 U.S.C. 804, because they are likely to result in (1) an annual effect on the economy of $100 million or more; (2) a major increase in costs or prices for consumers, individual industries, or federal, State or local government agencies, or geographic regions; or (3) significant adverse effects on competition, employment, investment, productivity, innovation, or on the ability of United States-based enterprises to compete with foreign-based enterprises in domestic or export markets.

Unfunded Mandates Reform Act

For purposes of the Unfunded Mandates Reform Act of 1995 (Pub. L. 104–4), as well as Executive Order 12875, these final regulations do not include any federal mandate that may result in expenditures by state, local, or tribal governments, nor does it include mandates which may impose an annual burden of $100 million or more on the private sector.

Federalism Statement – Department of Labor and Department of Health and Human Services

Executive Order 13132 outlines fundamental principles of federalism, and requires the adherence to specific criteria by federal agencies in the process of their formulation and implementation of policies that have "substantial direct effects" on the States, the relationship between the national government and States, or on the distribution of power and responsibilities among the various levels of government. Federal agencies promulgating regulations that have these federalism implications must consult with State and local officials, and describe the extent of their consultation and the nature of the concerns of State and local officials in the preamble to the regulation.

In the Departments' view, these final regulations have federalism implications, because they have substantial direct effects on the States, the relationship between the national government and States, or on the distribution of power and responsibilities among various levels of government. However, in the Departments' view, the federalism implications of these final regulations are substantially mitigated because, with respect to health insurance issuers, the vast majority of States have enacted laws, which meet or exceed the federal HIPAA standards prohibiting discrimination based on health factors.

In general, through section 514, ERISA supersedes State laws to the extent that they relate to any covered employee benefit plan, and preserves State laws that regulate insurance, banking, or securities. While ERISA prohibits States from regulating a plan as an insurance or investment company or bank, HIPAA added a new preemption provision to ERISA (as well as to the PHS Act) narrowly preempting State requirements for group health insurance coverage. With respect to the HIPAA nondiscrimination provisions, States may continue to apply State law requirements except to the extent that such requirements prevent the application of the portability, access, and renewability requirements of HIPAA, which include HIPAA's nondiscrimination requirements provisions that are the subject of this rulemaking.

In enacting these new preemption provisions, Congress intended to preempt State insurance requirements only to the extent that those requirements prevent the application of the basic protections set forth in HIPAA. HIPAA's Conference Report states that the conferees intended the narrowest preemption of State laws with regard to health insurance issuers. H.R. Conf. Rep. No. 736, 104th Cong. 2d Session 205 (1996). State insurance laws that are more stringent than the federal requirements are unlikely to "prevent the application of" the HIPAA nondiscrimination provisions, and be preempted. Accordingly, States have significant latitude to impose requirements on health insurance issuers that are more restrictive than the federal law.

Guidance conveying this interpretation was published in the **Federal Register** on April 8, 1997. (62 FR 16904) and on December 30, 2004 (T.D. 9166, 2005–1 C.B. 558 [62 FR 78720]). These final regulations clarify and implement the statute's minimum standards and do not significantly reduce the discretion given the States by the statute. Moreover, the Departments understand that the vast majority of States have requirements that meet or exceed the minimum requirements of the HIPAA nondiscrimination provisions.

HIPAA provides that the States may enforce the provisions of HIPAA as they pertain to issuers, but that the Secretary of Health and Human Services must enforce any provisions that a State fails to substantially enforce. To date, HHS has had occasion to enforce the HIPAA nondiscrimination provisions in only two States and currently enforces the nondiscrimination provisions in only one State in accordance with that State's specific request to do so. When exercising its responsibility to enforce provisions of HIPAA, HHS works cooperatively with the State for the purpose of addressing the State's concerns and avoiding conflicts with the exercise of State authority.[8] HHS has developed procedures to implement its enforcement responsibilities, and to afford the States the maximum opportunity to enforce HIPAA's requirements in the first instance. HHS's procedures address the handling of reports that States may not be enforcing HIPAA's requirements, and the mechanism for allocating enforcement responsibility between the States and HHS. In compliance with Executive Order 13132's requirement that agencies examine closely any policies that may have federalism implications or limit the policy making discretion of the States, DOL and HHS have engaged in numerous efforts to consult with and work cooperatively with affected State and local officials.

For example, the Departments sought and received input from State insurance regulators and the National Association of Insurance Commissioners (NAIC). The NAIC is a non-profit corporation established by the insurance commissioners of the 50 States, the District of Columbia, and the four U.S. territories. In most States the Insurance Commissioner is appointed by the Governor, in approximately 14 States the insurance commissioner is an elected official. Among other activities, it provides a forum for the development of uniform policy when uniformity is appropriate. Its members meet, discuss, and offer solutions to mutual problems. The NAIC sponsors quarterly meetings to provide a forum for the exchange of ideas, and in-depth consideration of insurance issues by regulators, industry representatives, and consumers. CMS and Department of Labor staff have attended the quarterly meetings consistently to listen to the concerns of the State Insurance Departments regarding HIPAA issues, including the nondiscrimination provisions. In addition to the general discussions, committee meetings and task groups, the NAIC sponsors the standing CMS/DOL meeting on HIPAA issues for members during the quarterly conferences. This meeting provides CMS and the Department of Labor with the opportunity to provide updates on regulations, bulletins, enforcement actions and outreach efforts regarding HIPAA.

In addition, the Departments specifically consulted with the NAIC in developing these final regulations. Through the NAIC, the Departments sought and received the input of State insurance departments regarding certain insurance rating practices and late enrollment issues. The Departments employed the States' insights on insurance rating practices in developing the provisions prohibiting "list-billing," and their experience with late enrollment in crafting the regulatory provision clarifying the relationship between the nondiscrimination provisions and late enrollment. Specifically, the regulations clarify that while late enrollment, if offered by a plan, must be available to all similarly situated individuals regardless of any health factor, an individual's status as a late enrollee is not itself within the scope of any health factor.

The Departments have also cooperated with the States in several ongoing outreach initiatives, through which information on HIPAA is shared among federal regulators, State regulators, and the regulated community. In particular, the Department of Labor has established a Health Benefits Education Campaign with more than 70 partners, including CMS, the NAIC and many business and consumer groups. CMS has sponsored conferences with the States — the Consumer Outreach and Advocacy conferences in March 1999 and June 2000 and the Implementation and Enforcement of HIPAA National State-federal Conferences in August 1999, 2000, 2001, 2002, and 2003. Furthermore, both the Department of Labor and CMS Web sites offer links to important State Web sites and other resources, facilitating coordination between the State and federal regulators and the regulated community.

Throughout the process of developing these regulations, to the extent feasible within the specific preemption provisions of HIPAA, the Departments have attempted to balance the States' interests in regulating health insurance issuers, and Congress's intent to provide uniform minimum protections to consumers in every State. By doing so, it is the Departments' view that they have complied with the requirements of Executive Order 13132.

Pursuant to the requirements set forth in section 8(a) of Executive Order 13132, and by the signatures affixed to these regulations, the Departments certify that the Employee Benefits Security Administration and the Centers for Medicare & Medicaid Services have complied with the requirements of Executive Order 13132 for the attached final regulation, Final Rules for Nondiscrimination in Health Coverage in the Group Market (RIN 1210–AA77 and RIN 0938–AI08), in a meaningful and timely manner.

Unified Analysis of Costs and Benefits

1. Introduction

HIPAA's nondiscrimination provisions generally prohibit group health plans and group health insurance issuers from discriminating against individuals on the basis of health factors. The primary effect and intent of the provision is to increase access to affordable group health coverage for individuals with health problems.

[8] This authority applies to insurance issued with respect to group health plans generally, including plans covering employees of church organizations. Thus, this discussion of federalism applies to all group health insurance coverage that is subject to the PHS Act, including those church plans that provide coverage through a health insurance issuer (but not to church plans that do not provide coverage through a health insurance issuer).

This effect, and the economic costs and benefits attendant to it, primarily flows from the statutory provisions of HIPAA that this regulation implements. However, the statute alone leaves room for varying interpretations of exactly which practices are prohibited or permitted at the margin. These regulations draw on the Departments' authority to clarify and interpret HIPAA's statutory nondiscrimination provisions in order to secure the protections intended by Congress for plan participants and beneficiaries. The Departments crafted them to satisfy this mandate in as economically efficient a manner as possible, and believe that the economic benefits of the regulations justify their costs. The analysis underlying this conclusion takes into account both the effect of the statute and the impact of the discretion exercised in the regulations.

The nondiscrimination provisions of the HIPAA statute and of these regulations generally apply to both group health plans and group health insurance issuers. Economic theory predicts that issuers will pass their costs of compliance back to plans, and that plans may pass some or all of issuers' and their own costs of compliance to participants. This analysis is carried out in light of this prediction.

These final regulations are needed to clarify and interpret the HIPAA nondiscrimination provisions under section 702 of ERISA, section 2702 of the PHS Act, and section 9802 of the Code, and to ensure that group health plans and group health insurance issuers do not discriminate against individual participants or beneficiaries based on any health factors with respect to health care coverage and premiums. The 2001 interim rules provided additional guidance to explain the application of the statute to benefits, to clarify the relationship between the HIPAA nondiscrimination provisions and the HIPAA preexisting condition exclusion limitations, to explain the applications of these provisions to premiums, to describe similarly situated individuals, to explain the application of the provisions to actively at work and nonconfinement clauses, to clarify that more favorable treatment of individuals with medical needs generally is permitted, and to describe plans' and issuers' obligations with respect to plan amendments.[9] These final regulations clarify the relationship between the source-of-injury rules and the timing of a diagnosis of a medical condition and add an example to illustrate how the benefits rules apply to the carryover feature of HRAs.

The proposed rules on wellness programs were issued in order to ensure that the exception for wellness programs would not contravene HIPAA's nondiscrimination provisions. With respect to wellness programs, these final regulations clarify some ambiguities in the proposed rules, make some changes in terminology and organization, and add a description of wellness programs not required to satisfy additional standards. The final rules also set the maximum reward for wellness programs that require satisfaction of a standard at 20 percent of the cost of single coverage (with additional provisions related to rewards that apply also to classes of dependents), where the proposed rules had stated the limit in terms of a range of percentages.

Because the 2001 interim rules and proposed regulations on wellness programs were originally issued as separate rulemaking actions, the Departments estimated their economic impacts separately. The costs and benefits of the statutory nondiscrimination provisions and the 2001 interim rules are again described separately from the wellness program provisions here, due to both differing baselines for the measurement of impact, and to reliance on different types of information and assumptions in the analyses.

2. Costs and Benefits of HIPAA's Nondiscrimination Provisions

The Departments have evaluated the impacts of HIPAA's nondiscrimination provisions. The nondiscrimination provisions of the 2001 interim final rules were estimated to result in costs of about $20 million to amend plans, revise plan informational materials, and notify employees previously denied coverage on the basis of a health factor of enrollment opportunities. Because these costs were associated with one-time activities that were required to be completed by the applicability date of the 2001 interim rules, these costs have been fully defrayed.

The primary statutory economic benefits associated with the HIPAA nondiscrimination provisions derive from increased access to affordable group health plan coverage for individuals whose health factors had previously restricted their participation in such plans. Expanding access entails both benefits and costs. Newly-covered individuals, who previously had to purchase similar services out-of-pocket, reap a simple and direct financial gain. In addition, these individuals may be induced to consume more (or different) health care services, reaping a benefit which has financial value, and which in some cases will produce additional indirect benefits both to the individual (improved health) and possibly to the economy at large.[10]

Inclusion of these newly-covered individuals, though, will increase both premiums and claims costs incurred by group health plans. Economic theory predicts that these costs will ultimately be shifted

[9] The Departments' estimate of the economic impact of the 2001 interim final regulations was published at 66 FR 1393 (January 8, 2001). These one-time costs were already absorbed by plans and issuers and are not discussed in this analysis. In fact, the only notice requirement in the 2001 interim final regulations was deleted from the final regulations because the time period for compliance has passed, with one small exception. Certain self-insured, nonfederal governmental plans that had opted out of the HIPAA nondiscrimination provisions under Section 2721 (b)(2) of the PHS Act and that have since decided to opt back in may be required to send a notice to individuals previously denied coverage due to a health factor. However, to date, only approximately 550 such plans have notified CMS that they are opting-out of the HIPAA nondiscrimination provisions and CMS does not receive information regarding a plan's decision to opt back in. The Departments estimate that the number of plans having done this is very small and, therefore, estimate that the impact of the notice provision on such plans is too small to calculate.

[10] Individuals without health insurance are less likely to get preventive care and less likely to have a regular source of care. A lack of health insurance generally increases the likelihood that needed medical treatment will be forgone or delayed. Forgoing or delaying care increases the risk of adverse health outcomes. These adverse outcomes in turn generate higher medical costs, which are often shifted to public funding sources (and therefore to taxpayers) or to other payers. They also erode productivity and the quality of life. Improved access to affordable group health coverage for individuals with health problems under HIPAA's nondiscrimination provisions will lead to more insurance coverage, timelier and fuller medical care, better health outcomes, and improved productivity and quality of life. This is especially true for the individuals most affected by HIPAA's nondiscrimination provisions — those with adverse health conditions. Denied insurance, individuals in poorer health are more likely to suffer economic hardship, to forgo badly needed care for financial reasons, and to suffer adverse health outcomes as a result. For them, gaining insurance is more likely to mean gaining economic security, receiving timely, quality care, and living healthier, more productive lives. For an extensive discussion of the consequences of uninsurance, see: "The Uninsured and their Access to Health Care" (2004). *The Kaiser Commission on Medicaid and the Uninsured*, November; "Insuring America's Health", (2004). *Institute of Medicine*; "Health Policy and the Uninsured" (2004) edited by Catherine G. McLaughlin. Washington, DC: Urban Institute Press; Miller, Wilhelmine *et al* (2004) "Covering the Uninsured: What is it Worth," *Health Affairs*, March: w157–w167.

to all plan participants or employees, either through an increased share of insurance costs, or lowered compensation.[11] If the number of newly-covered individuals is small relative to the total number of plan participants and costs are distributed evenly, then the increased burden for each individual should be minimal. However, it is unclear how previously-covered individuals will respond to subsequent changes in their benefits package and if their response will have unforeseen economic costs.[12] The HIPAA nondiscrimination cost is estimated to be substantial. Annual group health plan costs average approximately $7,100 per-participant,[13] and it is likely that average costs would be higher for individuals who had been denied coverage due to health factors. Prior to HIPAA's enactment, less than one-tenth of one percent of employees, or roughly 120,000 in today's labor market, were denied employment-based coverage annually because of health factors.[14] A simple assessment suggests that the total cost of coverage for such employees could be $850 million. However, this estimated statutory transfer is small relative to the overall cost of employment-based health coverage. Group health plans will spend over $620 billion this year to cover approximately 174 million employees and their dependents.[15] Estimated costs under HIPAA's nondiscrimination provisions represent a very small fraction of one percent of total group health plan expenditures.

3. Costs and Benefits of Finalizing the 2001 Interim Rules

Prohibiting Discrimination

Many of the provisions of these regulations serve to specify more precisely than the statute alone exactly what practices are prohibited by HIPAA as unlawful discrimination in eligibility or employee premiums among similarly situated employees. For example, under the regulations, eligibility generally may not be restricted based on an individual's participation in risky activities, confinement to an institution, or absence from work on an individual's enrollment date due to illness. The regulations provide that various plan features including waiting periods and eligibility for certain benefits constitute rules for eligibility which may not vary across similarly situated individuals based on health factors. They also provide that plans may not reclassify employees based on health factors in order to create separate groups of similarly situated individuals among which discrimination would be permitted.

All of these provisions have the effect of clarifying and ensuring certain participants' right to freedom from discrimination in eligibility and premium amounts, thereby securing their access to affordable group health plan coverage. The costs and benefits attributable to these provisions resemble those attendant to HIPAA's statutory nondiscrimination provisions. Securing participants' access to affordable group coverage provides economic benefits by reducing the numbers of uninsured and thereby improving health outcomes. The regulations entail a shifting of costs from the employees whose rights are secured (and/or from other parties who would otherwise pay for their health care) to plan sponsors (or to other plan participants if sponsors pass those costs back to them).

The Departments lack any basis on which to distinguish these benefits and costs from those of the statute itself. It is unclear how many plans were engaging in the discriminatory practices targeted for prohibition by these regulatory provisions. Because these provisions operate largely at the margin of the statutory requirements, it is likely that the effects of these provisions were far smaller than the similar statutory effects. The Departments are confident, however, that by securing employees' access to affordable coverage at the margin, the regulations, like the statute, have yielded benefits that justify costs.

Clarifying Requirements

Additional economic benefits derive directly from the improved clarity provided by the regulations. The regulation provides clarity through both its provisions and its examples of how those provisions apply in various circumstances. By clarifying employees' rights and plan sponsors' obligations under HIPAA's nondiscrimination provisions, the regulations reduce

[11] The voluntary nature of the employment-based health benefit system in conjunction with the open and dynamic character of labor markets make explicit as well as implicit negotiations on compensation a key determinant of the prevalence of employee benefits coverage. It is likely that 80% to 100% of the cost of employee benefits is borne by workers through reduced wages (see for example Jonathan Gruber and Alan B. Krueger, "The Incidence of Mandated Employer-Provided Insurance: Lessons from Workers Compensation Insurance," *Tax Policy and Economy* (1991); Jonathan Gruber, "The Incidence of Mandated Maternity Benefits," *American Economic Review*, Vol. 84 (June 1994), pp. 622-641; Lawrence H. Summers, "Some Simple Economics of Mandated Benefits," *American Economic Review*, Vol. 79, No. 2 (May 1989); Louise Sheiner, "Health Care Costs, Wages, and Aging," Federal Reserve Board of Governors working paper, April 1999; and Edward Montgomery, Kathryn Shaw, and Mary Ellen Benedict, "Pensions and Wages: An Hedonic Price Theory Approach," *International Economic Review*, Vol. 33 No. 1, Feb. 1992.). The prevalence of benefits is therefore largely dependent on the efficacy of this exchange. If workers perceive that there is the potential for inappropriate denial of benefits they will discount their value to adjust for this risk. This discount drives a wedge in the compensation negotiation, limiting its efficiency. With workers unwilling to bear the full cost of the benefit, fewer benefits will be provided. The extent to which workers perceive a federal regulation supported by enforcement authority to improve the security and quality of benefits, the differential between the employers costs and workers willingness top accept wage offsets is minimized.

[12] Research shows that while the share of employers offering insurance is generally stable and eligibility rates have only declined slightly over time, the overall increase in uninsured workers is due to the decline in worker take-up rates, which workers primarily attribute to cost. Research on elasticity of coverage, however, has focused on getting uninsured workers to adopt coverage (which appears to require large subsidies) rather than covered workers opting out of coverage. This makes it difficult to ascertain the loss in coverage that would result from a marginal increase in costs. (See, for example, David M. Cutler "Employee Costs and the Decline in Health Insurance Coverage" NBER Working Paper #9036. July 2002; Gruber, Jonathon and Ebonya Washington. "Subsidies to Employee Health Insurance Premiums and the Health Insurance Market" NBER Working Paper #9567. March 2003; and Cooper, PF and J. Vistnes. "Workers' Decisions to Take-up Offered Insurance Coverage: Assessing the Importance of Out-of-Pocket Costs" Med Care 2003, 41 (7 Suppl): III35–43.) Finally, economic discussions on elasticity of insurance tend to view coverage as a discrete concept and does not consider that the value of coverage may have also changed.

[13] Departments' tabulations using the 2005 Kaiser Family Foundation's Employer Health Benefits Annual Survey. Average employee premium is a weighted average of premiums for single, family, and employee-plus-one health plans. The estimate for Employee-Plus-One health premiums was derived using the 2003 MEPS-IC, as was the share of employees in each type of plans. Participants are defined as the workers or primary policy holders.

[14] Departments' tabulations off the February 1997 Current Population Survey (CPS), Contingent Worker Supplement. The estimate was projected to reflect current labor market conditions by assuming the same share of the employed, civilian force would be affected and using the 2004 CPS table, "Employment status of the civilian noninstitutional population, 1940 to date."

[15] The Departments' estimate is based on the Office of the Actuary at the Centers for Medicare and Medicaid Services (CMS) projected measure of total personal health expenditures by private health insurance in 2005. This total ($707.0 billion) is then multiplied by the share of privately insured individuals covered by employer-sponsored health insurance in 2004 as estimated by the 2005 March CPS (88 percent).

uncertainty and costly disputes over these rights and obligations. Greater clarity promotes employers' and employees' common understanding of the value of group health plan benefits and confidence in the security and predictability of those benefits, thereby improving labor market efficiency and fostering the establishment and continuation of group health plans by employers.

Impact of the Final Rules

As noted earlier in this preamble, the Departments have not modified the 2001 interim rules in any way that would impact the original cost estimates or the magnitude of the statutory transfers. Accordingly, no impact is attributable to these final regulations when measured against the baseline of the interim final rules. The provisions of the 2001 interim rules offer the appropriate baseline for this measurement because these rules were generally applicable for plan years beginning on or after July 1, 2001.

4. Costs and Benefits of the Rules Applicable to Wellness Programs

By contrast with the nondiscrimination regulatory provisions issued as interim final rules, the provisions relating to wellness programs were issued as proposed rules. This final regulation will not become effective until its applicability date.

Under the final regulation, health plans generally may vary employee premium contributions or benefit levels across similarly situated individuals based on a health factor only in connection with wellness programs. The final regulation establishes five requirements for wellness programs that vary premiums or benefits based on participation in the program and condition a reward involving premiums or benefits on satisfaction of a standard related to a health factor. These requirements will, therefore, apply to only a subset of all wellness programs.

Available literature, together with comments received by the Departments, demonstrate that well-designed wellness programs can deliver benefits well in excess of their costs. For example, the U.S. Centers for Disease Control and Prevention estimate that implementing proven clinical smoking cessation interventions can save one year of life for each $2,587 invested.[16] In addition to reduced mortality, benefits of effective wellness programs can include reduced absenteeism, improved productivity, and reduced medical costs.[17] The requirements of the final regulation were crafted to accommodate and not impair such beneficial programs, while combating discrimination in eligibility and premiums for similarly situated individuals as intended by Congress.

Estimation of the economic impacts of the requirements is difficult because data on affected plans' current practices are incomplete, and because plans' approaches to compliance with the requirements and the effects of those approaches will vary and cannot be predicted. Nonetheless, the Departments endeavored to consider the impacts fully and to develop estimates based on reasonable assumptions.

The Departments estimate that 1.6 percent of large plans and 1.2 percent of small plans currently vary employee premium contributions across similarly situated individuals due to participation in a wellness program that provides rewards based on satisfaction of a standard related to a health factor.[18] This amounts to 30,000 plans covering 1.1 million participants. According to survey data reported by Hewitt Associates,[19] just less than one-half as many plans vary benefit levels across similarly situated individuals as vary premiums. This amounts to 13,000 plans covering 460,000 participants. The Departments considered the effect of each of the five requirements on these plans. For purposes of its estimates, the Departments assumed that one-half of the plans in the latter group are also included in the former, thereby estimating that 37,000 plans covering 1.3 million participants will be subject to the five requirements for wellness programs.

Limit on Reward

Under the first requirement, any reward, whether applicable to employee premiums or benefit levels, must not exceed 20 percent of the total premium for employee-only coverage under the plan (with additional provisions related to rewards that apply also to classes of dependents). This percentage is the highest of the three alternative percentages suggested in the proposed rule, and the award limit used for purposes of the analysis of the proposed rule, which was 15 percent — the midpoint of the three alternative percentages suggested in the proposal. The estimates here also reflect increases in average annual premiums and the numbers of plans and participants since publication of the proposed rules.

The Departments lack representative data on the magnitude of the rewards applied by affected plans today. One consultant practicing in this area suggested that wellness incentive premium discounts ranged from about 3 percent to 23 percent, with an average of about 11 percent.[20] This suggests that most affected plans, including some whose discounts are somewhat larger than average, already comply with the first requirement and will not need to reduce the size of the rewards they apply. It appears likely, however, that perhaps a few thousand plans covering approximately one hundred thousand

[16] Cromwell, J., W. J. Bartosch, M. C. Fiore, V. Hasselblad and T. Baker . "Cost-Effectiveness of the Clinical Practice Recommendations in the AHCPR Guideline for Smoking Cessation." *Journal of the American Medical Association*, vol. 278 (December 3, 1997): 1759–66.

[17] The benefits of employer wellness programs are well documented. One study found the annual per participant savings to be $613 while private companies have reported returns of as much as $4.50 in lowered medical expenses for every dollar spent on health programs. (See for example, Gregg M. State *et al*, "Quantifiable Impact of the Contract for Health Wellness: Health Behaviors, Health Care Costs, Disability and Workers' Compensation," *Journal of Occupational and Environmental Medicine* (2003), vol. 45 (2): 109–117; Morgan O'Rourke & Laura Sullivan, "A Health Return on Employee Investment" *Risk Management* (2003), vol. 50 (11): 34–38; American Association of Health Plans and Health Insurance Association of America "The Cost Savings of Disease Management Programs: Report on a Study of Health Plans," November, 2003; Rachel Christensen, "Employment-Based Health Promotion and Wellness Programs" EBRI Notes (2001), vol. 22 (7): 1–6; and Steven G. Aldana "Financial Impact of Wellness Programs: A Comprehensive Review of the Literature," *American Journal of Health Promotions* (2001), vol. 15 (5): 296–320.)

[18] Estimates are based on a 1993 survey of employers by the Robert Wood Johnson Foundation. More recent estimates are unavailable.

[19] Hewitt Associates, July 2003.

[20] This estimate was made in 1998, shortly after the 1997 interim final rule was published. Since then, it appears that wellness programs advocates have been advising health plans to offer premium discounts in the range of 5 to 11 percent, well below the proposed ceiling. For a full discussion, see Larry Chapman's, "Increasing Participation in Wellness Programs," *National Wellness Institute Members 'Ask the Expert,'* July/August 2004.

participants will need to reduce the size of their rewards in order to comply with the first requirement.

The Departments considered the potential economic effects of requiring these plans to reduce the size of their rewards. These effects are likely to include a shifting of costs between plan sponsors and participants, as well as new economic costs and benefits. Shifts in costs will arise as plans reduce rewards where necessary. Plan sponsors can exercise substantial control over the size and direction of these shifts. Limiting the size of rewards restricts only the differential treatment between participants who satisfy wellness program standards and those who do not. It does not, for example, restrict plans sponsors' flexibility to determine the overall respective employer and employee shares of base premiums. Possible outcomes include a shifting of costs to plan sponsors from participants who satisfy wellness program standards, from plan sponsors to participants who do not satisfy the standards, from participants who satisfy the standards to those who do not, or some combination of these.

The Departments developed a very rough estimate of the total amount of costs that might derive from this requirement. The Departments' estimate assumes that (1) all rewards take the form of employee premium discounts; (2) discounts are distributed evenly within both the low-to-average range and the average-to-high range, and are distributed across these ranges such that their mean equals the assumed average; and (3) 70 percent of participants qualify for the discount. The 4,000 affected plans could satisfy this requirement by reducing the premium discount for the 100,000 participants who successfully complete a certified wellness program. When applied to the 2005 average annual employee-only premium of $4,024,[21] discounts range from $115 to $920, with an average of $460. The maximum allowable discount based on 20 percent of current premium is $805. Reducing all discounts greater than $805 to that amount will result in an average annual reduction of about $57. Applying this reduction to the 100,000 participants assumed to be covered by 4,000 plans affected by the limit results in an estimate of the aggregate cost at $6 million.

New economic costs and benefits may arise if changes in the size of rewards result in changes in participant behavior. Net economic welfare might be lost if some wellness programs' effectiveness is eroded, but the magnitude and incidence of such effects is expected to be negligible. Consider a wellness program that discounts premiums for participants who take part in an exercise program. It is plausible that, at the margin, a few participants who would take part in order to obtain an existing discount will not take part to obtain a somewhat lower discount. This effect is expected to be negligible, however. Reductions in discounts are likely to average about $57 annually, which is very small when spread over biweekly pay periods. Moreover, the final regulation limits only rewards applied to similarly situated individuals in the context of a group health plan. It does not restrict plan sponsors from encouraging healthy lifestyles in other ways, such as by varying life insurance premiums.

On the other hand, net economic welfare likely will be gained in instances where large premium differentials would otherwise have served to discourage enrollment in health plans by employees who did not satisfy wellness program requirements.

The Departments believe that the net economic gains from prohibiting rewards so large that they could discourage enrollment based on health factors justify any net losses that might derive from the negligible reduction of some employees' incentive to participate in wellness programs.

<u>*Reasonable Design*</u>

Under the second requirement, the program must be reasonably designed to promote health or prevent disease. The Departments believe that a program that is not so designed would not provide economic benefits, but would serve merely to shift costs from plan sponsors to targeted individuals based on health factors. Comments received by the Departments and available literature on employee wellness programs, however, suggest that existing wellness programs generally satisfy this requirement. As was stated in the analysis of the proposed rule, this requirement therefore is not expected to compel plans to modify existing wellness programs or entail additional economic costs.

<u>*Annual Opportunity to Qualify*</u>

Although this requirement was included in the proposal within the requirement for reasonable design, it has been reorganized as a separate provision in these final regulations. At the time of the proposal, the Departments assumed that most plans satisfied the requirements for reasonable design, such that they would not be required to modify existing programs. Accordingly, no cost was attributed to the reasonable design requirements when taken together. The Departments did request comments on this assumption, but received no additional information in response. Accordingly, the Departments have not attributed a cost to this provision of the final regulations.

<u>*Uniform Availability*</u>

The fourth requirement provides that where rewards are conditioned on satisfaction of a standard related to a health factor, rewards must be available to all similarly situated individuals. A reward is not available to all similarly situated individuals unless the program allows for a reasonable alternative standard if the otherwise applicable initial standard is unreasonably difficult to achieve due to a medical condition or medically inadvisable for the individual to meet. In particular, the program must offer any such individual the opportunity to satisfy a reasonable alternative standard. Comments received by the Departments and available literature on employee wellness programs suggest that some wellness programs do not currently satisfy this requirement and will have to be modified. The Departments estimate that among employers that provide incentives for employees to participate in wellness programs, nine percent require employees to achieve a low risk behavior to qualify for the incentive, 53 percent require a pledge of compliance, and 55 percent require participation in a program.[22]

[21] Average based on the Kaiser Family Foundation/Health Research and Education Trust *Survey of Employer-Sponsored Health Benefits, 2005.*

[22] Hewitt Associates, July, 2003. The sum of these shares exceeds 100 percent due to some employers using multiple criteria to determine compliance.

Depending on the nature of the wellness program, it might be unreasonably difficult due to a medical condition or medically inadvisable for at least some plan participants to achieve the behavior or to comply with or participate in the program.

The Departments identified three broad types of economic impact that might arise from this requirement. First, affected plans will incur some economic cost to make available reasonable alternative standards. Second, additional economic costs and benefits may arise depending on the nature of alternatives provided, individuals' use of these alternatives, and any changes in the affected individuals' behavioral and health outcomes. Third, some costs may be shifted from individuals who would fail to satisfy programs' initial standards, but who will satisfy reasonable alternative standards once available (and thereby qualify for associated rewards), to plan sponsors (or to other participants in their plans if plan sponsors elect to pass these costs back to all participants).

The Departments note that some plans that offer rewards to similarly situated individuals based on their ability to meet a standard related to a health factor (and are therefore subject to the requirement) may not need to provide alternative standards. The requirement provides that alternative standards need not be specified or provided until a participant for whom it is unreasonably difficult due to a medical condition or medically inadvisable to satisfy the initial standard seeks such an alternative. Some wellness programs' initial standards may be such that no participant would ever find them unreasonably difficult to satisfy due to a medical condition or medically inadvisable to attempt. The Departments estimate that 3,000 potentially affected plans have initial wellness program standards that might be unreasonably difficult for some participants to satisfy due to a medical condition or medically inadvisable to attempt.[23] Moreover, because alternatives need not be made available until they are sought by qualified plan participants, it might be possible for some plans to go for years without needing to make available an alternative standard. This could be particularly likely for small plans.[24]

The Departments estimate that as many as 27 percent of participants in plans with rewards that are based on meeting a standard related to a health factor, or 344,000 individuals, might fail to satisfy wellness programs' initial standards because they are unreasonably difficult due to a medical condition or medically inadvisable to meet.[25] Of these, only about 30,000 are in the 3,000 plans assumed to apply standards that might be unreasonably difficult due to a medical condition or medically inadvisable for some plan participants to satisfy. The standards would in fact be unreasonably difficult or medically inadvisable to satisfy for some subset of these individuals — roughly two-thirds, or 19,000 by the Departments' estimate.[26] Of these, it is assumed that between 5,000 and 19,000 of those individuals that seek alternative standards are able to satisfy them.[27]

The cost associated with establishing alternative standards is unknown. However, the regulation does not prescribe a particular type of alternative standard that must be provided. Instead, it permits plan sponsors flexibility to provide any reasonable alternative, or to waive the standard, for individuals for whom the initial standard is unreasonably difficult due to a medical condition or medically inadvisable to meet. The Departments expect that plan sponsors will select alternatives that entail the minimum net costs possible. Plan sponsors may select low-cost alternatives, such as requiring an individual for whom it would be unreasonably difficult to quit smoking (and thereby qualify for a non-smoker discount) to attend a smoking cessation program that is available at little or no cost in the community, or to watch educational videos or review educational literature. Plan sponsors presumably will select higher-cost alternatives only if they thereby derive offsetting benefits, such as a higher smoking cessation success rate.

Although there is considerable uncertainty in these estimates, it seems reasonable to assume that the net cost sponsors will incur in the provision of alternatives, including new economic costs and benefits, will not exceed the cost of providing discounts (or waiving surcharges) for all plan participants who qualify for alternatives, which is estimated at between $2 million and $9 million.[28] Other economic costs and benefits might arise where alternative standards are made available. For example, some individuals might receive a discount for satisfying alternative standards that turn out to be less beneficial to overall health than the initial standard

[23] Estimate is based on both the share of plans in the 2003–04 Hewitt survey stating that certain health factors or lifestyle choices affect employees' benefit coverage and the share of employers requiring employees to achieve a lower-risk behavior to earn incentives. These measures are then combined with the number of workers in the civilian labor force (from 2003 estimates of the Bureau of Labor Statistics (BLS) suffering from these maladies (as provided by the Centers for Disease Control (CDC) 2004 *Health* and the National Center for Statistics and Analysis (NCSA) 2004 estimates of seatbelt use), by demographic group.

[24] The most common standards that would be implemented by this provision of the wellness program rules pertain to smoking, blood pressure, and cholesterol levels, according to the Hewitt survey. Based on data from the CDC, NCSA and BLS, the Departments estimate that among plans with five participants, about one-fourth will not contain any smokers, one-third will not contain participants with high blood pressure and two-fifths will not contain any with high cholesterol. Approximately 97 percent of all plans with potentially difficult initial wellness program standards have fewer than 100 participants.

[25] This estimate is considerably lower than that offered in the proposal due to a difference in the format of the data reported in the 2001 and 2003 Hewitt surveys, and the Departments' original adjustment for data reported in the 2001 survey as, "not provided." The Departments believe in light of the 2003 data that the adjustments thought to be appropriate at the time overestimated the number of plans with standards that might be unreasonably difficult or medically inadvisable to meet, resulting in more instances in which alternative standards might be established and met, and greater magnitudes of transfers for individuals who would newly attain rewards. The Departments have revised their assumptions to account for a smaller number of plans with standards unreasonably difficult or medically inadvisable to meet, and a correspondingly larger number of participants who will already have been satisfying these standards. Accordingly, this results in a reduction of the estimates of transfers in connection with establishing reasonable alternative standards.

[26] Having previously determined the share of the working class population suffering from various maladies using CDC, NCSA and BLS estimates and how, according to the Hewitt survey, these conditions are factored into wellness programs, the Departments were able to estimate that 26.8 percent of plan participants may initially fail to satisfy program standards. Since the Hewitt study went on to state that 9 percent of employers surveyed required participants to meet the standard in order to receive premium discounts, it was then concluded that 2.3 percent *may* have difficulty meeting the standards and 1.5 percent *will* have difficulty meeting the standards.

[27] No independent estimates of those satisfying alternative standards were available, so the Departments created an upper bound which assumes all individuals for whom the standards are unreasonably difficult seek and satisfy an alternative standard, and a lower bound which assumes half of those for whom the standards are unreasonably difficult seek an alternative, and half of those are able to satisfy it.

[28] These estimates are the product of the range of numbers of individuals who might newly attain rewards and the average premium reward. It is likely that many plan sponsors will find more cost effective ways to satisfy this requirement, and that the true net cost to them will therefore be smaller than this.

might have been, resulting in a net loss of economic welfare. In other cases, the satisfaction of an alternative standard might produce the desired health improvement, which would represent a net gain in economic welfare.

Although outcomes are uncertain, the Departments note that plan sponsors have strong motivation to identify and provide alternative standards that have positive net economic effects. They will be disinclined to provide alternatives that worsen behavioral and health outcomes, or that make financial rewards available absent meaningful efforts by participants to improve their health habits and health. Instead they will be inclined to provide alternatives that sustain or reinforce plan participants' incentive to improve their health habits and health, and/or that help participants make such improvements. It therefore seems likely that gains in economic welfare from this requirement will equal or justify losses. The Departments anticipate that the requirement to provide reasonable alternative standards will reduce instances where wellness programs serve only to shift costs to higher risk individuals and increase instances where programs succeed at helping individuals with higher health risks improve their health habits and health.

Disclosure Regarding Reasonable Alternative Standards

The fifth requirement provides that plan materials describing wellness program standards that are related to a health factor must disclose the availability of reasonable alternative standards. Under some wellness programs, an individual must satisfy a standard related to a health factor in order to qualify for the reward.

Plans offering wellness programs under which an individual must satisfy a standard related to a health factor in order to qualify for the reward must disclose in all plan materials describing the terms of the program the availability of a reasonable alternative standard. The regulations provide sample language for this disclosure. An actual description of the alternative standard is not required in such materials. In plan materials that merely mention that a wellness program is available but do not describe its terms, this disclosure of the availability of an alternative standard is not required. The Departments generally account elsewhere for plans' cost of updating such materials to reflect changes in plan provisions as required under various disclosure requirements and as is part of usual business practice. This particular requirement is expected to represent a negligible fraction of the ongoing cost of updating plans' materials, and is not separately accounted for here.

Statutory Authority

The Department of the Treasury final rule is adopted pursuant to the authority contained in sections 7805 and 9833 of the Code (26 U.S.C. 7805, 9833).

The Department of Labor final rule is adopted pursuant to the authority contained in sections 29 U.S.C. 1027, 1059, 1135, 1161–1168, 1169, 1181–1183, 1181 note, 1185, 1185a, 1185b, 1191, 1191a, 1191b, and 1191c, sec. 101(g), Public Law 104–191, 110 Stat. 1936; sec. 401(b), Public Law 105–200, 112 Stat. 645 (42 U.S.C. 651 note); Secretary of Labor's Order 1–2003, 68 FR 5374 (Feb. 3, 2003).

The Department of Health and Human Services final rule is adopted pursuant to the authority contained in sections 2701 through 2763, 2791, and 2792 of the PHS Act (42 U.S.C. 300gg through 300gg–63, 300gg–91, and 300gg–92), as added by HIPAA (Public Law 104–191, 110 Stat. 1936), and amended by the Mental Health Parity Act (MHPA) and the Newborns' and Mothers' Health Protection Act (NMHPA) (Public Law 104–204, 110 Stat. 2935), and the Women's Health and Cancer Rights Act (WHCRA) (Public Law 105–277, 112 Stat. 2681–436).

* * * * *

Adoption of Amendments to the Regulations

Internal Revenue Service
26 CFR Chapter I

Accordingly, 26 CFR Part 54 is amended as follows:

PART 54 — PENSION EXCISE TAXES

Paragraph 1. The authority citation for part 54 is amended by removing the citation for §54.9802–1T to read, in part, as follows:

Authority: 26 U.S.C. 7805. * * *

§54.9802–1T [Removed]

Par. 2. Section 54.9802–1T is removed.

Par. 3. Section 54.9802–1 is revised to read as follows:

§54.9802–1 Prohibiting discrimination against participants and beneficiaries based on a health factor.

(a) *Health factors.* (1) The term *health factor* means, in relation to an individual, any of the following health status-related factors:

(i) Health status;

(ii) Medical condition (including both physical and mental illnesses), as defined in §54.9801–2;

(iii) Claims experience;

(iv) Receipt of health care;

(v) Medical history;

(vi) Genetic information, as defined in §54.9801–2 of this chapter;

(vii) Evidence of insurability; or

(viii) Disability.

(2) Evidence of insurability includes —

(i) Conditions arising out of acts of domestic violence; and

(ii) Participation in activities such as motorcycling, snowmobiling, all-terrain vehicle riding, horseback riding, skiing, and other similar activities.

(3) The decision whether health coverage is elected for an individual (including the time chosen to enroll, such as under special enrollment or late enrollment) is not, itself, within the scope of any health factor. (However, under §54.9801–6, a plan must treat special enrollees the same as similarly situated individuals who are enrolled when first eligible.)

(b) *Prohibited discrimination in rules for eligibility* — (1) *In general.* (i) A group health plan may not establish any rule for eligibility (including continued eligibility) of any individual to enroll for benefits under the terms of the plan that discriminates based on any health factor that relates to that individual or a dependent of that individual. This rule is subject to the provisions of paragraph (b)(2) of this section (explaining how this rule applies to benefits), paragraph (b)(3) of this section (allowing plans to impose certain preexisting condition exclusions), paragraph (d) of this section (containing rules for establishing groups of similarly situated individuals), paragraph (e) of this section (relating to nonconfinement, actively-at-work, and other service requirements), paragraph (f) of this section (relating to wellness programs), and paragraph (g) of this section (permitting favorable treatment of individuals with adverse health factors).

(ii) For purposes of this section, rules for eligibility include, but are not limited to, rules relating to —

(A) Enrollment;

(B) The effective date of coverage;

(C) Waiting (or affiliation) periods;

(D) Late and special enrollment;

(E) Eligibility for benefit packages (including rules for individuals to change their selection among benefit packages);

(F) Benefits (including rules relating to covered benefits, benefit restrictions, and cost-sharing mechanisms such as coinsurance, copayments, and deductibles), as described in paragraphs (b)(2) and (3) of this section;

(G) Continued eligibility; and

(H) Terminating coverage (including disenrollment) of any individual under the plan.

(iii) The rules of this paragraph (b)(1) are illustrated by the following examples:

Example 1. (i) *Facts.* An employer sponsors a group health plan that is available to all employees who enroll within the first 30 days of their employment. However, employees who do not enroll within the first 30 days cannot enroll later unless they pass a physical examination.

(ii) *Conclusion.* In this *Example 1*, the requirement to pass a physical examination in order to enroll in the plan is a rule for eligibility that discriminates based on one or more health factors and thus violates this paragraph (b)(1).

Example 2. (i) *Facts.* Under an employer's group health plan, employees who enroll during the first 30 days of employment (and during special enrollment periods) may choose between two benefit packages: an indemnity option and an HMO option. However, employees who enroll during late enrollment are permitted to enroll only in the HMO option and only if they provide evidence of good health.

(ii) *Conclusion.* In this *Example 2*, the requirement to provide evidence of good health in order to be eligible for late enrollment in the HMO option is a rule for eligibility that discriminates based on one or more health factors and thus violates this paragraph (b)(1). However, if the plan did not require evidence of good health but limited late enrollees to the HMO option, the plan's rules for eligibility would not discriminate based on any health factor, and thus would not violate this paragraph (b)(1), because the time an individual chooses to enroll is not, itself, within the scope of any health factor.

Example 3. (i) *Facts.* Under an employer's group health plan, all employees generally may enroll within the first 30 days of employment. However, individuals who participate in certain recreational activities, including motorcycling, are excluded from coverage.

(ii) *Conclusion.* In this *Example 3*, excluding from the plan individuals who participate in recreational activities, such as motorcycling, is a rule for eligibility that discriminates based on one more health factors and thus violates this paragraph (b)(1).

Example 4. (i) *Facts.* A group health plan applies for a group health policy offered by an issuer. As part of the application, the issuer receives health information about individuals to be covered under the plan. Individual *A* is an employee of the employer maintaining the plan. *A* and *A*'s dependents have a history of high health claims. Based on the information about *A* and *A*'s dependents, the issuer excludes *A* and *A*'s dependents from the group policy it offers to the employer.

(ii) *Conclusion.* See *Example 4* in 29 CFR 2590.702(b)(1) and 45 CFR 146.121(b)(1) for a conclusion that the exclusion by the issuer of *A* and *A*'s dependents from coverage is a rule for eligibility that discriminates based on one or more health factors and violates rules under 29 CFR 2590.702(b)(1) and 45 CFR 146.121(b)(1) similar to the rules under this paragraph (b)(1). (If the employer is a small employer under 45 CFR 144.103 (generally, an employer with 50 or fewer employees), the issuer also may violate 45 CFR 146.150, which requires issuers to offer all the policies they sell in the small group market on a guaranteed available basis to all small employers and to accept every eligible individual in every small employer group.) If the plan provides coverage through this policy and does not provide equivalent coverage for *A* and *A*'s dependents through other means, the plan violates this paragraph (b)(1).

(2) *Application to benefits* — (i) *General rule.* (A) Under this section, a group health plan is not required to provide coverage for any particular benefit to any group of similarly situated individuals.

(B) However, benefits provided under a plan must be uniformly available to all similarly situated individuals (as described in paragraph (d) of this section). Likewise, any restriction on a benefit or benefits must apply uniformly to all similarly situated individuals and must not be directed at individual participants or beneficiaries based on any health factor of the participants or beneficiaries (determined based on all the relevant facts and circumstances). Thus, for example, a plan may limit or exclude benefits in relation to a specific disease or condition, limit or exclude benefits for certain types of treatments or drugs, or limit or exclude benefits based on a determination of whether the benefits are experimental or not medically necessary, but only if the benefit limitation or exclusion applies uniformly to all similarly situated individuals and is not directed at individual participants or beneficiaries based on any health factor of the participants or beneficiaries. In addition, a plan may impose annual, lifetime, or other limits on benefits and may require the satisfaction of a deductible, copayment, coinsurance, or other cost-sharing requirement in order to obtain a benefit if the limit or cost-sharing requirement applies uniformly to all similarly situated individuals and is not directed at individual participants or beneficiaries based on any health factor of the participants or beneficiaries. In the case of a cost-sharing requirement, see also paragraph (b)(2)(ii) of this section, which permits variances in the application of a cost-sharing mechanism made available under a wellness program. (Whether any plan provision or practice with respect to benefits complies with this paragraph (b)(2)(i) does not affect whether the provision or practice is permitted under ERISA, the Americans with Disabilities Act, or any other law, whether State or Federal.)

(C) For purposes of this paragraph (b)(2)(i), a plan amendment applicable to all individuals in one or more groups of similarly situated individuals under the plan and made effective no earlier than the first day of the first plan year after the amendment is adopted is not considered to be directed at any individual participants or beneficiaries.

(D) The rules of this paragraph (b)(2)(i) are illustrated by the following examples:

Example 1. (i) *Facts.* A group health plan applies a $500,000 lifetime limit on all benefits to each participant or beneficiary covered under the plan. The limit is not directed at individual participants or beneficiaries.

(ii) *Conclusion.* In this *Example 1*, the limit does not violate this paragraph (b)(2)(i) because $500,000 of benefits are available uniformly to each participant and beneficiary under the plan and because the limit is applied uniformly to all participants and beneficiaries and is not directed at individual participants or beneficiaries.

Example 2. (i) *Facts.* A group health plan has a $2 million lifetime limit on all benefits (and no other lifetime limits) for participants covered under the plan. Participant *B* files a claim for the treatment of AIDS. At the next corporate board meeting of the plan sponsor, the claim is discussed. Shortly thereafter, the plan is modified to impose a $10,000 lifetime limit on benefits for the treatment of AIDS, effective before the beginning of the next plan year.

(ii) *Conclusion.* The facts of this *Example 2* strongly suggest that the plan modification is directed at *B* based on *B*'s claim. Absent outweighing evidence to the contrary, the plan violates this paragraph (b)(2)(i).

Example 3. (i) A group health plan applies for a group health policy offered by an issuer. Individual *C* is covered under the plan and has an adverse health condition. As part of the application, the issuer receives health information about the individuals to be covered, including information about *C*'s adverse health condition. The policy form offered by the issuer generally provides benefits for the adverse health condition that *C* has, but in this case the issuer offers the plan a policy modified by a rider that excludes benefits for *C* for that condition. The exclusionary rider is made effective the first day of the next plan year.

(ii) *Conclusion.* See *Example 3* in 29 CFR 2590.702(b)(2)(i) and 45 CFR 146.121(b)(2)(i) for a conclusion that the issuer violates rules under 29 CFR 2590.702(b)(2)(i) and 45 CFR 146.121(b)(2)(i) similar to the rules under this paragraph (b)(2)(i) because benefits for *C*'s condition are available to other individuals in the group of similarly situated individuals that includes *C* but are not available to *C*. Thus, the benefits are not uniformly available to all similarly situated individuals. Even though the exclusionary rider is made effective the first day of the next plan year, because the rider does not apply to all similarly situated individuals, the issuer violates the rules under 29 CFR 2590.702(b)(2)(i) and 45 CFR 146.121(b)(2)(i). If the plan provides coverage through this policy and does not provide equivalent coverage for *C* through other means, the plan violates this paragraph (b)(2)(i).

Example 4. (i) *Facts.* A group health plan has a $2,000 lifetime limit for the treatment of temporomandibular joint syndrome (TMJ). The limit is applied uniformly to all similarly situated individuals and is not directed at individual participants or beneficiaries.

(ii) *Conclusion.* In this *Example 4*, the limit does not violate this paragraph (b)(2)(i) because $2,000 of benefits for the treatment of TMJ are available uniformly to all similarly situated individuals and a plan may limit benefits covered in relation to a specific disease or condition if the limit applies uniformly to all similarly situated individuals and is not directed at individual participants or beneficiaries. (This example does not address whether the plan provision is permissible under the Americans with Disabilities Act or any other applicable law.)

Example 5. (i) *Facts.* A group health plan applies a $2 million lifetime limit on all benefits. However, the $2 million lifetime limit is reduced to $10,000 for any participant or beneficiary covered under the plan who has a congenital heart defect.

(ii) *Conclusion.* In this *Example 5*, the lower lifetime limit for participants and beneficiaries with a congenital heart defect violates this paragraph (b)(2)(i) because benefits under the plan are not uniformly available to all similarly situated individuals and the plan's lifetime limit on benefits does not apply uniformly to all similarly situated individuals.

Example 6. (i) *Facts.* A group health plan limits its benefits for prescription drugs to those listed on a drug formulary. The limit is applied uniformly to all similarly situated individuals and is not directed at individual participants or beneficiaries.

(ii) *Conclusion.* In this *Example 6*, the exclusion from coverage of drugs not listed on the drug formulary does not violate this paragraph (b)(2)(i) because benefits for prescription drugs listed on the formulary are uniformly available to all similarly situated individuals and because the exclusion of drugs not listed on the formulary applies uniformly to all similarly situated individuals and is not directed at individual participants or beneficiaries.

Example 7. (i) *Facts.* Under a group health plan, doctor visits are generally subject to a $250 annual deductible and 20 percent coinsurance requirement. However, prenatal doctor visits are not subject to any deductible or coinsurance requirement. These rules are applied uniformly to all similarly situated individuals and are not directed at individual participants or beneficiaries.

(ii) *Conclusion.* In this *Example 7*, imposing different deductible and coinsurance requirements for prenatal doctor visits and other visits does not violate this paragraph (b)(2)(i) because a plan may establish different deductibles or coinsurance requirements for different services if the deductible or coinsurance requirement is applied uniformly to all similarly situated individuals and is not directed at individual participants or beneficiaries.

Example 8. (i) *Facts.* An employer sponsors a group health plan that is available to all current employees. Under the plan, the medical care expenses of each employee (and the employee's dependents) are reimbursed up to an annual maximum amount. The maximum reimbursement amount with respect to an employee for a year is $1500 multiplied by the number of years the employee has participated in the plan, reduced by the total reimbursements for prior years.

(ii) *Conclusion.* In this *Example 8*, the variable annual limit does not violate this paragraph (b)(2)(i). Although the maximum reimbursement amount for a year varies among employees within the same group of similarly situated individuals based on prior claims experience, employees who have participated in the plan for the same length of time are eligible for the same total benefit over that length of time (and the restriction on the maximum reimbursement amount is not directed at any individual participants or beneficiaries based on any health factor).

(ii) *Exception for wellness programs.* A group health plan may vary benefits, including cost-sharing mechanisms (such as a deductible, copayment, or coinsurance), based on whether an individual has met the standards of a wellness program that satisfies the requirements of paragraph (f) of this section.

(iii) *Specific rule relating to source-of-injury exclusions.* (A) If a group health plan generally provides benefits for a type of injury, the plan may not deny benefits otherwise provided for treatment of the injury if the injury results from an act of domestic violence or a medical condition (including both physical and mental health conditions). This rule applies in the case of an injury resulting from a medical condition even if the condition is not diagnosed before the injury.

(B) The rules of this paragraph (b)(2)(iii) are illustrated by the following examples:

Example 1. (i) *Facts.* A group health plan generally provides medical/surgical benefits, including benefits for hospital stays, that are medically necessary. However, the plan excludes benefits for self-inflicted injuries or injuries sustained in connection with attempted suicide. Because of depression, Individual *D* attempts suicide. As a result, *D* sustains injuries and is hospitalized for treatment of the injuries. Under the exclusion, the plan denies *D* benefits for treatment of the injuries.

(ii) *Conclusion.* In this *Example 1*, the suicide attempt is the result of a medical condition (depression). Accordingly, the denial of benefits for the treatments of *D*'s injuries violates the requirements of this paragraph (b)(2)(iii) because the plan provision excludes benefits for treatment of an injury resulting from a medical condition.

Example 2. (i) *Facts.* A group health plan provides benefits for head injuries generally. The plan also has a general exclusion for any injury sustained while participating in any of a number of recreational activities, including bungee jumping. However, this exclusion does not apply to any injury that results from a medical condition (nor from domestic violence). Participant *E* sustains a head injury while bungee jumping. The injury did not result from a medical condition (nor from domestic violence). Accordingly, the plan denies benefits for *E*'s head injury.

(ii) *Conclusion.* In this *Example 2*, the plan provision that denies benefits based on the source of an injury does not restrict benefits based on an act of domestic violence or any medical condition. Therefore, the provision is permissible under this paragraph (b)(2)(iii) and does not violate this section. (However, if the plan did not allow *E* to enroll in the plan (or applied different rules for eligibility to *E*) because *E* frequently participates in bungee jumping, the plan would violate paragraph (b)(1) of this section.)

(3) *Relationship to §54.9801–3.* (i) A preexisting condition exclusion is permitted under this section if it —

(A) Complies with §54.9801–3;

(B) Applies uniformly to all similarly situated individuals (as described in paragraph (d) of this section); and

(C) Is not directed at individual participants or beneficiaries based on any health factor of the participants or beneficiaries. For purposes of this paragraph (b)(3)(i)(C), a plan amendment relating to a preexisting condition exclusion applicable to all individuals in one or more groups of similarly situated individuals under the plan and made effective no earlier than the first day of the first plan year after the amendment is adopted is not considered to be directed at any individual participants or beneficiaries.

(ii) The rules of this paragraph (b)(3) are illustrated by the following examples:

Example 1. (i) *Facts.* A group health plan imposes a preexisting condition exclusion on all individuals enrolled in the plan. The exclusion applies to conditions for which medical advice, diagnosis, care, or treatment was recommended or received within the six-month period ending on an individual's enrollment date. In addition, the exclusion generally extends for 12 months after an individual's enrollment date, but this 12-month period is offset by the number of days of an individual's creditable coverage in accordance with §54.9801–3. There is nothing to indicate that the exclusion is directed at individual participants or beneficiaries.

(ii) *Conclusion.* In this *Example 1*, even though the plan's preexisting condition exclusion discriminates against individuals based on one or more health factors, the preexisting condition exclusion does not violate this section because it applies uniformly to all similarly situated individuals, is not directed at individual participants or beneficiaries, and complies with §54.9801–3 (that is, the requirements relating to the six-month look-back period, the 12-month (or 18-month) maximum exclusion period, and the creditable coverage offset).

Example 2. (i) *Facts.* A group health plan excludes coverage for conditions with respect to which medical advice, diagnosis, care, or treatment was recommended or received within the six-month period ending on an individual's enrollment date. Under the plan, the preexisting condition exclusion generally extends for 12 months, offset by creditable coverage. However, if an individual has no claims in the first six months following enrollment, the remainder of the exclusion period is waived.

(ii) *Conclusion.* In this *Example 2*, the plan's preexisting condition exclusions violate this section because they do not meet the requirements of this paragraph (b)(3); specifically, they do not apply uniformly to all similarly situated individuals. The plan provisions do not apply uniformly to all similarly situated individuals because individuals who have medical claims during the first six months following enrollment are not treated the same as similarly situated individuals with no claims during that period. (Under paragraph (d) of this section, the groups cannot be treated as two separate groups of similarly situated individuals because the distinction is based on a health factor.)

(c) *Prohibited discrimination in premiums or contributions* — (1) *In general.* (i) A group health plan may not require an individual, as a condition of enrollment or continued enrollment under the plan, to pay a premium or contribution that is greater than the premium or contribution for a similarly situated individual (described in paragraph (d) of this section) enrolled in the plan based on any health factor that relates to the individual or a dependent of the individual.

(ii) Discounts, rebates, payments in kind, and any other premium differential mechanisms are taken into account in determining an individual's premium or contribution rate. (For rules relating to cost-sharing mechanisms, see paragraph (b)(2) of this section (addressing benefits).)

(2) *Rules relating to premium rates* — (i) *Group rating based on health factors not restricted under this section.* Nothing in this section restricts the aggregate amount that an employer may be charged for coverage under a group health plan.

(ii) *List billing based on a health factor prohibited.* However, a group health plan may not quote or charge an employer (or an individual) a different premium for an individual in a group of similarly situated individuals based on a health factor. (But see paragraph (g) of this section permitting favorable treatment of individuals with adverse health factors.)

(iii) *Examples.* The rules of this paragraph (c)(2) are illustrated by the following examples:

Example 1. (i) *Facts.* An employer sponsors a group health plan and purchases coverage from a health insurance issuer. In order to determine the premium rate for the upcoming plan year, the issuer reviews the claims experience of individuals covered under the plan. The issuer finds that Individual *F* had significantly higher claims experience than similarly situated individuals in the plan. The issuer quotes the plan a higher per-participant rate because of *F*'s claims experience.

(ii) *Conclusion.* See *Example 1* in 29 CFR 2590.702(c)(2) and 45 CFR 146.121(c)(2) for a conclusion that the issuer does not violate the provisions of 29 CFR 2590.702(c)(2) and 45 CFR 146.121(c)(2) similar to the provisions of this paragraph (c)(2) because the issuer blends the rate so that the employer is not quoted a higher rate for *F* than for a similarly situated individual based on *F*'s claims experience.

Example 2. (i) *Facts.* Same facts as *Example 1*, except that the issuer quotes the employer a higher premium rate for *F*, because of *F*'s claims experience, than for a similarly situated individual.

(ii) *Conclusion.* See *Example 2* in 29 CFR 2590.702(c)(2) and 45 CFR 146.121(c)(2) for a conclusion that the issuer violates provisions of 29 CFR 2590.702(c)(2) and 45 CFR 146.121(c)(2) similar to the provisions of this paragraph (c)(2). Moreover, even if the plan purchased the policy based on the quote but did not require a higher participant contribution for *F* than for a similarly situated individual, see *Example 2* in 29 CFR 2590.702(c)(2) and 45 CFR 146.121(c)(2) for a conclusion that the issuer would still violate 29 CFR 2590.702(c)(2) and 45 CFR 146.121(c)(2) (but in such a case the plan would not violate this paragraph (c)(2)).

(3) *Exception for wellness programs.* Notwithstanding paragraphs (c)(1) and (2) of this section, a plan may vary the amount of premium or contribution it requires similarly situated individuals to pay based on whether an individual has met the standards of a wellness program that satisfies the requirements of paragraph (f) of this section.

(d) *Similarly situated individuals.* The requirements of this section apply only within a group of individuals who are treated as similarly situated individuals. A plan may treat participants as a group of similarly situated individuals separate from beneficiaries. In addition, participants may be treated as two or more distinct groups of similarly situated individuals and beneficiaries may be treated as two or more distinct groups of similarly situated individuals in accordance with the rules of this paragraph (d). Moreover, if individuals have a choice of two or more benefit packages, individuals choosing one benefit package may be treated as one or more groups of similarly situated individuals distinct from individuals choosing another benefit package.

(1) *Participants.* Subject to paragraph (d)(3) of this section, a plan may treat participants as two or more distinct groups of similarly situated individuals if the distinction between or among the groups of participants is based on a *bona fide* employment-based classification consistent with the employer's usual business practice. Whether an employment-based classification is *bona fide* is determined on the basis of all the relevant facts and circumstances. Relevant facts and circumstances include whether the employer uses the classification for purposes independent of qualification for health coverage (for example, determining eligibility for other employee benefits or determining other terms of employment). Subject to paragraph (d)(3) of this section, examples of classifications that, based on all the relevant facts and circumstances, may be *bona fide* include full-time versus part-time status, different geographic location, membership in a collective bargaining unit, date of hire, length of service, current employee versus former employee status, and different occupations. However, a classification based on any health factor is not a *bona fide* employment-based classification, unless the requirements of paragraph (g) of this section are satisfied (permitting favorable treatment of individuals with adverse health factors).

(2) *Beneficiaries.* (i) Subject to paragraph (d)(3) of this section, a plan may treat beneficiaries as two or more distinct groups of similarly situated individuals if the distinction between or among the

groups of beneficiaries is based on any of the following factors:

(A) A *bona fide* employment-based classification of the participant through whom the beneficiary is receiving coverage;

(B) Relationship to the participant (for example, as a spouse or as a dependent child);

(C) Marital status;

(D) With respect to children of a participant, age or student status; or

(E) Any other factor if the factor is not a health factor.

(ii) Paragraph (d)(2)(i) of this section does not prevent more favorable treatment of individuals with adverse health factors in accordance with paragraph (g) of this section.

(3) *Discrimination directed at individuals.* Notwithstanding paragraphs (d)(1) and (2) of this section, if the creation or modification of an employment or coverage classification is directed at individual participants or beneficiaries based on any health factor of the participants or beneficiaries, the classification is not permitted under this paragraph (d), unless it is permitted under paragraph (g) of this section (permitting favorable treatment of individuals with adverse health factors). Thus, if an employer modified an employment-based classification to single out, based on a health factor, individual participants and beneficiaries and deny them health coverage, the new classification would not be permitted under this section.

(4) *Examples.* The rules of this paragraph (d) are illustrated by the following examples:

Example 1. (i) *Facts.* An employer sponsors a group health plan for full-time employees only. Under the plan (consistent with the employer's usual business practice), employees who normally work at least 30 hours per week are considered to be working full-time. Other employees are considered to be working part-time. There is no evidence to suggest that the classification is directed at individual participants or beneficiaries.

(ii) *Conclusion.* In this *Example 1*, treating the full-time and part-time employees as two separate groups of similarly situated individuals is permitted under this paragraph (d) because the classification is *bona fide* and is not directed at individual participants or beneficiaries.

Example 2. (i) *Facts.* Under a group health plan, coverage is made available to employees, their spouses, and their dependent children. However, coverage is made available to a dependent child only if the dependent child is under age 19 (or under age 25 if the child is continuously enrolled full-time in an institution of higher learning (full-time students)). There is no evidence to suggest that these classifications are directed at individual participants or beneficiaries.

(ii) *Conclusion.* In this *Example 2*, treating spouses and dependent children differently by imposing an age limitation on dependent children, but not on spouses, is permitted under this paragraph (d). Specifically, the distinction between spouses and dependent children is permitted under paragraph (d)(2) of this section and is not prohibited under paragraph (d)(3) of this section because it is not directed at individual participants or beneficiaries. It is also permissible to treat dependent children who are under age 19 (or full-time students under age 25) as a group of similarly situated individuals separate from those who are age 25 or older (or age 19 or older if they are not full-time students) because the classification is permitted under paragraph (d)(2) of this section and is not directed at individual participants or beneficiaries.

Example 3. (i) *Facts.* A university sponsors a group health plan that provides one health benefit package to faculty and another health benefit package to other staff. Faculty and staff are treated differently with respect to other employee benefits such as retirement benefits and leaves of absence. There is no evidence to suggest that the distinction is directed at individual participants or beneficiaries.

(ii) *Conclusion.* In this *Example 3*, the classification is permitted under this paragraph (d) because there is a distinction based on a *bona fide* employment-based classification consistent with the employer's usual business practice and the distinction is not directed at individual participants and beneficiaries.

Example 4. (i) *Facts.* An employer sponsors a group health plan that is available to all current employees. Former employees may also be eligible, but only if they complete a specified number of years of service, are enrolled under the plan at the time of termination of employment, and are continuously enrolled from that date. There is no evidence to suggest that these distinctions are directed at individual participants or beneficiaries.

(ii) *Conclusion.* In this *Example 4*, imposing additional eligibility requirements on former employees is permitted because a classification that distinguishes between current and former employees is a *bona fide* employment-based classification that is permitted under this paragraph (d), provided that it is not directed at individual participants or beneficiaries. In addition, it is permissible to distinguish between former employees who satisfy the service requirement and those who do not, provided that the distinction is not directed at individual participants or beneficiaries. (However, former employees who do not satisfy the eligibility criteria may, nonetheless, be eligible for continued coverage pursuant to a COBRA continuation provision or similar State law.)

Example 5. (i) *Facts.* An employer sponsors a group health plan that provides the same benefit package to all seven employees of the employer. Six of the seven employees have the same job title and responsibilities, but Employee *G* has a different job title and different responsibilities. After *G* files an expensive claim for benefits under the plan, coverage under the plan is modified so that employees with *G*'s job title receive a different benefit package that includes a lower lifetime dollar limit than in the benefit package made available to the other six employees.

(ii) *Conclusion.* Under the facts of this *Example 5*, changing the coverage classification for *G* based on the existing employment classification for *G* is not permitted under this paragraph (d) because the creation of the new coverage classification for *G* is directed at *G* based on one or more health factors.

(e) *Nonconfinement and actively-at-work provisions* — (1) *Nonconfinement provisions* — (i) *General rule.* Under the rules of paragraphs (b) and (c) of this section, a plan may not establish a rule for eligibility (as described in paragraph (b)(1)(ii) of this section) or set any individual's premium or contribution rate based on whether an individual is confined to a hospital or other health care institution. In addition, under the rules of paragraphs (b) and (c) of this section, a plan may not establish a rule for eligibility or set any individual's premium or contribution rate based on an individual's ability to engage in normal life activities, except to the extent permitted under paragraphs (e)(2)(ii) and (3) of this section (permitting plans, under certain circumstances, to distinguish among employees based on the performance of services).

(ii) *Examples.* The rules of this paragraph (e)(1) are illustrated by the following examples:

Example 1. (i) *Facts.* Under a group health plan, coverage for employees and their dependents generally becomes effective on the first day of employment. However, coverage for a dependent who is confined to a hospital or other health care institution does not become effective until the confinement ends.

(ii) *Conclusion.* In this *Example 1*, the plan violates this paragraph (e)(1) because the plan delays the effective date of coverage for dependents based on confinement to a hospital or other health care institution.

Example 2. (i) *Facts.* In previous years, a group health plan has provided coverage through a group health insurance policy offered by Issuer *M*. However, for the current year, the plan provides coverage through a group health insurance policy offered by Issuer *N*. Under Issuer *N*'s policy, items and services provided in connection with the confinement of a dependent to a hospital or other health care institution are not covered if the confinement is covered under an extension of benefits clause from a previous health insurance issuer.

(ii) *Conclusion.* See *Example 2* in 29 CFR 2590.702(e)(1) and 45 CFR 146.121(e)(1) for a conclusion that Issuer *N* violates provisions of 29 CFR 2590.702(e)(1) and 45 CFR 146.121(e)(1) similar to the provisions of this paragraph (e)(1) because the group health insurance coverage restricts benefits based on whether a dependent is confined to a hospital or other health care institution that is covered under an extension of benefits from a previous issuer. See *Example 2* in 29 CFR 2590.702(e)(1) and 45

CFR 146.121(e)(1) for the additional conclusions that under State law Issuer *M* may also be responsible for providing benefits to such a dependent; and that in a case in which Issuer *N* has an obligation under 29 CFR 2590.702(e)(1) or 45 CFR 146.121(e)(1) to provide benefits and Issuer *M* has an obligation under State law to provide benefits, any State laws designed to prevent more than 100% reimbursement, such as State coordination-of-benefits laws, continue to apply.

(2) *Actively-at-work and continuous service provisions* — (i) *General rule*. (A) Under the rules of paragraphs (b) and (c) of this section and subject to the exception for the first day of work described in paragraph (e)(2)(ii) of this section, a plan may not establish a rule for eligibility (as described in paragraph (b)(1)(ii) of this section) or set any individual's premium or contribution rate based on whether an individual is actively at work (including whether an individual is continuously employed), unless absence from work due to any health factor (such as being absent from work on sick leave) is treated, for purposes of the plan, as being actively at work.

(B) The rules of this paragraph (e)(2)(i) are illustrated by the following examples:

Example 1. (i) *Facts*. Under a group health plan, an employee generally becomes eligible to enroll 30 days after the first day of employment. However, if the employee is not actively at work on the first day after the end of the 30-day period, then eligibility for enrollment is delayed until the first day the employee is actively at work.

(ii) *Conclusion*. In this *Example 1*, the plan violates this paragraph (e)(2) (and thus also violates paragraph (b) of this section). However, the plan would not violate paragraph (e)(2) or (b) of this section if, under the plan, an absence due to any health factor is considered being actively at work.

Example 2. (i) *Facts*. Under a group health plan, coverage for an employee becomes effective after 90 days of continuous service; that is, if an employee is absent from work (for any reason) before completing 90 days of service, the beginning of the 90 day period is measured from the day the employee returns to work (without any credit for service before the absence).

(ii) *Conclusion*. In this *Example 2*, the plan violates this paragraph (e)(2) (and thus also paragraph (b) of this section) because the 90-day continuous service requirement is a rule for eligibility based on whether an individual is actively at work. However, the plan would not violate this paragraph (e)(2) or paragraph (b) of this section if, under the plan, an absence due to any health factor is not considered an absence for purposes of measuring 90 days of continuous service.

(ii) *Exception for the first day of work*. (A) Notwithstanding the general rule in paragraph (e)(2)(i) of this section, a plan may establish a rule for eligibility that requires an individual to begin work for the employer sponsoring the plan (or, in the case of a multiemployer plan, to begin a job in covered employment) before coverage becomes effective, provided that such a rule for eligibility applies regardless of the reason for the absence.

(B) The rules of this paragraph (e)(2)(ii) are illustrated by the following examples:

Example 1. (i) *Facts*. Under the eligibility provision of a group health plan, coverage for new employees becomes effective on the first day that the employee reports to work. Individual *H* is scheduled to begin work on August 3. However, *H* is unable to begin work on that day because of illness. *H* begins working on August 4, and *H*'s coverage is effective on August 4.

(ii) *Conclusion*. In this *Example 1*, the plan provision does not violate this section. However, if coverage for individuals who do not report to work on the first day they were scheduled to work for a reason unrelated to a health factor (such as vacation or bereavement) becomes effective on the first day they were scheduled to work, then the plan would violate this section.

Example 2. (i) *Facts*. Under a group health plan, coverage for new employees becomes effective on the first day of the month following the employee's first day of work, regardless of whether the employee is actively at work on the first day of the month. Individual *J* is scheduled to begin work on March 24. However, *J* is unable to begin work on March 24 because of illness. *J* begins working on April 7 and *J*'s coverage is effective May 1.

(ii) *Conclusion*. In this *Example 2*, the plan provision does not violate this section. However, as in *Example 1*, if coverage for individuals absent from work for reasons unrelated to a health factor became effective despite their absence, then the plan would violate this section.

(3) *Relationship to plan provisions defining similarly situated individuals*. (i) Notwithstanding the rules of paragraphs (e)(1) and (2) of this section, a plan may establish rules for eligibility or set any individual's premium or contribution rate in accordance with the rules relating to similarly situated individuals in paragraph (d) of this section. Accordingly, a plan may distinguish in rules for eligibility under the plan between full-time and part-time employees, between permanent and temporary or seasonal employees, between current and former employees, and between employees currently performing services and employees no longer performing services for the employer, subject to paragraph (d) of this section. However, other Federal or State laws (including the COBRA continuation provisions and the Family and Medical Leave Act of 1993) may require an employee or the employee's dependents to be offered coverage and set limits on the premium or contribution rate even though the employee is not performing services.

(ii) The rules of this paragraph (e)(3) are illustrated by the following examples:

Example 1. (i) *Facts*. Under a group health plan, employees are eligible for coverage if they perform services for the employer for 30 or more hours per week or if they are on paid leave (such as vacation, sick, or bereavement leave). Employees on unpaid leave are treated as a separate group of similarly situated individuals in accordance with the rules of paragraph (d) of this section.

(ii) *Conclusion*. In this *Example 1*, the plan provisions do not violate this section. However, if the plan treated individuals performing services for the employer for 30 or more hours per week, individuals on vacation leave, and individuals on bereavement leave as a group of similarly situated individuals separate from individuals on sick leave, the plan would violate this paragraph (e) (and thus also would violate paragraph (b) of this section) because groups of similarly situated individuals cannot be established based on a health factor (including the taking of sick leave) under paragraph (d) of this section.

Example 2. (i) *Facts*. To be eligible for coverage under a *bona fide* collectively bargained group health plan in the current calendar quarter, the plan requires an individual to have worked 250 hours in covered employment during the three-month period that ends one month before the beginning of the current calendar quarter. The distinction between employees working at least 250 hours and those working less than 250 hours in the earlier three-month period is not directed at individual participants or beneficiaries based on any health factor of the participants or beneficiaries.

(ii) *Conclusion*. In this *Example 2*, the plan provision does not violate this section because, under the rules for similarly situated individuals allowing full-time employees to be treated differently than part-time employees, employees who work at least 250 hours in a three-month period can be treated differently than employees who fail to work 250 hours in that period. The result would be the same if the plan permitted individuals to apply excess hours from previous periods to satisfy the requirement for the current quarter.

Example 3. (i) *Facts*. Under a group health plan, coverage of an employee is terminated when the individual's employment is terminated, in accordance with the rules of paragraph (d) of this section. Employee *B* has been covered under the plan. *B* experiences a disabling illness that prevents *B* from working. *B* takes a leave of absence under the Family and Medical Leave Act of 1993. At the end of such leave, *B* terminates employment and consequently loses coverage under the plan. (This termination of coverage is without regard to whatever rights the employee (or members of the employee's family) may have for COBRA continuation coverage.)

(ii) *Conclusion*. In this *Example 3*, the plan provision terminating *B*'s coverage upon *B*'s termination of employment does not violate this section.

Example 4. (i) *Facts*. Under a group health plan, coverage of an employee is terminated when the employee ceases to perform services for the employer sponsoring the plan, in accordance with the rules of paragraph (d) of this section. Employee *C* is laid off for three months. When the layoff begins, *C*'s coverage under the plan is terminated. (This termination of coverage is without regard to whatever rights the employee (or members of the employee's family) may have for COBRA continuation coverage.)

(ii) *Conclusion*. In this *Example 4*, the plan provision terminating *C*'s coverage upon the cessation of *C*'s performance of services does not violate this section.

(f) *Wellness programs*. A wellness program is any program designed to promote health or prevent disease. Paragraphs (b)(2)(ii) and (c)(3) of this section provide exceptions to the general prohibitions against discrimination based on a health factor for plan provisions that vary benefits (including cost-sharing mechanisms) or the premium or contribution for similarly situated individuals in connection with a wellness program that satisfies the requirements of this paragraph (f). If none of the conditions for obtaining a reward under a wellness program is based on an individual satisfying a standard that is related to a health factor, paragraph (f)(1) of this section clarifies that the wellness program does not violate this section if participation in the program is made available to all similarly situated individuals. If any of the conditions for obtaining a reward under a wellness program is based on an individual satisfying a standard that is related to a health factor, the wellness program does not violate this section if the requirements of paragraph (f)(2) of this section are met.

(1) *Wellness programs not subject to requirements*. If none of the conditions for obtaining a reward under a wellness program is based on an individual satisfying a standard that are related to a health factor (or if a wellness program does not provide a reward), the wellness program does not violate this section, if participation in the program is made available to all similarly situated individuals. Thus, for example, the following programs need not satisfy the requirements of paragraph (f)(2) of this section, if participation in the program is made available to all similarly situated individuals:

(i) A program that reimburses all or part of the cost for memberships in a fitness center.

(ii) A diagnostic testing program that provides a reward for participation and does not base any part of the reward on outcomes.

(iii) A program that encourages preventive care through the waiver of the copayment or deductible requirement under a group health plan for the costs of, for example, prenatal care or well-baby visits.

(iv) A program that reimburses employees for the costs of smoking cessation programs without regard to whether the employee quits smoking.

(v) A program that provides a reward to employees for attending a monthly health education seminar.

(2) *Wellness programs subject to requirements*. If any of the conditions for obtaining a reward under a wellness program are based on an individual satisfying a standard that is related to a health factor, the wellness program does not violate this section if the requirements of this paragraph (f)(2) are met.

(i) The reward for the wellness program, coupled with the reward for other wellness programs with respect to the plan that require satisfaction of a standard related to a health factor, must not exceed 20 percent of the cost of employee-only coverage under the plan. However, if, in addition to employees, any class of dependents (such as spouses or spouses and dependent children) may participate in the wellness program, the reward must not exceed 20 percent of the cost of the coverage in which an employee and any dependents are enrolled. For purposes of this paragraph (f)(2), the cost of coverage is determined based on the total amount of employer and employee contributions for the benefit package under which the employee is (or the employee and any dependents are) receiving coverage. A reward can be in the form of a discount or rebate of a premium or contribution, a waiver of all or part of a cost-sharing mechanism (such as deductibles, copayments, or coinsurance), the absence of a surcharge, or the value of a benefit that would otherwise not be provided under the plan.

(ii) The program must be reasonably designed to promote health or prevent disease. A program satisfies this standard if it has a reasonable chance of improving the health of or preventing disease in participating individuals and it is not overly burdensome, is not a subterfuge for discriminating based on a health factor, and is not highly suspect in the method chosen to promote health or prevent disease.

(iii) The program must give individuals eligible for the program the opportunity to qualify for the reward under the program at least once per year.

(iv) The reward under the program must be available to all similarly situated individuals.

(A) A reward is not available to all similarly situated individuals for a period unless the program allows —

(*1*) A reasonable alternative standard (or waiver of the otherwise applicable standard) for obtaining the reward for any individual for whom, for that period, it is unreasonably difficult due to a medical condition to satisfy the otherwise applicable standard; and

(*2*) A reasonable alternative standard (or waiver of the otherwise applicable standard) for obtaining the reward for any individual for whom, for that period, it is medically inadvisable to attempt to satisfy the otherwise applicable standard.

(B) A plan or issuer may seek verification, such as a statement from an individual's physician, that a health factor makes it unreasonably difficult or medically inadvisable for the individual to satisfy or attempt to satisfy the otherwise applicable standard.

(v) (A) The plan must disclose in all plan materials describing the terms of the program the availability of a reasonable alternative standard (or the possibility of waiver of the otherwise applicable standard) required under paragraph (f)(2)(iv) of this section. However, if plan materials merely mention that a program is available, without describing its terms, this disclosure is not required.

(B) The following language, or substantially similar language, can be used to satisfy the requirement of this paragraph (f)(2)(v): "If it is unreasonably difficult due to a medical condition for you to achieve the standards for the reward under this program, or if it is medically inadvisable for you to attempt to achieve the standards for the reward under this program, call us at [insert telephone number] and we will work with you to develop another way to qualify for the reward." In addition, other examples of language that would satisfy this requirement are set forth in *Examples 3*, *4*, and *5* of paragraph (f)(3) of this section.

(3) *Examples*. The rules of paragraph (f)(2) of this section are illustrated by the following examples:

Example 1. (i) *Facts*. An employer sponsors a group health plan. The annual premium for employee-only coverage is $3,600 (of which the employer pays $2,700 per year and the employee pays $900 per year). The annual premium for family coverage is $9,000 (of which the employer pays $4,500 per year and the employee pays $4,500 per year). The plan offers a wellness program with an annual premium rebate of $360. The program is available only to employees.

(ii) *Conclusion*. In this *Example 1*, the program satisfies the requirements of paragraph (f)(2)(i) of this section because the reward for the wellness program, $360, does not exceed 20 percent of the total annual cost of employee-only coverage, $720. ($3,600 x 20% = $720.) If any class of dependents is allowed to participate in the program and the employee is enrolled in family coverage, the plan could offer the employee a reward of up to 20 percent of the cost of family coverage, $1,800. ($9,000 x 20% = $1,800.)

Example 2. (i) *Facts*. A group health plan gives an annual premium discount of 20 percent of the cost of employee-only coverage to participants who adhere to a wellness program. The wellness program consists solely of giving an annual cholesterol test to participants. Those participants who achieve a count under 200 receive the premium discount for the year.

(ii) *Conclusion*. In this *Example 2*, the program fails to satisfy the requirement of being available to all similarly situated individuals because some participants may be unable to achieve a cholesterol count of under 200 and the plan does not make available a reasonable alternative standard or waive the cholesterol standard. (In addition, plan materials describing the program are required to disclose the availability of a reasonable alternative standard (or the possibility of waiver of the otherwise applicable standard) for obtaining the premium discount. Thus, the premium discount violates paragraph (c) of this section because it may require an individual to pay a higher premium based on a health factor of the individual than is required of a similarly situated individual under the plan.

Example 3. (i) *Facts*. Same facts as *Example 2*, except that the plan provides that if it is unreasonably difficult due to a medical condition for a participant to achieve the targeted cholesterol count (or if it is medically inadvisable for a participant to attempt to achieve the targeted cholesterol count) within a 60-day period, the plan will make available a reasonable alternative standard that takes the relevant medical condition into account. In addition, all plan materials describing the terms of the program include the following statement: "If it is unreasonably difficult due to a medical condition for you to achieve a cholesterol count under 200, or if it is medically inadvisable for you to attempt to achieve a count under 200, call us at the number below and we will work with you to develop another way to get the discount." Individual *D* begins a diet and exercise program but is unable to achieve a cholesterol count under 200 within the prescribed period. *D*'s doctor determines *D* requires prescription medication to achieve a medically advisable cholesterol count. In addition, the doctor determines that *D* must be monitored through periodic blood tests to continually reevaluate *D*'s health status. The plan accommodates *D* by making the discount available to *D*, but only if *D* follows the advice of *D*'s doctor's regarding medication and blood tests.

(ii) *Conclusion*. In this *Example 3*, the program is a wellness program because it satisfies the five requirements of paragraph (f)(2) of this section. First, the program complies with the limits on rewards under a program. Second, it is reasonably designed to promote health or prevent disease. Third, individuals eligible for the program are given the opportunity to qualify for the reward at least once per year. Fourth, the reward under the program is available to all similarly situated individuals because it accommodates individuals for whom it is unreasonably difficult due to a medical condition to achieve the targeted count (or for whom it is medically inadvisable to attempt to achieve the targeted count) in the prescribed period by providing a reasonable alternative standard. Fifth, the plan discloses in all materials describing the terms of the program the availability of a reasonable alternative standard. Thus, the premium discount does not violate this section.

Example 4. (i) Facts. A group health plan will waive the $250 annual deductible (which is less than 20 percent of the annual cost of employee-only coverage under the plan) for the following year for participants who have a body mass index between 19 and 26, determined shortly before the beginning of the year. However, any participant for whom it is unreasonably difficult due to a medical condition to attain this standard (and any participant for whom it is medically inadvisable to attempt to achieve this standard) during the plan year is given the same discount if the participant walks for 20 minutes three days a week. Any participant for whom it is unreasonably difficult due to a medical condition to attain either standard (and any participant for whom it is medically inadvisable to attempt to achieve either standard) during the year is given the same discount if the individual satisfies an alternative standard that is reasonable in the burden it imposes and is reasonable taking into consideration the individual's medical situation. All plan materials describing the terms of the wellness program include the following statement: "If it is unreasonably difficult due to a medical condition for you to achieve a body mass index between 19 and 26 (or if it is medically inadvisable for you to attempt to achieve this body mass index) this year, your deductible will be waived if you walk for 20 minutes three days a week. If you cannot follow the walking program, call us at the number above and we will work with you to develop another way to have your deductible waived." Due to a medical condition, Individual *E* is unable to achieve a BMI of between 19 and 26 and is also unable to follow the walking program. *E* proposes a program based on the recommendations of *E*'s physician. The plan agrees to make the discount available to *E* if *E* follows the physician's recommendations.

(ii) *Conclusion*. In this *Example 4*, the program satisfies the five requirements of paragraph (f)(2) of this section. First, the program complies with the limits on rewards under a program. Second, it is reasonably designed to promote health or prevent disease. Third, individuals eligible for the program are given the opportunity to qualify for the reward at least once per year. Fourth, the reward under the program is available to all similarly situated individuals because it generally accommodates individuals for whom it is unreasonably difficult due to a medical condition to achieve (or for whom it is medically inadvisable to attempt to achieve) the targeted body mass index by providing a reasonable alternative standard (walking) and it accommodates individuals for whom it is unreasonably difficult due to a medical condition (or for whom it is medically inadvisable to attempt) to walk by providing an alternative standard that is reasonable for the individual. Fifth, the plan discloses in all materials describing the terms of the program the availability of a reasonable alternative standard for every individual. Thus, the waiver of the deductible does not violate this section.

Example 5. (i) *Facts*. In conjunction with an annual open enrollment period, a group health plan provides a form for participants to certify that they have not used tobacco products in the preceding twelve months. Participants who do not provide the certification are assessed a surcharge that is 20 percent of the cost of employee-only coverage. However, all plan materials describing the terms of the wellness program include the following statement: "If it is unreasonably difficult due to a health factor for you to meet the requirements under this program (or if it is medically inadvisable for you to attempt to meet the requirements of this program), we will make available a reasonable alternative standard for you to avoid this surcharge." It is unreasonably difficult for Individual *F* to stop smoking cigarettes due to an addiction to nicotine (a medical condition). The plan accommodates *F* by requiring *F* to participate in a smoking cessation program to avoid the surcharge. *F* can avoid the surcharge for as long as *F* participates in the program, regardless of whether *F* stops smoking (as long as *F* continues to be addicted to nicotine).

(ii) *Conclusion*. In this *Example 5*, the premium surcharge is permissible as a wellness program because it satisfies the five requirements of paragraph (f)(2) of this section. First, the program complies with the limits on rewards under a program. Second, it is reasonably designed to promote health or prevent disease. Third, individuals eligible for the program are given the opportunity to qualify for the reward at least once per year. Fourth, the reward under the program is available to all similarly situated individuals because it accommodates individuals for whom it is unreasonably difficult due to a medical condition (or for whom it is medically inadvisable to attempt) to quit using tobacco products by providing a reasonable alternative standard. Fifth, the plan discloses in all materials describing the terms of the program the availability of a reasonable alternative standard. Thus, the premium surcharge does not violate this section.

Example 6. (i) *Facts*. Same facts as *Example 5*, except the plan accommodates *F* by requiring *F* to view, over a period of 12 months, a 12-hour video series on health problems associated with tobacco use. *F* can avoid the surcharge by complying with this requirement.

(ii) *Conclusion*. In this *Example 6*, the requirement to watch the series of video tapes is a reasonable alternative method for avoiding the surcharge.

(g) *More favorable treatment of individuals with adverse health factors permitted* — (1) *In rules for eligibility*. (i) Nothing in this section prevents a group health plan from establishing more favorable rules for eligibility (described in paragraph (b)(1) of this section) for individuals with an adverse health factor, such as disability, than for individuals without the adverse health factor. Moreover, nothing in this section prevents a plan from charging a higher premium or contribution with respect to individuals with an adverse health factor if they would not be eligible for the coverage were it not for the adverse health factor. (However, other laws, including State insurance laws, may set or limit premium rates; these laws are not affected by this section.)

(ii) The rules of this paragraph (g)(1) are illustrated by the following examples:

Example 1. (i) *Facts.* An employer sponsors a group health plan that generally is available to employees, spouses of employees, and dependent children until age 23. However, dependent children who are disabled are eligible for coverage beyond age 23.

(ii) *Conclusion.* In this *Example 1*, the plan provision allowing coverage for disabled dependent children beyond age 23 satisfies this paragraph (g)(1) (and thus does not violate this section).

Example 2. (i) *Facts.* An employer sponsors a group health plan, which is generally available to employees (and members of the employee's family) until the last day of the month in which the employee ceases to perform services for the employer. The plan generally charges employees $50 per month for employee-only coverage and $125 per month for family coverage. However, an employee who ceases to perform services for the employer by reason of disability may remain covered under the plan until the last day of the month that is 12 months after the month in which the employee ceased to perform services for the employer. During this extended period of coverage, the plan charges the employee $100 per month for employee-only coverage and $250 per month for family coverage. (This extended period of coverage is without regard to whatever rights the employee (or members of the employee's family) may have for COBRA continuation coverage.)

(ii) *Conclusion.* In this *Example 2*, the plan provision allowing extended coverage for disabled employees and their families satisfies this paragraph (g)(1) (and thus does not violate this section). In addition, the plan is permitted, under this paragraph (g)(1), to charge the disabled employees a higher premium during the extended period of coverage.

Example 3. (i) *Facts.* To comply with the requirements of a COBRA continuation provision, a group health plan generally makes COBRA continuation coverage available for a maximum period of 18 months in connection with a termination of employment but makes the coverage available for a maximum period of 29 months to certain disabled individuals and certain members of the disabled individual's family. Although the plan generally requires payment of 102 percent of the applicable premium for the first 18 months of COBRA continuation coverage, the plan requires payment of 150 percent of the applicable premium for the disabled individual's COBRA continuation coverage during the disability extension if the disabled individual would not be entitled to COBRA continuation coverage but for the disability.

(ii) *Conclusion.* In this *Example 3*, the plan provision allowing extended COBRA continuation coverage for disabled individuals satisfies this paragraph (g)(1) (and thus does not violate this section). In addition, the plan is permitted, under this paragraph (g)(1), to charge the disabled individuals a higher premium for the extended coverage if the individuals would not be eligible for COBRA continuation coverage were it not for the disability. (Similarly, if the plan provided an extended period of coverage for disabled individuals pursuant to State law or plan provision rather than pursuant to a COBRA continuation coverage provision, the plan could likewise charge the disabled individuals a higher premium for the extended coverage.)

(2) *In premiums or contributions.* (i) Nothing in this section prevents a group health plan from charging individuals a premium or contribution that is less than the premium (or contribution) for similarly situated individuals if the lower charge is based on an adverse health factor, such as disability.

(ii) The rules of this paragraph (g)(2) are illustrated by the following example:

Example. (i) *Facts.* Under a group health plan, employees are generally required to pay $50 per month for employee-only coverage and $125 per month for family coverage under the plan. However, employees who are disabled receive coverage (whether employee-only or family coverage) under the plan free of charge.

(ii) *Conclusion.* In this *Example*, the plan provision waiving premium payment for disabled employees is permitted under this paragraph (g)(2) (and thus does not violate this section).

(h) *No effect on other laws.* Compliance with this section is not determinative of compliance with any provision of ERISA (including the COBRA continuation provisions) or any other State or Federal law, such as the Americans with Disabilities Act. Therefore, although the rules of this section would not prohibit a plan from treating one group of similarly situated individuals differently from another (such as providing different benefit packages to current and former employees), other Federal or State laws may require that two separate groups of similarly situated individuals be treated the same for certain purposes (such as making the same benefit package available to COBRA qualified beneficiaries as is made available to active employees). In addition, although this section generally does not impose new disclosure obligations on plans, this section does not affect any other laws, including those that require accurate disclosures and prohibit intentional misrepresentation.

(*i*) *Applicability dates.* This section applies for plan years beginning on or after July 1, 2007.

Mark E. Matthews,
Deputy Commissioner for Services and Enforcement.

Approved June 22, 2006.

Eric Solomon,
Acting Deputy Assistant Secretary of the Treasury (Tax Policy).

(Filed by the Office of the Federal Register on December 12, 2006, 8:45 a.m., and published in the issue of the Federal Register for December 13, 2006, 71 F.R. 75013)

---

26 CFR 54.9802–2: Special rules for certain church plans.

T.D. 9299

DEPARTMENT OF THE TREASURY
Internal Revenue Service
26 CFR Part 54

Exception to the HIPAA Nondiscrimination Requirements for Certain Grandfathered Church Plans

AGENCY: Internal Revenue Service (IRS), Treasury.

ACTION: Final regulations.

SUMMARY: This document contains final regulations that provide guidance under section 9802(c) of the Internal Revenue Code relating to the exception for certain grandfathered church plans from the nondiscrimination requirements applicable to group health plans under section 9802(a) and (b). Final regulations (T.D. 9298) relating to the nondiscrimination requirements under section 9802(a) and (b) are being published elsewhere in this issue of the Bulletin. The regulations will generally affect sponsors of and participants in certain self-funded church plans that are group health plans, and the regulations provide plan sponsors and plan administrators with guidance necessary to comply with the law.

DATES: *Effective Date:* These regulations are effective February 12, 2006.

Applicability Date: These regulations apply for plan years beginning on or after July 1, 2007.

FOR FURTHER INFORMATION CONTACT: Russ Weinheimer at 202–622–6080 (not a toll-free number).

SUPPLEMENTARY INFORMATION:

Background

This document contains amendments to the Miscellaneous Excise Tax Regulations (26 CFR part 54) relating to the exception for certain grandfathered church plans from the nondiscrimination requirements applicable to group health plans. The nondiscrimination requirements applicable to group health plans were added to the Internal Revenue Code (Code), in section 9802, by the Health Insurance Portability and Accountability Act of 1996 (HIPAA), Public Law 104–191 (110 Stat. 1936). HIPAA also added similar nondiscrimination provisions applicable to group health plans and health insurance issuers (such as health insurance companies and health maintenance organizations) under the Employee Retirement Income Security Act of 1974 (ERISA), administered by the U.S. Department of Labor, and the Public Health Service Act (PHS Act), administered by the U.S. Department of Health and Human Services.

Final regulations relating to the HIPAA nondiscrimination requirements in paragraphs (a) and (b) of section 9802 of the Code are being published elsewhere in this issue of the Bulletin. Those regulations are similar to, and have been developed in coordination with, final regulations also being published today by the Departments of Labor and of Health and Human Services. Guidance under the HIPAA nondiscrimination requirements is summarized in a joint preamble to the final regulations.

The exception for certain grandfathered church plans was added to section 9802, in subsection (c), by section 1532 of the Taxpayer Relief Act of 1997, Public Law 105–34 (111 Stat. 788). A notice of proposed rulemaking on the exception for certain grandfathered church plans and a request for comments (REG–114083–00, 2001–1 C.B. 630) was published in the **Federal Register** of January 8, 2001. Two written comments were received. After consideration of the comments, the proposed regulations are adopted as amended by this Treasury decision.

Explanation and Summary of Comments

One comment was pleased with the guidance in the proposed rules and asked that they be published as final rules as soon as possible. The other comment explained why the statute needed this exception and suggested that the proposed regulations did nothing more than paraphrase the statute. Neither comment asked for any change in the proposed regulations.

These final regulations make no significant substantive change to the proposed regulations. An effective date has been supplied and references to the supplanted temporary regulations have been deleted, but otherwise no change has been made in the final regulations.

Special Analyses

It has been determined that this Treasury decision is not a significant regulatory action as defined in Executive Order 12866. Therefore, a regulatory assessment is not required. It also has been determined that section 553(b) of the Administrative Procedure Act (5 U.S.C. chapter 5) does not apply to these regulations, and because the regulations do not impose a collection of information requirement on small entities, the Regulatory Flexibility Act (5 U.S.C. chapter 6) does not apply. Therefore, a Regulatory Flexibility Analysis is not required. Pursuant to section 7805(f) of the Code, the notice of proposed rulemaking preceding these regulations was submitted to the Small Business Administration for comment on its impact on small business.

Drafting Information

The principal author of these regulations is Russ Weinheimer, Office of the Operating Division Counsel/Associate Chief Counsel (Tax Exempt and Government Entities). However, other personnel from the IRS and Treasury Department participated in their development.

* * * * *

Adoption of Amendments to the Regulations

Accordingly, 26 CFR part 54 is amended as follows:

PART 54 — PENSION EXCISE TAXES

Paragraph 1. The authority citation for part 54 is amended by adding an entry in numerical order to read, in part, as follows:

Authority: 26 U.S.C. 7805 * * *

Section 54.9802–2 also issued under 26 U.S.C. 9833. * * *

Par. 2. In §54.9801–1, paragraph (a) is revised to read as follows:

§54.9801–1 Basis and scope.

(a) *Statutory basis.* Sections 54.9801–1 through 54.9801–6, 54.9802–1, 54.9802–2, 54.9811–1T, 54.9812–1T, 54.9831–1, and 54.9833–1 (portability sections) implement Chapter 100 of Subtitle K of the Internal Revenue Code of 1986.

* * * * *

Par. 3. In §54.9801–2, the introductory text is amended to read as follows:

§54.9801–2 Definitions.

Unless otherwise provided, the definitions in this section govern in applying the provisions of §§54.9801–1 through 54.9801–6, 54.9802–1, 54.9802–2, 54.9811–1T, 54.9812–1T, 54.9831–1, and 54.9833–1.

* * * * *

Par. 4. Section 54.9802–2 is added to read as follows:

§54.9802–2 Special rules for certain church plans.

(a) *Exception for certain church plans*—(1) *Church plans in general.* A church plan described in paragraph (b) of this section is not treated as failing to meet the requirements of section 9802 or §54.9802–1 solely because the plan requires evidence of good health for coverage of individuals under plan provisions described in paragraph (b)(2) or (3) of this section.

(2) *Health insurance issuers.* See sections 2702 and 2721(b)(1)(B) of the

Public Health Service Act (42 U.S.C. 300gg–2 and 300gg–21(b)(1)(B)) and 45 CFR 146.121, which require health insurance issuers providing health insurance coverage under a church plan that is a group health plan to comply with nondiscrimination requirements similar to those that church plans are required to comply with under section 9802 and §54.9802–1 except that those nondiscrimination requirements do not include an exception for health insurance issuers comparable to the exception for church plans under section 9802(c) and this section.

(b) *Church plans to which this section applies*—(1) *Church plans with certain coverage provisions in effect on July 15, 1997.* This section applies to any church plan (as defined in section 414(e)) for a plan year if, on July 15, 1997 and at all times thereafter before the beginning of the plan year, the plan contains either the provisions described in paragraph (b)(2) of this section or the provisions described in paragraph (b)(3) of this section.

(2) *Plan provisions applicable to individuals employed by employers of 10 or fewer employees and self-employed individuals.* (i) A plan contains the provisions described in this paragraph (b)(2) if it requires evidence of good health of both —

(A) Any employee of an employer of 10 or fewer employees (determined without regard to section 414(e)(3)(C), under which a church or convention or association of churches is treated as the employer); and

(B) Any self-employed individual.

(ii) A plan does not contain the provisions described in this paragraph (b)(2) if the plan contains only one of the provisions described in this paragraph (b)(2). Thus, for example, a plan that requires evidence of good health of any self-employed individual, but not of any employee of an employer with 10 or fewer employees, does not contain the provisions described in this paragraph (b)(2). Moreover, a plan does not contain the provision described in paragraph (b)(2)(i)(A) of this section if the plan requires evidence of good health of any employee of an employer of fewer than 10 (or greater than 10) employees. Thus, for example, a plan does not contain the provision described in paragraph (b)(2)(i)(A) of this section if the plan requires evidence of good health of any employee of an employer with five or fewer employees.

(3) *Plan provisions applicable to individuals who enroll after the first 90 days of initial eligibility.* (i) A plan contains the provisions described in this paragraph (b)(3) if it requires evidence of good health of any individual who enrolls after the first 90 days of initial eligibility under the plan.

(ii) A plan does not contain the provisions described in this paragraph (b)(3) if it provides for a longer (or shorter) period than 90 days. Thus, for example, a plan requiring evidence of good health of any individual who enrolls after the first 120 days of initial eligibility under the plan does not contain the provisions described in this paragraph (b)(3).

(c) *Examples.* The rules of this section are illustrated by the following examples:

Example 1. (i) *Facts.* A church organization maintains two church plans for entities affiliated with the church. One plan is a group health plan that provides health coverage to all employees (including ministers and lay workers) of any affiliated church entity that has more than 10 employees. The other plan is Plan *O*, which is a group health plan that is not funded through insurance coverage and that provides health coverage to any employee (including ministers and lay workers) of any affiliated church entity that has 10 or fewer employees and any self-employed individual affiliated with the church (including a self-employed minister of the church). Plan *O* requires evidence of good health in order for any individual of a church entity that has 10 or fewer employees to be covered and in order for any self-employed individual to be covered. On July 15, 1997 and at all times thereafter before the beginning of the plan year, Plan *O* has contained all the preceding provisions.

(ii) *Conclusion.* In this *Example 1*, because Plan *O* contains the plan provisions described in paragraph (b)(2) of this section and because those provisions were in the plan on July 15, 1997 and at all times thereafter before the beginning of the plan year, Plan *O* will not be treated as failing to meet the requirements of section 9802 or §54.9802–1 for the plan year solely because the plan requires evidence of good health for coverage of the individuals described in those plan provisions.

Example 2. (i) *Facts.* A church organization maintains Plan *P*, which is a church plan that is not funded through insurance coverage and that is a group health plan providing health coverage to individuals employed by entities affiliated with the church and self-employed individuals affiliated with the church (such as ministers). On July 15, 1997 and at all times thereafter before the beginning of the plan year, Plan *P* has required evidence of good health for coverage of any individual who enrolls after the first 90 days of initial eligibility under the plan.

(ii) *Conclusion.* In this *Example 2*, because Plan *P* contains the plan provisions described in paragraph (b)(3) of this section and because those provisions were in the plan on July 15, 1997 and at all times thereafter before the beginning of the plan year, Plan *P* will not be treated as failing to meet the requirements of section 9802 or §54.9802–1 for the plan year solely because the plan requires evidence of good health for coverage of individuals enrolling after the first 90 days of initial eligibility under the plan.

(d) *Effective date.* This section is applicable to plan years beginning on or after July 1, 2007.

Par. 5. Section 54.9831–1 is amended by revising paragraphs (b) and (c)(1) to read as follows:

§54.9831–1 Special rules relating to group health plans.

* * * * *

(b) *General exception for certain small group health plans.* The requirements of §§54.9801–1 through 54.9801–6, 54.9802–1, 54.9802–2, 54.9811–1T, 54.9812–1T, and 54.9833–1 do not apply to any group health plan for any plan year if, on the first day of the plan year, the plan has fewer than two participants who are current employees.

(c) *Excepted benefits* — (1) *In general.* The requirements of §§54.9801–1 through 54.9801–6, 54.9802–1, 54.9802–2, 54.9811–1T, 54.9812–1T, and 54.9833–1 do not apply to any group health plan in relation to its provision of the benefits described in paragraph (c)(2), (3), (4), or (5) of this section (or any combination of these benefits).

* * * * *

Mark E. Matthews,
Deputy Commissioner for Services and Enforcement.

Approved June 22, 2006.

Eric Solomon,
Acting Deputy Assistant Secretary of the Treasury (Tax Policy).

(Filed by the Office of the Federal Register on December 12, 2006, 8:45 a.m., and published in the issue of the Federal Register for December 13, 2006, 71 F.R. 75055)

Part IV. Items of General Interest

Notice of Proposed Rulemaking by Cross-Reference to Temporary Regulations

Guidance Necessary to Facilitate Business Electronic Filing Under Section 1561

REG–161919–05

AGENCY: Internal Revenue Service (IRS), Treasury.

ACTION: Notice of proposed rulemaking by cross-reference to temporary regulations.

SUMMARY: In this issue of the Bulletin, the IRS is issuing temporary regulations (T.D. 9304) that affect component members of controlled groups of corporations and consolidated groups filing life-nonlife Federal income tax returns. They provide guidance regarding the apportionment of tax benefit items and the amount and type of information these members are required to submit with their returns. The text of those regulations also serves as the text of these proposed regulations.

DATES: Written or electronic comments, and a request for a public hearing, must be received by March 22, 2007.

ADDRESSES: Send submissions to: CC:PA:LPD:PR (REG–161919–05), Room 5203, Internal Revenue Service, P.O. Box 7604, Ben Franklin Station, Washington, DC 20044. Submissions may be hand-delivered Monday through Friday between the hours of 8 a.m. and 4 p.m. to CC:PA:LPD:PR (REG–161919–05), Courier's Desk, Internal Revenue Service, 1111 Constitution Avenue, NW, Washington, DC, or sent electronically, via the IRS internet site at *www.irs.gov/regs* or via the Federal eRulemaking Portal at *www.regulations.gov* (indicate IRS and REG–161919–05).

FOR FURTHER INFORMATION CONTACT: Concerning the proposed regulations, Grid Glyer, (202) 622–7930, concerning submissions of comments and requests for public hearings, Kelly Banks (202) 622–7180 (not toll-free numbers).

SUPPLEMENTARY INFORMATION:

Background and Explanation of Provisions

Temporary regulations in this issue of the Bulletin amend 26 CFR Part 1 to add §§1.1502–43T, 1.1561–1T, 1.1561–2T and 1.1561–3T, and amend §§1.1502–47T and 1.1563–1T. The text of those temporary regulations also serves as the text of these proposed regulations. The preamble to the temporary regulations explains the amendments.

Special Analyses

It has been determined that this notice of proposed rulemaking is not a significant regulatory action as defined in Executive Order 12866. Therefore, a regulatory assessment is not required. It has also been determined that section 553(b) of the Administrative Procedure Act (5 U.S.C. chapter 5) does not apply to the following proposed regulations, §§1.1561–1, 1.1561–3 and 1.1563–1, and because these regulations do not impose a collection of information on small entities, the Regulatory Flexibility Act (5 U.S.C. chapter 6) does not apply. With respect to the following proposed regulations, §§1.1502–43, 1.1502–47 and 1.1561–2, it is hereby certified that these regulations will not have a significant economic impact on a substantial number of small entities. This certification is based on the fact that these regulations primarily affect large corporations (which are members of either controlled or consolidated groups). Therefore, a regulatory flexibility analysis is not required. Pursuant to section 7805(f) of the Internal Revenue Code, this notice of proposed rulemaking will be submitted to the Chief Counsel for Advocacy of the Small Business Administration for comment on their impact on small business.

Comments and Requests for a Public Hearing

Before these proposed regulations are adopted as final regulations, consideration will be given to any written comments (a signed original and eight (8) copies) or electronic comments that are submitted timely to the IRS. All comments will be available for public inspection and copying. A public hearing may be scheduled if requested in writing by any person that timely submits written or electronic comments. If a public hearing is scheduled, notice of the date, time, and place for the public hearing will be published in the **Federal Register**.

Drafting Information

The principal author of these regulations is Grid Glyer of the Office of Associate Chief Counsel (Corporate). Other personnel from the Treasury Department and the IRS participated in their development.

* * * * *

Proposed Amendments to the Regulations

Accordingly, 26 CFR part 1 is proposed to be amended as follows:

PART 1—INCOME TAXES

Paragraph 1. The authority citation for part 1 continues to read, in part, as follows:

Authority: 26 U.S.C. 7805 * * *

Par. 2. Section 1.1502–43 is amended by revising paragraph (d) and adding paragraph (e) to read as follows:

§1.1502–43 Consolidated accumulated earnings tax.

[The text of the proposed amendment to §1.1502–43 is the same as the text for §1.1502–43T published elsewhere in this issue of the Bulletin].

Par. 3. Section 1.1502–47 is amended by revising paragraph (s) and adding paragraph (t) to read as follows:

§1.1502–47 Consolidated returns by life-nonlife groups.

[The text of the proposed amendment to §1.1502–47 is the same as the text for §1.1502–47T published elsewhere in this issue of the Bulletin].

Par. 4. Section 1.1561–1 is added to read as follows:

§1.1561–1 General rules regarding certain tax benefits available to the component members of a controlled group of corporations.

[The text of the proposed §1.1561–1 is the same as the text for §1.1561–1T published elsewhere in this issue of the Bulletin].

Par. 5. Section 1.1561–2 is amended by revising paragraphs (a), (b), (c) and (d) and adding paragraph (f) to read as follows:

§1.1561–2 Determination of amount of tax benefits.

[The text of the proposed amendment to §1.1561–2 is the same as the text for 1.1561–2T published elsewhere in this issue of the Bulletin].

Par. 6. Section 1.1561–3 is added to read as follows:

§1.1561–3 Allocating the section 1561(a) tax items.

[The text of the proposed §1.1561–3 is the same as the text for §1.1561–3T published elsewhere in this issue of the Bulletin].

Par. 7. Section 1.1563–1 is added to read as follows:

§1.1563–1 Definition of controlled group of corporations and component members.

[The text of the proposed §1.1563–1 is the same as the text for §1.1563–1T published elsewhere in this issue of the Bulletin].

Mark E. Matthews,
Deputy Commissioner for Services and Enforcement.

(Filed by the Office of the Federal Register on December 21, 2006, 8:45 a.m., and published in the issue of the Federal Register for December 22, 2006, 71 F.R. 76955)

Treatment of Services Under Section 482; Allocation of Income and Deductions From Intangibles; Stewardship Expense; Correction

Announcement 2007–10

AGENCY: Internal Revenue Service (IRS), Treasury.

ACTION: Correction to final and temporary regulations.

SUMMARY: This document contains corrections to final and temporary regulations (T.D. 9278, 2006–34 I.R.B. 256) that was published in the **Federal Register** on Friday, August 4, 2006 (71 FR 44466) regarding the treatment of controlled services transactions under section 482 and the allocation of income from intangibles, in particular with respect to contributions by a controlled party to the value of an intangible owned by another controlled party. This document also contains corrections to final and temporary regulations that modify the regulations under section 861 concerning stewardship expenses to be consistent with the changes made to the regulations under section 482.

EFFECTIVE DATE: These corrections are effective on January 1, 2007.

FOR FURTHER INFORMATION CONTACT: Thomas A. Vidano, (202) 435–5265, or Carol B. Tan (202) 435–5159, for matters relating to section 482, and David F. Bergkuist, (202) 622–3850, for matters relating to stewardship expenses (not toll-free numbers).

SUPPLEMENTARY INFORMATION:

Background

The final and temporary regulations (T.D. 9278) that are the subject of these corrections is under sections 482 and 861 of the Internal Revenue Code.

Need for Correction

As published, final and temporary regulations (T.D. 9278) contain errors that may prove to be misleading and are in need of clarification.

Correction of Publication

Accordingly, final and temporary regulations (T.D. 9278) that were the subject of FR Doc. 06–6497 are corrected as follows.

1. On page 44466, column 1, in the heading, the subject "Treatment of Services Under Section 482; Allocation of Income and Deductions From Intangibles; Stewardship Expense" is corrected to read "Treatment of Services Under Section 482; Allocation of Income and Deductions From Intangibles; and Apportionment of Stewardship Expense".

2. On page 44470, column 2, in the preamble under the paragraph heading "5. Comparable Profits Method for Services—Temp. Treas. Reg. § 1.482–9T(f)", fifth line from the top of the column, the language "assets play a greater role in general" is corrected to read "assets play a greater role in generating".

3. On page 44475, column 3, in the preamble under the paragraph heading "Services Subject to a Qualified Cost Sharing Arrangement—Temp. Treas. Reg. § 1.482–9T(m)(3)," fourth line from the top of the column, the language "two provisions, the rule § 1.482–" is corrected to read "two provisions, the rule in § 1.482–".

Cynthia Grigsby,
Senior Federal Register Liaison Officer, Legal Processing Division, Associate Chief Counsel (Procedure and Administration).

(Filed by the Office of the Federal Register on December 21, 2006, 8:45 a.m., and published in the issue of the Federal Register for December 22, 2006, 71 F.R. 76913)

Treatment of Services Under Section 482 Allocation of Income and Deductions From Intangibles Stewardship Expense; Correction

Announcement 2007–11

AGENCY: Internal Revenue Service (IRS), Treasury.

ACTION: Correction to notice of proposed rulemaking by cross-reference to temporary regulations, notice of proposed rulemaking, and notice of public hearing.

SUMMARY: This document contains corrections to a notice of proposed rulemaking by cross-reference to temporary regulations, notice of proposed rulemaking, and notice of public hearing (REG–146893–02, 2006–34 I.R.B. 317) that was published in the **Federal Register** on Friday, August 4, 2006 (71 FR 44247) relating to the treatment of controlled services transactions under section 482. These regulations also provide guidance regarding the allocation of income from intangibles, in particular with respect to contributions by a controlled party to the value of an intangible owned by another controlled party, as it relates to controlled services transactions, and modify the regulations under section 861 concerning stewardship expenses to be consistent with the changes made to the regulations under section 482.

FOR FURTHER INFORMATION CONTACT: Thomas A. Vidano, (202) 435–5265, or Carol B. Tan (202) 435–5159, for matters relating to section 482, and David F. Bergkuist, (202) 622–3850, for matters relating to stewardship expenses (not toll-free numbers).

SUPPLEMENTARY INFORMATION:

Background

The notice of proposed rulemaking (REG–146893–02, REG–115037–00 and REG–138603–03) by cross-reference to temporary regulations that is the subject of this correction is under section 482 and 861 of the Internal Revenue Code.

Need for Correction

As published, the notice of proposed rulemaking (REG–146893–02, REG–115037–00 and REG–138603–03) by cross-reference to temporary regulations contains errors that may prove to be misleading and are in need of clarification.

Correction of Publication

Accordingly, the notice of proposed rulemaking (REG–146893–02, REG–138603–03 and REG–115037–00) by cross-reference to temporary regulations that were the subject of FR Doc. 06–6674, is corrected as follows:

1. On page 44247, column 2, in the heading, the subject "Treatment of Services Under Section 482 Allocation of Income and Deductions From Intangibles Stewardship Expense" is corrected to read, "Treatment of Services Under Section 482; Allocation of Income and Deductions From Intangibles; and Apportionment of Stewardship Expense".

2. On page 44248, column 2, instructional Par. 3., number 2 is corrected to read as follows:

"2. Paragraphs (d)(3)(ii)(C), *Example 4*, *Example 5*, *Example 6* and (j)(6) are added."

§ 1.482–1 [Corrected]

3. On page 44248, column 3, § 1.482–1(j), lines 2 and 3, the language "amendment to § 1.482–1(j) is the same as the text of § 1.482–1T(j)(1) and (2)" is corrected to read "amendment to § 1.482–1(j)(6) is the same as the text of § 1.482–1T(j)(6)".

§ 1.482–8 [Corrected]

4. On page 44249, column 2, § 1.482–8(a), line 1, the language "(a) *Example 10. Cost of services plus*" is corrected to read "(b) * * * *Example 10. Cost of services plus*".

5. On page 44249, column 2, § 1.482–8, paragraph (b) following *Example 12.* is removed.

§ 1.482–9 [Corrected]

6. On page 44249, column 2, § 1.482–9(m)(6), last line, the language "operation as defined in § 1.482–8". is corrected to read "operation as defined in the proposed § 1.482–8.".

§ 1.861–8 [Corrected]

7. On page 44249, column 3, § 1.861–8(f)(4), line 3, the language "same as the text of § 1.861–8T(c)(4)(i)" is corrected to read "same as the text of § 1.861–8T(f)(4)(i)".

8. On page 44249, column 3, § 1.861–8(h), line 3, the language "as the text of § 1.861–8T(h)(1) published" is corrected to read "as the text of § 1.861–8T(h) published".

Cynthia Grigsby,
Senior Federal Register Liaison Officer,
Legal Processing Division,
Associate Chief Counsel
(Procedure and Administration).

(Filed by the Office of the Federal Register on December 21, 2006, 8:45 a.m., and published in the issue of the Federal Register for December 22, 2006, 71 F.R. 46956)

Application of Separate Limitations to Dividends From Noncontrolled Section 902 Corporations; Correction

Announcement 2007–12

AGENCY: Internal Revenue Service (IRS), Treasury.

ACTION: Correcting amendments.

SUMMARY: This document contains corrections to final and temporary regulations (T.D. 9260, 2006–23 I.R.B. 1001) that were published in the **Federal Register** on Tuesday, April 25, 2006 (71 FR 24516) concerning the application of separate foreign tax credit limitations to dividends received from noncontrolled section 902 corporations under section 904(d)(4).

DATES: These corrections are effective April 25, 2006.

FOR FURTHER INFORMATION CONTACT: Ginny Chung (202) 622–3850 (not a toll-free call).

SUPPLEMENTARY INFORMATION:

Background

The final and temporary regulations (T.D. 9260) that are the subject of these corrections are under sections 902, 904, and 964 of the Internal Revenue Code.

Need for Correction

As published, T.D. 9260 contains errors that may prove to be misleading and are in need of clarification.

* * * * *

Correction of Publication

Accordingly, 26 CFR part 1 is corrected by making the following correcting amendments:

PART 1—INCOME TAXES

Paragraph 1. The authority for part 1 is amended and continues to read in part:

Authority: 26 U.S.C. 7805 * * *

Par. 2. Section 1.902–1 is amended by adding a heading to paragraph (a)(4)(i) introductory text and revising the heading for paragraph (c)(8) to read as follows:

§ 1.902–1 Credit for domestic corporate shareholder of a foreign corporation for foreign income taxes paid by the foreign corporation.

(a) * * *

(4) *Third- or lower-tier corporation—(i) Third-tier corporation.* * * *

* * * * *

(c) * * *

(8) *Effect of certain liquidations, reorganizations, or similar transactions on certain foreign taxes paid or accrued in taxable years beginning on or before August 5, 1997.*

* * *

* * * * *

Par. 3. Section 1.902–1T is amended by revising the first sentence of paragraph (a)(7) to read as follows:

§ 1.902–1T Credit for domestic corporate shareholder of a foreign corporation for foreign income taxes paid by the foreign corporation (temporary).

(a) * * *

(7) * * * The term *foreign income taxes* means income, war profits, and excess profits taxes as defined in § 1.902–1(a), and taxes included in the term income, war profits, and excess profits taxes by reason of section 903, that are imposed by a foreign country or a possession of the United States, including any such taxes deemed paid by a foreign corporation under this section. * * *

* * * * *

Par. 4. Section 1.902–2 is amended by revising the first sentence of paragraph (a)(1) to read as follows:

§ 1.902–2 Treatment of deficits in post-1986 undistributed earnings and pre-1987 accumulated profits of a first- or lower-tier corporation for purposes of computing an amount of foreign taxes deemed paid under § 1.902–1.

(a) * * * (1) * * *For purposes of computing foreign income taxes deemed paid under § 1.902–1(b) with respect to dividends paid by a first- or lower-tier corporation, when there is a deficit in the post-1986 undistributed earnings of that corporation and the corporation makes a distribution to shareholders that is a dividend or would be a dividend if there were current or accumulated earnings and profits, then the post-1986 deficit shall be carried back to the most recent pre-effective date taxable year of the first- or lower-tier corporation with positive accumulated profits computed under section 902. * * *

* * * * *

Par. 5. Section 1.904–0 is amended by adding the entries for paragraphs (o)(1) and (o)(2) under § 1.904–5 to read as follows:

§ 1.904–0 Outline of regulations provisions for section 904.

* * * * *

§ 1.904–5 Look-through rules as applied to controlled foreign corporations and other entities.

* * * * *

(o) * * *

(1) Rules for controlled foreign corporations and other look-through entities.

(2) Rules for noncontrolled section 902 corporations.

* * * * *

Par. 6. Section 1.904–4 is amended by revising paragraph (c)(4) introductory text and adding paragraphs (c)(4)(i) through (c)(4)(iii) to read as follows:

§ 1.904–4 Separate application of section 904 with respect to certain categories of income.

* * * * *

(c) * * *

(3) and (4) [Reserved]. For further guidance, see § 1.904–4T(c)(3) and (4) introductory text.

(4)(i) *Income from sources within the QBU's country of operation.* Passive income from sources within the QBU's country of operation shall be treated as one item of income.

(ii) *Income from sources without the QBU's country of operation.* Passive income from sources without the QBU's country of operation shall be grouped on the basis of the tax imposed on that income as provided in § 1.904–4T(c)(3)(i) through (iv).

(iii) *Determination of the source of income.* For purposes of this paragraph (c)(4), income will be determined to be from sources within or without the QBU's country of operation under the laws of the foreign country of the payor of the income.

* * * * *

Par. 7. Section 1.904–5 is amended by revising paragraphs (a) introductory text and (a)(1) and adding *Examples 4* and *5* to paragraph (i)(5) to read as follows:

§ 1.904–5 Look-through rules as applied to controlled foreign corporations and other entities.

(a) and (a)(1) [Reserved]. For further guidance, see § 1.904–5T(a) introductory text and (a)(1).

* * * * *

(i) * * *

(5) * * *

Examples 4 and *5* [Reserved]. For further guidance, see § 1.904–5T(i)(5) *Examples 4* and *5*.

* * * * *

Par. 8. Section 1.904(f)–12T is amended by revising the heading for paragraph (g)(1) to read as follows:

§ 1.904(f)–12T Transition rules (temporary).

* * * * *

(g) * * * (1) *Recapture of separate limitation loss or overall foreign loss in a separate category for dividends from a noncontrolled section 902 corporation.*

* * *

* * * * *

Par. 9. Section 1.964–1 is amended by:

1. Redesignating paragraphs (a) introductory text, (a)(1), (a)(2) and (a)(3) as paragraphs (a)(1) introductory text, (a)(1)(i), (a)(1)(ii) and (a)(1)(iii), respectively.

2. Designating the undesignated text following newly-designated paragraph (a)(1)(iii) as paragraph (a)(2).

3. Removing the comma following the word "shall" from newly designated paragraph (a)(1) introductory text.

4. Removing the last sentence in newly-designated paragraph (a)(1)(i).

5. Revising newly-designated paragraph (a)(2), and the text of paragraphs

(b)(1) introductory text and (c)(1) introductory text.

The revisions read as follows:

§ 1.964–1 Determination of the earnings and profits of a foreign corporation.

(a) * * *

(2) *Required adjustments.* The computation described in paragraph (a)(1) of this section shall be made in the foreign corporation's functional currency (determined under section 985 and the regulations under that section) and may be made by following the procedures described in paragraphs (a)(1)(i) through (a)(1)(iii) of this section in an order other than the one listed, as long as the result so obtained would be the same. In determining earnings and profits, or the deficit in earnings and profits, of a foreign corporation under section 964, the amount of an illegal bribe, kickback, or other payment (within the meaning of section 162(c), as amended by section 288 of the Tax Equity and Fiscal Responsibility Act of 1982 in the case of payments made after September 3, 1982, and these regulations) paid after November 3, 1976, by or on behalf of the corporation during the taxable year of the corporation directly or indirectly to an official, employee, or agent in fact of a government shall not be taken into account to decrease such earnings and profits or to increase such deficit. No adjustment shall be required under paragraph (a)(1)(ii) or (iii) of this section unless it is material. Whether an adjustment is material depends on the facts and circumstances of the particular case, including the amount of the adjustment, its size relative to the general level of the corporation's total assets and annual profit or loss, the consistency with which the practice has been applied, and whether the item to which the adjustment relates is of a recurring or merely a nonrecurring nature. For the treatment of earnings and profits whose distribution is prevented by restrictions and limitations imposed by a foreign government, see section 964(b) and these regulations. For rules for determining the earnings and profits (or deficit in earnings and profits) of a foreign corporation for taxable years beginning before January 1, 1987, for purposes of sections 951 through 964, see 26 CFR 1.964–1(a) (revised as of April 1, 2006).

(b) * * *(1) * * * The accounting principles to be applied in making the adjustments required by paragraph (a)(1)(ii) of this section shall be those accounting principles generally accepted in the United States for purposes of reflecting in the financial statements of a domestic corporation the operations of its foreign affiliates, including the following:

* * * * *

(c) * * *(1) * * *The tax accounting standards to be applied in making the adjustments required by paragraph (a)(1)(iii) of this section shall be the following:

* * * * *

Par. 10. Section 1.964–1T is amended by revising the first sentence of paragraph (c)(2) and the last sentence of paragraph (c)(5)(i) to read as follows:

§ 1.964–1T Determination of the earnings and profits of a foreign corporation (temporary).

* * * * *

(c) * * *

(2) * * * For the first taxable year of a foreign corporation beginning after April 25, 2006, in which such foreign corporation first qualifies as a controlled foreign corporation (as defined in section 957 or 953) or a noncontrolled section 902 corporation (as defined in section 904(d)(2)(E)), any method of accounting or taxable year allowable under this section may be adopted, and any election allowable under this section may be made, by such foreign corporation or on its behalf notwithstanding that, in previous years, its books or financial statements were prepared on a different basis, and notwithstanding that such election is required by the Internal Revenue Code or regulations to be made in a prior taxable year. * * *

* * * * *

(5) * * *(i) * * * In the event that the United States shareholders of the controlled foreign corporation do not, in the aggregate, own (within the meaning of section 958(a)) more than 50 percent of the total combined voting power of all classes of the stock of such foreign corporation entitled to vote, the controlling United States shareholders of the controlled foreign corporation shall be all those United States shareholders who own (within the meaning of section 958(a)) stock of such corporation.

* * * * *

Cynthia Grigsby,
Senior Federal Register Liaison Officer,
Publications and Regulations Branch,
Legal Processing Division,
Associate Chief Counsel
(Procedure and Administration).

(Filed by the Office of the Federal Register on December 22, 2006, 8:45 a.m., and published in the issue of the Federal Register for December 26, 2006, 71 F.R. 77264)

Part I. Rulings and Decisions Under the Internal Revenue Code of 1986

Section 61.—Gross Income Defined

26 CFR 1.61–1: Gross income.
(Also § 817; § 1.817–5.)

Investor control and general public; taxation of variable contracts; insurance and annuities. This ruling effectively excludes classes of beneficial ownership from the definition of "general public" as defined in Rev. Rul. 81–225, 1981–2 C.B. 12, for purposes of investor control analysis. Investor control analysis is used to determine who owns (and is taxed on) income generated inside of variable contracts (*e.g.*, variable life insurance contracts or variable annuity contracts). Rev. Ruls. 81–225 and 2003–92 clarified and amplified.

Rev. Rul. 2007–7

ISSUE

Is the holder of a variable annuity or life insurance contract treated as the owner, for federal income tax purposes, of an interest in a regulated investment company that funds the variable contract solely because interests in the same regulated investment company are also available to investors described in § 1.817–5(f)(3) of the Income Tax Regulations?

FACTS

A, an individual, purchases a variable contract (within the meaning of § 817(d) of the Internal Revenue Code) from *IC*, a life insurance company subject to tax under Part 1 of Subchapter L. All assets funding the contract are held in a segregated asset account that invests in *RIC*, a regulated investment company. All the beneficial interests in *RIC* are held by one or more segregated asset accounts of *IC*, or by investors described in § 1.817–5(f)(3). Public access to *RIC* is available exclusively either through the purchase of a variable contract, or to investors described in § 1.817–5(f)(3).

LAW AND ANALYSIS

In Rev. Rul. 2003–92, 2003–2 C.B. 350, a taxpayer purchased a variable "annuity" contract. The segregated asset account on which the contract was based was divided into 10 sub-accounts, each of which invested in a partnership. Interests in each partnership were sold in private placement offerings to qualified purchasers. The ruling concludes that, because interests in the partnerships were available for purchase by the general public, the taxpayer is considered the owner for federal tax purposes of the interests in the partnerships held by the sub-accounts. The same analysis applies in the case of a variable life insurance contract. Rev. Rul. 2003–92 clarified and amplified Rev. Rul. 81–225, 1981–2 C.B. 12, which concluded that the policyholder is considered the owner of mutual fund shares that fund a variable "annuity" contract where those shares are also available directly or indirectly to the general public.

Section 817(h) and § 1.817–5 set forth diversification requirements for segregated asset accounts on which variable contracts are based. Section 817(h)(4) and § 1.817–5(f) provide a look-through rule for determining whether those diversification requirements are met. The look-through rule applies to a regulated investment company, partnership, or trust, but only if (A) all the beneficial interests in the investment company, partnership, or trust are held by one or more segregated asset accounts of one or more insurance companies, and (B) public access to the investment company, partnership or trust is available exclusively through the purchase of a variable contract. Under § 1.817–5(f)(3), the following four categories of beneficial interest are ignored for purposes of determining whether these two requirements are satisfied:

(1) Interests held by the general account of a life insurance company or a corporation related to a life insurance company, but only if the return on such interests is computed in the same manner as the return on an interest held by a segregated asset account is computed, there is no intent to sell such interests to the public, and a segregated asset account of such life insurance company also holds or will hold a beneficial interest in the investment company, partnership, or trust;

(2) Interests held by a manager, or a corporation related to the manager, of the investment company, partnership or trust, but only if the holding of the interests is in connection with the creation or management of the investment company, partnership or trust, the return on such interest is computed in the same manner as the return on an interest held by a segregated asset account is computed, and there is no intent to sell such interests to the public;

(3) Interests held by the trustee of a qualified pension or retirement plan; or

(4) Interests held by the public, or treated as owned by the policyholders pursuant to Rev. Rul. 81–225, but only if (A) the investment company, partnership or trust was closed to the public in accordance with Rev. Rul. 82–55, 1982–1 C.B. 12, or (B) all the assets of the segregated asset account are attributable to premium payments made by policyholders before September 26, 1981, to premium payments made in connection with a qualified pension or retirement plan, or to any combination of such premium payments.

The investors described in § 1.817–5(f)(3) are not members of the "general public" as that term is used in Rev. Rul. 2003–92 and Rev. Rul. 81–225. In the present case, all the beneficial interests in *RIC* are held by one or more segregated asset accounts of *IC*, or by investors described in § 1.817–5(f)(3), and public access to *RIC* is available exclusively either through the purchase of a variable contract, or to investors described in § 1.817–5(f)(3). Accordingly, interests in *RIC* are not available to the "general public" as that term is used in Rev. Rul. 2003–92 and Rev. Rul. 81–225, and *A* is not treated as the owner of an interest in a regulated investment company that funds the variable contract.

HOLDING

The holder of a variable annuity or life insurance contract is not treated as the owner of an interest in a regulated investment company that funds the variable contract solely because interests in the same regulated investment company are also available to investors described in § 1.817–5(f)(3).

EFFECT ON OTHER REVENUE RULING(S)

Rev. Rul. 81–225, 1981–2 C.B. 12, and Rev. Rul. 2003–92, 2003–2 C.B. 350, are hereby clarified and amplified.

DRAFTING INFORMATION

The principal author of this revenue ruling is Chris Lieu of the Office of Chief Counsel (Financial Institutions & Products). For further information regarding this revenue ruling, contact Chris Lieu at (202) 622–3970 (not a toll-free call).

Section 357.—Assumption of Liability

26 CFR 1.357–2: Liabilities in excess of basis.

Section 357(c). Section 357(c)(1) of the Code does not apply to transactions that qualify as reorganizations described in sections 368(a)(1)(A), (C), (D), or (G), and to which section 351 applies, provided certain requirements are satisfied. Rev. Ruls. 75–161 and 76–188 obsoleted. Rev. Rul. 78–330 modified.

Rev. Rul. 2007–8

ISSUE

Does § 357(c)(1) of the Internal Revenue Code apply to transactions that qualify as reorganizations described in §§ 368(a)(1)(A), (C), (D) (provided the requirements of § 354(b)(1) are satisfied), or (G) (provided the requirements of § 354(b)(1) are satisfied) and to which § 351 applies?

FACTS

Situation 1. A, an individual, owned all of the stock of corporation X and corporation Y. Y acquired all of the assets of X in exchange for an amount of Y stock constituting § 368(c) control and the assumption by Y of X's liabilities. Pursuant to the plan, X liquidated and distributed the Y stock to A. At the time of the acquisition, the sum of the X liabilities assumed by Y exceeded X's total adjusted basis in the property transferred to Y. Further, the value of X's assets transferred to Y exceeded the amount of X's liabilities assumed by Y, and, immediately after the exchange, the value of Y's assets exceeded the amount of Y's liabilities. The transaction qualified as a reorganization described in § 368(a)(1)(D) and as an exchange to which § 351 applied.

Situation 2. A, an individual, owned all of the stock of corporation X. B, an individual unrelated to A, owned all of the stock of corporation Y. Y acquired all of the assets of X in exchange for Y voting stock and the assumption by Y of X's liabilities. Pursuant to the plan, X liquidated and distributed the Y voting stock to A. At the time of the acquisition, the sum of the X liabilities assumed by Y exceeded X's total adjusted basis in the property transferred to Y. Further, the value of X's assets transferred to Y exceeded the amount of X's liabilities assumed by Y, and, immediately after the exchange, the value of Y's assets exceeded the amount of Y's liabilities. Simultaneously, and as part of the overall plan, B contributed property to Y in exchange for additional Y stock so that immediately after the transaction, B held more than 50 percent of the vote and of the value of all the stock of Y. The Y stock issued to X along with the Y stock issued to and held by B immediately after the transaction constituted § 368(c) control of Y. The transfer by X of all of its assets to Y in exchange for Y voting stock and assumption of liabilities, followed by the liquidation of X, qualified as a reorganization described in § 368(a)(1)(C). Further, X's transfer of assets to Y in exchange for Y voting stock along with B's transfer of property to Y in exchange for additional Y stock was an exchange to which § 351 applied.

LAW AND ANALYSIS

Section 357(a) provides that if, as part of the consideration in an exchange to which § 351 or § 361 applies, a liability of the taxpayer is assumed by another party to the exchange then such assumption shall not be treated as money or other property. However, in the case of certain exchanges, § 357(c)(1) provides that the transferor is required to recognize gain if the sum of the amount of liabilities assumed exceeds the total of the adjusted basis of the property transferred. Prior to the enactment of The American Jobs Creation Act of 2004 (Public Law 108–357, 188 Stat. 1418) (the Jobs Act), § 357(c)(1) applied in the case of an exchange (A) to which § 351 applied, or (B) to which § 361 applied by reason of a plan of reorganization within the meaning of § 368(a)(1)(D). The Jobs Act amended § 357(c)(1)(B), limiting the application of § 357(c)(1) to exchanges to which § 351 applies, or to which § 361 applies by reason of a plan of reorganization within the meaning of § 368(a)(1)(D) with respect to which stock or securities of the corporation to which the assets are transferred are distributed in a transaction that qualifies under § 355. Thus, as amended, § 357(c) no longer applies to an acquisitive § 368(a)(1)(D) reorganization – *i.e.*, one that satisfies the requirements of § 354(b)(1).

The legislative history to the Jobs Act amendment to § 357(c)(1)(B) explains Congress's intent in removing acquisitive § 368(a)(1)(D) reorganizations from the application of § 357(c)(1), as follows:

> The Committee believes that . . . the [transferee] should be permitted to assume liabilities of the [transferor] without application of the rule of section 357(c). This is because in an acquisitive reorganization under section 368(a)(1)(D), the transferor must generally transfer substantially all of its assets to the acquiring corporation and then go out of existence. Assumption of its liabilities by the acquiring corporation thus does not enrich the transferor corporation, which ceases to exist, and whose liability was limited to its assets in any event, by corporate form. The Committee believes that it was appropriate to conform the treatment of acquisitive reorganizations under section 368(a)(1)(D) to that of other acquisitive reorganizations.

S. Rep. No. 192, 108th Cong., 1st Sess. 185 (2003).

The Jobs Act amendment to § 357(c)(1)(B) excluded acquisitive § 368(a)(1)(D) reorganizations from the application of § 357(c)(1), because in such transactions the transferor ceases to exist and cannot be enriched by the assumption of its liabilities. The Jobs Act legislative history states that the amendment was made to conform the treatment of § 368(a)(1)(D) acquisitive reorganizations to the treatment of other acquisitive reorganizations. Therefore, the intent of the Jobs Act amendment to § 357(c)(1)(B) was to exclude reorganizations from the application of § 357(c)(1) unless described in § 357(c)(1)(B), regardless of whether such reorganizations are also exchanges to which § 351 applies.

In the transactions set forth in both Situation 1 and Situation 2, the transferor corporation ceases to exist and, therefore, cannot be enriched as a result of the assumption of its liabilities. In accordance with the above reasoning, in both Situation 1 and Situation 2, § 357(c)(1) does not apply to X's transfer of assets to Y in exchange for Y stock and assumption of X's liabilities notwithstanding the fact that such transfers were also exchanges to which § 351 applied.

In addition, under § 368(a)(3)(C), if a reorganization qualifies under § 368(a)(1)(G) and under any other subparagraph of § 368(a)(1) or under § 332 or § 351, then, other than for purposes of § 357(c)(1), the transaction will be treated as qualifying only under § 368(a)(1)(G). However, because § 357(c)(1) is no longer applicable to a transaction that qualifies as a reorganization described in § 368(a)(1)(A), (C), or (D) (provided the requirements of § 354(b)(1) are satisfied), it is also no longer applicable to a reorganization described in § 368(a)(1)(G) (provided the requirements of § 354(b)(1) are satisfied), regardless of whether § 351 applies.

HOLDING

Section 357(c)(1) does not apply to transactions that qualify as reorganizations described in §§ 368(a)(1)(A), (C), (D) (provided the requirements of § 354(b)(1) are satisfied), or (G) (provided the requirements of § 354(b)(1) are satisfied) and to which § 351 applies.

EFFECT ON OTHER REVENUE RULING

Rev. Rul. 75–161, 1975–1 C.B. 114, and Rev. Rul. 76–188, 1976–1 C.B. 99, are obsolete. Rev. Rul. 78–330, 1978–2 C.B. 147, is modified to the extent it holds that § 357(c)(1) is applicable to a transaction that qualifies as a reorganization described in § 368(a)(1)(A) or (D) (that satisfies the requirements of § 354(b)(1)).

DRAFTING INFORMATION

The principal author of this revenue ruling is Rebecca O. Burch of the Office of Associate Chief Counsel (Corporate). For further information regarding this revenue ruling, contact Rebecca O. Burch at (202) 622–7550 (not a toll-free call).

Section 446.—General Rule for Methods of Accounting

26 CFR 1.446–1: General rule for methods of accounting.

T.D. 9307

DEPARTMENT OF THE TREASURY Internal Revenue Service 26 CFR Part 1

Changes in Computing Depreciation

AGENCY: Internal Revenue Service (IRS), Treasury.

ACTION: Final and temporary regulations.

SUMMARY: This document contains regulations relating to a change in computing depreciation or amortization as well as a change from a nondepreciable or nonamortizable asset to a depreciable or amortizable asset (or *vice versa*). Specifically, these regulations provide guidance to any taxpayer that makes a change in depreciation or amortization on whether such a change is a change in method of accounting under section 446(e) of the Internal Revenue Code and on the application of section 1016(a)(2) in determining whether the change is a change in method of accounting.

DATES: *Effective Date:* These regulations are effective December 28, 2006.

Applicability Dates: For dates of applicability, see §§1.167(e)–1(e), 1.446–1(e)(4), and 1.1016–3(j).

FOR FURTHER INFORMATION CONTACT: Douglas H. Kim, (202) 622–3110 (not a toll-free number).

SUPPLEMENTARY INFORMATION:

Background

This document contains amendments to 26 CFR part 1. On January 2, 2004, the IRS and Treasury Department published temporary regulations (T.D. 9105, 2004–1 C.B. 419) in the **Federal Register** (69 FR 5) relating to the application of section 446(e) of the Internal Revenue Code (Code) and §1.167(e)–1 to a change in depreciation or amortization and the application of section 1016(a)(2) in determining whether a change in depreciation or amortization is a change in method of accounting. On the same date, the IRS published a notice of proposed rulemaking (REG–126459–03, 2004–1 C.B. 437) cross-referencing the temporary regulations in the **Federal Register** (69 FR 42). No public hearing was requested or held. Several comments responding to the notice of proposed rulemaking were received. After consideration of all the comments, the proposed regulations are adopted as amended by this Treasury decision, and the corresponding temporary regulations are removed. The revisions are discussed here in this preamble.

Section 1400N(d), which was added to the Code by section 101(a) of the Gulf Opportunity Zone Act of 2005, Public Law 109–135 (119 Stat. 2577), generally allows a 50-percent additional first year depreciation deduction for qualified Gulf Opportunity Zone property. The final regulations reflect the enactment of section 1400N(d).

Explanation of Provisions

Scope

The final regulations provide the changes in depreciation or amortization (depreciation) for property for which depreciation is determined under section 167, 168, 197, 1400I, 1400L(b), 1400L(c), or 1400N(d), or former section 168, of the Code that are, and those changes that are not, changes in method of accounting under section 446(e). The final regulations also clarify that the rules in §1.167(e)–1 with respect to a change in the depreciation method made without the consent of the Commissioner apply only to property for which depreciation is determined under section 167 (other than under section 168, 1400I, 1400L, or 1400N(d), or former section 168). Additionally, the final regulations provide that section 1016(a)(2) does not permanently affect a taxpayer's lifetime income for purposes of determining whether a change in depreciation is a change in method of accounting under section 446(e) and §1.446–1(e).

I. *Changes in Depreciation Method under Section 167*

The final regulations retain the rules contained in the temporary regulations providing that the rules in §1.167(e)–1 with respect to a change in depreciation method under §1.167(e)–1(b), (c), and (d) made without the consent of the Commissioner apply only to property for which depreciation is determined under section 167 (other than under section 168, 1400I, 1400L, or 1400N(d), or former section 168). No comments were received suggesting changes to these rules.

II. *Changes in Depreciation That Are, and Are Not, a Change in Method of Accounting Under Section 446(e)*

The final regulations provide rules on the changes in depreciation that are, and are not, a change in method of accounting under section 446(e).

A. *Changes in Depreciation That Are Changes in Method of Accounting*

The final regulations retain the rules contained in the temporary regulations providing the changes in depreciation that are a change in method of accounting under section 446(e). These changes are a change in the treatment of an asset from nondepreciable or nonamortizable to depreciable or amortizable, or *vice versa*. Additionally, a correction to require depreciation in lieu of a deduction for the cost of depreciable or amortizable assets that had been consistently treated as an expense in the year of purchase, or *vice versa*, is a change in method of accounting. Further, changes in computing depreciation generally are a change in method of accounting, including a change in the depreciation method, period of recovery, or convention of a depreciable or amortizable asset, and a change to or from claiming the additional first year depreciation deduction provided by section 168(k), 1400L(b), or 1400N(d) under certain circumstances.

No comments were received suggesting changes to these rules. However, a commentator inquired whether a calendar-year taxpayer that has not claimed the 30-percent additional first year depreciation for qualified property acquired after September 10, 2001, and placed in service prior to January 1, 2002, may claim the 30-percent additional first year depreciation by requesting a change in method of accounting. To claim the 30-percent additional first year depreciation for this property, Rev. Proc. 2003–50, 2003–2 C.B. 119, provides that the taxpayer had to file an amended return on or before December 31, 2003, or file a Form 3115, "*Application for Change in Accounting Method*," with the taxpayer's timely filed 2003 Federal tax return. If the taxpayer did not file this amended return or Form 3115, the taxpayer has made the deemed election not to deduct the additional first year depreciation for the 2001 taxable year. Accordingly, the taxpayer's change to claiming the 30-percent additional first year depreciation for qualified property placed in service in the taxable year that included September 11, 2001, is not a change in method of accounting under the temporary and final regulations. Instead, the taxpayer must file a request for a letter ruling to revoke the election.

Another commentator questioned whether the temporary regulations affected the procedures for obtaining consent to make a change in method of accounting. The regulations did not change these procedures and, accordingly, the rules in §1.446–1(e)(3) apply to a change in depreciation that is a change in method of accounting. Other commentators inquired whether a change in depreciation due to a posting or mathematical error, or a change in underlying facts, is a change in method of accounting. A change in depreciation due to a posting or mathematical error, or a change in underlying facts, is not a change in method of accounting because the rules in §1.446–1(e)(2)(ii)(*a*) and (*b*) also apply to a change in depreciation. Accordingly, the final regulations clarify this point.

B. *Changes in Depreciation That Are Not Changes in Method of Accounting*

The final regulations retain the rule contained in the temporary regulations that a change in method of accounting does not include an adjustment in the useful life of a depreciable or amortizable asset for which depreciation is determined under section 167 (other than under section 168, 1400I, 1400L, or 1400N(d), or former section 168). This rule does not apply, however, if a taxpayer is changing to or from a useful life (or recovery period or amortization period) that is specifically assigned by the Code, the regulations under the Code, or other guidance published in the Internal Revenue Bulletin. Several commentators questioned whether the useful life exception from change in method of accounting treatment that was in effect before the issuance of the temporary regulations has any remaining application. Section 1.446–1(e)(2)(ii)(*b*), as in effect before the issuance of the temporary regulations (see §1.446–1(e) as contained in 26 CFR part 1 edition revised as of April 1, 2003), provided that a change in the method of accounting does not include an adjustment in the useful life of a depreciable asset. The rule still applies but is limited by the temporary and final regulations to only a depreciable or amortizable asset for which depreciation is determined under section 167 (other than under section 168, 1400I, 1400L, or 1400N(d), or former section 168) and to only an adjustment in useful life that is not specifically assigned by the Code, the regulations under the Code, or other guidance published in the Internal Revenue Bulletin.

The final regulations also retain the rules contained in the temporary regulations of when an adjustment in useful life that is not a change in method of accounting is implemented. The final regulations clarify that these rules apply regardless of whether the adjustment in useful life is initiated by the IRS or a taxpayer. Furthermore, the final regulations clarify that in implementing an adjustment in useful life that is not a change in method of accounting, no section 481 adjustment is required or permitted.

The final regulations retain the rule contained in the temporary regulations providing that the making of a late depreciation election or the revocation of a timely valid depreciation election is not a change in method of accounting, except as otherwise provided by the Code, the regulations under the Code, or other guidance published in the Internal Revenue Bulletin. A commentator inquired whether a late section 179 election may be made by requesting a change in method of accounting. Under section 179 and the regulations under section 179, a late section 179 election generally is made by submitting a request for a letter ruling. However, for a taxable year beginning after 2002 and before 2010, a taxpayer may make a section 179 election by filing an amended return. Accordingly, the IRS and Treasury Department have included a cross-reference to section 179(c) and §1.179–5.

The final regulations retain the rule contained in the temporary regulations providing that any change in the placed-in-service date of a depreciable or amortizable asset is not treated as a change in method of accounting. The final regulations, however, clarify that this rule does not apply when the Code, the regulations under the Code, or other guidance published in the Internal Revenue Bulletin, provide that a change in placed-in-service date is treated as a change in method of accounting. A commentator requested that the final regulations clarify what constitutes a change in placed-in-service date. To illustrate the rule, the IRS and Treasury Department provided additional clarification in the final regulations. For example, the final regulations provide that if a taxpayer changes the placed-in-service date of a depreciable or amortizable asset because the taxpayer incorrectly determined the date on which the asset was placed in service, this change is not a change in method of accounting. However, if a taxpayer incorrectly determines that a depreciable or amortizable asset is nondepreciable property and later changes the treatment of the asset to depreciable property, this change is not a change in the placed-in-service date of the asset but is a change from nondepreciable to depreciable property and, therefore, the change is a change in method of accounting. The final regulations also clarify that a change in the convention of a depreciable or amortizable asset is not a change in the placed-in-service date of the asset and, therefore, is a change in method of accounting. Additionally, the final regulations provide examples illustrating what constitutes a change in placed-in-service date.

The final regulations retain the rules contained in the temporary regulations as to how and when a change in placed-in-service date that is not a change in method of accounting is implemented. The final regulations also clarify that these rules apply regardless of whether the change in placed-in-service date is made by the IRS or a taxpayer. Finally, the final regulations provide that in implementing a change in placed-in-service date that is not a change in method of accounting, no section 481 adjustment is required or permitted.

C. *Item Being Changed*

The final regulations retain the rule contained in the temporary regulations providing that for purposes of a change in depreciation, the item being changed is the depreciation treatment of each individual depreciable or amortizable asset or the depreciation treatment of each vintage account with respect to a depreciable asset for which depreciation is determined under §1.167(a)–11 (CLADR). Because general asset accounts and mass asset accounts are similar to vintage accounts, the final regulations clarify that the item is the depreciable treatment of each general asset account with respect to a depreciable asset for which general asset account treatment has been elected under section 168(i)(4) or the item is the depreciation treatment of each mass asset account with respect to a depreciable asset for which mass asset account treatment has been elected under former section 168(d)(2)(A). The final regulations also retain the rule contained in the temporary regulations providing that a change in depreciation under section 167 (other than under section 168, 1400I, 1400L, or 1400N(d), or former section 168) is permitted only with respect to all assets in a particular account (as defined in §1.167(a)–7) or vintage account.

D. *Effective Dates*

Several commentators questioned the application of the effective date of the temporary regulations. In response, the IRS, in Chief Counsel Notice 2004–007 (CC–2004–007, January 28, 2004) and Chief Counsel Notice 2004–024 (CC–2004–024, July 12, 2004) (see *www.irs.gov/foia*), clarified that the temporary regulations apply to property placed in service in a taxable year ending on or after December 30, 2003. In accordance with this clarification, the final regulations apply only to a change in depreciation made by a taxpayer for a depreciable or amortizable asset placed in service by the taxpayer in a taxable year ending on or after December 30, 2003, regardless of whether or not the change in depreciation is a change in method of accounting. Additionally, the examples in the final regulations relating to a change in depreciation have been revised to reflect this effective date.

III. *Application of Section 1016(a)(2) to a Change in Method of Accounting*

The final regulations contain the same rule as the temporary regulations, providing that section 1016(a)(2) does not permanently affect a taxpayer's lifetime income for purposes of determining whether a change in depreciation for property subject to section 167, 168, 1400I, 1400L, or 1400N(d), or former section 168, is a change in method of accounting under section 446(e) and the regulations under section 446(e). No comments were received suggesting changes to this rule.

Special Analyses

It has been determined that this Treasury decision is not a significant regulatory action as defined in Executive Order 12866. Therefore, a regulatory assessment is not required. It has also been determined that section 553(b) of the Administrative Procedure Act (5 U.S.C. chapter 5) does not apply to these regulations and, because these regulations do not impose on small entities a collection of information requirement, the Regulatory Flexibility Act (5 U.S.C. chapter 6) does not apply. Therefore, a Regulatory Flexibility Analysis is not required. Pursuant to section 7805(f) of the Code, the notice of proposed rulemaking was submitted to the Chief Counsel for Advocacy of the Small Business Administration for comment on its impact on small business.

Drafting Information

The principal author of these regulations is Douglas H. Kim, Office of Associate Chief Counsel (Passthroughs and

Special Industries). However, other personnel from the IRS and Treasury Department participated in their development.

* * * * *

Adoption of Amendments to the Regulations

Accordingly, 26 CFR part 1 is amended as follows:

PART 1—INCOME TAXES

Paragraph 1. The authority citation for part 1 continues to read in part as follows:

Authority: 26 U.S.C. 7805 * * *

Par. 2. Section 1.167(e)–1 is amended by revising paragraphs (a) and (e) to read as follows:

§1.167(e)–1 Change in method.

(a) *In general.* (1) Any change in the method of computing the depreciation allowances with respect to a particular account (other than a change in method permitted or required by reason of the operation of former section 167(j)(2) and §1.167(j)–3(c)) is a change in method of accounting, and such a change will be permitted only with the consent of the Commissioner, except that certain changes to the straight line method of depreciation will be permitted without consent as provided in former section 167(e)(1), (2), and (3). Except as provided in paragraphs (c) and (d) of this section, a change in method of computing depreciation will be permitted only with respect to all the assets contained in a particular account as defined in §1.167(a)–7. Any change in the percentage of the current straight line rate under the declining balance method, for example, from 200 percent of the straight line rate to any other percent of the straight line rate, or any change in the interest factor used in connection with a compound interest or sinking fund method, will constitute a change in method of depreciation. Any request for a change in method of depreciation shall be made in accordance with section 446(e) and the regulations under section 446(e). For rules covering the use of depreciation methods by acquiring corporations in the case of certain corporate acquisitions, see section 381(c)(6) and the regulations under section 381(c)(6).

(2) Paragraphs (b), (c), and (d) of this section apply to property for which depreciation is determined under section 167 (other than under section 168, section 1400I, section 1400L(c), under section 168 prior to its amendment by the Tax Reform Act of 1986 (100 Stat. 2121), or under an additional first year depreciation deduction provision (for example, section 168(k), 1400L(b), or 1400N(d))) of the Internal Revenue Code.

* * * * *

(e) *Effective date.* This section applies on or after December 30, 2003. For the applicability of regulations before December 30, 2003, see §1.167(e)–1 in effect prior to December 30, 2003 (§1.167(e)–1 as contained in 26 CFR part 1 edition revised as of April 1, 2003).

§1.167(e)–1T [Removed]

Par. 3. Section 1.167(e)–1T is removed.

Par. 4. Section 1.168(i)–4 is amended as follows:

1. Paragraph (f) is amended by removing the language "§1.446–1T (e)(2)(ii)(*d*)(*3*)(*ii*)" at the end of the paragraph and adding "§1.446–1(e)(2)(ii)(*d*)(*3*)(*ii*)" in its place.

2. Paragraph (g)(2)(ii) is amended by removing the language "as modified by Rev. Proc. 2004–11, 2004–1 C.B. 311."

Par. 5. Section 1.168(i)–6T is amended as follows:

1. Paragraph (k)(2)(i) is amended by removing the language "§1.446–1T (e)(3)(ii)" and adding "§1.446–1(e)(3)(ii)" in its place.

2. The last sentence in paragraph (k)(2)(ii) is amended by removing the language "§1.446–1T(e)(3)(ii)" and adding "§1.446–1(e)(3)(ii)" in its place.

Par. 6. Section 1.446–1 is amended by revising paragraphs (e)(2)(ii)(*a*), (e)(2)(ii)(*b*), (e)(2)(ii)(*d*), (e)(2)(iii), and (e)(4) to read as follows:

§1.446–1 General rule for methods of accounting.

* * * * *

(e) * * *

(2) * * *

(ii) (*a*) A change in the method of accounting includes a change in the overall plan of accounting for gross income or deductions or a change in the treatment of any material item used in such overall plan. Although a method of accounting may exist under this definition without the necessity of a pattern of consistent treatment of an item, in most instances a method of accounting is not established for an item without such consistent treatment. A material item is any item that involves the proper time for the inclusion of the item in income or the taking of a deduction. Changes in method of accounting include a change from the cash receipts and disbursement method to an accrual method, or *vice versa*, a change involving the method or basis used in the valuation of inventories (see sections 471 and 472 and the regulations under sections 471 and 472), a change from the cash or accrual method to a long-term contract method, or *vice versa* (see §1.460–4), certain changes in computing depreciation or amortization (see paragraph (e)(2)(ii)(*d*) of this section), a change involving the adoption, use or discontinuance of any other specialized method of computing taxable income, such as the crop method, and a change where the Internal Revenue Code and regulations under the Internal Revenue Code specifically require that the consent of the Commissioner must be obtained before adopting such a change.

(*b*) A change in method of accounting does not include correction of mathematical or posting errors, or errors in the computation of tax liability (such as errors in computation of the foreign tax credit, net operating loss, percentage depletion, or investment credit). Also, a change in method of accounting does not include adjustment of any item of income or deduction that does not involve the proper time for the inclusion of the item of income or the taking of a deduction. For example, corrections of items that are deducted as interest or salary, but that are in fact payments of dividends, and of items that are deducted as business expenses, but that are in fact personal expenses, are not changes in method of accounting. In addition, a change in the method of accounting does not include an adjustment with respect to the addition to a reserve for bad debts. Although such adjustment may involve the question of the proper time for the taking of a deduction, such items are traditionally corrected by adjustment in the current and future years. For the treatment of the adjustment of the addition to a bad debt reserve (for example, for banks under section 585 of the Internal Revenue Code), see the regulations under section 166 of the Internal Revenue Code. A change in the method of accounting also does not include a change in treatment resulting from a change in underlying facts. For further guidance on changes involving depreciable or amortizable assets, see paragraph (e)(2)(ii)(*d*) of this section and §1.1016–3(h).

* * * * *

(*d*) *Changes involving depreciable or amortizable assets*—(1) *Scope*. This paragraph (e)(2)(ii)(*d*) applies to property subject to section 167, 168, 197, 1400I, 1400L(c), to section 168 prior to its amendment by the Tax Reform Act of 1986 (100 Stat. 2121) (former section 168), or to an additional first year depreciation deduction provision of the Internal Revenue Code (for example, section 168(k), 1400L(b), or 1400N(d)).

(*2*) *Changes in depreciation or amortization that are a change in method of accounting*. Except as provided in paragraph (e)(2)(ii)(*d*)(*3*) of this section, a change in the treatment of an asset from nondepreciable or nonamortizable to depreciable or amortizable, or *vice versa*, is a change in method of accounting. Additionally, a correction to require depreciation or amortization in lieu of a deduction for the cost of depreciable or amortizable assets that had been consistently treated as an expense in the year of purchase, or *vice versa*, is a change in method of accounting. Further, except as provided in paragraph (e)(2)(ii)(*d*)(*3*) of this section, the following changes in computing depreciation or amortization are a change in method of accounting:

(*i*) A change in the depreciation or amortization method, period of recovery, or convention of a depreciable or amortizable asset.

(*ii*) A change from not claiming to claiming the additional first year depreciation deduction provided by, for example, section 168(k), 1400L(b), or 1400N(d), for, and the resulting change to the amount otherwise allowable as a depreciation deduction for the remaining adjusted depreciable basis (or similar basis) of, depreciable property that qualifies for the additional first year depreciation deduction (for example, qualified property, 50-percent bonus depreciation property, qualified New York Liberty Zone property, or qualified Gulf Opportunity Zone property), provided the taxpayer did not make the election out of the additional first year depreciation deduction (or did not make a deemed election out of the additional first year depreciation deduction; for further guidance, for example, see Rev. Proc. 2002–33, 2002–1 C.B. 963, Rev. Proc. 2003–50, 2003–2 C.B. 119, Notice 2006–77, 2006–40 I.R.B. 590, and §601.601(d)(2)(ii)(*b*) of this chapter) for the class of property in which the depreciable property that qualifies for the additional first year depreciation deduction (for example, qualified property, 50-percent bonus depreciation property, qualified New York Liberty Zone property, or qualified Gulf Opportunity Zone property) is included.

(*iii*) A change from claiming the 30-percent additional first year depreciation deduction to claiming the 50-percent additional first year depreciation deduction for depreciable property that qualifies for the 50-percent additional first year depreciation deduction, provided the property is not included in any class of property for which the taxpayer elected the 30-percent, instead of the 50-percent, additional first year depreciation deduction (for example, 50-percent bonus depreciation property or qualified Gulf Opportunity Zone property), or a change from claiming the 50-percent additional first year depreciation deduction to claiming the 30-percent additional first year depreciation deduction for depreciable property that qualifies for the 30-percent additional first year depreciation deduction, including property that is included in a class of property for which the taxpayer elected the 30-percent, instead of the 50-percent, additional first year depreciation deduction (for example, qualified property or qualified New York Liberty Zone property), and the resulting change to the amount otherwise allowable as a depreciation deduction for the property's remaining adjusted depreciable basis (or similar basis). This paragraph (e)(2)(ii)(*d*)(*2*)(*iii*) does not apply if a taxpayer is making a late election or revoking a timely valid election under the applicable additional first year depreciation deduction provision of the Internal Revenue Code (for example, section 168(k), 1400L(b), or 1400N(d)) (see paragraph (e)(2)(ii)(*d*)(*3*)(*iii*) of this section).

(*iv*) A change from claiming to not claiming the additional first year depreciation deduction for an asset that does not qualify for the additional first year depreciation deduction, including an asset that is included in a class of property for which the taxpayer elected not to claim any additional first year depreciation deduction (for example, an asset that is not qualified property, 50-percent bonus depreciation property, qualified New York Liberty Zone property, or qualified Gulf Opportunity Zone property), and the resulting change to the amount otherwise allowable as a depreciation deduction for the property's depreciable basis.

(*v*) A change in salvage value to zero for a depreciable or amortizable asset for which the salvage value is expressly treated as zero by the Internal Revenue Code (for example, section 168(b)(4)), the regulations under the Internal Revenue Code (for example, §1.197–2(f)(1)(ii)), or other guidance published in the Internal Revenue Bulletin.

(*vi*) A change in the accounting for depreciable or amortizable assets from a single asset account to a multiple asset account (pooling), or *vice versa*, or from one type of multiple asset account (pooling) to a different type of multiple asset account (pooling).

(*vii*) For depreciable or amortizable assets that are mass assets accounted for in multiple asset accounts or pools, a change in the method of identifying which assets have been disposed. For purposes of this paragraph (e)(2)(ii)(*d*)(*2*)(*vii*), the term *mass assets* means a mass or group of individual items of depreciable or amortizable assets that are not necessarily homogeneous, each of which is minor in value relative to the total value of the mass or group, numerous in quantity, usually accounted for only on a total dollar or quantity basis, with respect to which separate identification is impracticable, and placed in service in the same taxable year.

(*viii*) Any other change in depreciation or amortization as the Secretary may designate by publication in the **Federal Register** or in the Internal Revenue Bulletin (see §601.601(d)(2) of this chapter).

(*3*) *Changes in depreciation or amortization that are not a change in method of accounting*. Section 1.446–1(e)(2)(ii)(*b*) applies to determine whether a change in depreciation or amortization is not a change in method of accounting. Further, the following changes in depreciation or amortization are not a change in method of accounting:

(*i*) *Useful life*. An adjustment in the useful life of a depreciable or amortizable asset for which depreciation is determined under section 167 (other than under section 168, section 1400I, section 1400L(c), former section 168, or an additional first year depreciation deduction provision of the Internal Revenue Code (for example, section 168(k), 1400L(b), or 1400N(d))) is not a change in method of accounting. This paragraph (e)(2)(ii)(*d*)(*3*)(*i*) does not apply if a taxpayer is changing to or from a useful life (or recovery period or amortization period) that is specifically assigned by the Internal Revenue Code (for example, section 167(f)(1), section 168(c), section 168(g)(2) or (3), section 197), the regulations under the Internal Revenue Code, or other guidance published in the Internal Revenue Bulletin and, therefore, such change is a change in method of accounting (unless paragraph (e)(2)(ii)(*d*)(*3*)(*v*) of this section applies). See paragraph (e)(2)(ii)(*d*)(*5*)(*iv*) of this section for determining the taxable year in which to correct an adjustment in useful life that is not a change in method of accounting.

(*ii*) *Change in use*. A change in computing depreciation or amortization allowances in the taxable year in which the use of an asset changes in the hands of the same taxpayer is not a change in method of accounting.

(*iii*) *Elections*. Generally, the making of a late depreciation or amortization election or the revocation of a timely valid depreciation or amortization election is not a change in method of accounting, except as otherwise expressly provided by the Internal Revenue Code, the regulations under the Internal Revenue Code, or other guidance published in the Internal Revenue Bulletin. This paragraph (e)(2)(ii)(*d*)(*3*)(*iii*) also applies to making a late election or revoking a timely valid election made under section 13261(g)(2) or (3) of the Revenue Reconciliation Act of 1993 (107 Stat. 312, 540) (relating to amortizable section 197 intangibles). A taxpayer may request consent to make a late election or revoke a timely valid election by submitting a request for a private letter ruling. For making or revoking an election under section 179 of the Internal Revenue Code, see section 179(c) and §1.179–5.

(*iv*) *Salvage value*. Except as provided under paragraph (e)(2)(ii)(*d*)(*2*)(*v*) of this section, a change in salvage value of a depreciable or amortizable asset is not treated as a change in method of accounting.

(*v*) *Placed-in-service date*. Except as otherwise expressly provided by the Internal Revenue Code, the regulations under the Internal Revenue Code, or other guidance published in the Internal Revenue Bulletin, any change in the placed-in-service date of a depreciable or amortizable asset is not treated as a change in method of accounting. For example, if a taxpayer changes the placed-in-service date of a depreciable or amortizable asset because the taxpayer incorrectly determined the date on which the asset was placed in service, such a change is a change in the placed-in-service date of the asset and, therefore, is not a change in method of accounting. However, if a taxpayer incorrectly determines that a depreciable or amortizable asset is nondepreciable property and later changes the treatment of the asset to depreciable property, such a change is not a change in the placed-in-service date of the asset and, therefore, is a change in method of accounting under paragraph (e)(2)(ii)(*d*)(*2*) of this section. Further, a change in the convention of a depreciable or amortizable asset is not a change in the placed-in-service date of the asset and, therefore, is a change in method of accounting under paragraph (e)(2)(ii)(*d*)(*2*)(*i*) of this section. See paragraph (e)(2)(ii)(*d*)(*5*)(*v*) of this section for determining the taxable year in which to make a change in the placed-in-service date of a depreciable or amortizable asset that is not a change in method of accounting.

(*vi*) Any other change in depreciation or amortization as the Secretary may designate by publication in the **Federal Register** or in the Internal Revenue Bulletin (see §601.601(d)(2) of this chapter).

(*4*) *Item being changed*. For purposes of a change in depreciation or amortization to which this paragraph (e)(2)(ii)(*d*) applies, the item being changed generally is the depreciation treatment of each individual depreciable or amortizable asset. However, the item is the depreciation treatment of each vintage account with respect to a depreciable asset for which depreciation is determined under §1.167(a)–11 (class life asset depreciation range (CLADR) property). Similarly, the item is the depreciable treatment of each general asset account with respect to a depreciable asset for which general asset account treatment has been elected under section 168(i)(4) or the item is the depreciation treatment of each mass asset account with respect to a depreciable asset for which mass asset account treatment has been elected under former section 168(d)(2)(A). Further, a change in computing depreciation or amortization under section 167 (other than under section 168, section 1400I, section 1400L(c), former section 168, or an additional first year depreciation deduction provision of the Internal Revenue Code (for example, section 168(k), 1400L(b), or 1400N(d))) is permitted only with respect to all assets in a particular account (as defined in §1.167(a)–7) or vintage account.

(*5*) *Special rules*. For purposes of a change in depreciation or amortization to which this paragraph (e)(2)(ii)(*d*) applies—

(*i*) *Declining balance method to the straight line method for MACRS property*. For tangible, depreciable property subject to section 168 (MACRS property) that is depreciated using the 200-percent or 150-percent declining balance method of depreciation under section 168(b)(1) or (2), a taxpayer may change without the consent of the Commissioner from the declining balance method of depreciation to the straight line method of depreciation in the first taxable year in which the use of the straight line method with respect to the adjusted depreciable basis of the MACRS property as of the beginning of that year will yield a depreciation allowance that is greater than the depreciation allowance yielded by the use of the declining balance method. When the change is made, the adjusted depreciable basis of the MACRS property as of the beginning of the taxable year is recovered through annual depreciation allowances over the remaining recovery period (for further guidance, see section 6.06 of Rev. Proc. 87–57, 1987–2 C.B. 687, and §601.601(d)(2)(ii)(*b*) of this chapter).

(*ii*) *Depreciation method changes for section 167 property*. For a depreciable or amortizable asset for which depreciation is determined under section 167 (other than under section 168, section 1400I, section 1400L(c), former section 168, or an additional first year depreciation deduction provision of the Internal Revenue Code (for example, section 168(k), 1400L(b), or 1400N(d))), see §1.167(e)–1(b), (c), and (d) for the changes in depreciation method that are permitted to be made without the consent of the Commissioner. For CLADR property, see §1.167(a)–11(c)(1)(iii) for the changes in depreciation method for CLADR property that are permitted to be made without the consent of the Commissioner. Further, see §1.167(a)–11(b)(4)(iii)(*c*) for how to correct an incorrect classification or characterization of CLADR property.

(*iii*) *Section 481 adjustment*. Except as otherwise expressly provided by the Internal Revenue Code, the regulations under the Internal Revenue Code, or other guidance published in the Internal Revenue Bulletin, no section 481 adjustment is required or permitted for a change from one permissible method of computing depreciation or amortization to another permissible method of computing depreciation or amortization for an asset because this change is implemented by either a cut-off method (for further guidance, for example, see section 2.06 of Rev. Proc. 97–27, 1997–1 C.B. 680, section 2.06 of Rev. Proc. 2002–9, 2002–1 C.B. 327, and §601.601(d)(2)(ii)(*b*) of this chapter) or a modified cut-off method (under which the adjusted depreciable basis of the asset as of the beginning of the year of change is recovered using the new permissible method of accounting), as appropriate. However, a change from an impermissible method of computing depreciation or amortization to a permissible method of computing depreciation or amortization for an asset results in a section 481 adjustment. Similarly, a change in the treatment of an asset from nondepreciable or nonamortizable to depreciable or amortizable (or *vice versa*) or a change in the treatment of an asset from expensing to depreciating (or *vice versa*) results in a section 481 adjustment.

(*iv*) *Change in useful life*. This paragraph (e)(2)(ii)(*d*)(*5*)(*iv*) applies to an adjustment in the useful life of a depreciable or amortizable asset for which depreciation is determined under section 167 (other than under section 168, section 1400I, section 1400L(c), former section 168, or an additional first year depreciation deduction provision of the Internal Revenue Code (for example, section 168(k), 1400L(b), or 1400N(d))) and that is not a change in method of accounting under paragraph (e)(2)(ii)(*d*) of this section. For this adjustment in useful life, no section 481 adjustment is required or permitted. The adjustment in useful life, whether initiated by the Internal Revenue Service (IRS) or a taxpayer, is corrected by adjustments in the taxable year in which the conditions known to exist at the end of that taxable year changed thereby resulting in a redetermination of the useful life under §1.167(a)–1(b) (or if the period of limitation for assessment under section 6501(a) has expired for that taxable year, in the first succeeding taxable year open under the period of limitation for assessment), and in subsequent taxable years. In other situations (for example, the useful life is incorrectly determined in the placed-in-service year), the adjustment in the useful life, whether initiated by the IRS or a taxpayer, may be corrected by adjustments in the earliest taxable year open under the period of limitation for assessment under section 6501(a) or the earliest taxable year under examination by the IRS but in no event earlier than the placed-in-service year of the asset, and in subsequent taxable years. However, if a taxpayer initiates the correction in useful life, in lieu of filing amended Federal tax returns (for example, because the conditions known to exist at the end of a prior taxable year changed thereby resulting in a redetermination of the useful life under §1.167(a)–1(b)), the taxpayer may correct the adjustment in useful life by adjustments in the current and subsequent taxable years.

(*v*) *Change in placed-in-service date*. This paragraph (e)(2)(ii)(*d*)(*5*)(*v*) applies to a change in the placed-in-service date of a depreciable or amortizable asset that is not a change in method of accounting under paragraph (e)(2)(ii)(*d*) of this section. For this change in placed-in-service date, no section 481 adjustment is required or permitted. The change in placed-in-service date, whether initiated by the IRS or a taxpayer, may be corrected by adjustments in the earliest taxable year open under the period of limitation for assessment under section 6501(a) or the earliest taxable year under examination by the IRS but in no event earlier than the placed-in-service year of the asset, and in subsequent taxable years. However, if a taxpayer initiates the change in placed-in-service date, in *lieu* of filing amended Federal tax returns, the taxpayer may correct the placed-in-service date by adjustments in the current and subsequent taxable years.

(iii) *Examples*. The rules of this paragraph (e) are illustrated by the following examples:

Example 1. Although the sale of merchandise is an income producing factor, and therefore inventories are required, a taxpayer in the retail jewelry business reports his income on the cash receipts and disbursements method of accounting. A change from the cash receipts and disbursements method of accounting to the accrual method of accounting is a change in the overall plan of accounting and thus is a change in method of accounting.

Example 2. A taxpayer in the wholesale dry goods business computes its income and expenses on the accrual method of accounting and files its Federal income tax returns on such basis except for real estate taxes which have been reported on the cash receipts and disbursements method of accounting. A change in the treatment of real estate taxes from the cash receipts and disbursements method to the accrual method is a change in method of accounting because such change is a change in the treatment of a material item within his overall accounting practice.

Example 3. A taxpayer in the wholesale dry goods business computes its income and expenses on the accrual method of accounting and files its Federal income tax returns on such basis. Vacation pay has been deducted in the year in which paid because the taxpayer did not have a completely vested vacation pay plan, and, therefore, the liability for payment did not accrue until that year. Subsequently, the taxpayer adopts a completely vested vacation pay plan that changes its year for accruing the deduction from the year in which payment is made to the year in which the liability to make the payment now arises. The change for the year of deduction of the vacation pay plan is not a change in method of accounting but results, instead, because the underlying facts (that is, the type of vacation pay plan) have changed.

Example 4. From 1968 through 1970, a taxpayer has fairly allocated indirect overhead costs to the value of inventories on a fixed percentage of direct costs. If the ratio of indirect overhead costs to direct costs increases in 1971, a change in the underlying facts has occurred. Accordingly, an increase in the percentage in 1971 to fairly reflect the increase in the relative level of indirect overhead costs is not a change in method of accounting but is a change in treatment resulting from a change in the underlying facts.

Example 5. A taxpayer values inventories at cost. A change in the basis for valuation of inventories from cost to the lower of cost or market is a change in an overall practice of valuing items in inventory. The change, therefore, is a change in method of accounting for inventories.

Example 6. A taxpayer in the manufacturing business has for many taxable years valued its inventories at cost. However, cost has been improperly computed since no overhead costs have been included in valuing the inventories at cost. The failure to allocate an appropriate portion of overhead to the value of inventories is contrary to the requirement of the Internal Revenue Code and the regulations under the Internal Revenue Code. A change requiring appropriate allocation of overhead is a change in method of accounting because it involves a change in the treatment of a material item used in the overall practice of identifying or valuing items in inventory.

Example 7. A taxpayer has for many taxable years valued certain inventories by a method which provides for deducting 20 percent of the cost of the inventory items in determining the final inventory valuation. The 20 percent adjustment is taken as a "reserve for price changes." Although this method is not a proper method of valuing inventories under the Internal Revenue Code or the regulations under the Internal Revenue Code, it involves the treatment of a material item used in the overall practice of valuing inventory. A change in such practice or procedure is a change of method of accounting for inventories.

Example 8. A taxpayer has always used a base stock system of accounting for inventories. Under this system a constant price is applied to an assumed constant normal quantity of goods in stock. The base stock system is an overall plan of accounting for inventories which is not recognized as a proper method of accounting for inventories under the regulations. A change in this practice is, nevertheless, a change of method of accounting for inventories.

Example 9. In 2003, A1, a calendar year taxpayer engaged in the trade or business of manufacturing knitted goods, purchased and placed in service a building and its components at a total cost of $10,000,000 for use in its manufacturing operations. A1 classified the $10,000,000 as nonresidential real property under section 168(e). A1 elected not to deduct the additional first year depreciation provided by section 168(k) on its 2003 Federal tax return. As a result, on its 2003, 2004, and 2005 Federal tax returns, A1 depreciated the $10,000,000 under the general depreciation system of section 168(a), using the straight line method of depreciation, a 39-year recovery period, and the mid-month convention. In 2006, A1 completes a cost segregation study on the building and its components and identifies items that cost a total of $1,500,000 as section 1245 property. As a result, the $1,500,000 should have been classified in 2003 as 5-year property under section 168(e) and depreciated on A1's 2003, 2004, and 2005 Federal tax returns under the general depreciation system, using the 200-percent declining balance method of depreciation, a 5-year recovery period, and the half-year convention. Pursuant to paragraph (e)(2)(ii)(*d*)(*2*)(*i*) of this section, A1's change to this depreciation method, recovery period, and convention is a change in method of accounting. This method change results in a section 481 adjustment. The useful life exception under paragraph (e)(2)(ii)(*d*)(*3*)(*i*) of this section does not apply because the assets are depreciated under section 168.

Example 10. In 2003, B, a calendar year taxpayer, purchased and placed in service new equipment at a total cost of $1,000,000 for use in its plant located outside the United States. The equipment is 15-year property under section 168(e) with a class life of 20 years. The equipment is required to be depreciated under the alternative depreciation system of section 168(g). However, B incorrectly depreciated the equipment under the general depreciation system of section 168(a), using the 150-percent declining balance method, a 15-year recovery period, and the half-year convention. In 2010, the IRS examines B's 2007 Federal income tax return and changes the depreciation of the equipment to the alternative depreciation system, using the straight line method of depreciation, a 20-year recovery period, and the half-year convention. Pursuant to paragraph (e)(2)(ii)(*d*)(*2*)(*i*) of this section, this change in depreciation method and recovery period made by the IRS is a change in method of accounting. This method change results in a section 481 adjustment. The useful life exception under paragraph (e)(2)(ii)(*d*)(*3*)(*i*) of this section does not apply because the assets are depreciated under section 168.

Example 11. In May 2003, C, a calendar year taxpayer, purchased and placed in service equipment for use in its trade or business. C never held this equipment for sale. However, C incorrectly treated the equipment as inventory on its 2003 and 2004 Federal tax returns. In 2005, C realizes that the equipment should have been treated as a depreciable asset. Pursuant to paragraph (e)(2)(ii)(*d*)(*2*) of this section, C's change in the treatment of the equipment from inventory to a depreciable asset is a change in method of accounting. This method change results in a section 481 adjustment.

Example 12. Since 2003, D, a calendar year taxpayer, has used the distribution fee period method to amortize distributor commissions and, under that method, established pools to account for the distributor commissions (for further guidance, see Rev. Proc. 2000–38, 2000–2 C.B. 310, and §601.601(d)(2)(ii)(*b*) of this chapter). A change in the accounting of distributor commissions under the distribution fee period method from pooling to single asset accounting is a change in method of accounting pursuant to paragraph (e)(2)(ii)(*d*)(*2*)(*vi*) of this section. This method change results in no section 481 adjustment because the change is from one permissible method to another permissible method.

Example 13. Since 2003, E, a calendar year taxpayer, has accounted for items of MACRS property that are mass assets in pools. Each pool includes only the mass assets that are placed in service by E in the same taxable year. E is able to identify the cost basis of each asset in each pool. None of the pools are general asset accounts under section 168(i)(4) and the regulations under section 168(i)(4). E identified any dispositions of these mass assets by specific identification. Because of changes in E's recordkeeping in 2006, it is impracticable for E to continue to identify disposed mass assets using specific identification. As a result, E wants to change to a first-in, first-out method under which the mass assets disposed of in a taxable year are deemed to be from the pool with the earliest placed-in-service year in existence as of the beginning of the taxable year of each disposition. Pursuant to paragraph (e)(2)(ii)(*d*)(*2*)(*vii*) of this section, this change is a change in method of accounting. This method change results in no section 481 adjustment because the change is from one permissible method to another permissible method.

Example 14. In August 2003, F, a calendar year taxpayer, purchased and placed in service a copier for use in its trade or business. F incorrectly classified the copier as 7-year property under section 168(e). F elected not to deduct the additional first year depreciation provided by section 168(k) on its 2003 Federal tax return. As a result, on its 2003 and 2004 Federal tax returns, F depreciated the copier under the general depreciation system of section 168(a), using the 200-percent declining balance method of depreciation, a 7-year recovery period, and the half-year convention. In 2005, F realizes that the copier is 5-year property and should have been depreciated on its 2003 and 2004 Federal tax returns under the general depreciation system using a 5-year recovery period rather than a 7-year recovery period. Pursuant to paragraph (e)(2)(ii)(*d*)(*2*)(*i*) of this section, F's change in recovery period from 7 to 5 years is a change in method of accounting. This method change results in a section 481 adjustment. The useful life exception under paragraph (e)(2)(ii)(*d*)(*3*)(*i*) of this section does not apply because the copier is depreciated under section 168.

Example 15. In 2004, G, a calendar year taxpayer, purchased and placed in service an intangible asset that is not an amortizable section 197 intangible and that is not described in section 167(f). G amortized the cost of the intangible asset under section 167(a) using the straight line method of depreciation and a determinable useful life of 13 years. The safe harbor useful life of 15 or 25 years under §1.167(a)–3(b) does not apply to the intangible asset. In 2008, because of changing conditions, G changes the remaining useful life of the intangible asset to 2 years. Pursuant to paragraph (e)(2)(ii)(*d*)(*3*)(*i*) of this section, G's change in useful life is not a change in method of accounting because the intangible asset is depreciated under section 167 and G is not changing to or from a useful life that is specifically assigned by the Internal Revenue Code, the regulations under the Internal Revenue Code, or other guidance published in the Internal Revenue Bulletin.

Example 16. In July 2003, H, a calendar year taxpayer, purchased and placed in service "off-the-shelf" computer software and a new computer. The cost of the new computer and computer software are separately stated. H incorrectly included the cost of this software as part of the cost of the computer, which is 5-year property under section 168(e). On its 2003 Federal tax return, H elected to depreciate its 5-year property placed in service in 2003 under the alternative depreciation system of section 168(g) and H elected not to deduct the additional first year depreciation provided by section 168(k). The class life for a computer is 5 years. As a result, because H included the cost of the computer software as part of the cost of the computer hardware, H depreciated the cost of the software under the alternative depreciation system, using the straight line method of depreciation, a 5-year recovery period, and the half-year convention. In 2005, H realizes that the cost of the software should have been amortized under section 167(f)(1), using the straight line method of depreciation, a 36-month useful life, and a monthly convention. H's change from 5-years to 36-months is a change in method of accounting because H is changing to a useful life that is specifically assigned by section 167(f)(1). The change in convention from the half-year to the monthly convention also is a change in method of accounting. Both changes result in a section 481 adjustment.

Example 17 On May 1, 2003, I2, a calendar year taxpayer, purchased and placed in service new equipment at a total cost of $500,000 for use in its business. The equipment is 5-year property under section 168(e) with a class life of 9 years and is qualified property under section 168(k)(2). I2 did not place in service any other depreciable property in 2003. Section 168(g)(1)(A) through (D) do not apply to the equipment. I2 intended to elect the alternative depreciation system under section 168(g) for 5-year property placed in service in 2003. However, I2 did not make the election. Instead, I2 deducted on its 2003 Federal tax return the 30-percent additional first year depreciation attributable to the equipment and, on its 2003 and 2004 Federal tax returns, depreciated the remaining adjusted depreciable basis of the equipment under the general depreciation system under 168(a), using the 200-percent declining balance method, a 5-year recovery period, and the half-year convention. In 2005, I2 realizes its failure to make the alternative depreciation system election in 2003 and files a Form 3115, "*Application for Change in Accounting Method*," to change its method of depreciating the remaining adjusted depreciable basis of the 2003 equipment to the alternative depreciation system. Because this equipment is not required to be depreciated under the alternative depreciation system, I2 is attempting to make an election under section 168(g)(7). However, this election must be made in the taxable year in which the equipment is placed in service (2003) and, consequently, I2 is attempting to make a late election under section 168(g)(7). Accordingly, I2's change to the alternative depreciation system is not a change in accounting method pursuant to paragraph (e)(2)(ii)(*d*)(*3*)(*iii*) of this section. Instead, I2 must submit a request for a private letter ruling under §301.9100–3 of this chapter, requesting an extension of time to make the alternative depreciation system election on its 2003 Federal tax return.

Example 18. On December 1, 2004, J, a calendar year taxpayer, purchased and placed in service 20 previously-owned adding machines. For the 2004 taxable year, J incorrectly classified the adding machines as items in its "suspense" account for financial and tax accounting purposes. Assets in this suspense account are not depreciated until reclassified to a depreciable fixed asset account. In January 2006, J realizes that the cost of the adding machines is still in the suspense account and reclassifies such cost to the appropriate depreciable fixed asset account. As a result, on its 2004 and 2005 Federal tax returns, J did not depreciate the cost of the adding machines. Pursuant to paragraph (e)(2)(ii)(*d*)(*2*) of this section, J's change in the treatment of the adding machines from nondepreciable assets to depreciable assets is a change in method of accounting. The placed-in-service date exception under paragraph (e)(2)(ii)(*d*)(*3*)(*v*) of this section does not apply because the adding machines were incorrectly classified in a nondepreciable suspense account. This method change results in a section 481 adjustment.

Example 19. In December 2003, K, a calendar year taxpayer, purchased and placed in service equipment for use in its trade or business. However, K did not receive the invoice for this equipment until January 2004. As a result, K classified the equipment on its fixed asset records as being placed in service in January 2004. On its 2004 and 2005 Federal tax returns, K depreciated the cost of the equipment. In 2006, K realizes that the equipment was actually placed in service during the 2003 taxable year and, therefore, depreciation should have began in the 2003 taxable year instead of the 2004 taxable year. Pursuant to paragraph (e)(2)(ii)(*d*)(*3*)(*v*) of this section, K's change in the placed-in-service date of the equipment is not a change in method of accounting.

* * * * *

(4) *Effective date*—(i) *In general*. Except as provided in paragraphs (e)(3)(iii) and (e)(4)(ii) of this section, paragraph (e) of this section applies on or after December 30, 2003. For the applicability of regulations before December 30, 2003, see §1.446–1(e) in effect prior to December 30, 2003 (§1.446–1(e) as contained in 26 CFR part 1 edition revised as of April 1, 2003).

(ii) *Changes involving depreciable or amortizable assets*. With respect to paragraph (e)(2)(ii)(*d*) of this section, paragraph (e)(2)(iii) *Examples 9* through *19* of this section, and the language "certain changes in computing depreciation or amortization (see paragraph (e)(2)(ii)(*d*) of this section)" in the last sentence of paragraph (e)(2)(ii)(*a*) of this section—

(A) For any change in depreciation or amortization that is a change in method of accounting, this section applies to such a change in method of accounting made by a taxpayer for a depreciable or amortizable asset placed in service by the taxpayer in a taxable year ending on or after December 30, 2003; and

(B) For any change in depreciation or amortization that is not a change in method of accounting, this section applies to such a change made by a taxpayer for a depreciable or amortizable asset placed in service by the taxpayer in a taxable year ending on or after December 30, 2003.

§1.446–1T [Removed]

Par. 7. Section 1.446–1T is removed.

Par. 8. Section 1.1016–3 is amended by revising paragraphs (h) and (j) to read as follows:

§1.1016–3 Exhaustion, wear and tear, obsolescence, amortization, and depletion for periods since February 28, 1913.

* * * * *

(h) *Application to a change in method of accounting*. For purposes of determining whether a change in depreciation or amortization for property subject to section 167, 168, 197, 1400I, 1400L(c), to section 168 prior to its amendment by the Tax Reform Act of 1986 (100 Stat. 2121) (former section 168), or to an additional first year depreciation deduction provision of the Internal Revenue Code (for example, section 168(k), 1400L(b), or 1400N(d)) is a change in method of accounting under section 446(e) and the regulations under section 446(e), section 1016(a)(2) does not permanently affect a taxpayer's lifetime income.

* * * * *

(j) *Effective date*—(1) *In general*. Except as provided in paragraph (j)(2) of this section, this section applies on or after December 30, 2003. For the applicability of regulations before December 30, 2003, see §1.1016–3 in effect prior to December 30, 2003 (§1.1016–3 as contained in 26 CFR part 1 edition revised as of April 1, 2003).

(2) *Depreciation or amortization changes*. Paragraph (h) of this section applies to a change in depreciation or amortization for property subject to section 167, 168, 197, 1400I, 1400L(c), to former section 168, or to an additional first year depreciation deduction provision of the Internal Revenue Code (for example, section 168(k), 1400L(b), or 1400N(d)) for taxable years ending on or after December 30, 2003.

§1.1016–3T [Removed]

Par. 9. Section 1.1016–3T is removed.

Kevin M. Brown,
Deputy Commissioner for Services and Enforcement.

Approved December 21, 2006.

Eric Solomon,
Assistant Secretary of the Treasury (Tax Policy).

(Filed by the Office of the Federal Register on December 22, 2006, 8:45 a.m., and published in the issue of the Federal Register for December 28, 2006, 71 F.R. 78066)

Section 863.—Special Rules for Determining Source

26 CFR 1.863–8: Source of income derived from space and ocean activity under section 863(d).

T.D. 9305

DEPARTMENT OF THE TREASURY
Internal Revenue Service
26 CFR Parts 1 and 602

Source of Income From Certain Space and Ocean Activities; Source of Communications Income

AGENCY: Internal Revenue Service (IRS), Treasury.

ACTION: Final regulations.

SUMMARY: This document contains final regulations under section 863(d) governing the source of income from certain space and ocean activities. It also contains final regulations under section 863(a), (d), and (e) governing the source of income from certain communications activities. In addition, this document contains final regulations under section 863(a) and (b), amending the regulations in §1.863–3 to conform those regulations to these final regulations. The final regulations primarily affect persons who derive income from activities conducted in space, or on or under water not within the jurisdiction of a foreign country, possession of the United States, or the United States (in international water). The final regulations also affect persons who derive income from transmission of communications.

DATES: *Effective Date:* These regulations are effective December 27, 2006.

Applicability Date: For dates of applicability, see §1.863–8(h) and §1.863–9(l).

FOR FURTHER INFORMATION CONTACT: H. Michael Huynh, (202) 435–5161 (not a toll-free number).

SUPPLEMENTARY INFORMATION:

Paperwork Reduction Act

The collections of information contained in these final regulations have been reviewed and approved by the Office of Management and Budget (OMB) in accordance with the Paperwork Reduction Act of 1995 (44 U.S.C. 3507(d)) under control number 1545–1718.

The collections of information in these final regulations are in §§1.863–8(g) and 1.863–9(k). This information is required by the IRS to monitor compliance with the Federal tax rules for determining the source of income from space or ocean activities, or from transmission of communications.

An agency may not conduct or sponsor, and a person is not required to respond to, a collection of information unless the collection of information displays a valid control number assigned by the Office of Management and Budget.

The estimated annual burden per respondent is 5 hours.

Comments concerning the accuracy of this burden estimate and suggestions for reducing this burden should be sent to the Internal Revenue Service, Attn: IRS Reports Clearance Officer, SE:W:CAR:MP:T:T:SP, Washington, DC 20224, and to the Office of Management and Budget, Attn: Desk Officer for the Department of the Treasury, Office of Information and Regulatory Affairs, Washington, DC 20503.

Books or records relating to a collection of information must be retained as long as their contents may become material in the administration of any internal revenue law. Generally, tax returns and tax return information are confidential, as required by 26 U.S.C. 6103.

Background

Congress enacted section 863(d) and (e) as part of the Tax Reform Act of 1986, Pub. L. No. 99–514, 100 Stat. 2085. Section 863(d) governs the source of income derived from space or ocean activities. Section 863(e) governs the source of income derived from international communications activities.

The Treasury Department and the IRS published a notice of proposed rulemaking (REG–106030–98, 2001–1 C.B. 820) in the **Federal Register** on January 17, 2001 (66 FR 3903), which provided proposed regulations under section 863(a), (b), (d), and (e) (the 2001 proposed regulations). The Treasury Department and the IRS received numerous written comments on the 2001 proposed regulations and held a public hearing on May 23, 2001. Since that time, the aerospace, telecommunications, and related industries have experienced substantial technological evolution and significant business change and consolidation. In addition, the American Jobs Creation Act of 2004 (AJCA), Pub. L. No. 108–357, 118 Stat. 1418, enacted a number of materially relevant statutory changes that affect the treatment of space and ocean income for purposes of the foreign tax credit and subpart F rules.

In light of the extensive written comments, industry evolution, and AJCA changes, the Treasury Department and the IRS felt that it was appropriate to repropose these regulations to reflect these changes and to provide another opportunity for comment. Consequently, the Treasury Department and the IRS published another notice of proposed rulemaking in the **Federal Register** on September 19, 2005 (REG–106030–98, 2005–2 C.B. 739 [70 FR 54859]), which withdrew the 2001 proposed regulations and provided new proposed regulations under section 863(a), (b), (d), and (e) (the proposed regulations). The proposed regulations provided two sets of rules: one in §1.863–8 for determining the source of income from space or ocean activities, the other in §1.863–9 for determining the source of income from communications activities.

A public hearing on the proposed regulations was scheduled for December 15, 2005, but was ultimately cancelled because no one requested to speak. A few written comments, however, were received. These comments uniformly praised the proposed regulations as an improvement over the 2001 proposed regulations and generally were supportive of much of the proposed regulations. However, commentators suggested a few additional changes. After consideration of these comments, the proposed regulations are adopted as final regulations, as amended by this Treasury decision. The revisions to regulations governing the source of income from space or ocean activities and the source of income from communications activities are discussed in section A and section B, respectively, of this preamble.

Summary of Comments and Explanation of Revisions

A. *Space or Ocean Activity under Section 863(d)*

Section 863(d) governs the source of income from certain space or ocean activities. In general, section 863(d)(1) provides that, except as provided in regulations, any income derived from a space or ocean activity (space and ocean income) is income from sources within the United States (U.S. source income) if derived by a United States person and is income from sources without the United States (foreign source income) if derived by a foreign person. Section 863(d)(2)(A)(i) defines space activity to include any activity conducted in space. Section 863(d)(2)(A)(ii) defines ocean activity to include any activity conducted on or under water not within the jurisdiction (as recognized by the United States) of a foreign country, possession of the United States, or the United States. Section 863(d)(2)(B) excludes three types of activities from the definition of space or ocean activity. Space or ocean activity does not include any activity giving rise to transportation income governed by section 863(c), international communications income governed by section 863(e), or income with respect to mines, oil and gas wells, or other natural deposits to the extent within the United States or any foreign country or possession of the United States (as defined in section 638). See Section 863(d)(2)(B).

Section 1.863–8 of the proposed regulations generally provided rules for determining the source of income derived from space or ocean activity under section 863(d). Section 1.863–8(b)(1) of the proposed regulations reflected the general source rule under section 863(d)(1) that a United States person's space and ocean income is U.S. source income. Pursuant to the grant of regulatory authority under section 863(d)(1), however, the proposed regulations provided an exception to this general rule. Under that exception, a United States person's space and ocean income is foreign source income (and therefore not sourced on the basis of citizenship or residency) to the extent the income, based on all the facts and circumstances, is attributable to functions performed, resources employed, or risks assumed in a foreign country or countries.

For a foreign person, proposed §1.863–8(b)(2) reflected the general source rule under section 863(d)(1) that a foreign person's space and ocean income is foreign source income. Pursuant to regulatory authority under section 863(d)(1), however, the proposed regulations contained two exceptions to this general rule, one for controlled foreign corporations (CFCs), the other for foreign persons engaged in a U.S. trade or business. The proposed regulations generally sourced space and ocean income derived by a CFC, like that of a United States person, as U.S. source income. However, also like the rule for a United States person, a CFC's space and ocean income is foreign source income to the extent the income, based on all the facts and circumstances, is attributable to functions performed, resources employed, or risks assumed in a foreign country or countries. For a foreign person, other than a CFC, engaged in a trade or business within the United States, space and ocean income is U.S. source income to the extent it is attributable to functions performed, resources employed, or risks assumed within the United States.

In addition to the general source rules for United States and foreign persons, the proposed regulations provided special rules, applicable to both United States and foreign persons, for income from services, certain sales of property, and communications activities (other than international communications activities). These special rules, as well as modifications to the proposed regulations, are discussed below.

1. *Activities performed outside space and international water*

Section 1.863–8 of the proposed regulations provided source rules only for income from space or ocean activity. Thus, in some cases, income derived from a transaction must be allocated between space and ocean income and other income.

For example, §1.863–8(b)(3)(ii)(C) of the proposed regulations provided that when property is produced both in space or international water and outside space and international water, gross income allocable to production activity is allocated to production occurring in space or international water and production occurring outside space and international water based on where functions are performed, resources are employed, or risks are assumed. The proposed regulations also provided a similar analysis of functions performed, resources employed, or risks assumed to allocate income in the case of performance of services. See Prop. Treas. Reg. §1.863–8(d)(2). Under the proposed regulations, only the amount allocated to production or performance of a service occurring in space or international water is treated as space and ocean income (character rule). The source of gross income allocated to production or performance of a service occurring in space or international water is then determined under the rules of proposed §1.863–8(b)(1) or (2), as applicable (source rule).

Section 1.863–8(b)(1) of the proposed regulations reflected the general source rule that a United States person's space and ocean income is U.S. source income. Proposed §1.863–8(b)(2) reflected the general source rule that a foreign person's space and ocean income is foreign source income. Both proposed §1.863–8(b)(1) and (2), however, provided exceptions to their respective general source rules. As discussed above, under the exceptions, a United States person's space and ocean income may be foreign source income and a foreign person's space and ocean income may be U.S. source income based on where functions are performed, resources are employed, or risks are assumed.

One commentator noted that in some situations, the allocation of income derived from a transaction to determine space and ocean income based on functions performed, resources employed, or risks assumed presumably would remove the subsequent need to further analyze functions performed, resources employed, or risks assumed within a country to determine the source of the space and ocean income. In other words, the very act of determining the character of income seems to also determine the source of such income.

The Treasury Department and the IRS agree with the commentator that use of the same standard to classify the transaction as space or ocean activity and to source the space and ocean income may be duplicative in some cases. However, there are other cases where a transaction with some land-based activity may be classified in its entirety as a space or ocean activity (for example, a lease of a satellite), but the income may be partially U.S. source and partially foreign source under the source rules of proposed §1.863–8(b)(1) and (2) based on functions performed, resources employed, or risks assumed within the United States or a foreign country. Consequently, the character and source rules are not always duplicative.

Thus, the extent to which the character rules overlap with the source rules is particular to the type of transaction involved. The Treasury Department and the IRS recognize that the overlap in the character and source rules may produce equivalent results. But, the overlap is necessary to provide taxpayers and the IRS with workable rules. As a result, the final regulations do not follow this comment as a general matter.

Nonetheless, a conforming amendment has been made to the lease transaction in *Example 1* in §1.863–8(f) of the final regulations to more clearly illustrate how the rules work. That example illustrates that the transaction involved is first classified in its entirety as a space or ocean activity, and then the resulting space and ocean income is subjected to the source rules. The space and ocean income is sourced as foreign source income to the extent the income, based on all the facts and circumstances, is attributable to functions performed, resources employed, or risks assumed in a foreign country or countries.

2. *Activities performed by another person*

Section 1.863–8(a) of the proposed regulations provided that a taxpayer will not be considered to derive income from space or ocean activity if such activity is performed by another person. The approach under §1.863–8(a) of the proposed regulations, providing that a taxpayer derives income from a space or ocean activity only if it conducts such activity directly, is consistent with the approach adopted in the §1.863–3 regulations governing the source of income from certain sales of inventory. See, *e.g.*, Treas. Reg. §1.863–3(c) ("[T]he only production activities that are taken into account for purposes of §§1.863–1, 1.863–2, and this section are those conducted directly by the taxpayer.").

Accordingly, commentators believed that this provision assured that a content provider that retains a satellite operator to transmit programming abroad would not derive space and ocean income based on attribution of the satellite operator's activity. The Treasury Department and the IRS agree.

One commentator noted, however, that *Examples 2* and *4* in §1.863–8(f) of the proposed regulations seem to indicate that this is not what was intended. In *Example 2*, the taxpayer, an Internet service provider, transmits information requested by its customer, in part using satellite capacity leased from a third party. *Example 2* concludes that the service performed by the taxpayer is considered space activity to the extent the value of the service is attributable to functions performed, resources employed, and risks assumed in space. In *Example 4*, the taxpayer uses satellite capacity acquired from a third party to deliver programming services directly to its customers' televisions sets. *Example 4* concludes that the taxpayer's delivery of programming and other services is considered space activity to the extent the value of the delivery transaction is attributable to performance in space. In the commentator's view, the results reached in the examples conflict with the provision stating that activities performed by another person are not attributable to the taxpayer.

The Treasury Department and the IRS do not believe that *Examples 2* and *4* of §1.863–8(f) of the proposed regulations produce the result that the commentator raised. In *Examples 2* and *4*, the taxpayer performed the transmission or delivery activities using satellite capacity leased or acquired from a third party. Both *Examples 2* and *4* correctly conclude that the taxpayers derived space and ocean income from their own activities rather than from activities of another person. Thus, the examples do not, in fact, conflict with the text of the proposed regulations. Nevertheless, the Treasury Department and the IRS are concerned that *Examples 2* and *4* have been misinterpreted as suggesting that activities performed by another person may be attributable to the taxpayer in certain situations. This was not the intent of these examples. Consequently, *Examples 2* and *4* in §1.863–8(f) of the final regulations have been modified to make clear that the taxpayers in the examples *directly* engage in a space activity by performing the uplink (transmitting to the satellite) and downlink functions.

These examples differ from cases in which the taxpayer is a mere content provider that derives income either from the creation of content or from the creation and delivery of content, but in either case contracts with another person to deliver the content via satellite. Pursuant to §1.863–8(a) of the final regulations, content providers of this type would not derive space and ocean income because the delivery of the content via satellite is performed by another person. This would be the result even though the value of the customer contract includes a payment to the content provider for space or ocean activity. To clarify the distinction between these situations and *Examples 2* and *4*, a new *Example 5* has been added to the final regulations. That example involves a content provider that does not derive space and ocean income because the taxpayer does not directly perform any space or ocean activity.

3. *Income characterization rules for income from services and the de minimis exception*

Under §1.863–8(b)(4) of the proposed regulations, to the extent a service is characterized as space or ocean activity, the source of gross income derived from such transaction is determined under proposed §1.863–8(b)(1) or (2), as applicable. Section 1.863–8(d)(2)(ii)(B) of the proposed regulations provided, however, that if the taxpayer can demonstrate, based on all the facts and circumstances, that the value of the service attributable to performance in space or international water is *de minimis*, such service will not be treated as space or ocean activity. The *de minimis* rule was adopted to address taxpayers' concerns about potential confusion in qualifying for the "facilitation exception" under the 2001 proposed regulations. One commentator stated that the *de minimis* rule simply replaced one vague standard with another, as neither *Example 3* in §1.863–8(f) of the proposed regulations nor the text of the proposed regulations provides any guidance as to when activities performed in space or international water would be *de minimis* under a facts and circumstances approach.

The Treasury Department and the IRS recognize that issues of interpretation may arise in any facts and circumstances approach. Nevertheless, the Treasury Department and the IRS generally have refrained from adopting the alternative approach, to wit, adopting precise definitions and quantitative measures for a *de minimis* standard. Moreover, the inclusion of a precise definition and quantitative measures for determining *de minimis* value could raise equal, if not greater, concerns in terms of the quantitative threshold and other issues. Thus, the final regulations retain the *de minimis* standard for determining whether a taxpayer has space and ocean income. If the value of the service attributable to space or ocean activity is *de minimis* based on the facts and circumstances, the taxpayer will not derive space and ocean income. Nevertheless, the Treasury Department and the IRS agree that more guidance could be provided as to the application of the retained *de minimis* rule. Accordingly, *Examples 3* and *8* in §1.863–8(f) of the final regulations (*Example 7* in the proposed regulations) provide clearer illustrations of when activities performed in space or international water would be considered *de minimis* for this purpose and when those types of activities would not be considered *de minimis*.

4. *Source rules for income from certain sales of property*

The proposed regulations provided special rules for income from certain sales of property, either when any production occurs in space or international water, or when the sale occurs in space or international water. In either case, section 863(d) and the proposed regulations applied to determine the source of income from the sales of property, and the rules of sections 861(a)(6), 862(a)(6), 863(a), 863(b), and 865 apply only to the extent provided in the proposed regulations.

a. Sales of Property Produced in the United States and Sold in Space or International Water

Section 1.863–8(b)(3)(ii) of the proposed regulations provided that when the taxpayer both produces property and sells such property, one-half of the taxpayer's gross income will be considered income allocable to production activity and one-half of such gross income will be considered income allocable to sales activity. Taxpayers generally must then apply the rules of section 863(d) and the proposed regulations to determine the source of income allocable to production activity and sales activity.

For production activity, the source of gross income allocable to production occurring in space or international water is generally based on the citizenship or residence of the taxpayer, applying the rules of proposed §1.863–8(b)(1) or (2), as applicable. The source of gross income allocable to production occurring outside space and international water is determined under section 863(b) rather than section 863(d). See Prop. Treas. Reg. §1.863–8(b)(3)(ii)(B) (referencing Treas. Reg. §1.863–3(c)(1)).

As for sales activity, when property is sold in space or international water, the source of gross income allocable to sales activity is generally based on the citizenship or residence of the taxpayer, applying the rules of proposed §1.863–8(b)(1) or (2), as applicable. An exception to this general rule applied in cases when the property sold is inventory, within the meaning of section 1221(a)(1), and is sold in space or international water for use, consumption, or disposition outside space, international water, and the United States. In that case, the source of gross income allocable to sales activity is determined under Treas. Reg. §1.861–7(c) and §1.863–3(c)(2). Treas. Reg. §1.861–7(c) and §1.863–3(c)(2) generally provide for foreign source income where the seller's rights, title, and interest in the property are transferred to the buyer (the title passage rule) outside the United States and the property is not sold for use, consumption, or disposition in the United States. Treas. Reg. §1.861–7(c) and §1.863–3(c)(2) also applied to property sold outside space and international water. See Prop. Treas. Reg. §1.863–8(b)(3)(ii)(D).

One commentator believed that because certain U.S. manufacturers, such as U.S. satellite manufacturers, produce property that is sold in space or international water for use, consumption, or disposition in space or international water, they are at a disadvantage relative to U.S. manufacturers of other export property because the former may have U.S. source income with respect to income allocable to sales activity, while the latter may have foreign source income from sales activity.

In response to comments on the 2001 proposed regulations, proposed §1.863–8(b)(1) was revised to provide that space and ocean income will be foreign source income to the extent the space and ocean income is attributable to functions performed, resources employed, or risks assumed in a foreign country or countries. The Treasury Department and the IRS believe that this change may in many cases mitigate concerns about U.S. manufacturers potentially deriving 100 percent U.S. source income in these cases. Moreover, the Treasury Department and the IRS believe that the rules under the proposed regulations for determining the source of income allocable to sales activity are consistent with legislative intent to assert primary tax jurisdiction over income earned by United States persons that is not subject to foreign tax. See S. REP. NO. 99–313, 1986–3 C.B. 357–358 ("[T]he committee believes the United States should assert primary tax jurisdiction over income earned by its residents that is not within any foreign country's taxing jurisdiction....Moreover, when a U.S. taxpayer conducts activities in space or international waters, foreign countries generally do not tax the income. Thus, the foreign tax credit limitation is inflated by income that is not within any foreign country's tax jurisdiction."). Based on the legislative history, the Treasury Department and the IRS believe that sales of property in space or international water — with the exception of sales of inventory property in space or international water for use, consumption, or disposition outside space, international water, and the United States — should be considered space or ocean activity and that the source of income from such sales activity should be determined under section 863(d). As a result, no changes were made in response to this comment.

b. Purchased Versus Produced Property Sold for Use, Consumption, or Disposition in the United States

One commentator questioned the appropriateness of differences in determining the source of sales income depending on whether the taxpayer produced or purchased the property sold. Under the proposed regulations, when property produced by the taxpayer is sold in space or international water, the source of gross income allocable to sales activity is generally based on the citizenship or residence of the taxpayer, applying the rules of proposed §1.863–8(b)(1) or (2), as applicable (and not the title passage rule) — subject to the foregoing inventory exception for property that will be used, consumed, or disposed of outside space, international water, and the United States. A slightly different rule applied to sales of property that had been purchased by the taxpayer. While the proposed regulations also provided that, for purchased property, the source of gross income allocable to sales activity is generally based on the citizenship or residence of the taxpayer, the inventory exception for purchased property only required that the property be used, consumed, or disposed of outside space and international water.

The inventory exceptions for produced and purchased property were intended to produce different results when inventory property is used, consumed, or disposed of in the United States. In such case, the source of produced inventory property sales income is generally based on the citizenship or residence of the taxpayer, applying the rules of proposed §1.863–8(b)(1) or (2), because the inventory exception did not extend to produced property sold for use, consumption, or disposition in the United States. In contrast, the source of purchased inventory property sales income is generally based on title passage under Treas. Reg. §1.861–7(c) because the inventory exception did extend to purchased property even if it was sold for use, consumption, or disposition in the United States. The Treasury Department and the IRS believe that this difference between the produced and purchased property rules in the space and ocean context is consistent with the difference in the rules for sales of produced and purchased property outside the space and ocean context. In particular, under section 863(a) and (b) and the regulations thereunder, if property is produced in the United States and sold for use, consumption, or disposition in the United States, the place of sale will be presumed to be the United States, and income attributable to the sales activity will be U.S. source income. See §1.863–3(c)(2). There is, however, no comparable rule for purchased property under section 862(a)(6) or the regulations thereunder. Thus, the final regulations simply continue in the space and ocean context the varying treatment elsewhere for sales of purchased property and sales of produced property.

In response to comments, however, the produced and purchased property rules have been modified to be similar in structure and style, to better reflect and highlight the differences between these two rules.

5. *Allocations*

Taxpayers must allocate gross income under paragraphs (b)(1) and (b)(2) of proposed §1.863–8 among U.S., foreign, and space or ocean activities. Under proposed §1.863–8(b)(3)(ii)(C), allocations are also made between production activity occurring in space or international water and that occurring outside space and international water. Finally, allocations are also made under proposed §1.863–8(b)(4) between services performed in space or international water and services performed outside space and international water. In performing these allocations, the proposed regulations generally provided that taxpayers should consider the relative value of functions performed, resources employed, or risks assumed in different locations. Moreover, the preamble to the proposed regulations provided that allocations should be based generally on section 482 principles. Commentators noted that little guidance is given as to the mechanics of allocation other than the statement that the principles of section 482 should be used. Commentators stated that allocation of gross income based on section 482 principles will result in added expense, uncertainty, and extra burden on multinational taxpayers who are already required to undertake and update functional analyses and satisfy substantial documentation requirements.

While the final regulations were not changed in response to these comments, the Treasury Department and the IRS believe that some clarification is warranted. In suggesting the use of section 482 principles as a guide, the Treasury Department and the IRS intend for taxpayers to adopt a reasonable approach to the allocations required in this area. Taxpayers know their businesses and will generally be in the best position to fashion a reasonable method that most reliably reflects the relative value of functions performed, resources employed, and risks assumed in different locations. In the preamble to the proposed regulations, the Treasury Department and the IRS solicited comments on alternative methods of allocation for particular industries and criteria that could be used to evaluate the reasonableness of such methods. No such comments were received. One commentator noted, however, that the proposed regulations perhaps reflected what taxpayers in these industries have already been doing in order to determine the character and source of their space and ocean income. Consequently, the Treasury Department and the IRS believe that allocations of gross income based on functions performed, resources employed, and risks assumed are appropriate in these circumstances.

6. *Separation of a single transaction and aggregation of multiple transactions*

Paragraphs (d)(1)(i) and (d)(1)(ii) of §1.863–8 of the proposed regulations provided that for purposes of determining space or ocean activity, the Commissioner may separate parts of a single transaction or combine separate transactions into a single transaction. One commentator stated that this is a "one-way" street, as only the Commissioner has the authority to separate or combine transactions for purposes of the proposed regulations.

The final regulations do not change this rule. The Treasury Department and the IRS believe taxpayers are not inappropriately disadvantaged by this rule because taxpayers generally have the ability to structure their transactions in line with the economic prospects of their businesses. In addition, the Commissioner's ability to separate or combine transactions is not unfettered. Rather, the Commissioner may only separate or combine transactions to better reflect the value of functions performed, resources employed, or risks assumed. A taxpayer can always protect itself against recharacterization by adopting an arrangement that appropriately reflects the economic realities of a transaction or series of transactions. The taxpayer is clearly in the best position at the outset to structure its arrangements in this manner. In addition, taxpayers traditionally are not permitted to restructure retroactively the form of their completed transactions. Thus, the Treasury Department and the IRS believe that the limited "one-way" rule is appropriate in this case.

7. *Income derived from the leasing of shipping cargo containers*

One commentator requested that the Treasury Department and the IRS make clear that the final regulations under section 863(d) do not apply to income derived from the leasing of shipping cargo containers and that such income should be treated as rental income, sourced under sections 861 and 862. This commentator noted that valid arguments also exist for treating income derived from the leasing of shipping cargo containers as transportation income; however, in the commentator's view, the most appropriate treatment is rental income treatment, sourced under sections 861 and 862.

The treatment of income derived from the leasing of shipping cargo containers is not covered by these final regulations. Instead, the Treasury Department and the IRS intend to address the treatment of such income explicitly in separate guidance. That guidance may apply section 863(c), section 863(d), or other provisions to source income derived from the leasing of shipping cargo containers. Any such guidance will be prospective in nature. Until such time, the treatment of such income will be determined under existing law.

B. *Communications Activity under Section 863(a), (d), and (e)*

Section 863(e) governs the source of income from international communications activities (international communications income). International communications income is defined in section 863(e)(2) as income derived from the transmission of communications or data between the United States and a foreign country (or possession of the United States). Section 863(e)(1)(A) provides that any international communications income of a United States person is sourced 50 percent in the United States and 50 percent outside the United States (50/50 source rule). Section 863(e)(1)(A) does not provide for any statutory or regulatory exceptions to this 50/50 source rule. In contrast, section 863(e)(1)(B)(i) provides that any international communications income of a foreign person is sourced outside the United States, except as provided in regulations or in section 863(e)(1)(B)(ii). The exception under section 863(e)(1)(B)(ii) provides that if a foreign person maintains an office or other fixed place of business in the United States, any international communications income attributable to such office or other fixed place of business is U.S. source income.

Section 1.863–9 of the proposed regulations generally provided rules for determining the source of international communications income under section 863(e) and other communications income under section 863(a) and (d). Proposed §1.863–9(b)(1) reflected the rule under section 863(e)(1)(A) that a United States person's international communications income is 50 percent U.S. source income and 50 percent foreign source income. Proposed §1.863–9(b)(2) reflected the general rule under section 863(e)(1)(B) that a foreign person's international communications income is foreign source income.

Consistent with the statutory exception under section 863(e)(1)(B)(ii), proposed §1.863–9(b)(2)(iii) provided that any international communications income derived by a foreign person, other than a CFC, that is attributable to an office or other fixed place of business of the foreign person in the United States is U.S. source income. International communications income is attributable to an office or other fixed place of business to the extent of functions performed, resources employed, or risks assumed by the office or other fixed place of business. In addition to the statutory exception under section 863(e)(1)(B)(ii), section 863(e)(1)(B) provides general regulatory authority to depart from the general 100 percent foreign source rule for foreign persons. Thus, pursuant to this regulatory authority, the proposed regulations contained additional exceptions to the general rule applicable to foreign persons. In particular, the proposed regulations provided that international communications income derived by a CFC is 50 percent U.S. source income and 50 percent foreign source income (the same as for United States persons). The proposed regulations also provided that international communications income derived by a foreign person, other than a CFC, engaged in a trade or business within the United States is income from sources within the United States to the extent the income, based on all the facts and circumstances, is attributable to functions performed, resources employed, or risks assumed within the United States.

In addition to the general source rules for international communications income of United States and foreign persons, the proposed regulations also provided rules, applicable to both United States and foreign persons, for income from U.S. communications, foreign communications, space/ocean communications, and communications where endpoints are indeterminate. These rules, as well as modifications to the proposed regulations, are discussed below.

1. *Income characterization rules for communications income*

Section 1.863–9(h)(3) of the proposed regulations provided that the type of communications activity (and thus the applicable source rule) is determined by identifying the two points between which the taxpayer is paid to transmit the communication. For United States and foreign persons, U.S. communications income is entirely U.S. source income. A taxpayer derives U.S. communications income when the taxpayer is paid to transmit between two points in the United States or between the United States and a point in space or international water. In contrast, foreign communications income is entirely foreign source income for United States and foreign persons. A taxpayer derives foreign communications income when the taxpayer is paid to transmit between two points in a foreign country or countries (or a possession or possessions of the United States), between a foreign country and a possession of the United States, or between a foreign country (or a possession of the United States) and a point in space or international water. Finally, the proposed regulations provided different source rules for international communications income of United States and foreign persons. See section B.3 of this preamble for further discussion. A taxpayer derives international communications income when the taxpayer is paid to transmit between a point in the United States and a point in a foreign country (or a possession of the United States). When a taxpayer cannot establish the two points between which the taxpayer is paid to transmit the communication, §1.863–9(f) of the proposed regulation provided a default source rule under which all the income derived by the taxpayer from such communications activity is U.S. source income.

Commentators stated that the treatment of communications income as U.S. source income when the endpoints are indeterminate is overbroad and harsh, particularly as it relates to foreign taxpayers. Commentators also stated that taxpayers would have to commit significant resources to develop the technology necessary to identify the endpoints of communications. One commentator stated that it is unclear that a reliable system can be created at any expense to establish the endpoints of the transmission under all circumstances. Commentators suggested instead the use of any reasonable method to establish the endpoints between which a taxpayer is paid to transmit the communications. One commentator suggested that the Treasury Department and the IRS consider employing the Industry Issue Resolution Program or Prefiling Agreement Program as aids in the administration of a reasonable method rule.

The Treasury Department and the IRS solicited comments on the challenges to identifying the endpoints of communications in specific industries or situations, as well as suggestions for rules that are responsive to these particular challenges. The Treasury Department and the IRS also solicited comments on methods to establish the endpoints of a communication that may be reasonable for particular industries, as well as criteria that may be appropriate to evaluate the reasonableness of such methods. In response, one commentator submitted examples of reasonable methods to establish the endpoints between which a taxpayer is paid to transmit the communications. The examples relied on statistical reports of data such as minutes used, areas of transmission, port locations, and transport charges. This commentator noted that current federal regulations already require telecommunications companies to submit some of these reports to certain governmental agencies, for example, the Federal Communications Commission.

In light of the potential complexity in identifying the type of communications activity and in response to comments, the final regulations provide that a taxpayer may satisfy the requirement that the taxpayer establish the two points between which the taxpayer is paid to transmit, and bears the risk of transmitting, the communication by using any consistently applied reasonable method to establish one or both endpoints. In doing so, the taxpayer carries the burden of proof and must establish that the method used is reasonable (taking into account all of the facts and circumstances) and is consistently applied. In satisfying its burden of proof, a taxpayer will need to maintain reasonable records of communications activities. Depending on the facts and circumstances, methods based on, for example, records of port or transport charges, customer billing records, a satellite footprint, or records of termination fees made pursuant to an international settlement agreement may be reasonable. In addition, practices used by taxpayers to classify or categorize certain communications activity in connection with preparation of statements and analyses for the use of management, creditors, minority shareholders, joint ventures, or other parties or governmental agencies in interest may be reliable indicators of the reasonableness of the method chosen, but need not be accorded conclusive weight by the Commissioner. Furthermore, in evaluating the reasonableness of the method chosen, consideration will be given to all the facts and circumstances, including whether the endpoints would otherwise be identifiable absent this reasonable method provision.

Along with resultant changes made to the text of the final regulations, several examples have been added to §1.863–9(j) of the final regulations that illustrate instances where the taxpayer may be able to use reasonable methods to determine the endpoints between which the taxpayer is paid to transmit the communications.

2. *The paid-to-do rule with respect to foreign-originating communications*

Under the proposed regulations, a taxpayer derives income from a certain type of communications activity (for example, foreign communications or international communications) only if the taxpayer is paid to transmit, and bears the risk of transmitting (the paid-to-do rule), the communications of such type. See Prop. Treas. Reg. §1.863–9(h)(2) and (3). This is the case even if the taxpayer contracts out the transmission function.

Commentators stated that application of the paid-to-do rule in all instances would give rise to results that are inconsistent with Congressional intent and may result in excessive amounts of U.S. source income. One commentator noted that in some cases, while it is clear that a communication originated in a foreign country and that a U.S. telecommunications company is paid to terminate the foreign-originating traffic in the United States, it is unclear exactly where the U.S. telecommunications company picked up the communication. This lack of clarity often may be due to legal restrictions in certain foreign countries on ownership of capacity and carriage of transmissions by non-nationals. It can also be due to the fact that the international settlement agreements under which major international telecommunications carriers operate often do not specify where the traffic is picked up or handed off, and in some cases the hand-off point is specified by reference to a mid-point convention, even though the transmission signal, from a technical standpoint, travels from end-to-end with no real points in-between. The commentator further stated that at the time section 863(e) was enacted, U.S. carriers were generally not allowed to own and operate facilities in foreign countries; specifically, no U.S. carrier could carry a foreign-to-U.S. or U.S.-to-foreign transmission end-to-end. Thus, concluded the commentator, Congress focused on the endpoints of the communications rather than where the activities constituting the transmission of communications take place. The commentator suggested a rule that would provide that when a taxpayer is paid to transmit foreign-originating communications from a point outside the United States to a point in the United States, the taxpayer should be deemed to have been paid to transmit the communications from a point in the foreign country in which the communication originated.

Upon further consideration, the Treasury Department and the IRS believe that the paid-to-do rule may be over-inclusive in certain cases. Accordingly, the final regulations provide that international communications income also includes income derived from communications activity when the taxpayer is paid to transmit foreign-originating communications (communications with a beginning point in a foreign country or a possession of the United States) from a point in space or international water to a point in the United States. Also, a new example has been added to §1.863–9(j) of the final regulations to illustrate the changes made in the final regulations with respect to foreign-originating communications.

The changes made in the final regulations only affect communications that originate in a foreign country (or a possession of the United States) and does not affect communications that originate in space, international water, or the United States. The Treasury Department and the IRS continue to believe that communications activity is most appropriately characterized based on the two points between which the taxpayer is paid to transmit, and bears the risk of transmitting, the communication.

3. *Determining the source of communications income based on functions performed, resources employed, or risks assumed in a foreign country or countries*

As discussed above, the proposed regulations provided that the source of communications income is largely dependant on the type of communications activity and the citizenship or residence of the taxpayer. However, the proposed regulations provided for two instances where (in addition to the type of communications activity and the citizenship or residence of the taxpayer) the source of communications income may depend on functions performed, resources employed, or risks assumed. First, the proposed regulations provided that international communications income derived by a foreign person, other than a CFC, that is attributable to an office or other fixed place of business of the foreign person in the United States is U.S. source income. The proposed regulations provided that international communications income is attributable to an office or other fixed place of business to the extent of functions performed, resources employed, or risks assumed by the office or other fixed place of business. Second, the proposed regulations provided that international communications income derived by a foreign person, other than a CFC, engaged in a trade or business within the United States is income from sources within the United States to the extent the income, based on all the facts and circumstances, is attributable to functions performed, resources employed, or risks assumed within the United States.

Commentators suggested that the final regulations also provide for similar rules that would source communications income as foreign source income based on functions performed, resources employed, or risks assumed in a foreign country or countries. For example, one commentator suggested that the source of international and U.S. communications income derived by any United States or foreign person (including branches, partnerships, and disregarded entities) engaged in a trade or business in a foreign country or countries is income from sources without the United States to the extent the income, based on all the facts and circumstances, is attributable to functions performed, resources employed, or risks assumed in such foreign country or countries.

While the Treasury Department and the IRS recognize that commentators' suggestion to provide for a source rule based on functions performed, resources employed, or risks assumed in a foreign country or countries is reasonable, as explained below, the Treasury Department and the IRS believe that the statute and legislative history preclude such an option.

a. International Communications Income

Consistent with section 863(e)(1)(A), proposed §1.863–9(b)(1) provided that international communications income of a United States person is 50 percent U.S. source income and 50 percent foreign source income. One commentator suggested that it may be appropriate, in certain situations, to depart from the 50/50 source rule to provide special rules for foreign activities. According to the commentator, as a result of local regulatory requirements, U.S.-based international telecommunications providers often need to conduct portions of their international business through locally formed entities, and such entities are fully subject to foreign tax on their income. The commentator therefore concluded that a source rule for international communications income based on functions performed, resources employed, or risks assumed in a foreign country or countries is not only equitable but also consistent with treatment accorded to foreign persons having a U.S. fixed placed of business or engaged in a U.S. trade or business.

The Treasury Department and the IRS recognize that a source rule based on functions performed, resources employed, or risks assumed may be a reasonable alternative to the 50/50 source rule. Nonetheless, they continue to believe that the 50/50 source rule is the method that must be used to determine the source of a United States person's international communications income. This is because section 863(e)(1)(A) provides for an explicit 50/50 source rule for those persons without exception. In contrast, section 863(e)(1)(B) provides that a foreign person's international communications income is generally sourced outside the United States, except as provided in regulations. The Treasury Department and the IRS believe that the express grant of regulatory authority in the case of foreign persons and the omission of any such authority in the case of United States persons indicate that Congress intended the 50/50 sourcing rule be applied to United States persons without regulatory modification. There is nothing in the statute or legislative history that clearly demonstrates a different intention. In contrast, section 863(e)(1)(B)(ii) provides for a special source rule with respect to foreign persons with an office or other fixed place of business in the United States. A similar rule is not provided with respect to a United States person's foreign activities. Thus, Congress chose a rule that sourced international communications income of foreign persons in certain instances based on the place of their activities, but expressly chose the 50/50 method to source international communications income of United States persons, regardless of the place of their activities.

The Treasury Department and the IRS recognize that the statute does not require strict application of the 50/50 source rule for CFCs. Section 863(e)(1)(B) only provides that the international communications income of a foreign person is foreign source income, except as provided in regulations. Consistent with and in light of this regulatory authority, however, the Treasury Department and the IRS believe that the 50/50 source rule is the most appropriate method to determine the source of a CFC's international communications income. This approach addresses the concern of the Treasury Department and the IRS that United States persons may use CFCs to obtain benefits that are inconsistent with the purposes of section 863(e). Consequently, the rules for determining the source of international communications income derived by a CFC should be the same as the rules for determining the source of such income if it is derived by a United States person. In addition, the Treasury Department and the IRS believe that the 50/50 source rule for CFCs, as opposed to the 100 percent U.S. source rule that was originally proposed as part of the 2001 proposed regulations, should limit the potential for multiple levels of taxation that commentators raised with respect to those prior proposed regulations.

b. U.S. Communications Income

Section 1.863–9(c) of the proposed regulations provided that income derived by a United States or foreign person from U.S. communications activity is entirely from sources within the United States. One commentator noted that a foreign person deriving income from the transmission of communications between a point in the United States and another point in the United States or between a point in the United States and a point in space or international water has 100 percent U.S. source income, even if much or all of the activity involved is outside the United States. In contrast, under the space and ocean rules, a foreign person has U.S. source income only to the extent the income is attributable to functions performed, resources employed, or risks assumed within the United States. Commentators therefore suggested modification of the 100 percent U.S. source rule for U.S. communications income derived by United States and foreign persons to take into account foreign activities.

The Treasury Department and the IRS recognize that a source rule based on functions performed, resources employed, or risks assumed may be a reasonable alternative to the 100 percent U.S. source rule for U.S. communications. Nonetheless, the Treasury Department and the IRS believe that Congress did not intend such an option. The legislative history indicates that if a communication is between two points within the United States, the "income attributable thereto is to be sourced *entirely* as U.S. source income." S. REP. NO. 99–313, 1986–3 C.B. 359 (emphasis added). Congress intended such a result "even if the communication is routed through a satellite located in space, regardless of the satellite's location." *Id.* Thus, the legislative history clearly provides that Congress intended that U.S. communications income be sourced entirely as U.S. source income.

4. *International communications income derived by a foreign person (other than a CFC)*

Proposed §1.863–9(b)(2) reflected the general rule under section 863(e)(1)(B) that a foreign person's international communications income is foreign source income. Consistent with the statutory exception under section 863(e)(1)(B)(ii), proposed §1.863–9(b)(2)(iii) provided that any international communications income derived by a foreign person, other than a CFC, that is attributable to an office or other fixed place of business of the foreign person in the United States is U.S. source income. International communications income is attributable to an office or other fixed place of business to the extent of functions performed, resources employed, or risks assumed by the office or other fixed place of business. Pursuant to the grant of regulatory authority under section 863(e)(1)(B), the proposed regulations provided other exceptions to the general rule for foreign persons. The first exception is the 50/50 source rule for CFCs under §1.863–9(b)(2)(ii) of the proposed regulations, as discussed above. The second exception was provided in §1.863–9(b)(2)(iv) of the proposed regulations and applied to foreign persons other than CFCs. Section 1.863–9(b)(2)(iv) of the proposed regulations provided that international communications income derived by a foreign person, other than a CFC, engaged in a trade or business within the United States, that is attributable to functions performed, resources employed, or risks assumed within the United States is U.S. source income. One commentator noted that it is unclear why a separate rule is needed for a fixed place of business in the United States and a U.S. trade or business because international communications income attributable to a fixed place of business in the United States should also be attributable to functions performed, resources employed and risks assumed within the United States.

As indicated, the office or other fixed place of business rule under §1.863–9(b)(2)(iii) of the proposed regulations was derived from the statutory language of section 863(e), while the trade or business rule under §1.863–9(b)(2)(iv) of the proposed regulations was derived from the express grant of regulatory authority to source international communications income of foreign persons as other than foreign source. The Treasury Department and the IRS recognize that in most situations, the latter trade or business rule would indeed subsume the former fixed place of business rule, but still believe that the later rule serves an important function. The trade or business rule addresses the concern of the Treasury Department and the IRS that a foreign person could avoid a U.S. fixed place of business under section 863(e)(1)(B)(ii), yet engage in significant communications activity in the United States. The Treasury Department and the IRS believe that Congress intended that a foreign person engaged in substantial business in the United States be subject to U.S. tax on that communications activity.

5. *Allocations*

Section 1.863–9(h)(1)(ii) of the proposed regulations provided that to the extent that a taxpayer's transaction consists in part of non-*de minimis* communications activity and in part of non-*de minimis* non-communications activity, each part of the transaction must be treated as a separate transaction. Gross income is then allocated to each communications activity transaction and each non-communications activity transaction to the extent the income, based on all the facts and circumstances, is attributable to functions performed, resources employed, or risks assumed in each such activity. Moreover, the Treasury Department and the IRS suggested in the preamble to the proposed regulations that allocations of gross income should be based generally on section 482 principles. One commentator stated that the complexities inherent in allocating income, based on section 482 principles, between the separated transactions are significant.

While the final regulations were not changed in response to this comment, as in the case of allocations for space and ocean income, the Treasury Department and the IRS believe that some clarification is warranted. In suggesting the use of section 482 principles as a guide, the Treasury Department and the IRS intend for taxpayers to adopt a reasonable approach to the allocations required in this area. Taxpayers know their businesses and will generally be in the best position to fashion a reasonable method that most reliably reflects the relative value of functions performed, resources employed, and risks assumed in different locations. In the preamble to the proposed regulations, the Treasury Department and the IRS solicited comments on alternative methods of allocation for particular industries and criteria that could be used to evaluate the reasonableness of such methods. No such comments were received. One commentator noted, however, that the proposed regulations perhaps reflected what taxpayers in these industries have already been doing in order to determine the character and source of their communications income. Consequently, as in the case of space and ocean income, the Treasury Department and the IRS believe that allocations of gross income based on functions performed, resources employed, and risks assumed are appropriate in these circumstances.

Special Analyses

It has been determined that this Treasury decision is not a significant regulatory action as defined in Executive Order 12866. Therefore, a regulatory assessment pursuant to that Order is not required. It has also been determined that section 553(b) of the Administrative Procedure Act (5 U.S.C. chapter 5) does not apply to these regulations. Pursuant to the Regulatory Flexibility Act (5 U.S.C. chapter 6), it is hereby certified that the collection of information in these regulations will not have a significant economic impact on a substantial number of small entities. This certification is based on the fact that the rules provided in these regulations principally affect large multinational corporations that pay foreign taxes on income derived from substantial foreign operations and that use these and any other applicable source rules in determining their foreign tax credit. Accordingly, a Regulatory Flexibility Act assessment is not required. Pursuant to section 7805(f) of the Internal Revenue Code, the NPRM preceding these regulations were submitted to the Chief Counsel for Advocacy of the Small Business Administration for comment on their impact on small business.

Drafting Information

The principal author of these regulations is H. Michael Huynh of the Office of the Associate Chief Counsel (International). However, other personnel from the Treasury Department and the IRS participated in their development.

* * * * *

Adoption of Amendments to the Regulations

Accordingly, 26 CFR parts 1 and 602 are amended as follows:

PART 1—INCOME TAXES

Paragraph 1. The authority citation for part 1 is amended by adding entries in numerical order to read, in part, as follows:

Authority: 26 U.S.C. 7805 * * *

Section 1.863–8 also issued under 26 U.S.C. 863(a), (b) and (d). * * *

Section 1.863–9 also issued under 26 U.S.C. 863(a), (d) and (e). * * *

Par. 2. Section 1.863–3 is amended by:

1. Adding a sentence after the first sentence in paragraph (a)(1).

2. Adding a sentence at the end of paragraph (c)(1)(i)(A).

3. Adding a sentence after the first sentence in paragraph (c)(2).

The additions read as follows:

§1.863–3 Allocation and apportionment of income from certain sales of inventory.

(a) * * * (1) * * * To determine the source of income from sales of property produced by the taxpayer, when the property is either produced in whole or in part in space or on or under water not within the jurisdiction (as recognized by the United States) of a foreign country, possession of the United States, or the United States (in international water), or is sold in space or international water, the rules of §1.863–8 apply, and the rules of this section do not apply except to the extent provided in §1.863–8. * * *

* * * * *

(c) * * * (1) * * * (i) * * * (A) * * * For rules regarding the source of income when production takes place, in whole or in part, in space or international water, the rules of §1.863–8 apply, and the rules of this section do not apply except to the extent provided in §1.863–8.

* * * * *

(2) * * * Notwithstanding any other provision, for rules regarding the source of income when a sale takes place in space or international water, the rules of §1.863–8 apply, and the rules of this section do not apply except to the extent provided in §1.863–8. * * *

* * * * *

Par. 3. Sections 1.863–8 and 1.863–9 are added to read as follows:

§1.863–8 Source of income derived from space and ocean activity under section 863(d).

(a) *In general.* Income of a United States or a foreign person derived from space and ocean activity (space and ocean income) is sourced under the rules of this section, notwithstanding any other provision, including sections 861, 862, 863, and 865. A taxpayer will not be considered to derive income from space or ocean activity, as defined in paragraph (d) of this section, if such activity is performed by another person, subject to the rules for the treatment of consolidated groups in §1.1502–13.

(b) *Source of gross income from space and ocean activity*—(1) *Space and ocean income derived by a United States person.* Space and ocean income derived by a United States person is income from sources within the United States. However, space and ocean income derived by a United States person is income from sources without the United States to the extent the income, based on all the facts and circumstances, is attributable to functions performed, resources employed, or risks assumed in a foreign country or countries.

(2) *Space and ocean income derived by a foreign person*—(i) *In general.* Space and ocean income derived by a person other than a United States person is income from sources without the United States, except as otherwise provided in this paragraph (b)(2).

(ii) *Space and ocean income derived by a controlled foreign corporation.* Space and ocean income derived by a controlled foreign corporation within the meaning of section 957 (CFC) is income from sources within the United States. However, space and ocean income derived by a CFC is income from sources without the United States to the extent the income, based on all the facts and circumstances, is attributable to functions performed, resources employed, or risks assumed in a foreign country or countries.

(iii) *Space and ocean income derived by foreign persons engaged in a trade or business within the United States.* Space and ocean income derived by a foreign person (other than a CFC) engaged in a trade or business within the United States is income from sources within the United States to the extent the income, based on all the facts and circumstances, is attributable to functions performed, resources employed, or risks assumed within the United States.

(3) *Source rules for income from certain sales of property*—(i) *Sales of purchased property.* When a taxpayer sells purchased property in space or international water, the source of gross income from the sale generally will be determined under paragraph (b)(1) or (2) of this section, as applicable. However, if such property is inventory property within the meaning of section 1221(a)(1) (inventory property) and is sold for use, consumption, or disposition outside space and international water, the source of income from the sale will be determined under §1.861–7(c).

(ii) *Sales of property produced by the taxpayer*—(A) *General.* If the taxpayer both produces property and sells such property, the taxpayer must allocate gross income from such sales between production activity and sales activity under the 50/50 method. Under the 50/50 method, one-half of the taxpayer's gross income will be considered income allocable to production activity, and the source of that income will be determined under paragraph (b)(3)(ii)(B) or (C) of this section. The remaining one-half of such gross income will be considered income allocable to sales activity, and the source of that income will be determined under paragraph (b)(3)(ii)(D) of this section.

(B) *Production only in space or international water, or only outside space and international water.* When production occurs only in space or international water, income allocable to production activity is sourced under paragraph (b)(1) or (2) of this section, as applicable. When production occurs only outside space and international water, income allocable to production activity is sourced under §1.863–3(c)(1).

(C) *Production both in space or international water and outside space and international water.* When property is produced both in space or international water and outside space and international water, gross income allocable to production activity must be allocated to production occurring in space or international water and production occurring outside space and international water. Such gross income is allocated to production activity occurring in space or international water to the extent the income, based on all the facts and circumstances, is attributable to functions performed, resources employed, or risks assumed in space or international water. The balance of such gross income is allocated to production activity occurring outside space and international water. The source of gross income allocable to production activity in space or international water is determined under paragraph (b)(1) or (2) of this section, as applicable. The source of gross income allocated to production activity occurring outside space and international water is determined under §1.863–3(c)(1).

(D) *Source of income allocable to sales activity.* When property produced by the taxpayer is sold outside space and international water, the source of gross income allocable to sales activity will be determined under §§1.861–7(c) and 1.863–3(c)(2). When property produced by the taxpayer is sold in space or international water, the source of gross income allocable to sales activity generally will be determined under paragraph (b)(1) or (2) of this section, as applicable. However, if such property is inventory property within the meaning of section 1221(a)(1) and is sold in space or international water for use, consumption, or disposition outside space, international water, and the United States, the source of gross income allocable to sales activity will be determined under §§1.861–7(c) and 1.863–3(c)(2).

(4) *Special rule for determining the source of gross income from services.* To the extent a transaction characterized as the performance of a service constitutes a space or ocean activity, as determined under paragraph (d)(2)(ii) of this section, the source of gross income derived from such transaction is determined under paragraph (b)(1) or (2) of this section.

(5) *Special rule for determining source of income from communications activity (other than income from international communications activity).* Space and ocean activity, as defined in paragraph (d) of this section, includes activity that occurs in space or international water that is characterized as a communications activity as defined in §1.863–9(h)(1) (other than international communications activity). The source of space and ocean income that is also communications income as defined in §1.863–9(h)(2) (but not space/ocean communications income as defined in §1.863–9(h)(3)(v)) is determined under the rules of §1.863–9(c), (d), and (f), as applicable, rather than under paragraph (b) of this section. The source of space and ocean income that is also space/ocean communications income as defined in §1.863–9(h)(3)(v) is determined under the rules of paragraph (b) of this section. See §1.863–9(e).

(c) *Taxable income.* When a taxpayer allocates gross income under paragraph (b)(1), (b)(2), (b)(3)(ii)(C), or (b)(4) of this section, the taxpayer must allocate expenses, losses, and other deductions as prescribed in §§1.861–8 through 1.861–14T to the class or classes of gross income that include the income so allocated in each case. A taxpayer must then apply the rules of §§1.861–8 through 1.861–14T to apportion properly amounts of expenses, losses, and other deductions so allocated to such gross income between gross income from sources within the United States and gross income from sources without the United States.

(d) *Space and ocean activity*—(1) *Definition*—(i) *Space activity.* In general, space activity is any activity conducted in space. For purposes of this section, space means any area not within the jurisdiction (as recognized by the United States) of a foreign country, possession of the United States, or the United States, and not in international water. For purposes of determining space activity, the Commissioner may separate parts of a single transaction into separate transactions or combine separate transactions as part of a single transaction. Paragraph (d)(3) of this section lists specific exceptions to the general definition of space activity. Activities that constitute space activity include but are not limited to—

(A) Performance and provision of services in space, as defined in paragraph (d)(2)(ii) of this section;

(B) Leasing of equipment located in space, including spacecraft (for example, satellites) or transponders located in space;

(C) Licensing of technology or other intangibles for use in space;

(D) Production, processing, or creation of property in space, as defined in paragraph (d)(2)(i) of this section;

(E) Activity occurring in space that is characterized as communications activity (other than international communications activity) under §1.863–9(h)(1);

(F) Underwriting income from the insurance of risks on activities that produce space income; and

(G) Sales of property in space (see §1.861–7(c)).

(ii) *Ocean activity.* In general, ocean activity is any activity conducted on or under water not within the jurisdiction (as recognized by the United States) of a foreign country, possession of the United States, or the United States (collectively, in international water). For purposes of determining ocean activity, the Commissioner may separate parts of a single transaction into separate transactions or combine separate transactions as part of a single transaction. Paragraph (d)(3) of this section lists specific exceptions to the general definition of ocean activity. Activities that constitute ocean activity include but are not limited to—

(A) Performance and provision of services in international water, as defined in paragraph (d)(2)(ii) of this section;

(B) Leasing of equipment located in international water, including underwater cables;

(C) Licensing of technology or other intangibles for use in international water;

(D) Production, processing, or creation of property in international water, as defined in paragraph (d)(2)(i) of this section;

(E) Activity occurring in international water that is characterized as communications activity (other than international communications activity) under §1.863–9(h)(1);

(F) Underwriting income from the insurance of risks on activities that produce ocean income;

(G) Sales of property in international water (see §1.861–7(c));

(H) Any activity performed in Antarctica;

(I) The leasing of a vessel that does not transport cargo or persons for hire between ports-of-call (for example, the leasing of a vessel to engage in research activities in international water); and

(J) The leasing of drilling rigs, extraction of minerals, and performance and provision of services related thereto, except as provided in paragraph (d)(3)(ii) of this section.

(2) *Determining a space or ocean activity*—(i) *Production of property in space or international water.* For purposes of this section, production activity means an activity that creates, fabricates, manufactures, extracts, processes, cures, or ages property within the meaning of section 864(a) and §1.864–1.

(ii) *Special rule for performance of services*—(A) *General.* Except as provided in paragraph (d)(2)(ii)(B) of this section, if a transaction is characterized as the performance of a service, then such service will be treated as a space or ocean activity in its entirety when any part of the service is performed in space or international water. Services are performed in space or international water if functions are performed, resources are employed, or risks are assumed in space or international water, regardless of whether performed by personnel, equipment, or otherwise.

(B) *Exception to the general rule.* If the taxpayer can demonstrate the value of the service attributable to performance occurring in space or international water, and the value of the service attributable to performance occurring outside space and international water, then such service will be treated as space or ocean activity only to the extent of the activity performed in space or international water. The value of the service is attributable to performance occurring in space or international water to the extent the performance of the service, based on all the facts and circumstances, is attributable to functions performed, resources employed, or risks assumed in space or international water. In addition, if the taxpayer can demonstrate, based on all the facts and circumstances, that the value of the service attributable to performance in space and international water is *de minimis*, such service will not be treated as space or ocean activity.

(3) *Exceptions to space or ocean activity.* Space or ocean activity does not include the following types of activities:

(i) Any activity giving rise to transportation income as defined in section 863(c).

(ii) Any activity with respect to mines, oil and gas wells, or other natural deposits, to the extent the mines, wells, or natural deposits are located within the jurisdiction (as recognized by the United States) of any country, including the United States and its possessions.

(iii) Any activity giving rise to international communications income as defined in §1.863–9(h)(3)(ii).

(e) *Treatment of partnerships.* This section is applied at the partner level.

(f) *Examples.* The following examples illustrate the rules of this section:

Example 1. Space activity—activity occurring on land and in space—(i) *Facts.* S, a United States person, owns satellites in orbit. S leases one of its satellites to A. S, as lessor, will not operate the satellite. Part of S's performance as lessor in this transaction occurs on land. Assume that the combination of S's activities is characterized as the lease of equipment.

(ii) *Analysis.* Because the leased equipment is located in space, the transaction is defined in its entirety as space activity under paragraph (d)(1)(i) of this section. Income derived from the lease will be sourced under paragraph (b)(1) of this section. Under paragraph (b)(1) of this section, S's space income is sourced outside the United States to the extent the income, based on all the facts and circumstances, is attributable to functions performed, resources employed, or risks assumed in a foreign country or countries.

Example 2. Space activity—(i) *Facts.* X is an Internet service provider. X offers a service that permits a customer (C) to connect to the Internet via a telephone call, initiated by the modem of C's personal computer, to a control center. X transmits information requested by C to C's personal computer, in part using satellite capacity leased by X from S. X performs the uplink and downlink functions. X charges its customers a flat monthly fee. Assume that neither X nor S derive international communications income within the meaning of §1.863–9(h)(3)(ii). In addition, assume that X is able to demonstrate, pursuant to paragraph (d)(2)(ii)(B) of this section, the extent to which the value of the service is attributable to functions performed, resources employed, and risks assumed in space.

(ii) *Analysis.* Under paragraph (d)(2)(ii) of this section, the service performed by X constitutes space activity to the extent the value of the service is attributable to functions performed, resources employed, and risks assumed in space. To the extent the service performed by X constitutes space activity, the source of X's income from the service transaction is determined under paragraph (b) of this section. To the extent the service performed by X does not constitute space or ocean activity, the source of X's income from the service is determined under sections 861, 862, and 863, as applicable. To the extent that X derives space and ocean income that is also communications income within the meaning of §1.863–9(h)(2), the source of X's income is determined under paragraph (b) of this section and §1.863–9(c), (d), and (f), as applicable, as provided in paragraph (b)(5) of this section. S derives space and ocean income that is also communications income within the meaning of §1.863–9(h)(2), and the source of S's income is therefore determined under paragraph (b) of this section and §1.863–9(c), (d), and (f), as applicable, as provided in paragraph (b)(5) of this section.

Example 3. Services as space activity—de minimis value attributable to performance occurring in space—(i) *Facts.* R owns a retail outlet in the United States. R engages S to provide a security system for R's premises. S operates its security system by transmitting images from R's premises directly to a satellite, and from the satellite to a group of S employees located in Country B, who monitor the premises by viewing the transmitted images. The satellite is used as a medium of delivery and not as a method of surveillance. O provides S with transponder capacity on O's satellite, which S uses to transmit those images. Assume that S's transaction with R is characterized as the performance of a service. Assume that O's provision of transponder capacity is also viewed as the provision of a service. Assume also that S is able to demonstrate, pursuant to §1.863–9(h)(1), that the value of the transaction with R attributable to communications activities is *de minimis*.

(ii) *Analysis.* S derives income from providing monitoring services. S can demonstrate, pursuant to paragraph (d)(2)(ii) of this section, that based on all the facts and circumstances, the value of S's service transaction attributable to performance in space is *de minimis*. Thus, S is not treated as engaged in a space activity, and none of S's income from the service transaction is space income. In addition, because S demonstrates that the value of the transaction with R attributable to communications activities is *de minimis*, S is not required under §1.863–9(h)(1)(ii) to treat the transaction as separate communications and non-communications transactions, and none of S's gross income from the transaction is treated as communications income within the meaning of §1.863–9(h)(2). O's provision of transponder capacity is viewed as the provision of a service. Based on all the facts and circumstances, the value of O's service transaction attributable to performance in space is not *de minimis*. Thus, O's activity will be considered space activity, pursuant to paragraph (d)(2)(ii) of this section, to the extent the value of the services transaction is attributable to performance in space (unless O's activity in space is international communications activity). To the extent that O derives communications income, the source of such income is determined under paragraph (b) of this section and §1.863–9(b), (c), (d), and (f), as applicable, as provided in paragraph (b)(5) of this section. R does not derive any income from space activity.

Example 4. Space activity—(i) *Facts.* L, a domestic corporation, offers programming and certain other services to customers located both in the United States and in foreign countries. Assume that L's provision of programming and other services in this *Example 4* is characterized as the provision of a service, and that no part of the service transaction occurs in space or international water. Assume that the delivery of the programming constitutes a separate transaction also characterized as the performance of a service. L uses satellite capacity acquired from S to deliver the programming service directly to customers' television sets. L performs the uplink and downlink functions, so that part of the value of the delivery transaction derives from functions performed and resources employed in space. Assume that these contributions to the value of the delivery transaction occurring in space are not considered *de minimis* under paragraph (d)(2)(ii)(B) of this section. Customer C pays L to provide and deliver programming to C's residence in the United States. Assume S's provision of satellite capacity in this *Example 4* is viewed as the provision of a service, and also that S does not derive international communications income within the meaning of §1.863–9(h)(3)(ii).

(ii) *Analysis.* S's activity will be considered space activity. To the extent that S derives space and ocean income that is also communications income under §1.863–9(h)(2), the source of S's income is determined under paragraph (b) of this section and §1.863 9(c), (d), and (f), as applicable, as provided in paragraph (b)(5) of this section. On these facts, L's activities are treated as two separate service transactions: the provision of programming (and other services), and the delivery of programming. L's income derived from provision of programming and other services is not income derived from space activity. L's delivery of programming and other services is considered space activity, pursuant to paragraph (d)(2)(ii) of this section, to the extent the value of the delivery transaction is attributable to performance in space. To the extent that the delivery of programming is treated as a space activity, the source of L's income derived from the delivery transaction is determined under paragraph (b)(1) of this section, as provided in paragraph (b)(4) of this section. To the extent that L derives space and ocean income that is also communications income within the meaning of §1.863–9(h)(2), the source of such income is determined under paragraph (b) of this section and §1.863–9(b), (c), (d), (e), and (f), as applicable, as provided in paragraph (b)(5) of this section.

Example 5. Space activity—(i) *Facts.* The facts are the same as in *Example 4*, except that L does not deliver the programming service directly but instead engages R, a domestic corporation specializing in content delivery, to deliver by transmission its programming. For all portions of a transmission which require satellite capacity, R, in turn, contracts out such functions to S. S performs the uplink and downlink functions, so that part of the value of the delivery transaction derives from functions performed and resources employed in space.

(ii) *Analysis.* L's activity will not be considered space activity because none of L's activity occurs in space. Thus, L does not derive any space and ocean income. L does, however, derive communications income within the meaning of §1.863–9(h)(2). This is the case even though L does not perform the transmission function because L is paid by Customer C to transmit, and bears the risk of transmitting, the communications or data. To the extent that L's activity consists in part of non-*de minimis* communications and non-*de minimis* non-communications activity, each part of the transaction must be treated as a separate transaction and gross income is allocated accordingly under §1.863–9(h)(1)(ii). In addition, L must also allocate expenses, losses, and other deductions, for example, payments to R, to the class or classes of gross income that include the income so allocated. R's activity will not be considered space activity. Since R contracts out all of the functions involving satellite capacity to S, no part of R's activity occurs in space. Thus, R does not derive any space and ocean income. R does, however, derive communications income within the meaning of §1.863–9(h)(2). This is the case even though R does not perform the transmission function because R is paid by L to transmit, and bears the risk of transmitting, the communications or data. S's activity will be considered space activity. To the extent that S derives space and ocean income that is also communications income within the meaning of §1.863–9(h)(2), the source of such income is determined under paragraph (b) of this section and §1.863–9(b), (c), (d), (e), and (f), as applicable, as provided in paragraph (b)(5) of this section.

Example 6. Space activity—treatment of land activity—(i) *Facts.* S, a United States person, offers remote imaging products and services to its customers. In year 1, S uses its satellite's remote sensors to gather data on certain geographical terrain. In year 3, C, a construction development company, contracts with S to obtain a satellite image of an area for site development work. S pulls data from its archives and transfers to C the images gathered in year 1, in a transaction that is characterized as a sale of the data. S's rights, title, and interest in the data pass to C in the United States. Before transferring the images to C, S uses computer software in its land-based office to enhance the images so that the images can be used.

(ii) *Analysis.* The collection of data and creation of images in space is characterized as the creation of property in space. Because S both produces and sells the data, S must allocate gross income from the sale of the data between production activity and sales activity under the 50/50 method of paragraph (b)(3)(ii)(A). The source of S's income allocable to production activity is determined under paragraph (b)(3)(ii)(C) of this section because production activities occur both in space and on land. The source of S's income attributable to sales activity is determined under paragraph (b)(3)(ii)(D) of this section (by reference to §1.863–3(c)(2)) as U.S. source income because S's rights, title, and interest in the data pass to C in the United States.

Example 7. Use of intangible property in space—(i) *Facts.* X acquires a license to use a particular satellite slot or orbit, which X sublicenses to C. C pays X a royalty.

(ii) *Analysis.* Because the royalty is paid for the right to use intangible property in space, the source of the royalty paid by C to X is determined under paragraph (b) of this section.

Example 8. Performance of services—(i) *Facts.* E, a domestic corporation, operates satellites with sensing equipment that can determine how much heat and light particular plants emit and reflect. Based on the data, E will provide F, a U.S. farmer, a report analyzing the data, which F will use in growing crops. E analyzes the data from offices located in the United States. Assume that E's combined activities are characterized as the performance of services.

(ii) *Analysis.* Based on all the facts and circumstances, the value of E's service transaction attributable to performance in space is not *de minimis*. Thus, E's activities will be considered space activities, pursuant to paragraph (d)(2)(ii) of this section, to the extent the value of E's service transaction is attributable to performance in space. To the extent E's service transaction constitutes a space activity, the source of E's income derived from the service transaction will be determined under paragraph (b)(4) of this section, by reference to paragraph (b)(1) of this section. To the extent that E's service transaction does not constitute a space or ocean activity, the source of E's income derived from the service transaction is determined under sections 861, 862, and 863, as applicable.

Example 9. Separate transactions—(i) *Facts.* The same facts as *Example 8*, except that E provides the raw data to F in a transaction characterized as a sale of a copyrighted article. In addition, E provides an analysis in the form of a report to F. The price F pays E for the raw data is separately stated.

(ii) *Analysis.* To the extent that the provision of raw data and the analysis of the data are each treated as separate transactions, the source of income from the production and sale of data is determined under paragraph (b)(3)(ii) of this section. The provision of services would be analyzed in the same manner as in *Example 8*.

Example 10. Sale of property in international water—(i) *Facts.* T purchased and owns transatlantic cable that lies in international water. T sells the cable to B, with T's rights, title, and interest in the cable passing to B in international water. Assume that the transatlantic cable is not inventory property within the meaning of section 1221(a)(1).

(ii) *Analysis.* Because T's rights, title, and interest in the property pass to B in international water, the sale takes place in international water under §1.861–7(c), and the sale transaction is ocean activity under paragraph (d)(1)(ii) of this section. The source of T's sales income is determined under paragraph (b)(3)(i) of this section, by reference to paragraph (b)(1) or (2) of this section.

Example 11. Sale of property in space—(i) *Facts.* S, a United States person, manufactures a satellite in the United States and sells it to a customer who is not a United States person. S's rights, title, and interest in the satellite pass to the customer in space.

(ii) *Analysis.* Because S's rights, title, and interest in the satellite pass to the customer in space, the sale takes place in space under §1.861–7(c), and the sale transaction is space activity under paragraph (d)(1)(i) of this section. The source of income derived from the sale of the satellite in space is determined under paragraph (b)(3)(ii) of this section, with the source of income allocable to production activity determined under paragraphs (b)(3)(ii)(A) and (B) of this section, and the source of income allocable to sales activity determined under paragraphs (b)(3)(ii)(A) and (D) of this section. Under paragraph (b)(1) of this section, S's space income is sourced outside the United States to the extent the income, based on all the facts and circumstances, is attributable to functions performed, resources employed, or risks assumed in a foreign country or countries.

Example 12. Sale of property in space—(i) *Facts.* S has a right to operate from a particular position (satellite slot or orbit) in space. S sells the right to operate from that position to P. Assume that the sale of the satellite slot is characterized as a sale of property and that S's rights, title, and interest in the satellite slot pass to P in space.

(ii) *Analysis.* The sale of the satellite slot takes place in space under §1.861–7(c) because S's rights, title, and interest in the satellite slot pass to P in space. The sale of the satellite slot is space activity under paragraph (d)(1)(i) of this section, and income or gain from the sale is sourced under paragraph (b)(3)(i) of this section, by reference to paragraph (b)(1) or (2) of this section.

Example 13. Source of income of a foreign person—(i) *Facts.* FP, a foreign corporation that is not a CFC, derives income from the operation of satellites. FP operates ground stations in the United States and in foreign Country FC. Assume that FP is considered engaged in a trade or business within the United States based on FP's operation of the ground station in the United States.

(ii) *Analysis.* Under paragraph (b)(2)(iii) of this section, FP's space income is sourced in the United States to the extent the income, based on all the facts and circumstances, is attributable to functions performed, resources employed, or risks assumed within the United States.

Example 14. Source of income of a foreign person—(i) *Facts.* FP, a foreign corporation that is not a CFC, operates remote sensing satellites in space to collect data and images for its customers. FP uses an independent agent, A, in the United States who provides marketing, order-taking, and other customer service functions. Assume that FP is considered engaged in a trade or business within the United States based on A's activities on FP's behalf in the United States.

(ii) *Analysis.* Under paragraph (b)(2)(iii) of this section, FP's space income is sourced in the United States to the extent the income, based on all the facts and circumstances, is attributable to functions performed, resources employed, or risks assumed within the United States.

(g) *Reporting and documentation requirements*—(1) *In general.* A taxpayer making an allocation of gross income under paragraph (b)(1), (b)(2), (b)(3)(ii)(C), or (b)(4) of this section must satisfy the requirements in paragraphs (g)(2), (3), and (4) of this section.

(2) *Required documentation.* In all cases, a taxpayer must prepare and maintain documentation in existence when its return is filed regarding the allocation of gross income and allocation and apportionment of expenses, losses, and other deductions, the methodologies used, and the circumstances justifying use of those methodologies. The taxpayer must make available such documentation within 30 days upon request.

(3) *Access to software.* If the taxpayer or any third party used any computer software, within the meaning of section 7612(d), to allocate gross income, or to allocate or apportion expenses, losses, and other deductions, the taxpayer must make available upon request—

(i) Any computer software executable code, within the meaning of section 7612(d), used for such purposes, including an executable copy of the version of the software used in the preparation of the taxpayer's return (including any plug-ins, supplements, etc.) and a copy of all related electronic data files. Thus, if software subsequently is upgraded or supplemented, a separate executable copy of the version used in preparing the taxpayer's return must be retained;

(ii) Any related computer software source code, within the meaning of section 7612(d), acquired or developed by the taxpayer or a related person, or primarily for internal use by the taxpayer or such person rather than for commercial distribution; and

(iii) In the case of any spreadsheet software or similar software, any formulae or links to supporting worksheets.

(4) *Use of allocation methodology.* In general, when a taxpayer allocates gross income under paragraph (b)(1), (b)(2), (b)(3)(ii)(C), or (b)(4) of this section, it does so by making the allocation on a timely filed original return (including extensions). However, a taxpayer will be permitted to make changes to such allocations made on its original return with respect to any taxable year for which the statute of limitations has not closed as follows:

(i) In the case of a taxpayer that has made a change to such allocations prior to the opening conference for the audit of the taxable year to which the allocation relates or who makes such a change within 90 days of such opening conference, if the IRS issues a written information document request asking the taxpayer to provide the documents and such other information described in paragraphs (g)(2) and (3) of this section with respect to the changed allocations and the taxpayer complies with such request within 30 days of the request, then the IRS will complete its examination, if any, with respect to the allocations for that year as part of the current examination cycle. If the taxpayer does not provide the documents and information described in paragraphs (g)(2) and (3) of this section within 30 days of the request, then the procedures described in paragraph (g)(4)(ii) of this section shall apply.

(ii) If the taxpayer changes such allocations more than 90 days after the opening conference for the audit of the taxable year to which the allocations relate or the taxpayer does not provide the documents and information with respect to the changed allocations as requested in accordance with paragraphs (g)(2) and (3) of this section, then the IRS will, in a separate cycle, determine whether an examination of the taxpayer's allocations is warranted and complete any such examination. The separate cycle will be worked as resources are available and may not have the same estimated completion date as the other issues under examination for the taxable year. The IRS may ask the taxpayer to extend the statute of limitations on assessment and collection for the taxable year to permit examination of the taxpayer's method of allocation, including an extension limited, where appropriate, to the taxpayer's method of allocation.

(h) *Effective date.* This section applies to taxable years beginning on or after December 27, 2006.

§1.863–9 Source of income derived from communications activity under section 863(a), (d), and (e).

(a) *In general.* Income of a United States or a foreign person derived from each type of communications activity, as defined in paragraph (h)(3) of this section, is sourced under the rules of this section, notwithstanding any other provision including sections 861, 862, 863, and 865. Notwithstanding that a communications activity would qualify as space or ocean activity under section 863(d) and the regulations thereunder, the source of income derived from such communications activity is determined under this section, and not under section 863(d) and the regulations thereunder, except to the extent provided in §1.863–8(b)(5).

(b) *Source of international communications income*—(1) *International communications income derived by a United States person.* Income derived from international communications activity (international communications income) by a United States person is one-half from sources within the United States and one-half from sources without the United States.

(2) *International communications income derived by foreign persons*—(i) *In general.* International communications income derived by a person other than a United States person is, except as otherwise provided in this paragraph (b)(2), wholly from sources without the United States.

(ii) *International communications income derived by a controlled foreign corporation.* International communications income derived by a controlled foreign corporation within the meaning of section 957 (CFC) is one-half from sources within the United States and one-half from sources without the United States.

(iii) *International communications income derived by foreign persons with a fixed place of business in the United States.* International communications income derived by a foreign person, other than a CFC, that is attributable to an office or other fixed place of business of the foreign person in the United States is from sources within the United States. The principles of section 864(c)(5) apply in determining whether a foreign person has an office or fixed place of business in the United States. See §1.864–7. International communications income is attributable to an office or other fixed place of business to the extent of functions performed, resources employed, or risks assumed by the office or other fixed place of business.

(iv) *International communications income derived by foreign persons engaged in a trade or business within the United States.* International communications income derived by a foreign person (other than a CFC) engaged in a trade or business within the United States is income from sources within the United States to the extent the income, based on all the facts and circumstances, is attributable to functions performed, resources employed, or risks assumed within the United States.

(c) *Source of U.S. communications income.* Income derived by a United States or foreign person from U.S. communications activity is from sources within the United States.

(d) *Source of foreign communications income.* Income derived by a United States or foreign person from foreign communications activity is from sources without the United States.

(e) *Source of space/ocean communications income.* The source of income derived by a United States or foreign person from space/ocean communications activity is determined under section 863(d) and the regulations thereunder.

(f) *Source of communications income when taxpayer cannot establish the two points between which the taxpayer is paid to transmit the communication.* Income derived by a United States or foreign person from communications activity, when the taxpayer cannot establish the two points between which the taxpayer is paid to transmit the communication as required in paragraph (h)(3)(i) of this section, is from sources within the United States.

(g) *Taxable income.* When a taxpayer allocates gross income under paragraph (b)(2)(iii), (b)(2)(iv), or (h)(1)(ii) of this section, the taxpayer must allocate expenses, losses, and other deductions as prescribed in §§1.861–8 through 1.861–14T to the class or classes of gross income that include the income so allocated in each case. A taxpayer must then apply the rules of §§1.861–8 through 1.861–14T properly to apportion amounts of expenses, losses, and other deductions so allocated to such gross income between gross income from sources within the United States and gross income from sources without the United States. For amounts of expenses, losses, and other deductions allocated to gross income derived from international communications activity, when the source of income is determined under the 50/50 method of paragraph (b)(1) or (b)(2)(ii) of this section, taxpayers generally must apportion expenses, losses, and other deductions between sources within the United States and sources without the United States *pro rata* based on the relative amounts of gross income from sources within the United States and gross income from sources without the United States. However, the preceding sentence shall not apply to research and experimental expenditures qualifying under §1.861–17, which are to be allocated and apportioned under the rules of that section.

(h) *Communications activity and income derived from communications activity*—(1) *Communications activity*—(i) *General rule*. For purposes of this part, *communications activity* consists solely of the delivery by transmission of communications or data (communications). Delivery of communications other than by transmission (for example, by delivery of physical packages and letters) is not communications activity within the meaning of this section. Communications activity also includes the provision of capacity to transmit communications. Provision of content or any other additional service provided along with, or in connection with, a non-*de minimis* communications activity must be treated as a separate non-communications activity unless *de minimis*. Communications activity or non-communications activity will be treated as *de minimis* to the extent, based on the facts and circumstances, the value attributable to such activity is *de minimis*.

(ii) *Separate transaction*. To the extent that a taxpayer's transaction consists in part of non-*de minimis* communications activity and in part of non-*de minimis* non-communications activity, each such part of the transaction must be treated as a separate transaction. Gross income is allocated to each such communications activity transaction and non-communications activity transaction to the extent the income, based on all the facts and circumstances, is attributable to functions performed, resources employed, or risks assumed in each such activity.

(2) *Income derived from communications activity. Income derived from communications activity* (communications income) is income derived from the delivery by transmission of communications, including income derived from the provision of capacity to transmit communications. Income may be considered derived from a communications activity even if the taxpayer itself does not perform the transmission function, but in all cases, the taxpayer derives communications income only if the taxpayer is paid to transmit, and bears the risk of transmitting, the communications.

(3) *Determining the type of communications activity*—(i) *In general*. Whether income is derived from international communications activity, U.S. communications activity, foreign communications activity, or space/ocean communications activity is determined by identifying the two points between which the taxpayer is paid to transmit the communication. The taxpayer must establish the two points between which the taxpayer is paid to transmit, and bears the risk of transmitting, the communication. Whether the taxpayer contracts out part or all of the transmission function is not relevant. A taxpayer may satisfy the requirement that the taxpayer establish the two points between which the taxpayer is paid to transmit, and bears the risk of transmitting, the communication by using any consistently applied reasonable method to establish one or both endpoints. In evaluating the reasonableness of such method, consideration will be given to all the facts and circumstances, including whether the endpoints would otherwise be identifiable absent this reasonable method provision and the reliability of the data. Depending on the facts and circumstances, methods based on, for example, records of port or transport charges, customer billing records, a satellite footprint, or records of termination fees made pursuant to an international settlement agreement may be reasonable. In addition, practices used by taxpayers to classify or categorize certain communications activity in connection with preparation of statements and analyses for the use of management, creditors, minority shareholders, joint ventures, or other parties or governmental agencies in interest may be reliable indicators of the reasonableness of the method chosen, but need not be accorded conclusive weight by the Commissioner. In all cases, the method chosen to establish the two points between which the taxpayer is paid to transmit, and bears the risk of transmitting, the communication must be supported by sufficient documentation to permit verification by the Commissioner.

(ii) *Income derived from international communications activity. Income derived by a taxpayer from international communications activity* (international communications income) is income derived from communications activity, as defined in paragraph (h)(2) of this section, when the taxpayer is paid to transmit—

(A) Between a point in the United States and a point in a foreign country (or a possession of the United States); or

(B) Foreign-originating communications (communications with a beginning point in a foreign country or a possession of the United States) from a point in space or international water to a point in the United States.

(iii) *Income derived from U.S. communications activity. Income derived by a taxpayer from U.S. communications activity* (U.S. communications income) is income derived from communications activity, as defined in paragraph (h)(2) of this section, when the taxpayer is paid to transmit—

(A) Between two points in the United States; or

(B) Between the United States and a point in space or international water, except as provided in paragraph (h)(3)(ii)(B) of this section.

(iv) *Income derived from foreign communications activity. Income derived by a taxpayer from foreign communications activity* (foreign communications income) is income derived from communications activity, as defined in paragraph (h)(2) of this section, when the taxpayer is paid to transmit—

(A) Between two points in a foreign country or countries (or a possession or possessions of the United States);

(B) Between a foreign country and a possession of the United States; or

(C) Between a foreign country (or a possession of the United States) and a point in space or international water.

(v) *Income derived from space/ocean communications activity. Income derived by a taxpayer from space/ocean communications activity* (space/ocean communications income) is income derived from communications activity, as defined in paragraph (h)(2) of this section, when the taxpayer is paid to transmit between a point in space or international water and another point in space or international water.

(i) *Treatment of partnerships*. This section is applied at the partner level.

(j) *Examples*. The following examples illustrate the rules of this section:

Example 1. Income derived from non-communications activity—remote data base access—(i) *Facts*. D provides its customers in various foreign countries with access to its data base, which contains information on certain individuals' health care insurance coverage. Customer C obtains access to D's data base by placing a call to D's telephone number. Assume that C's telephone service, used to access D's data base, is provided by a third party, and that D assumes no responsibility for the transmission of the information via telephone.

(ii) *Analysis*. D is not paid to transmit communications and does not derive income from communications activity within the meaning of paragraph (h)(2) of this section. Rather, D derives income from provision of content or provision of services to its customers. Therefore, the rules of this section do not apply to determine the source of D's income.

Example 2. Income derived from U.S. communications activity—U.S. portion of international communication—(i) *Facts*. TC, a local telephone company, receives an access fee from an international carrier for picking up a call from a local telephone customer and delivering the call to a U.S. point of presence (POP) of the international carrier. The international carrier picks up the call from its U.S. POP and delivers the call to a foreign country.

(ii) *Analysis*. TC is not paid to carry the transmission between the United States and a foreign country. TC is paid to transmit a communication between two points in the United States. TC derives U.S. communications income as defined in paragraph (h)(3)(iii) of this section, which is sourced under paragraph (c) of this section as U.S. source income.

Example 3. Income derived from international communications activity—underwater cable—(i) *Facts*. TC, a domestic corporation, owns an underwater fiber optic cable. Pursuant to contracts, TC makes available to its customers capacity to transmit communications via the cable. TC's customers then solicit telephone customers and arrange to transmit the telephone customers' calls. The cable runs in part through U.S. waters, in part through international waters, and in part through foreign country waters.

(ii) *Analysis*. TC derives international communications income as defined in paragraph (h)(3)(ii) of this section because TC is paid to make available capacity to transmit communications between the United States and a foreign country. Because TC is a United States person, TC's international communications income is sourced under paragraph (b)(1) of this section as one-half from sources within the United States and one-half from sources without the United States.

Example 4. Income derived from international communications activity—satellite—(i) *Facts*. S, a United States person, owns satellites in orbit and uplink facilities in Country X, a foreign country. B, a resident of Country X, pays S to deliver B's programming from S's uplink facility, located in Country X, to a downlink facility in the United States owned by C, a customer of B.

(ii) *Analysis*. S derives international communications income under paragraph (h)(3)(ii) of this section because S is paid to transmit the communications between a beginning point in a foreign country and an endpoint in the United States. Because S is a United States person, the source of S's international communications income is determined under paragraph (b)(1) of this section as one-half from sources within the United States and one-half from sources without the United States.

Example 5. The paid-to-do rule—foreign communications via domestic route—(i) *Facts*. TC is paid to transmit communications from Toronto, Canada, to Paris, France. TC transmits the communications from Toronto to New York. TC pays another communications company, IC, to transmit the communications from New York to Paris.

(ii) *Analysis*. Under the *paid-to-do* rule of paragraph (h)(3)(i) of this section, TC derives foreign communications income under paragraph (h)(3)(iv) of this section because TC is paid to transmit communications between two points in foreign countries, Toronto and Paris. Under paragraph (h)(3)(i) of this section, the character of TC's communications activity is determined without regard to the fact that TC pays IC to transmit the communications for some portion of the delivery path. IC has international communications income under paragraph (h)(3)(ii) of this section because IC is paid to transmit the communications between a point in the United States and a point in a foreign country.

Example 6. The paid-to-do rule—domestic communication via foreign route—(i) *Facts*. TC is paid to transmit a call between two points in the United States, but routes the call through Canada.

(ii) *Analysis*. Under paragraph (h)(3)(i) of this section, the character of income derived from communications activity is determined by the two points between which the taxpayer is paid to transmit, and bears the risk of transmitting, the communications, without regard to the path of the transmission between those two points. Thus, under paragraph (h)(3)(iii) of this section, TC derives income from U.S. communications activity because it is paid to transmit the communications between two U.S. points.

Example 7. The paid-to-do rule—foreign-originating communications—(i) *Facts*. Under an international settlement agreement, G, a Country X international carrier, pays T to receive all calls originating in Country X that are bound for the United States and to terminate such calls in the United States. Due to Country X legal restrictions, the international settlement agreement specifies that G carries the transmission to a point outside the territory of Country X and that T carries the foreign-originating transmission from such point to the destined point in the United States. T, in turn, contracts out with another communications company, S, to transmit the U.S. portion of the communications. Tracing and identifying the endpoints of each transmission is not possible or practical. T does, however, keep records of termination fees received from G for terminating the foreign-originating calls.

(ii) *Analysis*. T derives communications income as defined in paragraph (h)(2) of this section. Based on all the facts and circumstances, T can establish that T is paid to transmit, and bears the risk of transmitting, foreign-originating calls from a point in space or international water to a point in the United States using a reasonable method to establish the endpoints, assuming that this method is consistently applied. In this case, T can reasonably establish that T is paid to receive foreign-originating calls and terminate such calls in the United States based on the records of termination fees pursuant to an international settlement agreement. Under paragraph (h)(3)(ii)(B) of this section, a taxpayer derives income from international communications activity when the taxpayer is paid to transmit foreign-originating communications from space or international water to the United States. Thus, under paragraph (h)(3)(ii)(B) of this section, T derives income from international communications. If, based on all the facts and circumstances, T could reasonably trace and identify the endpoints, then T would have to directly establish that each call originated in a foreign country. Assuming T is able to do so, the rest of the analysis in this *Example 7* remains the same. Under paragraph (h)(3)(iii) of this section, S derives income from U.S. communications activity because S is paid to transmit the communications between two U.S. points.

Example 8. Indeterminate endpoints—prepaid telephone calling cards—(i) *Facts*. S purchases capacity from TC to transmit telephone calls. S sells prepaid telephone calling cards that give customers access to TC's telephone lines for a certain number of minutes. Assume that S cannot establish the endpoints of its customers' telephone calls, even under the reasonable method rule of paragraph (h)(3) of this section.

(ii) *Analysis*. S derives communications income as defined in paragraph (h)(2) of this section because S makes capacity to transmit communications available to its customers. In this case, S cannot establish the two points between which the communications are transmitted. Therefore, S's communications income is U.S. source income, as provided by paragraph (f) of this section.

Example 9. Reasonable methods—minutes of use data on long distance calling plans—(i) *Facts*. B provides both domestic and international long distance services in a calling plan for a limited number of minutes for a set amount each month. Tracing and identifying the endpoints of each transmission is not possible or practical. B is, however, able to establish that the calling plan generated $10,000 of revenue for 25,000 minutes based on reports derived from customer billing records. Based on minutes of use data in these reports, B is able to establish that of the total 25,000 minutes, 60 percent or 15,000 minutes were for U.S. long distance calls and 40 percent or 10,000 minutes were for international calls.

(ii) *Analysis*. B derives communications income as defined in paragraph (h)(2) of this section. Based on all the facts and circumstances, B can establish the two points between which B is paid to transmit, and bears the risk of transmitting, the communications using a reasonable method to establish the endpoints, assuming that this method is consistently applied. In this case, B can reasonably establish that 60 percent of the income derived from the long distance calling plan is U.S. communications income and 40 percent is international communications income based on the minutes of use data derived from customer billing records to establish the endpoints of the communications. If, based on all the facts and circumstances, B could reasonably trace and identify the endpoints, then B would have to directly identify the endpoints between which B is paid to transmit the communications.

Example 10. Reasonable methods—system design—(i) *Facts*. D operates satellites which are designed to transmit signals through two separate ranges of signal frequencies (bands). Due to technological limitations, requirements, and practicalities, one band is designed to only transmit signals within the United States. The other band is designed to transmit signals between foreign countries and the United States. D cannot trace and identify the endpoints of each individual transmission. D does, however, track the total transmission through each band and the total income derived from transmitting signals through each band.

(ii) *Analysis.* D derives communications income as defined in paragraph (h)(2) of this section. Based on all the facts and circumstances, D can establish the two points between which D is paid to transmit, and bears the risk of transmitting, the communications using a reasonable method to establish endpoints, assuming that this method is consistently applied. In this case, D can reasonably establish that income derived from transmissions through the first band is U.S. communications income and income derived from transmissions through the second band is international communications income based on the design of the bands to establish the endpoints of the communications.

Example 11. Reasonable methods—port locations—(i) *Facts.* X provides its customer, C, with a virtual private network (VPN) so that C's U.S. headquarter office can connect and communicate with offices in the United States, Country X, Country Y, and Country Z. Assume that the VPN is only for communications with the U.S. headquarter office. X cannot trace and identify the endpoints of each transmission. C pays X a set amount each month for the entire service, regardless of the magnitude of the usage or the geographic points between which C uses the service.

(ii) *Analysis.* X derives communications income as defined in paragraph (h)(2) of this section. Based on the facts and circumstances, X can establish the two points between which X is paid to transmit, and bears the risk of transmitting, the communications using a reasonable method to establish endpoints, assuming that this method is consistently applied. In this case, X can reasonably establish that one-fourth of the income derived from the VPN service is U.S. communications income and three-fourths is international communications income based on the location of the VPN ports to establish the endpoints of the communications.

Example 12. Indeterminate endpoints—Internet access—(i) *Facts.* B, a domestic corporation, is an Internet service provider. B charges its customer, C, a monthly lump sum for Internet access. C accesses the Internet via a telephone call, initiated by the modem of C's personal computer, to one of B's control centers, which serves as C's portal to the Internet. B transmits data sent by C from B's control center in France to a recipient in England, over the Internet. B does not maintain records as to the beginning and endpoints of the transmission.

(ii) *Analysis.* B derives communications income as defined in paragraph (h)(2) of this section. The source of B's communications income is determined under paragraph (f) of this section as income from sources within the United States because B cannot establish the two points between which it is paid to transmit the communications.

Example 13. De minimis non-communications activity—(i) *Facts.* The same facts as in *Example 12.* Assume in addition that B replicates frequently requested sites on B's own servers, solely to speed up response time. Assume that B's replication of frequently requested sites would be considered a *de minimis* non-communications activity under this section.

(ii) *Analysis.* On these facts, because B's replication of frequently requested sites would be considered a *de minimis* non-communications activity, B is not required to treat the replication activity as a separate non-communications activity transaction under paragraph (h)(1) of this section. B derives communications income under paragraph (h)(2) of this section. The character and source of B's communications income are determined by demonstrating the points between which B is paid to transmit the communications, under paragraph (h)(3)(i) of this section.

Example 14. Income derived from communications and non-communications activity—bundled services—(i) *Facts.* A, a domestic corporation, offers customers local and long distance phone service, video, and Internet services. Customers pay a flat monthly fee plus 10 cents a minute for all long-distance calls, including international calls.

(ii) *Analysis.* Under paragraph (h)(1)(ii) of this section, to the extent that A's transaction with its customer consists in part of non-*de minimis* communications activity and in part of non-*de minimis* non-communications activity, each such part of the transaction must be treated as a separate transaction. A's gross income from the transaction is allocated to each such communications activity transaction and non-communications activity transaction in accordance with paragraph (h)(1)(ii) of this section. To the extent A can establish that it derives international communications income as defined in paragraph (h)(3)(ii) of this section, A would determine the source of such income under paragraph (b)(1) of this section. If A cannot establish the points between which it is paid to transmit communications, as required by paragraph (h)(3)(i) of this section, A's communications income is from sources within the United States, as provided by paragraph (f) of this section.

Example 15. Income derived from communications and non-communications activity—(i) *Facts.* B, a domestic corporation, is paid by D, a cable system operator in Foreign Country, to provide television programs and to transmit the television programs to Foreign Country. Using its own satellite transponder, B transmits the television programs from the United States to downlink facilities owned by D in Foreign Country. D receives the transmission, unscrambles the signals, and distributes the broadcast to D's customers in Foreign Country. Assume that B's provision of television programs is a non-*de minimis* non-communications activity, and that B's transmission of television programs is a non-*de minimis* communications activity.

(ii) *Analysis.* Under paragraph (h)(1)(ii) of this section, B must treat its communications and non-communications activities as separate transactions. B's gross income is allocated to each such separate communications and non-communications activity transaction in accordance with paragraph (h)(1)(ii) of this section. Income derived by B from the transmission of television programs to D's Foreign Country downlink facility is international communications income as defined in paragraph (h)(3)(ii) of this section because B is paid to transmit communications from the United States to a foreign country.

Example 16. Income derived from foreign communications activity—(i) *Facts.* S provides satellite capacity to B, a broadcaster located in Australia. B beams programming from Australia to the satellite. S's satellite picks the communications up in space and beams the programming over a footprint covering Southeast Asia.

(ii) *Analysis.* S derives communications income as defined in paragraph (h)(2) of this section. S's income is characterized as foreign communications income under paragraph (h)(3)(iv) of this section because S picks up the communication in space, and beams it to a footprint entirely covering a foreign area. Under paragraph (d) of this section, S's foreign communications income is from sources without the United States. If S were beaming the programming over a satellite footprint that covered area both in the United States and outside the United States, S would be required to allocate the income derived from the different types of communications activity.

(k) *Reporting and documentation requirements*—(1) *In general.* A taxpayer making an allocation of gross income under paragraph (b)(2)(iii), (b)(2)(iv), or (h)(1)(ii) of this section must satisfy the requirements in paragraphs (k)(2), (3), and (4) of this section.

(2) *Required documentation.* In all cases, a taxpayer must prepare and maintain documentation in existence when its return is filed regarding the allocation of gross income, and allocation and apportionment of expenses, losses, and other deductions, the methodologies used, and the circumstances justifying use of those methodologies. The taxpayer must make available such documentation within 30 days upon request.

(3) *Access to software.* If the taxpayer or any third party used any computer software, within the meaning of section 7612(d), to allocate gross income, or to allocate or apportion expenses, losses, and other deductions, the taxpayer must make available upon request—

(i) Any computer software executable code, within the meaning of section 7612(d), used for such purposes, including an executable copy of the version of the software used in the preparation of the taxpayer's return (including any plug-ins, supplements, etc.) and a copy of all related electronic data files. Thus, if software subsequently is upgraded or supplemented, a separate executable copy of the version used in preparing the taxpayer's return must be retained;

(ii) Any related computer software source code, within the meaning of section 7612(d), acquired or developed by the taxpayer or a related person, or primarily for internal use by the taxpayer or such person rather than for commercial distribution; and

(iii) In the case of any spreadsheet software or similar software, any formulae or links to supporting worksheets.

(4) *Use of allocation methodology.* In general, when a taxpayer allocates gross income under paragraph (b)(2)(iii), (b)(2)(iv), or (h)(1)(ii) of this section, it does so by making the allocation on a timely filed original return (including extensions). However, a taxpayer will be permitted to make changes to such allocations made on its original return with respect to any taxable year for which the statute of limitations has not closed as follows:

(i) In the case of a taxpayer that has made a change to such allocations prior to the opening conference for the audit of the taxable year to which the allocation relates or who makes such a change within 90 days of such opening conference, if the IRS issues a written information document request asking the taxpayer to provide the documents and such other information described in paragraphs (k)(2) and (3) of this section with respect to the changed allocations and the taxpayer complies with such request within 30 days of the request, then the IRS will complete its examination, if any, with respect to the allocations for that year as part of the current examination cycle. If the taxpayer does not provide the documents and information described in paragraphs (k)(2) and (3) of this section within 30 days of the request, then the procedures described in paragraph (k)(4)(ii) of this section shall apply.

(ii) If the taxpayer changes such allocations more than 90 days after the opening conference for the audit of the taxable year to which the allocations relate or the taxpayer does not provide the documents and information with respect to the changed allocations as requested in accordance with paragraphs (k)(2) and (3) of this section, then the IRS will, in a separate cycle, determine whether an examination of the taxpayer's allocations is warranted and complete any such examination. The separate cycle will be worked as resources are available and may not have the same estimated completion date as the other issues under examination for the taxable year. The IRS may ask the taxpayer to extend the statute of limitations on assessment and collection for the taxable year to permit examination of the taxpayer's method of allocation, including an extension limited, where appropriate, to the taxpayer's method of allocation.

(l) *Effective date.* This section applies to taxable years beginning on or after December 27, 2006.

PART 602—OMB CONTROL NUMBERS UNDER THE PAPERWORK REDUCTION ACT

Par. 4. The authority citation for part 602 continues to read as follows:

Authority: 26 U.S.C. 7805.

Par. 5. In §602.101 paragraph (b) is amended by adding an entry to the table in numerical order, §§1.863–8 and 1.863–9, to read as follows:

§602.101 OMB Control numbers.

* * * * *

(b) * * *

CFR part or section where identified and described	Current OMB control No.
* * * * *	
1.863–8	1545–1718
1.863–9	1545–1718
* * * * *	

Kevin M. Brown,
Acting Deputy Commissioner for Services and Enforcement.

Approved December 21, 2006.

Eric Solomon,
Acting Secretary of the Treasury (Tax Policy).

(Filed by the Office of the Federal Register on December 26, 2006, 8:45 a.m., and published in the issue of the Federal Register for December 27, 2006, 71 F.R. 77594)

Section 6664.—Definitions and Special Rules

26 CFR 1.6664–1: Accuracy-related and fraud penalties; definitions, effective date and special rules.

T.D. 9309

DEPARTMENT OF THE TREASURY
Internal Revenue Service
26 CFR Part 1

Qualified Amended Returns

AGENCY: Internal Revenue Service (IRS), Treasury.

ACTION: Final regulations and removal of temporary regulations.

SUMMARY: This document contains final regulations that state the rules relating to qualified amended returns by providing circumstances that end the period within which a taxpayer may file an amended return that constitutes a qualified amended return. The IRS uses qualified amended returns to determine whether an underpayment exists that is potentially subject to the accuracy-related penalty on underpayments. Among other things, these final regulations provide that the period for filing a qualified amended return is terminated once the IRS has served a John Doe summons on a third party with respect to the taxpayer's tax liability. In addition, for taxpayers who have claimed tax benefits from undisclosed listed transactions, the regulations provide that the period for filing a qualified amended return is terminated once the IRS requests information related to the transaction that is required to be included on a list under section 6112 from any person who made a tax statement to or for the benefit of the taxpayer, or any person who gave material aid, assistance, or advice to the taxpayer. The regulations also provide that the date on which published guidance is issued announcing a settlement initiative for a listed transaction in which penalties, in whole or in part, are compromised or waived is an additional date by which a taxpayer must file a qualified amended return.

DATES: *Effective Date:* These regulations are effective January 9, 2007.

Applicability Dates: For dates of applicability, see §1.6664–1(b)(3).

FOR FURTHER INFORMATION CONTACT: Laura Urich Daly, 202–622–4940 (not a toll-free number).

SUPPLEMENTARY INFORMATION:

Background

This document contains Final Regulations under 26 CFR part 1 relating to qualified amended returns. Temporary regulations (T.D. 9186, 2005–1 C.B. 790) relating to qualified amended returns were published in the **Federal Register** (70 FR 10037) on March 2, 2005. A notice of proposed rulemaking (REG–122847–04, 2005–1 C.B. 804) cross-referencing the temporary regulations was published in the **Federal Register** (70 FR 10062) for the same day. A correction (70 FR 36345) and a correcting amendment (published as Announcement 2005–53, 2005–2 C.B. 258 [70 FR 36344]) to the regulations were published in the **Federal Register** on June 23, 2005, and a correction to the correction was published in the **Federal Register** (70 FR 43635) on July 28, 2005. No written or electronic comments were received from the public in response to the notice of proposed rulemaking and no public hearing was requested or held. The proposed regulations are adopted as amended by this Treasury decision, and the corresponding temporary regulations are removed. The revisions are discussed below.

Explanation of Revisions

The final regulations clarify the applicability date of the regulations. Under the Special Rules section, the sentence in the proposed and temporary regulations regarding disclosure pursuant to §1.6011–4 was removed in these final regulations because it could be incorrectly interpreted to provide relief from the section 6707A penalty. These final regulations are not intended to have any effect upon the applicability of the section 6707A penalty. In addition, examples one, four, five, six, and seven in the proposed and temporary regulations were further clarified. Finally, example eight in the proposed and temporary regulations was removed as unnecessary.

No other substantive revisions were made to the proposed and temporary regulations or the corrections to those regulations. These final regulations do, however, include revisions to the table of contents to the regulations under section 6664.

Special Analyses

It has been determined that this Treasury decision is not a significant regulatory action as defined in Executive Order 12866. Therefore, a regulatory assessment is not required. It has also been determined that section 553(b) of the Administrative Procedure Act (5 U.S.C. chapter 5) does not apply to these regulations, and because the regulation does not impose a collection of information on small entities, the Regulatory Flexibility Act (5 U.S.C. chapter 6) does not apply. Pursuant to section 7805(f) of the Internal Revenue Code, the notice of proposed rulemaking preceding this regulation was submitted to the Chief Counsel for Advocacy of the Small Business Administration for comment on its impact on small businesses.

Drafting Information

The principal author of this regulation is Laura Urich Daly, Office of the Associate Chief Counsel (Procedure & Administration), Administrative Provisions and Judicial Practice Division.

* * * * *

Adoption of Amendments to the Regulations

Accordingly, 26 CFR part 1 is amended as follows:

PART 1—INCOME TAXES

Paragraph 1. The authority citation for part 1 continues to read in part as follows:

Authority: 26 U.S.C. 7805 * * *

Par. 2. Section 1.6664–0 is amended by adding entries for §§1.6664–1(b)(3) and 1.6664–2(c)(3)(i), (ii) and (5), and revising the entry for §1.6664–2(c)(4) to read as follows:

§1.6664–0 Table of contents.

* * * * *

§1.6664–1 Accuracy-related and fraud penalties; definitions, effective date and special rules.

* * * * *

(b) * * *

(3) Qualified amended returns.

§1.6664–2 Underpayment.

* * * * *

(c) * * *

(3) * * *

(i) General rule.

(ii) Undisclosed listed transactions.

(4) Special rules.

(5) Examples.

* * * * *

Par. 3. Section 1.6664–1 is amended by:

1. Revising the section heading.

2. Adding paragraph (b)(3).

The revision and addition read as follows:

§1.6664–1 Accuracy-related and fraud penalties; definitions, effective date and special rules.

* * * * *

(b) * * *

(3) *Qualified amended returns.* Sections 1.6664–2(c)(1), (c)(2), (c)(3)(i)(A), (c)(3)(i)(B), (c)(3)(i)(C), (c)(3)(i)(D)(2), (c)(3)(i)(E), and (c)(4) are applicable for amended returns and requests for administrative adjustment filed on or after March

2, 2005. Sections 1.6664–2(c)(3)(i)(D)(*1*) and (c)(3)(ii)(B) and (C) are applicable for amended returns and requests for administrative adjustment filed on or after April 30, 2004. The applicability date for §1.6664–2(c)(3)(ii)(A) varies depending upon which event occurs under §1.6664–2(c)(3)(i). For purposes of §1.6664–2(c)(3)(ii)(A), the date described in §1.6664–2(c)(3)(i)(D)(*1*) is applicable for amended returns and requests for administrative adjustment filed on or after April 30, 2004. For purposes of §1.6664–2(c)(3)(ii)(A), the dates described in §1.6664–2(c)(3)(i)(A), (B), (C), (D)(*2*), and (E) are applicable for amended returns and requests for administrative adjustment filed on or after March 2, 2005. Section 1.6664–2(c)(1) through (c)(3), as contained in 26 CFR part 1 revised as of April 1, 2004 and as modified by Notice 2004–38, 2004–1 C.B. 949, applies with respect to returns and requests for administrative adjustment filed on or after April 30, 2004 and before March 2, 2005. Section 1.6664–2(c)(1) through (3), as contained in 26 CFR part 1 revised as of April 30, 2004, applies with respect to returns and requests for administrative adjustment filed before April 30, 2004.

§1.6664–1T [Removed]

Par. 4. Section 1.6664–1T is removed.

Par. 5. Section 1.6664–2(c) is revised to read as follows:

§1.6664–2 Underpayment.

* * * * *

(c) *Amount shown as the tax by the taxpayer on his return*—(1) *Defined.* For purposes of paragraph (a) of this section, the *amount shown as the tax by the taxpayer on his return* is the tax liability shown by the taxpayer on his return, determined without regard to the items listed in paragraphs (b)(1), (2), and (3) of this section, except that it is reduced by the excess of—

(i) The amounts shown by the taxpayer on his return as credits for tax withheld under section 31 (relating to tax withheld on wages) and section 33 (relating to tax withheld at source on nonresident aliens and foreign corporations), as payments of estimated tax, or as any other payments made by the taxpayer with respect to a taxable year before filing the return for such taxable year, over

(ii) The amounts actually withheld, actually paid as estimated tax, or actually paid with respect to a taxable year before the return is filed for such taxable year.

(2) *Effect of qualified amended return.* The *amount shown as the tax by the taxpayer on his return* includes an amount shown as additional tax on a qualified amended return (as defined in paragraph (c)(3) of this section), except that such amount is not included if it relates to a fraudulent position on the original return.

(3) *Qualified amended return defined*—(i) *General rule.* A *qualified amended return* is an amended return, or a timely request for an administrative adjustment under section 6227, filed after the due date of the return for the taxable year (determined with regard to extensions of time to file) and before the earliest of—

(A) The date the taxpayer is first contacted by the Internal Revenue Service (IRS) concerning any examination (including a criminal investigation) with respect to the return;

(B) The date any person is first contacted by the IRS concerning an examination of that person under section 6700 (relating to the penalty for promoting abusive tax shelters) for an activity with respect to which the taxpayer claimed any tax benefit on the return directly or indirectly through the entity, plan or arrangement described in section 6700(a)(1)(A);

(C) In the case of a pass-through item (as defined in §1.6662–4(f)(5)), the date the pass-through entity (as defined in §1.6662–4(f)(5)) is first contacted by the IRS in connection with an examination of the return to which the pass-through item relates;

(D)(*1*) The date on which the IRS serves a summons described in section 7609(f) relating to the tax liability of a person, group, or class that includes the taxpayer (or pass-through entity of which the taxpayer is a partner, shareholder, beneficiary, or holder of a residual interest in a REMIC) with respect to an activity for which the taxpayer claimed any tax benefit on the return directly or indirectly.

(*2*) The rule in paragraph (c)(3)(i)(D)(*1*) of this section applies to any return on which the taxpayer claimed a direct or indirect tax benefit from the type of activity that is the subject of the summons, regardless of whether the summons seeks the production of information for the taxable period covered by such return; and

(E) The date on which the Commissioner announces by revenue ruling, revenue procedure, notice, or announcement, to be published in the Internal Revenue Bulletin (see §601.601(d)(2) of this chapter), a settlement initiative to compromise or waive penalties, in whole or in part, with respect to a listed transaction. This rule applies only to a taxpayer who participated in the listed transaction and for the taxable year(s) in which the taxpayer claimed any direct or indirect tax benefits from the listed transaction. The Commissioner may waive the requirements of this paragraph or identify a later date by which a taxpayer who participated in the listed transaction must file a qualified amended return in the published guidance announcing the listed transaction settlement initiative.

(ii) *Undisclosed listed transactions.* An *undisclosed listed transaction* is a transaction that is the same as, or substantially similar to, a listed transaction within the meaning of §1.6011–4(b)(2) (regardless of whether §1.6011–4 requires the taxpayer to disclose the transaction) and was neither previously disclosed by the taxpayer within the meaning of §1.6011–4 or §1.6011–4T, nor disclosed under Announcement 2002–2, 2002–1 C.B. 304, (see §601.601(d)(2)(ii) of this chapter) by the deadline therein. In the case of an *undisclosed listed transaction* for which a taxpayer claims any direct or indirect tax benefits on its return (regardless of whether the transaction was a listed transaction at the time the return was filed), an amended return or request for administrative adjustment under section 6227 will not be a *qualified amended return* if filed on or after the earliest of–

(A) The dates described in paragraph(c)(3)(i) of this section;

(B) The date on which the IRS first contacts any person regarding an examination of that person's liability under section 6707(a) with respect to the undisclosed listed transaction of the taxpayer; or

(C) The date on which the IRS requests, from any person who made a tax statement to or for the benefit of the taxpayer or from any person who gave the taxpayer material aid, assistance, or advice as described in section 6111(b)(1)(A)(i) with respect to the taxpayer, the information required to be included on a list under section 6112 relating to a transaction that was the same as, or substantially similar to, the undisclosed listed transaction, regardless of whether the taxpayer's information is required to be included on that list.

(4) *Special rules.* (i) A qualified amended return includes an amended return that is filed to disclose information pursuant to §1.6662–3(c) or §1.6662–4(e) and (f) even though it does not report any additional tax liability. See §1.6662–3(c), §1.6662–4(f), and §1.6664–4(c) for rules relating to adequate disclosure.

(ii) The Commissioner may by revenue procedure prescribe the manner in which the rules of paragraph (c) of this section regarding qualified amended returns apply to particular classes of taxpayers.

(5) *Examples.* The following examples illustrate the provisions of paragraphs (c)(3) and (c)(4) of this section:

Example 1. T, an individual taxpayer, claimed tax benefits on its 2002 Federal income tax return from a transaction that is substantially similar to the transaction identified as a listed transaction in Notice 2002–65, 2002–2 C.B. 690 (Partnership Entity Straddle Tax Shelter). T did not disclose his participation in this transaction on a Form 8886, "*Reportable Transaction Disclosure Statement*," as required by §1.6011–4. On June 30, 2004, the IRS requested from P, T's material advisor, an investor list required to be maintained under section 6112. The section 6112 request, however, related to the type of transaction described in Notice 2003–81, 2003–2 C.B. 1223 (Tax Avoidance Using Offsetting Foreign Currency Option Contracts). T did not participate in (within the meaning of §1.6011–4(c)) a transaction described in Notice 2003–81. T may file a qualified amended return relating to the transaction described in Notice 2002–65 because T did not claim a tax benefit with respect to the listed transaction described in Notice 2003–81, which is the subject of the section 6112 request.

Example 2. The facts are the same as in *Example 1*, except that T's 2002 Federal income tax return reflected T's participation in the transaction described in Notice 2003–81. As of June 30, 2004, T may not file a qualified amended return for the 2002 tax year.

Example 3. (i) Corporation X claimed tax benefits from a transaction on its 2002 Federal income tax return. In October 2004, the IRS and Treasury Department identified the transaction as a listed transaction. In December 2004, the IRS contacted P concerning an examination of P's liability under section 6707(a) (as in effect prior to the amendment to section 6707 by section 816 of the American Jobs Creation Act of 2004 (the Jobs Act), Public Law 108–357 (118 Stat. 1418)). P is the organizer of a section 6111 tax shelter (as in effect prior to the amendment to section 6111 by section 815 of the Jobs Act) who provided representations to X regarding tax benefits from the transaction, and the IRS has contacted P about the failure to register that transaction. Three days later, X filed an amended return.

(ii) X's amended return is not a qualified amended return, because X did not disclose the transaction before the IRS contacted P. X's amended return would have been a qualified amended return if it was submitted prior to the date on which the IRS contacted P.

Example 4. The facts are the same as in *Example 3* except that, instead of contacting P concerning an examination under section 6707(a), in December 2004, the IRS served P with a John Doe summons described in section 7609(f) relating to the tax liability of participants in the type of transaction for which X claimed tax benefits on its return. X cannot file a qualified amended return after the John Doe summons has been served regardless of when, or whether, the transaction becomes a listed transaction.

Example 5. On November 30, 2003, the IRS served a John Doe summons described in section 7609(f) on Corporation Y, a credit card company. The summons requested the identity of, and information concerning, United States taxpayers who, during the taxable years 2001 and 2002, had signature authority over Corporation Y's credit cards issued by, through, or on behalf of certain offshore financial institutions. Corporation Y complied with the summons, and identified, among others, Taxpayer B. On May 31, 2004, before the IRS first contacted Taxpayer B concerning an examination of Taxpayer B's Federal income tax return for the taxable year 2002, Taxpayer B filed an amended return for that taxable year, that showed an increase in Taxpayer B's Federal income tax liability. Under paragraph (c)(3)(i)(D) of this section, the amended return is not a qualified amended return because it was not filed before the John Doe summons was served on Corporation Y.

Example 6. The facts are the same as in *Example 5*. Taxpayer B continued to maintain the offshore credit card account through 2003 and filed an original tax return for the 2003 taxable year claiming tax benefits attributable to the existence of the account. On March 21, 2005, Taxpayer B filed an amended return for the taxable year 2003, that showed an increase in Taxpayer B's Federal income tax liability. Under paragraph (c)(3)(i)(D) of this section, the amended return is not a qualified amended return because it was not filed before the John Doe summons for 2001 and 2002 was served on Corporation Y, and the return reflects benefits from the type of activity that is the subject of the John Doe summons.

Example 7. (i) On November 30, 2003, the IRS served a John Doe summons described in section 7609(f) on Corporation Y, a credit card company. The summons requested the identity of, and information concerning, United States taxpayers who, during the taxable years 2001 and 2002, had signature authority over Corporation Y's credit cards issued by, through, or on behalf of certain offshore financial institutions. Taxpayer C did not have signature authority over any of Corporation Y's credit cards during either 2001 or 2002 and, therefore, was not a person described in the John Doe summons.

(ii) In 2003, Taxpayer C first acquired signature authority over a Corporation Y credit card issued by an offshore financial institution. Because Taxpayer C did not have signature authority during 2001 or 2002 over a Corporation Y credit card issued by an offshore financial institution, and was therefore not covered by the John Doe summons served on November 30, 2003, Taxpayer C's ability to file a qualified amended return for the 2003 taxable year is not limited by paragraph (c)(3)(i)(D) of this section.

* * * * *

§1.6664–2T [Removed]

Par. 6. Section 1.6664–2T is removed.

Mark E. Matthews,
Deputy Commissioner for Services and Enforcement.

Approved December 21, 2006.

Eric Solomon,
Assistant Secretary of the Treasury (Tax Policy).

(Filed by the Office of the Federal Register on January 8, 2007, 8:45 a.m., and published in the issue of the Federal Register for January 9, 2007, 72 F.R. 902)

Part III. Administrative, Procedural, and Miscellaneous

Description of Benefits Permitted to be Provided in Qualified Defined Benefit Plans

Notice 2007–14

I. PURPOSE

The Treasury Department and the Internal Revenue Service are considering guidance under §§ 401(a) and 411 of the Internal Revenue Code to provide clarification regarding the types of benefits that are permitted to be provided in a qualified defined benefit plan. The guidance under consideration would initially be issued in the form of proposed regulations. This notice describes the guidance under consideration and requests comments on the issues raised in Part III of this notice.

II. BACKGROUND

Section 401(a) provides rules for qualified pension plans, profit-sharing plans, and stock bonus plans. Section 1.401–1(a)(2) of the Income Tax Regulations provides that a qualified pension plan (*i.e.*, a qualified defined benefit plan or money purchase pension plan) is a definite written program and arrangement which is communicated to the employees and which is established and maintained by an employer to provide for the livelihood of the employees or their beneficiaries after the retirement of such employees through the payment of benefits. Under § 1.401 1(b)(1)(i), a qualified pension plan must be established and maintained by an employer primarily to provide systematically for the payment of definitely determinable benefits for employees over a period of years, usually for life, after retirement.[1]

Retirement benefits in a qualified defined benefit plan usually are measured by, and based on, factors such as years of service and compensation. A qualified defined benefit plan (or other qualified pension plan) also may provide certain non-retirement benefits, such as disability benefits and incidental death benefits. Under § 1.401–1(b)(1)(i), a qualified pension plan is not permitted to provide for the payment of benefits not customarily included in a pension plan, such as layoff benefits.[2]

Section 411(d)(6)(A) generally provides that a plan is treated as not satisfying the requirements of § 411 if the accrued benefit of a participant is decreased by a plan amendment. Section 411(d)(6)(B) provides that a plan amendment that has the effect of eliminating or reducing an early retirement benefit or a retirement-type subsidy, or eliminating an optional form of benefit, with respect to benefits attributable to service before the amendment is treated as impermissibly reducing accrued benefits. For a retirement-type subsidy, this protection applies only with respect to an employee who satisfies the preamendment conditions for the subsidy (either before or after the amendment).

Not all types of benefits permitted to be provided in a qualified defined benefit plan are protected from cutback under § 411(d)(6). In this respect, the 1984 Senate Finance Committee Report regarding section 301(a) of the Retirement Equity Act of 1984, Public Law 98–397 (98 Stat. 1426) (REA), which extended § 411(d)(6) anti-cutback protection to optional forms of benefit, early retirement benefits, and retirement-type subsidies, provides, in part:

> The bill provides that the term "retirement-type subsidy" is to be defined by Treasury regulations. The committee intends that under these regulations, a subsidy that continues after retirement is generally to be considered a retirement-type subsidy. The committee expects, however, that a qualified disability benefit, a medical benefit, a social security supplement, a death benefit (including life insurance), or a plant shutdown benefit (that does not continue after retirement age) will not be considered a retirement-type subsidy. The committee expects that Treasury regulations will prevent the recharacterization of retirement-type benefits as benefits that are not protected by the provision.

S. Rep. No. 98–575, at 30.

Sections 1.411(d)–3 and 1.411(d)–4, which were amended on August 12, 2005 (T.D. 9219, 2005–2 C.B. 538 [70 FR 47109]), provide rules relating to § 411(d)(6) protected benefits. Section 1.411(d)–4, Q&A–1(d), specifies that certain benefits, including ancillary benefits, are not protected from reduction or elimination under § 411(d)(6)(B). Section 1.411(d)–3 also includes rules relating to ancillary benefits. Section 1.411(d)–3(b)(3)(i) provides that § 411(d)(6) does not provide protection for benefits that are ancillary benefits, other rights and features, or any other benefits that are not described in § 411(d)(6).

Section 1.411(d)–3(g)(2) defines the term "ancillary benefit" as:

(1) a social security supplement under a defined benefit plan (other than a QSUPP as defined in § 1.401(a)(4)–12));

(2) a benefit payable under a defined benefit plan in the event of disability (to the extent that the benefit exceeds the benefit otherwise payable), but only if the total benefit payable in the event of disability does not exceed the maximum qualified disability benefit, as defined in § 411(a)(9);

(3) a life insurance benefit;

(4) a medical benefit described in § 401(h);

(5) a death benefit under a defined benefit plan other than a death benefit which is part of an optional form of benefit; or

(6) a plant shutdown benefit or other similar benefit in a defined benefit plan that does not continue past retirement age and does not affect the payment of the accrued benefit, but only to the extent that such plant shutdown benefit or other similar benefit is permitted in a qualified pension plan.

Section 1.411(d)–3(g) defines other key terms relating to the anti-cutback rules, including "retirement-type subsidy" and "retirement-type benefit." Section 1.411(d)–3(g)(6)(iv) defines the term "retirement-type subsidy" as the excess, if

[1] The regulations under § 401(a) provide separate rules for profit-sharing plans and stock bonus plans. *See* § 1.401–1(a)(2) and (b)(1)(ii) and (iii).

[2] Section 1.401–1(b)(1)(i) specifies that other benefits not customarily included in a pension plan include benefits for sickness, accident, hospitalization, or medical expenses (except medical benefits described in § 401(h) as defined in § 1.401–14(a)).

any, of the actuarial present value of a retirement-type benefit, over the actuarial present value of the accrued benefit commencing at normal retirement age or at actual commencement date, if later, with both such actuarial present values determined as of the date the retirement-type benefit commences. Section 1.411(d)–3(g)(6)(iii) defines the term "retirement-type benefit" as the payment of a distribution alternative with respect to an accrued benefit or the payment of any other benefit under a defined benefit plan (including a QSUPP as defined in § 1.401(a)(4)–12) that is permitted to be in a qualified pension plan, continues after retirement, and is not an ancillary benefit.

Under § 1.411(d)–4, Q&A–6, a plan may limit the availability of § 411(d)(6) protected benefits to employees who meet objective conditions that are ascertainable, specifically set forth in the plan, and not subject to employer discretion.[3] Q&A–6 provides examples of permissible objective conditions. Section 1.411(d)–4, Q&A–7 generally provides that a plan is not permitted to be amended to add objective conditions with respect to a § 411(d)(6) protected benefit that has already accrued. However, a plan amendment does not violate § 411(d)(6) to the extent that it applies to benefits that accrue after the amendment. Therefore, an amendment adding objective conditions to a § 411(d)(6) protected benefit is permitted with respect to benefits that accrue after the applicable amendment date.[4]

Section 411(a) provides that a qualified plan must provide that an employee's right to his normal retirement benefit is nonforfeitable upon the attainment of normal retirement age, and also provides vesting requirements with respect to an employee's accrued benefit. Under § 411(a)(9), the term "normal retirement benefit" is defined as the greater of the early retirement benefit under the plan or the benefit under the plan commencing at normal retirement age. Section 411(b)(1) provides anti-backloading rules governing the accrual of benefits under a defined benefit plan, to ensure that the minimum vesting rules of § 411(a) are not circumvented through a plan formula under which accruals are inappropriately deferred.

Section 905(b) of the Pension Protection Act of 2006 ("PPA '06), enacted on August 17, 2006, added § 401(a)(36), which provides that, for plan years beginning after December 31, 2006, a pension plan will not fail to qualify under § 401(a) solely because the plan provides that a distribution may be made to an employee who has attained age 62 and who is not separated from employment at the time of the distribution.

III. GUIDANCE UNDER CONSIDERATION

Treasury and the Service have become concerned that certain qualified defined benefit plans may include nontraditional benefits that are not subject to the protections of § 411 and other qualification rules of § 401(a). Examples of the types of benefits for which this concern arises include: (1) benefits that are payable only upon the involuntary termination of an employee or in other limited circumstances that are unrelated to retirement; and (2) benefits that could exceed the amount of the accrued benefit payable under the plan. If these benefits are contingent on future events that are not reasonably and reliably predictable on an actuarial basis, it is difficult to determine compliance with the incidental benefit requirements.[5] Moreover, there may be a risk that, in effect, if the contingent event on which the benefit is conditioned occurs, such a benefit could become a substantial or even the primary benefit that plan participants expect to receive. Such benefits also may not be the types of benefits that have been customarily included in qualified pension plans. Benefits payable only upon an employee's involuntary separation from service also raise questions regarding whether the availability of the benefits is based on conditions that are within the employer's control, and whether such benefits circumvent the vesting and anti backloading protections of § 411, as well as the definitely determinable benefits requirement of § 401(a). In addition, such benefits may not be among the type of benefits that are intended to receive the tax benefits generally applicable to qualified plan benefits.

Treasury and the Service believe that guidance to clarify the application of the requirements of §§ 401(a) and 411 to these types of benefits may be appropriate in light of the regulations under § 411(d)(6) that were issued in 2005. The § 1.411(d)–3 definitions of an ancillary benefit, a retirement-type benefit, and a retirement-type subsidy depend, in part, on whether a benefit is permitted to be provided in a qualified defined benefit plan. However, current guidance does not directly address whether certain benefits, such as benefits which are similar to plant shutdown benefits that do not continue after retirement or benefits payable solely upon involuntary separation, are permitted to be provided in a qualified pension plan. Thus, Treasury and the Service are considering whether to propose guidance that would clarify the types of benefits that are permitted to be provided in qualified defined benefit plans.

The guidance under consideration may include the following:

A. *Permitted benefits.* The guidance might provide that, in addition to the payment of retirement-type benefits (including retirement-type subsidies), the only benefit payments that are permitted to be provided under a qualified defined benefit plan are the payment of the ancillary benefits specifically identified in § 1.411(d)–3(g)(2).

B. *Plant shutdown benefits and similar ancillary benefits.* With respect to a plant shutdown benefit, the guidance might require that the benefit be payable as a result of an objectively defined plant shutdown event, such as an event that requires notice under the Worker Adjustment and Retraining Notification Act of 1988 (WARN), 29 U.S.C. section 2102. For benefits that are similar to plant shutdown benefits and that do not continue past retirement age, the guidance might set forth the extent to which there are any such "similar benefits," as described in

[3] A plan provision that permits an employer to deny a participant a § 411(d)(6) protected benefit for which the participant is otherwise eligible through the exercise of discretion violates the requirements of § 411(d)(6). See § 1.411(d)–4, Q&A–4. Similarly, pursuant to § 1.411(d)–4, Q&A–6(b), a plan cannot condition the availability of § 411(d)(6) protected benefits on objective conditions that are within the employer's discretion.

[4] The term *applicable amendment date* means the later of the effective date of a plan amendment or the date the amendment is adopted. *See* § 1.411(d)–3(g)(4).

[5] In the case of benefits which are contingent on events that are reasonably and reliably predictable on an actuarial basis (*e.g.*, death), the probability that those contingencies will occur is taken into account in determining whether retirement benefits are the primary benefit under the plan (*i.e.*, whether nonretirement benefits provided under the plan are merely incidental).

§ 1.411(d)–3(g)(2)(vi), that are permitted to be provided in a qualified defined benefit plan.

The guidance also might clarify that an ancillary plant shutdown benefit, as described in § 1.411(d)–3(g)(2)(vi), is permitted to be provided in a qualified defined benefit plan only if the amount payable in any year prior to retirement does not exceed the amount payable annually under the participant's accrued benefit expressed as an annual benefit commencing at normal retirement age and that the benefit may not be paid in a shorter or longer alternative form of payment. Under such a rule, for example, if a plan participant who is below the plan's normal retirement age of 65 had an accrued benefit payable as a life annuity at age 65 of $1,000 a month, the plan would be permitted to provide an ancillary plant shutdown benefit payable as a temporary annuity in an amount up to $1,000 a month. In such a case, the ancillary plant shutdown benefit would be paid to the plan participant up until the annuity starting date for payment of the participant's accrued benefit under the plan (*e.g.*, age 65 or some earlier age when the participant commences payment of the participant's accrued benefit in the form of a qualified joint and survivor annuity or elects an alternative optional form). This illustration of an ancillary plant shutdown benefit is different from a subsidized early retirement benefit payable on the occurrence of a plant shutdown.[6]

C. *Contingent accruals and early retirement benefits*. The guidance might also provide that, except for the payment of the accrued benefit in an optional form, a retirement-type benefit (and thus a retirement-type subsidy) is permitted to be provided in a qualified defined benefit plan only if the amount of the benefit is no greater than the unreduced accrued benefit provided under the plan. The guidance might also clarify the extent to which additional accruals are permitted, taking into account the backloading and vesting rules under § 411, if those accruals arise by reason of an event other than attainment of a specified age, performance of service, receipt or derivation of compensation, or the occurrence of death or disability (*e.g.*, if those additional accruals arise upon involuntary termination of employment). The guidance also might clarify the extent to which early retirement benefits (*i.e.*, benefits payable before normal retirement age, but after severance from employment, that are not ancillary benefits) payable as a result of a plant shutdown event, an involuntary termination of employment, or another event similarly under the control of the employer are permitted to be provided in a qualified defined benefit plan.

IV. EFFECTIVE DATE

It is anticipated that the guidance under consideration in this notice would be prospective. No implication is intended that the consideration of these issues affects the application of current law.

V. COMMENTS REQUESTED

Comments regarding the guidance under consideration described in Part III of this notice are requested. Of particular interest to Treasury and the Service are comments regarding the extent to which qualified defined benefit plans currently offer the types of benefits described in Part III of this notice, and comments regarding any appropriate transition rules that should be included in the guidance.

Written comments should be submitted by May 13, 2007. Send submissions to CC:PA:LPD:PR, (Notice 2007–14), Room 5203, Internal Revenue Service, PO Box 7604, Ben Franklin Station, Washington, D.C. 20044. Comments may also be hand delivered Monday through Friday between the hours of 8:30 a.m. and 4:00 p.m. to: Internal Revenue Service, CC:PA:LPD:PR, (Notice 2007–14), Courier's Desk, Internal Revenue Service, 1111 Constitution Avenue, N.W., Washington, DC. Alternatively, comments may be submitted via the Internet at *notice.comments@irscounsel.treas.gov* (Notice 2007–14). All comments will be available for public inspection.

DRAFTING INFORMATION

The principal authors of this notice are Pamela R. Kinard and Preston Rutledge of the Office of the Division Counsel/Associate Chief Counsel (Tax Exempt and Government Entities) and Kathleen Herrmann of the Employee Plans, Tax Exempt and Government Entities Division. For further information regarding this notice, contact Ms. Kinard at (202) 622–6060 or Mr. Rutledge at (202) 622–6090 (not toll-free numbers).

Closing Agreements for Certain Life Insurance and Annuity Contracts that Fail to Meet the Requirements of Section 817(h), 7702 or 7702A (As Applicable)

Notice 2007–15

SECTION 1. PURPOSE

This notice requests comments on how the Internal Revenue Service (the Service) might improve the procedures for obtaining closing agreements to correct inadvertent failures of life insurance or annuity contracts to satisfy the requirements of §§ 817(h), 7702 or 7702A of the Internal Revenue Code (Code), as applicable. This notice also provides four draft model closing agreements for comment.

SECTION 2. BACKGROUND

.01 *Qualification as a life insurance contract under § 7702.* (1) Section 7702 defines the term "life insurance contract" for all purposes of the Code. Section 7702(a) provides that a "life insurance contract" is any contract that is a life insurance contract under the applicable law, but only if such contract either (1) meets the cash value accumulation test of § 7702(b), or (2) meets the guideline premium requirements of § 7702(c) and falls within the cash value corridor of § 7702(d). (For flexible premium life insurance contracts issued before January 1, 1985, § 101(f)(1) provides that any amount paid by reason of death of the insured under a flexible premium life insurance contract issued before January 1, 1985, is excluded from gross income only if, under the contract, the sum of the premiums does not exceed the guideline premium limitation as of such time.)

[6] An example of a subsidized early retirement benefit is the unreduced early retirement benefit described in *Bellas v. CBS, Inc.*, 221 F.3d 517 (3d. Cir. 2000), *cert. denied*, 531 U.S. 1104 (2001) (holding that an early retirement benefit that is more valuable than an actuarially reduced normal retirement benefit and that is payable on occurrence of an unpredictable contingent event is a retirement-type subsidy, and therefore is protected under § 204(g) of the Employee Retirement Income Security Act of 1974).

(2) Charges for benefits that are qualified additional benefits (QABs) within the meaning of § 7702(f)(5) are subject to the expense charge rule of § 7702(C)(3)(B)(ii) for purposes of determining whether a contract satisfies the cash value accumulation test or the guideline premium requirements, as applicable. Section 7702(b)(2)(B); Rev. Rul. 2005–6, 2005–1 C.B. 471.

(3) Section 7702(f)(8) provides that if a taxpayer establishes to the satisfaction of the Secretary that the requirements of § 7702(a) were not met due to reasonable error, and reasonable steps are being taken to remedy that error, the Secretary may waive such failure.

(4) Section 7702(g)(1)(A) provides that if at any time a contract that is a life insurance contract under the applicable law does not meet the definition of a life insurance contract under § 7702(a), the income on the contract for any taxable year of the policyholder shall be treated as ordinary income received or accrued by the policyholder during such year. Further, § 7702(g)(1)(C) provides that if, during any taxable year of the policyholder, a contract that is a life insurance contract under the applicable law ceases to meet the definition of life insurance contract under § 7702(a), the income on the contract for all prior taxable years is treated as received or accrued during the taxable year in which such cessation occurs.

.02 *Diversification requirement for variable contracts.* (1) Section 817(d) defines the term "variable contract" to mean a contract that (1) provides for the allocation of all or part of the amounts received under the contract to an account that, pursuant to state law or regulation, is segregated from the general asset accounts of the company, and (2) provides for the payment of annuities, or is a life insurance contract, or provides for funding of insurance on retired lives. In the case of an annuity contract or a contract that provides funding of insurance on retired lives, the amounts paid in or the amounts paid out are required to reflect the investment return and the market value of the segregated asset account. In the case of a life insurance contract, the amount of the death benefit (or the period of coverage) must be adjusted on the basis of the investment return and the market value of the segregated asset account.

(2) Section 817(h) provides that for purposes of §§ 72 and 7702(a), a variable contract (other than a pension plan contract) that is otherwise described in § 817, and that is based on a segregated asset account, is not treated as an annuity, endowment, or life insurance contract for any period (and any subsequent period) for which the investments made by such account are not adequately diversified.

(3) Section 1.817–5(a)(2) of the Income Tax Regulations provides that the investments of a segregated asset account are treated as satisfying the diversification requirements of § 1.817–5(b) for one or more periods if (1) the issuer or holder of a variable contract based on the account shows that the failure to satisfy the diversification requirements was inadvertent; (2) the investments of the account satisfy the diversification requirements within a reasonable time after discovery of the failure; and (3) the issuer or holder agrees to make such adjustments or pay such amounts as the Commissioner may require.

.03 *Treatment of Modified Endowment Contracts.* (1) Section 7702A defines a modified endowment contract (MEC) as a contract that meets the requirement of § 7702 but fails to meet the 7-pay test of § 7702A(b), or that is received in exchange for a contract that is a MEC. Under § 7702A(b), a contract fails to meet the 7-pay test if the accumulated amount paid under the contract at any time during the first seven contract years exceeds the sum of the net level premiums that would have been paid on or before that time if the contract provided for paid-up future benefits after the payment of seven level annual premiums.

(2) Section 7702A(c)(1) provides that determinations under the 7-pay test are made by applying the rules of §§ 7702(b)(2) and 7702(e), with modifications. Under this provision, charges for QABs are accounted for under the expense charge rule of § 7702(c)(3)(B)(ii).

(3) Section 72(e)(10) provides that a MEC is subject to the rules of § 72(e)(2)(B) (which taxes non-annuity distributions on an income-out-first basis) and § 72(e)(4)(A) (which generally treats loans, assignments, or pledges of any portion of the value of a MEC as non-annuity distributions). Further, under § 72(v), an amount received under a MEC may be subject to a 10% additional tax.

.04 *Authority to enter into closing agreements.* Under the authority of § 7121, the Service may enter into a closing agreement with a taxpayer in respect of any internal revenue tax for any taxable period.

SECTION 3. EXISTING CORRECTION PROCEDURES

To remedy the significant unforeseen tax consequences for holders of contracts that fail these provisions, the Service provides procedures for issuers of these failed contracts to enter into closing agreements with the Service.

(1) In Rev. Rul. 91–17, 1991–1 C.B. 190, *amplified by* Rev. Proc. 92–25, 1992–1 C.B. 741, an insurance company issued contracts that qualified as life insurance, endowment, and annuity contracts under the applicable law, but otherwise failed to meet the definition of life insurance contracts under § 7702(a) or the diversification requirements of § 817(h). The ruling concludes that the income on the contracts is a non-periodic distribution for which the insurance company is subject to certain recordkeeping, reporting, withholding and deposit obligations. In addition, if the company's failure to meet those obligations was not due to reasonable cause, the company could be subject to various penalties under the Code. Rev. Rul. 91–17 provides that the Service will waive civil penalties for failure to satisfy the reporting, withholding, and deposit requirements for income deemed received under § 7702(g) if (a) the insurance company requests and receives a waiver of the failure to meet the definition of a life insurance contract pursuant to § 7702(f)(8); (b) the insurance company satisfies the conditions of § 1.817–5(a)(2)(i)-(iii) of the regulations; or (c) the insurance company requests and, in a timely manner, executes a closing agreement under which the company agrees to pay an amount based on the amount of tax that would have been owed by the policyholders if they were treated as receiving the income on the contracts, and any interest with regard to such tax. Notice 99–48, 1999–2 C.B. 429, provides the tax rates to be used to compute the amount of tax that would have been owed by the policyholders if they were treated as receiving the income on the contracts.

(2) Rev. Proc. 92–25, 1992–1 C.B. 741, provides a procedure by which an issuer of a variable contract seeking relief under § 1.817–5(a)(2) of the regulations may request to enter into a closing agreement with the Service. Under the procedure, an issuer of the failed contracts may remedy the failure by paying an amount based on the tax and interest that the policyholder would be required to pay. A model closing agreement was provided.

(3) Rev. Proc. 2001–42, 2001–2 C.B. 212, *modified and amplified by* Rev. Proc. 2007–19, page 515, this Bulletin, provides the procedure by which an issuer may remedy an inadvertent non-egregious failure to comply with the MEC rules under § 7702A. Under this procedure, an issuer may remedy such a failure by paying an amount based on the overages on the unintended MECs and the tax and interest that the policyholder would be required to pay on those overages, based on proxy earnings and tax rates. A model closing agreement was provided. Rev. Proc. 2007–19 simplified Rev. Proc. 2001–42 by making it easier for issuers to locate indices used to compute proxy earnings rates, and by permitting electronic filing of templates that are required under the procedure.

(4) Rev. Rul. 2005–6, 2005–1 C.B. 471, provides that for purposes of determining whether a contract qualifies as a life insurance contract under § 7702 or as a MEC under § 7702A, charges for QABs are taken into account under the expense charge rule of § 7702(c)(3)(B)(ii). The revenue ruling provides three alternatives for issuers of life insurance contracts that do not account for QABs under the expense charge rule. Alternative C, which applies after February 7, 2006, provides that an issuer whose compliance system does not properly account for charges for QABs may request a closing agreement under certain terms. Under this alternative, the amount required to be paid is based on the number of contracts for which relief is requested.

SECTION 4. DRAFT MODEL CLOSING AGREEMENTS

Four draft model closing agreements are set forth in Exhibits A through D. Exhibit A would correct inadvertent failures to satisfy the guideline premium requirements of § 7702. Exhibit B would correct failures to satisfy the requirements of § 7702 or the requirements of § 7702A due to improper accounting for charges for QABs. *See* Rev. Rul. 2005–6, Alternative C. Exhibits C and D would update the model closing agreements previously provided in Rev. Proc. 2001–42 (for inadvertent MECs) and Rev. Proc. 92–25 (for inadvertent failures to satisfy the diversification requirements of § 817(h)).

SECTION 5. REQUEST FOR COMMENTS

.01 *In general.* Because additional changes to the existing procedures may be warranted, the Service invites comments on how the various correction procedures in general may be simplified.

.02 *Draft model closing agreements.* The Service requests comments on the model closing agreements that are included in this notice as Exhibits A, B, C, and D. The Service will consider all comments before issuing final model closing agreements.

.03 *Other matters.* In addition to the general matters described in section 5.01 and 5.02, the Service requests comments in the following specific areas:

(a) Under what circumstances, if any, should the Service retain the discretion to negotiate different terms and conditions for failures that otherwise would be covered by the final model closing agreement?

(b) Would additional model closing agreements be useful to remedy other failures involving life insurance or annuity contracts, such as the failure of a life insurance contract to satisfy the cash value accumulation test of § 7702(b), or the failure of an annuity contract to contain the distribution provisions required under § 72(s)? If so, please describe the specific failures.

(c) Could the process for obtaining a waiver of reasonable errors under § 7702(f)(8) be simplified? If so, please describe.

(d) Do the three alternatives set forth in Rev. Rul. 2005–6 provide an appropriate model for remedies of other errors under § 7702 that would have been considered reasonable within the meaning of § 7702(f)(8) before, but not after, the Service published guidance on the underlying legal issue?

(e) Could the amounts that are required to be paid under the model closing agreements be determined more simply, without altering the incentives already in place for complying with §§ 72, 817(h), 7702 and 7702A and for coming forward voluntarily once errors are discovered? For example, do the existing procedures require issuers to produce information not otherwise generated in the normal course of administering the contracts? Are there circumstances in which the amount paid under the model closing agreements would more appropriately be determined based on factors other than total income on the contract?

(f) Do the amounts required to be paid under the model closing agreements strike an appropriate balance between making the government whole for the tax that otherwise would be due, and encouraging voluntary compliance with the underlying provisions once an error is discovered? If lesser amounts might be appropriate in some circumstances, what are those circumstances and how should those amounts be limited?

(g) Should each model closing agreement contain language to the effect the agreement is null and void if the taxpayer does not remit the required payment and undertake the required corrective actions within the time frames set forth in the agreement? Do the time frames in the draft model closing agreements allow taxpayers enough time to satisfy their obligations under those agreements?

.04 *Address for submitting comments.* Written comments on the issues addressed in this notice may be submitted to the Office of the Associate Chief Counsel (Financial Institutions and Products), Attention: Melissa S. Luxner (Notice 2007–15), room 3552, CC:FIP:4, Internal Revenue Service, 1111 Constitution Avenue, NW, Washington, DC 20224. Alternatively, taxpayers may submit comments electronically to *Notice.Comments@irscounsel.treas.gov*. The Service requests any comments by June 12, 2007.

SECTION 6. PENDING REQUESTS FOR CLOSING AGREEMENTS

The Service will continue to process closing agreements under §§ 72, 817(h), 7702 and 7702A under existing procedures until those procedures are modified by publication in the Internal Revenue Bulletin.

DRAFTING INFORMATION

The principal author of this notice is Melissa S. Luxner of the Office of Associate Chief Counsel (Financial Institutions & Products). For further information regarding this notice, contact Melissa S. Luxner at (202) 622–3970 (not a toll-free call).

EXHIBIT A

Effective as of date executed by Internal

Revenue Service ____________________

CLOSING AGREEMENT AS TO FINAL DETERMINATION
COVERING SPECIFIC MATTERS
UNDER SECTION 7702

THIS CLOSING AGREEMENT ("Agreement") is made pursuant to § 7121 of the Internal Revenue Code (the "Code") by and between ***[Insert Taxpayer Name, Address and EIN]*** ("Taxpayer") and the Commissioner of Internal Revenue (the "Service").

WHEREAS,

A. Taxpayer is the issuer of one or more contracts that were intended to qualify as life insurance contracts under § 7702.

B. Pursuant to Rev. Rul. 91–17, 1991–1 C.B. 190, *amplified by* Rev. Proc. 92–25, 1992–1 C.B. 741, as supplemented by Notice 99–48, 1999–2 C.B. 429, the Service under certain circumstances will waive civil penalties for failure of a taxpayer to satisfy the reporting, withholding and deposit requirements for income received or deemed received under § 7702(g).

C. By letter dated ***[Insert date]*** Taxpayer submitted to the Service, pursuant to Rev. Proc. 2006–1, 2006–1 I.R.B. 1 ***[or successor Rev. Proc., if applicable]***, a request for this Agreement covering ***[Insert number]*** of Taxpayer's life insurance contracts identified on Exhibit A attached to this Agreement (the "Contracts").

D. Taxpayer intended that each of the Contracts meet the definition of life insurance contract under § 7702. For each Contract, however, Taxpayer accepted and retained premiums that exceeded the Contract's guideline premium limitations under § 7702(c)(2) ***[or § 101(f), if applicable]***. As a result, each of the Contracts identified on Exhibit A failed to satisfy the requirements of § 7702.

E. The Service has determined that the errors described in C above which caused the Contracts to fail to satisfy the requirements of § 7702 were not reasonable errors within the meaning of § 7702(f)(8) ***[or § 101(f)(3)(H), if applicable]***, but are eligible for relief under Rev. Rul. 91–17.

F. Taxpayer represents to the Service that:

(1) With respect to Contracts under which the "death benefit," within the meaning of Notice 99–48, 1999–2 C.B. 429, is less than $50,000, the aggregate "income on the contract," within the meaning of § 7702(g)(1), through ***[Insert date]***, is ***$_[insert amount]***. The aggregate "income on the contract" for each year of failure is:

Year	Amount
	Total

(2) With respect to Contracts under which the "death benefit," within the meaning of Notice 99–48, is equal to or exceeds $50,000 but is less than $180,000, the aggregate "income on the contract," within the meaning of § 7702(g)(1), through ***[Insert date]***, is ***$ [insert amount]***. The aggregate "income on the contract" for each year of failure is:

Year	Amount
	Total

(3) With respect to Contracts under which the "death benefit," within the meaning of Notice 99–48, is equal to or exceeds $180,000, the aggregate income on the contract," within the meaning of § 7702(g)(1), through ***[Insert date]***, is ***$ [insert amount]***. The aggregate "income on the contract" for each year of failure is:

Year	Amount
	Total

G. With respect to Contracts under which the death benefit is less than $50,000, the tax (determined at a tax rate of 15 percent) that would have been owed by the Contract holders if they were treated as receiving the income on the Contracts set forth in E(1) above is ***$ [insert amount]***. With respect to Contracts under which the death benefit is equal to or exceeds $50,000 but is less than $180,000, the tax (determined at a rate of 28 percent) that would have been owed by the Contract holders if they were treated as receiving the income on the Contracts set forth in E(2) above is ***$ [insert amount]***. With respect to Contracts under which the death benefit is equal to or exceeds $180,000, the tax (determined at a tax rate of 36 percent) that would have been owed by the Contract holders if they were treated as receiving the income on the Contracts set forth in E(3) above is ***$ [insert amount]***.

The total tax that would have been owed by the Contract holders if they were treated as receiving the income on the Contracts is ***$ [insert amount]***. Interest on the total tax through ***[Insert date]*** is ***$ [insert amount]***. The two amounts total ***$ [insert amount]***.

H. To ensure that the Contracts qualify as life insurance contracts under § 7702(a), Taxpayer and the Service have entered into this Agreement.

NOW THEREFORE IT IS HEREBY FURTHER DETERMINED AND AGREED BETWEEN TAXPAYER AND THE SERVICE AS FOLLOWS:

1. In consideration for the agreement of the Service as set forth in Section 2 below, Taxpayer agrees as follows:

(A) Taxpayer will pay the Service the amount of ***$ [insert amount]*** at the time and in the manner described in Section 3 below.

(B) The amount paid pursuant to Section 1(A) above is not deductible, nor is such amount refundable, subject to credit or offset, or otherwise recoverable from the Service.

(C) For purposes of Taxpayer's complying with its reporting and withholding obligations under the Code,

(i) neither the investment in the contract for purposes of § 72, nor the premiums paid for purposes of § 7702 ***[or § 101(f), if applicable]***, on any Contract can be increased by any portion of the amount set forth in Section 1(A) above. If any such increases are made, they are entitled to no effect.

(ii) neither the investment in the contract for purposes of § 72, nor the premiums paid, for purposes of § 7702 ***[or §101(f), if applicable]***, on any Contract can be increased by any portion of the amount which Taxpayer represents to be the income on the contract for all of the Contracts in the aggregate. If any such increases are made, they are entitled to no effect.

(D) With respect to each Contract that is in force on the effective date of this Agreement, to the extent necessary in order to bring such Contract into compliance with § 7702 ***[or §101(f), if applicable]***:

(i) If the sum of the premiums paid as of the effective date of this Agreement exceeds the guideline premium limitation as of such date, Taxpayer will take the following corrective action:

(a) Increase the death benefit to not less than an amount that will ensure compliance with § 7702 ***[or §101(f), if applicable]***, or

(b) Refund to the Contract holder the amount of such excess, with interest at the Contract's interest crediting rate; or

(ii) If the sum of the premiums paid as of the effective date of this Agreement does not exceed the guideline premium limitation as of such date, Taxpayer will take no corrective action.

(E) With respect to any Contract which terminated by reason of the death of the insured and (i) prior to the date this Agreement is executed by the Service and Taxpayer and (ii) at a time when the premiums paid exceeded the guideline premium limitation for the Contract, Taxpayer will pay the Contract holder or the Contract holder's estate such excess, with interest at the Contract's interest crediting rate.

2. In consideration of the agreement of Taxpayer set forth in Section 1 above, the Service agrees as follows:

(A) To treat each Contract that is still in force as of the effective date of this Agreement as having satisfied the requirements of § 7702 **[or § 101(f), if applicable]** during the period from the date of issuance of the Contract through and including the later of (i) the date of the execution of this Agreement by the Service; or (ii) the date of any corrective action described in Section 1(D) above;

(B) To treat each Contract that terminated prior to the effective date of this Agreement as having satisfied the requirements of § 7702 **[or 101(f), if applicable]** during the period from date of issuance of the Contract through and including the date of the Contract's termination;

(C) To treat the failures described above, and any corrective action described in Section 1(D) or 1(E) above, as having no effect on the date the Contract was issued or entered into;

(D) To treat any amount paid prior to the effective date of this Agreement to any beneficiary under a Contract by reason of the death of the insured as paid under a life insurance contract for purposes of the exclusion from gross income under § 101(a)(1);

(E) To waive civil penalties for failure of Taxpayer to satisfy the reporting, withholding, or deposit requirements for income deemed received by Contract holders under § 7702; and

(F) To treat no portion of the amount described in Section 1(A) above as income to the Contract holders.

3. Any action required of Taxpayer in Section 1(D) or 1(E) above shall be taken by Taxpayer no later than ninety (90) days after the date of execution of this Agreement by the Service. Payment of the amount described in Section 1(A) above shall be made within thirty (30) days after the date of execution of this Agreement by the Service by check payable to the "United States Treasury," delivered together with a copy of this executed Agreement to Internal Revenue Service, Receipt and Control Stop 31, 201 W. Rivercenter Blvd., Covington, KY 41011.

4. This Agreement is, and shall be construed as being, for the benefit of Taxpayer. Contract holders covered by this Agreement are intended beneficiaries of this Agreement. This Agreement shall not be construed as creating any liability of Taxpayer to the Contract holders.

5. Neither the Service nor Taxpayer shall endeavor by litigation or other means to attack the validity of this Agreement.

6. This Agreement may not be cited or relied upon as precedent in the disposition of any other matter.

NOW THIS CLOSING AGREEMENT FURTHER WITNESSETH, that the Service and Taxpayer mutually agree that the matters so determined shall be final and conclusive, except as follows:

1. The matter to which this Agreement relates may be reopened in the event of fraud, malfeasance, or misrepresentation of material facts set forth herein.

2. This Agreement is subject to sections of the Code that expressly provide that effect be given to their provisions notwithstanding any other law or rule of law except § 7122.

3. This Agreement is subject to any legislation enacted subsequent to the date of execution hereof if the legislation provides that it is effective with respect to closing agreements.

IN WITNESS WHEREOF, the parties have subscribed their names to these presents in triplicate.

[Insert Taxpayer name]

Date Signed: ____________________ By: ____________________

Title: ____________________

COMMISSIONER OF INTERNAL REVENUE

Date Signed: ____________________ By: ____________________

Title: ____________________

EXHIBIT B

Effective as of date executed by Internal

Revenue Service ____________________

CLOSING AGREEMENT AS TO FINAL DETERMINATION
COVERING SPECIFIC MATTERS
UNDER REV. RUL. 2005–6

THIS CLOSING AGREEMENT ("Agreement") is made pursuant to § 7121 of the Internal Revenue Code (the "Code") by and between ***[Insert Taxpayer Name, Address and EIN]*** ("Taxpayer") and the Commissioner of Internal Revenue (the "Service").

WHEREAS,

A. Taxpayer is the issuer of one or more contracts that were intended to qualify as life insurance contracts under § 7702 and that provided qualified additional benefits (QABs) within the meaning of § 7702(f)(5).

B. Pursuant to Rev. Rul. 2005–6, 2005–1 C.B. 471, the Service under certain circumstances will waive civil penalties for failure of a taxpayer to satisfy the reporting, withholding and deposit requirements for income received or deemed received under § 7702(g).

C. By letter dated ***[Insert date]*** Taxpayer submitted to the Service, pursuant to Rev. Proc. 2006–1, 2006–1 I.R.B. 1 ***[or successor Rev. Proc., if applicable]***, a request for this Agreement covering ***[Insert number]*** of Taxpayer's life insurance contracts identified on Exhibit A attached to this Agreement (the "Contracts").

D. Taxpayer intended that each of the Contracts meet the definition of a life insurance contract under § 7702 and not be a modified endowment contract (MEC) within the meaning of § 7702A. Taxpayer, however, maintained a compliance system for the contracts that did not account properly for charges for qualified additional benefits (QABs) under § 7702(c)(3)(B)(ii). As a result, the Contracts identified in Exhibit A failed to satisfy the requirements of § 7702 or § 7702A, as applicable.

E. The Service has determined that the errors described in C above qualify the issuer for the remedy described in Rev. Rul. 2005–6.

F. To ensure that the Contracts qualify as life insurance contracts under § 7702(a), Taxpayer and the Service have entered into this Agreement.

NOW THEREFORE IT IS HEREBY FURTHER DETERMINED AND AGREED BETWEEN TAXPAYER AND THE SERVICE AS FOLLOWS:

1. In consideration for the agreement of the Service as set forth in Section 2 below, Taxpayer agrees as follows:

(A) To pay the Service the amount of ***$ [insert amount]*** at the time and in the manner described in Section 3 below.

(B) The amount paid pursuant to Section 1(A) above is not deductible, nor is such amount refundable, subject to credit or offset, or otherwise recoverable from the Service.

(C) For purposes of Taxpayer's complying with its reporting and withholding obligations under the Code,

(i) neither the investment in the contract for purposes of § 72, nor the premiums paid for purposes of § 7702, on any Contract can be increased by any portion of the amount set forth in Section 1(A) above. If any such increases are made, they are entitled to no effect.

(ii) neither the investment in the contract for purposes of § 72, nor the premiums paid, for purposes of § 7702, on any Contract can be increased by any portion of the amount which Taxpayer represents to be the income on the contract for all of the Contracts in the aggregate. If any such increases are made, they are entitled to no effect.

(D) With respect to each Contract that is in force on the effective date of this Agreement, to the extent necessary in order to bring such Contract into compliance with § 7702:

(i) If the sum of the premiums paid as of the effective date of this Agreement exceeds the amount necessary to keep the contracts in compliance with the requirements of § 7702, Taxpayer will take the following corrective action:

(a) Increase the death benefit to not less than an amount that will ensure compliance with § 7702, or

(b) Refund to the Contract holder the amount of such excess, with interest at the Contract's interest crediting rate; or

(ii) If the sum of the premiums paid as of the effective date of this Agreement does not exceed the amount necessary to keep the contracts in compliance with the requirements of § 7702, Taxpayer will take no corrective action.

(E) With respect to any Contract which terminated by reason of the death of the insured and (i) prior to the date this Agreement is executed by the Service and Taxpayer and (ii) at a time when the premiums paid exceeded the guideline premium limitation for the Contract, Taxpayer will pay the Contract holder or the Contract holder's estate such excess, with interest at the Contract's interest crediting rate.

2. In consideration of the agreement of Taxpayer set forth in Section 1 above, the Service agrees as follows:

(A) To treat each Contract that is still in force as of the effective date of this Agreement as having satisfied the requirements of § 7702 ***[and § 7702A, if applicable]***, during the period from the date of issuance of the Contract through and including the later of (i) the date of the execution of this Agreement by the Service, or (ii) the date of any corrective action described in Section 1(D) above;

(B) To treat each Contract that terminated prior to the effective date of this Agreement as having satisfied the requirements of § 7702 ***[and § 7702A, if applicable]*** during the period from date of issuance of the Contract through and including the date of the Contract's termination;

(C) To treat the failures described above, and any corrective action described in Section 1(D) or 1(E) above, as having no effect on the date the Contract was issued or entered into;

(D) To treat any amount paid prior to the effective date of this Agreement to any beneficiary under a Contract by reason of the death of the insured as paid under a life insurance contract for purposes of the exclusion from gross income under § 101(a)(1);

(E) To waive civil penalties for failure of Taxpayer to satisfy the reporting, withholding, or deposit requirements for income deemed received by Contract holders under § 7702 ***[and § 7702A, if applicable]***; and

(F) To treat no portion of the amount described in Section 1(A) above as income to the Contract holders.

3. Any action required of Taxpayer in Section 1(D) or 1(E) above shall be taken by Taxpayer no later than ninety (90) days after the date of execution of this Agreement by the Service. Payment of the amount described in Section 1(A) above shall be made within thirty (30) days after the date of execution of this Agreement by the Service by check payable to the "United States Treasury" delivered together with a copy of this executed Agreement, to Internal Revenue Service, Receipt and Control Stop 31, 201 W. Rivercenter Blvd., Covington, KY 41011.

4. This Agreement is, and shall be construed as being, for the benefit of Taxpayer. Contract holders covered by this Agreement are intended beneficiaries of this Agreement. This Agreement shall not be construed as creating any liability of Taxpayer to the Contract holders.

5. Neither the Service nor Taxpayer shall endeavor by litigation or other means to attack the validity of this Agreement.

6. This Agreement may not be cited or relied upon as precedent in the disposition of any other matter.

NOW THIS CLOSING AGREEMENT FURTHER WITNESSETH, that the Service and Taxpayer mutually agree that the matters so determined shall be final and conclusive, except as follows:

1. The matter to which this Agreement relates may be reopened in the event of fraud, malfeasance, or misrepresentation of material facts set forth herein.

2. This Agreement is subject to sections of the Code that expressly provide that effect be given to their provisions notwithstanding any other law or rule of law except § 7122.

3. This Agreement is subject to any legislation enacted subsequent to the date of execution hereof if the legislation provides that it is effective with respect to closing agreements.

IN WITNESS WHEREOF, the parties have subscribed their names to these presents in triplicate.

[Insert Taxpayer name]

Date Signed: ____________________ By: ____________________

Title: ____________________

COMMISSIONER OF INTERNAL REVENUE

Date Signed: ______________ By: ______________

Title: ______________

EXHIBIT C

Effective as of date executed by Internal

Revenue Service ______________

CLOSING AGREEMENT AS TO FINAL DETERMINATION
COVERING SPECIFIC MATTERS
UNDER SECTION 7702A

THIS CLOSING AGREEMENT ("Agreement") is made pursuant to § 7121 of the Internal Revenue Code (the "Code") by and between ***[Insert Taxpayer name, address, and EIN]*** ("Taxpayer") and the Commissioner of Internal Revenue (the "Service").

WHEREAS,

A. Taxpayer is the issuer of one or more life insurance contracts under § 7702;

B. Pursuant to Rev. Proc. 2001–42, 2001–2 C.B. 212, an issuer under certain circumstances may remedy an inadvertent non-egregious failure to comply with the modified endowment contract rules under § 7702A.

C. By letter dated ***[Insert date]***, Taxpayer submitted to the Service, pursuant to Rev. Proc. 2006–1, 2006–1 I.R.B. 1 ***[or successor Rev. Proc., if applicable]***, a request for this Agreement covering ***[Insert number]*** modified endowment contracts identified on Exhibit A attached to this Agreement (the "Contracts").

D. Taxpayer intended that each of the Contracts not be a modified endowment contract (MEC) under § 7702A. Taxpayer represents that the Contract[s] is [are] not described in Sec. 4.02 of Rev. Proc. 2001–42.

E. The Service has determined that the contracts identified on Exhibit A are eligible for relief under Rev. Proc. 2001–42.

F. Taxpayer represents that the cumulative "overage earnings," within the meaning of Sec. 3.06 of Rev. Proc. 2001–42, for the Contract[s] equal $ ***[Insert amount]***.

G. Taxpayer represents that the total of the amounts determined under Sec. 5.03(1)(a), (b), and (c) of Rev. Proc. 2001–42, after taking the special rule in Sec. 5.03(2) of that revenue procedure into account, with regard to the Contract[s] are $ ***[Insert amount]***, $ ***[Insert amount]***, and $ ***[Insert amount]***, respectively.

H. To ensure that the Contract[s] is/are not treated as [a] modified endowment contract[s], Taxpayer and the Service have entered into this Agreement.

NOW THEREFORE, IT IS HEREBY FURTHER DETERMINED AND AGREED BETWEEN TAXPAYER AND THE SERVICE AS FOLLOWS:

1. In consideration for the agreement of the Service as set forth in Section 2 below, Taxpayer agrees as follows:

(A) Taxpayer will pay to the Service the amount of $ ***[Insert amount]*** at the time and in the manner described in Section 3 below.

(B) The amount paid pursuant to Section 1(A) above is not deductible by Taxpayer, nor is such amount refundable, subject to credit or offset, or otherwise recoverable by Taxpayer from the Service.

(C) For purposes of Taxpayer's complying with its reporting and withholding obligations under the Code,

(i) neither the investment in the contract for purposes of § 72, nor the premiums paid for purposes of § 7702, on any Contract can be increased by any portion of the amount set forth in Section 1(A) above. If any such increases are made, they are entitled to no effect.

(ii) neither the investment in the contract for purposes of § 72, nor the premiums paid, for purposes of § 7702, on any Contract can be increased by any portion of the amount which Taxpayer represents to be the income on the contract for all of the Contracts in the aggregate. If any such increases are made, they are entitled to no effect.

(D) To bring Contract[s] for which the testing period (as defined in Sec. 3.01 of Revenue Procedure 2001–42) will not have expired on or before the date 90 days after the execution of this Agreement into compliance with § 7702A, either by an increase in death benefit[s] or the return of the excess premiums and earnings thereon to the contract holder[s].

2. In consideration of the agreement of Taxpayer set forth in Section 1 above, the Service agrees as follows:

(A) To treat each Contract as having satisfied the requirements of § 7702A during the period from the date of issuance of the Contract through and including the later of—

(i) date of the execution of this Agreement, and

(ii) the date of the corrective actions described in Section 1(D) above;

(B) To treat the corrective action described in 1(D) above as having no effect on the date the Contract was issued or entered into;

(C) To waive civil penalties for failure of Taxpayer to satisfy the reporting, withholding, and/or deposit requirements for income subject to tax under § 72(e)(10) that was received or deemed received by a contract holder under a Contract in a calendar year ending prior to the date of execution of this Agreement; and

(D) To treat no portion of the sum described in Section 1(A) above as income to the Contract holders.

3. The actions required of Taxpayer in Section 1(D) above shall be taken by Taxpayer no later than ninety (90) days after the date of execution of this Agreement by the Service. Payment of the amount described in Section 1(A) above shall be made within thirty (30) days of the date of execution of this Agreement by the Service by check payable to the "United States Treasury," delivered together with a copy of this executed Agreement to Internal Revenue Service, Receipt & Control Stop 31, 201 W. Rivercenter Blvd., Covington, KY 41011.

4. This Agreement is, and shall be construed as being, for the benefit of Taxpayer. The Contract holders covered by this Agreement are intended beneficiaries of this Agreement. This Agreement shall not be construed as creating any liability of an issuer to the Contract holders.

5. Neither the Service nor Taxpayer shall endeavor by litigation or other means to attack the validity of this Agreement.

6. This Agreement may not be cited or relied upon as precedent in the disposition of any other matter.

NOW THIS CLOSING AGREEMENT FURTHER WITNESSETH, that Taxpayer and the Service mutually agree that the matters so determined shall be final and conclusive, except as follows:

1. The matter to which this Agreement relates may be reopened in the event of fraud, malfeasance, or misrepresentation of material facts set forth herein.

2. This Agreement is subject to sections of the Code that expressly provide that effect be given to their provisions notwithstanding any other law or rule of law except § 7122.

3. This Agreement is subject to any legislation enacted subsequent to the date of execution hereof if the legislation provides that it is effective with respect to closing agreements.

IN WITNESS WHEREOF, the parties have subscribed their names to these presents in triplicate.

[Insert Taxpayer name]

Date Signed: ______________________ By: ______________________

Title: ______________________

COMMISSIONER OF INTERNAL REVENUE

Date Signed: ____________________ By: ____________________

Title: ____________________

EXHIBIT D

Effective as of date executed by Internal

Revenue Service ____________________

CLOSING AGREEMENT AS TO FINAL DETERMINATION
COVERING SPECIFIC MATTERS
UNDER SECTION 817(h)

THIS CLOSING AGREEMENT ("Agreement"), is made pursuant to § 7121 of the Internal Revenue Code (the "Code") by and between ***[Insert Taxpayer, Name, Address and EIN]*** (Taxpayer") and the Commissioner of Internal Revenue (the "Service").

WHEREAS,

A. Taxpayer is the issuer of one or more variable contracts, as defined in § 817(d) (without regard to § 817(h)), which are based, in whole or in part, on a segregated asset account (the "Account") and that provide for the allocation of amounts received under the variable contracts to the Account.

B. Pursuant to Rev. Proc. 92–25, 1992–1 C.B. 741, the Service may treat the investments of a segregated asset account on which a variable contract is based as satisfying the diversification requirements of § 817(h) and § 1.817–5(b) of the Income Tax Regulations for periods during which there was an inadvertent failure to diversify.

C. By letter dated ***[Insert date,]*** Taxpayer submitted to the Service, pursuant to Rev. Proc. 2006–1, 2006–1 I.R.B. 1 ***[or successor Rev. Proc., if applicable]***, a request for this Agreement that the ***[Insert account name]*** be treated as adequately diversified under § 817(h) for the period ***[Insert period of nondiversification]*** ("the period of nondiversification").

D. Taxpayer intended that Account be adequately diversified within the meaning of § 817 and § 1.817–5(b). The failure of the investments of the Account to satisfy the requirements of § 1.817–5(b) for the period of nondiversification was inadvertent.

E. The Service has determined that the failure of Account to satisfy the requirements of § 817(h) is eligible for relief under Rev. Proc. 92–25.

F. Taxpayer represents that the failure of the investments of the Account to satisfy the requirements of § 1.817–5(b) was discovered on ***[Insert date]***, and the investments came into compliance with those requirements on ***[Insert date]***.

G. The "income on the contract," within the meaning of § 1.817–5(a)(2) and § 7702(g)(l)(B) (without regard to § 7701(g)(l)(C)), for all contracts based on the Account during the period of non-diversification in the aggregate totals $***[Insert amount]*** for the ***[Insert account name]***.

H. The sum of the amounts computed in sections 4.02(1)(A) and (B) and 4.02(2)(A) of Rev. Proc. 92–25 is $ ***[Insert amount]***. The sum of the interest amounts computed in sections 4.02(1)(C) and 4.02(2)(A) of Rev. Proc. 92–25 is $ ***[Insert amount]***.

I. To ensure that variable contracts that provide for the allocation of amounts received thereunder to the Account are treated as annuity, endowment, or life insurance contracts, as applicable, Taxpayer and the Service have entered into this Agreement.

NOW THEREFORE, IT IS HEREBY FURTHER DETERMINED AND AGREEED BETWEEN TAXPAYER AND THE SERVICE AS FOLLOWS:

1. In consideration for the agreement of the Service as set forth in Section 2 below, Taxpayer agrees as follows:

(A) Taxpayer will pay the Service the amount of $ ***[Insert amount]*** at the time and in the manner described in Section 3 below.

(B) The amount paid pursuant to Section 1(A) above is not deductible, nor is such amount refundable, subject to credit or offset, or otherwise recoverable from the Service;

(C) For purposes of Taxpayer's complying with its reporting and withholding obligations under the Code,

(i) neither the investment in the contract for purposes of § 72, nor the premiums paid for purposes of § 7702 ***[or § 101(f), if applicable]***, on any Contract can be increased by any portion of the amount set forth in Section 1(A) above. If any such increases are made, they are entitled to no effect.

(ii) neither the investment in the contract for purposes of § 72, nor the premiums paid, for purposes of § 7702 ***[or §101(f), if applicable]***, on any Contract can be increased by any portion of the amount which Taxpayer represents to be the income on the contract for all of the Contracts in the aggregate. If any such increases are made, they are entitled to no effect.

2. In consideration of the agreement of Taxpayer set forth in Section 1 above, the Service agrees as follows:

(A) To treat the investments of the Account as adequately diversified for purposes of § 817(h) during the period of nondiversification; and

(B) To treat no portion of the amounts described in Section 1(A) above as income to the Contract holders.

3. Payment of the sum described in section 1(A) above shall be made within thirty (30) days of the date of execution of this Agreement by the Service. This payment must be made by check payable to the "United States Treasury," delivered, together with a copy of this executed Agreement, to Internal Revenue Service Center, Receipt and Control Stop 31, 201 W. Rivercenter Blvd., Covington, KY 41011.

4. This Agreement is, and shall be construed as being, for the benefit of Taxpayer. Holders of contracts based on the Account are intended beneficiaries of this Agreement. This Agreement shall not be construed as creating any liability of Taxpayer to the holders of the contracts based on the Account.

5. Neither the Service nor Taxpayer shall endeavor by litigation or other means to attack the validity of this Agreement.

6. This Agreement may not be cited or relied upon as precedent in the disposition of any other matter.

NOW THIS CLOSING AGREEMENT FURTHER WITNESSETH, that the Service and Taxpayer mutually agree that the matters so determined shall be final and conclusive, except as follows:

1. The matter to which this Agreement relates may be reopened in the event of fraud, malfeasance, or misrepresentation of material facts set forth herein.

2. This Agreement is subject to sections of the Code that expressly provide that effect be given to their provisions notwithstanding any other law or rule of law except § 7122.

3. This Agreement is subject to any legislation enacted subsequent to the date of execution hereof if the legislation provides that it is effective with respect to closing agreements.

IN WITNESS WHEREOF, the parties have subscribed their names to these presents in triplicate.

[Insert Taxpayer name]

Date Signed: ________________ By: ________________

Title: ________________

COMMISSIONER OF INTERNAL REVENUE

Date Signed: ________________ By: ________________

Title: ________________

26 CFR § 301.7121: Closing agreements.
(Also Part I, section 7702A.)

Rev. Proc. 2007–19

SECTION 1. PURPOSE

This revenue procedure modifies the procedure by which an issuer of a life insurance contract may remedy an inadvertent non-egregious failure to comply with the modified endowment contract rules under § 7702A of the Internal Revenue Code. Rev. Proc. 2001–42, 2001–2 C.B. 212, is modified and amplified.

SECTION 2. BACKGROUND

.01 *Definition of a modified endowment contract*

(1) Section 7702A(a) provides that a life insurance contract is a modified endowment contract ("MEC") if the contract—

(a) is entered into on or after June 21, 1988, and fails to meet the "7-pay test" of § 7702A(b), or

(b) is received in exchange for a contract described in paragraph (a) of this section 2.01(1).

(2) A contract fails to meet the 7-pay test if the accumulated amount paid under the contract at any time during the first 7 contract years exceeds the sum of the net level premiums which would have to be paid on or before such time if the contract were to provide for paid-up "future benefits" (as defined in §§ 7702A(c)(3) and 7702(f)(4)) after the payment of 7 level annual premiums.

.02 *Tax treatment of amounts received under a MEC.* Section 72(e)(10) provides that a MEC is subject to the rules of § 72(e)(2)(B), which tax non-annuity distributions on an income-out-first basis, and the rules of § 72(e)(4)(A) (as modified by §§ 72(e)(10)(A)(ii) and 72(e)(10)(B)), which generally deem loans and assignments or pledges of any portion of the value of a MEC to be non-annuity distributions. Moreover, under § 72(v), the portion of any annuity or non-annuity distribution received under a MEC that is includible in gross income is subject to a 10% additional tax unless the distribution is made on or after the date on which the taxpayer attains age 59½, is attributable to the taxpayer's becoming disabled (within the meaning of § 72(m)(7)), or is part of a series of substantially equal periodic payments (not less frequently than annually) made for the life (or life expectancy) of the taxpayer or the joint lives (or joint life expectancies) of such taxpayer and the taxpayer's beneficiary.

.03 *Rev. Proc. 2001–42.* The Internal Revenue Service ("Service") is aware of situations in which, as a result of inadvertent non-egregious failures to comply with the MEC rules, life insurance premiums are collected which exceed the 7-pay limit provided by § 7702A(b). This can produce significant unforeseen tax consequences for the contract holders. To allow issuers to remedy such situations, Rev. Proc. 2001–42 sets forth the circumstances under which the Service will enter into closing agreements which provide that contracts identified in the closing agreements will not be treated as MECs. Under Rev. Proc. 2001–42, an issuer must provide information about the contracts that are subject to the closing agreement, including a template for each contract setting forth the cumulative amounts paid under the contract, the contract's cumulative 7-pay premium, the overage, if any, for each contract year, the earnings rate applicable for each contract year, and the overage earnings for each contract year. In addition, the issuer must agree to pay under the closing agreement an amount based on the contract's overage, overage earnings, and tax and interest thereon.

.04 *Need for changes to Rev. Proc. 2001–42.* During the 5 years it has administered Rev. Proc. 2001–42, the Service has become aware of a number of changes that would make it easier for issuers to use that procedure to seek relief. The Service has determined that the General Account Total Return would be more accessible to taxpayers if based on Moody's Seasoned Corporate Aaa and Baa Bond Yields, rather than on the indices provided in Rev. Proc. 2001–42; similarly, the Bond Fund Total Return would be more accessible if the Merrill Lynch Corporate Bond Master Bond Index, Total Return, were instead identified as the Merrill Lynch U.S. Corporate Master Index (C0A0); the Service has the capacity to process electronic exhibits in connection with requests for closing agreements involving life insurance contracts (*see, e.g.*, Notice 2005–35, 2005–1 C.B. 1087); and, the Service has changed the address to which payments under Rev. Proc. 2001–42 must be sent.

SECTION 3. CHANGES TO EXISTING PROCEDURE

.01 *General Account Total Return.* Rev. Proc. 2001–42, section 3.07(2), is modified to provide that the General Account Total Return is the arithmetic average (weighted on a 50–50 basis) of the following two rates: (1) Moody's Seasoned Corporate Aaa Bond Yield, frequency annual; and (2) Moody's Seasoned Corporate Baa Bond Yield, frequency annual. Both rates are published by Moody's Investors Service, Inc., or any successor thereto, and are publicly available at *www.federalreserve.gov*. Under this methodology, the General Account Total Return for 2005 would be (5.23 + 6.06)/2 = 5.645. Section 3.07(2) is further modified to include the following tables setting forth the General Account Total Return as so determined for the years 1988 through 2005:

Year	General Account Total Return	Year	General Account Total Return
1988	10.2%	1997	7.6%
1989	9.7%	1998	6.9%
1990	9.8%	1999	7.4%
1991	9.2%	2000	8.0%
1992	8.6%	2001	7.5%
1993	7.5%	2002	7.2%
1994	8.3%	2003	6.2%
1995	7.8%	2004	6.1%
1996	7.7%	2005	5.6%

.02 *Variable Contracts Earnings Rate Table*. Rev. Proc. 2001–42, section 3.07(3), is modified by substituting the following earnings rate table for that which appears in section 3.07. This table supplements the existing table by providing earnings rates for the years 2001 through 2005:

Year	Variable contracts Earnings rate	Year	Variable contracts Earnings rate
1988	13.5%	1997	17.8%
1989	17.4%	1998	19.7%
1990	1.4%	1999	12.8%
1991	25.4%	2000	-5.5%
1992	5.9%	2001	-7.1%
1993	13.9%	2002	-14.1%
1994	-1.0%	2003	19.6%
1995	23.0%	2004	6.9%
1996	14.3%	2005	2.1%

.03 *Bond Fund Total Return*. Rev. Proc. 2001–42, section 3.07(6), is modified to provide that the Bond Fund Total Return is (a) the "calendar year percentage return" (as defined in section 3.07(7) of Rev. Proc. 2001–42) represented by the end-of-year values of the Merrill Lynch U.S. Corporate Master Index (C0A0), as published by Merrill Lynch & Company, Inc., or any successor thereto, less (b) 1.0 percentage point. The Merrill Lynch U.S. Corporate Master Index (C0A0) is publicly available at *www.mlindex.ml.com*. Under this methodology, the Bond Fund Total Return for 2005 would be ((1546.511–1516.602)/1516.602) – .01 = 0.9721 percent.

.04 *Address for Payment*. The address set forth in Rev. Proc. 2001–42, section 5.04, for payment of the amount required under a closing agreement concerning inadvertent MECs is modified to read as follows: Internal Revenue Service, Receipt & Control Stop 31, 201 W. Rivercenter Blvd., Covington, KY 41011.

.05 *Electronic Submissions*. A new section 5.06 is added to Rev. Proc. 2001–42 to read as follows:

".06 *Electronic submissions*. The information required under this revenue procedure may be submitted to the Service electronically, in read-only format, on a CD-ROM. Adobe Portable Document format is a suitable format. Other formats may be arranged on a case-by-case basis. The issuer must provide a total of 3 CD-ROMs, one for each of the three (3) copies of the closing agreement."

.06 *Additional changes to Rev. Proc. 2001–42*. The Service is aware that additional changes to Rev. Proc. 2001–42 may be warranted. Notice 2007–15, page 503, this Bulletin, requests comments on a variety of issues affecting closing agreements for life insurance products, including inadvertent MECs. The Service will continue to process closing agreements under the provisions of Rev. Proc. 2001–42, as modified by this revenue procedure, until Rev. Proc. 2001–42 is replaced or further modified by publication in the Internal Revenue Bulletin.

SECTION 4. PAPERWORK REDUCTION ACT

The collections of information in Rev. Proc. 2001–42 have been previously reviewed and approved by the Office of Management and Budget in accordance with the Paperwork Reduction Act (44 U.S.C. 3507) under control number 1545–1752. This revenue procedure does not make substantive changes to those collections of information.

SECTION 5. EFFECTIVE DATE

This revenue procedure is effective for submissions received after January 26, 2007, the date this revenue procedure was made available to the public.

SECTION 6. EFFECT ON OTHER DOCUMENTS

Rev. Proc. 2001–42 is modified and amplified.

DRAFTING INFORMATION

The principal author of this revenue procedure is Katherine A. Hossofsky of the Office of the Associate Chief Counsel (Financial Institutions & Products). For further information regarding this revenue procedure, please contact Ms. Hossofsky at (202) 622–8435 (not a toll-free call).

---

26 CFR 601.105: Examination of returns and claims for refund, credit or abatement; determination of correct tax liability.
(Also: Part I, §§ 6011, 6111, 6112; 1.6011–4, 301.6112–1.)

Rev. Proc. 2007–20

SECTION 1. PURPOSE

This revenue procedure provides that certain transactions with contractual protection are not reportable transactions for purposes of the disclosure rules under § 1.6011–4(b)(4) of the Income Tax Regulations. However, these transactions may be reportable transactions for purposes of the disclosure rules under § 1.6011–4(b)(2), (b)(3), (b)(5), (b)(6), or (b)(7).

SECTION 2. BACKGROUND

.01 Section 1.6011–4 requires a taxpayer that participates in a reportable transaction to disclose the transaction in accordance with the procedures provided in § 1.6011–4. Under § 1.6011–4(b), one category of reportable transaction is a transaction with contractual protection. A transaction with contractual protection is defined in § 1.6011–4(b)(4). Generally, a transaction with contractual protection is a transaction involving a fee that is refundable if all or part of the intended tax consequences from the transaction are not sustained or a transaction involving a fee that is contingent on the taxpayer's realization of the tax benefits from the transaction.

.02 Section 1.6011–4(b)(8)(i) provides that a transaction will not be considered a reportable transaction, or will be excluded from any individual category of reportable transaction, if the Commissioner makes a determination by published guidance that the transaction is not subject to the reporting requirements of § 1.6011–4.

SECTION 3. SCOPE

This revenue procedure applies to taxpayers that may be required to disclose reportable transactions under § 6011, material advisors that may be required to disclose reportable transactions under § 6111, and material advisors that may be required to maintain lists under § 6112. This revenue procedure also applies for purposes of § 4965.

SECTION 4. APPLICATION

.01 *In general*. The definition of a transaction with contractual protection includes references to "tax consequences" and "tax benefits." For purposes of § 1.6011–4, "tax" is defined as "Federal income tax." § 1.6011–4(c)(5). Accordingly, § 1.6011–4(b)(4) does not apply to transactions in which the refundable or contingent fees are based on the taxpayer's liability for taxes other than federal income taxes.

.02 *Exceptions*. The following transactions are not taken into account in determining whether a transaction is a transaction with contractual protection under § 1.6011–4(b)(4):

(1) Transactions in which the refundable or contingent fee is related to the work opportunity credit under § 51 of the Internal Revenue Code.

(2) Transactions in which the refundable or contingent fee is related to the welfare-to-work credit under § 51A.

(3) Transactions in which the refundable or contingent fee is related to the Indian employment credit under § 45A(a).

(4) Transactions in which the refundable or contingent fee is related to the low-income housing credit under § 42(a).

(5) Transactions in which the refundable or contingent fee is related to the new markets tax credit under § 45D(a).

(6) Transactions in which the refundable or contingent fee is related to the empowerment zone employment credit under § 1396(a).

(7) Transactions in which the refundable or contingent fee is related to the renewal community employment credit under § 1400H.

(8) Transactions in which the refundable or contingent fee is related to the employee retention credit under § 1400R(a), (b), or (c).

SECTION 5. EFFECT ON OTHER DOCUMENTS

This document modifies and supersedes Rev. Proc. 2004–65, 2004–2 C.B. 965.

SECTION 6. EFFECTIVE DATE

This revenue procedure is effective January 26, 2007, the date this revenue procedure was released to the public. The exceptions under section 4.02(1) through (3) apply to transactions that are entered into on or after January 1, 2003. The exceptions under section 4.02(4) through (8) apply to all transactions, regardless of when the transaction was entered into, that otherwise would have to have been disclosed under § 1.6011–4(b)(4) on or after January 1, 2006.

SECTION 7. DRAFTING INFORMATION

The principal author of this revenue procedure is Charles Wien of the Office of Associate Chief Counsel (Passthroughs & Special Industries). For further information regarding this revenue procedure, contact Mr. Wien at (202) 622–3070 (not a toll-free call).

Part IV. Items of General Interest

Income and Currency Gain or Loss With Respect to a Section 987 QBU; Correction

Announcement 2007–4

AGENCY: Internal Revenue Service (IRS), Treasury.

ACTION: Correction to notice of proposed rulemaking.

SUMMARY: This document contains corrections to a notice of proposed rulemaking (REG–208270–86, 2006–42 I.R.B. 698) that was published in the **Federal Register** on Thursday, September 7, 2006 (71 FR 52876), regarding the determination of the items of income or loss of a taxpayer with respect to a section 987 qualified business unit as well as the timing, amount character and source of any section 987 gain or loss.

FOR FURTHER INFORMATION CONTACT: Sheila Ramaswamy, (202) 622–3870 (not a toll-free number).

SUPPLEMENTARY INFORMATION:

Background

The notice of proposed rulemaking (REG–208270–86) that is the subject of these corrections is under section 987 of the Internal Revenue Code.

Need for Correction

As published, the notice of proposed rulemaking (REG–208270–86) contains errors that may prove to be misleading and are in need of clarification.

Correction of Publication

Accordingly, the notice of proposed rulemaking (REG–208270–86), that was the subject of FR Doc. 06–7250, is corrected as follows:

1. On page 52879, second column, in the preamble under the paragraph heading "*E. Concerns Regarding the 1991 Proposed Regulations: Notice 2000–20,*" the sixteenth line following the formula, the language "DE. The DE conducts mineral" is corrected to read "DE. The DE conducts mineral extraction in Country X".

2. On page 52886, first column, in the preamble under the paragraph heading "*C. Section 1.987–3 Determination of the Items of Section 987 Taxable Income or Loss of an Owner of a Section 987 QBU,*" the eighth line, the language "under other provisions are not taken" is corrected to read "under other provisions of the Code or regulations are not taken".

3. On page 52886, second column, under the paragraph heading "*C. Section 1.987–3 Determination of the Items of Section 987 Taxable Income or Loss of an Owner of a Section 987 QBU,*" first full paragraph, ninth line from the bottom of the paragraph, the language "rates for amount realized and adjusted" is corrected to read "rates for the amount realized and adjusted".

4. On page 52886, second column, under the paragraph heading "*C. Section 1.987–3 Determination of the Items of Section 987 Taxable Income or Loss of an Owner of a Section 987 QBU,*" second full paragraph, fifth line, the language "Generally the amount realized and" is corrected to read "Generally, the amount realized and adjusted".

§ 1.987–1 [Corrected]

5. On page 52895, second column, § 1.987–1(b)(7), paragraph (ii)(B) of *Example 1*, fifth line from the bottom of the paragraph, the language "neither the activities of DE1 or DE2 are" is corrected to read "the activities of DE1 are not".

§ 1.987–2 [Corrected]

6. On page 52899, first column, § 1.987–2(c)(9), lines 2 and 3, the language "illustrate the principles of this paragraph (c). For purposes of these" is corrected to read "illustrate the principles of paragraph (b) of this section and this paragraph (c). For purposes of these".

7. On page 52899, second column, § 1.987–2(c)(9), paragraph (ii)(B) of *Example 1*, last line, the language "section 988 to X as a result of the loan." is corrected to read "section 988 to X as a result of the disregarded loan."

8. On page 52899, third column, § 1.987–2(c)(9), paragraph (ii)(A) of *Example 3*, line 3, the language "Federal tax purposes and therefore is a" is corrected to read "Federal income tax purposes and therefore is a".

9. On page 52900, first column, § 1.987–2(c)(9), paragraph (ii)(C) of *Example 4*, line 3, the language "regarded for U.S. Federal tax purposes. As a" is corrected to read "regarded for U.S. Federal income tax purposes. As a".

10. On page 52900, second column, § 1.987–2(c)(9), paragraph (ii)(A) of *Example 7*, line 1, the language "(ii) *Analysis*. (A) For Federal tax purposes" is corrected to read "(ii) *Analysis*. (A) For Federal income tax purposes".

11. On page 52901, third column, § 1.987–2(d)(2), line 3, the language "described in section 988(c)(1)(i) and (ii)" is corrected to read "described in section 988(c)(1)(B)(i) and (ii)".

§ 1.987–3 [Corrected]

12. On page 52902, third column, § 1.987–3(e)(2), line 5, the language "described in section 988(c)(1)(A)(i) and" is corrected to read "described in section 988(c)(1)(B)(i) and".

13. On page 52904, first column, § 1.987–3(f) *Example 3.*, the fourth line from the bottom of the paragraph, the language "section and § 1.987–1(c)(3) €8,000 x $1=" is corrected to read "section and § 1.987–1(c)(3) (€8,000 x $1=".

§ 1.987–6 [Corrected]

14. On page 52911, first column, § 1.987–6(c) *Example*, lines 5 through 10 from the bottom of the column, the language "of this section, Sf7,500 (Sf750,000/Sf1,000,000 x Sf10,000) of the section 987 gain will be treated as foreign source general limitation income which is not subpart F income and Sf2,500 (Sf250,000/Sf1,000,000 x Sf10,000) will" is corrected to read "of this section, Sf7,500 ((Sf750,000/Sf1,000,000) x Sf10,000) of the section 987 gain will be treated as foreign source general limitation income which is not subpart F income and Sf2,500 ((Sf250,000/Sf1,000,000) x Sf10,000) will".

Cynthia E. Grigsby,
Senior Federal Register Liaison Officer,
Publications and Regulations Branch,
Legal Processing Division,
Associate Chief Counsel
(Procedure and Administration).

(Filed by the Office of the Federal Register on December 26, 2006, 8:45 a.m., and published in the issue of the Federal Register for December 27, 2006, 71 F.R. 77654)

Deletions From Cumulative List of Organizations Contributions to Which are Deductible Under Section 170 of the Code

Announcement 2007–13

The names of organizations that no longer qualify as organizations described in section 170(c)(2) of the Internal Revenue Code of 1986 are listed below.

Generally, the Service will not disallow deductions for contributions made to a listed organization on or before the date of announcement in the Internal Revenue Bulletin that an organization no longer qualifies. However, the Service is not precluded from disallowing a deduction for any contributions made after an organization ceases to qualify under section 170(c)(2) if the organization has not timely filed a suit for declaratory judgment under section 7428 and if the contributor (1) had knowledge of the revocation of the ruling or determination letter, (2) was aware that such revocation was imminent, or (3) was in part responsible for or was aware of the activities or omissions of the organization that brought about this revocation.

If on the other hand a suit for declaratory judgment has been timely filed, contributions from individuals and organizations described in section 170(c)(2) that are otherwise allowable will continue to be deductible. Protection under section 7428(c) would begin on February 12, 2007, and would end on the date the court first determines that the organization is not described in section 170(c)(2) as more particularly set forth in section 7428(c)(1). For individual contributors, the maximum deduction protected is $1,000, with a husband and wife treated as one contributor. This benefit is not extended to any individual, in whole or in part, for the acts or omissions of the organization that were the basis for revocation.

Hawaii Credit Counseling Service
Honolulu, HI
Lighthouse Credit Foundation, Inc.
Largo, FL

Foundations Status of Certain Organizations

Announcement 2007–14

The following organizations have failed to establish or have been unable to maintain their status as public charities or as operating foundations. Accordingly, grantors and contributors may not, after this date, rely on previous rulings or designations in the Cumulative List of Organizations (Publication 78), or on the presumption arising from the filing of notices under section 508(b) of the Code. This listing does *not* indicate that the organizations have lost their status as organizations described in section 501(c)(3), eligible to receive deductible contributions.

Former Public Charities. The following organizations (which have been treated as organizations that are not private foundations described in section 509(a) of the Code) are now classified as private foundations:

3TO, Sunnyvale, CA
According to His Riches Corporation, Washington, DC
ActiVote America, Inc., Carmel, IN
Africa Tent Evangelism, Inc., Lubbock, TX
African Aids Prevention and Medical Assistance Foundation, Charlotte, NC
All Faith Youth Outreach Program, Inc., Montgomery, AL
Alliance Preparatory High School, Rancho Cucamonga, CA
AMOR, Inc., Queens, NY
Animal Resource Center, Inc., Slinger, WI
Answer Evangelistic Ministries, Inc., San Antonio, TX
Arch Angel Arts Center, Rochelle, VA
Aventis Behring Foundation for Research and Advancement of Patient Health, King of Prussia, PA
Bamboo Village Hawaii, Inc., Kurtistown, HI
Begin Again Ministries, Inc., Springfield, MO
Bethel Ministries, Inc., Huachuca City, AZ
Better Days Ahead, Inc., Houston, TX
B.F. Walker & Associates, Inc., Atlanta, GA
BHPS PTO, Inc., Tallahassee, FL
Blessed Through You, Inc., Odenton, MD
Breaking the Cycle, Inc., Smyrna, GA
Bucklin Community Better Life Foundation, Bucklin, KS
Building Doorways, Andover, MN
Bullock Foundation, Inc., Charlotte, NC
Butte Ski Club, Butte, MT
Called to Serve, Troy, MI
Cardiology P.C. Research Foundation, Birmingham, AL
Casa Del Sol Mobile Home Corporation, Davis, CA
CECN Foundation, Nacogdoches, TX
Center for Civil War Living History, Inc., Roanoke, VA
Center for Regional Economic Strategies, Dayton, OH
Central Washington Community Wellness Foundation, Ellensburg, WA
Changed Lives Seminars and Ministry, Memphis, TN
Chillicothe 757 Colts Baseball, Chillicothe, OH
Christian Life School Foundation, Kenosha, WI
Christian Rationalism Redeemer Center Correspondent, Inc., Waterbury, CT
Clarence & Lynn Wolfe Foundation, Searcy, AR
Columbus Georgia Wheelchair Athletic Association, Columbus, GA
Community Finance Corporation, Tucson, AZ
Community Healing Arts Center, Inc., Florence, MA
Community Health Resource, Inc., Hogansville, GA
Community Transportation Agency, Inc., Wilmington, DE
Conrad Charitable Foundation, Northville, MI
Consciousness, Inc., Milwaukee, WI
Coptic Legal Foundation, Glendale, CA
Council for Educational Improvement, Santa Fe, NM
Cri-Du-Chat Research Foundation, Cumming, GA
Danielle Dawn Smalley Foundation, Inc., Crandall, TX

Danish American Language Foundation, St. Charles, IL
Danita Corbitt Memorial Scholarship, Inc., Rossville, GA
Developmental Education & Research, Inc., Chandler, AZ
Diamonds in the Rough, New Orleans, LA
Disabled First, Oceanside, CA
Disabled Traveler, Lapeer, MI
Do2Learn Foundation, Inc., Raleigh, NC
Doctor William H. Huger Home Charitable Trust, Charleston, SC
Dragon Fly After School Program, Cambridge, MA
Duxbury Recreation Foundation, Inc., Duxbury, MA
Eagle Feather Publishing and Research Institute, Austin, TX
El Leon Literary Arts, Inc., Berkeley, CA
Enchantment House Community Services, Incorporated, Missouri City, TX
Energy Farm, Jackson, MS
Energy for the Future, Rancho Cordova, CA
Engineers Rod & Gun Club Charities, Ottawa, IL
Eucalyptus View, Inc., Escondido, CA
Faithful Servant Ministries, Alvord, TX
Family Images, Inc., New York, NY
Family Unity World Wide, Rockmart, GA
First Baptist Faith Foundation, Hilton Head, SC
For the Love of Homeless Pets, Inc., Hialeah Gardens, FL
Foundation for Consumers Construction Assistance, Inc., Bethany, OK
Foundation for in Home Care, Incorporated, Chattanooga, TN
Foundation for Integrative Therapies, Washington, DC
Foundation for Professional Excellence in the Community College, Austin, TX
Foundation for the Re-Entry of Ex-Offenders, Inc., (Free), Clinton, OH
Freedom Watch, Inc., Miami, FL
Gente Ayudando Gente S A, Houston, TX
Georgia Advocate Health Partners, Inc., Atlanta, GA
Grace Baptist Chapel Community Development Corporation, Bronx, NY
Grace Community Development Corporation, Memphis, TN
Grapevine Center for Communication Arts, Inc., Bloomfield, CT
Hair Angels Foundation, Inc., Carmel, IN
Healing the Environment, Inc., Thayne, WI
Hearts of Peace Foundation, Boulder, CO
Hope Foundation, Incorporated, Gaithersburg, MD
Housing & Community Synergy, Inc., Anaheim, CA
Howard Family Foundation, Inc., Los Angeles, CA
Human Services Projects, Inc., Park Forest, IL
Idaho Clean Air Foundation, Inc., Sandpoint, ID
Imani Support Services, Inc., Birmingham, AL
In His Rest Ministries, Anacortes, WA
Inner City Youth Computer Network, Philadelphia, PA
Inspirational Family Enrichment Association, Inc., Inkster, MI
Institute for the Advancement of Contemporary Chinese Architecture, Ltd., Oyster Bay, NY
Institute of Media Research, Inc., Cambridge, MA
Institute United for the Study and Defense Against Racism Toward Chinese People, Inc., Flushing, NY
Interdisciplinary Artists Aggregation, Inc., Santa Cruz, CA
International Justice Center, Inc., Suwanee, GA
International Latino Womens Congress, Philadelphia, PA
Isbell Home, Inc., Gadsden, AL
Jack and Elizabeth Gellman Torah Foundation, Inc., Amherst, NY
Jewishlinks, Inc., San Mateo, CA
Jo Saltkill Ministries, Inc., Ft. Worth, TX
John J. Barcklow Foundation, Inc., Springfield, VA
Kathedral Community Development, Inc., Tampa, FL
Kinderhudson Corporation, Nyack, NY
Ladwin Corp., San German, PR
Lafontaine Christian Church Scholarship Fund, Omaha, NE
Land Conservancy, Inc., Fairfield, NJ
Lark Second Chance, Harvey, IL
Laws of Life Expression Contest, Inc., Greensboro, NC
L D P Memorial Fund, Inc., Elizabeth, NJ
Linda Parham Ministries, Inc., Worcester, MA
Long March Foundation, Inc., New York, NY
Love for Life Foundation of Philippine American Physicians in America, Ledyard, CT
Lyceum Corporation, Dallas, TX
Making a Difference Foundation, Los Angeles, CA
Mapua Alumni Foundation, Inc., Yorba Linda, CA
Maridon Museum, Butler, PA
Marion Regional Healthcare Foundation, Mullins, SC
Mauldin Scholarship Charitable Trust, North Little Rock, AR
Metropolitan Community Housing and Development Organization, Inc., Baton Rouge, LA
Mirandette Martial Arts Center, Inc., Kentwood, MI
Moscow Directors' Art Theatre Studio of New York, New York, NY
Mount Pleasant Outreach Ministries, Inc., Atlanta, GA
Movement is Life, Inc., Detroit, MI
Moving Transit Through LA, Los Angeles, CA
NBCAR Historic District, Dothan, AL
Neurotherapy Research Association, Inc., Chevy Chase, MD
New Beginning Home Preparing for the Future, Winston Salem, NC
New Dimension Theatre Studio, Inc., Edgewater, NJ
New Vision Generational Learning Center, Kalamazoo, MI
Nickel of Hope, Cedar Hill, TX
Nile Vintage Group, Inc., Brooklyn, NY
Non Profit Secretarial Service NPSS, Inc., Houston, TX
North Coast Alliance, Cambria, CA
North Florida Housing, Inc., Newberry, FL
Note Worthy Outreach, Inc., Mission, KS
Notoriety, Inc., Irvine, CA
N.P.R.S.C., Inc., New Port Richey, FL
Nutritional Biomedicine Research Institute, Inc., Aspen, CO
Officeplease Foundation, Glen Ellen, CA
On Target of North Carolina, Inc., Kernersville, NC
Osseo Community Foundation, Osseo, MN
Our Father's House, Inc., Goose Creek, SC
Oxford Muse, Pearland, TX
Particle Economics Research Institute, Eastsound, WA
Partnership for Health, Healing & Community, Saco, ME
Perpetual Help Unlimited, Chicago, IL
Pineland Farms, Inc., New Gloucester, ME

Place of Hope Dog Rescue Foundation, Valentine, AZ
Pokagon Fund, Inc., New Buffalo, MI
Preventive Care for Productive Lives, Inc., Potomac, MD
Professionals Network of Florida, Inc., Jupiter, FL
Project Jakana, Ukiah, CA
Radar, Inc., Reno, NV
Rational Living Foundation, Inc., Tampa, FL
Real Estate Education Foundation, Albuquerque, NM
Rhonda Joy Edwards Vansant Foundation, Inc., Portland, OR
Rock Springs Community Center, Mullin, TX
Rockville Striders Youth Track Club, Inc., Rockville, MD
Rozie Wilson White Agency, Inc., Cedar Hill, TX
Ruthmere Foundation, Inc., Elkhart, IN
Sea Life Studies, Inc., Morro Bay, CA
Seeds of Hope, Corralitos, CA
Senior Citizens Foundation, Inc., Deming, NM
Serv Behavioral Health Systems, Inc., West Trenton, NJ
Share the Warmth, Inc., Evansville, IN
Sharing the Journey, Toledo, OH
Sharon Sockwell-Clark Mission Foundation, Inc., Bergheim, TX
Shield of Faith Out Reach Ministries, Inc., Atlanta, GA
Shirley A. Cunningham Jr. Family Foundation, Inc., Georgetown, KY
Show Low Housing Coalition, Inc., Show Low, AZ
Sibley House, Nuevo, CA
Silence the Violence, Inc., Brooklyn, NY
Snow Cloud Farm, Inc., Asheville, NC
Solutions Community Outreach, Inc., Houston, TX
South Central Urban Ministries, Inc., Nashville, TN
Southwest Psychoanalytic Foundation, Tucson, AZ
Spirit Investigations, Inc., Nashville, TN
Spotlight Fashion Group, Spartanburg, SC
SRDS, Sartell, MN
SS&W Enterprise, Inc., Philadelphia, PA
St. Augustine Foundation, Ltd., Yonkers, NY
St. Claude Community Family Center, River Ridge, LA
Stewart W. and Willma C. Hoyt Foundation, Binghamton, NY
Stratford Festival Theater, Inc., Fairfield, CT
Sundance Farm, Inc., Inman, KS
Supporting Parents Educational Dreams, Inc., Portland, OR
Tallship Michigan, Franklin, MI
Talons & Tails, Inc., Bunnell, FL
Tarlow Family Foundation, Inc., St. Louis, MO
Temple Broadcasting Communication, Inc., Simpsonville, SC
Texas Panhandle Film Commission, Amarillo, TX
Thomasville Initiative, Thomasville, NC
Titusville Friends of the Arts, Hydetown, PA
To God be the Glory Ministries, St. Louis, MO
Tony J. Ferry Ministries, Rehoboth, MA
Trail Corps Academy, Silverthorne, CO
United Charities of America, San Angelo, TX
Upward Bound Youth Foundation, Inc., Clearwater, FL
Veneto Org, Washington, DC
Virtuous Women Under Construction, Los Angeles, CA
VNA Foundation, Inc., Syracuse, NY
Walk-Ons, Inc., Salt Lake City, UT
Well Ministries, Inc., Wings Mills, MD
West Piedmont Workforce Investment Board, Martinsville, VA
Wishing Well Foundation of America, Inc., Palmetto Bay, FL
Women and Wisdom Foundation, Inc., Greensboro, NC
Women of Faith Ministries and Gods Associates, Indianapolis, IN
Women of Light Foundation, Inc., Potomac, MD
Workers Housing Corporation, San Juan, PR
WOW Community Outreach, Inc., Birmingham, AL
W.W.O.C.B. — "We Want Our Children Back" Community Organization of Athens, Athens, AL
Xristos Association, Inc., South Holland, IL
Yonkers Partnership Housing Development Fund Corporation, Yonkers, NY
Youth Determined to Succeed Y.D.T.S., Inc., Pittsburgh, PA
Youth Excelling Socially, Inc., Little Rock, AR
Youth of Promise, Irvine, CA

If an organization listed above submits information that warrants the renewal of its classification as a public charity or as a private operating foundation, the Internal Revenue Service will issue a ruling or determination letter with the revised classification as to foundation status. Grantors and contributors may thereafter rely upon such ruling or determination letter as provided in section 1.509(a)–7 of the Income Tax Regulations. It is not the practice of the Service to announce such revised classification of foundation status in the Internal Revenue Bulletin.

Treatment of Payments in Lieu of Taxes Under Section 141

Announcement 2007–19

AGENCY: Internal Revenue Service (IRS), Treasury.

ACTION: Cancellation of notice of public hearing on proposed rulemaking.

SUMMARY: This document cancels a public hearing on proposed regulations (REG–136806–06, 2006–47 I.R.B. 950) modifying the standards for treating payments in lieu of taxes (PILOTs) as generally applicable taxes for purposes of the private security or payment test under section 141.

DATES: The public hearing, originally scheduled for February 13, 2007 at 10 a.m. is cancelled.

FOR FURTHER INFORMATION CONTACT: Kelly Banks of the Publications and Regulations Branch, Legal Processing Division, Associate Chief Counsel (Procedure and Administration) at (202) 622–0392 (not a toll-free number).

SUPPLEMENTARY INFORMATION: A notice of proposed rulemaking and notice of public hearing that appeared in the **Federal Register** on Thursday, October 19, 2006 (71 FR 61693), announced that a public hearing was scheduled for February 13, 2007, at 10 a.m. in the IRS Auditorium, New Carrollton Federal Building, 5000 Ellin Road, Lanham, MD 20706. Subsequently, a notice of change of location of public hearing was published in the **Federal Register** on Tuesday, December 26, 2006, (published as Announcement 2007–6, 2007–4 I.R.B. 376 [71 FR 77352]) changing the location to the IRS Auditorium, Internal Revenue Building, 1111 Constitution Avenue, NW, Washington, DC. The subject of the public hearing is under section 141 of the Internal Revenue Code.

The public comment period for these regulations expired on January 16, 2007. The notice of proposed rulemaking and notice of public hearing instructed those interested in testifying at the public hearing to submit a request to speak and an outline of the topics to be addressed. As of Tuesday, January 23, 2007, no one has requested to speak. Therefore, the public hearing scheduled for February 13, 2007, is cancelled.

LaNita Van Dyke,
Branch Chief,
Publications and Regulations Branch,
Legal Processing Division,
Associate Chief Counsel
(Procedure and Administration).

(Filed by the Office of the Federal Register on January 29, 2007, 8:45 a.m., and published in the issue of the Federal Register for January 30, 2007, 72 F.R. 4220)

Part I. Rulings and Decisions Under the Internal Revenue Code of 1986

Section 337.—Nonrecognition for Property Distributed to Parent in Complete Liquidation of Subsidiary

Section 337(d)(1) provides for consolidated return regulations implementing the repeal of the *General Utilities* doctrine. These regulations, previously contained in §§1.337(d)–1 and 1.337(d)–2, are now proposed under §1.1502–36. See REG-157711-02, page 537.

Section 362.—Basis to Corporations

Section 362(e)(2) addresses loss duplication. However, proposed regulations provide special rules to suspend application of 362(e)(2) in the consolidated return setting while investment basis adjustments operate to address loss duplication. See REG-157711-02, page 537.

Section 671.—Trust Income, Deductions, and Credits Attributable to Grantors and Others as Substantial Owners

26 CFR 1.671–5: Reporting for widely held fixed investment trusts.

T.D. 9308

DEPARTMENT OF THE TREASURY
Internal Revenue Service
26 CFR Part 1

Reporting Rules for Widely Held Fixed Investment Trusts

AGENCY: Internal Revenue Service (IRS), Treasury.

ACTION: Final regulations and removal of the temporary regulations.

SUMMARY: This document contains final regulations amending §1.671–5 which provides reporting rules for widely held fixed investment trusts (WHFITs). These final regulations clarify and simplify reporting for trustees and middlemen of non-mortgage widely held fixed investment trusts (NMWHFITs). These final regulations also provide temporary safe harbor reporting rules for widely held mortgage trusts (WHMTs) that are outside the WHMT safe harbor. The preamble to these regulations also provides that trustees of WHFITs are to indicate on the Form 1041, "*U.S. Income Tax Return for Estates and Trusts*," filed for a WHFIT's 2006 calendar year that the return is a final return.

DATES: *Effective Date:* These regulations are effective December 29, 2006.

Applicability Date: For date of applicability, see §1.671–5(n).

FOR FURTHER INFORMATION CONTACT: Faith Colson, (202) 622–3060 (not a toll-free number).

SUPPLEMENTARY INFORMATION:

Paperwork Reduction Act

The collection of information contained in these final regulations has been previously reviewed and approved by the Office of Management and Budget in accordance with the Paperwork Reduction Act of 1995 (44 U.S.C. 3507) under control number 1545–1540. The collection of information in these final regulations is in §1.671–5. This information is required to be reported to beneficial owners of trust interests to enable them to correctly report their share of the items of income, deduction, and credit of the WHFIT in which they have invested. This information is also required to be reported to the IRS to enable the IRS to verify that trustees and middlemen are accurately reporting information to beneficial owners of trust interests and that beneficial owners are properly reporting their ownership of a trust interest.

An agency may not conduct or sponsor, and a person is not required to respond to, a collection of information unless it displays a valid control number.

The estimated annual burden per recordkeeper varies from 1 to 4 hours, depending on individual circumstances, with an estimated average of 2 hours. Comments concerning the accuracy of this burden estimate should be sent to the Internal Revenue Service, Attn: IRS Reports Clearance Officer, SE:W:CAR:MP:T:T:SP, Washington, DC 20224, and to the Office of Management and Budget, Attn: Desk Officer for the Department of Treasury, Office of Information and Regulatory Affairs, Washington, DC 20503.

Books or records relating to a collection of information must be retained as long as their contents might become material in the administration of any internal revenue law. Generally, tax returns and tax return information are confidential, as required by 26 U.S.C. 6103.

Background

This document contains amendments to 26 CFR part 1. On January 24, 2006, the Internal Revenue Service (IRS) and the Treasury Department published the WHFIT reporting rules in the **Federal Register** (T.D. 9241, 2006–7 I.R.B. 427 [71 FR 4002]) under §1.671–5 (WHFIT reporting rules). On August 3, 2006, in response to comments received subsequent to the publication of the WHFIT reporting rules, the IRS and the Treasury Department published final and temporary regulations (T.D. 9279, 2006–36 I.R.B. 355 [71 FR 43968]) (temporary regulations) as well as proposed regulations that, in part, cross-referenced the temporary regulations (71 FR 43998) (proposed regulations) (REG–125071–06, 2006–36 I.R.B. 375) in the **Federal Register**. No public hearing was requested or held with respect to the temporary or proposed regulations. Written comments responding to those regulations were received. After consideration of the comments, the proposed regulations, with certain revisions, are adopted as final regulations by this Treasury decision, and the corresponding temporary regulations are removed. The comments and the revisions are discussed in this preamble.

Summary of Comments and Explanation of Revisions

I. *Application of the WHFIT Reporting Rules to NMWHFITs*

A. *The Qualified NMWHFIT Exception*

Trustees and middlemen of NMWHFITs that satisfy the qualified NMWHFIT exception in §1.671–5(c)(2)(iv)(E) are excepted from reporting information regarding market discount and bond premium, and are permitted to use the simplified reporting for sales and dispositions of trust assets in §1.671–5(c)(2)(iv)(B) and the simplified reporting rules for sales or redemptions of trust interests in §1.671–5(c)(2)(v)(C). The temporary regulations provide that the qualified NMWHFIT exception is satisfied if the calendar year for which the trustee is reporting begins before January 1, 2011, and the NMWHFIT meets any of the following requirements: (1) the NMWHFIT has a start-up date as defined in §1.671–5(b)(19) before February 23, 2006; (2) the registration statement for the NMWHFIT becomes effective under the Securities Act of 1933, as amended (15 U.S.C. 77a, *et. seq.*) (Securities Act of 1933) and trust interests are offered for sale to the public before February 23, 2006; or (3) the registration statement of the NMWHFIT becomes effective under the Securities Act of 1933 and trust interests are offered for sale to the public on or after February 23, 2006 and before July 31, 2006, and the NMWHFIT is fully funded before October 1, 2006. These final regulations retain this amendment to the WHFIT reporting rules. Additionally, commentators on the temporary regulations expressed concern that certain trusts that otherwise satisfy the eligibility requirements for the qualified NMWHFIT exception would be disqualified because additional assets are deposited into the trust pursuant to a distribution reinvestment program. These final regulations clarify that for the purpose of determining whether a NMWHFIT is fully funded before October 1, 2006, deposits to the NMWHFIT pursuant to a distribution reinvestment program that is consistent with the requirements of §301.7701–4(c) will be disregarded.

Commentators have also expressed concern regarding NMWHFITs that hold debt instruments (fixed income trusts) that were originated before the WHFIT reporting rules were published in the **Federal Register**. Commentators are concerned because the simplified reporting permitted under the exception terminates after December 31, 2010, and many fixed income trusts will be unable to comply with the WHFIT reporting rules once the simplified reporting permitted under the qualified NMWHFIT exception terminates because these NMWHFITs generally are not able to engage in *pro-rata* sales of trust assets to effect redemptions. Commentators have requested that these NMWHFITs be permanently permitted to report consistent with the qualified NMWHFIT exception. In response, these regulations amend §1.671–5(c)(2)(iv)(E) to eliminate the requirement that the trustee must be reporting for a year that begins before January 1, 2011 for the NMWHFIT to be eligible for the simplified reporting. Accordingly, NMWHFITs that satisfy the qualified NMWHFIT exception and continue in existence after December 31, 2010 may report under the simplified reporting permitted under the exception until those NMWHFITs terminate.

B. *Simplified Reporting of Sales and Redemptions of Trust Interests*

With respect to the sale or redemption of a trust interest, section 1.671–5(c)(2)(v) of the WHFIT reporting rules requires trustees and middlemen to provide information regarding the sales assets proceeds (as defined in §1.671–5(b)(17)) or the redemption assets proceeds (as defined in §1.671–5(b)(14)) as well as the income that is attributable to a redeeming, selling or purchasing beneficial owner up to the date of the sale or redemption of a trust interest. Section 1.671–5(c)(2)(v)(C) excepts a NMWHFIT from the requirement to provide information to enable requesting persons to differentiate between income and proceeds if substantially all the NMWHFIT's income is comprised of dividends (equity trusts) and the NMWHFIT is required by its governing document to distribute the cash held for distribution by the NMWHFIT at least monthly. The temporary regulations, and these final regulations revise §1.671–5(c)(2)(v)(C) to provide that a NMWHFIT will be considered to have satisfied the requirement that it distribute the cash held for distribution monthly notwithstanding the fact that, although the governing document requires monthly distributions, the governing document of the NMWHFIT also permits the trustee to forego making its normally required monthly distribution if the cash held for distribution is less than 0.1 percent of the net asset value of the trust (aggregate fair market value of the trust's assets less the trust's liabilities) as of the date that the amount of the monthly distribution is required to be determined.

Commentators have indicated that it will be extremely difficult for a certain class of NMWHFITs that are not equity trusts to comply with §1.671–5(c)(2)(v). These NMWHFITs hold assets that produce income that is treated as interest income, not dividend income, for Federal income tax purposes. The assets of these NMWHFITs, however, are similar to assets that produce dividend income in that the assets are traded on a recognized exchange or securities market in such a way that the price of the assets is determined without a component attributable to accrued interest. As with NMWHFITs that hold assets that produce dividend income, it is difficult for the trustees and middlemen of these NMWHFITs to determine the income attributable to a redeeming, selling, or purchasing beneficial owner between trust distribution dates. For these reasons, the final regulations provide that NMWHFITs that hold assets that produce income that is treated as interest income for Federal income tax purposes will also qualify for the simplified reporting under §1.671–5(c)(2)(v)(C) but only if the assets are traded on a recognized exchange or securities market in such a way that the price of the assets is determined without a component attributable to accrued interest.

C. *Simplified Reporting for Sales and Dispositions by Certain NMWHFITs*

In addition to the qualified NMWHFIT exception, the WHFIT reporting rules provide that the trustees of NMWHFITs that meet the general *de minimis* test in §1.671–5(c)(2)(iv)(D)(*1*) are only required, under §1.671–5(c)(2)(iv)(B), to provide information regarding the amount of trust sales proceeds distributed to a beneficial owner. A NMWHFIT meets the general *de minimis* test if trust sales proceeds (as defined in §1.671–5(b)(21)) for the calendar year are not more than five percent of the net asset value of the trust as of the later of January 1 of the year for which the trustee is reporting or the start-up date. The reason for the *de minimis* exception, as stated in the preamble to the WHFIT reporting rules, is that the IRS and the Treasury Department believe that if a NMWHFIT only sells or disposes of assets infrequently, although there may be some deferral of gains and losses if sales and dispositions are not fully reported, the deferral is acceptable, in light of the burden of fully, accurately reporting the sales and dispositions.

Commentators on the WHFIT reporting rules reported that trustees of NMWHFITs frequently have to sell trust assets to obtain cash to effect redemptions and that, because of those sales, many NMWHFITs will not be able to meet the general *de minimis* test in §1.671–5(c)(2)(iv)(D)(*1*). Commentators on the WHFIT reporting rules requested that those regulations be amended to provide for reduced reporting where this will have little or no compliance impact. In response to those comments, the temporary regulations provide a number of modifications to the NMWHFIT reporting rules as applied to certain sales and dispositions of trust assets by NMWHFITs. Those modifications, as well as additional modification made by these final regulations, include:

1. *NMWHFIT Final Calendar Year Exception*

Section 1.671–5T(c)(2)(iv)(F) of the temporary regulations provides that all NMWHFITs qualify for the simplified reporting in §1.671–5T(c)(2)(iv)(B) in the final calendar year of the NMWHFIT, regardless of whether the NMWHFIT has otherwise satisfied the general *de minimis* test, provided that a beneficial owner cannot roll over its investment in the NMWHFIT to another WHFIT. Commentators on the temporary regulations requested that the IRS and Treasury Department clarify that a taxable roll-over would not preclude a trustee from reporting under the final year exception. Accordingly, these regulations remove the reference to a roll-over and instead require that, to be eligible for the final year exception, beneficial owners of trust interests must exchange their trust interests for cash or be treated as having exchanged their trust interests for cash for Federal income tax purposes upon the termination of the trust.

2. *Pro-rata Sales to Effect Redemptions Exception*

Section 1.671–5T(c)(2)(iv)(G) of the temporary regulations provides that a *pro-rata* sale of a trust asset to effect a redemption is not required to be reported under §1.671–5. The temporary regulations describe a *pro-rata* sale of a trust asset as occurring when (1) a trust interest holder tenders one or more trust interests for redemption; (2) the trustee sells the *pro-rata* share of a trust asset that is deemed to be owned by the trust interest holder as a result of the trust interest holder's ownership of the trust interest or interests tendered for redemption; (3) the trustee engages in the sale solely to obtain cash that is immediately distributed to the redeeming trust interest holder as a result of the redemption; and (4) the redemption is reported as required under §1.671–5(c)(2)(v).

Commentators on the temporary regulations have requested that the *pro-rata* sales to effect a redemption exception in the temporary regulations be adjusted to accommodate economic and practical issues that trustees confront in executing sales of trust assets to effect redemptions. These commentators requested that the *pro-rata* sales to effect a redemption exception be revised to provide the trustee with some flexibility regarding the time period in which the trustee has to execute sales following the tender of trust interests for redemptions and to permit trustees to aggregate sales of assets from several redemptions for the purpose of testing whether the asset sales have been *pro-rata*. In response, the final regulations provide that *pro-rata* sales to effect redemptions occur when (i) one or more trust interests are tendered for redemption; (ii) the trustee identifies the *pro-rata* share of the trust assets deemed to be owned by the trust interest or interests tendered for redemption, and sells those assets as soon as practicable; (iii) proceeds from the sale of the identified assets are used solely to effect redemptions; and (iv) the redemptions are reported as required under §1.671–5(c)(2)(v) by the trustee.

Additionally, the final regulations provide that the trustee may compare the aggregate of the *pro-rata* share of the trust assets deemed to be owned by the trust interests tendered for redemption and the sales of assets sold to effect redemptions to determine the *pro-rata* sales of assets to effect redemptions for a calendar month. Further, if the aggregate *pro-rata* share of the assets deemed to be owned by the redeemed trust interests for the month equals a fractional share, the trustee may round that amount to the next whole share for the purpose of determining the *pro-rata* sales to effect a redemption for the calendar month.

3. *De minimis Test Modifications*

Section 1.671–5T(b)(21) of the temporary regulations provides an amended definition of trust sales proceeds that excludes the gross proceeds paid to a NMWHFIT for a *pro-rata* sale of a trust asset to effect a redemption. The effect of this change in the definition of trust sales proceeds is to exclude the proceeds from *pro-rata* sales of trust assets to effect redemptions when determining whether a trust has met the general *de minimis* test. Since only the proceeds from non *pro-rata* sales of trust assets are considered for purposes of determining whether a NMWHFIT meets the general *de minimis* test, more trusts will meet the general *de minimis* test and qualify for the reduced reporting in §1.671–5(c)(2)(iv)(B). This amended definition is adopted by these final regulations.

Commentators on the temporary regulations requested that the final regulations also except certain other trust sales proceeds for the purpose of determining whether a NMWHFIT has met the general *de minimis* test if these sales are fully reported under §1.671–5(c)(2)(iv)(A) (the general reporting rules for sales and dispositions). These sales and dispositions include corporate reorganizations and restructurings for which the trust receives cash, the sale of securities received by the trust in corporate reorganizations and restructurings (including conversions of closed-end investment companies to open-end investment companies), principal prepayments, bond calls, bond maturities, and the sale of securities by the trustee as required by the governing document or applicable law governing fiduciaries in order to maintain the sound investment character of the trust, and any other non-volitional dispositions.

The IRS and the Treasury Department agree that this exclusion may be appropriate but are concerned that there may be some potential for abuse if trustees can choose to fully report some of these sales and not fully report other sales. Accordingly, the final regulations provide that the trust sales proceeds from these sales and dispositions may be excluded when determining whether the general *de minimis* test has been met, provided that the trustee consistently reports all such sales or dispositions, other than certain small excepted sales or dispositions (described in §1.671–5(c)(2)(iv)(D)(*4*)(*iii*)), under §1.671–5(c)(2)(iv)(A) during the life of the WHFIT.

The regulations currently provide that a WHFIT meets the general *de minimis* test in §1.671–5(c)(2)(iv)(D)(*1*) for its initial year if trust sales proceeds equal five percent or less of the net fair market value of the trust assets as of the start-up date. The start-up date is defined as the date when substantially all of the assets have been deposited with the trustee. Commentators suggested that the regulations provide trustees with an alternative date for measuring whether the *de minimis* test has been met for the initial trust year. They suggested that trustees be permitted to measure whether the *de minimis* test has been met by using the net fair market value of the trust's assets as of the date of the last deposit of trust assets into the NMWHFIT (not including any deposit of assets into the NMWHFIT pursuant to a distribution reinvestment program), not to exceed 90 days after the date the registration statement of the WHFIT becomes effective under the Securities Act of 1933. The final regulations adopt this suggestion.

The special WHMT *de minimis* test in §1.671–5(c)(2)(iv)(D)(*2*) of the WHFIT reporting rules was added to the WHFIT reporting rules in response to comments from the WHMT industry indicating that WHMT trustees would have difficulty applying the general *de minimis* test because it would be extremely difficult for the trustee to determine the fair market value of the mortgages held by the WHMT on an annual basis, as required under the general *de minimis* test. Under the special WHMT *de minimis* test, trustees of certain WHMTs are permitted to determine whether the *de minimis* test has been met using the outstanding principal balance of the mortgages of the trust as of January 1 rather than the net fair market value of the trust's assets. A commentator suggested that this *de minimis* test be expanded so that all WHFITs with hard to value debt instruments be permitted to use this *de minimis* test. In response, the IRS and Treasury Department request that trustees of WHFITs that hold hard to value debt instruments and that believe the application of the WHMT *de minimis* test to the instruments held by the WHFIT for which the trustees act would be useful, submit additional comments on this issue. The final regulations amend §1.671–5(c)(2)(iv)(D)(*2*) to provide that the application of the special *de minimis* test may be expanded by revenue ruling or other published guidance.

4. *Non Taxable Exchanges of Assets*

Commentators suggested that the final regulations provide an exception to the reporting rules for sales and dispositions of trust assets for exchanges of trust assets that result from non taxable corporate reorganizations. The final regulations adopt this suggestion.

D. *Market Discount*

Commentators requested amendments to the information required to be reported under the NMWHFIT safe harbor with respect to market discount. If a NMWHFIT is required to provide information regarding market discount under the general rules in §1.671–5(c)(2)(vii), the NMWHFIT safe harbor provides that a trustee's requirement to provide information regarding market discount is satisfied by providing information regarding the portion of the trust that the assets sold represented. Assuming that a trust interest holder purchased its interest at a discount, it was contemplated that the trust interest holder would allocate the same portion of its discount to the sale as the assets represented to the NMWHFIT.

This information was incomplete, however, with respect to a NMWHFIT holding debt instruments with original issue discount (OID). Under both the general provisions (§1.671–5(c)(2)(ii)(A) and (vii)) and the safe harbor (§1.671–5(f)(1)(vii) and (viii)), OID information and market discount information are required to be calculated and provided separately. Accordingly, for beneficial owners to determine the amount of market discount an owner must allocate to a particular sale or disposition of a debt instrument by the NMWHFIT, §1.671–5(f)(1)(viii)(A) is amended with respect to NMWHFITs that hold debt instruments with OID, to include a requirement that trustees provide a list of the aggregate adjusted issue prices of the debt instruments held by the NMWHFIT per trust interest as of the start-up date or the measuring date (as defined in §1.671–5(c)(2)(iv)(D)(*1*)) whichever will provide the more accurate information, as well as of January 1 of each subsequent year of the NMWHFIT. The IRS and the Treasury Department expect that beneficial owners of trust interests will use the adjusted issue price for the trust's debt instruments per trust interest for the year in which the beneficial owner purchased its interest to determine whether a trust interest has market discount.

II. *Applicability of the WHFIT Reporting Rules to WHMTs*

A. *Temporary WHMT safe harbor for WHMTs that hold interests in a REMIC, hold interests in another WHFIT, or hold or issue stripped interests*

The WHFIT reporting rules include a safe harbor for WHMTs that directly hold mortgages (as defined in §1.671–5(b)(11)) and issue trust interests that represent an equal *pro-rata* right to payments of interest and principal on the underlying mortgages. WHMTs that hold or issue stripped interests, hold interests in another WHFIT, or hold interests in a REMIC, are not eligible to report under the WHMT safe harbor. The IRS and the Treasury Department received comments expressing concern about the application of the WHFIT reporting rules to WHMTs that are outside the WHMT safe harbor because trustees and middlemen of these WHMTs are required to comply with the general WHFIT reporting rules in §1.671–5(c).

The commentators contended that some of the information required to be reported under the general information rules would be burdensome to obtain and moreover, is not required by beneficial owners to accurately report the tax consequences of owning a trust interest. In response to these concerns, pending the issuance of additional WHMT safe harbors, these final regulations provide a temporary safe harbor for all WHMTs that are outside the WHMT safe harbor in §1.671–5(g) of the WHFIT reporting rules because they hold or issue stripped interests, hold interests in a REMIC or hold an interest in another WHMT. Under the safe harbor, a trustee will be deemed to satisfy the requirements of §1.671–5(c)(1) if the trustee calculates and provides trust information in a manner that enables a requesting person to provide trust information to a beneficial owner of a trust interest that enables the owner to reasonably accurately report the tax consequences of its ownership of a trust interest on the Federal income tax return of the beneficial owner.

Additionally, in order to be deemed to have satisfied the requirements of §1.671–5(c)(1), the trustee must provide information regarding market discount and original issue discount (OID) that is calculated in any reasonable manner consistent with section 1272(a)(6). Pending the issuance of additional guidance, it is intended that this safe harbor except trustees from any penalties that may apply for not fully complying with paragraph (c) of the WHFIT reporting rules where it can be shown that full compliance with paragraph (c) is unnecessary in order to provide trust interest holders with appropriate information. A trustee or middleman required to provide information to the IRS under §1.671–5(d) and to beneficial owners under paragraph §1.671–5(e) may satisfy those obligations by calculating and providing trust information consistent with the information provided by the trustee under this safe harbor.

B. *Application of the requirement to provide market discount and OID information for existing WHMTs*

Section 1.671–5(c)(2)(ii)(A) requires a trustee of a WHFIT to provide information regarding OID. Commentators have expressed concern regarding the application of this requirement to existing WHMTs because the historical information that would enable the trustee to provide OID information has never been provided or maintained by the trustee or the persons responsible for information reporting. Commentators contend that it is unlikely that these trustees will be able to comply with this requirement for existing WHMTs. The IRS and the Treasury Department recognize that, in some cases, the information necessary for a WHMT to comply with this provision may not be available. If it can be demonstrated that a trustee of a WHMT with a start up date on or after August 13, 1998 and on or before January 24, 2006, has attempted in good faith, but without success, to obtain the historical information required to provide OID information, the IRS will not impose any penalties that would apply under §1.671–5(l) of the WHFIT reporting rules (redesignated §1.671–5(m) by these final regulations) as a result of a trustee's failure to comply with the requirement to provide OID information. Further, §1.671–5(c)(2)(ii)(A) of these final regulations excepts a trustee of a WHMT with a start up date prior to August 13, 1998 from the requirement to provide OID information. For purposes of calculating the market discount fraction under the WHMT safe harbor in §1.671–5(g)(1)(v), these trustees may assume that the WHMT is holding mortgages that were issued without OID.

The WHMT safe harbor provisions for calculating OID information in §1.671–5(g)(i)(iv) and market discount information in §1.671–5(g)(1)(v) require trustees to use the prepayment assumption used in pricing the original issue of trust interests. Commentators have indicated that trustees of existing WHMTs may not know the prepayment assumption used in pricing the original issue of trust interests. In response, the safe harbor is amended to provide that if the trustee does not know the prepayment assumption used in pricing the original issue of trust interests for a WHMT with a start-up date prior to January 24, 2006, and the trustee makes a good faith effort without success to obtain the prepayment assumption, the trustee may use any reasonable prepayment assumption when calculating OID and market discount information for that WHMT.

III. *Requirement to Register and Continued Consideration of a WHFIT Directory*

Prior to the publication of the WHFIT reporting rules, commentators expressed concern that middlemen would not be able to identify a client's investment as an investment in a WHFIT and suggested that the IRS publish a directory or list of WHFITs that would include the name and CUSIP number of each WHFIT, along with the name, address and telephone number of the WHFIT's representative. Commentators noted that a publicly available directory or list would assist middlemen and brokers in identifying a client's investment as an investment in a WHFIT and in locating the WHFIT's representative. The WHFIT reporting rules did not provide for a directory and instead, required the trustee to identify a representative of the trust to provide trust information in a publication generally read by and available to requesting persons, in the trust's prospectus, or on the trustee's Internet website.

Following the publication of the WHFIT reporting rules, additional comments were received regarding the need for a directory of WHFITs. In response to those comments, the proposed regulations indicated that the IRS and Treasury Department considered expanding Publication 938, "*Real Estate Mortgage Investment Conduits (REMICs) Reporting Information (And Other Collateralized Debt Obligations (CDOs))*," or creating a separate publication to list WHMT trustees and NMWHFITs. The IRS and Treasury Department continue to consider how a directory of WHFITs could be implemented. Pending the publication of such a directory, trustees must provide information regarding a trust representative in the manner provided in the WHFIT reporting rules.

IV. *Form 1041 Reporting*

A trustee of a WHFIT must indicate on the Form 1041 filed for the 2006 calendar year that the return is a final return.

Effective Date

These final amendments are effective December 29, 2006. In general, these final regulations are applicable to the reporting required under §1.671–5 as of January 1, 2007 (see §1.671–5(m) (redesignated §1.671–5(n) by these final regulations)) and will be applied as though these amendments were included in the WHFIT reporting rules. The IRS and the Treasury Department are aware that some trustees and middlemen were unable to complete updates to their computer and information reporting systems to comply with the WHFIT reporting rules until the amendments to the WHFIT reporting rules included in these regulations are finalized. Accordingly, the IRS will not impose any penalties that would apply under §1.671–5(l) (redesignated §1.671–5(m) by these final regulations) of the WHFIT reporting rules as a result of the failure to comply with the WHFIT reporting rules as amended by these final regulations with respect to the 2007 calendar year in cases where a trustee or middleman was unable to change its information reporting systems to comply with the WHFIT reporting rules because of uncertainty regarding the application of certain provisions of those rules pending the publication of these final regulations. For example, penalties will not be imposed on a trustee of a NMWHFIT that reports the amount of trust sales proceeds distributed to trust interest holders for the 2007 calendar year under §1.671–5(c)(2)(iv)(B) even though the trustee is unable to determine whether the NMWHFIT has met the *de minimis* test for the 2007 calendar year, provided that the trustee's failure to determine whether a NMWHFIT has met the *de minimis* test results from the trustee's inability to alter its existing information reporting systems by January 1, 2007, to capture the necessary information. As an additional example, penalties will not be imposed on the trustees or the middlemen of WHMTs that are unable to comply with certain provisions of the WHFIT reporting rules with respect to the 2007 calendar year because those trustees and middlemen were not able to change their existing reporting systems to comply with the WHFIT reporting rules pending the publication of these final regulations.

Special Analyses

It has been determined that these final regulations are not a significant regulatory action as defined in Executive Order 12866. Therefore, a regulatory assessment is not required. It is hereby certified that this regulation will not have a significant economic impact on a substantial number of small entities. This certification is based on the fact that the regulations will not have a significant economic impact on small entities because the reporting burdens in these regulations will fall primarily on large brokerage firms, large banks, and other large entities acting as trustees or middlemen, most of which are not small entities within the meaning of the Regulatory Flexibility Act (5 U.S.C. chapter 6). Thus, a substantial number of small entities are not expected to be affected. Therefore, a Regulatory Flexibility Analyses under the Regulatory Flexibility Act (5 U.S.C. chapter 6) is not required. Pursuant to section 7805(f) of the Internal Revenue Code, the notice of proposed rulemaking preceding this regulation was submitted to the Chief Counsel for Advocacy of the Small Business Administration for comment on its impact on small business.

Drafting Information

The principal author of these regulations is Faith Colson, Office of Associate Chief Counsel (Passthroughs & Special Industries). However, other personnel from the IRS and the Treasury Department participated in their development.

* * * * *

Adoption of Amendments to the Regulations

Accordingly, 26 CFR part 1 is amended as follows:

PART 1—INCOME TAXES

Paragraph 1. The authority citation for part 1 continues to read, in part, as follows:

Authority: 26 U.S.C. 7805 * * *

Par. 2. Section 1.671–5 is amended by:

1. Revising paragraph (a) by redesignating entries for paragraphs (h), (j), (k), (l), and (m) as entries for paragraphs (j), (k), (l), (m) and (n) and adding a new entry for paragraph (h).

2. Revising paragraphs (b)(5), (b)(8), (b)(21), (c)(2)(ii)(A), (c)(2)(iv), (c)(2)(v), (c)(2)(vi), (c)(2)(vii), (d)(2)(ii)(C), (d)(2)(ii)(F), (d)(2)(ii)(G), (f)(1), (f)(1)(i)(A), (f)(1)(viii)(A), (f)(2)(viii)(A), (f)(3)(i)(A)(*1*), (f)(3)(i)(B)(*5*), (f)(3)(i)(B)(*9*), (f)(3)(ii)(B)(*4*)(*i*), (f)(3)(ii)(B)(*5*), (f)(3)(ii)(B)(*6*), (g)(1)(iv)(A)(*2*), and (g)(1)(v)(A).

3. Redesignating paragraphs (h), (j), (k), (l), and (m) as (j), (k), (l), (m) and (n) respectively.

4. Adding new paragraph (h).

The additions and revisions read as follows:

§1.671–5 Reporting for widely held fixed investment trusts.

(a) * * *

(h) Additional safe harbors.

(1) Temporary safe harbors.

(2) Additional safe harbors provided by other published guidance.

* * * * *

(b) * * *

(5) The *cash held for distribution* is the amount of cash held by the WHFIT (other than trust sales proceeds and proceeds from sales described in paragraphs (c)(2)(iv)(D)(*4*), (G), and (H) of this section) less reasonably required reserve funds as of the date that the amount of a distribution is required to be determined under the WHFIT's governing document.

* * * * *

(8) An *in-kind redemption* is a redemption in which a beneficial owner receives a *pro-rata* share of each of the assets of the WHFIT that the beneficial owner is deemed to own under section 671. For example, for purposes of this paragraph (b)(8), if beneficial owner A owns a one percent interest in a WHFIT that holds 100 shares of X corporation stock, so that A is considered to own a one percent interest in each of the 100 shares, A's *pro-rata* share of the X corporation stock for this purpose is one share of X corporation stock.

* * * * *

(21) *Trust sales proceeds* equal the amount paid to a WHFIT for the sale or disposition of an asset held by the WHFIT, including principal payments received by the WHFIT that completely retire a debt instrument (other than a final scheduled principal payment) and *pro-rata* partial principal prepayments described under §1.1275–2(f)(2). Trust sales proceeds do not include amounts paid for any interest income that would be required to be reported under §1.6045–1(d)(3). Trust sales

proceeds also do not include amounts paid to a NMWHFIT as the result of *pro-rata* sales of trust assets to effect a redemption described in paragraph (c)(2)(iv)(G) of this section or the value of assets received as a result of a tax-free corporate reorganization as described in paragraph (c)(2)(iv)(H) of this section.

* * * * *

(c) * * *

(2) * * *

(ii) * * *

(A) All items of gross income (including OID, except that OID is not required to be included for a WHMT that has a start-up date (as defined in paragraph (b)(19) of this section) prior to August 13, 1998).

* * * * *

(iv) *Asset sales and dispositions*. The trustee must report information regarding sales and dispositions of WHFIT assets as required in this paragraph (c)(2)(iv). For purposes of this paragraph (c)(2)(iv), a payment (other than a final scheduled payment) that completely retires a debt instrument (including a mortgage held by a WHMT) or a *pro-rata* prepayment on a debt instrument (see §1.1275–2(f)(2)) held by a WHFIT must be reported as a full or partial sale or disposition of the debt instrument. *Pro-rata* sales of trust assets to effect redemptions, as defined in paragraph (c)(2)(iv)(G) of this section, or exchanges of trust assets as the result of a corporate reorganization under paragraph (c)(2)(iv)(H) of this section, are not reported as sales or dispositions under this paragraph (c)(2)(iv).

(A) *General rule*. Except as provided in paragraph (c)(2)(iv)(B) (regarding the exception for certain NMWHFITs) or paragraph (c)(2)(iv)(C) (regarding the exception for certain WHMTs) of this section, the trustee must report with respect to each sale or disposition of a WHFIT asset—

(*1*) The date of each sale or disposition;

(*2*) Information that enables a requesting person to determine the amount of trust sales proceeds (as defined in paragraph (b)(21) of this section) attributable to a beneficial owner as a result of each sale or disposition; and

(*3*) Information that enables a beneficial owner to allocate, with reasonable accuracy, a portion of the owner's basis in its trust interest to each sale or disposition.

(B) *Exception for certain NMWHFITs*. If a NMWHFIT meets paragraph (c)(2)(iv)(D)(*1*) (regarding the general *de minimis* test), paragraph (c)(2)(iv)(E) (regarding the qualified NMWHFIT exception), or paragraph (c)(2)(iv)(F) (regarding the NMWHFIT final calendar year exception) of this section, the trustee is not required to report under paragraph (c)(2)(iv)(A) of this section. Instead, the trustee must report sufficient information to enable a requesting person to determine the amount of trust sales proceeds distributed to a beneficial owner during the calendar year with respect to each sale or disposition of a trust asset. The trustee also must provide requesting persons with a statement that the NMWHFIT is permitted to report under this paragraph (c)(2)(iv)(B).

(C) *Exception for certain WHMTs*. If a WHMT meets either the general or the special *de minimis* test of paragraph (c)(2)(iv)(D) of this section for the calendar year, the trustee is not required to report under paragraph (c)(2)(iv)(A) of this section. Instead, the trustee must report information to enable a requesting person to determine the amount of trust sales proceeds attributable to a beneficial owner as a result of the sale or disposition. The trustee also must provide requesting persons with a statement that the WHMT is permitted to report under this paragraph (c)(2)(iv)(C).

(D) *De minimis tests*—(*1*) *General WHFIT de minimis test*. The general WHFIT *de minimis* test is satisfied if trust sales proceeds for the calendar year are not more than five percent of the net asset value of the trust (aggregate fair market value of the trust's assets less the trust's liabilities) as of the later of January 1 and the start-up date (as defined paragraph (b)(19) of this section); or, if the trustee chooses, the later of January 1 and the measuring date. The measuring date is the date of the last deposit of assets into the WHFIT (not including any deposit of assets into the WHFIT pursuant to a distribution reinvestment program), not to exceed 90 days after the date the registration statement of the WHFIT becomes effective under the Securities Act of 1933.

(*2*) *Special WHMT de minimis test*. A WHMT that meets the asset requirement of paragraph (g)(1)(ii)(E) of this section satisfies the special WHMT *de minimis* test in this paragraph (c)(2)(iv)(D)(*2*) if trust sales proceeds for the calendar year are not more than five percent of the aggregate outstanding principal balance of the WHMT (as defined in paragraph (g)(1)(iii)(D) of this section) as of the later of January 1 of that year or the trust's start-up date. For purposes of applying the special WHMT *de minimis* test in this paragraph (c)(2)(iv)(D)(*2*), amounts that result from the complete or partial payment of the outstanding principal balance of the mortgages held by the trust are not included in the amount of trust sales proceeds. The IRS and the Treasury Department may provide by revenue ruling, or by other published guidance, that the special *de minimis* test of this paragraph (c)(2)(iv)(D)(*2*) may be applied to WHFITs holding debt instruments other than those described in paragraph (g)(1)(ii)(E) of this section.

(*3*) *Effect of clean-up call*. If a WHFIT fails to meet either *de minimis* test described in this paragraph (c)(2)(iv)(D) solely as the result of a clean-up call, as defined in paragraph (b)(6) of this section, the WHFIT will be treated as having met the *de minimis* test.

(*4*) *Exception for certain fully reported sales*—(*i*) *Rule*. If a trustee of a NMWHFIT reports the sales described in paragraph (c)(2)(iv)(D)(*4*)(*ii*) of this section as provided under paragraph (c)(2)(iv)(A) of this section (regardless of whether the general *de minimis* test in paragraph (c)(2)(iv)(D)(*1*) of this section is satisfied for a particular calendar year) consistently throughout the life of the WHFIT, a trustee may exclude the trust sales proceeds received by the WHFIT as a result of those sales from the trust sales proceeds used to determine whether a WHFIT has satisfied the general *de minimis* test in paragraph (c)(2)(iv)(D)(*1*) of this section.

(*ii*) *Applicable sales and dispositions*. This paragraph (c)(2)(iv)(D)(*4*) applies to sales and dispositions resulting from corporate reorganizations and restructurings for which the trust receives cash, the sale of assets received by the trust in corporate reorganizations and restructurings (including conversions of closed-end investment companies to open-end investment companies), principal prepayments, bond calls, bond maturities, and the sale of securities by the trustee as required by the governing document or applicable law governing fiduciaries in order to maintain the sound investment character of the trust, and any other nonvolitional dispositions of trust assets.

(*iii*) *Certain small sales and dispositions*. If the amount of trust sales proceeds from a sale or disposition described in paragraph (c)(2)(iv)(D)(*4*)(*ii*) of this section is less than .01 percent of the net fair market value of the WHFIT as determined for applying the *de minimis* test for the calendar year, the trustee is not required to report the sale or disposition under paragraph (c)(2)(iv)(A) of this section provided the trustee includes the trust sales proceeds, received for purposes of determining whether the trust has met the general *de minimis* test of paragraph (c)(2)(iv)(D)(*1*) of this section.

(E) *Qualified NMWHFIT exception*. The qualified NMWHFIT exception is satisfied if—

(*1*) The NMWHFIT has a start-up date (as defined in paragraph (b)(19) of this section) before February 23, 2006;

(*2*) The registration statement of the NMWHFIT becomes effective under the Securities Act of 1933, as amended (15 U.S.C. 77a, *et. seq.*) and trust interests are offered for sale to the public before February 23, 2006; or

(*3*) The registration statement of the NMWHFIT becomes effective under the Securities Act of 1933 and trust interests are offered for sale to the public on or after February 23, 2006, and before July 31, 2006, and the NMWHFIT is fully funded before October 1, 2006. For purposes of determining whether a NMWHFIT is fully funded under this paragraph (c)(2)(iv)(E), deposits to the NMWHFIT after October 1, 2006, that are made pursuant to a distribution reinvestment program that is consistent with the requirements of §301.7701–4(c) of this chapter are disregarded.

(F) *NMWHFIT final calendar year exception*. The NMWHFIT final calendar year exception is satisfied if—

(*1*) The NMWHFIT terminates on or before December 31 of the year for which the trustee is reporting;

(*2*) Beneficial owners exchange their interests for cash or are treated as having exchanged their interests for cash upon termination of the trust; and

(*3*) The trustee makes reasonable efforts to engage in *pro-rata* sales of trust assets to effect redemptions.

(G) *Pro-rata sales of trust assets to effect a redemption*—(1) *Rule*. *Pro-rata* sales of trust assets to effect redemptions are not required to be reported under this paragraph (c)(2)(iv).

(2) *Definition*. *Pro-rata* sales of trust assets to effect redemptions occur when—

(*i*) One or more trust interests are tendered for redemption;

(*ii*) The trustee identifies the *pro-rata* shares of the trust assets that are deemed to be owned by the trust interest or interests tendered for redemption (See paragraph (b)(8) of this section for a description of how *pro-rata* is to be applied for purposes of this paragraph (c)(2)(iv)(G)) and sells those assets as soon as practicable;

(*iii*) Proceeds from the sales of the assets identified in paragraph (c)(2)(iv)(G)(*2*)(*ii*) of this section are used solely to effect redemptions; and

(*iv*) The redemptions are reported as required under paragraph (c)(2)(v) of this section by the trustee.

(*3*) *Additional rules* (*i*) *Calendar month aggregation*. The trustee may compare the aggregate *pro-rata* share of the assets deemed to be owned by the trust interests tendered for redemption during the calendar month with the aggregate sales of assets to effect redemptions for the calendar month to determine the *pro-rata* sales of trust assets to effect redemptions for the calendar month. If the aggregate *pro-rata* share of an asset deemed to be owned by the trust interests tendered for redemption for the month is a fractional amount, the trustee may round that number up to the next whole number for the purpose of determining the *pro-rata* sales to effect redemptions for the calendar month;

(*ii*) *Sales of assets to effect redemptions may be combined with sales of assets for other purposes*. Sales of assets to effect redemptions may be combined with the sales of assets to obtain cash for other purposes but the proceeds from the sales of assets to effect redemptions must be used solely to provide cash for redemptions and the sales of assets to obtain cash for other purposes must be reported as otherwise provided in this paragraph (c)(2)(iv). For example, if a trustee sells assets and the proceeds are used by the trustee to pay trust expenses, these amounts are to be included in the amounts reported under paragraph (c)(2)(iv)(A) or (B), as appropriate.

(*4*) *Example*—(*i*) *January 1, 2008*. Trust has one million trust interests and all interests have equal value and equal rights. The number of shares of stock in corporations A through J and the *pro-rata* share of each stock that a trust interest is deemed to own as of the January 1, 2008, is as follows:

STOCK	TOTAL SHARES	PER TRUST INTEREST
A	24,845	.024845
B	28,273	.028273
C	35,575	.035575
D	13,866	.013866
E	25,082	.025082
F	39,154	.039154
G	16,137	.016137
H	14,704	.014704
I	17,436	.017436
J	31,133	.031133

(*ii*) *Transactions of January 2, 2008*. On January 2, 2008, 50,000 trust interests are tendered for redemption. The deemed *pro-rata* ownership of stocks A through J represented by the 50,000 redeemed trust interests and the stocks sold to provide cash for the redemptions are set out in the following table:

STOCK	DEEMED PRO-RATA OWNERSHIP	SHARES SOLD
A	1,242.25	1,242
B	1,413.65	1,413
C	1,778.75	1,779
D	693.30	694
E	1,254.10	1,254
F	1,957.70	1,957
G	806.85	807
H	735.20	735
I	871.80	872
J	1,556.65	1,557

(*iii*) *Transactions on January 15 through 17, 2008*. On January 15, 2008, 10,000 trust interests are tendered for redemption. Trustee lends money to Trust for redemptions. On January 16, B merges into C at a rate of .55 per share. On January 17, Trustee sells stock to obtain cash to be reimbursed the cash loaned to Trust to effect the redemptions. The *pro-rata* share of the stock deemed to be owned by the 10,000 redeemed trust interests and the stock sold by the trustee to effect the redemptions are set out in the following table:

STOCK	DEEMED PRO-RATA OWNERSHIP	SHARES SOLD
A	248.45	249
B	0	0
C	511.25	512
D	138.66	138
E	250.82	251
F	391.54	392
G	161.37	162
H	147.04	148
I	174.36	174
J	311.33	311

(*iv*) *Transactions on January 28 and 29, 2008*. On January 28, 2008, the value of the H stock is $30.00 per share and Trustee, pursuant to Trust's governing document, sells the H stock to preserve the financial integrity of Trust and receives $414,630. Trustee intends to report this sale under paragraph (c)(2)(iv)(A) of this section and to distribute the proceeds of the sale *pro-rata* to trust interest holders on Trust's next scheduled distribution date. On January 29, 2008, while trustee still holds the proceeds from the January 28 sale, 10,000 trust interests are tendered for redemption. The *pro-rata* share of the stock deemed to be owned by the 10,000 redeemed trust interests and the stock sold by the trustee to effect the redemptions are set out in the following table:

STOCK	DEEMED PRO-RATA OWNERSHIP	SHARES SOLD
A	248.45	248
B	0	0
C	511.25	511
D	138.66	139
E	250.82	251
F	391.54	391
G	161.37	161
H	0 Share of cash proceeds: $4,458.39	0

STOCK	DEEMED PRO-RATA OWNERSHIP	SHARES SOLD
I	174.36	175
J	311.33	312

(*v*) *Monthly amounts*. To determine the *pro-rata* sales to effect redemptions for January, trustee compares the aggregate *pro-rata* share of stocks A through J (rounded to the next whole number) deemed to be owned by the trust interests tendered for redemption during the month of January with the sales of stocks A through J to effect redemptions:

STOCK	DEEMED PRO-RATA OWNERSHIP	SHARES SOLD
A	1740	1739
B	0	0
C	3579	3579
D	971	971
E	1756	1756
F	2741	2741
G	1130	1130
H	883	883
I	1221	1221
J	2180	2180

(*vi*) *Pro-rata sales to effect redemptions for the month of January*. For the month of January, the deemed *pro-rata* ownership of shares of stocks A through J equal or exceed the sales of stock to effect redemptions for the month. Accordingly, all of the sales to effect redemptions during the month of January are considered to be *pro-rata* and are not required to be reported under this paragraph (c)(2)(iv).

(H) *Corporate Reorganizations*. The exchange of trust assets for other assets of equivalent value pursuant to a tax free corporate reorganization is not required to be reported as a sale or disposition under this paragraph (c)(2)(iv).

(v) *Redemptions and sales of WHFIT interests*—(A) *Redemptions*—(*1*) *In general*. Unless paragraph (c)(2)(v)(C) of this section applies, for each date on which the amount of a redemption proceeds for the redemption of a trust interest is determined, the trustee must provide information to enable a requesting person to determine—

(*i*) The redemption proceeds (as defined in paragraph (b)(15) of this section) per trust interest on that date;

(*ii*) The redemption asset proceeds (as defined in paragraph (b)(14) of this section) per trust interest on that date; and

(*iii*) The gross income that is attributable to the redeeming beneficial owner for the portion of the calendar year that the redeeming beneficial owner held its interest (including income earned by the WHFIT after the date of the last income distribution).

(*2*) *In kind redemptions*. The value of the assets received with respect to an in-kind redemption (as defined in paragraph (b)(8) of this section) is not required to be reported under this paragraph (c)(2)(v)(A). Information regarding the income attributable to a redeeming beneficial owner must, however, be reported under paragraph (c)(2)(v)(A)(*1*)(*iii*) of this section.

(B) *Sale of a trust interest*. Unless paragraph (c)(2)(v)(C) of this section applies, if a secondary market for interests in the WHFIT is established, the trustee must provide, for each day of the calendar year, information to enable requesting persons to determine—

(*1*) The sale assets proceeds (as defined in paragraph (b)(17) of this section) per trust interest on that date; and

(*2*) The gross income that is attributable to a selling beneficial owner and to a purchasing beneficial owner for the portion of the calendar year that each held the trust interest.

(C) *Simplified Reporting for Certain NMWHFITs*—(*1*) *In general*. The trustee of a NMWHFIT described in paragraph (c)(2)(v)(C)(*2*) of this section is not required to report the information described in paragraph (c)(2)(v)(A) of this section (regarding redemptions) or (c)(2)(v)(B) of this section (regarding sales). However, the trustee must report to requesting persons, for each date on which the amount of redemption proceeds to be paid for the redemption of a trust interest is determined, information that will enable requesting persons to determine the redemption proceeds per trust interest on that date. The trustee also must provide requesting persons with a statement that this paragraph applies to the NMWHFIT.

(*2*) *NMWHFITs that qualify for the exception*. This paragraph (c)(2)(v)(C) applies to a NMWHFIT if—

(*i*) Substantially all the assets of the NMWHFIT produce income that is treated as interest income (but only if these assets trade on a recognized exchange or securities market without a price component attributable to accrued interest) or produce dividend income (as defined in section 6042(b) and the regulations under that section). (Trust sales proceeds and gross proceeds from sales described in paragraphs (c)(2)(iv)(G) and (H) of this section are ignored for the purpose of determining if substantially all of a NMWHFIT's assets produce dividend or the interest income described in this paragraph); and

(*ii*) The qualified NMWHFIT exception of paragraph (c)(2)(iv)(E) of this section is satisfied, or the trustee is required by the governing document of the NMWHFIT to determine and distribute all cash held for distribution (as defined in paragraph (b)(5) of this section) no less frequently than monthly. A NMWHFIT will be considered to have satisfied this paragraph (c)(2)(v)(C)(*2*)(*i*) notwithstanding that the governing document of the NMWHFIT permits the trustee to forego making a required monthly or more frequent distribution, if the cash held for distribution is less than 0.1 percent of the aggregate net asset value of the trust as of the date specified in the governing document for calculating the amount of the monthly distribution.

(vi) *Information regarding bond premium.* The trustee generally must report information that enables a beneficial owner to determine, in any manner that is reasonably consistent with section 171, the amount of the beneficial owner's amortizable bond premium, if any, for each calendar year. However, if a NMWHFIT meets the general *de minimis* test in paragraph (c)(2)(iv)(D)(*1*) of this section, the qualified NMWHFIT exception of paragraph (c)(2)(iv)(E) of this section, or the NMWHFIT final calendar year exception of paragraph (c)(2)(iv)(F) of this section, the trustee of the NMWHFIT is not required to report information regarding bond premium.

(vii) *Information regarding market discount.* The trustee generally must report information that enables a beneficial owner to determine, in any manner reasonably consistent with section 1276 (including section 1276(a)(3)), the amount of market discount that has accrued during the calendar year. However, if a NMWHFIT meets the general *de minimis* test in paragraph (c)(2)(iv)(D) of this section, the qualified NMWHFIT exception of paragraph (c)(2)(iv)(E) of this section, or the NMWHFIT final calendar year exception of paragraph (c)(2)(iv)(F) of this section, the trustee of such NMWHFIT is not required to provide information regarding market discount.

* * * * *

(d) * * *

(2) * * *

(ii) * * *

(C) *Gross income.* All items of gross income of the WHFIT attributable to the TIH for the calendar year (including OID (unless the exception for certain WHMTs applies (see paragraph (c)(2)(ii)(A) of this section)) and all amounts of income attributable to a selling, purchasing, or redeeming TIH for the portion of the calendar year that the TIH held its interest (unless paragraph (c)(2)(v)(C) of this section (regarding an exception for certain NMWHFITs) applies));

* * * * *

(F) *Reporting Redemptions.* All redemption asset proceeds (as defined in paragraph (b)(14) of this section) paid to the TIH for the calendar year, if any, or, if paragraph (c)(2)(v)(C) of this section (regarding an exception for certain NMWHFITs) applies, all redemption proceeds (as defined in paragraph (b)(15) of this section) paid to the TIH for the calendar year;

(G) *Reporting sales of a trust interest on a secondary market.* All sales asset proceeds (as defined in paragraph (b)(17) of this section) paid to the TIH for the sale of a trust interest or interests on a secondary market established for the NMWHFIT for the calendar year, if any, or, if paragraph (c)(2)(v)(C) of this section (regarding an exception for certain NMWHFITs) applies, all sales proceeds (as defined in paragraph (b)(18) of this section) paid to the TIH for the calendar year; and

* * * * *

(f) *Safe harbor for providing information for certain NMWHFITs*—(1) *Safe harbor for trustee reporting of NMWHFIT information.* The trustee of a NMWHFIT that meets the requirements of paragraph (f)(1)(i) of this section is deemed to satisfy paragraph (c)(1)(i) of this section, if the trustee calculates and provides WHFIT information in the manner described in this paragraph (f) and provides a statement to a requesting person giving notice that information has been calculated in accordance with this paragraph (f)(1).

(i) *In general*—(A) *Eligibility to report under this safe harbor.* Only NMWHFITs that meet the requirements set forth in paragraphs (f)(1)(i)(A)(*1*) and (*2*) of this section may report under this safe harbor. For purposes of determining whether the requirements of paragraph (f)(1)(i)(A)(*1*) of this section are met, trust sales proceeds and gross proceeds from sales described in paragraphs (c)(2)(iv)(G) and (H) of this section are ignored.

(*1*) Substantially all of the NMWHFIT's income is from dividends or interest; and

(*2*) All trust interests have identical value and rights.

* * * * *

(viii) *Reporting market discount information under the safe harbor*—(A) *In general*—(*1*) *Trustee required to provide market discount information.* If the trustee is required to provide information regarding market discount under paragraph (c)(2)(vii) of this section, the trustee must provide—

(*i*) The information required to be provided under paragraph (f)(1)(iv)(A)(*1*)(*iii*) of this section; and

(*ii*) If the NMWHFIT holds debt instruments with OID, a list of the aggregate adjusted issue prices of the debt instruments per trust interest calculated as of the start-up date or measuring date (see paragraph (c)(2)(iv)(D)(*4*) of this section) (whichever provides more accurate information) and as of January 1 for each subsequent year of the NMWHFIT.

(*2*) *Trustee not required to provide market discount information.* If the trustee is not required to provide market discount information under paragraph (c)(2)(vii) of this section (because the NMWHFIT meets the general *de minimis* test of paragraph (c)(2)(iv)(D)(*1*) of this section, the qualified NMWHFIT exception of paragraph (c)(2)(iv)(E) of this section, or the NMWHFIT final year exception of paragraph (c)(2)(iv)(F) of this section), the trustee is not required under this paragraph (f) to provide any information regarding market discount.

* * * * *

(2) * * *

(viii) * * *

(A) Except as provided in paragraph (f)(2)(viii)(B) of this section, the trustee or middleman must provide the TIH with the information provided under paragraph (f)(1)(viii) of this section.

(3) * * *

(i) * * *

(A) * * *

(*1*) Trust is a NMWHFIT that holds common stock in ten different corporations and has 100 trust interests outstanding. The start-up date for Trust is December 15, 2006, and Trust's registration statement under the Securities Act of 1933 became effective after July 31, 2006. Trust terminates on March 15, 2008. The agreement governing Trust requires Trust to distribute cash held by Trust reduced by accrued but unpaid expenses on April 15, July 15, and October 15 of the 2007 calendar year. The agreement also provides that the trust interests will be redeemed by the Trust for an amount equal to the value of the trust interest, as of the close of business, on the day the trust interest is tendered for redemption. There is no reinvestment plan. A secondary market for interests in Trust will be created by Trust's sponsor and Trust's sponsor will provide Trustee with a list of dates on which sales occurred on this secondary market.

(B) * * *

(*5*) On June 1, 2007, Trustee sells shares of stock for $1000x to preserve the soundness of the trust. The stock sold on June 1, 2007, equaled 20% of the aggregate fair market value of the assets held by Trust on the start-up date of Trust. Trustee has chosen not to report sales described in paragraph (c)(2)(iv)(*4*)(*ii*) of Trust's assets under paragraph (c)(2)(iv)(D)(*4*) of this section.

* * * * *

(*9*) On December 10, 2007, *J* tenders a trust interest to Trustee for redemption through Broker1. Trustee determines that the amount of the redemption proceeds to be paid for a trust interest that is tendered for redemption on December 10, 2007 is $116x, of which $115x represents the redemption asset proceeds. Trustee pays this amount to Broker1 on *J*'s behalf. On December 12, 2007, trustee engages in a non *pro-rata* sale of shares of common stock for $115x to effect *J*'s redemption of a trust interest. The stock sold on December 12, 2007, equals 2% of the aggregate fair market value of all the assets of Trust as of the start-up date.

* * * * *

(ii) * * *

(B) * * *

(*4*) * * * (i) *Application of the de minimis test*. The aggregate fair market value of the assets of Trust as of January 1, 2007, was $10,000x. During the 2007 calendar year, Trust received trust sales proceeds of $1115x. The trust sales proceeds received by Trust for the 2007 calendar year equal 11.15% of Trust's fair market value as of January 1, 2007. Accordingly, the *de minimis* test is not satisfied for the 2007 calendar year. The qualified NMWHFIT exception in paragraph (c)(2)(iv)(E) of this section and the NMWHFIT final calendar year exception in (c)(2)(iv)(F) of this section also do not apply to Trust for the 2007 calendar year.

* * * * *

(*5*) *Reporting redemptions*. Because Trust is not required to make distributions at least as frequently as monthly, and Trust does not satisfy the qualified NMWHFIT exception in paragraph (c)(2)(iv)(E) of this section, the exception in paragraph (c)(2)(v)(C) does not apply to Trust. To satisfy the requirements of paragraph (f)(1) of this section, Trustee provides a list of dates for which the redemption proceeds to be paid for the redemption of a trust interest was determined for the 2007 calendar year and the redemptions asset proceeds paid for each date. During 2007, Trustee only determined the amount of redemption proceeds paid for the redemption of a trust interest once, for December 10, 2007 and the redemption asset proceeds determined for that date was $115x.

(*6*) *Reporting sales of trust interests*. Because trust is not required to make distributions at least as frequently as monthly, and Trust does not satisfy the qualified NMWHFIT exception in paragraph (c)(2)(iv)(E) of this section, the exception in paragraph (c)(2)(v)(C) of this section does not apply to Trust. Sponsor, in accordance with the trust agreement, provides Trustee with a list of dates on which sales on the secondary market occurred. To satisfy the requirements of paragraph (f)(1) of this section, Trustee provides requesting persons with a list of dates on which sales on the secondary market occurred and the amount of cash held for distribution, per trust interest, on each date. The first sale during the 2007 calendar year occurred on September 30, 2007, and the amount of cash held for distribution, per trust interest, on that date is $1.35x. The second sale occurred on December 10, 2007, and the amount of cash held for distribution, per trust interest, on that date is $1.00x.

(g) * * *

(1) * * *

(iv) * * * (A) * * *

(*2*) In calculating the daily portion of OID, the trustee must use the prepayment assumption used in pricing the original issue of trust interests. If the WHMT has a start-up date prior to January 24, 2006, and the trustee, after a good faith effort to ascertain that information, does not know the prepayment assumption used in pricing the original issue of trust interests, the trustee may use any reasonable prepayment assumption to calculate OID provided it continues to use the same prepayment assumption consistently thereafter.

* * * * *

(v) * * * (A) * * *

(*3*) *Computing the total amount of stated interest remaining to be paid and the total remaining OID at the beginning of the month*. To compute the total amount of stated interest remaining to be paid to the WHMT as of the beginning of the month and the total remaining OID as of the beginning of the month, the trustee must use the prepayment assumption used in pricing the original issue of trust interests. If the WHMT has a start-up date prior to January 24, 2006, and the trustee, after a good faith effort to ascertain that information, does not know the prepayment assumption used in pricing the original issue of trust interests, the trustee may use any reasonable prepayment assumption to calculate these amounts provided it continues to use the same prepayment assumption consistently thereafter.

* * * * *

(h) *Additional safe harbors*—(1) *Temporary safe harbor for WHMTs*—(i) *Application*. Pending the issuance of additional guidance, the safe harbor in this paragraph applies to trustees and middlemen of WHMTs that are not eligible to report under the WHMT safe harbor in paragraph (g) of this section because they hold interests in another WHFIT, in a REMIC, or hold or issue stripped interests.

(ii) *Safe harbor*. A trustee is deemed to satisfy the requirements of paragraph (c) of this section, if the trustee calculates and provides trust information in a manner that enables a requesting person to provide trust information to a beneficial owner of a trust interest that enables the owner to reasonably accurately report the tax consequences of its ownership of a trust interest on its federal income tax return. Additionally, to be deemed to satisfy the requirements of paragraph (c) of this section, the trustee must calculate and provide trust information regarding market discount and OID by any reasonable manner consistent with section 1272(a)(6). A middleman or a trustee may satisfy its obligation to furnish information to the IRS under paragraph (d) of this section and to the trust interest holder under paragraph (e) of this section by providing information consistent with the information provided under this paragraph by the trustee.

(2) *Additional safe harbors provided by other published guidance*. The IRS and the Treasury Department may provide additional safe harbor reporting procedures for complying with this section or a specific paragraph of this section by other published guidance (see §601.601(d)(2) of this chapter).

* * * * *

(m) *Penalties for failure to comply*—(1) *In general*. Every trustee or middleman who fails to comply with the reporting obligations imposed by this section is subject to penalties under sections 6721, 6722, and any other applicable penalty provisions.

(2) *Penalties not imposed on trustees and middlemen of certain WHMTs for failure to report OID*. Penalties will not be imposed as a result of a failure to provide OID information for a WHMT that has a start-up date on or after August 13, 1998 and on or before January 24, 2006, if the

trustee of the WHMT does not have the historic information necessary to provide this information and the trustee demonstrates that it has attempted in good faith, but without success, to obtain this information. For purposes of calculating a market discount fraction under paragraph (g)(1)(v) of this section, for a WHMT described in this paragraph, it may be assumed that the WHMT is holding mortgages that were issued without OID. A trustee availing itself of this paragraph must include a statement to that effect when providing information to requesting persons under paragraph (c) of these regulations.

* * * * *

§1.671–5T [Removed]

Par. 3. Section 1.671–5T is removed.

Kevin M. Brown,
Deputy Commissioner for Services and Enforcement.

Approved December 21, 2006.

Eric Solomon,
Assistant Secretary (Tax Policy).

(Filed by the Office of the Federal Register on December 26, 2006, 10:22 a.m., and published in the issue of the Federal Register for December 29, 2006, 71 F.R. 78351)

Section 1502.—Regulations

Consolidated corporate returns, unified rule for loss on subsidiary stock. See REG-157711-02, page 537.

Part III. Administrative, Procedural, and Miscellaneous

Estimated Tax Penalty for Citizens or Residents of the United States Living Abroad

Notice 2007–16

Section 1: Purpose

This notice addresses the foreign earned income exclusion and housing cost amount for certain citizens and residents of the United States living abroad as modified by the Tax Increase Prevention and Reconciliation Act of 2005, Pub. L. No. 109–222, 120 Stat. 345, (TIPRA). This notice provides that, under certain circumstances, the Internal Revenue Service (Service) will waive section 6654 penalties for underpayment of estimated tax by certain citizens and residents of the United States living abroad.

Section 2: Background

Generally, the Internal Revenue Code requires individuals to pay federal income tax as they earn income. To the extent these taxes are not withheld from an individual's wages, an individual taxpayer must pay estimated taxes in four installments. Section 6654(a) of the Code provides for an addition to tax where a taxpayer fails to make a sufficient and timely payment of "estimated tax."

In general, estimated taxes are required in four installments and the amount of any required installment shall be 25 percent of the "required annual payment." *See* section 6654(c) and (d)(1)(A). The term "required annual payment" means the lesser of 90 percent of tax shown on the return for the taxable year (or, if no return is filed, 90 percent of tax for such year), or 100 percent of tax shown on the return of the individual for the preceding taxable year if the adjusted gross income (AGI) shown on the return of the individual for the preceding taxable year is less than or equal to $150,000. If the AGI shown on the return of the individual for the preceding taxable year exceeds $150,000, the required annual payment is 110 percent of tax shown on that return.

If the preceding taxable year was not a taxable year of 12 months or if the individual did not file a return for such preceding taxable year, the required annual payment is 90 percent of tax shown on the return for the current taxable year. *See* section 6654(d)(1)(B).

Section 911(a) of the Code allows a qualified individual to elect to exclude from U.S. gross income the foreign earned income and housing cost amount of that individual. Prior to the enactment of TIPRA, the maximum amount of foreign earned income that could be excluded under section 911 in 2006 was $80,000. The housing cost amount that an individual could exclude under section 911 was the taxpayer's "reasonable" housing expenses over a floor equal to 16% of the salary of a GS–14 federal worker. The exclusions for foreign earned income and housing cost amounts operated like other exclusions in the Code and were ignored when determining the tax rate applicable to non-excluded income.

On May 17, 2006, TIPRA was enacted into law. Section 515 of TIPRA made several changes to section 911 of the Code. First, TIPRA increased the foreign earned income exclusion cap by indexing it for inflation after 2005. Thus, the amount of foreign earned income that may be excluded in 2006 is $82,400. Second, TIPRA modified the housing cost amount by changing the manner in which the floor is calculated and by generally imposing a cap equal to 30% of the maximum amount of the taxpayer's foreign earned income exclusion. Third, TIPRA imposed a "stacking" rule on the amounts excluded under section 911, so that income not excluded by section 911 is subject to the same rate of tax as would have been applicable had the taxpayer not elected the section 911 exclusion. Thus, an individual with $82,400 of excluded income and $20,000 of taxable income will be taxed at rates that apply to taxable income in the range of $82,400 to $102,400 (25% or 28%), rather than $0 to $20,000 (10% or 15%).

Section 3: Transitional Penalty Relief for Underpayment of Estimated Taxes

The TIPRA changes to section 911 were enacted in May 2006, but they are effective for taxable years beginning after December 31, 2005. Therefore, taxpayers relying on the law as it existed prior to the retroactive change may have underpaid their estimated tax liabilities for 2006.

Section 6654(e)(3) authorizes the Service to waive section 6654 penalties for underpayments of estimated tax in unusual circumstances to the extent its imposition would be against equity and good conscience. Pursuant to this authority, the Service will waive the section 6654 penalty for calendar year 2006 for an underpayment of estimated tax to the extent that the underpayment is attributable to the modifications made by section 515 of TIPRA. This waiver is available only to qualified individuals who file a Form 2555, *Foreign Earned Income*, or Form 2555–EZ, *Foreign Earned Income Exclusion*, with their timely filed Form 1040, *U.S. Individual Income Tax Return*, or Form 1040X, *Amended U.S. Individual Income Tax Return*.

Section 4: Contact Information

The principal author of this notice is Karen E. Briscoe of the Office of Associate Chief Counsel (Procedure & Administration). For further information regarding this notice, contact Mrs. Briscoe at (202) 622–8117 (not a toll-free call).

Part IV. Items of General Interest

Notice of Proposed Rulemaking

Unified Rule for Loss on Subsidiary Stock

REG–157711–02

AGENCY: Internal Revenue Service (IRS), Treasury.

ACTION: Notice of proposed rulemaking.

SUMMARY: This document contains proposed regulations under sections 358, 362(e)(2) and 1502 of the Internal Revenue Code (Code). The regulations apply to corporations filing consolidated returns. The regulations implement aspects of the repeal of the *General Utilities* doctrine by redetermining members' bases in subsidiary stock and requiring certain reductions in subsidiary stock basis on a transfer of the stock. The regulations also promote the clear reflection of income by redetermining members' bases in subsidiary stock and reducing the subsidiary's attributes to prevent the duplication of loss. Additionally, the regulations provide guidance limiting the application of section 362(e)(2) with respect to transactions between members of a consolidated group.

DATES: Written or electronic comments or a request for a public hearing must be received by April 23, 2007.

ADDRESSES: Send submissions to: CC:PA:LPD:PR (REG–157711–02), room 5203, Internal Revenue Service, PO Box 7604, Ben Franklin Station, Washington, DC 20044. Submissions may be hand-delivered Monday through Friday between the hours of 8 a.m. and 4 p.m. to CC:PA:LPD:PR (REG–157711–02), Courier's Desk, Internal Revenue Service, 1111 Constitution Avenue, N.W., Washington, DC, or sent electronically, via the IRS Internet site at *www.irs.gov/regs* or via the Federal eRulemaking Portal at *www.regulations.gov* (IRS/REG–157711–02).

FOR FURTHER INFORMATION CONTACT: Concerning the proposed regulations, Theresa Abell (202) 622–7700 or Phoebe Bennett (202) 622–7770; concerning submissions of comments, Richard Hurst, *Richard.A.Hurst@irscounsel.treas.gov*, (202) 622–7180 (not toll-free numbers).

SUPPLEMENTARY INFORMATION:

Paperwork Reduction Act

The collection of information contained in this notice of proposed rulemaking has been submitted to the Office of Management and Budget for review in accordance with the Paperwork Reduction Act of 1995 (44 U.S.C. 3507(d)). Comments on the collection of information should be sent to the **Office of Management and Budget**, Attn: Desk Officer for the Department of the Treasury, Office of Information and Regulatory Affairs, Washington, DC 20503, with copies to the Internal Revenue Service, Attn: IRS Reports Clearance Officer, SE:W:CAR:MP:T:T:SP, Washington, DC 20224. Comments on the collection of information should be received by March 26, 2007.

Comments are specifically requested concerning:

Whether the proposed collection of information is necessary for the proper performance of the functions of the IRS, including whether the information will have practical utility;

The accuracy of the estimated burden associated with the proposed collection of information;

How the quality, utility, and clarity of the information to be collected may be enhanced;

How the burden of complying with the proposed collection of information may be minimized, including through the application of automated collection techniques or other forms of information technology; and

Estimates of capital or start-up costs and costs of operation, maintenance, and purchase of services to provide information.

The collection of information in these proposed regulations is in §§1.1502–13(e)(4)(v) and 1.1502–36(d)(6). The respondents are corporations filing consolidated returns. The collection of information is required to allow a corporation to preserve a subsidiary's attributes by foregoing a stock loss. The collection of information is required to obtain a benefit.

Estimated total annual reporting and/or recordkeeping burden: 25 hours.

Estimated average annual burden per respondent and/or recordkeeper: 15 minutes.

Estimated number of respondents and/or recordkeepers: 100.

Estimated annual frequency of responses: Once.

An agency may not conduct or sponsor, and a person is not required to respond to, a collection of information unless it displays a valid control number assigned by the Office of Management and Budget.

Books or records relating to the collection of information must be retained as long as their contents may become material in the administration of any Internal Revenue law. Generally, tax returns and tax return information are confidential, as required by 26 U.S.C. 6103.

Background

The discussion in this preamble begins with an overview of the history of the regulatory attempts to address both the circumvention of *General Utilities* repeal and the duplication of loss by consolidated groups, in particular, in §1.1502–20 (the Loss Disallowance Rule, or LDR). The discussion then turns to *Rite Aid Corp. v. United States*, 255 F.3d 1357 (Fed. Cir. 2001), which rejected the loss duplication rule in the LDR. Section A.4 of this preamble discusses the immediate administrative responses to *Rite Aid*. Section A.5 of this preamble discusses the legislative response to *Rite Aid*. Following the *Rite Aid* decision, the IRS and Treasury Department undertook a study to reconsider the issues addressed by §1.1502–20. Section B of this preamble discusses the various issues considered in that study, including both the original noneconomic and duplicated stock loss specifically addressed by the LDR and certain related issues with which the Internal Revenue Service and Treasury Department have grown concerned since the LDR was promulgated. Section C of this preamble describes the various approaches that were considered to address noneconomic stock loss and sets forth the conclusions reached regarding each. Section D of this preamble describes the various approaches that were considered to address loss duplication and sets forth the conclusions reached regarding each. Section E of this preamble describes the various approaches that were considered to address the noneconomic and duplicated loss that can arise from the general operation of the investment adjustment system and sets forth the conclusions reached regarding each. Section F of this preamble describes the specific provisions of this proposed regulation §1.1502–36. Section G of this preamble discusses the proposed removal of §§1.337(d)–1, 1.337(d)–2, and 1.1502–35.

The IRS and Treasury Department are also proposing regulations to address the application of section 362(e)(2) to members of consolidated groups. These proposed regulations are described in section H of this preamble.

Finally, the IRS and Treasury Department are proposing various technical and administrative revisions to the consolidated return regulations. These proposed regulations are described in section I of this preamble.

The IRS and Treasury Department request comments on the proposed regulations and other approaches that could be adopted, as well as other issues currently under study. See section J of this preamble for further discussion of comments requested.

A. *History of General Utilities Repeal and Loss Disallowance under §1.1502–20.*

1. *The repeal of the General Utilities doctrine.*

In 1986, Congress enacted section 337(d), which directs the Secretary to prescribe such regulations as may be necessary or appropriate to carry out the repeal of the *General Utilities* doctrine (*GU* repeal). See Tax Reform Act of 1986, Public Law 99–514 (100 Stat. 2085 (1986)). The legislative history states that Congress was concerned that the *General Utilities* doctrine allowed "assets to leave corporate solution and to take a stepped-up basis in the hands of the transferee without the imposition of a corporate-level tax" and thus "tend[ed] to undermine the corporate income tax." H.R. Rep. No. 99–426, 99th Cong., 1st Sess. 282 (1985). The *General Utilities* doctrine and *GU* repeal are discussed extensively in the Treasury Decisions referenced in this preamble; in addition, see generally, H.R. Rep. No. 99–426 at 274–282 for a discussion of the history of the *General Utilities* doctrine; see also *General Utilities & Operating Co. v. Helvering*, 296 U.S. 200 (1935).

2. *The administrative response to GU repeal: §1.1502–20.*

The IRS and Treasury Department first responded to *GU* repeal by issuing Notice 87–14, 1987–1 C.B. 445, which set forth the intent to promulgate regulations affecting adjustments to members' bases in stock of any subsidiary acquired when the subsidiary held an appreciated asset. Notice 87–14 indicated that, in general, adjustments to subsidiary stock basis would not reflect gains on such assets. Thus, Notice 87–14 implied that a tracing-based regime would be adopted to determine adjustments to members' bases in shares of subsidiary stock.

After several years of study, the IRS and Treasury Department concluded that any approach relying on the identification and tracing of appreciation on particular assets, while theoretically accurate, would impose substantial administrative burdens on taxpayers and on the government. See T.D. 8294, 1990–1 C.B. 66 [55 FR 9426, 9428] (March 14, 1990). As a result, the tracing-based approach envisioned in Notice 87–14 was implemented only in regulations promulgated under section 337(d). Those regulations applied only for the period of time between the issuance of Notice 87–14 and the effective date of final regulations under §1.1502–20 (February 1, 1991). See T.D. 8364, 1991–2 C.B. 43 [56 FR 47379] (September 19, 1991), §§1.337(d)–1 and 1.337(d)–2 (as contained in 26 CFR part 1 revised as of April 1, 1991).

In lieu of tracing, the LDR used certain operating presumptions to determine the extent to which investment adjustments would be permitted to give rise to allowable stock loss. Because the LDR only disallowed loss, noneconomic investment adjustments were able to increase stock basis and thus reduce gain without limitation. As a result, the LDR reduced the duplication of gain in the tax system. The IRS and Treasury Department considered the reduction of gain duplication an important balance to the imprecision inherent in the LDR's use of irrebuttable presumptions.

The study following the issuance of Notice 87–14 led the IRS and Treasury Department to consider the issue of loss duplication by members of consolidated groups. Their conclusion was that loss duplication was inappropriate in the consolidated setting. Further, the IRS and Treasury Department recognized that there were administrative advantages to addressing both issues in a single integrated rule. Thus, unlike the regulations under section 337(d), the LDR was at once directed at both the circumvention of *GU* repeal through the use of noneconomic stock loss and the duplication of loss. See T.D. 8294 and T.D. 8364.

3. *The Rite Aid opinion.*

Ten years after the promulgation of the LDR, the validity of the duplicated loss component of the LDR was considered in *Rite Aid, supra.* Under the duplicated loss component of the LDR, Rite Aid had been disallowed a deduction for an economic loss on subsidiary stock solely because the stock loss could be duplicated by the subsidiary after it left the group. The Federal Circuit stated that the Secretary's authority to change the application of a Code provision to a consolidated group was limited to situations in which the change was necessary to address a problem created by the filing of a consolidated return. Because duplicated stock loss occurs and is allowable in the separate return setting, the court concluded that the duplicated loss component of the LDR was not addressing a problem arising from the filing of a consolidated return. Accordingly, the court held that the Secretary did not have the authority to change the Code rule allowing a deduction for the stock loss.

4. *The administrative response to Rite Aid.*

In response to the *Rite Aid* decision, on February 19, 2002, the IRS announced that it would not continue to litigate the validity of the duplicated loss rule in §1.1502–20. See Notice 2002–11, 2002–1 C.B. 526.

On March 7, 2002, the IRS and Treasury Department promulgated §1.1502–20T(i) (to suspend the application of the LDR) and §1.337(d)–2T (to provide an interim rule addressing noneconomic stock loss). See T.D. 8984, 2002–1 C.B. 668 [67 FR 11034] (March 12, 2002). Concurrently with the promulgation of §§1.337(d)–2T and 1.1502–20T(i), the IRS issued Notice 2002–18, 2002–1 C.B. 644, announcing that loss duplication regulations would also be promulgated. Following the publication of T.D. 8984, the IRS and Treasury Department undertook a study of the issues underlying both noneconomic and duplicated loss on subsidiary stock.

In general, §1.337(d)–2T disallowed stock loss and reduced stock basis (to value) upon the disposition or deconsolidation of subsidiary stock by a member of a consolidated group. However, under §1.337(d)–2T(c)(2), loss disallowance and basis reduction were avoided to the extent the taxpayer could establish that the loss or basis "is not attributable to the recognition of built-in gain on the disposition of an asset." Section 1.337(d)–2T(c)(2) defined the term "built-in gain" as gain that is "attributable, directly or indirectly, in whole or in part, to any excess of value over basis that is reflected, before the disposition of the asset, in the basis of the share, directly or indirectly, in whole or in part."

On March 14, 2003, the IRS and Treasury Department promulgated §1.1502–35T as an interim measure to address the problem of loss duplication in consolidated groups. See T.D. 9048, 2003–1 C.B. 644 [68 FR 12287] (March 14, 2003). In the preamble to T.D. 9048, the IRS and Treasury Department announced that the issues addressed in §1.1502–35T were still under study. The provisions of §1.1502–35 are discussed in more detail in section D.1 of this preamble.

Further guidance on the interim rules was issued August 25, 2004, in the form of Notice 2004–58, 2004–2 C.B. 520. In Notice 2004–58, the IRS announced that it would accept the "basis disconformity" method as an alternative approach to determining whether stock loss or basis was attributable to "built-in gain" within the meaning of §1.337(d)–2T.

Under the basis disconformity method described in Notice 2004–58, stock loss or basis is treated as attributable to built-in gain to the extent of the least of (i) the net positive investment adjustment applied to the stock basis (disregarding distributions), (ii) the aggregate gain (net of directly related expenses) recognized on asset dispositions by the subsidiary, and (iii) the disconformity amount (generally, the amount by which the basis of the share exceeds the share's proportionate interest in the subsidiary's net inside asset basis; for this purpose, net inside asset basis is defined as the excess of the sum of the subsidiary's money, asset basis, loss carryforwards, and deferred deductions over its liabilities). Notice 2004–58 also requested comments on the general scope of *GU* repeal and on other approaches that could be adopted to safeguard the purposes of *GU* repeal in the consolidated return context.

5. *The legislative response to Rite Aid.*

Congress responded to the *Rite Aid* opinion on October 22, 2004, in the American Jobs Creation Act (the AJCA), Public Law No. 108–357 (118 Stat. 1418 (2004)). In the AJCA, Congress added a sentence at the end of section 1502 of the Code, so that the section now reads:

> The Secretary shall prescribe such regulations as he may deem necessary in order that the tax liability of any affiliated group of corporations making a consolidated return and of the each corporation in the group, both during and after the period of affiliation, may be returned, determined, computed, assessed, collected, and adjusted, in such manner as clearly to reflect the income tax liability and the various factors necessary for the determination of such liability, and in order to prevent avoidance of such tax liability. In carrying out the preceding sentence, the Secretary may prescribe rules that are different from the provisions of chapter 1 that would apply if such corporations filed separate returns.

In the legislative history to the AJCA, Congress stated that the Secretary is authorized to change the application of a Code provision when the Secretary determines it is necessary to clearly reflect the income tax liability of the group and each corporation in the group, both during and after the period of affiliation. See H.R. Conf. Rep. No. 108–755, 108th Cong., 2d Sess. 653 (2004). Congress thus rejected the suggestion in the *Rite Aid* opinion that the Secretary's authority to change the general application of the Code is limited to promulgating regulations that address problems created by the filing of a consolidated return.

In the AJCA legislative history, Congress also spoke to the proper scope of future regulations. Regarding the promulgation of regulations addressing noneconomic stock loss, Congress stated that "presumptions and other simplifying conventions" could be used to prevent the circumvention of *GU* repeal. See H.R. Conf. Rep. No. 108–755, fn. 595. In addition, Congress indicated two acceptable methods for addressing loss duplication by group members. The first would disallow subsidiary stock loss to the extent it duplicates losses that remain available to the group. The second would reduce the subsidiary's attributes in order to prevent the subsidiary from using losses outside the group, to the extent the losses duplicate stock loss. But Congress also stated its intention that the result of the *Rite Aid* decision is to be preserved. The IRS and Treasury Department interpret this statement to mean that regulations addressing loss duplication by consolidated groups must not disallow a deduction for an economic loss on subsidiary stock solely because the stock loss duplicates unrecognized or unabsorbed losses that later could be used outside the group.

6. *Further administrative response to Rite Aid.*

On March 3, 2005, the IRS and Treasury Department finalized §1.337(d)–2. See T.D. 9187, 2005–1 C.B. 778 [70 FR 10319] (March 3, 2005). In T.D. 9187, the IRS and Treasury Department stated that the issues addressed in §1.337(d)–2 were still under study and that an alternative approach would be proposed. On March 14, 2006, the IRS and Treasury Department finalized §1.1502–35. See T.D. 9254, 2006–13 I.R.B. 662 [71 FR 13008] (March 14, 2006). In T.D. 9254, the IRS and Treasury Department stated that both noneconomic and duplicated loss were still under study, and that regulations would be proposed adopting a singe integrated approach to addressing both issues. The results of that study and the proposed integrated approach are described below in sections D through H of this preamble.

B. *Issues Considered in the Post-Rite Aid Study.*

1. *GU repeal and noneconomic investment adjustments under the LDR.*

Section 337(d) generally directs the Secretary to prescribe regulations to prevent the circumvention of *GU* repeal and, in particular, section 337(d)(1) directs the Secretary to promulgate regulations to prevent the circumvention of *GU* repeal through the use of the consolidated return regulations. Congress' concern stems from the general operation of the investment adjustment system of §1.1502–32.

The purpose of the investment adjustment system is to promote the clear reflection of the group's income. See §1.1502–32(a)(1). One of the principal ways that the investment adjustment system promotes clear reflection is by preventing a subsidiary's items of income, gain, deduction and loss from giving rise to duplicative gain or loss on the subsidiary's stock. To that end, the investment adjustment system adjusts members' bases in shares of subsidiary stock to reflect such items once they have been taken into account by the group. See T.D. 8560, 1994–2 C.B. 200 [59 FR 41666] (August 15, 1994).

Example 1. Economic adjustment to stock basis prevents duplication. P, the common parent of a consolidated group, purchases all 100 outstanding shares of S common stock for $100 cash, taking a basis of $1 in each share. At the time, S owns one asset, A1, with a basis and value of $100. Later, the value of A1 increases to $150. S sells A1 to a nonmember for $150 and recognizes a $50 gain, which the P group takes into account. Under the investment adjustment system, P increases its basis in its S stock to reflect the $50 taken into account by the group. As a result, the basis of each share increases to $1.50, its fair market value. P can then sell all or any portion of its S stock for its fair market value without recognizing duplicative gain on the disposition.

The result in *Example 1* is that the group takes its economic gain into account only once, on the disposition of S's asset, and not again on the subsequent disposition of the S stock. Thus the group's income is clearly reflected and there is no circumvention of *GU* repeal.

The investment adjustment system is not a tracing regime. Rather, it is a presumptive regime based on certain operating assumptions. A principal assumption is that all of a subsidiary's items taken into account represent economic accruals (of gain or loss) to the group. Another principal assumption is that all such items accrue equally to all outstanding shares, at least within a class. When these assumptions correspond to the facts of a particular situation, as in *Example 1*, the investment adjustment system produces appropriate results: stock basis, which reflects only the investment in the stock, increases to reflect economic accrual (the group's return on its stock investment), and, as a result, stock basis can then shelter that return on the group's investment, protecting it from being taken into account again when the stock is sold.

The assumptions, however, do not correspond to the facts of all situations. For example, if stock of a subsidiary is purchased for its fair market value when the subsidiary holds appreciated assets, the items of income or gain generated when that appreciation is recognized do not represent an economic accrual on the group's investment (because the appreciation was already reflected in the basis of the stock). Nevertheless, the presumptive rules of the investment adjustment system treat such items as economic accruals and include them in the investment adjustment to be applied to the basis of the stock.

Example 2. Noneconomic adjustment to stock basis creates noneconomic stock loss. Assume the same facts as in *Example 1* except that P does not purchase the stock of S until the value of A1 has increased to $150. Accordingly, P purchases the stock for $150, taking a basis of $1.50 in each share. As in *Example 1*, when S sells A1, the investment adjustment system again increases P's basis in its S stock to reflect the $50 taken into account by the group. As a result, P's basis in each of its shares increases to $2, even though the fair market value of each share remains $1.50. If P were then to sell all or some portion of the S stock for its fair market value, P would recognize a $.50 loss on each share ($50 loss in the aggregate).

In this situation, a deduction for the stock loss would be inappropriate because neither the group nor its members have suffered any economic loss. If P were allowed to deduct that noneconomic loss, the deduction would offset the gain recognized on S's asset and, effectively, eliminate the corporate-level tax on the gain on S's asset. This is the circumvention of *GU* repeal that concerned Congress in 1986.

At the time Notice 87–14 was issued, the IRS and Treasury Department had identified the creation of noneconomic stock loss in situations similar to those illustrated in *Example 2*. Thus, Notice 87–14 referred specifically to investment adjustments attributable to the disposition of assets that, at the time of the acquisition of the subsidiary stock, had a fair market value in excess of adjusted basis. For that reason, §1.337(d)–1, which implemented Notice 87–14, disallowed subsidiary stock loss unless the taxpayer could show that the loss was not attributable to the recognition of appreciation on assets owned, directly or indirectly, by a subsidiary when it became a member.

2. *Duplicated loss and the clear reflection of group income under the LDR.*

In the study that followed the issuance of Notice 87–14, the IRS and Treasury Department also considered the issue of loss duplication by members of a consolidated group. The specific concern of the IRS and Treasury Department was the loss duplication that occurs when an economic loss is reflected in both a member's basis in subsidiary stock and in the subsidiary's assets or operations, and the loss is first recognized with respect to the stock.

Example 3. Duplication of loss. P forms S by contributing $110 to S in exchange for all 100 outstanding shares of S stock. S uses the cash to purchase an asset, A1. The value of A1 later declines to $10. If P were then to sell all or some portion of the S stock for its fair market value, P would recognize a $1 loss on each share.

In this situation, even though P would have recognized the group's economic loss on its disposition of the S stock, the loss continues to be reflected in the basis of A1. As a result, that loss would remain available for use by P (if the stock sale did not deconsolidate S) or S (if the stock sale deconsolidated S). Upon the disposition of A1, the group's single economic loss would thus be recognized and taken into account more than once by the group and its members or former members.

In contrast, if the duplicated loss had first been taken into account with respect to A1, the investment adjustment system would have prevented a duplicative benefit to the group and its members by reducing P's basis in S stock by the amount of the loss. In that case, the group would have enjoyed the tax benefit attributable to the loss, but that benefit would not remain available for another use by the group and its members or former members.

The IRS and Treasury Department concluded that the duplication of a group's tax benefit (represented by a single economic loss) distorts income without regard to whether the duplicated loss is taken into account first with respect to the subsidiary's stock or first with respect to the subsidiary's assets and operations. The IRS and Treasury Department further concluded that, even if the duplicated loss is used by a former member outside the group, that duplicative use distorts the income of the group and its members. Accordingly, the IRS and Treasury Department decided to promulgate regulations that would complement the investment adjustment system by addressing the stock-first recognition of a duplicated loss and that such regulations would apply to both deconsolidating and nondeconsolidating dispositions. Recognizing the administrative benefits of addressing both noneconomic and duplicated stock loss in a single integrated rule, the IRS and Treasury Department promulgated the LDR as a single rule with components directed at both.

The method adopted by the LDR to address loss duplication was the disallowance of stock loss (or reduction of stock basis) that duplicated unrecognized inside loss, such as that illustrated in *Example 3.* However, groups had several mechanisms available to recognize or preserve the inside loss and thereby avoid loss disallowance (by eliminating loss duplication). Inside losses could be recognized through an actual asset sale or a deemed asset sale under section 338(h)(10), and, following the sale, the subsidiary's unabsorbed losses would be available to the group. In addition, the LDR allowed the common parent to elect to reattribute the subsidiary's losses (to itself) under §1.1502–20(g). If the group chose not to exercise those options, then the stock loss was denied, but the inside loss was preserved for a nonduplicative use by the subsidiary, in or out of the group.

At the time the LDR was promulgated, the duplication potential illustrated in *Example 3* was the principal form of loss duplication with which the IRS and Treasury Department were concerned. Thus it is the only form of loss duplication specifically addressed by the LDR. The anti-abuse rule in the LDR did, however, provide a limited mechanism for expanding the scope of that provision.

3. *Noneconomic and duplicated loss resulting from investment adjustments allocated to shares with disparate bases.*

Since the promulgation of the LDR, the IRS and Treasury Department have become increasingly concerned with the noneconomic and duplicated loss potential arising from the interaction of §1.1502–32 and the disparate reflection of gain or loss in members' bases in individual shares of subsidiary stock.

As discussed in section B.1 of this preamble, the investment adjustment system is a presumptive regime that allocates a subsidiary's items of income, gain, deduction, and loss taken into account by the group. It operates in accordance with the assumption that all such items reflect economic accruals to all shares equally within each class. When its underlying assumptions correspond to the facts of a particular situation, the investment adjustment system produces appropriate results, as illustrated in *Example 1.* But when its underlying assumptions do not correspond to the facts of a situation because shares held by members have disparate bases, the general operation of the investment adjustment system can give rise to both noneconomic and duplicated loss on individual shares of subsidiary stock.

Example 4. Noneconomic loss. P and M (a member of the P group) form S by contributing property to S in exchange for all 100 outstanding shares of S stock. P contributes A1, with a basis and value of $80, in exchange for 80 shares of S stock. M contributes A2, with a basis of $0 and a value of $20, to S in exchange for 20 shares of S stock. S then sells A2 for $20 and recognizes a $20 gain that is taken into account by the group. As a result, the basis of each share increases by $.20. P's basis in each of its shares is then $1.20 (or, $96 in the aggregate), and M's basis in each of its shares is then $.20 (or, $4 in the aggregate), even though the value of each share remains $1. P then sells all or some portion of its shares to X, a nonmember, and, under general principles of tax law, recognizes a $.20 noneconomic loss on each share, effectively eliminating up to $16 of the gain on A2.

Example 5(a). Duplicated loss, inside recognition precedes stock disposition. P forms S with $100 and receives all 50 shares of S common stock. S uses the $100 to buy A1, which then declines in value to $50. P contributes another $50 for a second 50 shares of common stock. S then sells A1 and recognizes a loss of $50 that is taken into account on the P group return. The absorption of the $50 loss results in a $.50 reduction to the basis of each share (original and newly issued). P then sells all or some portion of the original shares to X for $1 each (each with a basis of $1.50) and recognizes a $.50 loss on each share (up to $25 total). Although the $50 asset loss and the $25 stock loss both reflect an economic loss of the group, they are both reflecting the same loss. The group has actually experienced only $50 of economic loss. Therefore, the $.50 loss recognized on each of the original shares (up to $25 total) is duplicative.

Example 5(b). Duplicated loss, stock disposition precedes inside recognition. The facts are the same as in *Example 5(a)*, except that, before S sells A1, P sells 20 of its original 50 shares to X for $20 (aggregate basis $40), recognizing a $20 loss that is taken into account on the P group return, and S remains a member of the group. S then sells A1, recognizing a $50 loss that is taken into account on the P group return. Although the $50 asset loss and the $20 stock loss both reflect an economic loss of the group, they are both reflecting the same loss. As in *Example 5(a)*, the group has actually experienced only $50 of economic loss. Therefore, $20 of the recognized loss is duplicative. Alternatively, if P sold all its original 50 shares, P would recognize a $50 loss even though the entire $50 group loss would remain available to S for a duplicative use against its separate year income.

The IRS and Treasury Department recognize that, in each case where the disproportionate reflection of an item in a particular share causes an inappropriate stock loss, whether noneconomic or duplicated, that loss is offset by unrecognized gain in other shares. However, that gain can be deferred indefinitely or even eliminated by the group. Accordingly, the IRS and Treasury Department do not believe that the system is appropriately balanced in such cases.

The IRS and Treasury Department further recognize that these issues could be addressed by adopting a tracing-based approach to the allocation of investment adjustments. However, the complexity and burden of a tracing-based approach would render such an approach generally inadministrable for consolidated taxpayers and for the government. As a result, the system would be prone to error and, in practice, inconsistently applied. Moreover, the IRS and Treasury Department continue to believe that the assumptions on which the investment adjustment system is based are appropriate for typical commercial transactions, as the IRS and Treasury Department understand that typically subsidiaries have only common stock outstanding, that their stock is wholly owned by group members, and that members' bases in shares of subsidiary stock are uniform, as under the facts of *Example 1.* See section E.2 of the preamble of CO–30–92, 1992–2 C.B. 627 [57 FR 53634, 53639] (November 12, 1992).

Because a tracing-based approach to the allocation of investment adjustments would not be administrable, the IRS and Treasury Department are not considering revising the investment adjustment system to adopt such an approach. Instead, the IRS and Treasury Department have considered various presumptive approaches that could be adopted to mitigate the creation of noneconomic and duplicated loss when members hold subsidiary stock with disparate bases. The approaches considered and decisions reached are discussed in section E of this preamble.

4. *Redetermination events: changes in the extent that unrecognized gain or loss is effectively reflected in the basis of individual shares.*

Because the investment adjustment system adjusts the basis of each share in accordance with its proportionate interest in S's assets and operations, the relationship between a share's basis and its allocable portion of unrecognized appreciation or depreciation determines the extent to which such amounts are effectively reflected in the basis of the share. This relationship, however, is not fixed at the time that stock is acquired. The reason is that there are many transactions, referred to here as redetermination events, that alter either the basis of a share or the interest it represents. These events generally occur in one of three types of situations.

a. *Stock basis is reallocated.*

The relationship between the basis of a share and the interest represented by the share can be altered whenever stock basis is reallocated among shares, including when it is allocated to shares of stock of other members.

Example 6. Intragroup spin-off. P forms S by contributing $100 to S in exchange for all the stock of S. S purchases two assets, A1 and A2, for $50 each. Subsequently, A1 appreciates to $75 and A2 depreciates to $25. In a transaction qualifying under sections 355 and 368(a)(1)(D), S transfers A2 to C in exchange for all of the C stock and S then distributes all the C stock to P. Under section 358 and §1.358–2, P's basis in the S stock is allocated among the S and C stock in proportion to the value of the stock of S and C. As a result, P's basis in its S stock is $75 (75/100 x $100) and P's basis in its C stock is $25 (25/100 x $100). S sells A1 for $75, recognizing a $25 gain that is taken into account on the P group return. P's basis in its S stock increases by $25, from $75 to $100. P then sells its S stock for $75 and recognizes a $25 loss.

In this *Example 6*, after the reallocation of stock basis, P's basis in its S stock reflects the unrecognized appreciation on A1, just as P's basis in its S stock reflected unrecognized appreciation on A1 in *Example 2*. As a result, P's reallocated S stock basis protects the appreciation on A1 from being recognized as both asset gain and stock gain. Increasing P's basis in its S stock to reflect the recognition of S's gain on A1 is not only unnecessary, it inflates stock basis and thereby gives rise to either noneconomic loss or noneconomic reduction of gain when the stock is sold.

Basis reallocations, and the consequences described, can occur for a number of reasons, including, for example, under rules like §1.1502–32(c)(4) (cumulative redetermination of investment adjustments) and §1.1502–35(b) (basis redetermination to reduce disparity) and the corresponding provision in these proposed regulations.

b. *Capital transactions expand or contract the subsidiary's pool of assets.*

The relationship between the basis of a share and the nature of the interest represented by the share can also be altered by capital transactions that have no effect on the basis or value of outstanding shares, but that nevertheless alter the interest represented by those share. Some common examples arise in the context of section 351 exchanges, even though, as illustrated in *Example 7(a)*, a section 351 exchange in its simplest form cannot give rise to stock basis that reflects unrecognized appreciation.

Example 7(a). Contribution of appreciated asset in section 351 exchange. P forms S by contributing an asset, A1, to S in exchange for all 80 outstanding shares of S stock. The basis of A1 is $40 and its value is $80. S sells A1 and recognizes a $40 gain that is taken into account by the P group. As a result, P's aggregate basis in its S shares is increased by $40, from $40 to $80. Subsequently, P sells its S stock for $80, the stock's fair market value, and recognizes $0 on the sale. The group is thus taxed once on its $40 economic gain.

In *Example 7(a)*, P holds appreciated S stock and S holds an appreciated asset, but that appreciation is not reflected in either P's basis in its S stock or S's basis in its asset. Each share has a basis of $.50 and an interest in 1/80 of S's asset, A1, which has $40 of unrecognized appreciation (allocable $.50 to each share). If this relationship between P's basis in its S shares and the interest represented by the shares remains constant, as in *Example 7(a)*, the investment adjustment system produces appropriate results. But if there is a change in that relationship, the underlying assumptions of the investment adjustment system may no longer correspond to the facts of the situation and, as a result, the general operation of the system could produce inappropriate results. Such changes can occur whenever S acquires property in exchange for additional shares of its stock.

Example 7(b). Contribution of appreciated asset in subsequent section 351 exchange creates disconformity in original shares. The facts are the same as in *Example 7(a)*, except that, before A1 is sold, P contributes a second asset, A2, to S in exchange for an additional 20 shares of S stock. A2 has a basis of $0 and a value of $20. S sells both assets and recognizes a $60 gain that is taken into account by the P group. As a result, P's basis in its original shares increases by $48 ($.60 per share), from $40 to $88 (or, from $.50 to $1.10 per share), and P's basis in its new shares increases by $12, from $0 to $12 (or, from $0 to $.60 per share). P then sells 20 of its original shares (basis of $22) for $20, their fair market value, and recognizes a $2 loss.

In *Example 7(b)*, P's basis in the original S stock reflected no unrecognized appreciation when the stock was issued. After the second contribution, however, P's basis in those shares reflects a portion of the unrecognized appreciation on A2. The reason is that each share represents an interest in S's entire pool of assets. When the pool changes, the nature of the interest represented by the shares changes, even though the share's basis and value remain constant. Thus, in *Example 7(b)*, while each original share's basis ($.50) and value ($1) remain constant, the interest represented by each share changed from 1/80 of an asset with unrecognized appreciation of $40 (or, $.50 per share), to 1/100 of assets with unrecognized appreciation of $60 (or, $.60 per share). This shift causes the basis of each original share to reflect $.10 of unrecognized appreciation. When the gain is recognized, $.10 of the gain allocated to each original share under the investment adjustment system is a noneconomic increase in the share's basis. That increase will give rise to noneconomic stock loss or gain reduction. Although this (noneconomic) allocation of the (economic) item results in an offsetting stock gain on the basis of the new shares, that gain can be indefinitely deferred and even eliminated.

The principles that increase the reflection of unrecognized appreciation in the original shares in *Example 7(b)* can also cause the reflection of unrecognized appreciation in the basis of shares that are received in exchange for property that is not appreciated, including cash. Although such shares would have a substituted basis (which generally precludes the reflection of unrecognized appreciation, as illustrated in *Example 7(a)*), the reflection of unrecognized appreciation is prevented only if the shares represent, wholly and solely, the transferee's interest in its transferred property. If there are previously issued shares outstanding, or if other shares are issued in the exchange, the shares represent an interest in a pool of assets that includes more than the transferred assets. As a result, the interest represented by each such share may be significantly different from what it would be if the subsidiary held only the transferred property.

Example 7(c). Multiple transferors in single section 351 exchange. The facts are the same as in *Example 7(a)*, except that, when P contributes A1 to S in exchange for 80 shares of S stock, M (another member in the group), also contributes $20 cash to S in exchange for 20 shares of S stock. S sells A1 for $80 and recognizes a $40 gain that is taken into account by the group. Accordingly, P's aggregate basis in its shares increases by $32 (80/100 x $40), from $40 to $72, and M's aggregate basis in its shares increases by $8 (20/100 x $40), from $20 to $28. M then sells its shares for $20, their fair market value, and recognizes an $8 noneconomic loss.

Similar changes in the extent to which unrecognized amounts are reflected in basis can occur whenever the subsidiary's pool of assets is increased or decreased by a capital transaction. The reason is that the interest represented by each share, and thus the relationship between a share's basis and the interest represented by the share, changes whenever the subsidiary's pool of assets changes. Such transactions include acquisitive reorganizations (if new shares are issued) and redemptions.

c. *Assets are acquired with a basis that reflects unrecognized appreciation.*

The relationship between the basis of a share and the nature of the interest represented by the share can also be altered by transactions in which S acquires assets with a basis that reflects unrecognized appreciation, such as stock of a new member. The reason is that, after the lower-tier acquisition, the S shares have an interest in unrecognized appreciation and the investment adjustment system will increase the basis of the S shares when those lower-tier items are recognized.

Example 8. Acquisition of lower-tier subsidiary with appreciated assets. P forms S by contributing $100 to S in exchange for all the stock of S. S then purchases all the stock of T for $100 when T holds one asset, A1, with a basis of $0 and a value of $100. T sells A1, recognizing a $100 gain that is taken into account on the P group return. As a result, both S's basis in its T stock and P's basis in its S stock are increased by $100, from $100 to $200. P then sells its S stock, recognizing a $100 loss.

The result is the same noneconomic loss illustrated in *Example 2*.

d. *Other redetermination events.*

The IRS and Treasury Department expect that other transactions and events can alter the extent to which unrecognized asset appreciation is reflected in stock basis. Accordingly, the preceding discussion is not intended to present an exhaustive list of possible redetermination events.

e. *Conclusions regarding redetermination events.*

The IRS and Treasury Department recognize that redetermination events occur as the result of *bona fide* business transactions engaged in frequently and routinely throughout the time a share is held by any member of the group, and that these transactions are typically not tax-structured transactions. Still, these events generate a significant potential for noneconomic stock loss or gain reduction that facilitates the circumvention of *GU* repeal. Accordingly, the IRS and Treasury Department believe that all such events, whether described in this preamble or not, must be taken into account in any model that is adopted to address the circumvention of *GU* repeal.

Nevertheless, the IRS and Treasury Department recognize, and are concerned that, the factual analysis necessary to identify all redetermination events for all members' shares would be an extensive, complex, difficult, and, therefore, expensive undertaking and, as such, would impose a substantial burden on both taxpayers and the government. Moreover, the nature of the undertaking would make it prone to error and, as a result, the rule would be unevenly administered and similarly situated taxpayers would not be similarly treated.

The IRS and Treasury Department recognize that redetermination events can also create or increase the extent to which the basis of an individual share duplicates an inside loss. However, because duplicated loss is measured at the time that a stock loss is either recognized or preserved for later use, loss duplication rules by their operation account for redetermination events. Accordingly, regulations addressing loss duplication do not generally require specific provisions to address redetermination events.

C. *Methods Considered to Implement GU Repeal.*

The IRS and Treasury Department considered a number of approaches to address the circumvention of *GU* repeal independently from the issue of loss duplication. The approaches fall into two broad categories: tracing-based and presumptive approaches.

1. *Tracing-based methods.*

Under a tracing-based method, the extent to which a member can enjoy the benefit of subsidiary stock basis attributable to the recognition of an item of income or gain is determined by the extent to which the recognized item is reflected in the basis of the share and thus already protected from duplicative recognition on a later disposition of the stock. The IRS and Treasury Department continue to believe that tracing is a theoretically correct method for implementing *GU* repeal in the consolidated return setting and so considered various tracing-based proposals.

a. *Pure tracing.*

In general, a tracing approach would look solely to the connection between a subsidiary's recognized items and any appreciation reflected in stock basis in order to determine the extent to which the group will be allowed the benefit of stock basis attributable to those items. However, such an approach would require taxpayers to create and maintain (and the IRS to examine) records to establish:

- the identity of every "tainted asset," that is, every asset held by the subsidiary and any lower-tier subsidiaries on every "measuring date," which includes the date on which the member (or its predecessor) purchased the share and all subsequent dates on which the subsidiary has a redetermination event;

- the "tainted appreciation," that is, the appreciation on each tainted asset held by the subsidiary and any lower-tier subsidiaries on each measuring date; and
- the extent to which tainted appreciation is recognized, whether as income or gain, and included in an adjustment to the basis of the share.

In addition, to fully benefit from a tracing regime, taxpayers would need to create and maintain similar records for tainted assets with unrecognized depreciation on a measuring date, because the recognition of that depreciation would be allowed to reduce the amount of recognized appreciation treated as tainted.

These records would have to be created and maintained for each share of stock of each subsidiary and each share of lower-tier subsidiary stock held by a subsidiary on each measuring date. In addition, these records would need to be created and maintained not just for subsidiaries, but for all corporations the stock of which is acquired by a member, because the information would be necessary if the corporation becomes a member at some later date.

In administering the various temporary and final regulations promulgated as loss limitation rules under §1.337(d)–1 and §1.337(d)–2, the IRS has found that taxpayers encounter substantial difficulty in attempting to satisfy these requirements.

To begin, taxpayers are generally unable to accurately identify all of a subsidiary's tainted assets. One reason is simply the vast number of assets implicated. Another reason is that many assets are accounted for in mass accounts and thus cannot be separately identified. Problems are exacerbated if appropriate records are not created contemporaneously; taxpayers have found this a particular concern when subsidiaries have been acquired with inadequate records.

Furthermore, the commonplace nature of many redetermination events makes it difficult to identify all such dates. For example, many taxpayers routinely issue stock when a member contributes cash or property to a subsidiary, even if the issuance of stock would not be required for section 351 to apply, and each such occurrence is a redetermination event.

Valuation also imposes significant financial and administrative burdens on both taxpayers and the government. These problems are exacerbated because the corporation's assets are not themselves the subject of an arms-length transaction and, in most cases, the date on which the assets are actually valued is long after the stock transaction.

The most problematic aspect of tracing, however, has typically been establishing the connection, or lack thereof, between items taken into account by the group and particular amounts of tainted appreciation. If much time has elapsed between a measuring date and the disposition of a tainted asset, or if an asset is held in a mass account, this can be difficult or even impossible. If tainted appreciation is recognized as income earned through the wasting or consumption of the appreciation, instead of as gain on the disposition of the asset, there are additional difficulties. In those cases, tracing is possible only if the tainted appreciation generates an identifiable stream of income. However, this is frequently not the case. For example, intangible assets, like patents or goodwill, are the source of significant tainted appreciation and they typically do not generate identifiable income streams.

i. *Conclusions regarding tracing.*

For all the reasons set forth in this preamble, the IRS and Treasury Department have again, as in 1990, concluded that tracing is not a viable method for preventing the circumvention of *GU* repeal in consolidation. This conclusion, while arguably based on theoretical concerns in 1990, is now based on several years of administering §1.337(d)–2 (in both its temporary and final form) as a tracing regime. The IRS found that the difficulties encountered, by taxpayers and the government alike, in administering §1.337(d)–2 as a tracing-based rule were overwhelmingly greater than those encountered in administering it as a presumption-based rule under the basis disconformity method permitted under Notice 2004–58. Accordingly, the IRS and Treasury Department are not proposing to adopt a tracing-based approach.

ii. *Tracing in other contexts.*

The IRS and Treasury Department recognize that tracing-based regimes are used to implement other provisions in the Code. For example, section 382(h), which prescribes the tax treatment of built-in items recognized by a corporation that has had an ownership change, and section 1374, which prescribes the tax treatment of built-in items recognized by an S corporation that was formerly a C corporation, both use tracing-based regimes. Further, the IRS and Treasury Department are proposing regulations implementing section 362(e)(2) in a consolidated return context that require certain items to be traced. See section H of this preamble.

The tracing regimes appropriate for those sections, however, do not present compliance and administrative concerns of the scope and magnitude presented by a tracing regime appropriate for *GU* repeal in the consolidated setting for at least three reasons.

To begin, both sections 382(h) and 1374 apply only for a limited period of time—five years in the case of section 382(h) and ten years in the case of section 1374—and so whatever burden is imposed is more limited in nature.

More importantly, sections 382(h) and 1374 are generally concerned only with the unrecognized appreciation and depreciation in a pool of assets held by a corporation on a single date—the date the C corporation converts to an S corporation or the date the S corporation acquires assets of a C corporation in the case of section 1374, and the date a corporation has an ownership change in the case of section 382(h). Similarly, section 362(e)(2) is only concerned with net unrecognized depreciation in a pool of assets on the date of the transaction to which section 362(e)(2) applies. But the ability to circumvent *GU* repeal using the consolidated return provisions can be created any time the subsidiary has a redetermination event. Thus, any rule implementing *GU* repeal in the consolidated context, unlike rules implementing sections 362(e)(2), 382(h), and 1374, must trace the pool of assets held on all measuring dates, and not just the pool of assets held when subsidiary stock is acquired (or when assets are transferred).

Finally, unlike regulations implementing *GU* repeal, regulations implementing those other sections do not need to take into account the changing relationship between the basis in a particular share of stock and the unrecognized appreciation and depreciation in the corporation's assets.

For these reasons, any tracing-based regime appropriately implementing *GU* repeal in the consolidated setting would be much more expansive and complex, and therefore much less administrable, than the tracing regimes appropriately implementing sections 382(h) or 1374 (or proposed to implement section 362(e)(2)).

b. *Modified tracing.*

The IRS and Treasury Department considered several approaches that could be adopted to modify a tracing model by limiting the extent to which tracing would be required, in order to mitigate the administrative burdens of a pure tracing model.

i. *Exclusion for items attributable to after-acquired assets.*

Several commentators have suggested an approach, generally called the "after-acquired asset exception," which allows taxpayers to identify assets acquired after the acquisition of subsidiary stock, in order to treat any gain realized on those assets as economic to the group. In general, all other items of gain and income would be deemed to be noneconomic, that is, attributable to the recognition of appreciation that was already reflected in basis. Stock loss would be allowed only to the extent that stock basis was attributable to the amounts deemed economic to the group. In response to concerns raised by the IRS and Treasury Department about redetermination events, the proposal was modified to provide that only assets acquired after the latest measuring date would be treated as giving rise to economic amounts. The principal advantage of this approach is that it identifies some untainted items with no need for valuation.

To begin, the IRS and Treasury Department are concerned with the burden and error potential presented by the need to identify all redetermination events. Moreover, because these events can occur with considerable frequency in the ordinary course of business, it is unlikely that a great deal of time will typically elapse between the last redetermination date and the date of a stock disposition. Thus, the amount of gain recognized on an asset acquired and sold during such periods of time will not likely be significant. As a result, it appears unlikely that this approach would afford much relief to taxpayers (in terms of administrative burden or reducing the disallowance amount) or to the government (in terms of administrative burden).

Furthermore, in order to implement *GU* repeal appropriately, such an approach must take into account not only gains, but also losses, recognized on after-acquired assets. But the identification of such losses imposes an additional administrative burden that taxpayers have no incentive to facilitate. In any event, a requirement to take losses into account could be easily manipulated by the timing and structuring of redetermination events.

ii. *Exclusion for items recognized after prescribed period of time.*

Several commentators also suggested a tracing-based approach that would apply to investment adjustments taken into account only during a prescribed period of time following the acquisition of a share. The chief advantage to this approach is that, regardless how burdensome the administration of the rule, it would not extend indefinitely.

Like the proposed after-acquired-asset approach, however, this approach would need to take redetermination events into account. The tracing period would then begin again on the date of each redetermination event. Thus, like the after-acquired-asset exception, this approach is unlikely to afford much relief to taxpayers (in terms of administrative or tax burden) or the government (in terms of administrative burden) because the period for tracing may never close.

Moreover, the IRS and Treasury Department are concerned that such an approach does not adequately respond to *GU* repeal. The reason is that noneconomic investment adjustments circumvent *GU* repeal whenever they are taken into account. Thus, the IRS and Treasury Department continue to believe that, in the absence of any direction from Congress, such as in the case of section 1374, imposing time limits on the implementation of *GU* repeal would be inappropriate. See T.D. 8294.

iii. *Exclusion for basis conforming acquisitions.*

Commentators have also suggested adopting a tracing-based approach that excepted any stock acquired in either a section 351 exchange or a qualified stock purchase for which an election was made under section 338. The rationale for this approach is that, by operation of statute, the basis of stock acquired in these transactions can reflect no unrecognized appreciation.

The IRS and Treasury Department agree that, in certain circumstances, the structure of a stock acquisition will, by operation of law, preclude the reflection of unrecognized appreciation in stock basis. The IRS and Treasury Department are concerned, however, that many acquisitions under section 351 or section 338 actually do not preclude the reflection of unrecognized asset appreciation in stock basis. For example, if subsidiary stock is acquired in a section 351 exchange in multiple transactions or by multiple transferors, as illustrated in *Example 7(b)* and *Example 7(c)*, respectively, the basis of the shares received can reflect unrecognized appreciation. Similarly, because only 80 percent of the stock of a subsidiary need be acquired to elect section 338 treatment, the basis of up to 20 percent of a subsidiary's shares may reflect unrecognized appreciation. Moreover, even if the initial acquisition precludes the reflection of unrecognized gain, once there is a redetermination event, the form of the acquisition no longer prevents the reflection of unrecognized appreciation in stock basis. Thus, very few, if any, such transactions would ultimately qualify for this exception.

Thus, like the two previously described approaches to modified tracing, this approach has the inaccuracy and burden associated with identifying redetermination dates and a limited potential for relief to either taxpayers or the government.

iv. *Conclusions regarding modified tracing.*

Each approach considered would increase the administrative burden significantly without significantly increasing precision or relief. Accordingly, the IRS and Treasury Department are not proposing to adopt any of these approaches.

2. *Hybrid tracing-presumptive model: asset tracing.*

The IRS and Treasury Department also considered a hybrid tracing-presumptive approach that would identify all assets held when a share is acquired and on each redetermination date thereafter (again, the "tainted assets") and then presume all items of income, gain, deduction, and loss traced to those assets to be tainted. The intent was to design an approach that would be more precise than either a modified tracing or purely presumptive approach, while being more administrable than a pure tracing-based approach. The chief advantages of this approach are that it may enhance precision and, like the after-acquired asset exception described in section C.1.b.i of this preamble, may eliminate any need for valuation.

However, like the modified tracing approaches described above, this approach would require the identification of all redetermination events. Furthermore, it would require the identification of all assets held at the time of each such event and the tracing of those assets to particular investment adjustments. Thus, it presents even more complexity, burden, and expense than the modified tracing regimes considered. Furthermore, the IRS and Treasury Department are concerned that this approach could be easily abused, either by the manipulation of redetermination dates or the use of intercompany transactions to make valuation elective. (That is, taxpayers could selectively engage in intercompany transactions so that, in effect, some assets would be valued and not others.)

Finally, the IRS and Treasury Department are not convinced that the approach in fact significantly enhances the precision of a pure presumptive model in light of the fact that there is no actual valuation (and therefore no actual determination that there was any gain reflected in stock basis).

For all these reasons, the IRS and Treasury Department concluded that the potential advantages of this hybrid tracing-presumptive approach are outweighed by its disadvantages. Accordingly, the IRS and Treasury Department are not proposing to adopt this approach.

3. *Presumptive-based models.*

Recognizing that even the hybrid tracing-presumptive model would present significant burden and imprecision, the IRS and Treasury Department considered various presumptive models that, like the LDR, would eliminate all elements of tracing. A principal advantage of such approaches is that they are readily administrable by both taxpayers and the IRS. Thus, the rules can apply uniformly and consistently, with the result that similarly situated taxpayers will be similarly treated, increasing the overall fairness of the system. The elimination of any tracing element, however, increases the importance of limitations, where appropriate, on the nature and amount of items treated as noneconomic to a share. The approaches considered are discussed in this section C.3 and in section C.4 of this preamble.

a. *Basis disconformity under Notice 2004–58.*

One model considered was the basis disconformity model described in Notice 2004–58, presently available as a method to avoid disallowance under §1.337(d)–2. As noted in section A.4 of this preamble, the basis disconformity model treats as built-in gain (within the meaning of §1.337(d)–2) the smallest of three amounts. The first is the basis disconformity amount (which identifies the minimum amount of built-in gain that could be reflected in the share), the second is the net positive adjustment amount (which identifies the actual amount of stock basis attributable to the consolidated return system), and the total gains on property dispositions (which responds to the definition of the term built-in gain in §1.337(d)–2). A significant advantage of this approach is that both taxpayers and the IRS find it readily administrable with information that taxpayers are already required to maintain.

However, the Notice 2004–58 basis disconformity model, because it is an interpretation of the current loss limitation rule in §1.337(d)–2, reflects limitations that inhibit the extent to which the rule addresses the circumvention of *GU* repeal and promotes the clear reflection of group income. For example, the model did not account for the consumption of unrecognized appreciation reflected in stock basis (the "wasting asset" problem). Thus, if unrealized gain reflected in stock basis was recognized as income (for example through a lease, instead of a disposition of the property), the resulting noneconomic stock loss was not disallowed under the current rule. In addition, the model did not address the problem of basis disparity. (See, for example, *Example 4*.)

A more significant concern, however, is that the basis disconformity approach is underinclusive in that it can only address noneconomic stock loss to the extent of net appreciation reflected in stock basis, which is, by its nature, reduced by unrecognized depreciation reflected in basis. As a result, a potentially significant amount of noneconomic stock loss remained unaddressed, particularly in deconsolidating dispositions of subsidiary stock.

Example 9. Unrecognized loss reflected in stock basis. P purchases all the outstanding stock of S for $150. At the time, S owns one asset, A1, with a basis of $25 and value of $100, and one asset, A2, with a basis of $100 and a value of $50. S sells A1 to a nonmember for $100 and recognizes a $75 gain, which the P group takes into account. Under the investment adjustment system, P increases its basis in the S stock by $75, to $225, to reflect the $75 taken into account by the group. If P then sells the S stock for $150 (its fair market value), P will recognize a $75 loss. Under the basis disconformity approach, only $25, the excess of P's S stock basis ($225) over S's net inside asset basis ($100 cash plus S's $100 basis in A2, or, $200), of the $75 gain is treated as a noneconomic investment adjustment. Thus, although the entire loss is noneconomic, only $25 of that loss would be disallowed under this approach.

b. *Modified basis disconformity.*

The IRS and Treasury Department considered several modifications to the basis disconformity model, all of which were intended to address the underinclusivity of that model. One approach suggested by commentators would mitigate the wasting assets concern by first, for a prescribed period of time, treating the sum of all property gains and, up to the disconformity amount, all income as noneconomic (and thus included in the disallowance amount). After the prescribed time, all gains and income would be treated as noneconomic, but only to the extent of the disconformity amount. Other approaches considered reflected variations on this suggestion.

The IRS and Treasury Department recognize that the model described, and any similar models, would be readily administrable, but are concerned that such a model would not adequately preserve the group's ability to deduct economic loss sustained by the group. The reason is that stock loss could be attributable to economic investment adjustments (adjustments attributable to the recognition of items of income and gain that were not reflected in stock basis) that were followed by economic loss (attributable to a decline in the value of the subsidiary's assets). For example, assume that P contributed an asset to S (basis and value of $10), the asset appreciated and S sold it for $100 (recognizing a $90 gain that increased P's basis in S stock to $100), S reinvested the $100 in an asset that declined in value to $10, and P then sold the stock for $10. P would recognize a $90 loss that would be disallowed because S had a $90 gain on the disposition of an asset. Yet the entire loss was an economic loss. As a result, the IRS and Treasury Department are concerned that the result in *Rite Aid* (that the group receive the tax benefit of its economic loss) would not be adequately protected.

Ultimately, the IRS and Treasury Department concluded that the basis disconformity model in Notice 2004–58 would not be modified, but that elements of the model would be incorporated in a new approach.

4. *The presumptions and simplifying conventions adopted in these proposed regulations.*

a. *Loss limitation model.*

As discussed in section A.2 of this preamble, when the IRS and Treasury Department rejected a tracing approach in favor of the presumptive approach in 1990, the decision was made to balance the use of irrebuttable presumptions by adopting a loss limitation model. Under a loss limitation model, losses attributable to noneconomic investment adjustments are disallowed, but gain reduction (or elimination) attributable to noneconomic investment adjustments is not. The IRS and Treasury Department believed that allowing noneconomic gain reduction not only balanced the benefits and burdens of the presumptive approach, it also provided the considerable advantage of reducing gain duplication in consolidated groups.

Example 10. Noneconomic gain reduction, elimination of gain duplication. P purchases all the stock of S for $150 when S holds one asset, A1, with a basis of $100. S sells A1 for $150, recognizing $50 of gain. S uses the $150 proceeds from the sale of A1 to purchase A2. The value of A2 appreciates to $200, and P then sells its S stock for $200.

If the investment adjustment system did not adjust stock basis for items attributable to appreciation reflected in basis, P's basis in S stock would remain $150 and, when P sells the S stock, P would recognize a gain of $50 (reflecting the $50 appreciation in A2). When S sells A2, S would recognize the same $50 of economic gain a second time. However, because P's basis in S is increased by the $50 gain recognized on the sale of A1, P will recognize no gain or loss on its sale of S stock. The gain on A2 is therefore taxed once, when there is a recognition event with respect to A2.

These proposed regulations adopt a loss limitation model for the same reasons such a model was adopted in 1990, in the regulations promulgated under section 337(d) and the LDR (to balance the use of a presumptive approach).

However, the LDR, as well as §§1.337(d)–1 and 1.337(d)–2, applied the loss limitation model by disallowing loss recognized on the disposition of subsidiary stock and reducing basis on the deconsolidation of subsidiary stock. The IRS and Treasury Department recognize that the effect of a loss disallowance rule can be achieved by applying a basis reduction rule immediately before the disposition of loss stock. Modifying the loss limitation model to reduce basis in all cases simplifies the structure of the rule by avoiding the need for two distinct rules.

b. *Amount of basis reduction.*

The IRS and Treasury Department considered two basic approaches to determining the amount of basis reduction. One would be determined with reference to a share's adjusted basis and the other would be determined with reference to the disconformity between the share's basis and its allocable portion of the subsidiary's attributes.

i. *Adjusted purchase price cap.*

Under this approach, the basis of a transferred loss share would be reduced by the amount that the subsidiary's items increased the share's basis, but only to the extent of the adjusted purchase price. For purposes of this rule, the adjusted purchase price would be defined as the holder's original basis in the stock, adjusted to take into account all redetermination events. The rationale for this rule is that the adjusted purchase price represents the maximum amount of unrecognized gain that could be reflected in stock basis. However, this cap does not establish that, in fact, there was any appreciation reflected in stock basis and, therefore, it could prove to be substantially overinclusive.

The IRS and Treasury Department considered several rules that could be combined with the adjusted purchase price cap in order to mitigate its potential for overinclusiveness. One approach would combine this cap with the asset tracing model described in this preamble. Another approach would combine this cap with rules that treat income items as included in the basis reduction amount under a different rate (for example, using a declining percentage over time) or amount (for example, using an annual income cap, perhaps based on a percentage of the gross items). The IRS and Treasury Department ultimately concluded that the limitations either imposed unacceptable burdens (because of the need to identify redetermination dates and trace assets) or did not significantly increase the theoretical soundness of the approach, and that the potential for overinclusiveness prevented the approach from responding adequately to the Congressional mandate to preserve the result in *Rite Aid*.

ii. *Modified adjusted purchase price cap.*

To address the potential overinclusivity of the adjusted purchase price cap, the IRS and Treasury Department considered modifying the rule by reducing the cap by the basis of any tainted assets sold at a gain. The rationale for this modification is that the maximum potential amount of appreciation reflected in basis is reduced by the basis of tainted assets as they are sold. While this modification reduced the potential for overinclusiveness in a theoretically sound manner, it exacerbated the administrative difficulties by requiring not only the identification of all redetermination dates, but also of all assets held on such dates. Moreover, the IRS and Treasury Department ultimately concluded that the basic premise (that the limitation represented the maximum possible noneconomic income) remained an inadequate response to the Congressional directive that the group be allowed to deduct its economic loss.

iii. *Disconformity cap.*

This model would also reduce basis by the amount that the subsidiary's items increased the share's basis, but only to the extent of the disconformity amount. For this purpose, the disconformity amount would generally be the same as the basis disconformity amount described in Notice 2004–58. The rationale for this limitation is that the disconformity amount identifies the minimum amount of unrecognized appreciation actually reflected in the basis of a share of subsidiary stock at the relevant time. Thus, although the amount of such appreciation could actually be considerably greater (as in *Example 9*), and could even be equal to the adjusted purchase price (assuming a subsidiary was purchased with no basis in any of its assets), it is not lower. Not only does the disconformity cap have the advantage of identifying an amount of appreciation actually reflected in stock basis, it allows for the computation of that amount with information taxpayers are already required to know. Additionally, it avoids the need to identify redetermination events because, by computing disconformity immediately before a transfer, this approach automatically takes the effect of all such events into account.

iv. *Modified disconformity cap.*

Because the use of a disconformity cap raises significant potential for underinclusivity, as illustrated in *Example 9*, the IRS and Treasury Department considered increasing the disconformity cap by the amount of unrecognized loss on any tainted assets held by the subsidiary. The rationale for this increase is that those losses could prevent an equal amount of recognized tainted appreciation from being treated as noneconomic. Thus, the rule would not undermine the theoretical foundation of the disconformity cap.

However, this approach would require the identification of redetermination dates, as well as the identification and valuation of all assets held on the last such date. Recognizing the imprecision inherent in this approach, the IRS and Treasury Department considered increasing the disconformity cap by only a discounted portion of those unrecognized losses. The IRS and Treasury Department concluded that this approach would introduce burden and imprecision much greater than the potential benefit obtained by increasing the cap on basis reductions, at least in the majority of commercially typical cases.

The IRS and Treasury Department also considered implementing this modification not as a general rule, but only as an anti-abuse rule, so that it would apply only in circumstances that indicated a significant amount of tainted income or gain might be sheltered by unrecognized loss on tainted assets. For example, such a rule could require an increase to the disconformity cap if there was a significant loss in stock, if the subsidiary recognized significant gain shortly before stock sale, or if the stock was held for only a short period of time before it was sold. The IRS and Treasury Department were concerned, however, that the increased uncertainty and burden introduced by such an approach could not be justified in light of the protections against manipulation that exist in the Code and other rules of law. For example, see sections 269, 362(e)(2), and 482, as well as various anti-avoidance and anti-abuse provisions in the regulations, including these proposed regulations.

v. *Disconformity cap with duplication rule.*

In considering the structural potential for underinclusivity in the disconformity cap, the IRS and Treasury Department observed that the recognition of noneconomic gains in excess of the disconformity amount causes the subsidiary's unrecognized losses to be expressed in stock basis. The facts of *Example 9* illustrate this point. In that example, P purchased S for $150 when S held A1 (basis $25, value $100) and A2 (basis $100, value $50). S sold A1 and recognized $75 gain, which increased P's basis in S to $225. P then sold the S stock and recognized a $75 loss. At the time of the stock sale, S's net asset basis was $200 (the $100 received for A1 and the basis of A2), which exceeds the value of the stock by $50. Thus, the basis disconformity amount is $25 (the excess of the $225 stock basis over the $200 net asset basis), and so (although there is a $75 recognized gain), only $25 is disallowed. However, at that point, S's $200 net asset basis exceeds S's $150 value by $50. The $50 of unrecognized loss on A2 is reflected in both P's basis in S stock and S's basis in its assets. That is, the loss on A2 has been duplicated. As a result, the underinclusivity of the disconformity cap can be measured and addressed as duplicated loss.

The IRS and Treasury Department recognize that addressing this loss as a duplicated loss allows taxpayers to accelerate the benefit of a subsidiary's unrecognized losses (that is, obtain the benefit of the loss without a recognition event with respect to its loss assets). However, this approach allows taxpayers the benefit of their economic loss while limiting any arguably excessive benefit to the ability to accelerate inside loss. In the end, loss duplication is prevented. (The IRS and Treasury Department have long recognized that it is appropriate for a group to offset recognized built-in gains and losses, see §§1.337(d)–1 and 1.337(d)–2, as promulgated in 1990 and again as temporary and final regulations following the *Rite Aid* decision).

vi. *Conclusion.*

In light of the concerns raised by any method that would reduce basis beyond the disconformity amount, the IRS and Treasury Department have concluded that the amount of basis reduction should be limited to the disconformity amount and that combining the disconformity cap with a loss duplication rule to address its underinclusivity provides the most appropriate balancing of interests. Under this approach, the group's economic loss is appropriately protected and neither the group nor its members will receive more than one benefit for the subsidiary's economic loss.

c. *Items applied to reduce basis.*

i. *Character of items applied to reduce basis.*

In general, the IRS and Treasury Department have concluded, and commentators have generally agreed, that all gains on property dispositions, as well as various gain equivalents, should be fully available to reduce basis under a presumptive rule.

Questions arose, however, regarding whether income items should also be fully available to reduce basis. The reasons for these questions center on the general difficulty of tracing income items (which is limited in the best of circumstances) and the observation that the likelihood of a particular income item being attributable to tainted appreciation generally decreases over time. Accordingly, the IRS and Treasury Department considered several proposals to limit both the amount and the rate of inclusion for income items.

All of these approaches would segregate income that could be traced to particular appreciation reflected in stock basis and treat those amounts in the same manner as items of gain. The net income remaining would be applied to reduce basis according to prescribed limits. For example, one proposal would apply net income to reduce basis for a prescribed period of time following a measuring date, but, after that time, net income would be so applied only according to a declining percentage.

The IRS and Treasury Department are concerned, however, that the approaches considered could be readily manipulated, for example, by converting gain into income that cannot be readily traced to particular assets or by delaying the recognition of income items until after the applicable time period. Therefore, any such rule would inappropriately influence the structure of business transactions and, at the same time, fail to provide adequate protection for *GU* repeal. In addition, the need to account for redetermination dates would add complexity and diminish the potential relief afforded under any such approach. Moreover, the IRS and Treasury Department identified no theoretical basis for any particular rule and were concerned that the increased precision may be more perceived than real.

ii. *Capital transfers.*

Adjustments to reflect transfers of capital, whether contributions or distributions, are not adjustments attributable to the recognition of appreciation or depreciation. Accordingly, these adjustments do not increase or decrease the extent to which stock basis is noneconomic or facilitates the circumvention of *GU* repeal. For that reason, such amounts are not taken into account in determining the extent to which subsidiary stock basis is subject to reduction.

Commentators have suggested that the nature of an intercompany cancellation of indebtedness is similar to that of a capital contribution and thus should not be taken into account in determining basis reduction. The IRS and Treasury Department recognize that this may often be the case, but are concerned that, under some circumstances, this may not be the case. Because it will be administratively very difficult to identify situations in which intercompany cancellation of indebtedness is not similar to a capital contribution, and to distinguish intercompany cancellation of indebtedness from other arguably similar cases, these proposed regulations treat items related to intercompany cancellation of indebtedness like all other items of income or loss. However, the IRS and Treasury Department continue to study the issue and invite further comments.

d. *Netting of items from different tax periods.*

Under the LDR, there was no cross-year netting of investment adjustments. Positive investment adjustments were taken into account in determining the loss disallowance amount, negative investment adjustments were not. The IRS and Treasury Department have reconsidered whether items from different tax periods should be considered together in determining basis reduction.

The IRS and Treasury Department recognize that the particular circumvention of *GU* repeal at issue here is a product of the manner in which the investment adjustment system adjusts stock basis to reflect a subsidiary's amounts that are taken into account by the group. Thus, the IRS and Treasury Department have concluded that the appropriate measure of the concern must take into account the net extent to which the basis of a share has been increased or decreased by the investment adjustment system. Whether a loss is taken into account in the same year in which a gain is taken into account or in a separate year does not change the net effect of the investment adjustment system. Thus, unlike the LDR, these proposed regulations allow netting of all investment adjustments made to a share for all periods.

e. *Summary and conclusions.*

Only a presumptive approach can eliminate the substantial administrative burdens imposed by the tracing based and hybrid regimes discussed above. As a result, only a presumptive approach can be applied consistently among taxpayers and thus achieve the overall fairness necessary to these regulations. Importantly, if presumptions are rebuttable, the administrative burdens associated with a tracing system are not avoided. In fact, they are exacerbated, because taxpayers will feel it necessary to be prepared to establish, and the government will then need to be prepared to examine, returns using both systems. Accordingly, the proposed regulations reflect a presumptive approach that does not permit the rebuttal of its operating presumptions. As noted in section A.5 of this preamble, Congress has specifically sanctioned the use of presumptions and other simplifying conventions to address the circumvention of *GU* repeal.

To balance the use of irrebuttable presumptions, the proposed regulations adopt several provisions that are intended to enhance their overall fairness and theoretical soundness. First, the proposed regulations adopt the disconformity amount as the maximum amount of potential stock basis reduction. The reason, as discussed, is that only the disconformity amount both establishes the fact that the taxpayer had unrealized gain reflected in stock basis and identifies the minimum amount of such gain. Second, the proposed regulations include all items taken into account, from all years, in the determination of the basis reduction amount. Thus, basis is not reduced for certain amounts (such as capital transfers) that cannot be attributable to noneconomic investment adjustments. In addition, by presuming all items of income, gain, deduction and loss as attributable to appreciation or depreciation reflected in basis, the proposed regulations avoid the administrative burden and other concerns inherent in various tracing and hybrid approaches. Moreover, by presuming all items to be reflected in basis, the benefits and burdens inherent in the use of irrebuttable presumptions are fairly balanced between taxpayers and the government. Presuming all items of income and gain are noneconomic favors the fisc, while presuming all items of deduction and loss are noneconomic favors taxpayers.

D. *Loss Duplication.*

The IRS and Treasury Department continue to believe that a group's income is distorted when the group enjoys more than one tax benefit from an economic loss. Further, the IRS and Treasury Department believe that a subsidiary's use of a group loss in a separate return year, after the group has already recognized the benefit of the loss, distorts the subsidiary's separate year income.

Moreover, the IRS and Treasury Department do not believe that the manner or order in which a group takes its losses into account affects the extent to which loss duplication is inappropriate. Thus, loss duplication is inappropriate and must be addressed whether arising in situations like that illustrated in *Example 3* (loss reflected in both stock and assets) or in *Example 5* (duplication attributable to disparate stock basis). In addition, loss duplication is inappropriate and must be addressed whether the group chooses to recognize loss first as an inside loss, on the subsidiary's assets and operations (which is addressed by §1.1502–32), or as a stock loss (which is currently addressed, at least partially, by §1.1502–35).

Accordingly, the IRS and Treasury Department have returned to a fundamental premise of the LDR and again concluded that a loss duplication rule that operates without regard to members' continued affiliation is a necessary complement to the investment adjustment system. The IRS and Treasury Department have also concluded that such a rule must also address the potential for loss duplication presented when loss is disproportionately reflected in the bases of individual shares.

Importantly, as noted in section A.5 of this preamble, Congress has indicated that it, too, views the prevention of loss duplication, including in deconsolidating stock dispositions, as an area that is appropriately addressed by regulation. See H.R. Conf. Rep. No. 108–755 at 652.

Therefore, the IRS and Treasury Department have reviewed the current rules and considered alternative approaches to address the duplication of loss.

1. *Reconsideration of §1.1502–35.*

Loss duplication is currently addressed in §1.1502–35. That rule generally applies whenever there is a disposition of loss shares of subsidiary stock. To address the loss duplication problems arising when loss is disproportionately reflected in stock basis, the rule first redetermines members' bases to reduce that disparity (to address the problems illustrated in *Example 5*). Different rules apply depending on the subsidiary's status as a group member following the stock disposition. If the subsidiary remains a member, the full blending rule of §1.1502–35(b)(1) applies and all members' bases in shares of the subsidiary's stock are combined and then allocated evenly to preferred (to value) and then to common (equally). If the subsidiary ceases to be a member, the basis redetermination rule of §1.1502–35(b)(2) applies and members' bases are redetermined to reduce loss on all members' shares. However, this rule only redetermines basis to the extent of items of deduction and loss included in negative adjustments applied to nonloss shares. As under the full blending rule, redetermination under this rule first reduces or eliminates loss on preferred shares and then equalizes members' bases in common shares.

The potential for loss duplication following the redetermination of members' bases is addressed only if the subsidiary remains a member of the group. In that case, stock loss (to the extent of loss duplication) is suspended, the suspended loss is reduced as the subsidiary's items of deduction and loss are taken into account, and any suspended loss remaining when the subsidiary ceases to be a member is allowed at that time. The regulation does not address the duplication of loss when the subsidiary ceases to be a member, other than to prevent the reimportation of duplicated losses back into the group.

The IRS and Treasury Department understand that certain administrability concerns have arisen under §1.1502–35. For example, taxpayers have commented that the rules relating to the suspension of loss in nondeconsolidating dispositions and the treatment of reimported losses present substantial compliance issues. The experience of the IRS is consistent with those comments.

Moreover, the IRS and Treasury Department have reconsidered the appropriateness of allowing subsidiaries to duplicate group losses after the period of consolidation. Under this approach, former members can use group losses (that have already been used by the group) to offset their separate year income. This duplicative use of group losses distorts the former member's separate income. Under section 1502, consolidated return regulations are directed to promote the clear reflection of not only the income of a group, but also of its members, including former members. Accordingly, as in 1990, the IRS and Treasury Department have concluded that a group loss, once used by the group, should not be available to a former member for a second, duplicative use outside the group.

For these reasons, the IRS and Treasury Department propose to remove §1.1502–35 and replace it with a more easily administered and more comprehensive approach to addressing loss duplication among members of a consolidated group.

2. *Other methods considered for addressing loss duplication.*

As discussed in section D of this preamble, the IRS and Treasury Department have concluded that loss duplication is an inappropriate distortion of income (of either a group or its members, including former members) regardless of the subsidiary's status after a transfer of its stock. Accordingly, these proposed regulations address loss duplication in both nondeconsolidating and deconsolidating stock transfers. Several approaches were considered.

a. *Disallowance of stock loss.*

As a general matter, the IRS and Treasury Department believe that disallowing duplicative stock loss better implements single entity principles because it results in the recognition of the subsidiaries' economic gain or loss on its assets and operations, instead of on its stock. However, to preserve the result in *Rite Aid*, stock loss could only be disallowed for nondeconsolidating transfers and additional rules would be necessary to address both the loss remaining in the group and the duplication of loss in deconsolidating transfers (which could not be subject to the loss disallowance rule). Thus, a rule implementing this approach would need to include a provision comparable to §1.1502–35(c), which taxpayers and the IRS have found to present significant compliance issues. In addition, this approach would need to include a provision to address loss duplication in deconsolidating transfers.

b. *Loss duplication accounts.*

The IRS and Treasury Department also considered an approach that would allow stock loss, but identify the amount of loss duplication and create a suspended account to limit the deductibility of items as they are taken into account. One advantage of this approach is that it only requires one set of rules to address both nondeconsolidating and deconsolidating transfers. This approach also has the advantage of increasing the precision in identifying (and disallowing) losses that are actually duplicated.

However, unless the rule were to use presumptions to treat items as chargeable against the loss duplication account, it would present considerable tracing issues. In addition, this approach raises administrability issues comparable to those associated with the loss suspension regime in §1.1502–35(c). These difficulties are exacerbated by the need to have the account follow the subsidiary, possibly through subsequent acquisitions, until the account is eliminated.

The IRS and Treasury Department are also concerned that, because this approach would reduce or eliminate duplication only when inside losses were recognized, taxpayers could avoid the effect of the rule by waiting until assets appreciated before disposing of them. To mitigate this concern, the rule could require the subsidiary to take into account the duplication account, either ratably over time or at some specified time, but this could give rise to income in the absence of any loss duplication.

c. *Attribute reduction.*

The IRS and Treasury Department also considered a presumptive rule that would identify the extent of duplicated loss and then reduce the subsidiary's attributes by that amount. This approach, like the loss duplication account, has the advantage of needing only one set of rules to govern both deconsolidating and nondeconsolidating transfers. It has the added advantage of being similar to regimes that are already familiar to taxpayers, such as the attribute reduction rules of sections 108 and 1017, and §1.1502–28. Although attribute reduction could be based on valuation, like the rule in section 362(e)(2), the IRS and Treasury Department believe that mandatory valuation would present a significant administrative burden and expense for both taxpayers and the IRS.

d. *Conclusions.*

The IRS and Treasury Department have concluded that the complexity, administrative burden, and expense of the loss disallowance and the loss duplication account approaches outweighed their respective advantages. Accordingly, these proposed regulations adopt an attribute reduction rule. The IRS and Treasury Department recognize that the attribute reduction approach allows taxpayers to accelerate economic losses of the subsidiary, but believe that this approach best preserves the result in *Rite Aid* while addressing loss duplication. In general, the approach adopted operates as an irrebuttable presumption, to avoid the burden of mandatory valuation in all cases, but taxpayers continue to have several mechanisms available to structure their transactions to permit valuation (for example, by using actual or deemed asset sales).

3. *Gain duplication.*

Notwithstanding the conclusions regarding duplication of loss, for the reasons set forth in the LDR preambles, the IRS and Treasury Department have tentatively concluded that adequate protections, and the incentive to use them, already exist to prevent the duplication of gain. See T.D. 8294, T.D. 8364 and T.D. 8984. For example, see sections 332, 336(e) (which is the subject of another current guidance project), and 338(h)(10). Accordingly, the duplication of gain is not addressed in these proposed regulations, except as a result of the adoption of a loss disallowance model. The IRS and Treasury Department continue to study the issues, however, and invite further comment. See section J of this preamble for further discussion of the issues on which comments are requested.

E. *Noneconomic and Duplicated Loss from Investment Adjustment System.*

For all the reasons discussed in this preamble, the IRS and Treasury Department believe that the approaches to noneconomic and duplicated loss that are adopted in these proposed regulations represent the best approach to the (original) noneconomic and duplicated loss concerns described in sections B.1 and B.2 of this preamble. However, those rules alone do not adequately address the problem of noneconomic and duplicated loss attributable to investment adjustments applied to shares of stock with disparate bases. This is the concern described in section B.3 of this preamble and illustrated in *Example 4* and *Example 5*, as well as *Example 7(b)* and *Example 7(c)*.

The IRS and Treasury Department believe it is essential to address this concern. One reason is that stock basis would be inappropriately eliminated when, in cases like *Example 4*, there is noneconomic loss on one share because appreciated assets were contributed to a corporation in exchange for other shares. In those cases, the noneconomic loss should not be allowed, but a rule that only prevents that loss does not address the problem that there is insufficient basis on the shares received in the exchange. The result would be noneconomic gain on the sale of those shares. An equally important reason is that loss could otherwise be duplicated when, in cases like *Example 5*, loss is disproportionately reflected in the basis of some shares. Although regulations could prevent duplication in such cases (by eliminating inside loss to the full extent of duplicated stock loss), allowing a deduction for disproportionate stock loss in such cases permits the acceleration of a disproportionate amount of inside loss. To the extent that loss is disproportionately reflected in the basis of an individual share, acceleration is generally unwarranted and should be prevented to the extent possible. Accordingly, the IRS and Treasury Department have considered various approaches to mitigating these effects.

1. *Revise investment adjustment system to adopt a tracing approach.*

The IRS and Treasury Department recognize that one approach to this problem would be to revise the investment adjustment system so that it would allocate subsidiaries' items of income, gain, deduction, and loss to their shares in accordance with the actual reflection of those items in the each share's basis. This approach would be similar to the section 704(c) regime applicable to partnerships. However, this approach is a tracing model and, as discussed in section C of this preamble, the IRS and Treasury Department do not believe that tracing is administrable in the consolidated setting.

Moreover, as noted above, the IRS and Treasury Department continue to believe that the presumptive-based rules of §1.1502–32 are not only administrable, but appropriate in the vast majority of cases because typically subsidiary stock is common stock owned entirely by members with uniform bases. Where subsidiaries have issued preferred stock, it is generally section 1504(a)(4) stock. In addition, the investment adjustment system contains some guidance for situations that do not reflect the general assumptions on which the rules are based (*for example*, the cumulative redetermination rule in §1.1502–32(c)(4)). In such cases, tracing would be unnecessary. Moreover, the IRS and Treasury Department do not believe that typical commercial transactions generally require groups to alter a subsidiary's capital structure in a manner that would require tracing. Accordingly, the IRS and Treasury Department are not considering revising the investment adjustment system to implement a tracing regime.

2. *Presumptive approaches to reduce basis disparity.*

The two presumptive approaches considered to reduce basis disparity were a full blending rule similar to that in §1.1502–35(b)(1) and a rule that would redetermine investment adjustments made under §1.1502–32, similar to the rule in §1.1502–35(b)(2).

a. *Full basis blending.*

Under the full basis blending approach, all members' bases are aggregated and then allocated among members' shares in a manner that results in the elimination of loss on preferred shares and of basis disparity on all other shares, at least within each class. As a result, members' bases are aligned with the operating premises of the investment adjustment system.

Full basis blending not only mitigates the effects of previous noneconomic investment adjustments, addressing the concern illustrated in *Example 4* and *Example 5(a)*, it also prevents the acceleration of disproportionate amounts of unrecognized loss, addressing the concern illustrated in *Example 5(b)*.

A full basis blending rule is, however, a significant departure from the rules generally applicable under the Code. Commentators have suggested that this departure from generally applicable law may be more significant than is warranted in light of the extent to which the concerns can be addressed under the investment adjustment redetermination approach described in this preamble.

b. *Redetermination of investment adjustments previously made to stock basis.*

The investment adjustment redetermination approach is less a departure from Code provisions as it is a departure from the general operation of §1.1502–32. In general, this approach would reallocate investment adjustments previously applied to members' bases in subsidiary stock with the goal of reducing, to the greatest extent possible, the disparity in members' bases in subsidiary stock. Thus, like the full blending approach, this approach would bring members' bases closer into alignment with the assumptions underlying the investment adjustment system. However, it would do so to a more limited extent than the full blending rule and in a manner that is less of a departure from general Code rules.

i. *Recomputation of individual investment adjustments.*

Presently, §1.1502–35(b)(2) addresses duplicated loss by redetermining investment adjustments when there is a deconsolidating disposition of subsidiary stock. To achieve the greatest reduction in basis disparity possible, §1.1502–35(b)(2) in effect deconstructs investment adjustments in order to remove negative items (that is, items of deduction and expense) from adjustments to the bases of gain shares and then apply those items to reduce members' bases in loss shares. Taxpayers have raised concerns with the complexity and administrability of this approach. The IRS has observed compliance and audit difficulties with this approach.

Accordingly, the IRS and Treasury Department have reconsidered whether this general approach, redetermining investment adjustments, could be adopted in a simpler form. The principal method considered was a presumptive reallocation of entire investment adjustments (exclusive of distributions), instead of the individual items that comprise them. The approach is similar to that used in the cumulative redetermination rule of §1.1502–32(c)(4). A significant advantage to this simplified approach is that it is readily administered with information that taxpayers are already required to know (§1.1502–32 already requires taxpayers to determine investment adjustments exclusive of distributions).

The IRS and Treasury Department recognize that this general approach, in whichever form adopted, does not address the acceleration illustrated in *Example 5(b)* to the extent that full blending would. However, this approach is less disruptive to the general determination of basis.

ii. *Reallocations to loss shares that are not transferred.*

Presently, §1.1502–35(b)(2) reallocations can result in the reduction of any member's basis in a loss share of subsidiary stock. The IRS and Treasury Department have reconsidered whether reallocated investment adjustments should be applied to reduce loss on shares that are not transferred in the transaction.

The IRS and Treasury Department have concluded that reallocating investment adjustments to reduce the basis of only transferred loss shares better implements the loss disallowance model. The reason is that this approach allows subsidiary stock basis to remain intact until there is a taxable disposition, deconsolidation, or worthlessness of the share, thereby permitting that basis to enjoy the full protection of subsequent appreciation as long as it remains in the group and otherwise subject to the consolidated return system. This approach has the added benefit of affording the maximum potential to eliminate disparate reflection of loss on transferred shares because all the reallocations are directed to transferred shares. As a result, this approach reduces the amount of loss that can be accelerated (as illustrated in *Example 5(b)*).

iii. *Reallocations of positive and negative investment adjustments.*

Under the basis redetermination rule in §1.1502–35(b)(2), only negative items are reallocated. However, the sole purpose of §1.1502–35, and thus the basis redetermination rules in §1.1502–35(b), is to address the duplication of loss. (The full blending approach of §1.1502–35(b)(1) addresses noneconomic loss attributable to basis disparity as well as loss duplication, but only incidentally as a result of its broad operation.) The IRS and Treasury Department believe that, although it is appropriate for a rule addressing only loss duplication to reallocate just negative items (or negative investment adjustments), a rule addressing both noneconomic and duplicated loss must reallocate both negative and positive items (or investment adjustments). As illustrated in *Example 4* and *Example 5*, reallocations of both positive and negative amounts are necessary to prevent the noneconomic and duplicated stock loss that results from the disparate reflection of unrecognized gain and to do so without causing inappropriate results to taxpayers (specifically, noneconomic gain).

For the foregoing reasons, the IRS and Treasury Department have concluded that the reallocation of both positive and negative adjustments is appropriate and necessary to balance the use of a presumptive system. Accordingly, these proposed regulations provide for the reallocation of both positive and negative investment adjustments to minimize the potential over- and under-application of the noneconomic and duplicated loss rules.

Explanation of Provisions

F. *Explanation of the Proposed Regulations.*

1. *Overview.*

The proposed regulation consists of three principal rules that apply when a member transfers a loss share of subsidiary stock. The first rule redetermines members' bases in subsidiary stock by reallocating §1.1502–32 adjustments (to adjust for disproportionate reflection of gains and losses in the bases of members' shares). The second rule reduces members' bases in transferred loss shares (but not below value) by the net positive amount of all investment adjustments applied to the bases of those shares, but only to the extent of the share's disconformity amount (to address noneconomic stock loss). The third rule reduces the subsidiary's attributes to prevent the duplication of a loss recognized on, or preserved in the basis of, transferred stock.

The three rules generally apply in the order described. If members transfer stock of multiple subsidiaries in one transaction, the basis redetermination and basis reduction rules apply first with respect to transfers of loss shares of stock of the subsidiaries at the lowest tier and then successively to transferred shares at each next higher tier. These rules are not applied at any tier until any gain or loss recognized (even if disallowed) on lower-tier transfers and any items resulting from lower-tier adjustments (whether required by the basis redetermination or basis reduction rule or otherwise) are taken into account and reflected in stock basis. After the basis redetermination and reallocation rules have applied with respect to all transferred loss shares, the attribute reduction rule applies with respect to the highest-tier transferred loss shares. The attribute reduction rule then applies successively with respect to transferred loss shares at each next lower tier.

For purposes of these proposed regulations, a transfer of stock includes any event in which gain or loss would be recognized (but for these proposed regulations), the holder of a share and the subsidiary cease to be members of the same group, a nonmember acquires an outstanding share from a member, or the share is treated as worthless. This rule allows the proposed regulations to prescribe one integrated set of rules that implements a loss limitation approach and that can be applied to all loss shares, regardless of the event giving rise to the application of the section.

2. *The basis redetermination rule.*

When a member transfers a share of subsidiary (S) stock and, after the application of all other provisions of the Code and regulations, the share is a loss share, this rule subjects all members' shares of S stock to redetermination.

Under the basis redetermination rule, investment adjustments (exclusive of distributions) that were previously applied to members' bases in S stock are generally reallocated in a manner that, to the greatest extent possible, first eliminates loss on preferred shares and then eliminates basis disparity on all shares. The rule moves both positive and negative adjustments, and so addresses both noneconomic and duplicated losses. Because it generally requires adjustments to be made to reduce disparity, it brings members' bases closer in line with the fundamental principals underlying the investment adjustment system. As a result, there is less likelihood for later noneconomic or duplicated loss attributable to the investment adjustment system.

The rule operates by first removing positive investment adjustments (up to the amount of the loss) from the bases of transferred loss shares. Then, to the extent of any remaining loss on the transferred shares, negative investment adjustments are removed from shares that are not transferred loss shares and applied to reduce the loss on transferred loss shares. The positive adjustments removed from the transferred loss shares are allocated and applied only after the negative items have been reallocated. The reason is to preserve the most flexibility possible in reallocating positive adjustments, in order to minimize disparity to the greatest extent. Thus, the operation of these rules has the effect of removing basis from transferred loss shares and using it to reduce disparity in members' bases in S shares.

Redetermination is limited in several respects. First, because the premise of the rule is that the original allocation of an item did not represent the most economically appropriate allocation of the item, redeterminations under the rule are limited to allocations of investment adjustments that could have been made at the time an item was taken into account. Accordingly, no adjustments can be reallocated to shares that were not held by members in the year taken into account, as members' shares would not have been able to receive those adjustments in the original allocation.

A related limitation on reallocation is that an investment adjustment cannot be reallocated except to the extent that the full effect of the reallocation can be accomplished. Thus, an investment adjustment can not be reallocated to the extent the resulting basis has previously been taken into account (including at a higher tier). This rule guards against double benefits from an adjustment (for example, by not allowing positive adjustments to be moved from, or negative adjustments be moved to, shares after the item would have affected basis that was taken into account in recognizing gain or loss). It also guards against the loss of a benefit (for example, by not allocating positive adjustments to previously transferred shares that can no longer benefit from the basis).

The principle purpose of the rule is to reduce loss on transferred shares. However, because its secondary purpose is to decrease disconformity to the greatest extent possible, in certain fact patterns, the application of the rule will actually increase loss on some shares. Importantly, in no fact patterns will the application of the rule create gain on shares. Overall, the rule has no effect on the aggregate amount of gain or loss on members' bases in subsidiary stock.

In the basis reallocation rule, and in several other provisions of the proposed regulations, there is a direction to allocate items in a manner that reduces disparity to the greatest extent possible. The regulations do not, however, prescribe the manner in which such determinations are to be made. The IRS and Treasury Department intend that taxpayers have flexibility in choosing the methods and formulas to be employed in making these determinations and the IRS will respect any reasonable method or formula so employed.

The IRS and Treasury Department recognize that the redetermination of basis imposes a certain administrative burden. Thus, the rule contains two safe harbors that excuse taxpayers from reallocating basis in situations in which redetermination is deemed unnecessary. One safe harbor is for situations in which redetermination would have no ultimate effect on the basis of any share held by a member. This happens, for example, if only common stock is outstanding and there is no disparity in the bases of the shares. In such a case, any redetermination would result in the same bases the members had before redetermination. The second safe harbor is for situations in which the group disposes of its entire interest in the subsidiary to an unrelated person in one or more fully taxable transactions. In such a case, the group recognizes all the gains and losses on the shares and so obtains no benefit from the disparate reflection of gain or loss. Transfers that are excepted from basis redetermination, like transfers of shares that remain loss shares after application of the rule, are then subject to the basis reduction rule.

3. *The basis reduction rule.*

If, after basis redetermination, any member's transferred share is a loss share (even if the share only became a loss share as a result of the application of the basis redetermination rule), the basis of that share is subject to reduction under this rule. This rule is intended to eliminate stock loss that is presumed noneconomic. It operates by reducing the basis of each transferred loss share (but not below value) by the lesser of the share's disconformity amount and its net positive adjustment.

A share's disconformity amount is the excess of its basis over its allocable portion of S's net inside attributes, determined at the time of the transfer. This amount identifies the net amount of unrealized appreciation reflected in the basis of the share. Because the disconformity amount is computed at the time of the transfer, the disconformity amount reflects the effects of all prior redetermination events.

The term net inside attributes is defined as the sum of S's loss carryovers, deferred deductions, cash, and asset basis, reduced by S's liabilities. This computation is used in both this basis reduction rule and the attribute reduction rule described in section F.4 of this preamble. Both rules do, however, have special provisions that modify the computation of net inside attributes if S holds lower-tier subsidiary stock. See sections F.3.a and F.4.a of this preamble for a discussion of rules relating to the stock of lower-tier subsidiaries for purposes of basis reduction and attribute reduction, respectively.

A share's net positive adjustment is computed as the greater of zero and the sum of all investment adjustments (excluding distributions) applied to the basis of the transferred loss share, including by reason of prior basis reallocations. All items of income, gain, deduction, and loss are included fully in the net positive adjustment amount. This rule identifies the extent to which basis has been increased by the investment adjustment provisions for items of income, gain, deduction and loss (whether taxable or not) that have been taken into account by the group.

a. *Special rules applicable when S holds stock of lower-tier subsidiary.*

For purposes of computing the disconformity amount, if S holds stock of a lower-tier subsidiary (S1) that was not transferred in the transaction, S's net inside attribute amount is computed by treating S's basis in S1 stock as "tentatively reduced" by the lesser of the S1 share's net positive adjustment and its disconformity amount. This reduction is made only for purposes of determining basis reduction to the S share, and has no other effect. The purpose of this adjustment is to prevent S1's recognized items from giving rise to noneconomic loss in S stock, for example, when S1 recognizes gain that is already reflected (indirectly) in P's basis in S shares. This problem is illustrated in *Example 8* (subsidiary holding lower-tier subsidiary stock with a basis that reflects lower-tier unrecognized appreciation).

When determining the disconformity amount of a share of subsidiary stock, no tentative reduction is made to the basis of lower-tier shares that were transferred in the transaction (without regard to whether S retained the shares after the transaction, such as when S1 is transferred because S and S1 cease to be members of the same group but S continues to hold S1 stock). The reason is that the basis reduction rule applies directly to each transfer, starting with the lowest-tier transfer, and so any noneconomic loss in S stock that was attributable to S1's items has been eliminated by the time that the basis reduction rule applies to the S Stock. In addition, the tentative basis reduction rule does not apply to shares that are lower tier to any shares that were transferred in the transaction. The application of the rule to those shares is unnecessary because, when the basis reduction rule applied to S1, it eliminated any inappropriate effects from items that tiered up from subsidiaries that were lower tier to S1.

4. *The attribute reduction rule.*

If any transferred share remains a loss share after application of the basis reduction rule, the subsidiary's attributes (including the consolidated attributes attributable to the subsidiary) are subject to reduction. The attribute reduction rule addresses the duplication of loss by members of consolidated groups. This rule is intended to insure that the group does not recognize more than one loss with respect to a single economic loss regardless of whether the group chooses to dispose of the subsidiary stock before or after the subsidiary recognizes the loss with respect to its assets or operations.

Under this rule, S's attributes are reduced by the "attribute reduction amount," which is computed as the lesser of the net stock loss and the aggregate inside loss. This amount reflects the total amount of unrecognized loss that is reflected in both the basis of the S stock and S's attributes. Net stock loss is the excess of the sum of the bases (after application of the basis reduction rule) of all S shares transferred by members in the same transaction over the value of such shares. S's aggregate inside loss is the excess of S's net inside attributes over the value of all of the S shares. The term net inside attributes generally has the same meaning as in the basis reduction rule, subject to special rules for lower-tier subsidiaries (see section F.4.a of this preamble).

Unlike comparable provisions in §1.1502–35 and the LDR, this rule does not limit its application to a share's proportionate interest in the subsidiary's aggregate inside loss. The reason is that when a member recognizes a stock loss, or preserves a stock loss for later recognition (for example, when the share is retained but deconsolidated), the member enjoys (or preserves for later use) the benefit of the entire amount of that stock loss. If basis is uniform, the amount of stock loss will reflect a proportionate interest in the subsidiary's unrecognized loss. But if basis is disparate, the loss on a particular share can reflect any amount, even all, of the subsidiary's unrecognized loss. In either case, the potential loss duplication equals the entire amount by which the stock loss is duplicated in the subsidiary's attributes. Accordingly, the proposed regulations reduce attributes to that extent. This prevents the duplication (but not acceleration) of loss otherwise available in situations similar to *Example 5(b)* by reducing S's attributes by the entire amount by which the stock loss duplicates the aggregate inside loss.

A principal goal of this regulation is to address the issues of noneconomic and duplicated stock loss in a manner that is as readily administrable as possible, by taxpayers and the government. For that reason, the proposed regulations generally avoid imposing valuation requirements whenever possible. However, the proposed regulations do, to the extent possible, use readily available information to identify the location and amount of loss, to avoid knowingly creating gain. The order in which attributes are reduced reflects these principles.

After S's attribute reduction amount is determined, it is first applied to reduce or eliminate items that represent actual realized losses, such as operating loss carryovers, capital loss carryovers, and deferred deductions. If S's attribute reduction amount exceeds those items, the excess is then applied to reduce or eliminate the loss in the basis of property that is publicly traded (other than subsidiary stock, which is subject to special rules). The reason that the basis of publicly traded property, unlike that of other assets, is only reduced by the amount of loss reflected in the basis of the property is that such property can be readily and easily valued. Finally, if any attribute reduction amount remains after eliminating those attributes, it is applied to reduce or eliminate the basis in assets, other than publicly traded property (which then reflects no loss) and other than cash and equivalents (which also reflect no loss). This reduction is made proportionately according to the basis in each property.

The proposed regulations provide a special rule that applies to the extent a subsidiary has liabilities that have not been taken into account as of the time of the transfer. Under the general rule, if the attribute reduction amount exceeds attributes available for reduction, that excess attribute reduction amount has no further effect. However, a special rule applies if the attribute reduction amount exceeds the attributes available for reduction and the subsidiary has a liability that has not been taken into account. Typically this will happen when cash or other liquid assets are held to fund future expenses related to the liability. Because the assets held by S do not reflect attributes that can be reduced, loss can be duplicated later, when the liability is taken into account. To prevent the duplication of loss in such cases, the excess attribute reduction amount is suspended and applied to prevent the deduction or capitalization of payments later made by S or another person with respect to the liability.

a. *Special rules applicable when S holds stock of lower-tier subsidiary.*

When S holds stock of lower-tier subsidiaries, the attribute reduction amount is computed in a manner that identifies the maximum potential amount of loss duplication and attributes are reduced to that extent. However, the rule incorporates two restrictions to prevent excessive reduction of attributes that could otherwise result from this approach. These rules are set forth in this section 4.a.

First, to facilitate the computation of S's attribute reduction amount, all of S's shares of S1 stock are treated as a single share (generally referred to as the S1 stock). To identify the maximum potential duplication, the computation of the attribute reduction amount is made treating S's basis in S1 stock as its "deemed basis" in that stock. The proposed regulations define deemed basis as the greater of S's actual aggregate basis in the S1 shares (adjusted for any gain or loss recognized on a transfer of the S1 shares) and the S1 shares' allocable portion of S1's net inside attributes. For example, assume P owns all the stock of S with a basis of $150, S owns all the stock of S1 with a basis of $100, and S1 owns an asset with a basis of $150. S's deemed basis in S1 stock is $150, the greater of $100 (S's actual basis in S1 stock) and $150 (the S1 shares' allocable portion of S1's net inside attribute amount), which is the maximum amount of inside loss that S can recognize. The proposed regulation uses deemed basis not only to identify the maximum potential amount of loss duplication ($150 in the example), but also to reduce attributes on the assumption that taxpayers will act in their best interest when deciding how lower-tier attributes will be recognized (subject to certain limits discussed in this section F.4.a).

S's deemed basis in S1 stock is also used for purposes of allocating S's attribute reduction amount between S's S1 stock and S's other attributes. However, for this purpose, deemed basis is treated as reduced by certain amounts that, by their nature, do not reflect loss. These excluded amounts include the value of S1 shares transferred in the transaction and the portion of S1's cash, S1's cash equivalents, and the value of S1's publicly traded property (net of S1's liabilities) that is attributable to S's nontransferred shares of S1 stock. The excluded amounts also include the corresponding amounts with respect to all shares of stock of lower-tier subsidiaries. These modifications prevent nonloss assets from inappropriately increasing the allocation of attribute reduction to S1 stock.

The attribute reduction amount allocated to S's block of S1 stock is then apportioned and applied to reduce the bases of S's individual shares of S1 stock in a manner that, to the greatest extent possible, reduces disparity. This general rule is subject to two modifications. First, no allocated amount is apportioned to any transferred S1 share if gain or loss is recognized on the transfer of that share. The reason is that the recognition of gain or loss (even if not allowed) establishes that the basis of that share does not reflect (or no longer reflects) unrecognized loss. This modification thus directs attribute reduction to other shares that are the source of the potential duplication. The second modification is that no allocated amount that is apportioned to any transferred S1 share is to be applied to reduce the basis of the share below its value. This modification prevents attribute reduction from knowingly creating gain on such shares.

To fully implement the loss duplication rule, any portion of S's attribute reduction amount that is allocated to S1 stock, whether or not it is apportioned or applied to reduce the basis of any S1 shares, tiers down and becomes an attribute reduction amount of S1. The attribute reduction rules then apply to reduce S1's attributes in the same manner that they apply S's attribute reduction amount to reduce S's attributes. However, because the attribute reduction amount represents the maximum potential amount of duplication in the lower-tier subsidiary, the proposed regulations include two modifications to prevent the reduction of attributes beyond the amount necessary to eliminate duplicated loss.

The first modification is the conforming limit rule, which prevents the tier down of attribute reduction from reducing S1's net inside attributes below the sum of the value of the S1 shares transferred by members and the aggregate bases that members have in nontransferred S1 stock (after any reduction to those shares by the direct application of S's attribute reduction amount).

The second modification is the basis restoration rule. This rule applies after the attribute reduction rule has been applied with respect to all transfers and all resulting reductions (whether as a result of direct or tier-down attribute reduction) have been given effect. This rule reverses stock basis reductions made by the attribute reduction rule, but only to the extent necessary to conform inside (net inside attributes) and outside (stock) basis at each tier, taking into account the effect of any prior section 362(e)(2) transactions. Because net inside attributes can be a negative number, stock basis may be a negative number even after basis restoration. In such cases, the basis of the share will remain an excess loss account in the hands of the owning member after the transaction (the regulations specifically provide that the excess loss account created by this rule is not taken into account under §1.1502–19). Basis restoration adjustments are made at each tier, but they do not give rise to any upper-tier adjustments.

With these two modifications, the attribute reduction rule can reduce lower-tier attributes in an amount that eliminates the full duplication potential reflected in S's basis in S1 stock and S1's net inside attributes without creating a noneconomic gain in the corresponding attribute.

b. *Election to reduce stock basis and/or reattribute loss.*

Finally, the attribute reduction rule contains an elective provision under which groups can reduce the potential for loss duplication and thereby reduce or completely avoid attribute reduction under these regulations. Under this rule, the common parent of a group can elect to reduce stock basis, reattribute attributes, or do some combination of basis reduction and attribute reattribution in order to prevent the reduction of attributes otherwise required under these proposed regulations. The total amount that can be the subject of the election is limited to the amount that S's attributes would otherwise be subject to reduction.

The election to reattribute attributes can only be made if S ceases to be a member of the P group as a result of the transfer. The reason is that the election is not intended to be merely a mechanism for changing location of items within a group (and its continuing members). The election can be made with respect to loss carryforwards and deferred deductions of S or any of S's lower-tier subsidiaries, but only to the extent and in the order that such attributes would otherwise have been reduced under the attribute reduction rule. However, P may only reattribute attributes of lower-tier subsidiaries that would otherwise be reduced as a result of tier-down attribute reduction to the extent that the reattribution does not create an excess loss account in the stock of any lower-tier subsidiary. When this election is made, P is treated as succeeding to the attributes as though it had acquired them in a section 381(a) transaction.

Proposed regulations under §1.1502–32 treat the reattributed attributes as absorbed and tiering up to reduce the basis of shares such that the full amount tiers up through the transferred S shares for which the election is made. This amount is allocated to shares in the chain with positive basis in a manner that reduces the disparity in the basis of the shares to the greatest extent possible. However, this amount is not allocated to any lower-tier subsidiary shares that were transferred in a transfer in which gain or loss was recognized. The IRS and Treasury Department recognize and are concerned with the potential complexity of this election and request comments regarding both the administrability and the benefit of the election, particularly as it relates to attributes of lower-tier subsidiaries.

Although the maximum amount of the election is computed by tentatively applying the attribute reduction rule to S, the election is actually given effect immediately before the application of the attribute reduction rule. Thus, to the extent loss duplication has not been eliminated by the election, the attribute reduction rules apply in their general manner.

5. *Over-ride provisions.*

These proposed regulations contain two over-ride provisions. One, found in the general introductory provisions of the proposed regulation, requires that the provisions of these proposed regulations be interpreted and applied in accordance with their stated purposes. The other, an anti-abuse and anti-avoidance rule, provides that "appropriate adjustments" will be made if a taxpayer acts with a view to avoid the purposes of this section or use this section to avoid another rule of law. The anti-abuse rule includes several examples that illustrate general principles. The examples are not intended to specify particular transactions that will be treated as abusive in all cases or to prevent the IRS from treating other transactions as abusive. This rule is an important safeguard to ensure that only transfers made in the ordinary course of business enjoy the benefits and avoid the burdens arising from the principles adopted in these proposed regulations.

6. *Special rules for section 362(e)(2) transactions.*

The IRS and Treasury Department recognize that adjustments made pursuant to section 362(e)(2) (see discussion in section H of this preamble) alter the extent to which comparisons of stock basis, net inside attributes, and value can identify both the amount of unrecognized appreciation reflected in stock basis and the amount of duplicated loss. For example, a reduction to asset basis under section 362(e)(2)(A) increases the disconformity amount of the shares received in the transaction subject to section 362(e)(2), but this amount does not represent unrealized appreciation reflected in stock basis. Further, the reduction to asset basis under section 362(e)(2)(A) decreases the amount of loss duplication that can exist with respect to the shares received in the transaction subject to section 362(e)(2). Similarly, if stock basis is reduced pursuant to an election under section 362(e)(2)(C), there is an increase in the subsidiary's net inside attribute amount that reduces the disconformity amount of all shares and increases aggregate inside loss, even though there has been neither a decrease in the amount of unrealized appreciation reflected in stock basis nor an increase in duplicated loss.

Accordingly, to adjust for distortions resulting from basis reduction under section 362(e)(2)(A), the proposed regulations adjust the disconformity amount of the shares received in the transaction to which section 362(e)(2) applied by an amount equal to the amount the basis of such shares would have been reduced had an election under section 362(e)(2)(C) been made. Further, for purposes of computing the attribute reduction amount on a transfer of any shares received in the section 362(e)(2) transaction, and applying the conforming limitation on the application of tier-down attribute reduction, the basis in such shares is reduced by an amount equal to the amount the basis of such shares would have been reduced had an election under section 362(e)(2)(C) been made. Similarly, to adjust for distortions resulting from basis reduction under section 362(e)(2)(C), for purposes of computing any share's disconformity amount or the subsidiary's aggregate inside loss, and for purposes of determining any stock basis restoration, the proposed regulations reduce S's net inside attribute amount by an amount equal to the amount S's attributes would have been reduced under section 362(e)(2)(A) had no election under section 362(e)(2)(C) been made. Further, the regulations indicate that the special application of section 362(e)(2) to intercompany transactions must be taken into account, so these adjustments only apply to the extent section 362(e)(2) has actually resulted in some basis reduction.

The IRS and Treasury Department recognize that the computations in these proposed regulations may need to take other items into account. Accordingly, the proposed regulations provide that the Commissioner will make appropriate adjustments to account for changes in the relationship between stock basis, net inside attributes, and value that are not the result of either §1.1502–32 or these proposed regulations and that are not otherwise adjusted under these proposed regulations. In addition, the proposed regulations provide that taxpayers may seek a written determination regarding the treatment of comparable items or adjustments.

7. *Special rules considered but not adopted.*

a. *Discounting of losses that are limited by section 382 or other provisions.*

The IRS and Treasury Department considered whether losses could be included in the computation of the net inside attribute amount at a reduced rate if their use was limited, for example, by section 382. Ultimately no administrable and precise method was identified for determining the extent to which losses could be considered properly excluded (or included at a reduced rate), except in the most extreme cases. Accordingly, the proposed regulations do not provide special rules for limited losses. As a result, losses are fully included in net inside attributes.

The IRS and Treasury Department recognize that this approach is extremely favorable to taxpayers as it reduces the disconformity amount (and thus the extent to which stock basis may be reduced) with the only potential cost being the elimination of the losses under the attribute reduction rule. The IRS and Treasury Department believe that this taxpayer-favorable result, when produced in the ordinary course of business, is not an inappropriate result as part of the overall balance reached by these regulations. Taxpayers that engage in transactions that have no *bona fide* purpose other than to acquire limited losses to avoid the purposes of the proposed regulations, however, will be subject to the anti-avoidance rule and the benefits of the transaction will be eliminated.

b. *Exceptions for basis conforming acquisitions.*

Practitioners had suggested that any proposed regulations addressing noneconomic loss contain an exception for transactions such as section 351 exchanges and acquisitions subject to a section 338 election. These proposed regulations do not explicitly contain such an exception. One reason is that such an exception would introduce the complexity and burden of identifying all redetermination events. A more important reason, however, is that such an exception is unnecessary under the basis disconformity model because, by measuring disconformity immediately before the transfer of loss shares, this rule automatically excludes situations from basis reduction when there is inside/outside conformity. Thus, the effect of this suggestion is accomplished and no special rules are necessary.

c. *Shadow account for reduced basis.*

The proposed regulations do not contain a mechanism, suggested by practitioners, for restoring basis to transferred shares that are retained by a member and later sold at a gain (for example, when a member retains S shares but S ceases to be a member). The IRS and Treasury Department are concerned that such a rule would add undue complexity to the regulatory scheme. Moreover, such a rule would be inconsistent with a fundamental principle underlying these proposed regulations, specifically, that a transfer (as defined in these proposed regulations) is the appropriate time for these proposed regulations to apply. Thus, the basis reduction rules do not permanently reduce the basis of lower-tier subsidiary stock unless the stock is transferred in the transaction. And, moreover, similar to the general application of other provisions of the Code and regulations, subsequent events should not reverse the effects of such application.

8. *Effective date.*

The proposed regulations would be applicable as of the date they are published as final regulations in the **Federal Register**.

G. *Sections 1.337(d)–1, 1.337(d)–2, and 1.1502–35.*

Because proposed §1.1502–36 addresses both noneconomic and duplicated loss on subsidiary stock, the IRS and Treasury Department are also proposing the removal of §§1.337(d)–1, 1.337(d)–2, and 1.1502–35, except to the extent necessary to address losses suspended under §1.1502–35(c) and losses reimported under §1.1502–35(g)(3).

Additionally, the IRS and Treasury Department intend to publish temporary regulations that will modify the anti-abuse provisions of §1.1502–35. First, the temporary regulations will restate the loss reimportation rule as a principle-based rule. This change responds to comments received about the administrability of the current provision. Second, the temporary regulations will modify the loss reimportation rule to provide that a duplicated loss on subsidiary stock is subject to the loss reimportation rule even if the group deconsolidates the subsidiary before selling loss shares of the subsidiary stock. These modifications are reflected in these proposed regulations.

These proposed regulations also revise several regulations solely to reflect the removal of §§1.337(d)–1, 1.337(d)–2, and 1.1502–35 (other than with respect to loss suspension and loss reimportation), and the addition of §1.1502–36.

The proposed regulations described in this section G would be applicable as of the date they are published as final regulations in the **Federal Register**.

H. *Suspension of Section 362(e)(2) in Consolidation.*

1. *Background.*

As part of the AJCA, Congress enacted section 362(e)(2) to address certain instances of loss duplication. Very generally, that provision provides that if loss property is transferred to a corporation in a section 351 exchange (or as a capital contribution or paid-in surplus), the transferee's aggregate basis in the assets will be limited to the properties' fair market value. However, section 362(e)(2) also permits the parties to elect to limit the basis of the stock received (or treated as received) in the exchange to its fair market value, so that the loss is preserved in the basis of the transferred property. Section 362(e)(2)(C). See REG–110405–05, 2006–48 I.R.B. 1004 [71 FR 62067] (October 23, 2006), ("the 2006 proposal") for a more detailed explanation of the general application of section 362(e)(2).

Practitioners have questioned whether it is necessary to apply section 362(e)(2) to intercompany transactions where there is a consolidated return rule addressing loss duplication. The IRS and Treasury Department recognize that loss duplication in consolidated groups is generally addressed by §1.1502–32 (when losses are recognized on a subsidiary's assets or operations) and, currently, by §1.1502–35 (or by this proposed §1.1502–36 when it is finalized). In general, the IRS and Treasury believe that these regulations together address loss duplication in a manner that is most consistent with single entity principles. Nevertheless, the IRS and Treasury Department are concerned that, if section 362(e)(2) were not to apply to intercompany transfers, members of consolidated groups may be able to reduce gain under circumstances that separate taxpayers could not. Accordingly, the IRS and Treasury Department have tentatively concluded that section 362(e)(2) should be applied to intercompany transactions. However, the IRS and Treasury are concerned with the administrative burden imposed by section 362(e)(2) and are continuing to study whether its provisions should be applicable to such transfers. Comments are invited on this issue.

2. *Suspension of section 362(e)(2) for intercompany transactions.*

Although the IRS and Treasury Department have tentatively concluded that section 362(e)(2) should remain applicable to transfers between members of a consolidated group, as noted, the IRS and Treasury Department are concerned with the significant complexity and administrative burden that section 362(e)(2) adds in the consolidated return context. For example, if an election is made to reduce stock basis under section 362(e)(2)(C), a portion of the items attributable to the transferred loss assets can produce duplicative reductions unless traced and treated as duplicative of the section 362(e)(2) reduction to stock basis.

Moreover, the IRS and Treasury Department recognize that basis reductions are not necessary in intercompany section 362(e)(2) transactions as long as duplication can effectively be eliminated by the general operation of the investment adjustment system. Accordingly, these proposed regulations would suspend application of section 362(e)(2) until the occurrence of a "section 362(e)(2) application event," and then apply the principles of section 362(e)(2) only to the extent the investment adjustment system has not eliminated and can no longer effectively eliminate any remaining duplication. The IRS and Treasury Department expect that this suspension will often effectively eliminate the application of section 362(e)(2) to most intercompany transactions.

Nevertheless, in order to apply section 362(e)(2) upon the occurrence of a section 362(e)(2) application event, the group must determine the extent to which an intercompany transaction resulted in loss duplication that would have been prevented by section 362(e)(2), and track the extent to which this duplication is effectively eliminated while the transferor and the transferee are members. Accordingly, these proposed regulations require the group to identify the amount and location of basis in the transferred assets that would have been eliminated had section 362(e)(2)(A) applied at the time of the intercompany transaction. This is the amount of the net built-in loss that is duplicated as a result of the section 362(e)(2) transaction. The regulations refer to this amount of duplication as the "section 362(e)(2) amount."

The duplicated loss is reflected in both the transferor's basis in the transferee stock (or securities), and in the transferee's basis in the property received. The duplication is initially reflected in the basis of the transferee stock (or securities) to the extent the basis would have been reduced under section 362(e)(2)(C), if such an election was made and section 362(e)(2) was not suspended by these temporary regulations. The duplication is also initially reflected in the transferee's basis in the property received to the extent the basis of such property would have been reduced under section 362(e)(2)(A) if no election was made under section 362(e)(2)(C) and section 362(e)(2) was not suspended by these temporary regulations. Over time this amount can be reflected in other attributes of the transferee (such as unabsorbed losses) to the extent such attributes are attributable to the transferee's basis in the property received.

3. *Elimination of the section 362(e)(2) amount.*

Because the investment adjustment system reduces stock basis as a subsidiary's attributes are taken into account, the duplication is eliminated to this extent, and the section 362(e)(2) amount must be eliminated to this extent. Further, if the basis of the stock (or securities) received in the intercompany section 362(e)(2) transaction is reduced as the result of a section 362(e)(2)(C) election, as a result of attribute reduction under these proposed regulations, or is otherwise eliminated without the recognition of gain or loss, the duplication is similarly eliminated. Accordingly, these types of basis reductions result in an elimination of all or a portion of the section 362(e)(2) amount. The proposed regulations provide specific guidance regarding how much of any remaining section 362(e)(2) amount is reflected in the basis of the subsidiary's stock (or securities) or the subsidiary's attributes as the section 362(e)(2) amount is eliminated.

4. *Application of section 362(e)(2) to intercompany transactions.*

Upon the occurrence of a section 362(e)(2) application event, the regulations apply section 362(e)(2) only to the extent necessary. A section 362(e)(2) application event occurs when all or a portion of the duplicated amount can no longer be effectively eliminated by the operation of the investment adjustment system, and can involve either the stock (or securities) of the transferee or the assets transferred in the intercompany section 362(e)(2) transaction. Such an event is defined to include any transfer (as defined in proposed §1.1502–36) of the transferee's stock received in the exchange, any satisfaction of a security received in the exchange, any transaction in which a nonmember acquires any of the transferred assets with substituted basis or succeeds to any attributes attributable to such basis, or any other transaction the result of which prevents all or a portion of any remaining section 362(e)(2) amount reflected in stock basis and attributes from being effectively eliminated by the operation of the investment adjustment system when taken into account.

Further, if the transferor and the transferee in the intercompany section 362(e)(2) transaction continue to be members of the same group (including as members of another group), the investment adjustment system can continue to effectively eliminate the duplication. Accordingly, these proposed regulations provide a subgroup exception implicit in the definition of section 362(e)(2) application events that allows the transferor and transferee to become members of a new group without triggering the application of section 362(e)(2). In such a case, the transferor and transferee will continue to track the section 362(e)(2) amount reflected in stock basis and attributes, and apply these provisions upon the occurrence of a section 362(e)(2) event.

Given the fact that section 362(e)(2) is applied in this context only to the extent necessary, the scope of its application varies slightly depending upon the type of section 362(e)(2) application event that occurs. If the application event involves a transaction in which a nonmember acquires some or all of the transferee's attributes that reflect a section 362(e)(2) amount, section 362(e)(2) applies to the extent such attributes reflect all or part of any remaining section 362(e)(2) amount. In such a case, the resulting reduction in attributes is applied to the attributes involved in the application event that reflect the section 362(e)(2) amount. If the application event involves all or part of the transferee stock (or securities) received in the section 362(e)(2) transaction, section 362(e)(2) applies to the extent such stock (or securities) reflect all or part of any remaining section 362(e)(2) amount. Further, in this case, the resulting reduction in attributes is applied proportionately to the transferee's attributes that reflect the section 362(e)(2) amount (based on the relative section 362(e)(2) amount reflected). The reduction in the transferee's attributes is not a noncapital, nondeductible expense.

As is provided in section 362(e)(2)(C), the transferor and transferee may elect to reduce the basis in the transferee stock (or securities) received in the intercompany section 362(e)(2) transaction instead of reducing the transferee's attributes. Similar to the provisions of the proposed regulations under section 362(e)(2), the reduction in the basis of the transferee stock (or securities) received in the intercompany section 362(e)(2) transaction is equal to the amount of the reduction in the transferee's attributes absent the election. Further, if this election is made, the type of section 362(e)(2) application event dictates which shares (or securities) receive the basis reduction. If the application event involves a transaction in which a nonmember acquires some or all of the transferee's attributes, the reduction is applied proportionately to all of the transferee stock (or securities) held by members immediately before the application event (based on the relative section 362(e)(2) amount reflected). However, if the application event involves all or a part of the transferee stock (or securities) received in the intercompany section 362(e)(2) transaction, the reduction is applied proportionately to the stock (or securities) so involved (based on the relative section 362(e)(2) amount reflected). The reduction in the basis of the stock of the transferee as a result of this election is treated as a nondeductible basis recovery item.

Under the proposed regulations, the election to reduce stock basis (in lieu of attributes) under section 362(e)(2)(C) may be made for the intercompany transaction on either the group return for the year of the intercompany section 362(e)(2) transaction or the year in which the first section 362(e)(2) application event occurs. In either case, the election has effect only if and to the extent there is a section 362(e)(2) application event, is irrevocable once made, and applies to all section 362(e)(2) application events with respect to such intercompany section 362(e)(2) transaction (even if the application event occurs at a time when the transferor and transferee are members of another consolidated group).

5. *Special allocations under §1.1502–32.*

The proposed regulations also include a special allocation provision in §1.1502–32 that requires all items taken into account by a group (including tier-ups of such amounts) that reflect a section 362(e)(2) amount to be allocated entirely to members' shares. In other words, such items are allocated as if any shares held by nonmembers were not outstanding. The reason for these special allocation rules is to prevent the general §1.1502–32 allocation of items to dilute the elimination of duplication where shares of subsidiary stock are held by nonmembers.

6. *Other considerations.*

In the 2006 proposal, the IRS and Treasury Department proposed regulations that would provide that the tracing rules in §1.358–2(a)(2) will not apply to stock received in a section 362(e)(2) transaction if the transferor and transferee elect to apply section 362(e)(2)(C). The IRS and Treasury requested comments regarding whether that treatment is appropriate. As noted in section H.4 of this preamble, these proposed regulations would allow the making of a section 362(e)(2)(C) election to be deferred until the year of the first section 362(e)(2) application event. The IRS and Treasury Department are aware of the potential difficulty and administrative burden associated with retroactively not applying the provisions of §1.358–2(a)(2). The IRS and Treasury Department continue to study this issue, and invite comments regarding whether the proposed revision to §1.358–2(a)(2)(viii) regarding section 362(e)(2)(C) elections should apply to intercompany transactions.

These proposed regulations would be applicable as of the date they are published as final regulations in the **Federal Register**.

I. *Other Revisions to the Consolidated Return Regulations.*

The IRS and Treasury Department are also proposing various technical and administrative revisions to the consolidated return regulations.

1. *Removal of §1.1502–13(f)(6)(ii).*

Section 1.1502–13(f)(6)(ii) prevents a member from recognizing gain on the qualified disposition of parent stock. However, §1.1502–13(f)(6)(ii) only applies to dispositions of parent stock occurring prior to May 16, 2000. Thus, the provision has no current applicability. Nevertheless, gain on dispositions of parent stock occurring on or after May 16, 2000, may qualify to be prevented by §1.1032–3, which has fewer conditions to its application than did §1.1502–13(f)(6)(ii). To avoid confusion, the IRS and Treasury Department propose replacing the current provisions in §1.1502–13(f)(6)(ii) (and references to that provision) with a reference to §1.1032–3.

2. *Modification of exception to definition of deconsolidation in §1.1502–19.*

Section 1.1502–19 provides rules for the determination and recapture of excess loss accounts. In general, an excess loss account is recaptured (taken into account) when there is a disposition of the stock to which the account relates. Section 1.1502–19(c) defines the term disposition for purposes of §1.1502–19. Under that section, the term disposition includes transfers, cancellations, deconsolidations, and worthlessness. The term deconsolidation is defined in §1.1502–19(c)(1)(ii).

In general, the termination of a consolidated group will give rise to the deconsolidation of the members of the group. However, §1.1502–19(c)(3)(i)(A) provides that, if a group terminates because a member of another group has acquired either the assets of the common parent of the terminating group (in a reorganization described in section 381(a)(2)) or the stock of the common parent, the members of the acquired group that become members of the acquiror's group are not treated as deconsolidated. Thus, there is no recapture of excess loss accounts in the shares of stock of subsidiaries of the acquired group that, after the acquisition, are held by a member of the acquiring group.

The exception to deconsolidation treatment in §1.1502–19(c)(3)(i)(A) (and therefore to the recapture of excess loss accounts) is warranted because its conditions ensure that the consolidated return provisions will continue to apply to the members of the acquired group. Thus, the provisions of §1.1502–19 are able to continue to regulate the determination and recapture of the excess loss accounts. However, for the continued application of the consolidated return provisions to the acquired group, it is only necessary that the acquiror be a member of a group following the acquisition. Its status prior to the acquisition is immaterial. The IRS and Treasury Department have therefore decided to revise the rule in §1.1502–19(c)(3)(i)(A) to require only that the acquiror be a member of a group following the qualified acquisition.

Thus, under the proposed regulations, the exception to deconsolidation treatment provided in §1.1502–19(c)(3)(i)(A) would be available when the acquisition is by a stand-alone corporation or a member of an affiliated, nonconsolidated group.

3. *Clarification of "substantially all" standard in §1.1502–19(c)(1)(iii)(A).*

Section 1.1502–19(c)(1)(iii) defines the term "worthless" for purposes of excess loss account recapture (resulting in the inclusion of the excess loss account in income). The definition of worthlessness in §1.1502–19(c)(1)(iii) is adopted for determining the time when subsidiary stock with positive basis may be treated as worthless (and therefore deductible). See §1.1502–80(c).

Section 1.1502–19(c)(1)(iii)(A) generally provides that a share of subsidiary stock will be treated as worthless when substantially all the subsidiary's assets are treated as disposed of, abandoned, or destroyed for federal tax purposes. This provision prevents an excess loss account from being included in income (and a worthless stock deduction from being taken) until the subsidiary's activities have been taken into account by the group. As a result, the group's income is clearly reflected and single entity treatment is promoted.

The current regulations do not, however, define the term "substantially all" for purposes of §1.1502–19(c)(1)(iii)(A). Particular concerns have arisen because the term is used in many other areas of tax law, most notably in the area of corporate reorganizations. Because different policies are operative in those areas, the thresholds appropriate in those areas are not necessarily appropriate for purposes of §1.1502–19(c)(1)(iii)(A) and the consolidated return provisions that incorporate it.

The IRS and Treasury Department believe that the single entity purpose of these consolidated return provisions is best effected by treating a subsidiary's stock as worthless only once the subsidiary has recognized all items of income, gain, deduction, and loss attributable to its assets and operations. Accordingly, these proposed regulations clarify §1.1502–19(c)(1)(iii)(A) by providing that stock of a subsidiary will be treated as worthless when the subsidiary has disposed of, abandoned, or destroyed (for Federal tax purposes) all its assets other than its corporate charter and those assets, if any, that are necessary to satisfy state law minimum capital requirements to maintain corporate existence.

4. *Triangular reorganizations that are also group structure changes.*

Sections 1.1502–30 and 1.1502–31 provide special rules for determining the basis of stock following, respectively, a triangular reorganization and a group structure change. The provisions both generally adopt net asset basis rules, but, in the case of a triangular reorganization, taxpayers can elect other rules in certain transactions. The regulations do not specify whether a group structure change that is also a triangular reorganization is subject to the basis rules applicable to group structure changes (under §1.1502–31) or to triangular reorganizations (under §1.1502–30). Because it is appropriate to conform the basis of the stock of the former common parent to its net asset basis in the case of any group structure change, the IRS and Treasury Department intend the rules of §1.1502–31 to control the determination of stock basis when a transaction is a group structure change, without regard to whether the transaction is also a triangular reorganization. Accordingly, the proposed regulations add a rule to clarify that §1.1502–31 governs the determination of basis in all cases to which it applies, even those that also qualify as triangular reorganizations.

5. *Allocations of investment adjustments to prevent or minimize excess loss accounts.*

Under §1.1502–32(c)(2)(i), positive investment adjustments allocated to a member's shares of a class of common stock are allocated first to equalize and eliminate excess loss accounts and then equally to all the member's other shares in that class. In the case of a negative adjustment, that section provides for the reduction of a member's positive basis in shares of a class of common stock before the creation or increase of an excess loss account in any such share. However, the current rule does not require that negative adjustments must be made first to equalize excess loss accounts before applying them equally to all shares. The proposed regulations add such a provision in order to better reflect the member's investment in its shares of subsidiary stock.

6. *Expired losses and attribute reduction under §1.1502–28.*

Section 1.1502–32(b)(3)(ii)(C)(*2*) provides that, if the amount of a discharge of indebtedness exceeds the amount of the related attribute reduction under §1.1502–28, that excess is treated as applying to reduce attributes to the extent of certain expired losses. In general, this section only applies to losses that expired without tax benefit, that were taken into account as noncapital, nondeductible expenses when they expired, and that would have been reduced had they not expired. The effect of this rule is to create a positive adjustment to the extent of the expired losses. The purpose of the rule, as stated in T.D. 8560, is to more fully integrate expired losses into the investment adjustment system.

As currently written, however, the rule does not explicitly state whether this special treatment of expired losses is available to all members' expired losses or only to the debtor-subsidiary's expired losses. Allowing such treatment for all members' expired losses is beyond the intended scope of relief and undermines the purpose of sections 108 and 1017, and §1.1502–28. Accordingly, §1.1502–32(b)(3)(ii)(C)(*2*) is revised to state explicitly that such treatment is intended only for the debtor-subsidiary's expired losses. The regulation is also revised to clarify that all available attributes, not just those of the debtor-subsidiary, must be reduced before this special rule for certain expired losses can apply.

7. *Applicability of other rules of law, anti-duplicative adjustments rules.*

Many of the consolidated return rules include provisions stating that other rules of law continue to apply. These provisions are generally unnecessary in light of §1.1502–80(a), which provides that the provisions of the Code continue to apply to taxpayers filing a consolidated return unless specifically provided otherwise in the consolidated return regulations. However, these provisions often also contain statements that the consolidated return provisions modify other rules of law and that duplicative adjustments should not be made as a result of the consolidated return provisions. To simplify the regulations and remove any potential negative implication from the absence of such a provision in a particular provision, these proposed regulations incorporate all of these principles in §1.1502–80(a) and remove similar provisions from other sections of the consolidated return regulations.

8. *Retention of, and nonsubstantive revisions to, §1.1502–80(c).*

Section 1.1502–80(c) provides that subsidiary stock is not treated as worthless until the earlier of the time that the subsidiary ceases to be a member of the group and the time that the stock is worthless within the meaning of §1.1502–19(c)(1)(iii). This rule, with its companion rule postponing the inclusion in income of excess loss accounts, prevents a group from recognizing any amount (whether loss or gain) on subsidiary stock until the subsidiary has taken into account all of its operating income, gain, deduction, and loss. Thus, the rule promotes single entity treatment by enabling the group to continue treating its investment in subsidiary stock as an investment in the subsidiary's assets and operations until the subsidiary has either taken all of its items into account or ceased to be a member of the group.

Following the *Rite Aid* decision, practitioners have submitted comments suggesting that §1.1502–80(c) should be removed from the consolidated return regulations. The suggestion was based on the observation that §1.1502–80(c) prevented inappropriate disallowance under the LDR and, since the LDR no longer applies to stock dispositions, §1.1502–80(c) is no longer necessary. While it is correct that there is no longer an LDR-based justification for the rule in §1.1502–80(c), the LDR was neither the only nor the principal purpose for the rule. The principal purpose of the rule was, and is, to promote single entity treatment. And, with its companion rule governing the inclusion of excess loss accounts, this rule continues to do that.

In addition, the IRS and Treasury Department recognize that, to the extent a subsidiary's attributes would survive a worthlessness event (for example, when a subsidiary survives and is owned by its creditors following a bankruptcy), §1.1502–80(c) benefits the group by postponing the time that the subsidiary's stock is treated as worthless. Because section 382(g)(4)(D) could subject S's losses to a zero section 382 limitation if P were to treat S's stock as worthless during bankruptcy, a court might prevent P from treating S's stock as worthless in an earlier year, effectively denying P any worthlessness deduction. See *In re Prudential Lines, Inc.*, 928 F.2d 565 (2d Cir. 1991), *cert. denied*, 112 S.Ct. 82 (1991).

Accordingly, the IRS and Treasury Department have rejected the suggestion to remove §1.1502–80(c). The proposed regulations do, however, revise the language of the current rule solely for the purpose of clarifying its operation. No substantive change is intended.

9. *Effective dates.*

The proposed regulations described in this section I would be applicable as of the date they are published as final regulations in the **Federal Register**.

J. *Request for Comments.*

As described in this preamble, many approaches and combinations of approaches were considered with respect to both noneconomic and duplicated loss and, although the IRS and Treasury Department believe the approach adopted in these proposed regulations best responds to and balances the Congressional mandates, comments are requested concerning both the approach adopted in these proposed regulations and other possible approaches.

As noted in section D of this preamble, the IRS and Treasury Department are continuing to study, and invite comments on, the issue of gain duplication by consolidated groups. Comments are specifically requested concerning the circumstances under which gain duplication should be addressed and the mechanisms that could be adopted to do so. For example, comments could address whether a gain duplication rule could or should parallel the approach to loss duplication suggested in the proposed regulations, or whether some other approach would be more appropriate or administrable. Comments are also requested regarding limitations that may be necessary or appropriate to address concerns such as attribute churning and conversion. In addition, comments are requested concerning the noneconomic reduction of stock gain (that is, the appropriateness of the continued use of a loss disallowance model) and the reduction of noneconomic stock gain (that is, the reduction of basis through the absorption of built-in losses or net built-in losses), and the extent to which it would be appropriate to address gain duplication without addressing these issues.

As noted in section H of this preamble, the IRS and Treasury Department are continuing to study the application of section 362(e)(2) in the consolidated setting. Comments are specifically requested concerning the general application of section 362(e)(2) to intercompany transactions, as well as the administrability and appropriateness of the proposed rules suspending the application of section 362(e)(2) to intercompany transactions and specially allocating items attributable to intercompany section 362(e)(2) transactions.

Although these regulations are generally proposed to be applicable when published as final regulations in the **Federal Register**, the IRS and Treasury Department invite comments regarding the extent to which it would be appropriate and desirable to allow taxpayers to elect to apply these provisions retroactively.

Special Analyses

It has been determined that this notice of proposed rulemaking is not a significant regulatory action as defined in Executive Order 12866. Therefore, a regulatory assessment is not required. It is hereby certified that these regulations will not have a significant economic impact on a substantial number of small entities. This certification is based on the fact that these regulations primarily will affect affiliated groups of corporations that have elected to file consolidated returns, which tend to be larger entities. Therefore, a Regulatory Flexibility Analysis under the Regulatory Flexibility Act (5 U.S.C. chapter 6) is not required. Pursuant to section 7805(f), this regulation has been submitted to the Chief Counsel for Advocacy of the Small Business Administration for comment on its impact on small business.

Comments and Requests for Public Hearing

Before these proposed regulations are adopted as final regulations, consideration will be given to any written (a signed original and eight (8) copies) or electronic comments that are submitted timely to the IRS. The IRS and Treasury Department request comments on the clarity of the proposed regulations and how they can be made easier to understand. All comments will be available for public inspection and copying. A public hearing will be scheduled if requested in writing by any person that timely submits written comments. If a public hearing is scheduled, notice of the date, time, and place for the public hearing will be published in the **Federal Register**.

Drafting Information

The principal authors of these regulations are Theresa Abell and Phoebe Bennett of the Office of Associate Chief Counsel (Corporate). However, other personnel from the IRS and Treasury Department participated in their development.

* * * * *

Proposed Amendments to the Regulations

Accordingly, 26 CFR part 1 is proposed to be amended as follows:

PART 1—INCOME TAXES

Paragraph 1. The authority citation for part 1 is amended by adding an entry in numerical order to read in part as follows:

Authority: 26 U.S.C. 7805 * * *

Section 1.1502–36 also issued under 26 U.S.C. 1502 * * *

Section 1.1502–36 also issued under 26 U.S.C. 337(d). * * *

§1.337(d)–1 [Removed]

Par. 2. Section 1.337(d)–1 is removed.

§1.337(d)–2 [Removed]

Par. 3. Section 1.337(d)–2 is removed.

Par. 4. Section 1.358–6 is amended by:

1. Revising paragraph (e).

2. Adding new paragraph (f)(3).

The revision and addition read as follows:

§1.358–6 Stock basis in certain triangular reorganizations.

* * * * *

(e) *Cross-reference regarding triangular reorganizations involving members of a consolidated group.* For rules relating to stock basis adjustments made as a result of a triangular reorganization in which P and S, or P and T, as applicable, are, or become, members of a consolidated group, see §1.1502–30. However, if a transaction is a group structure change, even if it is also a triangular reorganization, stock basis adjustments are determined under §1.1502–31.

* * * * *

(f) * * *

(3) *Special rule for triangular reorganizations involving members of a consolidated group.* Paragraph (e) of this section shall apply to all transfers on or after the date these regulations are published as final regulations in the **Federal Register**.

Par. 5. Section 1.1502–13 is amended by:

1. Revising paragraphs (a)(4), (f)(6)(ii), and (j)(5)(i)(A).

2. Adding new paragraph (e)(4).

3. Revising the last sentence of paragraph (f)(6)(iv)(A).

4. Removing the second sentence in paragraph (f)(6)(v).

5. Adding a new last sentence to paragraph (l)(1).

The revisions and additions read as follows:

§1.1502–13 Intercompany transactions.

(a) * * *

(4) *Application of other rules of law.* See §1.1502–80(a) regarding the general applicability of other rules of law and a limitation on duplicative adjustments.

* * * * *

(e) * * *

(4) *Intercompany section 362(e)(2) transactions*—(i) *Purpose and scope.* This paragraph (e)(4) provides simplifying rules for intercompany transactions that are subject to section 362(e)(2) (intercompany section 362(e)(2) transactions). The purpose of this paragraph (e)(4) is to suspend the application of section 362(e)(2) during the period of time that the duplication resulting from the intercompany section 362(e)(2) transaction (the section 362(e)(2) amount, as defined in paragraph (e)(4)(ii)(A) of this section) can effectively be eliminated by the operation of the investment adjustment provisions of §1.1502–32. The amount and location of this duplication is identified and tracked while in the consolidated group. When this duplication can no longer effectively be eliminated by the investment adjustment provisions, the principles of section 362(e)(2) apply to the extent necessary to eliminate all or a portion of any remaining section 362(e)(2) amount (as defined in paragraph (e)(4)(ii)(B) of this section) reflected in B's attributes or stock. For purposes of this paragraph (e)(4), any reference to B stock received in an intercompany section 362(e)(2) transaction refers to B stock or B securities received (or deemed received) without the recognition of gain or loss.

(ii) *Identification and elimination of section 362(e)(2) amount*—(A) *Section 362(e)(2) amount.* The *section 362(e)(2) amount* is the amount of duplication resulting from an intercompany section 362(e)(2) transaction, and is equal to the amount by which B's basis in the assets received in an intercompany section 362(e)(2) transaction would have, but for the application of this paragraph (e)(4), been eliminated under section 362(e)(2)(A) (absent an election under section 362(e)(2)(C)). Such amount is initially reflected in both the basis of the B stock received in the transaction and B's basis in the assets received. Each share of B stock initially reflects the section 362(e)(2) amount to the extent the basis would have been reduced under section 362(e)(2)(C) if such an election was made and this paragraph (e)(4) did not apply. B's basis in each asset received initially reflects the section 362(e)(2) amount to the extent the basis in such asset would have been reduced under section 362(e)(2)(A) if no election was made under section 362(e)(2)(C) and this paragraph (e)(4) did not apply. However, over time the section 362(e)(2) amount may be reflected in B's basis in assets, deferred items, or other unabsorbed losses (B's attributes).

(B) *Remaining section 362(e)(2) amount.* The *remaining section 362(e)(2) amount* is the portion of the section 362(e)(2) amount that has not been eliminated.

(C) *Elimination of section 362(e)(2) amount*—*(1) Elimination caused by reduction in B's attributes.* The section 362(e)(2) amount is eliminated as B's attributes that reflect the section 362(e)(2) amount are taken into account by the group (including as a result of attribute reduction under paragraph (e)(4)(iv) of this section, or §1.1502–36(d) to the extent it did not reduce the basis in B stock that reflects the section 362(e)(2) amount). The portions of B's attributes that reflect a section 362(e)(2) amount are generally taken into account by the group proportionately. However, because any reduction in B's attributes under paragraph (e)(4)(iv) of this section is applied to reduce attributes that reflect the section 362(e)(2) amount, the section 362(e)(2) amount is eliminated to the extent of the full amount of such reduction. If the section 362(e)(2) amount is eliminated because B's attributes that reflect the section 362(e)(2) amount are taken into account, each share of B stock received in the intercompany section 362(e)(2) transaction that is held by a member is treated as proportionately reflecting the remaining section 362(e)(2) amount (based on the section 362(e)(2) amount reflected before the elimination).

(*2*) *Elimination caused by reduction in basis in B stock.* The section 362(e)(2) amount is also eliminated to the extent the basis in B stock that reflects the section 362(e)(2) amount is reduced under paragraph (e)(4)(v) of this section, is reduced under §1.1502–36(d), or is otherwise eliminated (other than under §1.1502–32) without the recognition of gain or loss. The portion of the basis in a share of B stock that reflects a section 362(e)(2) amount is so reduced or eliminated before any other portion of the basis in such a share. If the section 362(e)(2) amount is eliminated as provided in this paragraph (e)(4)(ii)(C)(*2*), each of B's attributes that reflected the section 362(e)(2) amount is treated as proportionately reflecting the remaining section 362(e)(2) amount (based on the section 362(e)(2) amount reflected before the elimination).

(iii) *Section 362(e)(2) application event.* A section 362(e)(2) application event is any transaction or event that results in—

(A) A transfer (within the meaning of §1.1502–36(f)(11)) of any of the B stock that was received in the intercompany section 362(e)(2) transaction;

(B) Any satisfaction (actual or deemed) of a security received in an intercompany section 362(e)(2) transaction without the recognition of gain or loss;

(C) Any nonmember holding an asset with a substituted basis that reflects all or a portion of the remaining section 362(e)(2) amount or succeeding to an attribute that reflects all or a portion of the remaining section 362(e)(2) amount; or

(D) Any other transaction the result of which prevents all or a portion of any remaining section 362(e)(2) amount reflected in stock basis or attributes from being effectively eliminated by the operation of the investment adjustment provisions of §1.1502–32 when taken into account.

(iv) *General rule.* In the case of an intercompany section 362(e)(2) transaction, no adjustment to B's attributes shall be made under section 362(e)(2) until immediately before a section 362(e)(2) application event (as defined in paragraph (e)(4)(iii) of this section). At that time, unless an election is made under paragraph (e)(4)(v) of this section, B reduces its attributes that reflect the remaining section 362(e)(2) amount as provided in this paragraph (e)(4)(iv).

(A) *Amount of reduction.* If the application event involves B's attributes that reflect all or a portion of the remaining section 362(e)(2) amount, the amount of the reduction is equal to the remaining section 362(e)(2) amount reflected in the attributes so involved. If the application event involves all or a portion of the B stock received in the intercompany section 362(e)(2) transaction, the amount of the reduction is equal to the remaining section 362(e)(2) amount reflected in the B stock so involved.

(B) *Application of reduction.* If the application event involves B's attributes that reflect all or a portion of the remaining section 362(e)(2) amount, the reduction is applied to reduce each attribute so involved by the full amount of the remaining section 362(e)(2) amount reflected in each such attribute. If the application event involves all or a portion of the B stock received in the intercompany section 362(e)(2) transaction, the reduction is applied proportionately (based on the remaining section 362(e)(2) amount reflected in each attribute prior to reduction) to all of B's attributes that reflect the remaining section 362(e)(2) amount.

(C) *Effect of the reduction.* Any reduction to B's attributes under this paragraph (e)(4)(iv) is not a noncapital, nondeductible expense described in §1.1502–32(b)(2)(iii).

(v) *Election to reduce the basis in B stock.* In lieu of reducing B's attributes as provided in paragraph (e)(4)(iv) of this section, S and B may elect to reduce the basis in the B stock received in the intercompany section 362(e)(2) transaction as provided in this paragraph (e)(4)(v).

(A) *Amount of reduction.* The basis in the B stock is reduced by an amount equal to the amount B would otherwise be required to reduce its attributes under paragraph (e)(4)(iv) of this section.

(B) *Application of reduction.* If the application event involves B's attributes that reflect all or a portion of the remaining section 362(e)(2) amount, the reduction is applied proportionately (based on the remaining section 362(e)(2) amount reflected in the B stock prior to reduction) to all of the B stock received in the intercompany section 362(e)(2) transaction that is held by members immediately before the application event. If the application event involves all or a portion of the B stock received in the intercompany section 362(e)(2) transaction, the reduction is applied proportionately (based on the remaining section 362(e)(2) amount reflected in the B stock prior to reduction) to the B stock so involved. Any reduction in the basis of the B stock under this paragraph (e)(4)(v) is applied immediately before the section 362(e)(2) application event.

(C) *Effect of the reduction.* Any reduction to the basis of the B stock under this paragraph (e)(4)(v) is a nondeductible basis recovery item described in §1.1502–32(b)(3)(iii)(B).

(D) *Election.* The election is made in the manner described in regulations implementing section 362(e)(2). The election must be made for an intercompany section 362(e)(2) transaction on or with the group return for either the year in which the intercompany section 362(e)(2) transaction or the first section 362(e)(2) application event occurs. The election is irrevocable and applicable for all section 362(e)(2) application events with respect to such intercompany section 362(e)(2) transaction (even if the event occurs while S and B are members of another consolidated group). If the election is made on or with the return for the year of the intercompany section 362(e)(2) transaction, it has effect only if and to the extent there is a remaining section 362(e)(2) amount when there is a section 362(e)(2) application event.

(vi) *Examples.* The application of this paragraph (e)(4) is illustrated by the following examples:

Example 1. Section 362(e)(2) amount reflected in asset basis. (i) *Facts.* P owns the sole outstanding share of S stock. S owns Asset 1 with a basis of $100 and a value of $20. On January 1, year 1, S contributes Asset 1 to newly formed B in exchange for 10 shares of B stock in a transaction to which section 351 applies. At the end of year 1, B's only item is a $10 depreciation deduction with respect to Asset 1, which gives rise to a $10 loss that is absorbed by the group.

On January 1, year 2, S sells all 10 shares of B stock for $18. After applying and giving effect to all generally applicable rules of law, S's basis in each share of B stock is $9 (the original $10 basis reduced by $1 loss attributable to the depreciation on Asset 1). No election is made under section 362(e)(2)(C).

(ii) *Suspension of section 362(e)(2) in year 1.* S's contribution of Asset 1 to B is an intercompany transaction to which section 362(e)(2) applies. Under the general rules of section 362(e)(2)(A), B's basis in Asset 1 would be reduced by $80 to its value, $20. However, as described in this paragraph (e)(4), the transfer is an intercompany section 362(e)(2) transaction and therefore, under paragraph (e)(4)(iv) of this section, no adjustment is made under section 362(e)(2) until there is a section 362(e)(2) application event. The $80 reduction that B would have had in its basis in Asset 1 is a section 362(e)(2) amount described in paragraph (e)(4)(ii)(A) of this section. This amount is reflected ratably in S's basis in the 10 shares of B stock, and in B's basis in Asset 1. There is no section 362(e)(2) application event in year 1 and so there is no section 362(e)(2) adjustment in year 1.

(iii) *Application of section 362(e)(2) on sale of B stock.* S's sale of the B stock is a transfer within the meaning of §1.1502–36(f)(11) and therefore a section 362(e)(2) application event under paragraph (e)(4)(iii)(A) of this section. Accordingly, under paragraphs (e)(4)(iv)(A) and (e)(4)(iv)(B) of this section, because the section 362(e)(2) application event was caused by the transfer of B stock received in the intercompany section 362(e)(2) transaction, B must reduce its basis in Asset 1 that reflects the remaining section 362(e)(2) amount by an amount equal to the remaining section 362(e)(2) amount reflected in the B stock involved in the application event. Because S sold all of the B stock received in the intercompany section 362(e)(2) transaction and this stock reflects all of the section 362(e)(2) amount, B must reduce its basis in Asset 1 by the full amount of the remaining section 362(e)(2) amount immediately before the application event. Although there was originally an $80 section 362(e)(2) amount, $8 of that amount ($80/$100 x $10) was eliminated under paragraph (e)(4)(ii)(C)(*1*) of this section when the loss attributable to the depreciation deduction on Asset 1 was absorbed in year 1. Thus, at the time of the sale, the remaining section 362(e)(2) amount is only $72 ($80 less $8), and B's basis in Asset 1 is reduced by such amount, to $18. Under paragraph (e)(4)(iv)(C) of this section, the reduction in the basis of Asset 1 is not a noncapital, nondeductible expense described in §1.1502–32(b)(2)(iii) and so has no effect on S's basis in its B shares. See §1.1502–36 for additional rules relating to loss on shares of subsidiary stock.

Example 2. Section 362(e)(2) amount reflected in unabsorbed loss. (i) *Facts.* The facts are the same as in *Example 1*, except that during year 1 B sells Asset 1 to an unrelated nonmember for $20, and recognizes an $80 loss that is not absorbed by the group.

(ii) *Suspension of section 362(e)(2) in year 1.* As in paragraph (ii) of *Example 1*, S's contribution of Asset 1 to B is an intercompany section 362(e)(2) transaction, the section 362(e)(2) amount is $80, and there is no section 362(e)(2) adjustment in year 1. This amount is reflected ratably in S's basis in the 10 shares of B stock, and initially in B's basis in Asset 1. Further, because the $80 loss recognized on the sale of Asset 1 is not absorbed by the group, at the end of year 1 the remaining section 362(e)(2) amount is $80, reflected ratably in S's basis in the 10 shares of B stock, and in B's unabsorbed $80 loss.

(iii) *Application of section 362(e)(2) on sale of B stock.* As in paragraph (iii) of *Example 1*, S's sale of the 10 shares of B stock is a section 362(e)(2) application event that involves all of the B stock received in the intercompany section 362(e)(2) transaction. Accordingly, immediately before the application event, B must reduce the unabsorbed loss carryover that reflects the remaining section 362(e)(2) amount by an amount equal to the remaining section 362(e)(2) amount reflected in the B stock involved in the application event, $80 (all of the remaining section 362(e)(2) amount). The reduction of the loss carryover is not a noncapital, nondeductible expense described in §1.1502–32(b)(2)(iii) and so has no effect on S's basis in its B shares. See §1.1502–36 for additional rules relating to loss on shares of subsidiary stock.

Example 3. Section 362(e)(2) amount reflected in unabsorbed loss, partial application. (i) *Facts.* The facts are the same as in *Example 2*, except that on January 1, year 2, S only sells two shares of the B stock to an unrelated nonmember for $4.

(ii) *Suspension of section 362(e)(2) in year 1.* S's contribution of Asset 1 to B is an intercompany section 362(e)(2) transaction, the section 362(e)(2) amount is $80, and there is no section 362(e)(2) adjustment in year 1. This amount is reflected ratably in S's basis in the 10 shares of B stock, and initially in B's basis in Asset 1. Further, because the $80 loss recognized on the sale of Asset 1 is not absorbed by the group, at the end of year 1 the remaining section 362(e)(2) amount is $80, reflected ratably in S's basis in the 10 shares of B stock, and in B's unabsorbed $80 loss.

(iii) *Application of section 362(e)(2) on sale of B stock.* S's sale of two of the shares of B stock is a section 362(e)(2) application event that involves two shares of the B stock received in the intercompany section 362(e)(2) transaction. Accordingly, immediately before the application event, B must reduce the unabsorbed loss carryover that reflects the remaining section 362(e)(2) amount by an amount equal to the remaining section 362(e)(2) amount reflected in the B stock involved in the application event, $16 ($8 of the remaining section 362(e)(2) amount reflected in each share). The loss carryover is reduced from $80 to $64. This reduction is not a noncapital, nondeductible expense described in §1.1502–32(b)(2)(iii) and so has no effect on S's basis in its B shares. Additionally, under paragraph (e)(4)(ii)(C)(*1*) of this section, $16 of the remaining section 362(e)(2) amount is eliminated, and, thereafter, the $64 remaining section 362(e)(2) amount is ratably reflected in S's basis in the remaining 8 shares of B stock and in B's $64 loss carryover. Because no election is made under section 362(e)(2)(C) in the year of the intercompany section 362(e)(2) transaction or in the year of the stock sale, the first section 362(e)(2) application event, no such election can be made with respect to the remaining shares received in the intercompany section 362(e)(2)(C) transaction. See §1.1502–36 for additional rules relating to loss on shares of subsidiary stock.

(iv) *Application of section 362(e)(2) on sale of B stock, section 362(e)(2)(C) election.* If S and B elect under paragraph (e)(4)(v) of this section to reduce S's basis in the B stock received in the intercompany section 362(e)(2) transaction, under paragraph (e)(4)(v)(A) of this section S will reduce its basis in the B stock by $16 (an amount equal to the amount that B would otherwise be required to reduce its loss carryover, or the remaining section 362(e)(2) amount reflected in the two shares of B stock sold). Under paragraph (e)(4)(v)(B) of this section, this $16 reduction is applied proportionately to the two shares of B stock sold immediately before the application event, reducing the basis of each share to $2. The reduction in the basis of the two B shares sold is a nondeductible basis recovery item described in §1.1502–32(b)(3)(iii)(B), and will affect P's basis in its share of S stock. Additionally, under paragraph (e)(4)(ii)(C)(*2*) of this section, $16 of the remaining section 362(e)(2) amount is eliminated, and, thereafter, the $64 remaining section 362(e)(2) amount is ratably reflected in S's basis in the remaining 8 shares of B stock and in B's $80 loss carryover. S recognizes no gain or loss on the sale of these two shares of B stock. Under paragraph (e)(4)(v)(D) of this section, S and B's election to reduce S's basis in the B stock is irrevocable and applicable to all future section 362(e)(2) application events with respect to this intercompany section 362(e)(2) transaction, such as subsequent dispositions of B stock to an unrelated nonmember.

Example 4. Section 362(e)(2) amount reflected in unabsorbed loss, subgroup exception. (i) *Facts.* The facts are the same as in *Example 3*, except that S does not sell any shares of B stock, and on January 1, year 2, P sells the sole share of the S stock to P1, the common parent of another consolidated group.

(ii) *Suspension of section 362(e)(2) in year 1.* S's contribution of Asset 1 to B is an intercompany section 362(e)(2) transaction, the section 362(e)(2) amount is $80, and there is no section 362(e)(2) adjustment in year 1. This amount is reflected ratably in S's basis in the 10 shares of B stock, and initially in B's basis in Asset 1. Further, because the $80 loss recognized on the sale of Asset 1 is not absorbed by the group, at the end of year 1 the remaining section 362(e)(2) amount is $80, reflected ratably in S's basis in the 10 shares of B stock, and in B's unabsorbed $80 loss.

(iii) *No section 362(e)(2) application event on sale of S stock.* P's sale of the S stock is not an application event described in paragraph (e)(4)(iii) of this section. Further, because S and B continue to be members of the same consolidated group, there is no transfer (within the meaning of §1.1502–36(f)(11)) of the 10 shares of B stock. Accordingly, there is no application event and, under paragraph (e)(4)(iv) of this section, no section 362(e)(2) adjustment is required. However, adjustments will be required if a section 362(e)(2) application event occurs at a time when there is a remaining section 362(e)(2) amount.

* * * * *

(f) * * *

(6) * * *

(ii) *Gain stock.* For dispositions of P stock occurring before May 16, 2000, see §1.1502–13(f)(6)(ii) as contained in 26 CFR part 1 in effect on April 1, 2000. For dispositions of P stock occurring on or after May 16, 2000, see §1.1032–3.

* * * * *

(iv) * * * (A) * * * If P grants M an option to acquire P stock in a transaction meeting the requirements of §1.1032–3, M is treated as having purchased the option from P for fair market value with cash contributed to M by P.

* * * * *

(j) * * *

(5) * * * (i) * * *

(A) The acquisition of either the assets of the common parent of the terminating group in a reorganization described in section 381(a)(2), or the stock of the common parent of the terminating group; or

* * * * *

(l) * * * (1) * * * Paragraphs (a)(4), (e)(4), (f)(6)(ii), (f)(6)(iv)(A), and (j)(5)(i)(A) of this section apply to all transfers on or after the date these regulations are published as final regulations in the **Federal Register**.

* * * * *

Par. 6. Section 1.1502–19 is amended by:

1. Revising paragraphs (a)(3), (c)(1)(iii)(A), and (c)(3)(i)(A).

2. Adding a new last sentence to paragraph (h)(1).

The revisions and addition read as follows:

§1.1502–19 Excess loss accounts.

(a) * * *

(3) *Application of other rules of law.* See §1.1502–80(a) regarding the general applicability of other rules of law and a limitation on duplicative adjustments. In addition, for purposes of this section, the definitions in §1.1502–32 apply.

* * * * *

(c) * * *

(1) * * *

(iii) * * *

(A) All of S's assets (other than its corporate charter and those assets, if any, necessary to satisfy state law minimum capital requirements to maintain corporate existence) are treated as disposed of, abandoned, or destroyed for Federal income tax purposes (for example, under section 165(a) or §1.1502–80(c), or, if S's asset is stock of a lower-tier member, the stock is treated as disposed of under this paragraph (c)). An asset of S is not considered to be disposed of or abandoned to the extent the disposition is in complete liquidation of S under section 332 or is in exchange for consideration (other than in satisfaction of indebtedness);

* * * * *

(3) * * * (i) * * *

(A) The acquisition of either the assets of the common parent of the terminating group in a reorganization described in section 381(a)(2), or the stock of the common parent of the terminating group; or

* * * * *

(h) * * * (1) * * * Paragraphs (a)(3), (c)(1)(iii)(A), and (c)(3)(i)(A) of this section apply to all transfers on or after the date these regulations are published as final regulations in the **Federal Register**.

* * * * *

§1.1502–20 [Removed]

Par. 7. Section 1.1502–20 is removed.

Par. 8. Section 1.1502–21 is amended by:

1. Removing the last sentence of paragraph (b)(1).

2. Removing paragraph (b)(3)(v).

3. Revising paragraphs (b)(2)(ii)(A), (b)(2)(iv)(B)(*2*), (h)(6), and (h)(8).

4. Adding new paragraph (h)(1)(iii).

The revisions and addition read as follows:

§1.1502–21 Net operating losses.

* * * * *

(b) * * *

(2) * * *

(ii) *Special rules*—(A) *Year of departure from group.* If a corporation ceases to be a member during a consolidated return year, net operating loss carryovers attributable to the corporation are first carried to the consolidated return year, then are subject to reduction under section 108 and §1.1502–28 (regarding discharge of indebtedness income that is excluded from gross income under section 108(a)), and then are subject to reduction under §1.1502–36 (regarding transfers of loss shares of subsidiary stock). Only the amount that is neither absorbed nor reduced under section 108 and §1.1502–28 or under §1.1502–36 may be carried to the corporation's first separate return year. For rules concerning a member departing a subgroup, see paragraph (c)(2)(vii) of this section.

* * * * *

(iv) * * *

(B) * * *

(*2*) *Special rules*—(*i*) *Carryback to a separate return year.* If a portion of the CNOL attributable to a member for a taxable year is carried back to a separate return year, the percentage of the CNOL attributable to each member, as of immediately after such portion of the CNOL is carried back, is recomputed pursuant to paragraph (b)(2)(iv)(B)(*2*)(*v*) of this section.

(*ii*) *Excluded discharge of indebtedness income.* If during a taxable year a member realizes discharge of indebtedness income that is excluded from gross income under section 108(a) and such amount reduces any portion of the CNOL attributable to any member pursuant to section 108 and §1.1502–28, the percentage of the CNOL attributable to each member as of immediately after the reduction of attributes pursuant to sections 108 and 1017, and §1.1502–28, shall be recomputed pursuant to paragraph (b)(2)(iv)(B)(*2*)(*v*) of this section.

(*iii*) *Departing member.* If during a taxable year a member that had a separate net operating loss for the year of the CNOL ceases to be a member, the percentage of the CNOL attributable to each member as of the first day of the following consolidated return year shall be recomputed pursuant to paragraph (b)(2)(iv)(B)(*2*)(*v*) of this section.

(*iv*) *Reduction of attributes for stock loss.* If during a taxable year a member does not cease to be a member of the group and any portion of the CNOL attributable to any member is reduced pursuant to §1.1502–36, the percentage of the CNOL attributable to each member immediately after the reduction of attributes pursuant to §1.1502–36 shall be recomputed pursuant to paragraph (b)(2)(iv)(B)(*2*)(*v*) of this section.

(*v*) *Recomputed percentage.* The recomputed percentage of the CNOL attributable to each member shall equal the unabsorbed CNOL attributable to the member at the time of the recomputation divided by the sum of the unabsorbed CNOL attributable to all of the members at the time of the recomputation. For purposes of the preceding sentence, a CNOL that is reduced pursuant to section 108 and §1.1502–28, or under §1.1502–36, or that is otherwise permanently disallowed or eliminated, shall be treated as absorbed.

(*vi*) *Examples*. For purposes of the examples in this section, unless otherwise stated, all groups file consolidated returns, all corporations have calendar taxable years, the facts set forth the only corporate activity, value means fair market value and the adjusted basis of each asset equals its value, all transactions are with unrelated persons, and the application of any limitation or threshold under section 382 is disregarded. * * *

* * * * *

(h) * * * (1) * * *

(iii) Paragraphs (b)(2)(ii)(A) and (b)(2)(iv)(B)(*2*) of this section apply to taxable years the original return for which the due date (without regard to extensions) is on or after the date these regulations are published as final regulations in the **Federal Register**.

* * * * *

(6) *Certain prior periods*. Paragraphs (b)(1), (b)(2)(iv)(A), (b)(2)(iv)(B)(*1*), and (c)(2)(vii) of this section shall apply to taxable years for which the due date of the original return (without regard to extensions) is after March 21, 2005. Sections 1.1502–21T(b)(1), (b)(2)(iv), and (c)(2)(vii), as contained in 26 CFR part 1 revised as of April 1, 2004, shall apply to taxable years for which the due date of the original return (without regard to extensions) is on or before March 21, 2005, and after August 29, 2003. For taxable years for which the due date of the original return (without regard to extensions) is on or before August 29, 2003, see paragraphs (b)(1), (b)(2)(ii)(A), (b)(2)(iv), and (c)(2)(vii) of this section and §1.1502–21T(b)(1) as contained in 26 CFR part 1 revised as of April 1, 2003.

* * * * *

(8) *Losses treated as expired under §1.1502–35(f)(1)*. For rules regarding losses treated as expired under §1.1502–35(f) on and after March 10, 2006, see §1.1502–21(b)(3)(v) as contained in 26 CFR part 1 in effect on April 1, 2006. For rules regarding losses treated as expired before March 10, 2006, see §1.1502–21T(h)(8) as contained in 26 CFR part 1 in effect on April 1, 2005.

Par. 9. Section 1.1502–30 is amended by:

1. Revising paragraph (b)(4).

2. Adding a new second sentence to paragraph (c).

The revision and addition read as follows:

§1.1502–30 Stock basis after certain triangular reorganizations.

* * * * *

(b) * * *

(4) *Application of other rules of law*. If a transaction otherwise subject to this section is also a group structure change subject to §1.1502–31, the provisions of §1.1502–31 and not this section apply to determine stock basis. See §1.1502–80(a) regarding the general applicability of other rules of law and a limitation on duplicative adjustments. See §1.1502–80(d) for the non-application of section 357(c) to P.

* * * * *

(c) * * * However, paragraph (b)(4) of this section applies to reorganizations occurring on or after the date these regulations are published as final regulations in the **Federal Register**.

* * * * *

Par. 10. Section 1.1502–31 is amended by:

1. Revising paragraph (a)(2).

2. Adding a new last sentence to paragraph (h)(1).

The revision and addition read as follows:

§1.1502–31 Stock basis after a group structure change.

(a) * * *

(2) *Application of other rules of law*. If a transaction subject to this section is also a triangular reorganization otherwise subject to §1.1502–30, the provisions of this section and not those of §1.1502–30 apply to determine stock basis. See §1.1502–80(a) regarding the general applicability of other rules of law and a limitation on duplicative adjustments.

* * * * *

(h) * * * (1) * * * In addition, paragraph (a)(2) of this section applies to group structure changes that occurred on or after the date these regulations are published as final regulations in the **Federal Register**.

* * * * *

Par. 11. Section 1.1502–32 is amended by:

1. Revising paragraphs (a)(2), (b)(3)(ii)(C)(*2*), (b)(3)(iii)(C), (b)(3)(iii)(D), (c)(1), (c)(2)(i), the first sentence in paragraph (c)(2)(ii)(A) introductory text, the first sentence in paragraph (c)(3), and the first sentence in paragraph (c)(4)(i) introductory text.

2. Adding new paragraph (h)(9).

The revisions and addition read as follows:

§1.1502–32 Investment adjustments.

(a) * * *

(2) *Application of other rules of law*. See §1.1502–80(a) regarding the general applicability of other rules of law and a limitation on duplicative adjustments.

* * * * *

(b) * * *

(3) * * *

(ii) * * *

(C) * * *

(*2*) *Expired loss carryovers*. If the amount of the discharge exceeds the amount of the attribute reduction under sections 108 and 1017, and §1.1502–28, the excess nevertheless is treated as applied to reduce tax attributes to the extent a loss carryover attributable to S expired without tax benefit, the expiration was taken into account as a noncapital, nondeductible expense under paragraph (b)(3)(iii) of this section, and the loss carryover would have been reduced had it not expired.

* * * * *

(iii) * * *

(C) *Loss suspended under §1.1502–35(c)*. For losses suspended by §1.1502–35(c) prior to the date these regulations are published as final regulations in the **Federal Register**, see §1.1502–32(b)(3)(iii)(C) as contained in 26 CFR part 1 revised as of April 1, 2006.

(D) *Reimported losses disallowed under §1.1502–35*. Any loss or deduction the use of which is disallowed pursuant to §1.1502–35(b) (other than duplicating items that are carried back to a consolidated return year of the group), and with respect to which no waiver described in paragraph (b)(4) of this section is filed, is treated as a noncapital, nondeductible expense incurred during the taxable year that such loss would otherwise be absorbed. For losses or deductions disallowed under §1.1502–35(g)(3)(iii) prior to the date these regulations are published as final regulations in the **Federal Register**, see §1.1502–32(b)(3)(iii)(D) as contained in 26 CFR part 1 revised as of April 1, 2006.

* * * * *

(c) *Allocation of adjustments among shares of stock*—(1) *In general*—(i) *Distributions*. The portion of the adjustment under paragraph (b) of this section that is described in paragraph (b)(2)(iv) of this section (negative adjustments for distributions) is allocated to the shares of S stock to which the distribution relates.

(ii) *Special allocations in the case of certain loss transfers and reallocations of investment adjustments subject to prior use limitation*—(A) *Losses attributable to transfers subject to section 362(e)(2)*—(*1*) *In general*. If a nonmember holds shares of S stock, any amounts that directly or indirectly reflect a section 362(e)(2) amount (as defined in §1.1502–13(e)(4)(ii)(A)) are allocated to members' shares of S stock under the general principles of this paragraph (c), except that such allocations are made as though the shares of S stock held by nonmembers were not outstanding.

(*2*) *Example*. The application of this paragraph (c) is illustrated by the following example:

Example. (i) *Facts*. P owns four of the five outstanding shares of the stock of M. X, a nonmember, owns the remaining outstanding share of M stock. On January 1, year 1, M contributes Asset 1 to S, a newly formed subsidiary, in exchange for five shares of S stock in a transaction to which section 351 applies. At the time of the transfer, M's basis in Asset 1 is $100 and its value is $20. At the end of year 1, S's only item is a $10 depreciation deduction with respect to Asset 1, which gives rise to a $10 loss that is absorbed by the group. At the beginning of year 2, M sells one of its S shares to X for $3.60, and M and S elect to reduce M's basis in the S stock under §1.1502–13(e)(4)(v) by the amount of the remaining section 362(e)(2) amount ($72) (computed in paragraph (iii)(C) of this *Example*) reflected in the share. See §1.1502–13(e)(4). Accordingly, M's basis in the S share is reduced by $14.40 (the portion of the $72 remaining section 362(e)(2) amount reflected in the share (computed in paragraph (iii)(C) of this *Example*)), to $3.60. M recognizes no gain or loss on the sale of the S share. At the end of year 2, S's only item is an additional $10 depreciation deduction with respect to Asset 1, which gives rise to an additional $10 loss that is absorbed by the group. At the end of year 2, M's only item is a $14.40 nondeductible basis recovery item resulting from the election to reduce its basis in the S share. See, §1.1502–13(e)(4)(v)(C).

(ii) *Application of section 362(e)(2) and §1.1502–13(e)(4) to the transfer of Asset 1*. M's contribution of Asset 1 to S is a transaction described in section 362(e)(2). Under the general rules of section 362(e)(2)(A), S's basis in Asset 1 would be limited to its value ($20) and would thus be reduced by $80, from $100 to $20. However, the transfer is an intercompany section 362(e)(2) transaction and therefore, under §1.1502–13(e)(4)(iv), no adjustment is made to S's basis in Asset 1 under section 362(e)(2) until there is a section 362(e)(2) application event (within the meaning of §1.1502–13(e)(4)(iii)). There is no section 362(e)(2) application event in year 1 and so there is no section 362(e)(2) adjustment in year 1. The $80 reduction that S would have had in its basis in Asset 1 is a section 362(e)(2) amount described in §1.1502–13(e)(4)(ii)(A). This $80 section 362(e)(2) amount is initially reflected ratably ($16 per share) in M's basis in each of the five shares of S stock received in the transaction, and in S's basis in Asset 1. Further, under §1.1502–13(e)(4)(ii)(C)(*1*), the section 362(e)(2) amount reflected in an attribute is generally eliminated proportionately as the attribute is taken into account. Accordingly, $8 ($80/$100 x $10) of the year 1 Asset 1 depreciation deduction is attributable to the section 362(e)(2) amount.

(iii) *Treatment of year 1 item*. (A) *Allocation of item among shares of S stock*. Although no adjustment is made under section 362(e)(2) during year 1, if any shares of S stock are held by nonmembers, any items taken into account that are attributable to the section 362(e)(2) amount must be specially allocated under the rules of this paragraph (c)(1)(ii). Because M owns all the shares of S stock, the special allocation rules of this paragraph (c)(1)(ii) have no application to the allocation of S's depreciation deduction to M's shares. Accordingly, the entire $10 of depreciation on Asset 1 is included in the remaining adjustment to the S shares under the general rules in paragraphs (c)(2) through (c)(4) of this section. As a result, $2 is allocated to, and decreases the basis in, each share of S stock held by M from $20 to $18.

(B) *Allocation of tiered-up item among shares of M stock*. Under paragraph (a)(3)(iii) of this section, adjustments to M's basis in S stock tier up and are taken into account in determining adjustments to higher-tier stock. However, because X, a nonmember, holds a share of M stock, any portion of the tiering-up adjustment that is attributable to a section 362(e)(2) amount is specially allocated under this paragraph (c)(1)(ii). In this case, $8 of the adjustment to M's basis in S stock (80/100 x $10) is attributable to a section 362(e)(2) amount and thus $8 of the tiered-up adjustment is indirectly attributable to a section 362(e)(2) amount. As a result, $8 of the tiered-up adjustment must be allocated as though X's share of M stock was not outstanding. Accordingly, $2 (1/4) of the $8 of the tiered-up adjustment is allocated to each of P's four shares of M stock and no portion of that amount is allocated to X's share of M stock. However, the remaining $2 of the tiered-up adjustment not attributable to a section 362(e)(2) amount is included in the remaining adjustment allocated to all outstanding shares under the general rules in paragraphs (c)(2) through (c)(4) of this section. Thus, $.40 (1/5) of the $2 of the tiered-up adjustment is allocated to each outstanding share. (Although $.40 is allocated to X's share of M stock, that allocation does not affect X's basis in the share because X is not a member of the group. See paragraph (c)(1)(iv) of this section.) The allocation of the tiered up year 1 item is thus:

Item	Allocation	
	P's shares of M stock (4/5)	X's share of M stock (1/5)
Tiered-up section 362(e)(2) amount ($8 of the $10 depreciation on Asset 1)	$8.00 ($2.00 per share)	N/A
Tiered-up non-section 362(e)(2) amount ($2 of the $10 depreciation on Asset 1)	$1.60 ($.40 per share)	$.40 ($.40 per share)
Total allocation:	$9.60 ($2.40 per share)	$.40 ($.40 per share)

(C) *Remaining section 362(e)(2) amount.* After the year 1 items have been taken into account, the remaining section 362(e)(2) amount with respect to the S shares is $72 ($80 less $8 eliminated due to Asset 1 depreciation being taken into account). Under §1.1502–13(e)(4)(ii)(C)(*1*), this $72 remaining section 362(e)(2) amount is reflected proportionately in the five S shares held by M, or $14.40 per share.

(iv) *Treatment of year 2 items.* (A) *Elimination of a portion of the section 362(e)(2) amount.* Under §1.1502–13(e)(4)(ii)(C)(*2*), S's remaining section 362(e)(2) amount is eliminated to the extent of the reduction in M's basis in the S stock under §1.1502–13(e)(4)(v). Accordingly, S's remaining section 362(e)(2) amount is reduced by $14.40, to $57.60. This remaining section 362(e)(2) amount is reflected proportionately in the four remaining S shares held by M, or $14.40 per share.

(B) *Allocation of item among shares of S stock.* Because X owns a share of S stock in year 2, the special allocation rule in paragraph (c)(1)(ii) of this section applies to the allocation of the portion of the year 2 depreciation deduction attributable to a section 362(e)(2) amount. Under that rule, $6.40 (57.60/90 x $10) of the item attributable to a section 362(e)(2) amount must be allocated as though only the four shares of S stock held by M were outstanding. Accordingly, $1.60 (1/4) of the $6.40 of the $10 depreciation deduction is allocated to each of M's four shares of S stock and no portion of that amount is allocated to X's share of S stock. However, the remaining $3.60 of the $10 depreciation deduction not attributable to a section 362(e)(2) amount is included in the remaining adjustment allocated to all outstanding shares under the general rules in paragraphs (c)(2) through (c)(4) of this section. Thus, $.72 (1/5) of the $3.60 of the $10 depreciation deduction is allocated to each outstanding S share. (Although $.72 is allocated to X's share of S stock, that allocation does not affect X's basis in the share because X is not a member of the group. See paragraph (c)(1)(iv) of this section.) The allocation of S's year 2 item is thus:

Item	Allocation	
	M's shares of S stock (4/5)	X's share of S stock (1/5)
Section 362(e)(2) amount ($6.40 of the $10 depreciation on Asset 1)	$6.40 ($1.60 per share)	N/A
Non-section 362(e)(2) amount ($3.60 of the $10 depreciation on Asset 1)	$2.88 ($.72 per share)	$.72 ($.72 per share)
Total allocation:	$9.28 ($2.32 per share)	$.72 ($.72 per share)

(C) *Adjustments to the basis of shares of M stock.* The adjustment to the basis of M stock includes two items: M's $14.40 nondeductible basis recovery item resulting from the reduction in M's basis in the S stock under §1.1502–13(e)(4)(v); and $9.28 tiered-up adjustment from the adjustment made to its basis in the S stock. The full amount of the $14.40 nondeductible basis recovery item, and $6.40 of the $9.28 tiered-up adjustment is attributable to the section 362(e)(2) amount. Therefore $20.80 ($14.40 plus $6.40) must be allocated entirely to P's shares of M stock. Accordingly, $5.20 (1/4) of the $20.80 is allocated to each of P's four shares of M stock. The remaining $2.88 of the tiered-up adjustment not attributable to a section 362(e)(2) amount is included in the remaining adjustment allocated to all outstanding shares under the general rules in paragraphs (c)(2) through (c)(4) of this section. Thus, approximately $.58 (1/5) of the $2.88 of the tiered-up adjustment is allocated to each outstanding share. (Although approximately $.58 is allocated to X's share of M stock, that allocation does not affect X's basis in the share because X is not a member of the group. See paragraph (c)(1)(iv) of this section.) The allocation of M's year 2 items is thus:

Item	Allocation	
	P's shares of M stock (4/5)	X's share of M stock (1/5)
Nondeductible basis recovery ($14.40 reduction in S stock basis)	$14.40 ($3.60 per share)	N/A
Tiered-up section 362(e)(2) amount ($6.40 of the $9.28 tiered-up adjustment)	$6.40 ($1.60 per share)	N/A
Tiered-up non-section 362(e)(2) amount ($2.88 of the $9.28 tiered-up adjustment)	$2.30 (approx. $.58 per share)	$.58 (approx. $.58 per share)
Total allocation:	$23.10 (approx. $5.78 per share)	$.58 (approx. $.58 per share)

(D) *No duplicative adjustments to the basis of shares of M stock.* A portion of the $2.88 of the tiered-up adjustment not attributable to a section 362(e)(2) amount duplicates a portion of the $14.40 nondeductible basis recovery item resulting from the reduction in M's basis in the S stock under §1.1502–13(e)(4)(v). Consequently, under §1.1502–80(a), such portion of the tiered-up adjustment is not applied to reduce P's basis in its shares of M stock. The election to reduce M's basis in the S stock eliminated $14.40 of the remaining section 362(e)(2) amount. Accordingly, at the S level, $1.60 ($14.40/$90 x $10) of the Asset 1 year 2 depreciation deduction is associated with this amount. This portion was allocated to all outstanding shares of S stock under the general rules in paragraphs (c)(2) through (c)(4) of this section ($.32 per share ($1.60/5)). At the M level, $1.28 (4 x $.32) of the tiered-up non-section 362(e)(2) amount reflects depreciation on this $14.40 of Asset 1 basis. So, at the M level, approximately $.26 ($1.28/5) of this tiered-up amount is allocated to each outstanding share. This approximately $.26 per share amount would duplicate a portion of the $14.40 nondeductible basis recovery item if it were applied to reduce P's basis in the M shares. Accordingly, although approximately $5.78 of the items are allocated to each M share held by P, P's basis in each share of M stock is only reduced by approximately $5.52 ($5.78 less $.26).

(B) *Losses reattributed pursuant to an election under §1.1502–36(d)(6).* If a member transfers (within the meaning of §1.1502–36(f)(11)) loss shares of S stock and the common parent elects under §1.1502–36(d)(6) to reattribute S attributes, the resulting noncapital, nondeductible expense is allocated to all loss shares of S stock transferred by members in the transaction in proportion to the loss in the shares, and such amount tiers up to any higher tiers under the general rules of this section. If lower-tier subsidiary attributes that would otherwise be reduced as a result of tier-down attribute reduction under §1.1502–36(d)(5)(ii)(D) are reattributed, the resulting noncapital, nondeductible expense is allocated to the shares of the lower-tier subsidiary (and any tier up of such amount is allocated to the shares of higher tier subsidiaries) that will cause the full amount of this expense to be applied to reduce the basis of the loss shares of S stock transferred by members in the transaction. However, this noncapital, nondeductible expense (and any tier up of such amount) is not allocated to shares (other than S shares) transferred in a transfer in which gain or loss was recognized. Further, this noncapital, nondeductible expense (and any tier up of such amount) is allocated among lower-tier shares with positive basis in a manner that reduces the disparity in the basis of the shares to the greatest extent possible. The tier up of this amount is allocated to the loss shares of S stock transferred by members in the transaction in proportion to the loss in the shares, and such amount tiers up to any higher tiers under the general rules of this section. For example, suppose P owns M1, P and M1 own M2, M2 owns S, M1 and S own S1, and M1 and S1 own S2. If S sells a portion of the S1 shares at a gain and M2 sells all of the S stock at a net loss (after adjusting the basis for the gain recognized by S on the sale of the S1 shares), and P elects under §1.1502–36(d)(6) to reattribute attributes of S2, the resulting noncapital, nondeductible expense is allocated entirely to the S2 shares held by S1, the tier up of this amount is allocated entirely to the S1 shares held by S (excluding the S1 shares sold), and the tier up of this amount is allocated to the loss shares of S stock sold by M2. This amount then tiers up from M2 to M1 and P, and from M1 to P under the general rules of this section.

(C) *Reallocations of investment adjustments subject to prior use limitation.* If the reallocation of an investment adjustment under §1.1502–36(b)(2) is subject to the limitation in §1.1502–36(b)(2)(iii)(B)(*2*) due to prior use, no amount of such reallocation (including as a tiered-up amount) shall be allocated to any share whose prior use resulted in the application of the limitation.

(iii) *Remaining adjustment.* The *remaining adjustment* is that portion of the adjustment described in paragraphs (b)(2)(i) through (b)(2)(iii) of this section (adjustments for taxable income or loss, tax-exempt income, and noncapital, nondeductible expenses) that is not specially allocated under paragraph (c)(1)(ii) of this section. The remaining adjustment is allocated among the shares of S stock as provided in paragraphs (c)(2) through (c)(4) of this section. If the remaining adjustment is positive, it is allocated first to any preferred stock to the extent provided in paragraph (c)(3) of this section, and then to the common stock as provided in paragraph (c)(2) of this section. If the remaining adjustment is negative, it is allocated only to common stock as provided in paragraph (c)(2) of this section.

(iv) *Nonmember shares.* No adjustment under this section that is allocated to a share for the period it is owned by a nonmember affects the basis of the share.

(v) *Cross-references.* See paragraph (c)(4) of this section for the reallocation of adjustments, and paragraph (d) of this section for definitions. See §1.1502–19(d) for special allocations of basis determined or adjusted under the Code with respect to excess loss accounts.

(2) *Common stock*—(i) *Allocation within a class.* The remaining adjustment described in paragraph (c)(1)(iii) of this section that is allocable to a class of common stock generally is allocated equally to each share within the class. However, if a member has an excess loss account in shares of a class of common stock at the time of a positive remaining adjustment, the portion of the adjustment allocable to the member with respect to the class is allocated first to equalize and eliminate that member's excess loss account and then to increase equally its basis in the shares of that class. Similarly, any negative remaining adjustment is allocated first to reduce the member's positive basis in shares of the class before creating or increasing its excess loss account. After positive basis is eliminated, any remaining portion of the negative adjustment is allocated first to equalize, to the greatest extent possible, and then to increase equally, the member's excess loss accounts in the shares of that class. Distributions and any adjustments or determinations under the Internal Revenue Code (for example, under section 358, including any modifications under §1.1502–19(d)) are taken into account before the allocation is made under this paragraph (c)(2)(i).

(ii) *Allocation among classes*—(A) *General rule.* If S has more than one class of common stock, the extent to which the remaining adjustment described in paragraph (c)(1)(iii) of this section is allocated to each class is determined, based on consistently applied assumptions, by taking into account the terms of each class and all other facts and circumstances relating to the overall economic arrangement. * * *

* * * * *

(3) *Preferred stock.* If the remaining adjustment described in paragraph (c)(1)(iii) of this section is positive, it is allocated to preferred stock to the extent required (when aggregated with prior allocations to the preferred stock during the period that S is a member of the consolidated group) to reflect distributions described in section 301 (and all other distributions treated as dividends) to which the preferred stock becomes entitled, and arrearages arising, during the period that S is a member of the consolidated group. * * *

* * * * *

(4) *Cumulative redetermination*—(i) *General rule.* A member's basis in each share of S preferred and common stock must be redetermined whenever necessary to determine the tax liability of any person. See paragraph (b)(1) of this section. The redetermination is made by reallocating S's adjustments described in paragraphs (c)(1)(ii) and (c)(1)(iii) of this section (adjustments for specially allocated losses and remaining adjustments, respectively) for each consolidated return year (or other applicable period) of the group by taking into account all of the facts and circumstances affecting allocations under this paragraph (c) as of the redetermination date with respect to all of S shares. * * *

* * * * *

(h) * * *

(9) *Allocations of investment adjustments, including adjustments attributable to certain loss transfers; certain conforming amendments.* Paragraphs (a)(2), (b)(3)(ii)(C)(*2*), (b)(3)(iii)(C), (b)(3)(iii)(D), (c)(1), (c)(2)(i), (c)(2)(ii)(A), (c)(3), and (c)(4)(i) of this section are applicable on or after

the date these regulations are published as final regulations in the **Federal Register**.

* * * * *

Par. 12. Section 1.1502–33 is amended by:

1. Revising paragraph (a)(2).
2. Adding a new last sentence to paragraph (j)(1).

The revision and addition read as follows:

§1.1502–33 Earnings and profits.

(a) * * *

(2) *Application of other rules of law.* See §1.1502–80(a) regarding the general applicability of other rules of law and a limitation on duplicative adjustments.

* * * * *

(j) * * * (1) * * * However, paragraph (a)(2) of this section applies with respect to determinations of the earnings and profits of a member in consolidated return years beginning on or after the date these regulations are published as final regulations in the **Federal Register**.

* * * * *

Par. 13. Section 1.1502–35 is amended by:

1. Revising paragraphs (a), (b) and (h).
2. Removing and reserving paragraphs (f) and (g).
3. Adding new paragraph (l).

The revisions and addition read as follows:

§1.1502–35 Transfers of subsidiary stock and deconsolidations of subsidiaries.

(a) *Losses on subsidiary stock transferred or deconsolidated prior to the date that these regulations are published as final regulations in the* ***Federal Register***. If a member disposed of a loss share of stock of a subsidiary (S), or if S ceased to be a member (deconsolidated) when any member held loss shares of S stock, and if the disposition or deconsolidation occurred prior to the date that these regulations are published as final regulations in the **Federal Register**, see §1.1502–35, as contained in 26 CFR part 1, revised as of April 1, 2007. For transfers and deconsolidations on or after the date that these regulations are published as final regulations in the **Federal Register**, see §1.1502–36.

(b) *Anti-loss reimportation rule applicable on or after the date that these regulations are published as final regulations in the* ***Federal Register***—(1) *Conditions for application.* This paragraph (b) applies when—

(i) A member of a group (the selling group) recognized and was allowed a loss with respect to a share of stock of S, a subsidiary or former subsidiary in the selling group;

(ii) That stock loss was duplicated (in whole or in part) in S's attributes (duplicating items) at the earlier of the time that the loss was recognized or that S ceased to be a member; and

(iii) Within ten years of the date that S ceased to be a member, there is a reimportation event. For this purpose, a reimportation event is any event after which a duplicating item becomes directly or indirectly reflected in the attributes of any member of the selling group, including S, or, if not reflected in the attributes, would be properly taken into account by any member of the selling group (for example, as the result of a carryback) (reimported items).

(2) *Effect of application.* Immediately before the time that a reimported item (or any portion of a reimported item) would be properly taken into account (but for the application of this paragraph (b)), such item (or such portion of the item) is reduced to zero and no deduction or loss is allowed, directly or indirectly, with respect to that item.

(3) *Operating rules.* For purposes of this paragraph (b)—

(i) The terms "member", "subsidiary", and "group" include their predecessors and successors to the extent necessary to effectuate the purposes of this section;

(ii) The determination of whether a loss is duplicative is made under the principles of §1.1502–35, as contained in 26 CFR part 1, revised as of April 1, 2006; and

(iii) The reduction of a reimported item (other than duplicating items that are carried back to a consolidated return year of the selling group) is a noncapital, nondeductible expense with in the meaning of §1.1502–32(b)(2)(iii).

(4) *Period of applicability.* The provisions of this paragraph (b) apply to a reimported item if its related stock loss is recognized on or after the date that these regulations are published as final regulations in the **Federal Register**. The provisions of this paragraph (b) (other than paragraph (b)(1)(i)) also apply to a reimportation event if its related stock loss is recognized on or after March 7, 2002, and is recognized in either a disposition (described in paragraph (g)(3)(i)(A) of this section, as contained in 26 CFR part 1, revised as of January 1, 2007) or a disposition otherwise subject to this section. For prior law, see paragraph (g)(3) of this section, as contained in 26 CFR part 1, revised as of January 1, 2007.

* * * * *

(h) *Application of other rules of law.* See §1.1502–80(a) regarding the general applicability of other rules of law and a limitation on duplicative adjustments.

* * * * *

(l) *Effective date.* Paragraphs (a), (b), and (h) of this section apply with respect to stock transfers, deconsolidations of subsidiaries, determinations of worthlessness, and stock dispositions on or after the date these regulations are published as final regulations in the **Federal Register**. For rules applicable prior to the date these regulations are published as final regulations in the **Federal Register**, see §1.1502–35 as contained in 26 CFR part 1 in effect on April 1, 2007.

§1.1502–35T [Removed]

Par. 14. Section 1.1502–35T is removed.

Par. 15. Section 1.1502–36 is added to read as follows:

§1.1502–36 Unified rule for loss on subsidiary stock.

(a) *In general*—(1) *Scope.* This section provides rules for adjusting members' bases in stock of a subsidiary (S) and for reducing S's attributes when a member (M) transfers a loss share of S stock. See paragraph (f) of this section for definitions of the terms used in this section, including *transfer* and *loss share*.

(2) *Purpose.* The rules in this section have two principal purposes. The first is to prevent the consolidated return provisions from reducing a group's consolidated taxable income through the creation of noneconomic loss on S stock. The second is to prevent members (including former members) of the group from collectively obtaining more than one tax benefit from a single economic loss. Additional purposes are set forth in other paragraphs

of this section. The rules of this section must be interpreted and applied in a manner that is consistent with and reasonably carries out the purposes of this section.

(3) *Overview*—(i) *General application of section.* This section applies when M transfers a share of S stock and, after giving effect to all applicable rules of law other than this section, the share is a loss share. Paragraph (b) of this section applies first to require certain redeterminations of all members' bases in shares of S stock. If the transferred share is a loss share after any basis redetermination required by paragraph (b) of this section, paragraph (c) of this section applies to require certain reductions in M's basis in the transferred loss share. If the transferred share is a loss share after any reduction required by paragraph (c) of this section, paragraph (d) of this section applies to require certain reductions in S's attributes. Paragraphs (e), (f), and (g) of this section provide general operating rules (predecessor/successor rules, effects of prior section 362(e)(2) transactions), definitions, and an anti-abuse rule, respectively.

(ii) *Stock of multiple subsidiaries transferred in the transaction*—(A) *Order of application*—(*1*) *Transferred shares in lowest tier.* If shares of stock of more than one subsidiary are transferred in a transaction and no transferred shares of stock of the lowest-tier subsidiary (S2) are loss shares, any gain recognized with respect to the S2 shares immediately adjusts members' bases in subsidiary stock under the principles of §1.1502–32. However, if any of the transferred S2 shares are loss shares, first paragraph (b) of this section and then paragraph (c) of this section apply with respect to the S2 shares. After giving effect to any adjustments required under paragraphs (b) and (c) of this section, gain or loss is computed on all transferred S2 shares. Any adjustments under paragraphs (b) and (c) of this section, any gain or loss recognized on transferred S2 shares (whether allowed or disallowed), and any other related or resulting adjustments are then applied to adjust members' bases in subsidiary stock under the principles of §1.1502–32.

(*2*) *Application of paragraphs (b) and (c) of this section to higher-tier stock.* After giving effect to any lower-tier adjustments described in paragraph (a)(3)(ii)(A)(*1*) of this section, transfers in the next higher tier in which shares are transferred, and then in each next higher tier successively, are subject to the treatment described in paragraph (a)(3)(ii)(A)(*1*).

(*3*) *Application of paragraph (d) of this section.* After paragraphs (b) and (c) of this section have been applied with respect to all transferred loss shares and after giving effect to all adjustments (whether required by paragraphs (b) and (c) of this section, by the recognition of gain on a transfer, or otherwise), paragraph (d) of this section applies with respect to the highest-tier shares that are then transferred loss shares. Paragraph (d) then applies with respect to transferred loss shares in each next lower tier successively.

(B) *Example.* The rules of this paragraph (a)(3) are illustrated by the following example:

Example. M owns all the outstanding shares of S stock and one of the two outstanding shares of S2 stock, S owns all the outstanding shares of S1 stock, and S1 owns the other outstanding share of S2 stock. As part of one transaction, M sells all the S shares and its S2 share, and S1 sells its S2 share. The sales are to unrelated individuals, S and S1 do not elect to file a consolidated return after the transaction, the S and S1 shares are loss shares and the S2 shares are gain shares. Each share is transferred within the meaning of this section, the S and S2 shares because S and S2 cease to be owned by M, and M and S1, respectively, as a result of taxable dispositions, and the S1 shares because S and S1 cease to be members of the same group. This section applies to the transfer of the S and S1 (loss) shares, but not to the transfer of the S2 (gain) shares. Accordingly, immediately before the transaction, after giving effect to other rules of law, the following occurs. First, the gain recognized on the transferred S2 shares tiers up to adjust members' bases in all upper-tier subsidiary shares under the principles of §1.1502–32. Then, if S's transferred S1 shares are still loss shares, paragraphs (b) and (c) of this section apply to those shares. The loss on the S1 shares is not recognized in the transfer (because there is no taxable disposition of the shares) and so only the adjustments to the bases of the S1 shares required by paragraphs (b) and (c) of this section tier up to adjust M's basis in the S stock. Then, if M's transferred shares of S stock are still loss shares, paragraphs (b) and (c) of this section apply with respect to those shares. If, after giving effect to any adjustments under paragraphs (b) and (c) of this section, any of the S shares are still loss shares, paragraph (d) of this section applies with respect to the transfer of those shares. If any transferred S1 shares are still loss shares after the application of paragraph (d) of this section with respect to the transfer of S shares, paragraph (d) applies with respect to the transfer of the S1 shares.

(4) *Other rules of law and coordination with deferral and disallowance provisions.* This section applies and has effect immediately upon the transfer of a loss share even if the loss is deferred, disallowed, or otherwise not taken into account under any other applicable rules of law. For example, if M sells loss shares of S stock to another member in an intercompany transaction, every member's bases in shares of S stock and all of S's attributes may be adjusted under this section even though M's loss is deferred under §§1.267(f)–1 and 1.1502–13, and S remains a member. See §1.1502–80(a) regarding the general applicability of other rules of law and a limitation on duplicative adjustments.

(5) *Nomenclature, factual assumptions adopted in this section.* Unless otherwise stated, for purposes of this section, the following nomenclature and assumptions are adopted. P is the common parent of a consolidated group and X is a nonmember of the P group. If a corporation has preferred stock outstanding, it is stock described in section 1504(a)(4). The examples set forth the only facts and activities relevant to the example. All transactions are between unrelated persons and are independent of each other. Tax liabilities and their effect, and the application of any loss disallowance or deferral provision of the Code or regulations, including but not limited to section 267, are disregarded. All persons report on a calendar year basis and use the accrual method of accounting. All parties comply with filing and other requirements of this section and all other provisions of the Code and regulations.

(b) *Basis redetermination to reduce disparity*—(1) *In general*—(i) *Purpose and scope.* The rules of this paragraph (b) reduce (but do not increase) the extent to which there is disparity in members' bases in shares of S stock. These rules are intended to prevent the operation of the investment adjustment system from creating noneconomic or duplicated loss when members hold S shares with disparate bases, and they operate by reallocating previously applied investment adjustments. The provisions of this paragraph (b) do not alter the aggregate amount of basis in shares of S stock held by members or the aggregate amount of investment adjustments applied to shares of S stock.

(ii) *Exemptions from basis redetermination*—(A) *No potential for redetermination.* Notwithstanding the general rule in paragraph (b)(2) of this section, basis redetermination will not be required if redetermination would not result in a change to any member's basis in any share of S stock. For example, if S has only one class of stock outstanding and there is no disparity in members' bases in S shares, no member's basis would be changed by the application of this paragraph (b). Accordingly, under this paragraph (b)(1)(ii)(A), no redetermination would be required. Similarly, if S has preferred and common stock outstanding, there is no gain or loss on any member's preferred shares, and there is no disparity in members' bases in the common stock, no member's basis would be changed by the application of this paragraph (b). Accordingly, under this paragraph (b)(1)(ii)(A), no redetermination would be required.

(B) *Disposition of entire interest.* Notwithstanding the general rule in paragraph (b)(2) of this section, basis redetermination will not be required if, within the group's taxable year in which the transfer occurs, every share of S stock held by a member is transferred to a nonmember in one or more fully taxable transactions.

(iii) *Transfers of stock of subsidiaries at multiple tiers.* If stock of subsidiaries at multiple tiers is transferred in a transaction, see paragraph (a)(3)(ii) of this section regarding the order of application of this section.

(iv) *Investment adjustment.* For purposes of this paragraph (b), the term *investment adjustment* means the adjustment for items described in §1.1502–32(b)(2), excluding §1.1502–32(b)(2)(iv) (distributions). The term includes all such adjustments reflected in the basis of the share, whether originally applied directly by §1.1502–32 or otherwise. The term therefore includes investment adjustments reallocated to the share, and it does not include investment adjustments reallocated from the share, whether pursuant to this section or any other provision of law. It also includes the proportionate amount of investment adjustments reflected in the basis of a share after the basis is apportioned among shares, for example in a transaction qualifying under section 355.

(2) *Basis redetermination rule.* If M transfers a loss share of S stock, all members' bases in all their shares of S stock are subject to redetermination under this paragraph (b). The adjustments are made in accordance with the following:

(i) *Decreasing the bases of transferred loss shares*—(A) *Removing positive investment adjustments from transferred loss shares.* M's basis in each of its transferred loss shares of S stock is first reduced, but not below value, by removing positive investment adjustments previously applied to the basis of the share. The positive investment adjustments removed from transferred loss shares are reallocated under paragraph (b)(2)(ii) of this section after negative investment adjustments are reallocated under paragraph (b)(2)(i)(B) of this section.

(B) *Reallocating negative investment adjustments.* If a transferred share is still a loss share after applying paragraph (b)(2)(i)(A) of this section, M's basis in the share is reduced, but not below value, by reallocating and applying negative investment adjustments to the transferred loss share from shares held by members that are not transferred loss shares. Reductions under this paragraph (b)(2)(i)(B) are made first to M's bases in transferred loss shares of S preferred stock and then to M's bases in transferred loss shares of S common stock.

(ii) *Increasing the bases of gain preferred and all common shares*—(A) *Preferred stock.* After the application of paragraph (b)(2)(i) of this section, the positive investment adjustments removed from transferred loss shares are reallocated and applied to increase, but not above value, members' bases in gain shares of S preferred stock.

(B) *Common stock.* Any positive investment adjustments removed from transferred loss shares and not applied to S preferred shares are then reallocated and applied to increase members' bases in shares of S common stock. Reallocations are made to shares of common stock without regard to whether a particular share is a loss share or a transferred share, and without regard to the share's value.

(iii) *Operating rules*—(A) *In general.* All reallocations (both to and from members' shares of S stock) are made in a manner that reduces basis disparity among shares of preferred stock and among shares of common stock to the greatest extent possible (that is, causes the ratio of the basis to the value of each member's share to be as equal as possible).

(B) *Limits on reallocation*—(*1*) *Restriction to outstanding shares.* Investment adjustments can only be reallocated to shares that were held by members in the period to which the adjustment is attributable.

(*2*) *Limitation by prior use of allocation*—(*i*) *In general.* In order to prevent the reallocation of investment adjustments from either increasing or decreasing members' aggregate bases in subsidiary stock, no investment adjustment (positive or negative) may be reallocated under this paragraph (b)(2) to the extent that it was (or would have been) used prior to the time that it would otherwise be reallocated under this paragraph (b)(2). For this purpose, an investment adjustment was used (or would have been used) to the extent that it was reflected in (or would have been reflected in) the basis of a share of subsidiary stock and the basis of that share has already been taken into account, directly or indirectly, in determining income, gain, deduction, or loss (including by affecting the application of this section to a prior transfer of subsidiary stock) or in determining the basis of any property that is not subject to §1.1502–32. However, notwithstanding the general rule, if the prior use was in an intercompany transaction, an investment adjustment may be reallocated to the extent that §1.1502–13 has prevented the gain or loss on the transaction from being taken into account. (In that case, appropriate adjustments must be made to the prior intercompany transaction.) Further, if an investment adjustment was reflected in (or would have been reflected in) the basis of a share that has been taken into account, but the basis of that share would not change as a result of the reallocation (for example, because the reallocation would be among shares that are all lower-tier to the share with the previously used basis), the investment adjustment may be reallocated. See §1.1502–32(c)(1)(ii)(C) regarding special allocations applicable if the reallocation of an investment adjustment is limited under this paragraph (b)(2)(iii)(B)(*2*).

(*ii*) *Example.* The application of this paragraph (b)(2)(iii)(B)(*2*) is illustrated by the following example:

Example. (i) *Facts.* P owns all 20 shares of M stock, and 10 shares of S stock. M owns the remaining 10 shares of S stock. In year 1, S recognizes $200 of income that results in a $10 positive investment adjustment being allocated to each share of S stock. The group does not recognize any other items. The $100 positive adjustment to M's basis in the S stock tiers up, and results in a $5 positive adjustment to each share of M stock. In year 2, P sells one share of M stock and recognizes a gain. In year 3, M sells one loss share of S stock, and paragraph (b) of this section applies and requires a reallocation of the year 1 positive investment adjustment.

(ii) *Application of limitation by prior use.* M's basis in the transferred loss share of S stock reflects a $10 positive investment adjustment attributable to S's year 1 income. Under the general rule of this paragraph (b), that $10 would be subject to reallocation to reduce basis disparity. However, that $10 adjustment had originally tiered up to adjust P's basis in its M shares and, as a result, $.50 of that adjustment was reflected in P's basis in each share of M stock. When P sold the share of M stock, the basis of that share (including the tiered up $.50) was used in determining the gain on the sale. Accordingly, $.50 of the $10 investment adjustment originally allocated to the S share that tiered-up to the M share was previously used and therefore cannot be reallocated in a manner that would (if it were the original allocation) affect the basis of the sold share. Thus, taking into account the special allocations in §1.1502–32(c)(1)(ii)(C), up to $9.50 of the adjustment to M's transferred S share could be allocated to P's shares of S stock (leaving $.50 on M's transferred S share, all of which would be treated as tiered up to P's transferred M share). Alternatively, all $10 could be reallocated to M's other S shares (because the tier up to P's M shares would have been the same regardless which of M's shares of S stock were adjusted.)

(iii) *Application of limitation where adjustment would have been used.* The facts are the same as in paragraph (i) of this *Example* except that M does not sell any shares of S stock and, in year 3, P sells a loss share of S stock. As in paragraph (i) of this *Example*, when P sold the share of M stock, the basis of that share was used in determining the gain on the share. When P sells the loss share of S stock, the $10 positive investment adjustment from S's year 1 income cannot be reallocated in a manner that, if it were the original adjustment, would have caused any amount to be reflected in the basis of the transferred share. If this $10 positive investment adjustment had originally been allocated to the S shares held by M, $.50 of the $10 investment adjustment would have tiered up to the M share that P sold, would have been reflected in P's basis, and would have been used in determining the gain or loss on the sale. Accordingly, taking into account the special allocations in §1.1502–32(c)(1)(ii)(C), up to $9.50 of the $10 adjustment to P's transferred S share could be allocated to M's shares of S stock (all of which would tier up to P's 19 retained M shares). Alternatively, all $10 could be reallocated to P's other S shares.

(C) *Order of reallocation.* In general, reallocations are made first with respect to the earliest available adjustments. However, the overall application of this paragraph (b) to a transaction must be made in a manner that reduces basis disparity to the greatest extent possible.

(3) *Examples.* The general application of this paragraph (b) is illustrated by the following examples:

Example 1. Transfer of stock received in section 351 exchange. (i) *Redetermination to prevent noneconomic loss.* (A) *Facts.* For many years, P has owned two assets, Asset 1 and Asset 2. On January 1, year 1, P receives four shares of S common stock (the Block 1 shares) in exchange for Asset 1, which has a basis and value of $80. The exchange qualifies under section 351 and, therefore, under section 358, P's aggregate basis in the Block 1 shares is $80 ($20 per share). On July 1, year 1, P receives another share of S common stock (the Block 2 share) in exchange for Asset 2, which has a basis of $0 and value of $20. This exchange also qualifies as a section 351 exchange and, under section 358, P's basis in the Block 2 share is $0. P's Block 1 and Block 2 shares are the only outstanding shares of S stock. On October 1, year 1, S sells Asset 2 for $20. On December 31, year 1, P sells one of its Block 1 shares for $20. After applying and giving effect to all generally applicable rules of law (other than this section), P's basis in each Block 1 share is $24 (P's original $20 basis increased under §1.1502–32 by $4 (the share's allocable portion of the $20 gain recognized on the sale of Asset 2)). In addition, P's basis in its Block 2 share is $4 (P's original $0 basis increased under §1.1502–32 by $4 (the share's allocable portion of the $20 gain recognized on the sale of Asset 2)). P's sale of the Block 1 share is a transfer of a loss share and therefore subject to the provisions of this section.

(B) *Basis redetermination under this paragraph (b).* Under this paragraph (b), P's bases in all its shares of S stock are subject to redetermination. First, paragraph (b)(2)(i)(A) of this section applies to reduce P's basis in the transferred loss share, but not below value, by removing positive investment adjustments applied to the basis of the share. Accordingly, P's basis in the transferred Block 1 share is reduced by $4 (the amount of the positive investment adjustment applied to the share), from $24 to $20. No further reduction to the basis of the share is required under this paragraph (b) because the basis of the share is then equal to value. Under paragraph (b)(2)(ii)(B) of this section, the positive investment adjustment removed from the transferred loss share is reallocated and applied to increase P's bases in its S shares in a manner that reduces basis disparity to the greatest extent possible. Accordingly, the $4 positive investment adjustment removed from the Block 1 share is reallocated and applied to the basis of the Block 2 share, increasing it from $4 to $8.

(C) *Application of paragraphs (c) and (d) of this section.* Because P's sale of the Block 1 share is no longer a transfer of a loss share after the application of this paragraph (b), paragraphs (c) and (d) of this section do not apply.

(ii) *Redetermination to prevent duplicated loss.* (A) *Facts.* The facts are the same as in paragraph (i)(A) of this *Example 1*, except that, at the time of the second contribution, the value of Asset 1 had declined to $20 and so, instead of contributing Asset 2, P contributed Asset 3 to S in exchange for the Block 2 share. At the time of that exchange, Asset 3 had a basis and value of $5. On October 1, year 1, S sells Asset 1 for $20, recognizing a $60 loss that is absorbed by the group. On December 31, year 1, P sells one of its Block 1 shares for $5. After applying and giving effect to all generally applicable rules of law (other than this section), P's basis in each Block 1 share is $8 (P's original $20 basis decreased under §1.1502–32 by $12 (the share's allocable portion of the $60 loss recognized on the sale of Asset 1)). P's basis in its Block 2 share is an excess loss account of $7 (its original basis of $5 reduced by $12, the share's portion of the loss recognized on Asset 1). P's sale of the Block 1 share is a transfer of a loss share and therefore subject to the provisions of this section.

(B) *Basis redetermination under this paragraph (b).* Under this paragraph (b), P's bases in all its shares of S stock are subject to redetermination. There are no positive investment adjustments and so there is no adjustment under paragraph (b)(2)(i)(A) of this section. However, under paragraph (b)(2)(i)(B) of this section, P's basis in the transferred Block 1 share is reduced, but not below value, by reallocating negative investment adjustments from shares that are not transferred loss shares. In total, there were $48 of negative investment adjustments applied to shares that are not transferred loss shares. Accordingly, P's basis in the Block 1 share is reduced by $3, from $8 to its value of $5. Under paragraph (b)(2)(i)(B) of this section, the negative investment adjustments applied to the transferred share are reallocated from (and therefore cause an increase in the basis of) S shares that are not transferred loss shares in a manner that reduces basis disparity to the greatest extent possible. Accordingly, the $3 negative investment adjustment reallocated and applied to the transferred Block 1 share is reallocated entirely from the Block 2 share, increasing the basis in the Block 2 share from an excess loss account of $7 to an excess loss account of $4.

(C) *Application of paragraphs (c) and (d) of this section.* Because P's sale of the Block 1 share is no longer a transfer of a loss share after the application of this paragraph (b), paragraphs (c) and (d) of this section do not apply.

(iii) *Nonapplicability of redetermination rule to sale of entire interest.* The facts are the same as in paragraph (ii)(A) of this *Example 1*, except that, on December 31, year 1, P sells all its shares of S stock for $25. Under paragraph (b)(1)(ii)(B) of this section, this paragraph (b) does not apply to redetermine P's basis in its S shares because every S share held by a member is transferred to a nonmember in a fully taxable transaction. However, the sale of the Block 1 shares is a transfer of loss shares and therefore subject to paragraphs (c) and (d) of this section. Paragraphs (c)(7) and (d)(3)(i)(A) of this section apply netting principles to prevent adjustments under either paragraph (c) or paragraph (d) of this section.

Example 2. Redetermination increases basis of transferred loss share. (i) *Facts.* On January 1, year 1, P owns all 10 outstanding shares of S common stock. Five of the shares have a basis of $20 per share (the Block 1 shares) and five of the shares have a basis of $10 per share (the Block 2 shares). S's only asset, Asset 1, has a basis of $50. S has no other attributes. On October 1, year 1, S sells Asset 1 for $100. On December 31, year 2, S sells one Block 1 share and one Block 2 share to X for $10 per share. After applying and giving effect to all generally applicable rules of law (other than this section), P's basis in each Block 1 share is $25 (P's original $20 basis increased under §1.1502–32 by $5 (the share's allocable portion of the $50 gain recognized on the sale of Asset 1)), and P's basis in each Block 2 share is $15 (P's original $10 basis increased by $5). P's sale of the Block 1 and Block 2 shares is a transfer of loss shares and therefore subject to the provisions of this section.

(ii) *Basis redetermination under this paragraph (b).* Under this paragraph (b), P's bases in all its shares of S stock are subject to redetermination. First, paragraph (b)(2)(i)(A) of this section applies to reduce P's basis in the transferred Block 1 and Block 2 shares, but not below value, by removing the positive investment adjustments applied to the bases of the transferred loss shares. Accordingly, the basis of the Block 1 share is reduced by $5, from $25 to $20. The basis of the Block 2 share is also reduced by $5, from $15 to $10. (Although the Block 1 share is still a loss share, there is no reduction to its basis under paragraph (b)(2)(i)(B) of this section because there were no negative investment adjustments to shares that are not transferred loss shares.) Next, paragraph (b)(2)(ii)(B) of this section applies to reallocate and apply the $10 of positive investment adjustments removed from the transferred loss shares to increase P's bases in its S shares in a manner that reduces basis disparity to the greatest extent possible. Accordingly, of the $10 positive investment adjustments to be reallocated, $6 is reallocated and applied to the basis of the Block 2 share (increasing it from $10 to $16) and $4 is reallocated and applied equally to the basis of each of the four retained Block 2 shares (increasing the basis of each from $15 to $16). After giving effect to the reallocations under this paragraph (b), P's basis in each retained Block 1 share is $25, P's basis in the transferred Block 1 share is $20, and P's basis in each Block 2 share is $16.

(iii) *Application of paragraph (c) of this section.* After the application of this paragraph (b), P's sale of the Block 1 and Block 2 shares is still a transfer of loss shares and, accordingly, subject to paragraph (c) of this section. No adjustment is required to the basis of the Block 1 share under paragraph (c) of this section because, after its basis is redetermined under this paragraph (b), the net positive adjustment to the basis of the share is $0. See paragraph (c)(3) of this section. However, paragraph (c) of this section reduces P's basis in the transferred Block 2 share (by the lesser of its net positive adjustment and its disconformity amount, or $6, from $16 to $10, its value).

(iv) *Application of paragraph (d) of this section.* After the application of paragraph (c) of this section, P's sale of the Block 1 share is still a transfer of a loss share and, accordingly, subject to paragraph (d) of this section. No adjustment is required under paragraph (d) of this section because there is no aggregate inside loss. See paragraph (d)(3)(iii) of this section. Because P's sale of the Block 2 share is no longer a transfer of a loss share after the application of paragraph (c) of this section, paragraph (d) of this section does not apply to the transfer of the Block 2 share.

Example 3. Application to outstanding common and preferred shares. (i) *Facts.* P owns all the stock of M and all eight outstanding shares of S common stock. S also has two shares of nonvoting preferred stock outstanding; the preferred shares have a $100 annual, cumulative preference as to dividends (per share). M owns one of the preferred shares (PS1) and P owns the other (PS2). On January 1, year 1, the bases and values of the outstanding S shares are:

	Preferred		Common							
	PS1 (M)	PS2 (P)	CS1 (P)	CS2 (P)	CS3 (P)	CS4 (P)	CS5 (P)	CS6 (P)	CS7 (P)	CS8 (P)
Basis	1250	975	1025	710	550	400	375	250	215	100
Value	1000	1000	375	375	375	375	375	375	375	375

As of January 1, year 1, there are no arrearages on the preferred stock. In year 1, S has a $1100 capital loss and $100 of ordinary income. The loss is absorbed by the group and the resulting negative adjustment of $1000 is allocable entirely to the common stock. See §1.1502–32(c)(1).

In year 2, S has $700 of ordinary income and a $100 ordinary loss. Also, on October 1, year 2, S declares a dividend of $200 ($100 with respect to each of the preferred shares). Thus, there is a net positive investment adjustment for year 2 of $400. See §1.1502–32(b)(2). Under §1.1502–32(c)(1), a negative adjustment of $100 is first allocated to each of the preferred shares to reflect the dividend declaration. Then, $400 of the $600 remaining adjustment (the adjustment computed without taking distributions into account) is allocated $200 to each of the preferred shares to reflect its entitlement to dividends accruing in year 1 and year 2. See §1.1502–32(c)(3). (The year 2 investment adjustment to each preferred share is therefore a positive $100.) Finally, under §1.1502–32(c)(2), the remaining $200 of the investment adjustment is allocated to the common stock, equally to all outstanding shares. After applying and giving effect to all generally applicable rules of law (other than this section), the adjusted bases and the values of the shares as of January 1, year 3, are:

	Preferred		Common							
	PS1 (M)	PS2 (P)	CS1 (P)	CS2 (P)	CS3 (P)	CS4 (P)	CS5 (P)	CS6 (P)	CS7 (P)	CS8 (P)
Basis	1250	975	1025	710	550	400	375	250	215	100
Year 1 §1.1502–32 adjustments	N/A	N/A	-125	-125	-125	-125	-125	-125	-125	-125
Year 2 §1.1502–32 adjustments	+100	+100	+25	+25	+25	+25	+25	+25	+25	+25
Adjusted basis	1350	1075	925	610	450	300	275	150	115	0
Value	1100	1100	275	275	275	275	275	275	275	275
Unrecognized gain/(loss)	(250)	25	(650)	(335)	(175)	(25)	0	125	160	275

On January 1, year 3, M sells PS1 for $1100 and P sells CS2 for $275. The sales of PS1 and CS2 are transfers of loss shares and therefore subject to the provisions of this section.

(ii) *Basis redetermination under this paragraph (b).* Under this paragraph (b), all members' bases in shares of S stock are subject to redetermination in accordance with the following:

(A) *Removing positive investment adjustments from transferred loss shares.* First, paragraph (b)(2)(i)(A) of this section applies to reduce M's basis in PS1 and P's basis in CS2, but not below value, by removing the positive investment adjustments applied to the bases of the shares. Accordingly, M's basis in PS1 is reduced by $200 (the investment adjustment applied to the share without regard to the distribution), from $1350 to $1150, and P's basis in CS2 is reduced by $25, from $610 to $585.

(B) *Reallocating negative investment adjustments from shares that are not transferred loss shares.* Because the transferred shares remain loss shares after the removal of positive investment adjustments, their bases are further reduced under paragraph (b)(2)(i)(B) of this section, but not below value, by negative investment adjustments applied to shares that are not transferred loss shares. Reallocations are made first to preferred shares and then to the common shares, in a manner that reduces basis disparity to the greatest extent possible. The remaining loss on PS1 is $50, the remaining loss on CS2 is $310, and the total amount of negative investment adjustments applied to shares that are not transferred loss shares is $875 (the sum of the adjustments made to all common shares other than CS2). Thus, $50 of negative investment adjustments are reallocated to the basis of PS1 and $310 of negative investment adjustments are reallocated to the basis of CS2, reducing each to its value ($1100 and $275, respectively). The negative investment adjustments are reallocated from the shares that are not transferred loss shares in a manner that reduces basis disparity to the greatest extent possible. Accordingly, of the $360 reallocated negative investment adjustments, $125 is reallocated from each of CS7 and CS8, and $110 is reallocated from CS6. As a result, the basis of CS6 increases to $260, the basis of CS7 increases to $240, and the basis of CS8 increases to $125.

(C) *Increasing basis by reallocated positive investment adjustments.* Under paragraph (b)(2)(ii)(A) of this section, the $225 of positive investment adjustments removed from the transferred loss shares are then reallocated and applied to increase the basis of preferred shares, but not above value. Accordingly, $25 of that amount is reallocated to PS2, increasing its basis from $1075 to $1100, its value. The remaining $200 is allocated among the common shares in a manner that reduces basis disparity to the greatest extent possible. Accordingly, of the $200 positive investment adjustment that is reallocated to common shares, $150 is reallocated to CS8, $35 is reallocated to CS7, and $15 is reallocated to CS6, increasing the basis of each to $275.

(D) *Summary of reallocation adjustments.* The adjustments made under this paragraph (b) are therefore:

	Preferred		Common							
	PS1 (M)	PS2 (P)	CS1 (P)	CS2 (P)	CS3 (P)	CS4 (P)	CS5 (P)	CS6 (P)	CS7 (P)	CS8 (P)
Adjusted basis before redetermination	1350	1075	925	610	450	300	275	150	115	0
Removing positive adjustments from transferred loss shares	-200			-25						
Reallocating negative adjustments	-50			-310				+110	+125	+125
Applying positive adjustments removed from transferred shares		+25						+15	+35	+150
Basis after redetermination	1100	1100	925	275	450	300	275	275	275	275
Value	1100	1100	275	275	275	275	275	275	275	275
Gain/(loss)	0	0	(650)	0	(175)	(25)	0	0	0	0

(iii) *Application of paragraphs (c) and (d) of this section.* Because M's sale of PS1 and P's sale of CS2 are no longer transfers of loss shares after the application of this paragraph (b), paragraphs (c) and (d) of this section do not apply.

(iv) *Higher-tier effects.* The adjustments made to PS1 give rise to a $250 nondeductible basis recovery item (a noncapital, nondeductible expense under §1.1502–32(b)(3)(iii)(B)) that will be included in the year 3 investment adjustment to be applied to reduce P's basis in its M stock.

(c) *Stock basis reduction to prevent noneconomic loss*—(1) *In general.* The rules of this paragraph (c) reduce M's basis in a transferred share of S stock in order to prevent noneconomic stock loss and thereby promote the clear reflection of the group's income. The effect of these rules is to limit the reduction to M's basis in the S share to the amount of net unrealized appreciation reflected in the share's basis immediately before the transfer. These rules also limit the reduction to M's basis in the S share to the portion of the share's basis that is attributable to investment adjustments made pursuant to the consolidated return regulations.

(2) *Basis reduction rule*—(i) *In general.* If M transfers a share of S stock and, after the application of paragraph (b) of this section, the share is a loss share, M's basis in the share is reduced, but not below value, by the lesser of—

(A) The share's net positive adjustment (see paragraph (c)(3) of this section); and

(B) The share's disconformity amount (see paragraph (c)(4) of this section).

(ii) *Transactions that adjusted stock or asset basis.* See paragraph (e)(2) of this section for special rules that may apply if a prior transaction, such as an exchange subject to section 362(e)(2), adjusted the basis in any share of S stock or S's attributes in a manner that altered a share's disconformity amount.

(iii) *Transfers of stock of subsidiaries at multiple tiers.* If stock of subsidiaries at multiple tiers is transferred in a transaction, see paragraph (a)(3)(ii) of this section regarding the order of application of this section.

(3) *Net positive adjustment.* A share's *net positive adjustment* is the greater of—

(i) Zero; and

(ii) The sum of all investment adjustments reflected in the basis of the share. The term investment adjustment has the same meaning as in paragraph (b)(1)(iv) of this section.

(4) *Disconformity amount.* A share's *disconformity amount* is the excess, if any, of—

(i) M's basis in the share; over

(ii) The share's allocable portion of S's net inside attribute amount (as defined in paragraph (c)(5) of this section).

(5) *Net inside attribute amount.* S's *net inside attribute amount* is determined as of the time immediately before the transfer, taking into account all applicable rules of law other than this section (except as specifically provided otherwise in this section). S's net inside attribute amount is the sum of S's net operating and capital loss carryovers, deferred deductions, money, and basis in assets other than money (for this purpose, S's basis in any share of lower-tier subsidiary stock is S's basis in that share, adjusted to reflect any gain or loss recognized in the transaction and any other related or resulting adjustments), reduced by the amount of S's liabilities. See paragraph (f) of this section for definitions of the terms "allocable portion", "deferred deduction", "liability", and "loss carry-

over". See paragraph (c)(6) of this section for special rules regarding the computation of S's net inside attribute amount for purposes of this paragraph (c) if S holds stock of a subsidiary.

(6) *Determination of S's net inside attribute amount if S owns stock of a lower-tier subsidiary*—(i) *Overview*. If a loss share of S stock is transferred when S holds a share of stock of another subsidiary (S1) and the S1 share is not transferred in the same transaction, S's net inside attribute amount is determined by treating S's basis in its S1 share as tentatively reduced under this paragraph (c)(6). The purpose of this rule is to reduce the extent to which S1's investment adjustments increase noneconomic loss on S stock (as a result of S1's recognition of items that are indirectly reflected in members' bases in S stock).

(ii) *General rule for nontransferred shares of lower-tier subsidiary*. Solely for purposes of determining the disconformity amount of a share of S stock, S's basis in a share of S1 stock is treated as reduced by the share's tentative reduction amount. The tentative reduction amount is the lesser of the S1 share's net positive adjustment and the S1 share's disconformity amount, computed under the principles of paragraphs (c)(3) and (c)(4) of this section, respectively.

(iii) *Multiple tiers of nontransferred shares*. If S directly or indirectly owns non-transferred shares of stock of subsidiaries in multiple tiers, then, subject to the limitations in paragraph (c)(6)(iv) of this section (regarding nontransferred shares that are lower-tier to transferred shares), the rules of this paragraph (c)(6) first apply to determine the tentatively reduced basis of stock of the subsidiary at the lowest tier. These rules then apply successively to determine the tentatively reduced basis of nontransferred shares of stock of subsidiaries at each next higher tier that is lower tier to S. The tentative reductions are treated as noncapital, nondeductible expenses that tier up under the principles of §1.1502–32, tentatively reducing the basis of stock and the net positive adjustments of subsidiaries that are lower tier to S.

(iv) *Nonapplicability of tentative basis reduction rule to transferred shares*. The tentative basis reduction rule in this paragraph (c)(6) does not apply to any share of stock of a lower-tier subsidiary (S1) that is transferred in the same transaction in which the S share is transferred. Further, for purposes of determining the S share's disconformity amount, the tentative basis reduction rule in this paragraph (c)(6) does not apply with respect to stock of any other subsidiary (S2) to the extent it is lower tier to the transferred S1 share. However, the tentative basis reduction rule may apply to S2 stock for purposes of computing the disconformity amount of the transferred S1 share. The purpose of this rule is to prevent tentative adjustments under this paragraph (c)(6) to the extent that this paragraph (c) has already applied to shares of subsidiary stock, without regard to whether the basis of those shares was reduced under this paragraph (c).

(v) *Example*. The rules of this paragraph (c)(6) are illustrated by the following example:

Example. (i) *Facts*. P owns the sole outstanding share of S stock, S owns the sole outstanding share of S1 stock, S1 owns the sole outstanding share of S2 stock, S2 owns the sole outstanding share of S3 stock, and S3 owns the sole outstanding share of S4 stock. The S and S1 shares are loss shares, and the S3 share is a gain share. In one transaction, P sells its S share to X, S1 issues new shares in an amount that prevents S and S1 from being members of the same group, and S2 sells the S3 share to an unrelated individual. S1 and S2 elect to file a consolidated return following the transaction, as do S3 and S4.

(ii) *General applicability of section*. The transaction is a transfer of the S and S3 shares (by reason of the sales) and of the S1 share (because S and S1 cease to be members of the same group). The transfer of the S3 share is not a transfer of a loss share and so this section does not apply to that transfer. This section does, however, apply to the transfer of the S and S1 loss shares. Under paragraph (a)(3)(ii)(A) of this section, the application of this section begins with the application of paragraph (b) to the transfer of the loss share of S1 stock, the lowest-tier subsidiary the stock of which is transferred in the transaction.

(iii) *Application of paragraphs (b) and (c) to transfer of S1 stock*. First, the gain recognized on the transfer of S3 stock tiers up to adjust the basis of each upper-tier share. Then, because the transferred S1 share is still a loss share under these facts, paragraph (b) of this section applies to S's transfer of S1 stock. However, no adjustment is required under paragraph (b) of this section because redetermination would change no member's basis in a share (members hold only one share of S1 stock). See paragraph (b)(1)(ii)(A) of this section. The S1 share is still a loss share and so it is then subject to the provisions of this paragraph (c). In determining basis reduction under this paragraph (c), the disconformity amount of the S1 share is computed by treating S1's basis in S2 stock as tentatively reduced under this paragraph (c)(6). In determining the disconformity amount of the S1 share, this tentative reduction rule has no application with respect to S2's basis in the S3 share (because the S3 share is transferred in the transaction) or with respect to S3's basis in the S4 share (because the S4 stock is lower tier to the transferred S3 share). After the application of this paragraph (c) to the transfer of the S1 share, paragraph (b) of this section applies to P's transfer of the S share if the share is still a loss share.

(iv) *Application of section to transfer of S stock*. First, assuming the S share has remained a loss share, paragraph (b) of this section applies to P's transfer of S stock. However, no adjustment is required under paragraph (b) of this section, either because there is no potential for redetermination (members hold only one share of S stock) or because P transfers the group's entire interest in S to a nonmember in a fully taxable transaction. See, respectively, paragraphs (b)(1)(ii)(A) and (b)(1)(ii)(B) of this section. The transferred share is still a loss share and therefore subject to the provisions of this paragraph (c). In determining the disconformity amount of the S share, S's net inside attributes are determined by taking into account S's actual basis in the S1 stock. The tentative reduction rule of this paragraph (c)(6) does not apply to S's basis in the S1 share because the S1 share is transferred in the transaction. All other shares are lower tier to the transferred S1 share and are therefore not subject to tentative reduction for purposes of determining the disconformity amount of the S share.

(7) *Netting of gains and losses taken into account*—(i) *General rule*. Solely for purposes of computing the basis reduction required under this paragraph (c), the basis of each transferred loss share of S stock is treated as reduced proportionately (as to loss) by the amount of gain taken into account by members with respect to all transferred gain shares of S stock, provided that—

(A) The gain and loss shares are transferred in the same transaction; and

(B) The gain is taken into account in the year of the transaction.

(ii) *Example*. The netting rule of this paragraph (c)(7) is illustrated by the following example:

Example. *Disposition of gain and loss shares*. (i) *Facts*. P owns the only two outstanding shares of S common stock. Share A has a basis of $54 and Share B has a basis of $100. In the same transaction, P sells the two S shares to X for $60 each. P realizes a gain of $6 on Share A and a loss of $40 on Share B. P's sale of Share B is a transfer of a loss share and therefore subject to the provisions of this section. (No adjustment is required under paragraph (b) of this section because P transfers the group's entire interest in S to a nonmember in a fully taxable transaction. See paragraph (b)(1)(ii)(B) of this section.) The transfer is then subject to the provisions of this paragraph (c). However, for this purpose, P treats its basis in Share B as reduced by the $6 gain taken into account with respect to Share A. Thus, solely for purposes of computing the basis reduction required with respect to P's basis in Share B, P's basis in Share B is treated as $94 ($100 less $6). If, after the application of this paragraph (c), the sale of Share B is still a transfer of a loss share, then the transfer is subject to paragraph (d) of this section. (Although the basis of Share B is not reduced by gain for purposes of paragraph (d) of this section, paragraph (d)(3)(i)(A) of this section applies netting principles to limit adjustments under paragraph (d) of this section.)

(ii) *Allocation of gain amount to determine net loss.* The facts are the same as in paragraph (i) of this *Example*, except that, in addition to Share A and Share B, a third share of S stock, Share C, is outstanding. P's basis in Share C is $80. P sells all three shares of S stock to X for $60 each. P's sales of Share B and Share C are transfers of loss shares and therefore subject to the provisions of this section. (No adjustment is required under paragraph (b) of this section because P transfers the group's entire interest in S to a nonmember in a fully taxable transaction. See paragraph (b)(1)(ii)(B) of this section.) The transfer is then subject to the provisions of this paragraph (c). However, for this purpose, P treats its bases in Share B and Share C as reduced by the $6 gain taken into account on Share A. The gain is allocated to Share B and Share C proportionately based on the amount of loss in each share. Thus, $4 of gain ($40/$60 x $6) is treated as allocated to Share B and $2 of gain ($20/$60 x $6) is treated as allocated to Share C. Accordingly, P computes the basis reduction required under this paragraph (c) by treating its basis in Share B as $96 ($100 less $4) and its basis in Share C as $78 ($80 less $2). If, after the application of this paragraph (c), the sales of Share B and Share C are still transfers of loss shares, then the transfers are subject to paragraph (d) of this section. (Although the bases of Share B and Share C are not reduced by gain for purposes of paragraph (d) of this section, paragraph (d)(3)(i)(A) of this section applies netting principles to limit adjustments under paragraph (d) of this section.)

(iii) *Disposition of stock with deferred gain.* The facts are the same as in paragraph (i) of this *Example*, except that P sells the gain share to a member. Under §1.1502–13, P's gain recognized on Share A is not taken into account in the taxable year of the transfer and therefore cannot be treated as reducing P's loss recognized on Share B.

(8) *Examples.* The application of this paragraph (c) is illustrated by the following examples.

Example 1. Appreciation reflected in stock basis at acquisition. (i) *Appreciation recognized as gain.* (A) *Facts.* On January 1, year 1, P purchases the sole outstanding share of S stock for $100. At that time, S owns two assets, Asset 1 with a basis of $0 and a value of $40, and Asset 2 with a basis and value of $60. In year 1, S sells Asset 1 for $40. On December 31, year 1, P sells its S share for $100. After applying and giving effect to all generally applicable rules of law (other than this section), P's basis in the S share is $140 (P's original $100 basis increased under §1.1502–32 to reflect the $40 gain recognized on the sale of Asset 1). P's sale of the S share is a transfer of a loss share and therefore subject to the provisions of this section.

(B) *Application of paragraph (b) of this section.* No adjustment is required under paragraph (b) of this section, either because redetermination would change no member's basis in a share (members hold only one share of S stock) or because P transfers the group's entire interest in S to a nonmember in a fully taxable transaction. See, respectively, paragraphs (b)(1)(ii)(A) and (b)(1)(ii)(B) of this section. After the application of paragraph (b) of this section, P's sale of the S share is still a transfer of a loss share and therefore subject to this paragraph (c).

(C) *Basis reduction under this paragraph (c).* Under this paragraph (c), P's basis in the S share is reduced, but not below value, by the lesser of the share's net positive adjustment and disconformity amount. The share's net positive adjustment is the greater of zero and the sum of all investment adjustments applied to the basis of the share, computed without taking distributions into account. There are no distributions. The only investment adjustment to the share is the $40 adjustment attributable to the gain recognized on the sale of Asset 1. Thus, the share's net positive adjustment is $40. The share's disconformity amount is the excess, if any, of its basis ($140) over its allocable portion of S's net inside attribute amount. S's net inside attribute amount is the sum of S's money ($40 from the sale of Asset 1) and S's basis in Asset 2 ($60), or $100. The share is the only outstanding S share and so its allocable portion of the $100 net inside attribute amount is the entire $100. Thus, the share's disconformity amount is $40, the excess of $140 over $100. The lesser of the net positive adjustment ($40) and the share's disconformity amount ($40) is $40. Accordingly, the basis in the share is reduced by $40, from $140 to $100, immediately before the sale.

(D) *Application of paragraph (d) of this section.* Because P's sale of the S share is no longer a transfer of a loss share after the application of this paragraph (c), paragraph (d) of this section does not apply.

(ii) *Appreciation recognized as income (instead of gain).* The facts are the same as in paragraph (i)(A) of this *Example 1*, except that, instead of selling Asset 1, the value of Asset 1 is consumed in the production of $40 of income in year 1 (reducing the value of Asset 1 to $0). Because the net positive adjustment includes items of income as well as items of gain, the results are the same as those described in paragraph (i) of this *Example 1*.

(iii) *Post-acquisition appreciation eliminates stock loss.* The facts are the same as in paragraph (i)(A) of this *Example 1* except that, in addition, the value of Asset 2 increases to $100 before the stock is sold. As a result, P sells the S share for $140. Because P's sale of the S share is not a transfer of a loss share, this section does not apply to the transfer, notwithstanding that P's basis in the S share was increased by the gain recognized on Asset 1.

(iv) *Distributions.* (A) *Facts.* The facts are the same as in paragraph (i)(A) of this *Example 1* except that, in addition, S distributes a $10 dividend before the end of year 1. As a result, the value of the share decreases and P sells the share for $90. After applying and giving effect to all generally applicable rules of law (other than this section), P's basis in the S share is $130 (P's original $100 basis increased by $30 under §1.1502–32 (the net of the $40 gain recognized on the sale of Asset 1 and the $10 dividend declared and distributed)). P's sale of the S share is a transfer of a loss share and therefore subject to the provisions of this section.

(B) *Application of paragraph (b) of this section.* No adjustment is required under paragraph (b) of this section, either because redetermination would change no member's basis in a share (members hold only one share of S stock) or because P transfers the group's entire interest in S to a nonmember in a fully taxable transaction. See, respectively, paragraphs (b)(1)(ii)(A) and (b)(1)(ii)(B) of this section. After the application of paragraph (b) of this section, P's sale of the S share is still a transfer of a loss share and therefore subject to this paragraph (c).

(C) *Basis reduction under this paragraph (c).* Under this paragraph (c), P's basis in the S share is reduced, but not below value, by the lesser of the share's net positive adjustment and disconformity amount. The share's net positive adjustment is $40 (the sum of all investment adjustments applied to the basis of the share, computed without taking distributions into account). The share's disconformity amount is the excess of its basis ($130) over its allocable portion of S's net inside attribute amount. S's net inside attribute amount is the sum of S's money ($30, the $40 sale proceeds minus the $10 distribution) and S's basis in Asset 2 ($60), or $90. The share is the only outstanding S share and so its allocable portion of the $90 net inside attribute amount is the entire $90. The lesser of the share's net positive adjustment ($40) and its disconformity amount ($40) is $40. Accordingly, the basis in the share is reduced by $40, from $130 to $90, immediately before the sale.

(D) *Application of paragraph (d) of this section.* Because P's sale of the S share is no longer a transfer of a loss share after the application of this paragraph (c), paragraph (d) of this section does not apply.

Example 2. Loss of appreciation reflected in basis. (i) *Facts.* On January 1, year 1, P purchases the sole outstanding share of S stock for $100. At that time, S owns two assets, Asset 1 with a basis of $0 and a value of $40, and Asset 2 with a basis and value of $60. The value of Asset 1 declines to $0 and P sells its S share for $60. After applying and giving effect to all generally applicable rules of law (other than this section), P's basis in the S share remains $100. P's sale of the S share is a transfer of a loss share and therefore subject to the provisions of this section.

(ii) *Application of paragraph (b) of this section.* No adjustment is required under paragraph (b) of this section, either because redetermination would change no member's basis in a share (members hold only one share of S stock) or because P transfers the group's entire interest in S to a nonmember in a fully taxable transaction. See, respectively, paragraphs (b)(1)(ii)(A) and (b)(1)(ii)(B) of this section. After the application of paragraph (b) of this section, P's sale of the S share is still a transfer of a loss share and therefore subject to this paragraph (c).

(iii) *Basis reduction under this paragraph (c).* Under this paragraph (c), P's basis in the S share ($100) is reduced immediately before the sale, but not below value ($60), by the lesser of the share's net positive adjustment and disconformity amount. There were no adjustments to P's basis in the share and so the share's net positive adjustment is $0. Thus, although the share's disconformity amount is $40 (the excess of P's basis in the share ($100) over the share's allocable portion of S's net inside attribute amount ($60)), no basis reduction is required under this paragraph (c).

(iv) *Application of paragraph (d) of this section.* After the application of this paragraph (c), P's sale of the S share is still a transfer of a loss share, and, accordingly, subject to paragraph (d) of this section. No adjustment is required under paragraph (d) of this section because there is no aggregate inside loss. See paragraph (d)(3)(iii) of this section.

Example 3. Items accruing after S becomes a member. (i) *Recognition of loss accruing after S becomes a member.* (A) *Facts.* On January 1, year 1, P purchases the sole outstanding share of S stock for $100. At that time, S owns two assets, Asset 1, with a basis of $0 and a value of $40, and Asset 2, with a basis and value of $60. In year 1, S sells Asset 1 for $40. Also in year 1, the value of Asset 2 declines and S sells Asset 2 for $20. On December 31, year 1, P sells its S share for $60. After applying and giving effect to all generally applicable rules of law (other than this section), P's basis in the S share is $100 (P's original $100 basis, unadjusted under §1.1502–32 because the $40 gain recognized on the sale of Asset 1 offsets the $40 loss on the sale of Asset 2). P's sale of the S share is a transfer of a loss share and therefore subject to the provisions of this section.

(B) *Application of paragraph (b) of this section.* No adjustment is required under paragraph (b) of this section, either because redetermination would change no member's basis in a share (members hold only one share of S stock) or because P transfers the group's entire interest in S to a nonmember in a fully taxable transaction. See, respectively, paragraphs (b)(1)(ii)(A) and (b)(1)(ii)(B) of this section. After the application of paragraph (b) of this section, P's sale of the S share is still a transfer of a loss share and therefore subject to this paragraph (c).

(C) *Basis reduction under this paragraph (c).* Under this paragraph (c), P's basis in the S share ($100) is reduced immediately before the sale, but not below value ($60), by the lesser of the share's net positive adjustment and disconformity amount. The share's net positive adjustment is $0. Thus, although the share has a disconformity amount of $40 (the excess of P's basis in the share ($100) over the share's allocable portion of S's net inside attribute amount ($60)), no basis reduction is required under this paragraph (c).

(D) *Application of paragraph (d) of this section.* After the application of this paragraph (c), P's sale of the S share is still a transfer of a loss share, and, accordingly, subject to paragraph (d) of this section. No adjustment is required under paragraph (d) of this section because there is no aggregate inside loss. See paragraph (d)(3)(iii) of this section.

(ii) *Recognition of gain accruing after S becomes a member.* (A) *Facts.* The facts are the same as in paragraph (i)(A) of this *Example 3*, except that neither P nor S sells anything in year 1. In addition, in year 2, the value of Asset 1 declines to $0, the value of Asset 2 returns to $60, and S creates Asset 3 (with a basis of $0). In year 3, S sells Asset 3 for $40. On December 31, year 3, P sells its S share for $100. After applying and giving effect to all generally applicable rules of law (other than this section), P's basis in the S share is $140 (P's original $100 basis increased under §1.1502–32 to reflect the $40 gain recognized on the sale of Asset 3 in year 3).

(B) *Application of paragraph (b) of this section.* No adjustment is required under paragraph (b) of this section, either because redetermination would change no member's basis in a share (members hold only one share of S stock) or because P transfers the group's entire interest in S to a nonmember in a fully taxable transaction. See, respectively, paragraphs (b)(1)(ii)(A) and (b)(1)(ii)(B) of this section. After the application of paragraph (b) of this section, P's sale of the S share is still a transfer of a loss share and therefore subject to this paragraph (c).

(C) *Basis reduction under this paragraph (c).* Under this paragraph (c), P's basis in the S share ($140) is reduced immediately before the sale, but not below value ($100), by the lesser of the share's net positive adjustment and disconformity amount. The share's net positive adjustment is $40 (the year 3 investment adjustment). The share's disconformity amount is the excess of its basis ($140) over its allocable portion of S's net inside attribute amount. S's net inside attribute amount is $100, the sum of S's money ($40 from the sale of Asset 3) and its basis in its assets ($60 (the sum of Asset 1's basis of $0 and Asset 2's basis of $60)). S's $100 net inside attribute amount is allocable entirely to the sole outstanding S share. Thus, the share's disconformity amount is the excess of $140 over $100, or $40. The lesser of the share's net positive adjustment ($40) and its disconformity amount ($40) is $40. Accordingly, the basis in the share is reduced by $40, from $140 to $100, immediately before the sale.

(D) *Application of paragraph (d) of this section.* Because P's sale of the S share is no longer a transfer of a loss share after the application of this paragraph (c), paragraph (d) of this section does not apply.

(iii) *Recognition of income earned after S becomes a member.* The facts are the same as in paragraph (ii)(A) of this *Example 3*, except that instead of creating Asset 3, S earns $40 of income from services provided in year 3. Because the net positive adjustment includes items of income as well as items of gain, the results are the same as those described in paragraph (ii) of this *Example 3*.

Example 4. Computing the disconformity amount. (i) *Unrecognized loss reflected in stock basis.* (A) *Facts.* P owns the sole outstanding share of S stock with a basis of $100. S owns two assets, Asset 1 with a basis of $20 and a value of $60, and Asset 2 with a basis of $60 and a value of $40. In year 1, S sells Asset 1 for $60. On December 31, year 1, P sells the S share for $100. After applying and giving effect to all generally applicable rules of law (other than this section), P's basis in the S share is $140 (P's original $100 basis increased under §1.1502–32 to reflect the $40 gain recognized on the sale of Asset 1). P's sale of the S share is a transfer of a loss share and therefore subject to the provisions of this section.

(B) *Application of paragraph (b) of this section.* No adjustment is required under paragraph (b) of this section, either because redetermination would change no member's basis in a share (members hold only one share of S stock) or because P transfers the group's entire interest in S to a nonmember in a fully taxable transaction. See, respectively, paragraphs (b)(1)(ii)(A) and (b)(1)(ii)(B) of this section. After the application of paragraph (b) of this section, P's sale of the S share is still a transfer of a loss share and therefore subject to this paragraph (c).

(C) *Basis reduction under this paragraph (c).* Under this paragraph (c), P's basis in the S share ($140) is reduced immediately before the sale, but not below value ($100), by the lesser of the share's net positive adjustment and disconformity amount. The share's net positive adjustment is $40 (the year 1 investment adjustment). The share's disconformity amount is the excess of its basis ($140) over its allocable portion of S's net inside attribute amount. S's net inside attribute amount is the sum of S's money ($60 from the sale of Asset 1) and S's basis in Asset 2 ($60), or $120. S's net inside attribute amount is allocable entirely to the sole outstanding S share. Thus, the share's disconformity amount is the excess of $140 over $120, or $20. The lesser of the share's net positive adjustment ($40) and its disconformity amount ($20) is $20. Accordingly, the basis in the share is reduced by $20, from $140 to $120, immediately before the sale.

(D) *Application of paragraph (d) of this section.* After the application of this paragraph (c), P's sale of the S share is still a transfer of a loss share, and, accordingly, subject to paragraph (d) of this section. Paragraph (d) of this section reduces the basis of Asset 2 by $20 because the loss is duplicated.

(ii) *Loss carryover.* The facts are the same as in paragraph (i)(A) of this *Example 4*, except that Asset 2 has a basis of $0 (rather than $60) and S has a $60 loss carryover (as defined in paragraph (f)(6) of this section). The analysis of the application of this paragraph (c) is the same here as in paragraph (i)(C) of this *Example 4*. Furthermore, the analysis of the application of this paragraph (c) would also be the same if the $60 loss carryover were subject to a section 382 limitation from a prior ownership change, or if, instead, it were subject to the limitation in §1.1502–21(c) on losses carried from separate return limitation years. However, under each alternative fact pattern, paragraph (d) of this section reduces the loss carryover by $20 because the loss is duplicated.

(iii) *Liabilities.* The facts are the same as in paragraph (i)(A) of this *Example 4*, except that S borrows $100 before P sells the S share. S's net inside attribute amount remains $120, computed as the sum of S's money ($160 ($60 from the sale of Asset 1 plus the $100 borrowed cash)) plus S's basis in Asset 2 ($60), minus its liabilities ($100). Thus, the S share's disconformity amount remains the excess of $140 over $120, or $20. The results are the same as in paragraph (i) of this *Example 4*.

Example 5. Computing the allocable portion of the net inside attribute amount. (i) *Facts.* On January 1, year 1, P owns all five outstanding shares of S stock with a basis of $20 per share. S owns Asset with a basis of $0. In year 1, S sells Asset for $100. On December 31, year 1, P sells one of its S shares, Share 1, for $20. After applying and giving effect to all generally applicable rules of law (other than this section), P's basis in Share 1 is $40 (P's original $20 basis increased by $20 under §1.1502–32 to reflect the share's allocable portion of the $100 gain recognized on the sale of Asset). P's sale of Share 1 is a transfer of a loss share and therefore subject to the provisions of this section.

(ii) *Application of paragraph (b) of this section.* No adjustment is required under paragraph (b) of this section because redetermination would change no member's basis in a share (S has only one class of stock outstanding and there is no disparity in the basis of the shares). See paragraph (b)(1)(ii)(A) of this section. After the application of paragraph (b) of this section, P's sale of Share 1 is still a transfer of a loss share and therefore subject to this paragraph (c).

(iii) *Basis reduction under this paragraph (c).* Under this paragraph (c), P's basis in Share 1 ($40) is reduced immediately before the sale, but not below value ($20), by the lesser of the share's net positive adjustment and disconformity amount. Share 1's net positive adjustment is $20 (the year 1 investment adjustment). Share 1's disconformity amount is the excess of its basis ($40) over its allocable portion of S's net inside attribute amount. S's net inside attribute amount is the sum of S's money ($100 from the sale of Asset), and Share 1's allocable portion of S's net inside attribute amount is $20 (1/5 x $100). Thus, Share 1's disconformity amount is the excess of $40 over $20, or $20. The lesser of the share's net positive adjustment ($20) and its disconformity amount ($20) is $20. Accordingly, the basis in the share is reduced by $20, from $40 to $20, immediately before the sale.

(iv) *Application of paragraph (d) of this section.* Because P's sale of Share 1 is no longer a transfer of a loss share after the application of this paragraph (c), paragraph (d) of this section does not apply.

Example 6. Liabilities. (i) *In general.* (A) *Facts.* On January 1, year 1, P purchases the sole outstanding share of S stock for $100. At that time, S owns Asset, with a basis of $0 and value of $100, and $100 cash. S also has a $100 liability. In year 1, S distributes $60 to P and earns $20. The value of Asset declines to $60 and, on December 31, year 1, P sells the S share for $20. After applying and giving effect to all generally applicable rules of law (other than this section), P's basis in the S share is $60 (P's original $100 basis decreased under §1.1502–32 by $40 (the net of the $60 distribution and the $20 income earned)). P's sale of the S share is a transfer of a loss share and therefore subject to the provisions of this section.

(B) *Application of paragraph (b) of this section.* No adjustment is required under paragraph (b) of this section, either because redetermination would change no member's basis in a share (members hold only one share of S stock) or because P transfers the group's entire interest in S to a nonmember in a fully taxable transaction. See, respectively, paragraphs (b)(1)(ii)(A) and (b)(1)(ii)(B) of this section. After the application of paragraph (b) of this section, P's sale of the S share is still a transfer of a loss share and therefore subject to this paragraph (c).

(C) *Basis reduction under this paragraph (c).* Under this paragraph (c), P's basis in the S share ($60) is reduced immediately before the sale, but not below value ($20), by the lesser of the share's net positive adjustment and disconformity amount. The share's net positive adjustment is $20 (the year 1 investment adjustment computed without taking the distribution into account). The share's disconformity amount is the excess of its basis ($60) over its allocable portion of S's net inside attribute amount. S's net inside attribute amount is negative $40, computed as the sum of S's money ($60 ($100 minus the $60 distribution plus the $20 income earned)) plus S's basis in Asset ($0), minus S's liability ($100). S's net inside attribute amount is allocable entirely to the sole outstanding S share. Thus, the share's disconformity amount is the excess of $60 over negative $40, or $100. The lesser of the share's net positive adjustment ($20) and its disconformity amount ($100) is $20. Accordingly, the basis in the share is reduced by $20, from $60 to $40, immediately before the sale.

(D) *Application of paragraph (d) of this section.* After the application of this paragraph (c), the S share is still a loss share and, accordingly, S's attributes are subject to reduction under paragraph (d) of this section. No adjustment is required under paragraph (d) of this section, however, because there is no aggregate inside loss. See paragraph (d)(3)(iii) of this section.

(ii) *Excluded cancellation of indebtedness income—insufficient attributes available for reduction required by sections 108 and 1017, and §1.1502–28.* (A) *Facts.* The facts are the same as in paragraph (i)(A) of this *Example 6*, except that P does not sell the S share. Instead, in year 4, Asset is destroyed in a fire and S spends its $60 on deductible expenses that are not absorbed by the group. S's loss becomes part of the consolidated net operating loss (CNOL). In year 5, S becomes insolvent and S's debt is discharged. Because of S's insolvency, S's discharge of indebtedness income is excluded under section 108 and, as a result, S's attributes are subject to reduction under sections 108 and 1017, and §1.1502–28. S's only attribute is the portion of the CNOL attributable to S ($60) and it is reduced to $0. There are no other consolidated attributes. In year 5, the S stock becomes worthless under section 165(g), taking into account the provisions of §1.1502–80(c). After applying and giving effect to all generally applicable rules of law (other than this section), P's basis in the S share is $60 (P's original $100 basis decreased under §1.1502–32 by the year 1 investment adjustment of $40 (the net of the $60 distribution and the $20 income earned). The investment adjustment for year 5 is $0 ($60 tax exempt income from the excluded COD applied to reduce attributes minus $60 noncapital, nondeductible expense from the reduction of S's portion of the CNOL). Under paragraph (f)(11)(i)(D) of this section, a share is transferred on the last day of the taxable year during which it becomes worthless under section 165(g), taking into account the provisions of §1.1502–80(c). Accordingly, P transfers a loss share of S stock on December 31, year 5, and the transfer is therefore subject to the provisions of this section.

(B) *Application of paragraph (b) of this section.* No adjustment is required under paragraph (b) of this section because redetermination would change no member's basis in a share. See paragraph (b)(1)(ii)(A) of this section. After the application of paragraph (b) of this section, P's transfer of the S share is still a transfer of a loss share and therefore subject to this paragraph (c).

(C) *Basis reduction under this paragraph (c).* Under this paragraph (c), P's basis in its S share ($60) is reduced immediately before the sale, but not below value ($0), by the lesser of the share's net positive adjustment and disconformity amount. The share's net positive adjustment is $20 (the year 1 investment adjustment computed without taking the distribution into account). The share's disconformity amount is the excess of its basis ($60) over its allocable portion of S's net inside attribute amount. S's net inside attribute amount is $0 (S's basis in Asset). (The attribute reduction required under sections 108 and 1017 and §1.1502 28 is given effect before the application of this section; therefore, S's portion of the CNOL was eliminated under section 108 and §1.1502–28.) S's net inside attribute amount is allocable entirely to the sole outstanding S share. Thus, the share's disconformity amount is the excess of $60 over $0, or $60. The lesser of the share's net positive adjustment ($20) and its disconformity amount ($60) is $20. Accordingly, the basis in the share is reduced by $20, from $60 to $40, immediately before the transfer.

(D) *Application of paragraph (d) of this section.* After the application of this paragraph (c), the S share is still a loss share, and, accordingly, S's attributes are subject to reduction under paragraph (d) of this section. No adjustment is required under paragraph (d) of this section, however, because there is no aggregate inside loss. See paragraph (d)(3)(iii) of this section.

(iii) *Excluded cancellation of indebtedness income—full attribute reduction under sections 108 and 1017, and §1.1502–28 (using attributes attributable to another member).* (A) *Facts.* The facts are the same as in paragraph (ii)(A) of this *Example 6* except that P loses the $60 distributed in year 1 and the loss is not absorbed by the group. Thus, as of December 31, year 5, the CNOL is $120, attributable $60 to S and $60 to P. As a result, under §1.1502–28(a)(4), after the portion of the CNOL attributable to S is reduced to $0, the remaining $40 of excluded COD applies to the portion of the CNOL attributable to P, reducing it from $60 to $20. After applying and giving effect to all generally applicable rules of law (other than this section), P's basis in the S share at the end of year 5 is $100 (P's original $100 basis decreased under §1.1502–32 by $40 at the end of year 1 and then increased under §1.1502–32 by $40 at the end of year 5 ($100 tax exempt income from the excluded COD applied to reduce attributes minus $60 noncapital, nondeductible expense from the reduction of S's portion of the CNOL). Under paragraph (f)(11)(i)(D) of this section, a share is transferred on the last day of the taxable year during which it becomes worthless under section 165(g), taking into account the provisions of §1.1502–80(c). Accordingly, P transfers a loss share of S stock on December 31, year 5, and the transfer is therefore subject to the provisions of this section.

(B) *Application of paragraph (b) of this section.* No adjustment is required under paragraph (b) of this section because redetermination would change no member's basis in a share. See paragraph (b)(1)(ii)(A) of this section. After the application of paragraph (b) of this section, P's transfer of the S share is still a transfer of a loss share and therefore subject to this paragraph (c).

(C) *Basis reduction under this paragraph (c).* Under this paragraph (c), P's basis in the S share ($100) is reduced immediately before the sale, but not below value ($0), by the lesser of the share's net positive adjustment and disconformity amount. The share's net positive adjustment is $60 (the sum of the year 1 investment adjustment computed without taking the distribution into account ($20) and the year 5 investment adjustment ($40)). The share's disconformity amount is the excess of its basis ($100) over its allocable portion of S's net inside attribute amount. S's net inside attribute amount is $0 (S's basis in Asset). S's net inside attribute amount is allocable entirely to the sole outstanding S share. The share's disconformity amount is therefore $100. The lesser of the share's net positive adjustment ($60) and its disconformity amount ($100) is $60. Accordingly, P's basis in the share is reduced by $60, from $100 to $40, immediately before the transfer.

(D) *Application of paragraph (d) of this section.* After the application of this paragraph (c), the S share is still a loss share, and, accordingly, S's attributes are subject to reduction under paragraph (d) of this section. No adjustment is required under paragraph (d) of this section, however, because there is no aggregate inside loss. See paragraph (d)(3)(iii) of this section.

Example 7. Lower-tier subsidiary (no transfer of lower-tier stock). (i) *Facts.* P owns the sole outstanding share of S stock with a basis of $160. S owns two assets, Asset A with a basis and value of $100, and the sole outstanding share of S1 stock with a basis of $60. S1 owns one asset, Asset 1, with a basis of $20 and value of $60. In year 1, S1 sells Asset 1 to X for $60, recognizing $40 of gain. On December 31, year 1, P sells its S share to Y, a member of another consolidated group, for $160. After applying and giving effect to all generally applicable rules of law (other than this section), P's basis in the S share is $200 (P's original $160 basis increased under §1.1502–32 by $40 (to reflect the tiering up of the increase to S's basis in the S1 share under §1.1502–32 by $40 (to reflect the gain recognized on S1's sale of Asset 1)). P's sale of the S share is a transfer of a loss share and therefore subject to the provisions of this section. (S does not transfer the S1 share because S and S1 are members of the same group following the transfer. See paragraph (f)(11) of this section.)

(ii) *Application of paragraph (b) of this section.* No adjustment is required under paragraph (b) of this section, either because redetermination would change no member's basis in a share (members hold only one share of S stock) or because P transfers the group's entire interest in S to a nonmember in a fully taxable transaction. See, respectively, paragraphs (b)(1)(ii)(A) and (b)(1)(ii)(B) of this section. After the application of paragraph (b) of this section, P's sale of the S share is still a transfer of a loss share and therefore subject to this paragraph (c).

(iii) *Basis reduction under this paragraph (c).* (A) *In general.* Under this paragraph (c), P's basis in the S share ($200) is reduced immediately before the sale, but not below value ($160), by the lesser of the share's net positive adjustment and disconformity amount. The S share's net positive adjustment is $40. The share's disconformity amount is the excess, if any, of the basis of the share ($200) over the share's allocable portion of S's net inside attribute amount. S's net inside attribute amount is the sum of S's basis in Asset A ($100) plus S's basis in the S1 share.

(B) *S's basis in the S1 share.* Although S's actual basis in the S1 share is $100 (S's original $60 basis increased by S1's year 1 positive $40 investment adjustment), for purposes of computing the S share's disconformity amount, S's basis in the S1 share is tentatively reduced by the lesser of the S1 share's net positive adjustment and its disconformity amount. The S1 share's net positive adjustment is $40 (the year 1 investment adjustment). The S1 share's disconformity amount is the excess, if any, of its basis ($100) over its allocable portion of S1's net inside attribute amount. S1's net inside attribute amount is $60 (its cash received on the sale of Asset 1) and it is entirely attributable to S's S1 share. The S1 share's disconformity amount is therefore the excess of $100 over $60, or $40. The lesser of the S1 share's net positive adjustment ($40) and its disconformity amount ($40) is $40. Accordingly, for purposes of computing the disconformity amount of the S share, S's basis in its S1 share is tentatively reduced by $40, from $100 to $60.

(C) *The disconformity amount of P's S share.* S's net inside attribute amount is treated as the sum of its basis in Asset A ($100) and its (tentatively reduced) basis in its S1 share ($60), or $160. S's net inside attribute amount is allocable entirely to P's S share. Thus, the S share's disconformity amount is the excess of $200 over $160, or $40.

(D) *Amount of reduction.* P's basis in its S share is reduced by the lesser of the S share's net positive adjustment ($40) and disconformity amount ($40), or $40. Accordingly, P's basis in the S share is reduced by $40, from $200 to $160, immediately before the sale.

(E) *Effect on S's basis in its S1 share.* The transaction has no effect on S's basis in the S1 share. Thus, S owns the S1 share with a basis of $100, S's original $60 basis in the share plus the $40 adjustment for the gain recognized on the sale of Asset 1 in year 1.

(iv) *Application of paragraph (d) of this section.* Because P's sale of the S share is no longer a transfer of a loss share after the application of this paragraph (c), paragraph (d) of this section does not apply.

(d) *Attribute reduction to prevent duplication of loss*—(1) *In general.* The rules of this paragraph (d) reduce S's attributes to the extent they duplicate a net loss on shares of S stock transferred by members in a single transaction. This rule furthers single entity principles by preventing S from using deductions and losses to the extent that the group or its members (including former members) have either used, or preserved for later use, a corresponding loss in S shares. This rule applies without regard to whether S ceases to be a member after the transfer of its shares.

(2) *Attribute reduction rule*—(i) *General.* If a transferred share is a loss share after the application of paragraph (c) of this section, S's attributes are reduced by S's attribute reduction amount. S's attribute reduction amount is determined under paragraph (d)(3) of this section and applied in accordance with the provisions of paragraphs (d)(4), (d)(5), and (d)(6) of this section.

(ii) *Transfers of stock of subsidiaries at multiple tiers.* If stock of subsidiaries at multiple tiers is transferred in a transaction, this paragraph (d) (other than paragraph (d)(6) to the extent necessary to make the election to reattribute attributes) applies only after paragraphs (b) and (c) of this section have applied with respect to all transfers of loss shares. See paragraph (a)(3)(ii) of this section regarding the order of application of this section.

(3) *Attribute reduction amount*—(i) *General.* S's *attribute reduction amount* is the lesser of—

(A) The net stock loss (see paragraph (d)(3)(ii) of this section); and

(B) S's aggregate inside loss (see paragraph (d)(3)(iii) of this section).

(ii) *Net stock loss.* The *net stock loss* is the excess, if any, of—

(A) The aggregate basis of all shares of S stock transferred by members in the transaction (taking into account any adjustments required under paragraphs (b) and (c) of this section, any gain or loss recognized at lower tiers, and any other related or resulting adjustments); over

(B) The aggregate value of those shares.

(iii) *Aggregate inside loss*—(A) *General.* S's *aggregate inside loss* is the excess, if any, of—

(*1*) S's net inside attribute amount; over

(*2*) The value of all outstanding shares of S stock.

(B) *Net inside attribute amount.* S's *net inside attribute amount* generally has the same meaning as in paragraph (c)(5) of this section. However, if S holds stock of a lower-tier subsidiary, the provisions of paragraph (d)(5) of this section (and not the provisions of paragraph (c)(6) of this section) modify the computation of S's net inside attribute amount for purposes of this paragraph (d).

(iv) *Transactions that adjusted stock or asset basis.* See paragraph (e)(2) of this section for special rules that may apply if a prior transaction, such as an exchange subject to section 362(e)(2), adjusted the basis in any share of S stock or S's attributes in a manner that altered the potential for loss duplication.

(v) *Lower-tier subsidiaries.* See paragraph (d)(5) of this section for special rules relating to the application of this paragraph (d) if S owns shares of stock of a subsidiary.

(4) *Application of attribute reduction*—(i) *Attributes available for reduction.* S's attributes available for reduction under this paragraph (d) are—

(A) *Category A.* Net operating loss carryovers;

(B) *Category B.* Capital loss carryovers;

(C) *Category C.* Deferred deductions;

(D) *Category D.* Basis in publicly traded property (other than stock of a subsidiary), but only to the extent of the amount, if any, that each such property's basis exceeds its value; and

(E) *Category E.* Basis of assets excluding—

(*1*) Money and cash equivalents, and

(*2*) The basis of publicly traded property (other than stock of a subsidiary).

(ii) *Rules of application*—(A) *In general.* S's attribute reduction amount is allocated and applied to reduce the attributes in each category in the order that the categories are set forth in paragraph (d)(4)(i) of this section. If the amount to be allocated and applied to any category equals or exceeds the amount of attributes in the category, the attributes in that category are reduced to zero and any excess is then allocated and applied to the attributes in the next category. If the amount to be allocated and applied is less than the amount of attributes in any category other than Category A or Category B, it is allocated and applied proportionately to all attributes in the category based on the amount of each attribute. If the amount to be allocated and applied to attributes in Category E exceeds the amount of attributes in that category, then—

(*1*) To the extent of any liabilities of S (or a lower-tier subsidiary) that are not taken into account for tax purposes before the transfer, such excess is suspended and allocated and applied proportionately to reduce any amounts that would be deductible or capitalizable as a result of such liabilities later being taken into account by S or another person; solely for purposes of this paragraph (d)(4)(ii)(A)(*1*), *liability* means any liability or obligation that would be required to be capitalized as an assumed liability by a person that purchased all of S's assets and assumed all of S's liabilities in a single transaction; and

(*2*) To the extent such excess is greater than any amount suspended by paragraph (d)(4)(ii)(A)(*1*) of this section, it is disregarded and has no further effect.

(B) *Order of reduction of loss carryovers.* With respect to attributes in Category A and Category B, the attribute reduction amount is applied first to reduce losses carried from the first taxable year in which a loss carryover arose, and then to reduce loss carryovers that arose in each next successive year.

(C) *Time and effect of attribute reduction.* In general, the reduction of attributes is effective immediately before the transaction in which there is a transfer of a loss share of S stock. If the reduction to a member's basis in a share of S stock exceeds the basis of that share, the excess is an excess loss account to which the member owning the share succeeds (and such excess loss account is not taken into account under §1.1502–19 or otherwise as a result of the transaction). The reductions to attributes required under this paragraph (d)(4), including by reason of paragraph (d)(5)(ii)(D) of this section (tier down of attribute reduction amounts to lower-tier subsidiaries), are not noncapital, nondeductible expenses described in §1.1502–32(b)(2)(iii). Accordingly, such reductions have no effect on the basis of stock of upper-tier subsidiaries.

(5) *Special rules applicable if S holds stock of a lower-tier subsidiary (S1) immediately before a transfer of loss shares of S stock*—(i) *Computation of S's attribute reduction amount.* For purposes of determining S's attribute reduction amount under paragraph (d)(3) of this section—

(A) *Single share.* All of S's shares of S1 stock held immediately before the transaction (whether or not transferred in, or held by S immediately after, the transaction) are treated as a single share (generally referred to as the S1 stock); and

(B) *Deemed basis.* S's basis in its S1 stock is treated as its *deemed basis* in the stock, which is equal to the greater of—

(*1*) The sum of S's basis in each share of S1 stock (adjusted to reflect any gain or loss recognized on the transfer of any S1 shares in the transaction, whether allowed or disallowed); and

(*2*) The portion of S1's net inside attribute amount allocable to S's shares of S1 stock.

(C) *Multiple tiers.* If S owns (directly or indirectly) stock of subsidiaries in multiple tiers (whether or not transferred in, or held by S, directly or indirectly, immediately after, the transaction), S's deemed basis in such stock is determined first with respect to shares of stock of the lowest-tier subsidiary or subsidiaries. Deemed basis is then determined with respect to the basis of stock of subsidiaries in each next higher tier.

(ii) *Allocation and application of S's attribute reduction amount*—(A) *Allocation of attribute reduction amount between S1 stock and other assets.* For purposes of allocating S's attribute reduction amount, S's basis in S1 stock is treated as equal to its deemed basis in the S1 stock (determined under paragraph (d)(5)(i)(B) of this section), reduced by—

(*1*) The value of S's transferred shares of S1 stock,

(*2*) The excess of the sum of S1's money, S1's cash equivalents, the value of S1's publicly traded property (other than stock of a subsidiary) and S1's transferred shares of lower-tier subsidiary (S2) stock, and all corresponding S2 amounts (net of S2's liabilities) that are allocable to S1's nontransferred shares of S2 stock, over the total amount of S1's liabilities, to the extent that such excess is allocable to S's nontransferred shares of S1 stock, and

(*3*) The corresponding amounts with respect to shares of stock of all lower tier subsidiaries.

(B) *Application of attribute reduction amount to S's S1 stock.* The attribute reduction amount allocated to S's S1 stock (the allocated amount) is apportioned among, and applied to reduce S's bases in, S's individual S1 shares in accordance with the following—

(*1*) No allocated amount is apportioned to a share of transferred S1 stock if gain or loss is recognized on its transfer;

(*2*) The allocated amount is apportioned among all of S's other shares of S1 stock in a manner that, when applied to those shares, reduces the disparity in S's bases in the S1 shares to the greatest extent possible;

(*3*) The allocated amount that is apportioned to any S1 share transferred in a transfer in which no gain or loss was recognized is applied only to the extent necessary to reduce the basis of that share to, but not below, the value of the share; and

(*4*) The allocated amount that is apportioned to S1 shares not transferred in the transaction is applied to reduce the bases of such shares without limitation.

(C) *Further effects of allocated amount.* Any portion of the allocated amount that is not applied to reduce S's basis in a share of S1 stock has no effect on any other attributes of S, it is not a noncapital, nondeductible expense of S, and it does not cause S to recognize income or gain. However, as provided in paragraph (d)(5)(ii)(D) of this section, such amounts continue to be part of the allocated amount for purposes of the tier down rule in paragraph (d)(5)(ii)(D) of this section.

(D) *Tier down of attribute reduction amount*—(*1*) *General rule.* The portion of

S's attribute reduction amount that is allocated to S1 stock (the allocated amount) is an attribute reduction amount of S1. Thus, subject to the basis conforming limitation in paragraph (d)(5)(ii)(D)(*2*) of this section, the allocated amount applies to reduce S1's attributes under the provisions of this paragraph (d). The allocated amount is an attribute reduction amount of S1 that must be allocated to S1's assets even if its application to S's basis in S1 stock is limited under paragraph (d)(5)(ii)(B) of this section and even if its application to S1's attributes is limited under paragraph (d)(5)(ii)(D)(*2*) of this section.

(*2*) *Conforming limitation on reduction of lower-tier subsidiary's attributes.* Notwithstanding the general rule in paragraph (d)(5)(ii)(D)(*1*) of this section, and subject to any modification in paragraph (e)(2) of this section, the application of S's attribute reduction amount to S1's attributes (the tier down amount) is limited such that, when combined with any attribute reduction amount computed with respect to a transfer of S1 stock, the total amount of reduction to S1's attributes does not exceed the excess of—

(*i*) The portion of S1's net inside attributes that is allocable to all S1 shares held by members immediately before the transaction; over

(*ii*) The sum of the value of all S1 shares transferred by members in the transaction and the sum of all members' bases in any other shares of S1 stock held immediately before the transaction (after any reduction under this section, including this paragraph (d)).

(iii) *Stock basis restoration.* After this paragraph (d) has applied with respect to all shares of subsidiary stock transferred in the transaction, basis is restored under this paragraph (d)(5)(iii). In general, under this paragraph (d)(5)(iii), reductions otherwise required under paragraph (d)(5)(ii)(B) of this section are reversed to the extent necessary to restore members' bases in subsidiary stock to conform the basis of each member's share of subsidiary stock to the share's allocable portion of the subsidiary's net inside attribute amount as defined in paragraph (c)(5) of this section, without regard to paragraph (c)(6) of this section. The restoration adjustments are first made at the lowest tier and then at each next higher tier successively. Restoration adjustments do not tier up to affect the bases of higher-tier shares. Rather, restoration is computed and applied separately at each tier. For purposes of this rule–

(A) A subsidiary's net inside attribute amount is determined by treating the basis in stock of a lower-tier subsidiary as the actual basis of the stock, as adjusted under this section;

(B) The net inside attribute amount is treated as decreased by any attribute reduction amount suspended under paragraph (d)(4)(ii)(A)(*1*) of this section (liabilities not taken into account); and

(C) If a subsidiary received property in a prior intercompany section 362(e)(2) transaction and the stock of such subsidiary was reduced as the result of an election under section 362(e)(2)(C) (taking into account the provisions of §1.1502–13(e)(4)), the net inside attribute amount must be reduced as provided in paragraph (e)(2) of this section.

(6) *Elections to reduce the potential for loss duplication*—(i) *In general.* Notwithstanding the general operation of this paragraph (d), the common parent of the group of which S is a member immediately before the transaction (P) may make an irrevocable election to reduce the potential for loss duplication, and thereby avoid or reduce attribute reduction. Under this paragraph (d)(6), P may elect to reduce members' bases in transferred loss shares of S stock, or reattribute S's attributes (including attributes of lower-tier subsidiaries) to the extent such attributes would otherwise be subject to reduction under this paragraph (d), or both. The combined amount of stock basis reduction and reattribution of attributes may not exceed S's attribute reduction amount, tentatively computed without regard to any election under this paragraph (d)(6).

(ii) *Order of application*—(A) *Stock of one subsidiary transferred in the transaction.* If shares of stock of only one subsidiary are transferred in the transaction, any stock basis reduction and reattribution of attributes (including from lower-tier subsidiaries) is deemed to occur immediately before the application of this paragraph (d), based on the tentatively computed attribute reduction amount. If a transferred share is still a loss share after giving effect to this election, the provisions of this paragraph (d) then apply with respect to that share.

(B) *Stock of multiple subsidiaries transferred in the transaction.* If shares of stock of more than one subsidiary are transferred in the transaction and elections under this paragraph (d)(6) are made with respect to transfers of stock of subsidiaries in multiple tiers, effect is given to the elections from the lowest tier to the highest tier in the manner provided in this paragraph (d)(6)(ii)(B). The scope of the election for the transfer at the lowest tier is determined by tentatively applying paragraph (d) with respect to the transferred loss shares of this lowest-tier subsidiary immediately after applying paragraphs (b) and (c) of this section to the stock of such subsidiary. The effect of any stock basis reduction or reattribution of losses immediately tiers up (under the principles of §1.1502–32) to adjust members' bases in all higher-tier shares. The process is repeated for elections for each next higher-tier transfer.

(iii) *Special rules for reattribution elections*—(A) *In general.* Because the reattribution election is intended to provide the group a means to retain certain S attributes, and not to change the location of attributes where S continues to be a member, the election to reattribute attributes may only be made if S becomes a nonmember (within the meaning of §1.1502–19(c)(2)) as a result of the transaction. The election to reattribute S's attributes can only be made for attributes in Category A, Category B, and Category C. Attributes subject to the election will be reattributed to P in the same order, manner, and amount that they would otherwise be reduced under paragraph (d)(4) of this section. P succeeds to reattributed attributes as if such attributes were succeeded to in a transaction described in section 381(a). Any owner shift of the subsidiary (including any deemed owner shift resulting from section 382(g)(4)(D) or section 382(l)(3)) in connection with the transaction is not taken into account under section 382 with respect to the reattributed attributes. The reattribution of S's attributes is a noncapital, nondeductible expense described in §1.1502–32(b)(2)(iii). See §1.1502–32(c)(1)(ii)(B) regarding special allocations applicable to such noncapital, nondeductible expense. If P elects to reattribute S attributes (including attributes of a lower-tier subsidiary) and reduce S stock basis, the reattribution is given effect before the stock basis reduction.

(B) *Insolvency limitation.* If S, or any higher-tier subsidiary, is insolvent within the meaning of section 108(d)(3) at the time of the transfer, S's losses may be reattributed only to the extent they exceed the sum of the separate insolvencies of any subsidiaries (taking into account only S and its higher-tier subsidiaries) that are insolvent. For purposes of determining insolvency, liabilities owed to higher-tier members are not taken into account, and stock of a subsidiary that is limited and preferred as to dividends and that is not owned by higher-tier members is treated as a liability to the extent of the amount of preferred distributions to which the stock would be entitled if the subsidiary were liquidated on the date of the disposition.

(C) *Limitation on reattribution from lower-tier subsidiaries.* P's ability to reattribute attributes of lower-tier subsidiaries is limited under this paragraph (d)(6)(iii)(C) in order to prevent circular computations of the attribute reduction amount. Accordingly, attributes that would otherwise be reduced as a result of tier down attribute reduction under paragraph (d)(5)(ii)(D) of this section may only be reattributed to the extent that the reduction in the basis of any lower-tier subsidiary stock resulting from the noncapital, nondeductible expense (as allocated under §1.1502–32(c)(1)(ii)(B)) will not create an excess loss account in any such stock.

(iv) *Special rules for stock basis reduction elections.* An election to reduce basis in S stock is effective for all members' bases in loss shares of S stock that are transferred in the transaction. The reduction is allocated among all such shares in proportion to the amount of loss on each share. This reduction in S stock basis is a noncapital, nondeductible expense of the transferring member. The attribute reduction amount (determined under paragraph (d)(3)(i) of this section) is treated as reduced by the amount of any reduction in the basis of the S stock under this paragraph (d)(6). Accordingly, the election to reduce stock basis under this paragraph (d)(6) is treated as reducing or eliminating the duplication even if the shares of S stock are loss shares after giving effect to the election.

(v) *Form and manner of election.* An election under this paragraph (d)(6) is made in the form of a statement titled "Section 1.1502–36 Election to Reattribute Attributes," "Section 1.1502–36 Election to Reduce Stock Basis," or "Section 1.1502–36 Election to Reattribute Attributes and Reduce Stock Basis," as applicable. The statement must include the name and employer identification number of the subsidiary the stock of which is transferred, the name and employer identification number of any lower-tier subsidiary whose attributes are reattributed, and the amount by which the group is electing to reattribute attributes and/or reduce stock basis. The statement must be included on or with the group's timely filed original return for the taxable year of the transfer of the subsidiary stock to which the election relates.

(7) *Examples.* The application of this paragraph (d) is illustrated by the following examples:

Example 1. Computation of attribute reduction amount. (i) *Transfer of all S shares.* (A) *Facts.* P owns all 100 of the outstanding shares of S stock with a basis of $2 per share. S owns land with a basis of $100, has a $120 loss carryover, and has no liabilities. Each share has a value of $1. P sells 30 of the S shares to X for $30. As a result of the sale, P and S cease to be members of the same group. Accordingly, P transfers all 100 S shares. See paragraphs (f)(11)(i)(A) and (f)(11)(i)(B) of this section. P's transfer of the S shares is a transfer of loss shares and therefore subject to the provisions of this section.

(B) *Application of paragraphs (b) and (c) of this section.* No adjustment is required under paragraph (b) of this section because redetermination would not change any member's basis in an S share (there is only one class of stock outstanding and there is no disparity in the bases of the shares). See paragraph (b)(1)(ii)(A) of this section. No adjustment is required under paragraph (c) of this section because the net positive adjustment is $0. See paragraph (c)(3) of this section. Thus, after the application of paragraph (c) of this section, P's transfer of the S shares is still a transfer of loss shares and, accordingly, subject to this paragraph (d).

(C) *Attribute reduction under this paragraph (d).* Under this paragraph (d), S's attributes are reduced by S's attribute reduction amount. Paragraph (d)(3) of this section provides that S's attribute reduction amount is the lesser of the net stock loss and S's aggregate inside loss. The net stock loss is the excess of the aggregate bases of the transferred shares ($200) over the aggregate value of the transferred shares ($100), or $100. S's aggregate inside loss is the excess of its net inside attribute amount ($220, the sum of the $100 basis of the land and the $120 loss carryover) over the value of all outstanding S shares ($100), or $120. The attribute reduction amount is therefore the lesser of the net stock loss ($100) and the aggregate inside loss ($120), or $100. Under paragraph (d)(4) of this section, S's $100 attribute reduction amount is allocated and applied to reduce S's $120 loss carryover to $20. Under paragraph (d)(4)(ii)(C) of this section, the reduction of the loss carryover is not a noncapital, nondeductible expense and has no effect on P's basis in the S stock.

(ii) *Transfer of less than all S shares.* (A) *Facts.* The facts are the same as in paragraph (i)(A) of this *Example 1*, except that P only sells 20 S shares to X. P's sale of the 20 S shares is a transfer of loss shares and therefore subject to the provisions of this section.

(B) *Application of paragraphs (b) and (c) of this section.* No adjustment is required under paragraph (b) or paragraph (c) of this section for the reasons set forth in paragraph (i)(B) of this *Example 1*. Thus, after the application of paragraph (c) of this section, P's transfer of the S shares is still a transfer of loss shares and, accordingly, subject to this paragraph (d).

(C) *Attribute reduction under this paragraph (d).* Under this paragraph (d), S's attributes are reduced by S's attribute reduction amount. Paragraph (d)(3) of this section provides that S's attribute reduction amount is the lesser of the net stock loss and S's aggregate inside loss. The net stock loss is the excess of the aggregate bases of the transferred shares ($40) over the aggregate value of the transferred shares ($20), or $20. S's aggregate inside loss is the excess of its net inside attribute amount ($220) over the value of all outstanding S shares ($100), or $120. The attribute reduction amount is therefore the lesser of the net stock loss ($20) and the aggregate inside loss ($120), or $20. Under paragraph (d)(4) of this section, S's $20 attribute reduction amount is allocated and applied to reduce S's $120 loss carryover to $100. Under paragraph (d)(4)(ii)(C) of this section, the reduction of the loss carryover is not a noncapital, nondeductible expense and has no effect on P's basis in the S stock.

Example 2. Proportionate allocation of attribute reduction amount. (i) *Facts.* P owns the sole outstanding share of S stock with a basis of $150. S owns land with a basis of $100, a factory with a basis of $20, and rental property with a basis of $30. P sells its S share for $90. P's sale of the S share is a transfer of a loss share and therefore subject to the provisions of this section.

(ii) *Application of paragraphs (b) and (c) of this section.* No adjustment is required under paragraph (b) of this section, either because redetermination would not change any member's basis in a share (members hold only one share of S stock) or because P transfers the group's entire interest in S to a nonmember in a fully taxable transaction. See, respectively, paragraphs (b)(1)(ii)(A) and (b)(1)(ii)(B) of this section. No adjustment is required under paragraph (c) of this section because the net positive adjustment is $0. See paragraph (c)(3) of this section. Thus, after the application of paragraph (c) of this section, P's sale of the S share is still a transfer of a loss share and, accordingly, subject to this paragraph (d).

(iii) *Attribute reduction under this paragraph (d).* Under paragraph (d)(3) of this section, S's attribute reduction amount is determined to be $60, the lesser of the net stock loss ($60) and S's aggregate inside loss ($60, the excess of S's $150 net inside attribute amount (the $100 basis of the land plus the $20 basis of the factory plus the $30 basis of the rental property) over the $90 value of the S share). Under paragraph (d)(4) of this section, the $60 attribute reduction amount is allocated and applied proportionately to reduce S's attributes as follows:

Available attributes	Attribute amount	Allocable portion of attribute reduction amount	Adjusted attribute amount
Category E			
Basis of land	$100	(100/150 x $60) $40	$60
Basis of factory	$20	(20/150 x $60) $8	$12
Basis of rental property	$30	(30/150 x $60) $12	$18
Total attributes	$150	$60	$90

Example 3. Publicly traded property. (i) *Facts.* The facts are the same as in paragraph (i) of *Example 2*, except that, instead of the factory and rental property, S holds two shares of publicly traded stock, Share X (basis and value of $20) and Share Y (basis of $30 and value of $5). P's sale of the S share is a transfer of a loss share and therefore subject to the provisions of this section.

(ii) *Application of paragraphs (b) and (c) of this section.* No adjustment is made under paragraph (b) or paragraph (c) of this section for the reasons set forth in paragraph (ii) of Example 2. Thus, after the application of paragraph (c) of this section, P's sale of the S share is still a transfer of a loss share and, accordingly, subject to this paragraph (d).

(iii) *Attribute reduction under this paragraph (d).* Under paragraph (d)(3) of this section, S's attribute reduction amount is determined to be $60, the lesser of the net stock loss ($60) and S's aggregate inside loss ($60, the excess of S's $150 net inside attribute amount (the $20 basis of Share X plus the $30 basis of Share Y plus the $100 basis of the land) over the $90 value of the S share). Although S has $150 of attributes, S's attributes available for reduction include the basis of publicly traded property only to the extent it exceeds the value of the property. That loss on publicly traded property is a Category D attribute. S's attribute reduction amount is allocated and applied to reduce S's attributes as follows:

Available attributes	Attribute amount	Application of attribute reduction amount	Adjusted attribute amount
Category D			
Loss in Share Y	$25	$25	$0
Category E			
Basis of land	$100	$35	$65
Total attributes	$125	$60	$65

Attributes after application of paragraph (d)	
Attribute	Amount
Basis of Share X	$20
Basis of Share Y	$5
Basis of land	$65

Example 4. Attributes attributable to liability not taken into account. (i) *S operates one business.* (A) *Facts.* On January 1, year 1, P forms S by exchanging $100 and land with a basis of $50 for the sole outstanding share of S stock. In year 1, S earns $500, spends $100 to build a factory on its land, and purchases $450 of publicly traded property. S also earns a section 38 general business credit of $50. However, pollution generated by S's business gives rise to a substantial environmental remediation liability under Federal law. Before any amounts have been taken into account with respect to the environmental remediation liability, P sells its S share to X for $150. At the time of the sale, the value of the publicly traded property was $450. If X had purchased S's assets and assumed S's liabilities directly, X would have been required to capitalize any expenses related to environmental remediation. After giving effect to all other provisions of law, P's basis in the S share is $650 (the original basis of $150 increased by the $500 of income earned). The sale is therefore a transfer of a loss share of subsidiary stock and subject to this section.

(B) *Application of paragraphs (b) and (c) of this section.* No adjustment is required under paragraph (b) of this section, either because redetermination would not change any member's basis in a share (P holds only one share of S stock) or because P transfers the group's entire interest in S to a nonmember in a fully taxable transaction. See, respectively, paragraphs (b)(1)(ii)(A) and (b)(1)(ii)(B) of this section. No adjustment to basis is made under paragraph (c) of this section because, although the net positive adjustment is $500, the disconformity amount is $0. See paragraph (c)(3) of this section. Thus, after the application of paragraph (c) of this section, P's sale of the S share is still a transfer of a loss share and, accordingly, subject to this paragraph (d).

(C) *Attribute reduction under this paragraph (d).* Under paragraph (d)(3) of this section, S's attribute reduction amount is the lesser of the net stock loss ($500) and the aggregate inside loss. The aggregate inside loss is $500, computed as the excess of S's net inside attribute amount ($650, the sum of $100 (basis in factory), $50 (basis in land), $450 (basis in publicly traded property), and $50 (cash remaining after purchases)) over the value of the S share ($150). Thus, S's attribute reduction amount is $500, the lesser of the net stock loss ($500) and the aggregate inside loss ($500). Under paragraph (d)(4) of this section, S's $500 attribute reduction amount is allocated and applied to reduce S's attributes as follows:

Available attributes	Attribute amount	Allocable portion of attribute reduction amount	Adjusted attribute amount
Category D			
Loss on publicly traded property	$0	$0	$0
Category E			
Basis of factory	$100	$100	$0
Basis of land	$50	$50	$0

Under the general rule of this paragraph (d), the remaining $350 attribute reduction amount would have no further effect (and would not be applied to reduce S's general business tax credit). However, S has a liability that has not been taken into account, and, therefore, under paragraph (d)(4)(ii)(A)(*1*) of this section, the remaining $350 attribute reduction amount is suspended and allocated and applied to reduce any amounts that would be deductible or capitalizable as a result of the liability later being taken into account. If the liability is satisfied for an amount that is less than $350, under paragraph (d)(4)(ii)(A)(*2*) the remaining portion of that $350 is disregarded and has no further effect.

(ii) *S operates more than one business.* (A) *Facts.* The facts are the same as in paragraph (i)(A) of *Example 4*, except that S operates a business providing environmental remediation services. Prior to P's sale of the S share, S transfers its environmental remediation services business and its $50 of cash to S1 in exchange for the sole outstanding share of S1 stock. (S's basis in the assets transferred in connection with the environmental remediation business is $0.)

(B) *Application of paragraphs (b) and (c) of this section.* No adjustment is made under paragraph (b) or paragraph (c) of this section for the reasons set forth in paragraph (i)(B) of this *Example 4*. Thus, after the application of paragraph (c) of this section, P's sale of the S share is still a transfer of a loss share and, accordingly, subject to this paragraph (d).

(C) *Attribute reduction under this paragraph (d).* (*1*) *Computation of attribute reduction amount.* Under paragraph (d)(3) of this section, S's attribute reduction amount is the lesser of the net stock loss ($500) and the aggregate inside loss. The aggregate inside loss is the excess of S's net inside attribute amount over the value of the S share. Under paragraph (d)(5)(i)(B) of this section, S's net inside attribute amount is determined by using S's deemed basis in the S1 share ($50, the greater of its basis ($50) and S1's net inside attribute amount ($50)). Accordingly, S's net inside attribute amount is $650 (the sum of $100 (basis in factory), $50 (basis in land), $450 (basis in publicly traded property), and $50 (deemed basis in S1 stock). The aggregate inside loss is $500, computed as the excess of S's net inside attribute amount ($650) over the value of the S share ($150). Thus, S's attribute reduction amount is $500, computed as the lesser of the net stock loss ($500) and the aggregate inside loss ($500).

(*2*) *Allocation, apportionment, and application of attribute reduction amount.* Under paragraphs (d)(4) and (d)(5)(ii) of this section, S's $500 attribute reduction amount is allocated proportionately (by basis) between its assets and the S1 share. Under paragraph (d)(5)(ii)(A) of this section, for this purpose, S's basis in its S1 share is its deemed basis ($50) reduced by S1's cash ($50), or, $0. As a result, no portion of S's attribute reduction amount is allocated to the S1 share and the entire attribute reduction amount is allocated as set forth in paragraph (i)(C) of this *Example 4*. In addition, as in paragraph (i)(C) of this *Example 4*, under paragraph (d)(4)(ii)(A)(*1*) of this section, the remaining $350 excess attribute reduction amount is suspended and applied to the extent of S's environmental remediation liability to reduce any amounts that would be deductible or capitalizable as a result of such liability later being taken into account. Alternatively, assume that S1 had liabilities for employee medical expenses that had not been taken into account for tax purposes, the $350 excess attribute reduction amount would be suspended and then allocated and applied as S's and S1's liabilities are taken into account. In either case, under paragraph (d)(4)(ii)(A)(*2*) of this section, to the extent the suspended amount exceeds the liabilities taken into account, that excess is disregarded and has no further effect.

Example 5. Wholly owned lower-tier subsidiary (no lower-tier transfer). (i) *Application of conforming limitation.* (A) *Facts.* P owns the sole outstanding share of S stock with a basis of $250. S owns Asset with a basis of $100 and the only two outstanding shares of S1 stock (Share A has a basis of $40 and Share B has a basis of $60). S1 owns Asset 1 with a basis of $50. P sells its S share to P1, the common parent of another consolidated group, for $50. The sale is a transfer of a loss share and therefore subject to this section.

(B) *Application of paragraphs (b) and (c) of this section.* No adjustment is required under paragraph (b) of this section, either because redetermination would not change any member's basis in a share (members hold only one share of S stock) or because P transfers the group's entire interest in S to a nonmember in a fully taxable transaction. See, respectively, paragraphs (b)(1)(ii)(A) and (b)(1)(ii)(B) of this section. No adjustment is required under paragraph (c) of this section because, although there is a $50 disconformity amount, the net positive adjustment is $0. See paragraph (c)(3) of this section. Thus, after the application of paragraph (c) of this section, P's sale of the S share is still a transfer of a loss share and, accordingly, subject to this paragraph (d).

(C) *Attribute reduction under this paragraph (d).* (*1*) *Computation of attribute reduction amount.* Under paragraph (d)(3) of this section, S's attribute reduction amount is the lesser of P's net stock loss and S's aggregate inside loss. P's net stock loss is $200 ($250 basis minus $50 value). S's aggregate inside loss is the excess of S's net inside attribute amount over the value of the S share. Under paragraphs (d)(3)(iii)(B) and (d)(5)(i) of this section, S's net inside attribute amount is $200, computed as the sum of S's basis in Asset ($100) and its deemed basis in the S1 stock (treated as a single share) ($100, computed as the greater of S's $100 total basis in the S1 shares and S1's $50 basis in Asset 1). S's aggregate inside loss is therefore $150 ($200 net inside attribute amount minus $50 value of the S share). Accordingly, S's attribute reduction amount is $150, the lesser of the net stock loss ($200) and the aggregate inside loss ($150).

(*2*) *Allocation, apportionment, and application of S's attribute reduction amount.* Under paragraphs (d)(4) and (d)(5)(ii) of this section, S's $150 attribute reduction amount is allocated proportionately (by basis) between Asset (basis $100) and the S1 stock (treated as a single share) (deemed basis $100). Accordingly, $75 of the attribute reduction amount ($100/$200 x $150) is allocated to Asset and $75 of the attribute reduction amount ($100/$200 x $150) is allocated to the S1 stock. The $75 allocated to Asset is applied to reduce S's basis in Asset to $25. The $75 allocated to the S1 stock is first apportioned between the shares in a manner that reduces disparity to the greatest extent possible. Thus, of the total $75 allocated to the S1 stock, $27.50 is apportioned to Share A and $47.50 is apportioned to Share B. The application of the apportioned amounts reduces the basis of each share to $12.50. As a result, immediately after the allocation, apportionment, and application of S's attribute reduction amount, S's basis in Asset is $25 and S's basis in each of the S1 shares is $12.50.

(*3*) *Tier down of S's attribute reduction amount, application of conforming limitation.* Under paragraph (d)(5)(ii)(D) of this section, any portion of S's attribute reduction amount allocated to S1 stock is an attribute reduction amount of S1 (regardless of the extent, if any, to which it is apportioned and applied to reduce the basis of any shares of S1 stock). Under the general rules of this paragraph (d), the $75 allocated to the S1 stock would be applied to reduce S1's basis in Asset 1 to $0. However, under paragraph (d)(5)(ii)(D)(*2*) of this section, S1's attributes can be reduced by only $25 as a result of tier down attribute reduction, the excess of the portion of S1's net inside attribute amount that is allocable to all S1 shares held by members immediately before the transaction ($50) over the sum of the aggregate value of S1 shares transferred by members in the transaction (none) and the aggregate amount of members' bases in nontransferred S1 shares, after reduction under this paragraph ($25). Thus, of S1's $75 tier down attribute reduction amount, only $25 is applied to reduce S1's basis in Asset 1, from $50 to $25. The remaining $50 of allocated amount has no further effect.

(*4*) *Basis restoration.* Under paragraph (d)(5)(iii) of this section, after this paragraph (d) has been applied with respect to all transfers of subsidiary stock, any reduction made to the basis of a share of subsidiary stock under paragraph (d)(5)(ii)(B) of this section is reversed to the extent necessary to conform the basis of that share to the share's allocable portion of the subsidiary's net inside attribute amount. S1's net inside attribute amount after the application of this paragraph (d) is $25 and thus each of the two S1 share's allocable portion of S1's net inside attribute amount is $12.50. Accordingly, the basis of each share (as reduced by this paragraph (d)) is already conformed with its allocable portion of S1's net inside attribute amount and no restoration will be required or permitted under paragraph (d)(5)(iii) of this section.

(ii) *Application of basis restoration rule.* (A) *Facts.* The facts are the same as in paragraph (i)(A) of this *Example 5*, except that S's basis in Share A is $15 and S's basis in Share B is $35, and S1's basis in Asset 1 is $100.

(B) *Basis redetermination and basis reduction under paragraphs (b) and (c) of this section.* No adjustment is required under paragraph (b) or paragraph (c) of this section for the reasons set forth in paragraph (i)(B) of this *Example 5.* Thus, after the application of paragraph (c) of this section, P's transfer of the S share is still a transfer of a loss share and, accordingly, subject to this paragraph (d).

(C) *Attribute reduction under this paragraph (d).* (*1*) *Computation of attribute reduction amount.* Under paragraph (d)(3) of this section, S's attribute reduction amount is the lesser of P's net stock loss and S's aggregate inside loss. P's net stock loss is $200 ($250 basis minus $50 value). S's aggregate inside loss is the excess of S's net inside attribute amount over the value of the S share. Under paragraphs (d)(3)(iii)(B) and (d)(5)(i) of this section, S's net inside attribute amount is $200, computed as the sum of S's basis in Asset ($100) and its deemed basis in the S1 stock (treated as a single share) ($100, computed as the greater of S's $50 total basis in the S1 shares and S1's $100 basis in Asset 1). S's aggregate inside loss is therefore $150 ($200 net inside attribute amount minus $50 value of the S share). Accordingly, S's attribute reduction amount is $150, the lesser of the net stock loss ($200) and the aggregate inside loss ($150).

(*2*) *Allocation, apportionment, and application of S's attribute reduction amount.* Under paragraphs (d)(4) and (d)(5)(ii) of this section, S's $150 attribute reduction amount is allocated proportionately (by basis) between Asset (basis $100) and the S1 stock (treated as a single share) (deemed basis $100). Accordingly, $75 of the attribute reduction amount ($100/$200 x $150) is allocated to Asset and $75 of the attribute reduction amount ($100/$200 x $150) is allocated to the S1 stock. The $75 allocated to Asset is applied to reduce S's basis in Asset to $25. The $75 allocated to the S1 stock is first apportioned between the shares in a manner that reduces disparity to the greatest extent possible. Thus, of the total $75 allocated to the S1 stock, $27.50 is apportioned to Share A and $47.50 is apportioned to Share B. The application of the apportioned amounts reduces the basis of each share to an excess loss account of $12.50. As a result, immediately after the allocation, apportionment, and application of S's attribute reduction amount, S's basis in Asset is $25 and S's basis in each of the S1 shares is an excess loss account of $12.50.

(*3*) *Tier down of S's attribute reduction amount, application of limitation.* Under paragraph (d)(5)(ii)(D) of this section, any portion of S's attribute reduction amount allocated to S1 stock is an attribute reduction amount of S1 (regardless of the extent, if any, to which it is apportioned and applied to reduce the basis of any shares of S1 stock). Accordingly, under the general rules of this paragraph (d), the $75 allocated to the S1 stock is applied to reduce S1's basis in Asset 1 from $100 to $25.

(*4*) *Basis restoration.* Under paragraph (d)(5)(iii) of this section, after this paragraph (d) has been applied with respect to all transfers of subsidiary stock, any reduction made to the basis of a share of subsidiary stock under paragraph (d)(5)(ii)(B) of this section is reversed to the extent necessary to conform the basis of that share to the share's allocable portion of the subsidiary's net inside attribute amount. S1's net inside attribute amount after the application of this paragraph (d) is $25 and thus each of the two S1 share's allocable portion of S1's net inside attribute amount is $12.50. Accordingly, the reductions to Share A and to Share B under this paragraph (d) are reversed to restore the basis of each share to $12.50. Thus, $25 of the $27.50 attribute reduction applied to reduce the basis of Share A and $25 of the $47.50 attribute reduction applied to reduce the basis of Share B are reversed, restoring the basis of each share to $12.50.

Example 6. Multiple blocks of lower-tier subsidiary stock outstanding. (i) *Excess loss account taken into account (transfer of upper-tier share causes disposition within the meaning of §1.1502–19(c)(1)(ii)(B)).* (A) *Facts.* P owns the sole outstanding share of S stock with a basis of $200. S holds all five outstanding shares of S1 common stock (shares A, B, C, D, and E). S has an excess loss account of $20 in share A and a positive basis of $20 in each of the other shares. The only investment adjustment applied to any S1 share was a negative $20 investment adjustment applied to share A when it was the only outstanding share, and this amount tiered up and adjusted P's basis in the S share. S1 owns one asset with a basis of $250. P sells its S share to P1, the common parent of a consolidated group, for $20. The sale of the S share is a disposition of share A under §1.1502–19(c)(1)(ii)(B) (after the transaction, S1 will no longer be a member of the P group). Under paragraph (a)(3)(i) of this section, before the application of this section, S's excess loss account in share A is taken into account, increasing S's basis in share A to $0 and P's basis in its S share to $220. After giving effect to the recognition of the excess loss account, P's sale of the S share is a transfer of a loss share and therefore subject to the provisions of this section.

(B) *Basis redetermination and basis reduction under paragraphs (b) and (c) of this section.* No adjustment is made under paragraph (b) of this section, either because redetermination would change no member's basis in a share (members hold only one share of S stock) or because P transfers the group's entire interest in S to a nonmember in a fully taxable transaction. See, respectively, paragraphs (b)(1)(ii)(A) and (b)(1)(ii)(B) of this section. No adjustment is made under paragraph (c) of this section because, even though there is a disconformity amount of $120, the net positive adjustment is zero. See paragraph (c)(3) of this section. Thus, after the application of paragraph (c) of this section, P's sale of the S share remains a transfer of a loss share and, accordingly, subject to this paragraph (d).

(C) *Attribute reduction under this paragraph (d).* (*1*) *Computation of attribute reduction amount.* Under paragraph (d)(3) of this section, S's attribute reduction amount is the lesser of P's net stock loss and S's aggregate inside loss. P's net stock loss is $200 (the S share's $220 basis minus its $20 value). S's aggregate inside loss is the excess of S's net inside attribute amount over the value of the S share. Under paragraphs (d)(3)(iii)(B) and (d)(5)(i) of this section, S's net inside attribute amount is $250, S's deemed basis in the S1 stock (treated as a single share) ($250, computed as the greater of S's $80 total basis in the S1 shares ($0 basis of share A plus $20 of basis in each of the four other shares) and S1's $250 basis in its asset). S's aggregate inside loss is therefore $230 ($250 net inside attribute amount minus $20 value of the S share). Accordingly, S's attribute reduction amount is $200, the lesser of the net stock loss ($200) and the aggregate inside loss ($230).

(*2*) *Allocation, apportionment, and application of S's attribute reduction amount.* Under paragraphs (d)(4) and (d)(5)(ii) of this section, S's $200 attribute reduction amount is allocated entirely to the S1 stock (treated as a single share) and then apportioned among the shares in a manner that reduces disparity to the greatest extent possible. Thus, $24 is apportioned to share A and $44 is apportioned to each of the other shares. Because there is no transfer of the S1 shares, the apportioned amounts are applied fully to reduce the basis of each share to an excess loss account of $24.

(*3*) *Tier down of S's attribute reduction amount.* Under paragraph (d)(5)(ii)(D) of this section, the $200 of S's attribute reduction amount allocated to the S1 shares is an attribute reduction amount of S1 (regardless of the extent, if any, to which it is apportioned and applied to reduce the basis of any shares of S1 stock). Accordingly, under the general rules of this paragraph (d), S1's $200 attribute reduction amount is allocated and applied to reduce S1's basis in its asset from $250 to $50.

(*4*) *Basis restoration.* Under paragraph (d)(5)(iii) of this section, after this paragraph (d) has been applied with respect to all transfers of subsidiary stock, any reduction made to the basis of a share of subsidiary stock under paragraph (d)(5)(ii)(B) of this section is reversed to the extent necessary to conform the basis of that share to the share's allocable portion of the subsidiary's net inside attribute amount. S1's net inside attribute amount after the application of this paragraph (d) is $50 and thus each of the five S1 share's allocable portion of S1's net inside attribute amount is $10. Accordingly, the reductions to the bases of S1 stock under this paragraph (d) are reversed to restore (to the extent possible) the basis of each share to $10. Thus, $24 of the $24 attribute reduction applied to reduce the basis of share A is reversed, restoring the basis of share A to $0, and $34 of the $44 attribute reduction applied to reduce the basis of each other share is reversed, restoring the basis of each of those shares to $10.

(ii) *Sale of gain share to member.* (A) *Facts.* The facts are the same as in paragraph (i)(A) of this *Example 6*, except that P owns shares A, B, C, and D, S owns share E, S has a liability of $20, and S1's basis in its asset is $500. Also, as part of the transaction, S sells share E to P for $40. Unlike under the facts of paragraph (i)(A) of this *Example 6*, there is no disposition of share A within the meaning of §1.1502–19(c)(1)(ii)(B) (because the share continues to be held by P, and S1 continues to be a member of the P group). As a result, the share A excess loss account is not taken into account. Although S's sale of share E is a transfer of that share, the share is not a loss share and thus the transfer is not subject to this section. P's sale of the S share, however, is a transfer of a loss share and therefore subject to the provisions of this section.

(B) *Transfer in lowest tier (gain share).* S's sale of share E is the lowest tier transfer in the transaction. Under paragraph (a)(3)(ii)(A)(*1*) of this section, because there are no transfers of loss shares at that tier, no adjustments are required under paragraphs (b) and (c) of this section. However, S's gain recognized on the transfer of share E is computed and immediately adjusts members' bases in subsidiary stock under the principles of §1.1502–32 (because P and S are not members of the same group immediately after the transaction, the sale is not subject to §1.1502–13). Accordingly, P's basis in its S share is increased by $20, from $200 to $220.

(C) *Transfers in next higher (the highest) tier (application of paragraphs (b) and (c) of this section).* The next higher tier transfer is P's sale of the S stock. Because the sale is a transfer of a loss share, first paragraph (b) of this section and then paragraph (c) of this section apply to the transfer. No adjustments are required under paragraph (b), either because there is no potential for redetermination (members hold only one share of S stock) or because P transfers the group's entire interest in S to a nonmember in a fully taxable transaction. See, respectively, paragraphs (b)(1)(ii)(A) and (b)(1)(ii)(B) of this section. Under paragraph (c) of this section, P's basis in its S share is decreased by $20, the lesser of the disconformity amount ($200, computed as the excess of stock basis ($220) over S's net inside attribute amount ($20, the $40 value of the transferred share E minus the $20 liability)) and the net positive adjustment ($20). Thus, after the application of paragraph (c) of this section, P's basis in the S share is $200, and the sale remains a transfer of a loss share. There are no higher tier transfers and, therefore, P's transfer of the S share is then subject to this paragraph (d).

(D) *Attribute reduction under this paragraph (d).* (*1*) *Computation of attribute reduction amount.* Under paragraph (d)(3) of this section, S's attribute reduction amount is the lesser of P's net stock loss and S's aggregate inside loss. After the application of paragraph (c) of this section, P's net stock loss is $180 (the S share's $200 basis minus its $20 value). S's aggregate inside loss is the excess of S's net inside attribute amount over the value of the S share. Under paragraphs (d)(3)(iii)(B) and (d)(5)(i) of this section, S's net inside attribute amount is $80, computed as $100 (S's deemed basis in share E (the greater of S's basis in share E, adjusted for the gain recognized, ($40) and share E's allocable portion of S1's net inside attribute amount ($100, representing 1/5 of S1's $500 basis in its asset))) minus S's liability ($20). Accordingly, S's net aggregate inside loss is $60 ($80 net inside attribute amount minus $20 value of the S stock). S's attribute reduction amount is therefore the lesser of $180 and $60, or $60.

(*2*) *Allocation, apportionment, and application of S's attribute reduction amount.* Under paragraphs (d)(4) and (d)(5)(ii) of this section, S's $60 attribute reduction amount is allocated entirely to its S1 stock, share E. However, under paragraph (d)(5)(ii)(B)(*1*) of this section, none of the allocated amount is apportioned to, or applied to reduce the basis of share E, because share E was transferred in a transfer in which gain or loss was recognized. Under paragraph (d)(5)(ii)(C) of this section, the $60 allocated amount not apportioned to share E has no effect on S or S's attributes.

(*3*) *Tier down of S's attribute reduction amount.* Notwithstanding the fact that no portion of the allocated amount was apportioned to or applied to reduce the basis of share E, the entire $60 allocated amount tiers down and is an attribute reduction amount of S1. See paragraphs (d)(5)(ii)(C) and (d)(5)(ii)(D) of this section. Under the general rules of this paragraph (d), S1's $60 attribute reduction amount is allocated and applied to reduce S1's basis in its asset from $500 to $440.

(*4*) *Basis restoration.* Under paragraph (d)(5)(iii) of this section, after this paragraph (d) has been applied with respect to all transfers of subsidiary stock, any reduction made to the basis of a share of subsidiary stock under paragraph (d)(5)(ii)(B) of this section is reversed to the extent necessary to conform the basis of that share to the share's allocable portion of the subsidiary's net inside attribute amount. No reduction was made to the basis of any share of subsidiary stock under paragraph (d)(5)(ii)(B) of this section. Therefore, no stock basis is increased under the basis restoration rule in paragraph (d)(5)(iii) of this section.

Example 7. Allocation of attribute reduction if lower-tier subsidiary has nonloss assets or liabilities. (i) *S1 holds cash.* (A) *Facts.* P owns the sole outstanding share of S stock with a basis of $800. S owns Asset 1 with a basis of $400 and the sole outstanding share of S1 stock with a basis of $300. S1 holds Asset 2 with a basis of $50, and $100 cash. P sells its S share to P1, the common parent of a consolidated group, for $100.

(B) *Application of paragraphs (b) and (c) of this section.* No adjustment is required under paragraph (b) of this section, either because redetermination would change no member's basis in a share (members hold only one share of S stock) or because P transfers the group's entire interest in S to a nonmember in a fully taxable transaction. See, respectively, paragraphs (b)(1)(ii)(A) and (b)(1)(ii)(B) of this section. No adjustment is required under paragraph (c) of this section because the net positive adjustment is $0. See paragraph (c)(3) of this section. Thus, after the application of paragraph (c) of this section, P's sale of the S share is still a transfer of a loss share and, accordingly, subject to this paragraph (d).

(C) *Attribute reduction under this paragraph (d).* (*1*) *Computation of attribute reduction amount.* Under paragraph (d)(3) of this section, S's attribute reduction amount is the lesser of P's net stock loss and S's aggregate inside loss. P's net stock loss is $700 (the S share's $800 basis minus its $100 value). S's aggregate inside loss is the excess of S's net inside attribute amount over the value of the S share. Under paragraphs (d)(3)(iii)(B) and (d)(5)(i) of this section, S's net inside attribute amount is the sum of its basis in Asset 1 of $400 and its deemed basis in the S1 share. S's deemed basis in the S1 share is $300, the greater of S's basis in the S1 share ($300) and S1's net inside attribute amount ($150, S1's $50 basis in Asset 2 plus S1's $100 cash). Therefore, S's net inside attribute amount is $700 and S's aggregate inside loss is $600 ($700 net inside attribute amount less $100 value). S's attribute reduction amount is $600, the lesser of the net stock loss ($700) and the aggregate inside loss ($600).

(*2*) *Allocation, apportionment, and application of S's attribute reduction amount.* Under paragraphs (d)(4) and (d)(5)(ii)(A) of this section, S's $600 attribute reduction amount is allocated proportionately (by basis) between S's basis in Asset 1 ($400) and its deemed basis in the S1 share. For purposes of allocating the attribute reduction amount, S's deemed basis in the S1 share is reduced by S1's $100 cash (from $300 to $200). Thus, the $600 is allocated $400 to Asset 1 ($400/$600 x $600) and $200 to the S1 share ($200/$600 x $600). The $400 allocated to Asset 1 is applied to reduce S's basis in Asset 1 to $0. The $200 allocated to the S1 share is apportioned and applied to reduce S's basis in the S1 share to $100.

(*3*) *Tier down of S's attribute reduction amount.* Under paragraph (d)(5)(ii)(D) of this section, any portion of S's attribute reduction amount allocated to the S1 stock is an attribute reduction amount of S1 (regardless of the extent, if any, to which it is apportioned and applied to reduce the basis of any shares of S1 stock). Accordingly, under the general rules of this paragraph (d), the $200 allocated to the S1 share is an attribute reduction amount of S1 that is allocated and applied entirely to reduce S1's basis in Asset 2 from $50 to $0. The remaining $150 S1 attribute reduction amount is disregarded and has no further effect.

(*4*) *Basis restoration.* Under paragraph (d)(5)(iii) of this section, after this paragraph (d) has been applied with respect to all transfers of subsidiary stock, any reduction made to the basis of a share of subsidiary stock under paragraph (d)(5)(ii)(B) of this section is reversed to the extent necessary to conform the basis of that share to the share's allocable portion of the subsidiary's net inside attribute amount. S1's net inside attribute amount after the application of this paragraph (d) is $100 and thus the S1 share's allocable portion of S1's net inside attribute amount is $100. Accordingly, the basis of the share (as reduced by this paragraph (d)) is already conformed with its allocable portion of S1's net inside attribute amount and no restoration will be required or permitted under paragraph (d)(5)(iii) of this section.

(ii) *S1 borrows cash.* The facts are the same as in paragraph (i)(A) of this *Example 7* except that S1 borrows $50 from X, an unrelated person, immediately before P sells the S share. The computation of the attribute reduction amount is the same as in paragraph (i)(C) of this *Example 7* (because the $50 cash from the loan proceeds and the $50 liability offset in the computation of S's net inside attribute amount). However, under paragraph (d)(5)(ii)(A) of this section, for purposes of allocating the attribute reduction amount, deemed basis is reduced by the amount of

S1's cash, but only to the extent it exceeds S1's liabilities. S1's cash ($150, the original $100 plus the $50 loan proceeds) exceeds its liability ($50) by $100, so S's deemed basis in the S1 share is reduced by $100 (from $300 to $200) for allocation purposes. The results are the same as in paragraph (i) of this *Example 7*.

(iii) *S1 borrows cash and invests in non-publicly traded property*. (A) *Facts*. The facts are the same as in paragraph (ii) of this *Example 7* except that S1 uses its $150 (the original $100 plus the $50 loan proceeds) to purchase Asset 3, an asset that is not publicly traded.

(B) *Application of paragraphs (b) and (c) of this section*. No adjustment is required under paragraph (b) or paragraph (c) of this section for the reasons set forth in paragraph (i)(B) of this *Example 7*. Thus, after the application of paragraph (c) of this section, P's sale of the S share is still a transfer of a loss share and, accordingly, subject to this paragraph (d).

(C) *Attribute reduction under this paragraph (d)*. (*1*) *Computation of attribute reduction amount*. The attribute reduction amount is the same as computed in paragraph (i)(C)(*1*) of this *Example 7* (because $50 of the basis in S1's assets and the $50 liability offset in the computation of S1's net inside attribute amount of $150).

(*2*) *Allocation, apportionment, and application of S's attribute reduction amount*. Under paragraphs (d)(4) and (d)(5)(ii)(A) of this section, S's $600 attribute reduction amount is allocated proportionately (by basis) between S's basis in Asset 1 ($400) and its deemed basis in the S1 share. For purposes of allocating the attribute reduction amount, deemed basis is only reduced for allocation purposes by cash, cash equivalents, and the value of publicly traded property (reduced by liabilities). Thus, there is no reduction to the basis of the S1 share for purposes of allocating the attribute reduction amount. Accordingly, S's $600 attribute reduction amount is allocated $343 ($400/$700 x $600) to Asset 1 and $257 ($300/$700 x $600) to the S1 share.

(*3*) *Tier down of S's attribute reduction amount, application of conforming limitation*. Under paragraph (d)(5)(ii)(D) of this section, any portion of S's attribute reduction amount allocated to the S1 stock is an attribute reduction amount of S1 (regardless of the extent, if any, to which it is apportioned and applied to reduce the basis of any shares of S1 stock). Thus, the entire $257 of S's attribute reduction amount allocated to the S1 share is an attribute reduction amount of S1. Under the general rules of this paragraph (d), the entire amount is allocated to, and would be applied to reduce, S1's bases in Asset 2 and Asset 3, reducing the basis of each asset to $0. However, under paragraph (d)(5)(ii)(D)(*2*) of this section, the reduction is limited to the excess of S1's net inside attribute amount ($150) over S's basis in the S1 share after reduction under this paragraph (d) ($43). Thus, of the $257 attribute reduction amount allocated to the S1 share, only $107 is applied proportionately to reduce S1's bases in Asset 2 by $26.75 ($50/$200 x $107), to $23.25, and Asset 3 by $80.25 ($150/$200 x $107), to $69.75. The remaining $150 S1 attribute reduction amount is disregarded and has no further effect.

(*4*) *Basis restoration*. Under paragraph (d)(5)(iii) of this section, after this paragraph (d) has been applied with respect to all transfers of subsidiary stock, any reduction made to the basis of a share of subsidiary stock under paragraph (d)(5)(ii)(B) of this section is reversed to the extent necessary to conform the basis of that share to the share's allocable portion of the subsidiary's net inside attribute amount. S1's net inside attribute amount after the application of this paragraph (d) is $43 ($23.25 basis in Asset 2 plus $69.75 basis in Asset 3 minus $50 liability) and thus the S1 share's allocable portion of S1's net inside attribute amount is $43. Accordingly, the basis of the share (as reduced by this paragraph (d)) is already conformed with its allocable portion of S1's net inside attribute amount and no restoration will be required or permitted under paragraph (d)(5)(iii) of this section.

Example 8. Election to reduce stock basis or reattribute attributes under paragraph (d)(6) of this section. (i) *Deconsolidating sale*. (A) *Facts*. P owns the sole outstanding share of M stock with a basis of $1,000. M owns all 100 outstanding shares of S stock with a basis of $2.10 per share ($210 total). M sells all its S shares to X for $1 per share (total $100) and makes no election under paragraph (d)(6) of this section. At the time of the sale, S has no liabilities and the following:

Category	Attribute	Attribute amount
Category A	NOL	$10
Category E	Basis of Asset 1	$20
	Basis of Asset 2	$180
	Total Category E	$200

(B) *Application of paragraphs (b) and (c) of this section*. No adjustment is made under paragraph (b) of this section, either because redetermination would change no member's basis in a share (S has only one class of stock outstanding and there is no disparity in the basis of the shares) or because P transfers the group's entire interest in S to a nonmember in a fully taxable transaction. See, respectively, paragraphs (b)(1)(ii)(A) and (b)(1)(ii)(B) of this section. No adjustment is required under paragraph (c) of this section because the net positive adjustment is $0. See paragraph (c)(3) of this section. Thus, after the application of paragraph (c) of this section, M's transfer of the S shares is still a transfer of loss shares and, accordingly, subject to this paragraph (d).

(C) *Attribute reduction under this paragraph (d)*. (*1*) *Computation of attribute reduction amount*. Under paragraph (d)(3) of this section, S's attribute reduction amount is the lesser of the net stock loss ($110, P's aggregate basis in the transferred S shares ($210) less the aggregate value of the transferred shares ($100)) and S's aggregate inside loss. S's aggregate inside loss is $110 (S's $210 net inside attribute amount (the $10 NOL plus the $20 basis of Asset 1 plus the $180 basis of Asset 2) less the $100 value of all outstanding S shares). Thus, the attribute reduction amount is $110.

(*2*) *Application of attribute reduction amount*. S's $110 attribute reduction amount is applied as follows:

Category	Attribute	Attribute amount	Allocation of attribute reduction amount	Adjusted attribute amount
Category A	NOL	$10	$10	$0
Category E	Basis of Asset 1	$20	(20/200 x $100) $10	$10
	Basis of Asset 2	$180	(180/200 x $100) $90	$90
	Total Category E	$200	$100	$100

(D) *Results*. The P group realizes a $110 loss on M's sale of the S shares, which reduces P's basis in the M share from $1,000 to $890. The reduction of S's attributes is not a noncapital, nondeductible expense of S and does not tier up to reduce the basis of the S shares or M share. Immediately after the transaction, the entities own the following:

Entity	Asset	Basis
P	M share	$890
X	100 S shares	$100
S	Asset 1	$10
	Asset 2	$90

(E) *Election to reduce stock basis.* The facts are the same as in paragraph (i)(A) of this *Example 8* except that P elects under paragraph (d)(6) of this section to reduce M's bases in the S shares by the full attribute reduction amount of $110, in lieu of S reducing its attributes. The election is effective for all transferred loss shares and is allocated to such shares in proportion to the loss in each share. Accordingly, the basis of each of the 100 transferred shares is reduced from $2.10 to $1.00. After giving effect to the election, the S shares are not loss shares and this section has no further application to the transfer. The reduction of M's bases in the S shares pursuant to the election under paragraph (d)(6) of this section is a noncapital, nondeductible expense of M that will reduce P's basis in the M share. See paragraph (d)(6)(iv) of this section. Immediately after the transaction, the entities own the following:

Entity		Basis/Attribute
P	M share	$890
X	100 S shares	$100
S	NOL	$10
	Asset 1	$20
	Asset 2	$180

(F) *Election to reattribute losses.* The facts are the same as in paragraph (i)(A) of this *Example 8* except that P elects under paragraph (d)(6) of this section to reattribute S's attributes. Although S's attribute reduction amount is $110, P can only reattribute attributes in Category A, Category B, and Category C. P can therefore elect to reattribute $10 of attributes (the NOL), and, as a result, will reduce S's NOL to $0. The reattribution of the $10 NOL is a noncapital, nondeductible expense of S, and under §1.1502–32(c)(1)(ii)(B) this expense is allocated to the loss shares of S stock sold in proportion to the loss in the shares, or $.10 per share. Further, this expense tiers up under the general rules of §1.1502–32 and reduces P's basis in the M stock by $10. After giving effect to the election, the P group would realize a $100 loss on M's sale of the S shares. M could recognize the $100 stock loss (in which case S's basis in Asset 1 and Asset 2 would be reduced to $10 and $90, respectively, as in paragraph (i)(C)(*2*) of this *Example 8*) or P could elect to reduce M's basis in the S shares by all or any portion of the $100 stock loss (in which case S's attribute reduction amount would be reduced by the amount of the reduction in the basis of the S stock, and S's basis in Asset 1 and Asset 2 would be reduced proportionately).

(ii) *Nondeconsolidating sale.* (A) *Facts.* The facts are the same as in paragraph (i)(A) of this *Example 8*, except that M only sells 20 S shares (for a total of $20).

(B) *Application of paragraphs (b) and (c) of this section.* No adjustment is required under paragraph (b) or paragraph (c) of this section for the reasons set forth in paragraph (i)(B) of this *Example 8*. Thus, after the application of paragraph (c) of this section, M's sale of the S shares is still a transfer of loss shares and, accordingly, subject to this paragraph (d).

(C) *Attribute reduction under this paragraph (d).* (*1*) *Computation of attribute reduction amount.* Under paragraph (d)(3) of this section, S's attribute reduction amount is the lesser of the net stock loss ($22, P's aggregate basis in the transferred S shares ($42) less the aggregate value of the transferred shares ($20)) and S's $110 aggregate inside loss (as calculated in paragraph (i)(C)(*1*) of this *Example 8*). Thus, the attribute reduction amount is $22.

(*2*) *Application of attribute reduction amount.* S's $22 attribute reduction amount is applied as follows:

Category	Attribute	Attribute amount	Allocation of attribute reduction amount	Adjusted attribute amount
Category A	NOL	$10	$10	$0
Category E	Basis of Asset 1	$20	(20/200 x $12) $1.20	$18.80
	Basis of Asset 2	$180	(180/200 x $12) $10.80	$169.20
	Total Category E	$200	$12	$188

(D) *Results.* The P group realizes a $22 loss on M's sale of the S shares, which reduces P's basis in the M share from $1,000 to $978. The reduction of S's attributes is not a noncapital, nondeductible expense of S and does not tier up to reduce the bases of the S shares or M share. Immediately after the transaction, the entities have the following:

Entity	Asset	Basis
P	M share	$978
X	20 S shares	$20
S	Asset 1	$18.80
	Asset 2	$169.20

(E) *Election to reduce stock basis.* The facts are the same as in paragraph (ii)(A) of this *Example 8*, except that P elects under paragraph (d)(6) of this section to reduce M's bases in the S shares by the full attribute reduction amount of $22, in lieu of S reducing its attributes. The election is effective for all transferred loss shares and is allocated to such shares in proportion to the loss in each share. Accordingly, the basis of each of the 20 transferred shares is reduced from $2.10 to $1.00. The P group realizes no loss on M's sale of the S shares. The reduction of M's basis in the S shares pursuant to the election under paragraph (d)(6) of this section is a noncapital, nondeductible expense of M that will reduce P's basis in the M share. Immediately after the transaction, the entities have the following:

Entity		Basis/Attribute
P	M share	$978
X	20 S shares	$20
S	NOL	$10
	Asset 1	$20
	Asset 2	$180

(F) *Election to reattribute attributes.* The facts are the same as in paragraph (ii)(A) of this *Example 8*. Because S remains a member of the P group following M's sale of S stock, P cannot elect under paragraph (d)(6) of this section to reattribute any portion of S's attributes in lieu of attribute reduction.

Example 9. Transfers at multiple tiers, gain and loss shares. (i) *Facts.* P owns the sole outstanding share of S stock with a basis of $700. S owns Asset 1 (basis of $170) and all ten outstanding shares of S1 common stock ($170 basis in share 1, $10 basis in share 2, and $15 basis in each of share 3 through share 10). S1 owns the sole outstanding share of S2 ($0 basis), the sole outstanding share of S3 ($60 basis), and the sole outstanding share of S4 ($100 basis). S2's sole asset is Asset 2 ($75 basis). S3's sole asset is Asset 3 ($75 basis). S4's sole asset is Asset 4 ($80 basis). In one transaction, P sells its S share to P1 (the common parent of a different consolidated group) for $240, S sells S1 share 1 to X for $20, S transfers S1 share 2 to a partnership in a section 721 transaction, and S1 sells its S2 share to Y for $50. No election is made under paragraph (d)(6) to reduce stock basis or reattribute attributes.

(ii) *Transfer in lowest tier (only gain share).* S1's sale of the S2 share is a transfer of the S2 share and that is the lowest tier in which there is a transfer. There is no transfer of a loss share at that tier, and thus this section does not apply to that transfer. The gain recognized on the transfer of the S2 share is computed and is applied to adjust the bases of members' shares of subsidiary stock under the principles of §1.1502–32. Accordingly, $5 is allocated to each of S1 shares, increasing the basis of share 1 to $175, the basis of share 2 to $15, and the basis of each other share to $20. The $50 applied to S's bases in S1 shares then tiers up to increase P's basis in the S share from $700 to $750.

(iii) *Transfers in next higher tier (loss share).* S's sale of the S1 share 1 and S's transfer of the S1 share 2 to a partnership are both transfers of stock in the next higher tier. However, only the S1 share 1 is a loss share and so this section only applies with respect to the transfer of that share.

(A) *Basis redetermination under paragraph (b) of this section.* Under paragraph (b)(2)(i)(A) of this section, members' bases in S1 shares are redetermined by first removing the positive investment adjustments applied to the bases of transferred loss shares. Accordingly, the $5 positive investment adjustment applied to the basis of S1 share 1 is removed, reducing the basis of S1 share 1 from $175 to $170. Because there were no negative adjustments made to the bases of S1 shares, there are no negative adjustments that can be reallocated to further reduce the basis of S1 share 1. Finally, under paragraph (b)(2)(ii)(B), the positive investment adjustment removed from S1 share 1 is reallocated and applied to increase the bases of other S1 shares in a manner that reduces disparity to the greatest extent possible. Accordingly, the entire $5 is reallocated and applied to increase the basis of S1 share 2, from $15 to $20. After basis is redetermined under paragraph (b) of this section, S1 share 1 is still a loss share and therefore subject to basis reduction under paragraph (c) of this section.

(B) *Basis reduction under paragraph (c) of this section.* No adjustment is required to the basis of S1 share 1 under paragraph (c) of this section because, although the disconformity amount is $149 (the excess of the $170 stock basis over the share's $21 allocable portion of S1's net inside attribute amount ($210, determined under paragraph (c)(5) of this section as S1's basis in the stock of S2 (adjusted for the gain recognized) ($50), S3 ($60), and S4 ($100))), the share's net positive adjustment is $0 (because the $5 positive investment adjustment originally allocated to S1 share 1 was reallocated to S1 share 2 under paragraph (b) of this section). See paragraph (c)(3) of this section.

(C) *Computation of loss, adjustments to stock basis.* S recognizes a loss of $150 on the sale of the S1 share 1 ($170 adjusted basis minus $20 amount realized). P's basis in its S share is therefore decreased by the $150 loss recognized by S (on the sale of the S1 share) and increased by the $50 gain that tiered up from S1 (as a result of S1's sale of the S2 share). Following these adjustments, P's basis in the S share is $600 and the sale of the S share is still a transfer of a loss share.

(iv) *Transfer in highest tier (loss share).* The sale of the S share is a transfer in the next higher tier, which is the highest tier in this transaction. Because the sale is a transfer of a loss share, it is subject to this section.

(A) *Basis redetermination and basis reduction under paragraphs (b) and (c) of this section.* No adjustment is required under paragraph (b) of this section, either because there is no potential for redetermination (members hold only one share of S stock) or because P transfers the group's entire interest in S to a nonmember in a fully taxable transaction. See, respectively, paragraphs (b)(1)(ii)(A) and (b)(1)(ii)(B) of this section. In addition, no adjustment is required under paragraph (c) of this section because, although the disconformity amount is $230 (the excess of the $600 stock basis over the $370 allocable portion of S's net inside attribute amount ($370, determined under paragraph (c)(5) of this section as S's basis in the stock of S1 (adjusted for the loss recognized) ($200) and Asset 1 ($170))), the share's net positive adjustment is $0. See paragraph (c)(3) of this section. Accordingly, the sale of the S share is still a transfer of a loss share. Because there are no higher-tier loss shares transferred in the transaction, this paragraph (d) then applies with respect to the transfer of the S share.

(B) *Attribute reduction under this paragraph (d).* *(1) Computation of S's attribute reduction amount.* Under paragraph (d)(3) of this section, S's attribute reduction amount is the lesser of P's net stock loss and S's aggregate inside loss. P's net stock loss is $360 (the S share's $600 adjusted basis minus $240 amount realized). S's aggregate inside loss is the excess of S's net inside attribute amount over the value of the S share. S's net inside attribute amount is the sum of its bases in its assets, treating its S1 shares as a single share (the S1 stock) and treating S's deemed basis in the S1 stock as its basis in that stock. Under paragraph (d)(5)(i)(C) of this section, when subsidiaries are owned in multiple tiers, deemed basis is first determined for shares at the lowest tier, and then for stock in each next higher tier. S1's deemed basis in the S2 stock is $75 (the greater of $50 (S1's basis in the S2 share ($0) increased by the $50 gain recognized) and $75 (S2's basis in Asset 2)). S1's deemed basis in the S3 stock is $75 (computed as the greater of $60 (S1's basis in the S3 share) and $75 (S3's basis in Asset 3)). S1's deemed basis in the S4 stock is $100 (computed as the greater of $100 (S1's basis in the S4 share) and $80 (S4's basis in Asset 4)). Accordingly, S1's net inside attribute amount is $250 ($75 deemed basis in the S2 stock plus $75 deemed basis in the S3 stock plus $100 deemed basis in the S4 stock). S's deemed basis in the S1 stock is the greater of the sum of S's actual basis in each share of S1 stock (adjusted for any gain or loss recognized) and S1's net inside attribute amount. S's actual basis in the S1 stock, adjusted for the loss recognized, is $200 (the sum of S's $170 basis in the S1 share 1 and S's $20 basis in each other S1 share, reduced by the $150 loss recognized). Thus, S's deemed basis in the S1 stock is $250, the greater of $200 (aggregate basis in S1 shares, adjusted for loss recognized) and $250 (S1's net inside attribute amount). As a result, S's net inside attribute amount is $420, the sum of $250 (S's deemed basis in S1 stock) and $170 (S's basis in Asset 1). Accordingly, the aggregate inside loss is $180, the excess of S's net inside attribute amount ($420) over the value of all of the S stock ($240). S's attribute reduction amount is therefore $180, the lesser of the net stock loss ($360) and the aggregate inside loss ($180).

(2) *Allocation, apportionment, and application of S's attribute reduction amount.* Under paragraphs (d)(4) and (d)(5)(ii) of this section, S's $180 attribute reduction amount is allocated proportionately (by basis) between Asset 1 and its S1 stock. Under paragraph (d)(5)(ii)(A) of this section, for purposes of allocating S's $180 attribute reduction amount, S's deemed basis in the S1 stock is reduced by the value of any transferred S1 shares (and other items that are not relevant here). Additionally, for this purpose, S's deemed basis in S1 stock is reduced by S's nontransferred S1 shares' allocable portion of the value of S1's transferred shares of each lower-tier subsidiary's stock (and other items that are not relevant here). Accordingly, for purposes of allocating S's attribute reduction amount, S's deemed basis in the S1 stock must be reduced by $80 (the $40 value of the two transferred S1 shares, and S's eight nontransferred S1 shares' $40 allocable portion of the $50 value of the transferred S2 share), to $170. Thus, $90 of the attribute reduction amount ($170/$340 x $180) is allocated to Asset 1 and $90 of the attribute reduction amount ($170/$340 x $180) is allocated to the S1 stock. Under paragraph (d)(5)(ii)(B)(*1*) of this section, none of the $90 allocated to the S1 stock is apportioned to share 1 because loss is recognized on the transfer of share 1. Under paragraph (d)(5)(ii)(B)(*2*) of this section, the $90 allocated amount is apportioned among the other nine shares of S1 stock in a manner that reduces disparity to the greatest extent possible. Accordingly, of the total $90 allocated amount, $10 is apportioned to each of the remaining shares of S1 stock. Under paragraph (d)(5)(ii)(B)(*3*) of this section, however, an apportioned amount cannot be applied to reduce the basis of a transferred share below its value. Because the basis of share 2 is already equal to its value, none of the $10 apportioned to share 2 is applied to reduce its basis. The amounts apportioned to the remaining S1 shares, however, are applied to reduce the bases of those shares without limitation, reducing the basis of each from $20 to $10. As a result, immediately after the allocation and application of S's attribute reduction amount, S's basis in Asset 1 is $80 ($170 minus $90), its basis in share 1 is $170, its basis in share 2 is $20, and its basis in each other share of S1 stock is $10. Under paragraph (d)(5)(ii)(D) of this section, the entire $90 of S's attribute reduction amount that was allocated to the S1 stock is an attribute reduction amount of S1, regardless of the fact that none of the allocated amount was apportioned to share 1 and none of the amount apportioned to share 2 was applied to reduce the basis of share 2.

(v) *Attribute reduction under this paragraph (d) in next lower tier.* (A) *Computation of S1's attribute reduction amount.* S's sale of share 1 is a transfer of a loss share and is in the next lower tier. Thus, this paragraph (d) next applies with respect to S's transfer of share 1. S1's attribute reduction amount will include both the $90 attribute reduction amount that tiered down from S and any attribute reduction amount resulting from the application of this paragraph (d) with respect to S's transfer of the S1 share 1 (S1's direct attribute reduction amount). Under paragraph (d)(3) of this section, S1's direct attribute reduction amount is the lesser of the net stock loss on transferred S1 shares and S1's aggregate inside loss. The net stock loss on transferred S1 shares is $150, computed as the excess of S's $190 adjusted bases in transferred shares of S1 stock ($170 in share 1 plus $20 in share 2) over the value of those shares ($40). S1's aggregate inside loss is $50, the excess of S1's $250 net inside attribute amount (as calculated in paragraph (iv)(B)(*1*) of this *Example 10*) over the $200 value of all outstanding S1 shares (extrapolated from the amount realized on the sale of share 1). Therefore, S1's direct attribute reduction amount is $50, the lesser of the $150 net stock loss and S1's $50 aggregate inside loss. S1's total attribute reduction amount is thus $140, the sum of the $90 attribute reduction amount that tiered down from S and the $50 direct attribute reduction amount computed with respect to the transfer of share 1.

(B) *Allocation, apportionment, and application of S1's attribute reduction amount.* Under paragraphs (d)(4) and (d)(5)(ii) of this section, S1's $140 attribute reduction amount is allocated proportionately (by basis) among the S2 stock, the S3 stock, and the S4 stock. As described in paragraph (iv)(B)(*2*) of this *Example 10*, under paragraph (d)(5)(ii)(A) of this section, for purposes of allocating S1's $140 attribute reduction amount, S1's deemed basis in the S2 stock is reduced by the value of the transferred S2 share. Accordingly, for purposes of allocating S1's attribute reduction amount, S1's deemed basis in the S2 stock must be reduced by $50 (the value of the transferred S2 share), to $25. Thus, $17.50 of S1's attribute reduction amount ($25/$200 x $140) is allocated to the S2 stock, $52.50 of S1's attribute reduction amount ($75/$200 x $140) is allocated to the S3 stock, and $70 of S1's attribute reduction amount ($100/$200 x $140) is allocated to the S4 stock. Under paragraph (d)(5)(ii)(B)(*1*) of this section, none of the amount allocated to S2 stock is apportioned to the S2 share because gain was recognized on the transfer of the S2 share. However, the $52.50 allocated to the S3 stock is apportioned and applied to reduce the basis in the S3 share, from $60 to $7.50, and the $70 allocated to the S4 stock is apportioned and applied to reduce the basis of the S4 share, from $100 to $30. (Note: Although the conforming limitation in paragraph (d)(5)(ii)(D)(*2*) of this section limits the application of tier down attribute reduction such that the total amount of attribute reduction applied to reduce S1's attributes does not exceed $130 (the excess of S1's $250 net inside attribute amount over $120, the value of the transferred S1 shares ($40) plus the basis of the nontransferred S1 shares after reduction ($80)), this limitation does not apply because only $122.50 ($52.50 plus $70) of attribute reduction is applied to reduce S1's attributes.) Under paragraph (d)(5)(ii)(D) of this section, the attribute reduction amount allocated to the S2 stock, the S3 stock, and the S4 stock becomes an attribute reduction amount of S2, S3, and S4, respectively (even though the amount allocated to S2 stock was not apportioned or applied to reduce the basis of the S2 share).

(vi) *Attribute reduction under this paragraph (d) in lowest tier.* Although the sale of the S2 share is a transfer of subsidiary stock at the next lower tier, the S2 share is not a loss share. Thus, this paragraph (d) does not apply with respect to that transfer. However, S2, S3, and S4 have attribute reduction amounts that tiered down from S1 and that are applied to reduce attributes under the provisions of this paragraph (d).

(A) *Tier down of S1's attribute reduction amount to S2.* Under the general rules of this paragraph (d), S2's $17.50 attribute reduction amount is allocated and applied to reduce S2's basis in Asset 2 from $75 to $57.50.

(B) *Tier down of S1's attribute reduction amount to S3.* Under the general rules of this paragraph (d), S3's $52.50 of attribute reduction amount is allocated and applied to reduce S3's basis in Asset 3 from $75 to $22.50.

(C) *Tier down of S1's attribute reduction amount to S4, application of conforming limitation.* Under the general rules of this paragraph (d), S4's $70 attribute reduction amount is allocated to, and would be applied to reduce, S4's basis in Asset 4. However, under paragraph (d)(5)(ii)(D)(*2*) of this section, the reduction is limited to the excess of S4's net inside attribute amount ($80) over the basis of the S4 share ($30, after reduction under this paragraph (d)). As a result, only $50 (the excess of $80 over $30) of S4's $70 attribute reduction amount is applied to S4's basis in Asset 4, reducing it from $80 to $30. The remaining $20 of S4's attribute reduction amount is disregarded and has no further effect.

(vii) *Application of basis restoration rule.* After all adjustments required under this paragraph (d) have been given effect, reductions made to the basis of subsidiary stock under this paragraph (d) are subject to reversal under the basis restoration rule in paragraph (d)(5)(iii) of this section. Under this rule, adjustments are reversed (and basis is restored) only to the extent necessary to conform the basis of each share with its allocable portion of the subsidiary's net inside attribute amount. The restoration adjustments are first made at the lowest tier and then at each next higher tier successively.

(A) *Basis restoration at lowest tier.* No restoration is permitted with respect to the S2 share because the basis of the S2 share was not reduced under paragraph (d)(5)(ii)(B) of this section. S3's net inside attribute amount ($22.50, after reduction under this paragraph (d)) exceeds S1's basis in the S3 share ($7.50, after reduction under this paragraph (d)) by $15. To conform S1's basis in the S3 share to S3's net inside attribute amount, the $52.50 reduction to the basis of the S3 share under paragraph (d)(5)(ii)(B) of this section is reversed by $15 (restoring basis to $22.50). The restoration of S1's basis in the S3 share does not tier up to affect the basis in stock of any other subsidiary. S1's basis in the S4 share ($30, after reduction under this paragraph (d)) is already conformed with S4's net inside attribute amount ($30, after reduction under this paragraph (d)) and no restoration will be required or permitted under paragraph (d)(5)(iii) of this section.

(B) *Basis restoration at next higher tier.* Each share of S1 stock has an allocable portion of S1's net inside attribute amount equal to $10.25 (1/10 x $102.50, the sum of S1's adjusted bases in its S2 stock ($50, $0 plus $50 gain recognized), S3 stock ($22.50 after restoration), and S4 stock ($30)). Neither S's basis in S1 share 1 nor S's basis in S1 share 2 was reduced under this paragraph (d). Accordingly, the basis of neither share is subject to restoration under paragraph (d)(5)(iii) of this section. However, S's basis in each of its other shares of S1 stock was reduced by $10, from $20 to $10. Accordingly, the reduction to the basis of each of those shares is reversed to the extent of $.25, to restore the basis of each such share to $10.25 (its allocable portion of S1's net inside attribute amount).

(vii) *Results.* After the application of this section, P recognizes a loss of $360 on the sale of the S share, S recognizes a loss of $150 on the sale of S1 share 1, and S1 recognizes a $50 gain on the sale of the S2 share. Immediately after the transaction, the entities each directly own the following:

Entity	Asset	Basis	Value
P1	S share	$240	$240
P	Proceeds of the sale of S share	$240	$240
S	Proceeds of sale of Share 1 of S1 stock	$20	$20
	Partnership interest received for Share 2	$20	$20
	Shares 3 through 10 of S1 stock	$82 ($10.25 per share)	
S1	Proceeds of sale of S2 share	$50	$50
	The S3 share	$22.50	
	The S4 share	$30	
S2	Asset 2	$57.50	
S3	Asset 3	$22.50	
S4	Asset 4	$30	
X	Share 1 of S1 stock	$20	$20
Y	The S2 share	$50	$50
Partnership	Share 2 of S1 stock	$20	$20

(e) *Operating rules*—(1) *Predecessors, successors.* This section applies to predecessor or successor persons, groups, and assets to the extent necessary to effectuate the purposes of this section.

(2) *Adjustments for prior transactions that altered stock basis or other attributes.* In certain situations, M's basis in S stock or S's attributes are adjusted in a manner that alters the relationship between stock basis and inside attributes. Such adjustments affect the extent to which this relationship identifies unrecognized asset gain reflected in stock basis and the extent to which loss is duplicated. The provisions of this paragraph (e)(2) modify the computations in paragraphs (c) and (d) of this section to adjust for the effects of such adjustments.

(i) *Reductions to S's basis in assets or other attributes pursuant to section 362(e)(2)(A).* If S's attributes have been reduced under section 362(e)(2) (taking into account the provisions of §1.1502–13(e)(4)), then the disconformity amount of the S shares received (or deemed received) in the transaction to which section 362(e)(2) applied is reduced by the amount that the basis in such shares would have been reduced under section 362(e)(2)(C) (taking into account the provisions of §1.1502–13(e)(4)) had such an election been made. In addition, for purposes of determining the attribute reduction amount under paragraph (d) of this section resulting from the transfer of any S shares received (or deemed received) in a transaction to which section 362(e)(2) applied, and for purposes of applying paragraph (d)(5)(ii)(D)(*2*) of this section (conforming limitation) to S, the basis in such shares is treated as reduced by the amount the basis in such shares would have been reduced under section 362(e)(2)(C) (taking into account the provisions of §1.1502–13(e)(4)) had such an election been made.

(ii) *Reductions to the basis of any share of S stock pursuant to an election under section 362(e)(2)(C).* If the basis of any share of S stock has been reduced as the result of an election under section 362(e)(2)(C) (taking into account the provisions of §1.1502–13(e)(4)), then, for purposes of computing either any S share's disconformity amount or S's aggregate inside loss, and for purposes of applying paragraph (d)(5)(iii) of this section (stock basis restoration) to S, S's net inside attribute amount is reduced by the amount that S's attributes would have been reduced under section 362(e)(2)(A) (taking into account the provisions of §1.1502–13(e)(4)) in the absence of an election under section 362(e)(2)(C) (taking into account the provisions of §1.1502–13(e)(4)).

(iii) *Other adjustments*. The Commissioner shall make such adjustments as appropriate if the relationship between a member's basis in a share of S stock and the share's allocable portion of S's net inside attributes has been altered, other than by the operation of §1.1502–32 or this section, provided that such change is not otherwise addressed in this section. Taxpayers may request a written determination from the Commissioner determining that other adjustments to M's basis in S stock or S's attributes are to be adjusted in a manner consistent with the principles of this paragraph (e)(2) for purposes of making the computations under paragraphs (c) and (d) of this section.

(iv) *Example*. The application of this paragraph (e)(2) is illustrated by the following example:

Example. Adjustments for intercompany section 362(e)(2) transaction. (i) *Adjustments for reduction of S's basis in assets*. (A) *Facts*. In an intercompany section 362(e)(2) transaction (within the meaning of §1.1502–13(e)(4)(i)), P contributes Asset 1 to newly formed S in exchange for the sole outstanding share of S stock. At the time of the contribution, P's basis in Asset 1 was $100 and its value was $20. Accordingly, S's basis in Asset 1 would have been reduced by $80 under section 362(e)(2) and that $80 is a section 362(e)(2) amount within the meaning of §1.1502–13(e)(4)(ii)(A). P sells the S share for $20 in year 3. As of the time of the sale, no portion of the section 362(e)(2) amount has been taken into account and thus the entire $80 is a remaining section 362(e)(2) amount reflected in S's basis in Asset 1 and P's basis in the share of S stock. P's sale of the S share is a section 362(e)(2) application event within the meaning of §1.1502–13(e)(4)(iii) and therefore, immediately before the sale, S's basis in Asset 1 is reduced by $80 pursuant to section 362(e)(2) and §1.1502–13(e)(4)(iv). Under §1.1502–13(e)(4)(iv)(C), this reduction is not a noncapital, nondeductible expense described in §1.1502–32(b)(2)(iii), and does not affect P's basis in the S share. The sale is also a transfer of a loss share and therefore subject to the provisions of this section.

(B) *Application of paragraph (b) of this section*. No adjustment is required under paragraph (b) of this section, either because there is no potential for redetermination (members hold only one share of S stock) or because P transfers the group's entire interest in S to a nonmember in a fully taxable transaction. See, respectively, paragraphs (b)(1)(ii)(A) and (b)(1)(ii)(B) of this section. After the application of paragraph (b) of this section, P's sale of the S share is still a transfer of a loss share and therefore subject to paragraph (c) of this section.

(C) *Basis reduction under paragraph (c) of this section*. In determining the reduction of basis under paragraph (c) of this section, the share's disconformity amount is reduced by $80, the amount that the basis in the S share would have been reduced under §1.1502–13(e)(4)(v) had such an election been made. The disconformity amount (and the net positive adjustment) are $0 and so no basis adjustment will be made under paragraph (c) of this section. The transferred share is still a loss share and so is therefore subject to paragraph (d) of this section.

(D) *Attribute reduction under paragraph (d) of this section*. In determining the attribute reduction amount under paragraph (d)(3) of this section, P's basis in the transferred share is treated as reduced by $80, the amount that the basis in the S share would have been reduced under §1.1502–13(e)(4)(v) had such an election been made. As a result, P recognizes an $80 loss on the sale of the S stock, but, for purposes of applying paragraph (d) of this section, the net stock loss and, therefore, the attribute reduction amount are $0.

(ii) *Adjustments for election to reduce stock basis under section 362(e)(2)(C)*. The facts are the same as in paragraph (i) of this *Example*, except that P and S elect to reduce P's basis in the S share by $80 under §1.1502–13(e)(4)(v). As a result, the basis of Asset 1 remains $100 and, immediately before the sale of the S stock, P's basis in the S share is reduced to $20. Because the share is then not a loss share, this section does not apply to the transfer. If, instead, the share were sold for less than $20, it would be a loss share and the transfer would be subject to this section. In that case, for purposes of computing the S share's disconformity amount, S's aggregate inside loss, and applying paragraph (d)(5)(iii) of this section, S's net inside attributes would be treated as reduced by $80, the amount that S's attributes would have been reduced under §1.1502–13(e)(4)(iv) had the election under §1.1502–13(e)(4)(v) not been made.

(3) *Plural, singular*. All terms used in this section include both the plural and singular as the context may require.

(f) *Definitions*. In addition to the definitions in other paragraphs of this section and in §1.1502–1, the following definitions apply for purposes of this section.

(1) *Allocable portion* has the same meaning as in §1.1502–32(b)(4)(iii)(B). Thus, for example, within a class of stock, each share has the same allocable portion of the net inside attribute amount and, if there is more than one class of stock, the net inside attribute amount is allocated to each class by taking into account the terms of each class and all other facts and circumstances relating to the overall economic arrangement.

(2) *Deferred deduction* means any deduction for expenses or loss that would be taken into account under general tax accounting principles as of the time of the transfer of the share, but that is nevertheless not taken into account immediately after the transfer by reason of the application of a deferral provision. Such provisions include, for example, sections 267(f) and 469, and §1.1502–13. *Deferred deduction* also includes equivalent amounts, such as negative adjustments under section 475 (mark to market accounting method for dealers in securities) and section 481 (adjustments required by changes in method of accounting).

(3) *Distribution* has the same meaning as in §1.1502–32(b)(3)(v).

(4) *Higher tier, lower tier*. A subsidiary (S1) (and its shares of stock) is *higher tier* with respect to another subsidiary (S2) (and its shares of stock) if investment adjustments made to the bases of shares of S2 stock under §1.1502–32 affect the investment adjustments made to the bases of shares of S1 stock. A subsidiary (S1) (and its shares of stock) is *lower tier* with respect to another subsidiary (S) (and its shares of stock) if investment adjustments made to the bases of shares of S1 stock affect the investment adjustments made to the bases of shares of S stock. The term lowest-tier subsidiary generally refers to a subsidiary that owns no stock of another subsidiary. The term highest-tier subsidiary generally refers to a subsidiary the stock of which is not lower tier to any shares transferred in the transaction.

(5) *Liability* means a liability that has been incurred within the meaning of section 461(h), except to the extent otherwise provided in paragraph (d)(4)(ii)(A)(*1*) of this section.

(6) *Loss carryover* means any net operating or capital loss carryover attributable to S that is or, under the principles of §1.1502–21, would be carried to S's first taxable year, if any, following the year of the transfer.

(7) *Loss share, gain share*. A *loss share* is a share of stock with a basis that exceeds its value. A *gain share* is a share of stock with a value that exceeds its basis.

(8) *Preferred stock, common stock*. *Preferred stock* and *common stock* have the same meanings as in §1.1502–32(d)(2) and (3), respectively.

(9) *Publicly traded property*. Property is *publicly traded property* if it is traded on an established market within the meaning of §1.1273–2(f).

(10) *Transaction* includes all the steps taken pursuant to the same plan or arrangement.

(11) *Transfer*—(i) *Definition*. Except as provided in paragraph (f)(11)(ii) of this section, for purposes of this section, M

transfers a share of S stock on the earliest of—

(A) The date that M ceases to own the share as a result of a transaction in which, but for the application of this section, M would recognize gain or loss with respect to the share;

(B) The date that M and S cease to be members of the same group;

(C) The date that a nonmember acquires the share from M; and

(D) The last day of the taxable year during which the share becomes worthless under section 165(g), taking into account the provisions of §1.1502–80(c).

(ii) *Excluded transactions*. Notwithstanding paragraph (f)(11)(i) of this section, M does not transfer a share of S stock if—

(A) M ceases to own the share as a result of a section 381(a) transaction in which any member acquires assets from S or in which S acquires assets from M, provided that, in either case, M recognizes no gain or loss with respect to the share; or

(B) M ceases to own the share as a result of a distribution of the share to a nonmember in a transaction to which section 355 applies, provided M does not recognize any gain or loss with respect to the share as a result of the distribution of the share.

(12) *Value* means the amount realized, if any, or otherwise the fair market value.

(g) *Anti-abuse rule*—(1) *General rule*. If a taxpayer acts with a view to avoid the purposes of this section or to apply the rules of this section to avoid the purposes of any other rule of law, appropriate adjustments will be made to carry out the purposes of this section or such other rule of law.

(2) *Examples*. The following examples illustrate the principles of the anti-abuse rule in this paragraph (g). No implication is intended regarding the potential applicability of any other anti-abuse rules:

Example 1. Stuffing gain asset to eliminate loss. (i) *Facts*. On January 1, year 1, P owns Asset 1 with a basis of $0 and a value of $100. On that same date, P purchases the sole outstanding share of S stock for $100. At that time, S owns Asset 2 with a basis of $0 and a value of $100. In year 1, S sells Asset 2 for $100. In year 2, with a view to avoiding the basis reduction rule in paragraph (c) of this section upon the sale of the S share, P contributes Asset 1 to S in a transaction to which section 351 applies and receives an additional share of S stock with a basis of $0 under section 358. On December 31, year 2, P sells its two S shares for $200. After applying and giving effect to all generally applicable rules of law (other than this section), P's basis in the original share of S stock is $200 (P's original $100 basis, increased by $100 under §1.1502–32 to reflect the $100 gain recognized on the sale of Asset 2), and P's basis in the other share of S stock is $0.

(ii) *Analysis*. Absent the application of this paragraph (g), P would not recognize any net gain or loss on the sale of the two S shares. Under paragraph (c)(7) of this section, for purposes of computing the basis reduction required by paragraph (c) of this section, P's basis in the original share of S stock would be treated as reduced by the gain recognized on the other share of S stock. Further, P would not recognize any net stock loss within the meaning of paragraph (d)(3)(ii) of this section. Accordingly, this section would not apply to the transfer of the S shares. However, because P contributed Asset 1 to S with a view to avoiding the basis reduction rule in paragraph (c) of this section, the contribution of Asset 1 is disregarded for purpose of applying this section. Accordingly, this section applies to the sale of the S share without regard to the contribution of Asset 1, and the basis of the original S share is reduced by $100 under paragraph (c) of this section. P recognizes no gain or loss on the sale of the original S share, and $100 of gain on the sale of the other S share.

Example 2. Loss Trafficking. (i) *Facts*. On January 1, year 1, P purchases the sole outstanding share of S stock for $100. At that time, S owns one asset, Asset 1, with a basis of $0 and a value of $100. In year 1, S sells Asset 1 for $100 and, with a view to eliminating the disconformity amount, S purchases the sole outstanding share of X stock, a corporation with a $100 NOL and an asset with a basis and value of $1, from an unrelated party for $1. In year 2, X is liquidated into S in a transaction to which section 332 applies. On December 31, year 2, P sells its S share for $100. After applying and giving effect to all generally applicable rules of law (other than this section), P's basis in the S share is $200 (P's original $100 basis, increased under §1.1502–32 to reflect the $100 gain recognized on the sale of Asset 1). P's sale of the S share is a transfer of a loss share and therefore subject to the provisions of this section.

(ii) *Analysis*. No adjustment is required under paragraph (b) of this section, either because there is no potential for redetermination (members hold only one share of S stock) or because P transfers the group's entire interest in S to a nonmember in a fully taxable transaction. See, respectively, paragraphs (b)(1)(ii)(A) and (b)(1)(ii)(B) of this section. Under paragraph (c) of this section, P's basis in the S share ($200) is reduced, but not below the share's value ($100), by the lesser of the share's net positive adjustment and disconformity amount. The share's net positive adjustment is the greater of zero and the sum of all investment adjustments applied to the basis of the share, computed without taking distributions into account. There are no distributions. The only investment adjustment to the S share is the $100 positive adjustment attributable to the gain recognized on the sale of Asset 1. The share's net positive adjustment is therefore $100. The share's disconformity amount is the excess, if any, of its basis ($200) over its allocable portion of S's net inside attribute amount. Because S purchased the X stock and liquidated X with a view to avoiding the purposes of this section (to utilize X's attributes to minimize the disconformity amount of the S loss share), the attributes acquired from X are disregarded for purposes of applying this section. Accordingly, S's net inside attribute amount is limited to S's money ($100 from the sale of Asset 1, less $1 for the purchase of the X stock), or $99. The loss share's allocable portion of the $99 net inside attribute amount is $99. The loss share's disconformity amount is therefore the excess of $200 over $99, or $101. The lesser of the share's net positive adjustment ($100) and disconformity amount ($101) is $100. As a result, the basis in the loss share is reduced by $100, and P recognizes no gain or loss on the sale of the S share.

Example 3. Use of a partnership to prevent current attribute reduction. (i) *Facts*. P owns 100 shares of S stock with a basis of $10 each. S owns Asset 1 with a basis of $1000 and a value of $100. In year 1, with a view to preventing a current reduction in the basis of Asset 1, S and M form a partnership. S contributes Asset 1 and M contributes Asset 2. On December 31, year 1, P sells 20 S shares for $1 each. After applying paragraph (c) of this section, P's basis in each transferred S share is still $10, and P recognizes a $180 loss (a $9 loss on each transferred S share).

(ii) *Analysis*. No adjustment is required under paragraph (b) of this section because S has only one class of stock outstanding and there is no disparity in the bases of the shares. See paragraph (b)(1)(ii)(A) of this section. No adjustment is required under paragraph (c) of this section because the net positive adjustment is $0. See paragraph (c)(3) of this section. Absent the application of this paragraph (g), under paragraph (d) of this section S's attribute reduction amount of $180 would be applied to reduce S's basis in the partnership interest. Because S acted with a view to avoiding a current reduction in the basis of Asset 1 under paragraph (d) of this section, this section is applied by treating S as if it held Asset 1 at the time of the stock sale.

Example 4. Creation of an intercompany receivable to mitigate attribute reduction. (i) *Facts*. P owns 100 shares of S stock each with equal basis that exceeds value. S owns cash and Asset 1 with a basis that exceeds value. In year 1, with a view to mitigating a reduction in the basis of Asset 1, S lends the cash to M. On December 31, year 1, P sells 20 S shares and recognizes a loss.

(ii) *Analysis*. No adjustment is required under paragraph (b) of this section because S has only one class of stock outstanding and there is no disparity in the bases of the shares. See paragraph (b)(1)(ii)(A) of this section. No adjustment is required under paragraph (c) of this section because the net positive adjustment is $0. See paragraph (c)(3) of this section. Absent the application of this paragraph (g), under paragraph (d) of this section S's attribute reduction amount would be applied to proportionately reduce the basis in S's assets. Accordingly, S's basis in both its intercompany receivable and Asset 1 would be reduced. Because S acted with a view to mitigating the reduction in the basis of Asset 1 under paragraph (d) of this section, this section is applied without regard to the intercompany receivable. Accordingly, S's basis in Asset 1 is reduced by the full attribute reduction amount.

(h) *Effective date*. This section applies to all transfers on or after the date these regulations are published as final regulations in the **Federal Register**. For rules applicable on and after March 10, 2006, and before the date these regulations are published as final regulations in the **Federal Register**, see §§1.1502–35 and 1.337(d)–2 as contained in 26 CFR part 1 in effect on January 1, 2007. For rules applicable on and after March 3, 2005 and before March 10, 2006, see §§1.337(d)–2T, 1.1502–20 and 1.1502–35T as contained in 26 CFR part 1 in effect on April 1, 2005. For rules applicable before March 3, 2005, see §§1.337(d)–2T, 1.1502–20, and 1.1502–35T as contained in 26 CFR part 1 in effect on April 1, 2004.

Par. 16. Section 1.1502–80 is amended by:

1. Revising paragraphs (a) and (c).
2. Adding new paragraph (g).

The revisions and addition read as follows:

§1.1502–80 Applicability of other provisions of law.

(a) *In general.* The Internal Revenue Code, or other law, shall be applicable to the group to the extent the regulations do not exclude its application. To the extent not excluded, other rules operate in addition to, and may be modified by, these regulations. Thus, for example, in a transaction to which section 381(a) applies, the acquiring corporation will succeed to the tax attributes described in section 381(c). Furthermore, sections 269 and 482 apply for any consolidated year. However, in a recognition transaction otherwise subject to section 1001, for example, the rules of section 1001 continue to apply, but may be modified by the intercompany transaction regulations under §1.1502–13. Nothing in these regulations shall be interpreted or applied to require an adjustment to a member's basis in subsidiary stock or other attributes to the extent the adjustment would have the effect of duplicating another adjustment required under the Code or other rule of law, including other provisions of these regulations.

* * * * *

(c) *Deferral of section 165*—(1) *General rule.* Subsidiary stock is not treated as worthless under section 165 until immediately before the earlier of the time—

(i) The stock is worthless within the meaning of §1.1502–19(c)(1)(iii); and

(ii) The subsidiary for any reason ceases to be a member of the group.

(2) *Cross reference.* See §1.1502–36 for additional rules relating to stock loss.

* * * * *

(g) *Effective dates.* Paragraphs (a) and (c) of this section are applicable on or after the date these regulations are published as final regulations in the **Federal Register**.

Par. 17. Section 1.1502–91 is amended by revising paragraph (h)(2) to read as follows:

§1.1502–91 Application of section 382 with respect to a consolidated group.

* * * * *

(h) * * *

(2) *Disposition of stock or an intercompany obligation of a member.* Gain or loss recognized by a member on the disposition of stock (including stock described in section 1504(a)(4) and §1.382–2T(f)(18)(ii) and (iii)) of another member is treated as a recognized gain or loss for purposes of section 382(h)(2) (unless disallowed) even though gain or loss on such stock was not included in the determination of a net unrealized built-in gain or loss under paragraph (g)(1) of this section. Gain or loss recognized by a member with respect to an intercompany obligation is treated as recognized gain or loss only to the extent (if any) the transaction gives rise to aggregate income or loss within the consolidated group. The first sentence of this paragraph (h)(2) is applicable on or after the date these regulations are published as final regulations in the **Federal Register**.

* * * * *

Par. 18. For each section listed in the table, remove the language in the "Remove" column and add in its place the language in the "Add" column as set forth below:

Section	Remove	Add
§1.267(f)–1(k)	§1.337(d)–2; §1.1502–35	§1.1502–36
§1.597–4(g)(2)(v)	§§1.337(d)–2 and 1.1502–35(f)	§1.1502–36
§1.1502–11(b)(3)(ii)(c)	§§1.337(d)–2 and 1.1502–35	§1.1502–36
§1.1502–12(r)	§§1.337(d)–2 and 1.1502–35	§1.1502–36
§1.1502–15(b)(2)(iii)	§§1.337(d)–2, 1.1502–35, or	§1.1502–36
§1.1502–32(b)(3)(iii)(B)	§1.1502–35(b) or (f)(2)	

Mark E. Matthews,
Deputy Commissioner for Services and Enforcement.

(Filed by the Office of the Federal Register on January 16, 2007, 10:51 a.m., and published in the issue of the Federal Register for January 23, 2007, 72 F.R. 2963)

Update to Revenue Procedure 2001–31, Filing Summary of Archer MSAs, Electronically

Announcement 2007–15

The Tax Relief and Healthcare Act of 2006 (P.L. 109–432) requires trustee/custodians to file Form 8851, *Summary of Archer MSAs.* Revenue Procedure 2001–31 contains procedures for filing Form 8851. Currently, this revenue procedure is being revised but will not be available by March 20, 2007, the due date of Form 8851. Numerous changes are being made to the revenue procedure. This announcement details the major changes so filers can use this announcement along with Revenue Procedure 2001–31 to file

Form 8851 electronically. The changes are:

- The name of the Martinsburg Computing Center was changed to Enterprise Computing Center – Martinsburg (ECC-MTB).

- The due date for filing Forms 8851 was changed to March 20, 2007. This date is effective for both filing periods, January 1, 2005 through June 20, 2005 and January 1, 2006 through June 20, 2006. A separate transmission is required for each filing period.

- ECC-MTB no longer accepts magnetic media for the filing of Forms 8851. The only acceptable method for those with over 250 forms is electronic filing via the Filing Information Returns System (FIRE) at *http://fire.irs.gov*. For more information regarding the FIRE system, refer to Publication 3609, *Filing Information Returns Electronically*, which can be downloaded from *www.irs.gov*. Filers of Form 8851 must call ECC-MTB toll-free at 1–866–455–7438, ext. 3 for log-on instructions.

If you have questions concerning the filing of Form 8851, *Summary of Archer MSAs*, please contact the Internal Revenue Service ECC-MTB toll-free at 866–455–7438.

Emancipation Day Holiday Filing and Payment Extension

Announcement 2007–16

Taxpayers across the nation have until Tuesday, April 17, 2007, to file their 2006 returns and pay any taxes due. Taxpayers have extra time to file and pay because April 15 falls on a Sunday in 2007, and the following day, Monday, April 16, is Emancipation Day, a legal holiday in the District of Columbia. This means the entire country has an April 17 deadline. Previously, the April 17 deadline applied just to individuals in the District of Columbia and six eastern states who are served by an IRS processing facility in Massachusetts, where Patriots Day will be observed on April 16, 2007.

By law, filing and payment deadlines that fall on a Saturday, Sunday or legal holiday are timely satisfied if met on the next business day. Under I.R.C. § 7503, holidays observed in the District of Columbia have impact nationwide on tax issues, not just in the District of Columbia. Under city legislation, April 16 is a holiday in the District of Columbia. See § 301.7503–1(b), Proc. & Admin. Regs.; D.C. Code § 28–2701; D.C. LEGIS 16–91.

Among the tax-filing and payment requirements affected by this change, the April 17, 2007 deadline will apply to any of the following:

2006 federal individual income tax returns, whether filed electronically or on paper;

Requests for an automatic six-month tax-filing extension, whether submitted electronically or on Form 4868;

Tax year 2006 balance due payments, whether made electronically (direct debit or credit card) or by check;

Tax-year 2006 contributions to a Roth or traditional IRA;

Individual estimated tax payments for the first quarter of 2007, whether made electronically or by check; and

Individual refund claims for tax year 2003, where the regular three-year statute of limitations is expiring.

Other tax-filing and payment requirements affected by this change are described in IRS Publication 509, *Tax Calendars for 2007*, available at the IRS web site at *http://www.irs.gov/publications/p509/index.html*.

Exclusion From Gross Income of Previously Taxed Earnings and Profits and Adjustments to Basis of Stock in Controlled Foreign Corporations and of Other Property; Correction

Announcement 2007–17

AGENCY: Internal Revenue Service (IRS), Treasury.

ACTION: Correction to notice of proposed rulemaking.

SUMMARY: This document corrects notice of proposed rulemaking (REG–121509–00, 2006–40 I.R.B. 602) that was published in the **Federal Register** on Tuesday, August 29, 2006 (71 FR 51155). The document contains proposed regulations that provide guidance relating to the exclusion from gross income of previously taxed earnings and profits under section 959 of the Internal Revenue Code (Code) and related basis adjustments under section 961 of the Code.

FOR FURTHER INFORMATION CONTACT: Ethan Atticks, (202) 622–3840 (not a toll-free number).

SUPPLEMENTARY INFORMATION:

Background

The notice of proposed rulemaking (REG–121509–00) that is the subject of these corrections is under sections 959 and 961 of the Internal Revenue Code.

Need for Correction

As published, REG 121509–00 contains errors that may prove to be misleading and are in need of clarification.

Correction of Publication

Accordingly, the notice of proposed rulemaking (REG–121509–00), that was the subject of FR Doc. 06–7195, is corrected as follows:

1. On page 51155, column 1, in the preamble, under the paragraph heading "Background", the last paragraph of the column, third line, the language, "sections 959 and 961. Section 959(a)(1)" is

corrected to read "sections 959, 961, and 1502. Section 959(a)(1)".

2. On page 51156, column 1, in the preamble, the last paragraph of the column, fifth line from bottom, the language "109–222), which provides for look-" is corrected to read "109–222), which generally provides for look-".

3. On page 51156, column 3, in the preamble, under paragraph heading "2. Shareholder PTI Accounts", sixth line, the language "directly, or indirectly under section" is corrected to read "directly or indirectly under section".

4. On page 51157, column 1, in the preamble, under paragraph heading "3. Successors in Interest", second paragraph, sixteenth line, the language "corporation from a person that is not a" is corrected to read "corporation from any person, including a person that is not a".

5. On page 51157, column 1, in the preamble, under paragraph heading "*B. CFC-Level Exclusion Under Section 959(b)*", first line of first paragraph, the language "The earnings and profits of a CFC" is corrected to read "Section 959(b) provides an exclusion pursuant to which the earnings and profits of a CFC".

6. On page 51157, column 1, in the preamble, under paragraph heading "*B. CFC-Level Exclusion Under Section 959(b)*", first paragraph, third line from the bottom of the paragraph, the language "rules regarding cross-chain sales of" is corrected to read "to provide guidance regarding cross-chain sales of".

7. On page 51157, column 2, in the preamble, first paragraph of the column, ninth line, the language "section 951(a)) and a $100 of non-" is corrected to read "section 951(a)) and $100x of non-".

8. On page 51157, column 2, in the preamble, first paragraph of the column, last line, the language "$91x ((70% x $30) + (70% x $100))." is corrected to read "$91x ((70% x $30x) + (70% x $100x)).".

9. On page 51157, column 2, in the preamble, second paragraph of the column, third line, the language "accordingly, provides that, the amount" is corrected to read "accordingly, provides that the amount".

10. On page 51157, column 2, in the preamble, second paragraph of the column, eleventh line, the language "of section 958(a)) in the lower-tier and" is corrected to read "of section 958(a)) in the lower- and".

11. On page 51157, column 2, in the preamble, fourth paragraph of the column, seventh line, the language "CFC from a person who was not taxed" is corrected to read "CFC from a person that was not taxed".

12. On page 51157, column 3, in the preamble, first paragraph of the column, eighth line, the language "inclusion is still $100. In contrast, Prop." is corrected to read "inclusion is still $100x. In contrast, Prop.".

13. On page 51157, column 3, in the preamble, under the paragraph heading "1. Shareholder-Level Accounting of PTI", last line of the column, the language "shareholder who owns the stock or by" is corrected to read "shareholder that owns the stock or by".

14. On page 51158, column 2, in the preamble, under the paragraph heading "a. Dollar Basis Pooling Election", first paragraph of the column, ninth to fifteenth lines, the language "to a distribution of PTI. Notice 88–71, 1988–2 C.B. 374, makes this pooled approach available to taxpayers for purposes of section 986(c) at the taxpayer's election, but it does not provide guidance as to how this election is made. The proposed regulations" is corrected to read "to a distribution of PTI. The proposed regulations make this pooled approach available to taxpayers for purposes of section 986(c) at the taxpayer's election. The proposed regulations".

15. On page 51158, column 3, in the preamble, under paragraph heading "4. Adjustment of Shareholder PTI Accounts", second paragraph, tenth line, the language "corporation. Next, a shareholder's PTI" is corrected to read "corporation. Second, a shareholder's PTI".

16. On page 51160, column 1, in the preamble, under paragraph heading "b. Shareholder That Is a Member of a Consolidated Group", first paragraph, seventh line from the bottom of the first paragraph, the language "consolidated group who own stock in" is corrected to read "consolidated group that own stock in".

17. On page 51160, column 1, in the preamble, second paragraph, eleventh line, the language "taxable year who own stock in the" is corrected to read "taxable year that own stock in the".

18. On page 51161, column 3, in the preamble, under paragraph heading "*A. Coordination of Shareholder-Level and Corporate-Level Accounts*", ninth line, the language "PTI information is to be shared between" is corrected to read "PTI information is to be shared among".

19. On page 51161, column 3, in the preamble, thirteenth line, the language "are necessary, and if so, how they" is corrected to read "are necessary and, if so, how they".

20. On page 51162, column 3, in the preamble, under paragraph heading "*F. Section 961(c) Basis Adjustments*", first line of the paragraph, the language "Section 961(c) is by its terms only" is corrected to read "Section 961(c) is only".

§ 1.959–1 [Corrected]

21. On page 51163, column 3, § 1.959–1(a), second line of the column, the language "except that such distributions shall" is corrected to read "except that such distribution shall".

22. On page 51164, column 1, § 1.959–1(b)(2), first paragraph of the column, fifth and sixth lines, the language "any) that are attributable to section 951(a) inclusions." is corrected to read "any).".

23. On page 51164, column 1, § 1.959–1(b)(3), second paragraph of the column, third line, the language "income with respect to the previously" is corrected to read "a United States shareholder's income with respect to the previously".

24. On page 51164, column 1, § 1.959–1(b)(4)(iii), second line from the bottom of the paragraph, the language "corporations are members of the same" is corrected to read "if both the first mentioned corporation and the covered shareholder are members of the same".

25. On page 51165, column 1, § 1.959–1(d)(3), second paragraph of the column, first line, the language "The application of this paragraph" is corrected to read "*Examples*. The application of this paragraph".

26. On page 51165, column 1, § 1.959–1(d)(3), *Example 1.*, paragraph heading, the language "*Shareholder previously taxed earnings and profits account.*" is corrected to read "*Shareholder's previously taxed earnings and profits account.*".

27. On page 51165, column 1, § 1.959–1(d)(3)(i), eighth and ninth lines, the language "currency. FC earns $100x of subpart F income in year 1 and $100x of non-subpart" is corrected to read "cur-

rency. In year 1, FC earns \$100x of subpart F income and \$100x of non-subpart F".

§ 1.959–2 [Corrected]

28. On page 51165, column 2, § 1.959–2(a)(1), fourth line from the bottom of the paragraph, the language "income of such distributee CFC also" is corrected to read "income of such upper-tier CFC also".

29. On page 51165, column 3, § 1.959–2(a)(2), paragraph (i) of *Example 2.*, second line from the bottom of the paragraph, the language "2, and FC had no earnings for year 2 other" is corrected to read "2, and FC had no earnings and profits for year 2 other".

30. On page 51165, column 3, § 1.959–2(a)(2), paragraph (ii) of *Example 3.*, eighth and ninth lines, the language "DP's *pro rata* share of the remaining \$50, or \$35 (\$50 x 70%), is included in DP's gross" is corrected to read "DP's *pro rata* share of the remaining \$50x, or \$35x (\$50x x 70%), is included in DP's gross".

31. On page 51166, column 1, § 1.959–2(a)(2), paragraph (ii) of *Example 3.*, first paragraph of the column, first line, the language "reduced to \$0, however, as a result of the" is corrected to read "reduced to \$0, as a result of the".

32. On page 51166, column 1, § 1.959–2(b)(2), third paragraph of the column, first line, the language "The application of this paragraph" is corrected to read "*Example.* The application of this paragraph".

§ 1.959–3 [Corrected]

33. On page 51166, column 3, § 1.959–3(b)(3)(i), third paragraph of the column, fifth through twelfth lines, the language "earnings and profits in the year in which such amounts are included in gross income of a United States shareholder under section 951(a) and are reclassified as to category of earnings and profits in the year in which such amounts would be so included but for the provisions of" is corrected to read "earnings and profits in the taxable year of the foreign corporation in which such amounts are included in the gross income of a United States shareholder under section 951(a) and are reclassified as to category of earnings and profits in the taxable year of the foreign corporation in which such amounts would be so included in the gross income of a United States shareholder under section 951(a) but for the provisions of".

34. On page 51167, column 2, § 1.959–3(c)(1), third paragraph of the column, fourth line, the language "are distributed by a foreign corporation" is corrected to read "are distributed by a foreign corporation to another foreign corporation".

35. On page 51167, column 2, § 1.959–3(c)(1), fourteenth line, the language "included in the foreign corporation's" is corrected to read "included in the distributee foreign corporation's".

36. On page 51167, column 2, § 1.959–3(c)(2), fourth paragraph of the column, first line, the language "The application of this paragraph" is corrected to read "*Example.* The application of this paragraph".

37. On page 51172, column 3, § 1.959–3(g)(4), paragraph (i) of *Example 1.*, first paragraph of the column, fourth line from the bottom of the paragraph, the language "earnings and profits on its stock Class A" is corrected to read "earnings and profits on its Class A".

38. On page 51173, column 3, § 1.959–3(g)(4), paragraph (i) of *Example 5.*, third line, the language "on its stock Class A stock consisting of a" is corrected to read " on its Class A stock consisting of a".

39. On page 51174, column 3, § 1.959–3(h)(3)(i), third paragraph of the column, fourth line from the bottom of the paragraph, the language "§§ 1.959–1 and this section shall apply" is corrected to read "§ 1.959–1 and this section shall apply".

40. On page 51175, column 1, § 1.959–3(h)(4)(i), fourth paragraph of the column, fifth line from the bottom of the paragraph, the language "§§ 1.959–1 and this section shall" is corrected to read "§ 1.959–1 and this section shall".

41. On page 51175, column 1, § 1.959–3(h)(4)(ii), fifth paragraph of the column, first line, the language "The application of this paragraph" is corrected to read "*Example.* The application of this paragraph".

§ 1.961–2 [Corrected]

42. On page 51177, column 1, § 1.961–2(d), paragraph (i) of *Example 3.*, third paragraph of the column, third line from the bottom of the paragraph, the language "December 31, of year 1. In year 2, DP has a" is corrected to read "December 31 of year 1. In year 2, DP has a".

§ 1.961–3 [Corrected]

43. On page 51177, column 2, § 1.961–3(a)(1), first paragraph of the column, second line from the bottom of the paragraph, the language "shareholders gross income under" is corrected to read "shareholder's gross income under".

44. On page 51177, column 3, § 1.961–3(b)(1), third paragraph of the column, twelfth line, the language "than wholly owned by a single United" is corrected to read "than wholly indirectly owned by a single United".

LaNita Van Dyke,
Chief, Publications and Regulations Branch,
Legal Processing Division,
Associate Chief Counsel
(Procedure and Administration).

(Filed by the Office of the Federal Register on December 7, 2006, 8:45 a.m., and published in the issue of the Federal Register for December 8, 2006, 71 F.R. 71116)

Flat Rate Supplemental Wage Withholding; Correction

Announcement 2007–20

AGENCY: Internal Revenue Service (IRS), Treasury.

ACTION: Correcting amendment.

SUMMARY: This document contains correction to final regulations (T.D. 9276, 2006–37 I.R.B. 423) that were published in the **Federal Register** on Tuesday, July 25, 2006 (71 FR 42049), amending the regulations that provide for determining the amount of income tax withholding on supplemental wages. These regulations apply to all employers and others making supplemental wage payments to employees.

DATES: The correction is effective January 1, 2007.

FOR FURTHER INFORMATION CONTACT: A. G. Kelley, (202) 622–6040 (not a toll-free number).

SUPPLEMENTARY INFORMATION:

Background

The final regulations that are the subject of this correction are under sections 3401 and 3402 of the Internal Revenue Code.

Need for Correction

As published, final regulations (T.D. 9276) contain an error that may prove to be misleading and is in need of clarification.

* * * * *

Correction of Publication

Accordingly, 26 CFR part 31 is corrected by making the following correcting amendment:

PART 31—EMPLOYMENT TAXES AND COLLECTION OF INCOME TAX AT SOURCE

Paragraph 1. The authority citation for part 31 continues to read, in part, as follows:

Authority: 26 U.S.C. 7805 * * *

Par. 2. Section 31.3402(g)–1(a)(8) is amended by revising the last sentence of *Example 3* paragraph (iv). The revision reads as follows:

§ 31.3402(g)–1 Supplemental wage payments.

(a) * * *

(8) * * *

Example 3. * * *

(iv) * * * If R elects to use optional flat rate withholding provided under paragraph(a)(7)(iii)(F) of this section, withholding would be calculated at 25 percent of the $1,000,000 portion of the payment and would be $250,000.

* * * * *

LaNita Van Dyke,
Chief, Publications and Regulations Branch, Legal Processing Division, Associate Chief Counsel (Procedure and Administration).

(Filed by the Office of the Federal Register on January 25, 2007, 8:45 a.m., and published in the issue of the Federal Register for January 26, 2007, 72 F.R. 3734)

Part I. Rulings and Decisions Under the Internal Revenue Code of 1986

Section 412.—Minimum Funding Standards

26 CFR 1.412(l)(7)–1: Mortality tables used to determine current liability.

T.D. 9310

DEPARTMENT OF THE TREASURY
Internal Revenue Service
26 CFR Part 1

Updated Mortality Tables for Determining Current Liability

AGENCY: Internal Revenue Service (IRS), Treasury.

ACTION: Final regulations.

SUMMARY: This document contains final regulations providing mortality tables to be used in determining current liability for purposes of applying certain pension funding requirements. These regulations affect sponsors, administrators, participants, and beneficiaries of certain retirement plans.

DATES: *Effective Date:* These regulations are effective February 2, 2007.

Applicability Date: These regulations apply for plan years beginning on or after January 1, 2007.

FOR FURTHER INFORMATION CONTACT: Bruce Perlin or Linda Marshall at (202) 622–6090 (not a toll-free number).

SUPPLEMENTARY INFORMATION:

Background

Section 412 of the Internal Revenue Code provides minimum funding requirements with respect to certain defined benefit pension plans.[1] Title I of the Pension Protection Act of 2006 (PPA), Pub. L. No. 109–280, 120 Stat. 780, makes extensive changes to the rules of section 412, generally applicable to plan years beginning on or after January 1, 2008. Except as otherwise stated, all references to section 412 in this document refer to section 412 without regard to the amendments made by Title I of PPA.

Section 412(l) provides additional funding requirements for certain defined benefit pension plans, based in part on a plan's unfunded current liability, as defined in section 412(l)(8). Pursuant to section 412(c)(6), if the otherwise applicable minimum funding requirement exceeds the plan's full funding limitation (defined in section 412(c)(7) as the excess of a specified measure of plan liability over the plan assets), then the minimum funding requirement for the year is reduced by that excess. Under section 412(c)(7)(E), the full funding limitation cannot be less than the excess of 90% of the plan's current liability (including the expected increase in current liability due to benefits accruing during the plan year) over the value of the plan's assets. For this purpose, the term *current liability* generally has the same meaning given that term under section 412(l)(7).

Section 412(l)(7)(C)(ii) provides that, for purposes of determining current liability in plan years beginning on or after January 1, 1995, the mortality table used is the table prescribed by the Secretary. Under section 412(l)(7)(C)(ii)(I), the initial mortality table used in determining current liability under section 412(l)(7) must be based on the prevailing commissioners' standard table (described in section 807(d)(5)(A)) used to determine reserves for group annuity contracts issued on January 1, 1993. For purposes of section 807(d)(5), Rev. Rul. 92–19, 1992–1 C.B. 227, specifies the prevailing commissioners' standard table used to determine reserves for group annuity contracts issued on January 1, 1993, as the 1983 Group Annuity Mortality Table (1983 GAM). Accordingly, Rev. Rul. 95–28, 1995–1 C.B. 74, sets forth two gender-specific mortality tables, based on 1983 GAM, for purposes of determining current liability for participants and beneficiaries (other than disabled participants).

Section 412(l)(7)(C)(iii)(I) specifics that the Secretary is to establish different mortality tables to be used to determine current liability for individuals who are entitled to benefits under the plan on account of disability. One such set of tables is to apply to individuals whose disabilities occur in plan years beginning before January 1, 1995, and a second set of tables for individuals whose disabilities occur in plan years beginning on or after such date. Under section 412(l)(7)(C)(iii)(II), the separate tables for disabilities that occur in plan years beginning after December 31, 1994, apply only with respect to individuals who are disabled within the meaning of title II of the Social Security Act and the regulations thereunder. Rev. Rul. 96–7, 1996–1 C.B. 59, sets forth the mortality tables established under section 412(l)(7)(C)(iii).

Under section 412(l)(7)(C)(ii)(III), the Secretary is required to periodically (at least every 5 years) review any tables in effect under that subsection and, to the extent necessary, by regulation update the tables to reflect the actual experience of pension plans and projected trends in such experience. Section 412(l)(7)(C)(ii)(II) provides that the updated tables are to take into account the results of available independent studies of mortality of individuals covered by pension plans. Pursuant to section 412(l)(7)(C)(ii)(II), any new mortality tables prescribed by regulation can be effective no earlier than the first plan year beginning after December 31, 1999. Under section 412(l)(10), increases in current liability arising from the adoption of such a new mortality table are required to be amortized over a 10-year period.

Notice 2003–62, 2003–2 C.B. 576, was issued as part of the periodic review by the IRS and the Treasury Department of the mortality tables used in determining current liability under section 412(l)(7). At the time Notice 2003–62 was issued, the IRS and the Treasury Department were

[1] Section 302 of the Employee Retirement Income Security Act of 1974, as amended (ERISA) sets forth funding rules that are parallel to those in section 412 of the Code. Under section 101 of Reorganization Plan No. 4 of 1978 (43 FR 47713) and section 302 of ERISA, the Secretary of the Treasury has interpretive jurisdiction over the subject matter addressed in these regulations for purposes of ERISA, as well as the Code. Thus, these final Treasury regulations issued under section 412 of the Code apply as well for purposes of section 302 of ERISA.

aware of two reviews of mortality experience for retirement plan participants undertaken by the Retirement Plans Experience Committee of the Society of Actuaries (the UP–94 Study and the RP–2000 Mortality Tables Report),[2] and commentators were invited to submit any other independent studies of pension plan mortality experience. Notice 2003–62 also requested the submission of studies regarding projected trends in mortality experience. With respect to projecting mortality improvements, the IRS and the Treasury Department requested comments regarding the advantages and disadvantages of reflecting these trends on an ongoing basis through the use of generational, modified generational, or sequentially static mortality tables.

The IRS and the Treasury Department have reviewed the mortality tables that are used for purposes of determining current liability for participants and beneficiaries (other than disabled participants). The existing mortality table for determining current liability (1983 GAM) was compared to independent studies of mortality of individuals covered by pension plans, after reflecting projected trends for mortality improvement through 2007. The comparison indicated that the 1983 GAM is no longer appropriate for determining current liability.

Based on this review of the 1983 GAM compared to more recent mortality experience, the IRS and the Treasury Department have determined that updated mortality tables based on the RP–2000 Mortality Tables Report should be used to determine current liability for participants and beneficiaries (other than disabled participants).[3]

On December 2, 2005, the IRS issued proposed regulations under section 412(l)(7) (REG–124988–05, 2005–2 C.B. 1186 [70 FR 72260]) setting forth mortality tables, proposed to be effective for plan years beginning on or after January 1, 2007, to be used for nondisabled pension plan participants. The proposed regulations would have required plans of 500 or more participants to use separate mortality tables (derived from the RP–2000 mortality tables) for nonannuitant and annuitant periods. These separate tables were developed by projecting mortality improvement from a base year of 2007 over the period of the approximate expected duration of liabilities (7 years for the annuitant tables and 15 years for the nonannuitant tables). Small plans, defined as those with fewer than 500 participants (including both active and inactive participants), would have been permitted to use a combined table that applies the same mortality rates to both annuitants and nonannuitants. The proposed regulations provided for updated tables to be issued annually reflecting a new base year and using the projection factors described in the proposed regulations, to reflect expected improvements in mortality. Two comments on the proposed regulation were received, and no public hearing was requested or held.

On August 17, 2006, PPA was enacted. PPA contains a comprehensive revision of the minimum funding requirements for single employer plans, based on the calculation of a funding target that replaces the current liability calculation under section 412(l). These minimum funding provisions of PPA are generally effective for plan years beginning after December 31, 2007. Under section 430(h)(3)(A) as enacted in PPA, the Secretary is directed to prescribe by regulation the mortality tables used in determining present value or making any computation under the funding rules. The specifications for developing the mortality tables under section 430(h)(3)(A) are the same as the specifications set forth in section 412(l)(7)(C)(ii)(III).

Explanation of Provisions

These regulations set forth the mortality tables to be used under section 412(l)(7)(C)(ii) to determine current liability for participants and beneficiaries (other than disabled participants) for plan years beginning on or after January 1, 2007. These mortality tables are the same mortality tables that were published for 2007 in the proposed regulations, and are based on the tables contained in the RP–2000 Mortality Tables Report. The IRS and the Treasury Department have reviewed the RP–2000 mortality tables and the accompanying report published by the Society of Actuaries, and have determined that the RP–2000 mortality tables form the best available basis for predicting mortality of pension plan participants and beneficiaries (other than disabled participants) based on pension plan experience and expected trends. As under the mortality tables applicable for earlier plan years, the mortality tables set forth in these regulations are gender-distinct because of significant differences between expected male mortality and expected female mortality.

Of the two comments received on the proposed regulations, one commentator stated that requiring separate annuitant and nonannuitant mortality tables adds complexity without increasing accuracy. According to this commentator, the complexity could be avoided without loss of accuracy by using the RP–2000 blended table. This commentator suggested that, if separate annuitant and nonannuitant mortality tables are required, they should not be required to be used before 2008. The other commentator agreed with the use of separate annuitant and nonannuitant tables.

In a change from the proposed regulations, the IRS and the Treasury Department have chosen to permit all plans to use a blended table for 2007 rather than require the use of separate annuitant and nonannuitant tables. This decision was made because of the sweeping changes made to the minimum funding requirements for single employer plans by PPA that will generally become effective in 2008. The IRS and the Treasury Department believe that using separate annuitant and nonannuitant tables results in a more accurate measure of a plan's current liability. However, in view of the sweeping PPA changes and the resulting need to overhaul actuarial valuation systems, it was determined that all plans (and not just small plans) should be permitted to use the combined mortal-

[2] The UP–94 Study, prepared by the UP–94 Task Force of the Society of Actuaries, was published in the Transactions of the Society of Actuaries, Vol. XLVII (1995), p. 819. The RP–2000 Mortality Table Report was released in July, 2000. Society of Actuaries, RP–2000 Mortality Tables Report, at *http://www.soa.org/ccm/content/research-publications/experience-studies-tools/the-rp–2000-mortality-tables/*.

[3] Because of the enactment of PPA, the IRS and Treasury Department are not planning to complete a review of the section 412(l)(7)(C)(iii) mortality tables for disabled participants pursuant to section 412(l)(7)(C)(ii)(III). The IRS and Treasury Department will review recent mortality experience and expected trends for disabled participants to determine what mortality tables should be used for disabled participants under section 430(h)(3)(D) as added by PPA.

ity tables for the 2007 plan year.[4] It is expected that proposed regulations under section 430(h)(3)(A) providing mortality tables for purposes of determining present value under section 430 will require large plans to use separate annuitant and nonannuitant tables to achieve a more accurate measure of the present value of plan benefits.

If the separate tables for annuitants and nonannuitants are used, the nonannuitant mortality table is applied to determine the probability of survival for a nonannuitant for the period before the nonannuitant is projected to commence receiving benefits. The annuitant mortality table is applied to determine the present value of benefits for each annuitant, and for each nonannuitant for the period after which the nonannuitant is projected to commence receiving benefits. For purposes of this section, an annuitant means a plan participant who has commenced receiving benefits and a nonannuitant means a plan participant who has not yet commenced receiving benefits (*e.g.*, an active employee or a terminated vested participant). Thus, for example, with respect to a 45-year-old active participant who is projected to commence receiving an annuity at age 55, current liability would be determined using the nonannuitant mortality table for the period before the participant attains age 55 (*i.e.*, so that the probability of an active male participant living from age 45 to the age of 55 for the table that applies in plan years beginning in 2007 is 98.59%) and the annuitant mortality table for the period ages 55 and above. Similarly, if a 45-year-old terminated vested participant is projected to commence an annuity at age 65, current liability would be determined using the nonannuitant mortality table for the period before the participant attains age 65 and the annuitant mortality table for ages 65 and above. A participant whose benefit has partially commenced is treated as an annuitant with respect to the portion of the benefit which has commenced and a nonannuitant with respect to the balance of the benefit.

As under the proposed regulations, the annuitant and nonannuitant tables were developed by applying projected mortality improvements to the annuitant and nonannuitant tables from the RP–2000 Mortality Tables Report. Mortality improvement was projected forward from the base year of 2007 by 7 years for annuitants and 15 years for nonannuitants, to approximate an average expected duration of liabilities. The projection factors used are from Mortality Projection Scale AA, which was also recommended for use in the UP–94 Study and RP–2000 Mortality Tables Report.

The blended table provided under these regulations was constructed in the same manner as under the proposed regulations, by applying the nonannuitant/annuitant weighting factors published in the RP–2000 Mortality Tables Report. However, because the RP–2000 Mortality Tables Report does not provide weighting factors before age 50 or after age 70, the IRS and the Treasury Department have extended the table of weighting factors for ages 41 through 50 (ages 45–50 for females) and for ages 70 through 79 in order to develop the blended table.

For most plans, these regulations will be in effect only for the 2007 plan year because the minimum funding requirements enacted in PPA will replace the currently applicable minimum funding requirements for plan years beginning on or after January 1, 2008. For plans that remain subject to the pre-PPA requirements of section 412 after the 2007 plan year (see sections 104 through 106 of PPA), these regulations require that the mortality tables that will be provided pursuant to section 430(h)(3)(A) are to be used as the mortality tables that apply for determining current liability under section 412 for those later plan years.

Applicability Date

These regulations apply to plan years beginning on or after January 1, 2007.

Special Analyses

It has been determined that this Treasury Decision is not a significant regulatory action as defined in Executive Order 12866. Therefore, a regulatory assessment is not required. It also has been determined that section 553(b) of the Administrative Procedure Act (5 U.S.C. chapter 5) does not apply to these regulations, and because the regulation does not impose a collection of information on small entities, the Regulatory Flexibility Act (5 U.S.C. chapter 6) does not apply. Pursuant to section 7805(f) of the Code, the notice of proposed rulemaking preceding these regulations was submitted to the Small Business Administration for comment on its impact on small business.

Drafting Information

The principal authors of these regulations are Bruce Perlin and Linda S. F. Marshall, Office of Division Counsel/Associate Chief Counsel (Tax Exempt and Government Entities). However, other personnel from the IRS and Treasury Department participated in the development of these regulations.

* * * * *

Adoption of Amendments to the Regulations

Accordingly, 26 CFR part 1 is amended as follows:

PART 1—INCOME TAXES

Paragraph 1. The authority citation for part 1 continues to read, in part, as follows:

Authority: 26 U.S.C. 7805 * * *

Par. 2. Section 1.412(l)(7)–1 is added to read as follows:

§1.412(l)(7)–1 Mortality tables used to determine current liability.

(a) *In general.* The mortality tables set forth in paragraph (d) of this section are to be used in determining current liability under section 412(l)(7) for participants and beneficiaries (other than disabled participants) for plan years beginning in 2007. For plan years beginning on or after January 1, 2008, the mortality tables described in section 430(h)(3)(A) are to be used in determining current liability under section 412(l)(7) for participants and beneficiaries (other than disabled participants).

(b) *Separate tables for annuitants and nonannuitants.* The separate tables for annuitants and nonannuitants are used unless the plan applies the optional combined table pursuant to paragraph (c) of this section. If these separate tables are used, the

[4] For most single employer plans, these regulations will be in effect only for the plan year beginning in 2007 because changes to section 412 made by PPA will eliminate the need for single employer plans to calculate current liability for plan years beginning on or after January 1, 2008. However, sections 104 through 106 of PPA provide later effective dates for the PPA changes to section 412 with respect to certain plans, and therefore those plans will continue to be required to determine current liability for some plan years beginning on or after January 1, 2008.

nonannuitant mortality table is applied to determine the probability of survival for a nonannuitant for the period before the nonannuitant is projected to commence receiving benefits. The annuitant mortality table is applied to determine the present value of benefits for each annuitant, and for each nonannuitant for the period after which the nonannuitant is projected to commence receiving benefits. For purposes of this section, an annuitant means a plan participant who has commenced receiving benefits and a nonannuitant means a plan participant who has not yet commenced receiving benefits (*e.g.*, an active employee or a terminated vested participant). Thus, for example, with respect to a 45-year-old active participant who is projected to commence receiving an annuity at age 55, current liability would be determined using the nonannuitant mortality table for the period before the participant attains age 55 (*i.e.*, so that the probability of an active male participant living from age 45 to the age of 55 for the table that applies in plan years beginning in 2007 is 98.59%) and the annuitant mortality table for the period ages 55 and above. Similarly, if a 45-year-old terminated vested participant is projected to commence an annuity at age 65, current liability would be determined using the nonannuitant mortality table for the period before the participant attains age 65 and the annuitant mortality table for ages 65 and above. For purposes of this section, a participant whose benefit has partially commenced is treated as an annuitant with respect to the portion of the benefit which has commenced and a nonannuitant with respect to the balance of the benefit.

(c) *Optional combined tables.* As an alternative to the separate tables specified for annuitants and nonannuitants as described in paragraph (b) of this section, the optional combined table, which applies the same mortality rates to both annuitants and nonannuitants, can be used.

(d) *Mortality tables for 2007.* As set forth in paragraph (a) of this section, the following tables are to be used for determining current liability for plan years beginning during 2007 in accordance with the rules of this section.

Age	MALE	MALE	MALE	FEMALE	FEMALE	FEMALE
	Non-Annuitant Table	Annuitant Table	Optional Combined Table	Non-Annuitant Table	Annuitant Table	Optional Combined Table
1	0.000408	0.000408	0.000408	0.000366	0.000366	0.000366
2	0.000276	0.000276	0.000276	0.000239	0.000239	0.000239
3	0.000229	0.000229	0.000229	0.000178	0.000178	0.000178
4	0.000178	0.000178	0.000178	0.000133	0.000133	0.000133
5	0.000163	0.000163	0.000163	0.000121	0.000121	0.000121
6	0.000156	0.000156	0.000156	0.000113	0.000113	0.000113
7	0.000150	0.000150	0.000150	0.000106	0.000106	0.000106
8	0.000138	0.000138	0.000138	0.000094	0.000094	0.000094
9	0.000134	0.000134	0.000134	0.000090	0.000090	0.000090
10	0.000136	0.000136	0.000136	0.000090	0.000090	0.000090
11	0.000140	0.000140	0.000140	0.000092	0.000092	0.000092
12	0.000146	0.000146	0.000146	0.000095	0.000095	0.000095
13	0.000154	0.000154	0.000154	0.000099	0.000099	0.000099
14	0.000167	0.000167	0.000167	0.000109	0.000109	0.000109
15	0.000176	0.000176	0.000176	0.000119	0.000119	0.000119
16	0.000186	0.000186	0.000186	0.000127	0.000127	0.000127
17	0.000197	0.000197	0.000197	0.000135	0.000135	0.000135
18	0.000207	0.000207	0.000207	0.000138	0.000138	0.000138
19	0.000217	0.000217	0.000217	0.000136	0.000136	0.000136
20	0.000226	0.000226	0.000226	0.000134	0.000134	0.000134
21	0.000239	0.000239	0.000239	0.000132	0.000132	0.000132
22	0.000251	0.000251	0.000251	0.000133	0.000133	0.000133
23	0.000267	0.000267	0.000267	0.000138	0.000138	0.000138
24	0.000282	0.000282	0.000282	0.000144	0.000144	0.000144
25	0.000301	0.000301	0.000301	0.000152	0.000152	0.000152
26	0.000331	0.000331	0.000331	0.000164	0.000164	0.000164
27	0.000342	0.000342	0.000342	0.000171	0.000171	0.000171
28	0.000352	0.000352	0.000352	0.000180	0.000180	0.000180
29	0.000369	0.000369	0.000369	0.000190	0.000190	0.000190
30	0.000398	0.000398	0.000398	0.000212	0.000212	0.000212
31	0.000447	0.000447	0.000447	0.000257	0.000257	0.000257
32	0.000503	0.000503	0.000503	0.000293	0.000293	0.000293
33	0.000565	0.000565	0.000565	0.000323	0.000323	0.000323
34	0.000629	0.000629	0.000629	0.000349	0.000349	0.000349
35	0.000692	0.000692	0.000692	0.000372	0.000372	0.000372
36	0.000753	0.000753	0.000753	0.000394	0.000394	0.000394

Age	MALE Non-Annuitant Table	MALE Annuitant Table	MALE Optional Combined Table	FEMALE Non-Annuitant Table	FEMALE Annuitant Table	FEMALE Optional Combined Table
37	0.000810	0.000810	0.000810	0.000415	0.000415	0.000415
38	0.000844	0.000844	0.000844	0.000439	0.000439	0.000439
39	0.000875	0.000875	0.000875	0.000465	0.000465	0.000465
40	0.000904	0.000904	0.000904	0.000506	0.000506	0.000506
41	0.000936	0.000963	0.000936	0.000555	0.000555	0.000555
42	0.000974	0.001081	0.000975	0.000611	0.000611	0.000611
43	0.001018	0.001258	0.001021	0.000672	0.000672	0.000672
44	0.001071	0.001493	0.001079	0.000738	0.000738	0.000738
45	0.001131	0.001788	0.001146	0.000788	0.000791	0.000788
46	0.001185	0.002142	0.001211	0.000839	0.000896	0.000840
47	0.001244	0.002554	0.001286	0.000889	0.001054	0.000893
48	0.001304	0.003026	0.001366	0.000962	0.001265	0.000972
49	0.001368	0.003557	0.001457	0.001039	0.001528	0.001059
50	0.001434	0.004146	0.001557	0.001149	0.001844	0.001184
51	0.001500	0.004226	0.001636	0.001272	0.001962	0.001312
52	0.001570	0.004254	0.001754	0.001442	0.002173	0.001496
53	0.001681	0.004312	0.001932	0.001637	0.002445	0.001714
54	0.001803	0.004369	0.002134	0.001861	0.002771	0.001969
55	0.001986	0.004514	0.002508	0.002117	0.003155	0.002314
56	0.002217	0.004749	0.003020	0.002414	0.003608	0.002755
57	0.002488	0.005069	0.003464	0.002696	0.004088	0.003170
58	0.002803	0.005501	0.003990	0.002947	0.004588	0.003583
59	0.003095	0.005972	0.004529	0.003223	0.005156	0.004066
60	0.003421	0.006539	0.005177	0.003521	0.005780	0.004640
61	0.003860	0.007284	0.006030	0.003838	0.006450	0.005354
62	0.004244	0.008024	0.006929	0.004170	0.007168	0.006148
63	0.004746	0.008989	0.008099	0.004513	0.007932	0.007084
64	0.005154	0.009947	0.009159	0.004862	0.008758	0.007996
65	0.005553	0.011015	0.010377	0.005213	0.009662	0.009018
66	0.006073	0.012379	0.011951	0.005559	0.010640	0.010192
67	0.006447	0.013705	0.013349	0.005896	0.011690	0.011323
68	0.006650	0.014940	0.014641	0.006220	0.012838	0.012522
69	0.006974	0.016504	0.016231	0.006528	0.014126	0.013843
70	0.007115	0.017971	0.017689	0.006818	0.015607	0.015309
71	0.008002	0.019884	0.019606	0.007450	0.017078	0.016784
72	0.009777	0.022078	0.021822	0.008714	0.018995	0.018716
73	0.012439	0.024592	0.024371	0.010610	0.020819	0.020577
74	0.015988	0.027435	0.027256	0.013139	0.023074	0.022872
75	0.020425	0.031057	0.030919	0.016299	0.025117	0.024967
76	0.025749	0.034615	0.034523	0.020092	0.027673	0.027570
77	0.031961	0.039054	0.038999	0.024516	0.030911	0.030846
78	0.039059	0.044018	0.043992	0.029573	0.034074	0.034043
79	0.047046	0.049617	0.049610	0.035261	0.037618	0.037610
80	0.055919	0.055919	0.055919	0.041582	0.041582	0.041582
81	0.063476	0.063476	0.063476	0.046024	0.046024	0.046024
82	0.071926	0.071926	0.071926	0.051021	0.051021	0.051021
83	0.080176	0.080176	0.080176	0.056651	0.056651	0.056651
84	0.090433	0.090433	0.090433	0.063006	0.063006	0.063006
85	0.100383	0.100383	0.100383	0.071188	0.071188	0.071188
86	0.111295	0.111295	0.111295	0.080522	0.080522	0.080522
87	0.125051	0.125051	0.125051	0.091080	0.091080	0.091080
88	0.140385	0.140385	0.140385	0.101448	0.101448	0.101448
89	0.155142	0.155142	0.155142	0.114246	0.114246	0.114246
90	0.173400	0.173400	0.173400	0.126258	0.126258	0.126258
91	0.188868	0.188868	0.188868	0.138648	0.138648	0.138648
92	0.207683	0.207683	0.207683	0.151126	0.151126	0.151126
93	0.224037	0.224037	0.224037	0.165722	0.165722	0.165722

Age	MALE	MALE	MALE	FEMALE	FEMALE	FEMALE
	Non-Annuitant Table	Annuitant Table	Optional Combined Table	Non-Annuitant Table	Annuitant Table	Optional Combined Table
94	0.240367	0.240367	0.240367	0.177747	0.177747	0.177747
95	0.260098	0.260098	0.260098	0.189133	0.189133	0.189133
96	0.276058	0.276058	0.276058	0.199703	0.199703	0.199703
97	0.291564	0.291564	0.291564	0.212246	0.212246	0.212246
98	0.310910	0.310910	0.310910	0.220832	0.220832	0.220832
99	0.325614	0.325614	0.325614	0.228169	0.228169	0.228169
100	0.339763	0.339763	0.339763	0.234164	0.234164	0.234164
101	0.358628	0.358628	0.358628	0.244834	0.244834	0.244834
102	0.371685	0.371685	0.371685	0.254498	0.254498	0.254498
103	0.383040	0.383040	0.383040	0.266044	0.266044	0.266044
104	0.392003	0.392003	0.392003	0.279055	0.279055	0.279055
105	0.397886	0.397886	0.397886	0.293116	0.293116	0.293116
106	0.400000	0.400000	0.400000	0.307811	0.307811	0.307811
107	0.400000	0.400000	0.400000	0.322725	0.322725	0.322725
108	0.400000	0.400000	0.400000	0.337441	0.337441	0.337441
109	0.400000	0.400000	0.400000	0.351544	0.351544	0.351544
110	0.400000	0.400000	0.400000	0.364617	0.364617	0.364617
111	0.400000	0.400000	0.400000	0.376246	0.376246	0.376246
112	0.400000	0.400000	0.400000	0.386015	0.386015	0.386015
113	0.400000	0.400000	0.400000	0.393507	0.393507	0.393507
114	0.400000	0.400000	0.400000	0.398308	0.398308	0.398308
115	0.400000	0.400000	0.400000	0.400000	0.400000	0.400000
116	0.400000	0.400000	0.400000	0.400000	0.400000	0.400000
117	0.400000	0.400000	0.400000	0.400000	0.400000	0.400000
118	0.400000	0.400000	0.400000	0.400000	0.400000	0.400000
119	0.400000	0.400000	0.400000	0.400000	0.400000	0.400000
120	1.000000	1.000000	1.000000	1.000000	1.000000	1.000000

(e) *Effective date.* This section applies for plan years beginning on or after January 1, 2007.

Linda M. Kroening,
Acting Deputy Commissioner for Services and Enforcement.

Approved January 26, 2007.

Eric Solomon,
Assistant Secretary of the Treasury (Tax Policy).

(Filed by the Office of the Federal Register on February 1, 2007, 8:45 a.m., and published in the issue of the Federal Register for February 2, 2007, 72 F.R. 4955)

Section 472.—Last-in, First-out Inventories

26 CFR 1.472–1: Last-in, first-out inventories.

LIFO; price indexes; department stores. The December 2006 Bureau of Labor Statistics price indexes are accepted for use by department stores employing the retail inventory and last-in, first-out inventory methods for valuing inventories for tax years ended on, or with reference to, December 31, 2006.

Rev. Rul. 2007–11

The following Department Store Inventory Price Indexes for December 2006 were issued by the Bureau of Labor Statistics (BLS). The indexes are accepted by the Internal Revenue Service, under § 1.472–1(k) of the Income Tax Regulations and Rev. Proc. 86–46, 1986–2 C.B. 739, for appropriate application to inventories of department stores employing the retail inventory and last-in, first-out inventory methods for tax years ended on, or with reference to, December 31, 2006.

The Department Store Inventory Price Indexes are prepared on a national basis and include (a) 23 major groups of departments, (b) three special combinations of the major groups — soft goods, durable goods, and miscellaneous goods, and (c) a store total, which covers all departments, including some not listed separately, except for the following: candy, food, liquor, tobacco, and contract departments.

BUREAU OF LABOR STATISTICS, DEPARTMENT STORE
INVENTORY PRICE INDEXES BY DEPARTMENT GROUPS
(January 1941 = 100, unless otherwise noted)

	Groups	Dec. 2005	Dec. 2006	Percent Change From Dec. 2005 to Dec. 2006[1]
1.	Piece Goods	467.2	448.2	-4.1
2.	Domestics and Draperies	506.3	476.6	-5.9
3.	Women's and Children's Shoes	659.5	667.5	1.2
4.	Men's Shoes	862.7	889.6	3.1
5.	Infants' Wear	568.5	561.2	-1.3
6.	Women's Underwear	547.0	547.6	0.1
7.	Women's Hosiery	337.9	345.8	2.3
8.	Women's and Girls' Accessories	558.5	542.4	-2.9
9.	Women's Outerwear and Girls' Wear	350.8	356.8	1.7
10.	Men's Clothing	527.4	519.6	-1.5
11.	Men's Furnishings	560.6	571.4	1.9
12.	Boys' Clothing and Furnishings	394.0	387.5	-1.6
13.	Jewelry	842.7	872.7	3.6
14.	Notions	801.0	822.8	2.7
15.	Toilet Articles and Drugs	1000.7	1014.0	1.3
16.	Furniture and Bedding	602.9	597.4	-0.9
17.	Floor Coverings	614.5	622.1	1.2
18.	Housewares	697.7	685.7	-1.7
19.	Major Appliances	205.0	209.5	2.2
20.	Radio and Television	37.7	34.0	-9.8
21.	Recreation and Education[2]	77.4	76.1	-1.7
22.	Home Improvements[2]	136.7	141.2	3.3
23.	Automotive Accessories[2]	117.0	122.1	4.4
Groups 1–15: Soft Goods		548.0	551.3	0.6
Groups 16–20: Durable Goods		375.7	370.0	-1.5
Groups 21–23: Misc. Goods[2]		93.0	93.8	0.9
	Store Total[3]	487.2	488.2	0.2

[1]Absence of a minus sign before the percentage change in this column signifies a price increase.

[2]Indexes on a January 1986 = 100 base.

[3]The Store Total index covers all departments, with the following exceptions: candy, food, liquor, tobacco, as well as contract departments.

DRAFTING INFORMATION

The principal author of this revenue ruling is John Roman Faron of the Office of Associate Chief Counsel (Income Tax and Accounting). For further information regarding this revenue ruling, contact Mr. Faron at (202) 622–8142 (not a toll-free call).

Part III. Administrative, Procedural, and Miscellaneous

Definition of Party and Allocation of Net Income or Proceeds for Purposes of Section 4965

Notice 2007–18

I Purpose

This notice provides guidance under section 4965 of the Internal Revenue Code ("Code") to tax-exempt entities described in section 4965(c) that may be parties to prohibited tax shelter transactions. This notice also provides guidance to tax-exempt entities described in sections 4965(c)(1), (2), and (3) (referred to herein as Non-Plan Entities) subject to tax under section 4965(a) regarding the allocation to various periods of net income or proceeds attributable to a prohibited tax shelter transaction. In particular, this notice responds to written comments requesting guidance regarding the definition of the term "party to a prohibited tax shelter transaction" for purposes of section 4965 and related disclosure provisions and regarding the appropriate treatment of net income or proceeds received prior to the effective date of the section 4965(a) tax.

II Background

The Tax Increase Prevention and Reconciliation Act of 2005 ("TIPRA"), Pub. L. No. 109–222, 120 Stat. 345, enacted on May 17, 2006, designates certain transactions as prohibited tax shelter transactions and includes new entity-level and manager-level excise taxes and disclosure rules applicable to prohibited tax shelter transactions to which a tax-exempt entity is a party. TIPRA creates new section 4965 and amends sections 6033(a)(2), 6011(g), and 6652(c)(3) of the Code.

A. Imposition of Excise Tax on Certain Tax-Exempt Entities

Section 4965(a) requires Non-Plan Entities to pay an excise tax "for the taxable year in which the entity becomes [a party to a prohibited tax shelter transaction] and any subsequent taxable year in the amount determined under [section 4965(b)]." Non-Plan Entities include those entities described in section 4965(c)(1) through (3) — *i.e.*, entities described in section 501(c), 501(d), section 170(c) (other than the United States), and Indian tribal governments (within the meaning of section 7701(a)(40)). Section 4965(e)(1) defines the term "prohibited tax shelter transaction" to mean (1) "any listed transaction," and (2) "any prohibited reportable transaction." A "listed transaction" is defined by cross-reference to section 6707A(c)(2). A "prohibited reportable transaction" means any confidential transaction under Treas. Reg. § 1.6011–4(b)(3) or any transaction with contractual protection under Treas. Reg. § 1.6011–4(b)(4) which is a reportable transaction as defined by section 6707A(c)(1). Pursuant to Revenue Procedure 2007–20, 2007–7 I.R.B. 517 (Feb. 2, 2007), transactions in which the refundable or contingent fee is related to tax credits under sections 42 and 45D of the Code will not be treated as reportable transactions for purposes of Treas. Reg. § 1.6011–4(b)(4) and, thus, will not be subject to section 4965.

B. General Computation Rule

Section 4965(b)(1) provides that, for a transaction other than a "subsequently listed transaction" as defined in section 4965(e)(2), the amount of the excise tax imposed on the Non-Plan Entity is computed based on the greater of (1) the entity's net income "for the taxable year" attributable to the transaction or (2) 75 percent of the proceeds "received by the entity for the taxable year" which are attributable to the transaction.

C. Computation Rule for Subsequently Listed Transactions

Section 4965(e)(2) defines the term "subsequently listed transaction" as any transaction to which a tax-exempt entity is a party and which is determined by the Secretary to be a listed transaction at any time after the entity has become a party to the transaction, provided, however, that the transaction was not a prohibited reportable transaction at the time the entity became a party to the transaction.

Section 4965(b)(1) provides that, for a subsequently listed transaction, the amount of the excise tax is based on the greater of (1) the entity's net income for the taxable year which is attributable to the prohibited tax shelter transaction and is "properly allocable" to the period beginning on the later of the date the transaction is identified as a listed transaction or the first day of the taxable year, or (2) 75 percent of the proceeds received by the entity for the taxable year which are attributable to the prohibited tax shelter transaction and which are "properly allocable" to the period beginning on the later of the date the transaction is identified as a listed transaction or the first day of the taxable year.

D. Effective Date

Section 516(d) of TIPRA provides that section 4965 generally applies to taxable years ending after the date of enactment with respect to transactions entered into before, on, or after that date. However, "no tax under section 4965(a) . . . shall apply with respect to income or proceeds that are properly allocable to any period ending on or before the date which is 90 days after the date of enactment." The 90th day after the date of enactment was August 15, 2006.

Section 4965(f) authorizes the Secretary to promulgate regulations providing guidance "regarding the determination of the allocation of net income or proceeds of a tax-exempt entity attributable to a transaction to various periods, including before and after the listing of the transaction or the date which is 90 days after the date of the enactment of this section."

On July 11, 2006, the Internal Revenue Service ("Service") released Notice 2006–65, 2006–31 I.R.B. 102, which alerted taxpayers to the new provisions and solicited comments regarding these provisions. The Service received numerous written comments in response to Notice 2006–65. Many of the comments requested guidance regarding the circumstances under which a tax-exempt entity will be considered a "party" to a prohibited tax shelter transaction, as well as how the Service intends to exercise its allocation authority under section 4965(f), particularly with respect to transactions entered into prior to the enactment of section 4965.

The Service and the Treasury Department intend to issue further guidance under section 4965 and the related statutory provisions. Pending the issuance of further guidance, taxpayers may rely upon the guidance in this notice.

III Definition of Party

A. In General

For purposes of sections 4965, 6033(a)(2) and 6011(g), a tax-exempt entity is a party to a transaction if it (1) facilitates the transaction by reason of its tax-exempt, tax indifferent or tax-favored status; or (2) is identified in published guidance, by type, class or role, as a party to a prohibited tax shelter transaction.

Published guidance may identify which tax-exempt entities, by type, class or role, will not be treated as a party to a prohibited tax shelter transaction for purposes of sections 4965, 6033(a)(2) and 6011(g).

B. Examples

Example 1. A tax-exempt entity enters into a transaction ("Transaction A") with an S corporation. Transaction A is the same as or substantially similar to the transaction identified by the Secretary as a listed transaction in Notice 2004–30, 2004–1 C.B. 828. The tax-exempt entity's role in Transaction A is similar to the role of the exempt party, as described in Notice 2004–30. The tax-exempt entity purportedly receives the S corporation stock and, due to the tax-exempt entity's tax-exempt status, aids the S corporation and its shareholders in avoiding taxable income. The tax-exempt entity facilitates Transaction A by reason of its tax-exempt, tax indifferent or tax-favored status. Accordingly, the tax-exempt entity is a party to Transaction A for purposes of sections 4965, 6033(a)(2) and 6011(g).

Example 2. A tax-exempt entity is a partner in a partnership. The partnership has a number of other taxable and tax-exempt partners. The partnership enters into a number of transactions, including a transaction ("Transaction B") which is the same as or substantially similar to the transaction identified by the Secretary as a listed transaction in Notice 2002–35, 2002–1 C.B. 992 (as clarified and modified by Notice 2006–16, 2006–9 I.R.B. 538). The partnership participates in Transaction B in a role similar to the role of T, as described in Notice 2002–35, *i.e.*, the role of the taxpayer receiving the purported tax benefits from the transaction. The tax and economic consequences from Transaction B to the other partners are not dependent on the tax-exempt entity's tax-exempt, tax indifferent or tax-favored status. Accordingly, the tax-exempt entity does not facilitate Transaction B by reason of its tax-exempt, tax indifferent or tax-favored status. The tax-exempt entity also has not been identified, by type, class or role, as a party to a prohibited tax shelter transaction in published guidance. Therefore, the tax-exempt entity is not a party to Transaction B for purposes of sections 4965, 6033(a)(2) and 6011(g).

The IRS and Treasury Department recognize that "party" as used in section 4965 applies more broadly than the term is defined for purposes of this interim notice. Accordingly, the IRS and Treasury Department will propose regulations that will define "party" under section 4965 to include a tax-exempt entity that enters into a prohibited tax shelter transaction that reduces such entity's liability for applicable Federal taxes (*i.e.*, employment taxes, excise taxes, and in appropriate cases unrelated business income tax).

IV Net Income and Proceeds

A. In general

For purposes of section 4965(a), the amount and the timing of the net income and proceeds attributable to the prohibited tax shelter transaction will be computed in a manner consistent with the substance of the transaction. In determining the substance of listed transactions, the Service will look to, among other items, the listing guidance and any subsequent published guidance relating to the transaction.

B. Allocation of net income / proceeds to a taxable year

In general, for purposes of section 4965(a), the net income and proceeds attributable to a prohibited tax shelter transaction must be allocated to a particular taxable year in a manner consistent with the Non-Plan Entity's established method of accounting for Federal income tax purposes. If the Non-Plan Entity has not established a method of accounting for Federal income tax purposes, the Non-Plan Entity must use the cash receipts and disbursements method of accounting ("cash method") provided for in section 446 of the Code to determine the amount and timing of net income and proceeds attributable to a prohibited tax shelter transaction solely for purposes of section 4965(a). If a Non-Plan Entity has established a method of accounting other than the cash method, the Non-Plan Entity may nevertheless use the cash method of accounting to determine the amount of the net income and proceeds attributable to a prohibited tax shelter transaction entered into prior to the date of enactment of section 4965 and allocable to pre- and post-enactment periods.

If a Non-Plan Entity has not established a taxable year for Federal income tax purposes, the entity's taxable year for the purpose of determining the amount and timing of net income and proceeds attributable to a prohibited tax shelter transaction will be deemed to be the annual period the entity has used in keeping its books and records.

Any net income or proceeds attributable to a prohibited tax shelter transaction allocated to a taxable year ending on or before August 15, 2006 under this section IV, will not be subject to the excise tax imposed by section 4965(a).

C. Examples

Example 3. In 1999, X, a calendar year Non-Plan Entity using the cash method of accounting, entered into a lease-in/lease-out transaction ("LILO") substantially similar to the transaction described in Notice 2000–15, 2000–1 C.B. 826 (describing Rev. Rul. 99–14, 1999–1 C.B. 835, superseded by Rev. Rul. 2002–69, 2002–2 C.B. 760). In 1999, X purported to lease property to Y pursuant to a "head lease," and Y purported to lease the property back to X pursuant to a "sublease" of a shorter term. In form, X received $268M as an advance payment of head lease rent. Of this amount, $200M had been, in form, financed by a nonrecourse loan obtained by Y. X deposited the $200M with a "debt payment undertaker." This served to defease both a portion of X's rent obligation under its sublease and Y's repayment obligation under the nonrecourse loan. Of the remainder of the $268M advance head lease rent payment, X deposited $54M with an "equity payment undertaker." This served to defease the remainder of X's rent obligation under the sublease. This amount inures to the benefit of Y and enables Y to recover its investment in the transaction and a return on that investment. In substance, the $54M is a loan from Y to X. X retained the remaining $14M of the advance head lease rent payment. In substance, this represents an accommodation fee for X's participation in the transaction.

According to the substance of the transaction, the head lease, sublease and nonrecourse debt will be ignored for Federal income tax purposes. Therefore, any net income or proceeds resulting from these elements of the transaction will not be considered net income or proceeds attributable to the LILO transaction for purposes of section 4965(a).

Under X's established cash basis method of accounting, any net income and proceeds received in 1999 and attributable to the LILO transaction are allocated to X's December 31, 1999, tax year for purposes of section 4965. Because the 1999 tax year is before the effective date of TIPRA, X will not be subject to any excise tax under section 4965 for the amounts received in 1999.

D. Special rule relating to taxable years that include August 16, 2006

In the case of the taxable year that includes August 16, 2006 ("the transition year"), the Service will treat the period beginning on the first day of the transition year and ending on August 15, 2006, and the period beginning on August 16, 2006, and ending on the last day of the transition year as short taxable years. This treatment is solely for purposes of allocating net income or proceeds under section 4965, and the Non-Plan Entity does not file tax returns with respect to these short taxable years or otherwise take the short taxable year into account for Federal tax purposes. Accordingly, the net income or proceeds that are properly allocated to the transition year in accordance with this section IV will be treated as follows:

- as allocable to the period ending on or before August 15, 2006, (and accordingly not subject to tax under section 4965(a)) to the extent such net income or proceeds would have been properly taken into account in accordance with this section IV by the Non-Plan Entity in the deemed short year ending on August 15, 2006; and
- as allocable to the period beginning after August 15, 2006, (and accordingly subject to tax under section 4965(a)) to the extent such net income or proceeds would have been properly taken into account in accordance with this section IV by the Non-Plan Entity in the short year beginning August 16, 2006.

Example 4. B, a Non-Plan Entity using the cash method of accounting, has an annual accounting period that ends on December 31, 2006. B became a party to a prohibited tax shelter transaction on March 15, 2006. On that date, B received a payment of $600,000 as an accommodation fee for its involvement in the transaction. B received no other proceeds or income attributable to this transaction in 2006. Under B's method of accounting, the payment received by B on March 15, 2006, is taken into account in the deemed short year ending on August 15, 2006. Accordingly, solely for purposes of section 4965, the payment is treated as allocable solely to a period ending on or before August 15, 2006, and is not subject to the excise tax imposed by section 4965(a).

Example 5. The facts are the same as in Example 4, above, except that B received an additional payment of $400,000 on September 30, 2006. Under B's method of accounting, the payment received by B on September 30, 2006, is taken into account in the deemed short year beginning on August 16, 2006. Accordingly, solely for purposes of section 4965, the payment is treated as allocable to a period beginning after August 15, 2006, and is subject to the excise tax imposed by section 4965(a).

V Request For Comments

The Service anticipates issuing further guidance under section 4965 and related statutory provisions and invites comments from the public regarding all aspects of these provisions and, in particular, regarding the definition of the term "party to a prohibited tax shelter transaction" for purposes of section 4965 and related disclosure provisions, the appropriate method for allocating net income or proceeds (including, specifically, with respect to governments) to various periods, including pre- and post-listing periods for subsequently listed transactions, and the definition of the term "proceeds" for section 4965 purposes. Written comments should be submitted by March 23, 2007. Send submissions to: CC:PA:LPD:PR (Notice 2007–18), Room 5203, Internal Revenue Service, POB 7604, Ben Franklin Station, Washington, DC 20044. Submissions may be hand delivered Monday through Friday between the hours of 8 a.m. and 4 p.m. to: CC:PA:LPD:PR (Notice 2007–18), Courier's Desk, Internal Revenue Service, 1111 Constitution Avenue, NW, Washington, DC. Alternatively, taxpayers may submit comments electronically to *notice.comments@irscounsel.treas.gov* (Notice 2007–18).

VI Drafting Information

The principal author of this notice is Galina Kolomietz of the Office of Division Counsel/Associate Chief Counsel (Tax-Exempt and Government Entities). For further information regarding this notice, contact Ms. Kolomietz at (202) 622–6070 (not a toll-free call).

Weighted Average Interest Rates Update

Notice 2007–20

This notice provides guidance as to the corporate bond weighted average interest rate and the permissible range of interest rates specified under § 412(b)(5)(B)(ii)(II) of the Internal Revenue Code. In addition, it provides guidance as to the interest rate on 30-year Treasury securities under § 417(e)(3)(A)(ii)(II).

CORPORATE BOND WEIGHTED AVERAGE INTEREST RATE

Sections 412(b)(5)(B)(ii) and 412(l)(7)(C)(i), as amended by the Pension Funding Equity Act of 2004 and by the Pension Protection Act of 2006, provide that the interest rates used to calculate current liability and to determine the required contribution under § 412(l) for plan years beginning in 2004 through 2007 must be within a permissible range based on the weighted average of the rates of interest on amounts invested conservatively in long term investment grade corporate bonds during the 4-year period ending on the last day before the beginning of the plan year.

Notice 2004–34, 2004–1 C.B. 848, provides guidelines for determining the corporate bond weighted average interest rate and the resulting permissible range of interest rates used to calculate current liability. That notice establishes that the corporate bond weighted average is based on the monthly composite corporate bond rate derived from designated corporate bond indices. The methodology for determining the monthly composite corporate bond rate as set forth in Notice 2004–34 continues to apply in determining that rate. See Notice 2006–75, 2006–36 I.R.B. 366.

The composite corporate bond rate for January 2007 is 5.89 percent. Pursuant to Notice 2004–34, the Service has determined this rate as the average of the monthly yields for the included corporate bond indices for that month.

The following corporate bond weighted average interest rate was determined for plan years beginning in the month shown below.

Month	For Plan Years Beginning in: Year	Corporate Bond Weighted Average	90% to 100% Permissible Range
February	2007	5.79	5.21 to 5.79

30-YEAR TREASURY SECURITIES INTEREST RATE

Section 417(e)(3)(A)(ii)(II) defines the applicable interest rate, which must be used for purposes of determining the minimum present value of a participant's benefit under § 417(e)(1) and (2), as the annual rate of interest on 30-year Treasury securities for the month before the date of distribution or such other time as the Secretary may by regulations prescribe. Section 1.417(e)–1(d)(3) of the Income Tax Regulations provides that the applicable interest rate for a month is the annual interest rate on 30-year Treasury securities as specified by the Commissioner for that month in revenue rulings, notices or other guidance published in the Internal Revenue Bulletin.

The rate of interest on 30-year Treasury securities for January 2007 is 4.85 percent. The Service has determined this rate as the monthly average of the daily determination of yield on the 30-year Treasury bond maturing in February 2036.

Drafting Information

The principal authors of this notice are Paul Stern and Tony Montanaro of the Employee Plans, Tax Exempt and Government Entities Division. For further information regarding this notice, please contact the Employee Plans' tax payer assistance telephone service at 877–829–5500 (a toll-free number), between the hours of 8:30 a.m. and 4:30 p.m. Eastern time, Monday through Friday. Mr. Stern may be reached at 202–283–9703. Mr. Montanaro may be reached at 202–283–9714. The telephone numbers in the preceding sentences are not toll-free.

Study on Donor Advised Funds and Supporting Organizations

Notice 2007–21

PURPOSE

This notice invites public comments in connection with a study being conducted by the Department of the Treasury (the Treasury) and the Internal Revenue Service (the Service) on the organization and operation of donor advised funds (as defined in § 4966(d)(2) of the Internal Revenue Code (Code)) and of supporting organizations described in § 509(a)(3). This study is required by § 1226 of the Pension Protection Act of 2006, Pub. L. No. 109–280, 120 Stat. 780 (2006) (the PPA).

BACKGROUND

Charitable organizations described in § 501(c)(3) are classified under § 509 as either public charities or private foundations, depending on their exempt purposes, the sources of their financial support, or their manner of operation. Private foundations, which typically derive their support from, and are often controlled by, a small number of donors, are subject to a number of anti-abuse rules and excise taxes not applicable to public charities. In addition, contributions to private foundations are subject to lower charitable deduction limits than are contributions to public charities.

Supporting Organizations

Under § 509(a)(3), a supporting organization is a § 501(c)(3) charitable organization that is classified as a public charity, not as a private foundation, as a result of the supporting organization's close relationship to one or more organizations described in §§ 509(a)(1) or 509(a)(2) (referred to in regulations under section 509(a)(3) as "publicly supported organizations"). To qualify as a supporting organization under § 509(a)(3), an organization must satisfy three requirements:

(A) the organization must be organized and at all times thereafter operated exclusively for the benefit of, to perform the functions of, or to carry out the purposes of one or more specified publicly supported organizations;

(B) the organization must be operated, supervised, or controlled by or in connection with one or more publicly supported organizations; and

(C) the organization must not be controlled directly or indirectly by one or more disqualified persons (as defined in § 4946) other than foundation managers and other than one or more publicly supported organizations.

Section 1.509(a)–4 of the Income Tax Regulations provides that the second requirement is met if the supporting organization has one of three relationships with one or more publicly supported organizations. A "Type I" supporting organization is "operated, supervised, or controlled by" a publicly supported organization. This relationship is comparable to that of a parent and subsidiary in that one or more publicly supported organizations can direct the policies, programs or activities of the supporting organization. A "Type II" supporting organization is "supervised or controlled in connection with" one or more publicly supported organizations. In this relationship, the supporting organization and the publicly supported organization(s) are under common supervision or control. A "Type III" supporting organization is "operated in connection with" a publicly supported organization. An organization will qualify as a Type III supporting organization only if it meets certain tests designed to ensure that the organization will be responsive to, and significantly involved in the operations of, the publicly supported organization(s). Under the PPA, this previously informal nomenclature used to describe the relationship between a supporting organization and its publicly supported organizations is incorporated into new §§ 4942(g)(4), 4943(f)(5) and (6), and 4966(d)(4).

Donor Advised Funds

Prior to the PPA, the term donor advised fund was not defined in the Code. However, the term generally was understood to refer to separate funds or accounts established and maintained by public charities to receive contributions from a single donor or a group of donors. The charities had ultimate authority over how the assets in each account were invested and distributed, but the donors, or individuals selected by the donors, were permitted to provide nonbinding recommendations regarding account distributions and/or investments. Donor advised funds often were compared to component funds of certain community trusts. See §§ 1.170A–9(e)(10) and (11).

The PPA adds new § 4966(d)(2), which defines a donor advised fund as a fund or account that is owned and controlled by a sponsoring organization, separately identified by reference to contributions of a donor or donors, and with respect to which the donor or a person appointed or designated by the donor (donor advisor) has or reasonably expects to have advisory privileges with respect to the distribution or investment of the assets in the fund. The term donor advised fund does not include a fund or account (1) that makes distributions only to a single identified organization or governmental entity, or (2) with respect to which a donor advises a sponsoring organization regarding grants for travel, study or similar purposes, provided that certain requirements are met.

A sponsoring organization is defined under new § 4966(d)(1) as a § 170(c) organization that is not a governmental organization (referenced in §§ 170(c)(1) and (2)(A)) or a private foundation and maintains one or more donor advised funds.

Supporting Organizations and Donor Advised Funds as Alternatives to Private Foundations

Traditionally, supporting organizations and donor advised funds have offered donors certain advantages relative to private foundations, such as the possibility of a higher charitable contribution deduction and the avoidance of certain limitations that apply to private foundations, including the § 4941 self-dealing rules, the § 4942 annual payout requirements, and the § 4943 business holdings limits. Although certain advantages remain, new rules enacted as part of the PPA add certain requirements for deductibility of charitable contributions to donor advised funds and impose new restrictions on the operations of donor advised funds and supporting organizations.

New Rules Affecting Supporting Organizations and Donor Advised Funds under the PPA

The PPA contains several provisions intended to improve the accountability of donor advised funds and supporting organizations (see §§ 1226, 1231–1235 and 1241–1245 of the PPA). Those PPA provisions add §§ 4966 and 4967 to the Code, and amend §§ 170, 508, 509, 2055, 2522, 4942, 4943, 4945, 4958, and 6033 of the Code. For a description of some of the new rules, see Notice 2006–109, 2006–51 I.R.B. 1121 (December 18, 2006).

The new rules affecting supporting organizations include: excise taxes on certain payments to a substantial contributor or a related person and on the entire amount of any loan to a disqualified person (§ 4958(c)(3)); the extension of § 4958 to transactions between a supported organization and a person who is a disqualified person of a supporting organization (§ 4958(f)); a grant of regulatory authority to adopt a new payout requirement for certain Type III supporting organizations (PPA § 1241(d)); limits on the permitted business holdings of certain supporting organizations (§ 4943(f)); organizational and operational requirements (§ 509(f)); and reporting requirements (§§ 6033(a)(3)(B) and 6033(l)). In addition, new rules apply to certain private foundations that make grants to certain supporting organizations (§§ 4942(g)(4) and 4945(d)(4)(A)).

The new rules affecting donor advised funds include: definitions of the terms "sponsoring organization" and "donor advised fund" (§ 4966(d)); excise taxes on certain taxable distributions from a donor advised fund (§ 4966(c)); excises taxes on donors, advisors, or related persons who receive certain benefits as a result of a distribution from a donor advised fund (or who advise as to such a distribution) (§ 4967); excise taxes on payments from a donor advised fund to any donor, advisor, or a related person (§§ 4958(c)(2) and 4958(f)(1)(E)); the extension of § 4958 to transactions between the sponsoring organization and certain investment advisors or related persons (§§ 4958(f)(1)(F) and 4958(f)(8)); limits on permitted business holdings (§ 4943(e)); substantiation requirements (§§ 170(f)(18), 2055(e)(5) and 2522(c)(5)); and reporting and disclosure requirements for sponsoring organizations (§§ 508(f) and 6033(k)).

Deductible Charitable Contributions

Generally, an income tax deduction is allowed under § 170 for a charitable contribution made in the year the deduction is claimed, subject to certain limitations and substantiation requirements. *See, e.g., U.S. v. American Bar Endowment*, 477 U.S. 105 (1986); §§ 1.170A–1(a) and 1.170A–13. Charitable contributions also may be deductible for gift or estate tax purposes. §§ 2522 and 2055. Under the PPA, a taxpayer may deduct a contribution to a donor advised fund only if the sponsoring organization receiving the contribution is one of certain specified types, and the taxpayer making the contribution obtains an acknowledgement from the sponsoring organization that the organization has exclusive legal control over the property contributed. §§ 170(f)(18), 2522(c)(5), and 2055(e)(5).

ISSUES IDENTIFIED FOR FURTHER STUDY UNDER THE PPA

In discussing § 1226 of the PPA, the Technical Explanation prepared by the Joint Committee on Taxation states, in part, "Elsewhere in the bill, provision is made for new rules with respect to donor advised funds and supporting organizations. Many issues arise under current law with respect to such organizations, some of which are addressed in the bill and some of which would benefit from additional study."[1]

Section 1226 of the PPA provides that the Secretary shall undertake a study on the organization and operation of donor advised funds and supporting organizations,

[1] Joint Committee on Taxation, *Technical Explanation of H.R. 4, The "Pension Protection Act of 2006," as Passed by the House on July 28, 2006 and as Considered by the Senate on August 3, 2006*, (JCX–38–06), August 3, 2006, at 333.

and that the study shall specifically consider:

(1) whether the deductions allowed for income, gift, or estate taxes for charitable contributions to sponsoring organizations of donor advised funds or to supporting organizations are appropriate in consideration of (i) the use of contributed assets (including the type, extent, and timing of such use) or (ii) the use of the assets of such organizations for the benefit of the person making the charitable contribution (or a person related to such person),

(2) whether donor advised funds should be required to distribute for charitable purposes a specified amount (whether based on the income or assets of the fund) in order to ensure that the sponsoring organization with respect to the fund is operating consistent with the purposes or functions constituting the basis for its exemption under § 501 or its status as an organization described in § 509(a),

(3) whether the retention by donors to donor advised funds or supporting organizations of rights or privileges with respect to amounts transferred to such organizations (including advisory rights or privileges with respect to the making of grants or the investment of assets) is consistent with the treatment of such transfers as completed gifts that qualify for a deduction for income, gift, or estate taxes, and

(4) whether any of the issues described above also are issues with respect to other forms of charities or charitable donations.

REQUEST FOR PUBLIC COMMENTS

To assist in performing the required study, the Treasury and the Service request comments on the specific issues identified above and other issues relevant to the study. In particular, the Treasury and the Service request comments with respect to the following:

1. What are the advantages and disadvantages of donor advised funds and supporting organizations to the charitable sector, donors, sponsoring organizations, and supported organizations, compared to private foundations and other charitable giving arrangements?

2. How should the amount and availability of a charitable contribution deduction for a transfer of assets to a donor advised fund or a supporting organization, and the tax-exempt status or foundation classification of the donee, be determined if:

a. the transferred assets are paid to, or used for the benefit of, the donor or persons related to the donor (including, for example, salaries and other compensation arrangements, loans, or any other personal benefits or rights)?

b. the donor has investment control over the transferred assets?

c. there is an expectation that the donor's "advice" will be followed, or will be the sole or primary consideration, in determining distributions from, or investment of the assets in, the supporting organization or the donor advised fund?

d. the donor or the donee has option rights (*e.g.*, puts, calls, or rights of first refusal) with respect to the transferred assets?

e. the transferred assets are appreciated real, personal, or intangible property that is not readily convertible to cash?

3. What are the effects or the expected effects of the PPA provisions (including the § 4958 excess benefit transaction tax amendments applicable to donor advised funds and supporting organizations) on the practices and behavior of donors, donor advised funds, sponsoring organizations, supporting organizations and supported organizations?

4. What would be appropriate payout requirements, and why, for:

a. donor advised funds?

b. funds that are excepted from donor advised fund treatment by statute or by the authority of the Secretary, but for which the donor retains meaningful rights with respect to the investment or use of the transferred amounts?

c. supporting organizations?

d. any other types of charities?

5. What are the advantages and disadvantages of perpetual existence of donor advised funds or supporting organizations?

6. What other types of charitable giving arrangements give rise to any of the above issues?

Section 1226 of the PPA provides that, not later than August 16, 2007, the Secretary shall submit to the Congress a report on the study. Comments should refer to Notice 2007–21 and be submitted by April 9, 2007, to:

Internal Revenue Service
P. O. Box 7604
Ben Franklin Station
Washington, D.C. 20044
Attn: CC:PA:LPD:PR
Room 5203

Alternatively, comments may be submitted electronically via e-mail to *Notice.Comments@irscounsel.treas.gov*. The comments you submit will be available for public inspection and copying.

DRAFTING INFORMATION

The principal authors of this notice are Robert Fontenrose of the Exempt Organizations, Tax Exempt and Government Entities Division, and Susan J. Kassell of the Office of Associate Chief Counsel (Income Tax & Accounting). For further information regarding exempt organization issues, contact Mr. Fontenrose at (202) 283–9484 (not a toll-free call). For further information regarding charitable contribution issues, contact Ms. Kassell at (202) 622–5020 (not a toll-free call).

---

26 CFR 601.105: Examination of returns and claims for refund, credit, or abatement; determination of correct tax liability.
(Also: Part 1, §§ 6011, 6111, 6662A, 6707, 6707A.)

Rev. Proc. 2007–21

SECTION 1. PURPOSE

This revenue procedure provides guidance to persons against whom a penalty under section 6707 or 6707A of the Internal Revenue Code is assessed, and who may request rescission of all or any portion of that penalty from the Commissioner of the Internal Revenue Service if the penalty is with respect to a reportable transaction other than a listed transaction. This revenue procedure describes the procedures for requesting rescission, including the deadline by which a person must request rescission; the information the person must provide in the rescission request; the factors that weigh in favor of and against granting rescission; where the person must submit the rescission request; and the rules governing requests for additional information from the person requesting rescission.

SECTION 2. BACKGROUND

.01 Section 6011 and the regulations thereunder require a taxpayer that has participated in a reportable transaction to disclose certain information with respect to the reportable transaction with its tax return. Section 1.6011–4(b) of the Income Tax Regulations enumerates and describes the categories of reportable transactions. One category of reportable transactions is a transaction that is the same as, or substantially similar to, one of the types of transactions that the Internal Revenue Service has determined to be a tax avoidance transaction and has identified by notice, regulation, or other form of published guidance as a "listed transaction." Treas. Reg. § 1.6011–4(b)(2).

.02 The American Jobs Creation Act of 2004, Pub. L. No. 108–357, 118 Stat. 1418 (the Act), was enacted on October 22, 2004. Section 811 of the Act added section 6707A to the Code to provide a monetary penalty for the failure to include on any return or statement any information required to be disclosed under section 6011 with respect to a reportable transaction. Section 6707A(b)(1) provides that the penalty for failure to include information with respect to a reportable transaction, other than a listed transaction, is $10,000 in the case of a taxpayer that is a natural person, and $50,000 in any other case. Section 6707A(b)(2) provides that for a listed transaction, the penalty is increased to $100,000 in the case of a taxpayer that is a natural person, and $200,000 in any other case.

.03 Section 816 of the Act amended section 6707 to provide for the imposition of a penalty on a material advisor who is required to file a return under section 6111(a) with respect to any reportable transaction, and who fails to file a timely return or who files a false or incomplete return with respect to the reportable transaction. Section 6707(b)(1) provides that the penalty for failing to file a timely return or filing a false or incomplete return with respect to any reportable transaction other than a listed transaction is $50,000. Section 6707(b)(2) provides that the penalty with respect to any listed transaction equals the greater of (1) $200,000, or (2) 50 percent of the gross income derived by the material advisor with respect to aid, assistance, or advice that is provided with respect to the listed transaction before the date the return is filed under section 6111. If the penalty is with respect to a listed transaction and the failure or action subject to the penalty was intentional, the penalty is the greater of (1) $200,000, or (2) 75 percent of the gross income derived by the material advisor with respect to aid, assistance, or advice that is provided with respect to the listed transaction before the date the return is filed under section 6111.

.04 Section 6707A(d)(1) grants the Commissioner authority to rescind all or a portion of any penalty imposed under section 6707A if (1) the violation relates to a reportable transaction that is not a listed transaction and (2) rescission of the penalty would promote compliance with the requirements of the Code and effective tax administration. Section 6707A(d)(2) provides that the Commissioner's determination whether to rescind the penalty may not be reviewed in any judicial proceeding. The legislative history to section 6707A provides that "the IRS Commissioner or his delegate can rescind (or abate) the penalty." H.R. Conf. Rep. No. 755, 108th Cong., 2d Sess. at 373 (2004). Section 6707(c) provides that the rescission provisions of section 6707A(d) shall also apply to any penalty imposed on a material advisor under section 6707.

.05 Section 6707A(e) requires a person that is required to file periodic reports under section 13 or 15(d) of the Securities Exchange Act of 1934, or is required to be consolidated with another person for purposes of those reports, to disclose in those reports for the periods specified by the Secretary, the requirement to pay the penalties set forth in section 6707A(e)(2) (*i.e.*, certain penalties under section 6662(h) and penalties under section 6662A(c), section 6707A(b)(2), or section 6707A(e)). If the person fails to disclose the requirement to pay the penalties, then section 6707A(e) requires that the failure be treated as a failure to disclose a listed transaction for which an additional section 6707A penalty applies. Because a penalty imposed under section 6707A(e) is treated as a penalty imposed with respect to a listed transaction, the penalty is not subject to rescission. *See* Rev. Proc. 2005–51, 2005–2 C.B. 296.

.06 Section 812 of the Act, which added section 6662A to the Code, provides that a 20-percent accuracy-related penalty may be imposed on any "reportable transaction understatement," as defined in section 6662A(b). Section 6662A(c) increases the penalty rate to 30 percent for the portion of any reportable transaction understatement with respect to which the relevant facts affecting the tax treatment of the reportable transaction were not adequately disclosed in accordance with regulations prescribed under section 6011. If the Commissioner (or the Commissioner's delegate) rescinds the penalty under section 6707A, then the taxpayer is treated as meeting the reportable transaction disclosure requirements of the regulations under section 6011, and the 30-percent penalty rate under section 6662A(c) does not apply. *See* I.R.C. § 6664(d)(2).

.07 Section 812 of the Act also added section 6664(d) to the Code, which provides a reasonable cause exception to the section 6662A reportable transaction understatement penalty. Generally, this exception cannot apply to any reportable transaction understatement unless, among other things, the relevant facts affecting the tax treatment of the reportable transaction are adequately disclosed in accordance with the regulations prescribed under section 6011. If the Commissioner (or the Commissioner's delegate) rescinds the penalty under section 6707A for failure to include reportable transaction information with a return or statement, then the taxpayer is treated as meeting the reportable transaction disclosure requirements of the regulations under section 6011, and the taxpayer has satisfied that prerequisite to establishing the reasonable cause exception to the reportable transaction understatement penalty under section 6662A. *See* I.R.C. § 6664(d)(2). Satisfying that one element of section 6664, however, will not alone establish reasonable cause.

.08 Section 903 of the Act amended section 6404(g)(2) to provide an exception to the general rule that interest and certain penalties will be suspended if the Secretary fails to provide a taxpayer with timely notice of an adjustment to the taxpayer's liability. Under section 6404(g)(2)(E), interest and certain penalties will not be suspended with respect to any listed transaction as defined in section 6707A(c). Also, under section 6404(g)(2)(E), interest and certain penalties will not be suspended with respect to any reportable transaction (other than a listed transaction) that the taxpayer did not disclose as required by regulations under section 6011. If the penalty imposed under section 6707A is rescinded under the provisions of section 6707A(d), then the taxpayer is treated as meeting the reportable transaction disclosure requirements of the regulations under section 6011 for purposes of section 6404(g)(2)(E).

.09 Notice 2005–11, 2005–1 C.B. 493, provides that, in determining whether rescission of the penalty under 6707A would promote compliance with the requirements of the Code and effective tax administration, the Commissioner (or the Commissioner's delegate) will take into account all of the relevant facts and circumstances, including: (1) whether the taxpayer has a history of complying with the tax laws; (2) whether the violation results from an unintentional mistake of fact; and (3) whether imposing the penalty would be against equity and good conscience. Further, Notice 2005–11 provides that the Commissioner's determination whether to rescind a penalty in whole or in part is not reviewable by the IRS Office of Appeals or any court. Notice 2005–11 is effective until further guidance is issued in the form of regulations or other guidance that explicitly supersedes Notice 2005–11.

SECTION 3. SCOPE

This revenue procedure applies to any person against whom a penalty under section 6707 or 6707A is assessed and who may also request rescission of all or a portion of the penalty from the Commissioner. A person may only request rescission of a penalty under section 6707 or 6707A if the violation relates to a reportable transaction other than a listed transaction. Further guidance will be issued providing pre-assessment administrative appeal rights to persons against whom the IRS proposes to assess a penalty under section 6707 or 6707A.

SECTION 4. APPLICATION

.01 *When rescission request must be made.* In accordance with sections 6707A(d) and 6707(c), a person (*i.e.*, a taxpayer under section 6707A or material advisor under section 6707) requesting rescission of a penalty assessed under either section 6707A or section 6707 must request rescission in writing within 30 days after the date the Service sends notice and demand for payment of the penalty pursuant to section 6303. If the person pays the penalty (not including interest) in full prior to the Service sending notice and demand for payment, the person must request rescission in writing within 30 days from the date of payment. The Service will apply sections 7502 and 7503 to determine whether a request for rescission is timely. A person may request rescission only after filing with the Service the complete return or statement required under section 6011 or 6111, as applicable. Additionally, in order to request rescission, a person must have exhausted the administrative remedies available within the IRS Office of Appeals regarding the proposed assessment of the penalty unless the person has agreed in writing to the assessment of the penalty and has agreed not to file or prosecute a claim for refund or credit of the penalty, administratively or through litigation, other than by requesting rescission. The method of requesting rescission that is provided in this revenue procedure is the exclusive method of requesting rescission. A person may not request rescission through a refund claim, in a collection due process hearing, or through any other avenue for approaching the Service.

.02 *Information required in rescission request.* The written request for rescission must include: (1) the name, address, telephone number, and Taxpayer Identification Number, as applicable, of the person against whom the relevant penalty is imposed; (2) the amount of the penalty imposed; (3) a copy of the complete return or statement required under section 6011 or 6111, as applicable, that the person filed with the Service; (4) a copy of the notice and demand for payment or a statement that the person made payment in full prior to receiving notice and demand; (5) a copy of the agreement to the assessment of the penalty and not to file or prosecute a claim for refund or credit of the penalty, if applicable; (6) a statement of the facts and circumstances relating to the violation, which includes the Code section under which the penalty was determined (*i.e.*, section 6707(a) or section 6707A(a)), the reason(s) the original return or statement was not timely filed or was incomplete, a description of the safeguards the person had in place to ensure the proper filing of the return or statement, any remedial measures the person has taken to prevent future violations, and any other facts or circumstances relevant to how rescission would promote compliance with the requirements of the Code and effective tax administration, including the factors listed under section 4.04 of this revenue procedure; (7) a statement of the person's history of compliance with the tax law over the past 10 years, including but not limited to, identification of any penalties that the Service assessed against the person with respect to any reportable transaction and compliance with any requirement to disclose a reportable transaction; (8) for a penalty assessed under section 6707A, copies of all offerings and promotional materials that the taxpayer received with respect to the reportable transaction involved in the rescission request; (9) a statement providing the identity of related parties (as defined in section 267(b)) to the transaction, the identity of tax exempt entities involved in the transaction, and parties to any designation agreement, if applicable; and (10) the following declaration signed by the person requesting rescission: "Under penalties of perjury, I declare that I have examined this rescission request, and to the best of my knowledge and belief the information in this rescission request is true, correct, and complete."

.03 *Information that will expedite the rescission request.* Including some or all of the following information in a rescission request will expedite processing of the request: (1) a copy of the notice of proposed assessment (*e.g.*, 30-day letter and Form 4549, *Income Tax Examination Changes*); (2) the name, telephone number, and address of the IRS revenue agent that examined the person with respect to the applicable penalty; and (3) the name, telephone number, and address of the IRS appeals officer that considered the proposed penalty assessment, if applicable.

.04 *Factors that weigh in favor of granting rescission.* In determining whether rescission would promote compliance with the requirements of the Code and effective tax administration, the Commissioner (or the Commissioner's delegate) will take into account the following list of factors that weigh in favor of granting rescission. This is not an exclusive list and no single factor will be determinative of whether to grant rescission in any particular case. Rather, the Commissioner (or the Commissioner's delegate) will consider and weigh all relevant factors, regardless of whether the factor is included in this list.

(A) The person, upon becoming aware of its failure to disclose or report a reportable transaction properly, filed a complete and proper, albeit untimely, Form 8886 or 8264 (or any successor forms), as applicable. For a penalty assessed under section 6707A, this factor will weigh strongly in favor of rescission provided that (i) the taxpayer files the Form 8886 prior to the date the Service first contacts the taxpayer (including contacts by the Service with any partnership in which the taxpayer is a partner, any S corporation in which the taxpayer is a shareholder, or any trust in which the taxpayer is a beneficiary) concerning a tax examination for the tax period in which the taxpayer participated in the reportable transaction and (ii) other circumstances suggest that the taxpayer did not delay filing an untimely but properly completed Form 8886 until after the Service had taken steps to identify the taxpayer's participation in the reportable transaction in question. For a penalty assessed under section 6707, this factor will weigh strongly in favor of rescission provided that the material advisor files the form required under section 6111 prior to the earlier of the date that any taxpayer files a Form 8886 identifying the material advisor with respect to the reportable transaction in question or the date the Service contacts the material advisor concerning the reportable transaction.

(B) The failure to properly disclose was due to an unintentional mistake of fact that existed despite the person's reasonable attempts to ascertain the correct facts with respect to the transaction.

(C) The person has an established history of properly disclosing other reportable transactions and complying with other tax laws, including compliance with any requests made under section 6112, if applicable.

(D) The person demonstrates that the failure to include on any return or statement any information required to be disclosed under section 6011 or section 6111 arose from events beyond the person's control.

(E) The person cooperates with the Service by providing timely information with respect to the transaction at issue that the Commissioner (or the Commissioner's delegate) may request in consideration of the rescission request. In considering whether a person cooperates with the Service, the Commissioner (or the Commissioner's delegate) may take into account whether the person complies with requests for additional information described in section 4.09 of this revenue procedure.

(F) Assessment of the penalty would weigh against equity and good conscience, including whether the person demonstrates that there was reasonable cause for, and the person acted in good faith with respect to, the failure to timely file or to include on any return any information required to be disclosed under section 6011 or section 6111. For a penalty assessed under section 6707A, an important factor in determining reasonable cause and good faith is the extent of the taxpayer's efforts to ensure that persons who prepared the taxpayer's return were informed of the taxpayer's participation in the reportable transactions. For a penalty assessed under section 6707, an important factor in determining reasonable cause and good faith is the extent of the material advisor's efforts to determine whether there was a requirement to file the return required under section 6111. The presence of reasonable cause, however, will not necessarily be determinative of whether to grant rescission.

.05 *Absence of factors described in section 4.04 weigh against rescission.* The absence of facts establishing the factors described in section 4.04 of this revenue procedure weigh against granting rescission. The absence of any one of these factors, however, will not necessarily be determinative of whether to grant rescission.

.06 *Factors not considered.* In determining whether to grant rescission, the Commissioner (or the Commissioner's delegate) will not consider doubt as to liability for, or collectibility of, the penalties. For example, the Commissioner (or the Commissioner's delegate) will not consider whether the taxpayer will suffer "economic hardship," as defined in Treas. Reg. § 301.6343–1(b)(4), if rescission is not granted.

.07 *Effect of rescission request on collection.* A person need not pay the section 6707 or 6707A penalty assessed prior to requesting rescission. The Service, however, will not suspend collection efforts solely because a person has made a rescission request.

.08 *Where rescission request must be submitted.* The written request for rescission should be sent to the following address:

Internal Revenue Service
LM:PQA:JC:1953(RR)
Large & Mid-Size Business Division
110 West 44th St., 3rd Floor
New York, NY 10036

The person must send the written request to the above address prior to the date specified in section 4.01 of this revenue procedure.

.09 *Request for additional information.* After receiving the rescission request, the Service may make a written request seeking additional information and documents relating to the transaction, such as marketing materials and tax opinions, from the person requesting rescission. Requested information must be submitted to the Service within 30 days of the date of mailing of the request for additional information by the Service. The Service may grant an extension of time for good cause to persons who request additional time within the 30-day period. A person's failure to provide the requested information within the applicable time period may weigh against rescission. Meritless claims of privilege may weigh against rescission. Further, the examining revenue agent and other Service employees involved with the examination may be asked to review and comment on the rescission request.

SECTION 5. PAPERWORK REDUCTION ACT

The collection of information contained in this revenue procedure has been reviewed and approved by the Office of Management and Budget in accordance with the Paperwork Reduction Act (44 U.S.C. § 3507) under control number 1545–2047.

An agency may not conduct or sponsor, and a person is not required to respond to, a collection of information unless the collection of information displays a valid OMB control number.

The collection of information in this revenue procedure is in section 4. This information is required to administer the provisions of sections 6707(c) and 6707A(d) and determine whether the Service should rescind penalties otherwise applicable. The likely respondents are taxpayers and material advisors who are subject to a penalty under section 6707 or 6707A.

The estimated total annual reporting or recordkeeping burden is 3865.5 hours.

The estimated annual burden per respondent/recordkeeper varies from 3 to 6 hours, depending on individual circumstances, with an estimated average of 4.5 hours. The estimated number of respondents or recordkeepers is 859.

The estimated annual frequency of responses (used for reporting requirements only) is 1.

Books or records relating to a collection of information must be retained as long as their contents may become material in the administration of any internal revenue law. Generally, tax returns and tax return information are confidential, as required by 26 U.S.C. § 6103.

SECTION 6. EFFECTIVE DATE

This revenue procedure is effective for any rescission request that relates to a section 6707 or 6707A penalty for which notice and demand, or payment, is made after October 22, 2004.

SECTION 7. DRAFTING INFORMATION

The principal author of this revenue procedure is Matthew S. Cooper of the Office of the Associate Chief Counsel (Procedure and Administration), Administrative Provisions & Judicial Practice Division. For further information regarding this revenue procedure, contact Matthew S. Cooper at (202) 622–4940 (not a toll-free call).

Part IV. Items of General Interest

Notice of Proposed Rulemaking

Release of Lien or Discharge of Property

REG–159444–04

AGENCY: Internal Revenue Service (IRS), Treasury.

ACTION: Notice of proposed rulemaking.

SUMMARY: This document contains proposed regulations related to release of lien and discharge of property under sections 6325, 6503, and 7426 of the Internal Revenue Code (Code). The proposed regulations update existing regulations and contain procedures for processing a request made by a property owner for discharge of a Federal tax lien from his property, under section 6325(b)(4). The proposed regulations also clarify the impact of these procedures on sections 6503(f)(2) and 7426(a)(4) and (b)(5). The proposed regulations reflect the enactment of sections 6325(b)(4), 6503(f)(2), and 7426(a)(4) by the IRS Restructuring and Reform Act of 1998.

DATES: Written or electronic comments and requests for a public hearing must be received by April 11, 2007.

ADDRESSES: Send submissions to: CC:PA:LPD:PR (REG–159444–04), room 5203, Internal Revenue Service, POB 7604, Ben Franklin Station, Washington, DC 20044. Submissions may be hand-delivered Monday through Friday between the hours of 8 a.m. and 4 p.m. to CC:PA:LPD:PR (REG–159444–04), Courier's Desk, Internal Revenue Service, 1111 Constitution Avenue, NW, Washington, DC 20224. Alternatively, taxpayers may submit comments electronically to the IRS Internet site at *www.irs.gov/regs* or via the Federal eRulemaking Portal at *www.regulations.gov* (IRS-REG–159444–04).

FOR FURTHER INFORMATION CONTACT: Concerning the regulations, Debra A. Kohn, (202) 622–7985; concerning submissions of comments and the hearing, Richard A. Hurst, Publications and Regulations Specialist, at *Richard.A.Hurst@irscounsel.treas.gov* or (202) 622–7180 (not toll-free numbers).

SUPPLEMENTARY INFORMATION:

Background

This document contains proposed amendments to the Procedure and Administration Regulations (26 CFR part 301) under sections 6325, 6503, and 7426 of the Code. Section 6325(b)(4) was enacted by section 3106(a) of the IRS Restructuring and Reform Act of 1998 (RRA 1998), Pub. L. No. 105–206 (112 Stat. 685). Section 6503(f)(2) was enacted by section 3106(b)(3) of RRA 1998. Sections 7426(a)(4) and (b)(5) were enacted by section 3106(b)(1) of RRA 1998. These provisions of RRA 1998 provide a statutory mechanism for a person other than the person against whom the underlying tax was assessed, upon furnishing a deposit or bond, to obtain a discharge of the Federal tax lien from property owned by him, and for the IRS or the courts to determine the disposition of the deposit or bond amount.

The provisions added by RRA 1998 were enacted in response to *United States v. Williams*, 514 U.S. 527 (1995). In *Williams*, the Supreme Court held that a third party who paid another person's tax liability under protest had standing to bring a civil suit for refund pursuant to 28 U.S.C. 1346(a)(1), which waives the Government's sovereign immunity with respect to refund suits for Federal taxes alleged to have been erroneously or illegally assessed or collected. The Government argued in *Williams* that section 1346(a)(1) was intended to afford a remedy only to the person against whom a tax is assessed, and not a third party in this situation. In rejecting this argument, the Supreme Court reasoned that the plaintiff in *Williams*, who was not the taxpayer and who needed a discharge of the Federal tax lien in order to sell her property, had no effective remedy other than to pay the tax giving rise to the lien and to institute a refund suit. Sections 6325(b)(4), 6503(f)(2), and 7426(a)(4) and (b)(5) afford such a remedy to an owner of the property in this situation if the owner is not the person whose unsatisfied liability gave rise to the lien (a third-party owner). In light of the addition of these provisions to the Code, the continuing applicability of *Williams* is extremely limited, as the IRS has noted in other published guidance. See Rev. Rul. 2005–50, 2005–2 C.B. 124 (2005).

The current Code of Federal Regulations contains both temporary and final regulations under sections 6325, 6503, and 7426. Neither the temporary regulations nor the final regulations reflect the amendments to the Code made by RRA 1998. These proposed regulations, if adopted as final, would constitute permanent regulations that would incorporate the amendments made by RRA 1998 by replacing the existing temporary regulations and updating the existing final regulations under sections 6325, 6503, and 7426. In particular, these proposed regulations contain procedures for processing a request for a certificate of discharge of a Federal tax lien under section 6325(b)(4). In addition, these proposed regulations clarify the impact of these procedures on the collection limitations period tolling provisions of section 6503(f)(2) and on the judicial remedy provisions of sections 7426(a)(4) and (b)(5).

The proposed regulations also incorporate, with updates, the language of the existing temporary regulations relating to release of lien under section 6325(a), while withdrawing the existing temporary regulations. Changes to the language of the existing temporary regulations have been made to account for the IRS's acceptance of additional forms of payment since the temporary regulations became effective in 1983. Although section 7805(e)(2) provides that temporary regulations expire after three years, this provision applies only to temporary regulations issued after November 20, 1988. Since the temporary regulations relevant here were issued prior to that date, they are not subject to the three-year statutory limit. The proposed regulations provide that the existing temporary regulations under section 6325(a) are removed as of the date the proposed regulations become effective as final regulations.

The existing permanent and temporary regulations do not account for the current organizational structure of the IRS. The existing permanent regulations under sections 6325 and 6503(f) employ the title "district director," in numerous instances, in indicating the highest official of a local office of the IRS. That title was used under an organizational structure of the IRS that no longer exists. In order to account for the IRS's current organizational structure and to allow for future reorganizations of the IRS, the proposed regulations remove the title "district director" throughout §§301.6325–1 and 301.6503(f)–1, and replace that title with the term "appropriate official." Section 301.6325–1(h) and Section 301.6503(f)–1(c) of the proposed regulations state that as used throughout section 301.6325–1 and section 301.6503(f)–1, respectively, the term "appropriate official" means the official or office identified in the relevant IRS Publication, or if such official is not so identified, the Secretary or his delegate. In this context, the relevant publication is either IRS Publication 1450, "*Instructions on How to Request a Certificate of Release of Federal Tax Lien*," or IRS Publication 783, "*Instructions on How to Apply for a Certificate of Discharge of Property From Federal Tax Lien*."

Explanation of Provisions

I. *In General*

Under section 6325(a), the Secretary shall issue a certificate of release of a Federal tax lien within 30 days of finding that the liability for the underlying tax either has been fully satisfied or has become legally unenforceable, or if an appropriate bond has been furnished to and accepted by the Secretary.

Under section 6325(b)(4)(A), the Secretary shall issue a certificate of discharge of property from a Federal tax lien if the owner of the property requests the issuance of a certificate of discharge and either deposits an amount of money "equal to the value of the interest of the United States (as determined by the Secretary) in the property" or furnishes an acceptable bond in a like amount. Section 6325(b)(4)(D) renders section 6325(b)(4)(A) inapplicable "if the owner of the property is the person whose unsatisfied liability gave rise to the lien." This means that if undivided interests in the property at issue are owned by both the taxpayer and another person, neither the taxpayer nor the other person may obtain a discharge of the property from the Federal tax lien under section 6325(b)(4).

Under section 6325(b)(4)(B), the Secretary shall refund the amount deposited, with interest, or release the bond furnished, "to the extent that the Secretary determines that" either: (i) the unsatisfied liability giving rise to the lien "can be satisfied from a source other than such property"; or (ii) the value of the interest of the United States in the property "is less than the Secretary's prior determination of such value." Section 7426(a)(4) allows a person who has obtained a certificate of discharge under section 6325(b)(4) to bring a civil action in Federal district court against the United States "for a determination of whether the value of the interest of the United States (if any) in such property is less than the value determined by the Secretary." This action must be filed within 120 days after the date the certificate of discharge is issued. Section 7426(a)(4) states that "[n]o other action may be brought by such person for such a determination." Section 7426(b)(5) provides that if the Federal district court determines that the Secretary's determination of the value of the interest of the United States in the property under section 6325(b)(4) exceeds the value of such interest, the court shall grant a judgment ordering a refund of the deposit amount, or a release of the bond, to the extent that the amount furnished exceeds the value determined by the court.

Section 6325(b)(4)(C) states that if no action is filed under section 7426(a)(4) within the specified 120-day period, the Secretary shall, within 60 days after the expiration of that period: (i) apply the deposit, or collect on the bond, to the extent necessary to satisfy the liability secured by the lien; and (ii) refund, with interest, any portion of the deposit not used to satisfy such liability.

Section 6503(f)(2) suspends the running of the period provided in section 6502 for collecting an assessed tax liability from the time a person becomes entitled to a certificate of discharge under section 6325(b)(4) until 30 days after: (A) the earliest date on which the Secretary no longer holds any amount as a deposit or bond provided under section 6325(b)(4) because the deposit or bond either has been used to satisfy the unpaid tax liability or has been refunded or released; or (B) the date a judgment secured under section 7426(b)(5) becomes final. Suspension of the running of the collection limitations period under section 6503(f)(2) applies only with respect to the amount of the assessment equal to the value of the interest of the United States in the subject property, plus interest, penalties, and certain other additions to tax.

II. *Release of Lien*

Section 6325(a) provides that the Secretary shall issue a certificate of release of lien within 30 days of the satisfaction of certain conditions. Section 301.6325–1(a)(1) and (2) of the existing permanent regulations state that the Secretary "may" issue a certificate of release if such conditions are met. These proposed regulations change the word "may" to "shall" in the appropriate instances, and incorporate the 30-day requirement contained in the existing temporary regulations, consistent with section 6325(a).

Much of the remainder of the language of §401.6325–1(a) of the temporary regulations is essentially the same as the language of §301.6325–1(a) of the existing permanent regulations. Therefore, the remaining language need not be incorporated into these proposed regulations. The language of §401.6325–1(b), dealing with notices of Federal tax lien that also contain certificates of release that become effective as of a prescribed date, survives as an addition to §301.6325–1(a). The language of §401.6325–1(c), defining the phrase *satisfaction of the tax liability* for purposes of section 6325(a)(1), also survives as an addition to §301.6325–1(a). The language of §401.6325–1(d), defining the phrase *proof of full payment* for purposes of §401.6325–1(a), survives as part of a new subsection of the permanent regulations addressing payment via credit and debit cards and electronic funds transfers, consistent with 26 CFR §§31.6302–1(h)(8) and 301.6311–2(a). The language of §401.6325–1(e), dealing with Federal tax liens listing multiple tax liabilities, and the language of §401.6325–1(f), dealing with the requirements of a valid request for a certificate of release, is incorporated into the permanent regulations.

III. *Discharge of Property under Section 6325(b)(4)*

A. *Issuance of the certificate of discharge*

Section 6325(b)(4)(A) requires the Secretary to issue a certificate of discharge of a third-party owner's property from a Federal tax lien if the third-party owner meets certain requirements. The proposed regulations state that a certificate of discharge must be issued under section 6325(b)(4) if the third-party owner submits a proper request and either deposits an appropriate amount or furnishes an acceptable bond.

1. Request of third-party owner

Section 301.6325–1(b)(4) provides that a person seeking a certificate of discharge under section 6325(b) must submit an application in writing to the local IRS official responsible for collection of the tax at issue, and that the application must contain such information as the official may require. Section 301.6325–1(b)(4) as currently written applies to only certificates of discharge under section 6325(b)(1) through (3). The proposed regulations extend the applicability of the language of §301.6325–1(b)(4) (redesignated as §301.6325–1(b)(5)) to a request for a certificate of discharge under section 6325(b)(4) and indicate that the request should be submitted to the appropriate IRS official or office.

New §301.6325–1(b)(5) of the proposed regulations states that a request for a certificate of discharge made by a third-party owner will be viewed as a request under section 6325(b)(4), and not as a request made under section 6325(b)(2), unless the third-party owner expressly states otherwise in writing. Similarly, any amount the IRS receives from a third-party owner following a discharge request will be viewed as a deposit made under section 6325(b)(4)(A), rather than as a payment under section 6325(b)(2), unless the third-party owner in writing expressly states otherwise, and expressly waives the right to file a civil suit in Federal district court for a refund of the amount received in writing.

The waiver provisions included in the proposed regulations generally protect the third-party owner in that a certificate of discharge granted under section 6325(b)(4), unlike one granted under section 6325(b)(2), affords a third-party owner the right to pursue a civil action under section 7426(a)(4) regarding the IRS's determination of the value of its lien. Amounts paid under section 6325(b)(2) do not constitute deposits and are immediately credited to the taxpayer's account once paid by the taxpayer or another person.

2. Value of the interest of the United States (as determined by the Secretary) in the property

Section 6325(b)(4)(A) and (D) requires the Secretary to issue a certificate of discharge of a third-party owner's property from a Federal tax lien if the third-party owner either deposits with the Secretary an amount "equal to the value of the interest of the United States (as determined by the Secretary)" or furnishes a bond acceptable to the IRS in a like amount. The proposed regulations provide that the deposit should be made or the bond should be furnished to the appropriate IRS official or office.

Section 301.6325–1(b)(2)(iii) indicates that in determining the value of the interest of the United States under section 6325(b)(2), the appropriate official "shall give consideration to the value of the property and the amount of all liens and encumbrances thereon having priority over the Federal tax lien. In determining the value of the property, the [appropriate official] may, in his discretion, give consideration to the forced sale value of the property in appropriate cases."

The proposed regulations state that this language applies to the determination of the value of the United States' interest in a third-party owner's property under section 6325(b)(4) and provide that the appropriate official shall make the determination.

B. *Processing the deposit*

Section 6325(b)(4)(B) states that the Secretary shall refund the amount deposited, with interest at the overpayment rate determined under section 6621, and shall release the bond, to the extent that the Secretary determines that either: (i) the unsatisfied tax liability giving rise to the lien can be satisfied from a source other than the third-party owner's property; or (ii) the value of the United States' interest in the property is less than the Secretary's prior determination of such value.

The proposed regulations specify that any request for a refund of deposit or release of bond under section 6325(b)(4)(B) must be made in writing and must contain the information required by the appropriate IRS Publication. The proposed regulations also clarify that the phrase "unsatisfied liability giving rise to the lien" contained in section 6325(b)(4)(B)(i) refers to the entire tax liability listed on the notice of Federal tax lien, not just the portion of the liability equal to the value of the United States' interest in the third-party owner's property. The proposed regulations, in addition, indicate that the Secretary is afforded discretion as to whether he should make a determination, and if he does so, in determining whether a deposit should be refunded or a bond released under section 6325(b)(4)(B).

As discussed in part IV of this preamble, a third-party owner wishing to file a civil suit for disposition of his deposit or bond is required by section 7426(a)(4) to do so within 120 days of issuance of the certificate of discharge. Consistent with this limitation period for filing suit, the proposed regulations allow the same 120-day period for the IRS to make any administrative determination regarding refund of deposit or release of bond under section 6325(b)(4)(B). During that 120-day period, the third-party owner may request a refund of deposit or release of bond administratively under section 6325(b)(4)(B), file a civil suit in district court under section 7426(a)(4), or both.

IV. *Civil Action by Person Other Than Taxpayer for Substitution of Value*

Section 7426(a)(4) provides that a person to whom a certificate of discharge has been issued under section 6325(b)(4) with respect to any property may, within 120 days after the day the certificate is issued, bring a civil action in Federal district court for "a determination of whether the value of the interest of the United States (if any) in such property is less than the value determined by the Secretary."

A. *Allowable basis for judicial determination*

The existing permanent regulations under section 7426 do not address the cause of action afforded by section 7426(a)(4). The proposed regulations clarify that the only allowable basis for a judicial determination under section 7426(a)(4) is that the value of the interest of the United States in the third-party owner's property is less than the value as determined by the Secretary under section 6325(b)(4)(A)(i). This follows from the express language of section 7426(a)(2) and is the case despite the fact that an additional basis for reevaluation of the Secretary's original determination – that the tax liability underlying the lien can be satisfied from another source – is provided under section 6325(b)(4)(B)(i).

B. *Exclusivity of remedy*

The proposed regulations emphasize that section 7426(a)(4) provides the only judicial remedy available to a third-party owner whose property is subject to a Federal tax lien to obtain a refund of the deposit or bond provided in exchange for a discharge of the lien from the property.

Section 7426(a)(4) explicitly provides that: "No other action may be brought by such person [to whom a certificate of discharge is issued under section 6325(b)(4)] for such a determination." Additionally, by the terms of section 7426(a)(4), a third-party owner must obtain a certificate of discharge under section 6325(b)(4) (and not under section 6325(b)(2)) to have standing to pursue the remedy offered by section 7426(a)(4).

C. *No tolling of 120-day period*

The proposed regulations state that an administrative request for refund of deposit or release of bond made under section 6325(b)(4)(B) does not affect the running of the 120-day period for bringing a civil suit under section 7426(a)(4). The statutory scheme makes the standing of a third-party owner to bring suit under section 7426(a)(4) independent of, rather than related to, events that might occur under section 6325(b)(4)(B). Thus, an administrative request for refund of deposit or release of bond under section 6325(b)(4)(B) is not a prerequisite to filing an action under section 7426(a)(4), and the 120-day period of section 7426(a)(4) will not be tolled by an administrative request for refund of deposit or release of bond made under section 6325(b)(4)(B).

D. *Court's authority to issue judgment*

The proposed regulations under section 7426 address section 7426(b)(5), which authorizes a Federal district court to decide whether the Secretary's determination of the value of the United States' interest in a third-party owner's property exceeds the actual value of its interest, and, if so, to grant a judgment ordering refund of all or part of the third-party owner's deposit accordingly.

V. *Secretary's Use of Deposit or Bond if Judicial Action Not Filed*

Section 6325(b)(4)(C) instructs the Secretary how to process the third-party owner's deposit or bond if the third-party owner does not institute suit under section 7426(a)(4) within the statutorily prescribed 120-day period. Under section 6325(b)(4)(C), the Secretary has 60 days after expiration of the 120-day period to: (i) apply the amount deposited (or collect on the bond furnished) "to the extent necessary to satisfy the unsatisfied liability secured by the lien"; and (ii) refund, with interest at the overpayment rate, any portion of the amount deposited "which is not used to satisfy such liability." Thus, the statute affords the Secretary a total of 180 days after issuing the certificate of discharge to complete processing of the third-party owner's deposit or bond.

The proposed regulations specify that the IRS may take these actions even after 180 days have passed. Prohibiting the IRS from either applying or refunding the deposit once the 180-day period has elapsed would prevent the IRS from ever relinquishing a deposit thereafter, in effect requiring IRS personnel to retain amounts deposited despite, in many cases, being aware that the amounts should be applied to outstanding tax liabilities or returned to third-party owners.

However, because section 6325(b)(4)(C) reflects Congress's intent that the deposit or bond be processed within 60 days after expiration of the 120-day period for bringing suit (or 180 days after the date a certificate of discharge is issued under section 6325(b)(4)(A)), the proposed regulations state that the deposit or bond will be deemed to have been processed as of the 60th day after expiration of the 120-day period for purposes of applying payments to the taxpayer's account. This means that if the IRS has not either applied or refunded any part of the deposit within the 180-day period, the IRS will be prohibited from charging the taxpayer interest and penalties on an outstanding liability to which the deposit should have been applied under section 6325(b)(4)(C)(i). On the other hand, the IRS will pay the third-party owner interest at the overpayment rate on any refund that should have been paid under section 6325(b)(4)(C)(ii) within the 60-day period until the refund is actually paid.

VI. *Suspension of Running of Period of Limitation*

Section 6503(f)(2) states that in the case of any assessment for which a lien was made on any property, the running of the period for collecting the assessed tax liability, under section 6502, shall be suspended from the date any person becomes entitled to a certificate of discharge with respect to the property under section 6325(b)(4) until the date which is 30 days after the earlier of: (A) the earliest date on which the Secretary no longer holds any amount as a deposit or bond provided under section 6325(b)(4) with respect to the property, because the deposit or bond either has been used to satisfy the unpaid tax or has been refunded; or (B) the date that a judgment secured under section 7426(b)(5) becomes final. Suspension of the running of the collection limitations period under section 6503(f)(2) applies only with respect to the amount of the assessment equal to the value of the interest of the United States in the subject property, plus interest, penalties and certain other additions to tax.

The proposed regulations under section 6503 address the suspension of the running of the period for collecting a tax liability provided by section 6503(f)(2).

Section 6325(b)(4)(A) provides that the Secretary shall issue a certificate of discharge when the third-party owner makes a request and deposits an appropriate amount or furnishes an acceptable bond. The proposed regulations state that the suspension of the running of the collection statute of limitations begins on the date a deposit or bond in the amount determined by the Secretary is received by the appropriate official under section 6325(b)(4)(A), as that is the date the third-party owner becomes entitled to a certificate of discharge under that provision.

Assuming that no judgment is obtained under section 7426(b)(5), section 6503(f)(2)(A) ties the end of the period for suspension of the running of the collection statute to the ultimate disposition of the third-party owner's deposit or bond, which is addressed by section 6325(b)(4)(B) and (C). The proposed regulations state that the suspension ends 30 days after the date the appropriate official no longer holds the deposit or bond by reason of taking actions prescribed under section 6325(b)(4)(B) and (C).

Because section 6325(b)(4)(C) contemplates that the deposit or bond will be processed within 60 days after the expiration of 120 days after the date the Secretary issues the certificate of discharge, as discussed in the previous section, the regulations state that the deposit or bond is deemed processed no later than that date for purposes of section 6503(f)(2)(A). This means that if the deposit or bond is not processed within the 180-day period, the running of the collection statute ceases to be suspended as of 90 days (60 days + the 30 days afforded by section 6503(f)(2)) after the 120-day period ends. Thus, the period for collection resumes running under section 6503(f)(2)(A) 31 days after the 180 days have passed.

Section 6503(f)(2)(B) ties the end of the suspension period to the finality of a judgment obtained under section 7426(b)(5). The proposed regulations state that if a judgment is obtained under section 7426(b)(5), the suspension of the running of the collection statute ends 30 days after all appeals of that judgment, if any, have been exhausted.

Proposed Effective Date

These regulations are proposed to apply to any release of lien or discharge of property that is requested after the date that these regulations are published as final regulations in the **Federal Register**.

Special Analyses

It has been determined that this notice of proposed rulemaking is not a significant regulatory action as defined in Executive Order 12866. Therefore, a regulatory assessment is not required. It also has been determined that section 553(b) of the Administrative Procedure Act (5 U.S.C. chapter 5) does not apply to these regulations, and because these regulations do not impose collection of information on small entities, the Regulatory Flexibility Act (5 U.S.C. chapter 6) does not apply. Pursuant to section 7805(f) of the Code, this notice of proposed rulemaking will be submitted to the Chief Counsel for Advocacy of the Small Business Administration for comment on its impact on small business.

Comments and Requests for Public Hearing

Before these proposed regulations are adopted as final regulations, consideration will be given to any written comments (a signed original and eight (8) copies) or electronic comments that are timely submitted to the IRS. The IRS and Treasury Department request comments on the clarity of the proposed rules and how they may be made easier to understand. All comments will be available for public inspection and copying. A public hearing will be scheduled if requested in writing by any person that timely submits written comments. If a public hearing is scheduled, notice of the date, time, and place for the public hearing will be published in the **Federal Register**.

Drafting Information

The principal author of these regulations is Debra A. Kohn of the Office of the Associate Chief Counsel (Procedure and Administration). However, other personnel from the IRS and Treasury Department participated in their development.

* * * * *

Proposed Amendments to the Regulations

Accordingly, 26 CFR part 301 is proposed to be amended as follows:

PART 301—PROCEDURE AND ADMINISTRATION

Paragraph 1. The authority citation for part 301 continues to read, in part, as follows:

Authority: 26 U.S.C. 7805 * * *

Par. 2. Section 301.6325–1 is amended as follows:

1. Paragraphs (a) and (b)(1)(i), (b)(2)(i), and (b)(2)(ii) are revised.

2. Paragraph (b)(2)(iii) is redesignated as paragraph (b)(6) and revised.

3. Paragraph (b)(4) is redesignated as paragraph (b)(5) and revised.

4. A new paragraph (b)(4) is added.

5. Paragraphs (c)(1) and (c)(2) are amended by removing the language "district director" and adding the language "appropriate official" in its place, wherever it appears.

6. The first sentence of paragraph (d)(1) is amended by removing the language "A district director" and adding the language "The appropriate official" in its place, by removing the word "Code" and adding the language "Internal Revenue Code" in its place, and by removing the language "the district director" and adding the language "the appropriate official" in its place. The third sentence is amended by removing the language "a district director" and adding the language "the appropriate official" in its place, and removing the language "the district director" and adding "the appropriate official" in its place.

7. Paragraph (d)(2)(i) is amended by removing the language "A district director" and adding the language "The appropriate official" in its place, by removing the word "Code" and adding the language "Internal Revenue Code" in its place, and by removing the language "the district director" and adding the language "the appropriate official" in its place.

8. Paragraph (d)(2)(ii), *Examples 1* through *4*, are amended by removing the language "district director" and adding the language "appropriate official" in its place, wherever it appears.

9. Paragraphs (d)(3) and (d)(4) are amended by removing the language "district director" and adding the language "appropriate official" in its place, wherever it appears.

10. The first sentence of paragraph (e) is amended by removing the language "a district director" and adding the language "the appropriate official" in its place, and by removing the language "the district director" and adding the language "the appropriate official" in its place. The third and fourth sentences are amended by removing the language "district director"

and adding the language "appropriate official" in its place.

11. Paragraphs (f)(1) and (f)(2)(i) are amended by removing the language "a district director" and adding the language "the appropriate official" in its place, paragraph (f)(2)(i)(*b*) is amended by removing the language "the district director" and adding the language "the appropriate official" in its place, and paragraph (f)(3) is amended by removing the word "Code" and adding the language "Internal Revenue Code" in its place.

12. Paragraphs (h), (i), and (j) are added.

The revisions and additions read as follows:

§301.6325–1 Release of lien or discharge of property.

(a) *Release of lien*—(1) *Liability satisfied or unenforceable.* The appropriate official shall issue a certificate of release for a filed notice of Federal tax lien, no later than 30 days after the date on which he finds that the entire tax liability listed in such notice of Federal tax lien either has been fully satisfied (as defined in paragraph (a)(4) of this section) or has become legally unenforceable. In all cases, the liability for the payment of the tax continues until satisfaction of the tax in full or until the expiration of the statutory period for collection, including such extension of the period for collection as is agreed to.

(2) *Bond accepted.* The appropriate official shall issue a certificate of release of any tax lien if he is furnished and accepts a bond that is conditioned upon the payment of the amount assessed (together with all interest in respect thereof), within the time agreed upon in the bond, but not later than 6 months before the expiration of the statutory period for collection, including any agreed upon extensions. For provisions relating to bonds, see sections 7101 and 7102 and §§301.7101–1 and 301.7102–1.

(3) *Certificate of release for a lien which has become legally unenforceable.* The appropriate official shall have the authority to file a notice of Federal tax lien which also contains a certificate of release pertaining to those liens which become legally unenforceable. Such release will become effective as a release as of a date prescribed in the document containing the notice of Federal tax lien and certificate of release.

(4) *Satisfaction of tax liability.* For purposes of paragraph (a)(1) of this section, satisfaction of the tax liability occurs when—

(i) The appropriate official determines that the entire tax liability listed in a notice of Federal tax lien has been fully satisfied. Such determination will be made as soon as practicable after tender of payment; or

(ii) The taxpayer provides the appropriate official with proof of full payment (as defined in paragraph (a)(5) of this section) with respect to the entire tax liability listed in a notice of Federal tax lien together with the information and documents set forth in paragraph (a)(7) of this section. See paragraph (a)(6) of this section if more than one tax liability is listed in a notice of Federal tax lien.

(5) *Proof of full payment.* As used in paragraph (a)(4)(ii) of this section, the term *proof of full payment* means—

(i) An internal revenue cashier's receipt reflecting full payment of the tax liability in question;

(ii) A canceled check in an amount sufficient to satisfy the tax liability for which the release is being sought;

(iii) A record, made in accordance with procedures prescribed by the Commissioner, of proper payment of the tax liability by credit or debit card or by electronic funds transfer; or

(iv) Any other manner of proof acceptable to the appropriate official.

(6) *Notice of a Federal tax lien which lists multiple liabilities.* When a notice of Federal tax lien lists multiple tax liabilities, the appropriate official shall issue a certificate of release when all of the tax liabilities listed in the notice of Federal tax lien have been fully satisfied or have become legally unenforceable. In addition, if the taxpayer requests that a certificate of release be issued with respect to one or more tax liabilities listed in the notice of Federal tax lien and such liability has been fully satisfied or has become legally unenforceable, the appropriate official shall issue a certificate of release. For example, if a notice of Federal tax lien lists two separate liabilities and one of the liabilities is satisfied, the taxpayer may request the issuance of a certificate of release with respect to the satisfied tax liability and the appropriate official shall issue a release.

(7) *Taxpayer requests.* A request for a certificate of release with respect to a notice of Federal tax lien shall be submitted in writing to the appropriate official. The request shall contain the information required in the appropriate IRS Publication.

(b) *Discharge of specific property from the lien*—(1) *Property double the amount of the liability.* (i) The appropriate official may, in his discretion, issue a certificate of discharge of any part of the property subject to a Federal tax lien imposed under chapter 64 of the Internal Revenue Code if he determines that the fair market value of that part of the property remaining subject to the Federal tax lien is at least double the sum of the amount of the unsatisfied liability secured by the Federal tax lien and of the amount of all other liens upon the property which have priority over the Federal tax lien. In general, fair market value is that amount which one ready and willing but not compelled to buy would pay to another ready and willing but not compelled to sell the property.

* * * * *

(2) *Part payment; interest of United States valueless*—(i) *Part payment.* The appropriate official may, in his discretion, issue a certificate of discharge of any part of the property subject to a Federal tax lien imposed under chapter 64 of the Internal Revenue Code if there is paid over to him in partial satisfaction of the liability secured by the Federal tax lien an amount determined by him to be not less than the value of the interest of the United States in the property to be so discharged. In determining the amount to be paid, the appropriate official will take into consideration all the facts and circumstances of the case, including the expenses to which the Government has been put in the matter. In no case shall the amount to be paid be less than the value of the interest of the United States in the property with respect to which the certificate of discharge is to be issued.

(ii) *Interest of the United States valueless.* The appropriate official may, in his discretion, issue a certificate of discharge of any part of the property subject to the Federal tax lien if he determines that the interest of the United States in the property to be so discharged has no value.

(3) *Discharge of property by substitution of proceeds of sale.* The appropriate official may, in his discretion, issue

a certificate of discharge of any part of the property subject to a Federal tax lien imposed under chapter 64 of the Internal Revenue Code if such part of the property is sold and, pursuant to a written agreement with the appropriate official, the proceeds of the sale are held, as a fund subject to the Federal tax liens and claims of the United States, in the same manner and with the same priority as the Federal tax liens or claims had with respect to the discharged property. This paragraph does not apply unless the sale divests the taxpayer of all right, title, and interest in the property sought to be discharged. Any reasonable and necessary expenses incurred in connection with the sale of the property and the administration of the sale proceeds shall be paid by the applicant or from the proceeds of the sale before satisfaction of any Federal tax liens or claims of the United States.

(4) *Right of substitution of value*—(i) *Issuance of certificate of discharge to property owner who is not the taxpayer.* If an owner of property subject to a Federal tax lien imposed under chapter 64 of the Internal Revenue Code submits an application for a certificate of discharge pursuant to paragraph (b)(5) of this section, the appropriate official shall issue a certificate of discharge of such property after the owner either deposits with the appropriate official an amount equal to the value of the interest of the United States in the property, as determined by the appropriate official pursuant to paragraph (b)(6) of this section, or furnishes an acceptable bond in a like amount. This paragraph does not apply if any owner of the property is the person whose unsatisfied liability gave rise to the Federal tax lien. Thus, if the property is owned by both the taxpayer and another person, neither the taxpayer nor the other person may obtain a certificate of discharge of the property under this paragraph.

(ii) *Refund of deposit and release of bond.* The appropriate official may, in his discretion, determine that either the entire unsatisfied tax liability listed on the notice of Federal tax lien can be satisfied from a source other than the property sought to be discharged, or the value of the interest in the United States is less than the prior determination of such value. The appropriate official shall refund the amount deposited with interest at the overpayment rate determined under section 6621 or release the bond furnished to the extent that he makes this determination.

(iii) *Refund request.* If a property owner desires an administrative refund of his deposit or release of the bond, the owner shall file a request in writing with the appropriate official. The request shall contain such information as the appropriate IRS Publication may require. The request must be filed within 120 days after the date the certificate of discharge is issued. A refund request made under this paragraph neither is required nor is effective to extend the period for filing an action in court under section 7426(a)(4).

(iv) *Internal Revenue Service's use of deposit if court action not filed.* If no action is filed under section 7426(a)(4) for refund of the deposit or release of the bond within the 120-day period specified therein, the appropriate official shall, within 60 days after the expiration of the 120-day period, apply the amount deposited or collect on such bond to the extent necessary to satisfy the liability listed on the notice of Federal tax lien, and shall refund, with interest at the overpayment rate determined under section 6621, any portion of the amount deposited that is not used to satisfy the liability. If the appropriate official has not completed the application of the deposit to the unsatisfied liability before the end of the 60-day period, the deposit will be deemed to have been applied to the unsatisfied liability as of the 60th day.

(5) *Application for certificate of discharge.* Any person desiring a certificate of discharge under this paragraph (b) shall submit an application in writing to the appropriate official. The application shall contain the information required by the appropriate IRS Publication. For purposes of this paragraph (b), any application for certificate of discharge made by a property owner who is not the taxpayer, and any amount submitted pursuant to the application, will be treated as an application for discharge and a deposit under section 6325(b)(4) unless the owner of the property submits a statement, in writing, that the application is being submitted under another paragraph of section 6325 and not under section 6325(b)(4), and the owner in writing waives the rights afforded under paragraph (b)(4), including the right to seek judicial review.

(6) *Valuation of interest of United States.* For purposes of paragraphs (b)(2) and (b)(4) of this section, in determining the value of the interest of the United States in the property, or any part thereof, with respect to which the certificate of discharge is to be issued, the appropriate official shall give consideration to the value of the property and the amount of all liens and encumbrances thereon having priority over the Federal tax lien. In determining the value of the property, the appropriate official may, in his discretion, give consideration to the forced sale value of the property in appropriate cases.

* * * * *

(h) As used in this section, the term *appropriate official* means either the official or office identified in the relevant IRS Publication or, if such official or office is not so identified, the Secretary or his delegate.

(i) *Temporary regulations removed.* The provisions of §401.6325–1 of this chapter are removed on the date these regulations are published as final regulations in the **Federal Register**.

(j) *Effective date.* This section applies to any release of lien or discharge of property that is requested after these regulations are published as final regulations in the **Federal Register**.

Par. 3. Section 301.6503(f)–1 is amended as follows:

1. The section heading is revised.
2. The undesignated paragraph is designated as paragraph (a) and a paragraph heading is added.
3. In newly designated paragraph (a), the language "a district director" is removed and the language "the appropriate official" is added in its place, the language "the district director" is removed and the language "the appropriate official" is added in its place, and in the *Example* the language "district director" is removed and the language "appropriate official" is added in its place, wherever it appears.
4. Paragraphs (b), (c), and (d) are added.

The revisions and additions read as follows:

§301.6503(f)–1 Suspension of running of period of limitation; wrongful seizure of property of third-party owner and

discharge of wrongful lien for substitution of value.

(a) *Wrongful seizure.* * * *

(b) *Discharge of wrongful lien for substitution of value.* If a person other than the taxpayer submits a request in writing for a certificate of discharge for a filed Federal tax lien under section 6325(b)(4), the running of the period of limitations on collection after assessment under section 6502 for any liability listed in such notice of Federal tax lien shall be suspended for a period equal to the period beginning on the date the appropriate official receives a deposit or bond in the amount specified in §301.6325–1(b)(4)(i) and ending on the date that is 30 days after the earlier of—

(1) The date the appropriate official no longer holds, or is deemed to no longer hold, within the meaning of paragraph (b)(4)(iv) of this section, any amount as a deposit or bond by reason of taking such actions as prescribed in sections 6325(b)(4)(B) and (C); or

(2) The date the judgment secured under section 7426(b)(5) becomes final.

(c) As used in this section, the term *appropriate official* means either the official or office identified in the relevant IRS Publication or, if such official or office is not so identified, the Secretary or his delegate.

(d) *Effective date.* This section applies to any request for a certificate of discharge made after these regulations are published as final regulations in the **Federal Register**.

Par. 4. In §301.7426–1, paragraphs (a)(4), (b)(5), and (d) are added.

§301.7426–1 Civil actions by persons other than taxpayers.

(a) * * *

(4) *Substitution of value.* A person who obtains a certificate of discharge under section 6325(b)(4) with respect to any property may, within 120 days after the day on which the certificate is issued, bring a civil action against the United States in a district court of the United States for a determination of whether the value of the interest of the United States (if any) in such property is less than the value determined by the appropriate official. A civil action under this provision shall be the exclusive judicial remedy for a person other than the taxpayer who obtains a certificate of discharge for a filed notice of Federal tax lien.

(b) * * *

(5) *Substitution of value.* If the court determines that the determination by the appropriate official of the value of the interest of the United States in the property exceeds the actual value of such interest, the court may grant a judgment ordering a refund of the amount deposited, or a release of the bond, to the extent that the aggregate of those amounts exceeds the value as determined by the court.

* * * * *

(d) Paragraphs (a)(4) and (b)(5) of this section apply to any request for a certificate of discharge made after these regulations are published as final regulations in the **Federal Register**.

Mark E. Matthews,
Deputy Commissioner
for Services and Enforcement.

(Filed by the Office of the Federal Register on January 10, 2007, 8:45 a.m., and published in the issue of the Federal Register for January 11, 2007, 72 F.R. 1301)

Compliance Resolution Program for Employees Other Than Corporate Insiders for Additional 2006 Taxes Arising Under § 409A Due to the Exercise of Stock Rights

Announcement 2007–18

The Internal Revenue Service announces a compliance resolution program (the Program) that permits employers to pay the additional taxes arising under § 409A of the Internal Revenue Code due to the exercise of certain discounted stock options and stock appreciation rights (stock rights) in 2006. The Program provides a means to minimize the burdens of compliance on employees who are not corporate insiders, while ensuring that all applicable taxes are paid. As described in more detail below, the Program:

- Applies only to discounted stock rights exercised during 2006.
- Applies only to employees and former employees who are not subject to the disclosure requirements under section 16(a) of the Securities Exchange Act of 1934 (a non-insider), and were not subject to such requirements at the date of grant of the stock right.
- Requires full payment by the employer of the applicable § 409A taxes arising from the exercise of the stock right.
- Provides relief for the employees from the requirement to pay the § 409A taxes.
- Does not affect an employer's obligation to report the compensation income and wages arising from the exercise of the stock right on the Form W–2, in Box 1, 3 and 5, and to apply the appropriate employment taxes, and does not affect an employee's obligation to report such compensation income on the Form 1040 and pay the applicable income tax (other than the additional § 409A taxes).
- Requires treatment of the employer's payment of the employee's § 409A taxes as an additional payment of compensation to the employee in the employee's taxable year in which the payment is made.
- Requires notice to employees and to the IRS of the employer's participation in the Program.

Employers that wish to participate in this Program must notify the IRS no later than February 28, 2007 of their intent to participate, and must notify affected employees within 15 days of providing the notification to the IRS.

Section 1. Background

A. Section 409A

Section 409A was added to the Code by § 885 of the American Jobs Creation Act of 2004, Public Law 108–357 (118 Stat. 1418). Section 409A generally provides that, unless certain requirements are met, amounts deferred under a nonqualified deferred compensation plan for all taxable years are currently includible in gross income to the extent not subject to a substantial risk of forfeiture and not previously included in gross income. In addition, the amount includible in income under § 409A is subject to certain additional taxes discussed below (referred to as § 409A taxes).

On December 20, 2004, the IRS issued Notice 2005–1, 2005–1 C.B. 274, setting forth initial guidance on the application of § 409A, and supplying transition guidance in accordance with the statutory provisions. A notice of proposed rulemaking (REG–158080–04, 2005–2 C.B. 786 [70 FR 57930]) was published in the Federal Register on October 4, 2005. The preamble to the proposed regulations clarified and extended certain provisions of the transition guidance provided in Notice 2005–1, generally through December 31, 2006. On October 4, 2006, the IRS issued Notice 2006–79, 2006–43 I.R.B. 763, which further clarified and extended certain provisions of the transition guidance through December 31, 2007.

Pursuant to Notice 2006–100, 2006–51 I.R.B. 1109, issued on November 30, 2006, service recipients generally are required to report amounts includible under § 409A for 2006 on a timely filed Form W–2 or 1099, as applicable. Service providers are required to report amounts includible under § 409A for the service provider's 2006 tax year and to pay any taxes due in accordance with the requirements of Notice 2006–100.

B. Application of § 409A to Certain Discounted Stock Rights

The IRS has become aware of numerous instances in which stock options were issued with an exercise price less than the fair market value of the underlying stock on the date of grant or in which stock appreciation rights were issued under which the compensation payable upon exercise of such right was more than the excess of the fair market value of the stock subject to such right on the date of exercise over the fair market value of such stock on the date of grant of such right (collectively such options and rights are referred to as discounted stock rights). In many cases, the discount resulted from a discrepancy between the purported grant date and the actual grant date. In some cases, the employee exercised the stock right during 2006.

Such discounted stock rights, to the extent they were issued or became earned and vested on or after January 1, 2005, are generally treated as providing nonqualified deferred compensation subject to § 409A. By contrast, a stock option granted with an exercise price that can never be less than the fair market value of the underlying stock on the date of grant, and that does not include any additional deferral feature, generally is not subject to § 409A, and the exercise of such stock option does not implicate § 409A. Similarly, a stock appreciation right that does not provide compensation in excess of the difference between the fair market value of the stock subject to such right on the date of exercise and the fair market value of such stock on the date of grant of such right, and that does not include any additional deferral feature, generally is not subject to § 409A, and the exercise of such stock right does not implicate § 409A.

C. Consequences Under § 409A of the Exercise of Certain Discounted Stock Rights in 2006

In the absence of affirmative steps taken before the exercise of a stock right to avoid a violation of § 409A, the exercise of a discounted stock right during 2006, where the term of the stock right otherwise extended beyond 2006, generally is treated as an impermissible payment of nonqualified deferred compensation under § 409A. Such an impermissible payment generally triggers adverse Federal income tax consequences under § 409A for the service provider, and reporting requirements for the service recipient, with respect to the stock rights that were exercised and with respect to any additional amounts that are treated as deferred under the same plan for purposes of § 409A under the applicable plan aggregation rules. Such tax consequences include immediate income inclusion; an additional 20% income tax (in accordance with § 409A(a)(1)(B)(i)(II)) on the amounts required to be so included (the 20% tax); and a second additional tax (in accordance with § 409A(a)(1)(B)(ii)) equal to the interest on unpaid taxes from the year of initial deferral (or if later, the first year the deferred amount was not subject to a substantial risk of forfeiture), calculated at the underpayment rate plus 1% (the interest tax).

Notice 2006–100 provides that where there is a required income inclusion under § 409A in the service provider's tax year 2006, the plan aggregation rules apply in determining the amount required to be included in income. For purposes of participation in, and the relief provided by, the Program, taxpayers may assume, in the case of a violation involving a stock right, that the plan aggregation rules apply only to aggregate all amounts deferred under stock rights subject to § 409A held by the employee with respect to whom the violation occurred. In the case of an unexercised stock right, Notice 2006–79 permits the service recipient to substitute for such a stock right a stock right that is not subject to § 409A. In the case of certain stock rights granted to a service provider who was subject to the disclosure requirements of section 16(a) of the Securities Exchange Act of 1934 on the date of grant of the stock right, the substitution was required to be completed by December 31, 2006. For other service providers, the substitution must be completed by December 31, 2007. If a taxpayer utilizes the available transition rules to exclude a right to an amount (including an unexercised stock right) from coverage under § 409A, then the amount is treated as always having been excluded from coverage under § 409A. Accordingly, the amount is not required to be aggregated for purposes of determining the amount includible in income under § 409A in 2006. If the right to the amount is not excluded from coverage under § 409A by the applicable deadline, the right to the amount will remain subject to the plan aggregation rules regardless of whether the right to the amount is, or is amended to be, compliant with the requirements of § 409A. However, because a stock right may be removed from coverage under § 409A retroactively, any income inclusion under § 409A with respect to an unexercised stock right due to the plan aggregation rules will not be treated as income for any of the service provider's taxable years before the 2007 tax year.

Section 2. Scope of Program

This Program addresses only the additional § 409A taxes for the employee's 2006 tax year resulting from the exercise of an applicable stock right (discussed below), and the information reporting requirements related to such § 409A taxes. The Program does not address other consequences that may arise from the grant or exercise of a stock right with an exercise price less than the fair market value of the underlying stock on the date of grant. Accordingly, the Program does not address the employer's obligation to report the compensation income arising from the exercise of the stock right on the 2006 Form W–2, in Box 1, 3 and 5, as appropriate, and to apply the appropriate employment taxes to the payment of wages. The Program also does not address the employee's obligation to report such compensation income on the Form 1040 and pay the applicable income tax (other than any additional § 409A taxes). The Program also does not address the non-§ 409A tax consequences, including employment tax and information reporting consequences, that may arise from a failure of a purported incentive stock option to meet the requirements of § 422, or the application of § 162(m) to an employer's otherwise available deduction for compensation expense with respect to the exercise of a stock right.

Section 3. Eligibility Requirements

This Program is available to an employer that granted applicable stock rights that were subject to the requirements of § 409A because the exercise price was below the fair market value of the underlying stock on the date of grant, where such stock rights were exercised during the employee's 2006 tax year. For this purpose, an applicable stock right means any stock right granted in connection with the performance of services by an employee other than a stock right granted to an employee who is subject to the disclosure requirements of section 16(a) of the Securities Exchange Act of 1934 as of the date the employer provides a notice of intent to participate in the program under section 4.A or who was subject to such disclosure requirements on the date of grant of such stock right.

Section 4. Terms of Participation in the Program

If an employer complies with all of the requirements in this section 4 with respect to an employee, the employer and the employee will be eligible for the relief set forth in section 5 of this announcement.

A. Notice to the IRS of Intent to Participate

An employer must submit to the IRS by February 28, 2007 a notice of the employer's intent to participate in the Program. The notice of intent to participate must state, under penalties of perjury, the following:

> [Insert name of the employer and taxpayer identification number] hereby provides notice to the IRS of its intent to participate in the Program described in Announcement 2007–18. [Insert name] is the person for the IRS to contact regarding the participation of [Insert name of the employer] in the Program, and may be contacted at [Insert address and phone number]. *Choose either sentence A or sentence B. Sentence A.* [Insert name of the employer] hereby certifies that [Insert name of the employer] is not under examination by the IRS. *Sentence B.* [Insert name of the employer] hereby certifies that [Insert name of the employer] is under examination by the IRS and is providing a copy of this notice of intent to participate in the Program to the examining revenue agent.

An employer must also submit a Form 2848, *Power of Attorney and Declaration of Representative*, as appropriate. For information regarding the submission of this notice, see section 6 of this announcement.

B. Notices to Affected Employees and IRS

i. Notice to Affected Employees of Intent to Participate

No later than 15 days after the employer submits the notice of intent to participate described in section 4.A of this announcement, an employer must provide a notice to all employees that the employer reasonably anticipates may be affected by the employer's participation in the Program. Such notice must provide the following information:

(i) the employer has notified the IRS of the employer's intent to participate in the Program (the Program must be specifically referred to in the notice to employees as the program set forth in Announcement 2007–18, Compliance Resolution Program for Employees Other than Corporate Insiders for Additional 2006 Taxes Arising Under § 409A due to the Exercise of Stock Rights);

(ii) the employer intends to provide further notice to the employee on or before July 15, 2007 certifying that the employer has made a further submission to the IRS that to the best of its information, knowledge, and belief, satisfies the requirements of this announcement, or certifying that the employer has not made such a further submission;

(iii) the employer's participation in the Program may affect the employee's Federal income tax obligations solely with respect to the additional taxes imposed under § 409A of the Internal Revenue Code due to the exercise of discounted stock options or stock appreciation rights, but does not affect the employee's obligation to report on Form 1040 the compensation income arising from the exercise that is shown on the Form W–2 (or W–2c, if applicable) provided to the employee or to pay the applicable Federal taxes (other than the additional § 409A taxes).

The notice to affected employees may provide additional information that is not inconsistent with the required information. The notice must be provided directly to the individual employee, but may be provided electronically. If an employer provides such notices to employees that the employer reasonably anticipates may be affected by the employer's participation in the Program, and subsequently determines that an exercise of a stock right by an additional employee is eligible to be included in this Program, the employer may include such additional employee and exercise in a further submission without providing the notices required by this Section 4.B, provided all other requirements of this announcement are met with respect to such additional employee.

ii. Second Notice to IRS

No later than 15 days after the employer submits the notice of intent to participate described in section 4.A of this announcement, the employer must provide a notice to the IRS stating the number of employees to whom the notices required by section 4.B.i of this announcement were provided.

C. Employer's Further Submission of Information and Payment to the IRS

An employer must make a further submission of information and payment (a further submission) to the IRS by June 30, 2007 meeting all of the requirements of this section 4.C.

i. Information

An employer must include in the further submission to the IRS the following information, signed under penalties of perjury:

a. The employer's name and taxpayer identification number.

b. A list of employees for whom the employer is remitting the § 409A taxes due (the 20% tax and the interest tax) under section 4.C.ii below, including each such employee's taxpayer identification number.

c. For each identified employee, an identification of each stock right exercise resulting in the § 409A taxes, including information that specifically identifies the specific stock right that was exercised, the date of exercise, the exercise price, the fair market value of the underlying shares on the date of exercise, and the number of shares purchased or, in the case of a stock appreciation right, the number of shares used to calculate the payment made.

d. For each identified stock right exercise for each identified employee, the amount of § 409A taxes remitted, including the manner in which such § 409A taxes were calculated.

ii. Remittance of All § 409A Taxes Due

a. Remittance of Taxes

With respect to an exercise of a stock right subject to § 409A by an employee during 2006, the employer must remit to the IRS by June 30, 2007, an amount equal to the full amount of the additional tax liability of the employee under § 409A that results from such exercise. Such additional tax consists of the 20% tax and the interest tax described below. For purposes of determining the § 409A taxes, the amount of income includible under § 409A must be determined in accordance with applicable guidance under § 409A. With respect to such exercise of a stock right, an employer is treated as having remitted an amount equal to the full amount of the additional tax liability if the employer remits substantially all of the additional tax liability based upon a reasonable, good faith interpretation of the applicable guidance. Where it is determined that an employer has failed to submit substantially all of the additional tax liability that results from the exercise of a stock right subject to § 409A during 2006 based upon a reasonable, good faith interpretation of the applicable guidance, neither the employer nor the employee is entitled to any relief under this announcement with respect to the § 409A taxes resulting from the exercise of such stock right.

b. Calculation of the 20% tax

For purposes of this Program, the amount of the 20% tax equals 20% of the excess of the fair market value of the stock on the date of exercise over the sum of the exercise price paid by the employee and any other amount paid by the employee for the stock right. See Notice 2006–100.

c. Calculation of the Interest Tax

For purposes of this Program, the amount of the interest tax equals the amount of interest at the underpayment rate plus 1% on the underpayment of Federal income tax that would have occurred had the portion of the amount deferred under the stock right as of December 31, 2005, that was not subject to a substantial risk of forfeiture (as defined for purposes of § 409A) as of December 31, 2005, been includible in gross income as of December 31, 2005. For this purpose, the amount deferred under the stock right as of December 31, 2005 equals the excess of the fair market value of the underlying stock on December 31, 2005 over the sum of the exercise price and any other amount paid by the employee for the stock right. For purposes of this Program, employers must calculate the underpayment based on the highest marginal Federal income tax rate in effect for 2005 (35%). For purposes of determining the applicable interest, the underpayment is treated as due on April 17, 2006, and the interest runs from that date through the earlier of April 17, 2007 or the date the further submission is sent to the IRS with payment.

d. Additional Amount Due for Taxes Remitted After April 17, 2007

For payments sent to the IRS after April 17, 2007, the amount required to be submitted is increased by an amount equal to the underpayment interest rate applied to the amount that would otherwise be due on April 17, 2007 through the date the further submission (with payment) is sent to the IRS.

iii. Section 409A Tax Payments Constitute Compensation to the Employee

The payment of the § 409A taxes due as part of this Program constitutes additional compensation income to the employee for the employee's taxable year in which such payment is made. Accordingly, the employer must represent under penalties of perjury that the employer is treating such payment as additional compensation to the employee for the taxable year of such employee in which such payment is made, in accordance with this section iii. With respect to any employee for whom a payment of § 409A taxes has been made as part of the further submission, no relief shall be provided under this announcement with respect to the exercise of a stock right by such employee during 2006 if it is determined that the employer has failed to treat such payments as additional compensation for the taxable year of such employee in which such payment is made, in accordance with this section iii.

Payments made on behalf of an employee or former employee to cover § 409A taxes are wages for Federal Insurance Contributions Act (FICA), Federal Unemployment Tax Act (FUTA), and Federal income tax withholding purposes for the employee's taxable year in which the payment is made. Such wages, as well as any additional wages resulting from the employer's payment of the employee's share of FICA tax and income tax without withholding such amounts from the employee, must be reported on Form 941, *Employer's QUARTERLY Federal Tax Return*, and in box 1, 3 and 5 of the employee's Form W–2, *Wage and Tax Statement*, for the year in which the payment is made. See Rev. Rul. 58–113, 1958–1 C.B. 362, and Rev. Proc. 81–48, 1981–2 C.B. 623, for methods of computing gross wages when paying FICA and Federal income tax withholding on behalf of an employee.

iv. Further Representations by the Employer

The further submission must include the following representations by the employer, signed under penalties of perjury:

a. In accordance with section 4.B.i of this announcement, the employer provided the notices of the employer's intent to participate in the Program to all employees the employer reasonably anticipated would be affected by the employer's participation in the program by no later than 15 days after the employer submitted its notice of intent to participate in the Program to the IRS.

b. With respect to any employee for which a payment of § 409A taxes has been made as part of the further submission, the employer has made reasonable, good faith efforts to identify all exercises of a stock right by such employee during 2006 that resulted in the inclusion of income under § 409A, applying a reasonable, good faith interpretation of the applicable guidance under § 409A, has listed all such identified exercises of a stock right in its further submission, and has accurately calculated and paid the § 409A taxes resulting from such identified exercises of a stock right in accordance with this announcement.

c. The employer will, upon a written request from an affected employee, disclose to the employee any portion of such information that is relevant to the employee's 2006 Federal income tax return, including information the employee reasonably needs to respond to an information request from the IRS, an examination, or tax litigation involving issues related to the exercise of a stock right and the application of § 409A.

D. Notice to Affected Employees of the Employer's Further Submission

An employer must provide a notice to all employees to whom a notice was provided pursuant to section 4.B.i, and any additional employees that are listed in the employer's further submission to the IRS, by no later than July 15, 2007, certifying the following:

(i) the employer has made a further submission under the Program, that is specifically referenced as the program provided under Announcement 2007–18, Compliance Resolution Program for Employees Other than Corporate Insiders for Additional 2006 Taxes Arising Under § 409A due to the Exercise of Stock Rights, that to the best of the employer's information, knowledge and belief, satisfies the requirements of this announcement, and that such further submission (a) includes the employee and makes payment of such employee's § 409A taxes addressed by this announcement or (b) does not include the employee because the employer has concluded that the employee does not owe any § 409A taxes addressed by this announcement, or

(ii) the employer has failed to make a further submission under the Program, that is specifically referenced as the program provided under Announcement 2007–18, Compliance Resolution Program for Employees Other than Corporate Insiders for Additional 2006 Taxes Arising Under § 409A due to the Exercise of Stock Rights, and the employee is therefore liable for any applicable § 409A taxes.

The notice to affected employees may provide additional information that is not inconsistent with the required information. The notice must be provided directly to the individual employee, but may be provided electronically.

Section 5. Scope of Relief

A. Employer's Information Reporting Requirements

If an employer complies fully with the provisions of section 4 with respect to an exercise of a stock right by an employee, the employer will not be required to report the § 409A inclusion amount with respect to such stock right exercise in box 12 of Form W–2 using code Z. If an employer complies fully with the provisions of section 4 with respect to an exercise of a stock right by an employee, but has already reported the § 409A inclusion amount with respect to such exercise of a stock right by an employee in box 12 of Form W–2 using Code Z, the employer may provide a Form W–2c that does not report the § 409A inclusion amount in box 12 of Form W–2c using Code Z, and such employer will not be subject to any penalties under § 6721 or § 6722 of the Code. Nothing in this Program relieves the employer of any information reporting requirements with respect to an employee or an exercise of a stock right that was not identified in the employer's further submission. Nothing in this announcement or Program affects the employer's obligation to report the amount that would be required, without regard to § 409A, to be included in income and wages due to the exercise of a stock right, and to withhold and pay the applicable employment taxes, or the employee's obligations to include such amounts in income and pay Federal taxes on them (other than § 409A taxes).

B. Employee's § 409A Taxes

If an employer complies fully with the provisions of section 4 of this announcement with respect to amounts includible in income under § 409A due to the exercise of an applicable stock right by an employee during 2006, the employee will not be required to pay the § 409A taxes on the applicable Federal income tax return for the 2006 tax year with respect to such amounts includible in income under § 409A. Nothing in this Program relieves the employee of any § 409A taxes with respect to an exercise of a stock right that was not identified in the employer's further submission, or relieves the employee or employer of any other tax, including Federal income tax and employment taxes that would otherwise arise from the exercise of the stock right. In addition, nothing in this Program addresses or relieves the employee of any § 409A taxes due to participation in a nonqualified deferred compensation plan, other than the exercise of an applicable stock right in 2006.

An employee who received a notice of application under section 4.B.i of this announcement, and who files a return before finding out that, due to a failure by the employer to comply with the requirements for relief set forth in this announcement, the employee is not relieved of the duty to report and pay § 409A taxes, will be treated as having had reasonable cause and as having acted in good faith with respect to the portion of any underpayment that is due to the employee's failure to timely pay § 409A taxes arising from the exercise of an applicable stock right in 2006, and will not be subject to penalties for the 2006 tax year under § 6654 for any estimated tax underpayment attributable to such failure. An employee who received a notice of application under section 4.B.i of this announcement, requested an extension of time to file a return, and files a timely income tax return on extension after learning that he or she is not relieved of the duty to report and pay § 409A taxes due to a failure by the employer to comply with the requirements for relief set forth in this announcement, will not be subject to penalties under § 6651(a)(2) or § 6654 for the failure to timely pay § 409A taxes arising from the exercise of an applicable stock right in 2006, provided such § 409A taxes are paid with the filed return.

C. An Employer's Failure to Comply with Representations or Other Actions Required under the Program

Information and representations required under this Program are material, and an employer who knowingly makes a false statement or representation will be deemed to have failed to make a further submission under the Program so that no relief under this Program is available to the employer or any employee. Except as provided in paragraph 5.B with respect to certain penalties, no relief is provided under this Program with respect to an employer or to an employee if the employer fails to comply with the requirements of this announcement, provided that the Commissioner may, in his sole discretion, determine that the employer has substantially complied with the requirements of this announcement with respect to some or all of the employees identified by the employer and that, accordingly, such employer and some or all of such employees are entitled to the relief provided under this announcement.

D. An Employer's or Employee's State and Local Information Reporting, Filing and Tax Requirements

Nothing in this Program relieves the employer or employee of any requirements regarding information reporting, filing of tax returns, or the payment of any taxes, to the extent such requirements relate to any state or local tax. This includes any state or local tax information reporting requirement which relates to the Form W–2.

Section 6. Procedures for Submission of Notices and Further Submissions to the IRS

A. Submissions to the IRS

A notice of intent to participate in the Program in accordance with section 4.A of this announcement, a second notice to the IRS in accordance with section 4.B.ii of this announcement, or a further submission in accordance with section 4.C of this announcement, shall be submitted to the following address:

Internal Revenue Service
Attn: Announcement 2007–18
2001 Butterfield Road
LMSB Team 1160
Downers Grove, IL 60515

B. Requests for Further Information and Withdrawals of Applications and Further Submissions

The IRS reserves the right to request further information from an employer at any time following the employer's submission of a notice of intent to participate in the Program. In addition, nothing in this announcement or Program limits or otherwise affects the IRS's right to request further information, to examine a taxpayer's federal tax return, and except as otherwise explicitly provided in this announcement and Program, to assess any unpaid taxes, penalties or interest.

The employer retains the right to withdraw a notice of intent to participate or a further submission at any time on or before June 30, 2007, provided that notices are provided under section 4.D of this announcement that reflect the withdrawal. The employer also retains the right to modify a further submission at any time on or before June 30, 2007, provided that a modification after April 17, 2007 involving the payment of additional § 409A taxes is subject to the requirement of an additional amount due for further submissions after April 17, 2007 with respect to the additional § 409A taxes identified in the modification, and provided that notices are provided under section 4.D of this announcement that reflect the modification. Where an employer withdraws a submission on or before June 30, 2007, the employer is entitled to a return of the funds submitted to the IRS, without interest. Where an employer modifies a further submission in a manner that reduces the § 409A taxes covered by the further submission, the employer may obtain a return of amounts previously submitted to the IRS consistent with such modification, without interest, provided such modification is submitted on or before June 30, 2007. After June 30, 2007, an employer may obtain a return of any amount paid to the IRS with respect to an employee pursuant to the announcement if the employer demonstrates that the employee for whom the § 409A taxes were paid has paid the § 409A taxes in full.

For information about this announcement, call (630) 493–5167 (not a toll-free number).

Flat Rate Supplemental Wage Withholding; Correction

Announcement 2007–21

AGENCY: Internal Revenue Service (IRS), Treasury.

ACTION: Correcting amendment.

SUMMARY: This document contains corrections to final regulations (T.D. 9276, 2006–37 I.R.B. 423) that were published in the **Federal Register** on Tuesday, July 25, 2006 (71 FR 42049), amending the regulations that provide for determining the amount of income tax withholding on supplemental wages. These regulations apply to all employers and others making supplemental wage payments to employees.

DATES: The correction will be effective January 1, 2007.

FOR FURTHER INFORMATION CONTACT: A. G. Kelley, (202) 622–6040 (not a toll-free number).

SUPPLEMENTARY INFORMATION:

Background

The final regulations that are the subject of these corrections are under sections 3401 and 3402 of the Internal Revenue Code.

Need for Corrections

As published, final regulations (T.D. 9276) contain errors that may prove to be misleading and are in need of clarification.

* * * * *

Correction of Publication

Accordingly, 26 CFR part 31 is corrected by making the following correcting amendments:

PART 31—EMPLOYMENT TAXES AND COLLECTION OF INCOME TAX AT SOURCE

Paragraph 1. The authority citation for part 31 continues to read, in part, as follows:

Authority: 26 U.S.C. 7805 * * *

Par. 2. Section 31.3402(g)–1(a)(8) is amended by revising the fifth sentence of *Example 1* paragraph (iii), the fifth sentence of *Example 3* paragraph (i), the last sentence of *Example 3* paragraph (iv) and the third sentence of *Example 3* paragraph (vi). The revisions read as follows:

§ 31.3402(g)–1 Supplemental wage payments.

(a) * * *

(8) * * *

Example 1. * * *

(iii) * * * If Y elected to withhold income tax using paragraph (a)(7) of this section, Y would withhold on the $400,000 component at 25 percent (pursuant to paragraph (a)(7)(iii)(F) of this section), which would result in $100,000 tax withheld. * * *

* * * * *

Example 3. (i) * * * Unrelated company U pays D sick pay as an agent of the employer R and such sick pay is supplemental wages pursuant to § 31.3401(a)–1(b)(8)(i)(*b*)(*2*). * * *

* * * * *

(iv) * * * If R elects to use optional flat rate withholding provided under paragraph (a)(7)(iii)(f) of this section, withholding would be calculated at 25 percent of the $1,000,000 portion of the payment and would be $250,000.

* * * * *

(vi) * * * If U elects to withhold income tax at the flat rate provided under paragraph (a)(7)(iii)(F) of this section, withholding on the $50,000 of sick pay would be calculated at 25 percent of the $50,000 payment and would be $12,500. * * *

* * * * *

LaNita Van Dyke,
Chief, Publications and Regulations Branch,
Legal Processing Division,
Associate Chief Counsel
(Procedure and Administration).

(Filed by the Office of the Federal Register on December 26, 2006, 8:45 a.m., and published in the issue of the Federal Register for December 27, 2006, 71 F.R. 77612)

Income Attributable to Domestic Production Activities; Correction

Announcement 2007–22

AGENCY: Internal Revenue Service (IRS), Treasury.

ACTION: Correcting amendment.

SUMMARY: This document contains corrections to final regulations (T.D. 9263, 2006–25 I.R.B. 1063) which were published in the **Federal Register** on Thursday, June 1, 2006, (71 FR 31268), relating to the deduction for income attributable to domestic production activities under section 199 of the Internal Revenue Code (Code).

DATES: This correction is effective June 1, 2006.

FOR FURTHER INFORMATION CONTACT: Paul Handleman or Lauren Ross Taylor at (202) 622–3040 (not a toll-free number).

SUPPLEMENTARY INFORMATION:

Background

The final regulations (T.D. 9263) that are subject to this correction are under section 199 of the Internal Revenue Code.

Need for Correction

On June 1, 2006, final regulations (T.D. 9263) were published in the **Federal Register** at 71 FR 31268. These regulations contain errors that may prove to be misleading and are in need of clarification.

* * * * *

Correction of Publication

Accordingly, 26 CFR Part 1 is corrected by making the following correcting amendments:

PART 1—INCOME TAXES

Paragraph 1. The authority citation for part 1 continues to read, in part, as follows:

Authority: 26 U.S.C. 7805 * * *

§ 1.199–1 [Corrected]

Par. 2. Section 1.199–1(b)(1) is amended by revising the first sentence of the paragraph to read as follows:

§ 1.199–1 Income attributable to domestic production activities.

* * * * *

(b) * * *

(1) *In general.* For purposes of paragraph (a) of this section, the definition of taxable income under section 63 applies, except that taxable income (or alternative minimum taxable income, if applicable) is determined without regard to section 199 and without regard to any amount excluded from gross income pursuant to section 114 or pursuant to section 101(d) of the American Jobs Creation Act of 2004, Public Law 108–357 (118 Stat. 1418) (Act). * * *

* * * * *

§ 1.199–2 [Corrected]

Par. 3. Section 1.199–2 is amended by revising the first sentence of paragraph (a)(3)(ii) and the last sentence of paragraph (e)(3) to read as follows:

§ 1.199–2 Wage limitation.

(a) * * *

(3) * * *

(ii) *Corrected return filed to correct a return that was filed within 60 days of the due date.* If a corrected information return (Return B) is filed with SSA on or before the 60th day after the due date (including extensions) of Return B to correct an information return (Return A) that was filed with SSA on or before the 60th day after the due date (including extensions) of the information return (Return A) and paragraph (a)(3)(iii) of this section does not apply, then the wage information on Return B must be included in determining W–2 wages. * * *

* * * * *

(e) * * *

(3) * * * For example, see Rev. Proc. 2006–22, 2006–23 I.R.B. 1033. (See § 601.601(d)(2) of this chapter).

§ 1.199–3 [Corrected]

Par. 4. Section 1.199–3(l)(4)(iv)(A) is amended by revising the first sentence of the paragraph to read as follows:

§ 1.199–3 Domestic production gross receipts.

* * * * *

(l) * * *

(4) * * *

(iv) * * *

(A) * * * *DPGR*. Notwithstanding paragraphs (l)(4)(i), (ii), and (iii) of this section, if less than 5 percent of a taxpayer's gross receipts derived from a sale, exchange, or other disposition of utilities are attributable to the transmission or distribution of the utilities and the storage of potable water after completion of treatment of the potable water, then the gross receipts derived from the lease, rental, license, sale, exchange, or other disposition of the utilities that are attributable to the transmission and distribution of the utilities and the storage of potable water after completion of treatment of the potable water may be treated as being DPGR (assuming all other requirements of this section are met). * * *

* * * * *

§ 1.199–4 [Corrected]

Par. 5. Section 1.199–4(d)(6) is amended by revising paragraph (i) of *Examples 1* and *2* to read as follows:

§ 1.199–4 Costs allocable to domestic production gross receipts.

* * * * *

(d) * * *

(6) * * *

Example 1. * * *

(i) *Facts.* X, a United States corporation that is not a member of an expanded affiliated group (EAG) (as defined in § 1.199–7), engages in activities that generate both DPGR and non-DPGR. All of X's production activities that generate DPGR are within Standard Industrial Classification (SIC) Industry Group AAA (SIC AAA). All of X's production activities that generate non-DPGR are within SIC Industry Group BBB (SIC BBB). X is able to specifically identify CGS allocable to DPGR and to non-DPGR. X incurs $900 of research and experimentation expenses (R&E) that are deductible under section 174, $300 of which are performed with respect to SIC AAA and $600 of which are performed with respect to SIC BBB. None of the R&E is legally mandated R&E as described in § 1.861–17(a)(4) and none of the R&E is included in CGS. X incurs section 162 selling expenses that are not includible in CGS and are definitely related to all of X's gross income. For 2010, the adjusted basis of X's assets is $5,000, $4,000 of which generates gross income attributable to DPGR and $1,000 of which generates gross income attributable to non-DPGR. For 2010, X's taxable income is $1,380 based on the following Federal income tax items: * * *

* * * * *

Example 2. * * *

(i) *Facts.* The facts are the same as in *Example 1* except that X owns stock in Y, a United States corporation, equal to 75% of the total voting power of stock of Y and 80% of the total value of stock in Y. X and Y are not members of an affiliated group as defined in section 1504(a). Accordingly, the rules of § 1.861–14T do not apply to X's and Y's selling expenses, R&E, and charitable contributions. X and Y are, however, members of an affiliated group for purposes of allocating and apportioning interest expense (see § 1.861–11T(d)(6)) and are also members of an EAG. For 2010, the adjusted basis of Y's assets is $45,000, $21,000 of which generates gross income attributable to DPGR and $24,000 of which generates gross income attributable to non-DPGR. All of Y's activities that generate DPGR are within SIC Industry Group AAA (SIC AAA). All of Y's activities that generate non-DPGR are within SIC Industry Group BBB (SIC BBB). None of X's and Y's sales are to each other. Y is not able to specifically identify CGS allocable to DPGR and non-DPGR. In this case, because CGS is definitely related under the facts and circumstances to all of Y's gross receipts, apportionment of CGS between DPGR and non-DPGR based on gross receipts is appropriate. For 2010, Y's taxable income is $1,910 based on the following Federal income tax items: * * *

* * * * *

§ 1.199–6 [Corrected]

Par. 6. Section 1.199–6 is amended as follows:

1. The last sentence of paragraph (g) is revised.

2. The last sentence of *Example 2* (i) in paragraph (m) is revised.

The revisions read as follows:

§ 1.199–6 Agricultural and horticultural cooperatives.

* * * * *

(g) *Written notice to patrons.* * * * The cooperative must report the amount of the patron's section 199 deduction on Form 1099–PATR, "*Taxable Distributions Received From Cooperatives*," issued to the patron.

* * * * *

(m) * * *

Example 2. (i) * * * Cooperative X must report the amount of Patron A's section 199 deduction on Form 1099–PATR, "*Taxable Distributions Received From Cooperatives*," issued to Patron A for the calendar year 2008.

* * * * *

§ 1.199–7 [Corrected]

Par. 7. Section 1.199–7 is amended as follows:

1. By revising paragraph (a)(4), *Example 3*.

2. By revising paragraph (e), *Example 10* (i).

The revisions read as follows:

§ 1.199–7 Expanded affiliated groups.

(a) * * *

(4) * * *

Example 3. The facts are the same as in *Example 2* except that rather than reselling the machinery, B rents the machinery to unrelated persons and B takes the gross receipts attributable to the rental of the machinery into account under its methods of accounting in 2007, 2008, and 2009. In addition, as of the close of business on December 31, 2008, A and B cease to be members of the same EAG. With respect to the machinery acquired from C and the unrelated persons, B's gross receipts attributable to the rental of the machinery in 2007, 2008, and 2009 are non-DPGR because no member of the EAG MPGE the machinery and because C does not qualify as an EAG partnership. With respect to machinery acquired from A, B's gross receipts in 2007 and 2008 attributable to the rental of the machinery are DPGR because at the time B takes into account the gross receipts derived from the rental of the machinery under its methods of accounting, B is a member of the same EAG as A and B is treated as conducting A's previous MPGE activities. However, with respect to the rental receipts in 2009, because A and B are not members of the same EAG in 2009, B's rental receipts are non-DPGR.

* * * * *

(e) * * *

Example 10. (i) *Facts.* Corporation P owns all of the stock of Corporations S and T, and P, S, and T file a consolidated Federal income tax return on a calendar year basis. In 2007, P MPGE QPP in the

United States at a cost of $1,000. On November 30, 2007, P sells the QPP to S for $2,500. On February 28, 2008, P disposes of 60% of the stock of S. On June 30, 2008, S sells the QPP to an unrelated person for $3,000.

* * * * *

§ 1.199–8 [Corrected]

Par. 8. Section 1.199–8 is amended by revising paragraph (h) to read as follows:

§ 1.199–8 Other rules.

* * * * *

(h) *Disallowed losses or deductions.* Except as provided by publication in the Internal Revenue Bulletin (see § 601.601(d)(2)(ii)(*b*) of this chapter), losses or deductions of a taxpayer that otherwise would be taken into account in computing the taxpayer's section 199 deduction are taken into account only if and to the extent the deductions are not disallowed by section 465 or 469, or any other provision of the Code. If only a portion of the taxpayer's share of the losses or deductions is allowed for a taxable year, the proportionate share of those allowable losses or deductions that are allocated to the taxpayer's qualified production activities, determined in a manner consistent with sections 465 and 469, and any other applicable provision of the Code, is taken into account in computing QPAI for purposes of the section 199 deduction for that taxable year. To the extent that any of the disallowed losses or deductions are allowed in a later year, the taxpayer takes into account a proportionate share of those losses or deductions in computing its QPAI for that later taxable year. Losses or deductions of the taxpayer that are disallowed for taxable years beginning on or before December 31, 2004, are not taken into account in a later year for purposes of computing the taxpayer's QPAI and the wage limitation of section 199(d)(1)(A)(iii) under § 1.199–9 for that taxable year, regardless of whether the losses or deductions are allowed for other purposes. For taxpayers that are partners in partnerships, see § 1.199–9(b)(2). For taxpayers that are shareholders in S corporations, see § 1.199–9(c)(2).

* * * * *

§ 1.199–9 [Corrected]

Par. 9. Section 1.199–9(b)(6) is amended as follows:

1. By revising *Example 1* paragraphs (i), (iii)(B)(*1*), and the seventh sentence of (iii)(B)(*2*).

2. By revising *Example 2* paragraphs (i), and (iii)(B)(*1*), and the table following (iii)(B)(*3*).

3. Paragraph (h) is revised.

The revisions read as follows:

§ 1.199–9 Application of section 199 to pass-thru entities for taxable years beginning on or before May 17, 2006, the enactment date of the Tax Increase Prevention and Reconciliation Act of 2005.

* * * * *

(b) * * *

(6) * * *

Example 1. * * * (i) *Partnership Federal income tax items.* X and Y, unrelated United States corporations, are each 50% partners in PRS, a partnership that engages in production activities that generate both DPGR and non-DPGR. X and Y share all items of income, gain, loss, deduction, and credit 50% each. Both X and Y are engaged in a trade or business. PRS is not able to specifically identify CGS allocable to DPGR and non-DPGR. In this case, because CGS is definitely related under the facts and circumstances to all of PRS's gross income, apportionment of CGS between DPGR and non-DPGR based on gross receipts is appropriate. For 2006, the adjusted basis of PRS's business assets is $5,000, $4,000 of which generate gross income attributable to DPGR and $1,000 of which generate gross income attributable to non-DPGR. For 2006, PRS has the following Federal income items: * * *

* * * * *

(iii) * * *

(B) * * * (*1*) For 2006, in addition to the activities of PRS, Y engages in production activities that generate both DPGR and non-DPGR. Y is able to specifically identify CGS allocable to DPGR and to non-DPGR. For 2006, the adjusted basis of Y's non-PRS assets attributable to its production activities that generate DPGR is $8,000 and to other production activities that generate non-DPGR is $2,000. Y has no other assets. Y has the following Federal income tax items relating to its non-PRS activities: * * *

(*2*) * * * Y has $1,290 of gross income attributable to DPGR ($3,000 DPGR ($1,500 from PRS and $1,500 from non-PRS activities) — $1,710 CGS ($810 from PRS and $900 from non-PRS activities)). * * *

* * * * *

Example 2. * * * (i) *Partnership items of income, gain, loss, deduction or credit.* X and Y, unrelated United States corporations each of which is engaged in a trade or business, are partners in PRS, a partnership that engages in production activities that generate both DPGR and non-DPGR. Neither X nor Y is a member of an affiliated group. X and Y share all items of income, gain, loss, deduction, and credit 50% each. All of PRS's domestic production activities that generate DPGR are within Standard Industrial Classification (SIC) Industry Group AAA (SIC AAA). All of PRS's production activities that generate non-DPGR are within SIC Industry Group BBB (SIC BBB). PRS is not able to specifically identify CGS allocable to DPGR and to non-DPGR and, therefore, apportions CGS to DPGR and non-DPGR based on its gross receipts. PRS incurs $900 of research and experimentation expenses (R&E) that are deductible under section 174, $300 of which are performed with respect to SIC AAA and $600 of which are performed with respect to SIC BBB. None of the R&E is legally mandated R&E as described in § 1.861–17(a)(4) and none is included in CGS. PRS incurs section 162 selling expenses (that include W–2 wage expense) that are not includible in CGS and are definitely related to all of PRS's gross income. For 2006, PRS has the following Federal income tax items: * * *

* * * * *

(iii) * * *

(B) * * * (*1*) For 2006, in addition to the activities of PRS, Y engages in domestic production activities that generate both DPGR and non-DPGR. With respect to those non-PRS activities, Y is not able to specifically identify CGS allocable to DPGR and to non-DPGR. In this case, because CGS is definitely related under the facts and circumstances to all of Y's non-PRS gross receipts, apportionment of CGS between DPGR and non-DPGR based on Y's non-PRS gross receipts is appropriate. For 2006, Y has the following non-PRS Federal income tax items: * * *

* * * * *

(*3*) * * *

DPGR ($4,500 DPGR ($1,500 from PRS and $3,000 from non-PRS activities))	$4,500
CGS ($600 from sales of products by PRS and $1,500 from non-PRS activities)	(2,100)
Section 162 selling expenses (including W–2 wages) ($420 from PRS + $540 from non-PRS activities) x ($4,500 DPGR/$9,000 total gross receipts)	(480)
Section 174 R&E-SIC AAA ($150 from PRS and $300 from non-PRS activities)	(450)
Section 174 R&E-SIC BBB ($300 from PRS + $450 from non-PRS activities) x ($1,500 DPGR/$6,000 total gross receipts allocated to SIC BBB ($1,500 from PRS and $4,500 from non-PRS activities))	(188)
Y's QPAI	1,282

* * * * *

(h) * * * Except as provided in paragraph (i) of this section regarding qualifying in-kind partnerships and paragraph (j) of this section regarding EAG partnerships, an owner of a pass-thru entity is not treated as conducting the qualified production activities of the pass-thru entity, and *vice versa*. This rule applies to all partnerships, including partnerships that have elected out of subchapter K under section 761(a). Accordingly, if a partnership MPGE QPP within the United States, or produces a qualified film or produces utilities in the United States, and distributes or leases, rents, licenses, sells, exchanges, or otherwise disposes of such property to a partner who then, without performing its own qualifying MPGE or other production, leases, rents, licenses, sells, exchanges, or otherwise disposes of such property, then the partner's gross receipts from this latter lease, rental, license, sale, exchange, or other disposition are treated as non-DPGR. In addition, if a partner MPGE QPP within the United States, or produces a qualified film or produces utilities in the United States, and contributes or leases, rents, licenses, sells, exchanges, or otherwise disposes of such property to a partnership which then, without performing its own qualifying MPGE or other production, leases, rents, licenses, sells, exchanges, or otherwise disposes of such property, then the partnership's gross receipts from this latter disposition are treated as non-DPGR.

* * * * *

Guy R. Traynor,
Federal Register Liaison,
Legal Processing Division,
Associate Chief Counsel
(Procedure & Administration).

(Filed by the Office of the Federal Register on December 29, 2006, 8:45 a.m., and published in the issue of the Federal Register for January 3, 2007, 72 F.R. 5)

Part I. Rulings and Decisions Under the Internal Revenue Code of 1986

Section 106.—Contributions by Employer to Accident and Health Plans

A notice provides guidance on rollovers from health Flexible Spending Arrangements (health FSAs) and Health Reimbursement Arrangements (HRAs) to Health Savings Accounts (HSAs). See Notice 2007-22, page 670.

Section 223.—Health Savings Accounts

A notice provides guidance on rollovers from health Flexible Spending Arrangements (health FSAs) and Health Reimbursement Arrangements (HRAs) to Health Savings Accounts (HSAs). See Notice 2007-22, page 670.

Section 263.—Capital Expenditures

A revenue procedure provides administrative guidance permitting the use of a "Net Consideration Method" of accounting for certain patent cross licensing arrangements. Under the method, only cash and other non-patent-right consideration are taken into account for withholding and capitalization purposes. See Rev. Proc. 2007-23, page 675.

Section 263A.—Capitalization and Inclusion in Inventory Costs of Certain Expenses

A revenue procedure provides administrative guidance permitting the use of a "Net Consideration Method" of accounting for certain patent cross licensing arrangements. Under the method, only cash and other non-patent-right consideration are taken into account for withholding and capitalization purposes. See Rev. Proc. 2007-23, page 675.

Section 367.—Foreign Corporations

26 CFR 1.367(a)–3: Treatment of transfers of stock or securities to foreign corporations.

T.D. 9311

DEPARTMENT OF THE TREASURY
Internal Revenue Service
26 CFR Parts 1 and 602

Certain Transfers of Stock or Securities by U.S. Persons to Foreign Corporations

AGENCY: Internal Revenue Service (IRS), Treasury.

ACTION: Final and temporary regulations.

SUMMARY: This document contains final and temporary regulations under section 367(a) of the Internal Revenue Code (Code) regarding gain recognition agreements. The final regulations are necessary to update cross-references in the current regulations. The temporary regulations are necessary to respond to comments requested in Notice 2005–74. The regulations primarily affect U.S. persons that transfer stock or securities to foreign corporations or corporations engaged in transactions that affect existing gain recognition agreements. The text of these temporary regulations also serves as the text of the proposed regulations (REG–147144–06) set forth in the notice of proposed rulemaking on this subject published elsewhere in this issue of the Bulletin.

DATES: *Effective Date:* These regulations are effective February 5, 2007.

Applicability Dates: For dates of applicability, see §§1.367(a)–3T(f) and 1.367(a)–8T(h).

ADDRESSES: Send submissions to: CC:PA:LPD:PR (REG–147144–06), room 5203, Internal Revenue Service, PO Box 7604, Ben Franklin Station, Washington, DC 20044. Submissions may be hand-delivered Monday through Friday between the hours of 8 a.m. and 4 p.m. to CC:PA:LPD:PR (REG–147144–06), Courier's Desk, Internal Revenue Service, 1111 Constitution Avenue, NW, Washington, DC, or sent electronically, via the IRS Internet site at *www.irs.gov/regs* or via the Federal eRulemaking Portal at *www.regulations.gov* (IRS REG–147144–06).

FOR FURTHER INFORMATION CONTACT: Daniel McCall, (202) 622–3860 (not a toll-free number).

SUPPLEMENTARY INFORMATION:

Paperwork Reduction Act

These temporary regulations are being issued without prior notice and public procedure pursuant to the Administrative Procedure Act (5 U.S.C. 553). For this reason, the collections of information contained in these regulations have been reviewed and pending receipt and evaluation of public comments, approved by the Office of Management and Budget in accordance with the Paperwork Reduction Act of 1995 (44 U.S.C. 3507(d)) under control number 1545–2056. Response to these collections of information is mandatory.

An agency may not conduct or sponsor, and a person is not required to respond to, a collection of information, unless the collection of information displays a valid control number.

For further information concerning this collection of information, and where to submit comments on the collection of information and the accuracy of the estimated burden, and suggestions for reducing the burden, please refer to the preamble to the cross-referencing notice of proposed rulemaking (REG–147144–06) published elsewhere in this issue of the Bulletin.

Books and records relating to these collections of information must be retained as long as their contents may become material in the administration of any internal revenue law. Generally, tax returns and tax return information are confidential, as required by 26 U.S.C. 6103.

Background

Section 367(a)(1) provides that if, in connection with any exchange described in section 332, 351, 354, 356, or 361, a United States person (U.S. transferor) transfers property to a foreign corporation (transferee foreign corporation), such foreign corporation shall not, for purposes of determining the extent to which gain shall be recognized on such transfer, be considered to be a corporation. Section 367(a)(2), (3) and (6) provides exceptions to this general rule and grants regulatory authority to provide additional exceptions and to limit the statutory exceptions.

Exceptions to the general rule of section 367(a)(1) for certain transfers by a U.S. transferor of the stock or securities of a corporation (transferred corporation) to a transferee foreign corporation are provided in §1.367(a)–3 (initial transfer). In some cases, these exceptions require, among other things, that the U.S. transferor file a gain recognition agreement (GRA), as provided in §1.367(a)–8. Section 1.367(a)–3(b)(1)(ii) and (c)(1)(iii)(B). Pursuant to a GRA, the U.S. transferor agrees, among other things, to include in income the gain realized, but not recognized, on the initial transfer of the stock or securities, and pay any applicable interest, upon certain events (triggering events) that occur before the close of the fifth full taxable year following the year of the initial transfer. Section 1.367(a)–8(b)(1)(iii) and (3)(i).

Section 1.367(a)–8(e)(1) and (2) provides that dispositions of the stock or securities of the transferred corporation are generally triggering events. Similarly, §1.367(a)–8(e)(3) provides that dispositions of substantially all (within the meaning of section 368(a)(1)(C)) of the assets of the transferred corporation are generally treated as deemed dispositions of the stock or securities of the transferred corporation and therefore are also triggering events. Finally, dispositions of stock of the transferee foreign corporation can also be triggering events. See §1.367(a)–8(f)(2)(ii).

Notwithstanding these rules, §1.367(a)–8 provides that various nonrecognition transactions are not triggering events if certain requirements are satisfied. For example, §1.367(a)–8(g) provides exceptions for certain transactions involving the U.S. transferor, the transferee foreign corporation, and the transferred corporation. Although these exceptions clearly contemplate some nonrecognition transactions, the current regulations are unclear whether, and if so how, the exceptions apply to various asset reorganizations involving section 361 exchanges by the U.S. transferor, the transferee foreign corporation, and the transferred corporation.

Section 1.367(a)–8 also provides that certain nonrecognition transactions are not triggering events because the GRA is terminated without further effect. For example, §1.367(a)–8(h)(3) lists certain nonrecognition transactions that terminate the GRA, provided that immediately after the transaction the basis in the transferred stock is not greater than the U.S. transferor's basis in the stock that, immediately before the initial transfer, necessitated the GRA.

On September 28, 2005, the IRS and the Treasury Department issued Notice 2005–74, 2005–2 C.B. 726, see §601.601(d)(2), which announced the intention to amend the regulations under section 367(a) to address the effect on GRAs of certain asset reorganizations involving the U.S. transferor, the transferee foreign corporation, and the transferred corporation. The notice was issued in response to comments that the current regulations do not adequately address various asset reorganizations involving the U.S. transferor, the transferee foreign corporation, and the transferred corporation. Notice 2005–74 addressed the most common of these reorganizations and requested comments on other transactions (for example, certain upstream and downstream reorganizations).

Notice 2005–74 generally provided that, if particular requirements are satisfied, certain asset reorganizations of the U.S. transferor, the transferee foreign corporation, or the transferred corporation will not constitute triggering events. A key premise of the notice was that the covered transactions involved situations where the ability to collect tax is sufficiently preserved in the event of a subsequent trigger of the GRA (that is, the obligor under the GRA remains unchanged as a result of the asset reorganization). In light of taxpayer comments and further study, however, the IRS and Treasury Department have determined that there are additional instances where the ability to collect tax after these asset reorganizations and certain other nonrecognition transactions (as defined in section 7701(a)(45)) is sufficiently preserved so that these transactions also should not constitute a triggering event if particular requirements are met. The IRS and Treasury Department also have concluded that other portions of the current section 367(a) regulations addressing GRAs should be revised.

Explanation of Provisions

A. *Overview*

The temporary regulations adopt the rules announced in Notice 2005–74, with a number of modifications discussed below. Notice 2005–74 only provided guidance on a particular range of transactions, namely certain asset reorganizations, that are insufficiently addressed in the current regulations. The temporary regulations respond to comments and provide guidance on the effect on GRAs of transactions that are not addressed in the current regulation or Notice 2005–74. The temporary regulations also make additional changes to the existing regulations. For example, the temporary regulations modify and clarify procedural requirements attendant to entering into GRAs. Finally, the temporary regulations reorganize the current regulation so that distinct paragraphs address triggering events, exceptions to triggering events, and events that terminate a GRA. The IRS and Treasury Department continue to consider issuing additional public guidance that further revises §1.367(a)–8.

B. *Effect of Certain Asset Reorganizations and Nontaxable Liquidations on Gain Recognition Agreements*

1. *Transfers of transferee foreign corporation stock by U.S. transferor*

a) *Asset reorganizations*

Notice 2005–74 provided that if, in a section 361 transaction, a U.S. transferor transfers all or a portion of the stock or securities of the transferee foreign corporation to an acquiring domestic corporation (successor U.S. transferor) pursuant to certain asset reorganizations, the exchanges made pursuant to the asset reorganization will trigger the gain recognition agreement, unless various conditions are satisfied. These conditions are: (1) the U.S. transferor must have been a member of a consolidated group (original consolidated group) at the time of the initial transfer and the common parent of such group (original common parent) entered into the original GRA; (2) immediately after the asset reorganization, the successor U.S. transferor is a member of the original consolidated group (consolidation continuity requirement); and (3) the original common parent enters into a new GRA with respect to the transfer subject to the original GRA, modified by substituting the successor U.S. transferor for the original U.S. transferor. A notice of the asset reorganization also must be provided with the successor U.S. transferor's next annual certification.

For this purpose, an asset reorganization is defined as a reorganization described in section 368(a)(1) involving the transfer of assets by a corporation to another corporation pursuant to section 361, except that such term shall include reorganizations described in section 368(a)(1)(D) or (G) only if the requirements of section 354(b)(1)(A) and (B) are met.

The IRS and Treasury Department received several comments that the consolidation continuity requirement was unduly restrictive because it focused on maintaining the same obligor for a GRA following the asset reorganization. Commentators asserted that an equal or better ability to collect the tax due as a result of a triggering event subsequent to such a reorganization may be preserved in certain instances where the consolidation continuity requirement would not be satisfied. However, these same commentators noted that if there were no consolidation continuity requirement, such that a U.S. transferor that is a member of a consolidated group at the time of the initial transfer could be acquired in a later asset reorganization by a corporation (successor corporation) that is not a member of such group without triggering the GRA, the actions of the successor corporation could inappropriately affect the liability of the original consolidated group under the GRA. As a result, the commentators requested that the consolidation continuity requirement be curtailed or eliminated, while at the same time not inappropriately exposing the original consolidated group to the liabilities arising from the actions of the successor corporation.

The IRS and Treasury Department generally agree with these views. Therefore, the temporary regulations eliminate the consolidation continuity requirement and address concerns about the liability of a consolidated group that disposes of a U.S. transferor subject to a GRA.

Specifically, the temporary regulations provide that when a U.S. transferor transfers all or a portion of the stock of the transferee foreign corporation to an acquiring corporation in an asset reorganization, the exchanges made pursuant to the reorganization will not be triggering events and the GRA will terminate without further effect, but only if certain requirements are satisfied. These requirements ensure that the ability to collect tax is sufficiently preserved and that the terms of the GRA are administrable.

First, the acquiring corporation (successor U.S. transferor) must be a domestic corporation, and the successor U.S. transferor or the common parent of the consolidated group of which the successor U.S. transferor is a member (as applicable) must enter into a new GRA to recognize gain with respect to the initial transfer during the remaining term of the original GRA (with certain modifications).

Second, with its next certification, the successor U.S. transferor must provide to the IRS the new GRA, notice of the transaction, and Form 8838 (*Consent To Extend the Time To Assess Tax Under Section 367 – Gain Recognition Agreement*) to extend the period of assessment of tax on the initial transfer.

Third, unless the successor U.S. transferor is a member of the same consolidated group of which the U.S. transferor was a member immediately before the asset reorganization, the person entering into the new GRA must elect that, if the new GRA is triggered in whole or in part, the person will include the required amount in the year of the triggering event (as opposed to the year of the initial transfer). Requiring an inclusion in these circumstances only in the year of a subsequent triggering event when the U.S. transferor is no longer owned by the same consolidated group is necessary, among other reasons, because the successor U.S. transferor may not have existed in the year of the initial transfer. In such a case, the successor U.S. transferor would not be able to amend a return for the year of the initial transfer to include any tax due as a result of a subsequent triggering event. Moreover, the requirement is appropriate even if the successor U.S. transferor did exist in the year of the initial transfer because its tax year for the year of the initial transfer may be closed. In sum, this requirement assures the GRA rules are administrable and that the ability to collect tax is sufficiently preserved. If these requirements are met, the original GRA will terminate without further effect.

The IRS and Treasury Department have decided to eliminate the consolidation continuity requirement because these three requirements adequately address the government's concern in this area by, among other things, preserving the ability to collect the tax due as a result of a triggering event subsequent to a covered asset reorganization. In many asset reorganizations, the successor U.S. transferor will have an equal or greater ability to pay the tax due in the case of a subsequent triggering event than would the original U.S. transferor. Furthermore, the current regulations generally do not impose any financial or other requirements on the ability of a U.S. transferor to enter into a GRA. But see §1.367(a)–8(d) (imposing a security requirement in certain situations). Consequently, the IRS and Treasury Department believe that even if in some circumstances an acquisition of a U.S. transferor may affect the ability to collect the tax due as a result of a subsequent triggering event (for example, the U.S. transferor is acquired from a consolidated group by another consolidated group whose value is less than that of the original consolidated group), the requirements above nonetheless sufficiently preserve the ability to collect the tax that would be due if the new GRA were triggered and ensure that the terms of the GRA are administrable.

As described in this section, the temporary regulations require that the acquirer be a domestic corporation because, among other reasons, the IRS and Treasury Department are concerned that if a foreign acquirer is allowed to enter into a new GRA, it may be difficult for the IRS to collect any tax due in the event of a subsequent trigger of the GRA. However, the IRS and Treasury Department continue to study whether it would be appropriate to allow a domestic corporate shareholder of the U.S. transferor to enter into a new GRA when a U.S. transferor is acquired by a foreign corporation in an asset reorganization under conditions similar to those provided in §1.367(a)–3T(e). The IRS and Treasury Department welcome more detailed comments on specific approaches that could extend these rules to foreign acquisitions of the U.S. transferor.

b) *Nontaxable liquidations*

The current regulations provide that, if a corporate U.S. transferor liquidates in a transaction that qualifies under sections 332 and 337, the GRA is triggered unless (1) the U.S. transferor filed a consolidated income tax return with a U.S. parent corporation both in the year of the initial transfer and the year of the liquidation, and (2) the common parent enters into a new GRA, with certain modifications. Section 1.367(a)–8(f)(2)(ii).

The temporary regulations provide a similar rule. However, the temporary regulations eliminate the consolidation continuity requirement, so the U.S. transferor is no longer required to be a member of the same consolidated group in the year of the initial transfer and the year of the liquidation. Consequently, the temporary regulations provide that where a U.S. transferor disposes of the stock of the foreign transferee corporation in a liquidation that qualifies under sections 332 and 337, the disposition will not constitute a triggering event provided that: (1) the distributee (successor U.S. transferor) is a domestic corporation described in section 332(b)(1); (2) the successor U.S. transferor or, if the successor U.S. transferor is a member of a consolidated group, the common parent of the successor U.S. transferor's group, enters into a new GRA covering the remaining term of the original GRA (with certain modifications); (3) where the successor U.S. transferor is not a member of the original consolidated group immediately after the liquidation, the person entering into the GRA agrees that if there is a subsequent triggering event, the taxpayer will recognize the gain in the year of the triggering event (as opposed to the year of the initial transfer); and (4) the successor U.S. transferor provides, with its next annual certification, Form 8838 to extend the period of assessment of the tax on the initial transfer. If these conditions are satisfied, the original GRA will terminate without further effect.

For reasons similar to those discussed above in the context of asset reorganizations involving the U.S. transferor, the IRS and Treasury Department believe that the temporary regulations sufficiently address the government's concerns in this area, including preserving the ability to collect tax due as a result of a subsequent triggering event. As a result, it is not necessary for the U.S. transferor to be a member of the same consolidated group in the year of the transfer and the year of the liquidation. In addition, the IRS and Treasury Department believe that it is appropriate to require an inclusion in the year of a subsequent triggering event if the successor U.S. transferor was not a member of a consolidated group with the U.S. transferor immediately before the liquidation for reasons similar to those discussed regarding asset reorganizations involving the U.S. transferor.

2. *Transfers of transferred corporation stock or securities by transferee foreign corporation in an asset reorganization*

Notice 2005–74 provided that if, in a section 361 transaction, a transferee foreign corporation transfers stock or securities of a transferred corporation to a foreign acquiring corporation in an asset reorganization, the exchanges made pursuant to the reorganization will be a triggering event, unless certain conditions are met. These conditions require that the U.S. transferor, common parent, or new common parent corporation, as applicable, enter into a new GRA, with certain modifications. In addition, the U.S. transferor also is required to provide the new GRA and a notice of the asset reorganization with its next annual certification.

For purposes of this rule, Notice 2005–74 retained the same definition of asset reorganization as used for the provision dealing with transfers of transferee corporation stock, with certain modifications. Specifically, Notice 2005–74 excludes the following asset reorganizations: (1) triangular asset reorganizations described in §1.358–6(b); and (2) asset reorganizations where, after the reorganization, the same corporation is both the transferee foreign corporation (or successor transferee foreign corporation, as applicable) and the transferred corporation (or the successor transferred corporation, as applicable).

The temporary regulations generally incorporate these rules and provide that if the above conditions are satisfied the original GRA will terminate without further effect. However, even if these conditions are satisfied, the temporary regulations provide specific gain recognition rules if the transferee foreign corporation transfers stock or securities of the transferred corporation in an asset reorganization and the U.S. transferor recognizes gain under section 356(a)(1). See section C of this preamble.

As noted in this preamble, Notice 2005–74 excluded from the definition of the term asset reorganization any triangular asset reorganizations of the transferee foreign corporation and transferred corporation and certain upstream and downstream reorganizations. In response to comments and upon further study by the IRS and Treasury Department, the temporary regulations address the treatment of triangular asset reorganizations of the transferee foreign corporation and certain upstream and downstream reorganizations. See sections G and H of this preamble.

3. *Transfers of substantially all of a transferred corporation's assets*

Notice 2005–74 provides that if a transferred corporation transfers substantially all its assets in an asset reorganization, the exchanges made pursuant to the reorganization will be a triggering event, unless certain conditions are met. These conditions require that the U.S. transferor, U.S. parent corporation or new U.S. parent corporation, as applicable, enters into a new GRA, with certain modifications. The U.S. transferor also is required to provide the new GRA and the notice of the asset reorganization with its next annual certification. The definition of asset reorganization is the same as that used in asset reorganizations involving the transferee foreign corporation.

The temporary regulations generally incorporate these rules and provide that if these conditions are met, the original

GRA will terminate without further effect. However, even if these conditions are satisfied, the temporary regulations provide specific gain recognition rules (described in section C of this preamble) if the transferred corporation transfers substantially all of its assets in an asset reorganization and the transferee foreign corporation recognizes gain under section 356(a)(1). In addition, although the definition of asset reorganization excludes triangular asset reorganizations and downstream mergers of the transferee foreign corporation, the temporary regulations address the tax treatment of these transactions. See sections G and H of this preamble.

C. *Special Rules Regarding Nonrecognition Transactions Involving Money or Other Property*

The current regulations provide that certain nonrecognition transactions are not triggering events if particular requirements are satisfied. However, commentators have stated that the current regulations provide that certain nonrecognition transactions at the transferee foreign corporation or transferred corporation level in which any money or other property (as described in sections 351(b) or 356(a)) is received in exchange are triggering events without exception. These commentators assert that it is not appropriate to trigger an entire GRA as a result of receiving a relatively minor amount of "boot" in the nonrecognition transaction. These commentators also note that the current regulations do not address clearly the treatment of transfers of transferee foreign corporation stock by a U.S. transferor in a nonrecognition transaction in which the U.S. transferor receives boot.

The IRS and Treasury Department agree that the receipt of boot under section 351(b) or 356(a)(1) in connection with the disposition of transferred corporation stock or securities, or substantially all of a transferred corporation's assets, should not automatically trigger all the gain under a GRA. Accordingly, the temporary regulations provide that if certain conditions are met, the entire GRA will not be triggered when a transferee foreign corporation disposes of transferred corporation stock or securities in a nonrecognition transaction simply because the transferee foreign corporation receives boot.

However, the IRS and Treasury Department believe that the GRA should be triggered to the extent that gain would be recognized in such a transaction by a transferee foreign corporation or a transferred corporation, before taking into account basis increases that may apply to the stock or securities disposed of as a result of triggering the GRA. The current, as well as the temporary regulations, provide that if a U.S. transferor is required to recognize gain because of a triggering event, then certain basis increases are allowed as of the date of the initial transfer. Therefore, in determining the amount of gain that is recognized under the GRA in such a transaction, the temporary regulations provide that the U.S. transferor first must recognize that amount of gain that the transferee foreign corporation or transferred corporation would have recognized under 351(b) or 356(a)(1), before taking into account the basis increases that are allowed under the regulations as of the date of the initial transfer. Second, if the U.S. transferor has not recognized all the gain realized, but not recognized, on the initial transfer, then its new GRA will reflect any remaining unrecognized gain on the initial transfer. Third, after the consequences of the transaction are determined under the temporary regulations, then the taxpayer must determine the amount of gain, if any, that the transferee foreign corporation or transferred corporation must recognize under 351(b) or 356(a)(1). In determining the amount to be recognized, the basis of the stock disposed of shall reflect the basis increase allowed as a result of the gain recognized under the GRA by the U.S. transferor.

This special rule limiting recognition of gain in otherwise nonrecognition transactions involving boot applies only if the U.S. transferor complies with the otherwise applicable requirements of the exception to recognizing all of the gain subject to the GRA when there is a triggering event. This special rule is intended to require the U.S. transferor to recognize only an appropriate amount of income, without automatically triggering the entire GRA.

The IRS and Treasury Department also believe that additional guidance is needed on the treatment of transfers of transferee foreign corporation stock by a U.S. transferor in a nonrecognition exchange in which the U.S. transferor receives boot. Therefore, the temporary regulations treat the disposition of transferee foreign corporation stock in a nonrecognition transaction by the U.S. transferor when the U.S. transferor receives money or other property as described in section 351(b) or 356(a) as a termination of the GRA in whole or in part. Consequently, if a new GRA is filed, then the U.S. transferor will recognize gain under the new GRA in the event of a subsequent triggering event in the amount of the gain realized, but not recognized, in the initial transfer less any gain recognized by the U.S. transferor under section 351(b) and 356(a)(1) in connection with the nonrecognition transaction. If, however, a new GRA is not filed in connection with the nonrecognition transaction, then the original GRA is triggered, and the U.S. transferor must recognize the gain that was realized, but not recognized, on the initial transfer less any gain recognized by the U.S. transferor under section 351(b) or 356(a)(1) in connection with the nonrecognition transaction.

D. *Effect of Consolidation and Deconsolidation on Gain Recognition Agreements*

Commentators noted that the current regulation does not adequately address the effect on GRAs of certain transactions involving consolidated groups. For example, the commentators noted that it is not clear what effect a U.S. transferor becoming a member of a consolidated group has on an existing GRA. The current regulations do provide, however, that if a U.S. transferor is a member of a consolidated group at the time of the initial transfer and ceases to be a member of the group during the term of the GRA, the common parent of such group that entered into the GRA continues to be liable under the original GRA. Section 1.367(a)–8(b)(5)(ii). Several commentators have raised concerns that such a result is not appropriate because the actions of an acquirer could unilaterally affect the liability of the original consolidated group under the GRA.

The IRS and Treasury Department agree that the effect of these transactions needs to be clarified and rationalized. Accordingly, in response to these concerns, the temporary regulations provide specific rules addressing these transactions. In particular, the IRS and Treasury Department believe that the U.S. parent corporation of a consolidated group should not continue to be liable under a GRA with respect to a U.S. transferor that is no longer a member of such group.

The temporary regulations provide that when a U.S. transferor becomes a member of a consolidated group (including a transaction where it joins such a group after being a member of another consolidated group) the transaction is a triggering event unless certain conditions are met. If these conditions are satisfied, the original GRA is terminated without further effect. These conditions require the U.S. parent corporation of the consolidated group that the U.S. transferor joins (1) to enter into a new GRA for the remaining term of the original GRA and (2) to elect to recognize gain in the taxable year of any subsequent triggering event (as opposed to the year of the initial transfer). A notice of the consolidation transaction must also be filed with the next annual certification. The IRS and Treasury Department believe that these requirements ensure that a GRA remains in effect after a U.S. transferor joins a consolidated group. These requirements are also consistent with §1.1502–77(a), which provides that the common parent is the sole agent for each member of the consolidated group.

In addition, the temporary regulations also cover situations in which a U.S. transferor ceases to be a member of a consolidated group and does not become a member of a new consolidated group. In these cases, the transaction is a triggering event, unless certain conditions are met. If these conditions are satisfied, the original GRA is terminated without further effect. These conditions require the U.S. transferor (1) to enter into a new GRA for the remaining term of the original gain recognition agreement and (2) to elect that in the event of a subsequent triggering event the U.S. transferor will recognize gain in the year of the triggering event. The U.S. transferor must also provide notice of the deconsolidation with the next annual certification.

E. *U.S. Transferor Goes Out of Existence in a Transaction Giving Rise to a Gain Recognition Agreement*

The current regulation provides that when a U.S. transferor goes out of existence in a transaction giving rise to a GRA, gain generally qualifies for nonrecognition treatment only if the U.S. transferor is owned by a single U.S. parent corporation, the U.S. transferor and its parent corporation file a consolidated Federal income tax return for the taxable year that includes the transfer, and the parent of the consolidated group enters into a GRA. Section 1.367(a)–8(f)(2)(i). The current regulation provides that a U.S. transferor that is controlled by five or fewer domestic corporations may request a ruling that the transaction qualifies for nonrecognition treatment. Section 1.367(a)–8(f)(2)(i).

Notice 2005–74, in turn, provides a rule that treats all members of the U.S. parent's consolidated group for the taxable year that includes the transfer as a single corporation for purposes of §1.367(a)–8(f)(2)(i). Thus, a U.S. transferor that is not directly owned by a single U.S. parent corporation may still qualify for nonrecognition, without requesting a ruling, when the U.S. transferor goes out of existence in a transaction giving rise to a GRA, if it is indirectly wholly owned by members of a consolidated group.

The IRS and Treasury Department believe it is necessary to provide additional guidance on how GRAs are entered into when a U.S. transferor is controlled by multiple corporate shareholders with which the U.S. transferor does not join in filing a consolidated return. Moreover, the IRS and Treasury Department believe that in this area a single rule should apply both in consolidated and nonconsolidated situations. As a result, the temporary regulations provide unified rules, replacing both the current regulations and Notice 2005–74, in situations in which a U.S. transferor goes out of existence in a transaction giving rise to a GRA.

The temporary regulations generally provide that when a U.S. transferor goes out of existence in a transaction giving rise to a GRA, the gain may qualify for nonrecognition treatment if (1) the requirements of section 367(a)(5) and any regulations under that paragraph are satisfied such that five or fewer domestic corporations control the U.S. transferor and appropriate basis adjustments are made, (2) the requirements of §1.367(a)–3(c)(1) are satisfied if the transferred corporation is domestic, (3) all domestic corporate shareholders of the U.S. transferor that own at least five percent of either the total voting power or the total fair market value of the stock of the transferee foreign corporation immediately after the transaction enter into GRAs with respect to their *pro rata* share of the gain in the transferred stock or securities that designate such domestic corporate shareholders as U.S. transferors for purposes of §§1.367(a)–3(b) and (c) and 1.367(a)–8T, and (4) all domestic corporate shareholders that enter into GRAs elect to recognize any gain upon a subsequent trigger of the GRA in the year of the triggering event.

The temporary regulations eliminate the current regulation's option to request a private letter ruling because guidance is now provided on how GRAs are entered into by five or fewer domestic corporations that control a U.S. transferor satisfying section 367(a)(5). In addition, the temporary regulations clarify that the terms of section 367(a)(5) must be satisfied (along with other requirements) to avoid gain recognition on the U.S. transferor's section 361 transfer of stock or securities to a foreign acquiring corporation. Therefore, the rule in Notice 2005–74 treating consolidated group members as a single corporation is incorporated by reference to section 367(a)(5), which provides that all members of the same affiliated group are treated as one corporation. Lastly, because these rules address how gain recognition may be avoided under section 367(a)(1) on the initial transfer itself, rather than the effect of subsequent transactions on existing GRAs, these rules have been removed from §1.367(a)–8 and included instead in §1.367(a)–3T(e).

F. *Transfers of Transferred Corporation's Assets*

Under the current regulations, dispositions of substantially all of the assets of the transferred corporation (within the meaning of section 368(a)(1)(C)) are generally treated as deemed dispositions of the stock or securities of the transferred corporation and therefore are triggering events. Section 1.367(a)–8(e)(3). In Revenue Ruling 57–518, 1957–2 C.B. 253, see §601.601(d)(2), the IRS stated that what constitutes "substantially all of the properties" as the term is used in section 368(a)(1)(C) "will depend upon the facts and circumstances in each case rather than upon any particular percentage." However, Revenue Procedure 77–37, 1977–2 C.B. 568, see §601.601(d)(2), provides that for ruling purposes, the transfer by a corporation of 70 percent of its gross assets or 90 percent of its assets net of liabilities will generally be deemed to be a transfer of substantially all of the assets of a corporation.

Commentators have noted that defining substantially all by reference to section 368(a)(1)(C) may not be appropriate in the context of the GRA rules. The IRS and Treasury Department, however, generally believe that defining "substantially all" for these purposes by reference to the definition of the term under section 368(a)(1)(C) is appropriate. Nonetheless, the IRS and Treasury Department believe that it is important to clarify the scope of the term "substantially all," as used in the current regulation and the temporary regulations. One commentator suggested that if a transferred corporation disposes of less than 70 percent of its gross assets or 90 percent of its assets net of liabilities, the transfer will not be treated as a disposition of substantially all of the assets of the transferred corporation for purposes of §1.367(a)–8(e)(3), and thus, such a disposition would not trigger a GRA. This suggestion is not correct. If, upon considering the facts and circumstances, a transferred corporation has disposed of substantially all its assets, such a transaction is a triggering event, even if the transferred corporation disposes of less than 70 percent of a corporation's gross assets or 90 percent of its assets net of liabilities. The "substantially all" safe harbor provided in Revenue Procedure 77–37 is intentionally high so that the IRS does not need to engage in a factually detailed analysis before issuing a letter ruling. As a result, in the context of GRAs, the Revenue Procedure's threshold does not mean that a disposition of substantially all the assets does not occur upon the disposition of a lesser amount of assets. Therefore, the temporary regulations provide that whether a transferred corporation has disposed of substantially all of its assets is determined under all the facts and circumstances.

G. *Transactions that Terminate the GRA*

1. *Taxable dispositions of transferee foreign corporation stock*

Section 1.367(a)–8(h)(1) provides that a GRA will terminate, in whole or in part, as a result of certain taxable dispositions of the transferee foreign corporation stock by the U.S. transferor. A key premise for this termination rule is that the basis in the transferee foreign corporation stock received by the U.S. transferor in the initial transfer is assumed to reflect the basis in the transferred stock or securities.

The IRS and Treasury Department continue to believe this termination rule is appropriate. As a result, the temporary regulations generally retain this rule. However, the temporary regulations modify the termination rule to ensure that a GRA terminates only when the transferee foreign corporation stock disposed of in fact reflects the basis of the transferred stock or securities. This termination rule only applies to transferee foreign corporation stock that is received (or deemed received) in the initial transfer. The IRS and Treasury Department understand that in some cases, taxpayers may take the position that the basis in the transferee foreign corporation stock does not reflect the basis of the transferred stock or securities. For example, taxpayers may take the position that the basis in such transferee foreign corporation stock received also reflects the basis of other property that had a built-in loss when it was transferred to the transferee foreign corporation. Thus, the termination rule in the temporary regulations will apply only when the basis of the transferee foreign corporation stock received (or deemed received) in the initial transfer properly reflects the sum of the aggregate basis of the transferred stock or securities immediately before the initial transfer, plus any increase in the basis of such stock or securities as a result of recognizing gain on the transfer. In addition, for purposes of this basis determination, basis increases to the transferee foreign corporation stock as a result of income inclusions (for example, pursuant to section 961) shall not be taken into account.

In cases where the basis of the relevant transferee foreign corporation stock exceeds the basis of the transferred stock or securities, however, the temporary regulations allow the U.S. transferor to take advantage of this termination rule if it elects to reduce its basis in the transferee foreign corporation stock such that it does not exceed the basis it had in the transferred stock or securities. If the U.S. transferor makes this election, the basis reduction will be effective immediately before the taxable disposition that terminates the GRA. In addition, if the U.S. transferor makes this election, it may increase its basis in other stock of the transferee foreign corporation it holds, if any, by a corresponding amount but not above the fair market value of such stock.

Similar rules apply in the case of partial dispositions of transferee foreign corporation stock and dispositions of transferee foreign corporation stock in nonrecognition transactions in which a portion of the realized gain is recognized.

2. *Certain inbound distributions or transfers of the transferred stock*

Section 1.367(a)–8(h)(3) provides that a distribution of the transferred stock in a transaction qualifying under section 355 or sections 332 and 337 will terminate the GRA if the U.S. transferor's basis in the transferred stock or securities that it receives in the section 355 or 332 and 337 transaction does not exceed the basis the U.S. transferor had in the transferred stock or securities immediately before the initial transfer. In response to comments, however, the temporary regulations allow the U.S. transferor to take advantage of this termination rule if it elects to reduce the basis of the transferred stock or securities if the basis exceeds the basis the U.S. transferor had in the transferred stock or securities immediately before the initial transfer. For purposes of this basis determination, basis increases to the transferred stock as a result of income inclusions (for example, pursuant to section 961) shall not be taken into account. If the U.S. transferor elects to reduce basis in the transferred stock or securities it receives, the U.S. transferor shall increase its basis in other transferee foreign corporation stock (if any) by a corresponding amount but not above the fair market value of such stock.

Although the temporary regulations generally provide that a GRA terminates in certain section 332 liquidations of the transferee foreign corporation, the IRS and Treasury Department are studying to what extent this rule should apply when the transferee foreign corporation has a minority shareholder and therefore recognizes gain under section 336 in connection with the section 332 liquidation. As noted in the request for comments, although the IRS and Treasury Department generally believe it is appropriate to terminate entirely the GRA in a section 332 liquidation, in other circumstances it may not be appropriate. For example, if after an initial transfer, a wholly-owned transferee foreign corporation issues a minority interest to a foreign shareholder, completely terminating the GRA upon a section 332 liquidation of the transferee foreign corporation does not account for the fact that the U.S. transferor has indirectly disposed of up to 20 percent of its interest in the transferred stock or securities. Therefore, when the temporary regulations are finalized, the IRS and Treasury Department may address the effect that section 336 gain has on a gain recognition agreement when a transferee foreign corporation with a minority shareholder liquidates under section 332.

The temporary regulations expand the current rule to terminate GRAs when certain U.S. persons other than the original U.S. transferor receive the stock or securities that was transferred in the initial transfer. For example, if the transferred corporation is distributed to a domestic corporation or U.S. individual other than the U.S. transferor in a section 355 "split off," the GRA would terminate if the domestic corporation or U.S. individual receives the transferred stock or securities with a basis that is not greater than the basis the U.S. transferor had in the transferred stock or securities immediately before the initial transfer.

Finally, and in response to comments requested in Notice 2005–74, the temporary regulations also expand the current rule to provide that the GRA will terminate in additional transactions where the U.S. transferor or a domestic corporation receives the transferred stock or securities with a basis that is not greater than the basis the U.S. transferor had in the transferred stock or securities immediately before the initial transfer. These transactions are upstream asset reorganizations where the U.S. transferor acquires the assets of the transferee foreign corporation, downstream asset reorganizations where the transferred corporation acquires the assets of the transferee foreign corporation, and certain other asset reorganizations where a domestic corporation acquires the assets of the transferee foreign corporation. Consequently, the temporary regulations generally provide that the GRA terminates in particular circumstances when the transferred stock or securities are held with the correct basis by certain U.S. persons, even if the U.S. person is not the original U.S. transferor.

However, the IRS and Treasury Department believe that it is not appropriate for the GRA to terminate when the transferred stock or securities may then be disposed of, directly or indirectly, by a foreign shareholder without being subject to U.S. tax. Therefore, this termination rule is limited to section 332 liquidations, section 355 distributions, and asset reorganizations where the domestic corporation that holds the transferred stock or securities after the transaction is either the U.S. transferor or a member of the same consolidated group of which the U.S. transferor is then a member. The IRS and Treasury Department continue to study whether it would be appropriate to expand the scope of the rule to transactions where the acquirer is not a member of the same consolidated group of which the U.S. transferor is then a member and request comments regarding such a rule.

H. *Triangular Reorganizations of Transferee Foreign Corporation and Transferred Corporation*

Notice 2005–74 provides rules that allow a U.S. transferor to avoid gain recognition on certain asset reorganizations of the transferee foreign corporation and transferred corporation. However, Notice 2005–74 restricts the definition of "asset reorganization" to exclude triangular asset reorganizations of the transferee foreign corporation and transferred corporation.

In response to comments and after further study, the temporary regulations address the treatment of certain triangular asset reorganizations. Specifically, they provide that if the transferee foreign corporation or transferred corporation is acquired in a triangular asset reorganization, the exchanges made pursuant to the reorganization will not be triggering events if certain requirements are satisfied. For purposes of this rule, a triangular asset reorganization is limited to a transaction in which the acquiring subsidiary is foreign. The additional requirements are as follows. First, the U.S. transferor or common parent must enter into a new GRA to recognize gain with respect to the initial transfer during the remaining term of the original GRA, with certain modifications. In the case of a triangular asset reorganization of the transferee foreign corporation, the U.S. transferor also must make certain designations depending on whether the parent corporation of the foreign acquiring subsidiary is foreign or domestic and depending on the type of triangular asset reorganization. Finally, the U.S. transferor must provide notice of the transaction with its next annual certification.

I. *Other Changes*

The current regulations refer to "stock of the transferred corporation" in some paragraphs but refer to "stock or securities of the transferred corporation" in other paragraphs. The temporary regulations refer to "stock or securities of the transferred corporation" because either stock or securities, or both, may be subject to a GRA when transferred to a transferee foreign corporation by a U.S. person. In contrast, the temporary regulations generally refer only to stock, and not securities, of the transferee foreign corporation. The rules applying to a disposition of the transferee foreign corporation are concerned primarily with transactions in which the U.S. transferor loses or decreases its control of the transferee foreign corporation, which does not occur when a U.S. transferor disposes of securities of the transferee foreign corporation.

The current regulation provides a reasonable cause exception to triggering a GRA when the person required to file the GRA fails to comply in any material respect with the terms of a GRA, or when the person fails to meet the timeliness requirement for submitting a GRA. The temporary regulations retain this reasonable cause exception but provide additional guidance on how the person should submit a request for reasonable cause relief. The temporary regulations also provide that the Area Director or Director of Field Operations, as applicable, shall notify the person in writing within 120 days of the filing if the person will be granted reasonable cause relief or if additional time is required to make the determination. The 120-day period runs from the date that the IRS notifies the person that its request has been received. Once this period begins, the person shall be deemed to have established reasonable cause if it is not again notified within 120 days.

Effective Dates

With the exception of the special boot rules described in section C of this preamble, these temporary regulations apply to GRAs filed with respect to transfers of stock or securities occurring on or after March 7, 2007. The boot rules described in section C of this preamble apply to GRAs filed with respect to transfers of stock or securities occurring on or after 180 days after February 5, 2007. However, GRAs that are filed after March 7, 2007 in connection with transactions entered into pursuant to a contract that was binding before February 5, 2007 are not subject to these regulations, but taxpayers may elect to apply the rules of these regulations to such a GRA. For all open years, taxpayers may apply rules of these regulations that were not already effective under §1.367(a)–8 to GRAs filed before March 7, 2007. Similar effective date rules are provided for those transfers discussed in section E of this preamble (regarding a U.S. transferor that goes out of existence in a transaction giving rise to a GRA).

Special Analyses

It has been determined that this Treasury Decision is not a significant regulatory action as defined in Executive Order 12866. Therefore, a regulatory assessment is not required. It has also been determined that 5 U.S.C. 553(b) and (d) do not apply to these regulations. For applicability of the Regulatory Flexibility Act, please refer to the cross-referenced notice of proposed rulemaking published elsewhere in this Bulletin. Pursuant to section 7805(f) of the Internal Revenue Code, this regulation has been submitted to the Chief Counsel for Advocacy of the Small Business Administration for comment on its impact on small business.

Request for Comments

The IRS and Treasury Department are considering issuing subsequent public guidance to address additional issues under section 367(a). Accordingly, comments are requested regarding the application of §1.367(a)–8, including whether other transactions should be excepted from being treated as triggering events pursuant to rules similar to those contained in the temporary regulations. For example, comments are requested as to the most appropriate treatment of divisive reorganizations qualifying under section 368(a)(1)(D) or (G), involving the U.S. transferor corporation, the transferee foreign corporation, and the transferred corporation. Comments also are requested on how a GRA is affected by a subsequent transaction to which section 304 applies involving transferee foreign corporation stock or transferred corporation stock. The IRS and Treasury Department believe that the rules in the temporary regulations generally deal with many transactions to which section 304 applies but request specific comments on any issues raised.

In addition, the IRS and Treasury Department request comments on the rule in §1.367(a)–8T(b)(3)(iii), which imposes interest on the additional tax, if any, that is required to be paid as a result of a triggering event. Specifically, comments are requested on whether interest should be imposed even when no additional tax is ultimately due as a result of a triggering event because, for example, a taxpayer has sufficient net operating losses to offset the tax that would otherwise be due as a result of a triggering event. If an interest charge is not required in such a case, a taxpayer may be viewed as inappropriately benefiting from deferring the realized but unrecognized gain on the initial transfer until a later year. However, there are other instances where the current regulations clearly permit such a benefit (for example, under §1.367(a)–8(h)(1)(i) in certain taxable dispositions of the stock of the transferee foreign corporation).

As described in section B.1.a of this preamble, comments are requested on whether a GRA should not be triggered, if certain conditions similar to those provided in §1.367(a)–3T(e) are met, when a U.S. transferor is acquired by a foreign corporation in an asset reorganization. Specifically, the IRS and Treasury Department request comments on how to reconcile the terms of the GRA that would be filed pursuant to §1.367(a)–3T(e) with the terms of a new GRA that would be filed to avoid triggering the original GRA. For example, the transferee foreign corporation under the outstanding GRA (and under the new GRA filed to avoid triggering the outstanding GRA) would be the transferred corporation with respect to the GRA filed pursuant to §1.367(a)–3T(e).

Finally, and as described in section G.2 of this preamble, the IRS and Treasury Department are studying to what extent the GRA termination rule should apply when the transferee foreign corporation liquidates in a transaction described in section 332 but also recognizes gain under section 336 because of a minority shareholder. Comments are requested on how the termination rule should address such a transaction, taking into consideration potentially different results depending on whether the minority shareholder is also subject to a GRA or is, for example, instead a foreign person who was issued transferee foreign corporation stock after the initial transfer.

For information on how to submit comments or request a public hearing, see the section "Comments and Requests for a Public Hearing," set forth in the notice of proposed rulemaking published elsewhere in this issue of the Bulletin.

Drafting Information

The principal author of these temporary regulations is Daniel McCall of the Office of Associate Chief Counsel (International). However, other personnel from the IRS and the Treasury Department participated in their development.

* * * * *

Amendments to the Regulations

Accordingly, 26 CFR parts 1 and 602 are amended as follows:

PART 1—INCOME TAXES

Paragraph 1. The authority citation for part 1 is amended by adding new entries to read as follows:

Authority: 26 U.S.C. 7805* * *

Section 1.367(a)–3T(e) also issued under 367(a) and (b).* * *

Section 1.367(a)–8T also issued under 367(a) and (b).* * *

Par. 2. For each entry in the table in the "Section" column, remove the language in the "Remove" column and add the language in the "Add" column in its place.

Section	Remove	Add
1.367(a)–3(d)(3), Example 1(ii), fourth sentence	§1.367(a)–8(e)	§1.367(a)–8T(d)(1)
1.367(a)–3(d)(3), Example 1(ii), fourth sentence	§1.367(a)–8(b)(1)(vii)	§1.367(a)–8T(b)(1)(vii)
1.367(a)–3(d)(3), Example 1(ii), fifth sentence	§1.367(a)–8(b)(1)(vii)	§1.367(a)–8T(b)(1)(vii)
1.367(a)–3(d)(3), Example 1A(ii), first sentence	§1.367(a)–8(a)(3)	§1.367(a)–8T(a)(3)
1.367(a)–3(d)(3), Example 4(i), first sentence	§1.367(a)–8(e)(3)(i)	§1.367(a)–8T(d)(2)
1.367(a)–3(d)(3), Example 4(ii), first sentence	§1.367(a)–8(e)(3)(i)	§1.367(a)–8T(d)(2)
1.367(a)–3(d)(3), Example 4(ii), second sentence	§1.367(a)–8(h)(2), because A and W filed a consolidated Federal income tax return prior to the transaction,	§1.367(a)–8T(g)(2), because A owned an amount of stock in W described in section 1504(a)(2) immediately before the transaction,
1.367(a)–3(d)(3), Example 6(ii), last sentence	§1.367(a)–8(e)(3)(i)	§1.367(a)–8T(d)(2)
1.367(a)–3(d)(3), Example 7A(ii), last sentence	§1.367(a)–8(b)(5)	§1.367(a)–8T(b)(5)
paragraph (d)(3), Example 7A(ii), last sentence	and (e)(3)(i).	and V satisfies the requirements contained in §1.367(a)–8T(e)(1)(iii).
1.367(a)–3(d)(3), Example 8(ii), second to last sentence	§1.367(a)–8(e)(3)(i)	§1.367(a)–8T(d)(2)
1.367(a)–3(d)(3), Example 11(ii), sixth sentence	§1.367(a)–8(e)	§1.367(a)–8T(d)(1)
1.367(a)–3(d)(3), Example 11(ii), sixth sentence	§1.367(a)–8(b)(1)(vii)	§1.367(a)–8T(b)(1)(vii)
1.367(a)–3(e)(1)(A), first sentence	(e)	(g)
1.367(a)–3(e)(1)(F), third sentence	(g)	(j)
1.367(a)–3(e)(2), first sentence	(e)(1) and (g)	(g)(1) and (j)
1.367(a)–3(e)(2), second sentence	(e)(2)	(g)(2)
1.367(a)–3(e)(2)(G), first sentence	(e)(1)(G)	(g)(1)(G)
1.367(a)–3(g)(1), first sentence	(g)(2)	(j)(2)
1.367(a)–3(g)(2)(i), first sentence	(g)(2)(iii), (g)(2)(iv)	(j)(2)(iii), (j)(2)(iv)
1.367(a)–3(g)(2)(ii), first sentence	(g)(2)(iii) or (iv)	(j)(2)(iii) or (iv)
1.367(a)–3(g)(2)(ii), fourth sentence	§1.367(a)–3(f)	§1.367(a)–3(h)
1.367(a)–3(g)(2)(iii), first sentence	(g)(2)(ii)	(j)(2)(ii)
1.367(a)–3(g)(2)(iv), first sentence	(g)(2)(i) and (ii)	(j)(2)(i) and (ii)
1.367(b)–4(b)(1)(iii), Example 4(i), last sentence	§1.367(a)–8(f)(2)	§1.367(a)–3T(e)

Par. 3. Section 1.367(a)–3 is amended as follows:

1. The second sentence of paragraph (a) is revised.

2. The first sentence of paragraph (d)(2)(iii) is revised.

3. Paragraph (d)(2)(iv) is revised.

4. The title and introductory text of paragraph (d)(2)(v) is revised.

5. The last two sentences of paragraph (d)(3), *Example 1A*(ii) are revised.

6. The last two sentences of paragraph (d)(3), *Example 5A*(ii) are revised.

7. The first and second sentences of paragraph (d)(3), *Example 7*(ii) are revised.

8. The third sentence of paragraph (d)(3), *Example 7A*(ii) is revised.

9. The last sentence of paragraph (d)(3), *Example 9*(ii) is revised.

10. The title of paragraph (d)(3), *Example 10* is revised.

11. The third sentence of paragraph (d)(3), *Example 12*(ii) is revised.

12. Redesignating paragraphs (e), (f), and (g) as paragraphs (g), (h), and (j), respectively.

13. Adding new paragraphs (e) and (i).

The revisions and addition read as follows:

§1.367(a)–3 Treatment of transfers of stock or securities to foreign corporations.

(a) * * * In general, a transfer of stock or securities by a U.S. person to a foreign corporation that is described in section 351, 354 (including a reorganization described in section 368(a)(1)(B) and including an indirect stock transfer described in paragraph (d) of this section), 356 or section 361(a) or (b) is subject to section 367(a)(1) and, therefore, is treated as a taxable exchange, unless one of the exceptions set forth in paragraph (b) of this section (regarding transfers of foreign stock or securities), paragraph (c) of this section (regarding transfers of domestic stock or securities), or paragraph (e) of this section (regarding transfers of stock or securities in a section 361 exchange) applies. * * *

* * * * *

(d) * * *

(2)(iii) * * * For purposes of determining the amount of gain that a U.S. person is required to include in income as a result of a triggering event, see §1.367(a)–8T(b)(3)(i) and (d).

(iv) * * * The U.S. transferor's agreement to recognize gain, as provided in §1.367(a)–8, shall include appropriate provisions consistent with the principles of §1.367(a)–3 and §1.367(a)–8, including, for example, as an additional triggering event an indirect disposition of the transferred stock or securities. For example, in the case of a triangular section 368(a)(1)(B) reorganization described in paragraph (d)(1)(iii)(A) of this section, a triggering event shall include an indirect disposition of the transferred stock or securities by the transferee foreign corporation, such as a disposition of the stock of the acquiring corporation (either foreign or domestic) by the transferee foreign corporation. In the case of a triangular section 368(a)(1)(B) reorganization described in paragraph (d)(1)(iii)(B) of this section, a disposition of the stock of the acquiring corporation by the domestic issuing corporation in a taxable transaction shall, for example, terminate the gain recognition agreement if the principles of §1.367(a)–8T(g)(1)(i)(A) and (B) are satisfied. See *Examples 5* and *5A* of this section.

(v) *Determination of whether substantially all of the transferred corporation's assets are disposed of.* For purposes of applying §1.367(a)–8T(d)(2) to determine whether substantially all of the assets of the transferred corporation have been disposed of, the following assets shall be taken into account (but only if such assets are not fully taxable under section 367 in the taxable year that includes the indirect transfer)—

* * * * *

(3) * * *

Example 1A. * * *

(ii) * * * If A leaves the P group, the gain recognition agreement would be triggered pursuant to §1.367(a)–8T(d)(4), unless the exception provided under §1.367(a)–8T(e)(8) applies.

* * * * *

Example 5A * * *

(ii) * * * If Y sold substantially all of its assets (within the meaning of section 368(a)(1)(C)), the gain recognition agreement would be terminated because U owned an amount of stock in Y described in section 1504(a)(2) immediately before the transaction and Y is a domestic corporation. See §1.367(a)–8T(g)(2). In addition, if F disposed of the stock of S in a taxable transaction the gain recognition agreement would be terminated if the principles of §1.367(a)–8T(g)(1)(i)(A) and (B) are satisfied.

* * * * *

Example 7. * * *

(ii) * * * The disposition by R, the transferred corporation, of substantially all of its assets would terminate the gain recognition agreement if the assets were disposed of in a taxable transaction because V owned an amount of stock in Z described in section 1504(a)(2) immediately before the transaction, and R is a domestic corporation. See §1.367(a)–8T(g)(2). Because the assets were transferred in an exchange to which section 351 applies, such transfer does not trigger the gain recognition agreement if V complies with the requirements contained in §1.367(a)–8T(e)(1)(iii). * * *

Example 7A. * * *

(ii) * * * Thus, the gain recognition agreement would terminate because V owned an amount of stock in Z described in section 1504(a)(2) immediately before the transaction, and R is a domestic corporation. See §1.367(a)–8T(g)(2).* * *

* * * * *

Example 9. * * *

(ii) * * * To determine whether there is a triggering event under §1.367(a)–8T(d)(2), both the Business A assets in M and the Business B assets in R must be considered.

Example 10. Concurrent application of asset transfer and indirect stock transfer rules in section 368(a)(1)(A)/(a)(2)(D) reorganization—(i) Facts. * * *

* * * * *

Example 12. * * *

(ii) * * * E's transfer of its N stock could qualify for nonrecognition treatment if D satisfies the requirements in §1.367(a)–3T(e).* * *

* * * * *

(e) [Reserved]. For further guidance, see §1.367(a)–3T(e).

(f) [Reserved]. For further guidance, see §1.367(a)–3T(f).

* * * * *

(i) [Reserved].

* * * * *

Par. 4. Section 1.367(a)–3T is added to read as follows:

§1.367(a)–3T Treatment of transfers of stock or securities to foreign corporations (temporary).

(a) through (d) [Reserved]. For further guidance, see §1.367(a)–3(a) through (d).

(e) *Transfers by a domestic corporation to a foreign corporation in a section 361 exchange*—(1) *General rule.* Notwithstanding paragraphs (b) and (c) of this section, if the U.S. transferor is a domestic corporation that transfers stock or securities to a foreign corporation in a section 361 exchange that would otherwise be subject to section 367(a)(1) under paragraph (a) of this section, such transfer shall not be subject to section 367(a)(1) if—

(i) The conditions set forth in the second sentence of section 367(a)(5) and any regulations under that section have been satisfied, such that, for example, the U.S. transferor is controlled (within the meaning of section 368(c)) by 5 or fewer domestic corporations and appropriate basis adjustments are made;

(ii) In the case of transferred property that is stock or securities of a domestic corporation, the conditions set forth in paragraph (c) of this section are satisfied;

(iii) All domestic corporate shareholders of the U.S. transferor immediately before the transaction that own 5 percent or more (applying the attribution rules of section 318, as modified by section 958(b)) of the total voting power or the total fair market value of the stock of the transferee foreign corporation immediately after the transaction enter into gain recognition agreements as provided in §1.367(a)–8T with respect to their *pro rata* share (determined by the relative fair market value of the U.S. transferor stock or securities owned) of the gain that was realized but not recognized on the transfer of the stock or securities of the transferred corporation that, in addition to the terms of §1.367(a)–8T(b), designate such domestic corporate shareholders as U.S. transferors for purposes of paragraphs (b) and (c) of this section and §1.367(a)–8T; and

(iv) All domestic corporate shareholders that enter into gain recognition agreements pursuant to paragraph (e)(1)(iii) of this section make the election described in §1.367(a)–8T(b)(1)(vii).

(2) *Certain triangular asset reorganizations*. If a transaction described in paragraph (e)(1) of this section qualifies as a triangular asset reorganization described in §1.358–6(b)(2)(i) through (iii), or in sections 368(a)(1)(G) and (a)(2)(D), the principles of §1.367(a)–3(d)(2)(iv) shall apply with respect to any gain recognition agreements filed in connection with such transaction.

(3) *Example*. The provisions of paragraph (e)(1) of this section are illustrated in the following example:

Example. (i) *Facts*. US1 and US2, domestic corporations, own 60% and 40%, respectively, of the fair market value of UST, also a domestic corporation. US1 and US2 are not members of the same consolidated group and are unrelated. UST owns 100% of FC, a foreign corporation. In year 1, UST transfers 100% of the stock of FC to FA, a foreign corporation, in a reorganization described in section 368(a)(1)(A) after which US1 and US2 own 6% and 4%, respectively, of the stock of FA. At the time of the initial transfer, the section 1248 amount with respect to the FC stock is $0. The notice requirement under §1.367(b)–1(c) is satisfied. Section 7874 does not apply to FA's acquisition of the stock of FC. US1 and US2 satisfy the conditions set forth in the second sentence of section 367(a)(5), including making appropriate basis adjustments. Pursuant to paragraph (e)(1) of this section, US1 enters into a gain recognition agreement to recognize its *pro rata* share of the gain realized but not recognized on UST's transfer of the stock of FC to FA, designates itself as a U.S. transferor for purposes of paragraph (b) of this section and §1.367(a)–8T, and makes the election described in §1.367(a)–8T(b)(1)(vii). US2 does not enter into a gain recognition agreement with respect to its *pro rata* share of the gain realized but not recognized on UST's transfer of the stock of FC to FA because US2 owns less than 5 percent of the stock of FA. In year 4, FA sells 30% of the FC stock for cash.

(ii) *Result*. Because the requirements of paragraph (e)(1)(i) through (iv) of this section are satisfied, the transfer of the FC stock by UST to FA in the year 1 reorganization is not subject to section 367(a)(1). In addition, because FA partially disposes of the stock of FC in year 4, US1 must recognize 30% of its *pro rata* share of the gain realized but not recognized on the initial transfer of the FC stock to FA pursuant to §1.367(a)–8T(d)(1)(iii). The proportion of gain recognized by US1 is determined by reference to the relative fair market value of the UST stock owned by US1 at the time of the initial transfer. Thus, US1 must include 18% of the gain realized, but not recognized, on the initial transfer (the 30% of the transferred property that was disposed of multiplied by the amount of gain subject to the gain recognition agreement (corresponding to the 60% of the fair market value of UST stock that US1 held immediately before the initial transfer)), and pay any applicable interest.

(iii) *Alternate facts*. The facts are the same as in paragraph (i) of this *Example*, except that US1 and US2 are members of a consolidated group in which USP is the common parent. US2 is also a 5-percent transferee shareholder as a result of applying the attribution rules of section 318, as modified by section 958(b). The result is the same as in paragraph (ii) of this *Example*, except that under §1.367(a)–8T(a)(3)(i)(A) USP files gain recognition agreements on behalf of both US1 and US2. Thus, US1 and US2 must include in income in year 4 18% and 12%, respectively, of the gain realized, but not recognized, on the initial transfer (the 30% of the transferred property that was disposed of multiplied by the amount of gain subject to the gain recognition agreement (corresponding to the 60% and 40% of the fair market value of UST stock that US1 and US2, respectively, held immediately before the initial transfer)), and pay any applicable interest.

(f) *Effective date*—(1) *General rule*. The rules of this §1.367(a)–3T(e) apply to transfers of stock or securities occurring on or after March 7, 2007. However, these rules do not apply to transfers of stock or securities occurring on or after March 7, 2007, if such transfer was entered into pursuant to a written agreement which was (subject to customary conditions) binding before February 5, 2007, and at all times thereafter. Solely for purposes of this paragraph (f), a transfer described in the preceding sentence shall be deemed to be a transfer occurring before March 7, 2007. For matters covered in this section for periods before March 7, 2007 but on or after July 20, 1998, the rule of §1.367(a)–8(f)(2)(i) (see 26 CFR part 1, revised April 1, 2006) applies.

(2) *Transfers before effective date*—(i) *General rule*. Taxpayers may apply the rules of §1.367(a)–3T(e) to transfers before March 7, 2007 and after July 20, 1998, for all open taxable years ending on or after July 20, 1998. This paragraph (f)(2)(i) applies only to rules in §1.367(a)–3T(e) that were not already effective under the rules of §1.367(a)–8(f)(2)(i).

(ii) *Special filing rule*. This paragraph (f)(2)(ii) provides the time and manner in which taxpayers may apply paragraph (f)(2)(i) of this section. Notwithstanding the rules provided in §1.367(a)–8T(a)(2), all agreements, certifications, or other information related to the gain recognition agreement that should have been filed on or before March 7, 2007 with respect to a transfer shall be treated as having been timely filed, provided they are attached to a Federal income tax return amending the taxpayer's Federal income tax return for the taxable year in which they should have been attached. The amended return described in the preceding sentence must be filed before August 6, 2007. A taxpayer that wishes to apply paragraph (f)(2)(i) of this section but that fails to meet the filing requirement described in the preceding sentence must request reasonable cause relief as provided in §1.367(a)–8T(e)(10).

(3) *Expiration*. The applicability of this section expires on or before February 1, 2010.

* * * * *

Par. 5. Section 1.367(a)–8 is amended by revising paragraphs (a) through (i) to read as follows:

§1.367(a)–8 Gain recognition agreement requirements.

(a) through (i) [Reserved]. For further guidance, see §1.367(a)–8T(a) through (h).

Par. 6. Section 1.367(a)–8T is added to read as follows:

§1.367(a)–8T Gain recognition agreement requirements (temporary).

(a) *In general.* This section specifies the terms and conditions for an agreement to recognize gain entered into pursuant to §§1.367(a)–3(b) through (d) and 1.367(a)–3T(e) to qualify for nonrecognition treatment under section 367(a).

(1) *Definitions.* The following definitions apply for purposes of this section:

(i) *Asset reorganization.* Except as otherwise provided in this paragraph (a)(1)(i), the term *asset reorganization* means a reorganization described in section 368(a)(1) involving the transfer of assets by a corporation to another corporation pursuant to section 361, except that such term shall include reorganizations described in section 368(a)(1)(D) or (G) only if the requirements of section 354(b)(1)(A) and (B) are met. For purposes of paragraphs (e)(3)(ii) and (e)(3)(iii) of this section, the following reorganizations are excluded from the term "asset reorganization":

(A) Triangular asset reorganizations described in §1.358–6(b)(2)(i) through (iii) or in sections 368(a)(1)(G) and (a)(2)(D). For rules applicable to triangular asset reorganizations described in §1.358–6(b)(2)(i) through (iii) or in sections 368(a)(1)(G) and (a)(2)(D), see paragraph (e)(4) of this section.

(B) Asset reorganizations where, after the reorganization, the same corporation is both the transferee foreign corporation (or successor transferee foreign corporation, as applicable) and the transferred corporation (or the successor transferred corporation, as applicable); for example, the acquisition of the transferee foreign corporation's assets by the transferred corporation in a reorganization described in section 368(a)(1). For rules applicable to certain upstream and downstream reorganizations involving the transferee foreign corporation and transferred corporation, see paragraphs (e)(6) and (g)(3) of this section.

(ii) The term *common parent* means a corporation that controls an affiliated group of corporations that files its Federal income tax returns on a consolidated basis.

(iii) The term *consolidated group* has the meaning set forth in §1.1502–1(h).

(iv) The term *disposition* means any transfer that would constitute a disposition for any purpose of the Internal Revenue Code and the regulations thereunder. It also includes an indirect disposition of the stock of the transferred corporation as described in §1.367(a)–3(d). It does not, however, include a redemption of stock under section 302(d) to the extent the redemption is treated as a distribution to which section 301(c)(1) applies.

(v) The term *gain recognition agreement* means an agreement described in paragraph (b) of this section.

(vi) The term *initial transfer* means a transfer in connection with which a gain recognition agreement is filed in connection with an exchange described in §§1.367(a)–3(b) through (d) and 1.367(a)–3T(e).

(vii) The term *nonrecognition transaction* means any disposition of property in a transaction in which gain or loss is not recognized in whole or in part for purposes of subtitle A.

(viii) The term *transferee foreign corporation* means the foreign corporation the stock of which is received in an exchange described in section 367(a) by a U.S. transferor.

(ix) *Transferred corporation.* Other than in the case of an indirect stock transfer, the term *transferred corporation* means the corporation the stock or securities of which are transferred by a U.S. transferor to a foreign corporation in an exchange described in section 367(a)(1). In the case of an indirect stock transfer, the term *transferred corporation* has the meaning set forth in §1.367(a)–3(d)(2)(ii).

(x) The term *triggering event* means an event described in paragraph (d) of this section, except as provided in paragraphs (e) (exceptions to triggering events) and (g) (terminations of gain recognition agreements) of this section.

(xi) The term *U.S. transferor* means a U.S. person (as defined in §1.367(a)–1T(d)(1)) that transfers stock or securities of the transferred corporation in exchange for stock or securities of the transferee foreign corporation in an exchange described in section 367(a). For the application of the rules of this section to indirect transfers involving partnerships and interests therein, see §1.367(a)–1T(c)(3).

(2) *Filing requirements for gain recognition agreements.* A U.S. transferor's gain recognition agreement must be attached to, and filed by the due date (including extensions) of, the U.S. transferor's income tax return for the taxable year that includes the date of the initial transfer, except that if the U.S. transferor is a member of a consolidated group for the taxable year in which the transfer was made, the agreement must be attached to the consolidated group's tax return. If a new gain recognition agreement is entered into pursuant to an exception in paragraph (e) of this section, the agreement must be attached to, and filed by the due date (including extensions) of, the applicable income tax return for the taxable year that includes the date of the triggering event. If the timeliness requirement of this paragraph (a)(2) is not satisfied, see paragraph (e)(10) of this section.

(3) *Who must sign*—(i) *General rule.* The gain recognition agreement must be signed under penalties of perjury by the appropriate party corresponding to the following categories of U.S. transferor. A gain recognition agreement may also be signed by an agent authorized to do so under a general or specific power of attorney.

(A) In the case of a corporate U.S. transferor, a responsible officer, except that if the U.S. transferor (or successor U.S. transferor designated in a new gain recognition agreement entered into under paragraph (e) of this section) is a member, but not the common parent of a consolidated group for the taxable year in which the transfer was made (or for the taxable year in which a new gain recognition agreement is entered into under paragraph (e) of this section) the agreement must be entered into by the common parent and signed by a responsible officer of such common parent.

(B) In the case of an individual U.S. transferor (including a partner who is treated as a U.S. transferor by virtue of §1.367(a)–1T(c)(3)), the individual.

(C) In the case of a trust or estate, a trustee, executor, or equivalent fiduciary.

(D) In the case of a bankruptcy case under Title 11, United States Code, a debtor in possession or trustee.

(ii) *Signature requirement.* When a gain recognition agreement, certification, or other information is required under this section to be attached to and filed by the due date (including extensions) of a U.S. Federal income tax return and signed under penalties of perjury by the person who signs the return, the attachment and filing of an unsigned copy is considered to satisfy such requirement, provided the taxpayer retains the original in its records in the manner specified by §1.6001–1(e).

(b) *Gain recognition agreement*—(1) *Contents*. The gain recognition agreement must set forth the following information, with the heading "GAIN RECOGNITION AGREEMENT UNDER §1.367(a)–8T" and with paragraphs labeled to correspond with the numbers set forth as follows:

(i) A statement that the document submitted constitutes the U.S. transferor's agreement to recognize gain in accordance with the requirements of this section.

(ii) A description of the property transferred as described in paragraph (b)(2) of this section.

(iii) The U.S. transferor's agreement to recognize gain, as described in paragraph (b)(3) of this section.

(iv) A waiver of the period of limitations as described in paragraph (b)(4) of this section.

(v) An agreement to file with the U.S. transferor's tax returns for the five full taxable years following the year of the initial transfer a certification as described in paragraph (b)(5) of this section.

(vi) A statement that arrangements have been made in connection with the transferred property to ensure that the U.S. transferor will be informed of any triggering events.

(vii) A statement as to whether, if all or a portion of the gain recognition agreement is triggered under paragraph (d) of this section, the taxpayer elects to include the required amount in the year of the triggering event rather than in the year of the initial transfer.

(2) *Description of property transferred*. (i) The agreement shall include a description of each property transferred by the U.S. transferor, an estimate of the fair market value of the property as of the date of the initial transfer, a statement of the cost or other basis of the property and any adjustments thereto, and the date on which the property was acquired by the U.S. transferor.

(ii) The U.S. transferor must provide the following information:

(A) The type or class, amount, and characteristics of the stock or securities transferred, as well as the name, address, and place of incorporation of the issuer of the stock or securities, and the percentage (by voting power and value) that the stock (if any) represents of the total stock outstanding of the transferred corporation.

(B) The name, address and place of incorporation of the transferee foreign corporation, and the percentage of stock (by voting power and value) that the U.S. transferor received or will receive in the transaction.

(C) If stock or securities are transferred pursuant to §1.367(a)–3T(e), a statement that the conditions set forth in the second sentence of section 367(a)(5) and any regulations under that section have been satisfied, and an explanation of any basis or other adjustments made pursuant to section 367(a)(5) and any regulations under that paragraph.

(D) If the transferred corporation is a domestic corporation, the taxpayer identification number of the transferred corporation, together with a statement describing whether, and if so, how, section 7874 applies to the transfer, and a statement that all of the requirements of §1.367(a)–3(c)(1) are satisfied.

(E) If the transferred corporation is a foreign corporation, a statement as to whether the U.S. transferor was a section 1248 shareholder, as defined in §1.367(b)–2(b), of the transferred corporation immediately before the exchange, and, if so, a statement as to whether the U.S. transferor is a section 1248 shareholder with respect to the transferee foreign corporation stock received, and whether any reporting requirements or other rules contained in regulations under section 367(b) are applicable, and, if so, whether they have been satisfied.

(F) If the transaction involved the transfer of assets other than stock or securities and the transaction was subject to the indirect stock transfer rules of §1.367(a)–3(d), a statement as to whether the reporting requirements under section 6038B have been satisfied with respect to the transfer of property other than stock or securities, and an explanation of whether gain was recognized under section 367(a)(1) and whether section 367(d) was applicable to the transfer of such assets, or whether any tangible assets qualified for nonrecognition treatment under section 367(a)(3) (as limited by section 367(a)(5) and §§1.367(a)–4T through 1.367(a)–6T).

(3) *Terms of agreement*—(i) *General rule*. If before the close of the fifth full taxable year (not less than 60 months) following the close of the taxable year of the initial transfer, there is a triggering event, then, unless an election is made under paragraph (b)(1)(vii) of this section, by the 90th day thereafter the U.S. transferor must file an amended Federal income tax return for the year of the initial transfer and recognize thereon the gain realized, but not recognized, upon the initial transfer, with interest. If an election under paragraph (b)(1)(vii) of this section was made, then, if a triggering event occurs, the U.S. transferor must include the gain realized, but not recognized, on the initial transfer in income on its Federal income tax return for the taxable year that includes the date of the triggering event. In accordance with paragraph (b)(3)(iii) of this section, interest must be paid on any additional tax due. If a taxpayer properly makes the election under paragraph (b)(1)(vii) of this section but later fails to include in income the gain realized, but not recognized, on the initial transfer, the Commissioner may, in his discretion, include the gain in the taxpayer's income in the year of the initial transfer.

(ii) *Offsets*. No special limitations apply with respect to net operating losses, capital losses, credits against tax, or similar items.

(iii) *Reporting of interest and gain*. If additional tax is required to be paid pursuant to paragraph (b)(3)(i) of this section, then interest must be paid on that amount at the rates determined under section 6621 with respect to the period between the date that was prescribed for filing the U.S. transferor's Federal income tax return for the year of the initial transfer and the date on which the additional tax for that year is paid. If the election in paragraph (b)(1)(vii) of this section is made, a taxpayer should include the amount of gain as taxable income on its Federal income tax return (together with other income or loss items) and include the amount of interest in its payment (or reduce the amount of any refund due by the amount of the interest). A taxpayer must also attach to its Federal income tax return a separate schedule with the heading "Calculation of Section 367 Tax and Interest," on which the amount of tax attributable to the gain and the interest required to be paid under this section are separately identified and calculated.

(iv) *Basis adjustments*—(A) *Transferee foreign corporation.* If a U.S. transferor is required to recognize gain under this section as a result of a triggering event, then the transferee foreign corporation's basis in the transferred stock or securities shall be increased (as of the date of the initial transfer) by the amount of gain required to be recognized (but not by any tax or interest required to be paid on such amount) by the U.S. transferor.

(B) *U.S. transferor.* If a U.S. transferor is required to recognize gain as a result of a triggering event, then the U.S. transferor's basis in the stock of the transferee foreign corporation received (or deemed received) in the initial transfer shall be increased by the amount of gain required to be recognized (as of the date of the initial transfer) (but not by any tax or interest required to be paid on such amount).

(C) *Other adjustments.* Other appropriate adjustments to basis that are consistent with the principles of this paragraph (b)(3)(iv) may be made if the U.S. transferor is required to recognize gain under this section. In no case, however, shall the transferred corporation's net asset basis be increased as a result of the U.S. transferor recognizing gain under this section as a result of a triggering event.

(D) *Example.* The principles of this paragraph (b)(3) are illustrated by the following example:

Example. (i) *Facts.* D, a domestic corporation owning 100 percent of the stock of S, a foreign corporation, transfers all of the S stock to F, a foreign corporation, in an exchange described in section 368(a)(1)(B). The section 1248 amount with respect to the S stock at the time of the transfer is $0. In the exchange, D receives 20 percent of the voting stock of F. The transaction is subject to both sections 367(a) and (b). See §§1.367(a)–3(b) and 1.367(b)–1(a). All of the requirements of §1.367(a)–3(b)(1) are satisfied, and D enters into a gain recognition agreement to qualify for nonrecognition treatment and does not make the election contained in paragraph (b)(1)(vii) of this section. Two years after the initial transfer, F transfers all of the S stock to F1, a foreign corporation, in an exchange to which section 351 applies, and D complies with the requirements of paragraph (e)(1)(ii) of this section. Four years after the initial transfer, D transfers its entire 20 percent interest in F's voting stock to a domestic partnership in exchange for an interest in the partnership and complies with the requirements of paragraph (e)(1)(i) of this section. D complies with the notice requirement under §1.367(b)–1(c) for each transaction subject to section 367(b). Because D complies with the requirements of paragraph (e) for each transaction that would otherwise be a triggering event, D is not required to recognize the gain that was realized, but not recognized, on the initial transfer. Five years after the initial transfer, S disposes of substantially all (as described in paragraph (d)(2) of this section) of its assets, and D is required by the terms of the gain recognition agreement to recognize all the gain that it realized on the initial transfer of the stock of S.

(ii) *Result.* As a result of the triggering event and paragraph (b)(3)(iv) of this section, the amount of gain required to be recognized as a result of S's disposition of substantially all its assets (but not the tax or interest required to be paid on such amount) is reflected by an increased basis (as of the date of the initial transfer) in D's partnership interest, the partnership's interest in the 20 percent voting stock of F, F's stock of F1, and F1's stock of S. S, however, is not permitted to increase its basis in its assets for purposes of determining the direct or indirect U.S. tax results, if any, on the sale of its assets.

(4) *Waiver of period of limitation.* The U.S. transferor must file, with the gain recognition agreement, a waiver of the period of limitation on assessment of tax upon the gain realized on the initial transfer. The waiver shall be executed on Form 8838 "*Consent To Extend the Time To Assess Tax Under Section 367—Gain Recognition Agreement*" and shall extend the period for assessment of such tax to a date not earlier than the eighth full taxable year following the taxable year of the initial transfer. The waiver shall also contain such other terms with respect to assessment as may be considered necessary by the Commissioner to ensure the assessment and collection of the correct tax liability for each year for which the waiver is required. The waiver must be signed by a person who would be authorized to sign the agreement pursuant to the provisions of paragraph (a)(3) of this section.

(5) *Annual certification.* The U.S. transferor must file with its income tax return for each of the five full taxable years following the taxable year of the initial transfer a certification that there has not been a triggering event, and a description of any exception under paragraph (e) of this section if such an exception is relied upon for the position that there has not been a triggering event. The U.S. transferor must include with its annual certification a statement describing any dispositions of assets by the transferred corporation that are not made in the ordinary course of business. The annual certification pursuant to this paragraph (b)(5) must be signed by a person who would be authorized to sign the agreement pursuant to the provisions of paragraph (a)(3) of this section.

(c) *Use of security.* The U.S. transferor may be required to furnish a bond or other security that satisfies the requirements of §301.7101–1 of this chapter if the Area Director, Field Examination, Small Business/Self Employed or the Director of Field Operations, Large and Mid-Size Business (Director) determines that such security is necessary to ensure the payment of any tax on the gain realized, but not recognized, upon the initial transfer. Such bond or security generally will be required only if the stock or securities transferred are a principal asset of the U.S. transferor and the Director has reason to believe that a disposition of the stock or securities may be contemplated.

(d) *Triggering events.* If there is a triggering event described in this paragraph (d) during the term of the gain recognition agreement, the U.S. transferor must include in income the gain realized, but not recognized, upon the initial transfer as provided in paragraph (b)(3)(i) of this section. In addition, the U.S. transferor must pay any interest required by paragraph (b)(3)(iii) of this section. See §1.367(a)–3(d)(2)(iv) for additional triggering events when a gain recognition agreement has been filed in connection with an indirect stock transfer. Except to the extent provided in paragraphs (e) and (g) of this section, if any of the following events occur during the term of the gain recognition agreement, it shall constitute a triggering event:

(1) *Disposition of stock or securities of the transferred corporation*—(i) *In general.* A disposition, in whole or in part, by the transferee foreign corporation (or any other person) of the transferred stock or securities received by the transferee foreign corporation in the initial transfer. For purposes of this section, a reference to transferred stock or securities shall also include stock or securities of the transferred corporation the basis of which is determined (directly or indirectly) in whole or in part, by reference to the basis of the stock or securities transferred in the initial transfer. A disposition of all or a portion of the stock or securities of the transferred corporation by installment sale is treated as a disposition of the stock or securities in the year of the installment sale.

(ii) *Example.* The provisions of this paragraph (d)(1)(i) are illustrated by the following example:

Example. Interaction between trigger of gain recognition agreement and subpart F rules—(i) *Facts.* USP, a domestic corporation, owns all of the stock of two foreign corporations, CFC1 and CFC2. USP's section 1248 amount with respect to CFC2 is $30. USP has a basis of $50 in its stock of CFC2; the stock of CFC2 has a fair market value of $100. In a transaction described in sections 351 and 368(a)(1)(B), USP transfers the stock of CFC2 to CFC1 in exchange for additional stock of CFC1 with a basis of $50. The transaction is subject to both sections 367(a) and (b). See §§1.367(a)–3(b) and 1.367(b)–1(a). To qualify for nonrecognition treatment under section 367(a), USP enters into a gain recognition agreement for $50 under this section. No election under paragraph (b)(1)(vii) of this section is made. USP also complies with the notice requirement under §1.367(b)–1(c). Two years after the initial transfer, CFC1 sells the stock of CFC2 for $120. At the time of the sale, the section 1248 amount with respect to the CFC2 stock continues to be $30. The $70 of gain recognized on the sale of CFC2 stock would give rise to a $70 subpart F inclusion to USP under section 951(a)(1)(A).

(ii) *Result*—(A) *Trigger of gain recognition agreement with no election.* CFC1's sale of CFC2 stock is a triggering event. As a result, USP must amend its return for the year of the initial transfer and include $50 in income (as well as pay any applicable interest), $30 of which will be recharacterized as a dividend pursuant to section 1248. Under paragraph (b)(3)(iv) of this section, as of the date of the initial transfer, CFC1 has a basis of $100 in its CFC2 stock, and USP has a basis in its CFC1 stock of $100. As a result of the sale of CFC2 stock by CFC1, USP will have a $20 subpart F inclusion under section 951(a)(1)(A).

(B) *Trigger of gain recognition agreement with election.* Assume the same facts as in paragraph (i) of this *Example*, except that USP elected under paragraph (b)(1)(vii) of this section to include the amount of gain realized, but not recognized, on the initial transfer, $50, in the year of the triggering event rather than in the year of the initial transfer. The result is the same as above, except that USP will include the $50 of gain on its tax return for the year of the triggering event, together with interest. For purposes of determining the amount of the $50 gain characterized as a dividend pursuant to section 1248, if any, of the $50 inclusion, USP will take into account the section 1248 amount of CFC2 at the time of the disposition in the year of the triggering event.

(iii) *Partial dispositions.* If the transferee foreign corporation or any other person disposes of only a portion of the stock or securities of the transferred corporation, then the U.S. transferor is required to recognize only a proportionate amount of the gain realized, but not recognized, upon the initial transfer. The proportion required to be recognized shall be determined by reference to the fair market value of the transferred stock or securities disposed of and the total fair market value of the transferred stock or securities immediately before the disposition.

(2) *Disposition of substantially all of the transferred corporation's assets.* A disposition of substantially all of the transferred corporation's assets (including stock in a subsidiary corporation or an interest in a partnership) by the transferred corporation or any other person. Solely for purposes of this section, the term *substantially all* has the meaning provided under section 368(a)(1)(C). Accordingly, the determination of whether substantially all of the transferred corporation's assets have been disposed of shall be made under all the facts and circumstances. For purposes of this paragraph (d)(2), dispositions of stock in connection with an asset reorganization of a corporation all or a portion the stock of which is owned by the transferred corporation, or a liquidation of a corporation the stock of which is owned by the transferred corporation in an amount satisfying the requirements of section 1504(a)(2) and to which sections 332 and 337 apply, shall not be taken into account. If the initial transfer was an indirect stock transfer, see §1.367(a)–3(d)(2)(v). If the transferred corporation is a domestic corporation, see paragraph (g)(2) of this section. For an example of when a disposition of substantially all the transferred corporation's assets by a person other than the transferred corporation is a triggering event under this paragraph (d)(2), see paragraph (e)(6)(ii) of this section.

(3) *Disposition of the stock of the transferee foreign corporation*—(i) *General rule.* A disposition in whole or in part, by the U.S. transferor of the stock of the transferee foreign corporation that is received (or deemed received) in the initial transfer. For purposes of this section, a reference to stock described in the preceding sentence shall also include stock of the transferee foreign corporation the basis of which is determined, directly or indirectly, in whole or in part, by reference to the basis of the stock of the transferee foreign corporation that is received (or deemed received) in the initial transfer.

(ii) *Partial dispositions.* If the U.S. transferor disposes of only a portion of the stock of the transferee foreign corporation that is received (or deemed received) in the initial transfer, then the U.S. transferor is required to recognize only a proportionate amount of the gain realized, but not recognized, upon the initial transfer. The proportion required to be recognized shall be determined by reference to the fair market value of the transferee foreign corporation stock disposed of and the total fair market value of the transferee foreign corporation stock immediately before the disposition.

(4) *Deconsolidation.* A U.S. transferor that is a member of a consolidated group ceases to be a member of the consolidated group, other than by reason of an acquisition of the assets of the U.S. transferor in a transaction to which section 381(a) applies, or by reason of joining a new consolidated group as part of the same transaction. However, in the case of a transaction to which section 381(a) applies, see paragraph (d)(3) of this section (providing that a triggering event includes a disposition of the stock of the transferee foreign corporation).

(5) *Consolidation.* A U.S. transferor becomes a member of a consolidated group.

(6) *Individual U.S. transferor becomes a non-citizen nonresident.* A U.S. transferor that is an individual loses U.S. citizenship, or a U.S. transferor that is a long-term resident ceases to be taxed as a lawful permanent resident (as defined in section 877(e)(2)). Immediately before the date that the U.S. transferor loses U.S. citizenship or ceases to be taxed as a long-term resident, the gain recognition agreement will be triggered. No additional inclusion is required under section 877 with respect to the transferred stock or securities, and a gain recognition agreement under section 877 may not be used to avoid taxation under section 367(a) resulting from the trigger of the section 367(a) gain recognition agreement.

(7) *Death of an individual; trust or estate goes out of existence.* An individual U.S. transferor dies, or a U.S. transferor that is a trust or estate goes out of existence.

(8) *Failure to comply.* The failure to comply in any material respect with the requirements of this section or with the terms of a gain recognition agreement (for example, a failure to file an annual certification or Form 8838). Such a material failure to comply shall extend the period for assessment of tax until three years after the date on which the Director of Field Operations or Area Director receives actual notice of the failure to comply.

(e) *Exceptions.* Notwithstanding paragraph (d) of this section, the following events shall not constitute triggering events:

(1) *Certain nonrecognition transactions*—(i) *Dispositions of stock of the transferee foreign corporation by the U.S. transferor*—(A) *Transfers to a corporation or partnership.* Except to the extent provided in paragraph (g)(1)(iv) of this section, a disposition of stock of the transferee foreign corporation by the U.S. transferor in an exchange to which section 351, 354 (but only in a reorganization described in section 368(a)(1)(B)), or 721 applies, will not be a triggering event under paragraph (d)(3) of this section, and the original gain recognition agreement shall terminate without further effect, if the U.S. transferor complies with requirements similar to those contained in paragraph (e)(1)(ii) of this section, providing for notice and an agreement to recognize gain in the case of a direct or indirect disposition of the stock previously held by the U.S. transferor. See paragraph (e)(3)(i) of this section for dispositions of the transferee foreign corporation stock in certain asset reorganizations.

(B) *Liquidations of the U.S. transferor under sections 332 and 337.* The disposition of the transferee foreign corporation stock pursuant to a liquidation of the U.S. transferor under sections 332 and 337 will not be a triggering event under paragraph (d)(3) of this section, and the original gain recognition agreement shall terminate without further effect, if the following conditions are satisfied:

(*1*) The distributee is a domestic corporation described in section 332(b)(1).

(*2*) The domestic distributee corporation (successor U.S. transferor) enters into a new gain recognition agreement pursuant to which it agrees to recognize gain (during the remaining term of the original gain recognition agreement), with respect to the initial transfer, modified by substituting the successor U.S. transferor in place of the original U.S. transferor, and agreeing to treat the successor U.S. transferor as the original U.S. transferor for purposes of this section. If, however, in connection with a liquidation described in section 332, the U.S. transferor recognizes gain under section 336 with respect to a portion of the stock of the transferee foreign corporation, and the conditions described in paragraph (g)(1) of this section are satisfied, the new gain recognition agreement that the successor U.S. transferor enters into shall reflect the gain realized, but not recognized, on the initial transfer (subject to adjustment for prior partial dispositions) less that proportion corresponding to gain recognized under section 336. The proportion is determined by reference to the relative fair market values of the transferee foreign corporation stock received (or deemed received) in the initial transfer on which the U.S. transferor recognized gain under section 336 and the total fair market value of the transferee foreign corporation stock received (or deemed received) by the U.S. transferor in the initial transfer that is distributed by the U.S. transferor in the liquidation.

(*3*) The successor U.S. transferor makes the election described in paragraph (b)(1)(vii) of this section. However, if the U.S. transferor was a member of a consolidated group in the year of the initial transfer, and the successor U.S. transferor is also a member of the original consolidated group immediately after the liquidation, no such election must be made.

(*4*) The successor U.S. transferor provides with its next annual certification (described in paragraph (b)(5) of this section) the new gain recognition agreement, a notice of the liquidation, and Form 8838 to extend the period for assessment of the tax on the initial transfer to a date not earlier than the eighth full taxable year following the taxable year of the initial transfer.

(ii) *Transfers of stock or securities of the transferred corporation by the transferee foreign corporation to a corporation or partnership.* Except to the extent provided in paragraph (f)(1)(i) of this section, a disposition of stock or securities of the transferred corporation by the transferee foreign corporation in an exchange to which section 351, 354 (but only in a reorganization described in section 368(a)(1)(B)), or 721 applies, will not be a triggering event described in paragraph (d)(1) of this section, and the original gain recognition agreement shall terminate without further effect, if the following conditions are satisfied:

(A) The transferee foreign corporation receives (or is deemed to receive) in exchange for the property disposed of, stock in a corporation, or an interest in a partnership, that acquired the transferred stock or securities (or receives stock in a corporation that controls the corporation acquiring the transferred stock or securities in the case of a triangular section 368(a)(1)(B) reorganization).

(B) The U.S. transferor provides a notice of the transfer with its next annual certification under paragraph (b)(5) of this section, setting forth—

(*1*) A full description of the transfer;

(*2*) The applicable nonrecognition provision; and

(*3*) The name, address, and taxpayer identification number (if any) of the new transferee of the transferred stock or securities.

(C) The U.S. transferor provides with its next annual certification a new gain recognition agreement pursuant to which it agrees to recognize gain (during the remaining term of the original gain recognition agreement) with respect to the initial transfer, and in which it agrees that any of the following events also constitutes a triggering event:

(*1*) A disposition of the stock or securities or partnership interest that the transferee foreign corporation received in exchange for the transferred stock or securities (other than in a disposition which itself qualifies under the rules of paragraph (e) of this section).

(*2*) The corporation or partnership that acquired the transferred stock or securities disposes of such property (other than in a disposition which itself qualifies under the rules of paragraph (e) of this section).

(*3*) Any other disposition that has the effect of an indirect disposition of the transferred stock or securities.

(iii) *Transfers of the transferred corporation's assets to a corporation or partnership.* Except to the extent provided in paragraph (f)(1)(ii) of this section, a disposition of substantially all of the transferred corporation's assets by the transferred corporation in an exchange to which section 351, 354 (but only in a reorganization described in section 368(a)(1)(B)—for example, where stock in a subsidiary corporation comprises substantially all of the transferred corporation's assets), or 721 applies, will not be a triggering event under paragraph (d)(2) of this section, and the original gain recognition agreement shall terminate without further effect, if the transferred corporation receives (or is deemed to receive) in exchange for all or a portion of its assets stock in a corporation or an interest in a partnership that acquired the assets of the transferred corporation (or receives stock in a corporation that controls the corporation acquiring the assets) and the U.S. transferor complies with requirements similar to those contained in paragraph (e)(1)(ii) of this section, (providing for notice and an agreement to recognize gain in the case of a direct or indirect disposition of the assets previously held by the transferred corporation). See paragraph (e)(3)(iii) of this section for dispositions of substantially all of the transferred corporation's assets in certain asset reorganizations.

(2) *Recapitalizations*—(i) *Transferred corporation.* Except to the extent provided in paragraph (f)(1) of this section, a transaction described in section 368(a)(1)(E) of the transferred corporation will not be a triggering event under paragraph (d)(1) of this section. The description of this exception that is required to be filed with the annual certification under paragraph (b)(5) of this section must include a description of the type or class, amount, and characteristics of the stock or securities that the transferred corporation issued in the reorganization.

(ii) *Transferee foreign corporation.* A section 368(a)(1)(E) reorganization of the transferee foreign corporation will not be a triggering event under paragraph (d)(3) of this section. The description of this exception that is required to be filed with the annual certification under paragraph (b)(5) of this section must include a description of the type or class, amount, and characteristics of the stock or securities that the transferee foreign corporation issued in the reorganization. See paragraph (g)(1) of this section for rules regarding the recognition of gain by the U.S. transferor in connection with nonrecognition exchanges.

(3) *Certain asset reorganizations*—(i) *Transfers of transferee foreign corporation's stock by U.S. transferor.* Except to the extent provided in paragraph (g)(1)(iv) of this section, if the U.S. transferor transfers all or a portion of the stock of the transferee foreign corporation to a domestic acquiring corporation (successor U.S. transferor) pursuant to an asset reorganization, the exchanges made pursuant to such asset reorganization will not be triggering events described in paragraph (d)(3) of this section, and the original gain recognition agreement shall terminate without further effect, if the following conditions are satisfied:

(A) The common parent of the original consolidated group, successor U.S. transferor, or new common parent, as applicable, enters into a new gain recognition agreement pursuant to which the successor U.S. transferor agrees to recognize gain (during the remaining term of the original gain recognition agreement) with respect to the initial transfer, modified by substituting the successor U.S. transferor in place of the original U.S. transferor and agreeing to treat the successor U.S. transferor as the original U.S. transferor for purposes of this section.

(B) The successor U.S. transferor or new common parent, as applicable, makes the election described in paragraph (b)(1)(vii) of this section. However, if the U.S. transferor was a member of a consolidated group in the year of the initial transfer, and the successor U.S. transferor is also a member of the original consolidated group immediately after the asset reorganization, no such election must be made.

(C) The successor U.S. transferor provides with its next annual certification (described in paragraph (b)(5) of this section)—

(*1*) The new gain recognition agreement;

(*2*) A notice of the transfer setting forth a full description of the transfer (including the date of such transfer), and the successor U.S. transferor's name, address, and taxpayer identification number; and

(*3*) Form 8838 to extend the period for assessment of the tax on the initial transfer to a date not earlier than the eighth full taxable year following the taxable year of the initial transfer.

(ii) *Transfers of transferred corporation stock or securities by transferee foreign corporation to a foreign acquiring corporation.* Except to the extent provided in paragraph (f)(1) of this section, if the transferee foreign corporation transfers all or a portion of the stock or securities of the transferred corporation to a foreign acquiring corporation (successor transferee foreign corporation) in an asset reorganization, the exchanges made pursuant to such reorganization will not be triggering events described in paragraph (d)(1) or (d)(3) of this section, and the original gain recognition agreement shall terminate without further effect, if the following conditions are satisfied:

(A) The U.S. transferor or common parent, as applicable, enters into a new gain recognition agreement pursuant to which the U.S. transferor agrees to recognize gain (during the remaining term of the original gain recognition agreement), with respect to the initial transfer, substituting the successor transferee foreign corporation in place of the original transferee foreign corporation, and agreeing to treat the successor transferee foreign corporation as the original transferee foreign corporation for purposes of this section.

(B) The U.S. transferor provides with its next annual certification (described in paragraph (b)(5) of this section) the new gain recognition agreement and a notice of the transfer setting forth a full description of the transfer (including the date of such transfer), and the successor transferee foreign corporation's name, address, and taxpayer identification number (if any).

(iii) *Transfers of substantially all of the transferred corporation's assets.* Except to the extent provided in paragraph (f)(2) of this section, if the transferred corporation transfers substantially all of its assets to an acquiring corporation (successor transferred corporation) pursuant to an asset reorganization, the exchanges made pursuant to such asset reorganization will not be triggering events under paragraph (d)(1) or (d)(2) of this section, and the original gain recognition agreement shall terminate without further effect, if the following conditions are satisfied:

(A) The U.S. transferor or common parent, as applicable, enters into a new gain recognition agreement pursuant to which the U.S. transferor agrees to recognize gain (during the remaining term of the original gain recognition agreement), with respect to the initial transfer, modified by—

(*1*) Substituting the successor transferred corporation in place of the original transferred corporation and agreeing to treat the successor transferred corporation as the original transferred corporation for purposes of this section; and

(*2*) Treating only the assets acquired by the successor transferred corporation from the original transferred corporation pursuant to the asset reorganization as the assets subject to the triggering event rules under paragraph (d)(2) of this section.

(B) The U.S. transferor provides with its next annual certification (described in paragraph (b)(5) of this section) the new gain recognition agreement and a notice of the transfer setting forth a full description of the transfer (including the date of such transfer), and the successor transferred corporation's name, address, and taxpayer identification number (if any).

(iv) *Example*. The rules of paragraph (e)(3) of this section are illustrated by the following examples:

Example 1. (i) *Facts*. UST, a domestic corporation incorporated under the laws of State A, owns 100% of the stock of TFD, a foreign corporation. In year 1, UST transfers all of the TFD stock to TFC, a foreign corporation, in an exchange to which section 351 applies. In the exchange, UST receives 100% of the stock of TFC. The transaction is subject to both sections 367(a) and (b). See §§1.367(a)–3(b) and 1.367(b)–1(a). All of the requirements of §1.367(a)–3(b)(1) are satisfied, and UST enters into a gain recognition agreement. UST also complies with the notice requirement under §1.367(b)–1(c). In year 3, UST transfers its assets in a section 361(a) exchange to USA, a newly formed domestic corporation incorporated under the laws of State B, in exchange for stock of USA, and UST distributes such stock to its shareholders in a transaction described in section 368(a)(1)(F).

(ii) *Result*. The transfer of the TFC stock by UST to USA pursuant to the section 368(a)(1)(F) reorganization is a triggering event under paragraph (d)(3) of this section. If, however, UST complies with the requirements contained in paragraph (e)(3)(i) of this section, the transfer will not be a triggering event.

(iii) *Alternate facts*. The facts are the same as in paragraph (i) of this *Example 1*, except that the acquiring corporation is foreign instead of domestic. Because paragraph (e)(3)(i) of this section provides an exception to a triggering event under paragraph (d)(3) of this section only if the acquiring corporation in the asset reorganization is a domestic corporation, the section 368(a)(1)(F) reorganization is a triggering event without exception. See also section 367(a)(5) and §§1.367(a)–1T(f) and 1.367(a)–3T(e) (providing that certain corporate shareholders of a U.S. transferor may enter into a gain recognition agreement when the U.S. transferor goes out of existence in a section 361 initial transfer).

Example 2. (i) *Facts*. UST, a domestic corporation, owns 100% of the stock of three foreign corporations, FC1, FC2 and FC3. In year 1, USP transfers 100% of the stock of FC1 to FC2 in an exchange to which section 351 applies. The transaction is subject to both sections 367(a) and (b). See §§1.367(a)–3(b) and 1.367(b)–1(a). All of the requirements of §1.367(a)–3(b)(1) are satisfied, and UST enters into a gain recognition agreement. UST also complies with the notice requirement under §1.367(b)–1(c). In year 4, in a reorganization described in section 368(a)(1)(D), FC2 transfers all of its assets, including the stock of FC1, to FC3 in exchange for FC3 stock. FC2 transfers the FC3 stock to UST in exchange for FC2 stock held by UST, and the FC2 stock is canceled.

(ii) *Analysis*. The transfer of FC1 stock to FC3 and the exchange of FC2 stock for FC3 stock by UST pursuant to the reorganization described in section 368(a)(1)(D) are triggering events under paragraphs (d)(1) and (d)(3) of this section. If, however, UST complies with the requirements contained in paragraph (e)(3)(ii) of this section, the transfers will not be triggering events.

Example 3. (i) *Facts*. UST, a domestic corporation, owns 100% of the stock of two foreign corporations, FC1 and FC2. In year 1, UST transfers 100% of the stock of FC1 to FC2 in an exchange to which section 351 applies. The transaction is subject to both sections 367(a) and (b). See §§1.367(a)–3(b) and 1.367(b)–1(a). All of the requirements of §1.367(a)–3(b)(1) are satisfied, and UST enters into a gain recognition agreement. UST also complies with the notice requirement under §1.367(b)–1(c). In year 4, in a reorganization described in section 368(a)(1)(C), FC1 transfers all of its assets to FC3, an unrelated foreign corporation, in exchange for FC3 stock. FC1 transfers the FC3 stock to FC2 in exchange for the FC1 stock held by FC2 and the FC1 stock is canceled.

(ii) *Analysis*. FC1's transfer of all of its assets to FC3 and FC2's exchange of FC1 stock for FC3 stock pursuant to the reorganization described in section 368(a)(1)(C) are triggering events under paragraphs (d)(2) and (d)(1) of this section, respectively. If, however, UST complies with the requirements contained in paragraph (e)(3)(iii) of this section, the transfers will not be triggering events.

(4) *Certain triangular reorganizations*—(i) *Triangular asset reorganizations of the transferee foreign corporation*. For purposes of this paragraph (e)(4), the term *triangular asset reorganization* means a triangular reorganization described in §1.358–6(b)(2)(i) through (iii) or in sections 368(a)(1)(G) and (a)(2)(D) where the acquiring subsidiary is foreign. Except to the extent provided in paragraph (f)(1) or (g)(1)(iv) of this section, the exchanges made pursuant to a triangular asset reorganization of the transferee foreign corporation will not be triggering events under paragraph (d)(1) or (d)(3) of this section, and the original gain recognition agreement shall terminate without further effect, if the following conditions are satisfied:

(A) The U.S. transferor or common parent, as applicable, enters into a new gain recognition agreement pursuant to which the U.S. transferor agrees to recognize gain (during the remaining term of the original gain recognition agreement), with respect to the initial transfer, and in which the U.S. transferor agrees to—

(*1*) If the parent corporation of the foreign acquiring subsidiary is foreign, treat such foreign parent as the original transferee foreign corporation for purposes of this section and treat as a triggering event a disposition of the stock of the foreign acquiring subsidiary, or, in the case of a reorganization described in section 368(a)(2)(E), the corporation originally identified as the transferee foreign corporation; and

(*2*) If the parent corporation of the foreign acquiring subsidiary is domestic, treat the foreign acquiring subsidiary as the original transferee foreign corporation for purposes of this section, and apply the principles of paragraph (g) of this section to taxable dispositions by the domestic parent corporation of the foreign acquiring subsidiary or, in the case of a reorganization described in section 368(a)(2)(E), the corporation originally identified as the transferee foreign corporation. In the case of a reorganization described in section 368(a)(2)(E) where the transferee foreign corporation is the merged corporation, rather than the surviving corporation, then the surviving corporation shall be treated as the transferee foreign corporation for purposes of this section.

(B) The U.S. transferor provides with its next annual certification (described in paragraph (b)(5) of this section) the new gain recognition agreement and a notice of the transfer setting forth a full description of the transfer (including the date of such transfer) and the name, address, and taxpayer identification number (if any) for the parent corporation of the foreign acquiring subsidiary.

(ii) *Triangular asset reorganizations of the transferred corporation*. Except to the extent provided in paragraph (f)(1) or (f)(2) of this section, the exchanges made pursuant to a triangular asset reorganization of the transferred corporation will not be triggering events in paragraph (d)(1) or (d)(2) of this section, and the original gain recognition agreement shall terminate without further effect, if the following conditions are satisfied:

(A) The U.S. transferor or common parent, as applicable, enters into a new gain recognition agreement pursuant to which the U.S. transferor agrees to recognize gain (during the remaining term of the original gain recognition agreement), in accordance with the rules of paragraph (b) of this section, with respect to the initial transfer, and in which the U.S. transferor agrees to—

(*1*) Treat a disposition of the stock of the acquiring parent as a triggering event;

(*2*) If the reorganization is a triangular C reorganization or a reorganization described in section 368(a)(2)(D), treat a disposition of the stock of the foreign acquiring subsidiary as a triggering event; and

(*3*) If the reorganization is described in section 368(a)(2)(E) and the merged corporation is the transferred corporation, treat a disposition of the stock of the surviving corporation as a triggering event.

(B) The U.S. transferor provides with its next annual certification (described in paragraph (b)(5) of this section) the new gain recognition agreement and a notice of the transfer setting forth a full description of the transfer (including the date of such transfer) and the name, address, and taxpayer identification number (if any) for the parent corporation of the foreign acquiring subsidiary.

(5) *Compulsory transfers*. A compulsory transfer under §1.367(a)–4T(f)(2) that is not reasonably foreseeable by the U.S. transferor is not a triggering event under paragraphs (d)(1) through (d)(3) of this section.

(6) *Certain liquidations and upstream reorganizations of the transferred corporation into the transferee foreign corporation*—(i) *General rule*. A transfer of assets by the transferred corporation to the transferee foreign corporation pursuant to a liquidation described in section 332, where the transferee foreign corporation is described in section 332(b)(1), or pursuant to a reorganization described in section 368(a), and related exchanges of stock or securities of the transferred corporation will not be triggering events under paragraph (d)(1) or (d)(2) of this section. The description of this exception that is required to be filed with the annual certification under paragraph (b)(5) of this section must include a description of the transaction. In such a case, the original gain recognition agreement shall continue to apply during the remainder of its term. If, however, in connection with a liquidation described in section 332, the transferred corporation recognizes gain under section 336 with respect to a portion of its assets, such assets shall be treated as disposed of for purposes of paragraph (d)(2) of this section.

(ii) *Example*. The principles of this paragraph (e)(6) are illustrated by the following example:

Example. (i) *Facts*. UST, a domestic corporation, owns 100 percent of the stock of TFD, a foreign corporation. UST transfers all of the TFD stock to newly-formed TFC, a foreign corporation, in an exchange to which section 351 applies. In the exchange, UST receives 100 percent of the voting stock of TFC. The transaction is subject to both sections 367(a) and (b). See §§1.367(a)–3(b) and 1.367(b)–1(a). All of the requirements of §1.367(a)–3(b)(1) are satisfied, and UST enters into a gain recognition agreement to qualify for nonrecognition treatment and does not make the election described in paragraph (b)(1)(vii) of this section. UST also complies with the notice requirement under §1.367(b)–1(c). Two years after the initial transfer, TFD liquidates into TFC in a transaction described in sections 332 and 337, and UST complies with the requirements of this paragraph (e)(6). Four years after the initial transfer, TFC disposes of substantially all of the assets previously held by TFD.

(ii) *Result*. Because paragraph (d)(2) of this section provides that a disposition of substantially all of the transferred corporation's assets by any person is a triggering event, TFC's disposition of substantially all of the assets previously held by TFD is a triggering event. Under the terms of the gain recognition agreement, UST must amend its return for the year of the initial transfer and include in income the gain realized, but not recognized, on the initial transfer of the stock of TFD to TFC, and pay any interest charge.

(7) *Death of an individual U.S. transferor*. If the U.S. transferor is an individual and such individual dies, the individual's death will not be a triggering event under paragraph (d)(7) of this section, if—

(i) The person winding up the affairs of the U.S. transferor retains, for the duration of the waiver of the statute of limitations relating to the gain recognition agreement, assets to meet any possible liability of the U.S. transferor under the duration of the gain recognition agreement;

(ii) The person winding up the affairs of the U.S. transferor provides security as provided under paragraph (c) of this section for any possible liability of the U.S. transferor under the gain recognition agreement; or

(iii) The person winding up the affairs of the U.S. transferor obtains a ruling from the Internal Revenue Service providing for successors to the U.S. transferor under the gain recognition agreement.

(8) *Deconsolidation*. A deconsolidation described in paragraph (d)(4) of this section will not be a triggering event, and the original gain recognition agreement shall terminate without further effect, if the following conditions are satisfied:

(i) The U.S. transferor enters into a new gain recognition agreement pursuant to which the U.S. transferor agrees to recognize gain (during the remaining term of the original gain recognition agreement) with respect to the initial transfer and makes the election described in paragraph (b)(1)(vii) of this section.

(ii) The U.S. transferor provides with its next annual certification (described in paragraph (b)(5) of this section) notice of the deconsolidation.

(9) *Consolidation*. A consolidation described in paragraph (d)(5) of this section will not be a triggering event, and the original gain recognition agreement shall terminate without further effect, if the following conditions are satisfied:

(i) The common parent of the consolidated group that includes the U.S. transferor immediately after the consolidation enters into a new gain recognition agreement pursuant to which the U.S. transferor agrees to recognize gain (during the remaining term of the original gain recognition agreement) with respect to the initial transfer and in which it makes the election described in paragraph (b)(1)(vii) of this section.

(ii) The U.S. transferor provides with its next annual certification (described in paragraph (b)(5) of this section) a notice of the consolidation.

(10) *Reasonable cause exception for failure to comply*—(i) *Request for relief*. A failure to comply described in paragraph (d)(8) of this section will not be a triggering event, and the timeliness requirement with respect to a gain recognition agreement shall be considered satisfied notwithstanding a failure to file the agreement in a timely manner, if the person required to file the gain recognition agreement, annual certification, or Form 8838 is able to demonstrate to the Area Director, Field Examination, Small Business/Self Employed or the Director of Field Operations, Large and Mid-Size Business (Director) having jurisdiction of the taxpayer's tax return for the taxable year, that such failure was due to reasonable cause and not willful neglect. In determining whether the person has reasonable cause, the Director shall consider whether the person acted reasonably and in good faith. Whether the person acted reasonably and in good faith will be determined after considering all the facts and circumstances. The Director shall notify the person in writing within 120 days of

the filing if it is determined that the failure to comply was not due to reasonable cause, or if additional time will be needed to make such determination. For this purpose, the 120-day period shall begin to run on the date the Service notifies the person in writing that the request has been received and assigned for review. Once such period commences, if the person is not again notified within 120 days, then the person shall be deemed to have established reasonable cause. The reasonable cause exception of this paragraph (e)(10) shall apply only if, once the person becomes aware of the failure to file or comply with the agreement, the person complies with the requirements of paragraph (e)(10)(ii) of this section.

(ii) *Requirements for reasonable cause relief*—(A) *Time of submission*. Requests for reasonable cause relief will only be considered if once the person becomes aware of the failure to file or comply with the agreement, the person attaches all the documents that should have been filed, as well as a complete written statement setting forth the reasons for the failure to timely comply, to an amended return that amends the return to which the documents should have been attached pursuant to the rules of section 367(a) and the regulations under that paragraph.

(B) *Notice requirement*. In addition to the requirement of paragraph (e)(10)(ii)(A) of this section, the person must provide a copy of the amended return and all required attachments to the Director as follows:

(*1*) If the taxpayer is under examination for any taxable year when the person requests relief, the taxpayer must provide a copy of the amended return and attachments to the personnel conducting the examination.

(*2*) If the taxpayer is not under examination for any taxable year when the person requests relief, the taxpayer must provide a copy of the amended return and attachments to the Director having jurisdiction over the taxpayer's return.

(f) *Gain recognized in connection with certain nonrecognition transactions*—(1) *Dispositions of transferred stock or securities*—(i) *General rule*. If a disposition of the transferred stock or securities occurs in connection with a nonrecognition transaction described in paragraph (e)(1)(ii), (e)(2)(i), (e)(3)(ii), (e)(3)(iii), or (e)(4) of this section and gain is recognized by the transferee foreign corporation in connection with the transaction (for example, under sections 351(b) or 356(a)(1)), the U.S. transferor must recognize gain pursuant to the gain recognition agreement as determined under paragraph (f)(1)(ii) of this section. This paragraph (f)(1)(i) shall not apply to the extent that the gain recognized is treated as a dividend under section 356(a)(2).

(ii) *Method for determining amount of gain to be recognized*. The portion of the gain recognition agreement that must be recognized under paragraph (f)(1)(i) of this section, if any, is the gain that would be recognized by the transferee foreign corporation on such disposition (but not in excess of the amount of the gain recognition agreement). For purposes of this paragraph (f)(1)(ii), the gain that would be recognized in the nonrecognition transactions listed in paragraph (f)(1)(i) of this section by the transferee foreign corporation shall be calculated before taking into account any basis increase that may apply under paragraph (b)(3)(iv) of this section as a result of the gain that the U.S. transferor is required to recognize. If the amount of gain that the transferee foreign corporation would be required to recognize is less than the amount of the gain subject to the gain recognition agreement, then the new gain recognition agreement filed pursuant to paragraph (e)(1)(ii), (e)(2)(i), (e)(3)(ii), (e)(3)(iii), or (e)(4) of this section shall provide that the U.S. transferor shall recognize the remaining portion of the gain that was realized, but not recognized, on the initial transfer if a subsequent triggering event occurs.

(iii) *Example*. The rule of this paragraph (f)(1) is illustrated by the following example:

Example. (i) *Facts*. UST, a domestic corporation owning 100% of the stock of TFD, a foreign corporation, transfers all of the TFD stock to newly-formed TFC, a foreign corporation, in an exchange to which section 351 applies. In the exchange, UST receives 100% of the stock of TFC. The transaction is subject to both sections 367(a) and (b). See §§1.367(a)–3(b) and 1.367(b)–1(a). All of the requirements of §1.367(a)–3(b)(1) are satisfied, and UST enters into a gain recognition agreement to qualify for nonrecognition treatment and does not make the election contained in paragraph (b)(1)(vii) of this section. UST also complies with the notice requirement under §1.367(b)–1(c). At the time of the initial transfer, UST has a basis of $50 in the stock of TFD, which has a fair market value of $100. Thus, the amount of gain subject to the gain recognition agreement is $50. Two years after the initial transfer, TFC and X, an unrelated domestic corporation, form CFC, a foreign corporation. TFC transfers the stock of TFD to CFC in an exchange to which section 351 applies. UST also complies with the notice requirement under §1.367(b)–1(c). At the time of the transfer, TFC's basis in the TFD stock equals $50 and the fair market value remains $100. In the exchange, TFC receives 25% of the stock of CFC and $35 of cash. Before taking into account adjustments made under paragraph (b)(3)(iv) of this section, TFC would recognize $35 of gain under section 351(b). X transfers property to CFC in exchange for the remaining 75% of the CFC stock. Under paragraph (d)(1) of this section, TFC's disposition of the TFD stock is a triggering event. However, UST complies with the requirements of paragraph (e)(1)(ii) of this section providing for an exception to the triggering event.

(ii) *Result*. Under paragraph (f)(1)(ii) of this section, pursuant to the terms of the gain recognition agreement, UST must recognize $35 of the $50 gain realized, but not recognized, on the initial transfer. The new gain recognition agreement that UST files pursuant to paragraph (e)(1)(ii)(C) of this section will reflect the $15 that remains of the gain realized, but not recognized, on the initial transfer. Under paragraph (b)(3)(iv)(A) of this section, TFC's basis in the TFD stock is increased (as of the date of the initial transfer) by $35 to $85. Under paragraph (b)(3)(iv)(B) of this section, UST's basis in the TFC stock is also increased by $35. Finally, after taking account of adjustments under paragraph (b)(3)(iv) of this section, TFC must recognize $15 of gain under section 351(b).

(2) *Dispositions of substantially all of the transferred corporation's assets*. If a disposition of substantially all of the assets of the transferred corporation occurs in connection with a nonrecognition transaction described in paragraph (e)(1)(iii), (e)(3)(iii), or (e)(4)(ii) of this section and gain is recognized on such disposition (for example, under section 351(b) or 356(a)(1)), the U.S. transferor must recognize gain pursuant to the gain recognition agreement to the extent of such gain recognized (but not in excess of the gain realized, but not recognized, on the initial transfer). This paragraph (f)(2) shall not apply to the extent that recognized gain is treated as a dividend under section 356(a)(2).

(g) *Transactions that terminate the gain recognition agreement or reduce the amount of gain required to be recognized pursuant to a gain recognition agreement*. Notwithstanding paragraph (d) of this section, the following events shall not constitute triggering events and instead shall either terminate the gain recognition agreement, or reduce the amount of gain required to be recognized pursuant to a gain recognition agreement:

(1) *Taxable disposition of stock of the transferee foreign corporation by U.S. transferor*—(i) *General rule*. If the U.S. transferor disposes of all the stock of the transferee foreign corporation that is received (or deemed received) in the initial transfer, then the gain recognition agreement shall terminate without further effect if—

(A) Immediately before the disposition, the aggregate basis of the transferee foreign corporation stock disposed of does not exceed the sum of the aggregate basis of the transferred stock or securities immediately before the initial transfer plus any increase in the basis of such stock or securities as a result of the recognition of gain on the initial transfer. For purposes of this paragraph (g)(1)(i)(A), an increase in basis of the stock disposed of as a result of an income inclusion with respect to such stock (for example, pursuant to section 961) shall not be taken into account; and

(B) All realized gain (if any) in the stock disposed of is recognized currently and included in taxable income as a result of the disposition.

(ii) *Partial dispositions*—(A) *General rule*. If the U.S. transferor disposes of a portion of the stock of the transferee foreign corporation that is received (or deemed received) in the initial transfer in a transaction that satisfies the conditions described in paragraphs (g)(1)(i)(A) and (B) of this section, such disposition will not be a triggering event and the gain recognition shall remain in effect. For purposes of determining whether the condition described in paragraph (g)(1)(i)(A) of this section is satisfied, however, the aggregate basis of the stock of the transferee foreign corporation disposed of is compared to the aggregate basis of the transferred stock or securities exchanged for such stock at the time of the initial transfer.

(B) *Subsequent triggering event*. If the gain recognition agreement is triggered after a disposition described in paragraph (g)(1)(ii)(A) of this section, the U.S. transferor shall be required to recognize only a proportionate amount of the gain subject to the gain recognition agreement that otherwise would be required to be recognized on a subsequent triggering event. Except as provided in paragraph (g)(1)(iv) of this section, the proportion required to be recognized shall be determined by reference to the percentage of stock (based on relative fair market value) of the transferee foreign corporation received (or deemed received) in the initial transfer that is retained by the U.S. transferor.

(iii) The rule of paragraph (g)(1)(ii) of this section is illustrated by the following example:

Example. (i) *Facts*. A, a United States citizen, owns 100% of the outstanding stock of foreign corporation X. In a transaction to which section 351 applies, A exchanges his stock in X (and other assets) for 100% of the outstanding stock of foreign corporation Y. The transaction is subject to both sections 367(a) and (b). See §§1.367(a)–3(b) and 1.367(b)–1(a). A enters into a gain recognition agreement, makes the election contained in paragraph (b)(1)(vii) of this section, and also complies with the notice requirement under §1.367(b)–1(c). In the second year following the initial transfer, A disposes of 60% of the fair market value of the stock of Y, and the requirements of paragraphs (g)(1)(i)(A) and (B) are met with respect to such disposition. In the fourth year following the initial transfer, Y disposes of 50% of the fair market value of the stock of X.

(ii) *Result*. The disposition of 60% of the stock of Y is not a triggering event, and the gain recognition agreement continues in effect. The disposition of X stock, however, is a triggering event under paragraph (d)(1)(i) of this section. As a result of the subsequent disposition of 50% of the stock of X, under paragraphs (d)(1)(iii) and (g)(1)(ii)(B) of this section, A is required to include in income in the year of such disposition 20% (40% of the fair market value of Y multiplied by 50% of the fair market value of X) of the gain that A realized but did not recognize on the initial transfer of the X stock to Y, and pay any applicable interest.

(iv) *Certain nonrecognition transactions*. The rules described in these paragraphs (g)(1)(iv)(A) through (C) apply if the U.S. transferor disposes of all or a portion of the stock of the transferee foreign corporation received (or deemed received) in the initial transfer pursuant to a nonrecognition transaction described in paragraph (e)(1)(i), (e)(2)(ii), (e)(3)(i), or (e)(3)(ii) of this section, the condition described in paragraph (g)(1)(i)(A) of this section is satisfied with respect to such disposition, and gain is recognized in connection with the disposition (for example, under sections 351(b), 356(a)(1), or 336). If, however, only a portion of the stock of the transferee corporation stock is disposed of pursuant to this paragraph (g)(1)(iv), then for purposes of determining whether the condition described in paragraph (g)(1)(i)(A) of this section is satisfied, the aggregate basis of the stock disposed of is compared to the aggregate basis of the transferred stock or securities exchanged for such stock at the time of the initial transfer.

(A) *U.S. transferor files new gain recognition agreement*. This paragraph (g)(1)(iv)(A) applies if the U.S. transferor (or successor U.S. transferor, as applicable) enters into a new gain recognition agreement as provided in paragraph (e)(1)(i), (e)(3)(i), or (e)(3)(ii) of this section, as applicable. In such a case, the amount of gain subject to the new gain recognition agreement shall equal the amount of gain realized, but not recognized, on the initial transfer, less any gain recognized by the U.S. transferor in connection with the nonrecognition transaction. If the amount of gain recognized on the transfer is equal to or greater than the amount of gain realized, but not recognized, on the initial transfer, then the original gain recognition agreement shall terminate without further effect.

(B) *U.S. transferor does not file a new gain recognition agreement*. This paragraph (g)(1)(iv)(B) applies if the U.S. transferor (or successor U.S. transferor, as applicable) fails to enter into a new gain recognition agreement as provided in paragraph (e)(1)(i), (e)(3)(i), or (e)(3)(ii) of this section, as applicable. In such a case, the amount required to be recognized by the U.S. transferor pursuant to the gain recognition agreement shall be the amount of gain realized, but not recognized, on the initial transfer, less any gain recognized by the U.S. transferor in connection with the nonrecognition transaction.

(C) *Special rule for recapitalizations*. Because paragraph (e)(2)(ii) of this section does not require the U.S. transferor to enter into a new gain recognition agreement, the amount of gain subject to the gain recognition agreement shall equal the amount of gain realized, but not recognized, on the initial transfer, less any gain recognized by the U.S. transferor in connection with the nonrecognition transaction described in paragraph (e)(2)(ii) of this section.

(v) *Election to reduce basis*—(A) *General rule*. For purposes of paragraphs (g)(1)(i), (ii) and (iv) of this section, the U.S. transferor may elect to reduce its aggregate basis in the stock disposed of effective immediately before the disposition such that the condition described in paragraph (g)(1)(i)(A) is satisfied. If an election is made pursuant to this paragraph (g)(1)(v), the U.S. transferor may increase its basis in other stock of the transferee foreign corporation it holds, if any, by a corresponding amount but not above the fair market value of such stock.

(B) *Election.* The election pursuant to this paragraph (g)(1)(v) is made by filing with the U.S. transferor's income tax return for the taxable year in which the disposition of the transferee foreign corporation stock occurs, a statement setting forth the following information, with the heading "Election to Reduce Stock Basis Under §1.367(a)–8T(g)(1)(v)":

(*1*) A description of the transferee foreign corporation stock that the U.S. transferor has disposed of.

(*2*) An estimate of the fair market value of the stock as of the date of the disposition.

(*3*) A comparison of the basis of the transferee foreign corporation stock before and after the election that is made pursuant to this paragraph (g)(1)(v).

(*4*) The date on which the transferee foreign corporation stock was disposed of by the U.S. transferor.

(vi) The rules of paragraph (g)(1) of this section are illustrated by the following examples:

Example 1. (i) *Facts.* USP, a domestic corporation, owns 100% of the stock of two foreign corporations, FC1 and FC2. The basis and fair market value of the FC1 stock is $100 and $90, respectively. The basis and fair market value of the FC2 stock is $0 and $100, respectively. USP also owns land that has a basis and fair market value of $10. In year 1, USP transfers 100% of the stock of FC1 and FC2 and the land to FC3, a newly formed foreign corporation, in exchange for 20 shares of FC3 stock. The transfer of the stock of FC1 and FC2 qualifies under section 351 and section 368(a)(1)(B). The transfer of the land qualifies under section 351. The transfer of the FC2 stock is subject to both section 367(a) and (b). See §§1.367(a)–3(b) and 1.367(b)–1(a). Pursuant to §1.367(a)–3(b)(1)(ii) and this section, USP enters into a gain recognition agreement with respect to the $100 of gain in the FC2 stock and complies with the notice requirement under §1.367(b)–1(c). USP takes the position that its basis in each of the 20 shares of FC3 stock received in the transfer equals $5.5 (($100+$0+10)/20). In year 3, USP sells 100% of its FC3 stock to an unrelated person for cash.

(ii) *Result.* The disposition of the FC3 stock is a triggering event described in paragraph (d)(3) of this section. The disposition does not terminate the gain recognition agreement pursuant to paragraph (g)(1)(i) of this section because USP takes the position that the basis of each of the 10 shares of FC3 stock it received in exchange for the FC2 stock in the initial transfer equals $5.5. Thus, the total basis in the 10 shares received for the FC2 stock equals $55, which exceeds the $0 basis USP had in the FC2 stock it transferred to FC3 in the initial transfer. As a result, the condition described in paragraph (g)(1)(i)(A) of this section is not satisfied. USP may, however, elect to reduce its basis in 10 of the FC3 shares it disposes of from $5.5 to $0, and increase its basis in its remaining 10 shares of FC2 stock by $5.5, pursuant to paragraph (g)(1)(v) of this section. As a result, the condition described in paragraph (g)(1)(i)(A) of this section would be satisfied, the disposition would not be a triggering event, and the gain recognition would terminate without further effect.

Example 2. (i) *Facts.* USP, a domestic corporation, owns 100% of the stock of FC1, a foreign corporation. The basis and fair market value of the FC1 stock is $0 and $80, respectively. In year 1, USP transfers 100% of the stock of FC1 to FC2, a newly formed foreign corporation, in exchange for 20 shares of FC2 stock. The transfer of the stock of FC1 qualifies under section 351 and section 368(a)(1)(B). The transfer of the FC1 stock is subject to both section 367(a) and (b). See §§1.367(a)–3(b) and 1.367(b)–1(a). Pursuant to §1.367(a)–3(b)(1)(ii) and this section, USP enters into a gain recognition agreement with respect to the $80 of gain in the FC1 stock and complies with the notice requirement under §1.367(b)–1(c). USP's basis and fair market value in the FC2 stock it receives at the time of the transfer is $0 and $80, respectively. In year 3, when the fair market value of the FC2 stock continues to equal $80, USP transfers land that has a basis and fair market value of $20 to FC2 in a transfer that qualifies under section 351, but does not receive additional shares of FC2 in connection with such transfer. In year 5, USP sells 100% of its FC2 stock to an unrelated person for cash.

(ii) *Result.* The disposition of the FC3 stock is a triggering event described in paragraph (d)(3) of this section. The disposition would not terminate the gain recognition agreement pursuant to paragraph (g)(1)(i) of this section if the basis in each of the 20 FC2 shares that USP sells equals $1 ($20/20 shares) because immediately before the disposition the basis in the FC2 shares received for the FC1 shares exceeds the basis of the FC1 shares at the time of the initial transfer. As a result, the condition described in paragraph (g)(1)(i)(A) of this section would not be satisfied. USP may, however, elect to adjust its basis in its FC2 shares such that 16 of the shares have zero basis (reflecting the basis of the FC1 stock) and 4 of the shares have $20 of basis (reflecting the basis of the land). In such a case, the condition described in paragraph (g)(1)(i)(A) of this section would be satisfied, the disposition would not be a triggering event, and the gain recognition agreement would terminate without further effect.

(2) *Certain dispositions by a domestic transferred corporation of substantially all of its assets.* If, immediately before the initial transfer, the U.S. transferor owned an amount of stock in the transferred corporation described in section 1504(a)(2), and the transferred corporation is domestic, then the gain recognition agreement shall terminate without further effect if the transferred corporation disposes of substantially all of its assets in a transaction in which all realized gain is recognized currently. If an indirect stock transfer necessitated the filing of the gain recognition agreement, such agreement shall terminate if, immediately before the indirect transfer, the U.S. transferor owned an amount of stock in the acquired corporation described in section 1504(a)(2) (or, in the case of a section 368(a)(1)(A) and (a)(2)(E) reorganization described in §1.367(a)–3(d)(1)(ii), the U.S. transferor owned an amount of stock in the acquiring corporation described in section 1504(a)(2)) and the transferred corporation disposes of substantially all of its assets (taking into account §1.367(a)–3(d)(2)(v)) in a transaction in which all realized gain is recognized currently.

(3) *Distribution or transfer by transferee foreign corporation of stock or securities of transferred corporation under section 337, 355 or 361*—(i) *Scope.* This paragraph (g)(3) applies if the transferee foreign corporation distributes or transfers the stock or securities that initially necessitated the filing of the gain recognition agreement (and any additional stock received after the initial transfer) pursuant to any of the following transactions:

(A) A liquidating distribution to the U.S. transferor or a domestic corporation that is a member of the same consolidated group of which the U.S. transferor is then a member and that qualifies under sections 332 and 337, if such domestic distributee corporation is described in section 332(b)(1).

(B) A distribution to the U.S. transferor, a domestic corporation that is a member of the same consolidated group of which the U.S. transferor is a member, or an individual that is a United States person, that qualifies under section 355.

(C) A transfer to the U.S. transferor or a domestic corporation that is a member of the same consolidated group of which the U.S. transferor is then a member and to which section 361 applies (but, if in connection with a reorganization described in section 368(a)(1)(D) or (G), only if the requirements of section 354(b)(1)(A) and (B) are met).

(ii) *General rule.* If a distribution or transfer is described in paragraph (g)(3)(i) of this section, the gain recognition agreement shall terminate without further effect, provided that immediately after such distribution or transfer the basis in the transferred stock or securities in the hands of the domestic corporation or individual, as applicable, does not exceed the basis that the U.S. transferor had in the transferred stock or securities immediately before the initial transfer. For purposes of this paragraph (g)(3)(ii), only the basis in the stock or securities transferred shall be taken into account, and increases to stock basis as a result of income inclusions with respect to stock (for example, pursuant to section 961) shall not be taken into account. In the case of a transaction described in paragraph (g)(3)(i)(B) of this section, any reductions or redistributions of stock basis under §1.367(b)–5(c)(2) or (4), respectively, shall be made before applying the rules of this paragraph (g)(3)(ii).

(iii) *Election to reduce basis in stock or securities of transferred corporation.* For purposes of paragraph (g)(3)(ii) of this section, the domestic corporation or individual, as applicable, may elect to reduce the basis in the stock or securities transferred to equal the basis the U.S. transferor had in the corresponding transferred stock or securities immediately before the initial transfer, such that the gain recognition agreement shall terminate without further effect. If such an election is made, the domestic corporation or individual may increase its basis in other stock of the transferred corporation it holds, if any, by a corresponding amount but not above the fair market value of such stock.

(iv) *Election.* The election pursuant to paragraph (g)(3)(iii) of this section is made by filing with the domestic corporation's or individual's income tax return for the taxable year in which the distribution or transfer occurs, a statement setting forth the following information, with the heading "Election to Reduce Stock Basis Under §1.367(a)–8T(g)(3)(iii)":

(*1*) A description of the stock or securities received.

(*2*) An estimate of the fair market value of the stock or securities as of the date of their receipt.

(*3*) A statement comparing the basis of the stock or securities before and after the election.

(*4*) The date on which the stock or securities were received.

(v) *Examples.* The rules of paragraph (g)(3) of this section are illustrated by the following examples:

Example 1. (i) *Facts.* USP, a domestic corporation, owns 100% of the stock of two foreign corporations, FC1 and FC2. FC1 has 10 shares of stock issued and outstanding. In year 1, when the basis and fair market value of the FC1 stock is $0 and $90, respectively, USP transfers its 10 shares of FC1 stock to FC2 in an exchange to which section 351 applies. The transaction is subject to both sections 367(a) and (b). See §§1.367(a)–3(b) and 1.367(b)–1(a). Pursuant to §1.367(a)–3(b)(1)(ii) and this section, USP enters into a gain recognition agreement with respect to such transfer. USP also complies with the notice requirement under §1.367(b)–1(c). In year 2, FC2 transfers land with a basis and fair market value of $10 to FC1 in exchange for one newly issued share of FC1 stock. In year 4, FC2 distributes all of its FC1 stock to USP in a liquidating distribution that qualifies under sections 332 and 337.

(ii) *Result.* In determining whether the gain recognition agreement entered into by USP is terminated under paragraph (g)(3) of this section, or in the alternative triggered under paragraph (d)(1) of this section, only the stock of FC1 transferred by USP to FC2 in year 1 is considered. Thus, the basis in the one share of FC1 stock issued to FC2 in year 2 in exchange for land is not taken into account. If instead of FC1 actually issuing another share of stock to FC2 in exchange for the land, FC1 was deemed to issue stock to FC2 in such exchange, then the gain recognition agreement would terminate only if USP elects to adjust the basis in its FC1 shares such that nine of the shares have zero basis and one of the shares has $10 of basis.

Example 2. (i) *Facts.* USP, a domestic corporation, owns 100% of the stock of two foreign corporations, FC and FD. In year 1, USP transfers 100% of the stock of FC to FD in an exchange to which section 351 applies. The transaction is subject to both sections 367(a) and (b). See §§1.367(a)–3(b) and 1.367(b)–1(a). At the time of the initial transfer, USP has a basis of $80 in its stock of FC; the stock of FC has a fair market value of $100. USP's basis in its stock of FD, and the fair market value of the FD stock, are both $100. Pursuant to §1.367(a)–3(b)(1)(ii) and this section, USP enters into a gain recognition agreement with respect to the initial transfer. USP also complies with the notice requirement under §1.367(b)–1(c). In year 4, FD distributes all of the stock of FC to USP in a *pro rata* distribution to which section 355 applies. At the time of the distribution, the fair market value of the FC stock has increased to $200, while the fair market value of the FD stock has remained $100. Under section 358, USP allocates its $180 predistribution basis in its FD stock between the FD stock and FC stock according to the stock blocks' relative fair market values, yielding a $60 basis in the FD stock and a $120 basis in the FC stock. Immediately before the distribution, USP's section 1248 amount with respect to FC and FD is zero.

(ii) *Result.* The distribution of FC stock is a triggering event under paragraph (d)(1) of this section. The distribution does not terminate the gain recognition agreement under paragraph (g)(3) of this section because after the distribution, USP's basis of $120 in the FC stock exceeds the $80 basis that USP had in the FC stock at the time of the initial transfer. If, however, USP elects to reduce its basis in the FC stock it receives to $80, then the condition described in paragraph (g)(3) of this section will be satisfied, and the gain recognition agreement will terminate without further effect. In addition, the $40 of basis that USP elected to reduce is redistributed to the stock of FD, the result of which is that USP has a basis of $100 in its FD stock.

(h) *Effective date*—(1) *General rule*—(i) *Gain recognition agreements filed for transfers on or after effective date.* With the exception of paragraph (f) of this section, the rules of this section apply to gain recognition agreements filed with respect to transfers of stock or securities under Treas. Reg. §§1.367(a)–3(b) through (d) and 1.367(a)–3T(e) occurring on or after March 7, 2007. The rules of paragraph (f) of this section apply to gain recognition agreements filed with respect to transfers of stock or securities under Treas. Reg. §§1.367(a)–3(b) through (d) and 1.367(a)–3T(e) occurring on or after August 6, 2007. However, the rules of this section do not apply to gain recognition agreements filed with respect to such a transfer of stock or securities occurring on or after March 7, 2007, if such transfer was entered into pursuant to a written agreement which was (subject to customary conditions) binding before February 5, 2007, and at all times thereafter. Solely for purposes of this paragraph (h), a transfer described in the preceding sentence shall be deemed to be a transfer occurring before March 7, 2007 to which the rules of §1.367(a)–8 (see 26 CFR part 1, revised April 1, 2006) apply. See paragraph (h)(2)(iii) of this section for the ability to apply the rules of this section with respect to gain recognition agreements filed before March 7, 2007.

(ii) *Gain recognition agreements filed for transfers before effective date.* For matters covered in this section for periods before March 7, 2007 but on or after July 20, 1998, the corresponding rules of §1.367(a)–8 (see 26 CFR part 1, revised April 1, 2006) apply. For matters covered in this section for periods before July 20, 1998, the corresponding rules of §1.367(a)–3T(g) (see 26 CFR part 1, revised April 1, 1998) and Notice 87–85, 1987–2 C.B. 395; (see §601.601(d)(2)(ii) of this chapter) apply. In addition, if a U.S. transferor entered into a gain recognition agreement for transfers before July 20, 1998, then the rules of §1.367(a)–3T(g) (see 26 CFR part 1, revised April 1, 1998) continue to apply in lieu of this section in the event of any direct or indirect nonrecognition transfer of the same property. See also, §1.367(a)–3(h).

(2) *Applicability to gain recognition agreements filed before effective date*—(i) *General rule.* This paragraph (h)(2)(i) applies only to rules in this regulation §1.367(a)–8T that were not already effective under the rules of §1.367(a)–8 (see 26 CFR part 1, revised April 1, 2006). Taxpayers may apply all or part of these regulations to gain recognition agreements filed with respect to transfers of stock or securities, for all open years, on or after July 20, 1998. If a taxpayer failed to file a gain recognition agreement with respect to a transfer of stock or securities on or after July 20, 1998 and before March 7, 2007, the taxpayer must first obtain reasonable cause relief under §1.367(a)–8(c)(2) to file the gain recognition agreement before the taxpayer may apply this paragraph (h)(2)(i).

(ii) *Special filing rule for tax year ending before effective date.* This paragraph (h)(2)(ii) provides the time and manner in which taxpayers may apply paragraph (h)(2)(i) of this section. Notwithstanding the rules provided in §1.367(a)–8T(a)(2), all agreements, certifications, or other information related to such gain recognition agreement that should have been filed on or before March 7, 2007 shall be treated as having been timely filed, provided they are attached to a Federal income tax return amending the taxpayer's Federal income tax return for the taxable year in which they should have been attached. The amended return described in the preceding sentence must be filed before August 6, 2007. A taxpayer that wishes to apply paragraph (h)(2)(i) of this section but that fails to meet the filing requirement described in the preceding sentence must request reasonable cause relief as provided in paragraph (e)(10) of this section.

(iii) *Tax year ending after effective date.* A taxpayer that entered into a gain recognition agreement to which §1.367(a)–8 (see 26 CFR part 1, revised April 1, 2006) applies may apply the rules of this section in a tax year ending on or after March 7, 2007 by attaching the agreement, certification, or other information related to such gain recognition agreement that the rules of this section require in accordance with the rules of this section and with the time and manner rules provided in §1.367(a)–8T(a)(2).

(iv) *Examples.* The rules of paragraph (h)(2) of this section are illustrated by the following examples:

Example 1. (i) *Facts.* USP, a domestic corporation, owns 100% of the stock of two foreign corporations, FC and FD. In 2003, USP transfers 100% of the stock of FC to FD in an exchange to which section 351 applies. The transaction is subject to both sections 367(a) and (b). See §§1.367(a)–3(b) and 1.367(b)–1(a). Pursuant to §1.367(a)–3(b)(1)(ii) and this section, USP enters into a gain recognition agreement with respect to the initial transfer. USP also complies with the notice requirement under §1.367(b)–1(c). In 2005, FD distributes all of the stock of FC to USP in a *pro rata* distribution to which section 355 applies. Under section 358, USP's basis in its FC stock exceeds the basis that USP had in FC immediately before the initial transfer.

(ii) *Result.* Under paragraph (h)(1)(ii) of this section, the rules of §1.367(a)–8 apply because the gain recognition agreement was filed before March 7, 2007. As a result of the year 2005 transaction, under §1.367(a)–8(e)(1), USP is required to recognize all of the gain subject to the gain recognition agreement, and pay any applicable interest. The gain recognition agreement does not terminate under §1.367(a)–8(h)(3) because USP's basis in its FC stock immediately after the section 355 distribution exceeds the basis USP had in the FC stock immediately before the initial transfer. However, paragraph (g)(3)(iii) of this section provides a rule that would allow USP to elect to reduce its basis in the FC stock such that the conditions in paragraph (g)(3) of this section would be satisfied and the gain recognition agreement would terminate without further effect. Under paragraph (h)(2)(i) of this section, USP may apply paragraph (g)(3)(iii) of this section to the 2005 transaction, if 2005 is an open year, because the rule provided in paragraph (g)(3)(iii) of this section was not already effective under §1.367(a)–8. Under paragraph (h)(2)(ii) of this section, USP must submit the documents required under paragraph (g)(3)(iii) of this section to a Federal income tax return amending its 2005 Federal income tax return before August 6, 2007.

Example 2. (i) *Facts.* UST, a domestic corporation, owns 100% of the stock of two foreign corporations, TFC and TFD. In 2003, USP transfers 100% of the stock of TFD to TFC in an exchange to which section 351 applies. The transaction is subject to both sections 367(a) and (b). See §§1.367(a)–3(b) and 1.367(b)–1(a). All of the requirements of §1.367(a)–3(b)(1) are satisfied, and UST enters into a gain recognition agreement. UST also complies with the notice requirement under §1.367(b)–1(c). In 2005, TFC transfers its TFD stock to F1, also a foreign corporation, in an exchange to which section 351 applies. UST does not file a new gain recognition agreement under §1.367(a)–8(g)(2).

(ii) *Result.* Under paragraph (h)(1)(ii) of this section, the rules of §1.367(a)–8 apply because the gain recognition agreement was filed before March 7, 2007. Under §1.367(a)–8(e), UST must recognize the gain realized, but not recognized, on its initial transfer of TFD stock. Paragraph (h)(2)(i) of this section does not apply because the rule in paragraph (e)(1)(ii) of this section was already effective under §1.367(a)–8(g)(2). Therefore, UST's only recourse from recognizing the gain subject to the gain recognition agreement is the reasonable cause exception provided in §1.367(a)–8(c)(2).

(3) *Expiration.* The applicability of this section expires on or before February 1, 2010.

PART 602—OMB CONTROL NUMBERS UNDER THE PAPERWORK REDUCTION ACT

Par. 7. The authority citation for part 602 continues to read as follows:

Authority: 26 U.S.C. 7805.

Par. 8. In §602.101, paragraph (b) is revised by adding an entry for §1.367(a)–8T in numerical order to the table to read as follows:

§602.101 OMB Control numbers.

* * * * *

CFR part or section where identified and described	Current OMB control No.
* * * * *	
1.367(a)–8T	1545–2056
* * * * *	

Kevin M. Brown,
Deputy Commissioner for Services and Enforcement.

Approved January 31, 2007.

Eric Solomon,
Assistant Secretary of the Treasury (Tax Policy).

(Filed by the Office of the Federal Register on February 1, 2007, 8:52 a.m., and published in the issue of the Federal Register for February 5, 2007, 72 F.R. 5174)

Section 807.—Rules for Certain Reserves

Insurance companies; interest rate tables. Prevailing state assumed interest rates are provided for the determination of reserves under section 807 of the Code for contracts issued in 2006 and 2007. Rev. Rul. 92–19 supplemented in part.

Rev. Rul. 2007–10

For purposes of § 807(d)(4) of the Internal Revenue Code, for taxable years beginning after December 31, 2005, this ruling supplements the schedules of prevailing state assumed interest rates set forth in Rev. Rul. 92–19, 1992–1 C.B. 227. This information is to be used by insurance companies in computing their reserves for (1) life insurance and supplementary total and permanent disability benefits, (2) individual annuities and pure endowments, and (3) group annuities and pure endowments. As § 807(d)(2)(B) requires that the interest rate used to compute these reserves be the greater of (1) the applicable federal interest rate, or (2) the prevailing state assumed interest rate, the table of applicable federal interest rates in Rev. Rul. 92–19 is also supplemented.

Following are supplements to schedules A, B, C, and D to Part III of Rev. Rul. 92–19, providing prevailing state assumed interest rates for insurance products with different features issued in 2006 and 2007, and a supplement to the table in Part IV of Rev. Rul. 92–19, providing the applicable federal interest rates under § 807(d) for 2006 and 2007. This ruling does not supplement Parts I and II of Rev. Rul. 92–19.

This is the fifteenth supplement to the interest rates provided in Rev. Rul. 92–19. Earlier supplements were published in Rev. Rul. 93–58, 1993–2 C.B. 241 (interest rates for insurance products issued in 1992 and 1993); Rev. Rul. 94–11, 1994–1 C.B. 196 (1993 and 1994); Rev. Rul. 95–4, 1995–1 C.B. 141 (1994 and 1995); Rev. Rul. 96–2, 1996–1 C.B. 141 (1995 and 1996); Rev. Rul. 97–2, 1997–1 C.B. 134 (1996 and 1997); Rev. Rul. 98–2, 1998–2 C.B. 259 (1997 and 1998); Rev. Rul. 99–10, 1999–1 C.B. 671 (1998 and 1999); Rev. Rul. 2000–17, 2000–1 C.B. 842 (1999 and 2000); Rev. Rul. 2001–11, 2001–1 C.B. 780 (2000 and 2001); Rev. Rul. 2002–12, 2002–1 C.B. 624 (2001 and 2002); Rev. Rul. 2003–24, 2003–1 C.B. 557 (2002 and 2003); Rev. Rul. 2004–14, 2004–1 C.B. 511 (2003 and 2004); Rev. Rul. 2005–29, 2005–1 C.B. 1080 (2004 and 2005); and Rev. Rul. 2006–25, 2006–20 I.R.B. 882 (May 15, 2006) (2005 and 2006).

Part III. Prevailing State Assumed Interest Rates — Products Issued in Years After 1982.*

Schedule A

STATUTORY VALUATION INTEREST RATES
BASED ON THE 1980 AMENDMENTS TO THE
NAIC STANDARD VALUATION LAW

A. Life insurance valuation:

Guarantee Duration (years)	Calendar Year of Issue 2007
10 or fewer	4.50**
More than 10 but not more than 20	4.25**
More than 20	4.00**

Source: Rates calculated from the monthly averages, ending June 30, 2006, of Moody's Composite Yield on Seasoned Corporate Bonds.

* The terms used in the schedules in this ruling and in Part III of Rev. Rul. 92–19 are those used in the Standard Valuation Law; the terms are defined in Rev. Rul. 92–19.

** As these rates exceed the applicable federal interest rate for 2007 of 3.97 percent, the valuation interest rate to be used for this product under § 807 is the applicable rate specified in this table.

Part III, Schedule B

STATUTORY VALUATION INTEREST RATES
BASED ON THE 1980 AMENDMENTS TO THE
NAIC STANDARD VALUATION LAW

B. Single premium immediate annuities and annuity benefits involving life contingencies arising from other annuities with cash settlement options and from guaranteed interest contracts with cash settlement options:

Calendar Year of Issue	Valuation Interest Rate
2006	5.25*

Source: Rates calculated from the monthly averages, ending June 30, 2006, of Moody's Composite Yield on Seasoned Corporate Bonds (formerly known as Moody's Corporate Bond Yield Average — Monthly Average Corporates). The terms used in this schedule are those used in the Standard Valuation Law as defined in Rev. Rul. 92–19.

*As this prevailing state assumed interest exceeds the applicable federal interest rate for 2006 of 3.98 percent, the valuation interest rate of 5.25 percent is to be used for this product under § 807.

STATUTORY VALUATION INTEREST RATES
BASED ON NAIC STANDARD VALUATION LAW
FOR **2006** CALENDAR YEAR BUSINESS
GOVERNED BY THE 1980 AMENDMENTS

C. Valuation interest rates for other annuities and guaranteed interest contracts that are valued on an issue year basis:

Cash Settlement Options?	Future Interest Guarantee?	Guarantee Duration (years)	Valuation Interest Rate (%) For Plan Type A	B	C
Yes	Yes	5 or fewer	5.25	4.75	4.50
		More than 5, but not more than 10	5.25	4.75	4.50
		More than 10, but not more than 20	4.75	4.50	4.25*
		More than 20	4.25*	4.00*	4.00*
Yes	No	5 or fewer	5.50	4.75	4.50
		More than 5, but not more than 10	5.25	4.75	4.50
		More than 10, but not more than 20	5.00	4.50	4.50
		More than 20	4.50*	4.25*	4.25*
No	Yes or No	5 or fewer	5.25		
		More than 5, but not more than 10	5.25	NOT APPLICABLE	
		More than 10, but not more than 20	4.75		
		More than 20	4.25*		

Source: Rates calculated from the monthly averages, ending June 30, 2006, of Moody's Composite Yield on Seasoned Corporate Bonds.

*As these rates exceed the applicable federal interest rate for 2006 of 3.98 percent, the valuation interest rate to be used for this product under § 807 is the applicable rate specified in the above table.

STATUTORY VALUATION INTEREST RATES
BASED ON NAIC STANDARD VALUATION LAW
FOR **2006** CALENDAR YEAR BUSINESS
GOVERNED BY THE 1980 AMENDMENTS

D. Valuation interest rates for other annuities and guaranteed interest contracts that are contracts with cash settlement options and that are valued on a change in fund basis:

Cash Settlement Options?	Future Interest Guarantee?	Guarantee Duration (years)	Valuation Interest Rate For Plan Type A	B	C
Yes	Yes	5 or fewer	5.75	5.50	4.50
		More than 5, but not more than 10	5.50	5.50	4.50
		More than 10, but not more than 20	5.25	5.25	4.50
		More than 20	4.75	4.75	4.25*
Yes	No	5 or fewer	5.75	5.50	4.75
		More than 5, but not more than 10	5.75	5.50	4.75
		More than 10, but not more than 20	5.50	5.25	4.50
		More than 20	4.75	4.75	4.25*

Source: Rates calculated from the monthly averages, ending June 30, 2006, of Moody's Composite Yield on Seasoned Corporate Bonds.

*As the applicable federal interest rate for 2006 of 3.98 percent is less than the prevailing state assumed interest rate, the valuation interest rate to be used for this product under § 807 is the applicable rate specified in the above table.

Part IV. Applicable Federal Interest Rates

TABLE OF
APPLICABLE FEDERAL INTEREST RATES
FOR PURPOSES OF § 807

Year	Interest Rate
2006	3.98
2007	3.97

Sources: Rev. Rul. 2004–106, 2004–2 C.B. 893, for the 2005 rate; Rev. Rul. 2005–77, 2005–2 C.B. 1071, for the 2006 rate; and Rev. Rul. 2006–61, 2006–49 I.R.B. 1028 (Dec. 11, 2006) for the 2007 rate.

EFFECT ON OTHER REVENUE RULINGS

Rev. Rul. 92–19 is supplemented by the addition to Part III of that ruling of prevailing state assumed interest rates under § 807 for certain insurance products issued in 2006 and 2007 and is further supplemented by an addition to the table in Part IV of Rev. Rul. 92–19 listing applicable federal interest rates. Parts I and II of Rev. Rul. 92–19 are not affected by this ruling.

DRAFTING INFORMATION

The principal author of this revenue ruling is Josephine H. Firehock of the Office of Associate Chief Counsel (Financial Institutions and Products). For further information regarding this revenue ruling, contact her at (202) 622–3970 (not a toll-free call).

Section 1441.—Withholding of Tax on Nonresident Aliens

A revenue procedure provides administrative guidance permitting the use of a "Net Consideration Method" of accounting for certain patent cross licensing arrangements. Under the method, only cash and other non-patent-right consideration are taken into account for withholding and capitalization purposes. See Rev. Proc. 2007-23, page 675.

Part II. Treaties and Tax Legislation

Subpart A.—Tax Conventions and Other Related Items

U.S.-Island of Jersey Reciprocal Exemption Agreement

Announcement 2007–23

The United States and the United Kingdom of Great Britain and Northern Ireland (on behalf of the Bailiwick of Jersey) have exchanged diplomatic notes evidencing a reciprocal exemption agreement for income from the international operation of ships for taxable years beginning on or after January 1, 1997. The diplomatic notes reproduced herein contain the terms of the reciprocal exemptions.

The principal author of this announcement is Patricia Bray of the Office of Associate Chief Counsel (International). For further information regarding this announcement, contact Patricia Bray at (202) 622–3880 (not a toll-free call).

The text of the agreement is as follows.

Note No : 195/97

Her Britannic Majesty's Embassy presents its compliments to the Department of State and has the honour to refer to the United States' Diplomatic Note dated 15 July 1997 concerning the proposed agreement with the Government of the United Kingdom of Great Britain and Northern Ireland, (on behalf of the Bailiwick of Jersey), to exempt from income tax, on a reciprocal basis, income derived by residents of Jersey and the United States of America from the international operation of ships.

The British Embassy, on behalf of the Government of the United Kingdom of Great Britain and Northern Ireland, hereby confirms that the proposals set out by the Department of State are acceptable. This Note, together with the Department of State's Note of 15 July 1997, shall therefore constitute an agreement between the Government of the United States of America and the Government of the United Kingdom of Great Britain and Northern Ireland which will enter into force on 12 November 1997, and shall have effect with respect to taxable years beginning on or after 1 January 1997.

British Embassy
Washington DC
12 November 1997

BRITISH EMBASSY
WASHINGTON

The Department of State wishes to propose to the British Embassy that the Government of the United States of America and the Government of the United Kingdom of Great Britain and Northern Ireland, on behalf of the Balliwick of Jersey, conclude an agreement to exempt from income tax, on a reciprocal basis, income derived by residents of Jersey and the United States from the international operation of ships. The terms of the agreement are as follows:

1. The Government of the United States of America, in accordance with sections 872(b)(1) and 883(a)(i) of the Internal Revenue Code, agrees to exempt from tax gross income derived from the international operation of ships by Jersey residents and corporations organized in Jersey. This exemption is granted on the basis of equivalent exemptions granted by Jersey to United States residents and to corporations organized in the United States.

2. In the case of a corporation, the exemption shall apply only if the corporation meets either of the following conditions:

   (a) the corporation's stock is primarily and regularly traded on an established securities market in Jersey, another country which grants an equivalent exemption to United States corporations, or the United States; or

   (b) more than 50 percent of the value of the corporation's stock is owned, directly or indirectly, by individuals who are residents of

Jersey, or of a country which grants an equivalent exemption to United States corporations or by acorporation organized in a country which grants an equivalent exemption to U.S. corporations and whose stock is primarily and regularly traded on an established securities market in that country, another country which grants an equivalent exemption to U.S. corporations, or the United States.

3. For purposes of subparagraph (b) of paragraph 2, the States of Jersey shall be treated as an individual resident of Jersey. For the purposes of the exemption from United States tax, subparagraphs (a) and (b) of paragraph 2 shall be considered to be satisfied if the corporation is a "controlled foreign corporation" under the Internal Revenue Code.

4. In this agreement, the expression "corporation organized in Jersey" means a corporation registered in Jersey.

5. Gross income includes all income derived from the international operation or chartering of ships, including income from the rental of ships on a full (time or voyage) basis and income from the rental of containers and related equipment which is incidental to the international operation of ships. It also includes income from the rental on a bareboat basis of ships used for international transport and income from the disposition of ships which is incidental to income from the international operation of ships.

6. Either Government may terminate this agreement by giving written notice of termination through diplomatic channels.

If the proposals set out above are acceptable to the British Embassy, the Department of State proposes that the present Note together with the British Embassy's reply in that sense shall constitute an agreement between the Government of the United States of America and the Government of the United Kingdom of Great Britain and Northern Ireland which shall enter into force on the date of the British Embassy's reply, and shall have effect with respect to taxable years beginning on or after January 1, 1997.

Department of State,
Washington. JUL 15 1997

Part III. Administrative, Procedural, and Miscellaneous

Health Savings Accounts

Notice 2007–22

This notice provides guidance on rollovers from health Flexible Spending Arrangements (health FSAs) and Health Reimbursement Arrangements (HRAs) to Health Savings Accounts (HSAs) under amendments to the Internal Revenue Code by section 302 of the Health Opportunity Patient Empowerment Act of 2006 (the Act) included in the Tax Relief and Health Care Act of 2006, enacted December 20, 2006, Pub. L. No. 109–432. The guidance also provides special transition relief for rollovers completed before March 15, 2007. It is anticipated that additional guidance will be published later under this provision.

As discussed in detail below, the new rules provide, in limited circumstances, for certain amounts in a health FSA or HRA to be rolled over into an HSA and for the rollover to receive favorable tax treatment. Generally, under the new rules, all of the following conditions must be satisfied in order to receive the favorable tax treatment:

- By plan year end—
    - The plan must be amended
    - The employee must elect the rollover
    - The year-end balance must be frozen
- The funds must be transferred by the employer within two and a half months after the end of the plan year and result in a zero balance in the health FSA or HRA.

Under special transition relief provided in this notice for amounts remaining at the end of 2006, however:

- There is no requirement to freeze the year-end balance in the health FSA or HRA, and
- The amendment, election, and transfer must be completed by March 15, 2007.

BACKGROUND

Eligible individuals, as defined in § 223(c)(1) of the Code, may contribute to HSAs. In general, these are individuals who, as of the first day of the month, are covered by a high deductible health plan (HDHP) and by no other health plan that is not an HDHP (with the exception of certain disregarded coverage, including permitted insurance). An individual covered by a general purpose health FSA or general purpose HRA is not eligible to contribute to an HSA. See Rev. Rul. 2004–45, 2004–1 C.B. 971. If a general purpose health FSA allows reimbursements for expenses incurred during a grace period following the end of the plan year, an otherwise eligible individual participating in the health FSA is generally not eligible to make contributions to an HSA until the first day of the first month following the end of the grace period. The maximum duration of a grace period is until the fifteenth day of the third month following the end of a plan year. See Notice 2005–42, 2005–1 C.B. 1204. Prior to the Act, this rule applied even if the individual's health FSA had no unused benefits as of the end of the prior year (*i.e.*, the balance in the health FSA was zero as of the last day of the plan year). Notice 2005–86, 2005–2 C.B. 1075. However, coverage by an HSA-compatible health FSA or HRA (limited-purpose health FSA or HRA, post-deductible health FSA or HRA, retirement HRA, or suspended HRA), does not affect an employee's eligibility to contribute to an HSA, including coverage during a health FSA grace period. See Rev. Rul. 2004–45.

HEALTH OPPORTUNITY PATIENT EMPOWERMENT ACT OF 2006 — GENERAL RULES

Section 302(a) of the Act provides for "qualified HSA distributions" before January 1, 2012. A qualified HSA distribution is a direct distribution of an amount from a health FSA or HRA to an HSA. The distribution (rollover to an HSA) must not exceed the lesser of the balance in the health FSA or HRA (1) on September 21, 2006, or (2) as of the date of the distribution. Thus, an individual who was not covered by a health FSA or HRA on September 21, 2006 may not elect a qualified HSA distribution. Similarly, an individual who participated in a health FSA with one employer on September 21, 2006, and participates in a health FSA with a second employer after that date, may not elect a qualified HSA distribution with respect to the second employer's health FSA.

A qualified HSA distribution must be contributed directly to the HSA trustee by the employer. Qualified HSA distributions may be made from general purpose health FSAs and HRAs, as well as from HSA-compatible health FSAs and HRAs. Only one qualified HSA distribution is allowed with respect to each health FSA or HRA of an individual. Qualified HSA distributions are not taken into account in applying the annual limit for HSA contributions. Qualified HSA distributions are treated as rollovers and thus, are not deductible.

If the individual fails to remain HSA-eligible during the testing period following the distribution, the amount of the rollover is included in gross income and is subject to an additional 10 percent tax. For this purpose, the testing period is defined as the period beginning with the month in which the qualified HSA distribution is contributed to the HSA and ending on the last day of the 12th month following that month. It is not required that an employee be an eligible individual with HDHP coverage in order to have a qualified HSA distribution made on the employee's behalf. However, if an employee is not an eligible individual immediately following the qualified HSA distribution, the amount of the distribution is included in the employee's income and subject to an additional 10 percent tax.

Section 302(b) of the Act provides that only certain health FSA coverage during a grace period is treated as disregarded coverage for the purpose of determining an individual's eligibility to contribute to an HSA. Under new § 223(c)(1)(B)(iii) of the Code, coverage during a grace period by a general purpose health FSA is disregarded if (1) the balance in the health FSA at the end of the prior plan year is zero or (2) the individual makes a qualified HSA distribution of any balance remaining at the end of the plan year to an HSA.

Section 302(b) of the Act only applies to health FSA coverage during a grace period following a plan year. Thus, health FSA coverage during the plan year is not disregarded, regardless of whether the health FSA balance is reduced to zero during the plan year by a qualified HSA distribution or otherwise.

QUALIFIED HSA DISTRIBUTIONS

If an employer wants to provide qualified HSA distributions, the employer must amend the health FSA or HRA written plan. In order to comply with the comparability rules in § 4980G of the Code, the amended plan must offer qualified HSA distributions to any otherwise eligible individual covered by the employer's HDHP. See new § 106(e)(5)(B) of the Code. However, there is no requirement that the health FSA or HRA be terminated in order to provide a qualified HSA distribution. Health FSAs and HRAs must satisfy the nondiscrimination requirements in § 105(h) of the Code.

A qualified HSA distribution may be made at any time prior to January 1, 2012. However, even if the qualified HSA distribution reduces the balance of an FSA or HRA to zero, the health FSA or HRA coverage does not end. If the FSA or HRA is not HSA-compatible, employees can become eligible individuals only after transfers at the end of the plan year of the FSA or HRA that result in either disregarded coverage under 302(b) of the Act, or the termination of the HRA coverage at the end of the plan year. Consequently, qualified HSA distributions from health FSAs or HRAs that are not HSA-compatible and that take place at any time other than the end of a plan year, generally result in the inclusion of the distribution in income and the imposition of an additional 10 percent tax.

The amendments in the Act do not change the requirement that unused amounts remaining at the end of a health FSA's plan year must be forfeited in the absence of a grace period. Notice 2005–42. Thus, if a health FSA does not have a grace period, unused amounts remaining at the end of the plan year are forfeited and generally cannot be transferred through a qualified HSA distribution to an HSA after the end of the plan year. Although the unused amounts can be distributed to an HSA before the end of the plan year, because the health FSA coverage continues until the end of the plan year, an individual covered by the health FSA is not an eligible individual immediately after the qualified HSA distribution, and thus any such qualified HSA distribution is included in income and subject to an additional 10 percent tax. Similarly, an individual without HDHP coverage after a distribution is not an eligible individual after the distribution and thus the qualified HSA distribution is included in income and subject to an additional 10 percent tax. Unless a participant has a change in status as provided in Treas. Reg. § 1.125–4(a), health FSA elections may not be changed during a plan year. Prop. Treas. Reg. § 1.125–1, Q & A–15.

BALANCES DETERMINED ON CASH BASIS

For all purposes, balances are determined on a cash basis. Cash basis means the balance as of any date, without taking into account expenses incurred that have not been reimbursed as of that date. Thus, pending claims, claims submitted, claims received or claims under review that have not been paid as of a date are not taken into account for purposes of determining the account balance as of that date. In addition, the balance as of any date of a health FSA is determined by applying the uniform coverage rule (*i.e.*, maximum reimbursement available for the plan year reduced for prior reimbursements paid as of the date for the same plan year). See Prop. Treas. Reg. § 1.125–2, Q&A 7(b)(2).

HDHP COVERAGE BEGINNING AFTER 1ST DAY OF THE MONTH

An employee who begins HDHP coverage after the first day of the month is not an eligible individual until the first day of the next month. If a qualified HSA distribution is made on behalf of such an employee before the first day of the next month, the employee is not an eligible individual as of the date of the qualified HSA distribution and the amount of the distribution is included in the employee's income and subject to an additional 10 percent tax. Thus, if an employee begins HDHP coverage after the first day of the month, any qualified HSA distribution on behalf of the individual made on or after the first day of the next month avoids immediate inclusion in income.

CONSEQUENCES OF FAILING TO ROLL OVER ENTIRE BALANCE OF GENERAL PURPOSE HEALTH FSA OR GENERAL PURPOSE HRA

An employee with a balance in a health FSA with a grace period or HRA at the end of a plan year is not treated as an eligible individual for HSA purposes on the first day of the immediately following plan year if a qualified HSA distribution does not result in a zero balance in the health FSA or HRA. Because the employee is covered under a health plan that is not an HDHP during the testing period, the amount of the qualified HSA distribution is included in the employee's gross income in the year of the distribution and is subject to a 10 percent additional tax. However, an employee with a balance in an HSA-compatible health FSA or HRA at the end of a plan year remains an eligible individual, if otherwise eligible, regardless of whether a qualified HSA distribution is made.

ADDITIONAL TAX FOR FAILURE TO REMAIN AN ELIGIBLE INDIVIDUAL

If an individual ceases to be an eligible individual during the testing period, the amount of the qualified HSA distribution is included in the gross income of the individual and subject to an additional 10 percent tax. Failing to remain an eligible individual does not require the withdrawal of the qualified HSA distribution, and the amount is not an excess contribution. However, any HSA withdrawal not used for qualified medical expenses is included in income and subject to an additional 10 percent tax (with certain exceptions), regardless of whether the HSA received a qualified HSA distribution that was previously included in the account beneficiary's income and subject to the additional tax. See § 223(f)(4)(B).

PERMANENT RULE — INDIVIDUALS WITH A ZERO BALANCE IN GENERAL PURPOSE HEALTH FSA ON THE LAST DAY OF PLAN YEAR

Under the Act, if an individual has a zero balance in a general purpose health

FSA, as determined on a cash basis, on the last day of the health FSA plan year, the individual does not fail to be an eligible individual as of the first day of the immediately following health FSA plan year because of coverage during a health FSA grace period.

PERMANENT RULE — INDIVIDUALS WITH A ZERO BALANCE IN GENERAL PURPOSE HRA ON THE LAST DAY OF PLAN YEAR

An individual with a zero balance in a general purpose HRA, determined on a cash basis, on the last day of the HRA plan year, does not fail to be an eligible individual on the first day of the immediately following HRA plan year, so long as (1) effective on the first day of the immediately following HRA plan year, the employee elects to waive participation in the HRA, or (2) effective on or before the first day of the following HRA plan year, the employer terminates the general purpose HRA with respect to all employees, or (3) effective on or before the first day of the following HRA plan year, with respect to all employees, the employer converts the general purpose HRA to an HSA-compatible HRA, as described in Rev. Rul. 2004–45.

PERMANENT RULE — PLAN-YEAR-END ROLLOVERS FROM GENERAL PURPOSE HEALTH FSA OR GENERAL PURPOSE HRA TO HSA

An employee with a balance in a general purpose health FSA with a grace period or general purpose HRA at the end of a health FSA or HRA plan year (plan year) is treated as an eligible individual for HSA purposes as of the first day of the first month in the immediately following plan year that the individual has HDHP coverage on the first day of the month if:

(1) the employer amends the health FSA or HRA written plan effective by the last day of the plan year to allow a qualified HSA distribution,

(2) a qualified HSA distribution from the health FSA or HRA has not been previously made on behalf of the employee with respect to that particular health FSA or HRA,

(3) the employee has HDHP coverage as of the first day of the month during which the qualified HSA distribution occurs, and is otherwise an eligible individual,

(4) the employee elects by the last day of the plan year to have the employer make a qualified HSA distribution from the health FSA or HRA to the HSA of the employee,

(5) the health FSA or HRA makes no reimbursements to the employee after the last day of the plan year,

(6) the employer makes the qualified HSA distribution directly to the HSA trustee by the fifteenth day of the third calendar month following the end of the immediately preceding plan year, but after the employee becomes HSA-eligible,

(7) the qualified HSA distribution from the health FSA or HRA does not exceed the lesser of the balance of the health FSA or HRA on (a) September 21, 2006, or (b) the date of the distribution, and

(8)(a) after the qualified HSA distribution there is a zero balance in the health FSA or HRA, and the employee is no longer a participant in any non-HSA compatible health plan or (b) effective on or before the date of the first qualified HSA distribution the general purpose health FSA or general purpose HRA written plan is converted to an HSA-compatible health FSA or HRA, as described in Rev. Rul. 2004–45, for all participants.

TRANSITION RULE — QUALIFIED HSA DISTRIBUTIONS FROM GENERAL PURPOSE HEALTH FSA AND GENERAL PURPOSE HRA BEFORE MARCH 15, 2007

An employee with a balance in a general purpose health FSA with a grace period or general purpose HRA after December 31, 2006 is treated as an eligible individual for HSA purposes as of the first day of the first month in 2007 that the employee has HDHP coverage on the first day of the month if:

(1) the employer amends the health FSA or HRA written plan effective on or before March 15, 2007, to allow a qualified HSA distribution,

(2) a qualified HSA distribution from the health FSA or HRA has not been previously made on behalf of the employee with respect to that particular health FSA or HRA,

(3) the employee has HDHP coverage as of the first day of the month during which the qualified HSA distribution occurs, and is otherwise an eligible individual,

(4) the employee elects on or before March 15, 2007, to have the employer make a qualified HSA distribution from the health FSA or HRA to the HSA of the employee,

(5) the qualified HSA distribution from the health FSA or HRA does not exceed the lesser of the balance of the respective health FSA or HRA on (a) September 21, 2006, or (b) the date of the distribution,

(6) the employer makes the qualified HSA distribution directly to the HSA trustee by March 15, 2007, but after the employee becomes HSA-eligible, and

(7)(a) after the qualified HSA distribution there is a zero balance in the health FSA or HRA, and the employee is no longer a participant in any non-HSA compatible health plan or (b) effective on or before the date of the first qualified HSA distribution, the general purpose health FSA or general purpose HRA written plan is converted to an HSA-compatible health FSA or HRA, as described in Rev. Rul. 2004–45, for all participants.

EXAMPLES

The following examples illustrate these rules. All references to balances in the following examples are determined on a cash basis. All grace periods satisfy the requirements of Notice 2005–42. It is assumed in the examples that, for purposes of § 106(e)(3)(B) and § 223(f)(4)(B), no employees are disabled.

Permanent Rule Examples

Example 1. For 2007, Employer Z has a calendar year general purpose health FSA with a grace period ending March 15, 2008. For 2007, Employee A timely elects salary reduction of $500 for the general purpose health FSA. Employer Z offers employees the option of electing HDHP coverage for the plan year beginning January 1, 2008. On or before December 31, 2007, A elects HDHP coverage beginning January 1, 2008. On December 31, 2007, A has a zero balance in the health FSA. A is otherwise an eligible individual on January 1, 2008.

A does not fail to be an eligible individual on January 1, 2008 merely because of the health FSA grace period.

Example 2. For 2007, Employer Y has a calendar year general purpose health FSA with a grace period ending on March 15, 2008. Employer Y offers employees the option of electing HDHP coverage for the plan year beginning January 1, 2008.

Before January 1, 2008, Employer Y amends the health FSA to allow for qualified HSA distributions. The amended plan allows an employee electing HDHP coverage to also elect to have any health FSA balance at year-end, determined on a cash basis, contributed directly to an HSA trustee for the employee. For this purpose, the year-end balance is the balance of the health FSA without regard to any expenses incurred but not paid. Under the amendment, if an employee elects the qualified HSA distribution, the employee cannot submit any additional claims after December 31, 2007, regardless of when the underlying expense was incurred nor are any claims paid after December 31, 2007 even if submitted prior to December 31, 2007.

Employee B has a balance of $950 in the health FSA on September 21, 2006, and a balance of $700 on December 31, 2007. On or before December 31, 2007, B elects HDHP coverage beginning January 1, 2008. B also elects to have a qualified HSA distribution of the $700 remaining in the health FSA on December 31, 2007. Employer Y contributes $700 to an HSA on behalf of B on or before March 15, 2008. B is otherwise an eligible individual as of January 1, 2008.

Employee C has a balance of $850 on December 31, 2007. On or before December 31, 2007, C elects HDHP coverage for 2008. C does not elect to have a qualified HSA distribution of the $850 remaining in the health FSA on December 31, 2007. C is otherwise an eligible individual.

B does not fail to be an eligible individual as of January 1, 2008 because after the qualified HSA distribution B has a zero balance in the health FSA. C is an eligible individual on April 1, 2008.

Example 3. For 2007, Employer W has a calendar year general purpose HRA. Employer W offers employees the option of electing HDHP coverage for the plan year beginning January 1, 2008.

Before January 1, 2008, Employer W amends the HRA to allow for qualified HSA distributions. The amended HRA allows an employee electing HDHP coverage for the plan year to also elect to have the lesser of the balance in the HRA on September 21, 2006 or the HRA balance at year-end, determined on a cash basis, contributed directly to an HSA trustee for the employee. For this purpose, the year-end balance is the balance of the HRA without regard to any expenses incurred but not paid. Under the amendment, if an employee elects the qualified HSA distribution, the employee cannot submit any additional claims after December 31, 2007, regardless of when the underlying expense was incurred, nor will the HRA reimburse any claim submitted but unpaid as of December 31, 2007. The amendment also provides that an employee who elects a qualified HSA distribution may also elect to waive participation in the HRA.

Employee D has a balance of $300 in the HRA on September 21, 2006, and a balance of $175 on December 31, 2007. On or before December 31, 2007, D elects HDHP coverage for 2008. D also elects to have a qualified HSA distribution of the $175 remaining in the HRA on December 31, 2007, and to waive participation in the HRA effective after December 31, 2007. Employer W contributes $175 to an HSA on behalf of D on or before March 15, 2008. D is otherwise an eligible individual as of January 1, 2008.

Employee E has a balance of $300 in the HRA on September 21, 2006, and a balance of $550 on December 31, 2007. On or before December 31, 2007, E elects HDHP coverage for 2008. E also elects to have a qualified HSA distribution of the $300 that was in the HRA on September 21, 2006. Employer W contributes $300 to an HSA on behalf of E on March 15, 2008. E is otherwise an eligible individual as of January 1, 2008.

Employee F has a balance of $400 in the HRA on September 21, 2006. On or before December 31, 2007, F elects HDHP coverage for 2008. On June 15, 2008, F has a balance of $275 in the HRA, and elects to have a qualified HSA distribution of the $275. Employer W contributes $275 to an HSA on behalf of F on August 20, 2008. F is otherwise an eligible individual as of January 1, 2008.

D does not fail to be an eligible individual as of January 1, 2008 because after the qualified HSA distribution D has a zero balance in the HRA and does not participate in any non-HSA compatible HRA. E fails to be an eligible individual after the qualified HSA distribution, because E has a balance exceeding zero in the HRA after the distribution. E must include $300 in gross income in 2008, as well as pay an additional 10 percent tax. F fails to be an eligible individual after the qualified HSA distribution, because F remains a participant in an HRA that is not HSA-compatible until the end of the HRA plan year. The result is the same regardless of whether F waived participation in the HRA after June 15, 2008. Thus, F must include $275 in gross income in 2008, as well as pay an additional 10 percent tax.

Example 4. The same facts as *Example 3*, except Employer W converted the general purpose HRA to an HSA-compatible retirement HRA for all employees effective January 1, 2008.

Employee G has a balance of $275 in the HRA on September 21, 2006, and a balance of $700 on December 31, 2007. On or before December 31, 2007, G elects HDHP coverage beginning January 1, 2008. G is otherwise an eligible individual as of January 1, 2008. G also elects to have a qualified HSA distribution of the $275 that was in the HRA on September 21, 2006. Employer W contributes $275 to an HSA on behalf of G on or before March 15, 2008. G has a balance of $425 in a retirement HRA and remains an active employee.

G is an eligible individual as of January 1, 2008, because the HRA G participates in is HSA-compatible.

Example 5. Employer V has a fiscal year general purpose health FSA with a grace period. The fiscal year of the health FSA is October 1 — September 30. The grace period ends on December 15. For the plan year beginning October 1, 2007, Employer V offers employees the option of electing HDHP coverage.

In December 2006, Employer V amends the health FSA to allow for qualified HSA distributions. The amended plan allows an employee electing HDHP coverage for the plan year to also elect to have any health FSA balance at the end of the plan year, determined on a cash basis, contributed directly to an HSA trustee for the employee. For this purpose, the plan-year-end balance is the balance of the health FSA without regard to any expenses incurred but not paid. If an employee elects the qualified HSA distribution, the employee cannot submit any additional claims after September 30, 2007, regardless of when the underlying expense was incurred. The health FSA does not reimburse claims submitted but unpaid as of September 30, 2007.

Employee H has a balance of $600 in the health FSA on September 21, 2006, and a balance of $500 on September 30, 2007. On or before September 30, 2007, H elects HDHP coverage for the plan year beginning October 1, 2007. H also elects to have a qualified HSA distribution of the $500 remaining in the health FSA on September 30, 2007. Employer V contributes $500 to an HSA on behalf of H on or before December 15, 2007. H is otherwise an eligible individual as of October 1, 2007.

H does not fail to be an eligible individual as of October 1, 2007 because after the qualified HSA distribution H has a zero balance in the health FSA.

Example 6. The same facts as *Example 5*, except Employer V has a limited purpose health FSA.

Employee I has a balance of $2,000 in the limited purpose health FSA on September 21, 2006, and a balance of $3,000 on September 30, 2007. On or before September 30, 2007, I elects HDHP coverage for the plan year beginning October 1, 2007. I also elects to have a qualified HSA distribution of $2,000 that was in the health FSA on September 21, 2006. Employer V contributes $2,000 to an HSA on behalf of I on or before December 15, 2007. I has a balance of $1,000 in a limited purpose health FSA. I is otherwise an eligible individual as of October 1, 2007.

I does not fail to be an eligible individual because I participates in an HSA-compatible health FSA.

Example 7. For 2007, Employer U has a calendar year general purpose health FSA with a grace period ending on March 15, 2008. Employer U has a fiscal year health plan that begins July 1, 2007. For the plan year beginning July 1, 2007, Employer U offers employees the option of electing HDHP coverage.

Before January 1, 2008, Employer U amends the health FSA to allow for qualified HSA distributions. The amended plan allows an employee electing HDHP coverage to also elect to have any health FSA balance at year-end, determined on a cash basis, contributed directly to an HSA trustee for the employee. For this purpose, the year-end balance is the balance of the health FSA without regard to any expenses incurred but not paid. Under the amendment, if an employee elects the qualified HSA distribution, the employee cannot submit any additional claims after December 31, 2007, regardless of when the underlying expense was incurred. The health FSA does not pay claims submitted but unpaid as of December 31, 2007.

Employee J has a balance of $500 in the health FSA on September 21, 2006, and a balance of $400 on June 30, 2007. On or before June 30, 2007, J elects HDHP coverage for the immediately following health plan year. J also elects to have a qualified HSA distribution of $400 that was in the health FSA on June 30, 2007. Employer U contributes $400 to an HSA on behalf of J on or before September 15, 2007. J is an otherwise eligible individual as of July 1, 2007.

J fails to be an eligible individual after the distribution because J's participation in a health FSA is not disregarded coverage until January 1, 2008, even though the qualified HSA distribution reduces the balance of the health FSA to zero. J must include $400 in his gross income for 2007, and pay an additional 10 percent tax. J is an eligible individual on January 1, 2008.

Example 8. For 2007, Employer T has a calendar year general purpose health FSA with a grace period ending on March 15, 2008. Employer T offers employees the option of electing HDHP coverage for the plan year beginning January 15, 2008.

Before January 1, 2008, Employer T amends the health FSA to allow for qualified HSA distributions. The amended plan allows an employee electing HDHP coverage to also elect to have any health FSA balance at year-end, determined on a cash basis, contributed directly to an HSA trustee for the employee. For this purpose, the year-end balance is the balance of the health FSA without regard to any expenses incurred but not paid. Under the amendment, if an employee elects the qualified HSA distribution, the employee cannot submit any additional claims after December 31, 2007, regardless of when the underlying expense was incurred. The health FSA does not pay claims submitted but unpaid as of December 31, 2007.

Employee K has a balance of $1,000 in the health FSA on September 21, 2006, and a balance of $700 on December 31, 2007. On or before December 31, 2007, K elects HDHP coverage for the plan year beginning January 15, 2008. K also elects to have a qualified HSA distribution of the $700 remaining in the health FSA on December 31, 2007. Employer T contributes $700 to an HSA on behalf of K after February 1, 2008, but before March 15, 2008. K is otherwise an eligible individual as of January 15, 2008.

Employee L has a balance of $175 in the health FSA on September 21, 2006, and a balance of $150 on December 31, 2007. On or before December 31, 2007, L elects HDHP coverage for the plan year beginning January 15, 2008. L also elects to have a qualified HSA distribution of the $150 remaining in the health FSA on December 31, 2007. Employer T contributes $150 to an HSA on behalf of L on January 25, 2008.

K does not fail to be an eligible individual because K has a zero balance in the health FSA after the qualified HSA distribution. K is eligible to contribute to the HSA as of February 1, 2008. L is not an eligible individual at the time of the distribution because L does not have HDHP coverage on the first day of January. L must include $150 in gross income in 2008, and pay an additional 10 percent tax. As of February 1, 2008, L is an eligible individual because L has HDHP coverage and no other health plan coverage that is not an HDHP, is not enrolled in Medicare, and cannot be claimed as a dependent on another person's tax return.

Transition Rule Examples

Example 9. For 2006, Employer S has a calendar year general purpose health FSA with a grace period ending on March 15, 2007. Employer S offers employees the option of electing HDHP coverage for the plan year beginning January 1, 2007.

Employer S amends the health FSA to allow for qualified HSA distributions. The amended plan allows an employee electing HDHP coverage to also elect to have any health FSA balance at year-end, determined on a cash basis, contributed directly to an HSA trustee for the employee. For this purpose, the year-end balance is the balance of the health FSA without regard to any expenses incurred but not paid. During the period from January 1, 2007 to March 15, 2007, an employee electing HDHP coverage for 2007 may elect a qualified HSA distribution of the health FSA balance. The amount of the qualified HSA distribution is determined on a cash basis on the date of the distribution.

Employee M has a balance of $850 on December 31, 2006. On or before December 31, 2006, M elects HDHP coverage beginning January 1, 2007. M does not elect to have a qualified HSA distribution of the $850 remaining in the health FSA on December 31, 2006. M incurred $850 of § 213(d) expenses after January 1 and the health FSA reimbursed M for that amount. M's health FSA balance is zero on January 22, 2007. M is otherwise an eligible individual as of January 1, 2007.

Employee N has a balance of $800 in the health FSA on September 21, 2006, and a balance of $200 on December 31, 2006. On or before December 31, 2006, N elects HDHP coverage beginning January 1, 2007. During January 2007, the health FSA reimburses N for $50 in § 213(d) medical expenses. On February 12, 2007, N elects to have a qualified HSA distribution of the remaining health FSA balance of $150. Employer S contributes $150 to an HSA on behalf of N on or before March 15, 2007. N is otherwise an eligible individual as of January 1, 2007.

Employee O has a balance of $300 in the health FSA on September 21, 2006, and a balance of $175 on December 31, 2006. On or before December 31, 2006, O elects HDHP coverage for 2007. On or before March 15, 2007, O also elects to have a qualified HSA distribution of the $175 remaining in the health FSA on December 31, 2006. Employer S contributes $175 to an HSA on behalf of O on or before March 15, 2007. O is otherwise an eligible individual as of January 1, 2007.

M has disqualifying coverage by the health FSA until April 1, 2007 because M neither had a zero balance in the FSA on December 31, 2006 nor did M have a zero balance following a qualified HSA distribution on or before March 15, 2007. N is an eligible individual as of January 1, 2007 because after the qualified HSA distribution N has a zero balance in a health FSA. O is an eligible individual as of January 1, 2007, because after the qualified HSA distribution O has a zero balance in a health FSA.

Example 10. The same facts as *Example 9*, except M and N incurred their respective $850 and $50 in § 213(d) medical expenses in December 2006. M and N submitted the expenses and were reimbursed from the health FSA for the expenses after January 1, 2007 and before February 1, 2007. On February 12, 2007, N elects to have a qualified HSA distribution of the remaining health FSA balance of $150. Employer S contributes $150 to an HSA on behalf of N on or before March 15, 2007. N is otherwise an eligible individual as of January 1, 2007.

M has disqualifying coverage by the health FSA until April 1, 2007, because M neither has a zero balance in the FSA on December 31, 2006 nor did M have a zero balance following a qualified HSA distribution on or before March 15, 2007. N is an eligible individual as of January 1, 2007 because after the qualified HSA distribution N has a zero balance in a health FSA.

Examples of Additional 10 Percent Tax

Example 11. Employee P, who is 32 years old, has HDHP coverage as of January 1, 2008. P elects to have a qualified HSA distribution on or before December 31, 2007. On or before March 15, 2008, P's employer contributes $250 from a general purpose health FSA to an HSA on behalf of P in a qualified HSA distribution meeting the requirements of section 302 of the Act and this notice. Following the qualified HSA distribution, P has a balance of zero in the general purpose health FSA.

In July 2008, P terminates employment with Employer R, and begins employment with Employer Q. Employer Q does not offer an HDHP. P obtains health coverage under a low deductible health plan, and ceases to be an eligible individual for HSA purposes. P must include the $250 qualified HSA distribution in his gross income for 2008, and pay an additional 10 percent tax under § 106(e)(3) of the Code. P does not have to withdraw the $250 from his HSA, and the amounts in the HSA may grow tax-free.

Example 12. The same facts as *Example 11*, except in February 2009, P uses $200 from his HSA for a nonqualified medical expense. The $200 is included in P's gross income for 2009 and is subject to an additional 10 percent tax under § 223(f)(4) of the Code.

Example 13. The same facts as *Example 12*, except P uses $200 from his HSA for a qualified medical expense. The $200 is not included in P's gross income, and there is no additional tax.

NO EFFECT ON HSA ESTABLISHMENT DATE

Qualified medical expenses for HSA purposes are only expenses incurred after the HSA is established. Notice 2004–2, 2004–1 C.B. 269, Q&A–26. While this notice provides that certain individuals are treated as eligible individuals as of the first day of the plan year, those rules do not treat an HSA as established before the actual establishment of the HSA.

State trust law determines when an HSA is established. Most state trust laws require that for a trust to exist, an asset must be held in trust; thus, most state trust laws require that a trust must be funded to be established.

REPORTING

Amounts transferred through a qualified HSA distribution are not reported in box 12 of Form W–2. Employers are not responsible for reporting whether an employee receiving a qualified HSA distribution remains an eligible individual during the testing period. However, employers must report qualified HSA distributions as rollover contributions to the HSA trustee, and the HSA trustee must report the qualified HSA distribution as a rollover contribution on Form 5498–SA.

EFFECTIVE DATE

The provision in the Act allowing qualified HSA distributions from health FSAs and HRAs is effective on or after December 20, 2006, and before January 1, 2012.

EFFECT ON OTHER DOCUMENTS

Published guidance under § 105(b) states that if any person has the right to receive cash or any other taxable or nontaxable benefit under a health FSA or HRA, other than the reimbursement of § 213(d) medical expenses of the employee, employee's spouse or employee's dependents, then all distributions made from the arrangement are included in the employee's gross income, even amounts paid to reimburse medical care. See Rev. Rul. 2006–36, 2006–36 I.R.B. 353; Rev. Rul. 2005–24, 2005–1 C.B. 892; Rev. Rul. 2003–102, 2003–2 C.B. 559; Notice 2002–45, 2002–2 C.B. 93; Rev. Rul. 2002–41, 2002–2 C.B. 75; Rev. Rul. 69–141, 1969–1 C.B. 48. New § 106(e) provides that a health FSA or HRA will not fail to satisfy the requirements of §§ 105 or 106 merely because the plan provides for a qualified HSA distribution. Amounts rolled into an HSA may be used for purposes other than reimbursing the § 213(d) medical expenses of the employee, spouse or dependents. Accordingly, Rev. Rul. 2006–36, Rev. Rul. 2005–24, Rev. Rul. 2003–102, Notice 2002–45, Rev. Rul. 2002–41, and Rev. Rul. 69–141 are modified with respect to qualified HSA distributions described in § 106(e). In addition, Notice 2005–86, 2005–2 C.B. 1075, is modified effective as of December 20, 2006.

DRAFTING INFORMATION

The principal author of this notice is Leslie R. Paul of the Office of Division Counsel/Associate Chief Counsel (Tax Exempt and Government Entities). For further information regarding this notice, contact Ms. Paul at (202) 622–6080 (not a toll-free call).

---

26 CFR 601.702: Publication, public inspection, and specific requests for records.
(Also: Part I, Section 6103(p)(2).)

Rev. Proc. 2007–22

SECTION 1. PURPOSE

This revenue procedure modifies the payment procedures for user fees applicable to the processing of Form 8802, *Application for United States Residency Certification*, to allow for the electronic payment of such fees effective April 2, 2007.

SECTION 2. BACKGROUND

Form 8802 is used to request Form 6166, a letter that the applicant may use as proof of the applicant's status as a resident of the United States to claim benefits under an income tax treaty or an exemption from a value added tax (VAT) imposed by a foreign country.

Rev. Proc. 2006–35, 2006–37 I.R.B. 434, announced that a new user fee charge will apply to process all requests for residency certification on Form 8802. Section 3.01 of the revenue procedure describes the fee schedule, and section 3.02 provides that the fee must be paid by check or money order to the United States Treasury in U.S. dollars.

Notice 2006–90, 2006–42 I.R.B. 688, modified Rev. Proc. 2006–35, by delaying the effective date of the user fee charge for processing Form 8802 until November 1, 2006.

Recognizing the administrative advantages to both taxpayers and the IRS of alternative payment methods, the IRS is making arrangements to allow for the electronic payment of these fees.

SECTION 3. PROCEDURES

Effective for Forms 8802 submitted on or after April 2, 2007, payment of user fees for Form 8802 may be made electronically to the IRS. The specific instructions for making payments electronically will be included in the next version of Form 8802 and its accompanying instructions, to be issued in March 2007. All further changes and modifications to these payment procedures will be reflected in Form 8802 and its accompanying instructions.

SECTION 4. INQUIRIES

For information regarding processing of Form 8802 and the user fees, contact Mr. Robert Hergenhan of Wage and Investment, Customer Account Service, Accounts Management at (215) 516–6685 (not a toll-free call).

SECTION 5. EFFECT ON OTHER DOCUMENTS

Effective February 9, 2007, Rev. Proc. 2006–35, as modified by Notice 2006–90, is further modified.

SECTION 6. EFFECTIVE DATE

This revenue procedure is effective February 9, 2007.

SECTION 7. DRAFTING INFORMATION

The principal author of this revenue procedure is Ms. Quyen P. Huynh of the Office of Associate Chief Counsel (International). For further information regarding this revenue procedure, contact Quyen P. Huynh at (202) 622–3880 (not a toll-free call).

---

26 CFR 1.1441–1: Requirement for deduction and withholding of tax on payments to foreign persons.
(Also: Part I, §§ 263, 263A.)

Rev. Proc. 2007–23

SECTION 1. PURPOSE

This revenue procedure provides administrable tax rules under domestic and international provisions of the Internal Revenue Code for certain patent cross licensing arrangements. This revenue procedure is issued in response to comments and requests for guidance in connection with Notice 2006–34, 2006–14 I.R.B. 705. In general, and as described below, this revenue procedure provides rules permitting taxpayers to change to, or continue to use, the Net Consideration Method described in section 5 of this revenue procedure for a qualified patent cross licensing arrangement (QPCLA) described in section 4 of this revenue procedure. This revenue procedure does not provide rules concerning the treatment of cross licensing arrangements that are not QPCLAs.

SECTION 2. DEFINITIONS

.01 *Application.* The definitions contained in this section 2 apply only for purposes of this revenue procedure.

.02 *Cross Licensing Arrangement.* A "cross licensing arrangement" is a contractual arrangement between two or more parties that own intellectual property under which each party grants to the other a license of specified intellectual property that is properly characterized as a license under applicable U.S. tax law principles.

.03 *Consideration.* The term "consideration" means, with respect to a cross licensing arrangement, any license rights, cash, or other consideration paid or received pursuant to the arrangement.

.04 *Controlled.* The term "controlled" has the same meaning as in § 1.482–1(i)(4) of the Income Tax Regulations.

SECTION 3 . BACKGROUND

.01 *Request for Comments.* Notice 2006–34 requested comments, information, and documents on cross licensing arrangements, including the: (i) business circumstances in which the arrangements arise; (ii) legal and factual means for distinguishing between different types of, or uses for, the arrangements; (iii) means for sourcing income from the arrangements; (iv) means for valuing cross-licensed rights; (v) financial accounting treatment of the arrangements; and (vi) foreign tax treatment of the arrangements.

.02 *Comments.* In response to the requests for information contained in Notice 2006–34, several commentators stated that many cross licensing arrangements are entered into primarily to provide each party with unfettered use of its own patents. In this way, the parties seek "freedom to operate" or the freedom to use their own intellectual property without threat of costly patent litigation from the potentially competing patent claims of the other party. These arrangements may be worded to insure "patent exhaustion" (that is, they are worded to confer rights to make, have made, import, sell, lease, use, or otherwise dispose of patented products). Commentators also stated that the use of cross licensing arrangements in this context would not typically include the transfer of other technology, such as know-how, copyright, or trademark rights. Commentators also indicated that these arrangements may or may not involve cash payments. These arrangements generally are nonexclusive.

Commentators indicated that parties to a cross licensing arrangement entered into to avoid patent litigation typically do not attempt to value the underlying patents prior to entering into the arrangement beyond a broad relative judgment that is reflected in the amount of cash payments, if any, between the parties.

Commentators pointed to the particular circumstances of patent law. Reports offered by the U.S. Patent and Trademark Office (USPTO) indicate drastic increases in the numbers of patents applied for and granted over the last 50 years. For instance, in 1950 the USPTO received 74,108 patent applications and granted 47,847 patents; by 2000, the USPTO received 315,015 patent applications and granted 175,455 patents. United States Patent and Trademark Office, *Table of Annual U.S. Patent Activity Since 1790, available at http://www.uspto.gov/web/offices/ac/ido/oeip/taf/h_counts.pdf.* At the same time, commentators indicated that a large number of patent infringement suits are filed each year with large associated costs. Commentators indicated that businesses, when faced with a potential "patent thicket," often choose to negotiate and enter into cross licensing arrangements rather than face uncertain results and expenses that might accompany patent litigation.

Commentators also described other technology sharing business arrangements that may involve a shared business purpose and the sharing of intellectual property beyond patent rights. In addition to providing information regarding the different uses for cross licensing and other technology sharing arrangements, commentators stated their view that, under established tax law principles, the execution of a cross licensing arrangement without any cash payment is not an income recognition event that would trigger withholding tax.

Commentators also indicated that attempting to value any rights granted under a cross licensing arrangement, or to source any income arising therefrom, would be extremely difficult, likely incorporating all of the uncertainties of both patent law and tax law. Commentators indicated that, under U.S. generally accepted accounting principles, profit or loss is generally reported with respect to cross licenses and similar arrangements only to the extent of any cash payments. Commentators said that several policy objectives, including maintaining U.S. competitiveness in the global marketplace in light of foreign taxation rules, would be hindered if an amount in excess of any cash received under a cross licensing arrangement were subject to withholding.

For all these reasons, commentators urged that only cash received under a cross licensing arrangement should be subject to withholding.

.03 *Applicable Law.*

Section 61(a) of the Internal Revenue Code provides the general rule that, except as otherwise provided by law, gross income includes all income from whatever source derived.

Section 162 permits a taxpayer to deduct all the ordinary and necessary expenses paid or incurred during the taxable year in carrying on any trade or business.

Section 263(a) provides that no deduction shall be allowed for any amount paid out for new buildings or for permanent improvements or betterments made to increase the value of any property or estate.

Section 263A provides that in the case of any property to which § 263A applies, the direct costs of such property and such property's proper share of those indirect costs (including taxes), part or all of which are allocable to such property shall, in the case of property which is inventory in the hands of the taxpayer, be included in inventory costs and, in the case of any other property, shall be capitalized. With certain exceptions, § 263A applies to real or tangible personal property produced by the taxpayer and real or personal property described in § 1221(a)(1) which is acquired by the taxpayer for resale.

In relevant part, §§ 871(a) and 881(a) impose a 30-percent tax on U.S. source fixed or determinable annual or periodical gains, profits, and income (FDAP) received by nonresident aliens and foreign corporations to the extent such FDAP is not effectively connected with the conduct of a trade or business within the United States. Royalties, whether paid in one lump sum or periodically, constitute

FDAP. *Commissioner v. Wodehouse*, 337 U.S. 369, 392 (1949); see also §§ 1.871–7(b)(1) and 1.1441–2(b).

Section 1441(a) provides the general rule that all payors having the control, receipt, custody, disposal or payment of items described in § 1441(b) must deduct and withhold a tax equal to 30 percent on payments of certain items of income to nonresident aliens to the extent that such items constitute gross income from sources within the United States. Section 1441(b) provides that these items of income include interest, dividends, rent, salaries, wages, premiums, annuities, compensations, remunerations and emoluments or other fixed or determinable annual or periodical gains, profits, and income. Section 1442(a) provides that, in the case of foreign corporations subject to taxation under subtitle A of the Code, there shall be deducted and withheld at the source in the same manner and on the same items of income as is provided in § 1441 a tax equal to 30 percent thereof.

Section 861(a)(4) provides that rentals or royalties from property located in the United States or from any interest in such property, including rentals or royalties for the use of or for the privilege of using in the United States patents, copyrights, secret processes and formulas, good will, trade marks, trade brands, franchises, and other like property, shall be treated as income from sources within the United States.

Section 862(a)(4) provides that rentals or royalties from property located without the United States or from any interest in such property, including rentals or royalties for the use of or for the privilege of using without the United States patents, copyrights, secret processes and formulas, good will, trade marks, trade brands, franchises, and other like property, shall be treated as income from sources without the United States.

Section 863(a) provides that items of gross income, expenses, losses, and deductions, other than those specified in §§ 861(a) and 862(a), shall be allocated or apportioned to sources within or without the United States, under regulations prescribed by the Secretary.

Section 863(b) provides that, in the case of gross income derived from sources partly within and partly without the Unites States, the taxable income may first be computed by deducting the expenses, losses, or other deductions apportioned or allocated thereto and a ratable part of any expenses, losses, or other deductions which cannot definitely be allocated to some item or class of gross income. The section further provides that the portion of such taxable income attributable to sources within the United States may be determined by processes or formulas of general apportionment prescribed by the Secretary.

Sections 871(b) and 882 provide that when a nonresident alien individual or a foreign corporation is engaged in a trade or business within the United States, the individual or corporation is taxable at U.S. graduated tax rates on taxable income which is effectively connected with the conduct of a trade or business within the United States (ECI). Section 864(c) provides specific rules for determining the income, gain, or loss treated as ECI.

Section 1031(a)(1) provides generally that no gain or loss is recognized on the exchange of property held for productive use in a trade or business or for investment if such property is exchanged solely for property of like kind which is to be held either for productive use in a trade or business or for investment. For § 1031 to apply, a taxpayer must have realized gain or loss from a disposition of property, as described in § 1001. While a sale or other disposition of a patent generally gives rise to a gain or loss under § 1001, the mere grant of a patent license does not because it is not a sale or other disposition of property within the meaning of § 1001(a). Similarly, gain or loss under § 1001 does not arise in the case of mutual grants of licenses. Thus, § 1031 has no application to a QPCLA addressed in this revenue procedure.

In general, the foregoing rules regarding inclusion, deduction, sourcing, and withholding operate independently as to each item of gross income and expense.

.04 *Administrability Issues*. The Treasury Department (Treasury) and the Internal Revenue Service (IRS) recognize that QPCLAs entered into by uncontrolled parties to pursue their businesses free from potential patent infringement claims raise many difficult issues for both taxpayers and the IRS. In light of the large number of patent applications and grants, and the difficulty and cost of resolving patent infringement disputes, it is often very difficult to ascertain the validity and scope of patent rights without incurring significant expense, which may include the cost of litigation. Thus, this unique interaction of patent and tax law creates administrative challenges for the taxation of QPCLAs.

For instance, while valuation of intellectual property is always difficult, valuation of patent rights is exceedingly difficult where the parties enter into the cross licensing arrangement to avoid or settle patent infringement disputes. Uncertainty in the patent law increases the difficulties of reaching a valuation when the parties enter into a cross licensing arrangement to avoid the costs and risks of determining their ultimate patent rights by litigation.

Similarly, the sourcing of gross income from QPCLAs entered into to avoid or settle patent infringement disputes may present administrative problems. In those arrangements, the difficulty in tracing the location and use of intangibles to a particular jurisdiction in the absence of objective benchmarks (for example, if a QPCLA did not provide for per-unit cash royalties based on sales of products) may make it difficult to allocate income to a particular source.

For these reasons, Treasury and the IRS have determined that, in the interest of sound tax administration, taxpayers are not required to take into account amounts other than the "net consideration" as defined in section 5.02 of this revenue procedure for QPCLAs described in section 4 of this revenue procedure.

SECTION 4. QUALIFIED PATENT CROSS LICENSING ARRANGEMENT (QPCLA)

A QPCLA is a nonexclusive, nontransferable patent cross licensing arrangement among uncontrolled parties, the subject matter of which is limited to the parties' present or future patent rights, as specified in the arrangement. If the parties to an arrangement also engage in more than *de minimis* licensing or other transfer of other intangible property (including copyrights, trademarks, and know how) pursuant to the arrangement, the arrangement is not a QPCLA. The determination of whether the licensing or other transfer of other intangible property is *de minimis* is determined under all the facts and circumstances.

SECTION 5. NET CONSIDERATION METHOD

.01 *Scope.* The Net Consideration Method provided in this section 5 may be used for a QPCLA by any taxpayer without regard to whether the taxpayer has made a payment of income subject to withholding with respect to the QPCLA.

.02 *Net Consideration.* For purposes of this section, "net consideration" is defined as the amount of consideration other than license rights and *de minimis* other intangible property received in the taxable year by a party pursuant to the arrangement, reduced by the amount of consideration other than license rights and *de minimis* other intangible property paid in the taxable year by the party pursuant to the arrangement.

.03 *Financial Statement Conformity.* A taxpayer may not use the Net Consideration Method discussed in this section for a QPCLA unless the taxpayer takes into account only the "net consideration", as defined in subsection 5.02 of this revenue procedure, for such arrangement on its audited financial statements (if any), or similar statement in the case of a foreign corporation, for all years ending after February 14, 2007, that the net consideration method is used for tax purposes.

.04 *Use of Net Consideration Method.* A taxpayer choosing to use the Net Consideration Method must apply the Net Consideration Method as provided in sections 5.05 and 5.06 of this revenue procedure. The use of the Net Consideration Method will be presumed to clearly reflect a taxpayer's income.

.05 *Withholding.* Under the Net Consideration Method, only the net consideration transferred between the parties to a QPCLA during a taxable year will be taken into account for withholding purposes. The Net Consideration Method applies whether the QPCLA is entered into in advance of, during, or after a patent dispute.

.06 *Capitalization.* Under the Net Consideration Method, only the net consideration transferred between the parties to a QPCLA during a taxable year will be taken into account for capitalization purposes under § 263(a) or § 263A of the Code.

.07 *Example.* X, a domestic corporation, and Y, a foreign corporation, each hold patents potentially implicated by the manufacture and sale of product P. In addition, each actively engages in the manufacture and sale of product P on a global basis. Y does not have income effectively connected with a U.S. trade or business. In 2007, X and Y enter into a QPCLA with respect to their respective patents. In accordance with the terms of the QPCLA, $20 million is paid by X to Y. The only consideration for the QPCLA taken into account on X's financial statements is the $20 million payment made by X to Y. X may use the Net Consideration Method to determine its withholding obligations and the amount subject to capitalization for federal income tax purposes.

Under the Net Consideration Method, only the $20 million payment made by X under the QPCLA is treated as income to Y for withholding purposes. Therefore, withholding under § 1442 will apply only with respect to the portion of the $20 million payment by X attributable to U.S. sources under § 861(a)(4). Further, only the $20 million payment by X is subject to capitalization under § 263(a) or § 263A.

SECTION 6. CHANGE IN ACCOUNTING METHOD

A change in the reporting of a QPCLA to the Net Consideration Method described in section 5 of this revenue procedure is a change in method of accounting within the meaning of §§ 446 and 481 and the regulations issued thereunder. Accordingly, a taxpayer that wishes to change its treatment for a QPCLA to the Net Consideration Method must obtain the consent of the Commissioner under §§ 446(e) and 1.446–1(e)(3).

SECTION 7. EFFECTIVE DATE

In general, the rules described in this revenue procedure apply to a QPCLA entered into on or after February 14, 2007.

SECTION 8. QPCLAS ENTERED INTO PRIOR TO THIS REVENUE PROCEDURE

Use of the Net Consideration Method described in section 5 of this revenue procedure for a QPCLA entered into prior to February 14, 2007 will not be raised as an issue by the IRS. If a taxpayer uses the Net Consideration Method described in section 5 of this revenue procedure for one or more QPCLAs entered into prior to February 14, 2007, and its use of that method is an issue under consideration (within the meaning of section 3.09 of Rev. Proc. 2002–9, 2002–1 C.B. 327, or its successor) in examination, in appeals, or before the U.S. Tax Court, that issue will not be further pursued by the IRS.

SECTION 9. COMMENTS

.01 *Comments Requested.* The Treasury and IRS request comments on the definition of a QPCLA and whether the Net Consideration Method also should extend to other types of cross licensing arrangements and, if so, under what conditions.

For example, comments are requested on the tax treatment of cross licensing arrangements for the joint development of intellectual property discussed in comments in response to Notice 2006–34. Such cross licensing arrangements are not within the definition of a QPCLA because the parties to such arrangements also engage in more than *de minimis* licensing or other transfer of other intangible property pursuant to the arrangements. The Treasury and IRS are considering, however, whether it may be appropriate to extend similar tax treatment to those arrangements. See § 1.482–7(g)(2) and (g)(8), Examples 4 and 5.

.02 *Submission of Comments.* Written comments may be submitted to the Office of Associate Chief Counsel (International), Attention: John E. Hinding (Revenue procedure 2007–23), CC:INTL:6, Internal Revenue Service, 1111 Constitution Avenue, N.W., Washington, DC 20224. Alternatively, taxpayers may submit comments electronically to *revenue procedure.comments@irscounsel.treas.gov*. Please include "Revenue Procedure 2007–23" in the subject line of any electronic communications. Comments will be available for public inspection and copying.

SECTION 10. DRAFTING INFORMATION

The principal authors of this revenue procedure are John E. Hinding of the Office of Associate Chief Counsel (International) and Martin Scully, Jr. of the Office of Associate Chief Counsel (Income Tax & Accounting). However, other personnel from the IRS and Treasury participated in their development. For comments or questions regarding the international provisions applicable to cross licenses covered by this revenue procedure, contact John E. Hinding at 202–435–5265 (not a toll-free call). For comments or questions regarding the domestic provisions applicable to cross licenses covered by this revenue procedure, contact Martin Scully, Jr. at 202–622–8066 (not a toll-free call).

Part IV. Items of General Interest

Notice of Proposed Rulemaking by Cross-Reference to Temporary Regulations

Certain Transfers of Stock or Securities by U.S. Persons to Foreign Corporations

REG–147144–06

AGENCY: Internal Revenue Service (IRS), Treasury.

ACTION: Notice of proposed rulemaking by cross-reference to temporary regulations.

SUMMARY: In this issue of the Bulletin, the IRS is issuing temporary regulations (T.D. 9311) under section 367(a) of the Internal Revenue Code (Code) regarding gain recognition agreements. These regulations are necessary to respond to comments requested in Notice 2005–74. The regulations primarily affect U.S. persons that transfer stock or securities to foreign corporations or corporations engaged in transactions that affect existing gain recognition agreements. The text of those regulations also serves as the text of these proposed regulations. The preamble to the temporary regulations explains the temporary regulations and these proposed regulations.

DATES: Written or electronic comments and requests for a public hearing must be received by May 7, 2007.

ADDRESSES: Send submissions to: CC:PA:LPD:PR (REG–147144–06), room 5203, Internal Revenue Service, PO Box 7604, Ben Franklin Station, Washington, DC 20044. Submissions may be hand-delivered Monday through Friday between the hours of 8 a.m. and 4 p.m. to CC:PA:LPD:PR (REG–147144–06), Courier's Desk, Internal Revenue Service, 1111 Constitution Avenue, NW, Washington, DC, or sent electronically, via the IRS Internet site at *www.irs.gov/regs* or via the Federal eRulemaking Portal at *www.regulations.gov* (IRS REG–147144–06).

FOR FURTHER INFORMATION CONTACT: Concerning the proposed regulations, Daniel McCall, (202) 622–3860; concerning submissions of comments, requests for a public hearing, and/or to be placed on the building access list to attend a hearing, contact Richard Hurst at (202) 622–7180 (not toll-free numbers).

SUPPLEMENTARY INFORMATION:

Paperwork Reduction Act

The collections of information contained in this notice of proposed rulemaking have been submitted to the Office of Management and Budget for review in accordance with the Paperwork Reduction Act of 1995 (44 U.S.C. 3507(d)). Comments on the collection of information should be sent to the **Office of Management and Budget**, Attn: Desk Officer for the Department of the Treasury, Office of Information and Regulatory Affairs, Washington, DC 20503, with copies to the **Internal Revenue Service**, Attn: IRS Reports Clearance Officer, SE:W:CAR:MP:T:T:SP, Washington, DC 20224. Comments on the collection of information should be received by May 7, 2007.

Comments are specifically requested concerning:

Whether the proposed collections of information are necessary for the proper performance of the functions of the Internal Revenue Service, including whether the information will have practical utility;

The accuracy of the estimated burden associated with the proposed collection of information;

How the quality, utility, and clarity of the information to be collected may be enhanced;

How the burden of complying with the proposed collections of information may be minimized, including through the application of automated collection techniques or other forms of information technology; and

Estimates of capital and start-up costs of operation, maintenance, and purchase of service to provide information.

The collections of information in this proposed regulation is in §1.367(a)–8(b)(3)(iii), (e)(1) through (e)(8), and (g). Responses to these collections of information are required to prevent triggering gain recognition agreements—for example, by submitting new gain recognition agreements or by submitting elections to reduce basis in certain stock. Responses are also required to facilitate electronic filing. These regulations include a rule requiring that gain or interest due under section 367(a) be included in a schedule that can be attached to a taxpayer's electronically-filed return. Response to these collections of information is mandatory. The likely respondents are large corporations.

Estimated total annual reporting burden: 240.

Estimated average annual burden hours per respondent: from 1 hour to 2 hours, depending on individual circumstances.

Estimated number of respondents: 170.

An agency may not conduct or sponsor, and a person is not required to respond to, a collection of information, unless the collection of information displays a valid control number assigned by the Office of Management and Budget.

Books or records relating to these collections of information must be retained as long as their contents may become material in the administration of any internal revenue law. Generally, tax returns and tax return information are confidential, as required by 26 U.S.C. 6103.

Background and Explanation of Provisions

Temporary regulations in this issue of the Bulletin amend the Income Tax Regulations (26 CFR part 1) relating to section 367(a) of the Internal Revenue Code (Code) and gain recognition agreements. The text of those regulations also serves as the text of these proposed regulations. The preamble to the temporary regulations explains the temporary regulations and these proposed regulations.

Special Analyses

It has been determined that this notice of proposed rulemaking is not a significant regulatory action as defined in Executive Order 12866. Therefore, a regulatory assessment is not required.

It is hereby certified that the collections of information contained in these regulations will not have a significant economic impact on a substantial number of small entities. Accordingly, a regulatory flexibility analysis is not required. These regulations primarily will affect United States persons that are large corporations engaged in cross-border corporate transactions. Thus, the number of affected small entities—in whichever of the three categories defined in the Regulatory Flexibility Act (small businesses, small organizations, and small governmental jurisdictions)—will not be substantial. The IRS and Treasury Department estimate that small organizations and small governmental jurisdictions are likely to be affected only insofar as they might hold a portfolio interest in stock or securities and in the unlikely event that they transfer such stock or securities to a foreign corporation. While a certain number of small entities may transfer stock or securities to a foreign corporation in connection with an acquisition or reorganization, the IRS and Treasury Department do not anticipate the number to be substantial. Furthermore, the IRS and Treasury Department estimate that those small entities that are affected by the regulations will likely face a burden of approximately two hours at an hourly rate of $200. Considering that the collections of information enable taxpayers to defer or avoid the recognition of potentially large amounts of gain that is subject to a gain recognition agreement, IRS and Treasury believe that $400 is not a significant economic impact. Comments about the accuracy of this certification may be submitted to the addresses provided in the preamble. Pursuant to section 7805(f) of the Internal Revenue Code, this regulation has been submitted to the Chief Counsel for Advocacy of the Small Business Administration for comment on its impact on small business.

Comments and Requests for a Public Hearing

Before these proposed regulations are adopted as final regulations, consideration will be given to any written comments (a signed original and eight (8) copies) or electronic comments that are submitted timely to the IRS. The IRS and Treasury Department specifically request comments on the clarity of the proposed rules and how they can be made easier to understand. For additional requests for comments, see the section "Request for Comments," in the preamble to the cross-referenced temporary regulations of this issue of the Bulletin. All comments will be available for public inspection and copying. A public hearing will be scheduled if requested in writing by any person that timely submits written comments. If a public hearing is scheduled, notice of the date, time, and place for the public hearing will be published in the **Federal Register**.

Drafting Information

The principal author of these proposed regulations is Daniel McCall of the Office of Associate Chief Counsel (International). However, other personnel from the IRS and the Treasury Department participated in their development.

* * * * *

Proposed Amendments to the Regulations

Accordingly, 26 CFR part 1 is proposed to be amended as follows:

PART 1—INCOME TAXES

Paragraph 1. The authority citation for part 1 is amended by adding new entries to read as follows:

Authority: 26 U.S.C. 7805* * *

Section 1.367(a)–3T(e) also issued under 367(a) and (b).* * *

Section 1.367(a)–8T also issued under 367(a) and (b).* * *

Par. 2. Section 1.367(a)–3 is amended by revising paragraphs (e) and (f) to read as follows:

§1.367(a)–3 Treatment of transfers of stock or securities to foreign corporations.

* * * * *

(e) [The text of this proposed amendment is the same as the text of §1.367(a)–3T(e) published elsewhere in this issue of the Bulletin].

(f) [The text of this proposed amendment is the same as the text of §1.367(a)–3T(f) published elsewhere in this issue of the Bulletin].

* * * * *

Par. 3. Section 1.367(a)–8 is revised to read as follows:

§1.367(a)–8 Gain recognition agreement requirements.

[The text of proposed §1.367(a)–8 is the same as the text of §1.367(a)–8T published elsewhere in this issue of the Bulletin.]

Kevin M. Brown,
Deputy Commissioner for Services and Enforcement.

(Filed by the Office of the Federal Register on February 1, 2007, 10:34 a.m., and published in the issue of the Federal Register for February 5, 2007, 72 F.R. 5228)

Archer Medical Savings Accounts — Trustees' Reports on the Number of Archer MSAs Established Between January 1, 2005 and June 30, 2005 and Between January 1, 2006 and June 30, 2006

Announcement 2007–24

PURPOSE

The purpose of this announcement is to notify trustees and custodians that they must report to the Internal Revenue Service (IRS) the number of Archer MSAs established (1) between January 1, 2005 and June 30, 2005 and (2) between January 1, 2006 and June 30, 2006. Trustees must report this information to IRS on separate Forms 8851 for 2005 and 2006, no later than March 20, 2007. Form 8851 (revised 2007) is currently available at *www.irs.gov*.

Archer Medical Savings Accounts (Archer MSAs)

Archer MSAs are authorized by section 220 of the Internal Revenue Code. The Tax Relief and Health Care Act of 2006 § 117, Pub. Law. No. 109–432, amends sections 220(j)(4), (5) of the Code to require that trustees of Archer MSAs report the number of Archer MSAs established (1) between January 1, 2005 and June 30, 2005 and (2) between January 1, 2006 and June 30, 2006. Trustees must report this information to IRS by March 20, 2007. Archer MSAs will terminate if the number of individuals establishing Archer MSAs exceeds certain numerical limits. If these limitations are exceeded in 2005 or 2006, April 19, 2007 will be a "cut-off date" after which, in general, no new Archer MSAs can be established. IRS will publish no later than April 19, 2007 the number of Archer MSAs established and whether April 19, 2007 is a "cut-off date."

Questions regarding this announcement may be directed to Shoshanna Tanner in the Office of Division Counsel/Associate Chief Counsel (Tax Exempt and Government Entities) at (202) 622–6080 (not a toll-free number).

Corporate Reorganizations; Distributions Under Sections 368(a)(1)(D) and 354(b)(1)(B)

Announcement 2007–25

AGENCY: Internal Revenue Service (IRS), Treasury.

ACTION: Final and temporary regulations; correction notice.

SUMMARY: This document contains corrections to temporary regulations (T.D. 9303, 2007–5 I.R.B. 379) that was published in the **Federal Register** on Tuesday, December 19, 2006 (71 FR 75879) regarding the qualification of certain transactions as reorganizations described in section 368(a)(1)(D).

DATES: These corrections are effective December 19, 2006.

FOR FURTHER INFORMATION CONTACT: Bruce A. Decker at (202) 622–7550 (not a toll-free number).

SUPPLEMENTARY INFORMATION:

Background

The temporary regulations (T.D. 9303) that is the subject of these corrections are under sections 368 and 354 of the Internal Revenue Code.

Need for Correction

As published, the temporary regulations (T.D. 9303) contain errors that may prove to be misleading and are in need of correction.

Correction of Publication

Accordingly, the temporary regulations (T.D. 9303) that was the subject of FR Doc. E6–21565, is corrected as follows:

1. On page 75879, column 1, in the preamble, under the caption "SUMMARY:", line 9, the language "securities of the acquiring corporation is" is corrected to read "securities of the acquiring corporation are."

2. On page 75880, column 1, in the preamble, under the paragraph heading "Background", first full paragraph of the column, line 5, the language "its operating assets to Y for $34x dollars," is corrected to read "its operating assets to Y for $34x,."

3. On page 75880, column 1, in the preamble, under the paragraph heading "Background", second full paragraph of the column, line 7, the language "requirements of section 354 and 356, is corrected to read "requirements of sections 354 and 356,."

4. On page 75881, column 1, in the preamble, under the paragraph heading "Special Analyses", line 7 from the bottom of the paragraph, the language "published elsewhere in this **Federal**" is corrected to read "published elsewhere in this issue of the **Federal**."

* * * * *

PART 1—INCOME TAXES

Paragraph 1. The authority citation for part 1 continues to read in part as follows:

Authority: 26 U.S.C. 7805 * * *

§ 1.368–2T [Corrected]

Par. 2. Section 1.368–2T is amended by revising paragraph (l)(1) to read as follows:

§ 1.368–2T Definition of terms (temporary).

* * * * *

(l) * * *

1) *General rule.* In order to qualify as a reorganization under section 368(a)(1)(D), a corporation (transferor corporation) must transfer all or part of its assets to another corporation (transferee corporation) and immediately after the transfer the transferor corporation, or one or more of its shareholders (including persons who were shareholders immediately before the transfer), or any combination thereof, must be in control of the transferee corporation; but only if, in pursuance of the plan, stock or securities of the transferee corporation are distributed in a transaction which qualifies under section 354, 355, or 356.

* * * * *

LaNita Van Dyke,
*Chief, Publications and Regulations Branch,
Legal Processing Division,
Office of Associate Chief Counsel
(Procedure and Administration).*

(Filed by the Office of the Federal Register on January 23, 2007, 8:45 a.m., and published in the issue of the Federal Register for January 24, 2007, 72 F.R. 3057)

Corporate Reorganizations; Distributions Under Sections 368(a)(1)(D) and 354(b)(1)(B); Correction Notice

Announcement 2007–26

AGENCY: Internal Revenue Service (IRS), Treasury.

ACTION: Notice of proposed rulemaking by cross-reference to temporary regulations; Correction notice.

SUMMARY: This document contains corrections to notice of proposed rulemaking by cross-reference to temporary regulations (REG–125632–06, 2007–5 I.R.B. 415) that was published in the **Federal Register** on Tuesday, December 19, 2006 (71 FR 75898) providing guidance regarding the qualification of certain transactions as reorganizations described in section 368(a)(1)(D) where no stock and/or securities of the acquiring corporation are issued and distributed in the transaction.

FOR FURTHER INFORMATION CONTACT: Bruce A. Decker at (202) 622–7550 (not a toll-free number).

SUPPLEMENTARY INFORMATION:

Background

The notice of proposed rulemaking by cross-reference to temporary regulations (REG–125632–06) that is the subject of these corrections are under sections 368 and 354 of the Internal Revenue Code.

Need for Correction

As published, notice of proposed rulemaking by cross-reference to temporary regulations (REG–125632–06) contains errors that may prove to be misleading and are in need of clarification.

Correction of Publication

Accordingly, the notice of proposed rulemaking by cross-reference to temporary regulations (REG–125632–06) that was the subject of FR Doc. E6–21572, is corrected as follows:

On page 75898, column 3, in the preamble, under the caption "SUMMARY:", line 9, the language "acquiring corporation is issued and" is corrected to read "acquiring corporation are issued and."

LaNita Van Dyke,
Chief, Publications and Regulations Branch,
Legal Processing Division,
Office of Associate Chief Counsel (Procedure and Administration).

(Filed by the Office of the Federal Register on January 23, 2007, 8:45 a.m., and published in the issue of the Federal Register for January 24, 2007, 72 F.R. 3087)

Extension of Deadline for Settlement Offered to Certain Foreign Embassy Staff

Announcement 2007–28

Following is a copy of the News Release issued by the Office of Deputy Commissioner, International on February 13, 2007 (IR–2007–34).

IRS Extends Deadline for Settlement Offered to Certain Foreign Embassy Staff

IR–2007–34, Feb. 13, 2007

WASHINGTON — The Internal Revenue Service will extend until March 30 the deadline for current and former U.S.-based employees of foreign embassies, consular offices and missions and international organizations to participate in a one-time settlement initiative to resolve outstanding tax matters related to their employment.

The deadline for participating in the offer, first announced November 17, had originally been February 20. Following requests from several embassies, the date is being extended to make certain those wishing to participate in the initiative have the opportunity to do so.

The offer is open to employees of those organizations who are U.S. citizens, green-card holders and foreign employees who have U.S. tax obligations. Accredited diplomatic personnel are generally exempt from income taxes on their wages under international treaties or agreements.

The IRS estimates that as many as half of these employees subject to U.S. tax either fail to report their wages, claim deductions they are not entitled to, incorrectly establish SEP/IRA retirement plans, fail to pay self-employment tax or fail to file tax returns at all.

To participate, employees must submit amended or original tax returns, which properly reflect their income and expenses, for tax years 2003, 2004 and 2005.

Failure to act now could mean facing a costly audit process in the future. Foreign embassy, consular office or international organization employees who fail to come forward may be subject to IRS audits and penalties which could cover more than just three years.

Additional guidance on the extension will be announced soon and will be posted on *IRS.gov*.

Part I. Rulings and Decisions Under the Internal Revenue Code of 1986

Section 42.—Low-Income Housing Credit

The adjusted applicable federal short-term, mid-term, and long-term rates are set forth for the month of March 2007. See Rev. Rul. 2007-15, page 687.

Section 101.—Certain Death Benefits

26 CFR 1.101–1: Exclusion from gross income of proceeds of life insurance contracts payable by reason of death.
(Also § 671.)

Transfer for value and grantor trusts; life insurance. This ruling treats the grantor of a grantor trust as the owner of a life insurance contract that is owned by the trust for purposes of determining whether a transfer of a contract (a) is a transfer for valuable consideration, and (b) if so, is a transfer to the insured within the meaning of section 101(a)(2)(B) of the Code.

Rev. Rul. 2007–13

ISSUE

Is the grantor who is treated for federal income tax purposes as the owner of a trust that owns a life insurance contract on the grantor's life treated as the owner of the contract for purposes of determining whether a transfer of the contract (a) is a transfer for a valuable consideration within the meaning of § 101(a)(2) of the Internal Revenue Code, and (b) if so, is a transfer to the insured within the meaning of § 101(a)(2)(B)?

FACTS

Situation 1. *TR1* and *TR2* are grantor trusts, both of which are treated as wholly owned by *G* under subpart E of Part I of subchapter J of the Internal Revenue Code. *TR2* owns a life insurance contract upon the life of *G*. *TR2* transfers the life insurance contract to *TR1* in exchange for cash.

Situation 2. The facts are the same as in Situation 1, except that *TR2* is not a grantor trust.

LAW AND ANALYSIS

Section 61 defines gross income as all income from whatever source derived, including gains derived from dealings in property.

Section 101(a)(1) provides that, except as otherwise provided in §§ 101(a)(2), 101(d), and 101(f), gross income does not include amounts received under a life insurance contract if such amounts are received by reason of the death of the insured.

Section 101(a)(2) provides, generally, that if a life insurance contract, or any interest therein, is transferred for a valuable consideration, the exclusion from gross income provided by § 101(a)(1) shall not exceed an amount equal to the sum of the actual value of the consideration and the premiums and other amounts subsequently paid by the transferee.

The term "transfer for a valuable consideration" is defined for purposes of § 101(a)(2) in § 1.101–1(b)(4) of the Income Tax Regulations as any absolute transfer for value of a right to receive all or a part of the proceeds of a life insurance policy.

Section 101(a)(2)(B) provides that § 101(a)(2) does not apply to a transfer of a life insurance contract or any interest therein to the insured, to a partner of the insured, to a partnership in which the insured is a partner, or to a corporation in which the insured is a shareholder or officer.

In Rev. Rul. 85–13, 1985–1 C.B. 184, a grantor acquired the corpus of a trust in exchange for the grantor's unsecured promissory note. The ruling concludes that the grantor is considered to have borrowed the corpus of the trust and, as a result, is treated as the owner of the trust under § 675(3). Because the grantor is treated as the owner of the trust, the grantor is deemed the owner of the trust assets for federal income tax purposes. In addition, because the grantor is therefore considered to own the purported consideration both before and after the transaction, the exchange of a promissory note for the trust assets is not recognized as a sale for federal income tax purposes.

In Situation 1, because *G* is treated as the owner of both *TR1* and *TR2* for federal income tax purposes, *G* is treated as the owner of all the assets of both trusts, including both the life insurance contract and the cash received for it, both before and after the exchange. Accordingly, in Situation 1 there has been no transfer of the contract within the meaning of § 101(a)(2).

In Situation 2, because *G* is treated as the owner of all the assets of *TR1* but not of *TR2* for federal income tax purposes, *G* is treated as the owner of the cash (but not the life insurance contract) before the exchange, and as the owner of the life insurance contract (but not the cash) after the exchange. Accordingly, in Situation 2 there has been a transfer of the life insurance contract for a valuable consideration within the meaning of § 101(a)(2). Nevertheless, the transfer for value limitations of § 101(a)(2) do not apply, because the transfer to *TR1* is treated as a transfer to *G*, the insured, within the meaning of § 101(a)(2)(B).

HOLDING

The grantor who is treated for federal income tax purposes as the owner of a trust that owns a life insurance contract on the grantor's life is treated as the owner of the contract for purposes of applying the transfer for value limitations of § 101(a)(2). Accordingly, in Situation 1, the transfer of a life insurance contract between two grantor trusts that are treated as wholly owned by the same grantor is not a transfer for a valuable consideration within the meaning of § 101(a)(2); in Situation 2, the transfer of a life insurance contract to a grantor trust that is treated as wholly owned by the insured is a transfer to the insured within the meaning of § 101(a)(2)(B) and is therefore excepted from the transfer for value limitations under § 101(a)(2).

DRAFTING INFORMATION

The principal author of this revenue ruling is Chris Lieu of the Office of Associate Chief Counsel (Financial Institutions & Products). For further information regarding this revenue ruling, contact Chris Lieu at (202) 622–3970 (not a toll-free call).

Section 280G.—Golden Parachute Payments

Federal short-term, mid-term, and long-term rates are set forth for the month of March 2007. See Rev. Rul. 2007-15, page 687.

Section 382.—Limitation on Net Operating Loss Carryforwards and Certain Built-In Losses Following Ownership Change

The adjusted applicable federal long-term rate is set forth for the month of March 2007. See Rev. Rul. 2007-15, page 687.

Section 404.—Deduction for Contributions of an Employer to an Employees' Trust or Annuity Plan and Compensation Under a Deferred-Payment Plan

This revenue ruling provides guidance on when a taxpayer using an accrual method of accounting incurs a liability under section 461 for payroll taxes on deferred compensation. See Rev. Rul. 2007-12, page 685.

Section 412.—Minimum Funding Standards

The adjusted applicable federal short-term, mid-term, and long-term rates are set forth for the month of March 2007. See Rev. Rul. 2007-15, page 687.

Section 461.—General Rule for Taxable Year of Deduction

26 CFR 1.461–1: General rule for taxable year of deduction.
(Also § 404.)

Payroll taxes on deferred compensation. This ruling provides guidance on when a taxpayer using an accrual method of accounting incurs a liability under section 461 of the Code for payroll taxes on deferred compensation. Rev. Rul. 69–587 revoked. Rev. Rul. 96–51 amplified.

Rev. Rul. 2007–12

ISSUE

If the all events test and recurring item exception of § 461 of the Internal Revenue Code are otherwise met, may an accrual method taxpayer treat its Federal Insurance Contributions Act (FICA) and Federal Unemployment Tax Act (FUTA) tax liability as incurred in Year 1 if the compensation to which the tax liability relates is deferred compensation that is deductible under § 404 in Year 2?

FACTS

X, a corporation, uses an accrual method of accounting and files its federal income tax returns on a calendar year basis. As of the end of Year 1, X has a fixed liability to pay compensation for services provided by X's employees during Year 1. As of the end of Year 1, all events have occurred to establish the fact of X's liability for the taxes ("payroll taxes") owed under §§ 3111 (the employer's share of FICA taxes) and 3301 (FUTA taxes) related to the compensation, and the amount of the payroll tax liability can be determined with reasonable accuracy. X properly adopted the recurring item exception under § 1.461–5 of the Income Tax Regulations as a method of accounting with respect to the payroll taxes. X pays the payroll taxes either (1) in Year 1 or (2) before the earlier of September 15 of Year 2 or the date X files a timely (including extensions) federal income tax return for Year 1. Therefore, under § 461, the payroll taxes generally would be treated as incurred by X in Year 1. However, the compensation to which the payroll taxes relate is deferred compensation that is properly deductible under § 404 in Year 2.

LAW AND ANALYSIS

Section 404(a) provides, in relevant part, that if compensation is paid or accrued by an employer on account of any employee under a plan deferring the receipt of such compensation, and is otherwise deductible under Chapter 1, the compensation is deductible pursuant to the rules, and subject to the limitations, of § 404.

Section 404(a)(5) provides, in part, that if the plan of compensation is not described in § 404(a)(1), (2), or (3), the compensation deductible under § 404 is deductible in the taxable year in which an amount attributable to the compensation is includible in the gross income of the employee participating in the plan. Furthermore, § 404(a)(5) provides that for purposes of § 404, any vacation pay that is treated as deferred compensation is deductible in the employer's taxable year that it is paid to the employee.

Section 1.404(b)–1T Q&A 2 provides, in part, that for purposes of § 404(a), a plan, or method or arrangement, defers the receipt of compensation or benefits to the extent it is one under which an employee receives compensation or benefits more than a brief period of time after the end of the employer's taxable year in which the services creating the right to such compensation or benefits are performed. A plan, or method or arrangement shall be presumed to be one deferring the receipt of compensation for more than a brief period of time after the end of an employer's taxable year to the extent that compensation is received after the 15th day of the 3rd calendar month after the end of the employer's taxable year in which the related services are rendered.

Section 461(a) provides that the amount of any deduction or credit must be taken for the taxable year that is the proper taxable year under the method of accounting used in computing taxable income.

Section § 1.461–1(a)(2)(i) provides that, under an accrual method of accounting, a liability is incurred, and is generally taken into account for federal income tax purposes, in the taxable year in which (1) all the events have occurred that establish the fact of the liability, (2) the amount of the liability can be determined with reasonable accuracy, and (3) economic performance has occurred with respect to the liability (the "all events test"). *See also* § 1.446–1(c)(1)(ii)(A).

Section 1.461–4(d)(2)(i) provides that in general, if the liability of a taxpayer arises out of the providing of services to the taxpayer by another person, economic performance occurs as the services are provided. Section 1.461–4(d)(2)(iii) provides that with respect to employee benefits which arise out of the provision of services to the taxpayer, the economic performance requirement is satisfied to the extent that any amount is otherwise deductible under § 404. Section 1.461–4(g)(6) provides generally that, if a taxpayer is liable to pay a tax, economic performance occurs as the tax is paid to the governmental authority that imposed it.

Section 1.461–5(b)(1) provides a recurring item exception to the general rule of economic performance. Under the recurring item exception, a liability is treated as incurred for a taxable year if: (i) at the end of the taxable year, all events have occurred that establish the fact of the liability and the amount can be determined with reasonable accuracy; (ii) economic performance occurs on or before the earlier of (a) the date that the taxpayer files a return (including extensions) for the taxable year, or (b) the 15th day of the 9th calendar month after the close of the taxable year; (iii) the liability is recurring in nature; and (iv) either the amount of the liability is not material or accrual of the liability in the taxable year results in better matching of the liability against the income to which it relates than would result from accrual of the liability in the taxable year in which economic performance occurs. Section 1.461–5(b)(5)(ii) provides that, in the case of a liability for taxes, the matching requirement of the recurring item exception is deemed satisfied.

Rev. Rul. 69–587, 1969–2 C.B. 108, concludes that, under the all events test of § 461, an accrual method employer generally may not deduct payroll taxes payable with respect to bonuses and vacation pay accrued but unpaid at year-end until the taxable year in which the bonuses and vacation pay are paid.

Rev. Rul. 96–51, 1996–2 C.B. 36, concludes that, under the all events test, an accrual method employer may deduct in Year 1 its otherwise deductible payroll taxes imposed on year-end wages properly accrued in Year 1 but paid in Year 2, provided the employer satisfies the requirements of the recurring item exception in § 1.461–5 with respect to those taxes. However, Rev. Rul. 96–51 does not address the application of § 404 because the year-end wages were paid before the 15th day of the 3rd calendar month after the end of Year 1.

In general, § 404 applies to compensation paid or accrued by an employer on account of any employee under a plan deferring the receipt of such compensation. An employer's liability for payroll taxes does not represent compensation paid or accrued by an employer on account of any employee. Therefore, § 404 does not control the deductibility of an employer's liability for payroll taxes, even if the payroll tax liability relates to a deferred compensation liability subject to the deduction rules of § 404. Accordingly, § 404 does not alter the timing of the accrual of X's payroll tax liability under § 461.

HOLDING

If the all events test and recurring item exception of § 461 are otherwise met, an accrual basis taxpayer may treat its payroll tax liability as incurred in Year 1, regardless of whether the compensation to which the liability relates is deferred compensation that is deductible under § 404 in Year 2.

EFFECT ON OTHER DOCUMENTS

Rev. Rul. 96–51 is amplified. Rev. Rul. 69–587 is revoked.

APPLICATION

A change in treatment of payroll tax liabilities associated with deferred compensation to comply with this revenue ruling is a change in method of accounting within the meaning of §§ 446 and 481 and the regulations issued thereunder. Accordingly, a taxpayer that wants to change its treatment of payroll taxes associated with deferred compensation to comply with this revenue ruling must obtain the consent of the Commissioner under § 446(e) and § 1.446–1(e)(2)(i).

DRAFTING INFORMATION

The principal author of this revenue ruling is Martin L. Osborne of the Office of Associate Chief Counsel (Income Tax and Accounting). For further information regarding this revenue ruling, contact Mr. Osborne at (202) 622–7900 (not a toll-free call).

Section 467.—Certain Payments for the Use of Property or Services

The adjusted applicable federal short-term, mid-term, and long-term rates are set forth for the month of March 2007. See Rev. Rul. 2007-15, page 687.

Section 468.—Special Rules for Mining and Solid Waste Reclamation and Closing Costs

The adjusted applicable federal short-term, mid-term, and long-term rates are set forth for the month of March 2007. See Rev. Rul. 2007-15, page 687.

Section 482.—Allocation of Income and Deductions Among Taxpayers

Federal short-term, mid-term, and long-term rates are set forth for the month of March 2007. See Rev. Rul. 2007-15, page 687.

Section 483.—Interest on Certain Deferred Payments

The adjusted applicable federal short-term, mid-term, and long-term rates are set forth for the month of March 2007. See Rev. Rul. 2007-15, page 687.

Section 642.—Special Rules for Credits and Deductions

Federal short-term, mid-term, and long-term rates are set forth for the month of March 2007. See Rev. Rul. 2007-15, page 687.

Section 807.—Rules for Certain Reserves

The adjusted applicable federal short-term, mid-term, and long-term rates are set forth for the month of March 2007. See Rev. Rul. 2007-15, page 687.

Section 846.—Discounted Unpaid Losses Defined

The adjusted applicable federal short-term, mid-term, and long-term rates are set forth for the month of March 2007. See Rev. Rul. 2007-15, page 687.

Section 932.—Coordination of United States and Virgin Islands Income Taxes

A notice provides interim rules concerning the statute of limitations on assessment for individuals claiming to be *bona fide* residents of the U.S. Virgin Islands. See Notice 2007-19, page 689.

Section 1274.—Determination of Issue Price in the Case of Certain Debt Instruments Issued for Property

(Also Sections 42, 280G, 382, 412, 467, 468, 482, 483, 642, 807, 846, 1288, 7520, 7872.)

Federal rates; adjusted federal rates; adjusted federal long-term rate and the long-term exempt rate. For purposes of sections 382, 642, 1274, 1288, and other sections of the Code, tables set forth the rates for March 2007.

Rev. Rul. 2007–15

This revenue ruling provides various prescribed rates for federal income tax purposes for March 2007 (the current month). Table 1 contains the short-term, mid-term, and long-term applicable federal rates (AFR) for the current month for purposes of section 1274(d) of the Internal Revenue Code. Table 2 contains the short-term, mid-term, and long-term adjusted applicable federal rates (adjusted AFR) for the current month for purposes of section 1288(b). Table 3 sets forth the adjusted federal long-term rate and the long-term tax-exempt rate described in section 382(f). Table 4 contains the appropriate percentages for determining the low-income housing credit described in section 42(b)(2) for buildings placed in service during the current month. Finally, Table 5 contains the federal rate for determining the present value of an annuity, an interest for life or for a term of years, or a remainder or a reversionary interest for purposes of section 7520.

REV. RUL. 2007–15 TABLE 1

Applicable Federal Rates (AFR) for March 2007

		Period for Compounding		
	Annual	*Semiannual*	*Quarterly*	*Monthly*
Short-term				
AFR	5.06%	5.00%	4.97%	4.95%
110% AFR	5.58%	5.50%	5.46%	5.44%
120% AFR	6.09%	6.00%	5.96%	5.93%
130% AFR	6.61%	6.50%	6.45%	6.41%
Mid-term				
AFR	4.86%	4.80%	4.77%	4.75%
110% AFR	5.35%	5.28%	5.25%	5.22%
120% AFR	5.84%	5.76%	5.72%	5.69%
130% AFR	6.34%	6.24%	6.19%	6.16%
150% AFR	7.33%	7.20%	7.14%	7.09%
175% AFR	8.58%	8.40%	8.31%	8.26%
Long-term				
AFR	5.01%	4.95%	4.92%	4.90%
110% AFR	5.52%	5.45%	5.41%	5.39%
120% AFR	6.03%	5.94%	5.90%	5.87%
130% AFR	6.54%	6.44%	6.39%	6.36%

REV. RUL. 2007–15 TABLE 2

Adjusted AFR for March 2007

		Period for Compounding		
	Annual	*Semiannual*	*Quarterly*	*Monthly*
Short-term adjusted AFR	3.58%	3.55%	3.53%	3.52%
Mid-term adjusted AFR	3.71%	3.68%	3.66%	3.65%
Long-term adjusted AFR	4.18%	4.14%	4.12%	4.10%

REV. RUL. 2007–15 TABLE 3 Rates Under Section 382 for March 2007	
Adjusted federal long-term rate for the current month	4.18%
Long-term tax-exempt rate for ownership changes during the current month (the highest of the adjusted federal long-term rates for the current month and the prior two months.)	4.18%

REV. RUL. 2007–15 TABLE 4 Appropriate Percentages Under Section 42(b)(2) for March 2007	
Appropriate percentage for the 70% present value low-income housing credit	8.15%
Appropriate percentage for the 30% present value low-income housing credit	3.49%

REV. RUL. 2007–15 TABLE 5 Rate Under Section 7520 for March 2007	
Applicable federal rate for determining the present value of an annuity, an interest for life or a term of years, or a remainder or reversionary interest	5.8%

Section 1288.—Treatment of Original Issue Discount on Tax-Exempt Obligations

The adjusted applicable federal short-term, mid-term, and long-term rates are set forth for the month of March 2007. See Rev. Rul. 2007-15, page 687.

Section 6501.—Limitations on Assessment and Collection

A notice provides interim rules concerning the statute of limitations on assessment for individuals claiming to be *bona fide* residents of the U.S. Virgin Islands. See Notice 2007-19, page 689.

Section 7520.—Valuation Tables

The adjusted applicable federal short-term, mid-term, and long-term rates are set forth for the month of March 2007. See Rev. Rul. 2007-15, page 687.

Section 7654.—Coordination of United States and Certain Possession Individual Income Taxes

A notice provides interim rules concerning the statute of limitations on assessment for individuals claiming to be *bona fide* residents of the U.S. Virgin Islands. See Notice 2007-19, page 689.

Section 7872.—Treatment of Loans With Below-Market Interest Rates

The adjusted applicable federal short-term, mid-term, and long-term rates are set forth for the month of March 2007. See Rev. Rul. 2007-15, page 687.

Part III. Administrative, Procedural, and Miscellaneous

Statute of Limitations on Assessment Concerning Certain Individuals Filing Income Tax Returns With the U.S. Virgin Islands

Notice 2007–19

SECTION 1. PURPOSE

This notice provides interim rules under sections 932(c) and 7654(e) concerning the statute of limitations on assessment of the U.S. income tax liability (if any) of a U.S. citizen or resident alien who takes the position that he or she is a *bona fide* resident of the U.S. Virgin Islands and the U.S. filing obligations of such an individual. This notice also announces that the Treasury Department and Internal Revenue Service (IRS) intend to issue regulations under sections 932(c) and 7654(e). Finally, this notice announces that the Treasury Department and the IRS are studying the feasibility of an automatic exchange of information program with the U.S. Virgin Islands Bureau of Internal Revenue concerning income tax information of individual taxpayers. Such a program for the timely exchange of equivalent data in a form compatible with IRS systems may eliminate the reporting requirements set forth in the interim rules. Until the regulations are issued, taxpayers may rely on this notice.

SECTION 2. INTERIM RULES

Under the authority of section 7654(e), an income tax return filed with the U.S. Virgin Islands by a U.S. citizen or resident alien (USVI Form 1040) will be deemed to be a U.S. income tax return of that individual for purposes of section 6501(a), provided that the individual is a covered person. The term "covered person" means a U.S. citizen or resident alien who takes the position that he or she is a *bona fide* resident of the U.S. Virgin Islands, files USVI Form 1040 with the U.S. Virgin Islands, and has less than $75,000 of gross income for the taxable year. For purposes of this notice, gross income means the total amount of income from whatever source derived, before any exclusions or deductions (for example, disregarding any applicable U.S. Virgin Islands tax benefits authorized under section 934(b)). Gross income does not include income of the individual's spouse.

For example, assume that C, a U.S. citizen and calendar year taxpayer who has less than $75,000 of gross income for 2006, takes the position that he is a *bona fide* resident of the U.S. Virgin Islands and files USVI Form 1040 for 2006 on March 12, 2007 with the U.S. Virgin Islands. C does not file Form 1040, *U.S. Individual Income Tax Return* (U.S. Form 1040), with the IRS. C is a covered person. Under these circumstances, the 3-year period of limitations under section 6501(a) will expire on April 15, 2010, and the IRS will make no further assessment of income tax for A's 2006 taxable year after that date except as otherwise authorized by section 6501.

With respect to a U.S. citizen or resident alien who takes the position that he or she is a *bona fide* resident of the U.S. Virgin Islands for a taxable year but who has gross income of $75,000 or more (referred to as a non-covered person), a U.S. Form 1040 filed by the non-covered person with the IRS, on which the non-covered person reports no gross income and no taxable income, will be treated as an income tax return described in section 6501(a).

This notice imposes a new annual information reporting requirement under section 7654 for non-covered persons. The Treasury Department and the IRS intend to issue a new form titled *Bona Fide Residence-Based Return Position* for purposes of this new information reporting requirement. Until this form is issued, a non-covered person will meet the information reporting requirement by attaching a statement to U.S. Form 1040 reporting no gross income and no taxable income. The statement should be titled "Bona Fide Residence-Based Return Position" and must set forth the following information.

1. The non-covered person's name, social security number, and address as reported on U.S. Form 1040.

2. A statement affirming the non-covered person's *bona fide* residence in the U.S. Virgin Islands as defined in Treas. Reg. § 1.937–1(b) and a brief summary of the facts on which it is based.

3. An affirmation that the non-covered person has properly filed a U.S. Virgin Islands individual income tax return, a statement of the total tax liability reported on USVI Form 1040, and the amount of gross income reported on such return (adding back any applicable territorial tax benefits authorized under section 934(b)).

4. The following declaration signed and dated by the individual: "Under penalties of perjury, I declare that I have examined this statement and the accompanying attachments and to the best of my knowledge and belief, they are true, correct, and complete."

For example, assume that on March 12, 2007, N, a U.S. citizen and calendar year taxpayer with at least $75,000 of gross income for 2006, files U.S. Form 1040 (2006) with the IRS, taking the position that he does not have any gross income or taxable income for U.S. income tax purposes (as reported on lines 22 and 43, respectively) under section 932(c)(4). N attaches a Bona Fide Residence-Based Return Position statement. As a result of filing U.S. Form 1040, the 3-year period of limitations under section 6501(a) will expire on April 15, 2010, and the IRS will make no further assessment of income tax for N's 2006 taxable year after that date except as otherwise authorized by section 6501.

U.S. Forms 1040 with attached Bona Fide Residence-Based Return Position statements must be filed with the Internal Revenue Service Center, P.O. Box 331 Drop Point S–607, Bensalem, PA 19020–8517. Failure to file the Bona Fide Residence-Based Position statement is subject to a penalty under section 6688. If a non-covered person and his or her spouse filed a joint USVI Form 1040, then they may file a jointly executed U.S. Form 1040 but must attach a separate Bona Fide Residence-Based Return Position statement for each spouse who is a non-covered person.

SECTION 3. EFFECTIVE DATE

This notice applies for taxable years ending on or after December 31, 2006. Taxpayers also may choose to apply this notice to a taxable year ending before

December 31, 2006 as specified in this section 3.

A non-covered person may choose to apply this notice to a taxable year ending before December 31, 2006 by filing U.S. Form 1040 with the IRS at the address provided in section 2, reporting no gross income and no taxable income for that taxable year. Although a Bona Fide Residence-Based Position statement need not be filed for a taxable year ending before December 31, 2006, the non-covered person should clearly note on the first page of U.S. Form 1040 the applicable taxable year and that U.S. Form 1040 is being filed in accordance with this notice.

For example, assume that on March 16, 2007, J, a U.S. citizen and calendar year taxpayer with at least $75,000 of gross income for taxable year 2003, files U.S. Form 1040 with the IRS, taking the position that for taxable year 2003 she does not have any gross income or taxable income for U.S. income tax purposes under section 932(c)(4). J clearly marks U.S. Form 1040 as applying to her taxable year ending December 31, 2003 and as being filed in accordance with Notice 2007–19. Under these circumstances, the 3-year period of limitations under section 6501(a) for taxable year 2003 will expire on March 16, 2010, and the IRS will make no further assessment of income tax for J's 2003 taxable year after that date except as otherwise authorized by section 6501.

A covered person may choose to apply this notice to a taxable year ending before December 31, 2006 by providing documentation upon examination that establishes to the satisfaction of the Commissioner that the taxpayer is a covered person. Because the USVI Form 1040 filed with the U.S. Virgin Islands is deemed to be a covered person's U.S. Form 1040, the covered person's statute of limitations under section 6501(a) will begin to run on the date USVI Form 1040 is filed with the U.S. Virgin Islands.

SECTION 4. PAPERWORK REDUCTION ACT

The collection of information contained in this notice has been reviewed and approved by the Office of Management and Budget in accordance with the Paperwork Reduction Act (44 U.S.C. 3507) under control number 1545–2063.

An agency may not conduct or sponsor, and a person is not required to respond to, a collection of information unless the collection of information displays a valid OMB control number.

The collection of information in this notice is in section 2. This information is required to determine if a taxpayer satisfies the requirements of *bona fide* residence in the U.S. Virgin Islands under section 937(a). The information will be used to determine if a taxpayer satisfies his or her U.S. income tax filing requirements. The collection of information is voluntary. The likely respondents are individuals.

The estimated total annual reporting burden is 42,500 hours.

The estimated annual burden per respondent varies from 4 to 6 hours, depending on individual circumstances, with an estimated average of 5 hours. The estimated number of respondents is 8,500.

The estimated frequency of responses: annually.

Books or records relating to a collection of information must be retained as long as their contents may become material in the administration of any internal revenue law. Generally, tax returns and tax return information are confidential, as required by 26 U.S.C. 6103.

SECTION 5. DRAFTING INFORMATION

The principal author of this notice is J. David Varley of the Office of Associate Chief Counsel (International). For further information regarding this notice, contact Mr. Varley at (202) 435–5262 (not a toll-free call).

2007 Calendar Year Resident Population Estimates

Notice 2007–23

This notice informs (1) state and local housing credit agencies that allocate low-income housing tax credits under § 42 of the Internal Revenue Code and (2) states and other issuers of tax-exempt private activity bonds under § 141, of the proper population figures to be used for calculating the 2007 calendar year population-based component of the state housing credit ceiling (Credit Ceiling) under § 42(h)(3)(C)(ii), the 2007 calendar year volume cap (Volume Cap) under § 146, and the 2007 volume limit (Volume Limit) under § 142(k)(5).

The population figures both for the population-based component of the Credit Ceiling and for the Volume Cap are determined by reference to § 146(j). That section provides generally that determinations of population for any calendar year are made on the basis of the most recent census estimate of the resident population of a state (or issuing authority) released by the U.S. Census Bureau before the beginning of such calendar year. Section 142(k)(5) provides that the Volume Limit is based on the State population.

The population-based component of the Credit Ceiling and the Volume Cap are adjusted for inflation pursuant to §§ 42(h)(3)(H) and 146(d)(2), respectively. The adjustments for the 2007 calendar year were published in Rev. Proc. 2006–53, 2006–48 I.R.B. 996. Section 3.08 of Rev. Proc. 2006–53 provides that, for calendar year 2007, the amounts used under § 42(h)(3)(C)(ii) to calculate the Credit Ceiling is the greater of $1.95 multiplied by the State population (see the resident population figures provided below) or $2,275,000. Further, section 3.16 of Rev. Proc. 2006–53 provides that the amounts used under § 146(d)(1) to calculate the Volume Cap for calendar year 2007 is the greater of $85 multiplied by the State population (see the resident population figures provided below) or $256,235,000.

The proper population figures for calculating the Credit Ceiling, the Volume Cap, and the Volume Limit for the 2007 calendar year are the estimates of the resident population of the 50 states, the District of Columbia, and Puerto Rico released by the U.S. Census Bureau on December 22, 2006, in Press Release CB06–187. The proper population figures for calculating the Credit Ceiling, the Volume Cap, and the Volume Limit for the 2007 calendar year for the insular areas (American Samoa, Guam, Northern Mariana Islands, and U.S. Virgin Islands) are the figures released electronically by the U.S. Census Bureau on July 17, 2003, and referenced in Census Bureau Tip Sheet TP03–16, dated August 8, 2003. For convenience, these estimates are reprinted below.

Resident Population Figures	
Alabama	4,599,030
Alaska	670,053
American Samoa	57,794
Arizona	6,166,318
Arkansas	2,810,872
California	36,457,549
Colorado	4,753,377
Connecticut	3,504,809
Delaware	853,476
D.C.	581,530
Florida	18,089,888
Georgia	9,363,941
Guam	171,019
Hawai	1,285,498
Idaho	1,466,465
Illinois	12,831,970
Indiana	6,313,520
Iowa	2,982,085
Kansas	2,764,075
Kentucky	4,206,074
Louisiana	4,287,768
Maine	1,321,574
Maryland	5,615,727
Massachusetts	6,437,193
Michigan	10,095,643
Minnesota	5,167,101
Mississippi	2,910,540
Missouri	5,842,713
Montana	944,632
Nebraska	1,768,331
Nevada	2,495,529
New Hampshire	1,314,895
New Jersey	8,724,560
New Mexico	1,954,599
New York	19,306,183
North Carolina	8,856,505
North Dakota	635,867
Northern Mariana Islands	82,459
Ohio	11,478,006
Oklahoma	3,579,212
Oregon	3,700,758

Pennsylvania	12,440,621
Puerto Rico	3,927,776
Rhode Island	1,067,610
South Carolina	4,321,249
South Dakota	781,919
Tennessee	6,038,803
Texas	23,507,783
U.S. Virgin Islands	108,605
Utah	2,550,063
Vermont	623,908
Virginia	7,642,884
Washington	6,395,798
West Virginia	1,818,470
Wisconsin	5,556,506
Wyoming	515,004

The principal authors of this notice are Christopher J. Wilson, Office of the Associate Chief Counsel (Passthroughs and Special Industries) and Timothy L. Jones, Office of the Division Counsel/Associate Chief Counsel (Tax-Exempt and Government Entities). For further information regarding this notice, contact Mr. Wilson at (202) 622–3040 (not a toll-free call).

Note. This revenue procedure will be reproduced as the next revision of IRS Publication 1167, General Rules and Specifications for Substitute Forms and Schedules.

Rev. Proc. 2007–24

TABLE OF CONTENTS

PART 1 – INTRODUCTION TO SUBSTITUTE FORMS

PART 2 – GENERAL GUIDELINES FOR SUBMISSIONS AND APPROVALS

Part 1
Introduction to Substitute Forms

Section 1.1 – Overview of Revenue Procedure 2007–24

1.1.1 Purpose

The purpose of this revenue procedure is to provide guidelines and general requirements for the development, printing, and approval of substitute tax forms. Approval will be based on these guidelines. After review and approval, submitted forms will be accepted as substitutes for official IRS forms.

1.1.2 Unique Forms

Certain unique specialized forms require the use of other additional publications to supplement this publication. See Part 4.

1.1.3 Scope

The IRS accepts quality substitute tax forms that are consistent with the official forms and do not have an adverse impact on our processing. The IRS Substitute Forms Unit administers the formal acceptance and processing of these forms nationwide. While this program deals primarily with paper documents, it also reviews for approval other processing and filing forms such as those used in electronic filing.

Only those substitute forms that comply fully with the requirements are acceptable. This revenue procedure is updated as required to reflect pertinent tax year form changes and to meet processing and/or legislative requirements.

1.1.4 Forms Covered by This Revenue Procedure

The following types of forms are covered by this revenue procedure:

- IRS tax forms and their related schedules,
- Worksheets as they appear in instruction packages,
- Applications for permission to file returns electronically and forms used as required documentation for electronically filed returns,
- Powers of Attorney,
- Over-the-counter estimated tax payment vouchers, and
- Forms and schedules relating to partnerships, exempt organizations, and employee plans.

1.1.5 Forms Not Covered by This Revenue Procedure

The following types of forms are not covered by this revenue procedure:

- W-2 and W-3 (see Publication 1141 for information on these forms),
- W-2c and W-3c (see Publication 1223 for information on these forms),
- 941 and Schedule B (Form 941) (see Publication 4436 for information on these forms),
- 1096, 1098 series, 1099 series, 5498 series, W-2G, and 1042-S (see Publication 1179 for information on these forms),
- Federal Tax Deposit (FTD) coupons, which may not be reproduced,
- Forms 1040-ES (OCR) and 1041-ES (OCR), which may not be reproduced,
- Forms 5500, 5500-EZ, and associated schedules (see the Department of Labor website at *www.dol.gov* for information on these forms),
- Forms 8717 and 8905, bar-coded forms requiring separate approval,
- Requests for information or documentation initiated by the IRS,
- Forms used internally by the IRS,

- State tax forms,
- Forms developed outside the IRS, and
- General Instructions and Specific Instructions (not reviewed by the Substitute Forms Program Unit).

Section 1.2 – IRS Contacts

1.2.1 Where To Send Substitute Forms

Send your substitute forms for approval to the following offices (do not send forms with taxpayer data):

Form	Office and Address
BSA Forms (FINCEN Family and TD F 90-22 Family other than TD F 90-22.1)	IRS Computing Center BSA Compliance Branch P.O. Box 32063 Detroit, MI 48232-0063
5500, 5500-EZ, and Schedules A through E, G, H, I, P, R, SSA, and T for Form 5500	Check EFAST information at the Department of Labor's website at *www.efast.dol.gov*
8717 and 8905	*Joanna.H.Weber@irs.gov*
All others (except W-2, W-2c, W-3, W-3c, 941, Schedule B (Form 941), 1096, 1098, 1099, 5498, W-2G, and 1042-S)	Internal Revenue Service Attn: Substitute Forms Program SE:W:CAR:MP:T:T:SP 1111 Constitution Avenue, NW Room 6406 Washington, DC 20224

In addition, the Substitute Forms Program Unit can be contacted via email at **taxforms@irs.gov* (the asterisk must be included in the address). Please enter "Substitute Forms" on the subject line.

For questions about Forms W-2 and W-3, refer to IRS Publication 1141, General Rules and Specifications for Substitute Forms W-2 and W-3. For Forms W-2c and W-3c, refer to IRS Publication 1223, General Rules and Specifications for Substitute Forms W-2c and W-3c. For Forms 941 and Schedule B (Form 941), refer to IRS Publication 4436, General Rules and Specifications for Substitute Form 941 and Schedule B (Form 941). For Forms 1096, 1098, 1099, 5498, W-2G, and 1042-S, refer to IRS Publication 1179, General Rules and Specifications for Substitute Forms 1096, 1098, 1099, 5498, W-2G, and 1042-S.

Section 1.3 – What's New

1.3.1 What's New

The following changes have been made to the Revenue Procedure for tax year 2006.

- We combined Sections 4.1 and 4.2 in order to reduce duplication.
- Because Forms 8717 and 8905 now contain bar coding, substitutes of these forms must be forwarded to *Joanna.H.Weber@irs.gov*.
- The Exhibits section has been changed and updated.

Section 1.4 – Definitions

1.4.1
Substitute Form

A tax form (or related schedule) that differs in any way from the official version and is intended to replace the form that is printed and distributed by the IRS. This term also covers those approved substitute forms exhibited in this revenue procedure.

1.4.2
Printed/Preprinted Form

A form produced using conventional printing processes, or a printed form which has been reproduced by photocopying or a similar process.

1.4.3
Preprinted Pin-Fed Form

A printed form that has marginal perforations for use with automated and high-speed printing equipment.

1.4.4
Computer Prepared Substitute Form

A preprinted form in which the taxpayer's tax entry information has been inserted by a computer, computer printer, or other computer-type equipment such as word processing equipment.

1.4.5
Computer Generated Substitute Tax Return or Form

A tax return or form that is entirely designed and printed using a computer printer such as a laser printer, etc., on plain white paper. This return or form must conform to the physical layout of the corresponding IRS form, although the typeface may differ. The text should match the text on the officially printed form as closely as possible. Condensed text and abbreviations will be considered on a case-by-case basis.

Exception. All jurats (perjury statements) must be reproduced verbatim.

1.4.6
Manually Prepared Form

A preprinted reproduced form in which the taxpayer's tax entry information is entered by an individual using a pen, pencil, typewriter, or other non-automated equipment.

1.4.7
Graphics

Parts of a printed tax form that are not tax amount entries or required text. Examples of graphics are line numbers, captions, shadings, special indicators, borders, rules, and strokes created by typesetting, photographics, photocomposition, etc.

1.4.8
Acceptable Reproduced Form

A legible photocopy of an original form.

1.4.9
Supporting Statement (Supplemental Schedule)

A document providing detailed information to support a line entry on an official or approved substitute form and filed with (attached to) a tax return.

Note. A supporting statement is not a tax form and does not take the place of an official form.

1.4.10
Specific Form Terms

The following specific terms are used throughout this revenue procedure in reference to all substitute forms: format, sequence, line reference, item caption, and data entry field.

1.4.11
Format

The overall physical arrangement and general layout of a substitute form.

1.4.12
Sequence

Sequence is an integral part of the total format requirement. The substitute form should show the same numeric and logical placement order of data, as shown on the official form.

1.4.13
Line Reference

The line numbers, letters, or alphanumerics used to identify each captioned line on an official form. These line references are printed to the immediate left of each caption and/or data entry field.

1.4.14
Item Caption

The text on each line of a form, which identifies the data required.

1.4.15
Data Entry Field

Designated areas for the entry of data such as dollar amounts, quantities, responses and checkboxes.

1.4.16
Advance Draft

A draft version of a new or revised form may be posted to the IRS website for information purposes. Substitute forms may be submitted based on these advance drafts, but any company that receives forms approval based on these early drafts is responsible for monitoring and revising forms to mirror any revisions in the final forms provided by the IRS.

Section 1.5 – Agreement

1.5.1
Important Stipulation of This Revenue Procedure

Any person or company who uses substitute forms and makes all or part of the changes specified in this revenue procedure agrees to the following stipulations.

- The IRS presumes that any required changes are made in accordance with these procedures and will not be disruptive to the processing of the tax return.
- Should any of the changes be disruptive to the IRS's processing of the tax return, the person or company agrees to accept the determination of the IRS as to whether the form may continue to be filed.
- The person or company agrees to work with the IRS in correcting noted deficiencies. Notification of deficiencies may be made by any combination of fax, letter, email, or phone contact and may include the return of unacceptable forms for the re-submission of acceptable forms.

Part 2
General Guidelines for Submissions and Approvals

Section 2.1 – General Specifications for Approval

2.1.1
Overview

If you produce any tax forms using IRS guidelines on permitted changes, you can generate your own substitutes without further approval. If your changes are more extensive, you must get IRS approval before using substitute forms. More extensive changes can include the use of typefaces and sizes other than those found on the official form and the condensing of line item descriptions to save space.

2.1.2
Email Submissions

The Substitute Forms Program now accepts substitute forms submissions via email. The email address is **taxforms@irs.gov* (the asterisk must be included in the address). Please include "PDF Submissions" on the subject line.

Follow these guidelines.

- Your submission should include all the forms you wish to submit in one attached pdf file. **Do not email each form individually.**
- An approval check sheet listing the forms you are submitting should always be included in the pdf file along with the forms.
- Small (fewer than 15 forms), rather than large, submissions should expedite processing. The optimal submission should contain 15 forms.
- Emailing pdf submissions will not expedite review and approval. The pdf submissions will be assigned a control number and put in queue along with mailed-in paper submissions.
- Optimize pdf files before submitting.
- The maximum allowable email attachment is 2.5 megabytes.
- The Substitute Forms Unit accepts zip files.
- To alleviate delays during the peak time of September through December, submit advance draft forms as early as possible.

If the guidelines are not followed, you may need to resubmit.

In addition to submitting forms via email, you may continue to send your submissions to:

Internal Revenue Service
SE:W:CAR:MP:T:T:SP
Attn: Substitute Forms Program
1111 Constitution Avenue, NW
Room 6406
Washington, DC 20224

2.1.3
Expediting the Process

Follow these basic guidelines for expediting the process.

- Always include a check sheet for the Substitute Forms Unit's response.
- Follow Publication 1167 for general substitute form guidelines. Follow the specialized publications produced by the Substitute Forms Unit for other specific forms.
- To spread out the workload, send in draft versions of substitute forms when they are posted. **Note.** Be sure to make any changes to approved drafts before releasing final versions.

2.1.4
Schedules

Schedules are considered to be an integral part of a complete tax return. A schedule may be included as part of a form or printed separately.

2.1.5
Examples of Schedules That Must Be Submitted with the Return

Form 706, United States Estate (and Generation-Skipping Transfer) Tax Return, is an example of this situation. Its Schedules A through U have pages numbered as part of the basic return. For Form 706 to be approved, the entire form including Schedules A through U must be submitted.

2.1.6
Examples of Schedules That Can Be Submitted Separately

However, Schedules 1, 2, and 3 of Form 1040A are examples of schedules that can be submitted separately. Although printed by the IRS as a supplement to Form 1040A, none of these schedules are required to be filed with Form 1040A. These schedules may be separated from Form 1040A and submitted as substitute forms.

2.1.7
Use and Distribution of Unapproved Forms

The IRS is continuing a program to identify and contact tax return preparers, forms developers, and software publishers who use or distribute unapproved forms that do not conform to this revenue procedure. The use of unapproved forms hinders the processing of the returns.

Section 2.2 – Highlights of Permitted Changes and Requirements

---

2.2.1
Methods of Reproducing Internal Revenue Service Forms

Official IRS tax forms are supplied by the IRS. These forms may be provided in the taxpayer's tax package or over-the-counter. Forms can also be picked up at many IRS offices, post offices, or libraries, and are available on CD-ROM and online at *www.irs.gov*.

There are methods of reproducing IRS printed tax forms suitable for use as substitutes without prior approval.

- You can photocopy most tax forms and use them instead of the official ones. The entire substitute form, including entries, must be legible.
- You can reproduce any current tax form as cut sheets, snap sets, and marginally punched, pin-fed forms as long as you use an official IRS version as the master copy.
- You can reproduce a form that requires a signature as a valid substitute form. Many tax forms (including returns) have a taxpayer signature requirement as part of the form layout. The jurat/perjury statement/signature line areas must be retained and worded exactly as on the official form. The requirement for a signature, by itself, does not prohibit a tax form from being properly computer-generated.

Section 2.3 – Vouchers

2.3.1
Overview

All payment vouchers (Forms 940-V, 940-EZ(V), 941-V, 943-V, 945-V, 1040-V, and 2290-V) must be reproduced in conjunction with their forms. Substitute vouchers must be the same size as the officially printed vouchers. Vouchers that are prepared for printing on a laser printer may include a scan line.

2.3.2
Scan Line Specifications

	NNNNNNNNN	AA	AAAA	NN	N	NNNNNN	NNN
Item:	A	B	C	D	E	F	G

A. Social Security Number/Employer Identification Number (SSN/EIN) has 9 numeric spaces.

B. Check Digits have 2 alpha spaces.

C. Name Control has 4 alphanumeric spaces.

D. Master File Tax (MFT) Code has 2 numeric spaces (see below).

E. Taxpayer Identification Number (TIN) Type has 1 numeric space (see below).

F. Tax Period has 6 numeric spaces in year/month format (YYYYMM).

G. Transaction Code has 3 numeric spaces.

2.3.3
MFT Code

Code Number for Forms:

- 1040 family – 30;
- 940/940-EZ – 10;
- 941 – 01;
- 943 – 11;
- 945 – 16; and
- 2290 – 60.

2.3.4
TIN Type

Type Number for:

- Form 1040 family – 0; and
- Forms 940, 940-EZ, 941, 943, 945, and 2290 – 2.

2.3.5
Voucher Size

The voucher size must be exactly 8.0″ x 3.25″ (Forms 1040-ES and 1041-ES must be 7.625″ x 3.0″). The document scan line must be vertically positioned 0.25 inches from the bottom of the scan line to the bottom of the voucher. The last character on the right of the scan line must be placed 3.5 inches from the right leading edge of the document. The minimum required horizontal clear space between characters is .014 inches. The line to be scanned must have a clear band 0.25 inches in height from top to bottom of the scan line, and from border to border of the document. "Clear band" means no printing except for dropout ink.

2.3.6
Print and Paper Weight

Vouchers must be imaged in black ink using OCR A, OCR B, or Courier 10. These fonts may not be mixed in the scan line. The horizontal character pitch is 10 CPI. The preferred paper weight is 20 to 24 pound OCR bond.

2.3.7
Specifications for Software Developers

Certain vouchers may be reproduced for use in the IRS lockbox system. These include the 1040-V, 1040-ES, the 940 family, and 2290 vouchers. Software developers must follow these specific guidelines to produce scannable vouchers strictly for lockbox purposes. Also see Exhibit C.

- The total depth must be 3.25 inches.
- The scan line must be .5 inches from the bottom edge and 1.75 inches from the left edge of the voucher and left-justified.
- Software developers vouchers must be 8.5 inches wide (instead of 8 inches with a cut line). Therefore, no vertical cut line is required.
- Scan line positioning must be exact.
- Do not use the over-the-counter format voucher and add the scan line to it.
- All scanned data must be in 12-point OCR A font.
- The 4-digt NACTP ID code should be placed under the payment indicator arrow.
- Windowed envelopes must not display the scan line in order to avoid disclosure and privacy issues.

Note. All software developers must ensure that their software uses OCR A font so taxpayers will be able to print the vouchers in the correct font.

2.3.8
Specific Line Positions

Follow these line specifications for entering taxpayer data in the lockbox vouchers.

	Start Row	Start Column	Width	End Column
Line Specifications for Taxpayer Data:				
Taxpayer Name	56	6	36	41
Taxpayer Address, Apt.	57	6	36	41
Taxpayer City, State, ZIP	58	6	36	41
Line Specifications for Mail To Data:				
Mail Address	57	43	38	80
Mail City, State, ZIP	58	43	38	80
Line Specifications for:				
Scan Line	63	26	n/a	n/a

2.3.9
How to Get Approval

To receive approval, please send 50 voucher samples yearly, by December 8, for testing to the following address.

Internal Revenue Service
Attn: Doris Bethea, C5-163
5000 Ellin Rd.
Lanham, MD 20706

For further information, contact Doris Bethea, *Doris.E.Bethea@irs.gov*, at 202-283-0218.

Section 2.4 – Restrictions on Changes

2.4.1 What You Cannot Do to Forms Suitable for Substitute Tax Forms

You cannot, without prior IRS approval, change any IRS tax form or use your own (non-approved) versions including graphics, unless specifically permitted by this revenue procedure.

You cannot adjust any of the graphics on Forms 1040, 1040A, and 1040EZ (except in those areas specified in Part 5 of this revenue procedure) without prior approval from the IRS Substitute Forms Unit.

You cannot use your own preprinted label on tax returns filed with the IRS unless you fully comply with the criteria specified in Section 3.6.3 on the use of pre-addressed IRS labels.

Section 2.5 – Guidelines for Obtaining IRS Approval

2.5.1 Basic Requirements

Preparers who submit substitute privately designed, privately printed, computer generated, or computer prepared tax forms must develop these substitutes using the guidelines established in this part. These forms, unless excepted by the revenue procedure, must be approved by the IRS before being filed.

2.5.2 Conditional Approval Based on Advanced Drafts

The IRS cannot grant final approval of your substitute form until the official form has been published. However, the IRS posts advance draft forms in the "Tax Professionals" area of its website at:

www.irs.gov/taxpros/lists/0,,id=97782,00.html

We encourage submission of proposed substitutes of these advance draft forms and will grant conditional approval based solely on these early drafts. These advance drafts are subject to significant change before forms are finalized. If these advance drafts are used as the basis for your substitute forms, you will be responsible for subsequently updating your final forms to agree with the final official version. These revisions need not be submitted for further approval.

Note. Approval of forms based on advance drafts will not be granted after the final version of an official form is published.

2.5.3 Submission Procedures

Follow these general guidelines when submitting substitute forms for approval.

- Any alteration of forms must be within the limits acceptable to the IRS. It is possible that, from one filing period to another, a change in law or a change in internal need (processing, audit, compliance, etc.) may change the allowable limits for the alteration of the official form.

- When specific approval of any substitute form (other than those specified in Part 1, Section 1.2 – IRS Contacts) is desired, a sample of the proposed substitute form should be forwarded for consideration via email or by letter to the Substitute Forms Unit at the address shown in Section 1.2.
- Schedules and forms (for example, Forms 3468, 4136, etc.) that can be used with more than one type of return (for example, 1040, 1041, 1120, etc.) should be submitted only once for approval, regardless of the number of different tax returns with which they may be associated. Also, all pages of multi-page forms or returns should be submitted in the same package.

2.5.4
Approving Offices

Because only the Substitute Forms Unit is authorized to approve substitute forms, unnecessary delays may occur if forms are sent to the wrong office. The Substitute Forms Unit may then coordinate the response with the initiator responsible for revising that particular form. Such coordination may include allowing the initiator to officially approve the form. No IRS office is authorized to allow deviations from this revenue procedure.

2.5.5
IRS Review of Software Programs, etc.

The IRS does not review or approve the logic of specific software programs, nor does the IRS confirm the calculations on the forms produced by these programs. The accuracy of the program remains the responsibility of the software package developer, distributor, or user.

The Substitute Forms Unit is primarily concerned with the pre-filing quality review of the final forms that are expected to be processed by IRS field offices. For this purpose, you should submit forms without including any taxpayer information such as names, addresses, monetary amounts, etc.

2.5.6
When To Send Proposed Substitutes

Proposed substitutes, which are required to be submitted per this revenue procedure, should be sent as much in advance of the filing period as possible. This is to allow adequate time for analysis and response.

2.5.7
Accompanying Statement

When submitting sample substitutes, you should include an accompanying statement that lists each form number and its changes from the official form (position, arrangement, appearance, line numbers, additions, deletions, etc.). With each of the items you should include a detailed reason for the change.

When requesting approval, please include a check sheet. Check sheets expedite the approval process. The check sheet may look like the example in Exhibit D displayed in the back of this procedure or may be one of your own design. Please include your fax number on the check sheet.

2.5.8
Approval/Non-Approval Notice

The Substitute Forms Unit will fax the check sheet or an approval letter to the originator if a fax number has been provided, unless:

- The requester has asked for an email response or for a formal letter, or
- Significant corrections to the submitted forms are required.

Notice of approval may impose qualifications before using the substitutes. Notices of unapproved forms may specify the changes required for approval and require re-submission of the form(s) in question. Telephone contact is used when appropriate.

2.5.9 Duration of Approval

Most signature tax returns and many of their schedules and related forms have the tax (liability) year printed in the upper right corner. Approvals for these annual forms are usually good for one calendar year (January through December of the year of filing). Quarterly tax forms in the 940 series and Form 720 require approval for any quarter in which the form has been revised.

Because changes are usually made to an annual form every year, each new filing season generally requires a new submission of a substitute form. Very rarely is updating the preprinted year the only change made to an annual form.

2.5.10 Limited Continued Use of an Approved Change

Limited changes approved for one tax year may be allowed for the same form in the following tax year. Examples are the use of abbreviated words, revised form spacing, compressed text lines, and shortened captions, etc., which do not change the integrity of lines or text on the official forms.

If substantial changes are made to the form, new substitutes must be submitted for approval. If only minor editorial changes are made to the form, it is not subject to review. It is the responsibility of each vendor who has been granted permission to use substitute forms to monitor and revise forms to mirror any revisions to official forms made by the Service. If there are any questions, please contact the Substitute Forms Unit.

2.5.11 When Approval Is Not Required

If you received written approval for a specific change on a form last year, you may make the same change this year if the item is still present on the official form.

- The new substitute form does not have to be submitted to the IRS and written approval is not required.
- However, the new substitute form must conform to the official current year IRS form in other respects: date, Office of Management and Budget (OMB) approval number, attachment sequence number, Paperwork Reduction Act Notice statement, arrangement, item caption, line number, line reference, data sequence, etc.
- The new substitute must also comply with changes to this revenue procedure. The procedure may have eliminated, added to, or otherwise changed the guideline(s) that affected the change approved in the prior year.
- An approved change is authorized only for the period from a prior tax year substitute form to a current tax year substitute form.

Exception. Forms with temporary, limited, or interim approvals (or with approvals that state a change is not allowed in any other tax year) are subject to review in subsequent years.

2.5.12 Continuous-Use Forms

Forms without preprinted tax years are called "continuous-use" forms. Continuous-use forms are revised when a legislative change affects the form or a change will facilitate processing. These forms may have revision dates that are valid for longer than one year.

2.5.13 IRS Website Posting Schedule

A schedule of print dates (for annual and quarterly forms) and most current revision dates (for continuous-use forms) are maintained on the IRS website. The Tax Products Posting Schedule can be found at *www.irs.gov/formspubs/article/0,,id=103641,00.html*. See Section 4.2.2.

2.5.14
Required Copies

Generally, you must send us one copy of each form being submitted for approval. However, if you are producing forms for different computer systems (for example, IBM compatible vs. Macintosh) or different types of printers (for example, laser vs. inkjet), and these forms differ **significantly** in appearance, submit one copy for each type of system or printer.

2.5.15
Requestor's Responsibility

Following receipt of an initial approval for a substitute forms package or a software output program to print substitute forms, it is the responsibility of the originator (designer or distributor) to provide client firms or individuals with forms that meet the IRS's requirements for continuing acceptability. Examples of this responsibility include:

- Using the prescribed print paper, font size, legibility, state tax data deletion, etc., and
- Informing all users of substitute forms of the legal requirements of the Paperwork Reduction Act Notice, which is generally found in the instructions for the official IRS forms.

2.5.16
Source Code

The Substitute Forms Unit will assign a unique source code to each firm that submits substitute paper forms for approval. This source code will be a permanent identifier that should be used on every submission by a particular firm.

The source code consists of three alpha characters and should generally be printed at the bottom left margin area on the first page of every approved substitute form.

Section 2.6 – Office of Management and Budget (OMB) Requirements for All Substitute Forms

---

2.6.1
OMB Requirements for All Substitute Forms

There are legal requirements of the Paperwork Reduction Act of 1995 (The Act). Public Law 104-13 requires the following.

- OMB approves all IRS tax forms that are subject to the Act.
- Each IRS form contains (in the upper right corner) the OMB number, if assigned.
- Each IRS form (or its instructions) states why the IRS needs the information, how it will be used, and whether or not the information is required to be furnished to the IRS.

This information must be provided to every user of official or substitute IRS forms or instructions.

2.6.2
Application of the Paperwork Reduction Act

On forms that have been assigned OMB numbers:

- All substitute forms must contain in the upper right corner the OMB number that is on the official form, and
- The required format is: OMB No. 1545-XXXX (Preferred) or OMB # 1545-XXXX (Acceptable).

2.6.3
Required Explanation to Users

You must inform the users of your substitute forms of the IRS use and collection requirements stated in the instructions for official IRS forms.

- If you provide your users or customers with the official IRS instructions, each form must retain either the Paperwork Reduction Act Notice (or Disclosure, Privacy Act, and Paperwork Reduction Act Notice), or a reference to it as the IRS does on the official forms (usually in the lower left corner of the forms).

- This notice reads, in part, “We ask for the information on this form to carry out the Internal Revenue laws of the United States....”

Note. If no IRS instructions are provided to users of your forms, the exact text of the Paperwork Reduction Act Notice (or Disclosure, Privacy Act, and Paperwork Reduction Act Notice) must be furnished separately or on the form.

2.6.4 Finding the OMB Number and Paperwork Reduction Act Notice

The OMB number and the Paperwork Reduction Act Notice, or references to it, may be found printed on an official form (or its instructions). The number and the notice are included on the official paper format and in other formats produced by the IRS (for example, compact disc (CD) or Internet download).

Part 3 Physical Aspects and Requirements

Section 3.1 – General Guidelines for Substitute Forms

3.1.1 General Information

The official form is the standard. Because a substitute form is a variation from the official form, you should know the requirements of the official form for the year of use before you modify it to meet your needs. The IRS provides several means of obtaining the most frequently used tax forms. These include the Internet and CD-ROM (see Part 4).

3.1.2 Design

Each form must follow the design of the official form as to format arrangement, item caption, line numbers, line references, and sequence.

3.1.3 State Tax Information Prohibited

Generally, state tax information must not appear on the federal tax return, associated form, or schedule that is filed with the IRS. Exceptions occur when amounts are claimed on, or required by, the federal return (for example, state and local income taxes, on Schedule A of Form 1040).

3.1.4 Vertical Alignment of Amount Fields

IF a form is to be...	THEN...
Manually prepared	1. The entry column must have a vertical line or some type of indicator in the amount field to separate dollars from cents. 2. The cents column must be at least 3/10″ wide.
Computer generated	1. Vertically align the amount entry fields where possible. 2. Use one of the following amount formats: a) 0,000,000, or b) 0,000,000.00.

IF a form is to be...	THEN...
Computer prepared	1. You may remove the vertical line in the amount field that separates dollars from cents. 2. Use one of the following amount formats: a) 0,000,000, or b) 0,000,000.00.

3.1.5 Attachment Sequence Number

Many individual income tax forms have a required "attachment sequence number" located just below the year designation in the upper right corner of the form. The IRS uses this number to indicate the order in which forms are to be attached to the tax return for processing. Some of the attachment sequence numbers may change from year to year.

The following applies to computer prepared forms.

- The sequence number may be printed in no less than 12-point boldface type and centered below the form's year designation.
- The sequence number may also be placed following the year designation for the tax form and separated with an asterisk.
- The actual number may be printed without labeling it the "Attachment Sequence Number."

3.1.6 Assembly of Forms

If developing software or forms for use by others, please inform your customers/clients that the order in which the forms are arranged may affect the processing of the package. A return must be arranged in the order indicated below.

IF the form is...	THEN the sequence is...
1040	• Form 1040, and • Schedules and forms in attachment sequence number order.
Any other tax return (Form 1120, 1120S, 1065, 1041, etc.)	• The tax returns, • Directly associated schedules (Schedule D, etc.), • Directly associated forms, • Additional schedules in alphabetical order, and • Additional forms in numerical order.

Supporting statements should then follow in the same sequence as the forms they support. Additional information required should be attached last.

In this way, the forms are received in the order in which they must be processed. If you do not send returns to us in order, processing may be delayed.

3.1.7 Paid Preparer's Information and Signature Area

On Forms 1040EZ, 1040A, 1040, and 1120, etc., the "Paid Preparer's Use Only" area may not be rearranged or relocated. You may, however, add three extra lines to the paid preparer's address area without prior approval. This applies to other tax forms as well.

3.1.8 Some Common Reasons for Requiring Changes to Substitute Forms

Some reasons that substitute form submissions may require changes include the following.

- Failing to preprint certain amounts in entry spaces.
- Shading areas incorrectly.
- Failing to include a reference to the location of the Paperwork Reduction Act Notice.
- Not including parentheses for losses.
- Not including "Attach Statement" when appropriate.
- Including line references or entry spaces that don't match the official form.

- Printing text that is different from the official form.
- Altering the jurat.

Section 3.2 – Paper

3.2.1 Paper Content

The paper must be:

- Chemical wood writing paper that is equal to or better than the quality used for the official form,
- At least 18 pound (17″ x 22″, 500 sheets), or
- At least 50 pound offset book (25″ x 38″, 500 sheets).

3.2.2 Paper with Chemical Transfer Properties

There are several kinds of paper prohibited for substitute forms. These are:

1. Carbon-bonded paper, and
2. Chemical transfer paper except when the following specifications are met:
    a. Each ply within the chemical transfer set of forms must be labeled, and
    b. Only the top ply (ply one and white in color), the one that contains chemical on the back only (coated back), may be filed with the IRS.

3.2.3 Example

A set containing three plies would be constructed as follows: ply one (coated back), "Federal Return, File with IRS"; ply two (coated front and back), "Taxpayer's copy"; and ply three (coated front), "Preparer's copy."

The file designation, "Federal Return, File with IRS" for ply one, must be printed in the bottom right margin (just below the last line of the form) in 12-point boldface type.

It is not mandatory, but recommended, that the file designation "Federal Return, File with IRS" be printed in a contrasting ink for visual emphasis.

3.2.4 Carbon Paper

Do not attach any carbon paper to any return you file with the IRS.

3.2.5 Paper and Ink Color

We prefer that the color and opacity of paper substantially duplicates that of the original form. This means that your substitute must be printed in black ink and may be on white or on the colored paper the IRS form is printed on. Forms 1040A and 1040 substitute reproductions may be in black ink without the colored shading. The only exception to this rule is Form 1041-ES, which should always be printed with a very light gray shading in the color screened area. This is necessary to assist us in expeditiously separating this form from the very similar Form 1040 ES.

3.2.6
Page Size

Substitute or reproduced forms and computer prepared/generated substitutes may be the same size as the official form or they may be the standard commercial size (8½″ x 11″). The thickness of the stock cannot be less than .003 inches.

Section 3.3 – Printing

3.3.1
Printing Medium

The private printing of all substitute tax forms must be by conventional printing processes, photocopying, computer graphics, or similar reproduction processes.

3.3.2
Legibility

All forms must have a high standard of legibility as to printing, reproduction, and fill-in matter. Entries of taxpayer data may be no smaller than eight points. The IRS reserves the right to reject those with poor legibility. The ink and printing method used must ensure that no part of a form (including text, graphics, data entries, etc.) develops "smears" or similar quality deterioration. This standard must be followed for any subsequent copies or reproductions made from an approved master substitute form, either during preparation or during IRS processing.

3.3.3
Type Font

Many federal tax forms are printed using "Helvetica" as the basic type font. We request that you use this type font when composing substitute forms.

3.3.4
Print Spacing

Substitute forms should be printed using a 6 lines/inch vertical print option. They should also be printed horizontally in 10 pitch pica (that is, 10 print characters per inch) or 12 pitch elite (that is, 12 print positions per inch).

3.3.5
Image Size

The image size of a printed substitute form should be as close as possible to that of the official form. You may omit any text on both computer prepared and computer generated forms that is solely instructional.

3.3.6
Title Area Changes

To allow a large top margin for marginal printing and more lines per page, the title line(s) for all substitute forms (not including the form's year designation and sequence number, when present), may be photographically reduced by 40 percent or reset as one line of type. When reset as one line, the type size may be no smaller than 14-point. You may omit "Department of the Treasury, Internal Revenue Service" and all reference to instructions in the form's title area.

3.3.7
Remove Government Printing Office Symbol and IRS Catalog Number

When privately printing substitute tax forms, the Government Printing Office (GPO) symbol and/or jacket number must be removed. In the same place using the same type size, print the Employer Identification Number (EIN) of the printer or designer or the IRS assigned source code. (We prefer this last number be printed in the lower left area of the first page of each form.) Also, remove the IRS Catalog Number (Cat. No.) and the recycle symbol if the substitute is not produced on recycled paper.

3.3.8
Printing on One Side of Paper

While it is preferred that both sides of the paper be used for substitutes and reproduced forms, resulting in the same page arrangement as that of the official form or schedule, the IRS will accept your forms if only one side of the paper is used.

3.3.9
Photocopy Equipment

The IRS does not undertake to approve or disapprove the specific equipment or process used in reproducing official forms. Photocopies of forms must be entirely legible and satisfy the conditions stated in this and other revenue procedures.

3.3.10
Reproductions

Reproductions of official forms and substitute forms that do not meet the requirements of this revenue procedure may not be filed instead of the official forms. Illegible photocopies are subject to being returned to the filer for re-submission of legible copies.

3.3.11
Removal of Instructions

You may remove references to instructions. No prior approval is needed.

Exception. The words "For Paperwork Reduction Act Notice, see instructions" must be retained or a similar statement indicating the location of the Notice must be provided on each form.

Section 3.4 – Margins

3.4.1
Margin Size

The format of a reproduced tax form when printed on the page must have margins on all sides at least as large as the margins on the official form. This allows room for IRS employees to make necessary entries on the form during processing.

- A 1/2-inch to 1/4-inch margin must be maintained across the top, bottom, and both sides of all substitute forms.
- The marginal, perforated strips containing pin-fed holes must be removed from all forms prior to filing with the IRS.

3.4.2
Marginal Printing

Prior approval is not required for the marginal printing allowed when printed on an official form or on a photocopy of an official form.

- With the exception of the actual tax forms (for example, Forms 1040, 1040A, 1040EZ, 1120, 940, 941, etc.), you may print in the left vertical margin and in the left half of the bottom margin.
- Printing is never allowed in the top right margin of the tax form (for example, Forms 1040, 1040A, 1040EZ, 1120, 940, 941, etc.). The Service uses this area to imprint a Document Locator Number for each return. There are no exceptions to this requirement.

Section 3.5 – Examples of Approved Formats

3.5.1
Examples of Approved Formats From the Exhibits

Two sets of exhibits (Exhibits A-1 and 2; B-1 and 2) at the end of this revenue procedure are examples of how these guidelines may be used. Vertical spacing is six (6) lines to the inch. A combination of upper-case and lower-case print font is acceptable in producing substitute forms.

The same logic may be applied to any IRS form that is normally reproducible as a substitute form, with the exception of the tax return forms as discussed elsewhere.

Note. These exhibits may be from a prior year and are not to be used as current substitute forms.

Section 3.6 – Miscellaneous Information for Substitute Forms

3.6.1 Filing Substitute Forms

To be acceptable for filing, a substitute form must print out in a format that will allow the filer to follow the same instructions as for filing official forms. These instructions are in the taxpayer's tax package or in the related form instructions. The form must be legible, must be on the appropriately sized paper, and must include a jurat where one appears on the published form.

3.6.2 Caution to Software Publishers

The IRS has received returns produced by software packages with approved output where either the form heading was altered or the lines were spaced irregularly. This produces an illegible or unrecognizable return or a return with the wrong number of pages. We realize that many of these problems are caused by individual printer differences but they may delay input of return data and, in some cases, generate correspondence to the taxpayer. Therefore, in the instructions to the purchasers of your product, both individual and professional, please stress that their returns will be processed more efficiently if they are properly formatted. This includes:

- Having the correct form numbers and titles at the top of the return, and
- Submitting the same number of pages as if the form were an official IRS form with the line items on the proper pages.

3.6.3 Use Pre-Addressed IRS Label

If you are a practitioner filling out a return for a client or a software publisher who prints instruction manuals, stress the use of the pre-addressed label provided in the tax package the IRS sent to the taxpayer, when available. The use of this label (or its precisely duplicated label information) is extremely important for the efficient, accurate, and economical processing of a taxpayer's return. Labeled returns indicate that a taxpayer is an established filer and permits the IRS to automatically accelerate processing of those returns. This results in quicker refunds, less manual review by IRS functions, and greater accuracy in names, addresses, and postal deliveries.

3.6.4 Caution to Producers of Software Packages

If you are producing a software package that generates name and address data onto the tax return, do not under any circumstances program either the IRS preprinted check digits or a practitioner derived name control to appear on any return prepared and filed with the IRS.

3.6.5 Programming to Print Forms

Whenever applicable:

- Use only the following label information format for single filers:
  JOHN Q. PUBLIC
  310 OAK DRIVE
  HOMETOWN, STATE 94000

- Use only the following information for joint filers:
JOHN Q. PUBLIC
MARY I. PUBLIC
310 OAK DRIVE
HOMETOWN, STATE 94000

Part 4
Additional Resources

Section 4.1 – Guidance From Other Revenue Procedures

4.1.1
General

The IRS publications listed below provide guidance for substitute tax forms not covered in this revenue procedure. The publications are available only on the IRS website. Identify the requested document by the IRS publication number.

- Publication 1141, General Rules and Specifications for Substitute Forms W-2 and W-3.
- Publication 1179, General Rules and Specifications for Substitute Forms 1096, 1098, 1099, 5498, W-2G, and 1042-S.
- Publication 1187, Specifications for Filing Forms 1042-S, Foreign Person's U.S. Source Income Subject to Withholding, Electronically or Magnetically.
- Publication 1220, Specifications for Filing Forms 1098, 1099, 5498, and W-2G Electronically or Magnetically.
- Publication 1223, General Rules and Specifications for Substitute Forms W-2c and W-3c.
- Publication 1239, Specifications for Filing Form 8027, Employer's Annual Information Return of Tip Income and Allocated Tips, Electronically or Magnetically.
- Publication 1345, Handbook for Authorized IRS *e-file* Providers of Individual Income Tax Returns.
- Publication 1345-A, Filing Season Supplement for Authorized IRS *e-file* Providers.
- Publication 4436, General Rules and Specifications for Substitute Form 941 and Schedule B (Form 941).

Section 4.2 – Electronic Tax Products

4.2.1
The IRS Website

Copies of tax forms with instructions, publications, draft forms, fillable forms, prior year forms and publications, and other tax-related information may be found on the IRS website at *www.irs.gov.*

4.2.2
Tax Products Posting Schedule

The IRS website provides a Tax Products Posting Schedule for the official forms released for use by taxpayers. The schedule has three parts.

- Anticipated print dates of annual returns.
- Anticipated print dates of quarterly returns.
- Last revision dates and target print dates for continuous-use forms.

The site address is *www.irs.gov/formspubs/article/0,,id=103641,00.html*. The site will be updated weekly during peak printing periods and as necessary at other times. The planned dates are subject to change.

Section 4.3 – Federal Tax Forms on CD-ROM

4.3.1 Information About Federal Tax Forms CD-ROM

The CD-ROM contains over 3,000 tax forms and publications for small businesses, return preparers, and others who frequently need current or prior year tax products. Most current tax forms on the CD-ROM may be filled in electronically, then printed out for submission and saved for recordkeeping. Other products on the CD-ROM include the Internal Revenue Bulletins, Tax Supplements, and Internet resources for the tax professional with links to the World Wide Web.

4.3.2 System Requirements and How To Order the Federal Tax Forms CD-ROM

For system requirements, contact the National Technical Information Service (NTIS) help desk at 703-487-4608. Prices are subject to change.

The cost of the CD if purchased via the Internet at *http://www.irs.gov/cdorders* from NTIS, is $35 (with no handling fee).

If purchased using the following methods, the cost for each CD is $35 (plus a $5 handling fee). These methods are:

- By phone – 1-877-CDFORMS (1-877-233-6767),
- By fax – 703-605-6900,
- By mail using the order form contained in IRS Publication 1045 (Tax Professionals Guide), and
- By mail to:
  National Technical Information Service
  5285 Port Royal Road
  Springfield, VA 22161

Part 5
Requirements for Specific Tax Returns

Section 5.1 – Tax Returns (Forms 1040, 1040A, 1120, etc.)

5.1.1 Acceptable Forms

Tax forms (such as Forms 1040, 1040A, and 1120) require a signature and establish tax liability. Computer generated versions are acceptable under the following conditions.

- These substitute forms must be printed on plain white paper.
- Substitute forms must conform to the physical layout of the corresponding IRS form although the typeface may differ. The text should match the text on the officially published form as closely as possible. Condensed text and abbreviations will be considered on a case-by-case basis.
  Caution. All jurats (perjury statements) must be reproduced verbatim. No text can be added, deleted, or changed in meaning.
- Various computer graphic print media such as laser printing, inkjet printing, etc., may be used to produce the substitute forms.
- The substitute form must be the same number of pages and contain the same line text as the official form.
- All substitute forms must be submitted for approval prior to their original use. You do not need approval for a substitute form if its only change is the preprinted year and you had received a prior year approval letter.

  Exception. If the approval letter specifies a one time exception for your form, the next year's form must be approved.

5.1.2
Prohibited Forms

The following are prohibited.

- Computer generated tax forms (for example, Form 1040, etc.) on lined or color barred paper.
- Tax forms that differ from the official IRS forms in a manner that makes them not standard or unable to process.

5.1.3
Changes Permitted to Forms 1040 and 1040A

Certain changes (listed in Sections 5.2 through 5.4) are permitted to the graphics of the form without prior approval, but these changes apply to only acceptable preprinted forms. Changes not requiring prior approval are good only for the annual filing period, which is the current tax year. Such changes are valid in subsequent years only if the official form does not change.

5.1.4
Other Changes Not Listed

All changes not listed in Sections 5.2 through 5.4 require approval from the IRS before the form can be filed.

Section 5.2 – Changes Permitted to Graphics (Forms 1040A and 1040)

5.2.1
Adjustments

You may make minor vertical and horizontal spacing adjustments to allow for computer or word processing printing. This includes widening the amount columns or tax entry areas if the adjustments comply with other provisions stated in revenue procedures. No prior approval is needed for these changes.

5.2.2
Name and Address Area

The horizontal rules and instructions within the name and address area may be removed and the entire area left blank. No line or instruction can remain in the area. However, the statement regarding use of the IRS label should be retained. The heavy ruled border (when present) that outlines the name, address area, and social security number must not be removed, relocated, expanded, or contracted.

5.2.3
Required Format

When the name and address area is left blank, the following format must be used when printing the taxpayer's name and address. Otherwise, unless the taxpayer's preprinted label is affixed over the information entered in this area, the lines must be filled in as shown below.

- 1st name line (35 characters maximum).
- 2nd name line (35 characters maximum).
- In-care-of name line (35 characters maximum).
- City, state (25 characters maximum), one blank character, and ZIP code.

5.2.4
Conventional Name and Address Data

When there is no in-care-of name line, the name and address will consist of only three lines (single filer) or four lines (joint filer). Name and address (joint filer) with no in-care-of name line:

JOHN Z. JONES
MARY I. JONES
1234 ANYWHERE ST., APT. 111
ANYTOWN, STATE 12321

5.2.5
Example of In-Care-Of Name Line

Name and address (single filer) with in-care-of name line:

JOHN Z. JONES
C/O THOMAS A. JONES
4311 SOMEWHERE AVE.
SAMETOWN, STATE 54345

5.2.6
SSN and Employer Identification Number (EIN) Area

The vertical lines separating the format arrangement of the SSN/EIN may be removed. When the vertical lines are removed, the SSN and EIN formats must be 000-00-0000 or 00-0000000, respectively.

5.2.7
Cents Column

- You may remove the vertical rule that separates the dollars from the cents.
- All entries in the amount column should have a decimal point following the whole dollar amounts whether or not the vertical line that separates the dollars from the cents is present.
- You may omit printing the cents, but all amounts entered on the form must follow a consistent format. You are strongly urged to round off the figures to whole dollar amounts, following the official form instructions.
- When several amounts are summed together, the total should be rounded off after addition (that is, individual amounts should not be rounded off for computation purposes).
- When printing money amounts, you must use one of the following formats:
  (a) 0,000,000.;
  (b) 0,000,000.00.
- When there is no entry for a line, leave the line blank.

5.2.8
"Paid Preparer's Use Only" Area

On all forms, the paid preparer's information area may not be rearranged or relocated. You may add three lines and remove the horizontal rules in the preparer's address area.

Section 5.3 – Changes Permitted to Form 1040A Graphics

5.3.1
General

No prior approval is needed for the following changes (for use with computer prepared forms only).

5.3.2
Line 4 of Form 1040A

This line may be compressed horizontally (to allow for same line entry for the name of the qualifying child) by using the following caption: "Head of household; child's name" (name field).

5.3.3
Other Lines

Any line with text that takes up two or more vertical lines may be compressed to one line by using contractions, etc., and by removing instructional references.

5.3.4 Page 2 of Form 1040A

All lines must be present and numbered in the order shown on the official form. These lines may also be compressed.

5.3.5 Color Screening

It is not necessary to duplicate the color screening used on the official form. A substitute Form 1040A may be printed in black and white only with no color screening.

5.3.6 Other Changes Prohibited

No other changes to the Form 1040A graphics are allowed without prior approval except for the removal of instructions and references to instructions.

Section 5.4 – Changes Permitted to Form 1040 Graphics

5.4.1 General

No prior approval is needed for the following changes (for use with computer prepared forms only). Specific line numbers in the following headings may have changed due to tax law changes.

5.4.2 Line 4 of Form 1040

This line may be compressed horizontally (to allow for a larger entry area for the name of the qualifying child) by using the following caption: "Head of household; child's name" (name field).

5.4.3 Line 6c of Form 1040

The vertical lines separating columns (1) through (4) may be removed. The captions may be shortened to allow a one line caption for each column.

5.4.4 Other Lines

Any other line with text that takes up two or more vertical lines may be compressed to one line by using contractions, etc., and by removing instructional references.

5.4.5 Line 21 – Other Income

The fill-in portion of this line may be expanded vertically to three lines. The amount entry box must remain a single entry.

5.4.6 Line 44 of Form 1040 – Tax

You may change the line caption to read "Tax" and computer print the words "Total includes tax from" and either "Form(s) 8814" or "Form 4972." If both forms are used, print both form numbers. This specific line number may have changed.

5.4.7 Line 55 of Form 1040 – Other Credits

You may change the caption to read: "Other credits from Form" and computer print only the form(s) that apply.

5.4.8
Color Screening

It is not necessary to duplicate the color screening used on the official form. A substitute Form 1040 may be printed in black and white only with no color screening.

5.4.9
Other Changes Prohibited

No other changes to the Form 1040 graphics are permitted without prior approval except for the removal of instructions and references to instructions.

Part 6
Format and Content of Substitute Returns

Section 6.1 – Acceptable Formats for Substitute Forms and Schedules

6.1.1
Exhibits and Use of Acceptable Formats

Exhibits of acceptable formats for Schedule A, usually attached to the Form 1040, and Form 2106-EZ are shown in the exhibits section of this revenue procedure.

- If your computer generated forms appear exactly like the exhibits, no prior authorization is needed.
- You may computer generate forms not shown here, but you must design them by following the manner and style of those in the exhibits section.
- Take care to observe other requirements and conditions in this revenue procedure. The IRS encourages the submission of all proposed forms covered by this revenue procedure.

6.1.2
Instructions

The format of each substitute form or schedule must follow the format of the official form or schedule as to item captions, line references, line numbers, sequence, form arrangement and format, etc. Basically, try to make the form look like the official one, with readability and consistency being primary factors. You may use periods and/or other similar special characters to separate the various parts and sections of the form. Do not use alpha or numeric characters for these purposes. All line numbers and items must be printed even though an amount is not entered on the line.

6.1.3
Line Numbers

When a line on an official form is designated by a number or a letter, that designation (reference code) must be used on a substitute form. The reference code must be printed to the left of the text of each line and immediately preceding the data entry field, even if no reference code precedes the data entry field on the official form. If an entry field contains multiple lines and shows the line references once on the left and right side of the form, use the same number of line references on the substitute form.

In addition, the reference code that is immediately before the data field must either be followed by a period or enclosed in parentheses. There also must be at least two blank spaces between the period or the right parenthesis and the first digit of the data field. (See example below.)

6.1.4
Decimal Points

A decimal point (that is, a period) should be used for each money amount regardless of whether the amount is reported in dollars and cents or in whole dollars, or whether or not the vertical line that separates the dollars from the cents is present. The decimal points must be vertically aligned when possible.

Example:

5 STATE & LOCAL INC. TAXES..............	5.	495.00
6 REAL ESTATE TAXES...........................	6.	
7 PERSONAL PROPERTY TAXES...........	7.	198.00
or		
5 STATE & LOCAL INC. TAXES..............	(5)	495.00
6 REAL ESTATE TAXES...........................	(6)	
7 PERSONAL PROPERTY TAXES............	(7)	198.00

6.1.5
Multi-Page Forms

When submitting a multi-page form, send all its pages in the same package.

Exception. If you will not be producing certain pages, please note that in your cover letter.

Section 6.2 – Additional Instructions for All Forms

6.2.1
Use of Your Own Internal Control Numbers and Identifying Symbols

You may show the computer prepared internal control numbers and identifying symbols on the substitute if using such numbers or symbols is acceptable to the taxpayer and the taxpayer's representative. Such information must not be printed in the top 1/2 inch clear area of any form or schedule requiring a signature. Except for the actual tax return form (Forms 1040, 1120, 940, 941, etc.), you may print in the left vertical and bottom left margins. The bottom left margin you may use extends 3 1/2 inches from the left edge of the form.

6.2.2
Descriptions for Captions, Lines, etc.

Descriptions for captions, lines, etc., appearing on the substitute forms may be limited to one print line by using abbreviations and contractions, and by omitting articles, prepositions, etc. However, sufficient key words must be retained to permit ready identification of the caption, line, or item.

6.2.3
Determining Final Totals

Explanatory detail and/or intermediate calculations for determining final line totals may be included on the substitute. We prefer that such calculations be submitted in the form of a supporting statement. If intermediate calculations are included on the substitute, the line on which they appear may not be numbered or lettered. Intermediate calculations may not be printed in the right column. This column is reserved only for official numbered and lettered lines that correspond to the ones on the official form. Generally, you may choose the format for intermediate calculations or subtotals on supporting statements to be submitted.

6.2.4
Instructional Text on the Official Form

Text on the official form, which is solely instructional (for example, "See instructions," etc.), may generally be omitted from the substitute form.

6.2.5
Mixing Forms on the Same Page Prohibited

You may not show more than one form or schedule on the same printout page. Both sides of the paper may be printed for multi-page official forms, but it is unacceptable to intermix single page schedules of forms except for Schedules A and B (Form 1040), which are printed back to back by the IRS.

For instance, Schedule E can be printed on both sides of the paper because the official form is multi-page, with page 2 continued on the back. However, do not print Schedule E on the front page and Schedule SE on the back, or Schedule A on the front and Form 8615 on the back, etc. Both pages of a substitute form must match the official form. The back page may be left blank if the back page of the official form contains only the instructions.

6.2.6 Identifying Substitutes

Identify all computer prepared substitutes clearly. Print the form designation 1/2 inch from the top margin and 1 1/2 inches from the left margin. Print the title centered on the first line of print. Print the taxable year and, where applicable, the sequence number on the same line 1/2 inch to 1 inch from the right margin. Include the taxpayer's name and SSN on all forms and attachments. Also, print the OMB number as reflected on the official form.

6.2.7 Negative Amounts

Negative (or loss) amount entries should be enclosed in brackets or parentheses or include a minus sign. This assists in accurate computation and input of form data. The IRS pre-prints parentheses in negative data fields on many official forms. These parentheses should be retained or inserted on printouts of affected substitute forms.

Part 7
Miscellaneous Forms and Programs

Section 7.1 – Specifications for Substitute Schedules K-1

7.1.1 Requirements for Schedules K-1 That Accompany Forms 1041, 1065, 1065-B, and 1120S

Because of significant changes to improve processing, prior approval is now required for substitute Schedules K-1 that accompany Form 1041 (for estates and trusts), Form 1065 (for partnerships), Form 1065-B (for electing large partnerships), or Form 1120S (for S corporations). Substitute Schedules K-1 should be as close as possible to exact replicas of copies of the official IRS schedules and follow the same process for submitting other substitute forms and schedules. Before releasing their substitute forms, software vendors are responsible for making any subsequent changes that have been made to the final official IRS forms after the draft forms have been posted.

You must include all information on the form. Submit Schedules K-1 to the IRS at **taxforms@irs.gov* with "Attn: Substitute Forms" on the subject line or at:

Internal Revenue Service
Attn: Substitute Forms Program
SE:W:CAR:MP:T:T:SP
1111 Constitution Avenue, NW
Room 6406
Washington, D.C. 20224

Include the 6-digit form ID code in the upper right of Schedules K-1 of Forms 1041, 1065, and 1120S.

- 661106 for Form 1041,
- 651106 for Form 1065, and
- 671106 for Form 1120S.

Please allow white space around the 6-digit code.

Schedules K-1 that accompany Forms 1041, 1065, 1065-B, or 1120S must meet all specifications. The specifications include, but are not limited to, the following requirements.

- You will no longer be able to produce Schedules K-1 that contain only those lines or boxes that taxpayers are required to use. All lines must be included.
- The words "*See attached statement for additional information." must be preprinted in the lower right hand side on Schedules K-1 of Forms 1041, 1065, and 1120S.
- All K-1s that are filed with the IRS should be printed on standard 8.5" x 11" paper (the international standard (A4) of 8.27" x 11.69" may be substituted).
- Each recipient's information must be on a separate sheet of paper. Therefore, you must separate all continuously printed substitutes, by recipient, before filing with the IRS.
- No carbon copies or pressure-sensitive copies will be accepted.
- The Schedule K-1 must contain the name, address, and SSN or EIN of both the entity (estate, trust, partnership, or S corporation) and the recipient (beneficiary, partner, or shareholder).
- The Schedule K-1 must contain the tax year, the OMB number, the schedule number (K-1), the related form number (1041, 1065, 1065-B, or 1120S), and the official schedule name in substantially the same position and format as shown on the official IRS schedule.
- The Schedule K-1 must contain all the line items as shown on the official form, except for the instructions, if any are printed on the back of the official Schedule K-1.
- The line items or boxes must be in the same order and arrangement as those on the official form.
- The amount of each recipient's share of each item must be shown. Furnishing a total amount of each item and a percentage (or decimal equivalent) to be applied to such total amount by the recipient does not satisfy the law and the specifications of this revenue procedure.
- State or local tax-related information may not be included on the Schedules K-1 filed with the IRS.
- The entity may have to pay a penalty if substitute Schedules K-1 are filed that do not conform to specifications.
- Additionally, the IRS may consider the Schedules K-1 that do not conform to specifications as not being able to process and may return Forms 1041, 1065, 1065-B, or 1120S to the entity to be filed correctly.

Schedules K-1 that are 2-D bar-coded will continue to require prior approval from the IRS (see Sections 7.1.3 through 7.1.5).

7.1.2 Special Requirements for Recipient Copies of Schedules K-1

Standardization for reporting information is required for recipient copies of substitute Schedules K-1 of Forms 1041, 1065, 1065-B, and 1120S. Uniform visual standards are provided to increase compliance by allowing recipients and practitioners to more easily recognize a substitute Schedule K-1. The entity must furnish to each recipient a copy of Schedule K-1 that meets the following requirements.

- Include the 6-digit form ID code in the upper right of Schedules K-1 of Forms 1041, 1065, and 1120S.
  - 661106 for Form 1041,
  - 651106 for Form 1065, and
  - 671106 for Form 1120S.

  Please allow white space around the 6-digit code.
- You will no longer be able to produce Schedules K-1 that contain only those lines or boxes that taxpayers are required to use. All lines must be included.
- Both pages 1 and 2 of Schedules K-1 of Forms 1065 and 1120S must be provided to each recipient.
- The words "*See attached statement for additional information." must be preprinted in the lower right hand side on Schedules K-1 of Forms 1041, 1065, and 1120S.
- The Schedule K-1 must contain the name, address, and SSN or EIN of both the entity and recipient.

- The Schedule K-1 must contain the tax year, the OMB number, the schedule number (K-1), the related form number (1041, 1065, 1065-B, or 1120S), and the official schedule name in substantially the same position and format as shown on the official IRS schedule.
- All applicable amounts and information required to be reported must be titled and numbered in the same manner as shown on the official IRS schedule. The line items or boxes must be in the same order and arrangement and must be numbered like those on the official IRS schedule.
- The Schedule K-1 must contain all items required for use by the recipient. The instructions to the schedule must identify the line or box number and code, if any, for each item as shown in the official IRS schedule.
- The amount of each recipient's share of each item must be shown. Furnishing a total amount of each line item and a percentage (or decimal equivalent) to be applied to such total amount by the recipient does not satisfy the law and the specifications of this revenue procedure.
- Instructions to the recipient that are substantially similar to those on or accompanying the official IRS schedule must be provided to aid in the proper reporting of the items on the recipient's income tax return. Where items are not reported to a recipient because they do not apply, the related instructions may be omitted.
- The quality of the ink or other material used to generate recipients' schedules must produce clearly legible documents. In general, black chemical transfer inks are preferred.
- In order to assure uniformity of substitute Schedules K-1, the paper size should be standard 8.5" x 11" (the international standard (A4) of 8.27" x 11.69" may be substituted.)
- The paper weight, paper color, font type, font size, font color, and page layout must be such that the average recipient can easily decipher the information on each page.
- State or local tax-related information may be included on recipient copies of substitute Schedules K-1. All non-tax-related information should be separated from the tax information on the substitute schedule to avoid confusion for the recipient.
- The legend "Important Tax Return Document Enclosed" must appear in a bold and conspicuous manner on the outside of the envelope that contains the substitute recipient copy of Schedule K-1.
- The entity may have to pay a penalty if a substitute Schedule K-1 furnished to any recipient does not conform to the specifications of this revenue procedure and results in impeding processing.

7.1.3 Requirements for Schedules K-1 with Two-Dimensional (2-D) Bar Codes

In an effort to reduce the burden of manually transcribing tax documents, improve quality, and increase government efficiency, the IRS is pleased to provide specifications for 2-D bar-coded substitute Schedules K-1 for Forms 1041, 1065, and 1120S. The IRS encourages voluntary participation in adding 2-D barcoding.

Note. If software vendors do not want to produce bar-coded Schedules K-1, they may produce the official IRS Schedules K-1 but cannot use the expedited process for approving bar-coded K-1s and their parent returns as outlined in Section 7.1.5.

In addition to the requirements in Sections 7.1.1 and 7.1.2, the bar-coded Schedules K-1 must meet the following specifications.

- The bar code should print in the space labeled "For IRS Use Only" on each Schedule K-1. The entire bar code must print within the "For IRS Use Only" box surrounded by a white space of at least 1/4 inch.
- Bar codes must print in PDF 417 format.
- The bar codes must always be in the specified format with every field represented by at least a field delimiter (carriage return). Leaving out a field in a bar code will cause every subsequent field to be misread.
- Be sure to include the 6 digit form ID code in the upper right of Schedules K-1 of Forms 1041, 1065, and 1120S.
    - 661106 for Form 1041,

- 651106 for Form 1065, and
- 671106 for Form 1120S.

Please allow white space around the 6-digit code.

7.1.4 Approval Process for Bar-Coded Schedules K-1

Prior to releasing commercially available tax software that creates bar-coded Schedules K-1, the printed schedule and the bar code must both be tested. Bar code testing must be done using the final official IRS Schedule K-1. Bar code approval requests must be resubmitted for any subsequent changes to the official IRS form that would affect the bar code. Below are instructions and a sequence of events that will comprise the testing process.

- The IRS has released the final Schedule K-1 bar-code specifications by publishing them on the IRS.gov website (see *http://www.irs.gov/efile/article/0,,id=129859,00.html*).
- The IRS will publish a set of test documents that will be used to test the ability of tax preparation software to create bar codes in the correct format.
- Software developers will submit two identical copies of the test documents – one to the IRS and one to a contracted testing vendor.
- The IRS will use one set to ensure the printed schedules comply with standard substitute forms specifications.
- If the printed forms fail to meet the substitute form criteria, the IRS will inform the software developer of the reason for noncompliance.
- The software developer must resubmit the Schedule(s) K-1 until they pass the substitute forms criteria.
- The testing vendor will review the bar codes to ensure they meet the published bar-code specifications.
- If the bar code(s) does not meet published specifications, the testing vendor will contact the software developer directly informing them of the reason for noncompliance.
- Software developers must submit new bar-coded schedules until they pass the bar-code test.
- When the bar code passes, the testing vendor will inform the IRS that the developer has passed the bar-code test and the IRS will issue an overall approval for both the substitute form and the bar code.
- After receiving this consolidated response, the software vendor is free to release software for tax preparation as long as any subsequent revisions to the schedules do not change the fields.
- Find the mailing address for the testing vendor below. Separate and simultaneous mailings to the IRS and the vendor will reduce testing time.

7.1.5 Procedures for Reducing Testing Time

In order to help provide incentives to the software development community to participate in the Schedule K-1 2-D project, the IRS has committed to expediting the testing of bar-coded Schedules K-1 and their associated parent returns. To receive this expedited service, follow the instructions below.

- Mail the parent returns (Forms 1065, 1120S, 1041) and associated bar-coded Schedule(s) K-1 to the appropriate address below in a separate package from all other approval requests.

Internal Revenue Service
Attn: Bar-Coded K-1
SE:W:CAR:MP:T:T:SP
1111 Constitution Avenue, NW
Room 6406
Washington, D.C. 20224

- Mail one copy of the parent form(s) and Schedule(s) K-1 to the IRS and another copy to the testing vendor at the address below.

  Northrop Grumman Information Tech
  Attn: Bill Philpot, Product Assurance Manager
  1800 Alexander Bell Drive
  Suite 300
  Reston, VA 20191
  Phone: 703-453-1200

- Include multiple email and phone contact points in the packages.
- While the IRS can expedite bar-coded Schedules K-1 and their associated parent returns, it cannot expedite the approval of non-associated tax returns.

Section 7.2 – Procedures for Printing IRS Envelopes

7.2.1 Procedures for Printing IRS Envelopes

Organizations are permitted to produce substitute tax return envelopes. Use of substitute return envelopes that comply with the requirements set forth in this section will assist in delivery of mail by the U.S. Postal Service and facilitate internal sorting at the Internal Revenue Service Centers.

Use the following 5-digit ZIP codes when mailing returns to the IRS Service Centers:

Service Center	ZIP Code
Atlanta, GA	39901
Kansas City, MO	64999
Austin, TX	73301
Philadelphia, PA	19255
Memphis, TN	37501
Andover, MA	05501
Cincinnati, OH	45999
Ogden, UT	84201
Fresno, CA	93888

7.2.2 Sorting Returns by Form Type

Sorting returns by form type is accomplished by the preprinted bar codes on return envelopes included in each specific type of form or package mailed to the taxpayers. The 32 bit bar code on the left of the address on each envelope identifies the type of form the taxpayer is filing, and it assists in consolidating like returns for processing. Failure to use the envelopes furnished by the IRS results in additional processing time and effort, and possibly delays the timely deposit of funds, processing of returns, and issuance of refund checks.

7.2.3 ZIP+4 or 9-Digit ZIP Codes

The IRS will not furnish or sell bulk quantities of preprinted tax return envelopes to taxpayers or tax practitioners. A suitable alternative has been developed that will accommodate the sorting needs of both the IRS and the United States Postal Service (USPS). The alternative is based on the use of ZIP+4, or 9-digit ZIP codes, for mailing various types of tax returns to the IRS Service Centers. The IRS uses the last four digits to identify and sort the various form types into separate groups for processing. The list of 4-digit extensions with the related form designations is provided below.

ZIP+4	Package
XXXXX-0002	1040
XXXXX-0005	941
XXXXX-0006	940
XXXXX-0008	943
XXXXX-0011	1065
XXXXX-0012	1120
XXXXX-0013	1120S
XXXXX-0014	1040EZ
XXXXX-0015	1040A
XXXXX-0027	990
XXXXX-0031	2290

7.2.4 Guidelines for Having Envelopes Preprinted

You may use the preparers' company names, addresses, and logos as long as you do not interfere with the clear areas. The government recommends that the envelope stocks have an average opacity of not less than 89 percent and contain a minimum of 50 percent waste paper. Use of carbon based ink is essential for effective address and bar-code reading. Envelope construction can be of side seam or diagonal seam design. The government recommends that the size of the envelope should be 5 3/4 inches by 9 inches. Continuous pin-fed construction is not desirable, but is permissible, if the glued edge is at the top. This requirement is firm because mail opening equipment is designed to open the bottom edge of each envelope.

7.2.5 Envelopes/ZIP Codes

The above procedures or guidelines are written for the user having envelopes preprinted. Many practitioners may not wish to have large quantities of envelopes with differing ZIP codes/form designations preprinted due to low volume, warehousing, waste, etc. In this case, the practitioner can type or machine print the addresses with the appropriate ZIP codes to accommodate sorting. If the requirements/guidelines outlined in this section cannot be met, then use only the appropriate 5-digit service center ZIP code.

Section 7.3 – Guidelines for Substitute Forms 8655

7.3.1
Increased Standardization for Forms 8655

Increased standardization for reporting information on substitute Forms 8655 is now required to aid in processing and for compliance purposes. Please follow the guidelines in Section 7.3.2.

7.3.2
Requirements for Substitute Forms 8655

Please follow these specific requirements when producing substitute Forms 8655.

- The first line of the title must be "Reporting Agent Authorization."
- If you want to include a reference to "State Limited Power of Attorney," it can be in parentheses under the title. "State" must be the first word within the parentheses.
- You must include "Form 8655" on the form.
- While the line numbers do not have to match the official form, the sequence of the information must be in the same order.
- The size of any variable data must be printed in a font no smaller than 10-point.
- For adequate disclosure checks, the following must be included for each taxpayer:
  (a) Name,
  (b) EIN, and
  (c) Address.
- At this time, Form 944 will not be required if Form 941 is checked. Only those forms that the reporting agent company supports need to be listed.
- The jurat must be identical with the exception of references to line numbers.
- A contact name and number for the reporting agent is not required.
- Line 17, or the equivalent line, must include two checkboxes.
- Any state information included should be contained in a separate section of the substitute form. Preferably this information will be in the same area as line 19 of the official form.
- All substitute Forms 8655 must be approved by the Substitute Forms Unit as outlined in the Form 8655 specifications in Publication 1167.
- If you have not already been assigned a 3-letter source code, you will be given one when your substitute form is approved. This source code should be included in the lower left corner of the form.

Part 8
Alternative Methods of Filing

Section 8.1 – Forms for Electronically Filed Returns

8.1.1
Electronic Filing Program

Electronic filing is a method by which qualified filers transmit tax return information directly to an IRS Service Center in the format of the official IRS forms. The IRS accepts both refund and balance-due individual tax returns that are filed electronically.

8.1.2
Applying to Participate in IRS *e-file*

Anyone wishing to participate in IRS *e-file* of tax returns must submit an *e-file* application. The application can be completed and submitted electronically on the IRS website at *www.irs.gov* or by filing Form 8633, Application to Participate in the IRS *e-file* Program.

8.1.3
Mailing Instructions

IF submitting Form 8633 by...	THEN mail it to...
Regular mail	Internal Revenue Service Andover Submission Processing Center Attn: EFU Acceptance - Testing Stop 983 P.O. Box 4099 Woburn, MA 01888-4099
Overnight mail	Internal Revenue Service Andover Submission Processing Center Attn: EFU Acceptance - Testing Stop 983 310 Lowell Street Andover, MA 05501-0001

8.1.4
Obtaining the Taxpayer Signature

Form 8453, U.S. Individual Income Tax Declaration for an IRS *e-file* Return, is the signature document for an electronically filed 1040, 1040A, or 1040EZ return not filed with an electronic signature. Form 8453, which serves as a transmittal for associated nonelectronic (paper) documents such as Forms 3115, 5713, 8283, and 8332, is a one-page form and can only be approved through the Substitute Forms Program in that format. Form 8453-OL serves the same purpose for taxpayers filing through online services. For specific information about electronic filing, refer to Publication 1345, Handbook for Authorized IRS *e-file* Providers of Individual Income Tax Returns.

8.1.5
Guidelines for Preparing Substitute Forms in the Electronic Filing Program

A participant in the electronic filing program, who wants to develop a substitute form should follow the guidelines throughout this publication and send a sample form for approval to the Substitute Forms Unit at the address in Part 1. If you do not prepare Substitute Form 8453 using a font in which all IRS wording fits on a single page, the form will not be accepted.

Note. Use of unapproved forms could result in suspension of the participant from the electronic filing program.

Section 8.2 – Effect on Other Documents

8.2.1
Effect on Other Documents

This revenue procedure supersedes Revenue Procedure 2005–74, 2005–2 C.B. 1098.

Exhibit A-1 (Preferred Format)

SCHEDULES A&B (Form 1040)

Department of the Treasury
Internal Revenue Service

Schedule A—Itemized Deductions

(Schedule B is on back)

▶ Attach to Form 1040. ▶ See Instructions for Schedules A&B (Form 1040).

OMB No. 1545-0074

2006

Attachment Sequence No. **07**

Name(s) shown on Form 1040 | Your social security number

Medical and Dental Expenses		**Caution.** Do not include expenses reimbursed or paid by others.		
	1	Medical and dental expenses (see page A-1)	1	
	2	Enter amount from Form 1040, line 38 [2]		
	3	Multiply line 2 by 7.5% (.075)	3	
	4	Subtract line 3 from line 1. If line 3 is more than line 1, enter -0-		4
Taxes You Paid (See page A-3.)	5	State and local income taxes	5	
	6	Real estate taxes (see page A-3)	6	
	7	Personal property taxes	7	
	8	Other taxes. List type and amount ▶	8	
	9	Add lines 5 through 8		9
Interest You Paid (See page A-3.)	10	Home mortgage interest and points reported to you on Form 1098	10	
	11	Home mortgage interest not reported to you on Form 1098. If paid to the person from whom you bought the home, see page A-3 and show that person's name, identifying no., and address ▶	11	
Note. Personal interest is not deductible.	12	Points not reported to you on Form 1098. See page A-4 for special rules	12	
	13	Investment interest. Attach Form 4952 if required. (See page A-4.)	13	
	14	Add lines 10 through 13		14
Gifts to Charity If you made a gift and got a benefit for it, see page A-4.	15	Gifts by cash or check. If you made any gift of $250 or more, see page A-5	15	
	16	Other than by cash or check. If any gift of $250 or more, see page A-5. You **must** attach Form 8283 if over $500	16	
	17	Carryover from prior year	17	
	18	Add lines 15 through 17		18
Casualty and Theft Losses	19	Casualty or theft loss(es). Attach Form 4684. (See page A-6.)		19
Job Expenses and Certain Miscellaneous Deductions (See page A-6.)	20	Unreimbursed employee expenses—job travel, union dues, job education, etc. Attach Form 2106 or 2106-EZ if required. (See page A-6.) ▶	20	
	21	Tax preparation fees	21	
	22	Other expenses—investment, safe deposit box, etc. List type and amount ▶	22	
	23	Add lines 20 through 22	23	
	24	Enter amount from Form 1040, line 38 [24]		
	25	Multiply line 24 by 2% (.02)	25	
	26	Subtract line 25 from line 23. If line 25 is more than line 23, enter -0-		26
Other Miscellaneous Deductions	27	Other—from list on page A-7. List type and amount ▶		27
Total Itemized Deductions	28	Is Form 1040, line 38, over $150,500 (over $75,250 if married filing separately)? ☐ **No.** Your deduction is not limited. Add the amounts in the far right column for lines 4 through 27. Also, enter this amount on Form 1040, line 40. ☐ **Yes.** Your deduction may be limited. See page A-7 for the amount to enter. ▶		28
	29	If you elect to itemize deductions even though they are less than your standard deduction, check here ▶ ☐		

For Paperwork Reduction Act Notice, see Form 1040 instructions. **Schedule A (Form 1040) 2006**

Exhibit A-2 (Acceptable Format)

SCHEDULES A&B (Form 1040)

Department of the Treasury
Internal Revenue Service

Schedule A—Itemized Deductions

▶ Attach to Form 1040. ▶ See Instructions for Schedules A&B (Form 1040).

OMB No. 1545-0074

2006

Attachment Sequence No. 07

Name(s) shown on Form 1040 | **Your social security number**

Medical and Dental Expenses		**Caution.** Do not include expenses reimbursed or paid by others.		
	1	Medical and dental expenses (see page A-1)	1	
	2	Enter amount from Form 1040, line 38 [2]		
	3	Multiply line 2 by 7.5% (.075)	3	
	4	Subtract line 3 from line 1. If line 3 is more than line 1, enter -0-		4
Taxes You Paid (See page A-3.)	5	State and local income taxes	5	
	6	Real estate taxes (see page A-3)	6	
	7	Personal property taxes	7	
	8	Other taxes. List type and amount ▶	8	
	9	Add lines 5 through 8		9
Interest You Paid (See page A-3.)	10	Home mortgage interest and points reported to you on Form 1098	10	
	11	Home mortgage interest not reported to you on Form 1098. If paid to the person from whom you bought the home, see page A-3 and show that person's name, identifying no., and address ▶	11	
Note. Personal interest is not deductible.	12	Points not reported to you on Form 1098. See page A-4 for special rules	12	
	13	Investment interest. Attach Form 4952 if required. (See page A-4.)	13	
	14	Add lines 10 through 13		14
Gifts to Charity If you made a gift and got a benefit for it, see page A-4.	15	Gifts by cash or check. If you made any gift of $250 or more, see page A-5	15	
	16	Other than by cash or check. If any gift of $250 or more, see page A-5. You **must** attach Form 8283 if over $500	16	
	17	Carryover from prior year	17	
	18	Add lines 15 through 17		18
Casualty and Theft Losses	19	Casualty or theft loss(es). Attach Form 4684. (See page A-6.)		19
Job Expenses and Certain Miscellaneous Deductions (See page A-6.)	20	Unreimbursed employee expenses—job travel, union dues, job education, etc. Attach Form 2106 or 2106-EZ if required. (See page A-6.) ▶	20	
	21	Tax preparation fees	21	
	22	Other expenses—investment, safe deposit box, etc. List type and amount ▶	22	
	23	Add lines 20 through 22	23	
	24	Enter amount from Form 1040, line 38 [24]		
	25	Multiply line 24 by 2% (.02)	25	
	26	Subtract line 25 from line 23. If line 25 is more than line 23, enter -0-		26
Other Miscellaneous Deductions	27	Other—from list on page A-7. List type and amount ▶		27
Total Itemized Deductions	28	Is Form 1040, line 38, over $150,500 (over $75,250 if married filing separately)? ☐ **No.** Your deduction is not limited. Add the amounts in the far right column for lines 4 through 27. Also, enter this amount on Form 1040, line 40. ☐ **Yes.** Your deduction may be limited. See page A-7 for the amount to enter. ▶		28
	29	If you elect to itemize deductions even though they are less than your standard deduction, check here ▶ ☐		

For Paperwork Reduction Act Notice, see Form 1040 instructions. **Schedule A (Form 1040) 2006**

Exhibit B-1 (Preferred Format)

Form **2106-EZ**

Department of the Treasury
Internal Revenue Service

Unreimbursed Employee Business Expenses

▶ Attach to Form 1040 or Form 1040NR.

OMB No. 1545-0074

2006

Attachment Sequence No. **54A**

Your name	Occupation in which you incurred expenses	**Social security number**
		: :

You May Use This Form Only if All of the Following Apply.

- You are an employee deducting ordinary and necessary expenses attributable to your job. An ordinary expense is one that is common and accepted in your field of trade, business, or profession. A necessary expense is one that is helpful and appropriate for your business. An expense does not have to be required to be considered necessary.
- You **do not** get reimbursed by your employer for any expenses (amounts your employer included in box 1 of your Form W-2 are not considered reimbursements for this purpose).
- If you are claiming vehicle expense, you are using the standard mileage rate for 2006.

Caution: *You can use the standard mileage rate for 2006* ***only if: (a)*** *you owned the vehicle and used the standard mileage rate for the first year you placed the vehicle in service,* ***or (b)*** *you leased the vehicle and used the standard mileage rate for the portion of the lease period after 1997.*

Part I Figure Your Expenses

1	Vehicle expense using the standard mileage rate. Complete Part II and multiply line 8a by 44.5¢ (.445) . . .	1	
2	Parking fees, tolls, and transportation, including train, bus, etc., that **did not** involve overnight travel or commuting to and from work . . .	2	
3	Travel expense while away from home overnight, including lodging, airplane, car rental, etc. **Do not** include meals and entertainment . . .	3	
4	Business expenses not included on lines 1 through 3. **Do not** include meals and entertainment . . .	4	
5	Meals and entertainment expenses: $________ × 50% (.50) (Employees subject to Department of Transportation (DOT) hours of service limits: Multiply meal expenses incurred while away from home on business by 75% (.75) instead of 50%. For details, see instructions.)	5	
6	**Total expenses.** Add lines 1 through 5. Enter here and on **Schedule A (Form 1040), line 20** (or on **Schedule A (Form 1040NR, line 9).** (Armed Forces reservists, fee-basis state or local government officials, qualified performing artists, and individuals with disabilities: See the instructions for special rules on where to enter this amount.) . . .	6	

Part II Information on Your Vehicle. Complete this part **only** if you are claiming vehicle expense on line 1.

7 When did you place your vehicle in service for business use? (month, day, year) ▶ .... / .... / ....

8 Of the total number of miles you drove your vehicle during 2006, enter the number of miles you used your vehicle for:

a Business .... **b** Commuting (see instructions) .... **c** Other ....

9 Do you (or your spouse) have another vehicle available for personal use? . . . ☐ **Yes** ☐ **No**

10 Was your vehicle available for personal use during off-duty hours? . . . ☐ **Yes** ☐ **No**

11a Do you have evidence to support your deduction?. . . . ☐ **Yes** ☐ **No**

b If "Yes," is the evidence written?. . . . ☐ **Yes** ☐ **No**

For Paperwork Reduction Act Notice, see page 4. Form **2106-EZ** (2006)

Exhibit B-2 (Acceptable Format)

Form **2106-EZ** Department of the Treasury Internal Revenue Service	**Unreimbursed Employee Business Expenses** ▶ Attach to Form 1040 or Form 1040NR.	OMB No. 1545-0074 **2006** Attachment Sequence No. **54A**
Your name	Occupation in which you incurred expenses	**Social security number**

You May Use This Form Only if All of the Following Apply.

- You are an employee deducting ordinary and necessary expenses attributable to your job. An ordinary expense is one that is common and accepted in your field of trade, business, or profession. A necessary expense is one that is helpful and appropriate for your business. An expense does not have to be required to be considered necessary.
- You **do not** get reimbursed by your employer for any expenses (amounts your employer included in box 1 of your Form W-2 are not considered reimbursements for this purpose).
- If you are claiming vehicle expense, you are using the standard mileage rate for 2006.

Caution: *You can use the standard mileage rate for 2006* ***only if:*** ***(a)*** *you owned the vehicle and used the standard mileage rate for the first year you placed the vehicle in service,* ***or*** ***(b)*** *you leased the vehicle and used the standard mileage rate for the portion of the lease period after 1997.*

Part I **Figure Your Expenses**

1	Vehicle expense using the standard mileage rate. Complete Part II and multiply line 8a by 44.5¢ (.445)	1	
2	Parking fees, tolls, and transportation, including train, bus, etc., that **did not** involve overnight travel or commuting to and from work	2	
3	Travel expense while away from home overnight, including lodging, airplane, car rental, etc. **Do not** include meals and entertainment	3	
4	Business expenses not included on lines 1 through 3. **Do not** include meals and entertainment	4	
5	Meals and entertainment expenses: $ ________ × 50% (.50) (Employees subject to Department of Transportation (DOT) hours of service limits: Multiply meal expenses incurred while away from home on business by 75% (.75) instead of 50%. For details, see instructions.)	5	
6	**Total expenses.** Add lines 1 through 5. Enter here and on **Schedule A (Form 1040), line 20** (or on **Schedule A (Form 1040NR, line 9).** (Armed Forces reservists, fee-basis state or local government officials, qualified performing artists, and individuals with disabilities: See the instructions for special rules on where to enter this amount.)	6	

Part II **Information on Your Vehicle.** Complete this part **only** if you are claiming vehicle expense on line 1.

7 When did you place your vehicle in service for business use? (month, day, year) ▶ .... / .... / ....

8 Of the total number of miles you drove your vehicle during 2006, enter the number of miles you used your vehicle for:

a Business .... **b** Commuting (see instructions) .... **c** Other ....

9 Do you (or your spouse) have another vehicle available for personal use? ☐ Yes ☐ No

10 Was your vehicle available for personal use during off-duty hours? ☐ Yes ☐ No

11a Do you have evidence to support your deduction?. ☐ Yes ☐ No

b If "Yes," is the evidence written?. ☐ Yes ☐ No

For Paperwork Reduction Act Notice, see page 4. Form **2106-EZ** (2006)

Exhibit C
Software Developers Voucher

Form **1040-ES** Department of the Treasury Internal Revenue Service	**Estimated Tax for Individuals**	OMB No. 1545-0074 **2007**

(Cut here)

Form **1040-ES**	**2007**	**Payment Voucher 1**

File only if you are making a payment of estimated tax by check or money order. Mail this voucher with your check or money order payable to the **"United States Treasury."** Write your social security number and "2007 Form 1040-ES" on your check or money order. Do not send cash. Enclose, but do not staple or attach, your payment with this voucher.

Calendar year -- Due April 16, 2007	
Amount of estimated tax you are paying by check or money order.	1,425

XXXX

William T THOMAS
511 JONATHAN CAROL BLVD
JEWELL, OH 43530

PO Box 970006
St Louis, MO 63197-0006

400011018 HT THOM 30 0 200712 430

Exhibit D

Check Sheet of IRS Substitute Forms 20 :
Submitted on

Company: . . . .
Contact: . . . .
Phone: . . . .
Fax: . . . .
Source Code: . . . .

Form Number	Approved With Corrections	Must Be Resubmitted	Approved	Comments

Authorized Name: ______________________________
Title: ______________________________
Reviewer's Name: ______________________________
Telephone: ______________________________
Date: ______________________________

Part IV. Items of General Interest

AJCA Modifications to the Section 6112 Regulations

Announcement 2007–27

AGENCY: Internal Revenue Service (IRS), Treasury.

ACTION: Notice of public hearing on proposed rulemaking.

SUMMARY: This document provides notice of a public hearing on proposed rulemaking (REG–103043–05, 2006–49 I.R.B. 1063) relating to the obligation of material advisors to prepare and maintain lists with respect to reportable transactions under section 6112.

DATES: The public hearing is being held on Tuesday, March 20, 2007, at 10:00 a.m. The IRS must receive outlines of the topics to be discussed at the public hearing by March 6, 2007.

ADDRESSES: The public hearing is being held in the IRS Auditorium, Internal Revenue Service Building, 1111 Constitution Avenue, NW, Washington, DC 20224. Due to building security procedures, visitors must enter at the Constitution Avenue entrance. In addition, all visitors must present photo identification to enter the building.

Mail outlines to CC:PA:LPD:PR (REG–103043–05), room 5205, Internal Revenue Service, POB 7604, Ben Franklin Station, Washington, DC 20044. Submissions may be hand-delivered Monday through Friday between the hours of 8:00 a.m. and 4:00 p.m. to CC:PA:LPD:PR (REG–103043–05), Couriers Desk, Internal Revenue Service, 1111 Constitution Avenue, NW, Washington, DC or sent electronically via the Federal erulemaking Portal at *www.regulations.gov* (IRS-REG–103043–05).

FOR FURTHER INFORMATION CONTACT: Concerning submissions of comments, the hearing and/or to be placed on the building access list to attend the hearing Kelly Banks at (202) 622–7180 (not a toll-free number).

SUPPLEMENTARY INFORMATION:

The subject of the public hearing is the notice of proposed rulemaking (REG–103043–05) that was published in the **Federal Register** on Thursday, November 2, 2006 (71 FR 64501). The notice also announced that a hearing will be scheduled if requested by the public in writing by January 31, 2007.

The rules of 26 CFR 601.601 apply to the hearing. A period of 10 minutes is allotted to each person for presenting oral comments. After the deadline has passed, persons who have submitted written comments and wish to present oral comments at the hearing must submit an outline of the topics to be discussed and the amount of time to be devoted to each topic (a signed original and eight (8) copies) by March 6, 2007.

The IRS will prepare an agenda containing the schedule of speakers. Copies of the agenda will be made available free of charge, at the hearing. Because of access restrictions, the IRS will not admit visitors beyond the immediate entrance area more than 30 minutes before the hearing starts. For information about having your name placed on the building access list to attend the hearing, see the "FOR FURTHER INFORMATION CONTACT" section of this document.

LaNita Van Dyke,
Branch Chief,
Publications and Regulations Branch,
Legal Processing Division,
Associate Chief Counsel
(Procedure and Administration).

(Filed by the Office of the Federal Register on February 14, 2007, 8:45 a.m., and published in the issue of the Federal Register for February 15, 2007, 72 F.R. 7361)

AJCA Modifications to the Section 6011 Regulations

Announcement 2007–29

AGENCY: Internal Revenue Service (IRS), Treasury.

ACTION: Notice of public hearing on proposed rulemaking.

SUMMARY: This document provides notice of a public hearing on proposed rulemaking (REG–103038–05, 2006–49 I.R.B. 1049) relating to the disclosure of reportable transactions under section 6011.

DATES: The public hearing is being held on Tuesday, March 20, 2007, at 10:00 a.m. The IRS must receive outlines of the topics to be discussed at the public hearing by March 6, 2007.

ADDRESSES: The public hearing is being held in the IRS Auditorium, Internal Revenue Service Building, 1111 Constitution Avenue, NW, Washington, DC 20224. Due to building security procedures, visitors must enter at the Constitution Avenue entrance. In addition, all visitors must present photo identification to enter the building.

Mail outlines to CC:PA:LPD:PR (REG–103038–05), room 5205, Internal Revenue Service, POB 7604, Ben Franklin Station, Washington, DC 20044. Submissions may be hand-delivered Monday through Friday between the hours of 8:00 a.m. and 4:00 p.m. to CC:PA:LPD:PR (REG–103038–05), Couriers Desk, Internal Revenue Service, 1111 Constitution Avenue, NW, Washington, DC or sent electronically via the Federal erulemaking Portal at *www.regulations.gov* (IRS-REG–103038–05).

FOR FURTHER INFORMATION CONTACT: Concerning submissions of comments, the hearing and/or to be placed on the building access list to attend the hearing Kelly Banks at (202) 622–7180 (not a toll-free number).

SUPPLEMENTARY INFORMATION:

The subject of the public hearing is the notice of proposed rulemaking (REG–103038–05) that was published in the **Federal Register** on Thursday, November 2, 2006 (71 FR 64488).

The rules of 26 CFR 601.601(a)(3) apply to the hearing.

A period of 10 minutes is allotted to each person for presenting oral comments. After the deadline has passed, persons who have submitted written comments and wish to present oral comments at the hearing must submit an outline of the topics to be discussed and the amount of time to be devoted to each topic (a signed original and eight (8) copies) by March 6, 2007.

The IRS will prepare an agenda containing the schedule of speakers. Copies of the agenda will be made available free of charge at the hearing. Because of access restrictions, the IRS will not admit visitors beyond the immediate entrance area more than 30 minutes before the hearing starts. For information about having your name placed on the building access list to attend the hearing, see the "FOR FURTHER INFORMATION CONTACT" section of this document.

LaNita Van Dyke,
Branch Chief,
Publications and Regulations Branch,
Legal Processing Division,
Associate Chief Counsel
(Procedure and Administration).

(Filed by the Office of the Federal Register on February 14, 2007, 8:45 a.m., and published in the issue of the Federal Register for February 15, 2007, 72 F.R. 7360)

AJCA Modifications to the Section 6111 Regulations

Announcement 2007–30

AGENCY: Internal Revenue Service (IRS), Treasury.

ACTION: Notice of public hearing on proposed rulemaking.

SUMMARY: This document provides notice of a public hearing on proposed rulemaking (REG–103039–05, 2006–49 I.R.B. 1057) relating to the disclosure of reportable transactions by material advisors under section 6111.

DATES: The public hearing is being held on Tuesday, March 20, 2007, at 10:00 a.m. The IRS must receive outlines of the topics to be discussed at the public hearing by March 6, 2007.

ADDRESSES: The public hearing is being held in the IRS Auditorium, Internal Revenue Service Building, 1111 Constitution Avenue, NW, Washington, DC 20224. Due to building security procedures, visitors must enter at the Constitution Avenue entrance. In addition, all visitors must present photo identification to enter the building.

Mail outlines to CC:PA:LPD:PR (REG–103039–05), room 5205, Internal Revenue Service, POB 7604, Ben Franklin Station, Washington, DC 20044. Submissions may be hand-delivered Monday through Friday between the hours of 8:00 a.m. and 4:00 p.m. to CC:PA:LPD:PR (REG–103039–05), Couriers Desk, Internal Revenue Service, 1111 Constitution Avenue, NW, Washington, DC or sent electronically via the Federal erulemaking Portal at *www.regulations.gov* (IRS-REG–103039–05).

FOR FURTHER INFORMATION CONTACT: Concerning submissions of comments, the hearing and/or to be placed on the building access list to attend the hearing Kelly Banks at (202) 622–7180 (not a toll-free number).

SUPPLEMENTARY INFORMATION:

The subject of the public hearing is the notice of proposed rulemaking (REG–103039–05) that was published in the **Federal Register** on Thursday, November 2, 2006 (71 FR 64496). The notice also announced that a hearing will be scheduled if requested by the public in writing by January 31, 2007.

The rules of 26 CFR 601.601 apply to the hearing.

A period of 10 minutes is allotted to each person for presenting oral comments. After the deadline has passed, persons who have submitted written comments and wish to present oral comments at the hearing must submit an outline of the topics to be discussed and the amount of time to be devoted to each topic (a signed original and eight (8) copies) by March 6, 2007.

The IRS will prepare an agenda containing the schedule of speakers. Copies of the agenda will be made available free of charge at the hearing. Because of access restrictions, the IRS will not admit visitors beyond the immediate entrance area more than 30 minutes before the hearing starts. For information about having your name placed on the building access list to attend the hearing, see the "FOR FURTHER INFORMATION CONTACT" section of this document.

LaNita Van Dyke,
Branch Chief,
Publications and Regulations Branch,
Legal Processing Division,
Associate Chief Counsel
(Procedure and Administration).

(Filed by the Office of the Federal Register on February 14, 2007, 8:45 a.m., and published in the issue of the Federal Register for February 15, 2007, 72 F.R. 7360)

Nondiscrimination and Wellness Programs in Health Coverage in the Group Market; Correction

Announcement 2007–32

AGENCY: Internal Revenue Service (IRS), Treasury.

ACTION: Correcting amendments.

SUMMARY: This document contains correction to final regulations (T.D. 9298, 2007–6 I.R.B. 434) that were published in the **Federal Register** on Wednesday, December 13, 2006 (71 FR 75014) governing the provisions prohibiting discrimination based on a health factor for group health plans and issuers of health insurance coverage offered in connection with a group health plan.

DATES: The correction is effective February 12, 2007.

FOR FURTHER INFORMATION CONTACT: Russ Weinheimer, (202) 622–6080 (not a toll-free number).

SUPPLEMENTARY INFORMATION:

Background

The correction notice that is the subject of this document is under section 9802 of the Internal Revenue Code.

Need for Correction

As published, final regulations (T.D. 9298) contain errors that may prove to be misleading and are in need of clarification.

* * * * *

Correction of Publication

Accordingly, 26 CFR part 54 is corrected by making the following correcting amendments:

PART 54—PENSION EXCISE TAXES

Paragraph 1. The authority citation for part 54 continues to read, in part, as follows:

Authority: 26 U.S.C. 7805 * * *

Par. 2. Section 54.9802–1(b)(2)(i)(D) is amended by revising paragraph (ii) of *Example 4*.

Par. 3. Section 54.9802–1(f)(1) is amended by revising the first sentence of the paragraph. The revisions read as follows:

§ 54.9802–1 Prohibiting discrimination against participants and beneficiaries based on a health factor.

* * * * *

(b) * * *

(2) * * *

(i) * * *

(D) * * *

Example 4. * * *

(ii) *Conclusion.* In this *Example 4*, the limit does not violate this paragraph (b)(2)(i) because $2,000 of benefits for the treatment of TMJ are available uniformly to all similarly situated individuals and a plan may limit benefits covered in relation to a specific disease or condition if the limit applies uniformly to all similarly situated individuals and is not directed at individual participants or beneficiaries. (This example does not address whether the plan provision is permissible under the Americans with Disabilities Act or any other applicable law.)

* * * * *

(f) * * *

(1) * * * If none of the conditions for obtaining a reward under a wellness program are based on an individual satisfying a standard that is related to a health factor (or if a wellness program does not provide a reward), the wellness program does not violate this section, if participation in the program is made available to all similarly situated individuals. * * *

* * * * *

LaNita Van Dyke,
Chief, Publications and Regulations Branch,
Legal Processing Division,
Associate Chief Counsel
(Procedure and Administration).

(Filed by the Office of the Federal Register on February 21, 2007, 8:45 a.m., and published in the issue of the Federal Register for February 22, 2007, 72 F.R. 7929)

Part I. Rulings and Decisions Under the Internal Revenue Code of 1986

Section 181.—Treatment of Certain Qualified Film and Television Productions

26 CFR 1.181–1T: Deduction for qualified film and television production costs (temporary).

T.D. 9312

DEPARTMENT OF THE TREASURY
Internal Revenue Service
26 CFR Parts 1 and 602

Section 181 — Deduction for Qualified Film and Television Production Costs

AGENCY: Internal Revenue Service (IRS), Treasury.

ACTION: Temporary regulation.

SUMMARY: This document contains temporary regulations relating to deductions for the cost of producing film and television productions under section 181. These temporary regulations reflect changes to the law made by the American Jobs Creation Act of 2004 and the Gulf Opportunity Zone Act of 2005, and affect taxpayers that produce films and television productions within the United States. The text of these temporary regulations also serves as the text of the proposed regulations (REG–115403–05) set forth in the notice of proposed rulemaking on this subject in this issue of the Bulletin.

DATES: *Effective Date:* These regulations are effective February 9, 2007.

Applicability Dates: For dates of applicability, see §1.181–6T.

FOR FURTHER INFORMATION CONTACT: Bernard P. Harvey, (202) 622–3110 (not a toll-free number).

SUPPLEMENTARY INFORMATION:

Paperwork Reduction Act

These temporary regulations are being issued without prior notice and public procedure pursuant to the Administrative Procedure Act (5 U.S.C. 553). For this reason, the collections of information contained in these regulations have been reviewed and, pending receipt and evaluation of public comments, approved by the Office of Management and Budget under control number 1545–2059. Responses to these collections of information are required to obtain a tax benefit.

An agency may not conduct or sponsor, and a person is not required to respond to, a collection of information unless the collection of information displays a valid OMB control number.

For further information concerning this collection of information, and where to submit comments on the collection of information and the accuracy of the estimated burden, and suggestions for reducing this burden, please refer to the preamble of the cross-referencing notice of proposed rulemaking published in this issue of the Bulletin.

Books or records relating to a collection of information must be retained as long as their contents may become material in the administration of any internal revenue law. Generally, tax returns and tax return information are confidential, as required by 26 U.S.C. 6103.

Background

This document contains amendments to 26 CFR part 1 to provide regulations under section 181 of the Internal Revenue Code of 1986 (Code). Section 181 was added to the Code by section 244 of the American Jobs Creation Act of 2004, Public Law No. 108–357 (118 Stat. 1418) (Oct. 22, 2004), and was modified by section 403(e) of the Gulf Opportunity Zone Act of 2005, Public Law No. 109–135 (119 Stat. 2577) (Dec. 21, 2005).

Explanation of Provisions

For several years, independent filmmakers and television producers have moved production activities from the United States to other countries. Frequently, this has been motivated by credits and other incentives offered by foreign governments to attract the economic benefits gained by hosting these productions. Congress enacted section 181 to make domestic production more attractive to these taxpayers.

Section 181 permits the owner of a qualified film or television production to elect to deduct production costs in the year the costs are paid or incurred in lieu of capitalizing the costs and recovering them through depreciation allowances if the aggregate costs do not exceed $15 million for each qualifying production ($20 million if a significant amount of the production costs are incurred in certain designated areas) (the "production cost limit"). A film or television production is a qualified film or television production if 75 percent of the total compensation of the production is compensation for services performed in the United States by actors, directors, producers, and other relevant production personnel (the "75 percent test").

Allowance of Deduction

The deduction under section 181 is allowed for the cost of producing qualified film and television productions for which principal photography begins after October 22, 2004, and before January 1, 2009. Production costs incurred before or after this period may be deducted so long as principal photography commences during the period.

Section 181 refers to "the taxpayer" who makes the election and takes the deduction. The temporary regulations provide that only the owner of the film or television production may elect to deduct production costs under section 181. Under the regulations, the owner of the production is deemed to be the person or persons otherwise required to capitalize production costs into the basis of the film or television production under section 263A (or the person or persons that would be required to capitalize production costs if subject to section 263A).

The production costs that must be taken into account (for both the amount of the deduction and for the production cost limit) are the amounts that, absent section 181, are required to be capitalized under section 263A (or the amounts that would be required to be capitalized if the taxpayer was subject to section 263A). Although a film's budget might be evidence that the production costs will not exceed the production cost limit, the budget is not the same as production costs for purposes of section 181. All production costs eligible to be deducted under section 181 are subject to the production cost limit. Under the temporary regulations, distribution costs are specifically excluded from the definition of production costs under section 181, consistent with the exclusion of distribution costs under section 263A.

Section 181 does not require the production to be placed in service in order for the producer to begin deducting production costs, and there is no requirement that the production ever be placed in service or completed. However, the temporary regulations require that, at the time the election is made and in any year that a deduction is claimed, a taxpayer must have a reasonable basis for believing that the production will be set for production (as defined in American Institute of Certified Public Accountants Statement of Position 00–2), will be a qualified film or television production upon completion, and will not exceed the production cost limit. For example, a taxpayer that has developed a shooting script, has a well-documented budget, and has obtained financing on the basis of these facts is in a good position to determine whether it has a reasonable basis to claim the deduction.

The temporary regulations treat the cost of acquiring a production as a production cost. This rule is premised upon the understanding that under section 1245, the seller would recapture upon the sale of the production any section 181 deduction that the seller had claimed. In the case of a sale between related parties, the purchaser must treat the greater of the acquisition cost or the seller's production cost as the purchaser's production cost for purposes of the production cost limit, notwithstanding that the purchaser's deduction under section 181 is based on the purchaser's actual acquisition cost.

In the film industry, once a prospective producer has determined the estimated budget for a production, it usually must obtain financing from a bank or other lender to cover at least part of the production cost. The producer may incur up-front costs in obtaining such financing. The producer's pre-sale agreements with distributors may be used as collateral for this financing. Generally, the financier will be repaid directly by these distributors upon delivery of the finished production. In addition, the financier will usually require that the producer obtain a completion guarantee (often referred to as a completion bond) as a condition of the loan. The completion guarantee is a guarantee that, if the production costs exceed the budgeted costs or the loan proceeds are mishandled, the film will still be completed and/or the financier will be made whole. A completion guarantee can be satisfied in a number of ways. For example, the guarantor may loan funds to the producer to finish the production, may finish the production itself (although this is rare), or may reimburse the financier for the amount loaned to the producer (plus interest and other charges). Generally, the producer must pay an up-front amount in order to obtain a completion guarantee.

The temporary regulations provide that the costs of obtaining financing, including premium costs for completion guarantees, are production costs that are subject to the production cost limit and are deductible under section 181. In addition, if the completion guarantor loans additional funds to the producer and the funds are expended by the producer to complete the production, or if the completion guarantor incurs additional production costs on its own behalf, the additional funds are production costs under section 181.

Participations and residuals (P&R) are defined in section 167(g)(7)(B), as costs with respect to an item of property described in section 167(g)(6), the amount of which by contract varies with the amount of income earned in connection with the property. In the context of film and television production, participations are payments to actors, directors, and other talent based on a contractually-defined measure of future income from the production. Residuals are payments made pursuant to collective-bargaining agreements, such as those of the directors' and actors' guilds, based upon non-theatrical sales, under terms that differ between video, free television, and pay television sales. Participations are generally paid by the producer but may be assumed by a third-party distributor. On the other hand, residuals are generally paid by a distributor out of its gross receipts from the production. Industry accounting generally treats participation payments made by distributors as a reduction in the producer's profit rather than a production cost, and generally treats residual payments made by distributors as a distribution cost.

Various comments were received with respect to the treatment of P&R under section 181. Some comments suggested that taxpayers be permitted to elect to deduct participation payments (rather than capitalizing those payments into the basis of the production) under the income forecast method rather than section 181. Other comments suggested that Congress, by specifically excluding P&R costs paid or incurred by the taxpayer from the definition of "qualified compensation" in section 181(d)(3), intended these costs to be excluded from the production cost limit in section 181(a)(2). Comments received also suggested that P&R costs should be excluded for purposes of determining whether the production cost limit is exceeded, but nonetheless should be deductible production costs under section 181.

In addition, various comments expressed concerns about productions being subsequently disqualified if P&R costs are included in determining if the production cost limit is exceeded. For example, a taxpayer forecasts its production costs (including a reasonable amount of P&R costs based upon projected income from the production) and based upon this forecast the taxpayer determines it has a reasonable basis for making an election under section 181. However, if an unexpectedly large amount of P&R is later paid as a result of production earnings being much greater than was initially expected, with the result that the total production cost exceeds the production cost limit, the production would become disqualified from treatment under section 181.

The temporary regulations provide that P&R costs are considered production costs for purposes of the production cost limit. The IRS and Treasury Department recognize that P&R costs are costs that are generally subject to capitalization under section 263A (see §1.263A–1(e)(2) and §1.263A–1(e)(3)). Nonetheless, an explicit reference to P&R costs is provided in the temporary regulations in order to avoid any uncertainty with respect to these costs.

The IRS and Treasury Department believe that the statute requires P&R costs to be included in the production cost limit. For example, the statute specifically provides that participations and residuals are excluded from the definition of compensation for purposes of determining whether the production was a qualified film or television production, as defined in section 181(d)(1). This explicit exclusion is not found in the production cost limit of section 181(a)(2) or elsewhere in section 181.

In addition, the IRS and Treasury Department are concerned that if P&R costs were excluded from the definition of production costs under section 181, section 181(b) could cause them to be nondeductible under any provision of the Internal Revenue Code. Specifically, section 181(b) states that no depreciation or amortization deduction other than the deduction provided under section 181 is allowed for the basis of a qualified film or television production for which an election has been made. Therefore, if P&R costs were excluded from the definition of production costs under section 181, a taxpayer wishing to expense P&R costs under the holding of *Associated Patentees*, 4 T.C. 979 (1945), may be barred from doing so under section 181(b), as the holding in that case is explicit that a deduction under *Associated Patentees* is a depreciation deduction of basis.

Additionally, the IRS and Treasury Department are concerned that a blanket exclusion of participations from the definition of production costs would allow taxpayers to manipulate the total production cost (and avoid the production cost limit) by structuring compensation as participation payments. Commentators argued that this potential abuse could be mitigated with an anti-abuse rule that treats only those participations that are disguised non-contingent or guaranteed payments, where the talent incurs minimal risk of non-payment (for example, participations with a payment priority over distribution cost repayment and/or production financing cost repayment) as production costs subject to the production cost limit, but does not treat other participation costs as production costs.

The IRS and Treasury Department considered excluding from the amount to be taken into consideration as production costs any residuals (payments to actors' or directors' guilds based on gross income from exploitation in secondary markets) that are paid by the distributor or other third party, under the theory that these payments are costs of exploiting the finished production. However, the same argument could be advanced for participations contingent on income, notwithstanding that most participations are taken in lieu of compensation for services (normally a production cost). In addition, a payment of residuals by a third party is still made on the producer's behalf, and the producer remains the party with ultimate liability for the payment. Thus, the temporary regulations provide that P&R costs are production costs that are deductible under section 181 and are included in the production cost limit.

Section 181(a)(2)(B) provides a higher production cost limit for a qualified film or television production "the aggregate cost of which is significantly incurred" in a designated area. Designated areas include areas eligible for designation as low-income communities or certain distressed counties and isolated areas. However, neither the statute nor its legislative history provides a definition for "significantly incurred," nor do they explain how the standard should be applied. However, Congress' stated intent in enacting section 181 was to encourage economic activity in these designated areas. Accordingly, the temporary regulations provide two different tests for establishing when production costs have been significantly incurred in a designated area. One test is based upon production costs while the other is based upon days of production. Under the first of these tests, the temporary regulations establish a 20 percent threshold for the "significantly incurred" standard (similar to the rules of §1.199–3(g)(3)). This test compares production costs incurred in first-unit principal photography that takes place in a designated area to all production costs incurred for first-unit principal photography. First-unit principal photography typically films the primary actors, whereas second-unit principal photography typically films shots that establish location or context (exteriors of buildings, crowds, cars passing). Production costs of principal photography include, for example, compensation to actors, directors and other production personnel, location costs, camera rental and insurance, and catering. This 20 percent test is based upon production costs incurred in first-unit principal photography and ignores all other production costs such as preproduction, editing, and postproduction costs for purposes of the "significantly incurred" requirement. These other production costs often greatly exceed principal photography costs, and must be incurred where adequate production facilities exist (and it is likely that few such facilities are available in the designated areas). The IRS and Treasury Department believe that if all production costs were taken into consideration in determining whether the 20 percent "significantly incurred" threshold had been met, very few films would qualify for the higher production cost limit, even if a substantial amount of principal photography occurred in a designated area. However, we request comments regarding whether the exclusion of preproduction, editing, and postproduction costs will unfairly impact taxpayers.

Comments were received requesting that consideration be given to developing a "significantly incurred" test based upon the number of days of principal photography. The temporary regulations adopt this suggestion and provide, as an alternative to the 20 percent cost-based test, a "significantly incurred" test based upon the total number of days of principal photography. Under this test, if at least 50 percent of the total days of principal photography take place in a designated area, the production will be deemed to have satisfied the "significantly incurred" requirement of section 181(a)(2)(B). This 50 percent test may provide a simpler computation than the 20 percent cost-based test and avoids issues such as the allocation of salaries to specific days of principal photography.

A taxpayer intending to utilize the $20 million production cost limit under section 181(a)(2)(B) must maintain records adequate to demonstrate that it has a reasonable basis under the "significantly incurred" standard to support reliance on the higher dollar limitation.

Election

The Conference report underlying section 181 provides that, until the Secretary publishes specific guidance, taxpayers may make a valid election under section 181 by claiming the deduction on the taxpayer's return for the year that production costs are first incurred. H.R. Conf.

Rep. 108–755. The IRS published the section 181 election requirements in Notice 2006–47, 2006–20 I.R.B. 892, May 15, 2006. See §601.601(d)(2)(ii)(*b*). The notice also includes transition rules for taxpayers that incurred costs during the period prior to October 22, 2004 (the enactment of section 181) for productions that qualify under section 181 (that is, productions for which principal photography began on or after October 22, 2004). The temporary regulations provide the same election requirements and transition rules, along with a requirement that the taxpayer have a reasonable basis for claiming the deduction.

Many films are owned by a passthrough entity with more than one owner. The temporary regulations provide that if the production is owned by a partnership, the election is made at the partnership level.

Section 181(c)(2) provides that an election under section 181 may not be revoked without the consent of the Secretary. However, the election is effectively revoked if the production costs exceed the production cost limit or if the production fails to be a qualified film or television production. In recognition of the concerns expressed by commentators over the inclusion of P&R costs in the definition of production costs under section 181, and the fact that the requirements of section 181 may ultimately not be met notwithstanding a prior reasonable basis for believing otherwise, the temporary regulations permit taxpayers to revoke a section 181 election by filing a statement with the return for the taxable year in which the revocation is effective identifying the production for which the election is revoked. The return for that taxable year must also report compliance with the recapture provisions discussed in "Special Rules" in this preamble.

Qualified Film or Television Production (definitions)

Both the Senate report and the Conference report underlying section 181 state that "the provision defines a qualified film or television production as any production of a motion picture (whether released theatrically or directly to video cassette or any other format); miniseries, scripted, dramatic television episode; or movie of the week" that satisfies the 75 percent test. The definition provided in the Senate report and the Conference report arguably would exclude productions that do not fall within these delineated categories, such as reality programming, documentaries, sports programs, news programs, variety shows, game shows, live performances, interview and talk shows, commercials and "infomercials," religious/inspirational programming, educational programming, exercise shows, training videos, and others. Comments were received noting that it appeared from the legislative history that Congress intended for the provision to apply only to a motion picture, miniseries, scripted dramatic television episode, or movie of the week. Notwithstanding the legislative history, section 181(d)(2) itself defines a production as "property described in section 168(f)(3)." Section 168(f)(3) property is "any film or video tape." Accordingly, the temporary regulations adopt the broader statutory definition provided in section 168(f)(3) and specifically define a production under section 181 to include any film or video tape production the production cost of which is subject to capitalization under section 263A.

Once a film or television production is released or broadcast, the taxpayer may face additional costs to prepare the production for foreign distribution, rebroadcast (for example, editing a theatrical film for television), or release to the home video market. Consistent with the approach taken under the income forecast method (see section 167(g)(5)(A)(ii)), these costs are not treated as production costs of the film or television production for purposes of the production cost limit under section 181(a)(2), and no deduction may be taken under section 181 for such costs.

Section 181(d)(1) compares qualified compensation to total compensation in applying the 75 percent test. Although qualified compensation is defined by section 181(d)(3)(A) as compensation for services performed in the United States by actors, directors, producers, and other relevant production personnel, the 75 percent test compares this amount to the "total compensation of the production." In order to be consistent with the definition provided for in section 181(d)(3)(A), the temporary regulations define "total compensation of the production" as the total amount of compensation paid for services performed anywhere by actors, directors, producers, and other relevant production personnel in the production of the film or television production. In addition, the temporary regulations specifically provide that the terms compensation and qualified compensation include compensation paid to persons who are not directly employed by the producer.

The term *qualified compensation* is defined as compensation for services by various participants performed "in the United States." The definition of "United States" in section 7701(a)(9) includes the 50 states and the District of Columbia. Although the goal of section 181 is to encourage economic activity within the United States as defined in section 7701(a)(9), the use of a standard based upon principal photography requires the use of a slightly broader definition that takes into account that the physical act of principal photography may take place on land, at sea, or in the air. Consequently, the temporary regulations provide that a service is performed in the United States for purposes of the 75 percent test if the principal photography to which the service relates occurs within the fifty states, the District of Columbia, the territorial waters of the continental United States, or the airspace or space above the continental United States and its territorial waters.

There are some services related to a production that may physically take place at a variety of places outside the control and knowledge of the producer (for example, training, rehearsal, and pre- and post-production). However, the producer has direct or indirect control and knowledge of the shooting location of principal photography with which these other services are associated. Therefore, the IRS and Treasury Department believe that as a general rule the 75 percent test should be based upon the locations where principal photography occurs.

In this regard, the temporary regulations provide a special rule for animated productions. Although these productions may have a "principal photography" analogue, the production process is completely different and the majority of the work of the "talent" is performed independent of the actual frame photography. Computer-generated animation is not photographed at all. Hand-drawn animated films involve the creation of a storyboard (sketches of the story action) by the principal artists. Once the storyboards are approved, individual frames showing important moments in the action called "keyframes" are created by the principal artists, after which the frames in between these frames (the "in-betweens") are produced by assistant animators. These in-betweens are frequently outsourced overseas. Background art is created separately. The animation frames are transferred to plastic cels with a copier or, in some cases, are hand painted on the cels (or both). The cels are then photographed against the background art. Voice acting, music, and Foley (sound effects) are recorded independently. All of these elements are then combined into the finished film.

The production process for computer animation is similar, except that the principal artists work directly with computer programmers to create keyframe images in the animation software. In-between work is less likely to be outsourced, as the computer can generate most in-between frames from the keyframes themselves. Background art can be created within the computer program or scanned in from physical artwork. Post-production is generally done completely in the digital realm, and the final product is output to disc.

The temporary regulations apply the 75 percent test to animated productions based upon the production locations for (at least) the keyframe animation, the in-between animation, the animation photography, and the recording of the voice acting performances instead of the location where principal photography takes place. A separate rule is provided for productions that combine animation and live action, taking into account the production locations for the animation functions in addition to the location of principal photography.

Special Rules

The version of the legislation that became section 181 (as originally passed by the Senate) provided a deduction for production costs up to $15 million, and allowed production costs in excess of $15 million to be depreciated using the straight-line method over a 36-month period. Jumpstart Our Business Strength (JOBS) Act, S. 1637, 108th Cong. §321 (2003). The depreciation provision was removed in conference, with the result that the deduction does not apply to qualified film or television productions with an aggregate production cost in excess of $15 million ($20 million if a significant amount of the production costs are incurred in designated areas.) Section 181 is silent as to what should happen when a production appears to meet the requirements of section 181 in the year the election is first made, but fails to meet those requirements thereafter (for example, when the production cost exceeds $15 million, or when the production no longer meets the 75 percent test).

The temporary regulations provide a recapture provision that requires the recapture of any production costs previously deducted under section 181 in the year the election is voluntarily revoked or the production fails to meet the requirements of section 181. For property already placed in service, the taxpayer must include in income the difference between the aggregate amount claimed under section 181 and the depreciation that would have been otherwise allowable with respect to the production in the same years. For a production not yet placed in service, the taxpayer must include in income the aggregate amount claimed under section 181. The structure of the recapture provision is intended in part to alleviate concerns that including P&R in the definition of production costs under section 181 would cause taxpayers to completely forgo the benefits of section 181. Under the temporary regulations, a taxpayer with a reasonable belief that it is producing a qualified film or television production, and that the production cost will not exceed the production cost limit, will be permitted to elect to currently deduct production costs under section 181 with the understanding that a recapture may be required in a later year if circumstances or expectations change. A taxpayer that is required to recapture previously deducted production costs under section 181 will nonetheless be permitted to deduct otherwise allowable depreciation expenses in future years.

Prior to the technical correction enacted in the Gulf Opportunity Zone Act of 2005, a taxpayer could potentially incur production costs, deduct the production costs under section 181 against ordinary income, then sell the film after holding it for one year and report the proceeds (including the gain attributable to the basis reduction from the section 181 deduction) as a long-term capital gain, effectively converting ordinary income to capital gain. This potential "tax flip," existed because, as originally enacted, the statute did not specify that the deduction under section 181 is a deduction for depreciation or amortization, or state that it is subject to recapture under section 1245. The technical correction specifically treats a deduction under section 181 as a deduction for depreciation or amortization that is subject to recapture under section 1245, and the temporary regulations follow this rule.

Effective Date

The temporary regulations apply to qualified film and television productions with respect to which principal photography or, in the case of an animated production, in-between animation, commenced on or after February 9, 2007 and before January 1, 2009.

Effect on Other Documents

The following publications are modified as of February 9, 2007:

Notice 2006–47, 2006–20 I.R.B. 892, is modified by removing section B.2. in the INTERIM PROVISIONS of Notice 2006–20.

Rev. Proc. 2002–9, 2002–1 C.B. 327, is modified and amplified to include the automatic changes in methods of accounting in §1.181–2T(d)(2) and (e)(1) in the APPENDIX of Rev. Proc. 2002–9.

Special Analyses

It has been determined that this Treasury decision is not a significant regulatory action as defined in Executive Order 12866. Therefore, a regulatory assessment is not required. It also has been determined that section 553(b) and (d) of the Administrative Procedure Act (5 U.S.C. chapter 5) does not apply to these regulations. For applicability of the Regulatory Flexibility Act (5 U.S.C. chapter 6), please refer to the Special Analyses section of the preamble to the cross-reference notice of proposed rulemaking published in this issue of the Bulletin. Pursuant to section 7805(f) of the Code, these regulations have been submitted to the Chief Counsel for Advocacy of the Small Business Administration for comment on its impact on small business.

Drafting Information

The principal author of these regulations is Bernard P. Harvey, Office of Associate Chief Counsel (Passthroughs and Special Industries). However, other personnel from the IRS and Treasury Department participated in their development.

* * * * *

Amendments to the Regulations

Accordingly, 26 CFR parts 1 and 602 are amended as follows:

PART 1—INCOME TAXES

Paragraph 1. The authority citation for part 1 continues to read, in part, as follows:

Authority: 26 U.S.C. 7805 * * *

Par. 2. Sections 1.181–0T through 1.181–6T are added to read as follows:

§1.181–0T Table of contents (temporary).

This section lists the table of contents for §§1.181–1T through 1.181–6T.

§1.181–1T Deduction for qualified film and television production costs (temporary).

(a) *Deduction*—(1) *In general.* The owner (as defined in paragraph (a)(2) of this section) of any film or television production (as defined in §1.181–3T(b)) that the owner reasonably expects will be, upon completion, a qualified film or television production (as defined in §1.181–3T(a)) for which the production costs (as defined in paragraph (a)(3) of this section) will not be in excess of the production cost limit of paragraph (b) of this section may elect to treat all production costs incurred by the owner as an expense that is deductible in the taxable year in which the costs are paid (in the case of a taxpayer who uses the cash method of accounting) or incurred (in the case of a taxpayer who uses the accrual method of accounting). This deduction is subject to recapture if the owner's expectations prove to be inaccurate. This section provides rules for determining who is the owner of a production, what is a production cost, and the maximum production cost that may be incurred for a production for which an election is made under section 181 of the Internal Revenue Code (Code). Section 1.181–2T provides rules for making the election under section 181. Section 1.181–3T provides definitions and rules concerning qualified film and television productions. Section 1.181–4T provides special rules, including rules for recapture of the deduction. Section 1.181–5T provides examples of the application of §§1.181–1T through 1.181–4T, while §1.181–6T provides the effective date of §§1.181–1T through 1.181–5T.

(2) *Owner.* For purposes of this section and §§1.181–2T through 1.181–6T, the owner of a production is any taxpayer that is required under section 263A to capitalize costs paid or incurred in producing the production into the cost basis of the production, or that would be required to do so if section 263A applied to that taxpayer. A taxpayer that obtains only a limited license or right to exploit a production, or receives an interest or profit participation in a production as compensation for services, generally is not an owner of the production for purposes of this section and §§1.181–2T through 1.181–6T.

(3) *Production costs.* (i) The term *production costs* means all costs paid or incurred by the owner in producing or acquiring a production that are required, absent the provisions of section 181, to be capitalized under section 263A, or that would be required to be capitalized if section 263A applied to the owner. These production costs specifically include, but are not limited to, participations and residuals, compensation paid for services,

compensation paid for property rights, non-compensation costs, and costs paid or incurred in connection with obtaining financing for the production (for example, premiums paid or incurred to obtain a completion bond for the production).

(ii) Production costs do not include costs paid or incurred to distribute or exploit a production (including advertising and print costs).

(iii) Production costs do not include the costs to prepare a new release or new broadcast of an existing film or video after the initial release or initial broadcast of the film or video (for instance, the preparation of a DVD release of a theatrically-released film, or the preparation of an edited version of a theatrically-released film for television broadcast). Costs paid or incurred to prepare a new release or a new broadcast of a film or video that has previously been released or broadcast, therefore, are not taken into account for purposes of paragraph (b) of this section, and may not be deducted under this paragraph (a).

(iv) If a production (or any right or interest in a production) is acquired from any person bearing a relationship to the taxpayer described in section 267(b) or section 707(b)(1), and the costs paid or incurred to acquire the production are less than the seller's production cost, the purchaser must treat the seller's production cost as a production cost of the acquired production for purposes of determining whether the aggregate production cost paid or incurred with respect to the production exceeds the applicable production cost limit imposed under paragraphs (b)(1) and (b)(2) of this section. Notwithstanding this paragraph (a)(3)(iv), the taxpayer's deduction under section 181 is limited to the taxpayer's acquisition cost of the production plus any further production costs incurred by the taxpayer.

(v) The provisions of this paragraph (a) apply notwithstanding the provisions of section 167(g)(7)(D).

(b) *Limit on amount of production cost and amount of deduction*—(1) *In general.* Except as provided under paragraph (b)(2) of this section, the deduction permitted under section 181 does not apply in the case of any production, the production cost of which exceeds $15,000,000.

(2) *Higher limit for productions in certain areas*—(i) *In general.* This section is applied by substituting $20,000,000 for $15,000,000 in the case of any production the aggregate production cost of which is significantly incurred in an area eligible for designation as—

(A) A low income community under section 45D; or

(B) A distressed county or isolated area of distress by the Delta Regional Authority established under 7 U.S.C section 2009aa–1.

(ii) *Significantly incurred.* The aggregate production cost of a production is significantly incurred within one or more areas specified in paragraph (b)(2)(i) of this section if—

(A) At least 20 percent of the total production cost incurred in connection with first-unit principal photography for the production is incurred in connection with first-unit principal photography that takes place in such areas; or

(B) At least 50 percent of the total number of days of first-unit principal photography for the production consists of days during which first-unit principal photography takes place in such areas.

(iii) *Animated film and television productions.* For purposes of an animated film or television production, the aggregate production cost of the production is significantly incurred within one or more areas specified in paragraph (b)(2)(i) of this section if—

(A) At least 20 percent of the total production cost incurred in connection with keyframe animation, in-between animation, animation photography, and the recording of voice acting performances for the production is incurred in connection with such activities that take place in such areas; or

(B) At least 50 percent of the total number of days of keyframe animation, in-between animation, animation photography, and the recording of voice acting performances for the production consists of days during which such activities take place in such areas.

(iv) *Productions incorporating both live action and animation.* For purposes of a production incorporating both live action and animation, the aggregate production cost of the production is significantly incurred within one or more areas specified in paragraph (b)(2)(i) of this section if—

(A) At least 20 percent of the total production cost incurred in connection with first-unit principal photography, keyframe animation, in-between animation, animation photography, and the recording of voice acting performances for the production is incurred in connection with such activities that take place in such areas; or

(B) At least 50 percent of the total number of days of first unit principal photography, keyframe animation, in-between animation, animation photography, and the recording of voice acting performances for the production consists of days during which such activities take place in such areas.

(v) *Records required.* A taxpayer intending to utilize the higher production cost limit under paragraph (b)(2)(i) of this section must maintain records adequate to demonstrate qualification under this paragraph (b)(2).

(c) *No other depreciation or amortization deduction allowed.* (1) Except as provided in paragraph (c)(2) of this section, an owner that elects to deduct production costs under section 181 with respect to a production may not deduct production costs for that production under any provision of the Code other than section 181 unless §1.181–4T(a) applies to the production. In addition, except as provided in paragraph (c)(2) of this section, an owner that has, in a previous taxable year, deducted any production cost of a production under a provision of the Code other than section 181 is ineligible to make an election with respect to that production under section 181.

(2) An owner may make an election under section 181 despite prior deductions claimed for amortization of the cost of acquiring or developing screenplays, scripts, story outlines, motion picture production rights to books and plays, and other similar properties for purposes of potential future development or production of a production under any provision of the Code if such costs were incurred before the first taxable year in which an election could be made under §1.181–2T(a). However, the production cost of the production does not include costs that a taxpayer has begun to amortize prior to the time that the production is set for production (for further guidance, see Rev. Proc. 2004–36, 2004–1 C.B. 1063, and §601.601(d)(2)(ii)(*b*) of this chapter).

§1.181–2T Election (temporary).

(a) *Time and manner of making election.* (1) Except as provided in paragraph (e) of this section, a taxpayer electing to deduct the production cost of a production under section 181 must do so in the time and manner described in this paragraph (a). Except as provided in paragraphs (a)(2) and (e) of this section, the election must be made by the due date (including extensions) for filing the taxpayer's Federal income tax return for the first taxable year in which production costs (as defined in §1.181–1T(a)(3)) have been paid or incurred. See §301.9100–2 of this chapter for a six-month extension of this period in certain circumstances. The election under section 181 is made separately for each production produced by the owner.

(2) An owner may not make an election under paragraph (a)(1) of this section until the first taxable year in which the owner reasonably expects (based on all of the facts and circumstances) that—

(i) The production will be set for production and will, upon completion, be a qualified film or television production; and

(ii) The aggregate production cost paid or incurred with respect to the production will, at no time, exceed the applicable production cost limit set forth under §1.181–1T(b) of the regulations.

(3) If the election under this paragraph (a) is made in a taxable year subsequent to the taxable year in which production costs were first paid or incurred because paragraph (a)(2) of this section was not satisfied until such subsequent taxable year, the election must be made in the first such taxable year, and any production costs incurred prior to the taxable year in which the taxpayer makes the election are treated as production costs (except as provided in §1.181–1T(c)(2)) that are deductible under §1.181–1T(a) in the taxable year paragraph (a)(2) of this section is first satisfied and the election is made.

(b) *Election by entity.* In the case of a production owned by an entity, the election is made by the entity. For example, the election is made for each member of a consolidated group by the common parent of the group, for each partner by the partnership, or for each shareholder by the S corporation. The election must be made by the due date (including extensions) for filing the return for the later of the taxable year of the entity in which production costs are first paid or incurred or the first taxable year in which §1.181–2T(a)(2) is satisfied.

(c) *Information required*—(1) *Initial election.* For each production to which the election applies, the taxpayer must attach a statement to the return stating that the taxpayer is making an election under section 181 and providing—

(i) The name (or other unique identifying designation) of the production;

(ii) The date production costs were first paid or incurred with respect to the production;

(iii) The amount of production costs (as defined in §1.181–1T(a)(3)) paid or incurred with respect to the production during the taxable year (including costs described in §1.181–2T(a)(3));

(iv) The aggregate amount of qualified compensation (as defined in §1.181–3T(d)) paid or incurred with respect to the production during the taxable year (including costs described in §1.181–2T(a)(3));

(v) The aggregate amount of compensation (as defined in §1.181–3T(c)) paid or incurred with respect to the production during the taxable year (including costs described in §1.181–2T(a)(3));

(vi) If the owner expects that the total production cost of the production will be significantly paid or incurred in (or, if applicable, if a significant portion of the total number of days of principal photography will occur in) one or more of the areas specified in §1.181–1T(b)(2)(i), the identity of the area or areas, the amount of production costs paid or incurred (or the number of days of principal photography engaged in) for the applicable activities described in §1.181–1T(b)(2)(ii), (iii), or (iv), as applicable, that take place within such areas (including costs described in §1.181–2T(a)(3)), and the total production cost paid or incurred (or the total number of days of principal photography engaged in) for such activities (whether or not they take place in such areas), for the taxable year (including costs described in §1.181–2T(a)(3)); and

(vii) A declaration that the owner reasonably expects (based on all of the facts and circumstances at the time the election was filed) both that the production will be set for production (or has been set for production) and will be a qualified film or television production, and that the aggregate production cost of the production paid or incurred will not, at any time, exceed the applicable dollar amount set forth under §1.181–1T(b).

(2) *Subsequent taxable years.* If the owner pays or incurs additional production costs in any taxable year subsequent to the taxable year in which production costs are first deducted under section 181, the owner must attach a statement to its Federal income tax return for that subsequent taxable year providing—

(i) The name (or other unique identifying designation) of the production;

(ii) The date the production costs were first paid or incurred;

(iii) The amount of production costs paid or incurred by the owner with respect to the production during the taxable year;

(iv) The amount of qualified compensation paid or incurred with respect to the production during the taxable year;

(v) The aggregate amount of compensation paid or incurred with respect to the production during the taxable year, and the aggregate amount of compensation paid or incurred with respect to the production in all prior taxable years;

(vi) If the owner expects that the total production cost of the production will be significantly paid or incurred in (or, if applicable, if a significant portion of the total number of days of principal photography will occur in) one or more of the areas specified in §1.181–1T(b)(2)(i), the identity of the area or areas, the amount of production costs paid or incurred (or the number of days of principal photography engaged in) for the applicable activities described in §1.181–1T(b)(2)(ii), (iii), or (iv), as applicable, that take place within such areas, and the total production cost paid or incurred (or the number of days of principal photography engaged in) for such activities (whether or not they take place in such areas), for the taxable year; and

(vii) A declaration that the owner continues to reasonably expect (based on all of the facts and circumstances at the time the election was filed) both that the production will be set for production (or has been set for production) and will be a qualified film or television production, and that the aggregate production cost of the production paid or incurred will not, at any time, exceed the applicable dollar amount set forth under §1.181–1T(b).

(3) *Deductions by more than one owner.* If more than one taxpayer will claim deductions under section 181 with respect to the production for the taxable year, each owner (but not the members of an entity who are issued a Schedule K–1 by the entity with respect to their interest in the production) must provide a list of the names and taxpayer identification numbers of all such taxpayers, the dollar amount that each such taxpayer is entitled to deduct under section 181, and the information required by paragraphs (c)(1)(iii) through (vi) and (c)(2)(iii) through (vi) of this section for all owners.

(d) *Revocation of election*—(1) *In general.* An election made under this section may not be revoked without the consent of the Secretary.

(2) *Consent granted.* The Secretary's consent to revoke an election under this section with respect to a particular production will be granted if the owner—

(i) Files a Federal income tax return in which the owner complies with the recapture provisions of §1.181–4T(a) to recapture the amount described in §1.181–4T(a)(3); and

(ii) Attaches a statement to the owner's return clearly indicating the name (or other unique identifying designation) of the production, and stating that the election under section 181 with respect to that production is being revoked pursuant to §1.181–2T(d)(2).

(e) *Transition rules*—(1) *Costs first paid or incurred prior to October 23, 2004.* If a taxpayer begins principal photography of a production after October 22, 2004, but first paid or incurred production costs before October 23, 2004, the taxpayer is entitled to make an election under this section with respect to those costs. If, before June 15, 2006, the taxpayer filed its Federal tax return for the taxable year in which production costs were first paid or incurred, and if the taxpayer wants to make a section 181 election for that taxable year, the taxpayer may make the election either by—

(i) Filing an amended Federal tax return for the taxable year in which production costs were first paid or incurred, and for all subsequent affected taxable year(s), on or before November 15, 2006, provided that all of these years are open under the period of limitations for assessment under section 6501(a); or

(ii) Filing a Form 3115, "*Application for Change in Accounting Method*," for the first or second taxable year ending on or after December 31, 2005, in accordance with the administrative procedures issued under §1.446–1(e)(3)(ii) for obtaining the Commissioner's automatic consent to a change in accounting method (for further guidance, for example, see Rev. Proc. 2002–9, 2002–1 C.B. 327, and §601.601(d)(2)(ii)(*b*) of this chapter). This change in method of accounting results in a section 481 adjustment. Further, any limitations on obtaining the automatic consent of the Commissioner do not apply to a taxpayer seeking to change its method of accounting under this paragraph (e)(1). Moreover, the taxpayer must include on line 1a of the Form 3115 the designated automatic accounting method change number "100".

(2) Returns filed after June 14, 2006, and before March 12, 2007. If, after June 14, 2006, and before March 12, 2007, the owner of a film or television production filed its original Federal income tax return for a taxable year ending after October 22, 2004, without making an election under section 181 for production costs first paid or incurred after October 22, 2004, and if the taxpayer wants to make an election under section 181 for production costs first paid or incurred during that taxable year, the taxpayer must make the election within the time provided by paragraph (a) of this section and in the manner provided in paragraph (c)(1) of this section, except that the election statement attached to the return must include the information required in paragraphs (c)(1)(i) through (vi) of this section.

(3) *Information required.* If, in accordance with paragraph (e)(1) of this section, the taxpayer is making an election for a prior taxable year by filing amended Federal tax return(s), the statement and information required by paragraphs (c)(1) and (c)(2) of this section must be attached to each amended return. If, in accordance with paragraph (e)(1) of this section, the taxpayer is making a section 181 election for a prior taxable year by filing a Form 3115 for the first or second taxable year ending on or after December 31, 2005, the statement and information required by paragraphs (c)(1) and (c)(2) of this section must be attached to the Form 3115. For purposes of the preceding sentence, the amount of the cost or compensation paid or incurred for the production must only include the amount paid or incurred in taxable years prior to the year of change (for further guidance on year of change, see section 5.02 of Rev. Proc. 2002–9 and §601.601(d)(2)(ii)(*b*) of this chapter).

§1.181–3T Qualified film or television production (temporary).

(a) *In general.* The term *qualified film or television production* means any production (as defined in paragraph (b) of this section) if not less than 75 percent of the total amount of compensation (as defined in paragraph (c) of this section) paid with respect to the production is qualified compensation (as defined in paragraph (d) of this section).

(b) *Production*—(1) *In general.* Except as provided in paragraph (b)(3) of this section, for purposes of this section and §§1.181–1T, 1.181–2T, 1.181–4T, 1.181–5T, and 1.181–6T, a film or television production (or production) means any film or video (including digital video) production the production cost of which is subject to capitalization under section 263A, or that would be would be subject to capitalization if section 263A applied to the owner of the production.

(2) *Special rules for television productions.* Each episode of a television series is a separate production to which the rules, limitations, and election requirements of this section and §§1.181–1T, 1.181–2T, 1.181–4T, 1.181–5T, and 1.181–6T apply. A taxpayer may elect to deduct production costs under section 181 only for the first 44 episodes of a television series (including pilot episodes). A television series may include more than one season of programming.

(3) *Exception for certain sexually explicit productions.* A production does not include property with respect to which records are required to be maintained under 18 U.S.C. 2257. Section 2257 of Title 18 requires maintenance of certain records with respect to any book, magazine, periodical, film, videotape, or other matter that—

(i) Contains one or more visual depictions made after November 1, 1990, of active sexually explicit conduct; and

(ii) is produced in whole or in part with materials that have been mailed or shipped in interstate or foreign commerce, or is shipped or transported or is intended for shipment or transportation in interstate or foreign commerce.

(c) *Compensation*. The term *compensation* means, for purposes of this section and §1.181–2T(c), all payments made by the owner (whether paid directly by the owner or paid indirectly on the owner's behalf) for services performed by actors (as defined in paragraph (f)(1) of this section), directors, producers, and other relevant production personnel (as defined in paragraph (f)(2) of this section) with respect to the production. Indirect payments on the owner's behalf include, for example, payments by a partner on behalf of an owner that is a partnership, payments by a shareholder on behalf of an owner that is a corporation, and payments by a contract producer on behalf of an owner. Payments for services include all elements of compensation as provided for in §1.263A–1(e)(2)(i)(B) and (3)(ii)(D). Compensation is not limited to wages reported on Form W–2, "*Wage and Tax Statement*," and includes compensation paid to independent contractors. However, solely for purposes of paragraph (a) of this section, the term "compensation" does not include participations and residuals (as defined in section 167(g)(7)(B)). See §1.181–1T(a)(3) for additional rules concerning participations and residuals.

(d) *Qualified compensation*. The term *qualified compensation* means, for purposes of this section and §1.181–2T(c), all payments made by the owner (whether paid directly by the owner or paid indirectly on the owner's behalf) paid for services performed in the United States (as defined in paragraph (f)(3) of this section) by actors, directors, producers, and other relevant production personnel with respect to the production. A service is performed in the United States for purposes of this paragraph (d) if the principal photography to which the compensated service relates occurs within the United States and the person performing the service is physically present in the United States. For purposes of an animated film or animated television production, the location where production activities such as keyframe animation, in-between animation, animation photography, and the recording of voice acting performances are performed is considered in lieu of the location of principal photography. For purposes of a production incorporating both live action and animation, the location where production activities such as keyframe animation, in-between animation, animation photography, and the recording of voice acting performances for the production is considered in addition to the location of principal photography.

(e) *Special rule for acquired productions*. A taxpayer who acquires an unfinished production from a prior owner must take into account all compensation paid by or on behalf of the seller and any previous owners in determining if the production is a qualified film or television production as defined in paragraph (a) of this section. Any owner seeking to deduct as a production cost either the cost of acquiring a production or any subsequent production costs should obtain from the seller detailed records concerning the compensation paid with respect to the production in order to demonstrate the eligibility of the production under section 181.

(f) *Other definitions*. The following definitions apply for purposes of this section and §§1.181–1T, 1.181–2T, 1.181–4T, 1.181–5T, and 1.181–6T:

(1) *Actors*. The term *actors* includes players, newscasters, or any other persons who are compensated for their performance or appearance in a production.

(2) *Production personnel*. The term *production personnel* includes, for example, writers, choreographers, and composers providing services during production, casting agents, camera operators, set designers, lighting technicians, make-up artists, and others who are compensated for providing services directly related to producing the production.

(3) *United States*. The term *United States* includes the 50 states, the District of Columbia, the territorial waters of the continental United States, the airspace or space over the continental United States and its territorial waters, and the seabed and subsoil of those submarine areas that are adjacent to the territorial waters of the continental United States and over which the United States has exclusive rights, in accordance with international law, with respect to the exploration and exploitation of natural resources. The term United States does not include possessions and territories of the United States (or the airspace or space over these areas).

§1.181–4T Special rules (temporary).

(a) *Recapture*—(1) *Applicability*. The rules of this paragraph (a) apply notwithstanding whether a taxpayer has satisfied the requirements of §1.181–2T(d). A taxpayer that, with respect to a production, claimed a deduction under section 181 in any taxable year in an amount in excess of the amount that would be allowable as a deduction for that year in the absence of section 181 must recapture deductions as provided for in paragraph (a)(3) of this section for the production in the first taxable year in which—

(i) The aggregate production cost of the production exceeds the applicable production cost limit under §1.181–1T(b);

(ii) The owner no longer reasonably expects (based on all of the facts and circumstances at the time the election was filed) both that the production will be set for production (or has been set for production) and will be a qualified film or television production, and that the aggregate production cost of the production paid or incurred will not, at any time, exceed the applicable dollar amount set forth under §1.181–1T(b); or

(iii) the taxpayer revokes the election pursuant to §1.181–2T(d).

(2) *Principal photography not commencing prior to January 1, 2009*. If a taxpayer claims a deduction under section 181 with respect to a production for which principal photography does not commence prior to January 1, 2009, the taxpayer must recapture deductions as provided for in paragraph (a)(3) of this section in the taxpayer's taxable year that includes December 31, 2008.

(3) *Amount of recapture*. A taxpayer subject to recapture under this §1.181–4T must, in the taxable year in which recapture is triggered, include in the taxpayer's gross income and add to the taxpayer's adjusted basis in the property—

(i) For a production that is placed in service in a taxable year prior to the taxable year in which recapture is triggered, the difference between the aggregate amount claimed as a deduction under section 181 with respect to the production in all such prior taxable years and the aggregate depreciation deductions that would have been allowable with respect to the property for such prior taxable years (or that the taxpayer could have elected to deduct in the taxable year that the property was placed in service) with respect to the production under the taxpayer's method of accounting; or

(ii) For a production that has not been placed in service, the aggregate amount claimed as a deduction under section 181 with respect to the production in all such prior taxable years.

(b) *Recapture under section 1245*. For purposes of recapture under section 1245, any deduction allowed under section 181 is treated as a deduction allowable for amortization.

§1.181–5T Examples (temporary).

The following examples illustrate the application of §§1.181–1T through 1.181–4T:

Example 1. X, a corporation using a calendar taxable year, is a producer of films. X is the owner (within the meaning of §1.181–1T(a)(2)) of film ABC. X incurs production costs in year 1, but does not commence principal photography for film ABC until year 2. In year 1, X reasonably expects, based on all of the facts and circumstances, that film ABC will be set for production and will be a qualified film or television production, and that at no time will the production cost of film ABC exceed the applicable production cost limit of §1.181–1T(b). Provided that X satisfies all other requirements of §§1.181–1T through 1.181–4T and §1.181–6T, X may deduct in year 1 the production costs for film ABC that X incurred in year 1.

Example 2. The facts are the same as in *Example 1*. In year 2, X begins, but does not complete, principal photography for film ABC. Most of the scenes that X films in year 2 are shot outside the United States and, as of December 31, year 2, less than 75 percent of the total compensation paid with respect to film ABC is qualified compensation. Nevertheless, X still reasonably expects, based on all of the facts and circumstances, that film ABC will be a qualified film or television production, and that at no time will the production cost of film ABC exceed the applicable production cost limit of §1.181–1T(b). Provided that X satisfies all other requirements of §§1.181–1T through 1.181–4T and §1.181–6T, X may deduct in year 2 the production costs for film ABC that X incurred in year 2.

Example 3. The facts are the same as in *Example 2*. In year 3, X continues, but does not complete, production of film ABC. Due to changes in the expected production cost of film ABC, X no longer expects film ABC to qualify under section 181. X files a statement with its return for year 3 identifying the film and stating that X revokes its election under section 181. X includes in income in year 3 the deductions claimed in year 1 and in year 2 as provided for in §1.181–4T. X has successfully revoked its election pursuant to §1.181–2T(d).

Example 4. The facts are the same as in *Example 2*. In year 3, X completes production of film ABC at a cost of $14.5 million and places it into service. ABC is an unexpected success in year 4, causing participation payments to drive the total production cost of film ABC above $15 million in year 4. X includes in income in year 4 as recapture under §1.181–4T(a) the difference between the deductions claimed in year 1, year 2, and year 3, and the deductions that it would have claimed under the income forecast method described in section 167(g) of the Internal Revenue Code, a method that was allowable for the film in year 3 (the year the film was placed in service). Because X calculated the recapture amount by comparing actual deductions to deductions under the income forecast method, X must use this method to calculate deductions for film ABC for year 4 and in subsequent taxable years.

§1.181–6T Effective date (temporary).

(a) *In general*. (1) Section 181 applies to productions commencing after October 22, 2004, and shall not apply to productions commencing after December 31, 2008. Except as provided in paragraphs (b) and (c) of this section, §§1.181–1T through 1.181–5T apply to productions, the first day of principal photography for which occurs on or after February 9, 2007, and before January 1, 2009. In the case of an animated production, this paragraph (a) should be applied by substituting "in-between animation" in place of "principal photography". Productions involving both animation and live-action photography may use either standard.

(2) The applicability of §§1.181–1T through 1.181–5T expires on February 8, 2010.

(b) *Application of regulation project REG–115403–05 to pre-effective date productions*. A taxpayer may apply §§1.181–1T through 1.181–5T to productions, the first day of principal photography (or "in-between" animation) for which occurs after October 22, 2004, and before February 9, 2007, provided that the taxpayer applies all provisions in §§1.181–1T through 1.181–5T to the productions.

(c) *Special rules for returns filed for prior taxable years*. If before March 12, 2007, an owner of a film or television production began principal photography (or "in-between" animation) for the production after October 22, 2004, and filed its original Federal income tax return for the year such costs were first paid or incurred without making an election under section 181 for the costs of the production, and if the taxpayer wants to make an election under section 181 for such taxable year, see §1.181–2T(e) for the time and manner of making the election.

PART 602—OMB CONTROL NUMBERS UNDER THE PAPERWORK REDUCTION ACT

Par. 3. The authority citation for part 602 continues to read as follows:

Authority: 26 U.S.C. 7805.

Par. 4. In §602.101, paragraph (b) is amended by adding the following entry in numerical order to the table to read as follows:

§602.101 OMB Control numbers.

* * * * *

(b) * * *

CFR part or section where identified and described	Current OMB Control No.
* * * * *	
1.181–1T and 1.181–2T	1545–2059
* * * * *	

Kevin M. Brown,
Deputy Commissioner for Services and Enforcement.

Approved February 1, 2007.

Eric Solomon,
Assistant Secretary of the Treasury (Tax Policy).

(Filed by the Office of the Federal Register on February 8, 2007, 8:45 a.m., and published in the issue of the Federal Register for February 9, 2007, 72 F.R. 6155)

Section 7805.—Rules and Regulations

26 CFR 301.7805–1: Rules and regulations.

Obsolete revenue rulings. As part of the Service's continuing program of reviewing previously published guidance, this ruling publishes a list of rulings and actions relating to decisions of the Tax Court that are obsolete. Rev. Rul. 54–19 obsoleted in part. Rev. Ruls. 55–132, 56–462, 56–518, 57–505, 58–370, 58–500, 69–212, and 71–477 obsoleted.

Rev. Rul. 2007–14

The Internal Revenue Service is continuing its program of reviewing guidance (including revenue rulings, revenue procedures, notices, and actions relating to decisions of the Tax Court) published in the Internal Revenue Bulletin to identify items that are obsolete because (1) the applicable statutory provisions have been changed or repealed; (2) the matter is specifically covered by statute, regulations, or subsequent published position; or (3) the facts on which the position is based no longer occur or are not sufficiently described to permit clear application of the current statute and regulations.

The following revenue ruling is partially obsolete. Rev. Rul. 54–19, 1954–1 C.B. 179, is obsolete with respect to the income tax conclusion, but not with respect to the estate tax conclusion.

In addition, the rulings listed below are obsolete.

Ruling No.	C.B. Citation
Rev. Rul. 55–132	1955–1 C.B. 213
Rev. Rul. 56–462	1956–2 C.B. 20
Rev. Rul. 56–518	1956–2 C.B. 25
Rev. Rul. 57–505	1957–2 C.B. 50
Rev. Rul. 58–370	1958–2 C.B. 14
Rev. Rul. 58–500	1958–2 C.B. 21
Rev. Rul. 69–212	1969–1 C.B. 34
Rev. Rul. 71–477	1971–2 C.B. 479

Furthermore, in light of the amendments to § 104(a)(2) of the Internal Revenue Code under § 1605 of the Small Business Job Protection Act of 1996, Pub. L. No. 104–188, 110 Stat. 1838 (1996), certain acquiescences to decisions are obsolete. These amendments make clear that Congress intended "that the exclusion from gross income [under § 104(a)(2)] only applies to damages received on account of a personal physical injury or physical sickness", and thus damages received on account of personal nonphysical injuries or nonphysical sickness generally would be required to be included in gross income. H.R. Conf. Rep. No. 737, 104th Cong., 2d Sess. 301 (1996), 1996–3 C.B. 1041. Consequently, acquiescences to the following decisions are withdrawn:

Hawkins v. Commissioner, 6 B.T.A. 1023 (1927), *acq.*, VII–1 C.B. 14 (1928).

McDonald v. Commissioner, 9 B.T.A. 1340 (1928), *acq.*, VII–2 C.B. 26 (1928).

DRAFTING INFORMATION

The principal author of this revenue ruling is Christina M. Glendening of the Office of Associate Chief Counsel (Income Tax and Accounting). For further information regarding this revenue ruling, contact Ms. Glendening at (202) 622–4920 (not a toll-free call).

Part III. Administrative, Procedural, and Miscellaneous

Modifications of Commercial Mortgage Loans Held by a REMIC

Notice 2007–17

I. PURPOSE

The Internal Revenue Service (IRS) and the Department of the Treasury (Treasury) receive many requests from the public to resolve issues through published guidance. Available resources limit the number of issues that can be addressed. As a result, publication of guidance on many important tax issues is often delayed. Illustrative of the requests for guidance received by the IRS and Treasury is a recent request for an expansion of the permitted types of modifications to loan obligations held by a real estate mortgage investment conduit ("REMIC"). This request relates to guidance in a narrow, technical area of the tax law, where the need for guidance is driven by market changes with which taxpayers may be more familiar than are the IRS and Treasury.

The IRS and Treasury have made, and continue to make, efforts to develop ways of publishing guidance in a more timely and efficient manner. As part of this effort, the IRS and Treasury anticipate the launch of a pilot program to solicit greater input from the public in the initial development of certain guidance projects.

Under this pilot program, the IRS and Treasury would publish a notice for each guidance project selected for the program. The notice would identify research, background documents, drafts of proposed guidance and other work products, and ask interested parties to provide them. These written submissions from the public will help the IRS and Treasury determine whether it is appropriate to publish guidance. If so, the IRS and Treasury expect that increased public participation in the preliminary stages of certain guidance development would provide a significant benefit to taxpayers by permitting IRS and Treasury to hasten the publication of a greater number of guidance projects. It is anticipated that notices issued under the pilot program would follow the model of this notice, relating to modifications of commercial loan obligations held by a REMIC.

As this and additional projects are completed, the IRS and Treasury will review and evaluate the pilot program. Comments on the program may be solicited, and IRS and Treasury will consider publishing guidelines for future projects.

As a model for the pilot program, the IRS and Treasury solicit input, in the specific format described below, on whether it is appropriate to amend existing income tax regulations to permit certain modifications to securitized commercial mortgage loans.

II. BACKGROUND

The REMIC provisions contained in Part IV of subchapter M of Chapter 1 of the Internal Revenue Code (sections 860A - 860G) provide for a pass-through vehicle that issues multiple classes of interests in pools of residential and commercial mortgage loans. All of the income from the mortgage loans in the REMIC is taxed to the holders of the regular and residual interests in the REMIC. Among the requirements for qualification are that the mortgage loans held by the REMIC must consist of "qualified mortgages" that are principally secured by an interest in real property. All of a REMIC's loans must be acquired on the startup day of the REMIC or within three months thereafter, except that the REMIC may exchange a defective loan for a "qualified replacement mortgage" for up to two years.

Section 1.860G–2(b)(1) of the Income Tax Regulations provides that, subject to certain exceptions described in section 1.860G–2(b)(3), if an obligation is significantly modified, then the modified obligation is treated as one that was newly issued in exchange for the unmodified obligation that it replaced. If such a significant modification occurs after the obligation has been contributed to the REMIC and the modified obligation is not a qualified replacement mortgage, the modified obligation will not be a qualified mortgage and the deemed disposition of the unmodified obligation will be a prohibited transaction under section 860F(a)(2). Section 1.860G–2(b)(2) defines a "significant modification" as any change in the terms of an obligation that would be treated as an exchange of obligations under section 1001 and the related regulations. The treatment of specific loan modifications as deemed exchanges is addressed in section 1.1001–3. Section 1.1001–3 defines a loan modification and provides that a modification that is significant will be treated as a deemed exchange of the original loan for a new loan.

Section 1.860G–2(b)(3) sets forth four types of loan modifications that are expressly permitted without regard to the section 1001 modification rules. The four permitted modifications are: (i) changes in the terms of the obligation occasioned by default or a reasonably foreseeable default; (ii) assumption of the obligation; (iii) waiver of a due-on-sale clause or a due on encumbrance clause; and (iv) conversion of an interest rate by a mortgagor pursuant to the terms of a convertible mortgage.

The present REMIC regulations were adopted in 1992 at a time when the mortgage-backed securities market involved primarily residential mortgage loans. Since the adoption of the REMIC regulations, the securitization of commercial real estate mortgages has become more common. The four types of modifications that are expressly permitted without regard to the section 1001 modification rules cover the most common changes affecting residential mortgage loans, but may not cover the range of likely changes in commercial mortgage loans.

To accommodate commercial mortgage loans, the IRS and Treasury are considering whether the present REMIC regulations should be amended to reflect the evolution of market practices in the mortgage-backed securities industry. In particular, the IRS and Treasury are considering whether the regulations should be amended to provide exceptions for certain modifications of commercial mortgage loans. In doing so, the IRS and Treasury are considering whether such changes would be consistent with the policy underlying existing regulatory provisions and Congressional intent in enacting the REMIC rules.

III. REQUEST FOR SUBMISSIONS

A. In General

The determination of whether to amend the REMIC rules requires extensive legal and policy analysis, as well as a better understanding of commercial mortgage securities industry practices. Consequently, the IRS and Treasury are requesting written submissions from taxpayers, industry associations, and other interested parties to aid the IRS and Treasury in determining whether it is appropriate to amend the REMIC regulations by expanding the list of permitted loan modifications to include certain modifications incurred in connection with commercial mortgages.

B. Format of Submissions

Submissions should include draft changes to the REMIC regulations and a policy memorandum. It is anticipated that the draft amendment will include proposed exceptions for new types of permissible loan modifications that reflect routine industry practices in connection with commercial mortgage loans.

The policy memorandum should discuss:

1. the evolution of market practices in the securitization of commercial mortgages in REMIC form;
2. the relevant REMIC policy considerations affecting restrictions on mortgage loan modifications;
3. the authority under current law for amending the regulations to include exceptions for commercial mortgages;
4. the relationship between the section 1001 modification rules and the separate REMIC modification rules;
5. an analysis of the extent to which the four existing exceptions for mortgages and any proposed exceptions for commercial mortgages constitute departures from the section 1001 modification rules;
6. the purpose and background of the four existing exceptions for modifications of mortgages in the REMIC modification rules (including policies that might favor allowing assumptions and waivers of due on sale clauses in programs intending to assist residential housing acquisitions (*e.g.*, tax-exempt single family housing bonds, VA & FHA insured mortgages));
7. examples of what are considered to be common changes requested by borrowers to the terms of commercial mortgages and an explanation of why such changes are requested by borrowers;
8. an explanation of each proposed exception for commercial mortgages, including (i) how each proposed exception is consistent with the underlying existing regulatory provisions and Congressional intent in enacting the REMIC rules, (ii) whether the proposed exception relates to a common change; and (iii) how each proposed exception would accommodate a legitimate business concern;
9. each proposed exception illustrated by one or more examples;
10. whether there are alternatives to resolve industry issues related to commercial mortgage loan modifications other than through amending the regulations and the feasibility of such alternatives (*e.g.*, drafting documents to permit certain changes to the terms of the commercial mortgage loan to avoid triggering a significant modification under section 1.1001–3);
11. identification of the types of taxpayers and other interested persons who are affected by the inability to modify commercial mortgage loans once the loan is placed in a REMIC and how they are affected;
12. an estimate of how many taxpayers and other interested persons are directly and indirectly affected by an inability to modify commercial mortgage loans;
13. potential consequences to the industry if changes are not made to the regulations to permit certain changes to the terms of the commercial mortgage loans; and
14. because some or all of the proposed exceptions for commercial mortgage loans will likely constitute a significant modification under section 1.1001–3, a discussion of the resulting tax consequences to the REMIC of deemed exchange treatment under section 1001 (*e.g.*, how would the existing REMIC rules treat a gain or loss from a deemed exchange).

C. Communication with Submitting Parties during the Drafting Process

Written submissions should fully develop the issues set forth in part III., B., above. A dialogue between submitting parties and IRS and Treasury personnel during the drafting process may help ensure that submissions are as comprehensive as possible. Consequently, the IRS and Treasury encourage submitting parties to contact or meet with IRS and Treasury personnel during the initial development of their submissions.

IV. IRS AND TREASURY REVIEW OF SUBMISSIONS

A. Meetings with a Submitting Party

A submitting party may be asked to meet informally with personnel from IRS and Treasury. These meetings are intended to be used to explore the proposals and the analysis supporting those proposals set forth in a written submission and to gather additional facts and information. Discussions at these meetings may focus on the legal and policy justifications for each proposal, relevant industry practices, and any other issues of concern raised by IRS and Treasury personnel. At the end of these meetings, the IRS and Treasury may request a submitting party to provide additional factual development or legal research. The IRS and Treasury may also request additional meetings to the extent necessary to clarify any remaining issues.

Any solicitation of input from interested persons will be done within the requirements of the Federal Advisory Committee Act. The IRS does not intend to form advisory committees during this process. Although input is welcome, interested parties will not be invited to enter into negotiations or to participate in the decision-making process with respect to the proposed resolution of any issue.

B. IRS and Treasury Review and Decision-Making

After IRS and Treasury personnel have met with submitting parties and have been provided with any additional information requested, IRS and Treasury personnel will further review all submitted material, and develop any additional legal and policy analysis. After the review process is completed, the IRS and Treasury will decide whether it is appropriate to publish guidance that permits certain modifications to commercial real estate loans. If guidance is appropriate, the IRS and Treasury intend to publish proposed amendments to the REMIC regulations permitting additional types of modifications to commercial real estate loans.

V. DEADLINE AND ADDRESS FOR SUBMISSIONS

Written submissions should be submitted no later than Monday, April 30, 2007, to Internal Revenue Service, CC:PA:LPD:RU (Notice 2007–17), room 5203, P.O. Box 7604, Ben Franklin Station, Washington, DC 20044. Submissions may be hand delivered between the hours of 8 a.m. and 4 p.m. to CC:PA:LPD:RU (Notice 2007–17), Courier's Desk, Internal Revenue Service, 1111 Constitution Avenue, NW, Washington, DC 20224. Alternatively, submissions may be submitted via the Internet at *Notice.Comments@irscounsel.treas.gov* (Notice 2007–17). All submissions will be available for public inspection and copying in their entirety. Therefore, submissions received by the IRS and Treasury should not include taxpayer-specific information of a confidential nature. Submissions should include the name and telephone number of a person to contact.

VI. DRAFTING INFORMATION

The principal author of this notice is Diana Imholtz of the Office of Associate Chief Counsel (Financial Institutions and Products). For further information regarding this notice, contact Ms. Imholtz at 202–622–3930 (not a toll-free call).

Reporting on Acquisitions of Interests in Insurance Contracts in Which Certain Tax-Exempt Organizations Hold an Interest

Notice 2007–24

PURPOSE

This notice invites public comments on draft IRS forms to implement a new information reporting requirement for charities and certain other entities with respect to certain structured insurance contracts explained below. Public comments are also invited with respect to a Congressionally mandated study being conducted by the Department of the Treasury (the Treasury) and the Internal Revenue Service (the Service). The new reporting requirements and study are required by section 6050V of the Internal Revenue Code (the Code), which was added by section 1211 of the Pension Protection Act of 2006, Pub. L. No. 109–280, 120 Stat. 780 (2006) (PPA). In general, section 1211 of the PPA imposes a new information reporting requirement on organizations (including certain government entities) to which contributions are deductible for Federal income, estate or gift tax purposes and which acquire an applicable insurance contract in a reportable acquisition after August 17, 2006, but on or before August 17, 2008. To enable these organizations to satisfy the requirements of section 6050V, the Treasury and the Service designed Form 8921, *Transactions Involving a Pool of Applicable Insurance Contracts*, and Form 8922, *Applicable Insurance Contract Information Return (For Tax-Exempt Organizations and Government Entities under Section 6050V)*. Copies of the draft forms, and their instructions, are attached to this notice. The information collected on the forms and the public comments will assist the Treasury and the Service in conducting the study mandated under section 1211 of the PPA.

BACKGROUND

Recently, there has been an increase in transactions involving the acquisition of life insurance contracts under arrangements in which both a tax-exempt organization and private investors have an interest in a contract. Under such arrangements, private investors often provide capital used to fund the purchase of the life insurance contracts (and, sometimes, annuity and endowment contracts). Both the private investors and the tax-exempt organization have an interest, directly or indirectly, in the contracts and receive cash, either while the contracts are in force or upon the death of the insured individual.

LEGISLATION

Section 6050V of the Code requires each applicable exempt organization that makes a reportable acquisition of an applicable insurance contract to file an information return at a prescribed time and in a prescribed form. The information reporting requirement applies to reportable acquisitions after August 17, 2006, but before August 17, 2008. Penalties under sections 6721 and 6724(d)(1)(B)(iv) apply to applicable exempt organizations that do not file an information return as required under section 6050V.

For purposes of section 6050V of the Code, an applicable exempt organization is generally a religious, charitable, scientific, literary, educational, amateur sports or similar organization, a fraternal society operating on a lodge system, a governmental organization (including an Indian Tribal Government), a Veterans' organization, a cemetery company, or an employee stock ownership plan. A reportable acquisition is the acquisition by an applicable exempt organization of a direct or indirect interest in an applicable insurance contract in any case in which the acquisition is a part of a structured transaction involving a pool of such contracts. An applicable insurance contract is any life insurance, annuity, or endowment contract in which both an applicable exempt organization and a person other than an applicable exempt organization have directly or indirectly held an interest (whether or not at the same time). Exceptions apply in the case of persons with an insurable interest in the insured independent of the applicable exempt organization, named beneficiaries, or in limited circumstances, trust beneficiaries or trustees. For example, under section 6050V(d)(2)(B)(ii), an insurance contract is not an applicable insurance contract if the applicable exempt organization's sole interest in the contract is as a named beneficiary.

The Treasury and the Service intend that Form 8921 will be used to report information to the Service about structured transactions under which there have been reportable acquisitions of applicable insurance contracts made by an applicable exempt organization. Form 8922 will be used to report information to the Service about the applicable insurance contracts that are part of a structured transaction required to be reported on a Form 8921.

Generally, on Form 8921, an applicable exempt organization would:

- Report information on the transaction itself, including information about the applicable exempt organization, other participants in the transaction, and the cash flows associated with the transaction.

- Assign a unique structured transaction identifier (STI) to each transaction as provided on the form and the instructions.

- Provide a description of the allocation formulas, interest rates, and other terms that govern the financial arrangement between the applicable exempt organization and the other participants in the transaction.

- Attach copies of documents related to the reportable acquisition, including any contracts covering the relationships between the applicable exempt organization and the persons other than the applicable exempt organization.

Generally, on Form 8922 an applicable exempt organization would:

- Report information on the underlying applicable insurance contracts, including information about the issuers of the contracts and the individuals insured under the contracts.

- Use the STI assigned on Form 8921 that specifically relates to the underlying applicable insurance contracts.

- Attach a representative copy of the applicable insurance contract.

It is anticipated that a separate Form 8922 will be required with respect to a single transaction if the transaction involves more than one issuer, or more than one type of applicable insurance contract.

In addition to imposing the new information reporting requirements, section 1211 of the PPA requires the Treasury and the Service to undertake a study on the use by applicable exempt organizations of applicable insurance contracts for the purpose of sharing with investors the benefits of the applicable exempt organization's insurable interest in individuals insured under such contracts. It also requires the Treasury and the Service to address in the study whether these activities are consistent with the tax-exempt status of certain applicable exempt organizations. The study may address whether such arrangements are or may be used to improperly shelter income from tax. The study will be based, in part, on information received from applicable exempt organizations on Forms 8921 and 8922 and the public comments. A report on the study is due to the Senate Finance Committee and the House Ways and Means Committee in 2009.

REQUESTS FOR PUBLIC COMMENT

The Treasury and the Service request comments on draft Forms 8921 and 8922. In addition to comments on the draft forms more generally, the Treasury and the Service specifically request comments on (i) the clarity of the forms and instructions and how they can be made easier to understand, (ii) the availability of the information that is requested on the forms without new or additional recordkeeping on the part of the filers, (iii) the relevance of the requested information to the study mandated by section 1211 of the PPA, (iv) the use of such structured insurance transactions to improperly shelter income from tax, (v) the meaning of the term "direct or indirect interest" in an applicable insurance contract, (vi) the meaning of the term "structured transaction involving a pool" of applicable insurance contracts, and (vii) the application of the unrelated business income tax under section 511 of the Code on the inside buildup of income.

The Treasury and the Service also request comments more generally to assist in the required study, especially on: (i) the purpose of transactions that are the subject of the study, other than to raise money for the applicable exempt organizations, (ii) the use of life insurance and annuity contracts by applicable exempt organizations in transactions that do not involve the participation of persons that are not tax-exempt, and (iii) in the case of an applicable insurance contract in which a charity, as defined under State law, has an interest, the appropriate treatment of amounts received by the charity as a death benefit in light of (A) the charity's role in the transaction, (B) how the charity financed the acquisition of its interest, (C) whether the charity's activities with respect to the contract are substantially related to the charity's exempt purpose or function, and (D) any other relevant factors.

Written comments on draft Forms 8921 and 8922 and the study mandated under section 1211 of the PPA should be sent to: CC:PA:LPD:PR (Notice 2007–24), Room 5203, Internal Revenue Service, P.O. Box 7604, Ben Franklin Station, Washington, D.C. 20044. Alternatively, comments may be hand delivered between the hours of 8:00 a.m. and 4:00 p.m. Monday to Friday to CC:PA:LPD:PR (Notice 2007–24), Courier's Desk, Internal Revenue Service, 1111 Constitution Avenue, NW, Washington, D.C. Comments may also be transmitted electronically via the following e-mail address: *Notice.Comments@irscounsel.treas.gov*. Please include "Notice 2007–24" in the subject line of any electronic communications.

All comments will be available for public inspection and copying. Because organizations will need to begin filing Forms 8921 and 8922 as soon as possible in 2007, comments, if any, on Forms 8921 and 8922 must be received by *March 16, 2007*.

Written comments on the study mandated under section 1211 of the PPA should be received by *August 22, 2007*.

DRAFTING INFORMATION

The principal author of this notice is Stephen J. Coleman of the Office of Associate Chief Counsel (Procedure & Administration). For further information regarding this notice, contact Stephen J. Coleman at (202) 622–4910 (not a toll-free call).

Form **8921**
(March 2007)
Department of the Treasury
Internal Revenue Service

Transaction Involving a Pool of Applicable Insurance Contracts

(For Tax-Exempt Organizations and Government Entities under Section 6050V)

OMB No. XXXX-XXXX

See instructions for the required filing date.

1 Structured transaction date	2 Structured transaction identifier (STI)	3 Amended Form 8921 ☐
/ /	—	

4 Name of organization — Taxpayer identification number (TIN)

Number and street (or P.O. Box if mail is not delivered to street address)

City or town, state or country, and ZIP+4

Internet address

State/Country in which organized

5 Organization's role in STI (check all that apply): ☐ Contract owner ☐ Contract Beneficiary ☐ Provide insurable interest ☐ Other

6 Check the appropriate box identifying your type of organization

- a ☐ Religious, charitable, scientific, literary, educational, amateur sports, or similar organization
- b ☐ Governmental organization
- c ☐ Fraternal society operating on a lodge system
- d ☐ Indian tribal government
- e ☐ Veterans' organization
- f ☐ Cemetery company
- g ☐ Employee stock ownership plan

7 Persons (other than your organization) known to hold (directly or indirectly) an interest in the applicable insurance contracts or who otherwise receive amounts from the section 6050V structured transaction. Do not include insureds. Attach additional sheets, if necessary.

a Name	b Address	c Role in structured transaction (Check all that apply.)	d Legal form	e Check if applicable
		☐ Lender ☐ Investor ☐ Broker/Advisor ☐ Contract Owner ☐ Contract Beneficiary ☐ Other ______	☐ Individual ☐ Corporation ☐ Partner ☐ Trust ☐ Government ☐ Other	Foreign ☐ Tax-Exempt ☐
		☐ Lender ☐ Investor ☐ Broker/Advisor ☐ Contract Owner ☐ Contract Beneficiary ☐ Other ______	☐ Individual ☐ Corporation ☐ Partner ☐ Trust ☐ Government ☐ Other	Foreign ☐ Tax-Exempt ☐
		☐ Lender ☐ Investor ☐ Broker/Advisor ☐ Contract Owner ☐ Contract Beneficiary ☐ Other ______	☐ Individual ☐ Corporation ☐ Partner ☐ Trust ☐ Government ☐ Other	Foreign ☐ Tax-Exempt ☐
		☐ Lender ☐ Investor ☐ Broker/Advisor ☐ Contract Owner ☐ Contract Beneficiary ☐ Other ______	☐ Individual ☐ Corporation ☐ Partner ☐ Trust ☐ Government ☐ Other	Foreign ☐ Tax-Exempt ☐

For Paperwork Reduction Act Notice, see separate instructions. Cat. No. 37732X Form **8921** (3-2007)

	Cash flows under the structured transaction		
	I Amounts to be paid or received within 2 years	II Amounts to be paid or received after 2 years	III Total amounts to be paid or received
8 Premiums or other consideration			
9 Insurance or annuity benefits **a** Death/endowment benefits			
b Annuity payments			
c Withdrawals/surrenders (see instructions)			
d Policy loans			
e Other insurance contract proceeds			
f Total. Add lines 12a through 12e			
10 Amounts received or to be received (directly or indirectly) by your organization from other participants in the structured transaction			
a Received from lenders			
b Received from investors			
c Received from other parties			
d Total. Add lines 13a through 13c			
11 Amounts paid or to be paid (directly or indirectly) by your organization to other participants in the structured transaction			
a Paid to lenders			
b Paid to investors			
c Paid to other parties (see instructions)			
d Total. Add lines 14a through 14c			

12 Describe the section 6050V structured transaction (see instructions). Continue on separate sheet(s), if necessary.

13 Attach copies of related documents, including any contracts governing the relationships between the applicable exempt organization and persons other than applicable exempt organizations that have directly or indirectly held an interest in the applicable insurance contracts, and promotional materials (including financial projections) provided to your organization, to your donors, or to other persons who have directly or indirectly held an interest in the applicable insurance contracts.

Please Sign Here

Under penalties of perjury, I declare that I have examined this return, including accompanying schedules and statements, and to the best of my knowledge and belief, it is true, correct, and complete.

Signature of authorized person | Date

Type or print name

Title | Telephone number ( )

Form **8921** (3-2007)

Printed on recycled paper

Form **8922** (March 2007) Department of the Treasury Internal Revenue Service

Applicable Insurance Contract Information Return

(For Tax-Exempt Organizations and Government Entities under Section 6050V)

OMB No. xxxx-xxxx

Part I A separate Form 8922 must be filed for each different issuer and for each different contract type and form. See instructions for the required filing date(s).

1 Structured transaction date	**2** Structured transaction identifier	**3a** Sequence number (see instructions)	**3b** Check if amended ☐
4 Name of organization		Taxpayer identification number (TIN)	
Number and street (or P.O. Box if mail is not delivered to street address)			Room/Suite
City or town, state or country, and ZIP+4			
5 Name of insurance contracts issuer		Taxpayer identification number (TIN)	
Number and street (or P.O. Box if mail is not delivered to street address)			Room/Suite
City or town, state or country, and ZIP+4			

6 Type of applicable insurance contract
- **a** ☐ Life insurance (including contracts with an endowment feature)
- **b** ☐ Deferred annuity
- **c** ☐ Immediate annuity

7 Contract form identifier ______________________

8a Owner(s) of the contracts: ☐ Your organization ☐ Other ______________

b Beneficiaries of the contracts: ☐ Your organization ☐ Other ______________

9a Are premiums fixed by the insurance contracts or at the discretion of the contract owners? ☐ Fixed ☐ Discretionary

b If fixed contracts, enter the premium term in year(s) ________ , or
c If for the life of the insured, check here ☐

10 Investment options (check all that apply):
☐ No option ☐ Guaranteed interest funds ☐ Bond or equity funds ☐ Other

11a Do the contracts endow? ☐ Yes ☐ No

b If "Yes," when? ☐ After ________ years, or ☐ at age ________ of the insured

For lines 12 through 15, check the boxes that apply.

12 ☐ Contracts have cash surrender values

13 ☐ Policy loans are available from these contracts

14 ☐ Partial cash withdrawals are available from these contracts

15 ☐ Contracts are immediate annuities: **a** Payments are ☐ fixed ☐ variable
b If payments are inflation indexed, check here ▶ ☐

16 Attach representative copy of the applicable insurance contract covered by this Form 8922.

For Paperwork Reduction Act Notice, see separate instructions. Cat. No. 37734T Form **8922** (3-2007)

17 List insureds or annuitants covered by the applicable insurance contracts to which this Form 8922 applies. Attach additional sheets if necessary.

a Insured or annuitant covered (see instructions)

1 **a** Name	**b** Social security number (SSN)	**c** Gender ☐ Male ☐ Female	**d** Age
e Relation to organization resulting in an insurable interest: ☐ Donor ☐ Other ▶		**f** Number of insured of	
2 Donations received within past 12 months from insureds	3 First-year premium or other consideration	4 Death or endowment benefit, if life insurance	5 Monthly annuity, if immediate annuity

b Insured or annuitant covered (see instructions)

1 **a** Name	**b** Social security number (SSN)	**c** Gender ☐ Male ☐ Female	**d** Age
e Relation to organization resulting in an insurable interest: ☐ Donor ☐ Other ▶		**f** Number of insured of	
2 Donations received within past 12 months from insureds	3 First-year premium or other consideration	4 Death or endowment benefit, if life insurance	5 Monthly annuity, if immediate annuity

c Insured or annuitant covered (see instructions)

1 **a** Name	**b** Social security number (SSN)	**c** Gender ☐ Male ☐ Female	**d** Age
e Relation to organization resulting in an insurable interest: ☐ Donor ☐ Other ▶		**f** Number of insured of	
2 Donations received within past 12 months from insureds	3 First-year premium or other consideration	4 Death or endowment benefit, if life insurance	5 Monthly annuity, if immediate annuity

d Insured or annuitant covered (see instructions)

1 **a** Name	**b** Social security number (SSN)	**c** Gender ☐ Male ☐ Female	**d** Age
e Relation to organization resulting in an insurable interest: ☐ Donor ☐ Other ▶		**f** Number of insured of	
2 Donations received within past 12 months from insureds	3 First-year premium or other consideration	4 Death or endowment benefit, if life insurance	5 Monthly annuity, if immediate annuity

e Insured or annuitant covered (see instructions)

1 **a** Name	**b** Social security number (SSN)	**c** Gender ☐ Male ☐ Female	**d** Age
e Relation to organization resulting in an insurable interest: ☐ Donor ☐ Other ▶		**f** Number of insured of	
2 Donations received within past 12 months from insureds	3 First-year premium or other consideration	4 Death or endowment benefit, if life insurance	5 Monthly annuity, if immediate annuity

Part I

Please Sign Here

Under penalties of perjury, I declare that I have examined this return, including accompanying schedules and statements, and to the best of my knowledge and belief, it is true, correct, and complete.

▶ Signature of authorized person — Date

▶ Type or print name

▶ Title — ( ) Telephone number

Form **8922** (3-2007)

Printed on recycled paper

Instructions for Forms 8921 and 8922

Department of the Treasury
Internal Revenue Service

(March 2007)

Section references are to the Internal Revenue Code unless otherwise noted.

General Instructions

Purpose of Forms

Generally, an applicable exempt organization must file a Form 8921 for each structured transaction under which it makes reportable acquisitions of applicable insurance contracts. The applicable exempt organization must file a Form 8922 for each type of insurance contract and each contract form that is issued as part of a structured transaction required to be reported on Form 8921. See *When and Where to File* below regarding the filing deadlines for Forms 8921 and 8922. For more information on the reporting requirements, see section 6050V. See *Definitions* below for terms used in these instructions.

Who Must File

Applicable exempt organizations must file Forms 8921 and 8922 if they acquire a direct or indirect interest in an applicable insurance contract after August 17, 2006, and on or before August 17, 2008. Form 8921 must be filed (regardless of the date the structured transaction was entered into) if any applicable insurance contract is acquired after August 17, 2006, and on or before August 17, 2008.

How to Complete Forms

In order to be considered complete, Forms 8921 and 8922 must be completed in their entirety with all required attachments. If the information required exceeds the space provided, attach additional sheets. The additional sheets must be in the same order as the lines to which they correspond. Include your organization's name and the structured transaction identifier (STI) at the top of each additional sheet.

Round off cents to whole dollars.

When and Where to File

If an applicable exempt organization makes a reportable acquisition after August 17, 2006, and on or before August 17, 2008, it must file a Form 8921 within 60 days of making the first such reportable acquisition relating to each structured transaction; however, no forms are required to be filed before May 1, 2007. A separate Form 8922 must be filed for each type of applicable insurance contract issued as part of the structured transaction and for each contract form. Contract forms differ if the contract terms (including premium, investment, or withdrawal options) differ.

If any information required by Form 8921 is unavailable at the time of its initial filing, or if any information already provided changes, then an amended Form 8921 must be filed by October 1, 2007 (with respect to changes effected on or before August 17, 2007), or by October 1, 2008 (with respect to changes effected on or before August 17, 2008, but after August 17, 2007).

Reportable acquisitions relating to each type or form of insurance contract must be reported on separate Forms 8922. If any information required by Form 8922 is unavailable at the time of initial filing, an amended Form 8922 must be filed. Forms 8922 must be filed according to the following schedule.

IF reportable acquisitions were made after...	AND on or before...	THEN file Form 8922 by...
August 17, 2006,	February 17, 2007,	May 1, 2007
February 17, 2007,	May 17, 2007,	August 1, 2007
May 17, 2007,	August 17, 2007,	November 1, 2007
August 17, 2007,	November 17, 2007,	February 1, 2008
November 17, 2007,	February 17, 2008,	May 1, 2008
February 17, 2008,	May 17, 2008,	August 1, 2008
May 17, 2008,	August 17, 2008,	October 31, 2008

Where to send. Send Forms 8921 and 8922 to the following address.

Internal Revenue Service
Ogden, UT 84201-0027

If filing using a private delivery service, send Forms 8921 and 8922 to the following address.

Internal Revenue Service
1973 N. Rulon White Blvd.
Ogden, UT 84404

Penalty

There is a monetary penalty under section 6721 for the failure to file a required Form 8921 or Form 8922 on or before the required filing date. See *When and Where to File*. Other penalties are imposed for the failure to include all information and required attachments, or for the inclusion of incorrect information. The penalty is generally $50 per failure, not to exceed $250,000 during any calendar year, but may be less in certain cases. See sections 6721 and 6724(d)(1)(B)(xiv).

If one or more failures are due to intentional disregard of the filing requirement (or the correct information reporting requirement), then the penalty per failure is the greater of (a) $100, or (b) 10% of the value of the benefit of any applicable insurance contract when information is required to be included on the return. In this case, the penalty imposed for such intentional disregard is not taken into account in applying any calendar year limitation. See section 6721(e).

No penalty shall be imposed for any failure if it is shown that such failure is due to reasonable cause and not to willful neglect. See section 6724(a).

Definitions

Applicable Exempt Organization

An applicable exempt organization is generally a religious, charitable, scientific, literary, educational, amateur sports or similar organization, a governmental organization, a fraternal society operating on a lodge system, a veterans' organization, an Indian tribal government, a cemetery company, or an employee stock ownership plan. See section 6050V(d)(3). The term "organization" when used in these instructions refers to an applicable exempt organization.

Applicable Insurance Contract

An applicable insurance contract is any life insurance, annuity, or endowment contract in which both an applicable exempt organization and a person other than an applicable exempt

Cat. No. 49348T

organization have directly or indirectly held an interest (whether or not at the same time). However, a contract is not an applicable insurance contract if:

- Each person directly or indirectly holding an interest in the contract (other than an applicable exempt organization) has an insurable interest in the contract's insured that is independent of the applicable exempt organization,
- The sole interest in the contract of each involved person is as a named beneficiary, or
- Under certain circumstances, the sole interest in the contract of each person other than an applicable exempt organization is a beneficiary of one or more trusts holding an interest in the contract, or a trustee who holds an interest in the contract solely in a fiduciary capacity. See section 6050V(d)(2).

Reportable Acquisition

A reportable acquisition is one in which an acquisition is made of a direct or indirect interest in an applicable insurance contract when the acquisition is a part of a structured transaction involving a pool of such contracts.

Structured Transaction

A structured transaction is any transaction in which an applicable exempt organization acquires a direct or indirect interest in a pool of applicable insurance contracts.

Structured Transaction Identifier (STI)

A structured transaction identifier, or STI, is a 13-digit number used to identify the structured transaction for which a Form 8921 is being filed. See instructions for Line 2 of Form 8921.

Specific Instructions for Form 8921

Part I

Line 1

Enter the date that your organization entered into the structured transaction.

Line 2

Enter a structured transaction identifier (STI). The STI is to be used to identify the section 6050V structured transaction for which this Form 8921 and related Forms 8922 are being filed. It should be entered in Line 2 of all Forms 8922 associated with this particular section 6050V structured transaction, on all additional sheets attached to Form 8921 or to Form 8922, and on all other required attachments to Form 8921 or Form 8922.

The STI consists of two parts. The first part (before the dash) is your organization's nine-digit taxpayer identification number. The second part of the STI is a four-digit sequence number that is unique for each structured transaction. For example, if this is the sole structured transaction entered into by your organization, enter 0001 as the sequence number. If your organization is a party to a second structured transaction, enter 0002 for that transaction.

Line 3

Check this box if this is an amended Form 8921. An amended form must be filed if there is any material change in the terms or relationships in a structured transaction. An amended form must also be filed in order to correct any errors in an initial Form 8921 filed by your organization.

Line 4

Enter the name, taxpayer identification number, mailing address, internet address, and the state or country in which your organization is organized.

Line 5

Check all boxes that describe your organization's role in the structured transaction.

Line 7

Columns a and b. Enter the name and mailing address of any person known to hold (directly or indirectly) an interest in the applicable insurance contracts or who otherwise have received or will receive amounts from the structured transaction being reported on this Form 8921. Do not include your organization. Do not list any insured, unless that person has an interest in the applicable insurance contracts or the structured transaction other than as an insured. Attach additional sheets, if necessary.

Column c. Check all the boxes that describe the role of that person in the structured transaction. If "Other" is checked, provide a description in the space provided.

Column d. Check the appropriate box that describes that person's legal form. If "Other" is checked, provide a description in the space below the check box.

Column e. Check the "Foreign" box if the person is a foreign entity not subject to U.S. federal income tax. Check the "Tax-Exempt" box if that person is an applicable exempt organization.

Cash flow under the structured transaction

For lines 8 through 11, follow the instructions below for *Column I, Column II, Column III,* and *Future amounts.*

Column I. Report amounts paid or received (or expected to be paid or received) prior to the second anniversary dates of the applicable insurance contracts.

Column II. Report amounts expected to be paid or received on or after the contracts' second anniversary dates.

Column III. Add the amounts in columns I and II and enter the total in column III.

Future amounts. Future amounts are to be estimated expected values, based on contract terms and/or amounts shown in promotional or other materials.

Line 8

Report the premiums or other considerations that have been paid or are expected to be paid with respect to the applicable insurance contracts covered by the structured transaction. Include amounts paid by your organization and amounts paid to insurers by other parties to the structured transaction.

Do not reduce gross premiums by amounts received as policyholder dividends, policy loans, cash value withdrawals, or policy surrenders.

Line 9

Report insurance or annuity benefit amounts received (or expected to be received) from the applicable insurance contracts covered by the structured transaction. Include all amounts to be received from the insurance contracts by any parties to the structured transaction.

Line 9c. Report amounts received (or expected to be received) as withdrawals of cash values, contract surrenders (net of any surrender charges or adjustments), or as policyholder dividends paid in cash or deposited in an interest bearing account. Do not include policyholder dividends used to buy supplemental insurance.

Line 9e. Report any other source of receipts associated with the applicable insurance contracts.

Combine all amounts from lines 9a through 9e and enter on line 9f.

Line 10

Report amounts received (or expected to be received) by your organization under the structured transaction. Include all amounts to be received by your organization from any other parties to the structured transaction. Any amounts paid by other parties directly to insurance companies as premiums or other consideration should also be included. Also treat any amounts paid by other parties directly to brokers, advisors, or similar parties as amounts received by your organization. See *Direct payments to brokers and similar persons* below.

Line 10b. Report amounts received or expected to be received from persons (other than lenders) that furnish funds in the anticipation of earning an investment return.

Line 10c. Report amounts received (or expected to be received) from persons other than lenders or investors (for example, brokers or advisors).

Lines 11a through 11d

Report amounts paid (or expected to be paid) under the structured transaction by your organization or directly from an applicable insurance contract. Include all amounts to be paid by your organization to any other parties to the structured transaction. Any amounts paid to other parties directly by insurance companies as benefits or other payments from applicable insurance contracts should also be included. Also treat any amounts paid by other parties directly to brokers, advisors, or similar parties as amounts paid by your organization. See *Direct payments to brokers and similar persons* below.

How to distribute amounts. Distribute amounts according to whomever ultimately receives payment. For example, if amounts are first paid to a trust or other account and are ultimately distributed to one or more investors and lenders, report the initial payment amount as being paid to the investors or lenders, respectively.

Line 11a. Report amounts paid (or expected to be paid) to persons participating as lenders in the structured transaction. Reported amounts should include both payments of interest and repayments of principal.

Line 11b. Report amounts paid (or expected to be paid) to persons (other than lenders) that furnish funds in the anticipation of earning an investment return. Reported amounts should include both earnings and payments of invested principal.

Line 11c. Report any amounts paid (or expected to be paid) to persons other than lenders or investors (for example, brokers or advisors).

Direct payments to brokers and similar persons

If persons to the structured transaction contribute to a trust or other arrangement that pays out fees or similar monies to brokers or other persons (without going through your organization or an applicable insurance contract), report these amounts as follows. Report the amounts as amounts received by your organization on the appropriate line 10(a) through 10(c). Also, include these amounts as funds paid by your organization to other parties (line 11(c)).

Line 12

Provide a description of the structured transaction. Include all facts that may be relevant to understanding the structure, economics, and tax consequences of the structured transaction. In particular:

- Identify the persons providing funds to pay insurance premiums and explain the determination of their share of such premiums;
- Report the aggregate anticipated death or annuity benefits amounts to be paid under the transaction and explain the allocation of these amounts to the parties to the structured transaction;
- State explicitly any percentages, formulas, interest rates, dollar amounts, etc. used to allocate the financial obligations of the interested persons and the distribution of earnings or insurance benefits to such persons; and
- Identify recipients or payers of any residual surplus or deficit.

If interest rates are fixed by contract, provide the specific rates and terms; if variable, identify the index(es) and spread(s).

Continue on separate sheet(s) if necessary.

Line 13

Attach copies of all documents related to the section 6050V structured transaction. Include any documents or contracts governing the relationships amongst any and all parties to the structured transaction. Attach all materials used to promote or inform about the structured transaction, including any financial projections, that were given to your organization, donors, prospective insureds, and other parties that had an interest in the structured transaction.

Part II

An authorized individual must sign and date the Form 8921 for your organization. Enter that individual's name, title, and telephone number in the spaces provided.

Specific Instructions for Form 8922

Part I

Line 1

Enter the date on which your organization entered into the structured transaction, as reported on line 1 of the filed Form 8921.

Line 2

Enter the STI assigned to the structured transaction for which this Form 8922 is being filed. See line 2 of the Specific Instructions for Form 8921. It should also be entered on all additional sheets attached to Form 8922 and on all other required attachments to Form 8922.

Line 3

An additional Form 8922 must be filed if there are additional reportable acquisitions relating to a given structured transaction that have not been reported on previously filed Forms 8922. Enter in line 3a a four-digit Form 8922 sequence number for this Form 8922. For example, if this is the initial Form 8922 associated with a Form 8921 (uniquely identified by its structured transaction identifier (STI)), enter 0001. Enter 0002 if this is the second Form 8922 filed with respect to the same Form 8921, and so forth. For the filing schedule for Forms 8922, see *When and Where to File* on page 1.

An amended Form 8922 must also be filed in order to correct any errors on previously filed Forms 8922. Enter the same Form 8922 sequence number on the amended form as was entered on the original. Check the box in line 3b if this is an amended Form 8922. Amended Forms 8922 should be filed in a timely manner upon discovery of the error(s).

Line 4

Enter the name, mailing address, and taxpayer identification number of your organization.

Line 5

Enter the name, mailing address, and taxpayer identification number of the issuer of the insurance contracts being reported on this Form 8922.

Line 6

Check the box that appropriately identifies the type of applicable insurance contract being reported on this Form 8922. An immediate annuity is a contract under which the first benefit payment is due in one payment intervals (for example, monthly) from the date of purchase. Under a deferred annuity, payments begin, if at all, at a later date.

Line 7

Enter a contract form identifier (number or name) that is used to identify the contract form being reported on this Form 8922. A Form 8922 need not be filed for each contract, but a Form 8922 must be filed for each different contract form. Contract forms differ if the contract terms (including premium, investment, or withdrawal options) differ. Use this identifier on any subsequent Form 8922 that reports additional contracts using that particular contract form.

Line 8a

Check the "Your organization" box if your organization is an owner of the contracts being reported on this Form 8922. If other persons are contract owners, check the "Other" box, and enter their names in the space provided to the right of the box.

Line 8b

Check the "Your organization" box if your organization is a beneficiary of the contracts being reported on this Form 8922. If other persons are contract beneficiaries, check the "other" box, and enter their names in the space provided to the right of the box.

Line 9

Check the "Fixed" box if premium obligations are fixed in amount and periodicity by the insurance contract. Check the "Discretionary" box if premium amounts and timing are determined at the discretion of the contract owner.

If premiums are fixed by contract, enter the premium term in years on line 9b. If the premiums are to be paid over the life of the insured(s), check box for the life of the insured.

Line 10

Identify the available investment options under the contract. Check all boxes that apply, even if one or more options are not chosen.

IF...	THEN check box for...
No specified investment option is available (for example, where only a guaranteed cash value schedule is specified), regardless of whether or not policyholder dividends may be paid.	No Option
Fixed or variable rates of interest are specified in the contract, but where there is no possibility that the market value of the contract cash value may fall due to changes in market pricing of shares.	Guaranteed Interest Funds
Investments in bond, equity, or blended funds are available, and where the cash value of the contract depends on the market value of the underlying investments.	Bonds or Equity Funds
The contract provides other types of investment options, including options that offer additional guarantees as to the contract cash value (for example, contracts that guarantee a fixed or variable floor on cash values in situations where the market value of the underlying investments declines).	Other

Lines 11a and 11b

Check the box in line 11a if the contracts have an endowment feature. If so, check the appropriate box in line 11b that best describes the feature, and enter the requested information. An endowment feature is one that pays a benefit if the insured survives to a specified date or age. The ability to receive the contract's cash value on demand is not an endowment feature.

Line 15

Complete these lines if the contract type is an immediate annuity. Check if the payments are fixed or variable. Payments are variable if dependent upon a fund value or other index (other than a price index).

Line 17

List the insureds covered by the applicable insurance contracts to which this Form 8922 pertains. Attach additional sheets if necessary.

Box 1e. Relation to organization resulting in an insurable interest. If the insured is a donor of your organization, and donor status provides an insurable status with respect to your organization in your state or other jurisdiction, then check the "Donor" box. Enter the total amount of donations received from the insured within the past 12 months prior to his or her becoming an insured in item 2. Otherwise, check the "Other" box and write a brief description of the relationship that establishes an insurable interest in the insured by your organization.

Box 1f. Number of insured. Enter the number of the insured for each contract. If the contract insures a single individual, enter "1 of 1." However, if a single contract covers more than one insured, list each insured separately, but consecutively, and enter the number of the insured. For example, if a life insurance contract is a "second-to-die policy," then list the two insureds consecutively, enter "1 of 2" for the first listed individual and "2 of 2" for the second listed individual. For policies with multiple insureds, enter the amounts for Boxes 3 to 5 on the line containing the first named insured.

Box 3. First-year premium or other consideration. Enter the premiums paid or due in the first policy year (that is, those premiums prior to the first policy anniversary date) on the applicable insurance contract for each named insured.

Box 4. Death or endowment benefit. If the applicable insurance contract is a life insurance contract, enter the amount of death or endowment benefits. If the amount of death benefit can change over time, enter the initial benefit amount.

Box 5. Monthly annuity. If the applicable insurance contract is an immediate annuity policy, enter the monthly annuity amount. If the annuity pays more or less frequently than monthly, enter the monthly equivalent amount. For example, if an annuity pays annually, enter one-twelfth of the annual amount.

Part II

An authorized individual must sign and date the Form 8922 for your organization. Enter that individual's name, title, and telephone number in the spaces provided.

Paperwork Reduction Act Notice You are not required to provide the information requested on a form that is subject to the Paperwork Reduction Act unless the form displays a valid OMB control number. Books or records relating to a form or its instructions must be retained as long as their contents may become material in the administration of any Internal Revenue law. Generally, tax returns and return information are confidential, as required by section 6103.

The time needed to complete and file these forms will vary depending on individual circumstances, such as the complexity of the section 6050V structured transaction and the number of individuals insured under the applicable insurance contracts. The estimated burden of applicable exempt organizations filing these forms is approved under the OMB control number XXXX-XXXX and is shown below.

Recordkeeping	Xhr., Y min.
Learning about the law or the form	X hr., Ymin.
Preparing, copying, assembling, and sending the form to the IRS	X hr., Ymin.

If you have comments concerning the accuracy of these time estimates or suggestions for making this form simpler, we would be happy to hear from you. You can write to the Internal Revenue Service, Tax Products Coordinating Committee, SE:W:CAR:MP:T:T:SP, 1111 Constitution Ave. NW, IR-6406, Washington, DC 20224. Do not send the forms to this address. Instead, see *When and Where to File* on page 1.

-4-

Revised Housing Cost Amounts Eligible for Exclusion or Deduction

Notice 2007–25

SECTION 1. PURPOSE

This notice provides modifications and additions to the adjusted limitations on housing expenses published in Notice 2006–87, 2006–43 I.R.B. 766, for purposes of section 911 of the Internal Revenue Code (Code).

SECTION 2. BACKGROUND

Notice 2006–87 provides an adjusted limitation on housing expenses for a qualified individual incurring housing expenses in 2006 in one or more of the identified high cost localities to use (in lieu of the otherwise applicable limitation of $24,720) in determining his or her housing expenses under section 911(c)(2)(A) of the Code. Notice 2006–87 also requests comments on the average housing costs for specific locations that differ significantly from the amounts provided in the notice.

In response to comments received on Notice 2006–87, the Internal Revenue Service (IRS) and the Treasury Department are publishing certain modifications and additions to the 2006 housing expense table in Notice 2006–87. The adjusted limitations on housing expenses provided in section 3 supersede and replace the adjusted limitations on housing expenses for 2006 for those specific locations provided in Notice 2006–87. The adjusted limitations on housing expenses provided in section 4 address locations within countries with high housing costs that were not identified in Notice 2006–87, and provide an adjusted limitation on housing expenses for 2006 for these locations. A complete table of the adjusted limitations on housing expenses for 2006 is available on the IRS website at *http://www.irs.gov/formspubs* under the link "What's Hot in forms and publications".

The IRS and the Treasury Department continue to work on guidance for housing expenses for 2007. Based on preliminary indications, the 2007 adjusted limitations on housing expenses for some locations may be lower than the 2006 adjusted limitations on housing expenses in Notice 2006–87 for those locations. The IRS and the Treasury Department intend to provide guidance for housing expenses for 2007 as soon as possible.

SECTION 3. MODIFIED ADJUSTED LIMITATIONS ON HOUSING EXPENSES FOR SPECIFIC LOCATIONS IDENTIFIED IN NOTICE 2006–87

Country	Location	Limitation on Housing Expenses (daily)	Limitation on Housing Expenses (full year)
Austria	Vienna	78.97	28,824
Bermuda	Bermuda	197.26	72,000
Japan	Nagoya	103.52	37,786
Japan	Osaka-Kobe	145.30	53,036
Norway	Oslo	83.76	30,573
Russia	Moscow	207.45	75,720
Ukraine	Kiev	89.98	32,844

SECTION 4. ADJUSTED LIMITATIONS ON HOUSING EXPENSES FOR LOCATIONS NOT INCLUDED IN NOTICE 2006–87

Country	Location	Limitation on Housing Expenses (daily)	Limitation on Housing Expenses (full year)
China	Beijing	131.51	48,000
China	Shanghai	147.95	54,000
India	Mumbai	156.19	57,011
India	New Delhi	73.75	26,920
Indonesia	Jakarta	103.49	37,776
Qatar	Doha	95.30	34,786
Saudi Arabia	Jeddah	84.02	30,667
Saudi Arabia	Riyadh	84.02	30,667

Country	Location	Limitation on Housing Expenses (daily)	Limitation on Housing Expenses (full year)
Switzerland	Zurich	105.20	38,398
Taiwan	Taipei	122.42	44,685
United Arab Emirates	Abu Dhabi	82.12	29,973
United Arab Emirates	Dubai	116.31	42,452
United Kingdom	Basingstoke	112.60	41,099
United Kingdom	Gibraltar	122.24	44,616
United Kingdom	Surrey	121.51	44,350

SECTION 5. EFFECT ON OTHER DOCUMENTS

Notice 2006–87 is modified and supplemented.

SECTION 6. EFFECTIVE DATE

This notice is effective for taxable years beginning on or after January 1, 2006.

SECTION 7. DRAFTING INFORMATION

The principal author of this notice is Paul J. Carlino of the Office of Associate Chief Counsel (International). For further information regarding this notice, contact Mr. Carlino at (202) 622–3840 (not a toll-free call).

---

26 CFR 601.105: Examination of returns and claims for refund, credit, or abatement; determination of correct tax liability.
(Also: Part 1, §§ 6011, 6662, 6662A, 6707A; 1.6011–4.)

Rev. Proc. 2007–25

SECTION 1. PURPOSE

This revenue procedure amplifies Rev. Proc. 2005–51, 2005–2 C.B. 296, which provides guidance to persons who may be required to pay certain penalties under sections 6662(h), 6662A, or 6707A of the Internal Revenue Code, and who may be required under section 6707A(e) to disclose those penalties on reports filed with the Securities and Exchange Commission ("SEC").

SECTION 2. BACKGROUND

.01 Section 6707A(e), as added by the American Jobs Creation Act of 2004, Pub. L. No. 108–357, 118 Stat. 1418, requires a person that is required to file periodic reports under section 13 or 15(d) of the Securities Exchange Act of 1934, or is required to be consolidated with another person for purposes of those reports, to disclose in those reports for the periods specified by the Secretary the requirement to pay the penalties set forth in section 6707A(e)(2).

.02 Section 4 of Rev. Proc. 2005–51 sets forth the report on which the disclosures must be made, the information that must be disclosed, and the deadlines by which persons must make the disclosures on reports filed with the SEC in order to avoid additional penalties under section 6707A(e).

.03 Section 4.01 of Rev. Proc. 2005–51 specifically provides that a person who files SEC Form 10–K, *Annual Report*, pursuant to section 13 or 15(d) of the Securities Exchange Act of 1934, either separately or consolidated with another person, must disclose in Item 3 (Legal Proceedings) of Form 10–K the requirement to pay any penalty specified in section 2.05 of Rev. Proc. 2005–51.

.04 After the issuance of Rev. Proc. 2005–51, questions arose regarding persons required to file periodic reports under section 13 or 15(d) of the Securities Exchange Act of 1934, or required to be consolidated with another person for purposes of those reports, but that file these periodic reports on a form other than a Form 10–K.

SECTION 3. SCOPE

This revenue procedure applies to any person required to pay any penalty described in section 2.05 of Rev. Proc. 2005–51 that is also required to file periodic reports under section 13 or 15(d) of the Securities Exchange Act of 1934 on a form other than a Form 10–K or is required to be consolidated with another person for purposes of those reports.

SECTION 4. APPLICATION

.01 A person who files Form 10–KSB, *Annual Report of Small Business Issuers*, pursuant to section 13 or 15(d) of the Securities Exchange Act of 1934, either separately or consolidated with another person, must disclose in Item 3 (Legal Proceedings) of Form 10–KSB the requirement to pay any penalty specified in section 2.05 of Rev. Proc. 2005–51.

.02 A person who files Form 11–K, *Annual Report of Employee Stock Purchase, Savings and Similar Plans*, must disclose in the Form 11–K, under the subheading "Legal Proceedings", the requirement to pay any penalty specified in section 2.05 of Rev. Proc. 2005–51.

.03 A person who files Form 20–F, *Annual Report of Foreign Private Issuers*, pursuant to section 13 or 15(d) of the Securities Exchange Act of 1934, either separately or consolidated with another person, must disclose in Item 8 (Financial Information) of Form 20–F, under the subheading "Legal Proceedings", the requirement to pay any penalty specified in section 2.05 of Rev. Proc. 2005–51.

.04 A person who files Form 40–F, *Annual Report of Certain Canadian Issuers*, pursuant to section 13 or 15(d) of the Securities Exchange Act of 1934, either separately or consolidated with another person, must disclose in the Annual Information Form filed as part of the Form 40–F, under the subheading "Legal Proceedings", the requirement to pay any penalty specified in section 2.05 of Rev. Proc. 2005–51.

.05 A person who files Form N–SAR, *Annual Report of Registered Investment Companies*, pursuant to section 13 or

15(d) of the Securities Exchange Act of 1934, either separately or consolidated with another person, must disclose in Sub-Item 77E (Legal Proceedings) of Form N–SAR the requirement to pay any penalty specified in section 2.05 of Rev. Proc. 2005–51.

.06 A person who files Form N–CSR, *Annual Report of Registered Investment Companies*, pursuant to section 13 or 15(d) of the Securities Exchange Act of 1934, either separately or consolidated with another person, must disclose in Item 1 (Reports to Stockholders) of Form N–CSR, under the subheading "Legal Proceedings", the requirement to pay any penalty specified in section 2.05 of Rev. Proc. 2005–51.

.07 The same procedures described in sections 4.02 and 4.03 of Rev. Proc. 2005–51 regarding the information that must be disclosed and the deadlines by which persons must make the disclosures on reports filed with the SEC that apply to Form 10–K apply to Forms 10–KSB, 11–K, 20–F, 40–F, N–SAR, and N–CSR, as applicable.

SECTION 5. EFFECT ON OTHER DOCUMENTS

Rev. Proc. 2005–51, 2005–2 C.B. 296, is amplified.

SECTION 6. PAPERWORK REDUCTION ACT

The collections of information in Rev. Proc. 2005–51 have been previously reviewed and approved by the Office of Management and Budget in accordance with the Paperwork Reduction Act (44 U.S.C. 3507) under control number 1545–1956. This revenue procedure does not make substantive changes to those collections of information.

An agency may not conduct or sponsor, and a person is not required to respond to, a collection of information unless the collection of information displays a valid OMB control number.

SECTION 7. EFFECTIVE DATE

This revenue procedure is effective for any penalty specified in section 2.05 of Rev. Proc. 2005–51 that relates to a return or statement the due date for which is after October 22, 2004.

SECTION 8. DRAFTING INFORMATION

The principal author of this revenue procedure is Matthew S. Cooper of the Office of the Associate Chief Counsel (Procedure & Administration). For further information regarding this revenue procedure, contact Matthew S. Cooper at (202) 622–4940 (not a toll-free call).

Part IV. Items of General Interest

Withdrawal of Notice of Proposed Rulemaking and Notice of Proposed Rulemaking

Agreements for Payment of Tax Liabilities in Installments

REG–100841–97

AGENCY: Internal Revenue Service (IRS), Treasury.

ACTION: Withdrawal of notice of proposed rulemaking and notice of proposed rulemaking.

SUMMARY: This document withdraws the notice of proposed rulemaking published in the **Federal Register** on December 31, 1997 (REG–100841–97, 1998–1 C.B. 588 [62 FR 68241]) and contains proposed regulations relating to the payment of tax liabilities in installments. The proposed regulations reflect changes to the law made by the Taxpayer Bill of Rights II, the Internal Revenue Service Restructuring and Reform Act of 1998, and the American Jobs Creation Act of 2004.

DATES: Written or electronic comments and requests for a public hearing must be received by June 4, 2007.

ADDRESSES: Send submissions to: CC:PA:LPD:PR (REG–100841–97), room 5203, Internal Revenue Service, POB 7604, Ben Franklin Station, Washington, DC 20044. Submissions may be hand delivered Monday through Friday between the hours of 8 a.m. and 4 p.m. to: CC:PA:LPD:PR (REG–100841–97), Courier's Desk, Internal Revenue Service, 1111 Constitution Avenue, NW, Washington, DC. Alternatively, taxpayers may submit comments electronically directly to the IRS Internet site at *www.irs.gov/regs* or via the Federal eRulemaking Portal at *www.regulations.gov* (indicate IRS and REG–100841–97).

FOR FURTHER INFORMATION CONTACT: Concerning the regulations, G. William Beard, (202) 622 3620; concerning submissions of comments or requests for a hearing, Kelly Banks, (202) 622–7180 (not toll-free numbers).

SUPPLEMENTARY INFORMATION:

Background

On December 31, 1997, a notice of proposed rulemaking (REG–100841–97; 62 FR 68241) reflecting changes made to section 6159 of the Internal Revenue Code (Code) by section 202 of the Taxpayer Bill of Rights II, Public Law 104–168 (110 Stat. 1452, 1457) was published in the **Federal Register**. That proposed rule was not acted upon prior to the enactment of the Internal Revenue Service Restructuring and Reform Act of 1998 (RRA 1998), Public Law 105–206, section 3462 (112 Stat. 685, 764), which made further amendments to section 6159. Section 843 of the American Jobs Creation Act of 2004 (AJCA), Public Law 108–357 (118 Stat. 1418, 1600), also made changes to section 6159. This document amends the prior notice of proposed rulemaking. It contains proposed amendments to the Procedure and Administration Regulations (26 CFR part 301) under section 6159 reflecting the amendment of the Code by RRA 1998, the Taxpayer Bill of Rights II, and the AJCA.

Installment Agreements under Section 6159

Consistent with its mission of applying the tax laws with integrity and fairness to all, the IRS generally expects that all taxpayers will pay the total amount due, regardless of amount, at the time the Code requires that the tax be paid. See Policy Statement P–5–2, Collecting Principles (Approved February 17, 2000), reprinted at IRM 1.2.1.5.2. When attempting to resolve a tax delinquency, the IRS will work with taxpayers to achieve full payment of all tax, penalties, and interest. Where payment in full cannot immediately be achieved, the IRS may allow taxpayers to pay over time through installment agreements.

Explanation of Provisions

The proposed regulations allow the IRS to enter into agreements for the full or partial payment of any unpaid tax in installments. The regulations provide rules for the submission of proposed installment agreements, the processing, acceptance, and rejection of such agreements by the IRS, the termination or modification of existing agreements, and the appeal of rejections, modifications, and terminations to the IRS Office of Appeals (Appeals). The majority of these provisions are unchanged from what was contained in the prior regulations or reflect longstanding IRS administrative practice. The rules regarding when a proposed installment agreement becomes pending, restrictions on collection activity while an agreement is pending or in effect, and the suspension of the statute of limitations for collection are nearly identical to the provisions in existing §301.6331–4. The only change was a clarification that the IRS will not be precluded from filing suit or a proof of claim in bankruptcy for the full amount of the liabilities owed, regardless of whether the installment agreement provides for full or partial payment of the liabilities at issue.

Taxpayers may request administrative review of IRS decisions to modify or terminate installment agreements pursuant to section 6159(e), added to the Code by section 202 of the Taxpayer Bill of Rights II. Taxpayers may appeal rejections of proposed installment agreements under section 7122(d), added to the Code by section 3462 of RRA 1998. The proposed regulations allow taxpayers to appeal a termination, modification, or rejection of an installment agreement to Appeals provided they request the appeal in the manner specified by the IRS.

The previous notice of proposed rulemaking contained a more detailed procedure for seeking review of decisions to terminate or modify agreements. That proposed regulation has not been adopted. These regulations contain a less detailed procedure because procedures for appealing differ depending on the IRS operating division handling the case, the size of the tax liability, or the type of tax at issue. For example, some taxpayers may be able to request an appeal by telephone while others will be required to submit a formal written request. See Publication 1660, *Collection Appeal Rights*.

The proposed regulations incorporate the provisions of section 6159(c), added to the Code by section 3467 of RRA 1998. That section requires the IRS to accept a proposed installment agreement for income taxes under certain circumstances. The regulations also incorporate section 3506 of RRA 1998, which requires the IRS to send each taxpayer with an installment agreement an annual statement showing the balance due at the beginning of the year, the payments made during the year, and the remaining balance due at the end of the year.

Section 843 of the AJCA amended section 6159(a) to allow the IRS to enter into installment agreements that provide for partial (as well as full) payment of a tax liability. The proposed regulations incorporate this change. Because a partial payment installment agreement could be confused with a compromise of the liability, the proposed regulations clarify that an installment agreement does not reduce the amount of taxes, interest, or penalties owed. *See* H. Rep. No. 108–755, 108th Cong., 2d Sess., 2005 U.S.C.C.A.N. 1341 (October 7, 2004).

The proposed regulations also clarify that the IRS may enter into an installment agreement that, by its terms, ends upon the expiration of the period of limitations on collection in section 6502 and §301.6502–1, or at some prior date. A partial payment installment agreement that ends prior to the expiration of the collection period of limitations would allow the IRS to collect the balance of the tax liability against any property belonging to the taxpayer or request the Department of Justice to institute a judicial action to reduce the liability to judgment or take other actions to enforce the federal tax lien. The proposed regulations do not limit the authority of the IRS to enter into partial payment installment agreements that run to the end of the collection period.

Section 843 of the AJCA amended section 6159(c) to exclude partial payment installment agreements from the scope of installment agreements that must be accepted by the IRS. The proposed regulations provide that installment agreements guaranteed under section 6159(c) must provide for the full payment of the liabilities.

Section 843 of the AJCA added new section 6159(d), requiring the IRS to review partial payment installment agreements every two years. (Former subsections (d) and (e) were redesignated (e) and (f).) The primary purpose of the review is to determine whether the financial condition of the taxpayer has significantly changed so as to warrant an increase in the value of the payments being made. *See* H. Rep. No. 108–755, 108th Cong., 2d Sess., 2005 U.S.C.C.A.N. 1341 (October 7, 2004). The proposed regulations reflect this requirement.

The proposed regulations clarify the application of payments made pursuant to installment agreements. Consistent with Revenue Procedure 2002–26, 2002–1 C.B. 746, all payments will be applied in the best interests of the Government, unless the installment agreement provides otherwise. Current regulations provide rules for when the IRS may terminate an agreement but do not expressly provide that a taxpayer and the IRS may agree to end an agreement. The proposed regulations clarify that an installment agreement may be terminated by agreement between the taxpayer and the IRS, or may be superceded by a new agreement.

Proposed Effective Date

These regulations are proposed to be effective upon publication in the **Federal Register** of the final regulations.

Special Analyses

It has been determined that this notice of proposed rulemaking is not a significant regulatory action as defined in Executive Order 12866. Therefore, a regulatory assessment is not required. It also has been determined that section 553(b) of the Administrative Procedure Act (5 U.S.C. chapter 5) does not apply to these regulations and, because these regulations do not impose a collection of information under the Paperwork Reduction Act (44 U.S.C. section 3501), the Regulatory Flexibility Act (5 U.S.C. chapter 6) does not apply to these regulations. Pursuant to section 7805(f) of the Code, this notice of proposed rulemaking will be submitted to the Chief Counsel for Advocacy of the Small Business Administration for comment on its impact on small business.

Comments and Requests for a Public Hearing

Before these proposed regulations are adopted as final regulations, consideration will be given to any written comments (a signed original and eight (8) copies) or electronic comments that are submitted timely to the IRS. The IRS generally requests any comments on the clarity of the proposed rule and how it may be made easier to understand. All comments will be available for public inspection and copying. A public hearing may be scheduled if requested in writing by a person that timely submits written or electronic comments. If a public hearing is scheduled, notice of the date, time, and place for the hearing will be published in the **Federal Register**.

Drafting Information

The principal author of these regulations is G. William Beard, Office of Associate Chief Counsel (Procedure and Administration), Collection, Bankruptcy & Summonses Division.

* * * * *

Withdrawal of Proposed Regulations

Accordingly, under the authority of 26 U.S.C. 7805, the notice of proposed rulemaking (REG–100841–97) that was published in the **Federal Register** on December 31, 1997 (62 FR 68241) is withdrawn.

Proposed Amendments to the Regulations

Accordingly, 26 CFR part 301 is proposed to be amended as follows:

PART 301—PROCEDURE AND ADMINISTRATION

Paragraph 1. The authority citation for part 301 continues to read in part as follows:

Authority: 26 U.S.C. 7805 * * *

Par. 2. Section 301.6159–0 is added to read as follows:

§301.6159–0 Table of contents.

This section lists the major captions that appear in the regulations under §301.6159–1.

§301.6159–1 Agreements for the payment of tax liabilities in installments.

(a) Authority.

(b) Procedures for submission and consideration of proposed installment agreements.

(c) Acceptance, form, and terms of installment agreements.

(d) Rejection of a proposed installment agreement.

(e) Modification or termination of installment agreements by the Internal Revenue Service.

(f) Effect of installment agreement or pending installment agreement on collection activity.

(g) Suspension of the statute of limitations on collection.

(h) Annual statement.

(i) Biannual review of partial payment installment agreements.

(j) Cross reference.

(k) Effective date.

Par. 3. Section 301.6159–1 is revised to read as follows:

§301.6159–1 Agreements for payment of tax liabilities in installments.

(a) *Authority.* The Commissioner may enter into a written agreement with a taxpayer that allows the taxpayer to make scheduled periodic payments of any tax liability if the Commissioner determines that such agreement will facilitate full or partial collection of the tax liability.

(b) *Procedures for submission and consideration of proposed installment agreements*—(1) *In general.* A proposed installment agreement must be submitted according to the procedures, and in the form and manner, prescribed by the Commissioner.

(2) *When a proposed installment agreement becomes pending.* A proposed installment agreement becomes pending when it is accepted for processing. The Internal Revenue Service (IRS) may not accept a proposed installment agreement for processing following reference of a case involving the liability that is the subject of the proposed installment agreement to the Department of Justice for prosecution or defense. The proposed installment agreement remains pending until the IRS accepts the proposal, the IRS notifies the taxpayer that the proposal has been rejected, or the proposal is withdrawn by the taxpayer. If a proposed installment agreement that has been accepted for processing does not contain sufficient information to permit the IRS to evaluate whether the proposal should be accepted, the IRS will request the taxpayer to provide the needed additional information. If the taxpayer does not submit the additional information that the IRS has requested within a reasonable time period after such a request, the IRS may reject the proposed installment agreement.

(3) *Revised proposals of installment agreements submitted following rejection.* If, following the rejection of a proposed installment agreement, the IRS determines that the taxpayer made a good faith revision of the proposal and submitted the revision within 30 days of the date of rejection, the provisions of this section shall apply to that revised proposal. If, however, the IRS determines that a revision was not made in good faith, the provisions of this section do not apply to the revision and the appeal period in paragraph (d)(3) of this section continues to run from the date of the original rejection.

(c) *Acceptance, form, and terms of installment agreements*—(1) *Acceptance of an installment agreement*—(i) *In general.* A proposed installment agreement has not been accepted until the IRS notifies the taxpayer or the taxpayer's representative of the acceptance. Except as provided in paragraph (c)(1)(iii) of this section, the Commissioner has the discretion to accept or reject any proposed installment agreement.

(ii) *Acceptance does not reduce liabilities.* The acceptance of an installment agreement by the IRS does not reduce the amount of taxes, interest, or penalties owed. (However, penalties may continue to accrue at a reduced rate pursuant to section 6651(h).)

(iii) *Guaranteed installment agreements.* In the case of a liability of an individual for income tax, the Commissioner shall accept a proposed installment agreement if, as of the date the individual proposes the installment agreement—

(A) The aggregate amount of the liability (not including interest, penalties, additions to tax, and additional amounts) does not exceed $10,000;

(B) The taxpayer (and, if the liability relates to a joint return, the taxpayer's spouse) has not, during any of the preceding five taxable years—

(*1*) Failed to file any income tax return;

(*2*) Failed to pay any required income tax; or

(*3*) Entered into an installment agreement for the payment of any income tax;

(C) The Commissioner determines that the taxpayer is financially unable to pay the liability in full when due (and the taxpayer submits any information the Commissioner requires to make that determination);

(D) The installment agreement requires full payment of the liability within three years; and

(E) The taxpayer agrees to comply with the provisions of the Internal Revenue Code for the period the agreement is in effect.

(2) *Form of installment agreements.* An installment agreement must be in writing. A written installment agreement may take the form of a document signed by the taxpayer and the Commissioner or a written confirmation of an agreement entered into by the taxpayer and the Commissioner that is mailed or personally delivered to the taxpayer.

(3) *Terms of installment agreements.* (i) Except as otherwise provided in this section, an installment agreement is effective from the date the IRS notifies the taxpayer or the taxpayer's representative of its acceptance until the date the agreement ends by its terms or until it is superceded by a new installment agreement.

(ii) By its terms, an installment agreement may end upon the expiration of the period of limitations on collection in section 6502 and §301.6502–1, or at some prior date.

(iii) As a condition to entering into an installment agreement with a taxpayer, the Commissioner may require that—

(A) The taxpayer agree to a reasonable extension of the period of limitations on collection; and

(B) The agreement contain terms that protect the interests of the Government.

(iv) Except as otherwise provided in an installment agreement, all payments made under the installment agreement will be applied in the best interests of the Government.

(v) While an installment agreement is in effect, the Commissioner may request, and the taxpayer must provide, a financial condition update at any time.

(vi) At any time after entering into an installment agreement, the Commissioner and the taxpayer may agree to modify or terminate an installment agreement or may agree to a new installment agreement that supercedes the existing agreement.

(d) *Rejection of a proposed installment agreement*—(1) *When a proposed installment agreement becomes rejected.* A proposed installment agreement has not been rejected until the IRS notifies the taxpayer or the taxpayer's representative of the rejection, the reason(s) for rejection, and the right to an appeal.

(2) *Independent administrative review.* The IRS may not notify a taxpayer or taxpayer's representative of the rejection of an installment agreement until an independent administrative review of the proposed rejection is completed.

(3) *Appeal of rejection of a proposed installment agreement.* The taxpayer may administratively appeal a rejection of a proposed installment agreement to the IRS Office of Appeals (Appeals) if, within the 30-day period commencing the day after the taxpayer is notified of the rejection, the taxpayer requests an appeal in the manner provided by the Commissioner.

(e) *Modification or termination of installment agreements by the Internal Revenue Service*—(1) *Inadequate information or jeopardy.* The Commissioner may terminate an installment agreement if the Commissioner determines that—

(i) Information which was provided to the IRS by the taxpayer or the taxpayer's representative in connection with the granting of the installment agreement was inaccurate or incomplete in any material respect; or

(ii) Collection of any liability to which the installment agreement applies is in jeopardy.

(2) *Change in financial condition, failure to timely pay an installment or another Federal tax liability, or failure to provide requested financial information.* The Commissioner may modify or terminate an installment agreement if—

(i) The Commissioner determines that the financial condition of a taxpayer that is party to the agreement has significantly changed; or

(ii) A taxpayer that is party to the installment agreement fails to—

(A) Timely pay an installment in accordance with the terms of the installment agreement;

(B) Pay any other Federal tax liability when the liability becomes due; or

(C) Provide a financial condition update requested by the Commissioner.

(3) *Notice.* Unless the Commissioner determines that collection of the tax is in jeopardy, the Commissioner will notify the taxpayer in writing at least 30 days prior to modifying or terminating an installment agreement pursuant to paragraph (e)(1) or (2) of this section. The notice provided pursuant to this section must briefly describe the reason for the intended modification or termination. Upon receiving notice, the taxpayer may provide information showing that the reason for the proposed modification or termination is incorrect.

(4) *Appeal of modification or termination of an installment agreement.* The taxpayer may administratively appeal the modification or termination of an installment agreement to Appeals if, following issuance of the notice required by paragraph (e)(3) of this section and prior to the expiration of the 30-day period commencing the day after the modification or termination is to take effect, the taxpayer requests an appeal in the manner provided by the Commissioner.

(f) *Effect of installment agreement or pending installment agreement on collection activity*—(1) *In general.* No levy may be made to collect a tax liability that is the subject of an installment agreement during the period that a proposed installment agreement is pending with the IRS, for 30 days immediately following the rejection of a proposed installment agreement, during the period that an installment agreement is in effect, and for 30 days immediately following the termination of an installment agreement. If, prior to the expiration of the 30-day period following the rejection or termination of an installment agreement, the taxpayer appeals the rejection or termination decision, no levy may be made while the rejection or termination is being considered by Appeals. This section will not prohibit levy to collect the liability of any person other than the person or persons named in the installment agreement.

(2) *Exceptions.* Paragraph (f)(1) of this section shall not prohibit levy if the taxpayer files a written notice with the IRS that waives the restriction on levy imposed by this section, the IRS determines that the proposed installment agreement was submitted solely to delay collection, or the IRS determines that collection of the tax to which the installment agreement or proposed installment agreement relates is in jeopardy.

(3) *Other actions by the IRS while levy is prohibited*—(i) *In general.* The IRS may take actions other than levy to protect the interests of the Government with regard to the liability identified in an installment agreement or proposed installment agreement. Those actions include, for example—

(A) Crediting an overpayment against the liability pursuant to section 6402;

(B) Filing or refiling notices of Federal tax lien; and

(C) Taking action to collect from any person who is not named in the installment agreement or proposed installment agreement but who is liable for the tax to which the installment agreement relates.

(ii) *Proceedings in court.* Except as otherwise provided in this paragraph (f)(3)(ii), the IRS will not refer a case to the Department of Justice for the commencement of a proceeding in court, against a person named in an installment agreement or proposed installment agreement, if levy to collect the liability is prohibited by paragraph (f)(1) of this section. Without regard to whether a person is named in an installment agreement or proposed installment agreement, however, the IRS may authorize the Department of Justice to file a counterclaim or third-party complaint in a refund action or to join that person in any other proceeding in which liability for the tax that is the subject of the installment agreement or proposed installment agreement may be established or disputed, including a suit against the United States under 28 U.S.C. 2410. In addition, the United States may file a claim in any bankruptcy proceeding or insolvency action brought by or against such person. If a person named in an installment agreement is joined in a proceeding, the United States obtains a judgment against that person, and the case is referred back to the IRS for collection, collection will continue to occur pursuant to the terms of the installment agreement. Notwithstanding the installment agreement, any claim or suit permitted will be for the full amount of the liabilities owed.

(g) *Suspension of the statute of limitations on collection.* The statute of limitations under section 6502 for collection of any liability shall be suspended during the period that a proposed installment agreement relating to that liability is pending with the IRS, for 30 days immediately following the rejection of a proposed installment agreement, and for 30 days immediately following the termination of an installment agreement. If, within the 30 days following the rejection or termination of an installment agreement, the taxpayer files an appeal with Appeals, the statute of limitations for collection shall be suspended while the rejection or termination is being considered by Appeals. The statute of limitations for collection shall continue to run if an exception under paragraph (f)(2) of this section applies and levy is not prohibited with respect to the taxpayer.

(h) *Annual statement.* The Commissioner shall provide each taxpayer who is party to an installment agreement under this section with an annual statement setting forth the initial balance owed at the beginning of the year, the payments made during the year, and the remaining balance as of the end of the year.

(i) *Biannual review of partial payment installment agreements.* The Commissioner shall perform a review of the taxpayer's financial condition in the case of a partial payment installment agreement at least once every two years. The purpose of this review is to determine whether the taxpayer's financial condition has significantly changed so as to warrant an increase in the value of the payments being made or termination of the agreement.

(j) *Cross reference.* Pursuant to section 6601(b)(1), the last day prescribed for payment is determined without regard to any installment agreement, including for purposes of computing penalties and interest provided by the Internal Revenue Code. For special rules regarding the computation of the failure to pay penalty while certain installment agreements are in effect, see section 6651(h) and §301.6651–1(a)(4).

(k) *Effective date.* This section is applicable on the date final regulations are published in the **Federal Register**.

Par. 4. Section 301.6331–4 is revised to read as follows:

§301.6331–4 Restrictions on levy while installment agreements are pending or in effect.

Cross-reference. For provisions relating to the making of levies while an installment agreement is pending or in effect, see §301.6159–1.

Mark E. Matthews,
Deputy Commissioner for Services and Enforcement.

(Filed by the Office of the Federal Register on March 2, 2007, 8:45 a.m., and published in the issue of the Federal Register for March 5, 2007, 72 F.R. 9712)

Notice of Proposed Rulemaking by Cross-Reference to Temporary Regulation

Section 181 — Deduction for Qualified Film and Television Production Costs

REG–115403–05

AGENCY: Internal Revenue Service (IRS), Treasury.

ACTION: Notice of proposed rulemaking by cross reference to temporary regulation.

SUMMARY: In this issue of the Bulletin, the IRS is issuing temporary regulations (T.D. 9312) under section 181 of the Internal Revenue Code relating to deductions for costs of producing qualified film and television productions. These temporary regulations reflect changes to the law made by the American Jobs Creation Act of 2004 and the Gulf Opportunity Zone Act of 2005, and affect taxpayers that produce films and television productions within the United States. This action is necessary to provide guidance for the application of section 181. The text of the temporary regulations also serves as the text of these proposed regulations. This document also provides notice of a public hearing on these proposed regulations.

DATES: Written comments and requests for a public hearing must be received by May 10, 2007.

ADDRESSES: Send submissions to: CC:PA:LPD:PR (REG–115403–05), room 5203, Internal Revenue Service, PO Box 7604, Ben Franklin Station, Washington, DC 20044. Submissions may be hand delivered Monday through Friday between the hours of 8 a.m. and 4 p.m. to: CC:PA:LPD:PR (REG–115403–05), Courier's Desk, Internal Revenue Service, 1111 Constitution Avenue, N.W., Washington, DC, or sent electronically, via the IRS Internet site at *www.irs.gov/regs* or via the Federal eRulemaking Portal at *http://www.Regulations.gov/* (IRS REG–115403–05).

FOR FURTHER INFORMATION CONTACT: Concerning the regulations, Bernard P. Harvey, (202) 622–3110; concerning submissions and to request a hearing, Kelly Banks, (202) 622–7180 (not toll-free numbers).

SUPPLEMENTARY INFORMATION:

Paperwork Reduction Act

The collections of information contained in this notice of proposed rulemaking have been submitted to the Office of Management and Budget for review in accordance with the Paperwork Reduction Act of 1995 (44 U.S.C. 3507(d)). Comments on the collections of information should be sent to the Office of Management and Budget, Attn: Desk Officer for the Department of the Treasury, Office of Information and Regulatory Affairs, Washington, DC 20503, with copies to the **Internal Revenue Service**, Attn: IRS Reports Clearance Officer, SE:W:CAR:MP:T:T:SP, Washington, DC 20224. Comments on the collection of information should be received by April 10, 2007. Comments are specifically requested concerning:

Whether the proposed collection of information is necessary for the proper performance of the functions of the Internal Revenue Service, including whether the information will have practical utility;

The accuracy of the estimated burden associated with the proposed collection of information;

How the quality, utility, and clarity of the information to be collected may be enhanced;

How the burden of complying with the proposed collection of information may be minimized, including through the application of automated collection techniques or other forms of information technology; and

Estimates of capital or start-up costs and costs of operation, maintenance, and purchase of service to provide information.

The collection of information in this proposed regulation is in §1.181–2T(c). This information is required to verify that the production cost of the film or television production for which the deduction under section 181 of the Internal Revenue Code is claimed does not exceed the statutory production cost limit, that at least 75 percent of the compensation from the production is compensation for services performed in the United States, that production costs deducted under section 181(a)(2)(B) are substantially incurred in the specific areas designated in section 181(a)(2)(B), and that, in situations in which more than one taxpayer is claiming a deduction for a single production, the total deduction for the production does not exceed the statutory limit. The collection of information is mandatory. The likely recordkeepers are business or other for-profit institutions, and small businesses or organizations.

Estimated total annual recordkeeping burden: 1,500 hours.

The estimated annual burden per recordkeeper varies from 2 to 4 hours, depending on individual circumstances, with an estimated average of 3 hours.

Estimated number of recordkeepers: 500.

An agency may not conduct or sponsor, and a person is not required to respond to, a collection of information unless it displays a valid control number assigned by the Office of Management and Budget.

Books or records relating to a collection of information must be retained as long as their contents may become material in the administration of any internal revenue law. Generally, tax returns and tax return information are confidential, as required by 26 U.S.C. 6103.

Background

The temporary regulations in this issue of the Bulletin contain amendments to 26 CFR part 1 to provide regulations under section 181 of the Internal Revenue Code of 1986 (Code). Section 181 was added to the Code by section 244 of the American Jobs Creation Act of 2004, Public Law No. 108–357 (118 Stat. 1418) (Oct. 22, 2004), and was modified by section 403(e) of the Gulf Opportunity Zone Act of 2005, Public Law No. 109–135 (119 Stat. 2577) (Dec. 21, 2005).

Explanation of Provisions

The temporary regulations in this issue of the Bulletin amend the Income Tax Regulations (26 CFR part 1) to add regulations under section 181 of the Internal Revenue Code of 1986 (Code). The text of the temporary regulations also serves as the text of these proposed regulations. The preamble to the temporary regulations explains these proposed regulations.

Special Analyses

It has been determined that this notice of proposed rulemaking is not a significant regulatory action as defined in Executive Order 12866. Therefore, a regulatory assessment is not required. It also has been determined that section 553(b) and (d) of the Administrative Procedure Act (5 U.S.C. chapter 5) does not apply to these regulations. It is hereby certified that this regulation will not have a significant economic impact on a substantial number of small entities. The proposed regulations impose a collection of information on small entities in order to demonstrate eligibility for tax benefits under the statute, and this collection of information will require recordkeeping. This collection of information is discussed elsewhere in this preamble. However, the recordkeeping required by this collection of information does not differ significantly from the recordkeeping that a taxpayer must perform in order to determine whether the taxpayer is eligible to claim a deduction under the statute. Consequently, the economic impact on small entities resulting from the recordkeeping required under this regulation is *de minimis*. Accordingly, a regulatory flexibility analysis is not required. We request comment on the accuracy of this certification. Pursuant to section 7805(f) of the Code, this regulation has been submitted to the Chief Counsel for Advocacy of the Small Business Administration for comment on its impact on small business.

Comments and Requests for a Public Hearing

Before these proposed regulations are adopted as final regulations, consideration will be given to any written comments (a signed original and eight (8) copies) or electronically generated comments that are submitted timely to the IRS. The IRS and Treasury Department generally request comments on the clarity of the proposed rule and how it may be made easier to understand. All comments will be available for public inspection and copying. A public hearing may be scheduled if requested in writing by a person who timely submits comments. If a public hearing is scheduled, notice of the date, time, and place for the hearing will be published in the **Federal Register**.

Drafting Information

The principal author of these regulations is Bernard P. Harvey, Office of Associate Chief Counsel (Passthroughs and Special Industries). However, other personnel from the IRS and Treasury Department participated in their development.

* * * * *

Proposed Amendments to the Regulations

Accordingly, 26 CFR part 1 is amended as follows:

PART 1—INCOME TAXES

Paragraph 1. The authority citation for part 1 continues read as follows:

Authority: 26 U.S.C. 7805 * * *

Par. 2. Sections 1.181–0 through 1.181–6 are added as follows:

§1.181-0 Table of contents.

[The text of this proposed section is the same as the text of §1.181-0T published elsewhere in this issue of the Bulletin.]

§1.181–1 Deduction for qualified film and television production costs.

[The text of this proposed section is the same as the text of §1.181–1T published elsewhere in this issue of the Bulletin.]

§1.181–2 Election.

[The text of this proposed section is the same as the text of §1.181–2T published elsewhere in this issue of the Bulletin.]

§1.181–3 Qualified film or television production.

[The text of this proposed section is the same as the text of §1.181–3T published elsewhere in this issue of the Bulletin.]

§1.181–4 Special rules.

[The text of this proposed section is the same as the text of §1.181–4T published elsewhere in this issue of the Bulletin.]

§1.181–5 Examples.

[The text of this proposed section is the same as the text of §1.181–5T published elsewhere in this issue of the Bulletin.]

§1.181–6 Effective date.

[The text of this proposed section is the same as the text of §1.181–6T published elsewhere in this issue of the Bulletin.]

Kevin M. Brown,
Deputy Commissioner for Services and Enforcement.

(Filed by the Office of the Federal Register on February 8, 2007, 8:45 a.m., and published in the issue of the Federal Register for February 9, 2007, 72 F.R. 6190)

Announcement and Report Concerning Advance Pricing Agreements

Announcement 2007–31

February 26, 2007

This Announcement is issued pursuant to § 521(b) of Pub. L. 106–170, the Ticket to Work and Work Incentives Improvement Act of 1999, which requires the Secretary of the Treasury to report annually to the public concerning Advance Pricing Agreements (APAs) and the APA Program. The first report covered calendar years 1991 through 1999. Subsequent reports covered separately each calendar year 2000 through 2005. This eighth report describes the experience, structure and activities of the APA Program during calendar year 2006. It does not provide guidance regarding the application of the arm's length standard.

Matthew W. Frank
Director, Advance Pricing Agreement Program

Background

Internal Revenue Code (IRC) § 482 provides that the Secretary may distribute, apportion, or allocate gross income, deductions, credits, or allowances between or among two or more commonly controlled businesses if necessary to reflect clearly the income of such businesses. Under the § 482 regulations, the standard to be applied in determining the true taxable income of a controlled business is that of a business dealing at arm's length with an unrelated business. The arm's length standard has also been adopted by the international community and is incorporated into the transfer pricing guidelines issued by the Organization for Economic Cooperation and Development (OECD). OECD, TRANSFER PRICING GUIDELINES FOR MULTINATIONAL ENTERPRISES AND TAX ADMINISTRATORS (1995). Transfer pricing issues by their nature are highly factual and have traditionally been one of the largest issues identified by the IRS in its audits of multinational corporations. The APA Program is designed to resolve actual or potential transfer pricing disputes in a principled, cooperative manner, as an alternative to the traditional examination process. An APA is a binding contract between the IRS and a taxpayer by which the IRS agrees not to seek a transfer pricing adjustment under IRC § 482 for a covered transaction if the taxpayer files its tax return for a covered year consistent with the agreed transfer pricing method (TPM). In 2006, the IRS and taxpayers executed 82 APAs and amended three APAs.

Since 1991, with the issuance of Rev. Proc. 91–22, 1991–1 C.B. 526, the IRS has offered taxpayers, through the APA Program, the opportunity to reach an agreement in advance of filing a tax return on the appropriate TPM to be applied to related party transactions. In 1996, the IRS issued internal procedures for processing APA requests. Chief Counsel Directives Manual (CCDM), ¶¶ 42.10.10 – 42.10.16 (November 15, 1996). Also in 1996, the IRS updated Rev. Proc. 91–22 with the release of Rev. Proc. 96–53, 1996–2 C.B. 375. In 1998, the IRS published Notice 98–65, 1998–2 C.B. 803, which set forth streamlined APA procedures for small business taxpayers. Then on July 1, 2004, the IRS updated and superseded both Rev. Proc. 96–53 and Notice 98–65 by issuing Rev. Proc. 2004–40, 2004–2 C.B. 50, effective for all APA requests filed on or after August 19, 2004.

On December 19, 2005, the IRS again updated the procedural rules for processing and administering APAs with the release of Rev. Proc. 2006–9, 2006–2 I.R.B. 278. Rev. Proc. 2006–9 supersedes Rev. Proc. 2004–40 and is effective for all APA requests filed on or after February 1, 2006.

Advance Pricing Agreements

An APA generally combines an agreement between a taxpayer and the IRS on an appropriate TPM for the transactions at issue (Covered Transactions) with an agreement between the U.S. and one or more foreign tax authorities (under the authority of the mutual agreement process of our income tax treaties) that the TPM is correct. With such a "bilateral" APA, the taxpayer ordinarily is assured that the income associated with the Covered Transactions will not be subject to double taxation by the U.S. and the foreign jurisdiction. It is the policy of the United States, as reflected in §§ 2.08 and 7 of Rev. Proc. 2006–9, to encourage taxpayers that enter the APA Program to seek bilateral or multilateral APAs when competent authority procedures are available with respect to the foreign country or countries involved. However, the IRS may execute an APA with a taxpayer without reaching a competent authority agreement (a "unilateral" APA).

A unilateral APA is an agreement between a taxpayer and the IRS establishing an approved TPM for U.S. tax purposes. A unilateral APA binds the taxpayer and the IRS, but does not prevent foreign tax administrations from taking different positions on the appropriate TPM for a transaction. As stated in § 7.07 of Rev. Proc. 2006–9, should a transaction covered by a unilateral APA be subject to double taxation as the result of an adjustment by a foreign tax administration, the taxpayer may seek relief by requesting that the U.S. Competent Authority consider initiating a mutual agreement proceeding pursuant to an applicable income tax treaty (if any).

When a unilateral APA involves taxpayers operating in a country that is a treaty partner, information relevant to the APA (including a copy of the APA and APA annual reports) may be provided to the treaty partner under normal rules and principles governing the exchange of information under income tax treaties.

The APA Program

An IRS team headed by an APA team leader is responsible for the consideration of each APA. As of December 31, 2006, the APA Program had 20 team leaders. The team leader is responsible for organizing the IRS APA team. The IRS APA team leader arranges meetings with the taxpayer, secures whatever information is necessary from the taxpayer to analyze the taxpayer's related party transactions and the available facts under the arm's length standard of IRC § 482 and the regulations thereunder, and leads the discussions with the taxpayer.

The APA team generally includes an economist, an international examiner, LMSB field counsel, and, in a bilateral case, a U.S. Competent Authority analyst who leads the discussions with the treaty partner. The economist may be from the APA Program or the IRS field organization. As of December 31, 2006, the APA Program had eight economists. The APA team may also include an LMSB International Technical Advisor, other LMSB exam personnel, and an Appeals Officer.

The APA Process

The APA process is voluntary. Taxpayers submit an application for an APA, together with a user fee as set forth in Rev. Proc. 2006–9, § 4.12. The APA process can be broken into five phases: (1) application; (2) due diligence; (3) analysis; (4) discussion and agreement; and (5) drafting, review, and execution.

(1) *Application*

In many APA cases, the taxpayer's application is preceded by a pre-file conference with the APA staff in which the taxpayer can solicit the informal views of the APA Program. Pre-file conferences can occur on an anonymous basis, although a taxpayer must disclose its identity when it applies for an APA. Taxpayers must file the appropriate user fee on or before the due date, including extensions, of the tax return for the first taxable year that the taxpayer proposes to be covered by the APA. (If the taxpayer receives an extension to file its tax return, it must file its user fee no later than the actual filing date of the return.) Many taxpayers file a user fee first and then follow up with a full application later. The procedures for pre-file conferences, user fees, and applications can be found in §§ 3 and 4 of Rev. Proc. 2006–9.

The APA application can be a relatively modest document for small businesses. Section 9 of Rev. Proc. 2006–9 describes the special APA procedures for small business taxpayers. For most taxpayers, however, the APA application is a substantial document filling several binders.

The application is assigned to an APA team leader who is responsible for the case. The APA team leader's first responsibility is to organize the APA team. This involves contacting the appropriate LMSB International Territory Manager to secure the assignment of an international examiner to the APA case and the LMSB Counsel's office to secure a field counsel lawyer. In a bilateral case, the U.S. Competent Authority will assign a U.S. Competent Authority analyst to the team. In a large APA case, the international examiner may invite his or her manager and other LMSB personnel familiar with the taxpayer to join the team. If the APA may affect taxable years in Appeals, the appropriate appellate conferee will be invited to join the team. In appropriate cases, the APA team leader contacts the Manager, LMSB International Technical Advisors, to determine whether to include a technical advisor on the team. The IRS APA team will generally include a technical advisor if the APA request concerns cost sharing, or a complex intangibles or services transaction. The APA team leader then distributes copies of the APA application to all team members and sets up an opening conference with the taxpayer. The APA office strives to hold this opening conference within 45 days of the assignment of the case to a team leader. At the opening conference, the APA team leader proposes a case plan designed, if feasible, to complete a unilateral APA or, in the case of a bilateral APA, the recommended U.S. negotiating position within 12 months from the date the full application is filed. The actual median and average times for completing unilateral APAs, recommended negotiating positions for bilateral APAs, and APAs for small business taxpayers are shown below in Tables 2, 5, and 11, respectively.

(2) <u>*Due Diligence*</u>

The APA team must satisfy itself that the relevant facts submitted by the taxpayer are complete and accurate. This due diligence aspect of the APA is vital to the process. It is because of this due diligence that the IRS can reach advance agreements with taxpayers in the highly factual setting of transfer pricing. Due diligence can proceed in a number of ways. Typically, the APA team leader will submit in advance of the opening conference a list of questions to the taxpayer for discussion at the conference. The opening conference may result in additional questions and an agreement to meet one or more times in the future. These questions and meetings are not an audit and are focused on the transfer pricing issues associated with the transactions in the taxpayer's application, or such other transactions that the taxpayer and the IRS may agree to add.

(3) <u>*Analysis*</u>

A significant part of the analytical work associated with an APA is done typically by the APA economist and/or an IRS field economist assigned to the case. The analysis may result in the need for additional information. Once the IRS APA team has completed its due diligence and analysis, it begins discussions with the taxpayer over the various aspects of the APA including the covered transactions, the TPM, the selection of comparable transactions, asset intensity and other adjustments, the appropriate critical assumptions, the APA term, and other key issues. The APA team leader will discuss particularly difficult issues with his or her managers, but generally the APA team leader is empowered to negotiate the APA.

(4) <u>*Discussion and Agreement*</u>

The discussion and agreement phase differs for bilateral and unilateral cases. In a bilateral case, the discussions proceed in two parts and involve two IRS offices — the APA Program and the U.S. Competent Authority. In the first part, the APA team will attempt to reach a consensus with the taxpayer regarding the recommended position that the U.S. Competent Authority should take in negotiations with its treaty partner. This recommended U.S. negotiating position is a paper drafted by the APA team leader and signed by the APA Director that provides the APA Program's view of the best TPM for the Covered Transaction, taking into account IRC § 482 and the regulations thereunder, the relevant tax treaty, and the U.S. Competent Authority's experience with the treaty partner.

The experience of the APA office and the U.S. Competent Authority is that APA negotiations are likely to proceed more rapidly with a foreign competent authority if the U.S. negotiating position is fully supported by the taxpayer. Consequently, the APA office works together with the taxpayer in developing the recommended U.S. negotiating position. On occasion, the APA team will agree to disagree with a taxpayer. In these cases, the APA office will send a recommended U.S. negotiating position to the U.S. Competent Authority that includes elements with which the taxpayer does not agree. This disagreement is noted in the paper. The APA team leader also solicits the views of the field members of the APA team, and, in the vast majority of APA cases, the international examiner, LMSB field counsel, and other IRS field team members concur in the position prepared by the APA team leader.

Once the APA Program completes the recommended U.S. negotiating position, the APA process shifts from the APA Program to the U.S. Competent Authority. The U.S. Competent Authority analyst assigned to the APA takes the recommended U.S. negotiating position and prepares the final U.S. negotiating position, which is then transmitted to the foreign competent authority. The negotiations with the foreign competent authority are conducted by the U.S. Competent Authority analyst, most often in face-to-face negotiating sessions conducted periodically throughout the year. At the request of the U.S. Competent Authority analyst, the APA team leader may continue to assist the negotiations.

In unilateral APA cases, the discussions proceed solely between the APA Program and the taxpayer. In a unilateral case, the taxpayer and the APA Program must reach agreement to conclude an APA. As in bilateral cases, the APA team leader almost always will achieve a consensus with the IRS field personnel assigned to the APA team regarding the final APA. The APA Program has a procedure in which the IRS field personnel are solicited formally for their concurrence in the final APA. This concurrence, or any item in disagreement, is noted in a memorandum prepared by the APA team leader that accompanies the final APA sent forward for review and execution.

(5) *Drafting, Review, and Execution*

Once the IRS and the taxpayer reach agreement, the drafting of the final APA generally takes little time because the APA Program has developed standard language that is incorporated into every APA. The current version of this language is found in Attachment A. APAs are reviewed by the APA Branch Chief and the APA Director. In addition, the team leader prepares a summary memorandum for the Associate Chief Counsel (International) (ACC(I)). On March 1, 2001, the ACC(I) delegated to the APA Director the authority to execute APAs on behalf of the IRS. *See* Chief Counsel Notice CC–2001–016. The APA is executed for the taxpayer by an appropriate corporate officer.

Model APA at Attachment A

[§ 521(b)(2)(B)]

Attachment A contains the current version of the model APA language.

The Current APA Office Structure, Composition, and Operation

In 2006, the APA office consisted of four branches with Branches 1 and 3 staffed with APA team leaders and Branch 2 staffed with economists. Branch 4, the APA West Coast branch, is headquartered in Laguna Niguel, California, with an additional office in San Francisco, and is staffed with both team leaders and economists.

Overall, the APA staff increased by seven, to 40 from 33, from the end of 2005 to the end of 2006. Three team leaders, three economists, and a branch chief were added to the Program.

As of December 31, 2006, the APA staff was as follows:

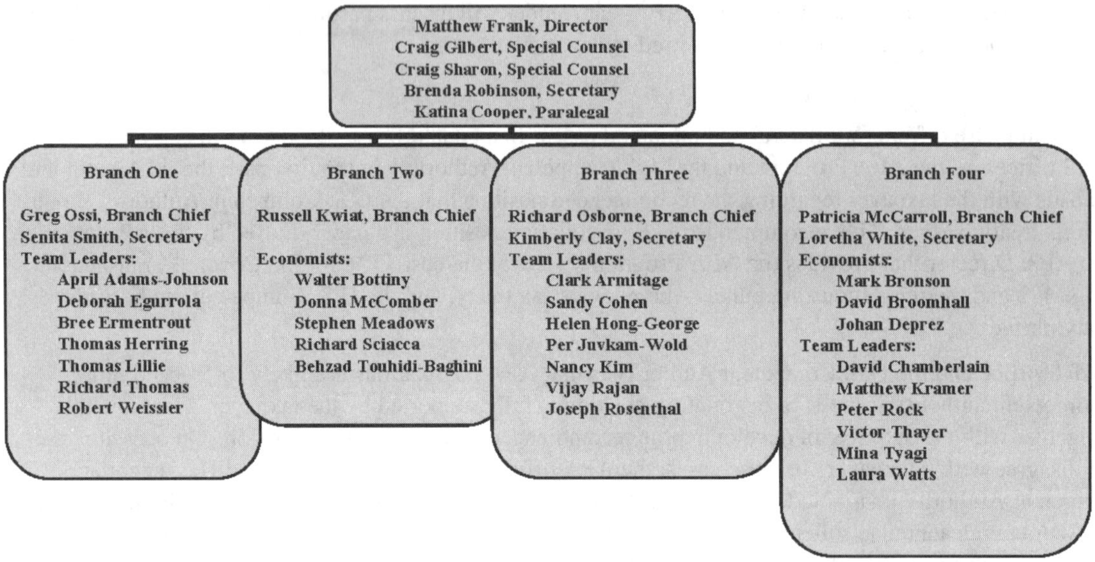

The staffing increase in 2006 was achieved through the hiring of eight persons and the addition of a second person detailed to the APA Program from the IRS Appeals Office. This hiring, most of which occurred mid-year, allowed the APA Program to realize a 6 percent increase in staffing in 2006 over 2005 measured by total work hours and a 12 percent increase in staffing for the second half of 2006 over the same period in 2005, again measured by total work hours. The change in APA staffing levels over the last six years is reflected in the table below.

Hours of APA attorneys, economists, and paralegal staff by year (excluding holiday and leave)

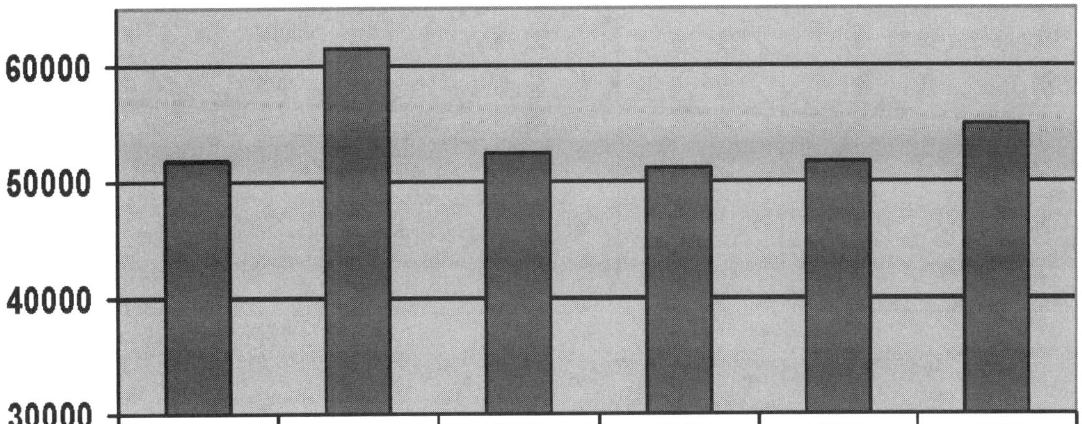

	2001	2002	2003	2004	2005	2006
APA staff hours	51820	61528	52495	51170	51744	54970

APA Issue/Industry Coordination Teams

In May 2005, the IRS Chief Counsel announced a series of initiatives to improve APA Program performance. One initiative was to increase specialization within the office by creating teams of select individuals to handle all cases of a particular type. The purpose was to increase efficiency, quality, and consistency.

The APA Program selected five categories of cases for specialization – cases involving cost sharing arrangements, financial products, the semiconductor industry, the automotive industry, and the pharmaceutical industry. These categories were selected because they each had a sufficient number of cases and commonality of issues to warrant their assignment to teams. Cases falling within these five categories have historically accounted for about 40 percent of the APA Program's case load (excluding Small Business Taxpayer ("SBT") cases) and more than half of its total case time. At the end of 2006, cases within these five categories account for 31 of the 90 non-SBT cases pending in the office that were either unilateral APAs or bilateral APAs that had not yet been forwarded to Competent Authority.

Staffing of the coordination teams at the end of 2006 is indicated below.

Auto & Auto Parts

Craig Sharon, Reviewer

Tom Herring, Team Leader
Per Juvkam-Wold, Team Leader
Vijay Rajan, Team Leader
Victor Thayer, Team Leader
Walt Bottiny, Principal Economist

Pharmaceuticals & Medical Devices

Craig Sharon, Reviewer

Clark Armitage, Team Leader
Tom Herring, Team Leader
Peter Rock, Team Leader
Victor Thayer, Team Leader
Stephen Meadows, Principal Economist

Cost Sharing

Patricia McCarroll, Reviewer

David Chamberlain, Team Leader
Matthew Kramer, Team Leader
Craig Sharon, Team Leader
Robert Weissler, Team Leader
Mark Bronson, Principal Economist

Financial Products

Richard Osborne, Reviewer

Clark Armitage, Team Leader
Per Juvkam-Wold, Team Leader
Donna McComber, Principal Economist

Semiconductors

Greg Ossi, Reviewer

April Adams-Johnson, Team Leader
Matthew Kramer, Team Leader
Vijay Rajan, Team Leader
Peter Rock, Team Leader
Behzad Touhidi-Baghini, Principal Economist

The APA Program is mindful that the purpose of the coordination effort is not to impose the same transfer pricing method on all taxpayers in an industry. The appropriate transfer pricing method remains a case-by-case determination, influenced by numerous factors that are not common to all companies operating in a particular industry. While the coordination effort may result in the APA Program promoting a common approach on some issues where appropriate, the Program expects that the greater industry familiarity developed through the coordination effort will also allow it to develop a more sophisticated understanding of issues that will permit more tailored approaches, thereby promoting more (appropriately) varied results than might otherwise be the case.

APA Training

In 2006, the APA office continued its training activities. Training sessions addressed APA-related current developments, new APA office practices and procedures, and international tax law issues. The training materials used for new hires are available to the public through the APA internet site at *http://www.irs.gov/businesses/corporations/article/0,,id=96221,00.html*. These materials do not constitute guidance on the application of the arm's length standard and are not to be relied upon or cited as precedent.

APA Program Statistical Data
[§ 521(b)(2)(C) and (E)]

The statistical information required under § 521(b)(2)(C) is contained in Tables 1 and 10 below; the information required under § 521(b)(2)(E) is contained in Tables 2 and 3 below:

TABLE 1: APA APPLICATIONS, EXECUTED APAs, AND PENDING APAs

	Unilateral	Bilateral	Multilateral	Year Total	Cumulative Total
APA applications filed during year 2006	42	67		109	1037
All APAs executed					
Year 2006	42	39	1	82	692
1991–2005	282	320	8	610	
APA renewals executed during year 2006	21	14		35	180
Revised or Amended APAs executed during year 2006	2	1		3	33
Pending requests for APAs	46	203		249	
Pending requests for new APAs	30	137		167	
Pending requests for renewal APAs	16	66		82	
APAs canceled or revoked	0	0		0	5
APAs withdrawn	3	13		16	121

TABLE 2: MONTHS TO COMPLETE APAs

Months to Complete Advance Pricing Agreements in Year 2006					
All New		All Renewals		All Combined	
Average	33.9	Average	27.5	Average	31.2
Median	35.3	Median	25.9	Median	28.1
Unilateral New		Unilateral Renewals		Unilateral Combined	
Average	22.0	Average	18.5	Average	20.3
Median	22.9	Median	17.4	Median	18.7
Bilateral/Multilateral New		Bilateral/Multilateral Renewals		Bilateral/Multilateral Combined	
Average	43.6	Average	40.9	Average	42.7
Median	45.4	Median	38.5	Median	43.7

TABLE 3: APA COMPLETION TIME – MONTHS PER APA

Months	Number of APAs	Months	Number of APAs	Months	Number of APAs	Months	Number of APAs
1		**18**	3	**35**	2	**52**	
2		**19**	2	**36**	1	**53**	1
3	1	**20**		**37**	1	**54**	1
4		**21**	2	**38**	3	**55**	1
5		**22**	1	**39**		**56**	1
6		**23**	8	**40**	2	**57**	
7		**24**	1	**41**	2	**58**	
8		**25**	1	**42**		**59**	1
9	2	**26**	2	**43**	1	**60**	
10	2	**27**	2	**44**	1	**61**	3
11	3	**28**	2	**45**	1	**62**	
12	1	**29**		**46**	2	**63**	
13	1	**30**	2	**47**		**64**	
14		**31**	1	**48**	2	**65**	1
15	6	**32**	1	**49**		**66**	
16	1	**33**	3	**50**	3	**67**	
17	1	**34**		**51**	3	**68**	

TABLE 4: RECOMMENDED NEGOTIATING POSITIONS

Recommended Negotiating Positions Completed in Year 2006	62

TABLE 5: MONTHS TO COMPLETE RECOMMENDED NEGOTIATING POSITIONS

New		**Renewal**		**Combined**	
Average	26.1	Average	26.5	Average	26.2
Median	23.9	Median	28.9	Median	23.9

TABLE 6: RECOMMENDED NEGOTIATING POSITIONS COMPLETION TIME – MONTHS PER APA

Months	Number	Months	Number	Months	Number	Months	Number
1		17	4	33	2	49	
2		18	3	34	3	50	
3		19		35		51	1
4		20	1	36		52	
5	1	21	3	37	1	53	
6		22	2	38		54	
7	2	23	5	39		55	1
8	1	24	6	40		56	
9		25	1	41	1	57	
10		26	1	42		58	1
11	2	27	1	43		59	
12		28	4	44	2	60	
13		29	2	45		61	
14		30	3	46		62	1
15	3	31	2	47		63	
16		32	2	48		64	

Tables 7 and 8 below show how long each APA request pending at the end of 2006 has been in the system as measured from the filing date of the APA submission. The numbers for pending unilateral and bilateral cases differ from the numbers in Table 1 because Tables 7 and 8 reflect only cases for which submissions have been received while Table 1 includes any case for which a user fee has been paid.

TABLE 7: UNILATERAL APAs – TIME IN INVENTORY – MONTHS PER APA

Months	Number of APAs	Months	Number of APAs	Months	Number of APAs	Months	Number of APAs
1	2	8	4	15	1	22	
2		9		16	1	23	2
3		10		17		24	1
4	2	11	5	18		25	
5	1	12	1	19		26	
6	2	13		20		27	
7	11	14		21	1	28	1

TABLE 8: BILATERAL APAs – TIME IN INVENTORY – MONTHS PER APA

Months	Number of APAs	Months	Number of APAs	Months	Number of APAs	Months	Number of APAs
1	1	**27**	5	**53**		**79**	
2		**28**	1	**54**	3	**80**	
3	10	**29**	4	**55**		**81**	
4	7	**30**	3	**56**	2	**82**	
5	3	**31**	3	**57**		**83**	
6	8	**32**	2	**58**	1	**84**	
7	7	**33**	6	**59**	2	**85**	
8	4	**34**	5	**60**		**86**	
9	1	**35**	2	**61**		**87**	
10	5	**36**		**62**		**88**	
11	7	**37**	1	**63**		**89**	2
12	5	**38**		**64**		**90**	
13	4	**39**		**65**		**91**	
14	7	**40**	4	**66**	1	**92**	
15	3	**41**		**67**	2	**93**	
16	5	**42**	2	**68**		**94**	
17	2	**43**	3	**69**		**95**	
18	1	**44**	1	**70**		**96**	
19	1	**45**	1	**71**	1	**97**	
20	5	**46**	1	**72**	2	**98**	
21	5	**47**		**73**		**99**	
22	5	**48**	3	**74**		**100-105**	1
23	9	**49**	1	**75**		**106-110**	
24		**50**	5	**76**		**111-115**	
25	2	**51**		**77**		**116-120**	1
26	4	**52**		**78**	1		

Of the 218 cases in the APA Program's inventory shown in Tables 7 and 8, 108 cases (all of which are reflected in Table 8) are bilateral cases that have been forwarded to the Competent Authority office for discussion with a treaty partner. This leaves 110 cases in the APA Program's active inventory at the end of 2006 that are either unilateral APAs (35 cases) or bilateral APAs for which the APA Program has not yet completed a recommended negotiating position (75 cases).

The table below shows the average age (in months) of the 110 active cases in inventory at the end of 2006, along with a comparison of the number of active cases and their average age at year-end for each year back to 2002. The table also shows the same information for cases that were at least 6 months old or 1 year old (the latter being a subset of the former) at the end of each year to allow comparison without potential distortions caused by year-to-year variations in the number of cases received in the latter half or during the course of the year.

TABLE 9: NUMBER AND AVERAGE AGE OF ACTIVE CASES IN INVENTORY AT YEAR-END

	2002	2003	2004	2005	2006
Active cases	80	106	130	133	110
Average age (months)	14.1	15.1	15.2	13.2	10.6
Active cases 6+ months	40	78	106	87	81
Average age (months)	25.5	19.4	17.8	18.5	13.0
Active cases 1+ year	22	46	60	55	32
Average age (months)	38.9	26.8	24.2	23.3	19.4

TABLE 10: SMALL BUSINESS TAXPAYER APAs

Small Business Taxpayer APAs Completed in Year 2006	**19**
New	10
Renewals	9
Unilateral	15
Bilateral	4

TABLE 11: MONTHS TO COMPLETE SMALL BUSINESS TAXPAYER APAs

Months to Complete Small Business Taxpayer APAs in Year 2006					
New		**Renewal**		**Combined**	
Average	24.2	Average	21.4	Average	22.9
Median	20.9	Median	21.2	Median	21.2

TABLE 12: INDUSTRIES COVERED[1]

Industry Involved – NAICS Codes	Number
Electronic equipment, appliance and component manufacturing – 335	10–12
Wholesale trade, durable goods – 421	10–12
Computer and electronic product manufacturing – 334	7–9
Chemical manufacturing – 325	4–6
Information service and data processing services – 514	4–6
Miscellaneous manufacturing – 339	4–6

[1] The categories in this table are drawn from the North American Industry Classification System (NAICS), which has replaced the U.S. Standard Industrial Classification (SIC) system. NAICS was developed jointly by the U.S., Canada, and Mexico to provide new comparability in statistics about business activity across North America.

Industry Involved – NAICS Codes — Continued	Number
Machinery manufacturing – 333	4–6
Food manufacturing – 311	1–3
Securities, commodity contracts and other intermediary and related activities – 523	1–3
Transportation equipment manufacturing – 336	1–3
Wholesale trade, nondurable goods – 422	1–3
Motor vehicle and parts dealers – 441	1–3
Beverage and tobacco manufacturing – 312	1–3
Fabricated metal manufacturing – 332	1–3
Sporting goods, hobby, book and music stores – 451	1–3
Food and beverage stores – 445	1–3
Air transportation – 481	1–3
Clothing and clothing accessories stores – 448	1–3
Broadcasting and telecommunications – 513	1–3
Plastics and rubber products manufacturing – 326	1–3
Petroleum and coal manufacturing – 324	1–3
Wood product manufacturing – 321	1–3
Water transportation – 483	1–3
Publishing industries – 511	1–3
Motion pictures and sound recording industries – 512	1–3

Trades or Businesses

[§ 521(b)(2)(D)(i)]

The nature of the relationships between the related organizations, trades, or businesses covered by APAs executed in 2006 is set forth in Table 13 below:

TABLE 13: NATURE OF RELATIONSHIPS BETWEEN RELATED ENTITIES

Relationship	Number of APAs
Foreign Parent – U.S. Subsidiary (-ies)	42
Unilateral	*21*
Bilateral	*21*
U.S. Parent – Foreign Subsidiary (-ies)	36
Unilateral	*15*
Bilateral	*21*
Foreign Company and U.S. branch(es)	0
Unilateral	*0*
Bilateral	*0*
Partnership	4
Unilateral	≤ 3
Bilateral	≤ 3

Relationship — Continued	Number of APAs
U.S. Company and non-U.S. branch(es)	0
Unilateral	*0*
Bilateral	*0*

Covered Transactions
[§ 521(b)(2)(D)(ii)]

The controlled transactions covered by APAs executed in 2006 are set forth in Table 14 and Table 15 below:

TABLE 14: TYPES OF COVERED TRANSACTIONS

Transaction Type	Number
Sale of tangible property into the U.S.	41
Use of intangible property by Non-U.S. entity	25
Sale of tangible property from the U.S.	18
Performance of services by Non-U.S. entity	16
Use of intangible property by U.S. entity	11
Performance of services by U.S. entity	11
R&D cost sharing – U.S. parent	≤ 3
R&D cost sharing – Non-U.S. parent	≤ 3
Financial products – U.S. parent	≤ 3
Other	≤ 3

TABLE 15: TYPES OF SERVICES INCLUDED IN COVERED TRANSACTIONS

Intercompany Services Involved in the Covered Transactions	Number
Distribution	24
Technical support services	20
Marketing	19
Logistical support	19
Administrative	19
Sales support	14
Product support	11
Management	11
Communication service	10
Purchasing	10
Research and development	7
Accounting	6
Headquarters costs	6
Manufacturing services	6

Intercompany Services Involved in the Covered Transactions — Continued	Number
Legal	4
Contract research & development	≤ 3
Warranty services	≤ 3
Assembly	≤ 3
Billing services	≤ 3
Testing and installation services	≤ 3

Business Functions Performed and Risks Assumed
[§ 521(b)(2)(D)(ii)]

The general descriptions of the business functions performed and risks assumed by the organizations, trades, or businesses whose results are tested in the Covered Transactions in the APAs executed in 2006 are set forth in Tables 16 and 17 below:

TABLE 16: FUNCTIONS PERFORMED BY THE TESTED PARTY

Functions Performed	Number
Distribution functions	64
Marketing functions	44
Manufacturing	41
Transportation and warehousing	30
Managerial, legal, accounting, finance, personnel, and other support services	29
Product assembly and/or packaging	25
Purchasing and materials management	24
Research and development	17
Technical training and tech support for sales staff (including sub-distributors)	17
Product testing and quality control	17
Product design and engineering	12
Licensing of intangibles	11
Product service (repairs, etc.)	11
Process engineering	7
Engineering and construction related services	5
Consulting services	≤ 3
Trading and risk management of financial products	≤ 3

TABLE 17: RISKS ASSUMED BY THE TESTED PARTY

Risks Assumed	Number
Market risks, including fluctuations in costs, demand, pricing, & inventory	89
Credit and collection risks	67
General business risks (*e.g.*, related to ownership of PP&E)	60

Risks Assumed — Continued	Number
Financial risks, including interest rates & currency	36
Product liability risks	32
R&D risks	17

Discussion

The majority of APAs have Covered Transactions that involve numerous business functions and risks. For instance, with respect to functions, companies that manufacture products typically conduct research and development, engage in product design and engineering, manufacture the product, market and distribute the product, and perform support functions such as legal, finance, and human resources services. Regarding risks, companies are subject to market risks, R&D risks, financial risks, credit and collection risks, product liability risks, and general business risks. In the APA evaluation process, a significant amount of time and effort is devoted to understanding how the functions and risks are allocated among the controlled group of companies that are party to the Covered Transactions.

In its APA submission, the taxpayer must provide a functional analysis. The functional analysis identifies the economic activities performed, the assets employed, the economic costs incurred, and the risks assumed by each of the controlled parties. The importance of the functional analysis derives from the fact that economic theory posits that there is a positive relationship between risk and expected return and that different functions provide different value and have different opportunity costs associated with them. It is important that the functional analysis go beyond simply categorizing the tested party as, say, a distributor. It should provide more specific information because, in the example of distributors, not all distributors undertake similar functions and risks.

The functional analysis is critical in determining the TPM (including the selection of comparables). In evaluating the functional analysis, the APA Program considers contractual terms between the controlled parties and the consistency of the conduct of the parties with respect to the allocation of risk. In accordance with the section 482 regulations, the APA Program also gives consideration to the ability of controlled parties to fund losses that might be expected to occur as a result of the assumption of risk. Another relevant factor considered in evaluating the functional analysis is the extent to which a controlled party exercises managerial or operational control over the business activities that directly influence the amount of income or loss realized. The section 482 regulations posit that parties at arm's length will ordinarily bear a greater share of those risks over which they have relatively more control.

In addition to the functional analysis, the APA evaluation process considers broader economic factors and conditions including the economic condition of the particular industry.

Related Organizations, Trades, or Businesses Whose Prices or Results are Tested to Determine Compliance with APA Transfer Pricing Methods
[§ 521(b)(2)(D)(iii)]

The related organizations, trades, or businesses whose prices or results are tested to determine compliance with TPMs prescribed in APAs executed in 2006 are set forth in Table 18 below:

TABLE 18: RELATED ORGANIZATIONS, TRADES, OR BUSINESSES WHOSE PRICES OR RESULTS ARE TESTED[2]

Type of Organization	Number
Multiple tested parties	37
U.S. distributor	31
U.S. provider of services	14
U.S. manufacturer	13
Non-U.S. manufacturer	12
Non U.S. distributor	10

[2] "Multiple tested parties" includes covered transactions that utilize profit splits, CUPs, and CUTs.

Type of Organization — Continued	Number
Non-U.S. provider of services	5
Non-U.S. licensee of intangible property	5
U.S. licensee of intangible property	≤ 3
U.S. dealer in financial products	≤ 3
U.S. participant in cost sharing agreement	≤ 3
Other	≤ 3

Transfer Pricing Methods and the Circumstances Leading to the Use of Those Methods
[§ 521(b)(2)(D)(iv)]

The TPMs used in APAs executed in 2006 are set forth in Tables 19–20 below:

TABLE 19: TRANSFER PRICING METHODS USED FOR TRANSFERS OF TANGIBLE AND INTANGIBLE PROPERTY[3]

TPM Used	Number
CPM: PLI is operating margin	25
Residual profit split	20
CPM: PLI is Berry ratio	11
CPM: PLI is markup on total costs	10
Unspecified method	8
CPM: PLI is gross margin	6
CUT (intangibles only)	≤ 3
Other profit split	≤ 3
CPM: PLI is other PLI	≤ 3
Cost Plus Method (tangibles only)	≤ 3
CUP (tangibles only) – not based on published market data	≤ 3
CPM: PLI is markup on other costs	≤ 3
Resale Price Method (tangibles only)	≤ 3
CPM: PLI is return on assets or capital employed	≤ 3
CUP (tangibles only) – based on published market data	≤ 3

TABLE 20: TRANSFER PRICING METHODS USED FOR SERVICES

TPM Used	Number
CPM: PLI is markup on total costs	11
Cost plus a markup	4
Cost with no markup	4

[3] Profit Level Indicators (PLIs) used with the Comparable Profit Method of Treas. Reg. § 1.482–5, and as used in these TPM tables, are as follows: (1) operating margin (ratio of operating profit to sales); (2) Berry ratio (ratio of gross profit to operating expenses); (3) gross margin (ratio of gross profit to sales); (4) markup on total costs (percentage markup on total costs); and (5) rate of return on assets or capital employed (ratio of operating profit to operating assets).

TPM Used — Continued	Number
CPM: PLI is operating margin	≤ 3
CPM: PLI is Berry ratio	≤ 3
Comparable Uncontrolled Transaction	≤ 3
Other	≤ 3

Discussion

The TPMs used in APAs completed during 2006 were based on the section 482 regulations. Under Treas. Reg. § 1.482–3, the arm's length amount for controlled transfers of tangible property may be determined using the Comparable Uncontrolled Price (CUP) method, the Resale Price Method, the Cost Plus Method, the Comparable Profits Method (CPM), or the Profit Split Method. Under Treas. Reg. § 1.482–4, the arm's length amount for controlled transfers of intangible property may be determined using the Comparable Uncontrolled Transaction (CUT) method, CPM, or the Profit Split Method. An "Unspecified Method" may be used for both tangible and intangible property if it provides a more reliable result than the enumerated methods under the best method rule of Treas. Reg. § 1.482–1(c). For transfers involving the provision of services, Treas. Reg. § 1.482–2(b) provides that services performed for the benefit of another member of a controlled group should bear an arm's length charge, either deemed to be equal to the cost of providing the services or an amount that would have been charged between independent parties. In addition, Treas. Reg. § 1.482–2(a) provides rules concerning the proper treatment of loans or advances.

Treas. Reg. § 1.482–7 provides rules for qualified cost sharing arrangements under which the parties agree to share the costs of development of intangibles in proportion to their shares of reasonably anticipated benefits. APAs involving cost sharing arrangements generally address both the method of allocating costs among the parties as well as determining the appropriate amount of the "buy-in" payment due for the transfer of pre-existing intangibles to the controlled participants. In 2006, the APA Program completed more than half a dozen cost sharing and/or buy-in APAs, including both outbound and inbound transactions. The majority of these were unilateral, but the APA Program also completed its recommendations on three additional bilateral cost sharing/buy-in cases and sent those on to Competent Authority. The methods used in the buy-in cases included valuations based on comparable uncontrolled transactions, on discounted cash flows, and on market capitalization. In addition, the Program is currently working on approximately half a dozen more cases involving cost sharing/buy-ins, split about evenly between bilateral and unilateral.

In reviewing the TPMs applicable to transfers of tangible and intangible property reflected in Table 19, the majority of the APAs followed the specified methods. However, several points should be made. The section 482 regulations note that for transfers of tangible property, the CUP method will generally be the most direct and reliable measure of an arm's length price for the Controlled Transaction if sufficiently reliable comparable transactions can be identified. Treas. Reg. § 1.482–3(b)(2)(ii)(A). It was the experience of the APA Program in 2006, that in the cases that came into the APA Program, sufficiently reliable CUP transactions were difficult to find.

Similar to the CUP method, for transfers of intangible property, the CUT method will generally provide the most reliable measure of an arm's length result if sufficiently reliable comparables may be found. Treas. Reg. § 1.482–4(c)(2)(ii). It has generally been difficult to identify external comparables, and APAs using the CUT method tend to rely on internal transactions between the taxpayer and unrelated parties. In 2006, three or fewer Covered Transactions utilized the CUT TPM.

The Cost Plus Method (tangibles only) and Resale Price Method were each applied in 2006 in three or fewer APAs. See Treas. Reg. § 1.482–3(c), (d).

The CPM is frequently applied in APAs. That is because reliable public data on comparable business activities of independent companies may be more readily available than potential CUP data, and comparability of resources employed, functions, risks, and other relevant considerations are more likely to exist than comparability of product. The CPM also tends to be less sensitive than other methods to differences in accounting practices between the tested party and comparable companies, *e.g.*, classification of expenses as cost of goods sold or operating expenses. Treas. Reg. § 1.482–3(c)(3)(iii)(B), and –3(d)(3)(iii)(B). In addition, the degree of functional comparability required to obtain a reliable result under the CPM is generally less than required under the Resale Price or Cost Plus methods because differences in functions performed often are reflected in operating expenses, and thus taxpayers performing different functions may have very different gross profit margins but earn similar levels of operating profit. Treas. Reg. § 1.482–5(c)(2).

Table 19 reflects more than 54 uses of the CPM (with varying PLIs) in Covered Transactions involving tangible or intangible property. In some APAs, the CPM was also used concurrently with other methods.

The CPM has proven to be versatile in part because of the various PLIs that can be used in connection with the method. Reaching agreement on the appropriate PLI has been the subject of much discussion in many of the cases, and it depends heavily on the facts and circumstances. Some APAs have called for different PLIs to apply to different parts of the Covered Transactions or with one PLI used as a check against the primary PLI.

The CPM was also used regularly with services as the Covered Transactions in APAs executed in 2006. There were at least 13 services Covered Transactions using the CPM method with various PLIs according to the specific facts of the taxpayers involved. Table 20 reflects the methods used to determine the arm's length results for APAs involving services transactions.

In 2006, 20 APAs involving tangible or intangible property used the Residual Profit Split Method. Treas. Reg. § 1.482–6(c)(3). In residual profit split cases, routine contributions by the controlled parties are allocated routine market returns, and the residual income is allocated among the controlled taxpayers based upon the relative value of their contributions of non-routine intangible property to the relevant business activity.

Profit splits have also been used in a number of financial product APAs in which the primary income-producing functions are performed in more than one jurisdiction.

Critical Assumptions

[§ 521(b)(2)(D)(v)]

Critical Assumptions used in APAs executed in 2006 are described in Table 21 below:

TABLE 21: CRITICAL ASSUMPTIONS

Critical Assumptions involving the following:	Number of APAs
Material changes to the business	82
Material changes to tax and/or financial accounting practices	82
Other financial ratio	7
Assets will remain substantially same	4
Cost allocations	4
Minimum sales volume	≤ 3
Changes in affiliated companies	≤ 3
Limit on product line revenues	≤ 3
Currency fluctuations	≤ 3
Material sales fluctuations	≤ 3
Catastrophic events	≤ 3
Limit on sales to related parties	≤ 3
Major regulatory changes	≤ 3
Sales territories substantially same	≤ 3
Profit projections hold	≤ 3
Other	4

Discussion

APAs include critical assumptions upon which their respective TPMs depend. A critical assumption is any fact (whether or not within the control of the taxpayer) related to the taxpayer, a third party, an industry, or business and economic conditions, the continued existence of which is material to the taxpayer's proposed TPM. Critical assumptions might include, for example, a particular mode of conducting business operations, a particular corporate or business structure, or a range of expected business volume. Rev. Proc. 2006–9, § 4.05. Failure to meet a critical assumption may render an APA inappropriate or unworkable. Most APAs contain only the standard critical assumption language set forth in Appendix B of the Model APA (Attachment A to this Announcement and Report). Where appropriate, additional critical assumption language may be added but the APA Program generally seeks to limit additional critical assumption language to objective, measurable benchmarks.

A critical assumption may change or fail to materialize due to changes in economic circumstances, such as a fundamental and dramatic change in the economic conditions of a particular industry. In addition, a critical assumption may change or fail to materialize due to a taxpayer's actions that are initiated for good faith business reasons, such as a change in business strategy, mode of conducting operations, or the cessation or transfer of a business segment or entity covered by the APA.

If a critical assumption has not been met, the APA may be revised by agreement of the parties. If such an agreement cannot be achieved, the APA is canceled. If a critical assumption has not been met, it requires taxpayer's notice to and discussion with the Service, and, in the case of a bilateral APA, competent authority consideration. Rev. Proc. 2006–9, § 11.05, 11.06.

Sources of Comparables, Selection Criteria, and the Nature of Adjustments to Comparables and Tested Parties
[§ 521(b)(2)(D)(v), (vi), and (vii)]

The sources of comparables, selection criteria, and rationale used in determining the selection criteria for APAs executed in 2006 are described in Tables 22 through 24 below. Various formulas for making adjustments to comparables are included as Attachment B.

TABLE 22: SOURCES OF COMPARABLES

Sources	Number of Times This Source Used
Compustat	73
Worldscope	19
Disclosure	13
Global Vantage	10
Mergent	7
Amadeus	5
Japanese Accounts and Data on Enterprises ("JADE")	4
Taxpayer's information on competition	4
Moody's	≤ 3
Other	6

TABLE 23: COMPARABLES SELECTION CRITERIA

Selection Criteria Considered	Number of Times This Criterion Used
Comparable functions	90
Comparable risks	71
Comparable industry	59
Comparable products	43
Comparable intangibles	38
Comparable terms	10

TABLE 24: ADJUSTMENTS TO COMPARABLES OR TESTED PARTIES

Adjustment	Number of Times Used
Balance sheet adjustments	
Inventory	64
Payables	62
Receivables	62
Property, plant, equipment	16
Other	≤ 3
Accounting adjustments	
LIFO to FIFO inventory accounting	29
Accounting reclassifications (*e.g.*, from COGS to operating expenses)	7
Marketing/ Procurement	≤ 3
Other	7
Profit level indicator adjustments (used to "back into" one PLI from another)	
Operating expense	≤ 3
Other	≤ 3
Miscellaneous adjustments	
Research & development	≤ 3
Advertising	≤ 3
Foreign exchange	≤ 3
Other	≤ 3

Discussion

At the core of most APAs are comparables. The APA Program works closely with taxpayers to find the best and most reliable comparables for each Covered Transaction. In some cases, CUPs or CUTs can be identified. In other cases, comparable business activities of independent companies are used in applying the CPM or a profit split method. Generally, in the APA Program's experience since 1991, CUPs and CUTs have been most often derived from the internal transactions of the taxpayer.

For profit-based methods in which comparable business activities or functions of independent companies are sought, the APA Program typically has selected them using a three-part process. First, a pool of potential comparables has been identified through broad searches. From this pool, companies having transactions that are clearly not comparable to those of the tested party have been eliminated through the use of quantitative and qualitative analyses, *i.e.*, quantitative screens and business descriptions. Then, based on a review of available descriptive and financial data, a set of comparable transactions or business activities of independent companies has been finalized. The comparability of the finalized set has then been enhanced through the application of adjustments.

Sources of Comparables

Comparables used in APAs can be U.S. or foreign, depending on the relevant market, the type of transaction being evaluated, the availability of relevant data, and the results of the functional and risk analyses. In general, comparables have been located by searching a variety of databases that provide data on U.S. publicly traded companies and on a combination of public and private non-U.S. companies. Table 22 shows the various databases and other sources used in selecting comparables for the APAs executed in 2006.

Although comparables were most often identified from the databases cited in Table 22, in some cases comparables were found from other sources, such as comparables derived internally from taxpayer transactions with third parties.

Selecting Comparables

Initial pools of potential comparables generally are derived from the databases using a combination of industry and keyword identifiers. Then, the pool is refined using a variety of selection criteria specific to the transaction or business activity being tested and the TPM being used.

The listed databases allow for searches by industrial classification, by keywords, or by both. These searches can yield a number of companies whose business activities may or may not be comparable to those of the entity being tested. Therefore, comparables based solely on industry classification or keyword searches are rarely used in APAs. Instead, the pool of comparables is examined closely, and companies are selected based on a combination of screens, business descriptions, and other information found in the companies' Annual Reports to shareholders and filings with the U.S. Securities and Exchange Commission (SEC).

Business activities are required to meet certain basic comparability criteria to be considered comparables. Functions, risks, economic conditions, and the property (product or intangible) and services associated with the transaction must be comparable. Determining comparability can be difficult – the goal has been to use comparability criteria restrictive enough to eliminate business activities that are not comparable, but yet not so restrictive as to have no comparables remaining. The APA Program normally has begun with relatively strict comparability criteria and then has relaxed them slightly if necessary to derive a pool of reliable comparables. A determination on the appropriate size of the comparables set, as well as the business activities that comprise the set, is highly fact-specific and depends on the reliability of the results.

In addition, the APA Program, consistent with the section 482 regulations, generally has looked at the results of comparables over a multi-year period. Often this has been a three-year or a five-year period, but other periods are sometimes used depending on the circumstances of the controlled transaction. Using a shorter period might result in the inclusion of comparables in different stages of economic development or use of atypical years of a comparable due to cyclical fluctuations in business conditions.

Many Covered Transactions have been tested with comparables that have been chosen using additional criteria and/or screens. These include sales level criteria and tests for financial distress and product comparability. These common selection criteria and screens have been used to increase the overall comparability of a group of companies and as a basis for further research. The sales level screen, for example, has been used to remove companies that, due to their size, might face fundamentally different economic conditions from those of the transaction or business activities being tested. In addition, APA analyses have incorporated selection criteria related to removing companies experiencing "financial distress" because of concerns that companies in financial distress often have experienced unusual circumstances that render them not comparable to the business activity being tested. These criteria include an unfavorable auditor's opinion, bankruptcy, failure to comply with financial obligations (*e.g.*, debt covenants), and, in certain circumstances, operating losses in a given number of years.

An additional important class of selection criteria is the development and ownership of intangible property. In some cases in which the business activity being tested is manufacturing, several criteria have been used to ensure, for example, that if the controlled entity does not own significant manufacturing intangibles or conduct research and development (R&D), then neither will the comparables. These selection criteria have included determining the importance of patents to a company or screening for R&D expenditures as a percentage of sales. Again, quantitative screens related to identifying comparables with significant intangible property generally have been used in conjunction with an understanding of the comparable derived from publicly available business information.

Selection criteria relating to asset comparability and operating expense comparability have also been used at times. A screen of property, plant, and equipment (PP&E) as a percentage of sales or assets, combined with a reading of a company's SEC filings, has been used to help ensure that distributors (generally lower PP&E) were not compared with manufacturers (generally higher PP&E), regardless of their industry classification. Similarly, a test involving the ratio of operating expenses to sales has helped to determine whether a company undertakes a significant marketing and distribution function.

Table 25 shows the number of times various screens were used in APAs executed in 2006:

TABLE 25: COMPARABILITY SCREENS

Comparability/Financial Distress Screen	Times Used
Comparability screens used	
Sales	48
R&D/ sales	43
Foreign sales/ total sales	15
Advertising expense/ sales	14
PP&E/ sales	6
SG&A/ sales	5
Non-startup or start-up	5
PP&E/ total assets	≤ 3
Operating expenses/ sales	≤ 3
Non-startup or startup	≤ 3
Government sales/ sales	≤ 3
Inventory/ sales	≤ 3
Intangible property/ total assets	≤ 3
Work in process inventory/ total inventory	≤ 3
Financial distress	
Bankruptcy	48
Losses in one or more years	33
Unfavorable auditor's opinion	31
Stopped filing public documents	≤ 3
No sales growth	≤ 3

Adjusting Comparables

After the comparables have been selected, the regulations require that "[i]f there are material differences between the controlled and uncontrolled transactions, adjustments must be made if the effect of such differences on prices or profits can be ascertained with sufficient accuracy to improve the reliability of the results." Treas. Reg. § 1.482–1(d)(2). In almost all cases involving income-statement-based PLIs used in the CPM or the Residual Profit Split Method, certain "asset intensity" or "balance sheet" adjustments for factors that have generally agreed-upon effects on profits are calculated. In addition, in specific cases, additional adjustments are performed to improve reliability.

The most common balance sheet adjustments used in APAs are adjustments for differences in accounts receivable, inventories, and accounts payable. The APA Program generally has required adjustments for receivables, inventory, and payables based on the principle that there is an opportunity cost for holding assets. For these assets, it is generally assumed that the cost is appropriately measured by the interest rate on short-term debt.

To compare the profits of two business activities with different relative levels of receivables, inventory, or payables, the APA Program estimates the carrying costs of each item and adjusts profits accordingly. Although different formulas have been used in specific APA cases, Attachment B presents one set of formulas used in many APAs. Underlying these formulas are the notions that (1) balance sheet items normally should be expressed as mid-year averages, (2) formulas should try to avoid using data items that are being tested by the TPM (for example, if sales are controlled, then the denominator of the balance sheet ratio should not be sales), (3) a short term interest rate should be used, and (4) an interest factor should recognize the average holding period of the relevant asset. During the course of 2006, the APA Program often used an interest rate equal to LIBOR (3 months) plus 200 basis points for purposes of calculating adjustments for accounts receivable and accounts payable for U.S. companies. However, the facts and circumstances surrounding a given case will ultimately determine the reliability of making balance sheet adjustments and the selection of the most reliable interest rate.

The APA Program also requires that data be compared on a consistent accounting basis. For example, although financial statements may be prepared on a first-in first-out (FIFO) basis, cross-company comparisons are less meaningful if one or more of the comparables use last-in first-out (LIFO) inventory accounting methods. This adjustment directly affects costs of goods sold and inventories, and therefore affects both profitability measures and inventory adjustments.

Still important in some cases is the adjustment for differences in relative levels of PP&E between a tested business activity and the comparables. Ideally, comparables and the business activity being tested will have fairly similar relative levels of PP&E, since major differences can be a sign of fundamentally different functions and risks. Typically, the PP&E adjustment is made using a medium term interest rate. During the course of 2006, the APA Program often used the Corporate Bonds (Moody's) Baa rate as the interest rate for purposes of calculating adjustments for inventory and PP&E for U.S. companies. Again, however, the facts and circumstances surrounding a given case will ultimately determine the reliability of making balance sheet adjustments and the selection of the most reliable interest rate.

Additional adjustments used less frequently include those for differences in other balance sheet items, operating expenses, R&D, or currency risk. Accounting adjustments, such as reclassifying items from cost of goods sold to operating expenses, are also made when warranted to increase reliability. Often, data are not available for both the controlled and uncontrolled transactions in sufficient detail to allow for these types of adjustments.

The adjustments made to comparables or tested parties in APAs executed in 2006 are reflected in Table 24 above.

Ranges, Targets, and Adjustment Mechanisms

[§ 521(b)(2)(D)(viii)–(ix)]

The types of ranges, targets, and adjustment mechanisms used in APAs executed in 2006 are described in Table 26 and 27 below.

TABLE 26: RANGES AND TARGETS[4]

Type of Range or Target	Number
Interquartile range	68
Specific point (royalty)	18
Specific point within CPM range (not floor or ceiling)	13
Full range	5
Floor (*i.e.*, result must be no less than x)	4
Specific point (profit split)	≤ 3
Specific point (CUP)	≤ 3
Ceiling (*i.e.*, result must be no more than x)	≤ 3
Narrower range within interquartile range	≤ 3
Other	5

[4] The numbers do not include TPMs with cost or cost-plus methodologies.

TABLE 27: ADJUSTMENT MECHANISMS

Adjustment mechanism	Number
Taxpayer makes an adjustment: to specified point or royalty rate	41
Taxpayer makes an adjustment: to closest edge of single year	28
Taxpayer makes an adjustment: to closest edge of multi-year average	20
Taxpayer makes an adjustment: to median of current year	12
Taxpayer makes an adjustment: to median of multi-year average	11
Taxpayer makes an adjustment: to other	≤ 3
Other	≤ 3

Discussion

Treas. Reg. § 1.482–1(e)(1) states that sometimes a pricing method will yield "a single result that is the most reliable measure of an arm's length result." Sometimes, however, a method may yield "a range of reliable results," called the "arm's length range." A taxpayer whose results fall within the arm's length range will not be subject to adjustment.

Under Treas. Reg. § 1.482–1(e)(2)(i), such a range is normally derived by considering a set of more than one comparable uncontrolled transaction of similar comparability and reliability. If these comparables are of very high quality, as defined in the section 482 regulations, then under Treas. Reg. § 1.482–1(e)(2)(iii)(A), the arm's length range includes the results of all of the comparables (from the least to the greatest). However, the APA Program has only rarely identified cases meeting the requirements for the full range. If the comparables are of lesser quality, then under Treas. Reg. § 1.482–1(e)(2)(iii)(B), "the reliability of the analysis must be increased, when it is possible to do so, by adjusting the range through application of a valid statistical method to the results of all of the uncontrolled comparables." One such method, the "interquartile range," is ordinarily acceptable, although a different statistical method "may be applied if it provides a more reliable measure." The "interquartile range" is defined as, roughly, the range from the 25th to the 75th percentile of the comparables' results. See Treas. Reg. § 1.482–1(e)(2)(iii)(C). The interquartile range was used 68 times in 2006.

Thirty-eight or more Covered Transactions reflected on Table 26 were tested against a single, specific result. Thirteen of these Covered Transactions involved a CPM in which the taxpayer agreed to a "point." Some APAs – deliberately infrequent – specify not a point or a range, but a "floor" or a "ceiling". When a floor is used, the tested party's result must be greater than or equal to some particular value. When a ceiling is used, the tested party's result must be less than or equal to some particular value. Four APAs executed in 2006 used a floor and three or fewer used a ceiling.

Some APAs look to a tested party's results over a period of years (multi-year averaging) to determine whether a taxpayer has complied with the APA. In 2006, rolling multi-year averaging was used for 15 Covered Transactions. Ten of those used three-year averages. Nine Covered Transactions used a cumulative multi-year average, while 18 Covered Transactions used term averages and three or fewer Covered Transactions used partial term averages.

Adjustments

Under Treas. Reg. § 1.482–1(e)(3), if a taxpayer's results fall outside the arm's length range, the Service may adjust the result "to any point within the arm's length range." Accordingly, an APA may permit or require a taxpayer to make an intercompany adjustment after the year's end to put the year's results within the range, or at the point specified by the APA. Similarly, to enforce the terms of an APA, the Service may make such an adjustment. When the APA specifies a range, the adjustment is sometimes to the closest edge of the range, and sometimes to another point such as the median of the interquartile range. Depending on the facts of each case, automatic adjustments are not always permitted. APAs may specify that in such a case there will be a negotiation between the competent authorities involved to determine whether and to what extent an adjustment should be made. APAs may permit automatic adjustments unless the result is far outside the range specified in the APA. Thus, APAs provide flexibility and efficiency, permitting adjustments when normal business fluctuations and uncertainties push the result somewhat outside the range.

Where a taxpayer's actual transactions do not comply with the TPM, a taxpayer must nonetheless report its taxable income in an amount consistent with the TPM (an APA primary adjustment), as further discussed in § 11.02 of Rev. Proc. 2006–9.

APA Term and Rollback Lengths
[§ 521(b)(2)(D)(x)]

The various term lengths for APAs executed in 2006 are set forth in Table 28 below:

TABLE 28: TERMS OF APAs

APA Term in Years	Number of APAs
1	0
2	1
3	6
4	3
5	46
6	8
7	9
8	6
9	1
10 or more	2

The number of rollback years to which an APA TPM was applied in 2006 is set forth in Table 29 below:

TABLE 29: NUMBER OF YEARS COVERED BY ROLLBACK OF APA TPM

Number of Rollback Years	Number of APAs
1	1
2	4
3	3
4	2
5 or more	5

Nature of Documentation Required
[§ 521(b)(2)(D)(xi)]

APAs executed in 2006 required that taxpayers provide various documents with their annual reports. These documents are described in Table 30 below:

TABLE 30: NATURE OF DOCUMENTATION REQUIRED

Documentation	Number of Times Required
Statement identifying all material differences between Taxpayer's business operations during APA Year and description of Taxpayer's business operations contained in Taxpayer's request for APA, or if there have been no such material differences, a statement to that effect	82
Description of any failure to meet Critical Assumptions or, if there have been none, a statement to that effect	82
Statement identifying all material changes in Taxpayer's accounting methods and classifications, and methods of estimation, from those described or used in Taxpayer's request for APA, or if there have been none, statement to that effect	82
Description of, reason for, and financial analysis of, any Compensating Adjustments with respect to APA Year, including means by which any Compensating Adjustment has been or will be satisfied	82
Financial analysis demonstrating Taxpayer's compliance with TPM	82
Organizational chart	82
Financial statements as prepared in accordance with US GAAP	71
Certified public accountant's opinion that financial statements present fairly financial position of Taxpayer and the results of its operations, in accordance with US GAAP	71
Financial statements as prepared in accordance with a foreign GAAP	15
Certified public accountant's opinion that financial statements present fairly financial position of Taxpayer and the results of its operations, in accordance with a foreign GAAP	11
Book to tax reconciliations	9
Schedule of costs and expenses (*e.g.*, intercompany allocations)	8
Certified public accountant's review of financial statements	8
Various work papers	7
United States income tax return	5
Profit & Loss statement	4
Changes in entity classifications	4
Changes in Taxpayer notice information	≤ 3
Description of special accounting treatment for certain income items	≤ 3
Reconciliation of foreign to US GAAP	≤ 3
Other	4

Approaches for Sharing of Currency or Other Risks
[§ 521(b)(2)(D)(xii)]

During 2006, there were 36 tested parties that faced financial risks, including interest rate and currency risks. In appropriate cases, APAs may provide specific approaches for dealing with currency risk, such as adjustment mechanisms and/or critical assumptions.

Efforts to Ensure Compliance with APAs

[§ 521(b)(2)(F)]

As described in Rev. Proc. 2006–9, § 11.01, APA taxpayers are required to file annual reports to demonstrate compliance with the terms and conditions of the APA. The filing and review of annual reports is a critical part of the APA process. Through annual report review, the APA Program monitors taxpayer compliance with the APA on a contemporaneous basis. Annual report review provides current information on the success or problems associated with the various TPMs adopted in the APA process.

All reports received by the APA office are tracked by one designated APA team leader who also has the primary responsibility for annual report review. Other APA team leaders and economists assist in this review, especially when the team leader who negotiated the case is available since that person will already be familiar with the relevant facts and terms of the agreement. Once received by the APA office, the annual report is sent out to the district personnel with exam jurisdiction over the taxpayer.

The statistics for the review of APA annual reports are reflected in Table 31 below. As of December 31, 2006, there were 256 pending annual reports. In 2006, 537 reports were closed.

TABLE 31: STATISTICS OF ANNUAL REPORTS

Number of APA annual reports pending as of December 31, 2006	256
Number of APA annual reports closed in Year 2006	537
Number of APA annual reports requiring adjustment in Year 2006	12
Number of taxpayers involved in adjustments	6
Number of APA annual report cases over one year old	93

ATTACHMENT A
Model APA – Based on Revenue Procedure 2006–9

ADVANCE PRICING AGREEMENT
between
[*Insert Taxpayer's Name*]
and
THE INTERNAL REVENUE SERVICE

PARTIES

The Parties to this Advance Pricing Agreement (APA) are the Internal Revenue Service (IRS) and [*Insert Taxpayer's Name*], EIN _______.

RECITALS

[*Insert Taxpayer Name*] is the common parent of an affiliated group filing consolidated U.S. tax returns (collectively referred to as "Taxpayer"), and is entering into this APA on behalf of itself and other members of its consolidated group.

Taxpayer's principal place of business is [*City, State*]. [*Insert general description of taxpayer and other relevant parties*].

This APA contains the Parties' agreement on the best method for determining arm's-length prices of the Covered Transactions under I.R.C. section 482, any applicable tax treaties, and the Treasury Regulations.

{If renewal, add} [Taxpayer and IRS previously entered into an APA covering taxable years ending _________ to _________, executed on _________.]

AGREEMENT

The Parties agree as follows:

1. *Covered Transactions.* This APA applies to the Covered Transactions, as defined in Appendix A.

2. *Transfer Pricing Method.* Appendix A sets forth the Transfer Pricing Method (TPM) for the Covered Transactions.

3. *Term.* This APA applies to Taxpayer's taxable years ending _______ through _______ (APA Term).

4. *Operation.*

a. Revenue Procedure 2006–9 governs the interpretation, legal effect, and administration of this APA.

b. Nonfactual oral and written representations, within the meaning of sections 10.04 and 10.05 of Revenue Procedure 2006–9 (including any proposals to use particular TPMs), made in conjunction with the APA Request constitute statements made in compromise negotiations within the meaning of Rule 408 of the Federal Rules of Evidence.

5. *Compliance.*

a. Taxpayer must report its taxable income in an amount that is consistent with Appendix A and all other requirements of this APA on its timely filed U.S. Return. However, if Taxpayer's timely filed U.S. Return for an APA Year is filed prior to, or no later than 60 days after, the effective date of this APA, then Taxpayer must report its taxable income for that APA Year in an amount that is consistent with Appendix A and all other requirements of this APA either on the original U.S. Return or on an amended U.S. Return filed no later than 120 days after the effective date of this APA, or through such other means as may be specified herein.

b. {*Insert when U.S. Group or Foreign Group contains more than one member.*} [This APA addresses the arm's-length nature of prices charged or received in the aggregate between Taxpayer and Foreign Participants with respect to the Covered Transactions. Except as explicitly provided, this APA does not address and does not bind the IRS with respect to prices charged or received, or the relative amounts of income or loss realized, by particular legal entities that are members of U.S. Group or that are members of Foreign Group.]

c. For each taxable year covered by this APA (APA Year), if Taxpayer complies with the terms and conditions of this APA, then the IRS will not make or propose any allocation or adjustment under I.R.C. section 482 to the amounts charged in the aggregate between Taxpayer and Foreign Participant[s] with respect to the Covered Transactions.

d. If Taxpayer does not comply with the terms and conditions of this APA, then the IRS may:

i. enforce the terms and conditions of this APA and make or propose allocations or adjustments under I.R.C. section 482 consistent with this APA;

ii. cancel or revoke this APA under section 11.06 of Revenue Procedure 2006–9; or

iii. revise this APA, if the Parties agree.

e. Taxpayer must timely file an Annual Report (an original and four copies) for each APA Year in accordance with Appendix C and section 11.01 of Revenue Procedure 2006–9. Taxpayer must file the Annual Report for all APA Years through the APA Year ending [insert year] by [insert date]. Taxpayer must file the Annual Report for each subsequent APA Year by [insert month and day] immediately following the close of that APA Year. (If any date falls on a weekend or holiday, the Annual Report shall be due on the next date that is not a weekend or holiday.) The IRS may request additional information reasonably necessary to clarify or complete the Annual Report. Taxpayer will provide such requested information within 30 days. Additional time may be allowed for good cause.

f. The IRS will determine whether Taxpayer has complied with this APA based on Taxpayer's U.S. Returns, Financial Statements, and other APA Records, for the APA Term and any other year necessary to verify compliance. For Taxpayer to comply with this APA, an independent certified public accountant must *{use the following or an alternative}* render an opinion that Taxpayer's Financial Statements present fairly, in all material respects, Taxpayer's financial position under U.S. GAAP.

g. In accordance with section 11.04 of Revenue Procedure 2006–9, Taxpayer will (1) maintain its APA Records, and (2) make them available to the IRS in connection with an examination under section 11.03. Compliance with this subparagraph constitutes compliance with the record-maintenance provisions of I.R.C. sections 6038A and 6038C for the Covered Transactions for any taxable year during the APA Term.

h. The True Taxable Income within the meaning of Treasury Regulations sections 1.482–1(a)(1) and (i)(9) of a member of an affiliated group filing a U.S. consolidated return will be determined under the I.R.C. section 1502 Treasury Regulations.

i. *{Optional for US Parent Signatories}* To the extent that Taxpayer's compliance with this APA depends on certain acts of Foreign Group members, Taxpayer will ensure that each Foreign Group member will perform such acts.

6. *Critical Assumptions*. This APA's critical assumptions, within the meaning of Revenue Procedure 2006–9, section 4.05, appear in Appendix B. If any critical assumption has not been met, then Revenue Procedure 2006–9, section 11.06, governs.

7. *Disclosure*. This APA, and any background information related to this APA or the APA Request, are: (1) considered "return information" under I.R.C. section 6103(b)(2)(C); and (2) not subject to public inspection as a "written determination" under I.R.C. section 6110(b)(1). Section 521(b) of Pub. L. 106–170 provides that the Secretary of the Treasury must prepare a report for public disclosure that includes certain specifically designated information concerning all APAs, including this APA, in a form that does not reveal taxpayers' identities, trade secrets, and proprietary or confidential business or financial information.

8. *Disputes*. If a dispute arises concerning the interpretation of this APA, the Parties will seek a resolution by the IRS Associate Chief Counsel (International) to the extent reasonably practicable, before seeking alternative remedies.

9. *Materiality*. In this APA the terms "material" and "materially" will be interpreted consistently with the definition of "material facts" in Revenue Procedure 2006–9, section 11.06(4).

10. *Section Captions*. This APA's section captions, which appear in *italics*, are for convenience and reference only. The captions do not affect in any way the interpretation or application of this APA.

11. *Terms and Definitions*. Unless otherwise specified, terms in the plural include the singular and vice versa. Appendix D contains definitions for capitalized terms not elsewhere defined in this APA.

12. *Entire Agreement and Severability*. This APA is the complete statement of the Parties' agreement. The Parties will sever, delete, or reform any invalid or unenforceable provision in this APA to approximate the Parties' intent as nearly as possible.

13. *Successor in Interest*. This APA binds, and inures to the benefit of, any successor in interest to Taxpayer.

14. *Notice*. Any notices required by this APA or Revenue Procedure 2006–9 must be in writing. Taxpayer will send notices to the IRS at the address and in the manner set forth in Revenue Procedure 2006–9, section 4.11. The IRS will send notices to:

Taxpayer Corporation
Attn: Jane Doe, Sr. Vice President (Taxes)
1000 Any Road
Any City, USA 10000
(phone: __________)

15. *Effective Date and Counterparts.* This APA is effective starting on the date, or later date of the dates, upon which all Parties execute this APA. The Parties may execute this APA in counterparts, with each counterpart constituting an original.

WITNESS,

The Parties have executed this APA on the dates below.

[Taxpayer Name in all caps]

By: ____ Date: ________, 20 _____
Jane Doe
Sr. Vice President (Taxes)

IRS

By: ____ Date: ________, 20 _____
Matthew W. Frank
Director, Advance Pricing Agreement Program

APPENDIX A

COVERED TRANSACTIONS AND TRANSFER PRICING METHOD (TPM)

1. Covered Transactions.

[*Define the Covered Transactions.*]

2. TPM.

{Note: If appropriate, adapt language from the following examples.}

[The Tested Party is __________.]

- **CUP Method**

The TPM is the comparable uncontrolled price (CUP) method. The Arm's Length Range of the price charged for __________ is between __________ and __________ per unit.

- **CUT Method**

The TPM is the CUT Method. The Arm's Length Range of the royalty charged for the license of __________ is between _____% and _____ % of [Taxpayer's, Foreign Participants', or other specified party's] Net Sales Revenue. [Insert definition of net sales revenue or other royalty base.]

- **Resale Price Method (RPM)**

The TPM is the resale price method (RPM). The Tested Party's Gross Margin for any APA Year is defined as follows: the Tested Party's gross profit divided by its sales revenue (as those terms are defined in Treasury Regulations sections 1.482–5(d)(1) and (2)) for that APA Year. The Arm's Length Range is between _____% and _____ %, and the Median of the Arm's Length Range is _____%.

• **Cost Plus Method**

The TPM is the cost plus method. The Tested Party's Cost Plus Markup is defined as follows for any APA Year: the Tested Party's ratio of gross profit to production costs (as those terms are defined in Treasury Regulations sections 1.482–3(d)(1) and (2)) for that APA Year. The Arm's Length Range is between ____% and ____%, and the Median of the Arm's Length Range is ____%.

• **CPM with Berry Ratio PLI**

The TPM is the comparable profits method (CPM). The profit level indicator is a Berry Ratio. The Tested Party's Berry Ratio is defined as follows for any APA Year: the Tested Party's gross profit divided by its operating expenses (as those terms are defined in Treasury Regulations sections 1.482–5(d)(2) and (3)) for that APA Year. The Arm's Length Range is between ______ and ______, and the Median of the Arm's Length Range is ______.

• **CPM using an Operating Margin PLI**

The TPM is the comparable profits method (CPM). The profit level indicator is an operating margin. The Tested Party's Operating Margin is defined as follows for any APA Year: the Tested Party's operating profit divided by its sales revenue (as those terms are defined in Treasury Regulations section 1.482–5(d)(1) and (4)) for that APA Year. The Arm's Length Range is between ____% and ____ %, and the Median of the Arm's Length Range is ____%.

• **CPM using a Three-year Rolling Average Operating Margin PLI**

The TPM is the comparable profits method (CPM). The profit level indicator is an operating margin. The Tested Party's Three-Year Rolling Average operating margin is defined as follows for any APA Year: the sum of the Tested Party's operating profit (within the meaning of Treasury Regulations section 1.482–5(d)(4) for that APA Year and the two preceding years, divided by the sum of its sales revenue (within the meaning of Treasury Regulations section 1.482–5(d)(1)) for that APA Year and the two preceding years. The Arm's Length Range is between ____% and ____%, and the Median of the Arm's Length Range is ____%.

• **Residual Profit Split Method**

The TPM is the residual profit split method. [*Insert description of routine profit level determinations and residual profit-split mechanism*].

[*Insert additional provisions as needed.*]

3. Application of TPM.

For any APA Year, if the results of Taxpayer's actual transactions produce a [price per unit, royalty rate for the Covered Transactions] [or] [Gross Margin, Cost Plus Markup, Berry Ratio, Operating Margin, Three-Year Rolling Average Operating Margin for the Tested Party] within the Arm's Length Range, then the amounts reported on Taxpayer's U.S. Return must clearly reflect such results.

For any APA year, if the results of Taxpayer's actual transactions produce a [price per unit, royalty rate] [or] [Gross Margin, Cost Plus Markup, Berry Ratio, Operating Margin, Three-Year Rolling Average Operating Margin for the Tested Party] outside the Arm's Length Range, then amounts reported on Taxpayer's U.S. Return must clearly reflect an adjustment that brings the [price per unit, royalty rate] [or] [Tested Party's Gross Margin, Cost Plus Markup, Berry Ratio, Operating Margin, Three-Year Rolling Average Operating Margin] to the Median.

For purposes of this Appendix A, the "results of Taxpayer's actual transactions" means the results reflected in Taxpayer's and Tested Party's books and records as computed under U.S. GAAP [*insert another relevant accounting standard if applicable*], with the following adjustments:

(a) [The fair value of stock-based compensation as disclosed in the Tested Party's audited financial statements shall be treated as an operating expense]; and

(b) To the extent that the results in any prior APA Year are relevant (for example, to compute a multi-year average), such results shall be adjusted to reflect the amount of any adjustment made for that prior APA Year under this Appendix A.

4. APA Revenue Procedure Treatment

If Taxpayer makes a primary adjustment under the terms of this Appendix A, Taxpayer may elect APA Revenue Procedure Treatment in accordance with section 11.02(3) of Revenue Procedure 2006–9.

[*Insert additional provisions as needed.*]

APPENDIX B

CRITICAL ASSUMPTIONS

This APA's critical assumptions are:

1. The business activities, functions performed, risks assumed, assets employed, and financial and tax accounting methods and classifications [and methods of estimation] of Taxpayer in relation to the Covered Transactions will remain materially the same as described or used in Taxpayer's APA Request. A mere change in business results will not be a material change.

[*Insert additional provisions as needed.*]

APPENDIX C

APA RECORDS AND ANNUAL REPORT

APA RECORDS

The APA Records will consist of:

1. All documents listed below for inclusion in the Annual Report, as well as all documents, notes, work papers, records, or other writings that support the information provided in such documents.

ANNUAL REPORT

The Annual Report will include two copies of a properly completed APA Annual Report Summary in the form of Exhibit E to this APA, one copy of the form bound with, and one copy bound separately from, the rest of the Annual Report. In addition, the Annual Report will include a table of contents and the information and exhibits identified below, organized as follows.

1. Statements that fully identify, describe, analyze, and explain:

a. All material differences between any of the U.S. Entities' business operations (including functions, risks assumed, markets, contractual terms, economic conditions, property, services, and assets employed) during the APA Year and the description of the business operations contained in the APA Request. If there have been no material differences, the Annual Report will include a statement to that effect.

b. All material changes in the U.S. Entities' accounting methods and classifications, and methods of estimation, from those described or used in Taxpayer's request for this APA. If any such change was made to conform to changes in U.S. GAAP (or other relevant accounting standards), Taxpayer will specifically identify such change. If there has been no material change in accounting methods and classifications or methods of estimation, the Annual Report will include a statement to that effect.

c. Any change to the Taxpayer notice information in section 14 of this APA.

d. Any failure to meet any critical assumption. If there has been no failure, the Annual Report will include a statement to that effect.

e. Any change to any entity classification for federal income tax purposes (including any change that causes an entity to be disregarded for federal income tax purposes) of any Worldwide Group member that is a party to the Covered Transactions or is otherwise relevant to the TPM.

f. The amount, reason for, and financial analysis of any compensating adjustments under paragraph 4 of Appendix A and Revenue Procedure 2006–9, section 11.02(3), for the APA Year, including but not limited to:

i. the amounts paid or received by each affected entity;

ii. the character (such as capital, ordinary, income, expense) and country source of the funds transferred, and the specific affected line item(s) of any affected U.S. Return; and

iii. the date(s) and means by which the payments are or will be made.

g. The amounts, description, reason for, and financial analysis of any book-tax difference relevant to the TPM for the APA Year, as reflected on Schedule M–1 or Schedule M–3 of the U.S. Return for the APA Year.

2. The Financial Statements, and any necessary account detail to show compliance with the TPM, with a copy of the independent certified public accountant's opinion required by paragraph 5(f) of this APA.

3. A financial analysis that reflects Taxpayer's TPM calculations for the APA Year. The calculations must reconcile with and reference the Financial Statements in sufficient account detail to allow the IRS to determine whether Taxpayer has complied with the TPM.

4. An organizational chart for the Worldwide Group, revised annually to reflect all ownership or structural changes of entities that are parties to the Covered Transactions or are otherwise relevant to the TPM.

5. A copy of the APA.

APPENDIX D

DEFINITIONS

The following definitions control for all purposes of this APA. The definitions appear alphabetically below:

Term	Definition
Annual Report	A report within the meaning of Revenue Procedure 2006–9, section 11.01.
APA	This Advance Pricing Agreement, which is an "advance pricing agreement" within the meaning of Revenue Procedure 2006–9, section 2.04.
APA Records	The records specified in Appendix C.
APA Request	Taxpayer's request for this APA dated ________, including any amendments or supplemental or additional information thereto.
Covered Transaction(s)	This term is defined in Appendix A.
Financial Statements	Financial statements prepared in accordance with U.S. GAAP and stated in U.S. dollars.
Foreign Group	Worldwide Group members that are not U.S. persons.
Foreign Participants	[name the foreign entities involved in Covered Transactions].
I.R.C.	The Internal Revenue Code of 1986, 26 U.S.C., as amended.
Pub. L. 106–170	The Ticket to Work and Work Incentives Improvement Act of 1999.
Revenue Procedure 2006–9	Rev. Proc. 2006–9, 2006–2 I.R.B. 278.
Transfer Pricing Method (TPM)	A transfer pricing method within the meaning of Treasury Regulations section 1.482–1(b) and Revenue Procedure 2006–9, section 2.04.
U.S. GAAP	U.S. generally-accepted accounting principles.
U.S. Group	Worldwide Group members that are U.S. persons.
U.S. Return	For each taxable year, the "returns with respect to income taxes under subtitle A" that Taxpayer must "make" in accordance with I.R.C. section 6012. {*Or substitute for partnership:* For each taxable year, the "return" that Taxpayer must "make" in accordance with I.R.C. section 6031.}
Worldwide Group	Taxpayer and all organizations, trades, businesses, entities, or branches (whether or not incorporated, organized in the United States, or affiliated) owned or controlled directly or indirectly by the same interests.

APPENDIX E

APA ANNUAL REPORT SUMMARY FORM

The APA Annual Report Summary on the next page is a required APA Record. The APA Team Leader has supplied some of the information requested on the form. Taxpayer is to supply the remaining information requested by the form and submit the form as part of its Annual Report.

APA Annual Report SUMMARY	**Department of the Treasury— Internal Revenue Service Office of Associate Chief Counsel (International) Advance Pricing Agreement Program**	APA no. ______ Team Leader ______ Economist ______ Intl Examiner ______ CA Analyst ______

APA Information	
	Taxpayer Name: ______
	Taxpayer EIN:______ NAICS:______
	APA Term: Taxable years ending ______ to ______.
	Original APA [ ] Renewal APA [ ]
	Annual Report due dates: ______, 200__ for all APA Years through APA Year ending in 200__; for each APA Year thereafter, on ______ [month and day] immediately following the close of the APA Year.
	Principal foreign country(ies) involved in covered transaction(s): ______
	Type of APA: [ ] unilateral [ ] bilateral with ______
	Tested party is [ ] US [ ] foreign [ ] both
	Approximate dollar volume of covered transactions (on an annual basis) involving tangible goods and services: [ ] N/A [ ] <$50 million [ ] $50–100 million [ ] $100–250 million [ ] $250–500 million [ ] >$500 million
	APA tests on (check all that apply): [ ] annual basis [ ] multi-year basis [ ] term basis
	APA provides (check all that apply) a: [ ] range [ ] point [ ] floor only [ ] ceiling only [ ] other ______
	APA provides for adjustment (check all that apply) to: [ ] nearest edge [ ] median [ ] other point

<table>
<tr><td>APA Annual Report Information
(to be completed by the Taxpayer)</td><td>APA date executed: ________________, 200__
This APA Annual Report Summary is for APA Year(s) ending in 200__ and was filed on ______, 200__
Check here [ ] if Annual Report was filed after original due date but in accordance with extension.
Has this APA been amended or changed? [ ] yes [ ] no Effective Date: ____________
Has Taxpayer complied with all APA terms and conditions? [ ] yes [ ] no
Were all the critical assumptions met? [ ] yes [ ] no
Has a Primary Compensating Adjustment been made in any APA Year covered by this Annual Report?
[ ] yes [ ] no If yes, which year(s): 200__
Have any necessary Secondary Compensating Adjustments been made? [ ] yes [ ] no
Did Taxpayer elect APA Revenue Procedure treatment? [ ] yes [ ] no
Any change to the entity classification of a party to the APA? [ ] yes [ ] no
Taxpayer notice information contained in the APA remains unchanged? [ ] yes [ ] no
Taxpayer's current US principal place of business: (City, State) ________________________</td></tr>
</table>

<table>
<tr><td rowspan="12">APA Annual Report Checklist of Key Contents
(to be completed by the Taxpayer)</td><td>Financial analysis reflecting TPM calculations</td><td>[ ] yes [ ] no</td></tr>
<tr><td>Financial statements showing compliance with TPM(s)</td><td>[ ] yes [ ] no</td></tr>
<tr><td>Schedule M–1 or M–3 book-tax differences</td><td>[ ] yes [ ] no</td></tr>
<tr><td>Current organizational chart of relevant portion of world-wide group</td><td>[ ] yes [ ] no</td></tr>
<tr><td>Attach copy of APA</td><td>[ ] yes [ ] no</td></tr>
<tr><td colspan="2">Other APA records and documents included:</td></tr>
<tr><td colspan="2">[The information required in the following section should be tailored to the particular case]</td></tr>
<tr><td>____________________</td><td>[ ] yes [ ] no</td></tr>
<tr><td>____________________</td><td>[ ] yes [ ] no</td></tr>
<tr><td>____________________</td><td>[ ] yes [ ] no</td></tr>
<tr><td>____________________</td><td>[ ] yes [ ] no</td></tr>
<tr><td>____________________</td><td>[ ] yes [ ] no</td></tr>
</table>

<table>
<tr><td rowspan="2">Contact Information</td><td>Authorized Representative</td><td>Phone Number</td><td>Affiliation and Address</td></tr>
<tr><td></td><td></td><td></td></tr>
</table>

ATTACHMENT B

FORMULAS FOR BALANCE SHEET ADJUSTMENTS

Definitions of Variables:

AP	=	average accounts payable
AR	=	average trade accounts receivable, net of allowance for bad debt
cogs	=	cost of goods sold
INV	=	average inventory, stated on FIFO basis
opex	=	operating expenses (general, sales, administrative, and depreciation expenses)
PPE	=	property, plant, and equipment, net of accumulated depreciation
sales	=	net sales
tc	=	total cost (cogs + opex, as defined above)
h	=	average accounts payable or trade accounts receivable holding period, stated as a fraction of a year
i	=	interest rate
t	=	entity being tested
c	=	comparable

Equations:

If Cost of Goods Sold is controlled (generally, sales in denominator of PLI):

Receivables Adjustment ("RA"): $RA = \{[(AR_t / sales_t) \times sales_c] - AR_c\} \times \{i/[1+(i \times h_c)]\}$

Payables Adjustment ("PA"): $PA = \{[(AP_t / sales_t) \times sales_c] - AP_c\} \times \{i/[1+(i \times h_c)]\}$

Inventory Adjustment ("IA"): $IA = \{[(INV_t / sales_t) \times sales_c] - INV_c\} \times i$

PP&E Adjustment ("PPEA"): $PPEA = \{[(PPE_t / sales_t) \times sales_c] - PPE_c\} \times i$

If Sales are controlled (generally, costs in the denominator of PLI):[5]

Receivables Adjustment ("RA"): $RA = \{[(AR_t / tc_t) \times tc_c] - AR_c\} \times \{i/[1+(i \times h_c)]\}$

Payables Adjustment ("PA"): $PA = \{[(AP_t / tc_t) \times tc_c] - AP_c\} \times \{i/[1+(i \times h_c)]\}$

Inventory Adjustment ("IA"): $IA = \{[(INV_t / tc_t) \times tc_c] - INV_c\} \times i$

PP&E Adjustment ("PPEA"): $PPEA = \{[(PPE_t / tc_t) \times tc_c] - PPE_c\} \times i$

Then Adjust Comparables as Follows:

adjusted $sales_c = sales_c + RA$

adjusted $cogs_c = cogs_c + PA - IA$

adjusted $opex_c = opex_c - PPEA$

[5] Depending on the specific facts, the equations below may use total costs ("tc") or cost of goods sold ("cogs").

Part I. Rulings and Decisions Under the Internal Revenue Code of 1986

Section 61.—Gross Income Defined

26 CFR 1.61–21: Taxation of fringe benefits.

Fringe benefits aircraft valuation formula. The Standard Industry Fare Level (SIFL) cents-per-mile rates and terminal charge in effect for the first half of 2007 are set forth for purposes of determining the value of noncommercial flights on employer-provided aircraft under section 1.61–21(g) of the regulations.

Rev. Rul. 2007–17

For purposes of the taxation of fringe benefits under section 61 of the Internal Revenue Code, section 1.61–21(g) of the Income Tax Regulations provides a rule for valuing noncommercial flights on employer-provided aircraft. Section 1.61–21(g)(5) provides an aircraft valuation formula to determine the value of such flights. The value of a flight is determined under the base aircraft valuation formula (also known as the Standard Industry Fare Level formula or SIFL) by multiplying the SIFL cents-per-mile rates applicable for the period during which the flight was taken by the appropriate aircraft multiple provided in section 1.61–21(g)(7) and then adding the applicable terminal charge. The SIFL cents-per-mile rates in the formula and the terminal charge are calculated by the Department of Transportation and are reviewed semi-annually.

The following chart sets forth the terminal charge and SIFL mileage rates:

Period During Which the Flight Is Taken	*Terminal Charge*	*SIFL Mileage Rates*
1/1/07 - 6/30/07	$37.92	Up to 500 miles = $.2075 per mile
		501–1500 miles = $.1582 per mile
		Over 1500 miles = $.1521 per mile

DRAFTING INFORMATION

The principal author of this revenue ruling is Kathleen Edmondson of the Office of Division Counsel/Associate Chief Counsel (Tax Exempt/Government Entities). For further information regarding this revenue ruling, contact Ms. Edmondson at (202) 622–0047 (not a toll-free call).

Section 368.—Definitions Relating to Corporate Reorganizations

26 CFR 1.368–2T: Definition of terms (temporary).

T.D. 9313

DEPARTMENT OF THE TREASURY
Internal Revenue Service
26 CFR Part 1

Corporate Reorganizations; Additional Guidance on Distributions Under Sections 368(a)(1)(D) and 354(b)(1)(B)

AGENCY: Internal Revenue Service (IRS), Treasury.

ACTION: Temporary regulations.

SUMMARY: This document contains temporary regulations amending §1.368–2T(l), which provides guidance regarding the qualification of certain transactions as reorganizations described in section 368(a)(1)(D) where no stock and/or securities of the acquiring corporation are issued and distributed in the transaction. These regulations clarify that the rules in §1.368–2T(l) are not intended to affect the qualification of related party triangular asset acquisitions as reorganizations described in section 368. These regulations affect corporations engaging in such transactions and their shareholders. The text of the temporary regulations also serves as the text of the proposed regulations (REG–157834–06) set forth in the notice of proposed rulemaking on this subject in this issue of the Bulletin.

DATES: *Effective Date:* These regulations are effective on March 1, 2007.

Applicability Date: For dates of applicability, see §1.368–2T(l)(4)(i).

FOR FURTHER INFORMATION CONTACT: Bruce A. Decker at (202) 622–7550 (not a toll-free number).

SUPPLEMENTARY INFORMATION:

Background

On December 19, 2006, the IRS and Treasury Department published temporary regulations (T.D. 9303, 2007–5 I.R.B. 379) under §1.368–2T(l) in the **Federal Register** (71 FR 75879) providing guidance regarding the qualification of certain transactions as reorganizations described in section 368(a)(1)(D) where no stock and/or securities of the acquiring corporation are issued and distributed in the transaction. Under the temporary regulations, in cases where it is determined that the same person or persons own, directly or indirectly, all of the stock of the transferor and transferee corporations in identical proportions, the distribution requirement under sections 368(a)(1)(D) and 354(b)(1)(B) will be treated as satisfied even though no stock is actually issued in the transaction.

In each case where it is determined that the same person or persons own all of the stock of the transferor and transferee corporations in identical proportions, a nominal share of stock of the transferee corporation will be deemed issued in addition to the actual consideration exchanged in the transaction. The nominal share of stock in the transferee corporation will then be deemed distributed by the transferor corporation to its shareholders and, in appropriate circumstances, further transferred to the extent necessary to reflect the actual ownership of the transferor and transferee corporations.

The IRS and Treasury Department have become aware that the temporary regulations may have unintended consequences regarding related party triangular asset acquisitions otherwise qualifying under section 368. Specifically, the temporary regulations may cause certain related party asset acquisitions that would otherwise qualify as tax-free triangular reorganizations to be treated as reorganizations described in section 368(a)(1)(D) with boot.

For example, the temporary regulations may cause a related party transaction that would otherwise qualify as a tax-free reorganization described in section 368(a)(1)(C) in which substantially all of the target corporation's properties are acquired solely in exchange for voting stock of the corporation in control of the acquiring corporation to also be described in section 368(a)(1)(D). If so, section 368(a)(2)(A) would preclude the transaction from being treated as described in section 368(a)(1)(C). Accordingly, the transaction would be treated as described only in section 368(a)(1)(D), and the voting stock of the corporation in control of the acquiring corporation would be treated as boot. Further, the temporary regulations may cause a related party transaction that would otherwise qualify as a tax-free reorganization described in section 368(a)(1)(A) by reason of section 368(a)(2)(D) from so qualifying because the deemed issuance of a nominal share of stock of the acquiring corporation would violate the requirements of section 368(a)(2)(D)(i). If so, the transaction would be treated as described only in section 368(a)(1)(D), and the stock of the corporation in control of the acquiring corporation would be treated as boot.

The IRS and Treasury Department did not intend for the temporary regulations to apply to such transactions.

Explanation of Provisions

These temporary regulations clarify and amend the temporary regulations (T.D. 9303) under §1.368–2T(l) by providing that the deemed issuance of the nominal share of stock of the transferee corporation in a transaction otherwise described in section 368(a)(1)(D) does not apply if the transaction otherwise qualifies as a triangular reorganization described in §1.358–6(b)(2) or section 368(a)(1)(G) by reason of section 368(a)(2)(D). Accordingly, if a transaction qualifies as a triangular reorganization described in §1.358–6(b)(2) or section 368(a)(1)(G) by reason of section 368(a)(2)(D) without regard to the temporary regulations, it will not be treated as a reorganization described in section 368(a)(1)(D).

Special Analyses

It has been determined that this Treasury decision is not a significant regulatory action as defined in Executive Order 12866. Therefore, a regulatory assessment is not required. It also has been determined that section 553(b) of the Administrative Procedure Act (5 U.S.C. chapter 5) does not apply to these regulations. For the applicability of the Regulatory Flexibility Act, please refer to the cross-reference notice of proposed rulemaking published elsewhere in this issue of the Bulletin. Pursuant to section 7805(f) of the Internal Revenue Code, these regulations were submitted to the Chief Counsel for Advocacy of the Small Business Administration for comment on their impact on small business.

Drafting Information

The principal author of these regulations is Bruce A. Decker of the Office of the Associate Chief Counsel (Corporate).

* * * * *

Amendments to the Regulations

Accordingly, 26 CFR part 1 is amended as follows:

PART 1—INCOME TAXES

Paragraph 1. The authority citation for part 1 continues to read as follows:

Authority: 26 U.S.C. 7805 * * *

Par. 2. Section 1.368–2T is amended by adding paragraph (l)(2)(iv) to read as follows:

§1.368–2T Definition of terms (temporary).

* * * * *

(l) * * *

(2) * * *

(iv) *Exception*. Paragraph (l)(2) of this section does not apply to a transaction otherwise described in §1.358–6(b)(2) or section 368(a)(1)(G) by reason of section 368(a)(2)(D).

* * * * *

Kevin M. Brown,
Deputy Commissioner for Services and Enforcement.

Approved February 21, 2007.

Eric Solomon,
Assistant Secretary of the Treasury (Tax Policy).

(Filed by the Office of the Federal Register on February 28, 2007, 8:45 a.m., and published in the issue of the Federal Register for March 1, 2007, 72 F.R. 9262)

Section 472.—Last-in, First-out Inventories

26 CFR 1.472–1: Last-in, first-out inventories.

LIFO; price indexes; department stores. The January 2007 Bureau of Labor Statistics price indexes are accepted for use by department stores employing the retail inventory and last-in, first-out inventory methods for valuing inventories for tax years ended on, or with reference to, January 31, 2007.

Rev. Rul. 2007–18

The following Department Store Inventory Price Indexes for January 2007 were issued by the Bureau of Labor Statistics. The indexes are accepted by the Internal

Revenue Service, under § 1.472–1(k) of the Income Tax Regulations and Rev. Proc. 86–46, 1986–2 C.B. 739, for appropriate application to inventories of department stores employing the retail inventory and last-in, first-out inventory methods for tax years ended on, or with reference to, January 31, 2007.

The Department Store Inventory Price Indexes are prepared on a national basis and include (a) 23 major groups of departments, (b) three special combinations of the major groups — soft goods, durable goods, and miscellaneous goods, and (c) a store total, which covers all departments, including some not listed separately, except for the following: candy, food, liquor, tobacco, and contract departments.

BUREAU OF LABOR STATISTICS, DEPARTMENT STORE INVENTORY PRICE INDEXES BY DEPARTMENT GROUPS
(January 1941 = 100, unless otherwise noted)

	Groups	Jan. 2006	Jan. 2007	Percent Change From Jan. 2006 to Jan. 2007[1]
1.	Piece Goods	436.7	434.9	-0.4
2.	Domestics and Draperies	506.9	475.2	-6.3
3.	Women's and Children's Shoes	671.3	645.4	-3.9
4.	Men's Shoes	868.1	875.2	0.8
5.	Infants' Wear	555.2	558.2	0.5
6.	Women's Underwear	545.6	551.7	1.1
7.	Women's Hosiery	341.3	344.7	1.0
8.	Women's and Girls' Accessories	555.4	537.2	-3.3
9.	Women's Outerwear and Girls' Wear	325.7	338.1	3.8
10.	Men's Clothing	516.8	514.5	-0.4
11.	Men's Furnishings	555.5	559.2	0.7
12.	Boys' Clothing and Furnishings	396.5	371.0	-6.4
13.	Jewelry	868.9	909.5	4.7
14.	Notions	794.2	817.1	2.9
15.	Toilet Articles and Drugs	1010.7	1004.5	-0.6
16.	Furniture and Bedding	603.9	597.1	-1.1
17.	Floor Coverings	611.0	613.7	0.4
18.	Housewares	699.4	689.4	-1.4
19.	Major Appliances	204.3	210.2	2.9
20.	Radio and Television	37.4	33.6	-10.2
21.	Recreation and Education[2]	77.3	76.3	-1.3
22.	Home Improvements[2]	138.0	141.3	2.4
23.	Automotive Accessories[2]	117.2	122.4	4.4
	Groups 1–15: Soft Goods	540.9	542.1	0.2
	Groups 16–20: Durable Goods	375.6	370.6	-1.3
	Groups 21–23: Misc. Goods[2]	93.1	93.9	0.9
	Store Total[3]	482.8	482.8	0.0

[1]Absence of a minus sign before the percentage change in this column signifies a price increase.

[2]Indexes on a January 1986 = 100 base.

[3]The store total index covers all departments, including some not listed separately, except for the following: candy, food, liquor, tobacco, and contract departments.

DRAFTING INFORMATION

The principal author of this revenue ruling is John Roman Faron of the Office of Associate Chief Counsel (Income Tax and Accounting). For further information regarding this revenue ruling, contact Mr. Faron at (202) 622–4930 (not a toll-free call).

Section 6621.—Determination of Rate of Interest

26 CFR 301.6621–1: Interest rate.

Interest rates; underpayments and overpayments. The rate of interest determined under section 6621 of the Code for the calendar quarter beginning April 1, 2007, will be 8 percent for overpayments (7 percent in the case of a corporation), 8 percent for underpayments, and 10 percent for large corporate underpayments. The rate of interest paid on the portion of a corporate overpayment exceeding $10,000 will be 5.5 percent.

Rev. Rul. 2007–16

Section 6621 of the Internal Revenue Code establishes the rates for interest on tax overpayments and tax underpayments. Under section 6621(a)(1), the overpayment rate is the sum of the federal short-term rate plus 3 percentage points (2 percentage points in the case of a corporation), except the rate for the portion of a corporate overpayment of tax exceeding $10,000 for a taxable period is the sum of the federal short-term rate plus 0.5 of a percentage point for interest computations made after December 31, 1994. Under section 6621(a)(2), the underpayment rate is the sum of the federal short-term rate plus 3 percentage points.

Section 6621(c) provides that for purposes of interest payable under section 6601 on any large corporate underpayment, the underpayment rate under section 6621(a)(2) is determined by substituting "5 percentage points" for "3 percentage points." See section 6621(c) and section 301.6621–3 of the Regulations on Procedure and Administration for the definition of a large corporate underpayment and for the rules for determining the applicable date. Section 6621(c) and section 301.6621–3 are generally effective for periods after December 31, 1990.

Section 6621(b)(1) provides that the Secretary will determine the federal short-term rate for the first month in each calendar quarter.

Section 6621(b)(2)(A) provides that the federal short-term rate determined under section 6621(b)(1) for any month applies during the first calendar quarter beginning after such month.

Section 6621(b)(2)(B) provides that in determining the addition to tax under section 6654 for failure to pay estimated tax for any taxable year, the federal short-term rate that applies during the third month following such taxable year also applies during the first 15 days of the fourth month following such taxable year.

Section 6621(b)(3) provides that the federal short-term rate for any month is the federal short-term rate determined during such month by the Secretary in accordance with § 1274(d), rounded to the nearest full percent (or, if a multiple of 1/2 of 1 percent, the rate is increased to the next highest full percent).

Notice 88–59, 1988–1 C.B. 546, announced that, in determining the quarterly interest rates to be used for overpayments and underpayments of tax under section 6621, the Internal Revenue Service will use the federal short-term rate based on daily compounding because that rate is most consistent with section 6621 which, pursuant to section 6622, is subject to daily compounding.

Rounded to the nearest full percent, the federal short-term rate based on daily compounding determined during the month of January 2007 is 5 percent. Accordingly, an overpayment rate of 8 percent (7 percent in the case of a corporation) and an underpayment rate of 8 percent are established for the calendar quarter beginning April 1, 2007. The overpayment rate for the portion of a corporate overpayment exceeding $10,000 for the calendar quarter beginning April 1, 2007, is 5.5 percent. The underpayment rate for large corporate underpayments for the calendar quarter beginning April 1, 2007, is 10 percent. These rates apply to amounts bearing interest during that calendar quarter.

Under section 6621(b)(2)(B), the 8 percent rate that applies to estimated tax underpayments for the first calendar quarter in 2007, as provided in Rev. Rul. 2006–63, 2006–52 I.R.B. 1143, also applies to such underpayments for the first 15 days in April 2007.

Interest factors for daily compound interest for annual rates of 5.5 percent, 7 percent, 8 percent, and 10 percent are published in Tables 16, 19, 21, and 25 of Rev. Proc. 95–17, 1995–1 C.B. 556, 570, 573, 575, and 579.

Annual interest rates to be compounded daily pursuant to section 6622 that apply for prior periods are set forth in the tables accompanying this revenue ruling.

DRAFTING INFORMATION

The principal author of this revenue ruling is Raymond Bailey of the Office of Associate Chief Counsel (Procedure & Administration). For further information regarding this revenue ruling, contact Mr. Bailey at (202) 622–4910 (not a toll-free call).

TABLE OF INTEREST RATES

PERIODS BEFORE JUL. 1, 1975 — PERIODS ENDING DEC. 31, 1986

OVERPAYMENTS AND UNDERPAYMENTS

PERIOD	RATE	In 1995–1 C.B. DAILY RATE TABLE
Before Jul. 1, 1975	6%	Table 2, pg. 557
Jul. 1, 1975—Jan. 31, 1976	9%	Table 4, pg. 559
Feb. 1, 1976—Jan. 31, 1978	7%	Table 3, pg. 558
Feb. 1, 1978—Jan. 31, 1980	6%	Table 2, pg. 557
Feb. 1, 1980—Jan. 31, 1982	12%	Table 5, pg. 560
Feb. 1, 1982—Dec. 31, 1982	20%	Table 6, pg. 560
Jan. 1, 1983—Jun. 30, 1983	16%	Table 37, pg. 591
Jul. 1, 1983—Dec. 31, 1983	11%	Table 27, pg. 581
Jan. 1, 1984—Jun. 30, 1984	11%	Table 75, pg. 629
Jul. 1, 1984—Dec. 31, 1984	11%	Table 75, pg. 629
Jan. 1, 1985—Jun. 30, 1985	13%	Table 31, pg. 585
Jul. 1, 1985—Dec. 31, 1985	11%	Table 27, pg. 581

TABLE OF INTEREST RATES

PERIODS BEFORE JUL. 1, 1975 — PERIODS ENDING DEC. 31, 1986 – Continued

OVERPAYMENTS AND UNDERPAYMENTS

PERIOD	RATE	In 1995–1 C.B. DAILY RATE TABLE
Jan. 1, 1986—Jun. 30, 1986	10%	Table 25, pg. 579
Jul. 1, 1986—Dec. 31, 1986	9%	Table 23, pg. 577

TABLE OF INTEREST RATES

FROM JAN. 1, 1987 — DEC. 31, 1998

	OVERPAYMENTS			UNDERPAYMENTS		
	RATE	1995–1 C.B. TABLE	PG	RATE	1995–1 C.B. TABLE	PG
Jan. 1, 1987—Mar. 31, 1987	8%	21	575	9%	23	577
Apr. 1, 1987—Jun. 30, 1987	8%	21	575	9%	23	577
Jul. 1, 1987—Sep. 30, 1987	8%	21	575	9%	23	577
Oct. 1, 1987—Dec. 31, 1987	9%	23	577	10%	25	579
Jan. 1, 1988—Mar. 31, 1988	10%	73	627	11%	75	629
Apr. 1, 1988—Jun. 30, 1988	9%	71	625	10%	73	627
Jul. 1, 1988—Sep. 30, 1988	9%	71	625	10%	73	627
Oct. 1, 1988—Dec. 31, 1988	10%	73	627	11%	75	629
Jan. 1, 1989—Mar. 31, 1989	10%	25	579	11%	27	581
Apr. 1, 1989—Jun. 30, 1989	11%	27	581	12%	29	583
Jul. 1, 1989—Sep. 30, 1989	11%	27	581	12%	29	583
Oct. 1, 1989—Dec. 31, 1989	10%	25	579	11%	27	581
Jan. 1, 1990—Mar. 31, 1990	10%	25	579	11%	27	581
Apr. 1, 1990—Jun. 30, 1990	10%	25	579	11%	27	581
Jul. 1, 1990—Sep. 30, 1990	10%	25	579	11%	27	581
Oct. 1, 1990—Dec. 31, 1990	10%	25	579	11%	27	581
Jan. 1, 1991—Mar. 31, 1991	10%	25	579	11%	27	581
Apr. 1, 1991—Jun. 30, 1991	9%	23	577	10%	25	579
Jul. 1, 1991—Sep. 30, 1991	9%	23	577	10%	25	579
Oct. 1, 1991—Dec. 31, 1991	9%	23	577	10%	25	579
Jan. 1, 1992—Mar. 31, 1992	8%	69	623	9%	71	625
Apr. 1, 1992—Jun. 30, 1992	7%	67	621	8%	69	623
Jul. 1, 1992—Sep. 30, 1992	7%	67	621	8%	69	623
Oct. 1, 1992—Dec. 31, 1992	6%	65	619	7%	67	621
Jan. 1, 1993—Mar. 31, 1993	6%	17	571	7%	19	573
Apr. 1, 1993—Jun. 30, 1993	6%	17	571	7%	19	573
Jul. 1, 1993—Sep. 30, 1993	6%	17	571	7%	19	573
Oct. 1, 1993—Dec. 31, 1993	6%	17	571	7%	19	573
Jan. 1, 1994—Mar. 31, 1994	6%	17	571	7%	19	573
Apr. 1, 1994—Jun. 30, 1994	6%	17	571	7%	19	573
Jul. 1, 1994—Sep. 30, 1994	7%	19	573	8%	21	575
Oct. 1, 1994—Dec. 31, 1994	8%	21	575	9%	23	577
Jan. 1, 1995—Mar. 31, 1995	8%	21	575	9%	23	577
Apr. 1, 1995—Jun. 30, 1995	9%	23	577	10%	25	579
Jul. 1, 1995—Sep. 30, 1995	8%	21	575	9%	23	577
Oct. 1, 1995—Dec. 31, 1995	8%	21	575	9%	23	577
Jan. 1, 1996—Mar. 31, 1996	8%	69	623	9%	71	625
Apr. 1, 1996—Jun. 30, 1996	7%	67	621	8%	69	623
Jul. 1, 1996—Sep. 30, 1996	8%	69	623	9%	71	625
Oct. 1, 1996—Dec. 31, 1996	8%	69	623	9%	71	625
Jan. 1, 1997—Mar. 31, 1997	8%	21	575	9%	23	577
Apr. 1, 1997—Jun. 30, 1997	8%	21	575	9%	23	577
Jul. 1, 1997—Sep. 30, 1997	8%	21	575	9%	23	577
Oct. 1, 1997—Dec. 31, 1997	8%	21	575	9%	23	577

TABLE OF INTEREST RATES

FROM JAN. 1, 1987 — DEC. 31, 1998 – Continued

	OVERPAYMENTS			UNDERPAYMENTS		
		1995–1 C.B.			1995–1 C.B.	
	RATE	TABLE	PG	RATE	TABLE	PG
Jan. 1, 1998—Mar. 31, 1998	8%	21	575	9%	23	577
Apr. 1, 1998—Jun. 30, 1998	7%	19	573	8%	21	575
Jul. 1, 1998—Sep. 30, 1998	7%	19	573	8%	21	575
Oct. 1, 1998—Dec. 31, 1998	7%	19	573	8%	21	575

TABLE OF INTEREST RATES

FROM JANUARY 1, 1999 — PRESENT

NONCORPORATE OVERPAYMENTS AND UNDERPAYMENTS

	RATE	1995–1 C.B. TABLE	PAGE
Jan. 1, 1999—Mar. 31, 1999	7%	19	573
Apr. 1, 1999—Jun. 30, 1999	8%	21	575
Jul. 1, 1999—Sep. 30, 1999	8%	21	575
Oct. 1, 1999—Dec. 31, 1999	8%	21	575
Jan. 1, 2000—Mar. 31, 2000	8%	69	623
Apr. 1, 2000—Jun. 30, 2000	9%	71	625
Jul. 1, 2000—Sep. 30, 2000	9%	71	625
Oct. 1, 2000—Dec. 31, 2000	9%	71	625
Jan. 1, 2001—Mar. 31, 2001	9%	23	577
Apr. 1, 2001—Jun. 30, 2001	8%	21	575
Jul. 1, 2001—Sep. 30, 2001	7%	19	573
Oct. 1, 2001—Dec. 31, 2001	7%	19	573
Jan. 1, 2002—Mar. 31, 2002	6%	17	571
Apr. 1, 2002—Jun. 30, 2002	6%	17	571
Jul. 1, 2002—Sep. 30, 2002	6%	17	571
Oct. 1, 2002—Dec. 31, 2002	6%	17	571
Jan. 1, 2003—Mar. 31, 2003	5%	15	569
Apr. 1, 2003—Jun. 30, 2003	5%	15	569
Jul. 1, 2003—Sep. 30, 2003	5%	15	569
Oct. 1, 2003—Dec. 31, 2003	4%	13	567
Jan. 1, 2004—Mar. 31, 2004	4%	61	615
Apr. 1, 2004—Jun. 30, 2004	5%	63	617
Jul. 1, 2004—Sep. 30, 2004	4%	61	615
Oct. 1, 2004—Dec. 31, 2004	5%	63	617
Jan. 1, 2005—Mar. 31, 2005	5%	15	569
Apr. 1, 2005—Jun. 30, 2005	6%	17	571
Jul. 1, 2005—Sep. 30, 2005	6%	17	571
Oct. 1, 2005—Dec. 31, 2005	7%	19	573
Jan. 1, 2006—Mar. 31, 2006	7%	19	573
Apr. 1, 2006—Jun. 30, 2006	7%	19	573
Jul. 1, 2006—Sep. 30, 2006	8%	21	575
Oct. 1, 2006—Dec. 31, 2006	8%	21	575
Jan. 1, 2007—Mar. 31, 2007	8%	21	575
Apr. 1, 2007— Jun. 30, 2007	8%	21	575

TABLE OF INTEREST RATES

FROM JANUARY 1, 1999 — PRESENT

CORPORATE OVERPAYMENTS AND UNDERPAYMENTS

	OVERPAYMENTS			UNDERPAYMENTS		
	RATE	1995–1 C.B. TABLE	PG	RATE	1995–1 C.B. TABLE	PG
Jan. 1, 1999—Mar. 31, 1999	6%	17	571	7%	19	573
Apr. 1, 1999—Jun. 30, 1999	7%	19	573	8%	21	575
Jul. 1, 1999—Sep. 30, 1999	7%	19	573	8%	21	575
Oct. 1, 1999—Dec. 31, 1999	7%	19	573	8%	21	575
Jan. 1, 2000—Mar. 31, 2000	7%	67	621	8%	69	623
Apr. 1, 2000—Jun. 30, 2000	8%	69	623	9%	71	625
Jul. 1, 2000—Sep. 30, 2000	8%	69	623	9%	71	625
Oct. 1, 2000—Dec. 31, 2000	8%	69	623	9%	71	625
Jan. 1, 2001—Mar. 31, 2001	8%	21	575	9%	23	577
Apr. 1, 2001—Jun. 30, 2001	7%	19	573	8%	21	575
Jul. 1, 2001—Sep. 30, 2001	6%	17	571	7%	19	573
Oct. 1, 2001—Dec. 31, 2001	6%	17	571	7%	19	573
Jan. 1, 2002—Mar. 31, 2002	5%	15	569	6%	17	571
Apr. 1, 2002—Jun. 30, 2002	5%	15	569	6%	17	571
Jul. 1, 2002—Sep. 30, 2002	5%	15	569	6%	17	571
Oct. 1, 2002—Dec. 31, 2002	5%	15	569	6%	17	571
Jan. 1, 2003—Mar. 31, 2003	4%	13	567	5%	15	569
Apr. 1, 2003—Jun. 30, 2003	4%	13	567	5%	15	569
Jul. 1, 2003—Sep. 30, 2003	4%	13	567	5%	15	569
Oct. 1, 2003—Dec. 31, 2003	3%	11	565	4%	13	567
Jan. 1, 2004—Mar. 31, 2004	3%	59	613	4%	61	615
Apr. 1, 2004—Jun. 30, 2004	4%	61	615	5%	63	617
Jul. 1, 2004—Sep. 30, 2004	3%	59	613	4%	61	615
Oct. 1, 2004—Dec. 31, 2004	4%	61	615	5%	63	617
Jan. 1, 2005—Mar. 31, 2005	4%	13	567	5%	15	569
Apr. 1, 2005—Jun. 30, 2005	5%	15	569	6%	17	571
Jul. 1, 2005—Sep. 30, 2005	5%	15	569	6%	17	571
Oct. 1, 2005—Dec. 31, 2005	6%	17	571	7%	19	573
Jan. 1, 2006—Mar. 31, 2006	6%	17	571	7%	19	573
Apr. 1, 2006—Jun. 30, 2006	6%	17	571	7%	19	573
Jul. 1, 2006—Sep. 30, 2006	7%	19	573	8%	21	575
Oct. 1, 2006—Dec. 31, 2006	7%	19	573	8%	21	575
Jan. 1, 2007—Mar. 31, 2007	7%	19	573	8%	21	575
Apr. 1, 2007—Jun. 30, 2007	7%	19	573	8%	21	575

TABLE OF INTEREST RATES FOR
LARGE CORPORATE UNDERPAYMENTS

FROM JANUARY 1, 1991 — PRESENT

	RATE	1995–1 C.B. TABLE	PG
Jan. 1, 1991—Mar. 31, 1991	13%	31	585
Apr. 1, 1991—Jun. 30, 1991	12%	29	583
Jul. 1, 1991—Sep. 30, 1991	12%	29	583
Oct. 1, 1991—Dec. 31, 1991	12%	29	583
Jan. 1, 1992—Mar. 31, 1992	11%	75	629
Apr. 1, 1992—Jun. 30, 1992	10%	73	627
Jul. 1, 1992—Sep. 30, 1992	10%	73	627
Oct. 1, 1992—Dec. 31, 1992	9%	71	625
Jan. 1, 1993—Mar. 31, 1993	9%	23	577
Apr. 1, 1993—Jun. 30, 1993	9%	23	577

TABLE OF INTEREST RATES FOR
LARGE CORPORATE UNDERPAYMENTS

FROM JANUARY 1, 1991 — PRESENT – Continued

	RATE	1995–1 C.B. TABLE	PG
Jul. 1, 1993—Sep. 30, 1993	9%	23	577
Oct. 1, 1993—Dec. 31, 1993	9%	23	577
Jan. 1, 1994—Mar. 31, 1994	9%	23	577
Apr. 1, 1994—Jun. 30, 1994	9%	23	577
Jul. 1, 1994—Sep. 30, 1994	10%	25	579
Oct. 1, 1994—Dec. 31, 1994	11%	27	581
Jan. 1, 1995—Mar. 31, 1995	11%	27	581
Apr. 1, 1995—Jun. 30, 1995	12%	29	583
Jul. 1, 1995—Sep. 30, 1995	11%	27	581
Oct. 1, 1995—Dec. 31, 1995	11%	27	581
Jan. 1, 1996—Mar. 31, 1996	11%	75	629
Apr. 1, 1996—Jun. 30, 1996	10%	73	627
Jul. 1, 1996—Sep. 30, 1996	11%	75	629
Oct. 1, 1996—Dec. 31, 1996	11%	75	629
Jan. 1, 1997—Mar. 31, 1997	11%	27	581
Apr. 1, 1997—Jun. 30, 1997	11%	27	581
Jul. 1, 1997—Sep. 30, 1997	11%	27	581
Oct. 1, 1997—Dec. 31, 1997	11%	27	581
Jan. 1, 1998—Mar. 31, 1998	11%	27	581
Apr. 1, 1998—Jun. 30, 1998	10%	25	579
Jul. 1, 1998—Sep. 30, 1998	10%	25	579
Oct. 1, 1998—Dec. 31, 1998	10%	25	579
Jan. 1, 1999—Mar. 31, 1999	9%	23	577
Apr. 1, 1999—Jun. 30, 1999	10%	25	579
Jul. 1, 1999—Sep. 30, 1999	10%	25	579
Oct. 1, 1999—Dec. 31, 1999	10%	25	579
Jan. 1, 2000—Mar. 31, 2000	10%	73	627
Apr. 1, 2000—Jun. 30, 2000	11%	75	629
Jul. 1, 2000—Sep. 30, 2000	11%	75	629
Oct. 1, 2000—Dec. 31, 2000	11%	75	629
Jan. 1, 2001—Mar. 31, 2001	11%	27	581
Apr. 1, 2001—Jun. 30, 2001	10%	25	579
Jul. 1, 2001—Sep. 30, 2001	9%	23	577
Oct. 1, 2001—Dec. 31, 2001	9%	23	577
Jan. 1, 2002—Mar. 31, 2002	8%	21	575
Apr. 1, 2002—Jun. 30, 2002	8%	21	575
Jul. 1, 2002—Sep. 30, 2002	8%	21	575
Oct. 1, 2002—Dec. 31, 2002	8%	21	575
Jan. 1, 2003—Mar. 31, 2003	7%	19	573
Apr. 1, 2003—Jun. 30, 2003	7%	19	573
Jul. 1, 2003—Sep. 30, 2003	7%	19	573
Oct. 1, 2003—Dec. 31, 2003	6%	17	571
Jan. 1, 2004—Mar. 31, 2004	6%	65	619
Apr. 1, 2004—Jun. 30, 2004	7%	67	621
Jul. 1, 2004—Sep. 30, 2004	6%	65	619
Oct. 1, 2004—Dec. 31, 2004	7%	67	621
Jan. 1, 2005—Mar. 31, 2005	7%	19	573
Apr. 1, 2005—Jun. 30, 2005	8%	21	575
Jul. 1, 2005—Sep. 30, 2005	8%	21	575
Oct. 1, 2005—Dec. 31, 2005	9%	23	577
Jan. 1, 2006—Mar. 31, 2006	9%	23	577
Apr. 1, 2006—Jun. 30, 2006	9%	23	577
Jul. 1, 2006—Sep. 30, 2006	10%	25	579
Oct. 1, 2006—Dec. 31, 2006	10%	25	579
Jan. 1, 2007—Mar. 31, 2007	10%	25	579
Apr. 1, 2007—Jun. 30, 2007	10%	25	579

TABLE OF INTEREST RATES FOR CORPORATE OVERPAYMENTS EXCEEDING $10,000

FROM JANUARY 1, 1995 — PRESENT

	RATE	1995–1 C.B. TABLE	PG
Jan. 1, 1995—Mar. 31, 1995	6.5%	18	572
Apr. 1, 1995—Jun. 30, 1995	7.5%	20	574
Jul. 1, 1995—Sep. 30, 1995	6.5%	18	572
Oct. 1, 1995—Dec. 31, 1995	6.5%	18	572
Jan. 1, 1996—Mar. 31, 1996	6.5%	66	620
Apr. 1, 1996—Jun. 30, 1996	5.5%	64	618
Jul. 1, 1996—Sep. 30, 1996	6.5%	66	620
Oct. 1, 1996—Dec. 31, 1996	6.5%	66	620
Jan. 1, 1997—Mar. 31, 1997	6.5%	18	572
Apr. 1, 1997—Jun. 30, 1997	6.5%	18	572
Jul. 1, 1997—Sep. 30, 1997	6.5%	18	572
Oct. 1, 1997—Dec. 31, 1997	6.5%	18	572
Jan. 1, 1998—Mar. 31, 1998	6.5%	18	572
Apr. 1, 1998—Jun. 30, 1998	5.5%	16	570
Jul. 1, 1998—Sep. 30, 1998	5.5%	16	570
Oct. 1, 1998—Dec. 31, 1998	5.5%	16	570
Jan. 1, 1999—Mar. 31, 1999	4.5%	14	568
Apr. 1, 1999—Jun. 30, 1999	5.5%	16	570
Jul. 1, 1999—Sep. 30, 1999	5.5%	16	570
Oct. 1, 1999—Dec. 31, 1999	5.5%	16	570
Jan. 1, 2000—Mar. 31, 2000	5.5%	64	618
Apr. 1, 2000—Jun. 30, 2000	6.5%	66	620
Jul. 1, 2000—Sep. 30, 2000	6.5%	66	620
Oct. 1, 2000—Dec. 31, 2000	6.5%	66	620
Jan. 1, 2001—Mar. 31, 2001	6.5%	18	572
Apr. 1, 2001—Jun. 30, 2001	5.5%	16	570
Jul. 1, 2001—Sep. 30, 2001	4.5%	14	568
Oct. 1, 2001—Dec. 31, 2001	4.5%	14	568
Jan. 1, 2002—Mar. 31, 2002	3.5%	12	566
Apr. 1, 2002—Jun. 30, 2002	3.5%	12	566
Jul. 1, 2002—Sep. 30, 2002	3.5%	12	566
Oct. 1, 2002—Dec. 31, 2002	3.5%	12	566
Jan. 1, 2003—Mar. 31, 2003	2.5%	10	564
Apr. 1, 2003—Jun. 30, 2003	2.5%	10	564
Jul. 1, 2003—Sep. 30, 2003	2.5%	10	564
Oct. 1, 2003—Dec. 31, 2003	1.5%	8	562
Jan. 1, 2004—Mar. 31, 2004	1.5%	56	610
Apr. 1, 2004—Jun. 30, 2004	2.5%	58	612
Jul. 1, 2004—Sep. 30, 2004	1.5%	56	610
Oct. 1, 2004—Dec. 31, 2004	2.5%	58	612
Jan. 1, 2005—Mar. 31, 2005	2.5%	10	564
Apr. 1, 2005—Jun. 30, 2005	3.5%	12	566
Jul. 1, 2005—Sep. 30, 2005	3.5%	12	566
Oct. 1, 2005—Dec. 31, 2005	4.5%	14	568
Jan. 1, 2006—Mar. 31, 2006	4.5%	14	568
Apr. 1, 2006—Jun. 30, 2006	4.5%	14	568
Jul. 1, 2006—Sep. 30, 2006	5.5%	16	570
Oct. 1, 2006—Dec. 31, 2006	5.5%	16	570
Jan. 1, 2007—Mar. 31, 2007	5.5%	16	570
Apr. 1, 2007—Jun. 30, 2007	5.5%	16	570

Part III. Administrative, Procedural, and Miscellaneous

Weighted Average Interest Rates Update

Notice 2007–27

This notice provides guidance as to the corporate bond weighted average interest rate and the permissible range of interest rates specified under § 412(b)(5)(B)(ii)(II) of the Internal Revenue Code. In addition, it provides guidance as to the interest rate on 30-year Treasury securities under § 417(e)(3)(A)(ii)(II).

CORPORATE BOND WEIGHTED AVERAGE INTEREST RATE

Sections 412(b)(5)(B)(ii) and 412(l)(7)(C)(i), as amended by the Pension Funding Equity Act of 2004 and by the Pension Protection Act of 2006, provide that the interest rates used to calculate current liability and to determine the required contribution under § 412(l) for plan years beginning in 2004 through 2007 must be within a permissible range based on the weighted average of the rates of interest on amounts invested conservatively in long term investment grade corporate bonds during the 4-year period ending on the last day before the beginning of the plan year.

Notice 2004–34, 2004–1 C.B. 848, provides guidelines for determining the corporate bond weighted average interest rate and the resulting permissible range of interest rates used to calculate current liability. That notice establishes that the corporate bond weighted average is based on the monthly composite corporate bond rate derived from designated corporate bond indices. The methodology for determining the monthly composite corporate bond rate as set forth in Notice 2004–34 continues to apply in determining that rate. See Notice 2006–75, 2006–36 I.R.B. 366.

The composite corporate bond rate for February 2007 is 5.85 percent. Pursuant to Notice 2004–34, the Service has determined this rate as the average of the monthly yields for the included corporate bond indices for that month.

The following corporate bond weighted average interest rate was determined for plan years beginning in the month shown below.

For Plan Years Beginning in: Month	Year	Corporate Bond Weighted Average	90% to 100% Permissible Range
March	2007	5.80	5.22 to 5.80

30-YEAR TREASURY SECURITIES INTEREST RATE

Section 417(e)(3)(A)(ii)(II) defines the applicable interest rate, which must be used for purposes of determining the minimum present value of a participant's benefit under § 417(e)(1) and (2), as the annual rate of interest on 30-year Treasury securities for the month before the date of distribution or such other time as the Secretary may by regulations prescribe. Section 1.417(e)–1(d)(3) of the Income Tax Regulations provides that the applicable interest rate for a month is the annual interest rate on 30-year Treasury securities as specified by the Commissioner for that month in revenue rulings, notices or other guidance published in the Internal Revenue Bulletin.

The rate of interest on 30-year Treasury securities for February 2007 is 4.82 percent. The Service has determined this rate as the average of the yield on the 30-year Treasury bond maturing in February 2036 determined each day through February 7, 2007, and the yield on the 30-year Treasury bond maturing in February 2037 determined each day for the balance of the month.

Drafting Information

The principal authors of this notice are Paul Stern and Tony Montanaro of the Employee Plans, Tax Exempt and Government Entities Division. For further information regarding this notice, please contact the Employee Plans' taxpayer assistance telephone service at 877–829–5500 (a toll-free number), between the hours of 8:30 a.m. and 4:30 p.m. Eastern time, Monday through Friday. Mr. Stern may be reached at 202–283–9703. Mr. Montanaro may be reached at 202–283–9714. The telephone numbers in the two preceding sentences are not toll-free.

---

26 CFR 601.201: Rulings and determination letters. (Also: Part I, §§ 25, 103, 143.)

Rev. Proc. 2007–26

SECTION 1. PURPOSE

This revenue procedure provides issuers of qualified mortgage bonds, as defined in section 143(a) of the Internal Revenue Code, and issuers of mortgage credit certificates, as defined in section 25(c), with (1) the nationwide average purchase price for residences located in the United States, and (2) average area purchase price safe harbors for residences located in statistical areas in each state, the District of Columbia, Puerto Rico, the Northern Mariana Islands, American Samoa, the Virgin Islands, and Guam.

SECTION 2. BACKGROUND

.01 Section 103(a) provides that, except as provided in section 103(b), gross income does not include interest on any state or local bond. Section 103(b)(1) provides that section 103(a) shall not apply to any private activity bond that is not a "qualified bond" within the meaning of section 141. Section 141(e) provides, in part, that the term "qualified bond" means any private activity bond if such bond (1) is a qualified mortgage bond under section 143, (2) meets the volume cap requirements under section 146, and (3) meets the applicable requirements under section 147.

.02 Section 143(a)(1) provides that the term "qualified mortgage bond" means a bond that is issued as part of a qualified mortgage issue. Section 143(a)(2)(A) provides that the term "qualified mortgage issue" means an issue of one or more bonds by a state or political subdivision thereof, but only if: (i) all proceeds of the issue (exclusive of issuance costs and a reasonably required reserve) are to be used to finance owner-occupied residences; (ii) the issue meets the requirements of subsections (c), (d), (e), (f), (g), (h), (i), and (m)(7) of section 143; (iii) the issue does not meet the private business tests of paragraphs (1) and (2) of section 141(b); and (iv) with respect to amounts received more than 10 years after the date of issuance, repayments of $250,000 or more of principal on mortgage financing provided by the issue are used by the close of the first semiannual period beginning after the date the prepayment (or complete repayment) is received to redeem bonds that are part of the issue.

Average Area Purchase Price

.03 Section 143(e)(1) provides that an issue of bonds meets the purchase price requirements of section 143(e) if the acquisition cost of each residence financed by the issue does not exceed 90 percent of the average area purchase price applicable to such residence. Section 143(e)(5) provides that, in the case of a targeted area residence (as defined in section 143(j)), section 143(e)(1) shall be applied by substituting 110 percent for 90 percent.

.04 Section 143(e)(2) provides that the term "average area purchase price" means, with respect to any residence, the average purchase price of single-family residences (in the statistical area in which the residence is located) that were purchased during the most recent 12-month period for which sufficient statistical information is available. Under sections 143(e)(3) and (4), respectively, separate determinations are to be made for new and existing residences, and for two-, three-, and four-family residences.

.05 Section 143(e)(2) provides that the determination of the average area purchase price for a statistical area shall be made as of the date on which the commitment to provide the financing is made or, if earlier, the date of the purchase of the residence.

.06 Section 143(k)(2)(A) provides that the term "statistical area" means (i) a metropolitan statistical area (MSA), and (ii) any county (or the portion thereof) that is not within an MSA. Section 143(k)(2)(C) further provides that if sufficient recent statistical information with respect to a county (or portion thereof) is unavailable, the Secretary may substitute another area for which there is sufficient recent statistical information for such county (or portion thereof). In the case of any portion of a State which is not within a county, section 143(k)(2)(D) provides that the Secretary may designate as a county any area that is the equivalent of a county. Section 6a.103A–1(b)(4)(i) of the Temporary Income Tax Regulations (issued under section 103A of the Internal Revenue Code of 1954, the predecessor of section 143) provides that the term "State" includes a possession of the United States and the District of Columbia.

.07 Section 6a.103A–2(f)(5)(i) provides that an issuer may rely upon the average area purchase price safe harbors published by the Department of the Treasury for the statistical area in which a residence is located. Section 6a.103A–2(f)(5)(i) further provides that an issuer may use an average area purchase price limitation different from the published safe harbor if the issuer has more accurate and comprehensive data for the statistical area.

Qualified Mortgage Credit Certificate Program

.08 Section 25(c) permits a state or political subdivision to establish a qualified mortgage credit certificate program. In general, a qualified mortgage credit certificate program is a program under which the issuing authority elects not to issue an amount of private activity bonds that it may otherwise issue during the calendar year under section 146, and in their place, issues mortgage credit certificates to taxpayers in connection with the acquisition of their principal residences. Section 25(a)(1) provides, in general, that the holder of a mortgage credit certificate may claim a federal income tax credit equal to the product of the credit rate specified in the certificate and the interest paid or accrued during the tax year on the remaining principal of the indebtedness incurred to acquire the residence. Section 25(c)(2)(A)(iii)(III) generally provides that residences acquired in connection with the issuance of mortgage credit certificates must meet the purchase price requirements of section 143(e).

Income Limitations for Qualified Mortgage Bonds and Mortgage Credit Certificates

.09 Section 143(f) imposes limitations on the income of mortgagors for whom financing may be provided by qualified mortgage bonds. In addition, section 25(c)(2)(A)(iii)(IV) provides that holders of mortgage credit certificates must meet the income requirement of section 143(f). Generally, under sections 143(f)(1) and 25(c)(2)(A)(iii)(IV), the income requirement is met only if all owner-financing under a qualified mortgage bond and all mortgage credit certificates issued under a qualified mortgage credit certificate program are provided to mortgagors whose family income is 115 percent or less of the applicable median family income. Section 143(f)(5), however, generally provides for an upward adjustment to the percentage limitation in high housing cost areas. High housing cost areas are defined in section 143(f)(5)(C) as any statistical area for which the housing cost/income ratio is greater than 1.2.

.10 Under section 143(f)(5)(D), the housing cost/income ratio with respect to any statistical area is determined by dividing (a) the applicable housing price ratio for such area by (b) the ratio that the area median gross income for such area bears to the median gross income for the United States. The applicable housing price ratio is the new housing price ratio (new housing average area purchase price divided by the new housing average purchase price for the United States) or the existing housing price ratio (existing housing average area purchase price divided by the existing housing average purchase price for the United States), whichever results in the housing cost/income ratio being closer to 1.

Average Area and Nationwide Purchase Price Limitations

.11 Average area purchase price safe harbors for each state, the District of Columbia, Puerto Rico, the Northern Mariana Islands, American Samoa, the Virgin Islands, and Guam were last published in Rev. Proc. 2006–17, 2006–14 I.R.B. 709.

.12 The nationwide average purchase price limitation was last published in section 4.02 of Rev. Proc. 2006–17. Guidance with respect to the United States and area median gross income figures that are to be used in computing the housing cost/income ratio described in section 143(f)(5) was last published in Rev. Proc. 2006–20, 2006–17 I.R.B. 841.

.13 This revenue procedure uses FHA loan limits for a given statistical area to calculate the average area purchase price safe harbor for that area. FHA sets limits on the dollar value of loans it will insure based on median home prices and conforming loan limits established by the Federal Home Loan Mortgage Corporation. In particular, FHA sets an area's loan limit at 95 percent of the median home sales price for the area, subject to certain floors and caps measured against conforming loan limits.

.14 To calculate the average area purchase price safe harbors in this revenue procedure, the FHA loan limits are adjusted to take into account the differences between average and median purchase prices. Because FHA loan limits do not differentiate between new and existing residences, this revenue procedure contains a single average area purchase price safe harbor for both new and existing residences in a statistical area. The Treasury Department and the Internal Revenue Service have determined that FHA loan limits provide a reasonable basis for determining average area purchase price safe harbors. If the Treasury Department and the Internal Revenue Service become aware of other sources of average purchase price data, including data that differentiate between new and existing residences, consideration will be given as to whether such data provide a more accurate method for calculating average area purchase price safe harbors.

.15 The average area purchase price safe harbors listed in section 4.01 of this revenue procedure are based on FHA loan limits released January 3, 2007. FHA loan limits are available for statistical areas in each state, the District of Columbia, Puerto Rico, the Northern Mariana Islands, American Samoa, the Virgin Islands, and Guam. See section 3.03 of this revenue procedure with respect to FHA loan limits revised after January 3, 2007.

.16 OMB Bulletin No. 03–04, dated and effective June 6, 2003, revised the definitions of the nation's metropolitan areas and recognized 49 new metropolitan statistical areas. The OMB bulletin no longer includes primary metropolitan statistical areas.

SECTION 3. APPLICATION

Average Area Purchase Price Safe Harbors

.01 Average area purchase price safe harbors for statistical areas in each state, the District of Columbia, Puerto Rico, the Northern Mariana Islands, American Samoa, the Virgin Islands, and Guam are set forth in section 4.01 of this revenue procedure. Average area purchase price safe harbors are provided for single-family and two to four-family residences. For each type of residence, section 4.01 of this revenue procedure contains a single safe harbor that may be used for both new and existing residences. Issuers of qualified mortgage bonds and issuers of mortgage credit certificates may rely on these safe harbors to satisfy the requirements of sections 143(e) and (f). Section 4.01 of this revenue procedure provides safe harbors for MSAs and for certain counties and county equivalents. If no purchase price safe harbor is available for a statistical area, the safe harbor for "ALL OTHER AREAS" may be used for that statistical area (except for Alaska, for which a separate safe harbor is provided for statistical areas not listed).

.02 If a residence is in an MSA, the safe harbor applicable to it is the limitation of that MSA. If an MSA falls in more than one state, the MSA is listed in section 4.01 of this revenue procedure under each state.

.03 If the FHA revises the FHA loan limit for any statistical area after January 3, 2006, an issuer of qualified mortgage bonds or mortgage credit certificates may use the revised FHA loan limit for that statistical area to compute (as provided in the next sentence) a revised average area purchase price safe harbor for the statistical area provided that the issuer maintains records evidencing the revised FHA loan limit. The revised average area purchase price safe harbor for that statistical area is computed by dividing the revised FHA loan limit by .76.

.04 If, pursuant to section 6a.103A–2(f)(5)(i), an issuer uses more accurate and comprehensive data to determine the average area purchase price for a statistical area, the issuer must make separate average area purchase price determinations for new and existing residences. Moreover, when computing the average area purchase price for a statistical area that is an MSA, as defined in OMB Bulletin No. 03–04, the issuer must make the computation for the entire applicable MSA. When computing the average area purchase price for a statistical area that is not an MSA, the issuer must make the computation for the entire statistical area and may not combine statistical areas. Thus, for example, the issuer may not combine two or more counties.

.05 If an issuer receives a ruling permitting it to rely on an average area purchase price limitation that is higher than the applicable safe harbor in this revenue procedure, the issuer may rely on that higher limitation for the purpose of satisfying the requirements of section 143(e) and (f) for bonds sold, and mortgage credit certificates issued, not more than 30 months following the termination date of the 12-month period used by the issuer to compute the limitation.

Nationwide Average Purchase Price

.06 Section 4.02 of this revenue procedure sets forth a single nationwide average purchase price for purposes of computing the housing cost/income ratio under section 143(f)(5).

.07 Issuers must use the nationwide average purchase price set forth in section 4.02 of this revenue procedure when computing the housing cost/income ratio under section 143(f)(5) regardless of whether they are relying on the average area purchase price safe harbors contained in this revenue procedure or using more accurate and comprehensive data to determine average area purchase prices for new and existing residences for a statistical area that are different from the published safe harbors in this revenue procedure.

.08 If, pursuant to section 6.02 of this revenue procedure, an issuer relies on the average area purchase price safe harbors contained in Rev. Proc. 2006–17, the issuer must use the nationwide average purchase price set forth in section 4.02 of Rev. Proc. 2006–17 in computing the housing cost/income ratio under section 143(f)(5). Likewise, if, pursuant to section 6.05 of this revenue procedure, an issuer relies on the nationwide average purchase price published in Rev. Proc. 2006–17, the issuer may not rely on the average area purchase price safe harbors published in this revenue procedure.

SECTION 4. AVERAGE AREA AND NATIONWIDE AVERAGE PURCHASE PRICES

.01 Average area purchase prices for single-family and two to four-family residences in MSAs, and for certain counties and county equivalents are set forth below. The safe harbor for "ALL OTHER AREAS" (found at the end of the table below) may be used for a statistical area that is not listed below.

STATE	MSA NAME	COUNTY NAME	SAFE HARBOR AVERAGE PRICE			
			1 LIVING UNIT	2 LIVING UNITS	3 LIVING UNITS	4 LIVING UNITS
AK	ANCHORAGE, AK (MSA)	ANCHORAGE	$335,592	$377,982	$459,276	$529,934
	NON-METRO	DENALI	$316,137	$404,668	$489,126	$607,879
	JUNEAU, AK (MICRO)	JUNEAU	$398,750	$449,118	$545,658	$629,605
	ANCHORAGE, AK (MSA)	MATANUSKA-SUSIT	$335,592	$377,982	$459,276	$529,934
	NON-METRO	SITKA	$431,250	$485,724	$590,132	$680,921
	NON-METRO	YAKUTAT CITY	$316,137	$404,668	$489,126	$607,879
AZ	FLAGSTAFF, AZ (MSA)	COCONINO	$437,500	$492,763	$598,684	$690,789
	PAYSON, AZ (MICRO)	GILA	$293,750	$337,168	$407,558	$506,495
	PHOENIX-MESA-SCOTTSDALE, AZ (MSA)	MARICOPA	$346,250	$389,987	$473,816	$546,711
	LAKE HAVASU CITY-KINGMAN, AZ (MICRO)	MOHAVE	$321,842	$362,500	$440,461	$508,224
	NON-METRO	NAVAJO	$265,000	$337,168	$407,558	$506,495
	TUCSON, AZ (MSA)	PIMA	$315,592	$355,461	$431,908	$506,495
	PHOENIX-MESA-SCOTTSDALE, AZ (MSA)	PINAL	$346,250	$389,987	$473,816	$546,711
	PRESCOTT, AZ (MSA)	YAVAPAI	$375,000	$422,368	$513,158	$592,105
CA	OAKLAND-FREMONT-HAYWARD, CA METROPOLITAN	ALAMEDA	$477,355	$611,117	$738,699	$918,021
	NON-METRO	ALPINE	$477,355	$611,117	$738,699	$918,021
	NON-METRO	AMADOR	$443,750	$506,842	$615,789	$710,526
	CHICO, CA (MSA)	BUTTE	$400,000	$450,526	$547,368	$631,579
	NON-METRO	CALAVERAS	$477,355	$550,461	$668,816	$774,671
	NON-METRO	COLUSA	$381,250	$429,408	$521,711	$601,974
	OAKLAND-FREMONT-HAYWARD, CA METROPOLITAN	CONTRA COSTA	$477,355	$611,117	$738,699	$918,021
	CRESCENT CITY, CA (MICRO)	DEL NORTE	$311,250	$350,566	$425,921	$506,495
	SACRAMENTO-ARDEN-ARCADE-ROSEVILLE, CA	EL DORADO	$477,355	$587,092	$713,289	$823,026
	FRESNO, CA (MSA)	FRESNO	$381,250	$429,408	$521,711	$601,974
	NON-METRO	GLENN	$283,750	$337,168	$407,558	$506,495
	EUREKA-ARCATA-FORTUNA, CA (MICRO)	HUMBOLDT	$393,750	$443,487	$538,816	$621,711
	EL CENTRO, CA (MSA)	IMPERIAL	$274,934	$337,168	$407,558	$506,495
	BISHOP, CA (MICRO)	INYO	$477,355	$542,039	$658,553	$759,868

STATE	MSA NAME	COUNTY NAME	SAFE HARBOR AVERAGE PRICE 1 LIVING UNIT	2 LIVING UNITS	3 LIVING UNITS	4 LIVING UNITS
	BAKERSFIELD, CA (MSA)	KERN	$368,750	$415,329	$504,605	$582,237
	HANFORD-CORCORAN, CA (MSA)	KINGS	$312,316	$351,766	$427,379	$506,495
	CLEARLAKE, CA (MICRO)	LAKE	$401,250	$451,934	$549,079	$633,553
	LOS ANGELES-LONG BEACH-GLENDALE, CA METROPOLITAN	LOS ANGELES	$477,355	$611,117	$738,699	$918,021
	MADERA, CA (MSA)	MADERA	$425,000	$478,684	$581,579	$671,053
	SAN FRANCISCO-SAN MATEO-REDWOOD CITY, CA	MARIN	$477,355	$611,117	$738,699	$918,021
	NON-METRO	MARIPOSA	$411,704	$464,605	$564,474	$651,316
	UKIAH, CA (MICRO)	MENDOCINO	$477,355	$563,158	$684,211	$789,474
	MERCED, CA (MSA)	MERCED	$471,557	$531,122	$645,288	$744,564
	NON-METRO	MONO	$477,355	$611,117	$738,699	$918,021
	SALINAS, CA (MSA)	MONTEREY	$477,355	$611,117	$738,699	$918,021
	NAPA, CA (MSA)	NAPA	$477,355	$611,117	$738,699	$918,021
	TRUCKEE-GRASS VALLEY, CA (MICRO)	NEVADA	$477,355	$611,117	$738,699	$918,021
	SANTA ANA-ANAHEIM-IRVINE, CA METROPOLITAN	ORANGE	$477,355	$611,117	$738,699	$918,021
	SACRAMENTO-ARDEN-ARCADE-ROSEVILLE, CA	PLACER	$477,355	$587,092	$713,289	$823,026
	NON-METRO	PLUMAS	$410,000	$461,789	$561,053	$647,368
	RIVERSIDE-SAN BERNARDINO-ONTARIO, CA (MSA)	RIVERSIDE	$477,355	$561,711	$682,500	$787,500
	SACRAMENTO-ARDEN-ARCADE-ROSEVILLE, CA	SACRAMENTO	$477,355	$587,092	$713,289	$823,026
	SAN JOSE-SUNNYVALE-SANTA CLARA, CA (MSA)	SAN BENITO	$477,355	$611,117	$738,699	$918,021
	RIVERSIDE-SAN BERNARDINO-ONTARIO, CA (MSA)	SAN BERNARDINO	$477,355	$561,711	$682,500	$787,500
	SAN DIEGO-CARLSBAD-SAN MARCOS, CA (MSA)	SAN DIEGO	$477,355	$611,117	$738,699	$918,021
	SAN FRANCISCO-SAN MATEO-REDWOOD CITY, CA	SAN FRANCISCO	$477,355	$611,117	$738,699	$918,021
	STOCKTON, CA (MSA)	SAN JOAQUIN	$477,355	$549,079	$667,105	$769,737
	SAN LUIS OBISPO-PASO ROBLES, CA (MSA)	SAN LUIS OBISPO	$477,355	$611,117	$738,699	$918,021
	SAN FRANCISCO-SAN MATEO-REDWOOD CITY, CA	SAN MATEO	$477,355	$611,117	$738,699	$918,021
	SANTA BARBARA-SANTA MARIA, CA (MSA)	SANTA BARBARA	$477,355	$611,117	$738,699	$918,021
	SAN JOSE-SUNNYVALE-SANTA CLARA, CA (MSA)	SANTA CLARA	$477,355	$611,117	$738,699	$918,021
	SANTA CRUZ-WATSONVILLE, CA (MSA)	SANTA CRUZ	$477,355	$611,117	$738,699	$918,021
	REDDING, CA (MSA)	SHASTA	$423,625	$477,136	$579,697	$668,882
	NON-METRO	SISKIYOU	$293,750	$337,168	$407,558	$506,495

STATE	MSA NAME	COUNTY NAME	SAFE HARBOR AVERAGE PRICE 1 LIVING UNIT	2 LIVING UNITS	3 LIVING UNITS	4 LIVING UNITS
	VALLEJO-FAIRFIELD, CA (MSA)	SOLANO	$477,355	$611,117	$738,699	$907,895
	SANTA ROSA-PETALUMA, CA (MSA)	SONOMA	$477,355	$611,117	$738,699	$918,021
	MODESTO, CA (MSA)	STANISLAUS	$477,355	$537,653	$653,222	$753,718
	YUBA CITY, CA (MSA)	SUTTER	$424,680	$478,325	$581,142	$670,549
	RED BLUFF, CA (MICRO)	TEHAMA	$293,750	$337,168	$407,558	$506,495
	VISALIA-PORTERVILLE, CA (MSA)	TULARE	$325,000	$366,053	$444,737	$513,158
	PHOENIX LAKE-CEDAR RIDGE, CA (MICRO)	TUOLUMNE	$437,500	$492,763	$598,684	$690,789
	OXNARD-THOUSAND OAKS-VENTURA, CA (MSA)	VENTURA	$477,355	$611,117	$738,699	$918,021
	SACRAMENTO-ARDEN-ARCADE-ROSEVILLE, CA	YOLO	$477,355	$587,092	$713,289	$823,026
	YUBA CITY, CA (MSA)	YUBA	$424,680	$478,325	$581,142	$670,549
CO	DENVER-AURORA, CO (MSA)	ADAMS	$405,750	$457,003	$555,237	$640,658
	DENVER-AURORA, CO (MSA)	ARAPAHOE	$405,750	$457,003	$555,237	$640,658
	NON-METRO	ARCHULETA	$263,487	$337,168	$407,558	$506,495
	BOULDER, CO (MSA)	BOULDER	$458,500	$516,416	$627,421	$723,947
	DENVER-AURORA, CO (MSA)	BROOMFIELD	$405,750	$457,003	$555,237	$640,658
	DENVER-AURORA, CO (MSA)	CLEAR CREEK	$405,750	$457,003	$555,237	$640,658
	DENVER-AURORA, CO (MSA)	DENVER	$405,750	$457,003	$555,237	$640,658
	DENVER-AURORA, CO (MSA)	DOUGLAS	$405,750	$457,003	$555,237	$640,658
	EDWARDS, CO (MICRO)	EAGLE	$477,355	$537,653	$653,222	$753,718
	COLORADO SPRINGS, CO (MSA)	EL PASO	$325,000	$366,053	$444,737	$513,158
	DENVER-AURORA, CO (MSA)	ELBERT	$405,750	$457,003	$555,237	$640,658
	NON-METRO	GARFIELD	$393,209	$442,878	$538,075	$620,857
	DENVER-AURORA, CO (MSA)	GILPIN	$405,750	$457,003	$555,237	$640,658
	NON-METRO	GRAND	$293,750	$337,168	$407,558	$506,495
	DENVER-AURORA, CO (MSA)	JEFFERSON	$405,750	$457,003	$555,237	$640,658
	DURANGO, CO (MICRO)	LA PLATA	$303,750	$342,118	$415,658	$506,495
	EDWARDS, CO (MICRO)	LAKE	$477,355	$537,653	$653,222	$753,718
	FORT COLLINS-LOVELAND, CO (MSA)	LARIMER	$312,500	$351,974	$427,632	$506,495
	DENVER-AURORA, CO (MSA)	PARK	$405,750	$457,003	$555,237	$640,658
	NON-METRO	PITKIN	$381,999	$488,975	$591,028	$734,521
	NON-METRO	ROUTT	$398,026	$448,303	$544,667	$628,462
	NON-METRO	SAN MIGUEL	$477,355	$611,117	$738,699	$918,021
	SILVERTHORNE, CO (MICRO)	SUMMIT	$431,250	$485,724	$590,132	$680,921
	COLORADO SPRINGS, CO (MSA)	TELLER	$325,000	$366,053	$444,737	$513,158
	GREELEY, CO (MSA)	WELD	$361,250	$406,882	$494,342	$570,395
CT	BRIDGEPORT-STAMFORD-NORWALK, CT (MSA)	FAIRFIELD	$477,355	$611,117	$738,699	$918,021
	HARTFORD-WEST HARTFORD-EAST HARTFORD, CT	HARTFORD	$439,125	$494,593	$600,908	$693,355
	TORRINGTON, CT (MICRO)	LITCHFIELD	$375,000	$422,368	$513,158	$592,105

STATE	MSA NAME	COUNTY NAME	SAFE HARBOR AVERAGE PRICE 1 LIVING UNIT	2 LIVING UNITS	3 LIVING UNITS	4 LIVING UNITS
	HARTFORD-WEST HARTFORD-EAST HARTFORD, CT	MIDDLESEX	$439,125	$494,593	$600,908	$693,355
	NEW HAVEN-MILFORD, CT (MSA)	NEW HAVEN	$385,625	$435,039	$528,553	$609,868
	NORWICH-NEW LONDON, CT (MSA)	NEW LONDON	$398,750	$449,118	$545,658	$629,605
	HARTFORD-WEST HARTFORD-EAST HARTFORD, CT	TOLLAND	$439,125	$494,593	$600,908	$693,355
DC	WASHINGTON-ARLINGTON-ALEXANDRIA, DC-VA-MD	DISTRICT OF COL	$477,355	$611,117	$738,699	$888,158
DE	DOVER, DE (MSA)	KENT	$350,395	$394,655	$479,487	$553,255
	WILMINGTON, DE-MD-NJ METROPOLITAN DIVISION	NEW CASTLE	$385,112	$433,758	$526,996	$608,072
	SEAFORD, DE (MICRO)	SUSSEX	$325,000	$366,053	$444,737	$513,158
FL	GAINESVILLE, FL (MSA)	ALACHUA	$269,000	$337,168	$407,558	$506,495
	JACKSONVILLE, FL (MSA)	BAKER	$387,500	$436,447	$530,263	$611,842
	PANAMA CITY-LYNN HAVEN, FL (MSA)	BAY	$331,250	$373,092	$453,289	$523,026
	PALM BAY-MELBOURNE-TITUSVILLE, FL (MSA)	BREVARD	$291,250	$337,168	$407,558	$506,495
	FORT LAUDERDALE-POMPANO BEACH-DEERFIELD	BROWARD	$477,355	$544,336	$661,343	$763,088
	PUNTA GORDA, FL (MSA)	CHARLOTTE	$295,012	$337,168	$407,558	$506,495
	JACKSONVILLE, FL (MSA)	CLAY	$387,500	$436,447	$530,263	$611,842
	NAPLES-MARCO ISLAND, FL (MSA)	COLLIER	$477,355	$563,017	$684,039	$789,276
	JACKSONVILLE, FL (MSA)	DUVAL	$387,500	$436,447	$530,263	$611,842
	PALM COAST, FL (MICRO)	FLAGLER	$287,500	$337,168	$407,558	$506,495
	GAINESVILLE, FL (MSA)	GILCHRIST	$269,000	$337,168	$407,558	$506,495
	TAMPA-ST. PETERSBURG-CLEARWATER, FL (MSA)	HERNANDO	$292,500	$337,168	$407,558	$506,495
	TAMPA-ST. PETERSBURG-CLEARWATER, FL (MSA)	HILLSBOROUGH	$292,500	$337,168	$407,558	$506,495
	SEBASTIAN-VERO BEACH, FL (MSA)	INDIAN RIVER	$281,250	$337,168	$407,558	$506,495
	ORLANDO-KISSIMMEE, FL (MSA)	LAKE	$338,750	$381,539	$463,553	$534,868
	CAPE CORAL-FORT MYERS, FL (MSA)	LEE	$356,250	$401,250	$487,500	$562,500
	SARASOTA-BRADENTON-VENICE, FL (MSA)	MANATEE	$442,237	$498,097	$605,166	$698,268
	PORT ST. LUCIE-FORT PIERCE, FL (MSA)	MARTIN	$364,000	$409,979	$498,105	$574,737
	MIAMI-MIAMI BEACH-KENDALL, FL METROPOLITAN	MIAMI-DADE	$477,355	$544,336	$661,343	$763,088
	KEY WEST-MARATHON, FL (MICRO)	MONROE	$477,355	$611,117	$738,699	$918,021
	JACKSONVILLE, FL (MSA)	NASSAU	$387,500	$436,447	$530,263	$611,842

STATE	MSA NAME	COUNTY NAME	SAFE HARBOR AVERAGE PRICE 1 LIVING UNIT	2 LIVING UNITS	3 LIVING UNITS	4 LIVING UNITS
	FORT WALTON BEACH-CRESTVIEW-DESTIN, FL (MSA)	OKALOOSA	$312,375	$351,833	$427,461	$506,495
	ORLANDO-KISSIMMEE, FL (MSA)	ORANGE	$338,750	$381,539	$463,553	$534,868
	ORLANDO-KISSIMMEE, FL (MSA)	OSCEOLA	$338,750	$381,539	$463,553	$534,868
	WEST PALM BEACH-BOCA RATON-BOYNTON BEACH	PALM BEACH	$477,355	$544,336	$661,343	$763,088
	TAMPA-ST. PETERSBURG-CLEARWATER, FL (MSA)	PASCO	$292,500	$337,168	$407,558	$506,495
	TAMPA-ST. PETERSBURG-CLEARWATER, FL (MSA)	PINELLAS	$292,500	$337,168	$407,558	$506,495
	LAKELAND, FL (MSA)	POLK	$270,000	$337,168	$407,558	$506,495
	SARASOTA-BRADENTON-VENICE, FL (MSA)	SARASOTA	$442,237	$498,097	$605,166	$698,268
	ORLANDO-KISSIMMEE, FL (MSA)	SEMINOLE	$338,750	$381,539	$463,553	$534,868
	JACKSONVILLE, FL (MSA)	ST. JOHNS	$387,500	$436,447	$530,263	$611,842
	PORT ST. LUCIE-FORT PIERCE, FL (MSA)	ST. LUCIE	$364,000	$409,979	$498,105	$574,737
	DELTONA-DAYTONA BEACH-ORMOND BEACH, FL (MSA)	VOLUSIA	$302,864	$341,121	$414,446	$506,495
	NON-METRO	WALTON	$477,355	$538,520	$654,276	$791,700
GA	ATLANTA-SANDY SPRINGS-MARIETTA, GA (MSA)	BARROW	$332,750	$374,782	$455,342	$525,395
	ATLANTA-SANDY SPRINGS-MARIETTA, GA (MSA)	BARTOW	$332,750	$374,782	$455,342	$525,395
	BRUNSWICK, GA (MSA)	BRANTLEY	$275,921	$337,168	$407,558	$506,495
	ATLANTA-SANDY SPRINGS-MARIETTA, GA (MSA)	BUTTS	$332,750	$374,782	$455,342	$525,395
	ATLANTA-SANDY SPRINGS-MARIETTA, GA (MSA)	CARROLL	$332,750	$374,782	$455,342	$525,395
	ATLANTA-SANDY SPRINGS-MARIETTA, GA (MSA)	CHEROKEE	$332,750	$374,782	$455,342	$525,395
	ATLANTA-SANDY SPRINGS-MARIETTA, GA (MSA)	CLAYTON	$332,750	$374,782	$455,342	$525,395
	ATLANTA-SANDY SPRINGS-MARIETTA, GA (MSA)	COBB	$332,750	$374,782	$455,342	$525,395
	ATLANTA-SANDY SPRINGS-MARIETTA, GA (MSA)	COWETA	$332,750	$374,782	$455,342	$525,395
	ATLANTA-SANDY SPRINGS-MARIETTA, GA (MSA)	DAWSON	$332,750	$374,782	$455,342	$525,395

STATE	MSA NAME	COUNTY NAME	SAFE HARBOR AVERAGE PRICE			
			1 LIVING UNIT	2 LIVING UNITS	3 LIVING UNITS	4 LIVING UNITS
	ATLANTA-SANDY SPRINGS-MARIETTA, GA (MSA)	DEKALB	$332,750	$374,782	$455,342	$525,395
	ATLANTA-SANDY SPRINGS-MARIETTA, GA (MSA)	DOUGLAS	$332,750	$374,782	$455,342	$525,395
	ATLANTA-SANDY SPRINGS-MARIETTA, GA (MSA)	FAYETTE	$332,750	$374,782	$455,342	$525,395
	ATLANTA-SANDY SPRINGS-MARIETTA, GA (MSA)	FORSYTH	$332,750	$374,782	$455,342	$525,395
	ATLANTA-SANDY SPRINGS-MARIETTA, GA (MSA)	FULTON	$332,750	$374,782	$455,342	$525,395
	BRUNSWICK, GA (MSA)	GLYNN	$275,921	$337,168	$407,558	$506,495
	ATLANTA-SANDY SPRINGS-MARIETTA, GA (MSA)	GWINNETT	$332,750	$374,782	$455,342	$525,395
	ATLANTA-SANDY SPRINGS-MARIETTA, GA (MSA)	HARALSON	$332,750	$374,782	$455,342	$525,395
	ATLANTA-SANDY SPRINGS-MARIETTA, GA (MSA)	HEARD	$332,750	$374,782	$455,342	$525,395
	ATLANTA-SANDY SPRINGS-MARIETTA, GA (MSA)	HENRY	$332,750	$374,782	$455,342	$525,395
	ATLANTA-SANDY SPRINGS-MARIETTA, GA (MSA)	JASPER	$332,750	$374,782	$455,342	$525,395
	ATLANTA-SANDY SPRINGS-MARIETTA, GA (MSA)	LAMAR	$332,750	$374,782	$455,342	$525,395
	BRUNSWICK, GA (MSA)	MCINTOSH	$275,921	$337,168	$407,558	$506,495
	ATLANTA-SANDY SPRINGS-MARIETTA, GA (MSA)	MERIWETHER	$332,750	$374,782	$455,342	$525,395
	ATLANTA-SANDY SPRINGS-MARIETTA, GA (MSA)	NEWTON	$332,750	$374,782	$455,342	$525,395
	ATLANTA-SANDY SPRINGS-MARIETTA, GA (MSA)	PAULDING	$332,750	$374,782	$455,342	$525,395
	ATLANTA-SANDY SPRINGS-MARIETTA, GA (MSA)	PICKENS	$332,750	$374,782	$455,342	$525,395
	ATLANTA-SANDY SPRINGS-MARIETTA, GA (MSA)	PIKE	$332,750	$374,782	$455,342	$525,395
	ATLANTA-SANDY SPRINGS-MARIETTA, GA (MSA)	ROCKDALE	$332,750	$374,782	$455,342	$525,395

STATE	MSA NAME	COUNTY NAME	SAFE HARBOR AVERAGE PRICE 1 LIVING UNIT	2 LIVING UNITS	3 LIVING UNITS	4 LIVING UNITS
	ATLANTA-SANDY SPRINGS-MARIETTA, GA (MSA)	SPALDING	$332,750	$374,782	$455,342	$525,395
	ATLANTA-SANDY SPRINGS-MARIETTA, GA (MSA)	WALTON	$332,750	$374,782	$455,342	$525,395
HI	HILO, HI (MICRO)	HAWAII	$593,750	$668,750	$812,500	$937,500
	HONOLULU, HI (MSA)	HONOLULU	$716,033	$865,929	$1,052,063	$1,213,918
	KAPAA, HI (MICRO)	KAUAI	$716,033	$851,776	$1,034,868	$1,194,079
	KAHULUI-WAILUKU, HI (MICRO)	MAUI	$716,033	$840,461	$1,021,184	$1,178,289
ID	BOISE CITY-NAMPA, ID (MSA)	ADA	$296,250	$337,168	$407,558	$506,495
	NON-METRO	BLAINE	$477,355	$584,276	$709,868	$819,079
	BOISE CITY-NAMPA, ID (MSA)	BOISE	$296,250	$337,168	$407,558	$506,495
	BOISE CITY-NAMPA, ID (MSA)	CANYON	$296,250	$337,168	$407,558	$506,495
	BOISE CITY-NAMPA, ID (MSA)	GEM	$296,250	$337,168	$407,558	$506,495
	COEUR D'ALENE, ID (MSA)	KOOTENAI	$286,250	$337,168	$407,558	$506,495
	BOISE CITY-NAMPA, ID (MSA)	OWYHEE	$296,250	$337,168	$407,558	$506,495
	JACKSON, WY-ID (MICRO)	TETON	$477,355	$611,117	$738,699	$918,021
	NON-METRO	VALLEY	$416,842	$469,495	$570,461	$658,224
IL	ST. LOUIS, MO-IL (MSA)	BOND	$281,250	$337,168	$407,558	$506,495
	ST. LOUIS, MO-IL (MSA)	CALHOUN	$281,250	$337,168	$407,558	$506,495
	ST. LOUIS, MO-IL (MSA)	CLINTON	$281,250	$337,168	$407,558	$506,495
	CHICAGO-NAPERVILLE-JOLIET, IL METROPOLITAN	COOK	$362,105	$407,845	$495,512	$571,745
	CHICAGO-NAPERVILLE-JOLIET, IL METROPOLITAN	DEKALB	$362,105	$407,845	$495,512	$571,745
	CHICAGO-NAPERVILLE-JOLIET, IL METROPOLITAN	DUPAGE	$362,105	$407,845	$495,512	$571,745
	CHICAGO-NAPERVILLE-JOLIET, IL METROPOLITAN	GRUNDY	$362,105	$407,845	$495,512	$571,745
	ST. LOUIS, MO-IL (MSA)	JERSEY	$281,250	$337,168	$407,558	$506,495
	CHICAGO-NAPERVILLE-JOLIET, IL METROPOLITAN	KANE	$362,105	$407,845	$495,512	$571,745
	CHICAGO-NAPERVILLE-JOLIET, IL METROPOLITAN	KENDALL	$362,105	$407,845	$495,512	$571,745
	LAKE COUNTY-KENOSHA COUNTY, IL-WI METROP	LAKE	$362,105	$407,845	$495,512	$571,745
	ST. LOUIS, MO-IL (MSA)	MACOUPIN	$281,250	$337,168	$407,558	$506,495
	ST. LOUIS, MO-IL (MSA)	MADISON	$281,250	$337,168	$407,558	$506,495
	CHICAGO-NAPERVILLE-JOLIET, IL METROPOLITAN	MCHENRY	$362,105	$407,845	$495,512	$571,745
	ST. LOUIS, MO-IL (MSA)	MONROE	$281,250	$337,168	$407,558	$506,495
	ST. LOUIS, MO-IL (MSA)	ST. CLAIR	$281,250	$337,168	$407,558	$506,495
	CHICAGO-NAPERVILLE-JOLIET, IL METROPOLITAN	WILL	$362,105	$407,845	$495,512	$571,745

STATE	MSA NAME	COUNTY NAME	SAFE HARBOR AVERAGE PRICE 1 LIVING UNIT	2 LIVING UNITS	3 LIVING UNITS	4 LIVING UNITS
IN	LOUISVILLE-JEFFERON COUNTY, KY-IN (MSA)	CLARK	$281,125	$337,168	$407,558	$506,495
	CINCINNATI-MIDDLETOWN, OH-KY-IN (MSA)	DEARBORN	$332,500	$374,500	$455,000	$525,000
	LOUISVILLE-JEFFERON COUNTY, KY-IN (MSA)	FLOYD	$281,125	$337,168	$407,558	$506,495
	CINCINNATI-MIDDLETOWN, OH-KY-IN (MSA)	FRANKLIN	$332,500	$374,500	$455,000	$525,000
	LOUISVILLE-JEFFERON COUNTY, KY-IN (MSA)	HARRISON	$281,125	$337,168	$407,558	$506,495
	GARY, IN METROPOLITAN DIVISION	JASPER	$362,105	$407,845	$495,512	$571,745
	GARY, IN METROPOLITAN DIVISION	LAKE	$362,105	$407,845	$495,512	$571,745
	GARY, IN METROPOLITAN DIVISION	NEWTON	$362,105	$407,845	$495,512	$571,745
	CINCINNATI-MIDDLETOWN, OH-KY-IN (MSA)	OHIO	$332,500	$374,500	$455,000	$525,000
	GARY, IN METROPOLITAN DIVISION	PORTER	$362,105	$407,845	$495,512	$571,745
	LOUISVILLE-JEFFERON COUNTY, KY-IN (MSA)	WASHINGTON	$281,125	$337,168	$407,558	$506,495
KS	KANSAS CITY, MO-KS (MSA)	FRANKLIN	$268,750	$337,168	$407,558	$506,495
	KANSAS CITY, MO-KS (MSA)	JOHNSON	$268,750	$337,168	$407,558	$506,495
	KANSAS CITY, MO-KS (MSA)	LEAVENWORTH	$268,750	$337,168	$407,558	$506,495
	KANSAS CITY, MO-KS (MSA)	LINN	$268,750	$337,168	$407,558	$506,495
	KANSAS CITY, MO-KS (MSA)	MIAMI	$268,750	$337,168	$407,558	$506,495
	KANSAS CITY, MO-KS (MSA)	WYANDOTTE	$268,750	$337,168	$407,558	$506,495
KY	CINCINNATI-MIDDLETOWN, OH-KY-IN (MSA)	BOONE	$332,500	$374,500	$455,000	$525,000
	CINCINNATI-MIDDLETOWN, OH-KY-IN (MSA)	BRACKEN	$332,500	$374,500	$455,000	$525,000
	LOUISVILLE-JEFFERON COUNTY, KY-IN (MSA)	BULLITT	$281,125	$337,168	$407,558	$506,495
	CINCINNATI-MIDDLETOWN, OH-KY-IN (MSA)	CAMPBELL	$332,500	$374,500	$455,000	$525,000
	CINCINNATI-MIDDLETOWN, OH-KY-IN (MSA)	GALLATIN	$332,500	$374,500	$455,000	$525,000
	CINCINNATI-MIDDLETOWN, OH-KY-IN (MSA)	GRANT	$332,500	$374,500	$455,000	$525,000
	LOUISVILLE-JEFFERON COUNTY, KY-IN (MSA)	HENRY	$281,125	$337,168	$407,558	$506,495
	LOUISVILLE-JEFFERON COUNTY, KY-IN (MSA)	JEFFERSON	$281,125	$337,168	$407,558	$506,495
	CINCINNATI-MIDDLETOWN, OH-KY-IN (MSA)	KENTON	$332,500	$374,500	$455,000	$525,000
	LOUISVILLE-JEFFERON COUNTY, KY-IN (MSA)	MEADE	$281,125	$337,168	$407,558	$506,495
	LOUISVILLE-JEFFERON COUNTY, KY-IN (MSA)	NELSON	$281,125	$337,168	$407,558	$506,495

STATE	MSA NAME	COUNTY NAME	SAFE HARBOR AVERAGE PRICE 1 LIVING UNIT	2 LIVING UNITS	3 LIVING UNITS	4 LIVING UNITS
	LOUISVILLE-JEFFERON COUNTY, KY-IN (MSA)	OLDHAM	$281,125	$337,168	$407,558	$506,495
	CINCINNATI-MIDDLETOWN, OH-KY-IN (MSA)	PENDLETON	$332,500	$374,500	$455,000	$525,000
	LOUISVILLE-JEFFERON COUNTY, KY-IN (MSA)	SHELBY	$281,125	$337,168	$407,558	$506,495
	LOUISVILLE-JEFFERON COUNTY, KY-IN (MSA)	SPENCER	$281,125	$337,168	$407,558	$506,495
	LOUISVILLE-JEFFERON COUNTY, KY-IN (MSA)	TRIMBLE	$281,125	$337,168	$407,558	$506,495
MA	BARNSTABLE TOWN, MA (MSA)	BARNSTABLE	$477,355	$577,237	$701,316	$809,211
	PROVIDENCE-NEW BEDFORD-FALL RIVER, RI-MA	BRISTOL	$416,250	$472,891	$571,567	$710,309
	NON-METRO	DUKES	$477,355	$611,117	$738,699	$918,021
	ESSEX COUNTY, MA METROPOLITAN DIVISION	ESSEX	$477,355	$606,728	$737,146	$850,554
	SPRINGFIELD, MA (MSA)	FRANKLIN	$273,500	$337,168	$407,558	$506,495
	SPRINGFIELD, MA (MSA)	HAMPDEN	$273,500	$337,168	$407,558	$506,495
	SPRINGFIELD, MA (MSA)	HAMPSHIRE	$273,500	$337,168	$407,558	$506,495
	CAMBRIDGE-NEWTON-FRAMINGHAM, MA METROPOLITAN	MIDDLESEX	$477,355	$606,728	$737,146	$850,554
	NON-METRO	NANTUCKET	$477,355	$611,117	$738,699	$918,021
	BOSTON-QUINCY, MA METROPOLITAN DIVISION	NORFOLK	$477,355	$606,728	$737,146	$850,554
	BOSTON-QUINCY, MA METROPOLITAN DIVISION	PLYMOUTH	$477,355	$606,728	$737,146	$850,554
	BOSTON-QUINCY, MA METROPOLITAN DIVISION	SUFFOLK	$477,355	$606,728	$737,146	$850,554
	WORCESTER, MA (MSA)	WORCESTER	$385,000	$488,975	$591,028	$734,521
MD	BALTIMORE-TOWSON, MD (MSA)	ANNE ARUNDEL	$477,355	$537,653	$653,222	$753,718
	BALTIMORE-TOWSON, MD (MSA)	BALTIMORE	$477,355	$537,653	$653,222	$753,718
	BALTIMORE-TOWSON, MD (MSA)	BALTIMORE CITY	$477,355	$537,653	$653,222	$753,718
	WASHINGTON-ARLINGTON-ALEXANDRIA, DC-VA-METROPOLITAN	CALVERT	$477,355	$611,117	$738,699	$888,158
	BALTIMORE-TOWSON, MD (MSA)	CARROLL	$477,355	$537,653	$653,222	$753,718
	WILMINGTON, DE-MD-NJ METROPOLITAN DIVISION	CECIL	$385,112	$433,758	$526,996	$608,072
	WASHINGTON-ARLINGTON-ALEXANDRIA, DC-VA-METROPOLITAN	CHARLES	$477,355	$611,117	$738,699	$888,158
	BETHESDA-GAITHERSBURG-FREDERICK, MD METROPOLITAN	FREDERICK	$477,355	$611,117	$738,699	$888,158
	NON-METRO	GARRETT	$437,500	$492,763	$598,684	$690,789

STATE	MSA NAME	COUNTY NAME	SAFE HARBOR AVERAGE PRICE 1 LIVING UNIT	2 LIVING UNITS	3 LIVING UNITS	4 LIVING UNITS
	BALTIMORE-TOWSON, MD (MSA)	HARFORD	$477,355	$537,653	$653,222	$753,718
	BALTIMORE-TOWSON, MD (MSA)	HOWARD	$477,355	$537,653	$653,222	$753,718
	NON-METRO	KENT	$327,089	$368,405	$447,596	$516,457
	BETHESDA-GAITHERSBURG-FREDERICK, MD METROPOLITAN	MONTGOMERY	$477,355	$611,117	$738,699	$888,158
	WASHINGTON-ARLINGTON-ALEXANDRIA, DC-VA-METROPOLITAN	PRINCE GEORGE'S	$477,355	$611,117	$738,699	$888,158
	BALTIMORE-TOWSON, MD (MSA)	QUEEN ANNE'S	$477,355	$537,653	$653,222	$753,718
	SALISBURY, MD (MSA)	SOMERSET	$296,250	$337,168	$407,558	$506,495
	LEXINGTON PARK, MD (MICRO)	ST. MARY'S	$371,053	$417,922	$507,755	$585,872
	EASTON, MD (MICRO)	TALBOT	$371,250	$418,145	$508,026	$599,342
	HAGERSTOWN-MARTINSBURG, MD-WV (MSA)	WASHINGTON	$362,500	$408,289	$496,053	$572,368
	SALISBURY, MD (MSA)	WICOMICO	$296,250	$337,168	$407,558	$506,495
	OCEAN PINES, MD (MICRO)	WORCESTER	$437,499	$492,761	$598,682	$690,787
ME	PORTLAND-SOUTH PORTLAND-BIDDEFORD, ME (MSA)	CUMBERLAND	$336,875	$379,428	$460,987	$531,908
	NON-METRO	HANCOCK	$272,500	$337,168	$407,558	$506,495
	NON-METRO	LINCOLN	$317,625	$357,746	$434,645	$506,495
	PORTLAND-SOUTH PORTLAND-BIDDEFORD, ME (MSA)	SAGADAHOC	$336,875	$379,428	$460,987	$531,908
	PORTLAND-SOUTH PORTLAND-BIDDEFORD, ME (MSA)	YORK	$336,875	$379,428	$460,987	$531,908
MI	NILES-BENTON HARBOR, MI (MSA)	BERRIEN	$298,750	$337,168	$408,816	$506,495
	KALAMAZOO-PORTAGE, MI (MSA)	KALAMAZOO	$285,625	$337,168	$407,558	$506,495
	WARREN-TROY-FARMINGTON HILLS, MI METROPOLITAN	LAPEER	$297,500	$337,168	$407,558	$506,495
	ADRIAN, MI (MICRO)	LENAWEE	$297,500	$337,168	$407,558	$506,495
	WARREN-TROY-FARMINGTON HILLS, MI METROPOLITAN	LIVINGSTON	$297,500	$337,168	$407,558	$506,495
	WARREN-TROY-FARMINGTON HILLS, MI METROPOLITAN	MACOMB	$297,500	$337,168	$407,558	$506,495
	MONROE, MI (MSA)	MONROE	$297,500	$337,168	$407,558	$506,495
	WARREN-TROY-FARMINGTON HILLS, MI METROPOLITAN	OAKLAND	$297,500	$337,168	$407,558	$506,495
	WARREN-TROY-FARMINGTON HILLS, MI METROPOLITAN	ST. CLAIR	$297,500	$337,168	$407,558	$506,495
	KALAMAZOO-PORTAGE, MI (MSA)	VAN BUREN	$285,625	$337,168	$407,558	$506,495
	ANN ARBOR, MI (MSA)	WASHTENAW	$344,875	$388,438	$471,934	$544,539

STATE	MSA NAME	COUNTY NAME	SAFE HARBOR AVERAGE PRICE			
			1 LIVING UNIT	2 LIVING UNITS	3 LIVING UNITS	4 LIVING UNITS
	DETROIT-LIVONIA-DEARBORN, MI METROPOLITAN	WAYNE	$297,500	$337,168	$407,558	$506,495
MN	MINNEAPOLIS-ST. PAUL-BLOOMINGTON, MN-WI	ANOKA	$331,250	$373,092	$453,289	$523,026
	MINNEAPOLIS-ST. PAUL-BLOOMINGTON, MN-WI	CARVER	$331,250	$373,092	$453,289	$523,026
	MINNEAPOLIS-ST. PAUL-BLOOMINGTON, MN-WI	CHISAGO	$331,250	$373,092	$453,289	$523,026
	MINNEAPOLIS-ST. PAUL-BLOOMINGTON, MN-WI	DAKOTA	$331,250	$373,092	$453,289	$523,026
	MINNEAPOLIS-ST. PAUL-BLOOMINGTON, MN-WI	HENNEPIN	$331,250	$373,092	$453,289	$523,026
	MINNEAPOLIS-ST. PAUL-BLOOMINGTON, MN-WI	ISANTI	$331,250	$373,092	$453,289	$523,026
	MINNEAPOLIS-ST. PAUL-BLOOMINGTON, MN-WI	RAMSEY	$331,250	$373,092	$453,289	$523,026
	MINNEAPOLIS-ST. PAUL-BLOOMINGTON, MN-WI	SCOTT	$331,250	$373,092	$453,289	$523,026
	MINNEAPOLIS-ST. PAUL-BLOOMINGTON, MN-WI	SHERBURNE	$331,250	$373,092	$453,289	$523,026
	MINNEAPOLIS-ST. PAUL-BLOOMINGTON, MN-WI	WASHINGTON	$331,250	$373,092	$453,289	$523,026
	MINNEAPOLIS-ST. PAUL-BLOOMINGTON, MN-WI	WRIGHT	$331,250	$373,092	$453,289	$523,026
MO	KANSAS CITY, MO-KS (MSA)	BATES	$268,750	$337,168	$407,558	$506,495
	KANSAS CITY, MO-KS (MSA)	CALDWELL	$268,750	$337,168	$407,558	$506,495
	KANSAS CITY, MO-KS (MSA)	CASS	$268,750	$337,168	$407,558	$506,495
	KANSAS CITY, MO-KS (MSA)	CLAY	$268,750	$337,168	$407,558	$506,495
	KANSAS CITY, MO-KS (MSA)	CLINTON	$268,750	$337,168	$407,558	$506,495
	ST. LOUIS, MO-IL (MSA)	CRAWFORD	$281,250	$337,168	$407,558	$506,495
	ST. LOUIS, MO-IL (MSA)	FRANKLIN	$281,250	$337,168	$407,558	$506,495
	KANSAS CITY, MO-KS (MSA)	JACKSON	$268,750	$337,168	$407,558	$506,495
	ST. LOUIS, MO-IL (MSA)	JEFFERSON	$281,250	$337,168	$407,558	$506,495
	KANSAS CITY, MO-KS (MSA)	LAFAYETTE	$268,750	$337,168	$407,558	$506,495
	ST. LOUIS, MO-IL (MSA)	LINCOLN	$281,250	$337,168	$407,558	$506,495
	KANSAS CITY, MO-KS (MSA)	PLATTE	$268,750	$337,168	$407,558	$506,495
	KANSAS CITY, MO-KS (MSA)	RAY	$268,750	$337,168	$407,558	$506,495
	ST. LOUIS, MO-IL (MSA)	ST. CHARLES	$281,250	$337,168	$407,558	$506,495
	ST. LOUIS, MO-IL (MSA)	ST. LOUIS	$281,250	$337,168	$407,558	$506,495
	ST. LOUIS, MO-IL (MSA)	ST. LOUIS CITY	$281,250	$337,168	$407,558	$506,495
	ST. LOUIS, MO-IL (MSA)	WARREN	$281,250	$337,168	$407,558	$506,495
	ST. LOUIS, MO-IL (MSA)	WASHINGTON	$281,250	$337,168	$407,558	$506,495
MT	MISSOULA, MT (MSA)	MISSOULA	$290,625	$337,168	$407,558	$506,495
NC	WILMINGTON, NC (MSA)	BRUNSWICK	$303,125	$341,414	$414,803	$506,495
	VIRGINIA BEACH-NORFOLK-NEWPORT NEWS, VA-NC (MSA)	CURRITUCK	$412,500	$464,605	$564,474	$651,316
	RALEIGH-CARY, NC (MSA)	FRANKLIN	$266,875	$337,168	$407,558	$506,495

STATE	MSA NAME	COUNTY NAME	SAFE HARBOR AVERAGE PRICE			
			1 LIVING UNIT	2 LIVING UNITS	3 LIVING UNITS	4 LIVING UNITS
	RALEIGH-CARY, NC (MSA)	JOHNSTON	$266,875	$337,168	$407,558	$506,495
	WILMINGTON, NC (MSA)	NEW HANOVER	$303,125	$341,414	$414,803	$506,495
	JACKSONVILLE, NC (MSA)	ONSLOW	$306,250	$344,934	$419,079	$506,495
	WILMINGTON, NC (MSA)	PENDER	$303,125	$341,414	$414,803	$506,495
	RALEIGH-CARY, NC (MSA)	WAKE	$266,875	$337,168	$407,558	$506,495
NH	MANCHESTER-NASHUA, NH (MSA)	HILLSBOROUGH	$401,875	$488,975	$591,028	$734,521
	CONCORD, NH (MICRO)	MERRIMACK	$277,500	$337,168	$407,558	$506,495
	ROCKINGHAM COUNTY-STRAFFORD COUNTY, NH METROPOLITAN	ROCKINGHAM	$477,355	$606,728	$737,146	$850,554
	ROCKINGHAM COUNTY-STRAFFORD COUNTY, NH METROPOLITAN	STRAFFORD	$477,355	$606,728	$737,146	$850,554
NJ	ATLANTIC CITY, NJ (MSA)	ATLANTIC	$425,000	$478,684	$581,579	$671,053
	NEW YORK-WHITE PLAINS-WAYNE, NY-NJ METROPOLITAN	BERGEN	$477,355	$611,117	$738,699	$918,021
	CAMDEN, NJ METROPOLITAN DIVISION	BURLINGTON	$385,112	$433,758	$526,996	$608,072
	CAMDEN, NJ METROPOLITAN DIVISION	CAMDEN	$385,112	$433,758	$526,996	$608,072
	OCEAN CITY, NJ (MSA)	CAPE MAY	$477,355	$558,934	$679,079	$783,553
	VINELAND-MILLVILLE-BRIDGETON, NJ (MSA)	CUMBERLAND	$405,000	$456,158	$554,211	$639,474
	NEWARK-UNION, NJ-PA METROPOLITAN DIVISION	ESSEX	$477,355	$611,117	$738,699	$918,021
	CAMDEN, NJ METROPOLITAN DIVISION	GLOUCESTER	$385,112	$433,758	$526,996	$608,072
	NEW YORK-WHITE PLAINS-WAYNE, NY-NJ METROPOLITAN	HUDSON	$477,355	$611,117	$738,699	$918,021
	NEWARK-UNION, NJ-PA METROPOLITAN DIVISION	HUNTERDON	$477,355	$611,117	$738,699	$918,021
	TRENTON-EWING, NJ (MSA)	MERCER	$439,550	$495,071	$601,489	$694,026
	EDISON, NJ METROPOLITAN DIVISION	MIDDLESEX	$477,355	$611,117	$738,699	$918,021
	EDISON, NJ METROPOLITAN DIVISION	MONMOUTH	$477,355	$611,117	$738,699	$918,021
	NEWARK-UNION, NJ-PA METROPOLITAN DIVISION	MORRIS	$477,355	$611,117	$738,699	$918,021
	EDISON, NJ METROPOLITAN DIVISION	OCEAN	$477,355	$611,117	$738,699	$918,021
	NEW YORK-WHITE PLAINS-WAYNE, NY-NJ METROPOLITAN	PASSAIC	$477,355	$611,117	$738,699	$918,021
	WILMINGTON, DE-MD-NJ METROPOLITAN DIVISION	SALEM	$385,112	$433,758	$526,996	$608,072
	EDISON, NJ METROPOLITAN DIVISION	SOMERSET	$477,355	$611,117	$738,699	$918,021

STATE	MSA NAME	COUNTY NAME	SAFE HARBOR AVERAGE PRICE 1 LIVING UNIT	2 LIVING UNITS	3 LIVING UNITS	4 LIVING UNITS
	NEWARK-UNION, NJ-PA METROPOLITAN DIVISION	SUSSEX	$477,355	$611,117	$738,699	$918,021
	NEWARK-UNION, NJ-PA METROPOLITAN DIVISION	UNION	$477,355	$611,117	$738,699	$918,021
	ALLENTOWN-BETHLEHEM-EASTON, PA-NJ (MSA)	WARREN	$402,192	$459,255	$557,974	$643,816
NM	LOS ALAMOS, NM (MICRO)	LOS ALAMOS	$318,750	$359,013	$436,184	$506,495
	FARMINGTON, NM (MSA)	SAN JUAN	$281,250	$337,168	$407,558	$506,495
	SANTA FE, NM (MSA)	SANTA FE	$381,999	$449,471	$546,086	$630,099
NV	CARSON CITY, NV (MSA)	CARSON CITY	$398,750	$449,118	$545,658	$629,605
	LAS VEGAS-PARADISE, NV (MSA)	CLARK	$400,000	$450,526	$547,368	$631,579
	GARDNERVILLE RANCHOS, NV (MICRO)	DOUGLAS	$477,355	$582,829	$708,158	$817,105
	ELKO, NV (MICRO)	ELKO	$325,000	$366,053	$444,737	$513,158
	ELKO, NV (MICRO)	EUREKA	$325,000	$366,053	$444,737	$513,158
	FERNLEY, NV (MICRO)	LYON	$331,250	$373,092	$453,289	$523,026
	PAHRUMP, NV (MICRO)	NYE	$325,000	$366,053	$444,737	$513,158
	RENO-SPARKS, NV (MSA)	STOREY	$477,355	$537,653	$653,222	$753,718
	RENO-SPARKS, NV (MSA)	WASHOE	$477,355	$537,653	$653,222	$753,718
NY	ALBANY-SCHENECTADY-TROY, NY (MSA)	ALBANY	$300,000	$337,895	$410,526	$506,495
	NEW YORK-WHITE PLAINS-WAYNE, NY-NJ METRO	BRONX	$477,355	$611,117	$738,699	$918,021
	POUGHKEEPSIE-NEWBURGH-MIDDLETOWN, NY (MSA)	DUTCHESS	$443,750	$499,803	$607,237	$700,658
	BUFFALO-NIAGARA FALLS, NY (MSA)	ERIE	$275,075	$337,168	$407,558	$506,495
	NEW YORK-WHITE PLAINS-WAYNE, NY-NJ METROPOLITAN	KINGS	$477,355	$611,117	$738,699	$918,021
	ROCHESTER, NY (MSA)	LIVINGSTON	$268,750	$337,168	$407,558	$506,495
	SYRACUSE, NY (MSA)	MADISON	$267,500	$337,168	$407,558	$506,495
	ROCHESTER, NY (MSA)	MONROE	$268,750	$337,168	$407,558	$506,495
	NASSAU-SUFFOLK, NY METROPOLITAN DIVISION	NASSAU	$477,355	$611,117	$738,699	$918,021
	NEW YORK-WHITE PLAINS-WAYNE, NY-NJ METROPOLITAN	NEW YORK	$477,355	$611,117	$738,699	$918,021
	BUFFALO-NIAGARA FALLS, NY (MSA)	NIAGARA	$275,075	$337,168	$407,558	$506,495
	SYRACUSE, NY (MSA)	ONONDAGA	$267,500	$337,168	$407,558	$506,495
	ROCHESTER, NY (MSA)	ONTARIO	$268,750	$337,168	$407,558	$506,495
	POUGHKEEPSIE-NEWBURGH-MIDDLETOWN, NY (MSA)	ORANGE	$443,750	$499,803	$607,237	$700,658
	ROCHESTER, NY (MSA)	ORLEANS	$268,750	$337,168	$407,558	$506,495
	SYRACUSE, NY (MSA)	OSWEGO	$267,500	$337,168	$407,558	$506,495
	NEW YORK-WHITE PLAINS-WAYNE, NY-NJ METRO	PUTNAM	$477,355	$611,117	$738,699	$918,021

STATE	MSA NAME	COUNTY NAME	SAFE HARBOR AVERAGE PRICE 1 LIVING UNIT	2 LIVING UNITS	3 LIVING UNITS	4 LIVING UNITS
	NEW YORK-WHITE PLAINS-WAYNE, NY-NJ METRO	QUEENS	$477,355	$611,117	$738,699	$918,021
	ALBANY-SCHENECTADY-TROY, NY (MSA)	RENSSELAER	$300,000	$337,895	$410,526	$506,495
	NEW YORK-WHITE PLAINS-WAYNE, NY-NJ METRO	RICHMOND	$477,355	$611,117	$738,699	$918,021
	NEW YORK-WHITE PLAINS-WAYNE, NY-NJ METRO	ROCKLAND	$477,355	$611,117	$738,699	$918,021
	ALBANY-SCHENECTADY-TROY, NY (MSA)	SARATOGA	$300,000	$337,895	$410,526	$506,495
	ALBANY-SCHENECTADY-TROY, NY (MSA)	SCHENECTADY	$300,000	$337,895	$410,526	$506,495
	ALBANY-SCHENECTADY-TROY, NY (MSA)	SCHOHARIE	$300,000	$337,895	$410,526	$506,495
	NASSAU-SUFFOLK, NY METROPOLITAN DIVISION	SUFFOLK	$477,355	$611,117	$738,699	$918,021
	KINGSTON, NY (MSA)	ULSTER	$406,250	$457,566	$555,921	$641,447
	ROCHESTER, NY (MSA)	WAYNE	$268,750	$337,168	$407,558	$506,495
	NEW YORK-WHITE PLAINS-WAYNE, NY-NJ METRO	WESTCHESTER	$477,355	$611,117	$738,699	$918,021
OH	ASHTABULA, OH (MICRO)	ASHTABULA	$290,797	$337,168	$407,558	$506,495
	CINCINNATI-MIDDLETOWN, OH-KY-IN (MSA)	BROWN	$332,500	$374,500	$455,000	$525,000
	CINCINNATI-MIDDLETOWN, OH-KY-IN (MSA)	BUTLER	$332,500	$374,500	$455,000	$525,000
	CANTON-MASSILLON, OH (MSA)	CARROLL	$277,500	$337,168	$407,558	$506,495
	CINCINNATI-MIDDLETOWN, OH-KY-IN (MSA)	CLERMONT	$332,500	$374,500	$455,000	$525,000
	CLEVELAND-ELYRIA-MENTOR, OH (MSA)	CUYAHOGA	$297,550	$337,168	$407,558	$506,495
	COLUMBUS, OH (MSA)	DELAWARE	$307,500	$346,342	$420,789	$506,495
	COLUMBUS, OH (MSA)	FAIRFIELD	$307,500	$346,342	$420,789	$506,495
	COLUMBUS, OH (MSA)	FRANKLIN	$307,500	$346,342	$420,789	$506,495
	CLEVELAND-ELYRIA-MENTOR, OH (MSA)	GEAUGA	$297,550	$337,168	$407,558	$506,495
	DAYTON, OH (MSA)	GREENE	$271,250	$337,168	$407,558	$506,495
	CINCINNATI-MIDDLETOWN, OH-KY-IN (MSA)	HAMILTON	$332,500	$374,500	$455,000	$525,000
	CLEVELAND-ELYRIA-MENTOR, OH (MSA)	LAKE	$297,550	$337,168	$407,558	$506,495
	COLUMBUS, OH (MSA)	LICKING	$307,500	$346,342	$420,789	$506,495
	CLEVELAND-ELYRIA-MENTOR, OH (MSA)	LORAIN	$297,550	$337,168	$407,558	$506,495
	COLUMBUS, OH (MSA)	MADISON	$307,500	$346,342	$420,789	$506,495
	CLEVELAND-ELYRIA-MENTOR, OH (MSA)	MEDINA	$297,550	$337,168	$407,558	$506,495
	DAYTON, OH (MSA)	MIAMI	$271,250	$337,168	$407,558	$506,495
	DAYTON, OH (MSA)	MONTGOMERY	$271,250	$337,168	$407,558	$506,495
	COLUMBUS, OH (MSA)	MORROW	$307,500	$346,342	$420,789	$506,495
	COLUMBUS, OH (MSA)	PICKAWAY	$307,500	$346,342	$420,789	$506,495

STATE	MSA NAME	COUNTY NAME	SAFE HARBOR AVERAGE PRICE 1 LIVING UNIT	2 LIVING UNITS	3 LIVING UNITS	4 LIVING UNITS
	AKRON, OH (MSA)	PORTAGE	$330,000	$371,684	$451,579	$521,053
	DAYTON, OH (MSA)	PREBLE	$271,250	$337,168	$407,558	$506,495
	CANTON-MASSILLON, OH (MSA)	STARK	$277,500	$337,168	$407,558	$506,495
	AKRON, OH (MSA)	SUMMIT	$330,000	$371,684	$451,579	$521,053
	COLUMBUS, OH (MSA)	UNION	$307,500	$346,342	$420,789	$506,495
	CINCINNATI-MIDDLETOWN, OH-KY-IN (MSA)	WARREN	$332,500	$374,500	$455,000	$525,000
OR	CORVALLIS, OR (MSA)	BENTON	$307,500	$346,342	$420,789	$506,495
	PORTLAND-VANCOUVER-BEAVERTON, OR-WA (MSA)	CLACKAMAS	$374,474	$421,776	$512,437	$591,316
	ASTORIA, OR (MICRO)	CLATSOP	$287,500	$337,168	$407,558	$506,495
	PORTLAND-VANCOUVER-BEAVERTON, OR-WA (MSA)	COLUMBIA	$374,474	$421,776	$512,437	$591,316
	BEND, OR (MSA)	DESCHUTES	$427,250	$481,218	$584,658	$674,605
	MEDFORD, OR (MSA)	JACKSON	$422,500	$475,868	$578,158	$667,105
	GRANTS PASS, OR (MICRO)	JOSEPHINE	$324,868	$365,904	$444,557	$512,961
	EUGENE-SPRINGFIELD, OR (MSA)	LANE	$331,250	$373,092	$453,289	$523,026
	NON-METRO	LINCOLN	$277,500	$337,168	$407,558	$506,495
	SALEM, OR (MSA)	MARION	$285,000	$337,168	$407,558	$506,495
	PORTLAND-VANCOUVER-BEAVERTON, OR-WA (MSA)	MULTNOMAH	$374,474	$421,776	$512,437	$591,316
	SALEM, OR (MSA)	POLK	$285,000	$337,168	$407,558	$506,495
	NON-METRO	TILLAMOOK	$297,500	$337,168	$407,558	$506,495
	PORTLAND-VANCOUVER-BEAVERTON, OR-WA (MSA)	WASHINGTON	$374,474	$421,776	$512,437	$591,316
	PORTLAND-VANCOUVER-BEAVERTON, OR-WA (MSA)	YAMHILL	$374,474	$421,776	$512,437	$591,316
PA	PITTSBURGH, PA (MSA)	ALLEGHENY	$327,500	$368,868	$448,158	$517,105
	PITTSBURGH, PA (MSA)	ARMSTRONG	$327,500	$368,868	$448,158	$517,105
	PITTSBURGH, PA (MSA)	BEAVER	$327,500	$368,868	$448,158	$517,105
	READING, PA (MSA)	BERKS	$300,000	$337,895	$410,526	$506,495
	PHILADELPHIA, PA METROPOLITAN DIVISION	BUCKS	$385,112	$433,758	$526,996	$608,072
	PITTSBURGH, PA (MSA)	BUTLER	$327,500	$368,868	$448,158	$517,105
	ALLENTOWN-BETHLEHEM-EASTON, PA-NJ (MSA)	CARBON	$402,192	$459,255	$557,974	$643,816
	STATE COLLEGE, PA (MSA)	CENTRE	$279,375	$337,168	$407,558	$506,495
	PHILADELPHIA, PA METROPOLITAN DIVISION	CHESTER	$385,112	$433,758	$526,996	$608,072
	PHILADELPHIA, PA METROPOLITAN DIVISION	DELAWARE	$385,112	$433,758	$526,996	$608,072
	PITTSBURGH, PA (MSA)	FAYETTE	$327,500	$368,868	$448,158	$517,105
	LANCASTER, PA (MSA)	LANCASTER	$383,250	$431,661	$524,447	$605,132
	ALLENTOWN-BETHLEHEM-EASTON, PA-NJ (MSA)	LEHIGH	$402,192	$459,255	$557,974	$643,816
	PHILADELPHIA, PA METROPOLITAN DIVISION	MONTGOMERY	$385,112	$433,758	$526,996	$608,072

STATE	MSA NAME	COUNTY NAME	SAFE HARBOR AVERAGE PRICE			
			1 LIVING UNIT	2 LIVING UNITS	3 LIVING UNITS	4 LIVING UNITS
	ALLENTOWN-BETHLEHEM-EASTON, PA-NJ (MSA)	NORTHAMPTON	$402,192	$459,255	$557,974	$643,816
	PHILADELPHIA, PA METROPOLITAN DIVISION	PHILADELPHIA	$385,112	$433,758	$526,996	$608,072
	NEWARK-UNION, NJ-PA METROPOLITAN DIVISION	PIKE	$477,355	$611,117	$738,699	$918,021
	PITTSBURGH, PA (MSA)	WASHINGTON	$327,500	$368,868	$448,158	$517,105
	PITTSBURGH, PA (MSA)	WESTMORELAND	$327,500	$368,868	$448,158	$517,105
	YORK-HANOVER, PA (MSA)	YORK	$424,587	$478,218	$581,014	$670,401
PR	SAN JUAN-CAGUAS-GUAYNABO, PR (MSA)	AGUAS BUENAS	$325,000	$366,053	$444,737	$513,158
	SAN JUAN-CAGUAS-GUAYNABO, PR (MSA)	AIBONITO	$325,000	$366,053	$444,737	$513,158
	SAN JUAN-CAGUAS-GUAYNABO, PR (MSA)	ARECIBO	$325,000	$366,053	$444,737	$513,158
	SAN JUAN-CAGUAS-GUAYNABO, PR (MSA)	BARCELONETA	$325,000	$366,053	$444,737	$513,158
	SAN JUAN-CAGUAS-GUAYNABO, PR (MSA)	BARRANQUITAS	$325,000	$366,053	$444,737	$513,158
	SAN JUAN-CAGUAS-GUAYNABO, PR (MSA)	BAYAMON	$325,000	$366,053	$444,737	$513,158
	SAN JUAN-CAGUAS-GUAYNABO, PR (MSA)	CAGUAS	$325,000	$366,053	$444,737	$513,158
	SAN JUAN-CAGUAS-GUAYNABO, PR (MSA)	CAMUY	$325,000	$366,053	$444,737	$513,158
	SAN JUAN-CAGUAS-GUAYNABO, PR (MSA)	CANOVANAS	$325,000	$366,053	$444,737	$513,158
	SAN JUAN-CAGUAS-GUAYNABO, PR (MSA)	CAROLINA	$325,000	$366,053	$444,737	$513,158
	SAN JUAN-CAGUAS-GUAYNABO, PR (MSA)	CATANO	$325,000	$366,053	$444,737	$513,158
	SAN JUAN-CAGUAS-GUAYNABO, PR (MSA)	CAYEY	$325,000	$366,053	$444,737	$513,158
	FAJARDO, PR (MSA)	CEIBA	$325,000	$366,053	$444,737	$513,158
	SAN JUAN-CAGUAS-GUAYNABO, PR (MSA)	CIALES	$325,000	$366,053	$444,737	$513,158
	SAN JUAN-CAGUAS-GUAYNABO, PR (MSA)	CIDRA	$325,000	$366,053	$444,737	$513,158
	SAN JUAN-CAGUAS-GUAYNABO, PR (MSA)	COMERIO	$325,000	$366,053	$444,737	$513,158
	SAN JUAN-CAGUAS-GUAYNABO, PR (MSA)	COROZAL	$325,000	$366,053	$444,737	$513,158
	SAN JUAN-CAGUAS-GUAYNABO, PR (MSA)	DORADO	$325,000	$366,053	$444,737	$513,158
	FAJARDO, PR (MSA)	FAJARDO	$325,000	$366,053	$444,737	$513,158
	SAN JUAN-CAGUAS-GUAYNABO, PR (MSA)	FLORIDA	$325,000	$366,053	$444,737	$513,158
	SAN JUAN-CAGUAS-GUAYNABO, PR (MSA)	GUAYNABO	$325,000	$366,053	$444,737	$513,158
	SAN JUAN-CAGUAS-GUAYNABO, PR (MSA)	GURABO	$325,000	$366,053	$444,737	$513,158

STATE	MSA NAME	COUNTY NAME	SAFE HARBOR AVERAGE PRICE 1 LIVING UNIT	2 LIVING UNITS	3 LIVING UNITS	4 LIVING UNITS
	SAN JUAN-CAGUAS-GUAYNABO, PR (MSA)	HATILLO	$325,000	$366,053	$444,737	$513,158
	SAN JUAN-CAGUAS-GUAYNABO, PR (MSA)	HUMACAO	$325,000	$366,053	$444,737	$513,158
	SAN JUAN-CAGUAS-GUAYNABO, PR (MSA)	JUNCOS	$325,000	$366,053	$444,737	$513,158
	SAN JUAN-CAGUAS-GUAYNABO, PR (MSA)	LAS PIEDRAS	$325,000	$366,053	$444,737	$513,158
	SAN JUAN-CAGUAS-GUAYNABO, PR (MSA)	LOIZA	$325,000	$366,053	$444,737	$513,158
	FAJARDO, PR (MSA)	LUQUILLO	$325,000	$366,053	$444,737	$513,158
	SAN JUAN-CAGUAS-GUAYNABO, PR (MSA)	MANATI	$325,000	$366,053	$444,737	$513,158
	SAN JUAN-CAGUAS-GUAYNABO, PR (MSA)	MAUNABO	$325,000	$366,053	$444,737	$513,158
	SAN JUAN-CAGUAS-GUAYNABO, PR (MSA)	MOROVIS	$325,000	$366,053	$444,737	$513,158
	SAN JUAN-CAGUAS-GUAYNABO, PR (MSA)	NAGUABO	$325,000	$366,053	$444,737	$513,158
	SAN JUAN-CAGUAS-GUAYNABO, PR (MSA)	NARANJITO	$325,000	$366,053	$444,737	$513,158
	SAN JUAN-CAGUAS-GUAYNABO, PR (MSA)	OROCOVIS	$325,000	$366,053	$444,737	$513,158
	SAN JUAN-CAGUAS-GUAYNABO, PR (MSA)	QUEBRADILLAS	$325,000	$366,053	$444,737	$513,158
	SAN JUAN-CAGUAS-GUAYNABO, PR (MSA)	RIO GRANDE	$325,000	$366,053	$444,737	$513,158
	SAN JUAN-CAGUAS-GUAYNABO, PR (MSA)	SAN JUAN	$325,000	$366,053	$444,737	$513,158
	SAN JUAN-CAGUAS-GUAYNABO, PR (MSA)	SAN LORENZO	$325,000	$366,053	$444,737	$513,158
	SAN JUAN-CAGUAS-GUAYNABO, PR (MSA)	TOA ALTA	$325,000	$366,053	$444,737	$513,158
	SAN JUAN-CAGUAS-GUAYNABO, PR (MSA)	TOA BAJA	$325,000	$366,053	$444,737	$513,158
	SAN JUAN-CAGUAS-GUAYNABO, PR (MSA)	TRUJILLO ALTO	$325,000	$366,053	$444,737	$513,158
	SAN JUAN-CAGUAS-GUAYNABO, PR (MSA)	VEGA ALTA	$325,000	$366,053	$444,737	$513,158
	SAN JUAN-CAGUAS-GUAYNABO, PR (MSA)	VEGA BAJA	$325,000	$366,053	$444,737	$513,158
	SAN JUAN-CAGUAS-GUAYNABO, PR (MSA)	YABUCOA	$325,000	$366,053	$444,737	$513,158
RI	PROVIDENCE-NEW BEDFORD-FALL RIVER, RI-MA	BRISTOL	$416,250	$472,891	$571,567	$710,309
	PROVIDENCE-NEW BEDFORD-FALL RIVER, RI-MA	KENT	$416,250	$472,891	$571,567	$710,309
	PROVIDENCE-NEW BEDFORD-FALL RIVER, RI-MA	NEWPORT	$416,250	$472,891	$571,567	$710,309
	PROVIDENCE-NEW BEDFORD-FALL RIVER, RI-MA	PROVIDENCE	$416,250	$472,891	$571,567	$710,309
	PROVIDENCE-NEW BEDFORD-FALL RIVER, RI-MA	WASHINGTON	$416,250	$472,891	$571,567	$710,309

STATE	MSA NAME	COUNTY NAME	SAFE HARBOR AVERAGE PRICE 1 LIVING UNIT	2 LIVING UNITS	3 LIVING UNITS	4 LIVING UNITS
SC	HILTON HEAD ISLAND-BEAUFORT, SC (MICRO)	BEAUFORT	$373,750	$420,961	$511,447	$590,132
	CHARLESTON-NORTH CHARLESTON, SC (MSA)	BERKELEY	$334,375	$376,612	$457,566	$527,961
	CHARLESTON-NORTH CHARLESTON, SC (MSA)	CHARLESTON	$334,375	$376,612	$457,566	$527,961
	CHARLESTON-NORTH CHARLESTON, SC (MSA)	DORCHESTER	$334,375	$376,612	$457,566	$527,961
	HILTON HEAD ISLAND-BEAUFORT, SC (MICRO)	JASPER	$373,750	$420,961	$511,447	$590,132
TN	NASHVILLE-DAVIDSON—MURFREESBORO, TN (MSA)	CANNON	$297,500	$337,168	$407,558	$506,495
	NASHVILLE-DAVIDSON—MURFREESBORO, TN (MSA)	CHEATHAM	$297,500	$337,168	$407,558	$506,495
	NASHVILLE-DAVIDSON—MURFREESBORO, TN (MSA)	DAVIDSON	$297,500	$337,168	$407,558	$506,495
	NASHVILLE-DAVIDSON—MURFREESBORO, TN (MSA)	DICKSON	$297,500	$337,168	$407,558	$506,495
	NASHVILLE-DAVIDSON—MURFREESBORO, TN (MSA)	HICKMAN	$297,500	$337,168	$407,558	$506,495
	NASHVILLE-DAVIDSON—MURFREESBORO, TN (MSA)	MACON	$297,500	$337,168	$407,558	$506,495
	NASHVILLE-DAVIDSON—MURFREESBORO, TN (MSA)	ROBERTSON	$297,500	$337,168	$407,558	$506,495
	NASHVILLE-DAVIDSON—MURFREESBORO, TN (MSA)	RUTHERFORD	$297,500	$337,168	$407,558	$506,495
	NASHVILLE-DAVIDSON—MURFREESBORO, TN (MSA)	SMITH	$297,500	$337,168	$407,558	$506,495
	NASHVILLE-DAVIDSON—MURFREESBORO, TN (MSA)	SUMNER	$297,500	$337,168	$407,558	$506,495
	NASHVILLE-DAVIDSON—MURFREESBORO, TN (MSA)	TROUSDALE	$297,500	$337,168	$407,558	$506,495
	NASHVILLE-DAVIDSON—MURFREESBORO, TN (MSA)	WILLIAMSON	$297,500	$337,168	$407,558	$506,495
	NASHVILLE-DAVIDSON—MURFREESBORO, TN (MSA)	WILSON	$297,500	$337,168	$407,558	$506,495
UT	PROVO-OREM, UT (MSA)	JUAB	$273,750	$337,168	$407,558	$506,495
	NON-METRO	KANE	$268,750	$337,168	$407,558	$506,495

STATE	MSA NAME	COUNTY NAME	SAFE HARBOR AVERAGE PRICE 1 LIVING UNIT	2 LIVING UNITS	3 LIVING UNITS	4 LIVING UNITS
	SALT LAKE CITY, UT (MSA)	SALT LAKE	$306,250	$344,934	$419,079	$506,495
	SALT LAKE CITY, UT (MSA)	SUMMIT	$306,250	$344,934	$419,079	$506,495
	SALT LAKE CITY, UT (MSA)	TOOELE	$306,250	$344,934	$419,079	$506,495
	PROVO-OREM, UT (MSA)	UTAH	$273,750	$337,168	$407,558	$506,495
	ST. GEORGE, UT (MSA)	WASHINGTON	$366,875	$413,217	$502,039	$579,276
VA	CHARLOTTESVILLE, VA (MSA)	ALBEMARLE	$399,375	$449,822	$546,513	$630,592
	WASHINGTON-ARLINGTON-ALEXANDRIA, DC-VA-METROPOLITAN	ALEXANDRIA	$477,355	$611,117	$738,699	$888,158
	RICHMOND, VA (MSA)	AMELIA	$344,375	$387,875	$471,250	$543,750
	WASHINGTON-ARLINGTON-ALEXANDRIA, DC-VA-METROPOLITAN	ARLINGTON	$477,355	$611,117	$738,699	$888,158
	RICHMOND, VA (MSA)	CAROLINE	$344,375	$387,875	$471,250	$543,750
	RICHMOND, VA (MSA)	CHARLES CITY	$344,375	$387,875	$471,250	$543,750
	CHARLOTTESVILLE, VA (MSA)	CHARLOTTESVILLE	$399,375	$449,822	$546,513	$630,592
	VIRGINIA BEACH-NORFOLK-NEWPORT NEWS, VA-METROPOLITAN	CHESAPEAKE	$412,500	$464,605	$564,474	$651,316
	RICHMOND, VA (MSA)	CHESTERFIELD	$344,375	$387,875	$471,250	$543,750
	WASHINGTON-ARLINGTON-ALEXANDRIA, DC-VA-METROPOLITAN	CLARKE	$477,355	$611,117	$738,699	$888,158
	RICHMOND, VA (MSA)	COLONIAL HEIGHT	$344,375	$387,875	$471,250	$543,750
	CULPEPER, VA (MICRO)	CULPEPER	$381,999	$448,442	$544,837	$628,658
	RICHMOND, VA (MSA)	CUMBERLAND	$344,375	$387,875	$471,250	$543,750
	RICHMOND, VA (MSA)	DINWIDDIE	$344,375	$387,875	$471,250	$543,750
	WASHINGTON-ARLINGTON-ALEXANDRIA, DC-VA-METROPOLITAN	FAIRFAX	$477,355	$611,117	$738,699	$888,158
	WASHINGTON-ARLINGTON-ALEXANDRIA, DC-VA-METROPOLITAN	FAIRFAX IND	$477,355	$611,117	$738,699	$888,158
	WASHINGTON-ARLINGTON-ALEXANDRIA, DC-VA-METROPOLITAN	FALLS CHURCH	$477,355	$611,117	$738,699	$888,158
	WASHINGTON-ARLINGTON-ALEXANDRIA, DC-VA-METROPOLITAN	FAUQUIER	$477,355	$611,117	$738,699	$888,158
	CHARLOTTESVILLE, VA (MSA)	FLUVANNA	$399,375	$449,822	$546,513	$630,592
	WINCHESTER, VA-WV (MSA)	FREDERICK	$475,000	$535,000	$650,000	$750,000
	WASHINGTON-ARLINGTON-ALEXANDRIA, DC-VA-METROPOLITAN	FREDERICKSBURG	$477,355	$611,117	$738,699	$888,158
	VIRGINIA BEACH-NORFOLK-NEWPORT NEWS, VA-METROPOLITAN	GLOUCESTER	$412,500	$464,605	$564,474	$651,316
	RICHMOND, VA (MSA)	GOOCHLAND	$344,375	$387,875	$471,250	$543,750
	CHARLOTTESVILLE, VA (MSA)	GREENE	$399,375	$449,822	$546,513	$630,592

STATE	MSA NAME	COUNTY NAME	SAFE HARBOR AVERAGE PRICE 1 LIVING UNIT	2 LIVING UNITS	3 LIVING UNITS	4 LIVING UNITS
	VIRGINIA BEACH-NORFOLK-NEWPORT NEWS, VA-METROPOLITAN	HAMPTON	$412,500	$464,605	$564,474	$651,316
	RICHMOND, VA (MSA)	HANOVER	$344,375	$387,875	$471,250	$543,750
	RICHMOND, VA (MSA)	HENRICO	$344,375	$387,875	$471,250	$543,750
	RICHMOND, VA (MSA)	HOPEWELL	$344,375	$387,875	$471,250	$543,750
	VIRGINIA BEACH-NORFOLK-NEWPORT NEWS, VA-METROPOLITAN	ISLE OF WIGHT	$412,500	$464,605	$564,474	$651,316
	VIRGINIA BEACH-NORFOLK-NEWPORT NEWS, VA-METROPOLITAN	JAMES CITY	$412,500	$464,605	$564,474	$651,316
	RICHMOND, VA (MSA)	KING AND QUEEN	$344,375	$387,875	$471,250	$543,750
	NON-METRO	KING GEORGE	$381,999	$448,442	$544,837	$628,658
	RICHMOND, VA (MSA)	KING WILLIAM	$344,375	$387,875	$471,250	$543,750
	WASHINGTON-ARLINGTON-ALEXANDRIA, DC-VA-METROPOLITAN	LOUDOUN	$477,355	$611,117	$738,699	$888,158
	RICHMOND, VA (MSA)	LOUISA	$344,375	$387,875	$471,250	$543,750
	WASHINGTON-ARLINGTON-ALEXANDRIA, DC-VA-METROPOLITAN	MANASSAS	$477,355	$611,117	$738,699	$888,158
	WASHINGTON-ARLINGTON-ALEXANDRIA, DC-VA-METROPOLITAN	MANASSAS PARK	$477,355	$611,117	$738,699	$888,158
	VIRGINIA BEACH-NORFOLK-NEWPORT NEWS, VA-METROPOLITAN	MATHEWS	$412,500	$464,605	$564,474	$651,316
	CHARLOTTESVILLE, VA (MSA)	NELSON	$399,375	$449,822	$546,513	$630,592
	RICHMOND, VA (MSA)	NEW KENT	$344,375	$387,875	$471,250	$543,750
	VIRGINIA BEACH-NORFOLK-NEWPORT NEWS, VA-METROPOLITAN	NEWPORT NEWS	$412,500	$464,605	$564,474	$651,316
	VIRGINIA BEACH-NORFOLK-NEWPORT NEWS, VA-METROPOLITAN	NORFOLK	$412,500	$464,605	$564,474	$651,316
	RICHMOND, VA (MSA)	PETERSBURG	$344,375	$387,875	$471,250	$543,750
	VIRGINIA BEACH-NORFOLK-NEWPORT NEWS, VA-METROPOLITAN	POQUOSON	$412,500	$464,605	$564,474	$651,316
	VIRGINIA BEACH-NORFOLK-NEWPORT NEWS, VA-METROPOLITAN	PORTSMOUTH	$412,500	$464,605	$564,474	$651,316
	RICHMOND, VA (MSA)	POWHATAN	$344,375	$387,875	$471,250	$543,750
	RICHMOND, VA (MSA)	PRINCE GEORGE	$344,375	$387,875	$471,250	$543,750
	WASHINGTON-ARLINGTON-ALEXANDRIA, DC-VA-METROPOLITAN	PRINCE WILLIAM	$477,355	$611,117	$738,699	$888,158
	RICHMOND, VA (MSA)	RICHMOND IND	$344,375	$387,875	$471,250	$543,750
	WASHINGTON-ARLINGTON-ALEXANDRIA, DC-VA-METROPOLITAN	SPOTSYLVANIA	$477,355	$611,117	$738,699	$888,158

STATE	MSA NAME	COUNTY NAME	SAFE HARBOR AVERAGE PRICE			
			1 LIVING UNIT	2 LIVING UNITS	3 LIVING UNITS	4 LIVING UNITS
	WASHINGTON-ARLINGTON-ALEXANDRIA, DC-VA-METROPOLITAN	STAFFORD	$477,355	$611,117	$738,699	$888,158
	VIRGINIA BEACH-NORFOLK-NEWPORT NEWS, VA-METROPOLITAN	SUFFOLK	$412,500	$464,605	$564,474	$651,316
	VIRGINIA BEACH-NORFOLK-NEWPORT NEWS, VA-METROPOLITAN	SURRY	$412,500	$464,605	$564,474	$651,316
	RICHMOND, VA (MSA)	SUSSEX	$344,375	$387,875	$471,250	$543,750
	VIRGINIA BEACH-NORFOLK-NEWPORT NEWS, VA-METROPOLITAN	VIRGINIA BEACH	$412,500	$464,605	$564,474	$651,316
	WASHINGTON-ARLINGTON-ALEXANDRIA, DC-VA-METROPOLITAN	WARREN	$477,355	$611,117	$738,699	$888,158
	VIRGINIA BEACH-NORFOLK-NEWPORT NEWS, VA-METROPOLITAN	WILLIAMSBURG	$412,500	$464,605	$564,474	$651,316
	WINCHESTER, VA-WV (MSA)	WINCHESTER	$475,000	$535,000	$650,000	$750,000
	VIRGINIA BEACH-NORFOLK-NEWPORT NEWS, VA-METROPOLITAN	YORK	$412,500	$464,605	$564,474	$651,316
VI	NON-METRO	ST. CROIX	$287,500	$337,168	$407,558	$506,495
	NON-METRO	ST. THOMAS	$318,750	$359,013	$436,184	$506,495
VT	BURLINGTON-SOUTH BURLINGTON, VT (MSA)	CHITTENDEN	$318,750	$359,013	$436,184	$506,495
	BURLINGTON-SOUTH BURLINGTON, VT (MSA)	FRANKLIN	$318,750	$359,013	$436,184	$506,495
	BURLINGTON-SOUTH BURLINGTON, VT (MSA)	GRAND ISLE	$318,750	$359,013	$436,184	$506,495
WA	WENATCHEE, WA (MSA)	CHELAN	$281,250	$337,168	$407,558	$506,495
	PORT ANGELES, WA (MICRO)	CLALLAM	$296,250	$337,168	$407,558	$506,495
	PORTLAND-VANCOUVER-BEAVERTON, OR-WA (MSA)	CLARK	$374,474	$421,776	$512,437	$591,316
	WENATCHEE, WA (MSA)	DOUGLAS	$281,250	$337,168	$407,558	$506,495
	OAK HARBOR, WA (MICRO)	ISLAND	$366,842	$413,179	$502,039	$579,276
	NON-METRO	JEFFERSON	$420,000	$473,053	$574,737	$663,158
	SEATTLE-BELLEVUE-EVERETT, WA METROPOLITAN	KING	$477,355	$542,039	$658,553	$759,868
	BREMERTON-SILVERDALE, WA (MSA)	KITSAP	$475,000	$535,000	$650,000	$750,000
	TACOMA, WA METROPOLITAN DIVISION	PIERCE	$477,355	$542,039	$658,553	$759,868
	NON-METRO	SAN JUAN	$477,355	$598,355	$726,974	$838,816
	MOUNT VERNON-ANACORTES, WA (MSA)	SKAGIT	$373,662	$420,862	$511,328	$589,993
	PORTLAND-VANCOUVER BEAVERTON, OR-WA (MSA)	SKAMANIA	$374,474	$421,776	$512,437	$591,316

STATE	MSA NAME	COUNTY NAME	SAFE HARBOR AVERAGE PRICE			
			1 LIVING UNIT	2 LIVING UNITS	3 LIVING UNITS	4 LIVING UNITS
	SEATTLE-BELLEVUE-EVERETT, WA METROPOLITAN	SNOHOMISH	$477,355	$542,039	$658,553	$759,868
	OLYMPIA, WA (MSA)	THURSTON	$344,505	$388,022	$471,429	$543,957
	BELLINGHAM, WA (MSA)	WHATCOM	$375,000	$422,368	$513,158	$592,105
WI	MADISON, WI (MSA)	COLUMBIA	$284,625	$337,168	$407,558	$506,495
	MADISON, WI (MSA)	DANE	$284,625	$337,168	$407,558	$506,495
	MADISON, WI (MSA)	IOWA	$284,625	$337,168	$407,558	$506,495
	LAKE COUNTY-KENOSHA COUNTY, IL-WI METROPOLITAN	KENOSHA	$362,105	$407,845	$495,512	$571,745
	MILWAUKEE- WAUKESHA-WEST ALLIS, WI (MSA)	MILWAUKEE	$287,375	$337,168	$407,558	$506,495
	MILWAUKEE-WAUKESHA-WEST ALLIS, WI (MSA)	OZAUKEE	$287,375	$337,168	$407,558	$506,495
	MINNEAPOLIS-ST. PAUL-BLOOMINGTON, MN-WI	PIERCE	$331,250	$373,092	$453,289	$523,026
	MINNEAPOLIS-ST. PAUL-BLOOMINGTON, MN-WI	ST. CROIX	$331,250	$373,092	$453,289	$523,026
	MILWAUKEE-WAUKESHA-WEST ALLIS, WI (MSA)	WASHINGTON	$287,375	$337,168	$407,558	$506,495
	MILWAUKEE-WAUKESHA-WEST ALLIS, WI (MSA)	WAUKESHA	$287,375	$337,168	$407,558	$506,495
WV	HAGERSTOWN-MARTINSBURG, MD-WV (MSA)	BERKELEY	$362,500	$408,289	$496,053	$572,368
	WINCHESTER, VA-WV (MSA)	HAMPSHIRE	$475,000	$535,000	$650,000	$750,000
	HAGERSTOWN-MARTINSBURG, MD-WV (MSA)	JEFFERSON	$477,355	$611,117	$738,699	$888,158
	HAGERSTOWN-MARTINSBURG, MD-WV (MSA)	MORGAN	$362,500	$408,289	$496,053	$572,368
WY	JACKSON, WY-ID (MICRO)	TETON	$477,355	$611,117	$738,699	$918,021
ALL OTHER AREAS			$263,368	$337,168	$407,558	$506,495

.02 The nationwide average purchase price (for use in the housing cost/income ratio for new and existing residences) is $269,600.

SECTION 5. EFFECT ON OTHER DOCUMENTS

Rev. Proc. 2006–17 is obsolete except as provided in section 6 of this revenue procedure.

SECTION 6. EFFECTIVE DATES

.01 Issuers may rely on this revenue procedure to determine average area purchase price safe harbors for commitments to provide financing or issue mortgage credit certificates that are made, or (if the purchase precedes the commitment) for residences that are purchased, in the period that begins on March 8, 2007, and ends on the date as of which the safe harbors contained in section 4.01 of this revenue procedure are rendered obsolete by a new revenue procedure.

.02 Notwithstanding section 5 of this revenue procedure, issuers may continue to rely on the average area purchase price safe harbors contained in Rev. Proc. 2006–17, with respect to bonds sold, or for mortgage credit certificates issued with respect to bond authority exchanged, before April 7, 2007, if the commitments to provide financing or issue mortgage credit certificates are made on or before May 7, 2007.

.03 Except as provided in section 6.04, issuers must use the nationwide average purchase price limitation contained in this revenue procedure for commitments to provide financing or issue mortgage credit certificates that are made, or (if the purchase precedes the commitment) for residences that are purchased, in the period that begins on March 8, 2007, and ends on the date when the nationwide average purchase price limitation is rendered obsolete by a new revenue procedure.

.04 Notwithstanding sections 5 and 6.03 of this revenue procedure, issuers may continue to rely on the nationwide average purchase price set forth in Rev. Proc. 2006–17 with respect to bonds sold, or for mortgage credit certificates issued with respect to bond authority exchanged, before April 7, 2007, if the commitments to provide financing or issue mortgage credit certificates are made on or before May 7, 2007.

SECTION 7. PAPERWORK REDUCTION ACT

The collection of information contained in this revenue procedure has been reviewed and approved by the Office of Management and Budget in accordance with the Paperwork Reduction Act (44 U.S.C. 3507) under control number 1545–1877.

An agency may not conduct or sponsor, and a person is not required to respond to, a collection of information unless the collection of information displays a valid OMB control number.

This revenue procedure contains a collection of information requirement in section 3.03. The purpose of the collection of information is to verify the applicable FHA loan limit that issuers of qualified mortgage bonds and qualified mortgage certificates have used to calculate the average area purchase price for a given metropolitan statistical area for purposes of section 143(e) and 25(c). The collection of information is required to obtain the benefit of using revisions to FHA loan limits to determine average area purchase prices. The likely respondents are state and local governments.

The estimated total annual reporting and/or recordkeeping burden is: 15 hours.

The estimated annual burden per respondent and/or recordkeeper: 15 minutes.

The estimated number of respondents and/or recordkeepers: 60.

Books or records relating to a collection of information must be retained as long as their contents may become material in the administration of any internal revenue law. Generally tax returns and tax return information are confidential, as required by 26 U.S.C. 6103.

SECTION 8. DRAFTING INFORMATION

The principal authors of this revenue procedure are David E. White and Timothy L. Jones of the Office of Division Counsel/Associate Chief Counsel (Tax Exempt & Government Entities). For further information regarding this revenue procedure, contact David E. White at (202) 622–3980 (not a toll-free call).

Part IV. Items of General Interest

Notice of Proposed Rulemaking by Cross-Reference to Temporary Regulations

Corporate Reorganizations; Additional Guidance on Distributions Under Sections 368(a)(1)(D) and 354(b)(1)(B)

REG–157834–06

AGENCY: Internal Revenue Service (IRS), Treasury.

ACTION: Notice of proposed rulemaking by cross-reference to temporary regulations.

SUMMARY: In this issue of the Bulletin, the IRS is issuing temporary regulations (T.D. 9313) that amend §1.368–2T(l), which provides guidance regarding the qualification of certain transactions as reorganizations described in section 368(a)(1)(D) where no stock and/or securities of the acquiring corporation are issued and distributed in the transaction. These regulations clarify that the rules in §1.368–2T(l) are not intended to affect the qualification of related party triangular asset acquisitions as reorganizations described in section 368. These regulations affect corporations engaging in such transactions and their shareholders. The text of those regulations also serves as the text of these proposed regulations.

DATES: Written or electronic comments and requests for a public hearing must be received by May 30, 2007.

ADDRESSES: Send submissions to: CC:PA:LPD:PR (REG–157834–06), Internal Revenue Service, PO Box 7604, Ben Franklin Station, Washington, DC 20044. Submissions may be hand delivered to CC:PA:LPD:PR (REG–157834–06), Courier Desk, Internal Revenue Service, 1111 Constitution Avenue, NW, Washington, DC, or sent electronically, via the IRS Internet site at *www.irs.gov/regs* or via the Federal eRulemaking Portal at *www.regulations.gov* (IRS REG–157834–06).

FOR FURTHER INFORMATION CONTACT: Concerning the proposed regulations, Bruce A. Decker, (202) 622–7550; concerning submission of comments, requests for a public hearing, and/or a publication and regulations specialist, Kelly Banks, (202) 622–7180.

SUPPLEMENTARY INFORMATION:

Background

Temporary regulations in this issue of the Bulletin amend 26 CFR part 1. The temporary regulations amend §1.368–2T(l), which provides guidance regarding the qualification of certain transactions as reorganizations described in section 368(a)(1)(D) where no stock and/or securities of the acquiring corporation are issued and distributed in the transaction. The text of those regulations also serves as the text of these proposed regulations. The preamble to the temporary regulations explains the amendments.

Explanation of Provisions

These regulations clarify that the rules in §1.368–2T(l) are not intended to affect the qualification of related party triangular asset acquisitions as reorganizations described in section 368.

Special Analyses

It has been determined that this notice of proposed rulemaking is not a significant regulatory action as defined in Executive Order 12866. Therefore, a regulatory assessment is not required. It also has been determined that section 553(b) of the Administrative Procedure Act (5 U.S.C. chapter 5) does not apply to these regulations, and because the regulations do not impose a collection of information on small entities, the Regulatory Flexibility Act (5 U.S.C. chapter 6) does not apply. Pursuant to section 7805(f) of the Internal Revenue Code, this notice of proposed rulemaking will be submitted to the Chief Counsel for Advocacy of the Small Business Administration for comment on its impact on small business.

Comments and Requests for a Public Hearing

Before these proposed regulations are adopted as final regulations, consideration will be given to any written (a signed original and eight (8) copies) or electronic comments that are submitted timely to the IRS. The IRS and Treasury Department request comments on the clarity of the proposed rules and how they can be made easier to understand. All comments will be available for public inspection and copying. A public hearing will be scheduled if requested in writing by any person that timely submits written comments. If a public hearing is scheduled, notice of the date, time, and place for the public hearing will be published in the **Federal Register**.

Drafting Information

The principal author of these regulations is Bruce A. Decker, Office of Associate Chief Counsel (Corporate).

* * * * *

Proposed Amendments to the Regulations

Accordingly, 26 CFR part 1 is proposed to be amended as follows:

PART 1—INCOME TAXES

Paragraph 1. The authority citation for part 1 continues to read as follows:

Authority: 26 U.S.C. 7805 * * *

Par. 2. Section 1.368–2 is amended by adding paragraph (l)(2)(iv) to read as follows:

§1.368–2 Definition of terms.

* * * * *

[The text of this proposed amendment to §1.368–2(l)(2)(iv) is the same as the text of §1.368–2T(l)(2)(iv) published elsewhere in this issue of the Bulletin.

Kevin M. Brown,
Deputy Commissioner for Services and Enforcement.

(Filed by the Office of the Federal Register on February 28, 2007, 8:45 a.m., and published in the issue of the Federal Register for March 1, 2007, 72 F.R. 9284)

Foundations Status of Certain Organizations

Announcement 2007–33

The following organizations have failed to establish or have been unable to maintain their status as public charities or as operating foundations. Accordingly, grantors and contributors may not, after this date, rely on previous rulings or designations in the Cumulative List of Organizations (Publication 78), or on the presumption arising from the filing of notices under section 508(b) of the Code. This listing does *not* indicate that the organizations have lost their status as organizations described in section 501(c)(3), eligible to receive deductible contributions.

Former Public Charities. The following organizations (which have been treated as organizations that are not private foundations described in section 509(a) of the Code) are now classified as private foundations:

7 Cord Ministries, Waco, TX
Abundant Life Family Services, Inc., Los Angeles, CA
Acting Out Foundation, Beachwood, OH
Ada A. Grant, Inc., Chicago, IL
Adelante Now Foundation, Albuquerque, NM
Agape Mission and Community Service Group, Inc., Birmingham, AL
Alta-Pasa Debutante Association, Fontana, CA
Amateur Division of the International Log Rolling Association, Onalaska, WI
American Academy of Continuing Medical Education, Inc., Skillman, NJ
Animal Lovers for Infinity, Inc., Boston, MA
Anishinabe Miikana Project, Inc., Red Lake, MN
Association of Iu Mien, San Jose, CA
Better World Services, Inc., Centreville, VA
B.G.B.B. Foundation, Inc. (bridging Gaps and Breaking Barriers), Nashville, TN
Bible Mission, La Quinta, CA
Biobehavioral Institute of Boston, Inc., Boston, MA
Black Hills Coalition of Standing Rock Enrollees, Rapid City, SD
Burningbush Pastoral Care Services, Inc., Plano, TX
Center for Community Stabilization, Rogers, AR
Changing Directions, Far Hills, NJ
Chesapeake Institutes for Behavioral Research, Glenn Allen, VA
Chuckie Goodnight Foundation, Inc., Brewster, KY
Civil War Landscapes Association, Chicago, IL
Claudine Carew Scholarship Fund, Williamsburg, VA
Community Education Network, Inc., Bethesda, MD
Computers for Kids, Inc., Bloomington, MN
Concerned Black Men of Cape Cod & The Islands, Inc., Provincetown, MA
Cooper Foundation, Elm City, NC
Counseling Ministries International, Inc., Ada, OK
Cross Atlantic Foundation, Inc., Lynbrook, NY
Dedicated Helper, Inglewood, CA
Divine Destiny, Inc., Chesapeake, VA
Dry Branch Community Life Center, Inc., Dry Branch, GA
Dunbar Township Science Center, Leisenring, PA
Education Sports Plus Foundation, Inc., Newton, NJ
Educational Opportunities, Inc., Chicago, IL
Family and Youth Achievement Center, Durham, NC
FATA Foundation, Coral Springs, FL
For This Cause, Oceano, CA
Fort Wayne Music Fest, Inc., Fort Wayne, IN
Foundation in Memory of Suel, Walnut, CA
Friends of Rain Forests in Myannar, Aberdeen, MD
Front Forty Productions, Inc., Verona, WI
Full Gospel Ministries, Ltd., Joshua Tree, CA
Genesis Protected Animal Refuge, Inc., Pikesville, MD
Georgia Motorcyclists Association, Inc., Atlanta, GA
Gloary, Inc., Delray Beach, FL
Global Information Freedom, Inc., Cary, NC
Global Vision Alliance, Orinda, CA
Good Shepherd International Miracle Center, Inc., Virginia Beach, VA
Greater Hope Community Development, Houston, TX
Greater Rome Chamber of Commerce Foundation, Rome, GA
Helen E. Popa Masters in Nursing Loan Fund, Austintown, OH
Hellenic American Education Foundation, Inc., Bayside, NY
Holographic Ecology, Inc., Santa Barbara, CA
IGBO Union of St. Louis, Inc., St. Louis, MO
Incredible Dreams Childcare and Learning Center, Incorporated, Chicago, IL
Indo-American Social Service Partners, Brooklyn, NY
Inspiration Community Service Center, Solon, OH
Institute of Modern Test Theory, Chicago, IL
Intercare Housing, Inc., Indianapolis, IN
Interfaith Partnership for Advocacy Reconciliation, Winston-Salem, NC
International Terrorism Awareness Coalition, Highstown, NJ
Joe Stephens Foundation, Houston, TX
Kidron Brook Ministries, Inc., Kernersville, NC
Kollel Ari Yerucham, New York, NY
Lakeland Cardinals Booster Club, Fox Lake, IL
Latino Cultural Center of Napa Valley, Napa, CA
Lincoln Park Youth in Touch, Incorporated, Hampton, VA
Mahoning Valley Renaissance Institute, Mineral Ridge, OH
Manjui Foundation, Inc., Baltimore, MD
Masjidullah Economic Community Corporation of America (M.E.C.C.A.), Philadelphia, PA
Mending Hoop Ranch & Reserve, Peebles, OH
Mental Health Alliance, Inc., Louisville, KY
Minor League Players Institute, Chicago, IL
Mirabal Sister Culture and Community Center, Inc., New York, NY
Montana Wildlife Recovery, Inc., Bozeman, MT
Museo Eduardo Carillo, Santa Cruz, CA
Natomas Education Foundation, Sacramento, CA
NBBJ Training Academy, Inc., Columbus, OH
Nerih, Inc., Aliquippa, PA
Night Hawk Foundation, Greenville, MS
Nursing Assistance Home Care Serv, Inc., Randallstown, MD

Passport for Godly Ling, Inc.,
Sante Fe, TX
Piscataway Township Education
Foundation, Piscataway, NJ
Pizza Family Ministries, Deltona, FL
Pneuma Ministries Community
Development, Inc., Meridianville, AL
Polish American Leadership Initiative,
Chicago, IL
Positive Strokes, Inc., Norman, OK
Quest Ministries International,
Hervey, LA
Restore Hope, Inc., Bronson, MI
Ronald J. Weiss Memorial Foundation,
Lagrangeville, NY
Self-Sufficient Families, Los Angeles, CA
Share the Love Center, Simi Valley, CA
Solutions Benefiting Life Institute, Ltd.,
Sudbury, MA
Sound Touches, Jefferson, GA
Southern California Indian Health
Coalition, Inc., Banning, CA
Talamm, Inc., Silver Spring, MD
Thomasville Boxing Association,
Thomasville, GA
Tower Educational Consulting Group,
Inc., Elyria, OH
Triune Project, Inc., Newport Beach, CA
Turning Point for Women and Children,
Goldsboro, NC
Underwater Learning Institute, Ltd.,
Baltimore, MD
US Chamber Foundation for Legal
Reform, Washington, DC
Victory Community Development, Inc.,
Bessemer, AL
Willoughby Hills Lions Club Scholarship
Fund, Willoughby Hills, OH
Wolf Point Development Corporation,
Wolf Point, MT
Women of Vision, Redondo Beach, CA

If an organization listed above submits information that warrants the renewal of its classification as a public charity or as a private operating foundation, the Internal Revenue Service will issue a ruling or determination letter with the revised classification as to foundation status. Grantors and contributors may thereafter rely upon such ruling or determination letter as provided in section 1.509(a)–7 of the Income Tax Regulations. It is not the practice of the Service to announce such revised classification of foundation status in the Internal Revenue Bulletin.

Deletions From Cumulative List of Organizations Contributions to Which are Deductible Under Section 170 of the Code

Announcement 2007–34

The names of organizations that no longer qualify as organizations described in section 170(c)(2) of the Internal Revenue Code of 1986 are listed below.

Generally, the Service will not disallow deductions for contributions made to a listed organization on or before the date of announcement in the Internal Revenue Bulletin that an organization no longer qualifies. However, the Service is not precluded from disallowing a deduction for any contributions made after an organization ceases to qualify under section 170(c)(2) if the organization has not timely filed a suit for declaratory judgment under section 7428 and if the contributor (1) had knowledge of the revocation of the ruling or determination letter, (2) was aware that such revocation was imminent, or (3) was in part responsible for or was aware of the activities or omissions of the organization that brought about this revocation.

If on the other hand a suit for declaratory judgment has been timely filed, contributions from individuals and organizations described in section 170(c)(2) that are otherwise allowable will continue to be deductible. Protection under section 7428(c) would begin on March 26, 2007, and would end on the date the court first determines that the organization is not described in section 170(c)(2) as more particularly set forth in section 7428(c)(1). For individual contributors, the maximum deduction protected is $1,000, with a husband and wife treated as one contributor. This benefit is not extended to any individual, in whole or in part, for the acts or omissions of the organization that were the basis for revocation.

American Education
Foundation International
San Francisco, CA
Ladder 12 Firefighters Fund, Inc.
New York, NY

Part I. Rulings and Decisions Under the Internal Revenue Code of 1986

Section 61.—Gross Income Defined

26 CFR 1.61–2: Compensation for services, including fees, commissions, and similar items.

Frivolous tax returns; wages not taxable income. This ruling discusses and refutes the frivolous position taken by some taxpayers that wages are not taxable income.

Rev. Rul. 2007–19

PURPOSE

The Internal Revenue Service (Service) is aware that some taxpayers are attempting to reduce or eliminate their federal income tax liability by claiming that compensation received in exchange for personal services is not taxable income. These taxpayers often attempt to avoid their federal income tax liability by failing to file federal income tax returns or by failing to report all income from wages or other compensation on their federal income tax return. They often furnish Forms W–4, *Employee's Withholding Allowance Certificate*, on which they claim excessive withholding allowances or claim complete exemption from withholding. In addition, they often claim deductions from gross income for personal, living and family expenditures in order to reduce the tax liability related to wages or other compensation.

The Service is aware that some promoters and return preparers are advising or recommending that taxpayers take these or other meritless positions. This revenue ruling emphasizes to taxpayers, promoters and return preparers that wages and other compensation received in exchange for personal services are taxable income subject to federal income tax. Any argument that such compensation is not taxable income has no merit and is frivolous.

The Service is committed to identifying taxpayers who attempt to avoid their federal tax obligations by taking frivolous positions. The Service will take vigorous enforcement action against these taxpayers and against promoters and return preparers who assist taxpayers in taking these frivolous positions. Frivolous returns and other similar documents submitted to the Service are processed through the Service's Frivolous Return Program. As part of this program, the Service determines whether taxpayers who have taken frivolous positions have filed all required tax returns; computes the correct amount of tax and interest due; and determines whether civil or criminal penalties should apply. The Service also determines whether civil or criminal penalties should apply to return preparers, promoters and others who assist taxpayers in taking frivolous positions and recommends whether an injunction should be sought to halt these activities. Other information about frivolous tax positions is available on the Service website at *www.irs.gov*.

ISSUE

Whether Taxpayer A may avoid federal income tax liability by maintaining that the Internal Revenue Code does not tax wages or other compensation received in exchange for personal services.

FACTS

Taxpayer A receives wages in exchange for personal services. Taxpayer A then does one or more of the following: (1) furnishes a Form W–4 to the employer on which Taxpayer A claims excessive withholding allowances or claims complete exemption from withholding; (2) fails to file a federal income tax return; (3) fails to report the wages on the federal income tax return; (4) claims a refund for any withheld income tax; or (5) claims deductions for personal, living and family expenditures to offset the wages reported on the federal income tax return. Taxpayer A claims that compensation received for personal services is not subject to federal income tax.

Arguments that wages are not subject to federal income tax take many forms including, but not limited to, the following:

1. A tax on wages is a direct tax subject to the provision in Article I, Section 2, Clause 3 of the Constitution that requires that direct taxes be apportioned among the states by population.

2. Money received in exchange for personal labor constitutes an equal, nontaxable exchange of property.

3. Taxable income from wages or other compensation for personal services can only be determined after deduction of the cost of providing the labor.

LAW AND ANALYSIS

1. Article 1, Section 2, Clause 3 of the United States Constitution states that "direct Taxes shall be apportioned among the several States which may be included within this Union, according to their respective Numbers . . . ." This statement has been used to support the argument that there is a constitutional impediment to the imposition of a direct tax on an individual's wages. The Sixteenth Amendment to the Constitution, ratified in 1913, provides that "[t]he Congress shall have power to lay and collect taxes on incomes, from whatever source derived, without apportionment among the several States, and without regard to any census or enumeration." The Sixteenth Amendment has been reviewed by the Supreme Court and upheld. *Brushaber v. Union Pacific Railroad Co.*, 240 U.S. 1 (1916). Thus, the imposition of income tax on wages, without apportionment among the states, is authorized. *See, e.g., Funk v. Commissioner*, 687 F.2d 264 (8th Cir. 1982); *Abrams v. Commissioner*, 82 T.C. 403 (1984).

Section 61(a) of the Internal Revenue Code defines gross income as income from whatever source derived, including (but not limited to) "compensation for services, including fees, commissions, fringe benefits, and similar items." I.R.C. § 61(a)(1). Courts consistently have upheld the determination that wages fall within section 61(a)(1)'s definition of compensation and, accordingly, constitute taxable income. *See, e.g., Ledford v. United States*, 297 F.3d 1378 (Fed. Cir. 2002); *United States v. Connor*, 898 F.2d 942 (3d Cir. 1990); *Casper v. Commissioner*, 805 F.2d 902 (10th Cir. 1986); *Connor v. Commissioner*, 770 F.2d 17 (2d Cir. 1985); *Lovell v. United States*, 755 F.2d 517 (7th Cir. 1984); *Perkins v. Commissioner*, 746 F.2d 1187 (6th Cir. 1984); *Funk v. Com-*

missioner, 687 F.2d 264 (8th Cir. 1982); *Lonsdale v. Commissioner*, 661 F.2d 71 (5th Cir. 1981); *Rowlee v. Commissioner*, 80 T.C. 1111 (1983).

In *United States v. Connor*, 898 F.2d at 943, the Third Circuit noted that "[e]very court which has ever considered the issue has unequivocally rejected the argument that wages are not income." All income received by a taxpayer is income under section 61 unless it is specifically exempted or excluded. *See Commissioner v. Glenshaw Glass Co.*, 348 U.S. 426, 429–30 (1955) ("Congress applied no limitations as to the source of taxable receipts, nor restrictive labels as to the intention of Congress to tax all gains except those specifically exempted.").

2. Some taxpayers claim that the payment of wages or other compensation in exchange for personal labor is a nontaxable exchange of property. These taxpayers sometimes rely on sections 83 or 1001 of the Internal Revenue Code to support this argument. Section 83 provides for the determination of the amount to be included in gross income and the timing of the inclusion when property is transferred to an employee or independent contractor in connection with the performance of services. Section 1001 provides for the determination of the amount and timing of the recognition of gain or loss from the sale or other disposition of property.

Courts have universally rejected the argument that labor is property that can be exchanged for wages or other compensation in a nontaxable transaction. *See Casper v. Commissioner*, 805 F.2d at 905; *Funk v. Commissioner*, 687 F.2d at 265. Courts recognize a distinction between selling labor and selling or exchanging property. *See Reading v. Commissioner*, 70 T.C. 730, 733–34 (1978), *aff'd*, 614 F.2d 159 (8th Cir. 1980). Further, the courts have concluded that a taxpayer has no tax basis in one's labor and, therefore, the full amount of the wages or other compensation received represents gain which may be taxed as income. *See, e.g., Casper*, 805 F.2d at 905; *Abrams*, 82 T.C. at 407; *Reading*, 70 T.C. at 733–34.

3. A related argument is that income from the sale of labor cannot be determined until the taxpayer's investment in that labor has been recovered. This argument has been repeatedly rejected. *See Rowlee*, 80 T.C. at 1120; *Reading*, 70 T.C. at 733–34. In *Reading*, the Tax Court examined the contention that gain must be realized for there to be income, analyzing the distinction recognized under federal tax law between producing a physical product and providing services. The court flatly rejected the idea that living expenses constitute the cost of "goods" sold for providing labor or services. *Reading*, 70 T.C. at 733–34. Thus, the court concluded that the gain from the sale of labor is the entire amount received and upheld the disallowance of deductions for personal living expenses.

Courts have uniformly rejected arguments that wages and other compensation for personal services are not taxable income. Accordingly, raising these arguments justifies the imposition of sanctions. *See Ledford v. United States*, 297 F.3d at 1381–82 (Fed. Cir. 2002); *Casper v. Commissioner*, 805 F.2d at 906; *Connor v. Commissioner*, 770 F.2d at 20.

HOLDING

1. Wages fall within the definition of income set forth in section 61(a)(1) of the Internal Revenue Code. Taxpayer A's wages and other compensation for services are income subject to federal income tax and must be reported on Taxpayer A's federal income tax return.

2. The payment of wages and other compensation for personal services is not an equal exchange of property. The full amount of wages received by Taxpayer A is subject to federal income tax and must be reported on Taxpayer A's federal income tax return.

3. Wages and other compensation received by Taxpayer A in exchange for personal services are subject to federal income tax without reduction of Taxpayer A's personal living expenses.

CIVIL AND CRIMINAL PENALTIES

The Service will challenge the claims of individuals who improperly attempt to avoid or evade their federal tax liability. In addition to liability for the tax due plus statutory interest, taxpayers who fail to file valid returns or pay tax based on arguments that wages and other compensation for personal services are exempt from federal income tax face substantial civil and criminal penalties. Potentially applicable civil penalties include: (1) the section 6662 accuracy-related penalties, which are generally equal to 20 percent of the amount of tax the taxpayer should have paid; (2) the section 6663 penalty for civil fraud, which is equal to 75 percent of the amount of tax the taxpayer should have paid; (3) the section 6702(a) penalty of $5,000 for a "frivolous tax return"; (4) the section 6702(b) penalty of $5,000 for submitting a "specified frivolous submission"; (5) the section 6651 additions to tax for failure to file a return, failure to pay the tax owed, and fraudulent failure to file a return; (6) the section 6673 penalty of up to $25,000 if the taxpayer makes frivolous arguments in the United States Tax Court; and (7) the section 6682 penalty of $500 for providing false information with respect to withholding.

Taxpayers relying on these frivolous positions also may face criminal prosecution under: (1) section 7201 for attempting to evade or defeat tax, the penalty for which is a significant fine and imprisonment for up to 5 years; (2) section 7203 for willful failure to file a return, the penalty for which is a significant fine and imprisonment for up to one year; (3) section 7206 for making false statements on a return, statement, or other document, the penalty for which is a significant fine and imprisonment for up to 3 years; or (4) other provisions of federal law.

Persons, including return preparers, who promote these frivolous positions and those who assist taxpayers in claiming tax benefits based on frivolous positions may face civil and criminal penalties and also may be enjoined by a court pursuant to sections 7407 and 7408. Potential penalties include: (1) a $250 penalty under section 6694 for each return or claim for refund prepared by an income tax return preparer who knew or should have known that the taxpayer's position was frivolous (or $1,000 for each return or claim for refund if the return preparer's actions were willful, intentional or reckless); (2) a penalty under section 6700 for promoting abusive tax shelters; (3) a $1,000 penalty under section 6701 for aiding and abetting the understatement of tax; and (4) criminal prosecution under section 7206, for which the penalty is a significant fine and imprisonment for up to 3 years, for assisting or advising about the preparation of a false return, statement or other document under the internal revenue laws.

DRAFTING INFORMATION

This revenue ruling was authored by the Office of Associate Chief Counsel (Procedure & Administration), Administrative Provisions and Judicial Practice Division. For further information regarding this revenue ruling, contact that office at (202) 622–7950 (not a toll-free call).

Section 168.—Accelerated Cost Recovery System

26 CFR 1.168(a)–1: Modified accelerated cost recovery system.

T.D. 9314

DEPARTMENT OF THE TREASURY
Internal Revenue Service
26 CFR Part 1

Depreciation of MACRS Property That is Acquired in a Like-Kind Exchange or As a Result of an Involuntary Conversion

AGENCY: Internal Revenue Service (IRS), Treasury.

ACTION: Final regulations and removal of temporary regulations.

SUMMARY: This document contains final regulations relating to the depreciation of property subject to the accelerated cost recovery system under section 168 of the Internal Revenue Code (MACRS property). Specifically, these final regulations provide guidance on how to depreciate MACRS property acquired in a like-kind exchange under section 1031 or as a result of an involuntary conversion under section 1033 when both the acquired and relinquished property are subject to MACRS in the hands of the acquiring taxpayer. These final regulations will affect taxpayers involved in a like-kind exchange under section 1031 or an involuntary conversion under section 1033. The corresponding temporary regulations are removed.

DATES: *Effective Dates:* These regulations are effective on February 26, 2007.

Applicability Dates: For dates of applicability, see §§1.168(a)–1(b), 1.168(b)–1(b), 1.168(d)–1(d)(3), 1.168(i)–1(l), 1.168(i)–6(k), and 1.168(k)–1(g)(3)(ii).

FOR FURTHER INFORMATION CONTACT: Patrick S. Kirwan, (202) 622–3110 (not a toll-free number).

SUPPLEMENTARY INFORMATION:

Background

This document contains amendments to 26 CFR part 1 under section 168 of the Internal Revenue Code (Code). Section 168 provides the depreciation deduction for tangible property generally placed in service after December 31, 1986.

On March 1, 2004, the IRS and the Treasury Department published in the **Federal Register** (69 FR 9529) temporary regulations (T.D. 9115, 2004–1 C.B. 680) relating to the depreciation allowable for tangible property of a character subject to the allowance for depreciation provided in section 167(a) that is generally placed in service after December 31, 1986, and is subject to section 168 (MACRS property) that is acquired in a like-kind exchange or as a result of involuntary conversion. On the same date the IRS published a notice of proposed rulemaking related to this topic in the **Federal Register** (REG–106590–00, REG–138499–02, 2004–1 C.B. 704 [69 FR 9560]). No public hearing on the regulations was requested or held. Several written comments to the notice of proposed rulemaking were received. After consideration of all the comments received, the proposed regulations are adopted as amended by this Treasury decision, and the corresponding temporary regulations are removed. The revisions to the proposed regulations are discussed in this preamble. Unless otherwise specifically stated, references to the temporary regulations are to T.D. 9115.

General Overview

Section 167 allows as a depreciation deduction a reasonable allowance for the exhaustion, wear, and tear of property used in a trade or business or held for the production of income. The depreciation allowable for depreciable tangible property placed in service after 1986 generally is determined under section 168. Section 1001 generally provides for the recognition of gain or loss on the sale or exchange of property. Under section 1031(a)(1), no gain or loss is recognized on an exchange of property held for productive use in a trade or business or for investment if the property is exchanged solely for property of like kind that is to be held either for productive use in a trade or business or for investment. Section 1031(b) provides that if an exchange would be within the provision of section 1031(a) were it not for the fact that the property received in the exchange consists not only of property permitted to be received in such an exchange, but also of other property or money, then the gain, if any, to the recipient shall be recognized, but in an amount not in excess of the sum of such money and the fair market value of such other property. Under section 1031(c), no loss from a transaction that also involves other property or money is recognized. Under section 1031(d), the basis of property acquired in an exchange described in section 1031 is the same as that of the property exchanged, decreased by the amount of any money received by the taxpayer and increased by the amount of gain (or decreased by the amount of loss) that was recognized on such exchange.

Section 1033(a)(1) provides that if property (as a result of its destruction in whole or in part, theft, seizure, or requisition or condemnation or threat or imminence thereof) is compulsorily or involuntarily converted into property similar or related in service or use to the property so converted, no gain is recognized. Under section 1033(b)(1), the basis of property acquired by the taxpayer in such a transaction is the basis of the converted property. Under section 1033(a)(2)(A), if property is compulsorily or involuntarily converted into money or into property not similar or related in service or use to the converted property, and, within the time frame described in section 1033(a)(2)(B), the taxpayer purchases other property that is related in service or use to the converted property or purchases stock in the acquisition of control of a corporation owning such property, then the taxpayer may elect to recognize gain only to the extent that the amount realized upon such conversion exceeds the cost of such other property or stock. Under section 1033(b)(2), if such an election is made, the basis of the replacement property acquired by the taxpayer generally is the cost of that property decreased by any gain not recognized by reason of section 1033(a)(2).

Summary of Comments and Explanation of Provisions

Scope

In general, the final regulations adopt the rules outlined in the proposed and temporary regulations with the addition of some clarifying language and examples provided in response to comments. The temporary regulations provided guidance as to how to determine the annual depreciation allowance under section 168 for replacement property acquired in a like-kind exchange or involuntary conversion. However, the temporary regulations did not apply to a like-kind exchange or involuntary conversion if the allowance for depreciation of either the relinquished or replacement property is computed under a depreciation system other than section 168 (MACRS), or for which a taxpayer made a valid election under section 168(f)(1) to exclude it from the application of MACRS. A commentator requested that the final regulations apply to all property acquired in a like-kind exchange or involuntary conversion. However, it is anticipated that the vast majority of like-kind exchanges and involuntary conversions occurring after the effective date of the final regulations will involve the exchange of MACRS property. In addition, there are differences between MACRS and other depreciation systems which would require the creation of additional rules which would only apply in a limited number of circumstances. Furthermore, certain types of property are statutorily excluded from being treated as MACRS property. Therefore, the final regulations do not adopt the commentator's suggestion. However, the final regulations allow a taxpayer to elect to treat the sum of the exchanged basis and excess basis of the replacement property as MACRS property that is placed in service at the time of replacement if the tangible depreciable property acquired by a taxpayer in a like-kind exchange or involuntary conversion replaces tangible depreciable property for which the taxpayer made a valid election under section 168(f)(1) to exclude it from the application of MACRS. For example, a taxpayer that exchanges a machine depreciated under the unit of production method for a used machine may depreciate under MACRS the sum of the exchanged basis and excess basis of the used machine (replacement property) as a machine placed in service at the time of replacement.

Optional Depreciation Tables

For taxpayers who wish to use the optional depreciation tables to determine the depreciation allowances for the replacement MACRS property instead of the formulas (for example, see section 6 of Rev. Proc. 87–57, 1987–2 C.B. 687, 692), the final regulations provide guidance on choosing the applicable optional table as well as how to modify the calculation for computing the depreciation allowances for the replacement MACRS property. A commentator noted that under the temporary regulations depreciation computed using the optional tables could be different than the depreciation computed using the formulas and suggested adopting a different transaction coefficient. The IRS and Treasury recognize that use of the optional depreciation tables may result in a different computation of depreciation. Nonetheless, the optional depreciation tables are intended to provide an alternative method of calculating depreciation for taxpayers. Furthermore, the transaction coefficient formula provided in the temporary regulations is consistent with transaction coefficient formulas provided in other depreciation guidance. Therefore, the final regulations retain the rules provided in the temporary regulations.

Depreciation Convention Provisions

Several comments were received about the application of the depreciation convention provisions under the temporary regulations. In response to these comments, several changes were made in the final regulations. Section 1.168(i)–6(c)(5)(ii)(A) was added in order to provide an explanation of the applicable convention separate from the explanation of the rule for determining the remaining recovery period for the replacement MACRS property. Section 1.168(i)–6(c)(4)(v) specifically addresses the convention that applies to the exchanged basis when the year of replacement is after the year of disposition and the relinquished MACRS property was placed in service in the year of disposition. Section 1.168(i)–6(c)(5)(i)(B) of the final regulations contains a new rule that provides that if, using the convention that applies to the relinquished MACRS property, the remaining recovery period of the relinquished MACRS property at the beginning of the year of disposition is less than the number of months between the first of that year and the time of disposition, the entire basis in the relinquished MACRS property is deductible in the year of disposition and the exchanged basis is zero. In light of this new rule, *Example 4* of §1.168(i)–6T(c)(6) of the temporary regulations has been replaced by *Example 5* of §1.168(i)–6(c)(6).

Deferred Exchanges

The temporary regulations did not permit a taxpayer to take depreciation on relinquished MACRS property during the period between the disposition of the relinquished MACRS property and the acquisition of the replacement MACRS property. A comment was received which noted that under the half-year convention if relinquished MACRS property is disposed of in year 1 and the replacement MACRS property is not acquired until year 2, the taxpayer would only be entitled to deduct a half-year of depreciation in each year. The IRS and Treasury Department recognize that this result could occur under the convention rules. However, similar results occur when property is disposed of and replaced in a transaction to which section 1031 or section 1033 do not apply. In addition, the IRS and Treasury Department believe that a taxpayer cannot depreciate property the taxpayer does not own. Therefore, the final regulations retain the rule provided in the temporary regulations with respect to this issue. The final regulations reserve on providing specific guidance as to whether an intermediary (such as an exchange accommodation titleholder) is entitled to depreciation.

Acquisition Prior to Disposition for an Involuntary Conversion

The temporary regulations allowed taxpayers to begin depreciating replacement property upon acquisition even if the acquisition occurs prior the disposition of the relinquished property if the replacement property is acquired to meet the requirements of section 1033(a)(2)(B) (acquisition under threat of condemnation). However, the temporary regulations also required taxpayers to include in taxable income any excess depreciation allowable on the unadjusted depreciable basis of the replacement MACRS property over the depreciation allowable on the excess basis of the replacement MACRS property from the date the replacement MACRS property was placed in service by the taxpayer to the time of disposition of the relinquished MACRS property. A comment was received suggesting that taxpayers be permitted to reduce the exchanged basis of the replacement property by the excess depreciation rather than requiring a taxpayer to recognize the excess depreciation as taxable income. This suggestion was not adopted in the final regulations because it would have the effect of inappropriately accelerating depreciation deductions for the replacement property.

Exchanges of Multiple Properties

The determination of the basis of property acquired in a like-kind exchange involving multiple properties is described in §1.1031(j)–1 and the determination of the basis of multiple properties acquired as a result of an involuntary conversion is described in §1.1033(b)–1. Commentators requested examples to show how the temporary regulations apply to the depreciation treatment of a like-kind exchange or an involuntary conversion involving multiple properties. Other commentators suggested that taxpayers be permitted to use any reasonable, consistent method of allocating basis among the properties. The IRS and Treasury Department believe that these comments concern the allocation of basis principles under sections 1031 and 1033, rather than the depreciation rules under section 168. Once basis in property is determined or allocated under section 1031 or section 1033, these final regulations would then apply for determining the depreciation allowable with respect to such basis. The IRS and Treasury Department believe that issues related to allocation of basis among multiple properties involved in like-kind exchanges or involuntary conversions for purposes of depreciation are beyond the scope of the final regulations. Therefore the final regulations do not address these issues. However, the IRS and Treasury Department intend to invite interested parties to submit written comments regarding whether additional published guidance is needed in this area, and to invite written comments that specifically propose or address possible resolutions to these issues.

Transactions Involving Nondepreciable Property

A commentator requested guidance as to how depreciation is calculated if the relinquished property was only partially used for business purposes. In response to this comment, the final regulations provide an example to show how depreciation is calculated on replacement property received in exchange for property that was used only partially for business purposes (see *Example 2* in §1.168(i)–6(d)(3)(iii)).

General Asset Accounts

Under the temporary regulations, general asset account treatment terminates for the relinquished MACRS property as of the first day of the year of disposition. Because this rule would require taxpayers to track each property in a general asset account, the IRS and Treasury Department requested comments on alternative methods to account for a like-kind exchange or involuntary conversion involving MACRS property contained in a general asset account when the replacement MACRS property has a longer recovery period or less accelerated depreciation method than the relinquished MACRS property or when the basis of the general asset account would change as a result of the like-kind exchange or involuntary conversion. No comments were received on this rule and no alternatives were suggested. Therefore, the regulations are adopted as proposed.

Effective Date

These final regulations generally apply to a like-kind exchange or an involuntary conversion of MACRS property for which the time of disposition and the time of replacement both occur after February 27, 2004. For a like-kind exchange or an involuntary conversion of MACRS property for which the time of disposition, the time of replacement, or both occur on or before February 27, 2004, a taxpayer may apply these final regulations or rely on prior guidance issued by the IRS.

Special Analyses

It has been determined that this Treasury decision is not a significant regulatory action as defined in Executive Order 12866. Therefore, a regulatory assessment is not required. It also has been determined that section 553(b) of the Administrative Procedure Act (5 U.S.C. chapter 5) does not apply to these regulations and, because these regulations do not impose a collection of information requirement on small entities, the Regulatory Flexibility Act (5 U.S.C. chapter 6) does not apply. Therefore, a Regulatory Flexibility Analysis is not required. Pursuant to section 7805(f) of the Code, the notice of proposed rulemaking preceding these final regulations was submitted to the Chief Counsel for Advocacy of the Small Business Administration for comment on its impact on small business.

Drafting Information

The principal author of these regulations is Patrick S. Kirwan, Office of the Associate Chief Counsel (Passthroughs and Special Industries). However, other personnel from the IRS and Treasury Department participated in their development.

* * * * *

Adoption of Amendments to the Regulations

Accordingly, 26 CFR part 1 is amended as follows:

PART 1—INCOME TAXES

Paragraph 1. The authority citation for part 1 continues to read in part as follows:

Authority: 26 U.S.C. 7805 * * *

Par. 2. Sections 1.168(a)–1 and 1.168(b)–1 are added to read as follows:

§1.168(a)–1 Modified accelerated cost recovery system.

(a) Section 168 determines the depreciation allowance for tangible property that is of a character subject to the allowance for depreciation provided in section 167(a) and that is placed in service after December 31, 1986 (or after July 31, 1986, if the taxpayer made an election under section 203(a)(1)(B) of the Tax Reform Act of 1986; 100 Stat. 2143). Except for property excluded from the application of section 168 as a result of section 168(f) or as a result of a transitional rule, the provisions of section 168 are mandatory for all eligible property. The allowance for depreciation under section 168 constitutes the amount of depreciation allowable under section 167(a). The determination of whether tangible property is property of a character subject to the allowance for depreciation is made under section 167 and the regulations under section 167.

(b) This section is applicable on and after February 27, 2004.

§1.168(b)–1 Definitions.

(a) *Definitions*. For purposes of section 168 and the regulations under section 168, the following definitions apply:

(1) *Depreciable property* is property that is of a character subject to the allowance for depreciation as determined under section 167 and the regulations under section 167.

(2) *MACRS property* is tangible, depreciable property that is placed in service after December 31, 1986 (or after July 31, 1986, if the taxpayer made an election under section 203(a)(1)(B) of the Tax Reform Act of 1986; 100 Stat. 2143) and subject to section 168, except for property excluded from the application of section 168 as a result of section 168(f) or as a result of a transitional rule.

(3) *Unadjusted depreciable basis* is the basis of property for purposes of section 1011 without regard to any adjustments described in section 1016(a)(2) and (3). This basis reflects the reduction in basis for the percentage of the taxpayer's use of property for the taxable year other than in the taxpayer's trade or business (or for the production of income), for any portion of the basis the taxpayer properly elects to treat as an expense under section 179, section 179C, or any similar provision, and for any adjustments to basis provided by other provisions of the Internal Revenue Code and the regulations under the Code (other than section 1016(a)(2) and (3)) (for example, a reduction in basis by the amount of the disabled access credit pursuant to section 44(d)(7)). For property subject to a lease, see section 167(c)(2).

(4) *Adjusted depreciable basis* is the unadjusted depreciable basis of the property, as defined in §1.168(b)–1(a)(3), less the adjustments described in section 1016(a)(2) and (3).

(b) *Effective date*. This section is applicable on or after February 27, 2004.

§§1.168(a)–1T and 1.168(b)–1T [Removed]

Par. 3. Sections 1.168(a)–1T and 1.168(b)–1T are removed.

Par. 4. Section 1.168(d)–1 is amended by revising the section heading and paragraphs (b)(3) and (d)(3) to read as follows:

§1.168(d)–1 Applicable conventions—half-year and mid-quarter conventions.

* * * * *

(b) * * *

(3) *Property placed in service and disposed of in the same taxable year*. (i) Under section 168(d)(3)(B)(ii), the depreciable basis of property placed in service and disposed of in the same taxable year is not taken into account in determining whether the 40-percent test is satisfied. However, the depreciable basis of property placed in service, disposed of, subsequently reacquired, and again placed in service, by the taxpayer in the same taxable year must be taken into account in applying the 40-percent test, but the basis of the property is only taken into account on the later of the dates that the property is placed in service by the taxpayer during the taxable year. Further, see §§1.168(i)–6(c)(4)(v)(B) and 1.168(i)–6(f) for rules relating to property placed in service and exchanged or involuntarily converted during the same taxable year.

(ii) The applicable convention, as determined under this section, applies to all depreciable property (except nonresidential real property, residential rental property, and any railroad grading or tunnel bore) placed in service by the taxpayer during the taxable year, excluding property placed in service and disposed of in the same taxable year. However, see §§1.168(i)–6(c)(4)(v)(A) and 1.168(i)–6(f) for rules relating to MACRS property that has a basis determined under section 1031(d) or section 1033(b). No depreciation deduction is allowed for property placed in service and disposed of during the same taxable year. However, see §1.168(k)–1(f)(1) for rules relating to qualified property or 50-percent bonus depreciation property, and §1.1400L(b)–1(f)(1) for rules relating to qualified New York Liberty Zone property, that is placed in service by the taxpayer in the same taxable year in which either a partnership is terminated as a result of a technical termination under section 708(b)(1)(B) or the property is transferred in a transaction described in section 168(i)(7).

* * * * *

(d) * * *

(3) *Like-kind exchanges and involuntary conversions*. The last sentence in paragraph (b)(3)(i) and the second sentence in paragraph (b)(3)(ii) of this section apply to exchanges to which section 1031 applies, and involuntary conversions to which section 1033 applies, of MACRS property for which the time of disposition and the time of replacement both occur after February 27, 2004.

§1.168(d)–1T [Removed]

Par. 5. Section 1.168(d)–1T is removed.

Par. 6. Section 1.168(i)–0 is amended as follows:

1. The entries for §1.168(i)–1(d)(2), (e)(3)(i), (e)(3)(v), (e)(3)(vi), (f), (f)(1), (f)(2), (f)(2)(i), (i), (j), and (l) are revised.

2. The entries for §1.168(i)–1(l)(1), (l)(2), and (l)(3) are added.

The revisions and additions read as follows:

§1.168(i)–0 Table of contents for the general asset account rules.

* * * * *

§1.168(i)–1 General asset accounts.

* * * * *

(d) * * *

(2) Special rule for passenger automobiles.

* * * * *

(e) * * *

(3) * * *

(i) In general.

* * * * *

(v) Transactions subject to section 1031 or 1033.

(vi) Anti-abuse rule.

* * * * *

(f) Assets generating foreign source income.

(1) In general.

(2) Source of ordinary income, gain, or loss.

(i) Source determined by allocation and apportionment of depreciation allowed.

* * * * *

(i) Identification of disposed or converted asset.

(j) Effect of adjustments on prior dispositions.

* * * * *

(l) Effective date.

(1) In general.

(2) Exceptions.

(3) Like-kind exchanges and involuntary conversions.

§1.168(i)–0T [Removed]

Par. 7. Section 1.168(i)–0T is removed.

Par. 8. Section 1.168(i)–1 is amended as follows:

1. Paragraphs (d)(2), (e)(3)(i), (e)(3)(iii)(B)(*4*), (e)(3)(v), (e)(3)(vi), (f)(1), (f)(2)(i), (i), (j), (l)(1), and (l)(3) are revised.

2. The first sentence in paragraph (l)(2)(ii)(B) is amended by removing the language "as modified by Rev. Proc. 2004–11, 2004–1 C.B. 311".

The revisions read as follows:

§1.168(i)–1 General asset accounts.

* * * * *

(d) * * *

(2) *Special rule for passenger automobiles.* For purposes of applying section 280F(a), the depreciation allowance for a general asset account established for passenger automobiles is limited for each taxable year to the amount prescribed in section 280F(a) multiplied by the excess of the number of automobiles originally included in the account over the number of automobiles disposed of during the taxable year or in any prior taxable year in a transaction described in paragraph (e)(3)(iii) (disposition of an asset in a qualifying disposition), (e)(3)(iv) (transactions subject to section 168(i)(7)), (e)(3)(v) (transactions subject to section 1031 or 1033), (e)(3)(vi) (anti-abuse rule), (g) (assets subject to recapture), or (h)(1) (conversion to personal use) of this section.

(e) * * *

(3) * * *

(i) *In general.* This paragraph (e)(3) provides the rules for terminating general asset account treatment upon certain dispositions. While the rules under paragraphs (e)(3)(ii) and (iii) of this section are optional rules, the rules under paragraphs (e)(3)(iv), (v), and (vi) of this section are mandatory rules. A taxpayer applies paragraph (e)(3)(ii) or (iii) of this section by reporting the gain, loss, or other deduction on the taxpayer's timely filed Federal income tax return (including extensions) for the taxable year in which the disposition occurs. For purposes of applying paragraph (e)(3)(iii) through (vi) of this section, see paragraph (i) of this section for identifying the unadjusted depreciable basis of a disposed asset.

* * * * *

(iii) * * *

(B) * * *

(*4*) A transaction, other than a transaction described in paragraphs (e)(3)(iv) (pertaining to transactions subject to section 168(i)(7)) and (e)(3)(v) (pertaining to transactions subject to section 1031 or 1033) of this section, to which a nonrecognition section of the Code applies (determined without regard to this section).

* * * * *

(v) *Transactions subject to section 1031 or section 1033*—(A) *Like-kind exchange or involuntary conversion of all assets remaining in a general asset account.* If all the assets, or the last asset, in a general asset account are transferred by a taxpayer in a like-kind exchange (as defined under §1.168–6(b)(11)) or in an involuntary conversion (as defined under §1.168–6(b)(12)), the taxpayer must apply this paragraph (e)(3)(v)(A) (instead of applying paragraph (e)(2), (e)(3)(ii), or (e)(3)(iii) of this section). Under this paragraph (e)(3)(v)(A), the general asset account terminates as of the first day of the year of disposition (as defined in §1.168(i)–6(b)(5)) and—

(*1*) The amount of gain or loss for the general asset account is determined under section 1001(a) by taking into account the adjusted depreciable basis of the general asset account at the time of disposition (as defined in §1.168(i)–6(b)(3)). The depreciation allowance for the general asset account in the year of disposition is determined in the same manner as the depreciation allowance for the relinquished MACRS property (as defined in §1.168(i)–6(b)(2)) in the year of disposition is determined under §1.168(i)–6. The recognition and character of gain or loss are determined in accordance with paragraph (e)(3)(ii)(A) of this section (notwithstanding that paragraph (e)(3)(ii) of this section is an optional rule); and

(*2*) The adjusted depreciable basis of the general asset account at the time of disposition is treated as the adjusted depreciable basis of the relinquished MACRS property.

(B) *Like-kind exchange or involuntary conversion of less than all assets remaining in a general asset account.* If an asset in a general asset account is transferred by a taxpayer in a like-kind exchange or in an involuntary conversion and if paragraph (e)(3)(v)(A) of this section does not apply to this asset, the taxpayer must apply this paragraph (e)(3)(v)(B) (instead of applying paragraph (e)(2), (e)(3)(ii), or (e)(3)(iii) of this section). Under this paragraph (e)(3)(v)(B), general asset account treatment for the asset terminates as of the first day of the year of disposition (as defined in §1.168(i)–6(b)(5)), and—

(*1*) The amount of gain or loss for the asset is determined by taking into account the asset's adjusted basis at the time of disposition (as defined in §1.168(i)–6(b)(3)). The adjusted basis of the asset at the time of disposition equals the unadjusted depreciable basis of the asset less the depreciation allowed or allowable for the asset, computed by using the depreciation method, recovery period, and convention applicable to the general asset account in which the asset was included. The depreciation allowance for the asset in the year of disposition is determined in the same manner as the depreciation allowance for the relinquished MACRS property (as defined in §1.168(i)–6(b)(2)) in the year of disposition is determined under §1.168(i)–6. The recognition and character of the gain or loss are determined in accordance with paragraph (e)(3)(iii)(A) of this section (notwithstanding that paragraph (e)(3)(iii) of this section is an optional rule); and

(*2*) As of the first day of the year of disposition, the taxpayer must remove the relinquished asset from the general asset account and make the adjustments to the general asset account described in paragraph (e)(3)(iii)(C)(*2*) through (*4*) of this section.

(vi) *Anti-abuse rule*—(A) *In general*. If an asset in a general asset account is disposed of by a taxpayer in a transaction described in paragraph (e)(3)(vi)(B) of this section, general asset account treatment for the asset terminates as of the first day of the taxable year in which the disposition occurs. Consequently, the taxpayer must determine the amount of gain, loss, or other deduction attributable to the disposition in the manner described in paragraph (e)(3)(iii)(A) of this section (notwithstanding that paragraph (e)(3)(iii)(A) of this section is an optional rule) and must make the adjustments to the general asset account described in paragraph (e)(3)(iii)(C)(*1*) through (*4*) of this section.

(B) *Abusive transactions*. A transaction is described in this paragraph (e)(3)(vi)(B) if the transaction is not described in paragraph (e)(3)(iv) or (e)(3)(v) of this section and the transaction is entered into, or made, with a principal purpose of achieving a tax benefit or result that would not be available absent an election under this section. Examples of these types of transactions include—

(*1*) A transaction entered into with a principal purpose of shifting income or deductions among taxpayers in a manner that would not be possible absent an election under this section in order to take advantage of differing effective tax rates among the taxpayers; or

(*2*) An election made under this section with a principal purpose of disposing of an asset from a general asset account in order to utilize an expiring net operating loss or credit. The fact that a taxpayer with a net operating loss carryover or a credit carryover transfers an asset to a related person or transfers an asset pursuant to an arrangement where the asset continues to be used (or is available for use) by the taxpayer pursuant to a lease (or otherwise) indicates, absent strong evidence to the contrary, that the transaction is described in this paragraph (e)(3)(vi)(B).

(f) * * *

(1) *In general*. This paragraph (f) provides the rules for determining the source of any income, gain, or loss recognized, and the appropriate section 904(d) separate limitation category or categories for any foreign source income, gain, or loss recognized, on a disposition (within the meaning of paragraph (e)(1) of this section) of an asset in a general asset account that consists of assets generating both United States and foreign source income. These rules apply only to a disposition to which paragraph (e)(2) (general disposition rules), (e)(3)(ii) (disposition of all assets remaining in a general asset account), (e)(3)(iii) (disposition of an asset in a qualifying disposition), (e)(3)(v) (transactions subject to section 1031 or 1033), or (e)(3)(vi) (anti-abuse rule) of this section applies.

(2) * * *

(i) *Source determined by allocation and apportionment of depreciation allowed*. The amount of any ordinary income, gain, or loss that is recognized on the disposition of an asset in a general asset account must be apportioned between United States and foreign sources based on the allocation and apportionment of the—

(A) Depreciation allowed for the general asset account as of the end of the taxable year in which the disposition occurs if paragraph (e)(2) of this section applies to the disposition;

(B) Depreciation allowed for the general asset account as of the time of disposition if the taxpayer applies paragraph (e)(3)(ii) of this section to the disposition of all assets, or the last asset, in the general asset account, or if all the assets, or the last asset, in the general asset account are disposed of in a transaction described in paragraph (e)(3)(v)(A) of this section; or

(C) Depreciation allowed for the disposed asset for only the taxable year in which the disposition occurs if the taxpayer applies paragraph (e)(3)(iii) of this section to the disposition of the asset in a qualifying disposition, if the asset is disposed of in a transaction described in paragraph (e)(3)(v)(B) of this section (like-kind exchange or involuntary conversion), or if the asset is disposed in a transaction described in paragraph (e)(3)(vi) of this section (anti-abuse rule).

* * * * *

(i) * * * A taxpayer may use any reasonable method that is consistently applied to the taxpayer's general asset accounts for purposes of determining the unadjusted depreciable basis of a disposed or converted asset in a transaction described in paragraph (e)(3)(iii) (disposition of an asset in a qualifying disposition), (e)(3)(iv) (transactions subject to section 168(i)(7)), (e)(3)(v) (transactions subject to section 1031 or 1033), (e)(3)(vi) (anti-abuse rule), (g) (assets subject to recapture), or (h)(1) (conversion to personal use) of this section.

(j) *Effect of adjustments on prior dispositions*. The adjustments to a general asset account under paragraph (e)(3)(iii), (e)(3)(iv), (e)(3)(v), (e)(3)(vi), (g), or (h)(1) of this section have no effect on the recognition and character of prior dispositions subject to paragraph (e)(2) of this section.

* * * * *

(l) * * *

(1) *In general*. Except as provided in paragraphs (l)(2) and (l)(3) of this section, this section applies to depreciable assets placed in service in taxable years ending on or after October 11, 1994. For depreciable assets placed in service after December 31, 1986, in taxable years ending before October 11, 1994, the Internal Revenue Service will allow any reasonable method that is consistently applied to the taxpayer's general asset accounts.

* * * * *

(3) *Like-kind exchanges and involuntary conversions*. This section applies for an asset transferred by a taxpayer in a like-kind exchange (as defined under §1.168–6(b)(11)) or in an involuntary conversion (as defined under §1.168–6(b)(12)) for which the time of disposition (as defined in §1.168(i)–6(b)(3)) and the time of replacement (as defined in §1.168(i)–6(b)(4)) both occur after February 27, 2004. For an asset transferred by a taxpayer in a like-kind exchange or in an involuntary conversion for which the time of disposition, the time of replacement, or both occur on or before February 27, 2004, see §1.168(i)–1 in effect prior to February 27, 2004 (§1.168(i)–1 as contained in

26 CFR part 1 edition revised as of April 1, 2003).

§1.168(i)–1T [Removed]

Par. 9. Section 1.168(i)–1T is removed.

Par. 10. Section 1.168(i)–5 is added to read as follows:

§1.168(i)–5 Table of contents.

This section lists the major paragraphs contained in §1.168(i)–6.

§1.168(i)–6 Like-kind exchanges and involuntary conversions.

§1.168(i)–5T [Removed]

Par. 11. Section 1.168(i)–5T is removed.

Par. 12. Section 1.168(i)–6 is added to read as follows:

§1.168(i)–6 Like-kind exchanges and involuntary conversions.

(a) *Scope*. This section provides the rules for determining the depreciation allowance for MACRS property acquired in a like-kind exchange or an involuntary conversion, including a like-kind exchange or an involuntary conversion of MACRS property that is exchanged or replaced with other MACRS property in a transaction between members of the same affiliated group. The allowance for depreciation under this section constitutes the amount of depreciation allowable under section 167(a) for the year of replacement and any subsequent taxable year for the replacement MACRS property and for the year of disposition of the relinquished MACRS property. The provisions of this section apply only to MACRS property to which §1.168(h)–1 (like-kind exchanges of tax-exempt use property) does not apply. Additionally, paragraphs (c) through (f) of this section apply only to MACRS property for which an election under paragraph (i) of this section has not been made.

(b) *Definitions.* For purposes of this section, the following definitions apply:

(1) *Replacement MACRS property* is MACRS property (as defined in §1.168(b)–1(a)(2)) in the hands of the acquiring taxpayer that is acquired for other MACRS property in a like-kind exchange or an involuntary conversion.

(2) *Relinquished MACRS property* is MACRS property that is transferred by the taxpayer in a like-kind exchange, or in an involuntary conversion.

(3) *Time of disposition* is when the disposition of the relinquished MACRS property takes place under the convention, as determined under §1.168(d)–1, that applies to the relinquished MACRS property.

(4) *Time of replacement* is the later of—

(i) When the replacement MACRS property is placed in service under the convention, as determined under this section, that applies to the replacement MACRS property; or

(ii) The time of disposition of the exchanged or involuntarily converted property.

(5) *Year of disposition* is the taxable year that includes the time of disposition.

(6) *Year of replacement* is the taxable year that includes the time of replacement.

(7) *Exchanged basis* is determined after the depreciation deductions for the year of disposition are determined under paragraph (c)(5)(i) of this section and is the lesser of—

(i) The basis in the replacement MACRS property, as determined under section 1031(d) and the regulations under section 1031(d) or section 1033(b) and the regulations under section 1033(b); or

(ii) The adjusted depreciable basis (as defined in §1.168(b)–1(a)(4)) of the relinquished MACRS property.

(8) *Excess basis* is any excess of the basis in the replacement MACRS property, as determined under section 1031(d) and the regulations under section 1031(d) or section 1033(b) and the regulations under section 1033(b), over the exchanged basis as determined under paragraph (b)(7) of this section.

(9) *Depreciable exchanged basis* is the exchanged basis as determined under paragraph (b)(7) of this section reduced by—

(i) The percentage of such basis attributable to the taxpayer's use of property for the taxable year other than in the taxpayer's trade or business (or for the production of income); and

(ii) Any adjustments to basis provided by other provisions of the Internal Revenue Code (Code) and the regulations under the Code (including section 1016(a)(2) and (3), for example, depreciation deductions in the year of replacement allowable under section 168(k) or 1400L(b)).

(10) *Depreciable excess basis* is the excess basis as determined under paragraph (b)(8) of this section reduced by—

(i) The percentage of such basis attributable to the taxpayer's use of property for the taxable year other than in the taxpayer's trade or business (or for the production of income);

(ii) Any portion of the basis the taxpayer properly elects to treat as an expense under section 179; and

(iii) Any adjustments to basis provided by other provisions of the Code and the regulations under the Code (including section 1016(a)(2) and (3), for example, depreciation deductions in the year of replacement allowable under section 168(k) or 1400L(b)).

(11) *Like-kind exchange* is an exchange of property in a transaction to which section 1031(a)(1), (b), or (c) applies.

(12) *Involuntary conversion* is a transaction described in section 1033(a)(1) or (2) that resulted in the nonrecognition of any part of the gain realized as the result of the conversion.

(c) *Determination of depreciation allowance*—(1) *Computation of the depreciation allowance for depreciable exchanged basis beginning in the year of replacement*—(i) *In general.* This paragraph (c) provides rules for determining the applicable recovery period, the applicable depreciation method, and the applicable convention used to determine the depreciation allowances for the depreciable exchanged basis beginning in the year of replacement. See paragraph (c)(5) of this section for rules relating to the computation of the depreciation allowance for the year of disposition and for the year of replacement. See paragraph (d)(1) of this section for rules relating to the computation of the depreciation allowance for depreciable excess basis. See paragraph (d)(4) of this section if the replacement MACRS property is acquired before disposition of the relinquished MACRS property in a transaction to which section 1033 applies. See paragraph (e) of this section for rules relating to the computation of the depreciation allowance using the optional depreciation tables.

(ii) *Applicable recovery period, depreciation method, and convention.* The recovery period, depreciation method, and convention determined under this paragraph (c) are the only permissible methods of accounting for MACRS property within the scope of this section unless the taxpayer makes the election under paragraph (i) of this section not to apply this section.

(2) *Effect of depreciation treatment of the replacement MACRS property by previous owners of the acquired property.* If replacement MACRS property is acquired by a taxpayer in a like-kind exchange or an involuntary conversion, the depreciation treatment of the replacement MACRS property by previous owners has no effect on the determination of depreciation allowances for the replacement MACRS property in the hands of the acquiring taxpayer. For example, a taxpayer exchanging, in a like-kind exchange, MACRS property for property that was depreciated under section 168 of the Internal Revenue Code of 1954 (ACRS) by the previous owner must use this section because the replacement property will become MACRS property in the hands of the acquiring taxpayer. In addition, elections made by previous owners in determining depreciation allowances for the replacement MACRS property have no effect on the acquiring taxpayer. For example, a taxpayer exchanging, in a like-kind exchange, MACRS property that the taxpayer depreciates under the general depreciation system of section 168(a) for other MACRS property that the previous owner elected to depreciate under the alternative depreciation system pursuant to section 168(g)(7) does not have to continue using the alternative depreciation system for the replacement MACRS property.

(3) *Recovery period and/or depreciation method of the properties are the same, or both are not the same*—(i) *In general.* For purposes of paragraphs (c)(3) and (c)(4) of this section in determining whether the recovery period and the depreciation method prescribed under section 168 for the replacement MACRS property are the same as the recovery period and the depreciation method prescribed under

section 168 for the relinquished MACRS property, the recovery period and the depreciation method for the replacement MACRS property are considered to be the recovery period and the depreciation method that would have applied under section 168, taking into account any elections made by the acquiring taxpayer under section 168(b)(5) or 168(g)(7), had the replacement MACRS property been placed in service by the acquiring taxpayer at the same time as the relinquished MACRS property.

(ii) *Both the recovery period and the depreciation method are the same.* If both the recovery period and the depreciation method prescribed under section 168 for the replacement MACRS property are the same as the recovery period and the depreciation method prescribed under section 168 for the relinquished MACRS property, the depreciation allowances for the replacement MACRS property beginning in the year of replacement are determined by using the same recovery period and depreciation method that were used for the relinquished MACRS property. Thus, the replacement MACRS property is depreciated over the remaining recovery period (taking into account the applicable convention), and by using the depreciation method, of the relinquished MACRS property. Except as provided in paragraph (c)(5) of this section, the depreciation allowances for the depreciable exchanged basis for any 12-month taxable year beginning with the year of replacement are determined by multiplying the depreciable exchanged basis by the applicable depreciation rate for each taxable year (for further guidance, for example, see section 6 of Rev. Proc. 87–57, 1987–2 C.B. 687, 692, and §601.601(d)(2)(ii)(*b*) of this chapter).

(iii) *Either the recovery period or the depreciation method is the same, or both are not the same.* If either the recovery period or the depreciation method prescribed under section 168 for the replacement MACRS property is the same as the recovery period or the depreciation method prescribed under section 168 for the relinquished MACRS property, the depreciation allowances for the depreciable exchanged basis beginning in the year of replacement are determined using the recovery period or the depreciation method that is the same as the relinquished MACRS property. See paragraph (c)(4) of this section to determine the depreciation allowances when the recovery period or the depreciation method of the replacement MACRS property is not the same as that of the relinquished MACRS property.

(4) *Recovery period or depreciation method of the properties is not the same.* If the recovery period prescribed under section 168 for the replacement MACRS property (as determined under paragraph (c)(3)(i) of this section) is not the same as the recovery period prescribed under section 168 for the relinquished MACRS property, the depreciation allowances for the depreciable exchanged basis beginning in the year of replacement are determined under this paragraph (c)(4). Similarly, if the depreciation method prescribed under section 168 for the replacement MACRS property (as determined under paragraph (c)(3)(i) of this section) is not the same as the depreciation method prescribed under section 168 for the relinquished MACRS property, the depreciation method used to determine the depreciation allowances for the depreciable exchanged basis beginning in the year of replacement is determined under this paragraph (c)(4).

(i) *Longer recovery period.* If the recovery period prescribed under section 168 for the replacement MACRS property (as determined under paragraph (c)(3)(i) of this section) is longer than that prescribed for the relinquished MACRS property, the depreciation allowances for the depreciable exchanged basis beginning in the year of replacement are determined as though the replacement MACRS property had originally been placed in service by the acquiring taxpayer in the same taxable year the relinquished MACRS property was placed in service by the acquiring taxpayer, but using the longer recovery period of the replacement MACRS property (as determined under paragraph (c)(3)(i) of this section) and the convention determined under paragraph (c)(4)(v) of this section. Thus, the depreciable exchanged basis is depreciated over the remaining recovery period (taking into account the applicable convention) of the replacement MACRS property.

(ii) *Shorter recovery period.* If the recovery period prescribed under section 168 for the replacement MACRS property (as determined under paragraph (c)(3)(i) of this section) is shorter than that of the relinquished MACRS property, the depreciation allowances for the depreciable exchanged basis beginning in the year of replacement are determined using the same recovery period as that of the relinquished MACRS property. Thus, the depreciable exchanged basis is depreciated over the remaining recovery period (taking into account the applicable convention) of the relinquished MACRS property.

(iii) *Less accelerated depreciation method*—(A) If the depreciation method prescribed under section 168 for the replacement MACRS property (as determined under paragraph (c)(3)(i) of this section) is less accelerated than that of the relinquished MACRS property at the time of disposition, the depreciation allowances for the depreciable exchanged basis beginning in the year of replacement are determined as though the replacement MACRS property had originally been placed in service by the acquiring taxpayer at the same time the relinquished MACRS property was placed in service by the acquiring taxpayer, but using the less accelerated depreciation method. Thus, the depreciable exchanged basis is depreciated using the less accelerated depreciation method.

(B) Except as provided in paragraph (c)(5) of this section, the depreciation allowances for the depreciable exchanged basis for any 12-month taxable year beginning in the year of replacement are determined by multiplying the adjusted depreciable basis by the applicable depreciation rate for each taxable year. If, for example, the depreciation method of the replacement MACRS property in the year of replacement is the 150-percent declining balance method and the depreciation method of the relinquished MACRS property in the year of replacement is the 200-percent declining balance method, and neither method had been switched to the straight line method in the year of replacement or any prior taxable year, the applicable depreciation rate for the year of replacement and subsequent taxable years is determined by using the depreciation rate of the replacement MACRS property as if the replacement MACRS property was placed in service by the acquiring taxpayer at the same time the relinquished MACRS property was placed in service by the acquiring taxpayer, until the 150-percent declining balance method has been switched to the straight line method. If, for example, the depreciation method of the replacement MACRS property is the straight line method, the applicable depreciation rate for the year of replacement is determined by using the remaining recovery period at the beginning of the year of disposition (as determined under this paragraph (c)(4) and taking into account the applicable convention).

(iv) *More accelerated depreciation method*—(A) If the depreciation method prescribed under section 168 for the replacement MACRS property (as determined under paragraph (c)(3)(i) of this section) is more accelerated than that of the relinquished MACRS property at the time of disposition, the depreciation allowances for the replacement MACRS property beginning in the year of replacement are determined using the same depreciation method as the relinquished MACRS property.

(B) Except as provided in paragraph (c)(5) of this section, the depreciation allowances for the depreciable exchanged basis for any 12-month taxable year beginning in the year of replacement are determined by multiplying the adjusted depreciable basis by the applicable depreciation rate for each taxable year. If, for example, the depreciation method of the relinquished MACRS property in the year of replacement is the 150-percent declining balance method and the depreciation method of the replacement MACRS property in the year of replacement is the 200-percent declining balance method, and neither method had been switched to the straight line method in the year of replacement or any prior taxable year, the applicable depreciation rate for the year of replacement and subsequent taxable years is the same depreciation rate that applied to the relinquished MACRS property in the year of replacement, until the 150-percent declining balance method has been switched to the straight line method. If, for example, the depreciation method is the straight line method, the applicable depreciation rate for the year of replacement is determined by using the remaining recovery period at the beginning of the year of disposition (as determined under this paragraph (c)(4) and taking into account the applicable convention).

(v) *Convention*. The applicable convention for the exchanged basis is determined under this paragraph (c)(4)(v).

(A) *Either the relinquished MACRS property or the replacement MACRS property is mid-month property*. If either the relinquished MACRS property or the replacement MACRS property is property for which the applicable convention (as determined under section 168(d)) is the mid-month convention, the exchanged basis must be depreciated using the mid-month convention.

(B) *Neither the relinquished MACRS property nor the replacement MACRS property is mid-month property*. If neither the relinquished MACRS property nor the replacement MACRS property is property for which the applicable convention (as determined under section 168(d)) is the mid-month convention, the applicable convention for the exchanged basis is the same convention that applied to the relinquished MACRS property. If the relinquished MACRS property is placed in service in the year of disposition, and the time of replacement is also in the year of disposition, the convention that applies to the relinquished MACRS property is determined under paragraph (f)(1)(i) of this section. If, however, relinquished MACRS property was placed in service in the year of disposition and the time of replacement is in a taxable year subsequent to the year of disposition, the convention that applies to the exchanged basis is the convention that applies in that subsequent taxable year (see paragraph (f)(1)(ii) of this section).

(5) *Year of disposition and year of replacement*. No depreciation deduction is allowable for MACRS property disposed of by a taxpayer in a like-kind exchange or involuntary conversion in the same taxable year that such property was placed in service by the taxpayer. If replacement MACRS property is disposed of by a taxpayer during the same taxable year that the relinquished MACRS property is placed in service by the taxpayer, no depreciation deduction is allowable for either MACRS property. Otherwise, the depreciation allowances for the year of disposition and for the year of replacement are determined as follows:

(i) *Relinquished MACRS property*—(A) *General rule*. Except as provided in paragraphs (c)(5)(i)(B), (c)(5)(iii), (e), and (i) of this section, the depreciation allowance in the year of disposition for the relinquished MACRS property is computed by multiplying the allowable depreciation deduction for the property for that year by a fraction, the numerator of which is the number of months (including fractions of months) the property is deemed to be placed in service during the year of disposition (taking into account the applicable convention of the relinquished MACRS property), and the denominator of which is 12. In the case of termination under §1.168(i)–1(e)(3)(v) of general asset account treatment of an asset, or of all the assets remaining, in a general asset account, the allowable depreciation deduction in the year of disposition for the asset or assets for which general asset account treatment is terminated is determined using the depreciation method, recovery period, and convention of the general asset account. This allowable depreciation deduction is adjusted to account for the period the asset or assets is deemed to be in service in accordance with this paragraph (c)(5)(i).

(B) *Special rule*. If, at the beginning of the year of disposition, the remaining recovery period of the relinquished MACRS property, taking into account the applicable convention of such property, is less than the period between the beginning of the year of disposition and the time of disposition, the depreciation deduction for the relinquished MACRS property for the year of disposition is equal to the adjusted depreciable basis of the relinquished MACRS property at the beginning of the year of disposition. If this paragraph applies, the exchanged basis is zero and no depreciation is allowable for the exchanged basis in the replacement MACRS property.

(ii) *Replacement MACRS property*—(A) *Remaining recovery period of the replacement MACRS property*. The replacement MACRS property is treated as placed in service at the time of replacement under the convention that applies to the replacement MACRS property as determined under this paragraph (c)(5)(ii). The remaining recovery period of the replacement MACRS property at the time of replacement is the excess of the recovery period for the replacement MACRS property, as determined under paragraph (c) of this section, over the period of time that the replacement MACRS property would have been in service if it had been placed in service when the relinquished

MACRS property was placed in service and removed from service at the time of disposition of the relinquished MACRS property. This period is determined by using the convention that applied to the relinquished MACRS property to determine the date that the relinquished MACRS property is deemed to have been placed in service and the date that it is deemed to have been disposed of. The length of time the replacement MACRS property would have been in service is determined by using these dates and the convention that applies to the replacement MACRS property.

(B) *Year of replacement is 12 months.* Except as provided in paragraphs (c)(5)(iii), (e), and (i) of this section, the depreciation allowance in the year of replacement for the depreciable exchanged basis is determined by—

(*1*) Calculating the applicable depreciation rate for the replacement MACRS property as of the beginning of the year of replacement taking into account the depreciation method prescribed for the replacement MACRS property under paragraph (c)(3) of this section and the remaining recovery period of the replacement MACRS property as of the beginning of the year of disposition as determined under this paragraph (c)(5)(ii);

(*2*) Calculating the depreciable exchanged basis of the replacement MACRS property, and adding to that amount the amount determined under paragraph (c)(5)(i) of this section for the year of disposition; and

(*3*) Multiplying the product of the amounts determined under paragraphs (c)(5)(ii)(B)(*1*) and (B)(*2*) of this section by a fraction, the numerator of which is the number of months (including fractions of months) the property is deemed to be in service during the year of replacement (in the year of replacement the replacement MACRS property is deemed to be placed in service by the acquiring taxpayer at the time of replacement under the convention determined under paragraph (c)(4)(v) of this section), and the denominator of which is 12.

(iii) *Year of disposition or year of replacement is less than 12 months.* If the year of disposition or the year of replacement is less than 12 months, the depreciation allowance determined under paragraph (c)(5)(ii)(A) of this section must be adjusted for a short taxable year (for further guidance, for example, see Rev. Proc. 89–15, 1989–1 C.B. 816, and §601.601(d)(2)(ii)(*b*) of this chapter).

(iv) *Deferred transactions*—(A) *In general.* If the replacement MACRS property is not acquired until after the disposition of the relinquished MACRS property, taking into account the applicable convention of the relinquished MACRS property and replacement MACRS property, depreciation is not allowable during the period between the disposition of the relinquished MACRS property and the acquisition of the replacement MACRS property. The recovery period for the replacement MACRS property is suspended during this period. For purposes of paragraph (c)(5)(ii) of this section, only the depreciable exchanged basis of the replacement MACRS property is taken into account for calculating the amount in paragraph (c)(5)(ii)(B)(*2*) of this section if the year of replacement is a taxable year subsequent to the year of disposition.

(B) *Allowable depreciation for a qualified intermediary.* [Reserved].

(v) *Remaining recovery period.* The remaining recovery period of the replacement MACRS property is determined as of the beginning of the year of disposition of the relinquished MACRS property. For purposes of determining the remaining recovery period of the replacement MACRS property, the replacement MACRS property is deemed to have been originally placed in service under the convention determined under paragraph (c)(4)(v) of this section but at the time the relinquished MACRS property was deemed to be placed in service under the convention that applied to it when it was placed in service.

(6) *Examples.* The application of this paragraph (c) is illustrated by the following examples:

Example 1. A1, a calendar-year taxpayer, exchanges Building M, an office building, for Building N, a warehouse in a like-kind exchange. Building M is relinquished in July 2004 and Building N is acquired and placed in service in October 2004. A1 did not make any elections under section 168 for either Building M or Building N. The unadjusted depreciable basis of Building M was $4,680,000 when placed in service in July 1997. Since the recovery period and depreciation method prescribed under section 168 for Building N (39 years, straight line method) are the same as the recovery period and depreciation method prescribed under section 168 for Building M (39 years, straight line method), Building N is depreciated over the remaining recovery period of, and using the same depreciation method and convention as that of, Building M. Applying the applicable convention, Building M is deemed disposed of on July 15, 2004, and Building N is placed in service on October 15, 2004. Thus, Building N will be depreciated using the straight line method over a remaining recovery period of 32 years beginning in October 2004 (the remaining recovery period of 32 years and 6.5 months at the beginning of 2004, less the 6.5 months of depreciation taken prior to the disposition of the exchanged MACRS property (Building M) in 2004). For 2004, the year in which the transaction takes place, the depreciation allowance for Building M is ($120,000)(6.5/12) which equals $65,000. The depreciation allowance for Building N for 2004 is ($120,000)(2.5/12) which equals $25,000. For 2005 and subsequent years, Building N is depreciated over the remaining recovery period of, and using the same depreciation method and convention as that of, Building M. Thus, the depreciation allowance for Building N is the same as Building M, namely $10,000 per month.

Example 2. B, a calendar-year taxpayer, placed in service Bridge P in January 1998. Bridge P is depreciated using the half-year convention. In January 2004, B exchanges Bridge P for Building Q, an apartment building, in a like-kind exchange. Pursuant to paragraph (k)(2)(i) of this section, B decided to apply §1.168(i)–6 to the exchange of Bridge P for Building Q, the replacement MACRS property. B did not make any elections under section 168 for either Bridge P or Building Q. Since the recovery period prescribed under section 168 for Building Q (27.5 years) is longer than that of Bridge P (15 years), Building Q is depreciated as if it had originally been placed in service in July 1998 and disposed of in July 2004 using a 27.5 year recovery period. Additionally, since the depreciation method prescribed under section 168 for Building Q (straight line method) is less accelerated than that of Bridge P (150-percent declining balance method), then the depreciation allowance for Building Q is computed using the straight line method. Thus, when Building Q is acquired and placed in service in 2004, its basis is depreciated over the remaining 21.5 year recovery period using the straight line method of depreciation and the mid-month convention beginning in July 2004.

Example 3. C, a calendar-year taxpayer, placed in service Building R, a restaurant, in January 1996. In January 2004, C exchanges Building R for Tower S, a radio transmitting tower, in a like-kind exchange. Pursuant to paragraph (k)(2)(i) of this section, C decided to apply §1.168(i)–6 to the exchange of Building R for Tower S, the replacement MACRS property. C did not make any elections under section 168 for either Building R or Tower S. Since the recovery period prescribed under section 168 for Tower S (15 years) is shorter than that of Building R (39 years), Tower S is depreciated over the remaining recovery period of Building R. Additionally, since the depreciation method prescribed under section 168 for Tower S (150% declining balance method) is more accelerated than that of Building R (straight line method), then the depreciation allowance for Tower S is also computed using the same depreciation method as Building R. Thus, Tower S is depreciated over the remaining 31 year recovery period of Building R using the straight line method of depreciation and the mid-month convention. Alternatively, C may elect under paragraph (i) of this section to treat Tower S as though it is placed in service in January 2004. In such case, C uses the applicable recovery period, depreciation method, and convention prescribed under section 168 for Tower S.

Example 4. (i) In February 2002, D, a calendar-year taxpayer and manufacturer of rubber products, acquired for $60,000 and placed in service Asset T (a special tool) and depreciated Asset T using the straight line method election under section 168(b)(5) and the mid-quarter convention over its 3-year recovery period. D elected not to deduct the additional first year depreciation for 3-year property placed in service in 2002. In June 2004, D exchanges Asset T for Asset U (not a special tool) in a like-kind exchange. D elected not to deduct the additional first year depreciation for 7-year property placed in service in 2004. Since the recovery period prescribed under section 168 for Asset U (7 years) is longer than that of Asset T (3 years), Asset U is depreciated as if it had originally been placed in service in February 2002 using a 7-year recovery period. Additionally, since the depreciation method prescribed under section 168 for Asset U (200-percent declining balance method) is more accelerated than that of Asset T (straight line method) at the time of disposition, the depreciation allowance for Asset U is computed using the straight line method. Asset U is depreciated over its remaining recovery period of 4.75 years using the straight line method of depreciation and the mid-quarter convention.

(ii) The 2004 depreciation allowance for Asset T is $7,500 ($20,000 allowable depreciation deduction for 2004) × 4.5 months ÷ 12).

(iii) The depreciation rate in 2004 for Asset U is 0.1951 (1 ÷ 5.125 years (the length of the applicable recovery period remaining as of the beginning of 2004)). Therefore, the depreciation allowance for Asset U in 2004 is $2,744 (0.1951 × $22,500 (the sum of the $15,000 depreciable exchanged basis of Asset U ($22,500 adjusted depreciable basis at the beginning of 2004 for Asset T, less the $7,500 depreciation allowable for Asset T for 2004) and the $7,500 depreciation allowable for Asset T for 2004) × 7.5 months ÷ 12).

Example 5. The facts are the same as in *Example 4* except that D exchanges Asset T for Asset U in June 2005, in a like-kind exchange. Under these facts, the remaining recovery period of Asset T at the beginning of 2005 is 1.5 months and, as a result, is less than the 5-month period between the beginning of 2005 (year of disposition) and June 2005 (time of disposition). Accordingly, pursuant to paragraph (c)(5)(i)(B) of this section, the 2005 depreciation allowance for Asset T is $2,500 ($2,500 adjusted depreciable basis at the beginning of 2005 ($60,000 original basis minus $17,500 depreciation deduction for 2002 minus $20,000 depreciation deduction for 2003 minus $20,000 depreciation deduction for 2004)). Because the exchanged basis of asset U is $0.00 no depreciation is allowable for asset U.

Example 6. On January 1, 2004, E, a calendar-year taxpayer, acquired and placed in service Canopy V, a gas station canopy. The purchase price of Canopy V was $60,000. On August 1, 2004, Canopy V was destroyed in a hurricane and was therefore no longer usable in E's business. On October 1, 2004, as part of the involuntary conversion, E acquired and placed in service new Canopy W with the insurance proceeds E received due to the loss of Canopy V. E elected not to deduct the additional first year depreciation for 5-year property placed in service in 2004. E depreciates both canopies under the general depreciation system of section 168(a) by using the 200-percent declining balance method of depreciation, a 5-year recovery period, and the half-year convention. No depreciation deduction is allowable for Canopy V. The depreciation deduction allowable for Canopy W for 2004 is $12,000 ($60,000 × the annual depreciation rate of .40 × ½ year). For 2005, the depreciation deduction for Canopy W is $19,200 ($48,000 adjusted basis x the annual depreciation rate of .40).

Example 7. The facts are the same as in *Example 6*, except that E did not make the election out of the additional first year depreciation for 5-year property placed in service in 2004. E depreciates both canopies under the general depreciation system of section 168(a) by using the 200-percent declining balance method of depreciation, a 5-year recovery period, and the half-year convention. No depreciation deduction is allowable for Canopy V. For 2004, E is allowed a 50-percent additional first year depreciation deduction of $30,000 for Canopy W (the unadjusted depreciable basis of $60,000 multiplied by .50), and a regular MACRS depreciation deduction of $6,000 for Canopy W (the depreciable exchanged basis of $30,000 multiplied by the annual depreciation rate of .40 × ½ year). For 2005, E is allowed a regular MACRS depreciation deduction of $9,600 for Canopy W (the depreciable exchanged basis of $24,000 ($30,000 minus regular 2003 depreciation of $6,000) multiplied by the annual depreciation rate of .40).

Example 8. In January 2001, F, a calendar-year taxpayer, places in service a paved parking lot, Lot W, and begins depreciating Lot W over its 15-year recovery period. F's unadjusted depreciable basis in Lot W is $1,000x. On April 1, 2004, F disposes of Lot W in a like-kind exchange for Building X, which is nonresidential real property. Lot W is depreciated using the 150 percent declining balance method and the half-year convention. Building X is depreciated using the straight-line method with a 39-year recovery period and using the mid-month convention. Both Lot W and Building X were in service at the time of the exchange. Because Lot W was depreciated using the half-year convention, it is deemed to have been placed in service on July 1, 2001, the first day of the second half of 2001, and to have been disposed of on July 1, 2004, the first day of the second half of 2004. To determine the remaining recovery period of Building X at the time of replacement, Building X is deemed to have been placed in service on July 1, 2001, and removed from service on July 1, 2004. Thus, Building X is deemed to have been in service, at the time of replacement, for 3 years (36 months=5.5 months in 2001 + 12 months in 2002 + 12 months in 2003 + 6.5 months in 2004) and its remaining recovery period is 36 years (39 - 3). Because Building X is deemed to be placed in service at the time of replacement, July 1, 2004, the first day of the second half of 2004, Building X is depreciated for 5.5 months in 2004. However, at the beginning of the year of replacement the remaining recovery period for Building X is 36 years and 6.5 months (39 years - 2 years and 5.5 months (5.5 months in 2001 + 12 months in 2002 + 12 months in 2003)). The depreciation rate for building X for 2004 is 0.02737 (= 1/(39-2-5.5/12)). For 2005, the depreciation rate for Building X is 0.02814 (= 1/(39-3-5.5/12)).

Example 9. The facts are the same as in *Example 8.* F did not make the election under paragraph (i) of this section for Building Y in the initial exchange. In January 2006, F exchanges Building Y for Building Z, an office building, in a like-kind exchange. F did not make any elections under section 168 for either Building Y or Building Z. Since the recovery period prescribed for Building Y as a result of the initial exchange (39 years) is longer than that of Building Z (27.5 years), Building Z is depreciated over the remaining 33 years of the recovery period of Building Y. The depreciation methods are the same for both Building Y and Building Z so F's exchanged basis in Building Z is depreciated over 33 years, using the straight-line method and the mid-month convention, beginning in January 2006. Alternatively, F could have made the election under paragraph (i) of this section. If F makes such election, Building Z is treated as placed in service by F when acquired in January 2006 and F would recover its exchanged basis in Building Z over 27.5 years, using the straight line method and the mid-month convention, beginning in January 2006.

(d) *Special rules for determining depreciation allowances*—(1) *Excess basis*—(i) *In general.* Any excess basis in the replacement MACRS property is treated as property that is placed in service by the acquiring taxpayer in the year of replacement. Thus, the depreciation allowances for the depreciable excess basis are determined by using the applicable recovery period, depreciation method, and convention prescribed under section 168 for the property at the time of replacement. However, if replacement MACRS property is disposed of during the same taxable year the relinquished MACRS property is placed in service by the acquiring taxpayer, no depreciation deduction is allowable for either MACRS property. See paragraph (g) of this section regarding the application of section 179. See paragraph (h) of this section regarding the application of section 168(k) or 1400L(b).

(ii) *Example.* The application of this paragraph (d)(1) is illustrated by the following example:

Example. In 1989, G placed in service a hospital. On January 16, 2004, G exchanges this hospital plus $2,000,000 cash for an office building in a like-kind exchange. On January 16, 2004, the hospital has an adjusted depreciable basis of $1,500,000. After the exchange, the basis of the office building is $3,500,000. Pursuant to paragraph (k)(2)(i) of this section, G decided to apply §1.168(i)–6 to the exchange of the hospital for the office building, the replacement MACRS property. The depreciable exchanged basis of the office building is depreciated in accordance with paragraph (c) of this section. The depreciable excess basis of $2,000,000 is treated as being placed in service by G in 2004 and, as a result, is depreciated using the applicable depreciation method, recovery period, and convention prescribed for the office building under section 168 at the time of replacement.

(2) *Depreciable and nondepreciable property*—(i) If land or other nondepreciable property is acquired in a like-kind exchange for, or as a result of an involuntary conversion of, depreciable property, the land or other nondepreciable property is not depreciated. If both MACRS and nondepreciable property are acquired in a like-kind exchange for, or as part of an involuntary conversion of, MACRS property, the basis allocated to the nondepreciable property (as determined under section 1031(d) and the regulations under section 1031(d) or section 1033(b) and the regulations under section 1033(b)) is not depreciated and the basis allocated to the replacement MACRS property (as determined under section 1031(d) and the regulations under section 1031(d) or section 1033(b) and the regulations under section 1033(b)) is depreciated in accordance with this section.

(ii) If MACRS property is acquired, or if both MACRS and nondepreciable property are acquired, in a like-kind exchange for, or as part of an involuntary conversion of, land or other nondepreciable property, the basis in the replacement MACRS property that is attributable to the relinquished nondepreciable property is treated as though the replacement MACRS property is placed in service by the acquiring taxpayer in the year of replacement. Thus, the depreciation allowances for the replacement MACRS property are determined by using the applicable recovery period, depreciation method, and convention prescribed under section 168 for the replacement MACRS property at the time of replacement. See paragraph (g) of this section regarding the application of section 179. See paragraph (h) of this section regarding the application of section 168(k) or 1400L(b).

(3) *Depreciation limitations for automobiles*—(i) *In general*. Depreciation allowances under section 179 and section 167 (including allowances under sections 168 and 1400L(b)) for a passenger automobile, as defined in section 280F(d)(5), are subject to the limitations of section 280F(a). The depreciation allowances for a passenger automobile that is replacement MACRS property (replacement MACRS passenger automobile) generally are limited in any taxable year to the replacement automobile section 280F limit for the taxable year. The taxpayer's basis in the replacement MACRS passenger automobile is treated as being comprised of two separate components. The first component is the exchanged basis and the second component is the excess basis, if any. The depreciation allowances for a passenger automobile that is relinquished MACRS property (relinquished MACRS passenger automobile) for the taxable year generally are limited to the relinquished automobile section 280F limit for that taxable year. In the year of disposition the sum of the depreciation deductions for the relinquished MACRS passenger automobile and the replacement MACRS passenger automobile may not exceed the replacement automobile section 280F limit unless the taxpayer makes the election under §1.168(i)–6(i). For purposes of this paragraph (d)(3), the following definitions apply:

(A) *Replacement automobile section 280F limit* is the limit on depreciation deductions under section 280F(a) for the taxable year based on the time of replacement of the replacement MACRS passenger automobile (including the effect of any elections under section 168(k) or section 1400L(b), as applicable).

(B) *Relinquished automobile section 280F limit* is the limit on depreciation deductions under section 280F(a) for the taxable year based on when the relinquished MACRS passenger automobile was placed in service by the taxpayer.

(ii) *Order in which limitations on depreciation under section 280F(a) are applied*. Generally, depreciation deductions allowable under section 280F(a) reduce the basis in the relinquished MACRS passenger automobile and the exchanged basis of the replacement MACRS passenger automobile, before the excess basis of the replacement MACRS passenger automobile is reduced. The depreciation deductions for the relinquished MACRS passenger automobile in the year of disposition and the replacement MACRS passenger automobile in the year of replacement and each subsequent taxable year are allowable in the following order:

(A) The depreciation deduction allowable for the relinquished MACRS passenger automobile as determined under paragraph (c)(5)(i) of this section for the year of disposition to the extent of the smaller of the replacement automobile section 280F limit and the relinquished automobile section 280F limit, if the year of disposition is the year of replacement. If the year of replacement is a taxable year subsequent to the year of disposition, the depreciation deduction allowable for the relinquished MACRS passenger automobile for the year of disposition is limited to the relinquished automobile section 280F limit.

(B) The additional first year depreciation allowable on the remaining exchanged basis (remaining carryover basis as determined under §1.168(k)–1(f)(5) or §1.1400L(b)–1(f)(5), as applicable) of the replacement MACRS passenger automobile, as determined under §1.168(k)–1(f)(5) or §1.1400L(b)–1(f)(5), as applicable, to the extent of the excess of the replacement automobile section 280F limit over the amount allowable under paragraph (d)(3)(ii)(A) of this section.

(C) The depreciation deduction allowable for the taxable year on the depreciable exchanged basis of the replacement MACRS passenger automobile determined under paragraph (c) of this section to the extent of any excess over the sum of the amounts allowable under paragraphs (d)(3)(ii)(A) and (B) of this section of the smaller of the replacement automobile section 280F limit and the relinquished automobile section 280F limit.

(D) Any section 179 deduction allowable in the year of replacement on the excess basis of the replacement MACRS passenger automobile to the extent of the excess of the replacement automobile section 280F limit over the sum of the amounts allowable under paragraphs (d)(3)(ii)(A), (B), and (C) of this section.

(E) The additional first year depreciation allowable on the remaining excess basis of the replacement MACRS passenger automobile, as determined under §1.168(k)–1(f)(5) or §1.1400L(b)–1(f)(5), as applicable, to the extent of the excess of the replacement automobile section 280F limit over the sum of the amounts allowable under paragraphs (d)(3)(ii)(A), (B), (C), and (D) of this section.

(F) The depreciation deduction allowable under paragraph (d) of this section for the depreciable excess basis of the replacement MACRS passenger automobile to the extent of the excess of the replacement automobile section 280F limit over the sum of the amounts allowable under paragraphs (d)(3)(ii)(A), (B), (C), (D), and (E) of this section.

(iii) *Examples*. The application of this paragraph (d)(3) is illustrated by the following examples:

Example 1. H, a calendar-year taxpayer, acquired and placed in service Automobile X in January 2000 for $30,000 to be used solely for H's business. In December 2003, H exchanges, in a like-kind exchange, Automobile X plus $15,000 cash for new Automobile Y that will also be used solely in H's business. Automobile Y is 50-percent bonus depreciation property for purposes of section 168(k)(4). Both automobiles are depreciated using the double declining balance method, the half-year convention, and a 5-year recovery period. Pursuant to §1.168(k)–1(g)(3)(ii) and paragraph (k)(2)(i) of this section, H decided to apply §1.168(i)–6 to the exchange of Automobile X for Automobile Y, the replacement MACRS property. The relinquished automobile section 280F limit for 2003 for Automobile X is $1,775. The replacement automobile section 280F limit for Automobile Y is $10,710. The exchanged basis for Automobile Y is $17,315 ($30,000 less total depreciation allowable of $12,685 (($3,060 for 2000, $4,900 for 2001, $2,950 for 2002, and $1,775 for 2003)). Without taking section 280F into account, the additional first year depreciation deduction for the remaining exchanged basis is $8,658 ($17,315 x 0.5). Because this amount is less than $8,935 ($10,710 (the replacement automobile section 280F limit for 2003 for Automobile Y) - $1,775 (the depreciation allowable for Automobile X for 2003)), the additional first year depreciation deduction for the exchanged basis is $8,658. No depreciation deduction is allowable in 2003 for the depreciable exchanged basis because the depreciation deductions taken for Automobile X and the remaining exchanged basis exceed the exchanged automobile section 280F limit. An additional first year depreciation deduction of $277 is allowable for the excess basis of $15,000 in Automobile Y. Thus, at the end of 2003 the adjusted depreciable basis in Automobile Y is $23,379 comprised of adjusted depreciable exchanged basis of $8,657 ($17,315 (exchanged basis) – $8,658 (additional first year depreciation for exchanged basis)) and of an adjusted depreciable excess basis of $14,723 ($15,000 (excess basis) - $277 (additional first year depreciation for 2003)).

Example 2. The facts are the same as in *Example 1*, except that H used Automobile X only 75 percent for business use. As such, the total allowable depreciation for Automobile X is reduced to reflect that the automobile is only used 75 percent for business. The total allowable depreciation of Automobile X is $9,513.75 ($2,295 for 2000 ($3,060 limit x .75), $3,675 for 2001 ($4,900 limit x .75), $2,212.50 for 2002 ($2,950 limit x .75), and $1,331.25 for 2003 ($1,775 limit x .75). However, under §1.280F–2T(g)(2)(ii)(A), the exchanged basis is reduced by the excess (if any) of the depreciation that would have been allowable if the exchanged automobile had been used solely for business over the depreciation that was allowable in those years. Thus, the exchanged basis, for purposes of computing depreciation, for Automobile Y is $17,315.

Example 3. The facts are the same as in *Example 1*, except that H placed in service Automobile X in January 2002, and H elected not to claim the additional first year depreciation deduction for 5-year property placed in service in 2002 and 2003. The relinquished automobile section 280F limit for Automobile X for 2003 is $4,900. Because the replacement automobile section 280F limit for 2003 for Automobile Y ($3,060) is less than the relinquished automobile section 280F limit for Automobile X for 2003 and is less than $5,388 (($30,000 (cost) - $3,060 (depreciation allowable for 2002)) x 0.4 x 6/12), the depreciation that would be allowable for Automobile X (determined without regard to section 280F) in the year of disposition, the depreciation for Automobile X in the year of disposition is limited to $3,060. For 2003 no depreciation is allowable for the excess basis and the exchanged basis in Automobile Y.

Example 4. AB, a calendar-year taxpayer, purchased and placed in service Automobile X1 in February 2000 for $10,000. X1 is a passenger automobile subject to section 280F(a) and is used solely for AB's business. AB depreciated X1 using a 5-year recovery period, the double declining balance method, and the half-year convention. As of January 1, 2003, the adjusted depreciable basis of X1 was $2,880 ($10,000 original cost minus $2,000 depreciation deduction for 2000, minus $3,200 depreciation deduction for 2001, and $1,920 depreciation deduction for 2002). In November 2003, AB exchanges, in a like-kind exchange, Automobile X1 plus $14,000 cash for new Automobile Y1 that will be used solely in AB's business. Automobile Y1 is 50-percent bonus depreciation property for purposes of section 168(k)(4) and qualifies for the expensing election under section 179. Pursuant to paragraph §1.168(k)–1(g)(3)(ii) and paragraph (k)(2)(i) of this section, AB decided to apply §1.168(i)–6 to the exchange of Automobile X1 for Automobile Y1, the replacement MACRS property. AB also makes the election under section 179 for the excess basis of Automobile Y1. AB depreciates Y1 using a five-year recovery period, the double declining balance method and the half-year convention. For 2003, the relinquished automobile section 280F limit for Automobile X1 is $1,775 and the replacement automobile section 280F limit for 2003 for Automobile Y1 is $10,710.

(i) The 2003 depreciation deduction for Automobile X1 is $576. The depreciation deduction calculated for X1 is $576 (the adjusted depreciable basis of Automobile X1 at the beginning of 2003 of $2,880 × 40% × ½ year), which is less than the relinquished automobile section 280F limit and the replacement automobile section 280F limit.

(ii) The additional first year depreciation deduction for the exchanged basis is $1,152. The additional first year depreciation deduction of $1,152 (remaining exchanged basis of $2,304 ($2,880 adjusted basis of Automobile X1 at the beginning of 2003 minus $576) × 0.5)) is less than the replacement automobile section 280F limit minus $576.

(iii) AB's MACRS depreciation deduction allowable in 2003 for the remaining exchanged basis of $1,152 is $47 (the relinquished automobile section 280F limit of $1,775 less the depreciation deduction of $576 taken for Automobile X1 less the additional first year depreciation deduction of $1,152 taken for the exchanged basis) which is less than the depreciation deduction calculated for the depreciable exchanged basis.

(iv) For 2003, AB takes a $1,400 section 179 deduction for the excess basis of Automobile Y1. AB must reduce the excess basis of $14,000 by the section 179 deduction of $1,400 to determine the remaining excess basis of $12,600.

(v) For 2003, AB is allowed a 50-percent additional first year depreciation deduction of $6,300 (the remaining excess basis of $12,600 multiplied by .50).

(vi) For 2003, AB's depreciation deduction for the depreciable excess basis is limited to $1,235. The depreciation deduction computed without regard to the replacement automobile section 280F limit is $1,260 ($6,300 depreciable excess basis x 0.4 x 6/12). However the depreciation deduction for the depreciable excess basis is limited to $1,235 ($10,710 (replacement automobile section 280F limit) - $576 (depreciation deduction for Automobile X1) - $1,152 (additional first year depreciation deduction for the exchanged basis) - $47 (depreciation deduction for exchanged basis) $1,400 (section 179 deduction) - $6,300 (additional first year depreciation deduction for remaining excess basis)).

(4) *Involuntary conversion for which the replacement MACRS property is acquired and placed in service before disposition of relinquished MACRS property*. If, in an involuntary conversion, a taxpayer acquires and places in service the replacement MACRS property before the date of disposition of the relinquished MACRS property, the taxpayer depreciates the unadjusted depreciable basis of the replacement MACRS property under section 168 beginning in the taxable year when the replacement MACRS property is placed in service by the taxpayer and by using the applicable depreciation method, recovery period, and convention prescribed under section 168 for the replacement MACRS property at the placed-in-service date. However, at the time of disposition of the relinquished MACRS property, the taxpayer determines the exchanged basis and the excess basis of the replacement MACRS property and begins to depreciate the depreciable exchanged basis of the replacement MACRS property in accordance with paragraph (c) of this section. The depreciable excess basis of the replacement MACRS property continues to be depreciated by the taxpayer in accordance with the first sentence of this paragraph (d)(4). Further, in the year of disposition of the relinquished MACRS property, the taxpayer must include in taxable income the excess of the depreciation deductions allowable on the unadjusted depreciable basis of the replacement MACRS property over the depreciation deductions that

would have been allowable to the taxpayer on the depreciable excess basis of the replacement MACRS property from the date the replacement MACRS property was placed in service by the taxpayer (taking into account the applicable convention) to the time of disposition of the relinquished MACRS property. However, see §1.168(k)–1(f)(5)(v) for replacement MACRS property that is qualified property or 50-percent bonus depreciation property and §1.1400L(b)–1(f)(5) for replacement MACRS property that is qualified New York Liberty Zone property.

(e) *Use of optional depreciation tables*—(1) *Taxpayer not bound by prior use of table.* If a taxpayer used an optional depreciation table for the relinquished MACRS property, the taxpayer is not required to use an optional table for the depreciable exchanged basis of the replacement MACRS property. Conversely, if a taxpayer did not use an optional depreciation table for the relinquished MACRS property, the taxpayer may use the appropriate table for the depreciable exchanged basis of the replacement MACRS property. If a taxpayer decides not to use the table for the depreciable exchanged basis of the replacement MACRS property, the depreciation allowance for this property for the year of replacement and subsequent taxable years is determined under paragraph (c) of this section. If a taxpayer decides to use the optional depreciation tables, no depreciation deduction is allowable for MACRS property placed in service by the acquiring taxpayer and subsequently exchanged or involuntarily converted by such taxpayer in the same taxable year, and, if, during the same taxable year, MACRS property is placed in service by the acquiring taxpayer, exchanged or involuntarily converted by such taxpayer, and the replacement MACRS property is disposed of by such taxpayer, no depreciation deduction is allowable for either MACRS property.

(2) *Determination of the depreciation deduction*—(i) *Relinquished MACRS property.* In the year of disposition, the depreciation allowance for the relinquished MACRS property is computed by multiplying the unadjusted depreciable basis (less the amount of the additional first year depreciation deduction allowed or allowable, whichever is greater, under section 168(k) or section 1400L(b), as applicable) of the relinquished MACRS property by the annual depreciation rate (expressed as a decimal equivalent) specified in the appropriate table for the recovery year corresponding to the year of disposition. This product is then multiplied by a fraction, the numerator of which is the number of months (including fractions of months) the property is deemed to be placed in service during the year of the exchange or involuntary conversion (taking into account the applicable convention) and the denominator of which is 12. However, if the year of disposition is less than 12 months, the depreciation allowance determined under this paragraph (e)(2)(i) must be adjusted for a short taxable year (for further guidance, for example, see Rev. Proc. 89–15, 1989–1 C.B. 816, and §601.601(d)(2)(ii)(*b*) of this chapter).

(ii) *Replacement MACRS property*—(A) *Determination of the appropriate optional depreciation table.* If a taxpayer chooses to use the appropriate optional depreciation table for the depreciable exchanged basis, the depreciation allowances for the depreciable exchanged basis beginning in the year of replacement are determined by choosing the optional depreciation table that corresponds to the recovery period, depreciation method, and convention of the replacement MACRS property determined under paragraph (c) of this section.

(B) *Calculating the depreciation deduction for the replacement MACRS property.* (*1*) The depreciation deduction for the taxable year is computed by first determining the appropriate recovery year in the table identified under paragraph (e)(2)(ii)(A) of this section. The appropriate recovery year for the year of replacement is the same as the recovery year for the year of disposition, regardless of the taxable year in which the replacement property is acquired. For example, if the recovery year for the year of disposition would have been year 4 in the table that applied before the disposition of the relinquished MACRS property, then the recovery year for the year of replacement is Year 4 in the table identified under paragraph (e)(2)(ii)(A) of this section.

(*2*) Next, the annual depreciation rate (expressed as a decimal equivalent) for each recovery year is multiplied by a transaction coefficient. The transaction coefficient is the formula (1 / (1 - x)) where x equals the sum of the annual depreciation rates from the table identified under paragraph (e)(2)(ii)(A) of this section (expressed as a decimal equivalent) corresponding to the replacement MACRS property (as determined under paragraph (e)(2)(ii)(A) of this section) for the taxable years beginning with the placed-in-service year of the relinquished MACRS property through the taxable year immediately prior to the year of disposition. The product of the annual depreciation rate and the transaction coefficient is multiplied by the depreciable exchanged basis (taking into account paragraph (e)(2)(i) of this section). In the year of replacement, this product is then multiplied by a fraction, the numerator of which is the number of months (including fractions of months) the property is deemed to be placed in service by the acquiring taxpayer during the year of replacement (taking into account the applicable convention) and the denominator of which is 12. However, if the year of replacement is the year the relinquished MACRS property is placed in service by the acquiring taxpayer, the preceding sentence does not apply. In addition, if the year of replacement is less than 12 months, the depreciation allowance determined under paragraph (e)(2)(ii) of this section must be adjusted for a short taxable year (for further guidance, for example, see Rev. Proc. 89–15, 1989–1 C.B. 816, and §601.601(d)(2)(ii)(*b*) of this chapter).

(iii) *Unrecovered basis.* If the replacement MACRS property would have unrecovered depreciable basis after the final recovery year (for example, due to a deferred exchange), the unrecovered basis is an allowable depreciation deduction in the taxable year that corresponds to the final recovery year unless the unrecovered basis is subject to a depreciation limitation such as section 280F.

(3) *Excess basis.* As provided in paragraph (d)(1) of this section, any excess basis in the replacement MACRS property is treated as property that is placed in service by the acquiring taxpayer at the time of replacement. Thus, if the taxpayer chooses to use the appropriate optional depreciation table for the depreciable excess basis in the replacement MACRS property, the depreciation allowances for the depreciable excess basis are determined by multiplying the depreciable excess basis by the annual depreciation rate (expressed as a

decimal equivalent) specified in the appropriate table for each taxable year. The appropriate table for the depreciable excess basis is based on the depreciation method, recovery period, and convention applicable to the depreciable excess basis under section 168 at the time of replacement. However, If the year of replacement is less than 12 months, the depreciation allowance determined under this paragraph (e)(3) must be adjusted for a short taxable year (for further guidance, for example, see Rev. Proc. 89–15, 1989–1 C.B. 816, and §601.601(d)(2)(ii)(*b*) of this chapter).

(4) *Examples*. The application of this paragraph (e) is illustrated by the following examples:

Example 1. J, a calendar-year taxpayer, acquired 5-year property for $10,000 and placed it in service in January 2001. J uses the optional tables to depreciate the property. J uses the half-year convention and did not make any elections for the property. In December 2003, J exchanges the 5-year property for used 7-year property in a like-kind exchange. Pursuant to paragraph (k)(2)(i) of this section, J decided to apply §1.168(i)–6 to the exchange of the 5-year property for the 7-year property, the replacement MACRS property. The depreciable exchanged basis of the 7-year property equals the adjusted depreciable basis of the 5-year property at the time of disposition of the relinquished MACRS property, namely $3,840 ($10,000 less $2,000 depreciation in 2001, $3,200 depreciation in 2002, and $960 depreciation in 2003). J must first determine the appropriate optional depreciation table pursuant to paragraph (c) of this section. Since the replacement MACRS property has a longer recovery period and the same depreciation method as the relinquished MACRS property, J uses the optional depreciation table corresponding to a 7-year recovery period, the 200% declining balance method, and the half-year convention (because the 5-year property was depreciated using a half-year convention). Had the replacement MACRS property been placed in service in the same taxable year as the placed-in-service year of the relinquished MACRS property, the depreciation allowance for the replacement MACRS property for the year of replacement would be determined using recovery year 3 of the optional table. The depreciation allowance equals the depreciable exchanged basis ($3,840) multiplied by the annual depreciation rate for the current taxable year (.1749 for recovery year 3) as modified by the transaction coefficient [1 / (1 - (.1429 + .2449))] which equals 1.6335. Thus, J multiplies $3,840, its depreciable exchanged basis in the replacement MACRS property, by the product of .1749 and 1.6335, and then by one-half, to determine the depreciation allowance for 2003, $549. For 2004, J multiples its depreciable exchanged basis in the replacement MACRS property determined at the time of replacement of $3,840 by the product of the modified annual depreciation rate for the current taxable year (.1249 for recovery year 4) and the transaction coefficient (1.6335) to determine its depreciation allowance of $783.

Example 2. K, a calendar-year taxpayer, acquired used Asset V for $100,000 and placed it in service in January 1999. K depreciated Asset V under the general depreciation system of section 168(a) by using a 5-year recovery period, the 200-percent declining balance method of depreciation, and the half-year convention. In December 2003, as part of the involuntary conversion, Asset V is involuntarily converted due to an earthquake. In October 2005, K purchases used Asset W with the insurance proceeds from the destruction of Asset V and places Asset W in service to replace Asset V. Pursuant to paragraph (k)(2)(i) of this section, K decided to apply §1.168(i)–6 to the involuntary conversion of Asset V with the replacement of Asset W, the replacement MACRS property. If Asset W had been placed in service when Asset V was placed in service, it would have been depreciated using a 7-year recovery period, the 200-percent declining balance method, and the half-year convention. K uses the optional depreciation tables to depreciate Asset V and Asset W. For 2003 (recovery year 5 on the optional table), the depreciation deduction for Asset V is $5,760 ((0.1152)($100,000)(1/2)). Thus, the adjusted depreciable basis of Asset V at the time of replacement is $11,520 ($100,000 less $20,000 depreciation in 1999, $32,000 depreciation in 2000, $19,200 depreciation in 2001, $11,520 depreciation in 2002, and $5,760 depreciation in 2003). Under the table that applied to Asset V, the year of disposition was recovery year 5 and the depreciation deduction was determined under the straight line method. The table that applies for Asset W is the table that applies the straight line depreciation method, the half-year convention, and a 7-year recovery period. The appropriate recovery year under this table is recovery year 5. The depreciation deduction for Asset W for 2005 is $1,646 (($11,520)(0.1429)(1/(1–0.5))(1/2)). Thus, the depreciation deduction for Asset W in 2006 (recovery year 6) is $3,290 ($11,520)(0.1428)(1/(1–0.5)). The depreciation deduction for 2007 (recovery year 7) is $3,292 (($11,520)(.1429)(1/(1-.5))). The depreciation deduction for 2008 (recovery year 8) is $3,292 ($11,520 less allowable depreciation for Asset W for 2005 through 2007 ($1,646 + $3,290 + $3,292)).

Example 3. L, a calendar-year taxpayer, placed in service used Computer X in January 2002 for $5,000. L depreciated Computer X under the general depreciation system of section 168(a) by using the 200-percent declining balance method of depreciation, a 5-year recovery period, and the half-year convention. Computer X is destroyed in a fire in March 2004. For 2004, the depreciation deduction allowable for Computer X equals $480 ([($5,000)(.1920)] x (1/2)). Thus, the adjusted depreciable basis of Computer X was $1,920 when it was destroyed ($5,000 unadjusted depreciable basis less $1,000 depreciation for 2002, $1,600 depreciation for 2003, and $480 depreciation for 2004). In April 2004, as part of the involuntary conversion, L acquired and placed in service used Computer Y with insurance proceeds received due to the loss of Computer X. Computer Y will be depreciated using the same depreciation method, recovery period, and convention as Computer X. L elected to use the optional depreciation tables to compute the depreciation allowance for Computer X and Computer Y. The depreciation deduction allowable for 2004 for Computer Y equals $384 ([$1,920 x (.1920)(1/(1-.52))] x (1/2)).

(f) *Mid-quarter convention*. For purposes of applying the 40-percent test under section 168(d) and the regulations under section 168(d), the following rules apply:

(1) *Exchanged basis*. If, in a taxable year, MACRS property is placed in service by the acquiring taxpayer (but not as a result of a like-kind exchange or involuntary conversion) and—

(i) In the same taxable year, is disposed of by the acquiring taxpayer in a like-kind exchange or an involuntary conversion and replaced by the acquiring taxpayer with replacement MACRS property, the exchanged basis (determined without any adjustments for depreciation deductions during the taxable year) of the replacement MACRS property is taken into account in the year of replacement in the quarter the relinquished MACRS property was placed in service by the acquiring taxpayer; or

(ii) In the same taxable year, is disposed of by the acquiring taxpayer in a like-kind exchange or an involuntary conversion, and in a subsequent taxable year is replaced by the acquiring taxpayer with replacement MACRS property, the exchanged basis (determined without any adjustments for depreciation deductions during the taxable year) of the replacement MACRS property is taken into account in the year of replacement in the quarter the replacement MACRS property was placed in service by the acquiring taxpayer; or

(iii) In a subsequent taxable year, disposed of by the acquiring taxpayer in a like-kind exchange or involuntary conversion, the exchanged basis of the replacement MACRS property is not taken into account in the year of replacement.

(2) *Excess basis*. Any excess basis is taken into account in the quarter the replacement MACRS property is placed in service by the acquiring taxpayer.

(3) *Depreciable property acquired for nondepreciable property*. Both the exchanged basis and excess basis of the replacement MACRS property described in paragraph (d)(2)(ii) of this section (depreciable property acquired for nondepreciable property), are taken into account for determining whether the mid-quarter convention applies in the year of replacement.

(g) *Section 179 election*. In applying the section 179 election, only the excess basis, if any, in the replacement MACRS property is taken into account. If the replacement MACRS property is described in paragraph (d)(2)(ii) of this section (depreciable property acquired for nondepreciable property), only the excess basis in the replacement MACRS property is taken into account.

(h) *Additional first year depreciation deduction.* See §1.168(k)–1(f)(5) (for qualified property or 50-percent bonus depreciation property) and §1.1400L(b)–1(f)(5) (for qualified New York Liberty Zone property).

(i) *Elections*—(1) *Election not to apply this section.* A taxpayer may elect not to apply this section for any MACRS property involved in a like-kind exchange or involuntary conversion. An election under this paragraph (i)(1) applies only to the taxpayer making the election and the election applies to both the relinquished MACRS property and the replacement MACRS property. If an election is made under this paragraph (i)(1), the depreciation allowances for the replacement MACRS property beginning in the year of replacement and for the relinquished MACRS property in the year of disposition are not determined under this section (except as otherwise provided in this paragraph). Instead, for depreciation purposes only, the sum of the exchanged basis and excess basis, if any, in the replacement MACRS property is treated as property placed in service by the taxpayer at the time of replacement and the adjusted depreciable basis of the relinquished MACRS property is treated as being disposed of by the taxpayer at the time of disposition. While the relinquished MACRS property is treated as being disposed of at the time of disposition for depreciation purposes, the election not to apply this section does not affect the application of sections 1031 and 1033 (for example, if a taxpayer does not make the election under this paragraph (i)(1) and does not recognize gain or loss under section 1031, this result would not change if the taxpayer chose to make the election under this paragraph (i)(1)). In addition, the election not to apply this section does not affect the application of sections 1245 and 1250 to the relinquished MACRS property. Paragraphs (c)(5)(i) (determination of depreciation for relinquished MACRS property in the year of disposition), (c)(5)(iii) (rules for deferred transactions), (g) (section 179 election), and (h) (additional first year depreciation deduction) of this section apply to property to which this paragraph (i)(1) applies. See paragraph (j) of this section for the time and manner of making the election under this paragraph (i)(1).

(2) *Election to treat certain replacement property as MACRS property.* If the tangible depreciable property acquired by a taxpayer in a like-kind exchange or involuntary conversion (the replacement property) replaces tangible depreciable property for which the taxpayer made a valid election under section 168(f)(1) to exclude it from the application of MACRS (the relinquished property), the taxpayer may elect to treat, for depreciation purposes only, the sum of the exchanged basis and excess basis, if any, of the replacement property as MACRS property that is placed in service by the taxpayer at the time of replacement. An election under this paragraph (i)(2) applies only to the taxpayer making the election and the election applies to both the relinquished property and the replacement property. If an election is made under this paragraph (i)(2), the adjusted depreciable basis of the relinquished property is treated as being disposed of by the taxpayer at the time of disposition. Rules similar to those provided in §§1.168(i)–6(b)(3) and (4) apply for purposes of determining the time of disposition and time of replacement under this paragraph (i)(2). While the relinquished property is treated as being disposed of at the time of disposition for depreciation purposes, the election under this paragraph (i)(2) does not affect the application of sections 1031 and 1033, and the application of sections 1245 and 1250 to the relinquished property. If an election is made under this paragraph (i)(2), rules similar to those provided in paragraphs (c)(5)(iii) (rules for deferred transactions), (g) (section 179 election), and (h) (additional first year depreciation deduction) of this section apply to property. Except as provided in paragraph (k)(3)(ii) of this section, a taxpayer makes the election under this paragraph (i)(2) by claiming the depreciation allowance as determined under MACRS for the replacement property on the taxpayer's timely filed (including extensions) original Federal tax return for the placed-in-service year of the replacement property as determined under this paragraph (i)(2).

(j) *Time and manner of making election under paragraph (i)(1) of this section*—(1) *In general.* The election provided in paragraph (i)(1) of this section is made separately by each person acquiring replacement MACRS property. The election is made for each member of a consolidated group by the common parent of the group, by the partnership (and not by the partners separately) in the case of a partnership, or by the S corporation (and not by the shareholders separately) in the case of an S corporation. A separate election under paragraph (i)(1) of this section is required for each like-kind exchange or involuntary conversion. The election provided in paragraph (i)(1) of this section must be made within the time and manner provided in paragraph (j)(2) and (3) of this section and may not be made by the taxpayer in any other manner (for example, the election cannot be made through a request under section 446(e) to change the taxpayer's method of accounting), except as provided in paragraph (k)(2) of this section.

(2) *Time for making election.* The election provided in paragraph (i)(1) of this section must be made by the due date (including extensions) of the taxpayer's Federal tax return for the year of replacement.

(3) *Manner of making election.* The election provided in paragraph (i)(1) of this section is made in the manner provided for on Form 4562, *Depreciation and Amortization*, and its instructions. If Form 4562 is revised or renumbered, any reference in this section to that form is treated as a reference to the revised or renumbered form.

(4) *Revocation.* The election provided in paragraph (i)(1) of this section, once made, may be revoked only with the consent of the Commissioner of Internal Revenue. Such consent will be granted only in extraordinary circumstances. Requests for consent are requests for a letter ruling and must be filed with the Commissioner of Internal Revenue, Washington, DC 20224. Requests for consent may not be made in any other manner (for example, through a request under section 446(e) to change the taxpayer's method of accounting).

(k) *Effective date*—(1) *In general.* Except as provided in paragraph (k)(3) of this section, this section applies to a like-kind exchange or an involuntary conversion of MACRS property for which the time of disposition and the time of replacement both occur after February 27, 2004.

(2) *Application to pre-effective date like-kind exchanges and involuntary conversions.* For a like-kind exchange or an involuntary conversion of MACRS property for which the time of disposition, the time of replacement, or both occur on or before February 27, 2004, a taxpayer may—

(i) Apply the provisions of this section. If a taxpayer's applicable Federal tax return has been filed on or before February 27, 2004, and the taxpayer has treated the replacement MACRS property as acquired, and the relinquished MACRS property as disposed of, in a like-kind exchange or an involuntary conversion, the taxpayer changes its method of accounting for depreciation of the replacement MACRS property and relinquished MACRS property in accordance with this paragraph (k)(2)(i) by following the applicable administrative procedures issued under §1.446–1(e)(3)(ii) for obtaining the Commissioner's automatic consent to a change in method of accounting (for further guidance, see Rev. Proc. 2002–9, 2002–1 C.B. 327, and §601.601(d)(2)(ii)(*b*) of this chapter); or

(ii) Rely on prior guidance issued by the Internal Revenue Service for determining the depreciation deductions of replacement MACRS property and relinquished MACRS property (for further guidance, for example, see Notice 2000–4, 2000–1 C.B. 313, and §601.601(d)(2)(ii)(*b*) of this chapter). In relying on such guidance, a taxpayer may use any reasonable, consistent method of determining depreciation in the year of disposition and the year of replacement. If a taxpayer's applicable Federal tax return has been filed on or before February 27, 2004, and the taxpayer has treated the replacement MACRS property as acquired, and the relinquished MACRS property as disposed of, in a like-kind exchange or an involuntary conversion, the taxpayer changes its method of accounting for depreciation of the replacement MACRS property and relinquished MACRS property in accordance with this paragraph (k)(2)(ii) by following the applicable administrative procedures issued under §1.446–1(e)(3)(ii) for obtaining the Commissioner's automatic consent to a change in method of accounting (for further guidance, see Rev. Proc. 2002–9, 2002–1 C.B. 327, and §601.601(d)(2)(ii)(*b*) of this chapter).

(3) *Like-kind exchanges and involuntary conversions where the taxpayer made the election under section 168(f)(1) for the relinquished property*—(i) *In general.* If the tangible depreciable property acquired by a taxpayer in a like-kind exchange or involuntary conversion (the replacement property) replaces tangible depreciable property for which the taxpayer made a valid election under section 168(f)(1) to exclude it from the application of MACRS (the relinquished property), paragraph (i)(2) of this section applies to such relinquished property and replacement property for which the time of disposition and the time of replacement (both as determined under paragraph (i)(2) of this section) both occur after February 26, 2007.

(ii) *Application of paragraph (i)(2) of this section to pre-February 26, 2007, like-kind exchanges and involuntary conversions.* If the tangible depreciable property acquired by a taxpayer in a like-kind exchange or involuntary conversion (the replacement property) replaces tangible depreciable property for which the taxpayer made a valid election under section 168(f)(1) to exclude it from the application of MACRS (the relinquished property), the taxpayer may apply paragraph (i)(2) of this section to the relinquished property and the replacement property for which the time of disposition, the time of replacement (both as determined under paragraph (i)(2) of this section), or both occur on or before February 26, 2007. If the taxpayer wants to apply paragraph (i)(2) of this section and the taxpayer's applicable Federal tax return has been filed on or before February 26, 2007, the taxpayer must change its method of accounting for depreciation of the replacement property and relinquished property in accordance with this paragraph (k)(3)(ii) by following the applicable administrative procedures issued under §1.446–1(e)(3)(ii) for obtaining the Commissioner's automatic consent to a change in method of accounting (for further guidance, see Rev. Proc. 2002–9, 2002–1 C.B. 327, and §601.601(d)(2)(ii)(*b*) of this chapter).

§1.168(i)–6T [Removed]

Par. 13. Section 1.168(i)–6T is removed.

Par. 14. Section 1.168(k)–1 is amended as follows:

1. The second and third sentences in paragraph (f)(5)(v)(B) are revised.

2. The last sentences in Example 1(i), Example 3(i), Example 4(i), and Example 5(i) in paragraph (f)(5)(vi) are revised.

3. Paragraph (g)(3)(ii) is revised.

The revisions read as follows:

§1.168(k)–1 Additional first year depreciation.

* * * * *

(f) * * *

(5) * * *

(v) * * *

(B) * * * However, at the time of disposition of the involuntarily converted MACRS property, the taxpayer determines the exchanged basis (as defined in §1.168(i)–6(b)(7)) and the excess basis (as defined in §1.168(i)–6(b)(8)) of the acquired MACRS property and begins to depreciate the depreciable exchanged basis (as defined in §1.168(i)–6(b)(9) of the acquired MACRS property in accordance with §1.168(i)–6(c). The depreciable excess basis (as defined in §1.168(i)–6(b)(10)) of the acquired MACRS property continues to be depreciated by the taxpayer in accordance with the first sentence of this paragraph (f)(5)(v)(B).

* * * * *

(vi) * * *

Example 1. (i) * * * Pursuant to paragraph (g)(3)(ii) of this section and §1.168(i)–6(k)(2)(i), EE decided to apply §1.168(i)–6 to the involuntary conversion of Canopy V1 with the replacement of Canopy W1, the acquired MACRS property.

* * * * *

Example 3. (i) * * * Pursuant to paragraph (g)(3)(ii) of this section and §1.168(i)–6(k)(2)(i), FF decided to apply §1.168(i)–6 to the exchange of Computer X2 for Computer Y2, the acquired MACRS property.

* * * * *

Example 4. (i) * * * Pursuant to paragraph (g)(3)(ii) of this section and §1.168(i)–6(k)(2)(i), GG decided to apply §1.168(i)–6 to the exchange of Equipment X3 for Equipment Y3, the acquired MACRS property.

* * * * *

Example 5. (i) * * * Pursuant to paragraph (g)(3)(ii) of this section and §1.168(i)–6(k)(2)(i), GG decided to apply §1.168(i)–6 to the exchange of Equipment Y3 for Equipment Z1, the acquired MACRS property.

* * * * *

(g) * * *

(3) * * *

(ii) Paragraphs (f)(5)(ii)(F)(*2*) and (f)(5)(v) of this section apply to a like-kind exchange or an involuntary conversion of MACRS property and computer software for which the time of disposition and the time of replacement both occur after February 27, 2004. For a like-kind exchange or an involuntary conversion of MACRS property for which the time of disposition, the time of replacement, or both occur on or before February 27, 2004, see §1.168(i)–6(k)(2)(ii). For a like-kind exchange or involuntary conversion of computer software for which the time of disposition, the time of replacement, or both occur on or before February 27, 2004, a taxpayer may rely on prior guidance issued by the Internal Revenue Service for determining the depreciation deductions of the acquired computer software and the exchanged or involuntarily converted computer software (for further guidance, see §1.168(k)–1T(f)(5) published in the **Federal Register** on September 8, 2003 (T.D. 9091, 2003–2 C.B. 939 [68 FR 53000])). In relying on such guidance, a taxpayer may use any reasonable, consistent method of determining depreciation in the year of disposition and the year of replacement.

* * * * *

Kevin M. Brown,
Deputy Commissioner for Services and Enforcement.

Approved February 23, 2007.

Eric Solomon,
Assistant Secretary of the Treasury (Tax Policy).

(Filed by the Office of the Federal Register on February 26, 2007, 3:25 p.m., and published in the issue of the Federal Register for March 1, 2007, 72 F.R. 9245)

Section 527.—Political Organizations

26 CFR 601.105: Examinations of returns and claims for refund, credit or abatement; determination of correct tax liability.

A revenue procedure sets forth the elements of a safe harbor under section 527(l) of the Internal Revenue Code for waiver of amounts due for failure to comply with certain reporting requirements due to reasonable cause but not willful neglect. See Rev. Proc. 2007-27, page 887.

Section 6011.—General Requirement of Return, Statement, or List

26 CFR 1.6011–1(a): General requirement of return, statement or list.
(Also: §§ 6012(a), 6020(b), 6072(a), 6151.)

Frivolous tax returns; voluntary compliance. This ruling discusses and refutes the frivolous position taken by some taxpayers that complying with the internal revenue laws is purely voluntary and that taxpayers are not legally required to file federal tax returns or pay federal tax because the filing of a tax return or the payment of tax is a matter of choice.

Rev. Rul. 2007–20

PURPOSE

The Internal Revenue Service (Service) is aware that some taxpayers assert that compliance with the internal revenue laws is purely voluntary, specifically, that they are not required to file federal tax returns or pay federal tax because the filing of a tax return or the payment of tax is a matter of choice. Taxpayers who take this position argue that the Form 1040 Series instructions provide that filing a return and paying tax are voluntary and not mandatory. Often quoting from the Supreme Court's opinion in *Flora v. United States*, 362 U.S. 145, 176 (1960), they claim that "[o]ur system of taxation is based upon voluntary assessment and payment, not upon distraint." Some of these taxpayers also contend that section 6020(b) of the Internal Revenue Code requires the Service to prepare a federal tax return for any person who does not file a return, which, according to these taxpayers, means that they are not required to file a return.

This revenue ruling emphasizes to taxpayers, promoters, and return preparers that the requirements to file a tax return and pay the tax that is due are not optional. Any position to the contrary has no merit and is frivolous.

The Service is committed to identifying taxpayers who attempt to avoid their federal tax obligations by taking frivolous positions. The Service will take vigorous enforcement action against these taxpayers and against promoters and return preparers who assist taxpayers in taking these frivolous positions. Frivolous returns and other similar documents submitted to the Service are processed through the Service's Frivolous Return Program. As part of this program, the Service determines whether taxpayers who have taken frivolous positions have filed all required tax returns, computes the correct amount of tax and interest due, and determines whether civil or criminal penalties should apply. The Service also determines whether civil or criminal penalties should apply to return preparers, promoters, and others who assist taxpayers in taking frivolous positions, and recommends whether an injunction should be sought to halt these activities. Other information about frivolous tax positions is available on the Service website at *www.irs.gov*.

ISSUE

Whether filing a tax return or paying tax is voluntary.

FACTS

Taxpayer A claims that he is not required to file a federal income tax return or pay income taxes because filing a return and paying tax are "voluntary" activities that he can legitimately opt not to do. Taxpayer A further claims that if a tax return is required, the Service must prepare it for the taxpayer.

LAW AND ANALYSIS

Effective tax administration relies on taxpayers willingly complying with the tax laws, but taxpayers do not have the right to choose whether the laws apply to them. References to a "voluntary" tax system in *Flora*, *supra*, and in Service publications, mean a system that allows taxpayers to determine, in the first instance, the correct amount of their tax and to report their liability on appropriate returns, rather than having the government make the determinations for them. *See Hibbs v. Winn*, 542 U.S. 88, 100 n.3 (2004) ("[T]he taxpayer, not the taxing authority, is the *first* party to make the relevant calculation of income taxes owed.") (Emphasis added). "Voluntary" in this context does not mean that taxpayers may opt out of the system. As stated in *United States v. Schiff*, 876 F.2d 272, 275 (2d Cir. 1989):

> To the extent that income taxes are said to be "voluntary," . . . they are only voluntary in that one files the returns and pays the taxes without the IRS first telling each individual the amount due and then forcing payment of that amount. The payment of income taxes is not optional, however, . . . and the average citizen knows that the payment of income taxes is legally required.

See also United States v. Middleton, 246 F.3d 825, 840–41 (6th Cir. 2001); *United States v. Raymond*, 228 F.3d 804, 812–13 (7th Cir. 2000); *United States v. Gerads*, 999 F.2d 1255, 1256 (8th Cir. 1993); *Wilcox v. Commissioner*, 848 F.2d 1007, 1008 (9th Cir. 1988); *United States v. Tedder*, 787 F.2d 540, 542 (10th Cir. 1986); *Moore v. Commissioner*, 722 F.2d 193, 196 (5th Cir. 1984); *Woods v. Commissioner*, 91 T.C. 88, 90 (1988).

Any suggestion that taxpayers may elect not to file returns or pay tax ignores the laws that affirmatively and unambiguously establish these requirements. Specifically, the requirement to pay income taxes is clearly established in section 1 of the Internal Revenue Code, which imposes a tax on the taxable income of individuals, estates, and trusts as determined by the tables set forth in that section, and section 11, which imposes a tax on the taxable income of corporations. The requirement to file an income tax return is explicitly stated in sections 6011(a), 6012(a), and 6072(a) and corresponding Treasury Regulations. In addition, section 6151 requires taxpayers to submit payment of their taxes with their tax returns. Under these provisions of the Code, any taxpayer who has received more than a statutorily determined amount of gross income during the tax year is required to file a return for the year and pay tax on the income.

Underscoring the fallacy of any position that filing a tax return or paying tax is voluntary is the existence of civil and criminal penalties for failing to file or pay. *See Helvering v. Mitchell*, 303 U.S. 391, 399 (1938) ("In assessing income taxes the Government relies primarily upon the disclosure by the taxpayer of the relevant facts . . . [on an] annual return [backed up by] . . . sanctions [that] may . . . be either criminal or civil.") If, as some taxpayers claim, reporting and paying taxes were optional, penalties for noncompliance would not exist and would not be routinely imposed and upheld.

Section 6651(a) imposes an addition to tax for failure to file a required tax return or pay tax unless the failure is due to reasonable cause and not willful neglect. Section 7203 imposes a criminal penalty (in addition to the civil penalty) for willfully failing to file a return or pay tax.

Finally, the Service is not obligated to make returns for taxpayers who fail to do so. Section 6020(b) merely provides the Service with a mechanism for determining the tax liability of a taxpayer who has not filed a return. Section 6020(b) does not require the Service to prepare a tax return in any case, and it does not excuse a taxpayer from the requirements to file and pay or from liability for unpaid taxes, plus civil and criminal penalties for the failure to file or pay.

HOLDING(S)

Taxpayer A must file income tax returns if the income threshold is met and must pay the correct amount of income taxes owed. Compliance with the internal revenue laws, including filing tax returns and paying tax, is not optional. Further, the Service's authority to prepare a return under section 6020(b) does not relieve a taxpayer of the obligation to file a tax return or pay tax. Any claim by Taxpayer A that one may lawfully opt not to file a return or pay tax is frivolous.

The Service will challenge the claims of individuals who improperly attempt to avoid or evade their federal tax liability.

CIVIL AND CRIMINAL PENALTIES

The position described above—that the law permits a taxpayer to choose not to file an income tax return or pay income taxes because these acts are voluntary—is a frivolous position for purposes of section 6702(c). The Service will challenge the claims of individuals who attempt to improperly avoid or evade their federal tax liability. In addition to liability for the tax due plus statutory interest, taxpayers who fail to file valid returns or pay taxes, face substantial civil and criminal penalties. Potentially applicable civil penalties include: (1) the section 6662 accuracy-related penalties, which are generally equal to 20 percent of the amount of tax the taxpayer should have paid; (2) the section 6663 penalty for civil fraud, which is equal to 75 percent of the amount of tax the taxpayer should have paid; (3) the section 6702(a) penalty of $5,000 for filing a document that purports to be a return and that contains a frivolous position or suggests a desire by the taxpayer to delay or impede the administration of federal tax laws; (4) the section 6702(b) penalty of $5,000 for submitting a "specified frivolous submission"; (5) the section 6651 additions to tax for failure to file a return, failure to pay the tax owed, and fraudulent failure to file a return; (6) the section 6673 penalty of up to $25,000 if the taxpayer makes frivolous arguments in the United States Tax Court; and (7) the section 6682 penalty of $500 for providing false information with respect to withholding.

Taxpayers relying on this frivolous position also may face criminal prosecution under: (1) section 7201 for attempting to evade or defeat tax, the penalty for which is a significant fine and imprisonment for up to 5 years; (2) section 7203 for willful failure to file a return, the penalty for which is a significant fine and imprisonment for up to a year; (3) section 7206 for making false statements on a return, statement, or other document, the penalty for which is a significant fine and imprisonment for up to 3 years; and (4) other federal laws as applicable.

Persons, including return preparers, who promote this frivolous position and those who assist taxpayers in claiming tax benefits based on frivolous positions may face civil and criminal penalties and also may be enjoined by a court pursuant to sections 7407 and 7408. Potential penalties include: (1) a $250 penalty under section 6694 for each return or claim for refund prepared by an income tax return preparer who knew or should have known that the taxpayer's position was frivolous (or $1,000 for each return or claim for refund if the return preparer's actions were willful, intentional, or reckless); (2) a penalty under section 6700 for promoting abusive tax shelters; (3) a $1,000 penalty under section 6701 for aiding and abetting the understatement of tax; (4) criminal prosecution under section 7206, for which the penalty is a significant fine and imprisonment for up to 3 years, for assisting with or advising on the preparation of a false return, statement, or other document under the internal revenue laws; and (5) other federal laws as applicable.

DRAFTING INFORMATION

This revenue ruling was authored by the Office of Associate Chief Counsel (Procedure & Administration), Administrative Provisions and Judicial Practice Division. For further information regarding this revenue ruling, contact that office at (202) 622–7950 (not a toll-free call).

Section 6203.—Method of Assessment

26 CFR 301.6203–1: Method of assessment.
(Also: § 6330.)

Frivolous tax returns; summary record of assessment. This ruling discusses and refutes the frivolous position taken by some taxpayers that before the IRS may collect overdue taxes, the IRS must provide taxpayers with a summary record of assessment made on a Form 23C, *Assessment Certificate-Summary Record of Assessments*, or on another particular form. These taxpayers claim that if a Form 23C is not provided, the assessment is invalid and the IRS may not collect any taxes due.

Rev. Rul. 2007–21

PURPOSE

The Internal Revenue Service (Service) is aware that some taxpayers are claiming that, before the Service may collect overdue taxes, the Service must provide taxpayers with a summary record of assessment made on a Form 23C, "*Assessment Certificate-Summary Record of Assessments*," that is signed by an authorized employee or officer. If a Form 23C is not provided, these taxpayers claim that the assessment is invalid, and, consequently, that the Service may not collect any taxes due.

This revenue ruling emphasizes to taxpayers, promoters, and return preparers that, although an assessment is recorded on a summary record of assessment, such as the Form 23C or its computer-generated equivalent, the Revenue Accounting Control System (RACS) Report 006, there is no legal requirement that a summary record of assessment be provided to a taxpayer before the Service may proceed with collection activity. Further, if a taxpayer requests proof that an assessment was made, the Service is not required to provide any particular form or information in any particular format to the taxpayer so long as the Service provides the information required by Treasury Regulation § 301.6203–1 to the taxpayer. Any position to the contrary has no merit and is frivolous.

The Service is committed to identifying taxpayers who attempt to avoid their federal tax obligations by taking frivolous positions. The Service will take vigorous enforcement action against these taxpayers and against promoters and return preparers who assist taxpayers in taking these frivolous positions. Frivolous returns and other similar documents submitted to the Service are processed through the Service's Frivolous Return Program. As part of this program, the Service determines whether taxpayers who have taken frivolous positions have filed all required tax returns, computes the correct amount of tax and interest due, and determines whether civil or criminal penalties should apply. The Service also determines whether civil or criminal penalties should apply to return preparers, promoters, and others who assist taxpayers in taking frivolous positions, and recommends whether an injunction should be sought to halt these activities. Other information about frivolous tax positions is available on the Service's website at *www.irs.gov*.

ISSUE

Whether the Service must provide a taxpayer with a summary record of assessment, such as a Form 23C, before collection may begin.

FACTS

Taxpayer A argues in a request for a collection due process hearing under section 6330 or 6320 of the Internal Revenue Code that, pursuant to section 6203 and Treasury Regulation § 301.6203–1, the Service must first provide the taxpayer with a summary record of assessment of taxes due before collection action may commence. Taxpayer A further argues that the record provided must include a Form 23C signed by an authorized Service official. In response, the Service provides Taxpayer A with a record of assessment on a Form 4340 ("*Certificate of Assessments, Payments, Other Specified Matters*"), MFTRA-X ("Master File Transcript"), or other similar document. Taxpayer A asserts these forms do not meet the legal requirements and until the Service produces a valid summary record of assessment, the Service is prohibited from collecting the assessed liability. According to Taxpayer A, the Appeals Officer conducting the collection due process hearing, in verifying under section 6330(c)(1) that the Service has complied with applicable law and procedure, may not rely on anything other than the Form 23C to determine, for purposes of the section 6330(c)(1) requirement, that a valid assessment was made.

LAW AND ANALYSIS

Section 6203 states that an assessment of tax (including interest, additions to tax, and assessable penalties) "shall be made by recording the liability of the taxpayer in the office of the Secretary in accordance with rules or regulations prescribed by the Secretary." The section also states that, when requested by a taxpayer, "the Secretary shall furnish the taxpayer a copy of the record of assessment." Treasury Regulation § 301.6203–1 specifies that an assessment is made "by an assessment officer signing the summary record of assessment," which "*through supporting records*" must include the "identification of the taxpayer, the character of the liability assessed, the taxable period, if applicable, and the amount of the assessment." Under the regulation, if a taxpayer requests a copy of the record of assessment, the Service will give the taxpayer "a copy of the pertinent parts of the assessment which set forth the name of the taxpayer, the date of assessment, the character of the liability assessed, the taxable period, if applicable, and the amounts assessed." The date of the assessment is the date the summary record is signed.

There is no requirement in the statute or regulation that the assessment be recorded on a specific form or that the taxpayer be provided with a certain form as a record of assessment.

Until its transition to computerized recordkeeping, the Service generally used Form 23C for the summary record of assessment, but it now uses, except in unusual circumstances, a computer-generated summary record of assessment known as the RACS Report 006. Both forms have been recognized as summary records of assessment within the meaning of section 6203. *See March v. Internal Revenue Service*, 335 F.3d 1186, 1188 (10th Cir. 2003). In *Roberts v. Commissioner*, 329 F.3d 1224, 1228 (11th Cir. 2003), the taxpayer argued that an assessment was invalid because the Service did not use Form 23C but instead used RACS Report 006. The court held that there was nothing in the law to show that the use of the RACS report was not in compliance with the statute and the regulation. The RACS report and the Form 23C are both signed by an assessment officer. The RACS report, like the Form 23C, provides, when coupled with "supporting records," the information set forth in Treasury Regulation § 301.6203–1.

In response to a taxpayer's request under section 6203 and the regulation for "a copy of the record of assessment," the Service is not required to provide any particular form or document and may choose among documents that contain the items of information listed in the regulation. Instead of a RACS report 006, which does not break out individual taxpayer information, the Service may provide Form 4340, "*Certificate of Assessments, Payments, Other Specified Matters*," or a MFTRA-X transcript (literal or plain-language transcript) of the taxpayer's account, either of which sets forth all of the information required by the regulation, because each identifies the taxpayer, states the character of the liabilities assessed, the tax period giving rise to the assessment, the amount of the assessment, and the date of assessment. *See Goodman v. United States*, 185 Fed. Appx. 725, 728 (10th Cir. 2006); *Roberts*, 329 F.3d at 1228; *Carillo v. Commissioner*, T.C. Memo. 2005–290; *Michael v. Commissioner*, T.C. Memo. 2003–26. In addition, an Appeals Officer is not required to obtain a Form 23C or other particular document in a collection due process hearing and may rely on a Form 4340 or MFTRA-X transcript to verify the validity of the assessment for purposes of section 6330(c)(1). *See Nestor v. Commissioner*, 118 T.C. 162 (2002); *Perez v. Commissioner*, T.C. Memo. 2002–274.

HOLDING

The Service is not required to provide Taxpayer A with a summary record of assessment before collecting any taxes due. An assessment is not invalid, and collection is not precluded, because the Service has not provided a summary record of assessment to the taxpayer.

Additionally, Taxpayer A's claim that the Service must produce a Form 23C or other record of assessment as proof of assessment is frivolous. If a taxpayer requests a copy of the record of assessment, the Service may produce the information in any form or format, provided the summary produced contains the information required by Treasury Regulation § 301.6203–1. Acceptable copies of the record of assessment include, but are not limited to, Forms 4340 and MFTRA-X transcripts. Further, the Form 4340, MFTRA-X transcript, or other similar documents may be used in a collection due process proceeding to verify the validity of an assessment under section 6330(c)(1).

The Service will challenge the claims of individuals who improperly attempt to avoid or evade their federal tax liability.

CIVIL AND CRIMINAL PENALTIES

The position described above, that the Service must provide a taxpayer with a summary record of assessment, such as a Form 23C, before collection or must provide a Form 23C in any collection proceeding is a frivolous position under section 6702. The Service will challenge the claims of individuals who attempt to improperly avoid or evade their federal tax liability. In addition to liability for the tax due plus statutory interest, taxpayers who insist upon receiving a Form 23C before complying with their tax obligations face substantial civil and criminal penalties. Potentially applicable civil penalties include: (1) the section 6702(b) $5,000 penalty for submitting a "specified frivolous submission"; (2) the section 6651(a)(3) addition to tax for failure to pay the tax owed; and (3) the section 6673 penalty of up to $25,000 if the taxpayer makes frivolous arguments in the United States Tax Court.

Taxpayers relying on this frivolous position also may face criminal prosecution under section 7201 for attempting to evade or defeat tax, the penalty for which is a significant fine and imprisonment for up to 5 years, or prosecution under other federal laws as applicable.

DRAFTING INFORMATION

This revenue ruling was authored by the Office of Associate Chief Counsel (Procedure & Administration), Administrative Provisions and Judicial Practice Division. For further information regarding this revenue ruling, contact that office at (202) 622–7950 (not a toll-free call).

Section 7701.—Definitions

26 CFR 301.7701–6(a): Person.
(Also: §§ 6012, 7203, 7343, 26 CFR 1.6012–1(a).)

Frivolous tax returns; citizens of a state. This ruling discusses and refutes the frivolous position taken by some taxpayers that they are not subject to federal income tax, or that their income is excluded from taxation, because either (1) they claim to have rejected or renounced United States citizenship and are citizens exclusively of a state (sometimes characterized as a "natural-born citizen" of a "sovereign state"), or (2) they are not persons as identified by the Internal Revenue Code.

Rev. Rul. 2007–22

PURPOSE

The Internal Revenue Service (Service) is aware that some taxpayers are claiming that they are not subject to federal income tax, or that their income is excluded from taxation, because: 1) the taxpayers have declared that they have rejected or renounced United States citizenship because the taxpayers are citizens exclusively of a

State (sometimes characterized as a "natural-born citizen" of a "sovereign state"); or 2) the taxpayers claim they are not persons as identified by the Internal Revenue Code. These taxpayers often furnish Forms W–4, *Employee's Withholding Allowance Certificate*, to their employers on which the taxpayers claim excessive withholding allowances or claim complete exemption from withholding. Based on these Forms W–4, federal income taxes are not withheld from wages paid. Alternatively, these taxpayers attempt to avoid their federal income tax liability by submitting a Form 4852, *Substitute for Form W–2, Wage and Tax Statement, or Form 1099–R, Distributions From Pensions, Annuities, Retirement or Profit-Sharing Plans, IRAs, Insurance Contracts, etc.*, to the Internal Revenue Service with a zero on the line for the amount of wages received. These taxpayers often either fail to file returns, or file returns showing no income and claiming a refund for any withheld income taxes. The Service is also aware that some promoters, including return preparers, market a book, package, kit, or other materials that claim to show taxpayers how they can avoid paying income taxes based on these and other meritless arguments.

This revenue ruling emphasizes to taxpayers, promoters and return preparers that all U.S. citizens and residents are subject to federal income tax. Any argument that a taxpayer's income is excluded from taxation because: 1) the taxpayer has rejected or renounced United States citizenship because the taxpayer is a citizen exclusively of a State (sometime characterized as a "natural-born citizen" of a "sovereign state"); or 2) the taxpayer is not a person as defined by the Internal Revenue Code and is, therefore, not subject to federal tax, has no merit and is frivolous.

The Service is committed to identifying taxpayers who attempt to avoid their federal tax obligations by taking frivolous positions. The Service will take vigorous enforcement action against these taxpayers and against promoters and return preparers who assist taxpayers in taking these frivolous positions. Frivolous returns and other similar documents submitted to the Service are processed through the Service's Frivolous Return Program. As part of this program, the Service determines whether taxpayers who have taken frivolous positions have filed all required tax returns; computes the correct amount of tax and interest due; and determines whether civil or criminal penalties should apply. The Service also determines whether civil or criminal penalties should apply to return preparers, promoters and others who assist taxpayers in taking frivolous positions, and recommends whether an injunction should be sought to halt these activities. Other information about frivolous tax positions is available on the Service website at *www.irs.gov*.

ISSUES

1. Whether a taxpayer may avoid federal income tax liability by maintaining that the taxpayer is not a citizen of the United States and, thus, is not subject to the federal income tax laws.

2. Whether a taxpayer may avoid federal income tax liability by claiming the taxpayer is not a "person" as defined by the Internal Revenue Code and, thus, is not subject to the federal income tax laws.

FACTS

Taxpayer A claims to be exempt from federal income tax because, as a "sovereign citizen" of Taxpayer A's state of residence, Taxpayer A is not a citizen or resident of the United States and is not subject to federal tax laws.

Taxpayer B claims that the Fourteenth Amendment, providing "[a]ll persons born or naturalized in the United States, and subject to the jurisdiction thereof, are citizens of the United States and of the State wherein they reside," applies only to freed slaves and their descendants, and that all other persons are solely citizens of their state of residence.

Taxpayer C claims not to be a United States citizen or a person subject to tax because Taxpayer C has not requested, obtained, or exercised any privilege from an agency of government.

Taxpayer D claims not to be a "person" or a "taxpayer" as defined by the Internal Revenue Code because Taxpayer D is a freeborn and natural individual and not subject to the jurisdiction of the United States.

The taxpayer often furnishes a Form W–4, *Employee's Withholding Allowance Certificate*, to the employer on which the taxpayer claims excessive withholding allowances or claims complete exemption from withholding. Based on this Form W–4, federal income taxes are not withheld from wages paid. Alternatively, the taxpayer prepares a Form 4852 (*Substitute for Form W–2*) showing no wages received.

The taxpayer either fails to file a return, or files a return reporting zero income and claiming a refund for all taxes withheld. The taxpayer then contends the taxpayer is not covered by the federal tax laws and is not subject to federal income tax because the taxpayer is not a citizen of the United States, or the taxpayer is not a person as defined by the Internal Revenue Code.

LAW AND ANALYSIS

1. Citizenship

The Fourteenth Amendment to the United States Constitution defines the basis for United States citizenship, stating that "[a]ll persons born or naturalized in the United States, and subject to the jurisdiction thereof, are citizens of the United States and of the State wherein they reside." The Fourteenth Amendment, therefore, establishes simultaneous state and federal citizenship. *See United States v. Cruikshank*, 92 U.S. 542, 549 (1875) ("The same person may be at the same time a citizen of the United States and a citizen of a State. . . ."); *In re Slaughter-House Cases*, 83 U.S. (16 Wall.) 36, 74 (1873) (A man "must reside within the State to make him a citizen of it, but it is only necessary that he should be born or naturalized in the United States to be a citizen of the Union"). The Fourteenth Amendment's granting of citizenship applies to all persons born or naturalized in the United States, regardless of race. *See, e.g., Bell v. State of Maryland*, 378 U.S. 226, 249 (1964) (Douglas, J., concurring) ("The Fourteenth Amendment also makes every person who is born here a citizen; and there is no second or third or fourth class of citizenship.").

Section 7701(a)(9) of the Internal Revenue Code states that "[t]he term 'United States' when used in a geographical sense includes only the States and the District of Columbia." Claims that individuals are not citizens of the United States but are solely citizens of a sovereign state and not subject to federal taxation have been uniformly rejected by the courts. *See, e.g., United States v. Hilgeford*, 7 F.3d 1340, 1342 (7th Cir. 1993) ("The defendant in this case apparently holds a sincere belief that he is a citizen of the mythical "Indiana State Republic" and for that reason is an alien beyond the jurisdictional reach of federal courts. This belief is, of course, incorrect."); *United States v. Gerads*, 999 F.2d 1255, 1256 (8th Cir. 1993) ("[We] reject appellants' contention that they are not citizens of the United States, but rather "Free Citizens of the Republic of Minnesota" and, consequently, not subject to taxation."); *O'Driscoll v. Internal Revenue Service*, 1991 U.S. Dist. LEXIS 9829, *5–6 (E.D. Penn. 1991) ("Despite plaintiff's linguistic gymnastics, he is a citizen of both the United States and Pennsylvania, and liable for federal taxes.").

Similarly, the individual states are part of the United States and income earned within them is fully subject to United States taxation. *See, e.g., Solomon v. Commissioner*, T.C. Memo. 1993–509 (responding to argument that all of petitioner's income was earned outside of the United States, the court held that "petitioner attempts to argue an absurd proposition, essentially that the State of Illinois is not part of the United States.").

2. Definition of Person

The Internal Revenue Code defines "person" and sets forth which persons are subject to federal taxes. Section 7701(a)(14) defines "taxpayer" as "any person" subject to any internal revenue tax, and section 7701(a)(1) defines "person" to include an individual, trust, estate, partnership, or corporation.

Arguments that an individual is not a "person" within the meaning of the Internal Revenue Code have been uniformly rejected by the courts as have arguments with respect to the term "individual." *See, e.g., United States v. Dawes*, 874 F.2d 746, 750–51 (10th Cir. 1989), *overruled on other grounds*, 895 F.2d 1577 (10th Cir. 1990) ("The contention that appellants are not taxpayers because they are 'free born, white, preamble, sovereign, natural, individual common law '*de jure*' citizens of Kansas' is frivolous. Individuals are 'persons' under the Internal Revenue Code and thus subject to *26 U.S.C. § 7203*."); *United States v. Studley*, 783 F.2d 934, 937 n.3 (9th Cir. 1986) (in holding that an individual is a person under the Internal Revenue Code, the court noted "this argument has been consistently and thoroughly rejected by every branch of the government for decades. Indeed advancement of such utterly meritless arguments is now the basis for serious sanctions imposed on civil litigants who raise them").

Courts have also uniformly rejected claims that a taxpayer is not a person subject to tax because the taxpayer did not request, obtain, or exercise any privileges of citizenship. *See, e.g., Lovell v. United States*, 755 F.2d 517, 519 (7th Cir. 1984) ("All individuals, natural or unnatural, must pay federal income tax on their wages, regardless of whether they received any 'privileges' from the government").

HOLDING

1. The Fourteenth Amendment of the United States Constitution establishes simultaneous state and federal citizenship. Therefore, an individual cannot reject citizenship in the United States in favor of state citizenship, or otherwise claim not to be a citizen of the United States for the purpose of avoiding federal tax liability. Furthermore, income earned within a state of the United States by a United States citizen or resident is taxable under federal tax laws. Accordingly, Taxpayer A and Taxpayer B are subject to federal income tax liability because they are citizens of the United States and citizens of the state in which they reside.

2. The term "person" as used by the Internal Revenue Code includes natural persons and individuals. Moreover, a taxpayer need not request, obtain, or exercise a privilege from an agency of the government to be a "person" within the meaning of the Internal Revenue Code. Therefore, Taxpayer C and Taxpayer D are subject to federal income tax liability.

CIVIL AND CRIMINAL PENALTIES

The Service will challenge the claims of individuals who improperly attempt to avoid or evade their federal tax liability. In addition to liability for the tax due plus statutory interest, taxpayers who fail to file valid returns or pay tax based on arguments that they are not citizens or persons as contemplated by the Internal Revenue Code and, thus, are not subject to federal tax face substantial civil and criminal penalties. Potentially applicable civil penalties include: (1) the section 6662 accuracy-related penalties, which are generally equal to 20 percent of the amount of tax the taxpayer should have paid; (2) the section 6663 penalty for civil fraud, which is equal to 75 percent of the amount of tax the taxpayer should have paid; (3) the section 6702(a) penalty of $5,000 for a "frivolous tax return"; (4) the section 6702(b) penalty of $5,000 for submitting a "specified frivolous submission"; (5) the section 6651 additions to tax for failure to file a return, failure to pay the tax owed, and fraudulent failure to file a return; (6) the section 6673 penalty of up to $25,000 if the taxpayer makes frivolous arguments in the United States Tax Court; and (7) the section 6682 penalty of $500 for providing false information with respect to withholding.

Taxpayers relying on these frivolous positions also may face criminal prosecution under: (1) section 7201 for attempting to evade or defeat tax, the penalty for which is a significant fine and imprisonment for up to 5 years; (2) section 7203 for willful failure to file a return, the penalty for which is a significant fine and imprisonment for up to 1 year; (3) section 7206 for making false statements on a return, statement, or other document, the penalty for which is a significant fine and imprisonment for up to 3 years or (4) other provisions of federal law.

Persons, including return preparers, who promote these frivolous positions and those who assist taxpayers in claiming tax benefits based on frivolous positions may face civil and criminal penalties and also may be enjoined by a court pursuant to sections 7407 and 7408. Potential penalties include: (1) a $250 penalty under section 6694 for each return or claim for refund prepared by an income tax return preparer who knew or should have known that the taxpayer's position was frivolous (or $1,000 for each return or claim for refund if the return preparer's actions were willful, intentional or reckless); (2) a penalty under section 6700 for promoting abusive tax shelters; (3) a $1,000 penalty under section 6701 for aiding and abetting the understatement of tax; and (4) criminal prosecution under section 7206, for which the penalty is a significant fine and imprisonment for up to 3 years, for assisting or advising about the preparation of a false return, statement or other document under the internal revenue laws.

DRAFTING INFORMATION

This revenue ruling was authored by the Office of Associate Chief Counsel (Procedure and Administration), Administrative Provisions and Judicial Practice Division. For further information regarding this revenue ruling, contact that office at (202) 622–7950 (not a toll-free call).

Part III. Administrative, Procedural, and Miscellaneous

Clean Renewable Energy Bonds

Notice 2007–26

SECTION 1. PURPOSE

This notice solicits applications for allocations of the national bond volume limitation authority ("volume cap") to issue tax credit bonds called "clean renewable energy bonds" ("CREBs") under section 54(f) of the Internal Revenue Code (the "Code") to finance eligible clean renewable energy projects described in section 45 of the Code. This notice also provides related guidance on the following: (1) eligibility requirements that a project must meet to be considered for a volume cap allocation; (2) application requirements and the application form for requests for volume cap allocations; (3) the method (generally, a "smallest-to-largest" method) that the Internal Revenue Service ("IRS") and the Treasury Department will use to allocate the volume cap; and (4) certain aspects of the applicable law regarding CREBs and expected regulatory guidance in this area.

Applications for volume cap allocations pursuant to this notice must be filed in accordance with this notice by the following application deadline: July 13, 2007.

This notice *modifies and supersedes* Notice 2005–98, 2005–2 C.B. 1211 (December 11, 2005), which provided guidance on CREBs in connection with the allocation process for the original volume cap authorization under section 54.

SECTION 2. BACKGROUND

Section 1303 of the Energy Tax Incentives Act of 2005, Pub. L. No. 109–58, 119 Stat. 594 (2005), added section 54 to the Code. Section 54 originally provided for a total national volume cap of $800 million for CREBs to finance eligible clean renewable energy projects and delegated to the Secretary of the Treasury the authority to allocate that volume cap, subject to the constraint that the Secretary could allocate no more than $500 million of that volume cap to qualified borrowers which were governmental bodies (with the balance to be allocated to qualified borrowers which were cooperative electric companies). Section 54 originally required that CREBs had to be issued by an expiration date of December 31, 2007.

Section 202 of the Tax Relief and Health Care Act of 2006, Pub. L. No. 109–432, 120 Stat. 2922 (2006) (the "2006 Act"), amended section 54 in three respects. First, the 2006 Act increased the total national volume cap for CREBs from $800 million to $1.2 billion. Second, the 2006 Act extended the expiration date for the issuance of CREBs under the total authorized national volume cap of $1.2 billion from December 31, 2007, to December 31, 2008. Third, the 2006 Act increased the maximum allocations or reallocations to qualified borrowers which are governmental bodies from $500 million to $750 million (with the balance to be allocated to cooperative electric companies).

Section 54(a) provides that a taxpayer that holds a CREB on one or more credit allowance dates of the bond occurring during any taxable year is allowed as a nonrefundable credit against Federal income tax for the taxable year an amount equal to the sum of the credits determined under section 54(b) with respect to such dates.

Section 54(b)(1) provides that the amount of the credit with respect to any credit allowance date is 25 percent of the annual credit. Section 54(b)(2) provides that the annual credit is the product of (1) the credit rate determined by the Secretary, multiplied by (2) the outstanding face amount of the bond.

Section 54(b)(3) provides that the Secretary shall determine daily a credit rate that shall apply to the first day on which there is a binding, written contract for the sale or exchange of a CREB. The credit rate for any day is the credit rate the Secretary estimates will permit the issuance of CREBs with a specified maturity or redemption date without discount and without interest cost to the issuer.

Section 54(b)(4) provides that the term "credit allowance date" means March 15, June 15, September 15, December 15, and the last day on which the bond is outstanding. Section 54(b)(5) generally provides that if a bond is issued or redeemed, or matures, during the 3-month period ending on a credit allowance date, then the amount of the credit for that credit allowance date is a ratable portion of the credit otherwise determined for that 3-month period.

Section 54(g) provides that gross income includes the amount of the credit allowed to the taxpayer under section 54 (without regard to section 54(c)) and the amount so included is treated as interest income.

Section 54(d) provides that a "clean renewable energy bond" or CREB means any bond issued as part of an issue if: (1) the bond is issued by a qualified issuer pursuant to an allocation by the Secretary to the issuer of a portion of the volume cap under section 54(f)(2); (2) 95 percent or more of the proceeds of the issue are to be used for capital expenditures incurred by qualified borrowers for one or more qualified projects; (3) the qualified issuer designates the bond for purposes of section 54 and the bond is in registered form; and (4) the issue meets certain requirements described in section 54(h) regarding the expenditure of bond proceeds, including a requirement that the issuer reasonably expects, as of the issue date, that at least 95 percent of the net proceeds will be expended within 5 years.

Section 54(j)(4) defines a "qualified issuer" as: (1) a CREB lender; (2) a cooperative electric company; or (3) a governmental body. Section 54(j)(2) provides that a "CREB lender" is a lender that is: (1) a cooperative that is owned by, or has outstanding loans to, 100 or more cooperative electric companies and was in existence on February 1, 2002; or (2) any affiliated entity controlled by such a lender. Section 54(j)(1) defines the term "cooperative electric company" as a mutual or cooperative electric company described in section 501(c)(12) or section 1381(a)(2)(C), or a not-for-profit electric utility that has received a loan or loan guarantee under the Rural Electrification Act. Section 54(j)(3) defines the term "governmental body" as any State, territory, possession of the United States, the District of Columbia, Indian tribal government, or any political subdivision thereof.

Section 54(j)(5) provides that a "qualified borrower" is: (1) a mutual or cooperative electric company described in section

501(c)(12) or 1381(a)(2)(C); or (2) a governmental body.

Section 54(d)(2) defines the term "qualified project" as any of the following qualified facilities (as determined under section 45(d) without regard to any placed in service date) owned by a qualified borrower: (1) a wind facility under section 45(d)(1); (2) a closed-loop biomass facility under section 45(d)(2); (3) an open-loop biomass facility under section 45(d)(3); (4) a geothermal or solar energy facility under section 45(d)(4); (5) a small irrigation power facility under section 45(d)(5); (6) a landfill gas facility under section 45(d)(6); (7) a trash combustion facility under section 45(d)(7); (8) a refined coal production facility under section 45(d)(8); and (9) a qualified hydropower facility under section 45(d)(9).

Section 54(f)(1), as amended by section 202(a)(1) of the 2006 Act, provides that the national volume cap is $1.2 billion. Section 54(f)(2), as amended by section 202(a)(2) of the 2006 Act, provides that the Secretary shall allocate the volume cap among qualified projects in such manner as the Secretary determines appropriate, except that the Secretary may not allocate more than $750 million of the national volume cap to finance qualified projects of qualified borrowers that are governmental bodies. The amendments to section 54 of the Code made by section 202 of the 2006 Act apply to bonds issued, and allocations or reallocations of volume cap made, after December 31, 2006.

Section 54(d)(2)(D) provides that, for purposes of section 54(d)(1)(B), which requires qualified borrowers to use at least 95 percent of the proceeds of an issue for capital expenditures for qualified projects, any action that a qualified borrower or qualified issuer takes that is within its control and that causes such proceeds to fail to be used for a qualified project is treated as failing to satisfy that requirement. Section 54(d)(2)(D) further provides that the Secretary shall prescribe regulations specifying remedial actions that may be taken (including conditions to taking such remedial actions) to prevent an action described in the preceding sentence from causing a bond to fail to be a CREB.

Section 54(k) generally requires that, for a CREB that is a pooled financing bond under section 149(f)(4)(A), borrowers must enter into written loan commitments before the issue date of the CREB.

Section 54(l)(5) requires that the qualified issuer pay and amortize an equal amount of the principal of an issue of CREBs during each calendar year that the issue is outstanding.

Section 54(e)(1) limits the term of a CREB to the maximum term determined by the Secretary under section 54(e)(2). Section 54(e)(2) provides that, during each calendar month, the Secretary shall determine the maximum term for CREBs issued in the following calendar month. The maximum term is the term the Secretary estimates will result in the present value of the obligation to repay the principal on the bond being equal to 50 percent of the face amount of the bond. Section 54(e)(2) further provides that such present value shall be determined (1) without regard to the requirement of section 54(l)(5) to amortize the principal of CREBs amortized ratably each year and (2) using a discount rate equal to the average annual interest rate of tax-exempt obligations having a term of 10 years or more that are issued during the month. If the term as so determined is not a multiple of a whole year, such term shall be rounded to the next highest whole year.

Section 54(i) generally provides that the arbitrage requirements of section 148 applicable to tax-exempt State or local bonds apply to CREBs.

Section 54(l)(6) requires issuers of CREBs to submit information reporting returns to the IRS similar to those required to be submitted under section 149(e) for tax-exempt State or local governmental bonds.

Notice 2006–7, 2006–10 I.R.B. 559 (March 6, 2006), provides guidance regarding certain definitions used for CREB purposes.

SECTION 3. APPLICATION REQUIREMENTS IN GENERAL

Each application for a CREBs volume cap allocation ("Application") must be prepared and submitted in accordance with this section. In order for an Application to comply with this section, among other things, the Application must be prepared in substantially the form attached to this notice as Appendix A, subject to such minor changes or variations as the IRS and the Treasury Department may approve in their discretion. This notice, including Appendix A, may be found on the IRS web site at *http://www.irs.gov/taxexemptbond/index.html* or *http://www.irs.gov/pub/irs-drop/*. By submitting an Application, the applicant agrees to comply with the requirements of this notice.

a. *Qualified issuer.* An Application must be submitted by a qualified issuer within the meaning of section 54(j)(4). A "qualified issuer" is: (1) a CREB lender (as defined in section 54(j)(2)); (2) a cooperative electric company (as defined in section 54(j)(1)); or (3) a governmental body (as defined in section 54(j)(3)). An Application must identify the qualified issuer and must demonstrate that the entity constitutes a qualified issuer within the meaning of section 54(j)(4).

b. *Signatures.* An Application must be signed and dated by, and must include the printed name and title of, an authorized official of the qualified issuer. For purposes of this notice, the term "authorized official of the qualified issuer" means an officer, board member, employee, or other official of the qualified issuer who is duly authorized to execute legal documents on behalf of the qualified issuer in connection with incurring debt of the qualified issuer (*e.g.*, a mayor, chairperson of a city council, chairperson of a board of directors, county or city administrator or manager, or chief financial officer), similar to the kind of duly authorized official of an issuer who would be authorized to execute documents in connection with an issuer's declaration of official intent to reimburse expenditures from the proceeds of a borrowing under § 1.150–2(e).

c. *Contact person.* An Application must designate one or more persons with knowledge regarding the project, whom the qualified issuer duly authorized to discuss with the IRS any information relating to the Application. The designation must include the designee's name, title, telephone number, fax number, and mailing address. If a designee is not an official or officer of the issuer, the Application must include an executed Form 8821 (*Tax Information Authorization*), authorizing the disclosure of taxpayer information specifically relating to the Application to the designee.

d. *Addresses.* An Application must be submitted in one of the following ways: (1) by hard copy in duplicate accompanied by a copy of the application in electronic format on compact disc ("CD") by mail to the Internal Revenue Service (IRS), Attention SE:T:GE:TEB, 1111 Constitution Avenue, NW, PE – 5N3, Washington, D.C. 20224; (2) by hard copy in duplicate accompanied by a copy of the application in electronic format on compact disc ("CD") by hand delivery Monday through Friday between the hours of 8 a.m. and 4 p.m. to the Courier's Desk, Internal Revenue Service, 1111 Constitution Avenue, NW, PE – 5N3, Washington, D.C., attention SE:T:GE:TEB; or (3) by electronic submission in PDF format of a copy of a signed original document to the IRS to *Tina.F.Hill@irs.gov*.

e. *Due date*. An Application must be filed with the IRS on or before the Application deadline of July 13, 2007.

f. *Project description*. Each Application must contain the information required by this subsection f.

(i) *Qualified borrower*. Each Application must identify the qualified borrower expected to own the qualified project. A "qualified borrower" is: (1) a mutual or cooperative electric company described in sections 501(c)(12) or 1381(a)(2)(C); or (2) a governmental body (as defined in section 54(j)(3)). The Application must demonstrate that the entity is a qualified borrower within the meaning of section 54(j)(5). If any bond is expected to be a pooled financing bond (within the meaning of section 149(f)(4)(A)), the Application must demonstrate that the qualified issuer will enter into a written loan commitment with each qualified borrower prior to the issue date of the issue of CREBs.

(ii) *Qualified project*. Each Application must describe in reasonable detail the project or projects to be financed with the proceeds of the CREBs. The Application must demonstrate that each project will constitute a "qualified project" under section 54(d)(2)(A). The Application must indicate the expected date that the acquisition and construction of each project will commence and the expected date that each project will be placed in service. The Application must contain a certification by an independent, licensed engineer that each project will meet the requirements for a qualified facility under section 45(d) (but without regard to section 45(d)(10) and to any placed in service date) and that the project will be technically viable and will produce electricity. If the project is a qualified hydropower facility under section 45(d)(9) producing incremental hydropower production (as defined under section 45(c)(8)(B)), then the certification also must state that the project consists only of efficiency improvements or additions to capacity that produce additional production as described in section 45(c)(8)(B) based on a methodology that would meet Federal Energy Regulatory Commission (FERC) standards. If the project is a qualified hydropower facility under section 45(d)(9) producing qualified hydropower production that is a nonhydroelectric dam under section 45(c)(8)(C), then the certification also must state that the facility, when constructed, will meet FERC licensing requirements and other applicable environmental, licensing and regulatory requirements.

(iii) *Prior allocations and related projects*. Each Application must describe the amount of CREB volume cap previously allocated to each project described in the Application and to any "related projects." For purposes of this notice and the Application, the term "related projects" means projects that are owned by the same qualified borrower, or a "related party" as defined in § 1.150–1(b), located on the same site, and integrated, interconnected, or directly or indirectly dependent on each other, based on all the facts and circumstances ("Related Projects").

(iv) *Location of project*. The Application must indicate the location of the project.

(v) *Regulatory approvals*. The Application must describe a plan to obtain all necessary Federal, state and local regulatory approvals for the project.

g. *Plan of financing*. The Application must contain a reasonably detailed description of the plan of financing for the project, including all reasonably expected sources and uses of financing and other funds, the status of such financing, the anticipated date of bond issuance, the sources of security and repayment for the bonds, the aggregate face amount of bonds expected to be issued for the project, and the issuer's reasonably expected schedule for spending proceeds of CREBs. If the qualified borrower intends to use the proceeds of CREBs, to refinance qualified projects with CREBs, or to reimburse amounts paid with respect to a qualified project, the Application must demonstrate that the requirements under section 54(d)(2)(B) and (C), respectively, will be met.

h. *Dollar amount of allocation requested*. The Application must specify the dollar amount of the volume cap requested.

SECTION 4. REQUIRED DECLARATIONS IN APPLICATIONS

Each Application submitted under this notice must include the following declaration signed and dated by an authorized official of the qualified issuer who has personal knowledge of the relevant facts and circumstances: "Under penalties of perjury, I declare that I have examined this document and, to the best of my knowledge and belief, all of the facts contained herein are true, correct, and complete."

SECTION 5. CONSENT TO DISCLOSURE OF ALLOCATION

In order to provide the public with information on how the volume cap authorized by Congress has been allocated and facilitate oversight of the CREB program, the IRS intends to publish the results of the allocation process. The information will be the most useful to the public if it identifies the specific allocations awarded. Pursuant to § 6103, consent is required in order for the Service to disclose identifying information with respect to applicants awarded an allocation. Therefore, the Service requests that each applicant submit with the Application a declaration, consenting to the disclosure by the Internal Revenue Service of the name of the applicant (issuer), the name of the borrower (if other than the issuer), the type and location of the project that is the subject of the Application, and the amount of the CREBs volume cap allocation for such project in the event the project receives an allocation. To provide valid consent, the declaration must be in the form set forth in Appendix B. An applicant is not required to provide a declaration consenting to disclosure in order to receive an allocation. The Service will not publish identifying information with respect to applications that are not awarded an allocation of volume cap.

SECTION 6. VOLUME CAP ALLOCATIONS AND METHODOLOGY

a. *In general.* Available CREB volume cap under section 54, as amended by the 2006 Act, and any "relinquished volume cap" (as defined in paragraph b. of this section) will be allocated in accordance with this section to qualified projects for which Applications meeting the requirements of this notice have been filed with the IRS on or before the Application deadline set forth in this notice. Projects for governmental bodies and mutual or cooperative electric companies described in sections 501(c)(12) or 1381(a)(2)(C) will be allocated the full amount of volume cap requested beginning with the project(s) for which the smallest dollar amount of volume cap has been requested and continuing with the project(s) for which the next-smallest dollar amount of volume cap has been requested until the total amount of volume cap has been exhausted. For this purpose, any amount of the volume cap previously allocated to a project will be taken into account by increasing the amount requested for the project in the Application submitted pursuant to this notice by the amount previously allocated to the project. All applications that meet the requirements described in this notice will be granted according to the methodology set forth above until all applications from governmental bodies have been granted, or up to a maximum of $750 million has been allocated to projects of qualified borrowers that are governmental bodies, whichever occurs first. The remaining volume cap will be allocated under the smallest-to-largest methodology described above to qualified projects of qualified borrowers that are not governmental bodies. For purposes of this section, all Related Projects will be treated as a single project.

b. *Relinquished volume cap.* For purposes of this notice, "relinquished volume cap" means volume cap previously allocated to a qualified issuer to finance a qualified project for which the IRS has received written notice from a duly authorized official of the qualified issuer before the due date for Applications under this notice which states that the qualified issuer will not issue CREBs pursuant to the allocation and is relinquishing such allocation.

SECTION 7. EXPECTED TEMPORARY REGULATIONS; EFFECTIVE DATES; RELIANCE ON NOTICE

The Treasury Department and the IRS expect to issue temporary and proposed regulations (the "Temporary Regulations") under section 54 to provide guidance to holders and issuers of CREBs on selected issues regarding the CREBs program, including potentially, among other matters, certain definitions, general CREBs program requirements, qualified projects, use and expenditure of proceeds, remedial actions, arbitrage investment restrictions, and information reporting applicable to CREBs. The Treasury Department and the IRS expect that the Temporary Regulations will apply to CREBs sold on or after June 13, 2007 with respect to interim guidance provided in this notice. Prior to the promulgation and effective date of the Temporary Regulations on CREBs under section 54, taxpayers may rely on the interim guidance provided in this notice and Notice 2006–7.

SECTION 8. MAXIMUM TERM

The maximum term for a CREB is determined under section 54(e)(2) by using a discount rate equal to 110 percent of the long-term adjusted AFR, compounded semi-annually, for the month in which the bond is sold. For purposes of this notice, a bond is "sold" on the first day on which there is a binding contract in writing for the sale or exchange of the bond. The maximum term for a CREB will be published daily by the Bureau of Public Debt on its Internet site for State and Local Government Series securities at: *https://www.treasurydirect.gov*.

SECTION 9. CREDIT RATE

For each issue of CREBs, a separate credit rate will apply to each of the level annual repayments of principal of the issue (each, a "principal maturity"). The credit rate for a principal maturity of an issue of CREBs is the applicable CREB credit rate for that principal maturity on the date that the issue of CREBs is sold, which applicable CREB credit rate is published for that day by the Bureau of Public Debt on its Internet site for State and Local Government Series securities at: *https://www.treasurydirect.gov*. The credit rates will be determined by the Treasury Department based on its estimate of the yield on outstanding AA rated corporate bonds of a similar maturity for the business day immediately prior to the date on which the issue is sold.

SECTION 10. INFORMATION REPORTING

Section 54(l)(6) requires issuers of CREBs to submit information reporting returns to the IRS similar to those required to be submitted under section 149(e) for tax-exempt State or local governmental bonds. These information reporting returns are required to be submitted at the same time and in the same manner as those under section 149(e) on such forms as shall be prescribed by the Commissioner of the IRS for such purpose. Pending further guidance from the IRS regarding the applicable forms to be used for such information reporting for CREBs, in the case of an issue of CREBs, the issuer must submit to the IRS an information return on Form 8038, *Information Return for Tax-Exempt Private Activity Bond Issues*, at the same time and in the same manner as required under section 149(e), with modifications as described below. Issuers of CREBs should complete Part II of Form 8038 by checking the box on Line 20(c) (Other) and writing "CREBs" in the space provided for the bond description. For purposes of this notice, the term "issue" has the meaning used for tax-exempt bond purposes in § 1.150–1(c).

SECTION 11. REMEDIAL ACTIONS

The Treasury Department and the IRS expect that the Temporary Regulations will provide that, for purposes of the requirement of section 54(d)(1)(B) that qualified borrowers use at least 95 percent of the proceeds of an issue of CREBs for capital expenditures for qualified projects, a "deliberate action" taken by a qualified issuer or qualified borrower may cause such proceeds to fail to be used for such qualified use. For this purpose, the term "deliberate action" will have the same meaning as used in § 1.141–2(d)(3), except that "section 54" will be substituted for "section 141" in § 1.141–2(d)(3)(i). The Treasury Department and the IRS further expect that the Temporary Regulations will provide that a deliberate action that otherwise would cause an issue of CREBs to fail to meet the requirements of section 54(d)(1)(B) will not be treated as a deliberate action if the issuer takes a "remedial action" which meets the requirements specified in the Temporary Regulations. In addition, the Treasury Department and the IRS expect that the Temporary Regulations will contain a "redemption or defeasance" remedial action and an "alternative use of disposition proceeds" remedial action similar, but not identical to, the remedial actions contained in § 1.141–12(d) and § 1.141–12(e).

SECTION 12. ARBITRAGE REQUIREMENTS

Section 54(i) generally requires that an issue of CREBs must satisfy the arbitrage investment restrictions under section 148 applicable to tax-exempt bonds with respect to proceeds of the issue. In general, under section 148, subject to various specific prompt spending exceptions and other exceptions, the arbitrage investment restrictions, including the yield restrictions and the arbitrage rebate requirement, apply broadly to gross proceeds of tax-exempt bonds. The Treasury Department and the IRS expect that, except as otherwise provided in this section 12, the arbitrage investment restrictions under section 148 and § 1.148–1 to § 1.148–11, inclusive, and the exceptions to those restrictions will apply to gross proceeds of CREBs to the same extent and in the same manner as they apply to gross proceeds of tax-exempt state or local governmental bonds the interest on which is excludable from gross income under section 103.

The Treasury Department and the IRS further expect that, in applying the arbitrage investment restrictions under section 148 to CREBs, the modifications to the general rules described in paragraphs a. through e. of this section 12, below, will apply.

a. *Cooperative electric companies treated like state or local governmental entities.* Cooperative electric companies under section 54(j)(1) will be treated as "governmental persons" under § 1.141–1(b) for purposes of (1) applying the arbitrage investment restrictions under section 148, including the program investment definition under § 1.148–1(b), and (2) determining whether CREBs are private activity bonds under section 141 in applying any particular arbitrage investment restriction that depends on whether bonds are private activity bonds,

b. *5-year temporary period exception to arbitrage yield restriction.* If an issue of CREBs meets the spending requirements of section 54(h)(1), then the proceeds of the issue of CREBs will be treated as qualifying for a 5-year temporary period exception to arbitrage yield restriction under § 1.148–2(e)(2) beginning on issue date of the issue.

c. *CREB credit disregarded in determining CREB yield for arbitrage purposes.* In determining the yield on an issue of CREBs for arbitrage purposes under § 1.148–4, the CREBs credit allowed under section 54(a) and the credit rate under section 54(b)(2)(A) will be disregarded.

d. *Non-AMT tax-exempt bond investment exception inapplicable.* In applying the arbitrage restrictions against investing gross proceeds of an issue of CREBs in higher yielding investments under section 148(a) and § 1.148–2, the exception to arbitrage yield restriction for investments of gross proceeds of tax-exempt bonds in specified non-AMT tax-exempt bond investments under section 148(b)(3) (relating to an exception to the definition of "investment property" for specified non-AMT tax-exempt bonds) and § 1.148–2(d)(2)(v) (relating to a corresponding exception to arbitrage yield limitations) will be inapplicable.

e. *Application of small issuer exception to the arbitrage rebate requirement.* In determining whether an issue of CREBs qualifies for the $5 million small issuer exception to the arbitrage rebate requirement (increased to $10 million for certain public school facilities) under section 148(f)(4)(D) and § 1.148–8, both CREBs and tax-exempt bonds the interest on which is excludable from gross income under section 103 (other than private activity bonds) that are reasonably expected to be issued or actually issued by the CREB issuer (and other applicable on-behalf-of entities and subordinate entities taken into account under that section) within a calendar year will be taken into account in measuring the applicable size limitation.

SECTION 13. MISCELLANEOUS REGULATORY GUIDANCE

The Treasury Department and the IRS expect that the Temporary Regulations will provide guidance on selected discrete issues that have arisen with respect to CREBs, including clarifying that: (1) in applying the reimbursement restrictions under section 54(d)(1)(C), the general reimbursement rules and exceptions in § 1.150–2 will apply; (2) joint ownership of projects financed with CREBs will be recognized in a manner similar to the recognition of joint ownership of output projects under the private activity bond restrictions on tax-exempt bonds under section 141; (3) in determining whether all or a part of a facility will be eligible to be a qualified project for CREBs purposes, allocation and accounting rules similar to those employed under section 141 for mixed-use projects will be applied; (4) for purposes of the requirement under section 54(d) to use 95 percent of the proceeds of an issue of CREBs for qualified costs to finance capital expenditures for qualified projects, proceeds used to finance a reserve or replacement fund (*e.g.*, a debt service reserve fund to secure the CREBs) will be treated as nonqualified costs and will be eligible for financing with CREBs only from the five percent nonqualified portion of the proceeds; and (5) except in limited circumstances involving certain refinancings to which section 54(d)(2)(B) applies and reimbursements to which section 54(d)(2)(C) applies, costs of acquiring existing facilities (as contrasted with costs of enhancements, repair, or rehabilitation of existing facilities) generally will be treated as nonqualified costs for purposes of the 95 percent use of proceeds test under section 54(d).

SECTION 14. EFFECT ON OTHER DOCUMENTS

This notice *modifies* and *supersedes* Notice 2005–98, 2005–2 C.B. 1211 (December 11, 2005), which provided guidance on CREBs in connection with the allocation process for the original volume cap authorization under section 54.

SECTION 15. DRAFTING INFORMATION

The principal authors of this notice are Zoran Stojanovic and Timothy Jones of the Office of Associate Chief Counsel (Tax Exempt & Government Entities). However, other personnel from the IRS and the Treasury Department participated in its development. For further information regarding this notice and the Application, contact Tina Hill at (202) 283–9774 (not a toll-free call).

APPENDIX A

APPLICATION FOR ALLOCATION OF CLEAN ENERGY RENEWABLE BOND VOLUME CAP

Internal Revenue Service

Washington, D.C.

Dear Sir or Madam:

The following constitutes the application ("Application") of (Name) (the "Applicant") for allocation of clean renewable energy bond ("CREB") volume cap under Section 54(f) of the Internal Revenue Code (the "Code") (unless otherwise noted, section references herein are to the Code) to finance the project described below. *(If a single Application is used to request CREB volume cap for more than one project, then all of the required information in the Application must be provided separately for each project.)*

1. **Name of Applicant/Issuer** ______________________

   Street Address ______________________

   City ______________ State ______________ Zip ______________

   Telephone Number ______________ Fax Number ______________

2. **Status of Issuer** – *(Select as appropriate)*

   The Applicant/Issuer is a "qualified issuer " under section 54(j)(4) because it is—

   (i) a "clean renewable energy lender" that is a cooperative owned by, or has outstanding loans to, 100 or more cooperative electrical companies and was in existence on February 1, 2002 or is an affiliate that is owned by such a lender, as demonstrated by the attached documents included as Exhibit D.

   (ii) a "cooperative electric company" that is a mutual or cooperative electric company described in section 501(c)(12) or section 1381(a)(2)(C), as demonstrated by the attached documents included as Exhibit D, including a copy of the determination letter previously obtained from the IRS, if any (or other relevant documents).

   (iii) a "governmental body" that is a State, territory, possession of the United States, District of Columbia, Indian tribal government, or any political subdivision of the foregoing, as demonstrated by the attached documents included as Exhibit D. *(Supporting documents are not required to be attached for governmental bodies that are general purpose governmental entities with substantial taxing, eminent domain,* ***and*** *police powers such as generally a county, city, municipality, township, or borough.)*

3. **Name of Borrower** ______________________

   Street Address ______________________

   City ______________ State ______________ Zip ______________

   Telephone Number ______________ Fax Number ______________

4. **Status of Borrower** – *(Select as appropriate)* The Borrower is a "qualified borrower" under section 54(j)(5) because it is—

   (i) a qualified borrower under section 54(j)(5)(A) that is a mutual or cooperative electric company under section 501(c)(12) or section 1381(a)(2)(C), as demonstrated by the attached documents included as Exhibit D, including a copy of the determination letter previously obtained from the IRS, if any (or other relevant documents).

(ii) a qualified borrower under section 54(j)(5)(B) that is a "governmental body" under section 54(j)(3)(B) and is a State, territory, possession of the United States, District of Columbia, Indian tribal government, or any political subdivision of the foregoing, as demonstrated by the attached documents included as Exhibit D. *(Supporting documents are not required to be attached for governmental bodies that are general purpose governmental entities with substantial taxing, eminent domain,* ***and*** *police powers such as generally a county, city, municipality, township, or borough.)*

5. **Name of Project.**

____

____

6. **Detailed Description of Project.** A reasonably detailed description of the project (the "Project") is set forth below or in attached Exhibit A, including reasonably expected costs of components, such as land, site prep, equipment, installation, other dedicated facilities such as transmission, and capacity:

7. **Qualified Project.** The Project is a "qualified project" within the meaning of section 54(d)(2)(A) of the Code, because it is a "qualified facility" (as determined under section 45(d) of the Code without regard to section 45(d)(10) and to any placed in service date) that is *(select as appropriate)*—

(1) a wind facility – a facility using wind to produce electricity;

(2) a closed-loop biomass facility – a facility using closed-loop biomass (as defined in section 45(c)) to produce electricity or, if owned by the taxpayer prior to January 1, 2008, a facility using closed-loop biomass to produce electricity which is modified to use closed-loop biomass to co-fire with coal, with other biomass, or with both, but only if the modification is approved under the Biomass Power for Rural Development Programs or is part of a pilot project of the Commodity Credit Corporation;

(3) an open-loop biomass facility – a facility using open-loop biomass (as defined in section 45(c)) to produce electricity and in the case of a facility using agricultural livestock waste nutrients, the nameplate capacity rating of which is not less than 150 kilowatts;

(4) a geothermal or solar energy facility – a facility using geothermal energy (as defined in section 45(c)) or solar energy to produce electricity (not including a facility described in section 48(a)(3) the basis of which is taken into account by the taxpayer for purposes of determining the energy credit under section 48 of the Code);

(5) a small irrigation power facility – a facility using small irrigation power (as defined in section 45(c)) to produce electricity;

(6) a landfill gas facility – a facility producing electricity from gas derived from the biodegradation of municipal solid waste (as defined in section 45(c));

(7) a trash combustion facility – a facility that burns municipal solid waste (as defined in section 45(c)) to produce electricity;

(8) a refined coal production facility – a facility producing refined coal (as defined in section 45(c)); or

(9) a qualified hydropower facility – a facility engaged in qualified hydropower production (as defined in section 45).

8. **Construction Commencement Date and Placed in Service Date.** The Borrower begun or expects to begin the construction, installation and equipping of the Project on ____________________. The Borrower expects that the Project will be placed into service on or before ____________________.

9. **Independent Engineer's Certificate:** *(If the Application is for more than one Project, a separate certificate must be included for each Project.)* Attached as Exhibit B hereto is a certification by an independent, licensed engineer to the effect that the Project will be a "qualified project" within the meaning of section 54(d)(2)(A) and a "qualified facility" within the meaning of section 45(d) of the Code (without regard to section 45(d)(10) of the Code and to any placed in service date) and that the project is technically viable and will produce electricity.

If the project is a **qualified hydropower facility —**

a. producing incremental hydropower production, then the engineering certificate also must state that the project consists only of efficiency improvements or additions to capacity that produce additional production as described in section 45(c)(8)(B) based on a methodology that would meet Federal Energy Regulatory Commission (FERC) standards; or *b.* that is a nonhydroelectric dam under section 45(c)(8)(C), then the engineering certificate also must state that the facility, when constructed, will meet FERC licensing requirements and other applicable environmental, licensing and regulatory requirements.

10. Location of the Project:

Project address or physical location (do not include postal box numbers or mailing address)

____

____

____

City ________________ State ________________ Zip __________

County where Project is located ________________________

11. Individual to contact for more information about the Project:

Individual Name ________________________

Company Name ________________________

Street Address ________________________

City ________________ State ________________ Zip __________

Telephone Number ________________________

Fax Number ________________________

(Include as appropriate) The contact person is not an authorized official or officer of the Issuer and a properly executed Form 8821 is included with this Application that authorizes the disclosure by the IRS of information that relates to this Application and the Project(s) described above to the contact person.

12. Regulatory Approvals. Identify each regulatory body, the action that must be taken, status of any pending action and the remaining timeframe required to obtain each required approval such as a FERC approval, or siting permits. The plan of the Applicant for obtaining such approvals is as follows: *(or attach an Exhibit)*

13. Plan of Financing. Include a reasonably detailed description of the plan of financing for the Project, including all reasonably expected sources and uses of financing and other funds, the status of such financing, the anticipated date of bond issuance, the sources of security and repayment for the bonds, the aggregate face amount of bonds expected to be issued for the Project, and the issuer's reasonably expected schedule for spending proceeds of CREBs. Attached as Exhibit C is a plan of financing for the Project.

14. Refinancings and Reimbursements. *(Include the following statements, as applicable.) [(For refinancings, include the following statement.)* The Issuer intends to use the proceeds of CREBs to refinance qualified projects in accordance with section 54(d)(2)(B).] [*(For reimbursements, include the following statement.)* The Issuer intends to use the proceeds of CREBs to reimburse costs of a qualified project in accordance with section 54(d)(2)(C).] *(In addition, the Issuer must demonstrate that the requirements of § 54(d)(2)(B) or (C), as applicable, will be met.)*

15. Dollar Amount of Allocation Requested for the Project. To finance the Project, the Applicant hereby requests a CREB allocation in the amount of $__________.

16. Prior Allocations for the Project or Related Project. *(If the Project or any Related Project (as defined in section 3.f(iii) of this Notice) previously received an allocation of CREBs volume cap, then this paragraph must include a statement to that effect.)*

[*If applicable, include the following statement:* On *(Insert date)*, the Project previously received a CREBs volume cap allocation in the amount of $__________. A copy of the IRS allocation letter for that allocation is attached.]

[*If applicable, include the following statement:* On *(Insert date)*, a Related Project previously received a CREBs volume cap allocation in the amount of $__________. A copy of the IRS allocation letter for that allocation is attached.]

17. Other allocation requests for Related Projects to the Project. Included below are descriptions of other projects that are Related Projects (as defined in paragraph 16 above) to the Project for which the applicant or other entities are applying for a CREB volume cap allocation. With respect to an applicant on a Related Project other than the Applicant, set forth below are the names, addresses, contact persons, and telephone numbers for any such applicant.

18. Pooled Financing Bonds. *(If the issuer expects to use the requested allocation of CREB volume cap as part of a pooled financing bond within the meaning of section 54(l)(2), then the issuer should include the undertaking noted below.)*

[The Applicant Issuer expects to use the requested allocation for CREBs volume cap in a pooled financing bond within the meaning of section 54(i)(2), and the Issuer expressly agrees that it will obtain a written loan commitment for all borrowers from the issue of CREBs to which the requested allocation relates before the issue date of that issue.]

I hereby certify that I am an authorized officer or official of the Applicant and am duly authorized to execute legal documents on behalf of the Applicant in connection with incurring debt and that I am duly authorized to execute legal documents on behalf of the Application in making this Application. Under penalties of perjury, I declare that (i) I have knowledge of the relevant facts and circumstances relating to this Application and the Project(s), (ii) I have examined this Application, and (iii) to the best of my knowledge and belief, all of the facts contained in this Application are true, correct and complete.

By: ______________________________

Name and Title: ______________________________

Date: ______________________________

EXHIBIT A

DESCRIPTION OF THE PROJECT (RESPONSE TO QUESTION 6 OF THE APPLICATION)

(Attached hereto)

EXHIBIT B

ENGINEER'S CERTIFICATE (RESPONSE TO QUESTION 9 OF THE APPLICATION)

(Attached hereto in substantially the form below)

Dated: ________________, 2007

This certificate is being provided to the Internal Revenue Service ("IRS") in connection with an application (the "Application") by [*Name of Applicant Issuer*: ________________________] (the "Issuer") to the IRS requesting an allocation of volume cap authority to issue clean renewable energy bonds ("CREBs") under section 54 of the Internal Revenue Code, as amended (the "Code"). The CREBs are being issued to make a loan to [*Name of qualified borrower*: ________________ (the "Borrower"), to finance the costs of certain clean renewable energy facilities described more particularly in the Application (the "Project"). The undersigned hereby certifies as follows:

1. I am an independent, licensed engineer, duly qualified to practice the profession of engineering under the laws of the State of ________________, and I am not an officer or employee of the Issuer or the Borrower.

2. I have reviewed the Application for a CREBs volume cap allocation (including the exhibits thereto) of the Issuer of even date herewith describing the Project. To the best of my knowledge, information, and belief, the Project will meet the requirements to be a "qualified project" under section 54(d)(2)(A) of the Code and correspondingly a "qualified facility" under section 45(d) of the Code, determined without regard to section 45(d)(10) of the Code and without regard to any placed in service date).

[*(Include as appropriate)* To the best of my knowledge, information, and belief, the Project is a qualified hydropower facility under section 45(d)(9)—

a. producing incremental hydropower production consisting only of efficiency improvements or additions to capacity that produce additional production as described in section 45(c)(8)(B) based on a methodology that would meet Federal Energy Regulatory Commission (FERC) standards. or

b. that is a nonhydroelectric dam under section 45(c)(8)(C) and the facility, when constructed, will meet FERC licensing requirements and other applicable environmental, licensing and regulatory requirements.]

3. To the best of my knowledge, information and belief, the Project is technically viable and when constructed will produce electricity.

IN WITNESS WHEREOF, I have hereunto affixed my official signature on the date of this Engineer's Certificate.

By: ______________________________

Seal and/or License number:

Name and Title: ______________________________

____

Company: ______________________________

EXHIBIT C

PLAN OF FINANCING (RESPONSE TO QUESTION 13 OF THE APPLICATION)

(Attached hereto)

EXHIBIT D

DOCUMENTS REGARDING ISSUER OR BORROWER ORGANIZATIONAL STATUS (RESPONSE TO QUESTION 2 OR 4 OF THE APPLICATION, AS APPLICABLE)

(Attached hereto)

APPENDIX B

CONSENT TO PUBLIC DISCLOSURE OF CERTAIN CLEAN RENEWABLE ENERGY BOND APPLICATION INFORMATION

In the event that the Application of [*(Insert name of applicant here)*: ______________________________] (the "Applicant") for an allocation of authority to issue clean renewable energy bonds ("CREBs") under section 54 of the Internal Revenue Code is approved, the undersigned authorized representative of the Applicant hereby consents to the disclosure by the Internal Revenue Service through publication of a Notice in the Internal Revenue Bulletin or a press release of the name of applicant (issuer), the name of the borrower (if other than the issuer), the type and location of the project that is the subject of the Application, and the amount of the allocation, if any, of volume cap authority to issue CREBs for such project. The undersigned understands that this information might be published, broadcast, discussed or otherwise disseminated in the public record.

This authorization shall become effective upon the execution thereof. Except to the extent disclosure is authorized herein, the returns and return information of the undersigned taxpayer are confidential and are protected by law under the Internal Revenue Code.

I certify that I have the authority to execute this consent to disclose on behalf of the taxpayer named below.

Date: ______________________________ Signature: ______________________________

Print name: ______________________________

Title: ______________________________

Name of Applicant-Taxpayer: ______________________________

Taxpayer Identification Number: ______________________________

Taxpayer's Address: ______________________________

____

____

Note: Treasury Regulations require that the Internal Revenue Service must receive this consent within 60 days after it is signed and dated.

Certain Deduction Limits Under the Pension Protection Act of 2006

Notice 2007–28

This notice provides guidance on certain of the changes made by the Pension Protection Act of 2006, Pub. L. 109–280 (PPA '06), to § 404 of the Internal Revenue Code (Code). Section 404 generally provides rules concerning the deduction for contributions to plans of deferred compensation. Some of the PPA '06 amendments to § 404 are effective for years beginning after December 31, 2005 (the 2006 changes) and others are effective for years beginning after December 31, 2007 (the 2008 changes). This notice provides guidance with respect to the 2006 changes and one related issue. Future guidance will be provided with respect to the 2008 changes.

Q–1. What changes to the rules of § 404 of the Code were made by PPA '06 for years beginning after December 31, 2005?

A–1. In general, PPA '06 amended § 404 to modify the deduction permitted for defined benefit pension plans under § 404(a)(1). PPA '06 also modified the combined limit on deductions for contributions to defined benefit plans and defined contribution plans with overlapping coverage as set forth in § 404(a)(7).

Q–2. To what years do the 2006 changes apply when the taxable year of the employer differs from the plan year of the plan?

A–2. The 2006 changes apply to taxable years of the employer beginning after December 31, 2005.

Under § 1.404(a)–14(c) of the Income Tax Regulations (regulations), if the plan year of the plan and the taxable year of the employer do not coincide, the deductible limit for the taxable year of the employer is permitted to be determined as any one of the following alternatives: (1) the deductible limit determined for the plan year beginning in the taxable year, (2) the deductible limit determined for the plan year ending in the taxable year, or (3) a weighted average of alternatives (1) and (2). A plan year used under any of these alternatives is referred to in this notice as an associated plan year.

The calculations of the deductible limit for a taxable year are based on the calculations with respect to an associated plan year or years and must reflect the law in effect for the taxable year. For example, with respect to the 2006 calendar taxable year, any associated plan year (*i.e.*, a plan year beginning in 2006 or plan year ending in 2006 that is used to determine the deductible limit for the 2006 taxable year) must reflect the 2006 changes. Thus, if the deductible limit is determined with respect to the plan year ending in 2006 (which begins in 2005), the calculation of the limit with respect to that plan year must reflect the use of an interest rate within the permissible corporate rate range (instead of an interest rate within the permissible 30-year Treasury rate range) (see Q&A–3 below) that was used for purposes of § 412, and must reflect the limitation based upon 150 percent of current liability (in place of the limitation based on 100 percent of current liability) under § 404(a)(1)(D). The funding method and other actuarial assumptions that were used for purposes of § 412 for that plan year must also be used for the calculations of the deductible limit.

As another example, in the case of a taxable year that is not the calendar year and that begins in 2005 and ends in 2006, and a plan year that is the calendar year, the deductible limit for any associated plan year must not reflect the 2006 changes. Thus, if the deductible limit for the taxable year beginning July 1, 2005, and ending June 30, 2006, is determined based upon the plan year beginning in the taxable year (the 2006 calendar plan year), the calculations of such limit must not reflect the limitation based on 150 percent of current liability (*i.e.*, must be limited to 100 percent of unfunded current liability) and may use the 30-year Treasury rate in place of the corporate rate.

Q–3. What changes to § 404(a)(1) of the Code were made by PPA '06 for years beginning after December 31, 2005?

A–3. In general, PPA '06 amended § 404(a)(1) of the Code for years beginning after December 31, 2005, to replace the limitation of § 404(a)(1)(D) based upon unfunded current liability with a limitation based on 150 percent of current liability (140 percent in the case of a multiemployer plan). In addition, PPA '06 eliminated the § 404(a)(1)(F) option to use any interest rate within 90 percent to 110 percent of the weighted average of the rates of interest on 30-year Treasury securities during the 4-year period ending on the last day before the beginning of the plan year (the permissible 30-year Treasury rate range) for purposes of determining current liability in determining the maximum deduction under § 404(a)(1) rather than an interest rate within the 90 percent to 100 percent of the weighted average of the rates of interest on amounts invested conservatively in long-term investment grade corporate bonds (the permissible corporate rate range). The current liability is determined pursuant to existing guidance, including, for example, Notice 90–11, 1990–1 C.B. 319.

Q–4. When determining the deductible limit in accordance with the 2006 changes, is the deductible limit determined as of the valuation date for the plan year?

A–4. Yes, the deductible limit is determined as of the valuation date for the plan year and is adjusted for interest to the earlier of the end of the plan year or the end of the taxable year of the employer (the "relevant date"). See, for example, § 1.404(a)–14(f)(3) of the regulations.

Q–5. What does § 404(a)(1)(D)(ii) provide and is the adoption of a new plan treated as a plan amendment for purposes of § 404(a)(1)(D)(ii)?

A–5. Section 404(a)(1)(D)(ii) provides that, in the case of a plan which has 100 or fewer participants for the plan year, unfunded current liability shall not include the liability attributable to benefit increases for highly compensated employees (as defined in § 414(q), "HCEs") resulting from a plan amendment which is made or becomes effective, whichever is later, within the last two years. For purposes of § 404(a)(1)(D)(ii), the adoption of a new plan will not be treated as a plan amendment only if the employer did not maintain a defined benefit plan covering any HCE covered by the new plan during the past 2 years. Thus, for an employer with a taxable year that is the calendar year, if an HCE was covered by a defined benefit plan of the employer at any time during 2004 or 2005, a new plan established during the 2006 taxable year that covers that HCE would be considered a plan amendment for purposes of § 404(a)(1)(D)(ii).

Q–6. What changes to § 404(a)(7) were made by PPA '06 for years beginning after December 31, 2005?

A–6. In general, PPA '06 amended § 404(a)(7) of the Code for years beginning after December 31, 2005, to exclude multiemployer plans from consideration and to provide that the combined limit of § 404(a)(7) only applies in the case of employer contributions to one or more defined contribution plans to the extent that such contributions exceed 6 percent of the compensation otherwise paid or accrued during the taxable year to the beneficiaries under the plan.

Q–7. Is a plan that contains a qualified cash or deferred arrangement described in § 401(k) taken into account for purposes of the combined limit of § 404(a)(7)?

A–7. Yes, a plan that contains a qualified cash or deferred arrangement described in § 401(k) is taken into account for purposes of the combined limit of § 404(a)(7). However, pursuant to § 404(n), elective deferrals as defined in § 402(g)(3) are not taken into account. Thus, matching contributions and nonelective employer contributions are taken into account in applying the limits of § 404(a), including the combined limit of § 404(a)(7). If elective deferrals are the only contributions under a defined contribution plan, then the plan is not taken into account in applying the limits of § 404(a)(7).

Q–8. How does the combined limit of § 404(a)(7) apply when employer contributions to defined contribution plans (other than elective deferrals) exceed 6 percent of compensation of participants in those plans?

A–8. When employer contributions to defined contribution plans (other than elective deferrals) exceed 6 percent of compensation of participants in those plans, the amount of employer contributions to defined contribution plans to which the combined limit of § 404(a)(7) applies is equal to the amount of employer contributions for the plan year less 6 percent of compensation of participants in those plans. Thus, the combined limit of § 404(a)(7) (*i.e.*, the greater of 25 percent of compensation, or the contributions to the defined benefit plan or plans to the extent such contributions do not exceed the amount necessary to satisfy the minimum funding standard for the defined benefit plans, treating a contribution that does not exceed the unfunded current liability as an amount necessary to satisfy the minimum funding standard for each defined benefit plan) applies to the total of employer contributions to defined benefit plans and employer contributions to defined contribution plans (other than elective deferrals), less 6 percent of compensation of participants in the defined contribution plans.

Q–9. How does the combined limit of § 404(a)(7) apply when employer contributions to defined contribution plans (other than elective deferrals) do not exceed 6 percent of compensation of participants in those plans?

A–9. When employer contributions to defined contribution plans (other than elective deferrals) do not exceed 6 percent of compensation of participants in those plans, the combined limit of § 404(a)(7) does not apply to any employer contributions to defined contribution plans. In such a case, the combined limit of § 404(a)(7) (*i.e.*, the greater of 25 percent of compensation, or the contributions to the defined benefit plan or plans to the extent such contributions do not exceed the amount necessary to satisfy the minimum funding standard for the defined benefit plans, treating a contribution that does not exceed the unfunded current liability as an amount necessary to satisfy the minimum funding standard for each defined benefit plan) applies only to contributions to the defined benefit plans.

Drafting Information

The principal author of this notice is James E. Holland, Jr. of the Employee Plans, Tax Exempt and Government Entities Division. For further information regarding this notice, contact Mr. Holland at (202) 283–9699 (not a toll-free number).

Request for Comments and Interim Guidance Regarding Allocation of Costs Under the Simplified Methods of Accounting Under § 263A

Notice 2007–29

The Internal Revenue Service and Treasury Department are studying the appropriateness of the use of negative amounts in computing additional costs for purposes of the simplified methods of accounting under § 263A of the Internal Revenue Code. This notice invites public comment on changes to the simplified production method under § 1.263A–2(b) and the simplified resale method under § 1.263A–3(d) of the Income Tax Regulations. This notice also provides interim guidance pending the publication of future guidance.

BACKGROUND

Section 471 provides the general rules for inventories and authorizes the Secretary to determine when the use of inventories are necessary to clearly reflect income and to determine the valuation methods that are acceptable for tax purposes. The regulations under § 471 provide the general rules for the valuation of inventories.

Section 263A was enacted under the Tax Reform Act of 1986, and prescribes uniform capitalization rules for property produced or held for resale. Under § 263A, producers of real or tangible personal property and resellers of real or personal property must capitalize the direct costs and a proper share of the indirect costs of the property. Section 263A requires capitalization of indirect costs but generally does not set forth methods for allocating indirect costs. Instead, in accordance with the legislative history, the regulations under § 263A generally provide that taxpayers must allocate indirect costs to property using detailed or specific cost allocation methods, including a specific identification method, the standard cost method, and methods using burden rates. Alternatively, taxpayers may use the simplified production method or simplified resale method (simplified methods), as applicable.

The legislative history to § 263A indicates that Congress desired the Service to adopt a flexible approach in the § 263A regulations by providing simplified methods and assumptions when the costs and burdens of compliance may outweigh the benefits. Accordingly, the simplified methods are intended to alleviate the administrative burden of complying with the capitalization rules of § 263A.

In general, the simplified methods determine aggregate amounts of additional § 263A costs allocable to ending inventory. Additional § 263A costs generally are those costs, other than interest, that were not capitalized under the taxpayer's method of accounting immediately prior to the effective date of § 263A, but that are required to be capitalized under § 263A. Under the simplified methods, additional § 263A costs allocable to ending inventory are determined by multiplying § 471 costs (generally, the costs other than interest the taxpayer capitalized under its method of accounting immediately prior to the effective date of § 263A) remaining on hand at year end by an absorption ratio consisting of a numerator of additional § 263A costs incurred during the taxable year over a denominator of § 471 costs incurred during the taxable year.

At the time the § 263A regulations were issued, some commentators expressed concern that the simplified methods, in particular the simplified production method, would result in allocation of an excessive amount of § 263A costs to raw materials inventories. They suggested that this result occurs because the simplified production method does not take into account the fact that fewer indirect costs are incurred with respect to raw materials that are normally held only a short period of time, compared to other items of inventory held longer. The final regulations did not adopt these recommendations because the simplified production method formula properly reflects the costs of raw materials that are purchased on the last day of the year, and incorporating the suggestions would have reduced the simplicity that the simplified production method was intended to provide.

More recently, controversy has arisen regarding the inclusion of negative amounts in additional § 263A costs and whether aggregate additional § 263A costs may be a negative number. A negative amount may occur, for example, when a taxpayer includes book costs greater than those required for tax purposes in the § 471 cost of inventory. For example, if a taxpayer included book depreciation in § 471 costs in accordance with § 1.471–11(c)(2)(iii)(*b*) and the book depreciation is greater than tax depreciation for the year, the taxpayer may have capitalized too much depreciation for purposes of § 263A and must reduce total § 263A costs by the excess. A negative amount may result if the taxpayer does not adjust its § 471 costs to remove this excess depreciation amount but instead makes a negative adjustment to its additional § 263A costs. Some taxpayers have reasoned that allowing negative amounts is consistent with the purpose of the simplified methods to alleviate the administrative burden of complying with the capitalization rules of § 263A and may reduce overcapitalization that sometimes results.

The Service and Treasury Department are aware of this viewpoint but are concerned that including negative amounts in additional § 263A costs may result in significant distortions in some situations. Including negative amounts in additional § 263A costs may undercapitalize amounts because the simplified production method formula may remove more of the cost from ending inventory than was actually remaining in ending inventory. Generally, this distortion is caused by the use of a different formula for removing the cost from ending inventory than the formula by which the cost was originally capitalized under § 471. The inclusion of raw materials in the simplified production method formula also may cause distortions. For example, including a negative amount for book depreciation greater than tax depreciation (excess depreciation) in the simplified production method formula may reduce ending inventory by more than the amount of excess depreciation actually remaining in ending inventory. In some circumstances this distortion may be a reversal of the overcapitalization of excess tax depreciation over book depreciation in prior years, and thus, may not be a cause for concern. However, the inclusion can cause significant, lasting distortion in situations in which the taxpayer has a tax basis much lower than book basis in depreciable property.

The Service and Treasury Department are considering amending the regulations under § 263A to prohibit the use of some or all negative amounts in computing additional § 263A costs under the existing simplified methods and to provide a new alternative simplified method of cost allocation under § 263A. The Service and Treasury Department will consider a new method that would allow negative amounts in computing additional § 263A costs, avoid requiring changes to existing systems for determining § 471 costs, but reduce distortions. One option under consideration would treat costs related to raw materials differently from those related to work-in-process or finished goods. Another option would create distinctions based upon the type of cost, with certain permanent items such as basis differences being allocated using a separate formula. Additionally, the Service and Treasury Department are considering whether special rules should be provided for smaller taxpayers to compute additional § 263A costs.

INTERIM GUIDANCE

Pending the issuance of additional published guidance, the Service will not challenge the inclusion of negative amounts in computing additional costs under § 263A or the permissibility of aggregate negative additional § 263A costs. These issues will not be raised in any taxable year ending on or before publication of the guidance, and, if already raised as an issue in examination or before Appeals or the Tax Court in a taxable year ending on or before March 12, 2007, the issue will not be pursued by the Service. In addition, pending further published guidance, the Service will not deny consent for changes in method of accounting solely on the basis that the proposed method involves the inclusion of negative amounts in computing additional costs under § 263A or the permissibility of aggregate negative additional § 263A costs. However, the Service will not grant a taxpayer permission to treat a cost as a negative additional § 263A cost unless the taxpayer already treats that cost as a § 471 cost. In other words, the Service will not approve a change in method of accounting to change the costs capitalized under § 471 to begin capitalizing a cost under § 471 and to remove the same cost from ending inventory by treating it as a negative additional § 263A cost. In addition, any taxpayers granted consent to make these changes will be required to conform their methods of accounting to any future published guidance.

REQUEST FOR COMMENTS

The Service and Treasury Department specifically request public comments on the following issues:

1. If only some negative amounts are appropriate in computing additional § 263A costs under the existing simplified methods, which costs should be allowed and under what circumstances? For example, should variances that were treated as top-side adjustments (aggregate adjustments to total ending inventory that are not allocated to each item or unit in ending inventory) before enactment of § 263A be treated differently from variances that first arose after enactment of § 263A? If negative amounts may be included in the numerator of the existing methods for some costs, should aggregate negative additional § 263A costs be prohibited or restricted? Should items that generate a permanent difference, such as basis differences, be allowed under the existing simplified methods, or should they be allocated using a different method?

2. If the use of negative amounts is restricted for certain costs or in certain situations as described in (1) above, what specific modifications should be made to the existing simplified methods to effect this result and how should the negative costs be allocated? Should a new, alternative simplified method be created to allocate the negative costs or all additional § 263A costs?

3. How might a new, alternative simplified method of allocating costs under § 263A be designed that could be used for all additional § 263A costs, positive or negative, in lieu of the existing simplified methods, that would treat costs related to raw materials (including raw material content of work-in-process and finished goods) differently from those related to work-in-process or finished goods (excluding raw material content) and achieve maximum simplicity while reducing distortions? In particular, comments are requested on (a) how costs, including variances and book-tax differences, should be allocated between raw materials, work-in-process and finished goods, (b) whether only purchasing costs should be allocated to raw materials, (c) whether purchasing, storage, and handling costs of raw materials should be allocated to raw materials, (d) whether § 471 costs should be adjusted for purchased raw materials in transit and beginning inventory, and (e) whether separate absorption ratios should be calculated for raw materials, work-in-process and finished goods, and, if so, how those ratios should be calculated.

4. Should the simplified methods be modified for small taxpayers and if so, how? In particular, how should any changes described above be applied to small taxpayers? What criteria should be used for determining whether a taxpayer is a small taxpayer?

Comments should be submitted in writing on or before July 2, 2007, and should include a reference to Notice 2007–29. Send submissions to: CC:PA:LDP:PR (Notice 2007–29), Room 5203, Internal Revenue Service, P.O. Box 7604, Ben Franklin Station, Washington, DC 20044. Submissions may be hand delivered Monday through Friday between the hours of 8 a.m. and 4 p.m. to: CC:PA:LPD:PR (Notice 2007–29), Courier's Desk, Internal Revenue Service, 1111 Constitution Avenue, N.W., Washington, DC. Alternatively, comments may be submitted electronically directly to the Service via the following e-mail address: *Notice.comments@irscounsel.treas.gov*. Please include "Notice 2007–29" in the subject line of any electronic communication. All materials submitted will be available for public inspection and copying.

DRAFTING INFORMATION

The principal author of this notice is W. Thomas McElroy, Jr. of the Office of the Associate Chief Counsel (Income Tax and Accounting). For further information concerning this notice, contact Mr. McElroy at (202) 622–4970 (not a toll-free number).

Frivolous Positions

Notice 2007–30

PURPOSE

Positions that are the same as or similar to the positions listed in this notice are identified as frivolous for purposes of the penalty for a "frivolous tax return" under section 6702(a) of the Internal Revenue Code and the penalty for a "specified frivolous submission" under section 6702(b). Persons who file a purported return of tax, including an original or amended return, based on one or more of these positions are subject to a penalty of $5,000 if the purported return of tax does not contain information on which the substantial correctness of the self-assessed determination of tax may be judged or contains information that on its face indicates the self-assessed determination of tax is substantially incorrect. Likewise, persons who submit a "specified submission" (namely, a request for a collection due process hearing or an application for an installment agreement, offer-in-compromise, or Taxpayer Assistance Order) based on one or more of the positions listed in this notice are subject to a penalty of $5,000. The penalty may also be applied if the purported return or any portion of the specified submission is not based on a position set forth in this notice, yet reflects a desire to delay or impede the administration of Federal tax laws for purposes of section 6702(a)(2)(B) or 6702(b)(2)(A)(ii).

BACKGROUND

Section 407 of Tax Relief and Health Care Act of 2006, Pub. L. No. 109–432, 120 Stat. 2922 (2006), amended section 6702 to increase the amount of the penalty for frivolous tax returns from $500 to $5,000 and to impose a penalty of $5,000 on any person who submits a "specified frivolous submission." A submission is a "specified frivolous submission" if it is a "specified submission" (defined in section 6702(b)(2)(B) as a request for a hearing under section 6320 or 6330 or an application under section 6159, 7122 or 7811) and any portion of the submission (i) is based on a position identified by the Secretary as frivolous or (ii) reflects a desire to delay or impede administration of the Federal tax laws. Section 6702 was further amended to add a new subsection (c) requiring the Secretary to prescribe a list of positions identified as frivolous. This notice contains the prescribed list.

DISCUSSION

Frivolous Positions. Positions that are the same as or similar to the following are frivolous.

1. Compliance with the internal revenue laws is voluntary or optional and not required by law, including arguments that:
   a. Filing a Federal tax or information return or paying tax is purely voluntary under the law, or similar arguments described as frivolous in Rev. Rul. 2007–20, 2007–14 I.R.B. 863.
   b. Nothing in the Internal Revenue Code imposes a requirement to file a return or pay tax, or that a person is not required to file a tax return or pay a tax unless the Internal Revenue Service responds to the person's questions, correspondence, or a request to identify a provision in the Code requiring the filing of a return or the payment of tax.
   c. There is no legal requirement to file a Federal income tax return because the instructions to Forms 1040, 1040A, or 1040EZ or the Treasury regulations associated with the filing of the forms do not display an OMB control number as required by the Paperwork Reduction Act of 1980, 44 U.S.C. § 3501 *et seq.*, or similar arguments described as frivolous in Rev. Rul. 2006–21, 2006–15 I.R.B. 745.
   d. Because filing a tax return is not required by law, the Service must prepare a return for a taxpayer who does not file one in order to assess and collect tax.
   e. A taxpayer has an option under the law to file a document or set of documents in lieu of a return or elect to file a tax return reporting zero taxable income and zero tax liability even if the taxpayer received taxable income during the taxable period for which the return is filed, or similar arguments described as frivolous in Rev. Rul. 2004–34, 2004–1 C.B. 619.
   f. An employer is not legally obligated to withhold income or employment taxes on employees' wages.
   g. A taxpayer may "untax" himself or herself at any time or revoke the consent to be taxed and thereafter not be subject to internal revenue taxes.
   h. Only persons who have contracted with the government by applying for a governmental privilege or benefit, such as holding a Social Security number, are subject to tax, and those who have contracted with the government may choose to revoke the contract at will.
   i. A taxpayer may lawfully decline to pay taxes if the taxpayer disagrees with the government's use of tax revenues, or similar arguments described as frivolous in Rev. Rul. 2005–20, 2005–1 C.B. 821.
   j. An administrative summons issued by the Service is *per se* invalid and compliance with a summons is not legally required.
2. The Internal Revenue Code is not law (or "positive law") or its provisions are ineffective or inoperative, including the sections imposing an income tax or requiring the filing of tax returns, because the provisions have not been implemented by regulations even though the provisions in question either (a) do not expressly require the Secretary to issue implementing regulations to become effective or (b) expressly require implementing regulations which have been issued.
3. A taxpayer's income is excluded from taxation when the taxpayer rejects or renounces United States citizenship because the taxpayer is a citizen exclusively of a State (sometimes characterized as a "natural-born citizen" of a "sovereign state"), that is claimed to be a separate country or otherwise not subject to the laws of the United States. This position includes the argument that the United States does not include all or a part of the physical territory of the 50 States and instead consists of only places such as the District of Columbia, Commonwealths and Territories (*e.g.*, Puerto Rico), and Federal enclaves (*e.g.*, Native American reservations and military installations), or similar arguments described as frivolous in Rev. Rul. 2004–28, 2004–1 C.B. 624, or Rev. Rul. 2007–22, 2007–14 I.R.B. 866.
4. Wages, tips, and other compensation received for the performance of personal services are not taxable income or are offset by an equivalent deduction for the personal services rendered, including an argument that a taxpayer has a "claim of right" to exclude the cost or value of the taxpayer's labor from income or that taxpayers have a basis in their labor equal to the fair market value of the wages they receive, or similar arguments described as frivolous in Rev. Rul. 2004–29, 2004–1 C.B. 627, or Rev. Rul. 2007–19, 2007–14 I.R.B. 843.
5. United States citizens and residents are not subject to tax on their wages or other income derived from sources

within the United States, as only foreign-based income or income received by nonresident aliens and foreign corporations from sources within the United States is taxable, and similar arguments described as frivolous in Rev. Rul. 2004–30, 2004–1 C.B. 622.

6. A taxpayer has been removed or redeemed from the Federal tax system though the taxpayer remains a United States citizen or resident, or similar arguments described as frivolous in Rev. Rul. 2004–31, 2004–1 C.B. 617.
7. Only certain types of taxpayers are subject to income and employment taxes, such as employees of the Federal government, corporations, nonresident aliens, or residents of the District of Columbia or the Federal territories, or similar arguments described as frivolous in Rev. Rul. 2006–18, 2006–15 I.R.B. 743.
8. Only certain types of income are taxable, for example, income that results from the sale of alcohol, tobacco, or firearms or from transactions or activities that take place in interstate commerce.
9. Federal income taxes are unconstitutional or a taxpayer has a constitutional right not to comply with the Federal tax laws for one of the following reasons:
   a. The First Amendment permits a taxpayer to refuse to pay taxes based on religious or moral beliefs.
   b. A taxpayer may withhold payment of taxes or the filing of a tax return until the Service or other government entity responds to a First Amendment petition for redress of grievances.
   c. Mandatory compliance with, or enforcement of, the tax laws invades a taxpayer's right to privacy under the Fourth Amendment.
   d. The requirement to file a tax return is an unreasonable search and seizure contrary to the Fourth Amendment.
   e. Income taxation, tax withholding, or the assessment or collection of tax is a "taking" of property without due process of law or just compensation in violation of the Fifth Amendment.
   f. The Fifth Amendment privilege against self-incrimination grants taxpayers the right not to file returns or the right to withhold all financial information from the Service.
   g. Mandatory or compelled compliance with the internal revenue laws is a form of involuntary servitude prohibited by the Thirteenth Amendment.
   h. Individuals may not be taxed unless they are "citizens" within the meaning of the Fourteenth Amendment.
   i. The Sixteenth Amendment was not ratified, has no effect, contradicts the Constitution as originally ratified, lacks an enabling clause, or does not authorize a non-apportioned, direct income tax.
   j. Taxation of income attributed to a trust, which is a form of contract, violates the constitutional prohibition against impairment of contracts.
   k. Similar constitutional arguments described as frivolous in Rev. Rul. 2005–19, 2005–1 C.B. 819.
10. A taxpayer is not a "person" within the meaning of section 7701(a)(14) or other provisions of the Internal Revenue Code, or similar arguments described as frivolous in Rev. Rul. 2007–22, 2007–14 I.R.B. 866.
11. Federal Reserve Notes are not taxable income when paid to a taxpayer because they are not gold or silver and may not be redeemed for gold or silver.
12. In a transaction using gold and silver coins, the value of the coins is excluded from income or the amount realized in the transaction is the face value of the coins and not their fair market value for purposes of determining taxable income.
13. A taxpayer with a home-based business may deduct as business expenses the costs of maintaining the taxpayer's household along with personal expenses, or similar arguments described as frivolous by Rev. Rul. 2004–32, 2004–1 C.B. 621.
14. A "reparations" tax credit exists, including arguments that African-American taxpayers may claim a tax credit on their Federal income tax returns as reparations for slavery or other historical mistreatment, that Native Americans are entitled to an analogous credit (or are exempt from Federal income tax on the basis of a treaty), or similar arguments described as frivolous in Rev. Rul. 2004–33, 2004–1 C.B. 628, or Rev. Rul. 2006–20, 2006–15 I.R.B. 746.
15. A Native American or other taxpayer who is not an employer engaged in a trade or business may nevertheless claim (for example, in an amount exceeding all reported income) the Indian Employment Credit under section 45A, which explicitly requires, among other criteria, that the taxpayer be an employer engaged in a trade or business to claim the credit.
16. A taxpayer's wages are excluded from Social Security taxes if the taxpayer waives the right to receive Social Security benefits, or a taxpayer is entitled to a refund of, or may claim a charitable-contribution deduction for, the Social Security taxes that the taxpayer has paid, or similar arguments described as frivolous in Rev. Rul. 2005–17, 2005–1 C.B. 823.
17. Taxpayers may reduce or eliminate their Federal tax liability by altering a tax return, including striking out the penalty-of-perjury declaration, or attaching documents to the return, such as a disclaimer of liability, or similar arguments described as frivolous in Rev. Rul. 2005–18, 2005–1 C.B. 817.
18. A taxpayer is not obligated to pay income tax because the government has created an entity separate and distinct from the taxpayer—a "straw man"—that is distinguishable from the taxpayer by some variation of the taxpayer's name, and any tax obligations are exclusively those of the "straw man," or similar arguments described as frivolous in Rev. Rul. 2005–21, 2005–1 C.B. 822.
19. Inserting the phrase "nunc pro tunc" on a return or other document filed with or submitted to the Service has a legal effect, such as reducing a tax-

payer's tax liability, or similar arguments described as frivolous in Rev. Rul. 2006–17, 2006–15 I.R.B. 748.

20. A taxpayer may avoid tax on income by attributing the income to a trust, including the argument that a taxpayer can put all of the taxpayer's assets into a trust to avoid income tax while still retaining substantial powers of ownership and control over those assets or that a taxpayer may claim an expense deduction for the income attributed to a trust, or similar arguments described as frivolous in Rev. Rul. 2006–19, 2006–15 I.R.B. 749.
21. A taxpayer may lawfully avoid income tax by sending income offshore, including depositing income into a foreign bank account.
22. By purchasing equipment and services for an inflated price (which may or may not have been actually paid), a taxpayer can use the section 44 Disabled Access Credit to reduce tax or generate a refund irrespective of whether the taxpayer is a small business that purchased the equipment or services to comply with the requirements of the Americans with Disabilities Act.
23. A taxpayer is allowed to buy or sell the right to claim a child as a qualifying child for purposes of the Earned Income Tax Credit.
24. An IRS Form 23C, *Assessment Certificate — Summary Record of Assessments*, is an invalid record of assessment for purposes of section 6203 and Treas. Reg. § 301.6203–1, the Form 23C must be personally signed by the Secretary of the Treasury for an assessment to be valid, the Service must provide a copy of the Form 23C to a taxpayer if requested before taking collection action, or similar arguments described as frivolous in Rev. Rul. 2007–21, 2007–14 I.R.B. 865.
25. A tax assessment is invalid because the assessment was made from a section 6020(b) substitute for return, which is not a valid return.
26. A statutory notice of deficiency is invalid because the taxpayer to whom the notice was sent did not file an income tax return reporting the deficiency or because the statutory notice of deficiency was unsigned or not signed by the Secretary of the Treasury or by someone with delegated authority.
27. A Notice of Federal Tax Lien is invalid because it is not signed by a particular official (such as by the Secretary of the Treasury), or because it was filed by someone without delegated authority.
28. The form or content of a Notice of Federal Tax Lien is controlled by or subject to a state or local law, and a Notice of Federal Tax Lien that does not comply in form or content with a state or local law is invalid.
29. A collection due process notice under section 6320 or 6330 is invalid if it is not signed by the Secretary of the Treasury or other particular official, or if no certificate of assessment is attached.
30. Verification under section 6330 that the requirements of any applicable law or administrative procedure have been met may only be based on one or more particular forms or documents (which must be in a certain format), such as a summary record of assessment, or that the particular forms or documents or the ones on which verification was actually determined must be provided to a taxpayer at a collection due process hearing.
31. A Notice and Demand is invalid because it was not signed, was not on the correct form (*e.g.*, a Form 17), or was not accompanied by a certificate of assessment when mailed.
32. The United States Tax Court is an illegitimate court or does not, for any purported constitutional or other reason, have the authority to hear and decide matters within its jurisdiction.
33. Federal courts may not enforce the internal revenue laws because their jurisdiction is limited to admiralty or maritime cases or issues.
34. Revenue Officers are not authorized to issue levies or Notices of Federal Tax Lien or to seize property in satisfaction of unpaid taxes.
35. A Service employee lacks the authority to carry out the employee's duties because the employee does not possess a certain type of identification or credential, for example, a pocket commission or a badge, or it is not in the correct form or on the right medium.
36. A person may represent a taxpayer before the Service or in court proceedings even if the person does not have a power of attorney from the taxpayer, has not been enrolled to practice before the Service, or has not been admitted to practice before the court.
37. A civil action to collect unpaid taxes or penalties must be personally authorized by the Secretary of the Treasury and the Attorney General.
38. A taxpayer's income is not taxable if the taxpayer assigns or attributes the income to a religious organization (a "corporation sole" or ministerial trust) claimed to be tax-exempt under section 501(c)(3), or similar arguments described as frivolous in Rev. Rul. 2004–27, 2004–1 C.B. 625.
39. The Service is not an agency of the United States government but rather a private-sector corporation or an agency of a State or Territory without authority to administer the internal revenue laws.
40. Any position described as frivolous in any revenue ruling or other published guidance in existence when the return adopting the position is filed with or the specified submission adopting the position is submitted to the Service.

Returns or submissions that contain positions not listed above, which on their face have no basis for validity in existing law, or which have been deemed frivolous in a published opinion of the United States Tax Court or other court of competent jurisdiction, may be determined to reflect a desire to delay or impede the administration of Federal tax laws and thereby subject to the $5,000 penalty.

The list of frivolous positions above will be periodically revised as required by section 6702(c).

DRAFTING INFORMATION

The principal author of this notice is the Office of Associate Chief Counsel (Procedure & Administration). For further information regarding this notice, contact the Office of Associate Chief Counsel (Procedure & Administration), Administrative Provisions & Judicial Practice Division, Branch 2, at (202) 622–4940 (not a toll-free call).

26 CFR 601.105: Examination of returns and claims for refund, credit or abatement; determination of correct tax liability.
(Also Part I, § 527.)

Rev. Proc. 2007–27

SECTION 1. BACKGROUND

.01 Section 527 of the Internal Revenue Code provides for the tax treatment of all political organizations. Section 527(e) provides that a political organization is an organization (whether or not incorporated) organized and operated primarily for the purpose of accepting contributions or making expenditures to influence, or attempt to influence, the selection, nomination, election, or appointment of any individual to any Federal, State, or local public office, office in a political party or the election of Presidential or Vice-Presidential electors.

.02 Under § 527(i), certain political organizations must file Form 8871, *Political Organization Notice of Section 527 Status*, within 24 hours of being established and within 30 days of any material change to information reported on Form 8871 to be treated as tax-exempt § 527 organizations. Until these political organizations file the form, their income (including income that would otherwise be treated as exempt function income) is subject to taxation pursuant to § 527(i)(4). See Section I of Rev. Rul. 2003–49, 2003–1 C.B. 903.

.03 Under § 527(j), certain tax-exempt political organizations must report periodically on Form 8872, *Political Organization Report of Contributions and Expenditures*, information about contributions received and expenditures made by the organizations. These reports are due either monthly or semi-annually in odd-numbered years and either monthly or quarterly in even-numbered years. In addition, certain pre- and post-election reports are required. Information required to be reported includes the names and addresses of contributors, and, for individual contributors, their occupations and employers. A tax-exempt political organization that fails to include the required information is liable under § 527(j)(1) for the payment of an amount equal to the amount of the contribution or expenditure multiplied by the highest corporate tax rate (currently 35%). See Section II of Rev. Rul. 2003–49, 2003–1 C.B. 903.

.04 Section 527(l) provides that the Internal Revenue Service may waive all or any portion of the tax assessed due to a failure to comply with § 527(i) or the amount imposed under § 527(j) if the failure was due to reasonable cause and not due to willful neglect. In establishing reasonable cause, the key factor to consider is the extent of the organization's effort to obtain and report the required information. If the organization establishes to the Service's satisfaction that there are significant mitigating factors with respect to the failure, the failure arose from events beyond the organization's control, or the organization has exercised the appropriate level of due diligence to obtain and report the required information, waiver is appropriate.

.05 Political organizations have requested guidance on what steps a political organization needs to take to establish that its failure to disclose required information was due to reasonable cause and not due to willful neglect.

SECTION 2. FORM 8872 SCHEDULE A SAFE HARBOR

.01 This revenue procedure provides a "safe harbor" for establishing that failure to report certain contributor information on Form 8872 was due to reasonable cause and not due to willful neglect, and therefore qualifies for relief under § 527(l)(2) of the Code. The safe harbor will apply only to those contributions for which a political organization establishes that it meets the requirements of the safe harbor. For example, if a political organization fails to report required information with respect to contribution X and contribution Y on a Form 8872, and the political organization meets the safe harbor criteria for contribution X, but not contribution Y, the organization qualifies for relief pursuant to the safe harbor with respect to contribution X, but not contribution Y. In addition, the safe harbor will not apply in situations where the organization fails to report the name of the contributor on Form 8872 by the time prescribed. For each contribution for which the requirements of the safe harbor are satisfied, the Service will waive the full amount imposed under section 527(j) with respect to the contribution.

.02 A failure to report the address of a contributor and, if the contributor is an individual, the occupation and employer of the contributor will be considered to be due to reasonable cause and not due to willful neglect provided that all of the following requirements are met:

(1) All fundraising solicitations by (or on behalf of) the tax-exempt political organization contain a clear request (in a conspicuous and easily recognizable format) for the contributor's address and, if the contributor is an individual, the contributor's occupation and employer (consistent with the instructions for Form 8872) and include a statement that the political organization is subject to Federal taxes and penalties if it fails to disclose this information to the Service. A fundraising solicitation includes any solicitation of contributions or gifts in written (including electronically such as via the internet or by facsimile or email) or printed form, by television or radio, or by telephone.

(2) For each contribution for which the contributor has not provided the required information, such as the contributor's address, occupation and employer, the tax-exempt political organization makes a written (including electronically such as via the internet or by facsimile or email) request, or an oral request memorialized in writing, to the contributor for the required information within 30 days of receipt of the contribution. The information request may thank the contributor for the contribution, but must not include material on any other subject or an additional solicitation. Each information request must include a statement that the tax-exempt political organization is subject to Federal taxes and penalties if it fails to disclose this information to the Service. In addition, each information request that is not oral or electronic must include a pre-addressed return envelope or postcard. Each oral or electronic information request must include the mailing or Internet address to which the required information should be submitted instead of a pre-addressed return envelope or postcard.

(3) If the contributor has not responded to the information request by the due date of the Form 8872 and in the tax-exempt political organization's records, including contributor records, fundraising records or previously filed Forms 8872, the tax-exempt political organization has information about the contributor that is requested by the Form

8872, the organization must report such information on the Form 8872.

(4) If any missing or corrected contributor information is received after the contribution has been disclosed on Form 8872, the tax-exempt political organization files an amended Form 8872 including the additional information within 30 days of receipt of the information, unless the information is received less than 30 days and more than 2 business days before an election, in which case the tax-exempt political organization files an amended Form 8872 including the additional information no later than 2 business days before the election.

(5) The tax-exempt political organization discloses all the required information on Forms 8872 with respect to at least 85 percent of the total dollar amount of contributions it received during the calendar year.

(6) The political organization keeps contemporaneous records sufficient to substantiate that it has complied with subparagraphs (1) through (5) in this section.

.03 Even if a tax-exempt political organization does not meet the requirements of the safe harbor, the Service still may exercise its authority under section 527(l) if it determines that the failure is due to reasonable cause and not willful neglect.

SECTION 3. REQUEST FOR COMMENTS

.01 The Service is considering whether to publish additional guidance concerning the application of § 527(l) to a political organization that fails to file a completed Form 8871 or Form 8872 in the time and manner prescribed. The Service requests public comment concerning (1) the need for additional guidance and (2) circumstances in which such a failure should be deemed to be due to reasonable cause and not due to willful neglect. For example, under § 6724 and the regulations thereunder, a failure to comply with certain information reporting requirements is deemed to be due to reasonable cause and not due to willful neglect if the filer acted in a responsible manner and either there are significant mitigating factors with respect to the failure or the failure arose from events beyond the filer's control. The regulations under § 6724 provide examples of acting in a responsible manner, significant mitigating factors and events beyond the organization's control. However, the Service recognizes that the reporting requirements under § 527 have significant public disclosure and timeliness concerns (particularly in relation to public disclosure prior to elections) that may differentiate them from other information reporting requirements. Thus, comments should address the following questions:

(1) In applying § 527(l), how might the factors similar to those in the regulations under § 6724 be adapted for purposes of § 527(l)?

(a) Are there any significant mitigating factors that are unique to failures to file Form 8871 or Form 8872 in the time and manner prescribed?

(b) Are there any events beyond the political organization's control that are unique to failures to file Form 8871 or Form 8872 in the time and manner prescribed?

(c) Are there any factors unique to political organizations that should be considered in determining whether a political organization acted in a responsible manner, both before and after a failure to file Form 8871 or Form 8872 in the time and manner prescribed?

(2) Are there any factors relevant to determining whether all or only a portion of the amounts assessed should be waived?

(3) What documentation should the political organization maintain to establish that any failure to file Form 8871 or Form 8872 in the time and manner prescribed was due to reasonable cause and not due to willful neglect?

(4) Are there factors that indicate relief under § 527(l) should not be granted?

.02 Public comments should be submitted in writing on or before July 2, 2007.

Comments should be sent to the following address:

Internal Revenue Service
SE:T:EO:RA:G (Rev. Proc. 2007–27)
P.O. Box 7604
Ben Franklin Station
Washington, DC 20044

Comments may be hand delivered to:

SE:T:EO:RA:G (Rev. Proc. 2007–27)
Courier's Desk
Internal Revenue Service
1111 Constitution Ave., NW
Washington, DC 20224

Comments may also be sent electronically via the Internet to *notice.comments@irscounsel.treas.gov*. Please include "Rev. Proc. 2007–27" in the subject line.

All comments will be available for public inspection.

SECTION 4. DRAFTING INFORMATION

The principal author of this notice is Judith E. Kindell of Exempt Organizations, Tax Exempt and Government Entities Division. For further information regarding this notice, contact Judith E. Kindell at (202) 283–8964 (not a toll-free call).

Part I. Rulings and Decisions Under the Internal Revenue Code of 1986

Section 42.—Low-Income Housing Credit

The adjusted applicable federal short-term, mid-term, and long-term rates are set forth for the month of April 2007. See Rev. Rul. 2007-23, page 889.

Section 280G.—Golden Parachute Payments

Federal short-term, mid-term, and long-term rates are set forth for the month of April 2007. See Rev. Rul. 2007-23, page 889.

Section 382.—Limitation on Net Operating Loss Carryforwards and Certain Built-In Losses Following Ownership Change

The adjusted applicable federal long-term rate is set forth for the month of April 2007. See Rev. Rul. 2007-23, page 889.

Section 412.—Minimum Funding Standards

The adjusted applicable federal short-term, mid-term, and long-term rates are set forth for the month of April 2007. See Rev. Rul. 2007-23, page 889.

Section 467.—Certain Payments for the Use of Property or Services

The adjusted applicable federal short-term, mid-term, and long-term rates are set forth for the month of April 2007. See Rev. Rul. 2007-23, page 889.

Section 468.—Special Rules for Mining and Solid Waste Reclamation and Closing Costs

The adjusted applicable federal short-term, mid-term, and long-term rates are set forth for the month of April 2007. See Rev. Rul. 2007-23, page 889.

Section 468B.—Special Rules for Designated Settlement Funds

A revised Initial Regulatory Flexibility Analysis discusses the impact on small businesses of proposed regulations relating to the current taxation of qualified escrow accounts, qualified trusts, and other escrow accounts, trusts, and funds used during deferred exchanges of like-kind property. The proposed regulations were published on February 6, 2006. See Announcement 2007-35, page 949.

Section 482.—Allocation of Income and Deductions Among Taxpayers

Federal short-term, mid-term, and long-term rates are set forth for the month of April 2007. See Rev. Rul. 2007-23, page 889.

Section 483.—Interest on Certain Deferred Payments

The adjusted applicable federal short-term, mid-term, and long-term rates are set forth for the month of April 2007. See Rev. Rul. 2007-23, page 889.

Section 642.—Special Rules for Credits and Deductions

Federal short-term, mid-term, and long-term rates are set forth for the month of April 2007. See Rev. Rul. 2007-23, page 889.

Section 807.—Rules for Certain Reserves

The adjusted applicable federal short-term, mid-term, and long-term rates are set forth for the month of April 2007. See Rev. Rul. 2007-23, page 889.

Section 846.—Discounted Unpaid Losses Defined

The adjusted applicable federal short-term, mid-term, and long-term rates are set forth for the month of April 2007. See Rev. Rul. 2007-23, page 889.

Section 1031.—Exchange of Property Held for Productive Use or Investment

26 CFR 1.1031(k)–1: Treatment of deferred exchanges.

A revised Initial Regulatory Flexibility Analysis discusses the impact on small businesses of proposed regulations relating to the current taxation of qualified escrow accounts, qualified trusts, and other escrow accounts, trusts, and funds used during deferred exchanges of like-kind property. The proposed regulations were published on February 6, 2006. See Announcement 2007-35, page 949.

Section 1274.—Determination of Issue Price in the Case of Certain Debt Instruments Issued for Property

(Also Sections 42, 280G, 382, 412, 467, 468, 482, 483, 642, 807, 846, 1288, 7520, 7872.)

Federal rates; adjusted federal rates; adjusted federal long-term rate and the long-term exempt rate. For purposes of sections 382, 642, 1274, 1288, and other sections of the Code, tables set forth the rates for April 2007.

Rev. Rul. 2007–23

This revenue ruling provides various prescribed rates for federal income tax purposes for April 2007 (the current month). Table 1 contains the short-term, mid-term, and long-term applicable federal rates (AFR) for the current month for purposes of section 1274(d) of the Internal Revenue Code. Table 2 contains the short-term, mid-term, and long-term adjusted applicable federal rates (adjusted AFR) for the current month for purposes of section 1288(b). Table 3 sets forth the adjusted federal long-term rate and the long-term tax-exempt rate described in section 382(f). Table 4 contains the appropriate percentages for determining the low-income housing credit described in section 42(b)(2) for buildings placed in service during the current month. Finally, Table 5 contains the federal rate for determining the present value of an annuity, an interest for life or for a term of years, or a remainder or a reversionary interest for purposes of section 7520.

REV. RUL. 2007–23 TABLE 1

Applicable Federal Rates (AFR) for April 2007

Period for Compounding

	Annual	*Semiannual*	*Quarterly*	*Monthly*
Short-term				
AFR	4.90%	4.84%	4.81%	4.79%
110% AFR	5.39%	5.32%	5.29%	5.26%
120% AFR	5.89%	5.81%	5.77%	5.74%
130% AFR	6.39%	6.29%	6.24%	6.21%
Mid-term				
AFR	4.61%	4.56%	4.53%	4.52%
110% AFR	5.08%	5.02%	4.99%	4.97%
120% AFR	5.54%	5.47%	5.43%	5.41%
130% AFR	6.02%	5.93%	5.89%	5.86%
150% AFR	6.96%	6.84%	6.78%	6.74%
175% AFR	8.14%	7.98%	7.90%	7.85%
Long-term				
AFR	4.81%	4.75%	4.72%	4.70%
110% AFR	5.30%	5.23%	5.20%	5.17%
120% AFR	5.78%	5.70%	5.66%	5.63%
130% AFR	6.28%	6.18%	6.13%	6.10%

REV. RUL. 2007–23 TABLE 2

Adjusted AFR for April 2007

Period for Compounding

	Annual	*Semiannual*	*Quarterly*	*Monthly*
Short-term adjusted AFR	3.50%	3.47%	3.46%	3.45%
Mid-term adjusted AFR	3.65%	3.62%	3.60%	3.59%
Long-term adjusted AFR	4.04%	4.00%	3.98%	3.97%

REV. RUL. 2007–23 TABLE 3

Rates Under Section 382 for April 2007

Adjusted federal long-term rate for the current month	4.04%
Long-term tax-exempt rate for ownership changes during the current month (the highest of the adjusted federal long-term rates for the current month and the prior two months.)	4.18%

REV. RUL. 2007–23 TABLE 4

Appropriate Percentages Under Section 42(b)(2) for April 2007

Appropriate percentage for the 70% present value low-income housing credit	8.10%
Appropriate percentage for the 30% present value low-income housing credit	3.47%

REV. RUL. 2007–23 TABLE 5 Rate Under Section 7520 for April 2007	
Applicable federal rate for determining the present value of an annuity, an interest for life or a term of years, or a remainder or reversionary interest	5.6%

Section 1288.—Treatment of Original Issue Discount on Tax-Exempt Obligations

The adjusted applicable federal short-term, mid-term, and long-term rates are set forth for the month of April 2007. See Rev. Rul. 2007-23, page 889.

Section 1503.—Computation and Payment of Tax

26 CFR 1.1503(d)–1: Definitions and special rules for filings under section 1503(d).

T.D. 9315

DEPARTMENT OF THE TREASURY
Internal Revenue Service
26 CFR Parts 1 and 602

Dual Consolidated Loss Regulations

AGENCY: Internal Revenue Service (IRS), Treasury.

ACTION: Final regulations.

SUMMARY: This document contains final regulations under section 1503(d) of the Internal Revenue Code (Code) regarding dual consolidated losses. Section 1503(d) generally provides that a dual consolidated loss of a dual resident corporation cannot reduce the taxable income of any other member of the affiliated group unless, to the extent provided in regulations, the loss does not offset the income of any foreign corporation. Similar rules apply to losses of separate units of domestic corporations. These final regulations address various dual consolidated loss issues, including exceptions to the general prohibition against using a dual consolidated loss to reduce the taxable income of any other member of the affiliated group.

DATES: *Effective Date:* These regulations are effective on March 19, 2007.

Applicability Dates: For dates of applicability, see §1.1503(d)–8.

FOR FURTHER INFORMATION CONTACT: Jeffrey P. Cowan, (202) 622–3860 (not a toll-free number).

SUPPLEMENTARY INFORMATION:

Paperwork Reduction Act

The collection of information contained in these final regulations has been reviewed and approved by the Office of Management and Budget in accordance with the Paperwork Reduction Act of 1995 (44 U.S.C. 3507(d)) under control number 1545–1946.

The collections of information in these final regulations are in §§1.1503(d)–1(c), 1.1503(d)–3(e), 1.1503(d)–4(e), 1.1503(d)–6(c), 1.1503(d)–6(d), 1.1503(d)–6(e), 1.1503(d)–6(f), 1.1503(d)–6(g), 1.1503(d)–6(h), and 1.1503(d)–6(j). This information is required for various reasons. The information under §1.1503(d)–1(c) notifies the IRS when a taxpayer asserts that it had reasonable cause for failing to comply with certain filing requirements under the regulations. The information under §1.1503(d)–4(e) indicates when the taxpayer attempts to rebut the amount of presumed tainted income. The information under the other provisions provides the IRS with various information regarding domestic use elections, exceptions to the domestic use limitation, triggering events, new domestic use agreements, original elector statements, annual certifications, and terminations of existing domestic use elections.

An agency may not conduct or sponsor, and a person is not required to respond to, a collection of information unless it displays a valid control number.

Books or records relating to a collection of information must be retained as long as their contents might become material in the administration of any internal revenue law. Generally, tax returns and tax return information are confidential, as required by 26 U.S.C. 6103.

Background

Congress enacted section 1503(d), as part of the Tax Reform Act of 1986, to prevent a dual resident corporation from using a single economic loss once to offset income that was subject to U.S. tax, but not foreign tax, and a second time to offset income subject to foreign tax, but not U.S. tax (double dip). In 1988, Congress extended the application of section 1503(d), by adding section 1503(d)(3) and (4), to apply the provisions to separate units of domestic corporations and to grant the Secretary authority to promulgate regulations to prevent the avoidance of section 1503(d) through the contribution of assets to a corporation with a dual consolidated loss after the loss was sustained. The IRS and Treasury Department issued temporary regulations under section 1503(d) in 1989 (T.D. 8261, 1989–2 C.B. 220) and final regulations in 1992 (T.D. 8434, 1992–2 C.B. 240), see §601.601(d)(2)(ii)(*b*). These final regulations were updated and amended over the next 11 years (current regulations).

On May 24, 2005, the IRS and Treasury Department published in the **Federal Register** a notice of proposed rulemaking (REG–102144–04, 2005–1 C.B. 1297 [70 FR 29868]). The proposed regulations addressed the following fundamental concerns arising under the current regulations: (1) the potential over- and under-application of the current regulations; (2) various issues arising in the application of the current regulations, particularly in light of the adoption of the entity classification regulations under §§301.7701–1 through 301.7701–3 (check-the-box regulations); and (3) the administrative burden of the current regulations. The public hearing with respect to the 2005 proposed regulations was cancelled because no request to speak was received. However, the IRS and Treasury Department received a number of written comments which are discussed in this preamble.

Summary of Comments and Explanation of Provisions

A. *Application of Section 1503(d) to Regulated Investment Companies and Real Estate Investment Trusts*

Under the current regulations, a dual resident corporation is a domestic corporation that is subject to an income tax of a foreign country on its worldwide income or on a residence basis. As a result, unless specifically exempted, certain entities that are domestic corporations, but not generally taxed at the entity level, may be subject to the current regulations. The current regulations provide that an S corporation, which is a domestic corporation, is not treated as a dual resident corporation. The proposed regulations, and these final regulations, provide that an S corporation is not treated as a domestic corporation and thus cannot be a dual resident corporation or own a separate unit.

Under the current regulations, as a domestic corporation, a regulated investment company (as defined in section 851) or a real estate investment trust (as defined in section 856) could be a dual resident corporation or own a separate unit. In the preamble to the proposed regulations, however, the IRS and Treasury Department requested comments as to whether regulated investment companies or real estate investment trusts should, like S corporations, be excluded from the application of the dual consolidated loss rules. One commentator suggested that regulated investment companies and real estate investment trusts should be subject to the dual consolidated loss rules, but would limit recapture pursuant to a domestic use agreement to situations where there was a foreign use and a section 381 transaction occurred.

The IRS and Treasury Department believe that subjecting regulated investment companies and real estate investment trusts to the dual consolidated loss rules is inappropriate. Section 1503(d) was intended to apply to domestic corporations that are subject to entity-level tax. Although regulated investment companies and real estate investment trusts are domestic corporations under the Code, unlike most domestic corporations these entities often do not pay tax at the entity level because they may deduct the amount of dividends paid to their shareholders from their own taxable income. Thus, under the final regulations regulated investment companies and real estate investment trusts are excluded from the definition of a domestic corporation and, as a result, are not subject to the dual consolidated loss rules.

B. *Separate Units*

(1) *Separate unit combination rule*

Section 1.1503–2(c)(3)(ii) of the current regulations provides that if two or more foreign branches located in the same foreign country are owned by a single domestic corporation and the losses of each branch are available to offset the income of the other branches under the tax laws of the foreign country, then the branches are treated as a single separate unit.

In response to comments that the current combination rule was unnecessarily limited and did not appropriately address the check-the-box regulations, the proposed regulations adopt a broader combination rule that, subject to certain requirements, combines all separate units of a single domestic corporation. One requirement for combining separate units, both under the current regulations and the proposed regulations, is that the losses of each separate unit are made available to offset the income of the other separate units under the tax laws of a single foreign country.

The combination rule in the proposed regulations does not combine dual resident corporations that are members of the same consolidated group, or separate units of multiple domestic corporations that are members of the same consolidated group. However, in the preamble to the proposed regulations, the IRS and Treasury Department requested comments as to whether combination was appropriate in these cases.

Numerous comments were received on the scope and application of the combination rule. Commentators uniformly recommended that the combination rule be expanded to include separate units that are located in or subject to tax in the same foreign country (same-country separate units) and that are owned by multiple domestic corporations that are members of the same consolidated group. The IRS and Treasury Department believe that combining same-country separate units of domestic corporations that are members of the same consolidated group is consistent with the policies underlying section 1503(d) because, in general, all of the items of income, gain, deduction, and loss of such combined separate units are taken into account in both the United States and the foreign country. Therefore, these final regulations expand the combination rule to apply to same-country separate units of multiple domestic corporations that are members of the same consolidated group.

Two commentators recommended that the combination rule be expanded to combine dual resident corporations that are members of the same consolidated group. The IRS and Treasury Department do not believe that Congress intended that multiple dual resident corporations be treated as a single domestic corporation for purposes of section 1503(d). Combining dual resident corporations and separate units would also add complexity because certain rules apply differently to dual resident corporations and separate units. As a result, the combination rule in these final regulations does not apply to dual resident corporations.

Nevertheless, it is important to note that a dual resident corporation will often carry on its activities through a foreign branch (as defined in §1.367(a)–6T(g)(1)) and, as a result, will be a domestic owner of a foreign branch separate unit. In these cases, the foreign branch separate unit through which it carries on its activities in the foreign country will be eligible for combination. In addition, in many cases, a significant number of the items of income, gain, deduction, and loss of a dual resident corporation that owns a foreign branch separate unit will be attributable to the foreign branch separate unit (and therefore will not be items of the dual resident corporation itself). As a result, not extending the combination rule to dual resident corporations should, as a practical matter, have limited effect.

One commentator recommended eliminating the proposed regulations' requirement that losses of each separate unit must be available to offset the income of other separate units under the tax laws of a single foreign country in order for them to combine. The IRS and Treasury Department believe that it is appropriate to remove this requirement, provided that the individual separate units are located, or subject to income tax on a worldwide or residence basis, in the same foreign country. This is the case because it is likely that all of the items of the combined separate unit will be recognized in both the United States and the foreign jurisdiction, without regard to whether such items are available for offset under the income tax laws of the foreign country. In addition, the IRS and Treasury Department believe that eliminating this requirement will reduce complexity, and will further refine the application of the rules. As a result, these final regulations eliminate this requirement from the combination rule.

Commentators also recommended making combination elective in certain situations. The IRS and Treasury Department believe that elective combination would add complexity and create administrative burdens. Therefore, this comment is not adopted.

The IRS and Treasury Department recognize that the expanded combination rule may necessitate that the basis of the stock of multiple domestic corporations, which are members of the same consolidated group, be adjusted to reflect the items of income, gain, deduction, and loss entering into the computation of the dual consolidated loss of a combined separate unit. These regulations provide guidance on the manner of such basis adjustments.

These final regulations also clarify that the separate unit combination rule generally applies for all purposes of section 1503(d). As a result, except as specifically provided in these regulations, any individual separate unit composing a combined separate unit loses its character as an individual separate unit. For example, in determining whether there is a triggering event as a result of the transfer of the assets of a combined separate unit, all of the assets of the combined separate unit are taken into account (rather than only the assets of any individual separate unit within the combined separate unit).

(2) *Definition of a foreign branch by reference to §1.367(a)–6T(g)*

One commentator stated that the reference in the current and proposed regulations to §1.367(a)–6T(g) for the definition of a foreign branch, which implicitly includes references to §1.367(a)–6T(g)(1) through (3), creates needless complexity. The IRS and Treasury Department generally agree with this comment. Accordingly, these final regulations clarify that a foreign branch is defined, in part, by reference to §1.367(a)–6T(g)(1), rather than by reference to §1.367(a)–6T(g).

(3) *Treaty exception to the definition of a foreign branch separate unit*

One commentator suggested that the definition of a foreign branch separate unit should not include a branch that would not be subject to income tax in a foreign jurisdiction either as a result of an income tax convention or because of the passive nature of the activities. This commentator explained that such an exclusion is appropriate because in these cases there would be no potential use of a branch loss for foreign tax purposes.

The IRS and Treasury Department agree that it is appropriate to exclude from the definition of a foreign branch separate unit certain business operations that, under an applicable income tax convention, would not be considered a permanent establishment. As a result, these final regulations include an exception to the definition of a foreign branch separate unit. The IRS and Treasury Department do not, however, believe an exception is appropriate where the business operations are not subject to tax in the foreign jurisdiction because of the passive nature of the activities. Such an exception would require the analysis of foreign law which, to the extent possible, should not be required under these rules.

(4) *Activities owned by a dual resident corporation or a hybrid entity*

One commentator requested clarification that home-country activities of a dual resident corporation or hybrid entity separate unit can qualify as a foreign branch separate unit. The IRS and Treasury Department agree that this clarification is warranted and these final regulations are modified accordingly.

C. *Elimination of the Consistency Rule*

As a result of the expansion of the separate unit combination rule in these final regulations, the IRS and Treasury Department believe that the consistency rule would have only limited application. Therefore, the consistency rule has been eliminated from these final regulations. The IRS and Treasury Department believe that eliminating the consistency rule will simplify the application of the dual consolidated loss rules and will eliminate various issues that arise under the rule.

D. *Domestic Reverse Hybrid Entities*

One commentator noted that the application of the current and proposed regulations to certain structures involving domestic reverse hybrid entities appears inconsistent with the underlying policies of section 1503(d). In a typical structure, a foreign corporation owns the majority of the interests in a partnership or limited liability company that elects to be treated as a corporation for U.S. tax purposes and, therefore, is subject to tax on its worldwide income in the United States, but is treated as a pass-through entity under foreign law (domestic reverse hybrid). The domestic reverse hybrid is the parent of a consolidated group, is the obligor on group indebtedness, and holds stock of other group members. This structure allows the interest expense of the domestic reverse hybrid to offset income of the foreign corporation, which is not subject to U.S. tax, and to offset income of the other members of the consolidated group, which is not subject to foreign tax.

The commentator noted that because the domestic reverse hybrid is neither a dual resident corporation (because it is not subject to tax on a residence basis or on its worldwide income in the foreign country, but is instead treated as a pass-through entity) nor a separate unit of a domestic corporation, the current and proposed regulations do not apply to the losses of the domestic reverse hybrid. The commentator asserted that this result is inconsistent with the policies underlying section 1503(d), which was adopted, in part, to ensure that domestic corporations were not put at a competitive disadvantage as compared to foreign corporations through the use of certain inbound acquisition structures. See

S. Rep. No. 99–313, 1986–3 C.B. Vol. 3 at 420, see §601.601(d)(2)(ii)(*b*). The commentator suggested that the scope of the final regulations be broadened to treat such entities as separate units, the losses of which are subject to the restrictions of section 1503(d). This change would, in effect, apply the provisions of section 1503(d) to a separate unit of a foreign corporation.

The IRS and Treasury Department recognize that this type of structure results in a double dip similar to that which Congress intended to prevent through the adoption of section 1503(d). However, the IRS and Treasury Department believe that a domestic reverse hybrid is neither a dual resident corporation nor a separate unit and, therefore, is not subject to section 1503(d). As a result, this comment is not adopted. However, the IRS and Treasury Department continue to study these and similar structures.

E. *Transparent Entities*

Section 1.1503–2(c)(3) and 1.1503–2(c)(4) of the current regulations define a separate unit of a domestic corporation as a foreign branch (within the meaning of §1.367(a)–6T(g)), and an interest in a partnership, trust, or hybrid entity. As a result, the current regulations potentially apply not only to entities that are subject to tax in a foreign country (for example, hybrid entities), but also to entities that are not subject to tax in a foreign country, and otherwise have no connection to a foreign jurisdiction (for example, a domestic partnership engaged in a U.S. trade or business).

The proposed regulations modify the definition of a separate unit to exclude interests in non-hybrid entity partnerships and non-hybrid entity grantor trusts. These interests were excluded because the IRS and Treasury Department believe that it is unlikely that losses and deductions attributable to these interests could be put to a foreign use (as that term is defined in the proposed regulations). However, the proposed regulations retain the rule that a domestic corporation can own a separate unit through a non-hybrid entity partnership or non-hybrid entity grantor trust.

Commentators noted that, as a result of this change, the proposed regulations may not sufficiently and consistently address the treatment of certain entities. Such an entity is a pass-through entity for U.S. tax purposes (for example, a disregarded entity, a partnership or a grantor trust), but is not a hybrid entity because it is not subject to tax on its worldwide income or on a residence basis in a foreign country. In addition, the entity would not be treated as a pass-through entity under the laws of the applicable foreign country. One example of such an entity (transparent entity) is a limited liability company organized in the United States that for U.S. tax purposes is a partnership or disregarded entity, but, for purposes of the applicable foreign country, is not viewed as a pass-through entity. Another example is a foreign entity that is a pass-through entity for U.S. tax purposes, is not subject to income tax in a foreign country as a corporation (or otherwise at the entity level) either on its worldwide income or on a residence basis (because, for example, it is organized in a foreign country that does not impose an income tax), and is not treated as a pass-through entity under the laws of the applicable foreign country.

The commentators noted that under the proposed regulations items of income, gain, deduction, and loss of a transparent entity that is a partnership for U.S. tax purposes would be taken into account in computing the dual consolidated loss of a dual resident corporation or hybrid entity separate unit that owns an interest in such entity, even though it is unlikely that the items are taken into account by the jurisdiction in which the dual resident corporation or hybrid entity is subject to tax. As a result, items of deduction or loss which are unlikely to be available for a double dip (because they are not taken into account by the foreign country in which the dual resident corporation or hybrid entity is subject to tax) could inappropriately result in a dual consolidated loss. The commentators further noted that items of income or gain which are unlikely to be taken into account by the foreign country could inappropriately reduce (or eliminate) a dual consolidated loss of the dual resident corporation or hybrid entity separate unit that owns an interest in such entity.

The IRS and Treasury Department believe that losses attributable to interests in transparent entities should not be subject to section 1503(d), but also believe that items attributable to these interests should not influence the calculation or use of a dual consolidated loss of a dual resident corporation or separate unit in a manner that is inconsistent with the purposes of section 1503(d). Accordingly, these final regulations provide four new rules that address transparent entities (and interests therein).

First, these final regulations provide a definition of a transparent entity that is consistent with the description and examples in the preceding discussion.

Second, rules are provided for attributing items of income, gain, deduction, and loss to interests in transparent entities. The rules applicable for attributing items to these interests are consistent with the rules for attributing items to hybrid entity separate units.

Third, these final regulations provide that items of income, gain, deduction, and loss attributable to interests in transparent entities are not considered when calculating whether a dual resident corporation that holds an interest in such entity has income or a dual consolidated loss. This modification ensures that in cases where the foreign country in which the dual resident corporation is subject to tax is unlikely to take into account items of the transparent entity, such items do not inappropriately affect the computation of income or a dual consolidated loss of the dual resident corporation. Similar rules apply for purposes of calculating the income or dual consolidated loss of a separate unit through which an interest in a transparent entity is owned (directly or indirectly).

Finally, an interest in a transparent entity will be treated as a domestic affiliate for purposes of determining whether there is a domestic use of a dual consolidated loss. This change prevents a dual consolidated loss from being used to offset the income of a transparent entity such that there is no inappropriate domestic use of the loss.

These final regulations do not treat transparent entities, or interests therein, as dual resident corporations or separate units and, as a result, do not cause such entities (or interests therein) to be subject to the limitations of section 1503(d). Instead, the rules aim to appropriately take into account such entities when applying the dual consolidated loss rules to dual resident corporations and separate units.

F. *Reasonable Cause Exception*

The current regulations require various filings to be included on a timely filed income tax return. In addition, taxpayers that fail to include these filings must request an extension of time to file under §§301.9100–1 through 301.9100–3. The proposed regulations eliminate the requirement that a taxpayer obtain an extension of time under §§301.9100–1 through 301.9100–3 and instead adopt a reasonable cause standard.

On January 31, 2006, the IRS and Treasury Department published Notice 2006–13, 2006–8 I.R.B. 496, see §601.601(d)(2)(ii)(*b*), announcing that taxpayers that must file agreements, statements, and other information under section 1503(d) may cure any late filings by applying a reasonable cause exception similar to the standard contained in the proposed regulations, until such time as the proposed regulations become final. In addition to allowing the use of the reasonable cause exception prior to the proposed regulations being published as final regulations in the **Federal Register**, the notice modifies the procedures for obtaining reasonable cause relief to ensure that requests for reasonable cause relief are handled in a timely and efficient manner.

These final regulations adopt the reasonable cause standard contained in the proposed regulations and Notice 2006–13, with certain modifications. See paragraph S(3) of this preamble for the application of the reasonable cause exception to losses that are subject to the current regulations.

G. *Foreign Use*

(1) *In general*

Section 1.1503–2(g)(2)(i) of the current regulations provides that, in order to elect relief from the general limitation on the use of a dual consolidated loss to offset income of a domestic affiliate ((g)(2)(i) election), the taxpayer must, among other things, certify that no portion of the losses, expenses, or deductions taken into account in computing the dual consolidated loss has been, or will be, used to offset the income of any other person under the income tax laws of a foreign country. If, contrary to this certification, there is such a use, the dual consolidated loss subject to the (g)(2)(i) election generally must be recaptured and reported as gross income.

The proposed regulations modify the definition of "use" and provide a rule based on "foreign use" in order to minimize the potential over- and under-application of the current regulations. The proposed regulations provide that a foreign use is deemed to occur only if two conditions are satisfied. The first condition is satisfied if any portion of a deduction or loss taken into account in computing the dual consolidated loss is made available under the income tax laws of a foreign country to offset or reduce, directly or indirectly, any item that is recognized as income or gain under such laws (including items of income or gain generated by the dual resident corporation or separate unit itself), regardless of whether income or gain is actually offset, and regardless of whether these items are recognized under U.S. tax principles. The second condition is satisfied if items that are (or could be) offset pursuant to the first condition are considered, under U.S. tax principles, to be items of: (1) a foreign corporation; or (2) a direct or indirect (for example, through a partnership) owner of an interest in a hybrid entity, provided such interest is not a separate unit.

(2) *Indirect foreign use*

As noted, the proposed regulations provide that a foreign use of a dual consolidated loss will occur when any item of deduction or loss, entering into the computation of the dual consolidated loss, is made available, directly or indirectly, to offset under foreign law, income of a foreign corporation or an owner of an interest in a hybrid entity that is not a separate unit. The proposed regulations do not provide comprehensive examples illustrating when an indirect use of a dual consolidated loss occurs. However, the provision was included in the proposed regulations to address transactions that are structured to avoid the application of section 1503(d) through, for example, the use of a back-to-back lending or conduit financing-type arrangements, or through the use of one or more hybrid instruments.

Commentators requested additional guidance regarding an indirect foreign use. In response to these comments, these final regulations clarify when an indirect foreign use is deemed to occur, include an exception to the general indirect foreign use rule for certain ordinary course transactions, and provide related examples.

The indirect foreign use rules are designed to limit an indirect use to situations in which taxpayers have engaged in transactions which have the effect of transferring an item of deduction or loss composing a dual consolidated loss to another entity for foreign tax purposes, so that it is made available to offset the income of a foreign corporation or the owner of an interest in an entity which is not a separate unit. In general, these rules are intended to target structured transactions that are designed to achieve a double dip that is contrary to the policies of section 1503(d), and are not intended to apply to ordinary business transactions.

(3) *Exceptions to foreign use*

The proposed regulations contain three exceptions to the definition of a foreign use, including an exception where there is no dilution of an interest in a separate unit. In the preamble to the proposed regulations, the IRS and Treasury Department request comments as to whether a *de minimis* exception should be provided to the dilution limitation. The preamble also states that a revenue procedure would be issued, in conjunction with the proposed regulations being published as final regulations in the **Federal Register**, that would provide additional exceptions (safe harbors) under which a triggering event would be deemed rebutted if various conditions were satisfied, including, in certain cases, a demonstration that there can be no foreign use of a significant portion of the dual consolidated loss.

The IRS and Treasury Department received a number of comments on transactions and situations that could be included in the list of safe harbors. One commentator suggested an exception whereby recapture would not be required following transactions outside the taxpayer's control. For example, this commentator suggested that a recapture of a dual consolidated loss should not occur following the conveyance or relinquishment of assets of a separate unit, or interests in a separate unit, to a foreign government.

Commentators also suggested that relief should be provided following certain transactions, similar to those mentioned in the preamble to the proposed regulations, where there is a *de minimis* potential for foreign use, a *de minimis* carryover of asset basis, and for which rebuttal would otherwise be difficult or impossible. According to these commentators, this safe harbor would apply to many common business transactions in which the policies underlying section 1503(d) would not be violated because of only a *de minimis* potential for foreign use.

Another commentator stated that an exception to foreign use would be appropriate where the taxpayer enters into a binding and irrevocable agreement with the tax authorities of a foreign country which ensures that no portion of the dual consolidated loss can be put to a foreign use in the foreign country. The commentator explained that, pursuant to such an arrangement, the taxpayer and the foreign tax authorities would agree that the foreign tax attributes of a dual resident corporation or separate unit (for example, loss carryforwards and asset basis) would be eliminated such that there would be no opportunity for a foreign use.

After considering these comments, the IRS and Treasury Department believe that it is appropriate to include certain safe harbors where a foreign use will be deemed not to occur. As a result, these final regulations (rather than a revenue procedure) set forth additional exceptions to the definition of a foreign use. These exceptions generally apply in cases where the potential for foreign use is *de minimis*, or where the transaction giving rise to a foreign use occurs as a result of events largely outside of the taxpayer's control.

These new exceptions to foreign use include a *de minimis* rule and rules that apply to certain transactions involving the carry over of asset basis and the assumption of liabilities. Another new exception applies to a transaction that qualifies for the multiple-party event exception to a triggering event (referred to as successor elector events under the proposed regulations) where the acquiring unaffiliated domestic owner or consolidated group owns, immediately after the transaction, less than 100 percent of the acquired assets or interests. Without this exception to foreign use, many transactions that would qualify for the multiple-party event exception would immediately result in a foreign use triggering event when the unaffiliated domestic corporation or consolidated group acquires between 90 and 100 percent of the assets or interests. Finally, these regulations modify the "no dilution" exception contained in the proposed regulations to, among other things, incorporate a *de minimis* exception.

These final regulations provide that the exceptions may be supplemented through subsequent guidance published in the Internal Revenue Bulletin, as appropriate. As a result, the IRS and Treasury Department request comments on additional transactions or situations that should be added as safe harbors. For example, additional comments are requested on arrangements with foreign tax authorities whereby foreign tax attributes could be eliminated to ensure that no portion of the dual consolidated loss can be put to a foreign use.

(4) *Ordering rules for determining a foreign use*

The current and proposed regulations provide rules for determining the order in which dual consolidated losses are used in cases where the laws of a foreign country provide for the foreign use of such loss, but do not provide applicable rules for determining the order in which these losses are used in a taxable year.

A commentator noted that in certain cases involving dual consolidated losses incurred in different taxable years, the ordering rules may result in losses being deemed to be made available for a foreign use resulting in recapture, even though there are other losses which, if deemed to be used, would not result in recapture. This commentator recommended that in these situations the losses be deemed to first be used in a manner that will not result in the recapture of a dual consolidated loss. The commentator also noted that this approach is consistent with the exception to foreign use contained in §1.1503(d)–1(b)(14)(iii)(B) of the proposed regulations where there is no foreign country rule for determining use. Finally, the commentator stated that losses that do give rise to a foreign use should be deemed to be used on a "last-in/first-out" basis. The IRS and Treasury Department believe these rules are appropriate and, as a result, these comments are adopted.

(5) *Mirror legislation*

The current regulations contain a mirror legislation rule that denies a taxpayer the ability to make an election to use a dual consolidated loss to offset the income of a domestic affiliate where the foreign country has enacted legislation that operates in a manner similar to section 1503(d), and, as a result, prohibits the taxpayer from claiming the dual consolidated loss in the foreign country. The mirror legislation rule was designed to prevent the revenue gain resulting from the disallowance of a double dip from inuring solely to the foreign country. Staff of the Joint Committee on Taxation, General Explanation of the Tax Reform Act of 1986, at 1065 - 66 (J. Comm. Print 1987), see §601.601(d)(2)(ii)(*b*); see also *British Car Auctions, Inc. v. United States*, 35 Fed. Cl. 123 (1996), *aff'd without op.*, 116 F.3d 1497 (Fed. Cir. 1997) (upholding the validity of the mirror legislation rule). The effect of the mirror legislation rule is that a dual consolidated loss may be disallowed in the United States and in the foreign country. In such cases, Congress intended for the Treasury Department to pursue a bilateral agreement with the foreign jurisdiction so that the loss could offset income of an affiliate in only one country.

The proposed regulations retain the mirror legislation rule and modify it to better take into account the policies underlying its adoption.

A number of comments were received on the scope and utility of the mirror legislation rule. Several commentators encouraged the IRS and the Treasury Department to pursue bilateral agreements where the dual consolidated loss is disallowed in both the United States and the foreign country.

The IRS and Treasury Department agree that such agreements are necessary and recently concluded a competent authority agreement on such matters with the United Kingdom on October 6, 2006 (the Agreement). For the text of the Agreement, see Announcement 2006–86, 2006–45 I.R.B. 842; see §601.601(d)(2)(ii)(*b*). The Agreement applies to dual consolidated losses attributable to certain UK permanent establishments that are otherwise subject to both section 1503(d) and mirror legislation enacted by the United Kingdom. In general, the Agreement provides that taxpayers can elect to use or relieve the loss in either the United Kingdom or the United States, but not both.

The IRS and Treasury Department believe that these final regulations and the Agreement appropriately refine and limit the scope of the mirror rule. In addition, the IRS and Treasury Department believe that the provisions of the Agreement can serve as a model for future competent authority agreements, if necessary, between the United States and its treaty partners which would further the Congressional intent with respect to the application of the mirror legislation rule. Accordingly, comments are requested on the provisions of the Agreement and on specific jurisdictions and considerations that should be taken into account in future agreements.

Commentators also suggested that a "stand-alone" exception to the mirror legislation rule be adopted. This exception would apply where filing a domestic use election with respect to a dual consolidated loss otherwise subject to the mirror legislation rule would not violate the policies of section 1503(d). According to the commentators, this is the case because the mirror legislation in the foreign country would not have the effect of forcing taxpayers to use the losses in the United States. The commentators suggested that the mirror legislation rule would not apply provided there is not a foreign affiliate to which the separate unit or dual resident corporation could put the dual consolidated loss to a foreign use. The commentators noted that in these situations, the mirror legislation does not result in the revenue loss inuring solely to the United States, because it is factually impossible for the loss to offset taxable income in the foreign country that is not also taken into account in the United States.

The IRS and Treasury Department generally agree with this comment. As a result, these final regulations contain a stand-alone exception to the mirror legislation rule.

H. *Elimination of a Dual Consolidated Loss After Certain Transactions*

Both the current and proposed regulations contain rules that eliminate a dual consolidated loss that is subject to the general restrictions under section 1503(d)(1) following certain transactions. In the case of a dual resident corporation, the dual consolidated loss is generally eliminated in transactions described in section 381(a) because the dual resident corporation ceases to exist. In the case of a separate unit, the dual consolidated loss is generally eliminated in transactions where the separate unit ceases to be a separate unit of its domestic owner (either through a transaction described in section 381(a) or otherwise). In these cases, and subject to the exceptions discussed in this preamble, after the transaction it is no longer possible for the dual resident corporation or separate unit to generate income that can be offset by the dual consolidated loss. As a result, any unused dual consolidated loss is eliminated.

Both the current and the proposed regulations provide exceptions to the general elimination rule in the case of certain transactions to which section 381(a) applies. These exceptions generally apply in cases where it is possible that income that is generated by the transferee corporation after the transaction is subject to tax in both the United States and the foreign country such that it is appropriate for the income to be offset by the dual consolidated loss that carries over to the transferee.

These final regulations make certain modifications to the elimination rules. For example, the rules are modified to reflect the expansion of the separate unit combination rule. Thus, these final regulations take into account transactions involving combined separate units that have more than one domestic owner. For example, a dual consolidated loss of a domestic owner that is attributable to a separate unit will not be eliminated under these final regulations if the separate unit continues to be a separate unit of any member of its domestic owner's consolidated group.

I. *Application of SRLY Limitation to a Former Dual Resident Corporation*

Section 1.1503(d)–3(c)(3) of the proposed regulations provides that a dual consolidated loss is treated as a loss incurred by a dual resident corporation or separate unit in a separate return limitation year (SRLY) and is generally subject to all the limitations of §1.1502–21(c). The proposed regulations provide that when determining the general SRLY limitation with respect to a dual resident corporation, the calculation of aggregate consolidated taxable income only includes income, gain, deduction, and loss generated in years in which the dual resident corporation is a resident (or is taxed on its worldwide income) in the same foreign country in which it was a resident (or was taxed on its worldwide income) during the year in which the dual consolidated loss was generated. See proposed §1.1503(d)–3(c)(3)(iii).

One commentator noted that this rule prevents the dual consolidated loss of a dual resident corporation from being taken into account by its consolidated group after the dual resident corporation ceases to be subject to tax on a residence basis (or on its worldwide income), regardless of whether the former dual resident corporation contributes taxable income to the consolidated taxable income of the group. The commentator stated that this result is inappropriate because it does not merely limit the use of a dual consolidated loss from offsetting the income of a domestic affiliate, but has the effect of limiting the use of a dual consolidated loss from offsetting the domestic corporation's own taxable income.

The IRS and Treasury Department agree with this comment. Section 1503(d)(1) provides that a dual consolidated loss of a corporation shall not reduce the taxable income of any other member of the affiliated group for the taxable year or for any other taxable year. However, the limitations of section 1503(d)(1) do not prevent the use of a dual consolidated loss to offset the income of the dual resident corporation that incurred the loss, even where the dual resident corporation ceases to be subject to tax in the foreign country. As a result, this rule is not contained in these final regulations. But see section 1503(d)(4) (relating to tainted assets contributed to a dual resident corporation).

J. *Effect of Section 1503(d) on Foreign Tax Credits*

Section 1503(d)(2) generally defines a dual consolidated loss to mean any net operating loss of a dual resident corporation or a separate unit. Section 172(c) generally defines a net operating loss as the excess of deductions over gross income. Section 164(a)(3) generally provides that foreign taxes are allowed as a deduction for the taxable year in which paid or accrued. However, section 275(a)(4) provides that no deduction is allowed for any such taxes, to the extent the taxpayer chooses to take to any extent the benefits of section 901 (which permits taxpayers to claim a credit for certain taxes paid or accrued during the taxable year to any foreign country or any possession of the United States).

Commentators asked whether a creditable foreign tax expenditure incurred by a dual resident corporation or separate unit, for which an election is made to claim a credit pursuant to section 901, may be subject to the limitations of section 1503(d)(1).

The IRS and Treasury Department recognize that policy concerns arise in certain transactions in which two or more parties claim a credit for the same foreign taxes. Although these policy concerns are similar to those arising under section 1503(d), the IRS and Treasury Department do not believe that Congress intended the limitations of section 1503(d) to apply to foreign taxes, so long as the foreign taxes do not enter into the computation of a net operating loss (that is, so long as an election is made to claim a credit for such taxes, in lieu of deducting them). As a result, under the terms of the statute, the limitations of section 1503(d) do not apply to creditable foreign tax expenditures incurred by a dual resident corporation or a separate unit, provided an election is made to claim a credit with respect to such expenditures in accordance with section 901 and the related regulations.

Even though section 1503(d) does not apply to foreign tax credits that are claimed by more than one person, the IRS and Treasury Department continue to study these transactions and, as appropriate, intend to address them in future published guidance under other provisions.

K. *Tainted Income Rule*

Section 1503(d)(4) grants the Secretary authority to prescribe such regulations as may be necessary or appropriate to prevent the avoidance of the purposes of section 1503(d) by contributing assets to the corporation with the dual consolidated loss after such loss is incurred. Section 1.1503–2(e) of the current regulations prevents the dual consolidated loss of a dual resident corporation that ceases being a dual resident corporation from offsetting the income from assets that are acquired by the dual resident corporation in a nonrecognition transaction, or as a contribution to capital, at any time during the three taxable years immediately preceding the taxable year in which the corporation ceases to be a dual resident corporation, or any time thereafter. The proposed regulations retained the tainted income rule, with certain modifications.

One commentator noted that the tainted income rule of the current and proposed regulations applies with respect to assets acquired by a dual resident corporation, regardless of whether such tainted assets were received from a member of the dual resident corporation's affiliated group. According to this commentator, because section 1503(d) was intended to prevent the use of a dual consolidated loss from offsetting the taxable income of any other member of the affiliated group, applying the tainted income rule where the tainted assets were not received from a member of the dual resident corporation's affiliated group is inconsistent with the policies underlying section 1503(d).

Section 1503(d)(4) grants the Secretary broad regulatory authority to implement the tainted income rule. In addition, the IRS and Treasury Department believe that adopting the rule suggested by the commentator would require the IRS to trace the source of tainted assets received (for example, to ensure that the rule cannot be avoided through the imposition of an intermediary entity, such as a partnership, or through indirect transfers of assets). Moreover, such a rule would be difficult for both taxpayers and the IRS to apply, and would increase complexity. Accordingly, the IRS and Treasury Department believe that the tainted income rule should continue to apply without regard to the source of the tainted assets. As a result, this comment is not adopted.

L. *Items Taken into Account in Computing Income or a Dual Consolidated Loss*

(1) *In general*

Section 1503(d)(2)(A) generally defines a dual consolidated loss to mean any net operating loss of a domestic corporation which is subject to an income tax of a foreign country on its income without regard to whether such income is from sources inside or outside such foreign country, or is subject to such a tax on a residence basis. Section 1503(d)(3) grants the Secretary broad authority to subject any loss of a separate unit of a domestic corporation to the limitations of section 1503(d). Because separate units are not themselves taxpayers, it is necessary to determine which items of income, gain, deduction, and loss of the domestic owner of the separate unit should be taken into account for purposes of calculating a dual consolidated loss.

Section 1.1503–2(d)(1)(ii) of the current regulations provides a limited rule for attributing items of a domestic owner to a separate unit. Under this rule, a separate unit must compute its income as if it were a separate domestic corporation that is a dual resident corporation, using only those items of income, expense, deduction, and loss that are otherwise attributable to such separate unit. For this purpose, only items of the domestic owner that are recognized for U.S. tax purposes are taken into account.

In response to requests for additional guidance in this area, the proposed regulations provide more detailed rules for determining the amount of income or dual consolidated loss of a separate unit. This determination depends on various factors, including the type of separate unit, the ownership structure, and the nature of the item. The determination generally turns on whether it is likely that the relevant foreign country would take into account the item (assuming the item is recognized) for tax purposes. This determination is solely for purposes of section 1503(d) and does not apply for any other purpose, such as attributing items under an applicable income tax treaty or under other Code sections such as section 884 or 987.

These final regulations adopt the attribution rules contained in the proposed regulations, with modifications.

(2) *Books and records*

The proposed regulations provide that, in general, the items of income, gain, deduction, and loss that are attributable to a hybrid entity (and, therefore, attributable to interests in the hybrid entity) are those that are properly reflected on its books and records, as adjusted to conform to

U.S. tax principles. The proposed regulations further provide that the principles of §1.988–4(b)(2) apply for purposes of making this determination.

One commentator asked whether §1.988–4(b)(2) is a strict booking rule, or whether it would instead permit taxpayers to take positions contrary to how items are reflected on the books and records if, under the facts and circumstances, the items were not appropriately reflected on the books and records. Another commentator stated that the clause "to the extent consistent with U.S. tax principles" in the proposed regulations created uncertainty.

In response to these comments, the final regulations clarify that only the Commissioner, and not the taxpayer, may make adjustments to the books and records where the booking practices are employed with a principle purpose of avoiding the principles of section 1503(d), including inconsistently treating the same or similar items of income, gain, deduction, and loss. In addition, these final regulations clarify that, in general, a domestic owner's items of income, gain, deduction, and loss are attributable to the domestic owner's hybrid entity separate unit, or interest in a transparent entity, to the extent such items are reflected on the hybrid entity or transparent entity's books and records (as defined in §1.989(a)–1(d)), as adjusted to conform to U.S. tax principles.

The books and records standard set forth in these final regulations is intended to be consistent with the more detailed approach for attributing items that was adopted in proposed §1.987–2(b) that was published on September 7, 2006 (REG–208270–86, 2006–42 I.R.B. 698 [71 FR 52875]). It is anticipated that when those regulations are published as final regulations in the **Federal Register**, that approach will, as appropriate, be incorporated into these regulations. The IRS and Treasury Department believe that applying consistent standards under these two provisions, where appropriate, would make the rules more administrable. Comments are requested as to whether the standard contained in the section 987 proposed regulations is appropriate for purposes of section 1503(d).

(3) *Attributing interest expense under the principles of §1.882–5*

The proposed regulations provide that the principles of §1.882–5, as modified, apply for purposes of determining the interest expense that is attributable to a foreign branch separate unit. In making this determination, and solely for this purpose, the domestic owner is treated as a foreign corporation, the foreign branch separate unit is treated as a trade or business within the United States, and assets other than those of the foreign branch separate unit are treated as assets that are not U.S. assets.

Two comments were received on the application of this rule. First, commentators stated that adopting the principles of §1.882–5 results in unnecessary complexity. These commentators suggested that, in lieu of using the principles of §1.882–5, the interest expense of a foreign branch separate unit be determined by reference to its books and records. Another commentator noted the rationale of using the principles of §1.882–5 as a general matter, but suggested that where the foreign country looks to the books and records of the foreign branch separate unit for purposes of computing the interest expense of the separate unit, it would be appropriate to use the books and records for purposes of section 1503(d).

The IRS and Treasury Department continue to believe that the principles of §1.882–5, as modified, serve as a reasonable proxy for determining the items of interest expense recognized for U.S. tax purposes that, if recognized by the foreign country, would be taken into account by the foreign country. Therefore, the principles of §1.882–5, as modified, are retained as the general rule for purposes of determining the interest expense that is attributable to a foreign branch separate unit.

However, to minimize complexity, the IRS and Treasury Department believe it is appropriate to use a books and records approach, where possible. Therefore, these final regulations provide an exception to the general rule such that interest expense is attributable to a foreign branch separate unit to the extent it is reflected on its books and records. This exception only applies if the foreign country in which the foreign branch is located determines, for purposes of computing the taxable income (or loss) under the laws of the foreign country, the interest expense of the foreign branch separate unit by taking into account only the items of interest expense reflected on the foreign branch separate unit's books and records. This rule will not apply, however, in cases where the foreign country does not use a strict booking approach for interest expense.

Finally, it is important to note that in all cases only items of interest expense, as determined for U.S. tax purposes, are taken into account. The treatment of interest expense in the foreign country is only relevant for purposes of determining the method under which items of interest expense (determined for U.S. tax purposes) is attributed to the foreign branch separate unit.

(4) *Treaty-based methods*

The proposed regulations provide that for purposes of determining the items of income, gain, deduction (other than interest), and loss that are taken into account in determining the taxable income or loss of a foreign branch separate unit, the principles of sections 864(c)(2) and (c)(4) as set forth in §§1.864–4(c) and 1.864–6 shall apply.

One commentator stated that domestic corporations operating foreign branch separate units should be allowed to attribute items to the foreign branch separate unit based on the method provided under an income tax treaty between the United States and the foreign country (or between two foreign countries if foreign branch operations are conducted by a hybrid entity outside its home country). The IRS and Treasury Department believe that this approach is inappropriate for two reasons. First, it would have the effect of attributing items recognized by the foreign jurisdiction, which may not be recognized as items for U.S. tax purposes. This would be inconsistent with section 1503(d), which defines a dual consolidated loss solely based on U.S. tax rules. Second, this approach would require the interpretation of foreign law, which the IRS and Treasury Department believe should be avoided, to the extent possible. Accordingly, this comment is not adopted.

(5) *Gain or loss recognized under section 987*

The proposed regulations do not provide whether gain or loss of a domestic owner recognized under section 987 as a result of a remittance or transfer is attributable to a separate unit for purposes of calculating income or dual consolidated loss, but instead request comments.

Commentators stated that gain or loss recognized under section 987 should not be attributable to a separate unit because in most cases the foreign country would not recognize such items since the income of the separate unit will be computed in the local currency. The IRS and Treasury Department agree with this comment. As a result, these final regulations provide that gain or loss recognized under section 987, as a result of a remittance or transfer, will not be taken into account for purposes of computing the income or dual consolidated loss of a separate unit.

(6) *Attributable to or taken into account*

The proposed regulations generally provide that items are attributable to a hybrid entity separate unit, but are taken into account by a foreign branch separate unit. The IRS and Treasury Department believe that the use of these different terms is unnecessary and may lead to confusion. As a result, these final regulations provide that items are attributable to a separate unit, regardless of whether the separate unit is a foreign branch separate unit or a hybrid entity separate unit.

M. *Basis Adjustments*

Section 1.1503–2(d)(3) of the current regulations contains special basis adjustment rules that override the normal investment adjustment rules under §1.1502–32 for stock of affiliated dual resident corporations and affiliated domestic owners owned by other members of the consolidated group. Similar rules apply to separate units arising from the ownership of an interest in a partnership. These special basis adjustment rules were included in the current regulations to prevent the indirect deduction of a dual consolidated loss. Although the proposed regulations retain these rules, the IRS and Treasury Department requested comments on whether the special basis adjustment rules should be retained.

A number of commentators recommended that the special basis adjustment rules be removed for several reasons. For example, the commentators noted that an indirect use, which the special basis rules were intended to prevent, may not occur for many years after the dual consolidated loss was incurred. In response to these comments, the special basis rules are not contained in these final regulations. Thus, the basis adjustment rules under §1.1502–32 shall apply without modification for purposes of determining the adjusted basis in the stock of a dual resident corporation or the stock of an affiliated domestic owner owned by other members of the consolidated group. These final regulations also contain rules to ensure consistent treatment for a partner's basis in a partnership interest that is a separate unit, or through which a separate unit is owned indirectly.

N. *Losses of a Foreign Insurance Company Treated as a Domestic Corporation*

(1) *In general*

Section 953(d) generally provides that a foreign corporation that would qualify to be taxed as an insurance company if it were a domestic corporation may, under certain circumstances, elect to be treated as a domestic corporation (section 953(d) company). Section 953(d)(3) provides that if a section 953(d) company is treated as a member of an affiliated group, any loss of such corporation is treated as a dual consolidated loss for purposes of section 1503(d), without regard to section 1503(d)(2)(B) (grant of regulatory authority to exclude losses which do not offset the income of foreign corporations from the definition of a dual consolidated loss).

The current regulations do not address the application of section 953(d)(3). In the proposed regulations, however, the definition of a dual resident corporation includes a section 953(d) company that is a member of an affiliated group. In addition, the proposed regulations clarify that a section 953(d) company may not make a domestic use election. These rules are consistent with section 953(d)(3).

In response to comments, these final regulations provide additional guidance on the application of the dual consolidated loss rules to section 953(d)(3) companies, including the treatment of separate units owned by such companies.

(2) *Transactions intended to avoid the limitations of sections 953(d)(3) and 1503(d)*

The IRS and Treasury Department understand that taxpayers may be implementing structures that result in the same overall tax consequences as structures that Congress intended to be subject to the loss limitation rules provided under sections 953(d)(3) and 1503(d). However, taxpayers may be taking the position that the structures are not subject to these loss limitation rules. For example, a foreign insurance company may, in lieu of making an election under section 953(d) and thus being subject to the limitations of sections 953(d)(3) and 1503(d), file a certificate of domestication in a state as a limited liability company. As a business entity with multiple charters, this entity would be treated as a domestic corporation for U.S. tax purposes under §301.7701–2(b)(9). Taxpayers may take the position that this entity would be entitled to the same benefits of a company that makes an election under section 953(d), without being subject to the limitations on the use of its losses that are imposed under sections 953(d)(3) and 1503(d).

The IRS and Treasury Department disagree with the taxpayer's characterization of these structures under current law. In addition, the IRS and Treasury Department believe the taxpayers' characterization of the structures is contrary to the policies underlying section 953(d). Accordingly, the IRS and Treasury Department are considering issuing regulations, which may be retroactive, that would clarify the application of section 953(d)(3) to these structures. These regulations would provide that if a foreign insurance company is eligible to make an election to be treated as a domestic corporation pursuant to section 953(d), but in lieu of making such election becomes a domestic corporation through other means (for example, by filing a certificate of domestication in a state as a limited liability company), then such company shall be subject to the limitations under sections 953(d)(3) and 1503(d) (without regard to paragraph (2)(B) thereof). The IRS and Treasury Department request comments regarding appropriate rules to address these structures and other structures that are intended to avoid the purposes of section 953(d)(3).

O. *All or Nothing Rule*

Under the current regulations a triggering event (other than a foreign use) generally can be rebutted only if no portion of the dual consolidated loss can be used by (or carries over to) another person under foreign law. See §1.1503–2(g)(2)(iii)(A)(*2*) through (*7*). Thus, even a *de minimis* foreign use will cause the entire amount of the dual consolidated loss to be recaptured and reported as income.

The proposed regulations retain this so-called all or nothing principle because the IRS and Treasury Department recognize that departing from it would lead to significant administrative burdens for the Commissioner and taxpayers. Although the all or nothing principle was retained, the IRS and Treasury Department requested comments regarding administrable alternatives that would not involve substantial analysis of foreign law.

Several comments were received with respect to this issue. A number of commentators stated that the final regulations should remove the all or nothing principle and allow for a *pro-rata* recapture such that, for example, the disposition of an individual separate unit, which is part of a combined separate unit, would not result in the entire recapture of the combined separate unit's dual consolidated loss, but only the portion of the loss attributable to the individual separate unit. Another commentator suggested removing the all or nothing rule and allowing a taxpayer to establish that the losses otherwise subject to recapture were not, in fact, used under foreign law. The commentator suggested that any concerns regarding an analysis of foreign law could be mitigated by requiring the taxpayer to provide certified copies of foreign tax returns and, in addition, where the foreign tax base differs substantially from the U.S. tax base, by adopting an apportionment methodology.

The IRS and Treasury Department continue to believe that, even under the approaches suggested by these commentators, departing from the all or nothing principle would lead to substantial administrative complexity. As a result, these comments are not adopted.

Another commentator suggested that the final regulations include a general *de minimis* rule for purposes of applying the triggering and recapture provisions. Under this approach, if a taxpayer could establish that less than a specific percentage of the dual consolidated loss is available for a foreign use, the taxpayer could avoid recapture altogether. However, in situations where the potential loss available for a foreign use exceeds the *de minimis* amount, the dual consolidated loss would be recaptured to the extent it was actually put to a foreign use.

The IRS and Treasury Department do not believe that a *de minimis* rule as described would be meaningful given that the Commissioner and taxpayers would be required to determine the actual amount of the dual consolidated loss available for foreign use, which poses the same administrative concerns as generally departing from the all or nothing principle (that is, a complex analysis of foreign law or complicated ordering, stacking, or tracing rules). As a result, this suggestion is not adopted.

Finally, commentators suggested that following certain events otherwise requiring recapture, a taxpayer should be allowed to reduce the amount of recapture by establishing that a portion of the dual consolidated loss is attributable to items of deduction or loss that, due to permanent differences between the U.S. and foreign tax law, do not give rise to a corresponding item of deduction or loss in the foreign country. The commentators cited items of deduction or loss composing the dual consolidated loss attributable to a basis step-up following a section 338 election, or attributable to a deduction arising from the amortization of goodwill or certain intangibles under section 197, as examples of such items.

The IRS and Treasury Department recognize that items of deduction or loss that are never taken into account in the foreign country cannot be put to a foreign use. However, the IRS and Treasury Department believe that the suggested approach would, in most situations, involve many items of deduction and loss and, as a result, would present the same concerns as are present in the other approaches discussed above. For example, if the deductions giving rise to a dual consolidated loss were the result of a step-up in basis following a section 338 election, but the various assets to which such basis attached had, prior to the election, a basis for foreign tax purposes, complex ordering and stacking rules would be required to determine that, in fact, no portion of the dual consolidated loss is attributable to the pre-existing foreign tax basis. In addition, this approach would require rules to distinguish a permanent (or base) difference from a timing difference, in order to ensure that the portion of the dual consolidated loss that is not being recaptured would not be available for a foreign use at some point in the future. As a result, such rules would add complexity and would be administratively burdensome. Accordingly, this comment is not adopted.

Although these comments are not adopted in the final regulations, the IRS and Treasury Department believe that the application of the all or nothing rule will be significantly reduced under these regulations as a result of the new exceptions to foreign use and the further reduction of the term of the certification period.

P. *Triggering Events and Related Rules*

(1) *Modification of exceptions to triggering events*

The proposed regulations contain exceptions to triggering events that generally apply where assets or interests sold or disposed of are acquired, directly or through certain wholly-owned pass-through entities, by members of the consolidated group that includes the dual resident corporation or separate unit, or by the unaffiliated domestic owner.

The final regulations generally retain these exceptions, but modify them to take into account the new exceptions to foreign use. For example, the exceptions are modified to include certain acquisitions by pass-through entities that are more than 90-percent owned (rather than wholly owned) by the consolidated group or unaffiliated domestic owner. These rules also address certain deemed transactions (for example, pursuant to Rev. Rul. 99–5, 1999–1 C.B. 434) to minimize the likelihood that they result in triggering events, where appropriate, see §601.601(d)(2)(ii)(*b*).

Finally, in response to comments discussed in section G(3) of this preamble, these regulations contain a new exception to triggering events that occur as a result of certain compulsory transfers.

(2) *Rebuttal*

Under the current regulations, taxpayers may rebut all but two of the triggering events such that there is no recapture of a certified dual consolidated loss (or related interest charge) as a result of a putative triggering event. In general, under the current regulations, a triggering event is rebutted if the taxpayer demonstrates to the satisfaction of the Commissioner that, depending on the triggering event, either: (1) the losses, expenses, or deductions of the dual resident corporation (or separate unit) cannot be used to offset income of another person under the laws of a foreign country; or (2) the transfer of assets did not result in a carryover under foreign law of the losses, expenses, or deductions of the dual resident corporation (or separate unit). See §1.1503–2(g)(2)(iii)(A)(*2*) through 1.1503–2(g)(2)(iii)(A)(*7*). The dual consolidated loss rules do not require recapture or an interest charge in such cases because there is no opportunity for any portion of the dual consolidated loss to be used to offset income of any other person under the income tax laws of a foreign country.

The proposed regulations generally retain the rebuttal standard contained in the current regulations, with modifications. Taxpayers may rebut a triggering event under the proposed regulations if it can be demonstrated, to the satisfaction of the Commissioner, that there can be no foreign use of the dual consolidated loss. However, unlike the current regulations that have different standards for different triggering events, the proposed regulations apply the same standard to all triggering events (other than a foreign use triggering event, which cannot be rebutted).

One commentator noted that the rebuttal standard of the proposed regulations is unnecessarily broad with respect to certain asset transfers. For example, according to this commentator, a triggering event cannot be rebutted under this standard where a separate unit transfers over 50 percent of its assets in a transaction that does not result in a loss carryover to the transferee under foreign law. This is the case because the separate unit would not be able to establish that the dual consolidated loss, which did not carry over to the transferee, could never be put to a foreign use. Accordingly, this commentator requested that the rebuttal standard for asset transfers contained in the current regulations be adopted in the final regulations.

The IRS and Treasury Department agree with this comment and these final regulations are modified accordingly.

Another commentator noted that neither the proposed nor current regulations specify how taxpayers must demonstrate that there can be no foreign use during the remaining certification period by any means. The commentator stated that this lack of specificity creates uncertainty and, as a result, requested additional guidance as to how the determination is to be made.

The IRS and Treasury Department believe that this demonstration can be made in a number of ways, including based on the taxpayer's interpretation of foreign law, on an opinion from local advisors, or on assurance from the local country tax authorities. In all cases, however, the determination must be made to the satisfaction of the Commissioner. These final regulations are modified accordingly.

(3) *Reduction of recapture amount*

The proposed regulations permit the elector to reduce the amount of the dual consolidated loss that must be recaptured upon a triggering event. The recapture amount can be reduced to the extent the elector demonstrates that the dual consolidated loss would have offset other income of the dual resident corporation or separate unit reported on a timely filed U.S. income tax return for any taxable year up to and including the taxable year of the triggering event if such loss had been subject to the limitation under §1.1503(d)–2(b) of the proposed regulations.

Commentators questioned the requirements for the reduction of the recapture amount. One commentator suggested that recapture should be reduced by the amount of subsequent income attributable to the dual resident corporation or separate unit, irrespective of the income or loss of other group members.

The IRS and Treasury Department recognize that the policies underlying the SRLY rules differ from those underlying section 1503(d). Although the SRLY rules do not provide for a reduction in recapture in all cases consistent with the views of this commentator, the IRS and Treasury Department continue to believe that the SRLY rules are a reasonable and appropriate mechanism for implementing the restrictions of section 1503(d)(1) in the vast majority of cases. Further, the IRS and Treasury Department believe that deviating from the SRLY mechanism would add considerable complexity to the rules and could lead to unintended consequences. As a result, this comment is not adopted. The IRS and Treasury Department will consider addressing the interaction of the SRLY rules with the recapture provisions in future guidance. Comments are requested as to alternative mechanisms that are more consistent with dual consolidated loss policy and that are not unduly complicated.

(4) *Interest due on recapture*

Under both the current regulations and these final regulations, taxpayers must pay an interest charge in connection with recapture that is computed under the rules of section 6601. In response to comments, these final regulations clarify that this interest charge is deductible to the same extent as interest under section 6601.

(5) *Treatment of recapture income under section 384*

One commentator requested clarification regarding a subsequent elector's agreement to treat potential recapture amounts as unrealized built-in gain for purposes of section 384(a). The commentator stated that it may be unclear as to whether section 384 must otherwise apply to the transaction, whether the thresholds of section 384 apply, and whether potential recapture income treated as unrealized built-in gain is subject to reduction for income earned by a separate unit or dual resident corporation.

The IRS and Treasury Department believe that potential recapture amounts should be treated as unrealized built-in gains for purposes of determining whether section 384 applies, but that the requirements and exceptions of section 384 otherwise apply. In addition, the potential recapture amount treated as unrealized built-in gain may be reduced by potential offset, as permitted under the regulations. These final regulations have been modified accordingly.

(6) *Reconstituted dual consolidated loss*

Both the current and proposed regulations contain a reconstituted loss provision. This rule generally provides that if a dual consolidated loss is recaptured as a result of a triggering event, the dual resident corporation or separate unit that incurred the loss is treated as having a net operating loss in an amount equal to the amount recaptured. The loss is reconstituted in the taxable year immediately following the year of the recapture and is subject to the general restrictions of section 1503(d). This rule is intended to put the taxpayer in the same approximate position it would have been in had it never made an election to use the dual consolidated loss.

These final regulations modify the proposed regulations' reconstituted loss rule to reflect the expansion of the separate unit combination rule and the rules that eliminate dual consolidated losses following certain transactions. In addition, the rule was modified to better take into account the interaction of the dual consolidated loss rules with the general loss carryover rules. For example, these final regulations provide that, other than with respect to the multiple-party event exception, a transfer of an interest in a separate unit by its domestic owner to another corporation cannot cause all or a portion of the dual consolidated loss of such separate unit to carry over to the acquiring corporation, absent the application of section 381.

Q. *Certification Period*

Section 1.1503–2(g)(2)(vi)(B) of the current regulations provides that if a (g)(2)(i) election is made with respect to a dual consolidated loss of a dual resident corporation or a hybrid entity separate unit, the consolidated group, unaffiliated dual resident corporation, or unaffiliated domestic owner, as the case may be, must file with its tax return an annual certification during the 15 year certification period. This filing permits the dual consolidated loss to be used in the United States to offset the income of a domestic affiliate but certifies that the losses or deductions that make up the dual consolidated loss have not been used to offset the income of another person under the tax laws of a foreign country. The current regulations do not require annual certifications for (g)(2)(i) agreements entered into with respect to dual consolidated losses of foreign branch separate units. The current regulations also provide that if there is a triggering event during the 15 year period following the year in which the dual consolidated loss was incurred (certification period), the taxpayer must recapture and report as income the amount of the dual consolidated loss, and pay an interest charge. §1.1503–2(g)(2)(iii)(A).

The proposed regulations reduce the certification period from 15 years to seven years, and expand the annual certification requirement to include dual consolidated losses of foreign branch separate units.

Commentators recommended that the certification period in the proposed regulations be further reduced to five years, because such five-year period would be sufficient to deter the types of double dips with which section 1503(d) is concerned, and would be consistent with time periods used under similar provisions (for example, the term of gain recognition agreements entered into under section 367(a)). The IRS and Treasury Department agree with this comment, and, as a result, the certification period in these final regulations is five years.

Another commentator asserted that extending the annual certification requirement to foreign branch separate units is both unnecessary and administratively burdensome and, as a result, such certification should not be included in these final regulations.

The IRS and Treasury Department continue to believe that the annual certification requirement improves taxpayer compliance and is beneficial in monitoring and deterring inappropriate double dips. In addition, the IRS and Treasury Department believe that, where appropriate, treating foreign branch separate units, hybrid entity separate units, and dual resident corporations consistently for purposes of section 1503(d) will reduce the administrative complexity of these regulations. As a result, this comment is not adopted.

R. *Other Comments and Modifications*

(1) *Information provided with domestic use election*

One commentator recommended that certain information provided with the domestic use election should not bind a taxpayer if the information is provided in good faith, but subsequently is determined to be erroneous. The IRS and Treasury Department believe that adopting this recommendation would be administratively burdensome. Accordingly, this comment is not adopted.

(2) *No possibility of foreign use*

One commentator noted that taxpayers may be eligible to demonstrate no possibility of foreign use, but still choose to enter into a domestic use agreement. The commentator explained that taxpayers may do so to avoid the cost and effort required to satisfy the no possibility of foreign use standard, recognizing that this demonstration would only be beneficial if there is a triggering event during the certification period. The commentator further stated that the taxpayer should nonetheless retain the ability to argue at a later time, when a foreign use may occur after a change in foreign law, that no dual consolidated loss existed in the year in which the loss was actually incurred. Thus, if there was a change in foreign law, taxpayers would not be penalized for being unable to rebut the triggering event in the current year (due to a change in foreign law) but could instead rely on the foreign law in effect for the year in which the loss was incurred.

The IRS and Treasury Department recognize that taxpayers may simply choose to file a domestic use election, rather than engage in additional efforts to demonstrate no possibility of foreign use. The IRS and Treasury Department believe that these final regulations provide ample opportunities for taxpayers willing to demonstrate no possibility of foreign use. Taxpayers have three opportunities to demonstrate no possibility of foreign use under the final regulations: first under §1.1503(d)–6(c) to be excepted from the domestic use limitation, second under §1.1503(d)–6(e)(2) to rebut a triggering event, and third under §1.1503(d)–6(j)(2) to terminate a domestic use agreement. Because of these opportunities and the administrative burdens that would ensue from taking into account changes in foreign law, this comment is not adopted.

S. *Effective Dates*

(1) *General rule*

Except as provided in this preamble, these final regulations apply to dual consolidated losses incurred in taxable years beginning on or after April 18, 2007. However, a taxpayer may apply these regulations, in their entirety, to dual consolidated losses incurred in taxable years beginning on or after January 1, 2007.

(2) *Certification period*

A number of commentators requested that the reduced certification period of these final regulations apply with respect to dual consolidated losses that are subject to the current regulations. The commentators asserted that the policies underlying the reduced certification period should apply equally to dual consolidated losses that are subject to the current regulations. Commentators also recommended that the reduced certification period contained in these final regulations apply to closing agreements entered into between taxpayers and the IRS pursuant to §1.1503–2(g)(2)(iv)(B)(*3*)(*i*) and Rev. Proc. 2000–42, 2000–2 C.B. 394, see §601.601(d)(2)(ii)(*b*).

The IRS and Treasury Department generally agree with these comments and these final regulations are modified accordingly.

(3) *Reasonable cause exception*

These final regulations adopt the reasonable cause procedure for purposes of curing all late filings as introduced in the proposed regulations, and subsequently modified by Notice 2006–13, 2006–8 I.R.B. 496, see §601.601(d)(2)(ii)(*b*). Moreover, these final regulations provide that the reasonable cause procedures supplant the current procedures for all untimely filings with respect to dual consolidated losses incurred under the current regulations as well, except with respect to requests for closing agreements. Taxpayers requiring relief to cure a late request for a closing agreement must continue to seek extensions of time under §§301.9100–1 through 301.9100–3 and Rev. Proc. 2000–42, 2000–2 C.B. 394, see §601.601(d)(2)(ii)(*b*). Taxpayers seeking relief for other late filings required in connection with such closing agreements must, however, use the reasonable cause procedure of these final regulations. Therefore, as a result of these changes, untimely filings under section 1503(d) and these regulations will no longer be eligible for the relief provided by §§301.9100–1 through 301.9100–3, regardless of whether such filings were required under the current regulations (except for certain closing agreements) or these final regulations.

(4) *Multiple-party event exception to triggering events*

These final regulations provide an exception to certain triggering events involving multiple parties. In general, the exceptions provided under these final regulations with respect to multiple-party events are similar to those provided under §1.1503–2(g)(2)(iv)(B)(*1*). The procedures required to satisfy these multiple-party event exceptions are also similar to those found in §1.1503–2(g)(2)(iv)(B)(*3*). One important difference is that these final regulations do not require (or permit) taxpayers to obtain closing agreements. These final regulations also provide a special effective date provision with respect to events described in §1.1503–2(g)(2)(iv)(B)(*1*) that occur after April 18, 2007, that are with respect to dual consolidated losses subject to the current regulations. Such events are not eligible for the exception described in §1.1503–2(g)(2)(iv)(B)(*1*) and thus are not eligible for a closing agreement as described in §1.1503–2(g)(2)(iv)(B)(*3*)(*i*). Instead, such events are eligible for the multiple-party event exception described in these final regulations and as modified by the special effective date provision of §1.1503(d)–8(b)(4). Taxpayers may, however, choose to apply the multiple-party exception to events described in §1.1503–2(g)(2)(iv)(B)(*1*)(*i*) through (*iii*) that occur after March 19, 2007 and on or before April 18, 2007.

(5) *Basis adjustments*

One commentator requested that the elimination of the special basis adjustments described in paragraph M of this preamble be applied retroactively. The commentator further requested that such retroactive application apply to adjustments that occurred in closed taxable years if the basis of the stock is relevant in an open taxable year.

The IRS and Treasury Department agree with this comment. As a result, these regulations provide that taxpayers may apply the basis adjustment rules of these final regulations for all taxable years if such adjustments affected tax basis that is relevant in an open taxable year.

(6) *Other provisions*

A number of commentators requested that the IRS and Treasury Department provide that taxpayers be allowed to electively apply other provisions of these regulations to dual consolidated losses that are subject to the current regulations.

The IRS and Treasury Department do not believe that it would be appropriate to allow taxpayers to selectively apply provisions of these regulations (other than those that the IRS and Treasury Department view as clarifications) retroactively, because it would lead to administrative complexity for the IRS and could lead to unintended results.

Effect on Other Documents

These final regulations obsolete Notice 2006–13, 2006–8 I.R.B. 496, see §601.601(d)(2)(ii)(*b*). These final regulations also obsolete Rev. Proc. 2000–42, 2000–2 C.B. 394, see §601.601(d)(2)(ii)(*b*), with respect to triggering events occurring after April 18, 2007.

Special Analyses

It has been determined that this Treasury decision is not a significant regulatory action as defined in Executive Order 12866. Therefore, a regulatory assessment is not required. It is hereby certified that these regulations will not have a significant economic impact on a substantial number of small entities. This certification is based on the fact that these regulations will primarily affect affiliated groups of corporations that also have a foreign affiliate, which tend to be larger businesses. Moreover, the number of taxpayers affected and the average burden are minimal. Therefore, a Regulatory Flexibility Analysis is not required. Pursuant to section 7805(f) of the Internal Revenue Code, the notice of proposed rulemaking preceding this regulation was submitted to the Chief Counsel for Advocacy of the Small Business for comment on its impact on small business.

Drafting Information

The principal authors of these regulations are Jeffrey P. Cowan, of the Office of the Associate Chief Counsel (International), and Christopher L. Trump, formerly of the Office of the Associate Chief Counsel (International). However, other personnel from the IRS and Treasury Department participated in their development.

* * * * *

Adoption of Amendments to the Regulations

Accordingly, 26 CFR parts 1 and 602 are amended as follows:

PART 1—INCOME TAXES

Paragraph 1. The authority citation for part 1 is amended by adding an entry in numerical order to read in part as follows:

Authority: 26 U.S.C. 7805 * * *

Section 1.1503(d) also issued under 26 U.S.C. 953(d) and 26 U.S.C. 1502.

§1.1502–21 [Amended]

Par. 2. In §1.1502–21, paragraph (c)(2)(v) is amended by removing the language "§1.1503–2" and adding "§§1.1503(d)–1 through 1.1503(d)–8" in its place.

§1.1503–2A [Removed]

Par. 3. Section 1.1503–2A is removed.

Par. 4. New §§1.1503(d)–0 through 1.1503(d)–8 are added to read as follows:

§1.1503(d)–0 Table of contents.

This section lists the captions contained in §§1.1503(d)–1 through 1.1503(d)–8.

(i) Certain section 368(a)(1)(F) reorganizations.

(ii) Acquisition of a dual resident corporation by another dual resident corporation.

(iii) Acquisition of a separate unit by a domestic corporation.

(A) Acquisition by a corporation that is not a member of the same consolidated group.

(B) Acquisition by a member of the same consolidated group.

(iv) Special rules for foreign insurance companies.

(e) Special rule denying the use of a dual consolidated loss to offset tainted income.

(1) In general.

(2) Tainted income.

(i) Definition.

(ii) Income presumed to be derived from holding tainted assets.

(3) Tainted assets defined.

(4) Exceptions.

(f) Computation of foreign tax credit limitation.

§1.1503(d)–5 Attribution of items and basis adjustments.

(a) In general.

(b) Determination of amount of income or dual consolidated loss of a dual resident corporation.

(1) In general.

(2) Exceptions.

(c) Determination of amount of income or dual consolidated loss attributable to a separate unit, and income or loss attributable to an interest in a transparent entity.

(1) In general.

(i) Scope and purpose.

(ii) Only items of domestic owner taken into account.

(iii) Separate application.

(2) Foreign branch separate unit.

(i) In general.

(ii) Principles of §1.882–5.

(iii) Exception where foreign country attributes interest expense solely by reference to books and records.

(3) Hybrid entity separate unit and an interest in a transparent entity.

(i) General rule.

(ii) Interests in certain disregarded entities, partnerships, and grantor trusts owned by a hybrid entity or transparent entity.

(4) Special rules.

(i) Allocation of items between certain tiered separate units and interests in transparent entities.

(A) Foreign branch separate unit.

(B) Hybrid entity separate unit or interest in a transparent entity.

(ii) Combined separate unit.

(iii) Gain or loss on the direct or indirect disposition of a separate unit or an interest in a transparent entity.

(A) In general.

(B) Multiple separate units or interests in transparent entities.

(iv) Inclusions on stock.

(v) Foreign currency gain or loss recognized under section 987.

(vi) Recapture of dual consolidated loss.

(d) Foreign tax treatment disregarded.

(e) Items generated or incurred while a dual resident corporation, a separate unit, or a transparent entity.

(f) Assets and liabilities of a separate unit or an interest in a transparent entity.

(g) Basis adjustments.

(1) Affiliated dual resident corporation or affiliated domestic owner.

(2) Interests in hybrid entities that are partnerships or interests in partnerships through which a separate unit is owned indirectly.

(i) Scope.

(ii) Determination of basis of partner's interest.

(3) Combined separate units.

§1.1503(d)–6 Exceptions to the domestic use limitation rule.

(a) In general.

(1) Scope and purpose.

(2) Absence of foreign affiliate or foreign consolidation regime.

(3) Foreign insurance companies treated as domestic corporations.

(b) Elective agreement in place between the United States and a foreign country.

(1) In general.

(2) Application to combined separate units.

(c) No possibility of foreign use.

(1) In general.

(2) Statement.

(d) Domestic use election.

(1) In general.

(2) No domestic use election available if there is a triggering event in the year the dual consolidated loss is incurred.

(e) Triggering events requiring the recapture of a dual consolidated loss.

(1) Events.

(i) Foreign use.

(ii) Disaffiliation.

(iii) Affiliation.

(iv) Transfer of assets.

(v) Transfer of an interest in a separate unit.

(vi) Conversion to a foreign corporation.

(vii) Conversion to a regulated investment company, a real estate investment trust, or an S corporation.

(viii) Failure to certify.

(ix) Cessation of stand-alone status.

(2) Rebuttal.

(i) General rule.

(ii) Certain asset transfers.

(iii) Reporting.

(iv) Examples.

(f) Triggering event exceptions.

(1) Continuing ownership of assets or interests.

(i) Disaffiliation as a result of a transaction described in section 381.

(ii) Continuing ownership by consolidated group.

(iii) Continuing ownership by unaffiliated dual resident corporation or unaffiliated domestic owner.

(2) Transactions requiring a new domestic use agreement.

(i) Multiple-party events.

(ii) Events resulting in a single consolidated group.

(iii) Requirements.

(A) New domestic use agreement.

(B) Statement filed by original elector.

(3) Certain transfers qualifying for the *de minimis* exception to foreign use.

(4) Deemed transactions as a result of certain transfers that do not result in a foreign use.

(5) Compulsory transfers.

(6) Subsequent triggering events.

(g) Annual certification reporting requirement.

(h) Recapture of dual consolidated loss and interest charge.

(1) Presumptive rules.

(i) Amount of recapture.

(ii) Interest charge.

(2) Reduction of presumptive recapture amount and presumptive interest charge.

(i) Amount of recapture.

(ii) Interest charge.

(3) Rules regarding multiple-party event exceptions to triggering events.

(i) Scope.

(ii) Original elector and prior subsequent electors not subject to recapture or interest charge.

(iii) Recapture tax amount and required statement.

(A) In general.

(B) Recapture tax amount.

(iv) Tax assessment and collection procedures.

(A) In general.

(B) Collection from original elector and prior subsequent electors; joint and several liability.

(C) Allocation of partial payments of tax.

(D) Refund.

(v) Definition of income tax liability.

(vi) Example.

(4) Computation of taxable income in year of recapture.

(i) Presumptive rule.

(ii) Exception to presumptive rule.

(5) Character and source of recapture income.

(6) Reconstituted net operating loss.

(i) General rule.

(ii) Exception.

(iii) Special rule for recapture following multiple-party event exception to a triggering event.

(i) [Reserved].

(j) Termination of domestic use agreement and annual certifications.

(1) Rebuttals, exceptions to triggering events, and recapture.

(2) Termination of ability for foreign use.

(i) In general.

(ii) Statement.

(3) Agreements filed in connection with stand-alone exception.

§1.1503(d)–7 Examples.

(a) In general.

(b) Presumed facts for examples.

(c) Examples.

§1.1503(d)–8 Effective dates.

(a) General rule.

(b) Special rules.

(1) Reduction of term of agreements filed under §§1.1503–2(g)(2)(i) or 1.1503–2T(g)(2)(i).

(2) Reduction of term of closing agreements entered into pursuant to §1.1503–2(g)(2)(iv)(B)(*3*)(*i*).

(3) Relief for untimely filings.

(i) General rule.

(ii) Closing agreements.

(iii) Pending requests for relief.

(4) Multiple-party event exception to triggering events.

(5) Basis adjustment rules.

§1.1503(d)–1 Definitions and special rules for filings under section 1503(d).

(a) *In general.* This section and §§1.1503(d)–2 through 1.1503(d)–8 provide rules concerning the determination and use of dual consolidated losses pursuant to section 1503(d). Paragraph (b) of this section provides definitions that apply for purposes of this section and §§1.1503(d)–2 through 1.1503(d)–8. Paragraph (c) of this section provides a reasonable cause exception and a signature requirement for filings.

(b) *Definitions.* The following definitions apply for purposes of this section and §§1.1503(d)–2 through 1.1503(d)–8:

(1) *Domestic corporation* means an entity classified as a domestic corporation under section 7701(a)(3) and (4) or otherwise treated as a domestic corporation by the Internal Revenue Code, including, but not limited to, sections 269B, 953(d), 1504(d), and 7874. However, solely for purposes of section 1503(d), the term domestic corporation shall not include a regulated investment company as defined in section 851, a real estate investment trust as defined in section 856, or an S corporation as defined in section 1361.

(2) *Dual resident corporation* means—

(i) A domestic corporation that is subject to an income tax of a foreign country on its worldwide income or on a residence basis. A corporation is taxed on a residence basis if it is taxed as a resident under the laws of the foreign country; and

(ii) A foreign insurance company that makes an election to be treated as a domestic corporation pursuant to section 953(d) and is treated as a member of an affiliated group for purposes of chapter 6, even if such company is not subject to an income tax of a foreign country on its worldwide income or on a residence basis. See section 953(d)(3).

(3) *Hybrid entity* means an entity that is not taxable as an association for Federal tax purposes, but is subject to an income tax of a foreign country as a corporation (or otherwise at the entity level) either on its worldwide income or on a residence basis.

(4) *Separate unit*—(i) *In general.* The term *separate unit* means either of the following that is carried on or owned, as applicable, directly or indirectly, by a domestic corporation (including a dual resident corporation):

(A) Except to the extent provided in paragraph (b)(4)(iii) of this section, a business operation outside the United States that, if carried on by a U.S. person, would constitute a foreign branch as defined in §1.367(a)–6T(g)(1) (foreign branch separate unit).

(B) An interest in a hybrid entity (hybrid entity separate unit).

(ii) *Separate unit combination rule.* Except as otherwise provided in this paragraph, if a domestic owner, or two or more domestic owners that are members of the same consolidated group, have two or more separate units (individual separate units), then all such individual separate units that are located (in the case of a foreign branch separate unit) or subject to an income tax either on their worldwide income or on a residence basis (in the case of a hybrid entity an interest in which is a hybrid entity separate unit) in the same foreign country shall be treated as one separate unit (combined separate unit). See §1.1503(d)–7(c) *Example 1.* Separate units of a foreign insurance company that is a dual resident corporation under paragraph (b)(2)(ii) of this section, however, shall not be combined with separate units of any other domestic corporation. Except as specifically provided in this section or §§1.1503(d)–2 through 1.1503(d)–8, any individual separate unit composing a combined separate unit loses its character as an individual separate unit.

(iii) *Business operations that do not constitute a permanent establishment.* A business operation carried on by a domestic corporation that is not a dual resident corporation shall not constitute a foreign branch separate unit, provided the business operation:

(A) Is not carried on indirectly through a hybrid entity or a transparent entity; and

(B) Is conducted in a country with which the United States has entered into an income tax convention and is not treated as a permanent establishment pursuant to that convention, or is not otherwise subject to tax on a net basis under that convention. See §1.1503(d)–7(c) *Example 2*.

(iv) *Foreign branch separate units held by dual resident corporations or hybrid entities in the same foreign country*. A foreign branch separate unit may be owned by a dual resident corporation, or through a hybrid entity (an interest in which is a separate unit), even where the foreign branch is located in the same foreign country that subjects such dual resident corporation or hybrid entity to tax on its worldwide income or on a residence basis. But see the rule under paragraph (b)(4)(ii) of this section that combines certain same-country hybrid entity separate units and foreign branch separate units. See also §1.1503(d)–7(c) *Example 1*.

(5) *Dual consolidated loss* means—

(i) In the case of a dual resident corporation, and except to the extent provided in §1.1503(d)–5(b), the net operating loss (as defined in section 172(c) and the related regulations) incurred in a year in which the corporation is a dual resident corporation; and

(ii) In the case of a separate unit, the net loss attributable to the separate unit under §1.1503(d)–5(c) through (e).

(6) *Subject to tax*. For purposes of determining whether a domestic corporation or another entity is subject to an income tax of a foreign country on its income, the fact that it has no actual income tax liability to the foreign country for a particular taxable year shall not be taken into account.

(7) *Foreign country* includes any possession of the United States.

(8) *Consolidated group* has the meaning provided in §1.1502–1(h).

(9) *Domestic owner* means—

(i) A domestic corporation (including a dual resident corporation) that has one or more separate units or interests in a transparent entity; and

(ii) In the case of a combined separate unit, a domestic corporation (including a dual resident corporation) that has one or more individual separate units that are treated as part of the combined separate unit under paragraph (b)(4)(ii) of this section.

(10) *Affiliated dual resident corporation* and *affiliated domestic owner* mean a dual resident corporation and a domestic owner, respectively, that is a member of a consolidated group.

(11) *Unaffiliated dual resident corporation*, *unaffiliated domestic corporation*, and *unaffiliated domestic owner* mean a dual resident corporation, domestic corporation, and domestic owner, respectively, that is not a member of a consolidated group.

(12) *Domestic affiliate* means—

(i) A member of an affiliated group, without regard to the exceptions contained in section 1504(b) (other than section 1504(b)(3)) relating to includible corporations;

(ii) A domestic owner;

(iii) A separate unit; or

(iv) An interest in a transparent entity, as defined in paragraph (b)(16) of this section.

(13) *Domestic use*. See §1.1503(d)–2.

(14) *Foreign use*. See §1.1503(d)–3.

(15) *Grantor trust* means a trust, any portion of which is treated as being owned by the grantor or another person under subpart E of subchapter J of this chapter.

(16) *Transparent entity*—(i) *In general*. The term *transparent entity* means an entity described in this paragraph (b)(16) where all or a portion of its interests are owned, directly or indirectly, by a domestic corporation. An entity is described in this paragraph (b)(16) if the entity—

(A) Is not taxable as an association for Federal tax purposes;

(B) Is not subject to income tax in a foreign country as a corporation (or otherwise at the entity level) either on its worldwide income or on a residence basis; and

(C) Is not a pass-through entity under the laws of the applicable foreign country. For purposes of applying the preceding sentence, the applicable foreign country is the foreign country in which the relevant foreign branch separate unit is located, or the foreign country that subjects the relevant hybrid entity (an interest in which is a separate unit) or dual resident corporation to an income tax either on its worldwide income or on a residence basis.

(ii) *Example*. A U.S. limited liability company (LLC) does not elect to be taxed as an association for Federal tax purposes and is not subject to income tax in a foreign country as a corporation (or otherwise at the entity level) either on its worldwide income or on a residence basis. The LLC is owned by a hybrid entity (an interest in which is a separate unit) that is the relevant hybrid entity. Provided the LLC is not treated as a pass-through entity by the applicable foreign country that subjects the relevant hybrid entity to an income tax either on its worldwide income or on a residence basis, the LLC would qualify as a transparent entity. See also §1.1503(d)–7(c) *Example 26*.

(17) *Disregarded entity* means an entity that is disregarded as an entity separate from its owner, under §§301.7701–1 through 301.7701–3 of this chapter, for Federal tax purposes.

(18) *Partnership* means an entity that is classified as a partnership, under §§301.7701–1 through 301.7701–3 of this chapter, for Federal tax purposes.

(19) *Indirectly*, when used in reference to ownership, means ownership through a partnership, a disregarded entity, or a grantor trust, regardless of whether the partnership, disregarded entity, or grantor trust is a U.S. person.

(20) *Certification period* means the period of time up to and including the fifth taxable year following the year in which the dual consolidated loss that is the subject of a domestic use agreement (as described in §1.1503(d)–6(d)(1)) was incurred.

(c) *Special rules for filings under section 1503(d)*—(1) *Reasonable cause exception*. A person that is permitted or required to file an election, agreement, statement, rebuttal, computation, or other information pursuant to section 1503(d) and these regulations, that fails to make such filing in a timely manner, shall be considered to have satisfied the timeliness requirement with respect to such filing if the person is able to demonstrate, to the Area Director, Field Examination, Small Business/Self Employed or the Director of Field Operations, Large and Mid-Size Business (Director) having jurisdiction of the taxpayer's tax return for the taxable year, that such failure was due to reasonable cause and not willful neglect. In determining whether the taxpayer has reasonable cause, the Director shall consider whether the taxpayer acted reasonably and in good faith. In general, the taxpayer must demonstrate that it exercised ordinary care and prudence in meeting its tax obligations but nonetheless did not comply with the prescribed duty within the prescribed time. Whether the taxpayer acted reasonably and in good faith will be determined after considering all the facts and circumstances. The Director shall notify the person in writing within 120 days of the filing if it is determined that the failure to comply was not due to reasonable cause, or if additional time will be needed to make such determination. For this purpose, the 120-day period shall begin on the date the taxpayer is notified in writing that the request has been received and assigned for review. If, once such period commences, the taxpayer is not again notified within 120 days, then the taxpayer shall be deemed to have established reasonable cause. The reasonable cause exception of this paragraph (c) shall only apply if, once the person becomes aware of its failure to file the election, agreement, statement, rebuttal, computation or other information in a timely manner, the person complies with the requirements of paragraph (c)(2) of this section.

(2) *Requirements for reasonable cause relief*—(i) *Time of submission.* Requests for reasonable cause relief will only be considered if once the person becomes aware of the failure to file the election, agreement, statement, rebuttal, computation or other information, the person attaches all the documents that should have been filed, as well as a written statement setting forth the reasons for the failure to timely comply, to an amended return that amends the return to which the documents should have been attached pursuant to the rules of section 1503(d) and these regulations.

(ii) *Notice requirement.* In addition to the requirements of paragraph (c)(2)(i) of this section, the taxpayer must provide a copy of the amended return and all required attachments to the Director as follows:

(A) If the taxpayer is under examination for any taxable year when the taxpayer requests relief, the taxpayer must provide a copy of the amended return and attachments to the personnel conducting the examination.

(B) If the taxpayer is not under examination for any taxable year when the taxpayer requests relief, the taxpayer must provide a copy of the amended return and attachments to the Director having jurisdiction of the taxpayer's return.

(3) *Signature requirement.* When an election, agreement, statement, rebuttal, computation, or other information is required pursuant to section 1503(d) and these regulations to be attached to and filed by the due date (including extensions) of a U.S. tax return and signed under penalties of perjury by the person who signs the return, the attachment and filing of an unsigned copy is considered to satisfy such requirement, provided the taxpayer retains the original in its records in the manner specified by §1.6001–1(e).

§1.1503(d)–2 Domestic use.

A *domestic use* of a dual consolidated loss shall be deemed to occur when the dual consolidated loss is made available to offset, directly or indirectly, the income of a domestic affiliate (other than the dual resident corporation or separate unit that, in each case, incurred the dual consolidated loss) in the taxable year in which the dual consolidated loss is recognized, or in any other taxable year, regardless of whether the dual consolidated loss offsets income under the income tax laws of a foreign country and regardless of whether any income that the dual consolidated loss may offset in the foreign country is, has been, or will be subject to tax in the United States. A domestic use shall be deemed to occur in the year the dual consolidated loss is included in the computation of the taxable income of a consolidated group, unaffiliated dual resident corporation, or an unaffiliated domestic owner, as applicable, even if no tax benefit results from such inclusion in that year. See §1.1503(d)–7(c) *Examples 2* through *4*.

§1.1503(d)–3 Foreign use.

(a) *Foreign use*—(1) *In general.* Except as provided in paragraph (c) of this section, a *foreign use* of a dual consolidated loss shall be deemed to occur when any portion of a deduction or loss taken into account in computing the dual consolidated loss is made available under the income tax laws of a foreign country to offset or reduce, directly or indirectly, any item that is recognized as income or gain under such laws and that is, or would be, considered under U.S. tax principles to be an item of—

(i) A foreign corporation as defined in section 7701(a)(3) and (a)(5); or

(ii) A direct or indirect owner of an interest in a hybrid entity, provided such interest is not a separate unit. See §1.1503(d)–7(c) *Examples 5* through *10* and *37*.

(2) *Indirect use*—(i) *General rule.* Except to the extent provided in paragraph (a)(2)(ii) of this section, an item of deduction or loss shall be deemed to be made available indirectly if—

(A) One or more items are taken into account as deductions or losses for foreign tax purposes, but do not give rise to corresponding items of income or gain for U.S. tax purposes; and

(B) The item or items described in paragraph (a)(2)(i)(A) of this section have the effect of making an item of deduction or loss composing the dual consolidated loss available for a foreign use as described in paragraph (a)(1) of this section.

(ii) *Exception.* The general rule provided in paragraph (a)(2)(i) of this section shall not apply if the consolidated group, unaffiliated domestic owner, or unaffiliated dual resident corporation demonstrates, to the satisfaction of the Commissioner, that the item or items described in paragraph (a)(2)(i)(A) of this section that gave rise to the indirect foreign use—

(A) Were not incurred, or taken into account, with a principal purpose of avoiding the provisions of section 1503(d). For purposes of this paragraph (a)(2)(ii), an item incurred or taken into account as interest for foreign tax purposes, but disregarded for U.S. tax purposes, shall be deemed to have been incurred, or taken into account, with a principal purpose of avoiding the provisions of section 1503(d). Similarly, for purposes of this paragraph (a)(2)(ii), an item incurred or taken into account as the result of an instrument that is treated as debt for foreign tax purposes and equity for U.S. tax purposes, shall be deemed to have been incurred, or taken into account, with a principal purpose of avoiding the provisions of section 1503(d); and

(B) Were incurred, or taken into account, in the ordinary course of the dual resident corporation's or separate unit's trade or business.

(iii) *Examples.* See §1.1503(d)–7(c) *Examples 6* through *8*.

(3) *Deemed use.* See paragraph (e) of this section for a deemed foreign use pursuant to the mirror legislation rule.

(b) *Available for use.* A foreign use shall be deemed to occur in the year in which any portion of a deduction or loss taken into account in computing the dual consolidated loss is made available for an offset described in paragraph (a) of this section, regardless of whether it actually offsets or reduces any items of income or gain under the income tax laws of the foreign country in such year, and regardless of whether any of the items that may be so offset or reduced are regarded as income under U.S. tax principles.

(c) *Exceptions*—(1) *In general*. Paragraphs (c)(2) through (9) of this section provide exceptions to the general definition of foreign use set forth in paragraphs (a) and (b) of this section. These exceptions only apply to a foreign use that occurs solely as a result of the conditions or circumstances described therein, and do not apply if a foreign use occurs in any other case or by any other means. For example, the exception under paragraph (c)(4) of this section (regarding certain interests in partnerships or grantor trusts) shall not apply where the item of deduction or loss is made available through a foreign consolidation regime (or similar method). In addition, these exceptions do not apply when attempting to demonstrate that no foreign use of a dual consolidated loss can occur in any other year by any means under §1.1503(d)–6(c), (e)(2)(i), or (j)(2). But see §1.1503(d)–6(e)(2)(ii), which takes into account the exception under paragraph (c)(7) of this section for purposes of rebutting certain asset transfers.

(2) *Election or merger required to enable foreign use*. Where the laws of a foreign country provide an election that would enable a foreign use, a foreign use shall be considered to occur only if the election is made. Similarly, where the laws of a foreign country would enable a foreign use through a sale, merger, or similar transaction, a foreign use shall be considered to occur only if the sale, merger, or similar transaction occurs.

(3) *Presumed use where no foreign country rule for determining use*. This paragraph (c)(3) applies if the losses or deductions composing the dual consolidated loss are made available under the laws of a foreign country both to offset income that would constitute a foreign use and to offset income that would not constitute a foreign use, and the laws of the foreign country do not provide applicable rules for determining which income is offset by the losses or deductions. In such a case, the losses or deductions shall be deemed to be made available to offset the income that does not constitute a foreign use, to the extent of such income, before being considered to be made available to offset the income that does constitute a foreign use. See §1.1503(d)–7(c) *Example 11*.

(4) *Certain interests in partnerships or grantor trusts*—(i) *General rule*. Except to the extent provided in paragraph (c)(4)(iii) of this section, this paragraph (c)(4)(i) applies to a dual consolidated loss attributable to an interest in a hybrid entity partnership or a hybrid entity grantor trust, or to a separate unit owned indirectly through a partnership or grantor trust. In such a case, a foreign use will not be considered to occur if the foreign use is solely the result of another person's ownership of an interest in the partnership or grantor trust, as applicable, and the allocation or carry forward of an item of deduction or loss composing such dual consolidated loss as a result of such ownership. See §1.1503(d)–7(c) *Example 13*.

(ii) *Combined separate unit*. This paragraph applies to a dual consolidated loss attributable to a combined separate unit that includes an individual separate unit to which paragraph (c)(4)(i) of this section would apply, but for the application of the separate unit combination rule provided under §1.1503(d)–1(b)(4)(ii). In such a case, paragraph (c)(4)(i) of this section shall apply to the portion of the dual consolidated loss of such combined separate unit that is attributable, as provided under §1.1503(d)–5(c) through (e), to the individual separate unit (otherwise described in paragraph (c)(4)(i) of this section) that is a component of the combined separate unit. See §1.1503(d)–7(c) *Example 14*.

(iii) *Reduction in interest*. The exception under paragraph (c)(4)(i) of this section shall not apply if, at any time following the year in which the dual consolidated loss is incurred, there is more than a *de minimis* reduction in the domestic owner's percentage interest in the partnership or grantor trust, as applicable, as described in paragraph (c)(5) of this section. In such a case, a foreign use shall be deemed to occur at the time the reduction in interest exceeds the *de minimis* amount. See §1.1503(d)–7(c) *Example 13*.

(5) *De minimis reduction of an interest in a separate unit*—(i) *General rule*. This paragraph applies to a *de minimis* reduction of a domestic owner's interest in a separate unit (including an interest described in paragraph (c)(4)(i) of this section). Except to the extent provided in paragraph (c)(5)(ii) of this section, no foreign use shall be considered to occur with respect to a dual consolidated loss as a result of an item of deduction or loss composing such dual consolidated loss being made available solely as a result of a reduction in the domestic owner's interest in the separate unit, as provided under paragraph (c)(5)(iii) of this section. See §1.1503(d)–7(c) *Example 5*.

(ii) *Limitations*. The exception provided in paragraph (c)(5)(i) of this section shall not apply if—

(A) During any 12-month period the domestic owner's percentage interest in the separate unit is reduced by 10 percent or more, as determined by reference to the domestic owner's interest at the beginning of the 12-month period; or

(B) At any time the domestic owner's percentage interest in the separate unit is reduced by 30 percent or more, as determined by reference to the domestic owner's interest at the end of the taxable year in which the dual consolidated loss was incurred.

(iii) *Reduction in interest*. The following rules apply for purposes of paragraphs (c)(4) and (5) of this section. A reduction of a domestic owner's interest in a separate unit shall include a reduction resulting from another person acquiring through sale, exchange, contribution, or other means, an interest in the foreign branch or hybrid entity, as applicable. A reduction may occur either directly or indirectly, including through an interest in a partnership, a disregarded entity, or a grantor trust through which a separate unit is carried on or owned. In the case of an interest in a hybrid entity partnership or a separate unit all or a portion of which is carried on or owned through a partnership, an interest in such separate unit (or portion of such separate unit) is determined by reference to the owner's interest in the profits or the capital in the separate unit. In the case of an interest in a hybrid entity grantor trust or a separate unit all or a portion of which is carried on or owned through a grantor trust, an interest in such separate unit (or portion of such separate unit) is determined by reference to the domestic owner's share of the assets and liabilities of the separate unit.

(iv) *Examples and coordination with exceptions to other triggering events*. See

§1.1503(d)–7(c) *Examples 5*, *13*, and *14*. See also §1.1503(d)–6(f)(3) and (f)(5) for rules that coordinate the *de minimis* exception to foreign use with exceptions to other triggering events described in §1.1503(d)–6(e)(1), and provide an exception to foreign use following certain compulsory transfers.

(6) *Certain asset basis carryovers*. No foreign use shall be considered to occur with respect to a dual consolidated loss solely as a result of items of deduction or loss composing such dual consolidated loss being made available as a result of the transfer of assets of a dual resident corporation or separate unit, provided—

(i) Such items of loss and deduction are made available solely as a result of the basis of the transferred assets being determined, under foreign law, in whole or in part by reference to the basis of the assets in the hands of the dual resident corporation or separate unit;

(ii) The aggregate adjusted basis, as determined under U.S. tax principles, of all the assets so transferred during any 12-month period is less than 10 percent of the aggregate adjusted basis, as determined under U.S. tax principles, of all the dual resident corporation's or separate unit's assets, determined by reference to the assets held at the beginning of such 12-month period; and

(iii) The aggregate adjusted basis, as determined under U.S. tax principles, of all the assets so transferred at any time is less than 30 percent of the aggregate adjusted basis, as determined under U.S. tax principles, of all the dual resident corporation's or separate unit's assets, determined by reference to the assets held at the end of the taxable year in which the dual consolidated loss was generated. See §1.1503(d)–7(c) *Example 15*.

(7) *Assumption of certain liabilities*—(i) *In general*. Except to the extent provided in paragraph (c)(7)(ii) of this section, no foreign use shall be considered to occur with respect to any dual consolidated loss solely as a result of an item of deduction or loss composing such dual consolidated loss being made available following the assumption of liabilities of a dual resident corporation or separate unit, provided such availability arises solely as the result of an item of deduction or loss incurred with respect to, or as a result of, such liabilities. See §1.1503(d)–7(c) *Example 16*.

(ii) *Ordinary course limitation*. Paragraph (c)(7)(i) of this section shall apply only to the extent the liabilities assumed were incurred in the ordinary course of the dual resident corporation's, or separate unit's, trade or business. For purposes of this paragraph, liabilities incurred in the ordinary course of a trade or business shall include debt incurred to finance the trade or business of the dual resident corporation or separate unit.

(8) *Multiple-party events*. This paragraph applies to a transaction that qualifies for the triggering event exception described in §1.1503(d)–6(f)(2)(i)(B) where the acquiring unaffiliated domestic corporation or consolidated group owns, directly or indirectly, more than 90 percent, but less than 100 percent, of the transferred assets or interests immediately after the transaction. In such a case, no foreign use shall be considered to occur with respect to a dual consolidated loss of the dual resident corporation or separate unit whose assets or interests were acquired, solely as a result of the less than 10 percent direct or indirect ownership of the acquired assets or interests by persons other than the acquiring unaffiliated domestic corporation or consolidated group, as applicable, immediately after the transaction. See §1.1503(d)–7(c) *Example 37*.

(9) *Additional guidance*. The Commissioner may provide, by guidance published in the Internal Revenue Bulletin, that certain events or transactions do or do not result in a foreign use. Such guidance may also modify the triggering events and rebuttals described in §1.1503(d)–6(e), and the exceptions thereto under §1.1503(d)–6(f), as appropriate.

(d) *Ordering rules for determining the foreign use of losses*. If the laws of a foreign country provide for the foreign use of losses of a dual resident corporation or a separate unit, but do not provide applicable rules for determining the order in which such losses are used in a taxable year, the following rules shall apply:

(1) Any net loss, or net income, that the dual resident corporation or separate unit has in a taxable year shall first be used to offset net income, or loss, recognized by its affiliates in the same taxable year before any carry over of its losses is considered to be used to offset any income from the taxable year.

(2) If under the laws of the foreign country the dual resident corporation or separate unit has losses from different taxable years, it shall be deemed to use first the losses which would not constitute a triggering event that would result in the recapture of a dual consolidated loss pursuant to §1.1503(d)–6(h). Thereafter, it shall be deemed to use first the losses from the most recent taxable year from which a loss may be carried forward or back for foreign law purposes.

(3) Where different losses or deductions (for example, capital losses and ordinary losses) of a dual resident corporation or separate unit incurred in the same taxable year are available for foreign use, the different losses shall be deemed to be used on a *pro rata* basis. See §1.1503(d)–7(c) *Example 12*.

(e) *Mirror legislation rule*—(1) *In general*. Except as provided in paragraph (e)(2) of this section and §1.1503(d)–6(b) (relating to agreements entered into between the United States and a foreign country), a foreign use shall be deemed to occur if the income tax laws of a foreign country would deny any opportunity for the foreign use of the dual consolidated loss in the year in which the dual consolidated loss is incurred (mirror legislation), determined by assuming that such foreign country had recognized the dual consolidated loss in such year, for any of the following reasons:

(i) The dual resident corporation or separate unit that incurred the loss is subject to income taxation by another country (for example, the United States) on its worldwide income or on a residence basis.

(ii) The loss may be available to offset income (other than income of the dual resident corporation or separate unit) under the laws of another country (for example, the United States).

(iii) The deductibility of any portion of a deduction or loss taken into account in computing the dual consolidated loss depends on whether such amount is deductible under the laws of another country (for example, the United States). See §1.1503(d)–7(c) *Examples 17* through *19*.

(2) *Stand-alone exception*—(i) *In general*. This paragraph (c)(2) applies if, in the absence of the mirror legislation described in paragraph (e)(1) of this section,

no item of deduction or loss composing the dual consolidated loss of such dual resident corporation or separate unit would otherwise be available for a foreign use in the taxable year in which such dual consolidated loss is incurred. This determination is made without regard to whether such availability is limited by election (or other similar procedure). However, for purposes of this paragraph (e)(2)(i), no item of deduction or loss composing the dual consolidated loss of a dual resident corporation or separate unit is considered to be made available for foreign use solely because the laws of a foreign country would enable a foreign use through a sale, merger, or similar transaction (provided no such sale, merger, or similar transaction actually occurs). In such a case, no foreign use shall be considered to occur pursuant to paragraph (e)(1) of this section with respect to the dual consolidated loss, provided the requirements of paragraph (e)(2)(ii) of this section are satisfied. See §1.1503(d)–7(c) *Examples 17* through *19*.

(ii) *Stand-alone domestic use agreement.* In order to qualify for the exception under paragraph (e)(2)(i) of this section, the consolidated group, unaffiliated dual resident corporation, or unaffiliated domestic owner, as the case may be, must enter into a domestic use agreement in accordance with the provisions of §1.1503(d)–6(d) and, in addition, must include the following items in such domestic use agreement:

(A) A statement that the document is also being submitted under the provisions of paragraph (e)(2) of this section.

(B) A certification that the conditions of paragraph (e)(2)(i) of this section are satisfied during the taxable year in which the dual consolidated loss is incurred.

(C) An agreement to include with each annual certification required under §1.1503(d)–6(g), a certification that the conditions described in paragraph (e)(2)(i) of this section are satisfied during the taxable year of each such certification.

(iii) *Termination of stand-alone domestic use agreement.* This paragraph (e)(2)(iii) applies to a consolidated group, unaffiliated dual resident corporation, or unaffiliated domestic owner, as the case may be, that entered into a domestic use agreement pursuant to paragraph (e)(2)(ii) of this section, with respect to a dual consolidated loss, and which subsequently makes an election pursuant to §1.1503(d)–6(b) (relating to agreements entered into between the United States and a foreign country) with respect to such dual consolidated loss. In such a case, the dual consolidated loss shall be subject to the election under §1.1503(d)–6(b) (and any related agreements, representations and conditions), and the domestic use agreement entered into pursuant to paragraph (e)(2)(ii) of this section shall terminate and have no further effect.

§1.1503(d)–4 Domestic use limitation and related operating rules.

(a) *Scope.* This section prescribes rules that apply when the general limitation on the domestic use of a dual consolidated loss under paragraph (b) of this section applies. Thus, the rules of this section do not apply when an exception to the domestic use limitation applies (for example, as a result of a domestic use election under §1.1503(d)–6(d)). In general, when the domestic use limitation applies, the dual consolidated loss of a dual resident corporation or separate unit is subject to the separate return limitation year (SRLY) provisions of §1.1502–21(c), as modified under this section. Paragraph (c) of this section provides rules that determine the effect of a dual consolidated loss on a consolidated group, an unaffiliated dual resident corporation, or an unaffiliated domestic owner. Paragraph (d) of this section provides rules that eliminate dual consolidated losses following certain transactions or events. Paragraph (e) of this section contains provisions that prevent dual consolidated losses from offsetting tainted income. Finally, paragraph (f) of this section provides rules for computing foreign tax credits.

(b) *Limitation on domestic use of a dual consolidated loss.* Except as provided in §1.1503(d)–6, the domestic use of a dual consolidated loss is not permitted. See §1.1503(d)–2 for the definition of a domestic use. See also §1.1503(d)–7(c) *Examples 2* through *4*.

(c) *Effect of a dual consolidated loss on a consolidated group, unaffiliated dual resident corporation, or unaffiliated domestic owner.* For any taxable year in which a dual resident corporation or separate unit has a dual consolidated loss that is subject to the domestic use limitation of paragraph (b) of this section, the following rules shall apply:

(1) *Dual resident corporation.* This paragraph (c)(1) applies to a dual consolidated loss of a dual resident corporation. The unaffiliated dual resident corporation, or consolidated group that includes the dual resident corporation, shall compute its taxable income (or loss), or consolidated taxable income (or loss), respectively, without taking into account those items of deduction and loss that compose the dual resident corporation's dual consolidated loss. For this purpose, the dual consolidated loss shall be treated as composed of a *pro rata* portion of each item of deduction and loss of the dual resident corporation taken into account in calculating the dual consolidated loss. The dual consolidated loss is subject to the limitations on its use contained in paragraph (c)(3) of this section and, subject to such limitations, may be carried over or back for use in other taxable years as a separate net operating loss carryover or carryback of the dual resident corporation arising in the year incurred. If the dual resident corporation owns a separate unit or an interest in a transparent entity, the limitations contained in paragraph (c)(3) of this section shall apply to the dual resident corporation as if the separate unit or interest in a transparent entity were a separate domestic corporation that filed a consolidated return with the unaffiliated dual resident corporation, or with the consolidated group of the affiliated dual resident corporation, as applicable.

(2) *Separate unit.* This paragraph (c)(2) applies to a dual consolidated loss that is attributable to a separate unit. The unaffiliated domestic owner of a separate unit, or the consolidated group of an affiliated domestic owner of a separate unit, shall compute its taxable income (or loss) or consolidated taxable income (or loss), respectively, without taking into account those items of deduction and loss that compose the separate unit's dual consolidated loss. For this purpose, the dual consolidated loss shall be treated as composed of a *pro rata* portion of each item of deduction and loss of the separate unit taken into account in calculating the dual consolidated loss. The dual consolidated loss is subject to the limitations contained in paragraph (c)(3) of this section as if the separate unit to which the dual consolidated loss is attributable

were a separate domestic corporation that filed a consolidated return with its unaffiliated domestic owner or with the consolidated group of its affiliated domestic owner, as applicable. Subject to such limitations, the dual consolidated loss may be carried over or back for use in other taxable years as a separate net operating loss carryover or carryback of the separate unit arising in the year incurred. See §1.1503(d)–7(c) *Examples 29* and *38*.

(3) *SRLY limitation.* The dual consolidated loss shall be treated as a loss incurred by the dual resident corporation or separate unit in a separate return limitation year and shall be subject to all of the limitations of §1.1502–21(c) (SRLY limitation), subject to the following modifications—

(i) Notwithstanding §1.1502–1(f)(2)(i), the SRLY limitation is applied to any dual consolidated loss of a common parent that is a dual resident corporation, or any dual consolidated loss attributable to a separate unit of a common parent;

(ii) The SRLY limitation is applied without regard to §1.1502–21(c)(2) (SRLY subgroup limitation) and 1.1502–21(g) (overlap with section 382);

(iii) For purposes of calculating the general SRLY limitation under §1.1502–21(c)(1)(i), the calculation of aggregate consolidated taxable income shall only include items of income, gain, deduction, and loss generated—

(A) In the case of a hybrid entity separate unit, in years in which the hybrid entity (an interest in which is a separate unit) is taxed as a corporation (or otherwise at the entity level) either on its worldwide income or as a resident in the same foreign country in which it was so taxed during the year in which the dual consolidated loss was generated; and

(B) In the case of a foreign branch separate unit, in years in which the foreign branch qualified as a separate unit in the same foreign country in which it so qualified during the year in which the dual consolidated loss was generated.

(iv) For purposes of calculating the general SRLY limitation under §1.1502–21(c)(1)(i), the calculation of aggregate consolidated taxable income shall not include any amount included in income pursuant to §1.1503(d)–6(h) (relating to the recapture of a dual consolidated loss).

(4) *Items of a dual consolidated loss used in other taxable years.* A *pro rata* portion of each item of deduction or loss that composes the dual consolidated loss shall be considered to be used when the dual consolidated loss is used in other taxable years. See §1.1503(d)–7(c) *Examples 29* and *38*.

(5) *Reconstituted net operating losses.* For additional rules and limitations that apply to reconstituted net operating losses, see §1.1503(d)–6(h)(6).

(d) *Elimination of a dual consolidated loss after certain transactions*—(1) *General rule.* In general, a dual resident corporation has a net operating loss (and, therefore, a dual consolidated loss) only if it sustains such loss, or succeeds to such loss as a result of acquiring the assets of a corporation that sustained the loss in a transaction described in section 381(a). Similarly, a net loss generally is attributable to a separate unit of a domestic owner (and therefore is a dual consolidated loss) only if the domestic owner incurs the deductions or losses, or succeeds to such deductions or losses in a transaction described in section 381(a). Except as provided in §1.1503(d)–6(h)(6)(iii), section 1503(d) and these regulations do not alter these general rules. Thus, the provisions of §§1.1503(d)–1 through 1.1503(d)–8 generally do not cause a corporation to have a dual consolidated loss if it did not sustain (or inherit) the loss. Instead, these regulations either eliminate a dual consolidated loss that a corporation sustained (or inherited), or prevent the carryover of a dual consolidated loss under section 381 that would ordinarily occur, as a result of certain transactions.

(i) *Transactions described in section 381(a).* This paragraph (d)(1)(i) applies to a dual consolidated loss of a dual resident corporation, or of a domestic owner attributable to a separate unit, that is subject to the domestic use limitation rule of paragraph (b) of this section. In such a case, and except as provided in paragraph (d)(2) of this section, the dual consolidated loss shall not carry over to another corporation in a transaction described in section 381(a) and, as a result, shall be eliminated. See §1.1503(d)–7(c) *Example 20*.

(ii) *Cessation of separate unit status.* This paragraph (d)(1)(ii) applies when a separate unit of an unaffiliated domestic owner ceases to be a separate unit of its domestic owner, or when a separate unit of an affiliated domestic owner ceases to be a separate unit with respect to its domestic owner and all other members of the affiliated domestic owner's consolidated group. In such a case, and except as provided in paragraph (d)(2)(iii) of this section, a dual consolidated loss of the domestic owner attributable to such separate unit, that is subject to the domestic use limitation of paragraph (b) of this section, shall be eliminated. For purposes of this paragraph (d)(1)(ii), a separate unit may cease to be a separate unit if, for example, such separate unit is terminated, dissolved, liquidated, sold, or otherwise disposed of. See §1.1503(d)–7(c) *Example 21*.

(2) *Exceptions*—(i) *Certain section 368(a)(1)(F) reorganizations.* Paragraph (d)(1)(i) of this section (relating to transactions described in section 381(a)) shall not apply to a dual consolidated loss of a dual resident corporation that undergoes a reorganization described in section 368(a)(1)(F) in which the resulting corporation is a domestic corporation. In such a case, the dual consolidated loss of the resulting corporation continues to be subject to the limitations of paragraphs (b) and (c) of this section, applied as if the resulting corporation incurred the dual consolidated loss.

(ii) *Acquisition of a dual resident corporation by another dual resident corporation.* If a dual resident corporation transfers its assets to another dual resident corporation in a transaction described in section 381(a), and the transferee corporation is a resident of (or is taxed on its worldwide income by) the same foreign country of which the transferor was a resident (or was taxed on its worldwide income), then paragraph (d)(1)(i) of this section shall not apply with respect to dual consolidated losses of the dual resident corporation, and income generated by the transferee may be offset by the carryover dual consolidated losses of the transferor, subject to the limitations of paragraphs (b) and (c) of this section applied as if the transferee incurred the dual consolidated loss. Dual consolidated losses of the transferor dual resident corporation may not, however, be used to offset income attributable to separate units or interests in transparent entities owned by the transferee because they constitute domestic affiliates under §1.1503(d)–1(b)(12)(iii) and (iv), respectively.

(iii) *Acquisition of a separate unit by a domestic corporation.* This paragraph (d)(2)(iii) provides exceptions to the general rules in paragraphs (d)(1)(i) and (ii) of this section that eliminate the dual consolidated loss of a domestic owner that is attributable to a separate unit following certain transactions or events. The exceptions set forth in this paragraph (d)(2)(iii) shall only apply where a domestic owner transfers its assets to a domestic corporation (transferee corporation) in a transaction described in section 381(a).

(A) *Acquisition by a corporation that is not a member of the same consolidated group*—(*1*) *General rule.* If a domestic owner transfers either an individual separate unit or a combined separate unit to a transferee corporation that is not a member of its consolidated group in a transaction described in section 381(a), and the transferee corporation, or a member of the transferee's consolidated group, is a domestic owner of the transferred separate unit immediately after the transaction, then paragraphs (d)(1)(i) and (ii) of this section shall not apply to such transfer. In addition, income of the transferee, or a member of the transferee's consolidated group, that is attributable to the transferred separate unit may be offset by the carryover dual consolidated losses of the transferor domestic owner that were attributable to the transferred separate unit, subject to the limitations of paragraphs (b) and (c) of this section applied as if the transferee incurred the dual consolidated losses and such losses were attributable to the separate unit. See §1.1503(d)–7(c) *Example 21*.

(*2*) *Combination with separate units of the transferee.* This paragraph (d)(2)(iii)(A)(*2*) applies to a transaction described in paragraph (d)(2)(iii)(A)(*1*) of this section where the transferred separate unit is combined with another separate unit of the transferee, or another member of the transferee's consolidated group, immediately after the transfer as provided under §1.1503(d)–1(b)(4)(ii). In such a case, income generated by the transferee, or another member of the transferee's consolidated group, that is attributable to the combined separate unit may be offset by the carryover dual consolidated losses that were attributable to the transferred separate unit, subject to the limitations of paragraphs (b) and (c) of this section, applied as if the transferee incurred the dual consolidated losses and such losses were attributable to the combined separate unit.

(B) *Acquisition by a member of the same consolidated group.* If an affiliated domestic owner transfers its assets to another member of its consolidated group in a transaction described in section 381(a), and the transferee corporation or another member of such consolidated group is a domestic owner of the separate unit to which the dual consolidated loss was attributable, then paragraphs (d)(1)(i) and (ii) of this section shall not apply. In addition, income generated by the transferee that is attributable to the transferred separate unit may be offset by the carryover dual consolidated losses that were attributable to the transferred separate unit, subject to the limitations of paragraphs (b) and (c) of this section, applied as if the transferee incurred the dual consolidated losses and such losses were attributable to the separate unit. See §1.1503(d)–7(c) *Example 21*.

(iv) *Special rules for foreign insurance companies.* See §1.1503(d)–6(a) for additional limitations that apply where the transferor is a foreign insurance company that is a dual resident corporation under §1.1503(d)–1(b)(2)(ii).

(e) *Special rule denying the use of a dual consolidated loss to offset tainted income*—(1) *In general.* Dual consolidated losses incurred by a dual resident corporation that are subject to the domestic use limitation rule under paragraph (b) of this section shall not be used to offset income it earns after it ceases to be a dual resident corporation to the extent that such income is tainted income.

(2) *Tainted income*—(i) *Definition.* For purposes of paragraph (e)(1) of this section, the term *tainted income* means—

(A) Income or gain recognized on the sale or other disposition of tainted assets; and

(B) Income derived as a result of holding tainted assets.

(ii) *Income presumed to be derived from holding tainted assets.* In the absence of evidence establishing the actual amount of income that is attributable to holding tainted assets, the portion of a corporation's income in a particular taxable year that is treated as tainted income derived as a result of holding tainted assets shall be an amount equal to the corporation's taxable income for the year (other than income described in paragraph (e)(2)(i)(A) of this section) multiplied by a fraction, the numerator of which is the fair market value of all tainted assets acquired by the corporation (determined at the time such assets were so acquired) and the denominator of which is the fair market value of the total assets owned by the corporation at the end of such taxable year. To establish the actual amount of income that is attributable to holding tainted assets, documentation must be attached to, and filed by the due date (including extensions) of, the domestic corporation's tax return or the consolidated tax return of an affiliated group of which it is a member, as the case may be, for the taxable year in which the income is generated. See §1.1503(d)–7(c) *Example 22*.

(3) *Tainted assets defined.* For purposes of paragraph (e)(2) of this section, tainted assets are any assets acquired by a domestic corporation in a nonrecognition transaction, as defined in section 7701(a)(45), any assets otherwise transferred to the corporation as a contribution to capital, or any assets otherwise received from a separate unit or a transparent entity owned by such domestic corporation, at any time during the three taxable years immediately preceding the taxable year in which the corporation ceases to be a dual resident corporation or at any time thereafter.

(4) *Exceptions.* Income derived from assets acquired by a domestic corporation shall not be subject to the limitation described in paragraph (e)(1) of this section, and in addition shall not be treated as tainted assets as defined in paragraph (e)(3) of this section, if—

(i) For the taxable year in which the assets were acquired, the corporation did not have a dual consolidated loss (or a carryforward of a dual consolidated loss to such year); or

(ii) The assets were acquired as replacement property in the ordinary course of business.

(f) *Computation of foreign tax credit limitation.* If a dual consolidated loss is subject to the domestic use limitation rule under paragraph (b) of this section, the consolidated group, unaffiliated dual resident corporation, or unaffiliated domestic owner shall compute its foreign tax credit limitation by applying the limitations of paragraph (c) of this section. Thus, the items constituting the dual consolidated loss are not taken into account until the year in which such items are absorbed.

§1.1503(d)–5 Attribution of items and basis adjustments.

(a) *In general.* This section provides rules for determining the amount of income or dual consolidated loss of a dual resident corporation. This section also provides rules for determining the income or dual consolidated loss attributable to a separate unit, as well as the income or loss attributable to an interest in a transparent entity. Paragraph (b) of this section provides rules with respect to dual resident corporations. Paragraph (c) of this section provides rules with respect to separate units and interests in transparent entities. These determinations are required for various purposes under section 1503(d). For example, it is necessary for purposes of applying the domestic use limitation rule under §1.1503(d)–4(b) to a dual consolidated loss, and for determining the extent to which a dual consolidated loss is available to offset income as provided under §1.1503(d)–4(c). These determinations are also necessary for purposes of determining whether the amount subject to recapture may be reduced pursuant to §1.1503(d)–6(h)(2). Paragraph (d) of this section provides rules with respect to the foreign tax treatment of items. Paragraph (e) of this section provides rules regarding the treatment of items where a dual resident corporation, separate unit, or transparent entity only qualified as such during a portion of a taxable year. Paragraph (f) of this section provides rules for determining the assets and liabilities of a separate unit. Finally, paragraph (g) of this section provides rules for making basis adjustments to stock of certain members of a consolidated group and to certain interests in partnerships. The rules in this section apply for purposes of §§1.1503(d)–1 through 1.1503(d)–7.

(b) *Determination of amount of income or dual consolidated loss of a dual resident corporation*—(1) *In general.* For purposes of determining whether a dual resident corporation has income or a dual consolidated loss for the taxable year, and except as provided in paragraph (b)(2) of this section, the dual resident corporation shall compute its income or dual consolidated loss taking into account only those items of income, gain, deduction, and loss from such year (including any items recognized by such corporation as a result of an election under section 338). In the case of an affiliated dual resident corporation, such calculation shall be made in accordance with the rules set forth in the regulations under section 1502 governing the computation of consolidated taxable income. See also paragraphs (d) and (e) of this section.

(2) *Exceptions.* For purposes of determining the income or dual consolidated loss of a dual resident corporation, the following shall not be taken into account—

(i) Any net capital loss of the dual resident corporation;

(ii) Any carryover or carryback losses; or

(iii) Any items of income, gain, deduction, and loss that are attributable to a separate unit or an interest in a transparent entity of the dual resident corporation.

(c) *Determination of amount of income or dual consolidated loss attributable to a separate unit, and income or loss attributable to an interest in a transparent entity*—(1) *In general*—(i) *Scope and purpose.* Paragraphs (c) through (e) of this section apply for purposes of determining the income or dual consolidated loss attributable to a separate unit, and the income or loss attributable to an interest in a transparent entity, for the taxable year. In the case of an affiliated domestic owner, this determination shall be made in accordance with the rules set forth in the regulations under section 1502 governing the computation of consolidated taxable income. These rules apply solely for purposes of section 1503(d).

(ii) *Only items of domestic owner taken into account.* The computation made under paragraphs (c) through (e) of this section shall be made using only those existing items of income, gain, deduction, and loss of the separate unit's or transparent entity's domestic owner (or owners, in the case of certain combined separate units), as determined for U.S. tax purposes. These items must be translated into U.S. dollars (if necessary) at the appropriate exchange rate provided under section 989(b), as modified by regulations. The computation shall be made as if the separate unit or interest in a transparent entity were a domestic corporation, using items that are attributable to the separate unit or interest in a transparent entity. However, for purposes of making this computation, net capital losses, and carryover or carryback losses, of the domestic owner shall not be taken into account. Items of income, gain, deduction, and loss that are otherwise disregarded for U.S. tax purposes shall not be regarded or taken into account for purposes of this section. See §1.1503(d)–7(c) *Examples 6* and *23* through *25*.

(iii) *Separate application.* The attribution rules of this section shall apply separately to each separate unit or interest in a transparent entity. Thus, an item of income, gain, deduction, or loss shall not be considered attributable to more than one separate unit or interest in a transparent entity. In addition, for purposes of this section items of income, gain, deduction, and loss attributable to a separate unit or an interest in a transparent entity shall not offset items of income, gain, deduction, and loss of another separate unit or interest in a transparent entity. See §1.1503(d)–7(c) *Example 24*. See also the separate unit combination rule in §1.1503(d)–1(b)(4)(ii).

(2) *Foreign branch separate unit*—(i) *In general.* Except to the extent provided in paragraph (c)(4) of this section, for purposes of determining the items of income, gain, deduction (other than interest), and loss of a domestic owner that are attributable to the domestic owner's foreign branch separate unit, the principles of section 864(c)(2), (c)(4), and (c)(5), as set forth in §1.864–4(c), and §§1.864–5 through 1.864–7, shall apply. The principles apply without regard to limitations imposed on the effectively connected treatment of income, gain, or loss under the trade or business safe harbors in section 864(b) and the limitations for treating foreign source income as effectively connected under section 864(c)(4)(D). Except as provided in paragraph (c)(2)(iii) of this section, for purposes of determining the domestic owner's interest expense that is attributable to a foreign branch separate unit, the principles of §1.882–5, as modified in paragraph (c)(2)(ii) of this section, shall apply. When applying the principles of section 864(c) (as modified by this paragraph) and §1.882–5 (as modified in paragraph (c)(2)(ii) of this section), the

foreign branch separate unit's domestic owner shall be treated as a foreign corporation, the foreign branch separate unit shall be treated as a trade or business within the United States, and the other assets of the domestic owner shall be treated as assets that are not U.S. assets.

(ii) *Principles of §1.882–5.* For purposes of paragraph (c)(2)(i) of this section, the principles of §1.882–5 shall be applied, subject to the following modifications—

(A) Except as otherwise provided in this section, only the assets, liabilities, and interest expense of the domestic owner shall be taken into account in the §1.882–5 formula;

(B) Except as provided under paragraph (c)(2)(ii)(C) of this section, a taxpayer may use the alternative tax book value method under §1.861–9(i) for purposes of determining the value of its U.S. assets pursuant to §1.882–5(b)(2) and its worldwide assets pursuant to §1.882–5(c)(2);

(C) For purposes of determining the value of a U.S. asset pursuant to §1.882–5(b)(2), and worldwide assets pursuant to §1.882–5(c)(2), the taxpayer must use the same methodology under §1.861–9T(g) (that is, tax book value, alternative tax book value, or fair market value) that the taxpayer uses for purposes of allocating and apportioning interest expense for the taxable year under section 864(e);

(D) Asset values shall be determined pursuant to §1.861–9T(g)(2); and

(E) For purposes of determining the step-two U.S. connected liabilities, the amounts of worldwide assets and liabilities under §1.882–5(c)(2)(iii) and (iv) must be determined in accordance with U.S. tax principles, rather than substantially in accordance with U.S. tax principles.

(iii) *Exception where foreign country attributes interest expense solely by reference to books and records.* The principles of §1.882–5 shall not apply if the foreign country in which the foreign branch separate unit is located determines, for purposes of computing taxable income (or loss) of a permanent establishment or branch of a nonresident corporation under the laws of the foreign country, the interest expense of the foreign branch separate unit by taking into account only the items of interest expense reflected on the foreign branch separate unit's books and records. In such a case, only those items of the domestic owner's interest expense reflected on the foreign branch separate unit's books and records (as provided in paragraph (c)(3)(i) of this section), adjusted to conform to U.S. tax principles, shall be attributable to the foreign branch separate unit. This paragraph shall not apply where the foreign country does not use a method of attributing interest based solely on the interest that is reflected on the books and records. For example, this paragraph does not apply if the foreign country uses a method for attributing interest expense similar to §1.882–5 or that set forth in the Organization for Economic Co-operation and Development Report on the Attribution of Profits to Permanent Establishments, Part II (Banks), December 2006. See *www.oecd.org.*

(3) *Hybrid entity separate unit and an interest in a transparent entity*—(i) *General rule.* This paragraph (c)(3) applies to determine the items of income, gain, deduction, and loss of a domestic owner that are attributable to a hybrid entity separate unit, or an interest in a transparent entity, of such domestic owner. Except to the extent provided in paragraph (c)(4) of this section, the domestic owner's items of income, gain, deduction, and loss are attributable to the extent they are reflected on the books and records of the hybrid entity or transparent entity, as applicable, as adjusted to conform to U.S. tax principles. See §1.1503(d)–7(c) *Examples 23* through *26*. For purposes of this paragraph (c)(3), the term "books and records" has the meaning provided under §1.989(a)–1(d). The treatment of items for foreign tax purposes, including under any type of foreign anti-deferral regime, is not relevant for purposes of determining whether items are reflected on the books and records of the entity, or for purposes of making adjustments to such items to conform to U.S. tax principles. The method described in the second sentence of this paragraph shall not apply to the extent that the Commissioner determines that booking practices are employed with a principal purpose of avoiding the principles of section 1503(d), including inconsistently treating the same or similar items of income, gain, deduction, and loss. In such a case, the Commissioner may reallocate the items of income, gain, deduction, and loss between or among a domestic owner, its hybrid entities, its transparent entities (and interests therein), its separate units, or any other entity, as applicable, in a manner consistent with the principles of section 1503(d) and which properly reflects income (or loss).

(ii) *Interests in certain disregarded entities, partnerships, and grantor trusts owned by a hybrid entity or transparent entity.* This paragraph (c)(3)(ii) applies if a hybrid entity or transparent entity to which paragraph (c)(3)(i) of this section applies owns, directly or indirectly (other than through a hybrid entity or transparent entity), an interest in an entity that is treated as a disregarded entity, partnership, or grantor trust for U.S. tax purposes, but is not a hybrid entity or a transparent entity. For example, the rules of this paragraph would apply when a hybrid entity holds an interest in a limited partnership created in the United States and, for both U.S. and foreign tax purposes the entity is considered a partnership. In such a case, and except to the extent provided in paragraph (c)(4) of this section, items of income, gain, deduction, and loss that are reflected on the books and records of such disregarded entity, partnership or grantor trust, as determined under paragraph (c)(3)(i) of this section, shall be treated as being reflected on the books and records of the hybrid entity or transparent entity for purposes of applying paragraph (c)(3)(i) of this section. See §1.1503(d)–7(c) *Example 26*.

(4) *Special rules.* The following special rules shall apply for purposes of attributing items to separate units or interests in transparent entities under this section:

(i) *Allocation of items between certain tiered separate units and interests in transparent entities*—(A) *Foreign branch separate unit.* This paragraph (c)(4)(i) applies where a hybrid entity or transparent entity owns directly or indirectly (other than through a hybrid entity or a transparent entity), a foreign branch separate unit. For purposes of determining items of income, gain, deduction, and loss of the domestic owner that are attributable to the domestic owner's foreign branch separate unit described in the preceding sentence, only items of income, gain, deduction, and loss that are attributable to the domestic owner's interest in the hybrid entity, or transparent entity, as provided in paragraph (c)(3) of this section, shall be taken into account. Further, only assets, liabilities, and activities of the domestic owner's interest in the hybrid entity or the transparent entity shall be taken into account under paragraph (c)(2) of this section when applying the principles of 864(c)(2), (c)(4), (c)(5) (as set forth in §1.864–4(c), and §§1.864–5 through 1.864–7), and §1.882–5 (as modified in paragraph (c)(2)(ii) of this section). See §1.1503(d)–7(c) *Examples 25* and *26*.

(B) *Hybrid entity separate unit or interest in a transparent entity*. For purposes of determining items of income, gain, deduction, and loss that are attributable to a hybrid entity separate unit or an interest in a transparent entity described in paragraph (c)(3) of this section, such items shall not be taken into account to the extent they are attributable to a foreign branch separate unit pursuant to paragraph (c)(4)(i)(A) of this section. See §1.1503(d)–7(c) *Examples 25* and *26*.

(ii) *Combined separate unit*. If two or more individual separate units defined in §1.1503(d)–1(b)(4)(i) are treated as one combined separate unit pursuant to §1.1503(d)–1(b)(4)(ii), the items of income, gain, deduction, and loss that are attributable to the combined separate unit shall be determined as follows:

(A) Items of income, gain, deduction, and loss are first attributed to each individual separate unit without regard to §1.1503(d)–1(b)(4)(ii), pursuant to the rules of paragraphs (c) through (e) of this section.

(B) The combined separate unit then takes into account all of the items of income, gain, deduction, and loss attributable to its individual separate units pursuant to paragraph (c)(4)(ii)(A) of this section. See §1.1503(d)–7(c) *Examples 25* and *26*.

(iii) *Gain or loss on the direct or indirect disposition of a separate unit or an interest in a transparent entity*—(A) *In general*. This paragraph (c)(4)(iii) applies for purposes of attributing items of income, gain, deduction, and loss that are recognized on the sale, exchange, or other disposition of a separate unit or an interest in a transparent entity (or an interest in a disregarded entity, partnership, or grantor trust that owns, directly or indirectly, a separate unit or an interest in a transparent entity). For purposes of this paragraph (c)(4)(iii), items taken into account on the sale, exchange, or other disposition include loss recapture income or gain under section 367(a)(3)(C) or 904(f)(3), and gain or loss recognized by the domestic owner as the result of an election under section 338. In cases where this paragraph (c)(4)(iii)(A) applies, items taken into account on the sale, exchange, or other disposition shall be attributable to the separate unit or the interest in the transparent entity to the extent of gain or loss that would have been recognized had the separate unit or transparent entity sold all its assets (as determined in paragraph (f) of this section) in a taxable exchange, immediately before the sale, exchange, or other disposition (deemed sale). For purposes of a deemed sale described in this paragraph (c)(4)(iii), the assets are treated as being sold for an amount equal to their fair market value, plus the assumption of the liabilities of the separate unit or interest in a transparent entity (as determined in paragraph (f) of this section). See §1.1503(d)–7(c) *Example 27*.

(B) *Multiple separate units or interests in transparent entities*. This paragraph (c)(4)(iii)(B) applies to a sale, exchange, or other disposition described in paragraph (c)(4)(iii)(A) of this section that results in more than one separate unit or interest in a transparent entity being, directly or indirectly, disposed of. In such a case, items of income, gain, deduction, and loss recognized on such sale, exchange, or other disposition are allocated and attributed to each separate unit or interest in a transparent entity, based on the relative gain or loss that would have been recognized by each separate unit or interest in a transparent entity pursuant to a deemed sale of their assets. See §1.1503(d)–7(c) *Example 28*.

(iv) *Inclusions on stock*. Any amount included in income of a domestic owner arising from ownership of stock in a foreign corporation (for example, under sections 78, 951, or 986(c)) through a separate unit, or interest in a transparent entity, shall be attributable to the separate unit or interest in a transparent entity, if an actual dividend from such foreign corporation would have been so attributed. See §1.1503(d)–7(c) *Example 24*.

(v) *Foreign currency gain or loss recognized under section 987*. Foreign currency gain or loss of a domestic owner recognized under section 987 as a result of a transfer or remittance shall not be attributable to a separate unit or an interest in a transparent entity.

(vi) *Recapture of dual consolidated loss*. If all or a portion of a dual consolidated loss that was attributable to a separate unit is included in the gross income of a domestic owner under the recapture provisions of §1.1503(d)–6(h), such amount shall be attributable to the separate unit that incurred the dual consolidated loss being recaptured. See §1.1503(d)–7(c) *Examples 38* and *40*.

(d) *Foreign tax treatment disregarded*. The fact that a particular item taken into account in computing the income or dual consolidated loss of a dual resident corporation or a separate unit, or the income or loss of an interest in a transparent entity, is not taken into account in computing income (or loss) subject to a foreign country's income tax shall not cause such item to be excluded from being taken into account under paragraph (b), (c), or (e) of this section.

(e) *Items generated or incurred while a dual resident corporation, a separate unit, or a transparent entity*. For purposes of determining the amount of the dual consolidated loss of a dual resident corporation for the taxable year, only the items of income, gain, deduction, and loss generated or incurred during the period the dual resident corporation qualified as such shall be taken into account. For purposes of determining the amount of income of a dual resident corporation for the taxable year, all the items of income, gain, deduction, and loss generated or incurred during the year shall be taken into account. For purposes of determining the amount of the income or dual consolidated loss attributable to a separate unit, or the income or loss attributable to an interest in a transparent entity, for the taxable year, only the items of income, gain, deduction, and loss generated or incurred during the period the separate unit or the interest in the transparent entity qualified as such shall be taken into account. For purposes of this paragraph (e), the allocation of items to periods shall be made under the principles of §1.1502–76(b).

(f) *Assets and liabilities of a separate unit or an interest in a transparent entity*. A separate unit or an interest in a transparent entity shall be treated as owning assets to the extent items of income, gain, deduction, and loss from such assets would be attributable to the separate unit or interest in the transparent entity under paragraphs

(c) through (e) of this section. Similarly, liabilities shall be treated as liabilities of a separate unit, or an interest in a transparent entity, to the extent interest expense incurred on such liabilities would be attributable to the separate unit, or the interest in a transparent entity, under paragraphs (c) through (e) of this section.

(g) *Basis adjustments*—(1) *Affiliated dual resident corporation or affiliated domestic owner.* If a member of a consolidated group owns stock in an affiliated dual resident corporation or an affiliated domestic owner that is a member of the same consolidated group, the member shall adjust the basis of the stock in accordance with the provisions of §1.1502–32. Corresponding adjustments shall be made to the stock of other members in accordance with the provisions of §1.1502–32. In the case where two or more individual separate units are treated as a combined separate unit pursuant to §1.1503(d)–1(b)(4)(ii), see paragraph (g)(3) of this section.

(2) *Interests in hybrid entities that are partnerships or interests in partnerships through which a separate unit is owned indirectly*—(i) *Scope.* This paragraph (g)(2) applies for purposes of determining the adjusted basis of an interest in—

(A) A hybrid entity that is a partnership; and

(B) A partnership through which a domestic owner indirectly owns a separate unit.

(ii) *Determination of basis of partner's interest.* The adjusted basis of an interest described in paragraph (g)(2)(i) of this section shall be adjusted in accordance with section 705 and this paragraph (g)(2). The adjusted basis shall not be decreased for any amount of a dual consolidated loss that is attributable to the partnership interest, or separate unit owned indirectly through the partnership interest, as applicable, that is not absorbed as a result of the application of §1.1503(d)–4(b) and (c). The adjusted basis shall, however, be decreased for the amount of such dual consolidated loss that is absorbed in a carryover or carryback taxable year. The adjusted basis shall be increased for any amount included in income pursuant to §1.1503(d)–6(h) as a result of the recapture of a dual consolidated loss that was attributable to the interest in the hybrid partnership, or separate unit owned indirectly through the partnership interest, as applicable.

(3) *Combined separate units.* This paragraph (g)(3) applies where two or more individual separate units of one or more affiliated domestic owners are treated as one combined separate unit pursuant to §1.1503(d)–1(b)(4)(ii). In such a case, a member owning stock in an affiliated domestic owner of the combined separate unit shall adjust the basis in the stock of such domestic owner as provided in paragraph (g)(1) of this section, and an affiliated domestic owner shall adjust its basis in a partnership, as provided in paragraph (g)(2) of this section, taking into account only those items of income, gain, deduction, or loss attributable to each individual separate unit, prior to combination. For purposes of this rule, if the dual consolidated loss attributable to a combined separate unit is subject to the domestic use limitation of §1.1503(d)–4(b), then for purposes of this paragraph (g) and §1.1502–32, the dual consolidated loss shall be allocated to an individual separate unit to the extent such individual separate unit contributed items of deduction or loss giving rise to the dual consolidated loss. In addition, if one or more affiliated domestic owners are required to recapture all or a portion of a dual consolidated loss pursuant to paragraph (h) of this section, such recapture amount shall be allocated to the affiliated domestic owner of the individual separate units composing the combined separate unit, to the extent such individual separate units contributed items of deduction or loss giving rise to the recaptured dual consolidated loss.

§1.1503(d)–6 Exceptions to the domestic use limitation rule.

(a) *In general*—(1) *Scope and purpose.* This section provides certain exceptions to the domestic use limitation rule of §1.1503(d)–4(b). Paragraph (b) of this section provides an exception for bilateral elective agreements. Paragraph (c) of this section provides rules regarding an exception that applies when there is no possibility of a foreign use. Paragraphs (d) through (h) of this section provide rules for an exception where a domestic use election is made. Paragraph (e) of this section provides rules with respect to triggering events, and paragraph (f) of this section provides rules regarding exceptions to triggering events. Paragraph (g) of this section provides rules with respect to the annual certification reporting requirement. Paragraph (h) of this section provides rules regarding the recapture of dual consolidated losses. Finally, paragraph (j) of this section provides rules regarding the termination of domestic use agreements and the annual certification requirement.

(2) *Absence of foreign affiliate or foreign consolidation regime.* The absence of a foreign affiliate or a foreign consolidation regime alone does not constitute an exception to the domestic use limitation rule. This is the case because it is still possible that all or a portion of the dual consolidated loss may be put to a foreign use. For example, there may be a foreign use with respect to an affiliate acquired in a year subsequent to the year in which the dual consolidated loss was incurred. In addition, a foreign use may occur in the absence of a foreign consolidation regime through a sale, merger, or similar transaction. See §1.1503(d)–7(c) *Example 2.*

(3) *Foreign insurance companies treated as domestic corporations.* The exceptions contained in this section shall not apply to losses of a foreign insurance company that is a dual resident corporation under §1.1503(d)–1(b)(2)(ii), or to losses attributable to any separate unit of such foreign insurance company. In addition, these exceptions shall not apply to losses described in the preceding sentence that, subject to the rules of §1.1503(d)–4(d), carry over to a domestic corporation pursuant to a transaction described in section 381(a).

(b) *Elective agreement in place between the United States and a foreign country*—(1) *In general.* The domestic use limitation rule of §1.1503(d)–4(b) shall not apply to a dual consolidated loss to the extent the consolidated group, unaffiliated dual resident corporation, or unaffiliated domestic owner, as the case may be, elects to deduct the loss in the United States pursuant to an agreement entered into between the United States and a foreign country that puts into place an elective procedure through which losses in a particular year may be used to offset income in only one country. This exception shall apply only if all the terms and conditions required under such agreement are satisfied, including any reporting or filing requirements. See §1.1503(d)–3(e)(2)(iii) for the effect of an agreement described in this paragraph on a stand-alone domestic use agreement.

(2) *Application to combined separate units*. This paragraph (b)(2) applies where two or more individual separate units are treated as one combined separate unit pursuant to §1.1503(d)–1(b)(4)(ii), and an agreement described in paragraph (b)(1) of this section would apply to at least one of the individual separate units. In such a case, and except to the extent provided in the agreement, the consolidated group, unaffiliated dual resident corporation, or unaffiliated domestic owner, as the case may be, may apply the agreement to the individual separate units, as applicable, provided the terms and conditions of the agreement are otherwise satisfied. See §1.1503(d)–7(c) *Example 19*.

(c) *No possibility of foreign use*—(1) *In general*. The domestic use limitation rule of §1.1503(d)–4(b) shall not apply to a dual consolidated loss if the consolidated group, unaffiliated dual resident corporation, or unaffiliated domestic owner, as the case may be—

(i) Demonstrates, to the satisfaction of the Commissioner, that no foreign use (as defined in §1.1503(d)–3) of the dual consolidated loss occurred in the year in which it was incurred, and that no foreign use can occur in any other year by any means; and

(ii) Prepares a statement described in paragraph (c)(2) of this section that is attached to, and filed by the due date (including extensions) of, its U.S. income tax return for the taxable year in which the dual consolidated loss is incurred. See §1.1503(d)–7(c) *Examples 2*, *30*, and *31*.

(2) *Statement*. The statement described in this paragraph (c)(2) must be signed under penalties of perjury by the person who signs the tax return. The statement must be labeled "No Possibility of Foreign Use of Dual Consolidated Loss Statement" at the top of the page and must include the following items, in paragraphs labeled to correspond with the items set forth in paragraphs (c)(2)(i) through (iv) of this section:

(i) A statement that the document is submitted under the provisions of paragraph (c) of this section.

(ii) The name, address, taxpayer identification number, and place and date of incorporation of the dual resident corporation, and the country or countries that tax the dual resident corporation on its worldwide income or on a residence basis, or, in the case of a separate unit, identification of the separate unit, including the name under which it conducts business, its principal activity, and the country in which its principal place of business is located. In the case of a combined separate unit, such information must be provided for each individual separate unit that is treated as part of the combined separate unit under §1.1503(d)–1(b)(4)(ii).

(iii) A statement of the amount of the dual consolidated loss at issue.

(iv) An analysis, in reasonable detail and specificity, of the treatment of the losses and deductions composing the dual consolidated loss under the relevant facts. The analysis must include the reasons supporting the conclusion that no foreign use of the dual consolidated loss can occur as described in paragraph (c)(1)(i) of this section. The analysis must be supported with official or certified English translations of the relevant provisions of foreign law. The analysis may, for example, be based on the taxpayer's interpretation of foreign law, on advice received from local tax advisers in an opinion, or on a ruling from local country tax authorities. In all cases, however, the determination must be made to the satisfaction of the Commissioner.

(d) *Domestic use election*—(1) *In general*. The domestic use limitation rule of §1.1503(d)–4(b) shall not apply to a dual consolidated loss if an election to be bound by the provisions of paragraphs (d) through (j) of this section is made by the consolidated group, unaffiliated dual resident corporation, or unaffiliated domestic owner, as the case may be (elector). In order to elect such relief, an agreement described in this paragraph (d)(1) (domestic use agreement) must be attached to, and filed by the due date (including extensions) of, the U.S. income tax return of the elector for the taxable year in which the dual consolidated loss is incurred. The domestic use agreement must be signed under penalties of perjury by the person who signs the return. If dual consolidated losses of more than one dual resident corporation or separate unit requires the filing of domestic use agreements by the same elector, the agreements may be combined in a single document, but the information required by paragraphs (d)(1)(ii) and (iv) of this section must be provided separately with respect to each dual consolidated loss. The domestic use agreement must be labeled "Domestic Use Election and Agreement" at the top of the page and must include the following items, in paragraphs labeled to correspond with the following:

(i) A statement that the document submitted is an election and an agreement under the provisions of paragraph (d) of this section.

(ii) The information required by paragraph (c)(2)(ii) of this section.

(iii) An agreement by the elector to comply with all of the provisions of paragraphs (d) through (j) of this section, as applicable.

(iv) A statement of the amount of the dual consolidated loss at issue.

(v) A certification that there has not been, and will not be, a foreign use (as defined in §1.1503(d)–3) during the certification period (as defined in §1.1503(d)–1(b)(20)).

(vi) A certification that arrangements have been made to ensure that there will be no foreign use of the dual consolidated loss during the certification period, and that the elector will be informed of any such foreign use of the dual consolidated loss during such period.

(vii) If applicable, a notification that an excepted triggering event under paragraph (f)(2) of this section has occurred with respect to the dual consolidated loss within the taxable year in which the loss is incurred. See paragraph (g) of this section for notification of excepted triggering events occurring during the certification period.

(2) *No domestic use election available if there is a triggering event in the year the dual consolidated loss is incurred*. Except as otherwise provided in this section, if a dual resident corporation or separate unit incurs a dual consolidated loss in a taxable year and a triggering event, as described in paragraph (e)(1) of this section, occurs (and no exception applies) with respect to the dual consolidated loss in such taxable year, then the consolidated group, unaffiliated dual resident corporation, or unaffiliated domestic owner, as the case may be, may not make a domestic use election with respect to such dual consolidated loss and the loss will be subject to the domestic use limitation rule of §1.1503(d)–4(b). See §1.1503(d)–7(c) *Examples 5* through

7. See also §1.1503(d)–4(d) for rules that eliminate a dual consolidated loss after certain transactions.

(e) *Triggering events requiring the recapture of a dual consolidated loss*—(1) *Events*. Except as provided under paragraphs (e)(2) (rebuttal of triggering events) and (f) (exceptions to triggering events) of this section, if there is a triggering event described in this paragraph (e)(1) with respect to a dual consolidated loss of a dual resident corporation or a separate unit during the certification period (as defined in §1.1503(d)–1(b)(20)), the elector will recapture and report as ordinary income the amount of such dual consolidated loss as provided in paragraph (h) of this section on its tax return for the taxable year in which the triggering event occurs (or, when the triggering event is a foreign use of the dual consolidated loss, the taxable year that includes the last day of the foreign taxable year during which such use occurs). In addition, the elector must pay any applicable interest charge required by paragraph (h) of this section. For purposes of this section, any of the following events shall constitute a triggering event:

(i) *Foreign use*. A foreign use (as defined in §1.1503(d)–3) of the dual consolidated loss. See §1.1503(d)–3(c) for exceptions to foreign use.

(ii) *Disaffiliation*. An affiliated dual resident corporation or affiliated domestic owner that incurred directly or through a separate unit, respectively, a dual consolidated loss that is subject to a domestic use election, ceases to be a member of the consolidated group that made the domestic use election. For purposes of this paragraph (e)(1)(ii), an affiliated dual resident corporation or affiliated domestic owner shall be considered to cease to be a member of the consolidated group if it is no longer a member of the group within the meaning of §1.1502–1(b), or if the group ceases to exist (for example, when the group no longer files a consolidated return). See §1.1503(d)–7(c) *Example 34*. Any consequences resulting from this triggering event (for example, recapture of a dual consolidated loss) shall be taken into account on the tax return of the consolidated group for the taxable year that includes the date on which the affiliated dual resident corporation or affiliated domestic owner ceases to be a member of the consolidated group. This paragraph (e)(1)(ii) shall not apply to an acquisition described in §1.1502–75(d)(3) where the consolidated group that includes the affiliated dual resident corporation or affiliated domestic owner, as applicable, is treated as remaining in existence.

(iii) *Affiliation*. An unaffiliated dual resident corporation or unaffiliated domestic owner becomes a member of a consolidated group. Any consequences resulting from this triggering event (for example, recapture of a dual consolidated loss) shall be taken into account on the tax return of the unaffiliated dual resident corporation or unaffiliated domestic owner for the taxable year that ends at the end of the day on which such corporation becomes a member of the consolidated group.

(iv) *Transfer of assets*. Fifty percent or more of the dual resident corporation's or separate unit's gross assets (measured by the fair market value of the assets at the time of such transaction or, for multiple transactions, at the time of the first transaction) is sold or otherwise disposed of in either a single transaction or a series of transactions within a twelve-month period. See §1.1503(d)–7(c) *Examples 5* and *35* through *37*. In determining whether fifty percent or more of such assets is sold or otherwise disposed of, any dispositions occurring in the ordinary course of the dual resident corporation's or separate unit's trade or business shall be disregarded. In addition, for purposes of this paragraph (e)(1)(iv), an interest in another separate unit and the shares of a dual resident corporation shall not be treated as assets of a separate unit or a dual resident corporation.

(v) *Transfer of an interest in a separate unit*. Fifty percent or more of the interest in a separate unit (measured by voting power or value at the time of such transaction, or for multiple transactions, at the time of the first transaction) of the domestic owner, as determined by reference to such domestic owner's percentage interest on the last day of the taxable year in which the dual consolidated loss was incurred, is sold or otherwise disposed of either in a single transaction or a series of transactions within a twelve-month period. See §1.1503(d)–7(c) *Examples 5* and *35* through *37*.

(vi) *Conversion to a foreign corporation*. An unaffiliated dual resident corporation, unaffiliated domestic owner, or hybrid entity an interest in which is a separate unit, that incurred the dual consolidated loss, becomes a foreign corporation (for example, as a result of a reorganization or an election to be classified as a corporation under §301.7701–3(c) of this chapter).

(vii) *Conversion to a regulated investment company, a real estate investment trust, or an S corporation*. An unaffiliated dual resident corporation or unaffiliated domestic owner elects to be a regulated investment company pursuant to section 851(b)(1), a real estate investment trust pursuant to section 856(c)(1), or an S corporation pursuant to section 1362(a).

(viii) *Failure to certify*. The elector fails to file a certification with respect to a dual consolidated loss as required under paragraph (g) of this section.

(ix) *Cessation of stand-alone status*. In the case of a dual consolidated loss that is subject to the stand-alone exception described in §1.1503(d)–3(e)(2), the conditions described in §1.1503(d)–3(e)(2)(i) are no longer satisfied. See §1.1503(d)–7(c) *Example 18*.

(2) *Rebuttal*—(i) *General rule*. An event described in paragraph (e)(1) of this section shall not constitute a triggering event if the elector demonstrates, to the satisfaction of the Commissioner, that there can be no foreign use (as defined in §1.1503(d)–3) of the dual consolidated loss during the remaining certification period by any means. See paragraph (j)(1) of this section for rules regarding the termination of domestic use agreements and annual certifications following rebuttals under this general rule.

(ii) *Certain asset transfers*. An event described in paragraph (e)(1)(iv) of this section shall not constitute a triggering event if the elector demonstrates, to the satisfaction of the Commissioner, that the transfer of assets did not result in a carryover under foreign law of the dual resident corporation's, or separate unit's, losses, expenses, or deductions to the transferee of the assets. For purposes of this determination, the exception to foreign use in §1.1503(d)–3(c)(7) shall be taken into account. Following rebuttal under this paragraph (e)(2)(ii), the domestic use agreement continues in effect.

(iii) *Reporting*. In order to satisfy the requirements of paragraph (e)(2)(i) or (ii) of this section, the elector must prepare a statement, labeled "Rebuttal of Triggering

Event" at the top of the page, that indicates that it is submitted under the provisions of this paragraph (e)(2). The statement must include the information described in paragraphs (c)(2)(ii) and (iii) of this section. The statement must also include the information described in paragraph (c)(2)(iv) of this section that supports the conclusions under paragraph (e)(2)(i) or (ii) of this section, as applicable. The statement must be attached to, and filed by the due date (including extensions) of, the elector's income tax return for the taxable year in which the presumed triggering event occurs.

(iv) *Examples.* See §1.1503(d)–7(c) *Examples 32* and *33*.

(f) *Triggering event exceptions*—(1) *Continuing ownership of assets or interests.* The following events shall not constitute triggering events, requiring the recapture of the dual consolidated loss under paragraph (h) of this section:

(i) *Disaffiliation as a result of a transaction described in section 381.* An affiliated dual resident corporation or affiliated domestic owner ceases to be a member of a consolidated group solely by reason of a transaction in which a member of the same consolidated group succeeds to the tax attributes of the dual resident corporation or domestic owner under the provisions of section 381.

(ii) *Continuing ownership by consolidated group.* This paragraph (f)(1)(ii) applies when assets of an affiliated dual resident corporation, or assets of, or interests in, a separate unit of an affiliated domestic owner are sold or otherwise disposed of. In such a case, the sale or disposition shall not be treated as a triggering event to the extent the assets or interests are acquired by one or more members of the consolidated group that includes the affiliated dual resident corporation or affiliated domestic owner, or by a partnership or a grantor trust, but only if immediately after the acquisition more than 90 percent of the partnership's or grantor trust's interests is owned, directly or indirectly, by members of such consolidated group.

(iii) *Continuing ownership by unaffiliated dual resident corporation or unaffiliated domestic owner.* This paragraph (f)(1)(iii) applies when assets of an unaffiliated dual resident corporation, or assets of, or interests in, a separate unit of an unaffiliated domestic owner, are sold or otherwise disposed of. In such a case, the sale or disposition shall not be a triggering event to the extent such assets or interests are acquired by the unaffiliated dual resident corporation, or unaffiliated domestic owner, as applicable, or by a partnership or grantor trust, but only if immediately after the acquisition more than 90 percent of the partnership's or grantor trust's interests is owned, directly or indirectly, by the unaffiliated dual resident corporation or unaffiliated domestic owner. For example, this paragraph (f)(1)(iii) applies when an unaffiliated domestic owner acquires direct ownership of the assets of a separate unit that it had immediately before owned indirectly through a partnership.

(2) *Transactions requiring a new domestic use agreement*—(i) *Multiple-party events.* If all the requirements of paragraph (f)(2)(iii) of this section are satisfied, the following events shall not constitute triggering events requiring the recapture of the dual consolidated loss under paragraph (h) of this section:

(A) An affiliated dual resident corporation or affiliated domestic owner becomes an unaffiliated domestic corporation or a member of a new consolidated group (other than in a transaction described in paragraph (f)(2)(ii)(B) of this section).

(B) Assets of a dual resident corporation or assets of, or interests in, a separate unit, are sold or otherwise disposed of in a transaction in which such assets or interests are acquired by an unaffiliated domestic corporation, one or more members of a new consolidated group, or by a partnership or grantor trust, but only if immediately after the sale or disposition more than 90 percent of the partnership's or grantor trust's interests is owned, directly or indirectly, by the unaffiliated domestic owner or by members of a new consolidated group, as applicable. See the related exception to foreign use provided under §1.1503(d)–3(c)(8). See also §1.1503(d)–7(c) *Examples 36* and *37*.

(ii) *Events resulting in a single consolidated group.* If the requirements of paragraph (f)(2)(iii)(A) of this section are satisfied, the following events shall not constitute triggering events requiring the recapture of the dual consolidated loss under paragraph (h) of this section:

(A) An unaffiliated dual resident corporation or unaffiliated domestic owner becomes a member of a consolidated group.

(B) A consolidated group ceases to exist as a result of a transaction described in §1.1502–13(j)(5)(i) (relating to acquisitions of the common parent of the consolidated group), other than a transaction in which any member of the terminating group, or the successor-in-interest of such member, is not a member of the surviving group immediately after the terminating group ceases to exist. See §1.1503(d)–7(c) *Example 34*.

(iii) *Requirements*—(A) *New domestic use agreement.* The unaffiliated domestic corporation or new consolidated group (subsequent elector) must file an agreement described in paragraph (d)(1) of this section (new domestic use agreement). The new domestic use agreement must be labeled "New Domestic Use Agreement" at the top of the page, and must be attached to and filed by the due date (including extensions) of, the subsequent elector's income tax return for the taxable year in which the event described in paragraph (f)(2)(i) or (f)(2)(ii) of this section occurs. The new domestic use agreement must be signed under penalties of perjury by the person who signs the return and must include the following items:

(*1*) A statement that the document submitted is an election and agreement under the provisions of paragraph (f)(2) of this section.

(*2*) An agreement to assume the same obligations with respect to the dual consolidated loss as the unaffiliated dual resident corporation, unaffiliated domestic owner, or consolidated group, as applicable, that filed the original domestic use agreement (original elector) with respect to that loss. In such a case, obligations of an elector provided under this section shall also be considered to be obligations of a subsequent elector.

(*3*) In the event of a transaction described in section 384(a) involving the subsequent elector, an agreement to treat any potential recapture amount under paragraph (h) of this section with respect to the dual consolidated loss as unrealized built-in gain for purposes of section 384(a), subject to any applicable exceptions (for example, the threshold requirements under section 382(h)(3)(B)). The potential recapture amount treated as unrealized built-in gain under this paragraph (f)(2)(iii)(A)(*3*) may be reduced to the extent permitted by paragraph (h)(2)(i) of this section.

(*4*) In the case of a multiple-party event described in paragraph (f)(2)(i) of this section, an agreement to be subject to the rules provided in paragraph (h)(3) of this section.

(*5*) The name, U.S. taxpayer identification number, and address of the original elector and prior subsequent electors, if any, with respect to the dual consolidated loss.

(B) *Statement filed by original elector.* In the case of a multiple-party event described in paragraph (f)(2)(i) of this section, the original elector must file a statement that is attached to and filed by the due date (including extensions) of its income tax return for the taxable year in which the event occurs. The statement must be labeled "Original Elector Statement" at the top of the page, must be signed under penalties of perjury by the person who signs the tax return, and must include the following items:

(*1*) A statement that the document submitted is an election and agreement under the provisions of paragraph (f)(2) of this section.

(*2*) An agreement to be subject to the rules provided in paragraph (h)(3) of this section.

(*3*) The name, U.S. taxpayer identification number, and address of the subsequent elector.

(3) *Certain transfers qualifying for the de minimis exception to foreign use.* If a transaction or event qualifies for the *de minimis* exception to foreign use described in §1.1503(d)–3(c)(5), the transaction or event shall not constitute a triggering event under paragraph (e)(1)(iv) (transfers of assets) or (v) (transfers of an interest in a separate unit) of this section. For purposes of the preceding sentence, the transaction or event shall include deemed transfers that occur as a result of the transaction or event. See, for example, deemed transfers occurring pursuant to Rev. Rul. 99–5, 1999–1 C.B. 434, see §601.601(d)(2)(ii)(*b*), and section 708 and the related regulations. See also §1.1503(d)–7 *Example 5.* This paragraph (f)(3) only applies if the entire transaction or event qualifies for the *de minimis* exception to foreign use. For example, if a domestic owner sells five percent of a separate unit to a foreign corporation, which would qualify for the *de minimis* exception to foreign use if it were the only transfer, but pursuant to the same transaction also sells 70 percent of the same separate unit to another corporation in a manner that results in a triggering event under paragraph (e)(1)(v) of this section, this paragraph shall not apply to prevent the transaction from resulting in a triggering event.

(4) *Deemed transactions as a result of certain transfers that do not result in a foreign use.* The rules in this paragraph (f)(4) apply where the assets of, or the interests in, a separate unit are transferred in a transaction that would not result in a foreign use and, but for resulting deemed transactions or events, would not result in a triggering event described in paragraph (e)(1) of this section. For purposes of this paragraph (f)(4), deemed transactions or events shall include transactions or events that are deemed to occur pursuant to Rev. Rul. 99–5 and section 708 and the related regulations. In such a case, the deemed transactions shall not result in a triggering event under paragraph (e)(1)(iv) (transfers of assets) or (v) (transfers of an interest in a separate unit) of this section. See also §1.1503(d)–7 *Example 35.*

(5) *Compulsory transfers.* Transfers of the assets or stock of a dual resident corporation, or of the assets or interests in a separate unit, shall not constitute a triggering event (including a foreign use that occurs as a result of, or following, the transfer) if such transfers are—

(i) Legally required by a foreign government as a necessary condition of doing business in a foreign country;

(ii) Compelled by a genuine threat of immediate expropriation by a foreign government; or

(iii) The result of the expropriation of assets by the foreign government.

(6) *Subsequent triggering events.* Any triggering event described in paragraph (e) of this section that occurs subsequent to one of the transactions described in this paragraph (f), and that itself does not meet any of the exceptions provided in this paragraph (f), shall require recapture under paragraph (h) of this section by the elector or subsequent elector, as applicable.

(g) *Annual certification reporting requirement.* Unless and until the domestic use agreement is terminated pursuant to paragraph (j) of this section, the elector must file a certification, labeled "Certification of Dual Consolidated Loss" at the top of the page, that is attached to, and filed by the due date (including extensions) of, its income tax return for each taxable year during the certification period. The certification must provide that there has been no foreign use of the dual consolidated loss. The certification must identify the dual consolidated loss to which it pertains by setting forth the elector's year in which the loss was incurred and the amount of such loss. In addition, the certification must warrant that arrangements have been made to ensure that there will be no foreign use of the dual consolidated loss and that the elector will be informed of any such foreign use. If applicable, the certification must include a notification that an excepted triggering event under paragraph (f)(2) of this section has occurred with respect to the dual consolidated loss within the taxable year being certified. If dual consolidated losses of more than one taxable year are subject to the rules of this paragraph (g), the certification for those years may be combined in a single document, but each dual consolidated loss must be separately identified. See §1.1503(d)–3(e)(2)(ii) for additional certifications required where taxpayers elect the stand-alone exception of §1.1503(d)–3(e)(2).

(h) *Recapture of dual consolidated loss and interest charge*—(1) *Presumptive rules*—(i) *Amount of recapture.* Except as otherwise provided in this section, upon the occurrence of a triggering event described in paragraph (e) of this section that does not meet any of the exceptions provided in paragraph (f) of this section, the dual resident corporation or domestic owner of the separate unit shall recapture as gross income the total amount of the dual consolidated loss to which the triggering event applies on its income tax return for the taxable year in which the triggering event occurs (or, when the triggering event is a foreign use of the dual consolidated loss, the taxable year that includes the last day of the foreign taxable year during which such foreign use occurs). See §1.1503(d)–5(c)(4)(vi) for rules with respect to the attribution of recapture income to a separate unit. See also §1.1503(d)–7 *Examples 38* through *40.*

(ii) *Interest charge*. In connection with the recapture, the elector shall pay an interest charge. An interest charge may be due even if the amount of recapture income is reduced to zero pursuant to paragraph (h)(2)(i) of this section. See §1.1503(d)–7(c) *Example 39*. Except as otherwise provided in this section, the amount of the interest shall be computed under the rules of section 6601(a) by treating the additional tax resulting from the recapture as though it had been due and unpaid as of the date for payment of the tax for the taxable year in which the taxpayer received a tax benefit from the dual consolidated loss. For purposes of this paragraph (h)(1)(ii), a tax benefit shall be considered to have arisen in a taxable year in which the losses or deductions taken into account in computing the dual consolidated loss reduced U.S. taxable income. For the purpose of computing the interest charge, the additional tax resulting from the recapture is determined by treating the recapture income as the last income earned in the year of recapture. The interest shall be computed to the date for payment of the tax for the year of recapture and the interest thus computed becomes a part of the tax liability for that taxable year. See section 6601 for the computation of interest on a tax liability that it is not paid timely. The recapture interest charge shall be deductible to the same extent as interest under section 6601.

(2) *Reduction of presumptive recapture amount and presumptive interest charge*—(i) *Amount of recapture*. The dual resident corporation or domestic owner may recapture an amount less than the total dual consolidated loss if the elector demonstrates, to the satisfaction of the Commissioner, the lesser amount described in this paragraph (h)(2)(i). The reduction in the amount of recapture is the amount by which the dual consolidated loss would have offset other taxable income reported on a timely filed U.S. income tax return for any taxable year up to and including the taxable year of the triggering event (or, when the triggering event is a foreign use of the dual consolidated loss, the taxable year that includes the last day of the foreign taxable year during which such foreign use occurs) if no domestic use election had been made for the loss such that it was subject to the domestic use limitation of §1.1503(d)–4(b) (and therefore subject to the limitation under §1.1503(d)–4(c)). For this purpose, the rules for attributing items of income, gain, deduction, and loss under §1.1503(d)–5 shall apply. An elector using this rebuttal rule must prepare a separate accounting showing the income for each year that would have offset the dual resident corporation's or separate unit's recapture amount if no domestic use election had been made for the dual consolidated loss. The separate accounting must be signed under penalties of perjury by the person who signs the elector's tax return, must be labeled "Reduction of Recapture Amount" at the top of the page, and must indicate that it is submitted under the provisions of this paragraph (h)(2)(i). The accounting must be attached to, and filed by the due date (including extensions) of, the elector's income tax return for the taxable year in which the triggering event occurs. See §1.1503(d)–7(c) *Examples 38* through *40*.

(ii) *Interest charge*. The interest charge imposed under this section may be reduced if the elector demonstrates, to the satisfaction of the Commissioner, that the net interest owed would have been less than that provided in paragraph (h)(1)(ii) of this section if the elector had filed an amended return for the taxable year in which the recaptured dual consolidated loss was incurred, and for any other affected taxable years up to and including the taxable year of recapture, if no domestic use election had been made for the dual consolidated loss such that it had been subject to the restrictions of §1.1503(d)–4(b) (and therefore subject to the limitations under §1.1503(d)–4(c)). An elector using this rebuttal rule must prepare a computation demonstrating the reduction in the net interest owed as a result of treating the dual consolidated loss as a loss subject to the restrictions of §1.1503(d)–4(b) (and therefore subject to the limitations under §1.1503(d)–4(c)). The computation must be labeled "Reduction of Interest Charge" at the top of the page and must indicate that it is submitted under the provisions of this paragraph (h)(2)(ii). The computation must be signed under penalties of perjury by the person who signs the elector's tax return, and must be attached to, and filed by the due date (including extensions) of, the elector's income tax return for the taxable year in which the triggering event occurs. See §1.1503(d)–7(c) *Examples 39* and *40*.

(3) *Rules regarding multiple-party event exceptions to triggering events*—(i) *Scope*. The rules of this paragraph (h)(3) apply when, after a triggering event described in paragraph (e) of this section with respect to which the requirements of paragraph (f)(2)(i) of this section were met (excepted event), a triggering event under paragraph (e) of this section occurs, and no exception applies to such triggering event under paragraph (f) of this section (subsequent triggering event). See §1.1503(d)–7(c) *Examples 36* and *37*.

(ii) *Original elector and prior subsequent electors not subject to recapture or interest charge*—(A) Except to the extent otherwise provided in this paragraph (h)(3), neither the original elector nor any prior subsequent elector shall be subject to the rules of this paragraph (h) with respect to dual consolidated losses subject to the original domestic use agreement.

(B) In the case of a dual consolidated loss with respect to which multiple excepted events have occurred, only the subsequent elector that owns the dual resident corporation or separate unit at the time of the subsequent triggering event shall be subject to the recapture rules of this paragraph (h). For purposes of this paragraph (h), the term prior subsequent elector refers to all other subsequent electors.

(iii) *Recapture tax amount and required statement*—(A) *In general*. If a subsequent triggering event occurs, the subsequent elector shall take into account the recapture tax amount as determined under paragraph (h)(3)(iii)(B) of this section. The subsequent elector must prepare a statement that computes the recapture tax amount, as provided under paragraph (h)(3)(iii)(B) of this section, with respect to the dual consolidated loss subject to the new domestic use agreement. This statement must be attached to, and filed by the due date (including extensions) of, the subsequent elector's income tax return for the taxable year in which the subsequent triggering event occurs (or, when the subsequent triggering event is a foreign use of the dual consolidated loss, the taxable year that includes the last day of the foreign taxable year during which such foreign use occurs). The statement must be signed under penalties of perjury by the person who signs the return. The statement must be labeled "Statement Identifying Liability" at the top and, in addition to the calculation of the recapture tax amount, must include the following items, in paragraphs labeled to correspond with the items set forth in paragraphs (h)(3)(iii)(A)(*1*) through (*3*) of this section:

(*1*) A statement that the document is submitted under the provisions of §1.1503(d)–6(h)(3)(iii).

(*2*) A statement identifying the amount of the dual consolidated losses at issue and the taxable years in which they were used.

(*3*) The name, address, and taxpayer identification number of the original elector and all prior subsequent electors.

(B) *Recapture tax amount.* The recapture tax amount equals the excess (if any) of—

(*1*) The income tax liability of the subsequent elector for the taxable year that includes the amount of recapture and related interest charge with respect to the dual consolidated losses that are recaptured as a result of the subsequent triggering event, as provided under paragraphs (h)(1) and (h)(2) of this section; over

(*2*) The income tax liability of the subsequent elector for such taxable year, computed by excluding the amount of recapture and related interest charge described in paragraph (h)(3)(iii)(B)(*1*) of this section.

(iv) *Tax assessment and collection procedures*—(A) *In general*—(*1*) *Subsequent elector.* An assessment identifying an income tax liability of the subsequent elector is considered an assessment of the recapture tax amount where the recapture tax amount is part of the income tax liability being assessed and the recapture tax amount is reflected in a statement attached to the subsequent elector's income tax return as provided under paragraph (h)(3)(iii) of this section.

(*2*) *Original elector and prior subsequent electors.* The assessment of the recapture tax amount as set forth in paragraph (h)(3)(iv)(A)(*1*) of this section shall be considered as having been properly assessed as an income tax liability of the original elector and of each prior subsequent elector, if any. The date of such assessment shall be the date the income tax liability of the subsequent elector was properly assessed. The Commissioner may collect all or a portion of such recapture tax amount from the original elector and/or the prior subsequent electors under the circumstances set forth in paragraph (h)(3)(iv)(B) of this section.

(B) *Collection from original elector and prior subsequent electors; joint and several liability*—(1) *In general.* If the subsequent elector does not pay in full the income tax liability that includes a recapture tax amount, the Commissioner may collect that portion of the unpaid balance of such income tax liability attributable to the recapture tax amount in full or in part from the original elector and/or from any prior subsequent elector, provided that the following conditions are satisfied with respect to such elector:

(*i*) The Commissioner properly has assessed the recapture tax amount pursuant to paragraph (h)(3)(iv)(A)(*1*) of this section.

(*ii*) The Commissioner has issued a notice and demand for payment of the recapture tax amount to the subsequent elector in accordance with §301.6303–1 of this chapter.

(*iii*) The subsequent elector has failed to pay all of the recapture tax amount by the date specified in such notice and demand.

(*iv*) The Commissioner has issued a notice and demand for payment of the unpaid portion of the recapture tax amount to the original elector, or prior subsequent elector (as the case may be), in accordance with §301.6303–1 of this chapter.

(*2*) *Joint and several liability.* The liability imposed under this paragraph (h)(3)(iv)(B) on the original elector and each prior subsequent elector shall be joint and several.

(C) *Allocation of partial payments of tax.* If the subsequent elector's income tax liability for a taxable period includes a recapture tax amount, and if such income tax liability is satisfied in part by payment, credit, or offset, such payment, credit or offset shall be allocated first to that portion of the income tax liability that is not attributable to the recapture tax amount, and then to that portion of the income tax liability that is attributable to the recapture tax amount.

(D) *Refund.* If the Commissioner makes a refund of any income tax liability that includes a recapture tax amount, the Commissioner shall allocate and pay the refund to each elector who paid a portion of such income tax liability as follows:

(*1*) The Commissioner shall first determine the total amount of recapture tax paid by and/or collected from the original elector and from any prior subsequent electors. The Commissioner shall then allocate and pay such refund to the original elector and prior subsequent electors, with each such elector receiving an amount of such refund on a *pro rata* basis, not to exceed the amount of recapture tax paid by and/or collected from such elector.

(*2*) The Commissioner shall pay the balance of such refund, if any, to the subsequent elector.

(v) *Definition of income tax liability.* Solely for purposes of paragraph (h)(3) of this section, the term *income tax liability* means the income tax liability imposed on a domestic corporation under Title 26 of the United States Code for a taxable year, including additions to tax, additional amounts, penalties, and any interest charge related to such income tax liability.

(vi) *Example.* See §1.1503(d)–7(c) *Example 36.*

(4) *Computation of taxable income in year of recapture*—(i) *Presumptive rule.* Except to the extent provided in paragraph (h)(4)(ii) of this section, for purposes of computing the taxable income for the year of recapture, no current, carryover or carryback losses may offset and absorb the recapture amount.

(ii) *Exception to presumptive rule.* The recapture amount included in gross income may be offset and absorbed by that portion of the elector's net operating loss carryover that is attributable to the dual resident corporation or separate unit that incurred the dual consolidated loss being recaptured, if the elector demonstrates, to the satisfaction of the Commissioner, the amount of such portion of the carryover. The principles of §1.1502–21(b)(2)(iv) shall apply for purposes of determining whether any portion of a net operating loss carryover is attributable to the dual resident corporation or separate unit. In the case of a separate unit, such determination shall be made by treating the separate unit as a domestic corporation and a member of the consolidated group composing its unaffiliated domestic owner, or members of the consolidated group of which its affiliated domestic owner is a member, as appropriate. An elector utilizing this rebuttal rule must prepare a computation demonstrating the amount of net operating loss carryover that, under this paragraph (h)(4)(ii), may absorb the recapture amount included in gross income. Such computation must be signed under penalties of perjury and attached to and filed by the due date (including extensions) of, the income tax return for the taxable year in which the triggering event occurs (or, when the triggering event is a foreign use of the dual consolidated loss, the taxable year that includes the last day of the foreign taxable year during which such foreign use occurs).

(5) *Character and source of recapture income.* The amount recaptured under this paragraph (h) shall be treated as ordinary income. Except as provided in the prior sentence, such income shall be treated, as applicable, as income from the same source, having the same character, and falling within the same separate category, for all purposes, including sections 904(d) and 907, to which the items of deduction or loss composing the dual consolidated loss were allocated and apportioned, as provided under sections 861(b), 862(b), 863(a), 864(e), 865, and the related regulations. For this determination, the *pro rata* computation of the items of deduction or loss composing the dual consolidated loss as described in §1.1503(d)–4(c)(4) shall apply. See §1.1503(d)–7(c) *Example 38.*

(6) *Reconstituted net operating loss*—(i) *General rule.* Except as provided in paragraphs (h)(6)(ii) and (iii) of this section, commencing in the taxable year immediately following the year in which the dual consolidated loss is recaptured, the dual resident corporation, or the domestic owner of the separate unit, that incurred the dual consolidated loss that is recaptured shall be treated as having a net operating loss (reconstituted net operating loss) in an amount equal to the amount actually recaptured under this paragraph (h). If a domestic corporation (transferee) acquires the assets of the dual resident corporation or domestic owner in a transaction described in section 381(a), the preceding sentence shall be applied by treating the transferee as the dual resident corporation or domestic owner, as applicable. In a case to which this paragraph (h)(6) applies, the transferee corporation shall be treated as having a reconstituted net operating loss in an amount equal to the amount actually recaptured under this paragraph (h). In no event, however, shall more than one corporation be treated as having a reconstituted net operating loss as a result of a single dual consolidated loss being recaptured. A reconstituted net operating loss of a domestic owner shall be attributable under §1.1503(d)–5 to the separate unit that incurred the dual consolidated loss that was recaptured. Moreover, a reconstituted net operating loss shall be subject to the domestic use limitation of §1.1503(d)–4(b) (and therefore subject to the limitation under §1.1503(d)–4(c)), without regard to the exceptions contained in paragraphs (b) through (d) of this section (relating to elective agreements in place between the United States and a foreign country, the ability to demonstrate no possibility of a foreign use, and a domestic use election, respectively). The reconstituted net operating loss shall be available only for carryover, under section 172(b), to taxable years following the taxable year of recapture. For purposes of determining the remaining carryover period, the reconstituted net operating loss shall be treated as if it had been recognized in the taxable year in which the dual consolidated loss that is the basis of the recapture amount was incurred. See §1.1503(d)–7(c) *Examples 36*, *38*, and *40.*

(ii) *Exception.* Paragraph (h)(6)(i) of this section shall not apply to the extent the dual consolidated loss that is the basis of the recapture amount would have been eliminated pursuant to §1.1503(d)–4(d) if no domestic use election had been made for such loss. See §1.1503(d)–7(c) *Example 40.*

(iii) *Special rule for recapture following multiple-party event exception to a triggering event.* This paragraph applies to an excepted event described in paragraph (f)(2)(i)(B) of this section that is followed by a subsequent triggering event requiring recapture as described in paragraph (f)(6) of this section. In such a case, the domestic corporation that owns, directly or indirectly, the assets of the dual resident corporation, or the assets of or the interests in a separate unit, immediately following the excepted event shall be treated as if it incurred the dual consolidated loss that is recaptured for purposes of applying paragraph (h)(6)(i) of this section. See §1.1503(d)–7(c) *Example 36.*

(i) [Reserved].

(j) *Termination of domestic use agreement and annual certifications*—(1) *Rebuttals, exceptions to triggering events, and recapture.* The domestic use agreement filed with respect to a dual consolidated loss shall terminate prior to the end of the certification period and have no further effect if—

(i) An elector is able to rebut the presumption of a triggering event pursuant to the general rule in paragraph (e)(2)(i) of this section;

(ii) An event described in paragraph (e)(1) of this section is not a triggering event as a result of the application of paragraphs (f)(2)(i) or (ii) (relating to events requiring a new domestic use agreement) of this section; this paragraph (j)(1)(ii) does not, however, apply to terminate the new domestic use agreement filed in connection with the event pursuant to paragraph (f)(2)(iii)(A) of this section. See also paragraph (h)(3)(iv) of this section regarding collection from the original elector and prior subsequent electors in certain cases; or

(iii) A dual consolidated loss is recaptured pursuant to paragraph (h) of this section. See §1.1503(d)–7(c) *Examples 32* through *34.*

(2) *Termination of ability for foreign use*—(i) *In general.* A domestic use agreement filed with respect to a dual consolidated loss shall terminate and have no further effect as of the end of a taxable year if the elector—

(A) Demonstrates, to the satisfaction of the Commissioner, that as of the end of such taxable year no foreign use (as defined in §1.1503(d)–3) of the dual consolidated loss can occur in any other year by any means; and

(B) Prepares a statement described in paragraph (j)(2)(ii) of this section that is attached to, and filed by the due date (including extensions) of, its U.S. income tax return for such taxable year.

(ii) *Statement.* The statement described in this paragraph (j)(2)(ii) must be signed under penalties of perjury by the person who signs the return. The statement must be labeled "Termination of Ability for Foreign Use" at the top of the page and must include the following information, in paragraphs labeled to correspond with the following:

(A) A statement that the document is submitted under the provisions of paragraph (j)(2) of this section.

(B) The information required by paragraph (c)(2)(ii) of this section.

(C) A statement of the amount of the dual consolidated loss at issue and the year in which such dual consolidated loss was incurred.

(D) The information described in paragraph (c)(2)(iv) of this section that supports the conclusion that no foreign use can occur as provided in paragraph (j)(2)(i)(A) of this section.

(3) *Agreements filed in connection with stand-alone exception.* See §1.1503(d)–3(e)(2)(iii) for the termination of domestic use agreements filed in connection with the stand-alone exception to the mirror legislation rule when a subsequent election is made under paragraph (b) of this section (relating to agreements entered into between the United States and a foreign country).

§1.1503(d)–7 Examples.

(a) *In general.* This section provides examples that illustrate the application of §§1.1503(d)–1 through 1.1503(d)–6. This section also provides facts that are presumed for such examples.

(b) *Presumed facts for examples.* For purposes of the examples in this section, unless otherwise indicated, the following facts are presumed:

(1) Each entity has only a single class of equity outstanding, all of which is held by a single owner.

(2) P, a domestic corporation and the common parent of the P consolidated group, owns S, a domestic corporation and a member of the P consolidated group.

(3) DRC_X, a domestic corporation, is subject to Country X tax on its worldwide income or on a residence basis, and is a dual resident corporation.

(4) $DE1_X$ and $DE2_X$ are both Country X entities, subject to Country X tax on their worldwide income or on a residence basis, and disregarded as entities separate from their owners for U.S. tax purposes. $DE3_Y$ is a Country Y entity, subject to Country Y tax on its worldwide income or on a residence basis, and disregarded as an entity separate from its owner for U.S. tax purposes. All the interests in $DE1_X$, $DE2_X$, and $DE3_Y$ constitute hybrid entity separate units.

(5) FB_X is a Country X business operation that, if carried on by a U.S. person, would constitute a foreign branch, as defined in §1.367(a)–6T(g)(1), and is a Country X foreign branch separate unit.

(6) Neither the assets nor the activities of an entity constitute a foreign branch separate unit.

(7) FS_X is a Country X entity that is subject to Country X tax on its worldwide income or on a residence basis and is classified as a foreign corporation for U.S. tax purposes.

(8) The applicable foreign country has a consolidation regime that—

(i) Includes as members of a consolidated group any commonly controlled branches and permanent establishments in such jurisdiction, and entities that are subject to tax in such jurisdiction on their worldwide income or on a residence basis; and

(ii) Allows the losses of members of consolidated groups to offset income of other members.

(9) There is no mirror legislation, within the meaning of §1.1503(d)–3(e)(1), in the applicable foreign country.

(10) There is no elective agreement described in §1.1503(d)–6(b) between the United States and the applicable foreign country.

(11) There is no income tax convention between the United States and the applicable foreign country.

(12) If a domestic use election, within the meaning of §1.1503(d)–6(d), is made, all the necessary filings related to such election are properly completed on a timely basis.

(13) If there is a triggering event requiring recapture of a dual consolidated loss, the amount of recapture is not reduced pursuant to §1.1503(d)–6(h)(2).

(14) There are no other items of income, gain, deduction, and loss. In addition, the United States and the applicable foreign country recognize the same items of income, gain, deduction, and loss in each taxable year.

(15) All taxpayers use the calendar year as their taxable year.

(c) *Examples.* The following examples illustrate the application of §§1.1503(d)–1 through 1.1503(d)–6:

Example 1. Separate unit combination rule. (i) *Facts.* P owns $DE3_Y$ which, in turn, owns $DE1_X$. $DE1_X$ owns FB_X. PRS, an entity treated as a partnership for both U.S. and Country X tax purposes, is owned 50 percent by P and 50 percent by an unrelated foreign person. PRS carries on a business operation in Country X that, if carried on by a U.S. person, would constitute a foreign branch within the meaning of §1.367(a)–6T(g)(1). In addition, P owns DRC_X, a member of the consolidated group of which P is the parent, which carries on business operations in Country X that constitute a foreign branch within the meaning of §1.367(a)–6T(g)(1). S owns $DE2_X$.

(ii) *Result.* Pursuant to §1.1503(d)–1(b)(4)(ii), the interest in $DE1_X$, the interest in $DE2_X$, FB_X, P's share of the Country X business operations carried on by PRS (which is owned by P indirectly through its interest in PRS), and DRC_X's Country X business operations are combined and treated as a single separate unit of the consolidated group of which P is the parent. This is the case regardless of whether the losses of each individual separate unit are made available to offset the income of the other individual separate units under Country X tax laws. Because DRC_X is a dual resident corporation, it is not combined and treated as part of this combined separate unit and, as a result, DRC_x's income or dual consolidated loss is not taken into account in determining the income or dual consolidated loss of the combined separate unit. In addition, P's interest in $DE3_Y$ is not combined and is another separate unit because it is subject to tax in Country Y, rather than Country X.

Example 2. Definition of a separate unit and application of domestic use limitation—foreign branch separate unit. (i) *Facts.* P carries on business operations in Country X that constitute a permanent establishment under the U.S.-Country X income tax convention. In year 1, a loss is attributable to P's Country X permanent establishment, as determined under §1.1503(d)–5.

(ii) *Result.* Under §§1.1503(d)–1(b)(4)(i)(A) and 1.367(a)–6T(g)(1), P's Country X permanent establishment constitutes a foreign branch separate unit. Therefore, the year 1 loss attributable to the foreign branch separate unit constitutes a dual consolidated loss pursuant to §1.1503(d)–1(b)(5)(ii). The dual consolidated loss rules apply to the dual consolidated loss even though there is no affiliate of the foreign branch separate unit in Country X, because it is still possible that all or a portion of the dual consolidated loss can be put to a foreign use. For example, there may be a foreign use with respect to a Country X affiliate acquired in a year subsequent to the year in which the dual consolidated loss was incurred. See §1.1503(d)–6(a)(2). Accordingly, unless an exception under §1.1503(d)–6 applies (such as a domestic use election), the year 1 dual consolidated loss attributable to P's Country X permanent establishment is subject to the domestic use limitation rule of §1.1503(d)–4(b). As a result, pursuant to §1.1503(d)–4(c), the year 1 dual consolidated loss cannot offset income of P that is not attributable to its Country X foreign branch separate unit, nor can it offset income of any other domestic affiliate. The loss can, however, offset income of the Country X foreign branch separate unit, subject to the application of §1.1503(d)–4(c). The result would be the same even if Country X did not have a consolidation regime that includes as members of consolidated groups Country X branches or permanent establishments of nonresident corporations. The dual consolidated loss rules apply even in the absence of a consolidation regime in the foreign country because it is possible that all or a portion of a dual consolidated loss can be put to a foreign use by other means, such as through a sale, merger, or similar transaction. See §1.1503(d)–6(a)(2).

(iii) *Alternative facts.* The facts are the same as in paragraph (i) of this *Example 2*, except that P's Country X business operations constitute a foreign branch as defined in §1.367(a)–6T(g)(1), but do not constitute a permanent establishment under the U.S.-Country X income tax convention. Although the activities carried on by P in Country X would otherwise constitute a foreign branch separate unit as described in §1.1503(d)–1(b)(4)(i)(A), the exception under §1.1503(d)–1(b)(4)(iii) applies because the activities do not constitute a permanent establishment under the U.S.-Country X income tax convention. Thus, the Country X business operations do not constitute a foreign branch separate unit, and the year 1 loss is not subject to the dual consolidated loss rules. If P instead carried on its Country X business operations through $DE1_X$, then the exception under §1.1503(d)–1(b)(4)(iii) would not apply because P carries on the business operations through a hybrid entity and, as a result, the business operations would constitute a foreign branch separate unit. Thus, in such a case the year 1 loss would be subject to the dual consolidated loss rules.

Example 3. Domestic use limitation—foreign branch separate unit owned through a partnership. (i) *Facts.* P and S organize a partnership, PRS_X, under the laws of Country X. PRS_X is treated as a partnership for both U.S. and Country X tax purposes. PRS_X owns FB_X. PRS_X earns U.S. source income that is unconnected with its FB_X branch operations, and such income is not subject to tax by Country X. In addition, such U.S. source income is not attributable to FB_X under §1.1503(d)–5.

(ii) *Result.* Under §1.1503(d)–1(b)(4)(i)(A), P's and S's shares of FB_X owned indirectly through their interests in PRS_X are individual foreign branch separate units. Pursuant to §1.1503(b)–1(b)(4)(ii), these individual separate units are combined and treated as a single separate unit of the consolidated group of which P is the parent. Unless an exception under §1.1503(d)–6 applies, any dual consolidated loss attributable to FB_X cannot offset income of P or S (other than income attributable to FB_X, subject to the application of §1.1503(d)–4(c)), including their distributive share of the U.S. source income earned through their interests in PRS_X, nor can it offset income of any other domestic affiliates.

Example 4. Definition of a separate unit and domestic use limitation—interest in hybrid entity partnership and indirectly owned foreign branch separate unit. (i) *Facts.* HPS_X is a Country X entity that is subject to Country X tax on its worldwide income. HPS_X is classified as a partnership for Federal tax purposes. P, S, and FS_X, are the sole partners of HPS_X. For U.S. tax purposes, P, S, and FS_X each has an equal interest in each item of HPS_X's profit or loss. HPS_X carries on operations in Country Y that, if carried on by a U.S. person, would constitute a foreign branch within the meaning of §1.367(a)–6T(g)(1).

(ii) *Result.* Under §1.1503(d)–1(b)(4)(i)(B), the partnership interests in HPS_X held by P and S are individual hybrid entity separate units. These individual separate units are combined into a single separate unit under §1.1503(d)–1(b)(4)(ii). In addition, P's and S's share of the Country Y operations owned indirectly through their interests in HPS_X are individual foreign branch separate units under §1.1503(d)–1(b)(4)(i)(B). These individual separate units are also combined into a single separate unit under §1.1503(d)–1(b)(4)(ii). Unless an exception under §1.1503(d)–6 applies, dual consolidated losses attributable to P's and S's combined interests in HPS_X can only be used to offset income attributable to their combined interests in HPS_X (other than income attributable to P's and S's combined interests in the Country Y foreign branch separate unit), subject to the application of §1.1503(d)–4(c). Similarly, dual consolidated losses attributable to P's and S's combined interests in the Country Y operations of HPS_X can only be used to offset income attributable to their combined interests in such Country Y operations, subject to the application of §1.1503(d)–4(c). Neither FS_X's interest in HPS_X, nor its share of the Country Y operations owned by HPS_X, is a separate unit because FS_X is not a domestic corporation.

Example 5. Foreign use—general rule and de minimis reduction exception. (i) *Facts.* P owns $DE1_X$. $DE1_X$ owns FS_X. In year 1, there is a $100x loss attributable to P's interest in $DE1_X$ that is a dual consolidated loss. Also in year 1, FS_X earns $200x of income. $DE1_X$ and FS_X file a Country X consolidated tax return. For Country X tax purposes, the year 1 $100x loss of $DE1_X$ is used to offset $100x of year 1 income generated by FS_X. Under Country X tax law, unused losses are carried forward and available to offset income in subsequent taxable years.

(ii) *Result.* The $100x loss attributable to P's interest in $DE1_X$ is available to, and in fact does, offset FS_X's income under the laws of Country X. In addition, under U.S. tax principles, such income is considered to be an item of FS_X, a foreign corporation. As a result, under §1.1503(d)–3(a), there has been a foreign use of the year 1 dual consolidated loss attributable to P's interest in $DE1_X$. Therefore, P cannot make a domestic use election with respect to the loss as provided under §1.1503(d)–6(d)(2), and such loss will be subject to the domestic use limitation rule of §1.1503(d)–4(b). The result would be the same even if FS_X, under Country X tax law, had no income against which the dual consolidated loss of $DE1_X$ could be offset (unless FS_X's ability to use the loss under Country X tax law requires an election, and no such election is made).

(iii) *Alternative facts.* The facts are the same as in paragraph (i) of this *Example 5*, except that FS_X cannot use the loss of $DE1_X$ under Country X tax law without an election, and no such election is made. Pursuant to the exception in §1.1503(d)–3(c)(2), there is no foreign use of the year 1 dual consolidated loss attributable to P's interest in $DE1_X$. In addition, P files a domestic use election with respect to the year 1 dual consolidated loss attributable to its interest in $DE1_X$ and, at the beginning of year 3, P sells its interest in $DE1_X$ to F, a Country Y entity that is a foreign corporation. The sale of the interest in $DE1_X$ to F results in a foreign use triggering event pursuant to §1.1503(d)–6(e)(1)(i) because, immediately after the sale, the loss attributable to the interest in $DE1_X$ carries over under Country X law and, therefore, is available under U.S. tax principles to offset income of the owner of the interest in $DE1_X$ which, in the hands of F, is not a separate unit. It is also a foreign use because the loss is available under U.S. tax principles to offset the income of F, a foreign corporation. See §1.1503(d)–3(a)(1). Finally, the transfer is a triggering event pursuant to §1.1503(d)–6(e)(1)(iv) and (v).

(iv) *Alternative facts.* The facts are the same as in paragraph (iii), of this *Example 5*, except that P only sells 5 percent of its interest in $DE1_X$ to F. Pursuant to Rev. Rul. 99–5, 1999–1 C.B. 434, see §601.601(d)(2)(ii)(b) of this chapter, the transaction is treated as if P sold 5 percent of its interest in each of $DE1_X$'s assets to F, and then immediately thereafter P and F transferred their interests in the assets of $DE1_X$ to a partnership in exchange for an ownership interest therein. The sale of the 5 percent interest in $DE1_X$ generally results in a foreign use triggering event because a portion of the dual consolidated loss carries over under Country X tax law and is available under U.S. tax principles to offset income of the owner of the interest in $DE1_X$, a hybrid entity, which in the hands of F is not a separate unit. It is also a foreign use because the loss is available under U.S. tax principles to offset the income of F, a foreign corporation. See §1.1503(d)–3(a)(1). However, pursuant to the exception under §1.1503(d)–3(c)(5) (relating to a *de minimis* reduction of an interest in a separate unit), such availability does not result in a foreign use. In addition, pursuant to §1.1503(d)–6(f)(1) and (3), the deemed transfers pursuant to Rev. Rul. 99–5 as a result of the sale are not treated as triggering events described in §1.1503(d)–6(e)(1)(iv) or (v).

Example 6. Foreign use and indirect foreign use—foreign reverse hybrid structure and disregarded payments. (i) *Facts.* P owns $DE1_X$. $DE1_X$ owns 99 percent and S owns 1 percent of FRH_X, a Country X partnership that elected to be treated as a corporation for U.S. tax purposes. FRH_X conducts a trade or business in Country X. In year 1, $DE1_X$ incurs interest expense on a third-party loan, which constitutes a dual consolidated loss attributable to P's interest in $DE1_X$. In year 1, for Country X tax purposes, $DE1_X$ takes into account its distributive share of income generated by FRH_X and offsets such income with its interest expense.

(ii) *Result.* In year 1, the dual consolidated loss attributable to P's interest in $DE1_X$ is available to, and in fact does, offset income recognized in Country X and, under U.S. tax principles, the income is considered to be income of FRH_X, a foreign corporation. Accordingly, pursuant to §1.1503(d)–3(a)(1), there is a foreign use of the dual consolidated loss. Therefore, P cannot make a domestic use election with respect to the year 1 dual consolidated loss attributable to its interest in $DE1_X$, as provided under §1.1503(d)–6(d)(2), and such loss will be subject to the domestic use limitation rule of §1.1503(d)–4(b).

(iii) *Alternative facts.* (A) The facts are the same as in paragraph (i) of this *Example 6*, except as follows. Instead of owning $DE1_X$, P owns $DE3_Y$ which, in turn, owns $DE1_X$. In addition, $DE3_Y$, rather than $DE1_X$, is the obligor on the third-party loan and therefore incurs the interest expense on such loan. Finally, $DE3_Y$ on-lends the loan proceeds from the third-party loan to $DE1_X$, and $DE1_X$ pays interest to $DE3_Y$ on such loan that is generally disregarded for U.S. tax purposes.

(B) Pursuant to §1.1503(d)–5(c)(1)(ii), for purposes of calculating income or a dual consolidated loss, $DE3_Y$ and $DE1_X$ do not take into account interest income or interest expense, respectively, with respect to amounts paid on the disregarded loan from $DE3_Y$ to $DE1_X$. As a result, such items neither create a dual consolidated loss with respect to the interest in $DE1_X$, nor do they reduce (or eliminate) the dual consolidated loss attributable to the interest in $DE3_Y$. Thus, in year 1, there is a dual consolidated loss attributable to P's interest in $DE3_Y$, but not to P's indirect interest in $DE1_X$.

(C) In year 1, interest expense paid by $DE1_X$ to $DE3_Y$ on the disregarded loan is taken into account as a deduction in computing $DE1_X$'s taxable income for Country X tax purposes, but does not give rise to a corresponding item of income or gain for U.S. tax purposes (because it is generally disregarded). In addition, such interest has the effect of making an item of deduction or loss composing the dual consolidated loss attributable to P's interest in $DE3_Y$ available for a foreign use. This is the case because it may reduce or offset items of deduction or loss composing the dual consolidated loss for foreign tax purposes, and creates another deduction or loss that may reduce or offset income of $DE1_X$ for foreign tax purposes that, under U.S. tax principles, is treated as income of FRH_X, a foreign corporation. Moreover, because the disregarded item is incurred or taken into account as interest for foreign tax purposes, it is deemed to have been incurred or taken into account with a principal purpose of avoiding the provisions of section 1503(d). Accordingly, there is an indirect foreign use of the year 1 dual consolidated loss attributable to P's interest in $DE3_Y$, and P cannot make a domestic use election with respect to such loss as provided under §1.1503(d)–6(d)(2). Thus, the loss will be subject to the domestic use limitation rule of §1.1503(d)–4(b).

Example 7. Indirect foreign use—hybrid instrument. (i) *Facts.* P owns $DE1_X$ which, in turn, owns FS_X. $DE1_X$ borrows cash from an unrelated lender and transfers the cash to FS_X in exchange for an instrument (hybrid instrument). The hybrid instrument is treated as equity for U.S. tax purposes and debt for Country X tax purposes. Interest expense on the loan from the unrelated lender results in a dual consolidated loss being attributable to P's interest in $DE1_X$ in year 1. $DE1_X$ does not elect under Country X law to consolidate with FS_X. In year 1, FS_X distributes its stock as a payment on the hybrid instrument to $DE1_X$. For U.S. tax purposes, such payment is excluded from P's gross income under section 305. However, for Country X tax purposes, such payment is treated as interest and gives rise to a deduction taken into account in computing FS_X's Country X tax liability; the payment also gives rise to interest income to $DE1_X$ for Country X tax purposes.

(ii) *Result.* The payment on the hybrid instrument does not give rise to an item of income or gain for U.S. tax purposes and therefore does not reduce (or eliminate) the dual consolidated loss attributable to P's interest in $DE1_X$. In addition, such payment is taken into account as a deduction in computing FS_X's taxable income for Country X tax purposes. Moreover, such payment has the effect of making an item of deduction or loss composing the dual consolidated loss attributable to P's interest in $DE1_X$ available for a foreign use. This is the case because it may reduce or offset items of deduction or loss composing the dual consolidated loss for foreign tax purposes, and creates a deduction that reduces or offsets income of FS_X for foreign tax purposes that, under U.S. tax principles, is income of a foreign corporation. Further, because the item is incurred, or taken into account, using an instrument that is treated as equity for U.S. tax purposes and debt for foreign tax purposes, it is deemed to have been engaged in with the principal purpose of avoiding the provisions of section 1503(d). As a result, there has been an indirect foreign use of the year 1 dual consolidated loss, and P cannot make a domestic use election with respect to such loss, as provided under §1.1503(d)–6(d)(2). Thus, the year 1 dual consolidated loss will be subject to the domestic use limitation rule of §1.1503(d)–4(b).

Example 8. No indirect foreign use—transaction entered into in the ordinary course of business. (i) *Facts.* P owns $DE1_X$ and FB_Y. FB_Y is a foreign branch separate unit located in Country Y. $DE1_X$ owns FB_X and FS_X. P's interest in $DE1_X$ and FB_X are combined and treated as a single separate unit (Country X separate unit) pursuant to §1.1503(d)–1(b)(4)(ii). Under Country X tax laws, $DE1_X$ elects to consolidate with FS_X. FB_Y engages in the business of providing services and, in connection with its ordinary course of business, provides services to unrelated third parties and to $DE1_X$. As compensation for services, $DE1_X$ makes a payment to FB_Y. Under Country X tax law, the payment is deductible. However, the payment is generally disregarded for U.S. tax purposes and, pursuant to §1.1503(d)–5(c)(1)(ii), is not taken into account in calculating the income or dual consolidated loss attributable to the Country X separate unit or FB_Y. In year 1, the Country X separate unit and FB_Y each has a dual consolidated loss. The dual consolidated loss attributable to the Country X separate unit is subject to the domestic use limitation under §1.1503(d)–4(b) because $DE1_X$ and FS_X elect to consolidate and, as a result, the dual consolidated loss is put to a foreign use.

(ii) *Result.* The payment made by $DE1_X$ to FB_Y in connection with the performance of services is taken into account as a deduction in computing $DE1_X$'s taxable income for Country X tax purposes, but does not give rise to an item of income or gain for U.S. tax purposes. In addition, such payment has the effect of making an item of deduction or loss composing the dual consolidated loss attributable to FB_Y available for a foreign use. This is the case because it may reduce or offset items of deduction or loss composing the dual consolidated loss of FB_Y for foreign tax purposes, and creates another deduction that reduces or offsets income of FS_X for foreign tax purposes (because $DE1_X$ and FS_X elect to file a consolidated return) that, under U.S. tax principles, is income of a foreign corporation. However, the transaction between $DE1_X$ and FB_Y was entered into in the ordinary course of FB_Y's trade or business. As a result, if P can demonstrate to the satisfaction of the Commissioner that the transaction was not entered into with a principal purpose of avoiding the provisions of section 1503(d), FB_Y's year 1 dual consolidated loss will not be treated as having been made available for an indirect foreign use. In such a case, P would be entitled to make a domestic use election with respect to such loss.

Example 9. Foreign use—dual resident corporation with hybrid entity joint venture. (i) *Facts.* P owns DRC_X, a member of the P consolidated group. DRC_X owns 80 percent of HPS_X, a Country X entity that is subject to Country X tax on its worldwide income. HPS_X is classified as a partnership for U.S. tax purposes. FS_X owns the remaining 20 percent of HPS_X. In year 1, DRC_X generates a \$100x net operating loss (without regard to items attributable to DRC_X's interest in HPS_X). Also in year 1, HPS_X generates \$100x of income, \$80x of which is attributable to DRC_X's interest in HPS_X. DRC_X and HPS_X file a consolidated tax return for Country X tax purposes, and HPS_X offsets its \$100x of income with the \$100x loss generated by DRC_X.

(ii) *Result.* DRC_X and its interest in HPS_X are not combined because DRC_X is a dual resident corporation and the combination rule under §1.1503(d)–1(b)(4)(ii) only applies to separate units. The \$100x year 1 net operating loss incurred by DRC_X (without regard to items attributable to DRC_X's interest in HPS_X) is a dual consolidated loss. In addition, HPS_X is a hybrid entity and DRC_X's interest in HPS_X is a hybrid entity separate unit; however, there is no dual consolidated loss attributable to such separate unit in year 1 (instead, there is \$80x of income attributable to such separate unit). DRC_X's year 1 dual consolidated loss offsets \$100x of income for Country X purposes, and \$20x of such income is, under U.S. tax principles, income of FS_X, which owns an interest in HPS_X that is not a separate unit (in addition, FS_X is a foreign corporation). As a result, pursuant to §1.1503(d)–3(a), there is a foreign use of the year 1 dual consolidated loss of DRC_X, and P cannot make a domestic use election with respect to such loss pursuant to §1.1503(d)–6(d)(2). Therefore, such loss will be subject to the domestic use limitation rule of §1.1503(d)–4(b). The result would be the same even if HPS_X, under Country X laws, had no income against which the dual consolidated loss could be offset (unless the ability to use the loss under Country X laws required an election, and no such election is made).

Example 10. Foreign use—foreign parent corporation. (i) *Facts.* F1 and F2, nonresident alien individuals, each owns 50 percent of FP_X, a Country X entity that is subject to Country X tax on its worldwide income. FP_X is classified as a foreign corporation for U.S. tax purposes. FP_X owns DRC_X. DRC_X is the parent of a consolidated group that includes as a member DS, a domestic corporation. In year 1, DRC_X incurs a dual consolidated loss of \$100x and, for Country X tax purposes, FP_X generates \$100x of income. In year 1, FP_X elects to consolidate with DRC_X for Country X tax purposes, and the \$100x year 1 loss of DRC_X is used to offset the income of FP_X under the laws of Country X. For U.S. tax purposes, the items of FP_X do not constitute items of income in year 1.

(ii) *Result.* The year 1 dual consolidated loss of DRC_X offsets the income of FP_X under the laws of Country X. Pursuant to §1.1503(d)–3(a), the offset constitutes a foreign use because the items constituting such income are considered under U.S. tax principles to be items of a foreign corporation. This is the case even though the United States does not recognize such items as income in year 1. Therefore, DRC_X cannot make a domestic use election with respect to its year 1 dual consolidated loss pursuant to §1.1503(d)–6(d)(2). As a result, such loss will be subject to the domestic use limitation rule of §1.1503(d)–4(b).

(iii) *Alternative facts.* The facts are the same as in paragraph (i) of this *Example 10*, except that FP_X is classified as a partnership for U.S. tax purposes. The result would be the same as in paragraph (ii) of this *Example 10*, because the offset of the income generated by FP_X is a foreign use pursuant to §1.1503(d)–3(a). This is the case because the items constituting such income are considered under U.S. tax principles to be items of F1 and F2, the owners of interests in FP_X (a hybrid entity), that are not separate units. Moreover, the result would be the same if F1 and F2 owned their interests in FP_X indirectly through another partnership.

Example 11. No foreign use—absence of foreign loss allocation rules. (i) *Facts.* P owns $DE1_X$ and DRC_X. DRC_X is a member of the P consolidated group and owns FS_X. $DE1_X$ owns FB_X. P's interest in $DE1_X$ and P's indirect interest in FB_X are individual separate units that are combined into a single separate unit (Country X separate unit) pursuant to §1.1503(d)–1(b)(4)(ii). In year 1, DRC_X incurs a $200x net operating loss and $200x of income is attributable to P's Country X separate unit. The $200x net operating loss incurred by DRC_X is a dual consolidated loss. FS_X also earns $200x of income in year 1. DRC_X, $DE1_X$, and FS_X file a Country X consolidated tax return. However, Country X has no applicable rules for determining which income is offset by DRC_X's year 1 $200x loss.

(ii) *Result.* Under §1.1503(d)–3(c)(3), DRC_X's $200x loss shall be treated as having been made available to offset the $200x of income attributable to P's Country X separate unit. P's Country X separate unit is not, under U.S. tax principles, a foreign corporation, and there is no interest in $DE1_X$ (which is a hybrid entity) that is not a separate unit. As a result, DRC_X's loss being made available to offset the income attributable to P's Country X separate unit is not considered a foreign use of such loss. Therefore, P can make a domestic use election with respect to DRC_X's year 1 dual consolidated loss.

(iii) *Alternative facts.* The facts are the same as in paragraph (i) of this *Example 11*, except that in year 1 only $150x of income is attributable to P's Country X separate unit. Because only $150x of income is attributed to P's Country X separate unit, $50x of DRC_X's year 1 dual consolidated loss is treated as being made available to offset the income of FS_X, a foreign corporation, and therefore constitutes a foreign use. As a result, DRC_X cannot make a domestic use election with respect to its year 1 dual consolidated loss pursuant to §1.1503(d)–6(d)(2), and such loss will be subject to the domestic use limitation rule of §1.1503(d)–4(b).

Example 12. No foreign use—absence of foreign loss usage ordering rules. (i) *Facts.* (A) P owns DRC_X, a member of the P consolidated group. DRC_X owns FS_X. Under the Country X consolidation regime, a consolidated group may elect in any given year to use all or a portion of the losses of one consolidated group member to offset income of other consolidated group members. If no such election is made in a year in which losses are generated by a consolidated member, such losses carry forward and are available, at the election of the consolidated group, to offset income of consolidated group members in subsequent taxable years. Country X law does not provide ordering rules for determining when a loss from a particular taxable year is used because, under Country X law, losses never expire. In addition, Country X law does not provide ordering rules for determining when a particular type of loss (for example, capital or ordinary) is used.

(B) In year 1, DRC_X incurs a capital loss of $80x which, under §1.1503(d)–5(b)(2), is not a dual consolidated loss. DRC_X also incurs a net operating loss of $80x in year 1 which is a dual consolidated loss. FS_X generates $60x of capital gain in year 1 which, for Country X purposes, can be offset by capital losses and net operating losses. Under the laws of Country X, DRC_X elects to use $60x of its total year 1 loss of $160x to offset the $60x of capital gain generated by FS_X in year 1; the remaining $100x of year 1 loss carries forward. In both year 2 and year 3, DRC_X incurs a net operating loss of $100x, while FS_X incurs no income or loss in years 2 and 3. DRC_X's $100x losses incurred in year 2 and year 3 are dual consolidated losses. Because DRC_X does not elect under the laws of Country X to use all or a portion of its year 2 or year 3 net operating losses of $100x to offset the income of other members of the Country X consolidated group, P is permitted to make (and in fact does make) a domestic use election with respect to both the year 2 and year 3 dual consolidated losses of DRC_X. In year 4, DRC_X has a net operating loss of $10x and FS_X generates $125x of income. Country X law permits, upon an election, FS_X's $125x of income generated in year 4 to be offset by losses (including carryover losses from prior years) of other group members. Accordingly, in year 4, DRC_X elects to use $125x of its accumulated losses to offset the $125x of year 4 income generated by FS_X.

(ii) *Result.* (A) Under the ordering rules of §1.1503(d)–3(d)(3), a *pro rata* amount of DRC_X's year 1 net operating loss ($30x) and capital loss ($30x) is considered to be used to offset FS_X's year 1 $60x capital gain. As a result, P cannot make a domestic use election with respect to DRC_X's year 1 $80x dual consolidated loss because a portion of such loss is put to a foreign use.

(B) DRC_X's $10x year 4 net operating loss is also a dual consolidated loss. Under the ordering rules of §1.1503(d)–3(d)(1), such loss is considered to be used to offset $10x of FS_X's year 4 $125x of income. Consequently, P cannot make a domestic use election with respect to such loss. Under the ordering rules of §1.1503(d)–3(d)(2), $50x of capital loss carryover and $50x of ordinary loss from year 1 will be considered to offset $100x of FS_X's year 4 income because the income is first deemed to have been offset by losses the use of which would not constitute a triggering event that would result in the recapture of a dual consolidated loss. The remaining $15x of FS_X's year 4 income is considered to be offset by losses from year 3 because it is the most recent taxable year from which a loss may be carried forward. Thus, a portion of the year 3 dual consolidated loss has been put to a foreign use and the entire year 3 dual consolidated loss is recaptured. However, none of DRC_X's $100x year 2 net operating loss will be deemed to offset FS_X's year 4 income. As a result, DRC_X's year 2 dual consolidated loss will not be recaptured.

Example 13. Exception to foreign use through partnership interest. (i) *Facts.* (A) P owns 80 percent of HPS_X, a Country X entity subject to Country X tax on its worldwide income. FS_Z, an unrelated foreign corporation, owns the remaining 20 percent of HPS_X. HPS_X is classified as a partnership for Federal tax purposes and carries on operations in Country X that, if carried on by a U.S. person, would constitute a foreign branch within the meaning of §1.367(a)–6T(g)(1). P's interest in HPS_X and P's indirect interest in the Country X branch are individual separate units that are combined into a single separate unit (Country X separate unit) pursuant to §1.1503(d)–1(b)(4)(ii).

(B) In year 1, HPS_X incurs a loss of $100x, $80x of which is attributable to P's Country X separate unit. The $80x of loss attributable to P's Country X separate unit constitutes a dual consolidated loss and P makes a domestic use election with respect to such loss. In year 2, HPS_X generates $50x of income, $40x of which is attributable to P's interest in the Country X separate unit. Under Country X income tax laws, the $100x of year 1 loss incurred by HPS_X is carried forward and offsets the $50x of income generated by HPS_X in year 2; the remaining $50x of loss is carried forward and is available to offset income generated by HPS_X in subsequent years. P and FS_Z maintain their ownership interests in HPS_X throughout years 1 and 2.

(ii) *Result.* In year 2, under the laws of Country X, the $100x of year 1 loss, which includes the $80x dual consolidated loss attributable to P's Country X separate unit, is made available to offset income of HPS_X. Such income is attributable to P's interest in HPS_X, which is a separate unit. Such income also is income of FS_Z, a foreign corporation that is an owner of an interest in HPS_X, which is not a separate unit. However, pursuant to §1.1503(d)–3(c)(4), there is no foreign use of the year 1 dual consolidated loss in year 2. This is the case because P's interest in HPS_X as of the end of year 1 has not been reduced by more than a *de minimis* amount, and the portion of the $80x dual consolidated loss was made available for a foreign use in year 2 solely as a result of FS_Z's ownership in HPS_X and the allocation or carry forward of the dual consolidated loss as a result of such ownership.

(iii) *Alternative facts.* The facts are the same as in paragraph (i) of this *Example 13*, except that P also owns FS_X. In addition, FS_X and HPS_X elect to file a consolidated return under Country X law. The exception to foreign use under §1.1503(d)–3(c)(4) does not apply because there is a foreign use other than by reason of the dual consolidated loss being made available as a result of FS_Z's ownership in HPS_X and the allocation or carry forward of the dual consolidated loss as a result of such ownership. That is, the exception does not apply because there is also a foreign use of the dual consolidated loss as a result of FS_X and HPS_X filing a consolidated return under Country X law.

(iv) *Alternative facts.* The facts are the same as in paragraph (i) of this *Example 13*, except that at the end of year 2, FS_Z contributes cash to HPS_X in exchange for additional equity of HPS_X. As a result of the contribution, FS_Z's interest in HPS_X increases from 20 percent to 30 percent, and P's interest in HPS_X decreases from 80 percent to 70 percent. P's interest in HPS_X is reduced within a single 12-month period by 12.5 percent (10/80), as compared to P's interest in HPS_X as of the beginning of such 12-month period. Accordingly, pursuant to §1.1503(d)–3(c)(4)(iii), the exception to foreign use provided under §1.1503(d)–3(c)(4)(i) does not apply. Therefore, in year 2 there is a foreign use of the $80x year 1 dual consolidated loss attributable to P's Country X separate unit. Such foreign use constitutes a triggering event in year 2 and the $80x year 1 dual consolidated loss is recaptured. Alternatively, if FS_Z were a domestic corporation, there would not be a foreign use of the \$80x year 1 dual consolidated loss because the loss would not be available to offset income that, under U.S. tax principles, is income of a foreign corporation or a direct or indirect owner of an interest in a hybrid entity that is not a separate unit.

Example 14. Exception to foreign use through partnership interest—combination rule. (i) *Facts.* (A) P and FS_X form PRS_X. P and FS_X each own 50 percent of PRS_X throughout years 1 and 2. PRS_X is treated as a partnership for both U.S. and Country X tax purposes. PRS_X owns DE_Y. DE_Y is a Country Y entity subject to Country Y tax on its worldwide income and disregarded as an entity separate from its owner for U.S. tax purposes. DE_Y conducts business operations in Country Y that, if carried on by a U.S. person, would constitute a foreign branch as defined in §1.367(a)–6T(g)(1). P's interest in the Country Y operations conducted by DE_Y is an individual foreign branch separate unit. P's interest in DE_Y, owned indirectly through PRS_X, is a hybrid entity individual separate unit. P also owns FB_Y, a Country Y foreign branch individual separate unit. Under §1.1503(d)–1(b)(4)(ii), FB_Y and P's indirect interests in DE_Y and DE_Y's Country Y business operations are treated as a combined separate unit (Country Y separate unit).

(B) In year 1, there is a \$100x loss attributable to the Country Y business operations conducted by DE_Y. Thus, there is a \$50x loss attributable to P's interest in DE_Y's Country Y business operations in year 1. Also in year 1, there is a \$200x loss attributable to FB_Y. No income or loss is attributable to P's interest in DE_Y in year 1. Under §1.1503(d)–5(c)(4)(ii), the dual consolidated loss attributable to P's combined Country Y separate unit is \$250x (\$50x loss attributable to P's indirect interest in DE_Y's Country Y operations, plus \$200x loss attributable to FB_Y). In year 2, neither DE_Y nor DE_Y's Country Y operations generates income or loss. Under Country Y law, the \$100x of year 1 loss incurred by DE_Y is carried forward and is available to offset income of DE_Y in year 2.

(ii) *Result.* As a result of the carryover of the year 1 \$100x loss (which includes \$50x of the year 1 dual consolidated loss) under Country Y law, a portion of such loss will be available to offset income of DE_Y that is attributable to P's interest in DE_Y owned indirectly through PRS_X. A portion of such loss will also be available to offset income of DE_Y that is attributable to FS_X's indirect ownership of DE_Y. Accordingly, under §1.1503(d)–3(a), there would be a foreign use of a portion of P's \$250x year 1 dual consolidated loss because it is available to offset an item of income of the owner of an interest in a hybrid entity, which is not a separate unit (there would also be a foreign use in this case because FS_X is a foreign corporation). However, there has not been a reduction of P's interest in DE_Y, DE_Y has not consolidated under the laws of Country Y, and there has not been any other foreign use of the dual consolidated losses. As a result, no foreign use occurs as a result of the carryforward pursuant to §1.1503(d)–3(c)(4)(i) and (ii).

Example 15. No foreign use—asset basis carryover exception. (i) *Facts.* P owns FB_X and FS_X. In year 1, there is a dual consolidated loss attributable to FB_X. P's items of income, gain, deduction, and loss that are taken into account in calculating FB_X's dual consolidated loss include depreciation deductions attributable to FB_X's assets. P makes a domestic use election under §1.1503(d)–6(d) with respect to the year 1 dual consolidated loss of FB_X. At the end of year 2, P contributes a portion of FB_X's assets to FS_X, in exchange for stock in FS_X. The aggregate adjusted basis of the assets transferred by P to FS_X is less than 10 percent of the aggregate adjusted basis of all of FB_X's assets held at the beginning of year 2. In addition, no other assets of FB_X are transferred during the certification period. Under Country X law, FS_X's basis in the transferred assets is determined by reference to P's basis in such assets. In addition, under Country X law, a portion of the depreciation deductions that were taken into account in year 1 for U.S. tax purposes, are taken into account in year 2 for Country X tax purposes.

(ii) *Result.* As a result of the transfer of assets from P to FS_X, a portion of the year 1 dual consolidated loss is available for a foreign use. This is the case because a portion of the basis in FB_X's assets, which gave rise to depreciation deductions that were taken into account in computing the year 1 dual consolidated loss, will give rise to a depreciation deduction under Country X laws that will be available, under U.S. tax principles, to offset the income of FS_X, a foreign corporation, in year 2. However, the aggregate adjusted basis of all the assets transferred by P to FS_X, within the 12-month period ending at the end of year 2, is less than 10 percent of the aggregate adjusted basis of all of FB_X's assets at the beginning of such 12-month period. Moreover, the aggregate adjusted basis of the assets transferred by P to FS_X at any time during the certification period is less than 30 percent of the aggregate adjusted basis of FB_X's assets held at the end of year 1. In addition, the item of deduction giving rise to the foreign use is being made available solely as a result of the adjusted basis of the transferred assets being determined in whole, or in part, by reference to the adjusted basis of such transferred assets in the hands of FB_X. As a result, this transfer will not result in a foreign use pursuant to §1.1503(d)–3(c)(6).

Example 16. No foreign use—liability assumption exception. (i) *Facts.* P owns FB_X. In year 1, there is a dual consolidated loss attributable to FB_X for which P makes a domestic use election under §1.1503(d)–6(d). The dual consolidated loss includes a deduction for salary expense that was deductible for U.S. tax purposes at the end of year 1, even though it was not paid until year 2. The deduction was incurred in the ordinary course of FB_X's trade or business. During year 2, and before the accrued salary expense liability was paid, P sells all the assets of FB_X to FS_X in exchange for cash and FS_X's assumption of the liabilities of the FB_X trade or business, including the obligation to pay the accrued salary expense. Under Country X law, the accrued salary expense of FB_X is deductible, and is taken into account for purposes of computing the taxable income of FB_X, when paid. FB_X pays the accrued salary expense after the sale of FB_X to FS_X.

(ii) *Result.* (A) As a result of FS_X's assumption of the FB_X liabilities, including the accrued salary expense, a portion of the dual consolidated loss is available for a foreign use in year 2. This is the case because the deduction that was taken into account in year 1 in computing the dual consolidated loss under U.S. tax principles will, under Country X tax law, be taken into account and will be available to offset the income of FS_X, a foreign corporation, in year 2. However, because this item of expense is made available solely as a result of the assumption of a liability of FB_X, and such liability was incurred in the ordinary course of FB_X's trade or business, there will not be a foreign use of the year 1 dual consolidated loss pursuant to §1.1503(d)–3(c)(7).

(B) The transfer of all the assets of FB_X to FS_X is a triggering event under §1.1503(d)–6(e)(1)(iv), unless P can rebut the triggering event under §1.1503(d)–6(e)(2). For purposes of determining whether, under §1.1503(d)–6(e)(2)(ii), the transfer of assets resulted in a carryover under foreign law of FB_X's losses, expenses, or deductions, the exception to foreign use for the assumption of liabilities is taken into account. However, the other exceptions to foreign use do not apply for this purpose (or for purposes of demonstrating that no foreign use of a dual consolidated loss can occur in any other year under §1.1503(d)–6(c), (e)(2)(i) or (j)(2)). See §1.1503(d)–3(c)(1). Provided the other requirements of §1.1503(d)–6(e)(2)(ii) and (iii) are satisfied, P may be able to rebut the occurrence of a triggering event upon the transfer of FB_X's assets to FS_X.

Example 17. Mirror legislation rule—dual resident corporation and hybrid entity separate unit. (i) *Facts.* P owns DRC_X, a member of the P consolidated group. DRC_X owns FS_X. In year 1, DRC_X incurs a \$100x net operating loss that is a dual consolidated loss. To prevent corporations like DRC_X from offsetting losses both against income of affiliates in Country X and against income of foreign affiliates under the tax laws of another country, Country X mirror legislation prevents a corporation that is subject to the income tax of another country on its worldwide income or on a residence basis from using the Country X form of consolidation. Accordingly, the Country X mirror legislation prevents the loss of DRC_X from being made available to offset income of FS_X.

(ii) *Result.* Under §1.1503(d)–3(e), because the losses of DRC_X are subject to Country X's mirror legislation, there is a deemed foreign use of DRC_X's year 1 dual consolidated loss. The stand-alone exception to the mirror rule in §1.1503(d)–3(e)(2) does not apply because, absent the mirror legislation, DRC_X's year 1 dual consolidated loss would be available for a foreign use (as defined in §1.1503(d)–3), without regard to whether such availability is limited by election or similar procedure. That is, absent the mirror legislation, all or a portion of the dual consolidated loss would be available to offset the income of FS_X under the Country X consolidation regime. This is the case even if Country X did not recognize DRC_X as having a loss in year 1. Therefore, P may not make a domestic use election with respect to DRC_X's year 1 dual consolidated loss pursuant to §1.1503(d)–6(d)(2).

(iii) *Alternative facts.* The facts are the same as in paragraph (i) of this *Example 17*, except that P owns $DE1_X$ (rather than DRC_X) and, in year 1, there is a \$100 dual consolidated loss attributable to P's interest in $DE1_X$ (rather than of DRC_X). The Country X mirror legislation only applies to Country X dual resident corporations and, therefore, does not apply to losses attributable to P's interest in $DE1_X$. As a result, the mirror legislation rule under §1.1503(d)–3(e) would not deny the opportunity of such loss from being put to a foreign use (for example, by offsetting the income of FS_X through the Country X consolidation regime). Therefore, a domestic use election can be made with respect to the dual consolidated loss (provided the conditions for such an election are otherwise satisfied).

Example 18. Mirror legislation rule—standalone foreign branch separate unit. (i) *Facts.* P owns FB_X. In year 1, there is a $100x dual consolidated loss attributable to FB_X. Country X enacted mirror legislation to prevent Country X branches and permanent establishments of nonresident corporations from offsetting losses both against income of Country X affiliates and against other income of its owner (or foreign affiliates thereof) under the tax laws of another country. The Country X mirror legislation prevents a Country X branch or permanent establishment of a nonresident corporation from offsetting its losses against the income of Country X affiliates if such losses may be deductible against income (other than income of the Country X branch or permanent establishment) under the laws of another country.

(ii) *Result.* In general, under §1.1503(d)–3(e), because the losses of FB_X are subject to Country X's mirror legislation, there is a deemed foreign use of FB_X's year 1 dual consolidated loss. However, in the absence of the Country X mirror legislation, no item of deduction or loss composing FB_X's year 1 dual consolidated loss would be available in the year incurred for a foreign use (as defined in §1.1503(d)–3), without regard to whether such availability is limited by election or otherwise. This is the case because there is no Country X entity through which the dual consolidated loss could be put to a foreign use (absent a sale, merger, or similar transaction involving FB_X). As a result, the stand-alone exception in §1.1503(d)–3(e)(2) may apply, provided P complies with the requirements of §1.1503(d)–3(e)(2)(ii). Accordingly, P may make a domestic use election with respect to the year 1 dual consolidated loss of FB_X pursuant to §1.1503(d)–6(d). If, however, any item of the dual consolidated loss would otherwise be available for a foreign use during the certification period (for example, as a result of P acquiring a foreign corporation that is organized under the laws of Country X such that losses of FB_X could be put to a foreign use through consolidation or similar means), then such loss would be recaptured pursuant to §1.1503(d)–6(e)(1)(ix).

(iii) *Alternative facts.* The facts are the same as in paragraph (i) of this *Example 18*, except that the Country X mirror legislation operates in a manner similar to the rules under section 1503(d). That is, it allows the taxpayer to elect to use the loss to either offset income of an affiliate in Country X, or income of an affiliate (or other income of the owner of the Country X branch or permanent establishment) in the other country, but not both. Because the Country X mirror legislation permits the taxpayer to choose to put the dual consolidated loss to a foreign use, it does not deny the opportunity to put the loss to a foreign use. Therefore, there is no deemed foreign use of the dual consolidated loss pursuant to §1.1503(d)–4(e) and a domestic use election can be made for such loss.

Example 19. Application of mirror legislation rule to combined separate unit. (i) *Facts.* P owns FB_X, FS_X, and $DE1_X$. In year 1, there is a $50x dual consolidated loss attributable to FB_X and $10x of income attributable to P's interest in $DE1_X$. FS_X has income of $100x. Pursuant to §1.1503(d)–1(b)(4)(ii), FB_X and P's interest in $DE1_X$ are combined and treated as a single separate unit (Country X separate unit) which has a year 1 dual consolidated loss of $40x. Country X enacted mirror legislation to prevent Country X branches or permanent establishments of nonresident corporations from offsetting losses both against income of Country X affiliates and against other income of its owner (or foreign affiliates thereof) under the tax laws of another country. The Country X mirror legislation prevents a Country X branch or permanent establishment of a nonresident corporation from offsetting its losses against the income of Country X affiliates if such losses may be deductible against income (other than income of the Country X branch or permanent establishment) under the laws of another country. However, the United States and Country X have entered into an agreement described in §1.1503(d)–6(b) pursuant to the U.S.-Country X income tax convention (mirror agreement). The mirror agreement applies to Country X foreign branch separate units of domestic corporations, but not to Country X hybrid entity separate units. The mirror agreement provides that neither the Country X mirror legislation nor the mirror legislation rule under §1.1503(d)–3(e) will apply to losses attributable to Country X foreign branch separate units, provided certain conditions and reporting requirements are satisfied (including a domestic use election, if the loss is to be used to offset income of a domestic affiliate). Thus, losses attributable to Country X foreign branch separate units can, subject to the requirements of the mirror agreement, be used to offset income of a domestic affiliate or a Country X affiliate (but not both).

(ii) *Result.* The Country X mirror legislation only applies to Country X foreign branch separate units and does not apply to hybrid entity separate units. In addition, if P complies with the terms and conditions of the mirror agreement, the Country X mirror legislation would not apply to FB_X. As a result, the income tax laws of Country X would not deny the opportunity of a loss of either individual separate unit that composes P's combined Country X separate unit from being put to a foreign use. Therefore, notwithstanding §1.1503(d)–3(e), a domestic use election can be made with respect to the dual consolidated loss attributable to P's Country X separate unit, provided the terms and conditions of the mirror agreement are satisfied. See §1.1503(d)–6(b)(2).

(iii) *Alternative facts.* The facts are the same as in paragraph (i) of this *Example 19*, except that the Country X mirror legislation also applies to losses attributable to $DE1_X$, but the mirror agreement does not apply to such losses. The mirror legislation rule would apply with respect to P's interest in $DE1_X$ and, as a result, there is a deemed foreign use of the dual consolidated loss attributable to the Country X separate unit and a domestic use election cannot be made for such loss. This is the case even though, pursuant to §1.1503(d)–5(c)(4)(ii)(A), P's interest in $DE1_X$ (which is subject to the Country X mirror legislation) does not, as an individual separate unit, have a dual consolidated loss in year 1. Further, the stand-alone exception to the mirror legislation rule in §1.1503(d)–3(e)(2) does not apply because, absent the mirror legislation, the Country X combined separate unit's dual consolidated loss would be available in the year incurred for a foreign use (as defined in §1.1503(d)–3) because it could be used to offset income of FS_X under the Country X consolidation regime. This is the case even if Country X requires an election to consolidate and no such election is made. The result would be the same even if Country X did not recognize $DE1_X$ as having a loss.

Example 20. Dual consolidated loss limitation after section 381 transaction—disposition of assets and subsequent liquidation of dual resident corporation. (i) *Facts.* P owns DRC_X, a member of the P consolidated group. In year 1, DRC_X incurs a dual consolidated loss and P does not make a domestic use election with respect to such loss. Under §1.1503(d)–4(b), DRC_X's year 1 dual consolidated loss is subject to the limitations under §1.1503(d)–4(c) and, therefore, may not be used to offset the income of P or S (or any other domestic affiliate) on the group's U.S. income tax return. At the beginning of year 2, DRC_X sells all of its assets for cash and distributes the cash to P pursuant to a liquidation that qualifies under section 332.

(ii) *Result.* In general, under section 381, P would succeed to, and be permitted to use, DRC_X's net operating loss carryover. However, §1.1503(d)–4(d)(1)(i) prohibits the dual consolidated loss of DRC_X from carrying over to P. Therefore, DRC_X's year 1 net operating loss carryover is eliminated.

Example 21. Dual consolidated loss limitation applied to a separate unit transferred in a section 381 transaction. (i) *Facts.* S owns $DE1_X$ which, in turn, owns FB_X. S's interest in $DE1_X$ and its indirect interest in FB_X are combined and treated as a single separate unit (Country X separate unit) pursuant to §1.1503(d)–1(b)(4)(ii). In year 1, a dual consolidated loss is attributable to the Country X separate unit, and P does not make a domestic use election with respect to such loss. Under §1.1503(d)–4(b), the year 1 dual consolidated loss attributable to the Country X separate unit may not be used to offset the income of P or S (other than income attributable to the Country X separate unit, subject to the application of §1.1503(d)–4(c)) on the group's consolidated U.S. income tax return (nor may it be used to offset the income of any other domestic affiliates). At the beginning of year 2, S transfers its entire interest in $DE1_X$, and thus its entire indirect interest in FB_X, to FS_X in a transaction described in section 381.

(ii) *Result.* Section 1.1503(d)–4(d)(1)(ii) provides that the dual consolidated loss attributable to a separate unit that is subject to the domestic use limitation under §1.1503(d)–4(b) is eliminated if the separate unit ceases to be a separate unit of its affiliated domestic owner and all other members of the affiliated domestic owner's separate group. As a result of the transfer of the Country X separate unit to FS_x, the Country X separate unit ceases to be a separate unit of S, and is not a separate unit of any other member of the P consolidated group. In addition, the exceptions in §1.1503(d)–4(d)(2)(iii) do not apply because FS_X is not a domestic corporation. Thus, the year 1 dual consolidated loss attributable to the Country X separate unit is eliminated.

(iii) *Alternative facts.* Assume the same facts as in paragraph (i) of this *Example 21*, except S transfers its assets to DC, a domestic corporation that is not a member of the P consolidated group, in a transaction described in section 381(a). Immediately after the transaction, the Country X separate unit is a separate unit of DC. Under §1.1503(d)–4(d)(1)(ii), the year 1 dual consolidated loss of the Country X separate unit would be eliminated because it ceases to be a separate unit of S, and is not a separate unit of any other member of the P consolidated group. However, because the transferee is a domestic corporation and the Country X separate unit is a separate unit in the hands of DC immediately after the transaction, the exception under §1.1503(d)–4(d)(2)(iii)(A) applies. As a result, the year 1 dual consolidated loss of the Country X separate unit is not eliminated and any income generated by DC that is attributable to the Country X separate unit following the transfer may be offset by the carryover dual consolidated losses attributable to the Country X separate unit, subject to the limitations of §1.1503(d)–4(b) and (c) applied as if DC generated the dual consolidated loss and such loss was attributable to the Country X separate unit.

(iv) *Alternative facts.* Assume the same facts as in paragraph (iii) of this *Example 21*, except that P owns $DE2_X$ and the interest in $DE2_X$ is combined with and therefore included in the Country X separate unit. In addition, a portion of the dual consolidated loss of the Country X separate unit is attributable to P's interest in $DE2_X$. Pursuant to §1.1503(d)–4(d)(2)(iii)(A), the result would be the same as in paragraph (iii) of this *Example 21*, with respect to the portion of the dual consolidated loss attributable to the combined separate unit that is succeeded to and taken into account by DC pursuant to section 381. The portion of the dual consolidated loss attributable to P's interest in $DE2_X$, however, does not carry over to DC but is retained by P and continues to be subject to the limitations of §1.1503(d)–4(b) and (c) with respect to P's interest in $DE2_X$.

(v) *Alternative facts.* Assume the same facts as in paragraph (iv) of this *Example 21*, except that DC is a member of the P consolidated group. Pursuant to §1.1503(d)–4(d)(2)(iii)(B), the dual consolidated loss of the Country X separate unit is not eliminated and income attributable to the Country X separate unit may continue to be offset by the dual consolidated loss that is succeeded to and taken into account by DC pursuant to section 381, subject to the limitations of §1.1503(d)–4(b) and (c). The result would be the same even if the interest in $DE1_X$ ceased to be a separate unit in the hands of DC (for example, because it dissolved under Country X law in connection with the transaction), provided P, or another member of the P consolidated group, continued to own a portion of the Country X separate unit.

Example 22. Tainted income. (i) *Facts.* P owns 100 percent of DRC_Z, a domestic corporation that is included as a member of the P consolidated group. DRC_Z conducts a business in the United States. During year 1, DRC_Z was managed and controlled in Country Z and therefore was subject to tax as a resident of Country Z and was a dual resident corporation. In year 1, DRC_Z incurred a dual consolidated loss of $200x, and P did not make a domestic use election with respect to such loss. As a result, such loss is subject to the domestic use limitation rule of §1.1503(d)–4(b). At the end of year 1, DRC_Z moved its management and control to the United States and, as a result, ceased being a dual resident corporation. At the beginning of year 2, P transferred asset A, a non-depreciable asset, to DRC_Z in exchange for common stock in a transaction that qualified for nonrecognition under section 351. At the time of the transfer, P's tax basis in asset A equaled $50x and the fair market value of asset A equaled $100x. The tax basis of asset A in the hands of DRC_Z immediately after the transfer equaled $50x pursuant to section 362. Asset A did not constitute replacement property acquired in the ordinary course of business. DRC_Z did not generate income or gain during years 2, 3, or 4. On June 30, year 5, DRC_Z sold asset A to a third party for $100x, its fair market value at the time of the sale, and recognized $50x of income on such sale. In addition to the $50x income generated on the sale of asset A, DRC_Z generated $100x of operating income in year 5. At the end of year 5, the fair market value of all the assets of DRC_Z was $400x.

(ii) *Result.* DRC_Z ceased being a dual resident corporation at the end of year 1. Therefore, its year 1 dual consolidated loss cannot be offset by tainted income. Asset A is a tainted asset because it was acquired in a nonrecognition transaction after DRC_Z ceased being a dual resident corporation (and was not replacement property acquired in the ordinary course of business). As a result, the $50x of income recognized by DRC_Z on the disposition of asset A is tainted income and cannot be offset by the year 1 dual consolidated loss of DRC_Z. In addition, absent evidence establishing the actual amount of tainted income, $25x of the $100x year 5 operating income of DRC_Z (($100x/$400x) x $100x) also is treated as tainted income and cannot be offset by the year 1 dual consolidated loss of DRC_Z under §1.1503(d)–4(e)(2)(ii). Therefore, $75x of the $150x year 5 income of DRC_Z constitutes tainted income and may not be offset by the year 1 dual consolidated loss of DRC_Z; however, the remaining $75x of year 5 income of DRC_Z may be offset by such dual consolidated loss. The result would be the same if, instead of P transferring asset A to DRC_Z, such asset was received from a separate unit or a transparent entity of DRC_Z.

Example 23. Treatment of disregarded item and books and records of a hybrid entity. (i) *Facts.* P owns $DE1_X$ which, in turn, owns FS_X. In year 1, P borrows from a third party and on-lends the proceeds to $DE1_X$. In year 1, P incurs interest expense attributable to the third-party loan. Also in year 1, $DE1_X$ incurs interest expense attributable to its loan from P, but such expense is generally disregarded for U.S. tax purposes because $DE1_X$ is disregarded as an entity separate from P. The third-party loan and related interest expense are reflected on the books and records of P (and not on the books and records of $DE1_X$). The loan from P to $DE1_X$ and related interest expense are reflected on the books and records of $DE1_X$. There are no other items of income, gain, deduction, or loss reflected on the books and records of $DE1_X$ in year 1.

(ii) *Result.* Because the interest expense on P's third-party loan is not reflected on the books and records of $DE1_X$, no portion of such expense is attributable to P's interest in $DE1_X$ pursuant to §1.1503(d)–5(c)(3) for purposes of calculating the year 1 dual consolidated loss, if any, attributable to such interest. In addition, even though P's interest in $DE1_X$ is treated as a separate domestic corporation for purposes of determining the amount of income or dual consolidated loss attributable to it pursuant to §1.1503(d)–5(c)(1)(ii), such treatment does not cause the interest expense incurred on the loan from P to $DE1_X$ that is generally disregarded for U.S. tax purposes to be regarded for purposes of calculating the year 1 dual consolidated loss, if any, attributable to P's interest in $DE1_X$. As a result, even though the disregarded interest expense is reflected on the books and records of $DE1_X$, it is not taken into account for purposes of calculating income or a dual consolidated loss. Therefore, there is no dual consolidated loss attributable to P's interest in $DE1_X$ in year 1.

Example 24. Dividend income attributable to a separate unit. (i) *Facts.* P owns $DE1_X$ which, in turn, owns FB_X. P's interest in $DE1_X$ and its indirect interest in FB_X are combined and treated as a single separate unit (Country X separate unit) pursuant to §1.1503(d)–1(b)(4)(ii). $DE1_X$ owns $DE3_Y$. $DE3_Y$ owns the stock of FS_X. P's Country X separate unit would, without regard to year 1 dividend income (or related section 78 gross-up) received from FS_X, have a dual consolidated loss of $75x in year 1. In year 1, FS_X distributes $50x to $DE3_Y$ that is taxable as a dividend. $DE3_Y$ distributes the same amount to $DE1_X$. P computes foreign taxes deemed paid on the dividend under section 902 of $25x and includes that amount in gross income under section 78.

(ii) *Result.* The $50x dividend is reflected on the books and records of $DE3_Y$ and, therefore, is attributable to P's interest in $DE3_Y$ pursuant to §1.1503(d)–5(c)(3)(i). In addition, the $25x section 78 gross-up is attributable to P's interest in $DE3_Y$ pursuant to §1.1503(d)–5(c)(4)(iv). The distribution of $50x from $DE3_Y$ to $DE1_X$ is generally disregarded for U.S. tax purposes and, therefore, does not give rise to an item that is taken into account for purposes of calculating income or a dual consolidated loss. This is the case even though the item would be reflected on the books and records of $DE1_X$. In addition, pursuant to §1.1503(d)–5(c)(1)(iii), each separate unit must calculate its own income or dual consolidated loss, and each item of income, gain, deduction, and loss must be taken into account only once. As a result, the dual consolidated loss of $75x attributable to P's Country X separate unit in year 1 is not reduced by the amount of dividend income attributable to P's indirect interest in $DE3_Y$.

Example 25. Items reflected on books and records of a combined separate unit. (i) *Facts.* P owns $DE1_X$ which, in turn, owns FB_X. P's interest in $DE1_X$ and its indirect interest in FB_X are combined and treated as a single separate unit (Country X separate unit) pursuant to §1.1503(d)–1(b)(4)(ii). The following items are reflected on the books and records of $DE1_X$ in year 1: sales, depreciation expense, a political contribution, royalty expense paid to P, repairs and maintenance expense paid to a third party, and Country X income tax expense. The amount of sales under U.S. tax principles equals the amount of sales reported for accounting purposes. The depreciation expense is calculated on a straight-line basis over the useful life of the asset for accounting purposes, but is subject to accelerated depreciation for U.S. tax purposes. In addition, the repairs and maintenance expense, which is deducted when paid for accounting purposes, is properly capitalized and amortized over five years for U.S. tax purposes. Finally, P elects to claim as a credit under section 901 the Country X income tax expense that was paid in year 1.

(ii) *Result.* (A) For purposes of determining the income or dual consolidated loss attributable to P's Country X separate unit, items of income, gain, deduction, and loss must first be attributed to the individual separate units (that is, P's interest in $DE1_X$ and its indirect interest in FB_X). For purposes of attributing items to P's interest in $DE1_X$, P's items that are reflected on $DE1_X$'s books and records, as adjusted to conform to U.S. tax principles, are taken into account. See §1.1503(d)–5(c)(3)(i). For purposes of attributing items (other than interest expense) to FB_X, the principles of section 864(c)(2), (c)(4), and (c)(5) (as set forth in §1.864–4(c) and §§1.864–5 through 1.864–7) must be applied and, for interest expense, the principles of §1.882–5, as modified under §1.1503(d)–5(c)(2)(ii), must be applied; however, for these purposes, pursuant to §1.1503(d)–5(c)(4)(i)(A), FB_X only takes into account items attributable to P's interest in $DE1_X$ and the assets, liabilities, and activities of such interest. In addition, to the extent such items are taken into account by FB_X, they are not taken into account in determining the items attributable to P's interest in $DE1_X$. §1.1503(d)–5(c)(4)(i)(B). Because P's interest in $DE1_X$ has no assets or liabilities, and conducts no activities, other than through its ownership of FB_X, all of the items that are reflected on the books and records of $DE1_X$, as adjusted to conform to U.S. tax principles, are attributable to FB_X; no items are attributable to P's interest in $DE1_X$.

(B) The items reflected on the books and records of $DE1_X$ must be adjusted to conform to U.S. tax principles. No adjustment is required to sales because the amount of sales under U.S. tax principles equals the amount of sales for accounting purposes. The amount of straight-line depreciation expense reflected on $DE1_X$'s books and records must be adjusted to reflect the amount of depreciation on the asset that is allowable for U.S. tax purposes. The political contribution is not taken into account because it is not deductible for U.S. tax purposes. Similarly, because the royalty expense is paid to P, and therefore is generally disregarded for U.S. tax purposes, it is not taken into account. The repair and maintenance expense that is deducted in year 1 for accounting purposes also must be adjusted to conform to U.S. tax principles. Thus, the repair and maintenance expense will be taken into account in computing the income or dual consolidated loss attributable to P's Country X separate unit over five years (even though no item related to such expense would be reflected on the books and records of $DE1_X$ for years 2 through 5). Finally, because P elected to claim as a credit the Country X foreign taxes paid during year 1, no deduction is allowed for such amount pursuant to section 275(a)(4) and, therefore, the Country X tax expense is not taken into account.

(C) Pursuant to §1.1503(d)–5(c)(4)(ii)(B), the combined Country X separate unit of P calculates its income or dual consolidated loss by taking into account all the items of income, gain, deduction, and loss that were separately attributable to P's interest in $DE1_X$ and FB_X. However, in this case, there are no items attributable to P's interest in $DE1_X$. Therefore, the items attributable to the Country X separate unit are the items attributable to FB_X.

Example 26. Items attributable to a combined separate unit. (i) *Facts.* P owns $DE1_X$. $DE1_X$ owns a 50 percent interest in PRS_Z, a Country Z entity that is classified as a partnership both for Country Z tax purposes and for U.S. tax purposes. FS_X, which is unrelated to P, owns the remaining 50 percent interest in PRS_Z. PRS_Z carries on operations in Country X that, if carried on by a U.S. person, would constitute a foreign branch as defined in §1.367(a)–6T(g)(1). Therefore, P's share of the Country X operations carried on by PRS_Z constitutes a foreign branch separate unit. PRS_Z also owns assets that do not constitute a part of its Country X branch, including all of the interests in TE_T, a disregarded entity. TE_T is an entity incorporated under the laws of Country T, a country that does not have an income tax. Under the laws of Country X, an interest holder of TE_T does not take into account on a current basis the interest holder's share of items of income, gain, deduction, and loss of TE_T.

(ii) *Result.* (A) Pursuant to §1.1503(d)–1(b)(4)(ii), P's interest in $DE1_X$, and P's indirect ownership of a portion of the Country X operations carried on by PRS_Z, are combined and treated as a single separate unit (Country X separate unit). Pursuant to §1.1503(d)–5(c)(4)(ii)(A), for purposes of determining P's items of income, gain, deduction, and loss attributable to the Country X separate unit, the items of P are first attributed to each separate unit that composes the Country X separate unit.

(B) Pursuant to §1.1503(d)–5(c)(2)(i), the principles of section 864(c)(2), (c)(4), and (c)(5) (as set forth in §1.864–4(c) and §§1.864–5 through 1.864–7), apply for purposes of determining P's items of income, gain, deduction (other than interest expense), and loss that are attributable to P's indirect interest in the Country X operations carried on by PRS_Z. For purposes of determining P's interest expense that is attributable to P's indirect interest in the Country X operations carried on by PRS_Z, the principles of §1.882–5, as modified under §1.1503(d)–5(c)(2)(ii), shall apply. For purposes of applying these rules, P is treated as a foreign corporation, the Country X operations carried on by PRS_Z are treated as a trade or business within the United States, and the assets of P (including its share of the PRS_Z assets, other than those of the Country X operations) are treated as assets that are not U.S. assets. In addition, because P carries on its share of the Country X operations through $DE1_X$, a hybrid entity, §1.1503(d)–5(c)(4)(i)(A) provides that only the items attributable to P's interest in $DE1_X$, and only the assets, liabilities, and activities of P's interest in $DE1_X$, are taken into account for purposes of this determination.

(C) TE_T is a transparent entity as defined in §1.1503(d)–1(b)(16) because it is not taxable as an association for Federal tax purposes, is not subject to income tax in a foreign country as a corporation (or otherwise at the entity level) either on its worldwide income or on a residence basis, and is not treated as a pass-through entity under the laws of Country X (the applicable foreign country). TE_T is not a pass-through entity under the laws of Country X because a Country X holder of an interest in TE_T does not take into account on a current basis the interest holder's share of items of income, gain, deduction, and loss of TE_T. For purposes of determining P's items of income, gain, deduction, and loss that are attributable to P's interest in TE_T, only those items of P that are reflected on the books and records of TE_T, as adjusted to conform to U.S. tax principles, are taken into account. §1.1503(d)–5(c)(3)(i). Because the interest in TE_T is not a separate unit, a loss attributable to such interest is not a dual consolidated loss and is not subject to section 1503(d) and these regulations. Items must nevertheless be attributed to the interests in TE_T. For example, such attribution is required for purposes of calculating the income or dual consolidated loss attributable to the Country X separate unit, and for purposes of applying the domestic use limitation under §1.1503(d)–4(b) to a dual consolidated loss attributable to the Country X separate unit.

(D) For purposes of determining P's items of income, gain, deduction, and loss that are attributable to P's interest in $DE1_X$, only those items of P that are reflected on the books and records of $DE1_X$, as adjusted to conform to U.S. tax principles, are taken into account. §1.1503(d)–5(c)(3)(i). For this purpose, $DE1_X$'s distributive share of the items of income, gain, deduction, and loss that are reflected on the books and records of PRS_Z, as adjusted to conform to U.S. tax principles, are treated as being reflected on the books and records of $DE1_X$, except to the extent such items are taken into account by the Country X operations of PRS_Z. See §1.1503(d)–5(c)(3)(ii) and (4)(i)(B). Because TE_T is a transparent entity, the items reflected on its books and records are not treated as being reflected on the books and records of $DE1_X$.

(E) Pursuant to §1.1503(d)–5(c)(4)(ii)(B), the combined Country X separate unit of P calculates its income or dual consolidated loss by taking into account all the items of income, gain, deduction, and loss that were separately attributable to P's interest in $DE1_X$ and the Country X operations of PRS_Z owned indirectly by P.

Example 27. Sale of separate unit by another separate unit. (i) *Facts.* P owns $DE3_Y$ which, in turn, owns $DE1_X$. $DE3_Y$ also owns other assets that do not constitute a foreign branch separate unit. $DE1_X$ owns FB_X. Pursuant to §1.1503(d)–1(b)(4)(ii), P's indirect interests in $DE1_X$ and FB_X are combined and treated as one Country X separate unit (Country X separate unit). $DE3_Y$ sells its interest in $DE1_X$ at the end of year 1 to an unrelated foreign person for cash. The sale results in an ordinary loss of $30x. Items of income, gain, deduction, and loss derived from the assets that gave rise to the $30x loss would be attributable to the Country X separate unit under §1.1503(d)–5(c) through (e). Without regard to the sale of $DE1_X$, no items of income, gain, deduction, and loss are attributable to P's Country X separate unit in year 1.

(ii) *Result.* Pursuant to §1.1503(d)–5(c)(4)(iii)(A), the $30x ordinary loss recognized on the sale is attributable to the Country X separate unit, and not P's interest in $DE3_Y$. This is the case because the Country X separate unit is treated as owning the assets that gave rise to the loss under §1.1503(d)–5(f). Thus, the loss attributable to the sale creates a year 1 dual consolidated loss attributable to the Country X separate unit. In addition, pursuant to §1.1503(d)–6(d)(2), P cannot make a domestic use election with respect to the dual consolidated loss because the sale of the interest in $DE1_X$ is a triggering event described in §1.1503(d)–6(e)(1)(iv) and (v). Further, although the year 1 dual consolidated loss would otherwise be subject to the domestic use limitation rule of §1.1503(d)–4(b), it is eliminated pursuant to §1.1503(d)–4(d)(1)(ii). Finally, if there were a dual consolidated loss attributable to P's interest in $DE3_Y$, the sale of the interest in $DE1_X$ would not be taken into account for purposes of determining whether there is an asset triggering event with respect to such dual consolidated loss under §1.1503(d)–6(e)(1)(iv).

Example 28. Gain on sale of tiered separate units. (i) *Facts.* P owns 75 percent of HPS_X, a Country X entity subject to Country X tax on its worldwide income. FS_X owns the remaining 25 percent of HPS_X. HPS_X is classified as a partnership for Federal tax purposes. HPS_X carries on operations in Country Y that, if carried on by a U.S. person, would constitute a foreign branch within the meaning of §1.367(a)–6T(g)(1). HPS_X also owns assets that do not constitute a part of its Country Y operations and would not themselves constitute a foreign branch within the meaning of §1.367(a)–6T(g)(1) if owned by a U.S. person. Neither HPS_X nor the Country Y operations has liabilities. P's indirect interest in the Country Y operations carried on by HPS_X, and P's interest in HPS_X, are each separate units. P sells its interest in HPS_X and recognizes a gain of $150x on such sale. Immediately prior to P's sale of its interest in HPS_X, P's portion of the assets of the Country Y operations (that is, assets the income, gain, deduction and loss from which would be attributable to P's Country Y foreign branch separate unit) had a built-in gain of $200x, and P's portion of HPS_X's other assets (that is, assets the income, gain, deduction and loss from which would be attributable to P's interest in HPS_X) had a built-in gain of $100x.

(ii) *Result.* Pursuant to §1.1503(d)–5(c)(4)(iii)(B), $100x of the total $150x of gain recognized ($200x/$300x x $150x) is attributable to P's indirect interest in its share of the Country Y operations carried on by HPS_X. Similarly, $50x of such gain ($100x/$300x x $150x) is attributable to P's interest in HPS_X.

Example 29. Effect on domestic affiliate. (i) *Facts.* (A) P owns $DE1_X$ which, in turn, owns FB_X. P's interest in $DE1_X$ and its indirect interest in FB_X are combined and treated as a single separate unit (Country X separate unit) pursuant to §1.1503(d)–1(b)(4)(ii). In years 1 and 2, the items of income, gain, deduction, and loss that are attributable to P's Country X separate unit pursuant to §1.1503(d)–5 are as follows:

Item	year 1	year 2
Sales income	$100x	$160x
Salary expense	($75x)	($75x)
Research and experimental expense	($50x)	($50x)
Interest expense	($25x)	($25x)
Income/(dual consolidated loss)	($50x)	$10x

(B) P does not make a domestic use election with respect to the year 1 dual consolidated loss attributable to its Country X separate unit. Pursuant to §1.1503(d)–4(b) and (c)(2), the year 1 dual consolidated loss of $50x is treated as a loss incurred by a separate domestic corporation and is subject to the limitations under §1.1503(d)–4(c)(3). The P consolidated group has $100x of consolidated taxable income in year 2.

(ii) *Result.* (A) P must compute its taxable income for year 1 without taking into account the $50x dual consolidated loss, pursuant to §1.1503(d)–4(c)(2). Such amount consists of a *pro rata* portion of the expenses that were taken into account in calculating the year 1 dual consolidated loss. Thus, the items of the dual consolidated loss that are not taken into account by P in computing its taxable income are as follows: $25x of salary expense ($75x/$150x x $50x); $16.67x of research and experimental expense ($50x/$150x x $50x); and $8.33x of interest expense ($25x/$150x x $50x). The remaining amounts of each of these items, together with the $100x of sales income, are taken into account by P in computing its taxable income for year 1 as follows: $50x of salary expense ($75x - $25x); $33.33x of research and experimental expense ($50x - $16.67x); and $16.67x of interest expense ($25x - $8.33x).

(B) Subject to the limitations provided under §1.1503(d)–4(c), the year 1 $50x dual consolidated loss is carried forward and is available to offset the $10x of income attributable to the Country X separate unit in year 2. Pursuant to §1.1503(d)–4(c)(4), a *pro rata* portion of each item of deduction or loss included in such dual consolidated loss is considered to be used to offset the $10x of income, as follows: $5x of salary expense ($25x/$50x x $10x); $3.33x of research and experimental expense ($16.67x/$50x x $10x); and $1.67x of interest expense ($8.33x/$50x x $10x). The remaining amount of each item shall continue to be subject to the limitations under §1.1503(d)–4(c).

Example 30. Exception to domestic use limitation—no possibility of foreign use because items are not deducted or capitalized under foreign law. (i) *Facts.* P owns $DE1_X$ which, in turn, owns FS_X. In year 1, the sole item of income, gain, deduction, and loss attributable to P's interest in $DE1_X$, as provided under §1.1503(d)–5, is $100x of interest expense paid on a loan to an unrelated lender. For Country X tax purposes, the $100x interest expense attributable to P's interest in $DE1_X$ in year 1 is treated as a repayment of principal and therefore cannot be deducted (at any time) or capitalized.

(ii) *Result.* The $100x of interest expense attributable to P's interest in $DE1_X$ constitutes a dual consolidated loss. However, because the sole item constituting the dual consolidated loss cannot be deducted or capitalized (at any time) for Country X tax purposes, P can demonstrate that there can be no foreign use of the dual consolidated loss at any time. As a result, pursuant to §1.1503(d)–6(c)(1), if P prepares a statement described in §1.1503(d)–6(c)(2) and attaches it to its timely filed tax return, the year 1 dual consolidated loss attributable to P's interest in $DE1_X$ will not be subject to the domestic use limitation rule of §1.1503(d)–4(b).

Example 31. No exception to domestic use limitation—inability to demonstrate no possibility of foreign use. (i) *Facts.* P owns $DE1_X$ which, in turn, owns FB_X. P's interest in $DE1_X$ and its indirect interest in FB_X are combined and treated as a single separate unit (Country X separate unit) pursuant to §1.1503(d)–1(b)(4)(ii). In year 1, the sole items of income, gain, deduction, and loss attributable to P's Country X separate unit, as provided under §1.1503(d)–5, are $75x of sales income and $100x of depreciation expense. For Country X tax purposes, $DE1_X$ also generates $75x of sales income in year 1, but the $100x of depreciation expense is not deductible until year 2.

(ii) *Result.* The year 1 $25x net loss attributable to P's interest in the Country X separate unit constitutes a dual consolidated loss. In addition, even though $DE1_X$ has positive income in year 1 for Country X tax purposes, P cannot demonstrate that there is no possibility of foreign use with respect to the Country X separate unit's dual consolidated loss as provided under §1.1503(d)–6(c)(1)(i). P cannot make such a demonstration because the depreciation expense, an item composing the year 1 dual consolidated loss, is deductible (in a later year) for Country X tax purposes and, therefore, may be available to offset or reduce income for Country X purposes that would constitute a foreign use. For example, if $DE1_X$ elected to be classified as a corporation pursuant to §301.7701–3(c) of this chapter effective as of the end of year 1, and the deferred depreciation expense were available for Country X tax purposes to offset year 2 income of $DE1_X$, an entity treated as a foreign corporation in year 2 for U.S. tax purposes, there would be a foreign use.

(iii) *Alternative facts.* (A) The facts are the same as in paragraph (i) of this *Example 31*, except as follows. In year 1, the sole items of income, gain, deduction, and loss attributable to P's Country X separate unit, as provided in §1.1503(d)–5, are $75x of sales income, $100x of interest expense, and $25x of depreciation expense. For Country X tax purposes, $DE1_X$ generates $75x of sales income in year 1; the $100x interest expense is treated as a repayment of principal and therefore cannot be deducted or capitalized (at any time); and the $25x of depreciation expense is not deductible in year 1, but is deductible in year 2.

(B) In year 1, the $50x net loss attributable to P's Country X separate unit constitutes a dual consolidated loss. Even though the $100x interest expense, a nondeductible and noncapital item for Country X tax purposes, exceeds the $50x year 1 dual consolidated loss attributable to P's Country X separate unit, P cannot demonstrate that there is no possibility of foreign use of the dual consolidated loss as provided under §1.1503(d)–6(c)(1)(i). P cannot make such a demonstration because the $25x depreciation expense, an item of deduction or loss composing the year 1 dual consolidated loss, is deductible under Country X law (in year 2) and, therefore, may be available to offset or reduce income for Country X tax purposes that would constitute a foreign use.

Example 32. Triggering event rebuttal—expiration of losses in foreign country. (i) *Facts.* P owns DRC_X, a member of the P consolidated group. In year 1, DRC_X incurs a dual consolidated loss of $100x. P makes a domestic use election with respect to DRC_X's year 1 dual consolidated loss and such loss therefore is included in the computation of the P group's consolidated taxable income. DRC_X has no income or loss in year 2 through year 5. In year 5, P sells the stock of DRC_X to FS_X. At the time of the sale of the stock of DRC_X, all of the losses and deductions that were included in the computation of the year 1 dual consolidated loss of DRC_X had expired for Country X tax purposes because the laws of Country X only provide for a three-year carryover period for such items.

(ii) *Result.* The sale of DRC_X to FS_X generally would be a triggering event under §1.1503(d)–6(e)(1)(ii), which would require DRC_X to recapture the year 1 dual consolidated loss (and pay an applicable interest charge) on the P consolidated group's tax return for the year that includes the date on which DRC_X ceases to be a member of the P consolidated group. However, upon adequate documentation that the losses and deductions have expired for Country X tax purposes, P can rebut the presumption that a triggering event has occurred pursuant to §1.1503(d)–6(e)(2)(i). If the triggering event presumption is rebutted, the domestic use agreement filed by the P consolidated group with respect to the year 1 dual consolidated loss of DRC_X is terminated and has no further effect pursuant to §1.1503(d)–6(j)(1)(i). If the presumptive triggering event is not rebutted, the domestic use agreement would terminate and have no further effect pursuant to §1.1503(d)–6(j)(1)(iii) because the dual consolidated loss would be recaptured.

Example 33. Triggering events and rebuttals—tax basis carryover transaction. (i) *Facts.* (A) P owns $DE1_X$. $DE1_X$'s sole asset is A, which it acquired at the beginning of year 1 for $100x. $DE1_X$ does not have any liabilities. For U.S. tax purposes, $DE1_X$'s tax basis in A at the beginning of year 1 is $100x and $DE1_X$'s sole item of income, gain, deduction, and loss for year 1 is a $20x depreciation deduction attributable to A. As a result, the $20x depreciation deduction constitutes a dual consolidated loss attributable to P's interest in $DE1_X$. P makes a domestic use election with respect to the year 1 dual consolidated loss.

(B) For Country X tax purposes, $DE1_X$ has a $100x tax basis in A at the beginning of year 1, but A is not a depreciable asset. As a result, $DE1_X$ does not have any items of income, gain, deduction, and loss in year 1 for Country X tax purposes.

(C) During year 2, P sells its interest in $DE1_X$ to FS_X for $80x. P's disposition of its interest in $DE1_X$ constitutes a presumptive triggering event under §1.1503(d)–6(e)(1)(iv) and (v) requiring the recapture of the year 1 $20x dual consolidated loss (plus the applicable interest charge). For Country X tax purposes, $DE1_X$ retains its tax basis of $100x in A following the sale.

(ii) *Result.* The year 1 dual consolidated loss is a result of the $20x depreciation deduction attributable to A. Although no item of deduction or loss was recognized by $DE1_X$ at the time of the sale for Country X tax purposes, the deduction composing the dual consolidated loss was retained by $DE1_X$ after the sale in the form of tax basis in A. As a result, a portion of the dual consolidated loss may be available to offset income for Country X tax purposes in a manner that would constitute a foreign use. For example, if $DE1_X$ were to dispose of A, the amount of gain recognized by $DE1_X$ would be reduced (or an amount of loss recognized by $DE1_X$ would be increased) and, therefore, an item composing the dual consolidated loss would be available, under U.S. tax principles, to reduce income of a foreign corporation (and an owner of an interest in a hybrid entity that is not a separate unit). Thus, P cannot demonstrate pursuant to §1.1503(d)–6(e)(2)(i) that there can be no foreign use of the year 1 dual consolidated loss following the triggering event, and must recapture the year 1 dual consolidated loss. Pursuant to §1.1503(d)–6(j)(1)(iii), the domestic use agreement filed by the P consolidated group with respect to the year 1 dual consolidated loss is terminated and has no further effect.

(iii) *Alternative facts.* The facts are the same as paragraph (i) of this *Example 33*, except that instead of P selling its interest in $DE1_X$ to FS_X, $DE1_X$ sells asset A to FS_X for $80x and, for Country X tax purposes, FS_X's tax basis in A immediately after the sale is $80x. P's disposition of Asset A constitutes a presumptive triggering event under §1.1503(d)–6(e)(1)(iv) requiring the recapture of the year 1 $20x dual consolidated loss (plus the applicable interest charge). For Country X tax purposes, FS_X's tax basis in A was not determined, in whole or in part, by reference to the basis of A in the hands of $DE1_X$. As a result, the deduction composing the dual consolidated loss will not give rise to an item of deduction or loss in the form of tax basis for Country X tax purposes (for example, when FS_X disposes of A). Therefore, P may be able to demonstrate (for example, by obtaining the opinion of a Country X tax advisor) pursuant to §1.1503(d)–6(e)(2)(i) that there can be no foreign use of the year 1 dual consolidated loss and, thus, would not be required to recapture the year 1 dual consolidated loss.

Example 34. Triggering event resulting in a single consolidated group where acquirer files a new domestic use agreement. (i) *Facts.* P owns DRC_X, a member of the P consolidated group. In year 1, DRC_X incurs a dual consolidated loss and P makes a domestic use election with respect to such loss. No member of the P consolidated group incurs a dual consolidated loss in year 2. At the end of year 2, T, the parent of the T consolidated group, acquires all the stock of P, and all the members of the P group, including DRC_X, become members of a consolidated group of which T is the common parent.

(ii) *Result.* (A) Under §1.1503(d)–6(f)(2)(ii)(B), the acquisition by T of the P consolidated group is not an event described in §1.1503(d)–6(e)(1)(ii) requiring the recapture of the year 1 dual consolidated loss of DRC_X (and the payment of an interest charge), provided that the T consolidated group files a new domestic use agreement described in §1.1503(d)–6(f)(2)(iii)(A). If a new domestic use agreement is filed, then pursuant to §1.1503(d)–6(j)(1)(ii), the domestic use agreement filed by the P consolidated group with respect to the year 1 dual consolidated loss of DRC_X is terminated and has no further effect.

(B) Assume that T files a new domestic use agreement and a triggering event occurs at the end of year 3. As a result, the T consolidated group must recapture the dual consolidated loss that DRC_X incurred in year 1 (and pay an interest charge), as provided in §1.1503(d)–6(h). Each member of the T consolidated group, including DRC_X and any former members of the P consolidated group, is severally liable for the additional tax (and the interest charge) due upon the recapture of the dual consolidated loss of DRC_X. In addition, pursuant to §1.1503(d)–6(j)(1)(iii), the new domestic use agreement filed by the T group with respect to the year 1 dual consolidated loss of DRC_X is terminated and has no further effect.

Example 35. Triggering event exceptions for certain deemed transfers. (i) *Facts.* P owns $DE1_X$. In year 1, there is a $100x dual consolidated loss attributable to P's interest in $DE1_X$. P files a domestic use agreement under §1.1503(d)–6(d) with respect to such loss. During year 2, P sells 33 percent of its interest in $DE1_X$ to T, an unrelated domestic corporation.

(ii) *Result.* Pursuant to Rev. Rul. 99–5, the transaction is treated as if P sold 33 percent of its interest in each of $DE1_X$'s assets to T and then immediately thereafter P and T transferred their interests in the assets of $DE1_X$ to a partnership in exchange for an ownership interest therein. Upon the transfer of 33 percent of P's interest to T, a domestic corporation, no foreign use occurs and, therefore, there is no foreign use triggering event. However, P's deemed transfer of 67 percent of its interest in the assets of $DE1_X$ to a partnership is nominally a triggering event under §1.1503(d)–6(e)(1)(iv). Because the initial transfer of 33 percent of $DE1_X$'s interest was to a domestic corporation and there is only a triggering event because of the deemed transfer under Rev. Rul. 99–5, the deemed asset transfer is not treated as resulting in a triggering event pursuant to §1.1503(d)–6(f)(4).

(iii) *Alternative facts.* The facts are the same as in paragraph (i) of this *Example 35*, except that P sells 60 percent (rather than 33 percent) of its interest in $DE1_X$ to T. The sale is a triggering event under §1.1503(d)–6(e)(1)(iv) and (v) without regard to the occurrence of a deemed transaction. Therefore, §1.1503(d)–6(f)(4) does not apply.

Example 36. Triggering event exception involving multiple parties. (i) *Facts.* P owns $DE1_X$ which, in turn, owns FB_X. P's interest in $DE1_X$ and its indirect interest in FB_X are combined and treated as a single separate unit (Country X separate unit) pursuant to §1.1503(d)–1(b)(4)(ii). In year 1, there is a $100x dual consolidated loss attributable to P's Country X separate unit and P makes a domestic use election with respect to such loss. No member of the P consolidated group incurs a dual consolidated loss in year 2. At the end of year 2, T, the parent of the T consolidated group, acquires all of P's interest in $DE1_X$ for cash.

(ii) *Result.* (A) Under §1.1503(d)–6(f)(2)(i)(B), the acquisition by T of the interest in $DE1_X$ is not an event described in §1.1503(d)–6(e)(1)(iv) or (v) requiring the recapture of the year 1 dual consolidated loss attributable to the Country X separate unit (and the payment of an interest charge), provided: (1) the T consolidated group files a new domestic use agreement described in §1.1503(d)–6(f)(2)(iii)(A) with respect to the year 1 dual consolidated loss of the Country X separate unit; and (2) the P consolidated group files a statement described in §1.1503(d)–6(f)(2)(iii)(B) with respect to the year 1 dual consolidated loss. If these requirements are satisfied, then pursuant to §1.1503(d)–6(j)(1)(ii) the domestic use agreement filed by the P consolidated group with respect to the year 1 dual consolidated loss is terminated and has no further effect (if these requirements are not satisfied such that the P consolidated group recaptures the dual consolidated loss, the domestic use agreement would terminate pursuant to §1.1503(d)–6(j)(1)(iii)).

(B) Assume a triggering event occurs at the end of year 3 that requires recapture by the T consolidated group of the year 1 dual consolidated loss, as well as the payment of an interest charge, as provided in §1.1503(d)–6(h). T continues to own the Country X separate unit after the triggering event. In that case, each member of the T consolidated group is severally liable for the additional tax (and the interest charge) due upon the recapture of the year 1 dual consolidated loss. The T consolidated group must prepare a statement that computes the recapture tax amount as provided under §1.1503(d)–6(h)(3)(iii). Pursuant to §1.1503(d)–6(h)(3)(iv)(A), the recapture tax amount is assessed as an income tax liability of the T consolidated group and is considered as having been properly assessed as an income tax liability of the P consolidated group. If the T consolidated group does not pay in full the income tax liability attributable to the recapture tax amount, the unpaid balance of such recapture tax amount may be collected from the P consolidated group in accordance with the provisions of §1.1503(d)–6(h)(3)(iv)(B). Pursuant to §1.1503(d)–6(j)(1)(iii), the new domestic use agreement filed by the T consolidated group is terminated and has no further effect. Finally, pursuant to §1.1503(d)–6(h)(6)(iii), T is treated as if it incurred the dual consolidated loss that is recaptured for purposes of applying §1.1503(d)–6(h)(6)(i). Thus, T has a reconstituted net operating loss equal to the amount of the year 1 dual consolidated loss that was recaptured, and such loss is attributable to the Country X separate unit (and subject to the rules and limitations under §1.1503(d)–6(h)(6)(i)). Because T is treated as if it incurred the year 1 dual consolidated loss, P shall not be treated as having a net operating loss under §1.1503(d)–6(h)(6)(i).

Example 37. No foreign use following multiple-party event exception to triggering event. (i) *Facts.* P owns $DE1_X$ which, in turn, owns FB_X. P's interest in $DE1_X$ and its indirect interest in FB_X are combined and treated as a single separate unit (Country X separate unit) pursuant to §1.1503(d)–1(b)(4)(ii). In year 1, there is a $100x dual consolidated loss attributable to P's Country X separate unit and P makes a domestic use election with respect to such loss. T, a domestic corporation unrelated to P, owns 95 percent of PRS, a partnership. FS_X owns the remaining 5 percent of PRS. At the beginning of year 3, PRS purchases 100 percent of the interest in $DE1_X$ from P for cash. For Country X tax purposes, the $100x loss incurred by $DE1_X$ in year 1 carries forward and is available to offset income of $DE1_X$ in subsequent years.

(ii) *Result.* P's sale of its interest in $DE1_X$ is a triggering event under §1.1503(d)–6(e)(1)(iv) and (v). However, if P and T comply with the requirements under §1.1503(d)–6(f)(2)(iii), the sale would qualify for the multiple-party event exception under §1.1503(d)–6(f)(2)(i). In addition, because the $100x loss of $DE1_X$ carries forward to subsequent years for Country X purposes and is available to offset income of $DE1_X$, there would be a foreign use of the dual consolidated loss immediately after the sale pursuant to §1.1503(d)–3(a)(1). This is the case because the dual consolidated loss would be available to offset or reduce income that is considered, under U.S. tax principles, to be an item of FS_X, a foreign corporation (it would also be a foreign use because FS_X is an indirect owner of an interest in a hybrid entity that is not a separate unit). However, there is no foreign use in this case as a result of FS_X's 5 percent interest in $DE1_X$ pursuant to §1.1503(d)–3(c)(8).

Example 38. Character and source of recapture income. (i) *Facts.* (A) P owns FB_X. In year 1, the items of income, gain, deduction, and loss that are attributable to FB_X for purposes of determining whether it has a dual consolidated loss are as follows:

Sales income	$100x
Salary expense	($75x)
Interest expense	($50x)
Dual consolidated loss	($25x)

(B) P makes a domestic use election with respect to the year 1 dual consolidated loss attributable to FB_X and, thus, the $25x dual consolidated loss is used to offset the P group's consolidated taxable income.

(C) Pursuant to §1.861–8, the $75x of salary expense incurred by FB_X is allocated and apportioned entirely to foreign source general limitation income. Pursuant to §1.861–9T, $25x of the $50x interest expense attributable to FB_X is allocated and apportioned to domestic source income, $15x of such interest expense is allocated and apportioned to foreign source general limitation income, and the remaining $10x of such interest expense is allocated and apportioned to foreign source passive income.

(D) During year 2, $5x of income is attributable to FB_X under the rules of §1.1503(d)–5, and the P consolidated group has $100x of consolidated taxable income. At the end of year 2, FB_X undergoes a triggering event described in §1.1503(d)–6(e)(1), and P continues to own FB_X following the triggering event. Pursuant to §1.1503(d)–6(h)(2)(i), P is able to demonstrate to the satisfaction of the Commissioner that the $25x dual consolidated loss attributable to FB_X in year 1 would have offset the $5x of income attributable to FB_X in year 2, if no domestic use election were made with respect to the year 1 loss such that it was subject to the limitations of §1.1503(d)–4(b) and (c).

(ii) *Result.* P must recapture and report as ordinary income $20x ($25x - $5x) of FB_X's year 1 dual consolidated loss, plus applicable interest. The $20x recapture income is attributable to FB_X pursuant to §1.1503(d)–5(c)(4)(vi). Pursuant to §1.1503(d)–6(h)(5), the recapture income is treated as ordinary income whose source and character (including section 904 separate limitation character) is determined by reference to the manner in which the recaptured items of expense or loss taken into account in calculating the dual consolidated loss were allocated and apportioned. Further, pursuant to §1.1503(d)–6(h)(5), the *pro rata* computation described in §1.1503(d)–4(c)(4) shall apply. Thus, the character and source of the recapture income is determined in the same proportion as each item of deduction or loss that contributed to the dual consolidated loss being recaptured. Accordingly, P's $20x of recapture income is characterized and sourced as follows: $4x of domestic source income (($25x/$125x) x $20x); $14.4x of foreign source general limitation income (($75x + $15x)/$125x) x $20x); and $1.6x of foreign source passive income (($10x/$125x) x $20x). Pursuant to §1.1503(d)–6(h)(6)(i), commencing in year 3, the $20x recapture amount is reconstituted and treated as a net operating loss incurred by FB_X in a separate return limitation year, subject to the limitation under §1.1503(d)–4(b) (and therefore subject to the restrictions of §1.1503(d)–4(c)). Pursuant to §1.1503(d)–6(j)(1)(iii), the domestic use agreement filed by the P consolidated group with respect to the year 1 dual consolidated loss of FB_X is terminated and has no further effect.

Example 39. Interest charge without recapture. (i) *Facts.* P owns $DE1_X$ which, in turn, owns FB_X. P's interest in $DE1_X$ and its indirect interest in FB_X are combined and treated as a single separate unit (Country X separate unit) pursuant to §1.1503(d)–1(b)(4)(ii). In year 1, a dual consolidated loss of $100x is attributable to P's Country X separate unit. P makes a domestic use election with respect to such loss and uses the loss to offset the P group's consolidated taxable income. In year 2, there is $100x of income attributable to P's Country X separate unit and the P consolidated group has $200x of consolidated taxable income. At the end of year 2, the Country X separate unit undergoes a triggering event within the meaning of §1.1503(d)–6(e)(1). P demonstrates, to the satisfaction of the Commissioner, that if no domestic use election were made with respect to the year 1 dual consolidated loss such that it was subject to the limitations of §1.1503(d)–4(b) and (c), the year 1 $100x dual consolidated loss would have been offset by the $100x of year 2 income.

(ii) *Result.* There is no recapture of the year 1 dual consolidated loss attributable to P's Country X separate unit because it is reduced to zero under §1.1503(d)–6(h)(2)(i). However, P is liable for one year of interest charge under §1.1503(d)–6(h)(1)(ii), even though P's recapture amount is zero. This is the case because the P consolidated group had the benefit of the dual consolidated loss in year 1, and the income that offset the recapture income was not recognized until year 2. Pursuant to §1.1503(d)–6(j)(1)(iii), the domestic use agreement filed by the P consolidated group with respect to the year 1 dual consolidated loss is terminated and has no further effect.

Example 40. Reduced recapture and interest charge, and reconstituted dual consolidated loss. (i) *Facts.* S owns $DE1_X$ which, in turn, owns FB_X. S's interest in $DE1_X$ and its indirect interest in FB_X are combined and treated as a single separate unit (Country X separate unit) pursuant to §1.1503(d)–1(b)(4)(ii). In year 1, there is a $100x dual consolidated loss attributable to S's Country X separate unit, and P earns $100x. P makes a domestic use election with respect to the Country X separate unit's year 1 dual consolidated loss. Therefore, the consolidated group is permitted to offset P's $100x of income with the Country X separate unit's $100x dual consolidated loss. In year 2, $30x of income is attributable to the Country X separate unit under the rules of §1.1503(d)–5 and such income is offset by a $30x net operating loss incurred by P in such year. In year 3, $25x of income is attributable to the Country X separate unit under the rules of §1.1503(d)–5, and P earns $15x of income. In addition, at the end of year 3 there is a foreign use of the year 1 dual consolidated loss that constitutes a triggering event. S continues to own the Country X separate unit after the triggering event.

(ii) *Result.* (A) Under the presumptive rule of §1.1503(d)–6(h)(1)(i), S must recapture $100x (plus applicable interest). However, under §1.1503(d)–6(h)(2)(i), S may be able to demonstrate that a lesser amount is subject to recapture. The lesser amount is the amount of the $100x dual consolidated loss that would have remained subject to §1.1503(d)–4(c) at the time of the foreign use triggering event if a domestic use election had not been made for such loss.

(B) Although the combined separate unit earned $30x of income in year 2, there was no consolidated taxable income in such year. As a result, as of the end of year 2 the $100x dual consolidated loss would continue to be subject to §1.1503(d)–4(c) if a domestic use election had not been made for such loss. However, the $30x earned in year 2 can be carried forward to subsequent taxable years and may reduce the recapture income to the extent of consolidated taxable income generated in subsequent years. In year 3, $25x of income was attributable to the Country X separate unit and P earns $15x of income. Thus, the P consolidated group has $40x of consolidated taxable income in year 3. As a result, the $100x of recapture income can be reduced by $40x. This is the case because if a domestic use election had not been made for the $100x year 1 dual consolidated loss such that it was subject to the limitations of §1.1503(d)–4(b) and (c), only $60x of the loss would have remained subject to such limitations at the time of the foreign use triggering event. Accordingly, if S can adequately document the lesser amount, the amount of recapture income is $60x ($100x - $40x). The $60x recapture income is attributable to the Country X separate unit pursuant to §1.1503(d)–5(c)(4)(vi).

(C) Pursuant to §1.1503(d)–6(h)(6)(i), commencing in year 4, the $60x recapture amount is reconstituted and treated as a net operating loss incurred by the Country X separate unit of S in a separate return limitation year, subject to the limitation under §1.1503(d)–4(b) (and therefore subject to the restrictions of §1.1503(d)–4(c)). The loss is only available for carryover to taxable years after year 3 (and is not available for carryback). The carryover period of the loss, for purposes of section 172(b), will start from year 1, when the dual consolidated loss that was subject to recapture was incurred. In addition, such reconstituted net operating loss is not eligible for the exceptions contained in §1.1503(d)–6(b) through (d). Pursuant to §1.1503(d)–6(j)(1)(iii), the domestic use agreement filed by the P consolidated group with respect to the year 1 dual consolidated loss of the Country X separate unit is terminated and has no further effect.

(iii) *Alternative facts.* The facts are the same as in paragraph (i) of this *Example 40*, except that the triggering event that occurs at the end of year 3 is a sale by S of its entire interest in $DE1_X$ to B, an unrelated domestic corporation. The sale does not qualify as a transaction described in section 381. The results are the same as in paragraph (ii) of this *Example 40*, except that pursuant to §1.1503(d)–6(h)(6)(ii) the $60x net operating loss is not reconstituted (with respect to either S or B). The loss is not reconstituted with respect to S because the Country X separate unit ceases to be a separate unit of S (or any other member of the consolidated group that includes S) and therefore would have been eliminated pursuant to §1.1503(d)–4(d)(1)(ii) if no domestic use election had been made with respect to such loss. The loss is not reconstituted with respect to B because B was not the domestic owner of the combined separate unit when the dual consolidated loss that is recaptured was incurred, and B did not acquire the Country X separate unit in a section 381 transaction.

§1.1503(d)–8 Effective dates.

(a) *General rule.* Except as provided in paragraph (b) of this section, this paragraph (a) provides the dates of applicability of §§1.1503(d)–1 through 1.1503(d)–7. Sections 1.1503(d)–1 through 1.1503(d)–7 shall apply to dual consolidated losses incurred in taxable years beginning on or after April 18, 2007. However, a taxpayer may apply §§1.1503(d)–1 through 1.1503(d)–7, in their entirety, to dual consolidated losses incurred in taxable years beginning on or after January 1, 2007, by filing its return and attaching to such return the domestic use agreements, certifications, or other information in accordance with these regulations. For purposes of this section, the term *application date* means either April 18, 2007, or, if the taxpayer applies these regulations pursuant to the preceding sentence, January 1, 2007. Section 1.1503–2 applies for dual consolidated losses incurred in taxable years beginning on or after October 1, 1992, and before the application date.

(b) *Special rules*—(1) *Reduction of term of agreements filed under §§1.1503 2(g)(2)(i) or 1.1503–2T(g)(2)(i).* If an agreement was filed (or subsequently treated as filed) under §§1.1503–2A(c)(3), 1.1503–2(g)(2)(i), or 1.1503–2T(g)(2)(i) and remains in effect (that is, the dual consolidated loss subject to the agreement has not been recaptured pursuant to §1.1503–2(g)(2)(vii)) as of the application date, such agreement will be considered by the Internal Revenue Service to apply only for any taxable year up to and including the fifth taxable year following the year in which the dual consolidated loss that is the subject of the agreement was incurred and thereafter will have no effect.

(2) *Reduction of term of closing agreements entered into pursuant to §1.1503–2(g)(2)(iv)(B)(3)(i).* Taxpayers subject to the terms of a closing agreement entered into with the Internal Revenue Service pursuant to §1.1503–2(g)(2)(iv)(B)(*3*)(*i*) or Rev. Proc. 2000–42, 2000–2 C.B. 394, see §601.601(d)(2)(ii)(*b*) of this chapter, will be deemed to have satisfied the closing agreement's fifteen-year certification period requirement if the five-year certification period specified in §1.1503(d)–1(b)(20) has elapsed, provided such closing agreement is still in effect as of the application date, and provided the dual consolidated losses have not been recaptured. For example, if a calendar year taxpayer that has a January 1, 2007, application date entered into a closing agreement with respect to a dual consolidated loss incurred in 2003 and, as of January 1, 2007, the closing agreement is still in effect and the dual consolidated loss subject to the closing agreement has not been recaptured, then the closing agreement's fifteen-year certification period will be deemed satisfied when the five-year certification period described in §1.1503(d)–1(b)(20) has elapsed. Thus, the dual consolidated loss will be subject to the recapture and certification provisions of the closing agreement in such a case only through December 31, 2008. Alternatively, if a calendar year taxpayer that has a January 1, 2007, application date entered into a closing agreement with respect to a dual consolidated loss incurred in 2000 and, as of January 1, 2007, the closing agreement is still in effect and the dual consolidated loss subject to the closing agreement has not been recaptured, then the certification period is deemed to be satisfied.

(3) *Relief for untimely filings.* Paragraphs (b)(3)(i) through (iii) of this section set forth the effective dates for rules that provide relief for the failure to make timely filings of an election, agreement, statement, rebuttal, computation, closing agreement, or other information, pursuant to section 1503(d) and these regulations.

(i) *General rule.* Except as provided in paragraphs (b)(3)(ii) and (iii) of this section, the reasonable cause relief standard of §1.1503(d)–1(c) applies for all untimely filings with respect to dual consolidated losses, including with respect to dual consolidated losses incurred in taxable years beginning before the application date.

(ii) *Closing agreements.* Solely with respect to closing agreements described in §1.1503–2(g)(2)(iv)(B)(*3*)(*i*) and Rev. Proc. 2000–42, taxpayers must request relief for untimely requests through the process provided under §§301.9100–1 through 301.9100–3 of this chapter. See paragraph (b)(4) of this section for rules that permit the multiple-party event exception, rather than closing agreements, for certain triggering events.

(iii) *Pending requests for relief.* Taxpayers that have letter ruling requests under §§301.9100–1 through 301.9100–3 of this chapter pending as of March 19, 2007, (other than requests under paragraph (b)(3)(ii) of this section) are not required to use the reasonable cause procedure under §1.1503(d)–1(c); however, if such taxpayers have not yet received a determination of their request, they may withdraw their request consistent with the procedures contained in Rev. Proc. 2007–1, 2007–1 I.R.B. 1, see §601.601(d)(2)(ii)(*b*) of this chapter, (or any succeeding document) and use the reasonable cause procedure set forth in §1.1503(d)–1(c). In that event, the Internal Revenue Service will refund the taxpayer's user fee.

(4) *Multiple-party event exception to triggering events.* This paragraph (b)(4) applies to events described in §1.1503–2(g)(2)(iv)(B)(*1*)(*i*) through (*iii*) that occur after April 18, 2007, and that are with respect to dual consolidated losses that were incurred in taxable years beginning on or after October 1, 1992, and before the application date. The events described in the previous sentence are not eligible for the exception described in §1.1503–2(g)(2)(iv)(B)(*1*), but instead are eligible for the multiple-party event exception described in §1.1503(d)–6(f)(2)(i), as modified by this paragraph (b)(4). Thus, such events are not eligible for a closing agreement described in §1.1503–2(g)(2)(iv)(B)(*3*)(*i*) and Rev. Proc. 2000–42. For purposes of applying §1.1503(d)–6(f)(2)(i) to transactions covered by this paragraph, agreements described in §1.1503–2(g)(2)(i) (rather than domestic use agreements) shall be filed, and subsequent triggering events and exceptions thereto have the meaning provided in §1.1503–2(g)(2)(iii)(A) and (iv) (other than the exception provided under §1.1503–2(g)(2)(iv)(B)(*1*)). For example, if a calendar year taxpayer that has a January 1, 2007, application date filed an election under §1.1503–2(g)(2)(i) with respect to a dual consolidated loss that was incurred in 2004, and a triggering event described in §1.1503–2(g)(2)(iv)(B)(*1*)(*ii*) occurs with respect to such dual consolidated loss after April 18, 2007, then the event is eligible for the multiple-party event exception under §1.1503(d)–6(f)(2)(i) (and not the exception under §1.1503–2(g)(2)(iv)(B)(*1*)). However, in order to comply with §1.1503(d)–6(f)(2)(iii)(A), the subsequent elector must file a new agreement described in §1.1503–2(g)(2)(i) (rather than a new domestic use agreement). In addition, for purposes of determining whether there is a subsequent triggering event, and exceptions thereto, pursuant to such new agreement, §1.1503–2(g)(2)(iii)(A) and (iv) (other than the exception provided under §1.1503–2(g)(2)(iv)(B)(*1*)) shall apply. Notwithstanding the general application of this paragraph (b)(4) to events described in §1.1503–2(g)(2)(iv)(B)(*1*)(*i*) through (*iii*) that occur after April 18, 2007, a taxpayer may choose to apply this paragraph (b)(4) to events described in §1.1503–2(g)(2)(iv)(B)(*1*)(*i*) through (*iii*) that occur after March 19, 2007, and on or before April 18, 2007.

(5) *Basis adjustment rules.* Taxpayers may apply the basis adjustment rules of §1.1503(d)–5(g) for all open years in which such basis is relevant, even if the basis adjustment is attributable to a dual consolidated loss incurred (or recaptured) in a closed taxable year. Taxpayers applying the provisions of §1.1503(d)–5(g), however, must do so consistently for all open years.

PART 602—OMB CONTROL NUMBERS UNDER PAPERWORK REDUCTION ACT

Par. 5. The authority citation for part 602 continues to read as follows:

Authority: 26 U.S.C. 7805.

Par. 6. In §602.101, paragraph (b) is amended by adding entries in numerical order to the table to read as follows:

§602.101 OMB Control numbers.

* * * * *

(b) * * *

CFR part or section where identified and described	Current OMB control No.
* * * * *	
1.1503(d)–1	1545–1946
1.1503(d)–3	1545–1946
1.1503(d)–4	1545–1946
1.1503(d)–5	1545–1946
1.1503(d)–6	1545–1946
* * * * *	

Kevin M. Brown,
Deputy Commissioner for Services and Enforcement.

Approved February 27, 2007.

Eric Solomon,
Assistant Secretary of the Treasury (Tax Policy).

(Filed by the Office of the Federal Register on March 16, 2007, 8:45 a.m., and published in the issue of the Federal Register for March 19, 2007, 72 F.R. 12901)

Section 7520.—Valuation Tables

The adjusted applicable federal short-term, mid-term, and long-term rates are set forth for the month of April 2007. See Rev. Rul. 2007-23, page 889.

Section 7872.—Treatment of Loans With Below-Market Interest Rates

The adjusted applicable federal short-term, mid-term, and long-term rates are set forth for the month of April 2007. See Rev. Rul. 2007-23, page 889.

Part III. Administrative, Procedural, and Miscellaneous

Common Mistakes on Tax Returns

Notice 2007–35

The purpose of this notice is to alert taxpayers about common mistakes made by individuals while preparing their federal income tax returns. These mistakes may result in taxpayers failing to fully pay their correct tax liabilities. In addition, these mistakes may result in delays in processing returns and receiving refunds. Taxpayers should carefully read all the instructions to the tax forms and schedules and review their entire return before filing. In addition, e-filing, either through the Service's Free File Program at *www.irs.gov* or through tax preparation software or a tax professional, will help reduce errors and speed refunds. Taxpayers who e-file and use direct deposit will generally receive their refunds in as little as two weeks.

Additional taxpayer resources, including answers to frequently asked questions, also can be found at *www.irs.gov*. Taxpayers can learn more about common mistakes and find an error checklist on page 64 of the Instructions to the 2006 Form 1040, *U.S. Individual Income Tax Return*; this information also is available at Tax Topic 303 on the internet at *www.irs.gov* and from the toll-free TeleTax number, 1–800–829–4477.

1. ***Choosing the wrong filing status.*** Taxpayers should confirm that the filing status (*i.e.*, single, married filing jointly, married filing separately, head of household, qualifying widow(er) with dependent child) selected on the return is correct. For example, taxpayers often incorrectly claim "head of household" filing status without meeting the requirements for that status. In addition to delaying the processing of the return and any refund, designating the wrong filing status on a return also may affect a taxpayer's eligibility for the Earned Income Credit. The Instructions to the 2006 Forms 1040, 1040–A, and 1040–EZ provide detailed information to assist taxpayers in choosing their correct filing status.

2. ***Failing to include or using incorrect Social Security numbers.*** The names and Social Security numbers for the taxpayer, taxpayer's spouse, dependents, and qualifying children for the Earned Income Credit or Child Tax Credit must be included on the return exactly as they appear on the Social Security cards.

3. ***Failing to use the correct forms and schedules.*** Taxpayers should review the instructions to all applicable forms and schedules to be sure they have correctly used, and accurately completed, each form or schedule.

4. ***Failing to sign and date the return.*** Taxpayers must sign and date their return under penalties of perjury. If the return is not signed, it will not be accepted as filed by the Service. If it is a joint return, both spouses must sign the return.

5. ***Claiming ineligible dependents.*** Taxpayers may claim a person as a dependent only if that person meets the legal definition of a dependent. Taxpayers should consult the Instructions to Form 1040 or 1040–A to confirm that a person qualifies as a dependent. Each dependent must have a valid Social Security number (or other Taxpayer Identification Number, as applicable), which must be included on the tax return. The failure to include a dependent's name and Social Security number, or claiming an ineligible dependent, may result in an underpayment of tax and/or a denial of the Earned Income Credit.

6. ***Failing to file for the Earned Income Credit.*** Taxpayers should review carefully the eligibility requirements for the Earned Income Credit, including income limits, before filing returns. For example, many military families may qualify for the credit because they can choose to include or exclude combat zone compensation in the income calculations, depending on which treatment is more favorable. Detailed instructions for claiming and computing the credit are contained in the Instructions to the Form 1040 (and the Instructions to Forms 1040–A and 1040–EZ), Fact Sheet 2006–15, and Publication 596 (*Earned Income Credit (EIC)*) and through links at 1040 Central at *www.irs.gov*.

7. ***Improperly claiming the Earned Income Credit.*** Taxpayers must have earned income from work to claim the Earned Income Credit. For example, a taxpayer whose sole income is from Temporary Assistance for Needy Families or Social Security benefits does not have earned income and is therefore ineligible for the credit. Detailed instructions for claiming and computing the credit are contained in the Instructions to the Form 1040 (and the Instructions to Forms 1040–A and 1040–EZ), Fact Sheet 2006–15, and Publication 596 (*Earned Income Credit (EIC)*) and through links at 1040 Central at *www.irs.gov*.

8. ***Failing to report and pay domestic payroll taxes.*** Taxpayers employing household workers, such as a house cleaner, an in-home caregiver, or a nanny, must report and pay payroll taxes for those individuals when the payments exceed certain threshold amounts. Failure to pay and report payroll taxes may result in the assessment of additional tax due, interest on the unpaid amounts, and penalties. The Instructions to the Form 1040, Publication 926 (*Household Employer's Tax Guide*), and Publication 15–A (*Employer's Supplemental Tax Guide*) contain detailed information to assist taxpayers in determining whether an individual providing household help is a household employee for whom the taxpayer must report and pay payroll taxes.

9. ***Failing to report income because it was not included on a Form W–2, Form 1099, or other information return.*** Taxpayers must include on their tax returns income reported on a third-party information reporting statement such as a Form W–2 or Form 1099, or other similar statement. But even if income was not reported on a third-party reporting statement, taxpayers must still report all income. Failure to report all income may result in the assessment of additional tax due, interest on the unpaid amounts, and penalties.

10. ***Treating employees as independent contractors.*** Employers may not treat an employee as an "independent contractor" to avoid paying and reporting payroll taxes. Employers who improperly treat an employee as an independent contractor may be liable for additional tax due, interest on the unpaid amounts, and penalties. Publication 15–A (*Employer's Supplemental Tax Guide*) contains detailed information to assist taxpayers in determin-

ing whether an individual is an employee or an independent contractor.

11. ***Failing to file a return when due a refund.*** Taxpayers must file a return to claim a refund of withheld taxes when a refund is due. Taxpayers will forfeit refunds of withheld tax if a return requesting a refund is not filed within three years of the due date.

12. ***Failing to check liability for the alternative minimum tax.*** Taxpayers should determine whether the alternative minimum tax, or AMT, applies. If a taxpayer is liable for AMT but does not include it on the return, the Service will determine the taxpayer's liability and may reduce or deny a requested refund or assess any additional tax due, interest on the unpaid amounts, and penalties.

13. ***Failing to request federal telephone excise tax.*** Taxpayers can request a one-time credit of $30 to $60 for federal excise taxes paid for long-distance or bundled (local and long-distance) telephone service billed after February 28, 2003, and before August 1, 2006, whether for landline, cell phone or Voice over Internet Protocol service. Alternatively, taxpayers can request a one-time credit for the actual amount of excise taxes paid during the period using Form 8913, *Credit for Federal Telephone Excise Tax Paid.* Detailed information is provided in the 2006 Form 1040, 1040–A, and 1040–EZ Instructions, Fact Sheet 2007–1, and the Telephone Excise Tax Refund page at *www.irs.gov*.

14. ***Failing to accurately use or compute the Schedule D Tax Worksheet or Qualified Dividends and Capital Gain Tax Worksheet.*** Taxpayers should determine which worksheet they should use when computing their tax. Failure to use the correct worksheet may result in a reduction or denial of a requested refund or an assessment of additional tax due, interest on the unpaid amounts, and penalties.

15. ***Failing to enter the correct amount of taxable Social Security benefits.*** Taxpayers should report not only the total amount of their Social Security benefits, but also the correct amount of taxable Social Security benefits. In addition to delaying the processing of the tax return and any refund, reporting the incorrect amount of taxable Social Security benefits may result in an assessment of additional tax due, interest on the unpaid amounts, and penalties.

16. ***Mailing a return to the wrong address.*** Taxpayers who file their income tax returns by mail should send the returns to the appropriate Internal Revenue Service Center based on where the taxpayer lives and whether the taxpayer is including a check or money order with the return. The Forms 1040, 1040–A, and 1040–EZ Instructions, as well as the "Where To File" resource available on *www.irs.gov*, list the applicable mailing addresses according to where the taxpayer resides. Taxpayers who receive one of the Form Series 1040 booklets in the mail may also use the pre-addressed envelope that is included in the booklet to mail the return, unless the taxpayer has moved to another area with a different filing location. Mailing an income tax return to the wrong Internal Revenue Service Center or otherwise misaddressing the return could delay the processing of the return and any refund.

The principal author of this notice is the Office of Associate Chief Counsel (Procedure & Administration), Administrative Provisions & Judicial Practice Division. For further information regarding this notice, contact that office at (202) 622–7800 (not a toll-free call).

Part IV. Items of General Interest

Notice of Proposed Rulemaking

Suspension of Statutes of Limitations in Third-Party and John Doe Summons Disputes and Expansion of Taxpayers' Rights to Receive Notice and Seek Judicial Review of Third-Party Summonses

REG–153037–01

AGENCY: Internal Revenue Service (IRS), Treasury.

ACTION: Notice of proposed rulemaking.

SUMMARY: This document contains proposed amendments to the regulations relating to third-party and John Doe summonses. These proposed regulations reflect amendments to sections 7603 and 7609 of the Internal Revenue Code of 1986 made by the Internal Revenue Service Restructuring and Reform Act of 1998, the Omnibus Budget Reconciliation Act of 1990, the Technical and Miscellaneous Revenue Act of 1988, and the Tax Reform Act of 1986, which were enacted subsequent to adoption of the current regulations. These proposed regulations provide guidance relating to the manner in which summonses may be served on third-party recordkeepers, the expanded class of third-party summonses subject to notice requirements and other procedures, and the suspension of periods of limitations if a court proceeding is brought involving a challenge to a third-party summons, or if a third party's response to a summons is not finally resolved within six months after service. These proposed regulations affect third parties who are served with a summons, taxpayers identified in a third-party summons, and other persons entitled to notice of a third-party summons.

DATES: Written comments and requests for a public hearing must be received by October 19, 2006.

ADDRESSES: Send submissions to: CC:PA:LPD:PR (REG–153037–01), room 5203, Internal Revenue Service, POB 7604, Ben Franklin Station, Washington, DC 20044. Alternatively, submissions may be hand delivered between the hours of 8 a.m. and 4 p.m. to: CC:PA:LPD:PR (REG–153037–01), Courier's Desk, Internal Revenue Service, 1111 Constitution Avenue, NW, Washington, DC. Comments may also be submitted electronically to *www.irs.gov/regs* or the Federal eRulemaking Portal at *www.regulations.gov* (IRS—REG–153037–01).

FOR FURTHER INFORMATION CONTACT: Elizabeth Rawlins at (202) 622–3630 (not a toll-free number).

SUPPLEMENTARY INFORMATION:

Background

This document contains proposed regulations amending the Procedure and Administration Regulations (26 CFR part 301) under sections 7603 and 7609 of the Internal Revenue Code of 1986 (Code). The proposed regulations reflect amendments to sections 7603 and 7609 enacted in the Internal Revenue Service Restructuring and Reform Act of 1998 (Public Law 105–206, 112 Stat. 685) (RRA 1998), the Technical and Miscellaneous Revenue Act of 1988 (Public Law 100–647, 102 Stat. 3343) (TAMRA 1988), and the Tax Reform Act of 1986 (Public Law 99–514, 100 Stat. 2085) (TRA 1986). The proposed regulations also reflect changes made to section 6503(j) in the Omnibus Budget Reconciliation Act of 1990 (Public Law 101–508, 104 Stat. 1388) (OBRA 1990).

Explanation of Provisions

In general, section 7609 provides that if a summons is served on a third party requiring the third party to give testimony or produce records relating to a taxpayer or other person identified in the summons, the Internal Revenue Service (IRS) must provide notice of the summons to the taxpayer and to any other person identified in the description of summoned records and testimony within three days of the date on which the summons was served, but no later than 23 days prior to the date fixed in the summons as the day on which the examination of the summoned person or materials is scheduled. Persons entitled to notice of a third-party summons are entitled to bring a proceeding to quash the summons by filing a petition in district court within 20 days after notice is given. Persons entitled to notice also may intervene in any proceeding to enforce the summons. During the pendency of a proceeding to quash a summons brought by the taxpayer, or during the pendency of a proceeding to enforce a summons in which the taxpayer has intervened, the periods of limitations on assessment and criminal prosecution are suspended. These periods of limitations are also suspended if the third-party's response to the summons remains unresolved six months after the summons is served, regardless of whether a proceeding has been brought with respect to the summons. These proposed regulations amend prior regulations relating to third-party summonses to reflect the statutory changes to sections 7603 and 7609 described below.

Notice of Third-Party Summonses

Section 7609(a) requires the IRS to provide notice of a third-party summons to the taxpayer being investigated and every person identified in the description of summoned records and testimony unless the summons is excepted from the notice requirements under section 7609(c)(2). Prior to RRA 1998, the IRS was required to provide notice of a third-party summons only if the summons was served on a third-party recordkeeper and the summons required the production of records made or kept of another person's business transactions or affairs (or testimony about such records). RRA 1998 expanded the types of third-party summonses to which the notice, intervention, and proceeding to quash procedures apply by removing the prior specifically-defined third-party recordkeeper limitation. The proposed regulations reflect the expansion of the notice procedures to all third-party summonses not excepted by section 7609(c)(2).

Exceptions to Notice, Intervention, and Proceeding to Quash Procedures

Section 7609(c)(2) provides that certain summonses, including summonses served on the person with respect to whose liability the summons was issued, third-party summonses issued to confirm or deny the existence of records, and summonses that require court approval before service, are excepted from the notice, intervention, and proceeding to quash provisions of subsections 7609(a) and (b). Two additional exceptions, relating to third-party summonses issued in aid of collection under section 7609(c)(2)(D) and summonses issued by a criminal investigator under section 7602(c)(2)(E), were the subject of recent statutory changes.

Prior to RRA 1998, former section 7609(c)(2)(B) broadly excepted from the notice requirements and other procedural rules a summons issued in aid of the collection of any person's liability. RRA 1998 narrowed the collection exception, now found in section 7609(c)(2)(D), to except only summonses issued in aid of the collection of either: (i) an assessment or judgment against the person with respect to whose liability the summons is issued, or (ii) the liability of a transferee or fiduciary of the liable person. Under section 7609(c)(2)(D), as amended, the IRS now must give notice of a third-party summons issued in aid of the collection of a person's potential liability for an unassessed tax. For example, the IRS must provide notice of a third-party summons to a potentially responsible person if the purpose of the third-party summons is to determine whether the person is liable for the trust fund recovery penalty under section 6672.

The exception from notice, intervention, and proceeding to quash procedures for summonses issued by a criminal investigator under section 7609(c)(2)(E) was added by RRA 1998. Section 7609(c)(2)(E) excepts third-party summonses issued by criminal investigators if the summoned third party is not a third-party recordkeeper, as that term is defined under new section 7603(b).

Third-Party Recordkeepers

Section 7603(b)(1) provides that third-party recordkeeper summonses may be served by certified or registered mail to the last known address of the third-party recordkeeper. Section 7603(b)(2) enumerates classes of persons that are third-party recordkeepers, including banks, credit card issuers, attorneys, accountants, and enrolled agents.

1. *When third-party recordkeeper status arises*

Prior to RRA 1998, third-party recordkeeper summonses were defined under former section 7609(a)(1) as summonses that were served on a third-party recordkeeper, *i.e.*, a person belonging to one of several enumerated classes of business occupations, for the production of records made or kept of another person's business transactions or affairs. Based on these requirements, existing §301.7609–2(b) provides that "[a] person is a 'third-party recordkeeper' with respect to a given set of records only if the person made or kept the records in the person's capacity as a third-party recordkeeper."

RRA 1998 amended section 7603, relating to service of summonses, by adding to new subsection (b) the enumerated classes of third-party recordkeepers, but did not incorporate the requirement of former section 7609(a)(1)(B) that the records of the business transactions or affairs be made or kept by the third-party recordkeeper in its capacity as such. There is no indication in the legislative history to RRA 1998 that Congress intended to alter the requirement under §301.7609–2(b) that the records of a third-party recordkeeper be made or kept in the third-party recordkeeper's capacity as such. Accordingly, the proposed regulations maintain the requirement under existing §301.7609–2(b).

2. *Owners or developers of computer software source code*

RRA 1998 added owners or developers of computer software source code to the enumerated classes of third-party recordkeepers under section 7603(b)(2). The proposed regulations define owners or developers of computer software source code as third-party recordkeepers if they are summoned to produce the source code or the programs and data to which the source code relates, whether or not they make or keep records of another person's business transactions or affairs.

Suspension of Periods of Limitations

1. *Suspension under section 7609(e)(1)*

Section 7609(e)(1) provides that the periods of limitations under section 6501 (relating to assessment and collection) and section 6531 (relating to criminal prosecution) are suspended if any person with respect to whose liability a third-party summons was issued (or the agent, nominee, or other person acting under the direction and control of such person), pursuant to section 7609(b), intervenes in a judicial proceeding to enforce a third-party summons or brings a proceeding to quash a third-party summons. The suspension continues for the period during which the proceeding, including appeals, is pending.

2. *Suspension under section 7609(e)(2)*

Section 7609(e)(2) provides that the periods of limitations under section 6501 and section 6531, are suspended if there is no final resolution of the third party's response to the summons within six months after service of such summons, regardless of whether the person with respect to whose liability the summons was issued has intervened in an enforcement proceeding or brought a proceeding to quash.

Suspension of the periods of limitations under section 7609(e)(2) begins six months after the summons is served and ends upon the final resolution of the summoned party's response. The proposed regulations describe the types of summonses to which the suspension of periods of limitations under section 7609(e)(2) apply and define final resolution.

a. *Summonses to which suspension under section 7609(e)(2) may apply*

Prior to RRA 1998, former section 7609(e)(2) suspended a taxpayer's periods of limitations if either a third-party recordkeeper's response to a summons, for which the taxpayer was entitled to receive notice under section 7609(a), or if a summoned person's response to a John Doe summons was not finally resolved within six months after the summons was served. Nothing in the legislative history to RRA 1998 suggests that Congress intended to expand the basic statutory structure of section 7609(e)(2) to encompass any summonses other than John Doe summonses and third-party summonses subject to the notice requirement of section 7609(a). Therefore, the proposed regulations provide that the periods of limitations are suspended under section 7609(e)(2) only with respect to third-party summonses to which the notice requirements of section 7609(a) apply, or to John Doe summonses for which taxpayers are entitled to notice of any statute suspension pursuant to section 7609(i)(4).

b. *Final resolution of a third party's response to a summons*

Section 7609(e)(2) provides that suspension of the periods of limitations ends on the date of final resolution of the third party's response to the summons. The purpose of section 7609(e)(2) is to suspend the periods of limitations if an investigation is delayed by a summoned person's failure to produce all of the summoned information within six months. Although final resolution is not defined in section 7609, nor is it elaborated on in the legislative history of that statute, the same term is found in section 6503(j), which suspends the period of limitations on assessment during a judicial enforcement period relating to designated and related summonses. Like section 7609(e)(2), section 6503(j) provides that the suspension period will not end until there is final resolution of the summoned person's response to the summons. The legislative history of section 6503(j) indicated that the term *final resolution* means, in cases in which a court proceeding is brought, that no court proceeding remains pending and the summoned party has complied with the summons to the extent the court required. Therefore, the proposed regulations define final resolution as occurring when the summoned person fully complies with the production required by the summons. If the summons is the subject of litigation, full compliance occurs when any order enforcing any part of the summons is fully complied with and all appeals are either disposed of or the period in which an appeal may be taken or a request for further review may be made has expired. The IRS will administratively create procedures by which taxpayers can inquire about the suspension of their periods of limitations under section 7609(e)(2).

Protections for and Duties of Summoned Third Parties

Section 7609(i)(3) provides that any summoned party who produces records or gives testimony in good faith reliance on an IRS certificate or court order is not liable to a customer or other person for disclosure of records or testimony in response to a third-party summons. RRA 1998 modified these provisions by extending protection to all recipients of third-party summonses subject to the notice requirements of section 7609(a) and by expanding the protection from liability to include the giving of testimony by a third party, in addition to the production of records. The proposed regulations reflect these statutory changes.

Notification Requirement for John Doe Summonses under Section 7609(i)(4)

Section 7609(i)(4) requires the recipient of a John Doe summons to notify the unnamed taxpayers to which the summons applies if those taxpayers' periods of limitations are suspended by operation of section 7609(e)(2), relating to the absence of a resolution to the summoned party's response six months after service of the summons.

The proposed regulations specify the time and the manner for providing the notice required under section 7609(i)(4). Notice must be given as soon as possible after the suspension of the periods of limitations and must be made in writing. The written notification may be hand delivered, sent to the address of the taxpayer last known by the summoned person to be valid, or transmitted by any electronic means. Failure by the summoned party to comply with the notice requirements of section 7609(i)(4) will not preclude the suspension of the periods of limitations pursuant to section 7609(e)(2).

Use of Informal Procedures not Precluded by Section 7609

Section 7609(j) provides that nothing in section 7609 shall be construed to limit the IRS's ability to obtain information through formal or informal procedures authorized by sections 7601 and 7602. The proposed regulations provide that section 7609 does not require the IRS to issue a third-party summons before conducting an informal inquiry of a third party or examining a third party's books, papers, records, or other data during an investigation.

Proposed Effective Dates

These amendments are proposed to be applicable on the date the final regulations are filed with the **Federal Register**.

Special Analyses

It has been determined that this notice of proposed rulemaking is not a significant regulatory action as defined in Executive Order 12866. Therefore, a regulatory assessment is not required. It also has been determined that section 553(b) of the Administrative Procedure Act (5 U.S.C. chapter 5) does not apply to these regulations and, because these regulations do not impose a collection of information under the Paperwork Reduction Act (44 U.S.C. section 3501), the Regulatory Flexibility Act (5 U.S.C. chapter 6) does not apply to these regulations. Pursuant to section 7805(f) of the Code, this notice of proposed rulemaking will be submitted to the Chief Counsel for Advocacy of the Small Business Administration for comment on its impact on small business.

Comments and Requests for a Public Hearing

Before these proposed regulations are adopted as final regulations, consideration will be given to any written comments (preferably a signed original and eight (8) copies) that are submitted timely to the IRS. The IRS and the Treasury Department specifically request comments on the clarity of the proposed rule and how it may be made easier to understand. All comments will be available for public inspection and copying. A public hearing may be scheduled if requested in writing by a person who timely submits written comments. If a public hearing is scheduled, notice of the date, time, and place for the hearing will be published in the **Federal Register**.

Drafting Information

The principal author of these regulations is Elizabeth Rawlins of the Office of the Associate Chief Counsel, Procedure and Administration (Collection, Bankruptcy and Summonses Division), Internal Revenue Service.

* * * * *

Proposed Amendment to the Regulations

Accordingly, 26 CFR part 301 is proposed to be amended as follows:

PART 301—PROCEDURE AND ADMINISTRATION

Paragraph 1. The authority citation for part 301 continues to read, in part, as follows:

Authority: 26 U.S.C. 7805 * * *

Par. 2. Section 301.7603–1 is revised to read as follows:

§301.7603–1 Service of summons.

(a) *In general*—(1) *Hand delivery or delivery to place of abode.* Except as otherwise provided in paragraph (a)(2) of this section, a summons issued under section 6420(e)(2), 6421(g)(2), 6427(j)(2), or 7602 shall be served by an attested copy delivered in hand to the person to whom it is directed, or left at such person's last and usual place of abode.

(2) *Summonses issued to third-party recordkeepers.* A summons issued under section 6420(e)(2), 6421(g)(2), 6427(j)(2), or 7602 for the production of records (or testimony about such records) by a third-party recordkeeper, as described in section 7603(b)(2) and §301.7603–2, may also be served by certified or registered mail to the third-party recordkeeper's last known address, as defined in §301.6212–2. If service to a third-party recordkeeper is made by certified or registered mail, the date of service is the date on which the summons is mailed.

(b) *Persons who may serve a summons.* The officers and employees of the Internal Revenue Service whom the Commissioner has designated to carry out the authority described in §301.7602–1(b) to issue a summons are authorized to serve a summons issued under section 6420(e)(2), 6421(g)(2), 6427(j)(2), or 7602.

(c) *Effect of certificate of service.* The certificate of service signed by the person serving the summons shall be evidence of the facts it states on the hearing of an application for the enforcement of the summons.

(d) *Sufficiency of description of summoned records.* When a summons requires the production of records, it shall be sufficient if such records are described with reasonable certainty.

(e) *Records.* For purposes of this section and §301.7603–2, the term *records* includes books, papers, or other data.

(f) *Effective date.* This section is applicable on the date final regulations are published in the **Federal Register**.

Par. 3. Section 301.7603–2 is added to read as follows:

§301.7603–2 Third-party recordkeepers.

(a) *Definitions*—(1) *Accountant.* A person is an accountant under section 7603(b)(2)(F) for purposes of determining whether that person is a third-party recordkeeper if, on the date the records described in the summons were created, the person was registered, licensed, or certified as an accountant under the authority of any state, commonwealth, territory, or possession of the United States, or of the District of Columbia.

(2) *Attorney.* A person is an attorney under section 7603(b)(2)(E) for purposes of determining whether that person is a third-party recordkeeper if, on the date the records described in the summons were created, the person was registered, licensed, or certified as an attorney under the authority of any state, commonwealth, territory, or possession of the United States, or of the District of Columbia.

(3) *Credit cards*—(i) *Person extending credit through credit cards.* The term *person extending credit through the use of credit cards or similar devices* under section 7603(b)(2)(C) generally includes any person who issues a credit card. The term does not include a seller of goods or services who honors credit cards issued by other parties but who does not extend credit through the use of credit cards or similar devices.

(ii) *Devices similar to credit cards.* An object is a device similar to a credit card under section 7603(b)(2)(C) only if it is physical in nature, such as a charge plate or similar device that may be tendered to obtain an extension of credit. Thus, a person who extends credit by requiring customers to sign sales slips without requiring the use of, or reference to, a physical object issued by that person is not a third-party recordkeeper under section 7603(b)(2)(C).

(iii) *Debit cards.* A debit card is not a credit card or similar device because a debit card is not tendered to obtain an extension of credit.

(4) *Enrolled agent.* A person is an enrolled agent under section 7603(b)(2)(I) for purposes of determining whether that person is a third-party recordkeeper if the person is enrolled as an agent authorized to practice before the Internal Revenue Service pursuant to Circular 230, 31 CFR Part 10.

(5) *Owner or developer of certain computer code and data.* An owner or developer of computer software source code under section 7603(b)(2)(J) is a third-party recordkeeper when summoned to produce a computer software source code (as defined in section 7612(d)(2)), or an executable code and associated data described in section 7612(b)(1)(A)(ii), even if that person did not make or keep records of another person's business transactions or affairs.

(b) *When third-party recordkeeper status arises*—(1) *In general.* Except as provided in paragraph (a)(5) of this section, a person listed in section 7603(b)(2) is a third-party recordkeeper for purposes of section 7609(c)(2)(E) and §301.7603–1 only if the summons served on that person seeks records (or testimony regarding such records) of a third party's business transactions or affairs and such recordkeeper made or kept the records in the capacity of a third-party recordkeeper. For instance, an accountant is not a third-party recordkeeper (by reason of being an accountant) with respect to the accountant's records of a sale of property by the accountant to another person. Similarly, a credit card issuer is not a third-party recordkeeper (by reason of being a person extending credit through the use of credit cards or similar devices) with respect to—

(i) Records relating to non-credit card transactions, such as a cash sale by the issuer to a holder of the issuer's credit card; or

(ii) Records relating to transactions involving the use of another issuer's credit card.

(2) *Examples.* The rules of paragraph (b)(1) of this section are illustrated by the following examples:

Example 1. V issues a credit card (the V card) that is honored by R, a retailer. When using the V card, C, a customer, signs a sales slip in triplicate. C, R, and V each retain one copy. Only the copy held by V is held by a third-party recordkeeper under section 7603(b)(2), even though R may issue its own credit card.

Example 2. R, a retailer, issues its own credit card (the R card) to C, a customer. When C makes a credit purchase from R using the R card, C signs a sales slip in duplicate. C and R each retain one copy. Because R keeps the copy in its capacity as credit card issuer, as well as in its capacity as a retailer, it is a third-party recordkeeper under section 7603(b)(2) with respect to its copy of the sales slip.

(c) *Effective date*. This section is applicable on the date the final regulations are published in the **Federal Register**.

Par. 4. Sections 301.7609–1 through 301.7609–5 are revised to read as follows:

§301.7609–1 Special procedures for third-party summonses.

(a) *In general*—(1) Section 7609 requires the Internal Revenue Service (IRS) to follow special procedures when summoning a third party's testimony, records, or computer software source code. Except as provided in §301.7609–2(b), the IRS must provide notice of a third-party summons to any person identified in the summons, other than the person summoned. A person entitled to notice of a third-party summons may intervene in any proceeding brought to enforce the summons or may bring a proceeding to quash the summons, regardless of whether they receive notice of the summons from the IRS pursuant to section 7609(a) and §301.7609–2.

(2) Neither section 7609 nor §301.7603–1, §301.7603–2, or §§301.7609–1 through 301.7609–5, limit the IRS's ability to obtain information, other than by summons, through formal or informal procedures authorized by sections 7601 and 7602.

(b) *Cross references*. See §301.7609–2 for rules relating to persons who must be notified of a third-party summons and exceptions to the notification requirements. See §301.7609–3 for rules relating to the rights and duties of summoned parties. See §301.7609–4 for rules relating to actions to quash a summons or to intervene in a summons enforcement proceeding. See §301.7609–5 for rules relating to the suspension of periods of limitations.

(c) *Records*. For purposes of §§301.7609–1 through 301.7609–5, the term "records" includes books, papers, or other data.

(d) *Effective date*. This section is applicable on the date the final regulations are published in the **Federal Register**.

§301.7609–2 Notification of persons identified in third-party summonses.

(a) *In general*—(1) *Persons entitled to notice*. Except as provided in §301.7609–2(b), the Internal Revenue Service (IRS) shall give notice of a third-party summons to any person, other than the person summoned, who is identified in the summons. The only persons so identified are the person with respect to whose liability the summons is issued and any other person identified in the description of summoned records or testimony. For example, if the IRS issues a summons to a bank with respect to the liability of C that requires the production of account records of A and B, both of whom are named in the summons, the IRS must notify A, B and C of the summons.

(2) *Time for providing notice*. If notice is required by this paragraph (a)(1), such notice must be given within three days of the date on which the summons is served on the third party, but no later than 23 days prior to the date fixed in the summons as the date on which the examination of the summoned person or records is scheduled.

(3) *Methods for serving notice*. Notice may be served by hand delivery to any person entitled to notice or by leaving notice at such person's last and usual place of abode. Notice also may be served by certified or registered mail to the person's last known address, as defined in §301.6212–2. If service to a person entitled to notice is made by certified or registered mail, the date of service is the date on which the notice is mailed.

(4) *Content of the notice*. Notice required to be given to any person entitled to notice must be accompanied by a copy of the summons that has been served and must include an explanation of the right to bring a proceeding to quash the summons. The copy of the summons accompanying the notice is not required to contain the attestation that appears pursuant to section 7603 on the copy of the summons served on the summoned person.

(b) *Exceptions*. The IRS is not required to provide notice to persons identified in the following third-party summonses:

(1) *Summons served on the taxpayer*. The IRS is not required to provide notice of a summons served on the person with respect to whose liability the summons was issued, or any officer or employee of such person.

(2) *Existence of records*. The IRS is not required to provide notice in the case of a summons issued to determine whether or not records of the business transactions or affairs of a person identified in the summons have been made or kept.

(3) *Numbered account or similar arrangement*. The IRS is not required to provide notice in the case of a summons issued solely to determine the identity of a person having a numbered account or similar arrangement with a bank or other institution. An account is a numbered account or similar arrangement within the meaning of this paragraph (b)(3) if it is an account through which a person may authorize transactions solely through the use of a number, symbol, code name, or other device not involving the disclosure of the person's identity. The term *person having a numbered account or similar arrangement* includes the person who opened the account and any person authorized to access the account or to receive records or statements concerning it.

(4) *Summonses in aid of the collection of liabilities*—(i) *In general*. The IRS is not required to provide notice in the case of a summons issued in aid of the collection of liabilities. A summons is in aid of the collection of liabilities within the meaning of this paragraph if it is issued in connection with the collection of—

(A) An assessment or judgment against the person with respect to whose liability the summons is issued; or

(B) The liability determined at law or in equity of any transferee or fiduciary of a person described in paragraph (b)(4)(i)(A) of this section.

(ii) *Examples*. The rules of paragraph (b)(4) of this section are illustrated by the following examples:

Example 1. A third-party summons is issued to a bank to determine the amount held in an account in the name of A, against whom unpaid income taxes have been assessed. Notice of the summons is not required to be given to A or any other persons identified in the summons because the summons is issued in connection with the collection of taxes that have been assessed.

Example 2. A third-party summons is issued to determine whether assessments should be made against A, who is potentially liable for a trust fund recovery penalty under section 6672 with respect to the assessed but unpaid withholding tax liability of employer E. The summons is captioned: In the matter of A. Notice of the summons must be provided to A and to any other persons identified in the summons because the summons was issued with respect to A's potential, unassessed liability under section 6672.

(5) *Summonses issued by a criminal investigator.* The IRS is not required to provide notice in the case of a summons issued by a criminal investigator to a person other than a third-party recordkeeper, as defined in section 7603(b). For purposes of section 7609(c)(2)(E), a summons issued by a criminal investigator is any summons issued as part of a criminal investigation by an IRS officer or employee having authority to conduct a criminal investigation and to issue a summons.

(6) *John Doe summons.* The IRS is not required to provide notice in the case of a John Doe summons issued under section 7609(f).

(7) *Summons issued pursuant to a court order to prevent spoliation of evidence.* The IRS is not required to provide notice in the case of a summons for which a court determines there is reasonable cause to believe the giving of notice may lead to attempts to conceal, destroy, or alter records relevant to the examination, to prevent communication of information from other persons through intimidation, bribery, or collusion, or to flee to avoid prosecution, testifying, or production of records.

(c) *Effective date.* This section is applicable on the date the final regulations are published in the **Federal Register**.

§301.7609–3 Duty of and protection for the summoned party.

(a) *Duty of the summoned party.* Upon receipt of a summons, the summoned party must begin to assemble the summoned records. The summoned party must be prepared to produce the summoned records on the date on which the summons states that they are to be examined, regardless of the institution or anticipated institution of a proceeding to quash or the summoned party's intervention in a proceeding to quash, as allowed under section 7609(b)(2)(C).

(b) *Disclosing summoned party not liable*—(1) *In general.* A summoned party, or an agent or employee thereof, who makes a disclosure of records or gives testimony as required by a summons in good faith reliance on the certificate of the Secretary (as defined in paragraph (b)(2) of this section) or an order of a court requiring production of records or giving of testimony, will not be liable for any claim arising from such disclosure brought by any customer, any party with respect to whose tax liability the summons was issued, or any other person.

(2) *Certificate of the Secretary.* The Secretary may issue to the summoned party a certificate if the person with respect to whose liability the summons was issued expressly consents to the examination of the records summoned and the taking of testimony. The Secretary also may issue to the summoned party a certificate stating that—

(i) The 20-day period within which a person entitled to notice of the summons may institute a proceeding to quash the summons has expired; and

(ii) No proceeding has been instituted within that period.

(c) *Reimbursement of costs.* Summoned third parties may be entitled to reimbursement of their costs of assembling and preparing to produce summoned records, to the extent allowed by section 7610 and §301.7610–1.

(d) *Notification of suspension of periods of limitations in connection with a John Doe summons*—(1) *Requirement of notification.* If any periods of limitations are suspended under section 7609(e)(2) and §301.7609–5(d) with respect to a John Doe summons described in section 7609(f), the summoned party is required under section 7609(i)(4) to provide notice of such suspension to all persons with respect to whose liability the summons was issued.

(2) *Content of notification.* A summoned party required to notify a person of the suspension of the periods of limitations shall provide the following information to such person—

(i) A John Doe summons was served on the summoned party seeking records that may be relevant to the person's tax liability;

(ii) The date on which the summons was served;

(iii) The tax period(s) to which the summons relates;

(iv) Six months has passed since service of the summons and the summoned party's response to the summons has not been finally resolved;

(v) The periods of limitations under section 6501 (relating to assessment and collection) and section 6531 (relating to criminal prosecution), have been suspended; and

(vi) The date on which suspension of the periods of limitations under sections 6501 and 6531 began.

(3) *Time and manner of notification.* The notification must be made in writing and may be delivered in person, by mail sent to the address last known by the summoned party, or by use of any electronic means of transmission. Notification should be made as soon as possible after the suspension of the periods of limitations begins. Failure by a summoned party to give notice of the suspension of periods of limitations as required by section 7609(i)(4) does not prevent the suspension of the periods of limitations under section 7609(e)(2).

(e) *Effective date.* This section is applicable on the date the final regulations are published in the **Federal Register**.

§301.7609–4 Right to intervene; right to institute a proceeding to quash.

(a) *Intervention in proceeding with respect to enforcement of a summons.* Under section 7609(b)(1), a person entitled to notice of a summons under section 7609(a) and §301.7609–2 is entitled to intervene in any proceeding brought under section 7604 with respect to the enforcement of that summons.

(b) *Right to institute a proceeding to quash*—(1) *In general.* Under section 7609(b), a person entitled to notice of a summons under section 7609(a) and §301.7609–2 may institute a proceeding to quash the summons in the United States district court for the district in which the summoned person resides or is found.

(2) *Requirements for a proceeding to quash.* To institute a proceeding to quash a summons, a person entitled to notice of the summons must, not later than the 20th day following the day the notice of the summons was served on or mailed to such person—

(i) File a petition to quash a summons in the name of the person entitled to notice of the summons in the proper district court;

(ii) Notify the Internal Revenue Service (IRS) by sending a copy of that petition to quash by registered or certified mail to the IRS employee and office designated in the notice of summons to receive the copy; and

(iii) Notify the summoned person by sending by registered or certified mail a copy of the petition to quash to the summoned person.

(3) *Failure to give timely notice.* If a person entitled to notice of the summons fails to give proper and timely notice to either the summoned person or the IRS in the manner described in this paragraph (b)(2) of this section, that person has failed to institute a proceeding to quash and the district court lacks jurisdiction to hear the proceeding. For example, if the person entitled to notice mails a copy of the petition to the summoned person, but fails to mail a copy of the petition to the designated IRS employee and office, the person entitled to notice has failed to institute a proceeding to quash. Similarly, if the person entitled to notice mails a copy of such petition to the summoned person but, instead of sending a copy of the petition by registered or certified mail to the designated IRS employee and office, the person entitled to notice provides the designated IRS employee and office the petition by some other means, the person entitled to notice has failed to institute a proceeding to quash.

(4) *Failure to institute a proceeding to quash.* If a person entitled to notice fails to institute a proceeding to quash within 20 days following the day the notice of the summons was served on or mailed to such person, the IRS may examine the summoned records and take summoned testimony following the 23rd day after notice of the summons was served on or mailed to the person entitled to notice.

(c) *Presumption no notice has been mailed.* Section 7609(b)(2)(B) permits a person entitled to notice to institute a proceeding to quash by filing a petition in district court and notifying both the IRS and the summoned person. Unless the person entitled to notice has notified both the IRS and the summoned person in the appropriate manner, the person entitled to notice has failed to institute a proceeding to quash. For the purpose of permitting the IRS to examine the summoned witnesses and records, it is presumed that the notification was not timely mailed if the copy of the petition was not delivered to the summoned person or to the person and office designated to receive the notice on behalf of the IRS within three days after the close of the 20-day period allowed for instituting a proceeding to quash.

(d) *Effective date.* This section is applicable on the date the final regulations are published in the **Federal Register**.

§301.7609–5 Suspension of periods of limitations.

(a) *In general.* Except in the case of a summons that is a designated or related summons described in section 6503(j), the following rules relating to the suspension of certain periods of limitations apply to all third-party summonses subject to the notice requirements of section 7609(a) and to all John Doe summonses subject to the requirements of section 7609(f).

(b) *Intervention in an action to enforce the summons*—(1) *In general.* If a person entitled to notice of a summons under section 7609(a) and §301.7609–2 with respect to whose liability the summons was issued, or such person's agent, nominee, or other person acting under the direction or control of the person entitled to notice, takes any action to intervene in a proceeding with respect to enforcement of such summons brought pursuant to section 7604, that person's periods of limitations under sections 6501 (relating to assessment and collection) and 6531 (relating to criminal prosecutions) for the tax period or periods that are the subject of the summons are suspended for the period during which such proceeding is pending.

(2) *Action to intervene.* A person entitled to notice takes any action to intervene in a proceeding to enforce a summons within the meaning of §301.7609–4(a) on the date when a motion to intervene is filed with the court.

(c) *Institution of a proceeding to quash a summons*—(1) *In general.* If a person entitled to notice of a summons under section 7609(a) and §301.7609–2 with respect to whose liability the summons was issued, or such person's agent, nominee, or other person acting under the direction or control of the such person, takes any action described in §301.7609–4(b) to institute a proceeding to quash such summons, that person's periods of limitations under sections 6501 and 6531 for the tax period or periods that are the subject of the summons are suspended for the period during which such proceeding is pending.

(2) *Action to institute a proceeding to quash a summons.* A person entitled to notice takes any action to institute a proceeding to quash if he or she files a petition to quash the summons in any district court, regardless of whether the timely filing requirements of section 7609(b)(2)(A) or the notice requirements of section 7609(b)(2)(B) are satisfied. For example, a person entitled to notice takes an action to institute a proceeding to quash a summons for purposes of this section if that person files a petition to quash the summons in district court and notifies the summoned person by sending a copy of the petition by registered or certified mail, but fails to mail a copy of that notice to the appropriate Internal Revenue Service (IRS) person and office.

(d) *Summoned party's failure to finally resolve the response to a summons after six months from service*—(1) *In general.* If a third party's response to a summons for which the IRS was required to provide notice to persons identified in the summons, or to a John Doe summons described in section 7609(f), is not finally resolved within six months after the date of service of the summons, the periods of limitations are suspended under sections 6501 and 6531, for the person with respect to whose liability the summons was issued and for any person whose identity is sought to be obtained by a John Doe summons, for the tax period or periods that are the subject of the summons. The suspension shall begin on the date which is six months after the service of the summons and shall end on the date on which there is a final resolution of the summoned party's response to the summons.

(2) *Example.* The rules of paragraph (d)(1) of this section are illustrated by the following example:

Example. A John Doe summons is issued on April 1, 2000, to the promoter of a tax shelter and seeks the names of all participants in the shelter in order to investigate the participants' income tax liabilities for 1997 and 1998. The district court approves service of the summons on April 30, 2000, and the summons is served on the promoter on May 1, 2000. The promoter does not provide the names of the participants. The periods of limitations for the participants' income tax liabilities and criminal prosecution for 1997 and 1998 are suspended under section 7609(e)(2) beginning on November 1, 2000, the date which is six months after the date the John Doe summons was served until the date on which the promoter's response to the summons is finally resolved.

(e) *Definitions*—(1) *Agent, nominee, etc.* A person is the agent, nominee, or other person of a person entitled to notice under section 7609(a) and §301.7609–2, and is acting under the direction or control of the person entitled to notice for purposes of section 7609(e)(1), if the person entitled to notice has the ability in fact or at law to cause the agent, nominee or other person, to take the actions permitted under section 7609(b).

(2) *Period during which a proceeding is pending*—(i) *Intervention in an enforcement proceeding*. The period during which the periods of limitations under sections 6501 and 6531 are suspended under section 7609(e)(1) begins on the date any person described in paragraph (b) of this section intervenes in an action to enforce the summons. The periods of limitations remain suspended until all appeals are disposed of, or until the expiration of the period during which an appeal may be taken or a request for further review may be made. The periods of limitations remain suspended for the period during which a proceeding is pending, regardless of compliance (or partial compliance) with the summons during that period. If, following issuance of an order to enforce a third-party summons, a collateral proceeding is brought challenging whether production made by the summoned party fully satisfied the court order and whether sanctions should be imposed against the summoned party for a failure to satisfy that order, the periods of limitations remain suspended until all appeals of the collateral proceeding are disposed of, or until the expiration of the period during which an appeal may be taken or a request for further review of the collateral proceeding may be made. Any collateral proceeding to the original proceeding shall be considered to be a continuation of the original proceeding.

(ii) *Proceeding to quash a summons*. The period during which the periods of limitations under sections 6501 and 6531 are suspended under section 7609(e)(1) begins on the date any person described in paragraph (c) of this section files a petition to quash the summons in district court. The periods of limitations remain suspended until all appeals are disposed of, or until expiration of the period in which an appeal may be taken or a request for further review may be made. The periods of limitations remain suspended for the period during which a proceeding is pending, regardless of compliance (or partial compliance) with the summons during that period.

(iii) *Examples*. The rules of paragraph (e)(2) are illustrated by the following examples:

Example 1. A revenue agent issues a summons to A, an accountant for B, requiring production of records relating to B's income tax liabilities for 1998. The summons is served on A on March 1, 2000. B files a petition to quash the summons in district court on March 15, 2000. The district court dismisses B's petition on July 1, 2000. B fails to appeal this decision by filing a notice of appeal within 60 days from the date of the district court's order of dismissal. The revenue agent notifies A that B did not appeal the district court's order. A turns over all of the records requested in the summons. The periods of limitations applicable to B for 1998 under sections 6501 and 6531 are suspended under section 7609(e)(1) from March 15, 2000, the date B filed a petition to quash, until August 30, 2000, the last day on which B could have filed a notice of appeal.

Example 2. A revenue agent issues a summons to A, an accountant for B, requiring production of records relating to B's income tax liabilities for 1999. The summons is served on A on June 1, 2001. B files an untimely petition to quash the summons in district court on June 30, 2001. The district court dismisses B's petition on July 31, 2001. B does not file an appeal of the district court's order. The periods of limitations applicable to B for 1999 under sections 6501 and 6531 are suspended under section 7609(e)(1) from June 30, 2001, the date B filed an untimely petition to quash, until September 29, 2001, the last day on which B could have filed a notice of appeal.

(3) *Final resolution of the summoned third party's response to a summons*. For purposes of section 7609(e)(2)(B), final resolution with respect to a summoned party's response to a third-party summons occurs when the summons or any order enforcing any part of the summons is fully complied with and all appeals are disposed of or the period in which an appeal may be taken or a request for further review may be made has expired. The determination of whether there has been full compliance will be made within a reasonable time, given the volume and complexity of the records produced, after the later of the giving of all testimony or the production of all records requested by the summons. If, following an enforcement order, collateral proceedings are brought challenging whether the production made by the summoned party fully satisfied the court order and whether sanctions should be imposed against the summoned party for a failing to do so, the suspension of the periods of limitations shall continue until the summons or any order enforcing any part of the summons is fully complied with and the decision in the collateral proceeding becomes final. A decision in a collateral proceeding becomes final when all appeals are disposed of or when the period in which an appeal may be taken or a request for further review may be made has expired.

(f) *Effective date*. This section is applicable on the date the final regulations are published in the **Federal Register**.

Mark E. Matthews,
Deputy Commissioner for Services and Enforcement.

(Filed by the Office of the Federal Register on July 20, 2006, 8:45 a.m., and published in the issue of the Federal Register for July 21, 2006, 71 F.R. 41377)

Escrow Accounts, Trusts, and Other Funds Used During Deferred Exchanges of Like-Kind Property

Announcement 2007–35

AGENCY: Internal Revenue Service (IRS), Treasury.

ACTION: Proposed Rulemaking; Revised Initial Regulatory Flexibility Analysis.

SUMMARY: This document contains a revised initial regulatory flexibility analysis relating to proposed regulations (REG–113365–04, 2006–10 I.R.B. 580) under section 468B of the Internal Revenue Code on the taxation and reporting of income earned on escrow accounts, trusts, and other funds used during deferred exchanges of like-kind property, and proposed regulations under section 7872 regarding below-market loans to facilitators of these exchanges. The proposed regulations affect taxpayers that engage in deferred like-kind exchanges and escrow holders, trustees, qualified intermediaries, and others that hold funds during deferred like-kind exchanges.

DATES: Written or electronic comments must be received by May 4, 2007.

ADDRESSES: Send submissions to CC:PA:LPD:PR (REG–113365–04), room 5203, Internal Revenue Service, POB 7604, Ben Franklin Station, Washington, DC 20044. Submissions may be hand delivered Monday through Friday between the hours of 8 a.m. and 4 p.m. to: CC:PA:LPD:PR (REG–113365–04), courier's desk, Internal Revenue Service, 1111 Constitution Avenue, NW, Washington, DC. Alternatively, taxpayers may submit electronic comments via the Federal eRulemaking Portal at *www.regulations.gov* (IRS-REG–113365–04).

FOR FURTHER INFORMATION CONTACT: Concerning the revised initial regulatory flexibility analysis and the proposed regulations under section 468B, Jeffrey Rodrick, (202) 622–4930; concerning the proposed regulations under section 7872, David Silber, (202) 622–3930; concerning submission of comments, Kelly Banks, (202) 622–3628 (not toll-free numbers).

SUPPLEMENTARY INFORMATION:

On February 7, 2006, a partial withdrawal of notice of proposed rulemaking, notice of proposed rulemaking, and notice of public hearing was published in the **Federal Register** (71 FR 6231). The initial regulatory flexibility analysis included in that notice of proposed rulemaking concluded that the number of transactions involving small businesses that will be affected and the full extent of the economic impact on small businesses could not be precisely determined and requested additional comments. This notice revises the initial regulatory flexibility analysis included in that notice of proposed rulemaking in response to comments provided in writing and at a public hearing. These comments asserted that the analysis did not adequately define the industry, determine the number of small businesses affected, describe the economic impact of the proposed regulations on small businesses, or discuss alternatives to the proposed rules that were considered and the bases for conclusions reached. The IRS and the Department of the Treasury have worked closely with the Small Business Administration's (SBA) Office of Advocacy (Advocacy) to obtain additional information from the affected industry to identify and quantify the small businesses affected and to determine the likely economic impact of the proposed regulations on small businesses. In a letter dated August 3, 2006, the president of the leading industry association for qualified intermediaries (QI), wrote that the association "believes we have or can develop information that would be helpful in this [impact-study] effort," and volunteered to provide this information to the IRS. The industry association surveyed its members based on questions developed by the IRS and the Department of the Treasury, and submitted a summary of the survey responses for consideration. The association, which according to its website has over 300 member companies (not all of which are QIs), received approximately 130 responses. Seventy-one respondents indicated they engage in the QI business exclusively, which represents 22 percent of the estimated number of 325 full-time QIs in the industry (as discussed in this notice, not all of which are small businesses). The summary of the survey responses submitted did not address a substantial number of the issues important to evaluating the effect of the proposed regulations on small business. The summary of the survey responses is available at *www.IRS.gov/regs.* This notice seeks additional comments and reiterates questions that will assist in assessing the economic impact of the proposed regulations on small businesses in the QI industry and in considering reasonable alternatives. The survey information provided is discussed in this revised initial regulatory flexibility analysis and will be considered further in the development of final regulations.

Revised Initial Regulatory Flexibility Analysis

Reasons for Action and Succinct Statement of the Objectives of, and Legal Basis for, the Proposed Rule

The proposed regulations are issued under the authority of section 7805, section 468B(g) (which provides that nothing in any provision of law shall be construed as providing that an escrow account, settlement fund, or similar fund is not subject to current income tax and that the Secretary shall prescribe regulations providing for the taxation of such accounts or funds whether as a grantor trust or otherwise), and section 7872.

Section 1.468B–6 of the Income Tax Regulations was included in proposed regulations issued in 1999 under section 468B(g) (the 1999 proposed regulations), and provided rules for the current taxation of income of a qualified escrow account or qualified trust used in a section 1031 deferred exchange of like-kind property. The 1999 proposed regulations included a facts and circumstances test to determine whether the taxpayer (the transferor or exchangor of the property), the QI, or a transferee is the owner of the assets in a qualified escrow account or qualified trust and must take into account all items of income, deduction, and credit (including capital gains and losses) of the account or trust. The 1999 proposed regulations further provided that, if a QI or transferee is the owner of the assets transferred, the transaction may be characterized as a below-market loan from the taxpayer to the owner to which section 7872 may apply. Under this proposed rule, if a QI or transferee is the owner of the assets, the transaction is a loan to which section 7872 generally applies if the loan is below-market.

Comments received on the 1999 proposed regulations reflected differing interpretations of the 1999 proposed regulations and disagreement on the proper rules for taxing these transactions. Some commentators interpreted the 1999 proposed regulations as allowing a QI to "own" the funds held in connection with the deferred like-kind exchange and never characterize the arrangement between the taxpayer and the QI as a loan.

Rules based on a facts and circumstances test are inherently difficult for taxpayers to apply and for the IRS to administer, and are subject to inconsistent application. Therefore, the 2006 proposed regulations eliminate the facts and circumstances test and propose specific rules that determine whether the income of an escrow account, trust, or fund used in a deferred like-kind exchange is taxed to the taxpayer or to an exchange facilitator, which is a QI, transferee, or other party that holds the exchange funds. These rules are intended to provide greater certainty for taxpayers, enhance administrability, and ensure consistent treatment of taxpayers.

Description and Estimate of the Number of Small Businesses to Which the Proposed Regulations Will Apply

The 2006 proposed regulations affect exchange facilitators that hold exchange funds for taxpayers engaging in deferred exchanges of like-kind property. Exchange facilitators may be large or small businesses (including individuals operating as sole proprietors). For this purpose, the SBA size standards set forth at 13 CFR 121.201 for North American Industry Classification System (NAICS) code 531390 (other activities related to real estate), define a business with annual gross receipts of up to $2 million as a small business. There is no NAICS code associated specifically with exchange facilitators or QIs. Although like-kind exchanges are not limited to real estate transactions, 70 percent of the respondents to the industry survey indicated that they use NAICS code 531390. Therefore, notwithstanding comments criticizing the use of NAICS code 531390 for purposes of determining the applicable size standard with respect to the 2006 proposed regulations, after consultation with Advocacy, the IRS and the Department of the Treasury have determined that NAICS code 531390 is appropriate for this industry. Accordingly, the applicable size standard for determining what constitutes a small business with respect to the 2006 proposed regulations is $2 million in annual gross receipts, the SBA's definition of a small business for NAICS code 531390.

The IRS and the Department of the Treasury estimate that there are approximately 325 businesses (primarily QIs) that are full-time exchange facilitators. This estimate is based on information originally provided by the industry association in connection with the development of the 2006 proposed regulations. The recent industry survey did not provide any additional information regarding this number. Seventy-one of 121 (58.7 percent) respondents to the survey indicated that they are engaged exclusively in the QI business, although it is unclear how many of these are small businesses. Although 84 percent of respondents reported having annual gross revenues (fees plus net retained interest, if any) from the QI business of $1.5 million or less (the previous size standard for NAICS code 531390) for the most recent year, it is unclear how many of this number are exclusively in the QI business. The survey also indicated that almost 90 percent of respondents have 10 or fewer employees (including owners active in the business), and nearly 70 percent have fewer than 5 employees. An estimate of the percentage of the QI industry that consists of small businesses is difficult to make based on the available information. The summary of the survey responses did not correlate information on annual gross revenues reported with information on the number of respondents engaged exclusively in the QI business. Nonetheless, it appears that a significant portion of the QI industry consists of small businesses under the SBA's size standard. Accordingly, the IRS and the Department of the Treasury continue to seek information regarding the number of small businesses engaged in the QI industry. Specific comments are requested from QIs engaged exclusively in that business indicating whether their annual gross receipts are $2 million or less, or more than $2 million.

Searches for information through the Department of Commerce and the SBA disclosed no data collected or maintained on QIs or exchange facilitators as an industry.

Description of Compliance Requirements and Estimate of the Classes of Small Businesses that Will Be Affected by the Compliance Requirements

Under the 2006 proposed regulations, exchange funds are treated as loaned by the taxpayer to the exchange facilitator unless all of the income earned is paid to the taxpayer. If the exchange funds are treated as loaned to the exchange facilitator, interest generally is imputed to the taxpayer under section 7872 unless the exchange facilitator pays sufficient interest. If a loan between the taxpayer and the exchange facilitator does not provide for sufficient interest and the loan is not otherwise exempt from section 7872, interest income is imputed to the taxpayer at the applicable Federal rate (AFR) (or the difference between the rate paid and the AFR). Therefore, exchange facilitators must keep records of the amount of income paid to the taxpayer and may be required to report the income on Form 1099.

Under section 7872 and the 2006 proposed regulations, if the exchange funds are treated as loaned from the taxpayer to the QI and the loan is a below-market loan, income is deemed transferred to the exchange facilitator as compensation and retransferred to the taxpayer as interest. The taxpayer's imputed interest income is not offset by a deduction for the taxpayer's imputed payment to the exchange facilitator because compensation paid to the exchange facilitator is a cost of acquiring the replacement property that must be capitalized and added to the property's basis. The exchange facilitator has income from the imputed compensation and an offsetting deduction for the interest deemed paid to the taxpayer.

Seventy percent of respondents to the industry survey reported that they engage in at least 100 exchange transactions a year. According to information provided by the industry association from an earlier survey of its members, over 92 percent of the small business respondents currently pay to the taxpayer at least 20 percent of the income earned on exchange funds, including accounts that commingle the exchange funds of multiple taxpayers. The IRS and the Department of the Treasury request additional comments providing more specific information to clarify these results. The information available suggests that an overwhelming majority of small businesses affected by the 2006 proposed regulations currently maintain records of the amount of income paid to the taxpayer and report the payments on Form 1099. Therefore, the IRS and the Department of the Treasury estimate that for most small businesses the 2006 proposed regulations should not increase significantly the compliance burden associated with keeping records and reporting income paid to the taxpayer.

Nonetheless, commentators have stated generally that complying with the 2006 proposed regulations would result in additional recordkeeping and reporting requirements. Fifty-eight percent of respondents to the recent industry survey indicated that the 2006 proposed regulations significantly will increase recordkeeping burdens and accounting costs, but the survey did not provide quantified data on the amount of any additional time or cost expected to result from the 2006 proposed regulations. Comments are requested estimating the annual number of transactions that will result in an increased recordkeeping and reporting burden, per transaction, under the 2006 proposed regulations, as well as the amount of time and additional cost that each additional recordkeeping and reporting burden would impose.

Commentators also have stated that accounting for individual taxpayers' earnings in commingled accounts would necessitate additional labor and system design costs that would fall disproportionately on small business QIs. The IRS and the Department of the Treasury have not received specific comments quantifying the effect of these costs on small businesses. Specific comments are requested estimating the amount of these costs.

Commentators have asserted that complying with the loan characterization rules of the 2006 proposed regulations will result in a substantial revenue loss and cause a large number of small businesses to fail or to reduce their workforces. They claimed that small business QIs would be disproportionately affected because the small business QIs predominantly apply a business model that would place them at a disadvantage under the 2006 proposed regulations.

In general, commentators have described two business models employed to facilitate deferred like-kind exchanges:

1. The exchange facilitator segregates the exchange funds in separate accounts, charges a separate fee for its services, and pays all earnings to the taxpayer, or

2. The exchange facilitator commingles the exchange funds, pays a portion of the earnings to the taxpayer and retains a portion of the earnings, or may retain all of the earnings. Some of these exchange facilitators also may charge a separate fee for their services. If a fee is charged, it is likely to be lower than the fee that would be charged if the exchange facilitator retains no earnings.

Some small businesses offer customers both forms of structuring the transaction. Comments from and discussions with industry members, however, have disclosed that the first model is employed most commonly by large businesses often "affiliated" (in the sense of having some level of corporate relationship and not necessarily within the meaning of section 1504) with banks. The second model also may be employed by large businesses but is used widely by independent, small business QIs. In the recent industry survey, 95.8 percent of respondents indicated that they are not affiliated with a bank, savings and loan company, brokerage firm, or similar financial institution.

The earlier industry survey indicated that 96 percent of the small business respondents retain at least a portion of the interest earned on the exchange funds. Commentators have stated that if these small businesses are required to impute interest on the exchange funds, taxpayers will demand that this interest be paid to them. According to commentators, to compensate for this loss of revenue these businesses will be required to change their business practices to pay all income to the taxpayer and to charge higher fees. Commentators further stated that absent charging higher fees, paying all interest to the taxpayer is expected to result in a reduction of revenues ranging from 10 to 80 percent. Specific comments are requested estimating the effect on revenues or profits of a change in business practices to pay all income to the taxpayer.

Some commentators have asserted that, in contrast, bank-affiliated QIs generally pay all the income to the taxpayer under their current business practices and therefore will not be required to change their business practices or charge higher fees as a result of the 2006 proposed regulations. These commentators claim that bank-affiliated QIs are able to pay all the income to the taxpayer and charge fees commensurate with the fees charged by independent QIs because bank-affiliated QIs are compensated through the receipt of fees paid by institutions in which the funds are deposited. Moreover, these commentators maintain that bank-affiliated QIs indirectly benefit when funds are deposited with related-party depositary institutions that invest deposited exchange funds and earn income that is not required to be paid to the taxpayer under the 2006 proposed regulations. If, as these commentators claim, bank-affiliated QIs would not be required to change their business model as a result of the 2006 proposed regulations, the commentators predict that the 2006 proposed regulations will cause many small business QIs to be disadvantaged in competing with bank-affiliated QIs. Specific comments are requested estimating the number of QIs that would change their business model as a result of the 2006 proposed regulations.

Significant Alternatives Considered

Various alternatives to the rules contained in the 2006 proposed regulations were considered. For example, retaining the facts and circumstances test of the 1999 proposed regulations was considered but rejected because the test is difficult for taxpayers to apply, lacks administrability, is subject to misinterpretation, and may result in inconsistent tax treatment of similarly-situated taxpayers.

Rules that would allow the exchange facilitator and taxpayer to determine which party will be taxed on the earnings were considered but regarded as lacking certainty and administrability and violating established tax principles. Rules that would tax the party that receives the income (and thus treat only income paid and not income retained by the QI as the taxpayer's taxable income) were considered but not adopted. Under some circumstances, a QI's retention of income earned by an exchange fund is properly characterized as a payment of compensation by the taxpayer for the QI's services. Therefore, under the appropriate circumstances, a rule that taxed only the QI on retained earnings would violate the doctrine of *Old Colony Trust v. Commissioner*, 279 U.S. 716 (1929), that a payment that satisfies the obligation of a taxpayer to a third party is includible in the income of the taxpayer.

A rule that would treat all the earnings of the exchange funds in all circumstances as the taxpayer's income was considered but lacked flexibility and did not conform in all cases to the substance of the transaction. Other alternatives were considered and not adopted because they were considered inconsistent with section 7872. In the legislative history to section 7872, Congress stated that when a service provider is permitted to retain customer funds without paying interest to the customer, and the benefit the service provider derives from the funds is in lieu of a fee for services, the transaction is a compensation-related loan under section 7872. H.R. Conf. Rep. No. 861, 98th Cong., 2d Sess. 1019 (1984) (1984–3 (Vol. 2) C.B. 272). Moreover, it was determined that exchange funds are not received in consideration for the sale or exchange of property (within the meaning of section 1274(c)(1)) or received as a deferred payment on account of a sale or exchange of property (within the meaning of section 483).

The industry survey indicates that 30 percent of respondents closed at least half of their deferred like-kind exchange transactions within 60 days or less. Only eight percent completed at least half of their transactions in more than 150 days. In addition, 42 percent of survey respondents reported that at least half of their transactions typically involve exchange funds of $250,000 or less, while about 8 percent of respondents reported that most of their transactions involve exchange funds in excess of $1 million. In light of this information, comments specifically are requested regarding the average duration of exchange transactions, the average dollar amount of exchange funds, and the appropriateness and nature of a *de minimis* rule that would except certain exchange transactions from the application of section 7872.

If exchange funds are characterized as loaned by the taxpayer to the exchange facilitator, interest may be imputed if the exchange facilitator does not pay sufficient interest to the taxpayer. To reduce the administrative burden of determining imputed interest, the 2006 proposed regulations provide a special AFR, equal to the investment rate on a 182-day Treasury bill, in lieu of the short-term AFR (which applies to loans of 3 years or less), to qualify as sufficient interest for purposes of determining whether interest must be imputed. This special AFR was intended to be a more accurate measure of a market rate of interest for these loans than the short-term AFR, and was expected to result in characterization of fewer transactions as below-market loans than if the short-term AFR were used. Commentators have stated that the special AFR is significantly higher than the market rate paid on funds held for the periods of time that exchange funds typically are held by QIs. They state, for example, that few if any QIs that pay less than all the income to the taxpayer pay an amount that is equal to or greater than the special AFR provided in the 2006 proposed regulations. Specific comments are requested identifying the rate of return typically earned by small business QIs on exchange funds, the interest rate QIs typically pay to taxpayers, and an appropriate rate for testing exchange facilitator loans for sufficient interest under section 7872.

Duplicative, Overlapping, and Conflicting Rules

The IRS and the Department of the Treasury are not aware of any duplicative, overlapping, or conflicting federal rules.

Kevin M. Brown,
Deputy Commissioner for Services and Enforcement.

(Filed by the Office of the Federal Register on March 19, 2007, 8:45 a.m., and published in the issue of the Federal Register for March 20, 2007, 72 F.R. 13055)

Expenses for Household and Dependent Care Services Necessary for Gainful Employment; Correction

Announcement 2007–36

AGENCY: Internal Revenue Service (IRS), Treasury.

ACTION: Correction to notice of proposed rulemaking.

SUMMARY: This document contains a correction to notice of proposed rulemaking (REG–139059–02, 2006–24 I.R.B. 1052) that was published in the Federal Register on Wednesday, May 24, 2006 (71 FR 29847) regarding the credit for expenses for household and dependent care services necessary for gainful employment.

FOR FURTHER INFORMATION CONTACT: Sara Shepherd, (202) 622–4960 (not a toll-free call).

SUPPLEMENTARY INFORMATION:

Background

The notice of proposed rulemaking (REG–139059–02) that is the subject of this correction is under section 21 of the Internal Revenue Code.

Need for Correction

As published, the notice of proposed rulemaking (REG–139059–02) contains an error that may prove to be misleading and is in need of correction.

* * * * *

Correction of Publication

Accordingly, the notice of proposed rulemaking (REG–139059–02), that was the subject of FR Doc. E6–7390, is corrected as follows:

PART 1—INCOME TAXES

Paragraph 1. The authority citation for part 1 continues to read in part as follows:

Authority: 26 U.S.C. 7805 * * *

§ 1.21–1 [Corrected]

Par. 2. On page 29851, column 1, Sec. 1.21–1 is amended by revising paragraph (b)(5)(ii) to read as follows:

§ 1.21–1 Expenses for household and dependent care services necessary for gainful employment.

* * * * *

(b) * * *

(5) * * *

(ii) Custodial parent allowed the credit. A child to whom this paragraph (b)(5) applies is the qualifying individual of only one parent in any taxable year and is the qualifying child of the custodial parent even if the noncustodial parent may claim the dependency exemption for that child for that taxable year. See section 152(e). The custodial parent is the parent with whom a child shared the same principal place of abode the greater portion of the calendar year. See section 152(e)(4)(A).

* * * * *

Guy R. Traynor,
Branch Chief, Publications and Regulations Branch, Legal Processing Division, Associate Chief Counsel (Procedure and Administration).

(Filed by the Office of the Federal Register on July 5, 2006, 8:45 a.m., and published in the issue of the Federal Register for July 6, 2006, 71 F.R. 38322)

Expenses for Household and Dependent Care Services Necessary for Gainful Employment; Correction

Announcement 2007–37

AGENCY: Internal Revenue Service (IRS), Treasury.

ACTION: Correction to notice of proposed rulemaking.

SUMMARY: This document contains a correction to notice of proposed rulemaking (REG–139059–02, 2006–24 I.R.B. 1052) that was published in the Federal Register on Wednesday, May 24, 2006 (71 FR 29847) regarding the credit for expenses for household and dependent care services necessary for gainful employment.

FOR FURTHER INFORMATION CONTACT: Sara Shepherd, (202) 622–4960 (not a toll-free call).

SUPPLEMENTARY INFORMATION:

Background

The notice of proposed rulemaking (REG–139059–02) that is the subject of this correction is under section 21 of the Internal Revenue Code.

Need for Correction

As published, the notice of proposed rulemaking (REG–139059–02) contains an error that may prove to be misleading and is in need of correction.

Correction of Publication

Accordingly, the notice of proposed rulemaking (REG–139059–02), that was the subject of FR Doc. E6–7390, is corrected as follows:

1. On page 29848, column 2, in the preamble under the paragraph heading "3. Special Rule for Children of Separated or Divorced Parents", line 4 from the bottom of the paragraph, the language "section 152(e)(3)(A) as the parent with" corrected to read "section 152(e)(4)(A) as the parent with."

Guy R. Traynor,
Branch Chief, Publications and Regulations Branch,
Legal Processing Division,
Associate Chief Counsel
(Procedure and Administration).

(Filed by the Office of the Federal Register on July 5, 2006, 8:45 a.m., and published in the issue of the Federal Register for July 6, 2006, 71 F.R. 38323)

Deletions From Cumulative List of Organizations Contributions to Which are Deductible Under Section 170 of the Code

Announcement 2007–38

The names of organizations that no longer qualify as organizations described in section 170(c)(2) of the Internal Revenue Code of 1986 are listed below.

Generally, the Service will not disallow deductions for contributions made to a listed organization on or before the date of announcement in the Internal Revenue Bulletin that an organization no longer qualifies. However, the Service is not precluded from disallowing a deduction for any contributions made after an organization ceases to qualify under section 170(c)(2) if the organization has not timely filed a suit for declaratory judgment under section 7428 and if the contributor (1) had knowledge of the revocation of the ruling or determination letter, (2) was aware that such revocation was imminent, or (3) was in part responsible for or was aware of the activities or omissions of the organization that brought about this revocation.

If on the other hand a suit for declaratory judgment has been timely filed, contributions from individuals and organizations described in section 170(c)(2) that are otherwise allowable will continue to be deductible. Protection under section 7428(c) would begin on April 9, 2007, and would end on the date the court first determines that the organization is not described in section 170(c)(2) as more particularly set forth in section 7428(c)(1). For individual contributors, the maximum deduction protected is $1,000, with a husband and wife treated as one contributor. This benefit is not extended to any individual, in whole or in part, for the acts or omissions of the organization that were the basis for revocation.

Quality Industrial Services
Snohomish, WA

Nazareth, Inc.
Cleveland Heights, OH

One Step Ahead Daycare, Inc.
Racine, WI

Gift America Program
Rockville, MD

The Patrick and Janet Hayes
Charitable Supporting Organization
Houston, TX

10th Life Foundation
Santa Barbara, CA

San Francisco Neighbors Resource Center
San Francisco, CA

Emerald Foundation, Inc.
Ojai, CA

Osterville Village Association
Osterville, MA

Further Extension of Deadline for Settlement Offered to Certain Foreign Embassy Staff

Announcement 2007–39

Following is a copy of the News Release issued by the Office of Deputy Commissioner, International, on March 22, 2007 (IR–2007–67).

IRS Further Extends Deadline for Settlement Offered To Certain Foreign Embassy Staff

IR–2007–67, Mar. 22, 2007

WASHINGTON — The Internal Revenue Service is providing a further extension, until June 30, 2007, of the deadline for current and former U.S.-based employees of foreign embassies, consular offices and missions and international organizations to participate in a one-time settlement initiative to resolve outstanding tax matters related to their employment.

Following requests from several embassies, the date is again being extended to make certain those wishing to participate in the initiative have the opportunity to do so.

The offer is open to employees of those organizations who are U.S. citizens, green-card holders and foreign employees who have tax obligations. Accredited diplomatic personnel are generally exempt from income taxes on their wages under the Internal Revenue Code and international treaties or agreements.

The IRS estimates that as many as half of these employees subject to U.S. tax fail to report their wages, claim deductions they are not entitled to, incorrectly establish SEP/IRA retirement plans, fail to pay self-employment tax or fail to file tax returns.

To participate, employees must submit amended or original tax returns for tax years 2004 and 2005 that properly reflect their income and expenses. Participants in the settlement will not be required to provide tax year 2003 returns, which was previously part of the settlement eligibility requirement. In addition, participants with erroneously established SEP/IRA plans will not be required to distribute amounts contributed to these SEP/IRAs for tax years prior to the 2004 tax year. This change follows discussions with embassies and provides consistency with the income tax portion of the settlement initiative.

IRS will remove the 2003 tax year issues from the settlement elections previously received from taxpayers.

IRS encourages those affected taxpayers to act quickly so to avoid a future audit process that could prove costly. Foreign embassy, consular office or international organization employees who fail to come forward may be subject to IRS audits and penalties which could cover more than just three years.

Part I. Rulings and Decisions Under the Internal Revenue Code of 1986

Section 42.—Low-Income Housing Credit

Low-income housing credit; satisfactory bond; "bond factor" amounts for the period January through June 2007. This ruling provides the monthly bond factor amounts to be used by taxpayers who dispose of qualified low-income buildings or interests therein during the period January through June 2007.

Rev. Rul. 2007–25

In Rev. Rul. 90–60, 1990–2 C.B. 3, the Internal Revenue Service provided guidance to taxpayers concerning the general methodology used by the Treasury Department in computing the bond factor amounts used in calculating the amount of bond considered satisfactory by the Secretary under § 42(j)(6) of the Internal Revenue Code. It further announced that the Secretary would publish in the Internal Revenue Bulletin a table of bond factor amounts for dispositions occurring during each calendar month.

Rev. Proc. 99–11, 1999–1 C.B. 275, established a collateral program as an alternative to providing a surety bond for taxpayers to avoid or defer recapture of the low-income housing tax credits under § 42(j)(6). Under this program, taxpayers may establish a Treasury Direct Account and pledge certain United States Treasury securities to the Internal Revenue Service as security.

This revenue ruling provides in Table 1 the bond factor amounts for calculating the amount of bond considered satisfactory under § 42(j)(6) or the amount of United States Treasury securities to pledge in a Treasury Direct Account under Rev. Proc. 99–11 for dispositions of qualified low-income buildings or interests therein during the period January through June 2007.

Table 1
Rev. Rul. 2007–25
Monthly Bond Factor Amounts for Dispositions Expressed
As a Percentage of Total Credits

	Calendar Year Building Placed in Service or, if Section 42(f)(1) Election Was Made, the Succeeding Calendar Year										
Month of Disposition	1993	1994	1995	1996	1997	1998	1999	2000	2001	2002	2003
Jan '07	17.39	32.44	45.52	56.97	66.95	69.23	71.86	74.74	78.09	81.82	85.82
Feb '07	17.39	32.44	45.52	56.97	66.95	69.08	71.70	74.56	77.89	81.60	85.57
Mar '07	17.39	32.44	45.52	56.97	66.95	68.92	71.53	74.39	77.71	81.40	85.33
Apr '07	17.39	32.44	45.52	56.97	66.95	68.77	71.37	74.22	77.52	81.19	85.11
May '07	17.39	32.44	45.52	56.97	66.95	68.62	71.22	74.05	77.35	81.00	84.89
Jun '07	17.39	32.44	45.52	56.97	66.95	68.47	71.06	73.89	77.17	80.81	84.68

Table 1 (cont'd)
Rev. Rul. 2007–25
Monthly Bond Factor Amounts for Dispositions Expressed
As a Percentage of Total Credits

	Calendar Year Building Placed in Service or, if Section 42(f)(1) Election Was Made, the Succeeding Calendar Year										
Month of Disposition	2004	2005	2006	2007							
Jan '07	89.79	93.41	96.70	97.21							
Feb '07	89.50	93.07	96.27	97.21							
Mar '07	89.22	92.75	95.89	97.21							
Apr '07	88.96	92.46	95.57	97.21							
May '07	88.72	92.18	95.28	97.21							
Jun '07	88.48	91.93	95.02	97.21							

For a list of bond factor amounts applicable to dispositions occurring during other calendar years, see: Rev. Rul. 98–3, 1998–1 C.B. 248; Rev. Rul. 2001–2, 2001–1 C.B. 255; Rev. Rul. 2001–53, 2001–2 C.B. 488; Rev. Rul. 2002–72, 2002–2 C.B. 759; Rev. Rul. 2003–117, 2003–2 C.B. 1051; Rev. Rul. 2004–100, 2004–2 C.B. 718; Rev. Rul. 2005–67, 2005–2 C.B. 771; and Rev. Rul. 2006–51, 2006–41 I.R.B. 632.

DRAFTING INFORMATION

The principal author of this revenue ruling is David McDonnell of the Office of Associate Chief Counsel (Passthroughs and Special Industries). For further information regarding this revenue ruling, contact Mr. McDonnell at (202) 622–3040 (not a toll-free call).

Section 199.—Income Attributable to Domestic Production Activities

26 CFR 1.199–3: Domestic production gross receipts.

T.D. 9317

DEPARTMENT OF THE TREASURY Internal Revenue Service 26 CFR Part 1

Computer Software Under Section 199(c)(5)(B)

AGENCY: Internal Revenue Service (IRS), Treasury.

ACTION: Final and temporary regulations.

SUMMARY: This document contains final regulations concerning the application of section 199 of the Internal Revenue Code, which provides a deduction for income attributable to domestic production activities. The final regulations are necessary to provide guidance regarding certain transactions involving online software and to clarify the rules regarding the application of section 199 to certain cooperatives. The regulations will affect taxpayers engaged in certain domestic production activities involving computer software and taxpayers engaged in certain domestic production activities in cooperative form.

DATES: *Effective Date:* These regulations are effective March 20, 2007.

Applicability Date: For dates of applicability, see §1.199–8(i)(4) and (i)(7).

FOR FURTHER INFORMATION CONTACT: Paul Handleman or Lauren Ross Taylor, (202) 622–3040 (not a toll-free number).

SUPPLEMENTARY INFORMATION:

Background

This document amends 26 CFR part 1 to provide rules relating to the deduction for income attributable to domestic production activities under section 199 of the Internal Revenue Code (Code). Section 199 was added to the Code by section 102 of the American Jobs Creation Act of 2004 (Public Law 108–357, 118 Stat. 1418), and amended by section 403(a) of the Gulf Opportunity Zone Act of 2005 (Public Law 109–135, 119 Stat. 25) and section 514 of the Tax Increase Prevention and Reconciliation Act of 2005 (Public Law 109–222, 120 Stat. 345). On June 1, 2006, the IRS and Treasury Department published in the **Federal Register** final regulations under section 199 (T.D. 9263, 2006–25 I.R.B. 1063 [71 FR 31268]). Also on June 1, 2006, the IRS and Treasury Department published in the **Federal Register** temporary and proposed regulations under section 199 providing guidance on certain transactions involving computer software (T.D. 9262, 2006–24 I.R.B. 1040 [71 FR 31074] and REG–111578–06, 2006–24 I.R.B. 1060 [71 FR 31128], respectively). Written and electronic comments responding to the temporary and proposed regulations were received. After consideration of the comments, the proposed regulations are adopted as amended by this Treasury decision.

General Overview

Section 199(a)(1) allows a deduction equal to 9 percent (3 percent in the case of taxable years beginning in 2005 or 2006, and 6 percent in the case of taxable years beginning in 2007, 2008, or 2009) of the lesser of (A) the qualified production activities income (QPAI) of the taxpayer for the taxable year, or (B) taxable income (determined without regard to section 199) for the taxable year (or, in the case of an individual, adjusted gross income (AGI)).

Qualified Production Activities Income

Section 199(c)(1) defines QPAI for any taxable year as an amount equal to the excess (if any) of (A) the taxpayer's domestic production gross receipts (DPGR) for such taxable year, over (B) the sum of (i) the cost of goods sold (CGS) that are allocable to such receipts; and (ii) other expenses, losses, or deductions (other than the deduction under section 199) that are properly allocable to such receipts.

Section 199(c)(4)(A)(i) defines DPGR, in part, to mean the taxpayer's gross receipts that are derived from any lease, rental, license, sale, exchange, or other disposition of qualifying production property (QPP) that was manufactured, produced, grown, or extracted (MPGE) by the taxpayer in whole or in significant part within the United States. Section 199(c)(5) defines QPP to mean: (A) tangible personal property; (B) any computer software; and (C) any property described in section 168(f)(4) (certain sound recordings).

Patrons of Certain Cooperatives

Section 199(d)(3)(A) provides that any person who receives a qualified payment from a specified agricultural or horticultural cooperative shall be allowed for the taxable year in which such payment is received a deduction under section 199(a) equal to the portion of the deduction allowed under section 199(a) to such cooperative which is (i) allowed with respect to the portion of the QPAI to which such payment is attributable, and (ii) identified by such cooperative in a written notice mailed to such person during the payment period described in section 1382(d).

Section 199(d)(3)(B) provides that the taxable income of a specified agricultural or horticultural cooperative shall not be reduced under section 1382 by reason of that portion of any qualified payment as does not exceed the deduction allowable under section 199(d)(3)(A) with respect to such payment.

Section 199(d)(3)(C) provides that, for purposes of section 199, the taxable income of a specified agricultural or horticultural cooperative shall be computed without regard to any deduction allowable under section 1382(b) or (c) (relating to patronage dividends, per-unit retain allocations, and nonpatronage distributions).

Section 199(d)(3)(E) provides that, for purposes of section 199(d)(3), the term *qualified payment* means, with respect to any person, any amount that (i) is described in section 1385(a)(1) or (3), (ii) is received by such person from a specified agricultural or horticultural cooperative, and (iii) is attributable to QPAI with respect to which a deduction is allowed to such cooperative under section 199(a).

Authority to Prescribe Regulations

Section 199(d)(8) authorizes the Secretary to prescribe such regulations as are necessary to carry out the purposes of section 199, including regulations that prevent more than one taxpayer from being allowed a deduction under section 199 with respect to any activity described in section 199(c)(4)(A)(i).

Temporary Regulations

Section 1.199–3T(i)(6)(ii) provides that gross receipts derived from customer and technical support, telephone and other telecommunication services, online services (such as Internet access services, online banking services, providing access to online electronic books, newspapers, and journals), and other similar services do not constitute gross receipts derived from a lease, rental, license, sale, exchange, or other disposition of computer software.

However, §1.199–3T(i)(6)(iii) provides two exceptions under which gross receipts derived by a taxpayer from providing computer software to customers for the customers' direct use while connected to the Internet will be treated as being derived from the lease, rental, license, sale, exchange, or other disposition of such computer software. Such gross receipts will be treated as DPGR if all the other requirements of section 199 are met (for example, the taxpayer MPGE computer software in whole or in significant part within the United States).

The exception in §1.199–3T(i)(6)(iii)(A) applies to a taxpayer that derives gross receipts from providing computer software to customers for the customers' direct use while connected to the Internet (online software) and also derives gross receipts from customers that are unrelated to the taxpayer from the lease, rental, license, sale, exchange, or other disposition of computer software affixed to a tangible medium or downloaded from the Internet. The exception in §1.199–3T(i)(6)(iii)(B) applies if a taxpayer derives gross receipts from providing online software and an unrelated person derives, on a regular and ongoing basis in the unrelated person's business, gross receipts from the lease, rental, license, sale, exchange, or other disposition of substantially identical software to its customers affixed to a tangible medium or by allowing its customers to download the substantially identical computer software from the Internet.

Section 1.199–3T(i)(6)(iv) defines substantially identical software as computer software that, from a customer's perspective, has the same functional result as the online software and has a significant overlap of features or purpose with the online software. Section 1.199–3T(i)(6)(iv)(B) provides a safe harbor under which all computer software games are deemed to be substantially identical software.

The exceptions outlined in §1.199–3T(i)(6)(iii) permit gross receipts derived from providing online software to be treated as gross receipts derived from the lease, rental, license, sale, exchange, or other disposition of software. However, because the rules for online software are exceptions, all other provisions of the temporary and final regulations do not necessarily apply to online software. Specifically, §1.199–3T(i)(6)(iv)(E) provides that the computer software maintenance agreement exception provided in §1.199–3(i)(4)(i)(B)(*5*) does not apply to online software. Section 1.199–3(i)(4)(i)(B)(*5*) provides that a taxpayer may include in DPGR, the gross receipts derived from services performed pursuant to a qualified computer software maintenance agreement.

Summary of Comments and Explanation of Provisions

A commentator suggested that the online software exceptions should apply to transactions where access to computer software is provided over any public or private communications network and not just the Internet. The final regulations adopt this suggestion.

A commentator suggested that the final regulations provide an example where computer software would not be considered substantially identical software. This suggestion has been adopted.

Commentators noted that, in the future, some computer software will only be available over the Internet. In addition, newly developed computer software provided over the Internet may not have a substantially identical counterpart. The IRS and Treasury Department recognize that the computer software industry is evolving and current industry trends may result in a more limited applicability of the online software exceptions provided in the final regulation. However, there are significant differences between transactions which provide customers with access to online software and transactions involving the transfer of software to customers affixed to a tangible medium or by download. Accordingly, in order to give meaning to the statutory language requiring a lease, rental, license, sale, exchange, or other disposition, the online software exceptions have been narrowly tailored and are intended to apply only to gross receipts derived from providing customers access to computer software for the customers' direct use while connected to the Internet and only when the taxpayer (or another person) also derives gross receipts from the lease, rental, license, sale, exchange, or other disposition of the computer software (or substantially identical software) affixed to a tangible medium or by download. The final regulations clarify that, with respect to online software, taxpayers are providing customers with access to the taxpayers' software as opposed to actually transferring the software to customers either affixed to a tangible medium or by allowing them to download the computer software from the Internet.

Commentators suggested that the rule in §1.199–3T(i)(6)(iv)(E), precluding the application of the qualified computer software maintenance provision to online software, be deleted because it places taxpayers providing access to online software at a competitive disadvantage with taxpayers providing computer software to customers either affixed to a tangible medium or by allowing them to download the computer software from the Internet. In addition, commentators suggest that the advertising exception in §1.199–3(i)(5) should be extended to include online software. The final regulations do not adopt these suggestions. As previously noted, the online software exceptions have been narrowly tailored and the IRS and Treasury Department do not believe the exceptions should be extended beyond gross receipts derived from providing customers access to computer software for the customers' direct use. Therefore, the final regulations do not extend the exception for qualified computer software maintenance agreements in §1.199–3(i)(4)(i)(B)(*5*) or the advertising exception in §1.199–3(i)(5) to online software.

The final regulations in §1.199–3(i)(5)(ii)(B) do, however, extend the advertising exception to computer software that is provided to customers either affixed to a tangible medium (for example, a disk or DVD) or by allowing them to download the computer software from the Internet. However, the advertising exception only applies to advertising placed or integrated into software that is either affixed to a tangible medium or provided through download and does not apply to advertising incorporated into online software. In addition, the IRS and Treasury Department have clarified that, except as otherwise provided in §1.199–3(i)(5)(ii), gross receipts derived from the lease, rental, license, sale, exchange, or other disposition of QPP, a qualified film, or utilities do not include advertising income or product-placement income.

A commentator expressed concern that the exception for qualified computer software maintenance agreements in §1.199–3(i)(4)(i)(B)(*5*) does not apply if the taxpayer separately offers maintenance in subsequent years. The mere fact that a taxpayer separately offers maintenance in subsequent years does not preclude eligibility for the exception.

A commentator interpreted the rule in §1.199–3T(i)(6)(iii)(E) as possibly treating gross receipts derived from the lease, rental, license, sale, exchange, or other disposition of future updates, cyclical releases, and rewrites of the underlying software as non-DPGR if the underlying software is online software. The rule in §1.199–3T(i)(6)(iii)(E) only provides that the qualified computer software maintenance agreement exception does not apply to online software. Therefore, to the extent a taxpayer providing online software derives gross receipts from the lease, rental, license, sale, exchange, or other disposition of future updates, cyclical releases, and rewrites of the underlying software, the gross receipts are DPGR assuming all the other requirements of §1.199–3 are met.

A commentator noted that *Example 6* in the temporary regulations concludes that the gross receipts derived from storage of customers' data and telephone support are non-DPGR. *Example 6* is silent as to the amount of gross receipts derived from the storage of customers' data and telephone support and does not address whether the *de minimis* exception in §1.199–3(i)(4)(i)(B)(*6*) is available. Numerous examples in the final regulations under section 199 also conclude that gross receipts are non-DPGR without reference to the *de minimis* exception in §1.199–3(i)(4)(i)(B)(*6*). However, assuming all the requirements are met, the *de minimis* exception in §1.199–3(i)(4)(i)(B)(*6*) can apply when an example concludes the gross receipts are non-DPGR.

The IRS and Treasury Department received a comment letter on the application of section 199 to agricultural and horticultural cooperatives under §1.199–6 of the final regulations (71 FR 31312) published on June 1, 2006. The commentator noted that the sentence in §1.199–6(h) stating that the cooperative may not apply section 199(d)(3) and §1.199–6 to any portion of the section 199 deduction that is not passed through to its patrons is inconsistent with section 199(d)(3) which has no such limitation. These final regulations amend §1.199–6(h) to remove the sentence.

In addition, consistent with the change to §1.199–6(h), these final regulations amend §1.199–6(l) to remove the phrase, "To the extent a cooperative passes through the section 199 deduction to a patron" and add the phrase, "by the patron."

The final regulations also amend §1.199–6(c) to clarify that a cooperative's QPAI is computed without taking into account any deduction allowable under section 1382(b) or (c) (relating to patronage dividends, per-unit retain allocations, and nonpatronage distributions).

Effective Date

Section 199 applies to taxable years beginning after December 31, 2004. These final regulations are applicable for taxable years beginning on or after March 20, 2007. In addition, §1.199–8(i)(1) provides that, in certain circumstances, a taxpayer may rely on the guidance in Notice 2005–14, 2005–1 C.B. 498, see §601.602(d)(2), the proposed regulations under section 199 that were published in the **Federal Register** on November 4, 2005 (REG–105847–05, 2005–2 C.B. 987 [70 FR 67220]), or the final regulations under section 199 that were published in the **Federal Register** on June 1, 2006 (71 FR 31268). Regardless of which guidance a taxpayer applies, the taxpayer may apply these final regulations to taxable years beginning after December 31, 2004, and before March 20, 2007.

Special Analyses

It has been determined that this Treasury decision is not a significant regulatory action as defined in Executive Order 12866. Therefore, a regulatory assessment is not required. It also has been determined that section 553(b) of the Administrative Procedure Act (5 U.S.C. chapter 5) does not apply to this regulation, and because the regulation does not impose a collection of information on small entities, the Regulatory Flexibility Act (5 U.S.C. chapter 6) does not apply. Pursuant to section 7805(f) of the Internal Revenue Code, the notice of proposed rulemaking preceding this regulation was submitted to the Chief Counsel for Advocacy of the Small Business Administration for comment on its impact on small business.

Drafting Information

The principal authors of these regulations are Paul Handleman and Lauren Ross Taylor, Office of the Associate Chief Counsel (Passthroughs and Special Industries), IRS. However, other personnel from the IRS and Treasury Department participated in their development.

* * * * *

Adoption of Amendments to the Regulations

Accordingly, 26 CFR part 1 is amended as follows:

PART 1—INCOME TAXES

Paragraph 1. The authority citation for part 1 continues to read in part as follows:

Authority: 26 U.S.C. 7805 * * *

Par. 2. Section 1.199–0 is amended by:

1. Revising the entries for §§1.199–3(i)(5)(i) and (ii), 1.199–3(i)(6)(ii) through (v), 1.199–6(c), and 1.199–8(i)(4).

2. Adding a new entry for §1.199–8(i)(7).

The revisions and addition read as follows:

§1.199–0 Table of contents.

* * * * *

§1.199–3 Domestic production gross receipts.

* * * * *

(i) * * *

(5) * * *

(i) In general.

(ii) Exceptions.

(A) Tangible personal property.

(B) Computer software.

(C) Qualified film.

* * * * *

(6) * * *

(ii) Gross receipts derived from services.

(iii) Exceptions.

(iv) Definitions and special rules.

(A) Substantially identical software.

(B) Safe harbor for computer software games.

(C) Regular and ongoing basis.

(D) Attribution.

(E) Qualified computer software maintenance agreements.

(F) Advertising income and product-placement income.

(v) Examples.

* * * * *

§1.199–6 Agricultural and horticultural cooperatives.

* * * * *

(c) Determining cooperative's qualified production activities income and taxable income.

* * * * *

§1.199–8 Other rules.

* * * * *

(i) * * *

(4) Computer software.

* * * * *

(7) Agricultural and horticultural cooperatives.

* * * * *

Par. 3. Section 1.199–3 is amended by:

1. Revising paragraphs (i)(5)(i) and (i)(5)(ii).

2. Removing the language "(i)(5)(ii)" each place it appears in paragraph (i)(5)(iii) and adding the language "(i)(5)(ii)(C)" in its place.

3. Revising paragraphs (i)(6)(ii), (i)(6)(iii), (i)(6)(iv), and (i)(6)(v).

The revisions read as follows:

§1.199–3 Domestic production gross receipts.

* * * * *

(i) * * *

(5) * * *

(i) *In general.* Except as provided in paragraph (i)(5)(ii) of this section, gross receipts derived from the lease, rental, license, sale, exchange, or other disposition of QPP, a qualified film, or utilities do not include advertising income and product-placement income.

(ii) *Exceptions*—(A) *Tangible personal property.* A taxpayer's gross receipts that are derived from the lease, rental, license, sale, exchange, or other disposition of newspapers, magazines, telephone directories, periodicals, and other similar printed publications that are MPGE in whole or in significant part within the United States include advertising income from advertisements placed in those media, but only if the gross receipts, if any, derived from the lease, rental, license, sale, exchange, or other disposition of the newspapers, magazines, telephone directories, or periodicals are (or would be) DPGR.

(B) *Computer software.* A taxpayer's gross receipts that are derived from the lease, rental, license, sale, exchange, or other disposition of computer software that is MPGE in whole or in significant part within the United States include advertising income and product-placement income with respect to that computer software, but only if the gross receipts, if any, derived from the lease, rental, license, sale, exchange, or other disposition of computer software are (or would be) DPGR. For this purpose, advertising income and product-placement income mean compensation for placing or integrating advertising or a product into the computer software. This paragraph (i)(5)(ii)(B) does not extend to the exceptions provided in paragraph (i)(6)(iii) of this section. See paragraph (i)(6)(iv)(F) of this section.

(C) *Qualified film.* A taxpayer's gross receipts that are derived from the lease, rental, license, sale, exchange, or other disposition of a qualified film include advertising income and product-placement income with respect to that qualified film, but only if the gross receipts, if any, derived from the lease, rental, license, sale, exchange, or other disposition of a qualified film are (or would be) DPGR. For this purpose, advertising income and product-placement income mean compensation for placing or integrating advertising or a product into the qualified film.

* * * * *

(6) * * *

(ii) *Gross receipts derived from services.* Gross receipts derived from customer and technical support, telephone and other telecommunication services, online services (such as Internet access services, online banking services, providing access to online electronic books, newspapers, and journals), and other similar services do not constitute gross receipts derived from a lease, rental, license, sale, exchange, or other disposition of computer software.

(iii) *Exceptions.* Notwithstanding paragraph (i)(6)(ii) of this section, if a taxpayer derives gross receipts from providing customers access to computer software MPGE in whole or in significant part by the taxpayer within the United States for the customers' direct use while connected to the Internet or any other public or private communications network (online software), then such gross receipts will be treated as being derived from the lease, rental, license, sale, exchange, or other disposition of computer software only if—

(A) The taxpayer also derives, on a regular and ongoing basis in the taxpayer's business, gross receipts from the lease, rental, license, sale, exchange, or other disposition to customers that are not related persons (as defined in paragraph (b)(1) of this section) of computer software that—

(*1*) Has only minor or immaterial differences from the online software;

(*2*) Has been MPGE by the taxpayer in whole or in significant part within the United States; and

(*3*) Has been provided to such customers either affixed to a tangible medium (for example, a disk or DVD) or by allowing them to download the computer software from the Internet; or

(B) Another person derives, on a regular and ongoing basis in its business, gross receipts from the lease, rental, license, sale, exchange, or other disposition of substantially identical software (as described in paragraph (i)(6)(iv)(A) of this section) (as compared to the taxpayer's online software) to its customers pursuant to an activity described in paragraph (i)(6)(iii)(A)(*3*) of this section.

(iv) *Definitions and special rules*—(A) *Substantially identical software*. For purposes of paragraph (i)(6)(iii)(B) of this section, *substantially identical software* is computer software that—

(*1*) From a customer's perspective, has the same functional result as the online software described in paragraph (i)(6)(iii) of this section; and

(*2*) Has a significant overlap of features or purpose with the online software described in paragraph (i)(6)(iii) of this section.

(B) *Safe harbor for computer software games*. For purposes of paragraph (i)(6)(iv)(A) of this section, all computer software games are deemed to be substantially identical software. For example, computer software sports games are deemed to be substantially identical to computer software card games.

(C) *Regular and ongoing basis*. For purposes of paragraph (i)(6)(iii) of this section, in the case of a newly-formed trade or business or a taxpayer in its first taxable year, the taxpayer is considered to be engaged in an activity described in paragraph (i)(6)(iii) of this section on a regular and ongoing basis if the taxpayer reasonably expects that it will engage in the activity on a regular and ongoing basis.

(D) *Attribution*. For purposes of paragraph (i)(6)(iii)(A) of this section—

(*1*) All members of an expanded affiliated group (as defined in §1.199–7(a)(1)) are treated as a single taxpayer; and

(*2*) In the case of an EAG partnership (as defined in §1.199–3T(i)(8)), the EAG partnership and all members of the EAG to which the EAG partnership's partners belong are treated as a single taxpayer.

(E) *Qualified computer software maintenance agreements*. Paragraph (i)(4)(i)(B)(*5*) of this section does not apply if the computer software is online software under paragraph (i)(6)(iii) of this section.

(F) *Advertising income and product-placement income*. Paragraph (i)(5)(ii)(B) of this section does not apply if the computer software is online software under paragraph (i)(6)(iii) of this section. If a taxpayer provides a customer with access to online software in conjunction with providing computer software to such customer either affixed to a tangible medium or by download, paragraph (i)(5)(ii)(B) of this section will only apply to compensation for the placement or integration of advertising or a product into the computer software transferred to such customer either affixed to the tangible medium or by download.

(v) *Examples*. The following examples illustrate the application of this paragraph (i)(6):

Example 1. L is a bank and produces computer software within the United States that enables its customers to receive online banking services for a fee. Under paragraph (i)(6)(ii) of this section, gross receipts derived from online banking services are attributable to a service and do not constitute gross receipts derived from a lease, rental, license, sale, exchange, or other disposition of computer software. Therefore, L's gross receipts derived from the online banking services are non-DPGR.

Example 2. M is an Internet auction company that produces computer software within the United States that enables its customers to participate in Internet auctions for a fee. Under paragraph (i)(6)(ii) of this section, gross receipts derived from online auction services are attributable to a service and do not constitute gross receipts derived from a lease, rental, license, sale, exchange, or other disposition of computer software. M's activities constitute the provision of online services. Therefore, M's gross receipts derived from the Internet auction services are non-DPGR.

Example 3. N provides telephone services, voicemail services, and e-mail services. N produces computer software within the United States that runs all of these services. Under paragraph (i)(6)(ii) of this section, gross receipts derived from telephone and related telecommunication services are attributable to a service and do not constitute gross receipts derived from a lease, rental, license, sale, exchange, or other disposition of computer software. Therefore, N's gross receipts derived from the telephone and other telecommunication services are non-DPGR.

Example 4. O produces tax preparation computer software within the United States. O derives, on a regular and ongoing basis in its business, gross receipts from both the sale to customers that are unrelated persons of O's computer software that has been affixed to a compact disc as well as from the sale to customers of O's computer software that customers have downloaded from the Internet. O also derives gross receipts from providing customers access to the computer software for the customers' direct use while connected to the Internet. The computer software sold on compact disc or by download has only minor or immaterial differences from the online software, and O does not provide any other goods or services in connection with the online software. Under paragraph (i)(6)(iii)(A) of this section, O's gross receipts derived from providing access to the online software will be treated as derived from the lease, rental, license, sale, exchange, or other disposition of computer software and are DPGR (assuming all the other requirements of this section are met).

Example 5. The facts are the same as in *Example 4*, except that O does not sell the tax preparation computer software to customers affixed to a compact disc or by download. In addition, one of O's competitors, P, derives, on a regular and ongoing basis in its business, gross receipts from the sale to customers of P's substantially identical tax preparation computer software that has been affixed to a compact disc as well as from the sale to customers of P's substantially identical tax preparation computer software that customers have downloaded from the Internet. Under paragraph (i)(6)(iii)(B) of this section, O's gross receipts derived from providing access to its tax preparation online software will be treated as derived from the lease, rental, license, sale, exchange, or other disposition of computer software and are DPGR (assuming all the other requirements of this section are met).

Example 6. Q produces payroll management computer software within the United States. For a fee, Q provides customers access to the payroll management computer software for the customers' direct use while connected to the Internet. This is Q's sole method of providing access to its payroll management computer software to customers. In conjunction with the payroll management computer software, Q provides storage of customers' data and telephone support. One of Q's competitors, R, derives, on a regular and ongoing basis in its business, gross receipts from the sale to customers of R's substantially identical payroll management software that has been affixed to a compact disc as well as from the sale to customers of R's substantially identical payroll management software that customers have downloaded from the Internet. Under paragraph (i)(6)(iii)(B) of this section, Q's gross receipts derived from providing access to its payroll management online software will be treated as derived from the lease, rental, license, sale, exchange, or other disposition of computer software and are DPGR (assuming all the other requirements of this section are met). However, Q's gross receipts derived from the fees that are properly allocable to the storage of customers' data and telephone support are non-DPGR.

Example 7. The facts are the same as in *Example 6*, except that R produces inventory computer software, not payroll management computer software. R's inventory computer software is not substantially identical software as defined in paragraph (i)(6)(iv)(A) of this section because R's inventory software, from a customer's perspective, does not have the same functional result as Q's payroll management computer software and does not have significant overlap of features or purpose with Q's payroll management computer software. No other person provides substantially identical software to customers affixed to a compact disc or by download. Under paragraph (i)(6)(ii) of this section, gross receipts derived from providing access to Q's payroll online software do not constitute gross receipts derived from a lease, rental, license, sale, exchange or other disposition of payroll computer software. Therefore, Q's gross receipts derived from the payroll management computer software are non-DPGR.

Example 8. S produces computer software games within the United States. S derives, on a regular and ongoing basis in its business, gross receipts from both the sale to customers that are not related to S of S's computer software games that have been affixed to a compact disc as well as from the sale to customers of S's computer software games that customers have downloaded from the Internet. S also derives gross receipts from providing customers access to the computer software games for the customers' direct use while connected to the Internet (online software games). The computer software games sold on compact disc or by download have only minor or immaterial differences from the online software games, and S does not provide any other goods or services in connection with the online software games. Under paragraph (i)(6)(iii)(A) of this section, S's gross receipts derived from providing customers access to its online software games will be treated as derived from the lease, rental, license, sale, exchange, or other disposition of computer software and are DPGR (assuming all the other requirements of this section are met).

Example 9. The facts are the same as in *Example 8*, except S's gross receipts also include advertising income from integrating advertisers' logos into the computer software games. Under paragraph (i)(5)(ii)(B) of this section, for S's computer software games sold affixed to a compact disc or by download, S's advertising income is treated as gross receipts derived from the sale of the computer software games and, therefore, is DPGR (assuming all the other requirements of this section are met). However, under paragraphs (i)(5)(i) and (i)(6)(iv)(F) of this section, for S's online software games, S's advertising income is not derived from the lease, rental, license, sale, exchange, or other disposition of computer software and, therefore, is non-DPGR.

Par. 4. Section 1.199–3T is amended by revising paragraphs (i)(1), (i)(2), (i)(3), (i)(4), (i)(5), and (i)(6) to read as follows:

§1.199–3T Domestic production gross receipts (temporary).

* * * * *

(i) *Derived from the lease, rental, license, sale, exchange or other disposition.*

(1) through (6) [Reserved]. For further guidance, see §1.199–3(i)(1) through (6).

* * * * *

Par. 5. Section 1.199–6 is amended by:

1. Revising paragraphs (c) and (l).

2. Removing the language "qualified production activities income (QPAI) (as defined in §1.199–1(c))" from paragraph (e) and adding "QPAI" in its place.

3. Removing the language "However, the cooperative may not apply section 199(d)(3) and this section to any portion of the section 199 deduction that is not passed through to its patrons." from paragraph (h).

The revisions read as follows:

§1.199–6 Agricultural and horticultural cooperatives.

* * * * *

(c) *Determining cooperative's qualified production activities income and taxable income.* For purposes of determining its section 199 deduction, the cooperative's qualified production activities income (QPAI) (as defined in §1.199–1(c)) and taxable income are computed without taking into account any deduction allowable under section 1382(b) or (c) (relating to patronage dividends, per-unit retain allocations, and nonpatronage distributions).

* * * * *

(l) *No double counting.* A qualified payment received by a patron of a cooperative is not taken into account by the patron for purposes of section 199.

Par. 6. Section 1.199–8 is amended by:

1. Revising paragraph (i)(4).

2. Adding new paragraph (i)(7).

The revision and addition read as follows:

§1.199–8 Other rules.

* * * * *

(i) * * *

(4) *Computer software.* Section 1.199–3(i)(5)(ii)(B) and (i)(6)(ii) through (v) are applicable for taxable years beginning on or after March 20, 2007. A taxpayer may apply §1.199–3(i)(5)(ii)(B) and (i)(6)(ii) through (v) to taxable years beginning after December 31, 2004, and before March 20, 2007.

* * * * *

(7) *Agricultural and horticultural cooperatives.* Section 1.199–6(c) is applicable for taxable years beginning on or after March 20, 2007. A taxpayer may apply §1.199–(6)(c) to taxable years beginning after December 31, 2004, and before March 20, 2007.

Par. 7. Section 1.199–8T is amended by revising paragraphs (i)(1), (i)(2), (i)(3), and (i)(4) to read as follows:

§1.199–8T Other rules (temporary).

* * * * *

(i) *Effective dates.* (1) through (4) [Reserved]. For further guidance, see §1.199–8(i)(1) through (4).

* * * * *

Kevin M. Brown,
Deputy Commissioner for Services and Enforcement.

Approved March 14, 2007.

Eric Solomon,
Assistant Secretary of the Treasury.

(Filed by the Office of the Federal Register on March 19, 2007, 8:45 a.m., and published in the issue of the Federal Register for March 20, 2007, 72 F.R. 12969)

Section 368.—Definitions Relating to Corporate Reorganizations

26 CFR 1.368–1: Purpose and scope of exception of reorganization exchanges.

T.D. 9316

DEPARTMENT OF THE TREASURY
Internal Revenue Service
26 CFR Part 1

Corporate Reorganizations; Guidance on the Measurement of Continuity of Interest

AGENCY: Internal Revenue Service (IRS), Treasury.

ACTION: Final and temporary regulations.

SUMMARY: This document contains final and temporary regulations that provide guidance regarding the satisfaction of the continuity of interest requirement for corporate reorganizations. These regulations affect corporations and their shareholders. The text of the temporary regulations also serves as the text of the proposed regulations (REG–146247–06) set forth in the notice of proposed rulemaking on this subject in this issue of the Bulletin.

DATES: *Effective Date:* These regulations are effective March 20, 2007.

Applicability Date: For dates of applicability, see §1.368–1T(e)(8)(ii).

FOR FURTHER INFORMATION CONTACT: Lisa S. Dobson at (202) 622–7790 (not a toll-free number).

SUPPLEMENTARY INFORMATION:

Background and Explanation of Provisions

The Internal Revenue Code of 1986 (Code) provides general nonrecognition treatment for reorganizations described in section 368 of the Code. In addition to complying with the statutory and certain other requirements, to qualify as a reorganization, a transaction generally must satisfy the continuity of interest (COI) requirement. COI requires that, in substance, a substantial part of the value of the proprietary interests in the target corporation be preserved in the reorganization.

On August 10, 2004, the IRS and Treasury Department published a notice of proposed rulemaking (REG–129706–04, 2004–2 C.B. 479) in the **Federal Register** (69 FR 48429) (2004 proposed regulations) identifying certain circumstances in which the determination of whether a proprietary interest in the target corporation is preserved would be made by reference to the value of the issuing corporation's stock on the day before there is an agreement to effect the potential reorganization. On September 16, 2005, the IRS and Treasury Department published final regulations in the **Federal Register** (T.D. 9225, 2005–2 C.B. 716 [70 FR 54631]) (2005 final regulations) which retained the general framework of the 2004 proposed regulations but made several modifications in response to the comments received regarding the proposed regulations. Specifically, the 2005 final regulations provide that in determining whether a proprietary interest in the target corporation is preserved, the consideration to be exchanged for the proprietary interests in the target corporation pursuant to a contract to effect the potential reorganization is valued on the last business day before the first date such contract is a binding contract (the signing date), if the contract provides for fixed consideration (the signing date rule).

After consideration of comments relating to the 2005 final regulations, the IRS and Treasury Department are revising those regulations as set forth in this Treasury decision. These temporary regulations provide guidance for measuring whether the COI requirement is satisfied. The following sections specifically describe the revisions.

A. *Applicability of the Signing Date Rule*

For purposes of determining whether COI is satisfied, the 2005 final regulations require the consideration to be exchanged for the proprietary interests in the target corporation to be valued on the last business day before the first date such contract is a binding contract, if such contract provides for fixed consideration. As noted in the preamble to the 2005 final regulations, the signing date rule is based on the principle that, where a binding contract provides for fixed consideration, the target corporation shareholders can generally be viewed as being subject to the economic fortunes of the issuing corporation as of the signing date. However, if the contract does not provide for fixed consideration, the signing date value of the issuing corporation stock is not relevant for purposes of determining the extent to which a proprietary interest in the target corporation is preserved.

These temporary regulations continue to apply the signing date rule where the contract provides for fixed consideration. If the contract does not provide for fixed consideration, the temporary regulations provide that the signing date rule is not applicable. Further, these temporary regulations clarify that where fixed consideration includes other property that is identified by value, that specified value is the value of such other property to be used in determining whether COI is satisfied.

B. *Definition of Fixed Consideration*

As noted above, the temporary regulations provide that the signing date rule only applies to contracts that provide for fixed consideration. These temporary regulations modify the definition of fixed consideration.

The 2005 final regulations provide four circumstances in which a contract will be treated as providing for fixed consideration. Generally, under the 2005 final regulations, a contract provides for fixed consideration if (1) the contract states the number of shares of the issuing corporation plus the amount of money and any other property to be exchanged for all proprietary interests in the target corporation; (2) the contract states the number of shares of the issuing corporation plus the amount of money and any other property to be exchanged for each proprietary interest in the target corporation; (3) the contract states the percentage of proprietary interests in the target corporation to be exchanged for stock of the issuing corporation; or (4) the contract states the percentage of each proprietary interest in the target corporation to be exchanged for stock of the issuing corporation.

These temporary regulations combine the first two circumstances into one sentence that defines fixed consideration. No substantive change to these two definitions of fixed consideration is intended with this amendment.

The target corporation shareholders are generally subject to the economic fortunes of the issuing corporation as of the signing date only if the contract specifies the number of shares of the issuing corporation to be exchanged for all or each proprietary interest in the target corporation. Accordingly, the temporary regulations provide that the signing date rule is applicable in these situations. The IRS and Treasury Department request comments regarding whether it is appropriate to include in the definition of fixed consideration a contract that specifies a fixed percentage of the shares of the issuing corporation to be exchanged for all or each proprietary interest in the target corporation.

The temporary regulations eliminate the third and fourth circumstances described in the 2005 final regulations from the definition of fixed consideration. Because these types of transactions do not specify the number of shares of the issuing corporation to be received in the exchange, the target corporation shareholders are not subject to the economic fortunes of the issuing corporation as of the signing date. These provisions were removed because, in such situations, applying the signing date rule may produce inappropriate results.

A commentator noted that a transaction in which a fixed percentage of target corporation shares is exchanged for issuing corporation shares could inappropriately be precluded from satisfying COI due to the application of the signing date rule. For example, if the number of the issuing corporation shares to be received by the target corporation shareholders depends on the value of the issuing corporation shares on the closing date, and the issuing corporation shares appreciate significantly between the signing date and the closing date, the signing date rule could prevent a transaction from satisfying COI notwithstanding the fact that a substantial part of the value of the proprietary interests in the target corporation is exchanged for proprietary interests in the issuing corporation.

Further, the temporary regulations continue to treat a contract that provides for a shareholder election between shares of the issuing corporation stock and the money or other property to be exchanged for the proprietary interests in the target corporation as a contract that provides for fixed consideration in the circumstances described below.

C. *Shareholder Elections*

The 2005 final regulations contain a rule generally stating that a contract that permits the target corporation shareholders to elect to receive stock and/or money and/or other property with respect to their target corporation stock will be treated as providing for fixed consideration if the contract also provides the minimum number of shares of the issuing corporation stock and the maximum amount of money or other property to be exchanged for all of the proprietary interests in the target corporation, the minimum percentage of the number of shares of each class of proprietary interests in the target corporation to be exchanged for stock of the issuing corporation, or the minimum percentage (by value) of the proprietary interests in the target corporation to be exchanged for stock of the issuing corporation. The 2005 final regulations further include two special rules prescribing certain assumptions to be made in the determination of whether COI is satisfied in shareholder election cases. For example, in the case in which the contract states the minimum number of shares of the issuing corporation stock and the maximum amount of money or other property to be exchanged for all of the proprietary interests in the target corporation, the determination of whether a proprietary interest in the target corporation is preserved is made by assuming the issuance of the minimum number of shares of each class of stock of the issuing corporation and the maximum amount of money or other property allowable under the contract and without regard to the number of shares of each class of stock of the issuing corporation and the amount of money or other property actually exchanged for proprietary interests in the target corporation.

These temporary regulations treat certain transactions that allow for shareholder elections as providing for fixed consideration regardless of whether the agreement specifies the maximum amount of money or other property, or the minimum amount of issuing corporation stock, to be exchanged in the transaction. As noted above, if the target corporation shareholders can generally be viewed as subject to the economic fortunes of the issuing corporation as of the signing date, it is appropriate to treat the contract as providing for fixed consideration and to apply the signing date rule. The IRS and Treasury Department believe that these circumstances exist in cases where the target corporation shareholders may elect to receive issuing corporation stock in exchange for their target corporation stock at an exchange rate based on the value of the issuing corporation stock on the signing date. For example, if the issuing corporation stock has a value of $1 per share on the last business date before the first date on which the contract is binding, and the agreement provides that the target corporation shareholders may exchange each share of target corporation stock for either $1 or issuing corporation stock (based on the signing date value), the target corporation shareholders that choose to exchange their target corporation stock for stock of the issuing corporation are subject to the economic fortunes of the issuing corporation with respect to such stock as of the signing date. Accordingly, the IRS and Treasury Department believe that it is appropriate in such a case to apply the signing date rule to value the stock of the issuing corporation for purposes of testing whether the transaction satisfies the COI requirement.

Additionally, the IRS and Treasury Department are concerned that the assumptions in the shareholder election rule in the 2005 final regulations may create confusion about whether COI is satisfied based on the delivery of stock that does not in fact preserve the target corporation shareholders' proprietary interest in the target corporation when such result was not intended. For example, the rule might appear to suggest that stock that is redeemed in connection with the potential reorganization will nonetheless be treated as preserving the target corporation shareholders' proprietary interests in the target corporation, although this result would be contrary to Treas. Reg. 1.368–1(e)(1). Further, these assumptions could prevent a transaction from satisfying COI even though a substantial part of the value of the proprietary interests in the target corporation is actually exchanged for proprietary interests in the issuing corporation.

Because of this potential for confusion, and because these assumptions are not relevant to the revised shareholder election provision, the temporary regulations remove the assumptions so that the determination of whether COI is preserved depends on the actual consideration exchanged. Example 9 of the Temporary Regulations has been modified to illustrate the revised rules regarding shareholder elections.

D. *Contract Modifications*

The 2005 final regulations generally provide that a modification of the contract results in a new signing date. However, the 2005 final regulations provide that a modification that has the sole effect of providing for the issuance of additional shares of issuing corporation stock to the target corporation shareholders will not be treated as a modification if the execution of the transaction pursuant to the original agreement would have resulted in the preservation of a substantial part of the value of the target corporation shareholders' proprietary interests in the target corporation if there had been no modification. One commentator suggested that this rule be broadened to include modifications that decrease the money or other property that will be delivered to the target corporation shareholders. These temporary regulations reflect this broadening.

Further, the IRS and Treasury Department believe that the signing date rule should also apply to provide certainty regarding the value of the issuing corporation stock used for purposes of testing COI if the transaction fails to qualify as a tax-free reorganization. For this reason, the IRS and Treasury Department believe that the exception to the modification rule should also be available for certain types of modifications if the transaction fails to satisfy COI at the time of the execution of the contract. Accordingly, these temporary regulations provide that certain contract modifications will not result in a new signing date if the terms of the original contract would have prevented the transaction from qualifying as a reorganization.

E. *Contingent Consideration*

The 2005 final regulations provide that contingent consideration will generally prevent a contract from being treated as providing for fixed consideration. However, the 2005 final regulations provide for a limited exception to that general rule. The exception applies to cases in which the contingent consideration consists solely of stock of the issuing corporation and the execution of the potential reorganization would have resulted in the preservation of a substantial part of the value of the target corporation shareholders' proprietary interests in the target corporation if none of the contingent consideration was delivered to the target shareholders. The IRS and Treasury Department received a number of comments regarding the effect of contingent consideration on the application of the signing date rule.

A number of commentators suggested that the scope of the exception should be expanded to include cases in which the delivery of the contingent consideration to the target corporation shareholders does not decrease the ratio of the value of the shares of issuing corporation stock to the value of the money or other property (determined as of the last business day before the first date there is a binding contract) to be delivered to the target corporation shareholders relative to the ratio of the value of the shares of the issuing corporation stock to the value of the money or other property (determined as of the last business day before the first date there is a binding contract) to be delivered to the target corporation shareholders if none of the contingent consideration were delivered to the target corporation shareholders. These temporary regulations modify and expand the applicability of the signing date rule to certain transactions that provide for contingent adjustments (*i.e.*, increases or decreases) to the consideration.

As described above, the signing date rule is based on the principle that, where a binding contract provides for fixed consideration, the target corporation shareholders can generally be viewed as being subject to the economic fortunes of the issuing corporation as of the signing date. The IRS and Treasury Department believe that where this principle holds true, the signing date rule should apply regardless of whether the transaction potentially qualifies as a reorganization, and regardless of whether the contract provides for certain contingent adjustments to the otherwise fixed consideration. Accordingly, these temporary regulations provide that, generally, a contract that otherwise qualifies as providing for fixed consideration will be treated as providing for fixed consideration even if it provides for contingent adjustments to the consideration, and regardless of whether the transaction would have satisfied COI in the absence of any contingent adjustments. However, if the terms of the contingent adjustments potentially prevent the target corporation shareholders from being subject to the economic fortunes of the issuing corporation as of the signing date, the contract will not be treated as providing for fixed consideration.

Accordingly, these temporary regulations provide that a contract will not be treated as providing for fixed consideration if it provides for contingent adjustments to the consideration that prevent (to any extent) the target shareholders from being subject to the economic benefits and burdens of ownership of the issuing corporation as of the signing date. For example, a contract will not be treated as providing for fixed consideration if it provides for contingent adjustments in the event that the value of the stock of the issuing corporation, the value of the assets of the issuing corporation, or the value of any surrogate for either the value of the stock of the issuing corporation or the assets of the issuing corporation increase or decrease after the last business day before the first date there is a binding contract, or if the terms of the contingent adjustment provide that any increase or decrease in the number of shares of the issuing corporation will be computed using any value of the issuing corporation shares after the last business day before the first date the contract is a binding contract.

F. *Anti-Dilution Provisions*

These temporary regulations also clarify that if the issuing corporation's capital structure is altered and the number of shares of the issuing corporation to be issued to the target corporation shareholders is altered pursuant to a customary anti-dilution clause, the signing date value of the issuing corporation's shares must be adjusted to take this alteration into account.

G. *Other Issues*

The IRS and Treasury Department continue to study other issues related to the determination of whether the COI requirement is satisfied.

Effective Date

These temporary regulations are effective March 20, 2007 and apply to transactions occurring pursuant to a binding contract entered into after September 16, 2005. These temporary regulations provide transitional relief for certain transactions occurring pursuant to a binding contract entered into after September 16, 2005, and on or before March 20, 2007. Parties to transactions within the scope of the transitional relief may elect to apply the 2005 final regulations instead of these temporary regulations. Certain parties must adopt consistent treatment to obtain this relief.

Special Analyses

It has been determined that this Treasury decision is not a significant regulatory action as defined in Executive Order 12866. Therefore, a regulatory assessment is not required. It has also been determined that 5 U.S.C. 553(b) and (d) do not apply to these regulations. For applicability of the Regulatory Flexibility Act, please refer to the cross-reference notice of proposed rulemaking published elsewhere in this issue of the Bulletin. Pursuant to section 7805(f) of the Internal Revenue Code, these regulations were submitted to the Chief Counsel for Advocacy of the Small Business Administration for comment on their impact on small business.

Drafting Information

The principal author of these regulations is Lisa S. Dobson of the Office of the Associate Chief Counsel (Corporate). However, other personnel from the IRS and Treasury Department participated in their development.

* * * * *

Amendments to the Regulations

Accordingly, 26 CFR part 1 is amended as follows:

PART 1—INCOME TAXES

Paragraph 1. The authority citation for part 1 continues to read, in part, as follows:

Authority: 26 U.S.C. 7805 * * *

Par. 2. Section 1.368–1 is amended by:

1. Revising paragraph (e)(2).

2. Revising and redesignating the text of paragraph (e)(8) as paragraph (e)(8)(i).

3. Adding paragraph (e)(8)(ii).

The revisions and addition read as follows:

§1.368–1 Purpose and scope of exception of reorganization exchanges.

* * * * *

(e) * * *

(2) [Reserved]. For further guidance, see §1.368–1T(e)(2).

* * * * *

(8) *Effective dates*—(i) *In general.* Paragraphs (e)(1) and (e)(3) through (e)(7) of this section apply to transactions occurring after January 28, 1998, except that they do not apply to any transaction occurring pursuant to a written agreement which is binding on January 28, 1998, and at all times thereafter. Paragraph (e)(1)(ii) of this section, however, applies to transactions occurring after August 30, 2000, unless the transaction occurs pursuant to a written agreement that is (subject to customary conditions) binding on that date and at all times thereafter. Taxpayers who entered into a binding agreement on or after January 28, 1998, and before August 30, 2000, may request a private letter ruling permitting them to apply the final regulations to their transaction. A private letter ruling will not be issued unless the taxpayer establishes to the satisfaction of the IRS that there is not a significant risk of different parties to the transaction taking inconsistent positions, for Federal tax purposes, with respect to the applicability of the final regulations to the transaction.

(ii) *Signing date rule.* [Reserved]. For further guidance, see §1.368–1T(e)(8)(ii).

Par. 3. Section 1.368–1T is added to read as follows:

§1.368–1T Purpose and scope of exception of reorganization exchanges (temporary).

(a) through (e)(1) [Reserved]. For further guidance, see §1.368–1(a) through (e)(1).

(e)(2) *Measuring continuity of interest.* (i) *In general.* In determining whether a proprietary interest in the target corporation is preserved, the consideration to be exchanged for the proprietary interests in the target corporation pursuant to a contract to effect the potential reorganization shall be valued on the last business day before the first date such contract is a binding contract, if such contract provides for fixed consideration. If a portion of the consideration provided for in such a contract consists of other property identified by value, then this specified value of such other property is used for purposes of determining the extent to which a proprietary interest in the target corporation is preserved. If the contract does not provide for fixed consideration, this paragraph (e)(2)(i) is not applicable.

(ii) *Binding contract*—(A) *In general.* A binding contract is an instrument enforceable under applicable law against the parties to the instrument. The presence of a condition outside the control of the parties (including, for example, regulatory agency approval) shall not prevent an instrument from being a binding contract. Further, the fact that insubstantial terms remain to be negotiated by the parties to the contract, or that customary conditions remain to be satisfied, shall not prevent an instrument from being a binding contract.

(B) *Modifications*—(*1*) *In general.* If a term of a binding contract that relates to the amount or type of the consideration the target shareholders will receive in a potential reorganization is modified before the closing date of the potential reorganization, and the contract as modified is a binding contract, the date of the modification shall be treated as the first date there is a binding contract.

(*2*) *Modification of a transaction that preserves continuity of interest.* Notwithstanding paragraph (e)(2)(ii)(B)(*1*) of this section, a modification of a term that relates to the amount or type of consideration the target shareholders will receive in a transaction that would have resulted in the preservation of a substantial part of the value of the target corporation shareholders' proprietary interests in the target corporation if there had been no modification will not be treated as a modification if—

(*i*) The modification has the sole effect of providing for the issuance of additional shares of issuing corporation stock to the target corporation shareholders;

(*ii*) The modification has the sole effect of decreasing the amount of money or other property to be delivered to the target corporation shareholders; or

(*iii*) The modification has the effect of decreasing the amount of money or other property to be delivered to the target corporation shareholders and providing for the issuance of additional shares of issuing corporation stock to the target corporation shareholders.

(*3*) *Modification of a transaction that does not preserve continuity of interest.* Notwithstanding paragraph (e)(2)(ii)(B)(*1*) of this section, a modification of a term that relates to the amount or type of consideration the target shareholders will receive in a transaction that would not have resulted in the preservation of a substantial part of the value of the target corporation shareholders' proprietary interests in the target corporation if there had been no modification will not be treated as a modification if—

(*i*) The modification has the sole effect of providing for the issuance of fewer shares of issuing corporation stock to the target corporation shareholders;

(*ii*) The modification has the sole effect of increasing the amount of money or other property to be delivered to the target corporation shareholders; or

(*iii*) The modification has the effect of increasing the amount of money or other property to be delivered to the target corporation shareholders and providing for the issuance of fewer shares of issuing corporation stock to the target corporation shareholders.

(C) *Tender offers*. For purposes of this paragraph (e)(2), a tender offer that is subject to section 14(d) of the Securities and Exchange Act of 1934 [15 U.S.C. 78n(d)(1)] and Regulation 14D (17 CFR 240.14d–1 through 240.14d–101) and is not pursuant to a binding contract, is treated as a binding contract made on the date of its announcement, notwithstanding that it may be modified by the offeror or that it is not enforceable against the offerees. If a modification (not pursuant to a binding contract) of such a tender offer is subject to the provisions of Regulation 14d–6(c) (17 CFR 240.14d–6(c)) and relates to the amount or type of the consideration received in the tender offer, then the date of the modification shall be treated as the first date there is a binding contract.

(iii) *Fixed Consideration*—(A) *In general*. A contract provides for fixed consideration if it provides the number of shares of each class of stock of the issuing corporation, the amount of money, and the other property (identified either by value or by specific description), if any, to be exchanged for all the proprietary interests in the target corporation, or to be exchanged for each proprietary interest in the target corporation. A contract that provides a target corporation shareholder with an election to receive a number of shares of stock of the issuing corporation and/or money and/or other property in exchange for all of the shareholder's proprietary interests in the target corporation, or each of the shareholder's proprietary interests in the target corporation, provides for fixed consideration if the determination of the number of shares of issuing corporation stock to be provided to the target corporation shareholder is determined using the value of the issuing corporation stock on the last business day before the first date there is a binding contract.

(B) *Contingent adjustments to the consideration*—(*1*) *In general*. Except as provided in paragraph (e)(2)(iii)(B)(*2*) of this section, a contract that provides for contingent adjustments to the consideration will be treated as providing for fixed consideration if it would satisfy the requirements of paragraph (e)(2)(iii)(A) of this section without the contingent adjustment provision.

(*2*) *Exceptions*. A contract will not be treated as providing for fixed consideration if the contract provides for contingent adjustments to the consideration that prevent (to any extent) the target corporation shareholders from being subject to the economic benefits and burdens of ownership of the issuing corporation stock after the last business day before the first date the contract is a binding contract. For example, a contract will not be treated as providing for fixed consideration if the contract provides for contingent adjustments to the consideration in the event that the value of the stock of the issuing corporation, the value of the assets of the issuing corporation, or the value of any surrogate for either the value of the stock of the issuing corporation or the assets of the issuing corporation increase or decrease after the last business day before the first date there is a binding contract; or in the event the contract provides for contingent adjustments to the number of shares of the issuing corporation stock to be provided to the target corporation shareholders computed using any value of the issuing corporation shares after the last business day before the first date there is a binding contract.

(C) *Escrows*. Placing part of the consideration to be exchanged for proprietary interests in the target corporation in escrow to secure target's performance of customary pre-closing covenants or customary target representations and warranties will not prevent a contract from being treated as providing for fixed consideration.

(D) *Anti-dilution clauses*. The presence of a customary anti-dilution clause will not prevent a contract from being treated as providing for fixed consideration. However, the absence of such a clause will prevent a contract from being treated as providing for fixed consideration if the issuing corporation alters its capital structure between the first date there is an otherwise binding contract to effect the transaction and the effective date of the transaction in a manner that materially alters the economic arrangement of the parties to the binding contract. If the number of shares of the issuing corporation to be issued to the target corporation shareholders is altered pursuant to a customary anti-dilution clause, the value of the shares determined under paragraph (e)(2)(i) of this section must be adjusted accordingly.

(E) *Dissenters' rights*. The possibility that some shareholders may exercise dissenters' rights and receive consideration other than that provided for in the binding contract will not prevent the contract from being treated as providing for fixed consideration.

(F) *Fractional shares*. The fact that money may be paid in lieu of issuing fractional shares will not prevent a contract from being treated as providing for fixed consideration.

(iv) *Valuation of new issuances*. For purposes of applying paragraph (e)(2)(i) of this section, any class of stock, securities, or indebtedness that the issuing corporation issues to the target corporation shareholders pursuant to the potential reorganization and that does not exist before the first date there is a binding contract to effect the potential reorganization is deemed to have been issued on the last business day before the first date there is a binding contract to effect the potential reorganization.

(v) *Examples*. For purposes of the examples in this paragraph (e)(2)(v), P is the issuing corporation, T is the target corporation, S is a wholly owned subsidiary of P, all corporations have only one class of stock outstanding, A is an individual, no transactions other than those described occur, and the transactions are not otherwise subject to recharacterization. The following examples illustrate the application of this paragraph (e)(2):

Example 1. Application of signing date rule. On January 3 of Year 1, P and T sign a binding contract pursuant to which T will be merged with and into P on June 1 of Year 1. Pursuant to the contract, the T shareholders will receive 40 P shares and $60 of cash in exchange for all of the outstanding stock of T. Twenty of the P shares, however, will be placed in escrow to secure customary target representations and warranties. The P stock is listed on an established market. On January 2 of Year 1, the value of the P stock is $1 per share. On June 1 of Year 1, T merges with and into P pursuant to the terms of the contract. On that date, the value of the P stock is $.25 per share. None of the stock placed in escrow is returned to P. Because the contract provides for the number of shares of P and the amount of money to be exchanged for all of the proprietary interests in T, under this paragraph (e)(2), there is a binding contract providing for fixed consideration as of January 3 of Year 1. Therefore, whether the transaction satisfies the continuity of interest requirement is determined by reference to the value of the P stock on January 2 of Year 1. Because, for continuity of interest purposes, the T stock is exchanged for $40 of P stock and $60 of cash, the transaction preserves a substantial part of the value of the proprietary interest in T. Therefore, the transaction satisfies the continuity of interest requirement.

Example 2. Treatment of forfeited escrowed stock. (i) *Escrowed stock.* The facts are the same as in *Example 1* except that T's breach of a representation results in the escrowed consideration being returned to P. Because the contract provides for the number of shares of P and the amount of money to be exchanged for all of the proprietary interests in T, under this paragraph (e)(2), there is a binding contract providing for fixed consideration as of January 3 of Year 1. Therefore, whether the transaction satisfies the continuity of interest requirement is determined by reference to the value of the P stock on January 2 of Year 1. Pursuant to paragraph (e)(1)(i) of §1.368–1, for continuity of interest purposes, the T stock is exchanged for $20 of P stock and $60 of cash, the transaction does not preserve a substantial part of the value of the proprietary interest in T. Therefore, the transaction does not satisfy the continuity of interest requirement.

(ii) *Escrowed stock and cash.* The facts are the same as in paragraph (i) of this *Example 2* except that the consideration placed in escrow consists solely of eight of the P shares and $12 of the cash. Because the contract provides for the number of shares of P and the amount of money to be exchanged for all of the proprietary interests in T, under this paragraph (e)(2), there is a binding contract providing for fixed consideration as of January 3 of Year 1. Therefore, whether the transaction satisfies the continuity of interest requirement is determined by reference to the value of the P stock on January 2 of Year 1. Pursuant to paragraph (e)(1)(i) of §1.368–1, for continuity of interest purposes, the T stock is exchanged for $32 of P stock and $48 of cash, and the transaction preserves a substantial part of the value of the proprietary interest in T. Therefore, the transaction satisfies the continuity of interest requirement.

Example 3. Redemption of stock received pursuant to binding contract. The facts are the same as in *Example 1* except that A owns 50 percent of the outstanding stock of T immediately prior to the merger and receives 10 P shares and $30 in the merger and an additional 10 P shares upon the release of the stock placed in escrow. In connection with the merger, A and S agree that, immediately after the merger, S will purchase any P shares that A acquires in the merger for $1 per share. Shortly after the merger, S purchases A's P shares for $20. Because the contract provides for the number of shares of P and the amount of money to be exchanged for all of the proprietary interests in T, under this paragraph (e)(2), there is a binding contract providing for fixed consideration as of January 3 of Year 1. Therefore, whether the transaction satisfies the continuity of interest requirement is determined by reference to the value of the P stock on January 2 of Year 1. In addition, S is a person related to P under paragraph (e)(4)(i)(A) of §1.368–1. Accordingly, A is treated as exchanging his T shares for $50 of cash. Because, for continuity of interest purposes, the T stock is exchanged for $20 of P stock and $80 of cash, the transaction does not preserve a substantial part of the value of the proprietary interest in T. Therefore, the transaction does not satisfy the continuity of interest requirement.

Example 4. Modification of binding contract—continuity not preserved. The facts are the same as in *Example 1* except that on April 1 of Year 1, the parties modify their contract. Pursuant to the modified contract, which is a binding contract, the T shareholders will receive 50 P shares (an additional 10 shares) and $75 of cash (an additional $15 of cash) in exchange for all of the outstanding T stock. On March 31 of Year 1, the value of the P stock is $.50 per share. Under this paragraph (e)(2), although there was a binding contract providing for fixed consideration as of January 3 of Year 1, terms of that contract relating to the consideration to be provided to the target shareholders were modified on April 1 of Year 1. The execution of the transaction without modification would have resulted in the preservation of a substantial part of the value of the target corporation shareholders' proprietary interests in the target corporation if there had been no modification. However, because the modified contract provides for additional P stock and cash to be exchanged for all the proprietary interests in T, the exception in paragraph (e)(2)(ii)(B)(*2*) of this section does not apply to preserve the original signing date. Therefore, whether the transaction satisfies the continuity of interest requirement is determined by reference to the value of the P stock on March 31 of Year 1. Because, for continuity of interest purposes, the T stock is exchanged for $25 of P stock and $75 of cash, the transaction does not preserve a substantial part of the value of the proprietary interest in T. Therefore, the transaction does not satisfy the continuity of interest requirement.

Example 5. Modification of binding contract disregarded—continuity preserved. The facts are the same as in *Example 4* except that, pursuant to the modified contract, which is a binding contract, the T shareholders will receive 60 P shares (an additional 20 shares as compared to the original contract) and $60 of cash in exchange for all of the outstanding T stock. In addition, on March 31 of Year 1, the value of the P stock is $.40 per share. Under this paragraph (e)(2), although there was a binding contract providing for fixed consideration as of January 3 of Year 1, terms of that contract relating to the consideration to be provided to the target shareholders were modified on April 1 of Year 1. Nonetheless, the modification has the sole effect of providing for the issuance of additional P shares to the T shareholders. In addition, the execution of the terms of the contract without regard to the modification would have resulted in the preservation of a substantial part of the value of the T shareholders' proprietary interest in T because, for continuity of interest purposes, the T stock would have been exchanged for $40 of P stock and $60 of cash. Pursuant to paragraph (e)(2)(ii)(B)(*2*) of this section, the modification is not treated as a modification for purposes of paragraph (e)(2)(ii)(B)(*1*) of this section. Accordingly, whether the transaction satisfies the continuity of interest requirement is determined by reference to the value of the P stock on January 2 of Year 1. Because, for continuity of interest purposes, the T stock is exchanged for $60 of P stock and $60 of cash, the transaction preserves a substantial part of the value of the proprietary interest in T. Therefore the transaction satisfies the continuity of interest requirement.

Example 6. New issuance. The facts are the same as in *Example 1*, except that, instead of cash, the T shareholders will receive a new class of P securities that will be publicly traded. In the aggregate, the securities will have a stated principal amount of $60 and bear interest at the average LIBOR (London Interbank Offered Rates) during the 10 days prior to the potential reorganization. If the T shareholders had been issued the P securities on January 2 of Year 1, the P securities would have had a value of $60 (determined by reference to the value of comparable publicly traded securities). Whether the transaction satisfies the continuity of interest requirement is determined by reference to the value of the P stock and the P securities to be issued to the T shareholders on January 2 of Year 1. Under paragraph (e)(2)(iv) of this section, for purposes of valuing the new P securities, they will be treated as having been issued on January 2 of Year 1. Because, for continuity of interest purposes, the T stock is exchanged for $40 of P stock and $60 of other property, the transaction preserves a substantial part of the value of the proprietary interest in T. Therefore, the transaction satisfies the continuity of interest requirement.

Example 7. Fixed consideration—continuity not preserved. On January 3 of Year 1, P and T sign a binding contract pursuant to which T will be merged with and into P on June 1 of Year 1. Pursuant to the contract, 60 shares of the T stock will be exchanged for $80 of cash and 40 shares of the T stock will be exchanged for 20 shares of P stock. On January 2 of Year 1, the value of the P stock is $1 per share. On June 1 of Year 1, T merges with and into P pursuant to the terms of the contract. This contract provides for fixed consideration and therefore whether the transaction satisfies the continuity of interest requirement is determined by reference to the value of the P stock on January 2 of Year 1. However, applying the signing date rule, the P stock represents only 20 percent of the value of the total consideration to be received by the T shareholders. Accordingly, based on the economic realities of the exchange, the transaction does not preserve a substantial part of the value of the proprietary interest in T. Therefore, the transaction does not satisfy the continuity of interest requirement.

Example 8. Anti-dilution clause. (i) *Absence of anti-dilution clause.* On January 3 of Year 1, P and T sign a binding contract pursuant to which T will be merged with and into P on June 1 of Year 1. Pursuant to the contract, the T shareholders will receive 40 P shares and $60 of cash in exchange for all of the outstanding stock of T. The contract does not contain a customary anti-dilution provision. The P stock is listed on an established market. On January 2 of Year 1, the value of the P stock is $1 per share. On April 10 of Year 1, P issues its stock to effect a stock split; each shareholder of P receives an additional share of P for each P share that it holds. On April 11 of Year 1, the value of the P stock is $.50 per share. Because

P altered its capital structure between January 3 and June 1 of Year 1 in a manner that materially alters the economic arrangement of the parties, under paragraph (e)(2)(iii)(D) of this section, the contract is not treated as a binding contract that provides for fixed consideration. Accordingly, whether the transaction satisfies the continuity of interest requirement cannot be determined by reference to the value of the P stock on January 2 of Year 1.

(ii) *Adjustment for anti-dilution clause*. The facts are the same as in paragraph (i) of this *Example 8* except that the contract contains a customary anti-dilution provision, and the T shareholders receive 80 P shares and $60 of cash in exchange for all of the outstanding stock of T. Under paragraph (e)(2)(iii)(D) of this section, the contract is treated as a binding contract that provides for fixed consideration as of January 3 of Year 1. Therefore, whether the transaction satisfies the continuity of interest requirement is generally determined by reference to the value of the P stock on January 2 of Year 1. However, under paragraph (e)(2)(iii)(D) of this section, the value of the P stock on January 2 of Year 1 must be adjusted to take the stock split into account. For continuity of interest purposes, the T stock is exchanged for $40 of P stock (($1 ÷ 2) x 80) and $60 of cash. Therefore, the transaction satisfies the continuity of interest requirement.

Example 9. Shareholder election. On January 3 of Year 1, P and T sign a binding contract pursuant to which T will be merged with and into P on June 1 of Year 1. On January 2 of Year 1, the value of the P stock and the T stock is $1 per share. Pursuant to the contract, at the shareholders' election, each share of T will be exchanged for cash of $1, or alternatively, P stock. The contract provides that the determination of the number of shares of P stock to be exchanged for a share of T stock is made using the value of the P stock on the last business day before the first date there is a binding contract (*i.e.*, $1 per share). Accordingly, the contract provides for fixed consideration, and the determination of whether the transaction satisfies the continuity of interest requirement is based on the number of shares of P stock the T shareholders receive in the exchange and by reference to the value of the P stock on January 2 of Year 1.

Example 10. Contingent adjustment based on the value of the issuing corporation stock—continuity not preserved. On January 3 of Year 1, P and T sign a binding contract pursuant to which T will be merged with and into P on June 1 of Year 1. On January 2 of Year 1, the value of the P stock is $1 per share. Pursuant to the contract, if the value of the P stock does not decrease after January 2 of Year 1, the T shareholders will receive 40 P shares and $60 of cash in exchange for all of the outstanding stock of T. Furthermore, the contract provides that the T shareholders will receive $.16 of additional P shares and $.24 for every $.01 decrease in the value of one share of P stock after January 2 of Year 1. On June 1 of Year 1, T merges with and into P pursuant to the terms of the contract. On that date, the value of the P stock is $.40 per share. Pursuant to the terms of the contract, the consideration is adjusted so that the T shareholders receive 24 more P shares ((60 x $.16)/$.40) and $14.40 more cash (60 x $.24) than they would absent an adjustment. Accordingly, at closing the T shareholders receive 64 P shares and $74.40 of cash. Because the contract provides that additional P shares and cash will be delivered to the T shareholders if the value of the stock of P decreases after January 2 of Year 1, under paragraph (e)(2)(iii)(B)(*2*) of this section, the contract is not treated as providing for fixed consideration, and therefore whether the transaction satisfies the continuity of interest requirement cannot be determined by reference to the value of the P stock on January 2 of Year 1. For continuity of interest purposes, the T stock is exchanged for $25.60 of P stock (64 x $.40) and $74.40 of cash and the transaction does not preserve a substantial part of the value of the proprietary interest in T. Therefore, the transaction does not satisfy the continuity of interest requirement.

Example 11. Contingent adjustment to boot based on the value of the target corporation stock—continuity not preserved. On January 3 of Year 1, P and T sign a binding contract pursuant to which T will be merged with and into P on June 1 of Year 1. On January 2 of Year 1, T has 100 shares outstanding, and each T share is worth $1. On January 2 of Year 1, each P share is worth $1. Pursuant to the contract, if the value of the T stock does not increase after January 3 of Year 1, the T shareholders will receive 40 P shares and $60 of cash in exchange for all of the outstanding stock of T. Furthermore, the contract provides that the T shareholders will receive $1 of additional cash for every $.01 increase in the value of one share of T stock after January 3 of Year 1. On June 1 of Year 1, the value of the T stock is $1.40 per share and the value of the P stock is $.75 per share. Pursuant to the terms of the contract, the consideration is adjusted so that the T shareholders receive $40 more cash (40 x $1) than they would absent an adjustment. Accordingly, at closing the T shareholders receive 40 P shares and $100 of cash. Because the contract provides the number of shares of P stock and the amount of money to be exchanged for all the proprietary interests in T, and the contingent adjustment to the cash consideration is not based on changes in the value of the P stock, P assets, or any surrogate thereof, after January 2 of Year 1, there is a binding contract providing for fixed consideration as of January 3 of Year 1. Therefore, whether the transaction satisfies the continuity of interest requirement is determined by reference to the value of the P stock on January 2 of Year 1. For continuity of interest purposes, the T stock is exchanged for $40 of P stock (40 x $1) and $100 of cash. Therefore, the transaction does not satisfy the continuity of interest requirement.

Example 12. Contingent adjustment to stock based on the value of the target corporation stock—continuity preserved. On January 3 of Year 1, P and T sign a binding contract pursuant to which T will be merged with and into P on June 1 of Year 1. On that date T has 100 shares outstanding, and each T share is worth $1. On January 2 of Year 1, each P share is worth $1. Pursuant to the contract, if the value of the T stock does not decrease after January 3 of Year 1, the T shareholders will receive 40 P shares and $60 of cash in exchange for all of the outstanding stock of T. Furthermore, the contract provides that the T shareholders will receive $.40 less P stock and $.60 less cash for every $.01 decrease in the value of one share of T stock after January 3 of Year 1. The contract also provides that the number of P shares by which the consideration will be reduced as a result of this adjustment will be determined based on the value of the P stock on January 2 of Year 1. On June 1 of Year 1, T merges with and into P pursuant to the terms of the contract. On that date, the value of the T stock is $.70 per share and the value of the P stock is $.75 per share. Pursuant to the terms of the contract, the consideration is adjusted so that the T shareholders receive 12 fewer P shares ((30 x $.40)/$1) and $18 less cash (30 x $.60) than they would absent an adjustment. Accordingly, at closing the T shareholders receive 28 P shares and $42 of cash. Because the contract provides for the number of shares of P stock and the amount of money to be exchanged for all of the proprietary interests in T, the contract does not provide for contingent adjustments to the consideration based on a change in value of the P stock, P assets, or any surrogate thereof, after January 2 of Year 1, and the adjustment to the number of P shares the T shareholders receive is determined based on the value of the P shares on January 2 of Year 1, there is a binding contract providing for fixed consideration as of January 3 of Year 1. Therefore, whether the transaction satisfies the continuity of interest requirement is determined by reference to the value of the P stock on January 2 of Year 1. For continuity of interest purposes, the T stock is exchanged for $28 of P stock (28 x $1) and $42 of cash. Therefore, the transaction satisfies the continuity of interest requirement.

(e)(3) through (7) [Reserved]. For further guidance, see §1.368–1(e)(3) through (7).

(8) *Effective dates*. (i) [Reserved]. For further guidance, see §1.368–1(e)(8)(i).

(ii) *Signing date rule*. Paragraph (e)(2) of this section applies to transactions occurring pursuant to binding contracts entered into after September 16, 2005. For transactions occurring pursuant to binding contracts entered into after September 16, 2005, and on or before March 20, 2007, the parties to the transaction may elect to apply the provisions of §1.368–1(e)(2) as contained in 26 CFR part 1, revised April 1, 2006, instead of the provisions of this paragraph (e)(2). However, the target corporation, the issuing corporation, the controlling corporation of the acquiring corporation if stock thereof is provided as consideration in the transaction, and any direct or indirect transferee of transferred basis property from any of the foregoing, may not elect to apply the provisions of §1.368–1(e)(2) as contained in 26 CFR part 1, revised April 1, 2006, unless all such taxpayers elect to apply the provisions of such regulations. This election requirement will be satisfied if none of the specified parties adopts inconsistent treatment.

The applicability of this section expires on or before March 19, 2010.

Kevin M. Brown,
Deputy Commissioner for Services and Enforcement.

Approved March 14, 2007.

Eric Solomon,
Assistant Secretary of the Treasury (Tax Policy).

(Filed by the Office of the Federal Register on March 19, 2007, 8:45 a.m., and published in the issue of the Federal Register for March 20, 2007, 72 F.R. 12974)

Section 446.—General Rule for Methods of Accounting

26 CFR 1.446–1: General rule for methods of accounting.

A revenue ruling holds that ICE Futures, which is a United Kingdom Recognised Investment Exchange, is a qualified board or exchange within the meaning of section 1256(g)(7)(C) of the Code. See Rev. Rul. 2007-26, page 970.

Section 481.—Adjustments Required by Changes in Method of Accounting

A revenue ruling holds that ICE Futures, which is a United Kingdom Recognised Investment Exchange, is a qualified board or exchange within the meaning of section 1256(g)(7)(C) of the Code. See Rev. Rul. 2007-26, page 970.

Section 932.—Coordination of United States and Virgin Islands Income Taxes

A notice provides interim rules regarding the statute of limitations on assessment and exchange of information concerning individuals claiming to be *bona fide* residents of the U.S. Virgin Islands. See Notice 2007-31, page 971.

Section 1256.—Section 1256 Contracts Marked to Market

(Also §§ 446, 481, 7805; 1.446–1, 301.7805–1.)

ICE Futures; United Kingdom. This ruling holds that ICE Futures, which is a United Kingdom Recognised Investment Exchange, is a qualified board or exchange within the meaning of section 1256(g)(7)(C) of the Code.

Rev. Rul. 2007–26

ISSUE

Is ICE Futures, which is a United Kingdom Recognised Investment Exchange, a qualified board or exchange within the meaning of section 1256(g)(7)(C) of the Internal Revenue Code?

LAW

Section 1256(g)(7) of the Code provides that the term "qualified board or exchange" means:

(A) a national securities exchange which is registered with the Securities and Exchange Commission,

(B) a domestic board of trade designated as a contract market by the Commodity Futures Trading Commission, or

(C) any other exchange, board of trade, or other market which the Secretary determines has rules adequate to carry out the purposes of section 1256.

HOLDING

The Internal Revenue Service determines that ICE Futures, which is a United Kingdom Recognised Investment Exchange, is a qualified board or exchange within the meaning of section 1256(g)(7)(C) of the Code.

EFFECTIVE DATE

Under the authority of section 7805(b)(8) of the Code, this revenue ruling is effective for ICE Futures Contracts (commodity futures contracts and futures contract options) entered into on or after April 1, 2007.

CHANGE IN METHOD OF ACCOUNTING

A change in the treatment of ICE Futures Contracts to comply with this revenue ruling is a change in method of accounting within the meaning of sections 446 and 481 of the Code and the regulations thereunder. The Commissioner grants consent to taxpayers to change to the section 1256 mark to market method for the first taxable year during which the taxpayer holds an ICE Futures Contract that was entered into on or after April 1, 2007. Such a taxpayer need not file a Form 3115, *Application for Change in Accounting Method.* ICE Futures Contracts that were entered into before April 1, 2007, are not covered by the change in method for which consent is granted. Because the change is being made on a "cut-off" basis, there is no potential omission or duplication of income or deductions, and therefore no adjustment under section 481 is required.

DRAFTING INFORMATION

The principal author of this revenue ruling is K. Scott Brown of the Office of Associate Chief Counsel (Financial Institutions and Products). For further information regarding this revenue ruling, contact Mr. Brown at (202) 622–3920 (not a toll-free call).

Section 6501.—Limitations on Assessment and Collection

A notice provides interim rules regarding the statute of limitations on assessment and exchange of information concerning individuals claiming to be *bona fide* residents of the U.S. Virgin Islands. See Notice 2007-31, page 971.

Section 7654.—Coordination of United States and Certain Possession Individual Income Taxes

A notice provides interim rules regarding the statute of limitations on assessment and exchange of information concerning individuals claiming to be *bona fide* residents of the U.S. Virgin Islands. See Notice 2007-31, page 971.

Section 7805.—Rules and Regulations

26 CFR 301.7805–1: Rules and regulations.

A revenue ruling holds that ICE Futures, which is a United Kingdom Recognised Investment Exchange, is a qualified board or exchange within the meaning of section 1256(g)(7)(C) of the Code. See Rev. Rul. 2007-26, page 970.

Part III. Administrative, Procedural, and Miscellaneous

Statute of Limitations and Exchange of Information Concerning Certain Individuals Filing Income Tax Returns With the U.S. Virgin Islands

Notice 2007–31

SECTION 1. PURPOSE

This notice announces that for taxable years ending on or after December 31, 2006, the U.S. federal statute of limitations for all U.S. citizens and residents claiming to be *bona fide* residents of the U.S. Virgin Islands generally will commence upon the filing of an income tax return with the U.S. Virgin Islands.

This notice amends and supplements Notice 2007–19, 2007–11 I.R.B. 689, which the Treasury Department and the Internal Revenue Service (IRS) issued on February 21, 2007. Notice 2007–19 provided interim rules under sections 932(c) and 7654(e) concerning the statute of limitations on assessment of the U.S. income tax liability (if any) of a U.S. citizen or resident alien who takes the position that he or she is a *bona fide* resident of the U.S. Virgin Islands and the U.S. filing obligations of such an individual. It also announced that the Treasury Department and the IRS were studying the feasibility of an automatic exchange of information program with the U.S. Virgin Islands and the elimination of the reporting requirements set forth in the notice.

Since the issuance of Notice 2007–19, the U.S. Virgin Islands Bureau of Internal Revenue (BIR) and the IRS have entered into a new working arrangement concerning the routine (automatic) exchange of information (the "Working Arrangement") under the Tax Implementation Agreement between the United States of America and the Virgin Islands dated February 24, 1987 (the "Implementation Agreement"). In light of the Working Arrangement, this notice also provides new interim rules under sections 932(c) and 7654(e) concerning the statute of limitations on assessment and U.S. filing obligations of certain individuals who file returns with the U.S. Virgin Islands. Finally, this notice announces that the Treasury Department and the IRS intend to issue regulations under sections 932(c) and 7654(e) that incorporate these new interim rules. Until the regulations are issued, taxpayers may rely on this notice (and when appropriate, may also rely on Notice 2007–19).

SECTION 2. EXCHANGE OF INFORMATION

On March 21, 2007, the IRS and BIR officials serving as the competent authorities of the United States and the U.S. Virgin Islands, respectively, entered into the Working Arrangement, which provides guidelines and procedures for the routine exchange of information under the Implementation Agreement. The Working Arrangement applies to taxable years ending on or after December 31, 2006. The Working Arrangement will be terminated if for any reason the Implementation Agreement is terminated. The Working Arrangement may also be terminated upon written notice by either the IRS or the BIR. The text of the Working Arrangement is attached.

SECTION 3. INTERIM RULES

Under the authority of section 7654(e), an individual income tax return filed under section 932(c)(2) with the U.S. Virgin Islands by a U.S. citizen or resident alien (USVI Form 1040) who takes the position that he or she is a *bona fide* resident of the U.S. Virgin Islands for the entire taxable year (or an individual who files a joint return for the taxable year with such an individual) will be deemed to be a U.S. income tax return of that individual for purposes of section 6501(a), provided that the IRS and BIR have entered into an agreement for the routine exchange of information satisfying the requirements of the Commissioner of the IRS. The Working Arrangement announced in section 2 of this notice satisfies this condition. Therefore, a return filed with the U.S. Virgin Islands under section 932(c)(2) will be deemed to be a U.S. income tax return for purposes of section 6501(a) as described in this paragraph. In the event that the Working Arrangement is terminated and in the absence of a successor agreement, the interim rules provided in Notice 2007–19 will apply.

For example, assume that N, a U.S. citizen and calendar year taxpayer, takes the position that he is a *bona fide* resident of the U.S. Virgin Islands for the 2006 taxable year. On March 30, 2007, N files USVI Form 1040 (2006) with the U.S. Virgin Islands. N does not file Form 1040, *U.S. Individual Income Tax Return* (U.S. Form 1040), with the IRS (as described previously in Notice 2007–19). Under these circumstances and the rules provided in this notice, the 3-year period of limitations under section 6501(a) will expire on April 15, 2010, and the IRS will make no further assessment of income tax for N's 2006 taxable year after that date except as otherwise authorized by section 6501.

SECTION 4. EFFECTIVE DATE

This notice applies for taxable years ending on or after December 31, 2006.

With respect to taxable years ending before December 31, 2006, the interim rules provided in Notice 2007–19 are still effective if a taxpayer so chooses. Consequently, a "non-covered person" within the meaning of Notice 2007–19 may choose to apply the interim rules of that notice to a taxable year ending before December 31, 2006, by filing U.S. Form 1040 with the IRS as provided in the notice. A "covered person" within the meaning of Notice 2007–19 who chooses to apply the interim rules of that notice to a taxable year ending before December 31, 2006, need only provide the documentation specified in the notice upon examination.

SECTION 5. DRAFTING INFORMATION

The principal author of this notice is J. David Varley of the Office of Associate Chief Counsel (International). For further information regarding this notice, contact Mr. Varley at (202) 435–5262 (not a toll-free call).

ATTACHMENT TO NOTICE 2007–31

WORKING ARRANGEMENT BETWEEN INTERNAL REVENUE SERVICE DEPUTY COMMISSIONER (INTERNATIONAL), LMSB AND BUREAU OF INTERNAL REVENUE UNITED STATES VIRGIN ISLANDS CONCERNING ROUTINE (AUTOMATIC) EXCHANGE OF INFORMATION

I. Introduction

This Working Arrangement between the competent authorities of the United States and the U.S. Virgin Islands (the "parties") sets forth the agreement of the parties with respect to an initiative to facilitate information sharing for tax administration purposes in conjunction with Internal Revenue Service (IRS) Notices 2007–19 and 2007–31.

II. Authority

The authority for this Working Arrangement is the Tax Implementation Agreement between the United States of America and the Virgin Islands dated February 24, 1987 (the "Implementation Agreement"). Pursuant to Article 4(2)(c) of the Implementation Agreement, this Working Arrangement expands the information to be routinely (automatically) exchanged by the U.S. Virgin Islands to the IRS under Article 4(2)(b) of the Implementation Agreement.

III. Purpose

This Working Arrangement serves to carry out the purposes of Notices 2007–19 and 2007–31, by establishing a new routine exchange of information program between the IRS and the U.S. Virgin Islands Bureau of Internal Revenue (BIR) concerning income tax information of certain taxpayers who file an income tax return with U.S. Virgin Islands under section 932(c)(2) of the Internal Revenue Code of 1986, as amended (the "Code"). The IRS will use the information to identify and examine such taxpayers and to encourage those taxpayers to comply with U.S. federal income tax laws and regulations. This Working Arrangement and any requests for information or information exchanged pursuant to it and the Implementation Agreement constitute tax convention information under Code section 6105.

IV. Procedures and Requirements

Unless otherwise agreed to by the parties or specified in the request for information, the parties agree as follows:

A. The IRS will specify the information to be provided by the BIR in a written request for information to the BIR.

B. The BIR will provide electronic files of the requested information, including all income tax returns with schedules, statements, and attachments. The electronic files will be saved, indexed, and transmitted by the BIR to the IRS in accordance with instructions provided in the request for information.

C. All income tax returns will be date stamped by the BIR in a clearly legible manner that does not obstruct any taxpayer information on the return.

D. The BIR will provide all requested information in accordance with the following schedule:

1. With respect to all income tax returns that are timely filed with the BIR, within 90 days after the original due date or, to the extent the taxpayer timely files pursuant to a valid extension, within 90 days after the extended due date.
2. With respect to all delinquent returns, amended returns, and any other requested information filed with the BIR and not covered by paragraph D.1. (above), within 90 days after the end of the calendar-year quarter during which the requested information was received by the BIR.

V. Disclosure, Safeguards, and Recordkeeping Requirements

A. All information obtained under this Working Arrangement must be safeguarded in accordance with the Implementation Agreement as well as the safeguards described in IRS Publication 1075, *Tax Information Security Guidelines for Federal, State, and Local Agencies.*

B. Nothing in this Working Arrangement will cause the IRS or BIR to disclose information that is normally protected by governmental, attorney/client, or attorney work product privileges consistent with applicable laws, or any other information that is prohibited from disclosure. *See* IRM Section 11.3.32.17, *Restrictions on Disclosure of Returns and Return Information.*

C. Neither the IRS nor the BIR will disclose return information that would identify a confidential informant or seriously impair any civil or criminal tax investigation.

D. To the extent the BIR withholds a tax return and/or return information pursuant to paragraphs B. or C. (above), the BIR will provide the IRS with a privilege log that explains in sufficient detail the reason(s) for withholding the information.

VI. Costs

Pursuant to Article 5(3) of the Implementation Agreement, the IRS and the BIR agree not to charge each other for the costs of reproduction of information routinely exchanged. Further, prior to making any claim for reimbursement of extraordinary costs incurred in providing assistance, the BIR will consult with and provide an estimate of such costs to the IRS.

VII. Third Party Rights

This Working Arrangement does not confer any rights or benefits on any third party.

VIII. Taxable Periods

This Working Arrangement applies to income tax returns and other information filed with the USVI for taxable years ending on or after December 31, 2006.

IX. Amendment or Termination

This Working Arrangement will become effective on the date of the last signature below and will remain in force until terminated. This Working Arrangement will terminate on the first of the following to occur:

A. Termination of the Implementation Agreement, in which event this Working Arrangement will automatically terminate on the date on which termination of the Implementation Agreement becomes effective pursuant to Article 9 of the Implementation Agreement; or

B. Mailing or other delivery of written notice of termination by the IRS or the BIR to the other party. However, not less than 30 days prior to delivering such written notice, the terminating party must advise the other party in writing of its reasons for wishing to terminate this Working Arrangement. A notice of termination will be effective with respect to taxable years ending on or after December 31st of the following year. For example, if the BIR provides written notice to the IRS on August 31, 2009, that it is exercising its rights under this termination clause, then the BIR will be relieved of its responsibilities under this Working Arrangement with respect to taxable years ending on or after December 31, 2010.

X. Limitations

The terms of this Working Arrangement are not intended to alter, amend, or rescind any provisions of U.S. federal law. Any provision of this Working Arrangement that conflicts with U.S. federal law will be null and void. Nor are the terms of this Working Arrangement intended to alter, amend, or rescind any provisions of the Implementation Agreement now in effect. In any situation where a conflict arises between the provisions of this Working Arrangement and the Implementation Agreement, the provisions of the latter will govern.

XI. Approvals

For the Virgin Islands Bureau of Internal Revenue:

____

By: Gizette L. Thomas
Acting Director
U.S. Virgin Islands Bureau of Internal Revenue
Signed at _______________, this ____ day of ________, 2007.

For the Internal Revenue Service:

____

By: Frank Y. Ng
Deputy Commissioner (International), LMSB
Internal Revenue Service
Signed at Washington, DC this ____ day of ________, 2007.

26 CFR 601.105: Examination of returns and claims for refund, credit, or abatement; determination of correct tax liability.
(Also: Part I, § 911, 1.911–1.)

Rev. Proc. 2007–28

SECTION 1. PURPOSE

.01 This revenue procedure provides information to any individual who failed to meet the eligibility requirements of § 911(d)(1) of the Internal Revenue Code because adverse conditions in a foreign country precluded the individual from meeting those requirements for taxable year 2006.

.02 This revenue procedure lists the countries for which the eligibility requirements of § 911(d)(1) are waived for taxable year 2006.

SECTION 2. BACKGROUND

.01 Section 911(a) of the Code allows a "qualified individual," as defined in § 911(d)(1), to exclude foreign earned income and housing cost amounts from gross income. Section 911(c)(4) of the Code allows a qualified individual to deduct housing cost amounts from gross income.

.02 Section 911(d)(1) of the Code defines the term "qualified individual" as an individual whose tax home is in a foreign country and who is (A) a citizen of the United States and establishes to the satisfaction of the Secretary of the Treasury that the individual has been a *bona fide* resident of a foreign country or countries for an uninterrupted period that includes an entire taxable year, or (B) a citizen or resident of the United States who, during any period of 12 consecutive months, is present in a foreign country or countries during at least 330 full days.

.03 Section 911(d)(4) of the Code provides an exception to the eligibility requirements of § 911(d)(1). An individual will be treated as a qualified individual with respect to a period in which the individual was a *bona fide* resident of, or was present in, a foreign country, if the individual left the country during a period for which the Secretary of the Treasury, after consultation with the Secretary of State, determines that individuals were required to leave because of war, civil unrest, or similar adverse conditions that precluded the normal conduct of business. An individual must establish that but for those conditions the individual could reasonably have been expected to meet the eligibility requirements.

.04 For 2006, the Secretary of the Treasury, in consultation with the Secretary of State, has determined that war, civil unrest, or similar adverse conditions precluded the normal conduct of business in the following countries beginning on the specified date:

	Date of Departure
Country	*On or after*
East Timor	May 23, 2006
Lebanon	July 27, 2006
Nepal	April 26, 2006

.05 Accordingly, for purposes of § 911 of the Code, an individual who left one of the foregoing countries on or after the specified departure date shall be treated as a qualified individual with respect to the period during which that individual was present in, or was a *bona fide* resident of, such foreign country, if the individual establishes a reasonable expectation of meeting the requirements of § 911(d) but for those conditions.

.06 To qualify for relief under § 911(d)(4) of the Code, an individual must have established residency, or have been physically present, in the foreign country on or prior to the date that the Secretary of the Treasury determines that individuals were required to leave the foreign country. Individuals who establish residency, or are first physically present, in the foreign country after the date that the Secretary prescribes shall not be treated as qualified individuals under § 911(d)(4) of the Code. For example, individuals who are first physically present or establish residency in East Timor after May 23, 2006, are not eligible to qualify for the exception provided in § 911(d)(4) of the Code for taxable year 2006.

SECTION 3. INQUIRIES

A taxpayer who needs assistance on how to claim this exclusion, or on how to file an amended return, should contact a local IRS Office or, for a taxpayer residing or traveling outside the United States, the nearest overseas IRS office.

SECTION 4. DRAFTING INFORMATION

The principal author of this revenue procedure is Kate Y. Hwa of the Office of Associate Chief Counsel (International). For further information regarding this revenue procedure, contact Ms. Hwa at (202) 622–3840 (not a toll-free call).

Part IV. Items of General Interest

Proposed Regulations and Notice of Public Hearing

Effect of Election on Corporation

REG–158677–05

AGENCY: Internal Revenue Service (IRS), Treasury.

ACTION: Proposed regulations and notice of public hearing.

SUMMARY: These proposed regulations clarify that if a bank is an S corporation within the meaning of section 1361(a)(1), its status as an S corporation does not affect the applicability of the special rules for banks under the Internal Revenue Code.

DATES: Written or electronic comments and requests for a public hearing must be received by November 22, 2006.

ADDRESSES: Send submissions to: CC:PA:LPD:PR (REG–158677–05), Room 5203, Internal Revenue Service, POB 7604, Ben Franklin Station, Washington, DC 20044. Alternatively, taxpayers may submit comments electronically via the IRS Internet site at *http://www.irs.gov/regs* or via the Federal eRulemaking Portal at *http://www.regulations.gov* (IRS—REG–158677–05). If a public hearing is requested, the public hearing will be held in the Auditorium, New Carrollton Federal Building, 5000 Ellin Road, Lanham, MD.

FOR FURTHER INFORMATION CONTACT: Concerning the proposed regulations, Laura Fields at (202) 622–3050; concerning submissions and requests for a hearing, *Richard.A.Hurst@irscounsel.treas.gov*, (202) 622–7180 (not toll-free numbers).

SUPPLEMENTARY INFORMATION:

Background

Section 1361(b)(2) describes corporations that are ineligible to be S corporations (ineligible corporations). Until 1996, section 1361(b)(2)(A) treated as ineligible corporations financial institutions to which section 585 applied (without regard to section 585(c)), which included primarily all banks within the meaning of section 581 (section 581 banks). In 1996, Congress revised section 1361(b)(2)(A) to allow certain banks to be S corporations. Under current section 1361(b)(2)(A), a section 581 bank is eligible to be an S corporation only if it does not use the reserve method of accounting for bad debts described in section 585, which is otherwise available to certain banks.

The proposed regulations address issues regarding the application, to S corporation banks, of the special rules applicable to banks under the Internal Revenue Code (Code) (the special bank rules).

First, questions have arisen regarding whether certain language in section 1363(b), enacted in 1982, may prevent S corporation banks from being subject to the special bank rules. Subject to certain exceptions, the general rule of section 1363(b) requires that "[t]he taxable income of an S corporation shall be computed in the same manner as in the case of an individual * * *." The special bank rules, however, apply only to corporations, because section 581 banks must be corporations for Federal tax purposes.

Second, questions have also arisen regarding the impact of section 1363(b)(4), which also pre-dates the 1996 legislation allowing banks to be S corporations. Section 1363(b)(4) applies section 291 to certain S corporations even if they would not otherwise be subject to it. Specifically, section 1363(b)(4) provides, "Section 291 shall apply if the S corporation (or any predecessor) was a C corporation for any of the 3 immediately preceding taxable years." Section 291(a)(3) and (e)(1)(B) is a special bank rule that reduces by 20 percent the amount allowable as a deduction with respect to the portion of a bank's interest expense that is allocable to qualified tax-exempt obligations as defined in section 265(b)(3)(B). This portion of a bank's interest expense is the amount that bears the same ratio to the taxpayer's interest expense as the taxpayer's average adjusted bases of those tax-exempt obligations bears to the taxpayer's average adjusted bases of all its assets.

Explanation of Provisions

The proposed regulations clarify that neither the general rule of section 1363(b), nor paragraph (4) of that section, prevents the special bank rules from applying to banks that are S corporations. When Congress allowed banks to become S corporations, it did not intend to deny them the benefits, or shield them from the burdens, ordinarily applicable to banks. This is reflected in the existing regulations under section 1361. See Sec. 1.1361–4(a)(3) ("If an S corporation is a bank, or if an S corporation makes a valid QSub election for a subsidiary that is a bank, any special rules applicable to banks under the Internal Revenue Code continue to apply separately to the bank parent or bank subsidiary * * * (except as other published guidance may apply section 265(b) and section 291(a)(3) and (e)(1)(B) not only to the bank parent or bank subsidiary but also to any QSub * * *).").

The only special bank rule that Congress made inapplicable to S corporation banks was the section 585 reserve method for bad debts. The restriction in section 1361(b)(2)(A) regarding use of that method would be superfluous if the special bank rules were rendered inapplicable by section 1363(b). The section 585 reserve method is available only to banks, and those banks must be corporations. In amending section 1361(b)(2)(A), therefore, Congress did not expect the pre-existing general rule of section 1363(b) to prevent the special bank rules from applying to S corporation banks. The section 585 reserve method is a special bank rule, and it would have been unnecessary for Congress to make that rule inapplicable to S corporation banks if the special bank rules did not apply to them generally because of section 1363(b).

Section 1363(b)(4) historically subjected certain nonbank S corporations to section 291 if the S corporation (or any predecessor) was a C corporation for any of the 3 immediately preceding taxable years, even if section 291 would not otherwise apply. Section 1363(b)(4) does not provide that section 291 shall not apply in any other circumstance. When Congress enacted section 1363(b)(4) in 1984, banks could not yet be S corporations, and thus section 1363(b)(4) had no applicability to section 291(a)(3) and (e)(1)(B) (which applies only to banks). After the 1996 amendments to subchapter S, the general rule of section 1363(b) does not prevent the special bank rules from applying to S corporations. Thus, if section 291(a)(3) and (e)(1)(B) applies to an S corporation bank in the absence of section 1363(b)(4), section 1363(b)(4) does not affect the continuing application to that bank of section 291(a)(3) and (e)(1)(B).

Effective Date

These regulations are proposed to apply to taxable years of corporations beginning on or after August 24, 2006. No inference should be drawn from this effective date regarding prior taxable years.

Special Analyses

It has been determined that this notice of proposed rulemaking is not a significant regulatory action as defined in Executive Order 12866. Therefore a regulatory assessment is not required. It has also been determined that section 553(b) of the Administrative Procedure Act (5 U.S.C. chapter 5) does not apply to these regulations, and because the regulation does not impose a collection of information on small entities, the Regulatory Flexibility Act (5 U.S.C. chapter 6) does not apply. Pursuant to section 7805(f) of the Code, these proposed regulations will be submitted to the Chief Counsel for Advocacy of the Small Business Administration for comment on its impact on small business.

Comments and Public Hearing

Before these proposed regulations are adopted as final regulations, consideration will be given to any written comments (a signed original and eight (8) copies) or electronic comments that are submitted timely to the IRS. The Treasury Department and the IRS specifically request comments on the clarity of the proposed rules and how they can be made easier to understand. All comments will be available for public inspection and copying. A public hearing will be scheduled if requested in writing by any person that timely submits written comments. If a public hearing is scheduled, notice of the date, time, and place for the public hearing will be published in the Federal Register.

Drafting Information

The principal author of these proposed regulations is Laura Fields, Office of the Associate Chief Counsel (Passthroughs and Special Industries), IRS. However, other personnel from the IRS and Treasury Department participated in their development.

* * * * *

Proposed Amendments to the Regulations

Accordingly, 26 CFR part 1 is proposed to be amended as follows:

PART 1—INCOME TAXES

Paragraph 1. The authority citation for part 1 continues to read, in part, as follows:

Authority: 26 U.S.C. 7805 * * *.

Par. 2. Paragraph (b) of Sec. 1.1363–1 is amended as follows:

1. Paragraph (b) is revised.

2. Paragraph (d) is amended by removing the language "This section applies" and adding the language "This section (except for paragraph (b)(2) of this section) applies" in its place.

3. The paragraph heading for (d) is revised.

4. A sentence is added at the end of paragraph (d).

The revision and additions read as follows:

§1.1363–1 Effect of election on corporation.

* * * * *

(b) *Computation of corporate taxable income*—(1) *In general.* The taxable income of an S corporation is computed as described in section 1363(b).

(2) *Treatment of banks.* Section 1363(b) (concerning computation of an S corporation's taxable income) does not affect an S corporation's status as a bank within the meaning of section 581, and it does not prevent the application to such an S corporation bank of any special rule applicable to banks under the Internal Revenue Code, such as sections 582(c) and 291(a)(3) and (e)(1)(B). See Sec. 1.1361–4(a)(3) regarding application under subchapter S of the special rules applicable to banks. Further, section 1363(b)(4) causes section 291 to apply to an S corporation if the S corporation (or any predecessor) was a C corporation for any of the three immediately preceding taxable years, but section 1363(b)(4) does not prevent section 291 from applying to an S corporation to which section 291 otherwise applies.

(3) *Example.* The following example illustrates the application of this paragraph (b)(2):

Example. (i) *Facts.* X is described in section 581 and is an S corporation. Neither X nor any of X's predecessors was a C corporation for any of the three immediately preceding taxable years. During the current taxable year, X sold debt instrument DI at a loss. At the time of the sale, X's holding period in DI was more than one year and, but for section 582(c), the loss on the sale of DI would be capital. During the same taxable year, X held debt instrument QD, which it acquired after August 7, 1986. QD is a qualified tax-exempt obligation within the meaning of section 265(b)(3)(B).

(ii) X is described in section 581, and section 1363(b) does not affect X's status under section 581. Accordingly, X qualifies as a bank within the meaning of section 581. Also, section 1363(b) does not prevent any special rule applicable to banks under the Internal Revenue Code from applying to X. Thus, section 582(c), which is a special rule applicable to banks, imposes ordinary character on the loss that X recognized from the sale of debt instrument DI.

(iii) Because QD is a qualified tax-exempt obligation that was acquired after August 7, 1986, section 265(b)(3)(A) causes QD to be treated for purposes of section 291(e)(1)(B) as having been acquired on that date. For that reason, if section 291(e)(1)(B) applies to X, a portion of the interest expense that X incurs during the taxable year is interest on indebtedness incurred or continued to purchase or carry qualified tax-exempt obligations and thus is a financial institution preference item. Section 291(a)(3) and (e)(1)(B) is a special rule applicable to banks, and thus section 1363(b) does not prevent section 291(a)(3) and (e)(1)(B) from applying to X unless some other authority prevents that result.

(iv) Section 1363(b)(4) does not prevent section 291 from applying in situations in which section 291 otherwise applies. Therefore, section 1363(b)(4) does not prevent section 291(a)(3) and (e)(1)(B) from applying to X. It is irrelevant that neither X nor any predecessor of X was a C corporation for any of the three immediately preceding taxable years. X's status as a bank under section 581 causes section 291(a)(3) and (e)(1)(B) to apply.

* * * * *

(d) *Effective dates.* * * * Paragraph (b)(2) of this section applies to taxable years of corporations beginning on or after August 24, 2006.

Mark E. Matthews,
Deputy Commissioner for Services and Enforcement.

(Filed by the Office of the Federal Register on August 23, 2006, 8:45 a.m., and published in the issue of the Federal Register for August 24, 2006, 71 F.R. 50007)

Notice of Proposed Rulemaking by Cross-Reference to Temporary Regulations

Corporate Reorganizations; Guidance on the Measurement of Continuity of Interest

REG–146247–06

AGENCY: Internal Revenue Service (IRS), Treasury.

ACTION: Notice of proposed rulemaking by cross-reference to temporary regulations.

SUMMARY: In this issue of the Bulletin, the IRS is issuing temporary regulations (T.D. 9316) that provide guidance regarding the satisfaction of the continuity of interest requirement for corporate reorganizations. The text of those regulations also serves as the text of these proposed regulations.

DATES: Written or electronic comments and requests for a public hearing must be received by June 18, 2007.

ADDRESSES: Send submissions to: CC:PA:LPD:PR (REG–146247–06), room 5203, Internal Revenue Service, PO Box 7604, Ben Franklin Station, Washington, DC 20044. Submissions may be hand-delivered Monday through Friday between the hours of 8 a.m. and 4 p.m. to CC:PA:LPD:PR (REG–146247–06), Courier's Desk, Internal Revenue Service, 1111 Constitution Avenue, NW, Washington, DC, or sent electronically, via the Federal eRulemaking Portal at *http://www.regulations.gov/* (IRS and REG–146247–06).

FOR FURTHER INFORMATION CONTACT: Concerning the proposed regulations, Lisa S. Dobson at (202) 622–7790; concerning submissions of comments and requests for a public hearing, Kelly Banks at (202) 622–0392 (not toll-free numbers).

SUPPLEMENTARY INFORMATION:

Background and Explanation of Provisions

Temporary regulations in this issue of the Bulletin amend the Income Tax Regulations (26 CFR part 1) relating to section 368, which provides for general nonrecognition treatment for reorganizations. In addition to complying with the statutory and certain other requirements, to qualify as a reorganization, a transaction generally must satisfy the continuity of interest (COI) requirement. COI requires that, in substance, a substantial part of the value of the proprietary interests in the target corporation be preserved in the reorganization. The text of those regulations also serves as the text of these proposed regulations. The preamble to the temporary regulations explains the amendments.

Special Analyses

It has been determined that this notice of proposed rulemaking is not a significant regulatory action as defined in Executive Order 12866. Therefore, a regulatory assessment is not required. It has also been determined that section 553(b) of the Administrative Procedure Act (5 U.S.C. chapter 5) does not apply to these regulations, and because the regulation does not impose a collection of information on small entities, the Regulatory Flexibility Act (5 U.S.C. chapter 6) does not apply. Pursuant to section 7805(f) of the Internal Revenue Code, this notice of proposed rulemaking will be submitted to the Chief Counsel for Advocacy of the Small Business Administration for comment on its impact on small business.

Comments and Requests for Public Hearing

Before the proposed regulations are adopted as final regulations, consideration will be given to any written comments (a signed original and eight (8) copies) or electronic comments that are submitted timely to the IRS. Comments are requested on all aspects of the proposed regulations. All comments will be available for public inspection and copying. A public hearing will be scheduled if requested in writing by any person that timely submits written comments. If a public hearing is scheduled, notice of the date, time, and place for the public hearing will be published in the **Federal Register**.

Drafting Information

The principal author of these regulations is Lisa S. Dobson of the Office of the Associate Chief Counsel (Corporate). However, other personnel from the IRS and Treasury Department participated in their development.

* * * * *

Proposed Amendments to the Regulations

Accordingly, 26 CFR part 1 is proposed to be amended as follows:

PART 1—INCOME TAXES

Paragraph 1. The authority citation for part 1 continues to read, in part, as follows:

Authority: 26 U.S.C. 7805 * * *

Par. 2. Section 1.368–1 is amended by:

1. Revising paragraph (e)(2).

2. Revising and redesignating the text of paragraph (e)(8) as paragraph (e)(8)(i).

3. Adding paragraph (e)(8)(ii).

The revisions and addition read as follows:

§1.368–1 Purpose and scope of exception of reorganization exchanges.

[The text of the proposed amendment to §1.368–1(e)(2) and (e)(8) is the same as the text of §1.368–1T(e)(2) and (e)(8) published elsewhere in this issue of the Bulletin].

Kevin M. Brown,
Deputy Commissioner for Services and Enforcement.

(Filed by the Office of the Federal Register on March 19, 2007, 8:45 a.m., and published in the issue of the Federal Register for March 20, 2007, 72 F.R. 13058)

Corporate Reorganizations; Additional Guidance on Distributions Under Sections 368(a)(1)(D) and 354(b)(1)(B); Correction

Announcement 2007–40

AGENCY: Internal Revenue Service (IRS), Treasury.

ACTION: Correcting amendment.

SUMMARY: This document contains corrections to temporary regulations (T.D. 9313, 2007–13 I.R.B. 805) that were published in the **Federal Register** on Thursday, March 1, 2007 (72 FR 9262) providing guidance regarding the qualification of certain transactions as reorganizations described in section 368(a)(1)(D) where no stock and/or securities of the acquiring corporation are issued and distributed in the transaction.

DATES: This correcting amendment is effective March 29, 2007.

FOR FURTHER INFORMATION CONTACT: Bruce A. Decker at (202) 622–7550 (not a toll-free number).

SUPPLEMENTARY INFORMATION:

Background

The temporary regulations that are the subjects of this correction are under section 368 of the Internal Revenue Code.

Need for Correction

As published, temporary regulations (T.D. 9313) contain an error that may prove to be misleading and is in need of clarification.

* * * * *

Correction of Publication

Accordingly, 26 CFR part 1 is corrected by making the following amendments:

PART 1—INCOME TAXES

Paragraph 1. The authority citation for part 1 continues to read, in part, as follows:

Authority: 26 U.S.C. 7805 * * *

Par. 2. Section 1.368–2T is amended by revising paragraph (l)(2)(iv) to read as follows:

§1.368–2T Definition of terms (temporary).

* * * * *

(l) * * *

(2) * * *

(iv) *Exception*. This paragraph (l)(2) of this section does not apply to a transaction otherwise described in §1.358–6(b)(2) or section 368(a)(1)(G) by reason of section 368(a)(2)(D).

* * * * *

LaNita Van Dyke,
Chief, Publications and Regulations Branch, Legal Processing Division, Associate Chief Counsel (Procedure and Administration).

(Filed by the Office of the Federal Register on March 28, 2007, 8:45 a.m., and published in the issue of the Federal Register for March 29, 2007, 72 F.R. 14678)

Announcement of Disciplinary Actions Involving Attorneys, Certified Public Accountants, Enrolled Agents, and Enrolled Actuaries — Suspensions, Censures, Disbarments, and Resignations

Announcement 2007-41

Under Title 31, Code of Federal Regulations, Part 10, attorneys, certified public accountants, enrolled agents, and enrolled actuaries may not accept assistance from, or assist, any person who is under disbarment or suspension from practice before the Internal Revenue Service if the assistance relates to a matter constituting practice before the Internal Revenue Service and may not knowingly aid or abet another person to practice before the Internal Revenue Service during a period of suspension, disbarment, or ineligibility of such other person.

To enable attorneys, certified public accountants, enrolled agents, and enrolled actuaries to identify persons to whom these restrictions apply, the Director, Office of Professional Responsibility, will announce in the Internal Revenue Bulletin their names, their city and state, their professional designation, the effective date of disciplinary action, and the period of suspension. This announcement will appear in the weekly Bulletin at the earliest practicable date after such action and will continue to appear in the weekly Bulletins for five successive weeks.

Consent Suspensions From Practice Before the Internal Revenue Service

Under Title 31, Code of Federal Regulations, Part 10, an attorney, certified public accountant, enrolled agent, or enrolled actuary, in order to avoid the institution or conclusion of a proceeding for his or her disbarment or suspension from practice before the Internal Revenue Service, may offer his or her consent to suspension from such practice. The Director, Office of Professional Responsibility, in his discretion, may suspend an attorney, certified public accountant, enrolled agent, or enrolled actuary in accordance with the consent offered.

The following individuals have been placed under consent suspension from practice before the Internal Revenue Service:

Name	Address	Designation	Date of Suspension
Hankinson, Eugene M.	Somerset, PA	CPA	Indefinite from November 15, 2006
Canzano, Richard M.	Winchester, MA	Attorney	Indefinite from November 20, 2006
Sims, Jr., Lionel	Houston, TX	CPA	Indefinite from November 20, 2006
Wendekier, Raymond J.	Patton, PA	Attorney	Indefinite from November 21, 2006
Golden, Larry	Hinesville, GA	CPA	Indefinite from November 28, 2006
Lane, David B.	Hanover, MA	Attorney	Indefinite from November 28, 2006
Brown, Arthur I.	Miami, FL	CPA	Indefinite from December 1, 2006
Frisk, Daniel J.	Fargo, ND	Attorney	Indefinite from December 1, 2006
Small, Kenneth A.	McMurray, PA	CPA	Indefinite from December 1, 2006
Vazquez, Sonya M.	Port Orchard, WA	CPA	Indefinite from December 1, 2006
Swistak, Anthony	Adams, MA	Enrolled Agent	Indefinite from December 6, 2006
Lenahan, Jr., Robert J.	Elizabeth, NJ	Attorney	Indefinite from December 11, 2006

Name	Address	Designation	Date of Suspension
Hayes, Richard A.	Havervill, MA	Attorney	Indefinite from December 14, 2006
Scheller, Stephen M.	Coppell, TX	CPA	Indefinite from December 15, 2006
Wilson, James M.	Berlin, NJ	CPA	Indefinite from December 15, 2006
Franzese, Joseph P.	Winthrop, MA	Attorney	Indefinite from December 18, 2006
Black, Charles C.	Marietta, GA	Attorney	Indefinite from January 1, 2007
Enright, III, Robert A.	Naples, FL	Attorney	Indefinite from January 1, 2007
Fromovitz, Norman M.	Brooklyn, NY	CPA	Indefinite from January 1, 2007
Saylor, Mary A.	Iowa City, IA	Enrolled Agent	Indefinite from January 1, 2007
Seeherman, Alan	Wynnewood, PA	CPA	Indefinite from January 1, 2007
Beistel, Theodore L.	Canton, OH	CPA	Indefinite from January 3, 2007
Myers, Robert J.	Fairport Harbor, OH	CPA	Indefinite from January 9, 2007
Burrus, Robert V.	Valparaiso, IN	CPA	Indefinite from January 22, 2007
Patterson, Douglas W.	Newburgh, IN	Attorney	Indefinite from January 31, 2007
Lang, Jeffrey H.	Fishers, IN	CPA	Indefinite from January 22, 2007
Chickering, David	Vermillion, SD	CPA	February 5, 2007 to November 4, 2007

Name	Address	Designation	Date of Suspension
Moss, Steve E.	Henderson, NC	CPA	Indefinite from February 5, 2007
Hazlip, Kevin	Orange Park, FL	Enrolled Agent	Indefinite from February 10, 2007
Adelson, Robert A.	Newton, MA	Attorney	Indefinite from February 15, 2007
Boyer, Daniel D.	North Judson, IN	CPA	Indefinite from February 15, 2007
LaRusso, Anthony J.	North Caldwell, NJ	Attorney	Indefinite from February 15, 2007
Martin, Spencer R.	Lancaster, PA	CPA	Indefinite from February 15, 2007
Hursh, Stephanie S.	Brush Prairie, WA	Enrolled Agent	Indefinite from February 20, 2007
Guidera, George C.	Weston, CT	Attorney	Indefinite from February 26, 2007
Ruth, Christopher A.	Cypress, CA	CPA	Indefinite from February 27, 2007
Elias, Lenard S.	El Cajon, CA	Enrolled Agent	Indefinite from March 1, 2007
Ikeji, Chuck	Orlando, FL	CPA	Indefinite from March 1, 2007
Lewis, Craig S.	Savannah, GA	CPA	Indefinite from March 1, 2007
Sloan, Eric R.	Brighton, MI	CPA	Indefinite from March 1, 2007
Gostomski, Michael	Stamford, CT	CPA	Indefinite from March 5, 2007
Hafer, Charles J.	Hamburg, PA	Enrolled Agent	Indefinite from March 5, 2007
Jones, Phillip G.	Andalusia, AL	Enrolled Agent	Indefinite from March 7, 2007

Name	Address	Designation	Date of Suspension
Agashiwala, Mahesh J.	New York, NY	CPA	Indefinite from March 22, 2007
Berndgen, Michael	Plantation, FL	CPA	Indefinite from April 1, 2007
Grahn, Charles R.	Indianapolis, IN	Attorney	Indefinite from April 1, 2007
Shaw, G. Joyce	Hebron, KY	Enrolled Agent	Indefinite from April 1, 2007
Pikaart, Jr., Edward H.	N. Branford, CT	CPA	Indefinite from April 10, 2007
Kelley, Richard S.	Beverly, MA	Attorney	Indefinite from May 1, 2007
Crabtree, Michael L.	San Dimas, CA	Enrolled Agent	Indefinite from May 15, 2007
Hausmann, Mark D.	Troy, NY	Attorney	Indefinite from May 15, 2007

Expedited Suspensions From Practice Before the Internal Revenue Service

Under Title 31, Code of Federal Regulations, Part 10, the Director, Office of Professional Responsibility, is authorized to immediately suspend from practice before the Internal Revenue Service any practitioner who, within five years from the date the expedited proceeding is instituted (1) has had a license to practice as an attorney, certified public accountant, or actuary suspended or revoked for cause or (2) has been convicted of certain crimes.

The following individuals have been placed under suspension from practice before the Internal Revenue Service by virtue of the expedited proceeding provisions:

Name	Address	Designation	Date of Suspension
Hatchett, William M.	Pontiac, MI	Attorney	Indefinite from November 13, 2006
Jacobs, Mark L.	Jackson Heights, NY	Attorney	Indefinite from November 21, 2006
Sylver, Peter T.	E. Longmeadow, MA	Attorney	Indefinite from November 21, 2006

Name	Address	Designation	Date of Suspension
Portlock, David R.	Pensacola, FL	Enrolled Agent	Indefinite from November 27, 2006
Ascher, Michael P.	North Port, FL	Attorney	Indefinite from November 28, 2006
Barrett, Norman W.	Dover, DE	CPA	Indefinite from November 28, 2006
Burd, Gene	Houston, TX	Attorney	Indefinite from November 28, 2006
Caceres, Carlos H.	Silver Spring, MD	Attorney	Indefinite from November 28, 2006
Carrabotta, Peter S.	Niles, IL	Attorney	Indefinite from November 28, 2006
Davis, Carleton W.	St. Louis, MO	Attorney	Indefinite from November 28, 2006
Frasier, Roland B.	Rancho Santa Fe, CA	Attorney	Indefinite from November 28, 2006
Hubbard, Edward	Chicago, IL	Attorney	Indefinite from November 28, 2006
Hynes, Richard W.	Brookline, MA	Attorney	Indefinite from November 28, 2006
Johnson, Barbara C.	Andover, MA	Attorney	Indefinite from November 28, 2006
Konas, Theodore V.	Lancaster, PA	CPA	Indefinite from November 28, 2006
Korson, Daniel M.	Muskegon, MI	CPA	Indefinite from November 28, 2006
Lee, III, Norman J.	Collegeville, PA	Attorney	Indefinite from November 28, 2006
Loiben, Alan A.	Skokie, IL	Attorney	Indefinite from November 28, 2006

Name	Address	Designation	Date of Suspension
McGarry, Thomas H.	Denver, CO	Attorney	Indefinite from November 28, 2006
Roberts, Quinton D.	Elkridge, MD	Attorney	Indefinite from November 28, 2006
Schofield, Peter L.	Spencer, MA	Attorney	Indefinite from November 28, 2006
Shultz, Ryan K.	Mitchell, NE	Attorney	Indefinite from November 28, 2006
Stenger, Jeanne P.	Temecula, CA	Attorney	Indefinite from November 28, 2006
Wood, Gary K.	Edina, MN	Attorney	Indefinite from November 28, 2006
Bakare, Adigun S.	Laurel, MD	Attorney	Indefinite from December 6, 2006
Biagini, Marc J.	Downers Grove, IL	Attorney	Indefinite from December 6, 2006
Birchall, Richard G.	Brewster, MA	Attorney	Indefinite from December 6, 2006
Brown, Edward E.	Indianapolis, IN	Attorney	Indefinite from December 6, 2006
Cunningham, Jr., Shirley A.	Ft. Lauderdale, FL	Attorney	Indefinite from December 6, 2006
Docherty, Scott R.	Branson West, MO	Attorney	Indefinite from December 6, 2006
Dressler, Peter P.	West Chicago, IL	Attorney	Indefinite from December 6, 2006
Henry, William J.	Irvington, NJ	Attorney	Indefinite from December 6, 2006
Hubbard, Cynthia A.	Geneva, IL	Attorney	Indefinite from December 6, 2006
Jackson, Jr., Donald H.	Hanover, MA	Attorney	Indefinite from December 6, 2006

Name	Address	Designation	Date of Suspension
Katz, Norman H.	Owings Mills, MD	Attorney	Indefinite from December 6, 2006
Lakin, Leonard S.	Wellesley Hills, MA	Attorney	Indefinite from December 6, 2006
McGreevy, Jacqueline K.	Carbondale, CO	Attorney	Indefinite from December 6, 2006
Zepp, Dale D.	Ferguson, MO	Attorney	Indefinite from December 6, 2006
Triplett, Austin H.	Homewood, IL	Attorney	Indefinite from December 11, 2006
Murphy, Patrick W.	Honolulu, HI	Attorney	Indefinite from December 11, 2006
Cronin, Jr., Edward M.	Cambridge, MA	Attorney	Indefinite from December 11, 2006
Christof, Kevin F.	Santa Monica, CA	Attorney	Indefinite from December 21, 2006
Heath, Kenneth J.	Canaan, VT	CPA	Indefinite from December 21, 2006
Madigan, Brian C.	Binghamton, NY	Attorney	Indefinite from December 21, 2006
Malloy, Terry P.	Tulsa, OK	Attorney	Indefinite from December 21, 2006
Baynes, Robert M.	Indianapolis, IN	CPA	Indefinite from December 27, 2006
Ceresa, Richard A.	Woodbridge, CA	CPA	Indefinite from December 27, 2006
Crews, Richard A.	Henderson, CO	Attorney	Indefinite from December 27, 2006
Menkveld, Paul G.	Tucson, AZ	Attorney	Indefinite from December 27, 2006
Worischeck, Joseph H.	Tempe, AZ	Attorney	Indefinite from December 27, 2006

Name	Address	Designation	Date of Suspension
Brown, Kirk P.	Pueblo, CO	Attorney	Indefinite from December 28, 2006
Dowling, Stanley W.	Scotts Valley, CA	CPA	Indefinite from December 28, 2006
Simmons, Henry L.	Greensboro, NC	CPA	Indefinite from December 28, 2006
Steele, Regina D.	San Diego, CA	Attorney	Indefinite from December 29, 2006
Craig, III, William A.	Austin, TX	Attorney	Indefinite from January 1, 2007
Acker, Thomas R.	Hollis Center, ME	Attorney	Indefinite from January 8, 2007
Baxter, Laura M.	Monee, IL	CPA	Indefinite from January 8, 2007
Herald, Sally J.	Cold Spring, KY	Attorney	Indefinite from January 8, 2007
Klapheke, II, William T.	Bowling Green, KY	Attorney	Indefinite from January 8, 2007
McCarthy, Charles C.	Encino, CA	Attorney	Indefinite from January 8, 2007
Bolling, Darius C.	Chicago, IL	CPA	Indefinite from January 10, 2007
Breitlauch, Linda	Saylorsburg, PA	Attorney	Indefinite from January 10, 2007
Coddington, Paul F.	Concord, NH	Attorney	Indefinite from January 10, 2007
Davis, Jr., William E.	Pinehurst, TX	CPA	Indefinite from January 10, 2007
Esola, Louis A.	Greensburg, PA	CPA	Indefinite from January 10, 2007
Finch, Judith A.	Walnut Creek, CA	Attorney	Indefinite from January 10, 2007

Name	Address	Designation	Date of Suspension
Jeing, Thomas C.	San Francisco, CA	Attorney	Indefinite from January 10, 2007
Ledbetter, Dean D.	Pelham, AL	CPA	Indefinite from January 10, 2007
McDiarmid, Katherine B.	Greensboro, NC	Attorney	Indefinite from January 10, 2007
Mills, George P.	Oceanside, CA	Attorney	Indefinite from January 10, 2007
Rather, James L.	Irvine, CA	Attorney	Indefinite from January 10, 2007
Rivera, Eduardo M.	Torrance, CA	Attorney	Indefinite from January 10, 2007
Stepovich, Michael A.	Fairbanks, AK	Attorney	Indefinite from January 10, 2007
Ulbrich, David L.	Woodland Hills, CA	CPA	Indefinite from January 10, 2007
Swanson, Todd-Ellis	Greenville, SC	CPA	Indefinite from January 20, 2007
Rubin, Deborah L.	Delray Beach, FL	Attorney	Indefinite from January 26, 2007
Wood, Brent E.	Cary, NC	Attorney	Indefinite from January 26, 2007
Currin, Samuel T.	Raleigh, NC	Attorney	Indefinite from February 7, 2007
Lupo, Robert N.	Weston, MA	Attorney	Indefinite from February 20, 2007
Taggart, Lawrence W.	El Cajon, CA	Attorney	Indefinite from March 7, 2007
Fife, III, James H.	Schererville, IN	Attorney	Indefinite from March 8, 2007
Katsis, Kevin G.	Riverside, IL	Attorney	Indefinite from March 8, 2007

Name	Address	Designation	Date of Suspension
O'Driscoll, Dennis M.	Quincy, MA	Attorney	Indefinite from March 8, 2007
Siever, Beth F.	Austin, TX	Attorney	Indefinite from March 8, 2007
Wheatley-Clark, Sheila R.	Houston, TX	CPA	Indefinite from March 8, 2007

Suspensions From Practice Before the Internal Revenue Service After Notice and an Opportunity for a Proceeding

Under Title 31, Code of Federal Regulations, Part 10, after notice and an opportunity for a proceeding before an administrative law judge, the following individuals have been placed under suspension from practice before the Internal Revenue Service:

Name	Address	Designation	Effective Date
Redmond, Debra	Gifford, PA	Enrolled Agent	Indefinite from March 5, 2007

Disbarments From Practice Before the Internal Revenue Service After Notice and an Opportunity for a Proceeding

Under Title 31, Code of Federal Regulations, Part 10, after notice and an opportunity for a proceeding before an administrative law judge, the following individuals have been disbarred from practice before the Internal Revenue Service:

Name	Address	Designation	Effective Date
Brookstein, Gary	Huntingdon Valley, PA	CPA	December 15, 2006
James T. Jubb	Baltimore, MD	CPA	December 15, 2006

Censure Issued by Consent

Under Title 31, Code of Federal Regulations, Part 10, in lieu of a proceeding being instituted or continued, an attorney, certified public accountant, enrolled agent, or enrolled actuary, may offer his or her consent to the issuance of a censure. Censure is a public reprimand.

The following individuals have consented to the issuance of a Censure:

Name	Address	Designation	Date of Censure
Zucker, Robert W.	Boca Raton, FL	CPA	November 14, 2006
Montgomery, David E.	Pleasanton, CA	Enrolled Agent	November 15, 2006

Name	Address	Designation	Date of Censure
Higgins, James M.	S. Boston, MA	Attorney	December 1, 2006
Pennington, Debra L.	Lees Summit, MO	Enrolled Agent	January 29, 2007
Goodwin, Steven C.	Concord, MA	Attorney	February 2, 2007
Francis, Andrew W.E.	Houston, TX	CPA	February 21, 2007
Griffin, Richard M.	Duluth, GA	CPA	February 28, 2007

Resignations of Enrolled Agents

Under Title 31, Code of Federal Regulations, Part 10, an enrolled agent, in order to avoid the institution or conclusion of a proceeding for his or her disbarment or suspension from practice before the Internal Revenue Service, may offer his or her resignation as an enrolled agent. The Director, Office of Professional Responsibility, in his discretion, may accept the offered resignation.

The Director, Office of Professional Responsibility, has accepted offers of resignation as an enrolled agent from the following individuals:

Name	Address	Date of Resignation
Filipski, Kenneth M.	Bakersfield, CA	April 16, 2007

Part I. Rulings and Decisions Under the Internal Revenue Code of 1986

Section 34.—Certain Uses of Gasoline and Special Fuels

A notice provides guidance on the credits and payments provided for renewable diesel and renewable diesel mixtures under sections 34, 40A, 6426, and 6427. See Notice 2007-37, page 1002.

Section 40A.—Biodiesel and Renewable Diesel Used as Fuel

A notice provides guidance on the credits and payments provided for renewable diesel and renewable diesel mixtures under sections 34, 40A, 6426, and 6427. See Notice 2007-37, page 1002.

Section 263A.—Capitalization and Inclusion in Inventory Costs of Certain Expenses

26 CFR 1.263A–1: Uniform capitalization of costs.

T.D. 9318

DEPARTMENT OF THE TREASURY
Internal Revenue Service
26 CFR Part 1

Guidance Regarding the Simplified Service Cost Method and the Simplified Production Method

AGENCY: Internal Revenue Service (IRS), Treasury.

ACTION: Final regulations and removal of temporary regulations.

SUMMARY: This document contains final regulations relating to the capitalization of costs under the simplified service cost method and the simplified production method provided by the Income Tax Regulations. For taxpayers that use the simplified service cost method or the simplified production method, the regulations clarify when self-constructed assets are produced on a routine and repetitive basis in the ordinary course of their businesses.

DATES: *Effective Date:* These regulations are effective on March 29, 2007.

Applicability Date: For dates of applicability, see §§1.263A–1(l) and 1.263A–2(f).

FOR FURTHER INFORMATION CONTACT: Steven J. Gee or Donna M. Crawford, (202) 622–4970 (not a toll-free number).

SUPPLEMENTARY INFORMATION:

Background

This document contains amendments to 26 CFR part 1. On August 2, 2005, the IRS and Treasury Department published in the **Federal Register** a notice of proposed rulemaking (REG–121584–05, 2005–2 C.B. 523 [70 FR 44535]) by cross reference to temporary regulations (T.D. 9217, 2005–2 C.B. 498 [70 FR 44467]) (collectively, the 2005 regulations) under section 263A of the Internal Revenue Code (Code). These regulations provide that self-constructed tangible personal property is considered produced on a routine and repetitive basis in the ordinary course of a taxpayer's trade or business for purposes of the simplified service cost method or the simplified production method when units of tangible personal property are mass-produced, that is, numerous substantially identical assets are manufactured within a taxable year using standardized designs and assembly line techniques, and the applicable recovery period of such assets under section 168(c) is not longer than 3 years.

The IRS and Treasury Department issued Rev. Proc. 2006–11, 2006–3 I.R.B. 309, see §601.601(d)(2)(ii)(*b*), which provides procedures by which a taxpayer changing its method of accounting to comply with §1.263A–1T or §1.263A–2T (issued under T.D. 9217) for its first taxable year ending on or after August 2, 2005, may request the consent of the Commissioner utilizing either the administrative procedures for requesting the advance consent of the Commissioner (for further guidance, for example, see Rev. Proc. 97–27, 1997–1 C.B. 680, as modified and amplified by Rev. Proc. 2002–19, 2002–1 C.B. 696, as amplified and clarified by Rev. Proc. 2002–54, 2002–2 C.B. 432, and §601.601(d)(2)(ii)(*b*)), or the administrative procedures for obtaining the automatic consent of the Commissioner (for further guidance, for example, see Rev. Proc. 2002–9, 2002–1 C.B. 327, as modified and clarified by Announcement 2002–17, 2002–1 C.B. 561, modified and amplified by Rev. Proc. 2002–19, 2002–1 C.B. 696, and amplified, clarified, and modified by Rev. Proc. 2002–54, 2002–2 C.B. 432, and §601.601(d)(2)(ii)(*b*)). These final regulations have been revised to be consistent with the procedures provided in Rev. Proc. 2006–11.

One written comment was received in response to the 2005 regulations. No requests to speak at a public hearing were received, and no hearing was held. After consideration of the comment, the proposed regulations under section 263A are adopted by this Treasury decision.

Summary of Comments

A commentator expressed the belief that the categories of property, as described in Notice 88–86, 1988–2 C.B. 401, see §601.601(d)(2)(ii)(*b*), eligible for the simplified service cost method and the simplified production method represent a reasonable balance between technical accuracy and simplification. The commentator opposed the requirements in the 2005 regulations that, to qualify for the category of property "produced on a routine and repetitive basis," the property must be mass-produced using standardized designs and assembly line techniques, and have an applicable recovery period of not longer than 3 years. The commentator argued that, with respect to electric utility companies, there is no sound tax policy to support limiting the application of the methods based on the manner in which self-constructed assets are produced or the number of years over which the self-constructed assets are depreciated. The commentator further stated that the preamble to the 2005 regulations did not explain why there may be a distortion of income from the use of the simplified methods, and why such a distortion justified distinctions based on the method of manufacturing and the recovery lives of property.

The simplified methods are less accurate and less precise than a facts and circumstances method and, thus, may capitalize more or less costs than a facts and circumstances method. Therefore, the simplified methods may cause distortions when compared to a more accurate facts and circumstances method. The amount of distortion may not be very large for assets that are mass produced, because the underlying assumption of the simplified methods that costs are incurred ratably across all the assets may be appropriate. Additionally, any distortion caused by the lack of precision quickly reverses if the assets to which the methods may be applied typically have a high turnover rate, that is, a short recovery period. Inventory production frequently meets one or both of these two criteria. The IRS and Treasury Department provided the simplified methods for inventory because the reduction in the burdens of complying with the uniform capitalization rules generally outweighed the possible distortion within the simplified methods.

Under temporary regulations published in the **Federal Register** on March 30, 1987 (T.D. 8131, 1987–1 C.B. 98 [52 FR 10052]) (1987 regulations), the simplified methods were available only to inventory and non-inventory property held by a taxpayer primarily for sale to customers in the ordinary course of the taxpayer's trade or business. The preamble to the 1987 regulations stated that the methods were "designed to alleviate the administrative burdens of complying with [section 263A] where mass production of assets occurs on a repetitive and routine basis, with a typically high 'turnover' rate for the produced assets." The preamble to the 1987 regulations stated that the simplified methods could not be utilized with respect to self-constructed assets because the simplified methods were not appropriate for use "in accounting for casual or occasional production of property."

In response to comments suggesting that the categories of property eligible for the simplified service cost method and the simplified production method be expanded to include other categories of property with similar characteristics, Notice 88–86 expanded the availability of the methods, in relevant part, to "property constructed by a taxpayer for use in its trade or business if, in the ordinary course of its production activities, the taxpayer produces such property on a routine and repetitive basis (that is, the taxpayer produces numerous items of such property within a taxable year)." The final regulations published in the **Federal Register** on August 9, 1993 (T.D. 8482, 1993–2 C.B. 77 [58 FR 42198]) included the new category from Notice 88–86. The addition of certain self-constructed assets was merely intended to add another category of property with characteristics similar to inventory (mass produced or high turnover) and was not an indication that the application of the simplified methods to the production, whether or not casual or occasional, of all self-produced assets was considered appropriate.

The IRS and Treasury Department continue to believe that to prevent distortion when applied to self-constructed property, the simplified service cost method and simplified production method should be limited to property that is mass produced and has a typically high "turnover" rate. Accordingly, the final regulations do not incorporate the commentator's suggestions. The regulations clarify, however, that property with a typically high "turnover" rate includes materials and supplies that are used and consumed within three years of being produced.

The IRS and Treasury Department recognize that the application of the uniform capitalization requirements to self-constructed property can be burdensome, particularly to small taxpayers. The IRS and Treasury Department will consider proposing simplified methods for self-constructed property for small taxpayers in future guidance under section 263A.

Additionally, a commentator indicated that for taxpayers that have both property that is eligible for the simplified methods and property that is ineligible for the simplified methods, the regulations do not provide specific procedures to determine how to allocate service costs and other indirect costs between the eligible property and the ineligible property. The IRS and Treasury Department agree that service costs and other indirect costs must be allocated to ineligible property as well as eligible property. However, prescribing specific procedures and methods for these allocations is beyond the scope of these regulations. The IRS and Treasury Department may address this issue in future guidance.

Special Analyses

It has been determined that this Treasury decision is not a significant regulatory action as defined in Executive Order 12866. Therefore, a regulatory assessment is not required. It also has been determined that section 553(b) of the Administrative Procedure Act (5 U.S.C. chapter 5) does not apply to these regulations, and because the regulations do not impose a collection of information on small entities, the Regulatory Flexibility Act (5 U.S.C. chapter 6) does not apply. Pursuant to section 7805(f) of the Code, the notice of proposed rulemaking that preceded these regulations was submitted to the Chief Counsel for Advocacy of the Small Business Administration for comment on its impact on small business.

Drafting Information

The principal author of these regulations is Scott Rabinowitz of the Office of Associate Chief Counsel (Income Tax and Accounting). However, other personnel from the IRS and Treasury Department participated in their development.

* * * * *

Adoption of Amendments to the Regulations

Accordingly, 26 CFR part 1 is amended as follows:

PART 1—INCOME TAXES

Paragraph 1. The authority citation for part 1 continues to read in part as follows:

Authority: 26 U.S.C. 7805 * * *

Par. 2. Section 1.263A–1 is amended by revising paragraphs (h)(2)(i)(D), (k) and (l) to read as follows:

§1.263A–1 Uniform capitalization of costs.

* * * * *

(h) * * *

(2) * * *

(i) * * *

(D) *Self-constructed tangible personal property produced on a routine and repet-*

itive basis—(*1*) *In general.* Self-constructed tangible personal property produced by the taxpayer on a routine and repetitive basis in the ordinary course of the taxpayer's trade or business. Self-constructed tangible personal property is produced by the taxpayer on a routine and repetitive basis in the ordinary course of the taxpayer's trade or business when units of tangible personal property (as defined in §1.263A–10(c)) are mass-produced, that is, numerous substantially identical assets are manufactured within a taxable year using standardized designs and assembly line techniques, and either the applicable recovery period of the property determined under section 168(c) is not longer than 3 years or the property is a material or supply that will be used and consumed within 3 years of being produced. For purposes of this paragraph (h)(2)(i)(D), the applicable recovery period of the assets will be determined at the end of the taxable year in which the assets are placed in service for purposes of §1.46–3(d). Subsequent changes to the applicable recovery period after the assets are placed in service will not affect the determination of whether the assets are produced on a routine and repetitive basis for purposes of this paragraph (h)(2)(i)(D).

(*2*) *Examples.* The following examples illustrate this paragraph (h)(2)(i)(D):

Example 1. Y is a manufacturer of automobiles. During the taxable year, Y produces numerous substantially identical dies and molds using standardized designs and assembly line techniques. The dies and molds have a 3-year applicable recovery period for purposes of section 168(c). Y uses the dies and molds to produce or process particular automobile components and does not hold them for sale. The dies and molds are produced on a routine and repetitive basis in the ordinary course of Y's business for purposes of this paragraph because the dies and molds are both mass-produced and have a recovery period of not longer than 3 years.

Example 2. Z is an electric utility that regularly manufactures and installs identical poles that are used in transmitting and distributing electricity. The poles have a 20-year applicable recovery period for purposes of section 168(c). The poles are not produced on a routine and repetitive basis in the ordinary course of Z's business for purposes of this paragraph because the poles have an applicable recovery period that is longer than 3 years.

* * * * *

(k) *Change in method of accounting*—(1) *In general.* A change in a taxpayer's treatment of mixed service costs to comply with paragraph (h)(2)(i)(D) of this section is a change in method of accounting to which the provisions of sections 446 and 481 and the regulations under those sections apply. See §1.263A–7. For a taxpayer's first taxable year ending on or after August 2, 2005, the taxpayer is granted the consent of the Commissioner to change its method of accounting to comply with paragraph (h)(2)(i)(D) of this section, provided the taxpayer follows the administrative procedures, as modified by paragraphs (k)(2) through (4) of this section, issued under §1.446–1(e)(3)(ii) for obtaining the Commissioner's automatic consent to a change in accounting method (for further guidance, for example, see Rev. Proc. 2002–9, 2002–1 C.B. 327, as modified and clarified by Announcement 2002–17, 2002–1 C.B. 561, modified and amplified by Rev. Proc. 2002–19, 2002–1 C.B. 696, and amplified, clarified, and modified by Rev. Proc. 2002–54, 2002–2 C.B. 432, and §601.601(d)(2)(ii)(*b*) of this chapter). For purposes of Form 3115, "*Application for Change in Accounting Method*," the designated number for the automatic accounting method change authorized by this paragraph (k) is "95." If Form 3115 is revised or renumbered, any reference in this section to that form is treated as a reference to the revised or renumbered form. Alternatively, notwithstanding the provisions of any administrative procedures that preclude a taxpayer from requesting the advance consent of the Commissioner to change a method of accounting that is required to be made pursuant to a published automatic change procedure, for its first taxable year ending on or after August 2, 2005, a taxpayer may request the advance consent of the Commissioner to change its method of accounting to comply with paragraph (h)(2)(i)(D) of this section, provided the taxpayer follows the administrative procedures, as modified by paragraphs (k)(2) through (5) of this section, for obtaining the advance consent of the Commissioner (for further guidance, for example, see Rev. Proc. 97–27, 1997–1 C.B. 680, as modified and amplified by Rev. Proc. 2002–19, 2002–1 C.B. 696, as amplified and clarified by Rev. Proc. 2002–54, 2002–2 C.B. 432, and §601.601(d)(2)(ii)(*b*) of this chapter). For the taxpayer's second and subsequent taxable years ending on or after August 2, 2005, requests to secure the consent of the Commissioner must be made under the administrative procedures, as modified by paragraphs (k)(3) and (4) of this section, for obtaining the Commissioner's advance consent to a change in accounting method.

(2) *Scope limitations.* Any limitations on obtaining the automatic consent or advance consent of the Commissioner do not apply to a taxpayer seeking to change its method of accounting to comply with paragraph (h)(2)(i)(D) of this section for its first taxable year ending on or after August 2, 2005.

(3) *Audit protection.* A taxpayer that changes its method of accounting in accordance with this paragraph (k) to comply with paragraph (h)(2)(i)(D) of this section does not receive audit protection if its method of accounting for mixed service costs is an issue under consideration at the time the application is filed with the national office.

(4) *Section 481(a) adjustment.* A change in method of accounting to conform to paragraph (h)(2)(i)(D) of this section requires a section 481(a) adjustment. The section 481(a) adjustment period is two taxable years for a net positive adjustment for an accounting method change that is made to conform to paragraph (h)(2)(i)(D) of this section.

(5) *Time for requesting change.* Notwithstanding the provisions of §1.446–1(e)(3)(i) and any contrary administrative procedure, a taxpayer may submit a request for advance consent to change its method of accounting to comply with paragraph (h)(2)(i)(D) of this section for its first taxable year ending on or after August 2, 2005, on or before the date that is 30 days after the end of the taxable year for which the change is requested.

(l) *Effective date.* Paragraphs (h)(2)(i)(D), (k), and (l) of this section apply for taxable years ending on or after August 2, 2005.

§1.263A–1T [Removed]

Par. 3. Section 1.263A–1T is removed.

Par. 4. Section 1.263A–2 is amended by revising paragraphs (b)(2)(i)(D), (e) and (f) to read as follows:

§1.263A–2 Rules relating to property produced by the taxpayer.

* * * * *

(b) * * *

(2) * * *

(i) * * *

(D) *Self-constructed tangible personal property produced on a routine and repetitive basis—(1) In general.* Self-constructed tangible personal property produced by the taxpayer on a routine and repetitive basis in the ordinary course of the taxpayer's trade or business. Self-constructed tangible personal property is produced by the taxpayer on a routine and repetitive basis in the ordinary course of the taxpayer's trade or business when units of tangible personal property (as defined in §1.263A–10(c)) are mass-produced, that is, numerous substantially identical assets are manufactured within a taxable year using standardized designs and assembly line techniques, and either the applicable recovery period of the property determined under section 168(c) is not longer than 3 years or the property is a material or supply that will be used and consumed within 3 years of being produced. For purposes of this paragraph (b)(2)(i)(D), the applicable recovery period of the assets will be determined at the end of the taxable year in which the assets are placed in service for purposes of §1.46–3(d). Subsequent changes to the applicable recovery period after the assets are placed in service will not affect the determination of whether the assets are produced on a routine and repetitive basis for purposes of this paragraph (b)(2)(i)(D).

(2) *Examples.* The following examples illustrate this paragraph (b)(2)(i)(D):

Example 1. Y is a manufacturer of automobiles. During the taxable year Y produces numerous substantially identical dies and molds using standardized designs and assembly line techniques. The dies and molds have a 3-year applicable recovery period for purposes of section 168(c). Y uses the dies and molds to produce or process particular automobile components and does not hold them for sale. The dies and molds are produced on a routine and repetitive basis in the ordinary course of Y's business for purposes of this paragraph because the dies and molds are both mass-produced and have a recovery period of not longer than 3 years.

Example 2. Z is an electric utility that regularly manufactures and installs identical poles that are used in transmitting and distributing electricity. The poles have a 20-year applicable recovery period for purposes of section 168(c). The poles are not produced on a routine and repetitive basis in the ordinary course of Z's business for purposes of this paragraph because the poles have an applicable recovery period that is longer than 3 years.

* * * * *

(e) *Change in method of accounting—*(1) *In general.* A change in a taxpayer's treatment of additional section 263A costs to comply with paragraph (b)(2)(i)(D) of this section is a change in method of accounting to which the provisions of sections 446 and 481 and the regulations under those sections apply. See §1.263A–7. For a taxpayer's first taxable year ending on or after August 2, 2005, the taxpayer is granted the consent of the Commissioner to change its method of accounting to comply with paragraph (b)(2)(i)(D) of this section, provided the taxpayer follows the administrative procedures, as modified by paragraphs (e)(2) through (4) of this section, issued under §1.446–1(e)(3)(ii) for obtaining the Commissioner's automatic consent to a change in accounting method (for further guidance, for example, see Rev. Proc. 2002–9, 2002–1 C.B. 327, as modified and clarified by Announcement 2002–17, 2002–1 C.B. 561, modified and amplified by Rev. Proc. 2002–19, 2002–1 C.B. 696, and amplified, clarified, and modified by Rev. Proc. 2002–54, 2002–2 C.B. 432, and §601.601(d)(2)(ii)(*b*) of this chapter). For purposes of Form 3115, "*Application for Change in Accounting Method*," the designated number for the automatic accounting method change authorized by this paragraph (e) is "95." If Form 3115 is revised or renumbered, any reference in this section to that form is treated as a reference to the revised or renumbered form. Alternatively, notwithstanding the provisions of any administrative procedures that preclude a taxpayer from requesting the advance consent of the Commissioner to change a method of accounting that is required to be made pursuant to a published automatic change procedure, for its first taxable year ending on or after August 2, 2005, a taxpayer may request the advance consent of the Commissioner to change its method of accounting to comply with paragraph (b)(2)(i)(D) of this section, provided the taxpayer follows the administrative procedures, as modified by paragraphs (e)(2) through (5) of this section, for obtaining the advance consent of the Commissioner (for further guidance, for example, see Rev. Proc. 97–27, 1997–1 C.B. 680, as modified and amplified by Rev. Proc. 2002–19, 2002–1 C.B. 696, as amplified and clarified by Rev. Proc. 2002–54, 2002–2 C.B. 432, and §601.601(d)(2)(ii)(*b*) of this chapter). For the taxpayer's second and subsequent taxable years ending on or after August 2, 2005, requests to secure the consent of the Commissioner must be made under the administrative procedures, as modified by paragraphs (e)(3) and (4) of this section, for obtaining the Commissioner's advance consent to a change in accounting method.

(2) *Scope limitations.* Any limitations on obtaining the automatic consent or advance consent of the Commissioner do not apply to a taxpayer seeking to change its method of accounting to comply with paragraph (b)(2)(i)(D) of this section for its first taxable year ending on or after August 2, 2005.

(3) *Audit protection.* A taxpayer that changes its method of accounting in accordance with this paragraph (e) to comply with paragraph (b)(2)(i)(D) of this section does not receive audit protection if its method of accounting for additional section 263A costs is an issue under consideration at the time the application is filed with the national office.

(4) *Section 481(a) adjustment.* A change in method of accounting to conform to paragraph (b)(2)(i)(D) of this section requires a section 481(a) adjustment. The section 481(a) adjustment period is two taxable years for a net positive adjustment for an accounting method change that is made to conform to paragraph (b)(2)(i)(D) of this section.

(5) *Time for requesting change.* Notwithstanding the provisions of §1.446–1(e)(3)(i) and any contrary administrative procedure, a taxpayer may submit a request for advance consent to change its method of accounting to comply with paragraph (b)(2)(i)D) of this section for its first taxable year ending on or after August 2, 2005, on or before the date that is 30 days after the end of the taxable year for which the change is requested.

(f) *Effective date.* Paragraphs (b)(2)(i)(D), (e), and (f) of this section apply for taxable years ending on or after August 2, 2005.

§1.263A–2T **[Removed]**

Par. 5. Section 1.263A–2T is removed.

Kevin M. Brown,
Deputy Commissioner for Services and Enforcement.

Approved March 20, 2007.

Eric Solomon,
Assistant Secretary of the Treasury (Tax Policy).

(Filed by the Office of the Federal Register on March 28, 2007, 8:45 a.m., and published in the issue of the Federal Register for March 29, 2007, 72 F.R. 14675)

Section 985.—Functional Currency

26 CFR 1.985–3: United States dollar approximate separate transactions method.

T.D. 9320

DEPARTMENT OF THE TREASURY Internal Revenue Service 26 CFR Part 1

United States Dollar Approximate Separate Transactions Method

AGENCY: Internal Revenue Service (IRS), Treasury.

ACTION: Final regulation.

SUMMARY: This document contains final regulations which provide the translation rates that must be used when translating into dollars certain items and amounts transferred by a qualified business unit (QBU) to its home office or parent corporation for purposes of computing dollar approximate separate transactions method (DASTM) gain or loss. This regulation is necessary to provide guidance under section 985 regarding the proper translation rates that must be used under the DASTM method. Taxpayers affected by these regulations are taxpayers with QBUs required to use the DASTM method of accounting described in §1.985–3.

DATES: *Effective Date:* This regulation is effective March 30, 2007.

Applicability Date: This regulation is applicable to any transfer, dividend, or distribution that is a return of capital that is made after March 8, 2005, and that gives rise to an adjustment under §1.985–3(d)(3).

FOR FURTHER INFORMATION CONTACT: Sheila Ramaswamy, at (202) 622–3870.

SUPPLEMENTARY INFORMATION:

Background

On July 13, 2006, a notice of proposed rulemaking (REG–118897–06, 2006–31 I.R.B. 120), United States Dollar Approximate Separate Transactions Method, was published in the **Federal Register** (71 FR 39604). The notice of proposed rulemaking proposed to amend §1.985–3(d)(3). No requests for a public hearing were received, and no public hearing was held. The IRS received no comments in response to the notice of proposed rulemaking. The proposed regulation is adopted without change by this Treasury decision.

Explanation of Provisions

For taxable years beginning after August 24, 1994, a U.S. taxpayer's QBU that would otherwise be required to use a hyperinflationary currency as its functional currency generally must use the dollar as its functional currency and must compute income or loss under the DASTM method of accounting described in §1.985–3. See §1.985–1(b)(2)(ii). Under the DASTM method of accounting, a QBU's income or loss for a taxable year is computed in U.S. dollars and adjusted to account for its DASTM gain or loss. See §1.985–3(b). A QBU's DASTM gain or loss for a taxable year is determined under §1.985–3(d) by first computing the QBU's change in net worth from the prior year. In computing the QBU's change in net worth, items whose dollar value fluctuates with changes in exchange rates are translated using the year-end exchange rate while items whose dollar value does not change with exchange rate fluctuations are translated using the exchange rate for the translation period in which the cost of the item was incurred. Specified adjustments are made to the QBU's change in net worth. Under §1.985–3(d)(3), one of the adjustments requires adding back to the change in net worth transactions that decrease the QBU's net worth without affecting the QBU's income or loss including dividend distributions, certain transfers, and returns of capital from the QBU to its home office or parent corporation. This final regulation provides the translation rate to be used in translating these items into dollars for purposes of computing DASTM gain or loss.

Under §1.985–3(d)(3), the applicable translation rate to be used generally depends upon whether the dollar value of the item transferred changes with fluctuations in exchange rates. Accordingly, the regulation provides that if the item giving rise to the adjustment is an asset which would be translated under §1.985–3(d)(5) at the exchange rate for the last translation period of the taxable year if it were on the QBU's year-end balance sheet, the item will be translated at the exchange rate on the date the item is transferred. However, if the item giving rise to the adjustment is an asset which would be translated under §1.985–3(d)(5) at the exchange rate for the translation period in which the cost of the item was incurred if it were on the QBU's year-end balance sheet, the item will be translated at the same historical rate.

Special Analyses

It has been determined that this Treasury decision is not a significant regulatory action as defined in Executive Order 12866. Therefore, a regulatory assessment is not required. It has been determined that sections 553(b) and (d) of the Administrative Procedure Act (5 U.S.C. chapter 5) do not apply to this regulation, and because this regulation does not impose a collection of information on small entities, the provisions of the Regulatory Flexibility Act (5 U.S.C. chapter 6) does not apply. Pursuant to section 7805(f) of the Internal Revenue Code, the notice of proposed rulemaking preceding this regulation was submitted to the Chief Counsel for Advocacy of the Small Business Administration for comment on its impact on small business.

Drafting Information

The principal author of this regulation is Sheila Ramaswamy, Office of Associate Chief Counsel (International). However, other personnel from the IRS and Treasury Department participated in their development.

* * * * *

Adoption of Amendment to the Regulations

Accordingly, 26 CFR part 1 is amended as follows:

PART 1—INCOME TAXES

Paragraph 1. The authority citation for part 1 continues to read in part as follows:

Authority: 26 U.S.C. 7805 * * *

Par. 2. Section 1.985–3 is amended by revising paragraph (d)(3) to read as follows:

§1.985–3 United States dollar approximate separate transactions method.

* * * * *

(d) * * *

(3) *Positive adjustments*—(i) *In general.* The items described in this paragraph (d)(3) are dividend distributions for the taxable year and any items that decrease net worth for the taxable year but that generally do not affect income or loss or earnings and profits (or a deficit in earnings and profits). Such items include a transfer to the home office of a QBU branch and a return of capital.

(ii) *Translation.* Except as provided by ruling or administrative pronouncement, items described in paragraph (d)(3)(i) of this section shall be translated into dollars as follows:

(A) If the item giving rise to the adjustment would be translated under paragraph (d)(5) of this section at the exchange rate for the last translation period of the taxable year if it were shown on the QBU's year-end balance sheet, such item shall be translated at the exchange rate on the date the item is transferred.

(B) If the item giving rise to the adjustment would be translated under paragraph (d)(5) of this section at the exchange rate for the translation period in which the cost of the item was incurred if it were shown on the QBU's year-end balance sheet, such item shall be translated at the same historical rate.

(iii) *Effective date.* Paragraph (d)(3)(ii) of this section is applicable for any transfer, dividend, or distribution that is a return of capital that is made after March 8, 2005, and that gives rise to an adjustment under this paragraph (d)(3).

* * * * *

Kevin M. Brown,
Deputy Commissioner for Services and Enforcement.

Approved March 20, 2007.

Eric Solomon,
Assistant Secretary for Tax Policy.

(Filed by the Office of the Federal Register on March 29, 2007, 8:45 a.m., and published in the issue of the Federal Register for March 30, 2007, 72 F.R. 15043)

Section 6426.—Credit for Alcohol Fuel, Biodiesel and Alternative Fuel Mixtures

A notice provides guidance on the credits and payments provided for renewable diesel and renewable diesel mixtures under sections 34, 40A, 6426, and 6427. See Notice 2007-37, page 1002.

Section 6427.—Fuels Not Used for Taxable Purposes

A notice provides guidance on the credits and payments provided for renewable diesel and renewable diesel mixtures under sections 34, 40A, 6426, and 6427. See Notice 2007-37, page 1002.

Part III. Administrative, Procedural, and Miscellaneous

Weighted Average Interest Rates Update

Notice 2007–32

This notice provides guidance as to the corporate bond weighted average interest rate and the permissible range of interest rates specified under § 412(b)(5)(B)(ii)(II) of the Internal Revenue Code. In addition, it provides guidance as to the interest rate on 30-year Treasury securities under § 417(e)(3)(A)(ii)(II).

CORPORATE BOND WEIGHTED AVERAGE INTEREST RATE

Sections 412(b)(5)(B)(ii) and 412(l)(7)(C)(i), as amended by the Pension Funding Equity Act of 2004 and by the Pension Protection Act of 2006, provide that the interest rates used to calculate current liability and to determine the required contribution under § 412(l) for plan years beginning in 2004 through 2007 must be within a permissible range based on the weighted average of the rates of interest on amounts invested conservatively in long term investment grade corporate bonds during the 4-year period ending on the last day before the beginning of the plan year.

Notice 2004–34, 2004–1 C.B. 848, provides guidelines for determining the corporate bond weighted average interest rate and the resulting permissible range of interest rates used to calculate current liability. That notice establishes that the corporate bond weighted average is based on the monthly composite corporate bond rate derived from designated corporate bond indices. The methodology for determining the monthly composite corporate bond rate as set forth in Notice 2004–34 continues to apply in determining that rate. See Notice 2006–75, 2006–36 I.R.B. 366.

The composite corporate bond rate for March 2007 is 5.84 percent. Pursuant to Notice 2004–34, the Service has determined this rate as the average of the monthly yields for the included corporate bond indices for that month.

The following corporate bond weighted average interest rate was determined for plan years beginning in the month shown below.

For Plan Years Beginning in: Month	Year	Corporate Bond Weighted Average	90% to 100% Permissible Range
April	2007	5.80	5.22 to 5.80

30-YEAR TREASURY SECURITIES INTEREST RATE

Section 417(e)(3)(A)(ii)(II) defines the applicable interest rate, which must be used for purposes of determining the minimum present value of a participant's benefit under § 417(e)(1) and (2), as the annual rate of interest on 30-year Treasury securities for the month before the date of distribution or such other time as the Secretary may by regulations prescribe. Section 1.417(e)–1(d)(3) of the Income Tax Regulations provides that the applicable interest rate for a month is the annual interest rate on 30-year Treasury securities as specified by the Commissioner for that month in revenue rulings, notices or other guidance published in the Internal Revenue Bulletin.

The rate of interest on 30-year Treasury securities for March 2007 is 4.72 percent. The Service has determined this rate as the monthly average of the daily determination of yield on the 30-year Treasury bond maturing in February 2037.

Drafting Information

The principal authors of this notice are Paul Stern and Tony Montanaro of the Employee Plans, Tax Exempt and Government Entities Division. For further information regarding this notice, please contact the Employee Plans' taxpayer assistance telephone service at 877–829–5500 (a toll-free number), between the hours of 8:30 a.m. and 4:30 p.m. Eastern time, Monday through Friday. Mr. Stern may be reached at 202–283–9703. Mr. Montanaro may be reached at 202–283–9714. The telephone numbers in the preceding sentences are not toll-free.

Guidance Regarding the Application of Section 409A to Split-Dollar Life Insurance Arrangements

Notice 2007–34

I. PURPOSE

This notice provides guidance regarding the application of section 409A of the Internal Revenue Code (Code) to split-dollar life insurance arrangements. This notice also provides that certain modifications of split-dollar life insurance arrangements necessary to comply with, or avoid application of, section 409A will not be treated as a material modification for purposes of § 1.61–22(j) of the Income Tax Regulations.

II. BACKGROUND

A. Section 409A

Section 409A was added to the Code by section 885 of the American Jobs Creation Act of 2004, Public Law 108–357, 118 Stat. 1418 (AJCA). Section 409A(a) generally provides that unless certain requirements are met, amounts deferred under a nonqualified deferred compensation plan for all taxable years are currently includible in gross income to the extent not subject to a substantial risk of forfeiture and not previously included in gross income. Section 409A(a) also provides rules under which deferrals of compensation will not result in such immediate and additional tax liability, including rules about the timing of initial elections to defer compensation, payments of deferred compensation, and changes to the time or form of a scheduled payment of previously deferred amounts.

Section 885(d) of the AJCA and § 1.409A–6 provide that section 409A of the Code generally applies to amounts deferred after December 31, 2004. Section 885(d) of the AJCA and § 1.409A–6 further provide that section 409A applies to earnings on deferred compensation only to the extent that section 409A applies to the deferred compensation. Section 885(d) of the AJCA and § 1.409A–6 also provide, however, that amounts deferred in taxable years beginning before January 1, 2005 are treated as amounts deferred in a taxable year beginning on or after such date if the plan under which the deferral is made is materially modified after October 3, 2004, except as permitted under transition guidance.

Notice 2005–1, 2005–1 C.B. 274, provides certain transition relief with respect to the application of section 409A. This relief was modified and partially extended in the preamble to the proposed regulations regarding the application of section 409A to nonqualified deferred compensation plans (REG–158080–04, 2005–2 C.B. 786 [70 Fed. Reg. 57930] (Oct. 4, 2005)). This relief was again modified and partially extended in Notice 2006–79, 2006–43 I.R.B. 763.

Because certain types of split-dollar life insurance arrangements provide for deferred compensation as defined under § 1.409A–1(b), the requirements of section 409A apply to such arrangements. Split-dollar life insurance arrangements that provide only death benefits (as defined in § 1.409A–1(a)(5)) to or for the benefit of the service provider are excluded from coverage under section 409A under the exception for death benefit plans contained in § 1.409A–1(a)(5). Similarly, arrangements that provide a legally binding right to amounts that are included in income in accordance with the exception for short-term deferrals under § 1.409A–1(b)(4) also do not provide for deferred compensation subject to section 409A to the extent so included.

B. Section 1.61–22 of the Income Tax Regulations

Section 1.61–22 provides rules for the taxation of a split-dollar life insurance arrangement. Section 1.61–22(j)(1)(i) provides that the regulations apply to any split-dollar life insurance arrangement entered into after September 17, 2003. Section 1.61–22(j)(2)(i) provides that, for purposes of the general effective date provision, if an arrangement entered into on or before September 17, 2003 is materially modified after September 17, 2003, the arrangement is treated as a new arrangement entered into on the date of the modification.

Section 1.61–22(j)(2)(ii) provides a non-exclusive list of changes that are not material modifications for this purpose. Section 1.61–22(j)(2)(iii) provides that the Commissioner, in revenue rulings, notices and other guidance published in the Internal Revenue Bulletin, may provide additional guidance with respect to other modifications that are not material for this purpose. This notice is intended to provide such additional guidance with respect to certain modifications related to split-dollar life insurance arrangements covered by section 409A.

Commentators expressed concerns about the impact of changes to a split-dollar life insurance arrangement to comply with section 409A, where the split-dollar life insurance arrangement was entered into on or before September 17, 2003 and is not otherwise subject to the regulations set forth in § 1.61–22. Commentators suggested that modifications necessary to comply with section 409A may cause the split-dollar life insurance arrangement to be treated as materially modified for purposes of § 1.61–22(j)(2). Comments were requested as to the scope of changes that would be necessary to comply with, or avoid application of, section 409A, and under what conditions those changes should not be treated as material modifications for purposes of § 1.61–22(j)(2). The Treasury Department and the IRS have considered all of the comments submitted in formulating this notice providing guidance under which certain modifications will not be treated as material modifications for purposes of § 1.61–22(j).

C. IRS Notice 2002–8

Notice 2002–8, 2002–1 C.B. 398, provides guidance regarding split-dollar life insurance arrangements entered into before the date of publication of final regulations (*i.e.*, before September 18, 2003). Specifically, Notice 2002–8, Part IV.2 provides that, for split-dollar life insurance arrangements entered into before September 18, 2003, in cases where the value of current life insurance protection is treated as an economic benefit provided by a sponsor to a benefited person under a split-dollar life insurance arrangement, the IRS will not treat the arrangement as having been terminated (and thus will not assert that there has been a transfer of property to the benefited person by reason of termination of the arrangement) for so long as the parties to the arrangement continue to treat and report the value of the life insurance protection as an economic benefit provided to the benefited person. This treatment will be accepted without regard to the level of the remaining economic interest that the sponsor has in the life insurance contract.

Notice 2002–8, Part IV.3 also provides that, for split-dollar life insurance arrangements entered into before September 18, 2003, the parties to the arrangement may treat premium or other payments by the sponsor as loans. In such cases, the IRS will not challenge reasonable efforts to comply with the requirements of sections 1271–1275 and section 7872 of the Code. To qualify for this treatment, all payments made by the sponsor from the inception of the arrangement (reduced by any repayments to the sponsor) before the first taxable year in which such payments are treated as loans for Federal tax purposes must be treated as loans entered into at the beginning of the first year in which such payments are treated as loans.

III. APPLICATION OF SECTION 409A TO SPLIT-DOLLAR LIFE INSURANCE ARRANGEMENTS

A. Section 409A Grandfathered Benefits

1. In General

Section 409A is not effective with respect to amounts deferred in taxable years beginning before January 1, 2005, unless the plan under which the amount was deferred is materially modified after October 3, 2004 (section 409A grandfathered benefits). For purposes of determining whether section 409A is applicable with respect to an amount, the amount is considered deferred before January 1, 2005 and therefore grandfathered from application of section 409A if, before January 1, 2005, the service provider had a legally binding right to be paid the amount, and the right to the amount was earned and vested. See § 1.409A–6(b).

Section 409A is effective with respect to earnings on amounts deferred only to the extent that section 409A is effective with respect to the amounts deferred. Accordingly, section 409A is not effective with respect to earnings on section 409A grandfathered benefits. See § 1.409A–6.

2. Determination of Section 409A Grandfathered and Non-Grandfathered Benefits under a Split-Dollar Life Insurance Arrangement

For purposes of applying § 1.409A–6, earnings on section 409A grandfathered benefits under a split-dollar life insurance arrangement include an increase in the policy cash value, or an increase in any portion of the policy cash value, that is attributable to the section 409A grandfathered benefits. For this purpose, earnings on section 409A grandfathered benefits do not include any increase in the policy cash value attributable to continued services performed, compensation earned, or premium payments or other contributions made on or after January 1, 2005.

Where benefits under a split-dollar life insurance arrangement have a component that is a section 409A grandfathered benefit and a component that is a section 409A non-grandfathered benefit, the calculation of the section 409A grandfathered component of the benefit may be made under any reasonable method that allocates increases in policy cash value attributable to the section 409A grandfathered benefit. For this purpose, a method will not be treated as reasonable if it allocates a disproportionate amount of policy costs and expenses to the section 409A non-grandfathered component.

For purposes of this section III.A.2, the use of the proportional allocation method described in this paragraph will be treated as a reasonable method. The proportional allocation method defines the section 409A grandfathered benefit (including grandfathered earnings) as of any valuation date as equal to the greater of:

1. the portion of the policy cash value at December 31, 2004 that was earned and vested (as defined in § 1.409A–6(b)) reduced by any amount securing an amount owed to the service recipient; and
2. an amount equal to the policy cash value on the valuation date multiplied by a fraction, the numerator of which is the sum of the grandfathered premiums actually paid on the policy and the denominator of which is the sum of all premiums actually paid on the policy by the valuation date.

For purposes of this paragraph, grandfathered premiums include both premiums actually paid on or before December 31, 2004 that were earned and vested (as defined in § 1.409A–6(b)) as of such date and premiums paid after such date pursuant to a legally binding right that was earned and vested (as defined in § 1.409A–6(b)) as of such date.

B. Arrangements Subject to § 1.61–22

This section III.B addresses a split-dollar life insurance arrangement, or a portion of a split-dollar life insurance arrangement, that is not grandfathered under § 1.409A–6, but is subject to the rules under § 1.61–22 (but not § 1.7872–15) (including an arrangement or portion thereof that defers compensation in taxable years beginning before January 1, 2005, if the arrangement is materially modified (within the meaning of § 1.409A–6(d)) after October 3, 2004). Except where such an arrangement provides for only a short-term deferral excluded from coverage under § 1.409A–1(b)(4), a split-dollar life insurance arrangement the taxation of which is governed by the rules of § 1.61–22(d) – (g) generally provides for deferred compensation if, under the terms of the arrangement and the relevant facts and circumstances, the service provider has a legally binding right during a taxable year of the service provider to compensation that, pursuant to the terms of the arrangement, is or may be includible in the income of the service provider in a later taxable year of the service provider.

A split-dollar life insurance arrangement does not constitute a nonqualified deferred compensation plan for purposes of section 409A to the extent the arrangement constitutes a death benefit plan. See § 1.409A–1(a)(5). For purposes of this section III.B, the right to compensation described as the cost of current life insurance protection in § 1.61–22(d)(2)(i) and (3) is treated as provided under a death benefit plan under § 1.409A–1(a)(5) and thus is excluded from the requirements of section 409A, even if additional economic benefits are available under the arrangement that are subject to the application of section 409A.

Accordingly, a split-dollar life insurance arrangement covered by this section III.B provides for deferred compensation for purposes of section 409A if, under the terms of the arrangement and the relevant facts and circumstances, the service provider has a legally binding right during a taxable year of the service provider to economic benefits described in § 1.61–22(d)(2)(ii) (policy cash value to which the service provider has current access within the meaning of § 1.61–22(d)(4)(ii)) or § 1.61–22(d)(2)(iii) (any other economic benefits provided to the service provider) that, pursuant to the terms of the arrangement, are payable to (or on behalf of) the service provider in a later taxable year of the service provider, and such legally binding right does not qualify as a short-term deferral for purposes of § 1.409A–1(b)(4). For purposes of the application of section 409A, the excess of the policy cash value over the aggregate premium payments is treated as earnings. See § 1.409A–3(e) for the treatment of earnings for purposes of satisfying the requirements of section 409A.

C. Arrangements Subject to § 1.7872–15.

This section III.C addresses any split-dollar life insurance arrangement, or portion of a split-dollar life insurance arrangement, that is not grandfathered under § 1.409A–6, but is subject to § 1.7872–15 (and not § 1.61–22) (including an arrangement or portion thereof that defers compensation in taxable years beginning before January 1, 2005, if the arrangement is materially modified (within the meaning of § 1.409A–6(d)) after October 3, 2004).

Split-dollar life insurance arrangements pursuant to which payments are treated as split-dollar loans under § 1.7872–15 generally will not give rise to deferrals of compensation within the meaning of section 409A. However, in certain situations, such an arrangement may give rise to deferrals of compensation for purposes of section 409A, for example, if amounts on a split-dollar loan are waived, cancelled, or forgiven.

D. Arrangements Grandfathered under § 1.61–22(j)

1. In General

This section III.D addresses a split-dollar life insurance arrangement, or a portion of a split-dollar life insurance arrangement, that is not grandfathered under § 1.409A–6, but is grandfathered under § 1.61–22 (and thus is not covered by § 1.61–22 or § 1.7872–15 unless materially modified).

A split-dollar life insurance arrangement addressed by this section III.D provides for deferred compensation for purposes of section 409A if, under the terms of the arrangement and the relevant facts and circumstances, the service provider has a legally binding right during a taxable year to compensation that pursuant to the terms of the arrangement is payable to (or on behalf of) the service provider in a later year (for example, upon termination of the split-dollar arrangement), and such legally binding right does not qualify as a short-term deferral for purposes of § 1.409A–1(b)(4), and is not treated as provided under a death benefit plan for purposes of § 1.409A–1(a)(5). Notice 2002–8 provides that, in cases where the value of current life insurance protection is treated as an economic benefit provided by a sponsor to a benefited person under a split-dollar life insurance arrangement, the IRS will not treat the arrangement as having been terminated for so long as the parties to the arrangement continue to treat and report the value of the life insurance protection as an economic benefit provided to the benefited person. In such cases, provided that all other requirements of Notice 2002–8 are satisfied, the IRS will not assert that there has been a transfer of property to the benefited person by reason of termination of the arrangement for purposes of section 409A. In addition, in such cases, the IRS will not treat the right to the economic benefit of current life insurance protection (within the meaning of Notice 2002–8) as deferred compensation for purposes of section 409A.

For split-dollar life insurance arrangements entered into before September 18, 2003, the parties to the arrangement may be eligible to treat premium or other payments by the sponsor as loans under either Part IV.3 or Part IV.4 of Notice 2002–8. In such a situation, the arrangement generally will not give rise to deferrals of compensation within the meaning of section 409A. However, in certain situations, the arrangement may give rise to deferrals of compensation for purposes of section 409A, for example, if all or a portion of the payments on the loans are waived, cancelled, or forgiven.

2. Additional Transition Relief under § 1.61–22(j)

For purposes of § 1.61–22(j), a modification of a split-dollar life insurance arrangement necessary to bring such arrangement into compliance with section 409A, or to avoid application of section 409A, will not be treated as a material modification of such arrangement. For this purpose, a modification of a split-dollar life insurance arrangement is considered necessary to bring such arrangement into compliance with section 409A only if each of the following requirements is met:

1. The service recipient or service provider participating in the split-dollar life insurance arrangement has made a determination, based upon a reasonable application of section 409A, the regulations, and other guidance, that section 409A is applicable to the arrangement, and that the arrangement does not comply with the requirements of section 409A;

2. The service recipient or service provider participating in the split-dollar life insurance arrangement has made a determination, based upon a reasonable application of section 409A, the regulations, and other guidance, that the modification causes the arrangement to comply with section 409A or results in section 409A no longer being applicable to the arrangement, or that the modification is a necessary part of a number of actions that together cause the arrangement to come into compliance with section 409A or result in section 409A no longer being applicable to the arrangement;

3. The modification to the arrangement consists solely of changes to the applicable definitions (such as, the definition of a separation from service or a disability) or changes to the payment timing requirements, including election provisions related to the time and form of payment, or changes to the conditions under which all or part of the benefit under the arrangement will be forfeited (such as, an acceleration of a vesting requirement), reasonably intended to conform the arrangement to the requirements of, or to qualify for an exclusion from, section 409A;

4. The modification establishes a time and form of payment, or establishes potential times and forms of payment that are consistent with times and forms of payment under which the benefits could have been paid under the terms of the arrangement before the modification (including through the exercise of service recipient or service provider discretion in accordance with the terms of the arrangement before modification); and

5. The modification does not materially enhance the value of the benefits to the service provider under the arrangement.

IV. CONTINUED APPLICATION OF SECTION 409A

This notice does not affect the application of section 409A, including the application of the treatment of certain plans that are materially modified after October 3, 2004 as subject to section 409A. In addition, this notice does not affect the application of any transition relief under section 409A. Final regulations under section 409A were released on April 10, 2007 (T.D. 9321, 72 Fed. Reg. 19234 (April 17, 2007)). The final regulations generally are applicable for taxable years beginning on or after January 1, 2008. However, taxpayers may rely on the final regulations for purposes of applying this notice to prior periods.

V. DRAFTING INFORMATION

The principal author of this notice is Stephen Tackney of the Office of Division Counsel/Associate Chief Counsel (Tax Exempt and Government Entities). However, other personnel from the Treasury Department and the IRS participated in its development. For further information regarding the application of section 409A, contact Stephen Tackney at (202) 927–9639 (not a toll-free call).

GO Zone Bonus Depreciation Additional Guidance

Notice 2007–36

SECTION 1. PURPOSE

This notice provides guidance with respect to the 50-percent additional first year depreciation deduction provided by § 1400N(d) of the Internal Revenue Code (GO Zone additional first year depreciation deduction) for specified Gulf Opportunity Zone extension property (GO Zone extension property). This notice also provides additional guidance with respect to the original use requirement described in § 1400N(d)(2)(A)(iii) for qualified Gulf Opportunity Zone property (GO Zone property), including GO Zone extension property.

SECTION 2. BACKGROUND

.01 Section 1400N(d) generally allows a 50-percent additional first year depreciation deduction for GO Zone property. The GO Zone additional first year depreciation deduction is allowable in the taxable year in which the GO Zone property is placed in service by the taxpayer.

.02 GO Zone property is depreciable property that meets all of the requirements provided in § 1400N(d)(2) and in section 2.02 of Notice 2006–77, 2006–40 I.R.B. 590. One of these requirements is that the original use of the property must commence with the taxpayer in the GO Zone on or after August 28, 2005. Another requirement is that the property must be placed in service by the taxpayer on or before December 31, 2007 (December 31, 2008, in the case of qualified nonresidential real property and residential rental property). Depreciable property described in § 1400N(d)(2)(B) and in section 2.03 of Notice 2006–77 is not eligible for the GO Zone additional first year depreciation deduction.

.03 Section 1400N(d)(6), added by section 120 of the Tax Relief and Health Care Act of 2006 (TRHCA), Pub. L. No. 109–432, 120 Stat. 2922, extends the placed-in-service date requirement for GO Zone extension property. Section 1400N(d)(6)(A) provides that in the case of any GO Zone extension property, § 1400N(d)(2)(A) is applied without regard to § 1400N(d)(2)(A)(v), which is the placed-in-service date requirement described in section 2.02 of this notice. Section 1400N(d)(6)(B) provides that Go Zone extension property is property substantially all of the use of which is in one or more specified portions of the GO Zone (as described in section 3 of this notice) and that is either (I) nonresidential real property or residential rental property that is placed in service by the taxpayer on or before December 31, 2010, or (II) in the case of a taxpayer who places a building described in (I) in service on or before December 31, 2010, property described in § 168(k)(2)(A)(i) if substantially all of the use of such property is in such building and such property is placed in service by the taxpayer not later than 90 days after such building is placed in service. In the case of any GO Zone extension property that is nonresidential real property or residential rental property, § 1400N(d)(6)(D) provides that the GO Zone additional first year depreciation deduction is applicable only to the extent of the adjusted basis of such property attributable to manufacture, construction, or production before January 1, 2010. For further guidance, see section 4 of this notice.

.04 The counties and parishes in Alabama, Louisiana, and Mississippi that comprise the GO Zone are listed on page 2 of IRS Publication 4492, *Information for Taxpayers Affected by Hurricanes Katrina, Rita, and Wilma*, under Gulf Opportunity (GO) Zone (Core Disaster Area). In defining GO Zone extension property, § 1400N(d)(6)(C) provides that the term "specified portions of the GO Zone" means those portions of the GO Zone that are in any county or parish that is identified by the Secretary as being a county or parish in which hurricanes occurring during 2005 damaged (in the aggregate) more than 60 percent of the housing units in such county or parish that were occupied (determined according to the 2000 Census). The Joint Committee on Taxation's explanation of TRHCA references the data compiled, and published on February 12, 2006, in Current Housing Unit Damage Estimates Hurricanes Katrina, Rita, and Wilma, which is available at *www.dhs.gov/xlibrary/assets/GulfCoast_HousingDamageEstimates_021206.pdf* in identifying the counties and parishes that qualify as specified portions of the GO Zone. *See* Staff of Joint Committee of Taxation, Technical Explanation of H.R. 6408, the "Tax Relief and Health Care Act of 2006," as Introduced in the House on December 7, 2006, at 40, n.52 (December 7, 2006). For further guidance, see section 3 of this notice.

.05 With respect to the original use requirement described in section 2.02 of this notice, section 2.02(3) of Notice 2006–77 provides that rules similar to the original use rules in § 1.168(k)–1(b)(3) of the Income Tax Regulations apply. In addition, used property will satisfy the original use requirement so long as the property has not been previously used within the GO Zone. The Treasury Department and the Internal Revenue Service have learned that taxpayers are uncertain how to apply the original use requirement to transactions involving reconditioned or rebuilt property in the GO Zone. This notice clarifies the application of the original use requirement in § 1400N(d)(2)(A)(iii) for GO Zone property, including GO Zone extension property.

SECTION 3. SPECIFIED PORTIONS OF THE GO ZONE

Solely for purposes of § 1400N(d)(6), the portions of the GO Zone that are the specified portions of the GO Zone are:

.01 Alabama: No counties.

.02 Louisiana: The parishes of Calcasieu, Cameron, Orleans, Plaquemines, St. Bernard, St. Tammany, and Washington.

.03 Mississippi: The counties of Hancock, Harrison, Jackson, Pearl River, and Stone.

SECTION 4. GO ZONE EXTENSION PROPERTY

.01 *Definition.* GO Zone extension property is depreciable property that meets all of the following requirements:

(1) Property that is described in § 1400N(d)(2)(A)(i), (ii), (iii), and (iv), and in sections 2.02(1), (2), (3), and (4) of Notice 2006–77 (as modified by section 5 of this notice);

(2) Property that is not described in § 1400N(d)(2)(B) and in section 2.03 of Notice 2006–77;

(3) Substantially all of the use of the property is in one or more specified portions of the GO Zone (as defined in section 3 of this notice). For purposes of this section 4.01(3), the term "substantially all" means 80 percent or more during each taxable year. If greater than 20 percent of the use of the property is outside the counties and parishes designated as being part of the specified portions of the GO Zone, then the property is not GO Zone extension property under § 1400N(d)(6); and

(4)(a) Property that is nonresidential real property (as defined in § 168(e)(2)(B)) or residential rental property (as defined in § 168(e)(2)(A)) and depreciated under § 168 and placed in service by the taxpayer on or before December 31, 2010; or

(b) In the case of a taxpayer that places in service on or before December 31, 2010, a building (as defined in § 1.48–1(e)(1)) that is described in section 4.01(4)(a) of this notice and is GO Zone extension property, property that is described in § 168(k)(2)(A)(i) and § 1.168(k)–1(b)(2)(i) if substantially all of the use of such property is in the building and such property is placed in service by the taxpayer not later than 90 calendar days after the building is placed in service by the taxpayer. For purposes of this section 4.01(4)(b), the term "substantially all" means 80 percent or more during each taxable year. If greater than 20 percent of the use of the property is not in the building, then the property is not GO Zone extension property. Further, land improvements that are not in the building (for example, the sidewalks surrounding the building) are not GO Zone extension property. Moreover, if the building that is described in section 4.01(4)(a) of this notice and is GO Zone extension property is a multi-story building and the floors of that building are placed in service by the taxpayer on different dates, the taxpayer must place in service the property described in this section 4.01(4)(b) not later than 90 calendar days after the entire building is placed in service by the taxpayer but not later than March 31, 2011.

.02 *Determination of Adjusted Basis Qualifying for the GO Zone Additional First Year Depreciation Deduction.*

(1) *Property described in § 1400N(d)(6)(B)(ii)(I) and section 4.01(4)(a) of this notice.*

(a) *In general.* In the case of GO Zone extension property described in § 1400N(d)(6)(B)(ii)(I) and section 4.01(4)(a) of this notice (GO Zone extension real property), § 1400N(d)(6)(D) provides that the GO Zone additional first year depreciation deduction is available only for the adjusted basis of such property attributable to manufacture, construction, or production before January 1, 2010. The amounts of adjusted basis of the property attributable to manufacture, construction, or production before January 1, 2010, are referred to as "progress expenditures."

(b) *Determination of progress expenditures.* For purposes of § 1400N(d)(6)(D), progress expenditures for GO Zone extension real property that is manufactured, constructed, or produced generally is the amount paid or incurred that is properly chargeable to capital account with respect to the property. The amount that is properly chargeable to capital account for purposes of § 1400N(d)(6)(D) also includes any other costs paid or incurred by the taxpayer, such as interest, or any other direct or indirect costs that are required to be capitalized under § 263A(a) and the regulations thereunder with respect to the manufacture, construction, or production of the property.

For GO Zone extension real property actually manufactured, constructed, or produced by the taxpayer, the amount paid or incurred by the taxpayer is properly chargeable to capital account at the time and to the extent that the amount is properly includible in computing basis of the property under the taxpayer's method of accounting, such as, for example, after the requirements of § 461 (including the economic performance requirement of § 461(h)) are satisfied.

In the case of GO Zone extension real property that is manufactured, constructed, or produced for the taxpayer by another person under a written binding contract (as defined in § 1.168(k)–1(b)(4)(ii)), the amount that is properly chargeable to capital account for purposes of § 1400N(d)(6)(D) includes any payments by the taxpayer under the contract that represent part of the purchase price of the property but only to the extent progress is made in manufacture, construction, or production of the property, or, to the extent costs are incurred by the taxpayer earlier than payments are made (determined on a cumulative basis for the property), any part of that price for which the taxpayer has satisfied the requirements of § 461 (including the economic performance requirement of § 461(h)). In the case of an accrual method taxpayer, the taxpayer has made a payment if the transaction would be considered a payment by a taxpayer using the cash receipts and disbursements method of accounting. Solely for purposes of this paragraph, the written binding contract must be entered into before the manufacture, construction, or production of the property to be delivered under the contract is completed.

With respect to GO Zone extension real property that is manufactured, constructed, or produced by another person and is purchased by the taxpayer after the manufacture, construction, or production of the property is completed, only the part of the purchase price attributable to the cost of manufacture, construction, or production of the GO Zone extension real property before January 1, 2010, is eligible for the GO Zone additional first year depreciation deduction.

(2) *Property described in § 1400N(d)(6)(B)(ii)(II) and section 4.01(4)(b) of this notice.* The progress expenditure rule in § 1400N(d)(6)(D) and section 4.02(1) of this notice does not apply to the GO Zone extension property described in § 1400N(d)(6)(B)(ii)(II) and section 4.01(4)(b) of this notice (GO Zone extension personal property). Accordingly, the unadjusted depreciable basis (as defined in § 1.168(b)–1(a)(3)) of such GO Zone extension personal property is eligible for the GO Zone additional first year depreciation deduction (assuming all requirements are met).

SECTION 5. ORIGINAL USE REQUIREMENT FOR THE GO ZONE ADDITIONAL FIRST YEAR DEPRECIATION DEDUCTION

.01 *In general*. For purposes of the GO Zone additional first year depreciation deduction, depreciable property will meet the requirements of § 1400N(d)(2)(A)(iii) if the original use of the property commences with the taxpayer in the GO Zone on or after August 28, 2005. Except as provided in rules similar to the original use rules in § 1.168(k)–1(b)(3)(iii) (sale-leaseback, syndication, and certain other transactions) and in § 1.168(k)–1(b)(3)(iv) (fractional interests in property), original use means the first use to which the property is put, whether or not that use corresponds to the use of the property by the taxpayer. Thus, additional capital expenditures paid or incurred by a taxpayer to recondition or rebuild property that is acquired by purchase or owned by the taxpayer satisfy the original use requirement because it is the first use to which the improvement is put.

The cost of reconditioned or rebuilt property does not satisfy the original use requirement because the reconditioned or rebuilt property has been previously used. However, for purposes of the GO Zone additional first year depreciation deduction, used property (including reconditioned or rebuilt property) will satisfy the original use requirement so long as the property has not been previously used within the GO Zone. Thus, unlike the rules in § 1.168(k)–1(b)(3)(i), the portion of the cost of reconditioned or rebuilt property that is attributable to the cost of capital expenditures that were not previously used within the GO Zone will satisfy the original use requirement, regardless of whether or not the underlying property (before being reconditioned or rebuilt) to which the capital expenditures relate was previously used either inside or outside of the GO Zone. The question of whether property is reconditioned or rebuilt property is a question of fact. For purposes of this section 5.01, property that contains used parts will not be treated as reconditioned or rebuilt if the cost of the used parts is not more than 20 percent of the total cost of the property, whether acquired or self-constructed.

Rules similar to the rules in § 1.168(k)–1(b)(3)(ii), (iii), and (iv) also apply for purposes of the original use requirement for the GO Zone additional first year depreciation deduction.

.02 *Examples*. The following examples illustrate the provisions of this section 5.

Example 1. In July 2005, *A*, a calendar-year taxpayer, placed in service a new building that is located in the GO Zone. During 2007, *A* incurs $2,000,000 of capital expenditures to renovate and expand such building. In October 2007, *A* places these capital expenditures in service for use in *A*'s trade or business. The $2,000,000 of capital expenditures incurred by *A* satisfies the original use requirement. Assuming all other requirements are met, *A* may claim the GO Zone additional first year depreciation deduction for the $2,000,000 of capital expenditures, regardless of whether the $2,000,000 is added to the basis of the building or is capitalized as a separate asset.

Example 2. In March 2007, *B*, a calendar-year taxpayer, purchases from *C* for $5,000,000 a damaged building that is located in the GO Zone and has been previously used in *C*'s trade or business. In August 2007, *B* incurs $4,000,000 of capital expenditures to renovate the building. In November 2007, *B* places the building in service for use in *B*'s trade or business. The $5,000,000 purchase price does not qualify for the GO Zone additional first year depreciation deduction because the building was previously used by *C* within the GO Zone and, therefore, the original use requirement is not met. However, the $4,000,000 of capital expenditures incurred by *B* satisfies the original use requirement. Assuming all other requirements are met, *B* may claim the GO Zone additional first year depreciation deduction for the $4,000,000 of capital expenditures, regardless of whether the $4,000,000 is added to the basis of the building or is capitalized as a separate asset.

Example 3. *D* owns a building in the GO Zone that was used in *D*'s trade or business prior to Hurricane Katrina. This building was badly damaged by Hurricane Katrina. Since that hurricane, the building has been closed. *D* incurs $3,000,000 of capital expenditures to renovate and improve the closed building. All of the $3,000,000 capital expenditures are components and properties not previously used in the GO Zone. Upon completion of the improvements in March 2007, *D* decides to sell the still-closed building instead of placing the renovated building in service. In May 2007, *D* sells the building to *E* for $8,000,000. At the time of the sale, the fair market value of the improvements made by *D* is $3,000,000. None of the improvements made by *D* were placed in service by *D* and, therefore, *D* could not take a depreciation deduction with respect to the improvements. In June 2007, *E* places the building (with the improvements) in service for use in *E*'s trade or business. Of *E*'s total cost of the building ($8,000,000), $5,000,000 is attributable to the part of the building previously used in the GO Zone and $3,000,000 is attributable to the improvements made by *D* that were not previously used in the GO Zone. Consequently, 62.5 percent of *E*'s total cost of the building is attributable to used components and property and, thus, *E* has purchased a reconditioned or rebuilt building. Of *E*'s total cost of the building ($8,000,000), $5,000,000 does not qualify for the GO Zone additional first year depreciation deduction because this amount is attributable to property previously used in the GO Zone. However, the remaining amount of $3,000,000 is for improvements that were not previously used in the GO Zone and, thus, satisfies the original use requirement. Assuming all other requirements are met, *E* may claim the GO Zone additional first year depreciation deduction for the $3,000,000 cost of the improvements.

Example 4. The facts are the same as in *Example 3*, except that *D* incurs $7,000,000 of capital expenditures to renovate and improve the closed building, all of the $7,000,000 capital expenditures are components and properties not previously used in the GO Zone, and the fair market value of these improvements at the time of the sale of the building to *E* is $7,000,000. Of *E*'s total cost of the building ($8,000,000), $1,000,000 is attributable to the part of the building previously used in the GO Zone and $7,000,000 is attributable to the improvements made by *D* that were not previously used in the GO Zone. Consequently, only 12.5 percent of *E*'s total cost of the building is attributable to used parts and, thus, *E* is treated as purchasing a new building (and not a reconditioned or rebuilt building). Thus, *E*'s total cost of the building ($8,000,000) satisfies the original use requirement. Assuming all other requirements are met, *E* may claim the GO Zone additional first year depreciation deduction for the $8,000,000 cost of the building.

SECTION 6. EFFECT ON OTHER DOCUMENTS

Section 2.02(3) of Notice 2006–77, 2006–40 I.R.B. 590, is clarified, modified, and amplified to read as provided in section 5 of this notice.

SECTION 7. DRAFTING INFORMATION

The principal author of this notice is Douglas H. Kim of the Office of Associate Chief Counsel (Passthroughs & Special Industries). For further information regarding this notice, contact Mr. Kim at (202) 622–3110 (not a toll-free call).

Renewable Diesel

Notice 2007–37

Section 1. PURPOSE

(a) This notice provides guidance on the credits and payments provided for renewable diesel and renewable diesel mixtures under §§ 34, 40A, 6426, and 6427 of the Internal Revenue Code. Section 1346 of the Energy Policy Act of 2005 (Pub. L. 109–58) made these credits and payments applicable to renewable diesel and renewable diesel mixtures beginning January 1, 2006. References to regulations in this notice are to the Manufacturers and Retailers Excise Tax Regulations.

(b) This notice addresses issues related to fuel produced by coprocessing biomass and petroleum feedstocks (coproduced fuel). The coprocessing of biomass and petroleum feedstocks typically involves the use of catalysts, but the Energy Policy Act and its legislative history do not specify whether a process that uses catalysts is a thermal depolymerization process for purposes of the Internal Revenue Code. In addition, it is not clear under the Energy Policy Act and its legislative history whether the portion of coproduced fuel attributable to biomass is sufficiently similar to the remainder of the coproduced fuel to treat the portion attributable to biomass as renewable diesel if the coproduced fuel as a whole satisfies Clean Air Act registration requirements and ASTM diesel standards applicable to renewable diesel.

(c) The Department of Energy has advised and the Department of the Treasury and the Internal Revenue Service have concluded based on that advice that thermal depolymerization should be defined generically and broadly to include processes that use heat and pressure, with or without the presence of catalysts. The Department of Energy has also indicated that coproduced fuel attributable to biomass is likely to be virtually indistinguishable from the crude-oil derived products in the coproduced fuel, with only minor differences at the molecular level, and the rules in this notice relating to coproduced fuel follow from this view.

Section 2. RENEWABLE DIESEL; RENEWABLE DIESEL MIXTURE

(a) *Renewable diesel*—(1) *In general. Renewable diesel* means diesel fuel that—

(i) Is derived from biomass (as defined in § 45K(c)(3)) using a thermal depolymerization process;

(ii) Meets the registration requirements for fuels and fuel additives established by the Environmental Protection Agency (EPA) under section 211 of the Clean Air Act (42 U.S.C. 7545); and

(iii) Meets the requirements of the American Society of Testing and Materials (ASTM) D975 or D396.

(2) *Thermal depolymerization* is a process for the reduction of complex organic materials through the use of pressure and heat to decompose long-chain polymers of hydrogen, oxygen, and carbon into short-chain hydrocarbons with a maximum length of around 18 carbon atoms. A process may qualify as thermal depolymerization even if catalysts are used in the process.

(3) *Treatment as biodiesel.* For purposes of the Code, Notice 2005–4, 2005–1 C.B. 289, and Notice 2005–62, 2005–2 C.B. 443, renewable diesel is treated as biodiesel except that—

(i) Renewable diesel is *diesel fuel* as defined in § 48.4081–1(c)(2);

(ii) The amount of the credit or payment allowable for renewable diesel is $1.00 per gallon;

(iii) The small biodiesel producer credit of § 40A(a)(3) does not apply; and

(iv) The Certificate for Biodiesel described in section 2 of Notice 2005–4 (as modified by Notice 2005–62) must indicate at all appropriate locations that the fuel to which the certificate relates is renewable diesel and state that the renewable diesel meets the requirements of paragraph (a)(1) of this section instead of the requirements for biodiesel that are described in the certificate.

(b) *Renewable diesel mixture*—(1) *In general. Renewable diesel mixture* means a mixture of renewable diesel and diesel fuel (other than renewable diesel) that contains at least 0.1 percent (by volume) of diesel fuel (other than renewable diesel). The term also includes diesel fuel described in section 3(a) of this notice. Any volume of kerosene in a renewable diesel mixture is disregarded in determining whether the renewable diesel mixture satisfies the 0.1 percent requirement. The diesel fuel in a renewable diesel mixture may be either dyed or undyed. However, taxpayers are reminded of the penalty in § 6715 for the willful alteration of the strength or composition of any dye in dyed fuel. Also see § 48.6715–1.

(2) *Treatment as biodiesel mixture.* For purposes of the Code, Notice 2005–4, and Notice 2005–62, a renewable diesel mixture is treated as a biodiesel mixture.

Section 3. COPRODUCTION

(a) *In general.* Fuel produced from biomass (as defined in § 45K(c)(3)) and petroleum feedstocks using a thermal depolymerization process is a renewable diesel mixture if such fuel—

(1) Has been registered by the EPA under section 211 of the Clean Air Act (42 U.S.C. 7545); and

(2) Meets the requirements of ASTM D975 or D396.

(b) *Amount of renewable diesel in mixture.* If fuel is treated as a renewable diesel mixture under section 3(a) of this notice, only the portion of the mixture attributable to biomass qualifies as renewable diesel used in the production of a renewable diesel mixture. A taxpayer claiming a credit or payment with respect to fuel treated as a renewable diesel mixture under section 3(a) of this notice must use generally accepted scientific practices to establish the portion of the fuel that is attributable to biomass.

Section 4. EFFECTIVE DATE

This notice is effective January 1, 2006.

Section 5. DRAFTING INFORMATION

The principal author of this notice is Frank Boland of the Office of Associate Chief Counsel (Passthroughs & Special Industries). For further information regarding this notice, please contact Frank Boland at (202) 622–3130 (not a toll-free call).

NOTE: Use this Revenue Procedure to prepare Form 8851, Summary of Archer MSAs, for submission to Internal Revenue Service (IRS) using the FIRE (Filing Information Returns Electronically) System. Electronic filing is the only filing option for filers with more than 250 forms. **Call the IRS Enterprise Computing Center — Martinsburg (ECC-MTB) toll-free at 1–866–455–7438 for log on procedures specific to Form 8851.**

26 CFR 601.602: Tax forms and instructions.

Rev. Proc. 2007–29

TABLE OF CONTENTS

Part A. General

Part B. Electronic Filing Specifications

Part C. Record Format Specifications and Record Layouts

Part A. General

.01 Numerous editorial changes were made to this revenue procedure. Major changes are emphasized by the use of *italics*. Filers are urged to read the revenue procedure in its entirety.

Sec. 1. Purpose

.01 The purpose of this revenue procedure is to provide the specifications under which trustees may file Form 8851, Summary of Archer MSAs, electronically.

.02 Comments concerning this revenue procedure, or suggestions for making it more helpful and user friendly, can be addressed to:

IRS-Enterprise Computing Center — Martinsburg
Information Reporting Program
Attn: 8851 Coordinator
240 Murall Drive
Kearneysville WV 25430

.03 It is unlawful to intentionally transmit a computer virus to the Internal Revenue Service. Violators may be subject to a fine and/or imprisonment.

Sec. 2. Nature of Changes

.01 This Revenue Procedure was completely revised since its last revision in 2001. Please review this Revenue Procedure in its entirety. This section only lists the major changes.

.02 The name of the Martinsburg Computing Center was changed to Enterprise Computing Center – Martinsburg (ECC-MTB).

.03 ECC-MTB no longer accepts magnetic media for the filing of Forms 8851. The only acceptable method for those with over 250 forms is electronic filing via the FIRE System (see Part B). Filers of Form 8851 must call ECC-MTB toll-free at 1–866–455–7438, extension 3 for log-on instructions.

.04 The FIRE System is now on the Internet at http://fire.irs.gov. Substantial changes were made to the FIRE System so review this information carefully.

.05 The due date for filing Forms 8851 was changed to March 20, 2007. This date is effective for both filing periods, January 1, 2005 through June 30, 2005, and January 1, 2006 through June 30, 2006. A separate transmission is required for each filing period.

Sec. 3. Where To File and How To Contact the IRS Enterprise Computing Center — Martinsburg

.01 Paper Forms 8851 are processed at IRS-Enterprise Computing Center — Martinsburg (IRS/ECC-MTB). Send forms and correspondence to ECC at the following address:

IRS-Enterprise Computing Center — Martinsburg
Information Reporting Program
Attn: 8851 Coordinator
240 Murall Drive
Kearneysville WV 25430

.02 Paper forms and publications should be requested by calling the "Forms Only Number" listed in your local telephone directory or by calling the IRS toll-free number **1–800–TAX–FORM (1–800–829–3676).** Forms and publications can also be obtained by using the IRS Web site *www.irs.gov*.

.03 The Information Reporting Program Customer Service Section (IRP/CSS), located at IRS/ECC-MTB, answers electronic, paper filing and tax law questions from the payer community relating to the filing of business information returns (Forms 8851, 1096, 1098, 1099, 5498, 8027, and W-2G). Inquiries dealing with backup withholding and reasonable cause requirements due to missing and incorrect taxpayer identification numbers are also addressed by IRP/CSS. Assistance is available year-round to payers, transmitters, and employers nationwide, Monday through Friday, 8:30 a.m. to 4:30 p.m. Eastern Standard Time, by calling toll-free **1–866–455–7438.** The Telecommunications Device for the Deaf **(TDD)** toll number is **304–267–3367.** Call as soon as questions arise to avoid the busy filing seasons. Recipients of information returns (payees) should continue to contact 1–800–829–1040 with any questions on how to report the information returns data on their tax returns.

.04 The telephone numbers for inquiries or electronic submissions are:

Information Reporting Program Customer Service Section

TOLL-FREE 1–866–455–7438 or outside the U.S. 1–304–263–8700

304–267–3367 — TDD
(Telecommunication Device for the Deaf)

304–264–5602 — Fax Machine

Electronic Filing — FIRE system
http://fire.irs.gov

TO OBTAIN FORMS:
1–800–TAX–FORM (1–800–829–3676)

www.irs.gov — IRS website access to forms

Sec. 4. Filing Requirements

.01 If you are required to report 250 or more Archer MSAs, you must file electronically. Even though a trustee may not meet the required filing threshold of 250 documents, IRS encourages the filing of the Form 8851 electronically. Filers who transmit their information electronically are considered to have satisfied the magnetic media filing requirements.

.02 The filing requirement applies individually to each reporting entity as defined by its separate Taxpayer Identification Number (TIN), (Social Security Number [SSN], or Employer Identification Number [EIN]). For example, if filing for a corporation with several branches or locations and each uses the same name and EIN, the filer must aggregate the total volume to be filed for that EIN and apply the filing requirement accordingly.

.03 For additional information on filing requirements, please refer to the instructions on Form 8851.

Sec. 5. Due Dates

.01 *The due dates for filing paper returns with IRS also apply to electronic filing. File Form 8851, postmarked no later than March 20, 2007 for each reporting period. The two reporting periods are January 1, 2005 through June 30, 2005 for 2005 and January 1, 2006 through June 30, 2006 for 2006.*

.02 When using a delivery service other than the U.S. Postal Service, if no date of shipment appears on the package or container, the date of receipt will be the date received at IRS/ECC-MTB. Notice 97–26, 1997–17 I.R.B. 6, provides rules for determining the date that is treated as the postmark date. For items delivered by a non-designated Private Delivery Service (PDS), the actual date of receipt by IRS/ECC-MTB will be used as the filing date. For items delivered by a designated PDS, but through a type of service not designated in Notice 2004–83, 2004–52 I.R.B. 1030, the actual date of receipt by IRS/ECC-MTB will be used as the filing date. The timely mailing rule also applies to furnishing statements to recipients and participants.

Note: Due to security regulations at ECC-MTB, the Internal Revenue police officers will only accept packages from PDSs or couriers from *8:00 a.m. to 3:00 p.m.*, Monday through Friday.

Sec. 6. Processing of Information Returns Electronically

.01 All data received at IRS/ECC-MTB for processing will be given the same protection as individual income tax returns (Form 1040). IRS/ECC-MTB will process the data and determine if the records are formatted and coded according to this revenue procedure.

.02 *If you are filing information for more than one trustee or tax year, each trustee or tax year must be transmitted separately.*

.03 Do not report duplicate information. If a filer submits returns electronically, identical paper documents must **not** be filed.

.04 If the data is formatted incorrectly, IRS/ECC-MTB will request a replacement file. When IRS/ECC-MTB requests a replacement file, it is because we encountered errors (not limited to format) and were unable to process the file. It is imperative that filers maintain backup copies and/or recreate capabilities for their information return files. Open all IRS/ECC-MTB correspondence immediately. Refer to Part B, Section 4, for detailed procedures for replacing files submitted electronically.

.05 IRS/ECC-MTB will work with the filers to identify and resolve processing problems. If contacted by IRS/ECC-MTB, please respond promptly. IRS/ECC-MTB may have information the filers need to correct their files.

Sec. 7. Effect on Paper Documents

.01 Electronic reporting eliminates the need to submit paper Forms 8851 to IRS.

.02 Even though the threshold for filing electronically is 250 or more MSAs, IRS encourages transmitters to submit all returns electronically.

.03 The address for filing paper Forms 8851 is:

IRS-Enterprise Computing Center — Martinsburg
Information Reporting Program
Attn: 8851 Coordinator
240 Murall Drive
Kearneysville, WV 25430

.04 In all instances, identify which accounts are for individuals that were previously uninsured or excludable account holders, if applicable.

Sec. 8. State Abbreviations

.01 The following state and U.S. territory abbreviations are to be used when developing the state code portion of address fields. This table provides state and territory abbreviations only, and does not represent those states participating in the Combined Federal/State Filing Program.

State	Code	State	Code	State	Code
Alabama	AL	Kentucky	KY	No. Mariana Islands	MP
Alaska	AK	Louisiana	LA	Ohio	OH
American Samoa	AS	Maine	ME	Oklahoma	OK
Arizona	AZ	Marshall Islands	MH	Oregon	OR
Arkansas	AR	Maryland	MD	Pennsylvania	PA
California	CA	Massachusetts	MA	Puerto Rico	PR
Colorado	CO	Michigan	MI	Rhode Island	RI
Connecticut	CT	Minnesota	MN	South Carolina	SC
Delaware	DE	Mississippi	MS	South Dakota	SD
District of Columbia	DC	Missouri	MO	Tennessee	TN
Federated States of Micronesia	FM	Montana	MT	Texas	TX
Florida	FL	Nebraska	NE	Utah	UT
Georgia	GA	Nevada	NV	Vermont	VT
Guam	GU	New Hampshire	NH	Virginia	VA
Hawaii	HI	New Jersey	NJ	(U.S.) Virgin Islands	VI
Idaho	ID	New Mexico	NM	Washington	WA
Illinois	IL	New York	NY	West Virginia	WV
Indiana	IN	North Carolina	NC	Wisconsin	WI
Iowa	IA	North Dakota	ND	Wyoming	WY
Kansas	KS				

.02 Filers must adhere to the city, state, and ZIP Code format for U.S. addresses in the "B" Record. This also includes American Samoa, Federated States of Micronesia, Guam, Marshall Islands, Northern Mariana Islands, Puerto Rico, and the U.S. Virgin Islands.

.03 When reporting APO/FPO addresses, use the following format:

EXAMPLE:

Payee Name	PVT Willard J. Doe
Mailing Address	Company F, PSC Box 100 167 Infantry REGT
Payee City	APO (or FPO)
Payee State	AE, AA, or AP*
Payee ZIP Code	098010100

*AE is the designation for ZIPs beginning with 090–098, AA for ZIP 340, and AP for ZIPs 962–966.

Sec. 9. Definition of Terms

Element	Description
Account Holder	The owner of the Archer MSA.
Employer Identification Number (EIN)	A nine-digit number assigned by IRS for Federal tax reporting purposes.
File	For the purpose of this revenue procedure, a file consists of all records submitted by a transmitter electronically.
Filer	Person or organization that prepares and submits files. May be the trustee and/or transmitter.
Replacement	An information return file sent by the filer **at the request of IRS/ECC-MTB** because of errors encountered while processing their original submission.

Note 1: Filers should never submit files to IRS/ECC-MTB marked "Replacement" unless IRS/ECC-MTB has requested a replacement file in writing or via the FIRE System.

Element	Description
Social Security Number (SSN)	A nine-digit number assigned by the Social Security Administration (SSA) to an individual for tax and wage reporting purposes.
Special Character	Any character that is not a numeric, an alpha, or a blank.
Taxpayer Identification Number (TIN)	May be either a Social Security Number (SSN) or an Employer Identification Number (EIN).
Transmitter Control Code (TCC)	The five-digit code "MSA01" assigned to all filers prior to submitting Forms 8851 electronically. This number is inserted in the "A" Record and must be present in the file.
Trustee	Person or organization that is the custodian of the Archer MSA and is required to file Form 8851.

Part B. Electronic Filing Specifications

Note: The FIRE System DOES NOT provide fill-in forms. Filers must program files according to the Record Layout Specifications contained in this publication. For a list of software providers, log on to *www.irs.gov* and go to the *Approved IRS e-file for Business Providers* link.

Sec. 1. General

.01 Electronic filing of Forms 1098, 1099, 5498, 8851 and W-2G information returns, originals, corrections, and replacements is offered as an alternative to paper filing. Payers who are under the filing threshold requirement, are encouraged to file electronically.

.02 All electronic filing of information returns are received at IRS/ECC-MTB via the FIRE (Filing Information Returns Electronically) System. To connect to the FIRE System, point your browser to *http://fire.irs.gov*. The system is designed to support the electronic filing of information returns only.

.03 The electronic filing of information returns is not affiliated with any other IRS electronic filing programs. Filers must obtain separate approval to participate in each program. Only inquiries concerning electronic filing of information returns should be directed to IRS/ECC-MTB.

.04 Files submitted to IRS/ECC-MTB electronically must be in standard ASCII code. Do not send paper forms with the same information as electronically submitted files. This would create duplicate reporting resulting in penalty notices.

Sec. 2. Advantages of Filing Electronically

Some of the advantages of filing electronically are:

(1) Paperless, no Form 4804 requirements.

(2) Security – Secure Socket Layer (SSL) 128-bit encryption.

(3) Results available within 5 workdays regarding the acceptability of the data transmitted. It is the filer's responsibility to log into the system and check results.

(4) Better customer service due to on-line availability of transmitter's files for research purposes.

Sec. 3. Electronic Filing Approval Procedure

.01 Filers **must** fax a Form 8851, Summary of Archer MSAs, to IRS/ECC-MTB **prior** to filing the Form(s) 8851 electronically. **Only** trustee information, information above line 'a', should be provided on the Form 8851 when filing electronically. Please annotate the Form 8851 with "Electronic Filing" to indicate the method of filing. The fax number is (304) 264–5602.

.02 *Filers* ***must*** *call ECC-MTB toll-free at 1–866–455–7438, extension 3* ***prior*** *to logging on to the FIRE System for procedures specific to filing Form 8851.*

.03 Electronic filers assign their own logon name and password and do not need prior or special approval.

.04 For all passwords, it is the user's responsibility to remember the password and not allow the password to be compromised. Passwords are user assigned at first logon and must be 8 alpha/numerics containing at least 1 uppercase, 1 lowercase, and 1 numeric. However, filers who forget their password or PIN, can call **toll-free 1–866–455–7438** for assistance. The FIRE System may require users to change their passwords on a yearly basis.

Sec. 4. Electronic Submissions

.01 Electronically filed information may be submitted to IRS/ECC-MTB 24 hours a day, 7 days a week. Technical assistance is available Monday through Friday between 8:30 a.m. and 4:30 p.m. Eastern time by calling **toll-free 1–866–455–7438, ext. 3.**

.02 The FIRE System will be down from 2 p.m. EST December 21, 2007, through January 2, 2008. This allows IRS/ECC-MTB to update its system to reflect current year changes.

.03 If you are sending files larger than 10,000 records electronically, data compression is encouraged. When transmitting files larger than 5 million records, please contact IRS/ECC-MTB for additional information. WinZip and PKZip are the only acceptable compression packages. IRS/ECC-MTB cannot accept self-extracting zip files or compressed files containing multiple files. The time required to transmit information returns electronically will vary depending upon the type of connection to the internet and if data compression is used. **The time required to transmit a file can be reduced up to 95 percent by using compression.**

.04 Transmitters may create files using self assigned file name(s). Files submitted electronically will be assigned a new unique file name by the FIRE System. The filename assigned by the FIRE System will consist of submission type (ORIG [original] and REPL [replacement]), the filer's TCC and a four-digit number sequence. The sequence number will be incremented for every file sent. For example, if it is your first original file for the calendar year and your TCC is MSA01, the IRS assigned filename would be ORIG.MSA01.0001. **Record the filename.** This information will be needed by ECC-MTB to identify the file, if assistance is required.

.05 If a file was submitted timely and is bad, the filer will have up to 60 days from the day the file was transmitted to transmit an acceptable replacement file. If an acceptable file is not received within 60 days, the payer could be subject to late filing penalties. This only applies to files originally submitted electronically.

- A **replacement** is an information return file sent by the filer because the CHECK FILE STATUS option on the FIRE System indicated the original file was bad. After the necessary changes have been made, the file must be transmitted through the FIRE System. (**See Note.**)

Note: Filers should never transmit anything to IRS/ECC-MTB as a "Replacement" file unless the CHECK FILE STATUS option on the FIRE System indicates the file is bad.

Sec. 5. PIN Requirements

.01 User will be prompted to create a PIN consisting of 10 numerics when establishing their initial logon name and password.

.02 The PIN is required each time an ORIGINAL or REPLACEMENT file is sent electronically and is permission to release the file. An authorized agent may enter their PIN, however, the payer is responsible for the accuracy of the returns. The payer will be liable for penalties for failure to comply with filing requirements. If you forget your PIN, please call **toll-free 1–866–455–7438, ext. 3** for assistance.

Sec. 6. Electronic Filing Specifications

.01 The FIRE System is designed exclusively for the filing of Forms 1042-S, 1098, 1099, 5498, 8027, 8851, and W-2G.

.02 The results of the electronic transmission will be available in the CHECK FILE STATUS area of the FIRE System within 5 business days. It is the filer's responsibility to verify the acceptability of files submitted by selecting the CHECK FILE STATUS option. Forms 1042-S and 8027 require a longer processing time.

Sec. 7. Connecting to the FIRE System

.01 Point your browser to *http://fire.irs.gov* to connect to the FIRE System.

.02 Filers should turn off their pop-up blocking software before transmitting their files.
.03 Before connecting, call ECC-MTB for specific log on procedures for Form 8851 (See Part A, Sec. 3.)
.04 Your browser must support SSL 128-bit encryption.
.05 Your browser must be set to receive "cookies". Cookies are used to preserve your User ID status.

<u>**First time connection to The FIRE System**</u> (If you have logged on previously, skip to Subsequent Connections to the FIRE System.)

Click ***"Create New Account".***

Fill out the registration form and click ***"Submit"***.

Enter your ***User ID*** (most users logon with their first and last name).

Enter and verify your ***password*** (the password is user assigned and must be 8 alpha/numerics, containing at least 1 uppercase, 1 lowercase and 1 numeric). FIRE may require you to change the password once a year.

Click ***"Create".***

If you receive the message **"Account Created"**, click ***"OK".***

Enter and verify your 10-digit self-assigned PIN (Personal Identification Number).

Click ***"Submit".***

If you receive the message **"Your PIN has been successfully created!",** click ***"OK".***

Read the bulletin(s) and/or click **"Click here to continue".**

<u>**Subsequent connections to The FIRE System**</u>

Click ***"Log On".***

Enter your ***User ID*** (most users logon with their first and last name).

Enter your ***password*** (the password is user assigned and is case sensitive).

Read the bulletin(s) and/or click **"Click here to continue".**

<u>**Uploading your file to the FIRE System**</u>

Options:

Click ***"Send Information Returns"***
Enter your ***TCC:***
Enter your ***EIN:***
Click ***"Submit".***

The system will then display the company name, address, city, state, ZIP code, phone number, contact and email address. This information will be used to contact or send correspondence (if necessary) regarding this transmission. Update as appropriate and/or Click ***"Accept".***

Click one of the following:

Original File
Replacement File
Click on the file to be replaced.

Enter your 10-digit PIN.
Click ***"Submit".***
Click ***"Browse"*** to locate the file and open it.
Click ***"Upload".***

Uploading your file to the FIRE System

When the upload is complete, the screen will display the total bytes received and tell you the name of the file you just uploaded.

If you have more files to upload for that TCC:

Click ***"File Another?";*** otherwise,

Click ***"Main Menu".***

It is your responsibility to check the acceptability of your file; therefore, be sure to check back into the system in 5 business days using the CHECK FILE STATUS option.

Checking your FILE STATUS

Menu:

Click ***"Check File Status".***

Enter your ***TCC:***

Enter your ***EIN:***

Click ***"Search".***

If "Results" indicate:

"Good, Not Released" and you agree with the "Count of Payees", you are finished with this file.

"Good, Released" — File has been released to our mainline processing.

"Bad" — Correct the errors and timely resubmit the file as a "replacement".

"Not yet processed" — File has been received, but we do not have results available yet. Please check back in a few days.

Click on the desired file for a detailed report of your transmission.

When you are finished, click on ***Main Menu.***

Click ***"Log Out".***

Close your Web Browser.

Part C. Record Format Specifications and Record Layouts

.01 In order to be acceptable, records within the file must be in the following sequence:

(a) A Trustee "A" Record

(b) Account Holder "B" Records

(c) Control Total "C" Record

.02 If you are filing for more than one trustee, each trustee **must** be reported on a separate file.

Sec. 1. The Trustee "A" Record — General Field Descriptions and Record Layout

.01 This record identifies the entity preparing and transmitting the file. The first record of a file MUST be a Trustee "A" Record. Otherwise, a replacement file will be requested. The "A" Record is a fixed length of 150 positions.

Record Name: Trustee "A" Record			
Positions	**Field Title**	**Length**	**Description and Remarks**
1	Record Type	1	**Required.** Enter "A".
2–10	Trustee TIN	9	Enter the Taxpayer Identification Number (TIN), either the Employer Identification Number (EIN) or the Social Security Number (SSN) of the Trustee.
11–50	Trustee Name	40	**Required.** Enter the trustee's name. Abbreviate if necessary to fit 40-character limit, and omit punctuation. Left-justify and blank fill.
51–90	Trustee Address	40	**Required.** Enter mailing address of the trustee. Street address should include number, street, apartment or suite number (or P.O. Box if mail is not delivered to street address). Abbreviate as needed to fit 40-character limit, and omit punctuation. Left-justify and blank fill.
91–119	Trustee City	29	**Required.** Enter the city or town of trustee. If applicable, enter APO or FPO only. Left-justify and blank fill.
120–121	Trustee State	2	**Required.** Enter the valid U.S. Postal Service state abbreviation. Refer to the chart of valid state abbreviations in Part A, Sec. 8.
122–130	Trustee ZIP Code	9	**Required.** Enter the ZIP code of the trustee for all U.S. addresses, U.S. territories or possessions, APO/FPO addresses. For trustees using a five-digit ZIP code, enter the ZIP code in the left-most five positions and zero fill the remaining four positions. For trustees outside the U.S., enter nine zeros only. Do NOT blank fill.
131–135	Transmitter Control Code	5	**Required.** Enter your five-digit Transmitter (TCC) Control Code, "MSA01." This is the TCC assigned to all filers who report Form(s) 8851 electronically.
136	Report Period	1	**Required.** Enter the last digit of the year for which the Form 8851 is being filed. For example, if reporting for tax year 2005, enter a '5' , enter a '6', if reporting for 2006, etc.
137–148	Blanks	12	Enter Blanks.
149–150	Blanks or Carriage Return/Line Feed	2	Enter blanks or Carriage Return/Line Feed(CR/LF).

Trustee "A" Record Layout

Record Type "A"	Trustee TIN	Trustee Name	Trustee Address	Trustee City
1	2–10	11–50	51–90	91–119

Trustee State	Trustee ZIP Code	Transmitter Control Code (TCC) "MSA01"	Report Period	Blanks	Blanks or Carriage Return/Line Feed
120–121	122–130	131–135	136	137–148	149–150

Sec. 2. The Account Holder "B" Record — General Field Descriptions and Record Layout

.01 The "B" record contains the account holder information. The format of the "B" record will remain constant and is a fixed length of 150 positions.

Record Name: Account Holder "B" Record			
Positions	**Field Title**	**Length**	**Description and Remarks**
1	Record Type	1	**Required.** Enter "B".
2–10	Account Holder's Identification Number (TIN)	9	**Required.** Enter the nine-digit Taxpayer Identification Number (TIN) (EIN or SSN) of the Account Holder. Do NOT enter blanks, hyphens, or alpha characters. A TIN consisting of all the same digit (e.g., 111111111) is not acceptable.
11–50	Account Holder Name	40	**Required.** Enter the name of the account holder. Abbreviate as needed. Left-justify and blank fill.
51	Previously Uninsured Indicator	1	**Required.** Enter a code from the list below to indicate whether or not the account holder was previously uninsured. For a definition of "Previously Uninsured", please see Form 8851. **Condition** — **Code** Previously uninsured — 1 Previously insured — 0
52	Excludable Indicator	1	**Required.** Enter a code from the list below to indicate whether the account holder is excludable. For a definition of "excludable", please see Form 8851. **Condition** — **Code** Excludable — 1 Not excludable — 0
53–148	Blanks	96	Enter blanks.
149–150	Blank or Carriage Return/Line Feed	2	Enter blanks or carriage return/line feed (CR/LF).

Account Holder "B" Record Layout

Record Type "B"	Account Holder TIN	Account Holder Name	Previously Uninsured Indicator
1	2–10	11–50	51

Excludable Indicator	Blanks	Blanks or Carriage Return/Line Feed
52	53–148	149–150

Sec. 3. The Control Total "C" Record — General Field Descriptions and Record Layout

.01 Enter a "C" Record after the last "B" Record submitted for a particular Trustee "A" Record. The "C" Record serves as a summary of the preceding "B" Records' data, and enables IRS to cross check the correctness of information received.

.02 A "C" Record is the last record on the file.

.03 Each "C" Record has a fixed length of 150 positions.

.04 If the field is not applicable, allow for the field by entering blanks or zeros as instructed.

Record Name: Control Total "C" Record			
Positions	**Field Title**	**Length**	**Description and Remarks**
1	Record Type	1	**Required.** Enter "C".
2–7	Number of Account Holders	6	**Required.** Enter the total number of account holders being reported. Right-justify and zero fill.
8–13	Previously Uninsured	6	Enter the total number of account holders that were previously uninsured. Right-justify and zero fill.
14–19	Excludable	6	Enter the total number of excludable account holders being reported. Right-justify and zero fill.
20–148	Blanks	129	Enter blanks.
149–150	Blank or Carriage Return/Line Feed	2	Enter blanks or carriage return/line feed (CR/LF).

Control Total "C" Record Layout

Record Type "C"	Number of Account Holders	Previously Uninsured	Excludable
1	2–7	8–13	14–19

Blanks	Blanks or Carriage Return/Line Feed (CR/LF)
20–148	149–150

Part IV. Items of General Interest

Notice of Proposed Rulemaking and Notice of Public Hearing

Determining the Amount of Taxes Paid for Purposes of Section 901

REG–156779–06

AGENCY: Internal Revenue Service (IRS), Treasury.

ACTION: Notice of proposed rulemaking and notice of public hearing.

SUMMARY: These proposed regulations provide guidance relating to the determination of the amount of taxes paid for purposes of section 901. The proposed regulations affect taxpayers that claim direct and indirect foreign tax credits. This document also provides notice of a public hearing.

DATES: Written or electronic comments must be received by June 28, 2007. Outlines of topics to be discussed at the public hearing scheduled for July 30, 2007, at 10 a.m. must be received by July 9, 2007.

ADDRESSES: Send submissions to CC:PA:LPD:PR (REG–156779–06), Room 5203, Internal Revenue Service, P.O. Box 7604, Ben Franklin Station, Washington, DC 20044. Submissions may be hand delivered Monday through Friday between the hours of 8 a.m. and 4 p.m. to CC:PA:LPD:PR (REG–156779–06), Courier's Desk, Internal Revenue Service, 1111 Constitution Avenue, N.W., Washington, D.C., or sent electronically via the Federal eRulemaking Portal at *www.regulations.gov* (IRS REG–156779–06). The public hearing will be held in the Auditorium of the Internal Revenue Building, 1111 Constitution Avenue, N.W., Washington, D.C.

FOR FURTHER INFORMATION CONTACT: Concerning submission of comments, the hearing, and/or to be placed on the building access list to attend the hearing, Kelly Banks (202) 622–7180; concerning the regulations, Bethany A. Ingwalson, (202) 622–3850 (not toll-free numbers).

SUPPLEMENTARY INFORMATION:

Background

Section 901 of the Internal Revenue Code (Code) permits taxpayers to claim a credit for income, war profits, and excess profits taxes paid or accrued (or deemed paid) during the taxable year to any foreign country or to any possession of the United States.

Section 1.901–2(a) of the regulations defines a tax as a compulsory payment pursuant to the authority of a foreign country to levy taxes, and further provides that a tax is an income, war profits, or excess profits tax if the predominant character of the tax is that of an income tax in the U.S. sense. Section 1.901–2(e) provides rules for determining the amount of tax paid by a taxpayer for purposes of section 901. Section 1.901–2(e)(5) provides that an amount paid is not a compulsory payment, and thus is not an amount of tax paid, to the extent that the amount paid exceeds the amount of liability under foreign law for tax. For purposes of determining whether an amount paid exceeds the amount of liability under foreign law for tax, §1.901–2(e)(5) provides the following rule:

> An amount paid does not exceed the amount of such liability if the amount paid is determined by the taxpayer in a manner that is consistent with a reasonable interpretation and application of the substantive and procedural provisions of foreign law (including applicable tax treaties) in such a way as to reduce, over time, the taxpayer's reasonably expected liability under foreign law for tax, and if the taxpayer exhausts all effective and practical remedies, including invocation of competent authority procedures available under applicable tax treaties, to reduce, over time, the taxpayer's liability for foreign tax (including liability pursuant to a foreign tax audit adjustment).

Section 1.901–2(e)(5) provides further that if foreign tax law includes options or elections whereby a taxpayer's liability may be shifted, in whole or part, to a different year, the taxpayer's use or failure to use such options or elections does not result in a noncompulsory payment, and that a settlement by a taxpayer of two or more issues will be evaluated on an overall basis, not on an issue-by-issue basis, in determining whether an amount is a compulsory amount. In addition, it provides that a taxpayer is not required to alter its form of doing business, its business conduct, or the form of any transaction in order to reduce its liability for tax under foreign law.

A. *U.S.-Owned Foreign Entities*

Commentators have raised questions regarding the application of §1.901–2(e)(5) to a U.S. person that owns one or more foreign entities. In particular, commentators have raised questions concerning the application of the regulation when one foreign entity directly or indirectly owned by a U.S. person transfers, pursuant to a group relief type regime, a net loss to another foreign entity, which may or may not also be owned by the U.S. person. Certain commentators have expressed concern that foreign taxes paid by the transferor in a subsequent tax year might not be compulsory payments to the extent the transferor could have reduced its liability for those foreign taxes had it chosen not to transfer the net loss in the prior year. This concern arises because the current final regulations apply on a taxpayer-by-taxpayer basis, obligating each taxpayer to minimize its liability for foreign taxes over time, even though the net effect of the loss surrender may be to minimize the amount of foreign taxes paid in the aggregate by the controlled group over time.

Similar questions and concerns arise when one or more foreign subsidiaries of a U.S. person reach a combined settlement with a foreign taxing authority that results in an increase in the amount of one foreign subsidiary's foreign tax liability and a decrease in the amount of a second foreign subsidiary's foreign tax liability.

B. *Certain Structured Passive Investment Arrangements*

The IRS and Treasury Department have become aware that certain U.S. taxpayers are engaging in highly structured transactions with foreign counterparties in order to generate foreign tax credits. These transactions are intentionally structured to create a foreign tax liability when, removed from the elaborately engineered structure, the basic underlying business transaction generally would result in significantly less, or even no, foreign taxes. In particular, the transactions purport to convert what would otherwise be an ordinary course financing arrangement between a U.S. person and a foreign counterparty, or a portfolio investment of a U.S. person, into some form of equity ownership in a foreign special purpose vehicle (SPV). The transaction is deliberately structured to create income in the SPV for foreign tax purposes, which income is purportedly subject to foreign tax. The parties exploit differences between U.S. and foreign law in order to permit the U.S. taxpayer to claim a credit for the purported foreign tax payments while also allowing the foreign counterparty to claim a foreign tax benefit. The U.S. taxpayer and the foreign counterparty share the cost of the purported foreign tax payments through the pricing of the arrangement.

Explanation of Provisions

The proposed regulations address the application of §1.901–2(e)(5) in cases where a U.S. person directly or indirectly owns one or more foreign entities and in cases in which a U.S. person is a party to a highly structured passive investment arrangement described in this preamble. The proposed regulations would treat as a single taxpayer for purposes of §1.901–2(e)(5) all foreign entities with respect to which a U.S. person has a direct or indirect interest of 80 percent or more. The proposed regulations would treat foreign payments attributable to highly structured passive investment arrangements as noncompulsory payments under §1.901–2(e)(5) and, thus, would disallow credits for such amounts.

A. *U.S.-Owned Foreign Entities*

Section 1.901–2(e)(5) requires a taxpayer to interpret and apply foreign law reasonably in such a way as to reduce, over time, the taxpayer's reasonably expected liability under foreign law for tax. This requirement ensures that a taxpayer will make reasonable efforts to minimize its foreign tax liability even though the taxpayer may otherwise be indifferent to the imposition of foreign tax due to the availability of the foreign tax credit. The purpose of this requirement is served if all foreign entities owned by such person, in the aggregate, satisfy the requirements of the regulation. Accordingly, for purposes of determining compliance with §1.901–2(e)(5), the proposed regulations would treat as a single taxpayer all foreign entities in which the same U.S. person has a direct or indirect interest of 80 percent or more. For this purpose, an interest of 80 percent or more means stock possessing 80 percent or more of the vote and value (in the case of a foreign corporation) or an interest representing 80 percent or more of the income (in the case of non-corporate foreign entities).

The proposed regulations provide that if one 80 percent-owned foreign entity transfers or surrenders a net loss for the taxable year to a second such entity pursuant to a foreign law group relief or similar regime, foreign tax paid by the transferor in a different tax year does not fail to be a compulsory payment solely because such tax would not have been due had the transferor retained the net loss and carried it over to such other year. Similarly, it provides that if one or more 80 percent-owned foreign entities enter into a combined settlement under foreign law of two or more issues, such settlement will be evaluated on an overall basis, not on an issue-by-issue or entity-by-entity basis, in determining whether an amount is a compulsory amount. The proposed regulations include examples to illustrate the proposed rule.

The IRS and Treasury Department intend to monitor structures involving U.S.-owned foreign groups, including those that would be covered by the proposed regulations, to determine whether taxpayers are utilizing such structures to separate foreign taxes from the related income. The IRS and Treasury Department may issue additional regulations in the future in order to address arrangements that result in the inappropriate separation of foreign tax and income.

B. *Certain Structured Passive Investment Arrangements*

The structured arrangements discovered and identified by the IRS and the Treasury Department can be grouped into three general categories: (1) U.S. borrower transactions, (2) U.S. lender transactions, and (3) asset holding transactions. The transactions, including the claimed U.S. tax results, are described in section B.1 of this preamble. Section B.2 of this preamble discusses the purpose of the foreign tax credit regime and explains why allowing a credit in the transactions is inconsistent with this purpose. Section B.3 of this preamble discusses comments the IRS and the Treasury Department have received on the transactions and describes the proposed regulations. The IRS is continuing to scrutinize the transactions under current law and intends to utilize all tools available to challenge the claimed U.S. tax results in appropriate cases.

1. *Categories of structured passive investment arrangements*

(a) *U.S. borrower transactions*

The first category consists of transactions in which a U.S. person indirectly borrows funds from an unrelated foreign counterparty. If a U.S. person were to borrow funds directly from a foreign person, the U.S. person generally would make nondeductible principal payments and deductible interest payments. The U.S. person would not incur foreign tax. The foreign lender generally would owe foreign tax on its interest income. In a structured financing arrangement, the U.S. borrower attempts to convert all or a portion of its deductible interest payments and, in certain cases, its nondeductible principal payments into creditable foreign tax payments. The U.S. borrower's foreign tax credit benefit is shared by the parties through the pricing of the arrangement. See *Example 1* of proposed §1.901–2(e)(5)(iv)(D).

In a typical structured financing arrangement, the loan is made indirectly through an SPV. The foreign lender's interest income (and, in many cases, other income) is effectively isolated in the SPV. The U.S. borrower acquires a direct or indirect interest in the SPV and asserts that it has a direct or indirect equity interest in the SPV for U.S. tax purposes. The U.S. borrower claims a credit for foreign taxes imposed on the income derived by the SPV. The U.S. borrower's purported equity interest may be treated as debt for foreign tax purposes or it may be treated as an equity interest that is owned by the foreign lender for foreign tax purposes. In either case, the foreign lender is treated as owning an equity interest in the SPV for foreign tax purposes, which entitles the foreign lender to receive tax-free distributions from the SPV.

For example, assume that a U.S. person seeks to borrow $1.5 billion from a foreign person. Instead of borrowing the funds directly, the U.S. borrower forms a corporation (SPV) in the same country as the foreign counterparty. The U.S. borrower contributes $1.5 billion to SPV in exchange for 100 percent of the stock of SPV. SPV, in turn, loans the entire $1.5 billion to a corporation wholly owned by the U.S. borrower. The U.S. borrower recovers its $1.5 billion by selling its entire interest in SPV to the foreign counterparty, subject to an obligation to repurchase the interest in five years for $1.5 billion. Each year, SPV earns $120 million of interest income from the U.S. borrower's subsidiary. SPV pays $36 million of foreign tax and distributes the remaining $84 million to the foreign counterparty.

The U.S. borrower takes the position that, for U.S. tax purposes, the sale-repurchase transaction is a borrowing secured by the SPV stock. Accordingly, the U.S. borrower asserts that it owns the stock of SPV for U.S. tax purposes and has an outstanding debt obligation to the foreign counterparty. It reports the distribution from SPV as dividend income and claims indirect credits under section 902 for the $36 million of foreign taxes paid by SPV. It includes in income the cash dividend of $84 million paid to the foreign counterparty, plus a section 78 gross-up amount of $36 million, for a total of $120 million. The U.S. borrower claims a deduction of $84 million as interest on its debt obligation to the foreign counterparty. In addition, the U.S. borrower's subsidiary claims an interest deduction of $120 million. In the aggregate, the U.S. borrower and its subsidiary claim a foreign tax credit of $36 million and an interest expense deduction (net of income inclusions) of $84 million.

For foreign tax purposes, the foreign counterparty owns the equity of SPV and is not subject to additional foreign tax upon receipt of the dividend. Thus, the net result is that the foreign jurisdiction receives foreign tax payments attributable to what is in substance the lender's interest income, which is consistent with the foreign tax results that would be expected from a direct borrowing.

Both parties benefit from the arrangement. The foreign lender obtains an after-foreign tax interest rate that is higher than the after-foreign tax interest rate it would earn on a direct loan. The U.S. borrower's funding costs are lower on an after-U.S. tax basis (though not on a pre-U.S. tax basis) because it has converted interest expense into creditable foreign tax payments.

The benefit to the parties is solely attributable to the reduction in the U.S. borrower's U.S. tax liability resulting from the foreign tax credits claimed by the U.S. borrower. The foreign jurisdiction benefits from the arrangement because the amount of interest received by SPV exceeds the amount of interest that would have been received by the foreign lender if the transaction had been structured as a direct loan. As a result, the amount paid by SPV to the foreign jurisdiction exceeds the amount of foreign tax the foreign jurisdiction would have imposed on the foreign lender's interest income in connection with a direct loan.

(b) *U.S. lender transactions*

The second category consists of transactions in which a U.S. person indirectly loans funds to an unrelated foreign counterparty. If a U.S. person were to loan the funds directly to the foreign person, the U.S. person generally would be subject to U.S. tax on its interest income and the borrower would receive a corresponding deduction for the interest expense. The U.S. person generally would not be subject to foreign tax other than, in certain circumstances, a gross basis withholding tax.

In a typical structured financing arrangement, the U.S. person advances funds to a foreign borrower indirectly through an SPV. The U.S. person asserts that its interest in the SPV is equity for U.S. tax purposes. Income of the foreign borrower (or another foreign counterparty) is effectively shifted into the SPV. The U.S. person receives cash payments from the SPV and claims a credit for foreign taxes imposed on the income recognized by the SPV for foreign tax purposes. The foreign tax credits eliminate all or substantially all of the U.S. tax the U.S. person would otherwise owe on its return and, in many cases, U.S. tax the U.S. person would otherwise owe on unrelated foreign source income. The economic cost of the foreign taxes is shared through the pricing of the arrangement. See *Example 4* of proposed §1.901–2(e)(5)(iv)(D).

For example, assume a U.S. person seeks to loan $1 billion to a foreign person. In lieu of a direct loan, the U.S. lender contributes $1 billion to a newly-formed corporation (SPV). The foreign counterparty contributes $2 billion to SPV, which is organized in the same country as the foreign counterparty. SPV contributes the total $3 billion to a second special purpose entity (RH), receiving a 99 percent equity interest in RH in exchange. The foreign counterparty owns the remaining 1 percent of RH. RH loans the funds to the foreign counterparty in exchange for a note that pays interest currently and a second zero-coupon note. RH is a corporation for U.S. tax purposes and a flow-through entity for foreign tax purposes.

Each year, the foreign counterparty pays $92 million of interest to RH, and RH accrues $113 million of interest on the zero-coupon note. RH distributes the $92 million of cash it receives to SPV. Because RH is a partnership for foreign tax purposes, SPV is required to report for foreign tax purposes 99 percent ($203 million) of the income recognized by RH. Because RH is a corporation for U.S. tax purposes, SPV recognizes only the cash distributions of $92 million for U.S. tax purposes. SPV pays foreign tax of $48 million on its net income (30 percent of $159 million, or $203 interest income less $44 million interest deduction) and distributes its remaining cash of $44 million to the U.S. lender.

The U.S. lender takes the position that it has an equity interest in SPV for U.S. tax purposes. It claims an indirect credit for the $48 million of foreign taxes paid by SPV. It includes in income the cash dividend of $44 million, plus a section 78 gross-up amount of $48 million. For foreign tax purposes, the U.S. lender's interest in SPV is debt, and the foreign borrower owns 100 percent of the equity of SPV. The foreign counterparty and SPV, in the aggregate, have a net deduction of $44 million for foreign tax purposes.

Both parties benefit from the transaction. The foreign borrower obtains "cheap financing" because the $44 million of cash distributed to the U.S. lender is less than the amount of interest it would have to pay on a direct loan with respect to which the U.S. lender would owe U.S. tax. The U.S. lender is better off on an after-U.S. tax basis because of the foreign tax credits, which eliminate the U.S. lender's U.S. tax on the "dividend" income.

The benefit to the parties is solely attributable to the reduction in the U.S. lender's U.S. tax liability resulting from the foreign tax credits claimed by the U.S. lender. The foreign jurisdiction benefits because the aggregate foreign tax result is a deduction for the foreign borrower that is less than the amount of the interest deduction the foreign borrower would have had upon a direct loan.

(c) *Asset holding transactions*

The third category of transactions ("asset holding transactions") consists of transactions in which a U.S. person that owns an income-producing asset moves the asset into a foreign taxing jurisdiction. For example, assume a U.S. person owns passive-type assets (such as debt obligations) generating an income stream that is subject to U.S. tax. In an asset holding transaction, the U.S. person transfers the assets to an SPV that is subject to tax in a foreign jurisdiction on the income stream. Ordinarily, such a transfer would not affect the U.S. person's after-tax position since the U.S. person could claim a credit for the foreign tax paid and, thereby, obtain a corresponding reduction in the amount of U.S. tax it would otherwise owe. In the structured transactions, however, the cost of the foreign tax is shared by a foreign person who obtains a foreign tax benefit by participating in the arrangement. Thus, the U.S. person is better off paying the foreign tax instead of U.S. tax because it does not bear the full economic burden of the foreign tax.

In a typical structured transaction, a foreign counterparty participates in the arrangement with the SPV. For example, the foreign counterparty may be considered to own a direct or indirect interest in the SPV for foreign tax purposes. The foreign counterparty's participation in the arrangement allows it to obtain a foreign tax benefit that it would not otherwise enjoy. The foreign counterparty compensates the U.S. person for this benefit in some manner. This compensation, which can be viewed as a reimbursement for a portion of the foreign tax liability resulting from the transfer of the assets, puts the U.S. person in a better after-U.S. tax position. See *Example 7* of proposed §1.901–2(e)(5)(iv)(D).

The benefit to the parties is solely attributable to the reduction in the U.S. taxpayer's U.S. tax liability resulting from the foreign tax credits claimed by the U.S. taxpayer. The foreign jurisdiction benefits because the foreign taxes purportedly paid by the SPV exceed the amount by which the foreign counterparty's taxes are reduced.

2. *Purpose of the foreign tax credit*

The purpose of the foreign tax credit is to mitigate double taxation of foreign source income. Because the foreign tax credit provides a dollar-for-dollar reduction in U.S. tax that a U.S. person would otherwise owe, the U.S. person generally is indifferent, subject to various foreign tax credit limitations, as to whether it pays foreign tax on its foreign source income (if fully offset by the foreign tax credit) or whether it pays U.S. (and no foreign) tax on that income.

The structured arrangements described in section B.1 of this preamble violate this purpose. A common feature of all these arrangements is that the U.S. person and a foreign counterparty share the economic cost of the foreign taxes claimed as credits by the U.S. person. This creates an incentive for the U.S. person to subject itself voluntarily to the foreign tax because there is a U.S. tax motivation to do so. The result is an erosion of the U.S. tax base in a manner that is not consistent with the purpose of the foreign tax credit provisions.

Although the foreign counterparty derives a foreign tax benefit in these arrangements, the foreign jurisdiction generally is made whole because of the payments to the foreign jurisdiction made by the special purpose vehicle. In fact, the aggregate amount of payments to the foreign jurisdictions in connection with these transactions generally exceeds the amount of foreign tax that would have been imposed in the ordinary course. Only the U.S. fisc experiences a reduction in tax payments as a result of the structured arrangements.

The IRS and Treasury Department recognize that often there is a business purpose for the financing or portfolio investment underlying the otherwise elaborately engineered transactions. However, it is inconsistent with the purpose of the foreign tax credit to permit a credit for foreign taxes that result from intentionally structuring a transaction to generate foreign taxes in a manner that allows the parties to obtain duplicate tax benefits and share the cost of the tax payments. The result in these structured arrangements is that both parties as well as the foreign jurisdiction benefit at the expense of the U.S. fisc.

3. *Comments and proposed regulations*

The IRS and Treasury Department have determined that it is not appropriate to allow a credit in connection with these highly engineered transactions where the U.S. taxpayer benefits by intentionally subjecting itself to foreign tax. The proposed regulations would revise §1.901–2(e)(5) to provide that an amount paid to a foreign country in connection with such an arrangement is not an amount of tax paid. Accordingly, under the proposed regulations, a taxpayer would not be eligible to claim a foreign tax credit for such a payment. For periods prior to the effective date of final regulations, the IRS will continue to utilize all available tools under current law to challenge the U.S. tax results claimed in connection with such arrangements, including the substance over form doctrine, the economic substance doctrine, debt-equity principles, tax ownership principles, existing §1.901–2(e), section 269, and the partnership anti-abuse rules of §1.701–2.

Certain commentators recommended that the IRS and Treasury Department adopt a broad anti-abuse rule that would deny a foreign tax credit in any case where allowance of the credit would be inconsistent with the purpose of the foreign tax credit regime. Other commentators recommended a narrower approach that would only deny foreign tax credits attributable to transactions that include particular features. The IRS and Treasury Department are concerned that a broad anti-abuse rule would create uncertainty for both taxpayers and the IRS. The IRS and Treasury Department have concluded that, at this time, a targeted rule denying foreign tax credits in arrangements similar to the arrangements described in section B.1 of this preamble is more appropriate.

For periods after the effective date of final regulations, the IRS and Treasury Department will continue to scrutinize other arrangements that are not covered by the regulations but are inconsistent with the purpose of the foreign tax credit. Such arrangements may include arrangements that are similar to arrangements described in the proposed regulations, but that do not meet all of the conditions included in the proposed regulations. The IRS will utilize all available tools, including those described above, to challenge the claimed U.S. tax results in appropriate cases. In addition, the IRS and Treasury Department may issue additional regulations in the future in order to address such other arrangements.

The proposed regulations would retain the general rule in the existing regulations that a taxpayer need not alter its form of doing business or the form of any transaction in order to reduce its foreign tax liability. However, the proposed regulations would provide that, notwithstanding the general rule, an amount paid to a foreign country (a "foreign payment") is not a compulsory payment, and thus is not an amount of tax paid, if the foreign payment is attributable to a structured passive investment arrangement. For this purpose, the proposed regulations would define a structured passive investment arrangement as an arrangement that satisfies six conditions. The six conditions consist of features that are common to the three types of arrangements identified in section B.1 of this preamble. The IRS and Treasury Department believe it is appropriate to treat foreign payments attributable to these arrangements as voluntary payments because such arrangements are intentionally structured to generate the foreign payment.

The first condition is that the arrangement utilizes an entity that meets two requirements (an "SPV"). The first requirement is that substantially all of the gross income (for United States tax purposes) of the entity is attributable to passive investment income and substantially all of the assets of the entity are assets held to produce such passive investment income. The second requirement is that there is a purported foreign tax payment attributable to income of the entity. The purported foreign tax may be paid by the entity itself, by the owner(s) of the entity (if the entity is treated as a pass-through entity under foreign law) or by a lower-tier entity (if the lower-tier entity is treated as a pass-through entity under U.S. law).

For purposes of this first requirement, passive investment income is defined as income described in section 954(c), with two modifications. The first modification is that if the entity is a holding company that owns a direct equity interest (other than a preferred interest) of 10 percent or more in another entity (a lower-tier entity) that is predominantly engaged in the active conduct of a trade or business (or substantially all the assets of which consist of qualifying equity interests in other entities that are predominantly engaged in the active conduct of a trade or business), passive investment income does not include income attributable to the interest in such lower-tier entity. This exception does not apply if there are arrangements under which substantially all of the opportunity for gain and risk of loss with respect to such interest in the lower-tier entity are borne by either the U.S. party or the counterparty (but not both). Accordingly, a direct equity interest in any such lower-tier entity is not held to produce passive investment income provided there are no arrangements under which substantially all of the entity's opportunity for gain and risk of loss with respect to the lower-tier entity are borne by either the U.S. party or the counterparty (but not both). This modification is based on the notion that an entity is not a passive investment vehicle of the type targeted by these regulations if the entity is a holding company for one or more operating companies. This modification ensures that a joint venture arrangement between a U.S. person and a foreign person is not treated as a passive investment arrangement solely because the joint venture is conducted through a holding company structure.

The second modification is that passive investment income is determined by disregarding sections 954(c)(3) and (c)(6) and by treating income attributable to transactions with the counterparties (described in this preamble) as ineligible for the exclusions under sections 954(h) and (i). Sections 954(c)(3) and (c)(6) provide exclusions for certain related party payments of dividends, interest, rents, and royalties. Those exclusions are not appropriate for these transactions because these transactions can be structured utilizing related party payments. The modifications to the application of sections 954(h) and (i) are intended to ensure that income derived from the counterparty cannot qualify for the exclusion from passive investment income, but will not prevent other income from qualifying for those exclusions. The IRS and Treasury Department intend that the structured financing arrangements described in this preamble do not qualify for the active banking, financing or insurance business exceptions to the definition of passive investment income. Comments are requested on whether further modifications or clarifications to the proposed regulations' definition of passive investment income are appropriate to ensure this result.

The requirement that substantially all of the assets of the entity produce passive investment income is intended to ensure that an entity engaged in an active trade or business is not treated as an SPV solely because, in a particular year, it derives only passive investment income.

The second overall condition is that a person (a "U.S. party") would be eligible to claim a credit under section 901(a) (including a credit for foreign taxes deemed paid under section 902 or 960) for all or a portion of the foreign payment if such payment were an amount of tax paid. Such eligibility to claim the credit could arise because the U.S. party would be treated as having paid or accrued the foreign payment for purposes of section 901 if it were an amount of tax paid. Alternatively, the U.S. party's eligibility to claim the credit could arise because the U.S. party owns an equity interest in the SPV or another entity that would be treated as having paid or accrued the foreign payment for purposes of section 901 if it were an amount of tax paid.

The third overall condition is that the foreign payment or payments are (or are expected to be) substantially greater than the amount of credits, if any, that the U.S. party would reasonably expect to be eligible to claim under section 901(a) if such U.S. party directly owned its proportionate share of the assets owned by the SPV other than through a branch, a permanent establishment or any other arrangement (such as an agency arrangement) that would subject the income generated by its share of the assets to a net basis foreign tax. For example, if the SPV owns a note that generates interest income with respect to which a foreign payment is made, but foreign law (including an applicable treaty) provides for a zero rate of withholding tax on interest paid to non-residents, the U.S. party would not reasonably expect to pay foreign tax for which it could claim foreign tax credits if it directly owned the note and directly earned the interest income.

The fourth condition is that the arrangement is structured in such a manner that it results in a foreign tax benefit (such as a credit, deduction, loss, exemption or a disregarded payment) for a counterparty or for a person that is related to the counterparty, but not related to the U.S. party.

The fifth condition is that the counterparty is a person (other than the SPV) that is unrelated to the U.S. party and that (i) directly or indirectly owns 10 percent or more of the equity of the SPV under the tax laws of a foreign country in which such person is subject to tax on the basis of place of management, place of incorporation or similar criterion or otherwise subject to a net basis foreign tax or (ii) acquires 20 percent or more of the assets of the SPV under the tax laws of a foreign country in which such person is subject to tax on the basis of place of management, place of incorporation or similar criterion or otherwise subject to a net basis foreign tax.

The sixth condition is that the U.S. and an applicable foreign country treat the arrangement differently under their respective tax systems. For this purpose, an applicable foreign country is any foreign country in which either the counterparty, a person related to the counterparty (but not related to the U.S. party) or the SPV is subject to net basis tax. To provide clarity and limit the scope of this factor, the proposed regulations provide that the arrangement must be subject to one of four specified types of inconsistent treatment. Specifically, the U.S. and the foreign country (or countries) must treat one or more of the following aspects of the arrangement differently, and the U.S. treatment of the inconsistent aspect must materially affect the amount of foreign tax credits claimed, or the amount of income recognized, by the U.S. party to the arrangement: (i) the classification of an entity as a corporation or other entity subject to an entity-level tax, a partnership or other flow-through entity or an entity that is disregarded for tax purposes; (ii) the characterization as debt, equity or an instrument that is disregarded for tax purposes of an instrument issued in the transaction; (iii) the proportion of the equity of the SPV (or an entity that directly or indirectly owns the SPV) that is considered to be owned directly or indirectly by the U.S. party and the counterparty; or (iv) the amount of taxable income of the SPV for one or more tax years during which the arrangement is in effect.

Under the proposed regulations, a foreign payment would not be a compulsory payment if it is attributable to an arrangement that meets the six conditions. The proposed regulations would treat a foreign payment as attributable to such an arrangement if the foreign payment is attributable to income of the SPV. Such foreign payments include a payment by the SPV, a payment by the owner of the SPV (if the SPV is a pass-through entity under foreign law) and a payment by a lower-tier entity that is treated as a pass-through entity under U.S. law. For this purpose, a foreign payment is not treated as attributable to the income of the SPV if the foreign payment is a gross basis withholding tax imposed on a distribution or payment from the SPV to the U.S. party. Such taxes could be considered to be noncompulsory payments because the U.S. party intentionally subjects itself to the taxes as part of the arrangement. However, the IRS and Treasury Department have determined that such taxes should not be treated as attributable to the arrangement because, among other reasons, the foreign counterparty generally does not derive a duplicative foreign tax benefit and, therefore, generally does not share the economic cost of such taxes.

The IRS and Treasury Department considered excluding all foreign payments with respect to which the economic cost is not shared from the definition of foreign payments attributable to the arrangement, but determined that such a rule would be difficult to administer. The IRS and Treasury Department request comments on whether it would be appropriate to exclude certain foreign payments from the definition of foreign taxes attributable to the structured passive investment arrangement. Comments should address the rationale and administrable criteria for identifying any such exclusions.

Certain commentators recommended that the proposed regulations include a requirement that the foreign tax credits attributable to the arrangement be disproportionate to the amount of taxable income attributable to the arrangement. This recommendation has not been adopted for three reasons. First, the IRS and Treasury Department were concerned that such a requirement would create too much uncertainty and would be unduly burdensome for taxpayers and the IRS. Second, the extent to which interest and other expenses, as well as returns on borrowed funds and capital, should be considered attributable to a particular arrangement is not entirely clear. A narrow view could present opportunities for manipulation, especially for financial institutions having numerous alternative placements of leverage for use within the group, while an expansive view could undercut the utility of such a test. Third, the fundamental concern in these transactions is that they create an incentive for taxpayers voluntarily to subject themselves to foreign tax. This concern exists irrespective of whether the particular arrangement generates a disproportionate amount of foreign tax credits.

The IRS and Treasury Department considered whether it would be appropriate to permit a taxpayer to treat a foreign payment attributable to an arrangement that meets the definition of a structured passive investment arrangement as an amount of tax paid, if the taxpayer can show that tax considerations were not a principal purpose for the structure of the arrangement. Alternatively, the IRS and Treasury Department considered whether it would be appropriate to treat a foreign payment as an amount of tax paid if a taxpayer shows that there is a substantial business purpose for utilizing a hybrid instrument or entity, which would not include reducing the taxpayer's after-tax costs or enhancing the taxpayer's after-tax return through duplicative foreign tax benefits. The IRS and Treasury Department determined not to include such a rule in these proposed regulations due to administrability concerns. Comments are requested, however, on whether the final regulations should include such a rule as well as how such a rule could be made to be administrable in practice, including what reasonably ascertainable evidence would be sufficient to establish such a substantial non-tax business purpose, or the lack of a tax-related principal purpose. Comments should also address whether it would be appropriate to adopt a broader anti-abuse rule and permit a taxpayer to demonstrate that it should not apply.

C. *Effective Date*

The regulations are proposed to be effective for foreign taxes paid or accrued during taxable years of the taxpayer ending on or after the date on which the final regulations are published in the **Federal Register**. No inference is intended regarding the U.S. tax consequences of structured passive investment arrangements prior to the effective date of the regulations.

Special Analyses

It has been determined that this notice of proposed rulemaking is not a significant regulatory action as defined in Executive Order 12866. Therefore, a regulatory assessment is not required. It also has been determined that section 553(b) of the Administrative Procedure Act (5 U.S.C. chapter 5) does not apply to these regulations, and because the regulations do not impose a collection of information on small entities, the Regulatory Flexibility Act (5 U.S.C. chapter 6), does not apply. Pursuant to section 7805(f) of the Internal Revenue Code, this regulation has been submitted to the Chief Counsel for Advocacy of the Small Business Administration for comment on its impact on small businesses.

Comments and Public Hearing

Before these proposed regulations are adopted as final regulations, consideration will be given to any written (a signed original and eight (8) copies) or electronic comments that are submitted timely to the IRS. The IRS and Treasury Department request comments on the clarity of the proposed regulations and how they can be made easier to understand. All comments will be available for public inspection and copying.

A public hearing has been scheduled for July 30, 2007, at 10 a.m. in the Internal Revenue Building, 1111 Constitution Avenue, N.W., Washington, D.C. All visitors must present photo identification to enter the building. Because of access restrictions, visitors will not be admitted beyond the immediate entrance area more than 30 minutes before the hearing starts. For information about having your name placed on the building access list to attend the hearing, see the "FOR FURTHER INFORMATION CONTACT" section of this preamble.

The rules of 26 CFR 601.601(a)(3) apply to the hearing. Persons who wish to present oral comments must submit electronic or written comments and an outline of the topics to be discussed and time to be devoted to each topic (a signed original and eight (8) copies) by July 9, 2007. A period of 10 minutes will be allotted to each person for making comments. An agenda showing the scheduling of the speakers will be prepared after the deadline for receiving outlines has passed. Copies of the agenda will be available free of charge at the hearing.

Drafting Information

The principal author of these regulations is Bethany A. Ingwalson, Office of Associate Chief Counsel (International). However, other personnel from the IRS and the Treasury Department participated in their development.

* * * * *

Proposed Amendments to the Regulations

Accordingly, 26 CFR part 1 is proposed to be amended as follows:

PART 1—INCOME TAXES

Paragraph 1. The authority citation for part 1 continues to read in part as follows:

Authority: 26 U.S.C. 7805 * * *

Par. 2. Section 1.901–2 is amended by adding paragraphs (e)(5)(iii) and (iv), and revising paragraph (h) to read as follows:

§1.901–2 Income, war profits, or excess profits tax paid or accrued.

* * * * *

(e)(5) * * *

(iii) *U.S.-owned foreign entities*—(A) *In general.* If a U.S. person described in section 901(b) directly or indirectly owns stock possessing 80 percent or more of the total voting power and total value of one or more foreign corporations (or, in the case of a non-corporate foreign entity, directly or indirectly owns an interest in 80 percent or more of the income of one or more such foreign entities), the group comprising such foreign corporations and entities (the "U.S.-owned group") shall be treated as a single taxpayer for purposes of paragraph (e)(5) of this section. Therefore, if one member of such a U.S.-owned group transfers or surrenders a net loss for the taxable year to a second member of the U.S.-owned group and the loss reduces the foreign tax due from the second member pursuant to a foreign law group relief or similar regime, foreign tax paid by the first member in a different year does not fail to be a compulsory payment solely because such tax would not have been due had the member that transferred or surrendered the net loss instead carried over the loss to reduce its own income and foreign tax liability in that year. Similarly, if one or more members of the U.S.-owned group enter into a combined settlement under foreign law of two or more issues involving different members of the group, such settlement will be evaluated on an overall basis, not on an issue-by-issue or entity-by-entity basis, in determining whether an amount is a compulsory amount. The provisions of this paragraph (e)(5)(iii) apply solely for purposes of determining whether amounts paid are compulsory payments of foreign tax and do not, for example, modify the provisions of section 902 requiring separate pools of post-1986 undistributed earnings and post-1986 foreign income taxes for each member of a qualified group.

(B) *Special rules.* All domestic corporations that are members of a consolidated group (as that term is defined in §1.1502–1(h)) shall be treated as one domestic corporation for purposes of this paragraph (e)(5)(iii). For purposes of this paragraph (e)(5)(iii), indirect ownership of stock or another equity interest (such as an interest in a partnership) shall be determined in accordance with the principles of section 958(a)(2), whether the interest is owned by a U.S. or foreign person.

(C) *Examples.* The following examples illustrate the rules of this paragraph (e)(5)(iii):

Example 1. (i) *Facts.* A, a domestic corporation, wholly owns B, a country X corporation. B, in turn, wholly owns several country X corporations, including C and D. B, C, and D participate in group relief in country X. Under the country X group relief rules, a member with a net loss may choose to surrender the loss to another member of the group. In year 1, C has a net loss of (1,000x) and D has net income of 5,000x for country X tax purposes. Pursuant to the group relief rules in country X, C agrees to surrender its year 1 net loss to D and D agrees to claim the net loss. D uses the net loss to reduce its year 1 net income to 4,000x for country X tax purposes, which reduces the amount of country X tax D owes in year 1 by 300x. In year 2, C earns 3,000x with respect to which it pays 900x of country X tax. Country X permits a taxpayer to carry forward net losses for up to ten years.

(ii) *Result*. Paragraph (e)(5)(i) of this section provides, in part, that an amount paid to a foreign country does not exceed the amount of liability under foreign law for tax if the taxpayer determines such amount in a manner that is consistent with a reasonable interpretation and application of the substantive and procedural provisions of foreign law (including applicable tax treaties) in such a way as to reduce, over time, the taxpayer's reasonably expected liability under foreign law for tax. Under paragraph (e)(5)(iii)(A) of this section, B, C, and D are treated as a single taxpayer for purposes of testing whether the reasonably expected foreign tax liability has been minimized over time, because A directly and indirectly owns 100 percent of each of B, C, and D. Accordingly, none of the 900x paid by C in year 2 fails to be a compulsory payment solely because C could have reduced its year 2 country X tax liability by 300x by choosing to carry forward its year 1 net loss to year 2 instead of surrendering it to D to reduce D's country X liability in year 1.

Example 2. (i) *Facts*. L, M, and N are country Y corporations. L owns 100 percent of the common stock of M, which owns 100 percent of the stock of N. O, a domestic corporation, owns a security issued by M that is treated as debt for country Y tax purposes and as stock for U.S. tax purposes. As a result, L owns 100 percent of the stock of M for country Y purposes while O owns 99 percent of the stock of M for U.S. tax purposes. L, M, and N participate in group relief in country Y. Pursuant to the group relief rules in country Y, M may surrender its loss to any member of the group. In year 1, M has a net loss of $10 million, N has net income of $25 million, and L has net income of $15 million. M chooses to surrender its year 1 net loss to L. Country Y imposes tax of 30 percent on the net income of country Y corporations. Accordingly, in year 1, the loss surrender has the effect of reducing L's country Y tax by $3 million. In year 1, N makes a payment of $7.5 million to country Y with respect to its net income of $25 million. If M had surrendered its net loss to N instead of L, N would have had net income of $15 million, with respect to which it would have owed only $4.5 million of country Y tax.

(ii) *Result*. M and N, but not L, are treated as a single taxpayer for purposes of paragraph (e)(5) of this section because O directly and indirectly owns 99 percent of each of M and N, but owns no direct or indirect interest in L. Accordingly, in testing whether M and N's reasonably expected foreign tax liability has been minimized over time, L is not considered the same taxpayer as M and N, collectively, and the $3 million reduction in L's year 1 country Y tax liability through the surrender to L of M's $10 million country Y net loss in year 1 is not considered to reduce M and N's collective country Y tax liability.

(iv) *Certain structured passive investment arrangements*—(A) *In general*. Notwithstanding paragraph (e)(5)(i) of this section, an amount paid to a foreign country (a "foreign payment") is not a compulsory payment, and thus is not an amount of tax paid, if the foreign payment is attributable to an arrangement described in paragraph (e)(5)(iv)(B) of this section. For purposes of this paragraph (e)(5)(iv), a foreign payment is attributable to an arrangement described in paragraph (e)(5)(iv)(B) of this section if the foreign payment is described in paragraph (e)(5)(iv)(B)(*1*)(*ii*) of this section.

(B) *Conditions*. An arrangement is described in this paragraph (e)(5)(iv)(B) if all of the following conditions are satisfied:

(*1*) *Special purpose vehicle (SPV)*. An entity that is part of the arrangement meets the following requirements:

(*i*) Substantially all of the gross income (for United States tax purposes) of the entity is passive investment income as defined in paragraph (e)(5)(iv)(C)(*4*) of this section, and substantially all of the assets of the entity are assets held to produce such passive investment income. As provided in paragraph (e)(5)(iv)(C)(*4*)(*ii*) of this section, passive investment income generally does not include income of a holding company from qualified equity interests in lower-tier entities that are predominantly engaged in the active conduct of a trade or business. Thus, except as provided in paragraph (e)(5)(iv)(C)(*4*)(*ii*) of this section, qualified equity interests of a holding company in such lower-tier entities are not held to produce passive investment income and the ownership of such interests will not cause the holding company to satisfy this paragraph (e)(5)(iv)(B)(*1*)(*i*).

(*ii*) There is a foreign payment attributable to income of the entity (as determined under the laws of the foreign country to which such foreign payment is made), including the entity's share of income of a lower-tier entity that is a branch or pass-through entity under the laws of such foreign country. A foreign payment attributable to income of an entity includes a foreign payment attributable to income that is required to be taken into account by an owner of the entity, if the entity is a branch or pass-through entity under the laws of such foreign country. A foreign payment attributable to income of an entity also includes a foreign payment attributable to income of a lower-tier entity that is a branch or pass-through entity for U.S. tax purposes. A foreign payment attributable to income of the entity does not include a withholding tax (within the meaning of section 901(k)(1)(B)) imposed on a distribution or payment from the entity to a U.S. party (as defined in paragraph (e)(5)(iv)(B)(*2*) of this section).

(*2*) *U.S. party*. A person (a "U.S. party") would be eligible to claim a credit under section 901(a) (including a credit for foreign taxes deemed paid under section 902 or 960) for all or a portion of the foreign payment described in paragraph (e)(5)(iv)(B)(*1*)(*ii*) of this section if the foreign payment were an amount of tax paid.

(*3*) *Direct investment*. The foreign payment or payments described in paragraph (e)(5)(iv)(B)(*1*)(*ii*) of this section are (or are expected to be) substantially greater than the amount of credits, if any, the U.S. party would reasonably expect to be eligible to claim under section 901(a) for foreign taxes attributable to income generated by the U.S. party's proportionate share of the assets owned by the SPV if the U.S. party directly owned such assets. For this purpose, direct ownership shall not include ownership through a branch, a permanent establishment or any other arrangement (such as an agency arrangement) that would result in the income generated by the U.S. party's proportionate share of the assets being subject to tax on a net basis in the foreign country to which the payment is made. A U.S. party's proportionate share of the assets of the SPV shall be determined by reference to such U.S. party's proportionate share of the total value of all of the outstanding interests in the SPV that are held by its equity owners and creditors.

(*4*) *Foreign tax benefit*. The arrangement is structured in such a manner that it results in a foreign tax benefit (such as a credit, deduction, loss, exemption or a disregarded payment) for a counterparty described in paragraph (e)(5)(iv)(B)(*5*) of this section or for a person that is related to the counterparty (determined under the principles of paragraph (e)(5)(iv)(C)(*6*) of this section by applying the tax laws of a foreign country in which the counterparty is subject to tax on a net basis) but is not related to the U.S. party (within the meaning of paragraph (e)(5)(iv)(C)(*6*) of this section).

(*5*) *Unrelated counterparty*. The arrangement involves a counterparty. A counterparty is a person (other than the SPV) that is not related to the U.S. party (within the meaning of paragraph (e)(5)(iv)(C)(*6*) of this section) and that meets one of the following conditions:

(*i*) The person is considered to own directly or indirectly 10 percent or more of the equity of the SPV under the tax laws of a foreign country in which the person is subject to tax on the basis of place of management, place of incorporation or similar criterion or otherwise subject to a net basis tax.

(*ii*) In a single transaction or series of transactions, the person directly or indirectly acquires 20 percent or more of the value of the assets of the SPV under the tax laws of a foreign country in which the person is subject to tax on the basis of place of management, place of incorporation or similar criterion or otherwise subject to a net basis tax. For purposes of determining the percentage of assets of the SPV acquired by the person, an asset of the SPV shall be disregarded if a principal purpose for transferring such asset to the SPV was to avoid this paragraph (e)(5)(iv)(B)(*5*)(*ii*).

(*6*) *Inconsistent treatment*. The U.S. and an applicable foreign country (as defined in paragraph (e)(5)(iv)(C)(*1*) of this section) treat one or more of the following aspects of the arrangement differently under their respective tax systems, and the U.S. treatment of the inconsistent aspect would materially affect the amount of income recognized by the U.S. party or the amount of credits claimed by the U.S. party if the foreign payment described in paragraph (e)(5)(iv)(B)(*1*)(*ii*) of this section were an amount of tax paid:

(*i*) The classification of the SPV (or an entity that has a direct or indirect ownership interest in the SPV) as a corporation or other entity subject to an entity-level tax, a partnership or other flow-through entity or an entity that is disregarded for tax purposes.

(*ii*) The characterization as debt, equity or an instrument that is disregarded for tax purposes of an instrument issued by the SPV (or an entity that has a direct or indirect ownership interest in the SPV) to the U.S. party, the counterparty or a person related to the U.S. party or the counterparty.

(*iii*) The proportion of the equity of the SPV (or an entity that directly or indirectly owns the SPV) that is considered to be owned directly or indirectly by the U.S. party and the counterparty.

(*iv*) The amount of taxable income of the SPV for one or more tax years during which the arrangement is in effect.

(C) *Definitions*—(*1*) *Applicable foreign country*. An *applicable foreign country* means each foreign country to which a foreign payment described in paragraph (e)(5)(iv)(B)(*1*)(*ii*) of this section is made or which confers a foreign tax benefit described in paragraph (e)(5)(iv)(B)(*4*) of this section.

(*2*) *Entity*. For purposes of paragraph (e)(5)(iv)(B)(*1*) and (e)(5)(iv)(C)(*4*) of this section, the term *entity* includes a corporation, trust, partnership or disregarded entity described in §301.7701–2(c)(2)(i) of this chapter.

(*3*) *Indirect ownership*. For purposes of paragraph (e)(5)(iv) of this section, indirect ownership of stock or another equity interest (such as an interest in a partnership) shall be determined in accordance with the principles of section 958(a)(2), whether the interest is owned by a U.S. or foreign entity.

(*4*) *Passive investment income*—(*i*) *In general*. For purposes of paragraph (e)(5)(iv) of this section, the term *passive investment income* means income described in section 954(c), as modified by this paragraph (e)(5)(iv)(C)(*4*)(*i*) and paragraph (e)(5)(iv)(C)(*4*)(*ii*) of this section. In determining whether income is described in section 954(c), sections 954(c)(3) and 954(c)(6) shall be disregarded, and sections 954(h) and (i) shall be taken into account by applying those provisions at the entity level as if the entity were a controlled foreign corporation (as defined in section 957(a)). In addition, for purposes of the preceding sentence, any income of an entity attributable to transactions with a person that would be a counterparty (as defined in paragraph (e)(5)(iv)(B)(*5*) of this section) if the entity were an SPV, or with other persons that are described in paragraph (e)(5)(iv)(B)(*4*) of this section and that are eligible for a foreign tax benefit described in such paragraph (e)(5)(iv)(B)(*4*), shall not be treated as qualified banking or financing income or as qualified insurance income, and shall not be taken into account in applying sections 954(h) and (i) for purposes of determining whether other income of the entity is excluded from section 954(c)(1) under section 954(h) or (i).

(*ii*) *Income attributable to lower-tier entities*. Except as provided in this paragraph (e)(5)(iv)(C)(*4*)(*ii*), income of an entity that is attributable to an equity interest in a lower-tier entity is passive investment income. If the entity is a holding company and directly owns a qualified equity interest in another entity (a "lower-tier entity") that is engaged in the active conduct of a trade or business and that derives more than 50 percent of its gross income from such trade or business, then none of the entity's income attributable to such interest is passive investment income, provided that there are no arrangements whereby substantially all of the entity's opportunity for gain and risk of loss with respect to such interest is borne by the U.S. party (or a related person) or the counterparty (or a related person), but not both parties. For purposes of the preceding sentence, an entity is a holding company, and is considered to be engaged in the active conduct of a trade or business and to derive more than 50 percent of its gross income from such trade or business, if substantially all of its assets consist of qualified equity interests in one or more entities, each of which is engaged in the active conduct of a trade or business and derives more than 50 percent of its gross income from such trade or business and with respect to which there are no arrangements whereby substantially all of the entity's opportunity for gain and risk of loss with respect to such interest is borne by the U.S. party (or a related person) or the counterparty (or a related person), but not both parties. For purposes of this paragraph (e)(5)(iv)(C)(*4*)(*ii*), a lower-tier entity that is engaged in a banking, financing, or similar business shall not be considered to be engaged in the active conduct of a trade or business unless the income derived by such entity would be excluded from section 954(c)(1) under section 954(h) or (i), determined by applying those provisions at the lower-tier entity level as if the entity were a controlled foreign corporation (as defined in section 957(a)). In addition, for purposes of the preceding sentence, any income of an entity attributable to transactions with a person that would be a counterparty (as defined in paragraph (e)(5)(iv)(B)(*5*) of this section) if the entity were an SPV, or with other persons that are described in paragraph (e)(5)(iv)(B)(*4*) of this section and that are eligible for a foreign tax benefit described in such paragraph (e)(5)(iv)(B)(*4*), shall not be treated as qualified banking or financing income or as qualified insurance income, and shall not be taken into account in applying sections 954(h) and (i) for purposes of determining whether other income of the entity is excluded from section 954(c)(1) under section 954(h) or (i).

(*5*) *Qualified equity interest*. With respect to an interest in a corporation, the term *qualified equity interest* means stock representing 10 percent or more of the total combined voting power of all classes of stock entitled to vote and 10 percent or more of the total value of the stock of the corporation or disregarded entity, but does not include any preferred stock (as defined in section 351(g)(3)). Similar rules shall apply to determine whether an interest in an entity other than a corporation is a qualified equity interest.

(*6*) *Related person*. Two persons are related for purposes of paragraph (e)(5)(iv) of this section if—

(*i*) One person directly or indirectly owns stock (or an equity interest) possessing more than 50 percent of the total value of the other person; or

(*ii*) The same person directly or indirectly owns stock (or an equity interest) possessing more than 50 percent of the total value of both persons.

(*7*) *Special purpose vehicle (SPV)*. For purposes of this paragraph (e)(5)(iv), the term *SPV* means the entity described in paragraph (e)(5)(iv)(B)(*1*) of this section.

(D) *Examples*. The following examples illustrate the rules of paragraph (e)(5)(iv) of this section. No inference is intended as to whether a taxpayer would be eligible to claim a credit under section 901(a) if a foreign payment were an amount of tax paid.

Example 1. U.S. borrower transaction. (i) *Facts*. A domestic corporation (USP) forms a country M corporation (Newco), contributing $1.5 billion in exchange for 100 percent of the stock of Newco. Newco, in turn, loans the $1.5 billion to a second country M corporation (FSub) wholly owned by USP. FSub is engaged in the active conduct of manufacturing and selling widgets and derives more than 50 percent of its gross income from such business. USP then sells its entire interest in Newco to a country M corporation (FP) for the original purchase price of $1.5 billion, subject to an obligation to repurchase the interest in five years for $1.5 billion. The sale has the effect of transferring ownership of the Newco stock to FP for country M tax purposes. The sale-repurchase transaction is structured in a way that qualifies as a collateralized loan for U.S. tax purposes. Therefore, USP remains the owner of the Newco stock for U.S. tax purposes. In year 1, FSub pays Newco $120 million of interest. Newco pays $36 million to country M with respect to such interest income and distributes the remaining $84 million to FP. Under country M law, the $84 million distribution is excluded from FP's income. FP is not related to USP within the meaning of paragraph (e)(5)(iv)(C)(*6*) of this section. Under an income tax treaty between country M and the U.S., country M does not impose country M tax on interest received by U.S. residents from sources in country M.

(ii) *Result*. The payment by Newco to country M is not a compulsory payment, and thus is not an amount of tax paid. First, Newco is an SPV because all of Newco's income is passive investment income described in paragraph (e)(5)(iv)(C)(*4*) of this section, Newco's only asset, a note, is held to produce such income, and the payment to country M is attributable to such income. Second, if the foreign payment were treated as an amount of tax paid, USP would be deemed to pay the foreign payment under section 902(a) and, therefore, would be eligible to claim a credit for such payment under section 901(a). Third, USP would not pay any country M tax if it directly owned Newco's loan receivable. Fourth, distributions from Newco to FP are exempt from tax under country M law. Fifth, FP is a counterparty because FP and USP are unrelated and FP owns more than 10 percent of the stock of Newco under country M law. Sixth, FP is the owner of 100 percent of Newco's stock for country M tax purposes, while USP is the owner of 100 percent of Newco's stock for U.S. tax purposes, and USP's ownership of the stock would materially affect the amount of credits claimed by USP if the payment to country M were an amount of tax paid. If the foreign payment were treated as an amount of tax paid, USP's ownership of the stock for U.S. tax purposes would make USP eligible to claim a credit for such amount under sections 901(a) and 902(a). Because the payment to country M is not an amount of tax paid, USP has dividend income of $84 million and is not deemed to pay any country M tax under section 902(a). USP also has interest expense of $84 million. FSub's post-1986 undistributed earnings are reduced by $120 million of interest expense.

Example 2. U.S. borrower transaction. (i) *Facts*. The facts are the same as in *Example 1*, except that FSub is a wholly-owned subsidiary of Newco. In addition, FSub agrees not to pay, and Newco and FP agree not to cause FSub to pay, dividends during the five-year period in which FP holds the Newco stock subject to the obligation of USP to repurchase the stock.

(ii) *Result*. The results are the same as in *Example 1*. Although Newco wholly owns FSub, which is engaged in the active conduct of manufacturing and selling widgets and derives more than 50 percent of its income from such business, income attributable to Newco's stock in FSub is passive investment income because there are arrangements whereby substantially all of Newco's opportunity for gain and risk of loss with respect to its stock in FSub is borne by USP. See paragraph (e)(iv)(C)(*4*)(*ii*) of this section. Accordingly, Newco's stock in FSub is held to produce passive investment income. Thus, Newco is an SPV because all of Newco's income is passive investment income described in paragraph (e)(5)(iv)(C)(*4*) of this section, Newco's assets are held to produce such income, and the payment to country M is attributable to such income.

Example 3. Active business; no SPV. (i) *Facts*. A, a domestic corporation, wholly owns B, a country X corporation engaged in the manufacture and sale of widgets. On January 1, 2008, C, also a country X corporation, loans $400 million to B in exchange for an instrument that is debt for U.S. tax purposes and equity for country X tax purposes. As a result, C is considered to own 20 percent of the stock of B for country X tax purposes. B loans $55 million to D, a country Y corporation wholly owned by A. For its 2008 tax year, B has $166 million of net income attributable to its sales of widgets and $3.3 million of interest income attributable to the loan to D. Country Y does not impose tax on interest paid to nonresidents. B makes a payment of $50.8 million to country X with respect to B's net income. Country X does not impose tax on dividend payments between country X corporations. A and C are not related within the meaning of paragraph (e)(5)(iv)(C)(*6*) of this section.

(ii) *Result*. B is not an SPV within the meaning of paragraph (e)(5)(iv)(B)(*1*) of this section because the amount of interest income received from D does not constitute substantially all of B's income and the $55 million loan to D does not constitute substantially all of B's assets. Accordingly, the $50.8 million payment to country X is not attributable to an arrangement described in paragraph (e)(5)(iv) of this section.

Example 4. U.S. lender transaction. (i) *Facts*. (A) A country X corporation (foreign bank) contributes $2 billion to a newly-formed country X corporation (Newco) in exchange for 100 percent of Newco's common stock. A U.S. bank (USB) contributes $1 billion to Newco in exchange for securities that are treated as stock of Newco for U.S. tax purposes and debt of Newco for country X tax purposes. The securities represent 10 percent of the total voting power of Newco. Newco contributes the entire $3 billion to a newly-formed country X entity (RH) in exchange for 99 percent of RH's equity. Foreign bank owns the remaining 1 percent of RH. RH is treated as a corporation for U.S. tax purposes and a partnership for country X tax purposes. RH loans the entire $3 billion it receives from Newco to foreign bank in exchange for a note that pays interest currently and a zero-coupon note. Under an income tax treaty between country X and the U.S., country X does not impose country X tax on interest received by U.S. residents from sources in country X. Country X does not impose tax on dividend payments between country X corporations. USB and the foreign bank are not related within the meaning of paragraph (e)(5)(iv)(C)(*6*) of this section.

(B) In year 1, foreign bank pays RH $92 million of interest and accrues $113 million of interest on the zero-coupon note. RH distributes the $92 million of cash it receives to Newco. Newco distributes $44 million to USB. Because RH is a partnership for country X purposes, Newco is required to report for country X purposes 99 percent ($203 million) of the income recognized by RH. Newco is entitled to interest deductions of $44 million for distributions to USB on the securities for country X tax purposes and, thus, has $159 million of net income for country X tax purposes. Newco makes a payment to country X of $48 million with respect to its net income. For U.S. tax purposes, Newco's post-1986 undistributed earnings pool for year 1 is $44 million ($92 million - $48 million). For country X tax purposes, foreign bank is entitled to interest expense deductions of $205 million.

(ii) *Result.* (A) The payment to country X is not a compulsory payment, and thus is not an amount of tax paid. First, Newco is an SPV because all of Newco's income is passive investment income described in paragraph (e)(5)(iv)(C)(*4*) of this section, Newco's sole asset, stock of RH, is held to produce such income, and the payment to country X is attributable to such income. Second, if the foreign payment were treated as an amount of tax paid, USB would be deemed to pay the $48 million under section 902(a) and, therefore, would be eligible to claim a credit under section 901(a). Third, USB would not pay any country X tax if it directly owned its proportionate share of Newco's asset, the 99 percent interest in RH, because under the U.S.-country X tax treaty country X would not impose tax on USB's distributive share of RH's interest income. Fourth, foreign bank is entitled to interest deductions under country X law for interest it pays and accrues to RH, and will receive tax-free dividends from Newco upon payment of the accrued interest. Fifth, foreign bank and USB are unrelated and foreign bank is considered to own more than 10 percent of Newco under country X law. Sixth, the U.S. and country X view several aspects of the transaction differently, and the U.S. treatment would materially affect the amount of credits claimed by USB if the country X payment were an amount of tax paid. If the country X payment were treated as an amount of tax paid, the equity treatment of the securities for U.S. tax purposes would make USB eligible to claim a credit for the payment under sections 901(a) and 902(a). Moreover, the fact that Newco recognizes a smaller amount of income for U.S. tax purposes than it does for country X tax purposes would increase the amount of credits USB would be eligible to claim upon receipt of the $44 million distribution. Because the $48 million payment to country X is not an amount of tax paid, USB has dividend income of $44 million. It is not deemed to pay tax under section 902(a).

(B) In addition, RH is an SPV because all of RH's income is passive investment income described in paragraph (e)(5)(iv)(C)(*4*) of this section, RH's sole assets, notes of foreign bank, are held to produce such income, and Newco's payment to country X is attributable to such income. Second, if the foreign payment were treated as an amount of tax paid, USB would be deemed to pay the $48 million under section 902(a) and, therefore, would be eligible to claim a credit under section 901(a). Third, USB would not pay any country X tax if it directly owned its proportionate share of RH's assets, notes of foreign bank, because under the U.S.-country X tax treaty country X would not impose tax on interest paid by foreign bank to USB. Fourth, foreign bank is entitled to interest deductions under country X law for interest it pays and accrues to RH, and will receive tax-free dividends from Newco upon payment of the accrued interest. Fifth, foreign bank and USB are unrelated and foreign bank is considered to own directly or indirectly more than 10 percent of RH under country X law. Sixth, the U.S. and country X view several aspects of the transaction differently, and the U.S. treatment would materially affect the amount of credits claimed by USB if the country X payment were an amount of tax paid. If the country X payment were treated as an amount of tax paid, the equity treatment of the Newco securities for U.S. tax purposes would make USB eligible to claim a credit for the payment under sections 901(a) and 902(a). Moreover, the entity classification of RH for U.S. tax purposes results in Newco recognizing a smaller amount of income for U.S. tax purposes than it does for country X tax purposes, which would increase the amount of credits USB would be eligible to claim upon receipt of the $44 million distribution. Because the $48 million payment to country X is not an amount of tax paid, USB has dividend income of $44 million. It is not deemed to pay tax under section 902(a).

Example 5. Active business; no SPV. (i) *Facts.* A, a country X corporation, and B, a domestic corporation, each contribute $1 billion to a newly-formed country X entity (C) in exchange for stock of C. C is treated as a corporation for country X purposes and a partnership for U.S. tax purposes. C contributes $1.95 billion to a newly-formed country X corporation (D) in exchange for 100 percent of D's stock. It loans its remaining $50 million to D. Accordingly, C's sole assets are stock and debt of D. D uses the entire $2 billion to engage in the business of manufacturing and selling widgets. For the 2015 tax year, D derives $300 million of income from its widget business and derives $2 million of interest income. For the 2015 tax year, C has dividend income of $200 million and interest income of $3.2 million with respect to its investment in D. Country X does not impose tax on dividends received by one country X corporation from a second country X corporation. C makes a payment of $960,000 to country X with respect to C's net income.

(ii) *Result.* C's dividend income is not passive investment income, and C's stock in D is not held to produce such income, because C owns at least 10 percent of D and D derives more than 50 percent of its income from the active conduct of its widget business. See paragraph (e)(5)(iv)(C)(*4*)(*ii*) of this section. As a result, less than substantially all of C's income is passive investment income and less than substantially all of C's assets are held to produce passive investment income. Accordingly, C is not an SPV within the meaning of paragraph (e)(5)(iv)(B)(*1*) of this section, and the $960,000 payment to country X is not attributable to an arrangement described in paragraph (e)(5)(iv) of this section.

Example 6. Active business; no SPV. (i) *Facts.* The facts are the same as in *Example 5*, except that instead of loaning $50 million to D, C contributes the $50 million to E in exchange for 10 percent of the stock of E. E is a country Y entity that in not engaged in the active conduct of a trade or business. Also, for the 2015 tax year, D pays no dividends to C, E pays $3.2 million in dividends to C, and C makes a payment of $960,000 to country X with respect to C's net income.

(ii) *Result.* C's dividend income attributable to its stock in E is passive investment income, and C's stock in E is held to produce such income. C's stock in D is not held to produce passive investment income because C owns at least 10 percent of D and D derives more than 50 percent of its income from the active conduct of its widget business. See paragraph (e)(5)(iv)(C)(*4*)(*ii*) of this section. As a result, less than substantially all of C's assets are held to produce passive investment income. Accordingly, C does not meet the requirements of paragraph (e)(5)(iv)(B)(*1*) of this section, and the $960,000 payment to country X is not attributable to an arrangement described in paragraph (e)(5)(iv) of this section.

Example 7. Asset holding transaction. (i) *Facts.* (A) A domestic corporation (USP) contributes $6 billion of country Z debt obligations to a country Z entity (DE) in exchange for all of the class A and class B stock of DE. A corporation unrelated to USP and organized in country Z (Fcorp) contributes $1.5 billion to DE in exchange for all of the class C stock of DE. DE uses the $1.5 billion contributed by Fcorp to redeem USP's class B stock. The class C stock is entitled to "all" income from DE. However, Fcorp is obligated immediately to contribute back to DE all distributions on the class C stock. USP and Fcorp enter into—

(*1*) A forward contract under which USP agrees to buy after five years the class C stock for $1.5 billion; and

(*2*) An agreement under which USP agrees to pay Fcorp interest at a below-market rate on $1.5 billion.

(B) For U.S. tax purposes, these steps create a secured loan of $1.5 billion from Fcorp to USP. Therefore, for U.S. tax purposes, USP is the owner of both the class A and class C stock. DE is a disregarded entity for U.S. tax purposes and a corporation for country Z tax purposes. In year 1, DE earns $400 million of interest income on the country Z debt obligations. DE makes a payment to country Z of $100 million with respect to such income and distributes the remaining $300 million to Fcorp. Fcorp contributes the $300 million back to DE. USP and Fcorp are not related within the meaning of paragraph (e)(5)(iv)(C)(*6*) of this section. Country Z does not impose tax on interest income derived by U.S. residents.

(C) Country Z treats Fcorp as the owner of the class C stock. Pursuant to country Z tax law, Fcorp is required to report the $400 million of income with respect to the $300 million distribution from DE, but is allowed to claim credits for DE's $100 million payment to country Z. For country Z tax purposes, Fcorp's contribution increases its basis in the class C stock. When the class C stock is later "sold" to USP for $1.5 billion, the increase in tax basis will result in a country Z tax loss for Fcorp. Each year, the amount of the basis increase (and, thus, the amount of the loss generated) will be approximately $300 million.

(ii) *Result.* The payment to country Z is not a compulsory payment, and thus is not an amount of tax paid. First, DE is an SPV because all of DE's income is passive investment income described in paragraph (e)(5)(iv)(C)(*4*) of this section, all of DE's assets are held to produce such income, and the payment to country Z is attributable to such income. Second, if the payment were treated as an amount of tax paid, USP would be eligible to claim a credit for such amount under section 901(a). Third, USP would not pay any country Z tax if it directly owned DE's assets. Fourth, Fcorp is entitled to claim a credit under country Z tax law for the payment and will recognize a loss under country Z law upon the "sale" of the class C stock. Fifth, Fcorp and USP are not related within the meaning of paragraph (e)(5)(iv)(C)(*6*) of this section and Fcorp is considered to own more than 10 percent of DE under country Z law. Sixth, the United States and country X view certain aspects of the transaction differently and the U.S. treatment would materially affect the amount of credits claimed by USP if the country Z payment were an amount of tax paid. USP's ownership of the class C stock for U.S. tax purposes would make USP eligible to claim a credit for the country Z payment if the payment were treated as an amount of tax paid.

* * * * *

(h) *Effective date.* Paragraphs (a) through (e)(5)(ii) and paragraph (g) of this section, §1.901–2A, and §1.903–1 apply to taxable years beginning after November 14, 1983. Paragraphs (e)(5)(iii) and (iv) of this section are effective for foreign taxes paid or accrued during taxable years of the taxpayer ending on or after the date on which these regulations are published as final regulations in the **Federal Register**.

Kevin M. Brown,
Deputy Commissioner for Services and Enforcement.

(Filed by the Office of the Federal Register on March 29, 2007, 8:45 a.m., and published in the issue of the Federal Register for March 30, 2007, 72 F.R. 15081)

Announcement of Disciplinary Actions Involving Attorneys, Certified Public Accountants, Enrolled Agents, and Enrolled Actuaries — Suspensions, Censures, Disbarments, and Resignations

Announcement 2007-41

Under Title 31, Code of Federal Regulations, Part 10, attorneys, certified public accountants, enrolled agents, and enrolled actuaries may not accept assistance from, or assist, any person who is under disbarment or suspension from practice before the Internal Revenue Service if the assistance relates to a matter constituting practice before the Internal Revenue Service and may not knowingly aid or abet another person to practice before the Internal Revenue Service during a period of suspension, disbarment, or ineligibility of such other person.

To enable attorneys, certified public accountants, enrolled agents, and enrolled actuaries to identify persons to whom these restrictions apply, the Director, Office of Professional Responsibility, will announce in the Internal Revenue Bulletin their names, their city and state, their professional designation, the effective date of disciplinary action, and the period of suspension. This announcement will appear in the weekly Bulletin at the earliest practicable date after such action and will continue to appear in the weekly Bulletins for five successive weeks.

Consent Suspensions From Practice Before the Internal Revenue Service

Under Title 31, Code of Federal Regulations, Part 10, an attorney, certified public accountant, enrolled agent, or enrolled actuary, in order to avoid the institution or conclusion of a proceeding for his or her disbarment or suspension from practice before the Internal Revenue Service, may offer his or her consent to suspension from such practice. The Director, Office of Professional Responsibility, in his discretion, may suspend an attorney, certified public accountant, enrolled agent, or enrolled actuary in accordance with the consent offered.

The following individuals have been placed under consent suspension from practice before the Internal Revenue Service:

Name	Address	Designation	Date of Suspension
Hankinson, Eugene M.	Somerset, PA	CPA	Indefinite from November 15, 2006
Canzano, Richard M.	Winchester, MA	Attorney	Indefinite from November 20, 2006
Sims, Jr., Lionel	Houston, TX	CPA	Indefinite from November 20, 2006

Name	Address	Designation	Date of Suspension
Wendekier, Raymond J.	Patton, PA	Attorney	Indefinite from November 21, 2006
Golden, Larry	Hinesville, GA	CPA	Indefinite from November 28, 2006
Lane, David B.	Hanover, MA	Attorney	Indefinite from November 28, 2006
Brown, Arthur I.	Miami, FL	CPA	Indefinite from December 1, 2006
Frisk, Daniel J.	Fargo, ND	Attorney	Indefinite from December 1, 2006
Small, Kenneth A.	McMurray, PA	CPA	Indefinite from December 1, 2006
Vazquez, Sonya M.	Port Orchard, WA	CPA	Indefinite from December 1, 2006
Swistak, Anthony	Adams, MA	Enrolled Agent	Indefinite from December 6, 2006
Lenahan, Jr., Robert J.	Elizabeth, NJ	Attorney	Indefinite from December 11, 2006
Hayes, Richard A.	Havervill, MA	Attorney	Indefinite from December 14, 2006
Scheller, Stephen M.	Coppell, TX	CPA	Indefinite from December 15, 2006
Wilson, James M.	Berlin, NJ	CPA	Indefinite from December 15, 2006
Franzese, Joseph P.	Winthrop, MA	Attorney	Indefinite from December 18, 2006
Black, Charles C.	Marietta, GA	Attorney	Indefinite from January 1, 2007
Enright, III, Robert A.	Naples, FL	Attorney	Indefinite from January 1, 2007

Name	Address	Designation	Date of Suspension
Fromovitz, Norman M.	Brooklyn, NY	CPA	Indefinite from January 1, 2007
Saylor, Mary A.	Iowa City, IA	Enrolled Agent	Indefinite from January 1, 2007
Seeherman, Alan	Wynnewood, PA	CPA	Indefinite from January 1, 2007
Beistel, Theodore L.	Canton, OH	CPA	Indefinite from January 3, 2007
Myers, Robert J.	Fairport Harbor, OH	CPA	Indefinite from January 9, 2007
Burrus, Robert V.	Valparaiso, IN	CPA	Indefinite from January 22, 2007
Patterson, Douglas W.	Newburgh, IN	Attorney	Indefinite from January 31, 2007
Lang, Jeffrey H.	Fishers, IN	CPA	Indefinite from January 22, 2007
Chickering, David	Vermillion, SD	CPA	February 5, 2007 to November 4, 2007
Moss, Steve E.	Henderson, NC	CPA	Indefinite from February 5, 2007
Hazlip, Kevin	Orange Park, FL	Enrolled Agent	Indefinite from February 10, 2007
Adelson, Robert A.	Newton, MA	Attorney	Indefinite from February 15, 2007
Boyer, Daniel D.	North Judson, IN	CPA	Indefinite from February 15, 2007
LaRusso, Anthony J.	North Caldwell, NJ	Attorney	Indefinite from February 15, 2007
Martin, Spencer R.	Lancaster, PA	CPA	Indefinite from February 15, 2007
Hursh, Stephanie S.	Brush Prairie, WA	Enrolled Agent	Indefinite from February 20, 2007

Name	Address	Designation	Date of Suspension
Guidera, George C.	Weston, CT	Attorney	Indefinite from February 26, 2007
Ruth, Christopher A.	Cypress, CA	CPA	Indefinite from February 27, 2007
Elias, Lenard S.	El Cajon, CA	Enrolled Agent	Indefinite from March 1, 2007
Ikeji, Chuck	Orlando, FL	CPA	Indefinite from March 1, 2007
Lewis, Craig S.	Savannah, GA	CPA	Indefinite from March 1, 2007
Sloan, Eric R.	Brighton, MI	CPA	Indefinite from March 1, 2007
Gostomski, Michael	Stamford, CT	CPA	Indefinite from March 5, 2007
Hafer, Charles J.	Hamburg, PA	Enrolled Agent	Indefinite from March 5, 2007
Jones, Phillip G.	Andalusia, AL	Enrolled Agent	Indefinite from March 7, 2007
Agashiwala, Mahesh J.	New York, NY	CPA	Indefinite from March 22, 2007
Berndgen, Michael	Plantation, FL	CPA	Indefinite from April 1, 2007
Grahn, Charles R.	Indianapolis, IN	Attorney	Indefinite from April 1, 2007
Shaw, G. Joyce	Hebron, KY	Enrolled Agent	Indefinite from April 1, 2007
Pikaart, Jr., Edward H.	N. Branford, CT	CPA	Indefinite from April 10, 2007
Kelley, Richard S.	Beverly, MA	Attorney	Indefinite from May 1, 2007
Crabtree, Michael L.	San Dimas, CA	Enrolled Agent	Indefinite from May 15, 2007

Name	Address	Designation	Date of Suspension
Hausmann, Mark D.	Troy, NY	Attorney	Indefinite from May 15, 2007

Expedited Suspensions From Practice Before the Internal Revenue Service

Under Title 31, Code of Federal Regulations, Part 10, the Director, Office of Professional Responsibility, is authorized to immediately suspend from practice before the Internal Revenue Service any practitioner who, within five years from the date the expedited proceeding is instituted (1) has had a license to practice as an attorney, certified public accountant, or actuary suspended or revoked for cause or (2) has been convicted of certain crimes.

The following individuals have been placed under suspension from practice before the Internal Revenue Service by virtue of the expedited proceeding provisions:

Name	Address	Designation	Date of Suspension
Hatchett, William M.	Pontiac, MI	Attorney	Indefinite from November 13, 2006
Jacobs, Mark L.	Jackson Heights, NY	Attorney	Indefinite from November 21, 2006
Sylver, Peter T.	E. Longmeadow, MA	Attorney	Indefinite from November 21, 2006
Portlock, David R.	Pensacola, FL	Enrolled Agent	Indefinite from November 27, 2006
Ascher, Michael P.	North Port, FL	Attorney	Indefinite from November 28, 2006
Barrett, Norman W.	Dover, DE	CPA	Indefinite from November 28, 2006
Burd, Gene	Houston, TX	Attorney	Indefinite from November 28, 2006
Caceres, Carlos H.	Silver Spring, MD	Attorney	Indefinite from November 28, 2006
Carrabotta, Peter S.	Niles, IL	Attorney	Indefinite from November 28, 2006
Davis, Carleton W.	St. Louis, MO	Attorney	Indefinite from November 28, 2006

Name	Address	Designation	Date of Suspension
Frasier, Roland B.	Rancho Santa Fe, CA	Attorney	Indefinite from November 28, 2006
Hubbard, Edward	Chicago, IL	Attorney	Indefinite from November 28, 2006
Hynes, Richard W.	Brookline, MA	Attorney	Indefinite from November 28, 2006
Johnson, Barbara C.	Andover, MA	Attorney	Indefinite from November 28, 2006
Konas, Theodore V.	Lancaster, PA	CPA	Indefinite from November 28, 2006
Korson, Daniel M.	Muskegon, MI	CPA	Indefinite from November 28, 2006
Lee, III, Norman J.	Collegeville, PA	Attorney	Indefinite from November 28, 2006
Loiben, Alan A.	Skokie, IL	Attorney	Indefinite from November 28, 2006
McGarry, Thomas H.	Denver, CO	Attorney	Indefinite from November 28, 2006
Roberts, Quinton D.	Elkridge, MD	Attorney	Indefinite from November 28, 2006
Schofield, Peter L.	Spencer, MA	Attorney	Indefinite from November 28, 2006
Shultz, Ryan K.	Mitchell, NE	Attorney	Indefinite from November 28, 2006
Stenger, Jeanne P.	Temecula, CA	Attorney	Indefinite from November 28, 2006
Wood, Gary K.	Edina, MN	Attorney	Indefinite from November 28, 2006
Bakare, Adigun S.	Laurel, MD	Attorney	Indefinite from December 6, 2006

Name	Address	Designation	Date of Suspension
Biagini, Marc J.	Downers Grove, IL	Attorney	Indefinite from December 6, 2006
Birchall, Richard G.	Brewster, MA	Attorney	Indefinite from December 6, 2006
Brown, Edward E.	Indianapolis, IN	Attorney	Indefinite from December 6, 2006
Cunningham, Jr., Shirley A.	Ft. Lauderdale, FL	Attorney	Indefinite from December 6, 2006
Docherty, Scott R.	Branson West, MO	Attorney	Indefinite from December 6, 2006
Dressler, Peter P.	West Chicago, IL	Attorney	Indefinite from December 6, 2006
Henry, William J.	Irvington, NJ	Attorney	Indefinite from December 6, 2006
Hubbard, Cynthia A.	Geneva, IL	Attorney	Indefinite from December 6, 2006
Jackson, Jr., Donald H.	Hanover, MA	Attorney	Indefinite from December 6, 2006
Katz, Norman H.	Owings Mills, MD	Attorney	Indefinite from December 6, 2006
Lakin, Leonard S.	Wellesley Hills, MA	Attorney	Indefinite from December 6, 2006
McGreevy, Jacqueline K.	Carbondale, CO	Attorney	Indefinite from December 6, 2006
Zepp, Dale D.	Ferguson, MO	Attorney	Indefinite from December 6, 2006
Triplett, Austin H.	Homewood, IL	Attorney	Indefinite from December 11, 2006
Murphy, Patrick W.	Honolulu, HI	Attorney	Indefinite from December 11, 2006
Cronin, Jr., Edward M.	Cambridge, MA	Attorney	Indefinite from December 11, 2006

Name	Address	Designation	Date of Suspension
Christof, Kevin F.	Santa Monica, CA	Attorney	Indefinite from December 21, 2006
Heath, Kenneth J.	Canaan, VT	CPA	Indefinite from December 21, 2006
Madigan, Brian C.	Binghamton, NY	Attorney	Indefinite from December 21, 2006
Malloy, Terry P.	Tulsa, OK	Attorney	Indefinite from December 21, 2006
Baynes, Robert M.	Indianapolis, IN	CPA	Indefinite from December 27, 2006
Ceresa, Richard A.	Woodbridge, CA	CPA	Indefinite from December 27, 2006
Crews, Richard A.	Henderson, CO	Attorney	Indefinite from December 27, 2006
Menkveld, Paul G.	Tucson, AZ	Attorney	Indefinite from December 27, 2006
Worischeck, Joseph H.	Tempe, AZ	Attorney	Indefinite from December 27, 2006
Brown, Kirk P.	Pueblo, CO	Attorney	Indefinite from December 28, 2006
Dowling, Stanley W.	Scotts Valley, CA	CPA	Indefinite from December 28, 2006
Simmons, Henry L.	Greensboro, NC	CPA	Indefinite from December 28, 2006
Steele, Regina D.	San Diego, CA	Attorney	Indefinite from December 29, 2006
Craig, III, William A.	Austin, TX	Attorney	Indefinite from January 1, 2007
Acker, Thomas R.	Hollis Center, ME	Attorney	Indefinite from January 8, 2007
Baxter, Laura M.	Monee, IL	CPA	Indefinite from January 8, 2007

Name	Address	Designation	Date of Suspension
Herald, Sally J.	Cold Spring, KY	Attorney	Indefinite from January 8, 2007
Klapheke, II, William T.	Bowling Green, KY	Attorney	Indefinite from January 8, 2007
McCarthy, Charles C.	Encino, CA	Attorney	Indefinite from January 8, 2007
Bolling, Darius C.	Chicago, IL	CPA	Indefinite from January 10, 2007
Breitlauch, Linda	Saylorsburg, PA	Attorney	Indefinite from January 10, 2007
Coddington, Paul F.	Concord, NH	Attorney	Indefinite from January 10, 2007
Davis, Jr., William E.	Pinehurst, TX	CPA	Indefinite from January 10, 2007
Esola, Louis A.	Greensburg, PA	CPA	Indefinite from January 10, 2007
Finch, Judith A.	Walnut Creek, CA	Attorney	Indefinite from January 10, 2007
Jeing, Thomas C.	San Francisco, CA	Attorney	Indefinite from January 10, 2007
Ledbetter, Dean D.	Pelham, AL	CPA	Indefinite from January 10, 2007
McDiarmid, Katherine B.	Greensboro, NC	Attorney	Indefinite from January 10, 2007
Mills, George P.	Oceanside, CA	Attorney	Indefinite from January 10, 2007
Rather, James L.	Irvine, CA	Attorney	Indefinite from January 10, 2007
Rivera, Eduardo M.	Torrance, CA	Attorney	Indefinite from January 10, 2007
Stepovich, Michael A.	Fairbanks, AK	Attorney	Indefinite from January 10, 2007

Name	Address	Designation	Date of Suspension
Ulbrich, David L.	Woodland Hills, CA	CPA	Indefinite from January 10, 2007
Swanson, Todd-Ellis	Greenville, SC	CPA	Indefinite from January 20, 2007
Rubin, Deborah L.	Delray Beach, FL	Attorney	Indefinite from January 26, 2007
Wood, Brent E.	Cary, NC	Attorney	Indefinite from January 26, 2007
Currin, Samuel T.	Raleigh, NC	Attorney	Indefinite from February 7, 2007
Lupo, Robert N.	Weston, MA	Attorney	Indefinite from February 20, 2007
Taggart, Lawrence W.	El Cajon, CA	Attorney	Indefinite from March 7, 2007
Fife, III, James H.	Schererville, IN	Attorney	Indefinite from March 8, 2007
Katsis, Kevin G.	Riverside, IL	Attorney	Indefinite from March 8, 2007
O'Driscoll, Dennis M.	Quincy, MA	Attorney	Indefinite from March 8, 2007
Siever, Beth F.	Austin, TX	Attorney	Indefinite from March 8, 2007
Wheatley-Clark, Sheila R.	Houston, TX	CPA	Indefinite from March 8, 2007

Suspensions From Practice Before the Internal Revenue Service After Notice and an Opportunity for a Proceeding

Under Title 31, Code of Federal Regulations, Part 10, after notice and an opportunity for a proceeding before an administrative law judge, the following individuals have been placed under suspension from practice before the Internal Revenue Service:

Name	Address	Designation	Effective Date
Redmond, Debra	Gifford, PA	Enrolled Agent	Indefinite from March 5, 2007

Disbarments From Practice Before the Internal Revenue Service After Notice and an Opportunity for a Proceeding

Under Title 31, Code of Federal Regulations, Part 10, after notice and an opportunity for a proceeding before an administrative law judge, the following individuals have been disbarred from practice before the Internal Revenue Service:

Name	Address	Designation	Effective Date
Brookstein, Gary	Huntingdon Valley, PA	CPA	December 15, 2006
James T. Jubb	Baltimore, MD	CPA	December 15, 2006

Censure Issued by Consent

Under Title 31, Code of Federal Regulations, Part 10, in lieu of a proceeding being instituted or continued, an attorney, certified public accountant, enrolled agent, or enrolled actuary, may offer his or her consent to the issuance of a censure. Censure is a public reprimand.

The following individuals have consented to the issuance of a Censure:

Name	Address	Designation	Date of Censure
Zucker, Robert W.	Boca Raton, FL	CPA	November 14, 2006
Montgomery, David E.	Pleasanton, CA	Enrolled Agent	November 15, 2006
Higgins, James M.	S. Boston, MA	Attorney	December 1, 2006
Pennington, Debra L.	Lees Summit, MO	Enrolled Agent	January 29, 2007
Goodwin, Steven C.	Concord, MA	Attorney	February 2, 2007
Francis, Andrew W.E.	Houston, TX	CPA	February 21, 2007
Griffin, Richard M.	Duluth, GA	CPA	February 28, 2007

Resignations of Enrolled Agents

Under Title 31, Code of Federal Regulations, Part 10, an enrolled agent, in order to avoid the institution or conclusion of a proceeding for his or her disbarment or suspension from practice before the Internal Revenue Service, may offer his or her resignation as an enrolled agent. The Director, Office of Professional Responsibility, in his discretion, may accept the offered resignation.

The Director, Office of Professional Responsibility, has accepted offers of resignation as an enrolled agent from the following individuals:

Name	Address	Date of Resignation
Filipski, Kenneth M.	Bakersfield, CA	April 16, 2007

Foundations Status of Certain Organizations

Announcement 2007–42

The following organizations have failed to establish or have been unable to maintain their status as public charities or as operating foundations. Accordingly, grantors and contributors may not, after this date, rely on previous rulings or designations in the Cumulative List of Organizations (Publication 78), or on the presumption arising from the filing of notices under section 508(b) of the Code. This listing does *not* indicate that the organizations have lost their status as organizations described in section 501(c)(3), eligible to receive deductible contributions.

Former Public Charities. The following organizations (which have been treated as organizations that are not private foundations described in section 509(a) of the Code) are now classified as private foundations:

Advanced Senior Assisted Living and Development of America, Inc., Detroit, MI
Adventurous Youth Organization, Beverly Hills, CA
Africans in America, Inc., New York, NY
Agape Life Institute, Austin, TX
Amercia Vive Foundation, Bell, CA
American Dream Project, Inc., Wayne, NJ
AMICA Institute, South Hampton, NY
Asian Community Media Institute, Inc., Saint Paul, MN
Association of Christian Professionals, Inc., Chicago, IL
Audax Theatre Group, New York, NY
Bay Area Ability Center, Incorporated, Bay City, MI
Berean Basketball Boosters, Wilmington, OH
Bergens Promise, Inc., Rochelle Park, NJ
Beta Community Services, Inc., II, Baton Rouge, LA
Brainstorm, West Chester, PA
Brooklyn Heritage, Inc., Brooklyn, NY
Camp Refuge, Columbia, SC
Carolina Housing Alliance, Inc., Taylors, SC
Children and Families of East Tennessee, Inc., Johnson City, TN
City Links 4charities, Inc., Orlando, FL
Coastal Renaissance Behavioral Health Services, Inc., Sarasota, FL
Coluntuno Charitable Foundation Co., Marblehead, MA
Community Staffing Resources, Inc., Woonsocket, RI
Covington Middle School Parent Network, Vancouver, WA
Creation Station Art Center, Inc., Copley, OH
Dabhar, Inc., Downey, CA
Dallas County Repeater Corporation, Dallas, TX
Down to Earth Ministries, Inc., Chippewa Falls, WI
Earle Action Community Development Corporation, Inc., Earle, AR
Echelon, Inc., Meridian, MS
El Roi, Inc., Brick, NJ
Emmanuel Ministries of Romania, Inc., Sumter, SC
Exceptional Resources, Banks, OR
Father Resource Network, Mill Valley, CA
Finer Things Academy, Inc., Youngstown, OH
Friends of Boy Scout Troop 224, Orinda, CA
Friends of the Ashford Community Park, Ashford, WA
Gifts of First Fruits Foundation, The Colony, TX
God's Children at Play, Los Angeles, CA
Grandslam, Inc., Kingsport, TN
Grenier Foundation, Newark, CA
Harambee Community Development Corporation, Inc., Cincinnati, OH
Hartford Baltimore County Cheerleading League, Inc., Baltimore, MD
Health & Fitness Foundation of America, Irvine, CA
Hilltop Camp, Richland Center, WI
His Love and Truth Ministries, Arcata, CA
Historic Hilger Homestead, Helena, MT
Institute for the Study of Ideologies and Literature, Minneapolis, MN
International Partnership for Health NFP, Chicago, IL
Jeffrey G. Loving Memorial Open Arms Free Medical Facility, Angel Fire, NM
Judahs House, Fresno, CA
Just Everyday Sisters Used Supernaturally, Gardena, CA
Juxtopia Group, Inc., Baltimore, MD
Kat Whirld, Inc., Greenfield, MA
Kaye Starr Singers Corporation, Layton, UT
Kerr Interfaith Disaster Response, Inc., Kerrville, TX
Kiwanis Club of West Jeffersons Reflections of Hope Foundation, Inc., Harvey, LA
Lander County Humane Society, Battle Mountain, NV
Life Ten Ten, Inc., Jersey City, NJ
Light House Christian Ministry, Corsicana, TX
Little Creek Special Equestrians, Inc., Centerpoint, IN

L O F S, Inc., Leap of Faith Services, Memphis, TN
Lost Coast Interpretive Association, Whitehorn, CA
Lumina Group of St. Louis, St. Louis, MO
Make It Public, Inc., San Francisco, CA
MH Community Service, Monterey Park, CA
Mike Scuch Memorial College Scholarship Fund, Staten Island, NY
Miracle Life Nisim Haim, Oak Park, MI
Modjeska Ranch Rescue, Silverrado, CA
National Association of Disabled Asian-American, Los Angeles, CA
National Visionary Leadership Project, Washington, DC
Native Veterans Association of Alaska, Anchorage, AK
Norman and Judith Jo Kreiss Family Foundation, San Diego, CA
North End Partnership Association, Mason City, IA
Northwest Alabama Education Partnership, Florence, AL
Old River Committee, Inc., Tracy, CA
One America Foundation, Inc., Baltimore, MD
Pomerelle Institute, Inc., Albion, ID
Raisin Hope Rescue & Rehabilitation, Raymond, WA
Recreation Trail Management, Loveland, OH
Redeemed Services, Inc., Los Angeles, CA
Rehema Adult Day Health Care Center, Pomona, CA
Research Nurse Association, Inc., Wellesley, MA
Resiliency for Action and Success, Orange Park, FL
Rock Christian, Inc., Bakersfield, CA
Save A Teen, Oregon City, OR
Save Our Strays, Inc., Newport News, VA
Sea of Dreams Foundation, Inc., Honolulu, HI
Sherit Isroel, Inc., Brooklyn, NY
Silver Lake Football Association, Everett, WA
Single Family Services, Las Vegas, NV
SIS (Stay in School), Inc., Chicago, IL
Society for Counter-Ordnance Technology, Charlottesville, VA
Somaliland Community of Metro Chicago, Chicago, IL
Spazi, Inc., Miami, FL
Sterling Youth Accountability Board, Patton, CA
Sunny Health Recovery Center, Inc., Fairbanks, AK
Sunshine Service Dogs, Inc., Luck, TX
Teach Me to Live Ecumenical Ministries, Makawao, HI
Thaddean Society, Elgin, IL
Thomas Hart Benton Catalogue Raisonne Foundation, Inc., New York, NY
True Divine Ministries, Cincinnati, OH
US Sailing Foundation of Marion County, Jensen Beach, FL
Valley Falcons Youth Athletic Club, Sylmar, CA
William J. Gallion, Captiva, FL
Wolverine Management Foundation, Los Angeles, CA
Wrightco Educational Foundation, Claysburg, PA
Youth Programs Unlimited, Inc., Antioch, CA

If an organization listed above submits information that warrants the renewal of its classification as a public charity or as a private operating foundation, the Internal Revenue Service will issue a ruling or determination letter with the revised classification as to foundation status. Grantors and contributors may thereafter rely upon such ruling or determination letter as provided in section 1.509(a)–7 of the Income Tax Regulations. It is not the practice of the Service to announce such revised classification of foundation status in the Internal Revenue Bulletin.

Deletions From Cumulative List of Organizations Contributions to Which are Deductible Under Section 170 of the Code

Announcement 2007–43

The names of organizations that no longer qualify as organizations described in section 170(c)(2) of the Internal Revenue Code of 1986 are listed below.

Generally, the Service will not disallow deductions for contributions made to a listed organization on or before the date of announcement in the Internal Revenue Bulletin that an organization no longer qualifies. However, the Service is not precluded from disallowing a deduction for any contributions made after an organization ceases to qualify under section 170(c)(2) if the organization has not timely filed a suit for declaratory judgment under section 7428 and if the contributor (1) had knowledge of the revocation of the ruling or determination letter, (2) was aware that such revocation was imminent, or (3) was in part responsible for or was aware of the activities or omissions of the organization that brought about this revocation.

If on the other hand a suit for declaratory judgment has been timely filed, contributions from individuals and organizations described in section 170(c)(2) that are otherwise allowable will continue to be deductible. Protection under section 7428(c) would begin on April 23, 2007, and would end on the date the court first determines that the organization is not described in section 170(c)(2) as more particularly set forth in section 7428(c)(1). For individual contributors, the maximum deduction protected is $1,000, with a husband and wife treated as one contributor. This benefit is not extended to any individual, in whole or in part, for the acts or omissions of the organization that were the basis for revocation.

EPASA-USA, Inc. Ridgewood, NY
Morocco and the Casbah Dance Experience, Inc. New York, NY
ABG Housing, Inc. Orlando, FL
The Credit Network, Inc. Silver Spring, MD
Global Mindlink Foundation, Inc. Coral Springs, FL
Credit Debt Solutions, Inc. Chevy Chase, MD
Skopos Charities, Inc. San Jose, CA
Douglas R. & Patricia B. McKinnon Charitable Supporting Organization Tomball, TX
The Dreamhouse Charity, Inc. Wilsonville, OR
Dads Place Ministries, Inc. Thurmont, MD
Potomac Forum, Ltd. Potomac, MD
Community Housing and Land Development, Inc. San Jose, CA
New Haven Shelter Rancho Palos Verdes, CA

Part I. Rulings and Decisions Under the Internal Revenue Code of 1986

Section 274.—Disallowance of Certain Entertainment, etc., Expenses

26 CFR 1.274–1: Disallowance of certain entertainment, etc., expenses.

Geographical areas included in North American area. This ruling contains an updated list of all geographical areas included in the North American area for purposes of section 274 of the Code. Rev. Rul. 2003–109 superseded.

Rev. Rul. 2007–28

ISSUE

Section 274(h) of the Internal Revenue Code (the "Code") limits deductions for expenses incurred in connection with a convention, seminar, or similar meeting held outside the "North American area." This revenue ruling contains an updated list of all geographical areas currently included in the North American area for purposes of section 274(h).

LAW AND ANALYSIS

Section 274(h) disallows deductions under section 162 for expenses allocable to attendance of an individual at a convention, seminar, or similar meeting (collectively, a "convention") held outside the "North American area" unless the taxpayer demonstrates that the location of the convention satisfies specified standards of reasonableness.

A geographical area may be included in the "North American area" for purposes of section 274(h) under one of the four provisions described below.

Section 274(h)(3)(A)

Section 274(h)(3)(A) defines the term "North American area" as the United States, its possessions, the Trust Territory of the Pacific Islands, Canada, and Mexico. Under section 7701(a)(9), the United States consists of the fifty states and the District of Columbia. The Internal Revenue Service treats the following as the possessions of the United States for this purpose: American Samoa, Baker Island, the Commonwealth of Puerto Rico, the Commonwealth of the Northern Mariana Islands, Guam, Howland Island, Jarvis Island, Johnston Island, Kingman Reef, the Midway Islands, Palmyra Atoll, the United States Virgin Islands, Wake Island, and other United States islands, cays, and reefs not part of the fifty states or the District of Columbia. The jurisdictions that formerly constituted the Trust Territory of the Pacific Islands — the Republic of the Marshall Islands, the Federated States of Micronesia, and the Republic of Palau — are now covered by the compacts with the United States described below.

The Compact of Free Association Act of 1985

The Compact of Free Association Act of 1985, Pub. L. No. 99–239, 99 Stat. 1770 (1986), went into effect on October 21, 1986, with respect to the Republic of the Marshall Islands, and on November 3, 1986, with respect to the Federated States of Micronesia. Section 405 of Title IV of the Compact provides that, for purposes of section 274(h)(3)(A) of the Code, the Republic of the Marshall Islands and the Federated States of Micronesia are included in the North American area.

The Compact of Free Association Between the United States and the Republic of Palau

The Compact of Free Association between the United States and the Republic of Palau, Pub. L. No. 99–658, 100 Stat. 3672 (1986), went into effect on October 1, 1994. Section 225(d) of Title II of the Compact with Palau provides that, for purposes of section 274(h)(3)(A) of the Code, Palau is included in the North American area.

Section 274(h)(6)

Section 274(h)(6)(A) provides that the term "North American area" includes any "beneficiary country" if, as of the time a convention begins: (i) there is in effect an agreement described in section 274(h)(6)(C) providing for the exchange of information between the United States and the beneficiary country; and (ii) there is not in effect a finding by the Secretary of the Treasury that the tax laws of the beneficiary country discriminate against conventions held in the United States.

Section 274(h)(6)(B) defines the term "beneficiary country" as a beneficiary country as defined in section 212(a)(1)(A) of the Caribbean Basin Economic Recovery Act, Pub. L. No. 98–67, 97 Stat. 384 (1983), and Bermuda. Under section 274(h)(6)(C)(i), to constitute an agreement that provides for the exchange of information between the United States and a beneficiary country, an agreement generally must provide:

> for the exchange of such information (not limited to information concerning nationals or residents of the United States or the beneficiary country) as may be necessary or appropriate to carry out and enforce the tax laws of the United States and the beneficiary country (whether criminal or civil proceedings), including information which may otherwise be subject to nondisclosure provisions of the local law of the beneficiary country such as provisions respecting bank secrecy and bearer shares.

Where an exchange of information agreement between a beneficiary country and the United States does not qualify as an agreement described in section 274(h)(6)(C)(i) or is not in effect within the meaning of section 274(h)(6)(A)(i), the beneficiary country is not included as part of the North American area under section 274(h)(6) for purposes of determining whether deductions are allowed for expenses incurred in connection with a convention.

Rev. Rul. 2003–109, 2003–2 C.B. 839, identified each of the following jurisdictions as a beneficiary country for which there was in effect an agreement with the United States as described in section 274(h)(6)(C)(i) and for which there was not in effect a finding by the Secretary of the Treasury that the tax laws of the beneficiary country discriminate against conventions held in the United States: Antigua and Barbuda, Barbados, Bermuda, Costa Rica, Dominica, Dominican Republic,

Grenada, Guyana, Honduras, Jamaica, Saint Lucia, and Trinidad and Tobago.

It has come to the attention of the Internal Revenue Service that the tax information exchange agreement signed by the United States and Saint Lucia on January 30, 1987, is not in effect within the meaning of section 274(h)(6)(A)(i) because the government of Saint Lucia has not enacted legislation to implement the agreement. Accordingly, Saint Lucia is not included in the North American area under section 274(h)(6), subject to the transition relief provided in the Holding below.

Since publication of Rev. Rul. 2003–109, three new qualifying agreements have entered into force. First, the "Agreement Between the Government of the United States of America and the Government of the Commonwealth of the Bahamas for the Provision of Information with Respect to Taxes and for Other Matters" entered into force on December 31, 2003. *See* Treas. News Release JS–1075 (December 31, 2003). However, under the agreement with the Bahamas, Article 2 ("Provision of Information with Respect to United States Taxes") did not take effect with respect to requests for information made by the United States in connection with a civil matter until January 1, 2006, and Article 5 ("Convention Tax Treatment") similarly did not take effect until January 1, 2006. Consequently, the Bahamas is included within the North American area under section 274(h)(6) as of January 1, 2006.

Second, the "Agreement Between the United States of America and the Kingdom of the Netherlands in Respect of Aruba for the Exchange of Information With Respect to Taxes" entered into force on September 13, 2004. *See* Treas. News Release JS–1914 (September 14, 2004). Therefore, Aruba is included within the North American area under section 274(h)(6) as of September 13, 2004.

Third, the "Agreement Between the Government of the United States of America and the Government of the Kingdom of the Netherlands in Respect of the Netherlands Antilles for the Exchange of Information With Respect to Taxes" entered into force on March 22, 2007. Therefore, the Netherlands Antilles is included within the North American area under section 274(h)(6) as of March 22, 2007.

Two other beneficiary countries — the Cayman Islands and the British Virgin Islands — have entered into tax information exchange agreements with the United States that are not of the type described in section 274(h)(6)(C)(i) because of certain limitations in the scope of those agreements. Accordingly, the Cayman Islands and the British Virgin Islands are not included as part of the North American area under section 274(h)(6).

HOLDING

For purposes of determining whether deductions are allowed for expenses incurred in connection with a convention, seminar, or similar meeting, the following areas are included in the "North American area" as of the effective date of section 274(h) except as otherwise indicated:

1. The fifty states of the United States and the District of Columbia;
2. The possessions of the United States, which for this purpose are American Samoa, Baker Island, the Commonwealth of Puerto Rico, the Commonwealth of the Northern Mariana Islands, Guam, Howland Island, Jarvis Island, Johnston Island, Kingman Reef, the Midway Islands, Palmyra Atoll, the United States Virgin Islands, Wake Island, and other United States islands, cays, and reefs not part of the fifty states or the District of Columbia;
3. Canada;
4. Mexico;
5. The Republic of the Marshall Islands;
6. The Federated States of Micronesia;
7. The Republic of Palau;

	For expenses incurred in attending a convention that began after:
8. Antigua and Barbuda	February 9, 2003
9. Aruba	September 12, 2004
10. Bahamas	December 31, 2005
11. Barbados	November 2, 1984
12. Bermuda	December 1, 1988
13. Costa Rica	February 11, 1991
14. Dominica	May 8, 1988
15. Dominican Republic	October 11, 1989
16. Grenada	July 12, 1987

17.	Guyana	August 26, 1992
18.	Honduras	October 9, 1991
19.	Jamaica	December 17, 1986
20.	Netherlands Antilles	March 21, 2007
21.	Trinidad and Tobago	February 8, 1990

The Internal Revenue Service will treat Saint Lucia as not included in the North American area under section 274(h)(6) with respect to conventions that begin after April 4, 2007, except with respect to expenses for which the taxpayer demonstrates a nonrefundable contractual obligation existing as of April 4, 2007.

This revenue ruling will be updated as future developments result in the inclusion of other areas in, or the exclusion of areas from, the North American area.

EFFECT ON OTHER DOCUMENTS

Rev. Rul. 2003–109 is superseded.

DRAFTING INFORMATION

The principal author of this revenue ruling is Denen Norfleet Boyce of the Office of Associate Chief Counsel (International), Branch 7. For further information regarding this revenue ruling, contact the principal author at (202) 435–5262 (not a toll-free call).

Section 280F.—Limitation on Depreciation for Luxury Automobiles; Limitation Where Certain Property Used for Personal Purposes

26 CFR 1.280F–7: Property leased after December 31, 1986.

This procedure provides owners and lessees of passenger automobiles (including electric automobiles) with tables detailing the limitations on depreciation deductions for automobiles first placed in service during calendar year 2007 and the amounts to be included in income for automobiles first leased during calendar year 2007. See Rev. Proc. 2007-30, page 1104.

Section 401.—Qualified Pension, Profit-Sharing, and Stock Bonus Plans

26 CFR 1.401(a)(9)–6: Required minimum distributions for defined benefit plans and annuity contracts.
26 CFR 1.401(k)–1: Certain cash or deferred arrangements.

To conform to the amendments to section 415 Income Tax Regulations, Q&A–13(c)(3) of section 1.401(a)(9)–6 is amended, and section 1.401(k)–1 is amended by adding paragraph (e)(8). See T.D. 9319, page 1041.

Section 415.—Limitations on Benefits and Contributions Under Qualified Plans

26 CFR 1.415(a)–1: General rules with respect to limitations on benefits and contributions under qualified plans.

T.D. 9319

DEPARTMENT OF THE TREASURY
Internal Revenue Service
26 CFR Parts 1 and 11

Limitations on Benefits and Contributions Under Qualified Plans

AGENCY: Internal Revenue Service (IRS), Treasury.

ACTION: Final regulations and removal of temporary regulations.

SUMMARY: This document contains final regulations under section 415 of the Internal Revenue Code (Code) regarding the limitations of section 415, including updates to the regulations for numerous statutory changes since comprehensive final regulations were last published under section 415. The final regulations also make conforming changes to regulations under sections 401(a), 401(a)(9), 401(k), 402, 416, and 457, and make other minor corrective changes to regulations under sections 401(a)(4), 414(s), 457, and 924. These regulations affect administrators of, participants in, and beneficiaries of qualified employer plans and certain other retirement plans.

DATES: *Effective Date:* These regulations are effective April 5, 2007.

Applicability Dates: These regulations generally apply for limitation years beginning on or after July 1, 2007. See §§1.401(k)–1(e)(8), 1.415(a)–1(g), 1.457–6(c)(2)(i), and 1.457–12 regarding the applicability dates of these regulations.

FOR FURTHER INFORMATION CONTACT: Vernon S. Carter at (202) 622–6060 or Linda S. F. Marshall at (202) 622–6090 (not toll-free numbers).

SUPPLEMENTARY INFORMATION:

Background

This document contains amendments to the Income Tax Regulations (26 CFR Parts 1 and 11) under section 415 of the Code relating to limitations on benefits and contributions under qualified plans. In addition, this document contains conforming amendments to the Income Tax Regulations under sections 401(a) (including section 401(a)(9)), 401(k), 402, 416, and 457, as well as minor corrective changes to the regulations under section 457 and changes to other regulations under sections 401(a) (including section 401(a)(4)), 414(s), and 924 to update cross-references to the final regulations under section 415.

Section 415 was added to the Code by the Employee Retirement Income Security Act of 1974 (88 Stat. 829), Public Law 93–406 (ERISA), and has been amended many times since. Section 415 provides a series of limits on benefits under qualified defined benefit plans and on contributions and other additions under qualified defined contribution plans. See also section 401(a)(16). Pursuant to section

415(a)(2), the limitations of section 415 also apply to section 403(b) annuity contracts and to simplified employee pensions described in section 408(k) (SEPs). In addition, the limitations of section 415 for defined contribution plans apply to contributions allocated to any individual medical account that is part of a pension or annuity plan established pursuant to section 401(h) and to amounts attributable to medical benefits allocated to an account under a welfare benefit fund established for a key employee pursuant to section 419A(d)(1).

Section 404(j) provides generally that, in computing the amount of any deduction for contributions under a qualified plan, benefits and annual additions in excess of the applicable limitations under section 415 are not taken into account. In addition, in computing the applicable limits on deductions for contributions to a defined benefit plan, and in computing the full funding limitation, an adjustment under section 415(d)(1) is not taken into account for any year before the year for which that adjustment first takes effect.

The definition of compensation that is used for purposes of section 415 is also used for a number of other purposes under the Code. Under section 219(b)(3), contributions on behalf of an employee to a plan described in section 501(c)(18) are limited to 25 percent of compensation as defined in section 415(c)(3). Section 404(a)(12) provides that, for various specified purposes in determining deductible limits under section 404, the term *compensation* includes amounts treated as participant's compensation under section 415(c)(3)(C) or (D). Pursuant to section 409(b)(3), for purposes of determining whether employer securities are allocated proportionately to compensation in accordance with the rules of section 409(b)(1), the amount of compensation paid to a participant for any period is the amount of such participant's compensation (within the meaning of section 415(c)(3)) for such period. Under section 414(q)(4), for purposes of determining whether an employee is a highly compensated employee within the meaning of section 414(q), the term compensation has the meaning given such term by section 415(c)(3). Section 414(s), which defines the term compensation for purposes of certain qualification requirements, generally provides that the term compensation has the meaning given such term by section 415(c)(3). Under section 416(c)(2), allocations to participants who are non-key employees under a top-heavy plan that is a defined contribution plan are required to be at least 3 percent of the participant's compensation (within the meaning of section 415(c)(3)). Pursuant to section 457(e)(5), the term *includible compensation*, which is used in limiting the amount that can be deferred for a participant under an eligible deferred compensation plan as defined in section 457(b), has the same meaning as the term participant's compensation under section 415(c)(3).

Comprehensive regulations regarding section 415 were last issued in 1981. See T.D. 7748, 1981–1 C.B. 259, published in the **Federal Register** on January 7, 1981 (46 FR 1687). Since then, changes to section 415 have been made in the Economic Recovery Tax Act of 1981, Public Law 97–34 (95 Stat. 320) (ERTA), the Tax Equity and Fiscal Responsibility Act of 1982, Public Law 97–248 (96 Stat. 623) (TEFRA), the Deficit Reduction Act of 1984, Public Law 98–369 (98 Stat. 494) (DEFRA), the Tax Reform Act of 1986, Public Law 99–514 (100 Stat. 2481) (TRA '86), the Technical and Miscellaneous Revenue Act of 1988, Public Law 100–647 (102 Stat. 3342) (TAMRA), the Uruguay Round Agreements Act of 1994, Public Law 103–465 (108 Stat. 4809) (GATT), the Small Business Job Protection Act of 1996, Public Law 104–188 (110 Stat. 1755) (SBJPA), the Community Renewal Tax Relief Act of 2000, Public Law 106–554 (114 Stat. 2763) (CRA), the Economic Growth and Tax Relief Reconciliation Act of 2001, Public Law 107–16 (115 Stat. 38) (EGTRRA), the Job Creation and Worker Assistance Act of 2002, Public Law 107–147 (116 Stat. 21) (JCWAA), the Pension Funding Equity Act of 2004, Public Law 108–218 (118 Stat. 596) (PFEA), the Working Families Tax Relief Act of 2004, Public Law 108–311 (118 Stat. 1166) (WFTRA), the Gulf Opportunity Zone Act of 2005, Public Law 109–135 (119 Stat. 2577) (GOZA), and the Pension Protection Act of 2006, Public Law 109–280 (120 Stat. 780) (PPA '06).

Although some limited changes to the regulations were made after 1981, most of the statutory changes made since that time are not reflected in the regulations, but in IRS notices, revenue rulings, and other guidance of general applicability, as follows:

- Notice 82–13, 1982–1 C.B. 360, (see §601.601(d)(2)) provides guidance on deductible employee contributions (including guidance under section 415) to reflect the addition of provisions relating to deductible employee contributions in ERTA.

- Notice 83–10, 1983–1 C.B. 536, (see §601.601(d)(2)) provides guidance on the changes to section 415 made by TEFRA. The TEFRA changes were extensive, and included reductions of the dollar limits on annual benefits under a defined benefit plan and annual additions under a defined contribution plan, changes to the age and form adjustments made in the application of the limits under a defined benefit plan, and rules regarding the deductibility of contributions with respect to benefits that exceed the applicable limitations of section 415.

- Notice 87–21, 1987–1 C.B. 458, (see §601.601(d)(2)) provides guidance on the changes to section 415 made by TRA '86. The TRA '86 changes modified the rules for the indexing of the dollar limit on annual additions under a defined contribution plan, the treatment of employee contributions as annual additions, and the rules for age adjustments under defined benefit plans, and added a phase-in of the section 415(b)(1)(A) dollar limitation over 10 years of participation, as well as rules permitting the limitations of section 415 to be incorporated by reference under the terms of a plan.

- Rev. Rul. 98–1, 1998–1 C.B. 249, (modifying and superseding Rev. Rul. 95–29, 1995–1 C.B. 81) (see §601.601(d)(2)) provides guidance regarding certain form and age adjustments under a defined benefit plan pursuant to changes made by GATT (as modified under SBJPA), including transition rules relating to those adjustments.

- Notice 99–44, 1999–2 C.B. 326, (see §601.601(d)(2)) provides guidance regarding the repeal under SBJPA of the limitation on the combination of a defined benefit plan and a defined contribution plan under former section 415(e).

- Notice 2001–37, 2001–1 C.B. 1340, (see §601.601(d)(2)) provides guidance regarding the inclusion of salary reduction amounts for qualified transportation fringe benefits in the definition of compensation for purposes of section 415, as provided under CRA.

- Rev. Rul. 2001–51, 2001–2 C.B. 427, (see §601.601(d)(2)) provides guidance relating to the increases in the limitations of section 415 for both defined benefit and defined contribution plans, which were enacted as part of EGTRRA.

- Rev. Rul. 2001–62, 2001–2 C.B. 632, (superseding Rev. Rul. 95–6, 1995–1 C.B. 80) (see §601.601(d)(2)) provides mortality tables to be used to make certain form adjustments to benefits under a defined benefit plan for purposes of applying the limitations of section 415, pursuant to the requirement to use a specified mortality table added by GATT.

- Notice 2002–2, 2002–1 C.B. 285, (see §601.601(d)(2)) provides guidance regarding the treatment of reinvested employee stock ownership plan (ESOP) dividends under section 415(c), to reflect changes made by SBJPA.

- Rev. Rul. 2002–27, 2002–1 C.B. 925, (see §601.601(d)(2)) provides guidance pursuant to which a definition of compensation can be used for purposes of applying the limitations of section 415 even if that definition treats certain specified amounts that may not be available to an employee in cash as subject to section 125 (and therefore included in compensation).

- Rev. Rul. 2002–45, 2002–2 C.B. 116, (see §601.601(d)(2)) provides guidance regarding the treatment of certain payments to defined contribution plans to restore losses resulting from actions by a fiduciary for which there is a reasonable risk of liability for breach of a fiduciary duty (including the treatment of those payments under section 415).

- Notice 2004–78, 2004–2 C.B. 879, (see §601.601(d)(2)) provides guidance regarding the actuarial assumptions that must be used for distributions with annuity starting dates occurring during plan years beginning in years 2004 and 2005 to determine whether an amount payable under a defined benefit plan in a form that is subject to the minimum present value requirements of section 417(e)(3) satisfies the requirements of section 415. This guidance reflects changes made in PFEA.

For copies of recently issued revenue procedures, revenue rulings, notices, and other guidance published in the Internal Revenue Bulletin or the Cumulative Bulletin, please visit the IRS website at *www.irs.gov*.

Some previously issued guidance has been superseded by subsequent statutory changes. For example, the simplified actuarial adjustment factors formerly permitted to be used to adjust certain forms of benefit for purposes of applying the limitations of section 415(b) pursuant to Rev. Rul. 80–253, 1980–2 C.B. 159, (see §601.601(d)(2)) were not permitted to be used after statutory changes imposed the use of specified actuarial assumptions to make these adjustments. In addition, the projected post-retirement adjustments to the section 415(b)(1)(B) compensation limit that were required to be taken into account for purposes of sections 404 and 412 under Rev. Rul. 81–195, 1981–2 C.B. 104, (see §601.601(d)(2)) were not required or permitted to be taken into account for those purposes following the addition of section 404(j) in TEFRA.

The Treasury Department and the IRS believe that a single restatement of the section 415 rules serves the interests of plan sponsors, third-party administrators, plan participants, and plan beneficiaries. On May 31, 2005, a notice of proposed rulemaking (REG–130241–04, 2005–2 C.B. 18) was published in the **Federal Register** (70 FR 31214) to issue new regulations under section 415 (the proposed regulations). The guidance items described in this preamble were reflected in the proposed regulations with some modifications. In addition, the proposed regulations reflected other statutory changes not previously addressed by guidance, and included some other changes and clarifications to the 1981 regulations. To the extent practicable, the preamble to the proposed regulations identified and explained substantive changes from the 1981 regulations or existing guidance.

Following publication of the proposed regulations, comments were received and a public hearing was held on August 17, 2005. Subsequently, Notice 2005–87, 2005–2 C.B. 1097, (see §601.601(d)(2)) was issued to address certain concerns about the effective date provisions of the proposed regulations. After consideration of the comments received, the proposed regulations are adopted by this Treasury decision, subject to a number of changes that are summarized in the preamble.

Explanation of Provisions

Overview

These regulations reflect the numerous statutory changes to section 415 and related provisions that have been made since 1981. Some of the statutory changes reflected in the regulations are as follows:

- The current statutory limitations under sections 415(b)(1)(A) and 415(c)(1) applicable for defined benefit and defined contribution plans, respectively, as most recently amended by EGTRRA.

- Changes to the rules for age adjustments to the applicable limitations under defined benefit plans, under which the dollar limitation is adjusted for commencement before age 62 or after age 65.

- Changes to the rules, including specification of parameters, for benefit adjustments under defined benefit plans.

- The phase-in of the dollar limitation under section 415(b)(1)(A) over 10 years of participation, as added by TRA '86.

- The addition of the section 401(a)(17) limitation on compensation that is permitted to be taken into account in determining plan benefits, as added by TRA '86, and the interaction of this requirement with the limitations under section 415.

- Exceptions to the compensation-based limitation under section 415(b)(1)(B) for governmental plans and multiemployer plans.

- Changes to the aggregation rules under section 415(f) under which multiemployer plans are not aggregated with single-employer plans for purposes of applying the compensation-based limitation of section 415(b)(1)(B) to a single-employer plan.

- The repeal under SBJPA of the section 415(e) combined limitation on participation in a defined benefit plan and a defined contribution plan.

- The changes to section 415(c) that were made in conjunction with the repeal under EGTRRA of the exclusion allowance under section 403(b)(2).

- The current rounding and base period rules for annual cost-of-living adjustments pursuant to section 415(d), as most recently amended in EGTRRA and WFTRA.

- Changes to section 415(c) under which certain types of arrangements are no longer subject to the limitations of section 415(c) (such as individual retirement accounts other than SEPs) and other types of arrangements have become subject to the limitations of section 415(c) (such as certain individual medical accounts).

- The inclusion in compensation (for purposes of section 415) of certain salary reduction amounts not included in gross income.

- The modification for distributions with annuity starting dates in plan years beginning in years 2004 and 2005 made by PFEA with respect to the interest rate assumptions in section 415(b)(2)(E) for converting certain forms of benefits to an actuarially equivalent straight life annuity.

- The following modifications to section 415 that were made by PPA '06: (i) changes to the interest rate assumptions in section 415(b)(2)(E) that are used for converting certain forms of benefits to an equivalent straight life annuity (section 303 of PPA '06); (ii) elimination of the active participation requirement in determining a participant's high-3 years of service in section 415(b)(3) (section 832 of PPA '06); (iii) exemption from the section 415(b)(1)(B) compensation limit for certain benefits provided under a defined benefit plan maintained by an organization described in section 3121(w)(3)(A) (section 867 of PPA '06); and (iv) expansion of the definition of qualified participant in section 415(b)(2)(H) to include certain participants in a defined benefit plan maintained by an Indian tribal government (section 906(b) of PPA '06).

These regulations provide specific rules regarding when amounts received following severance from employment are considered compensation for purposes of section 415, and when such amounts are permitted to be deferred pursuant to section 401(k) or section 457(b). These regulations generally provide that amounts received following severance from employment are not considered to be compensation for purposes of section 415, but provide exceptions for certain payments made by the later of 2½ months following severance from employment or the end of the year in which the severance occurs. These regulations include corresponding changes to the regulations under sections 401(k) and 457 that provide that amounts payable following severance from employment can only be deferred if those amounts are within these same exceptions.[1] The rule pursuant to which compensation received after severance from employment is not considered compensation for purposes of section 415 generally does not apply to payments to an individual in qualified military service. The rules governing amounts received following severance from employment are discussed in this preamble in more detail under the paragraph heading "Definition of compensation (§1.415(c)–2)."

Provisions of the Regulations

General rules (§1.415(a)–1)

Section 1.415(a)–1 of these regulations sets forth general rules relating to limitations under section 415 and provides an overview of the remaining regulations, including cross-references to special rules that apply to section 403(b) annuities, multiemployer plans, governmental plans, and plans that are not subject to the requirements of section 411. In addition, §1.415(a)–1 provides rules for a plan's incorporation by reference of the rules of section 415 pursuant to section 1106(h) of TRA '86 (including detailed guidelines regarding incorporation by reference of the annual cost-of-living adjustments to the statutory limits and the application of default rules), rules for plans maintained by more than one employer, a definition of the term "severance from employment," and rules that apply in other special situations. Section 1.415(a)–1 generally retains the rules set forth in the proposed regulations.

The proposed regulations eliminated the rule under the 1981 regulations under which a multiemployer plan could satisfy the limitations of section 415 separately with respect to benefits or contributions from each employer. Thus, the proposed regulations required the benefits or annual additions with respect to a participant under a multiemployer plan to satisfy the limitations of section 415 on an aggregate basis. Some commentators asked that the rule from the 1981 regulations be retained. The IRS and the Treasury Department have determined that there is no statutory basis for permitting disaggregation of a multiemployer plan for this purpose. Furthermore, statutory changes made since the issuance of the 1981 regulations have made this permissive disaggregation rule from the 1981 regulations less needed and more conducive to significant abuses. In EGTRRA (and as made permanent in PPA '06), multiemployer plans were exempted from the limitation for defined benefit plans based on high-3 average compensation. This change eliminated the need for multiemployer plans to obtain compensation information with respect to each participant from multiple participat-

[1] The proposed regulations also contained corresponding changes to regulations under section 403(b) with respect to amounts payable following severance from employment. These changes will be incorporated into regulations under section 403(b) when those regulations are finalized.

ing employers. In TRA '86, the phase-in period for the dollar limitation for defined benefit plans was changed from 10 years of service to 10 years of plan participation. As a result of this change, the permissive disaggregation rule from the 1981 regulations allows for the multiplication of section 415 limits within a multiemployer plan that could not be otherwise achieved by simply establishing separate single employer plans. Accordingly, these final regulations retain the rule from the proposed regulations that does not allow disaggregation of a multiemployer plan. In this regard, see the discussion under the paragraph heading "Definition of compensation (§1.415(c)–2)" for a rule that treats all employers contributing to a multiemployer plan as a single employer for purposes of the restriction on the recognition of compensation paid after severance from employment with an employer.

Section 1.415(a)–1(d)(3)(v) provides rules regarding a plan's incorporation by reference of cost-of-living increases in the applicable limitations pursuant to section 415(d), including default rules that apply in the absence of contrary plan provisions. In providing rules for incorporation by reference, the proposed regulations provided that annual increases in the applicable limitations pursuant to section 415(d) do not apply in limitation years beginning after the annuity starting date to a participant who has previously commenced receiving benefits unless the plan specifies that this annual increase applies to such a participant.

One commentator pointed out that this provision in the proposed regulations modified the default treatment under the 1981 regulations (which provide that adjustments to the applicable limitations are not made after a participant's separation from service unless the plan so provides). In response to this comment, the final regulations retain the rule from the 1981 regulations under which the section 415(d) annual increases in the applicable limitations do not apply with respect to a participant for increases that become effective after the participant's severance from employment with the employer maintaining the plan (or, if earlier, after the annuity starting date in the case of a participant who has commenced receiving benefits) unless the plan specifies that this annual increase applies to such a participant. Thus, annual increases in the applicable limitations apply to a participant who has severed from employment with the employer maintaining the plan or who has commenced receiving benefits only if the plan specifies that those annual increases apply to such a participant.

Limitations applicable to defined benefit plans (§ 1.415(b)–1)

Section 1.415(b)–1 of these regulations sets forth rules for applying the limitations on benefits under a defined benefit plan. Under these limitations, the annual benefit must not exceed the lesser of $160,000 (as adjusted pursuant to section 415(d)) and 100 percent of the participant's average compensation for the period of the participant's high-3 years of service. These regulations generally define the period of a participant's high-3 years of service as the period of 3 consecutive calendar years during which the employee had the greatest aggregate compensation from the employer. A retirement benefit payable in a form other than a straight life annuity is adjusted to an actuarially equivalent straight life annuity to determine the annual benefit payable under that form of distribution. In addition, the $160,000 dollar limitation under section 415(b)(1)(A) is actuarially adjusted for benefit payments that commence before age 62 or after age 65. Section 1.415(b)–1 generally retains the rules set forth in the proposed regulations except as indicated below.

The proposed regulations provided that, in addition to applying to benefits payable to participants and beneficiaries, the limitations of section 415(b) apply to accrued benefits (regardless of whether the benefit is vested) and benefits payable from an annuity contract distributed to a participant. Some commentators argued that it is inappropriate to apply the limitations of section 415(b) to a participant's accrued benefit in the case of a plan that is not subject to the requirements of section 411, since such a plan sometimes does not define an accrued benefit and benefits under such a plan can always be reduced if needed so that payments under the plan will satisfy the limitations of section 415. In response, these regulations provide that the rule applying section 415(b) to limit a participant's accrued benefit applies only to a plan that is subject to the requirements of section 411. However, a plan that is not subject to the requirements of section 411 is still subject to the requirements of section 415(b) with respect to the annual benefit payable to a participant at any time under the plan. As indicated in the preamble to the proposed regulations, where a participant's accrued benefit is computed pursuant to the fractional rule of section 411(b)(1)(C), the limitations of section 415(b) apply to the accrued benefit as of the end of the limitation year and, for ages prior to normal retirement age, are not required to be applied to the projected annual benefit commencing at normal retirement age from which the accrued benefit is computed.

A. Actuarial assumptions used to convert benefit to a straight life annuity

Pursuant to section 415(b)(2)(B) (which provides for benefits paid in a form other than a straight life annuity to be adjusted to an actuarially equivalent straight life annuity in accordance with Treasury regulations), these regulations provide rules under which a retirement benefit payable in any form other than a straight life annuity is converted to the straight life annuity that is actuarially equivalent to that other form to determine the annual benefit (which is used to demonstrate compliance with section 415) with respect to that form of distribution. These rules reflect statutory changes that specify the actuarial assumptions that are to be used for these equivalency calculations as well as published guidance that has been issued since the prior final regulations were published in 1981. The statutory changes reflected in these rules include, for plan years beginning in years 2004 and 2005, the use of a 5.5 percent interest rate for benefits that are subject to the present value rules of section 417(e)(3),[2] as set forth in PFEA, as well as the modifica-

[2] Section 417(e)(3) provides minimum present value requirements for certain forms of benefit payable from a defined benefit plan under which payments cannot be less than the amount calculated using a specified interest rate and a specified mortality table. For forms of benefit that are subject to the minimum present value rules of section 417(e)(3), the limitations of section 415(b) apply to limit the amount of a distribution even if those limitations result in a lower distribution than would otherwise be required under the rules of section 417(e)(3). See §1.417(e)–1(d)(1).

tions under section 303 of PPA '06 to the equivalency calculations for benefits that are subject to the present value rules of section 417(e)(3) (which are applicable to distributions with annuity starting dates in plan years beginning after December 31, 2005). In addition to setting forth rules for adjusting forms of benefit other than straight life annuities, these regulations permit the IRS to issue published guidance setting forth simplified methods for making these adjustments.

Under these regulations, the annual benefit is determined as the greater of the actuarially equivalent straight life annuity determined under the plan's actuarial assumptions or the actuarially equivalent straight life annuity determined under actuarial assumptions specified by statute. This methodology implements the policy reflected in section 415(b)(2)(E), under which the plan's determination that a straight life annuity and a particular optional form of benefit are actuarially equivalent is overridden only when the optional form of benefit under the plan is more valuable than the corresponding straight life annuity when the two forms are compared using the statutorily specified actuarial assumptions.

The rules in these regulations under which a retirement benefit payable in any form other than a straight life annuity is converted to a straight life annuity to determine the annual benefit with respect to that form of distribution generally follow the rules set forth in Rev. Rul. 98–1. However, the calculation of the actuarially equivalent straight life annuity determined using the plan's assumptions for actuarial equivalence has been simplified for a form of benefit that is not subject to the minimum present value rules of section 417(e)(3). Under the simplified calculation, instead of first determining the actuarial assumptions used under the plan and then applying those assumptions to convert an optional form of benefit to an actuarially equivalent straight life annuity, the regulations use the straight life annuity, if any, that is payable at the same age under the plan. This straight life annuity is then compared to the straight life annuity that is the actuarial equivalent of the optional form of benefit (determined using the standardized assumptions), and the larger of the two straight life annuities is used for purposes of demonstrating compliance with section 415.

This simplification has not been extended to forms of benefit that are subject to the minimum present value rules of section 417(e)(3), however, because under a plan those forms of benefit are often determined as the actuarial equivalent of the deferred annuity, rather than as the actuarial equivalent of the immediate straight life annuity. Instead, for a benefit paid in a form to which section 417(e)(3) applies, pursuant to section 415(b)(2)(E), the actuarially equivalent straight life annuity benefit generally is determined as the greatest of three annual amounts. The first is the annual amount of the straight life annuity commencing at the annuity starting date that has the same actuarial present value as the particular form of benefit payable, computed using the interest rate and mortality table, or tabular factor, specified in the plan for actuarial equivalence. The second is the annual amount of the straight life annuity commencing at the annuity starting date that has the same actuarial present value as the particular form of benefit payable, computed using a 5.5 percent interest assumption and the applicable mortality table for the distribution under §1.417(e)–1(d)(2). The third is the annual amount of the straight life annuity commencing at the annuity starting date that has the same actuarial present value as the particular form of benefit payable (computed using the applicable interest rate for the distribution under §1.417(e)–1(d)(3) and the applicable mortality table for the distribution under §1.417(e)–1(d)(2)), divided by 1.05. This rule reflects the amendment of section 415(b)(2)(E) by section 303 of PPA '06.

One commentator asked whether the rules regarding adjustments for forms of benefit that are subject to the minimum present value standards of section 417(e)(3) apply to plans that are not subject to the requirements of section 417. Section 415(b)(2)(E) applies based on the form of the benefit, and not the status of the plan, and therefore the final regulations provide that these rules also apply to plans that are not subject to the requirements of section 417.

Some commentators expressed concern that the examples illustrating the rules for actuarial adjustments converted optional forms of benefit into straight life annuities payable monthly, and they noted that had the conversion been to a straight life annuity payable on the first day of each year, the straight life annuity would have been smaller and therefore a greater benefit would have been permissible under section 415(b). Under section 415(b)(2)(B), the Secretary is delegated authority to prescribe regulations for adjusting a benefit so that it is equivalent to a benefit payable annually in the form of a straight life annuity. These regulations provide that if a benefit is payable in the form of a straight life annuity, no adjustment is made to account for differences in the timing of payments during a year (for example, no adjustment is made on account of the annuity being payable in annual or monthly installments). Thus, if the section 415(b) dollar limit for a limitation year is $180,000, a plan is not permitted to provide for 12 monthly payments of $15,583, which is actuarially equivalent to an annual benefit of $180,000 payable on the first day of the year. With respect to a benefit payable in a form other than a straight life annuity, the annual benefit is determined as the straight life annuity payable on the first day of each month that is actuarially equivalent to the benefit payable in such other form.

Some commentators expressed concerns regarding the application of these actuarial adjustments in the case of annuity forms of benefit that are increased automatically each year pursuant to plan terms. Commentators argued that, in testing such a form of benefit for compliance with section 415, increases to the section 415(b) limits pursuant to section 415(d) should be taken into account. Thus, commentators asserted that a form of benefit with an automatic increase feature should satisfy section 415(b) so long as payments made pursuant to the benefit during each limitation year are less than the section 415(b) limit in effect for the limitation year.

In response to these comments, these final regulations provide that, for a form of benefit that is not subject to the requirements of section 417(e)(3), no adjustments are made to reflect these automatic increases if certain requirements are satisfied. Specifically, the form of benefit without regard to the automatic increase feature must satisfy the requirements of section 415(b), and the plan must provide that in no event will the amount payable to a participant under the form of benefit in any limitation year be greater than the section 415(b) limit applicable at the annuity starting date, as increased in subsequent years pursuant to section 415(d). If these requirements are not satisfied, the annual benefit with respect to a benefit that is subject to automatic increases must reflect the value of these automatic increases under the rules described above.

B. Inclusion of social security supplements in annual benefit

As under the proposed regulations, these regulations clarify that a social security supplement is included in determining the annual benefit. Under section 415(b)(2)(B), the annual benefit does not include ancillary benefits that are not directly related to retirement benefits. However, because a social security supplement is payable upon retirement as a form of retirement income, it is a retirement benefit. Thus, a social security supplement is included in determining the annual benefit without regard to whether it is an ancillary benefit or a qualified social security supplement (QSUPP) within the meaning of §1.401(a)(4)–12.

C. Determination of high-3 average compensation

The proposed regulations contained two new provisions that would have had a significant effect on the determination of a participant's average compensation for the participant's high-3 consecutive years. The first provision changed a rule in the 1981 final regulations by restricting the compensation used for this purpose to compensation earned in periods during which the participant was an active participant in the plan. Pursuant to the amendment of section 415(b)(3) made by section 832 of PPA '06 (which eliminated the active participation requirement for purposes of determining average compensation for years beginning after December 31, 2005), this change has not been incorporated into the final regulations.

The second provision in the proposed regulations clarified the interaction of the requirements of section 401(a)(17) and the definition of compensation that must be used for purposes of determining a participant's average compensation for the participant's high-3 consecutive years. Because a plan is not permitted to base benefits on compensation in excess of the limitation under section 401(a)(17), a plan's definition of compensation used for purposes of applying the limitations of section 415 is not permitted to reflect compensation in excess of the limitation under section 401(a)(17). Thus, for example, where a participant commences receiving benefits in 2006 at age 75 (so that the age-adjusted dollar limitation could be as high as $390,953, depending on plan provisions), and the participant had compensation in excess of the applicable section 401(a)(17) limit for years 2003, 2004, and 2005, the participant's benefit under the plan is limited by the average compensation for his highest three years as limited by section 401(a)(17), which is $205,000 (the average of $200,000, $205,000, and $210,000).

Commentators objected to this second provision. These regulations retain this provision from the proposed regulations because the IRS and the Treasury Department believe that this interpretation is based on the best reading of applicable statutory requirements. However, these regulations include a grandfather provision under which a defined benefit plan is considered to satisfy the limitations of section 415(b) for a participant with respect to benefits accrued or payable under the plan as of the end of the limitation year that is immediately prior to the effective date of these final regulations for the plan pursuant to plan provisions (including plan provisions relating to the plan's limitation year) that were both adopted and in effect before April 5, 2007, but only if such plan provisions meet the requirements of statutory provisions, regulations, and other published guidance relating to section 415 in effect immediately before the effective date of these final regulations. In determining whether plan provisions meet the requirements of statutory provisions, regulations, and other published guidance relating to section 415 in effect immediately before the effective date of these final regulations, plan provisions are permitted to reflect compensation in excess of the section 401(a)(17) limit, and the benefits based on such compensation are eligible for the grandfather rules.

These regulations set forth rules for computing the limitation of section 415(b)(1)(B) of 100 percent of the participant's average compensation for the period of the participant's high-3 years of service for a participant who is employed with the employer for less than 3 consecutive calendar years. For such a participant, the period of the participant's high-3 years of service is the actual number of consecutive years of service (including fractions of years, but not less than one year). In such a case, the limitation of section 415(b)(1)(B) of 100 percent of the participant's average compensation for the period of the participant's high-3 years of service is computed by averaging the participant's compensation during the participant's longest consecutive period of service over the actual period of service (including fractions of years, but not less than one year). In a change from the proposed regulations, these regulations provide that, in the case of a participant who has had a severance from employment with the employer maintaining the plan and who is subsequently rehired by that employer, the period of the participant's high-3 years of service is calculated by excluding any years for which the participant performs no services for and receives no compensation from the employer maintaining the plan (the break period), and by treating the year of service immediately prior to and the year of service immediately after the break period as if the years were consecutive.

These regulations also modify the proposed regulations by providing a rule that applies in the case of an employee who is rehired after severing employment. If the plan provides for the adjustment of a participant's compensation limit in accordance with section 415(d) for limitation years following the limitation year in which the employee severs employment, the rehired employee's compensation limit under section 415(b) is the greater of 100 percent of the participant's average compensation for the period of the participant's high-3 years of service, as determined prior to the employee's severance from employment and as adjusted pursuant to section 415(d), or 100 percent of the participant's average compensation for the period of the participant's high-3 years of service, taking into account service both before and after rehire. This rule was added because a participant's compensation limit should not be lower than it would otherwise be merely because the participant in rehired.

D. Treatment of benefits paid partially in the form of a QJSA

Under section 415(b)(2)(B), the survivor annuity portion of any joint and survivor annuity that constitutes a qualified joint and survivor annuity (QJSA), as defined in section 417(b), is not taken into account in determining the annual benefit for purposes of applying the limitations of section 415(b). As under the proposed regulations, these regulations clarify how this exception from the limitations of section 415 for the survivor annuity portion of a QJSA applies to benefits paid partially in the form of a QJSA and partially in some other form. Under this clarification, the rule excluding the survivor portion of a QJSA from the annual benefit applies to the survivor annuity payments under the portion of a benefit that is paid in the form of a QJSA, even if another portion of the benefit is paid in some other form.

E. Dollar limitation applicable to early or late commencement

The determination of the age-adjusted dollar limitation under these regulations reflects the rules enacted in EGTRRA. As provided in Q&A–3 of Rev. Rul. 2001–51, this determination generally follows the same steps and procedures as those used in Rev. Rul. 98–1, except that such determination takes into account the increased defined benefit dollar limitation enacted by EGTRRA and the adjustments for early or late commencement are no longer based on social security retirement age. Applying rules that are similar to those that are used for determining actuarial equivalence among forms of benefits, these regulations generally use the plan's determinations for actuarial equivalence of early or late retirement benefits, but override those determinations where the use of the specified statutory assumptions results in a lower limit. This methodology is retained from the proposed regulations because the IRS and the Treasury Department believe that generally a plan's actuarial equivalence for section 415 purposes should be the same as actuarial equivalence for other purposes and because of the need to have an administrable rule when a plan uses factors that are not explicitly based on an interest rate and mortality table.

Some commentators expressed concern that these rules effectively result in no increase to the dollar limitation where a plan that is not subject to the requirements of section 411 does not increase the participant's benefit to reflect a delay in commencement beyond age 65. No change has been made to address this concern because the IRS and the Treasury Department believe it is not appropriate to increase the dollar limitation for commencement after age 65 where, under the plan terms, there is no increase to the participant's benefit on account of delayed commencement (so that any increase in a participant's benefit is solely on account of additional service or compensation). In response to other commentator concerns, these regulations provide that an actuarial increase to a participant's benefit for commencement after age 65 is taken into account for this purpose even if the actuarial increase offsets additional benefit accruals under the plan.

These regulations adopt rules for mortality adjustments used in computing the dollar limitation on a participant's annual benefit for distributions commencing before age 62 or after age 65 that are generally consistent with Notice 83–10 and Notice 87–21. Under these rules, to the extent that a forfeiture does not occur upon the participant's death before the annuity starting date, generally no adjustment is made to reflect the probability of the participant's death during the relevant time period (which is the period before age 62 or after age 65), and to the extent a forfeiture occurs upon the participant's death before the annuity starting date, an adjustment must be applied to reflect the probability of the participant's death during the relevant time period.

These regulations also provide a simplified method for applying these mortality adjustment rules. Under this simplified method, a plan is permitted to treat no forfeiture as occurring upon a participant's death if the plan does not charge participants for providing a qualified preretirement survivor annuity, but only if the plan applies this treatment for adjustments that apply both before age 62 and after age 65. This simplified method eliminates the need to determine the extent of a forfeiture upon death in the case where a plan provides for a qualified preretirement survivor annuity.

One commentator asked whether, for purposes of adjusting the dollar limit for commencement prior to age 62, a plan is permitted to make a mortality adjustment for ages below age 62, even if the plan does not provide for a forfeiture upon the participant's death before the annuity starting date where it is before age 62. Recognizing that mortality adjustments would result in a lower limit in such a case, these regulations permit such an adjustment to be made if the plan so provides.

Some commentators expressed concern that the application of the rules that adjust the section 415(b)(1)(A) dollar limit for pre-age 62 benefit commencement as set forth in the proposed regulations could result in the limit decreasing as a participant ages under certain circumstances. To address this concern, these regulations provide that, notwithstanding the generally applicable rules for age adjustments to the dollar limitation, the age-adjusted section 415(b)(1)(A) dollar limit does not decrease on account of an increase in age or the performance of additional service.

F. Nonapplication of adjustment to dollar limitation for early commencement with respect to police department and fire department employees

Consistent with section 415(b)(2)(G) and (H), as amended by section 906(b) of PPA '06, these regulations provide that the early retirement reduction does not apply to certain participants in plans of state, Indian tribal government, and local government units who are employees of a police department or fire department, or former members of the Armed Forces of the United States. This rule applies to any participant in a plan maintained by a state, Indian tribal government, or political subdivision thereof who is credited, for benefit accrual purposes, with at least 15 years of service as either (1) a full-time employee of any police department or fire department of the state, Indian tribal government, or political subdivision that provides police protection, firefighting services, or emergency medical services, or (2) a member of the Armed Forces of the United States. These regulations clarify that the application of this rule depends on whether the employer is a police department or fire department of the state, Indian tribal government, or political subdivision, rather than on the job classification of the individual participant. Also, this rule applies based on the function of an organization rather than based on the name of the organization.

G. Application of $10,000 exception

Pursuant to section 415(b)(4), the benefits payable with respect to a participant under a defined benefit plan satisfy the limitations of section 415(b) if the retirement benefits payable with respect to such a participant under the plan and all other defined benefit plans of the employer do not exceed $10,000 for the plan year or for any prior plan year, and the employer has not at any time maintained a defined contribution plan in which the participant participated. As under the proposed regulations, these regulations clarify that the alternative $10,000 limitation under section 415(b)(4) is applied to actual distributions made during each year. Thus, a distribution for a limitation year that exceeds $10,000 is not within the section 415(b)(4) alternative limitation (and therefore will not be excepted from the otherwise applicable limits of section 415(b)), even if the distribution is a single-sum distribution that is the actuarial equivalent of an accrued benefit with annual payments that are less than $10,000.

H. Exclusion of annual benefit attributable to mandatory employee contributions from annual benefit

These regulations retain the rules from the 1981 regulations that the annual benefit does not include the annual benefit attributable to mandatory employee contributions. For this purpose, the term *mandatory employee contributions* means amounts contributed to the plan by the employee that are required as a condition of employment, as a condition of participation in the plan, or as a condition of obtaining benefits (or additional benefits) under the plan attributable to employer contributions. See section 411(c)(2)(C). Employee contributions to a defined benefit plan that are not maintained in a separate account as described in section 414(k) constitute mandatory employee contributions (even if an employee can elect whether to make the contributions, and even if section 411 does not apply to the plan) because, depending upon the investment performance of plan assets, employer contributions may be needed to pay the portion of the participant's benefit that is conditioned upon these employee contributions. Any other employee contributions (plus earnings thereon) are treated as a separate defined contribution plan rather than as part of a defined benefit plan.

These regulations retain the rule from the 1981 regulations that the annual benefit attributable to mandatory employee contributions is determined under the rules of section 411(c) and regulations promulgated under section 411, regardless of whether section 411 applies to the plan. These regulations also clarify that the following are not treated as employee contributions: (1) contributions that are picked up by a governmental employer as provided under section 414(h)(2), (2) repayment of any loan made to a participant from the plan, and (3) repayment of any amount that was previously distributed. One commentator asked how to determine the annual benefit attributable to mandatory employee contributions under section 411(c) in the case of a plan that is not subject to the requirements of section 411 and 417, and suggested the use of the plan's factors for this purpose. This suggestion was not incorporated into these final regulations because the amount payable with respect to employee contributions that is in excess of the amount that would be payable with respect to such contributions using the rules of section 411(c) is effectively a subsidy that should be included in determining the participant's annual benefit under the plan. These regulations also provide that, for purposes of determining the accumulated contributions described in section 411(c)(2)(C), where the plan is not subject to the requirements of section 411, the plan must determine what would have been the applicable effective date of section 411(a)(2) as if section 411 applied to the plan, and in determining the annual benefit that is actuarially equivalent to these accumulated contributions, the plan must determine the interest rate that would have been required under section 417(e)(3) as if section 417 applied to the plan.

Another commentator asked why the repayment of an employee contribution is not treated as an employee contribution under this rule. No change to the regulations has been made to reflect this concern because, while the repayment is not treated as an employee contribution for purposes of section 415, the original employee contribution is still considered an employee contribution for this purpose.

I. Exclusion of annual benefit attributable to rollover contributions from annual benefit

These regulations clarify that the annual benefit does not include the annual benefit attributable to rollover contributions made to a defined benefit plan (that is, rollover contributions that are not maintained in a separate account that is treated as a separate defined contribution plan under section 414(k)). In such a case, the annual benefit attributable to rollover contributions is determined by applying the rules of section 411(c) and treating the rollover contributions as employee contributions (regardless of whether sections 411 and 417 apply to the plan). This will occur, for example, if a distribution is rolled over from a defined contribution plan to a defined benefit plan to provide an annuity distribution. Thus, in the case of rollover contributions from a defined contribution plan to a defined benefit plan to provide an annuity distribution, the annual benefit attributable to those rollover contributions for purposes of section 415 is determined by applying the rules of section 411(c), regardless of the assumptions used to compute the annuity distribution under the plan. Accordingly, in such a case, if the plan credits higher interest or uses more favorable factors than those specified in section 411(c) to determine the amount of annuity payments arising from a rollover contribution, the annual benefit under the plan reflects the excess of those annuity payments over the amounts that would be payable using the rules of section 411(c) because such excess is effectively a subsidy which is included in determining the participant's annual benefit under the plan.

These final regulations clarify that the rule that excludes the annual benefit attributable to rollover contributions applies to rollover contributions from an eligible retirement plan, as defined in section 402(c)(8)(B). Thus, the rule applicable to rollovers is not limited solely to rollovers from qualified plans.

Rollover contributions to an account that is treated as a separate defined contribution plan under section 414(k) do not give rise to an annual benefit because the separate account is not treated as a defined benefit plan under section 415(b). Furthermore, under the rules relating to defined contribution plans, these rollover contributions to a separate account are excluded from the definition of annual additions to a defined contribution plan.

J. Treatment of benefits transferred among plans and terminated plans

These regulations generally retain the provisions in the proposed regulations that modify the rules of the 1981 final regulations for determining the amount of transferred benefits that are excluded from the annual benefit under a defined benefit plan in the event of a transfer from another defined benefit plan. These modifications to the 1981 final regulations are designed to ensure that transferred benefits are not counted more than once when the transferor plan and the transferee plan are aggregated under section 415(f) and §1.415(f)–1, and to prevent the circumvention of the limitations of section 415(b) through benefit transfers to plans of unrelated employers. The rules of section 415(b) that apply upon a transfer of benefits between plans operate independently from the requirements of section 414(l), and compliance with the requirements of section 414(l) does not ensure compliance with these rules.

The proposed regulations provided that, if the transferee plan's benefits are required to be taken into account pursuant to section 415(f) and §1.415(f)–1 in determining whether the transferor plan satisfies the limitations of section 415(b) for that limitation year, then the transferred benefits are disregarded in determining the annual benefit under the transferor plan. The final regulations modify this rule. This modification is being made in conjunction with modifications to the proposed regulations with respect to the aggregation of plans among formerly affiliated employers (discussed in more detail under the heading "Aggregating plans (§1.415(f)–1)"). Generally, under the modified section 415(f) aggregation rules, there are situations in which only a portion of the benefits provided under plans maintained by formerly affiliated employers is taken into account when applying section 415 on an aggregated basis to each employer. Given this modification to the aggregation rules, the determination of whether transferred benefits are nonetheless treated as provided by the transferor plan is properly based on whether the transferred benefits are included in the portion of the transferee plan that is aggregated with the transferor plan. Thus, the final regulations provide that, to the extent the benefits transferred to a transferee plan are otherwise required to be taken into account pursuant to section 415(f) and §1.415(f)–1 in determining whether the transferor plan satisfies the limitations of section 415(b), the transferred benefits are not also treated as being provided under the transferor plan (because these benefits will be taken into account by the transferor plan when it is aggregated with the transferee plan).

The proposed regulations provided that where there has been a transfer of liabilities between plans and the transferee plan's benefits are not required to be taken into account pursuant to section 415(f) and §1.415(f)–1 in determining whether the transferor plan satisfies the limitations of section 415(b), the assets associated with those transferred liabilities (other than surplus assets) are treated by the transferor plan as distributed as a single-sum distribution. These final regulations modify this proposed transfer rule in two respects. First, for the reasons described in the paragraph above, this transfer rule is applicable only if the benefits transferred to the transferee plan are not otherwise required to be taken into account by the transferor plan pursuant to section 415(f) and §1.415(f)–1. Second, the final regulations modify this proposed rule in response to comments expressing concern with the administrative complexity associated with the calculation of the deemed single-sum distribution. Instead of treating the assets associated with the transferred liabilities as a deemed single-sum distribution, the final regulations treat the transferred liabilities as comprising a plan that must be aggregated with the transferor plan, that had terminated with sufficient assets to pay benefit liabilities under the plan and had purchased annuities to provide plan benefits.

Although such a transfer is treated as a plan termination in computing the annual benefit under the transferor plan, no corresponding adjustment to the annual benefit under the transferee plan is made to reflect the fact that some of the benefits provided under the transferee plan are attributable to the transfer. Thus, the actual benefit provided under the transferee plan is used to determine the annual benefit under the transferee plan even though the transferred amount is also included along with other benefits provided under the transferor plan in determining the participant's annual benefit under the transferor plan.

While some commentators expressed concern that this resulted in double counting of benefits, in most such cases, a participant whose benefits have been transferred would accrue no additional benefit under the transferor plan that would be required to be tested under the transferor plan (in combination with the transferred benefits). Furthermore, these rules prevent the transferor plan from avoiding the limitations of section 415 for participants by spinning off the participants' benefits to a plan of an unrelated employer and then accruing additional benefits for the participants. For example, without these rules, the benefit of an executive in a plan maintained by the executive's employer could be transferred to a plan maintained by a business that is owned by the executive and that is not aggregated with the executive's employer for purposes of section 415, and the executive could accrue an additional benefit up to the section 415 limits under the plan maintained by the executive's employer.

The final regulations provide rules specifying how to take into account benefits provided under a terminated plan. If a defined benefit plan is terminated with sufficient assets to pay accrued benefits and a participant in the plan has not yet commenced benefits under the plan, for purposes of satisfying section 415(b) with respect to the participant, the final regulations require that all other defined benefit plans maintained by the employer that maintained the terminated plan take into account the benefits provided pursuant to the annuities purchased to provide benefits under the terminated plan at each possible annuity starting date. The final regulations provide that if a defined benefit plan is terminated and there are not sufficient assets for the payment of the accrued benefit of all plan participants, all other defined benefit plans maintained by the employer that maintained the terminated plan are required to take into account the benefits that are actually provided under the terminated plan. For example, if the terminated plan is subject to Title IV of ERISA, the other plans maintained by the employer that maintained the terminated plan take into account the benefits that are provided by the Pension Benefit Guaranty Corporation. If the terminated plan was not subject to Title IV of ERISA, the other plans take into account the benefits that are actually paid by the terminated plan. The multiple annuity starting date rules apply to the extent that benefits from a terminated plan and an ongoing plan do not commence at the same time.

These regulations clarify that if a participant elects to transfer a distributable benefit to a defined benefit plan pursuant to §1.411(d)–4, A–3(c), the transfer is treated in the same manner as an amount that is distributed and then rolled over (specifically, the transferred benefit is treated by the transferor plan as a distribution, and the annual benefit provided by the transferee plan does not include the annual benefit attributable to the amount transferred). This rule applies regardless of whether the requirements of section 411 apply to the plan and, in the case of a transfer from a defined contribution plan that is not subject to the requirements of section 411 (such as a governmental plan) to a defined benefit plan, the rule applies even if the participant's benefits are not distributable from the defined contribution plan at the time of the transfer.

K. 10-year phase-in of limitations based on years of participation and years of service

As under the proposed regulations, these regulations provide rules for applying the 10-year phase-in of the dollar limitation based on years of participation in the plan, as added by TRA '86, and modify the rules set forth in the 1981 regulations for applying the 10-year phase-in of the compensation limit based on years of service. These regulations, like the proposed regulations, follow the guidance set forth in Notice 87–21 for applying the 10-year phase-in based on years of participation, and apply analogous rules for purposes of applying the 10-year phase-in based on years of service.

L. Exception to compensation-based limit for certain church plans

The final regulations also reflect the amendment of section 415(b)(11) by PPA '06. Under the amendment, the section 415(b)(1)(B) compensation-based limit that is generally applicable to defined benefit plans is not applicable to a participant in a plan maintained by a church described in section 3121(w)(3)(A) if the participant has never been a highly compensated employee (as defined in section 414(q)) of the church. These regulations provide that if such a participant later becomes a highly compensated employee of the church, the plan is not treated as failing to satisfy the compensation-based limit provided that no plan amendments increasing the participant's benefits are adopted in the year the participant becomes a highly compensated employee and there is no increase in the participant's accrued benefit derived from employer contributions in subsequent years.

Multiple annuity starting dates (§1.415(b)–2)

Section 1.415(b)–2 of the proposed regulations set forth rules for computing the annual benefit under one or more defined benefit plans in the case of multiple annuity starting dates. Multiple annuity starting dates exist, for example, where benefit distributions to a participant have previously commenced under a plan that is aggregated for purposes of section 415 with a plan for which the participant receives current accruals. In addition, the multiple annuity starting date rules apply for purposes of determining the annual benefit of a participant where a new distribution election is effective during the current limitation year with respect to a distribution that previously commenced. The multiple annuity starting date rules also apply when benefit payments are increased, unless the benefit increase complies with one of the safe harbors provided in the regulations.

Numerous commentators raised concerns regarding these rules. Based on these comments, the IRS and the Treasury Department have determined that revisions to these rules are needed before these rules are adopted in final form. Accordingly, these regulations reserve a place for regulations regarding multiple annuity starting dates. The IRS and the Treasury Department are developing new proposed regulations regarding multiple annuity starting dates, and corresponding revisions to regulations under §1.401(a)(9)–6.

In the interim, §1.415(b)–1 of these regulations provides that if a participant has or will have distributions commencing at more than one annuity starting date, the limitations of section 415 must be satisfied as of each of the annuity starting dates, taking into account the benefits that have been or will be provided at all of the annuity starting dates. In determining the annual benefit of a participant as of a particular annuity starting date, the plan is required to actuarially adjust past and future distributions with respect to the benefit that commenced at the other annuity starting dates.

Limitations applicable to defined contribution plans (§1.415(c)–1)

Section 1.415(c)–1 of these regulations sets forth rules that apply to limitations on annual additions under a defined contribution plan. Under these limitations, annual additions must not be greater than the lesser of $40,000 (as adjusted pursuant to section 415(d)) or 100 percent of the participant's compensation for the limitation year. The term *annual additions* generally means the sum for any year of employer contributions, employee contributions, and forfeitures. In addition to applying to qualified defined contribution plans, the limitations in section 415(c) and §1.415(c)–1 of the regulations apply to section 403(b) annuity contracts, simplified employee pensions described in section 408(k), mandatory employee contributions to qualified defined benefit plans, and contributions to certain medical benefit accounts.

These regulations reflect a number of statutory changes to section 415(c) that were made after the issuance of the 1981 regulations. Among these changes are the revised limitation amounts under section 415(c), the revised rules applicable to employee stock ownership plans, and the rules applying the limitations of section 415(c) to certain medical benefit accounts. These regulations also make some other changes to the 1981 regulations, as discussed below. Consistent with the change to section 403(b)(1) made in JCWAA, these regulations provide that the limitations under section 415(c) apply to any section 403(b) annuity contract, regardless of whether the contract satisfies the requirements of section 414(i) to be a defined contribution plan. Thus, the limitations under section 415(c) apply to a section 403(b) annuity contract even if the limitations of section 415(b) also apply to the contract. Section 415(b) applies to the contract if the contract is a church plan that is covered by the grandfather rule of section 251(e)(5) of TEFRA.

Consistent with Rev. Rul. 2002–45, the regulations provide that a restorative payment that is allocated to a participant's account does not give rise to an annual addition for any limitation year. For this purpose, restorative payments are payments made to restore losses to a plan resulting from actions by a fiduciary for which there is a reasonable risk of liability for breach of a fiduciary duty under Title I of ERISA, where plan participants who are similarly situated are treated similarly with respect to the payments. Commentators suggested that restorative payments should also include payments made to restore losses to a plan resulting from actions by a fiduciary for which there is a reasonable risk of liability for breach of a fiduciary duty under other applicable federal or state law, to take into account contributions under plans that are not subject to Title I of ERISA in appropriate circumstances. These regulations adopt this suggestion. Accordingly, payments to a defined contribution plan are restorative payments only if the payments are made in order to restore some or all of the plan's losses due to an action (or a failure to act) that creates a reasonable risk of liability for such a breach of fiduciary duty under Title I of ERISA or under other applicable federal or state law. The regulations specifically list certain payments that satisfy this rule, including payments to a plan made pursuant to a Department of Labor order or court-approved settlement to restore losses to a qualified defined contribution plan on account of the breach of fiduciary duty, and payments made pursuant to the Department of Labor's Voluntary Fiduciary Correction Program to restore losses to a qualified defined contribution plan on account of the breach of fiduciary duty.

As under the proposed regulations, these final regulations provide that the Commissioner may in appropriate cases, considering all of the facts and circumstances, treat transactions between the plan and the employer, transactions between the plan and the employee, or certain allocations to participants' accounts as giving rise to annual additions. For example, in general, the Commissioner will treat payments made to a plan by an employer or another party to make up for losses due merely to market fluctuations and other payments that are not made on account of a reasonable risk of liability for breach of a fiduciary duty under Title I of ERISA or other Federal or state law generally as contributions that give rise to annual additions. As under the proposed regulations, these regulations clarify that where an employee or employer transfers assets to a plan in exchange for consideration that is less than the fair market value of the assets transferred to the plan, there is an annual addition in the amount of the difference between the value of the assets transferred and the consideration.

For taxable employers, these regulations retain the rule under the 1981 regulations that an employer contribution is not treated as credited to a participant's account for a particular limitation year unless the contribution is actually made to the plan no later than 30 days after the end of the period described in section 404(a)(6) applicable to the taxable year with or within which the particular limitation year ends. The final regulations modify the corresponding rule for tax-exempt employers in the proposed regulations. Under the final regulations, a contribution to a plan by a tax-exempt employer is taken into account for a limitation year for purposes of section 415(c) if the contribution is credited to a participant's account no later than the 15th day of the tenth calendar month following the end of the calendar year or fiscal year (as applicable, depending on the basis on which the employer keeps its books) with or within which the particular limitation year ends. This date corresponds to the due date for Form 5500, "*Annual Return/Report of Employee Benefit Plan*," (with extensions) in cases in which the calendar or fiscal year coincides with the plan year and generally corresponds to the date for taxable employers who request filing extensions. The extent to which elective contributions constitute plan assets for purposes of the prohibited transaction provisions of section 4975 and Title I of ERISA is determined in accordance with regulations and rulings issued by the Department of Labor. See 29 CFR 2510.3–102.

The final regulations clarify that if the allocation of an annual addition is dependent under the terms of the plan upon the satisfaction of a condition that has not been satisfied by the date as of which the annual addition is allocated, then the annual addition is considered allocated as of the date the condition is satisfied. This is a change from the proposed regulations, under which this rule only applied if the allocation was dependent upon participation in the plan as of a particular date. Additionally, the final regulations clarify that an annual addition that is made pursuant to a corrective amendment that complies with the requirements of §1.401(a)(4)–11(g) is credited to the account of a participant for a particular limitation year if it is allocated to the participant's account under the terms of the corrective amendment as of any date within that limitation year.

These regulations clarify the operation of the special increased limitation applicable to church plans under section 415(c)(7). Under this rule, notwithstanding the generally applicable limitations, annual additions for a section 403(b) annuity contract for a year with respect to an individual who is a church employee are treated as not exceeding the limitation of section 415(c) if such annual additions for the year are not in excess of $10,000. However, the total amount of additions with respect to any participant that are permitted to be taken into account for purposes of this rule for all years may not exceed $40,000. The regulations also reflect a special rule for church employees performing services outside the United States, as amended by GOZA. Under this special rule, for any individual who is a church employee performing any services for the church outside the United States during the limitation year, additions for a section 403(b) annuity contract for any year are not treated as exceeding the limitations of section 415(c) if those annual additions for the year do not exceed $3,000 (but only if the individual's adjusted gross income does not exceed $17,000). These regulations clarify that the $40,000 cumulative total only applies to excesses over what would have been permitted to be contributed without regard to this special rule, and clarify the interaction between the generally applicable church employee rule and the rule for church employees performing services outside the United States.

As under the proposed regulations, these regulations do not include the correction methods for excess annual additions applicable under §1.415–6(b)(6) of the 1981 regulations. Conforming changes have been made to §1.401(a)–2(b), §1.401(a)(9)–5, A–9(b)(1), and §1.402(c)–2, A–4(a) to reflect this deletion.

Despite the deletion, the deleted correction methods are generally permitted under the Employee Plans Compliance Resolution System (EPCRS), Rev. Proc. 2006–27, 2006–22 I.R.B. 945 (see §601.601(d)(2)). In section 2.02(2) of Rev. Proc. 2006–27, comments were requested on whether the correction methods in former §1.415–6(b)(6), including the maintenance of suspense accounts, should be retained as options under EPCRS. Pending the issuance of further guidance that takes into account those comments, plans that are eligible for the Self-Correction Program under section 4 of Rev. Proc. 2006–27 may implement corrections using the methods in former §1.415–6(b)(6), but only if the requirements of section 9 of Rev. Proc. 2006–27 are satisfied, and those corrections will also be taken into account for purposes of the Voluntary Correction and Audit Closing Agreement Programs under EPCRS.

These regulations generally retain the rules under the 1981 regulations providing that a contribution to reduce accumulated funding deficiencies or a contribution made pursuant to a funding waiver relates to the limitation year of the initial funding obligation. However, these regulations, like the proposed regulations, provide that any interest paid by the employer with respect to such a contribution that is in excess of a reasonable amount is taken into account as an annual addition for the limitation year when the contribution is made (in contrast to the 1981 regulations, which required interest in excess of a reasonable amount to be taken into account as an annual addition for the limitation year for which the contribution was originally required). Rev. Rul. 78–223, 1978–1 C.B. 125, (see §601.601(d)(2)) provides a method for determining contributions required to amortize waived contributions under a defined contribution plan. The application of any of the methods described in Rev. Rul. 78–223 will result in reasonable interest payments for purposes of applying the rules of section 415 (provided that, if a fixed interest rate in excess of 5 percent is used to amortize waived contributions, the interest rate must be reasonable). Thus, for example, the actual yield method (under which the adjusted account balance is increased or decreased periodically at the actual rate of investment return experienced by the plan for such period) can be used for this purpose.

Definition of compensation (§1.415(c)–2)

Section 1.415(c)–2 of these regulations defines the term "compensation," which is defined in section 415(c)(3) and used for purposes of applying the limitations of section 415 as well as for various other purposes specified under the Internal Revenue Code. These regulations reflect a number of statutory changes to section 415(c)(3) that were made after the issuance of the 1981 regulations. Among these changes are the inclusion in compensation of certain deemed amounts for disabled participants and nontaxable elective amounts for deferrals under sections 401(k), 403(b), and 457, cafeteria plan elections under section 125, and qualified transportation fringe elections under section 132(f)(4). In addition to these changes, these regulations make some other changes to the 1981 regulations, as discussed in this preamble.

The proposed regulations provided specific guidelines regarding when amounts received following severance from employment are considered compensation for purposes of section 415. The proposed regulations provided that the following are types of post-severance payments that are not excluded from compensation because of timing if they are paid within 2½ months following severance from employment: (1) payments that, absent a severance from employment, would have been paid to the employee while the employee continued in employment with the employer and are regular compensation for services during the employee's regular working hours, compensation for services outside the employee's regular working hours (such as overtime or shift differential), commissions, bonuses, or other similar compensation; and (2) payments for accrued *bona fide* sick, vacation, or other leave, but only if the employee would have been able to use the leave if employment had continued.

Commentators made a number of suggestions regarding the post-severance compensation rules. Some commentators requested a lengthening of the 2½-month period to as long as a year, or exceptions from the 2½-month rule under certain circumstances (such as teacher pay that is paid on a 12-month basis for each 9-month school year, or residual payments that are made to entertainment industry employees years after the services are performed). Some commentators requested changes to the types of compensation that are permitted or required to be taken into account for ease of plan administration.

The final regulations lengthen the time during which certain post-severance payments are taken into account from the 2½-month period under the proposed regulations. The final regulations provide that in order for payments after severance from employment to be treated as compensation within the meaning of section 415(c)(3), payments made for services provided to a former employer must be made by the later of 2½ months after the severance from employment or the end of the limitation year that includes the date of severance from employment. In addition, a governmental plan (within the meaning of section 414(d)) is permitted to provide that the calendar year that includes the date of severance from employment is substituted for the limitation year that includes the date of severance from employment for this purpose.

The final regulations also provide that post-severance payments of accrued *bona fide* sick, vacation, and other leave that are paid within the timeframe described in the preceding paragraph are not included in compensation unless the plan specifically includes such payments. Additionally, the final regulations permit a plan to specify that a post-severance payment from a nonqualified unfunded deferred compensation plan may be included in compensation if the payment is made within the timeframe described in the preceding paragraph, but only if the payment would have been made at the same time if the employee had continued his or her employment and only to the extent that the payment is includible in the employee's gross income.

As under the proposed regulations, the rule under the final regulations generally excluding payments after severance from employment from compensation does not apply to payments to an individual who does not currently perform services for the employer by reason of qualified military service (as that term is used in section 414(u)(1)) to the extent those payments do not exceed the amounts the individual would have received if the individual had continued to perform services for the employer rather than entering qualified military service. The final regulations modify the proposed regulations by adding another exception to the post-severance timing rule for compensation paid to a permanently and totally disabled participant, provided certain conditions are satisfied. As provided under the proposed regulations, the final regulations also contain corresponding amendments to the regulations under sections 401(k) and 457 that provide that amounts received following severance from employment can be deferred only if they are considered compensation under the rules of section 415.

Whether a person has a severance from employment with the employer that maintains a plan is determined for purposes of section 415 in the same manner as under §1.401(k)–1(d)(2), except that for purposes of determining the employer of an employee, the rules of section 415(h) are taken into account (under which the phrase "more than 50 percent" is substituted for the phrase "at least 80 percent" each place it appears in section 1563(a)(1) for purposes of applying section 414(b) and (c)). Thus, an employee has a severance when the employee ceases to be an employee of the employer maintaining the plan, and an employee does not have a severance from employment if, in connection with a change of employment, the employee's new employer maintains the plan with respect to the employee. In addition, the determination of whether an employee ceases to be an employee of the employer maintaining the plan is based on all of the relevant facts and circumstances. In the case of a multiemployer plan, a payment after severance from employment from an employer for whom services were provided is considered to be compensation within the meaning of section 415(c)(3) as long as the individual receiving the payment is employed by any employer maintaining the multiemployer plan. Thus, in the case of a multiemployer plan, an employee is treated as having a severance from employment only when the employee is no longer providing services to any employer maintaining the multiemployer plan. This rule is consistent with the treatment of a multiemployer plan as a single plan that is not disaggregated for purposes of applying the limitations of section 415.

As noted above, the final regulations provide that a plan cannot take into account compensation in excess of the section 401(a)(17) limit. In addition, the final regulations provide that elective deferrals can only be made from compensation as defined in section 415(c)(3). However, in applying these two rules, a plan is not required to determine a participant's compensation on the basis of the earliest payments of compensation during a year.

Commentators also requested clarification as to the treatment of nonresident aliens under all of the alternative definitions of compensation that the regulations allow. Commentators had noted that the various alternative definitions of compensation permitted under the 1981 regulations could be interpreted as including compensation paid to nonresident aliens, but the commentators observed that this issue was not sufficiently clear.

These regulations provide that amounts paid to an individual as compensation for services do not fail to be treated as compensation merely because those amounts are not includible in the individual's gross income on account of the location of the services. Similarly, these regulations also provide that amounts paid to an individual as compensation for services do not fail to be treated as compensation merely because those amounts are paid by an employer with respect to which payments of compensation to the individual are excluded from gross income. Thus, for example, the determination of whether an amount is includible as compensation is made without regard to the exclusions from gross income under sections 872, 893, 894, 911, and 933.

Under these modified rules, an employee who is a nonresident alien with no United States sourced income is not prevented from participating in a qualified plan sponsored by the employee's employer on account of the limitations of section 415 that relate to the employee's compensation. These rules, however, do not modify other requirements with respect to such an employee's participation in a qualified plan, such as the rules relating to the entity that is properly entitled to a deduction for contributions made to the plan on account of the employee's participation.

These regulations also provide a rule of administrative convenience under which section 415 compensation does not include compensation paid to a nonresident alien, provided that the individual does not participate in the plan and the compensation is not effectively connected with the conduct of a trade or business within the United States, and only to the extent that the compensation is excludable from the individual's gross income either on account of the location of the services or because compensation paid by the employer is excludable from gross income. This is relevant for purposes of determining who is a key employee under the top heavy rules of section 416 and who is a highly compensated employee under the rules of section 414(q).

Like the proposed regulations, these final regulations generally retain the rules in the 1981 regulations regarding section 415 compensation and contributions to and distributions from plans of deferred compensation. Accordingly, these regulations provide that distributions from a plan of deferred compensation (whether or not qualified) are not compensation for section 415 purposes (but permit a plan to include as compensation amounts received by an employee pursuant to a nonqualified unfunded plan for the year in which the amounts are actually received) and provide that contributions made by an employer (other than elective contributions) to a plan of deferred compensation (whether or not qualified) are not compensation to the extent that the contributions are not includible in the income of the employee for the taxable year in which contributed. The final regulations clarify that section

415 compensation includes amounts that are includible in the gross income of an employee under the rules of section 409A or section 457(f)(1)(A) or because the amounts are constructively received by the employee. The final regulations also clarify that a plan is permitted to include as compensation amounts received by an employee pursuant to a nonqualified deferred compensation plan only to the extent such amounts are includible in gross income.

Cost-of-living adjustments (§1.415(d)–1)

Section 1.415(d)–1 of these regulations sets forth rules that apply to cost-of-living adjustments to the various limitations of section 415 pursuant to section 415(d). Section 415(d) provides for the dollar and compensation limitations on annual benefits and the dollar limitation on annual additions to be adjusted annually for increases in the cost of living based on adjustment procedures similar to the procedures used to adjust social security benefit amounts. These adjustments also apply for other purposes as specified in the Code. These regulations specify the manner in which these adjustments are determined each year, and reflect statutory changes to the adjustment methodology made after the 1981 regulations were issued. In addition, these regulations make several other changes to the 1981 regulations, as discussed in this preamble. Section 1.415(d)–1 generally retains the rules set forth in the proposed regulations except as indicated in this preamble.

These regulations specify the circumstances under which an adjusted limit is permitted to be applied to participants who have previously commenced receiving benefits under a defined benefit plan. Under these regulations, the adjusted dollar limitation is applicable to current employees who are participants in a defined benefit plan and is permitted to apply to former employees who have retired or otherwise terminated their service under the plan and have a nonforfeitable right to accrued benefits, regardless of whether they have actually begun to receive benefits. If a participant has commenced receiving benefits, the annual increase is only permitted to be applied to the extent that benefits have not been paid. Thus, for example, a plan cannot provide that this annual increase applies to a participant who has previously received the entire plan benefit in a single-sum distribution. However, a plan is permitted to provide for an increase in benefits to a participant to the extent the participant accrues additional benefits under the plan that could have been accrued without regard to the adjustment of the dollar limitation (including benefits that accrue as a result of a plan amendment) on or after the effective date of the adjusted limitation.

These regulations retain the safe harbor set forth in the proposed regulations under which the annual benefit will satisfy the limitations of section 415(b) for the current limitation year following an adjustment to benefit payments that is made to reflect the cost-of-living adjustment made pursuant to section 415(d). Under this safe harbor, if a plan incorporates by reference the annual section 415(d) cost-of-living adjustments to the limitations of section 415, a distribution that is increased solely as a result of the application of the section 415(d) cost-of-living adjustments to the applicable limits will be treated as continuing to satisfy the requirements of section 415(b) and is not subject to the multiple annuity starting date rules. In connection with the changes discussed in the following paragraph, this safe harbor has been relocated to §1.415(a)–1(d)(3)(v).

Commentators expressed concern that the safe harbor in the proposed regulations did not cover situations where benefits are increased periodically by plan amendments that reflect the section 415(d) cost-of-living adjustments. After consideration of these comments, the IRS and the Treasury Department have determined that additional safe harbors are appropriate. Accordingly, under these final regulations, if a plan is amended to apply the adjusted section 415(b) limits in accordance with either of two safe harbors, a distribution that is increased pursuant to the amendment will be treated as continuing to satisfy the requirements of section 415(b).

A plan amendment satisfies the first safe harbor if the employee has received one or more distributions that satisfy the requirements of section 415(b) before the date the adjustment to the applicable limits is effective, the increased distribution is solely as a result of the amendment of the plan to reflect the adjustment to the applicable limits pursuant to section 415(d), and the amounts payable to the employee on and after the effective date of the adjustment are not greater than the amounts that would otherwise be payable without regard to the adjustment, multiplied by a fraction determined for the limitation year, the numerator of which is the limitation under section 415(b) (which is the lesser of the applicable dollar limitation under section 415(b)(1)(A), as adjusted for age at commencement, and the applicable compensation-based limitation under section 415(b)(1)(B)) in effect for the distribution following the section 415(d) adjustment, and the denominator of which is such limitation under section 415(b) in effect for the distribution immediately before the section 415(d) adjustment.

A plan amendment satisfies the second safe harbor if the employee has received one or more distributions that satisfy the requirements of section 415(b) before the date on which the increased distribution is effective, and the amounts payable to the employee on and after the effective date for the increased distribution are not greater than the amounts that would otherwise be payable without regard to the increase, multiplied by the cumulative adjustment fraction. The cumulative adjustment fraction is equal to the product of all of the annual fractions (described in the first safe harbor) that would have applied after benefits commence if the plan had been amended each year to incorporate the section 415(d) adjustments to the applicable section 415(b) limits in accordance with the first safe harbor. In determining the cumulative adjustment fraction, if for the limitation year for which the adjustment in the section 415(b)(1)(A) dollar limit pursuant to EGTRRA is first effective (generally, the first limitation year beginning after December 31, 2001), the section 415(b)(1)(A) dollar limit applicable to a participant is less than the section 415(b)(1)(B) compensation limit, then the annual fraction for such year is 1.0.

Aggregating plans (§1.415(f)–1)

Section 1.415(f)–1 of these regulations sets forth rules for aggregating plans pursuant to section 415(f). Section 1.415(f)–1 generally retains the rules set forth in the proposed regulations except as indicated in this preamble. Under section 415(f) and these regulations, for purposes of applying the limitations of section 415(b) and (c), all defined benefit plans that have ever been maintained by an employer are treated as one defined benefit plan, and all defined contribution plans that have ever been maintained by an employer are treated as one defined contribution plan. The controlled group rules of section 414(b) and (c) (as modified by section 415(h)), the affiliated service group rules of section 414(m), and the leased employee rules of section 414(n) apply for purposes of determining whether a plan that is maintained by an entity other than the employer is considered maintained by the employer for purposes of applying the aggregation rules of section 415(f). These basic employer aggregation rules were also contained in the 1981 regulations.

One commentator noted that the proposed regulations incorrectly reflected the rules of section 415(h) (which applies a 50 percent standard in lieu of an 80 percent standard for purposes of applying the control rules) by applying those rules in determining whether two or more organizations are a brother-sister group of trades or businesses under common control under the rules in §1.414(c)–2(c). These final regulations provide that the rules of section 415(h) do not apply for this purpose.

These final regulations make various changes and clarifications to the 1981 regulations relating to aggregating plans. As under the proposed regulations, these final regulations clarify that an employer's plan must be aggregated with all plans maintained by a predecessor employer (see section 414(a)), regardless of whether any such plan is assumed by the employer.

As under the proposed regulations, the final regulations provide that a former employer is a predecessor employer with respect to a participant in a plan maintained by an employer if the employer maintains a plan under which the participant had accrued a benefit while performing services for the former employer, but only if that benefit is provided under the plan maintained by the employer. In addition, as under the proposed regulations, these final regulations provide pursuant to section 414(a)(2) that, with respect to an employer of a participant, a former entity that antedates the employer is a predecessor employer with respect to the participant if, under the facts and circumstances, the employer constitutes a continuation of all or a portion of the trade or business of the former entity. This will occur, for example, where formation of the employer constitutes a mere formal or technical change in the employment relationship and continuity otherwise exists in the substance and administration of the business operations of the former entity and the employer. See *Lear Eye Clinic, Ltd. v. Commissioner*, 106 T.C. 418, 425 (1996).

These final regulations make several other changes to the employer aggregation rules. These changes limit the extent to which a plan maintained by an employer must aggregate benefits accrued under a plan that was formerly maintained by the employer or that was maintained by an entity that was formerly affiliated with the employer under the employer aggregation rules of §1.415(a)–1(f)(1) and (2) (which provide that a plan maintained by any member of a controlled group of employers or an affiliated service group is deemed to be maintained by all members of the group). Under these final regulations, a "formerly affiliated plan" of an employer is treated as if it were a plan that terminated immediately prior to the "cessation of affiliation" with sufficient assets to pay benefit liabilities under the plan, and had purchased annuities to provide plan benefits. The final regulations define a formerly affiliated plan of an employer as a plan that, immediately prior to the cessation of affiliation, was actually maintained by one or more of the entities that constitute the employer (as determined under the employer affiliation rules of §1.415(a)–1(f)(1) and (2)), and that, immediately after the cessation of affiliation, is not actually maintained by any of the entities that constitute the employer (as determined under the employer affiliation rules of §1.415(a)–1(f)(1) and (2)). The final regulations define a cessation of affiliation as the event that causes an entity to no longer be aggregated with one or more other entities as a single employer under the employer affiliation rules (such as a sale of a subsidiary) or an event that causes a plan to not actually be maintained by any of the entities that constitute the employer (such as a transfer of sponsorship of a plan to an unrelated employer).

A similar rule is provided under these final regulations with respect to a plan (or portion of a plan) maintained by a predecessor employer that is not assumed by the successor employer. As under the proposed regulations, the final regulations provide that all plans ever maintained by an employer or predecessor employer are aggregated. For purposes of applying this aggregation rule, these final regulations limit the extent to which plans that are not maintained by an employer but that are maintained by the employer's predecessor employer are taken into account when aggregating the employer's plans. This limit provides that a plan that is not maintained by the employer and is maintained by the employer's predecessor employer is treated as if the plan terminated (with sufficient assets to pay benefit liabilities under the plan) immediately prior to the event giving rise to the predecessor employer relationship. The effect of these rules is that, for purposes of aggregating the predecessor employer's plans with plans maintained by the employer, benefits accrued after the transfer of benefits from the predecessor employer's plan to the employer's plan are excluded.

These final regulations also add a rule that prevents the double counting of a participant's benefit when applying the aggregation rules. For example, in aggregating defined benefit plans of a predecessor employer with the defined benefit plans of an employer following a transfer of benefits to the plan maintained by the employer from the plan maintained by the predecessor employer, the transferee plan (maintained by the employer) does not double count a participant's benefit by taking into account both the transferred benefits and the portion of the transferor plan (maintained by the predecessor employer) that is deemed to have terminated on account of the transfer pursuant to §1.415(b)–1(b)(3)(i)(B). Instead, the transferee plan includes the benefits that are actually provided under the transferee plan when applying the aggregation rule.

The proposed regulations provided rules for applying the requirements of section 415(f)(2) when an employer has more than one defined benefit plan. Pursuant to section 415(f)(2), the proposed regulations provided that the compensation limit of section 415(b)(1)(B) is applied separately with respect to each plan, and in applying the compensation limit to the aggregated plans, the plans calculate a participant's average compensation for the participant's high-3 years of service by taking into account compensation for all years of active participation in the aggregated plans. Because the requirements of section 415(f)(2) have been rendered moot by the amendment to section 415(b)(3) made by section 832 of PPA '06, these rules have not been incorporated into the final regulations.

These regulations provide rules for aggregating participation and service for purposes of the 10-year phase-in of the limitations on defined benefit plans. Under these rules, years of participation in all aggregated plans and years of service for employers maintaining all aggregated plans are counted for purposes of applying the 10-year phase-in rules.

These regulations clarify the aggregation rules that apply to section 403(b) annuity contracts, other plans of the employer, and plans of related employers, in light of changes made in EGTRRA. Generally, a section 403(b) annuity contract is not aggregated with plans that are maintained by the participant's employer because the section 403(b) annuity contract is deemed maintained by the participant and not the employer for purposes of section 415. However, if a participant on whose behalf a section 403(b) annuity contract is purchased is in control of any employer for a limitation year, the annuity contract for the benefit of the participant is treated as a defined contribution plan maintained by both the controlled employer and the participant for that limitation year and accordingly, the section 403(b) annuity contract is aggregated with all other defined contribution plans maintained by the employer. Accordingly, the employer that contributes to the section 403(b) annuity contract must obtain information from participants regarding employers controlled by those participants and plans maintained by those controlled employers to monitor compliance with applicable limitations to comply with applicable reporting and withholding obligations.

In general, under these regulations, the benefits provided by all plans maintained by all employers maintaining a multiemployer plan (as defined in section 414(f)) are taken into account in applying the limitations of section 415 to the multiemployer plan. However, a multiemployer plan is permitted to provide that, where a participating employer maintains both a plan which is not a multiemployer plan and a multiemployer plan, only the benefits provided by the employer under the multiemployer plan are aggregated with the benefits under the non-multiemployer plan. By contrast, when a multiple employer plan is aggregated with a single employer plan maintained by the same employer, all of the benefits provided by the multiple employer plan must be taken into account in determining whether the aggregated plans satisfy section 415. These regulations also provide that a multiemployer plan is not aggregated with any other multiemployer plan for purposes of determining any section 415 limitation. In addition, a multiemployer plan is not aggregated with any other non-multiemployer plan for purposes of applying the 100 percent of compensation benefit limit to non-multiemployer plans under section 415(b)(1)(B).

Disqualification of plans and trusts (§1.415(g)–1)

Section 1.415(g)–1 of these final regulations sets forth rules regarding disqualification of plans and trusts, including plans and trusts that are aggregated pursuant to §1.415(f)–1. In large part, §1.415(g)–1 of these regulations replicates the rules of §1.415–9 of the 1981 regulations regarding ordering rules for disqualifying plans and trusts that are aggregated for purposes of compliance with section 415. In addition, the final regulations provide rules for disqualification where an individual medical benefit account (as described in section 415(l)) and a post-retirement medical benefits account for key employees (as described in section 419A(d)) is aggregated with a qualified defined contribution plan for purposes of applying section 415(c). If the total of the annual additions under both plans exceeds those limitations for a particular limitation year, the qualified defined contribution plan (rather than the medical benefit account) is disqualified for the limitation year.

Limitation year (§1.415(j)–1)

Section 1.415(j)–1 of the regulations sets forth rules regarding limitation years that are used as the period for demonstrating compliance with section 415. Section 1.415(j)–1 generally retains the rules set forth in the proposed regulations except as indicated in this preamble. In addition to setting forth general rules that generally correspond to rules under the 1981 regulations, these regulations provide specific guidelines with respect to overlapping limitation years for aggregated plans. These rules reflect the guidance provided in Rev. Rul. 79–5, 1979–1 C.B. 165 (see §601.601(d)(2)). Where defined contribution plans with different limitations years are aggregated, the rules of section 415(c) must be applied with respect to each limitation year of each such plan. For each such limitation year, the requirements of section 415(c) are applied to annual additions that are made for that time period with respect to the participant under all aggregated plans. Similarly, where defined benefit plans with different limitation years are aggregated, the rules of section 415(b) must be applied with respect to each limitation year of each such plan. Thus, for example, the dollar limitation of section 415(b)(1)(A) applicable to the limitation year for each plan must be applied to annual benefits under all aggregated plans to determine whether the plan satisfies the requirements of section 415(b).

These final regulations add a rule that applies to a terminating defined contribution plan. If a defined contribution plan is terminated effective as of a date other than the last day of the plan's limitation year, the plan is deemed to have been amended to change its limitation year. As a result of this deemed amendment, the section 415(c)(1)(A) dollar limit must be pro-rated under the short limitation year rules.

Sections 415(m) and (n) (Sections 415(m) and (n)) have not been addressed in these regulations. Comments received concerning these provisions in response to the notice of proposed rulemaking that preceded these regulations will be considered for guidance at a later date.

Section 416 regulations

These regulations update the definition of compensation used for purposes of applying the top heavy rules of section 416. Pursuant to statutory amendments to the definition of compensation under section 415(c)(3) under SBJPA and CRA (which were generally effective for years beginning after December 31, 1997), these regulations update the alternative definition of compensation permitted under the section 416 regulations (which is based on compensation reported on Form W–2, "*Wage and Tax Statement*") to include amounts that would be included on Form W–2 but for an election under sections 125, 132(f)(4), 401(k), 403(b), 408(k), 408(p)(2)(A)(i), or 457(b).

Section 457 regulations

These regulations include revisions to the regulations under section 457 that are in addition to the revisions to reflect the treatment of compensation paid after severance from employment (§1.457–4(d)). The additional revisions do not include any substantive changes, but merely make clarifications, including revisions in an example illustrating the section 457 catch-up rules (§1.457–5(d) *Example* 2) and a change in the rules relating to unforeseeable emergencies to reflect revisions in the definition of a dependent (made under WFTRA, which modified the definition of the term "dependent" under section 152) (§1.457–6(c)).

Effective Dates

In general

These regulations generally apply to limitation years beginning on or after July 1, 2007. However, §1.401(k)–1(e)(8) applies with respect to compensation paid (or that would have been paid but for a cash or deferred election) in plan years beginning on or after July 1, 2007, and the amendment to §1.457–4(d) applies to taxable years beginning on or after December 31, 2001 (see §1.457–12). See §§1.457–6(c)(2)(i) and 1.457–12 for the applicability of the modifications to §§1.457–5, 1.457–6, and 1.457–10. In the case of a governmental plan (within the meaning of section 414(d)), §§1.415(a)–1, 1.415(b)–1, 1.415(c)–1, 1.415(c)–2, 1.415(d)–1, 1.415(f)–1, 1.415(g)–1, and 1.415(j)–1 apply to limitation years that begin more than 90 days after the close of the first regular legislative session of the legislative body with authority to amend the plan that begins on or after July 1, 2007. However, a governmental plan is permitted to apply the provisions of §§1.415(a)–1, 1.415(b)–1, 1.415(c)–1, 1.415(c)–2, 1.415(d)–1, 1.415(f)–1, 1.415(g)–1, and 1.415(j)–1 to limitation years beginning on or after July 1, 2007.

In response to commentator concerns, and as provided in Notice 2005–87, these regulations reflect revisions to the effective date provisions of the proposed regulations to expand the benefits that are grandfathered from the application of these regulations. Under these regulations, a defined benefit plan is considered to satisfy the limitations of section 415(b) for a participant with respect to benefits accrued or payable under the plan as of the end of the limitation year that is immediately prior to the effective date of these final regulations for the plan pursuant to plan provisions (including plan provisions relating to the plan's limitation year) that were both adopted and in effect before April 5, 2007, but only if such plan provisions meet the requirements of statutory provisions, regulations, and other published guidance in effect immediately before the effective date of these final regulations. For this purpose, plan provisions will not be treated as failing to satisfy the requirements of statutory provisions, regulations, and other published guidance in effect immediately before the effective date of these final regulations merely because the plan has not been amended to reflect changes to section 415(b) made by PFEA and PPA '06. In addition, for this purpose, plan provisions will not be treated as failing to satisfy the requirements of section 415(b)(1)(B) merely because the plan's definition of compensation for a limitation year that is used for purposes of applying the limitations of section 415(b)(1)(B) reflects compensation for a plan year that is in excess of the limitation under section 401(a)(17) that applies to that plan year. Thus, plans that were in compliance with the rules of section 415 as in effect for limitation years prior to the effective date of these regulations for the plan will not be disqualified based on benefits that arise pursuant to plan provisions that were both adopted and in effect before April 5, 2007, and that accrue prior to the effective date of these regulations for the plan, even if those benefits no longer comply with the requirements of section 415 as set forth under these final regulations. However, such a plan will not be permitted to provide for the accrual of additional benefits for a participant on or after the effective date of these regulations for the plan unless such additional benefits, together with the participant's other accrued benefits, comply with these regulations.

The preamble to the proposed regulations provided that, pending issuance of final regulations, taxpayers may rely on the modifications contained in the proposed regulations in §1.401(k)–1(e)(8), §1.415(c)–2(e), and §1.457–4(d) regarding post-severance compensation payments and other compensation timing rules. Accordingly, taxpayers may apply those proposed amendments for periods prior to the effective date of these final regulations. The final regulations also provide that taxpayers may apply the post-severance compensation payments and other compensation timing rules contained in the final regulations in §1.415(c)–2(e) for years prior to the effective date of these final regulations. This early application also is used for purposes of determining compensation in §§1.401(k)–1(e)(8) and 1.457–4(d).

Plan amendment timing

Generally, a provision of a plan that results in a failure of the plan to satisfy these final regulations is a disqualifying provision described in §1.401(b)–1(b)(3)(i). Therefore, the remedial amendment period rules of §1.401(b)–1 apply. For example, in the case of a plan with a calendar plan year and a calendar limitation year that is maintained by an employer with a calendar taxable year (and the plan is not a governmental plan), the plan's remedial amendment period with respect to a disqualifying plan provision as a result of these final regulations ends on the date prescribed by law for the filing of the employer's income tax return (including extensions) for the 2008 taxable year. In addition, special timing rules apply in the case of certain plan amendments made pursuant to changes made to section 415 by PFEA and PPA '06.

Under section 101(c) of PFEA (prior to amendment by PPA '06), a plan amendment to reflect the 5.5 percent interest rate assumption that is generally required to be used for distributions with annuity starting dates in plan years beginning in years 2004 and 2005 under section 101(b)(4) of PFEA (for determining the actuarially equivalent straight life annuity for a form of benefit that is subject to section 417(e)) must be made on or before the last day of the first plan year beginning on or after January 1, 2006. Section 301(c) of PPA '06 modified section 101(c) of PFEA by extending the due date for the amendment required under section 101(b)(4) of PFEA to on or before the last day of the first plan year beginning on or after January 1, 2008. Thus, pursuant to section 101(c) of PFEA (as amended by PPA '06), in the case of an amendment to a plan with a calendar year plan year to reflect the interest rate assumption specified by section 101(b)(4) of PFEA, the plan is treated as having been operated in accordance with its terms and the amendment does not violate section 411(d)(6), provided that the plan is operated in conformity with the amendment and the amendment is adopted no later than December 31, 2008.

Under section 1107 of PPA '06, a plan amendment that is made pursuant to PPA '06 (or a regulation issued by the Secretary under PPA '06) must be made on or before the last day of the first plan year beginning on or after January 1, 2009 (January 1, 2011, in the case of a governmental plan within the meaning of section 414(d)). Under section 1107 of PPA '06, if the plan is amended by such date and the plan is operated in conformity with the amendment, the plan is treated as having been operated in accordance with its terms and the amendment does not cause the plan to fail to meet the requirements of section 411(d)(6). A plan amendment is treated as an amendment that is made pursuant to a statutory amendment made by PPA '06 (or a regulation issued by the Secretary under PPA '06) if the amendment is: (i) a plan amendment to reflect the changes to the assumptions in section 415(b)(2)(E) that are used for converting certain forms of benefits to an equivalent straight life annuity in a limitation year beginning on or after January 1, 2006 (section 303 of PPA '06); (ii) a plan amendment to reflect the modifications to the purchase of permissive service credit rules of section 415(n) (section 821 of PPA '06); (iii) a plan amendment to incorporate the exemption from the section 415(b)(1)(B) compensation limit for certain benefits provided under a defined benefit plan maintained by an organization described in section 3121(w)(3)(A) (section 867 of PPA '06); and (iv) a plan amendment to reflect the expansion of the definition of qualified participant in section 415(b)(2)(H) to include certain participants in a defined benefit plan maintained by an Indian tribal government (section 906(b) of PPA '06). However, section 1107 of PPA '06 does not apply for other amendments required by these regulations, unless such amendments are pursuant to a provision of PPA '06 that did not amend section 415 (for example, section 906 of PPA '06, relating to the definition of governmental plan in section 414(d)). Accordingly, there is no extension of the remedial amendment period for such amendments, and such amendments are subject to the requirements of section 411(d)(6).

Special Analyses

It has been determined that this Treasury decision is not a significant regulatory action as defined in Executive Order 12866. Therefore, a regulatory assessment is not required. It has also been determined that section 553(b) of the Administrative Procedure Act (5 U.S.C. chapter 5) does not apply to these regulations, and because the regulations do not impose a collection of information on small entities, the Regulatory Flexibility Act (5 U.S.C. chapter 6) does not apply. Pursuant to section 7805(f) of the Code, the notice of proposed rulemaking that preceded these regulations was submitted to the Chief Counsel for Advocacy of the Small Business Administration for comment on its impact on small business.

Drafting Information

The principal authors of these regulations are Vernon S. Carter and Linda S. F. Marshall, Office of Division Counsel/Associate Chief Counsel (Tax Exempt and Government Entities), and Christopher A. Crouch, formerly of the Office of Division Counsel/Associate Chief Counsel (Tax Exempt and Government Entities). However, other personnel from the IRS and the Treasury Department participated in the development of these regulations.

* * * * *

Adoption of Amendments to the Regulations

Accordingly, 26 CFR parts 1 and 11 are amended as follows:

PART 1—INCOME TAXES

Paragraph 1. The authority citation for part 1 continues to read in part as follows:

Authority: 26 U.S.C. 7805 * * *

Par. 2. For each section set forth in the table, remove the text that appears in the column labeled "Remove" and add the text that appears in the column labeled "Add" in its place.

Regulation cite	Remove	Add
§1.401(a)–1(b)(1)(iii)	1.415–1(d)(1)	1.415(a)–1(d)(1)
§1.401(a)(4)–2(c)(2)(ii)	1.415–6(b)(2)(i)	1.415(c)–1(b)(4)
§1.414(s)–1(c)(2)	1.415–2(d)(2) and (d)(3)	1.415(c)–2(b) and (c)
§1.414(s)–1(c)(2)	1.415–2(d)(10) and (d)(11)	1.415(c)–2(d)(2), (d)(3) and (d)(4)
§1.414(s)–1(c)(2)	1.415–2(d)(13)	1.415(c)–2(d)(1)
§1.924(c)–1(d)(6)	Paragraphs (d)(1) and (2) of §1.415–2	1.415(c)–2(b) and (c)

Par. 3. Section 1.401(a)–2(b) is revised to read as follows:

§1.401(a)–2 Impossibility of diversion under qualified plan or trust.

* * * * *

(b) *Section 415 suspense account.* Notwithstanding paragraph (a) of this section, a plan, or trust forming part of a plan, may provide for the reversion to the employer, upon termination of the plan, of amounts contributed to the plan that exceed the limitations imposed under section 415(c), to the extent set forth in rules prescribed by the Commissioner in revenue rulings, notices, or other guidance published in the Internal Revenue Bulletin (see §601.601(d)(2) of this chapter).

Par. 4. Section 1.401(a)(9)–5, A–9(b)(1) is revised to read as follows:

§1.401(a)(9)–5 Required minimum distributions from defined contribution plans.

* * * * *

A–9. * * *

(b) * * *

(1) Elective deferrals (as defined in section 402(g)(3)) and employee contributions that, pursuant to rules prescribed by the Commissioner in revenue rulings, notices, or other guidance published in the Internal Revenue Bulletin (see §601.601(d)(2) of this chapter), are returned to the employee (together with the income allocable thereto) in order to comply with the section 415 limitations.

* * * * *

Par. 5. Section 1.401(k)–1 is amended by adding paragraph (e)(8) to read as follows:

§1.401(k)–1 Certain cash or deferred arrangements.

* * * * *

(e) * * *

(8) *Section 415 compensation required.* With respect to compensation that is paid (or would have been paid but for a cash or deferred election) in plan years beginning on or after July 1, 2007, a cash or deferred arrangement satisfies this paragraph (e) only if cash or deferred elections can only be made with respect to amounts that are compensation within the meaning of section 415(c)(3) and §1.415(c)–2. Thus, for example, the arrangement is not a qualified cash or deferred arrangement if an eligible employee who is not in qualified military service (as that term is defined in section 414(u)) and who is not permanently and totally disabled (as defined in section 22(c)(3)) can make a cash or deferred election with respect to an amount paid after severance from employment, unless the amount is paid by the later of 2½ months after severance from employment or the end of the year that includes the date of severance from employment and is described in §1.415(c)–2(e)(3)(ii) or (iii).

* * * * *

Par. 6. Section 1.402(c)–2, A–4(a) is revised to read as follows:

§1.402(c)–2 Eligible rollover distributions; questions and answers.

* * * * *

A–4: * * *

(a) Elective deferrals (as defined in section 402(g)(3)) and employee contributions that, pursuant to rules prescribed by the Commissioner in revenue rulings, notices, or other guidance published in the Internal Revenue Bulletin (see §601.601(d)(2) of this chapter), are returned to the employee (together with the income allocable thereto) in order to comply with the section 415 limitations.

* * * * *

§§1.415–1 through 1.415–10 [Removed]

Par. 7. Sections 1.415–1 through 1.415–10 are removed.

Par. 8. Section 1.415(a)–1 is added to read as follows:

§1.415(a)–1 General rules with respect to limitations on benefits and contributions under qualified plans.

(a) *Trusts.* Under sections 415 and 401(a)(16), a trust that forms part of a pension, profit-sharing, or stock bonus plan will not be qualified under section 401(a) if any of the following conditions exists:

(1) In the case of a defined benefit plan, the annual benefit with respect to any participant for any limitation year exceeds the limitations of section 415(b) and §1.415(b)–1.

(2) In the case of a defined contribution plan, the annual additions credited with respect to any participant for any limitation year exceed the limitations of section 415(c) and §1.415(c)–1.

(3) The trust has been disqualified under section 415(g) and §1.415(g)–1 for any year.

(b) *Certain annuities and accounts*—(1) *In general.* Under section 415, an employee annuity plan described in section 403(a), an annuity contract described in section 403(b), or a simplified employee pension described in section 408(k) will not be considered to be described in the otherwise applicable section if any of the following conditions exists:

(i) The annual benefit under a defined benefit plan with respect to any participant for any limitation year exceeds the limitations of section 415(b) and §1.415(b)–1.

(ii) The contributions and other additions credited under a defined contribution plan with respect to any participant for any limitation year exceed the limitations of section 415(c) and §1.415(c)–1.

(iii) The employee annuity plan, annuity contract, or simplified employee pension has been disqualified under section 415(g) and §1.415(g)–1 for any year.

(2) *Special rule for section 403(b) annuity contracts.* If the contributions and other additions under an annuity contract that otherwise satisfies the requirements of section 403(b) exceed the limitations of section 415(c) and §1.415(c)–1 with respect to any participant for any limitation year (regardless of whether the annuity contract is a defined contribution plan or a defined benefit plan), then the portion of the contract that includes such excess annual addition fails to be a section 403(b) annuity contract, and the remaining portion of the contract is a section 403(b) annuity contract. However, the status of the remaining portion of the contract as a section 403(b) annuity contract is not retained unless, for the year of the excess and each year thereafter, the issuer of the contract maintains separate accounts for each such portion. In addition, if the benefit under an annuity contract that is a defined benefit plan and that otherwise satisfies the requirements of section 403(b) exceeds the limitations of section 415(b) and §1.415(b)–1 with respect to any participant for any limitation year, then the contract fails to be a section 403(b) annuity contract.

(3) *Section 403(b) annuity contract.* For purposes of section 415 and regulations promulgated under section 415, the term *section 403(b) annuity contract*

includes arrangements that are treated as annuity contracts for purposes of section 403(b). Thus, such term includes custodial accounts described in section 403(b)(7) and retirement income accounts described in section 403(b)(9).

(c) *Regulations*—(1) *In general.* This section provides general rules regarding the application of section 415. For further rules regarding the application of section 415, see—

(i) Section 1.415(b)–1 (for general rules regarding the limits applicable to defined benefit plans);

(ii) Section 1.415(b)–2 (for special rules for defined benefit plans where a participant has multiple annuity starting dates);

(iii) Section 1.415(c)–1 (for general rules regarding the limits applicable to defined contribution plans);

(iv) Section 1.415(c)–2 (for rules regarding the definition of compensation for purposes of section 415);

(v) Section 1.415(d)–1 (for rules regarding cost-of-living adjustments to the various limits of section 415);

(vi) Section 1.415(f)–1 (for rules for aggregating plans for purposes of section 415);

(vii) Section 1.415(g)–1 (for rules regarding disqualification of plans that fail to satisfy the requirements of section 415); and

(viii) Section 1.415(j)–1 (for rules regarding limitation years).

(2) *Cross references to special rules for section 403(b) annuity contracts.* For special rules relating to section 403(b) annuity contracts, see—

(i) Section 1.415(c)–2(g)(1) and (3) (relating to the definition of compensation for section 403(b) annuity contracts);

(ii) Section 1.415(f)–1(f) (relating to rules for section 403(b) annuity contracts for purposes of aggregating plans);

(iii) Section 1.415(g)–1(b)(3)(iv)(C) (regarding disqualification of a section 403(b) annuity contract aggregated with a qualified defined contribution plan if the aggregated plans exceed the limitations of section 415(c));

(iv) Section 1.415(g)–1(c) (relating to the plan year for section 403(b) annuity contracts); and

(v) Section 1.415(j)–1(e) (relating to the limitation year for section 403(b) annuity contracts).

(3) *Cross references to special rules for governmental plans.* For special rules relating to governmental plans, see—

(i) Paragraph (f)(4) of this section (regarding permissive service credits);

(ii) Paragraph (g)(2) of this section (providing a delayed effective date for governmental plans);

(iii) Section 1.415(b)–1(a)(6)(i) (providing an exception from the compensation-based limit of section 415(b)(1)(B) for governmental plans);

(iv) Section 1.415(b)–1(a)(7)(ii) (regarding a special limitation for certain governmental plans making an election during 1990);

(v) Section 1.415(b)–1(b)(4) (regarding qualified governmental excess benefit arrangements);

(vi) Section 1.415(b)–1(d)(3) and (4) (regarding age adjustments to the dollar limit of section 415(b)(1)(A) for employees of police and fire departments and members of the Armed Forces of the United States, and for survivor and disability benefits);

(vii) Section 1.415(b)–1(g)(3) (regarding adjustments to applicable limitations for years of participation, and adjustments to applicable limitations for years of service for survivor and disability benefits under governmental plans);

(viii) Section 1.415(c)–1(b)(2)(ii) and (3)(iii) (regarding amounts not treated as annual additions under governmental plans); and

(ix) Section 1.415(c)–2(e)(5) (providing an alternative rule for inclusion of compensation after a severance from employment for governmental plans).

(4) *Cross references to special rules for multiemployer plans.* For special rules relating to multiemployer plans as defined in section 414(f), see—

(i) Paragraph (e) of this section (regarding benefits or contributions taken into account where a plan is maintained by more than one employer);

(ii) Paragraph (f)(5)(ii) of this section (providing a special definition of severance from employment for multiemployer plans);

(iii) Section 1.415(b)–1(a)(6)(ii) (providing an exception from the compensation-based limit for multiemployer plans);

(iv) Section 1.415(b)–1(f)(3) (regarding the application of the minimum $10,000 limitation on benefits in the case of a multiemployer plan);

(v) Section 1.415(f)–1(g) (providing special rules for aggregating multiemployer plans with other plans); and

(vi) Section 1.415(g)–1(b)(3)(ii) (regarding plan disqualification rules where a multiemployer plan is aggregated with a plan that is not a multiemployer plan and the aggregated plans exceed the limitations of section 415).

(5) *Cross references to special rules for plans that are not subject to the requirements of section 411.* For special rules relating to plans that are not subject to the requirements of section 411, see—

(i) Paragraph (d)(1) of this section and §1.415(b)–1(a)(7)(iii) (providing that the rule limiting accruals to the section 415(b) limits does not apply to plans that are not subject to the requirements of section 411); and

(ii) Section 1.415(b)–1(b)(2)(iii) (providing rules for applying the section 411(c) factors in determining the annual benefit attributable to employee contributions for plans that are not subject to the requirements of section 411).

(6) *Cross references to special rules for plans maintained by churches.* For special rules relating to plans maintained by churches as defined in section 3121(w)(3)(A), see §§1.415(b)–1(a)(6)(iv) and 1.415(b)–1(a)(7)(iv) (providing an exception from the compensation-based limit for participants who have never been a highly compensated employee of the church).

(d) *Plan provisions*—(1) *In general.* Although no specific plan provision is required under section 415 in order for a plan to establish or maintain its qualification, the plan provisions must preclude the possibility that any distribution under a defined benefit plan or annual addition under a defined contribution plan will exceed the limitations of section 415. In addition, a defined benefit plan that is subject to the requirements of section 411 must preclude the possibility that any accrual under the plan will exceed the limitations of section 415. A defined benefit plan may include provisions that automatically freeze or reduce the rate of benefit accrual (or limit the benefit payable in the case of a plan that is not subject to the requirements of section 411), and a defined contribution plan may include provisions that automatically limit the annual addition to a level necessary to prevent the limitations of section 415 from being exceeded with respect to any participant. For rules relating to this type of plan provision and the definitely determinable benefit requirement for pension plans, see §1.401(a)–1(b)(1)(iii). Because §1.401(a)–1(b)(1)(iii) requires that the operation of such a provision preclude discretion by the employer, if two defined benefit plans that are aggregated under the rules of section 415(f) would otherwise provide for aggregate benefits that might exceed the limits of section 415(b), the plan provisions must specify (without involving employer discretion) how benefits will be limited to prevent a violation of section 415(b).

(2) *Special rule for profit-sharing and stock bonus plans*. A provision of a profit-sharing or stock bonus plan that automatically freezes or reduces the amount of annual additions to ensure that the limitations of section 415 will not be exceeded must comply with the requirement set forth in §1.401–1(b)(1)(ii) or (iii) (as applicable) that such plans provide a definite predetermined formula for allocating the contributions made to the plan among the participants. If the operation of a provision that automatically freezes or reduces the amount of annual additions to ensure that the limitations of section 415 are not exceeded does not involve discretionary action on the part of the employer, the definite predetermined allocation formula requirement is not violated by the provision. If the operation of such a provision involves discretionary action on the part of the employer, the definite predetermined allocation formula requirement is violated. For example, if two profit-sharing plans of one employer otherwise provide for aggregate contributions which may exceed the limits of section 415(c), the plan provisions must specify (without involving employer discretion) under which plan contributions and allocations will be reduced to prevent an excess annual addition and how the reduction will occur.

(3) *Incorporation by reference*—(i) *In general*. A plan is permitted to incorporate by reference the limitations of section 415, and will not fail to meet the definitely determinable benefit requirement or the definite predetermined allocation formula requirement, whichever applies to the plan, merely because it incorporates the limits of section 415 by reference.

(ii) *Section 415 can be applied in more than one manner, but a statutory or regulatory default rule exists*. Where a provision of section 415 is permitted to be applied in more than one manner but is to be applied in a specified manner in the absence of contrary plan provisions (in other words, a default rule exists), if a plan incorporates the limitations of section 415 by reference with respect to that provision of section 415 and does not specifically vary from the default rule, then the default rule applies. With respect to a provision of section 415 for which a default rule exists, if the limitations of section 415 are to be applied in a manner other than using the default rule, the plan must specify the manner in which the limitation is to be applied in addition to generally incorporating the limitations of section 415 by reference. For example, if a plan generally incorporates the limitations of section 415 by reference and does not restrict the accrued benefits to which the amendments to section 415(b)(2)(E) made by the Uruguay Round Agreements Act of 1994, Public Law 103–465 (108 Stat. 4809) (GATT), apply (as permitted by Q&A–12 of Rev. Rul. 98–1, 1998–1 C.B. 249 (see §601.601(d)(2) of this chapter), which reflects the amendments to section 767 of GATT made by section 1449 of the Small Business Job Protection Act of 1996, Public Law 104–188 (110 Stat. 1755)), then the amendments to section 415(b)(2)(E) made by GATT apply to all benefits under the plan.

(iii) *Section 415 can be applied in more than one manner with no statutory or regulatory default*. If a limitation of section 415 may be applied in more than one manner, and if there is no governing principle pursuant to which that limitation is applied in the absence of contrary plan provisions, then the plan must specify the manner in which the limitation is to be applied in addition to generally incorporating the limitations of section 415 by reference. For example, if an employer maintains two profit-sharing plans, and if any participant participates in more than one such plan, then both plans must specify (in a consistent manner) under which of the employer's two profit-sharing plans annual additions must be reduced if aggregate annual additions would otherwise exceed the limitations of section 415(c)).

(iv) *Former requirements*. A plan is not permitted to incorporate by reference formerly applicable requirements of section 415 that are no longer in force (such as the limits of former section 415(e)).

(v) *Cost-of-living adjustments*—(A) *In general*. A plan is permitted to incorporate by reference the annual adjustments to the limitations of section 415 that are made pursuant to section 415(d). See §1.415(d)–1 for additional rules relating to cost-of-living adjustments under section 415(d).

(B) *Cost-of-living adjustments not included in accrued benefit until effective*. Notwithstanding that a plan incorporates the increases to the applicable limits under section 415(d) by reference, the accrued benefit of a participant for purposes of section 411 and any amount payable to a participant for purposes of §1.415(b)–1(a)(1) are not permitted to reflect increases pursuant to the annual increase under section 415(d) of the dollar limitation described in section 415(b)(1)(A) or the compensation limit described in section 415(b)(1)(B) for any period before the annual increase becomes effective. See §1.415(d)–1(a)(3) for rules relating to when the annual adjustments to the dollar and compensation limitations are effective. A plan amendment does not violate the requirements of section 411(d)(6) merely because it eliminates the incorporation by reference of the increases under section 415(d) with respect to increases that have not yet occurred.

(C) *Application of increase in defined benefit dollar limit to participants who have incurred a severance from employment or commenced receiving benefits*. If a plan incorporates by reference the annual adjustments to the limitations of section 415 pursuant to this paragraph (d)(3)(v), the plan will be treated as applying the section 415(d) cost-of-living adjustments to the maximum extent permitted under the safe harbor described in §1.415(d)–1(a)(5), except to the extent provided in this paragraph (d)(3)(v)(C). Thus, such a plan is not subject to the requirements of §1.415(b)–1(b)(1)(iii) (providing special rules for determining the annual benefit of an employee in the case of multiple annuity starting dates) with respect to benefit increases that result solely from an increase in the section 415(b) limits pursuant to section 415(d). If a plan incorporates by reference the annual adjustments to the limitations of section 415 pursuant to this paragraph (d)(3)(v), the annual increase under section 415(d) of the dollar limitation described in section 415(b)(1)(A) does not apply with respect to a participant if the increase is effective after the participant's severance from employment with the employer maintaining the plan (or, if earlier, after the annuity starting date in the case of a participant who has commenced receiving benefits), unless the plan specifies that this annual increase applies. Similarly, if a plan incorporates by reference the annual adjustments to the limitations of section 415 pursuant to this paragraph (d)(3)(v), the annual increase under section 415(d) of the compensation-based limitation described in section 415(b)(1)(B) does not apply with respect to a participant for increases that are effective after the participant's severance from employment with the employer maintaining the plan (or, if earlier, after the annuity starting date in the case of a participant who has commenced receiving benefits), unless the plan specifies that this annual increase applies.

(D) *Treatment of cost-of-living adjustments for funding and deduction purposes.* In general, the annual increase under section 415(d) of the dollar limitation described in section 415(b)(1)(A) and the compensation limitation described in section 415(b)(1)(B) is treated as a plan amendment, regardless of whether the plan reflects the increase automatically through operation of plan provisions in accordance with this paragraph (d)(3)(v) or the plan is amended to reflect the increase (pursuant to §1.415(d)–1(a)(5)). However, where a plan reflects the annual increase under section 415(d) of the dollar limitation described in section 415(b)(1)(A) or the compensation limitation described in section 415(b)(1)(B) automatically through operation of plan provisions pursuant to this paragraph (d)(3)(v), the funding method for the plan is permitted to provide for this annual increase to be treated as an experience loss for purposes of applying sections 404, 412, and 431.

(e) *Rules for plans maintained by more than one employer.* Except as provided in §1.415(f)–1(g)(2)(i) (regarding aggregation of multiemployer plans with plans other than multiemployer plans), for purposes of applying the limitations of section 415 with respect to a participant in a plan maintained by more than one employer, benefits and contributions attributable to such participant from all of the employers maintaining the plan must be taken into account. Furthermore, in applying the limitations of section 415 with respect to a participant in such a plan, the total compensation received by the participant from all of the employers maintaining the plan is taken into account under the plan, unless the plan specifies otherwise.

(f) *Special rules*—(1) *Affiliated employers.* Pursuant to section 414(b) and §1.414(b)–1, all employees of all corporations that are members of a controlled group of corporations (within the meaning of section 1563(a), as modified by section 1563(f)(5), and determined without regard to section 1563(a)(4) and (e)(3)(C)) are treated as employed by a single employer for purposes of section 415. Similarly, pursuant to section 414(c) and regulations promulgated under section 414(c), all employees of trades or businesses that are under common control are treated as employed by a single employer. Thus, any defined benefit plan or defined contribution plan maintained by any member of a controlled group of corporations (within the meaning of section 414(b)) or by any trade or business (whether or not incorporated) that is part of a group of trades or businesses that are under common control (within the meaning of section 414(c)) is deemed maintained by all such members or such trades or businesses. Pursuant to section 415(h), for purposes of section 415, sections 414(b) and 414(c) are applied by using the phrase "more than 50 percent" instead of the phrase "at least 80 percent" each place the latter phrase appears in section 1563(a)(1) and in the regulations under section 414(c) (except for purposes of determining whether two or more organizations are a brother-sister group of trades or businesses under common control under the rules in §1.414(c)–2(c)).

(2) *Affiliated service groups.* Any defined benefit plan or defined contribution plan maintained by any member of an affiliated service group (within the meaning of section 414(m)) is deemed maintained by all members of that affiliated service group.

(3) *Leased employees*—(i) *In general.* Pursuant to section 414(n), except as provided in paragraph (f)(3)(ii) of this section, with respect to any person (referred to as the recipient) for whom a leased employee (within the meaning of section 414(n)(2)) performs services, the leased employee is treated as an employee of the recipient, but contributions or benefits provided by the leasing organization that are attributable to services performed for the recipient are treated as provided under a plan maintained by the recipient.

(ii) *Exception for leased employees covered by safe harbor plans.* Pursuant to section 414(n)(5), the rule of paragraph (f)(3)(i) of this section does not apply to a leased employee with respect to services performed for a recipient if—

(A) The leased employee is covered by a plan that is maintained by the leasing organization and that meets the requirements of section 414(n)(5)(B); and

(B) Leased employees (determined without regard to this paragraph (f)(3)(ii)) do not constitute more than 20 percent of the recipient's nonhighly compensated workforce.

(4) *Permissive service credit under governmental plans.* See section 415(n) for rules regarding the application of the limitations of sections 415(b) and (c) where a participant makes contributions (including a transfer described in section 403(b)(13) or section 457(e)(17)) to a defined benefit governmental plan to purchase permissive service credit under the plan.

(5) *Definition of severance from employment*—(i) *General rule.* For purposes of this section and §§1.415(b)–1, 1.415(b)–2, 1.415(c)–1, 1.415(c)–2, 1.415(d)–1, 1.415(f)–1, 1.415(g)–1, and 1.415(j)–1, whether an employee has a severance from employment with the employer that maintains a plan is determined in the same manner as under §1.401(k)–1(d)(2) except that, for purposes of determining the employer of an employee, the modifications provided under section 415(h) (described in paragraph (f)(1) of this section) to the employer aggregation rules apply. Thus, an employee has a severance from employment when the employee ceases to be an employee of the employer maintaining the plan, and an employee does not have a severance from employment if, in connection with a change of employment, the employee's

new employer maintains such plan with respect to the employee. The determination of whether an employee ceases to be an employee of the employer maintaining the plan is based on all of the relevant facts and circumstances.

(ii) *Multiemployer plans.* A participant in a multiemployer plan (within the meaning of section 414(f)) is not treated as having incurred a severance from employment with the employer maintaining the multiemployer plan for purposes of this section and §§1.415(b)–1, 1.415(b)–2, 1.415(c)–1, 1.415(c)–2, 1.415(d)–1, 1.415(f)–1, 1.415(g)–1, and 1.415(j)–1 if the participant continues to be an employee of another employer maintaining the multiemployer plan.

(6) *Qualified domestic relations orders.* A benefit provided to an alternate payee (as defined in section 414(p)(8)) of a participant pursuant to a qualified domestic relations order (as defined in section 414(p)(1)(A)) is treated as if it were provided to the participant for purposes of applying the limitations of section 415. See §1.401(a)–13(g)(4)(iv).

(7) *Effect on other requirements.* Except as provided in §1.417(e)–1(d)(1), the application of section 415 does not relieve a plan from the obligation to satisfy other applicable qualification requirements. Accordingly, the terms of the plan must provide for the plan to satisfy section 415 as well as all other applicable requirements. For example, if a defined benefit plan has a normal retirement age of 62, and if a participant's benefit remains unchanged between the ages of 62 and 65 because of the application of the section 415(b)(1)(A) dollar limit, the plan satisfies the requirements of section 411 only if the plan either commences distribution of the participant's benefit at normal retirement age (without regard to severance from employment) or provides for a suspension of benefits at normal retirement age that satisfies the requirements of section 411(a)(3)(B) and 29 CFR 2530.203–3. Similarly, if the increase to a participant's benefit under a defined benefit plan in a year after the participant has attained normal retirement age is less than the actuarial increase to the participant's previously accrued benefit because of the application of the section 415(b)(1)(B) compensation limitation (which is not adjusted for commencement after age 65), the plan satisfies the requirements of section 411 only if the plan either commences distribution of the participant's benefit at normal retirement age (without regard to severance from employment) or provides for a suspension of benefits at normal retirement age that satisfies the requirements of section 411(a)(3)(B) and 29 CFR 2530.203–3.

(g) *Effective date*—(1) *General rule.* Except as otherwise provided, this section and §§1.415(b)–1, 1.415(c)–1, 1.415(c)–2, 1.415(d)–1, 1.415(f)–1, 1.415(g)–1, and 1.415(j)–1 apply to limitation years beginning on or after July 1, 2007.

(2) *Governmental plans.* In the case of a governmental plan as defined in section 414(d), this section and §§1.415(b)–1, 1.415(c)–1, 1.415(c)–2, 1.415(d)–1, 1.415(f)–1, 1.415(g)–1, and 1.415(j)–1 apply to limitation years that begin more than 90 days after the close of the first regular legislative session of the legislative body with authority to amend the plan that begins on or after July 1, 2007. A governmental plan is permitted to apply the provisions of this section and §§1.415(b)–1, 1.415(c)–1, 1.415(c)–2, 1.415(d)–1, 1.415(f)–1, 1.415(g)–1, and 1.415(j)–1 to limitation years beginning on or after July 1, 2007, provided the plan applies all the applicable provisions of this section and §§1.415(b)–1, 1.415(c)–1, 1.415(c)–2, 1.415(d)–1, 1.415(f)–1, 1.415(g)–1, and 1.415(j)–1 for such limitation years.

(3) *Option to apply regulations earlier.* A plan may apply the rules in §1.415(c)–2(e) regarding post-severance compensation payments for limitation years prior to the effective date described in paragraphs (g)(1) and (2) of this section. This early application affects the rules relating to the definition of compensation in §1.401(k)–1(e)(8) and §1.457–4(d).

(4) *Grandfather rule for preexisting benefits.* A defined benefit plan is considered to satisfy the limitations of section 415(b) for a participant with respect to benefits accrued or payable under the plan as of the end of the limitation year that is immediately prior to the effective date of final regulations under this section and §§1.415(b)–1, 1.415(c)–1, 1.415(c)–2, 1.415(d)–1, 1.415(f)–1, 1.415(g)–1, and 1.415(j)–1 (as provided under paragraph (g)(1) or (2) of this section) pursuant to plan provisions (including plan provisions relating to the plan's limitation year) that were both adopted and in effect before April 5, 2007, but only if such plan provisions meet the applicable requirements of statutory provisions, regulations, and other published guidance relating to section 415 in effect immediately before the effective date of final regulations under this section and §§1.415(b)–1, 1.415(c)–1, 1.415(c)–2, 1.415(d)–1, 1.415(f)–1, 1.415(g)–1, and 1.415(j)–1 (as provided under paragraph (g)(1) or (2) of this section). Plan provisions will not be treated as failing to satisfy these requirements merely because the plan has not been amended to reflect changes to section 415(b) made by the Pension Funding Equity Act of 2004, Public Law 108–218 (118 Stat. 596), and the Pension Protection Act of 2006, Public Law 109–280 (120 Stat. 780). In addition, plan provisions will not be treated as failing to satisfy these requirements merely because the plan's definition of compensation for a limitation year that is used for purposes of applying the limitations of section 415(b)(1)(B) reflects compensation for a plan year that is in excess of the limitation under section 401(a)(17) that applies to that plan year. If benefits under a plan are accrued after the applicable effective date under paragraph (g)(1) or (2) of this section, then the sum of the benefits grandfathered under the first sentence of this paragraph (g)(4) and benefits accrued after the applicable effective date must satisfy the requirements of section 415, taking into account the requirements of this section and §§1.415(b)–1, 1.415(c)–1, 1.415(c)–2, 1.415(d)–1, 1.415(f)–1, 1.415(g)–1, and 1.415(j)–1.

Par. 9. Section 1.415(b)–1 is added to read as follows:

§1.415(b)–1 Limitations for defined benefit plans.

(a) *General rules*—(1) *Maximum limitations.* Except as otherwise provided under this section, a defined benefit plan fails to satisfy the requirements of section 415(a) for a limitation year if, during the limitation year, either the annual benefit (as defined in paragraph (b)(1)(i) of this section) accrued by a participant (whether or not the benefit is vested) or the annual benefit payable to a participant at any time under the plan exceeds the lesser of—

(i) $160,000 (as adjusted pursuant to section 415(d), §1.415(d)–1(a), and this section); or

(ii) 100 percent of the participant's average compensation for the period of the participant's high-3 years of service (as adjusted pursuant to section 415(d), §1.415(d)–1(a), and this section).

(2) *Defined benefit plan.* For purposes of section 415 and regulations promulgated under section 415, a defined benefit plan is any plan, contract, or account to which section 415 applies pursuant to §1.415(a)–1(a) or (b) (or any portion thereof) that is not a defined contribution plan within the meaning of §1.415(c)–1(a)(2). In addition, a section 403(b) annuity contract that is not described in section 414(i) is treated as a defined benefit plan for purposes of section 415 and regulations promulgated under section 415.

(3) *Plan provisions.* As required in §1.415(a)–1(d)(1), in order to satisfy the limitations on benefits under this section, the plan provisions (including the provisions of any annuity) must preclude the possibility that any annual benefit exceeding these limitations will be accrued (except as provided in paragraph (a)(7)(iii) of this section), distributed, or otherwise payable in any optional form of benefit (including the normal form of benefit) at any time (from the plan, from an annuity contract that will make distributions to the participant on behalf of the plan, or from an annuity contract that has been distributed under the plan). Thus, for example, a plan that is subject to the requirements of section 411 will fail to satisfy the limitations of this section if the plan does not contain terms that preclude the possibility that any annual benefit exceeding these limitations will be accrued or payable in any optional form of benefit (including the normal form of benefit) at any time, even though no participant has actually accrued a benefit in excess of these limitations.

(4) *Adjustments to dollar limitation for commencement before age 62 or after age 65.* The age-adjusted section 415(b)(1)(A) dollar limit computed pursuant to paragraph (d) or (e) of this section is used in place of the dollar limitation described in section 415(b)(1)(A) and paragraph (a)(1)(i) of this section in the case of a benefit with an annuity starting date that occurs before the participant attains age 62 or after the participant attains age 65.

(5) *Average compensation for period of high-3 years of service*—(i) *In general.* Except as otherwise provided in this paragraph (a)(5), for purposes of applying the limitation on benefits described in this section, the period of a participant's high-3 years of service is the period of 3 consecutive calendar years (taking into account the rule in paragraph (a)(5)(iii) of this section) during which the employee had the greatest aggregate compensation (as defined in §1.415(c)–2) from the employer, and the average compensation for the period of a participant's high-3 years of service is determined by dividing the aggregate compensation for this period by 3. For purposes of this paragraph (a)(5), in determining a participant's high-3 years of service, the plan may use any 12-month period to determine a year of service instead of the calendar year, provided that it is uniformly and consistently applied in a manner that is specified under the terms of the plan. As provided under §1.415(c)–2(f), because a plan is not permitted to base benefits on compensation in excess of the limitation under section 401(a)(17), a plan's definition of compensation for a year that is used for purposes of applying the limitations of section 415 is not permitted to reflect compensation for a year that is in excess of the limitation under section 401(a)(17) that applies to that year. See §§1.401(a)(17)–1(a)(3)(i) and 1.401(a)(17)–1(b)(3)(ii) for rules regarding the effective date of increases in the section 401(a)(17) compensation limitation for a plan year and for a 12-month period other than the plan year.

(ii) *Short periods of service.* For a participant who is employed with an employer for less than 3 consecutive years, the period of the participant's high-3 years of service is the actual number of consecutive years of service (including fractions of years, but not less than one year). In such a case, the limitation of section 415(b)(1)(B) of 100 percent of the participant's average compensation for the period of the participant's high-3 years of service is computed by dividing the participant's compensation during the participant's longest consecutive period of service by the number of years in that period (including fractions of years, but not less than one year). The rule in paragraph (a)(5)(iii) of this section is used for purposes of determining a participant's consecutive years of service.

(iii) *Break in service.* In the case of a participant who has had a severance from employment with an employer that maintains the plan and who is subsequently rehired by the employer, the period of the participant's high-3 years of service is calculated by excluding all years for which the participant performs no services for and receives no compensation from the employer maintaining the plan (referred to as the break period), and by treating the year of service immediately prior to and the year of service immediately after the break period as if such years of service were consecutive. See §1.415(d)–1(a)(2)(iii) for a special rule for determining a rehired participant's section 415(b)(1)(B) compensation limit in the case of a plan that adjusts the compensation limit for limitation years after the limitation year in which the participant incurs a severance from employment.

(iv) *Examples.* For purposes of these examples, except as otherwise stated, the plan year and the limitation year are the calendar year, and the plan uses the calendar year for purposes of determining the period of high-3 years of service. In addition, except as otherwise stated, it is assumed that the plan's normal retirement age is 65, and all participants discussed in these examples have at least ten years of service with the employer and at least ten years of participation in the plan at issue. It is also assumed that none of the plans in the examples are governmental plans. The following examples illustrate the rules of this paragraph (a)(5):

Example 1. (i) *Facts.* Plan A, which was established on January 1, 2008, covers Participant M, who was hired on January 1, 1990. Participant M's compensation (as defined in §1.415(c)–2) from the employer maintaining the plan is $140,000 each year for 1990 through 1992, is $120,000 each year for 1993 through 2007, and is $165,000 for 2008 and 2009. Assume that for Plan A's 2008 and 2009 limitation years, the section 415(b)(1)(A) age-adjusted dollar limit for M is $185,000 and $190,000, respectively, prior to the reduction of the age-adjusted dollar limit pursuant to paragraph (g)(1) of this section (which requires a reduction in the dollar limit if a participant has less than 10 years of participation in the plan).

(ii) *Conclusion.* As of the end of the 2008 limitation year, the period of M's high-3 consecutive years of service runs from January 1, 1990, through December 31, 1992, and M's average compensation for this period is $140,000. Thus, the limitation under section 415(b)(1)(B) for the 2008 limitation year is $140,000. As of the end of the 2009 limitation year, the period of M's high-3 consecutive years of service runs from January 1, 2007, through December 31, 2009, and M's average compensation for this period is $150,000. Thus, the limitation under section 415(b)(1)(B) for the 2009 limitation year is $150,000.

Example 2. (i) *Facts.* Participant N is a participant in Plan B. N's compensation for 2008, 2009, and 2010 is $300,000 for each year. N's average compensation for the period of N's high-3 years of service (determined before the application of section 401(a)(17)) is $300,000, based on N's compensation for 2008, 2009, and 2010. For all years before 2008, Participant N's compensation was less than the then-applicable section 401(a)(17) limit. On January 1, 2011, N commences receiving benefits from Plan B at the age of 75, 10 years after attaining N's normal retirement age under Plan B, when the age-adjusted section 415(b)(1)(A) dollar limit for benefits commencing at that age is $293,453.

(ii) *Conclusion.* Pursuant to §1.415(c)–2(f) and section 401(a)(17), Plan B is not permitted to provide for a definition of compensation that includes compensation for a year that is in excess of the limitation under section 401(a)(17) that applies to that year. Accordingly, the limitation under section 415(b)(1)(B) based on N's average compensation for the period of N's high three years of service must not reflect compensation for a year that is in excess of the limitation under section 401(a)(17) that applies to that year. Thus, if the limitation under section 401(a)(17) for years beginning in 2008, 2009, and 2010 is $230,000, $235,000, and $240,000, respectively, then the limitation under section 415(b)(1)(B) based on N's average compensation for the period of N's high three years of service is $235,000.

Example 3. (i) *Facts.* The facts are the same as in *Example 2*, except that N commences receiving benefits from Plan B on January 1, 2008, at the age of 75, 10 years after attaining N's normal retirement age under Plan B. In addition, N's period of high three years of service is from January 1, 2003, through December 31, 2005, and N's average compensation for this period is $300,000. The section 401(a)(17) limits for 2003, 2004 and 2005 are $200,000, $205,000, and $210,000, respectively. As of December 31, 2007, pursuant to plan provisions adopted and in effect on January 1, 2007, N's accrued benefit under Plan B, payable in the form of a straight life annuity, actuarially adjusted to reflect commencement 10 years after normal retirement age, is $300,000. Plan B has not been amended during 2007, and that as of December 31, 2007, Plan B satisfied all of the requirements of section 415(b) with respect to N's accrued benefit, pursuant to statutory provisions, regulations, and other published guidance in effect immediately before the limitation year beginning on January 1, 2008.

(ii) *Conclusion.* Under §1.415(a)–1(g)(4), Plan B is considered to satisfy the section 415(b)(1)(B) compensation limit with respect to N's benefit payable at age 75 of $300,000 (which N accrued prior to January 1, 2008), for limitation years beginning after December 31, 2007. This is because §1.415(a)–1(g)(4) provides that plan provisions will not be treated as failing to satisfy the requirements of section 415(b)(1)(B) merely because the plan's definition of compensation that is used for purposes of applying the limitations of section 415(b)(1)(B) reflects compensation in excess of the section 401(a)(17) limitation for limitation years beginning before January 1, 2008. N, however, cannot accrue any additional benefits under Plan B for limitation years beginning after December 31, 2007, until N's section 415(b)(1)(B) compensation limit, as limited by §1.415(c)–2(f) and section 401(a)(17), increases above $300,000.

Example 4. (i) *Facts.* Participant O participates in Plan C, maintained by Employer X. Plan C does not adjust a participant's section 415(b)(1)(B) compensation limit for limitation years after the limitation year in which the participant incurs a severance from employment. Prior to separating from employment with X in 2010, O's average compensation for O's period of high-3 years of service is $50,000, based on O's compensation for 2007, 2008, and 2009, which was $50,000 for each year. O's compensation for 2010 was $45,000. O's compensation is $0 for 2011. In 2012, O is rehired by X and resumes participation in Plan C. O's compensation in 2012 is $45,000, and is $70,000 in 2013.

(ii) *Conclusion.* As of the end of the 2013 limitation year, O's average compensation for O's period of high-3 years of service is $53,333, based on O's compensation in 2010, 2012, and 2013. See paragraph (a)(5)(iii) of this section.

Example 5. (i) *Facts.* The facts are the same as in *Example 4*, except that, in accordance with §1.415(a)–1(d)(3)(v), Plan C incorporates by reference section 415(d) adjustments to a participant's section 415(b)(1)(B) compensation limit for limitation years after the limitation year in which the participant incurs a severance from employment. Assume that the annual adjustment factor described in §1.415(d)–1(a)(2)(ii) for 2011 through 2013 is 1.03 for each year. Thus, disregarding O's rehire by X, O's average compensation for O's period of high-3 years of service for the 2013 limitation year is equal to $54,636 ($50,000 * 1.03 * 1.03 * 1.03).

(ii) *Conclusion.* Under §1.415(d)–1(a)(2)(iii), O's average compensation for O's period of high-3 years of service for the 2013 limitation year is $54,636.

(6) *Exceptions from compensation limit.* The limit under paragraph (a)(1)(ii) of this section (100 percent of the participant's average compensation for the participant's high-3 years of service) does not apply to—

(i) A governmental plan (as defined in section 414(d));

(ii) A multiemployer plan (as defined in section 414(f));

(iii) A collectively bargained plan that is described in section 415(b)(7); or

(iv) A participant in a plan maintained by an organization described in section 3121(w)(3)(A) who has never been a highly compensated employee (within the meaning of section 414(q)) of the organization.

(7) *Special rules*—(i) *Total benefits not in excess of $10,000.* See section 415(b)(4) and paragraph (f) of this section for an exception from the limits of section 415(b)(1) and paragraph (a)(1) of this section with respect to retirement benefits that do not exceed $10,000 for the limitation year.

(ii) *Governmental plans electing during 1990.* For a special limitation applicable to certain governmental plans electing the application of this rule during the first plan year beginning after December 31, 1989, see section 415(b)(10).

(iii) *Defined benefit plans not subject to the requirements of section 411.* In the case of a defined benefit plan that is not subject to the requirements of section 411, the limitations described in this paragraph (a) are not required to be applied to the annual benefit accrued by a participant before the benefit is payable. However, such a defined benefit plan is subject to the limitations described in this paragraph (a) with respect to the annual benefit payable to a participant at any time under the plan.

(iv) *Application of compensation limitation exception to a church employee who becomes a highly compensated employee*—(A) *In general.* If a participant who was described in paragraph (a)(6)(iv) of this section for a prior limitation year later becomes a highly compensated employee (within the meaning of section 414(q)) of the organization that maintains the defined benefit plan, the plan is not treated as failing to satisfy the compensation-based limitation described in paragraph (a)(1)(ii) of this section with respect to the participant if the requirements of paragraph (a)(7)(iv)(B) of this section are satisfied with respect to the participant.

(B) *Limitation on accruals.* The requirements of this paragraph (a)(7)(iv)(B) are satisfied with respect to a participant if no plan amendments increasing the participant's benefits are adopted during the limitation year in which the participant first becomes a highly compensated employee (within the meaning of section 414(q)) of the organization that maintains the plan, and there is no increase in the participant's accrued benefit derived from employer contributions (including increases as a result of increased compensation or service) in subsequent limitation years.

(b) *Annual benefit*—(1) *In general*—(i) *Definition of annual benefit*—(A) *Straight life annuities.* For purposes of this section and §1.415(b)–2, the term *annual benefit* means a benefit that is payable in the form of a straight life annuity. A *straight life annuity* means an annuity payable in equal installments for the life of the participant that terminates upon the participant's death. Examples of benefits that are not in the form of a straight life annuity include an annuity with a post-retirement death benefit and an annuity providing a guaranteed number of payments. If a benefit is payable in the form of a straight life annuity, no adjustment is made to the benefit to account for differences in the timing of payments during a year (for example, no adjustment is made on account of the annuity being payable in annual or monthly installments).

(B) *Other benefit forms.* With respect to a benefit payable in a form other than a straight life annuity, the annual benefit is determined as the straight life annuity payable on the first day of each month that is actuarially equivalent to the benefit payable in such other form, determined under the rules of paragraph (c) of this section.

(ii) *Rules for determination of annual benefit.* The annual benefit does not include the annual benefit attributable to either employee contributions or rollover contributions (as described in sections 401(a)(31), 402(c)(1), 403(a)(4), 403(b)(8), 408(d)(3), and 457(e)(16)), determined pursuant to the rules of paragraph (b)(2) of this section. The treatment of transferred benefits is determined under the rules of paragraph (b)(3) of this section. Paragraph (b)(4) of this section discusses the treatment of qualified governmental excess benefit arrangements.

(iii) *Determination of annual benefit in the case of multiple annuity starting dates*—(A) *General rule.* If a participant has or will have distributions commencing at more than one annuity starting date, then the limitations of section 415 must be satisfied as of each of the annuity starting dates, taking into account the benefits that have been or will be provided at all of the annuity starting dates. This will happen, for example, where benefit distributions to a participant have previously commenced under a plan that is aggregated for purposes of section 415 with a plan under which the participant receives current accruals. In determining the annual benefit for such a participant as of a particular annuity starting date, the plan must actuarially adjust the past and future distributions with respect to the benefits that commenced at the other annuity starting dates. For limitation years to which §1.415(b)–2 applies, these adjustments must be made using the rules of §1.415(b)–2. For purposes of this paragraph (b)(1)(iii) and §1.415(b)–2, the determination of whether a new annuity starting date has occurred is made without regard to the rule of §1.401(a)–20, Q&A–10(d) (under which the commencement of certain distributions may not give rise to a new annuity starting date).

(B) *Scope of multiple annuity starting date rules.* The rules provided in this paragraph (b)(1)(iii) and §1.415(b)–2 apply for purposes of determining the annual benefit of a participant where a new distribution election is effective during the current limitation year with respect to a distribution that previously commenced. The rules of this paragraph (b)(1)(iii) and §1.415(b)–2 also apply for determining the annual benefit of a participant for purposes of applying the limitations of section 415(b) and this section where benefit payments are increased as a result of plan terms or a plan amendment applying a cost-of-living adjustment or similar benefit increase, unless the increase is described in paragraph (b)(1)(iii)(C) of this section.

(C) *Safe harbors for certain benefit increases.* An increase to benefit payments as a result of plan terms or a plan amendment applying a cost-of-living adjustment or similar benefit increase is described in this paragraph (b)(1)(iii)(C) if the increase—

(*1*) Has previously been accounted for as part of the annual benefit under the rules of paragraph (c) of this section;

(*2*) Is not required to be accounted for as part of the annual benefit, pursuant to the exception for certain automatic benefit increase features under paragraph (c)(5) of this section;

(*3*) Is pursuant to a plan provision that automatically incorporates section 415(d) cost-of-living adjustments under §1.415(a)–1(d)(3)(v); or

(*4*) Complies with one of the safe harbors described in §1.415(d)–1(a)(5) or (6) (providing safe harbors for annual and other periodic adjustments to distributions).

(2) *Determination of annual benefit attributable to employee contributions and rollover contributions*—(i) *In general.* If employee contributions (other than contributions described in paragraph (b)(2)(ii) of this section) or rollover contributions are made to the plan, the annual benefit attributable to these contributions is determined as provided in this paragraph (b)(2).

(ii) *Certain employee contributions disregarded.* For purposes of this paragraph (b)(2), the following are not treated as employee contributions:

(A) Contributions that are picked up by a governmental employer as provided under section 414(h)(2).

(B) Repayment of any loan made to a participant from the plan.

(C) Repayment of a previously distributed amount as described in section 411(a)(7)(B) in accordance with section 411(a)(7)(C).

(D) Repayment of a withdrawal of employee contributions as provided under section 411(a)(3)(D).

(E) Repayments that would have been described in paragraph (b)(2)(ii)(C) or (b)(2)(ii)(D) of this section except that the plan does not restrict the timing of repayments to the maximum extent permitted by section 411(a).

(iii) *Annual benefit attributable to mandatory employee contributions.* In the case of mandatory employee contributions as defined in section 411(c)(2)(C) and §1.411(c)–1(c)(4) (or contributions that would be mandatory employee contributions if section 411 applied to the plan), the annual benefit attributable to those contributions is determined by applying the factors applicable to mandatory employee contributions as described in section 411(c)(2)(B) and (C) and regulations promulgated under section 411 to those contributions to determine the amount of a straight life annuity commencing at the annuity starting date, regardless of whether the requirements of sections 411 and 417 apply to that plan. For purposes of applying such factors to a plan that is not subject to the requirements of section 411, the applicable effective date of section 411(a)(2) (which is used under §1.411(c)–1(c)(3) to determine the beginning date from which statutorily specified interest must be credited to mandatory employee contributions) must be determined as if section 411 applied to the plan, and in determining the annual benefit that is actuarially equivalent to these accumulated contributions, the plan must determine the interest rate that would have been required under section 417(e)(3) as if section 417 applied to the plan. See §1.415(c)–1(a)(2)(ii)(B) and (b)(3) for rules regarding treatment of mandatory employee contributions to a defined benefit plan as annual additions under a defined contribution plan.

(iv) *Voluntary employee contributions.* If voluntary employee contributions are made to the plan, the portion of the plan to which voluntary employee contributions are made is treated as a defined contribution plan pursuant to section 414(k) and, accordingly, is a defined contribution plan pursuant to §1.415(c)–1(a)(2)(i). Accordingly, the portion of a plan to which voluntary employee contributions are made is not a defined benefit plan within the meaning of paragraph (a)(2) of this section and is not taken into account in determining the annual benefit under the portion of the plan that is a defined benefit plan.

(v) *Annual benefit attributable to rollover contributions.* The annual benefit attributable to rollover contributions from an eligible retirement plan, as defined in section 402(c)(8)(B) (for example, a contribution received pursuant to a direct rollover under section 401(a)(31)(A)), is determined in the same manner as the annual benefit attributable to mandatory employee contributions if the plan provides for a benefit derived from the rollover contribution (other than a benefit derived from a separate account to be maintained with respect to the rollover contribution and actual earnings and losses thereon). Thus, in the case of rollover contributions from a defined contribution plan to a defined benefit plan to provide an annuity distribution, the annual benefit attributable to those rollover contributions for purposes of section 415(b) is determined by applying the rules of section 411(c) as described in paragraph (b)(2)(iii) of this section, regardless of the assumptions used to compute the annuity distribution under the plan and regardless of whether the plan is subject to the requirements of sections 411 and 417. Accordingly, in such a case, if the plan uses more favorable factors than those specified in section 411(c) to determine the amount of annuity payments arising from rollover contributions, the annual benefit under the plan would reflect the excess of those annuity payments over the amounts that would be payable using the factors specified in section 411(c). See §1.415(c)–1(b)(3)(i) for rules excluding rollover contributions maintained in a separate account that is treated as a defined contribution plan pursuant to section 414(k) from annual additions to a defined contribution plan.

(3) *Treatment of transferred benefits*—(i) *In general*—(A) *Treatment of transferor plan if transferred benefits are aggregated with transferor plan.* Except as provided in paragraph (b)(3)(ii) of this section, when there has been a transfer of benefits from one defined benefit plan to another plan, to the extent the benefits transferred to the transferee plan are otherwise required to be taken into account pursuant to section 415(f) and §1.415(f)–1 in determining whether the transferor plan satisfies the limitations of section 415(b) for a limitation year, the transferred benefits are not treated as being provided under the transferor plan. This will occur, for example, if the employer sponsoring the transferor plan and the employer sponsoring the transferee plan are in the same controlled group within the meaning of section 414(b).

(B) *Treatment of transferor plan if transferred benefits are not aggregated with transferor plan.* Except as provided in paragraph (b)(3)(ii) of this section, when there has been a transfer of benefits from one defined benefit plan to another plan, to the extent the benefits transferred to the transferee plan are not otherwise required to be taken into account pursuant to section 415(f) and §1.415(f)–1 in determining whether the transferor plan satisfies the limitations of section 415(b) for a limitation year, the transferred benefits are treated by the transferor plan as if such benefits were provided under annuities purchased to provide benefits under a plan that must be aggregated with the transferor plan and that terminated immediately prior to the transfer with sufficient assets to pay all benefit liabilities under the plan, in accordance with the rules of paragraph (b)(5)(i) of this section. This will occur, for example, in the case of a transfer of benefits between defined benefit plans maintained by employers that are not required to be aggregated under sections 414(b) and (c) (as modified by section 415(h)) or sections 414(m).

(C) *Treatment of transferee plan.* Except as provided in paragraph (b)(3)(ii) of this section, where there has been a transfer of benefits from one defined benefit plan to another defined benefit plan, the transferee plan must take into account the transferred benefits in determining whether it satisfies the limitations of section 415(b).

(ii) *Elective transfer of distributable benefit.* Where, as described in §1.411(d)–4, Q&A–3(c) (permitting certain elective transfers of distributable benefits), a distributable benefit is transferred to a defined benefit plan from either a defined contribution plan or a defined benefit plan, the amount transferred is treated as a benefit paid from the transferor plan, and the annual benefit provided by the transferee defined benefit plan does not include the annual benefit attributable to the amount transferred (determined as if the transferred amount were a rollover contribution subject to the rules of paragraph (b)(2)(v) of this section). The rule in the preceding sentence applies regardless of whether the requirements of section 411 apply to the plan and, in the case of a transfer from a defined contribution plan that is not subject to the requirements of section 411 (such as a governmental plan) to a defined benefit plan, the rule applies even if the participant's benefits are not distributable from the defined contribution plan at the time of the transfer.

(4) *Treatment of qualified governmental excess benefit arrangements.* Pursuant to section 415(m), in determining whether a governmental plan (as defined in section 414(d)) meets the requirements of this section, the annual benefit does not include benefits provided under a qualified governmental excess benefit arrangement, as defined in section 415(m)(3). Thus, the limitation of section 415(b) does not apply to benefits to the extent the benefits are provided under a qualified governmental excess benefit arrangement.

(5) *Treatment of benefits provided under a terminated plan*—(i) *Terminated plan with sufficient assets.* If a defined benefit plan is terminated with sufficient assets for the payment of the benefit liabilities of all plan participants and a participant in the plan has not yet commenced benefits under the plan, for purposes of satisfying section 415(b) with respect to the participant, all other defined benefit plans maintained by the employer that maintained the terminated plan are required to take into account the benefits provided pursuant to the annuities purchased to provide benefits under the terminated plan

at each possible annuity starting date. In such a case, see paragraph (b)(1)(iii) of this section for rules regarding the determination of a participant's annual benefit if the participant commences receiving benefits under the terminated plan.

(ii) *Terminated plan with insufficient assets*. If a defined benefit plan is terminated and there are not sufficient assets for the payment of the benefit liabilities of all plan participants, for purposes of satisfying section 415(b) with respect to a participant, all other defined benefit plans maintained by the employer that maintained the terminated plan are required to take into account the benefits that are actually provided to the participant under the terminated plan. For example, in the case of a plan that is subject to Title IV of the Employee Retirement Income Security Act of 1974 (88 Stat. 829), Public Law 93–406 (ERISA), and that terminates with insufficient assets for the payment of the benefit liabilities of all plan participants, all other defined benefit plans maintained by the employer that maintained the terminating plan must take into account benefits that are paid by the Pension Benefit Guaranty Corporation. In such a case, see paragraph (b)(1)(iii) of this section for rules regarding the determination of a participant's annual benefit if the participant commences receiving benefits under the terminated plan.

(iii) *Other guidance*. The Commissioner may provide guidance regarding the rules applicable to terminated plans (and plans that are deemed to have been terminated pursuant to paragraph (b)(3)(i)(B) of this section) in revenue rulings, notices, and other guidance published in the Internal Revenue Bulletin. See §601.601(d) of this chapter.

(c) *Adjustment to form of benefit for forms other than a straight life annuity*—(1) *In general*. This paragraph (c) provides rules for adjusting a form of benefit other than a straight life annuity to an actuarially equivalent straight life annuity beginning at the same time for purposes of determining the annual benefit described in paragraph (b) of this section. Paragraph (c)(2) of this section describes how to adjust a benefit paid in a form to which section 417(e)(3) does not apply. Paragraph (c)(3) of this section describes how to adjust a benefit paid in a form to which section 417(e)(3) applies. Paragraph (c)(4) of this section describes benefit forms for which no adjustment is required. Paragraph (c)(5) of this section provides an exception from the requirements of this paragraph (c) with respect to certain automatic benefit increase features. Paragraph (c)(6) of this section sets forth examples illustrating the application of this paragraph (c). The Commissioner may, in revenue rulings, notices, or other guidance published in the Internal Revenue Bulletin set forth simplified methods for adjusting a form of benefit other than a straight life annuity to an actuarially equivalent straight life annuity beginning at the same time for purposes of determining the annual benefit described in paragraph (b) of this section. See §601.601(d)(2) of this chapter.

(2) *Benefits paid in a form to which section 417(e)(3) does not apply*. For a benefit paid in a form to which section 417(e)(3) does not apply, the actuarially equivalent straight life annuity benefit is the greater of—

(i) The annual amount of the straight life annuity (if any) payable to the participant under the plan commencing at the same annuity starting date as the form of benefit payable to the participant; or

(ii) The annual amount of the straight life annuity commencing at the same annuity starting date that has the same actuarial present value as the form of benefit payable to the participant, computed using a 5 percent interest assumption and the applicable mortality table described in §1.417(e)–1(d)(2) for that annuity starting date.

(3) *Benefits paid in a form to which section 417(e)(3) applies*—(i) *In general*. Except as otherwise provided in this paragraph (c)(3), for a benefit paid in a form to which section 417(e)(3) applies, the actuarially equivalent straight life annuity benefit is the greatest of:

(A) The annual amount of the straight life annuity commencing at the annuity starting date that has the same actuarial present value as the particular form of benefit payable, computed using the interest rate and mortality table, or tabular factor, specified in the plan for actuarial equivalence;

(B) The annual amount of the straight life annuity commencing at the annuity starting date that has the same actuarial present value as the particular form of benefit payable, computed using a 5.5 percent interest assumption and the applicable mortality table for the distribution under §1.417(e)–1(d)(2); or

(C) The annual amount of the straight life annuity commencing at the annuity starting date that has the same actuarial present value as the particular form of benefit payable (computed using the applicable interest rate for the distribution under §1.417(e)–1(d)(3) and the applicable mortality table for the distribution under §1.417(e)–1(d)(2)), divided by 1.05.

(ii) *Special rule for distributions in plan years beginning in 2004 and 2005*. For a distribution to which section 417(e)(3) applies and which has an annuity starting date occurring in plan years beginning in 2004 or 2005, except as provided in section 101(d)(3) of the Pension Funding Equity Act of 2004, Public Law 108–218 (118 Stat. 596), the actuarially equivalent straight life annuity benefit is the greater of—

(A) The annual amount of the straight life annuity commencing at the annuity starting date that has the same actuarial present value as the particular form of benefit payable, computed using the interest rate and mortality table, or tabular factor, specified in the plan for actuarial equivalence; or

(B) The annual amount of the straight life annuity commencing at the annuity starting date that has the same actuarial present value as the particular form of benefit payable, computed using a 5.5 percent interest assumption and the applicable mortality table for the distribution under §1.417(e)–1(d)(2).

(4) *Certain benefit forms for which no adjustment is required*—(i) *In general*. For purposes of the adjustments described in this paragraph (c), the following benefits are not taken into account:

(A) Survivor benefits payable to a surviving spouse under a qualified joint and survivor annuity (as defined in section 417(b)) to the extent that such benefits would not be payable if the participant's benefit were not paid in the form of a qualified joint and survivor annuity.

(B) Ancillary benefits that are not directly related to retirement benefits, such as preretirement disability benefits not in excess of the qualified disability benefit, preretirement incidental death benefits (including a qualified preretirement survivor annuity), and post-retirement medical benefits.

(ii) *Rules of application*—(A) *Social security supplements*. Although a social security supplement described in section 411(a)(9) and §1.411(a)–7(c)(4) may be an ancillary benefit, it is included in determining the annual benefit because it is payable upon retirement and therefore is directly related to retirement income benefits.

(B) *Qualified joint and survivor annuities combined with other distributions*. If benefits are paid partly in the form of a qualified joint and survivor annuity (QJSA) and partly in some other form (such as a single-sum distribution), the rule of paragraph (c)(4)(i)(A) of this section (under which survivor benefits are not included in determining the annual benefit) applies to the survivor annuity payments under the portion of the benefit that is paid in the form of a QJSA.

(5) *Exception for certain automatic benefit increase features*—(i) *General rule*. Notwithstanding paragraph (b)(1)(i)(B) of this section, no adjustment is required to a benefit that is paid in a form that is not a straight life annuity to take into account the inclusion in that form of an automatic benefit increase feature, as described in paragraph (c)(5)(ii) of this section, if:

(A) The benefit is paid in a form to which section 417(e)(3) does not apply.

(B) The plan satisfies the requirements of paragraph (c)(5)(iii) of this section.

(ii) *Definition of automatic benefit increase feature*. An automatic benefit increase feature is included in a form of benefit if that form provides for automatic, periodic increases to the benefits paid in that form, such as a form of benefit that automatically increases the benefit paid under that form annually according to a specified percentage or objective index, or a form of benefit that automatically increases the benefit paid in that form to share favorable investment returns on plan assets.

(iii) *Requirements*. A plan satisfies the requirements of this paragraph (c)(5)(iii) with respect to a form of benefit that includes an automatic benefit increase feature if the form of benefit without regard to the automatic benefit increase feature satisfies the requirements of section 415(b) and this section, and the plan provides that in no event will the amount payable to the participant under the form of benefit in any limitation year be greater than the section 415(b) limit applicable at the annuity starting date (which is the lesser of the age-adjusted section 415(b)(1)(A) dollar limit described in paragraph (a)(1)(i) of this section or the section 415(b)(1)(B) compensation limit described in paragraph (a)(1)(ii) of this section), as increased in subsequent years pursuant to section 415(d) and §1.415(d)–1. If the form of benefit without regard to the automatic benefit increase feature is not a straight life annuity, then the preceding sentence is applied by reducing the section 415(b) limit applicable at the annuity starting date to an actuarially equivalent amount (determined using the assumptions specified in paragraph (c)(2)(ii) of this section) that takes into account the death benefits under the form of benefit (other than the survivor portion of a QJSA).

(6) *Examples*. The following examples illustrate the provisions of this paragraph (c). For purposes of these examples, except as otherwise stated, actuarial equivalence under the plan is determined using a 5 percent interest assumption and the mortality table that applies under section 417(e)(3) as of January 1, 2003. It is assumed for purposes of these examples that the interest rate that applies under section 417(e)(3) and §1.417(e)–1(d)(3) for relevant time periods is 5.25 percent and that the mortality table that applies under section 417(e)(3) and §1.417(e)–1(d)(2) for relevant time periods is the mortality table that applies under section 417(e)(3) as of January 1, 2003. In addition, it is assumed that all participants discussed in these examples have at least ten years of service with the employer and at least ten years of participation in the plan at issue, all payments other than a payment of a single sum are made monthly, on the first day of each calendar month, and each plan's normal retirement age is 65. The examples are as follows:

Example 1. (i) *Facts*. Plan A provides a single-sum distribution determined as the actuarial present value of the straight life annuity payable at the actual retirement date. Plan A provides that a participant's single sum is determined as the greater of the present value determined using the otherwise applicable actuarial assumptions of the plan and the present value determined using the applicable interest rate and the applicable mortality table for the distribution under section 417(e)(3). In accordance with §1.417(e)–1(d)(1), Plan A also provides that the single sum is not less than the actuarial present value of the accrued benefit payable at normal retirement age, determined using the applicable interest rate and the applicable mortality table under section 417(e)(3) and §1.417(e)–1(d). Participant M retires at age 65 with a benefit under the plan formula (and before the application of section 415) of $152,619 and elects to receive a distribution in the form of a single sum. Under the plan and before the application of section 415, the amount of the single sum is $1,800,002 (which is based on the 5 percent interest rate and applicable mortality table as of January 1, 2003, since that present value is greater than the present value that would have been determined using the applicable interest rate (5.25 percent) and the applicable mortality table (the January 1, 2003, table) for the distribution under section 417(e)(3)).

(ii) *Conclusion*. For purposes of this section, the annual benefit is the greatest of the annual amount of the actuarially equivalent straight life annuity commencing at the same age (determined using the plan's actuarial factors), the annual amount of the actuarially equivalent straight life annuity commencing at the same age (determined using a 5.5 percent interest assumption and the applicable mortality table for the distribution under §1.417(e)–1(d)(2)), and the annual amount of the actuarially equivalent straight life annuity commencing at the same age (determined using the applicable interest rate and applicable mortality table for the distribution under §§1.417(e)–1(d)(2) and (d)(3)) divided by 1.05. Based on the factors used in the plan to determine the actuarially equivalent lump sum (in this case, an interest rate of 5 percent and the applicable mortality table as of January 1, 2003), $1,800,002 payable as a single sum is actuarially equivalent to an immediate straight life annuity at age 65 of $152,619. A single sum payment of $1,800,002 is actuarially equivalent to an immediate straight life annuity at age 65 of $159,105, using a 5.5 percent interest assumption and the applicable mortality table under §1.417(e)–1(d)(2). Based on the applicable interest rate and the applicable mortality table for the distribution under §§1.417(e)–1(d)(2) and (d)(3), $1,800,002 payable as a single sum is actuarially equivalent to an immediate straight life annuity at age 65 of $155,853. $148,432 is the result when this annual amount is divided by 1.05. With respect to the single-sum distribution, M's annual benefit for purposes of section 415(b) is equal to the greatest of the three resulting amounts ($152,619, $159,105, and $148,432), or $159,105.

Example 2. (i) *Facts*. The facts are the same as in *Example 1*, except that Participant M elects to receive his benefit in the form of a 10-year certain and life annuity. Applying the plan's actuarial equivalence factors, the benefit payable in this form is $146,100.

(ii) *Conclusion*. Since the form of benefit elected by M is a form of benefit to which section 417(e)(3) does not apply, the annual benefit for purposes of this section is the greater of the annual amount of the plan's straight life annuity commencing at the same age or the annual amount of the actuarially equivalent straight life annuity commencing at the same age, determined using a 5 percent interest rate and the applicable mortality table described in §1.417(e)–1(d)(2) for that annuity starting date. In this case, the straight life annuity payable under the plan commencing at the same age is $152,619. Because the plan's factors for actuarial equivalence in this case are the same standardized actuarial factors required to be applied to determine the actuarially equivalent straight life annuity, the actuarially equivalent straight life annuity using the required standardized factors is also $152,619. With respect to the 10-year certain and life annuity distribution, M's annual benefit is equal to the greater of the two resulting amounts ($152,619 and $152,619), or $152,619.

Example 3. (i) *Facts.* The facts are the same as in *Example 1.* Participant M retires at age 62 with a benefit under the plan (before the application of section 415) of $100,000 (after application of the plan's early retirement factors) and a Social Security supplement of $10,000 per year payable until age 65. N chooses to receive the accrued benefit in the form of a straight life annuity. The Plan has no provisions under which the actuarial value of the Social Security supplement can be paid as a level annuity for life.

(ii) *Conclusion.* Because the form of benefit elected by M is a form of benefit to which section 417(e)(3) does not apply and because the plan does not provide for a straight life annuity beginning at age 62, the annual benefit for purposes of this section is the annual amount of the straight life annuity commencing at age 62 that is actuarially equivalent to the distribution stream of $110,000 for three years and $100,000 thereafter, where actuarial equivalence is determined using a 5 percent interest rate and the applicable mortality table described in §1.417(e)–1(d)(2) for the annuity starting date. In this case, the actuarially equivalent straight life annuity is $102,180. Accordingly, with respect to this distribution stream, N's annual benefit is equal to $102,180. The results are the same without regard to whether the Social Security supplement is a QSUPP (as defined in §1.401(a)(4)–12).

Example 4. (i) *Facts.* Plan B is a defined benefit plan that provides a benefit equal to 100 percent of a participant's average compensation for the period of the participant's high-3 years of service, payable as a straight life annuity. For a married participant who does not elect another form of benefit, the benefit is payable in the form of a joint and 100 percent survivor annuity benefit that is a QJSA within the meaning of section 417 and that is reduced from the straight life annuity. For purposes of determining the amount of this QJSA, the plan provides that the reduction is only half of the reduction that would normally apply under the actuarial assumptions specified in the plan for determining actuarial equivalence of optional forms. The plan also provides that a married participant can elect to receive the plan benefits as a straight life annuity, or in the form of a single sum distribution that is the actuarial equivalent of the joint and 100 percent survivor annuity determined using the applicable interest rate and the applicable mortality table under section 417(e)(3) and §1.417(e)–1(d). Participant O elects, with spousal consent, a single-sum distribution.

(ii) *Conclusion.* The special rule that disregards the value of the survivor portion of a QJSA set forth in paragraph (c)(4)(i) of this section only applies to a benefit that is payable in the form of a qualified joint and survivor annuity. Any other form of benefit must be adjusted to a straight life annuity in accordance with paragraph (c)(1) of this section. Accordingly, because the benefit payable under the plan in the form of a single-sum distribution is actuarially equivalent to a straight life annuity that is greater than 100 percent of a participant's average compensation for the period of the participant's high-3 years of service, the limitation of section 415(b)(1)(B) has been exceeded.

Example 5. (i) *Facts.* Plan C is a defined benefit plan that provides an option to receive the benefit in the form of a joint and 100 percent survivor annuity with a 10-year certain feature, where the survivor beneficiary is the participant's spouse.

(ii) *Conclusion.* Since this form of benefit is not subject to section 417(e)(3), for a participant at age 65, the annual benefit with respect to the joint and 100 percent survivor annuity with a 10-year certain feature is determined for purposes of this section as the greater of the annual amount of the straight life annuity payable to the participant under the plan at age 65 (if any), or the annual amount of the straight life annuity commencing at age 65 that has the same actuarial present value as the joint and 100 percent survivor annuity with a 10-year certain feature (but excluding the survivor annuity payments pursuant to paragraph (c)(4)(i)(A) of this section), computing using a 5 percent interest assumption and the applicable mortality table described in §1.417(e)–1(d)(2) for the annuity starting date. This latter amount is equal to the product of the annual payments under this optional form of benefit and the factor that provides for actuarial equivalence between a straight life annuity and a 10-year certain and life annuity (with no annuity for the survivor) computed using a 5 percent interest rate and the applicable mortality table described in §1.417(e)–1(d)(2) for the annuity starting date.

Example 6. (i) *Facts.* Plan E provides a benefit at age 65 of a straight life annuity equal to the lesser of 90 percent of the participant's average compensation for the period of the participant's high-3 years of service and $148,500. Upon retirement at age 65, the optional forms of benefit available to a participant include payment of a QJSA with annual payments equal to 50 percent of the annual payments under the straight life annuity, along with a single-sum distribution that is actuarially equivalent (determined as the greater of the single sum calculated using a 5 percent interest assumption and the section 417(e)(3)(A)(ii)(I) mortality table in effect on January 1, 2003, and the single sum calculated using the section 417(e)(3)(A)(ii)(II) applicable interest rate and the section 417(e)(3)(A)(ii)(I) applicable mortality table for the distribution) to 50 percent of the annual payments under the straight life annuity. Participant Q retires at age 65. Q's average compensation for the period of Q's high-3 years of service is $100,000. Q elects to receive a distribution in the optional form of benefit described above, under which the annual payments under the QJSA are $45,000 and the single-sum distribution is equal to $530,734. Q's spouse is 3 years younger than Q.

(ii) *Determination of annual benefit.* Q's annual benefit under Plan E for purposes of section 415(b) is determined as the sum of the annual benefit attributable to the QJSA portion of the distribution and the annual benefit attributable to the single-sum portion of the distribution.

(iii) *Annual benefit attributable to QJSA portion.* Because survivor benefits are not taken into account in determining the annual benefit attributable to the QJSA portion of the distribution, the annual benefit attributable to the QJSA portion of the distribution is determined as if that distribution were a straight life annuity of $45,000 per year commencing at age 65. Thus, no form adjustment is needed to determine the annual benefit attributable to the QJSA portion of the distribution, and the annual benefit attributable to the QJSA portion of the benefit is $45,000.

(iv) *Annual benefit attributable to single sum portion.* The annual benefit attributable to the single sum portion of the distribution is determined as the greatest of the annual amount of the actuarially equivalent straight life annuity commencing at the same age (determined using the plan's actuarial factors), the annual amount of the actuarially equivalent straight life annuity commencing at the same age (determined using a 5.5 percent interest assumption and the applicable mortality table under §1.417(e)–1(d)(2) for the distribution), and the annual amount of the actuarially equivalent straight life annuity commencing at the same age (determined using the applicable interest rate and applicable mortality table under section 417(e)(3) and §§1.417(e)–1(d)(2) and (d)(3) for the distribution) divided by 1.05. With respect to the single-sum distribution, the annual amount of the actuarially equivalent straight life annuity commencing at the same age determined using the plan's actuarial factors is equal to $45,954. The annual amount of the actuarially equivalent straight life annuity commencing at the same age determined using a 5.5 percent interest assumption and the applicable mortality table under §1.417(e)–1(d)(2) for the distribution is $46,912. The actuarially equivalent straight life annuity commencing at the same age determined using the applicable interest rate and the applicable mortality table under section 417(e)(3) and §§1.417(e)–1(d)(2) and (d)(3) for the distribution is equal to $45,954. This amount divided by 1.05 is equal to $43,766. Thus, the annual benefit attributable to the single sum portion of the benefit is $46,912.

(v) *Conclusion.* Q's annual benefit under the optional form of benefit for purposes of section 415(b) is equal to the sum of the annual benefit attributable to the QJSA portion of the distribution and the annual benefit attributable to the single sum portion of the distribution, or $91,912. Because Q's average compensation for the period of Q's high-3 years of service is $100,000, the distribution satisfies the compensation limit of section 415(b)(1)(B).

Example 7. (i) *Facts.* Plan D is a defined benefit plan with a normal retirement age of 65. The normal retirement benefit under Plan D (and the only life annuity available under Plan D) is a life annuity with a fixed increase of 2 percent per year. The increase applies to the benefit provided in the prior year and is thus compounded. The plan provides that the benefit is limited to the lesser of 84 percent of the participant's average compensation for the period of the participant's high-3 years of service or 84 percent of the age-adjusted section 415(b)(1)(A) dollar limit (which is assumed to be $180,000 at age 65). Plan D does not incorporate the section 415(d) cost-of-living adjustments to the section 415(b) limits for limitation years following the limitation year in which a participant incurs a severance from employment. Participant P's retires at age 65, at which time P's average compensation for the period of P's high-3 years of service is $165,000. Under Plan D, P commences receiving benefits in the form of a life annuity of $138,600 with a fixed increase of 2 percent per year.

(ii) *Conclusion.* Because Plan D does not provide for a straight life annuity and the form of benefit is not subject to section 417(e)(3), P's annual benefit for purposes of section 415(b) is the annual amount of the straight life annuity, commencing at age 65, that is actuarially equivalent to the distribution stream of $138,600 with a fixed increase of 2 percent per year, where actuarial equivalence is determined using a 5 percent interest rate and the applicable mortality table for the distribution under section 417(e)(3) and §1.417(e)–1(d)(2). In order to satisfy the requirements of section 415 and this section, this annual benefit must not exceed 100 percent of the average compensation for the period of the participant's high-3 years of service, or $165,000. Using a 5 percent interest rate and the section 417(e)(3) applicable mortality table for the distribution, the actuarially equivalent straight life annuity is $165,453, which exceeds $165,000. Accordingly, the plan fails to satisfy the compensation-based limitation of section 415(b)(1)(B).

Example 8. (i) *Facts.* The facts are the same as in *Example 7*, except that Plan D incorporates by reference the section 415(d) cost-of-living adjustments to the section 415(b) limits as described in §1.415(a)–1(d)(3)(v) and Plan D provides that the benefit is limited to the applicable section 415(b) limit. Under Plan D, P commences receiving benefits at age 65 in the form of a life annuity of $138,221 with a fixed increase of 2 percent per year.

(ii) *Conclusion.* Because Plan D does not provide for a straight life annuity and the form of benefit is not subject to section 417(e)(3), P's annual benefit for purposes of section 415(b) is the annual amount of the straight life annuity, commencing at age 65, that is actuarially equivalent to the distribution stream of $138,221 with a fixed increase of 2 percent per year, where actuarial equivalence is determined using a 5 percent interest rate and the applicable mortality table for P's annuity starting date under section 417(e)(3) and §1.417(e)–1(d)(2). In order to satisfy the requirements of section 415(b) and this section, this annual benefit must not exceed 100 percent of P's average compensation for the period of P's high-3 years of service, or $165,000. Using a 5 percent interest rate and the section 417(e)(3) applicable mortality table for the distribution, the actuarially equivalent straight life annuity is $165,000, which does not exceed $165,000. Accordingly, the plan satisfies the compensation-based limitation of section 415(b)(1)(B).

(iii) *Section 415(d) adjustments.* In addition to the fixed 2 percent per year automatic increase, P's benefit will be increased in limitation years following the limitation year in which P retires in accordance with the plan provisions that incorporate by reference the section 415(d) cost-of-living adjustments to the section 415(b) limits (or, if Plan D did not incorporate by reference the section 415(d) adjustments, P's benefit may be increased pursuant to plan amendments that comply with the safe harbors provided in §1.415(d)–1(a)(5) or (6)), and such increases will not cause P's benefit to violate the requirements of section 415(b). For example, if in a later limitation year the applicable section 415(b) limit is increased by 3 percent pursuant to section 415(d) and §1.415(d)–1, P's benefit payable under Plan D will be increased by both the fixed automatic 2 percent per year increase and by the 3 percent section 415(d) cost-of-living adjustment. The effect of the combined increases may result in P's benefits for a year exceeding the then applicable dollar limit under section 415(b), but the plan will not violate section 415(b).

Example 9. (i) *Facts.* The facts are the same as in *Example 7*, except that the plan provides that benefits are limited to the lesser of 100 percent of the participant's average compensation for the period of the participant's high-3 years of service or 100 percent of the age-adjusted section 415(b)(1)(A) dollar limit. Assume that P retires at age 65 with a benefit in the form of a life annuity of $165,000 per year with a fixed increase of 2 percent per year. Additionally, assume that Plan D incorporates by reference the section 415(d) cost-of-living adjustments to the section 415(b) limits as described in §1.415(a)–1(d)(3)(v) and the plan provides pursuant to paragraph (c)(5) of this section that in no event will a benefit payable from the plan, as increased by the fixed increase of 2 percent per year, be greater than the section 415(b) limit applicable as of the annuity starting date for the benefit (increased pursuant to the rules of section 415(d) and §1.415(d)–1).

(ii) *Conclusion.* The benefit payable to P at age 65 is not required to be adjusted to take into account the fixed increase of 2 percent per year. This is because the benefit payable to P satisfies the requirements of section 415(b) without regard to the fixed increase of 2 percent per year, and pursuant to paragraph (c)(5) of this section, the plan provides that the benefit payable to P, as increased by the fixed increase of 2 percent per year, will never be greater than the section 415(b) limit applicable as of P's annuity starting date (increased in subsequent limitation years pursuant to the rules of section 415(d) and §1.415(d)–1).

(iii) *Section 415(d) adjustments.* In addition to the fixed 2 percent per year automatic increase, P's benefit will be increased in limitation years following the limitation year in which P retires in accordance with the plan provisions that incorporate by reference the section 415(d) cost-of-living adjustments to the section 415(b) limits (or, if Plan D did not incorporate by reference the section 415(d) adjustments, P's benefit may be increased pursuant to plan amendments that comply with the safe harbors provided in §1.415(d)–1(a)(5) or (6)), and such increases will not cause P's benefit to violate the requirements of section 415(b). However, pursuant to paragraph (c)(5)(iii) of this section, P's benefit during any limitation year, as increased by the 2 percent per year automatic increase feature and any plan provisions that incorporate by reference the section 415(d) cost-of-living adjustments or any plan amendments that increase P's benefits, cannot exceed the then applicable section 415(b) limit (as increased pursuant to section 415(d) and §1.415(d)–1).

Example 10. (i) *Facts.* Employer T maintains a defined benefit plan. Under the terms of the plan, all benefits in pay status (other than single sum payments) are adjusted upwards or downwards annually depending on an annual comparison of actual return on plan assets and an assumed interest rate of 4 percent. Thus, the plan does not offer a straight life annuity form of benefit, and the plan must determine for purposes of applying the section 415(b) limits the actuarially equivalent straight life annuity for benefits provided under the plan.

(ii) *Conclusion.* Benefits under the plan are paid in a form to which section 417(e)(3) does not apply. In determining the actuarially equivalent straight life annuity of benefits that are subject to the annual investment performance adjustment, the plan must assume a 5 percent return on plan assets. See paragraph (c)(2) of this section. Therefore, in determining the actuarially equivalent straight life annuity, the plan must assume that the form of benefit payable under the plan will be an annuity that increases annually by a factor equal to 1.05 divided by 1.04. This increasing annuity is then converted to an actuarially equivalent straight life annuity under paragraph (c)(2) of this section using a 5 percent interest rate and the applicable mortality table described in §1.417(e)–1(d)(2) for the relevant annuity starting date.

Example 11. (i) *Facts.* R is a participant in a defined benefit plan maintained by R's employer. Under the terms of the plan, R must make contributions to the plan in a stated amount to accrue benefits derived from employer contributions.

(ii) *Conclusion.* R's contributions are mandatory employee contributions within the meaning of section 411(c)(2)(C) and, thus, the annual benefit attributable to these contributions is not taken into account for purposes of testing the annual benefit derived from employer contributions against the applicable limitation on benefits. However, these contributions are treated as contributions to a defined contribution plan maintained by R's employer for purposes of section 415(c). See §1.415(c)–1(a)(2)(ii)(B). Accordingly, with respect to the current limitation year, the limitation on benefits (as described in paragraph (a)(1) of this section) is applicable to the annual benefit attributable to employer contributions to the defined benefit plan, and the limitation on contributions and other additions (as described in §1.415(c)–1) is applicable to the portion of the plan treated as a defined contribution plan, which consists of R's mandatory contributions. These same limitations would also apply if, instead of providing for mandatory employee contributions, the plan permitted voluntary employee contributions, because the portion of the plan attributable to voluntary employee contributions and earnings thereon is treated as a defined contribution plan maintained by the employer pursuant to section 414(k), and thus is not subject to the limitations of section 415(b).

Example 12. (i) *Facts.* V is a participant in a defined benefit plan maintained by V's employer. Under the terms of the plan, V must make contributions to the plan in a stated amount to accrue benefits derived from employer contributions. V's contributions are mandatory employee contributions within the meaning of section 411(c)(2)(C). Thus, the annual benefit attributable to these contributions is not taken into account for purposes of testing the annual benefit derived from employer contributions against the applicable limitation on benefits. V terminates employment and receives a distribution from the plan that includes V's mandatory employee contributions. Subsequently, V resumes employment with the employer maintaining the plan. V recommences participation in the plan and repays the prior distribution from the plan (including the portion of the distribution that included V's prior mandatory employee contributions to the plan) with reasonable interest.

(ii) *Conclusion.* In determining V's annual benefit under the plan for purposes of applying the limitations of section 415(b), no portion of V's repayment of the prior distribution is treated as employee contributions. See paragraphs (b)(2)(ii)(C), (D) and (E) of this section. However, V's annual benefit under the plan is determined by excluding the portion of the annual benefit attributable to V's employee contributions to the plan made both prior to the first distribution and during V's subsequent recommencement of plan participation.

(d) *Adjustment to section 415(b)(1)(A) dollar limit for commencement before age 62*—(1) *General rule*—(i) *Calculation using statutory factors*. For a distribution with an annuity starting date that occurs before the participant attains the age of 62, the age-adjusted section 415(b)(1)(A) dollar limit generally is determined as the actuarial equivalent of the annual amount of a straight life annuity commencing at the annuity starting date that has the same actuarial present value as a deferred straight life annuity commencing at age 62, where annual payments under the straight life annuity commencing at age 62 are equal to the dollar limitation of section 415(b)(1)(A) (as adjusted pursuant to section 415(d) and §1.415(d)–1 for the limitation year), and where the actuarially equivalent straight life annuity is computed using a 5 percent interest rate and the applicable mortality table under §1.417(e)–1(d)(2) that is effective for that annuity starting date (and expressing the participant's age based on completed calendar months as of the annuity starting date). However, if the plan has an immediately commencing straight life annuity payable both at age 62 and the age of benefit commencement, then the age-adjusted section 415(b)(1)(A) dollar limit is equal to the lesser of—

(A) The limit as otherwise determined under this paragraph (d)(1)(i); and

(B) The amount determined under paragraph (d)(1)(ii) of this section.

(ii) *Calculation using plan factors*. The amount determined under this paragraph (d)(1)(ii) is equal to the section 415(b)(1)(A) dollar limit (as adjusted pursuant to section 415(d) and §1.415(d)–1 for the limitation year) multiplied by the ratio of the annual amount of the immediately commencing straight life annuity under the plan to the annual amount of the straight life annuity under the plan commencing at age 62, with both annual amounts determined without applying the rules of section 415.

(2) *Mortality adjustments*—(i) *In general*. For purposes of determining the actuarially equivalent amount described in paragraph (d)(1)(i) of this section, to the extent that a forfeiture does not occur upon the participant's death before the annuity starting date, no adjustment is made to reflect the probability of the participant's death between the annuity starting date and the participant's attainment of age 62, unless the plan provides for such an adjustment. To the extent that a forfeiture occurs upon the participant's death before the annuity starting date, an adjustment must be made to reflect the probability of the participant's death between the annuity starting date and the participant's attainment of age 62.

(ii) *No forfeiture deemed to occur where qualified preretirement survivor annuity payable*. For purposes of paragraphs (d)(2)(i) and (e)(2)(i) of this section, a plan is permitted to treat no forfeiture as occurring upon a participant's death if the plan does not charge participants for providing a qualified preretirement survivor annuity (QPSA) (as defined in section 417(c)) on the participant's death, but only if the plan applies this treatment both for adjustments before age 62 and adjustments after age 65. Thus, in such a case, the plan is permitted to provide that, in computing the adjusted dollar limitation under section 415(b)(1)(A), no adjustment is made to reflect the probability of a participant's death after the annuity starting date and before age 62 or after age 65 and before the annuity starting date.

(3) *Exception for certain participants of certain governmental plans*. Pursuant to section 415(b)(2)(G) and (H), no age adjustment is made to the dollar limit for commencement before age 62 for any qualified participant. For this purpose, a qualified participant is a participant in a defined benefit plan that is maintained by a state, Indian tribal government (as defined in section 7701(a)(40)), or any political subdivision of a state or Indian tribal government with respect to whom the service taken into account in determining the amount of the benefit under the defined benefit plan includes at least 15 years of service of the participant—

(i) As a full-time employee of any police department or fire department that is organized and operated by the state, Indian tribal government, or political subdivision maintaining such defined benefit plan to provide police protection, firefighting services, or emergency medical services for any area within the jurisdiction of such state, Indian tribal government, or political subdivision; or

(ii) As a member of the Armed Forces of the United States.

(4) *Exception for survivor and disability benefits under governmental plans*. Pursuant to section 415(b)(2)(I), no age adjustment is made to the dollar limit for commencement before age 62 for a distribution from a governmental plan (as defined in section 414(d)) on account of the participant's becoming disabled by reason of personal injuries or sickness, or as a result of the death of the participant.

(5) *Special rule for commercial airline pilots*. Pursuant to section 415(b)(9), no age adjustment is made to the dollar limit for early commencement on or after age 60 for a participant if—

(i) The participant is a commercial airline pilot;

(ii) The participant separates from service upon or after attaining age 60; and

(iii) As of the time of the participant's retirement, regulations prescribed by the Federal Aviation Administration require an individual to separate from service as a commercial airline pilot after attaining any age occurring on or after age 60 and before age 62.

(6) *No decrease in age-adjusted section 415(b)(1)(A) dollar limit on account of age or service*. Notwithstanding any other provision of this paragraph (d), the age-adjusted section 415(b)(1)(A) dollar limit applicable to a participant does not decrease on account of an increase in age or the performance of additional service.

(7) *Examples*. The following examples illustrate the application of this paragraph (d). For purposes of these examples, it is assumed that the dollar limitation under section 415(b)(1)(A) for all relevant years is $180,000, that the normal form of benefit under the plan is a straight life annuity payable beginning at age 65, and that all payments other than a payment of a single sum are made monthly, on the first day of each calendar month. The examples are as follows:

Example 1. (i) Plan A provides that early retirement benefits are determined by reducing the accrued benefit by 4 percent for each year that the early retirement age is less than age 65. Participant M retires at age 60 with exactly 30 years of service with a benefit (prior to the application of section 415) in the form of a straight life annuity of $100,000 payable at age 65, and is permitted to elect to commence benefits at any time between M's retirement and M's attainment of age 65. For example, M can elect to commence benefits at age 60 in the amount of $80,000, can wait until age 62 and commence benefits in the amount of $88,000, or can wait until age 65 and commence benefits in the amount of $100,000. Plan A provides a QPSA to all married participants without charge. Plan A provides (consistent with paragraph (d)(2)(ii) of this section) that, for purposes of adjusting the dollar limitation under section 415(b)(1)(A) for commencement before age 62 or after age 65, no forfeiture is treated as occurring upon a participant's death before retirement and, therefore, in computing the adjusted dollar limitation under section 415(b)(1)(A), no adjustment is made to reflect the probability of a participant's death after the annuity starting date and before age 62 or after age 65 and before the annuity starting date.

(ii) The age-adjusted section 415(b)(1)(A) dollar limit that applies for commencement of M's benefit at age 60 is the lesser of the section 415(b)(1)(A) dollar limit multiplied by the ratio of the annuity payable at age 60 to the annuity payable at age 62, or the straight life annuity payable at age 60 that is actuarially equivalent, using 5 percent interest and the applicable mortality table effective for that annuity starting date under section 417(e)(3)(A)(ii)(I) and §1.417(e)–1(d)(2), to the deferred annuity payable at age 62 of $180,000 per year. In this case, the age-adjusted section 415(b)(1)(A) dollar limit at age 60 is $156,229 (the lesser of $163,636 ($180,000* $80,000/$88,000) and $156,229 (the straight life annuity at age 60 that is actuarially equivalent to a deferred annuity of $180,000 commencing at age 62, determined using 5 percent interest and the applicable mortality table, without a mortality decrement for the period between 60 and 62)).

Example 2. (i) The facts are the same as in *Example 1*, except that participant M elects to retire at age 60, 6 months, and 21 days.

(ii) Under paragraph (d)(1)(i) of this section, M is treated as age 60 and 6 months (or, age 60.5). Absent the rule provided in paragraph (d)(6) of this section, the age-adjusted section 415(b)(1)(A) dollar limit that applies for commencement of M's benefit at age 60.5 is the lesser of the section 415(b)(1)(A) dollar limit multiplied by the ratio of the annuity payable at age 60.5 to the annuity payable at age 62, or the straight life annuity payable at age 60.5 that is actuarially equivalent, using 5 percent interest and the applicable mortality table for that annuity starting date under section 417(e)(3)(A)(ii)(I) and §1.417(e)–1(d)(2), to the deferred annuity payable at age 62 of $180,000 per year. The age-adjusted section 415(b)(1)(A) dollar limit at age 60.5 is $161,769 (the lesser of $167,727 ($180,000* $82,000/$88,000) and $161,769 (the straight life annuity at age 60.5 that is actuarially equivalent to a deferred annuity of $180,000 commencing at age 62, determined using 5 percent interest and the applicable mortality table, without a mortality decrement for the period between 60.5 and 62).

Example 3. (i) The facts are the same as in *Example 1*, except the plan provides that, if a participant has 30 or more years of service, no reduction applies for benefits commencing at age 62 and later.

(ii) Absent the rule provided in paragraph (d)(6) of this section, the age-adjusted section 415(b)(1)(A) dollar limit that applies for commencement of M's benefit at age 60 is the lesser of the section 415(b)(1)(A) dollar limit multiplied by the ratio of the annuity payable at age 60 to the annuity payable at age 62, or the straight life annuity payable at age 60 that is actuarially equivalent, using 5 percent interest and the applicable mortality table for that annuity starting date under section 417(e)(3)(A)(ii)(I) and §1.417(e)–1(d)(2), to the deferred annuity payable at age 62 of $180,000 per year. In this case, because M has 30 years of service and would be eligible for the unreduced early retirement benefit at age 62, the age-adjusted section 415(b)(1)(A) dollar limit at age 60 would be $144,000 (the lesser of $144,000 ($180,000* $80,000/$100,000) and $156,229 (the straight life annuity at age 60 that is actuarially equivalent to a deferred annuity of $180,000 commencing at age 62, determined using 5 percent interest and the applicable mortality table, without a mortality decrement for the period between 60 and 62).

(iii) However, at age 59 11/12 with 29 11/12 years of service, the age-adjusted section 415(b)(1)(A) dollar limit for M is $155,311 (the lesser of $162,955 ($180,000* $79,667/$88,000) and $155,311 (the straight life annuity at age 59 11/12 that is actuarially equivalent to a deferred annuity of $180,000 commencing at age 62, determined using 5 percent interest and the applicable mortality table, without a mortality decrement for the period between 59 and 62). Thus, after applying the rule provided in paragraph (d)(6) of this section, the age-adjusted section 415(b)(1)(A) dollar limit that applies for commencement of M's benefit at age 60 is $155,311.

Example 4. (i) The facts are the same as in *Example 1*, except that the plan provides that, if a participant has 30 or more years of service, then no reduction is made in early retirement benefits if the early retirement age is at least age 62 and, in the case of an early retirement age before age 62, the early retirement benefit is determined by reducing the accrued benefit by 4 percent for each year that the early retirement age is less than age 62.

(ii) The age-adjusted section 415(b)(1)(A) dollar limit that applies for commencement of M's benefit at age 60 is the lesser of the section 415(b)(1)(A) dollar limit multiplied by the ratio of the annuity payable at age 60 to the annuity payable at age 62, or the straight life annuity payable at age 60 that is actuarially equivalent, using 5 percent interest and the applicable mortality table for that annuity starting date under section 417(e)(3)(A)(ii)(I) and §1.417(e)–1(d)(2), to the deferred annuity payable at age 62 of $180,000 per year. In this case, because M has 30 years of service and would be eligible for the unreduced early retirement benefit at age 62, the age-adjusted section 415(b)(1)(A) dollar limit at age 60 is $156,229 (the lesser of $165,600 ($180,000* $92,000/$100,000) and $156,229 (the straight life annuity at age 60 that is actuarially equivalent to a deferred annuity of $180,000 commencing at age 62, determined using 5 percent interest and the applicable mortality table, without a mortality decrement for the period between 60 and 62).

Example 5. (i) The facts are the same as in *Example 1*, except that Participant M chooses to receive benefits in the form of a 10-year certain and life annuity under which payments are 97 percent of the periodic payments that would be made under the immediately commencing straight life annuity. Annual payments to M are 97 percent of $80,000, or $77,600. Additionally, M's average compensation for the period of M's high-3 years of service is $120,000. As in *Example 1*, the age-adjusted section 415(b)(1)(A) dollar limit at age 60 is $156,229.

(ii) In the case of a form of benefit to which section 417(e)(3) does not apply, the annual benefit for purposes of this section is the greater of the annual amount of the plan's straight life annuity commencing at the same age or the annual amount of the actuarially equivalent straight life annuity commencing at the same age, determined using a 5 percent interest rate and the applicable mortality table for that annuity starting date under section 417(e)(3)(A)(ii)(I) and §1.417(e)–1(d)(2). In this case, the straight life annuity payable under the plan commencing at the same age is $80,000. The annual amount of the straight life annuity that is actuarially equivalent to the $77,600 benefit payable as a 10-year certain and life annuity is determined by applying the required standardized factors (a 5 percent interest assumption and the applicable mortality under section 417(e)(3)(A)(ii)(I) and §1.417(e)–1(d)(2), and is $79,416. With respect to the 10-year certain and life annuity commencing at age 62, M's annual benefit is equal to the greater of the two resulting amounts ($80,000 and $79,416), or $80,000. Because M's annual benefit is less than the age-adjusted section 415(b)(1)(A) dollar limit and is less than the section 415(b)(1)(B) compensation limit, M's benefit satisfies section 415.

Example 6. (i) Participant O is a full-time civilian employee of the Harbor Police Division of the State of X Port Authority. The Harbor Police Division provides police protection services. O performs clerical services for the Harbor Police Division. O is a participant in the defined benefit plan that is maintained by the State of X with respect to whom the years of service taken into account in determining the amount of the benefit under the plan includes 10 years of service working for the Harbor Police Division and 5 years of service as a member of the Armed Forces of the United States.

(ii) For a distribution with an annuity starting date that occurs before O attains the age of 62, there is no age adjustment to the section 415(b)(1)(A) dollar limit.

Example 7. (i) Participant R is a full-time employee of the Emergency Medical Service Department of County Y (which is not a part of a police or fire department) who performs services as a driver of an ambulance. R is a participant in the defined benefit plan that is maintained by County Y with respect to whom the years of service taken into account in determining the amount of the benefit under the plan includes 15 years of service working for County Y. R does not have service credit for time in the Armed Forces of the United States.

(ii) The age adjustments to the limitations of section 415(b)(1)(A) pursuant to section 415(b)(2)(C) and (D) will apply if R commences receiving a distribution at an age to which either of those adjustments applies.

(e) *Adjustment to section 415(b)(1)(A) dollar limit for commencement after age 65*—(1) *General rule*—(i) *Calculation using statutory factors.* For a distribution with an annuity starting date that occurs after the participant attains the age of 65, the age-adjusted section 415(b)(1)(A) dollar limit generally is determined as the actuarial equivalent of the annual amount of a straight life annuity commencing at the annuity starting date that has the same actuarial present value as a straight life annuity commencing at age 65, where annual payments under the straight life annuity commencing at age 65 are equal to the dollar limitation of section 415(b)(1)(A) (as adjusted pursuant to section 415(d) and §1.415(d)–1 for the limitation year), and where the actuarially equivalent straight life annuity is computed using a 5 percent interest rate and the applicable mortality table under §1.417(e)–1(d)(2) that is effective for that annuity starting date (and expressing the participant's age based on completed calendar months as of the annuity starting date). However, if the plan has an immediately commencing straight life annuity payable as of the annuity starting date and an immediately commencing straight life annuity payable at age 65, then the age-adjusted section 415(b)(1)(A) dollar limit is equal to the lesser of—

(A) The limit as otherwise determined under this paragraph (e)(1)(i); and

(B) The amount determined under paragraph (e)(1)(ii) of this section.

(ii) *Calculation using plan factors*. The amount determined under this paragraph (e)(1)(ii) is equal to the section 415(b)(1)(A) dollar limit (as adjusted pursuant to section 415(d) and §1.415(d)–1 for the limitation year) multiplied by the adjustment ratio described in paragraph (e)(2)(i) of this section.

(2) *Adjustment ratio*—(i) *General rule*. For purposes of applying the rule of paragraph (e)(1)(ii) of this section, the adjustment ratio is equal to the ratio of the annual amount of the adjusted immediately commencing straight life annuity under the plan described in paragraph (e)(2)(ii) of this section to the adjusted age 65 straight life annuity described in paragraph (e)(2)(iii) of this section.

(ii) *Adjusted immediately commencing straight life annuity*. The adjusted immediately commencing straight life annuity that is used for purposes of paragraph (e)(2)(i) of this section is the annual amount of the immediately commencing straight life annuity payable to the participant, computed disregarding the participant's accruals after age 65 but including actuarial adjustments even if those actuarial adjustments are applied to offset accruals. For this purpose, the annual amount of the immediately commencing straight life annuity is determined without applying the rules of section 415.

(iii) *Adjusted age 65 straight life annuity*. The adjusted age 65 straight life annuity that is used for purposes of paragraph (e)(2)(i) of this section is the annual amount of the straight life annuity that would be payable under the plan to a hypothetical participant who is 65 years old and has the same accrued benefit (with no actuarial increases for commencement after age 65) as the participant receiving the distribution (determined disregarding the participant's accruals after age 65 and without applying the rules of section 415).

(3) *Mortality adjustments*—(i) *In general*. For purposes of determining the actuarially equivalent amount described in paragraph (e)(1)(i) of this section, to the extent that a forfeiture does not occur upon the participant's death before the annuity starting date, no adjustment is made to reflect the probability of the participant's death between the participant's attainment of age 65 and the annuity starting date. To the extent that a forfeiture occurs upon the participant's death before the annuity starting date, an adjustment must be made to reflect the probability of the participant's death between the participant's attainment of age 65 and the annuity starting date.

(ii) *No forfeiture deemed to occur where QPSA payable*. See paragraph (d)(2)(ii) of this section for a rule deeming no forfeiture to occur if the plan does not charge participants for providing a QPSA on the participant's death.

(4) *Examples*. The following examples illustrate the application of this paragraph (e):

Example 1. (i) Plan A provides that monthly benefits payable upon commencement after normal retirement age (which is age 65) are increased by 0.5 percent for each month of delay in commencement after attainment of normal retirement age. Plan A provides a QPSA to all married participants without charge. Plan A provides (consistent with paragraph (d)(2)(ii) of this section) that, for purposes of adjusting the dollar limitation under section 415(b)(1)(A) for commencement before age 62 or after age 65, no adjustment is made to reflect the probability of a participant's death between the annuity starting date and the participant's attainment of age 62 or between the age of 65 and the annuity starting date. The normal form of benefit under Plan A is a straight life annuity commencing at age 65. Plan A does not provide additional benefit accruals once a participant is credited with 30 years of service. Participant M was credited with 30 years of service under Plan A when M attained age 65. M retires at age 70 on January 1, 2008, with a benefit (prior to the application of section 415) that is payable monthly in the form of a straight life annuity of $195,000, which reflects the actuarial increase of 30 percent applied to the accrued benefit of $150,000. It is assumed that all payments under Plan A, other than a payment of a single sum, are made monthly, on the first day of each calendar month. It is also assumed that the dollar limit in 2008 is $185,000.

(ii) The age-adjusted section 415(b)(1)(A) dollar limit at age 70 is the lesser of the section 415(b)(1)(A) dollar limit multiplied by the ratio of the adjusted immediately commencing straight life annuity payable at age 70 (computed disregarding the rules of section 415 and accruals after age 65, but including actuarial adjustments) to the adjusted age 65 straight life annuity (computed disregarding the rules of section 415 and any accruals after age 65), or the straight life annuity payable at age 70 that is actuarially equivalent, using 5 percent interest and the applicable mortality table for that annuity starting date under section 417(e)(3)(A)(ii)(I) and §1.417(e)–1(d)(2), to the straight life annuity payable at age 65, where annual payments under the straight life annuity payable at age 65 are equal to the dollar limitation of section 415(b)(1)(A). In this case, the age-adjusted section 415(b)(1)(A) dollar limit at age 70 is $240,500 (the lesser of $240,500 ($185,000* $195,000/$150,000) and $271,444 (the straight life annuity at age 70 that is actuarially equivalent to an annuity of $185,000 commencing at age 65, determined using 5 percent interest and the applicable mortality table, without a mortality decrement for the period between 65 and 70)).

Example 2. (i) The facts are the same as in *Example 1*, except that Plan A does not limit benefit accruals to 30 years of credited service, and thus M accrues benefits between ages 65 and 70.

(ii) Since M's accruals after attaining age 65 are disregarded for purposes of determining the age-adjusted section 415(b)(1)(A) dollar limit applicable to M at age 70, the result is the same as in *Example 1*.

Example 3. (i) The facts are the same as in *Example 1*, except that Plan A does not limit benefit accruals to 30 years of credited service. However, benefit accruals after an employee has reached normal retirement age (age 65), are offset by the actuarial increase that the plan provides for commencement of benefits after normal retirement age.

(ii) The result is the same as in *Example 1*, even if the actuarial increases for post-age 65 benefit commencement provided under Plan A do or do not fully offset M's benefit accruals after attaining age 65. This is because benefit accruals after age 65 are disregarded for purposes of determining the age-adjusted section 415(b)(1)(A) dollar limit applicable to M after age 65.

(f) *Total annual payments not in excess of $10,000*—(1) *In general*. Pursuant to section 415(b)(4), the annual benefit (without regard to the age at which benefits commence) payable with respect to a participant under any defined benefit plan is not considered to exceed the limitations on benefits described in section 415(b)(1) and in paragraph (a)(1) of this section if—

(i) The benefits (other than benefits not taken into account in the computation of the annual benefit under the rules of paragraph (b) or (c) of this section) payable with respect to the participant under the plan and all other defined benefit plans of the employer do not in the aggregate exceed $10,000 (as adjusted under paragraph (g) of this section) for the limitation year, or for any prior limitation year; and

(ii) The employer (or a predecessor employer) has not at any time maintained a defined contribution plan in which the participant participated.

(2) *Computation of benefits for purposes of applying the $10,000 amount.* For purposes of paragraph (f)(1)(i) of this section, the benefits payable with respect to the participant under a plan for a limitation year reflect all amounts payable under the plan for the limitation year (other than benefits not taken into account in the computation of the annual benefit under the rules of paragraph (b) or (c) of this section), and are not adjusted for form of benefit or commencement date.

(3) *Special rule with respect to participants in multiemployer plans.* The special $10,000 exception set forth in paragraph (f)(1) of this section applies to a participant in a multiemployer plan described in section 414(f) without regard to whether that participant ever participated in one or more other plans maintained by an employer who also maintains the multiemployer plan, provided that none of such other plans were maintained as a result of collective bargaining involving the same employee representative as the multiemployer plan.

(4) *Special rule with respect to employee contributions.* Notwithstanding §§1.415(c)–1(a)(2)(ii)(B) and 1.415(c)–1(b)(3), mandatory employee contributions under a defined benefit plan described in paragraph (b)(2)(iii) of this section are not considered a separate defined contribution plan maintained by the employer for purposes of paragraph (f)(1)(ii) of this section. Thus, the special dollar limitation provided for in this paragraph (f) applies to a contributory defined benefit plan. Similarly, for purposes of this paragraph (f), an individual medical account under section 401(h) or an account for postretirement medical benefits established pursuant to section 419A(d)(1) is not considered a separate defined contribution plan maintained by the employer.

(5) *Examples.* The application of this paragraph (f) may be illustrated by the following examples. For purposes of these examples, it is assumed that each participant has 10 years of participation in the plan and service with the employer. The examples are as follows:

Example 1. (i) B is a participant in a defined benefit plan maintained by X Corporation, which provides for a benefit payable in the form of a straight life annuity beginning at age 65. B's average compensation for the period of B's high-3 years of service is $6,000. The plan does not provide for mandatory employee contributions, and at no time has B been a participant in a defined contribution plan maintained by X. With respect to the current limitation year, B's benefit under the plan (before the application of section 415) is $9,500.

(ii) Because annual payments under B's benefit do not exceed $10,000, and because B has at no time participated in a defined contribution plan maintained by X, the benefits payable under the plan are not considered to exceed the limitation on benefits otherwise applicable to B ($6,000).

(iii) This result would remain the same even if, under the terms of the plan, B's benefit of $9,500 were payable at age 60, or if the plan provided for mandatory employee contributions.

Example 2. (i) The facts are the same as in *Example 1*, except that the plan provides for a benefit payable in the form of a life annuity with a 10-year certain feature with annual payments of $9,500. Assume that, after the adjustment described in paragraph (c) of this section, B's actuarially equivalent straight life annuity (which is the annual benefit used for demonstrating compliance with section 415) for the current limitation year is $10,400.

(ii) For purposes of applying the special rule provided in this paragraph for total benefits not in excess of $10,000, there is no adjustment required if the retirement benefit payable under the plan is not in the form of a straight life annuity. Therefore, because B's retirement benefit does not exceed $10,000, B may receive the full $9,500 benefit without the otherwise applicable benefit limitations of this section being exceeded.

Example 3. (i) The facts are the same as in *Example 1*, except that the plan provides for a benefit payable in the form of a single sum and the amount of the single sum that is the actuarial equivalent of the straight life annuity payable to B ($9,500 annually), determined in accordance with the rules of section 417(e)(3) and §1.417(e)–1(d), is $95,000.

(ii) Because the amount payable to B for the limitation year would exceed $10,000, the rule of this paragraph (f) does not provide an exception from the generally applicable limits of section 415(b)(1) for the single-sum distribution. Thus, the otherwise applicable limits apply to the single-sum distribution, and a single-sum distribution of $95,000 would not satisfy the requirements of section 415(b). Limiting the single-sum distribution to $60,000 (the present value of the annuity that complies with the compensation-based limitation of section 415(b)(1)(B)) in order to satisfy section 415 would be an impermissible forfeiture under the requirements of section 411(a). Accordingly, the plan should not provide for a single-sum distribution in these circumstances.

(g) *Special rule for participation or service of less than 10 years*—(1) *Proration of dollar limit based on years of participation*—(i) *In general.* Pursuant to section 415(b)(5)(A), where a participant has less than 10 years of participation in the plan, the dollar limit described in paragraph (a)(1)(i) of this section (as adjusted pursuant to section 415(d), §1.415(d)–1, and paragraphs (d) and (e) of this section) is reduced by multiplying the otherwise applicable limitation by a fraction—

(A) The numerator of which is the number of years of participation in the plan (or 1, if greater); and

(B) The denominator of which is 10.

(ii) *Years of participation.* The following rules apply for purposes of determining a participant's years of participation for purposes of this paragraph (g)(1)—

(A) A participant is credited with a year of participation (computed to fractional parts of a year) for each accrual computation period for which the participant is credited with at least the number of hours of service (or period of service if the elapsed time method is used for benefit accrual purposes) required under the terms of the plan in order to accrue a benefit for the accrual computation period, and the participant is included as a plan participant under the eligibility provisions of the plan for at least one day of the accrual computation period. If these two conditions are met, the portion of a year of participation credited to the participant is equal to the amount of benefit accrual service credited to the participant for such accrual computation period. For example, if under the terms of a plan, a participant receives 1/10 of a year of benefit accrual service for an accrual computation period for each 200 hours of service, and the participant is credited with 1,000 hours of service for the period, the participant is credited with ½ a year of participation for purposes of section 415(b)(5)(A) and this paragraph (g)(1).

(B) A participant who is permanently and totally disabled within the meaning of section 415(c)(3)(C)(i) for an accrual computation period is credited with a year of participation with respect to that period for purposes of section 415(b)(5)(A) and this paragraph (g)(1).

(C) For a participant to receive a year of participation (or part thereof) for an accrual computation period for purposes of section 415(b)(5)(A) and this paragraph (g)(1), the plan must be established no later than the last day of such accrual computation period.

(D) No more than one year of participation may be credited for any 12-month period for purposes of section 415(b)(5)(A) and this paragraph (g)(1).

(2) *Proration of compensation limit and special rule for total annual payments less than $10,000 based on years of service*—(i) *In general*. Pursuant to section 415(b)(5)(B), where a participant has less than 10 years of service with the employer, the compensation limit described in paragraph (a)(1)(ii) of this section and the $10,000 amount under the special rule for small annual payments under paragraph (f) of this section are reduced by multiplying the otherwise applicable limitation by a fraction—

(A) The numerator of which is the number of years of service with the employer (or 1, if greater); and

(B) The denominator of which is 10.

(ii) *Years of service*—(A) *In general*. For purposes of applying this paragraph (g)(2), years of service must be determined on a reasonable and consistent basis. A plan is considered to be determining years of service on a reasonable and consistent basis for this purpose if, subject to the limits of paragraph (g)(2)(ii)(B) of this section, a participant is credited with a year of service (computed to fractional parts of a year) for each accrual computation period for which the participant is credited with at least the number of hours of service (or period of service if the elapsed time method is used for benefit accrual purposes) required under the terms of the plan in order to accrue a benefit for the accrual computation period.

(B) *Rules of application*. No more than one year of service may be credited for any 12-month period for purposes of section 415(b)(5)(B). In addition, only the participant's service with the employer or a predecessor employer (as defined in §1.415(f)–1(c)) may be taken into account in determining the participant's years of service for this purpose. Thus, if an employer does not maintain a former employer's plan, a participant's service with the former employer may be taken into account in determining the participant's years of service for purposes of this paragraph (g)(2) only if the former employer is a predecessor employer with respect to the employer pursuant to §1.415(f)–1(c)(2) (which defines predecessor employer to include, under certain circumstances, a former entity that antedates the employer).

(C) *Period of disability*. Notwithstanding the rules of paragraph (g)(2)(ii)(B) of this section, a plan is permitted to provide that a participant who is permanently and totally disabled within the meaning of section 415(c)(3)(C)(i) for an accrual computation period is credited with service with respect to that period for purposes of section 415(b)(5)(B).

(3) *Exception for survivor and disability benefits under governmental plans*. The requirements of this paragraph (g) (regarding participation or service of less than 10 years) do not apply to a distribution from a governmental plan (as defined in section 414(d)) on account of the participant's becoming disabled by reason of personal injuries or sickness, or as a result of the death of the participant.

(4) *Examples*. The provisions of this paragraph (g) may be illustrated by the following examples:

Example 1. (i) C begins employment with Employer A on January 1, 2005, at the age of 58. Employer A maintains only a noncontributory defined benefit plan which provides for a straight life annuity beginning at age 65 and uses the calendar year for the limitation and plan year. Employer A has never maintained a defined contribution plan. C becomes a participant in Employer A's plan on January 1, 2006, and works through December 31, 2011, when C is age 65. C begins to receive benefits under the plan in 2012. C's average compensation for the period of C's high-3 years of service is $40,000. Furthermore, under the terms of Employer A's plan, for purposes of computing C's nonforfeitable percentage in C's accrued benefit derived from employer contributions, C has only 7 years of service with Employer A (2005–2011).

(ii) Because C has only 7 years of service with Employer A at the time he begins to receive benefits under the plan, the maximum permissible annual benefit payable with respect to C is $28,000 ($40,000 multiplied by 7/10).

Example 2. (i) The facts are the same as in *Example 1*, except that C's average compensation for the period of his high-3 years of service is $8,000.

(ii) Because C has only 7 years of service with Employer A at the time he begins to receive benefits, the maximum benefit payable with respect to C would be reduced to $5,600 ($8,000 multiplied by 7/10). However, the special rule for total benefits not in excess of $10,000, provided in paragraph (f) of this section, is applicable in this case. Accordingly, C may receive an annual benefit of $7,000 ($10,000 multiplied by 7/10) without the benefit limitations of this section being exceeded.

Example 3. (i) Employer B maintains a defined benefit plan. Benefits under the plan are computed based on months of service rather than years of service. Accordingly, for purposes of applying the reduction based on years of service less than 10 to the limitations under section 415(b), the plan provides that the otherwise applicable limitation is multiplied by a fraction, the numerator of which is the number of completed months of service with the employer (but not less than 12 months), and the denominator of which is 120. The plan further provides that months of service are computed in the same manner for this purpose as for purposes of computing plan benefits.

(ii) The manner in which the plan applies the reduction based on years of service less than 10 to the limitations under section 415(b) is consistent with the requirements of this paragraph (g).

Example 4. (i) G begins employment with Employer D on January 1, 2003, at the age of 58. Employer D maintains a noncontributory defined benefit plan which provides for a straight life annuity beginning at age 65 and uses the calendar year for the limitation and plan year. G becomes a participant in Employer D's plan on January 1, 2004, and works through December 31, 2009, when G is age 65. G performs sufficient service to be credited with a year of service under the plan for each year during 2003 through 2009 (although G is not credited with a year of service for 2003 because G is not yet a plan participant). G begins to receive benefits under the plan during 2010. The plan's accrual computation period is the plan year. The plan provides that, for purposes of applying the rules of section 415(b)(5)(B), a participant is credited with a year of service (computed to fractional parts of a year) for each plan year for which the participant is credited with sufficient service to accrue a benefit for the plan year. G's average compensation for the period of G's high-3 years of service is $200,000. It is assumed for purposes of this example that the dollar limitation of section 415(b)(1)(A) for limitation years ending in 2010 is $195,000.

(ii) G has 7 years of service and 6 years of participation in the plan at the time G begins to receive benefits under the plan. Accordingly, the limitation under section 415(b)(1)(B) based on G's average compensation for the period of G's high-3 years of service that applies pursuant to the adjustment required under section 415(b)(5)(B) is $140,000 ($200,000 multiplied by 7/10), and the dollar limitation under section 415(b)(1)(A) that applies to G pursuant to the adjustment required under section 415(b)(5)(A) is $117,000 ($195,000 multiplied by 6/10).

(h) *Retirement Protection Act of 1994 transition rules*. For special rules affecting the actuarial adjustment for form of benefit under paragraph (c) of this section and the adjustment to the dollar limit for early or late commencement under paragraphs (d) and (e) of this section for certain plans adopted and in effect before December 8, 1994, see section 767(d)(3)(A) of the Uruguay Round Agreements Act of 1994, Public Law 103–465 (108 Stat. 4809) as amended by section 1449(a) of the Small Business Job Protection Act of 1996, Public Law 104–188 (110 Stat. 1755). The Commissioner may provide guidance regarding these special rules in revenue rulings, notices, and other guidance published in the Internal Revenue Bulletin. See §601.601(d) of this chapter.

Par. 10. Section 1.415(b)–2 is added and reserved.

§1.415(b)–2 Multiple annuity starting dates. [Reserved].

Par. 11. Section 1.415(c)–1 is added to read as follows:

§1.415(c)–1 Limitations for defined contribution plans.

(a) *General rules*—(1) *Maximum limitations.* Under section 415(c) and this section, to satisfy the provisions of section 415(a) for any limitation year, except as provided by paragraph (a)(3) of this section, the annual additions (as defined in paragraph (b) of this section) credited to the account of a participant in a defined contribution plan for the limitation year must not exceed the lesser of—

(i) $40,000 (adjusted pursuant to section 415(d) and §1.415(d)–1(b)); or

(ii) 100 percent of the participant's compensation (as defined in §1.415(c)–2) for the limitation year.

(2) *Defined contribution plan*—(i) *Definition.* For purposes of section 415 and regulations promulgated under section 415, the term *defined contribution plan* means a defined contribution plan within the meaning of section 414(i) (including the portion of a plan treated as a defined contribution plan under the rules of section 414(k)) that is—

(A) A plan described in section 401(a) which includes a trust which is exempt from tax under section 501(a);

(B) An annuity plan described in section 403(a); or

(C) A simplified employee pension described in section 408(k).

(ii) *Additional plans treated as defined contribution plans*—(A) *In general.* Contributions to the types of arrangements described in paragraphs (a)(2)(ii)(B) through (D) of this section are treated as contributions to defined contribution plans for purposes of section 415 and regulations promulgated under section 415.

(B) *Employee contributions to a defined benefit plan.* Mandatory employee contributions (as defined in section 411(c)(2)(C) and §1.411(c)–1(c)(4), regardless of whether the plan is subject to the requirements of section 411) to a defined benefit plan are treated as contributions to a defined contribution plan. For this purpose, contributions that are picked up by the employer as described in section 414(h)(2) are not considered employee contributions.

(C) *Individual medical benefit accounts under section 401(h).* Pursuant to section 415(l)(1), contributions allocated to any individual medical benefit account which is part of a pension or annuity plan established pursuant to section 401(h) are treated as contributions to a defined contribution plan.

(D) *Post-retirement medical accounts for key employees.* Pursuant to section 419A(d)(2), amounts attributable to medical benefits allocated to an account established for a key employee (any employee who, at any time during the plan year or any preceding plan year, is or was a key employee as defined in section 416(i)) pursuant to section 419A(d)(1) are treated as contributions to a defined contribution plan.

(iii) *Section 403(b) annuity contracts.* Annual additions under an annuity contract described in section 403(b) are treated as annual additions under a defined contribution plan for purposes of this section.

(3) *Alternative contribution limitations*—(i) *Church plans.* For alternative contribution limitations relating to church plans, see paragraph (d) of this section.

(ii) *Special rules for medical benefits.* For additional rules relating to certain medical benefits, see paragraph (e) of this section.

(iii) *Employee stock ownership plans.* For additional rules relating to employee stock ownership plans, see paragraph (f) of this section.

(b) *Annual additions*—(1) *In general*—(i) *General definition.* The term *annual addition* means, for purposes of this section, the sum, credited to a participant's account for any limitation year, of—

(A) Employer contributions;

(B) Employee contributions; and

(C) Forfeitures.

(ii) *Certain excess amounts treated as annual additions.* Contributions do not fail to be annual additions merely because they are excess contributions (as described in section 401(k)(8)(B)) or excess aggregate contributions (as described in section 401(m)(6)(B)), or merely because excess contributions or excess aggregate contributions are corrected through distribution.

(iii) *Direct transfers.* The direct transfer of a benefit or employee contributions from a qualified plan to a defined contribution plan does not give rise to an annual addition.

(iv) *Reinvested employee stock ownership plan dividends.* The reinvestment of dividends on employer securities under an employee stock ownership plan pursuant to section 404(k)(2)(A)(iii)(II) does not give rise to an annual addition.

(2) *Employer contributions*—(i) *Amounts treated as an annual addition.* For purposes of paragraph (b)(1)(i)(A) of this section, the term *annual addition* includes employer contributions credited to the participant's account for the limitation year and other allocations described in paragraph (b)(4) of this section that are made during the limitation year. See paragraph (b)(6) of this section for timing rules applicable to annual additions with respect to employer contributions.

(ii) *Amounts not treated as annual additions*—(A) *Certain restorations of accrued benefits.* The restoration of an employee's accrued benefit by the employer in accordance with section 411(a)(3)(D) or section 411(a)(7)(C) or resulting from the repayment of cashouts (as described in section 415(k)(3)) under a governmental plan (as defined in section 414(d)) is not considered an annual addition for the limitation year in which the restoration occurs. This treatment of a restoration of an employee's accrued benefit as not giving rise to an annual addition applies regardless of whether the plan restricts the timing of repayments to the maximum extent allowed by section 411(a).

(B)*Catch-up contributions.* A catch-up contribution made in accordance with section 414(v) and §1.414(v)–1 does not give rise to an annual addition.

(C) *Restorative payments.* A restorative payment that is allocated to a participant's account does not give rise to an annual addition for any limitation year. For this purpose, restorative payments are payments made to restore losses to a plan resulting from actions by a fiduciary for which there is reasonable risk of liability for breach of a fiduciary duty under Title I of the Employee Retirement Income Security Act of 1974 (88 Stat. 829), Public Law 93–406

(ERISA) or under other applicable federal or state law, where plan participants who are similarly situated are treated similarly with respect to the payments. Generally, payments to a defined contribution plan are restorative payments only if the payments are made in order to restore some or all of the plan's losses due to an action (or a failure to act) that creates a reasonable risk of liability for such a breach of fiduciary duty (other than a breach of fiduciary duty arising from failure to remit contributions to the plan). This includes payments to a plan made pursuant to a Department of Labor order, the Department of Labor's Voluntary Fiduciary Correction Program, or a court-approved settlement, to restore losses to a qualified defined contribution plan on account of the breach of fiduciary duty (other than a breach of fiduciary duty arising from failure to remit contributions to the plan). Payments made to a plan to make up for losses due merely to market fluctuations and other payments that are not made on account of a reasonable risk of liability for breach of a fiduciary duty under Title I of ERISA are not restorative payments and generally constitute contributions that give rise to annual additions under paragraph (b)(4) of this section.

(D) *Excess deferrals.* Excess deferrals that are distributed in accordance with §1.402(g)–1(e)(2) or (3) do not give rise to annual additions.

(3) *Employee contributions.* For purposes of paragraph (b)(1)(i)(B) of this section, the term *annual addition* includes mandatory employee contributions (as defined in section 411(c)(2)(C) and regulations promulgated under section 411) as well as voluntary employee contributions. The term *annual addition* does not include—

(i) Rollover contributions (as described in sections 401(a)(31), 402(c)(1), 403(a)(4), 403(b)(8), 408(d)(3), and 457(e)(16));

(ii) Repayments of loans made to a participant from the plan;

(iii) Repayments of amounts described in section 411(a)(7)(B) (in accordance with section 411(a)(7)(C)) and section 411(a)(3)(D) or repayment of contributions to a governmental plan (as defined in section 414(d)) as described in section 415(k)(3);

(iv) Repayments that would have been described in paragraph (b)(3)(iii) of this section except that the plan does not restrict the timing of repayments to the maximum extent permitted by section 411(a); or

(v) Employee contributions to a qualified cost of living arrangement within the meaning of section 415(k)(2)(B).

(4) *Transactions with plan.* The Commissioner may in an appropriate case, considering all of the facts and circumstances, treat transactions between the plan and the employer, transactions between the plan and the employee, or certain allocations to participants' accounts as giving rise to annual additions. Further, where an employee or employer transfers assets to a plan in exchange for consideration that is less than the fair market value of the assets transferred to the plan, there is an annual addition in the amount of the difference between the value of the assets transferred and the consideration. A transaction described in this paragraph (b)(4) may constitute a prohibited transaction with the meaning of section 4975(c)(1).

(5) *Contributions other than cash.* For purposes of this paragraph (b), a contribution by the employer or employee of property rather than cash is considered to be a contribution in an amount equal to the fair market value of the property on the date the contribution is made. For this purpose, the fair market value is the price at which the property would change hands between a willing buyer and a willing seller, neither being under any compulsion to buy or to sell and both having reasonable knowledge of relevant facts. In addition, a contribution described in this paragraph (b)(5) may constitute a prohibited transaction within the meaning of section 4975(c)(1).

(6) *Timing rules*—(i) *In general*—(A) *Date of allocation.* For purposes of this paragraph (b), an annual addition is credited to the account of a participant for a particular limitation year if it is allocated to the participant's account under the terms of the plan as of any date within that limitation year. Similarly, an annual addition that is made pursuant to a corrective amendment that complies with the requirements of §1.401(a)(4)–11(g) is credited to the account of a participant for a particular limitation year if it is allocated to the participant's account under the terms of the corrective amendment as of any date within that limitation year. However, if the allocation of an annual addition is dependent upon the satisfaction of a condition (such as continued employment or the occurrence of an event) that has not been satisfied by the date as of which the annual addition is allocated under the terms of the plan, then the annual addition is considered allocated for purposes of this paragraph (b) as of the date the condition is satisfied.

(B) *Date of employer contributions.* For purposes of this paragraph (b), employer contributions are not treated as credited to a participant's account for a particular limitation year unless the contributions are actually made to the plan no later than 30 days after the end of the period described in section 404(a)(6) applicable to the taxable year with or within which the particular limitation year ends. If, however, contributions are made by an employer exempt from Federal income tax (including a governmental employer), the contributions must be made to the plan no later than the 15th day of the tenth calendar month following the end of the calendar year or fiscal year (as applicable, depending on the basis on which the employer keeps its books) with or within which the particular limitation year ends. If contributions are made to a plan after the end of the period during which contributions can be made and treated as credited to a participant's account for a particular limitation year, allocations attributable to those contributions are treated as credited to the participant's account for the limitation year during which those contributions are made.

(C) *Date of employee contributions.* For purposes of this paragraph (b), employee contributions, whether voluntary or mandatory, are not treated as credited to a participant's account for a particular limitation year unless the contributions are actually made to the plan no later than 30 days after the close of that limitation year.

(D) *Date for forfeitures.* A forfeiture is treated as an annual addition for the limitation year that contains the date as of which it is allocated to a participant's account as a forfeiture.

(E) *Treatment of elective contributions as plan assets.* The extent to which elective contributions constitute plan assets for purposes of the prohibited transaction provisions of section 4975 and Title I of ERISA, is determined in accordance with regulations and rulings issued by the Department of Labor. See 29 CFR 2510.3–102.

(ii) *Special timing rules*—(A) *Corrective contributions.* For purposes of this section, if, in a particular limitation year, an employer allocates an amount to a participant's account because of an erroneous forfeiture in a prior limitation year, or because of an erroneous failure to allocate amounts in a prior limitation year, the corrective allocation will not be considered an annual addition with respect to the participant for that particular limitation year, but will be considered an annual addition for the prior limitation year to which it relates. An example of a situation in which an employer contribution might occur under the circumstances described in the preceding sentence is a retroactive crediting of service for an employee under 29 CFR 2530.200b–2(a)(3) in accordance with an award of back pay. For purposes of this paragraph (b)(6)(ii), if the amount so contributed in the particular limitation year takes into account actual investment gains attributable to the period subsequent to the year to which the contribution relates, the portion of the total contribution that consists of such gains is not considered as an annual addition for any limitation year.

(B) *Contributions for accumulated funding deficiencies and previously waived contributions*—(*1*) *Accumulated funding deficiency.* In the case of a defined contribution plan to which the rules of section 412 apply, a contribution made to reduce an accumulated funding deficiency will be treated as if it were timely made for purposes of determining the limitation year in which the annual additions arising from the contribution are made, but only if the contribution is allocated to those participants who would have received an annual addition if the contribution had been timely made.

(*2*) *Previously waived contributions.* In the case of a defined contribution plan to which the rules of section 412 apply and for which there has been a waiver of the minimum funding standard in a prior limitation year in accordance with section 412(d), that portion of an employer contribution in a subsequent limitation year which, if not for the waiver, would have otherwise been required in the prior limitation year under section 412(a) will be treated as if it were timely made (without regard to the funding waiver) for purposes of determining the limitation year in which the annual additions arising from the contribution are made, but only if the contribution is allocated to those participants who would have received an annual addition if the contribution had been timely made (without regard to the funding waiver).

(*3*) *Interest.* For purposes of determining the amount of the annual addition under paragraphs (b)(6)(ii)(B)(*1*) and (*2*) of this section, a reasonable amount of interest paid by the employer is disregarded. However, any interest paid by the employer that is in excess of a reasonable amount, as determined by the Commissioner, is taken into account as an annual addition for the limitation year during which the contribution is made.

(C) *Simplified employee pensions.* For purposes of this paragraph (b), amounts contributed to a simplified employee pension described in section 408(k) are treated as allocated to the individual's account as of the last day of the limitation year ending with or within the taxable year for which the contribution is made.

(D) *Treatment of certain contributions made pursuant to veterans' reemployment rights.* If, in a particular limitation year, an employer contributes an amount to an employee's account with respect to a prior limitation year and such contribution is required by reason of such employee's rights under chapter 43 of title 38, United States Code, resulting from qualified military service, as specified in section 414(u)(1), then such contribution is not considered an annual addition with respect to the employee for that particular limitation year in which the contribution is made, but, in accordance with section 414(u)(1)(B), is considered an annual addition for the limitation year to which the contribution relates.

(c) *Examples.* The following examples illustrate the rules of paragraphs (a) and (b) of this section:

Example 1. (i) P is a participant in a qualified profit-sharing plan maintained by his employer, ABC Corporation. The limitation year for the plan is the calendar year. P's compensation (as defined in §1.415(c)–2) for the current limitation year is $30,000.

(ii) Because the compensation limitation described in section 415(c)(1)(B) applicable to P for the current limitation year is lower than the dollar limitation described in section 415(c)(1)(A), the maximum annual addition which can be allocated to P's account for the current limitation year is $30,000 (100 percent of $30,000).

Example 2. (i) The facts are the same as in *Example 1*, except that P's compensation for the current limitation year is $140,000.

(ii) The maximum amount of annual additions that may be allocated to P's account in the current limitation year is the lesser of $140,000 (100 percent of P's compensation) or the dollar limitation of section 415(c)(1)(A) as in effect as of January 1 of the calendar year in which the current limitation year ends. If, for example, the dollar limitation of section 415(c)(1)(A) in effect as of January 1 of the calendar year in which the current limitation year ends is $45,000, then the maximum annual addition that can be allocated to P's account for the current limitation year is $45,000.

Example 3. (i) Employer N maintains a qualified profit-sharing plan that uses the calendar year as its plan year and its limitation year. N's taxable year is a fiscal year beginning June 1 and ending May 31. Under the terms of the profit-sharing plan maintained by N, employer contributions are made to the plan two months after the close of N's taxable year and are allocated as of the last day of the plan year ending within the taxable year (and are not dependent on the satisfaction of a condition). Thus, employer contributions for the 2008 calendar year limitation year are made on July 31, 2009 (the date that is two months after the close of N's taxable year ending May 31, 2009) and are allocated as of December 31, 2008.

(ii) Because the employer contributions are actually made to the plan no later than 30 days after the end of the period described in section 404(a)(6) with respect to N's taxable year ending May 31, 2009, the contributions will be considered annual additions for the 2008 calendar year limitation year.

Example 4. (i) The facts are the same as in *Example 3*, except that the plan year for the profit-sharing plan maintained by N is the 12-month period beginning on February 1 and ending on January 31. The limitation year continues to be the calendar year. Under the terms of the plan, an employer contribution which is made to the plan on July 31, 2009, is allocated to participants' accounts as of January 31, 2009.

(ii) Because the last day of the plan year is in the 2009 calendar year limitation year, and because, under the terms of the plan, employer contributions are allocated to participants' accounts as of the last day of the plan year, the contributions are considered annual additions for the 2009 calendar year limitation year.

Example 5. (i) XYZ Corporation maintains a profit-sharing plan to which a participant may make voluntary employee contributions for any year not to exceed 10 percent of the participant's compensation for the year. The plan permits a participant to make retroactive make-up contributions for any year for which the participant contributed less than 10 percent of compensation. XYZ uses the calendar year as the plan year and the limitation year. Under the terms of the plan, voluntary employee contributions are credited to a participant's account for a particular limitation year if such contributions are allocated to the participant's account as of any date within that limitation year. Participant A's compensation is as follows—

Limitation year	Compensation
2008	$30,000
2009	$32,000
2010	$34,000
2011	$36,000

(ii) Participant A makes no voluntary employee contributions during limitation years 2008, 2009, and 2010. On October 1, 2011, participant A makes a voluntary employee contribution of $13,200 (10 percent of A's aggregate compensation for limitation years 2008, 2009, 2010, and 2011 of $132,000). Under the terms of the plan, $3,000 of this 2011 contribution is allocated to A's account as of limitation year 2008; $3,200 is allocated to A's account as of limitation year 2009; $3,400 is allocated to A's account as of limitation year 2010, and $3,600 is allocated to A's account as of limitation year 2011.

(iii) Under the rule set forth in paragraph (b)(6)(i)(C) of this section, employee contributions will not be considered credited to a participant's account for a particular limitation year for section 415 purposes unless the contributions are actually made to the plan no later than 30 days after the close of that limitation year. Thus, A's voluntary employee contribution of $13,200 made on October 1, 2011, would be considered as credited to A's account only for the 2011 calendar year limitation year, notwithstanding the plan provisions.

(d) *Special rules relating to church plans*—(1) *Alternative contribution limitation*—(i) *In general*. Pursuant to section 415(c)(7)(A), notwithstanding the general rule of paragraph (a)(1) of this section, additions for a section 403(b) annuity contract for a year with respect to a participant who is an employee of a church or a convention or association of churches, including an organization described in section 414(e)(3)(B)(ii), when expressed as an annual addition to such participant's account, are treated as not exceeding the limitation of paragraph (a)(1) of this section if such annual additions for the year are not in excess of $10,000.

(ii) *$40,000 aggregate limitation*. With respect to any participant, the total amount of annual additions that are in excess of the limitation of paragraph (a)(1) of this section but, pursuant to the rule of paragraph (d)(1)(i) of this section, are treated as not exceeding that limitation (taking into account the rule of paragraph (d)(3) of this section) cannot exceed $40,000. Thus, the aggregate of annual additions for all limitation years that would exceed the limitation of this section but for this paragraph (d)(1) is limited to $40,000.

(2) *Years of service taken into account for duly ordained, commissioned, or licensed ministers or lay employees*. For purposes of this paragraph (d)—

(i) All years of service by an individual as an employee of a church, or a convention or association of churches, including an organization described in section 414(e)(3)(B)(ii), are considered as years of service for one employer; and

(ii) All amounts contributed for annuity contracts by each such church (or convention or association of churches) during such years for the employee are considered to have been contributed by one employer.

(3) *Foreign missionaries*. Pursuant to section 415(c)(7)(C), in the case of any individual described in paragraph (d)(1) of this section performing any services for the church outside the United States during the limitation year, additions for an annuity contract under section 403(b) for any year are not treated as exceeding the limitation of paragraph (a)(1) of this section if such annual additions for the year do not exceed $3,000. The preceding sentence shall not apply with respect to any taxable year to any individual whose adjusted gross income for such taxable year (determined separately and without regard to community property law) exceeds $17,000.

(4) *Church, convention or association of churches*. For purposes of this paragraph (d), the terms "church" and "convention or association of churches" have the same meaning as when used in section 414(e).

(5) *Examples*. The following examples illustrate the rules of this paragraph (d):

Example 1. (i) E is an employee of ABC Church earning $7,000 during each calendar year. E participates in a section 403(b) annuity contract maintained by ABC Church beginning in the year 2008. E's taxable year is the calendar year, and the limitation year for the plan coincides with the calendar year. ABC Church contributes $10,000 to be allocated to E's account under the plan for the year 2008.

(ii) Under paragraph (d)(1) of this section, this allocation is treated as not violating the limits established in paragraph (a)(1) of this section because it does not exceed $10,000. Moreover, since an annual addition of $10,000 would otherwise exceed the limitation of paragraph (a)(1) of this section by $3,000, $3,000 is counted toward the aggregate limitation specified in paragraph (d)(1)(ii) of this section for year 2008. Accordingly, ABC Church may make such allocations for 13 years (for example, for years 2008 through 2020) without exceeding the aggregate limitation of $40,000 specified in paragraph (d) of this section. For the fourteenth year, ABC Church could allocate only $8,000 to E's account (the sum of the $7,000 limitation computed under paragraph (a)(1)(ii) of this section and the remaining $1,000 of the $40,000 aggregate limitation under paragraph (d)(1)(ii) of this section on annual additions in excess of the limits under paragraph (a)(1) of this section).

Example 2. (i) F is an employee of XYZ Church and F's taxable year is the calendar year. F earns $2,000 during each calendar year for services he provides to XYZ Church, all of which are performed outside the United States during each calendar year. F participates in a section 403(b) annuity contract maintained by ABC Church beginning in the year 2008. The limitation year for the plan coincides with the calendar year. ABC Church contributes $10,000 to be allocated to F's account under the plan for the year 2008. F's adjusted gross income for each taxable year (determined separately and without regard to community property law) does not exceed $17,000.

(ii) Under paragraph (d)(1) of this section, this allocation is treated as not violating the limits established in paragraph (a)(1) of this section because it does not exceed $10,000. Moreover, since an annual addition of $10,000 would otherwise exceed the limitation of paragraph (a)(1) of this section by $7,000 (the excess of $10,000 over the greater of the $2,000 compensation limitation under section 415(c)(1)(B) or the $3,000 section 415(c)(7)(C) amount), XYZ Church may make such allocations for 5 years (for example, for years 2008 through 2012) without exceeding the aggregate limitation of $40,000 specified in paragraph (d) of this section. In year 2013, XYZ church may contribute $8,000 to be allocated to F's account under the plan (the sum of the $3,000 limitation computed under paragraph (d)(3) of this section and the remaining $5,000 of the $40,000 aggregate limitation under paragraph (d)(1)(ii) of this section on annual additions in excess of the limits under paragraph (a)(1) of this section). For years after 2013, pursuant to paragraph (d)(3) of this section, XYZ Church could allocate $3,000 per year to F's account.

(e) *Special rules for medical benefits*. The limit under paragraph (a)(1)(ii) of this section (100 percent of the participant's compensation for the limitation year) does not apply to—

(1) An individual medical benefit account (as defined in section 415(l)); or

(2) A post-retirement medical benefits account for a key employee (as defined in section 419A(d)(1)).

(f) *Special rules for employee stock ownership plans*—(1) *In general.* Special rules apply to employee stock ownership plans, as provided in paragraphs (f)(2) through (f)(4) of this section.

(2) *Determination of annual additions for leveraged employee stock ownership plans*—(i) *In general.* Except as provided in this paragraph (f) of this section, in the case of an employee stock ownership plan to which an exempt loan as described in §54.4975–7(b) of this chapter has been made, the amount of employer contributions that is considered an annual addition for the limitation year is calculated with respect to employer contributions of both principal and interest used to repay that exempt loan for the limitation year.

(ii) *Employer stock that has decreased in value.* A plan may provide that, in lieu of computing annual additions in accordance with paragraph (f)(2)(i) of this section, annual additions with respect to a loan repayment described in paragraph (f)(2)(i) of this section are determined as the fair market value of shares released from the suspense account on account of the repayment and allocated to participants for the limitation year if that amount is less than the amount determined in accordance with paragraph (f)(2)(i) of this section.

(3) *Exclusions from annual additions for certain employee stock ownership plans that allocate to a broad range of participants*—(i) *General rule.* Pursuant to section 415(c)(6), in the case of an employee stock ownership plan (as described in section 4975(e)(7)) that meets the requirements of paragraph (f)(3)(ii) of this section for a limitation year, the limitations imposed by this section do not apply to—

(A) Forfeitures of employer securities (within the meaning of section 409(l)) under such an employee stock ownership plan if such securities were acquired with the proceeds of a loan (as described in section 404(a)(9)(A)); or

(B) Employer contributions to such an employee stock ownership plan which are deductible under section 404(a)(9)(B) and charged against the participant's account.

(ii) *Employee stock ownership plans to which the special exclusion applies.* An employee stock ownership plan meets the requirements of this paragraph (f)(3)(ii) for a limitation year if no more than one-third of the employer contributions for the limitation year that are deductible under section 404(a)(9) are allocated to highly compensated employees (within the meaning of section 414(q)).

(4) *Gratuitous transfers under section 664(g)(1).* The amount of any qualified gratuitous transfer (as defined in section 664(g)(1)) allocated to a participant for any limitation year is not taken into account in determining whether any other annual addition exceeds the limitations imposed by this section, but only if the amount of the qualified gratuitous transfer does not exceed the limitations imposed by section 415.

Par. 12. Section 1.415(c)–2 is added to read as follows:

§1.415(c)–2 Compensation.

(a) *General definition.* Except as otherwise provided in this section, compensation from the employer within the meaning of section 415(c)(3), which is used for purposes of section 415 and regulations promulgated under section 415, means all items of remuneration described in paragraph (b) of this section, but excludes the items of remuneration described in paragraph (c) of this section. Paragraph (d) of this section provides safe harbor definitions of compensation that are permitted to be provided in a plan in lieu of the generally applicable definition of compensation. Paragraph (e) of this section provides timing rules relating to compensation. Paragraph (f) of this section provides rules regarding the application of the rules of section 401(a)(17) to the definition of compensation for purposes of section 415. Paragraph (g) of this section provides special rules relating to the determination of compensation, including rules for determining compensation for a section 403(b) annuity contract, rules for determining the compensation of employees of controlled groups or affiliated service groups, rules for disabled employees, rules relating to foreign compensation, rules regarding deemed section 125 compensation, rules for employees in qualified military service, and rules relating to back pay.

(b) *Items includible as compensation.* For purposes of applying the limitations of section 415, except as otherwise provided in this section, the term *compensation* means remuneration for services of the following types—

(1) The employee's wages, salaries, fees for professional services, and other amounts received (without regard to whether or not an amount is paid in cash) for personal services actually rendered in the course of employment with the employer maintaining the plan, to the extent that the amounts are includible in gross income (or to the extent amounts would have been received and includible in gross income but for an election under section 125(a), 132(f)(4), 402(e)(3), 402(h)(1)(B), 402(k), or 457(b)). These amounts include, but are not limited to, commissions paid to salespersons, compensation for services on the basis of a percentage of profits, commissions on insurance premiums, tips, bonuses, fringe benefits, and reimbursements or other expense allowances under a nonaccountable plan as described in §1.62–2(c).

(2) In the case of an employee who is an employee within the meaning of section 401(c)(1) and regulations promulgated under section 401(c)(1), the employee's earned income (as described in section 401(c)(2) and regulations promulgated under section 401(c)(2)), plus amounts deferred at the election of the employee that would be includible in gross income but for the rules of section 402(e)(3), 402(h)(1)(B), 402(k), or 457(b).

(3) Amounts described in section 104(a)(3), 105(a), or 105(h), but only to the extent that these amounts are includible in the gross income of the employee.

(4) Amounts paid or reimbursed by the employer for moving expenses incurred by an employee, but only to the extent that at the time of the payment it is reasonable to believe that these amounts are not deductible by the employee under section 217.

(5) The value of a nonstatutory option (which is an option other than a statutory option as defined in §1.421–1(b)) granted to an employee by the employer, but only to the extent that the value of the option is includible in the gross income of the employee for the taxable year in which granted.

(6) The amount includible in the gross income of an employee upon making the election described in section 83(b).

(7) Amounts that are includible in the gross income of an employee under the rules of section 409A or section 457(f)(1)(A) or because the amounts are constructively received by the employee.

(c) *Items not includible as compensation.* The term *compensation* does not include—

(1) Contributions (other than elective contributions described in section 402(e)(3), section 408(k)(6), section 408(p)(2)(A)(i), or section 457(b)) made by the employer to a plan of deferred compensation (including a simplified employee pension described in section 408(k) or a simple retirement account described in section 408(p), and whether or not qualified) to the extent that the contributions are not includible in the gross income of the employee for the taxable year in which contributed. In addition, any distributions from a plan of deferred compensation (whether or not qualified) are not considered as compensation for section 415 purposes, regardless of whether such amounts are includible in the gross income of the employee when distributed. However, if the plan so provides, any amounts received by an employee pursuant to a nonqualified unfunded deferred compensation plan are permitted to be considered as compensation for section 415 purposes in the year the amounts are actually received, but only to the extent such amounts are includible in the employee's gross income.

(2) Amounts realized from the exercise of a nonstatutory option (which is an option other than a statutory option as defined in §1.421–1(b)), or when restricted stock or other property held by an employee either becomes freely transferable or is no longer subject to a substantial risk of forfeiture (see section 83 and regulations promulgated under section 83).

(3) Amounts realized from the sale, exchange, or other disposition of stock acquired under a statutory stock option (as defined in §1.421–1(b)).

(4) Other amounts that receive special tax benefits, such as premiums for group-term life insurance (but only to the extent that the premiums are not includible in the gross income of the employee and are not salary reduction amounts that are described in section 125).

(5) Other items of remuneration that are similar to any of the items listed in paragraphs (c)(1) through (c)(4) of this section.

(d) *Safe harbor rules with respect to plan's definition of compensation*—(1) *In general.* Paragraphs (d)(2) through (4) of this section contain safe harbor definitions of compensation that are automatically considered to satisfy section 415(c)(3) if specified in the plan. The Commissioner may, in revenue rulings, notices, and other guidance of general applicability published in the Internal Revenue Bulletin (see §601.601(d)(2) of this chapter), provide additional definitions of compensation that are treated as satisfying section 415(c)(3).

(2) *Simplified compensation.* The safe harbor definition of compensation under this paragraph (d)(2) includes only those items specified in paragraph (b)(1) or (2) of this section and excludes all those items listed in paragraph (c) of this section.

(3) *Section 3401(a) wages.* The safe harbor definition of compensation under this paragraph (d)(3) includes wages within the meaning of section 3401(a) (for purposes of income tax withholding at the source), plus amounts that would be included in wages but for an election under section 125(a), 132(f)(4), 402(e)(3), 402(h)(1)(B), 402(k), or 457(b). However, any rules that limit the remuneration included in wages based on the nature or location of the employment or the services performed (such as the exception for agricultural labor in section 3401(a)(2)) are disregarded for this purpose.

(4) *Information required to be reported under sections 6041, 6051 and 6052.* The safe harbor definition of compensation under this paragraph (d)(4) includes amounts that are compensation under the safe harbor definition of paragraph (d)(3) of this section, plus all other payments of compensation to an employee by his employer (in the course of the employer's trade or business) for which the employer is required to furnish the employee a written statement under sections 6041(d), 6051(a)(3), and 6052. See §§1.6041–1(a), 1.6041–2(a)(1), 1.6052–1, and 1.6052–2, and also see §31.6051–1(a)(1)(i)(C) of this chapter. This safe harbor definition of compensation may be modified to exclude amounts paid or reimbursed by the employer for moving expenses incurred by an employee, but only to the extent that, at the time of the payment, it is reasonable to believe that these amounts are deductible by the employee under section 217.

(e) *Timing rules*—(1) *In general*—(i) *Payment during the limitation year.* Except as otherwise provided in this paragraph (e), in order to be taken into account for a limitation year, compensation within the meaning of section 415(c)(3) must be actually paid or made available to an employee (or, if earlier, includible in the gross income of the employee) within the limitation year. For this purpose, compensation is treated as paid on a date if it is actually paid on that date or it would have been paid on that date but for an election under section 125, 132(f)(4), 401(k), 403(b), 408(k), 408(p)(2)(A)(i), or 457(b).

(ii) *Payment prior to severance from employment.* Except as otherwise provided in this paragraph (e), in order to be taken into account for a limitation year, compensation within the meaning of section 415(c)(3) must be paid or treated as paid to the employee (in accordance with the rules of paragraph (e)(1)(i) of this section) prior to the employee's severance from employment with the employer maintaining the plan. See §1.415(a)–1(f)(5) for the definition of severance from employment.

(2) *Certain minor timing differences.* Notwithstanding the provisions of paragraph (e)(1)(i) of this section, a plan may provide that compensation for a limitation year includes amounts earned during that limitation year but not paid during that limitation year solely because of the timing of pay periods and pay dates if—

(i) These amounts are paid during the first few weeks of the next limitation year;

(ii) The amounts are included on a uniform and consistent basis with respect to all similarly situated employees; and

(iii) No compensation is included in more than one limitation year.

(3) *Compensation paid after severance from employment*—(i) *In general.* Any compensation described in paragraph (e)(3)(ii) of this section does not fail to be compensation (within the meaning of section 415(c)(3)) pursuant to the rule of paragraph (e)(1)(ii) of this section merely because it is paid after the employee's severance from employment with the employer maintaining the plan, provided the compensation is paid by the later of 2½ months after severance from employment with the employer maintaining the plan or the end of the limitation year that includes the date of severance from employment

with the employer maintaining the plan. In addition, the plan may provide that amounts described in paragraph (e)(3)(iii) of this section are included in compensation (within the meaning of section 415(c)(3)) if—

(A) Those amounts are paid by the later of 2½ months after severance from employment with the employer maintaining the plan or the end of the limitation year that includes the date of severance from employment with the employer maintaining the plan; and

(B) Those amounts would have been included in the definition of compensation if they were paid prior to the employee's severance from employment with the employer maintaining the plan.

(ii) *Regular pay after severance from employment.* An amount is described in this paragraph (e)(3)(ii) if—

(A) The payment is regular compensation for services during the employee's regular working hours, or compensation for services outside the employee's regular working hours (such as overtime or shift differential), commissions, bonuses, or other similar payments; and

(B) The payment would have been paid to the employee prior to a severance from employment if the employee had continued in employment with the employer.

(iii) *Leave cashouts and deferred compensation.* An amount is described in this paragraph (e)(3)(iii) if the amount is either—

(A) Payment for unused accrued *bona fide* sick, vacation, or other leave, but only if the employee would have been able to use the leave if employment had continued; or

(B) Received by an employee pursuant to a nonqualified unfunded deferred compensation plan, but only if the payment would have been paid to the employee at the same time if the employee had continued in employment with the employer and only to the extent that the payment is includible in the employee's gross income.

(iv) *Other post-severance payments.* Any payment that is not described in paragraph (e)(3)(ii) or (iii) of this section is not considered compensation under paragraph (e)(3)(i) of this section if paid after severance from employment with the employer maintaining the plan, even if it is paid within the time period described in paragraph (e)(3)(i) of this section. Thus, compensation does not include severance pay, or parachute payments within the meaning of section 280G(b)(2), if they are paid after severance from employment with the employer maintaining the plan, and does not include post-severance payments under a nonqualified unfunded deferred compensation plan unless the payments would have been paid at that time without regard to the severance from employment.

(4) *Salary continuation payments for military service and disabled participants.* The rule of paragraph (e)(1)(ii) of this section does not apply to payments to an individual who does not currently perform services for the employer by reason of qualified military service (as that term is used in section 414(u)(1)) to the extent those payments do not exceed the amounts the individual would have received if the individual had continued to perform services for the employer rather than entering qualified military service, but only if the plan so provides. In addition, the rule of paragraph (e)(1)(ii) of this section does not apply to compensation paid to a participant who is permanently and totally disabled (as defined in section 22(e)(3)) if the conditions set forth in paragraph (g)(4)(ii)(A) of this section are satisfied (applied by substituting a continuation of compensation for the continuation of contributions), but only if the plan so provides.

(5) *Special rule for governmental plans.* For purposes of applying the rules of paragraph (e)(3) of this section, a governmental plan (as defined in section 414(d)) may provide for the substitution of the calendar year in which the severance from employment with the employer maintaining the plan occurs for the limitation year in which the severance from employment with the employer maintaining the plan occurs.

(6) *Examples.* The provisions of this paragraph (e) are illustrated by the following examples:

Example 1. (i) *Facts.* Participant A was a common law employee of Employer X, performing services as a script writer for Employer X from January 1, 2005 to December 31, 2005. Pursuant to a collective bargaining agreement, Employer X, Employer Y and Employer Z maintain and contribute to Plan T, a multiemployer plan (as defined in section 414(f)) in which Participant A participates. Under the collective bargaining agreement, Participant A is entitled to residual payments whenever television shows that Participant A wrote are re-used commercially (These residual payments constitute compensation described in paragraph (b) of this section and do not constitute compensation described in paragraph (c) of this section.). In the year 2008, Participant A receives residual payments from Employer X for television programs using the scripts that Participant A wrote in the year 2005 that were rebroadcast in the year 2008. In the years 2006, 2007, and 2008, Participant A was a common law employee of Employer Y, and did not perform any services for Employer X.

(ii) *Conclusion.* The residual payments received from Employer X by Participant A in the year 2008 are compensation for purposes of section 415(c)(3). The payments are not treated as made after severance from employment because Plan T is a multiemployer plan (as defined in section 414(f)) and Participant A continues to be employed by an employer maintaining Plan T.

Example 2. (i) *Facts.* The facts are the same as in *Example 1*, except that Participant A: ceased employment with Employer Y in the year 2006; subsequently moved away from the area in which A formerly worked; performs no services as an employee for any employer; and commenced receiving distributions under Plan T in March, 2006.

(ii) *Conclusion.* Based on the facts and circumstances, A has ceased employment with any employer maintaining Plan T. Pursuant to paragraph (e)(1)(ii) of this section, compensation must be paid prior to an employee's severance from employment with the employer maintaining the plan. Accordingly, the residual payments received by Participant A in the year 2008 are not compensation for purposes of section 415(c)(3).

(f) *Interaction with section 401(a)(17).* Because a plan may not base allocations (in the case of a defined contribution plan) or benefits (in the case of a defined benefit plan) on compensation in excess of the limitation under section 401(a)(17), a plan's definition of compensation for a year that is used for purposes of applying the limitations of section 415 is not permitted to reflect compensation for a year that is in excess of the limitation under section 401(a)(17) that applies to that year. See §§1.401(a)(17)–1(a)(3)(i) and 1.401(a)(17)–1(b)(3)(ii) for rules regarding the effective date of increases in the section 401(a)(17) compensation limitation for a plan year and for a 12-month period other than the plan year.

(g) *Special rules*—(1) *Compensation for section 403(b) annuity contract.* In the case of an annuity contract described in section 403(b), the term *participant's compensation* means the participant's includible compensation determined under section 403(b)(3). Accordingly, the rules for determining a participant's compensation pursuant to section 415(c)(3) (other than section 415(c)(3)(E)) and this section do not apply to a section 403(b) annuity contract.

(2) *Employees of controlled groups of corporations, etc.* In the case of an employee of two or more corporations which are members of a controlled group of corporations (as defined in section 414(b) as modified by section 415(h)), the term *compensation* for such employee includes compensation from all employers that are members of the group, regardless of whether the employee's particular employer has a qualified plan. This special rule is also applicable to an employee of two or more trades or businesses (whether or not incorporated) that are under common control (as defined in section 414(c) as modified by section 415(h)), to an employee of two or more members of an affiliated service group as defined in section 414(m), and to an employee of two or more members of any group of employers who must be aggregated and treated as one employer pursuant to section 414(o).

(3) *Aggregation of section 403(b) annuity with qualified plan of controlled employer.* If a section 403(b) annuity contract is aggregated with a qualified plan of a controlled employer in accordance with §1.415(f)–1(f)(2), then, in applying the limitations of section 415(c) in connection with the aggregation of the section 403(b) annuity with a qualified plan, the total compensation from both employers is permitted to be taken into account.

(4) *Permanent and total disability of defined contribution plan participant*—(i) *In general*. Pursuant to section 415(c)(3)(C), if the conditions set forth in paragraph (g)(4)(ii) of this section are satisfied, then, in the case of a participant in any defined contribution plan who is permanently and totally disabled (as defined in section 22(e)(3)), the *participant's compensation* means the compensation the participant would have received for the year if the participant was paid at the rate of compensation paid immediately before becoming permanently and totally disabled, if such compensation is greater than the participant's compensation determined without regard to this paragraph (g)(4).

(ii) *Conditions for deemed disability compensation.* The rule of paragraph (g)(4)(i) of this section applies only if the following conditions are satisfied—

(A) Either the participant is not a highly compensated employee (as defined in section 414(q)) immediately before becoming disabled, or the plan provides for the continuation of contributions on behalf of all participants who are permanently and totally disabled for a fixed or determinable period;

(B) The plan provides that the rule of this paragraph (g)(4) (treating certain amounts as compensation for a disabled participant) applies with respect to the participant; and

(C) Contributions made with respect to amounts treated as compensation under this paragraph (g)(4) are nonforfeitable when made.

(5) *Foreign compensation, etc.*—(i) *In general.* Amounts paid to an individual as compensation for services do not fail to be treated as compensation under paragraphs (b)(1) and (2) of this section (and are not excluded from the definition of compensation pursuant to paragraph (c)(4) of this section) merely because those amounts are not includible in the individual's gross income on account of the location of the services. Similarly, compensation for services do not fail to be treated as compensation under paragraphs (b)(1) and (2) of this section (and are not excluded from the definition of compensation pursuant to paragraph (c)(4) of this section) merely because those amounts are paid by an employer with respect to which all compensation paid to the participant by such employer is excluded from gross income. Thus, for example, the determination of whether an amount is treated as compensation under paragraph (b)(1) or (2) of this section is made without regard to the exclusions from gross income under sections 872, 893, 894, 911, 931, and 933.

(ii) *Exclusion of non-participant compensation by the plan.* With respect to a nonresident alien who is not a participant in a plan, the plan may provide that the compensation described in paragraph (g)(5)(i) of this section is not treated as compensation for purposes of paragraphs (b)(1) and (b)(2) of this section to the extent the compensation is excludable from gross income and is not effectively connected with the conduct of a trade or business within the United States, but only if the plan applies this rule uniformly to all such employees. For purposes of this paragraph (g)(5)(ii), nonresident alien has the same meaning as in section 7701(b)(1)(B).

(6) *Deemed section 125 compensation*—(i) *General rule.* A plan is permitted to provide that deemed section 125 compensation (as defined in paragraph (g)(6)(ii) of this section) is compensation within the meaning of section 415(c)(3), but only if the plan applies this rule uniformly to all employees with respect to whom amounts subject to section 125 are included in compensation.

(ii) *Definition of deemed section 125 compensation.* Deemed section 125 compensation is an amount that is excludable from the income of the participant under section 106 that is not available to the participant in cash in lieu of group health coverage under a section 125 arrangement solely because that participant is not able to certify that the participant has other health coverage. Under this definition, amounts are deemed section 125 compensation only if the employer does not otherwise request or collect information regarding the participant's other health coverage as part of the enrollment process for the health plan.

(7) *Employees in qualified military service.* See section 414(u)(7) for special rules regarding compensation of employees who are in qualified military service within the meaning of section 414(u)(5).

(8) *Back pay.* Payments awarded by an administrative agency or court or pursuant to a *bona fide* agreement by an employer to compensate an employee for lost wages are compensation within the meaning of section 415(c)(3) for the limitation year to which the back pay relates, but only to the extent such payments represent wages and compensation that would otherwise be included in compensation under this section.

Par. 13. Section 1.415(d)–1 is added to read as follows:

§1.415(d)–1 Cost-of-living adjustments.

(a) *Defined benefit plans*—(1) *Dollar limitation*—(i) *Determination of adjusted limit.* Under section 415(d)(1)(A), the dollar limitation described in section 415(b)(1)(A) applicable to defined benefit plans is adjusted annually to take into account increases in the cost of living. The adjustment of the dollar limitation is made by multiplying the adjustment factor for the year, as described in paragraph (a)(1)(ii)(A) of this section, by $160,000, and rounding the result in accordance with paragraph (a)(1)(iii) of this section. The adjusted dollar limitation is prescribed by the Commissioner and published in the Internal Revenue Bulletin. See §601.601(d)(2) of this chapter.

(ii) *Determination of adjustment factor*—(A) *Adjustment factor.* The adjustment factor for a calendar year is equal to a fraction, the numerator of which is the value of the applicable index for the calendar quarter ending September 30 of the preceding calendar year, and the denominator of which is the value of such index for the base period. The applicable index is determined consistent with the procedures used to adjust benefit amounts under section 215(i)(2)(A) of the Social Security Act, Public Law 92–336 (86 Stat. 406), as amended. If, however, the value of that fraction is less than one for a calendar year, then the adjustment factor for the calendar year is equal to one.

(B) *Base period.* For the purpose of adjusting the dollar limitation pursuant to paragraph (a)(1)(ii)(A) of this section, the base period is the calendar quarter beginning July 1, 2001.

(iii) *Rounding.* Any increase in the $160,000 amount specified in section 415(b)(1)(A) which is not a multiple of $5,000 is rounded to the next lowest multiple of $5,000.

(2) *Average compensation for high-3 years of service limitation*—(i) *Determination of adjusted limit.* Under section 415(d)(1)(B), with regard to participants who have had a severance from employment with the employer maintaining the plan, the compensation limitation described in section 415(b)(1)(B) is permitted to be adjusted annually to take into account increases in the cost of living. For any limitation year beginning after the severance occurs, the adjustment of the compensation limitation is made by multiplying the annual adjustment factor (as defined in paragraph (a)(2)(ii) of this section) by the compensation limitation applicable to the participant in the prior limitation year. The annual adjustment factor is prescribed by the Commissioner and published in the Internal Revenue Bulletin. See §601.601(d)(2) of this chapter.

(ii) *Annual adjustment factor.* The annual adjustment factor for a calendar year is equal to a fraction, the numerator of which is the value of the applicable index for the calendar quarter ending September 30 of the preceding calendar year, and the denominator of which is the value of such index for the calendar quarter ending September 30 of the calendar year prior to that preceding calendar year. The applicable index is determined consistent with the procedures used to adjust benefit amounts under section 215(i)(2)(A) of the Social Security Act. If the value of the fraction described in the first sentence of this paragraph (a)(2)(ii) is less than one for a calendar year, then the adjustment factor for the calendar year is equal to one. In such a case, the annual adjustment factor for future calendar years will be determined in accordance with revenue rulings, notices, or other published guidance prescribed by the Commissioner and published in the Internal Revenue Bulletin. See §601.601(d)(2) of this chapter.

(iii) *Special rule for rehired employees.* If, after having a severance from employment with the employer maintaining the plan, an employee is rehired by the employer maintaining the plan, the employee's compensation limit under section 415(b)(1)(B) is the greater of—

(A) 100 percent of the participant's average compensation for the period of the participant's high-3 years of service, as determined prior to the employee's severance from employment with the employer maintaining the plan, as adjusted pursuant to paragraph (a)(2)(i) of this section (if the plan so provides); or

(B) 100 percent of the participant's average compensation for the period of the participant's high-3 years of service, with the period of the participant's high-3 years of service determined pursuant to §1.415(b)–1(a)(5)(iii).

(3) *Effective date of adjustment.* The adjusted dollar limitation applicable to defined benefit plans and the adjusted compensation limit applicable to a participant are effective as of January 1 of each calendar year and apply with respect to limitation years ending with or within that calendar year. However, benefit payments (and, in the case of plans that are subject to the requirements of section 411, accrued benefits for a limitation year) cannot exceed the currently applicable dollar limitation or compensation limitation (as in effect before the January 1 adjustment) prior to January 1. Thus, where there is an increase in the limitation under section 415(b)(1), any increase in a participant's benefits associated with the limitation increase is permitted to occur as of a date no earlier than January 1 of the calendar year for which the increase in the limitation is effective, and can only be applied for payments due on or after January 1 of such calendar year. For example, assume that a participant in a defined benefit plan is currently receiving a benefit in the form of a straight life annuity, payable monthly, in an amount equal to the section 415(b)(1)(A) dollar limit, and the defined benefit plan has a limitation year that runs from July 1 to June 30. If the plan is amended to reflect the section 415(d) increase to the section 415(b)(1)(A) dollar limit that is effective as of January 1, 2009, the associated increase in the participant's monthly benefit payments is only effective for payments due on or after January 1, 2009, and the participant's benefit cannot be increased to reflect the section 415(d) increase that is effective January 1, 2009, with respect to any monthly payment due prior to January 1, 2009.

(4) *Application of adjusted figure*—(i) *In general.* If the dollar limitation of section 415(b)(1)(A) or the compensation limitation of section 415(b)(1)(B) is adjusted pursuant to section 415(d) for a limitation year, the adjustment is applied as provided in this paragraph (a)(4).

(ii) *Application of adjusted limitations to benefits that have not commenced.* An adjustment to the dollar limitation of section 415(b)(1)(A) is permitted to be applied to a participant who has not commenced benefits before the date on which the adjustment is effective. Annual adjustments to the compensation limit of section 415(b)(1)(B) as described in paragraph (a)(2) of this section are permitted to be made for all limitation years that begin after the participant's severance from employment, and apply to distributions that commence after the effective dates of such adjustments. However, no adjustment to the compensation limit of section 415(b)(1)(B) is made for any limitation year that begins on or before the date of the participant's severance from employment with the employer maintaining the plan.

(iii) *Application of adjusted dollar limitation to remaining payments under benefits that have commenced.* With respect to a distribution of accrued benefits that commenced before the date on which an adjustment to the section 415(b)(1)(A) dollar limitation is effective, a plan is permitted to apply the adjusted limitations to that distribution, but only to the extent that benefits have not been paid. Thus, for example, a plan cannot provide that the adjusted dollar limitation applies to a participant who has previously received the entire plan benefit in a single-sum distribution. However, a plan can provide for an increase in benefits to a participant who accrues additional benefits under the plan that could have been accrued without regard to the adjustment of the dollar limitation (including benefits that accrue as a result of a plan amendment) on or after the effective date of the adjusted limitation.

(iv) *Manner of adjustment for benefits that have commenced.* If a plan is amended to increase benefits payable under the plan in accordance with paragraphs (a)(5) or (a)(6) of this section (or the plan is treated as applying paragraph (a)(5) of this section because the plan incorporates the section 415(d) cost-of-living adjustments automatically by reference pursuant to §1.415(a)–1(d)(3)(v)), or if benefits payable under the plan are increased pursuant to a form of benefit that is described in §1.415(b)–1(c)(5), then the distribution as increased will be treated as continuing to satisfy the requirements of section 415(b). If benefits payable under a plan are increased in a manner other than as described in the preceding sentence, the plan must satisfy the requirements of §1.415(b)–1(b)(1)(iii), treating the commencement of the additional benefit as the commencement of a new distribution that gives rise to a new annuity starting date.

(5) *Safe harbor for annual adjustments to distributions.* An amendment to a plan to incorporate adjustments to the section 415(b) limits that increases a distribution that has previously commenced is described in this paragraph (a)(5) if—

(i) The employee has received one or more distributions that satisfy the requirements of section 415(b) before the date the adjustment to the applicable limits is effective (as determined under paragraph (a)(3) of this section);

(ii) The increased distribution is solely as a result of the amendment of the plan to reflect the adjustment to the applicable limits pursuant to section 415(d); and

(iii) The amounts payable to the employee on and after the effective date of the adjustment (as determined under paragraph (a)(3) of this section) are not greater than the amounts that would otherwise be payable without regard to the adjustment, multiplied by a fraction determined for the limitation year, the numerator of which is the limitation under section 415(b) (which is the lesser of the applicable dollar limitation under section 415(b)(1)(A), as adjusted for age at commencement, and the applicable compensation-based limitation under section 415(b)(1)(B)) in effect with respect to the distribution taking into account the section 415(d) adjustment, and the denominator of which is the limitation under section 415(b) in effect for the distribution immediately before the adjustment.

(6) *Safe harbor for periodic adjustments to distributions*—(i) *General rule.* An amendment to a plan that increases a distribution that has previously commenced is made using the safe harbor methodology of this paragraph (a)(6) if—

(A) The employee has received one or more distributions that satisfy the requirements of section 415(b) before the date on which the increase is effective; and

(B) The amounts payable to the employee on and after the effective date of the increase are not greater than the amounts that would otherwise be payable without regard to the increase, multiplied by the cumulative adjustment fraction.

(ii) *Cumulative adjustment fraction.* The cumulative adjustment fraction for purposes of this paragraph (a)(6) is equal to the product of all of the fractions described in paragraph (a)(5)(iii) of this section that would have applied after benefits commence if the plan had been amended each year to incorporate the section 415(d) adjustments to the applicable section 415(b) limits and had otherwise satisfied the safe harbor methodology described in paragraph (a)(5) of this section. For purposes of the preceding sentence, if for the limitation year for which the increase to the section 415(b)(1)(A) dollar limitation pursuant to section 611(a)(1)(A) of the Economic Growth and Tax Relief Reconciliation Act of 2001 (115 Stat. 38), Public Law 107–16 (EGTRRA), is first effective (generally, the first limitation year beginning after December 31, 2001), the section 415(b)(1)(A) dollar limit applicable to a participant is less than the section 415(b)(1)(B) compensation limit for the participant, then the fraction described in paragraph (a)(5)(iii) of this section for that limitation year is 1.0.

(7) *Examples.* The following examples illustrate the application of this paragraph (a):

Example 1. (i) X is a participant in a qualified defined benefit plan maintained by X's employer. The plan has a calendar year limitation year. Under the terms of the plan, X is entitled to a benefit consisting of a straight life annuity equal to 100 percent of X's average compensation for the period of X's high-3 years of service. X's average compensation for the period of X's high-3 years of service is $50,000. X incurs a severance from employment with the employer maintaining the plan on October 3, 2007, at age 65 with a nonforfeitable right to the accrued benefit after more than 10 years of participation in the plan. X begins to receive annual benefit payments (payable monthly) of $50,000, commencing on November 1, 2007. The dollar limitation for the 2007 limitation year (as adjusted pursuant to section 415(d)) is $180,000. Assume that the dollar limitation for the 2008 limitation year (as adjusted pursuant to section 415(d)) is $185,000 and the annual adjustment factor for adjusting the compensation limitation of section 415(b)(1)(B) for the 2008 limitation year is 1.0334. Effective January 1, 2008, the plan is amended to incorporate these adjustments to the dollar and compensation limitations, and accordingly, X's annual benefit payment is increased, effective for payments due on or after January 1, 2008. Prior to the plan amendment incorporating the application of the adjusted dollar and compensation limitations, X has received one or more distributions that satisfy the requirements of section 415(b). In addition, the adjustment to X's annual benefit payments is solely on account of the plan amendment incorporating the adjusted limitations.

(ii) For the limitation year beginning January 1, 2008, the dollar limit applicable to X under section 415(b)(1)(A) is $185,000, and the compensation limit applicable to X under section 415(b)(1)(B) is $51,670 ($50,000 multiplied by the annual adjustment factor of 1.0334). Accordingly, the adjustment to X's benefit satisfies the safe harbor for cost-of-living adjustments under paragraph (a)(5) of this section if, after the adjustment, X's benefit payable in the 2008 limitation year is no greater than $50,000 multiplied by $51,670 (X's section 415(b) limitation for 2008)/$50,000 (X's section 415(b) limitation for 2007).

Example 2. (i) The facts are the same as in *Example 1*, except that X's average compensation for the period of X's high-3 consecutive years of service is $200,000. Consequently, X's annual benefit payments commencing on November 1, 2007, are limited to $180,000.

(ii) For the limitation year beginning January 1, 2008, the dollar limit applicable to X under section 415(b)(1)(A) is $185,000, and the compensation limit applicable to X under section 415(b)(1)(B) is $206,680 ($200,000 multiplied by the annual adjustment factor of 1.0334). Accordingly, the adjustment to X's benefit satisfies the safe harbor for cost-of-living adjustments under paragraph (a)(5) of this section if, after the adjustment, X's benefit payable in 2008 is no greater than $180,000 multiplied by $185,000 (X's section 415(b) limitation for 2008)/$180,000 (X's section 415(b) limitation for 2007).

Example 3. (i) X is a participant in Plan T, a qualified defined benefit plan maintained by X's employer. In the year 2008, X receives a single-sum distribution of X's entire accrued benefit under the plan. At the time that X receives the single-sum distribution, X's accrued benefit under Plan T is limited by the section 415(b)(1)(A) age-adjusted dollar limit. X accrues no further benefits under Plan T after X receives the single-sum distribution. In the 2009 limitation year, pursuant to section 415(d) and §1.415(d)–1, the section 415(b)(1)(A) dollar limit is increased.

(ii) In the 2009 limitation year, Plan T may not provide additional benefits to X on account of the increase in the section 415(b)(1)(A) dollar limit pursuant to section 415(d) and §1.415(d)–1.

Example 4. (i) X is a participant in Plan T, a qualified defined benefit plan maintained by X's employer, Employer S. Plan T has a calendar limitation year. In 2008, X incurs a severance from employment with Employer S and X commences receiving distributions from Plan T in the form of a single life annuity in an annual amount of $30,000. At the time that X commences receiving distributions from Plan T, X's accrued benefit under Plan T is limited by the section 415(b)(1)(B) compensation limit. In 2009, the annual adjustment factor described in paragraph (a)(2) of this section (which is the factor for adjusting the compensation limit described in section 415(b)(1)(B)) is 1.03. Employer S amends Plan T, effective as of January 1, 2009, to increase the annual benefit of all participants who, prior to January 1, 2009, incurred a severance from employment with Employer S and who have commenced receiving benefits from Plan T by a factor of 1.015. Assume that for limitation years prior to 2009, X's distributions from Plan T satisfy the requirements of section 415(b).

(ii) The increase in X's annual benefit pursuant to the amendment effective January 1, 2009, is within the safe harbor described in paragraph (a)(6) of this section. This is because the amount payable to X under Plan T for the 2009 limitation year and limitation years thereafter (as increased by the amendment effective January 1, 2009) is not greater than the product of the amount payable to X under Plan T for such limitation years (as determined without regard to the amendment increasing X's benefit effective January 1, 2009) and the cumulative adjustment fraction (which, in X's case, is 1.03). Thus, X's annual benefit, as increased by the amendment, is not determined pursuant to the rules of §1.415(b)–1(b)(1)(iii).

Example 5. (i) Participant P participated in Plan A, maintained by Employer M, for more than 10 years. Plan A uses a calendar year limitation year and Plan A automatically adjusts a participant's section 415(b)(1)(B) compensation limit for limitation years after the limitation year in which the participant incurs a severance from employment as described in §1.415(a)–1(d)(3)(v). Prior to separating from employment with M in 2010, P's average compensation for P's period of high-3 years while a participant in Plan A is $50,000, based on P's compensation for 2007, 2008, and 2009, which was $50,000 for each year. P's compensation for year 2010 was $45,000. In year 2012, P is rehired by M and resumes participation in Plan A. P's compensation in year 2012 is $45,000, and is $70,000 in year 2013. Assume that the annual adjustment factor described in §1.415(d)–1(a)(2)(ii) for the limitation years 2011 through 2013 is 1.03 for each year. Thus, disregarding P's rehire by M, P's average compensation for P's period of high-3 years while a participant in Plan A for the 2013 limitation year would be equal to $54,636 (or 1.03 * 1.03 * 1.03 * $50,000). See §1.415(b)–1(a)(5)(iii).

(ii) Under §1.415(d)–1(a)(2)(iii), P's average compensation for P's period of high-3 years while a participant in Plan A for the 2013 limitation year is $54,636.

(b) *Defined contribution plans*—(1) *In general.* Under section 415(d)(1)(C), the dollar limitation described in section 415(c)(1)(A) is adjusted annually to take into account increases in the cost of living. The adjusted dollar limitation is prescribed by the Commissioner and published in the Internal Revenue Bulletin. See §601.601(d)(2) of this chapter.

(2) *Determination of adjusted limit*—(i) *Base period.* The base period taken into account for purposes of adjusting the dollar limitation pursuant to paragraph (b)(2)(ii) of this section is the calendar quarter beginning July 1, 2001.

(ii) *Method of adjustment*—(A) *In general.* The dollar limitation is adjusted with respect to a calendar year based on the increase in the applicable index for the calendar quarter ending September 30 of the preceding calendar year over such index for the base period. Adjustment procedures similar to the procedures used to adjust benefit amounts under section 215(i)(2)(A) of the Social Security Act will be used.

(B) *Rounding.* Any increase in the $40,000 amount specified in section 415(c)(1)(A) which is not a multiple of $1,000 shall be rounded to the next lowest multiple of $1,000.

(iii) *Effective date of adjustment.* The adjusted dollar limitation applicable to defined contribution plans is effective as of January 1 of each calendar year and applies with respect to limitation years ending with or within that calendar year. Annual additions for a limitation year cannot exceed the currently applicable dollar limitation (as in effect before the January 1 adjustment) prior to January 1. However, after a January 1 adjustment is made, annual additions for the entire limitation year are permitted to reflect the dollar limitation as adjusted on January 1.

(c) *Application of rounding rules to other cost-of-living adjustments.* Pursuant to section 415(d)(4)(A), the $5,000 rounding methodology of paragraph (a)(1)(iii) of this section is used for purposes of any provision of chapter 1 of subtitle A of the Internal Revenue Code that provides for adjustments in accordance with section 415(d), except to the extent provided by that provision. Thus, the $5,000 rounding methodology of paragraph (a)(1)(iii) of this section is used for purposes of—

(1) Determining the level of compensation specified in section 414(q)(1)(B) that is used to determine whether an employee is a highly compensated employee;

(2) Calculating the amounts used pursuant to section 409(o)(1)(C) to determine the maximum period over which distributions from an employee stock ownership plan may be made without participant consent; and

(3) Determining the levels of compensation specified in §1.61–21(f)(5)(i) and (iii) used in determining whether an employee is a control employee of a nongovernmental employer for purposes of the commuting valuation rule of §1.61–21(f).

(d) *Implementation of cost-of-living adjustments.* A plan is permitted to be amended to reflect any of the adjustments described in this section at any time after those limitations become applicable. Alternatively, a plan is permitted to incorporate by reference any of the adjustments described in this section in accordance with the rules of §1.415(a)–1(d)(3)(v). Because the accrued benefit of a participant can reflect increases in the applicable limitations only after those increases become effective, a pattern of repeated plan amendments increasing annual benefits to reflect the increases in the section 415(b) limitations pursuant to section 415(d) does not result in any protection under section 411(d)(6) for future increases to reflect increases in the section 415(b) limitations pursuant to §1.411(d)–4, Q&A–1(c)(1). Thus, a plan does not violate the requirements of section 411(d)(6) merely because the plan has been amended annually for a number of years to increase annual benefits to reflect the increases in the section 415(b) limitations pursuant to section 415(d) and subsequently is not amended to reflect later increases in the section 415(b) limitations.

Par. 14. Section 1.415(f)–1 is added to read as follows:

§1.415(f)–1 Aggregating plans.

(a) *In general.* Except as provided in paragraph (g) of this section (regarding multiemployer plans), and taking into account the rules of paragraph (b)(2) (regarding the break-up of affiliated employers and affiliated service groups), paragraph (c) (regarding predecessor employers), and paragraph (d)(1) (regarding nonduplication rules) of this section, section 415(f) and this section require that for purposes of applying the limitations of sections 415(b) and (c) applicable to a participant for a particular limitation year—

(1) All defined benefit plans (without regard to whether a plan has been terminated) ever maintained by the employer (or a predecessor employer within the meaning of paragraphs (c)(1) and (c)(2) of this section) under which the participant has accrued a benefit are treated as one defined benefit plan;

(2) All defined contribution plans (without regard to whether a plan has been terminated) ever maintained by the employer (or a predecessor employer within the meaning of paragraphs (c)(1) and (c)(2) of this section) under which the participant receives annual additions are treated as one defined contribution plan; and

(3) All section 403(b) annuity contracts purchased by an employer (including plans purchased through salary reduction contributions) for the participant are treated as one section 403(b) annuity contract.

(b) *Affiliated employers, affiliated service groups, and leased employees*—(1) *General rule*. See §1.415(a)–1(f)(1) and (2) for rules regarding aggregation of employers in the case of affiliated employers and affiliated service groups. See §1.415(a)–1(f)(3) for rules regarding the treatment of leased employees.

(2) *Special rule in the case of the break-up of an affiliated employer or an affiliated service group*—(i) *In general*. A formerly affiliated plan of an employer is taken into account for purposes of applying paragraph (a) of this section to the employer, but the formerly affiliated plan is treated as if it had terminated immediately prior to the cessation of affiliation with sufficient assets to pay benefit liabilities under the plan, and had purchased annuities to provide plan benefits. See §1.415(b)–1(b)(5)(i) for rules determining annual benefits under a terminated defined benefit plan under which annuities are purchased to provide plan benefits.

(ii) *Definitions*. For purposes of this paragraph (b)(2), a *formerly affiliated plan of an employer* is a plan that, immediately prior to the cessation of affiliation, was actually maintained by one or more of the entities that constitute the employer (as determined under the employer affiliation rules described in §1.415(a)–1(f)(1) and (2)), and immediately after the cessation of affiliation, is not actually maintained by any of the entities that constitute the employer (as determined under the employer affiliation rules described in §1.415(a)–1(f)(1) and (2)). For purposes of this paragraph (b)(2), a *cessation of affiliation* means the event that causes an entity to no longer be aggregated with one or more other entities as a single employer under the employer affiliation rules described in §1.415(a)–1(f)(1) and (2) (such as the sale of a subsidiary outside a controlled group), or that causes a plan to not actually be maintained by any of the entities that constitute the employer under the employer affiliation rules of §1.415(a)–1(f)(1) and (2) (such as a transfer of plan sponsorship outside of a controlled group).

(c) *Predecessor employer*—(1) *Where plan is maintained by successor*. For purposes of section 415 and regulations promulgated under section 415, a former employer is a predecessor employer with respect to a participant in a plan maintained by an employer if the employer maintains a plan under which the participant had accrued a benefit while performing services for the former employer (for example, the employer assumed sponsorship of the former employer's plan, or the employer's plan received a transfer of benefits from the former employer's plan), but only if that benefit is provided under the plan maintained by the employer. In such a case, in applying the limitations of section 415 to a participant in a plan maintained by the employer, paragraph (a) of this section requires the plan to take into account benefits provided to the participant under plans that are maintained by the predecessor employer and that are not maintained by the employer. For this purpose, the formerly affiliated plan rules in paragraph (b)(2) of this section apply as if the employer and predecessor employer constituted a single employer under the rules described in §1.415(a)–1(f)(1) and (2) immediately prior to the cessation of affiliation (and as if they constituted two, unrelated employers under the rules described in §1.415(a)–1(f)(1) and (2) immediately after the cessation of affiliation) and cessation of affiliation was the event that gives rise to the predecessor employer relationship, such as a transfer of benefits or plan sponsorship.

(2) *Where plan is not maintained by successor*. With respect to an employer of a participant, a former entity that antedates the employer is a predecessor employer with respect to the participant if, under the facts and circumstances, the employer constitutes a continuation of all or a portion of the trade or business of the former entity. This will occur, for example, where formation of the employer constitutes a mere formal or technical change in the employment relationship and continuity otherwise exists in the substance and administration of the business operations of the former entity and the employer.

(d) *Special rules*—(1) *Nonduplication*. In applying the limitations of section 415 to a plan maintained by an employer, if the plan is aggregated with another plan pursuant to the aggregation rules of paragraph (a) of this section, a participant's benefits are not counted more than once in determining the participant's aggregate annual benefit or annual additions. For example, if a defined benefit plan is treated as if it terminated immediately prior to a cessation of affiliation under paragraph (b)(2) of this section, the plans maintained by the employer (as determined after the cessation of affiliation) that actually maintains the plan do not double count the annual benefit provided under the plan by aggregating under paragraph (a) of this section both the participant's annual benefit provided under the plan and the participant's annual benefit under the plan as a formerly affiliated plan (which is a plan that the employers formerly affiliated with the employer must take into account as a terminated plan under the rules of paragraph (b)(2) of this section). Instead, the plans maintained by the employer include the annual benefit provided to the participant under the actual plan that the employer maintains. Similarly, if a defined benefit plan maintained by an employer (the transferee plan) receives a transfer of benefits from a defined benefit plan maintained by a predecessor employer (the transferor plan) and the transfer is described in §1.415(b)–1(b)(3)(i)(B) (which requires the transferred benefits to be treated by the transferor plan as if the benefits were provided under a plan that must be aggregated with the transferor plan that terminated immediately prior to the transfer), the transferee plan does not double count the transferred benefits under paragraph (a) of this section by taking into account both the actual benefit provided under the transferee plan and the benefit provided under the deemed terminated plan that the predecessor employer is treated as maintaining (and that otherwise would have to be taken into account by the transferee plan under the predecessor employer aggregation rules of paragraph (a) of this section). Instead, the transferee plan takes into account the transferred benefits that are actually provided under the transferee plan (see §1.415(b)–1(b)(3)(i)(C)) and, pursuant to paragraph (c)(1) of this section, any nontransferred benefits provided under plans maintained by the predecessor employer with respect to a participant whose benefits have been transferred to the transferee plan.

(2) *Determination of years of participation for multiple plans.* If two or more defined benefit plans are aggregated under section 415(f) and this section for a particular limitation year, in applying the reduction for participation of less than ten years (as described in section 415(b)(5)(A)) to the dollar limitation under section 415(b)(1)(A), time periods that are counted as years of participation under any of the plans are counted in computing the limitation of the aggregated plans under this section.

(3) *Determination of years of service for multiple plans.* If two or more defined benefit plans are aggregated under section 415(f) and this section for a particular limitation year, in applying the reduction for service of less than ten years (as described in section 415(b)(5)(B)) to the compensation limitation under section 415(b)(1)(B), time periods that are counted as years of service under any of the plans are counted in computing the limitation of the aggregated plans under this section.

(e) *Previously unaggregated plans*—(1) *In general.* This paragraph (e) provides rules for those situations in which two or more existing plans, which previously were not required to be aggregated pursuant to section 415(f) and this section, are aggregated during a particular limitation year and, as a result, the limitations of section 415(b) or (c) are exceeded for that limitation year. Paragraph (e)(2) of this section provides rules for defined contribution plans that are first required to be aggregated pursuant to section 415(f) and this section in a plan year. Paragraph (e)(3) of this section provides rules for defined benefit plans that are first required to be aggregated pursuant to section 415(f) and this section, and for defined benefit plans under which a participant's benefit is frozen following aggregation.

(2) *Defined contribution plans.* Two or more defined contribution plans that are not required to be aggregated pursuant to section 415(f) and this section as of the first day of a limitation year do not fail to satisfy the requirements of section 415 with respect to a participant for the limitation year merely because they are aggregated later in that limitation year, provided that no annual additions are credited to the participant's account after the date on which the plans are required to be aggregated.

(3) *Defined benefit plans*—(i) *First year of aggregation.* Two or more defined benefit plans that are not required to be aggregated pursuant to section 415(f) and this section as of the first day of a limitation year do not fail to satisfy the requirements of section 415 for the limitation year merely because they are aggregated later in that limitation year, provided that no plan amendments increasing benefits with respect to the participant under either plan are made after the occurrence of the event causing the plan to be aggregated.

(ii) *All years of aggregation in which accrued benefits are frozen.* Two or more defined benefit plans that are required to be aggregated pursuant to section 415(f) and this section during a limitation year subsequent to the limitation year during which the plans were first aggregated do not fail to satisfy the requirements of section 415 with respect to a participant for the limitation year merely because they are aggregated if there have been no increases in the participant's accrued benefit derived from employer contributions (including increases as a result of increased compensation or service) under any of the plans within the period during which the plans have been aggregated.

(f) *Section 403(b) annuity contracts*—(1) *In general.* In the case of a section 403(b) annuity contract, except as provided in paragraph (f)(2) of this section, the participant on whose behalf the annuity contract is purchased is considered for purposes of section 415 to have exclusive control of the annuity contract. Accordingly, except as provided in paragraph (f)(2) of this section, the participant, and not the participant's employer who purchased the section 403(b) annuity contract, is deemed to maintain the annuity contract, and such a section 403(b) annuity contract is not aggregated with a qualified plan that is maintained by the participant's employer.

(2) *Special rules under which the employer is deemed to maintain the annuity contract*—(i) *In general.* Where a participant on whose behalf a section 403(b) annuity contract is purchased is in control of any employer for a limitation year as defined in paragraph (f)(2)(ii) of this section (regardless of whether the employer controlled by the participant is the employer maintaining the section 403(b) annuity contract), the annuity contract for the benefit of the participant is treated as a defined contribution plan maintained by both the controlled employer and the participant for that limitation year. Accordingly, where a participant on whose behalf a section 403(b) annuity contract is purchased is in control of any employer for a limitation year, the section 403(b) annuity contract is aggregated with all other defined contribution plans maintained by that employer. In addition, in such a case, the section 403(b) annuity contract is aggregated with all other defined contribution plans maintained by the employee or any other employer that is controlled by the employee. Thus, for example, if a doctor is employed by a non-profit hospital to which section 501(c)(3) applies and which provides him with a section 403(b) annuity contract, and the doctor also maintains a private practice as a shareholder owning more than 50 percent of a professional corporation, then any qualified defined contribution plan of the professional corporation must be aggregated with the section 403(b) annuity contract for purposes of applying the limitations of section 415(c) and §1.415(c)–1. For purposes of this paragraph (f)(2), it is immaterial whether the section 403(b) annuity contract is purchased as a result of a salary reduction agreement between the employer and the participant.

(ii) *Determination of when a participant is in control of an employer.* For purposes of paragraph (f)(2)(i) of this section, a participant is in control of an employer for a limitation year if, pursuant to §1.415(a)–1(f)(1) and (2), a plan maintained by that employer would have to be aggregated with a plan maintained by an employer that is 100 percent owned by the participant. Thus, for example, if a participant owns 60 percent of the common stock of a corporation, the participant is considered to be in control of that employer for purposes of applying paragraph (f)(2)(i) of this section.

(3) *Aggregation of section 403(b) annuity with qualified plan of controlled employer.* If a section 403(b) annuity contract is aggregated with a qualified plan of a controlled employer in accordance with paragraph (f)(2) of this section, the plans must satisfy the limitations of section 415(c) both separately and on an aggregate basis. In applying separately the limitations of section 415 to the qualified plan and to the section 403(b) annuity contract, compensation from the controlled employer may not be aggregated with compensation from the employer purchasing the section 403(b) annuity contract (that is, without regard to §1.415(c)–2(g)(3)).

(g) *Multiemployer plans*—(1) *Multiemployer plan aggregated with another multiemployer plan.* Pursuant to section 415(f)(3)(B), multiemployer plans, as defined in section 414(f), are not aggregated with other multiemployer plans for purposes of applying the limits of section 415.

(2) *Multiemployer plan aggregated with other plan*—(i) *Aggregation only for benefits provided by the employer.* Notwithstanding the rule of §1.415(a)–1(e), a multiemployer plan, as defined in section 414(f), is permitted to provide that only the benefits under that multiemployer plan that are provided by an employer are aggregated with benefits under plans maintained by that employer that are not multiemployer plans. If the multiemployer plan so provides, then, where an employer maintains both a plan which is not a multiemployer plan and a multiemployer plan, only the benefits under the multiemployer plan that are provided by the employer are aggregated with benefits under the employer's plans other than multiemployer plans (in lieu of including benefits provided by all employers under the multiemployer plan pursuant to the generally applicable rule of §1.415(a)–1(e)).

(ii) *Exception from aggregation for purposes of applying section 415(b)(1)(B) compensation limit.* Pursuant to section 415(f)(3)(A), a multiemployer plan, as defined in section 414(f), is not aggregated with any other plan that is not a multiemployer plan for purposes of applying the compensation limit of section 415(b)(1)(B) and §1.415(b)–1(a)(1)(ii).

(h) *Special rules for aggregating certain plans, etc.* If a plan, annuity contract or arrangement is subject to a special limitation in addition to, or instead of, the regular limitations described in section 415(b) or (c), and is aggregated under this section with a plan which is subject only to the regular section 415(b) or (c) limitations, the following rules apply:

(1) Each plan, annuity contract or arrangement which is subject to a special limitation must meet its own applicable limitation and each plan subject to the regular limitations of section 415 must meet its applicable limitation.

(2) The limitation for the aggregated plans is the larger of the applicable limitations for the separate plans.

(i) [Reserved.]

(j) *Examples.* The following examples illustrate the rules of this section. Except to the extent otherwise stated in an example, each entity is not and has never been affiliated with another entity under the employer affiliation rules of §1.415(a)–1(f)(1) and (2), each entity has never maintained a qualified plan (other than the plans specifically mentioned in the example), and the limitation year for each qualified plan is the calendar year.

Example 1. (i) *Facts.* M was formerly an employee of ABC Corporation and is currently an employee of XYZ Corporation. ABC maintains a qualified defined benefit plan (Plan ABC) and a qualified defined contribution plan in which M participates and XYZ maintains a qualified defined benefit plan (Plan XYZ) and a qualified defined contribution plan in which M participates. ABC Corporation owns 60 percent of XYZ Corporation.

(ii) *Treatment as a single employer.* ABC Corporation and XYZ Corporation are members of a controlled group of corporations within the meaning of section 414(b) as modified by section 415(h). Because ABC Corporation and XYZ Corporation are members of a controlled group of corporations within the meaning of section 414(b) as modified by section 415(h), M is treated as being employed by a single employer under §1.415(a)–1(f)(1).

(iii) *Plan aggregation.* Under paragraph (a)(1) of this section, the sum of M's annual benefit under Plan ABC and M's annual benefit under Plan XYZ is not permitted to exceed the limitations of section 415(b) and §1.415(b)–1; and, under paragraph (a)(2) of this section, the sum of the annual additions to M's account under the defined contribution plans maintained by ABC and XYZ may not exceed the limitations of section 415(c) and §1.415(c)–1. For purposes of determining the limitations of section 415(b) and §1.415(b)–1 for the aggregated plans, a year of service for either employer is considered as a year of service for purposes of §1.415(b)–1(g)(2) (phase-in rules for the compensation limit) and a year of participation under either plan is considered as a year of participation for purposes of §1.415(b)–1(g)(1) (phase-in rules for the dollar limit).

Example 2. (i) *Facts.* The facts are the same as in *Example 1*, except that ABC Corporation and XYZ Corporation do not maintain defined contribution plans. In addition, Participant O was formerly an employee of ABC Corporation and is currently an employee of XYZ Corporation. Participant O has an accrued benefit under the ABC Plan, but Participant O has no accrued benefit under the XYZ Plan. Effective January 1, 2010, ABC Corporation sells all of its shares of stock of XYZ Corporation to an unaffiliated entity, LMN Corporation (the 2010 stock sale). After the 2010 stock sale, XYZ Corporation continues to maintain Plan XYZ. LMN Corporation maintains a qualified defined benefit plan (Plan LMN). After the 2010 stock sale, M begins to accrue benefits under Plan LMN, but O does not participate in Plan LMN.

(ii) *Affiliated employer status of the corporations.* Immediately after the 2010 stock sale, ABC Corporation and XYZ Corporation are no longer members of a controlled group of corporations under section 414(b) (as modified by section 414(h)) and accordingly are no longer treated as a single employer under the employer affiliation rules of §1.415(a)–1(f)(1). Immediately after the 2010 stock sale, LMN Corporation and XYZ Corporation are members of a controlled group of corporations under section 414(b) (as modified by section 414(h)) and accordingly are treated as a single employer under the employer affiliation rules of §1.415(a)–1(f)(1).

(iii) *Treatment of plans maintained by ABC Corporation after the 2010 stock sale.* Under §1.415(a)–1(f)(1), any plan maintained by any member of a controlled group of corporations is deemed maintained by all members of the controlled group, and paragraph (a)(1) of this section requires that, for purposes of applying the limitations of section 415(b), all defined benefit plans ever maintained by an employer (as determined under the affiliation rules of §1.415(a)–1(f)(1) and (2)) are treated as one defined benefit plan. Therefore, defined benefit plans maintained by ABC Corporation must take into account the annual benefit of a participant provided under Plan XYZ in applying the limitations of section 415(b) to the participant because Plan XYZ is a plan that had once been maintained by ABC Corporation. However, beginning with the 2010 limitation year, the aggregation of the annual benefit accrued by a participant under Plan XYZ for purposes of testing defined benefit plans maintained by ABC Corporation is limited to the annual benefit accrued by the participant under Plan XYZ immediately prior to the 2010 stock sale. This is because paragraph (b)(2)(i) of this section provides that a formerly affiliated plan of an employer is treated as if it had terminated immediately prior to the cessation of affiliation with sufficient assets to pay benefit liabilities under the plan, and had purchased annuities to provide plan benefits. The 2010 stock sale is a cessation of affiliation under paragraph (b)(2)(ii) of this section because this event caused XYZ Corporation to no longer be affiliated with ABC Corporation under the employer affiliation rules of §1.415(a)–1(f)(1) and (2). Immediately after the 2010 stock sale, Plan XYZ is a formerly affiliated plan with respect to ABC Corporation under paragraph (b)(2)(ii) of this section because immediately prior to the cessation of affiliation, Plan XYZ was actually maintained by XYZ Corporation (which together with ABC Corporation constituted a single employer under the employer affiliation rules of §1.415(a)–1(f)(1) and (2)), and immediately after the cessation of affiliation, Plan XYZ is not actually maintained by ABC Corporation or any other entity affiliated with it.

(iv) *Application of rules to Participants M and O with respect to plans maintained by ABC Corporation after the 2010 stock sale.* In applying the limitations of section 415(b) to Participant M for the 2010 limitation year and later limitation years, Plan ABC must take into account the annual benefit provided under Plan ABC to Participant M and the annual benefit provided under Plan XYZ to Participant M, but treating Plan XYZ as if it had terminated immediately prior to the 2010 stock sale with sufficient assets to pay benefit liabilities under the plan, and had purchased annuities to provide plan benefits. The aggregation of Plan XYZ with Plan ABC is irrelevant for purposes of Participant O because Participant O does not have any accrued benefit under Plan XYZ (as determined prior to the 2010 stock sale).

(v) *Treatment of plans maintained by LMN Corporation and XYZ Corporation after the 2010 stock sale.* Under §1.415(a)–1(f)(1) and paragraph (a)(1) of this section, when applying the limitations of section 415(b) to a participant under Plans LMN and XYZ for the 2010 limitation year and later years, the annual benefit provided to the participant under Plans LMN, XYZ and ABC must be aggregated. Benefits under Plan ABC must be included in this aggregation because XYZ Corporation is deemed to have once maintained Plan ABC pursuant to §1.415(a)–1(f)(1), and since LMN Corporation and XYZ Corporation constitute a single employer under §1.415(a)–1(f)(1), paragraph (a)(1) of this section requires the aggregation of all defined benefit plans ever maintained by LMN Corporation and XYZ Corporation. However, in performing this aggregation, a participant's annual benefit under Plan ABC is limited to the annual benefit accrued by the participant immediately prior to the 2010 stock sale. This is because, pursuant to paragraph (b)(2)(i) of this section, Plan ABC is a formerly affiliated plan of LMN Corporation and XYZ Corporation.

(vi) *Application of rules to Participants M and O with respect to plans maintained by LMN Corporation and XYZ Corporation after the 2010 stock sale.* In applying the limitation of section 415(b) to Participant M for the 2010 limitation year and later limitation years, Plan LMN and Plan XYZ must take into account the annual benefit provided under Plans LMN and XYZ to Participant M and the annual benefit provided under Plan ABC to Participant M as if Plan ABC had terminated immediately prior to the 2010 stock sale with sufficient assets to pay benefit liabilities under the plan, and had purchased annuities to provide plan benefits. Participant O does not have an accrued benefit under Plan LMN or Plan XYZ, so the aggregation of Plan ABC with Plans LMN and XYZ is currently irrelevant with respect to Participant O. However, if Participant O were to ever participate in Plans LMN or XYZ after the 2010 stock sale, Participant O's annual benefit under Plan ABC (determined as if Plan ABC terminated immediately prior to the 2010 stock sale) would have to be aggregated with any annual benefit that Participant O accrues under Plan LMN or Plan XYZ.

(vii) *Application of nonduplication rule.* In applying paragraph (a)(1) of this section to plans maintained by ABC Corporation after 2010 stock sale, plans maintained by ABC Corporation do not take into account the deemed termination of Plan ABC since ABC Corporation maintains Plan ABC after the cessation of affiliation. Similarly, in applying paragraph (a)(1) of this section to plans maintained by LMN Corporation and XYZ Corporation after the 2010 stock sale, plans maintained by LMN Corporation and XYZ Corporation do not take into account the deemed termination of Plan XYZ since XYZ Corporation maintains Plan XYZ after the cessation of affiliation. See paragraph (d)(1) of this section.

Example 3. (i) *Facts.* The facts are the same as in *Example 2*, except that on January 1, 2009, Plan ABC transfers Participant M's benefit to Plan XYZ.

(ii) *Treatment of plans maintained by ABC Corporation.* Pursuant to §1.415(b)–1(b)(3)(i)(A), M's benefit that is transferred from Plan ABC to Plan XYZ is not treated as being provided under Plan ABC for the limitation year in which the transfer occurs (2009). This is because M's transferred benefit is otherwise required to be taken into account by Plan ABC for the 2009 limitation year since Plan XYZ must be aggregated with Plan ABC pursuant to paragraph (a)(1) of this section. This result does not change for the 2010 limitation year and later limitation years, where pursuant to paragraph (b)(2)(i) of this section, Plan XYZ becomes a formerly affiliated plan with respect to ABC Corporation due to the 2010 stock sale. Under paragraph (b)(2)(i) of this section, Plan XYZ (the formerly affiliated plan) is treated from the perspective of plans maintained by ABC Corporation (Plan ABC) as if Plan XYZ terminated immediately prior to the 2010 stock sale with sufficient assets to pay benefit liabilities under the plan, and had purchased annuities to provide plan benefits. However, the pre-2010 stock sale benefits of Plan XYZ include the January 1, 2009, transfer of Participant M's benefit. Thus, in the 2010 limitation year, M's transferred benefit is still otherwise required to be taken into account by Plan ABC on account of the aggregation of Plan XYZ with Plan ABC pursuant to paragraph (a)(1) of this section, and therefore the transferred benefit is not treated as being provided by Plan ABC.

(iii) *Treatment of plans maintained by LMN Corporation and XYZ Corporation.* Pursuant to §1.415(b)–1(b)(3)(i)(C), Participant M's benefit that is transferred to Plan XYZ from Plan ABC must be treated as provided under Plan XYZ for purposes of applying the limitations of section 415 to Plan XYZ with respect to Participant M for the limitation year in which the transfer occurs and later years. This result does not change on account of the 2010 stock sale. When applying the limitation of section 415 to Plans LMN and XYZ for the 2010 limitation year and later years, Plans LMN and XYZ must aggregate the annual benefit provided to a participant under each plan along with the participant's benefit under Plan ABC pursuant to §1.415(a)–1(f)(1) and paragraph (a)(1) of this section. However, under paragraph (b)(2)(i) of this section, for the 2010 limitation year and later years, this aggregation of M's Plan ABC benefit only includes the annual benefit attributable to a participant's accrued benefit under Plan ABC immediately prior to the 2010 stock sale, which (due to the 2009 transfer) is zero.

Example 4. (i) *Facts.* The facts are the same as in *Example 2*, except that on January 1, 2011, Plan ABC transfers Participant M's benefit to Plan XYZ.

(ii) *Treatment of plans maintained by ABC Corporation for the 2011 limitation year and later years.* Pursuant to §1.415(b)–1(b)(3)(i)(B), M's benefit that is transferred from Plan ABC to Plan XYZ during the 2011 limitation year is treated by Plan ABC for the 2011 limitation year and later years as if the transferred benefit were provided under a plan that must be aggregated with Plan ABC that terminated immediately prior to the transfer with sufficient assets to pay benefit liabilities under the plan, and had purchased annuities to provide plan benefits. This is because M's transferred benefit is not otherwise required to be taken into account by Plan ABC for the 2011 limitation year and later years pursuant to paragraphs (a)(1) and (b)(2)(i) of this section. While Plan ABC must take into account Participant M's annual benefit under Plan XYZ under paragraph (a)(1) of this section, Participant M's annual benefit for this purpose is limited under paragraph (b)(2)(i) of this section to M's accrued benefit under Plan XYZ immediately prior to the 2010 stock sale, and Participant M's pre-2010 stock sale accrued benefit under Plan XYZ excludes the 2011 transfer.

(iii) *Treatment of plans maintained by LMN Corporation and XYZ Corporation for the 2011 limitation year and later years.* Pursuant to §1.415(b)–1(b)(3)(i)(C), Participant M's benefit that is transferred to Plan XYZ from Plan ABC must be treated as provided under Plan XYZ for purposes of applying the limitations of section 415 to Plan XYZ with respect to Participant M for the limitation year in which the transfer occurs and later years. In applying the limitations of section 415(b) to Plans LMN and XYZ with respect to Participant M for the 2010 limitation year and later years, the annual benefit of Participant M under Plans ABC, LMN, and XYZ must be aggregated pursuant to §1.415(a)–1(f)(1) and paragraph (a)(1) of this section, but for this purpose, Participant M's benefit under Plan ABC is treated as if it were provided under a plan that terminated immediately prior to the cessation of affiliation of ABC Corporation and XYZ Corporation with sufficient assets to pay benefit liabilities under the plan, and had purchased an annuity to provide Participant M's benefits. (See paragraph (b)(2)(i) of this section and *Example 2*.) In applying the limitations of section 415(b) to Plans LMN and XYZ with respect to Participant M for the 2011 limitation year and later years, the annual benefit of Participant M under Plans ABC, LMN, and XYZ still must be aggregated pursuant to §1.415(a)–1(f)(1) and paragraph (a)(1) of this section. However, beginning with the 2011 limitation year, ABC Corporation is a predecessor employer with respect to LMN Corporation and XYZ Corporation with respect to Participant M on account of the transfer of benefits from Plan ABC to Plan XYZ, pursuant to paragraph (c)(1) of this section. Therefore, Plans LMN and XYZ must take into account benefits that Participant M accrued under Plan ABC after the January 1, 2010, cessation of affiliation of ABC Corporation and XYZ Corporation that were not transferred to Plan XYZ on January 1, 2011, pursuant to paragraphs (c)(1) and (d)(1) of this section. Since all of Participant M's benefit in Plan ABC is transferred to Plan XYZ on January 1, 2011, Participant M's annual benefit from Plan ABC for purposes of aggregating Plan ABC with Plans LMN and XYZ is zero.

Example 5. (i) *Facts*. The facts are the same as in *Example 2*, except that instead of the 2010 stock sale, XYZ Corporation sells some of its operating assets to LMN Corporation (and, under the facts and circumstances, the sale does not result in XYZ Corporation constituting a predecessor employer of LMN Corporation under the rules of paragraph (c)(2) of this section), and in connection with the asset sale, LMN Corporation assumes sponsorship of Plan XYZ in place of XYZ Corporation, effective January 1, 2010.

(ii) *Treatment of plans maintained by ABC Corporation and XYZ Corporation*. Pursuant to paragraph (a)(1) of this section, all defined benefit plans ever maintained by ABC Corporation and XYZ Corporation must be aggregated as a single defined benefit plan for purposes of applying the limitations of section 415(b). However, for purposes of determining the annual benefit under Plan XYZ for the 2010 limitation year and later years, the aggregation of a participant's benefit under Plan XYZ is limited to the participant's annual benefit accrued immediately prior to the January 1, 2010, transfer of sponsorship of Plan XYZ. This is because paragraph (b)(2)(i) of this section provides that a formerly affiliated plan of an employer is treated as if it were a plan that terminated immediately prior to the cessation of affiliation with sufficient assets to pay benefit liabilities under the plan, and had purchased annuities to provide plan benefits. The January 1, 2010, transfer of sponsorship of Plan XYZ is a cessation of affiliation under paragraph (b)(2)(ii) of this section because this event causes Plan XYZ to no longer actually be maintained by either ABC Corporation or XYZ Corporation. Effective immediately after the January 1, 2010, transfer of sponsorship, Plan XYZ is a formerly affiliated plan with respect to ABC Corporation and XYZ Corporation under paragraph (b)(2)(ii) of this section because immediately prior to the cessation of affiliation, Plan XYZ was actually maintained by XYZ Corporation, and immediately after the cessation of affiliation, Plan XYZ is not actually maintained by either XYZ Corporation or ABC Corporation. Therefore, in applying the limitation of section 415(b) to Participant M for the 2010 limitation year and later limitation years, Plan ABC must take into account the annual benefit provided under Plan ABC to Participant M and the annual benefit provided under Plan XYZ to Participant M as if Plan XYZ had terminated immediately prior to the 2010 stock sale with sufficient assets to pay benefit liabilities under the plan, and had purchased annuities to provide plan benefits. The aggregation of Plan XYZ with Plan ABC is irrelevant for purposes of Participant O because Participant O does not have any accrued benefit under Plan XYZ (as determined prior to the 2010 transfer of sponsorship).

(iii) *Treatment of plans maintained by LMN Corporation*. Under paragraph (a)(1) of this section, all defined benefit plans ever maintained by LMN Corporation or a predecessor employer must be aggregated as a single plan for purposes of applying the limitations of section 415(b). ABC Corporation and XYZ Corporation constitute a predecessor employer pursuant to paragraph (c)(1) of this section with respect to the participants who participate in Plan XYZ on the date of the transfer of sponsorship of Plan XYZ (the transferred participants) from XYZ Corporation to LMN Corporation, such as Participant M. This is because, effective with the January 1, 2010, transfer of sponsorship, LMN Corporation maintains a plan (Plan XYZ) under which the participants accrued a benefit while performing services for XYZ Corporation (which is in turn affiliated with ABC Corporation under §1.415(a)–1(f)(1)) and such benefits are provided under a plan maintained by LMN Corporation. Therefore, for the 2010 limitation year and later years, the annual benefit under Plan ABC of the transferred participants (such as Participant M) must be aggregated with the annual benefit provided to such participants under Plans XYZ and LMN for purposes of determining whether Plan LMN or Plan XYZ satisfies the limitations of section 415(b). However, the aggregation of the transferred participants' Plan ABC annual benefits is limited to the annual benefit accrued under Plan ABC immediately prior to January 1, 2010, transfer of sponsorship. This is because, pursuant to paragraph (c)(1) of this section, Plan ABC is treated from the perspective of plans maintained by LMN Corporation as if Plan ABC had terminated immediately prior to the transfer of sponsorship of Plan ABC to LMN Corporation with sufficient assets to pay benefit liabilities under the plan, and had purchased annuities to provide plan benefits. ABC Corporation and XYZ Corporation do not constitute a predecessor employer with respect to Participant O. Thus, if Participant O is a participant in Plan LMN or becomes a participant in Plan XYZ after the 2010 transfer of sponsorship, neither plan aggregates Participant O's Plan ABC benefits for purposes of satisfying section 415(b). In applying paragraph (a)(1) of this section to a participant, plans maintained by LMN Corporation do not double count the participant's annual benefit. See paragraph (d)(1) of this section. Thus, such plans do not aggregate the annual benefit provided under Plan XYZ with the annual benefit from the deemed termination of Plan XYZ that LMN Corporation's predecessor employer (which is ABC and XYZ Corporations) must take into account in applying paragraph (a)(1) of this section, and instead consider the annual benefit actually provided under Plan XYZ.

Example 6. (i) *Facts*. N is employed by a hospital which purchases an annuity contract described in section 403(b) on N's behalf for the current limitation year. N is in control of the hospital within the meaning of section 414(b) or (c), as modified by section 415(h). The hospital also maintains a qualified defined contribution plan during the current limitation year in which N participates.

(ii) *Conclusion*. Under section 415(k)(4), the hospital, as well as N, is considered to maintain the annuity contract. Accordingly, for N the sum of the annual additions under the qualified defined contribution plan and the annuity contract must satisfy the limitations of section 415(c) and §1.415(c)–1.

Example 7. (i) *Facts*. The facts are the same as in *Example 6*, except that instead of being in control of the hospital, N is the 100 percent owner of a professional corporation P, which maintains a qualified defined contribution plan in which N participates.

(ii) *Conclusion*. Under section 415(k)(4), the professional corporation, as well as N, is considered to maintain the annuity contract. Accordingly, the sum of the annual additions under the qualified defined contribution plan maintained by professional corporation P and the annuity contract must satisfy the limitations of section 415(c) and §1.415(c)–1. See §1.415(g)–1(b)(3)(iv)(C)(2) for an example of the treatment of a contribution to a section 403(b) annuity contract that exceeds the limits of section 415(c) by reason of the aggregation required by this section.

Example 8. (i) *Facts*. J is an employee of two corporations, N and M, each of which has employed J for more than 10 years. N and M are not required to be aggregated pursuant to section 415(f) and this section. Each corporation has a qualified defined benefit plan in which J has participated for more than 10 years. Each plan provides a benefit which is equal to 75 percent of a participant's average compensation for the period of the participant's high-3 years of service and is payable in the form of a straight life annuity beginning at age 65. J's average compensation for the period of his high-3 years of service from each corporation is $160,000. In July 2008, N Corporation becomes a wholly owned subsidiary of M Corporation.

(ii) *Plan aggregation analysis*. As a result of the acquisition of N Corporation by M Corporation, J is treated as being employed by a single employer under section 414(b). Therefore, because section 415(f)(1)(A) requires that all defined benefit plans of an employer be treated as one defined benefit plan, the two plans must be aggregated for purposes of applying the limitations of section 415. However, under paragraph (e)(3)(i) of this section, since the plans were not aggregated as of the first day of the 2008 limitation year (January 1, 2008), they will not be considered aggregated until the limitation year beginning January 1, 2009, provided that no plan amendment increasing benefits with respect to participant J is made after the acquisition of N by M.

(iii) *Application to Participant J*. J has a total benefit under the two plans of $240,000, which, as a result of the plan aggregation, is in excess of the section 415(b) limit. However, under paragraph (e)(3)(ii) of this section, the limitations of section 415(b) and §1.415(b)–1 applicable to J may be exceeded in this situation without plan disqualification so long as J's accrued benefit derived from employer contributions is not increased (that is, J's accrued benefit does not increase on account of increased compensation, service, participation, or other accruals) during the period within which the limitations are being exceeded.

Example 9. (i) *Facts*. A, age 30, owns all of the stock of X Corporation and also owns 10 percent of the stock of Z Corporation. F, A's father, directly owns 75 percent of the stock of Z Corporation. Both corporations have qualified defined contribution plans in which A participates. A's compensation (within the meaning of §1.415(c)–2) for 2008 is $20,000 from Z Corporation and $150,000 from

X Corporation. During the period January 1, 2008 through June 30, 2008, annual additions of $20,000 are credited to A's account under the plan of Z Corporation, while annual additions of $40,000 are credited to A's account under the plan of X Corporation. In both instances, the amount of annual additions represent the maximum allowable under section 415(c) and §1.415(c)–1. On July 15, 2008, F dies, and A inherits all of F's stock in Z in 2008.

(ii) *Conclusion.* As of July 15, 2008, A is considered to be in control of X and Z Corporations, and the two plans must be aggregated for purposes of applying the limitations of section 415. However, even though A's total annual additions for 2008 are $60,000, the limitations of section 415(c) and §1.415(c)–1 are not violated for 2008, provided no annual additions are credited to A's accounts after July 15, 2008 (the date that A is first in control of Z) for the remainder of the 2008 limitation year.

Example 10. (i) *Facts.* P is a key employee of employer XYZ who participates in a qualified defined contribution plan (Plan X). P is also provided post-retirement medical benefits, and XYZ has taken into account a reserve for those benefits under section 419A(c)(2). In the 2008 limitation year, P's compensation is $30,000 and P's annual additions under Plan X are $5,000. Pursuant to section 419A(d), a separate account is maintained for P, and that account is credited with an allocation of $32,000 for the 2008 limitation year. It is assumed that the section 415(c)(1)(A) dollar limit for 2008 is $46,000.

(ii) *Separate testing analysis.* Under paragraph (h)(1) of this section, Plan X and the individual medical account must separately satisfy the requirements of section 415(c), taking into account any special limit applicable to that arrangement. In this case, the contributions to Plan X separately satisfy the limitations of section 415(c). While the individual medical account is treated as a defined contribution plan subject to the rules of section 415(c), it is not subject to the 100 percent of compensation limit of section 415(c)(1)(B), so the contributions to that account satisfy the limitations of section 415(c).

(iii) *Aggregation analysis.* The sum of the annual additions under Plan X and the amounts contributed to the separate account on P's behalf must satisfy the requirements of section 415(c). Under paragraph (h)(2) of this section, the limit applicable to the aggregated plan is equal to the greater of the limits applicable to the separate plans. In this case, the limit applicable to the medical account is $46,000 (which is greater than the limit of $30,000 applicable to the qualified plan), so the limit that applies to the aggregated plan is $46,000, and the aggregated plan satisfies the requirements of section 415.

Par. 15. Section 1.415(g)–1 is added to read as follows:

§1.415(g)–1 Disqualification of plans and trusts.

(a) *Disqualification of plans*—(1) *In general.* Under section 415(g) and this section, with respect to a particular limitation year, a plan (and the trust forming part of the plan) is disqualified in accordance with the rules provided in paragraph (b) of this section, if the conditions described in paragraph (a)(2) or (a)(3) of this section apply. For purposes of this paragraph (a), the determination of whether a plan or a group of aggregated plans exceeds the limitations imposed by section 415 for a particular limitation year is, except as otherwise provided, made by taking into account the aggregation of plan rules provided in section 415(f) and §1.414(f)–1.

(2) *Defined contribution plans.* A plan is disqualified in accordance with the rules provided in paragraph (b) of this section if annual additions (as defined in §1.415(c)–1(b)) with respect to the account of any participant in a defined contribution plan maintained by the employer exceed the limitations of section 415(c) and §1.415(c)–1.

(3) *Defined benefit plans.* A plan is disqualified in accordance with the rules provided in paragraph (b) of this section if the annual benefit (as defined in §1.415(b)–1(b)(1)) of a participant in a defined benefit plan maintained by the employer exceeds the limitations of section 415(b) and §1.415(b)–1.

(b) *Rules for disqualification of plans and trusts*—(1) *In general.* If any plan (including a trust which forms part of such plan) is disqualified for a particular limitation year under the rules set forth in this paragraph (b), then the disqualification is effective as of the first day of the first plan year containing any portion of the particular limitation year.

(2) *Single plan.* In the case of a single qualified defined benefit plan (determined without regard to section 415(f) and §1.415(f)–1) maintained by the employer that provides an annual benefit (as defined in §1.415(b)–1(b)(1)) in excess of the limitations of section 415(b) and §1.415(b)–1 for any particular limitation year, such plan is disqualified in that limitation year. Similarly, if the employer only maintains a single defined contribution plan (determined without regard to section 415(f) and §1.415(f)–1) under which annual additions (as defined in §1.415(c)–1(b)) allocated to the account of any participant exceed the limitations of section 415(c) and §1.415(c)–1 for any particular limitation year, such plan is also disqualified in that limitation year.

(3) *Multiple plans*—(i) *In general.* If the limitations of section 415(b) and §1.415(b)–1, or section 415(c) and §1.415(c)–1, are exceeded for a particular limitation year with respect to any participant solely because of the application of the aggregation rules of section 415(f)(1) and §1.415(f)–1 (taking into account the rules of §1.415(a)–1(f)), then one or more of the plans is disqualified in accordance with the ordering rules set forth in paragraph (b)(3)(ii) of this section, applied in accordance with the rules of application set forth in paragraph (b)(3)(iii) of this section, subject to the special rules set forth in paragraph (b)(3)(iv) of this section, until, without regard to annual benefits or annual additions under the disqualified plan or plans, the remaining plans satisfy the applicable limitations of section 415.

(ii) *Ordering rules*—(A) *Disqualification of ongoing plans other than multiemployer plans.* If there are two or more plans that have not been terminated at any time including the last day of the particular limitation year, and if one or more of those plans is a multiemployer plan described in section 414(f), then one or more of the plans (as needed to satisfy the limitations of section 415) that has not been terminated and is not a multiemployer plan is disqualified in that limitation year. For purposes of the preceding sentence, the determination of whether a plan is a multiemployer plan described in section 414(f) is made as of the last day of the particular limitation year.

(B) *Disqualification of ongoing multiemployer plans.* If, after the application of paragraph (b)(3)(ii)(A) of this section, there are two or more plans and one or more of the plans has been terminated at any time including the last day of the particular limitation year, then one or more of the plans (as needed to satisfy the applicable limitations of section 415) that has not been so terminated (regardless of whether the plan is a multiemployer plan described in section 414(f)) is disqualified in that limitation year.

(iii) *Rules of application*—(A) *Employer elects which plan is disqualified.* If there are two or more plans of an employer within a group of plans one or more of which is to be disqualified pursuant to paragraph (b)(3)(ii)(A) or (B) of this section, then the employer may elect, in a manner determined by the Commissioner, which plan or plans are disqualified. If those two or more plans are involved because of the application of §1.415(a)–1(f), the employers involved may elect, in a manner determined by the Commissioner, which plan or plans are disqualified. However, the election described in the preceding sentence is not effective unless made by all of those employers.

(B) *Commissioner determines which plan is disqualified.* If the election described in paragraph (b)(3)(iii)(A) of this section is not made with respect to the two plans described in paragraph (b)(3)(iii)(A) of this section, then the Commissioner, taking into account all of the facts and circumstances, has the discretion to determine the plan that is disqualified in the particular limitation year. In making this determination, some of the factors that will be taken into account include, but are not limited to, the number of participants in each plan, the amount of benefits provided on an overall basis by each plan, and the extent to which benefits are distributed or retained in each plan.

(iv) *Special rules*—(A) *Simplified employee pensions.* If there are two or more plans one or more of which is to be disqualified pursuant to paragraph (b)(3)(ii)(A) or (B) of this section, and if one of the plans is a simplified employee pension (as defined in section 408(k)), then the simplified employee pension is not disqualified until all of the other plans have been disqualified. However, if one of the plans has been terminated, then the simplified employee pension is disqualified before the terminated plan. For purposes of this paragraph (b)(3)(iv)(A), the disqualification of a simplified employee pension means that the simplified employee pension is no longer described under section 408(k).

(B) *Aggregating medical accounts with defined contribution plans.* In the event that aggregating a medical account described in §1.415(c)–1(a)(2)(ii)(C) or (D) and a defined contribution plan other than such a medical account causes the limitations of section 415(c) and §1.415(c)–1 applicable to a participant to be exceeded for a particular limitation year, the defined contribution plan other than the medical account is disqualified for the limitation year.

(C) *Aggregating section 403(b) annuity contract and qualified defined contribution plan*—(*1*) *In general.* In the event that aggregating a section 403(b) annuity contract and a qualified defined contribution plan under the provisions of section 415(f)(1)(B) causes the limitations of section 415(c) and §1.415(c)–1 applicable to a participant under the aggregated defined contribution plans to be exceeded for a particular limitation year, the excess of the contributions to the annuity contract plus the annual additions to the qualified plan over such limitations is attributed to the annuity contract and therefore includable in the gross income of the participant for the taxable year with or within which that limitation year ends. See §1.415(a)–1(b)(2) for rules regarding the treatment of a contribution to a section 403(b) annuity contract that exceeds the limitations of section 415.

(*2*) *Example.* The following example illustrates the application of this paragraph (b)(3)(iv)(C). It is assumed for purposes of this example that the dollar limitation under section 415(c)(1)(A) that applies for all relevant limitation years is $45,000. The example is as follows:

Example. (i) N is employed by a hospital which purchases an annuity contract described in section 403(b) on N's behalf for the current limitation year. N is also the 100 percent owner of a professional corporation P that maintains a qualified defined contribution plan during the current limitation year in which N participates. (The facts of this example are the same as in §1.415(f)–1(j) *Example 7.*) N's compensation (within the meaning of §1.415(c)–2) from the hospital for the current limitation year is $150,000. For the current limitation year, the hospital contributes $30,000 for the section 403(b) annuity contract on N's behalf, which is within the limitations applicable to N under the annuity contract (specifically, the limit under the annuity contract is $45,000)). Professional corporation P also contributes $20,000 to the qualified defined contribution plan on N's behalf for the current limitation year (which represents the only annual additions allocated to N's account under the plan for such year), which is within the $45,000 limitation of section 415(c)(1) applicable to N under the plan.

(ii) Under section 415(k)(4), the professional corporation, as well as N, is considered to maintain the annuity contract. Accordingly, the sum of the annual additions under the qualified defined contribution plan maintained by professional corporation P and the annuity contract must satisfy the limitations of section 415(c) and §1.415(c)–1.

(iii) Because the total aggregate contributions ($50,000) exceed the section 415(c) limitation applicable to N ($45,000), $5,000 of the $30,000 contributed to the section 403(b) annuity contract is considered an excess contribution and therefore currently includable in N's gross income. The contract continues to be a section 403(b) annuity contract only if, for the current limitation year and all years thereafter, the issuer of the contract maintains separate accounts for each portion attributable to such excess contributions. See §1.415(a)–1(b)(2).

(c) *Plan year for certain annuity contracts and individual retirement plans.* For purposes of this section, unless the plan under which the annuity contract or individual retirement plan is provided specifies that a different twelve-month period is considered to be the plan year—

(1) An annuity contract described in section 403(b) is considered to have a plan year coinciding with the taxable year of the individual on whose behalf the contract has been purchased; and

(2) A simplified employee pension described in section 408(k) is considered to have a plan year coinciding with the year under the plan that is used pursuant to section 408(k)(7)(C).

Par. 16. Section 1.415(j)–1 is added to read as follows:

§1.415(j)–1 Limitation year.

(a) *In general.* Unless the terms of a plan provide otherwise, the limitation year, with respect to any qualified plan maintained by the employer, is the calendar year.

(b) *Alternative limitation year election.* The terms of a plan may provide for the use of any other consecutive twelve month period as the limitation year. This includes a fiscal year with an annual period varying from 52 to 53 weeks, so long as the fiscal year satisfies the requirements of section 441(f). A plan may only provide for one limitation year regardless of the number or identity of the employers maintaining the plan.

(c) *Multiple limitation years*—(1) *In general.* Where an employer maintains more than one qualified plan, those plans may provide for different limitation years. The rule described in this paragraph (c) also applies to a controlled group of employers (within the meaning of section 414(b) or (c), as modified by section 415(h)). If the plans of an employer (or a controlled group of employers whose plans are aggregated) have different limitation years, section 415 is applied in accordance with the rule of paragraphs (c)(2) and (3) of this section.

(2) *Testing rule for defined contribution plans.* If a participant is credited with annual additions in only one defined contribution plan, in determining whether the requirements of section 415(c) are satisfied, only the limitation year applicable to that plan is considered. However, if a participant is credited with annual addi-

tions in more than one defined contribution plan, each such plan satisfies the requirements of section 415(c) only if the limitations of section 415(c) are satisfied with respect to amounts that are annual additions for the limitation year with respect to the participant under the plan, plus amounts credited to the participant's account under all other plans required to be aggregated with the plan pursuant to section 415(f) and §1.415(f)–1 that would have been considered annual additions for the limitation year under the plan if they had been credited under the plan rather than an aggregated plan.

(3) *Testing rule for defined benefit plans.* If a participant has participated in only one defined benefit plan, in determining whether the requirements of section 415(b) are satisfied, only the limitation year applicable to that plan is considered. However, if a participant has participated in more than one defined benefit plan, a plan satisfies the requirements of section 415(b) only if the annual benefit under all plans required to be aggregated pursuant to section 415(f) and §1.415(f)–1 for the limitation year of that plan with respect to the participant satisfy the applicable limitations of section 415(b). Thus, for example, the dollar limitation of section 415(b)(1)(A) applicable to the limitation year for each plan must be applied to annual benefits under all aggregated plans to determine whether the plan satisfies the requirements of section 415(b).

(d) *Change of limitation year*—(1) *In general.* Once established, the limitation year may be changed only by amending the plan. Any change in the limitation year must be a change to a 12-month period commencing with any day within the current limitation year. For purposes of this section, the limitations of section 415 are to be applied in the normal manner to the new limitation year.

(2) *Application to short limitation period.* Where there is a change of limitation year, the limitations of section 415 are to be separately applied to a limitation period which begins with the first day of the current limitation year and which ends on the day before the first day of the first limitation year for which the change is effective. In the case of a defined contribution plan, the dollar limitation with respect to this limitation period is determined by multiplying the applicable dollar limitation for the calendar year in which the limitation period ends by a fraction, the numerator of which is the number of months (including any fractional parts of a month) in the limitation period, and the denominator of which is 12. In the case of a defined benefit plan, no adjustment is made to the section 415(b) limitations to reflect a short limitation period.

(3) *Deemed change of limitation year.* If a defined contribution plan is terminated effective as of a date other than the last day of the plan's limitation year, the plan is treated for purposes of this section as if the plan was amended to change its limitation year. Thus, the rules of this paragraph (d) apply to the terminating plan's final limitation year.

(e) *Limitation year for individuals on whose behalf section 403(b) annuity contracts have been purchased.* The limitation year of an individual on whose behalf a section 403(b) annuity contract has been purchased by an employer is determined in the following manner.

(1) If the individual is not in control of any employer (within the meaning of §1.415(f)–1(f)(2)(ii)), the limitation year is the calendar year. However, the individual may elect to change the limitation year to another twelve-month period. To do this, the individual must attach a statement to his or her income tax return filed for the taxable year in which the change is made. Any change in the limitation year must comply with the rules set forth in paragraph (d) of this section.

(2) If the individual is in control of an employer (within the meaning of §1.415(f)–1(f)(2)(ii)), the limitation year is the limitation year of that employer.

(f) *Limitation year for individuals on whose behalf individual retirement plans are maintained.* The limitation year of an individual on whose behalf an individual retirement plan (within the meaning of section 7701(a)(37)) is maintained is determined in the manner described in paragraph (e) of this section.

(g) *Examples.* The following examples illustrate the application of this section:

Example 1. (i) Participant M is employed by both Employer A and Employer B, each of which maintains a qualified defined contribution plan. M participates in both of these plans. The limitation year for Employer A's plan is January 1 through December 31, and the limitation year for Employer B's plan is April 1 through March 31. Employer A and Employer B are both corporations, and Corporation X owns 100 percent of the stock of Employer A and Employer B.

(ii) The two plans in which M participates are required under section 415(f) to be aggregated for purposes of applying the limitations of section 415(c) to annual additions made with respect to M. Thus, for example, for the limitation year of Employer A's plan that begins January 1, 2008, annual additions with respect to M that are subject to the limitations of section 415(c) include both amounts that are annual additions with respect to M under Employer A's plan for the period beginning January 1, 2008, and ending December 31, 2008, and amounts contributed to Employer B's plan with respect to M that would have been considered annual additions for the period beginning January 1, 2008, and ending December 31, 2008, under Employer A's plan if those amounts had instead been contributed to Employer A's plan.

Example 2. In 2008, an employer with a qualified defined contribution plan using the calendar year as the limitation year elects to change the limitation year to a period beginning July 1 and ending June 30. Because of this change, the plan must satisfy the limitations of section 415(c) for the limitation period beginning January 1, 2008, and ending June 30, 2008. In applying the limitations of section 415(c) to this limitation period, the amount of compensation taken into account may only include compensation for this period. Furthermore, the dollar limitation for this period is the otherwise applicable dollar limitation for calendar year 2008, multiplied by 6/12.

Par. 17. Section 1.416–1 is amended by revising Q&A T–21 to read as follows:

§1.416–1 Questions and answers on top heavy plans.

* * * * *

T–21. Q. For purposes of testing whether an individual has compensation of more than $150,000, what definition of compensation must be used?

A. The definition of compensation to be used is the definition in §1.415(c)–2, however, compensation must be determined for a plan year, not a limitation year. Alternatively, compensation that would be stated on an employee's Form W–2, "*Wage and Tax Statement,*" for the calendar year that ends with or within the plan year may be used, although amounts that would have been stated on the employee's Form W–2 but for an election under section 125, 132(f)(4), 401(k), 403(b), 408(k), 408(p)(2)(A)(i), or 457(b) must be included. A plan must use the same definition of compensation for all top-heavy plan purposes for which the definition in this Q and A must be used.

* * * * *

Par. 18. Section 1.457–4 is amended by revising paragraph (d) to read as follows:

§1.457–4 Annual deferrals, deferral limitations, and deferral agreements under eligible plans.

* * * * *

(d) *Deferrals after severance from employment, including sick, vacation, and back pay under an eligible plan*—(1) *In general.* An eligible plan may provide that a participant who has not had a severance from employment may elect to defer accumulated sick pay, accumulated vacation pay, and back pay under an eligible plan if the requirements of section 457(b) are satisfied. For example, the plan must provide, in accordance with paragraph (b) of this section, that these amounts may be deferred for any calendar month only if an agreement providing for the deferral is entered into before the beginning of the month in which the amounts would otherwise be paid or made available and the participant is an employee on the date the amounts would otherwise be paid or made available. For purposes of section 457, compensation that would otherwise be paid for a payroll period that begins before severance from employment is treated as an amount that would otherwise be paid or made available before an employee has a severance from employment. In addition, deferrals may be made for former employees with respect to compensation described in §1.415(c)–2(e)(3)(i) (relating to certain compensation paid by the later of 2 1/2 months after severance from employment or the end of the limitation year that includes the date of severance from employment). For this purpose, the calendar year is substituted for the limitation year. In addition, compensation described in §1.415(c)–2(e)(4), (g)(4), or (g)(7) (relating to compensation paid to participants who are permanently and totally disabled or compensation relating to qualified military service under section 414(u)), provided those amounts represent compensation described in §1.415(c)–2(e)(3)(i).

(2) *Examples.* The provisions of this paragraph (d) are illustrated by the following examples:

Example 1. (i) *Facts.* Participant G, who is age 62 in year 2007, is an employee who participates in an eligible plan providing a normal retirement age of 65 and a *bona fide* sick leave and vacation pay program of the eligible employer. Under the terms of G's employer's eligible plan and the sick leave and vacation pay program, G is permitted to make a one-time election to contribute amounts representing accumulated sick pay to the eligible plan. G has a severance from employment on January 12, 2008, at which time G's accumulated sick and vacation pay that is payable on March 15, 2008, totals $12,000. G elects, on February 4, 2008, to have the $12,000 of accumulated sick and vacation pay contributed to the eligible plan.

(ii) *Conclusion.* Under the terms of the eligible plan and the sick and vacation pay program, G may elect before March 1, 2008, to defer the accumulated sick and vacation pay because the agreement providing for the deferral is entered into before the beginning of the month in which the amount is currently available and the amount is *bona fide* accumulated sick and vacation pay, as described in §1.415(c)–2(e)(3)(ii), and that is payable by the later of 2 1/2 months after severance from employment or the end of the calendar year that includes the date of severance from employment by G. Thus, under this section and §1.415(c)–2(e)(3)(ii), the $12,000 is included in G's includible compensation for purposes of determining G's includible compensation in year 2008.

Example 2. (i) *Facts.* Same facts as in *Example 1*, except that G's severance from employment is on May 31, 2008, G's $12,000 of accumulated sick and vacation pay is payable on September 15, 2008 (which is by the later of 2 1/2 months after severance from employment or the end of the calendar year that includes the date of severance from employment by G), and G's election to defer the accumulated sick and vacation pay is made before May 1, 2008.

(ii) *Conclusion.* Under this section and §1.415(c)–2(e)(3)(ii), the $12,000 is included in G's includible compensation for purposes of determining G's includible compensation in year 2008.

Example 3. (i) *Facts.* Employer X maintains an eligible plan and a vacation leave plan. Under the terms of the vacation leave plan, employees generally accrue three weeks of vacation per year. Up to one week's unused vacation may be carried over from one year to the next, so that in any single year an employee may have a maximum of four weeks' vacation time. At the beginning of each calendar year, under the terms of the eligible plan (which constitutes an agreement providing for the deferral), the value of any unused vacation time from the prior year in excess of one week is automatically contributed to the eligible plan, to the extent of the employee's maximum deferral limitations. Amounts in excess of the maximum deferral limitations are forfeited.

(ii) *Conclusion.* The value of the unused vacation pay contributed to X's eligible plan pursuant to the terms of the plan and the terms of the vacation leave plan is treated as an annual deferral to the eligible plan for January of the calendar year. No amounts contributed to the eligible plan will be considered made available to a participant in X's eligible plan.

* * * * *

Par. 19. Section 1.457–5 is amended by revising paragraph (d) *Example 2* to read as follows:

§1.457–5 Individual limitation for combined annual deferrals under multiple eligible plans.

* * * * *

(d) * * *

Example 2. (i) *Facts.* Participant E, who will turn 63 on April 1, 2006, participates in four eligible plans during year 2006: Plan W which is an eligible governmental plan; and Plans X, Y, and Z which are each eligible plans of three different tax-exempt entities. For year 2006, the limitation that applies to Participant E under all four plans under §1.457–4(c)(1)(i)(A) is $15,000. For year 2006, the additional age 50 catch-up limitation that applies to Participant E under all four plans under §1.457–4(c)(2) is $5,000. Further, for year 2006, different limitations under §1.457–4(c)(3) and (c)(3)(ii)(B) apply to Participant E under each of these plans, as follows: under Plan W, the underutilized limitation under §1.457–4(c)(3)(ii)(B) is $7,000; under Plan X, the underutilized limitation under §1.457–4(c)(3)(ii)(B) is $2,000; under Plan Y, the underutilized limitation under §1.457–4(c)(3)(ii)(B) is $8,000; and under Plan Z, §1.457–4(c)(3) is not applicable since normal retirement age is 62 under Plan Z. Participant E's includible compensation is in each case in excess of any applicable deferral.

(ii) *Conclusion.* For purposes of applying this section to Participant E for year 2006, Participant E could elect to defer $23,000 under Plan Y, which is the maximum deferral limitation under §1.457–4(c)(1) through (3), and to defer no amount under Plans W, X, and Z. The $23,000 maximum amount is equal to the sum of $15,000 plus $8,000, which is the catch-up amount applicable to Participant E under Plan Y and which is the largest catch-up amount applicable to Participant E under any of the four plans for year 2006. Alternatively, Participant E could instead elect to defer the following combination of amounts: an aggregate total of $15,000 to Plans X, Y, and Z, if no contribution is made to Plan W; an aggregate total of $20,000 to any of the four plans; or $22,000 to Plan W and none to any of the other three plans.

(iii) If the underutilized amount under Plans W, X, and Y for year 2006 were in each case zero (because E had always contributed the maximum amount or E was a new participant) or an amount not in excess of $5,000, the maximum exclusion under this section would be $20,000 for Participant E for year 2006 ($15,000 plus the $5,000 age 50 catch-up amount), which Participant E could contribute to any of the plans.

Par. 20. Section 1.457–6 is amended by revising paragraphs (a) and (c) to read as follows:

§1.457–6 Timing of distributions under eligible plans.

(a) *In general.* Except as provided in paragraph (c) of this section (relating to distributions on account of an unforeseeable emergency), paragraph (e) of this section (relating to distributions of small accounts), §1.457–10(a) (relating to plan terminations), or §1.457–10(c) (relating to domestic relations orders), amounts deferred under an eligible plan may not be paid to a participant or beneficiary before the participant has a severance from employment with the eligible employer or when the participant attains age 70½, if earlier. For rules relating to loans, see paragraph (f) of this section. This section does not apply to distributions of excess amounts under §1.457–4(e). However, except to the extent set forth by the Commissioner in revenue rulings, notices, and other guidance published in the Internal Revenue Bulletin (see §601.601(d) of this chapter), this section applies to amounts held in a separate account for eligible rollover distributions maintained by an eligible governmental plan as described in §1.457–10(e)(2).

* * * * *

(c) *Rules applicable to distributions for unforeseeable emergencies*—(1) *In general.* An eligible plan may permit a distribution to a participant or beneficiary for an unforeseeable emergency. The distribution must satisfy the requirements of paragraph (c)(2) of this section.

(2) *Requirements*—(i) *Unforeseeable emergency defined.* An unforeseeable emergency must be defined in the plan as a severe financial hardship of the participant or beneficiary resulting from an illness or accident of the participant or beneficiary, the participant's or beneficiary's spouse, or the participant's or beneficiary's dependent (as defined in section 152, and, for taxable years beginning on or after January 1, 2005, without regard to section 152(b)(1), (b)(2), and (d)(1)(B)); loss of the participant's or beneficiary's property due to casualty (including the need to rebuild a home following damage to a home not otherwise covered by homeowner's insurance, such as damage that is the result of a natural disaster); or other similar extraordinary and unforeseeable circumstances arising as a result of events beyond the control of the participant or the beneficiary. For example, the imminent foreclosure of or eviction from the participant's or beneficiary's primary residence may constitute an unforeseeable emergency. In addition, the need to pay for medical expenses, including non-refundable deductibles, as well as for the cost of prescription drug medication, may constitute an unforeseeable emergency. Finally, the need to pay for the funeral expenses of a spouse or a dependent (as defined in section 152, and, for taxable years beginning on or after January 1, 2005, without regard to section 152(b)(1), (b)(2), and (d)(1)(B)) of a participant or beneficiary may also constitute an unforeseeable emergency. Except as otherwise specifically provided in this paragraph (c)(2)(i), the purchase of a home and the payment of college tuition are not unforeseeable emergencies under this paragraph (c)(2)(i).

(ii) *Unforeseeable emergency distribution standard.* Whether a participant or beneficiary is faced with an unforeseeable emergency permitting a distribution under this paragraph (c) is to be determined based on the relevant facts and circumstances of each case, but, in any case, a distribution on account of unforeseeable emergency may not be made to the extent that such emergency is or may be relieved through reimbursement or compensation from insurance or otherwise, by liquidation of the participant's assets, to the extent the liquidation of such assets would not itself cause severe financial hardship, or by cessation of deferrals under the plan.

(iii) *Distribution necessary to satisfy emergency need.* Distributions because of an unforeseeable emergency must be limited to the amount reasonably necessary to satisfy the emergency need (which may include any amounts necessary to pay for any federal, state, or local income taxes or penalties reasonably anticipated to result from the distribution).

* * * * *

Par. 21. Section 1.457–10 is amended by revising paragraph (b)(8) to read as follows:

§1.457–10 Miscellaneous provisions.

* * * * *

(b) * * *

(8) *Purchase of permissive service credit by plan-to-plan transfers from an eligible governmental plan to a qualified plan*—(i) *General rule.* An eligible governmental plan of a State may provide for the transfer of amounts deferred by a participant or beneficiary to a defined benefit governmental plan (as defined in section 414(d)), and no amount shall be includible in gross income by reason of the transfer, if the conditions in paragraph (b)(8)(ii) of this section are met. A transfer under this paragraph (b)(8) is not treated as a distribution for purposes of §1.457–6. Therefore, such a transfer may be made before severance from employment.

(ii) *Conditions for plan-to-plan transfers from an eligible governmental plan to a qualified plan.* A transfer may be made under this paragraph (b)(8) only if the transfer is either—

(A) For the purchase of permissive service credit (as defined in section 415(n)(3)(A)) under the receiving defined benefit governmental plan; or

(B) A repayment to which section 415 does not apply by reason of section 415(k)(3).

(iii) *Example.* The provisions of this paragraph (b)(8) are illustrated by the following example:

Example. (i) *Facts.* Plan X is an eligible governmental plan maintained by County Y for its employees. Plan X provides for distributions only in the event of death, an unforeseeable emergency, or severance from employment with County Y (including retirement from County Y). Plan S is a qualified defined benefit plan maintained by State T for its employees. County Y is within State T. Employee A is an employee of County Y and is a participant in Plan X. Employee A previously was an employee of State T and is still entitled to benefits under Plan S. Plan S includes provisions allowing participants in certain plans, including Plan X, to transfer assets to Plan S for the purchase of service credit under Plan S and does not permit the amount transferred to exceed the amount necessary to fund the benefit resulting from the service credit. Although not required to do so, Plan X allows Employee A to transfer assets to Plan S to provide a service benefit under Plan S.

(ii) *Conclusion.* The transfer is permitted under this paragraph (b)(8).

* * * * *

PART 11—TEMPORARY INCOME TAX REGULATIONS UNDER THE EMPLOYEE RETIREMENT INCOME SECURITY ACT OF 1974

Par. 22. The authority citation for part 11 continues to read in part as follows:

Authority: 26 U.S.C. 7805.* * *

§11.415(c)(4)–1 [Removed]

Par. 23. Section 11.415(c)(4)–1 is removed.

Kevin M. Brown,
Deputy Commissioner for Services and Enforcement.

Approved March 20, 2007.

Eric Solomon,
Assistant Secretary of the Treasury (Tax Policy).

(Filed by the Office of the Federal Register on April 4, 2007, 8:45 a.m., and published in the issue of the Federal Register for April 5, 2007, 72 F.R. 16877)

Section 457.—Deferred Compensation Plans of State and Local Governments and Tax-Exempt Organizations

26 CFR 1.457–4: Annual deferrals, deferral limitations, and deferral agreements under eligible plans.

To conform to the amendments to section 415 Income Tax Regulations, section 1.457–4 is amended by revising paragraph (d). Also, minor corrective changes are made to section 1.457–5(d), Example 2, section 1.457–6(a) and (c) and section 1.457–10(b)(8). See T.D. 9319, page 1041.

Section 472.—Last-in, First-out Inventories

26 CFR 1.472–1: Last-in, first-out inventories.

LIFO; price indexes; department stores. The February 2007 Bureau of Labor Statistics price indexes are accepted for use by department stores employing the retail inventory and last-in, first-out inventory methods for valuing inventories for tax years ended on, or with reference to, February 28, 2007.

Rev. Rul. 2007–27

The following Department Store Inventory Price Indexes for February 2007 were issued by the Bureau of Labor Statistics. The indexes are accepted by the Internal Revenue Service, under § 1.472–1(k) of the Income Tax Regulations and Rev. Proc. 86–46, 1986–2 C.B. 739, for appropriate application to inventories of department stores employing the retail inventory and last-in, first-out inventory methods for tax years ended on, or with reference to, February 28, 2007.

The Department Store Inventory Price Indexes are prepared on a national basis and include (a) 23 major groups of departments, (b) three special combinations of the major groups — soft goods, durable goods, and miscellaneous goods, and (c) a store total, which covers all departments, including some not listed separately, except for the following: candy, food, liquor, tobacco, and contract departments.

BUREAU OF LABOR STATISTICS, DEPARTMENT STORE INVENTORY PRICE INDEXES BY DEPARTMENT GROUPS
(January 1941 = 100, unless otherwise noted)

Groups	Feb. 2006	Feb. 2007	Percent Change From Feb. 2006 to Feb. 2007[1]
1. Piece Goods	437.4	427.9	-2.2
2. Domestics and Draperies	499.5	474.1	-5.1
3. Women's and Children's Shoes	678.8	655.3	-3.5
4. Men's Shoes	869.8	867.5	-0.3
5. Infants' Wear	563.8	566.3	0.4
6. Women's Underwear	538.4	554.1	2.9
7. Women's Hosiery	346.1	345.8	-0.1
8. Women's and Girls' Accessories	570.3	547.7	-4.0
9. Women's Outerwear and Girls' Wear	334.1	360.0	7.8
10. Men's Clothing	519.4	520.1	0.1
11. Men's Furnishings	556.4	566.4	1.8
12. Boys' Clothing and Furnishings	400.2	381.2	-4.7
13. Jewelry	857.6	917.0	6.9
14. Notions	793.6	807.2	1.7
15. Toilet Articles and Drugs	1010.6	1001.8	-0.9
16. Furniture and Bedding	602.0	603.9	0.3
17. Floor Coverings	614.1	615.0	0.1
18. Housewares	698.0	692.9	-0.7
19. Major Appliances	204.3	211.0	3.3
20. Radio and Television	37.3	33.5	-10.2
21. Recreation and Education[2]	77.3	76.4	-1.2
22. Home Improvements[2]	139.2	141.6	1.7
23. Automotive Accessories[2]	117.4	122.7	4.5
Groups 1–15: Soft Goods	543.7	552.2	1.6
Groups 16–20: Durable Goods	375.1	372.4	-0.7
Groups 21–23: Misc. Goods[2]	93.3	94.1	0.9
Store Total[3]	484.5	489.6	1.1

[1]Absence of a minus sign before the percentage change in this column signifies a price increase.

[2]Indexes on a January 1986 = 100 base.

[3]The store total index covers all departments, including some not listed separately, except for the following: candy, food, liquor, tobacco, and contract departments.

DRAFTING INFORMATION

The principal author of this revenue ruling is John Roman Faron of the Office of Associate Chief Counsel (Income Tax and Accounting). For further information regarding this revenue ruling, contact Mr. Faron at (202) 622–4930 (not a toll-free call).

Section 1502.—Regulations

26 CFR 1.1502–35: Transfers of subsidiary stock and deconsolidations of subsidiaries.

T.D. 9322

DEPARTMENT OF THE TREASURY
Internal Revenue Service
26 CFR Part 1

Anti-Avoidance and Anti-Loss Reimportation Rules Applicable Following a Loss on Disposition of Stock of Consolidated Subsidiaries

AGENCY: Internal Revenue Service (IRS), Treasury.

ACTION: Final and temporary regulations.

SUMMARY: This document contains final and temporary regulations under section 1502 of the Internal Revenue Code (Code). These regulations provide guidance to corporations filing consolidated returns. These regulations apply an anti-avoidance rule and revise an anti-loss reimportation rule that applies following a disposition of stock of a subsidiary at a loss. The text of the temporary regulations also serves as the text of the proposed regulations (REG–156420–06) set forth in the notice of proposed rulemaking on this subject in this issue of the Bulletin.

DATES: *Effective Date:* These regulations are effective April 10, 2007.

Applicability Date: For dates of applicability, see §§1.1502–32T(k) and 1.1502–35T(j)(2).

FOR FURTHER INFORMATION CONTACT: Theresa Abell (202) 622–7700 or Phoebe Bennett (202) 622–7770 (not toll-free numbers).

SUPPLEMENTARY INFORMATION:

Background and Explanation of Provisions

Section 1.1502–35 currently addresses loss duplication. The rule generally applies whenever there is a disposition of loss shares of subsidiary stock or a subsidiary is deconsolidated. The regulation includes several specific anti-abuse rules, including a rule intended to prevent a group from getting the benefit of a loss on the stock of one of its subsidiaries and then reimporting the same economic loss back into the group (or its successor) in order to claim a duplicative benefit from the one loss.

The current anti-loss reimportation rule generally disallows reimported losses that duplicate a loss recognized and allowed with respect to the disposition of subsidiary stock. The term "subsidiary" is defined in §1.1502–1(c) to mean a corporation that is a member of a consolidated group but is not the common parent of the group. Taxpayers have attempted to avoid the anti-loss reimportation rule by first deconsolidating a subsidiary and then selling loss shares of the subsidiary's stock. The loss on the stock is one that was reflected in the subsidiary's attributes at the time of the deconsolidation and is thus one that the anti-loss reimportation rule is intended to address. But because the sale occurs after the subsidiary ceases to be a member of the group, taxpayers take the position that the loss recognized is not with respect to "subsidiary" stock and therefore is not subject to the anti-loss reimportation rule. Thus, after obtaining the tax benefit of its economic loss (on the disposition of the stock), the group would be free to reimport the loss and then (directly or through a successor group) claim a second tax benefit for its one economic loss.

The IRS and Treasury Department believe that the duplication of a group loss distorts group income, and is therefore inappropriate, regardless of whether or not a duplicative recognition of the loss occurs while the subsidiary is a member. In either case, the group would obtain more than a single tax benefit for one economic loss. The IRS and Treasury Department recognize that such transactions remain subject to, and reimportation will be prevented by, other principles of law, such as the Step-Transaction Doctrine and other anti-avoidance rules of law. However, the IRS and Treasury Department have concluded that tax administration would be better served by revising the current anti-loss reimportation rule to address these situations more directly.

Accordingly, these final and temporary regulations revise the anti-loss reimportation rule to clarify that losses reflected in the basis of subsidiary stock at the time of deconsolidation may not be recognized and reimported into the group, regardless of whether the stock losses are recognized when the subsidiary is a member of the group. To discourage further structuring to avoid its purposes, the loss reimportation rule is also revised to replace the list of events that cause the application of the rule with a list of criteria that identify reimportation transactions that will be treated as subject to the rule.

In addition, the temporary regulations add a general anti-avoidance rule under §1.1502–35T(g)(6), which provides that appropriate adjustments will be made if a taxpayer acts with a view to avoid the purposes of §1.1502–35. The temporary regulations also remove §1.1502–35(h) (continued applicability of other rules of law) because it unnecessarily duplicates §1.1502–80(a), which provides that other rules of law apply to members of consolidated groups unless otherwise provided in the regulations.

The temporary regulations that revise the anti-loss reimportation rule apply to reimportation events that occur on or after

April 10, 2007 if they occur with respect to stock of a subsidiary sold on or after March 7, 2002, or with respect to stock of a subsidiary or former subsidiary sold on or after April 10, 2007. The temporary regulations provide a general anti-avoidance rule that applies on or after April 10, 2007.

Special Analyses

It has been determined that this Treasury decision is not a significant regulatory action as defined in Executive Order 12866. Therefore, a regulatory assessment is not required. These temporary regulations address situations in which taxpayers inappropriately attempt to recognize duplicative tax losses by attempting to avoid the application of the anti-loss reimportation rule. For this reason, it has been determined pursuant to 5 U.S.C. 553(b)(B) that prior notice and public procedure are impracticable and contrary to the public interest. For the same reason, it has been determined pursuant to 5 U.S.C. 553(d)(3) that good cause exists to make these temporary regulations effective upon the date of publication. For applicability of the Regulatory Flexibility Act (5 U.S.C. chapter 6) refer to the Special Analyses section of the preamble to the cross-reference notice of the proposed rulemaking published in this issue of the Bulletin. Pursuant to section 7805(f) of the Code, these temporary regulations will be submitted to the Chief Counsel for Advocacy of the Small Business Administration for comment on their impact on small business.

Drafting Information

The principal author of these regulations is Phoebe Bennett, Office of the Associate Chief Counsel (Corporate). However, other personnel from the IRS and Treasury Department participated in their development.

* * * * *

Adoption of Amendments to the Regulations

Accordingly, 26 CFR part 1 is amended as follows:

PART 1—INCOME TAXES

Paragraph 1. The authority citation for part 1 continues to read as follows:

Authority: 26 U.S.C. 7805 * * *

Sections 1.1502–32T and 1.1502–35T also issued under 26 U.S.C. 1502 * * *

Par. 2. Section 1.1502–32 is amended by revising paragraph (b)(3)(iii)(D) and adding paragraph (k) to read as follows:

§1.1502–32 Investment adjustments.

* * * * *

(b) * * *

(3) * * *

(iii) * * *

(D) [Reserved]. For further guidance, see §1.1502–32T(b)(3)(iii)(D).

* * * * *

(k) [Reserved]. For further guidance, see §1.1502–32T(k).

Par. 3. Section 1.1502–32T is amended by revising paragraphs (a) through (b)(3)(iii) and adding paragraph (k) to read as follows:

§1.1502–32T Investment adjustments (temporary).

(a) through (b)(3)(iii)(C) [Reserved]. For further guidance, see §1.1502–32(a) through (b)(3)(iii)(C).

(D) *Loss disallowed under §1.1502–35T(g)(3)(ii).* Any loss or deduction the use of which is disallowed pursuant to §1.1502–35T(g)(3)(ii) (other than duplicating items that are carried back to a consolidated return year of the group), and with respect to which no waiver described in paragraph (b)(4) of this section is filed, is treated as a noncapital, nondeductible expense incurred during the taxable year that such loss would otherwise be absorbed.

(b)(3)(iv) through (b)(4)(iii) [Reserved]. For further guidance, see §1.1502–32(b)(3)(iv) through (b)(4)(iii).

* * * * *

(k) *Effective date*—(1) *Applicability date.* Paragraph (b)(3)(iii)(D) of this section applies to any original consolidated Federal income tax return due (without extensions) after April 10, 2007.

(2) *Expiration date.* The applicability of paragraphs (b)(3)(iii)(D) and (k) of this section will expire on April 9, 2007.

Par. 4. Section 1.1502–35 is amended by:

1. Revising paragraphs (g)(3) and (h).
2. Adding new paragraph (g)(6).
3. Revising paragraph (j).

The revisions and additions read as follows:

§1.1502–35 Transfers of subsidiary stock and deconsolidations of subsidiaries.

* * * * *

(g) * * *

(3) [Reserved]. For further guidance, see §1.1502–35T(g)(3).

* * * * *

(6) [Reserved]. For further guidance, see §1.1502–35T(g)(6).

(h) [Reserved]. For further guidance, see §1.1502–35T(h).

* * * * *

(j) *Effective dates*—(1) *In general.* This section applies with respect to stock transfers, deconsolidations of subsidiaries, determinations of worthlessness, and stock dispositions on or after March 10, 2006. For rules applicable before March 10, 2006, see §1.1502–35T(j) as contained in 26 CFR part 1 in effect on January 1, 2006.

(2) [Reserved]. For further guidance, see §1.1502–35T(j)(2).

* * * * *

Par. 5. Section 1.1502–35T is amended by revising paragraphs (g)(3) and (h) and adding a new paragraph (g)(6) and revising paragraph (j) to read as follows:

§1.1502–35T Transfers of subsidiary stock and deconsolidations of subsidiaries (temporary).

* * * * *

(c)(4)(ii) through (g)(2) [Reserved]. For further guidance, see §1.1502–35(c)(4)(ii) through (g)(2).

(3) *Anti-loss reimportation rule*—(i) *Conditions for application.* This paragraph (g)(3) applies when—

(A) A member of a group (the selling group) recognized and was allowed a loss with respect to a share of stock of S, a subsidiary or former subsidiary of the selling group;

(B) That stock loss was duplicated (in whole or in part) in S's attributes (duplicating items) at the earlier of the time that the loss was recognized or that S ceased to be a member; and

(C) Within ten years of the date that S ceased to be a member, there is a reimportation event. For this purpose, a reimportation event is any event after which a duplicating item is a reimported item. A reimported item is any duplicating item that is reflected in the attributes of any member of the selling group, including S, or, if not reflected in the attributes, would be properly taken into account by any member of the selling group (for example as the result of a carryback) (a reimported item).

(ii) *Effect of application.* Immediately before the time that a reimported item (or any portion of a reimported item) would be properly taken into account (but for the application of this paragraph (g)(3)), such item (or such portion of the item) is reduced to zero and no deduction or loss is allowed, directly or indirectly, with respect to that item.

(iii) *Operating rules.* For purposes of this paragraph (g)(3)—

(A) The terms member, subsidiary, and group include their predecessors and successors to the extent necessary to effectuate the purposes of this section;

(B) The determination of whether a loss is duplicative is made under the principles of paragraph (d)(4) of this section; and

(C) The reduction of a reimported item (other than duplicating items that are carried back to a consolidated return year of the selling group) is a noncapital, nondeductible expense within the meaning of §1.1502–32(b)(3)(iii).

(g)(4) through (g)(5) [Reserved]. For further guidance, see §1.1502–35(g)(4) through (g)(5).

(6) *General anti-avoidance rule applicable on or after April 10, 2007.* If a taxpayer acts with a view to avoid the purposes of this section, appropriate adjustments will be made to carry out the purposes of this section.

(h) *Application of other rules of law.* See §1.1502–80(a) regarding the general applicability of other rules of law.

(i) [Reserved]. For further guidance, see §1.1502–35(i).

(j)(1) [Reserved]. For further guidance, see §1.1502–35(j)(1).

(2) *Transactions after April 10, 2007*—(i) *Effective date.* Paragraph (g)(3) of this section applies to reimported items if the related stock loss is recognized on or after April 10, 2007. Paragraph (g)(3) (other than paragraph (g)(3)(i)(A)) of this section also applies with respect to the duplication of subsidiary stock loss recognized in dispositions (described in §1.1502–35(g)(3)(i)(A), as contained in 26 CFR part 1, revised as of January 1, 2007) on or after March 7, 2002, if the reimportation event with respect to that loss occurs on or after April 10, 2007. For rules applicable to losses reimported before April 10, 2007, see §1.1502–35(g)(3), as contained in 26 CFR part 1 in effect on January 1, 2007. Paragraphs (g)(6) and (h) of this section apply on or after April 10, 2007. For rules applicable prior to April 10, 2007, see §1.1502–35 as contained in 26 CFR part 1 in effect on January 1, 2007.

(ii) *Expiration date.* The applicability of paragraphs (g)(3), (g)(6), and (h) of this section will expire on April 9, 2007.

* * * * *

Linda M. Kroening,
Acting Deputy Commissioner for Services and Enforcement.

Approved March 29, 2007.

Eric Solomon,
Assistant Secretary of the Treasury.

(Filed by the Office of the Federal Register on April 9, 2007, 8:45 a.m., and published in the issue of the Federal Register for April 10, 2007, 72 F.R. 17804)

Part III. Administrative, Procedural, and Miscellaneous

Nonconventional Source Fuel Credit, Section 45K Inflation Adjustment Factor, and Section 45K Reference Price

Notice 2007–38

SECTION 1. PURPOSE

This notice publishes the nonconventional source fuel credit, inflation adjustment factor, and reference price under § 45K of the Internal Revenue Code for calendar year 2006. These are used to determine the credit allowable under § 45K for fuel produced from a nonconventional source. The calendar year 2006 inflation-adjusted credit applies to the sales of barrel-of-oil equivalent of qualified fuels sold by a taxpayer to an unrelated person during the 2006 calendar year, the domestic production of which is attributable to the taxpayer.

SECTION 2. BACKGROUND

Section 45K(a) provides for a credit for producing fuel from a nonconventional source, measured in barrel-of-oil equivalent of qualified fuels, the production of which is attributable to the taxpayer and is sold by the taxpayer to an unrelated person during the tax year. The credit is equal to the product of $3.00 and the appropriate inflation adjustment factor.

Section 45K(b)(1) and (2) provides for a phase-out of the credit. The credit allowable under § 45K(a) must be reduced by an amount which bears the same ratio to the amount of the credit (determined without regard to § 45K(b)(1)) as the amount by which the reference price for the calendar year in which the sale occurs exceeds $23.50 bears to $6.00. The $3.00 in § 45K(a) and the $23.50 and $6.00 each must be adjusted by multiplying these amounts by the appropriate inflation adjustment factor.

Section 45K(c)(1), in part, defines the term "qualified fuels" to include gas produced from biomass and liquid, gaseous, or solid synthetic fuels produced from coal (including lignite), including such fuels when used as feedstocks.

Section 45K(d)(1) provides that the credit applies only to sales of qualified fuels the production of which is within the United States (within the meaning of § 638(1)) or a possession of the United States (within the meaning of § 638(2)).

Section 45K(d)(2)(A) requires that the Secretary, not later than April 1 of each calendar year, determine and publish in the Federal Register the inflation adjustment factor and the reference price for the preceding calendar year.

Section 45K(d)(2)(B) defines "inflation adjustment factor" for a calendar year as a fraction the numerator of which is the GNP implicit price deflator for the calendar year and the denominator of which is the GNP implicit price deflator for calendar year 1979. The term "GNP implicit price deflator" means the first revision of the implicit price deflator for the gross national product as computed and published by the Department of Commerce.

Section 45K(d)(2)(C) defines "reference price" to mean with respect to a calendar year the Secretary's estimate of the annual average wellhead price per barrel for all domestic crude oil the price of which is not subject to regulation by the United States.

Section 45K(d)(5) provides that the term "barrel-of-oil equivalent" with respect to any fuel generally means that amount of the fuel that has a Btu content of 5.8 million.

Section 45K(g)(1) provides that in the case of a facility for producing coke or coke gas, which was placed in service before January 1, 1993, or after June 30, 1998, and before January 1, 2010, § 45K(g) shall apply with respect to coke and coke gas produced in such facility and sold during the period beginning on the later of January 1, 2006, or the date that such facility is placed in service, and ending on the date which is 4 years after the date such period began.

Section 45K(g)(2)(B) provides that in determining the amount of credit allowable under § 45K solely by reason of § 45K(g), § 45K(d)(2)(B) shall be applied by substituting "2004" for "1979." Accordingly, for purposes of § 45K(g), the inflation adjustment factor for a calendar year is a fraction the numerator of which is the GNP implicit price deflator for the calendar year and the denominator of which is the GNP implicit price deflator for calendar year 2004.

Section 45K(g)(2)(D) provides that the phase-out of the credit under § 45K(b)(1) does not apply in the case of facilities producing coke or coke gas.

SECTION 3. REFERENCE PRICE

The reference price for calendar year 2006 is $59.68.

SECTION 4. INFLATION ADJUSTMENT AND CREDIT AMOUNT

.01 *Gas Produced from Biomass and Liquid, Gaseous, or Solid Synthetic Fuel Produced from Coal.*

In the case of gas produced from biomass and liquid, gaseous, or solid synthetic fuel produced from coal, the inflation adjustment factor for calendar year 2006 is 2.3429. Because the calendar year 2006 reference price exceeds $23.50 multiplied by the inflation adjustment factor, the credit per barrel equivalent of qualified fuel sold in calendar year 2006 is reduced by $2.31, which is the amount that bears the same ratio to the amount of the credit (determined without regard to § 45K(b)(1)) as the amount by which the reference price for the calendar year 2006 exceeds $23.50 (adjusted for inflation) bears to $6.00 (adjusted for inflation).

The phase-out amount is computed as follows:
($3.00 x 2.3429) x [($59.68 – ($23.50 x 2.3429)) / ($6.00 x 2.3429)] = $2.31.

The nonconventional source fuel credit under § 45K(a) is $4.72 per barrel-of-oil equivalent of qualified fuels [($3.00 x 2.3429) - $2.31].

.02 *Facilities for Producing Coke or Coke Gas.* In case of facilities producing coke or coke gas, the inflation adjustment factor for calendar year 2006 is 1.0605. The nonconventional source fuel credit is $3.18 per barrel-of-oil equivalent ($3.00 x 1.0605).

SECTION 5. DRAFTING INFORMATION CONTACT

The principal author of this notice is Jaime C. Park of the Office of Associate Chief Counsel (Passthroughs and Special

Industries). For further information regarding this notice, contact Ms. Park at (202) 622–3120 (not a toll-free call).

---

26 CFR 601.105: Examination of returns and claims for refund, credit, or abatement; determination of correct tax liability.
(Also: Part I, §§ 280F; 1.280F–7.)

Rev. Proc. 2007–30

SECTION 1. PURPOSE

.01. This revenue procedure provides: (1) limitations on depreciation deductions for owners of passenger automobiles first placed in service by the taxpayer during calendar year 2007, including a separate table of limitations on depreciation deductions for trucks and vans; and (2) the amounts to be included in income by lessees of passenger automobiles first leased by the taxpayer during calendar year 2007, including a separate table of inclusion amounts for lessees of trucks and vans.

.02. The tables detailing these depreciation limitations and lessee inclusion amounts reflect the automobile price inflation adjustments required by § 280F(d)(7).

.03. Section 280F(a)(1)(C), which directed the use of higher depreciation deduction limits for certain electric automobiles, was applicable only to property placed in service after December 31, 2001 and before January 1, 2007. Accordingly, separate tables are no longer provided for electric automobiles, and taxpayers should use the applicable table provided in this revenue procedure.

SECTION 2. BACKGROUND

.01. For owners of passenger automobiles, § 280F(a) imposes dollar limitations on the depreciation deduction for the year that the passenger automobile is placed in service by the taxpayer and each succeeding year. Section 280F(d)(7) requires the amounts allowable as depreciation deductions to be increased by a price inflation adjustment amount for passenger automobiles placed in service after 1988. The method of calculating this price inflation amount for trucks and vans placed in service in or after calendar year 2003 uses a different CPI "automobile component" (the "new trucks" component) than that used in the price inflation amount calculation for other passenger automobiles (the "new cars" component), resulting in somewhat higher depreciation deductions for trucks and vans. This change reflects the higher rate of price inflation that trucks and vans have been subject to since 1988. For purposes of this revenue procedure, the term "trucks and vans" refers to passenger automobiles that are built on a truck chassis, including minivans and sport utility vehicles (SUVs) that are built on a truck chassis.

.02. For leased passenger automobiles, § 280F(c) requires a reduction in the deduction allowed to the lessee of the passenger automobile. The reduction must be substantially equivalent to the limitations on the depreciation deductions imposed on owners of passenger automobiles. Under § 1.280F–7(a), this reduction requires the lessees to include in gross income an inclusion amount determined by applying a formula to the amount obtained from a table. There is a table for lessees of trucks and vans and a table for all other passenger automobiles. Each table shows inclusion amounts for a range of fair market values for each tax year after the passenger automobile is first leased.

SECTION 3. SCOPE

.01. The limitations on depreciation deductions in section 4.02(2) of this revenue procedure apply to passenger automobiles (other than leased passenger automobiles) that are placed in service by the taxpayer in calendar year 2007, and continue to apply for each tax year that the passenger automobile remains in service.

.02. The tables in section 4.03 of this revenue procedure apply to leased passenger automobiles for which the lease term begins during calendar year 2007. Lessees of such passenger automobiles must use these tables to determine the inclusion amount for each tax year during which the passenger automobile is leased. See Rev. Proc. 2002–14, 2002–1 C.B. 450, for passenger automobiles first leased before January 1, 2003, Rev. Proc. 2003–75, 2003–2 C.B. 1018, for passenger automobiles first leased during calendar year 2003, Rev. Proc. 2004–20, 2004–1 C.B. 642, for passenger automobiles first leased during calendar year 2004, Rev. Proc. 2005–13, 2005–1 C.B. 759, for passenger automobiles first leased during calendar year 2005, and Rev. Proc. 2006–18, 2006–1 C.B. 645, for passenger automobiles first leased during calendar year 2006.

SECTION 4. APPLICATION

.01. In General.

(1) Limitations on Depreciation Deductions for Certain Automobiles. The limitations on depreciation deductions for passenger automobiles placed in service by the taxpayer for the first time during calendar year 2007 are found in Tables 1 and 2 in section 4.02(2) of this revenue procedure. Table 1 of this revenue procedure provides limitations on depreciation deductions for a passenger automobile (other than a truck or van). Table 2 of this revenue procedure provides limitations on depreciation deductions for a truck or van.

(2) Inclusions in Income of Lessees of Passenger Automobiles. A taxpayer first leasing a passenger automobile during calendar year 2007 must determine the inclusion amount that is added to gross income using the tables in section 4.03 of this revenue procedure. The inclusion amount is determined using Table 3 in the case of a passenger automobile (other than a truck or van), and Table 4 in the case of a truck or van. In addition, the procedures of § 1.280F–7(a) must be followed.

.02. Limitations on Depreciation Deductions for Certain Automobiles.

(1) Amount of the Inflation Adjustment. Under § 280F(d)(7)(B)(i), the automobile price inflation adjustment for any calendar year is the percentage (if any) by which the CPI automobile component for October of the preceding calendar year exceeds the CPI automobile component for October 1987. The term "CPI automobile component" is defined in § 280F(d)(7)(B)(ii) as the "automobile component" of the Consumer Price Index for all Urban Consumers published by the Department of Labor (the CPI). The new car component of the CPI was 115.2 for October 1987 and 136.3 for October 2006. The October 2006 index exceeded the October 1987 index by 21.1. The Service has, therefore, determined that the automobile price inflation adjustment for 2007 for passenger automobiles (other than trucks and vans) is 18.32 percent (21.1/115.2 x

100%). This adjustment is applicable to all passenger automobiles (other than trucks and vans) that are first placed in service in calendar year 2007. The dollar limitations in § 280F(a) must therefore be multiplied by a factor of 0.1832, and the resulting increases, after rounding to the nearest $100, are added to the 1988 limitations to give the depreciation limitations applicable to passenger automobiles (other than trucks and vans) for calendar year 2007. To determine the dollar limitations applicable to trucks and vans first placed in service during calendar year 2007, the new truck component of the CPI is used instead of the new car component. The new truck component of the CPI was 112.4 for October 1987 and 141.4 for October 2006. The October 2006 index exceeded the October 1987 index by 29.0. The Service has, therefore, determined that the automobile price inflation adjustment for 2007 for trucks and vans is 25.80 percent (29.0/112.4 x 100%). This adjustment is applicable to all trucks and vans that are first placed in service in calendar year 2007. The dollar limitations in § 280F(a) must therefore be multiplied by a factor of 0.2580, and the resulting increases, after rounding to the nearest $100, are added to the 1988 limitations to give the depreciation limitations applicable to trucks and vans.

(2) Amount of the Limitation. For passenger automobiles placed in service by the taxpayer in calendar year 2007, Tables 1 and 2 contain the dollar amount of the depreciation limitation for each tax year. Use Table 1 for passenger automobiles placed in service by the taxpayer in calendar year 2007. Use Table 2 for trucks and vans placed in service by the taxpayer in calendar year 2007.

REV. PROC. 2007–30 TABLE 1

DEPRECIATION LIMITATIONS FOR PASSENGER AUTOMOBILES
PLACED IN SERVICE BY THE TAXPAYER DURING CALENDAR YEAR 2007

Tax Year	*Amount*
1st Tax Year	$3,060
2nd Tax Year	$4,900
3rd Tax Year	$2,850
Each Succeeding Year	$1,775

REV. PROC. 2007–30 TABLE 2

DEPRECIATION LIMITATIONS FOR TRUCKS AND VANS
PLACED IN SERVICE BY THE TAXPAYER DURING CALENDAR YEAR 2007

Tax Year	*Amount*
1st Tax Year	$3,260
2nd Tax Year	$5,200
3rd Tax Year	$3,050
Each Succeeding Year	$1,875

03. Inclusions in Income of Lessees of Passenger Automobiles.

The inclusion amounts for passenger automobiles first leased in calendar year 2007 are calculated under the procedures described in § 1.280F–7(a). Lessees of passenger automobiles other than trucks and vans should use Table 3 of this revenue procedure in applying these procedures, while lessees of trucks and vans should use Table 4 of this revenue procedure.

REV. PROC. 2007–30 TABLE 3 DOLLAR AMOUNTS FOR PASSENGER AUTOMOBILES (THAT ARE NOT TRUCKS OR VANS) WITH A LEASE TERM BEGINNING IN CALENDAR YEAR 2007						
Fair Market Value of Passenger Automobile		Tax Year During Lease				
Over	Not Over	1st	2nd	3rd	4th	5th & later
$15,500	$15,800	2	5	11	11	13
15,800	16,100	4	10	17	19	22
16,100	16,400	6	14	24	28	31
16,400	16,700	9	18	31	35	41
16,700	17,000	11	23	37	43	50
17,000	17,500	13	29	46	54	62
17,500	18,000	17	37	56	68	77
18,000	18,500	20	44	68	81	93
18,500	19,000	24	51	80	94	108
19,000	19,500	27	59	90	108	124
19,500	20,000	30	67	101	121	139
20,000	20,500	34	74	113	134	154
20,500	21,000	37	82	123	148	170
21,000	21,500	41	89	135	161	185
21,500	22,000	44	97	146	174	201
22,000	23,000	49	108	163	194	224
23,000	24,000	56	123	185	221	255
24,000	25,000	63	138	207	248	285
25,000	26,000	70	153	229	275	316
26,000	27,000	77	168	251	302	347
27,000	28,000	83	183	274	328	378
28,000	29,000	90	198	296	355	409
29,000	30,000	97	213	318	382	439
30,000	31,000	104	228	341	408	470
31,000	32,000	111	243	363	435	501
32,000	33,000	118	258	385	461	532
33,000	34,000	125	273	407	488	563
34,000	35,000	131	288	430	515	593
35,000	36,000	138	303	452	542	624
36,000	37,000	145	318	474	568	656
37,000	38,000	152	333	496	595	686
38,000	39,000	159	348	519	621	717
39,000	40,000	166	363	541	648	748
40,000	41,000	172	378	564	674	779
41,000	42,000	179	393	586	701	810
42,000	43,000	186	408	608	728	840
43,000	44,000	193	423	630	755	871
44,000	45,000	200	438	652	782	902
45,000	46,000	207	453	674	809	933
46,000	47,000	213	468	697	835	964
47,000	48,000	220	483	719	862	995
48,000	49,000	227	498	742	888	1,025
49,000	50,000	234	513	764	915	1,056
50,000	51,000	241	528	786	942	1,087
51,000	52,000	248	543	808	969	1,117
52,000	53,000	254	558	831	995	1,148
53,000	54,000	261	573	853	1,022	1,179
54,000	55,000	268	588	875	1,049	1,210
55,000	56,000	275	603	897	1,076	1,241
56,000	57,000	282	618	920	1,102	1,271
57,000	58,000	289	633	942	1,128	1,303
58,000	59,000	296	648	964	1,155	1,334
59,000	60,000	302	663	987	1,182	1,364

REV. PROC. 2007–30 TABLE 3

DOLLAR AMOUNTS FOR PASSENGER AUTOMOBILES
(THAT ARE NOT TRUCKS OR VANS)
WITH A LEASE TERM BEGINNING IN CALENDAR YEAR 2007

Fair Market Value of Passenger Automobile		Tax Year During Lease				
Over	Not Over	1st	2nd	3rd	4th	5th & later
60,000	62,000	313	685	1,020	1,222	1,411
62,000	64,000	326	716	1,064	1,276	1,472
64,000	66,000	340	746	1,108	1,329	1,534
66,000	68,000	354	775	1,154	1,382	1,595
68,000	70,000	367	806	1,198	1,435	1,657
70,000	72,000	381	836	1,242	1,489	1,719
72,000	74,000	395	865	1,287	1,543	1,780
74,000	76,000	408	896	1,331	1,596	1,842
76,000	78,000	422	926	1,376	1,649	1,903
78,000	80,000	436	955	1,421	1,703	1,965
80,000	85,000	460	1,008	1,498	1,796	2,074
85,000	90,000	494	1,083	1,610	1,929	2,228
90,000	95,000	528	1,158	1,721	2,063	2,382
95,000	100,000	562	1,233	1,833	2,196	2,536
100,000	110,000	614	1,346	1,999	2,396	2,767
110,000	120,000	682	1,496	2,222	2,663	3,075
120,000	130,000	750	1,646	2,444	2,931	3,383
130,000	140,000	819	1,796	2,667	3,197	3,692
140,000	150,000	887	1,946	2,890	3,464	4,000
150,000	160,000	956	2,096	3,112	3,731	4,308
160,000	170,000	1,024	2,246	3,335	3,998	4,616
170,000	180,000	1,093	2,396	3,557	4,266	4,924
180,000	190,000	1,161	2,546	3,780	4,532	5,233
190,000	200,000	1,229	2,696	4,003	4,799	5,541
200,000	210,000	1,298	2,846	4,225	5,067	5,848
210,000	220,000	1,366	2,996	4,448	5,333	6,157
220,000	230,000	1,435	3,146	4,671	5,600	6,465
230,000	240,000	1,503	3,296	4,893	5,867	6,774
240,000	and up	1,571	3,446	5,116	6,134	7,082

REV. PROC. 2007–30 TABLE 4

DOLLAR AMOUNTS FOR TRUCKS AND VANS
WITH A LEASE TERM BEGINNING IN CALENDAR YEAR 2007

Fair Market Value of Truck or Van		Tax Year During Lease				
Over	Not Over	1st	2nd	3rd	4th	5th and later
$16,400	$16,700	2	4	8	10	11
16,700	17,000	4	9	15	17	21
17,000	17,500	6	15	24	28	33
17,500	18,000	10	22	35	42	48
18,000	18,500	13	30	46	55	64
18,500	19,000	17	37	57	69	79
19,000	19,500	20	45	68	82	94
19,500	20,000	24	52	80	95	109
20,000	20,500	27	60	90	109	125
20,500	21,000	30	67	102	122	141
21,000	21,500	34	75	113	135	156
21,500	22,000	37	82	124	149	171
22,000	23,000	42	94	140	169	194
23,000	24,000	49	109	163	195	225
24,000	25,000	56	123	186	222	256

REV. PROC. 2007–30 TABLE 4 DOLLAR AMOUNTS FOR TRUCKS AND VANS WITH A LEASE TERM BEGINNING IN CALENDAR YEAR 2007						
Fair Market Value of Truck or Van		Tax Year During Lease				
Over	Not Over	1st	2nd	3rd	4th	5th and later
25,000	26,000	63	138	208	249	286
26,000	27,000	70	153	230	276	317
27,000	28,000	77	168	252	302	349
28,000	29,000	83	184	274	329	379
29,000	30,000	90	199	296	356	410
30,000	31,000	97	214	318	383	440
31,000	32,000	104	228	342	408	472
32,000	33,000	111	243	364	435	503
33,000	34,000	118	258	386	462	534
34,000	35,000	125	273	408	489	564
35,000	36,000	131	289	430	515	595
36,000	37,000	138	304	452	542	626
37,000	38,000	145	318	475	569	657
38,000	39,000	152	333	497	596	688
39,000	40,000	159	348	520	622	718
40,000	41,000	166	363	542	649	749
41,000	42,000	172	379	563	676	780
42,000	43,000	179	394	586	702	811
43,000	44,000	186	409	608	729	842
44,000	45,000	193	423	631	756	872
45,000	46,000	200	438	653	783	903
46,000	47,000	207	453	675	810	934
47,000	48,000	213	469	697	836	965
48,000	49,000	220	484	719	863	996
49,000	50,000	227	499	741	890	1,026
50,000	51,000	234	514	764	916	1,057
51,000	52,000	241	528	787	943	1,088
52,000	53,000	248	543	809	969	1,119
53,000	54,000	254	559	831	996	1,150
54,000	55,000	261	574	853	1,023	1,180
55,000	56,000	268	589	875	1,050	1,211
56,000	57,000	275	604	897	1,076	1,243
57,000	58,000	282	618	920	1,103	1,273
58,000	59,000	289	633	943	1,129	1,304
59,000	60,000	296	648	965	1,156	1,335
60,000	62,000	306	671	998	1,196	1,381
62,000	64,000	319	701	1,043	1,249	1,443
64,000	66,000	333	731	1,087	1,303	1,504
66,000	68,000	347	761	1,131	1,357	1,566
68,000	70,000	361	791	1,176	1,410	1,627
70,000	72,000	374	821	1,221	1,463	1,689
72,000	74,000	388	851	1,265	1,517	1,751
74,000	76,000	402	881	1,309	1,570	1,813
76,000	78,000	415	911	1,354	1,624	1,874
78,000	80,000	429	941	1,399	1,676	1,936
80,000	85,000	453	994	1,476	1,770	2,044
85,000	90,000	487	1,069	1,587	1,904	2,198
90,000	95,000	521	1,144	1,699	2,037	2,352
95,000	100,000	555	1,219	1,810	2,171	2,506
100,000	110,000	607	1,331	1,977	2,371	2,737
110,000	120,000	675	1,481	2,200	2,638	3,045
120,000	130,000	744	1,631	2,423	2,904	3,354
130,000	140,000	812	1,781	2,646	3,171	3,662
140,000	150,000	880	1,932	2,867	3,439	3,970
150,000	160,000	949	2,081	3,091	3,705	4,279
160,000	170,000	1,017	2,232	3,313	3,972	4,586

REV. PROC. 2007–30 TABLE 4 DOLLAR AMOUNTS FOR TRUCKS AND VANS WITH A LEASE TERM BEGINNING IN CALENDAR YEAR 2007						
Fair Market Value of Truck or Van		Tax Year During Lease				
Over	Not Over	1st	2nd	3rd	4th	5th and later
170,000	180,000	1,086	2,381	3,536	4,239	4,895
180,000	190,000	1,154	2,532	3,758	4,506	5,203
190,000	200,000	1,222	2,682	3,981	4,773	5,511
200,000	210,000	1,291	2,831	4,204	5,040	5,820
210,000	220,000	1,359	2,982	4,426	5,307	6,128
220,000	230,000	1,428	3,131	4,649	5,575	6,435
230,000	240,000	1,496	3,282	4,871	5,841	6,744
240,000	and up	1,565	3,431	5,095	6,108	7,052

SECTION 5. EFFECTIVE DATE

This revenue procedure applies to passenger automobiles (other than leased passenger automobiles) that are first placed in service by the taxpayer during calendar year 2007, and to leased passenger automobiles that are first leased by the taxpayer during calendar year 2007.

SECTION 6. DRAFTING INFORMATION

The principal author of this revenue procedure is Bernard P. Harvey of the Office of Associate Chief Counsel (Passthroughs & Special Industries). For further information regarding the depreciation limitations and lessee inclusion amounts in this revenue procedure, contact Bernard P. Harvey at (202) 622–3110 (not a toll-free call).

Part IV. Items of General Interest

Notice of Proposed Rulemaking by Cross-Reference to Temporary Regulations

Anti-Avoidance and Anti-Loss Reimportation Rules Applicable Following a Loss on Disposition of Stock of Consolidated Subsidiaries

REG–156420–06

AGENCY: Internal Revenue Service (IRS), Treasury.

ACTION: Notice of proposed rulemaking by cross-reference to temporary regulations.

SUMMARY: In this issue of the Bulletin, the IRS is issuing temporary regulations (T.D. 9322) under section 1502 of the Internal Revenue Code (Code). The temporary regulations provide guidance to corporations filing consolidated returns. The temporary regulations apply an anti-avoidance rule and revise an anti-loss reimportation rule that applies after a disposition of stock of a subsidiary at a loss. The text of those regulations also serves as the text of these proposed regulations.

DATES: Written or electronic comments or a request for a public hearing must be received by July 9, 2007.

ADDRESSES: Send submissions to CC:PA:LPD:PR (REG–156420–06), room 5203, Internal Revenue Service, PO Box 7604, Ben Franklin Station, Washington, DC 20044. Submissions may be hand-delivered Monday through Friday between the hours of 8 a.m. and 4 p.m. to CC:PA:LPD:PR (REG–156420–06), Courier's Desk, Internal Revenue Service, 1111 Constitution Avenue, NW, Washington, DC, or sent electronically via the Federal eRulemaking Portal at *www.regulations.gov* (IRS–REG–156420–06).

FOR FURTHER INFORMATION CONTACT: Concerning the proposed regulations, Theresa Abell (202) 622–7700 or Phoebe Bennett (202) 622–7770; concerning submission of comments and request for public hearing, Richard Hurst at *Richard.A.Hurst@irscounsel.treas.gov* or (202) 622–7180 (not toll-free numbers).

SUPPLEMENTARY INFORMATION:

Background and Explanation of Provisions

Temporary regulations in this issue of the Bulletin amend the Income Tax Regulations (26 CFR part 1) relating to section 1502. The temporary regulations provide guidance to corporations filing consolidated returns. The temporary regulations apply an anti-avoidance rule and revise an anti-loss reimportation rule that applies following a disposition of stock of a subsidiary at a loss. The text of those regulations also serves as the text of these proposed regulations. The preamble to the temporary regulations explains the amendments.

Special Analyses

It has been determined that this notice of proposed rulemaking is not a significant regulatory action as defined in Executive Order 12866. Therefore, a regulatory assessment is not required. It is hereby certified that these regulations will not have a significant economic impact on a substantial number of small entities. This certification is based on the fact that these regulations primarily will affect affiliated groups of corporations that have elected to file consolidated returns, which tend to be larger entities. Therefore, a Regulatory Flexibility Analysis under the Regulatory Flexibility Act (5 U.S.C. chapter 6) is not required. Pursuant to section 7805(f) of the Code, this notice of proposed rulemaking will be submitted to the Chief Counsel for Advocacy of the Small Business Administration for comment on its impact on small business.

Comments and Requests for Public Hearing

Before these proposed regulations are adopted as final regulations, consideration will be given to any written (a signed original and eight (8) copies) or electronic comments that are submitted timely to the IRS. The IRS and Treasury Department request comments on the clarity of the proposed rules and how they can be made easier to understand. All comments will be available for public inspection and copying. A public hearing will be scheduled if requested in writing by any person that timely submits written comments. If a public hearing is scheduled, notice of the date, time, and place for the public hearing will be published in the **Federal Register**.

Drafting Information

The principal author of these regulations is Phoebe Bennett, Office of the Associate Chief Counsel (Corporate). However, other personnel from the IRS and Treasury Department participated in their development.

* * * * *

Proposed Amendments to the Regulations

Accordingly, 26 CFR part 1 is proposed to be amended as follows:

PART 1—INCOME TAXES

Paragraph 1. The authority citation for part 1 is amended by adding an entry in numerical order to read as follows:

Authority: 26 U.S.C. 7805 * * *

Par. 2. Section 1.1502–32 is amended by revising paragraph (b)(3)(iii)(D) and adding paragraph (k) to read as follows:

§1.1502–32 Investment adjustments.

* * * * *

(b) * * *

(3) * * *

(iii) * * *

(D) [The text of the proposed amendment to §1.1502–32(b)(3)(iii)(D) is the same as the text of §1.1502–32T(b)(3)(iii)(D) published elsewhere in this issue of the Bulletin].

* * * * *

(k) [The text of the proposed amendment to §1.1502–32(k) is the same as the text of §1.1502–32T(k) published elsewhere in this issue of the Bulletin].

Par. 3. Section 1.1502–35 is amended by:

1. Revising paragraphs (g)(3) and (h).
2. Adding new paragraph (g)(6).
3. Paragraph (j) is revised.

The revisions and additions read as follows:

§1.1502–35 Transfers of subsidiary stock and deconsolidations of subsidiaries.

* * * * *

(g) * * *

(3) [The text of the proposed amendment to §1.1502–35(g)(3) is the same as the text of §1.1502–35T(g)(3) published elsewhere in this issue of the Bulletin].

* * * * *

(6) [The text of the proposed amendment to §1.1502–35(g)(6) is the same as the text of §1.1502–35T(g)(6) published elsewhere in this issue of the Bulletin].

(h) [The text of the proposed amendment to §1.1502–35(h) is the same as the text of §1.1502–35T(h) published elsewhere in this issue of the Bulletin].

* * * * *

(j) [The text of the proposed amendment to §1.1502–35(j) is the same as the text of §1.1502–35T(j) published elsewhere in this issue of the Bulletin].

* * * * *

Linda M. Kroening,
Acting Deputy Commissioner for Services and Enforcement.

(Filed by the Office of the Federal Register on April 9, 2007, 8:45 a.m., and published in the issue of the Federal Register for April 10, 2007, 72 F.R. 17814)

Announcement of Disciplinary Actions Involving Attorneys, Certified Public Accountants, Enrolled Agents, and Enrolled Actuaries — Suspensions, Censures, Disbarments, and Resignations

Announcement 2007-41

Under Title 31, Code of Federal Regulations, Part 10, attorneys, certified public accountants, enrolled agents, and enrolled actuaries may not accept assistance from, or assist, any person who is under disbarment or suspension from practice before the Internal Revenue Service if the assistance relates to a matter constituting practice before the Internal Revenue Service and may not knowingly aid or abet another person to practice before the Internal Revenue Service during a period of suspension, disbarment, or ineligibility of such other person.

To enable attorneys, certified public accountants, enrolled agents, and enrolled actuaries to identify persons to whom these restrictions apply, the Director, Office of Professional Responsibility, will announce in the Internal Revenue Bulletin their names, their city and state, their professional designation, the effective date of disciplinary action, and the period of suspension. This announcement will appear in the weekly Bulletin at the earliest practicable date after such action and will continue to appear in the weekly Bulletins for five successive weeks.

Consent Suspensions From Practice Before the Internal Revenue Service

Under Title 31, Code of Federal Regulations, Part 10, an attorney, certified public accountant, enrolled agent, or enrolled actuary, in order to avoid the institution or conclusion of a proceeding for his or her disbarment or suspension from practice before the Internal Revenue Service, may offer his or her consent to suspension from such practice. The Director, Office of Professional Responsibility, in his discretion, may suspend an attorney, certified public accountant, enrolled agent, or enrolled actuary in accordance with the consent offered.

The following individuals have been placed under consent suspension from practice before the Internal Revenue Service:

Name	Address	Designation	Date of Suspension
Hankinson, Eugene M.	Somerset, PA	CPA	Indefinite from November 15, 2006
Canzano, Richard M.	Winchester, MA	Attorney	Indefinite from November 20, 2006

Name	Address	Designation	Date of Suspension
Sims, Jr., Lionel	Houston, TX	CPA	Indefinite from November 20, 2006
Wendekier, Raymond J.	Patton, PA	Attorney	Indefinite from November 21, 2006
Golden, Larry	Hinesville, GA	CPA	Indefinite from November 28, 2006
Lane, David B.	Hanover, MA	Attorney	Indefinite from November 28, 2006
Brown, Arthur I.	Miami, FL	CPA	Indefinite from December 1, 2006
Frisk, Daniel J.	Fargo, ND	Attorney	Indefinite from December 1, 2006
Small, Kenneth A.	McMurray, PA	CPA	Indefinite from December 1, 2006
Vazquez, Sonya M.	Port Orchard, WA	CPA	Indefinite from December 1, 2006
Swistak, Anthony	Adams, MA	Enrolled Agent	Indefinite from December 6, 2006
Lenahan, Jr., Robert J.	Elizabeth, NJ	Attorney	Indefinite from December 11, 2006
Hayes, Richard A.	Havervill, MA	Attorney	Indefinite from December 14, 2006
Scheller, Stephen M.	Coppell, TX	CPA	Indefinite from December 15, 2006
Wilson, James M.	Berlin, NJ	CPA	Indefinite from December 15, 2006
Franzese, Joseph P.	Winthrop, MA	Attorney	Indefinite from December 18, 2006
Black, Charles C.	Marietta, GA	Attorney	Indefinite from January 1, 2007

Name	Address	Designation	Date of Suspension
Enright, III, Robert A.	Naples, FL	Attorney	Indefinite from January 1, 2007
Fromovitz, Norman M.	Brooklyn, NY	CPA	Indefinite from January 1, 2007
Saylor, Mary A.	Iowa City, IA	Enrolled Agent	Indefinite from January 1, 2007
Seeherman, Alan	Wynnewood, PA	CPA	Indefinite from January 1, 2007
Beistel, Theodore L.	Canton, OH	CPA	Indefinite from January 3, 2007
Myers, Robert J.	Fairport Harbor, OH	CPA	Indefinite from January 9, 2007
Burrus, Robert V.	Valparaiso, IN	CPA	Indefinite from January 22, 2007
Patterson, Douglas W.	Newburgh, IN	Attorney	Indefinite from January 31, 2007
Lang, Jeffrey H.	Fishers, IN	CPA	Indefinite from January 22, 2007
Chickering, David	Vermillion, SD	CPA	February 5, 2007 to November 4, 2007
Moss, Steve E.	Henderson, NC	CPA	Indefinite from February 5, 2007
Hazlip, Kevin	Orange Park, FL	Enrolled Agent	Indefinite from February 10, 2007
Adelson, Robert A.	Newton, MA	Attorney	Indefinite from February 15, 2007
Boyer, Daniel D.	North Judson, IN	CPA	Indefinite from February 15, 2007
LaRusso, Anthony J.	North Caldwell, NJ	Attorney	Indefinite from February 15, 2007
Martin, Spencer R.	Lancaster, PA	CPA	Indefinite from February 15, 2007

Name	Address	Designation	Date of Suspension
Hursh, Stephanie S.	Brush Prairie, WA	Enrolled Agent	Indefinite from February 20, 2007
Guidera, George C.	Weston, CT	Attorney	Indefinite from February 26, 2007
Ruth, Christopher A.	Cypress, CA	CPA	Indefinite from February 27, 2007
Elias, Lenard S.	El Cajon, CA	Enrolled Agent	Indefinite from March 1, 2007
Ikeji, Chuck	Orlando, FL	CPA	Indefinite from March 1, 2007
Lewis, Craig S.	Savannah, GA	CPA	Indefinite from March 1, 2007
Sloan, Eric R.	Brighton, MI	CPA	Indefinite from March 1, 2007
Gostomski, Michael	Stamford, CT	CPA	Indefinite from March 5, 2007
Hafer, Charles J.	Hamburg, PA	Enrolled Agent	Indefinite from March 5, 2007
Jones, Phillip G.	Andalusia, AL	Enrolled Agent	Indefinite from March 7, 2007
Agashiwala, Mahesh J.	New York, NY	CPA	Indefinite from March 22, 2007
Berndgen, Michael	Plantation, FL	CPA	Indefinite from April 1, 2007
Grahn, Charles R.	Indianapolis, IN	Attorney	Indefinite from April 1, 2007
Shaw, G. Joyce	Hebron, KY	Enrolled Agent	Indefinite from April 1, 2007
Pikaart, Jr., Edward H.	N. Branford, CT	CPA	Indefinite from April 10, 2007
Kelley, Richard S.	Beverly, MA	Attorney	Indefinite from May 1, 2007

Name	Address	Designation	Date of Suspension
Crabtree, Michael L.	San Dimas, CA	Enrolled Agent	Indefinite from May 15, 2007
Hausmann, Mark D.	Troy, NY	Attorney	Indefinite from May 15, 2007

Expedited Suspensions From Practice Before the Internal Revenue Service

Under Title 31, Code of Federal Regulations, Part 10, the Director, Office of Professional Responsibility, is authorized to immediately suspend from practice before the Internal Revenue Service any practitioner who, within five years from the date the expedited proceeding is instituted (1) has had a license to practice as an attorney, certified public accountant, or actuary suspended or revoked for cause or (2) has been convicted of certain crimes.

The following individuals have been placed under suspension from practice before the Internal Revenue Service by virtue of the expedited proceeding provisions:

Name	Address	Designation	Date of Suspension
Hatchett, William M.	Pontiac, MI	Attorney	Indefinite from November 13, 2006
Jacobs, Mark L.	Jackson Heights, NY	Attorney	Indefinite from November 21, 2006
Sylver, Peter T.	E. Longmeadow, MA	Attorney	Indefinite from November 21, 2006
Portlock, David R.	Pensacola, FL	Enrolled Agent	Indefinite from November 27, 2006
Ascher, Michael P.	North Port, FL	Attorney	Indefinite from November 28, 2006
Barrett, Norman W.	Dover, DE	CPA	Indefinite from November 28, 2006
Burd, Gene	Houston, TX	Attorney	Indefinite from November 28, 2006
Caceres, Carlos H.	Silver Spring, MD	Attorney	Indefinite from November 28, 2006
Carrabotta, Peter S.	Niles, IL	Attorney	Indefinite from November 28, 2006

Name	Address	Designation	Date of Suspension
Davis, Carleton W.	St. Louis, MO	Attorney	Indefinite from November 28, 2006
Frasier, Roland B.	Rancho Santa Fe, CA	Attorney	Indefinite from November 28, 2006
Hubbard, Edward	Chicago, IL	Attorney	Indefinite from November 28, 2006
Hynes, Richard W.	Brookline, MA	Attorney	Indefinite from November 28, 2006
Johnson, Barbara C.	Andover, MA	Attorney	Indefinite from November 28, 2006
Konas, Theodore V.	Lancaster, PA	CPA	Indefinite from November 28, 2006
Korson, Daniel M.	Muskegon, MI	CPA	Indefinite from November 28, 2006
Lee, III, Norman J.	Collegeville, PA	Attorney	Indefinite from November 28, 2006
Loiben, Alan A.	Skokie, IL	Attorney	Indefinite from November 28, 2006
McGarry, Thomas H.	Denver, CO	Attorney	Indefinite from November 28, 2006
Roberts, Quinton D.	Elkridge, MD	Attorney	Indefinite from November 28, 2006
Schofield, Peter L.	Spencer, MA	Attorney	Indefinite from November 28, 2006
Shultz, Ryan K.	Mitchell, NE	Attorney	Indefinite from November 28, 2006
Stenger, Jeanne P.	Temecula, CA	Attorney	Indefinite from November 28, 2006
Wood, Gary K.	Edina, MN	Attorney	Indefinite from November 28, 2006

Name	Address	Designation	Date of Suspension
Bakare, Adigun S.	Laurel, MD	Attorney	Indefinite from December 6, 2006
Biagini, Marc J.	Downers Grove, IL	Attorney	Indefinite from December 6, 2006
Birchall, Richard G.	Brewster, MA	Attorney	Indefinite from December 6, 2006
Brown, Edward E.	Indianapolis, IN	Attorney	Indefinite from December 6, 2006
Cunningham, Jr., Shirley A.	Ft. Lauderdale, FL	Attorney	Indefinite from December 6, 2006
Docherty, Scott R.	Branson West, MO	Attorney	Indefinite from December 6, 2006
Dressler, Peter P.	West Chicago, IL	Attorney	Indefinite from December 6, 2006
Henry, William J.	Irvington, NJ	Attorney	Indefinite from December 6, 2006
Hubbard, Cynthia A.	Geneva, IL	Attorney	Indefinite from December 6, 2006
Jackson, Jr., Donald H.	Hanover, MA	Attorney	Indefinite from December 6, 2006
Katz, Norman H.	Owings Mills, MD	Attorney	Indefinite from December 6, 2006
Lakin, Leonard S.	Wellesley Hills, MA	Attorney	Indefinite from December 6, 2006
McGreevy, Jacqueline K.	Carbondale, CO	Attorney	Indefinite from December 6, 2006
Zepp, Dale D.	Ferguson, MO	Attorney	Indefinite from December 6, 2006
Triplett, Austin H.	Homewood, IL	Attorney	Indefinite from December 11, 2006
Murphy, Patrick W.	Honolulu, HI	Attorney	Indefinite from December 11, 2006

Name	Address	Designation	Date of Suspension
Cronin, Jr., Edward M.	Cambridge, MA	Attorney	Indefinite from December 11, 2006
Christof, Kevin F.	Santa Monica, CA	Attorney	Indefinite from December 21, 2006
Heath, Kenneth J.	Canaan, VT	CPA	Indefinite from December 21, 2006
Madigan, Brian C.	Binghamton, NY	Attorney	Indefinite from December 21, 2006
Malloy, Terry P.	Tulsa, OK	Attorney	Indefinite from December 21, 2006
Baynes, Robert M.	Indianapolis, IN	CPA	Indefinite from December 27, 2006
Ceresa, Richard A.	Woodbridge, CA	CPA	Indefinite from December 27, 2006
Crews, Richard A.	Henderson, CO	Attorney	Indefinite from December 27, 2006
Menkveld, Paul G.	Tucson, AZ	Attorney	Indefinite from December 27, 2006
Worischeck, Joseph H.	Tempe, AZ	Attorney	Indefinite from December 27, 2006
Brown, Kirk P.	Pueblo, CO	Attorney	Indefinite from December 28, 2006
Dowling, Stanley W.	Scotts Valley, CA	CPA	Indefinite from December 28, 2006
Simmons, Henry L.	Greensboro, NC	CPA	Indefinite from December 28, 2006
Steele, Regina D.	San Diego, CA	Attorney	Indefinite from December 29, 2006
Craig, III, William A.	Austin, TX	Attorney	Indefinite from January 1, 2007
Acker, Thomas R.	Hollis Center, ME	Attorney	Indefinite from January 8, 2007

Name	Address	Designation	Date of Suspension
Baxter, Laura M.	Monee, IL	CPA	Indefinite from January 8, 2007
Herald, Sally J.	Cold Spring, KY	Attorney	Indefinite from January 8, 2007
Klapheke, II, William T.	Bowling Green, KY	Attorney	Indefinite from January 8, 2007
McCarthy, Charles C.	Encino, CA	Attorney	Indefinite from January 8, 2007
Bolling, Darius C.	Chicago, IL	CPA	Indefinite from January 10, 2007
Breitlauch, Linda	Saylorsburg, PA	Attorney	Indefinite from January 10, 2007
Coddington, Paul F.	Concord, NH	Attorney	Indefinite from January 10, 2007
Davis, Jr., William E.	Pinehurst, TX	CPA	Indefinite from January 10, 2007
Esola, Louis A.	Greensburg, PA	CPA	Indefinite from January 10, 2007
Finch, Judith A.	Walnut Creek, CA	Attorney	Indefinite from January 10, 2007
Jeing, Thomas C.	San Francisco, CA	Attorney	Indefinite from January 10, 2007
Ledbetter, Dean D.	Pelham, AL	CPA	Indefinite from January 10, 2007
McDiarmid, Katherine B.	Greensboro, NC	Attorney	Indefinite from January 10, 2007
Mills, George P.	Oceanside, CA	Attorney	Indefinite from January 10, 2007
Rather, James L.	Irvine, CA	Attorney	Indefinite from January 10, 2007
Rivera, Eduardo M.	Torrance, CA	Attorney	Indefinite from January 10, 2007

Name	Address	Designation	Date of Suspension
Stepovich, Michael A.	Fairbanks, AK	Attorney	Indefinite from January 10, 2007
Ulbrich, David L.	Woodland Hills, CA	CPA	Indefinite from January 10, 2007
Swanson, Todd-Ellis	Greenville, SC	CPA	Indefinite from January 20, 2007
Rubin, Deborah L.	Delray Beach, FL	Attorney	Indefinite from January 26, 2007
Wood, Brent E.	Cary, NC	Attorney	Indefinite from January 26, 2007
Currin, Samuel T.	Raleigh, NC	Attorney	Indefinite from February 7, 2007
Lupo, Robert N.	Weston, MA	Attorney	Indefinite from February 20, 2007
Taggart, Lawrence W.	El Cajon, CA	Attorney	Indefinite from March 7, 2007
Fife, III, James H.	Schererville, IN	Attorney	Indefinite from March 8, 2007
Katsis, Kevin G.	Riverside, IL	Attorney	Indefinite from March 8, 2007
O'Driscoll, Dennis M.	Quincy, MA	Attorney	Indefinite from March 8, 2007
Siever, Beth F.	Austin, TX	Attorney	Indefinite from March 8, 2007
Wheatley-Clark, Sheila R.	Houston, TX	CPA	Indefinite from March 8, 2007

Suspensions From Practice Before the Internal Revenue Service After Notice and an Opportunity for a Proceeding

Under Title 31, Code of Federal Regulations, Part 10, after notice and an opportunity for a proceeding before an administrative law judge, the following individuals have been placed under suspension from practice before the Internal Revenue Service:

Name	Address	Designation	Effective Date
Redmond, Debra	Gifford, PA	Enrolled Agent	Indefinite from March 5, 2007

Disbarments From Practice Before the Internal Revenue Service After Notice and an Opportunity for a Proceeding

Under Title 31, Code of Federal Regulations, Part 10, after notice and an opportunity for a proceeding before an administrative law judge, the following individuals have been disbarred from practice before the Internal Revenue Service:

Name	Address	Designation	Effective Date
Brookstein, Gary	Huntingdon Valley, PA	CPA	December 15, 2006
James T. Jubb	Baltimore, MD	CPA	December 15, 2006

Censure Issued by Consent

Under Title 31, Code of Federal Regulations, Part 10, in lieu of a proceeding being instituted or continued, an attorney, certified public accountant, enrolled agent, or enrolled actuary, may offer his or her consent to the issuance of a censure. Censure is a public reprimand.

The following individuals have consented to the issuance of a Censure:

Name	Address	Designation	Date of Censure
Zucker, Robert W.	Boca Raton, FL	CPA	November 14, 2006
Montgomery, David E.	Pleasanton, CA	Enrolled Agent	November 15, 2006
Higgins, James M.	S. Boston, MA	Attorney	December 1, 2006
Pennington, Debra L.	Lees Summit, MO	Enrolled Agent	January 29, 2007
Goodwin, Steven C.	Concord, MA	Attorney	February 2, 2007
Francis, Andrew W.E.	Houston, TX	CPA	February 21, 2007
Griffin, Richard M.	Duluth, GA	CPA	February 28, 2007

Resignations of Enrolled Agents

Under Title 31, Code of Federal Regulations, Part 10, an enrolled agent, in order to avoid the institution or conclusion of a proceeding for his or her disbarment or suspension from practice before the Internal Revenue Service, may offer his or her resignation as an enrolled agent. The Director, Office of Professional Responsibility, in his discretion, may accept the offered resignation.

The Director, Office of Professional Responsibility, has accepted offers of resignation as an enrolled agent from the following individuals:

Name	Address	Date of Resignation
Filipski, Kenneth M.	Bakersfield, CA	April 16, 2007

Section 7428(c) Validation of Certain Contributions Made During Pendency of Declaratory Judgment Proceedings

Announcement 2007–45

This announcement serves notice to potential donors that the organization listed below has recently filed a timely declaratory judgment suit under section 7428 of the Code, challenging revocation of its status as an eligible donee under section 170(c)(2).

Protection under section 7428(c) of the Code begins on the date that the notice of revocation is published in the Internal Revenue Bulletin and ends on the date on which a court first determines that an organization is not described in section 170(c)(2), as more particularly set forth in section 7428(c)(1).

In the case of individual contributors, the maximum amount of contributions protected during this period is limited to $1,000.00, with a husband and wife being treated as one contributor. This protection is not extended to any individual who was responsible, in whole or in part, for the acts or omissions of the organization that were the basis for the revocation. This protection also applies (but without limitation as to amount) to organizations described in section 170(c)(2) which are exempt from tax under section 501(a). If the organization ultimately prevails in its declaratory judgment suit, deductibility of contributions would be subject to the normal limitations set forth under section 170.

Patrick and Janet Hayes Charitable Supporting Organization
Houston, TX

Part I. Rulings and Decisions Under the Internal Revenue Code of 1986

Section 42.—Low-Income Housing Credit

The adjusted applicable federal short-term, mid-term, and long-term rates are set forth for the month of May 2007. See Rev. Rul. 2007-29, page 1223.

Section 280G.—Golden Parachute Payments

Federal short-term, mid-term, and long-term rates are set forth for the month of May 2007. See Rev. Rul. 2007-29, page 1223.

Section 382.—Limitation on Net Operating Loss Carryforwards and Certain Built-In Losses Following Ownership Change

The adjusted applicable federal long-term rate is set forth for the month of May 2007. See Rev. Rul. 2007-29, page 1223.

Section 409A.—Inclusion in Gross Income of Deferred Compensation Under Nonqualified Deferred Compensation Plans

26 CFR 1.409A–6: Application of section 409A and effective dates.

T.D. 9321

DEPARTMENT OF THE TREASURY
Internal Revenue Service
26 CFR Part 1

Application of Section 409A to Nonqualified Deferred Compensation Plans

AGENCY: Internal Revenue Service (IRS), Treasury.

ACTION: Final regulations.

SUMMARY: This document contains final regulations regarding the application of section 409A to nonqualified deferred compensation plans. The final regulations are necessary to clarify and explain the rules governing the application of section 409A to nonqualified deferred compensation plans. The regulations affect service providers receiving amounts of deferred compensation and the service recipients for whom the service providers provide services.

FOR FURTHER INFORMATION CONTACT: Stephen Tackney, (202) 927–9639 (not a toll-free number).

DATES: *Effective Date:* These regulations are effective April 17, 2007.

Applicability Dates: For dates of applicability, see §1.409A–6(b).

SUPPLEMENTARY INFORMATION:

Background

Section 409A was added to the Internal Revenue Code (Code) by section 885 of the American Jobs Creation Act of 2004, Public Law 108–357 (118 Stat. 1418). Section 409A generally provides that unless certain requirements are met, amounts deferred under a nonqualified deferred compensation plan for all taxable years are currently includible in gross income to the extent not subject to a substantial risk of forfeiture and not previously included in gross income. Section 409A also includes rules applicable to certain trusts or similar arrangements associated with a nonqualified deferred compensation plan, where such arrangements are located outside of the United States or are restricted to the provision of benefits in connection with a decline in the financial health of the sponsor.

On December 20, 2004, the IRS issued Notice 2005–1 (published as modified on January 6, 2005, in 2005–1 C.B. 274), setting forth initial guidance with respect to the application of section 409A, and supplying transition guidance pursuant to a statutory directive. A notice of proposed rulemaking (REG–158080–04, 2005–2 C.B. 786 [70 FR 57930]) was published in the **Federal Register** on October 4, 2005. See §601.601(a)(3). A public hearing was conducted on January 25, 2006. In addition, the IRS received written and electronic comments responding to the notice of proposed rulemaking. After consideration of all the comments, the proposed regulations are adopted as amended by this Treasury decision. The amendments are discussed in this preamble.

The Treasury Department and the IRS have also issued six additional notices providing transition guidance with respect to section 409A: (1) Notice 2005–94, 2005–2 C.B. 1208 (transition guidance with respect to 2005 reporting and withholding obligations); (2) Notice 2006–4, 2006–3 I.R.B. 307 (transition guidance with respect to certain outstanding stock rights); (3) Notice 2006–33, 2006–15 I.R.B. 754 (transition guidance with respect to the application of section 409A(b)); (4) Notice 2006–64, 2006–29 I.R.B. 88 (interim guidance regarding payments necessary to meet Federal conflict of interest requirements); (5) Notice 2006–79, 2006–43 I.R.B. 763 (additional transition relief); and (6) Notice 2006–100, 2006–51 I.R.B. 1109 (transition guidance with respect to 2005 and 2006 reporting and withholding obligations). See §601.601(d)(2). For a discussion of the continued applicability of these notices, see the **Effect on Other Documents** section of this preamble.

Explanation of Provisions and Summary of Comments

I. *Structure and Format of Regulations*

The final regulations generally adopt the structure and format of the proposed regulations. A table of contents has been included in the final regulations, as well as several additional sets of examples addressing various topics.

II. *Definition of Nonqualified Deferred Compensation Plan*

A. *Excluded plans*

The final regulations exclude the types of plans described in section 409A(d)(1) from the definition of a nonqualified deferred compensation plan, as well as certain other arrangements that were also set forth in the proposed regulations. Accordingly, the final regulations generally provide that a nonqualified deferred compensation plan for purposes of section 409A does not include a qualified plan, a *bona fide* sick leave or vacation plan, a disability plan, a death benefit plan, or certain medical expense reimbursement arrangements.

The final regulations clarify that the exemption from coverage under section 409A for certain welfare plans does not apply to medical expense reimbursements that constitute taxable income to the service provider. The coverage exemption applies only to arrangements that provide benefits that are excludable from gross income under section 105 or section 106.

Several commentators requested clarification of when a leave program will be treated as a *bona fide* sick leave or vacation leave plan for purposes of section 409A. Another commentator requested a clarification of the definition of a compensatory time plan. Because the definitions of these terms may raise issues and require coordination with the provisions of section 451, section 125, and, with respect to certain taxpayers, section 457, the final regulations do not address these issues.

Notice 2005–1, Q&A–6 provides that, until further guidance, taxpayers whose participation in a nonqualified deferred compensation plan would be subject to section 457(f) may rely on the definitions of *bona fide* vacation leave, sick leave, compensatory time, disability pay, or death benefit plan applicable for purposes of section 457(f) as also being applicable for purposes of section 409A. Until further guidance, such taxpayers may continue to rely on such definitions for purposes of section 409A.

One commentator requested that a qualified employer plan for purposes of the exclusion from section 409A include certain plans covered by section 402(d) (certain plans with a foreign-situs trust treated as qualified plans with respect to the taxation of the participants and beneficiaries) and retirement plans described in section 1022(i)(2) of the Employee Retirement Income Security Act of 1974, as amended (certain Puerto Rican retirement plans). The final regulations adopt this suggestion.

B. *Section 457 plans*

The final regulations provide that section 409A is not applicable to an eligible deferred compensation plan under section 457(b), but may be applicable to a deferred compensation plan that is subject to section 457(f). Commentators requested clarification of the application of the exception in the proposed regulations from the definition of deferred compensation referred to as the short-term deferral rule (described in section III.C.1 of this preamble) to a section 457(f) plan. As discussed below, a right to deferred compensation generally refers to a legally binding right in one taxable year to compensation that is or may be payable in a subsequent taxable year. For purposes of determining the time of payment, the term "payment" generally refers to an actual or constructive payment of cash or property. However, the final regulations provide that for purposes of the short-term deferral rule, an amount is treated as paid when it is included in income under section 457(f) whether or not an actual or constructive payment occurs. Accordingly, where the income inclusion under section 457(f) stems from the lapse of a substantial risk of forfeiture that is also treated as a substantial risk of forfeiture for purposes of section 409A, the amount included in income will be considered a short-term deferral for purposes of section 409A. However, the right to earnings on amounts that have previously been included under section 457(f) will be deferred compensation for purposes of section 409A unless the right to the earnings independently satisfies the requirements for an exclusion.

C. *Arrangements with independent contractors*

The final regulations provide that section 409A generally does not apply to an amount deferred under an arrangement between a service provider and an unrelated service recipient if during the service provider's taxable year in which the service provider obtains a legally binding right to the deferred amount the service provider is actively engaged in the trade or business of providing services (other than as an employee or as a director of a corporation), and provides significant services to two or more service recipients to which the service provider is not related and that are not related to one another.

The final regulations retain the safe harbor in the proposed regulations, under which a service provider is deemed to be providing significant services to two or more such service recipients for this purpose if the revenues generated from the services provided to any service recipient or group of related service recipients during such taxable year do not exceed 70 percent of the total revenues generated by the service provider from the trade or business of providing such services. Commentators expressed concern that the safe harbor did not permit independent contractors to know in advance whether the arrangements under which an independent contractor deferred compensation during a taxable year would be subject to section 409A. Commentators requested certain look-back periods, including the ability to use averaging over the previous three to five years, or to satisfy the 70 percent threshold over a certain portion of the previous three to five years. The Treasury Department and the IRS are concerned that the suggested rules would allow service providers to engage in strategic behavior to ensure that activity in certain years would be exempt from section 409A. Accordingly, the final regulations adopt an additional safe harbor that provides that a service provider that has actually met the 70 percent threshold in the three immediately previous years is deemed to meet the 70 percent threshold for the current year, but only if at the time the amount is deferred the service provider does not know or have reason to anticipate that the service provider will fail to meet the threshold in the current year.

In response to comments, the final regulations provide that if an independent contractor qualifies for the safe harbor for exclusion from coverage under section 409A with respect to arrangements with unrelated service recipients, an arrangement between the independent contractor and a service recipient related to the independent contractor will not be subject to section 409A if the arrangement, and the practices under the arrangement, are *bona fide*, arise in the ordinary course of business, and are substantially the same as the arrangements and practices (such as billing and collection practices) applicable to one or more unrelated service recipients to whom the independent contractor provides substantial services and that produce a majority of the total revenue that the independent contractor earns from the trade or business of providing such services during the year.

The final regulations further clarify that if at the time the legally binding right to the payment arose, the arrangement was not subject to section 409A because the service provider was an independent contractor that was eligible for this exclusion from coverage under section 409A, the amount deferred under the arrangement during that taxable year (and earnings credited to the deferred amount) will not become subject to section 409A in a later year if the service provider becomes an employee, independent contractor, or other type of service provider subject to the rules of section 409A.

Commentators also requested that a service recipient be permitted to rely upon a representation of an independent contractor that the independent contractor meets the exclusion requirements, so that a service recipient will know whether it is subject to the reporting requirements with respect to amounts deferred subject to section 409A. The Treasury Department and the IRS are continuing to study this issue.

D. *Anti-abuse rule*

If a principal purpose of a plan is to achieve a result with respect to a deferral of compensation that is inconsistent with the purposes of section 409A, the Commissioner may treat the plan as a nonqualified deferred compensation plan for purposes of section 409A.

III. *Definition of Deferral of Compensation*

A. *In general*

The final regulations provide that a nonqualified deferred compensation plan is a plan that provides for the deferral of compensation. The final regulations further provide that a plan generally provides for the deferral of compensation if, under its terms and the relevant facts and circumstances, a service provider has a legally binding right during a taxable year to compensation that, pursuant to its terms, is or may be payable to (or on behalf of) the service provider in a later year. For this purpose, an amount generally is payable at the time the service provider has a right to currently receive a transfer of cash or property, including a transfer of property includible in income under section 83, the economic benefit doctrine or section 402(b). Accordingly, a taxable transfer of an annuity contract is treated as a payment for purposes of section 409A.

The definition of deferral of compensation in the final regulations excludes the condition that the amount not be actually or constructively received and included in income during the taxable year, because that language might cause confusion with respect to the applicable rules governing deferral elections and the prohibition on the acceleration of payments. For example, if a service provider has made an irrevocable election to defer an amount of his or her salary to a future year, that amount is treated as deferred compensation regardless of whether the service recipient actually pays such amount to the service provider during the year in which the services are performed. Any early payment of the deferred compensation (or any right to receive such an early payment) generally would constitute an impermissible acceleration of the payment of the deferred amount.

For this purpose, a plan will be treated as providing for a payment to be made in a subsequent year whether the plan explicitly so provides (including through a service provider election) or the deferral condition is inherent in the terms of the contract. Where the parties have agreed that a payment will be made upon an event that could occur after the year in which the legally binding right to the payment arises, the plan generally will provide for a deferral of compensation (unless otherwise excluded under a specific exception, such as the short-term deferral rule).

For example, if a plan provides a service provider a right to a payment upon separation from service, the plan generally will result in a deferral of compensation regardless of whether the service provider separates from service and receives the payment in the same year as the grant, because under the plan the payment is conditioned upon an event that may occur after the year in which the legally binding right to the payment arises. Similarly, if an arrangement such as a stock option or stock appreciation right not otherwise excluded from coverage under section 409A provides a right to a payment for a term of years where the payment could be received during the short-term deferral period or a subsequent period but is not otherwise includible in income until paid, the arrangement will provide for deferred compensation even though the service provider could receive the payment during the short-term deferral period (for example, by exercising the stock option or stock appreciation right). However, where a plan does not specify a payment date, payment event or term of years, (or specifies a date or event certain to occur during the year in which the services are performed), the plan generally will not provide for the deferral of compensation if the service provider actually or constructively receives the payment within the short-term deferral period.

The proposed regulations provided that earnings on deferred amounts are generally treated as deferred compensation for purposes of section 409A. Under the final regulations, whether a deferred amount constitutes earnings on an amount deferred, or actual or notional income attributable to an amount deferred, is determined under the principles defining income attributable to the amount taken into account under §31.3121(v)(2)–1(d)(2).

A commentator requested clarification of whether a payment for a noncompetition agreement could be subject to section 409A. Because such a payment would occur in connection with the performance or nonperformance of services, and a covenant not to compete does not create a substantial risk of forfeiture for purposes of section 409A, a legally binding right obtained in one year to a payment in a subsequent year in connection with a noncompetition agreement generally would constitute deferred compensation.

B. *Legally binding right*

The regulations define deferral of compensation in the context of a legally binding right to a payment of compensation in a future taxable year. Commentators requested clarification of the standard that would be used to determine whether a service provider has a legally binding right. A legally binding right includes a contractual right that is enforceable under the applicable law or laws governing the contract. A legally binding right also includes an enforceable right created under other applicable law, such as a statute.

One commentator suggested that no legally binding right exists where the payment is made only upon the realization of gain from a particular investment. For example, the commentator argued that a bonus payable based upon the amount that a service provider obtains in selling property should not be treated as granting the service provider a legally binding right to the payment until the property is sold. In such a situation, however, the requirement that the property be sold is a condition to the right to the payment, but the right to the payment is still a legally binding right. The service recipient could not simply revoke the promise, sell the property, and not pay the bonus. However, the condition that the property be sold before the service provider becomes entitled to payment may constitute a substantial risk of forfeiture, depending on the specific facts and circumstances.

C. *Short-term deferrals*

1. *In general*

Subject to the modifications described in this section III.C of the preamble, the final regulations generally adopt the short-term deferral rule that was contained in the proposed regulations. Under the short-term deferral rule, a deferral of compensation does not occur for purposes of section 409A if the arrangement under which a payment is made does not provide for a deferred payment and the payment is made no later than the 15th day of the third month following the later of the end of the service provider's taxable year or the end of the service recipient's taxable year in which occurs the later of the time the legally binding right to the payment arises or the time such right first ceases to be subject to a substantial risk of forfeiture (subject to certain extensions for unforeseeable events). For this purpose, an arrangement provides for a deferred payment if it provides for a payment that will be made or completed after a date or an event that will or may occur later than the end of the 2$^1/_2$ month period described in the preceding sentence, either because of an affirmative election on the part of the service provider or service recipient or a deferral condition inherent in the terms of the contract (for example, that the amount will be paid upon the service provider's separation from service, which may occur in a future year).

Several commentators requested that additional flexibility be provided to allow payments to be short-term deferrals. By analogy to the rules in the proposed regulations concerning when payments of deferred compensation amounts are considered timely for purposes of the payment date rules, the commentators suggested that payments should qualify as short-term deferrals if made by the end of the year after the year in which a substantial risk of forfeiture lapses, rather than by the 15th day of the third month of that year. The final regulations do not adopt this suggestion. The short-term deferral rule is based on the historical treatment of certain payments paid within a short period following the end of a taxable year as not constituting deferred compensation. See §1.404(b)–1T, Q&A–2(b). That short period has been defined as ending on the 15th day of the third month following the end of the year, subject to certain extensions for unforeseeable events. Extending the payment date by which a short-term deferral could be paid would be inconsistent with this approach and the legislative history of section 409A (H.R. Conf. Rep. No. 108–755, at 735 (2004)), and accordingly is not adopted in the final regulations. However, the final regulations liberalize the standard under which a payment can be a short-term deferral even if it is delayed due to unforeseeable events. The proposed regulations provided generally that payment could be delayed if the payment would jeopardize the service recipient's solvency and such insolvency was unforeseeable at the time the service provider obtained the right to the payment. By contrast, the final regulations provide generally that payment may be delayed where the payment would jeopardize the ability of the service recipient to continue as a going concern.

Commentators asked how the short-term deferral rule applies to a series of payments scheduled to commence following the lapse of a substantial risk of forfeiture. The final regulations provide that the short-term deferral rule applies separately to each payment, applying the technical definition of "payment" set out in the regulations, provided that the entire payment is made during the short-term deferral period. Accordingly, where a payment has been designated as a separate payment, it may qualify as a short-term deferral (and thus not deferred compensation) even where the service provider has a right to subsequent payments under the same arrangement. In contrast, where a payment has not been designated as a separate payment (such as, for example, a life annuity payment or a series of installment payments treated as a single payment), any initial payments in the series will not be treated as a short-term deferral even if paid within the short-term deferral period. For a discussion of the definition of payment, see §1.409A–3.

Commentators suggested that a right to a reimbursement be treated as potentially subject to the short-term deferral rule, arguing that the right to the reimbursement payment is subject to a substantial risk of forfeiture that the service provider will not incur the expense. Commentators argued that the short-term deferral rule then could apply if the reimbursement payment were made within a short period following the occurrence of the expense. Generally, the risk that a service provider will fail to incur a reimbursable expense will not qualify as a substantial risk of forfeiture, so the short-term deferral rule will not be applicable. However, the final regulations provide considerable additional flexibility with regard to structuring reimbursement arrangements to meet the requirements of section 409A. For a discussion of these provisions, see section VII.B.2 of this preamble.

2. *Application to event-based payments*

Some commentators asked whether any payments based on a legally binding right arising in the year of a separation from service are excluded from coverage under section 409A, if paid by the end of the relevant short-term deferral period. For example, where an employee had accrued benefits under a defined benefit supplemental executive retirement plan (SERP) during his career that was payable immediately upon a separation from service, including an amount accrued in the year of separation from service, commentators asked whether the payment of the portion of the benefits accrued in that final year is excluded from coverage under section 409A if paid by March 15 of the year following the separation from service, because the amount is paid within a short period following the year the service provider obtains a vested legally binding right to the additional benefit accrual. (This generally would be of most concern to specified employees subject to the requirement of a six-month delay in payment following a separation from service.)

The analysis that applies in this situation is similar to that applied to the general definition of deferral of compensation, discussed in section III.A of this preamble. The short-term deferral rule does not provide an exclusion from the requirements of section 409A for such current-year benefit accruals because the rule does not apply to amounts of compensation subject to a deferral election. For this purpose, an election to defer includes either an affirmative election on the part of the service provider or a deferral condition inherent in the terms of the contract. Where the parties have agreed that a payment will be made upon an event that does not necessarily coincide with the lapsing of the substantial risk of forfeiture, and could occur at a time beyond the short-term deferral period, the arrangement provides for a deferral election such that the short-term deferral rule does not apply. Accordingly, in this example, because the benefits accrued in the final year of the SERP could have been paid upon an event occurring after the short-term deferral period (if, for example, the individual had not separated from service until a later year), the payment of the benefit accrued in the final year is subject to section 409A and is not a short-term deferral, even if paid by March 15 of the year following the separation from service.

Also, for example, if a plan that is not subject to section 457(f) provides that an amount is subject to a substantial risk of forfeiture until the completion of three years of service, and is payable upon a separation of service following the three years of service, the right to the amount is not a short-term deferral even if the service provider separates from service immediately after vesting in the right, because under the plan the payment is based upon an event other than the lapsing of the substantial risk of forfeiture and such event may occur in a year subsequent to the year in which the risk of forfeiture lapses.

Conversely, where a plan specifies no payment date or payment event, or specifies only the date at which the substantial risk of forfeiture lapses, the plan may qualify for the short-term deferral rule if the payment is made within the applicable short-term deferral period. However, such a plan generally would violate section 409A if the payment were made after the short-term deferral period.

As discussed in this preamble with respect to the general definition of deferred compensation, to implement the statutory scheme, including the applicable reporting and form requirements, taxpayers generally must be able to determine whether an arrangement provides for a deferral of compensation at the time the service provider obtains a legally binding right to the compensation. Although a plan need not specify a payment date to be a short-term deferral that is excluded from coverage under section 409A, the short-term deferral exclusion does not apply if the payment event or date is specified and will or may occur after the end of the short-term deferral period.

The preamble to the proposed regulations explained that where a plan requires that a payment be made on a date within the short-term deferral period, but the payment is made after the specified date and after the end of the short-term deferral period, the arrangement will be treated as a nonqualified deferred compensation plan, but the payment date will be treated as a specified date. Thus, under such an arrangement, if the service provider receives the payment after the specified date, but not later than the end of the year in which the specified date occurs, the payment generally will comply with section 409A. However, taxpayers should note that a provision requiring only that a payment be made on or before the end of the short-term deferral period may not qualify as a permissible specified date for this purpose, if under the facts and circumstances the payment could have been made in more than one taxable year. For a discussion of the application of the definition of a specified payment date to this type of plan, see section VII.B of this preamble.

For a discussion of when rights to compensation upon a separation from service for good reason may be treated as rights to compensation upon an involuntary termination, and the potential application of the short-term deferral exception to these arrangements, see section III.J.3 of this preamble.

D. *Stock options and stock appreciation rights*

1. *In general*

Subject to the modifications described in this preamble, the final regulations adopt the provisions of the proposed regulations excluding from coverage under section 409A statutory stock options and certain other stock rights. Generally under the regulations, nondiscounted stock options and nondiscounted stock appreciation rights issued on service recipient stock that do not include any additional deferral feature are excluded from section 409A.

2. *Statutory stock options*

The final regulations adopt the exclusion from coverage under section 409A for statutory stock options, including incentive stock options described in section 422 of the Code and options granted under an employee stock purchase plan described in section 423 of the Code. This exclusion applies regardless of whether the statutory stock option would be excluded if the same option were not treated as a statutory stock option. For example, an employee stock purchase plan described in section 423 offering a discounted purchase price is not a deferred compensation plan for purposes of section 409A.

Commentators requested clarification, however, of the treatment of a statutory stock option that is modified, or otherwise becomes ineligible to be treated as a statutory stock option. The final regulations adopt the rule set forth in the proposed regulations, and provide that at the time of such modification or event, the modification or other event is treated as the grant of a new option, or causes the option to be treated as having had a deferral feature from the date of grant, as applicable, for purposes of section 409A only if such modification or other event would have been so treated had the option been a nonstatutory stock option immediately before such modification or other event. For example, where an incentive stock option is modified through an extension of the option's term, the extended option will be treated as having had an additional deferral feature from the date of grant for section 409A purposes only if the same extension of a nonstatutory stock option would have resulted in such treatment.

Commentators also requested that the exclusion from coverage under section 409A for certain stock rights issued under plans meeting the requirements of section 423 (employee stock purchase plans) be extended to employee stock purchase plans offered by foreign employers that do not meet such requirements, where the shares are made available for purchase at a discount and substantially all of the participants are nonresident aliens. The legislative history does not provide a basis for extending the exception applicable to options meeting the requirements of section 423 to grants of discounted stock options not meeting the requirements of section 423. Accordingly, this suggestion is not adopted in the final regulations.

3. *Definition of service recipient stock*

The final regulations adopt the requirement in the proposed regulations that for the exclusion for certain stock rights to apply, the stock right must relate to service recipient stock. Commentators criticized the definition of service recipient stock contained in the proposed regulations as too restrictive. Generally such criticisms centered on two different aspects of the definition of service recipient stock in the proposed regulations – the classes of stock that may qualify as service recipient stock, and the issuer or issuers whose stock may constitute service recipient stock, where the service recipient is comprised of more than one entity.

a. *Classes of stock that may qualify as service recipient stock*

Commentators requested clarification and expansion of the classes of stock of a corporation that may constitute service recipient stock. Commentators generally focused on two issues. First, with respect to stock of a particular service recipient corporation, commentators requested that the stock right be permitted to relate to any class of common stock, regardless of whether another class of common stock of that corporation was publicly traded, and regardless of whether that class of common stock had the greatest aggregate value of all classes of common stock issued by that corporate entity. Subject to the restrictions governing certain preferences as to distributions, the final regulations generally provide that any class of common stock may be used, regardless of whether another class of common stock that could qualify as service recipient stock is publicly traded or has a higher aggregate value outstanding, and regardless of whether the class of stock is subject to transferability restrictions or buyback rights (provided such buyback rights reflect the fair market value of the stock at the time of purchase).

Second, commentators suggested narrowing the types of preferences on a class of common stock that would prohibit that class from being treated as service recipient stock. One commentator requested that the classes of stock permitted as service recipient stock include any class of stock that is widely held by non-service recipients. While it may be unlikely that a widely-held class of stock was created to facilitate an abusive avoidance of section 409A, it does not follow that service recipient stock rights issued on such stock necessarily would be consistent with the intended application of section 409A if, for example, holders of such class enjoyed preferences that would make such stock rights a suitable substitute for nonqualified deferred compensation.

To be treated as service recipient stock under the final regulations, a class of stock must qualify as common stock under section 305 of the Code. Accordingly, the final regulations provide that stock that is not common stock under section 305 is not service recipient stock for purposes of section 409A. However, the mere classification of a class of stock as common stock under section 305 is not sufficient for such stock to be treated as service recipient stock for purposes of section 409A. The Treasury Department and the IRS are concerned that classes of stock that are common stock under section 305 may provide preferences that could permit stock rights with respect to such stock to resemble traditional nonqualified deferred compensation, such that exclusion of such stock rights would permit the avoidance of section 409A.

Commentators suggested that a preference with respect to liquidation rights, without any other preferences such as a preferential right to dividends, should be permitted under the definition of service recipient stock. A holder of this class of stock would not be guaranteed any return, but rather would simply be guaranteed preferred distribution rights upon a complete liquidation of the service recipient. The final regulations generally adopt this suggestion.

With respect to other preferential rights, commentators were unable to provide a workable standard under which permissible preferences could be distinguished from impermissible preferences. Accordingly, the final regulations do not treat any stock including such preferences as service recipient stock. However, the Treasury Department and the IRS continue to study this area, and the final regulations authorize the publication of other additional guidance, should a workable standard be developed.

b. *Entities the stock of which may qualify as service recipient stock*

Commentators also requested an expansion of the class of entities the stock of which can qualify as service recipient stock where the service recipient is comprised of multiple entities. The Treasury Department and the IRS believe that the stock right exception under section 409A was intended to cover stock rights directly reflecting the enterprise value of the entity for which the service provider is providing services. Consistent with this approach, the final regulations provide that service recipient stock may include the stock of the corporation for which the service provider was providing services at the date of grant. In addition, the final regulations provide that service recipient stock may include stock of any corporation in a chain of organizations all of which have a controlling interest in another organization, beginning with the parent organization and ending with the organization for which the service provider was providing services at the date of grant of the stock right. Similarly to the proposed regulations, the final regulations provide that the term "controlling interest" has the same meaning as provided in §1.414(c)–2(b)(2)(i), except that where that regulation requires at least an 80 percent interest, the final regulations generally require only a 50 percent interest. In addition, where the use of such stock with respect to the grant of a stock right to such service provider is based upon legitimate business criteria, the final regulations generally require only a 20 percent interest. For purposes of determining ownership of an interest in an organization, the attribution rules of §1.414(c)–4 apply, and the exclusion rules of §1.414(c)–3 also apply. For example, under the final regulations, with respect to an employee of a subsidiary corporation, the common stock of the ultimate parent corporation, or of a subsidiary corporation anywhere in the chain of corporate ownership between the subsidiary that employed the employee and the ultimate parent corporation (a higher tier subsidiary), could qualify as service recipient stock for purposes of determining whether a stock right issued to such employee with respect to such stock was excluded from coverage under section 409A, provided that the 50 percent or 20 percent ownership standard, as applicable, was satisfied by each corporation in the chain.

The proposed regulations contained many requirements for using an ownership level of less than 50 percent. Commentators requested several simplifications of these requirements. In response, the final regulations no longer require a formal election by any corporation. Rather, each individual grant of a stock right is analyzed to determine whether the stock qualifies as service recipient stock with respect to a service provider at the time the stock right is granted. If a corporation owns at least 50 percent of the stock of one corporation and owns less than 50 percent of the stock of another corporation, and it intends to treat its stock as service recipient stock with respect to employees of both corporations, there is no requirement that a legitimate business criteria exist with respect to the issuance of stock rights on the parent corporation stock to service providers of the first such corporation. The legitimate business criteria standard applies only to stock rights issued to service providers of subsidiaries that are not majority-owned, because the test of legitimate business criteria relates to the actual issuance of a stock right to a particular service provider. Accordingly, a subsidiary may have more than one shareholder corporation the stock of which qualifies as service recipient stock with respect to a subsidiary employee such as, for example, where three entities each own a one-third interest in the subsidiary. However, with respect to each grant of a stock right on stock of a particular non-majority shareholder corporation to a service provider of a particular subsidiary, there must exist legitimate business criteria for issuing such a stock right. Even if legitimate business criteria exist with respect to the issuance of a stock right on stock of a particular shareholder corporation to a particular service provider, legitimate business criteria may or may not exist with respect to the issuance of a stock right to the same service provider on stock of another shareholder corporation.

The legitimate business criteria requirement is a facts and circumstances test, focusing generally on whether there is sufficient nexus between a particular service provider and the entity, the stock of which underlies the stock right granted to the service provider, for the grant to serve a legitimate non-tax business purpose. As provided in the preamble to the proposed regulations, if a corporation issued a stock right on its stock to a current employee of a joint venture in which the corporation was a venturer, and the employee was a former employee of the corporate venturer, generally the issuance would be based on legitimate business criteria. Similarly, if the corporate venturer issued such a right to an employee of the joint venture who it reasonably expected would become an employee of the corporate venturer in the future, generally the legitimate business criteria requirement would be met. By contrast, where an employee has no real nexus with a corporate venturer, such as generally happens when the corporate venturer is a passive investor in the service recipient, the use of the investor corporation stock as the stock underlying a stock right grant to that employee generally would not be based upon legitimate business criteria. Similarly, where a corporation holds only a minority interest in an entity that in turn holds a minority interest in the entity for which the employee performs services, such that the corporation holds only an insubstantial indirect interest in the entity receiving the services, legitimate business criteria generally would not exist for issuing a stock right on the corporation's stock to the employee.

The Treasury Department and the IRS remain concerned that the manipulation of the structure of a related group of corporations may be used to allow stock options or stock appreciation rights to mimic the characteristics of nonqualified deferred compensation, by compensating holders based on predictable amounts and investment returns unrelated to the enterprise value of an operating entity. Accordingly, the exception contained in the proposed regulations under which the stock of a corporation serving as investment vehicle is not considered service recipient stock has been retained. In addition, an anti-abuse rule has been added to address corporate structures, transactions, or stock right grants, a principal purpose of which is the avoidance of the application of section 409A to an arrangement otherwise providing deferred compensation. These corporate structures, transactions, and stock right grants generally will occur where the structure, transaction, or grant is intended to provide enhanced security for the value of the stock right as a means of providing deferred compensation, rather than as compensation related to an increase in the true enterprise value of the service recipient. The regulations provide that if an entity becomes a member of a group of corporations or other entities treated as a single service recipient, and the primary source of income or value of such entity arises from the provision of management services to other members of the service recipient group, if any stock rights are issued with respect to such entity it is presumed that such structure was established for purposes of avoiding the application of section 409A.

c. *Equity interests in certain non-corporate entities*

The final regulations permit certain equity interests in a non-stock mutual company to be treated analogously to equity interests in a corporation. Commentators requested that the definition of service recipient stock be expanded to cover interests in cooperatives and interests in the value of an Indian tribal enterprise. The regulations do not include such interests in the definition of service recipient stock, but provide the IRS authority to provide guidance expanding the definition of service recipient stock. For a discussion of the application of the exclusion for certain stock rights to rights issued on equity interests in entities taxed as partnerships, see section III.G of this preamble.

4. *Valuation*

a. *In general*

The final regulations provide that for the exclusion for stock rights to apply, the stock right must specify an exercise price of the stock right that may never be less than the fair market value of the underlying stock on the date the stock right is granted. For purposes of this discussion and the final regulations, the exercise price of a stock appreciation right refers to the base stock value from which the appreciation is measured for purposes of determining the compensation payable under the stock appreciation right (for example, a stock appreciation right providing for a payment of the excess of the fair market value of 100 shares over $100 would have a $1 per share exercise price).

Several commentators expressed concerns regarding the determination of the fair market value of the underlying stock. Some commentators requested that the valuation rules applicable to incentive stock options be applied for purposes of the exclusion from section 409A. Under those rules, if the stock option would otherwise fail to be an incentive stock option solely because the exercise price was less than the fair market value of the underlying stock as of the date of grant, generally the option is treated as an incentive stock option if the issuer attempted in good faith to set the exercise price at fair market value. See section 422(c)(1). The Treasury Department and the IRS believe that this is not the appropriate standard for determining whether stock rights are subject to section 409A. Incentive stock options are subject to strict limitations on the amount of such options that may be granted to a particular employee. See section 422(d). In contrast, there are no such limits applicable to nonstatutory stock options, and grants of nonstatutory stock options often far exceed the limitation applicable to incentive stock options. In addition, section 422(c)(1) explicitly provides for the good faith standard with respect to incentive stock options, while no such provisions exist within section 409A or its legislative history.

Commentators requested clarification of the consistency standard with respect to the use of a valuation method. Specifically, commentators asked whether one valuation method could be used for purposes of establishing the exercise price while another method could be used for purposes of determining the fair market value of the stock at the time of the payment (for example, to determine the amount of payment in the case of a stock appreciation right or a stock option where the stock is subject to repurchase by the service recipient). The final regulations clarify that consistency is not required, provided that each valuation method used otherwise meets the requirements of the final regulations. Accordingly, a service recipient may use one valuation method for purposes of establishing an exercise price, but another valuation method for purposes of establishing the payment amount (in the case of a stock appreciation right) or the buyback amount (in the case of a stock option where the underlying stock is subject to a buyback arrangement). However, once an exercise price has been established, the exercise price may not be changed through the retroactive use of another valuation method. In addition, where after the date of grant, but before the date of exercise, of the stock right, the service recipient stock to which the stock right relates becomes readily tradable on an established securities market, the service recipient must use a valuation method for stock readily tradable on an established securities market for purposes of determining the payment amount (in the case of a stock appreciation right) or the buyback amount (in the case of a stock option where the underlying stock is subject to a buyback arrangement).

b. *Valuation — stock readily tradable on an established securities market*

The final regulations adopt the rules under the proposed regulations governing valuation of stock readily tradable on an established securities market, generally requiring that the valuation of such stock be based upon the contemporaneous prices established in the securities market, subject to the modifications discussed in this preamble. Some commentators requested additional guidance with respect to when a stock will be treated as readily tradable. The final regulations adopt the same standard as that set forth in §1.280G–1, Q&A–6(e), that stock is treated as readily tradable if it is regularly quoted by brokers or dealers making a market in such stock.

With respect to the rules governing the valuation of stock that is readily tradable on an established securities market, commentators generally focused on the provision of the proposed regulations permitting the use of an average selling price during a specified period that is within 30 days before or 30 days after the date of grant. Specifically, comments concentrated on the requirement that the commitment to grant the stock right with an exercise price set using such an average selling price be irrevocable before the beginning of the specified period. Commentators questioned both the purpose of the requirement of the commitment to the valuation method, as well as the actions required to satisfy the rule if averaging were being used.

The rule was intended to prohibit the use of an average price, set on a lookback basis, to ensure a discounted exercise price. For example, if a corporation decided to grant a stock option on July 1, and it could set the exercise price using an average selling price for any period falling within the prior 30 days without having had a prior commitment to a specific averaging period, the corporation could simply look for the lowest price that occurred during the prior June. Furthermore, if the corporation were not committed to grant the stock option on July 1, the corporation could wait until its stock price began to rise and then grant an option using the selling price on a given day during the previous 30 days to provide a particular discount. Accordingly, the final regulations require that the commitment to grant the stock right with an exercise price set using such an average selling price be irrevocable before the beginning of the specified period. To satisfy this requirement, the service recipient must designate the recipient of the stock option, the number of shares the stock option will permit the holder of the stock option to purchase, and the method for determining the exercise price including the period over which the averaging will occur, before the beginning of the specified averaging period.

One commentator stated that the requirement of an irrevocable commitment to the averaging period could not be met under French law, because French law requires that the stock option exercise price be set based on the average trading price over the preceding 20 days and the commitment to the grant before the beginning of the period may be viewed as violating that requirement. The final regulations provide that where applicable foreign law requires that the compensatory stock right granted by the issuer must be priced based upon a specific price averaging method and period, a stock right granted in accordance with such applicable foreign law will be treated as meeting the requirement, provided that the averaging period may not exceed 30 days.

c. *Valuation – stock not readily tradable on an established securities market*

i. *In general*

The final regulations adopt the provisions in the proposed regulations relating to the valuation of stock not readily tradable on an established securities market, subject to the modifications discussed in this section III.C.4.c. Accordingly, a valuation of stock based upon a reasonable application of a reasonable valuation method is treated as reflecting the fair market value of the stock. To meet this standard, it is not necessary that a taxpayer demonstrate that the value was determined by an independent appraiser. Where the taxpayer can otherwise demonstrate that the valuation was determined by the reasonable application of a reasonable valuation method, the standard will be met.

One commentator requested that the factors to be considered in determining the fair market value of the stock should be modified to include consideration of any recent equity sales made by the corporation in arm's-length transactions. The final regulations adopt this suggestion.

The final regulations continue to require that in the case of a stock right issued with respect to stock that was not publicly traded at the time the right was issued, but becomes publicly traded before the right is exercised, the stock value for purposes of calculating the payment amount (in the case of a stock appreciation right) or the buyback amount (in the case of a stock option where the underlying stock is subject to a buyback agreement) must be based upon the rules governing stock that is publicly traded. This does not mean that the initial exercise price determined under the rules governing stock that is not publicly traded must be reset. Rather, this means only that the value at the time of exercise used to determine the payment amount or the buyback amount must be determined under the rules governing stock that is publicly traded. For example, if a service provider holds an excluded stock appreciation right with an exercise price of $1 that was fixed based on a valuation of the closely-held corporate stock at the time of grant, and before exercise the stock becomes readily tradable on an established securities market, the amount payable upon exercise must be the excess of the value of the stock based on its trading price over the $1 exercise price.

ii. *Safe harbor presumptions*

The final regulations adopt a presumption in specified circumstances that, for purposes of section 409A, a valuation of stock reflects the fair market value of the stock, rebuttable only by a showing that the valuation is grossly unreasonable. The presumption applies where the valuation is based upon an independent appraisal, a generally applicable repurchase formula (applicable for both compensatory and noncompensatory purposes) that would be treated as fair market value under section 83, or, in the case of illiquid stock of a start-up corporation, a valuation by a qualified individual or individuals applied at a time that the corporation did not otherwise anticipate a change in control event or public offering of the stock.

Many of the comments with respect to these presumptions related to the presumption applicable to illiquid stock of start-up corporations. As set forth in the proposed regulations, the start-up corporation presumption would not apply if the service recipient or service provider could reasonably anticipate, as of the time the valuation is applied, that the service recipient would undergo a change in control event or make a public offering of securities within the 12 months following the event to which the valuation is applied. Commentators suggested that a 12-month period is too long, because changes occur so rapidly in the business world that it often is difficult or impossible to predict so far in advance whether such an event will occur. Commentators suggested that the service provider should retain the benefit of the presumption unless the issuing corporation entered into a definitive agreement or filed its registration statement with the Securities and Exchange Commission within a period of 15 or 30 days after issuing the stock right.

The Treasury Department and the IRS believe that a 15-day or a 30-day period is too short. Although there is always a risk that a public offering will fail or that a corporate transaction will not occur, the Treasury Department and the IRS also believe that a person should reasonably be able to anticipate whether such a transaction will occur during a reasonable period before the transaction.

Accordingly, the final regulations provide that the start-up corporation presumption will not apply if at the time the valuation is made, the service recipient or service provider may reasonably anticipate that the service recipient will undergo a change in control event in the next 90 days or an initial public offering within the next 180 days. As under the proposed regulations, the rule in the final regulations is concerned with what the parties may reasonably anticipate at the time the stock right is issued.

Other comments requested examples of persons with sufficient knowledge, experience, and skill in valuing illiquid stock of a start-up corporation. Because knowledge, skill and training may be obtained in different ways, the final regulations do not provide specific examples. However, the regulations clarify that the standard to be applied is whether a reasonable individual, upon being apprised of such person's relevant knowledge, experience, education and training, would reasonably rely on the advice of such person with respect to valuation in deciding whether to accept an offer to purchase or sell the stock being valued. The final regulations also clarify that significant experience generally means at least five years of relevant experience in business valuation or appraisal, financial accounting, investment banking, private equity, secured lending, or other comparable experience in the line of business or industry in which the service recipient operates.

With respect to the presumption based upon a generally applicable buyback formula, some commentators requested that the presumption apply where the formula is applicable to all compensatory stock transactions, but not also applicable to all noncompensatory stock transactions. The final regulations do not adopt this suggestion. However, the final regulations clarify that to meet the requirements of the presumption, the buyback formula is required to be applicable to compensatory and noncompensatory transactions with the issuer or a person owning 10 percent or more of the stock of the issuer, but is not required to be applicable to transactions with other persons or transactions that are part of an arm's length transaction constituting the sale of all or substantially all of the stock of the issuer to an unrelated purchaser.

5. *Modification of a stock right*

The final regulations continue to apply certain rules addressing modifications, extensions and renewals of stock rights. Although these rules in many respects resemble the rules applicable to statutory stock options, the rules are not intended to incorporate the rules applicable to statutory stock options except where explicitly provided.

The final regulations generally retain the rules in the proposed regulations that generally treat extensions of the exercise period of a stock right as an additional deferral feature as of the date of grant of the right, with an exception for certain limited extensions following a separation from service. Commentators characterized these rules as unnecessarily restrictive. Specifically, commentators argued that the extension of a stock option upon the occurrence of a separation from service (often in connection with a program of layoffs) or a corporate transaction is a common practice, and that often these extensions cover periods longer than the limited period provided in the proposed regulations. In addition, commentators argued that the same substantive results could be obtained by specifying a longer term for the stock right and providing the service recipient the discretion to shorten the term, rather than providing discretion to extend a shorter term, and that the former approach would be permissible under the proposed regulations. In response, the final regulations provide that the extension of an option exercise period generally is not treated as an additional deferral feature or a modification of the stock option for section 409A purposes if the exercise period is not extended beyond the earlier of the original maximum term of the option or 10 years from the original date of grant of the stock right.

Many commentators also requested that the extension of the exercise period of a stock right not be treated as an additional deferral feature for purposes of section 409A, where at the time of the extension the fair market value of the underlying stock does not exceed the exercise price (an "underwater" option). Because the issuance of an otherwise identical option with an exercise period ending after the end of the exercise period of the underwater option would be excluded from coverage under section 409A, the final regulations provide that such an extension does not constitute an additional deferral feature.

The final regulations adopt the provisions in the proposed regulations regarding substitution or assumption of stock rights due to a corporate transaction, which are generally in accordance with the corresponding provisions governing incentive stock options. The final regulations clarify that the applicable corporate transactions for this purpose include only those transactions described in §1.424–1(a)(3). One commentator requested that the provision permitting substitutions of stock options be modified to reflect that a holder of a nonstatutory stock option is not required to be employed by the successor entity. The final regulations adopt this suggestion, so that a substituted nonstatutory stock option may be treated as a continuation of the initial option even where the holder of the option is not employed or otherwise providing services to the successor entity, provided the substitution otherwise meets the rules provided in the regulations.

6. *Other stock right issues*

The final regulations adopt certain definitions from the regulations governing statutory stock options, modified as appropriate for purposes of applying the rules under section 409A. These include the time and date of grant of an option (§1.421–1(c)), and the definitions of option (§1.421–1(a)), stock (§1.421–1(d)), exercise price (§1.424–1(e)), exercise (§1.421–1(f)), and transfer (§1.421–1(g)). These definitions apply by analogy to stock appreciation rights.

The final regulations adopt the rule that a right to a payment of accumulated dividend equivalents at the time of the exercise of a stock right generally will be treated as a reduction in the exercise price of the stock right, causing the stock right to be deferred compensation subject to the requirements of section 409A. The final regulations provide that an arrangement to accumulate and pay dividend equivalents the payment of which is not contingent upon the exercise of a stock right may be treated as a separate arrangement for purposes of section 409A. Such an arrangement generally will be required to comply with section 409A (unless it independently qualifies for an exception from coverage under section 409A), but will not affect whether the related stock right qualifies for the exclusion from coverage under section 409A. The right to the dividend equivalents may be set forth within the stock right plan or the individual stock right grant, or in a separate document, as long as the payment of the dividend equivalents is not contingent upon the exercise of the stock right.

Commentators also asked whether the exclusion of stock rights from coverage under section 409A would apply to tandem rights, meaning a stock right that combines a stock option right and a stock appreciation right, exercisable on an alternative basis. Similarly, commentators asked whether the substitution of a stock option for a stock appreciation right, or *vice versa*, where all the terms except the mode of payment upon exercise are similar, would be treated as a modification of a stock right. The application of section 409A generally is not affected by the medium of a taxable payment (for example, cash or stock). Accordingly, whether a stock right is expressed as a tandem arrangement under which the exercise of one right terminates the other right, or there is a substitution of a stock appreciation right for a stock option identical in all respects except for the medium of payment, generally does not impact whether the arrangement is excluded from coverage under section 409A.

Commentators requested further clarification of the application of section 409A to stock option gain deferrals. The ability to defer gain upon the exercise or exchange (including a purported forfeiture) of a stock right is incompatible with the exclusion of certain stock rights from the requirements of section 409A because such exclusion is predicated on the option not having any additional deferral feature. Accordingly, if an arrangement provides for a potential to defer the payment of cash or property upon the exercise or exchange of a stock right beyond the year the right is exercised or beyond the original term of the stock right, the arrangement provides for a deferral feature and must comply with the requirements of section 409A from the time the legally binding right granted by the award arises.

Because a stock option with a deferral feature is subject to section 409A regardless of whether the deferral feature is actually utilized, an option that includes a provision permitting deferral of option gain generally will not satisfy the time and form of payment rules under section 409A if the service provider can exercise the option in more than one taxable year. If a deferral feature is added to a preexisting option, the option will be treated as having included a deferral feature as of the original date of grant, generally resulting in a violation of section 409A.

However, the final regulations provide that a stock right will not be treated as having a deferral feature where the service recipient delays a payment because the making of the payment would violate applicable Federal, state, local, or foreign law or jeopardize the ability of the service recipient to continue as a going concern. Although these provisions permit the delay for purposes of section 409A, no inference should be drawn as to the Federal tax consequences of such a delay under any other section of the Code or Federal tax doctrine such as section 83, section 451, the constructive receipt doctrine, or the economic benefit doctrine.

Commentators requested that the definition of service recipient stock be expanded to include the stock of a corporation for which a service recipient provides substantial services, at least with respect to a service provider of the service recipient that is providing services to the corporation. The legislative history does not support such a broad interpretation of service recipient stock, and the final regulations do not adopt this suggestion.

E. *Restricted property*

The final regulations provide, as did the proposed regulations, that a grant of restricted property generally will not constitute a deferral of compensation for purposes of section 409A. Commentators requested that the regulations clarify that a vested right to receive nonvested property in a future year does not constitute deferred compensation. Commentators argued that a right to receive nonvested property is not truly vested. For example, commentators argued that a right to receive restricted stock that will be subject to a substantial risk of forfeiture until the service provider completes three years of future services cannot be a vested right. The final regulations adopt this suggestion, so long as the risk of forfeiture to which the stock is subject constitutes a substantial risk of forfeiture for purposes of section 409A.

Commentators specifically requested clarification of the circumstances under which a service provider may elect to be paid a bonus or other payment in the form of restricted stock, rather than cash. Generally an election between compensation alternatives, none of which provides for a deferral of compensation within the meaning of section 409A, will not cause the election to be subject to the section 409A timing restrictions. Thus, a choice between an award of restricted stock or stock options that are not subject to section 409A will not be governed by the section 409A election timing rules. However, where any of the alternatives involves a deferral of compensation subject to section 409A, the election must comply with the provisions of section 409A. In addition, no inference should be drawn as to the Federal tax consequences of such an election provision under any other section of the Code or Federal tax doctrine such as section 83, section 451, the constructive receipt doctrine, or the economic benefit doctrine.

F. *Section 402(b) trusts*

The final regulations continue to except from coverage under section 409A transfers of a beneficial interest in a trust, or a transfer to or from a trust, to the extent such a transfer is subject to section 402(b). The final regulations further clarify that a right to compensation required to be included in income under section 402(b)(4)(A) (alternative taxation of highly compensated employees of a section 402(b) trust that fails to meet the requirements of section 401(a)(26) or section 410(b)) also is not a deferral of compensation. However, a right to receive a benefit formulated as a right to a future contribution to a section 402(b) trust is similar to a right to receive property in a future taxable year, and generally would constitute deferred compensation.

G. *Arrangements between partnerships and partners*

The proposed regulations did not address the application of section 409A to arrangements between partnerships and partners, and these final regulations also do not address such arrangements. The statute and the legislative history of section 409A do not specifically address arrangements between partnerships and partners providing services to a partnership and do not explicitly exclude such arrangements from the application of section 409A. Commentators raised a number of issues, relating both to the scope of the arrangements subject to section 409A and the coordination of the provisions of subchapter K and section 409A with respect to those arrangements that are subject to section 409A. The Treasury Department and the IRS are continuing to analyze the issues raised in this area. Notice 2005–1, Q&A–7 provides interim guidance regarding the application of section 409A to arrangements between partnerships and partners. Until further guidance is issued, taxpayers may continue to rely on Notice 2005–1, Q&A–7 and sections II.E and VI.E of the preamble to the proposed regulations.

Notice 2005–1, Q&A–7 provided that until further guidance is issued for purposes of section 409A, taxpayers may treat the issuance of a partnership interest (including a profits interest) or an option to purchase a partnership interest, granted in connection with the performance of services under the same principles that govern the issuance of stock. For this purpose, taxpayers may apply the principles applicable to stock options or stock appreciation rights under these final regulations, as effective and applicable, to equivalent rights with respect to partnership interests.

Taxpayers also may continue to rely upon the explanation in the preamble to the proposed regulations regarding the application of section 409A to guaranteed payments for services described in section 707(c). As stated in that preamble, until further guidance is issued, section 409A will apply to guaranteed payments described in section 707(c) (and rights to receive such guaranteed payments in the future), only in cases where the guaranteed payment is for services and the partner providing services does not include the payment in income by the 15th day of the third month following the end of the taxable year of the partner in which the partner obtained a legally binding right to the guaranteed payment or, if later, the taxable year in which the right to the guaranteed payment is first no longer subject to a substantial risk of forfeiture.

Commentators raised issues concerning the application of the provision in Notice 2005–1, Q&A–7 stating that until further guidance is issued, taxpayers may treat arrangements providing for payments subject to section 736 (payments to a retiring partner or a deceased partner's successor in interest) as not being subject to section 409A, except that an arrangement providing for payments that qualify as payments to a partner under section 1402(a)(10) is subject to section 409A. Section 1402(a)(10) provides for an exception from the Self-Employment Contributions Act (SECA) tax for payments to a retired partner, provided that certain conditions are met. Specifically, the payments must be made pursuant to a written plan of the partnership, must be on account of the partner's retirement and must continue at least until the partner's death. In addition, to qualify for the exception, the partner must not have rendered services during the partnership's taxable year ending within or with the partner's taxable year in which the amounts were received, as of the close of the partnership's taxable year no obligation must exist from the other partners to such retired partner except with respect to retirement payments under such plan, and before the end of the partnership's taxable year such retired partner's share, if any, of the capital of the partnership must have been paid to him in full.

Commentators questioned the appropriateness of the inclusion of such arrangements under section 409A, because neither the statute nor the legislative history refers to section 1402(a)(10). However, the Treasury Department and the IRS believe it is appropriate for such arrangements to be subject to section 409A because such arrangements are purposefully created to provide deferred compensation, and do not raise issues regarding the coordination of the provisions of section 409A with the provisions of section 736, specifically the rules governing the classification of payments to a retired partner under section 736(a) (payments considered as distributive share or guaranteed payments) and section 736(b) (payments for interest in partnership).

However, further clarification and relief is provided concerning the application of the deferral election timing rules to these payments. Until further guidance is issued, for purposes of section 409A, taxpayers may treat the legally binding right to the payments excludible from SECA tax under section 1402(a)(10) as arising on the last day of the partner's taxable year before the partner's first taxable year in which such payments are excludible from SECA tax under section 1402(a)(10), and the services for which the payments are compensation as performed in the partner's first taxable year in which such payments are excludible from SECA tax under section 1402(a)(10). Accordingly, for purposes of section 409A, the time and form of payment of such amounts generally may be established, including through an election to defer by the partner, on or before the final day of the partner's taxable year immediately preceding the partner's first taxable year in which such payments are excludible from SECA tax under section 1402(a)(10). However, this interim relief does not apply a second time where an amount paid under an arrangement in one year has been excluded from SECA tax under section 1402(a)(10), and an amount paid in a subsequent year has not been excluded from SECA tax under section 1402(a)(10) because, for example, the partner performed services in that subsequent year.

H. *Foreign plans*

1. *Plans covered by an applicable treaty*

The proposed regulations provided an exclusion from the definition of a nonqualified deferred compensation plan for any scheme, trust, or arrangement maintained with respect to an individual where contributions made by or on behalf of such individual to such scheme, trust or arrangement are excludable for Federal income tax purposes under an applicable income tax treaty. The final regulations retain that exclusion and clarify that the exclusion applies to the extent contributions made by or on behalf of such individual to such scheme, trust, arrangement or plan, or credited allocations, accrued benefits, or earnings or other amounts constituting income, of such individual under such scheme, trust, arrangement or plan, are excludable by such individual for Federal income tax purposes pursuant to any bilateral income tax convention to which the United States is a party.

2. *Exclusion for benefits earned under a broad-based foreign retirement plan*

The proposed regulations contained an exclusion from coverage under section 409A for amounts deferred under a broad-based foreign retirement plan, subject to certain conditions, including that the service provider not be eligible to participate in a qualified employer plan, and that if the person is a U.S. citizen or lawful permanent resident, the exception only applies to nonelective deferrals of foreign earned income (as defined in section 911(b)(1)) that do not exceed the limits under section 415(b) and (c) that would be applicable if the plan were a qualified plan. Deferrals by participants that are nonresident aliens are not subject to the limitation based on section 415. The final regulations adopt this provision, subject to certain modifications.

Many of the commentators requested expansion of the exclusion for broad-based foreign retirement plans. One commentator requested that the exclusion apply to U.S. citizens working in the United States for a foreign employer. The Treasury Department and the IRS do not believe such an exception is justified. However, the exception for U.S. citizens or lawful permanent residents has been expanded to cover nonelective deferrals of foreign earned income as defined in section 911(b)(1) without regard to section 911(b)(1)(B)(iv) and without regard to the requirement that the income be attributable to services performed during the period described in section 911(d)(1)(A) or (B). Accordingly, the exception may now cover certain participation by a U.S. citizen or lawful permanent resident who works overseas during only part of a year, and therefore is not a *bona fide* resident of a foreign country for an uninterrupted period that includes an entire taxable year, or is not present in the foreign country at least 330 full days during a period of 12 consecutive months.

The regulations have also been modified to address nonqualified deferred compensation plans covering *bona fide* residents of a U.S. possession. Under the regulations a *bona fide* resident of a possession who participates in a broad-based foreign retirement plan is not subject to section 409A with respect to participation in such plan. In addition, a plan substantially all of the participants in which are *bona fide* residents of a possession is eligible to be treated as a broad-based foreign retirement plan, so that U.S. citizens and resident aliens (other than *bona fide* residents of a possession) who participate in such a plan may be eligible for the more limited exclusion for participation in a broad-based foreign retirement plan.

Another commentator requested that the exclusion apply to a plan that otherwise meets the requirements for the exclusion, regardless of whether the plan is sponsored by a foreign or U.S. employer. This suggestion has been adopted in the final regulations.

Other commentators requested further clarification and revision of certain of the requirements to qualify for the exclusion. One commentator requested a safe harbor treating any plan granted favorable tax treatment under the laws of a foreign jurisdiction as qualifying for the exclusion. The Treasury Department and the IRS believe this standard is both too broad and not administrable, and this suggestion has not been adopted in the final regulations.

Another commentator requested that the regulations provide a safe harbor percentage for determining whether substantially all of a foreign plan's participants are nonresident aliens. The final regulations do not adopt such a provision. However, the final regulations clarify that in determining whether substantially all of a foreign plan's participants are nonresident aliens or *bona fide* residents of a possession, only active participants are considered. For this purpose, active participants include individuals who, under the terms of the plan and without further amendment or action by the plan sponsor, are eligible to make or receive contributions or accrue benefits under the plan (even if the individual has elected not to participate in the plan).

A similar standard applies to the requirement that the individual not be eligible to participate in a qualified employer plan. The final regulations provide that a service provider will be treated as eligible to participate in a qualified employer plan if, under the plan's terms and without further amendment or action by the plan sponsor, the service provider is eligible to make or receive contributions or accrue benefits under the plan (even if the service provider has elected not to participate in the plan).

The final regulations also clarify that the exclusion for United States citizens and lawful permanent residents applies to nonelective deferrals even if elective deferrals are permitted under the same plan, provided that the amounts deferred through nonelective deferrals and earnings on such amounts are distinguishable from amounts deferred through elective deferrals and earnings on such amounts, such as through the use of separate accounts.

3. *Tax equalization payments*

The proposed regulations excluded from coverage under section 409A certain arrangements, referred to as tax equalization arrangements, that provide for payments intended to compensate the service provider for the excess of taxes actually imposed by a foreign jurisdiction on the compensation paid over the taxes that would be imposed if the compensation were subject solely to United States Federal income tax, subject to certain requirements. The final regulations adopt these provisions, subject to modifications. Based upon the comments received, the final regulations generally expand the exclusion in two respects. First, the final regulations extend the tax equalization payments exception to cover reimbursements of U.S. taxes that exceed foreign taxes. Second, the final regulations provide that the payment must be made by the end of the second taxable year of the service provider following the latest of the deadline for filing a U.S. Federal tax return or the deadline for filing foreign tax returns (or if a foreign return is not required to be filed, the due date for foreign tax payments) reflecting the compensation for which the tax equalization payment is provided.

Commentators also asked how such reimbursement agreements could address the potential for an audit or other tax controversy, both in the U.S. and abroad. The same issue arises with respect to tax gross-up payments in general. For a discussion of the treatment of the right to such payments, see section VII.B.4 of this preamble.

4. *Certain Limited Deferrals by Nonresident Aliens*

The proposed regulations provided an exception for amounts deferred by a nonresident alien under a foreign plan maintained by a foreign service recipient, to the extent the amounts deferred during the year did not exceed $10,000. The final regulations adopt this provision, subject to the modifications described in this preamble. In response to comments, the final regulations clarify that the exception applies to amounts deferred in that taxable year up to the specified limit, regardless of whether additional amounts are deferred. In making this modification, the exclusion provision has been moved from the section providing a definition of nonqualified deferred compensation plan (§1.409A–1(a)) to the section providing a definition of an amount deferred (§1.409A–1(b)). In addition, the final regulations clarify that this exception applies to earnings on amounts deferred that were subject to the exception, provided that the taxpayer can identify both the deferred amounts excepted and the applicable earnings. Finally, in response to comments requesting that the limit be increased and indexed, the final regulations increase the limit for the small deferral exception to the limit provided for elective deferrals under section 402(g).

The small deferral exception is intended to provide relief to service providers that are not U.S. citizens or lawful permanent residents, are participating in a foreign plan, and perform services in the U.S. for which they are compensated. In such cases, the nonresident alien may inadvertently defer a relatively small amount of compensation that would otherwise be subject to U.S. Federal income tax. This may occur where the service provider defers the compensation that the service provider would otherwise have been paid for a brief period of service in the United States, or where the service provider receives service or compensation credit for a brief period of service in the United States under a benefit formula of a nonqualified deferred compensation plan.

Some commentators requested that the exemption be extended to cover all amounts deferred by nonresident aliens under foreign plans to the extent the nonresident alien provides only temporary services in the U.S. Where the compensation earned by such a nonresident alien would be subject to U.S. income tax if paid when earned, the Treasury Department and the IRS do not believe that such a broad exception is warranted.

5. *Other Foreign Plans*

The final regulations adopt the exclusion in the proposed regulations for deferrals of amounts that would be excluded as foreign earned income under section 911 if the amounts had been paid out when earned. The final regulations clarify that the amount is limited to an amount equal to or less than the difference between the maximum section 911 exclusion for the year and the amount actually excluded for the year. Commentators requested that the exception for the deferral of amounts that would be excluded under section 911 be relaxed, so that U.S. expatriates who return for periods longer than 30 days or who earn compensation for services performed in the U.S. that is not excluded as foreign earned income, may also take advantage of the exception. This exception was not intended to address such plans. Rather, the provision was intended to provide relief from the section 409A requirements for U.S. expatriates who intend to work full-time outside the U.S. for compensation that is less than the exclusion amount under section 911, because it would severely disadvantage such workers to expect them to request that their potential foreign employers modify standard plans to accommodate them, or to expect such workers to otherwise be able to determine how to avoid or comply with section 409A.

Commentators pointed out, however, that earnings on deferred amounts, including increases in amounts deferred under a nonaccount balance plan solely due to the passage of time, may not be treated as earned income under section 911 and argued that, nonetheless, such amounts should not lower the amount otherwise available to be deferred under the exception. The final regulations generally provide that rights to earnings credited on amounts that qualify for this exception are also excepted from coverage under section 409A, provided that the earnings satisfy the definition of earnings in §1.409A–1(o).

I. *Indemnification arrangements*

The final regulations generally provide that the right to the payment of contingent amounts pursuant to a service recipient's indemnification for expenses incurred as a result of a legal claim for damages related to the service provider's performance as a service provider, to the extent permissible under applicable law, will not be treated as the right to deferred compensation. Similarly, a right to liability insurance coverage providing for such payments in the event of such a suit also will not be treated as providing for a deferral of compensation.

J. *Separation pay plans*

1. *In general*

The final regulations generally adopt the provisions addressing separation pay plans set forth in the proposed regulations, subject to certain modifications. The final regulations clarify that separation pay refers only to compensation to which the service provider's right is conditioned upon a separation from service (including a separation from service due to death or disability) and not to compensation the service provider could receive without separating from service (such as an amount also payable upon a change in control, as a result of an unforeseeable emergency, or on a date certain). For example, the right to a gross-up payment for taxes payable due to the application of section 280G will constitute separation pay if a separation from service is required to obtain the payment. The final regulations also clarify that a separation pay plan for purposes of section 409A, including for purposes of the plan aggregation rules, refers only to plans providing for payments of amounts of deferred compensation (disregarding the exceptions from the definition of deferred compensation for certain types of separation pay) where one of the conditions to the right to the payment is a separation from service. A right to a payment upon a separation from service that is not deferred compensation does not become subject to section 409A under the plan aggregation rule. For example, the accelerated vesting due to a separation from service of stock options excluded from coverage under section 409A would not constitute a separation pay plan or otherwise become subject to section 409A under the plan aggregation rules.

The final regulations generally retain and supplement the various exceptions from the definition of deferred compensation for certain types of separation pay, providing exceptions for (1) certain *bona fide* collectively bargained arrangements, (2) certain arrangements providing separation pay due solely to an involuntary separation from service or participation in a window program in limited amounts and for a limited period of time, (3) certain foreign separation pay arrangements, (4) certain reimbursement arrangements providing for expense reimbursements or in-kind benefits for a limited period of time following a separation from service, and (5) certain rights to limited amounts of separation pay. These exceptions from coverage under section 409A for specified separation pay plans may be used in combination. For example, the rights of an employee to the maximum amount available under the exception for separation payments made solely due to involuntary separation from service or participation in a window program, to reimbursements for reasonable moving expenses and outplacement expenses that meet the requirement for exclusion from coverage under section 409A, and to rights to payments that do not exceed the limit on elective deferrals under section 402(g) and accordingly qualify for the limited payment exception, may all be excluded from coverage under section 409A due to application of the various exceptions.

The final regulations continue to provide that any amount, or entitlement to any amount, that acts as a substitute for, or replacement of, amounts deferred under a separate nonqualified deferred compensation plan constitutes a payment of deferred compensation or deferral of compensation under the separate nonqualified deferred compensation plan. Commentators asked how this would apply where the service provider would otherwise forfeit a payment upon separation from service but a payment is made anyway, in whole or in part.

The regulations provide that if a separation from service is voluntary, it is presumed that the payment results from an acceleration of vesting followed by a payment of the deferred compensation that is subject to section 409A. Accordingly, any change in the payment schedule to accelerate or defer the payments would be subject to the rules of section 409A. The presumption that a right to a payment is not a new right, but is instead a right substituted for an existing nonvested right, may be rebutted by demonstrating that the service provider's right to the payment after the separation from service would have existed regardless of the forfeiture of the nonvested right. Factors indicating that a right would have existed regardless of the forfeiture include that the amount to which the service provider obtains a right is materially less than the present value of the forfeited amount multiplied by a fraction, the numerator of which is the period of service the service provider actually completed, and the denominator of which is the full period of service the service provider would have been required to complete to receive the full amount of the payment. Another factor is that the payment consists of a type of payment customarily made to service providers who separate from service with that service recipient and do not forfeit nonvested rights to deferred compensation (for example, a payment of accrued but unused leave or a payment for a release of potential claims).

2. *Separation pay due solely to involuntary separation from service or participation in a window program*

The final regulations generally continue the exception from coverage under section 409A in the proposed regulations for rights to payments available only upon an involuntary separation from service or participation in a window program, payable no later than the end of the second taxable year of the service provider following the year of the separation from service, and limited to an amount that is generally the lesser of two times the service provider's annual compensation or two times the limit on compensation set forth in section 401(a)(17). This exception only applies where the payment is available solely due to an involuntary separation from service of the service provider, or the service provider's participation in a window program, and not to a plan providing for a payment upon a voluntary separation from service or other event. For a discussion of when a separation from service for good reason may be treated as an involuntary separation from service, see section III.J.3 of this preamble.

Commentators requested that the exclusion continue to apply to payments up to the limit, even where the entire amount of the separation payments exceeds the limit. The final regulations adopt this rule. Accordingly, where a service provider is entitled to a payment that qualifies for the exception except that it exceeds the limit, only the excess over the limit will be subject to section 409A. The right to the payment up to the applicable limit will not be subject to section 409A, including the requirement that the payment be delayed for six months in the case of a specified employee, provided that such limited payment is otherwise required to be made, and is made, no later than the end of the second taxable year following the service provider's taxable year in which the separation from service occurs.

The final regulations clarify that for purposes of applying the section 401(a)(17) limit, the statutory limit applicable for the year of the separation from service occurs applies. The final regulations also clarify that for purposes of determining the service provider's annual rate of pay for the taxable year preceding the taxable year in which the separation from service occurs, an annual rate of pay based upon the service provider's taxable year immediately preceding the service provider's taxable year in which the separation from service occurs is used, adjusted for any increase during the year that was expected to continue indefinitely if the service provider had not separated from service. One commentator requested that the limit be set at twice the amount of compensation set forth under section 401(a)(17), regardless of the service provider's actual income. This suggestion has not been adopted in the final regulations.

3. *Definition of involuntary separation from service*

The proposed regulations provided an exclusion from coverage under section 409A that applied only to certain amounts paid solely because of an actual involuntary separation from service or participation in a window program. Many comments asked how to determine whether a separation from service is involuntary for this purpose. The final regulations contain a definition of involuntary separation from service and also apply this definition for purposes of the definition of a substantial risk of forfeiture, pursuant to which a payment that will not be made unless the service provider experiences an involuntary separation from service is subject to a substantial risk of forfeiture for purposes of section 409A. (See section V of this preamble).

The final regulations provide that whether a separation from service is involuntary is determined based on all the facts and circumstances. For this purpose, any characterization of the separation from service as voluntary or involuntary by the service provider and the service recipient in the documentation relating to the separation from service is rebuttably presumed to properly characterize the nature of the separation from service. For example, if a separation from service is characterized as voluntary, the presumption may be rebutted by demonstrating that absent the voluntary separation from service the service recipient would have terminated the service provider's services, and that the service provider had knowledge that the service provider would be so terminated.

Commentators requested that a separation from service for good reason be treated as an involuntary separation from service. The final regulations provide that where the right to a payment is contingent upon a voluntary separation from service following an occurrence that constitutes good reason for the service provider to terminate his or her services, the right may be treated as payable only upon an involuntary separation from service where the good reason condition is such that the service provider's separation from service effectively is an involuntary separation for purposes of section 409A. To be treated as an involuntary separation for purposes of section 409A, the avoidance of the requirements of section 409A must not be a purpose of the inclusion of any good reason condition in the plan or of the actions by the service recipient in connection with the satisfaction of a condition. In addition, such good reason condition must require actions taken by the service recipient resulting in a material negative change in the employment relationship, such as a material negative change in the duties to be performed, the conditions under which such duties are to be performed, or the compensation to be received. Additional factors that may be relevant to whether a purported separation from service for good reason is the result of a *bona fide* good reason condition not having as a principal purpose the avoidance of section 409A include the extent to which the payments upon a separation from service for good reason are in the same amount and are made at the same time and in the same form as payments available upon an actual involuntary separation from service, and whether the service provider is required to give the service recipient notice of the existence of the good reason condition and a reasonable opportunity to remedy the condition. Where a good reason condition is sufficient to be treated for purposes of section 409A as a condition requiring an involuntary separation from service, an amount payable on account of a separation from service for good reason will be treated the same as an amount payable on account of an actual involuntary separation from service.

The final regulations also provide a safe harbor under which a provision for a payment upon a voluntary separation from service for good reason will be treated for purposes of section 409A as providing for a payment upon an actual involuntary separation from service. Those conditions include that the amount be payable only if the service provider separates from service within a limited period of time not to exceed two years following the initial existence of the good reason condition, and that the amount, time and form of payment upon a voluntary separation from service for good reason be identical to the amount, time and form of payment upon an involuntary separation from service. In addition, the service provider must be required to provide notice of the existence of the good reason condition within a period not to exceed 90 days of its initial existence, and the service recipient must be provided a period of at least 30 days during which it may remedy the good reason condition. For these purposes, a good reason condition may consist of one or more of the following conditions arising without the consent of the service provider: (1) a material diminution in the service provider's base compensation; (2) a material diminution in the service provider's authority, duties, or responsibilities; (3) a material diminution in the authority, duties, or responsibilities of the supervisor to whom the service provider is required to report, including a requirement that a service provider report to a corporate officer or employee instead of reporting directly to the board of directors of a corporation (or similar entity with respect to an entity other than a corporation); (4) a material diminution in the budget over which the service provider retains authority; (5) a material change in geographic location at which the service provider must perform the services; or (6) any other action or inaction that constitutes a material breach of the terms of an applicable employment agreement.

4. *Collectively bargained plans*

Commentators requested an exception from coverage under section 409A to address certain plans providing for payments upon a voluntary separation from service, in the context of a collective bargaining agreement covering services performed for multiple employers. The Treasury Department and the IRS believe these issues are better addressed in the definition of separation from service. See section VII.C.2.b of this preamble.

5. *Treatment as a separate plan*

For purposes of the plan aggregation rules, the final regulations provide for separate treatment of plans providing for separation pay solely due to an involuntary separation from service or participation in a window program. This exception is intended to apply only where the amounts are payable solely due to an involuntary separation from service or participation in a window program, and not where the amounts may also become payable for some other reason, even where such payments actually are made due to an involuntary separation from service or participation in a window program. Accordingly, any amount that would be paid as a result of a voluntary separation from service will not be included in this category. An arrangement that does not provide for deferred compensation will not be aggregated with a deferred compensation plan under this rule, merely because the arrangement not providing for deferred compensation accelerates vesting or payment upon an involuntary separation from service (for example, the acceleration of the vesting of a stock option or stock appreciation right that is excluded from coverage under section 409A).

6. *Reimbursement and fringe benefit plans*

a. *In general*

The proposed regulations provided that certain plans under which a service recipient reimburses certain types of expenses (for example, reasonable moving expenses or reasonable outplacement expenses directly related to a termination of the service provider's services) actually incurred by a service provider (including certain in-kind benefits provided to the service provider) following a separation from service are not nonqualified deferred compensation plans for purposes of section 409A, if such reimbursements are available only for expenses incurred, and the reimbursements are made, during a limited period (generally not after the second taxable year of the service provider following the separation from service).

In response to questions from commentators, the final regulations clarify that a right to a benefit that is excludible from income will not be treated as a deferral of compensation for purposes of section 409A. Accordingly, for example, an arrangement to provide health coverage excludible from income under section 105 generally would not be subject to section 409A.

Many commentators requested increased flexibility to provide for reimbursement arrangements upon a separation from service, including certain requests to exempt broad categories of such arrangements, such as the continuation of any plan in which the service provider participated while performing services. The Treasury Department and the IRS believe that an exemption from coverage under section 409A is not appropriate in such circumstances, because such plans may provide for rights to significant amounts of deferred compensation over lengthy periods of time. However, the final regulations extend the limited period during which taxable reimbursements of medical expenses may be provided, to cover the period during which the service provider would be entitled (or would, but for such arrangement, be entitled) to continuation coverage under a group health plan of the service recipient under section 4980B (COBRA) if the service provider elected such coverage and paid the applicable premiums. In addition, the final regulations contain several provisions governing reimbursement plans (including plans providing in-kind benefits) that constitute nonqualified deferred compensation plans for purposes of section 409A, so that taxpayers will be able to design such arrangements to comply with the payment timing requirements of section 409A. For a discussion of these provisions, see section VII.B.2 of this preamble.

b. *Specific exceptions for post-separation reimbursement plans*

The final regulations continue to exclude from coverage under section 409A the reimbursement of certain expenses such as reasonable outplacement expenses and reasonable moving expenses for a limited period of time due to a separation from service, whether the separation from service is voluntary or involuntary. The final regulations, like the proposed regulations, require that the eligible expense must be incurred by the service provider no later than the end of the second year following the year in which the separation from service occurs. In response to questions from commentators, the final regulations clarify that the exception applies to the qualifying reimbursements available during the limited period of time, even if the plan extends beyond the limited period of time.

Several commentators requested that the limited period of time refer solely to the time the expense is incurred, and not the time the expense is reimbursed, to reflect the need for time to process the reimbursement request. Although the final regulations do not adopt this suggestion, the final regulations extend the period during which a service provider can receive a reimbursement payment by providing that such payments must be made not later than the end of the third year following the separation from service. This extension applies only to reimbursements of expenses incurred by the service provider. Where the service recipient provides in-kind benefits (as defined in the regulations), or the service recipient pays a third party to provide in-kind benefits, such benefits must be provided by the end of the second year following the separation from service.

Commentators also requested that the final regulations clarify the treatment of rights to a reimbursement of any loss incurred due to a sale of a residence. The regulations clarify that for this purpose, reasonable moving expenses include the reimbursement of an amount related to a loss incurred due to a sale of a primary residence, provided that the reimbursement does not exceed the loss actually incurred.

7. *Limited payments of separation pay*

The final regulations provide that, if not otherwise excluded, a taxpayer may treat a right or rights under a separation pay plan to a payment or payments of an aggregate amount not to exceed the applicable dollar amount under section 402(g)(1)(B) for the year of the separation from service as not providing for a deferral of compensation. Commentators raised questions concerning the calculation of the excluded amount, and requested an increase in the amount. The limited payment exception is intended to avoid the application of section 409A to incidental benefits often provided upon a separation from service, where the parties may not realize that the benefits are nonqualified deferred compensation. The exception is not intended to address extended or significant benefits. Accordingly, the final regulations do not substantially increase the amount of the exclusion. However, to permit the excluded amount to automatically reflect cost-of-living increases, the maximum exclusion now equals the maximum amount of an elective deferral permitted under section 402(g) for the year of the separation from service.

The aggregate amount refers to the aggregate amount of payments to which the service provider has a right or rights. The exclusion may be applied to any type of separation pay plan, but may apply only once with respect to amounts paid by a service recipient to a service provider. So, for example, if a service provider treats a right to a payment of separation pay equal to the applicable limit under section 402(g) in the first year following a separation from service as an excluded right, the right to the amount is not treated as a deferral of compensation regardless of when the amount is actually paid (though other provisions of the Code and the constructive receipt doctrine continue to apply). However, once the right is treated as excluded, the service provider may not treat any other right with respect to the service recipient, such as an additional right to a payment equal to the applicable limit under section 402(g) in the second year following the separation from service, as excluded under this exception.

K. *Non-taxable benefits*

The final regulations clarify that a legally binding right to receive a nontaxable benefit does not provide for a deferral of compensation for purposes of section 409A, unless the service provider has received the right in exchange for, or has the right to exchange the right for, an amount that will be includible in income (other than due to participation in a cafeteria plan described in section 125). In addition, because such benefits do not provide for a deferral of compensation, the plan aggregation rules will not result in taxation of other benefit plans merely because the terms of such nontaxable benefit arrangements would not comply with section 409A if the arrangement were covered by section 409A. For a discussion of the requirements for a taxable reimbursement plan to satisfy the payment timing requirements of section 409A, see section VII.B.2 of this preamble.

L. *Legal settlements*

Commentators requested clarification of the application of section 409A to amounts paid pursuant to litigation between the service provider and service recipient, including both court awards and *bona fide* settlements, and including amounts characterized as wages or otherwise treated as replacing compensation. The Treasury Department and the IRS believe that section 409A was not intended to govern settlements or awards resolving *bona fide* legal claims based on wrongful termination, employment discrimination, the Fair Labor Standards Act, or worker's compensation statutes, regardless of whether such claims arise under Federal, state, local, or foreign laws, even where settlements or awards pursuant to such claims are treated as compensation for Federal tax purposes. The final regulations generally treat such arrangements as not providing for deferred compensation for purposes of section 409A. In addition, the final regulations generally provide that section 409A does not apply to the payment of, or reimbursement for, attorney's fees incurred in connection with the enforcement of such a claim. However, the exception covers only rights arising from the *bona fide* claim, and is not intended to allow such settlements or awards to act as substitutes for, or to allow for the restructuring of, preexisting deferred compensation subject to section 409A. For example, a change to the timing of the payment of a pre-existing amount of deferred compensation as part of such a settlement would be subject to the rules governing accelerated payments and subsequent deferral elections. In addition, the payment of an amount upon the execution of a waiver of any or all of such claims does not necessarily indicate that the amounts are paid as an award or settlement of an actual *bona fide* claim. Rather, to qualify for the exception under this provision, the amounts must be paid with respect to an actual *bona fide* claim for damages under the applicable law. For a discussion of the treatment of settlements of *bona fide* disputes regarding the right to preexisting deferred compensation subject to section 409A, see section VIII.G of this preamble.

M. *Split-dollar life insurance arrangements*

Some commentators requested that split-dollar life insurance arrangements be excluded from coverage under section 409A. Split-dollar life insurance arrangements are often used as a method of providing deferred compensation and there is no indication in the statute or legislative history of any legislative intent that such arrangements be excluded from coverage under section 409A. In addition, like a promise to transfer property in the future, a promise to transfer an economic benefit in the future may provide for deferred compensation. Accordingly, a split-dollar life insurance arrangement may provide for deferred compensation, and whether a split dollar life insurance arrangement provides for deferred compensation must be determined through application of the general rules defining deferred compensation and a nonqualified deferred compensation plan. In response to requests for additional guidance, the Treasury Department and the IRS anticipate issuing a notice addressing the application of section 409A to split-dollar life insurance arrangements.

Commentators raised issues concerning the interplay between the modifications that may be needed to satisfy the requirements of section 409A and the effective date rules applicable to split-dollar life insurance arrangements under §1.61–22(j). Commentators pointed out that the modifications necessary to meet the requirements of section 409A and these regulations may cause the arrangement to be treated as a new arrangement under §1.61–22(j) and requested relief. The notice will also address this issue.

N. *Educational benefits*

Commentators requested an exclusion from coverage under section 409A for promises to provide future taxable educational benefits to service providers. These benefits typically would be provided as an inducement to provide a period of services. Commentators expressed concern that the amount and timing of the payment of such benefits would be difficult to ascertain, because the amount and timing of the payments would depend upon the service provider's decisions with respect to further education. The final regulations generally provide an exception from coverage under section 409A for rights to educational benefits, where the benefits consist solely of educational assistance (as defined for purposes of section 127(c)) provided solely for the education of the service provider.

IV. *Definition of Plan*

A. *Plan aggregation rules*

The proposed regulations generally provided that all amounts deferred with respect to a service provider under all plans of a service recipient falling within a particular category would be treated as deferred under a single plan. The enumerated categories included amounts deferred under account balance plans, amounts deferred under nonaccount balance plans, amounts deferred under separation pay plans providing payments due solely to an involuntary termination or participation in a window program, and amounts deferred under any other plan. The final regulations adopt these provisions, subject to certain modifications described in this preamble.

The final regulations provide that the bifurcation rules applicable to plans under §31.3121(v)(2)–1(c)(1)(iii)(B), which are permissive for purposes of the application of section 3121(v)(2), must be applied for purposes of the plan aggregation rules under section 409A. Accordingly, a portion of a nonqualified deferred compensation plan is a separate account balance plan if that portion otherwise qualifies as an account balance plan and the amount payable to service providers under that portion is determined independently of the amount payable under the other portion of the plan.

The final regulations also provide additional categories of plans for purposes of the aggregation rules. One category covers split-dollar life insurance arrangements. Another category is comprised of reimbursement plans, providing for the reimbursement of expenses incurred or the provision of in-kind benefits (as defined in the regulations), to the extent the right to such benefits or reimbursements, separately or in the aggregate, does not constitute a substantial portion of the overall compensation earned by the service provider for performing services for the service recipient, or the overall compensation received due to a separation from service. Stock rights that constitute nonqualified deferred compensation for purposes of section 409A also comprise a separate category.

The final regulations further provide for account balance plans to be subdivided into a category for elective plans and a category for nonelective plans. Plans will only be subdivided in this manner to the extent the amounts deferred under an elective deferral arrangement (and earnings on such amounts) may be separately identified. For this purpose, a right to a match on an elective deferral will not be treated as an elective deferral arrangement.

In an additional category, any amounts deferred under a foreign plan may be treated as deferred under a separate plan from any amounts deferred under a domestic plan, provided that the deferrals under the plan are deferrals of amounts that would be treated as modified foreign earned income (meaning foreign earned income as defined under section 911(b)(1) without regard to section 911(b)(1)(B)(iv) and without regard to the requirement that the income be attributable to services performed during the period described in section 911(d)(1)(A) or (B)) if paid to the service provider at the time the amount is first deferred, and provided further that the foreign plan is not substantially identical to a domestic plan in which the service provider participates. For this purpose, a foreign plan is a plan that the service recipient provides primarily to nonresident aliens or resident aliens classified as resident aliens solely under section 7701(b)(1)(A)(ii) (and not section 7701(b)(1)(A)(i)).

B. *Written plan requirement*

Commentators requested clarification and simplification of the provisions required to be included in writing in plan documents to comply with section 409A. As a general rule, the final regulations provide that to satisfy the requirement that a plan be in writing, the document or documents constituting the plan must specify, at the time an amount is deferred, the amount to which the service provider has a right to be paid (or, in the case of an amount determinable under an objective, nondiscretionary formula, the terms of such formula), and the payment schedule or payment triggering events that will result in a payment of the amount.

A plan must provide for the six-month delay requirement applicable to payments to specified employees upon a separation from service no later than the time the provision may become applicable to a separation from service of the specified employee. Accordingly, the plan must contain the provision by the time at which the employee becomes a specified employee (either because the stock of a component of the service recipient becomes publicly traded, or because the specified employee effective date has been reached for a list of specified employees that includes the employee). A provision applicable to a plan sponsored by a service recipient or a plan in which a specified employee participates is effective with respect to a specified employee only to the extent the provision is binding on the employee.

With respect to a deferral election, whether an initial or subsequent deferral election, the plan must specify no later than the time by which that election is required to be irrevocable the conditions under which that election may be made. With respect to permitted accelerations of a payment, the plan need not specify the conditions under which the accelerated payment will be made except as explicitly required in these regulations. However, the taxpayer must demonstrate that the acceleration of the payment complies with the requirements of section 409A and these regulations.

Commentators also requested clarification regarding whether the requirement that a plan be in writing also means that the plan must be contained in a single document. For purposes of this rule, the plan consists of all documents that together define the service provider's rights to the compensation. Accordingly, the terms of a plan document may be contained in more than one document including, for example, a deferral election document.

Commentators asked whether a savings clause would be sufficient to ensure compliance with section 409A, where the savings clause provides that each provision of the plan will be interpreted to be consistent with the requirements of section 409A and that any provision of the plan that does not satisfy such requirements will be of no force or effect. The final regulations provide that for purposes of determining the terms of a plan, general provisions of the plan that purport to nullify noncompliant plan terms, or to supply required specific plan terms, are disregarded. Accordingly, if a plan contains terms that do not meet the requirements of section 409A and these regulations, or fails to contain a plan term necessary to meet the requirements of section 409A and these regulations, the plan will violate the requirements of section 409A and these regulations regardless of whether the plan contains such a savings clause.

Several commentators requested that the Treasury Department and the IRS publish model amendments. Due to the complex and varied universe of deferred compensation plans, the Treasury Department and the IRS do not believe that it is feasible to publish model amendments at this time.

V. *Definition of Substantial Risk of Forfeiture*

A. *In general*

The final regulations generally adopt the definition of substantial risk of forfeiture set forth in the proposed regulations. Several commentators requested that the definition of substantial risk of forfeiture be the same as the definition of substantial risk of forfeiture in §1.83–3(c). However, the definition of substantial risk of forfeiture for purposes of compensatory transfers of property under section 83 reflects different policy concerns from those involved in section 409A, and there are also practical differences between transfers of restricted property and promises to pay deferred compensation. This is reflected in the provisions of section 409A(e)(5), directing the Secretary of the Treasury Department to issue regulations disregarding a substantial risk of forfeiture in cases where necessary to carry out the purposes of section 409A. Accordingly, the final regulations do not adopt this suggestion.

A right to an amount deferred may be subject to the satisfaction of two or more different conditions that each independently would be a substantial risk of forfeiture. In that case, the substantial risk of forfeiture generally would continue until all of such conditions had been met. Alternatively, a right to an amount deferred may be subject to the satisfaction of any of two or more different conditions that each independently would constitute a substantial risk of forfeiture. In that case, the substantial risk of forfeiture generally would lapse as soon as one of the conditions had been met.

The final regulations explicitly provide that a payment conditioned on an involuntary separation from service without cause may be treated as subject to a substantial risk of forfeiture if there is a substantial risk that the service provider will not be involuntarily separated from service without cause. Many of the comments relating to the definition of a substantial risk of forfeiture requested also that a benefit available only upon a separation from service for good reason be treated as subject to a substantial risk of forfeiture. Under the definition of an involuntary separation from service provided in the final regulations, the right to a payment upon a separation for service for good reason may, in certain circumstances, be treated as a right to a payment upon an involuntary separation from service. For a discussion of the definition of an involuntary separation from service, see section III.J.3 of this preamble.

Commentators requested that a requirement that an employee sign a release of claims to receive a benefit be treated as a substantial risk of forfeiture. Generally, conditions under the discretionary control of the service provider (other than the decision whether or not to continue providing services) are not treated as creating a substantial risk of forfeiture. Accordingly, the final regulations do not adopt this suggestion.

One commentator suggested that any right to a payment be treated as subject to a substantial risk of forfeiture until the amount of the payment is readily determinable, at least where the payment could be zero. The Treasury Department and the IRS do not believe that this standard is appropriate.

B. *Election between vested and nonvested rights*

The final regulations provide that an amount will not be considered subject to a substantial risk of forfeiture after the date or time at which the recipient otherwise could have elected to receive the amount of compensation, unless the present value of the amount purportedly subject to a substantial risk of forfeiture (disregarding, in calculating the present value, the risk of forfeiture) is materially greater than the present value of the vested amount the recipient otherwise could have elected to receive. For example, if a service provider can elect to receive, in lieu of a payment of current compensation, a bonus based upon a formula that would otherwise subject the bonus to a substantial risk of forfeiture, the bonus will be subject to a substantial risk of forfeiture for purposes of section 409A only if the present value of the amount of the bonus (disregarding the risk of forfeiture) is materially greater than the present value of the current compensation amount.

Some commentators asked whether this exception addressed the extension of a substantial risk of forfeiture as part of the negotiated extension of an employment contract. Commentators argued that rights a service provider obtains under a new or extended employment contract could be viewed as a right to an amount materially greater than the amount the service provider otherwise could have received. The final regulations clarify that for purposes of this rule, compensation the service provider would receive for continuing to perform services regardless of whether the service provider elected to receive the vested payment is not taken into account for purposes of determining whether the present value of the right to the nonvested payment is materially greater.

VI. *Initial Deferral Election Rules*

A. *In general*

The final regulations adopt the provisions contained in the proposed regulations relating to initial deferral elections, subject to the modifications described in this preamble.

The proposed regulations generally provided that in a nonelective plan, a service recipient may designate the time and form of payment on or before the date the service provider obtains a legally binding right to the payment. Commentators requested clarification of how the service recipient's discretion to designate a time and form of payment related to the requirement in the proposed regulations that a service provider's deferral election be irrevocable by the applicable deadline. Specifically, commentators requested that a deferral election by a service provider be treated as irrevocable, even if during the period during which the service recipient could have set the time and form of payment (that is, through the date the service recipient grants the service provider a legally binding right to the payment), the service recipient retains the right to override the service provider's deferral election and provide for deferral of a lesser or greater amount. The final regulations do not adopt this suggestion. If a service provider may make an initial deferral election, including an election as to the time and form of payment, the election must be irrevocable as of the date required under the rules governing such service provider elections. Accordingly, a plan may not provide for such an override, unless such override cannot occur after the deadline by which the service provider's election must be effective.

Many commentators requested a clarification of the rules with respect to a deferral of a discretionary bonus, where the legally binding right to the bonus does not arise until a year subsequent to the year in which services are performed. For example, an employer announces in 2010 that it will be awarding discretionary bonuses for services performed in 2011, and will decide which employees will receive bonuses and in what amounts at the beginning of 2012. Section 409A(a)(4) generally provides that compensation for services performed during a taxable year may be deferred at the service provider's election only if the election to defer such compensation is made not later than the close of the taxable year preceding the year in which the services are rendered. Accordingly, even where the bonus is discretionary such that the legally binding right to the bonus does not arise until after the period of services for which the bonus is paid has begun, a service provider's deferral election must occur before the year in which the period of services begins absent some other applicable exception (such as, for example, the deferral election rules related to performance-based compensation). The determination of the period of services for which compensation is earned is based on all the facts and circumstances, but may include periods of service before the date the service provider obtains a legally binding right to the compensation. Although not necessarily determinative, one of the factors taken into account in that determination is a designation by the service recipient of the period of services for which the compensation is earned.

B. *Nonelective deferrals*

Commentators pointed out that under the proposed regulations, a service recipient might be required to designate a time and form of payment with respect to a nonelective deferral at an earlier date than the service provider would have to make such a designation if an election had been provided to the service provider. Commentators requested that the service recipient be provided the same flexibility as the service provider in such cases. The final regulations generally adopt this suggestion, so that if the service provider has no election as to the time and form of payment of an amount of deferred compensation, the service recipient may set the time and form of payment on any date on or before the later of the latest date the service provider would have been permitted under these regulations to elect such time and form of payment if an election had been provided to the service provider, or the date the service recipient grants the legally binding right to the compensation. So, for example, where compensation is performance-based compensation, and the service recipient retains the discretion to establish the time and form of the payment, the plan generally could permit the service recipient to establish the time and form of the payment on or before the date six months before the end of the relevant performance period.

C. *Performance-based compensation*

The final regulations generally adopt the definition of performance-based compensation contained in the proposed regulations, subject to the modifications described in this preamble. The final regulations clarify that where a portion of an award would qualify as performance-based compensation if the portion were the sole amount available under the plan, that portion of the award will not fail to qualify as performance-based compensation merely because another portion of the award does not qualify as performance-based compensation, if the portion that would qualify as performance-based compensation is designated separately or otherwise separately identifiable under the terms of the plan and each portion is determined independently of the other.

Commentators asked whether in order to use the deferral rules regarding performance-based compensation, a service provider must be required to perform services during the entire performance period, or from the date the performance criteria are set through the end of the performance period. Commentators argued that because a payment cannot be substantially certain to be made at the time of the deferral election under the deferral election rules applicable to performance-based compensation, a service provider's ability to manipulate the timing of income inclusion under a performance-based compensation arrangement is limited. The final regulations require only that the service provider provide services from the later of the date the performance period starts or the date the performance criteria are established through the date the initial deferral election is made.

Commentators suggested that a provision in a plan for automatic payment to occur upon death, disability, or a change in control event (as defined for purposes of section 409A) should not result in a failure of the arrangement to qualify as performance-based compensation. The final regulations adopt this suggestion, provided that where such an event occurs before a deferral election has been made, the right to the payment will no longer be treated as performance-based compensation so that a deferral election may not be effective unless made in accordance with another applicable deferral election rule.

In response to comments, the requirement that a deferral election under the rule applicable to performance-based compensation be made before the compensation has become substantially certain to be paid has been modified, and now requires that the election be made before the amount is readily ascertainable. Where the right to a specified amount is subject to a performance requirement being met (for example, a right to a payment of $10,000 if a certain profit level is attained), the amount is treated as readily ascertainable when it is substantially certain that the performance requirement will be met. With respect to the right to an amount of compensation that varies based upon the level of performance, the payment, or any portion of the payment, is treated as readily ascertainable to the extent the amount or the payment is calculable and the performance requirement is substantially certain to be met. For this purpose, a right to a payment is bifurcated between the amount that is readily ascertainable and the amount that is not readily ascertainable. Accordingly, any minimum amount that is calculable and for which the performance requirement entitling the service provider to the payment is substantially certain to be met generally will be treated as readily ascertainable.

For example, a service recipient agrees to pay $100 for every additional widget meeting certain quality requirements that is produced in a calendar year in excess of 100 widgets. At the end of the six months, 125 widgets have been produced and no election to defer has been made. As of that date, the performance-based compensation with respect to which an election to defer can be made does not include the $2500 ((125-100) multiplied by $100) that is calculable and for which the performance requirement is substantially certain to be met. In addition, the performance-based compensation does not include any additional amount that the service provider is substantially certain to earn based on the number of additional widgets that the service provider is substantially certain to produce before the end of the year. However, the payment is bifurcated so that any additional amount that is not substantially certain to be paid may be treated as performance-based compensation such that an election to defer such compensation may be made.

Commentators requested clarification of the circumstances under which compensation, the amount of which is determined by reference to the value of service recipient stock, may qualify as performance-based compensation. The fair market value of stock at any given time generally incorporates the market's perception of the probability that the stock will increase or decrease in value. Accordingly, compensation payable for a service period that is equal to the value of a predetermined number of shares of stock, and is variable only to the extent that the value of such shares appreciates or depreciates, generally will not be performance-based compensation. However, if the right to such compensation is subject to a performance-based vesting requirement, such compensation may be performance-based compensation. Also, the attainment of a prescribed value for the service recipient (or a portion thereof), or a share of stock of the service recipient, may be used as a performance-based criterion, if it is a condition for receiving the compensation and the other requirements are met.

D. *Initial eligibility*

Section 409A(a)(4)(B)(ii) provides that in the case of the first year in which a service provider becomes eligible to participate in the plan, an initial deferral election may be made within 30 days after the date the service provider becomes eligible to participate in the plan, with respect to compensation for services to be performed subsequent to the election. The final regulations adopt the provisions implementing the initial eligibility deferral election rules set forth in the proposed regulations, subject to the following modifications.

Many of the commentators on the initial eligibility deferral election rule expressed concerns about the application of the plan aggregation rules. The proposed regulations provided that the plan aggregation rules would apply in determining whether a service provider was newly eligible for a plan, so that if a service provider was already participating in an arrangement that is required to be aggregated with the arrangement for which the service provider is initially eligible, the service provider would not be able to take advantage of the initial eligibility deferral election rule. Some commentators requested that the plan aggregation rules not apply for this purpose. However, the Treasury Department and the IRS believe that such a rule would result in the potential for the adoption of serial plans as a means to claim repeated initial eligibility and the ability thereby to make late deferral elections. In addition, such a rule would require difficult determinations of whether one plan was sufficiently dissimilar from another plan to qualify as a separate plan.

Other commentators requested that the plan aggregation rules apply, but that plans allowing elections between current and deferred compensation, or the part of a plan allowing such elections, be treated separately from nonelective plans or nonelective benefits in each category. The final regulations generally adopt this rule through the modifications to the plan aggregation rules described in section IV.A of this preamble.

Other comments focused on the application of the initial eligibility deferral election rule in the case of a rehire or a change in position within a service recipient. Commentators pointed out that under the standard in the proposed regulations, if an employee had not received a distribution after the initial termination of employment, or had transferred to a position not participating in the plan without receiving a distribution and then transferred back to a position participating in the plan, the rehired or returning employee would still retain the right to benefits under the plan and thus would not be able to use the initial eligibility deferral election rules. The final regulations provide that the initial eligibility deferral election rules are applicable to a service provider provided that the service provider has not been an active participant in the plan (applying the plan aggregation rules) for at least 24 months. For this purpose, a service provider is an active participant in the plan if, under the plan's terms and without further amendment or action by the plan sponsor, the service provider is eligible to accrue benefits under the plan (even if the service provider has elected not to participate in the plan), other than earnings on amounts previously deferred.

Commentators requested relief with respect to the timing rules for initial elections establishing the time and schedule of payments under nonelective excess benefit plans. Commentators noted that under such plans, a service provider often automatically becomes a participant when the service provider's benefits under the qualified plan become limited under the rules governing qualified plans. Because determining whether a service provider is a participant requires calculations, commentators observed that both the service provider and the service recipient may be unaware that the service provider has become a participant in the plan for some time after the service provider actually first becomes eligible. The final regulations generally provide that with respect to a nonelective excess benefit plan, a service provider is treated as initially eligible to participate in the plan as of the first day of the service provider's taxable year immediately following the first year the service provider accrues a benefit under such plan, so that an initial deferral election with respect to the time and form of payment may be effective for benefits accrued under the plan based on services performed during the taxable year immediately preceding the year in which the election is made. This rule may only be used once with respect to a service provider's participation in a plan.

E. *Initial deferral elections with respect to certain forfeitable rights*

The proposed regulations provided a rule for initial deferral elections with respect to certain forfeitable rights, generally intended to address *ad hoc* awards. Under the rule in the proposed regulations, if a legally binding right to a payment in a subsequent year is subject to a forfeiture condition requiring the service provider's continued services for a period of at least 12 months from the date the service provider obtains the legally binding right, an election to defer such compensation may be made on or before the 30th day after the service provider obtains the legally binding right to the compensation, provided that the election is made at least 12 months in advance of the earliest date at which the forfeiture condition could lapse. The final regulations retain this rule, subject to the modifications described in this preamble.

Commentators suggested that the requirement of at least a 12-month service period following the deferral election during which the right could be forfeited due to a separation from service be shortened to 11 months, because the combination of the 30-day election period plus the 12-month service period requirement generally resulted in a requirement of at least a 13-month performance period. The requirement of a 12-month service period after an election is made ensures that the election occurs while at least an entire year (12 months) of services is still required. This conforms in many respects to the general rule that the deferral election must be made in the year before the year in which the services are performed. Any shorter period would permit service providers to make deferral elections in the same taxable year in which all of the services are performed. The Treasury Department and the IRS do not believe that such a rule is consistent with the legislative intent.

The final regulations also provide that this rule is available even if the right to the compensation may vest earlier than 12 months following the election due to the service provider's death or disability, or due to a change in control event (as defined for purposes of section 409A) with respect to the service recipient. However, if death, disability, or a change in control event occurs and the condition lapses before the end of such 12-month period, a deferral election may be given effect only if the deferral election is permitted under the regulations without regard to this rule.

F. *Initial deferral election with respect to fiscal year compensation*

The final regulations retain the initial deferral election rule with respect to fiscal year compensation that was in the proposed regulations. The final regulations clarify that the rule with respect to the deferral of fiscal year compensation is based upon the service recipient's taxable year, regardless of whether the service recipient's taxable year is the calendar year or some other period. Accordingly, where a service recipient with a calendar year taxable year is providing fiscal year compensation to a service provider based upon a calendar year, a service provider with a non-calendar year taxable year generally could take advantage of the rule to defer such fiscal year compensation on or before the December 31 preceding the calendar year upon which the fiscal year compensation is based.

G. *Initial deferral elections with respect to commissions*

The final regulations continue to provide a special deferral election rule with respect to commission payments. These rules are intended to address concerns that, for many commission arrangements, it is difficult to determine when the services related to a particular commission payment began, so that it is difficult to apply the general rule that requires that a deferral election be made before the year in which any services are performed. This rule is not intended to address whether, absent such a deferral election, a particular commission arrangement would result in deferred compensation. Whether a commission arrangement otherwise provides for deferred compensation must be determined through the application of the general rules defining deferred compensation. However, where a commission arrangement requires that the service provider be providing services at the time of the payment to be entitled to the payment, the commission is paid in the normal course, and neither the service provider nor the service recipient has a right to specify a payment date, the arrangement generally will not provide for the deferral of compensation.

The final regulations generally adopt the deferral election rule set forth in the proposed regulations treating the services related to a commission payment as performed in the year in which the customer remits payment to the service recipient. For this purpose, the proposed regulations provided that commissions include only compensation contingent upon the service recipient receiving payment from an unrelated customer for the product or services provided.

Commentators asked that this rule be extended to cover arrangements under which the service recipient paid the commission based upon consummation of a transaction, regardless of whether the customer paid the service recipient for the service or good purchased from the service recipient. For example, commentators stated that in some industries the service recipient pays a salesperson commissions based on the amount of sales recorded, even though the customer is not obligated to pay the service recipient until a later date. The final regulations generally adopt this suggestion by permitting the taxable year in which the sale occurs to be substituted for the year in which the customer remits payment. However, to avoid manipulation of the deferral election timing rules, the taxable year of the sale may be used only if it is applied consistently to all similarly situated service providers.

Commentators also asked that this rule be extended to commissions earned due to the increase in value, or maintenance of overall value, of a pool of assets or accounts. In response, the final regulations provide that, for purposes of the initial deferral election rules, the services with respect to investment commission compensation are deemed to be performed over the 12 months immediately preceding the date as of which the overall value of the assets or asset accounts is determined for purposes of the calculation of the investment commission compensation. For this purpose, investment commission compensation means compensation earned by a service provider if a substantial portion of the services provided by such service provider to a service recipient consists of sales of financial products or the provision of other direct customer services to an unrelated customer with respect to customer assets or customer asset accounts. For this purpose, amounts will only be treated as investment commission compensation if the customer retains the right to terminate the customer relationship and transfer or withdraw the assets or asset accounts without undue delay (which may be subject to a reasonable notice period), the compensation paid by the service recipient to the service provider consists of a portion of the value of the overall assets or asset account balance, an amount substantially all of which is calculated by reference to the increase in the value of the overall assets or account balance during a specified period, or both, and the value of the overall assets or account balance and investment commission compensation is determined at least annually.

Commentators also requested that the exception for commissions be expanded to address arrangements involving customers related to either the service provider or the service recipient. The Treasury Department and the IRS are concerned that where arrangements involve related parties, there is the potential for manipulation of the timing of the payment and the commission, but also understand that many of such arrangements may not involve abuse. Therefore, the final regulations provide that the special rules with respect to commissions apply to arrangements involving a customer related to the service provider or the service recipient provided that substantial sales or substantial services occur between the service recipient and a significant number of unrelated customers, and the sales or service arrangement and the commission arrangement with respect to a customer related to either the service recipient or the service provider are *bona fide* and arise in the ordinary course of business, and both the terms and practices are substantially the same as the terms and practices applicable to customers to whom the service provider and service recipient are not related, and to whom, either individually or in the aggregate, the service recipient has made substantial sales or provided substantial services.

H. *Involuntary and voluntary separations from service*

The final regulations provide that with respect to separation pay paid upon an actual involuntary separation from service, where the service provider had no prior right to such separation pay, and where the separation pay is the subject of *bona fide*, arm's length negotiations, the initial deferral election may be made at any time before the service provider obtains a legally binding right to the payment. The final regulations expand this rule to include voluntary separations from service as well as involuntary separations, as long as all of the other conditions in the previous sentence are met. The exception addresses both a choice between a current and a deferred payment, and the establishment of the time and form of payment of deferred compensation.

The exception is intended to address legally binding rights to deferred compensation arising as part of the process of separating from service and not based upon previously existing legally binding rights. The exception is intended to alleviate concern that where such rights are expressed or calculated based on prior compensation or service, any election by the service provider as to the timing of the payment during the negotiation process could be viewed as a late initial deferral election made during or after the year in which the services were performed, and to avoid the potential for the plan aggregation rules to eliminate the ability to make an initial eligibility deferral election. The Treasury Department and the IRS have become aware that certain taxpayers have attempted to apply this provision to existing deferred compensation plans, believing that the exception allows new elections provided that the separation pay was the subject of *bona fide* negotiations. This application is inconsistent with the explicit provision of the proposed regulations and these final regulations. The provision does not address preexisting legally binding rights to deferred compensation, including legally binding rights that are subject to a substantial risk of forfeiture. Any change in the time and form of payments under those arrangements would be required to meet the rules governing subsequent deferral elections and accelerated payments (including any applicable relief provided during the transition period). For a discussion of the treatment of benefits forfeitable upon the separation from service, see section III.J.1 of this preamble.

I. *Elections to annualize recurring part-year compensation*

Commentators asked how the deferral election rules would apply to an election by certain employees providing services over less than a 12-month period to receive payments for services on an annualized basis. For example, teachers performing services during a school year running from September of one year through June of the next year often are provided an election to receive the compensation on an annualized basis over 12 months instead of during only the school year. This raises issues under the general initial deferral election rules under section 409A because the teacher is permitted to elect after the beginning of the calendar year to defer some of the compensation that would be paid in September through December of that year to a period in the subsequent year.

The final regulations provide that with respect to recurring part-year compensation, an election to defer all or a portion of the compensation to be earned during a particular period of service may be made at any time before the period of service begins, provided that no amounts are deferred under the election to a date after the last day of the 13th month following the first day of the performance period. For this purpose, recurring part-year compensation is defined as compensation paid for services rendered in a capacity that the service recipient reasonably anticipates will continue in subsequent years on similar terms and conditions, and will require services to be provided over successive service periods of less than 12 months, each of which begins in one taxable year of the service provider and ends in the next such taxable year. For example, a teacher earning compensation from September 15 of one year through June 30 of the subsequent year could elect to defer compensation earned during such period on any date on or before September 15 of the first year, provided that no amount deferred in accordance with this rule is deferred beyond October 31 of the following year. This exception may be applied to a particular amount of compensation only once, so that an amount deferred under this exception may not be deferred a second time through treatment of the amount as earned in a subsequent service period.

J. *USERRA*

The final regulations provide that the initial deferral election rules are deemed satisfied to the extent that a deferral election provided to a service provider is necessary to satisfy the requirements of the Uniformed Services Employment and Reemployment Rights Act of 1994, as amended, 38 U.S.C. 4301–4334. Similar relief has been provided with respect to changes in the time and form of payment and accelerations of payments.

VII. *Time and Form of Payment*

A. *In general*

The final regulations clarify that except as explicitly provided otherwise, a single time and form of payment must be designated with respect to each payment that is payable upon a payment event. For example, a plan must designate how an amount will be paid upon a change in control event, and generally cannot provide one time and form of payment upon a particular type of change in control event, and another time and form of payment upon another type of change in control event. The final regulations retain the rule, however, that permits a plan to provide for a different time and form of payment, depending upon whether the permissible payment event occurs before or after a specified date. In addition, the final regulations also provide for a limited ability to designate different times and forms of payment based upon the conditions under which a service provider's separation from service occurs. See section VII.C.5 of this preamble for a discussion of payments upon a separation from service.

The proposed regulations provide that for purposes of applying the payment rules, a payment will be treated as made on a fixed date or on a fixed schedule if the payment or payments are made by the end of the calendar year in which a specified fixed payment date, or due date of a payment under a fixed schedule, occurs or, if later, the 15th day of the third month following such fixed date or due date. The final regulations clarify that the same flexibility applies to making a payment on account of a payment event. So, for example, where a payment is scheduled to be made upon the death of a service provider whose taxable year is the calendar year, the payment is timely if made on or before the later of December 31 of the calendar year in which the death occurs, or the 15th day of the third month following the date of death. If the service provider's taxable year is not the calendar year, the final regulations specify that the service provider's taxable year is used for purposes of this rule.

Commentators also requested that where a payment is scheduled to be made on a fixed date, a service recipient be permitted to pay at any preceding date within the same calendar year. Commentators argued that if the regulations permitted a payment to be made later within the same calendar year because the amount would be reflected on the same income tax return in the case of an individual service provider, then the same rationale should permit payments to be made earlier in the same calendar year. Because the adoption of this provision would conflict with the administration of the rules governing subsequent deferrals, the final regulations do not adopt this suggestion.

The subsequent deferral rules require that any election to extend the deferral period must not be effective for at least one year after the date the payment is due. If a payment due on a specified date during a calendar year could always be made on January 1 or any subsequent date during the calendar year, then the one-year waiting period would have to begin to run on the previous January 1, regardless of the actual payment date the plan specified.

For example, if a plan specified December 31 as the payment date, but the payment could be made on January 1, then any subsequent deferral election would need to be made on or before January 1 of the preceding calendar year, making the deadline for a subsequent deferral election almost two years before the actual specified payment date. Such a rule would unduly burden service providers who cannot actually receive a payment before the date specified in the plan. However, to lower the potential for unintentional violations, the final regulations provide that a payment will be deemed made at the scheduled time of payment if made not earlier than 30 days before the scheduled date, provided that the service provider is not permitted, directly or indirectly, to designate the taxable year of the payment.

In addition, the final regulations continue to provide that a plan may designate an entire taxable year of the service provider, rather than a specific date, as the specified date of payment. If a plan provides only for the taxable year of payment, the payment may be made at any time during such year. For purposes of the subsequent deferral rules, the payment will be treated as scheduled to be paid on the first day of the service provider's taxable year.

Commentators also requested clarification of the treatment of deadlines for payment, where the plan does not designate a specific payment date or taxable year of the service provider. For example, commentators asked whether a provision requiring payment as soon as administratively feasible but in no event later than the 15th day of the third month following the end of the year would be treated as having a fixed date of payment. The final regulations provide that such a provision will be a specified payment date only if the period during which such payment may be made is restricted either to a specified taxable year of the service provider or a period of not more than 90 days and the service provider is not provided an election as to the taxable year of the payment. If a specific payment date is not established, the first possible date on which a payment could be made under the plan is the specified payment date for purposes of the rules relating to subsequent deferral elections. For example, a payment scheduled to be made at any time on or after January 1, 2008, and on or before July 1, 2008, to a service provider whose taxable year is the calendar year will be deemed to have a fixed payment date. For purposes of the subsequent deferral rules, January 1, 2008, is the specified payment date.

By contrast, a payment scheduled to be made to such a service provider at any time on or before July 1, 2008, would not be deemed to have a fixed payment date, because the payment could be made before January 1, 2008. In addition, a payment scheduled to be made to a service provider, for example, within 180 days of a separation from service generally will not provide for a specified time and form of payment under the final regulations, because it specifies neither the taxable year of the service provider in which the payment must be made following the separation from service, nor a period of 90 days or less following the separation from service in which the payment must be made. Because such a payment schedule would not provide an objective payment date based upon the separation from service event, the payment also would not be eligible for the relief provided for payments made by the later of the end of the taxable year of the service provider or the 15th day of the third month following the specified payment date. However, a plan provision providing that the payment will be made within 90 days of a separation from service generally will be treated as a specified payment date, and for purposes of the subsequent deferral rules the date of the separation from service will be treated as the scheduled payment date.

B. *Specified time or fixed schedule of payments*

1. *In general*

The final regulations generally adopt the rules defining a specified time or fixed schedule of payments, including the ability to designate a service provider's taxable year as the year of payment rather than a specific date. For example, a plan provision providing for payment within the service provider's taxable year that includes December 31, 2008, would be treated as a fixed date of payment.

2. *Reimbursement and in-kind benefit plans*

Many commentators requested additional guidance regarding ways in which rights to taxable reimbursements or in-kind benefits might be structured to meet the definition of a fixed schedule of payments. In response, the final regulations provide that a right to reimbursements or in-kind benefits will meet the requirement of a fixed time and form of payment if certain requirements are satisfied. For this purpose, a reimbursement plan must provide for the reimbursement of expenses incurred during an objectively prescribed period (including a period beginning or ending based upon a service provider's death), where the amount of reimbursable expenses incurred or in-kind benefits available in one taxable year of the service provider cannot affect the amount of reimbursable expenses or in-kind benefits available in a different taxable year. In addition, the reimbursement payment must be made by no later than the end of the service provider's taxable year following the taxable year in which the expense is incurred. Such reimbursement or in-kind benefit rights may not be subject to liquidation or exchange for another benefit.

For example, a right to a reimbursement of membership fees incurred for each of three specified and consecutive calendar years by a former employee, where the former employee is entitled to reimbursement of the expenses incurred each year without regard to the expenses incurred in a different year, and where the former employee cannot exchange the right for cash or any other benefit, generally will be treated as providing for a fixed time and form of payment if the plan requires that the reimbursement payment be made by no later than the end of the calendar year following the year in which the expense is incurred. In contrast, a right to reimbursement of membership fees of up to $30,000 over three years would not meet the requirement of a fixed time and form of payment, because the extent to which the former employee incurred the expense in the first year would affect the amount available for reimbursement in a subsequent year.

This rule applies similarly to the provision of in-kind benefits, such as a right to use a corporate vehicle or aircraft. The final regulations also provide a special rule for arrangements reimbursing medical expenses to permit certain aggregate limits on the benefits provided, such as lifetime maximums.

3. *Payment schedules with fixed or formula payment limitations*

Commentators asked whether payment schedules with fixed or objective formula limitations on the amount that may be paid during any particular period would meet the requirement of a fixed schedule or time and form of payment. Where the fixed or formula limitation is established on or before the date the time and form of payment is otherwise required to be set, the fixed or formula limitation is based on a fixed or nondiscretionary, objectively determinable formula limitation on the amount that may be paid in a particular period where all the factors relevant to the determination of such limit are beyond the control of the service provider and not subject to any exercise of discretion by the service recipient, and the plan specifies the time and form of payment of any additional amount due in excess of the fixed or formula limitation amount, the schedule will be deemed to be a fixed schedule of payments because it is not subject to manipulation. However, a change in the limits or a change in the allocation method for the payment of the unpaid excess amounts that will be paid after the original due dates due to application of the limit may constitute a subsequent deferral election or the acceleration of a payment. Similarly, where the total amount payable under a plan with multiple participants is limited, the time and form of payment requirement may be met if the plan specifies, from the date the time and form of payment is otherwise required to be set, the following: (1) a fixed or nondiscretionary, objectively determinable limit on the amount that may be paid in a particular period such that none of the factors relevant to the determination of such limit is in the control of the service provider or subject to the exercise of any discretion by the service recipient; (2) where there is an overall limitation on the aggregate amount that may be paid to a group of service providers during a specified period, a nondiscretionary, objectively determinable method to allocate the payments that can be made in accordance with the limitation among the service providers participating in the plan over which neither the service recipient nor any service provider retains control or discretion; and (3) the time and form of payment of any amount that will be paid after its original due date because of the formula limitation.

For example, a plan may provide that all payments to all participants under the plan in a given year may not exceed $1 million, provided that the plan must provide an objective, nondiscretionary method of currently allocating the $1 million of payments if the amounts otherwise payable exceed $1 million (such as proportionately to each participant based on the amount otherwise payable to such participant absent the limit), and specifies the time and form of payment of any amount not paid currently because of the limitation (such as at the earliest time possible without exceeding the applicable limitation for any subsequent year). However, a change in the limits or a change in the allocation method may constitute a subsequent deferral election or an acceleration of a payment.

Commentators also asked whether the same analysis would apply where the limit on a payment is calculated pursuant to a formula related to business performance, such as a specified percentage of cash flow for the period. A payment schedule may be conditioned on a formula limitation if the formula limitation is specified at the time the schedule of payments is otherwise required to be set, the limitation is nondiscretionary and objectively determinable based on the business performance of the service recipient, and the service provider retains no control over the determination or application of the formula limitation. For this purpose, a formula limitation based on profits or other *indicia* of general business performance is not treated as discretionary or in the control of the service recipient. Thus, a plan providing that the maximum payment during a year will equal no more than a set percentage of the service recipient's cash flow for the previous year generally would meet the requirement of a fixed time and form of payment. However, a change in the formula limitation may constitute a subsequent deferral election or an acceleration of a payment. For a discussion of schedules of payments based upon the timing of payments received by the service recipient, see section VII.B.6 of this preamble.

4. *Tax gross-up payments*

Commentators requested clarification of how section 409A applies to a right to a tax gross-up payment that provides the service provider with the right to a payment of taxes otherwise payable by the service provider as well as any additional taxes resulting from the service recipient's payment of the taxes. The final regulations provide that a right to a tax gross-up payment is a right to deferred compensation that satisfies the requirement of a fixed time and form of payment if the plan provides that the tax gross up payment will be made, and the payment is made, by the end of the service provider's taxable year next following the service provider's taxable year in which the related taxes are remitted to the taxing authority.

In addition, the final regulations provide that a right to the reimbursement of expenses incurred due to a tax audit or litigation, whether Federal, state, local, or foreign, satisfies the requirement of a fixed time and form of payment if the right to the reimbursement provides that payment will be made, and the payment is made, by the later of the end of the service provider's taxable year next following the year in which the taxes that are the subject of the audit or litigation are remitted to the taxing authority, or, if no taxes are to be remitted, the end of the service provider's taxable year next following the year in which the audit or litigation is completed. Nothing in the provisions relating to tax gross-up payments modifies the application of section 409A to any underlying compensation arrangement that results in the taxes that are subject to the tax gross-up arrangement.

5. *Payment schedules based on payments to the service recipient*

Commentators requested guidance on payment schedules contingent on the receipt of certain payments by the service recipient. For example, commentators requested clarification whether a plan requiring an annual payment equal to a percentage of certain accounts receivable collected during the prior 12-month period would qualify as a fixed time and form of payment. The ability to schedule payments based upon the time the service recipient receives a customer's payment raises issues regarding the ability to, in effect, create an impermissible event-based payment through characterizing the payment as a schedule (for example, a payment "schedule" that pays an amount every year if a specified transaction occurs in that year actually pays based on whether and when the transaction occurs, which is not a permissible payment event under section 409A). In addition, these arrangements raise issues regarding the ability of the service recipient (or service provider) to control the timing of the payment of deferred compensation through an ability to influence the timing of the payment by the customer. Accordingly, the final regulations generally provide that a schedule based upon the timing of payments to the service recipient is not a fixed schedule of payments. However, the final regulations also provide certain parameters under which such a plan may qualify as having a fixed time and form of payment. First, if the service recipient is comprised of more than one entity, the payments must be due from a person that is not one of such entities (for example, not a payment due from a subsidiary corporation to a parent corporation). Second, the payments must stem from *bona fide* and routine transactions in the ordinary course of business of the service recipient, and the service provider must not at the time such payments are due retain effective control over the service recipient, the person from whom the payments to the service recipient are due, or the collection of the payments. Third, the payment schedule must provide for a nondiscretionary, objective method of identifying the customer payments to the service recipient from which the amount of the payment is determined, and a nondiscretionary, objective schedule under which payments of the nonqualified deferred compensation will be made (for example, a payment every March 1 of 10 percent of the accounts receivable collected during the previous calendar year). Finally, the sales to which the payment relates must be of a type that the service recipient is in the trade or business of making and makes frequently, and either all such sales must be taken into account or there must be a legitimate, nontax business purpose for limiting the sales taken into account.

C. *Separation from service*

1. *In general*

The final regulations generally adopt the provisions in the proposed regulations defining the circumstances under which a separation from service is deemed to occur, subject to the modifications described in this preamble. Some commentators requested that the parties to a nonqualified deferred compensation plan be permitted to define when a separation from service occurs, at least if they apply the definition consistently. The Treasury Department and IRS believe that a definition of separation from service that is objectively determinable, nondiscretionary and predictable, and not subject to negotiations between the parties is necessary to properly implement the legislative intent behind section 409A. The definitions of separation from service suggested by the commentators do not meet this standard. For example, a plan that defines separation from service as the date a service provider is removed from a payroll would leave to the parties the discretion to determine a payment date by an action that may have little practical significance, especially when compared to the effect on the service provider's deferred compensation amounts. The Treasury Department and the IRS continue to believe that the definition of separation from service should be based upon an objective determination of whether the service provider continues to provide significant services to the service recipient.

2. *Employees*

a. *In general*

The proposed regulations provided that an employee separated from service with the employer if the employee died, retired, or otherwise had a termination of employment with the employer. Whether a termination of employment had occurred would be determined based on the facts and circumstances. The proposed regulations provided that where the facts and circumstances indicated that the employer and the employee did not intend for the employee to provide more than insignificant future services, the employee would be treated as having a separation from service. For this purpose, an employer and employee would not be presumed to have intended only insignificant services be provided if the employee continued providing services at a rate equal to at least 20 percent of the rate of the previous three years. Where an employee continued providing services in another capacity (for example, as an independent contractor), the employee would be deemed not to have a separation from service if the service provider continued providing services at a rate equal to at least 50 percent of the services provided during the previous three years. Different rules were provided for service providers who were not employees.

Commentators criticized this standard in various respects. The proposed regulations applied one presumption where an employee continued providing services as an independent contractor, and another where an employee continued providing services as an employee. Commentators asked why the same presumptions did not apply regardless of whether the employee purports to continue service (or separate from service) as an employee or purports to continue service (or separate from service) as an independent contractor. Commentators also suggested that the presumptions should be based on the intent of the employer and employee at the time of the purported separation from service (or purported continuation of services), rather than the actual subsequent conduct. Commentators also argued that the employer and employee could be found to have violated section 409A based on subsequent actual conduct, even where the parties had a *bona fide* belief that a separation from service had or had not occurred, but circumstances changed.

In response to these comments, the final regulations provide a simplified standard, applicable whether an employee continues to provide services as an employee or as an independent contractor. The general standard for determining whether the employee has terminated employment is based on whether the facts and circumstances indicate that the service recipient and employee reasonably anticipated either that no further services would be performed after a certain date or that the level of *bona fide* services the employee would perform after such date (whether as an employee or as an independent contractor) would permanently decrease to no more than 20 percent of the average level of *bona fide* services performed over the immediately preceding 36-month period (or the full period in which the employee provided services to the employer (whether as an employee or as an independent contractor) if the employee has been providing services for less than 36 months). For this purpose, periods during which the employee is on an unpaid *bona fide* leave of absence are disregarded (including for purposes of determining the relevant 36-month period), and periods during which the employee is on a paid *bona fide* leave of absence are treated as periods during which the employee provided services at the level at which the employee would have been required to perform services to receive the compensation if not on a *bona fide* leave of absence. Facts and circumstances to be considered in determining whether the employee and employer reasonably anticipated that the service provider's future services would be permanently reduced to less than 20 percent of the average level of *bona fide* services provided during the previous 36-month period include, but are not limited to, whether the employee continues to be treated as an employee for other purposes (such as continuation of salary and participation in employee benefit programs), whether similarly situated service providers have been treated consistently, and whether the employee is eligible to perform services for, and realistically available to perform services for, other employers in the same line of business.

To assist in applying this standard, certain rebuttable presumptions are provided. An employee generally will be presumed to have separated from service where the level of *bona fide* services performed (whether as an employee or an independent contractor) changes to a level equal to 20 percent or less of the average level of services provided during the previous 36 months (whether as an employee or an independent contractor). An employee will be presumed not to have separated from service where the level of *bona fide* services rendered continues at a level that is 50 percent or more of the average level of services provided during the previous 36 months. No presumption applies to a change to a level of services between 20 percent and 50 percent of the average level of services provided during the previous 36 months. For purposes of the presumption, the entire period during which the employee has provided services to the employer is substituted for 36 months if the employee has been providing services to the employer for less than 36 months, and periods during which the employee is on a *bona fide* leave of absence are treated in the same manner as such periods are treated for the general rule.

The presumptions are rebuttable, by demonstrating that the employer and the employee reasonably anticipated that as of a certain date the level of *bona fide* services would be reduced permanently to a level less than or equal to 20 percent of the average level of services provided during the immediately preceding 36-month period or full period in which the employee has provided services if the employee has been providing services to the employer for a period of less than 36 months (or that the level of *bona fide* services would not be so reduced). For example, an employee may demonstrate that the service recipient and employee anticipated that the employee would cease providing services, but that (subsequent to the original cessation of services) business circumstances such as termination of the employee's replacement caused the employee to return to employment. Although the employee's return to employment may cause the employee to be presumed to have continued in employment because the rehired employee is providing services at a rate equal to the rate at which he was providing services before the termination of employment, the facts and circumstances in this case would demonstrate that at the time the employee terminated employment, the employee and the service recipient reasonably anticipated that the employee would not provide any services in the future.

Similarly, where the loss of a business client of the employer results in a permanent reduction in the level of *bona fide* services performed by the employee of more than 80 percent, so that the employee would be presumed to have separated from service, the taxpayer may rebut the presumption that a separation from service occurred by showing that the employer and employee reasonably anticipated that the level of services would not be so reduced. The separation from service would then be deemed to occur at the time that the employer and employee reasonably anticipated that such reduction would continue.

Commentators requested additional flexibility to treat certain employees as having experienced a separation from service, even where the employee continues to provide services in a reduced capacity. This is often referred to as a phased retirement, in which an employee obtains retirement benefits despite continuing to provide services on a part-time or reduced basis. The Treasury Department and the IRS believe that providing flexibility to alter the definition of a separation from service after an amount has been deferred is inconsistent with the statute and legislative intent, and could be subject to manipulation.

However, the final regulations permit certain flexibility for a plan to define a separation from service as including a change to a reduced level of *bona fide* services, if the definition is specified no later than the time and form of payment are elected or otherwise specified. Specifically, the final regulations provide that rather than treating a separation from service as requiring an anticipated permanent reduction in the level of *bona fide* services to 20 percent or less of the average level of *bona fide* services provided in the immediately preceding 36 months, a plan may treat another level of anticipated permanent reduction in the level of *bona fide* services as a separation from service, provided that the level of permanent reduction required must be set forth in the plan as a specific percentage, and the anticipated permanently reduced level of *bona fide* services must be greater than 20 percent but less than 50 percent of the average level of *bona fide* services provided in the immediately preceding 36 months. The plan must specify the definition of separation from service on or before the date at which a separation from service is designated as a time of payment of an amount deferred, and once designated, any change to the definition of separation from service with respect to such amount deferred will be subject to the rules regarding subsequent deferrals and the acceleration of payments.

For example, on or before the time at which a plan must designate a time and form of payment for a deferred amount, the plan may specify that a separation from service will be deemed to occur at any time that the employee and employer reasonably anticipate that the *bona fide* level of services the employee will perform (whether as an employee or an independent contractor) will be permanently reduced to a level that is less than 50 percent of the average level of *bona fide* services the employee performed during the immediately preceding 36 months (or the entire period the employee has provided services if the employee has been providing services to the employer less than 36 months).

b. *Identification of the service recipient*

Commentators requested that the definition of the term service recipient be expanded for purposes of determining whether a separation from service has occurred. The final regulations generally adopt this suggestion, so that for purposes of determining whether a service provider has separated from service with an employer or other service recipient, the service recipient is defined as including all entities that would be treated as part of the group of entities comprising the service recipient under section 414(b) and (c) and the accompanying regulations, but substituting a 50 percent ownership level for the 80 percent ownership level in section 414(b) and (c) and the accompanying regulations. A plan may specify that a higher or lower percentage ownership level will be used, provided that the ownership level may not be higher than 80 percent or lower than 20 percent, and provided further that an ownership level of less than 50 percent may be used only where such use is based on legitimate business criteria. As discussed, the plan must specify the percentage on or before the date at which a separation from service is designated as a time of payment of the amount deferred, and where a plan changes the definition of separation from service with respect to amounts previously deferred, such a change will be subject to the rules governing changes to the time and form of payment, including the anti-acceleration provisions.

Commentators also requested special treatment with respect to the identification of the service recipient in instances where an amount is deferred pursuant to a *bona fide* collective bargaining agreement covering service with multiple employers, and the employee may be expected to perform services covered by the *bona fide* collective bargaining agreement for a number of different employers. Specifically, commentators expressed concern that an employee not be treated as having separated from service when a particular period of service with an employer is completed, if the employee has made herself available to perform services covered by the *bona fide* collective bargaining agreement for another employer. The final regulations generally provide that where the amount is deferred pursuant to a plan provided under a *bona fide* collective bargaining agreement covering services with multiple employers, and where service providers may reasonably anticipate providing services for more than one of the participating employers, the plan may define a separation from service in a manner that treats the service provider as not having separated from service when the service provider stops performing services for one employer covered by the agreement and provides services for another employer covered by the agreement. The final regulations also provide that the plan may not treat a service provider as having separated from service during periods where the service provider is not providing services but has made herself available to perform services for a participating employer, provided that the definition requires that the service provider be deemed to have separated from service no later than the end of any 12-month period in which the service provider has not provided services covered by the *bona fide* collective bargaining agreement to any employer.

c. *Bona fide leave*

Many of the comments with respect to the definition of separation from service for an employee concerned the treatment of *bona fide* leaves of absence. For purposes of determining whether a service provider has separated from service (and not for purposes of determining whether a vacation or sick leave plan is a *bona fide* vacation or sick leave plan), a *bona fide* leave of absence refers to a leave of absence where there is a reasonable expectation the service provider will return to service with the service recipient. The final regulations provide that an employment relationship is treated as continuing while the individual is on sick leave, or other *bona fide* leave of absence, if the period of such leave does not exceed six months, or if longer, so long as the individual retains a right to reemployment with the service recipient under an applicable statute or by contract. For example, where a tenured professor takes a leave of absence, but the professor retains a right to reemployment with the university as part of the professor's tenured status, the professor will not be deemed to have terminated from employment merely due to the leave of absence from the university. If the period of leave exceeds six months and the individual does not retain a right to reemployment under an applicable statute or by contract, the employment relationship is deemed to terminate on the first date immediately following such six-month period. However, the final regulations modify the provisions in the proposed regulations with respect to disability leave. With respect to disability leave, the employment relationship will be treated as continuing for a period of up to 29 months, unless otherwise terminated by the employer or the employee, regardless of whether the employee retains a contractual right to reemployment. For this purpose, disability leave refers to leave due to the employee's inability to perform the duties of his or her position of employment or any substantially similar position of employment by reason of any medically determinable physical or mental impairment that can be expected to result in death or can be expected to last for a continuous period of not less than six months.

d. *Salary continuation programs and terminal leave*

Commentators requested that salary continuation programs be permitted to delay the occurrence of a separation from service, where an employee continues to receive salary and benefits and is otherwise treated as an employee, although not required to perform any further meaningful services. Some commentators also requested this treatment for terminal leave, or leave intended to bridge a service provider to a separation from service date that would permit continuation of benefits or accrual of additional benefits under, for example, a qualified plan. The Treasury Department and the IRS believe that these types of actions are subject to manipulation and should not delay the time when a service provider is treated as having separated from service for purposes of section 409A. Accordingly, the final regulations do not recognize extensions of leave or salary and benefits as a means of delaying the date of separation from service for purposes of section 409A. In addition, terminal leave with no intent to return generally would not be treated as *bona fide* leave for purposes of the rule for employees addressing *bona fide* leave.

Commentators expressed concern that the service recipient may wish to continue providing certain employee benefits, including in-kind benefits and reimbursement plans, during a salary continuation or terminal leave period. With respect to the application of section 409A, such plans generally may be structured to avoid providing for the deferral of compensation, or to provide deferred compensation in compliance with the requirements of section 409A. See sections III.J.6 and VII.B.2 of this preamble. The definition of separation from service for purposes of section 409A is not applicable for purposes of other Code provisions, such as those provisions governing qualified retirement plans or non-taxable benefits.

e. *Rehires and suspensions of benefits*

Commentators also requested that the regulations address rehires, and specifically whether payments of deferred compensation could be suspended during a subsequent period of employment or other service until a subsequent separation from service. Such a suspension generally would violate the rules governing changes in the time and form of payment because payments would be delayed in a manner that does not satisfy the rules applicable to subsequent deferral elections. Neither the statutory language of section 409A nor the legislative history indicates any intent to permit such additional flexibility. Moreover, the Treasury Department and the IRS believe that suspension of benefits rules would add significant complexity to the administration of the Code section. However, many of the desired results of a suspension of benefits provision often may be obtained through deferrals of future compensation after rehire.

f. *Mergers and acquisitions*

Comments with respect to the application of the separation from service standard in the case of a merger or acquisition generally focused on two areas. First, commentators requested that the final regulations adopt permissive use of the rule generally referred to as the "same desk" rule, allowing the parties to an asset purchase agreement to decide whether employees of the selling corporation that continue in the same position with the purchaser of the assets will be treated as separating from service. The final regulations adopt a rule providing that where as part of a sale of assets by one service recipient (seller) to an unrelated service recipient (buyer), a service provider of the seller would otherwise experience a separation from service with the seller, the seller and the buyer may specify whether a service provider providing services to the seller immediately before the asset purchase transaction and providing services to the buyer after and in connection with the asset purchase transaction has experienced a separation from service, provided that the asset purchase transaction results from *bona fide*, arm's length negotiations, all service providers providing services to the seller immediately before the asset purchase transaction and providing services to the buyer after and in connection with the asset purchase transaction are treated consistently (regardless of position at the seller) for purposes of applying the provisions of any nonqualified deferred compensation plan, and such treatment is specified no later than the closing date of the asset purchase transaction. For this purpose, a sale of assets refers to a transfer of substantial assets, such as a plant or division or substantially all of the assets of a trade or business.

Second, commentators requested clarification whether a spin-off of a subsidiary could result in a separation from service of an employee of the subsidiary, where the nonqualified deferred compensation plan defines a separation from service as including any action resulting in the employee no longer being an employee of the controlled group of corporations including the parent corporation. Generally such a transaction would not result in a termination of employment for an employee of the subsidiary, because the employee is continuing employment with the same employer both before and after the transaction. However, the rules that provide a service recipient discretion to terminate and liquidate a plan following a change in control transaction afford taxpayers the flexibility to pay out their deferred compensation liabilities in particular circumstances. See section VIII.B of this preamble.

3. *Directors*

The final regulations provide generally that where a service provider provides services to a service recipient both as an employee and as an independent contractor, the service provider must separate from service both as an employee and as an independent contractor to be treated as having separated from service. But where a service provider provides services both as an employee and a member of the board of directors of a corporate service recipient, the services provided as a director are not taken into account for purposes of determining whether the service provider has a separation from service as an employee for purposes of a nonqualified deferred compensation plan in which the service provider participates in his or her capacity as an employee that is not aggregated with any plan in which the service provider participates as a director. Accordingly, where an employee-director participates in a separate plan as an employee, his or her termination of services as an employee will constitute a separation from service for purposes of the employee plan, regardless of whether he or she continues providing services as a director (and *vice versa*). However, if a non-employee director is also providing additional services as an independent contractor, he or she cannot have a separation from service for purposes of section 409A until he or she has separated from service both as a director and as an independent contractor.

4. *Delay for specified employees*

Section 409A(a)(2)(B) provides that with respect to a specified employee, a payment of nonqualified deferred compensation on account of separation from service may not occur before the date that is six months after the date of separation from service (or, if earlier, the date of death of the employee). For this purpose, a specified employee is a key employee of a corporation any stock of which is publicly traded on an established securities market or otherwise. With respect to identifying specified employees, the final regulations generally adopt the provisions set forth in the proposed regulations, subject to the modifications and clarifications described in this preamble.

a. *Identification of specified employees*

Several commentators asked whether an employee may be subject to the six-month delay requirement if the service recipient stock is publicly traded only on a foreign exchange or is traded on a U.S. exchange only as American depositary receipts or American depositary shares (ADRs). The final regulations define an established securities market for purposes of the six-month delay rule by reference to the rules in §1.897–1(m), which generally include foreign securities markets. Accordingly, the six-month delay may apply to an employee of a service recipient the stock of which is publicly traded solely on a foreign exchange, or is traded on a U.S. exchange only as ADRs. In the case of a service recipient comprised of multiple entities, this rule would apply if one of the entities had stock that was publicly traded on a foreign exchange.

Some commentators requested that the final regulations provide that specified employees are limited to common law employees, and do not include other individuals. Section 409A(a)(2)(B) defines a specified employee as a key employee as defined in section 416(i) (without regard to section 416(i)(5)). Accordingly, where an individual is treated as a key employee for purposes of section 416(i), that individual generally is a specified employee for purposes of section 409A.

Commentators requested clarification of how the definition of compensation under section 415 applies for purposes of identifying the key employees that may ultimately be specified employees. The final regulations clarify that the general definition of compensation under §1.415(c)–2(a), applied as if the service recipient were not using any safe harbor provided in §1.415(c)–2(d), any of the special timing rules provided in §1.415(c)–2(e), or any of the special rules provided in §1.415(c)–2(g), will be treated as the general definition of compensation for purposes of identifying specified employees. However, the final regulations also provide that a service recipient may use any available definition of compensation under section 415 and the accompanying regulations, including any available safe harbor and any available election under the timing rules or special rules, provided that the definition is applied consistently to all employees of the service recipient for purposes of identifying specified employees. A service recipient may elect to use such a definition of compensation regardless of whether another definition of compensation is being used for purposes of a qualified plan sponsored by the service recipient. However, once a list of specified employees has become effective, the service recipient cannot change the definition of compensation for purposes of identifying specified employees for the period with respect to which such list is effective. For a discussion of the methods for making an election regarding the definition of compensation, see section VII.C.4.e of this preamble.

Commentators requested clarification of the treatment of the compensation of certain nonresident alien employees. As discussed in the preceding paragraph, for purposes of identifying key employees, the general definition of compensation under §1.415(c)–2(a) applies. A service recipient may elect to apply the rule of §1.415–2(g)(5)(ii) and not treat as compensation certain compensation excludible from an employee's gross income on account of the location of the services or the identity of the employer that is not effectively connected with the conduct of a trade or business within the United States. If no such election is made, the provisions of §1.415(c)–2(g)(5)(i) would apply, requiring the treatment as compensation of certain compensation excludible from an employee's gross income due to the location of the services or the identity of the service recipient.

b. *Alternative methods for applying the six-month delay requirement*

Commentators expressed concern that an attempt to identify key employees could result in an underinclusive list. Rather than risk a violation, commentators suggested that service recipients be permitted to use an alternative method for determining employees subject to the six-month delay requirement, even where such alternative method may result in an over-inclusive list. A nonqualified deferred compensation plan may provide that all payments upon separation from service will commence six months after the separation from service, regardless of whether the service provider is a specified employee. In addition, the final regulations provide that a plan may use an alternative method identifying the service providers whose distributions will be subject to a six-month delay, provided that the alternative method is reasonably designed to include all specified employees, the alternative method is an objectively determinable standard providing no direct or indirect election to any service provider regarding the application of the rule, and the alternative method results in no more than 200 service providers being identified in the class as of any date. Use of such an alternative method to delay a payment in accordance with the rules governing the delay of payments to a specified employee will not be treated as a change in the time and form of payment for purposes of the subsequent deferral rules even if the service provider is not a specified employee when the payment is delayed. However, if the list fails to include any individual who is a specified employee and that individual has a right to a payment of deferred compensation upon a separation from service without the required six-month delay, the plan providing such right to such individual will not be in compliance with section 409A. For a discussion of the method of initiating an alternative method designation, see section VII.C.4.e of this preamble.

c. *Specified employee effective date issues*

Under the proposed regulations, the employees identified as of an identification date would become specified employees effective as of the first day of the fourth month following the identification date. Commentators stated that service recipients who could compile the list of specified employees more quickly should be permitted to make the list effective at an earlier date. The final regulations provide that the first day of the fourth month will be the specified employee effective date if the service recipient does not specify another date. However, the final regulations permit a service recipient to specify a specified employee effective date following the specified employee identification date upon which the new list of specified employees will become effective, provided that the specified employee effective date may not be later than the first day of the fourth month following the specified employee identification date. For example, an employer that designates December 31 as a specified employee identification date for purposes of identifying key employees for purposes of the six-month delay rule, may specify any subsequent date on or before the following April 1 as the first date of the 12-month period during which such list of key employees will be treated as specified employees. To prevent manipulation, any change to the specified employee effective date may not become applicable until 12 months following the change in such specified employee effective date.

The final regulations also clarify that the six-month delay requirement applies only where the service provider is a specified employee as of the date of separation from service, and does not become applicable if the service provider is not a specified employee as of the date of separation from service even if the service provider subsequently would have become a specified employee if the separation had not occurred.

d. *Corporate transactions*

In response to comments, the final regulations significantly alter the proposed rules governing the identification of specified employees following a corporate transaction, such as a merger or spin-off. Commentators requested clarification of the determination of the next applicable specified employee identification date following the corporate transaction. In addition, commentators generally objected to any rule that resulted in the treatment of more than 50 employees as specified employees due to a corporate transaction (in addition to 1-percent and 5-percent owners treated as specified employees). The final regulations generally permit service recipients to avoid this result, but also permit service recipients to simply combine the pre-transaction separate lists of specified employees where it is determined that such treatment would be administratively less burdensome. Service recipients can determine whether to combine such lists on a case-by-case basis, if there are multiple transactions during the same year.

With respect to mergers and acquisitions, the final regulations address combinations of two public corporations, and combinations of a public and a closely-held corporation. For purposes of the discussion of the rules regarding the treatment of the identification of specified employees following such a transaction, references to specified employees include specified employees determined under any permissible method that the entities participating in the transaction used immediately before the transaction. Where two public corporations merge and become one public corporation, or a public corporation becomes a subsidiary of another public corporation, the final regulations provide that the resulting service recipient's next specified employee identification date and the first specified employee effective date following the transaction is the specified employee identification date and specified employee effective date that the acquiring service recipient would have been required to use absent the merger. For the period after the date of the transaction and before the next specified employee effective date, the specified employee list of the resulting service recipient consists of the 50 most highly compensated service providers appearing on the combined lists of the two service recipients' specified employees in effect as of the date of the transaction, ranking such specified employees in order of the amount of compensation used to determine each specified employees' status as a specified employee, plus any 1-percent and 5-percent owners not otherwise included who would be treated as specified employees. Alternatively, however, the resulting service recipient may use any other reasonable method to determine its specified employees immediately after the transaction, provided that such method is adopted not later than 90 days after the merger and applied prospectively from the date of adoption. For a discussion of the procedures for adopting such a method, see section VII.C.4.e of this preamble.

Where a public corporation and a private corporation merge and become a public corporation, or where a private corporation becomes a subsidiary of a public corporation, the resulting service recipient's next specified employee identification date and specified employee effective date following the transaction will be the specified employee identification date and specified employee effective date that the pre-transaction public corporation would have been required to use absent such transaction. For the time period after the transaction and before the next specified employee effective date, the specified employees of the pre-transaction public service recipient immediately before the transaction will continue to be the specified employees of the resulting service recipient, and service providers of the pre-merger private service recipient will not become specified employees until the next specified employee effective date. Consequently, the nonqualified deferred compensation plans in which service providers of the formerly private service recipient participate will not be required to contain a plan term delaying a payment upon separation from service of such service providers, or to delay such a payment, until the next specified employee effective date.

The final regulations also address spin-off transactions. Where as part of a corporate transaction, a public service recipient becomes two separate public service recipients, the final regulations provide that the next specified employee identification date and specified employee effective date of each of the post-transaction service recipients is the specified employee identification date and specified employee effective date that the pre-transaction service recipient would have been required to use absent such transaction. For the period after the date of the transaction and before the next specified employee effective date, the specified employees of the pre-transaction service recipient immediately before the transaction continue to be the specified employees of the post-transaction service recipients.

The final regulations provide guidance on initial public offerings and other corporate transactions where all or part of a private service recipient becomes one or more public service recipients. In that case, except as discussed in this paragraph, each post-transaction public service recipient will have a December 31 specified employee identification date and an April 1 specified employee date. Alternatively, the new public service recipient may establish a different specified employee identification date and specified employee effective date, provided that the specified employee identification date and specified employee effective date must be established on or before the date of the initial public offering or other corporate transaction.

For the period between the date of the initial public offering or other corporate transaction and the first specified employee effective date, the list of specified employees of each post-transaction public service recipient is comprised of the service providers that at the time of the corporate transaction or public offering would have been classified as specified employees of the former private service recipient, had such service recipient adopted the same specified employee identification date and specified employee effective date as selected by such post-transaction public service recipient, and had such former private service recipient been a public service recipient as of such specified employee identification date.

e. *Alternatives for the identification of specified employees*

As discussed in this preamble, the final regulations provide certain default definitions for purposes of identifying specified employees, where the service recipient has not adopted another definition. These default rules include the following provisions: the specified employee identification date is December 31; the specified employee effective date is April 1; the general definition of compensation under §1.415(c)–2(a) will apply (without giving effect to any use of the special timing rules under §1.415(c)–2(e) or of a safe harbor definition of compensation under §1.415(c)–2(d)); and certain rules regarding the identification of specified employees after a merger of public service recipients or an initial public offering or other transaction involving a formerly nonpublic service recipient becoming a public service recipient will apply.

Alternatively, the final regulations also provide that the service recipient may use other permissible rules and definitions, provided that such alternatives become effective only in accordance with the rules and deadlines set forth in the final regulations. In addition, the final regulations permit a service recipient to use an alternative method for purposes of identifying specified employees, with certain limitations, and to make an election under §1.415(c)–2(g)(5)(i) regarding the treatment as compensation of certain compensation excludible from an employee's gross income due to the location of the services or the identity of the employer. For purposes of these rules, a service recipient may use one of these alternatives when all necessary corporate action has been taken to make such alternative binding for purposes of all affected deferred compensation plans in which service providers of the service recipient participate. Accordingly, as a practical matter, the service recipient may find it expedient either to specify the definition of specified employee in all of its nonqualified deferred compensation plans or to retain the discretion in all such plans to make such determinations and take any necessary corporate action in accordance with each such plan.

f. *Application of the six-month delay rule*

The final regulations reflect the statutory language that a plan may provide that a payment will be made, notwithstanding the six-month delay, upon the service provider's death. A commentator requested similar treatment for the occurrence of a disability, unforeseeable emergency, or change in control event during the six months following the separation from service. The Treasury Department and the IRS do not believe that the statute permits such flexibility, but rather categorically prohibits any distribution due to a separation from service during the six months following the separation from service except where the service provider dies. Accordingly, where a payment on account of a separation from service has been delayed because the service provider is a specified employee, the payment may not be accelerated due to disability, a change in control event, or an unforeseeable emergency. However, where a payment is made to a specified employee on account of disability, a change in control event, or an unforeseeable emergency (as defined for purposes of section 409A), the payment need not be delayed merely because the specified employee separates from service after incurring the disability or unforeseeable emergency, or after the change in control event.

Commentators further requested that various types of periodic benefit payments be excluded from the six-month delay requirement, even if such payments constitute a payment of deferred compensation. Commentators argued that the requirement to delay such payments would be excessively burdensome and impracticable, given the nature and amount of benefits generally available under such arrangements. The Treasury Department and the IRS are not convinced that periodic payment or reimbursement plans should be excluded from the six-month delay rule; otherwise, deferred compensation could simply be converted to such programs to avoid the delay. However, as clarified in the final regulations, certain plans that provide for reimbursements or in-kind benefits during the six months following a separation from service will not be treated as nonqualified deferred compensation plans under the rules governing separation pay plans. See section III.J.6 of this preamble.

The final regulations also provide that the required delay of a payment to a specified employee upon a separation of service is not violated where the payment is made before the end of the six-month period due to an acceleration of a payment in compliance with the provisions of the regulations permitting accelerated distributions due to a domestic relations order, to satisfy a Federal, state, local, or foreign ethics law, or to pay certain employment taxes (see section VIII of this preamble).

5. *Different times and forms of payment on separation from service under specified circumstances*

The final regulations continue to provide that a time and form of payment must be specified with respect to each permissible payment event. Under the proposed regulations, a second time and form of payment could be established for a payment due to a permissible payment event where the distinction was based upon the event occurring before or after a certain date, such as the service provider reaching a certain age. Commentators requested that different times and forms of payment be permitted if based upon different types of separations from service. The final regulations generally provide that the time and form of payment upon a separation from service may vary depending upon either or both of the following: (1) whether the separation from service occurs during a limited period of time not to exceed two years following a change in control event as defined for purposes of section 409A; or (2) whether the separation from service occurs before or after a specified date (for example, the attainment of a specified age), or before or after a combination of a specified date and a specified period of service determined under a predetermined objective formula or pursuant to the method for crediting service under a qualified plan sponsored by the service recipient. The addition or deletion of such a different time and form of payment applicable to an existing deferral is subject to the subsequent deferral election rules and the anti-acceleration rules.

D. *Disability*

The final regulations generally adopt the definition of disability and other provisions related to the payment of an amount upon a service provider becoming disabled contained in the proposed regulations, subject to the modifications described in this preamble. For this purpose, a participant is disabled if the participant is unable to engage in any substantial gainful activity by reason of any medically determinable physical or mental impairment that can be expected to result in death or can be expected to last for a continuous period of not less than 12 months, or is, by reason of any medically determinable physical or mental impairment that can be expected to result in death or can be expected to last for a continuous period of not less than 12 months, receiving income replacement benefits for a period of not less than 3 months under an accident and health plan covering employees of the participant's employer. The determination of whether a service provider is disabled may be made by any person, including the administrator of a disability insurance program, and the plan need not specify who will make the determination. However, the plan will be treated as complying with section 409A only if the disability required for a payment complies with the definition of disability under the regulations, and a payment due to a disability will be deemed to comply with section 409A only if the service provider has actually suffered a qualifying disability. The final regulations also provide that a plan may provide that a service provider will be deemed disabled if the service provider is determined to be totally disabled by the Social Security Administration or the Railroad Retirement Board.

Commentators raised questions concerning the ability to pay upon the occurrence of a disability that does not qualify as a disability under the statute, where as a result of the disability the service provider has a separation from service. Such a payment would not constitute a payment due to a disability that complied with section 409A. However, if the plan provided for a payment due to the separation from service, a payment would constitute a payment due to a separation from service regardless of whether the separation from service resulted from such a disability and regardless of whether the service provider's right to receive such payment was conditioned upon the service provider being disabled under such disability definition.

E. *Death*

Most of the comments with respect to amounts that are payable due to the death of a service provider related to whether a beneficiary of the service provider could be given the opportunity to elect a time and form of payment under a plan without violating section 409A. The final regulations clarify that elections with respect to the time and form of payment to a beneficiary are subject to the general rules governing subsequent deferrals and accelerated payments, including elections by either the service provider or the beneficiary (with an exception for amounts payable under a domestic relations order). However, a change in a beneficiary will not be treated as a change in the time and form of payment, if the change in the time of payment stems solely from the different life expectancy of the new beneficiary, such as in the case of a joint and survivor annuity. Commentators requested that beneficiaries be permitted a limited period of time in which to change the time and form of payment without being subject to the subsequent deferral and anti-acceleration provisions. The Treasury Department and the IRS do not believe that the statutory language supports this type of late deferral election or payment acceleration. Accordingly, these suggestions are not adopted in the final regulations.

F. *Change in ownership or effective control of a corporation*

The final regulations generally adopt the provisions contained in the proposed regulations with respect to the definition of a change in control event, as well as certain special rules with respect to payments upon a change in control event, subject to the modifications described in this preamble.

One commentator requested that the threshold for a change in the effective control of a corporation be lowered from 35 percent to 20 percent, especially for a public corporation. The legislative history of section 409A indicates that the definition of a change in control event is to be based upon, but more restrictive than, the definition provided in section 280G. H.R. Conf. Rep. No. 108–755, at 730 (2004). Given that §1.280G–1, Q&A–28(a)(1) provides for a 20 percent standard, the adoption of that standard is not appropriate in light of the legislative history. However, the final regulations lower the threshold to 30 percent.

One commentator requested guidance with respect to the application of the change in control provisions to non-stock, non-profit corporations. The Treasury Department and the IRS are considering whether such guidance is appropriate, and if so what types of changes could be treated as analogous to a change in control event involving a stock corporation. Until further guidance, a non-stock, non-profit corporation may apply the change in effective control provisions in §1.409A–3(i)(5) (relating to a change in the composition of the board of directors) by analogy to changes in the composition of its board of directors, trustees, or other governing body.

The final regulations continue to provide that in the case of a payment on account of certain change in control events (a change in ownership of a corporation or a change in the ownership of a substantial portion of a corporation's assets), compensation payable pursuant to the service recipient's purchase of service recipient stock or a service recipient stock right held by a service provider, or payment of amounts of deferred compensation calculated by reference to the value of service recipient stock, generally may be treated as complying with the requirements of section 409A if paid under the terms and conditions that govern the payments to shareholders or the service recipient in connection with the change in control event. The final regulations continue to require that such amounts be paid no later than five years after the change in control event. However, the final regulations also provide that where such compensation is made subject to a condition on payment that constitutes a substantial risk of forfeiture under section 409A (without regard to the prohibition on additions or extensions of forfeiture conditions), and such compensation is payable under the same terms and conditions as apply to payments made to shareholders generally with respect to stock of the service recipient, or to the service recipient itself, pursuant to the change in control event, for purposes of determining whether such compensation is a short-term deferral the requirements of the short-term deferral rule are applied as if the legally binding right to such compensation arose on the date that it became subject to the substantial risk of forfeiture. The regulations also provide rules under which certain pre-existing forfeiture conditions may be extended or modified in connection with such a change in control event.

G. *Unforeseeable emergency*

The final regulations apply the provisions set forth in section 409A(a)(2)(B)(ii) regarding payments upon an unforeseeable emergency. The final regulations provide that a distribution on account of unforeseeable emergency may not be made to the extent that such emergency is or may be relieved through reimbursement or compensation from insurance or otherwise, by liquidation of the service provider's assets, to the extent the liquidation of such assets would not cause severe financial hardship, or by cessation of deferrals under the plan. The final regulations clarify that for these purposes, the availability of payments under any qualified plan (including any assets available by obtaining a loan under a qualified plan), or under any other nonqualified deferred compensation plan due to the unforeseeable emergency, including plans that would be nonqualified deferred compensation plans for purposes of section 409A except due to the effective date of the statute, need not be considered in determining whether an emergency is or may be relieved through other means. Accordingly, a payment due to an unforeseeable emergency may be made pursuant to a nonqualified deferred compensation plan that is subject to section 409A even though the financial need could be satisfied through an available distribution or loan from a qualified plan, or from another nonqualified deferred compensation plan (including a grandfathered plan) due to the unforeseeable emergency.

Section 826 of the Pension Protection Act of 2006, Public Law 109–280 (120 Stat. 780) modified the rules governing payments upon an unforeseeable emergency. Specifically, section 826 requires that the Treasury Department and the IRS modify the rules for determining whether a service provider has had an unforeseeable emergency for purposes of section 409A(a)(2)(B)(ii) to provide that if an event would constitute a hardship under the plan if it occurred with respect to the service provider's spouse or dependent, such event will, to the extent permitted under a plan, constitute a hardship if it occurs with respect to a person who is a beneficiary under the plan with respect to the service provider. The final regulations reflect this modification.

H. *Multiple payment events*

The final regulations provide that a plan may provide for a payment based upon the earlier of, or the later of, a series of events, provided that each payment event would otherwise satisfy the requirements of section 409A. The final regulations also provide that for purposes of the subsequent deferral and acceleration rules, each payment event will be viewed separately for purposes of analyzing the effect of a change in the time and form of payment. For a discussion of the effect of the addition or deletion of a permissible payment event from such a list, see section IX.C of this preamble.

I. *Delay in payment by the service recipient*

Commentators requested that a service recipient be permitted to delay a payment, where the delay is due to *bona fide* business concerns such as cash flow considerations. Where a payment is delayed due to the operation of a pre-specified objective, nondiscretionary formula related to the business performance of the service recipient, the payment generally may be delayed (for example, where payments in any given year are limited to a certain percentage of cash flow) provided that the time for later payment is governed by the objective, nondiscretionary formula. See section VII.B.3 of this preamble. In addition, the final regulations provide that if at the time of a specified payment date the making of the payment would jeopardize the ability of the service recipient to continue as a going concern, the payment will be treated as made upon the specified payment date if the payment is made during the first taxable year of the service provider in which the making of the payment would not have such effect. This provision is not required to be explicitly provided in the plan.

Because this provision permits the service recipient to delay any payment the making of which would jeopardize the ability of the service recipient to continue as a going concern, the provision in the proposed regulations permitting a delay in payment required to avoid a violation of a loan covenant or similar contractual obligation, where such violation would cause material harm to the service recipient, has not been adopted in the final regulations. Rather, where the payment would result in a violation of a loan covenant or similar contractual obligation, and the violation would jeopardize the ability of the service recipient to continue as a going concern, the payment can be delayed under the general provision.

The final regulations adopt the provision of the proposed regulations that permits a delay in payment necessary to avoid the application of the deduction limitation under section 162(m), subject to the following modifications. First, a plan is not required to provide explicitly for such a delay. However, the final regulations require that where any payment in a service recipient's taxable year is delayed in accordance with this provision, then all payments that could be delayed in accordance with this provision must be delayed (though some payments may be delayed until after separation from service and others until the earliest taxable year in which the deduction limitation no longer applies). Second, except as provided in the next sentence, the regulations provide that the payment must be made either during the service provider's first taxable year in which the service recipient reasonably anticipates, or reasonably should anticipate, that if the service recipient makes such payment during such year such payment will not fail to be deductible because of section 162(m) or, if later, during the period beginning on the day the service provider separates from service and ending on the later of the last day of the service provider's taxable year in which the separation from service occurs or the 15th day of the third month following the separation from service. Finally, the final regulations provide that where the payment has been delayed until the service provider's separation from service, the six-month delay requirement for specified employees may apply. Although commentators argued that the six-month delay rule should not apply because the original payment would not have been subject to the rule, this same argument could be made with respect to any deferral election to have current compensation paid instead at a separation from service, and accordingly is not adopted in the final regulations.

J. *Disputed payments and refusals to pay*

The final regulations adopt the provisions in the proposed regulations with respect to disputed payments and refusals to pay, subject to certain modifications. If a payment is not made due to a service recipient's refusal to pay an amount, the amount generally will be treated as paid in a timely manner if the service provider makes reasonable, good faith efforts to collect the payment. This provision is intended to address not only intentional refusals to pay, but also inadvertent delays (but, in either case, only if there is no collusion between the service provider and service recipient). For example, where through oversight a service recipient fails to make a payment on the required payment date, the payment will be treated as made on the specified date if the service provider makes reasonable, good faith efforts to collect the payment, generally through providing timely notice to the service recipient that the payment is due and unpaid. For this purpose, efforts to collect the payment will be presumed not to be reasonable, good faith efforts if notice is not given to the service recipient within 90 days of the latest date upon which the payment could have been timely made in accordance with the terms of the plan and the regulations and, if not paid, further measures to enforce the payment are not taken within 180 days after such date. For a discussion of payments that are accelerated due to a settlement of a *bona fide* dispute as to the service provider's right to the payment, see section VIII.G of this preamble.

K. *Back-to-back arrangements*

The proposed regulations addressed certain arrangements under which an entity (the intermediate service recipient) receives services from a service provider and provides services to a client (the ultimate service recipient), and the time the intermediate service recipient is entitled to receive a payment for services rendered to the ultimate service recipient is controlled by the date on which the intermediate service recipient is obligated to make a payment of deferred compensation to the service provider. For example, assume an intermediate service recipient provides investment management services for a group of investors. Pursuant to a nonqualified deferred compensation plan, the intermediate service recipient has agreed to pay its employee a sum certain when the employee terminates employment. Under the intermediate service recipient's agreement with the investor group, the investors will pay the same sum certain to the intermediate service recipient when the employee terminates employment. The proposed regulations referred to these types of arrangements as back-to-back arrangements.

The final regulations adopt the proposed provisions that addressed back-to-back nonqualified deferred compensation arrangements, subject to the modifications described in this section. The final regulations clarify that the rules addressing back-to-back arrangements apply regardless of whether the arrangement between the service provider and the intermediate service recipient is actually subject to section 409A, as long as each arrangement that is part of the overall back-to-back scheme complies with the requirements of section 409A without regard to whether such arrangement is actually subject to section 409A. Accordingly, the accommodations afforded to back-to-back arrangements are only applicable to the extent that each arrangement satisfies the requirements of section 409A as if those requirements applied to each such arrangement (modified in accordance with the back-to-back rules).

Commentators also requested that, with respect to taxpayers providing management services that are not eligible for the exception from coverage for independent contractors with multiple unrelated customers, the exception from the general payment timing rules permitting certain back-to-back arrangements be expanded to include not only arrangements where the payment from an ultimate service recipient to the intermediate service recipient is based upon the timing of a required payment under a section 409A compliant plan from the intermediate service recipient to a service provider (a forward back-to-back arrangement), but also where the payment to the service provider is based upon a required payment under a section 409A compliant arrangement from the ultimate service recipient to the intermediate service recipient (a reverse back-to-back arrangement). For example, a service recipient that provides investment management services to an investor group may have an arrangement whereby the investors are required to pay all amounts due to the investment manager service recipient if the investor group terminates the client relationship, and the investment manager service recipient in turn has an agreement with an employee to pay the employee a certain percentage of the amount the investor group pays to the investment manager service recipient, following termination of the client relationship. The final regulations do not provide an exception from the requirements of section 409A for reverse back-to-back arrangements, but the Treasury Department and the IRS will continue to study the matter.

VIII. *Prohibition of Accelerated Payments*

A. *In general*

Section 409A(a)(3) provides that a plan may not permit the acceleration of the time or schedule of any payment under the plan, except as provided in regulations by the Secretary. The final regulations retain the provisions in the proposed regulations relating to accelerated payments, subject to the modifications described in this preamble.

The final regulations generally provide that a payment of an amount as a substitute for a payment of deferred compensation will be treated as a payment of the deferred compensation, including for purposes of the prohibition on accelerated payments. Where a payment of an amount results in an actual or potential reduction of, or an actual or potential current or future offset to, an amount of deferred compensation, or the service provider receives a loan the repayment of which is secured by or may be accomplished through an offset of a nonqualified deferred compensation benefit, then the payment or loan is a substitute for the deferred compensation and is treated as a payment of the deferred compensation itself. If a service provider's rights to deferred compensation are subject to anticipation, alienation, sale, transfer, assignment, pledge, encumbrance, attachment, or garnishment by creditors of the service provider or the service provider's beneficiary, such amounts are treated as having been paid to the service provider.

The receipt of a payment of compensation, or right to a payment of compensation, proximate to the purported forfeiture or voluntary relinquishment of a right to deferred compensation generally is treated as a substituted payment for the payment of the deferred compensation. For example, where the right to an amount of deferred compensation is purportedly relinquished or forfeited, and concurrently or subsequently the service provider receives a current bonus payment, the bonus payment will be presumed to be a substitute payment for the amount of deferred compensation. The presumption is rebuttable by a showing that the compensation paid would have been paid regardless of the relinquishment or forfeiture of the right to the deferred compensation. For a discussion of the application of this provision to amounts forfeitable upon a separation from service, see section III.J.1 of this preamble.

A plan may not provide discretion to a service provider regarding whether a payment will be accelerated under one of the rules permitting the acceleration of payments under specified circumstances (for example, to comply with a domestic relations order), including through the provision of an election. However, where a plan provides a service recipient discretion to accelerate payments under one of the rules permitting the acceleration of a payment, the failure to accelerate such a payment will not constitute a subsequent deferral election.

B. *Plan termination and liquidation*

The proposed regulations contained provisions permitting a service recipient to terminate and liquidate a nonqualified deferred compensation plan, including when the service recipient has declared bankruptcy, when the service recipient has participated in certain change in control events, or at the discretion of the service recipient, all subject to certain restrictions and limitations. Commentators expressed concern over the restrictions and limitations. Some comments reflected confusion as to the meaning of these terms in the context of section 409A. The termination and liquidation of a nonqualified deferred compensation plan involves both the amendment of the plan to cease deferrals under the plan and provide for payment of all benefits accrued under the plan, and the accelerated payment of benefits accrued under the plan.

Several comments suggested that the final regulations expand the circumstances under which a service recipient may terminate and liquidate a nonqualified deferred compensation plan. Generally these comments requested discretion in case of a change in business conditions or circumstances, resulting in the service recipient's desire to terminate and liquidate the plan. The final regulations expand the circumstances under which a sale of assets of a corporation will result in a separation from service. See section VII.C.2.f of this preamble. In addition, the final regulations continue to allow the service recipient to terminate and liquidate a plan during a defined period following a change in control event. Outside of these particular business events, the comments failed to provide an objective standard or category of changes in business conditions or circumstances that would provide a safeguard against the use of plan termination and liquidation provisions to circumvent the prohibition on accelerations. Accordingly, the final regulations do not expand the ability of a service recipient to exercise its discretion to terminate and liquidate a deferred compensation plan. However, the period of time during which a service recipient may not commence a new plan after terminating and liquidating a nonqualified deferred compensation plan has been shortened from five years to three years. Also, the final regulations provide that a discretionary plan termination and liquidation will not qualify for this exception if it is proximate to a downturn in the financial health of the service recipient.

The final regulations clarify the rules under which a deferred compensation plan may be terminated and liquidated upon a change in control event. Under the final regulations, the service recipient must, within the 30 days preceding or the 12 months following the change in control event, take all necessary action to terminate and liquidate the plan and such action must be irrevocable. In addition, for the plan to be treated as terminated and liquidated, all other arrangements that would be classified with the plan as a single plan if the same service provider participated in the plan and all the other arrangements must be terminated and liquidated, so that all service providers who are participants in the plan and all such other arrangements required to be terminated and liquidated must receive all amounts of compensation deferred under the terminated and liquidated plan and other arrangements within 12 months of the date the service recipient takes such irrevocable action to terminate and liquidate the arrangements. For purposes of the rule, the entities comprising the service recipient are determined immediately following the change in control event, and the rule only applies with respect to service providers for whom a change in control has occurred. For example, where the change in control event consists of a sale of a subsidiary corporation such that the subsidiary corporation is no longer treated as a single service recipient with the (former) parent corporation, the requirement to terminate and liquidate substantially similar arrangements applies only to the purchaser service recipient group of corporations that now owns the subsidiary corporation. In addition, the rule would apply only to the service providers that had experienced a change in control, generally consisting only of the service providers of the subsidiary corporation. Where the change in control event consists of an asset purchase, the applicable service recipient with discretion to terminate and liquidate the plan is deemed to be the entity retaining the deferred compensation liability after the transaction.

Some commentators asked whether the plan termination and liquidation rules apply if a plan is terminated and liquidated when the service provider has no vested right to a payment, and all payments are forfeited. Where the service recipient retained the unfettered discretion to terminate such a plan without paying benefits, the service provider may not have obtained a legally binding right to a payment. In addition, if a service provider forfeits benefits under a nonqualified deferred compensation plan in exchange for other taxable benefits, those benefits may be treated as a payment of amounts under the nonqualified deferred compensation plan.

C. *Conflicts of interest and ethics rules*

The proposed regulations contained a special accelerated payment rule to permit accelerated payments required to be made by a certificate of divestiture. Notice 2006–64, 2006–29 I.R.B. 88, see §601.601(d)(2), expanded this exception to address situations in which a letter is received from the Office of Government Ethics that divestiture of the deferred compensation is required. Several commentators requested an expansion of these rules.

The final regulations provide that a payment may be accelerated where necessary for a Federal officer or employee in the executive branch to comply with an ethics agreement with the Federal government. The final regulations also provide that a payment may be accelerated where reasonably necessary to avoid the violation of a Federal, state, local, or foreign conflict of interest law or ethics law (including where such payment is reasonably necessary to permit the service provider to participate in activities in the normal course of his or her position in which the service provider would otherwise not be able to participate under an applicable law). For this purpose, a payment will be reasonably necessary to avoid such a violation if the making of the payment is a necessary part of a combination of actions resulting in compliance with the applicable law. A payment may be considered necessary to avoid such a violation even though actions other than making the payment could also result in compliance with the applicable law. For example, as requested by several commentators, this provision would provide a public accounting firm the ability to accelerate payments where reasonably necessary to satisfy conflict of interest rules prescribed by the Securities and Exchange Commission. This paragraph is intended to address payments to service providers, as well as payments to a spouse or minor children where such payments are reasonably necessary to comply with the applicable law. For this purpose, foreign law is considered to be applicable only to foreign earned income from sources within the foreign country that promulgated such law.

D. *State and local taxes, RRTA tax and foreign taxes*

Commentators stated that certain state and local jurisdictions tax nonqualified deferred compensation plans under a different set of rules than the Federal income tax rules, typically by reference to the rules applicable to FICA taxes. Commentators also requested that accelerations be permitted to cover applicable RRTA taxes. Finally, commentators requested that accelerated payments be permitted to account for the tax laws of foreign jurisdictions that may not be consistent with the Federal income tax rules. The final regulations adopt the suggestions with respect to state and local taxes, RRTA taxes, and foreign taxes.

E. *Minimum distributions under section 280H(d)*

One commentator suggested that acceleration be permitted to allow a personal service corporation to make minimum distributions to avoid taxation under section 280H(d). The Treasury Department and the IRS believe that such a provision would give taxpayers excessive control over the payment of deferred amounts that would be inconsistent with the purposes of section 409A. Therefore, this suggestion was not adopted.

F. *Top hat plan rules*

Some commentators requested that the final regulations permit a service recipient to accelerate payments or cancel deferral elections with respect to a service provider who is not part of a select group of management or highly compensated employees for purposes of the exclusion from coverage under certain provisions of the Employee Retirement Income Security Act of 1974 relating to top hat plans. See, for example, 29 U.S.C. §1051(2). Given the current lack of clarity with respect to the scope of coverage of the top hat plan rules, and the actions required when a plan participant no longer satisfies the requirement to qualify for the top hat plan rules, the Treasury Department and the IRS are not confident that an exception to the anti-acceleration provisions based upon these rules is feasible. Accordingly, the final regulations do not adopt this suggestion.

G. *Settlements of bona fide disputes regarding the right to a payment*

Commentators requested relief for certain payments made as a settlement of a dispute as to a service provider's right to a deferred amount. For example, assume that a plan provides for a payment of deferred compensation upon a termination of an employee's employment other than for cause and the employee and employer have a *bona fide* dispute as to whether the employee was terminated for cause, and thus whether the service provider is entitled to any payment under the plan. The final regulations provide that payments may be accelerated, including acceleration to payment as a lump sum, where the right to such payments arises as part of a settlement between the service provider and the service recipient of a *bona fide* dispute as to the service provider's right to the deferred amount. The provision applies only to a deferred amount, the right to which is the subject of an arm's length settlement of a *bona fide* dispute between the service provider and the service recipient, and only to the portion of the deferred amount that is the subject of the *bona fide* dispute. The provision does not apply to disputes that relate only to when (and not whether) a payment is due. Whether a payment qualifies for the exception is based on the particular facts and circumstances. A payment will be presumed not to meet this exception unless the payment is subject to a substantial reduction in the value of the payment made in relation to the amount that would have been payable had there been no dispute as to the service provider's right to the payment. For this purpose, a reduction that is less than 25 percent of the present value of the deferred amount in dispute generally is not a substantial reduction. In addition, a payment will be presumed not to meet this exception if the payment is made proximate to a downturn in the financial health of the service recipient.

H. *Cashout rules*

Commentators requested various modifications to the cashout rules generally expanding the conditions under which a service recipient may exercise discretion to cash out a service provider's entire amount deferred under a plan. The final regulations generally provide that a service recipient may exercise such discretion at any time that a service provider's amount deferred under the plan is less than the applicable dollar amount under section 402(g)(1)(B) for that calendar year. For this purpose, the plan aggregation rules apply, so a service recipient may not use this rule to cash out an amount under one arrangement but not another arrangement where the two arrangements would be treated as one plan. The final regulations, unlike the proposed regulations, do not require that a service provider have separated from service for the service recipient to cash out the amount deferred. In addition, the plan does not need to be amended to provide this discretion to the service recipient. Finally, the amount has been changed from $10,000 to the limit on elective deferrals under section 402(g) to permit the amount to be adjusted for changes in the cost of living.

The final regulations also provide that a plan under which amounts are to be paid in installments may provide for immediate payment of all remaining installments if the present value of the deferred amount to be paid in the remaining installments falls below a predetermined amount, and such immediate payment will not constitute an accelerated payment for purposes of §1.409A–3(j)(1), provided that such feature (including the predetermined amount) is established no later than the latest time at which the time and form of payment is otherwise required to be established, and provided further that any change in such feature including the predetermined amount must comply with the requirements for a change in the time and form of payment.

I. *Other acceleration issues*

Commentators requested that a service recipient be permitted to cancel a service provider's deferral elections in two situations. First, commentators asked that such a cancellation be allowed when the service provider is transferred to a position that is not eligible to participate in the plan. The Treasury Department and the IRS are not confident that a standard can be established that would clearly distinguish a *bona fide* transfer to an ineligible position from a *pro forma* transfer designed to avoid the prohibition on accelerated payments, especially when the underlying plan is specific to the service provider, as in the case of an individual employment agreement, and accordingly the final regulations do not adopt this suggestion. Second, commentators asked that a service provider's deferral election be cancelled if the service provider becomes disabled. The final regulations permit the cancellation of the service provider's deferral election due to a disability, provided that for this purpose a disability is defined as any medically determinable physical or mental impairment resulting in the service provider's inability to perform the duties of his or her position or any substantially similar position, where such impairment can be expected to result in death or can be expected to last for a continuous period of not less than six months.

IX. *Subsequent Changes in the Time and Form of Payment*

A. *In general*

The final regulations clarify that the rules governing changes in the time and form of payment apply both to service providers and service recipients. Accordingly, a service provider, a service recipient, or both a service provider and a service recipient may have and exercise discretion to defer a deferred compensation payment after the time and form of payment have been specified, provided that such discretion is limited to changes that comply with the requirements of these regulations addressing subsequent changes in the time and form of payment.

B. *Annuities*

Many commentators requested clarification and expansion of the rules that allow taxpayers to treat actuarially equivalent life annuities as one form of payment, thereby allowing elections among such annuity forms at any time before the initial annuity payment without regard to the rules on subsequent deferral elections. The final regulations clarify the circumstances under which two actuarially equivalent life annuities may be treated as one form of payment.

The final regulations generally provide that certain specified features are ignored for purposes of determining whether a particular annuity is treated as a life annuity for purposes of the form of payment rules (but not for purposes of determining whether a life annuity with such a feature is actuarially equivalent to a life annuity without such a feature). The specified features include: (1) term certain features (under which annuity payments continue for the longer of the life of the annuitant or a fixed period of time); (2) pop-up provisions (under which payments increase upon the death of the beneficiary or another event that eliminates the right to a survivor annuity); (3) cash refund features (under which payment is provided upon the death of the last annuitant in an amount that is not greater than the excess of the present value of the annuity at the annuity starting date over the total of payments before the death of the last annuitant); (4) Social Security or Railroad Retirement leveling features (including leveling features related to early retirement, survivor or disability benefits); and (5) features applying a permissible cost-of-living index. Accordingly, a life annuity with any of the specified features may be treated as a life annuity without regard to the fact that the features cause the annuity to fail to satisfy the general definition for life annuities, for example, because the periodic payments are not substantially equal. However, the life annuity with such a feature may only be treated as the same form of payment as a life annuity without such a feature if the two life annuities are actuarially equivalent (taking into account the feature) and have the same initial payment date.

Commentators also raised issues concerning the availability of subsidized joint and survivor annuities. The final regulations provide that for purposes of the definition of a time and form of payment, a subsidized joint and survivor annuity is treated as actuarially equivalent to a single life annuity provided that, neither the annual lifetime annuity benefit nor the annual survivor benefit available under the joint and survivor annuity is greater than the annual lifetime annuity benefit available under the single life annuity. For example, a single life annuity providing $100 a month for the lifetime of the service provider may be treated as actuarially equivalent to a joint and survivor annuity providing up to $100 a month for the lifetime of the service provider and up to $100 a month to the surviving joint annuitant.

Commentators asked whether the actuarial assumptions and methods used to determine actuarial equivalency must be applied consistently. The final regulations clarify that in determining whether two life annuities are actuarially equivalent, the same actuarial assumptions and methods must be used in valuing each life annuity. This requirement applies over the entire term of the service provider's participation in the plan, such that the annuities must be actuarially equivalent at all times for the annuity options to be treated as one time and form of payment. However, provided the actuarial methods and assumptions are reasonable, there is no requirement that consistent actuarial assumptions and methods be used over the term of the service provider's participation in the plan. Accordingly, the plan may change the actuarial assumptions and methods used to determine the life annuity payments, provided that all of the actuarial assumptions and methods are reasonable. In addition, there is no requirement that the actuarial assumptions and methods used under a nonqualified deferred compensation plan be the same as those used in a qualified plan sponsored by the service recipient.

C. *Application to multiple payment events*

The final regulations continue to provide that the subsequent deferral and anti-acceleration rules generally will apply to the addition or deletion of a permissible payment event. Commentators asked for clarification of how these rules apply.

The Treasury Department and the IRS believe that a failure to provide for a payment event at death, disability or an unforeseeable emergency generally will result from oversight, and that the addition of such a provision generally would not be abusive. Accordingly, the final regulations provide that the addition of death, disability, or an unforeseeable emergency as a potentially earlier payment event is a permissible acceleration. This provision does not apply to the addition of death, disability, or an unforeseeable emergency as a potentially later payment event, such as through the addition of death as a payment event to a plan providing for a payment of deferred compensation on a fixed date, so that after the change the payment would be due on the later of the fixed date or death. Nor, for example, would it apply to an amendment of a plan to substitute a service provider's death as a new payment event, instead of a fixed payment date. In those cases, the rules governing subsequent deferral elections apply. In addition, the substitution of death as a payment event for an amount that is deferred compensation will not cause the plan to be treated as a death benefit plan not subject to section 409A, but the substitution or addition of a payment event other than death as a payment event in a death benefit plan may result in the plan being treated as providing for deferred compensation.

The anti-acceleration provisions apply to the addition of a specified date or fixed schedule, a change in control event, or separation from service as a potentially earlier payment event, including the substitution of one of these payment events for another payment event. In addition, the anti-acceleration provisions apply where a payment event is removed from a plan term requiring payment upon the latest of two or more payment events. The provisions governing subsequent deferral elections apply to all changes in the time and form of payment, whether resulting from the addition, deletion or substitution of another payment event. Commentators requested clarification of how this provision would apply where the events were not specified dates, such as the substitution of a change in control payment event for a separation from service event. In such a situation, to satisfy the rules governing subsequent deferrals, this substitution would only be permissible if the change were not effective for one year, and provided that the payment would only occur upon the later of a change in control event or at least five years following a separation from service.

D. *Application to domestic relations orders*

The final regulations provide that the rules governing changes in the time and form of payment do not apply to changes in the time and form of payment under the terms of a domestic relations order, to the extent the change in the time and form of payment applies to a payment that will be made to the alternate payee and not the service provider. Accordingly, for example, a domestic relations order generally may provide for a new time and form of payment to a spouse or former spouse of the service provider, or provide such spouse or former spouse discretion to determine the time and form of payment to such spouse or former spouse.

X. *Application to nonqualified deferred compensation plans linked to qualified plans and other arrangements*

A. *Plans linked to qualified plans and certain broad-based foreign retirement plans*

The final regulations generally adopt the relief provided in the proposed regulations with respect to the election-timing and the anti-acceleration rules for changes in the amount of benefits under a nonqualified deferred compensation plan that result from an election (or failure to elect) by a service provider, or an amendment by a service recipient, in respect of a subsidized or ancillary benefit under a qualified plan. In response to comments, this relief is similarly extended to certain broad-based foreign retirement plans. In addition, this relief is extended for benefit formulas that include a reduction for amounts credited to the service provider's account under a tax-qualified plan (which may include matching contributions) or certain broad-based foreign retirement plans that provide benefits expressed as an account balance.

In response to comments, the final regulations also clarify that the linked plan relief provided for elective deferrals (including designated Roth contributions) and matching type contributions is subject to two separate, additive limits and not a single, coordinated limit. In addition, the final regulations clarify that the section 402(g) dollar limits are increased by the limit on catch-up contributions under section 414(v) for any year in which the service provider qualifies for such increase.

Commentators raised issues concerning other types of plans under which a service provider must participate in a qualified plan to receive nonqualified deferred compensation. Specifically, commentators asked whether a plan could comply with section 409A if it provided that an employee must defer the maximum amount permissible under a qualified plan in order to defer any amount under a nonqualified deferred compensation plan. Where the service provider can change the service provider's election to defer the maximum amount permissible under the qualified plan during the taxable year, and thereby change or discontinue deferrals under a nonqualified deferred compensation plan, the service provider can effectively make a late election to defer (or not defer) amounts under the nonqualified plan. The final regulations generally do not provide any additional relief with respect to this type of plan. However, where the additional amounts deferred under the nonqualified deferred compensation plan reflect only matching contributions that would be available under the qualified plan absent the restrictions in the qualified plan intended to reflect limits on qualified plan contributions under sections 401(m) and 401(a)(17), the final regulations provide relief but solely with respect to the matching amount that could have been contributed to the qualified plan absent such limits.

Commentators also stated that the rules in the proposed regulations did not adequately address the impact of after-tax contributions. Specifically, commentators requested relief for service providers who change their after-tax contributions (other than designated Roth contributions) under a qualified plan during a year where such decrease causes a corresponding change in nonqualified plan elective deferrals. The final regulations provide some additional relief concerning matching or other contributions contingent upon the making of an after-tax contribution. However, other suggestions were not adopted in the final regulations, because the Treasury Department and the IRS are concerned that such plans may give the service provider excessive control over amounts deferred under a nonqualified deferred compensation plan, contrary to the statutory intent.

B. *Plans linked to cafeteria plans*

Commentators expressed concern that changes to elections under a section 125 cafeteria plan could change the amount of eligible compensation used for purposes of a benefit formula under a nonqualified deferred compensation plan and thereby create an impermissible deferral election or acceleration of payment under the nonqualified deferred compensation plan. The final regulations provide relief from the deferral election-timing and anti-acceleration rules for changes to section 125 elections properly made in accordance with the rules under section 125, to the extent that the change in the amount deferred under the nonqualified deferred compensation plan results solely from the application of the change in amount of eligible compensation resulting from the election change under the cafeteria plan to a benefit formula based upon the service provider's eligible compensation, and only to the extent that such change applies in the same manner as any other increase or decrease in the eligible compensation would apply to such benefit formula.

C. *Offsets*

i. *In general*

Some commentators requested clarification whether an arrangement under which a specified amount paid by a service recipient to a service provider reduces or offsets an amount that is payable to the service provider under a nonqualified deferred compensation plan will be treated as providing for an acceleration of a payment under the nonqualified deferred compensation plan. As an example, one commentator stated that a plan may require that any payout at separation from service of accrued leave that is determined to be in excess of the correct amount of such payment will be deducted from the amount due under a nonqualified deferred compensation plan, rather than repaid separately by the service provider. One commentator suggested that offsets be permitted for all service provider debts of a kind and in amounts customarily incurred in the ordinary course of the business relationship between the service provider and the service recipient.

The Treasury Department and the IRS believe that the unfettered discretion to settle debts between a service recipient and a service provider through offsets from payments of nonqualified deferred compensation is not consistent with the intent of the statute, because it creates opportunities to disguise accelerated payments of deferred compensation. Accordingly, amounts that currently or in the future may be offset against nonqualified deferred compensation are treated as payments of deferred compensation and may violate the anti-acceleration rules under section 409A. See section VIII.A of this preamble. However, the Treasury Department and the IRS agree that the ability to offset small routine debts against amounts payable under a nonqualified deferred compensation plan is useful so that service recipients can avoid the administrative burden involved in paying deferred compensation amounts to a service provider while at the same time attempting to collect small amounts owed by the same service provider. Accordingly, the final regulations provide that payments of deferred compensation may be offset by amounts owed to the service recipient by the service provider, where such debt is incurred in the ordinary course of the service relationship, to the extent the entire offset in any taxable year does not exceed $5,000 and the offset is taken at the same time and in the same amount as the debt otherwise would have been due from the service provider.

ii. *Social security benefits and disability benefits*

Commentators requested clarification of the treatment of nonqualified deferred compensation plans that offset benefits with payments received as Social Security benefits and disability benefits. A plan provision providing for a direct, dollar-for-dollar reduction of payments due under a nonqualified deferred compensation plan by the amount of payments received or receivable as Social Security benefits will not fail to provide for a fixed schedule of payments. However, the rule relates solely to direct reductions in deferred compensation benefits to reflect eligibility for, or payment of, Social Security benefits, and does not permit other changes in the time and form of benefit based upon a service provider's eligibility or elections related to Social Security benefits. A reduction in a nonqualified deferred compensation plan benefit equal to the amount receivable under a service recipient sponsored disability plan generally will be treated similarly, provided that a substantial number of service providers participate in the disability plan. However, to allow the payment schedule to qualify as a fixed schedule, the disability plan must be established before the date the service provider becomes disabled. In addition, any subsequent amendment to the disability plan or other change in the benefit payable under the disability plan may result in an acceleration of a payment or a subsequent deferral under the nonqualified deferred compensation plan unless the facts and circumstances establish otherwise (for example, because the amendment or change results from actions taken by an independent third party, such as an unrelated insurer that issued a disability insurance policy for such disability plan, over which the service recipient and service provider have no control, or an action of the service recipient with respect to the disability plan that is generally applicable to a substantial number of other service providers who participate in such disability plan and has a material effect on the disability benefits of such other service providers).

XI. *Statutory Effective Dates*

A. *Effective dates – earned and vested amounts*

As provided in section 885(d) of the American Jobs Creation Act of 2004, section 409A generally is effective for amounts deferred after December 31, 2004. The final regulations adopt the definition set forth in the proposed regulations of an amount deferred on or before December 31, 2004, for purposes of the effective date, subject to the modifications described in this preamble. The final regulations clarify that the grandfathered amount includes any account balance that is earned and vested, as well as the present value of any earned and vested right to future account credits, even if such amounts had not been credited to the account as of December 31, 2004. For example, if a service provider had a vested right on December 31, 2004, to have a bonus amount added to the service provider's account balance in a nonqualified deferred compensation plan, the service provider's grandfathered amount would include the amount of such bonus even though such amount was not calculated and credited to the account until some time in 2005.

B. *Effective dates — calculation of grandfathered amount*

One commentator requested that the grandfathered amount in a nonaccount balance plan be expressed in terms of the form of benefit under the plan. So, for example, where the normal benefit was expressed in the form of an annuity payable at a certain age, that is how the amount of the grandfathered benefit would also be expressed. The final regulations do not adopt this suggestion, but reach a similar result by providing that any actuarial assumptions and methods that were reasonable to use as of December 31, 2004, may continue to be used in subsequent years for purposes of determining the grandfathered amount.

C. *Material modifications*

Section 885(d)(2) of the American Jobs Creation Act of 2004 provides generally that amounts deferred in taxable years beginning before January 1, 2005, are treated as amounts deferred in a taxable year beginning on or after such date if the plan under which the deferral is made is materially modified after October 3, 2004. The final regulations adopt the definition set forth in the proposed regulations of a material modification for these purposes, subject to the changes described in this preamble.

For purposes of the definition of a material modification under the effective date rules, the final regulations incorporate the exclusions from the definition of a modification for purposes of the rules governing stock rights. For example, a change to a discounted grandfathered stock right that could be covered by section 409A if materially modified under the effective date rules, will not be treated as materially modified and subject to section 409A if the change would not be treated under the rules governing stock rights as a modification resulting in treatment as a new grant of a stock right or an extension resulting in treatment of the stock right as having had a deferral feature from the date of grant.

The final regulations provide that neither the amendment of a plan to include a provision allowing for a payment to a person other than the service provider due to the application of a domestic relations order, nor the making of a payment in compliance with a domestic relations order where a plan did not address the ability to make such a payment, is treated as a material modification for purposes of the grandfathering rules.

Commentators also requested that a grandfathered plan be permitted to remove a provision requiring a cancellation of deferrals for a prescribed period of time under all nonqualified deferred compensation plans to receive a distribution from the grandfathered plan, without resulting in a material modification. Commentators argued that because the enforcement of such a provision by cancelling a current deferral election generally would result in an immediate violation of section 409A, the inability to remove the requirement that the deferral election be cancelled effectively nullifies the grandfathered right. Under the final regulations, an amendment to a grandfathered plan that changes such a provision to require a cancellation of deferrals for the equivalent period of time beginning with the first possible date that such a cancellation would not result in a prohibited accelerated payment (generally the beginning of the subsequent calendar year for a service provider with a calendar year taxable year) will not constitute a material modification. For example, taxpayers may amend an early distribution provision that requires the immediate cessation of deferrals for 12 months to apply only to deferrals over the first 12 month period with respect to which the service provider can make a timely deferral election, for example, by prohibiting deferrals of compensation attributable to services performed during the service provider's next taxable year.

Commentators requested clarification of the effect of a material modification of a plan. The specific consequences of a material modification of a plan are being considered as part of the anticipated guidance related to income inclusion and calculation. However, the final regulations provide that for amounts deferred in taxable years beginning before January 1, 2005, under a plan that is materially modified after October 3, 2004, whether the plan complies with the requirements of section 409A is determined by reference to the terms of the plan in effect, and any actions taken under the plan, on and after the date of the material modification. Accordingly, where the materially modified plan is compliant with section 409A and these regulations immediately following the material modification, the material modification generally will not itself result in a violation.

XII. *Applicability date of final regulations*

A. *Existing transition relief.*

Nothing in this preamble or the final regulations is intended to restrict the otherwise applicable transition relief. For a description of the applicable transition relief, see Notice 2006–79, 2006–43 I.R.B. 763 (extension of certain transition relief through 2007), Notice 2006–64, 2006–29 I.R.B. 88 (transition relief applicable to certain accelerated payments necessary to comply with Federal ethics requirements), Notice 2006–33, 2006–15 I.R.B. 754 (transition rules with respect to section 409A(b)), Notice 2006–4, 2006–3 I.R.B. 307 (transition relief with respect to the valuation standards applicable to stock rights issued on or before the effective date of the final regulations for purposes of the exclusion from coverage under section 409A for certain stock rights), the preamble to the proposed regulations (extension of certain transition relief through 2006), and Notice 2005–1, 2005–1 C.B. 274 (initial transition relief). See §601.601(d)(2).

B. *Application of final regulations*

The final regulations are generally applicable January 1, 2008. For periods before January 1, 2008, the standards and transition rules set forth in Notice 2006–79 continue to apply. For further information regarding the transition relief for periods before the applicability date of the final regulations, see Notice 2006–79 and section XI of the preamble to the proposed regulations.

Commentators requested clarification of the impact of the final regulations becoming applicable January 1, 2008, on plans that continue to defer compensation on or after January 1, 2008. Specifically, commentators asked whether actions taken with respect to nonqualified deferred compensation plans that would not have resulted in income inclusion under section 409A before 2008 because such actions were consistent with applicable guidance, but would not be consistent with the final regulations, would need to be modified to avoid income inclusion under section 409A in 2008 and later years. The following sections discuss the effect of the final regulations with respect to the requirements necessary to comply with section 409A, including the various requirements necessary for a plan to be excluded from coverage under section 409A.

C. *Stock rights*

Many of the comments related to stock options and stock appreciation rights. Some commentators requested that section 409A not apply to any stock rights issued before the applicability date of the final regulations. Neither the statute nor the legislative history indicates an intent for such a broad exception. The Treasury Department and the IRS understand that certain aspects of the guidance on stock rights have changed. However, the final regulations generally expand the exclusion from coverage under section 409A for certain stock rights to eliminate many issues raised by the proposed regulations. In addition, with respect to certain types of stock rights, such as discounted stock options, the guidance has explicitly and consistently indicated that either rights that would be excluded from coverage under section 409A must be substituted for such rights or such rights must be modified to comply with section 409A. Accordingly, the final regulations do not adopt a categorical exclusion from coverage under section 409A of all stock rights issued before the issuance of the final regulations.

Commentators also asked whether a stock option must be repriced to avoid coverage under section 409A if the exercise price would be treated as having been set at fair market value under section 409A under the applicable guidance, but would not be treated as having been set at fair market value if the standard of the final regulations had been applicable. For this purpose, the guidance provided in Notice 2006–4, 2006–3 I.R.B. 307, see §601.601(d)(2), remains in effect. Notice 2006–4 provided certain standards applicable to stock rights issued before January 1, 2005, for determining whether the exercise price of such stock right would be treated as having been set at fair market value for purposes of the exclusion from coverage under section 409A for certain stock rights. As provided in Notice 2006–4, for stock rights issued before January 1, 2005, the standards applicable to incentive stock options under section 422 are applicable. Generally this means that where the sole reason the stock right would fail to qualify for the exclusion from coverage under section 409A is due to the exercise price not being set at or above fair market value, the exercise price will be treated as set at or above fair market value if based upon a good faith attempt by the issuer to set the exercise price at or above fair market value. As further explained in Notice 2006–4, for stock rights issued on or after January 1, 2005, but before January 1, 2008, the provisions of Notice 2005–1 will apply, generally requiring that fair market value for purposes of setting the exercise price of a stock right must be determined using a reasonable valuation method. In addition, for stock rights issued on any date before January 1, 2008, taxpayers may rely upon the provisions of the proposed or final regulations with regard to the determination of the fair market value of the underlying stock.

Commentators requested that taxpayers not be required to bring stock rights granted before January 1, 2008, into compliance with section 409A if such rights were properly treated as not being subject to section 409A under the applicable guidance, but instead be permitted to keep such rights outstanding and unmodified.

The final regulations significantly expand the permissible classes of stock and the permissible issuers of stock under the service recipient stock rule, and taxpayers may rely on the final regulations for periods before the effective date of the final regulations. In addition, with respect to stock rights issued before April 10, 2007, on stock that would have constituted service recipient stock under a reasonable good faith interpretation of the statute and applicable guidance, but would not constitute service recipient stock under the final regulations, such stock will continue to constitute service recipient stock for purposes of applying section 409A to such stock right until the exercise or termination of such right, or until the stock right is modified in a manner that is treated as the grant of a new right. However, for a stock right issued on or after April 10, 2007, stock subject to such stock right will not be treated as service recipient stock after December 31, 2007, unless such stock satisfies the requirements of the final regulations, and if the stock does not satisfy these requirements, such stock right will be required to be modified either to be excluded from coverage under section 409A, or to comply with the requirements of section 409A and these regulations.

Commentators also expressed concerns about modifications and extensions of stock rights that occur before January 1, 2008. Different concerns and arguments arise depending upon whether these modifications and extensions occurred on or before the enactment of the statute (October 23, 2004), on or before the issuance of Notice 2005–1 (December 20, 2004), on or before the issuance of the proposed regulations (September 30, 2005) or on or before the applicability date of the final regulations (January 1, 2008). The final regulations significantly expand the permissible types of modifications and extensions that will not result in treatment of the stock right as a new grant or as having had a deferral feature from the date of grant, and taxpayers may rely on these regulations for periods before the applicability date of the regulations. In addition, any modifications or extensions occurring before the enactment of the statute (October 23, 2004) will not be considered in determining whether the right is excluded from coverage under section 409A. Finally, any extension granted before April 10, 2007, solely in order to give the holder of a stock right an additional period of time within which to exercise the stock right beyond the time originally prescribed is disregarded for purposes of the rules treating certain extensions as deferral features from the time of grant. See §1.409A–1(b)(5)(v)(C).

D. *Initial deferral elections*

Commentators asked whether and to what extent the final regulations would impact initial deferral elections made before the applicability date of the final regulations. If a deferral election made before January 1, 2008, was consistent with the proposed regulations or the applicable transition guidance, the initial deferral election will be deemed to comply with the provisions of section 409A, regardless of whether the period of deferral extends beyond December 31, 2007.

In addition, commentators asked whether and to what extent the final regulations would impact programs established before the applicability date of the final regulations, where initial deferral elections have not been made by January 1, 2008. For example, commentators asked how section 409A would apply if a service recipient has interpreted a program as providing for performance-based compensation and permitted deferral elections to occur in 2008 or later in accordance with the rules governing deferrals of performance-based compensation, but such compensation does not qualify as performance-based compensation under the final regulations. For a program established before April 10, 2007, that under a reasonable, good faith interpretation of the statute and applicable guidance would have permitted an initial deferral election to be made after December 31, 2007, and on or before December 31, 2008, an initial deferral election will be deemed to comply with the initial deferral election rules if made by the deadline established in the plan. For a program established before April 10, 2007, that under a reasonable, good faith interpretation of the statute and applicable guidance would have permitted an initial deferral election be made after December 31, 2008, an initial deferral election will be deemed to comply with the initial deferral election rules if made by December 31, 2008.

E. *Designation of time and form of payment*

Notice 2005–1 and the preamble to the proposed regulations consistently provide that elections as to the time and form of payment of deferred compensation would need to be compliant with the final regulations by the time such regulations were applicable. Both Notice 2005–1 and the preamble to the proposed regulations provide detailed transition guidance, generally permitting service providers and service recipients to change the time and form of payment at any time through the end of the transition period. Accordingly, a payment scheme that violates the provisions of the final regulations will need to be brought into compliance with the final regulations in accordance with the transition relief.

F. *Service providers in pay status*

Commentators asked how the final regulations apply to service providers that are already in pay status, where the payment trigger is based upon a reasonable, good faith interpretation of the statute and applicable guidance but is not in compliance with the final regulations. This may occur where the service provider has already begun receiving payments before January 1, 2008, or where all events necessary to receive the payment have occurred before January 1, 2008. For example, a service provider may have been treated as having separated from service before January 1, 2008, under a reasonable, good faith interpretation of the statute, but would not be treated as having separated from service under the final regulations. Where payments have commenced before January 1, 2008, the plan may continue to make such payments consistent with the application of the plan terms at the time the payments commenced, or may halt such payments on or before December 31, 2007, and amend the time and form of any remaining payments to comply with the final regulations in accordance with the transition guidance provided. Where payments have not commenced by January 1, 2008, but all the events necessary to receive the payment have occurred, the plan may make payments in accordance with the application of the plan terms on December 31, 2007, or may amend the time and form of payments to comply with section 409A in accordance with the transition guidance provided. Similarly, where payments have not commenced on or before December 31, 2007, because the service provider was treated as not having separated from service under a reasonable, good faith interpretation, but under the final regulations the service provider would be treated as having separated from service on or before December 31, 2007, the plan must treat the service provider as having separated from service on a date on or after April 10, 2007, and on or before December 31, 2007. Nothing in this paragraph is to be construed to permit the continuation of any payment schedule based upon an application of section 409A on or before December 31, 2007, that failed to meet the requirements of the applicable transition guidance. In addition, nothing in this paragraph is intended to waive the application of the constructive receipt doctrine or section 451 with respect to any discretion provided to the service provider (or former service provider) with respect to the application of these provisions.

In addition, commentators asked how the final regulations would apply in the case of the six-month delay for specified employees of public corporations. Where a separation from service occurs on or before December 31, 2007, under circumstances that under a reasonable, good faith interpretation of the statute and applicable guidance would not result in application of the six-month delay requirement for a payment to a specified employee, the beginning or continuation of payments of deferred compensation on or after January 1, 2008, will not result in a violation of the six-month delay requirement for a payment to a specified employee.

XIII. *Additional Transition Relief*

A. *Collectively bargained plans*

Consistent with Notice 2006–79, §3.05, the final regulations provide that a nonqualified deferred compensation plan maintained pursuant to one or more collective bargaining agreements in effect on October 3, 2004, is not required to comply with the provisions of section 409A on or before the earlier of the date on which the last of such collective bargaining agreements terminates (determined without regard to any extension of any agreement after October 3, 2004) or December 31, 2009.

With respect to amounts deferred under a nonqualified deferred compensation plan maintained pursuant to one or more collective bargaining agreements in effect on October 3, 2004, the plan may provide, or be amended to provide, for new payment elections with respect to both the time and form of payment of such amounts, and the election or amendment will not be treated as a change in the time or form of payment under section 409A(a)(4) or an acceleration of a payment under section 409A(a)(3), provided that the plan is so amended and elections are made before the date on which section 409A first applies to such plan. A deferral election may be made with respect to an amount that is a short-term deferral within the meaning of §1.409A–1(b)(4), provided that the election is made before the date on which section 409A would apply to an amount deferred under such plan and before January 1 of the calendar year in which the amount would otherwise have been paid.

B. *Requirement to amend plans on or before December 31, 2007*

Where there have been deferrals of compensation under a plan as of January 1, 2008 but the deferred compensation has not been paid, the plan must be made compliant with section 409A on or before December 31, 2007, with respect to such deferred compensation. These amendments are required only to bring the document into compliance effective January 1, 2008, and are not required to reflect any amendments made or actions taken under the transition rules to the extent such amendments or actions do not affect the plan's compliance with section 409A and these regulations for periods on or after January 1, 2008. For example, if a plan contains a haircut provision permitting an immediate distribution contingent on the forfeiture of a certain portion of a deferred amount, the haircut provision need not be removed retroactively for periods before January 1, 2008, where the plan has been operated in compliance with the applicable transition guidance (and thus no payment pursuant to the haircut provision has been made after December 31, 2004). In addition, a plan need not be amended to be made compliant with section 409A with respect to amounts deferred under the plan that were paid on or before December 31, 2007, in compliance with the transition guidance. However, the taxpayer must be able to demonstrate that the plan was operated in compliance with the transition guidance, including demonstrating that amounts were deferred or paid in compliance with the transition rules. For example, where payments were made in conjunction with elections of payment dates by either the service recipient or service provider during the transition period, the taxpayer must be able to demonstrate that the elections were provided and made in accordance with the transition rules.

XIV. *Calculation and Timing of Income Inclusion Amounts, Reporting and Withholding*

A. *In general*

These regulations do not address the calculation and timing of amounts required to be included in income under section 409A(a). Nor do these regulations address the reporting and withholding requirements applicable to service recipients providing nonqualified deferred compensation covered by section 409A. The Treasury Department and the IRS intend to issue further guidance, including such transition guidance as may be appropriate with respect to the reporting and withholding requirements. See Notice 2006–100, 2006–51 I.R.B. 1109, for transition rules applicable to the reporting and withholding requirements for 2005 and 2006. See §601.601(d)(2).

B. *Operational violations during the transition period*

Commentators on the proposed regulations and Notice 2006–100 asked whether a service provider whose nonqualified deferred compensation plan violated section 409A in operation before January 1, 2008, would be required to include an amount in income under section 409A only in the taxable year of the service provider in which the operational failure occurred (assuming this was the only year of an operational failure), or in such year and all prior years beginning after December 31, 2004. Commentators argued that for years before the operational violation, the taxpayer could be treated as operating the plan in reasonable, good faith compliance with the statute and Notice 2005–1, and therefore should be required to include an amount in income under section 409A only for the year in which the operational violation occurred. For example, where a taxpayer exercised a discounted stock option covered by section 409A in 2006, commentators argued that the taxpayer should be treated as operating the plan in reasonable, good faith compliance with section 409A during 2005, so that the taxpayer would be required to include an amount in income as a result of the section 409A violation only to 2006.

Where an operational failure occurs in 2006 or 2007, and no operational failures occurred in any prior year, the taxpayer (including the service recipient) may report the amounts required to be included in income under section 409A as taxable income only in the year of the operational failure. In addition, where the violation results from a payment, a taxpayer may include the required amount in income only for the year in which such violation occurs, regardless of whether the portion of the deferred compensation plan under which such payment was made is ever amended to comply with the requirements of section 409A for periods before such payment. For example, where a taxpayer exercises a discounted stock option subject to section 409A in 2006, and there was no operational violation in 2005, the taxpayer may include an amount in income under section 409A for 2006, and the taxpayer will not be required to include an amount in income with respect to such stock option for 2005, even if the taxpayer does not amend the stock option to comply with section 409A for 2005. However, where all or part of the total amount deferred in the year of the violation was also an amount deferred in one or more prior years that was not subject to a substantial risk of forfeiture in such year, taxpayers are also required to calculate and pay any applicable tax under section 409A(a)(1)(B)(i)(I) (based on the amount of interest determined under section 409A(a)(1)(B)(ii)). For example, if the discounted stock right in the previous example was not subject to a substantial risk of forfeiture as of December 31, 2005, the taxpayer would be required to compute and report the additional tax under section 409A(a)(1)(B)(i)(I) on the taxpayer's 2006 return. For purposes of this paragraph, the service recipient should treat the application of section 409A in the same manner for purposes of income tax withholding and reporting obligations.

C. *Application of plan aggregation rules during the transition period*

Notice 2006–100 provides that where there is a required income inclusion under section 409A in 2006, the plan aggregation rules apply in determining the amount includible in income. Commentators asked whether the plan aggregation rules would apply where the taxpayer violates section 409A in 2006 with respect to one arrangement (the first arrangement), but retains the right to modify another arrangement (the second arrangement) to exclude a right to an amount provided under the second arrangement from coverage under section 409A, where the second arrangement would otherwise be aggregated with the first arrangement. For this purpose, if the legally binding right to the amount under the second arrangement ultimately is modified (including, where permitted by applicable guidance, by the substitution of another right for such right), so that the right to the amount is excluded from coverage under section 409A, then the right to the amount is treated as always having been excluded from coverage under section 409A. Accordingly, the amount payable under the second arrangement would not be required to be aggregated with the first arrangement for purposes of determining the amount includible in income under section 409A. However, if the right to the amount under the second arrangement is not timely modified to be excluded from coverage under section 409A, the right to the amount under the second arrangement will remain subject to the plan aggregation rules regardless of whether the second arrangement is, or is amended to be, compliant with the requirements of section 409A. In such a case, because the right to the amount under the second arrangement could have been modified to be excluded from coverage under section 409A, and would not have been subject to the plan aggregation rules, the violation with respect to the second arrangement is not treated as occurring until the first taxable year of the service provider during which the arrangement could not have been so modified.

For example, assume a taxpayer with a calendar year taxable year exercised a discounted stock right during 2006 in violation of section 409A and that the taxpayer held another unexercised discounted stock right described in Notice 2006–79, §3.07 (relating to certain stock rights issued to corporate insiders) that could have been modified by December 31, 2006, to be excluded from coverage (by exchanging such stock right for another stock right pursuant to the preamble to the proposed regulations). If the unexercised stock right was not so modified by December 31, 2006, it would violate section 409A on January 1, 2007. Alternatively, assume a second taxpayer exercised a discounted stock right in 2006 in violation of section 409A and that taxpayer held another unexercised discounted stock right (not described in Notice 2006–79, §3.07) that could have been modified by December 31, 2007, to be excluded from coverage. If the second taxpayer failed to timely modify such unexercised stock right, the unexercised stock right would violate section 409A on January 1, 2008.

D. *Failures to amend during the transition period to comply with the rules of section 409A*

Commentators asked how section 409A and these regulations would apply to a plan that was operated in compliance with the transition guidance through December 31, 2007, but is not amended to become compliant with section 409A and these regulations by December 31, 2007. For these purposes, the plan will be treated as failing to comply with the requirements of section 409A and these regulations as of January 1, 2008, so that no amounts will be required to be included in income under section 409A with respect to such a violation for any taxable year ending before January 1, 2008. However, this does not affect the application of the tax imposed by section 409A(a)(1)(B)(i)(I) to amounts that were deferred in taxable years ending before January 1, 2008, to the extent that such amounts were not subject to a substantial risk of forfeiture in one or more of such earlier taxable years.

XV. *Offshore Trusts and Arrangements with Financial Triggers*

These regulations do not address the application of section 409A(b), generally prohibiting the use of offshore trusts associated with nonqualified deferred compensation plans, and the use of triggers whereby amounts held in a trust or other arrangement become restricted to the use for payment of nonqualified deferred compensation upon an event related to the financial health of the service recipient. For transition guidance related to the application of section 409A(b) to certain outstanding arrangements, see Notice 2006–33, 2006–15 I.R.B. 754. See §601.601(d)(2). Taxpayers may continue to rely upon Notice 2006–33 until further guidance is issued.

Applicability Date

These regulations are applicable for taxable years beginning on or after January 1, 2008. Taxpayers may rely on the provisions of these final regulations for taxable years beginning before January 1, 2008.

Effect on Other Documents

Notice 2005–1, 2005–1 C.B. 274, is obsoleted for taxable years beginning on or after January 1, 2008, except for the following sections of the guidance which remain effective as modified by any other applicable guidance: Q&A–6 (application to arrangements covered by section 457); Q&A–7 (application to arrangements between a partnership and a partner of the partnership); and Q&A–24 through Q&A–38 (information reporting and withholding guidance). For a discussion of the effect of reliance upon Notice 2005–1 or the proposed regulations for taxable years beginning before January 1, 2008, for arrangements continuing into taxable years beginning on or after January 1, 2008, see section XII of this preamble. See §601.601(d)(2).

Notice 2006–4, 2006–3 I.R.B. 307, addressing certain stock rights issued before January 1, 2008, is superseded by these final regulations with respect to stock rights issued in taxable years of the service provider beginning on or after January 1, 2008. For a discussion of the effect of reliance upon Notice 2005–1, Notice 2006–4, or the proposed regulations for taxable years beginning before January 1, 2008, for stock rights remaining outstanding on or after January 1, 2008, see section XII of this preamble.

Notice 2006–33, 2006–15 I.R.B. 754, Notice 2006–79, 2006–43 I.R.B. 763, and Notice 2006–100, 2006–51 I.R.B. 1109, are not affected by these final regulations. Notice 2006–64, 2006–29 I.R.B. 88, is superseded by the final regulations effective for taxable years of a service provider beginning on or after January 1, 2008. See §601.601(d)(2).

Special Analyses

It has been determined that this Treasury decision is not a significant regulatory action as defined in Executive Order 12866. Therefore, a regulatory assessment is not required. It has also been determined that section 553(b) of the Administrative Procedure Act (5 U.S.C. chapter 5) does not apply to these regulations, and because the regulation does not impose a collection of information on small entities, the Regulatory Flexibility Act (5 U.S.C. chapter 6) does not apply. Pursuant to section 7805(f) of the Code, the notice of proposed rulemaking preceding these regulations was submitted to the Chief Counsel for Advocacy of the Small Business Administration for comment on its impact on small business.

Drafting Information

The principal author of these regulations is Stephen Tackney of the Office of Division Counsel/Associate Chief Counsel (Tax Exempt and Government Entities). However, other personnel from the IRS and the Treasury Department participated in their development.

* * * * *

Adoption of Amendments to the Regulations

Accordingly, 26 CFR part 1 is amended as follows:

PART 1—INCOME TAXES

Paragraph 1. The authority citation for part 1 continues to read in part as follows:

Authority: 26 U.S.C. 7805 * * *

Par. 2. Sections 1.409A–0 through 1.409A–6 are added to read as follows:

§1.409A–0 Table of contents.

This section lists captions contained in §§1.409A–1, 1.409A–2, 1.409A–3, 1.409A–4, 1.409A–5 and 1.409A–6.

§1.409A–1 Definitions and covered plans.

(3) Compensation payable pursuant to the service recipient's customary payment timing arrangement.
(4) Short-term deferrals.
(i) In general.
(ii) Certain delayed payments.
(iii) Examples.
(5) Stock options, stock appreciation rights, and other equity-based compensation.
(i) Stock rights.
(A) Nonstatutory stock options not providing for the deferral of compensation.
(B) Stock appreciation rights not providing for the deferral of compensation.
(C) Stock rights that may provide for the deferral of compensation.
(D) Feature for the deferral of compensation.
(E) Rights to dividends.
(ii) Statutory stock options.
(iii) Service recipient stock.
(A) In general.
(B) American depositary receipts.
(C) Mutual company units.
(D) Other entities.
(E) Eligible issuer of service recipient stock.
(*1*) In general.
(*2*) Investment vehicles.
(*3*) Corporate structures established or transactions undertaken for purposes of avoiding coverage under section 409A.
(*4*) Substitutions and assumptions by reason of a corporate transaction.
(iv) Determination of the fair market value of service recipient stock.
(A) Stock readily tradable on an established securities market.
(B) Stock not readily tradable on an established securities market.
(*1*) In general.
(*2*) Presumption of reasonableness.
(*3*) Use of alternative methods.
(v) Modifications, extensions, substitutions, and assumptions of stock rights.
(A) Treatment of modified and extended stock rights.
(B) Modification in general.
(C) Extensions.
(*1*) In general.
(*2*) Certain extensions before April 10, 2007.
(*3*) Examples.
(D) Substitutions and assumptions of stock rights by reason of a corporate transaction.
(E) Acceleration of date when exercisable.
(F) Discretionary added benefits.
(G) Change in underlying stock increasing value.
(H) Change in the number of shares purchasable.
(I) Rescission of changes.
(J) Successive modifications and extensions.
(K) Modifications and extensions in effect on October 23, 2004.
(vi) Meaning and use of certain terms.
(A) Option.
(B) Date of grant of option.
(C) Stock.
(D) Exercise price.
(E) Exercise.
(F) Transfer.
(G) Readily tradable.
(H) Application to stock appreciation rights.
(6) Restricted property, section 402(b) trusts, and section 403(c) annuities.
(i) In general.
(ii) Promises to transfer property.
(7) Arrangements between partnerships and partners. [Reserved]
(8) Certain foreign plans.
(i) Plans with respect to compensation covered by treaty or other international agreement.
(ii) Plans with respect to certain other compensation.
(iii) Tax equalization agreements.
(iv) Certain limited deferrals of a nonresident alien.
(v) Additional foreign plans.
(vi) Earnings.
(9) Separation pay plans.
(i) In general.
(ii) Collectively bargained separation pay plans.
(iii) Separation pay due to involuntary separation from service or participation in a window program.
(iv) Foreign separation pay plans.
(v) Reimbursements and certain other separation payments.
(A) In general.
(B) Medical benefits.
(C) In-kind benefits and direct service recipient payments.
(D) Limited payments.
(E) Limited period of time.
(vi) Window programs – definition.
(10) Certain indemnification and liability insurance plans.
(11) Legal settlements.
(12) Certain educational benefits.
(c) Plan.
(1) In general.
(2) Plan aggregation rules.
(i) In general.
(ii) Dual status.
(3) Establishment of plan.
(i) In general.
(ii) Initial deferral election provisions.
(iii) Subsequent deferral election provisions.
(iv) Payment accelerations.
(v) Six-month delay for specified employees.
(vi) Plan amendments.
(vii) Transition rule for written plan requirement.
(viii) Plan aggregation rules.
(d) Substantial risk of forfeiture.
(1) In general.
(2) Stock rights.
(3) Enforcement of forfeiture condition.
(i) In general.
(ii) Examples.
(e) Performance-based compensation.
(1) In general.
(2) Payments based upon subjective performance criteria.
(3) Equity-based compensation.
(f) Service provider.
(1) In general.
(2) Independent contractors.
(i) In general.
(ii) Related person.
(iii) Significant services.
(iv) Management services.
(v) Services provided to related persons.
(g) Service recipient.
(h) Separation from service.
(1) Employees.
(i) In general.
(ii) Termination of employment.
(2) Independent contractors.
(i) In general.
(ii) Special rule.
(3) Definition of service recipient and employer.
(4) Asset purchase transactions.
(5) Dual status.
(6) Collectively bargained plans covering multiple employers.
(i) Specified employee.
(1) In general.
(2) Definition of compensation.
(3) Specified employee identification date.

(4) Specified employee effective date.
(5) Alternative methods of satisfying the six-month delay rule.
(6) Corporate transactions.
(i) Mergers and acquisitions of public service recipients.
(ii) Mergers and acquisitions of non-public service recipients.
(iii) Spinoffs.
(iv) Public offerings and other corporate transactions.
(v) Alternative methods of compliance.
(7) Nonresident alien employees.
(8) Elections affecting the identification of specified employees.
(j) Nonresident alien.
(k) Established securities market.
(l) Stock right.
(m) Separation pay plan.
(n) Involuntary separation from service.
(1) In general.
(2) Separations from service for good reason.
(i) In general.
(ii) Safe harbor.
(3) Special rule for certain collectively bargained plans.
(o) Earnings.
(p) In-kind benefits.
(q) Application of definitions and rules.

§1.409A–2 Deferral elections.

(a) Initial elections as to the time and form of payment.
(1) In general.
(2) Service recipient elections.
(3) General rule.
(4) Initial deferral election with respect to short-term deferrals.
(5) Initial deferral election with respect to certain forfeitable rights.
(6) Initial deferral election with respect to fiscal year compensation.
(7) First year of eligibility.
(i) In general.
(ii) Eligibility to participate.
(iii) Application to excess benefit plans.
(8) Initial deferral election with respect to performance-based compensation.
(9) Nonqualified deferred compensation plans linked to qualified employer plans or certain other arrangements.
(10) Changes in elections under a cafeteria plan.
(11) Initial deferral election with respect to certain separation pay.
(12) Initial deferral election with respect to certain commissions.
(i) Sales commission compensation.
(ii) Investment commission compensation.
(iii) Commission compensation and related persons.
(13) Initial deferral election with respect to compensation paid for final payroll period.
(i) In general.
(ii) Transition rule.
(14) Elections to annualize recurring part-year compensation.
(15) USERRA rights.
(b) Subsequent changes in time and form of payment.
(1) In general.
(2) Definition of payments for purposes of subsequent changes in the time and form of payment.
(i) In general.
(ii) Life annuities.
(A) In general.
(B) Certain features disregarded.
(C) Subsidized joint and survivor annuities.
(D) Actuarial assumptions and methods.
(iii) Installment payments.
(iv) Transition rule.
(3) Beneficiaries.
(4) Domestic relations orders.
(5) Coordination with prohibition against acceleration of payments.
(6) Application to multiple payment events.
(7) Delay of payments under certain circumstances.
(i) Payments subject to section 162(m).
(ii) Payments that would violate Federal securities laws or other applicable law.
(iii) Other events and conditions.
(8) USERRA rights.
(9) Examples.
(c) Special rules for certain resident aliens.

§1.409A–3 Permissible payments.

(a) In general.
(b) Designation of payment upon a permissible payment event.
(c) Designation of alternative specified dates or payment schedules based upon date of permissible event.
(d) When a payment is treated as made upon the designated payment date.
(e) Designation of time and form of payment with respect to earnings.
(f) Substitutions.
(g) Disputed payments and refusals to pay.
(h) Special rule for certain resident aliens.
(i) Definitions and special rules.
(1) Specified time or fixed schedule.
(i) In general.
(ii) Payment schedules with formula and fixed limitations.
(A) Individual limitations.
(B) Limitations on aggregate payments to all participants in substantially identical plans.
(iii) Payment schedules determined by timing of payments received by the service recipient.
(iv) Reimbursement or in-kind benefit plans.
(A) General rule.
(B) Medical reimbursement arrangements.
(v) Tax gross-up payments.
(vi) Examples.
(2) Separation from service—required delay in payment to a specified employee pursuant to a separation from service.
(i) In general.
(ii) Application of payment rules to delayed payments.
(3) Unforeseeable emergency.
(i) Definition.
(ii) Amount of payment permitted upon an unforeseeable emergency.
(iii) Payments due to an unforeseeable emergency.
(4) Disability.
(i) In general.
(ii) Limited plan definition of disability.
(iii) Determination of disability.
(5) Change in the ownership or effective control of a corporation, or a change in the ownership of a substantial portion of the assets of a corporation.
(i) In general.
(ii) Identification of relevant corporation.
(A) In general.
(B) Majority shareholder.
(C) Example.
(iii) Attribution of stock ownership.
(iv) Special rules for certain delayed payments pursuant to a change in control event.
(A) Certain transaction-based compensation.

(B) Certain nonvested compensation.
(v) Change in the ownership of a corporation.
(A) In general.
(B) Persons acting as a group.
(vi) Change in the effective control of a corporation.
(A) In general.
(B) Multiple change in control events.
(C) Acquisition of additional control.
(D) Persons acting as a group.
(vii) Change in the ownership of a substantial portion of a corporation's assets.
(A) In general.
(B) Transfers to a related person.
(C) Persons acting as a group.
(6) Certain back-to-back arrangements.
(i) In general.
(ii) Example.
(j) Prohibition on acceleration of payments.
(1) In general.
(2) Application to multiple payment events.
(3) Beneficiaries.
(4) Exceptions.
(i) In general.
(ii) Domestic relations order.
(iii) Conflicts of interest.
(A) Compliance with ethics agreements with the Federal government.
(B) Compliance with ethics laws or conflicts of interest laws.
(iv) Section 457 plans.
(v) Limited cashouts.
(vi) Payment of employment taxes.
(vii) Payment upon income inclusion under section 409A.
(viii) Cancellation of deferrals following an unforeseeable emergency or hardship distribution.
(ix) Plan terminations and liquidations.
(x) Certain distributions to avoid a nonallocation year under section 409(p).
(xi) Payment of state, local, or foreign taxes.
(xii) Cancellation of deferral elections due to disability.
(xiii) Certain offsets.
(xiv) *Bona fide* disputes as to a right to a payment.
(5) Nonqualified deferred compensation plans linked to qualified employer plans or certain other arrangements.
(6) Changes in elections under a cafeteria plan.

§1.409A–4 Calculation of income inclusion. [Reserved]

§1.409A–5 Funding. [Reserved]

§1.409A–6 Application of section 409A and effective dates.

(a) Statutory application and effective dates.
(1) Application to amounts deferred.
(i) In general.
(ii) Collectively bargained plans.
(2) Identification of date of deferral for statutory effective date purposes.
(3) Calculation of amount of compensation deferred for statutory effective date purposes.
(i) Nonaccount balance plans.
(ii) Account balance plans.
(iii) Equity-based compensation plans.
(iv) Earnings.
(v) Definition of plan.
(4) Material modifications.
(i) In general.
(ii) Adoptions of new plans.
(iii) Suspension or termination of a plan.
(iv) Changes to investment measures – account balance plans.
(v) Stock rights.
(vi) Rescission of modifications.
(vii) Definition of plan.
(b) Regulatory applicability date.

§1.409A–1 Definitions and covered plans.

(a) *Nonqualified deferred compensation plan*—(1) *In general.* Except as otherwise provided in this paragraph (a), the term *nonqualified deferred compensation plan* means any plan (within the meaning of paragraph (c) of this section) that provides for the deferral of compensation (within the meaning of paragraph (b) of this section). Whether a plan provides for the deferral of compensation generally is determined at the time the service provider obtains a legally binding right to the compensation under the plan, and is not affected by any retroactive change to the plan to characterize the right as one that does not provide for the deferral of compensation. For example, amounts deferred under a nonqualified deferred compensation plan do not become an excluded death benefit if the plan is amended so that the amounts are payable only upon the death of the service provider. If a principal purpose of a plan is to achieve a result with respect to a deferral of compensation that is inconsistent with the purposes of section 409A, the Commissioner may treat the plan as a nonqualified deferred compensation plan for purposes of section 409A and the regulations thereunder.

(2) *Qualified employer plans.* The term *nonqualified deferred compensation plan* does not include a qualified employer plan. The term *qualified employer plan* means any of the following plans:

(i) Any plan described in section 401(a) and a trust exempt from tax under section 501(a) or that is described in section 402(d).

(ii) Any annuity plan described in section 403(a).

(iii) Any annuity contract described in section 403(b).

(iv) Any simplified employee pension (within the meaning of section 408(k)).

(v) Any simple retirement account (within the meaning of section 408(p)).

(vi) Any plan under which an active participant makes deductible contributions to a trust described in section 501(c)(18).

(vii) Any eligible deferred compensation plan (within the meaning of section 457(b)).

(viii) Any plan described in section 415(m).

(ix) Any plan described in §1022(i)(2) of the Employee Retirement Income Security Act of 1974, Public Law 93–406 (88 Stat. 829, 942) (Sept. 2, 1974) (ERISA).

(3) *Certain foreign plans*—(i) *Participation addressed by treaty.* With respect to an individual for a taxable year, the term *nonqualified deferred compensation plan* does not include any scheme, trust, arrangement, or plan maintained with respect to such individual, to the extent contributions made by or on behalf of such individual to such scheme, trust, arrangement, or plan, or credited allocations, accrued benefits, earnings, or other amounts constituting income, of such individual under such scheme, trust, arrangement, or plan, are excludable by such individual for Federal income tax purposes pursuant to any bilateral income tax convention, or other bilateral or multilateral agreement, to which the United States is a party.

(ii) *Participation by nonresident aliens, certain resident aliens, and bona fide residents of possessions.* With respect to an alien individual for a taxable year during which such individual is a nonresident alien, a resident alien classified as a resident alien solely under section 7701(b)(1)(A)(ii) (and not section 7701(b)(1)(A)(i)), or a *bona fide* resident of a possession (within the meaning of section 937(a)), the term *nonqualified deferred compensation plan* does not include any broad-based foreign retirement plan (within the meaning of paragraph (a)(3)(v) of this section).

(iii) *Participation by U.S. citizens and lawful permanent residents.* With respect to an individual for a given taxable year during which such individual is a U.S. citizen or a resident alien classified as a resident alien under section 7701(b)(1)(A)(i), other than an individual who is also a *bona fide* resident of a possession (within the meaning of section 937(a)), the term *nonqualified deferred compensation plan* does not include a broad-based foreign retirement plan (within the meaning of paragraph (a)(3)(v) of this section), but only with respect to a plan, or a portion of a plan where such portion may be distinguished, providing for nonelective deferrals of modified foreign earned income, and earnings with respect to such nonelective deferrals, and only to the extent that the amounts deferred under all such plans of the service recipient, or all portions of such plans, in which the service provider participates in such taxable year, do not exceed the applicable limits under section 415(b) (applied to nonaccount balance plans as defined in paragraph (c)(2)(i)(C) of this section) and section 415(c) (applied to account balance plans as defined in paragraph (c)(2)(i)(A) of this section) that would be applicable if such plans were plans subject to section 415 and the modified foreign earned income of such individual were treated as compensation for purposes of applying section 415(b) and (c). For purposes of this paragraph (a)(3)(iii), the term *modified foreign earned income* means foreign earned income as defined in section 911(b)(1) without regard to section 911(b)(1)(B)(iv) and without regard to the requirement that the income be attributable to services performed during the period described in section 911(d)(1)(A) or (B). The provisions of this paragraph (a)(3)(iii) do not apply to any individual with respect to any taxable year in which the individual is simultaneously eligible to participate in a broad-based foreign retirement plan and a qualified employer plan described in paragraph (a)(2) of this section. For purposes of this paragraph (a)(3)(iii), an individual is eligible to participate in a qualified employer plan if under the terms of the plan and without further amendment or action by the plan sponsor, the individual is eligible to make or receive contributions or accrue benefits under the plan (regardless of whether the individual has elected to participate in the plan).

(iv) *Plans subject to a totalization agreement and similar plans.* The term *nonqualified deferred compensation plan* does not include any social security system of a jurisdiction to the extent that benefits provided under or contributions made to the system are subject to an agreement entered into pursuant to section 233 of the Social Security Act (42 U.S.C. 433) with any foreign jurisdiction. In addition, the term *nonqualified deferred compensation plan* does not include a social security system of a foreign jurisdiction to the extent that benefits are provided under or contributions are made to a government-mandated plan as part of that foreign jurisdiction's social security system.

(v) *Broad-based foreign retirement plan.* The term *broad-based foreign retirement plan* means a scheme, trust, arrangement, or plan (regardless of whether sponsored by a U.S. person) that is written and that, in the case of an employer-maintained plan, satisfies the following conditions:

(A) The plan is nondiscriminatory insofar as the employees who, under the terms of the plan (alone or in combination with other comparable plans) and without further amendment or action by the employer, are eligible to make or receive contributions or accrue benefits under the plan other than earnings (regardless of whether the employee has elected to participate in the plan), are a wide range of employees, substantially all of whom are nonresident aliens, resident aliens classified as resident aliens solely under section 7701(b)(1)(A)(ii) (and not section 7701(b)(1)(A)(i)), or *bona fide* residents of a possession (within the meaning of section 937(a)), including rank and file employees.

(B) The plan (alone or in combination with other comparable plans) actually provides significant benefits for a substantial majority of such covered employees.

(C) The benefits actually provided under the plan to such covered employees are nondiscriminatory.

(D) The plan contains provisions or is the subject of tax law provisions or other legal restrictions that generally discourage employees from using plan benefits for purposes other than retirement or restrict access to plan benefits before separation from service, including (but not limited to), restricting in-service distributions except in events similar to an unforeseeable emergency (as defined in §1.409A–3(i)(3)(i)) or hardship (as defined for purposes of section 401(k)(2)(B)(i)(IV)), or for educational purposes or the purchase of a primary residence.

(4) *Section 457 plans.* A nonqualified deferred compensation plan under section 457(f) may constitute a nonqualified deferred compensation plan for purposes of this paragraph (a). The rules of section 409A apply to nonqualified deferred compensation plans separately and in addition to any requirements applicable to such plans under section 457(f). In addition, nonelective deferred compensation of non-employees described in section 457(e)(12) and a grandfathered plan or arrangement described in §1.457–2(k)(4) may constitute a nonqualified deferred compensation plan for purposes of this paragraph (a). The term *nonqualified deferred compensation plan* does not include a length of service award to a *bona fide* volunteer under section 457(e)(11)(A)(ii). For purposes of the application of section 409A to a plan to which section 457 applies, a payment under the plan generally means the provision of cash or property to the service provider, provided that for purposes of the application of the short-term deferral rule set forth in paragraph (b)(4) of this section, the inclusion in income of an amount under section 457(f) is treated as a payment of the amount.

(5) *Certain welfare benefits.* The term *nonqualified deferred compensation plan* does not include a plan, or a portion of a plan, to the extent that the plan provides *bona fide* vacation leave, sick leave, compensatory time, disability pay, or death benefits. For these purposes, the term "disability pay" and "death benefits" have the same meanings as provided

in §31.3121(v)(2)–1(b)(4)(iv)(C) of this chapter, provided that for purposes of this paragraph, such disability pay and death benefits may be provided through insurance and the lifetime benefits payable under the plan are not treated as including the value of any taxable term life insurance coverage or taxable disability insurance coverage provided under the plan. The term *nonqualified deferred compensation plan* also does not include any Archer Medical Savings Account as described in section 220, any Health Savings Account as described in section 223, or any other medical reimbursement arrangement, including a health reimbursement arrangement, that satisfies the requirements of section 105 and section 106 such that the benefits or reimbursements provided under such arrangement are not includible in income.

(b) *Deferral of compensation*—(1) *In general*. Except as otherwise provided in paragraphs (b)(3) through (b)(12) of this section, a plan provides for the deferral of compensation if, under the terms of the plan and the relevant facts and circumstances, the service provider has a legally binding right during a taxable year to compensation that, pursuant to the terms of the plan, is or may be payable to (or on behalf of) the service provider in a later taxable year. Such compensation is deferred compensation for purposes of section 409A, this section and §§1.409A–2 through 1.409A–6. A legally binding right to an amount that will be excluded from income when and if received does not constitute a deferral of compensation, unless the service provider has received the right in exchange for, or has the right to exchange the right for, an amount that will be includible in income (other than due to participation in a cafeteria plan described in section 125). A service provider does not have a legally binding right to compensation to the extent that compensation may be reduced unilaterally or eliminated by the service recipient or other person after the services creating the right to the compensation have been performed. However, if the facts and circumstances indicate that the discretion to reduce or eliminate the compensation is available or exercisable only upon a condition, or the discretion to reduce or eliminate the compensation lacks substantive significance, a service provider will be considered to have a legally binding right to the compensation. Whether the discretion to reduce or eliminate the compensation lacks substantive significance depends on all the relevant facts and circumstances. However, where the service provider to whom the compensation may be paid has effective control of the person retaining the discretion to reduce or eliminate the compensation, or has effective control over any portion of the compensation of the person retaining the discretion to reduce or eliminate the compensation, or is a member of the family (as defined in section 267(c)(4) applied as if the family of an individual includes the spouse of any member of the family) of the person retaining the discretion to reduce or eliminate the compensation, the discretion to reduce or eliminate the compensation will not be treated as having substantive significance. For this purpose, compensation is not considered subject to unilateral reduction or elimination merely because it may be reduced or eliminated by operation of the objective terms of the plan, such as the application of a nondiscretionary, objective provision creating a substantial risk of forfeiture. Similarly, a service provider does not fail to have a legally binding right to compensation merely because the amount of compensation is determined under a formula that provides for benefits to be offset by benefits provided under another plan (including a plan that is qualified under section 401(a)), or because benefits are reduced due to actual or notional investment losses, or, in a final average pay plan, subsequent decreases in compensation.

(2) *Earnings*. References to the deferral of compensation or deferred compensation include references to earnings. When the right to earnings is specified under the terms of the plan, the legally binding right to earnings arises at the time of the deferral of the compensation to which the earnings relate. A plan may provide that the time and form of payment of earnings is treated separately from the time and form of payment of the underlying compensation, so that, provided that the rules of section 409A are otherwise met, a plan may provide that earnings will be paid at a separate time or in a separate form from the payment of the underlying compensation. For the application of the deferral election rules to current payments of earnings and dividend equivalents, see §1.409A–3(e).

(3) *Compensation payable pursuant to the service recipient's customary payment timing arrangement*. A deferral of compensation does not occur solely because compensation is paid after the last day of the service provider's taxable year pursuant to the timing arrangement under which the service recipient normally compensates service providers for services performed during a payroll period described in section 3401(b), or with respect to a non-employee service provider, a period not longer than the payroll period described in section 3401(b) or if no such payroll period exists, a period not longer than the earlier of the normal timing arrangement under which the service provider normally compensates non-employee service providers or 30 days after the end of the service provider's taxable year.

(4) *Short-term deferrals*—(i) *In general*. A deferral of compensation does not occur under a plan with respect to any payment (as defined in §1.409A–2(b)(2)) that is not a deferred payment, provided that the service provider actually or constructively receives such payment on or before the last day of the applicable 2½ month period. The following rules apply for purposes of this paragraph (b)(4)(i):

(A) The applicable 2½ month period is the period ending on the later of the 15th day of the third month following the end of the service provider's first taxable year in which the right to the payment is no longer subject to a substantial risk of forfeiture or the 15th day of the third month following the end of the service recipient's first taxable year in which the right to the payment is no longer subject to a substantial risk of forfeiture.

(B) A payment is treated as actually or constructively received if the payment is includible in income, including if the payment is includible in income under section 83, the economic benefit doctrine, section 402(b), or section 457(f).

(C) A right to a payment that is never subject to a substantial risk of forfeiture is considered to be no longer subject to a substantial risk of forfeiture on the first date the service provider has a legally binding right to the payment.

(D) A payment is a deferred payment if it is made pursuant to a provision of a plan that provides for the payment to be made or completed on or after any date, or upon or after the occurrence of any event, that will or may occur later than the end of the applicable $2^1/_2$ month period, such as a separation from service, death, disability, change in control event, specified time or schedule of payment, or unforeseeable emergency, regardless of whether an amount is actually paid as a result of the occurrence of such a payment date or event during the applicable $2^1/_2$ month period. If a plan provides that the service provider or service recipient may make an election under the plan (including an election under §1.409A–2(a)(4)) of a different payment date, schedule, or event, such right is disregarded for this purpose. In such cases, whether a plan provides for a deferred payment is determined based on the payment date, schedule, or event that would apply if no such election were made, except that if the plan would not provide for a deferred payment absent such an election, and the service provider or service recipient makes such an election, whether the plan provides for a deferred payment is determined based upon the payment date, schedule, or event that the service provider or service recipient in fact elected.

(E) A stock right provides for a deferred payment if such right includes any provision pursuant to which the holder of the stock right will or may have the right to exercise the stock right after the applicable $2^1/_2$ month period.

(F) This paragraph (b)(4)(i) is applied separately to each payment (as defined in §1.409A–2(b)(2)) required to be made under a plan.

(G) If a plan provides for a deferred payment with respect to part of a payment (for example a life annuity or a series of installment amounts treated as a single payment), the plan provides for a deferred payment with respect to the entire payment.

(ii) *Certain delayed payments*. A payment that otherwise qualifies as a short-term deferral under paragraph (b)(4)(i) of this section but is made after the applicable $2^1/_2$ month period may continue to qualify as a short-term deferral if the taxpayer establishes that it was administratively impracticable to make the payment by the end of the applicable $2^1/_2$ month period and, as of the date upon which the legally binding right to the compensation arose, such impracticability was unforeseeable, or the taxpayer establishes that making the payment by the end of the applicable $2^1/_2$ month period would have jeopardized the ability of the service recipient to continue as a going concern, and provided further that the payment is made as soon as administratively practicable or as soon as the payment would no longer have such effect. For purposes of this paragraph (b)(4)(ii), an action or failure to act of the service provider or a person under the service provider's control, such as a failure to provide necessary information or documentation, is not an unforeseeable event. In addition, a payment that otherwise qualifies as a short-term deferral under paragraph (b)(4)(i) of this section but is made after the applicable $2^1/_2$ month period may continue to qualify as a short-term deferral if the taxpayer establishes that the service recipient reasonably anticipated that the service recipient's deduction with respect to such payment otherwise would not be permitted by application of section 162(m), and, as of the date the legally binding right to the payment arose, a reasonable person would not have anticipated the application of section 162(m) at the time of the payment, and provided further that the payment is made as soon as reasonably practicable following the first date on which the service recipient anticipates or reasonably should anticipate that, if the payment were made on such date, the service recipient's deduction with respect to such payment would no longer be restricted due to the application of section 162(m). For additional rules applicable to certain transaction-based compensation, see §1.409A–3(i)(5)(iv)(A).

(iii) *Examples*. The following examples illustrate the provisions of this paragraph (b)(4). In these examples, except as otherwise noted, each employee and each employer has a calendar year taxable year and each employee is an individual who is employed by the specified employer.

Example 1. On November 1, 2008, Employer Z awards a bonus to Employee A such that Employee A has a legally binding right to the payment as of November 1, 2008, that is not subject to a substantial risk of forfeiture. The bonus plan does not provide for a payment date or a deferred payment. The bonus plan will not be considered to have provided for a deferral of compensation if the bonus is paid or made available to Employee A on or before March 15, 2009.

Example 2. Employer Y has a taxable year ending August 31. On November 1, 2008, Employer Y awards a bonus to Employee B so that Employee B has a legally binding right to the payment as of November 1, 2008, that is not subject to a substantial risk of forfeiture. The bonus plan does not provide for a payment date or a deferred payment. The bonus plan will not be considered to have provided for a deferral of compensation if the bonus is paid or made available to Employee B on or before November 15, 2009.

Example 3. On November 1, 2008, Employer X awards a bonus to Employee C such that Employee C has a legally binding right to the payment as of November 1, 2008. Under the bonus plan, Employee C will forfeit the bonus unless Employee C continues performing services through December 31, 2010. The right to the payment is subject to a substantial risk of forfeiture through December 31, 2010. Employee C has the right to make a written election not later than December 31, 2009, to receive the bonus on or after December 31, 2015, but Employee C does not make such election. The bonus plan does not provide for a default payment date or a deferred payment in the absence of an election by Employee C. The bonus plan will not be considered to have provided for a deferral of compensation if the bonus is paid or made available to Employee C on or before March 15, 2011.

Example 4. On November 1, 2008, Employer W awards a bonus to Employee D such that Employee D has a legally binding right to the payment as of November 1, 2008. Under the bonus plan, the bonus will be determined based on services performed during the period from January 1, 2009 through December 31, 2010. The bonus is scheduled to be paid as a lump sum payment on February 15, 2011. Under the bonus plan, Employee D will forfeit the bonus unless Employee D continues performing services through the scheduled payment date (February 15, 2011). Provided that at all times before the scheduled payment date Employee D is required to continue to perform services to retain the right to the bonus, and the bonus is paid on or before March 15, 2012, the bonus plan will not be considered to have provided for a deferral of compensation.

Example 5. On November 1, 2008, Employer V awards a bonus to Employee E such that Employee E has a legally binding right to the payment as of November 1, 2008. Under the bonus plan, Employee E will forfeit the bonus unless Employee E continues performing services through December 31, 2010. Under the bonus plan, the bonus is scheduled to be paid as a lump sum payment on July 1, 2011. By specifying a payment date after the applicable $2^1/_2$ month period, the bonus plan provides for a deferred payment. The bonus plan provides for a deferral of compensation, and will not qualify as a short-term deferral regardless of whether the bonus is paid or made available on or before March 15, 2011 (and generally any payment before June 1, 2011 would constitute an impermissible acceleration of a payment).

Example 6. On November 1, 2008, Employer U awards a bonus to Employee F such that Employee F has a legally binding right to the payment as of November 1, 2008, that is not subject to a substantial risk of forfeiture. The bonus plan provides for a lump sum payment upon Employee F's separation from service. Because the separation from service is an event that may occur after the applicable $2^1/_2$ month period, the bonus plan provides for a deferred payment and therefore provides for a deferral of compensation. Accordingly, the bonus plan will not qualify as a short-term deferral regardless of whether Employee F separates from service and the bonus is paid or made available on or before March 15, 2009.

Example 7. On November 1, 2008, Employer T grants Employee G a legally binding right to the payment of a life annuity with the first annuity payment on November 1, 2013, provided that Employee G continues performing services for Employer T continuously through November 1, 2013. Because the life annuity is treated as a single payment, and because all payments of the life annuity may not occur during the applicable 2½ month period, the plan provides for a deferred payment and none of the amounts payable under the annuity will qualify as a short-term deferral, so that section 409A applies to all amounts that are payable under the plan.

Example 8. On November 1, 2008, Employer S grants Employee H a stock right providing for an exercise price less than the fair market value of the underlying stock on November 1, 2008. The stock right is subject to a substantial risk of forfeiture requiring services through November 1, 2010. The stock right becomes exercisable when the substantial risk of forfeiture lapses and expires on November 1, 2013. Employee H continues providing services through November 1, 2010, at which time the substantial risk of forfeiture lapses. The stock right provides for a deferred payment and will not qualify as a short-term deferral regardless of whether Employee H exercises the stock right on or before March 15, 2011.

(5) *Stock options, stock appreciation rights, and other equity-based compensation*—(i) *Stock rights*—(A) *Nonstatutory stock options not providing for the deferral of compensation.* An option to purchase service recipient stock does not provide for a deferral of compensation if—

(*1*) The exercise price may never be less than the fair market value of the underlying stock (disregarding lapse restrictions as defined in §1.83–3(i)) on the date the option is granted and the number of shares subject to the option is fixed on the original date of grant of the option;

(*2*) The transfer or exercise of the option is subject to taxation under section 83 and §1.83–7; and

(*3*) The option does not include any feature for the deferral of compensation other than the deferral of recognition of income until the later of the following:

(*i*) The exercise or disposition of the option under §1.83–7.

(*ii*) The time the stock acquired pursuant to the exercise of the option first becomes substantially vested (as defined in §1.83–3(b)).

(B) *Stock appreciation rights not providing for the deferral of compensation.* A right to compensation based on the appreciation in value of a specified number of shares of service recipient stock occurring between the date of grant and the date of exercise of such right (a stock appreciation right) does not provide for a deferral of compensation if—

(*1*) Compensation payable under the stock appreciation right cannot be greater than the excess of the fair market value of the stock (disregarding lapse restrictions as defined in §1.83–3(i)) on the date the stock appreciation right is exercised over an amount specified on the date of grant of the stock appreciation right (the stock appreciation right exercise price), with respect to a number of shares fixed on or before the date of grant of the right;

(*2*) The stock appreciation right exercise price may never be less than the fair market value of the underlying stock (disregarding lapse restrictions as defined in §1.83–3(i)) on the date the right is granted; and

(*3*) The stock appreciation right does not include any feature for the deferral of compensation other than the deferral of recognition of income until the exercise of the stock appreciation right.

(C) *Stock rights that may provide for the deferral of compensation.* An option to purchase stock other than service recipient stock, or a stock appreciation right with respect to stock other than service recipient stock, generally will provide for the deferral of compensation within the meaning of this paragraph (b). If under the terms of an option to purchase service recipient stock (other than an incentive stock option described in section 422 or a stock option granted under an employee stock purchase plan described in section 423), the exercise price is or could become less than the fair market value of the stock (disregarding lapse restrictions as defined in §1.83–3(i)) on the date of grant, the grant of the option generally will provide for the deferral of compensation within the meaning of this paragraph (b). If under the terms of a stock appreciation right with respect to service recipient stock, the compensation payable under the stock appreciation right is or could be any amount greater than, with respect to a predetermined number of shares, the excess of the fair market value of the stock (disregarding lapse restrictions as defined in §1.83–3(i)) on the date the stock appreciation right is exercised over the fair market value of the stock (disregarding lapse restrictions as defined in §1.83–3(i)) on the date of grant of the stock appreciation right, the grant of the stock appreciation right generally will provide for a deferral of compensation within the meaning of this paragraph (b).

(D) *Feature for the deferral of compensation.* To the extent a stock right provides a right other than the right to receive cash or stock on the date of exercise and such additional right would otherwise allow compensation to be deferred beyond the date of exercise, the entire arrangement (including the underlying stock right) provides for the deferral of compensation. For purposes of this paragraph (b)(5)(i), neither the right to receive substantially nonvested stock (as defined in §1.83–3(b)) upon the exercise of a stock right, nor the right to pay the exercise price with previously acquired shares, constitutes a feature for the deferral of compensation.

(E) *Rights to dividends.* For purposes of this paragraph (b)(5)(i), the right, directly or indirectly contingent upon the exercise of a stock right, to receive an amount equal to all or part of the dividends or other distributions (other than stock dividends described in paragraph (b)(5)(v)(H) of this section) declared and paid on the number of shares underlying the stock right between the date of grant and the date of exercise of the stock right constitutes an offset to the exercise price of the stock option or an increase in the amount payable under the stock appreciation right (generally causing such stock right to be subject to section 409A). A plan providing a right to dividends or other distributions declared and paid on the number of shares underlying a stock right, the payment of which is not contingent upon, or otherwise payable on, the exercise of the stock right, may provide for a deferral of compensation, but the existence of the right to receive such an amount will not be treated as a reduction to the exercise price of (or an increase to the compensation payable under) the stock right. Thus, a right to such dividends or distributions that is not contingent, directly or indirectly, upon the exercise of a stock right will not cause the related stock right to fail to satisfy the requirements of the exclusion from the definition of a deferral of compensation provided in paragraphs (b)(5)(i)(A) and (B) of this section.

(ii) *Statutory stock options.* The grant of an incentive stock option as described in section 422, or the grant of an option under an employee stock purchase plan described in section 423 (including the grant of an option with an exercise price discounted in accordance with section 423(b)(6) and the accompanying regulations), does not constitute a deferral of compensation. However, the exclusion for statutory stock options under this paragraph (b)(5)(ii) does not apply to a modification, extension, or renewal of a statutory option that is treated as the grant of a new option that is not a statutory option. See §1.424–1(e). In such event, the option is treated for purposes of this paragraph (b) as if it had been a nonstatutory stock option from the date of the original grant. Accordingly, if such modification, extension, or renewal of the stock option would have been treated as the grant of a new option or as causing the option to have had a deferral feature from the date of grant under paragraph (b)(5)(v) of this section, the modification, extension, or renewal of the stock option is treated as the grant of a new option or as causing the option to have had a deferral feature from the date of grant for purposes of this paragraph (b)(5).

(iii) *Service recipient stock*—(A) *In general*. Except as otherwise provided in paragraphs (b)(5)(iii)(B), (C), and (D) of this section, the term *service recipient stock* means a class of stock that, as of the date of grant, is common stock for purposes of section 305 and the regulations thereunder of a corporation that is an eligible issuer of service recipient stock (as defined in paragraph (b)(5)(iii)(E) of this section). Notwithstanding the foregoing, the term *service recipient stock* does not include a class of stock that has any preference as to distributions other than distributions of service recipient stock and distributions in liquidation of the issuer. The term *service recipient stock* also does not include any stock that is subject to a mandatory repurchase obligation (other than a right of first refusal), or a put or call right that is not a lapse restriction as defined in §1.83–3(i), if the stock price under such right or obligation is based on a measure other than the fair market value (disregarding lapse restrictions as defined in §1.83–3(i)) of the equity interest in the corporation represented by the stock.

(B) *American depositary receipts*. An American depositary receipt or American depositary share may constitute service recipient stock, to the extent that the stock traded on a foreign securities market to which the American depositary receipt or American depositary share relates qualifies as service recipient stock.

(C) *Mutual company units*. Mutual company units may constitute service recipient stock. For this purpose, the term *mutual company unit* means a fixed percentage of the overall value of a non-stock mutual company or association. For purposes of determining the value of the mutual company unit, the unit may be valued in accordance with the rules set forth in paragraph (b)(5)(iv)(B) of this section governing valuation of service recipient stock the shares of which are not traded on an established securities market, applied as if the mutual company were a stock corporation with one class of common stock and the number of shares of such stock determined according to such fixed percentage. For example, an appreciation right based on the appreciation of 10 mutual company units, where each unit is defined as one percent of the overall value of the mutual company, would be valued as if the appreciation right were based upon 10 shares of a corporation, with 100 shares of common stock (and no other class of stock), the shares of which are not readily tradable on an established securities market.

(D) *Other entities*. An interest in an entity other than a corporation or non-stock mutual company or association may constitute service recipient stock to the extent designated by the Commissioner in revenue procedures, notices, or other guidance published in the Internal Revenue Bulletin (see §601.601(d)(2) of this chapter).

(E) *Eligible issuer of service recipient stock*—(*1*) *In general*. The term *eligible issuer of service recipient stock* means only the corporation for which the service provider provides direct services on the date of grant of the stock right (if the entity receiving such services is a corporation), and any corporation in a chain of corporations or other entities in which each corporation or other entity has a controlling interest in another corporation or other entity in the chain, ending with the corporation or other entity that has a controlling interest in the corporation or other entity for which the service provider provides direct services on the date of grant of the stock right. For this purpose, the term *controlling interest* has the same meaning as provided in §1.414(c)–2(b)(2)(i), provided that the language "at least 50 percent" is used instead of "at least 80 percent" each place it appears in §1.414(c)–2(b)(2)(i). In addition, where the use of such stock with respect to the grant of a stock right to such service provider is based upon legitimate business criteria, the term *controlling interest* has the same meaning as provided in §1.414(c)–2(b)(2)(i), provided that the language "at least 20 percent" is used instead of "at least 80 percent" each place it appears in §1.414(c)–2(b)(2)(i). For purposes of determining ownership of an interest in an organization, the rules of §§1.414(c)–3 and 1.414(c)–4 apply. The determination of whether a grant is based on legitimate business criteria is based on the facts and circumstances, focusing primarily on whether there is a sufficient nexus between the service provider and the issuer of the stock right so that the grant serves a legitimate non-tax business purpose other than simply providing compensation to the service provider that is excluded from the requirements of section 409A. For example, stock of a corporation that owns an interest in a joint venture involving an operating business, used with respect to stock rights granted to service providers of the joint venture who are former service providers of such corporation, generally will constitute use of service recipient stock based upon legitimate business criteria, and therefore could constitute service recipient stock with respect to such service providers if the corporation owns at least 20 percent of the joint venture and the other requirements of this paragraph (b)(5)(iii) are met. Similarly, the legitimate business criteria requirement generally would be met if the corporate venturer issued such a right to an employee of the joint venture who it reasonably expected would in the future become an employee of the corporate venturer. However, where a service provider has no real nexus with a corporate venturer, such as generally happens when the corporate venturer is a passive investor in the service recipient joint venture, a stock right issued to that employee on the investor corporation's stock generally would not be based upon legitimate business criteria. Similarly, where a corporation holds only a minority interest in an entity that in turn holds a minority interest in the entity for which the service provider performs services, such that the corporation holds only an insubstantial indirect interest in the entity receiving the services, legitimate business criteria generally would not exist for issuing a stock right on the corporation's stock to the service provider.

(*2*) *Investment vehicles.* Notwithstanding the provisions of paragraph (b)(5)(iii)(E)(*1*) of this section, except as to a service provider providing services directly to such corporation, for purposes of this paragraph (b)(5), an eligible issuer of service recipient stock does not include any corporation whose primary purpose is to serve as an investment vehicle with respect to the corporation's minority ownership interests in entities other than the service recipient.

(*3*) *Corporate structures established or transactions undertaken for purposes of avoiding coverage under section 409A.* Notwithstanding the provisions of paragraph (b)(5)(iii)(E)(*1*) of this section, an eligible issuer of service recipient stock does not include any corporation within a group of entities treated as a single service recipient if a purpose of the establishment of the structure of the ownership, or a purpose of a significant transaction between or among two or more entities comprising a single service recipient, is to provide deferred compensation not subject to the application of section 409A. If an entity becomes a member of a group of corporations or other entities treated as a single service recipient, and the primary source of income or value of such entity arises from the provision of management services to other members of the service recipient group, it is presumed that such structure was established for purposes of avoiding the application of section 409A if any stock rights are issued with respect to such entity.

(*4*) *Substitutions and assumptions by reason of a corporate transaction.* If the requirements of paragraph (b)(5)(v)(D) of this section are met such that the substitution of a new stock right pursuant to a corporate transaction for an outstanding stock right, or the assumption of an outstanding stock right pursuant to a corporate transaction, would not be treated as the grant of a new stock right or a change in the form of payment for purposes of this section and §§1.409A–2 through 1.409A–6, the stock underlying the stock right that replaced the stock right that is substituted or assumed will be treated as service recipient stock for purposes of applying this paragraph (b)(5) to the replacement stock rights if such underlying stock otherwise satisfies the requirements of paragraph (b)(5)(iii)(A) of this section. For example, if by reason of a spinoff transaction (under which the stock of a subsidiary corporation is distributed to the stockholders of a distributing corporation), a stock option to purchase distributing corporation stock is replaced with a stock option to purchase distributing corporation stock and a stock option to purchase the spun off subsidiary corporation's stock (each otherwise satisfying the requirements of paragraph (b)(5)(iii)(A) of this section), and where such substitution is not treated as a modification of the original stock option pursuant to paragraph (b)(5)(v)(D) of this section, both the distributing corporation stock and the subsidiary corporation stock are treated as service recipient stock for purposes of applying this paragraph (b)(5) to the replacement stock options.

(iv) *Determination of the fair market value of service recipient stock*—(A) *Stock readily tradable on an established securities market.* For purposes of paragraph (b)(5)(i) of this section, in the case of service recipient stock that is readily tradable on an established securities market, the fair market value of the stock may be determined based upon the last sale before or the first sale after the grant, the closing price on the trading day before or the trading day of the grant, the arithmetic mean of the high and low prices on the trading day before or the trading day of the grant, or any other reasonable method using actual transactions in such stock as reported by such market. The determination of fair market value also may be determined using an average selling price during a specified period that is within 30 days before or 30 days after the applicable valuation date, provided that the program under which the stock right is granted, including a program with a single participant, must irrevocably specify the commitment to grant the stock right with an exercise price set using such an average selling price before the beginning of the specified period. For this purpose, the term *average selling price* refers to the arithmetic mean of such selling prices on all trading days during the specified period, or the average of such prices over the specified period weighted based on the volume of trading of such stock on each trading day during such specified period. To satisfy this requirement, the service recipient must designate the recipient of the stock right, the number and class of shares of stock that are subject to the stock right, and the method for determining the exercise price including the period over which the averaging will occur, before the beginning of the specified averaging period. Notwithstanding the forgoing provisions of this paragraph (b)(5)(iv)(A), where applicable foreign law requires that a compensatory stock right be priced based upon a specific price averaging method and period, a stock right granted in accordance with such applicable foreign law will be treated as meeting the requirements of this paragraph (b)(5)(iv)(A), provided that the averaging period does not exceed 30 days.

(B) *Stock not readily tradable on an established securities market*—(*1*) *In general.* For purposes of paragraph (b)(5)(i) of this section, in the case of service recipient stock that is not readily tradable on an established securities market, the fair market value of the stock as of a valuation date means a value determined by the reasonable application of a reasonable valuation method. The determination whether a valuation method is reasonable, or whether an application of a valuation method is reasonable, is made based on the facts and circumstances as of the valuation date. Factors to be considered under a reasonable valuation method include, as applicable, the value of tangible and intangible assets of the corporation, the present value of anticipated future cash-flows of the corporation, the market value of stock or equity interests in similar corporations and other entities engaged in trades or businesses substantially similar to those engaged in by the corporation the stock of which is to be valued, the value of which can be readily determined through nondiscretionary, objective means (such as through trading prices on an established securities market or an amount paid in an arm's length private transaction), recent arm's length transactions involving the sale or transfer of such stock or equity interests, and other relevant factors such as control premiums or discounts for lack of marketability and whether the valuation method is used for other purposes that have a material economic effect on the service recipient, its stockholders, or its creditors. The use of a valuation method is not reasonable if such valuation method does not take into consideration in applying its methodology all available information material to the value of the corporation. Similarly, the use of a value previously calculated under a valuation method is not reasonable as of a later date if such calculation fails to reflect information available after the date of the calculation that may materially affect the value of the corporation (for example, the resolution of material litigation or the issuance of a patent) or the value was calculated with respect to a date that is more than 12 months earlier than the date for which the valuation is being used. The service recipient's consistent use of a valuation method to determine the value of its stock or assets for other purposes, including for purposes unrelated to compensation of service providers, is also a factor supporting the reasonableness of such valuation method.

(*2*) *Presumption of reasonableness*. For purposes of this paragraph (b)(5)(iv)(B), the use of any of the following methods of valuation is presumed to result in a reasonable valuation, provided that the Commissioner may rebut such a presumption upon a showing that either the valuation method or the application of such method was grossly unreasonable:

(*i*) A valuation of a class of stock determined by an independent appraisal that meets the requirements of section 401(a)(28)(C) and the regulations as of a date that is no more than 12 months before the relevant transaction to which the valuation is applied (for example, the date of grant of a stock option).

(*ii*) A valuation based upon a formula that, if used as part of a nonlapse restriction (as defined in §1.83–3(h)) with respect to the stock, would be considered to be the fair market value of the stock pursuant to §1.83–5, provided that such stock is valued in the same manner for purposes of any nonlapse restriction applicable to the transfer of any shares of such class of stock (or any substantially similar class of stock) to the issuer or any person that owns stock possessing more than 10 percent of the total combined voting power of all classes of stock of the issuer (applying the stock attribution rules of §1.424–1(d)), other than an arm's length transaction involving the sale of all or substantially all of the outstanding stock of the issuer, and such valuation method is used consistently for all such purposes, and provided further that this paragraph (b)(5)(iv)(B)(*2*)(*ii*) does not apply with respect to stock subject to a stock right payable in stock, where the stock acquired pursuant to the exercise of the stock right is transferable other than through the operation of a nonlapse restriction.

(*iii*) A valuation, made reasonably and in good faith and evidenced by a written report that takes into account the relevant factors described in paragraph (b)(5)(iv)(B)(*1*) of this section, of illiquid stock of a start-up corporation. For this purpose, illiquid stock of a start-up corporation means service recipient stock of a corporation that has no material trade or business that it or any predecessor to it has conducted for a period of 10 years or more and has no class of equity securities that are traded on an established securities market (as defined in paragraph (k) of this section), where such stock is not subject to any put, call, or other right or obligation of the service recipient or other person to purchase such stock (other than a right of first refusal upon an offer to purchase by a third party that is unrelated to the service recipient or service provider and other than a right or obligation that constitutes a lapse restriction as defined in §1.83–3(i)), and provided that this paragraph (b)(5)(iv)(B)(*2*)(*iii*) does not apply to the valuation of any stock if the service recipient or service provider may reasonably anticipate, as of the time the valuation is applied, that the service recipient will undergo a change in control event as described in §1.409A–3(i)(5)(v) or §1.409A–3(i)(5)(vii) within the 90 days following the action to which the valuation is applied, or make a public offering of securities within the 180 days following the action to which the valuation is applied. For purposes of this paragraph (b)(5)(iv)(B)(*2*)(*iii*), a valuation will not be treated as made reasonably and in good faith unless the valuation is performed by a person or persons that the corporation reasonably determines is qualified to perform such a valuation based on the person's or persons' significant knowledge, experience, education, or training. Generally, a person will be qualified to perform such a valuation if a reasonable individual, upon being apprised of such knowledge, experience, education, and training, would reasonably rely on the advice of such person with respect to valuation in deciding whether to accept an offer to purchase or sell the stock being valued. For this purpose, significant experience generally means at least five years of relevant experience in business valuation or appraisal, financial accounting, investment banking, private equity, secured lending, or other comparable experience in the line of business or industry in which the service recipient operates.

(*3*) *Use of alternative methods*. For purposes of this paragraph (b)(5), a different valuation method may be used for each separate action for which a valuation is relevant, provided that a single valuation method is used for each separate action and, once used, may not retroactively be altered. For example, one valuation method may be used to establish the exercise price of a stock option, and a different valuation method may be used to determine the value at the date of the repurchase of stock pursuant to a put or call right. However, once an exercise price or amount to be paid has been established, the exercise price or amount to be paid may not be changed through the retroactive use of another valuation method. In addition, notwithstanding the foregoing, where after the date of grant, but before the date of exercise or transfer, of the stock right, the service recipient stock to which the stock right relates becomes readily tradable on an established securities market, the service recipient must use the valuation method set forth in paragraph (b)(5)(iv)(A) of this section for purposes of determining the payment at the date of exercise or the purchase of the stock, as applicable.

(v) *Modifications, extensions, substitutions, and assumptions of stock rights*—(A) *Treatment of modified and extended stock rights*. A modification of the terms of a stock right within the meaning of paragraph (b)(5)(v)(B) of this section is considered to be the grant of a new stock right. The new stock right may or may not constitute a deferral of compensation under paragraph (b)(5)(i) of this section, determined at the date of grant of the new stock right. If there is an extension of a stock right (within the meaning of paragraph (b)(5)(v)(C) of this section), the stock right is treated as having had an additional deferral feature from the original date of grant of the stock right, and therefore will be treated as a plan providing for the deferral of compensation from the original grant date for purposes of this paragraph (b).

(B) *Modification in general.* Except as otherwise provided in paragraph (b)(5)(v) of this section, the term *modification* means any change in the terms of the stock right (or change in the terms of the plan pursuant to which the stock right was granted or in the terms of any other agreement governing the stock right) that may provide the holder of the stock right with a direct or indirect reduction in the exercise price of the stock right regardless of whether the holder in fact benefits from the change in terms. A change in the terms of the stock right shortening the period during which the stock right is exercisable is not a modification. It is not a modification to add a feature providing the ability to tender previously acquired stock for the stock purchasable under the stock right, or to withhold or have withheld shares of stock to facilitate the payment of the exercise price or the employment taxes or required withholding taxes resulting from the exercise of the stock right. In addition, it is not a modification for the grantor to exercise discretion specifically reserved under a stock right with respect to the transferability of the stock right.

(C) *Extensions—(1) In general.* An extension of a stock right refers to the provision to the holder of an additional period of time within which to exercise the stock right beyond the time originally prescribed under the terms of the stock right, the conversion or exchange of a stock right for a legally binding right to compensation in a future taxable year, or the addition of any feature for the deferral of compensation not permitted in paragraph (b)(5)(i)(A)(*3*) of this section (in the case of a stock option) or not permitted in paragraph (b)(5)(i)(B)(*3*) of this section (in the case of a stock appreciation right) to the terms of the stock right, other than at a time when the exercise price of the stock right equals or exceeds the fair market value of the service recipient stock that could be purchased (in the case of an option) or the fair market value of the service recipient stock used to determine the payment to the service provider (in the case of a stock appreciation right), and includes a renewal of such right that has such effect. It is not an extension if the exercise period of a stock right is extended to a date no later than the earlier of the latest date upon which the stock right could have expired by its original terms under any circumstances or the 10th anniversary of the original date of grant of the stock right. If the exercise period of a stock right is extended at a time when the exercise price of the stock right equals or exceeds the fair market value of the service recipient stock that could be purchased (in the case of an option) or the fair market value of the service recipient stock used to determine the payment to the service provider (in the case of a stock appreciation right), it is not an extension of the original stock right. Instead, in such a case, the original stock right is treated as modified rather than extended and a new stock right is treated as having been granted for purposes of this section. In addition, it is not an extension of a stock right if the expiration of the stock right is tolled while the holder cannot exercise the stock right because such an exercise would violate an applicable Federal, state, local, or foreign law, or would jeopardize the ability of the service recipient to continue as a going concern, provided that the period during which the stock right may be exercised is not extended more than 30 days after the exercise of the stock right first would no longer violate an applicable Federal, state, local, and foreign laws or would first no longer jeopardize the ability of the service recipient to continue as a going concern. For this purpose, a provision of foreign law shall be considered applicable only to foreign earned income (as defined under section 911(b)(1) without regard to section 911(b)(1)(B)(iv) and without regard to the requirement that the income be attributable to services performed during the period described in section 911(d)(1)(A) or (B)) from sources within the foreign country that promulgated such law.

(*2*) *Certain extensions before April 10, 2007.* An extension of a stock right before April 10, 2007, solely in order to provide the holder of such stock right an additional period of time beyond the time originally prescribed under the terms of such stock right within which to exercise the stock right is disregarded for purposes of applying the rules contained in paragraph (b)(5)(v)(C)(*1*) of this section. For purposes of applying the rules contained in paragraph (b)(5)(v)(C)(*1*) of this section on and after April 10, 2007, such a stock right is treated as having specified at the date of grant the time within which to exercise such stock right that was prescribed under the terms of such stock right in effect on April 9, 2007. Nothing in this paragraph (b)(5)(v)(C)(*2*) affects any other action treated as the extension of a stock right, including the addition of a deferral feature.

(*3*) *Examples.* The following examples illustrate the provisions of this paragraph (b)(5)(v)(C). In the examples, each employee is an individual employed by the specified employer, and each employee and each employer has a calendar year taxable year.

Example 1. On July 1, 2009, Employer Z grants Employee A a nonstatutory stock option that does not provide for the deferral of compensation in accordance with paragraph (b)(5)(i)(A) of this section. The terms of the nonstatutory stock option provide that the exercise period of the stock option expires on the earlier of July 1, 2019, or 3 months after Employee A's separation from service. On July 1, 2011, Employee A separates from service. On the same day, Employee A and Employer Z change the exercise period of the option so that it expires on July 1, 2013. Because the exercise period of the stock right is not extended beyond July 1, 2019, the change is not an extension for purposes of this paragraph (b)(5)(v)(C).

Example 2. The facts are the same as in *Example 1* except that Employee A separates from service on July 1, 2018, and on the same day, Employee A and Employer Z change the exercise period of the option so that it expires on July 1, 2020. As of July 1, 2018, the fair market value of the underlying stock exceeds the exercise price. Because the exercise period of the stock right is extended beyond July 1, 2019, the change is an extension for purposes of this paragraph (b)(5)(v)(C).

Example 3. The facts are the same as in *Example 2* except that as of July 1, 2018, the fair market value of the underlying stock is less than the exercise price of the option. Because the exercise period of the stock right is extended at a time when the fair market value of the underlying stock is less than the exercise price, the change is not an extension for purposes of this paragraph (b)(5)(v)(C) and the change is treated as a modification of the option, resulting in the extension of the exercise period being treated as the grant of a new option on July 1, 2018.

Example 4. On July 1, 2009, Employer Y grants to Employee B a stock appreciation right with respect to 200 shares of Employer Y common stock that does not provide for the deferral of compensation in accordance with paragraph (b)(5)(i)(B) of this section. Upon exercise of the stock appreciation right, Employee B is entitled to receive the excess of the fair market value of a share of Employer Y common stock on the date of exercise over $100 (the fair market value of a share of Employer Y common stock on July 1, 2009), multiplied by the number of shares with respect to which Employee B is exercising the right. The exercise period of the right expires on the earlier of July 1, 2019, or 3 months after Employee B separates from service. Employee B cannot exercise the stock appreciation right with respect to more than 100 shares unless Employee B continues to be employed by Employer Y through June 30, 2014. On July 1, 2011, when the fair market value of a share of Employer Y common stock is $200, Employee B and Employer Y amend the stock appreciation right to provide that the right will be exercisable only during calendar year 2018, except that before January 1, 2017, Employee B may elect to designate calendar year 2023 or any subsequent calendar year before 2033 as the year in which the right will be exercisable. The amendment constitutes an extension of the stock appreciation right under paragraph (b)(5)(v)(C)(*1*) of this section. Under paragraph (b)(5)(v)(A) of this section, the stock appreciation right is treated as having had an additional deferral feature from the original date of grant (July 1, 2009) of the right, and therefore is treated as a plan providing for the deferral of compensation from that date. During the period from July 1, 2009, through June 30, 2011, the provisions of the stock appreciation right relating to the time and form of payment did not satisfy the requirements of §1.409A–3(a). Therefore, the stock appreciation right provides for a deferral of compensation that does not comply with section 409A.

(D) *Substitutions and assumptions of stock rights by reason of a corporate transaction.* If the requirements of §1.424–1 (without regard to the requirement described in §1.424–1(a)(2) that an eligible corporation be the employer of the optionee) would be met if the stock right were a statutory option, the substitution of a new stock right pursuant to a corporate transaction (as defined in §1.424–1(a)(3)) for an outstanding stock right or the assumption of an outstanding stock right pursuant to a corporate transaction will not be treated as the grant of a new stock right or a change in the form of payment for purposes of this section and §§1.409A–2 through 1.409A–6. For purposes of the preceding sentence, the requirement of §1.424–1(a)(5)(iii) will be deemed to be satisfied if the ratio of the exercise price to the fair market value of the shares subject to the stock right immediately after the substitution or assumption is not greater than the ratio of the exercise price to the fair market value of the shares subject to the stock right immediately before the substitution or assumption. In the case of a transaction described in section 355 in which the stock of the distributing corporation and the stock distributed in the transaction are both readily tradable on an established securities market immediately after the transaction, for purposes of this paragraph (b)(5)(v), the requirements of §1.424–1(a)(5) related to the fair market value of the stock may be satisfied by—

(*1*) Using the last sale before or the first sale after the specified date as of which such valuation is being made, the closing price on the last trading day before or the trading day of a specified date, the arithmetic mean of the high and low prices on the last trading day before or the trading day of such specified date, or any other reasonable method using actual transactions in such stock as reported by such market on a specified date, for the stock of the distributing corporation and the stock distributed in the transaction, provided the specified date is designated before such specified date, and such specified date is not more than 60 days after the transaction;

(*2*) Using the arithmetic mean of such market prices on trading days during a specified period designated before the beginning of such specified period, where such specified period is not longer than 30 days and ends no later than 60 days after the transaction; or

(*3*) Using an average of such prices during such prespecified period weighted based on the volume of trading of such stock on each trading day during such prespecified period.

(E) *Acceleration of date when exercisable.* Although with respect to a stock right not immediately exercisable in full, a change in the terms of the right solely to accelerate or delay, within the original term of the stock right, the time at which the stock right (or any portion of such stock right) may be exercised is not a modification for purposes of this section, with respect to a stock right subject to section 409A, such an acceleration may constitute an impermissible acceleration of a payment date under §1.409A–3(j) or a subsequent deferral under §1.409A–2(b).

(F) *Discretionary added benefits.* If a change to a stock right provides, either by its terms or in substance, that the holder may receive an additional benefit under the stock right at the future discretion of the grantor, and the addition of such benefit would constitute a modification or extension, then the addition of such discretion is a modification or extension at the time that the stock right is changed to provide such discretion.

(G) *Change in underlying stock increasing value.* A change in the terms of the stock subject to a stock right that increases the value of the stock is a modification of such stock right, except to the extent that a new stock right is substituted for such stock right by reason of the change in the terms of the stock in accordance with paragraph (b)(5)(v)(D) of this section.

(H) *Change in the number of shares purchasable.* If a stock right is amended solely to increase the number of shares subject to the stock right, the increase is not considered a modification of the stock right but is treated as the grant of a new additional stock right to which the additional shares are subject. Notwithstanding the previous sentence, if the exercise price and number of shares subject to a stock right are proportionally adjusted to reflect a stock split (including a reverse stock split) or stock dividend, and the only effect of the stock split or stock dividend is to increase (or decrease) on a *pro rata* basis the number of shares owned by each shareholder of the class of stock subject to the stock right, then there is no modification of the stock right if it is proportionally adjusted to reflect the stock split or stock dividend and the aggregate exercise price of the stock right is not less than the aggregate exercise price before the stock split or stock dividend.

(I) *Rescission of changes.* A change to the terms of a stock right (or change in the terms of the plan pursuant to which the stock right was granted or in the terms of any other agreement governing the right) is not considered a modification or extension of the stock right to the extent the change in the terms of the stock right is rescinded by the earlier of the date the stock right is exercised or the last day of the service provider's taxable year during which such change occurred. Thus, for example, if the terms of a stock right granted to an individual employee with a calendar year taxable year are changed on March 1 in a manner that would result in an extension of the stock right, and the change is rescinded on November 1 of the same year, and the stock right is not exercised before the change is rescinded, the stock right is not considered extended under this paragraph (b)(5)(v).

(J) *Successive modifications and extensions.* The rules of this paragraph (b)(5)(v) apply as well to successive modifications and extensions.

(K) *Modifications and extensions in effect on October 23, 2004.* For purposes of the application of section 409A and these regulations to a stock right, if a legally binding right to a modification or extension of such stock right existed on October 23, 2004, such modification or extension is disregarded, and the stock right is treated as if granted with the terms and conditions in effect on October 23, 2004.

(vi) *Meaning and use of certain terms*—(A) *Option*. The term *option* means the right or privilege of an individual to purchase stock from a corporation by virtue of an offer of the corporation continuing for a stated period of time, whether or not irrevocable, to sell such stock at a price determined under paragraph (b)(5)(vi)(D) of this section, such individual being under no obligation to purchase. While no particular form of words is necessary, the option must express an offer to sell at the option price, the maximum number of shares purchasable under the option, and the period of time during which the offer remains open. The term *option* includes a warrant that meets the requirements of this paragraph (b)(5)(vi)(A). An option may be granted as part of or in conjunction with an employee stock purchase plan or subscription contract. An option must be in writing (in paper or electronic form) provided that such writing is adequate to establish an option right or privilege that is enforceable under applicable law.

(B) *Date of grant of option*. (*1*) The language the *date of grant of the option*, and similar phrases, refer to the date when the granting corporation completes the corporate action necessary to create the legally binding right constituting the option. A corporate action creating the legally binding right constituting the option is not considered complete until the date on which the maximum number of shares that can be purchased under the option and the minimum exercise price are fixed or determinable, and the class of underlying stock and the identity of the service provider is designated. Ordinarily, if the corporate action provides for an immediate offer of stock for sale to a service provider, or provides for a particular date on which such offer is to be made, the date of the granting of the option is the date of such corporate action if the offer is to be made immediately, or the date provided as the date of the offer, as the case may be. However, an unreasonable delay in the giving of notice of such offer to the service provider will be taken into account as indicating that the corporation provided that the offer was to be made at the subsequent date on which such notice is given.

(*2*) If the corporation imposes a condition on the granting of an option (as distinguished from a condition governing the exercise of the option), such condition generally will be given effect in accordance with the intent of the corporation. However, if the grant of an option is subject to approval by stockholders, the date of grant of the option will be determined as if the option had not been subject to such approval. A condition that does not require corporate action, such as the approval of, or registration with, some regulatory or government agency, for example, a stock exchange or the Securities and Exchange Commission, is ordinarily considered a condition upon the exercise of the option unless the corporate action clearly indicates that the option is not to be granted until such condition has been satisfied.

(*3*) In general, a condition imposed upon the exercise of an option will not operate to make ineffective the granting of the option. For example, on June 1, 2008, Corporation A grants to X, an employee, an option to purchase 5,000 shares of the corporation's common stock, exercisable by X on or after June 1, 2009, provided X is employed by the corporation on June 1, 2009, and provided that A's profits during the fiscal year preceding the year of exercise exceed $200,000. Such an option is granted to X on June 1, 2008, and will be treated as outstanding as of such date.

(C) *Stock*. The term *stock* means capital stock of any class, including voting or nonvoting common or preferred stock. Except as otherwise provided, the term stock includes both treasury stock and stock of original issue. Special classes of stock authorized to be issued to and held by employees are within the scope of the term stock for this purpose, provided such stock otherwise possesses the rights and characteristics of capital stock.

(D) *Exercise price*. The term *exercise price* means the consideration in cash or property that, pursuant to the terms of the option, is the price at which the stock subject to the option is purchased. The term *exercise price* does not include any amounts paid as interest under a deferred payment plan or treated as interest.

(E) *Exercise*. The term *exercise*, when used in reference to an option, means the act of acceptance by the holder of the option of the offer to sell contained in the option. In general, the time of exercise is the time when there is a sale or a contract to sell between the corporation and the individual. A promise to pay the exercise price does not constitute an exercise of the option unless the holder of the option is subject to personal liability on such promise. An agreement or undertaking by the service provider to make payments under a stock purchase plan does not constitute the exercise of an option to the extent the payments made remain subject to withdrawal by or refund to the service provider.

(F) *Transfer*. The term *transfer*, when used in reference to the transfer to an individual of a share of stock pursuant to the exercise of an option, means the transfer of ownership of such share, or the transfer of substantially all the rights of ownership. Such transfer must, within a reasonable time, be evidenced on the books of the corporation. A transfer may occur even if a share of stock is subject to a substantial risk of forfeiture or is not otherwise transferable immediately after the date of exercise. A transfer does not fail to occur merely because, under the terms of the arrangement, the individual may not dispose of the share for a specified period of time, or the share is subject to a right of first refusal or a right to acquire the share at the share's fair market value at the time of the sale.

(G) *Readily tradable*. For purposes of this section and §§1.409A–2 through 1.409A–6, stock is treated as readily tradable if it is regularly quoted by brokers or dealers making a market in such stock.

(H) *Application to stock appreciation rights*. For purposes of this section and §§1.409A–2 through 1.409A–6, the definitions provided in paragraphs (b)(5)(vi)(A) through (G) of this section may be applied by analogy to the issuance of, exercise of, or payment upon the exercise of, a stock appreciation right.

(6) *Restricted property, section 402(b) trusts, and section 403(c) annuities*—(i) *In general*. If a service provider receives property from, or pursuant to, a plan maintained by a service recipient, there is no deferral of compensation merely because the value of the property is not includible in income by reason of the property being substantially nonvested (as defined in §1.83–3(b)), or is includible in income

solely due to a valid election under section 83(b). For purposes of this paragraph (b)(6)(i), a transfer of property includes the transfer of a beneficial interest in a trust or annuity plan, or a transfer to or from a trust or under an annuity plan, to the extent such a transfer is subject to section 83, section 402(b) or section 403(c). In addition, for purposes of this paragraph (b), a right to compensation income that will be required to be included in income under section 402(b)(4)(A) is not a deferral of compensation.

(ii) *Promises to transfer property*. A plan under which a service provider obtains a legally binding right to receive property in a future taxable year where the property will be substantially vested (as defined in §1.83–3(b)) at the time of transfer of the property may provide for the deferral of compensation and, accordingly, may constitute a nonqualified deferred compensation plan. A legally binding right to receive property in a future taxable year where the property will be substantially nonvested (as defined in §1.83–3(b)) at the time of transfer of the property will not provide for the deferral of compensation and, accordingly, will not constitute a nonqualified deferred compensation plan unless offered in conjunction with another legally binding right that constitutes a deferral of compensation.

(7) *Arrangements between partnerships and partners*. [Reserved.]

(8) *Certain foreign plans*—(i) *Plans with respect to compensation covered by treaty or other international agreement*. A plan in which a service provider participates does not provide for a deferral of compensation for purposes of this paragraph (b) to the extent that the compensation under the plan would have been excluded from gross income for Federal income tax purposes under the provisions of any bilateral income tax convention or other bilateral or multilateral agreement to which the United States is a party if the compensation had been paid to the service provider at the time that the legally binding right to the compensation first arose or, if later, the time that the legally binding right was no longer subject to a substantial risk of forfeiture.

(ii) *Plans with respect to certain other compensation*. A plan in which a service provider participates does not provide for a deferral of compensation for purposes of this paragraph (b) to the extent that compensation under the plan would not have been includible in gross income for Federal tax purposes if it had been paid to the service provider at the time that the legally binding right to the compensation first arose or, if later, the time that the legally binding right was no longer subject to a substantial risk of forfeiture, due to one of the following:

(A) The service provider was a nonresident alien at such time and the compensation would not have been includible in gross income under section 872.

(B) The service provider was a qualified individual (as defined in section 911(d)(1)) at such time, the compensation would have been foreign earned income within the meaning of section 911(b)(1) (without regard to section 911(b)(1)(B)(iv)) if paid at such time, and the amount of such compensation was equal to or less than the excess (if any) of the maximum exclusion amount under section 911(b)(2)(D) for such taxable year over the amount of foreign earned income actually excluded from gross income by such qualified individual for such taxable year under section 911(a)(1).

(C) The compensation would have been excludible from gross income under section 893.

(D) The compensation would have been excludible from gross income under section 931 or section 933.

(iii) *Tax equalization agreements*. A tax equalization agreement does not provide for a deferral of compensation if payments made under such tax equalization agreement are made no later than the end of the second taxable year of the service provider beginning after the taxable year of the service provider in which the service provider's U.S. Federal income tax return is required to be filed (including any extensions) for the year to which the compensation subject to the tax equalization payment relates, or, if later, the second taxable year of the service provider beginning after the latest such taxable year in which the service provider's foreign tax return or payment is required to be filed or made for the year to which the compensation subject to the tax equalization payment relates. Where such payments arise due to an audit, litigation or similar proceeding, the right to the payments will not be treated as resulting in a deferral of compensation if the payments are scheduled and made in accordance with the provisions of §1.409A–3(i)(1)(v) (timing of tax gross-up payments). For purposes of this paragraph (b)(8)(iii), the term *tax equalization agreement* refers to an agreement, method, program, or other arrangement that provides payments intended to compensate the service provider for some or all of the excess of the taxes actually imposed by a foreign jurisdiction on the compensation paid by the service recipient to the service provider over the taxes that would be imposed if the compensation were subject solely to United States Federal, state, and local income tax, or some or all of the excess of the United States Federal, state, and local income tax actually imposed on the compensation paid by the service to the service provider over the taxes that would be imposed if the compensation were subject solely to taxes in the foreign jurisdiction, provided that the payment made under such agreement, method, program, or other arrangement may not exceed such excess and the amount necessary to compensate for the additional taxes on the amount paid under the agreement, method, program, or other arrangement.

(iv) *Certain limited deferrals of a nonresident alien*. With respect to a nonresident alien, a foreign plan does not provide for a deferral of compensation if the amounts deferred under the foreign plan based upon services performed by the nonresident alien in the United States (including amounts deferred based upon service credits or compensation received due to services performed in the United States) do not exceed the applicable dollar amount under section 402(g)(1)(B) for the taxable year. If the amounts deferred under the foreign plan based upon the services performed by the nonresident alien in the United States exceed the applicable dollar amount, an amount of such deferrals equal to such amount is treated as not deferred under a nonqualified deferred compensation plan. For purposes of this paragraph (b)(8)(iv), the term *foreign plan* means a plan that, together with all substantially similar plans, is maintained by a service recipient for a substantial number of participants, substantially all of whom are nonresident aliens or resident aliens classified as resident aliens solely under section 7701(b)(1)(A)(ii) (and not section 7701(b)(1)(A)(i)).

(v) *Additional foreign plans.* A plan in which a service provider participates does not provide for a deferral of compensation for purposes of this paragraph (b) to the extent designated by the Commissioner in revenue procedures, notices, or other guidance published in the Internal Revenue Bulletin (see §601.601(d)(2) of this chapter).

(vi) *Earnings.* Earnings on compensation excluded from the definition of deferral of compensation pursuant to this paragraph (b)(8) are also not treated as a deferral of compensation.

(9) *Separation pay plans*—(i) *In general.* A plan that otherwise provides for a deferral of compensation under this paragraph (b) does not fail to provide a deferral of compensation merely because the right to payment of the compensation is conditioned upon a separation from service. However, paragraphs (b)(9)(ii), (iii), (iv), and (v) of this section provide rules concerning the extent to which certain separation pay plans do not provide for the deferral of compensation. The exceptions contained in paragraphs (b)(9)(ii), (iii), (iv), and (v) of this section may be used in combination, such that compensation under a plan that would be excepted under one of those paragraphs may be treated as excepted under another of those paragraphs, so that other compensation under a plan may be treated as excepted under the first of such paragraphs. Notwithstanding any other provision of this paragraph (b)(9), any payment or benefit, or entitlement to a payment or benefit, that acts as a substitute for, or replacement of, amounts deferred by the service recipient under a separate nonqualified deferred compensation plan constitutes a payment or a deferral of compensation under the separate nonqualified deferred compensation plan, and does not constitute a payment or deferral of compensation under a separation pay plan. If a service provider receives a payment at separation from service and also has a legally binding right to an amount of deferred compensation that would be forfeited upon the separation from service, whether the payment acts as an acceleration of vesting and substitute payment for the amount of deferred compensation forfeited, or whether the deferred compensation is treated as forfeited and the amount paid is treated as a separate payment of current compensation, is determined based on the facts and circumstances, provided that, where the separation from service is voluntary, it is presumed that the payment results from an acceleration of vesting followed by a payment of the deferred compensation that is subject to section 409A. Accordingly, any change in the payment schedule to accelerate or defer the payments would be subject to the rules of section 409A. The presumption that a right to a payment is not a new right, but is instead a right substituted for a pre-existing forfeited right, may be rebutted by demonstrating that the service provider would have obtained the right to the payment regardless of the forfeiture of the nonvested right. A factor indicating that the service provider would have obtained a right to a payment regardless of the forfeiture of the nonvested right is that the amount to which the service provider obtains a right is materially less than an amount equal to the present value of the forfeited amount multiplied by a fraction, the numerator of which is the period of service the service provider actually completed, and the denominator of which is the full period of service the service provider would have been required to complete to receive the full amount of the payment. For example, where a service provider is entitled to a future payment only if the service provider completes three years of service and at the time of termination the service provider has completed one year of service, the presumption could be rebutted if the payment to the service provider is materially less than the present value of one-third of the nonvested amount. Another such factor is that the payment to the service provider is of a type customarily made to service providers who separate from service with the service recipient and do not forfeit nonvested rights to deferred compensation (for example, a payment of accrued but unused leave or a payment for a release of actual or potential claims).

(ii) *Collectively bargained separation pay plans.* A separation pay plan does not provide for a deferral of compensation to the extent the plan is a collectively bargained separation pay plan that provides for separation pay only upon an involuntary separation from service or pursuant to a window program. Only the portion of the separation pay plan attributable to employees covered by a *bona fide* collective bargaining agreement is considered to be provided under a collectively bargained separation pay plan. A collectively bargained separation pay plan is a separation pay plan that meets the following conditions:

(A) The separation pay plan is contained within an agreement that the Secretary of Labor determines to be a collective bargaining agreement.

(B) The separation pay provided by the collective bargaining agreement was the subject of arm's length negotiations between employee representatives and one or more employers, and the agreement between employee representatives and one or more employers satisfies section 7701(a)(46).

(C) The circumstances surrounding the agreement evidence good faith bargaining between adverse parties over the separation pay to be provided under the agreement.

(iii) *Separation pay due to involuntary separation from service or participation in a window program.* A separation pay plan that is not described in paragraph (b)(9)(ii) of this section and that provides for separation pay only upon an involuntary separation from service (as defined in paragraph (n) of this section) or pursuant to a window program does not provide for a deferral of compensation to the extent that the separation pay, or portion of the separation pay, provided under the plan meets the following requirements:

(A) The separation pay (other than amounts described in paragraphs (b)(9)(iv) and (v) of this section) does not exceed two times the lesser of—

(*1*) The sum of the service provider's annualized compensation based upon the annual rate of pay for services provided to the service recipient for the taxable year of the service provider preceding the taxable year of the service provider in which the service provider has a separation from service with such service recipient (adjusted for any increase during that year that was expected to continue indefinitely if the service provider had not separated from service); or

(*2*) The maximum amount that may be taken into account under a qualified plan pursuant to section 401(a)(17) for the year in which the service provider has a separation from service.

(B) The plan provides that the separation pay described in paragraph (b)(9)(iii)(A) of this section must be paid no later than the last day of the second taxable year of the service provider following the taxable year of the service provider in which occurs the separation from service.

(iv) *Foreign separation pay plans.* A separation pay plan (including a plan providing payments upon a voluntary separation from service) does not provide for deferred compensation to the extent the plan provides for amounts of separation pay required to be provided under the applicable law of a foreign jurisdiction. For this purpose, a provision of foreign law shall be considered applicable only to foreign earned income (as defined under section 911(b)(1) without regard to section 911(b)(1)(B)(iv) and without regard to the requirement that the income be attributable to services performed during the period described in section 911(d)(1)(A) or (B)) from sources within the foreign country that promulgated such law.

(v) *Reimbursements and certain other separation payments*—(A) *In general.* To the extent a separation pay plan (including a plan providing payments upon a voluntary separation from service) entitles a service provider to payment by the service recipient of reimbursements that are not otherwise excludible from gross income, for expenses that the service provider could otherwise deduct under section 162 or section 167 as business expenses incurred in connection with the performance of services (ignoring any applicable limitation based on adjusted gross income), or of reasonable outplacement expenses and reasonable moving expenses actually incurred by the service provider and directly related to the termination of services for the service recipient, such plan does not provide for a deferral of compensation to the extent such rights apply during a limited period of time (regardless of whether such rights extend beyond the limited period of time). For purposes of this paragraph (b)(9)(v)(A), the reimbursement of reasonable moving expenses includes the reimbursement of all or part of any loss the service provider actually incurs due to the sale of a primary residence in connection with a separation from service.

(B) *Medical benefits.* To the extent a separation pay plan (including a plan providing payments due to a voluntary separation from service) entitles a service provider to reimbursement by the service recipient of payments of medical expenses incurred and paid by the service provider but not reimbursed by a person other than the service recipient and allowable as a deduction under section 213 (disregarding the requirement of section 213(a) that the deduction is available only to the extent that such expenses exceed 7.5 percent of adjusted gross income), such plan does not provide for a deferral of compensation to the extent such rights apply during the period of time during which the service provider would be entitled (or would, but for such plan, be entitled) to continuation coverage under a group health plan of the service recipient under section 4980B (COBRA) if the service provider elected such coverage and paid the applicable premiums.

(C) *In-kind benefits and direct service recipient payments.* A service provider's entitlement to in-kind benefits from the service recipient, or a payment by the service recipient directly to the person providing the goods or services to the service provider, is treated as not providing for a deferral of compensation for purposes of this paragraph (b), if a right to reimbursement by the service recipient for a payment for such benefits, goods, or services by the service provider would not be treated as providing for a deferral of compensation under this paragraph (b)(9)(v).

(D) *Limited payments.* If not otherwise excluded, a taxpayer may treat a right or rights under a separation pay plan to a payment or payments as not providing for a deferral of compensation to the extent such payments in the aggregate do not exceed the applicable dollar amount under section 402(g)(1)(B) for the year of the separation from service.

(E) *Limited period of time.* For purposes of paragraphs (b)(9)(v)(A) and (C) of this section, a limited period of time in which expenses may be incurred, or in-which in-kind benefits may be provided by the service recipient or a third party that the service recipient will pay, does not include periods beyond the last day of the second taxable year of the service provider following the taxable year of the service provider in which the separation from service occurred, provided that the period during which the reimbursements for such expenses must be paid may not extend beyond the third taxable year of the service provider following the taxable year of the service provider in which the separation from service occurred.

(vi) *Window programs — definition.* The term *window program* refers to a program established by a service recipient in connection with an impending separation from service to provide separation pay, where such program is made available by the service recipient for a limited period of time (no longer than 12 months) to service providers who separate from service during that period or to service providers who separate from service during that period under specified circumstances. A program will not be considered a window program if a service recipient establishes a pattern of repeatedly providing for similar separation pay in similar situations for substantially consecutive, limited periods of time. Whether the recurrence of these programs constitutes a pattern is determined based on the facts and circumstances. Although no one factor is determinative, relevant factors include whether the benefits are on account of a specific business event or condition, the degree to which the separation pay relates to the event or condition, and whether the event or condition is temporary or discrete or is a permanent aspect of the employer's business.

(10) *Certain indemnification and liability insurance plans.* A plan in which a service provider participates does not provide for a deferral of compensation for purposes of this paragraph (b) to the extent that the plan provides (to the extent permissible under applicable law), for the indemnification of, or the purchase of an insurance policy providing for payments of, all or part of the expenses incurred or damages paid or payable by a service provider with respect to a *bona fide* claim against the service provider or service recipient, including amounts paid or payable by the service provider upon the settlement of a *bona fide* claim against the service provider or service recipient, where such claim is based on actions or failures to act by the service provider in his or her capacity as a service provider of the service recipient.

(11) *Legal settlements.* An agreement to which a service provider is a party does not provide for a deferral of compensation for purposes of this paragraph (b) to the extent that the agreement provides for

amounts paid as settlements or awards resolving *bona fide* legal claims based on wrongful termination, employment discrimination, the Fair Labor Standards Act, or worker's compensation statutes, including claims under applicable Federal, state, local, or foreign laws, or for reimbursements or payments of reasonable attorneys fees or other reasonable expenses incurred by the service provider related to such *bona fide* legal claims, regardless of whether such settlements, awards, or reimbursement or payment of expenses pursuant to such claims are treated as compensation or wages for Federal tax purposes. Whether the execution of a waiver of any or all of such types of claims indicates that the amounts are paid as an award or settlement of an actual *bona fide* claim for damages under applicable law is determined based on the facts and circumstances. This paragraph (b)(11) does not apply to any deferred amounts that did not arise as a result of an actual *bona fide* claim for damages under applicable law, such as amounts that would have been deferred or paid regardless of the existence of such claim, even if such amounts are paid or modified as part of a settlement or award resolving an actual *bona fide* claim. For this purpose, a provision of foreign law shall be considered applicable only to foreign earned income (as defined under section 911(b)(1) without regard to section 911(b)(1)(B)(iv) and without regard to the requirement that the income be attributable to services performed during the period described in section 911(d)(1)(A) or (B)) from sources within the foreign country that promulgated such law.

(12) *Certain educational benefits.* A plan in which a service provider participates does not provide for a deferral of compensation to the extent the plan provides for taxable educational benefits. For purposes of this paragraph (b)(12), the term *educational benefits* refers solely to benefits provided to a service provider, consisting solely of educational assistance for the education of the service provider, as defined in section 127(c) and the accompanying regulations, and does not refer to any benefits provided for the education of any other person, including any spouse, child, or other family member of the service provider.

(c) *Plan*—(1) *In general*. The term *plan* includes any agreement, method, program, or other arrangement, including an agreement, method, program, or other arrangement that applies to one person or individual. A plan may be adopted unilaterally by the service recipient or may be negotiated or agreed to by the service recipient and one or more service providers or service provider representatives. An agreement, method, program, or other arrangement may constitute a plan regardless of whether it is an employee benefit plan under section 3(3) of ERISA, as amended (29 U.S.C. 1002(3)). The requirements of section 409A are applied as if a separate plan or plans is maintained for each service provider. For purposes of determining the terms of a plan, general provisions of the plan that purport to nullify noncompliant plan terms, or to supply any specific plan terms required by this section, §1.409A–2 or §1.409A–3, are disregarded.

(2) *Plan aggregation rules*—(i) *In general.* Except as otherwise provided, the following rules apply with respect to the application of this section and §§1.409A–2 through 1.409A–6 to deferrals of compensation with respect to a service provider:

(A) All deferrals of compensation at the election of that service provider under all plans of the service recipient that are account balance plans, except to the extent that the plan is described in paragraph (c)(2)(i)(D), (E), (F), (G), or (H) of this section, are treated as deferred under a single plan. For purposes of this paragraph, the term *account balance plan* means—

(*1*) An agreement, method, program, or other arrangement that is an account balance plan as defined in §31.3121(v)(2)–1(c)(1)(ii)(A) of this chapter, including mandatorily bifurcating the agreement, method, program, or other arrangement in accordance with the rules provided in §31.3121(v)–1(c)(1)(iii)(B) of this chapter; or

(*2*) An agreement, method, program, or other arrangement that would be described in paragraph (c)(2)(i)(A)(*1*) of this section if the service provider were an employee.

(B) All deferrals of compensation other than at the election of that service provider, including deferrals reflecting matching by the service recipient with respect to amounts a service provider elects to defer, under all plans of the service recipient that are account balance plans, except to the extent the plan is described in paragraph (c)(2)(i)(D), (E), (F), (G), or (H) of this section, are treated as deferred under a single plan. For purposes of this paragraph (c)(2)(i)(B), the term "account balance plan" has the same meaning as provided in paragraph (c)(2)(i)(A) of this section.

(C) All deferrals of compensation with respect to that service provider under all plans of the service recipient that are nonaccount balance plans, except to the extent such plan is described in paragraph (c)(2)(i)(D), (E), (F), (G), or (H) of this section, are treated as deferred under a single plan. For purposes of this paragraph (c)(2)(i)(C), the term *nonaccount balance plan* means—

(*1*) An agreement, method, program, or other arrangement that is a nonaccount balance plan as defined in §31.3121(v)(2)–1(c)(2)(i) of this chapter, including mandatorily bifurcating the agreement, method, program, or other arrangement in accordance with the rules provided in §31.3121(v)–1(c)(1)(iii)(B) of this chapter; or

(*2*) An agreement, method, program, or other arrangement that would be described in paragraph (c)(2)(i)(C)(*1*) of this section if the service provider were an employee.

(D) All deferrals of compensation with respect to that service provider under all separation pay plans (as defined in paragraph (m) of this section) of the service recipient to the extent an amount deferred under the plans is not described in paragraph (c)(2)(i)(E) of this section and is payable solely upon an involuntary separation from service within the meaning of paragraph (n) of this section or as a result of participation in a window program, are treated as deferred under a single plan.

(E) All deferrals of compensation with respect to that service provider under all plans of the service recipient to the extent such amounts deferred consist of rights to in-kind benefits or reimbursements of expenses, such as membership fees, or expenses related to aircraft or vehicle usage, to the extent that the right to the in-kind benefit or reimbursement, separately or in the aggregate, does not constitute a substantial portion of either the overall compensation earned by the service provider for performing services for the service recipient or the overall compensation received due to a separation from service, are treated as deferred under a single plan.

(F) All deferrals of compensation with respect to that service provider under all plans of the service recipient to the extent that the taxation of such compensation is governed by §1.61–22 or §1.7872–15 (split-dollar life insurance arrangements), or the taxation of such compensation would be governed by §1.61–22 or §1.7872–15 but for the operation of §1.61–22(j) (effective date provisions), are treated as deferred under a single plan.

(G) All deferrals of compensation with respect to that service provider under all agreements, methods, programs, or other arrangements of the service recipient to the extent the deferrals under the agreements, methods, programs, or other arrangements are deferrals of amounts that would be treated as modified foreign earned income (meaning foreign earned income as defined under section 911(b)(1) without regard to section 911(b)(1)(B)(iv) and without regard to the requirement that the income be attributable to services performed during the period described in section 911(d)(1)(A) or (B)) if paid to the service provider at the time the amount is first deferred, and provided further that substantially all the participants in such agreements, methods, programs, or other arrangements and any substantially similar agreements, methods, programs, or other arrangements are nonresident aliens and that the service provider does not participate in a substantially identical agreement, method, program, or other arrangement that does not meet the requirements of this paragraph (c)(2)(i)(G) (a domestic arrangement), are treated as deferred under a single plan.

(H) All deferrals of compensation with respect to that service provider under all plans of the service provider to the extent such plans are stock rights (as defined in paragraph (l) of this section) subject to section 409A, are treated as deferred under a single plan.

(I) All deferrals of compensation with respect to that service provider under all plans of the service recipient to the extent such plans are not described in paragraph (c)(2)(i)(A), (B), (C), (D), (E), (F), (G), or (H) of this section are treated as deferred under a single plan.

(ii) *Dual status*. Agreements, methods, programs, and other arrangements in which a service provider participates are not aggregated with other agreements, methods, programs, and other arrangements to the extent the service provider participates in one set of agreements, methods, programs, and other arrangements due to status as an employee of the service recipient (employee arrangements) and another set of agreements, methods, programs, and other arrangements due to status as an independent contractor of the service recipient (independent contractor arrangements). For example, where a service provider deferred amounts under an independent contractor arrangement while providing services as an independent contractor, and then becomes eligible for and defers amounts under a separate employee arrangement after being hired as an employee, the two arrangements will not be aggregated for purposes of this paragraph (c)(2). Where an employee also is a member of the board of directors of the service recipient (or a similar position with respect to a non-corporate service recipient), the arrangements under which the employee participates as a director (director arrangements) are not aggregated with employee arrangements, provided that the director arrangements are substantially similar to arrangements provided to service providers providing services only as directors (or similar positions with respect to non-corporate service recipients). For example, an employee director who participates in an employee arrangement and a director arrangement generally may treat the two arrangements as separate plans, provided that the director arrangement is substantially similar to arrangements providing benefits to non-employee directors. To the extent a plan in which an employee director participates is not substantially similar to arrangements in which non-employee directors participate, such plan is treated as an employee plan for purposes of this paragraph (c)(2). Director plans and independent contractor plans are aggregated for purposes of this paragraph (c)(2).

(3) *Establishment of plan*—(i) *In general*. A plan does not satisfy the requirements of section 409A and this section and §§1.409A–2 through 1.409A–3 and §§1.409A–5 through 1.409A–6, unless the plan is established and maintained by a service recipient in accordance with the requirements of this section, §§1.409A–2 through 1.409A–3 and §§1.409A–5 through 1.409A–6. For purposes of this paragraph (c)(3), a plan is established on the latest of the date on which it is adopted, the date on which it is effective, and the date on which the material terms of the plan are set forth in writing. The material terms of the plan may be set forth in writing in one or more documents. For purposes of this paragraph (c)(3)(i), a plan will be deemed to be set forth in writing if it is set forth in any other form that is approved by the Commissioner. The material terms of the plan include the amount (or the method or formula for determining the amount) of deferred compensation to be provided under the plan and the time and form of payment. Notwithstanding the foregoing, a plan will be deemed to be established as of the date the participant obtains a legally binding right to a deferral of compensation, provided that the plan is otherwise established under the rules of this paragraph (c)(3)(i) by the end of the taxable year of the service provider in which the legally binding right arises, or with respect to an amount not payable in the year immediately following the taxable year of the service provider in which the legally binding right arises (the subsequent year), the 15th day of the third month of the subsequent year.

(ii) *Initial deferral election provisions*. If a plan provides a service provider or a service recipient with an initial deferral election, the plan satisfies the requirements of this paragraph (c)(3) if the plan sets forth in writing, on or before the date the applicable election is required to be irrevocable to satisfy the requirements of §1.409A–2(a), the conditions under which such election may be made.

(iii) *Subsequent deferral election provisions*. If a plan permits a subsequent deferral election described in §1.409A–2(b), the plan satisfies the requirements of this paragraph (c)(3) if the plan sets forth in writing, on or before the date the election is required to be irrevocable to meet the requirements of §1.409A–2(b), the conditions under which such election may be made.

(iv) *Payment accelerations*. Except as explicitly provided in §1.409A–3, a plan is not required to set forth in writing the conditions under which a payment may be accelerated if such acceleration is permitted under §1.409A–3(j)(4).

(v) *Six-month delay for specified employees.* A plan must provide that distributions to a specified employee may not be made before the date that is six months after the date of separation from service or, if earlier, the date of death (the six-month delay rule). The six-month delay rule, required for payments due to the separation from service of a specified employee, must be written in the plan. A plan does not fail to be established and maintained merely because it does not contain the six-month delay rule when the service provider who has a right to compensation deferred under such plan is not a specified employee. However, such provision must be set forth in writing on or before the date such service provider first becomes a specified employee. In general, this means the provision must be set forth in writing on or before the specified employee effective date (as defined in paragraph (i)(3) of this section) for the first list of specified employees that includes such service provider.

(vi) *Plan amendments.* In the case of an amendment that increases the amount deferred under a nonqualified deferred compensation plan, the plan is not considered established with respect to the additional amount deferred until the plan, as amended, is established in accordance with paragraph (c)(3)(i) of this section.

(vii) *Transition rule for written plan requirement.* For purposes of this paragraph (c)(3), a legally enforceable unwritten plan that was adopted and effective before December 31, 2007, is treated as established under this section as of the later of the date on which it was adopted or became effective, provided that the material terms of the plan are set forth in writing on or before December 31, 2007.

(viii) *Plan aggregation rules.* The plan aggregation rules of paragraph (c)(2)(i) of this section do not apply to the requirements of this paragraph (c)(3). Accordingly, deferrals of compensation under an agreement, method, program, or other arrangement that fails to meet the requirements of section 409A solely due to a failure to meet the requirements of this paragraph (c)(3) are not aggregated with deferrals of compensation under other agreements, methods, programs, or other arrangements that meet such requirements.

(d) *Substantial risk of forfeiture*—(1) *In general.* Compensation is subject to a substantial risk of forfeiture if entitlement to the amount is conditioned on the performance of substantial future services by any person or the occurrence of a condition related to a purpose of the compensation, and the possibility of forfeiture is substantial. For purposes of this paragraph (d), a condition related to a purpose of the compensation must relate to the service provider's performance for the service recipient or the service recipient's business activities or organizational goals (for example, the attainment of a prescribed level of earnings or equity value or completion of an initial public offering). For purposes of this paragraph (d), if a service provider's entitlement to the amount is conditioned on the occurrence of the service provider's involuntary separation from service without cause, the right is subject to a substantial risk of forfeiture if the possibility of forfeiture is substantial. An amount is not subject to a substantial risk of forfeiture merely because the right to the amount is conditioned, directly or indirectly, upon the refraining from the performance of services. Except as provided with respect to certain transaction-based compensation under §1.409A–3(i)(5)(iv), the addition of any risk of forfeiture after the legally binding right to the compensation arises, or any extension of a period during which compensation is subject to a risk of forfeiture, is disregarded for purposes of determining whether such compensation is subject to a substantial risk of forfeiture. An amount will not be considered subject to a substantial risk of forfeiture beyond the date or time at which the recipient otherwise could have elected to receive the amount of compensation, unless the present value of the amount subject to a substantial risk of forfeiture (disregarding, in determining the present value, the risk of forfeiture) is materially greater than the present value of the amount the recipient otherwise could have elected to receive absent such risk of forfeiture. For this purpose, compensation that the service provider would receive for continuing to perform services regardless of whether the service provider elected to receive the amount that is subject to a substantial risk of forfeiture is not taken into account in determining whether the present value of the right to the amount subject to a substantial risk of forfeiture is materially greater than the amount the recipient otherwise could have elected to receive absent such risk of forfeiture. For example, a salary deferral generally may not be made subject to a substantial risk of forfeiture. But, for example, where a bonus plan provides an election between a cash payment or restricted stock units with a present value that is materially greater (disregarding the risk of forfeiture) than the present value of such cash payment and that will be forfeited absent continued services for a period of years, the right to the restricted stock units generally will be treated as subject to a substantial risk of forfeiture.

(2) *Stock rights.* A stock right is not subject to a substantial risk of forfeiture at the earlier of the first date the holder may exercise the stock right and receive cash or property that is substantially vested (as defined in §1.83–3(b)) or the first date that the stock right is not subject to a forfeiture condition that would constitute a substantial risk of forfeiture. Accordingly, a stock option that the service provider may exercise immediately and receive substantially vested stock is not subject to a substantial risk of forfeiture, even if the stock option automatically terminates upon the service provider's separation from service.

(3) *Enforcement of forfeiture condition*—(i) *In general.* In determining whether the possibility of forfeiture is substantial in the case of rights to compensation granted by a service recipient to a service provider that owns a significant amount of the total combined voting power or value of all classes of equity of the service recipient (where the service provider's ownership is determined with application of the attribution rules under section 318 if the service recipient is a corporation, or if the service recipient is an entity that is not a corporation, with application by analogy of the attribution rules under section 318), all relevant facts and circumstances will be taken into account in determining whether the probability of the service recipient enforcing such condition is substantial, including—

(A) The service provider's relationship to other equity holders and the extent of their control, potential control and possible loss of control of the service recipient;

(B) The position of the service provider in the service recipient and the extent to which the service provider is subordinate to other service providers;

(C) The service provider's relationship to the officers and directors of the service recipient (or similar positions with respect to a noncorporate service recipient);

(D) The person or persons who must approve the service provider's discharge; and

(E) Past actions of the service recipient in enforcing the restrictions.

(ii) *Examples*. The following examples illustrate the rules of paragraph (d)(3)(i) of this section:

Example 1. A service provider would be considered as having deferred compensation subject to a substantial risk of forfeiture, but for the fact that the service provider owns 20 percent of the single class of stock in the transferor corporation. If the remaining 80 percent of the class of stock is owned by an unrelated individual (or members of such an individual's family) so that the possibility of the corporation enforcing a restriction on such rights is substantial, then such rights are subject to a substantial risk of forfeiture.

Example 2. A service provider would be considered as having deferred compensation subject to a substantial risk of forfeiture, but for the fact that the service provider, who is president of the corporation, also owns 4 percent of the voting power of all the stock of a corporation. If the remaining stock is so diversely held by the public that the president, in effect, controls the corporation, then the possibility of the corporation enforcing a restriction on the right to deferred compensation of the president is not substantial, and such rights are not subject to a substantial risk of forfeiture.

(e) *Performance-based compensation*—(1) *In general*. The term *performance-based compensation* means compensation the amount of which, or the entitlement to which, is contingent on the satisfaction of preestablished organizational or individual performance criteria relating to a performance period of at least 12 consecutive months. Organizational or individual performance criteria are considered preestablished if established in writing by not later than 90 days after the commencement of the period of service to which the criteria relates, provided that the outcome is substantially uncertain at the time the criteria are established. Performance-based compensation may include payments based on performance criteria that are not approved by a compensation committee of the board of directors (or similar entity in the case of a non-corporate service recipient) or by the stockholders or members of the service recipient. Performance-based compensation does not include any amount or portion of any amount that will be paid either regardless of performance, or based upon a level of performance that is substantially certain to be met at the time the criteria is established. In addition, except as provided in paragraph (e)(3) of this section, compensation is not performance-based compensation merely because the amount of such compensation is determined by reference to the value of the service recipient or the stock of the service recipient. Where a portion of an amount of compensation would qualify as performance-based compensation if the portion were the sole amount available under the plan, that portion of the award will not fail to qualify as performance-based compensation if that portion is designated separately or otherwise separately identifiable under the terms of the plan, and the amount of each portion is determined independently of the other. Compensation may be performance-based compensation where the amount will be paid regardless of satisfaction of the performance criteria due to the service provider's death, disability, or a change in control event (as defined in §1.409A–3(i)(5)(i)), provided that a payment made under such circumstances without regard to the satisfaction of the performance criteria will not constitute performance-based compensation. For purposes of this paragraph (e)(1), a disability refers to any medically determinable physical or mental impairment resulting in the service provider's inability to perform the duties of his or her position or any substantially similar position, where such impairment can be expected to result in death or can be expected to last for a continuous period of not less than six months.

(2) *Payments based upon subjective performance criteria*. The term *performance-based compensation* includes payments based upon subjective performance criteria, provided that—

(i) The subjective performance criteria are *bona fide* and relate to the performance of the participant service provider, a group of service providers that includes the participant service provider, or a business unit for which the participant service provider provides services (which may include the entire organization); and

(ii) The determination that any subjective performance criteria have been met is not made by the participant service provider or a family member of the participant service provider (as defined in section 267(c)(4) applied as if the family of an individual includes the spouse of any member of the family), or a person under the effective control of the participant service provider or such a family member, and no amount of the compensation of the person making such determination is effectively controlled in whole or in part by the service provider or such a family member.

(3) *Equity-based compensation*. Compensation is performance-based compensation if it is based solely on an increase in the value of the service recipient, or a share of stock in the service recipient, after the date of a grant or award. However, compensation payable for a service period that is equal to the value of a predetermined number of shares of stock, and is variable only to the extent that the value of such shares appreciates or depreciates, generally will not be performance-based compensation. Notwithstanding the foregoing, the attainment of a prescribed value for the service recipient (or a portion thereof), or a share of stock in the service recipient, may be used as a preestablished organizational criterion for purposes of providing performance-based compensation, provided that the other requirements of paragraph (e)(1) of this section are satisfied. In addition, an award of equity-based compensation may constitute performance-based compensation if entitlement to the compensation is subject to a condition that would cause the award to otherwise qualify as performance-based compensation, such as a performance-based vesting condition. A provision that allows a service provider to defer compensation that would be realized upon the exercise of a stock right generally constitutes an additional deferral feature for purposes of the definition of a deferral of compensation under paragraph (b)(5) of this section.

(f) *Service provider*—(1) *In general*. The term *service provider* includes an individual, corporation, subchapter S corporation, partnership, personal service corporation (as defined in section 269A(b)(1)), noncorporate entity that would be a personal service corporation if it were a corporation, qualified personal service corporation (as defined in section 448(d)(2)), and noncorporate entity that would be a qualified personal service corporation if it were a corporation, for any taxable year in which such individual, corporation, subchapter S corporation, partnership, or other entity accounts for gross income from the performance of services under the cash receipts and disbursements method of accounting. The term *service provider* generally includes a person who has separated from service (a former service provider).

(2) *Independent contractors*—(i) *In general*. Except as otherwise provided in paragraph (f)(2)(iv) of this section, section 409A does not apply to an amount deferred under a plan between a service provider and service recipient with respect to a particular trade or business in which the service provider participates, including earnings credited to such deferred amount, if during the service provider's taxable year in which the service provider obtains a legally binding right to the payment of the amount deferred each of the following applies:

(A) The service provider is actively engaged in the trade or business of providing services, other than as an employee or as a member of the board of directors of a corporation (or similar position with respect to an entity that is not a corporation).

(B) The service provider provides significant services to two or more service recipients to which the service provider is not related and that are not related to one another (as defined in paragraph (f)(2)(ii) of this section).

(C) The service provider is not related to the service recipient, applying the definition of related person contained in paragraph (f)(2)(ii) of this section subject to the modification that the language "20 percent" is not used instead of "50 percent" each place "50 percent" appears in sections 267(b) and 707(b)(1).

(ii) *Related person*. For purposes of this paragraph (f)(2), a person is related to another person if the persons bear a relationship to each other that is specified in section 267(b) or 707(b)(1), subject to the modifications that the language "20 percent" is used instead of "50 percent" each place it appears in sections 267(b) and 707(b)(1), and section 267(c)(4) is applied as if the family of an individual includes the spouse of any member of the family; or the persons are engaged in trades or businesses under common control (within the meaning of section 52(a) and (b)). In addition, an individual is related to an entity if the individual is an officer of an entity that is a corporation, or holds a position substantially similar to an officer of a corporation with an entity that is not a corporation.

(iii) *Significant services*. Whether a service provider is providing significant services depends on the facts and circumstances of each case. However, for purposes of paragraph (f)(2)(i) of this section, a service provider who provides services to two or more service recipients to which the service provider is not related and that are not related to one another is deemed to be providing significant services to two or more of such service recipients for a given taxable year, if the revenues generated from the services provided to any service recipient or group of related service recipients during such taxable year do not exceed 70 percent of the total revenue generated by the service provider from the trade or business of providing such services. In addition, in the case of a service provider who has been providing services in a trade or business for a period of not less than three consecutive years, for purposes of paragraph (f)(2)(i) of this section, a service provider who provides services to two or more service recipients to which the service provider is not related and that are not related to one another is deemed to be providing significant services to two or more of such service recipients for a given taxable year if in each of the prior three taxable years the revenues generated from the services provided to any service recipient or group of related service recipients during such prior taxable years did not exceed 70 percent of the total revenue generated by the service provider from the trade or business of providing such services and, at the time an amount is deferred, the service provider does not know or have reason to anticipate that the revenues generated from the services provided to any service recipient or group of related service recipients during the current year will exceed 70 percent of the total revenue generated by the service provider from the trade or business of providing such services.

(iv) *Management services*. This paragraph (f)(2) does not apply to a service provider to the extent the service provider provides management services to a service recipient. For purposes of this paragraph (f)(2)(iv), the term *management services* means services that involve the actual or *de facto* direction or control of the financial or operational aspects of a trade or business of the service recipient, or investment management or advisory services provided to a service recipient whose primary trade or business includes the investment of financial assets (including investments in real estate), such as a hedge fund or a real estate investment trust.

(v) *Services provided to related persons*. Section 409A does not apply to an amount deferred under a plan that is a *bona fide* agreement, method, program, or other arrangement between a service provider and a related service recipient arising in the ordinary course of a particular trade or business in which the service provider is engaged to the extent that—

(A) The service provider provides services to the service recipient as an independent contractor;

(B) During the service provider's taxable year in which the amount is deferred, the service provider qualifies for the safe harbor provided in paragraph (f)(2)(iii) of this section with respect to such trade or business; and

(C) Such agreement, method, program, or other arrangement and the practices thereunder (including billing and collection practices), are substantially similar to the agreements, methods, programs, or other arrangements and practices applicable to one or more unrelated service recipients to whom the service provider provides substantial services and that produce a majority of the total revenue that the service provider earns from the trade or business of providing such services during the taxable year.

(g) *Service recipient*. Except as otherwise specifically provided in these regulations, the term *service recipient* means the person for whom the services are performed and with respect to whom the legally binding right to compensation arises, and all persons with whom such person would be considered a single employer under section 414(b) (employees of controlled group of corporations), and all persons with whom such person would be considered a single employer under section 414(c) (employees of partnerships, proprietorships, etc., under common control). For example, if the service provider is an employee, the service recipient generally is the employer (including all persons treated as a single employer under section 414(b) or (c)). Notwithstanding the foregoing, section 409A applies to a plan that provides for the deferral of compensation, even if the payment of the compensation is not made by the person for whom services are performed.

(h) *Separation from service*—(1) *Employees*—(i) *In general*. An employee separates from service with the employer if the employee dies, retires, or otherwise has a termination of employment with the employer. However, for purposes of this paragraph (h)(1), the employment relationship is treated as continuing intact while the individual is on military leave, sick leave, or other *bona fide* leave of absence if the period of such leave does not exceed six months, or if longer, so long as the individual retains a right to reemployment with the service recipient under an applicable statute or by contract. For purposes of this paragraph (h)(1), a leave of absence constitutes a *bona fide* leave of absence only if there is a reasonable expectation that the employee will return to perform services for the employer. If the period of leave exceeds six months and the individual does not retain a right to reemployment under an applicable statute or by contract, the employment relationship is deemed to terminate on the first date immediately following such six-month period. Notwithstanding the foregoing, where a leave of absence is due to any medically determinable physical or mental impairment that can be expected to result in death or can be expected to last for a continuous period of not less than six months, where such impairment causes the employee to be unable to perform the duties of his or her position of employment or any substantially similar position of employment, a 29-month period of absence may be substituted for such six-month period.

(ii) *Termination of employment*. Whether a termination of employment has occurred is determined based on whether the facts and circumstances indicate that the employer and employee reasonably anticipated that no further services would be performed after a certain date or that the level of *bona fide* services the employee would perform after such date (whether as an employee or as an independent contractor) would permanently decrease to no more than 20 percent of the average level of *bona fide* services performed (whether as an employee or an independent contractor) over the immediately preceding 36-month period (or the full period of services to the employer if the employee has been providing services to the employer less than 36 months). Facts and circumstances to be considered in making this determination include, but are not limited to, whether the employee continues to be treated as an employee for other purposes (such as continuation of salary and participation in employee benefit programs), whether similarly situated service providers have been treated consistently, and whether the employee is permitted, and realistically available, to perform services for other service recipients in the same line of business. An employee is presumed to have separated from service where the level of *bona fide* services performed decreases to a level equal to 20 percent or less of the average level of services performed by the employee during the immediately preceding 36-month period. An employee will be presumed not to have separated from service where the level of *bona fide* services performed continues at a level that is 50 percent or more of the average level of service performed by the employee during the immediately preceding 36-month period. No presumption applies to a decrease in the level of *bona fide* services performed to a level that is more than 20 percent and less than 50 percent of the average level of *bona fide* services performed during the immediately preceding 36-month period. The presumption is rebuttable by demonstrating that the employer and the employee reasonably anticipated that as of a certain date the level of *bona fide* services would be reduced permanently to a level less than or equal to 20 percent of the average level of *bona fide* services provided during the immediately preceding 36-month period or full period of services provided to the employer if the employee has been providing services to the service recipient for a period of less than 36 months (or that the level of *bona fide* services would not be so reduced). For example, an employee may demonstrate that the employer and employee reasonably anticipated that the employee would cease providing services, but that, after the original cessation of services, business circumstances such as termination of the employee's replacement caused the employee to return to employment. Although the employee's return to employment may cause the employee to be presumed to have continued in employment because the employee is providing services at a rate equal to the rate at which the employee was providing services before the termination of employment, the facts and circumstances in this case would demonstrate that at the time the employee originally ceased to provide services, the employee and the service recipient reasonably anticipated that the employee would not provide services in the future. Notwithstanding the foregoing provisions of this paragraph (h)(1)(ii), a plan may treat another level of reasonably anticipated permanent reduction in the level of *bona fide* services as a separation from service, provided that the level of reduction required must be designated in writing as a specific percentage, and the reasonably anticipated reduced level of *bona fide* services must be greater than 20 percent but less than 50 percent of the average level of *bona fide* services provided in the immediately preceding 36 months. The plan must specify the definition of separation from service on or before the date on which a separation from service is designated as a time of payment of the applicable amount deferred, and once designated, any change to the definition of separation from service with respect to such amount deferred will be subject to the rules regarding subsequent deferrals and the acceleration of payments. For purposes of this paragraph (h)(1)(ii), for periods during which an employee is on a paid *bona fide* leave of absence (as defined in paragraph (h)(1)(i) of this section) and has not otherwise terminated employment pursuant to paragraph (h)(1)(i) of this section, the employee is treated as providing *bona fide* services at a level equal to the level of services that the employee would have been required to perform to receive the compensation paid with respect to such leave of absence. Periods during which an employee is on an unpaid *bona fide* leave of absence (as defined in paragraph (h)(1)(i) of this section) and has not otherwise terminated employment pursuant to paragraph (h)(1)(i) of this section, are disregarded for purposes of this paragraph (h)(1)(ii) (including for purposes of determining the applicable 36-month (or shorter) period).

(2) *Independent contractors*—(i) *In general*. An independent contractor is considered to have a separation from service with the service recipient upon the expiration of the contract (or in the case of more than one contract, all contracts)

under which services are performed for the service recipient if the expiration constitutes a good-faith and complete termination of the contractual relationship. An expiration does not constitute a good faith and complete termination of the contractual relationship if the service recipient anticipates a renewal of a contractual relationship or the independent contractor becoming an employee. For this purpose, a service recipient is considered to anticipate the renewal of the contractual relationship with an independent contractor if it intends to contract again for the services provided under the expired contract, and neither the service recipient nor the independent contractor has eliminated the independent contractor as a possible provider of services under any such new contract. Further, a service recipient is considered to intend to contract again for the services provided under an expired contract if the service recipient's doing so is conditioned only upon incurring a need for the services, the availability of funds, or both.

(ii) *Special rule*. Notwithstanding paragraph (h)(2)(i) of this section, a plan is considered to satisfy the requirement described in §1.409A–3(a)(1) with respect to an amount payable upon a separation from service if, with respect to amounts payable to a service provider who is an independent contractor, the plan provides that—

(A) No amount will be paid to the service provider before a date at least 12 months after the day on which the contract expires under which the service provider performs services for the service recipient (or, in the case of more than one contract, all such contracts expire); and

(B) No amount payable to the service provider on that date will be paid to the service provider if, after the expiration of the contract (or contracts) and before that date, the service provider performs services for the service recipient as an independent contractor or an employee.

(3) *Definition of service recipient and employer*. For purposes of this paragraph (h), the term *service recipient* or *employer* means the service recipient as defined in paragraph (g) of this section, provided that in applying section 1563(a)(1), (2), and (3) for purposes of determining a controlled group of corporations under section 414(b), the language "at least 50 percent" is used instead of "at least 80 percent" each place it appears in section 1563(a)(1), (2), and (3), and in applying §1.414(c)–2 for purposes of determining trades or businesses (whether or not incorporated) that are under common control for purposes of section 414(c), "at least 50 percent" is used instead of "at least 80 percent" each place it appears in §1.414(c)–2. A plan may provide with respect to a deferral of compensation under the plan that in applying sections 1563(a)(1), (2), and (3) for purposes of determining a controlled group of corporations under section 414(b), another defined percentage greater than 50 percent, but not greater than 80 percent, is used instead of "at least 80 percent" at each place it appears in sections 1563(a)(1), (2), and (3), and in applying §1.414(c)–2 for purposes of determining trades or businesses (whether or not incorporated) that are under common control for purposes of section 414(c), another defined percentage greater than 50 percent, but not greater than 80 percent, is used instead of "at least 80 percent" at each place it appears in §1.414(c)–2. In addition, where the use of such definition of service recipient for purposes of determining a separation from service is based upon legitimate business criteria, the plan may provide that for purposes of a deferral of compensation under the plan that in applying sections 1563(a)(1), (2), and (3) for purposes of determining a controlled group of corporations under section 414(b), the language "at least 20 percent" or another defined percentage not less than 20 percent but not greater than 50 percent is used instead of "at least 80 percent" at each place it appears in sections 1563(a)(1), (2), and (3), and in applying §1.414(c)–2 for purposes of determining trades or businesses (whether or not incorporated) that are under common control for purposes of section 414(c), the language "at least 20 percent" or another defined percentage not less than 20 percent but not greater than 50 percent is used instead of "at least 80 percent" at each place it appears in §1.414(c)–2. Where a definition of service recipient or employer other than the definition provided in the first sentence of this paragraph (h)(3) (the 50 percent standard) is used, the plan must designate in writing the alternate definition no later than the last date at which the time and form of payment of the applicable amount deferred must be elected in accordance with §1.409A–2(a), and any change in the definition for such amounts deferred will constitute a change in the time and form of payment subject to the rules governing subsequent deferral elections under §1.409A–2(b) and the acceleration of payments under §1.409A–3(j).

(4) *Asset purchase transactions*. Where as part of a sale or other disposition of assets by one service recipient (seller) to an unrelated service recipient (buyer), a service provider of the seller would otherwise experience a separation from service with the seller, the seller and the buyer may retain the discretion to specify, and may specify, whether a service provider providing services to the seller immediately before the asset purchase transaction and providing services to the buyer after and in connection with the asset purchase transaction has experienced a separation from service for purposes of this paragraph (h), provided that the asset purchase transaction results from *bona fide*, arm's length negotiations, all service providers providing services to the seller immediately before the asset purchase transaction and providing services to the buyer after and in connection with the asset purchase transaction are treated consistently (regardless of position at the seller) for purposes of applying the provisions of any nonqualified deferred compensation plan, and such treatment is specified in writing no later than the closing date of the asset purchase transaction. For purposes of this paragraph (h)(4), references to a sale or other disposition of assets, or an asset purchase transaction, refer only to a transfer of substantial assets, such as a plant or division or substantially all the assets of a trade or business. For purposes of this paragraph (h)(4), whether a service recipient is related to another service recipient is determined under the rules provided in paragraph (f)(2)(ii) of this section.

(5) *Dual status*. If a service provider provides services both as an employee of a service recipient and as an independent contractor of a service recipient, the service provider must separate from service both as an employee and as an independent contractor to be treated as having separated from service. If a service provider ceases providing services as an independent contractor and begins providing services as an employee, or ceases providing

services as an employee and begins providing services as an independent contractor, the service provider will not be considered to have a separation from service until the service provider has ceased providing services in both capacities. Notwithstanding the foregoing, if a service provider provides services both as an employee of a service recipient and a member of the board of directors of a corporate service recipient (or an analogous position with respect to a non-corporate service recipient), the services provided as a director are not taken into account in determining whether the service provider has a separation from service as an employee for purposes of a nonqualified deferred compensation plan in which the service provider participates as an employee that is not aggregated with any plan in which the service provider participates as a director under paragraph (c)(2)(ii) of this section. In addition, if a service provider provides services both as an employee of a service recipient and a member of the board of directors of a corporate service recipient (or an analogous position with respect to a non-corporate service recipient), the services provided as an employee are not taken into account in determining whether the service provider has a separation from service as a director for purposes of a nonqualified deferred compensation plan in which the service provider participates as a director that is not aggregated with any plan in which the service provider participates as an employee under paragraph (c)(2)(ii) of this section.

(6) *Collectively bargained plans covering multiple employers*. Notwithstanding the foregoing provisions of this paragraph (h), to the extent a plan is established pursuant to a *bona fide* collective bargaining agreement covering services performed by employees for multiple employers, such plan may define a separation from service in a reasonable manner that treats the employee as not having separated from service during periods in which the employee is not providing services but is available to perform services covered by the collective bargaining agreement for one or more employers, provided that the definition also provides that the employee must be deemed to have separated from service at a specified date not later than the end of any period of at least 12 consecutive months during which the employee has not provided any services covered by the collective bargaining agreement to any participating employer. This paragraph (h)(6) applies only if the definition of separation from service provided by the collective bargaining agreement was the subject of arm's length negotiations between employee representatives and two or more employers, the agreement between employee representatives and such employers satisfies section 7701(a)(46), and the circumstances surrounding the agreement evidence good faith bargaining between adverse parties over such definition.

(i) *Specified employee*—(1) *In general*. The term *specified employee* means a service provider who, as of the date of the service provider's separation from service, is a key employee of a service recipient any stock of which is publicly traded on an established securities market or otherwise. For purposes of this paragraph (i)(1), a service provider is a key employee if the service provider meets the requirements of section 416(i)(1)(A)(i), (ii), or (iii) (applied in accordance with the regulations thereunder and disregarding section 416(i)(5)) at any time during the 12-month period ending on a specified employee identification date. If a service provider is a key employee as of a specified employee identification date, the service provider is treated as a key employee for purposes of this paragraph (i) for the entire 12-month period beginning on the specified employee effective date.

(2) *Definition of compensation*. For purposes of identifying a specified employee by applying the requirements of section 416(i)(1)(A)(i), (ii), and (iii), the definition of compensation under §1.415(c)–2(a) is used, applied as if the service recipient were not using any safe harbor provided in §1.415(c)–2(d), were not using any of the elective special timing rules provided in §1.415(c)–2(e), and were not using any of the elective special rules provided in §1.415(c)–2(g). Notwithstanding the foregoing, a service recipient may elect to use any available definition of compensation under section 415 and the regulations thereunder in accordance with the election requirements set forth in paragraph (i)(8) of this section, including any available safe harbor and any available election under the timing rules or special rules, provided that the definition is applied consistently to all employees of the service recipient for purposes of identifying specified employees. A service recipient may elect to use such an alternative definition regardless of whether another definition of compensation is being used for purposes of a qualified plan sponsored by the service recipient. However, once a list of specified employees has become effective, the service recipient cannot change the definition of compensation for purposes of identifying specified employees for the period with respect to which such list is effective.

(3) *Specified employee identification date*. Unless another date is designated in accordance with the requirements of this paragraph (i)(3) and paragraph (i)(8) of this section, the specified employee identification date is December 31. A service recipient may designate in accordance with the requirements of paragraph (i)(8) of this section any other date as the specified employee identification date, provided that a service recipient must use the same specified employee identification date with respect to all nonqualified deferred compensation plans, and any change to the specified employee identification date may not be effective for a period of at least 12 months. The service recipient may designate a specified employee identification date in each plan or in a separate document applicable to all plans, provided that the service recipient will not be treated as having designated a specified employee identification date before the designation is legally binding on the service recipient and all affected service providers. Any designation of a specified employee identification date made on or before December 31, 2007, may be applied to any separation from service occurring on or after January 1, 2005, unless and until subsequently changed pursuant to this paragraph (i)(3).

(4) *Specified employee effective date*. Unless another date is designated in accordance with the requirements of this paragraph (i)(4) and paragraph (i)(8) of this section, the specified employee effective date is the first day of the fourth month following the specified employee identification date. A service recipient may designate in accordance with the requirements of paragraph (i)(8) of this section any date following the specified employee identification date as the spec-

ified employee effective date, provided that such date may not be later than the first day of the fourth month following the specified employee identification date, and provided further that a service recipient must use the same specified employee effective date with respect to all nonqualified deferred compensation plans, and any change to the specified employee effective date may not be effective for a period of at least 12 months. The service recipient may designate a specified employee effective date through inclusion in each plan document or through a separate document applicable to all plans, provided that the service recipient will not be treated as having designated a specified employee effective date on any date before the designation is legally binding on the service recipient and all affected service providers. Any designation of a specified employee effective date made on or before December 31, 2007, may be applied to any separation from service occurring on or after January 1, 2005, unless and until subsequently changed pursuant to this paragraph (i)(4).

(5) *Alternative methods of satisfying the six-month delay rule*. A plan may provide, in accordance with the requirements of paragraph (i)(8) of this section, for an alternative method to identify service providers who will be subject to the six-month delay rule provided in section 409A(a)(2)(B)(i), provided that the alternative method is reasonably designed to include all specified employees (determined without respect to any available service recipient elections), the alternative method is an objectively determinable standard providing no direct or indirect election to any service provider regarding its application, and the alternative method results in either all service providers or no more than 200 service providers being identified in the class as of any date. Use of such an alternative method will not be treated as a change in the time and form of payment for purposes of §1.409A–2(b) (the subsequent deferral rules), even if the service provider is not a specified employee when the payment is delayed.

(6) *Corporate transactions*—(i) *Mergers and acquisitions of public service recipients*. If as a result of a corporate transaction, two or more separate service recipients, more than one of which has stock outstanding that is publicly traded on an established securities market or otherwise immediately before the transaction, become one service recipient, any stock of which is publicly traded on an established securities market or otherwise immediately after the transaction (resulting public service recipient), the resulting public service recipient's next specified employee identification date and specified employee effective date following the corporate transaction are the specified employee identification date and specified employee effective date that the acquiring service recipient would have been required to use absent such transaction. For this purpose, in the case of a corporate merger, the acquiring service recipient is the service recipient that included the surviving corporation in such merger, in the case of an acquisition by a corporation of the stock of another corporation, the acquiring service recipient is the service recipient that included the corporation that acquired such stock, and in all other cases, the surviving service recipient is determined on the basis of all of the facts and circumstances. For the period between the transaction and the next specified employee effective date, the list of specified employees of the resulting public service recipient is determined by combining the lists of specified employees of all service recipients participating in the transaction that were in effect at the date of the corporate transaction, ranking such specified employees in order of the amount of compensation used to determine each specified employee's status as a specified employee, and treating the top 50 of such specified employees, plus any employees described in section 416(i)(1)(ii) or section 416(i)(1)(iii) and the regulations thereunder (relating to 1-percent and 5-percent owners) who are not included in such top 50 specified employees, as specified employees for the period between the corporate transaction and the next specified employee effective date. Alternatively, the resulting service recipient may elect in accordance with the requirements of paragraph (i)(8) of this section to use any reasonable method to determine the specified employees of the resulting service recipient, including the use of an alternative method of compliance described in paragraph (i)(5) of this section, provided that such method is adopted no later than 90 days after the corporate transaction and applied prospectively from the date the method is adopted.

(ii) *Mergers and acquisitions of nonpublic service recipients*. If as part of a corporate transaction a service recipient that does not have outstanding stock that is publicly traded on an established securities market or otherwise immediately before the transaction (initial private service recipient), and a service recipient with stock outstanding that is publicly traded on an established securities market or otherwise immediately before the transaction (initial public service recipient), become a single service recipient having stock that is publicly traded on an established securities market or otherwise immediately after the transaction (resulting public service recipient), the resulting public service recipient's next specified employee identification date and specified employee effective date following the corporate transaction are the specified employee identification date and specified employee effective date that the initial public service recipient would have been required to use absent such transaction. For the period after the date of the corporate transaction and before the next specified employee effective date, the specified employees of the initial public service recipient immediately before the transaction continue to be the specified employees of the resulting public service recipient, and no service providers of the initial private service recipient are required to be treated as specified employees.

(iii) *Spinoffs*. If as part of a corporate transaction, a service recipient with stock outstanding that is publicly traded on an established securities market or otherwise immediately before the transaction (initial public service recipient), becomes two or more separate service recipients, each with stock outstanding that is publicly traded on an established securities market or otherwise immediately after the transaction (post-transaction public service recipients), the next specified employee identification date of each of the post-transaction public service recipients is the specified employee identification date that the initial public service recipient would have been required to use absent such transaction. For the period after the date of the corporate transaction and before the next specified employee effective date, the specified employees of the initial public service recipient immediately before the transaction continue to be the specified employees of the post-transaction public service recipients.

(iv) *Public offerings and other corporate transactions.* If as part of an initial public offering or corporate transaction not described in paragraph (i)(6)(ii) or (iii) of this section, a service recipient with no outstanding stock that is publicly traded on an established securities market or otherwise immediately before such offering or other transaction (initial private service recipient), becomes one or more service recipients with stock outstanding that is publicly traded on an established securities market or otherwise immediately after such offering or other transaction (post-transaction public service recipient), each post-transaction public service recipient has a specified employee identification date of December 31 and a specified employee effective date of April 1, effective retroactively to the December 31 and April 1 next preceding the offering or other transaction for purposes of identifying the specified employees between the corporation transaction and the next December 31. Alternatively, a post-transaction public service recipient may elect in accordance with the requirements of paragraph (i)(8) of this section, a specified employee identification date and specified employee effective date on or before the date of the offering or other transaction. If a public service recipient makes such an election, for the period after the offering or other transaction and before the next specified employee effective date, the specified employees of the post-transaction public service recipient consist of the service providers that at the time of the offering or other transaction would have been classified as specified employees of the initial private service recipient, had the initial private service recipient elected the same specified employee identification date and specified employee effective date as selected by the post-transaction public service recipient, and had such initial private service recipient had stock publicly traded on an established securities market or otherwise as of the specified employee identification date preceding the transaction.

(v) *Alternative methods of compliance.* For purposes of this paragraph (i)(6), references to specified employees as of a corporate transaction or offering include any specified employees identified through the use of an alternative method described in paragraph (i)(5) of this section, where the use of such alternative method was established and effective at the time of the corporate transaction or offering.

(7) *Nonresident alien employees.* For purposes of determining whether an employee meets the requirements of section 416(i)(1)(A)(i), (ii), or (iii) (applied in accordance with the regulations thereunder and disregarding section 416(i)(5)), and therefore is a key employee, the incorporation of the rules of §1.415(c)–2(g)(5) regarding the definition of compensation applies. Accordingly, the rule of §1.415(c)–2(g)(5)(i), generally requiring the treatment as compensation of certain compensation excludible from an employee's gross income due to the location of the services or the identity of the employer, applies. In addition, a service recipient may elect in accordance with paragraph (i)(8) of this section to apply the rule of §1.415(c)–2(g)(5)(ii) to not treat as compensation certain compensation excludible from an employee's gross income on account of the location of the services or the identity of the employer that is not effectively connected with the conduct of a trade or business within the United States. A service recipient may elect to apply the rule of §1.415–2(g)(5)(ii) regardless of whether the service recipient has elected to apply the rule to a qualified plan sponsored by the service recipient; however, once a list of specified employees has become effective, any election of the rule for that period may not be changed. Notwithstanding the foregoing, any election of the rule made before January 1, 2008, may be effective with respect to any specified employee identification date on or before December 31, 2007.

(8) *Elections affecting the identification of specified employees.* The elections described in paragraphs (i)(2) through (7) of this section are effective only as of the date that all necessary corporate action has been taken to make such elections binding for purposes of all affected nonqualified deferred compensation plans in which the service providers of the service recipient that would become a specified employee due to the application of such election participate. Where a taxpayer attempts to make an election under paragraph (i)(2), (3), (4), (5), (6), or (7) of this section but such election is not binding on all the affected nonqualified deferred compensation plans and applied consistently to all such service providers, the election is not effective and the rule under paragraph (i)(2), (3), (4), (5), (6), or (7) of this section, as applicable, that would apply absent an election is applicable for identifying specified employees.

(j) *Nonresident alien.* (1) Except as provided in paragraph (j)(2) of this section, the term *nonresident alien* means an individual who is—

(i) A nonresident alien within the meaning of section 7701(b)(1)(B); or

(ii) A dual resident taxpayer within the meaning of §301.7701(b)–7(a)(1) of this chapter with respect to any taxable year in which such individual is treated as a nonresident alien for purposes of computing the individual's U.S. income tax liability.

(2) The term *nonresident alien* does not include—

(i) A nonresident alien with respect to whom an election is in effect for the taxable year under section 6013(g) to be treated as a resident of the United States;

(ii) A former citizen or long-term resident (within the meaning of section 877(e)(2)) who expatriated after June 3, 2004, and has not complied with the requirements of section 7701(n); or

(iii) An individual who is treated as a citizen or resident of the United States for the taxable year under section 877(g).

(k) *Established securities market.* The term *established securities market* means an established securities market within the meaning of §1.897–1(m).

(l) *Stock right.* The term *stock right* means a stock option (other than an incentive stock option described in section 422 or an option granted pursuant to an employee stock purchase plan described in section 423) or a stock appreciation right.

(m) *Separation pay plan.* The term *separation pay plan* means any plan that provides separation pay or, where a plan provides both amounts that are separation pay and that are not separation pay, that portion of the plan that provides separation pay. The term *separation pay* means any deferral of compensation (before the application of the exclusions from the definition of a deferral of compensation set forth in paragraph (b)(9) of this section) that will not be paid under any circumstances unless the service provider has had a separation from service, whether voluntary or involuntary, including payments in the form of reimbursements of expenses incurred, and the provision of in-kind benefits. A deferral of compensation that the service provider may receive without a separation from service does not become separation pay merely because the service provider elects to receive or receives the payment after or upon a separation from service. A deferral of compensation does not fail to be separation pay merely because the payment is conditioned upon the execution of a release of claims, noncompetition or nondisclosure provisions, or other similar requirements. Notwithstanding the foregoing, any amount, or entitlement to any amount, that acts as a substitute for, or replacement of, amounts deferred by the service recipient under a nonqualified deferred compensation plan constitutes a payment of compensation or deferral of compensation under such nonqualified deferred compensation plan.

(n) *Involuntary separation from service*—(1) *In general.* An involuntary separation from service means a separation from service due to the independent exercise of the unilateral authority of the service recipient to terminate the service provider's services, other than due to the service provider's implicit or explicit request, where the service provider was willing and able to continue performing services. An involuntary separation from service may include the service recipient's failure to renew a contract at the time such contract expires, provided that the service provider was willing and able to execute a new contract providing terms and conditions substantially similar to those in the expiring contract and to continue providing such services. The determination of whether a separation from service is involuntary is based on all the facts and circumstances. Any characterization of the separation from service as voluntary or involuntary by the service provider and the service recipient in the documentation of the separation from service is presumed to properly characterize the nature of the separation from service. However, the presumption may be rebutted where the facts and circumstances indicate otherwise. For example, if a separation from service is designated as a voluntary separation from service or resignation, but the facts and circumstances indicate that absent such voluntary separation from service the service recipient would have terminated the service provider's services, and that the service provider had knowledge that the service provider would be so terminated, the separation from service is involuntary.

(2) *Separations from service for good reason*—(i) *In general.* Notwithstanding paragraph (n)(1) of this section, a service provider's voluntary separation from service will be treated for purposes of this section and §§1.409A–2 through 1.409A–6 as an involuntary separation from service if the separation from service occurs under certain limited *bona fide* conditions, where the avoidance of the requirements of section 409A is not a purpose of the inclusion of these conditions in the plan or of the actions by the service recipient in connection with the satisfaction of these conditions, and a voluntary separation from service under such conditions effectively constitutes an involuntary separation from service. Generally such conditions will be prespecified under an agreement to provide compensation upon a separation from service for good reason. Such a good reason (or a similar condition) must be defined to require actions taken by the service recipient resulting in a material negative change to the service provider in the service relationship, such as the duties to be performed, the conditions under which such duties are to be performed, or the compensation to be received for performing such services. Other factors taken into account in determining whether a separation from service for good reason effectively constitutes an involuntary separation from service include the extent to which the payments upon a separation from service for good reason are in the same amount and are to be made at the same time and in the same form as payments available upon an actual involuntary separation from service, and whether the service provider is required to give the service recipient notice of the existence of the condition that would result in treatment as a separation from service for good reason and a reasonable opportunity to remedy the condition.

(ii) *Safe harbor.* For purposes of this section and §§1.409A–2 through 1.409A–6, if a plan provides that a voluntary separation from service will be treated as an involuntary separation from service if the separation from service occurs under certain express conditions, a separation from service satisfying the conditions set forth in the plan will be treated as an involuntary separation from the service if the necessary conditions (or set of conditions) require the following:

(A) The separation from service must occur during a pre-determined limited period of time not to exceed two years following the initial existence of one or more of the following conditions arising without the consent of the service provider:

(*1*) A material diminution in the service provider's base compensation.

(*2*) A material diminution in the service provider's authority, duties, or responsibilities.

(*3*) A material diminution in the authority, duties, or responsibilities of the supervisor to whom the service provider is required to report, including a requirement that a service provider report to a corporate officer or employee instead of reporting directly to the board of directors of a corporation (or similar governing body with respect to an entity other than a corporation).

(*4*) A material diminution in the budget over which the service provider retains authority.

(*5*) A material change in the geographic location at which the service provider must perform the services.

(*6*) Any other action or inaction that constitutes a material breach by the service recipient of the agreement under which the service provider provides services.

(B) The amount, time, and form of payment upon the separation from service must be substantially identical to the amount, time and form of payment payable due to an actual involuntary separation from service, to the extent such a right exists.

(C) The service provider must be required to provide notice to the service recipient of the existence of the condition described in paragraph (n)(2)(ii)(A) of this section within a period not to exceed 90 days of the initial existence of the condition, upon the notice of which the service recipient must be provided a period of at least 30 days during which it may remedy the condition and not be required to pay the amount.

(3) *Special rule for certain collectively bargained plans.* Notwithstanding the foregoing, for purposes of this paragraph

(n), to the extent a plan is subject to a *bona fide* collective bargaining agreement covering services performed for multiple employers under which an employee must separate from service with all such employers in order to receive a payment, such plan may use any reasonable definition of involuntary separation from service, provided that such definition is consistent with any definition of a separation from service adopted under paragraph (h)(6) of this section, and provided further that the definition of an involuntary separation from service provided by the collective bargaining agreement was the subject of arm's length negotiations between employee representatives and two or more employers, the agreement between employee representatives and such employers satisfies section 7701(a)(46), and the circumstances surrounding the agreement evidence good faith bargaining between adverse parties over such definition.

(o) *Earnings*. Whether a deferred amount constitutes earnings on an amount deferred, or actual or notional income attributable to an amount deferred, is determined under the principles defining income attributable to the amount taken into account under §31.3121(v)(2)–1(d)(2) of this chapter. Accordingly, with respect to an account balance plan, earnings on an amount deferred generally include an amount credited on behalf of a service provider under the terms of the plan that reflects a rate of return that does not exceed either the rate of return on a predetermined actual investment or, if the income does not reflect the rate of return on a predetermined actual investment, a reasonable rate of interest. With respect to nonaccount balance plans, earnings on an amount deferred generally include an increase, due solely to the passage of time, in the present value of the future payments to which the service provider has obtained a legally binding right, the present value of which constituted the amount deferred (determined as of the date such amount was deferred), but only if the amount deferred was determined using reasonable actuarial assumptions and methods. A right to earnings on an amount deferred generally is treated as a right to a deferral of compensation for purposes of this section and §§1.409A–2 through 1.409A–6. However, for purposes of any provision of this section and §§1.409A–2 through 1.409A–6 referring to earnings on deferred compensation (or similar terms), the use of an unreasonable rate of return, or unreasonable actuarial assumptions and methods, generally will result in the treatment of some or all of such a right to deferred compensation as a right only to deferred compensation, and not a right to earnings on deferred compensation, so that the provision will not be applicable. With respect to plans that are neither account balance plans nor nonaccount balance plans, these rules apply by analogy.

(p) *In-kind benefits*. The term *in-kind benefits* refers to services provided to or on behalf of a service provider, such as financial planning services, or tangible personal or real property made available for use by or on behalf of the service provider, such as the use of an aircraft or vehicle, and does not refer to a transfer of property within the meaning of section 83 and the regulations thereunder, or a promise to transfer, or an option to purchase or receive, property in the future.

(q) *Application of definitions and rules*. The definitions and rules set forth in paragraphs (a) through (p) of this section apply for purposes of section 409A, this section, and §§1.409A–2 through 1.409A–6.

§1.409A–2 Deferral elections.

(a) *Initial elections as to the time and form of payment*—(1) *In general*. A plan that is, or constitutes part of, a nonqualified deferred compensation plan meets the requirements of section 409A(a)(4)(B) only if under the terms of the plan, compensation for services performed during a service provider's taxable year (the service year) may be deferred at the service provider's election only if the election to defer such compensation is made and becomes irrevocable not later than the latest date permitted in this paragraph (a). An election will not be considered to be revocable merely because the service provider or service recipient may make an election to change the time and form of payment pursuant to paragraph (b) of this section, or the service recipient may accelerate the time of payment pursuant to §1.409A–3(j)(4) (exceptions to prohibition on accelerated payments). Whether a plan provides a service provider an opportunity to elect the time or form of payment of compensation is determined based upon all the facts and circumstances surrounding the determination of the time and form of payment of the compensation. For purposes of this section, an election to defer includes an election as to the time of the payment, an election as to the form of the payment or an election as to both the time and the form of the payment, but does not include an election as to the medium of payment (for example, an election between a payment of cash or a payment of property). Except as otherwise expressly provided in this section, an election will not be considered made until such election becomes irrevocable under the terms of the applicable plan. Accordingly, a plan may provide that an election to defer may be changed at any time before the last permissible date for making such an election. Where a plan provides the service provider a right to make an initial deferral election, and further provides that the election remains in effect until terminated or modified by the service provider, the election will be treated as made as of the date such election becomes irrevocable as to compensation for services performed during the relevant service year. For example, where a plan provides that a service provider's election to defer a set percentage will remain in effect until changed or revoked, but that as of each December 31 the election becomes irrevocable with respect to salary payable in connection with services performed in the immediately following year, the initial deferral election with respect to salary payable with respect to services performed in the immediately following year will be deemed to have been made as of the December 31 upon which the election became irrevocable. For purposes of this paragraph (a), the reference to a service period or a performance period refers to the period of service for which the right to the compensation arises, and may include periods before the grant of a legally binding right to the compensation. For example, where a service recipient grants a bonus based upon services performed in the calendar year 2010, but retains the discretion to rescind the bonus until 2011 such that the promise of the bonus is not a legally binding right, the period of service or performance period to which the compensation relates is the calendar year 2010.

(2) *Service recipient elections.* A plan that provides for a deferral of compensation for services performed during a service provider's taxable year that does not provide the service provider with an opportunity to elect the time or form of payment of such compensation must designate the time and form of payment by no later than the later of the time the service provider first has a legally binding right to the compensation or, if later, the time the service provider would be required under this section to make such an election if the service provider were provided such an election. Such designation is treated as an initial deferral election for purposes of this section. Where a plan permits a service recipient to exercise discretion to disregard a service provider election as to the time or form of a payment, any service provider election that is subject to such discretion will be treated as revocable so long as such discretion may be exercised.

(3) *General rule.* A plan that is, or constitutes part of, a nonqualified deferred compensation plan meets the requirements of section 409A(a)(4)(B) if under the terms of the plan, compensation for services performed during a service provider's taxable year (the service year) may be deferred at the service provider's election only if the election to defer such compensation is made not later than the close of the service provider's taxable year next preceding the service year.

(4) *Initial deferral election with respect to short-term deferrals.* If a service provider has a legally binding right to a payment of compensation in a subsequent taxable year that, absent a deferral election, would be treated as a short-term deferral within the meaning of §1.409A–1(b)(4), an election to defer such compensation may be made in accordance with the requirements of paragraph (b) of this section, applied as if the amount were a deferral of compensation and the scheduled payment date for the amount were the date the substantial risk of forfeiture lapses. Notwithstanding the requirements of paragraph (b) of this section, such a deferral election may provide that the deferred amounts will be payable upon a change in control event (as defined in §1.409A–3(i)(5)) without regard to the five-year additional deferral requirement in paragraph (b) of this section.

(5) *Initial deferral election with respect to certain forfeitable rights.* If a service provider has a legally binding right to a payment in a subsequent year that is subject to a condition requiring the service provider to continue to provide services for a period of at least 12 months from the date the service provider obtains the legally binding right to avoid forfeiture of the payment, an election to defer such compensation may be made on or before the 30th day after the service provider obtains the legally binding right to the compensation, provided that the election is made at least 12 months in advance of the earliest date at which the forfeiture condition could lapse. For purposes of this paragraph (a)(5), a condition will not be treated as failing to require the service provider to continue to provide services for a period of at least 12 months from the date the service provider obtains the legally binding right merely because the condition immediately lapses upon the death or disability (as defined in §1.409A–3(i)(4)) of the service provider, or upon a change in control event (as defined in §1.409A–3(i)(5)), provided that if death, disability, or a change in control event occurs and the condition lapses before the end of such 12-month period, a deferral election may be given effect only if the deferral election is permitted under this section without regard to this paragraph (a)(5).

(6) *Initial deferral election with respect to fiscal year compensation.* In the case of a service recipient with a taxable year that is not the same as the taxable year of the service provider, a plan may provide that fiscal year compensation may be deferred at the service provider's election if the election to defer such compensation is made not later than the close of the service recipient's taxable year immediately preceding the first taxable year of the service recipient in which any services are performed for which such compensation is payable. For purposes of this paragraph (a)(6), the term *fiscal year compensation* means compensation relating to a period of service coextensive with one or more consecutive taxable years of the service recipient, of which no amount is paid or payable during the service recipient's taxable year or years constituting the period of service. For example, fiscal year compensation generally would include a bonus to an individual employee with a calendar year taxable year that is based on a service period consisting of the service recipient's two consecutive taxable years ending September 30, 2011, where the amount will be paid after the end of the second of such taxable years, but would not include either a bonus based on a service period consisting of one or more calendar years or salary that would otherwise be paid during such taxable years of the service recipient.

(7) *First year of eligibility*—(i) *In general.* In the case of the first year in which a service provider becomes eligible to participate in a plan, the service provider may make an initial deferral election within 30 days after the date the service provider becomes eligible to participate in such plan, with respect to compensation paid for services to be performed after the election. In the case of a plan that does not provide for service provider elections with respect to the time or form of a payment, the time and form of the payment must be specified on or before the date that is 30 days after the date the service provider first becomes eligible to participate in such plan. For compensation that is earned based upon a specified performance period (for example, an annual bonus), where a deferral election is made in the first year of eligibility but after the beginning of the performance period, the election must apply only to the compensation paid for services performed after the election. For this purpose, an election will be deemed to apply to compensation paid for services performed after the election if the election applies to no more than an amount equal to the total amount of the compensation for the performance period multiplied by the ratio of the number of days remaining in the performance period after the election over the total number of days in the performance period.

(ii) *Eligibility to participate.* For purposes of this paragraph (a)(7), a service provider is eligible to participate in a plan at any time during which, under the plan's terms and without further amendment or action by the service recipient, the service provider is eligible to accrue an amount of deferred compensation under the plan other than earnings on amounts previously deferred, even if the service provider has elected not to accrue (or has not elected to accrue) an amount of deferred compensation. Where a service provider has been paid all amounts deferred under a plan, and on and before the date of the last payment was not eligible to continue (or to elect to continue) to participate in the plan for periods after the last payment (other than through an election of a different time and form of payment with respect to the amounts paid), the service provider may be treated as initially eligible to participate in a plan as of the first date following such payment that the service provider becomes eligible to accrue an additional amount of deferred compensation. Where a service provider has ceased being eligible to participate in a plan (other than the accrual of earnings), regardless of whether all amounts deferred under the plan have been paid, and subsequently becomes eligible to participate in the plan again, the service provider may be treated as being initially eligible to participate in the plan if the service provider had not been eligible to participate in the plan (other than the accrual of earnings) at any time during the 24-month period ending on the date the service provider again becomes eligible to participate in the plan.

(iii) *Application to excess benefit plans.* For purposes of this paragraph (a)(7), a service provider is treated as initially eligible to participate in an excess benefit plan as of the first day of the service provider's taxable year immediately following the first year the service provider accrues a benefit under the excess benefit plan; and any election made within 30 days following such date is treated as applying to benefits accrued under such plan for services performed before the election. For purposes of this paragraph (a)(7), the term *excess benefit plan* means all nonqualified deferred compensation plans in which a service provider participates, to the extent such plans do not provide for an election between current compensation (including a short-term deferral) and deferred compensation and solely provide deferred compensation equal to the excess of the benefits the service provider would have accrued under a qualified employer plan (as defined in §1.409A–1(a)(2)) in which the service provider also participates, in the absence of one or more of the limits incorporated into the plan to reflect one or more of the limits on contributions or benefits applicable to the qualified employer plan under the Internal Revenue Code, over the benefits the service provider actually accrues under the qualified employer plan. For purposes of this paragraph (a)(7), once a service provider has accrued a benefit or deferred compensation under a plan in any year, the service provider will not become eligible for an initial deferral election based upon an accrual or deferral under an excess benefit plan in a subsequent year, even if the benefit or deferred compensation accrued in a previous year is forfeited or eliminated.

(8) *Initial deferral election with respect to performance-based compensation.* In the case of any performance-based compensation (as defined in §1.409A–1(e)), an initial deferral election may be made with respect to such performance-based compensation on or before the date that is six months before the end of the performance period, provided that the service provider performs services continuously from the later of the beginning of the performance period or the date the performance criteria are established through the date an election is made under this paragraph (a)(8), and provided further that in no event may an election to defer performance-based compensation be made after such compensation has become readily ascertainable. For purposes of this paragraph (a)(8), if the performance-based compensation is a specified or calculable amount, the compensation is readily ascertainable if and when the amount is first substantially certain to be paid. If the performance-based compensation is not a specified or calculable amount because, for example, the amount may vary based upon the level of performance, the compensation, or any portion of the compensation, is readily ascertainable when the amount is first both calculable and substantially certain to be paid. For this purpose, the performance-based compensation is bifurcated between the portion that is readily ascertainable and the amount that is not readily ascertainable. Accordingly, in general any minimum amount that is both calculable and substantially certain to be paid will be treated as readily ascertainable.

(9) *Nonqualified deferred compensation plans linked to qualified employer plans or certain other arrangements.* If a nonqualified deferred compensation plan provides that the amount deferred under the plan is determined under the formula for determining benefits under a qualified employer plan (as defined in §1.409A–1(a)(2)) or a broad-based foreign retirement plan (as defined in §1.409A–1(a)(3)(v)) maintained by the service recipient but applied without regard to one or more limitations applicable to the qualified employer plan under the Internal Revenue Code or to the broad-based foreign retirement plan under other applicable law, or that the amount deferred under the nonqualified deferred compensation plan is determined as an amount offset by some or all of the benefits provided under the qualified employer plan or the broad-based foreign retirement plan, an increase in amounts deferred under the nonqualified deferred compensation plan that results directly from changes in benefit limitations applicable to the qualified employer plan or the broad-based foreign retirement plan under the Internal Revenue Code or other applicable law does not constitute a deferral election under the nonqualified deferred compensation plan, provided that such operation does not otherwise result in a change in the time or form of a payment under the nonqualified deferred compensation plan, and provided further that such change in the amounts deferred under the nonqualified deferred compensation plan does not exceed that change in the amounts deferred under the qualified employer plan or the broad-based foreign retirement plan, as applicable. In addition, with respect to such a nonqualified deferred compensation plan, the following actions or failures to act will not constitute a deferral election under the nonqualified deferred compensation plan even if in accordance with the terms of the nonqualified deferred compensation plan, the actions or inactions result in an increase in the amounts deferred under the plan, provided that such actions or inactions do not otherwise affect the time or form of payment under the nonqualified deferred compensation plan and provided further that with respect to actions or inactions described in paragraphs (a)(9)(i) or (ii), the change in the amount deferred under the nonqualified deferred compensation plan does not exceed the change in the amounts deferred under the qualified employer plan or the broad-based foreign retirement plan, as applicable:

(i) A service provider's action or inaction under the qualified employer plan or broad-based foreign retirement plan with respect to whether to elect to receive a subsidized benefit or an ancillary benefit under the qualified employer plan or broad-based foreign retirement plan.

(ii) The amendment of a qualified employer plan or broad-based foreign retirement plan to add or remove a subsidized benefit or an ancillary benefit, or to freeze or limit future accruals of benefits under the qualified plan or freeze or limit future accruals of benefits or reduce existing benefits under the broad-based foreign retirement plan.

(iii) A service provider's action or inaction under a qualified employer plan with respect to elective deferrals and other employee pre-tax contributions subject to the contribution restrictions under section 401(a)(30) or section 402(g), including an adjustment to a deferral election under such qualified employer plan, provided that for any given taxable year, the service provider's action or inaction does not result in an increase in the amounts deferred under all nonqualified deferred compensation plans in which the service provider participates (other than amounts described in paragraph (a)(9)(iv) of this section) in excess of the limit with respect to elective deferrals under section 402(g)(1)(A), (B), and (C) in effect for the taxable year in which such action or inaction occurs.

(iv) A service provider's action or inaction under a qualified employer plan with respect to elective deferrals and other employee pre-tax contributions subject to the contribution restrictions under section 401(a)(30) or section 402(g), and after-tax contributions by the service provider to a qualified employer plan that provides for such contributions, that affects the amounts that are credited under one or more nonqualified deferred compensation plans as matching amounts or other similar amounts contingent on such elective deferrals, employee pre-tax contributions, or after-tax contributions, provided that the total of such matching or contingent amounts, as applicable, never exceeds 100 percent of the matching or contingent amounts that would be provided under the qualified employer plan absent any plan-based restrictions that reflect limits on qualified plan contributions under the Internal Revenue Code.

(10) *Changes in elections under a cafeteria plan.* A change in an election under a cafeteria plan does not constitute a deferral election with respect to an amount deferred under a nonqualified deferred compensation plan to the extent that the change in the amount deferred under the nonqualified deferred compensation plan results solely from the application of the change in amount eligible to be treated as compensation under the terms of the nonqualified deferred compensation plan resulting from the election change under the cafeteria plan, to a benefit formula under the nonqualified deferred compensation plan based upon the service provider's eligible compensation, and only to the extent that such change applies in the same manner as any other increase or decrease in compensation would apply to such benefit formula.

(11) *Initial deferral election with respect to certain separation pay.* In the case of separation pay (as defined in §1.409A–1(m)), where such separation pay is the subject of *bona fide*, arm's length negotiations at the time of the separation from service, an initial deferral election may be made at any time up to the time the service provider obtains a legally binding right to the payment. This paragraph (a)(11) does not apply to any separation pay to which the service provider obtained a legally binding right before the negotiations at the time of the separation from service, including a right to a payment subject to a condition such as that the service provider separate from service other than for cause. In the case of separation pay due to participation in a window program (as defined in §1.409A–1(b)(9)(vi)), an initial deferral election may be made at any time before the time the election to participate in the window program becomes irrevocable.

(12) *Initial deferral election with respect to certain commissions*—(i) *Sales commission compensation.* For purposes of this paragraph (a), a service provider earning sales commission compensation is treated as providing the services to which such compensation relates only in the service provider's taxable year in which the customer remits payment to the service recipient or, if applied consistently to all similarly situated service providers, the service provider's taxable year in which the sale occurs. For purposes of this paragraph (a)(12), the term *sales commission compensation* means compensation or portions of compensation earned by a service provider if a substantial portion of the services provided by such service provider to a service recipient consist of the direct sale of a product or service to an unrelated customer, the compensation paid by the service recipient to the service provider consists of either a portion of the purchase price for the product or service or an amount substantially all of which is calculated by reference to the volume of sales, and payment of the compensation is either contingent upon the service recipient receiving payment from an unrelated customer for the product or services or, if applied consistently to all similarly situated service providers, is contingent upon the closing of the sales transaction and such other requirements as may be specified by the service recipient before the closing of the sales transaction. For this purpose, a customer is treated as an unrelated customer only if the customer is not related to either the service provider or the service recipient. A person is treated as related to another person if the person would be treated as related to the other person under §1.409A–1(f)(2)(ii) or the person would be treated as providing management services to the other person under §1.409A–1(f)(2)(iv).

(ii) *Investment commission compensation.* For purposes of this paragraph (a), a service provider earning investment commission compensation is treated as providing the services to which such compensation relates over the 12 months preceding the date as of which the overall value of the assets or asset accounts is determined for purposes of the calculation of the investment commission compensation. For purposes of this paragraph (a)(12), the term *investment commission compensation* means the compensation or the portion of compensation earned by a service provider if a substantial portion of the services provided by such service provider to a service recipient to which such compensation relates consists of sales of financial products or other direct customer services to an unrelated customer with respect to customer assets or customer asset accounts, the customer retains the right to terminate the customer relationship and may move or liquidate the assets or asset accounts without undue delay (which may be subject to a reasonable notice period), such compensation consists of a portion of the value of the overall assets or asset account balance, an amount substantially all of which is calculated by reference to the increase in the value of the overall assets or account balance during a specified period, or both, and the value of the overall assets or account balance and investment commission compensation is determined at least annually. For this purpose, a customer is treated as an unrelated customer only if the customer is not related to either the service provider or the service recipient. A person is treated as related to another person if the person would be treated as related to the other person under §1.409A–1(f)(2)(ii) or the person would be treated as providing management services to the other person under §1.409A–1(f)(2)(iv).

(iii) *Commission compensation and related persons*. The rules of paragraphs (a)(12)(i) and (ii) of this section apply to sales commission compensation and investment commission compensation involving a related customer, provided that substantial sales from which commission compensation arises are made, or substantial services from which commission compensation arises are provided, to unrelated customers by the service recipient, the sales and service arrangement and the commission arrangement with respect to the related customer are *bona fide*, arise from the service recipient's ordinary course of business, and are substantially the same, both in terms and in practice, as the terms and practices applicable to unrelated customers (as defined in such paragraphs) to which individually or in the aggregate substantial sales are made or substantial services provided by the service recipient.

(13) *Initial deferral election with respect to compensation paid for final payroll period*—(i) *In general*. Unless a plan provides otherwise, compensation payable after the last day of the service provider's taxable year solely for services performed during the final payroll period described in section 3401(b) containing the last day of the service provider's taxable year or, with respect to a non-employee service provider, a period not longer than the payroll period described in section 3401(b), where such amount is payable pursuant to the timing arrangement under which the service recipient normally compensates service providers for services performed during a payroll period described in section 3401(b), or with respect to a non-employee service provider, a period not longer than the payroll period described in section 3401(b), is treated as compensation for services performed in the subsequent taxable year in which the payment is made. The preceding sentence does not apply to any compensation paid during such period for services performed during any period other than such final payroll period, such as a payment of an annual bonus. Any amendment of a plan after December 31, 2007, to add a provision providing for a differing treatment of such compensation may not be effective for 12 months from the date the amendment is executed and enacted.

(ii) *Transition rule*. For purposes of this paragraph (a)(13), a plan that was adopted and effective before December 31, 2007, whether written or unwritten, will be treated as designating such compensation for services performed in the taxable year in which the payroll period ends, unless otherwise set forth in writing before December 31, 2007.

(14) *Elections to annualize recurring part-year compensation*. In the case of a service provider receiving recurring part-year compensation, an election to defer all or a portion of the recurring part-year compensation to be earned during a particular service period is considered to meet the requirements of this paragraph (a) if the election is made before the services for which the recurring part-year compensation is paid begin, and the election does not defer payment of any of the recurring part-year compensation to a date beyond the last day of the 13th month following the first date of the service period. For purposes of this paragraph (a)(14), the term *recurring part-year compensation* means compensation paid for services rendered in a position that the service recipient and service provider reasonably anticipate will continue on similar terms and conditions in subsequent years, and will require services to be provided during successive service periods each of which comprises less than 12 months (for example, a teacher providing services during a school year comprised of 10 consecutive months), and each of which periods begins in one taxable year of the service provider and ends in the next such taxable year. The rules of this paragraph (a)(14) apply to a particular amount of compensation only once, so that an amount deferred under this rule may not again be treated as recurring part-year compensation for purposes of this paragraph and subject to a second deferral election under this paragraph (a)(14).

(15) *USERRA rights*. The requirements of this paragraph (a) are deemed satisfied to the extent an initial deferral election is provided to satisfy the requirements of the Uniformed Service Employment and Reemployment Rights Act of 1994, as amended, 38 U.S.C. 4301–4334.

(b) *Subsequent changes in time and form of payment*—(1) *In general*. A plan that permits under a subsequent election a delay in a payment or a change in the form of payment (a subsequent deferral election), including a subsequent deferral election made by a service provider or a service recipient, satisfies the requirements of section 409A(a)(4)(C) only if the conditions of this paragraph (b) are met. For purposes of this paragraph (b), except as otherwise expressly provided in this section, a subsequent deferral election is not considered made until such election becomes irrevocable under the terms of the plan. Accordingly, a plan may provide that a subsequent deferral election may be changed at any time before the last permissible date for making such a subsequent deferral election. Where a plan permits a subsequent deferral election, the requirements of this paragraph are satisfied only if the following conditions are met:

(i) The plan requires that such election not take effect until at least 12 months after the date on which the election is made.

(ii) In the case of an election related to a payment not described in §1.409A–3(a)(2) (payment on account of disability), §1.409A–3(a)(3) (payment on account of death), or §1.409A–3(a)(6) (payment on account of the occurrence of an unforeseeable emergency), the plan requires that the payment with respect to which such election is made be deferred for a period of not less than five years from the date such payment would otherwise have been paid (or in the case of a life annuity or installment payments treated as a single payment, five years from the date the first amount was scheduled to be paid).

(iii) The plan requires that any election related to a payment described in §1.409A–3(a)(4) (payment at a specified time or pursuant to a fixed schedule) be made not less than 12 months before the date the payment is scheduled to be paid (or in the case of a life annuity or installment payments treated as a single payment, 12 months before the date the first amount was scheduled to be paid).

(2) *Definition of payments for purposes of subsequent changes in the time or form of payment*—(i) *In general.* Except as provided in paragraphs (b)(2)(ii) and (iii) of this section, the term *payment* refers to each separately identified amount to which a service provider is entitled to payment under a plan on a determinable date, and includes amounts applied for the benefit of the service provider. An amount is separately identified only if the amount may be objectively determined under a nondiscretionary formula. For example, an amount identified as 10 percent of the account balance as of a specified payment date would be a separately identified amount. A payment includes the provision of any taxable benefit, including payment in cash or in kind. In addition, a payment includes, but is not limited to, the transfer, cancellation, or reduction of an amount of deferred compensation in exchange for benefits under a welfare benefit plan, a fringe benefit excludible under section 119 or section 132, or any other benefit that is excludible from gross income. For additional rules relating to the application of this paragraph (b) to amounts payable at a fixed time or pursuant to a fixed schedule, see §1.409A–3(i)(1).

(ii) *Life annuities*—(A) *In general.* The entitlement to a life annuity is treated as the entitlement to a single payment. Accordingly, an election to delay payment of a life annuity, or to change the form of payment of a life annuity, must be made at least 12 months before the scheduled commencement of the life annuity, and must defer the payment for a period of not less than five years from the originally scheduled commencement of the life annuity. For purposes of §1.409A–1, this section, and §§1.409A–3 through 1.409A–6, the term *life annuity* means a series of substantially equal periodic payments, payable not less frequently than annually, for the life (or life expectancy) of the service provider, or a series of substantially equal periodic payments, payable not less frequently than annually, for the life (or life expectancy) of the service provider, followed upon the death or end of the life expectancy of the service provider by a series of substantially equal periodic payments, payable not less frequently then annually, for the life (or life expectancy) of the service provider's designated beneficiary (if any). A change in designated beneficiary before any annuity payment has been made under the plan is not a change in the time or form of payment. A change in the form of a payment before any annuity payment has been made under the plan, from one type of life annuity to another type of life annuity with the same scheduled date for the first annuity payment, is not considered a change in the time and form of a payment, provided that the annuities are actuarially equivalent applying reasonable actuarial methods and assumptions. For purposes of this paragraph (b)(2)(ii), a requirement that a service provider obtain the consent of a spouse or other potential recipient of a survivor annuity to change a beneficiary or form of payment is disregarded, so that any annuity form that the service recipient could elect to receive with such consent is considered currently available.

(B) *Certain features disregarded.* Notwithstanding the foregoing provisions of this paragraph (b)(2)(ii), the following features are disregarded for purposes of determining whether a payment form is a life annuity within the meaning of this paragraph (b)(2)(ii), but are not disregarded for purposes of determining whether a life annuity is the actuarial equivalent of another life annuity except as otherwise provided in this paragraph (b)(2)(ii):

(*1*) Term certain features under which annuity payments continue for the longer of the life of the annuitant or a fixed period of time.

(*2*) Pop-up features under which payments increase upon the death of the beneficiary or another event that eliminates the right to a survivor annuity.

(*3*) Cash refund features under which payment is provided upon the death of the last annuitant in an amount that is not greater than the excess of the present value of the annuity at the annuity starting date over the total of payments before the death of the last annuitant.

(*4*) Features under which an annuity form of payment provides higher periodic payments before the expected commencement of benefits under the Social Security Act (42 U.S.C. ch. 7) or the Railroad Retirement Act (45 U.S.C. 231 *et. seq.*) and lower periodic payments after such expected commencement date, so that the combined periodic payments under the arrangement and the Social Security Act or the Railroad Retirement Act, as applicable, are approximately level before and after such expected commencement date (Social Security or Railroad Retirement leveling features).

(*5*) Features providing for an increase in the annuity payment in a manner described in §1.401(a)(9)–6, Q&A–14(a)(1) or (2) (eligible cost-of-living adjustments).

(C) *Subsidized joint and survivor annuities.* For purposes of this paragraph (b)(2)(ii), a joint and survivor annuity will not fail to be treated as actuarially equivalent to a single life annuity due solely to the value of a subsidized survivor annuity benefit, provided that the annual lifetime annuity benefit available to the service provider under the joint and survivor annuity is not greater than the annual lifetime annuity benefit available to the service provider under the single life annuity alternative, and provided that the annual survivor annuity benefit is not greater than the annual lifetime annuity benefit available to the service provider under the joint and survivor annuity.

(D) *Actuarial assumptions and methods.* For purposes of this paragraph (b)(2)(ii), at any given time the same actuarial assumptions and methods must be used in valuing each annuity payment option, in determining whether the payments are actuarially equivalent and such assumptions must be reasonable. This requirement applies over the entire term of the service provider's participation in the plan, such that the annuity payment must be actuarially equivalent at all times for the annuity payment options to be treated as one time and form of payment. There is no requirement that the same actuarial methods and assumptions be used over the term of a service provider's participation in a plan. Accordingly, a plan may change the actuarial assumptions and methods used to determine the life annuity payments provided that all of the actuarial assumptions and methods are reasonable.

(iii) *Installment payments.* The entitlement to a series of installment payments that is not a life annuity is treated as the entitlement to a single payment, unless the plan provides at all times with respect to the amount deferred that the right to the series of installment payments is to be treated as a right to a series of separate payments.

For purposes of §1.409A–1, this section, and §§1.409A–3 through 1.409A–6, a series of installment payments refers to an entitlement to the payment of a series of substantially equal periodic amounts to be paid over a predetermined period of years, except to the extent any increase (or decrease) in the amount reflects reasonable earnings (or losses) through the date the amount is paid. For this purpose, a series of installment payments over a predetermined period and a series of installment payments over a shorter or longer period, or a series of installment payments over the same predetermined period but with a different commencement date, are different times and forms of payment. Accordingly, a change in the predetermined period or the commencement date is a change in the time and form of payment. Notwithstanding the foregoing, a schedule of payments does not fail to be an installment payment solely because such plan provides for an immediate payment of all remaining installments if the present value of the deferred amount to be paid in the remaining installment payments falls below a predetermined amount, and the immediate payment of such amount does not constitute an accelerated payment for purposes of §1.409A–3(j), provided that such feature including the predetermined amount is established by no later than the time and form of payment is otherwise required to be established, and provided further that any change in such feature including the predetermined amount is a change in the time and form of payment.

(iv) *Transition rule.* For purposes of this section, a plan that was adopted and effective before December 31, 2007, whether written or unwritten, that fails to make a designation as to whether the entitlement to a series of payments is to be treated as an entitlement to a series of separate payments under paragraph (b)(2)(iii) of this section, may make such designation on or before December 31, 2007, provided such designation is set forth in writing on or before December 31, 2007.

(3) *Beneficiaries.* The rules of this paragraph (b) governing changes in the time and form of payment apply to elections by beneficiaries with respect to the time and form of payment, as well as elections by service providers or service recipients with respect to the time and form of payment to beneficiaries. An election to change the identity of a beneficiary does not constitute a change in the time and form of payment merely because the election changes the identity of the recipient of the payment, if the time and form of the payment is not otherwise changed. In addition, an election to change the identity of a beneficiary before the initial payment of a life annuity does not constitute a change in the time and form of payment if the change in the time of payments stems solely from the different life expectancy of the new beneficiary, such as in the case of a joint and survivor annuity.

(4) *Domestic relations orders.* The rules of this paragraph (b) governing changes in the time and form of payment do not apply to elections by individuals other than a service provider, with respect to payments to a person other than the service provider, to the extent such elections are reflected in, or made in accordance with, the terms of a domestic relations order (as defined in section 414(p)(1)(B)).

(5) *Coordination with prohibition against acceleration of payments.* For purposes of applying the prohibition against the acceleration of payments in §1.409A–3(j), the definition of payment is the same as the definition in paragraph (b)(2) of this section. Accordingly, a change in the form of a payment that results in a more rapid schedule for payments generally will not constitute an acceleration of a payment, if the change in the form of payment is made in compliance with the subsequent deferral rules. For example, a change in form from a 10-year installment payment treated as a single payment to a lump-sum payment would not constitute an acceleration if the change in the form of the payment is made in compliance with the requirements of paragraph (b)(1) of this section, generally meaning that the election to change to a lump-sum payment must be made at least 12 months before the installment payments were scheduled to commence and the lump-sum payment could not be made until at least five years after the date the installment payments were scheduled to commence. See §1.409A–3(j)(4)(i) with respect to situations in which the failure to accelerate a payment or the modification of a plan term relating to certain accelerated payments will not be subject to the rules of this paragraph (b).

(6) *Application to multiple payment events.* In the case of a plan that permits a payment upon each of a number of potential permissible payment events, such as the earlier of a fixed date or separation from service, the requirements of paragraph (b)(1) of this section are applied separately to each payment (as defined in paragraph (b)(2) of this section) due upon each payment event. Notwithstanding the foregoing, the addition or deletion of a permissible payment event to a plan under which amounts were previously deferred is subject to the rules of this paragraph (b) where the addition or deletion of the permissible payment event may result in a change in the time or form of payment of the amount deferred. For application of the rules governing accelerations of payments to the addition of a permissible payment event to amounts deferred, see §1.409A–3(j).

(7) *Delay of payments under certain circumstances.* A payment may be delayed to a date after the designated payment date under any of the circumstances described in this paragraph (b)(7), and the provision will not fail to meet the requirements of establishing a permissible payment event and the delay in the payment will not constitute a subsequent deferral election, so long as the service recipient treats all payments to similarly situated service providers on a reasonably consistent basis.

(i) *Payments subject to section 162(m).* A payment may be delayed to the extent that the service recipient reasonably anticipates that if the payment were made as scheduled, the service recipient's deduction with respect to such payment would not be permitted due to the application of section 162(m), provided that the payment is made either during the service provider's first taxable year in which the service recipient reasonably anticipates, or should reasonably anticipate, that if the payment is made during such year, the deduction of such payment will not be barred by application of section 162(m) or during the period beginning with the date of the service provider's separation from service and ending on the later of the last day of the taxable year of the service recipient in which the service provider separates from service or the 15th day of the third month following the service provider's separation from service, and provided further that where any scheduled payment to a specific service provider in a service recipient's taxable year is delayed in accordance with this paragraph, the delay in payment will be treated as a subsequent deferral election unless all scheduled payments to that service provider that could be delayed in accordance with this paragraph are also delayed. Where the payment is delayed to a date on or after the service provider's separation from service, the payment will be considered a payment upon a separation from service for purposes of the rules under §1.409A–3(i)(2) (payments to specified employees upon a separation from service) and, in the case of a specified employee, the date that is six months after a service provider's separation from service is substituted for any reference to a service provider's separation from service in the first sentence of this paragraph. No election may be provided to the service provider with respect to the timing of the payment under this paragraph (b)(7)(i).

(ii) *Payments that would violate Federal securities laws or other applicable law.* A payment may be delayed where the service recipient reasonably anticipates that the making of the payment will violate Federal securities laws or other applicable law; provided that the payment is made at the earliest date at which the service recipient reasonably anticipates that the making of the payment will not cause such violation. The making of a payment that would cause inclusion in gross income or the application of any penalty provision or other provision of the Internal Revenue Code is not treated as a violation of applicable law.

(iii) *Other events and conditions.* A service recipient may delay a payment upon such other events and conditions as the Commissioner may prescribe in generally applicable guidance published in the Internal Revenue Bulletin (see §601.601(d)(2) of this chapter). For additional rules applicable to certain delayed payments pursuant to a change in control event, see §1.409A–3(i)(5)(iv). For additional rules applicable to amounts payable because of an unforeseeable emergency, see §1.409A–3(i)(3).

(8) *USERRA rights.* The requirements of this paragraph (b) are deemed met to the extent an election to change the time or form of a payment of deferred compensation is provided to satisfy the requirements of the Uniformed Services Employment and Reemployment Rights Act of 1994, as amended, 38 U.S.C. 4301–4344.

(9) *Examples.* The following examples illustrate the application of the provisions of this section. For purposes of these examples, each employee is an individual with a calendar year taxable year, and is employed by the specified employer:

Example 1. Initial election to defer salary. Employer ZZ sponsors a plan under which Employee A may elect to defer a percentage of Employee A's salary. Employee A has participated in the plan in prior years. To satisfy the requirements of this section with respect to salary earned in calendar year 2008, if Employee A elects to defer any amount of such salary, the deferral election (including an election as to the time and form of payment) must be made no later than December 31, 2007.

Example 2. Designation of time and form of payment where an initial deferral election is not provided. Employer YY has a taxable year ending September 30. On July 1, 2008, Employer YY enters into a legally binding obligation to pay Employee B a $10,000 bonus. The amount is not subject to a substantial risk of forfeiture and does not qualify as performance-based compensation as described in §1.409A–1(e). Employer YY does not provide Employee B an election as to the time and form of payment. Unless the amount is to be paid in accordance with the short-term deferral rule of §1.409A–1(b)(4), Employer YY must specify the time and form of payment on or before July 1, 2008, to satisfy the requirements of this section.

Example 3. Initial election to defer bonus payable based on services during calendar year. Employer XX has a taxable year ending September 30. Employee C participates in a bonus plan under which Employee C is entitled to a bonus for services performed during the calendar year that, absent an election by Employee C, will be paid on March 15 of the following year. The amount is not subject to a substantial risk of forfeiture and does not qualify as performance-based compensation as described in §1.409A–1(e). If Employee C elects to defer the payment of the bonus with respect to services rendered during calendar year 2008, Employee C must elect the time and form of payment not later than December 31, 2007, to satisfy the requirements of this section.

Example 4. Initial election to defer bonus payable based on services during fiscal year other than calendar year. Employer WW has a taxable year ending September 30. Employee D participates in a bonus plan under which Employee D is entitled to a bonus for services performed during Employer WW's fiscal year that, absent an election by Employee D, will be paid on December 15 of the calendar year in which the fiscal year ends. The amount is not subject to a substantial risk of forfeiture and does not qualify as performance-based compensation as described in §1.409A–1(e). The amount qualifies as fiscal year compensation. If Employee D elects to defer the payment of the amount related to the fiscal year ending September 30, 2009, to satisfy the requirements of this section Employee D must elect the time and form of payment not later than September 30, 2008.

Example 5. Initial election to defer bonus payable only if service provider completes at least 12 months of services after the election. Employer VV has a calendar year taxable year. On March 1, 2008, Employer VV grants Employee E a $10,000 bonus, payable on March 1, 2010 (with reasonable interest), provided that Employee E continues performing services as an employee of Employer VV through March 1, 2010. The amount does not qualify as performance-based compensation as described in §1.409A–1(e), and Employee E already participates in another account balance nonqualified deferred compensation plan. Employee E may make an initial deferral election on or before March 31, 2008 (within 30 days after obtaining a legally binding right), because at least 12 months of additional services are required after the date of election for the risk of forfeiture to lapse.

Example 6. Initial election to defer bonus that would otherwise constitute a short-term deferral. The same facts as *Example 5*, except that Employee E does not make an initial deferral election on or before March 31, 2008. Because the right to the compensation would not be treated as a deferral of compensation pursuant to §1.409A–1(b)(4) absent a deferral election (because the arrangement would be treated as a short-term deferral), Employee E may make an initial deferral election provided that the election may not become effective for 12 months and must defer the payment at least 5 years from March 1, 2010 (the first date the payment could become substantially vested). Accordingly, Employee E may make an election before March 1, 2009, provided that the election defers the payment to a date on or after March 1, 2015 (other than a payment due to death, disability, unforeseeable emergency, or a change in control event).

Example 7. Initial election to defer sales commissions. Employer UU has a calendar year taxable year. As part of Employee F's services for Employer UU, Employee F sells refrigerators to customers unrelated to Employee F or Employer UU. Under the employment arrangement, Employee F is entitled to 10% of the sales price of any refrigerator Employee F sells, payable only upon the receipt of payment from the customer who purchased the refrigerator. For purposes of the initial deferral rule, Employee F is treated as performing the services related to each refrigerator sale in the calendar year in which each customer pays for the refrigerator.

Example 8. Initial election to defer renewal sales commissions. The same facts as *Example 7*, except that Employee F also sells warranties related to the refrigerators sold. Under the warranty arrangement, refrigerator warranty customers are entitled in a future year to extend the warranty for an additional cost to be paid at the time of the extension. Under Employee F's arrangement with Employer UU, Employee F is entitled to 10% of the amount paid for an extension of any warranty, payable upon the receipt of payment from the customer extending the warranty. For purposes of the initial deferral election rule, Employee F is treated as performing the services related to the amount paid for the extension of the warranty in the taxable year in which the customer pays for the warranty extension.

Example 9. Initial election to defer investment commissions. Employer TT is in the trade or business of managing financial assets for customer accounts. Customers who deposit funds in an account with Employer TT are entitled to remove the account balance of such account upon 60 days notice to Employer TT. Employee G sells financial products and provides continuing customer service to certain unrelated customers involving the deposit and maintenance of funds in customer accounts managed by Employer TT. Under the employment arrangement, Employee G is entitled to a set percentage of the aggregate value of the assets held in the accounts of customers to whom Employee G sold financial products and provides customer service. Under the arrangement, the aggregate value of the assets held in the accounts is determined as of June 30 of each year, and unless Employee G elects to defer the payment, the amount is payable to Employee G in a lump sum on December 31 of the year in which the valuation is made. Employee G has no control over the valuation of the assets held in the accounts, or the calculation of the amount due Employee G. For purposes of the initial deferral rule, Employee G is treated as providing the services to which a payment relates during the July 1 through June 30 period ending on the June 30 date as of which the assets held in the account are valued.

Example 10. Initial election to defer part-year compensation. Employee H provides services as a teacher to Employer SS, a school system. The period of services routinely begins on the second Monday of August of one year and ends on the first Friday of June of the subsequent year. Employer SS provides an election to Employee H to receive the compensation for the period of services ratably over the period beginning on the second Monday of August of one year and ending on the last day of August of the subsequent year. Because the compensation constitutes recurring part-year compensation, as defined in paragraph (a)(14) of this section, and because the schedule will provide that all of the recurring part-year compensation is paid no later than September 30 of the subsequent year, Employee H will be deemed to have made a timely deferral election with respect to such recurring part-year compensation if Employee H elects before the first day of the service period to have the recurring part-year compensation paid under such schedule.

Example 11. Initial election to defer negotiated separation pay. Employer RR decides to terminate Employee J's employment involuntarily. As part of the process of terminating Employee J, Employer RR enters into *bona fide*, arm's length negotiations with respect to the terms of Employee J's termination of employment. As part of the process, Employer RR offers Employee J an amount that is in addition to any amounts to which Employee J is otherwise entitled, payable either as a lump sum payment at the end of 3 years or in 3 annual payments starting at the date of termination of employment. The election of the time and form of payment by Employee J may be made at any time before Employee J accepts the offer and obtains a legally binding right to the additional amount. The election may not apply to any amount to which Employee J already had a legally binding right.

Example 12. Election of time and form of payments under a window program. Employer QQ establishes a window program, as defined in §1.409A–1(b)(9)(vi). Individuals who elect to terminate employment under the window program are entitled to receive an amount equal to 2 weeks pay multiplied by every year of service with Employer QQ. The individuals participating in the window program may elect to receive the payment as either a lump sum payment payable on the first day of the month after making the election to participate in the window program, or as a payment of 3 equal annual installments on each January 1 of the first 3 years following the election to participate in the window program. Employee K is eligible to participate in the window program. Employee K will be treated as making a timely deferral election if the election as to the time and form of payment is made on or before the date Employee K's election to participate in the window program becomes irrevocable.

Example 13. Initial election to defer salary earned during final payroll period beginning in one calendar year and ending in the subsequent calendar year. Employer PP pays the salary of its employees, including Employee L, on a bi-weekly basis. One bi-weekly payroll period runs from December 24, 2008, through January 6, 2009, with a scheduled payment date of January 13, 2009. Employer PP sponsors, and Employee L participates in, a nonqualified deferred compensation plan under which Employee L may defer a specified percentage of his annual salary. The plan does not specify that any salary compensation paid for the payroll period in which falls January 1 is to be treated as compensation for services performed during the year preceding the year in which falls that January 1. For purposes of applying the initial deferral election rules, Employee L is deemed to have performed the services for the payroll period December 24, 2008, through January 6, 2009, during the calendar year 2009.

Example 14. Application of deferral election rules and anti-acceleration rules to a nonqualified deferred compensation plan linked to a qualified plan. Employee M participates in a qualified retirement plan that is a defined benefit plan that offers a subsidized early retirement benefit to employees who have attained age 55 and completed 30 years of service. Employee M, who has attained age 55 and completed 30 years of service, also participates in a nonqualified deferred compensation plan, under which the benefit payable is calculated under a formula, with that benefit then reduced by any benefit that Employee M has accrued under the qualified retirement plan. In 2008, Employee M fails to elect the subsidized early retirement benefit under the qualified retirement plan, with the effect that the amounts payable under the nonqualified deferred compensation plan are increased by an amount equal to the reduction in the benefit payable under the qualified plan. In 2009, Employer NN amends the qualified retirement plan to increase benefits under the plan, resulting in a decrease in the amounts payable under the nonqualified deferred compensation plan equal to the increase in the benefit payable under the qualified plan. Neither of these actions constitutes a deferral election or an acceleration of a payment under the nonqualified deferred compensation plan.

Example 15. Subsequent deferral election. Employee N participates in a nonqualified deferred compensation plan. Employee N elects to be paid in a lump sum payment at the earlier of age 65 or separation from service. Employee N anticipates that he will work after age 65, and wishes to defer payment to a later date. Provided that Employee N continues in employment and makes the election by his 64th birthday, Employee N may elect to receive a lump sum payment at the earlier of age 70 or separation from service.

Example 16. Subsequent deferral election rule – change in form of payment from lump sum payment to life annuity. Employee P participates in a nonqualified deferred compensation plan. Employee P elects to be paid in a lump sum payment at age 65. Employee P wishes to change the payment form to a life annuity. Provided that Employee P makes the election on or before his 64th birthday, Employee P may elect to receive a life annuity commencing at age 70.

Example 17. Subsequent deferral election rule – change in form of payment from life annuity to lump sum payment. Employee Q participates in a nonqualified deferred compensation plan. Employee Q elects to be paid in a life annuity at age 65. Employee Q wishes to change the payment form to a lump sum payment. Provided that Employee Q makes the election on or before his 64th birthday, Employee Q may elect to receive a lump sum payment at age 70.

Example 18. Subsequent deferral election rule – installment payments designated as separate payments. Employee R, whose taxable year is the calendar year, participates in a nonqualified deferred compensation plan that provides for payment in a series of 5 equal annual amounts, each designated as a separate payment. The first payment is scheduled to be made on January 1, 2010. Provided that Employee R makes the election on or before January 1, 2009, Employee R may elect for the first payment scheduled to be made on January 1, 2010, to be made on January 1, 2015. If Employee R makes that election, but does not elect to defer the remaining payments, the remaining payments continue to be due upon January 1 of the 4 consecutive calendar years commencing on January 1, 2011.

Example 19. Subsequent deferral election rule – change in form of payment from installment payments not designated as separate payments to lump sum payment. Employee S participates in a nonqualified deferred compensation plan that provides for payment in a series of 5 equal annual amounts that are not designated as a series of 5 separate payments. The first amount is scheduled to be paid on January 1, 2010. Employee S wishes to receive the entire amount equal to the sum of all 5 of the amounts to be paid as a lump sum payment. Provided that Employee S makes the election on or before January 1, 2009, Employee S may elect to receive a lump sum payment on or after January 1, 2015.

Example 20. Subsequent deferral election rule – change in form of payment from installment payments designated as separate payments to lump sum payment. Employee T participates in a nonqualified deferred compensation plan that provides for payment in a series of 5 equal annual amounts each of which is designated as a separate payment. The first amount is scheduled to be paid on January 1, 2010. Employee T wishes to receive the entire amount equal to the sum of all 5 of the amounts in a single lump sum payment. Provided that Employee T makes the election on or before January 1, 2009, Employee T may elect to receive a lump sum payment on or after January 1, 2019.

Example 21. Subsequent deferral election rule – change in form of payment from one life annuity form to another life annuity form. Employee U participates in a nonqualified deferred compensation plan that permits Employee U to elect before Employee

U's separation from service whether to be paid in the form of a single life annuity beginning on the first day of the month following Employee U's separation from service, or an annuity beginning on the first day of the month following Employee U's separation from service under which annuity payments continue for Employee U's lifetime but not less than 10 years. The two types of annuities are actuarially equivalent at all times applying reasonable actuarial methods and assumptions. For purposes of this section, the two types of annuities are treated as a single form of payment. Accordingly, the election provided under the plan is not treated as providing a subsequent deferral election or accelerated payment, and an election by Employee U under the plan between the two annuity options made before the first scheduled payment date for an annuity payment is not treated as a subsequent deferral election or an acceleration of a payment.

Example 22. Subsequent deferral election rule – change in time of payment from payment at specified age to payment at later of specified age or separation from service. Employee V participates in a nonqualified deferred compensation plan that provides for a lump sum payment at age 65. Employee V wishes to modify the plan so that the deferred amount will be payable upon the later of Employee V's attainment of a specified age or separation from service. Provided that Employee V makes such election on or before his 64th birthday, Employee V may modify the plan so Employee V will receive a lump sum payment upon the later of age 70 or separation from service.

Example 23. Subsequent deferral election rule – change in time of payment from payment at separation from service to payment at later of separation from service or specified age. Employee W participates in a nonqualified deferred compensation plan that provides for a lump sum payment at separation from service. Employee W wishes to make the payment payable upon the later of separation from service or a predetermined age. Provided that Employee W makes such election on or before the date 1 year before a separation from service, Employee W may elect to receive a lump sum payment upon the later of the date 5 years following a separation from service or at a specified age.

Example 24. Subsequent deferral election rule – change in time of payment from payment at separation from service to payment at a change in control event. Employee X participates in a nonqualified deferred compensation plan that provides for a lump sum payment at separation from service. Employee X wishes to change the payment provision such that the payment is payable upon a change in control event. A change in the distribution provision to provide for a payment only upon a change in control event will violate the rules governing payment provisions, because the change could result in an acceleration if the change in control event occurs before Employee X separates from service, or a subsequent deferral if the change in control does not occur until after Employee X separates from service. However, provided that Employee X makes such election on or before the date 1 year before a separation from service, Employee X may elect to receive a payment upon the later of a change in control event or 5 years following a separation from service.

(c) *Special rules for certain resident aliens.* For the first taxable year of an individual in which such individual is a resident alien, a nonqualified deferred compensation plan is deemed to meet the requirements of paragraph (a) of this section if, with respect to compensation payable for services performed during that first taxable year or with respect to compensation the right to which is subject to a substantial risk of forfeiture as of the first day of that first taxable year, an initial deferral election is made by the end of such first taxable year, provided that the initial deferral election may not apply to amounts that have already been paid or made available to the service provider before the election is made. For any year after the first taxable year in which an individual is classified as a resident alien, this paragraph (c) does not apply, provided that a taxable year may again be treated as the first taxable year in which an individual is classified as a resident alien if such individual is classified as a resident alien in that taxable year and has not been classified as a resident alien for the three consecutive taxable years immediately preceding that taxable year.

§1.409A–3 Permissible payments.

(a) *In general.* The requirements of section 409A(a)(2)(A) are met only if the plan provides that an amount of deferred compensation under the plan may be paid only upon an event or at a time set forth in this paragraph (a):

(1) The service provider's separation from service (as defined in §1.409A–1(h) and in accordance with paragraph (i)(2) of this section).

(2) The service provider becoming disabled (in accordance with paragraph (i)(4) of this section).

(3) The service provider's death.

(4) A time or a fixed schedule specified under the plan (in accordance with paragraph (i)(1) of this section).

(5) A change in the ownership or effective control of the corporation, or in the ownership of a substantial portion of the assets of the corporation (in accordance with paragraph (i)(5) of this section).

(6) The occurrence of an unforeseeable emergency (in accordance with paragraph (i)(3) of this section).

(b) *Designation of payment upon a permissible payment event.* Except as otherwise specified in this section, a plan provides for the payment upon an event described in paragraph (a)(1), (2), (3), (5), or (6) of this section if the plan provides the date of the event is the payment date, or specifies another payment date that is objectively determinable and nondiscretionary at the time the event occurs. A plan may also provide that a payment upon an event described in paragraph (a)(1), (2), (3), (5), or (6) of this section is to be made in accordance with a schedule that is objectively determinable and nondiscretionary based on the date the event occurs and that would qualify as a fixed schedule under paragraph (i)(1) of this section if the payment event were instead a fixed date, provided that the schedule must be fixed at the time the permissible payment event is designated. In addition, a plan may provide that a payment, including a payment that is part of a schedule, is to be made during a designated taxable year of the service provider that is objectively determinable and nondiscretionary at the time the payment event occurs such as, for example, a schedule of three substantially equal payments payable during the first three taxable years following the taxable year in which a separation from service occurs. A plan may also provide that a payment, including a payment that is part of a schedule, is to be made during a designated period objectively determinable and nondiscretionary at the time the payment event occurs, but only if the designated period both begins and ends within one taxable year of the service provider or the designated period is not more than 90 days and the service provider does not have a right to designate the taxable year of the payment (other than an election that complies with the subsequent deferral election rules of §1.409A–2(b)). Where a plan provides for a period of more than one day following a payment event during which a payment may be made, such as within 90 days following the date of the event, the payment date for purposes of the subsequent deferral rules under §1.409A–2(b) is treated as the first possible date upon which a payment could be made under the terms of the plan. A plan may provide for payment upon the earliest or latest of more than one event or time, provided that each event or time is described in paragraphs (a)(1) through (6) of this section. For examples illustrating the provisions of this paragraph, see paragraph (i)(1)(vi) of this section.

(c) *Designation of alternative specified dates or payment schedules based upon date of permissible event.* Except as otherwise provided in this paragraph (c), a plan may designate only one time and form of payment upon the occurrence of each event described in paragraph (a)(1), (2), (3), (5), or (6) of this section. For example, a plan does not satisfy the requirements of this paragraph (c) if it provides for one payment date or schedule of payments if a specified event occurs on a Monday, but another payment date or schedule of payments if the event occurs on any other day of the week. However, a plan that provides for a payment upon an event described in paragraph (a)(2), (3), (5), or (6) of this section may allow for an alternative payment schedule if the event occurs on or before one (but not more than one) specified date, provided that the addition or deletion of such a different time and form of payment applicable to an existing deferral is subject to §1.409A–2(b) (subsequent deferral elections) and paragraph (j) of this section (accelerated payments). For example, a plan may provide that a service provider will receive a lump sum payment of the service provider's entire benefit under the plan on the first day of the month following a change in control event that occurs before the service provider attains age 55, but will receive 5 substantially equal annual payments commencing on the first day of the month following a change in control event that occurs on or after the service provider attains age 55. In the case of a plan that provides that a payment upon an event described in paragraph (a)(1) of this section (a payment upon a separation from service), a different time and form of payment may be designated with respect to a separation from service under each of the following conditions, provided that the addition or deletion of such a different time and form of payment applicable to an existing deferral is subject to §1.409A–2(b) and paragraph (j) of this section:

(1) A separation from service during a limited period of time not to exceed two years following a change in control event (as defined in paragraph (i)(5) of this section).

(2) A separation from service before or after a specified date (for example, the attainment of a specified age), or a separation from service before or after a combination of a specified date, such as attaining a specified age, and a specified period of service determined under a predetermined, nondiscretionary, objective formula or pursuant to the method for crediting service under a qualified plan sponsored by the service recipient.

(3) A separation from service not described in paragraphs (c)(1) or (c)(2) of this section.

(d) *When a payment is treated as made upon the designated payment date.* Except as otherwise specified in this section, a payment is treated as made upon the date specified under the plan (including a date specified under paragraph (a)(4) of this section) if the payment is made at such date or a later date within the same taxable year of the service provider or, if later, by the 15th day of the third calendar month following the date specified under the plan and the service provider is not permitted, directly or indirectly, to designate the taxable year of the payment. In addition, a payment is treated as made upon the date specified under the plan (including a date specified under paragraph (a)(4) of this section) and is not treated as an accelerated payment if the payment is made no earlier than 30 days before the designated payment date and the service provider is not permitted, directly or indirectly to designate the taxable year of the payment. For purposes of this paragraph, if the date specified is only a designated taxable year of the service provider, or a period of time during such a taxable year, the date specified under the plan is treated as the first day of such taxable year or the first day of the period of time during such taxable year, as applicable. The payment with respect to a stock right generally occurs upon the exercise of the stock right, so that where a stock right designates a fixed exercise date, the stock right will be deemed to have been paid at such date if the exercise and payment occur on such date or a later date within the same taxable year of the service provider or, if later, by the 15th day of the third calendar month following the exercise date specified under the plan. If calculation of the amount of the payment is not administratively practicable due to events beyond the control of the service provider (or service provider's beneficiary), the payment will be treated as made upon the date specified under the plan if the payment is made during the first taxable year of the service provider in which the calculation of the amount of the payment is administratively practicable. For purposes of this paragraph, the inability of a service recipient to calculate the amount or timing of a payment due to a failure of a service provider (or service provider's beneficiary) to provide reasonably available information necessary to make such calculation does not constitute an event beyond the control of the service provider. Similarly, if the making of the payment at the date specified under the plan would jeopardize the ability of the service recipient to continue as a going concern, the payment will be treated as made upon the date specified under the plan if the payment is made during the first taxable year of the service provider in which the making of the payment would not have such effect.

(e) *Designation of time and form of payment with respect to earnings.* A nonqualified deferred compensation plan that provides for actual or notional earnings to be credited on amounts of deferred compensation may specify, in accordance with the requirements of §1.409A–2(a) (initial deferral elections), that such earnings are treated separately from the right to the other amounts deferred under the plan for purposes of designating the time and form of payments under such plan, provided that to satisfy the requirements of this paragraph (e), actual or notional earnings must be credited at least annually. For these purposes, a right to dividend equivalents may be treated analogously to a right to actual or notional earnings on an amount of deferred compensation. For purposes of this paragraph (e), the term *dividend equivalents* means the right to an amount equal to all or a specified portion of dividends declared and paid, if any, on a specified number of shares of stock.

(f) *Substitutions.* Except as otherwise provided under these regulations, the payment of an amount as a substitute for a payment of deferred compensation will be treated as a payment of the deferred compensation. A forfeiture or voluntary relinquishment of an amount of deferred compensation will not be treated as a payment of the compensation, but there is no forfeiture or voluntary relinquishment for this purpose if an amount is paid, or a legally binding right to a payment is created, that acts as a substitute for the forfeited or voluntarily relinquished amount. Whether a payment or a right to a payment acts as a substitute for a payment of deferred compensation is determined based on all the facts and circumstances. However, where the payment of an amount results in an actual or potential reduction of, or current or future offset to, an amount of deferred compensation, or if the service provider receives a loan the repayment of which is secured by or may be accomplished through an offset of or a reduction in an amount deferred under a nonqualified deferred compensation plan, the payment or loan is a substitute for the deferred compensation. In addition, where a service provider's right to deferred compensation is made subject to anticipation, alienation, sale, transfer, assignment, pledge, encumbrance, attachment, or garnishment by creditors of the service provider or the service provider's beneficiary, the deferred compensation is treated as having been paid. For the treatment of certain offsets, see paragraph (j)(4)(xiii) of this section. Even where there is no explicit reduction or offset, the payment of an amount or creation of a new right to a payment proximate to the purported forfeiture or voluntary relinquishment of a right to deferred compensation is presumed to be a substitute for the deferred compensation. The presumption is rebuttable by a showing that the compensation paid would have been received regardless of the forfeiture or voluntary relinquishment of the right to deferred compensation. Factors indicating that a payment would have been received regardless of such forfeiture or voluntarily relinquishment include that the amount paid is materially less than the forfeited or relinquished amount, or consists of a type of payment customarily made in the ordinary course of business of the service recipient to service providers who do not forfeit or relinquish deferred compensation (for example, a payment of accrued but unused leave or a payment for a release of actual or potential claims). See §1.409A–1(b)(9)(i) with respect to certain separation pay plans.

(g) *Disputed payments and refusals to pay*. If a service recipient fails to make a payment in whole or in part as of the date specified under a plan, either intentionally or unintentionally, other than with the express or implied consent of the service provider, the payment will be treated as made upon the date specified under the plan if the service provider accepts the portion (if any) of the payment that the service recipient is willing to make (unless such acceptance will result in a relinquishment of the claim to all or part of the remaining amount), makes prompt and reasonable, good faith efforts to collect the remaining portion of the payment, and any further payment (including payment of a lesser amount that satisfies the obligation to make the payment) is made no later than the end of the first taxable year of the service provider in which the service recipient and the service provider enter into a legally binding settlement of such dispute, the service recipient concedes that the amount is payable, or the service recipient is required to make such payment pursuant to a final and nonappealable judgment or other binding decision. For purposes of this paragraph (g), efforts to collect the payment will be presumed not to be prompt, reasonable, good faith efforts, unless the service provider provides notice to the service recipient within 90 days of the latest date upon which the payment could have been timely made in accordance with the terms of the plan and these regulations, and unless, if not paid, the service provider takes further enforcement measures within 180 days after such latest date. For purposes of this paragraph (g), a service recipient is not treated as having failed to make a payment where pursuant to the terms of the plan the service provider is required to request payment, or otherwise provide information or take any other action, and the service provider has failed to take such action. In addition, for purposes of this paragraph (g), the service provider is deemed to have requested that a payment not be made, rather than the service recipient having failed to make such payment, where the service recipient's decision to refuse to make the payment is made by the service provider or a member of the service provider's family (as defined in section 267(c)(4) applied as if the family of an individual includes the spouse of any member of the family), or any person or group of persons over whom the service provider or service provider's family member has effective control, or any person any portion of whose compensation is controlled the service provider or service provider's family member.

(h) *Special rule for certain resident aliens*. An agreement, method, program, or other arrangement that is, or constitutes part of, a nonqualified deferred compensation plan is deemed to meet the requirements of this section with respect to any amount payable in the first taxable year of the service provider in which a service provider is a resident alien, and with respect to any amount payable in a subsequent taxable year if no later than the last day of the first taxable year of the service provider in which the service provider is a resident alien, the plan is amended as necessary so that the times and forms of payment of amounts payable in a subsequent year comply with the provisions of this section. For any year after the first taxable year of an individual in which the individual is a resident alien, this paragraph (h) does not apply, provided that a taxable year may again be treated as the first taxable year in which an individual is a resident alien if such individual has not been a resident alien for at least three consecutive taxable years immediately preceding the taxable year in which the service provider is again a resident alien.

(i) *Definitions and special rules*—(1) *Specified time or fixed schedule*—(i) *In general*. Amounts are payable at a specified time or pursuant to a fixed schedule if objectively determinable amounts are payable at a date or dates that are nondiscretionary and objectively determinable at the time the amount is deferred. An amount is objectively determinable for this purpose if the amount is specifically identified or if the amount may be determined at the time payment is due pursuant to an objective, nondiscretionary formula specified at the time the amount is deferred (for example, 50 percent of a specified account balance). Except as otherwise provided in paragraph (i)(1) of this section, an amount is not objectively determinable if the amount of the payment is based all or in part upon the occurrence of an event, including the consummation of a transaction by, or a payment of an amount to, a service recipient. If an amount is payable in a service provider's taxable year (or pursuant to a fixed schedule of taxable years of the service provider) that is designated at the time the amount is deferred and that is objectively determinable, the amount is treated as payable at a specified time (or pursuant to a fixed schedule), provided that for purposes of the application of the subsequent deferral rules contained in §1.409A–2(b), the specified time or fixed schedule of payments is deemed to refer to the first day of the relevant taxable year or years. A specified time or fixed schedule also includes the designation at the time the amount is deferred of a defined period or periods within the service provider's taxable year or taxable years that are objectively determinable, provided that no such defined period may begin within one taxable year and end within another taxable year, and provided further that for purposes of the application of the subsequent deferral rules contained in §1.409A–2(b), the specified time or fixed schedule of payments is deemed to refer to the first day of the relevant period in which the payment will be made. A plan may provide that a payment upon the lapse of a substantial risk of forfeiture is to be made in accordance with a fixed schedule that is objectively determinable based on the date the substantial risk of forfeiture lapses (disregarding any discretionary acceleration of the lapse of the substantial risk of forfeiture), provided that the schedule must be fixed on the date the time and form of payment are designated, and any change in the fixed schedule will constitute a change in the time and form of payment. For example, a plan that provides for a bonus payment subject to the condition that the service provider complete three years of service, and subject to the further condition that such requirement of continued services will lapse upon the occurrence of an initial public offering, which condition if applied alone would constitute a substantial risk of forfeiture, may provide that a service provider is entitled to substantially equal payments on each of the first three anniversaries of the date the substantial risk of forfeiture lapses (the earlier of three years of service or the date of an initial public offering).

(ii) *Payment schedules with formula and fixed limitations*—(A) *Individual limitations*. A schedule of payments does not fail to be a fixed schedule of payments where the amount of a payment or payments that may be paid at a specified time or during a specified period is limited by an objective nondiscretionary formula or a specified amount that is not under the effective control of the service provider and is not subject to the exercise of discretion by the service recipient, where such limitation is established on or before the date the time and form of payment is otherwise required to be set under these regulations, and the plan specifies the time and form of any payment that will be made or completed after its original payment date due to the application of the limitation. A change in the limitation or a change in the time and form of any payment that exceeds the limitation is subject to the requirements of §1.409A–2(b) (subsequent deferral elections) and paragraph (j) of this section (accelerated payments). For purposes of this paragraph, a plan provision that reduces a schedule of periodic payments on a dollar-for-dollar basis by the amount of Social Security payments received or receivable may be treated as a nondiscretionary, objective formula limitation, if such reduction does not otherwise affect the time of payment of the deferred compensation (other than a forfeiture due to the reduction), including changes based on the service provider's eligibility or elections related to Social Security benefits. Similarly, a plan provision that reduces a schedule of periodic payments on a dollar-for-dollar basis by the amount of *bona fide* disability pay (within the meaning of §1.409A–1(a)(5)) received or receivable may be treated as a nondiscretionary, objective formula limitation, if the disability payments are made pursuant to a plan sponsored by the service recipient that covers a substantial number of service providers and was established before the service provider became disabled, and if such reduction does not otherwise affect the time of payment of the deferred compensation (other than a forfeiture due to the reduction). Whether an amendment to, or other change in the benefit payable under, such *bona fide* disability plan results in an acceleration of a payment for purposes of paragraph (j) of this section or a subsequent election to delay the time or change the form of payment for purposes of §1.409A–2(b) is determined based on all of the relevant facts and circumstances.

(B) *Limitations on aggregate payments to all participants in substantially identical plans*. A schedule of payments does not fail to be a fixed schedule of payments where the amount of the aggregate payments that will be made during a specified period of time to all participants in substantially identical plans is limited by an objective nondiscretionary formula or specified amount that is not under the effective control of the service provider and is not subject to the exercise of discretion by the service recipient, where the limit is established on or before the date the time and form of payment of the amount deferred is otherwise required to be set under these regulations, the method of allocating payments among the participants where there is an overall limitation on the aggregate amount that may be paid to a group of service providers during a specified period is an objective nondiscretionary allocation method that is not under the effective control of the service provider and is not subject to the exercise of discretion by the service recipient, the method is established on or before the date the time and form of payment of the amount deferred is otherwise required to be set, and the plan specifies the time and form of any payment of any amount that will be paid after its original payment date due to the application of the limitation. A change in the limitation or a change in the time and form of payment of any payment that is not otherwise made at the scheduled payment date due to application of the formula limitation is subject to the requirements of §1.409A–2(b) (subsequent deferral elections) and paragraph (j) of this section (accelerated payments).

(iii) *Payment schedules determined by timing of payments received by the service recipient*. A payment schedule determined by reference to the timing of payments received by the service recipient (not including payments from one entity to another entity where both entities are treated as part of a single service recipient), meets the requirements of a specified date or fixed schedule of payments if the following conditions are met:

(A) The payments due to the service recipient arise from *bona fide* and routine transactions in the ordinary course of business of the service recipient.

(B) The service provider does not have effective control of the service recipient, the person from whom such amounts are due, or the collection of any of the amounts due to the service recipient.

(C) The payment schedule provides an objective, nondiscretionary method of identification of the payments to the service recipient from which the amount of the payment from the service recipient to the service provider is determined.

(D) The payment schedule provides an objective, nondiscretionary schedule under which the payments will be made to the service provider.

(E) The payments to the service recipient from which the amount of the payments from service recipient to the service provider are determined result from sales of a type that the service recipient is in the trade or business of making and makes frequently, and either all such sales by the service recipient are taken into account for purposes of determining the payment to the service provider, or there is a legitimate, non-tax business reason for identifying the specific sales taken into account.

(iv) *Reimbursement or in-kind benefit plans*—(A) *General rule.* A plan that provides for reimbursements of expenses incurred by a service provider, or in-kind benefits, meets the requirements of a specified date or fixed schedule of payments with respect to such reimbursements or benefits if the following conditions are met:

(*1*) The plan provides an objectively determinable nondiscretionary definition of the expenses eligible for reimbursement or of the in-kind benefits to be provided.

(*2*) The plan provides for the reimbursement of expenses incurred or for the provision of the in-kind benefits during an objectively and specifically prescribed period (including the lifetime of the service provider).

(*3*) The plan provides that the amount of expenses eligible for reimbursement, or in-kind benefits provided, during a service provider's taxable year may not affect the expenses eligible for reimbursement, or in-kind benefits to be provided, in any other taxable year.

(*4*) The reimbursement of an eligible expense is made on or before the last day of the service provider's taxable year following the taxable year in which the expense was incurred.

(*5*) The right to reimbursement or in-kind benefits is not subject to liquidation or exchange for another benefit.

(B) *Medical reimbursement arrangements.* Notwithstanding the foregoing, an arrangement providing for the reimbursement of expenses referred to in section 105(b) will not be deemed to fail to meet the requirements of paragraph (i)(1)(iv)(A)(*3*) of this section solely because the arrangement provides for a limit on the amount of expenses that may be reimbursed under such arrangement over some or all of the period in which the reimbursement arrangement remains in effect.

(v) *Tax gross-up payments.* A plan providing a right to a tax gross-up payment will be treated as providing for payment at a specified time or on a fixed schedule of payments if the plan provides that payment will be made, and the payment is made, by the end of the service provider's taxable year next following the service provider's taxable year in which the service provider remits the related taxes. For purposes of this paragraph (i)(1)(v), the term *tax gross-up payment* refers to a payment to reimburse the service provider in an amount equal to all or a designated portion of the Federal, state, local, or foreign taxes imposed upon the service provider as a result of compensation paid or made available to the service provider by the service recipient, including the amount of additional taxes imposed upon the service provider due to the service recipient's payment of the initial taxes on such compensation. In addition, a right to the reimbursement of expenses incurred due to a tax audit or litigation addressing the existence or amount of a tax liability, whether Federal, state, local, or foreign, satisfies the requirement of a fixed time and form of payment if the right to the reimbursement provides that payment will be made, and the payment is made, by the end of the service provider's taxable year following the service provider's taxable year in which the taxes that are the subject of the audit or litigation are remitted to the taxing authority, or where as a result of such audit or litigation no taxes are remitted, the end of the service provider's taxable year following the service provider's taxable year in which the audit is completed or there is a final and nonappealable settlement or other resolution of the litigation. Nothing in this paragraph (i)(1)(v) otherwise alters the application of section 409A to the underlying compensation arrangement or other arrangement that results in the taxes subject to the right to the tax gross-up payment.

(vi) *Examples.* The following examples (in which each employee is an individual whose taxable year is the calendar year) illustrate the principles of paragraphs (a), (b), (c), (d), and (i)(1) of this section:

Example 1. Employee A provides services as an employee of Employer Z, but is not a specified employee. Employee A participates in a nonqualified deferred compensation plan providing for a lump sum payment payable on or before December 31 of the calendar year in which Employee A separates from service. The plan provides for a payment upon a separation from service in compliance with this section.

Example 2. Employee B provides services as an employee of Employer Y, but is not a specified employee. Employee B participates in a nonqualified deferred compensation plan providing for a lump sum payment payable on or before the 90th day immediately following the date upon which Employee B separates from service. Employer Y retains the sole discretion to determine when during the 90-day period the payment will be made. Although the plan does not specify a period during one calendar year in which the payment will be made, the plan provides for a payment upon a separation from service in compliance with this section because the period over which the payment may be made is not longer than 90 days.

Example 3. Employee C provides services as an employee of Employer X, but is not a specified employee. Employee C participates in a nonqualified deferred compensation plan providing for a lump sum payment payable on or before the 180th day following the date upon which Employee C separates from service. Employer X retains the sole discretion to determine when during the 180-day period the payment will be made. Because the plan does not specify a period during one calendar year in which the payment will be made, and because the period over which the payment may be made is longer than 90 days, the plan does not provide for a payment upon a separation from service that complies with this section.

Example 4. Employee D provides services as an employee of Employer W, but is not a specified employee. Employee D participates in a nonqualified deferred compensation plan providing for 10 installment payments payable on the first 10 anniversaries of the date Employee D separates from service, provided that no installment payment in any year may be more than 1% of Employer W's net income for the previous calendar year, and provided further that the excess over such limit that would otherwise be payable but is not paid due to application of the limit will become payable as of the first installment payment date at which time such amount, in combination with any installment payment otherwise due Employee D, does not exceed 1% of Employer W's net income for the previous calendar year. Provided that Employee D does not retain effective control of the calculation of Employer W's net income or the amount that Employee D will not be paid due to application of the limit, the plan provides for a schedule of payments upon a separation from service that complies with this section.

Example 5. Employee E and Employee F provide services as employees of Employer V, but neither is a specified employee. Employee E and Employee F both participate in substantially identical nonqualified deferred compensation plans providing for 10 installment payments payable on the first 10 anniversaries of the date the respective employee separates from service, provided that the total amount of installment payments in any year may not be more than 1%

of Employer V's net income for the previous year, that where any payments are not made due to application of the limit the determination of the amount not paid to a particular employee will be made by applying the overall limit proportionately based upon the installment payment due the employee that year, and that the excess over such limit that would otherwise be payable but is not paid due to application of the limit will become payable as of the first installment payment date at which time such amount, in combination with any installment payments otherwise due the participants, does not exceed 1% of Employer V's net income for the previous calendar year. Provided that neither Employee E nor Employee F retains effective control of the calculation of Employer V's net income or the amount that the respective employee will not be paid due to application of the limit, the plan provides for a schedule of payments upon a separation from service that complies with this section.

Example 6. Employee G provides services as an employee of Employer U, but is not a specified employee. As a *bona fide* part of this employment relationship, Employee G provides professional services to clients of Employer U as part of the *bona fide*, ordinary course of Employer U's trade or business. Under an arrangement between Employee G and Employer U, Employer U agrees to pay Employee G upon Employee G's separation from service an amount equal to 5% of any amount collected from Company T, a client of Employer U for which Employee G performed services during his employment with Employer U, during the 36 months following Employee G's separation from service. Under the arrangement, the amounts due to Employee G based upon payments received by Employer U during any calendar year are payable to Employee G on April 1 of the subsequent calendar year. Provided that Employee G does not have effective control of Employer U, Company T, or the collection of any amounts due Employer Y from Company T, the arrangement provides for a schedule of payments upon a separation from service that complies with this section.

Example 7. Employee H provides services as an employee of Employer S, but is not a specified employee. Under a plan sponsored by Employer S, Employee H has a legally binding right upon a separation from service to the reimbursement of country club dues paid in the calendar year of the separation from service and each of the next 3 calendar years following the separation from service in an amount not to exceed $30,000 in any calendar year, provided that the amount of dues paid in any calendar year that are eligible for reimbursement equals only the amount actually expended during such calendar year, and the maximum amount available for reimbursement in any calendar year will not be increased or decreased to reflect the amount expended or reimbursed in a prior or subsequent calendar year. The plan further provides that any reimbursement must be paid to Employee H by December 31 of the calendar year following the year in which Employee H pays the country club dues. The reimbursement plan provides for a schedule of payments upon a separation from service that complies with this section.

Example 8. Employee J provides services as an employee of Employer Q, but is not a specified employee. Under a plan sponsored by Employer Q, Employee J has a legally binding right upon a separation from service to the reimbursement of country club dues paid during the calendar year in which the separation from service occurs and the next 3 calendar years in a total amount not to exceed $90,000. The plan further provides that any reimbursement must be paid to Employee J by December 31 of the calendar year following the year in which Employee J pays the country club dues. Because the reimbursement of a payment of country club dues in one calendar year may affect the amount of country club dues available for reimbursement in another calendar year, the plan does not provide for a schedule of payments upon a separation from service that complies with this section.

(2) *Separation from service—required delay in payment to a specified employee pursuant to a separation from service*—(i) *In general.* In the case of any service provider who is a specified employee (as defined in §1.409A–1(i)) as of the date of a separation from service, the requirements of paragraph (a)(1) of this section permitting a payment upon a separation from service are satisfied only if payments may not be made before the date that is six months after the date of separation from service (or, if earlier than the end of the six-month period, the date of death of the specified employee). For this purpose, a service provider who is not a specified employee as of the date of a separation from service will not be treated as subject to this requirement even if the service provider would have become a specified employee if the service provider had continued to provide services through the next specified employee effective date. Similarly, a service provider who is treated as a specified employee as of the date of a separation from service will be subject to this requirement even if the service provider would not have been treated as a specified employee after the next specified employee effective date had the specified employee continued providing services through the next specified employee effective date. Notwithstanding the foregoing, this paragraph (i)(2)(i) does not apply to a payment made under the circumstances described in paragraph (j)(4)(ii) (domestic relations order), (j)(4)(iii) (conflicts of interest), or (j)(4)(vi) (payment of employment taxes) of this section.

(ii) *Application of payment rules to delayed payments.* The required delay in payment is met if payments to which a specified employee would otherwise be entitled during the first six months following the date of separation from service are accumulated and paid on the first day of the seventh month following the date of separation from service, or if each payment to which a specified employee is otherwise entitled upon a separation from service is delayed by six months. A service recipient may retain discretion to choose which method will be implemented, provided that no direct or indirect election as to the method may be provided to the service provider. For an affected specified employee, a date upon which the plan or the service recipient designates that the payment will be made after the six-month delay is treated as a fixed payment date for purposes of paragraph (d) of this section once the separation from service has occurred.

(3) *Unforeseeable emergency*—(i) *Definition.* For purposes of §§1.409A–1 and 1.409A–2, this section, and §§1.409A–4 through 1.409A–6, an *unforeseeable emergency* is a severe financial hardship to the service provider resulting from an illness or accident of the service provider, the service provider's spouse, the service provider's beneficiary, or the service provider's dependent (as defined in section 152, without regard to section 152(b)(1), (b)(2), and (d)(1)(B)); loss of the service provider's property due to casualty (including the need to rebuild a home following damage to a home not otherwise covered by insurance, for example, not as a result of a natural disaster); or other similar extraordinary and unforeseeable circumstances arising as a result of events beyond the control of the service provider. For example, the imminent foreclosure of or eviction from the service provider's primary residence may constitute an unforeseeable emergency. In addition, the need to pay for medical expenses, including non-refundable deductibles, as well as for the costs of prescription drug medication, may constitute an unforeseeable emergency. Finally, the need to pay for the funeral expenses of a spouse, a beneficiary, or a dependent (as defined in section 152, without regard to section 152(b)(1), (b)(2), and (d)(1)(B)) may also constitute an unforeseeable emergency. Except as otherwise provided in this paragraph (i)(3)(i), the purchase of a home and the payment of college tuition are not unforeseeable emergencies. Whether a service provider is faced with an unforeseeable emergency permitting a distribution under this paragraph (i)(3)(i) is to be determined based on the relevant facts and circum-

stances of each case, but, in any case, a distribution on account of unforeseeable emergency may not be made to the extent that such emergency is or may be relieved through reimbursement or compensation from insurance or otherwise, by liquidation of the service provider's assets, to the extent the liquidation of such assets would not cause severe financial hardship, or by cessation of deferrals under the plan. A plan may provide for a payment upon a specific type or types of unforeseeable emergency, without providing for payment upon all unforeseeable emergencies, provided that any event upon which a payment may be made qualifies as an unforeseeable emergency.

(ii) *Amount of payment permitted upon an unforeseeable emergency.* Distributions because of an unforeseeable emergency must be limited to the amount reasonably necessary to satisfy the emergency need (which may include amounts necessary to pay any Federal, state, local, or foreign income taxes or penalties reasonably anticipated to result from the distribution). Determinations of amounts reasonably necessary to satisfy the emergency need must take into account any additional compensation that is available if the plan provides for cancellation of a deferral election upon a payment due to an unforeseeable emergency. See paragraph (j)(4)(viii) of this section. However, the determination of amounts reasonably necessary to satisfy the emergency need is not required to take into account any additional compensation that is available from a qualified employer plan as defined in §1.409A–1(a)(2) (including any amount available by obtaining a loan under the plan), or that due to the unforeseeable emergency is available under another nonqualified deferred compensation plan (including a plan that would provide for deferred compensation except due to the application of the effective date provisions under §1.409A–6). The payment may be made from any plan in which the service provider participates that provides for payment upon an unforeseeable emergency, provided that the plan under which the payment was made must be designated at the time of payment.

(iii) *Payments due to an unforeseeable emergency.* A service provider may retain discretion with respect to whether to apply for a payment upon an unforeseeable emergency, and a service recipient may retain discretion with respect to whether to make a payment available under the plan due to an unforeseeable emergency. A service provider who has experienced an unforeseeable emergency will not be treated as making a subsequent deferral election under §1.409A–2(b) (subsequent deferral election rules) if the service provider does not apply for or elect to receive a payment available under the plan. A service recipient will not be treated as making a subsequent deferral election under §1.409A–2(b) (subsequent deferral election rules) if the service recipient exercises its discretion not to make a payment otherwise available due to an unforeseeable emergency.

(4) *Disability*—(i) *In general.* For purposes of §§1.409A–1 and 1.409A–2, this section, and §§1.409A–4 through 1.409A–6, except as otherwise specifically provided, a service provider is considered disabled if the service provider meets one of the following requirements:

(A) The service provider is unable to engage in any substantial gainful activity by reason of any medically determinable physical or mental impairment that can be expected to result in death or can be expected to last for a continuous period of not less than 12 months.

(B) The service provider is, by reason of any medically determinable physical or mental impairment that can be expected to result in death or can be expected to last for a continuous period of not less than 12 months, receiving income replacement benefits for a period of not less than three months under an accident and health plan covering employees of the service provider's employer.

(ii) *Limited plan definition of disability.* A plan may provide for a payment upon any disability, and need not provide for a payment upon all disabilities, provided that any disability upon which a payment may be made under the plan complies with the provisions of this paragraph (i)(4).

(iii) *Determination of disability.* A plan may provide that a service provider will be deemed disabled if determined to be totally disabled by the Social Security Administration or Railroad Retirement Board. A plan may also provide that a service provider will be deemed disabled if determined to be disabled in accordance with a disability insurance program, provided that the definition of disability applied under such disability insurance program complies with the requirements of this paragraph (i)(4).

(5) *Change in the ownership or effective control of a corporation, or a change in the ownership of a substantial portion of the assets of a corporation*—(i) *In general.* Pursuant to section 409A(a)(2)(A)(v), a plan may permit a payment upon the occurrence of a change in the ownership of the corporation (as defined in paragraph (i)(5)(v) of this section), a change in effective control of the corporation (as defined in paragraph (i)(5)(vi) of this section), or a change in the ownership of a substantial portion of the assets of the corporation (as defined in paragraph (i)(5)(vii) of this section) (collectively referred to as a change in control event). To qualify as a change in control event, the occurrence of the event must be objectively determinable and any requirement that any other person or group, such as a plan administrator or compensation committee, certify the occurrence of a change in control event must be strictly ministerial and not involve any discretionary authority. The plan may provide for a payment on a particular type or types of change in control events, and need not provide for a payment on all such events, provided that each event upon which a payment is provided qualifies as a change in control event. For rules regarding the ability of the service recipient to terminate the plan and pay amounts of deferred compensation upon a change in control event, see paragraph (j)(4)(ix)(B) of this section.

(ii) *Identification of relevant corporation*—(A) *In general.* To constitute a change in control event with respect to the service provider, the change in control event must relate to—

(*1*) The corporation for whom the service provider is performing services at the time of the change in control event;

(*2*) The corporation that is liable for the payment of the deferred compensation (or all corporations liable for the payment if more than one corporation is liable) but only if either the deferred compensation is attributable to the performance of service by the service provider for such corporation (or corporations) or there is a *bona fide* business purpose for such corporation or corporations to be liable for such payment and, in either case, no significant purpose of making such corporation or corporations liable for such payment is the avoidance of Federal income tax; or

(*3*) A corporation that is a majority shareholder of a corporation identified in paragraph (i)(5)(ii)(A)(*1*) or (*2*) of this section, or any corporation in a chain of corporations in which each corporation is a majority shareholder of another corporation in the chain, ending in a corporation identified in paragraph (i)(5)(ii)(A)(*1*) or (*2*) of this section.

(B) *Majority shareholder.* For purposes of this paragraph (i)(5)(ii), a majority shareholder is a shareholder owning more than 50 percent of the total fair market value and total voting power of such corporation.

(C) *Example.* The following example illustrates the rules of this paragraph (i)(5)(ii):

Example. Corporation A is a majority shareholder of Corporation B, which is a majority shareholder of Corporation C. A change in ownership of Corporation B constitutes a change in control event to service providers performing services for Corporation B or Corporation C, and to service providers for which Corporation B or Corporation C is solely liable for payments under the plan (for example, former employees), but is not a change in control event as to Corporation A or any other corporation of which Corporation A is a majority shareholder unless the sale constitutes a change in the ownership of a substantial portion of Corporation A's assets (see paragraph (i)(5)(vii) of this section).

(iii) *Attribution of stock ownership.* For purposes of paragraph (i)(5) of this section, section 318(a) applies to determine stock ownership. Stock underlying a vested option is considered owned by the individual who holds the vested option (and the stock underlying an unvested option is not considered owned by the individual who holds the unvested option). For purposes of the preceding sentence, however, if a vested option is exercisable for stock that is not substantially vested (as defined by §1.83–3(b) and (j)), the stock underlying the option is not treated as owned by the individual who holds the option.

(iv) *Special rules for certain delayed payments pursuant to a change in control event*—(A) *Certain transaction-based compensation.* Payments of compensation related to a change in control event described in paragraph (i)(5)(v) of this section (change in the ownership of a corporation) or paragraph (i)(5)(vii) of this section (change in the ownership of a substantial portion of a corporation's assets), that occur because a service recipient purchases its stock held by the service provider or because the service recipient or a third party purchases a stock right held by a service provider, or that are calculated by reference to the value of stock of the service recipient (collectively, transaction-based compensation), may be treated as paid at a designated date or pursuant to a payment schedule that complies with the requirements of section 409A if the transaction-based compensation is paid on the same schedule and under the same terms and conditions as apply to payments to shareholders generally with respect to stock of the service recipient pursuant to a change in control event described in paragraph (i)(5)(v) of this section (change in the ownership of a corporation) or as apply to payments to the service recipient pursuant to a change in control event described in paragraph (i)(5)(vii) of this section (change in the ownership of a substantial portion of a corporation's assets), and to the extent that the transaction-based compensation is paid not later than five years after the change in control event, the payment of such compensation will not violate the initial or subsequent deferral election rules set out in §1.409A–2(a) and (b) solely as a result of such transaction-based compensation being paid pursuant to such schedule and terms and conditions. If before and in connection with a change in control event described in paragraph (i)(5)(v) or (i)(5)(vii) of this section, transaction-based compensation that would otherwise be payable as a result of such event is made subject to a condition on payment that constitutes a substantial risk of forfeiture (as defined in §1.409A–1(d), without regard to the provisions of that section under which additions or extensions of forfeiture conditions are disregarded) and the transaction-based compensation is payable under the same terms and conditions as apply to payments made to shareholders generally with respect to stock of the service recipient pursuant to a change in control event described in paragraph (i)(5)(v) of this section or to payments to the service recipient pursuant to a change in control event described in paragraph (i)(5)(vii) of this section, for purposes of determining whether such transaction-based compensation is a short-term deferral the requirements of §1.409A–1(b)(4) are applied as if the legally binding right to such transaction-based compensation arose on the date that it became subject to such substantial risk of forfeiture.

(B) *Certain nonvested compensation.* Notwithstanding the provisions of §1.409A–1(d) (definition of a substantial risk of forfeiture) that disregard the extension or modification of a condition for purposes of determining whether a condition on payment constitutes a substantial risk of forfeiture, a condition that is a substantial risk of forfeiture that otherwise would lapse as a result of a change in control event described in paragraph (i)(5)(v) or (i)(5)(vii) of this section may be extended or modified before and in connection with such event to provide for a condition on payment that will not lapse as a result of such change in control event, and such extended or modified condition will be treated as continuing to subject the amount to a substantial risk of forfeiture, provided that the transaction constituting the change in control event is a *bona fide* arm's length transaction between the service recipient or its shareholders and one or more parties who are unrelated to the service recipient and service provider (applying the rules of §1.409A–1(f)(2)(ii)) and the modified or extended condition to which the payment is subject would otherwise be treated as a substantial risk of forfeiture under §1.409A–1(d) (without regard to the provisions disregarding additions or extensions of forfeiture conditions). In such a case, the continued application of a fixed schedule of payments based upon the lapse of the substantial risk of forfeiture, so that payments commence upon the lapse of the modified or extended condition on payment, will not be treated as a change in the fixed schedule of payments for purposes of §1.409A–2(b) (subsequent deferral elections) or paragraph (j) of this section (prohibition on the acceleration of payments).

(v) *Change in the ownership of a corporation*—(A) *In general.* Except as provided in paragraph (i)(5)(vi)(C) of this section, a change in the ownership of a corporation occurs on the date that any one person, or more than one person acting as a group (as defined in paragraph (i)(5)(v)(B) of this section), acquires ownership of stock of the corporation that, together with stock held by such person or group, constitutes more than 50 percent of the total fair market value or total voting power of the stock of such corporation. A nonqualified deferred compensation plan may provide that amounts payable upon a change in the ownership of a corporation will be paid only if the conditions in the preceding sentence are satisfied but substituting a percentage specified in the plan that is higher than 50 percent for the words "50 percent" in the preceding sentence, but only if the provision is set forth in the plan no later than the date by which the time and form of payment must be established under §1.409A–2. However, if any one person, or more than one person acting as a group, is considered to own more than 50 percent of the total fair market value or total voting power of the stock of a corporation (or such higher percentage specified in accordance with the preceding sentence), the acquisition of additional stock by the same person or persons is not considered to cause a change in the ownership of the corporation (or to cause a change in the effective control of the corporation (within the meaning of paragraph (i)(5)(vi) of this section)). An increase in the percentage of stock owned by any one person, or persons acting as a group, as a result of a transaction in which the corporation acquires its stock in exchange for property will be treated as an acquisition of stock for purposes of this section. This section applies only when there is a transfer of stock of a corporation (or issuance of stock of a corporation) and stock in such corporation remains outstanding after the transaction (see paragraph (i)(5)(vii) of this section for rules regarding the transfer of assets of a corporation). See §1.280G–1, Q&A–27(d), *Example 1*, *Example 2*, *Example 5*, and *Example 6*.

(B) *Persons acting as a group*. For purposes of paragraph (i)(5)(v)(A) of this section, persons will not be considered to be acting as a group solely because they purchase or own stock of the same corporation at the same time, or as a result of the same public offering. However, persons will be considered to be acting as a group if they are owners of a corporation that enters into a merger, consolidation, purchase or acquisition of stock, or similar business transaction with the corporation. If a person, including an entity, owns stock in both corporations that enter into a merger, consolidation, purchase or acquisition of stock, or similar transaction, such shareholder is considered to be acting as a group with other shareholders only with respect to the ownership in that corporation before the transaction giving rise to the change and not with respect to the ownership interest in the other corporation. See §1.280G–1, Q&A–27(d), *Example 3* and *Example 4*.

(vi) *Change in the effective control of a corporation*—(A) *In general*. Notwithstanding that a corporation has not undergone a change in ownership under paragraph (i)(5)(v) of this section, a change in the effective control of the corporation occurs only on either of the following dates:

(*1*) The date any one person, or more than one person acting as a group (as determined under paragraph (i)(5)(v)(B) of this section), acquires (or has acquired during the 12-month period ending on the date of the most recent acquisition by such person or persons) ownership of stock of the corporation possessing 30 percent or more of the total voting power of the stock of such corporation. A nonqualified deferred compensation plan may provide that amounts payable upon an effective change in control of a corporation will be paid only if the conditions in the preceding sentence are satisfied but substituting a percentage specified in the plan that is higher than 30 percent for the word "30 percent" in the preceding sentence, but only if the percentage is set forth in the plan no later than the date by which the time and form of payment must be established under §1.409A–2).

(*2*) The date a majority of members of the corporation's board of directors is replaced during any 12-month period by directors whose appointment or election is not endorsed by a majority of the members of the corporation's board of directors before the date of the appointment or election, provided that for purposes of this paragraph (i)(5)(vi)(A) the term *corporation* refers solely to the relevant corporation identified in paragraph (i)(5)(ii) of this section for which no other corporation is a majority shareholder for purposes of that paragraph. For example, if Corporation A is a publicly held corporation with no majority shareholder, and Corporation A is the majority shareholder of Corporation B, which is the majority shareholder of Corporation C, the term *corporation* for purposes of this paragraph (i)(5)(vi)(A)(*2*) would refer solely to Corporation A. A nonqualified deferred compensation plan may provide that amounts payable upon a change in the effective control of a corporation will be paid only if the conditions in the first sentence of this paragraph are satisfied substituting a portion of the members of the corporation's board of directors that is higher than the words "a majority of the members of the corporation's board of directors" in the first sentence of this paragraph, but only if the higher portion is set forth in the plan no later than the date by which the time and form of payment must be established under §1.409A–2(a)).

(B) *Multiple change in control events*. A change in effective control may occur in a transaction in which one of the two corporations involved in the transaction has a change in control event under paragraph (i)(5)(v) or (i)(5)(vii) of this section. Thus, for example, assume Corporation P transfers more than 40 percent of the total gross fair market value of its assets to Corporation O in exchange for 35 percent of O's stock. P has undergone a change in ownership of a substantial portion of its assets under paragraph (i)(5)(vii) of this section and O has a change in effective control under this paragraph (i)(5)(vi).

(C) *Acquisition of additional control*. If any one person, or more than one person acting as a group, is considered to effectively control a corporation (within the meaning of this paragraph (i)(5)(vi)), the acquisition of additional control of the corporation by the same person or persons is not considered to cause a change in the effective control of the corporation (or to cause a change in the ownership of the corporation within the meaning of paragraph (i)(5)(v) of this section).

(D) *Persons acting as a group*. Persons will not be considered to be acting as a group solely because they purchase or own stock of the same corporation at the same time, or as a result of the same public offering. However, persons will be considered to be acting as a group if they are owners of a corporation that enters into a merger, consolidation, purchase or acquisition of stock, or similar business transaction with the corporation. If a person, including an entity, owns stock in both corporations that enter into a merger, consolidation, purchase or acquisition of stock, or similar transaction, such shareholder is considered to be acting as a group with other shareholders in a corporation only with respect to the ownership in that corporation before the transaction giving rise to the change and not with respect to the ownership interest in the other corporation. See §1.280G–1, Q&A–27(d), *Example 4*.

(vii) *Change in the ownership of a substantial portion of a corporation's assets*—(A) *In general*. A change in the ownership of a substantial portion of a corporation's assets occurs on the date that any one person, or more than one person acting as a group (as determined in paragraph (i)(5)(v)(B) of this section), acquires (or has acquired during the 12-month period ending on the date of the most recent acquisition by such person or persons) assets from the corporation that have a total gross fair market value equal to or more than 40 percent of the total gross fair market value of all of the assets of the corporation immediately before such acquisition or acquisitions (or such higher amount specified by the plan no later than the date by which the time and form of payment must be established under §1.409A–2). For this purpose, gross fair market value means the value of the assets of the corporation, or the value of the assets being disposed of, determined without regard to any liabilities associated with such assets.

(B) *Transfers to a related person*—(*1*) There is no change in control event under this paragraph (i)(5)(vii) when there is a transfer to an entity that is controlled by the shareholders of the transferring corporation immediately after the transfer, as provided in this paragraph (i)(5)(vii)(B). A transfer of assets by a corporation is not treated as a change in the ownership of such assets if the assets are transferred to—

(*i*) A shareholder of the corporation (immediately before the asset transfer) in exchange for or with respect to its stock;

(*ii*) An entity, 50 percent or more of the total value or voting power of which is owned, directly or indirectly, by the corporation;

(*iii*) A person, or more than one person acting as a group, that owns, directly or indirectly, 50 percent or more of the total value or voting power of all the outstanding stock of the corporation; or

(*iv*) An entity, at least 50 percent of the total value or voting power of which is owned, directly or indirectly, by a person described in paragraph (i)(5)(vii)(B)(*1*)(*iii*) of this section.

(*2*) For purposes of this paragraph (i)(5)(vii)(B) and except as otherwise provided in this paragraph (i), a person's status is determined immediately after the transfer of the assets. For example, a transfer to a corporation in which the transferor corporation has no ownership interest before the transaction, but that is a majority-owned subsidiary of the transferor corporation after the transaction is not treated as a change in the ownership of the assets of the transferor corporation.

(C) *Persons acting as a group*. Persons will not be considered to be acting as a group solely because they purchase assets of the same corporation at the same time. However, persons will be considered to be acting as a group if they are owners of a corporation that enters into a merger, consolidation, purchase or acquisition of assets, or similar business transaction with the corporation. If a person, including an entity shareholder, owns stock in both corporations that enter into a merger, consolidation, purchase or acquisition of assets, or similar transaction, such shareholder is considered to be acting as a group with other shareholders in a corporation only to the extent of the ownership in that corporation before the transaction giving rise to the change and not with respect to the ownership interest in the other corporation. See §1.280G–1, Q&A–27(d), *Example 4*.

(6) *Certain back-to-back arrangements*—(i) *In general*. This paragraph (i)(6) applies where a service provider is providing services to a service recipient (the intermediate service recipient), who in turn is providing services to another service recipient (the ultimate service recipient), the services provided by the service provider to the intermediate service recipient are closely related to the services provided by the intermediate service recipient to the ultimate service recipient, there is a nonqualified deferred compensation plan providing for payments by the ultimate service recipient to the intermediate service recipient (the ultimate service recipient plan), there is a nonqualified deferred compensation plan or other agreement, method, program, or other arrangement providing for payments of compensation by the intermediate service recipient to the service provider (the intermediate service recipient plan), and the intermediate service recipient plan provides for a payment upon the occurrence of an event described in paragraph (a)(1), (2), (3), (5), or (6) of this section. In such a case, notwithstanding the generally applicable limits on payments in paragraph (a) of this section, the ultimate service recipient plan may provide for a payment to the intermediate service recipient upon the occurrence of a payment event under the intermediate service recipient plan described in paragraph (a)(1), (2), (3), (5), or (6) of this section if the time and form of payment is defined as the same time and form of payment provided under the intermediate service recipient plan, the amount of the payment under the ultimate service recipient plan does not exceed the amount of the payment under the intermediate service recipient plan, and the ultimate service recipient plan and the intermediate service recipient plan otherwise satisfy the requirements of section 409A (regardless of whether such plan is subject to section 409A).

(ii) *Example*. The provisions of paragraph (i)(6)(i) of this section are illustrated by the following example:

Example. Company B (intermediate service recipient) provides services to Company C (ultimate service recipient). Employee A (service provider) provides services to Company B that are closely related to the services Company B provides to Company C. Pursuant to a nonqualified deferred compensation plan meeting the requirements of section 409A, Employee A is entitled to a payment of deferred compensation upon a separation from service with Company B (the intermediate service recipient plan). Under an arrangement between Company B and Company C (the ultimate service recipient plan), Company C agrees to pay an amount of deferred compensation to Company B upon Employee A's separation from service with Company B, in accordance with the time, form and amount of payment provided in the intermediate service recipient plan. Provided that the intermediate service recipient plan and the ultimate service recipient plan otherwise comply with the requirements of section 409A (regardless of whether such arrangements are subject to section 409A), Company C's payment to Company B of the amount due under the ultimate service recipient plan upon the separation from service of Employee A from Company B may constitute a permissible payment event for purposes of paragraph (a) of this section.

(j) *Prohibition on acceleration of payments*—(1) *In general*. Except as provided in paragraph (j)(4) of this section, a nonqualified deferred compensation plan may not permit the acceleration of the time or schedule of any payment or amount scheduled to be paid pursuant to the terms of the plan, and no such accelerated payment may be made whether or not provided for under the terms of such plan. For purposes of determining whether a payment of deferred compensation has been made, the rules of paragraph (f) of this section (substituted payments) apply. For purposes of this paragraph (j), an impermissible acceleration does not occur if payment is made in accordance with plan provisions or an election as to the time and form of payment in effect at the time of initial deferral (or added in accordance with the rules applicable to subsequent deferral elections under §1.409A–2(b)) pursuant to which payment is required to be made on an accelerated schedule as a result of an intervening event that is an event described in paragraph (a)(1), (2), (3), (5), or (6) of this section. For example, a plan may provide that a participant will receive six installment payments commencing at separation from service, and also provide that if the participant dies after such payments commence but before all payments have been made, all remaining amounts will be paid in a lump sum payment. Additionally, it is not an acceleration of the time or schedule of payment of a deferral of compensation if a service recipient waives or accelerates the satisfaction of a condition constituting a substantial risk of forfeiture applicable to such deferral of compensation, provided that the requirements of section 409A (including the requirement that the payment be made upon a permissible payment event) are otherwise satisfied with respect to such deferral of compensation. For example, if a nonqualified deferred compensation plan provides for a lump sum payment of the vested benefit upon separation from service, and the benefit vests under the plan only after 10 years of service, it is not a violation of the requirements of section 409A if the service recipient reduces the vesting requirement to five years of service, even if a service provider becomes vested as a result and receives a payment in connection with a separation from service before the service provider would have completed 10 years of service. However, if the plan in this example had provided for a payment at a fixed date, rather than at separation from service, the date of payment could not be accelerated due to the accelerated vesting. For the definition of a payment for purposes of this paragraph (j), see §1.409A–2(b)(5) (coordination of the subsequent deferral election rules with the prohibition on acceleration of payments). For other permissible payments, see §1.409A–2(b)(2)(iii) (certain immediate payments of remaining installments) and paragraph (d) of this section (certain payments made no more than 30 days before the designated payment date).

(2) *Application to multiple payment events.* Generally, the addition of a permissible payment event, the deletion of a permissible payment event, or the substitution of one permissible payment event for another permissible payment event, results in an acceleration of a payment if the addition, deletion, or substitution could result in the payment being made at an earlier date than such payment would have been made absent such addition, deletion, or substitution. Notwithstanding the previous sentence, the addition of death, disability (as defined in paragraph (i)(4) of this section), or an unforeseeable emergency (as defined in paragraph (i)(3) of this section), as a potentially earlier alternative payment event to an amount previously deferred will not be treated as resulting in an acceleration of a payment, even if such addition results in the payment being paid at an earlier time than such payment would have been made absent the addition of the payment event. However, the addition of such a payment event as a potentially later alternative payment event generally is subject to the rules governing changes in the time and form of payment (see §1.409A–2(b)).

(3) *Beneficiaries.* The rules of this paragraph (j) apply to elections by beneficiaries with respect to the time and form of payment, as well as elections by service providers or service recipients with respect to the time and form of payment to beneficiaries. An election to change the identity of a beneficiary does not constitute an acceleration of a payment merely because the election changes the identity of the recipient of the payment, if the time and form of the payment is not otherwise changed. In addition, an election before the commencement of a life annuity to change the identity of a beneficiary does not constitute an acceleration of a payment if the change in the time of payments stems solely from the different life expectancy of the new beneficiary, such as in the case of a joint and survivor annuity, and does not change the commencement date of the life annuity.

(4) *Exceptions*—(i) *In general.* Except as otherwise expressly provided, a plan may provide for the acceleration of a payment in accordance with paragraphs (j)(4)(ii) through (xiv) of this section, or may provide a service recipient discretion to accelerate payments in accordance with the provisions of paragraphs (j)(4)(ii) through (xiv) of this section. A plan may not provide a service provider discretion with respect to whether a payment will be accelerated, and a service recipient may not provide a service provider a direct or indirect election as to whether the service recipient's discretion to accelerate a payment will be exercised, even if such acceleration would be permitted under paragraphs (j)(4)(ii) through (xiv) of this section. Whether a service recipient has provided a service provider an election as to whether the service recipient's discretion to accelerate a payment will be exercised is determined based on all the facts and circumstances, including whether similarly situated service providers have been treated differently. Except as otherwise provided in paragraphs (j)(4)(ii) through (xiv) of this section, the plan need not set forth the exception in writing, and provided all other requirements of this section are met, the making of such a payment or the addition of a plan term permitting the making of such a payment will not constitute the acceleration of a payment, and the failure to make such a payment or the deletion or modification of a plan term permitting the making of such a payment will not be subject to the rules regarding a change in the time and form of payment under §1.409A–2(b).

(ii) *Domestic relations order.* A plan may provide for acceleration of the time or schedule of a payment under the plan to an individual other than the service provider, or a payment under such plan may be made to an individual other than the service provider, to the extent necessary to fulfill a domestic relations order (as defined in section 414(p)(1)(B)).

(iii) *Conflicts of interest*—(A) *Compliance with ethics agreements with the Federal government.* A plan may provide for acceleration of the time or schedule of a payment under the plan, or a payment may be made under a plan, to the extent necessary for any Federal officer or employee in the executive branch to comply with an ethics agreement with the Federal government.

(B) *Compliance with ethics laws or conflicts of interest laws.* A plan may provide for acceleration of the time or schedule of a payment under the plan, or a payment may be made under a plan, to the extent reasonably necessary to avoid the violation of an applicable Federal, state, local, or foreign ethics law or conflicts of interest law (including where such payment is reasonably necessary to permit the service provider to participate in activities in the normal course of his or her position in which the service provider would otherwise not be able to participate under an applicable rule). A payment is reasonably necessary to avoid the violation of a Federal, state, local, or foreign ethics law or conflicts of interest law if the payment is a necessary part of a course of action that results in compliance with a Federal, state, local, or foreign ethics law or conflicts of interest law that would be violated absent such course of action, regardless of whether other actions would also result in compliance with the Federal, state, local, or foreign ethics law or conflicts of interest law. For this purpose, a provision of foreign law is considered applicable only to foreign earned income (as defined under section 911(b)(1) without regard to section 911(b)(1)(B)(iv) and without regard to the requirement that the income be attributable to services performed during the period described in section 911(d)(1)(A) or (B)) from sources within the foreign country that promulgated such law.

(iv) *Section 457 plans.* A plan subject to section 457(f) may provide for an acceleration of the time or schedule of a payment to a service provider, or a payment may be made under such a plan, to pay Federal, state, local, and foreign income taxes due upon a vesting event, provided that the amount of such payment is not more than an amount equal to the Federal, state, local, and foreign income tax withholding that would have been remitted by the employer if there had been a payment of wages equal to the income includible by the service provider under section 457(f) at the time of the vesting.

(v) *Limited cashouts.* A plan may require or provide a service recipient discretion to require (or be amended to require or to provide a service recipient discretion to require), a mandatory lump sum payment of amounts deferred under the plan that do not exceed a specified amount, provided that such plan term or amendment is executed and effective, and any required exercise of service recipient discretion is evidenced in writing, no later than the date of such payment, and provided that—

(A) The payment results in the termination and liquidation of the entirety of the service provider's interest under the plan, including all agreements, methods, programs, or other arrangements with respect to which deferrals of compensation are treated as having been deferred under a single nonqualified deferred compensation plan under §1.409A–1(c)(2); and

(B) The payment is not greater than the applicable dollar amount under section 402(g)(1)(B).

(vi) *Payment of employment taxes.* A plan may provide for the acceleration of the time or schedule of a payment, or a payment may be made under the plan, to pay the Federal Insurance Contributions Act (FICA) tax imposed under section 3101, section 3121(a), and section 3121(v)(2), or the Railroad Retirement Act tax imposed under section 3201, section 3211, section 3231(e)(1), and section 3231(e)(8), where applicable, on compensation deferred under the plan (the FICA or RRTA amount). Additionally, a plan may provide for the acceleration of the time or schedule of a payment, or a payment may be made under the plan, to pay the income tax at source on wages imposed under section 3401 or the corresponding withholding provisions of applicable state, local, or foreign tax laws as a result of the payment of the FICA or RRTA amount, and to pay the additional income tax at source on wages attributable to the pyramiding section 3401 wages and taxes. However, the total payment under this acceleration provision must not exceed the aggregate of the FICA or RRTA amount, and the income tax withholding related to such FICA or RRTA amount.

(vii) *Payment upon income inclusion under section 409A.* A plan may provide for the acceleration of the time or schedule of a payment, or a payment under such plan may be made, at any time the plan fails to meet the requirements of section 409A and these regulations. Such payment may not exceed the amount required to be included in income as a result of the failure to comply with the requirements of section 409A and these regulations.

(viii) *Cancellation of deferrals following an unforeseeable emergency or hardship distribution.* A plan may provide for a cancellation of a service provider's deferral election, or such a cancellation may be made, due to an unforeseeable emergency or a hardship distribution pursuant to §1.401(k)–1(d)(3). The deferral election must be cancelled, not merely postponed or otherwise delayed. Accordingly, any later deferral election will be subject to the provisions governing initial deferral elections. See §1.409A–2(a).

(ix) *Plan terminations and liquidations.* A plan may provide for the acceleration of the time and form of a payment, or a payment under such plan may be made, where the acceleration of the payment is made pursuant to a termination and liquidation of the plan in accordance with one of the following:

(A) The service recipient's termination and liquidation of the plan within 12 months of a corporate dissolution taxed under section 331, or with the approval of a bankruptcy court pursuant to 11 U.S.C. §503(b)(1)(A), provided that the amounts deferred under the plan are included in the participants' gross incomes in the latest of the following years (or, if earlier, the taxable year in which the amount is actually or constructively received).

(*1*) The calendar year in which the plan termination and liquidation occurs.

(*2*) The first calendar year in which the amount is no longer subject to a substantial risk of forfeiture.

(*3*) The first calendar year in which the payment is administratively practicable.

(B) The service recipient's termination and liquidation of the plan pursuant to irrevocable action taken by the service recipient within the 30 days preceding or the 12 months following a change in control event (as defined in paragraph (i)(5) of this section), provided that this paragraph will only apply to a payment under a plan if all agreements, methods, programs, and other arrangements sponsored by the service recipient immediately after the time of the change in control event with respect to which deferrals of compensation are treated as having been deferred under a single plan under §1.409A–1(c)(2) are terminated and liquidated with respect to each participant that experienced the change in control event, so that under the terms of the termination and liquidation all such participants are required to receive all amounts of compensation deferred under the terminated agreements, methods, programs, and other arrangements within 12 months of the date the service recipient irrevocably takes all necessary action to terminate and liquidate the agreements, methods, programs, and other arrangements. Solely for purposes of this paragraph (j)(4)(ix)(B), where the change in control event results from an asset purchase transaction, the applicable service recipient with the discretion to liquidate and terminate the agreements, methods, programs, and other arrangements is the service recipient that is primarily liable immediately after the transaction for the payment of the deferred compensation.

(C) The service recipient's termination and liquidation of the plan, provided that—

(*1*) The termination and liquidation does not occur proximate to a downturn in the financial health of the service recipient;

(*2*) The service recipient terminates and liquidates all agreements, methods, programs, and other arrangements sponsored by the service recipient that would be aggregated with any terminated and liquidated agreements, methods, programs, and other arrangements under §1.409A–1(c) if the same service provider had deferrals of compensation under all of the agreements, methods, programs, and other arrangements that are terminated and liquidated;

(*3*) No payments in liquidation of the plan are made within 12 months of the date the service recipient takes all necessary action to irrevocably terminate and liquidate the plan other than payments that would be payable under the terms of the plan if the action to terminate and liquidate the plan had not occurred;

(*4*) All payments are made within 24 months of the date the service recipient takes all necessary action to irrevocably terminate and liquidate the plan; and

(*5*) The service recipient does not adopt a new plan that would be aggregated with any terminated and liquidated plan under §1.409A–1(c) if the same service provider participated in both plans, at any time within three years following the date the service recipient takes all necessary action to irrevocably terminate and liquidate the plan.

(D) Such other events and conditions as the Commissioner may prescribe in generally applicable guidance published in the Internal Revenue Bulletin (see §601.601(d)(2) of this chapter).

(x) *Certain distributions to avoid a nonallocation year under section 409(p).* A plan may provide for an acceleration of the time and form of a payment, or a payment may be made under such plan, to prevent the occurrence of a nonallocation year (within the meaning of section 409(p)(3)) in the plan year of an employee stock ownership plan next following the plan year in which such payment is made, provided that the amount distributed may not exceed 125 percent of the minimum amount of distribution necessary to avoid the occurrence of a nonallocation year. Solely for purposes of determining permissible distributions under this paragraph (j)(4)(x), synthetic equity (within the meaning of section 409(p)(6)(C) and §1.409(p)–1(f)) granted during the plan year of the employee stock ownership plan in which such payment is made is disregarded for purposes of determining whether the subsequent plan year would result in a nonallocation year.

(xi) *Payment of state, local, or foreign taxes.* A plan may provide for an acceleration of the time and form of a payment, or a payment may be made under such plan, to reflect payment of state, local, or foreign tax obligations arising from participation in the plan that apply to an amount deferred under the plan before the amount is paid or made available to the participant (the state, local, or foreign tax amount). Such payment may not exceed the amount of such taxes due as a result of participation in the plan. Such payment may be made by distributions to the participant in the form of withholding pursuant to provisions of applicable state, local, or foreign law or by distribution directly to the participant. Additionally, an arrangement may provide for the acceleration of the time or schedule of payment, or a payment may be made under such arrangement, to pay the income tax at source on wages imposed under section 3401 as a result of such payment and to pay the additional income tax at source on wages imposed under section 3401 attributable to such additional section 3401 wages and taxes. However, the total payment under this acceleration provision must not exceed the aggregate of the state, local, and foreign tax amount, and the income tax withholding related to such state, local, and foreign tax amount.

(xii) *Cancellation of deferral elections due to disability.* A plan may provide for a cancellation of a service provider's deferral election, or a cancellation of such election may be made, where such cancellation occurs by the later of the end of the taxable year of the service provider or the 15th day of the third month following the date the service provider incurs a disability. For purposes of this paragraph, a disability refers to any medically determinable physical or mental impairment resulting in the service provider's inability to perform the duties of his or her position or any substantially similar position, where such impairment can be expected to result in death or can be expected to last for a continuous period of not less than six months.

(xiii) *Certain offsets.* A plan may provide for the acceleration of the time or schedule of a payment, or a payment may be made under such plan, as satisfaction of a debt of the service provider to the service recipient, where such debt is incurred in the ordinary course of the service relationship between the service recipient and the service provider, the entire amount of reduction in any of the service recipient's taxable years does not exceed $5,000, and the reduction is made at the same time and in the same amount as the debt otherwise would have been due and collected from the service provider.

(xiv) *Bona fide disputes as to a right to a payment.* A plan may provide for the acceleration of the time or schedule of one or more payments, or a payment may be made under such plan, where such payments occur as part of a settlement between the service provider and the service recipient of an arm's length, *bona fide* dispute as to the service provider's right to the deferred amount. Discretion to accelerate payments, other than due to an arm's length settlement of a *bona fide* dispute as to the service provider's right to the deferred amount, is not permitted under this paragraph (j)(4)(xiv). Whether a payment qualifies for the exception under this paragraph is based on all relevant facts and circumstances. A payment will be presumed not to meet this exception unless the payment is subject to a substantial reduction in the value of the payment made in relation to the amount that would have been payable had there been no dispute as to the service provider's right to the payment. For this purpose, a reduction that is less than 25 percent of the present value of the deferred amount in dispute generally is not a substantial reduction. In addition, a payment will be presumed not to meet this exception if the payment is made proximate to a downturn in the financial health of the service recipient.

(5) *Nonqualified deferred compensation plans linked to qualified employer plans or certain other arrangements.* If a nonqualified deferred compensation plan provides that the amount deferred under the plan is the amount determined under the formula determining benefits under a qualified employer plan (as defined in §1.409A–1(a)(2)), or a broad-based foreign retirement plan (as defined in §1.409A–1(a)(3)(v)) maintained by the service recipient but applied without regard to one or more limitations applicable to the qualified employer plan under the Internal Revenue Code or to the broad-based foreign retirement plan under other applicable law, or that the amount deferred under the nonqualified deferred compensation plan is determined as an amount offset by some or all of the benefits provided under the qualified employer plan or broad-based foreign retirement plan, a decrease in amounts deferred under the nonqualified deferred compensation plan that results directly from changes in benefit limitations applicable to the qualified employer plan or the broad-based foreign retirement plan under the Internal Revenue Code or other applicable law does not constitute an acceleration of a payment under the nonqualified deferred compensation plan, provided that such operation does not otherwise result in a change in the time or form of a payment under the nonqualified deferred compensation plan, and provided further that the change in the amounts deferred under the nonqualified deferred compensation plan does not exceed such change in the amounts deferred under the qualified employer plan or the broad-based foreign retirement plan, as applicable. In addition, with respect to such a nonqualified deferred compensation plan, the following actions or failures to act will not constitute an acceleration of a payment under the nonqualified deferred compensation plan even if in accordance with the terms of the nonqualified deferred compensation plan, the actions or inactions result in a decrease in the amounts deferred under the plan, provided that such actions or inactions do not otherwise affect the time or form of payment under the nonqualified deferred compensation plan, and provided further that with respect to actions or inactions described in paragraphs (j)(5)(i) and (ii) of this section, the change in the amount deferred under the nonqualified deferred compensation plan does not exceed the change in the amounts deferred under the qualified employer plan or the broad-based foreign retirement plan, as applicable:

(i) A service provider's action or inaction under the qualified employer plan or broad-based foreign retirement plan with respect to whether to elect to receive a subsidized benefit or an ancillary benefit under the qualified employer plan or broad-based foreign retirement plan.

(ii) The amendment of a qualified employer plan or broad-based foreign retirement plan to increase benefits provided under such plan, or to add or remove a subsidized benefit or an ancillary benefit.

(iii) A service provider's action or inaction under a qualified employer plan with respect to elective deferrals and other employee pre-tax contributions subject to the contribution restrictions under section 401(a)(30) or section 402(g), including an adjustment to a deferral election under such qualified employer plan, provided that for any given taxable year, the service provider's action or inaction does not result in a decrease in the amounts deferred under all nonqualified deferred compensation plans in which the service provider participates (other than amounts described in paragraph (j)(5)(iv) of this section) in excess of the limit with respect to elective deferrals under section 402(g)(1)(A), (B), and (C) in effect for the taxable year in which such action or inaction occurs.

(iv) A service provider's action or inaction under a qualified employer plan with respect to elective deferrals and other employee pre-tax contributions subject to the contributions restrictions under section 401(a)(30) or section 402(g), and after-tax contributions by the service provider to a qualified employer plan that provides for such contributions, that affects the amounts that are credited under one or more nonqualified deferred compensation plans as matching amounts or other similar amounts contingent on such elective deferrals, pre-tax contributions, or after-tax contributions, provided that the total of such matching or contingent amounts, as applicable, never exceeds 100 percent of the matching or contingent amounts that would be provided under the qualified employer plan absent any plan-based restrictions that reflect limits on qualified plan contributions under the Internal Revenue Code.

(6) *Changes in elections under a cafeteria plan.* A change in an election under a cafeteria plan (as defined in section 125(d)) does not result in an accelerated payment of an amount deferred under a nonqualified deferred compensation plan to the extent that the change in the amount deferred under the nonqualified deferred compensation plan results solely from the application of the change in amount eligible to be treated as compensation under the terms of the nonqualified deferred compensation plan resulting from the election change under the cafeteria plan, to a benefit formula under the nonqualified deferred compensation plan based upon the service provider's eligible compensation, and only to the extent that such change applies in the same manner as any other increase or decrease in compensation would apply to such benefit formula.

§1.409A–4 Calculation of income inclusion. [Reserved].

§1.409A–5 Funding. [Reserved].

§1.409A–6 Application of section 409A and effective dates.

(a) *Statutory application and effective dates*—(1) *Application to amounts deferred*—(i) *In general.* Except as otherwise provided in this section, section 409A applies with respect to amounts deferred in taxable years beginning after December 31, 2004, and with respect to amounts deferred in taxable years beginning before January 1, 2005, if the plan under which the deferral is made is materially modified after October 3, 2004. For amounts deferred in taxable years beginning before January 1, 2005, under a plan that is materially modified after October 3, 2004, whether the plan complies with the requirements of section 409A and these regulations is determined by reference to the terms of the plan in effect as of, and any actions taken under the plan on or after, the date of the material modification. Section 409A is applicable with respect to earnings on amounts deferred only to the extent that section 409A is applicable with respect to the amounts deferred. Accordingly, section 409A does not apply with respect to earnings on amounts deferred before January 1, 2005, unless section 409A applies with respect to the amounts deferred. For this purpose, a right to earnings that is subject to a substantial risk of forfeiture (as defined in §1.83–3(c)) or a requirement to perform further services, on an amount deferred that is not subject to a substantial risk of forfeiture (as defined in §1.83–3(c)) or a requirement to perform further services, is not treated as earnings on the amount deferred, but a separate right to compensation. Except as otherwise provided in applicable guidance (see §601.601(d)(2) of this chapter), the provisions of §§1.409A–1 through 1.409A–5 and this section provide the exclusive means of identifying agreements, methods, programs, or other arrangements subject to section 409A, and the exclusive means of satisfying the requirements of section 409A with respect to such agreements, methods, programs, or other arrangements.

(ii) *Collectively bargained plans.* Section 409A does not apply with respect to amounts deferred under a plan maintained pursuant to one or more *bona fide* collective bargaining agreements in effect on October 3, 2004, for the period ending on the earlier of the date on which the last of such collective bargaining agreements terminates (determined without regard to any extension thereof after October 3, 2004) or December 31, 2009.

(2) *Identification of date of deferral for statutory effective date purposes.* For purposes of determining whether section 409A is applicable with respect to an amount, the amount is considered deferred before January 1, 2005, if before January 1, 2005, the service provider had a legally binding right to be paid the amount, and the right to the amount was earned and vested. For purposes of this paragraph (a)(2), a right to an amount was earned and vested only if the amount was not subject to a substantial risk of forfeiture (as defined in §1.83–3(c)) or a requirement to perform further services. Amounts to which the service provider did not have a legally binding right before January 1, 2005 (for example because the service recipient retained discretion to reduce the amount), will not be considered deferred before January 1, 2005. In addition, amounts to which the service provider had a legally binding right before January 1, 2005, but the right to which was subject to a substantial risk of forfeiture or a requirement to perform further services after December 31, 2004, are not considered deferred before January 1, 2005, for purposes of the effective date. Notwithstanding the foregoing, an amount to which the service provider had a legally binding right before January 1, 2005, but for which the service provider was required to continue performing services to retain the right only through the completion of the payroll period (as defined in §1.409A–1(b)(3)) that includes December 31, 2004, is not treated as subject to a requirement to perform further services (or a substantial risk of forfeiture) for purposes of the effective date. For purposes of this paragraph (a)(2), a stock option, stock appreciation right, or similar compensation that on or before December 31, 2004, was immediately exercisable for cash or substantially vested property (as defined in §1.83–3(b)) is treated as earned and vested, regardless of whether the right would terminate if the service provider ceased providing services for the service recipient.

(3) *Calculation of amount of compensation deferred for statutory effective date purposes*—(i) *Nonaccount balance plans.* The amount of compensation deferred before January 1, 2005, under a nonqualified deferred compensation plan that is a nonaccount balance plan (as defined in §1.409A–1(c)(2)(i)(C)), equals the present value of the amount to which the service provider would have been entitled under the plan if the service provider voluntarily terminated services without cause on December 31, 2004, and received a payment of the benefits available from the plan on the earliest possible date allowed under the plan to receive a payment of benefits following the termination of services, and received the benefits in the form with the maximum value. Notwithstanding the foregoing, for any subsequent taxable year of the service provider, the grandfathered amount may increase to equal the present value of the benefit the service provider actually becomes entitled to, in the form and at the time actually paid, determined under the terms of the plan (including applicable limits under the Internal Revenue Code), as in effect on October 3, 2004, without regard to any further services rendered by the service provider after December 31, 2004, or any other events affecting the amount of or the entitlement to benefits (other than a participant election with respect to the time or form of an available benefit). For purposes of calculating the present value of a benefit under this paragraph (c)(3)(i), reasonable actuarial assumptions and methods must be used. Whether assumptions and methods are reasonable for this purpose is determined as of each date the benefit is valued for purposes of determining the grandfathered benefit, provided that any reasonable actuarial assumptions and methods that were used by the service recipient with respect to such benefit as of December 31, 2004, will continue to be treated as reasonable assumptions and methods for purposes of calculating the grandfathered benefit. Actuarial assumptions and methods will be presumed reasonable if they are the same as those used to value benefits under a qualified plan sponsored by the service recipient the benefits under which are part of the benefit formula under, or otherwise impact the amount of benefits under, the nonaccount balance nonqualified deferred compensation plan.

(ii) *Account balance plans.* The amount of compensation deferred before January 1, 2005, under a nonqualified deferred compensation plan that is an account balance plan (as defined in §1.409A–1(c)(2)(i)(A)), equals the portion of the service provider's account balance as of December 31, 2004, the right to which was earned and vested (as defined in paragraph (a)(2) of this section) as of December 31, 2004, plus any future contributions to the account, the right to which was earned and vested (as defined in paragraph (a)(2) of this section) as of December 31, 2004, to the extent such contributions are actually made.

(iii) *Equity-based compensation plans.* For purposes of determining the amounts deferred before January 1, 2005, under an equity-based compensation plan, the rules of paragraph (a)(3)(ii) of this section governing account balance plans are applied except that the account balance is deemed to be the amount of the payment available to the service provider on December 31, 2004 (or that would be available to the service provider if the right were immediately exercisable) the right to which is earned and vested (as defined in paragraph (a)(2) of this section) as of December 31, 2004. For this purpose, the payment available to the service provider excludes any exercise price or other amount that must be paid by the service provider.

(iv) *Earnings*. Earnings on amounts deferred under a plan before January 1, 2005, include only income (whether actual or notional) attributable to the amounts deferred under a plan as of December 31, 2004, or to such income. For example, notional interest earned under the plan on amounts deferred in an account balance plan as of December 31, 2004, generally will be treated as earnings on amounts deferred under the plan before January 1, 2005. Similarly, an increase in the amount of payment available pursuant to a stock option, stock appreciation right, or other equity-based compensation above the amount of payment available as of December 31, 2004, due to appreciation in the underlying stock after December 31, 2004, or accrual of other earnings such as dividends, is treated as earnings on the amount deferred. In the case of a nonaccount balance plan, earnings include the increase, due solely to the passage of time, in the present value of the future payments to which the service provider has obtained a legally binding right, the present value of which constituted the amounts deferred under the plan before January 1, 2005. Thus, for each year, there will be an increase (determined using the same interest rate used to determine the amounts deferred under the plan before January 1, 2005) resulting from the shortening of the discount period before the future payments are made, plus, if applicable, an increase in the present value resulting from the service provider's survivorship during the year. However, an increase in the potential benefits under a nonaccount balance plan due to, for example, an application of an increase in compensation after December 31, 2004, to a final average pay plan or subsequent eligibility for an early retirement subsidy, does not constitute earnings on the amounts deferred under the plan before January 1, 2005.

(v) *Definition of plan*. For purposes of paragraphs (a)(1), (2), and (3) of this section, the term "plan" has the meaning provided in §1.409A–1(c), except that the plan aggregation rules do not apply for purposes of the actuarial assumptions and methods used in paragraph (a)(3)(i) of this section. Accordingly, different reasonable actuarial assumptions and methods may be used to calculate the amounts deferred by a service provider in two different agreements, methods, programs, or other arrangements each of which constitutes a nonaccount balance plan.

(4) *Material modifications*—(i) *In general*. Except as otherwise provided, a modification of a plan is a material modification if a benefit or right existing as of October 3, 2004, is materially enhanced or a new material benefit or right is added, and such material enhancement or addition affects amounts earned and vested before January 1, 2005. Such material benefit enhancement or addition is a material modification whether it occurs pursuant to an amendment or to the service recipient's exercise of discretion under the terms of the plan. For example, an amendment to a plan to add a provision that payments of deferred amounts earned and vested before January 1, 2005, may be allowed upon request if service providers are required to forfeit 20 percent of the amount of the payment (a haircut) would be a material modification to the plan. Similarly, a material modification would occur if a service recipient exercised discretion to accelerate vesting of a benefit under the plan to a date on or before December 31, 2004. However, it is not a material modification for a service recipient to exercise discretion over the time and manner of payment of a benefit to the extent such discretion is provided under the terms of the plan as of October 3, 2004. It is not a material modification for a service provider to exercise a right permitted under the plan as in effect on October 3, 2004. The amendment of a plan to bring the plan into compliance with the provisions of section 409A will not be treated as a material modification. However, a plan amendment or the exercise of discretion under the terms of the plan that materially enhances an existing benefit or right or adds a new material benefit or right will be considered a material modification even if the enhanced or added benefit would be permitted under section 409A. For example, the addition of a right to a payment upon an unforeseeable emergency of an amount earned and vested before January 1, 2005, would be considered a material modification. The reduction of an existing benefit is not a material modification. For example, the removal of a haircut provision generally would not constitute a material modification. The following modifications also are not material modifications for purposes of this paragraph (a)(4)(i):

(A) The establishment of or contributions to a trust or other arrangement from which benefits under the plan are to be paid is not a material modification of the plan, provided that the contribution to the trust or other arrangement would not otherwise cause an amount to be includible in the service provider's gross income.

(B) The modification of a provision requiring the immediate cancellation of a current deferral election, to require the cancellation of deferrals for the same length of time beginning with the first date at which the application of such cancellation would not violate section 409A (for example, the first date of the service provider's first taxable year following the cancellation).

(C) Compliance with a domestic relations order (as defined in §1.409A–3(j)(4)(ii)) with respect to payments to an individual other than the service provider, or an amendment to a plan to require compliance with a domestic relations order with respect to payments to an individual other than the service provider.

(D) The modification of a plan providing a life annuity form of payment to permit an election between the existing life annuity form of payment and other forms of annuity payments that would be treated as a single form of payment with the existing life annuity form of payment under §1.409A–2(b)(2)(ii).

(E) The modification of a grandfathered plan to add a limited cashout feature consistent with §1.409A–3(j)(4)(v) (exception to prohibition on accelerated payments).

(ii) *Adoptions of new plans*. It is presumed that the adoption of a new plan or the grant of an additional benefit under an existing plan after October 3, 2004, and before January 1, 2005, constitutes a material modification of a plan. However, the presumption may be rebutted by demonstrating that the adoption of the plan or grant of the additional benefit was consistent with the service recipient's historical compensation practices. For example, the presumption that the grant of a discounted stock option on November 1, 2004, is a material modification of a plan may be rebutted by demonstrating that the grant was consistent with the historic practice of granting substantially similar discounted stock options (both as to terms and amounts) each November for a significant number of years. Notwithstanding paragraph (a)(4)(i) of this section and this paragraph (a)(4)(ii), the grant of an additional benefit under an existing plan that consists of a deferral of additional compensation not otherwise provided under the plan as of October 3, 2004, will be treated as a material modification of the plan only as to the additional deferral of compensation, if the plan explicitly identifies the additional deferral of compensation and provides that the additional deferral of compensation is subject to section 409A. Accordingly, amendments to conform a plan to the requirements of section 409A with respect to deferrals under a plan occurring after December 31, 2004, will not constitute a material modification of the plan with respect to amounts deferred that are earned and vested on or before December 31, 2004, provided that there is no concurrent material modification with respect to the amount of, or rights to, amounts deferred that were earned and vested on or before December 31, 2004. Similarly, a grant of an additional benefit under a new plan adopted after October 3, 2004, and before January 1, 2005, will not be treated as a material modification of an existing plan to the extent that the new plan explicitly identifies additional deferrals of compensation and provides that the additional deferrals of compensation are subject to section 409A.

(iii) *Suspension or termination of a plan.* A cessation of deferrals under, or termination of, a plan, pursuant to the provisions of such plan, is not a material modification. Amending a plan to provide participants an election whether to terminate participation in a plan generally constitutes a material modification of the plan.

(iv) *Changes to investment measures—account balance plans.* With respect to an account balance plan (as defined in §1.409A–1(c)(2)(i)(A)), it is not a material modification to change a notional investment measure to, or to add to an existing investment measure, an investment measure that qualifies as a predetermined actual investment within the meaning of §31.3121(v)(2)–1(d)(2) of this chapter or, for any given taxable year, reflects a reasonable rate of interest (determined in accordance with §31.3121(v)(2)–1(d)(2)(i)(C) of this chapter). For this purpose, if with respect to an amount deferred for a period, a plan provides for a fixed rate of interest to be credited, and the rate is to be reset under the plan at a specified future date that is not later than the end of the fifth taxable year that begins after the beginning of the period, the rate is reasonable at the beginning of the period, and the rate is not changed before the reset date, then the rate will be treated as reasonable in all future periods before the reset date.

(v) *Stock rights.* The modification, extension, or renewal of a stock right will not constitute a material modification of the stock right, if the modification, extension, or renewal would not be treated as the grant of a new stock right under §1.409A–1(b)(5)(v)(A), and would not result in the stock right being treated as having had a deferral feature from the date of grant pursuant to §1.409A–1(b)(5)(v)(C).

(vi) *Rescission of modifications.* Any modification to the terms of a plan that would inadvertently result in treatment as a material modification under this section is not considered a material modification of the plan to the extent the modification in the terms of the plan is rescinded by the earlier of a date before the right is exercised (if the change grants a discretionary right) or the last day of the taxable year of the service provider during which such change occurred. Thus, for example, if a service recipient modifies the terms of a plan on March 1 to allow an individual employee to elect a new change in the time or form of payment without realizing that such a change constituted a material modification that would subject the plan to the requirements of section 409A, and the modification is rescinded on November 1, then if no change in the time or form of payment has been made pursuant to the modification before November 1, the plan is not considered materially modified under this section.

(vii) *Definition of plan.* For purposes of this paragraph (a)(4), the term "plan" has the same meaning provided in §1.409A–1(c), except that the plan aggregation rules of §1.409A–1(c)(2) do not apply.

(b) *Regulatory applicability date.* §1.409A–1, §1.409A–2, §1.409A–3 and this section are applicable for taxable years beginning on or after January 1, 2008.

Kevin M. Brown,
Deputy Commissioner for Services and Enforcement.

Approved March 20, 2007.

Eric Solomon,
Assistant Secretary of the Treasury.

(Filed by the Office of the Federal Register on April 10, 2007, 8:45 a.m., and published in the issue of the Federal Register for April 17, 2007, 72 F.R. 19234)

Section 412.—Minimum Funding Standards

The adjusted applicable federal short-term, mid-term, and long-term rates are set forth for the month of May 2007. See Rev. Rul. 2007-29, page 1223.

Section 467.—Certain Payments for the Use of Property or Services

The adjusted applicable federal short-term, mid-term, and long-term rates are set forth for the month of May 2007. See Rev. Rul. 2007-29, page 1223.

Section 468.—Special Rules for Mining and Solid Waste Reclamation and Closing Costs

The adjusted applicable federal short-term, mid-term, and long-term rates are set forth for the month of May 2007. See Rev. Rul. 2007-29, page 1223.

Section 482.—Allocation of Income and Deductions Among Taxpayers

Federal short-term, mid-term, and long-term rates are set forth for the month of May 2007. See Rev. Rul. 2007-29, page 1223.

Section 483.—Interest on Certain Deferred Payments

The adjusted applicable federal short-term, mid-term, and long-term rates are set forth for the month of May 2007. See Rev. Rul. 2007-29, page 1223.

Section 642.—Special Rules for Credits and Deductions

Federal short-term, mid-term, and long-term rates are set forth for the month of May 2007. See Rev. Rul. 2007-29, page 1223.

Section 807.—Rules for Certain Reserves

The adjusted applicable federal short-term, mid-term, and long-term rates are set forth for the month of May 2007. See Rev. Rul. 2007-29, page 1223.

Section 846.—Discounted Unpaid Losses Defined

The adjusted applicable federal short-term, mid-term, and long-term rates are set forth for the month of May 2007. See Rev. Rul. 2007-29, page 1223.

Section 1274.—Determination of Issue Price in the Case of Certain Debt Instruments Issued for Property

(Also Sections 42, 280G, 382, 412, 467, 468, 482, 483, 642, 807, 846, 1288, 7520, 7872.)

Federal rates; adjusted federal rates; adjusted federal long-term rate and the long-term exempt rate. For purposes of sections 382, 642, 1274, 1288, and other sections of the Code, tables set forth the rates for May 2007.

Rev. Rul. 2007–29

This revenue ruling provides various prescribed rates for federal income tax purposes for May 2007 (the current month). Table 1 contains the short-term, mid-term, and long-term applicable federal rates (AFR) for the current month for purposes of section 1274(d) of the Internal Revenue Code. Table 2 contains the short-term, mid-term, and long-term adjusted applicable federal rates (adjusted AFR) for the current month for purposes of section 1288(b). Table 3 sets forth the adjusted federal long-term rate and the long-term tax-exempt rate described in section 382(f). Table 4 contains the appropriate percentages for determining the low-income housing credit described in section 42(b)(2) for buildings placed in service during the current month. Finally, Table 5 contains the federal rate for determining the present value of an annuity, an interest for life or for a term of years, or a remainder or a reversionary interest for purposes of section 7520.

REV. RUL. 2007–29 TABLE 1

Applicable Federal Rates (AFR) for May 2007

Period for Compounding

	Annual	*Semiannual*	*Quarterly*	*Monthly*
Short-term				
AFR	4.85%	4.79%	4.76%	4.74%
110% AFR	5.34%	5.27%	5.24%	5.21%
120% AFR	5.83%	5.75%	5.71%	5.68%
130% AFR	6.33%	6.23%	6.18%	6.15%
Mid-term				
AFR	4.62%	4.57%	4.54%	4.53%
110% AFR	5.09%	5.03%	5.00%	4.98%
120% AFR	5.56%	5.48%	5.44%	5.42%
130% AFR	6.03%	5.94%	5.90%	5.87%
150% AFR	6.98%	6.86%	6.80%	6.76%
175% AFR	8.16%	8.00%	7.92%	7.87%
Long-term				
AFR	4.90%	4.84%	4.81%	4.79%
110% AFR	5.39%	5.32%	5.29%	5.26%
120% AFR	5.89%	5.81%	5.77%	5.74%
130% AFR	6.39%	6.29%	6.24%	6.21%

REV. RUL. 2007–29 TABLE 2

Adjusted AFR for May 2007

Period for Compounding

	Annual	*Semiannual*	*Quarterly*	*Monthly*
Short-term adjusted AFR	3.47%	3.44%	3.43%	3.42%
Mid-term adjusted AFR	3.61%	3.58%	3.56%	3.55%
Long-term adjusted AFR	4.11%	4.07%	4.05%	4.04%

REV. RUL. 2007–29 TABLE 3

Rates Under Section 382 for May 2007

Adjusted federal long-term rate for the current month	4.11%
Long-term tax-exempt rate for ownership changes during the current month (the highest of the adjusted federal long-term rates for the current month and the prior two months.)	4.18%

REV. RUL. 2007–29 TABLE 4

Appropriate Percentages Under Section 42(b)(2) for May 2007

Appropriate percentage for the 70% present value low-income housing credit	8.11%
Appropriate percentage for the 30% present value low-income housing credit	3.47%

REV. RUL. 2007–29 TABLE 5

Rate Under Section 7520 for May 2007

Applicable federal rate for determining the present value of an annuity, an interest for life or a term of years, or a remainder or reversionary interest	5.6%

Section 1288.—Treatment of Original Issue Discount on Tax-Exempt Obligations

The adjusted applicable federal short-term, mid-term, and long-term rates are set forth for the month of May 2007. See Rev. Rul. 2007-29, page 1223.

Section 7520.—Valuation Tables

The adjusted applicable federal short-term, mid-term, and long-term rates are set forth for the month of May 2007. See Rev. Rul. 2007-29, page 1223.

Section 7872.—Treatment of Loans With Below-Market Interest Rates

The adjusted applicable federal short-term, mid-term, and long-term rates are set forth for the month of May 2007. See Rev. Rul. 2007-29, page 1223.

Part III. Administrative, Procedural, and Miscellaneous

26 CFR 601.601: Rules and regulations.
(Also Part I, §§ 25, 103, 143; 1.25–4T, 1.103–1, 6a.103A–2.)

Rev. Proc. 2007–31

SECTION 1. PURPOSE

This revenue procedure provides guidance with respect to the United States and area median gross income figures that are to be used by issuers of qualified mortgage bonds, as defined in § 143(a) of the Internal Revenue Code, and issuers of mortgage credit certificates, as defined in § 25(c), in computing the housing cost/income ratio described in § 143(f)(5).

SECTION 2. BACKGROUND

.01 Section 103(a) provides that, except as provided in § 103(b), gross income does not include interest on any state or local bond. Section 103(b)(1) provides that § 103(a) shall not apply to any private activity bond that is not a qualified bond (within the meaning of § 141). Section 141(e) provides that the term "qualified bond" includes any private activity bond that (1) is a qualified mortgage bond, (2) meets the applicable volume cap requirements under § 146, and (3) meets the applicable requirements under § 147.

.02 Section 143(a)(1) provides that the term "qualified mortgage bond" means a bond that is issued as part of a "qualified mortgage issue". Section 143(a)(2)(A) provides that the term "qualified mortgage issue" means an issue of one or more bonds by a state or political subdivision thereof, but only if (i) all proceeds of the issue (exclusive of issuance costs and a reasonably required reserve) are to be used to finance owner-occupied residences; (ii) the issue meets the requirements of subsections (c), (d), (e), (f), (g), (h), (i), and (m)(7) of § 143; (iii) the issue does not meet the private business tests of paragraphs (1) and (2) of § 141(b); and (iv) with respect to amounts received more than 10 years after the date of issuance, repayments of $250,000 or more of principal on financing provided by the issue are used not later than the close of the first semi-annual period beginning after the date the prepayment (or complete repayment) is received to redeem bonds that are part of the issue.

.03 Section 143(f) imposes eligibility requirements concerning the maximum income of mortgagors for whom financing may be provided by qualified mortgage bonds. Section 25(c)(2)(A)(iii)(IV) provides that recipients of mortgage credit certificates must meet the income requirements of § 143(f). Generally, under §§ 143(f)(1) and 25(c)(2)(A)(iii)(IV), these income requirements are met only if all owner-financing under a qualified mortgage bond and all certified indebtedness amounts under a mortgage credit certificate program are provided to mortgagors whose family income is 115 percent or less of the applicable median family income. Under § 143(f)(6), the income limitation is reduced to 100 percent of the applicable median family income if there are fewer than three individuals in the family of the mortgagor.

.04 Section 143(f)(4) provides that the term "applicable median family income" means the greater of (A) the area median gross income for the area in which the residence is located, or (B) the statewide median gross income for the state in which the residence is located.

.05 Section 143(f)(5) provides for an upward adjustment of the income limitations in certain high housing cost areas. Under § 143(f)(5)(C), a high housing cost area is a statistical area for which the housing cost/income ratio is greater than 1.2. The housing cost/income ratio is determined under § 143(f)(5)(D) by dividing (a) the applicable housing price ratio by (b) the ratio that the area median gross income bears to the median gross income for the United States. The applicable housing price ratio is the new housing price ratio (new housing average purchase price for the area divided by the new housing average purchase price for the United States) or the existing housing price ratio (existing housing average area purchase price divided by the existing housing average purchase price for the United States), whichever results in the housing cost/income ratio being closer to 1. This income adjustment applies only to bonds issued, and nonissued bond amounts elected, after December 31, 1988. *See* § 4005(h) of the Technical and Miscellaneous Revenue Act of 1988, 1988–3 C.B. 1, 311 (1988).

.06 The Department of Housing and Urban Development (HUD) has computed the median gross income for the United States, the states, and statistical areas within the states. The income information was released to the HUD regional offices on March 20, 2007, and may be obtained by calling the HUD reference service at 1–800–245–2691. The income information is also available at HUD's World Wide Web site, *http:huduser.org/datasets/il.html*, which provides a menu from which you may select the year and type of data of interest. The Internal Revenue Service annually publishes the median gross income for the United States.

.07 The most recent nationwide average purchase prices and average area purchase price safe harbor limitations were published on March 26, 2007, in Rev. Proc. 2007–26, 2007–13 I.R.B. 814.

SECTION 3. APPLICATION

.01 When computing the housing cost/income ratio under § 143(f)(5), issuers of qualified mortgage bonds and mortgage credit certificates must use as the median gross income for the United States either (1) the $59,600 median gross income figure released to the HUD regional offices on March 8, 2006, or (2) the $59,000 median gross income figure released to the HUD regional offices on March 20, 2007. *See* § 2.06 of this revenue procedure.

.02 When computing the housing cost/income ratio under § 143(f)(5), issuers of qualified mortgage bonds and mortgage credit certificates generally must use the area median gross income figures released by HUD on March 20, 2007. *See* § 2.06 of this revenue procedure. However, for any area for which the March 20, 2007 income figure is lower than the income figure released by HUD on March 8, 2006 for the same area, issuers may use the higher figure released on March 8, 2006, when computing the housing cost/income ratio under § 143(f)(5).

SECTION 4. EFFECT ON OTHER REVENUE PROCEDURES

.01 Rev. Proc. 2006–20, 2006–17 I.R.B. 841, is obsolete except as provided in § 5.02 of this revenue procedure.

.02 This revenue procedure does not affect the effective date provisions of Rev. Rul. 86–124, 1986–2 C.B. 27. Those effective date provisions will remain operative at least until the Service publishes a new revenue ruling that conforms the approach to effective dates set forth in Rev. Rul. 86–124 to the general approach taken in this revenue procedure. However, when determining the income requirements under § 143(f), for any state or area for which the March 20, 2007 statewide or area median gross income figure is lower than the income figure released by HUD on March 8, 2006, for the same state or area, issuers may use the higher figure released on March 8, 2006, until 30 days after release by HUD of updated income limits.

SECTION 5. EFFECTIVE DATES

.01 Issuers must use the United States and area median gross income figures specified in § 3 of this revenue procedure for commitments to provide financing that are made, or (if the purchase precedes the financing commitment) for residences that are purchased, in the period that begins on March 20, 2007, and ends on the date when these United States and area median gross income figures are rendered obsolete by a new revenue procedure.

.02 Notwithstanding § 5.01 of this revenue procedure, issuers also may continue to rely on the United States and area median gross income figures specified in Rev. Proc. 2006–20 with respect to bonds originally sold and nonissued bond amounts elected not later than May 17, 2007, if the commitments or purchases described in § 5.01 are made not later than July 16, 2007. Issuers also may continue to rely on the United States and area median gross income figures specified in Rev. Proc. 2006–20, to the extent allowed under §§ 3.01 and 3.02 of this revenue procedure.

DRAFTING INFORMATION

The principal author of this revenue procedure is David White of the Office of Assistant Chief Counsel (Exempt Organizations/Employment Tax/Government Entities). For further information regarding this revenue procedure, contact Mr. White at (202) 622–3980 (not a toll-free call).

Part IV. Items of General Interest

Announcement of Disciplinary Actions Involving Attorneys, Certified Public Accountants, Enrolled Agents, and Enrolled Actuaries — Suspensions, Censures, Disbarments, and Resignations

Announcement 2007-41

Under Title 31, Code of Federal Regulations, Part 10, attorneys, certified public accountants, enrolled agents, and enrolled actuaries may not accept assistance from, or assist, any person who is under disbarment or suspension from practice before the Internal Revenue Service if the assistance relates to a matter constituting practice before the Internal Revenue Service and may not knowingly aid or abet another person to practice before the Internal Revenue Service during a period of suspension, disbarment, or ineligibility of such other person.

To enable attorneys, certified public accountants, enrolled agents, and enrolled actuaries to identify persons to whom these restrictions apply, the Director, Office of Professional Responsibility, will announce in the Internal Revenue Bulletin their names, their city and state, their professional designation, the effective date of disciplinary action, and the period of suspension. This announcement will appear in the weekly Bulletin at the earliest practicable date after such action and will continue to appear in the weekly Bulletins for five successive weeks.

Consent Suspensions From Practice Before the Internal Revenue Service

Under Title 31, Code of Federal Regulations, Part 10, an attorney, certified public accountant, enrolled agent, or enrolled actuary, in order to avoid the institution or conclusion of a proceeding for his or her disbarment or suspension from practice before the Internal Revenue Service, may offer his or her consent to suspension from such practice. The Director, Office of Professional Responsibility, in his discretion, may suspend an attorney, certified public accountant, enrolled agent, or enrolled actuary in accordance with the consent offered.

The following individuals have been placed under consent suspension from practice before the Internal Revenue Service:

Name	Address	Designation	Date of Suspension
Hankinson, Eugene M.	Somerset, PA	CPA	Indefinite from November 15, 2006
Canzano, Richard M.	Winchester, MA	Attorney	Indefinite from November 20, 2006
Sims, Jr., Lionel	Houston, TX	CPA	Indefinite from November 20, 2006
Wendekier, Raymond J.	Patton, PA	Attorney	Indefinite from November 21, 2006
Golden, Larry	Hinesville, GA	CPA	Indefinite from November 28, 2006

Name	Address	Designation	Date of Suspension
Lane, David B.	Hanover, MA	Attorney	Indefinite from November 28, 2006
Brown, Arthur I.	Miami, FL	CPA	Indefinite from December 1, 2006
Frisk, Daniel J.	Fargo, ND	Attorney	Indefinite from December 1, 2006
Small, Kenneth A.	McMurray, PA	CPA	Indefinite from December 1, 2006
Vazquez, Sonya M.	Port Orchard, WA	CPA	Indefinite from December 1, 2006
Swistak, Anthony	Adams, MA	Enrolled Agent	Indefinite from December 6, 2006
Lenahan, Jr., Robert J.	Elizabeth, NJ	Attorney	Indefinite from December 11, 2006
Hayes, Richard A.	Havervill, MA	Attorney	Indefinite from December 14, 2006
Scheller, Stephen M.	Coppell, TX	CPA	Indefinite from December 15, 2006
Wilson, James M.	Berlin, NJ	CPA	Indefinite from December 15, 2006
Franzese, Joseph P.	Winthrop, MA	Attorney	Indefinite from December 18, 2006
Black, Charles C.	Marietta, GA	Attorney	Indefinite from January 1, 2007
Enright, III, Robert A.	Naples, FL	Attorney	Indefinite from January 1, 2007
Fromovitz, Norman M.	Brooklyn, NY	CPA	Indefinite from January 1, 2007
Saylor, Mary A.	Iowa City, IA	Enrolled Agent	Indefinite from January 1, 2007

Name	Address	Designation	Date of Suspension
Seeherman, Alan	Wynnewood, PA	CPA	Indefinite from January 1, 2007
Beistel, Theodore L.	Canton, OH	CPA	Indefinite from January 3, 2007
Myers, Robert J.	Fairport Harbor, OH	CPA	Indefinite from January 9, 2007
Burrus, Robert V.	Valparaiso, IN	CPA	Indefinite from January 22, 2007
Patterson, Douglas W.	Newburgh, IN	Attorney	Indefinite from January 31, 2007
Lang, Jeffrey H.	Fishers, IN	CPA	Indefinite from January 22, 2007
Chickering, David	Vermillion, SD	CPA	February 5, 2007 to November 4, 2007
Moss, Steve E.	Henderson, NC	CPA	Indefinite from February 5, 2007
Hazlip, Kevin	Orange Park, FL	Enrolled Agent	Indefinite from February 10, 2007
Adelson, Robert A.	Newton, MA	Attorney	Indefinite from February 15, 2007
Boyer, Daniel D.	North Judson, IN	CPA	Indefinite from February 15, 2007
LaRusso, Anthony J.	North Caldwell, NJ	Attorney	Indefinite from February 15, 2007
Martin, Spencer R.	Lancaster, PA	CPA	Indefinite from February 15, 2007
Hursh, Stephanie S.	Brush Prairie, WA	Enrolled Agent	Indefinite from February 20, 2007
Guidera, George C.	Weston, CT	Attorney	Indefinite from February 26, 2007
Ruth, Christopher A.	Cypress, CA	CPA	Indefinite from February 27, 2007

Name	Address	Designation	Date of Suspension
Elias, Lenard S.	El Cajon, CA	Enrolled Agent	Indefinite from March 1, 2007
Ikeji, Chuck	Orlando, FL	CPA	Indefinite from March 1, 2007
Lewis, Craig S.	Savannah, GA	CPA	Indefinite from March 1, 2007
Sloan, Eric R.	Brighton, MI	CPA	Indefinite from March 1, 2007
Gostomski, Michael	Stamford, CT	CPA	Indefinite from March 5, 2007
Hafer, Charles J.	Hamburg, PA	Enrolled Agent	Indefinite from March 5, 2007
Jones, Phillip G.	Andalusia, AL	Enrolled Agent	Indefinite from March 7, 2007
Agashiwala, Mahesh J.	New York, NY	CPA	Indefinite from March 22, 2007
Berndgen, Michael	Plantation, FL	CPA	Indefinite from April 1, 2007
Grahn, Charles R.	Indianapolis, IN	Attorney	Indefinite from April 1, 2007
Shaw, G. Joyce	Hebron, KY	Enrolled Agent	Indefinite from April 1, 2007
Pikaart, Jr., Edward H.	N. Branford, CT	CPA	Indefinite from April 10, 2007
Kelley, Richard S.	Beverly, MA	Attorney	Indefinite from May 1, 2007
Crabtree, Michael L.	San Dimas, CA	Enrolled Agent	Indefinite from May 15, 2007
Hausmann, Mark D.	Troy, NY	Attorney	Indefinite from May 15, 2007

Expedited Suspensions From Practice Before the Internal Revenue Service

Under Title 31, Code of Federal Regulations, Part 10, the Director, Office of Professional Responsibility, is authorized to immediately suspend from practice before the Internal Revenue Service any practitioner who, within five years from the date the expedited proceeding is instituted (1) has had a license to practice as an attorney, certified public accountant, or actuary suspended or revoked for cause or (2) has been convicted of certain crimes.

The following individuals have been placed under suspension from practice before the Internal Revenue Service by virtue of the expedited proceeding provisions:

Name	Address	Designation	Date of Suspension
Hatchett, William M.	Pontiac, MI	Attorney	Indefinite from November 13, 2006
Jacobs, Mark L.	Jackson Heights, NY	Attorney	Indefinite from November 21, 2006
Sylver, Peter T.	E. Longmeadow, MA	Attorney	Indefinite from November 21, 2006
Portlock, David R.	Pensacola, FL	Enrolled Agent	Indefinite from November 27, 2006
Ascher, Michael P.	North Port, FL	Attorney	Indefinite from November 28, 2006
Barrett, Norman W.	Dover, DE	CPA	Indefinite from November 28, 2006
Burd, Gene	Houston, TX	Attorney	Indefinite from November 28, 2006
Caceres, Carlos H.	Silver Spring, MD	Attorney	Indefinite from November 28, 2006
Carrabotta, Peter S.	Niles, IL	Attorney	Indefinite from November 28, 2006
Davis, Carleton W.	St. Louis, MO	Attorney	Indefinite from November 28, 2006
Frasier, Roland B.	Rancho Santa Fe, CA	Attorney	Indefinite from November 28, 2006
Hubbard, Edward	Chicago, IL	Attorney	Indefinite from November 28, 2006

Name	Address	Designation	Date of Suspension
Hynes, Richard W.	Brookline, MA	Attorney	Indefinite from November 28, 2006
Johnson, Barbara C.	Andover, MA	Attorney	Indefinite from November 28, 2006
Konas, Theodore V.	Lancaster, PA	CPA	Indefinite from November 28, 2006
Korson, Daniel M.	Muskegon, MI	CPA	Indefinite from November 28, 2006
Lee, III, Norman J.	Collegeville, PA	Attorney	Indefinite from November 28, 2006
Loiben, Alan A.	Skokie, IL	Attorney	Indefinite from November 28, 2006
McGarry, Thomas H.	Denver, CO	Attorney	Indefinite from November 28, 2006
Roberts, Quinton D.	Elkridge, MD	Attorney	Indefinite from November 28, 2006
Schofield, Peter L.	Spencer, MA	Attorney	Indefinite from November 28, 2006
Shultz, Ryan K.	Mitchell, NE	Attorney	Indefinite from November 28, 2006
Stenger, Jeanne P.	Temecula, CA	Attorney	Indefinite from November 28, 2006
Wood, Gary K.	Edina, MN	Attorney	Indefinite from November 28, 2006
Bakare, Adigun S.	Laurel, MD	Attorney	Indefinite from December 6, 2006
Biagini, Marc J.	Downers Grove, IL	Attorney	Indefinite from December 6, 2006
Birchall, Richard G.	Brewster, MA	Attorney	Indefinite from December 6, 2006

Name	Address	Designation	Date of Suspension
Brown, Edward E.	Indianapolis, IN	Attorney	Indefinite from December 6, 2006
Cunningham, Jr., Shirley A.	Ft. Lauderdale, FL	Attorney	Indefinite from December 6, 2006
Docherty, Scott R.	Branson West, MO	Attorney	Indefinite from December 6, 2006
Dressler, Peter P.	West Chicago, IL	Attorney	Indefinite from December 6, 2006
Henry, William J.	Irvington, NJ	Attorney	Indefinite from December 6, 2006
Hubbard, Cynthia A.	Geneva, IL	Attorney	Indefinite from December 6, 2006
Jackson, Jr., Donald H.	Hanover, MA	Attorney	Indefinite from December 6, 2006
Katz, Norman H.	Owings Mills, MD	Attorney	Indefinite from December 6, 2006
Lakin, Leonard S.	Wellesley Hills, MA	Attorney	Indefinite from December 6, 2006
McGreevy, Jacqueline K.	Carbondale, CO	Attorney	Indefinite from December 6, 2006
Zepp, Dale D.	Ferguson, MO	Attorney	Indefinite from December 6, 2006
Triplett, Austin H.	Homewood, IL	Attorney	Indefinite from December 11, 2006
Murphy, Patrick W.	Honolulu, HI	Attorney	Indefinite from December 11, 2006
Cronin, Jr., Edward M.	Cambridge, MA	Attorney	Indefinite from December 11, 2006
Christof, Kevin F.	Santa Monica, CA	Attorney	Indefinite from December 21, 2006
Heath, Kenneth J.	Canaan, VT	CPA	Indefinite from December 21, 2006

Name	Address	Designation	Date of Suspension
Madigan, Brian C.	Binghamton, NY	Attorney	Indefinite from December 21, 2006
Malloy, Terry P.	Tulsa, OK	Attorney	Indefinite from December 21, 2006
Baynes, Robert M.	Indianapolis, IN	CPA	Indefinite from December 27, 2006
Ceresa, Richard A.	Woodbridge, CA	CPA	Indefinite from December 27, 2006
Crews, Richard A.	Henderson, CO	Attorney	Indefinite from December 27, 2006
Menkveld, Paul G.	Tucson, AZ	Attorney	Indefinite from December 27, 2006
Worischeck, Joseph H.	Tempe, AZ	Attorney	Indefinite from December 27, 2006
Brown, Kirk P.	Pueblo, CO	Attorney	Indefinite from December 28, 2006
Dowling, Stanley W.	Scotts Valley, CA	CPA	Indefinite from December 28, 2006
Simmons, Henry L.	Greensboro, NC	CPA	Indefinite from December 28, 2006
Steele, Regina D.	San Diego, CA	Attorney	Indefinite from December 29, 2006
Craig, III, William A.	Austin, TX	Attorney	Indefinite from January 1, 2007
Acker, Thomas R.	Hollis Center, ME	Attorney	Indefinite from January 8, 2007
Baxter, Laura M.	Monee, IL	CPA	Indefinite from January 8, 2007
Herald, Sally J.	Cold Spring, KY	Attorney	Indefinite from January 8, 2007
Klapheke, II, William T.	Bowling Green, KY	Attorney	Indefinite from January 8, 2007

Name	Address	Designation	Date of Suspension
McCarthy, Charles C.	Encino, CA	Attorney	Indefinite from January 8, 2007
Bolling, Darius C.	Chicago, IL	CPA	Indefinite from January 10, 2007
Breitlauch, Linda	Saylorsburg, PA	Attorney	Indefinite from January 10, 2007
Coddington, Paul F.	Concord, NH	Attorney	Indefinite from January 10, 2007
Davis, Jr., William E.	Pinehurst, TX	CPA	Indefinite from January 10, 2007
Esola, Louis A.	Greensburg, PA	CPA	Indefinite from January 10, 2007
Finch, Judith A.	Walnut Creek, CA	Attorney	Indefinite from January 10, 2007
Jeing, Thomas C.	San Francisco, CA	Attorney	Indefinite from January 10, 2007
Ledbetter, Dean D.	Pelham, AL	CPA	Indefinite from January 10, 2007
McDiarmid, Katherine B.	Greensboro, NC	Attorney	Indefinite from January 10, 2007
Mills, George P.	Oceanside, CA	Attorney	Indefinite from January 10, 2007
Rather, James L.	Irvine, CA	Attorney	Indefinite from January 10, 2007
Rivera, Eduardo M.	Torrance, CA	Attorney	Indefinite from January 10, 2007
Stepovich, Michael A.	Fairbanks, AK	Attorney	Indefinite from January 10, 2007
Ulbrich, David L.	Woodland Hills, CA	CPA	Indefinite from January 10, 2007
Swanson, Todd-Ellis	Greenville, SC	CPA	Indefinite from January 20, 2007

Name	Address	Designation	Date of Suspension
Rubin, Deborah L.	Delray Beach, FL	Attorney	Indefinite from January 26, 2007
Wood, Brent E.	Cary, NC	Attorney	Indefinite from January 26, 2007
Currin, Samuel T.	Raleigh, NC	Attorney	Indefinite from February 7, 2007
Lupo, Robert N.	Weston, MA	Attorney	Indefinite from February 20, 2007
Taggart, Lawrence W.	El Cajon, CA	Attorney	Indefinite from March 7, 2007
Fife, III, James H.	Schererville, IN	Attorney	Indefinite from March 8, 2007
Katsis, Kevin G.	Riverside, IL	Attorney	Indefinite from March 8, 2007
O'Driscoll, Dennis M.	Quincy, MA	Attorney	Indefinite from March 8, 2007
Siever, Beth F.	Austin, TX	Attorney	Indefinite from March 8, 2007
Wheatley-Clark, Sheila R.	Houston, TX	CPA	Indefinite from March 8, 2007

Suspensions From Practice Before the Internal Revenue Service After Notice and an Opportunity for a Proceeding

Under Title 31, Code of Federal Regulations, Part 10, after notice and an opportunity for a proceeding before an administrative law judge, the following individuals have been placed under suspension from practice before the Internal Revenue Service:

Name	Address	Designation	Effective Date
Redmond, Debra	Gifford, PA	Enrolled Agent	Indefinite from March 5, 2007

Disbarments From Practice Before the Internal Revenue Service After Notice and an Opportunity for a Proceeding

Under Title 31, Code of Federal Regulations, Part 10, after notice and an opportunity for a proceeding before an administrative law judge, the following individuals have been disbarred from practice before the Internal Revenue Service:

Name	Address	Designation	Effective Date
Brookstein, Gary	Huntingdon Valley, PA	CPA	December 15, 2006
James T. Jubb	Baltimore, MD	CPA	December 15, 2006

Censure Issued by Consent

Under Title 31, Code of Federal Regulations, Part 10, in lieu of a proceeding being instituted or continued, an attorney, certified public accountant, enrolled agent, or enrolled actuary, may offer his or her consent to the issuance of a censure. Censure is a public reprimand.

The following individuals have consented to the issuance of a Censure:

Name	Address	Designation	Date of Censure
Zucker, Robert W.	Boca Raton, FL	CPA	November 14, 2006
Montgomery, David E.	Pleasanton, CA	Enrolled Agent	November 15, 2006
Higgins, James M.	S. Boston, MA	Attorney	December 1, 2006
Pennington, Debra L.	Lees Summit, MO	Enrolled Agent	January 29, 2007
Goodwin, Steven C.	Concord, MA	Attorney	February 2, 2007
Francis, Andrew W.E.	Houston, TX	CPA	February 21, 2007
Griffin, Richard M.	Duluth, GA	CPA	February 28, 2007

Resignations of Enrolled Agents

Under Title 31, Code of Federal Regulations, Part 10, an enrolled agent, in order to avoid the institution or conclusion of a proceeding for his or her disbarment or suspension from practice before the Internal Revenue Service, may offer his or her resignation as an enrolled agent. The Director, Office of Professional Responsibility, in his discretion, may accept the offered resignation.

The Director, Office of Professional Responsibility, has accepted offers of resignation as an enrolled agent from the following individuals:

Name	Address	Date of Resignation
Filipski, Kenneth M.	Bakersfield, CA	April 16, 2007

Archer Medical Savings Accounts — Cut-Off Year

Announcement 2007–44

PURPOSE

Sections 220(i) and (j) of the Internal Revenue Code provide that if the number of Archer Medical Savings Account (Archer MSA) returns filed for 2005 or 2006 or a statutorily specified projection of the number of Archer MSA returns that will be filed for 2005 or 2006 exceeds 750,000, then April 19, 2007, is a "cut-off" date for the Archer MSA pilot project. The Internal Revenue Service (IRS) has determined the following: (1) The applicable number of Archer MSA returns filed for 2004 is 39,037 and the applicable number of Archer MSA returns projected to be filed for 2005 is 35,246 (after reduction in each case for statutorily specified exclusions, such as the exclusion for previously uninsured taxpayers). Consequently, 2005 is not a "cut-off" year for the Archer MSA pilot project. (2) The applicable number of Archer MSA returns filed for 2005 is 16,850 and the applicable number of Archer MSA returns projected to be filed for 2006 is 15,192 (after reduction in each case for statutorily specified exclusions, such as the exclusion for previously uninsured taxpayers). Consequently, April 19, 2007 is not a "cut-off" date and 2006 is not a "cut-off" year for the Archer MSA pilot project.

BACKGROUND

The Health Insurance Portability and Accountability Act of 1996 added section 220 to the Code to permit eligible individuals to establish Archer MSAs under a pilot project effective January 1, 1997. The pilot project, as amended by The Tax Relief and Health Care Act of 2006 (TRHCA), Pub. Law. No. 109–432, § 117, has a scheduled "cut-off" year of 2006, but may have an earlier "cut-off" date if the number of individuals who have established Archer MSAs exceeds certain numerical limitations. Trustees' reports for Archer MSAs established between (1) January 1, 2005 and June 30, 2005 and (2) January 1, 2006 and June 30, 2006, were due no later than March 20, 2007. IRS is required to publish a determination of whether 2005 or 2006 is a "cut-off" year no later than April 19, 2007. See sections 220(i) and (j) as amended by TRHCA; Ann. 2007–24, 2007–10 I.R.B. 681.

If a year is a "cut-off" year, section 220 (i)(1) generally provides that no individual will be eligible for a deduction or exclusion for Archer MSA contributions for any taxable year beginning after the "cut-off" year unless the individual (A) was an active Archer MSA participant for any taxable year ending on or before the close of the "cut-off" year, or (B) first became an active Archer MSA participant for a taxable year ending after the "cut-off" year by reason of coverage under a high deductible health plan of an Archer MSA-participating employer.

Section 220(j)(2)(A) provides that the numerical limitation for 2005 is exceeded if the number of Archer MSA returns filed on or before April 15, 2005, for taxable years ending with or within the 2004 calendar year, plus the Secretary's estimate of the number of Archer MSA returns for those taxable years which will be filed after April 15, 2005, exceeds 750,000.

Section 220(j)(2)(A) provides that the numerical limitation for 2006 is exceeded if the number of Archer MSA returns filed on or before April 15, 2006, for taxable years ending with or within the 2005 calendar year, plus the Secretary's estimate of the number of Archer MSA returns for those taxable years which will be filed after April 15, 2006, exceeds 750,000.

For this purpose, section 220(j)(2)(A) provides that a tax return is an Archer MSA return for a taxable year if any exclusion is claimed under section 106(b) or any deduction is claimed under section 220 for that taxable year. Section 220(j)(2)(B) provides, as an alternative test, that: (1) the numerical limitation for 2005 is also exceeded if the sum of 90 percent of the Archer MSA returns for 2004 plus the product of 2.5 and the number of Archer MSAs for taxable years beginning in 2005 that are established during the portion of 2005 preceding July 1 (based on reports by Archer MSA trustees and custodians), exceeds 750,000 and (2) the numerical limitation for 2006 is also exceeded if the sum of 90 percent of the Archer MSA returns for 2005 plus the product of 2.5 and the number of Archer MSAs for taxable years beginning in 2006 that are established during the portion of 2006 preceding July 1 (based on reports by Archer MSA trustees and custodians), exceeds 750,000.

Under section 220(j)(3), in determining whether any calendar year is a "cut-off" year, the Archer MSA of any previously uninsured individual is not taken into account. In addition, section 220(j)(4)(D) specifies that, to the extent practical, all Archer MSAs established by an individual are aggregated and two married individuals opening separate Archer MSAs are to be treated as having a single Archer MSA for purposes of determining the number of Archer MSAs.

2005 Not a Cut-Off Year

A total of 33,622 tax returns reporting an excludable or deductible contribution to an Archer MSA for the 2004 taxable year were filed by April 15, 2005. The number of taxpayers reported as being previously uninsured was not available. It has been estimated that an additional 5,415 tax returns reporting Archer MSA contributions for the 2005 taxable year have been or will be filed after April 15, 2005, including 0 taxpayers who were previously uninsured. Accordingly, it has been determined that there were 39,037 (33,622 plus 5,415) Archer MSA returns for 2005. As a result, 39,622 (39,622 minus 0) Archer MSA returns count toward the applicable statutory limitation for 2005 Archer MSA returns of 750,000.

Based on the Forms 8851 filed on or before March 20, 2007, by Archer MSA trustees and custodians, it has been determined that 45 taxpayers who did not have Archer MSA contributions for 2004 established Archer MSAs for 2005 during the portion of 2005 preceding July 1. Of this total, 0 taxpayers were reported by trustees and custodians as previously uninsured, and therefore are not taken into account in determining whether 2005 is a "cut-off" year. The alternative limitation for 2005 (90 percent of the applicable number of Archer MSA returns for 2004 plus the product of 2.5 and the number of applicable Archer MSAs established from January 1, 2005, through June 30, 2005) is 35,246 (90 percent of 39,037 plus 2.5 multiplied by 45), which is less than the statutory limit of 750,000. Thus, 2005 is not a "cut-off" year for the Archer MSA pilot project by reason of either the 2005 Archer MSA returns test of section 220(j)(2)(A) or the alternative test of section 220(j)(2)(B) of the Code.

2006 Not a Cut-Off Year

A total of 17,306 tax returns reporting an excludable or deductible contribution to an Archer MSA for the 2005 taxable year were filed by April 15, 2006. Of this total, 3,038 taxpayers were reported as being previously uninsured. It has been estimated that an additional 3,055 tax returns reporting Archer MSA contributions for the 2005 taxable year have been or will be filed after April 15, 2006, including 473 taxpayers who were previously uninsured. Accordingly, it has been determined that there were 20,361(17,306 plus 3,055) Archer MSA returns for 2006. Of this total, 3,511 (3,038 plus 473) were for taxpayers reported as being previously uninsured. As a result, 16,850 (20,361 minus 3,511) Archer MSA returns count toward the applicable statutory limitation for 2006 Archer MSA returns of 750,000.

Based on the Forms 8851 filed on or before March 20, 2007, by Archer MSA trustees and custodians, it has been determined that 11 taxpayers who did not have Archer MSA contributions for 2005 established Archer MSAs for 2006 during the portion of 2006 preceding July 1. Of this total, 0 taxpayers were reported by trustees and custodians as previously uninsured, and therefore are not taken into account in determining whether 2006 is a "cut-off" year. In addition, 0 taxpayers were reported by trustees and custodians as excludable from the count because his or her spouse also established an Archer MSA. Accordingly, the applicable number of Archer MSAs established from January 1, 2006, through June 30, 2006, is 11 (11 minus (0 plus 0)). The alternative limitation for 2006 (90 percent of the applicable number of Archer MSA returns for 2005 plus the product of 2.5 and the number of applicable Archer MSAs established from January 1, 2006, through June 30, 2006) is 15,192 (90 percent of 16,850 plus 2.5 multiplied by 11), which is less than the statutory limit of 750,000. Thus, 2006 is not a "cut-off" year for the Archer MSA pilot project by reason of either the 2006 Archer MSA returns test of section 220(j)(2)(A) or the alternative test of section 220(j)(2)(B) of the Code.

Questions regarding this announcement may be directed to Shoshanna Tanner in the Office of Division Counsel/Associate Chief Counsel (Tax Exempt and Government Entities) at (202) 622–6080 (not a toll-free number).

Deletions From Cumulative List of Organizations Contributions to Which are Deductible Under Section 170 of the Code

Announcement 2007–46

The names of organizations that no longer qualify as organizations described in section 170(c)(2) of the Internal Revenue Code of 1986 are listed below.

Generally, the Service will not disallow deductions for contributions made to a listed organization on or before the date of announcement in the Internal Revenue Bulletin that an organization no longer qualifies. However, the Service is not precluded from disallowing a deduction for any contributions made after an organization ceases to qualify under section 170(c)(2) if the organization has not timely filed a suit for declaratory judgment under section 7428 and if the contributor (1) had knowledge of the revocation of the ruling or determination letter, (2) was aware that such revocation was imminent, or (3) was in part responsible for or was aware of the activities or omissions of the organization that brought about this revocation.

If on the other hand a suit for declaratory judgment has been timely filed, contributions from individuals and organizations described in section 170(c)(2) that are otherwise allowable will continue to be deductible. Protection under section 7428(c) would begin on May 7, 2007, and would end on the date the court first determines that the organization is not described in section 170(c)(2) as more particularly set forth in section 7428(c)(1). For individual contributors, the maximum deduction protected is $1,000, with a husband and wife treated as one contributor. This benefit is not extended to any individual, in whole or in part, for the acts or omissions of the organization that were the basis for revocation.

World Project, Inc.
Brooklyn, NY
Izaak Walton League of America
Calumet Region Chapter
Dolton, IL
Greenbriar Club, Inc.
Clearwater, FL
Cunningham Family Foundation
West Jordan, UT
Roxbury Insurance Company
Los Angeles, CA
Wishes Are Forever Foundation
Salt Lake City, UT

Part I. Rulings and Decisions Under the Internal Revenue Code of 1986

Section 871.—Tax on Nonresident Alien Individuals

26 CFR 1.871–14: Rules relating to repeal of tax on interest of nonresident alien individuals and foreign corporations received from certain portfolio debt investments.

T.D. 9323

DEPARTMENT OF THE TREASURY
Internal Revenue Service
26 CFR Part 1

Revisions to Regulations Relating to Repeal of Tax on Interest of Nonresident Alien Individuals and Foreign Corporations Received From Certain Portfolio Debt Investments

AGENCY: Internal Revenue Service (IRS), Treasury.

ACTION: Final regulations.

SUMMARY: This document contains final regulations under sections 871 and 881 of the Internal Revenue Code (Code) relating to the exclusion from gross income of portfolio interest paid to a nonresident alien individual or foreign corporation. These regulations clarify how the portfolio interest rules apply with respect to interest paid to a partnership (or simple or grantor trust) that has foreign partners (or beneficiaries or owners). These regulations also retroactively remove the rule in Treasury Regulation §1.1441–1(b)(7)(iii) that would impose interest under section 6601 when no underlying tax liability is due.

DATES: *Effective Date:* These regulations are effective on April 12, 2007.

Applicability Dates: The regulations relating to the application of the 10-percent shareholder test for interest paid to partnerships applies to interest paid after April 12, 2007. However, taxpayers may choose to apply the rules in the final regulations to interest paid during any taxable year which is not closed by the period of limitations, provided they do so consistently with respect to all relevant partnerships during such years. The regulations removing the rule imposing interest and penalties on withholding agents when no underlying tax has in fact been imposed apply to payments made after December 31, 2000.

FOR FURTHER INFORMATION CONTACT: Kathryn Holman of the Office of the Associate Chief Counsel (International), (202) 622–3840 (not a toll-free call).

SUPPLEMENTARY INFORMATION:

Background

Section 871(a) of the Code imposes a tax of 30 percent on U.S. source fixed or determinable annual or periodic (FDAP) income, including interest, received by a nonresident alien individual to the extent the amount so received is not effectively connected with the conduct of a trade or business within the United States. Section 881(a) imposes a similar tax with respect to FDAP income, including interest, received by a foreign corporation. Both sections 871(h)(3)(A) and 881(c)(3)(B) provide, among other limitations, that portfolio interest does not include interest received by a 10-percent shareholder, as defined in section 871(h)(3)(B).

Explanation of Provisions and Summary of Comments

The IRS and the Treasury Department issued proposed regulations (REG–118775–06, 2006–28 I.R.B. 73) under sections 871(h) and 881(c) in the **Federal Register** (71 FR 34047) on June 13, 2006. The proposed regulations address the application of the 10-percent shareholder test when U.S. source interest is paid to a partnership that has a nonresident alien individual or foreign corporation as a partner. The proposed regulations provide that, for interest paid on obligations issued on or after the date that final regulations are published, the 10-percent shareholder test is to be applied only at the partner level and at the time that the withholding agent would otherwise be required to withhold.

No public hearing was requested or held. However, a few comments were received. After consideration of the comments, the proposed regulations are adopted in these final regulations, with two modifications. In addition, these final regulations implement section 5 of Notice 2006–99, 2006–46 I.R.B. 907 (See §601.601(d)(2) of this chapter), modifying §1.1441–1(b)(7)(iii), as discussed below.

1. *Time for Applying the 10-Percent Shareholder Test.*

The proposed regulations provide that the 10-percent shareholder test applies at the time the withholding agent would otherwise be required to withhold. The regulations then provide an example in which the test is stated to apply on the "earliest" of when the interest is distributed, the date the statement under section 6031(b) is mailed, or the due date for furnishing the statement. In order to make clear that the test may be applied on multiple dates (and not only on the date of a first partial distribution of such interest), the example has been rephrased. The example now states that the 10-percent shareholder test is applied when any distributions that include the interest are made to a foreign partner and, to the extent that a foreign partner's distributive share of the interest has not actually been distributed, on the earlier of the date that the statement required under section 6031(b) is mailed or otherwise provided to such partner, or the due date for furnishing such statement. This change conforms more closely to the language of §1.1441–5(c)(2).

2. *Effective Date of the Regulation.*

The new provisions set forth in the proposed regulations were proposed to apply to interest paid on obligations issued after the date that final regulations are published. One commentator stated that, in order to provide for consistency and to eliminate uncertainty and avoid possible disputes with respect to interest paid to partnerships prior to the date that the final regulations are published, the final regulations should apply to interest paid after July 18, 1984, with respect to obligations issued after July 18, 1984, the effective date of the portfolio interest provisions. Another commentator stated that the final regulations should apply to interest paid after the date the final regulations are issued.

The IRS and the Treasury Department agree that taxpayers should be able to apply the regulations to interest paid in certain prior taxable years. Accordingly, while the final regulations generally provide that the provisions relating to the 10-percent shareholder test for interest paid to partnerships are to apply to interest paid after the date the regulations are published as final regulations, the regulations also permit taxpayers to choose to apply the provisions to interest paid in any taxable year that is not closed by the period of limitations, provided that the taxpayer consistently applies the provisions to all relevant partnerships during such years.

3. *Interest Imposed When No Tax Due.*

Treasury Regulation §1.1441–1(b)(7)(iii) provides that a withholding agent that has failed to withhold tax other than based on reliance on the appropriate presumptions is not relieved from liability for interest under section 6601. It further provides that such liability exists even when there is no underlying tax that is ultimately shown to be due. That is, the regulation imposes an interest charge under section 6601 on a withholding agent for an amount of tax that has not in fact been imposed. Treasury Regulation §1.1441–1(b)(7)(v) sets forth two examples that illustrate the operation of this rule.

In Notice 2006–99, 2006–46 I.R.B. 907, the IRS and the Treasury Department announced their intention to remove the rule in Treasury Regulation §1.1441–1(b)(7)(iii), and the accompanying examples illustrating the rule in Treasury Regulation §1.1441–1(b)(7)(v), that impose interest under section 6601 when no underlying tax liability is imposed. Further, the notice announced that the IRS and the Treasury Department intend to clarify that, like interest, penalties that are computed based on underpayments of tax will not be imposed when no tax has in fact been imposed.

These final regulations retroactively remove, in accordance with Notice 2006–99, the rule in §1.1441–1(b)(7)(iii) that would impose interest and penalties based on hypothetical underpayments of tax when in fact no tax has been imposed. The examples illustrating this rule in Treasury Regulation §1.1441–1(b)(7) are also removed.

Special Analyses

It has been determined that these regulations are not a significant regulatory action as defined in Executive Order 12866. Therefore, a regulatory assessment is not required. It has also been determined that section 553(b) of the Administrative Procedure Act (5 U.S.C. chapter 5) does not apply to these regulations, and because the regulations do not impose a collection of information on small entities, the Regulatory Flexibility Act (5 U.S.C. chapter 6) does not apply. Pursuant to section 7805(f) of the Code, the proposed rulemaking preceding these regulations was submitted to the Chief Counsel for Advocacy of the Small Business Administration for comment on its impact on small business.

Drafting Information

The principal author of the proposed regulations is Kathryn Holman, Office of Associate Chief Counsel (International). However, other personnel from the IRS and the Treasury Department participated in their development.

* * * * *

Adoption of Amendments to the Regulations

Accordingly, 26 CFR part 1 is amended as follows:

PART 1—INCOME TAXES

Paragraph 1. The authority citation for part 1 continues to read in part as follows:

Authority: 26 U.S.C. 7805 * * *

Par. 2. Section 1.871–14 is amended as follows:

1. Paragraphs (g) and (h) are redesignated as paragraphs (h) and (i), respectively.

2. New paragraph (g) is added.

3. Paragraph (1) of newly-designated paragraph (i) is amended by adding two sentences at the end of the paragraph.

The additions read as follows:

§1.871–14 Rules relating to repeal of tax on interest of nonresident alien individuals and foreign corporations received from certain portfolio debt investments.

* * * * *

(g) *Portfolio interest not to include interest received by 10-percent shareholders*—(1) *In general.* For purposes of section 871(h), the term *portfolio interest* shall not include any interest received by a 10-percent shareholder.

(2) *Ten-percent shareholder*—(i) *In general.* The term *10-percent shareholder* means—

(A) In the case of an obligation issued by a corporation, any person who owns 10-percent or more of the total combined voting power of all classes of stock of such corporation entitled to vote; or

(B) In the case of an obligation issued by a partnership, any person who owns 10-percent or more of the capital or profits interest in such partnership.

(ii) *Ownership*—(A) *Stock ownership.* For purposes of paragraph (g)(2)(i)(A) of this section, *stock owned* means stock directly or indirectly owned and stock owned by reason of the attribution rules of section 318(a), as modified by section 871(h)(3)(C).

(B) *Ownership of partnership interest.* For purposes of paragraph (g)(2)(i)(B) of this section, rules similar to the rules in paragraph (g)(2)(ii)(A) of this section shall be applied in determining the ownership of a capital or profits interest in a partnership.

(3) *Application of 10-percent shareholder test to partners receiving interest through a partnership*—(i) *Partner level test.* Whether interest paid to a partnership and included in the distributive share of a partner that is a nonresident alien individual or foreign corporation is received by a 10 percent shareholder shall be determined by applying the rules of this paragraph (g) only at the partner level.

(ii) *Time at which 10-percent shareholder test is applied.* The determination of whether a nonresident alien individual or foreign corporation that is a partner in a partnership is a 10-percent shareholder under the rules of section 871(h)(3), section 881(c)(3), and this paragraph (g) with respect to interest paid to such partnership shall be made at the time that the withholding agent, absent the provisions of section 871(h), 881(c) and the rules of this paragraph, would otherwise be required to withhold under sections 1441 and 1442 with respect to such interest. For example, in the case of U.S. source interest paid by a domestic corporation to a domestic partnership or withholding foreign partnership (as defined in §1.1441–5(c)(2)), the 10-percent shareholder test is applied when any distributions that include the interest are made to a foreign partner and, to the extent that a foreign partner's distributive share of the interest has not actually been distributed, on the earlier of the date that the statement required under section 6031(b) is mailed or otherwise provided to such partner, or the due date for furnishing such statement. See §1.1441–5(b)(2) and (c)(2)(iii).

(4) *Application of 10-percent shareholder test to interest paid to a simple trust or grantor trust.* Whether interest paid to a simple trust or grantor trust and distributed to or included in the gross income of a nonresident alien individual or foreign corporation that is a beneficiary or owner of such trust, as the case may be, is received by a 10-percent shareholder shall be determined by applying the rules of this paragraph (g) only at the beneficiary or owner level. The 10-percent shareholder test is applied with respect to a nonresident alien individual or foreign corporation that is a beneficiary of a simple trust or an owner of a grantor trust at the time that a withholding agent, absent any exceptions, would otherwise be required to withhold under sections 1441 and 1442 with respect to such interest.

* * * * *

(i) * * * (1) * * * The rules of paragraph (g) apply to interest paid after April 12, 2007. Taxpayers may choose to apply the rules of paragraph (g) to interest paid in any taxable year not closed by the period of limitations as of April 12, 2007, provided they do so consistently for all relevant partnerships during such years.

Par. 3. Section 1.881–2 (a)(6) is added to read as follows:

§1.881–2 Taxation of foreign corporations not engaged in U.S. business.

(a) * * *

(6) Interest received by a foreign corporation pursuant to certain portfolio debt instruments is not subject to the flat tax of 30 percent described in paragraph (a)(1) of this section. For rules applicable to a foreign corporation's receipt of interest on certain portfolio debt instruments, see sections 871(h), 881(c), and §1.871–14.

* * * * *

Par. 4. Section 1.1441–1(b)(7) is amended as follows:

1. Paragraphs (b)(7)(iii) is revised.

2. Paragraph (b)(7)(v) is removed.

The revision reads as follows:

§1.1441–1 Requirement for the deduction and withholding of tax on payments to foreign persons.

* * * * *

(b) * * *

(7) * * *

(iii) *Liability for Interest and Penalties.* For payments made after December 31, 2000, if a withholding agent fails to deduct and withhold any tax imposed under sections 1441 or 1442, and the tax against which such tax may be credited under section 1462 is paid, then the amount of tax required to be deducted and withheld shall not be collected from the withholding agent. However, the withholding agent is not relieved from liability for interest or any penalties or additions to the tax otherwise applicable in respect of the failure to deduct and withhold. See section 1463. Further, in the event that a tax liability is assessed against the beneficial owner under section 871, 881, or 882 and interest under section 6601(a) is assessed against, and collected from, the beneficial owner, the interest charge imposed on the withholding agent shall be abated to that extent so as to avoid the imposition of a double interest charge.

* * * * *

Kevin M. Brown,
Deputy Commissioner for Services and Enforcement.

Approved March 30, 2007.

Eric Solomon,
Assistant Secretary of the Treasury (Tax Policy).

(Filed by the Office of the Federal Register on April 11, 2007, 8:45 a.m., and published in the issue of the Federal Register for April 12, 2007, 72 F.R. 18386)

Part III. Administrative, Procedural, and Miscellaneous

Disciplinary Actions Under Section 822 of the American Jobs Creation Act of 2004

Notice 2007–39

This notice provides guidance to practitioners, employers, firms, and other entities that may be subject to monetary penalties under 31 U.S.C. section 330. This notice also invites comments from the public regarding rules and standards relating to monetary penalties under 31 U.S.C. section 330.

BACKGROUND

In general, 31 U.S.C. section 330 authorizes the Secretary to regulate attorneys, certified public accountants, enrolled agents, enrolled actuaries, and others who practice before the Service. Regulations under section 330 are promulgated in 31 CFR part 10 and are reprinted as Treasury Department Circular No. 230.

Section 822 of the American Jobs Creation Act of 2004, Pub. L. No. 108–357, 118 Stat. 1418 (the Act), amended 31 U.S.C. section 330 to expand the sanctions that the Secretary may impose for certain prohibited conduct within the meaning of section 10.52 of Circular 230 to include monetary penalties. As amended by the Act, 31 U.S.C. section 330 authorizes the Secretary to impose sanctions, including monetary penalties, against a practitioner who is incompetent or disreputable, who fails to comply with the regulations prescribed under section 330, or who, with intent to defraud, willfully and knowingly misleads or threatens a client or potential client. The Secretary is also authorized to impose monetary penalties against an employer, firm, or other entity, if the practitioner was acting on its behalf in connection with the prohibited conduct giving rise to the penalties and the employer, firm, or other entity knew, or reasonably should have known, of the prohibited conduct.

Monetary penalties apply only with respect to prohibited conduct that occurs after October 22, 2004, the date of enactment of the Act. Under the Act, the aggregate monetary penalties cannot exceed the gross income derived (or to be derived) from the prohibited conduct giving rise to the penalties.

Monetary penalties may be imposed for a single act of prohibited conduct or for a pattern of misconduct. Monetary penalties may be imposed in addition to, or in lieu of, any suspension, disbarment, or censure of the practitioner. Monetary penalties are not, however, a "bargaining point" that a practitioner may offer to avoid suspension, disbarment, or censure if these sanctions are otherwise appropriate.

REQUIREMENTS FOR IMPOSITION OF MONETARY PENALTIES

Amount of the Monetary Penalty

The aggregate amount of the monetary penalty (or penalties) imposed by the Secretary for any prohibited conduct may not exceed the collective gross income derived by the practitioner and the employer, firm, or other entity in connection with such prohibited conduct. If a single act of prohibited conduct giving rise to a monetary penalty is an integral part of a larger engagement, the amount of the penalty will be limited by the "gross income derived (or to be derived)" from the larger engagement. In the event that the larger engagement began on or before October 22, 2004, the "gross income derived (or to be derived)" will be calculated, on a *pro rata* basis, to exclude amounts attributable to conduct occurring on or before October 22, 2004. In determining the amount of the monetary penalty (or penalties), the Secretary will consider amounts that the practitioner, employer, firm, or other entity could reasonably expect to realize, irrespective of whether the amounts have actually been received.

The Secretary has discretion to impose a monetary penalty in an amount less than the amount allowed by statute. In determining the amount of the penalty (or penalties), the Service will consider the level of culpability of the practitioner, firm, or other entity; whether the practitioner, firm, or other entity violated a duty owed to a client or prospective client; the actual or potential injury caused by the prohibited conduct; and the existence of aggravating or mitigating factors. Mitigating factors may include whether the practitioner, employer, firm, or other entity took prompt action to correct the noncompliance after the prohibited conduct was discovered; promptly ceased engaging in the prohibited conduct; attempted to rectify any harm caused by the prohibited conduct; or undertook measures to ensure that the prohibited conduct would not occur again in the future. In general, the Service will not impose monetary penalties in cases of minor technical violations, when there is little or no injury to a client, the public, or tax administration, and there is little likelihood of repeated similar misconduct.

The Secretary may impose separate penalties against the practitioner and against the employer, firm, or other entity for any prohibited conduct. Each separate penalty may not exceed the gross income derived by the practitioner and the employer, firm, or other entity, respectively.

Imposition of a Separate Monetary Penalty on an Employer, Firm, or Other Entity

If a practitioner acted on behalf of an employer, firm, or other entity in connection with prohibited conduct, the Secretary may impose a separate monetary penalty on the employer, firm, or other entity if the employer, firm, or other entity knew, or reasonably should have known, of the prohibited conduct.

A practitioner is considered to have acted on behalf of an employer, firm, or other entity if –

(1) An agency relationship existed between the practitioner and the employer, firm, or other entity;

(2) The purpose of the agency relationship was to provide services in connection with practice before the Internal Revenue Service (as defined in section 10.2(d) of Circular 230); and

(3) The prohibited conduct giving rise to the penalty arose in connection with the agency relationship.

An employer, firm, or other entity knows or reasonably should know of the prohibited conduct if –

(1) One or more members of the principal management (or officers) of the employer, firm, or other entity, or one or more members of the principal management (or

officers) of a branch office knows, or has information from which a person with similar experience and background would reasonably know, of the prohibited conduct; or

(2) The employer, firm, or other entity through willfulness, recklessness, or gross indifference (including ignoring facts that would lead a person of reasonable prudence and competence to investigate or ascertain) did not take reasonable steps to ensure compliance with Circular 230; and one or more individuals associated with the employer, firm, or other entity, in connection with their agency relationship with the employer, firm, or other entity, engages in prohibited conduct within the meaning of section 10.52 of Circular 230 that harms a client, the public, or tax administration, or a pattern or practice of failing to comply with Circular 230.

The following examples illustrate the above provisions:

Example 1: Attorney A specializes in tax planning and works out of a national accounting firm's headquarters. Attorney A is involved in the development of off-the-shelf tax planning strategies, including Strategy X. Attorney A has wide discretion over his day-to-day work product and rarely supervises other professionals at the firm. Attorney A rarely deals directly with clients as this work is handled by other firm partners or employees. Attorney A works directly with the firm's other attorneys, accountants and support staff across the country to market and fine-tune Strategy X. Clients of the firm are examined by the Service with respect to Strategy X, but Attorney A is not identified on any Form 2848 as a representative.

Attorney A reports to the director of the firm's tax practice. The director of the firm's tax practice provides general oversight as to Attorney A. The director of the firm's tax practice was aware of the strategies that Attorney A developed, including Strategy X, although he was not necessarily familiar with the technical tax details of each strategy. The director of the firm's tax practice also knew that Strategy X generated measurable revenue for the firm.

OPR determines that Attorney A engaged in prohibited conduct in violation of Circular 230 in the creation, promotion and marketing of Strategy X. Attorney A acted on behalf of the firm because an agency relationship existed between Attorney A and the firm, and the misconduct arose in connection with that agency relationship as Attorney A worked on behalf of the firm to promote Strategy X. The firm knew or had reason to know of the prohibited conduct in this situation. The director of the firm's tax practice, who is a member of principal management of the firm, had general knowledge that Attorney A developed the tax-advantaged strategies. Alternatively, in the absence of general knowledge, the director of the firm's tax practice would need to inquire into Strategy X because it added measurably to the firm's revenue. Both Attorney A and the firm are subject to a monetary penalty.

Example 2: Unenrolled Return Preparer B owns and operates her own firm that provides return preparation services to the public and also specializes in preparing Forms 656, *Offers In Compromise*. B's firm employs 10 attorneys, CPAs and enrolled agents (all practitioners) and 15 unenrolled return preparers. B supervises and directs all of her employees. B's firm is structured in such a manner so that the first and predominant contact for clients coming in from the public is with the unenrolled return preparers. The unenrolled return preparers assist clients with preparing Forms 656 that are later submitted directly to the Service. B does not review individual Forms 656 but has provided specific instructions to her staff regarding how to complete false and misleading Forms 656 in violation of Circular 230. In order to facilitate the submission to the Service of the false or misleading Forms 656, B's procedure is to authorize one of her 10 practitioners to submit a Form 2848 on behalf of a client much later in the process, well after submission of the Forms 656 in violation of Circular 230.

Although B is not a practitioner, the practitioner's actions in submitting the Forms 2848 are done on behalf of the firm pursuant to an agency relationship and occur in connection with prohibited conduct. B's firm is considered to know or have reason to know of the prohibited conduct because B, a member of principal management, instructed her staff regarding completion of the forms in violation of Circular 230. The practitioner's actions subject B's firm to a monetary penalty.

When determining if a monetary penalty should be imposed on an employer, firm, or other entity, the Secretary will consider factors in addition to whether the employer, firm, or other entity knew, or reasonably should have known, of the prohibited conduct (or whether the employer, firm or other entity did not use reasonable efforts to ensure compliance with Circular 230). For example, the Secretary will consider the gravity of the misconduct, any history of noncompliance by the employer, firm, or other entity, preventative measures in effect prior to the misconduct, and any corrective measures taken by the employer, firm, or other entity after the prohibited conduct was discovered, including measures to ensure that future prohibited conduct does not occur.

Additional Guidance and Request for Comments

The Service may issue additional guidance regarding the application of monetary penalties, including, but not limited to, the factors that the Service should consider when evaluating all the facts and circumstances of a particular case. The Service requests comments with respect to the appropriate factors to be considered when determining whether a monetary penalty is appropriate. Comments also are requested as to factors that the Service should consider in declining to impose a monetary penalty on an employer, firm, or other entity, including the weight given to adequate procedures in place for purposes of complying with Circular 230.

Additionally, in order to develop a penalty system that best encourages compliance with Circular 230, the Service requests comments regarding mitigating circumstances to consider when determining the amount of a monetary penalty. Mitigating circumstances could be considered, for example, in varying the amount of the penalty to correspond to the seriousness of the misconduct or pattern of misconduct. Mitigating circumstances could include, but not be limited to, the immediacy of the misconduct, history of misconduct, the existence of firm procedures, and corrective measures taken after discovery of the misconduct.

Interested parties are invited to submit comments by August 13, 2007. Comments should be submitted to: Internal Revenue Service, CC:PA:LPD:PR (Notice 2007–39), Room 5203, P.O. Box 7604, Ben Franklin Station, Washington, DC 20224. Alternatively, comments may be hand delivered Monday through Friday between the hours of 8:00 a.m. to 4:00 p.m. to: CC:PA:LPD:PR (Notice 2007–39), Courier's Desk, Internal Revenue Service, 1111 Constitution Avenue, N.W., Washington, DC. Comments may also be submitted electronically via the following e-mail address: *Notice.Comments@irscounsel.treas.gov*. Please include "Notice 2007–39" in the subject line of any electronic submissions.

DRAFTING INFORMATION

The principal author of this notice is Matthew Cooper of the Office of Associate Chief Counsel (Procedure & Administration), Administrative Provisions and Judicial Practice Division. For further information regarding this notice, contact Matthew Cooper at (202) 622–4940 (not a toll-free call).

Part IV. Items of General Interest

Notice of Proposed Rulemaking and Notice of Public Hearing

Section 1367 Regarding Open Account Debt

REG–144859–04

AGENCY: Internal Revenue Service (IRS), Treasury.

ACTION: Notice of proposed rulemaking and notice of public hearing.

SUMMARY: This document proposes amendments to the regulations relating to the treatment of open account debt between S corporations and their shareholders. These proposed regulations provide rules regarding the definition of open account debt and the adjustments in basis of any indebtedness of an S corporation to a shareholder under section 1367(b)(2) of the Internal Revenue Code (Code) for shareholder advances and repayments on advances of open account debt. The proposed regulations affect shareholders of S corporations and are necessary to provide guidance needed to comply with the applicable tax law. This document also provides notice of a public hearing.

DATES: Written or electronic comments and requests for a public hearing must be received by July 11, 2007. Outlines of topics to be discussed at the public hearing scheduled for July 31, 2007, at 10 a.m., must be received by July 10, 2007.

ADDRESSES: Send submissions to: CC:PA:LPD:PR (REG–144859–04), room 5203, Internal Revenue Service, PO Box 7604, Ben Franklin Station, Washington, DC 20044. Submissions also may be hand-delivered Monday through Friday between the hours of 8 a.m. and 4 p.m. to: CC:PA:LPD:PR (REG–144859–04), Courier's Desk, Internal Revenue Service, 1111 Constitution Avenue, NW, Washington, DC, or sent electronically via the Federal eRulemaking Portal at *http://www.regulations.gov* (IRS REG–144859–04). The public hearing will be held in the IRS Auditorium, Internal Revenue Building, 1111 Constitution Avenue, NW, Washington, DC.

FOR FURTHER INFORMATION CONTACT: Concerning the proposed regulations, Stacy L. Short or Deane M. Burke, (202) 622–3070; concerning submissions of comments, the hearing, and/or to be placed on the building access list to attend the hearing, Richard Hurst at (202) 622–2949 (TDD Telephone) (not toll-free numbers) and his e-mail address is *Richard.A.Hurst@irscounsel.treas.gov*, (202) 622–7180 (not toll-free numbers).

SUPPLEMENTARY INFORMATION:

Paperwork Reduction Act

The collections of information contained in this notice of proposed rulemaking have been submitted to the Office of Management and Budget for review in accordance with the Paperwork Reduction Act of 1995 (44 U.S.C. 3507). Comments on the collections of information should be sent to the Office of Management and Budget, Attention: Desk Officer for the Department of the Treasury, Office of Information and Regulatory Affairs, Washington, DC 20503, with copies to the Internal Revenue Service, Attention: IRS Reports Clearance Officer, SE:W:CAR:MP:T:T:SP, Washington, DC 20224.

The recordkeeping requirement in these proposed regulations is in §1.1367–2(a)(2)(i). This information must be maintained by the shareholder to ensure that the indebtedness of the S corporation to the shareholder continues to meet the definition of open account debt found in §1.1367–2(a)(2)(i). The recordkeepers will be S corporation shareholders who have open account debt.

The following estimates are an approximation of the average time expected to be necessary for a collection of information. They are based on the information that is available to the Internal Revenue Service. Individual recordkeepers may require greater or less time, depending on their particular circumstances.

Estimated total annual recordkeeping burden: 250 hours.

Estimated average annual burden: hours per recordkeeper varies from .75 to 1.25 hours, depending on individual circumstances, with an estimated average of 1 hour.

Estimated number of recordkeepers: 250.

Estimated annual frequency of recordkeeping: On occasion.

Background

This document proposes to amend §1.1367–2 of the Income Tax Regulations (26 CFR part 1) regarding the definition of open account debt and adjustments in basis of indebtedness for shareholder advances and repayments on advances of open account debt.

Section 1367(a)(1) provides that the basis of each shareholder's stock in an S corporation is increased by the shareholder's *pro rata* share of the S corporation's income (separately and nonseparately computed items of income) and the excess of the deductions for depletion over the basis of the property subject to depletion. Section 1367(a)(2) provides that the basis of each shareholder's stock in the S corporation is decreased by the shareholder's *pro rata* share of distributions not includible in income of the shareholder by reason of section 1368 (nontaxable distributions), losses and deductions (separately and non-separately computed losses), any expense of the corporation that is not deductible and not properly chargeable to capital account, and certain deductions for depletion for any oil and gas property held by the S corporation. Under section 1367(b)(2)(A), if for any taxable year the amounts specified in section 1367(a)(2) (other than distributions) exceed the amount which reduces the shareholder's basis to zero, such excess losses and deductions shall be applied to reduce (but not below zero) the shareholder's basis in any indebtedness of the S corporation to the shareholder. Section 1367(b)(2)(B) provides that if a shareholder's basis in indebtedness is reduced for any taxable year, any net increase (the amount by which the items described in section 1367(a)(1) exceed the items described in section 1367(a)(2)) for any subsequent taxable year is applied to restore the reduction in basis in indebtedness before any of the excess is used to increase basis in stock.

On January 3, 1994, the Treasury Department and the IRS published final regulations under section 1367 of the Code (T.D. 8508, 1994–1 C.B. 219 [59 FR 12], amended on December 22, 1999 (T.D. 8852, 2000–1 C.B. 253 [64 FR 71641])). Those final regulations relate, in part, to adjustments to basis in both stock of shareholders and indebtedness of an S corporation to its shareholders. Section 1.1367–2 of the Income Tax Regulations provides specific rules for required adjustments (reductions and restorations) to basis in any indebtedness of an S corporation to a shareholder. Section 1.1367–2(a) also provides that for purposes of adjustments to basis of indebtedness to shareholders, shareholder advances not evidenced by separate written instruments and repayments on the advances (open account debt) are treated as a single indebtedness. Further, §1.1367–2(a) provides that the basis of indebtedness of the S corporation to a shareholder is reduced as provided in §1.1367–2(b) and restored as provided in §1.1367–2(c). Thus, the basis adjustment rules under the final regulations apply to all indebtedness of an S corporation to a shareholder, whether the indebtedness is evidenced by a written instrument or is open account debt.

Section 1.1367–2(b) provides the rules for the reduction of basis of indebtedness of an S corporation to a shareholder. Generally, under §1.1367–2(b)(1), if the basis of a shareholder's stock in the S corporation has been reduced to zero under section 1367(a)(2), the excess of certain losses and deductions specified in section 1367(a)(2) is applied to reduce (but not below zero) the basis of any indebtedness of the S corporation to the shareholder held by the shareholder at the close of the S corporation's taxable year. Any indebtedness of the S corporation to the shareholder that has been satisfied by the S corporation, or disposed of or forgiven by the shareholder during the taxable year, is not held by the shareholder at the close of that year and is not subject to basis reduction. Further, §1.1367–2(b)(2) provides that if the interest of the shareholder in the S corporation is terminated during the taxable year, the rules in §1.1367–2(b) are applied to any indebtedness of the S corporation to the shareholder held by the shareholder immediately before the termination of the shareholder's interest in the S corporation. If a shareholder holds more than one indebtedness at the close of the taxable year (or, if applicable, immediately prior to the termination of the shareholder's interest in the corporation), the basis of each indebtedness is reduced under §1.1367–2(b)(3) in the same proportion that the basis of each indebtedness bears to the aggregate bases of the indebtedness of the S corporation to the shareholder.

Section 1.1367–2(c) provides the rules for restoring basis of indebtedness of an S corporation to a shareholder. Generally, under §1.1367–2(c)(1), if, for any taxable year of the S corporation, there has been a reduction in the basis of an indebtedness of the S corporation to a shareholder, any net increase in any subsequent taxable year of the S corporation is applied to restore that reduction. For purposes of §1.1367–2, a net increase is the amount by which the shareholder's *pro rata* share of S corporation items described in section 1367(a)(1) exceed the items described in section 1367(a)(2) for the taxable year. The restoration rules apply only to indebtedness held by the shareholder as of the beginning of the taxable year in which the net increase arises. Further, the reduction in basis of indebtedness must be restored before a net increase is used to restore the shareholder's basis in stock. The shareholder's basis in indebtedness may not be restored above the adjusted basis of the indebtedness under section 1016(a) (excluding any prior year's adjustments under section 1367), determined as of the beginning of the taxable year in which the net increase arises.

Under §1.1367–2(c)(2), if a shareholder holds more than one indebtedness as of the beginning of an S corporation's taxable year, any net increase is applied first to restore the reduction of basis in any indebtedness repaid (in whole or in part) in that taxable year to the extent necessary to offset any gain that would otherwise be realized on the repayment. Any remaining net increase is applied to restore each outstanding indebtedness in proportion to the amount that the basis of each outstanding indebtedness has been reduced and not restored.

Section 1.1367–2(d) provides rules for the time at which adjustments to basis of indebtedness under section 1367(b)(2) are effective. Generally, under §1.1367–2(d)(1) the amount of the adjustments to basis of indebtedness are determined and effective as of the close of an S corporation's taxable year. However, if the shareholder is not a shareholder in the S corporation at that time, the adjustments are effective immediately before the shareholder's interest in the S corporation is terminated. Moreover, if a debt is disposed of or repaid, in whole or in part, before the close of the taxable year, the basis of that debt is restored effective immediately before the disposition or the first repayment on the debt during the taxable year.

On August 25, 2005, the Tax Court issued its decision in *Brooks v. Commissioner*, TC Memo. 2005–204. In *Brooks*, the taxpayer borrowed money from a bank and advanced that money as open account debt to his S corporation in one taxable year and reduced basis in that open account debt for losses passed through to the taxpayer at the end of that same year. In the first few weeks of the subsequent taxable year, the S corporation repaid the open account debt (the taxpayer then repaid his debt for the borrowed money). Late in that subsequent year, the taxpayer advanced additional money (again, amounts borrowed from a bank) in an amount that offset the repayment of advances to avoid the recognition of gain from repayment of the indebtedness. Also, the taxpayer's advances increased the shareholder's basis in the indebtedness and allowed losses for that year to pass through to the taxpayer shareholder. Taxpayer and the S corporation made these repayments and advances for several taxable years and deferred indefinitely the recognition of income on any repayment of his open account debt.

The court in *Brooks* held "that the basis of the open account indebtedness is properly computed by netting at the close of the year advances of open account debt during the year and repayments of open account debt during the year."

Explanation of Provisions

The Treasury Department and the IRS believe that the concept of "open account debt" as defined in §1.1367–2(a) was intended to provide administrative simplicity for S corporations but was not intended to permit the deferral allowed in *Brooks*. The IRS and Treasury Department are proposing these amendments to narrow the definition of open account debt and to modify the rules for adjustments of basis in indebtedness for the more narrowly defined open account debt.

In these proposed regulations, open account debt is defined as shareholder advances not evidenced by separate written instruments for which the principal amount of the aggregate advances (net of repayments on the advances) does not exceed $10,000 at the close of any day during the S corporation's taxable year. Included within that definition are separate advances under a line of credit agreement if the advances are not evidenced by a separate written instrument. Open account debt is treated as a single indebtedness. This $10,000 limitation on open account debt for the purposes of the §1.1367–2 regulations is modeled after section 7872(c)(3) and the §1.7872–9 proposed regulations, which provide a $10,000 *de minimis* exception to the treatment of loans with below-market interest rates for compensation-related or corporation-shareholder loans.

Under these proposed regulations, to determine whether shareholder advances and repayments on the advances exceed the $10,000 aggregate principal threshold on any day during the S corporation's taxable year for open account debt, the shareholder will have to maintain a "running balance" of those advances and repayments, and the outstanding principal amount of the open account debt. If the resulting aggregate principal of the running balance does not exceed $10,000 at the close of any day during the S corporation's taxable year, the advances and repayments on advances would constitute open account debt, would be treated as a single indebtedness, and would be accounted for at the close of the taxable year (as explained in this preamble). However, if the resulting aggregate principal of the running balance exceeds $10,000 at the close of any day during the S corporation's taxable year, the entire principal amount of that indebtedness would no longer constitute open account debt effective at the close of the day on the date the amount of the running balance exceeds $10,000. This principal amount would be treated as indebtedness evidenced by a written instrument for that taxable year, and would be accounted for according to the timing rules in §1.1367–2(d) for that taxable year and subsequent taxable years. Any new shareholder advances not evidenced by a written instrument and repayments on those advances within the $10,000 aggregate principal threshold amount during the taxable year would constitute a new open account debt.

The proposed regulations also modify the manner in which repayments on open account debt are accounted for under the existing final §1.1367–2 regulations. These rules are separate from the maintenance of a running balance of the advances and repayments to determine if a shareholder has exceeded the $10,000 threshold amount. For purposes of accounting for open account debt, each shareholder, at the end of the S corporation's taxable year, must determine if that shareholder has made a net advance or received a net repayment on open account debt for that taxable year. To determine if a net advance or a net repayment has occurred, each shareholder, at the end of the S corporation's taxable year, must net all advances and repayments made during the year without regard to the outstanding principal amount of the open account debt. If, at the end of the taxable year, a net repayment exists, the net repayment must be taken into account effective at the close of the S corporation's taxable year under the general basis adjustment rules in the existing final §1.1367–2 regulations. If, at the end of the taxable year, a net advance exists, the net advance is combined with the outstanding aggregate principal balance of the existing open account debt and that amount is carried forward to the beginning of the subsequent taxable year as the outstanding aggregate principal amount of the open account debt. If at any time during the taxable year the resulting aggregate principal of the running balance exceeds the $10,000 threshold amount so the entire principal amount of the indebtedness no longer constitutes open account debt, the running balance must be reconciled effective at the close of the day the balance exceeds $10,000 to determine the aggregate principal amount of the indebtedness, and for the remainder of the taxable year that principal amount is treated in the same manner as indebtedness evidenced by a written instrument for the purposes of this section.

Proposed Effective Date

The regulations, as proposed, apply to any shareholder advances to the S corporation made on or after the date of publication of a Treasury decision adopting these rules as final regulations in the **Federal Register** and repayments on those advances by the S corporation.

Special Analyses

It has been determined that this notice of proposed rulemaking is not a significant regulatory action as defined in Executive Order 12866. Therefore, a regulatory assessment is not required. It also has been determined that section 553(b) of the Administrative Procedure Act (5 U.S.C. chapter 5) does not apply to these regulations. Because these regulations do not impose a collection of information on small entities, the Regulatory Flexibility Act (5 U.S.C. chapter 6) does not apply. Pursuant to section 7805(f) of the Code, this notice of proposed rulemaking will be submitted to the Chief Counsel for Advocacy of the Small Business Administration for comment on its impact on small business.

Comments and Public Hearing

Before these proposed regulations are adopted as final regulations, consideration will be given to any written comments (a signed original and eight (8) copies) or electronic comments that are submitted timely to the IRS. The IRS and the Treasury Department request comments on the clarity of the proposed rules and how they can be made easier to understand. All comments will be available for public inspection and copying.

A public hearing has been scheduled for July 31, 2007, beginning at 10 a.m. in the IRS Auditorium, Internal Revenue Building, 1111 Constitution Avenue, NW, Washington, DC. Due to building security procedures, visitors must enter at the Constitution Avenue entrance. In addition, all visitors must present photo identification to enter the building. Because of access restrictions, visitors will not be admitted beyond the immediate entrance area more than 30 minutes before the hearing starts. For information about having your name placed on the building access list to attend the hearing, see the "FOR FURTHER INFORMATION CONTACT" section of this preamble.

The rules of 26 CFR 606.601(a)(3) apply to the hearing. Persons who wish to present oral comments at the hearing must submit electronic or written comments and an outline of the topics to be discussed and time to be devoted to each topic (a signed original and eight (8) copies) by July 10, 2007. A period of 10 minutes will be allotted to each person for making comments. An agenda showing the scheduling of the speakers will be prepared after the deadline for receiving outlines has passed. Copies of the agenda will be available free of charge at the hearing.

Drafting Information

The principal authors of these regulations are Stacy L. Short and Deane M. Burke of the Office of the Associate Chief Counsel (Passthroughs and Special Industries), IRS.

* * * * *

Proposed Amendments to the Regulations

Accordingly, 26 CFR part 1 is proposed to be amended as follows:

PART 1—INCOME TAX

Paragraph 1. The authority citation for part 1 is amended by adding an entry in numerical order to read in part as follows:

Authority: 26 U.S.C. 7805 * * *

Section 1.1367–2 also issued under 26 U.S.C. 1367(b)(2).* * *

Par. 2. Section 1.1367–2 is amended as follows:

1. Paragraph (a) is revised and redesignated as paragraph (a)(1) and paragraph (a)(2) is added.

2. Paragraphs (c)(2) and (d)(1) are revised.

3. Paragraph (d)(2) is redesignated as paragraph (d)(3).

4. New paragraph (d)(2) is added.

5. Paragraph (e) is amended by adding *Examples 6* and *7*.

The revisions and additions read as follows:

§1.1367–2 Adjustments to basis of indebtedness to shareholder.

(a) *In general*—(1) *Adjustments under section 1367.* This section provides rules relating to adjustments required by subchapter S to the basis of indebtedness (including open account debt as described in paragraph (a)(2) of this section) of an S corporation to a shareholder. The basis of indebtedness of the S corporation to a shareholder is reduced as provided in paragraph (b) of this section and restored as provided in paragraph (c) of this section in accordance with the timing rules in paragraph (d) of this section.

(2) *Open Account Debt*—(i) *General rule.* The term *open account debt* means shareholder advances not evidenced by separate written instruments and repayments on the advances, the aggregate outstanding principal of which does not exceed $10,000 of indebtedness of the S corporation to the shareholder at the close of any day during the S corporation's taxable year. Advances and repayments on open account debt are treated as a single indebtedness. For purposes of determining if shareholder advances not evidenced by separate written instruments and repayments on those advances exceed an aggregate outstanding principal of $10,000, a shareholder must maintain a running daily balance of all advances and repayments on those advances and the outstanding principal amount of the open account debt at the close of each day during the S corporation's taxable year.

(ii) *Exception.* If a shareholder's running balance exceeds an aggregate outstanding principal amount of $10,000 at the close of any day during the S corporation's taxable year, effective on the close of the day on which the shareholder's running balance exceeds $10,000, the running balance must be reconciled to determine the aggregate principal amount of indebtedness. For the remainder of the taxable year, that aggregate principal amount of indebtedness is treated in the same manner as indebtedness evidenced by a separate written instrument for purposes of this section. For the remainder of that taxable year and subsequent taxable years, the indebtedness is not open account debt and is subject to all basis adjustment rules applicable to basis of indebtedness of an S corporation to a shareholder in this section.

* * * * *

(c) * * * (1) * * *

(2) *Multiple indebtedness.* If a shareholder holds more than one indebtedness (including any open account debt and any debt treated as a single indebtedness under paragraph (a)(2)(ii)) as of the beginning of an S corporation's taxable year, any net increase is applied first to restore the reduction of basis in any indebtedness repaid (in whole or in part) in that taxable year to the extent necessary to offset any gain that would otherwise be realized on the repayment. Any remaining net increase is applied to restore each outstanding indebtedness (including any open account debt and any debt treated as a single indebtedness under paragraph (a)(2)(ii) of this section) in proportion to the amount that the basis of each outstanding indebtedness has been reduced under section 1367(b)(2)(A) and paragraph (b) of this section and not restored under section 1367(b)(2)(B) and this paragraph (c).

(d) *Time at which adjustments to basis of indebtedness are effective*—(1) *In general.* Except as provided in paragraph (d)(2) of this section, the amounts of the adjustments to basis of indebtedness provided in section 1367(b)(2) and this section are determined as of the close of the S corporation's taxable year, and the adjustments are generally effective as of the close of the S corporation's taxable year. However, if the shareholder is not a shareholder in the S corporation at that time, these adjustments are effective immediately before the shareholder terminates his or her interest in the S corporation. If a debt (including any open account debt and any debt treated as a single indebtedness under paragraph (a)(2)(ii) of this section) is disposed of or repaid in whole or in part before the close of the taxable year, the basis of that indebtedness is restored under paragraph (c) of this section, effective immediately before the disposition or the first repayment on the debt (or the net repayment on open account debt) during the taxable year. To the extent any reduction of basis in indebtedness under paragraph (b) of this section that is disposed of or repaid (in whole or in part) during the taxable year is not restored completely under paragraph (c) of this section, gain is realized on the repayment effective immediately before the indebtedness is disposed of or repaid (in whole or in part).

(2) *Open account debt*—(i) *In general.* All advances and repayments on open account debt (as described in paragraph (a)(2)(i) of this section) during the taxable year are netted continuously as the advances and repayments occur. The amount of any net advance or net repayment on open account debt for the S corporation's taxable year is determined at the close of the taxable year. If the shareholder advances, and repayments on the advances, during the S corporation's taxable year result in a net advance or net repayment, the basis of the open account debt is reduced as provided in paragraph (b) of this section and restored as provided in paragraph (c) of this section effective at the close of the taxable year. To the extent any reduction of basis of open account debt under paragraph (b) of this section that is disposed of or repaid (in whole or in part) during the taxable year is not restored completely under paragraph (c) of this section, income is realized on the net repayment at the close of the taxable year in which the open account debt is disposed of or repaid (in whole or in part).

(ii) *Exception.* On the close of the day on which the shareholder's running balance exceeds an aggregate outstanding principal amount of $10,000, the shareholder's running balance is reconciled to determine an aggregate principal amount of indebtedness. The resulting aggregate principal amount of indebtedness is treated as the principal amount of a debt evidenced by a separate written instrument for the remainder of that taxable year and any subsequent taxable year, and is no longer subject to the open account debt provisions of this section.

* * * * *

(e) * * *

* * * * *

Example 6. Treatment of open account debt. (i) A has been the sole shareholder in Corporation S since 2000. In 2007, A advances S $8,000, which is not evidenced by a written instrument. The $8,000 advance is open account debt and remains outstanding at that amount during 2007. On December 31, 2007, the basis of A's stock is zero; and the basis of the open account debt is reduced under paragraph (b) of this section to $4,000. On April 1, 2008, S repays $3,000 of the open account indebtedness. On September 1, 2008, A advances S an additional $2,000, which is not evidenced by a written instrument. There is no net increase under paragraph (c) of this section in year 2007 or 2008.

(ii) At no time during the 2007 taxable year does the running balance of A's open account debt exceed $10,000. As of December 31, 2007, A's basis in the open account debt is reduced under paragraph (b) of this section to $4,000.

(iii) At no time during the 2008 taxable year does the running balance of A's open account debt exceed $10,000. On April 1, 2008, S's $3,000 repayment is applied to A's running balance for open account debt carried forward from 2007 in the amount of $8,000 to reduce the running balance to $5,000. On September 1, 2008, A's advance to S of $2,000, which is not evidenced by a written instrument, is applied to A's running balance to bring A's aggregate outstanding principal on A's open account indebtedness to $7,000.

(iv) At the close of the 2008 taxable year, the $3,000 April repayment S makes to A and A's $2,000 September advance are netted to result in a net repayment of $1,000 for the taxable year on A's $8,000 open account debt carried forward from 2007. Because there is no net increase in 2008, no basis of indebtedness is restored for the 2008 taxable year.

Example 7. Treatment of shareholder indebtedness not evidenced by a written instrument which exceeds $10,000. (i) The facts are the same as in *Example 6*, in addition to which, on February 1, 2008, S repays $1,000 of the open account debt and on March 1, 2008, A advances S $5,000, which is not evidenced by a written instrument.

(ii) At no time during the 2007 taxable year does the running balance of A's open account debt exceed $10,000. As of December 31, 2007, the basis of the open account debt is reduced under paragraph (b) of this section to $4,000.

(iii) The running balance of A's open account debt does exceed $10,000 during the 2008 taxable year. On February 1, 2008, S's $1,000 repayment is applied to A's running balance for open account debt carried forward from 2007 in the amount of $8,000 to reduce the running balance to $7,000. On March 1, 2008, A's advance to S of $5,000, which is not evidenced by a written instrument, is applied to A's running balance to bring A's aggregate outstanding principal on A's open account debt to $12,000. Because this amount exceeds the $10,000 threshold amount, effective at the close of the day on March 1, 2008, A's running balance must be reconciled to determine an aggregate principal amount of indebtedness.

(iv) As of March 1, 2008, S had made a $1,000 repayment on A's open account debt, and A had advanced an additional $5,000 which was not evidenced by a written instrument. To reconcile A's running balance, the $1,000 repayment and $5,000 advance are netted first to result in a $4,000 net advance that is then added with A's existing principal amount of open account debt of $8,000 to determine the aggregate principal amount of indebtedness of $12,000. As of March 1, 2008, S's indebtedness to A that is not evidenced by a written instrument has a principal balance of $12,000 and a basis of $8,000 ($4,000 basis on December 31, 2007 + $4,000 net advance). On April 1, 2008, S repays $3,000 of that new indebtedness.

(v) On September 1, 2008, A advances S an additional $2,000, which is not evidenced by a written instrument. The $2,000 advance is considered new open account debt. On December 31, 2008, A's basis in his stock is zero and the outstanding principal in the two remaining debts are as follows:

	3/1/08 principal	4/1/08 repayment	9/1/08 advance	12/31/08 principal
Indebtedness treated as if evidenced by written instrument	$12,000	$3,000		$9,000
Open account debt			$2,000	$2,000

Par. 3. Section 1.1367–3 is amended as follows:

1. The section heading is revised.
2. The first sentence of the paragraph is revised.
3. A new second and last sentence are added.

The revisions and additions read as follows:

§1.1367–3 Effective dates and transitional rules.

Section 1.1367–2(a), (c)(2), (d)(2), and (e) *Example 6* and *Example 7* apply to any shareholder advances to the S corporation made on or after the date these regulations are published as final regulations in the **Federal Register** and repayments on those advances by the S corporation.

Kevin M. Brown,
Deputy Commissioner for Services and Enforcement.

(Filed by the Office of the Federal Register on April 11, 2007, 8:45 a.m., and published in the issue of the Federal Register for April 12, 2007, 72 F.R. 18417)

Announcement of Disciplinary Actions Involving Attorneys, Certified Public Accountants, Enrolled Agents, and Enrolled Actuaries — Suspensions, Censures, Disbarments, and Resignations

Announcement 2007-41

Under Title 31, Code of Federal Regulations, Part 10, attorneys, certified public accountants, enrolled agents, and enrolled actuaries may not accept assistance from, or assist, any person who is under disbarment or suspension from practice before the Internal Revenue Service if the assistance relates to a matter constituting practice before the Internal Revenue Service and may not knowingly aid or abet another person to practice before the Internal Revenue Service during a period of suspension, disbarment, or ineligibility of such other person.

To enable attorneys, certified public accountants, enrolled agents, and enrolled actuaries to identify persons to whom these restrictions apply, the Director, Office of Professional Responsibility, will announce in the Internal Revenue Bulletin their names, their city and state, their professional designation, the effective date of disciplinary action, and the period of suspension. This announcement will appear in the weekly Bulletin at the earliest practicable date after such action and will continue to appear in the weekly Bulletins for five successive weeks.

Consent Suspensions From Practice Before the Internal Revenue Service

Under Title 31, Code of Federal Regulations, Part 10, an attorney, certified public accountant, enrolled agent, or enrolled actuary, in order to avoid the institution or conclusion of a proceeding for his or her disbarment or suspension from practice before the Internal Revenue Service, may offer his or her consent to suspension from such practice. The Director, Office of Professional Responsibility, in his discretion, may suspend an attorney, certified public accountant, enrolled agent, or enrolled actuary in accordance with the consent offered.

The following individuals have been placed under consent suspension from practice before the Internal Revenue Service:

Name	Address	Designation	Date of Suspension
Hankinson, Eugene M.	Somerset, PA	CPA	Indefinite from November 15, 2006
Canzano, Richard M.	Winchester, MA	Attorney	Indefinite from November 20, 2006
Sims, Jr., Lionel	Houston, TX	CPA	Indefinite from November 20, 2006
Wendekier, Raymond J.	Patton, PA	Attorney	Indefinite from November 21, 2006
Golden, Larry	Hinesville, GA	CPA	Indefinite from November 28, 2006
Lane, David B.	Hanover, MA	Attorney	Indefinite from November 28, 2006

Name	Address	Designation	Date of Suspension
Brown, Arthur I.	Miami, FL	CPA	Indefinite from December 1, 2006
Frisk, Daniel J.	Fargo, ND	Attorney	Indefinite from December 1, 2006
Small, Kenneth A.	McMurray, PA	CPA	Indefinite from December 1, 2006
Vazquez, Sonya M.	Port Orchard, WA	CPA	Indefinite from December 1, 2006
Swistak, Anthony	Adams, MA	Enrolled Agent	Indefinite from December 6, 2006
Lenahan, Jr., Robert J.	Elizabeth, NJ	Attorney	Indefinite from December 11, 2006
Hayes, Richard A.	Havervill, MA	Attorney	Indefinite from December 14, 2006
Scheller, Stephen M.	Coppell, TX	CPA	Indefinite from December 15, 2006
Wilson, James M.	Berlin, NJ	CPA	Indefinite from December 15, 2006
Franzese, Joseph P.	Winthrop, MA	Attorney	Indefinite from December 18, 2006
Black, Charles C.	Marietta, GA	Attorney	Indefinite from January 1, 2007
Enright, III, Robert A.	Naples, FL	Attorney	Indefinite from January 1, 2007
Fromovitz, Norman M.	Brooklyn, NY	CPA	Indefinite from January 1, 2007
Saylor, Mary A.	Iowa City, IA	Enrolled Agent	Indefinite from January 1, 2007
Seeherman, Alan	Wynnewood, PA	CPA	Indefinite from January 1, 2007

Name	Address	Designation	Date of Suspension
Beistel, Theodore L.	Canton, OH	CPA	Indefinite from January 3, 2007
Myers, Robert J.	Fairport Harbor, OH	CPA	Indefinite from January 9, 2007
Burrus, Robert V.	Valparaiso, IN	CPA	Indefinite from January 22, 2007
Patterson, Douglas W.	Newburgh, IN	Attorney	Indefinite from January 31, 2007
Lang, Jeffrey H.	Fishers, IN	CPA	Indefinite from January 22, 2007
Chickering, David	Vermillion, SD	CPA	February 5, 2007 to November 4, 2007
Moss, Steve E.	Henderson, NC	CPA	Indefinite from February 5, 2007
Hazlip, Kevin	Orange Park, FL	Enrolled Agent	Indefinite from February 10, 2007
Adelson, Robert A.	Newton, MA	Attorney	Indefinite from February 15, 2007
Boyer, Daniel D.	North Judson, IN	CPA	Indefinite from February 15, 2007
LaRusso, Anthony J.	North Caldwell, NJ	Attorney	Indefinite from February 15, 2007
Martin, Spencer R.	Lancaster, PA	CPA	Indefinite from February 15, 2007
Hursh, Stephanie S.	Brush Prairie, WA	Enrolled Agent	Indefinite from February 20, 2007
Guidera, George C.	Weston, CT	Attorney	Indefinite from February 26, 2007
Ruth, Christopher A.	Cypress, CA	CPA	Indefinite from February 27, 2007
Elias, Lenard S.	El Cajon, CA	Enrolled Agent	Indefinite from March 1, 2007

Name	Address	Designation	Date of Suspension
Ikeji, Chuck	Orlando, FL	CPA	Indefinite from March 1, 2007
Lewis, Craig S.	Savannah, GA	CPA	Indefinite from March 1, 2007
Sloan, Eric R.	Brighton, MI	CPA	Indefinite from March 1, 2007
Gostomski, Michael	Stamford, CT	CPA	Indefinite from March 5, 2007
Hafer, Charles J.	Hamburg, PA	Enrolled Agent	Indefinite from March 5, 2007
Jones, Phillip G.	Andalusia, AL	Enrolled Agent	Indefinite from March 7, 2007
Agashiwala, Mahesh J.	New York, NY	CPA	Indefinite from March 22, 2007
Berndgen, Michael	Plantation, FL	CPA	Indefinite from April 1, 2007
Grahn, Charles R.	Indianapolis, IN	Attorney	Indefinite from April 1, 2007
Shaw, G. Joyce	Hebron, KY	Enrolled Agent	Indefinite from April 1, 2007
Pikaart, Jr., Edward H.	N. Branford, CT	CPA	Indefinite from April 10, 2007
Kelley, Richard S.	Beverly, MA	Attorney	Indefinite from May 1, 2007
Crabtree, Michael L.	San Dimas, CA	Enrolled Agent	Indefinite from May 15, 2007
Hausmann, Mark D.	Troy, NY	Attorney	Indefinite from May 15, 2007

Expedited Suspensions From Practice Before the Internal Revenue Service

Under Title 31, Code of Federal Regulations, Part 10, the Director, Office of Professional Responsibility, is authorized to immediately suspend from practice before the Internal Revenue Service any practitioner who, within five years from the date the expedited proceeding is instituted (1) has had a license to practice as an attorney, certified public accountant, or actuary suspended or revoked for cause or (2) has been convicted of certain crimes.

The following individuals have been placed under suspension from practice before the Internal Revenue Service by virtue of the expedited proceeding provisions:

Name	Address	Designation	Date of Suspension
Hatchett, William M.	Pontiac, MI	Attorney	Indefinite from November 13, 2006
Jacobs, Mark L.	Jackson Heights, NY	Attorney	Indefinite from November 21, 2006
Sylver, Peter T.	E. Longmeadow, MA	Attorney	Indefinite from November 21, 2006
Portlock, David R.	Pensacola, FL	Enrolled Agent	Indefinite from November 27, 2006
Ascher, Michael P.	North Port, FL	Attorney	Indefinite from November 28, 2006
Barrett, Norman W.	Dover, DE	CPA	Indefinite from November 28, 2006
Burd, Gene	Houston, TX	Attorney	Indefinite from November 28, 2006
Caceres, Carlos H.	Silver Spring, MD	Attorney	Indefinite from November 28, 2006
Carrabotta, Peter S.	Niles, IL	Attorney	Indefinite from November 28, 2006
Davis, Carleton W.	St. Louis, MO	Attorney	Indefinite from November 28, 2006
Frasier, Roland B.	Rancho Santa Fe, CA	Attorney	Indefinite from November 28, 2006
Hubbard, Edward	Chicago, IL	Attorney	Indefinite from November 28, 2006

Name	Address	Designation	Date of Suspension
Hynes, Richard W.	Brookline, MA	Attorney	Indefinite from November 28, 2006
Johnson, Barbara C.	Andover, MA	Attorney	Indefinite from November 28, 2006
Konas, Theodore V.	Lancaster, PA	CPA	Indefinite from November 28, 2006
Korson, Daniel M.	Muskegon, MI	CPA	Indefinite from November 28, 2006
Lee, III, Norman J.	Collegeville, PA	Attorney	Indefinite from November 28, 2006
Loiben, Alan A.	Skokie, IL	Attorney	Indefinite from November 28, 2006
McGarry, Thomas H.	Denver, CO	Attorney	Indefinite from November 28, 2006
Roberts, Quinton D.	Elkridge, MD	Attorney	Indefinite from November 28, 2006
Schofield, Peter L.	Spencer, MA	Attorney	Indefinite from November 28, 2006
Shultz, Ryan K.	Mitchell, NE	Attorney	Indefinite from November 28, 2006
Stenger, Jeanne P.	Temecula, CA	Attorney	Indefinite from November 28, 2006
Wood, Gary K.	Edina, MN	Attorney	Indefinite from November 28, 2006
Bakare, Adigun S.	Laurel, MD	Attorney	Indefinite from December 6, 2006
Biagini, Marc J.	Downers Grove, IL	Attorney	Indefinite from December 6, 2006
Birchall, Richard G.	Brewster, MA	Attorney	Indefinite from December 6, 2006

Name	Address	Designation	Date of Suspension
Brown, Edward E.	Indianapolis, IN	Attorney	Indefinite from December 6, 2006
Cunningham, Jr., Shirley A.	Ft. Lauderdale, FL	Attorney	Indefinite from December 6, 2006
Docherty, Scott R.	Branson West, MO	Attorney	Indefinite from December 6, 2006
Dressler, Peter P.	West Chicago, IL	Attorney	Indefinite from December 6, 2006
Henry, William J.	Irvington, NJ	Attorney	Indefinite from December 6, 2006
Hubbard, Cynthia A.	Geneva, IL	Attorney	Indefinite from December 6, 2006
Jackson, Jr., Donald H.	Hanover, MA	Attorney	Indefinite from December 6, 2006
Katz, Norman H.	Owings Mills, MD	Attorney	Indefinite from December 6, 2006
Lakin, Leonard S.	Wellesley Hills, MA	Attorney	Indefinite from December 6, 2006
McGreevy, Jacqueline K.	Carbondale, CO	Attorney	Indefinite from December 6, 2006
Zepp, Dale D.	Ferguson, MO	Attorney	Indefinite from December 6, 2006
Triplett, Austin H.	Homewood, IL	Attorney	Indefinite from December 11, 2006
Murphy, Patrick W.	Honolulu, HI	Attorney	Indefinite from December 11, 2006
Cronin, Jr., Edward M.	Cambridge, MA	Attorney	Indefinite from December 11, 2006
Christof, Kevin F.	Santa Monica, CA	Attorney	Indefinite from December 21, 2006
Heath, Kenneth J.	Canaan, VT	CPA	Indefinite from December 21, 2006

Name	Address	Designation	Date of Suspension
Madigan, Brian C.	Binghamton, NY	Attorney	Indefinite from December 21, 2006
Malloy, Terry P.	Tulsa, OK	Attorney	Indefinite from December 21, 2006
Baynes, Robert M.	Indianapolis, IN	CPA	Indefinite from December 27, 2006
Ceresa, Richard A.	Woodbridge, CA	CPA	Indefinite from December 27, 2006
Crews, Richard A.	Henderson, CO	Attorney	Indefinite from December 27, 2006
Menkveld, Paul G.	Tucson, AZ	Attorney	Indefinite from December 27, 2006
Worischeck, Joseph H.	Tempe, AZ	Attorney	Indefinite from December 27, 2006
Brown, Kirk P.	Pueblo, CO	Attorney	Indefinite from December 28, 2006
Dowling, Stanley W.	Scotts Valley, CA	CPA	Indefinite from December 28, 2006
Simmons, Henry L.	Greensboro, NC	CPA	Indefinite from December 28, 2006
Steele, Regina D.	San Diego, CA	Attorney	Indefinite from December 29, 2006
Craig, III, William A.	Austin, TX	Attorney	Indefinite from January 1, 2007
Acker, Thomas R.	Hollis Center, ME	Attorney	Indefinite from January 8, 2007
Baxter, Laura M.	Monee, IL	CPA	Indefinite from January 8, 2007
Herald, Sally J.	Cold Spring, KY	Attorney	Indefinite from January 8, 2007
Klapheke, II, William T.	Bowling Green, KY	Attorney	Indefinite from January 8, 2007

Name	Address	Designation	Date of Suspension
McCarthy, Charles C.	Encino, CA	Attorney	Indefinite from January 8, 2007
Bolling, Darius C.	Chicago, IL	CPA	Indefinite from January 10, 2007
Breitlauch, Linda	Saylorsburg, PA	Attorney	Indefinite from January 10, 2007
Coddington, Paul F.	Concord, NH	Attorney	Indefinite from January 10, 2007
Davis, Jr., William E.	Pinehurst, TX	CPA	Indefinite from January 10, 2007
Esola, Louis A.	Greensburg, PA	CPA	Indefinite from January 10, 2007
Finch, Judith A.	Walnut Creek, CA	Attorney	Indefinite from January 10, 2007
Jeing, Thomas C.	San Francisco, CA	Attorney	Indefinite from January 10, 2007
Ledbetter, Dean D.	Pelham, AL	CPA	Indefinite from January 10, 2007
McDiarmid, Katherine B.	Greensboro, NC	Attorney	Indefinite from January 10, 2007
Mills, George P.	Oceanside, CA	Attorney	Indefinite from January 10, 2007
Rather, James L.	Irvine, CA	Attorney	Indefinite from January 10, 2007
Rivera, Eduardo M.	Torrance, CA	Attorney	Indefinite from January 10, 2007
Stepovich, Michael A.	Fairbanks, AK	Attorney	Indefinite from January 10, 2007
Ulbrich, David L.	Woodland Hills, CA	CPA	Indefinite from January 10, 2007
Swanson, Todd-Ellis	Greenville, SC	CPA	Indefinite from January 20, 2007

Name	Address	Designation	Date of Suspension
Rubin, Deborah L.	Delray Beach, FL	Attorney	Indefinite from January 26, 2007
Wood, Brent E.	Cary, NC	Attorney	Indefinite from January 26, 2007
Currin, Samuel T.	Raleigh, NC	Attorney	Indefinite from February 7, 2007
Lupo, Robert N.	Weston, MA	Attorney	Indefinite from February 20, 2007
Taggart, Lawrence W.	El Cajon, CA	Attorney	Indefinite from March 7, 2007
Fife, III, James H.	Schererville, IN	Attorney	Indefinite from March 8, 2007
Katsis, Kevin G.	Riverside, IL	Attorney	Indefinite from March 8, 2007
O'Driscoll, Dennis M.	Quincy, MA	Attorney	Indefinite from March 8, 2007
Siever, Beth F.	Austin, TX	Attorney	Indefinite from March 8, 2007
Wheatley-Clark, Sheila R.	Houston, TX	CPA	Indefinite from March 8, 2007

Suspensions From Practice Before the Internal Revenue Service After Notice and an Opportunity for a Proceeding

Under Title 31, Code of Federal Regulations, Part 10, after notice and an opportunity for a proceeding before an administrative law judge, the following individuals have been placed under suspension from practice before the Internal Revenue Service:

Name	Address	Designation	Effective Date
Redmond, Debra	Gifford, PA	Enrolled Agent	Indefinite from March 5, 2007

Disbarments From Practice Before the Internal Revenue Service After Notice and an Opportunity for a Proceeding

Under Title 31, Code of Federal Regulations, Part 10, after notice and an opportunity for a proceeding before an administrative law judge, the following individuals have been disbarred from practice before the Internal Revenue Service:

Name	Address	Designation	Effective Date
Brookstein, Gary	Huntingdon Valley, PA	CPA	December 15, 2006
James T. Jubb	Baltimore, MD	CPA	December 15, 2006

Censure Issued by Consent

Under Title 31, Code of Federal Regulations, Part 10, in lieu of a proceeding being instituted or continued, an attorney, certified public accountant, enrolled agent, or enrolled actuary, may offer his or her consent to the issuance of a censure. Censure is a public reprimand.

The following individuals have consented to the issuance of a Censure:

Name	Address	Designation	Date of Censure
Zucker, Robert W.	Boca Raton, FL	CPA	November 14, 2006
Montgomery, David E.	Pleasanton, CA	Enrolled Agent	November 15, 2006
Higgins, James M.	S. Boston, MA	Attorney	December 1, 2006
Pennington, Debra L.	Lees Summit, MO	Enrolled Agent	January 29, 2007
Goodwin, Steven C.	Concord, MA	Attorney	February 2, 2007
Francis, Andrew W.E.	Houston, TX	CPA	February 21, 2007
Griffin, Richard M.	Duluth, GA	CPA	February 28, 2007

Resignations of Enrolled Agents

Under Title 31, Code of Federal Regulations, Part 10, an enrolled agent, in order to avoid the institution or conclusion of a proceeding for his or her disbarment or suspension from practice before the Internal Revenue Service, may offer his or her resignation as an enrolled agent. The Director, Office of Professional Responsibility, in his discretion, may accept the offered resignation.

The Director, Office of Professional Responsibility, has accepted offers of resignation as an enrolled agent from the following individuals:

Name	Address	Date of Resignation
Filipski, Kenneth M.	Bakersfield, CA	April 16, 2007

List of Nonbank Trustees and Custodians

Announcement 2007–47

The following is a list of entities that have been approved by the Commissioner of the Internal Revenue Service, pursuant to § 1.408–2(e) of the Income Tax Regulations, to serve as a nonbank trustee or custodian. This list updates and supersedes the list published with Announcement 2006–45, 2006–31 I.R.B. 121.

Archer medical savings accounts (Archer MSAs) established under § 220 of the Internal Revenue Code, health savings accounts described in § 223, custodial accounts of retirement plans qualified under § 401, custodial accounts described in § 403(b)(7), trust or custodial accounts of individual retirement accounts (IRAs) established under §§ 408 and 408A (Roth IRAs), Coverdell education savings accounts described in § 530, and custodial accounts of eligible deferred compensation plans described in § 457(b) will not be tax exempt if the trustee or custodian of such accounts is not a bank (as defined in § 408(n)) (and in the case of Archer MSAs and health savings accounts, a bank within the meaning of § 408(n) or an insurance company within the meaning of § 816) or an approved nonbank trustee or custodian.

An entity that is not a bank (as defined in § 408(n)) (and in the case of Archer MSAs and health savings accounts a bank within the meaning of § 408(n) or an insurance company within the meaning of § 816) must receive approval from the Service to serve as a nonbank trustee or nonbank custodian. A prospective nonbank trustee or custodian must file a written application with the Commissioner of Internal Revenue demonstrating that the requirements of § 1.408–2(e)(2) through § 1.408–2(e)(7) of the regulations will be met. If the application is approved, a written notice of approval will be issued to the applicant. The notice of approval will state the day on which it becomes effective, and (except as otherwise provided therein) will remain effective until revoked by the Service or withdrawn by the applicant. Entities that have received such approval from the Service may also sponsor certain retirement plans, custodial accounts under § 403(b)(7) and individual retirement arrangements established under §§ 408 and 408A. (See, Rev. Proc. 2005–16, 2005–1 C.B. 674, and Rev. Proc. 87–50, 1987–2 C.B. 647, as modified.)

A prospective nonbank trustee or custodian may not accept any fiduciary account before such notice of approval becomes effective. In addition, a nonbank trustee or custodian may not accept a fiduciary account until after the plan administrator or the person for whose benefit the account is to be established is furnished with a copy of the written notice of approval issued to the applicant.

The continued reliance on a notice of approval is dependent upon the continued satisfaction of the nonbank trustee requirements set forth in the regulations. The notice of approval issued to an applicant will be revoked if the Commissioner determines that the applicant is unwilling or unable to administer fiduciary accounts in a manner consistent with the requirements of the regulations. Generally, the notice will not be revoked unless the Commissioner determines that the applicant has knowingly, willfully, or repeatedly failed to administer fiduciary accounts in a manner consistent with the requirements of the regulations, or has administered a fiduciary account in a grossly negligent manner.

The written notice of approval to serve as a nonbank trustee or nonbank custodian is not an endorsement of any investment made with respect to any retirement plan or arrangement handled by the approved nonbank trustee or custodian. The Internal Revenue Service does not review or approve investments.

If the trustee or custodian of an account described above is not a bank (and in the case of Archer MSAs and health savings accounts, a bank or an insurance company) or an approved nonbank trustee or nonbank custodian, the amounts held in such account (including earned interest) will be deemed distributed and includible in gross income in the year(s) the account's trustee or custodian was not a bank or, if applicable, an insurance company, or an approved nonbank trustee or nonbank custodian. Contributions made to such account are not deductible from gross income and will be disallowed if claimed on an income tax return.

This list of approved nonbank trustees and nonbank custodians includes their names, addresses, and the date each application was approved.

If an approved nonbank trustee or custodian believes that the information about it is incorrect, incomplete, or that it has been incorrectly omitted from this list, it may, on or before August 13, 2007, notify the Service in writing of any changes it proposes to the list. This notification should include a copy of the notice of approval.

The notification should be addressed to:

Internal Revenue Service
SE:T:EP:RA:T1
Announcement 2007–47
1111 Constitution Ave., NW — PE
Washington, DC 20224

Drafting Information

The principal author of this announcement is Calvin Thompson of the Employee Plans, Tax Exempt and Government Entities Division. Please contact Mr. Thompson at 202–283–9596 (not a toll-free number), if there are any questions regarding the publication of this list. Written inquiries concerning this announcement should be addressed to the Internal Revenue Service at the above address.

APPROVED Nonbank Trustees/Custodians as of December 31, 2006		
Name	Address	Approval Date
1. A.B. Culbertson & Co.	1250 Continental Plaza Fort Worth, TX 76102	5/15/1984
2. A.G. Becker & Co.	Chicago, IL	12/12/1979
3. A.G. Edwards & Sons, Inc.	One North Jefferson St. Louis, MO 63103	11/26/1980
4. ABN AMRO Securities LLC	55 East 52nd Street New York, NY 10022	9/7/2000
5. Adler, Coleman Clearing Corp.	20 Broad St. New York, NY 10005	4/7/1987

APPROVED Nonbank Trustees/Custodians as of December 31, 2006		
Name	Address	Approval Date
6. Advest, Inc.	280 Trumbull Street Hartford, CT 06103	1/24/1989
7. Aisel & Co.	20 Broad Street New York, NY 10005	4/26/1991
8. American Brokerage Services, Inc.	131 Lafayette Ave. Detroit, MI 48226	9/18/1991
9. American Capital Marketing, Inc. (FKA American General Capital)	2777 Allen Parkway Houston, TX 77215	6/25/1984
10. American Express Financial Corp.	200 AXP Financial Center Minneapolis, MN 55474	8/12/1977
11. American Heritage Life Ins. Co.	76 South Laura Street Jacksonville, FL 32202	12/11/1984
12. American Transtech, Inc.	8000 Baymeadows Way Jacksonville, FL 32256	8/15/1990
13. Ameritrade, Inc.	4211 South 102nd Street Omaha, NE 68127–1031	4/18/1984
14. Analytic Investment Management, Inc.	2222 Martin Street, Suite 230 Irvine, CA 92715–1454	5/9/1989
15. Aspen Partnership	1895 Claremont Road Hoffman Estates, IL 60195	10/25/1990
16. B.C. Ziegler & Co.	215 North Main Street West Bend, WI 53095	9/27/1985
17. Banc of America Securities LLC	100 North Tryon Street NC 1–007–20–01 Charlotte, NC 28255	4/30/2003
18. Banc One Capital Corporation	P.O. Box 18277 90 North High Street Columbus, OH 43218	2/24/1992
19. Bank Hapoulim B.M.	6501 Wilshire Blvd. Los Angeles, CA 90048	5/15/1986
20. Bank Julius Baer & Co., LTD	330 Madison Avenue New York, NY 10017	12/15/1988
21. Bank Leumi Le — Israel B.N. Western Hemisphere Regional Mgt.	242 Fifth Avenue New York, NY 10022	2/10/1982
22. Bartlett & Co.	36 East Fourth Street Cincinnati, OH 45202	2/1/1989
23. Bear, Stearns & Co., Inc.	5 Hanover Square New York, NY 10004	6/2/1986
24. Bear, Sterns Securities Corp.	2 Broadway, 12th Floor New York, NY 10004	6/24/1991
25. Berklee College of Music, Inc.	1140 Boylston Street Boston, MA 02110	5/9/1989
26. Bernard L. Madoff Investment Securities LLC	885 Third Avenue New York, NY 10022	7/7/2004
27. BISYS Fund Services, Inc.	3425 Stelzer Rd. Columbus, OH 43219	12/31/2003

APPROVED Nonbank Trustees/Custodians as of December 31, 2006		
Name	Address	Approval Date
28. Blunt Ellis & Loewi, Inc.	225 East Mason Street Milwaukee, WI 53202	1/25/1982
29. BNY Clearing Services, LLC (FKA Kemper Clearing Corporation)	111 East Kilbourn Ave. Milwaukee, WI 53202	8/21/1989
30. Boettcher & Company, Inc.	828 Seventeenth Street Denver, CO 80201	8/10/1987
31. Brown & Company Securities Corporation	20 Winthrop Square Boston, MA 02110	2/27/1985
32. Bruns, Nordeman, Rea & Co.	New York, NY	10/31/1977
33. Burke, Christensen & Lewis Securities, Inc.	120 S. La Salle Street Suite 940 Chicago, IL 60603	3/11/1986
34. Burton J. Vincent, Chesley & Co.	105 West Adams Street Chicago, IL 60603	3/25/1982
35. Butler Wick & Co., Inc.	City Center One Bldg. Youngstown, OH 44501	10/8/1992
36. BUYandHold Securities Corporation	110 Wall Street New York, NY 10005	10/5/2000
37. Carolina Securities Corp.	239 Fayetteville St. Mall Raleigh, NC 27602	8/29/1983
38. Chapin, Davis & Company, Inc.	3 Village Square, Cross Keys Baltimore, MD 21210	12/7/1983
39. Charles Schwab & Co., Inc.	101 Montgomery Street San Francisco, CA 94104	1/8/1982
40. Christian & Missionary Alliance	P.O. Box C Nyack, NY 10960	8/15/1985
41. CIBC World Markets Corporation	200 Liberty Street New York, NY 10281	7/26/1977
42. Citigroup Global Markets, Inc.	388 Greenwich St. New York, NY 10105	7/22/1985
43. City Securities Corp.	135 North Pennsylvania Street Indianapolis, IN 46204	12/21/1982
44. Commerce First Thrift	Midvale, UT 84047	5/25/1978
45. Commonwealth of Kentucky	105 Sea Hero Road, Suite 1 Frankfort, KY 40601–8862	6/5/2006
46. Comprehensive Investment Services, Inc.	One Moody Plaza Galveston, TX 77550	6/16/2000
47. Continental Trust Co.	17110 Dallas Parkway Suite 200 Dallas, TX 75248	2/22/1977
48. Croatian Fraternal Union Of America	100 Delaney Drive Pittsburgh, PA 15235	10/12/2006
49. D. A. Davidson & Co.	Davidson Building 8 Third Street North Great Falls, MT 59403	6/11/1982

APPROVED Nonbank Trustees/Custodians as of December 31, 2006		
Name	Address	Approval Date
50. D.J. St. Germain, Inc.	1500 Main Street Springfield, MA 01115	1/1/1977
51. Davenport & Co. of Virginia, Inc.	901 E. Cary Street Richmond, VA 23219	2/2/1987
52. Davenport & Company LLC	901 East Cary Street Richmond, VA 23219	3/31/1997
53. Deutsche Bank Securities Corp. d.b.a. C.J. Lawrence Deutsche	1290 Avenue of the Americas New York, NY 10104	3/14/1980
54. Deutsche Bank Securities, Inc.	1 South Street Baltimore, MD 21203	4/11/1994
55. Dougherty, Dawkins, Strand & Yost, Inc.	100 South Fifth Street Suite 2300 Minneapolis, MN 55402	2/22/1986
56. Dresdner Kleinwort Wasserstein Securities LLC	75 Wall Street New York, NY 10005	10/9/2002
57. Dreyfus Investment Services Corp.	Two Mellon Bank Center Pittsburgh, PA 15259	5/18/1989
58. Duncan-Williams, Inc.	5860 Ridgeway Center Parkway Memphis, TN 38120	12/13/1995
59. E*Trade Clearing LLC	10951 White Rock Road Rancho Cordova, CA 95670	9/3/2002
60. E*Trade Securities LLC	4500 Bohannon Drive Menlo Park, CA 94025	8/30/2002
61. E*Trade Securities, Inc.	480 California Avenue Palo Alto, CA 94306	2/1/1996
62. Eads Generoe Trust	St. Louis, MO	2/3/1977
63. Edward D. Jones & Co.	201 Progress Parkway Maryland Height, MO 63043	5/30/1985
64. El Paso Electric Co.	P.O. Box 982 El Paso, TX 79960	6/15/1983
65. Elan Investment Services, Inc.	777 East Wisconsin Avenue Milwaukee, WI 53282	12/21/1987
66. Emmett A. Larkin Co., Inc.	100 Bush Street San Francisco, CA 94104	4/17/1986
67. Eppler, Guerin & Turner, Inc.	2001 Bryan Tower, Suite 2300 Dallas, TX 75201	9/6/1984
68. EVEREN Securities, Inc.	77 West Wacker Drive Chicago, IL 60601–1694	11/19/1998
69. Fahnestock & Co., Inc. (FKA Edward A. Viner & Co.)	110 Wall Street New York, NY 10005	4/15/1982
70. Fechtor, Detwiler & Co., Inc.	155 Federal Street Boston, MA 02110	3/26/1982
71. Ferris, Baker Watts, Inc. (FKA Ferris & Company)	1720 Eye Street, NW Washington, DC 20006	12/4/1987

APPROVED Nonbank Trustees/Custodians as of December 31, 2006		
Name	Address	Approval Date
72. Fiduciary Services Corporation	310 Commercial Drive Savannah, GA 31406	10/2/2003
73. Financial Data Services, Inc.	400 Atrium Drive Somerset, NJ 08873	11/14/1990
74. First Albany Corp.	41 State Street Albany, NY 12207	9/26/1979
75. First Clearing Corporation	10700 Wheat First Drive Glen Allen, VA 23060	4/21/1999
76. First Clearing, LLC (FKA First Clearing Corporation)	10700 Wheat First Drive Glen Allen, VA 23060	5/30/2003
77. First Illinois Capital Corp.	424 7th Street Plaza 7 Rockford, IL 61110	5/27/1982
78. First Manhattan Co.	437 Madison Avenue New York, NY 10022	1/26/1990
79. First of Michigan Corporation	100 Renaissance Center 26th Floor Detroit, MI 48243	8/31/1994
80. Fiserv Securities, Inc.	One Commerce Square 2005 Market Street Philadelphia, PA 19103	11/15/1984
81. Fleet Clearing Corporation	67 Wall Street New York, NY 10005	12/3/1986
82. Fleet Norstar Securities, Inc.	14 Wall Street New York, NY 10005	8/30/1991
83. Fleet Securities, Inc.	26 Broadway New York, NY 10004	5/3/1983
84. Folger, Nolan, Fleming & Douglass	725 15th Street, N.W. Washington, DC 20015	9/16/1981
85. Freedom Capital Management Corporation	One Beacon Street Boston, MA 02108	8/29/1991
86. Freeman Welwood & Co., Inc.	1501 Fourth Avenue Suite 1700 Seattle, WA 98101	2/13/1996
87. General Conference of the Mennonite Brethren Churches, Board of Trustees	315 South Lincoln Hillsboro, KS 67063	3/8/1983
88. Goldman, Sachs & Co.	85 Broad Street New York, NY 10004	12/8/1982
89. Greater Beneficial Union of Pittsburgh	4254 Clairton Blvd. Pittsburgh, PA 15227–3394	9/24/2004
90. Greek Catholic Union of the U.S.A.	5400 Tuscarawas Rd. Beaver, PA 15009–9513	5/24/2000
91. Gruntal & Co., Inc.	14 Wall Street New York, NY 10005	6/13/1984
92. GuideStone Financial Services	2401 Cedar Springs Road Dallas, TX 75201–1498	4/10/2001

APPROVED Nonbank Trustees/Custodians as of December 31, 2006		
Name	Address	Approval Date
93. H&R Block Financial Advisors, Inc.	735 Griswold Street Detroit, MI 48226	12/8/1983
94. H.G. Wellington & Co., Inc.	14 Wall Street New York, NY 10005	9/13/1993
95. H.M. Payson & Co.	One Portland Square P.O. Box 31 Portland, ME 04112	8/20/1987
96. Halpert and Company, Inc.	284 Millburn Avenue Millburn, NJ 07041	4/17/1996
97. Hamilton Investments, Inc. (FKA Illinois Company, Inc.)	30 North La Salle Street Chicago, IL 60602	8/6/1982
98. Hampshire Funding, Inc.	One Granite Place P.O. Box 2005 Concord, NH 03301	5/26/1988
99. Hanifen, Imhoff Clearing Corp.	1125 17th Street Denver, CO 80217	4/22/1997
100. Hanifen, Imhoff, Inc.	1125 17th Street, Suite 1700 Denver, CO 80202	12/3/1985
101. Harrisdirect, LLC	Harborside Financial Center 501 Plaza II Jersey City, NJ 07311	5/1/2002
102. Hartford Life Insurance Co.	Hartford Plaza Hartford, CT 06106	3/3/1982
103. Hartford Securities Distribution Company	200 Hopmeadow Street Simsbury, CT 06089	3/9/2006
104. Hazlett, Burt & Watson, Inc.	1300 Chapline Street Wheeling, WV 26003	4/11/1995
105. HealthEquity, Inc.	5151 East Broadway Boulevard Suite 510 Tucson, AZ 85711	2/27/2006
106. Heartland Securities, Inc.	208 South LaSalle Street Chicago, IL 60604	3/6/1984
107. Henry Scott, Inc.	Philadelphia, PA	3/23/1982
108. Herzfeld & Stern, Inc.	30 Broad Street New York, NY 10004	12/12/1984
109. Herzog, Heine, Geduld, Inc.	26 Broadway New York, NY 10004	2/11/1982
110. Holt & Collins	188 Embarcadero Suite 760 San Francisco, CA 94105	9/8/1988
111. Home Life Financial Assurance Corporation	2400 West Bay Drive Largo, FL 33540	11/13/1986
112. Howard, Weil, Labouisse, Friedrichs, Inc.	1100 Paydrus Street Suite 900 New Orleans, LA 70163	12/28/1987

APPROVED Nonbank Trustees/Custodians as of December 31, 2006		
Name	Address	Approval Date
113. Huntleigh Securities Corporation	222 South Central Avenue St. Louis, MO 63102	10/22/1997
114. I.M. Simon & Co.	7730 Forsyth Blvd. Clayton, MO 63105	11/3/1981
115. iClearing, LLC	100 Wood Avenue South Iselin, NJ 08830	2/7/2001
116. Integrated Fund Services, Inc.	221 East Fourth Street Suite 300 Cincinnati, OH 45202	5/15/2003
117. Investment Advisers, Inc.	1100 Dain Tower Minneapolis, MN 55440	10/9/1981
118. ISDA Fraternal Association	419 Wood Street Pittsburgh, PA 15222	10/28/2004
119. Isler, Colling & McAdams	Portland, OR	10/5/1978
120. J.C. Bradford & Co.	330 Commerce Street Nashville, TN 37201	2/28/1982
121. J.J.B. Hilliard, W.L. Lyons, Inc.	Hilliard Lyons Center 501 South Fourth St. Louisville, KY 40202	2/11/1992
122. Jacob Engle Foundation, Inc. (The)	P.O. Box 1136 Upland, CA 91786	3/25/1983
123. Janney Montgomery Scott, Inc.	1801 Market Street Philadelphia, PA 19103	3/23/1982
124. Jefferson Pilot Investor Services, Inc.	100 North Greene Street Greensboro, NC 27401	10/22/1979
125. Jesup, Josephthal & Co., Inc.	One Whitehall Street New York, NY 10004	12/18/1990
126. John Hancock Clearing Corporation	200 Liberty Street New York, NY 10281	3/21/1991
127. John Hancock Mutual Life Insurance Company	John Hancock Place 200 Clarendon Street Boston, MA 02117	8/24/1993
128. Juran & Moody, Inc.	Minnesota Mutual Life Center 400 North Robert Street Suite 800 Saint Paul, MN 55101	5/27/1994
129. Kagin Numismatic Services, Ltd.	1000 Insurance Exchange Bldg. Des Moines, IA 50309	3/18/1980
130. KH Funding Company	10801 Lockwood Drive Suite 370 Silver Spring, MD 20901	2/13/2002
131. Kirkpatrick, Pettis, Smith, Polian, Inc.	1623 Farnam Street Suite 700 Omaha, NE 68102	8/18/1981
132. L.F. Rothchild, Unterberg, Towbin	55 Water Street New York, NY 10041	12/23/1985

APPROVED Nonbank Trustees/Custodians as of December 31, 2006		
Name	Address	Approval Date
133. Legg Mason Wood Walker, Inc.	111 S. Calvert Street P.O. Box 1476 Baltimore, MD 21203	6/4/1985
134. Lehman Brothers, Inc.	200 Vesey Street New York, NY 10285	12/20/2000
135. Lester Sumrall Evangelistic Association, Inc.	530 East Ireland Road South Bend, IN 46614	9/2/1988
136. Liberty Life Insurance Co.	P.O. Box 789 Greenville, SC 29602	9/3/1982
137. Manley, Bennett, McDonald & Co.	St. Louis, MO	1/1/1977
138. McDonald & Company Securities, Inc.	580 Walnut Street Cincinnati, OH 45202	12/15/1983
139. MEGA Life and Health Insurance Company	501 West Interstate 44 Service Road Oklahoma City, OK 73118	5/29/1991
140. Menold, Crawford, Hippler & Co.	23930 Michigan Ave. Dearborn, MI 40126	12/9/1988
141. Merrill, Lynch, Pierce, Fenner & Smith, Inc.	1700 Merrill Lynch Drive MSC 0703 Pennington, NJ 08534	8/3/1987
142. Merrimack Valley Investment, Inc.	367 Kingsbury Ave. Haverhill, MA 01830	9/28/1984
143. Mesirow Financial, Inc.	350 N. Clark Street Chicago, IL 60610	5/28/1982
144. Metropolitan Life Insurance Co.	One Madison Avenue New York, NY 10010	1/28/1987
145. Metropolitan Mortgage & Securities Corporation	W. 292 Sprague Ave. Spokane, WA 99204	11/10/1976
146. Mid-Ohio Securities Corp.	225 Burns Road Elyria, OH 44036	1/28/1983
147. Mid-States Enterprises, Inc.	Carroll, IA	12/30/1976
148. Miller Johnson & Kuehn, Inc.	5500 Wayzata Blvd. Minneapolis, MN 55416	11/15/2000
149. Milwaukee Company (The)	250 East Wisconsin Avenue Milwaukee, WI 53202	9/15/1986
150. MKI Securities Corp.	61 Broadway New York, NY 10006	4/17/1985
151. Money Management Associates	4922 Fairmont Avenue Bethesda, MD 20814	5/26/1987
152. Moody Bible Institute of Chicago	820 N. La Salle Boulevard Chicago, IL 60610–3284	4/25/2003
153. Moore & Schley, Cameron & Co.	Two Broadway New York, NY 10004	11/15/1977

APPROVED Nonbank Trustees/Custodians as of December 31, 2006		
Name	Address	Approval Date
154. Morgan Keegan & Company, Inc.	Morgan Keegan Tower Fifty Front Street Memphis, TN 38108	1/27/1982
155. Morgan Stanley & Co. Incorporated	1585 Broadway New York, NY 10036	3/22/2004
156. Morgan Stanley DW Inc.	1585 Broadway New York, NY 10036	5/29/1986
157. Mortgage Loan Services, Inc.	780 Lynnhaven Parkway Suite 200 Virginia Beach, VA 23452	3/15/1995
158. Moseley, Hallgarten, Estabrook & Weeden, Inc.	One New York Plaza New York, NY 10004	12/10/1985
159. Murphy Favre, Inc.	W. 601 Riverside 9th Floor Spokane, WA 99201	8/2/1976
160. Mutual Service Cooperative	Two Pine Tree Drive Arden Hills, MN 55112	6/6/1996
161. Myriad Corporation	1400 50th Street West Des Moines, IA 50265	7/20/1977
162. National Bank of Greece, S.A.	33 State Street Boston, MA 02109	2/4/1988
163. National Covenant Properties	5701 N. Francisco Dr. Chicago, IL 60625	6/30/1978
164. National Investor Services Corp.	44 Wall Street New York, NY 10005	3/18/1996
165. National Slovak Society of the U.S.A.	351 Valley Brook Road McMurray, PA 15317–3337	10/28/2004
166. Nationwide Advisory Services, Inc. (Nationwide Financial Services, Inc.)	One Nationwide Plaza Columbus, OH 43216	9/25/1985
167. Nationwide Credit Union	One Nationwide Plaza Columbus, OH 43216	4/13/1978
168. NBC Securities, Inc.	1927 First Avenue North Birmingham, AL 35203	7/16/1996
169. Neuberger & Berman	522 Fifth Ave. New York, NY 10036	10/4/1983
170. Newhard, Cook & Co.	300 North Broadway St. Louis, MO 63102	6/4/1985
171. Oberweis Securities, Inc.	841 North Lake Street Aurora, IL 60506	2/11/1985
172. Parker/Hunter, Inc.	600 Grant Street Pittsburgh, PA 15219	6/15/1990
173. Partnership Services, Inc.	5520 LBJ Freeway Suite 430 Dallas, TX 75240	3/31/1993
174. Peninsular Securities Co.	Waters Building Grand Rapids, MI 49503	1/28/1985

APPROVED Nonbank Trustees/Custodians as of December 31, 2006		
Name	Address	Approval Date
175. Penson Financial Services, Inc.	1700 Pacific Avenue Suite 1400 Dallas, TX 75201	6/9/2005
176. Perelman-Carley & Associates, Inc.	Twin Towers 3000 Farnam Street Omaha, NE 68131	1/13/1989
177. Perkins Coie LLP	1201 Third Avenue Suite 4800 Seattle, WA 98101–3099	8/2/2004
178. Pershing LLC	One Pershing Plaza Jersey City, NJ 07399	12/4/1985
179. Pflueger & Baerwald, Inc.	Mills Building 220 Montgomery Street Room 1000 San Francisco, CA 94104	11/9/1981
180. PFS Investments, Inc.	3120 Breckenridge Boulevard Duluth, GA 30199	9/28/1995
181. Pioneer Financial Services, Inc.	4233 Roanoke Road Kansas City, MO 64111	1/25/1985
182. Pioneer Investment Management USA	60 State Street Boston, MA 02109	2/21/1986
183. Piper Jaffray & Co.	Piper Jaffray Center 800 Nicollet Mall Minneapolis, MN 55402–7020	4/21/1982
184. Polish Falcons of America	615 Iron City Drive Pittsburgh, PA 15205–4397	11/3/2004
185. Prescott, Ball & Turben, Inc.	1331 Euclid Ave. Cleveland, OH 44115	1/27/1983
186. PrimeVest Financial Services, Inc.	400 First Street South St. Cloud, MN 56301–3600	12/8/1993
187. Principal Life Insurance Company	711 High Street Des Moines, IA 50392–0001	7/27/1988
188. PWMCO, LLC	310 South Michigan Avenue Chicago, IL 60604	1/6/2005
189. R. Rowland & Co., Inc.	St. Louis, MO	3/29/1984
190. R.G. Dickinson & Co.	200 Des Moines Building 405 6th Ave. Des Moines, IA 50309	7/20/1983
191. R.J. Steichen & Company	Midwest Plaza, Suite 100 801 Nicolett Mall Minneapolis, MN 55402–2526	5/21/1993
192. Raymond James & Associates, Inc.	880 Carillon Parkway P.O. Box 12749 St. Petersburg, FL 33733–2749	4/26/1982
193. Raymond James & Associates, Inc.	880 Carillon Parkway P.O. Box 12749 St. Petersburg, FL 33733–2749	3/8/1982

APPROVED Nonbank Trustees/Custodians as of December 31, 2006		
Name	Address	Approval Date
194. RBC Dain Rauscher, Inc.	Dain Rauscher Plaza 60 South Sixth Street Minneapolis, MN 55402–4422	3/2/1998
195. RBC Dain Rauscher, Inc.	Dain Rauscher Plaza 60 South Sixth Street Minneapolis, MN 55402–4422	1/22/1982
196. Regan MacKenzie, Incorporated	999 Third Avenue Suite 4300 Seattle, WA 98104	8/31/1989
197. Regions Investment Company, Inc.	2011 Fourth Avenue North Birmingham, AL 35203	7/20/2000
198. Reserve Management Company, Inc.	810 Seventh Avenue New York, NY 10019	10/18/1989
199. Robert W. Baird & Co., Inc.	777 East Wisconsin Avenue Milwaukee, WI 53202	6/10/2004
200. Robert W. Baird & Co., Inc.	777 E. Wisconsin Avenue Milwaukee, WI 53202	7/31/1986
201. Robinson-Humphrey Co., Inc. (The)	Two Peachtree Street, N.W. Atlanta, GA 30383	5/24/1982
202. Romano Bros. & Co.	820 Davis Street Evanston, IL 60201	9/28/1984
203. Rose & Company Investment Brokers, Inc.	141 West Jackson Blvd. Chicago, IL 60604	4/14/1982
204. Rotan Mosle, Inc.	1500 S. Tower Pennzoil Place P.O. Box 3226 Houston, TX 77001	5/6/1980
205. Rushmore Investment Brokers, Inc.	4922 Fairmont Avenue Bethesda, MD 20814	9/24/1986
206. Sanford C. Bernstein & Co., Inc.	767 Fifth Avenue New York, NY 10153	11/13/1986
207. Santa Ana City Employees Credit Union	800 West Santa Ana Blvd. Santa Ana, CA 92701	3/25/1982
208. Saturna Capital Corporation	101 Prospect Street Bellingham, WA 98227–2838	3/28/1991
209. SBCI Swiss Bank Corporation Investment Banking, Inc.	222 Broadway, 4th Floor New York, NY 10038	2/11/1992
210. SBM Financial Services, Inc.	8400 Normandale Lake Blvd. Suite 1150 Minneapolis, MN 55437	5/13/1995
211. Scott & Stringfellow, Inc. (FKA Craige, Inc.)	823 E. Main Street Richmond, VA 23219	5/5/1999
212. Scottsdale Securities, Inc.	12855 Flushing Meadow St. Louis, MO 63131	10/9/1996
213. Securities America, Inc.	7100 West Center Road Suite 500 Omaha, NE 68106–2798	9/21/2006

APPROVED Nonbank Trustees/Custodians as of December 31, 2006		
Name	Address	Approval Date
214. Securities Management Research, Inc.	Two Moody Plaza Galveston, TX 77550	6/22/1978
215. Security Management Company, LLC (Formerly, Security Management Co.)	700 SW Harrison Street Topeka, KS 66636–0001	8/14/1996
216. SG Cowen Securities Corporation	1221 Avenue of the Americas New York, NY 10020	6/30/1998
217. ShareBuilder Securities Corporation	1000 124th Avenue, NE Bellevue, WA 98005	4/15/2003
218. SMA Services, Inc.	35 Lakeshore Drive Birmingham, AL 35209	8/27/1998
219. Smith, Moore & Co.	400 Locust Street St. Louis, MO 63102	1/18/1983
220. Southwest Securities, Inc.	Renaissance Tower 1201 Elm Street Suite 4300 Dallas, TX 75270	12/9/1992
221. Spear Rees & Co.	505 North Brand Boulevard Sixteenth Floor Glendale, CA 91203	1/13/1988
222. Spear, Leeds & Kellog	120 Broadway New York, NY 10271	3/29/1996
223. State Bond and Mortgage Company	8500 Normandale Lake Boulevard Minneapolis, MN 55437	12/21/1990
224. State Employees Credit Union	801 Hillsborough Street P.O. Box 26807 Raleigh, NC 27611–6807	1/1/1977
225. State Farm Investment Management Corporation	One State Farm Plaza Bloomington, IL 61410	9/22/1999
226. Stephens, Inc.	111 Center Street Little Rock, AR 72201	12/4/1987
227. Stern Brothers & Co.	1100 Main Street, Suite 2200 Kansas City, MO 64199	12/15/1987
228. Sterne, Agee & Leach, Inc.	1500 Am South-Sonat Tower Birmingham, AL 35203	9/11/1981
229. Stifel, Nicolaus & Co., Inc.	500 North Broadway St. Louis, MO 63102	9/9/1981
230. Summit Discount Brokerage (FKA Lehigh Securities Corp.)	1457 MacArthur Road Lehigh Valley, PA 18002	4/4/1990
231. Sunpoint Securities, Inc.	911 W. Loop 281 Longview, TX 75604	4/1/1998
232. SunTrust Capital Markets, Inc.	3333 Peachtree Road, NE Atlanta, GA 30326	5/27/1982
233. Sutro & Company, Inc.	201 California Street San Francisco, CA 94111–5096	12/8/1988
234. Swiss American Securities, Inc.	100 Wall Street New York, NY 10005	12/2/1980

APPROVED Nonbank Trustees/Custodians as of December 31, 2006		
Name	Address	Approval Date
235. Texas First Securities Corporation	1360 Post Oak Blvd. Suite 120 Houston, TX 77056	11/17/1988
236. TIAA-CREF Individual & Institutional Services, Inc.	730 Third Avenue New York, NY 10017	9/9/2002
237. Tucker Anthony, Incorporated	One Beacon Street Boston, MA 02108	10/23/1980
238. UBS Financial Services, Inc. (FKA UBS Paine Webber, Inc.)	1285 Avenue of the Americas New York, NY 10019	5/12/1989
239. UBS Financial Services, Inc. (FKA UBS Paine Webber, Inc.)	1285 Avenue of the Americas New York, NY 10019	8/26/2004
240. Ukrainian National Association	2200 Route 10 Parsippany, NJ 07054	9/24/2004
241. Unified Financial Securities, Inc.	429 North Pennsylvania Indianapolis, IN 46204	10/28/1976
242. United of Omaha Life Insurance Co.	Mutual of Omaha Plaza Omaha, NE 68175	3/16/1982
243. Variable Annuity Life Insurance Company	2929 Allen Parkway Houston, TX 77019	3/16/2006
244. W.H. Reaves & Co., Inc.	30 Montgomery Street Jersey City, NJ 07302	12/7/1990
245. W.H. Turlington & Co.	509 East Center Street Lexington, NC 27292	11/3/1980
246. Wachovia Securities, Inc.	201 North Tryon Street Charlotte, NC 28202	4/6/1990
247. Wachovia Securities, LLC	901 East Byrd Street Richmond, VA 23219	7/1/2003
248. Wayne Hummer & Co.	300 South Wacker Drive Chicago, IL 60606	1/25/1983
249. Web Street Securities, Inc.	222 South Riverside Plaza 11th Floor Chicago, IL 60601	4/27/2000
250. Wedbush Morgan Securities	1000 Wilshire Boulevard Los Angeles, CA 90030	12/24/1984
251. Weiss, Peck & Greer	One New York Plaza New York, NY 10004	6/16/1982
252. Wells Advisors, Inc.	3885 Holcomb Bridge Road Norcross, GA 30092	3/20/1992
253. Wexford LLC Corporation	1 New York Plaza, 11th Floor New York, NY 10292	6/30/1998

APPROVED Nonbank Trustees/Custodians as of December 31, 2006		
Name	Address	Approval Date
254. Wheat, First Securities, Inc.	707 East Main Street P.O. Box 1357 Richmond, VA 23211	3/23/1983
255. William R. Hough & Co., Inc.	100 2nd Avenue South Suite 800 St. Petersburg, FL 33701	4/18/1995

Corporate Reorganizations; Additional Guidance on Distributions Under Sections 368(a)(1)(D) and 354(b)(1)(B); Correction

Announcement 2007–48

AGENCY: Internal Revenue Service (IRS), Treasury.

ACTION: Correcting amendment.

SUMMARY: This document contains a correction to temporary regulations (T.D. 9313, 2007–13 I.R.B. 805) that were published in the **Federal Register** on Thursday, March 1, 2007 (72 FR 9262) providing guidance regarding the qualification of certain transactions as reorganizations described in section 368(a)(1)(D) where no stock and/or securities of the acquiring corporation are issued and distributed in the transaction.

DATES: This correcting amendment is effective April 13, 2007.

FOR FURTHER INFORMATION CONTACT: Bruce A. Decker at (202) 622–7550 (not a toll-free number).

SUPPLEMENTARY INFORMATION:

Background

The temporary regulations that are the subject of this correction are under section 368 of the Internal Revenue Code.

Need for Correction

As published, temporary regulations (T.D. 9313) contain an error that may prove to be misleading and is in need of clarification.

* * * * *

Correction of Publication

Accordingly, 26 CFR part 1 is corrected by making the following amendment:

PART 1—INCOME TAXES

Paragraph 1. The authority citation for part 1 continues to read, in part, as follows:

Authority: 26 U.S.C. 7805 * * *

Par. 2. Section 1.368–2T is amended by revising paragraph (l)(2)(iv) to read as follows:

§1.368–2T Definition of terms (temporary).

* * * * *

(l) * * *

(2) * * *

(iv) *Exception.* This paragraph (l)(2) does not apply to a transaction otherwise described in section 1.358–6(b)(2) or section 368(a)(1)(G) by reason of section 368(a)(2)(D).

* * * * *

LaNita Van Dyke,
*Chief, Publications and Regulations Branch,
Legal Processing Division,
Associate Chief Counsel
(Procedure and Administration).*

(Filed by the Office of the Federal Register on April 12, 2007, 8:45 a.m., and published in the issue of the Federal Register for April 13, 2007, 72 F.R. 18575)

Part I. Rulings and Decisions Under the Internal Revenue Code of 1986

Section 118.—Contributions to the Capital of a Corporation

26 CFR 1.118–1: Contributions to the capital of a corporation.

Contributions to the capital of a corporation; nonshareholder contributions. This ruling provides that payments received by a corporation under the federal universal service support mechanisms do not represent a nonshareholder contribution to capital under section 118(a) of the Code. The federal universal service support mechanisms are funded by contributions from telecommunications carriers. Telecommunications carriers receive support payments to provide discounted telecommunications services or telecommunication services in high cost areas.

Rev. Rul. 2007–31

ISSUE

Is universal service support received by a corporation under the universal service support mechanisms a nonshareholder contribution to capital under section 118(a) of the Internal Revenue Code?

FACTS

The federal universal service support mechanisms are required by 47 U.S.C. § 254. The Federal Communication Commission (Commission) is required to establish periodically the services to be supported by federal universal service support mechanisms. 47 U.S.C. § 254(c)(1). The Commission has established that the following services be supported by federal universal service support mechanisms: (1) voice grade access to the public switched network; (2) local usage; (3) dual tone multi-frequency signaling or its functional equivalent; (4) single-party service or its functional equivalent; (5) access to emergency services; (6) access to operator services; (7) access to interexchange service; (8) access to directory assistance; and (9) toll limitations for qualifying low-income consumers. 47 C.F.R. § 54.101(a). An eligible telecommunications carrier must offer each of the services in order to receive federal universal service support. 47 C.F.R. § 54.101(b).

The Universal Service Administrative Company (Administrator) administers the federal universal service support mechanisms. 47 C.F.R. § 54.701. The Administrator is responsible for administering the following federal universal support mechanisms: (1) the high cost support mechanisms described in 47 C.F.R. part 54, subpart D; (2) the low income support mechanisms described in 47 C.F.R. part 54, subpart E; (3) the schools and libraries support mechanism described in 47 C.F.R. part 54, subpart F; (4) the rural health care support mechanism described in 47 C.F.R. part 54, subpart G; (5) the interstate access universal support mechanism described in 47 C.F.R. part 54, subpart J; and (6) the interstate common line support mechanism described in 47 C.F.R. part 54, subpart K. 47 C.F.R. § 54.702(a). The Administrator is responsible for billing contributors, collecting contributions to the universal service support mechanisms, and disbursing universal service support funds. 47 C.F.R. § 54.702(b).

The federal universal service support mechanisms are funded by contributions from telecommunications carriers. Every telecommunications carrier that provides interstate telecommunications services must contribute, on an equitable and nondiscriminatory basis, to the specific, predictable, and sufficient mechanisms established by the Commission to preserve and advance universal service. 47 U.S.C. § 254(d). Entities that provide interstate telecommunications services to the public, or to such classes of users as to be effectively available to the public, for a fee will be considered telecommunications carriers providing interstate telecommunications services and must contribute to the universal service support mechanisms. 47 C.F.R. § 54.706(a). Federal universal service contribution costs may be recovered through interstate telecommunications-related charges to end users. 47 C.F.R. § 54.712(a).

In order to receive support, an eligible telecommunications carrier first must provide the supported services. The universal service support provided pursuant to 47 C.F.R. part 54, subparts D, J, and K (identified above) ensures that consumers in all regions of the nation have access to and pay rates for telecommunication services that are reasonably comparable to those in urban areas. The universal service support provided by 47 C.F.R. part 54, subparts E, F, and G (identified above) allows carriers to provide discounted, or reduced, rates to low income consumers, schools and libraries, and rural health care providers. The amount of federal universal service support received depends on either the discount offered to the targeted customers or the cost of providing service (the carrier's revenue requirement) in high cost areas. For financial accounting purposes, the Commission requires all carriers to record their federal universal service support receipts as revenue.

All carriers that receive universal service support must use that support only for the provision, maintenance, and upgrading of facilities and services for which the universal service support is intended. 47 U.S.C. § 254(e) and 47 C.F.R. § 54.7. This includes, for example, the ability to use the funds to reduce intrastate rates, to cover operating expenses (billing and marketing expenses) associated with the supported services, and to upgrade the facilities for the supported services. Annual certifications are required to be filed with the Administrator and the Commission with respect to universal service support from certain universal service support mechanisms stating that all universal service support received from such mechanisms will be used only for the provision, maintenance, and upgrading of facilities and services for which the support is intended.

LAW AND ANALYSIS

Section 118(a) of the Code provides that in the case of a corporation, gross income does not include any contribution to the capital of the taxpayer. The committee reports accompanying the enactment of what is now section 118(a) indicate that the provision was intended to codify the existing law that had developed through administrative and court decisions on the subject. H.R. Rep. No. 1337, 83d Cong., 2d Sess. 17 (1954); S. Rep. No. 1622, 83d Cong., 2d Sess. 18 (1954).

Section 1.118–1 of the Income Tax Regulations includes within the meaning of a contribution to capital, a contribution by a nonshareholder and cites as examples of nonshareholder contributions to capital: the value of land and other property contributed to a corporation by a governmental unit or by a civic group for the purpose of inducing the corporation to locate its business in a particular community, or for the purpose of enabling the corporation to expand its operating facilities. However, the exclusion from gross income does not apply to any money or property transferred to the corporation in consideration for goods or services rendered.

In *Detroit Edison Co. v. Commissioner*, 319 U.S. 98 (1943), 1943 C.B. 1019, the Supreme Court held that payments by prospective customers to an electric power company that were used by the company to construct the facilities necessary to deliver electricity to the customers were not nonshareholder contributions to capital. The Court found that the motivation for the prospective customers' contributions was to obtain electric services from the power company and, therefore, the contributions were payment for services. 319 U.S. at 102, 1943 C.B. at 1021.

In contrast, *Brown Shoe Co. v. Commissioner*, 339 U.S. 583 (1950), 1950–1 C.B. 38, held that money and property contributions by community groups to induce a shoe company to locate or expand its factory operations in the contributing communities were nonshareholder contributions to capital. The Court reasoned that when the motivation of the contributors is to benefit the community at large and the contributors do not anticipate any direct benefit from their contributions, the contributions are nonshareholder contributions to capital. 339 U.S. at 591, 1950–1 C.B. at 41.

The Court again considered this issue in *United States v. Chicago, Burlington & Quincy R.R.*, 412 U.S. 401 (1973), 1973–2 C.B. 428. In that case, the Court set forth the following five characteristics of a nonshareholder contribution to capital: (1) the contribution must become a permanent part of transferee's working capital structure; (2) the contribution may not be compensation, such as a direct payment for a specific, quantifiable service provided for the transferor by the transferee; (3) the contribution must be bargained for; (4) the asset transferred foreseeably must result in benefit to the transferee in an amount commensurate with its value; and (5) the asset ordinarily, if not always, will be employed in or contribute to the production of additional income and its value assured in that respect. 412 U.S. at 413, 1973–2 C.B. at 432.

In reaching its conclusion that the improvements at issue did not qualify as contributions to capital, the Court reasoned:

> Although the assets were not payments for specific, quantifiable services performed by CB&Q for the Government as a customer, other characteristics of the transaction lead us to the conclusion that, despite this, the assets did not qualify as contributions to capital. The facilities were not in any real sense bargained for by CB&Q. Indeed, except for the orders by state commissions and the government subsidies, the facilities would not have been constructed at all.

412 U.S. at 413–14, 1973–2 C.B. at 432.

In *Texas & Pacific Railway Co. v. United States*, 286 U.S. 285 (1932), XI–1 C.B. 263, the Court held that payments received by a railroad company from the federal government did not constitute a contribution to capital and thus were includible in income. The Court noted the Transportation Act of 1920 provided for payments representing a guarantee of minimum operating income to compensate the railroad during the transition from federal control to private ownership. The Court reasoned that the payments did not represent capital contributions:

> Here they were to be measured by a deficiency in operating income, and might be used for the payment of dividends, of operating expenses, of capital charges, or for any other purpose .... The Government's payments were not in their nature bounties, but an addition to a depleted operating revenue consequent upon a federal activity.

286 U.S. at 290, XI–1 C.B. at 265.

In *Deason v. Commissioner*, 590 F.2d 1377 (5th Cir. 1979), the Fifth Circuit held that payments received from the Department of Labor for job training for unemployed individuals were not a contribution to capital under section 118. The court affirmed the opinion of the Tax Court, which concluded that irrespective of the public benefit of reduced unemployment that occurred as a result of the payments, the payments constituted direct compensation for training services and thus could not be considered a contribution to capital.

As provided in section 1.118–1 and stated by the Supreme Court in *Detroit Edison* and *Chicago, Burlington & Quincy R.R.*, compensation in exchange for a specific quantifiable service constitutes taxable income, not a capital contribution. Indeed, the Court in *Brown Shoe* premised its decision that inducement payments by community groups to a private corporation for relocating and building a factory constituted a capital contribution, based on the specific absence of customers and payment for services. Conversely, these are precisely the factors that are present in the universal service support. There is a clear nexus between the universal service support and the provision of universal telecommunications services by the carriers. The motivation underlying the universal service support is to compensate the carriers for the shortfall in operating income for providing services at a discount to certain customers and/or providing services to customers in high cost areas at below cost rates. The universal service support is predicated on the carriers providing the mandated universal service and is an integral part of the government's mandate to insure that universal service is provided.

In addition, the universal service support does not satisfy the five characteristics of a nonshareholder contribution to capital set forth in *Chicago, Burlington & Quincy R.R.*, because the universal service support: (1) does not necessarily become a permanent part of the carrier's working capital structure because the support is not limited to the acquisition of capital assets and can be used to pay current expenses; (2) is made for specific, quantifiable telecommunication services to telecommunication customers of the carrier; (3) is not bargained for because the universal service support mechanisms are a unilateral government program and the method of participation by carriers is mandated (despite any certification requirements); (4) does not benefit the carrier commensurate with the value of the support because the support payments merely maintain the carrier's viability; and (5) does not necessarily generate additional income for the carrier because the support is not limited to the acquisition of capital assets that will generate additional income for the carrier, but can be used to pay current expenses or to replace capital assets.

The holdings in *Texas Pacific* and *Deason* also are illustrative in this context. In *Texas Pacific*, the federal government provided payments to fulfill a statutory public purpose and yet because of the inherent nature of the transaction as reimbursement for deficiencies in operating income, the payments did not warrant capital contribution treatment. In *Deason*, the federal government made payments that served the public goal of reducing unemployment. Despite the existence of a public benefit derived from the payment, the court concluded that the payments were compensation for services and therefore ineligible as a capital contribution. Similarly, although a public purpose is served by payment of the universal service support, and the payor is not the consumer of the universal telecommunications services, the universal service support is nonetheless compensation to the carriers for the provision of universal telecommunications services.

HOLDING

Universal service support received by a corporation under the universal service support mechanisms is not a nonshareholder contribution to capital under section 118(a) of the Code.

DRAFTING INFORMATION

The principal author of this revenue ruling is David McDonnell of the Office of Associate Chief Counsel (Passthroughs and Special Industries). For further information regarding this revenue ruling, contact Mr. McDonnell at (202) 622–3040 (not a toll-free call).

Section 166.—Bad Debts

A revenue ruling providing guidance as to the period in which a bank that has elected the conformity method of accounting under regulations section 1.166–2(d)(3) can treat uncollected interest as worthless. See Rev. Rul. 2007-32, page 1278.

Section 199.—Income Attributable to Domestic Production Activities

26 CFR 199–9: Application of section 199 to pass-thru entities for taxable years beginning on or before May 17, 2006, the enactment date of the Tax Increase Prevention and Reconciliation Act of 2005.
(Also § 1.199–3T.)

Income attributable to domestic production activities; qualifying in-kind partnerships. This ruling provides that a partnership engaged in the extraction and processing of minerals within the United States is a qualifying in-kind partnership for purposes of section 199 of the Code. Each partner of a qualifying in-kind partnership is treated as having manufactured, produced, grown, or extracted (MPGE) property MPGE by the partnership that is distributed to that partner.

Rev. Rul. 2007–30

This revenue ruling designates the extraction and processing of minerals (as defined in § 1.611–1(d)(5) of the Income Tax Regulations) as an activity within § 1.199–9(i)(2)(iii) and § 1.199–3T(i)(7)(ii)(C) of the temporary Income Tax Regulations. A partnership engaged solely in an activity or industry designated by the Secretary will be a qualifying in-kind partnership under §§ 1.199–9(i)(2) and 1.199–3T(i)(7)(ii).

Pursuant to §§ 1.199–9(i)(1) and 1.199–3T(i)(7)(i), each partner of a qualifying in-kind partnership is treated as having manufactured, produced, grown, or extracted (MPGE) property MPGE by the partnership that is distributed to that partner.

Sections 1.199–9(i)(2) and 1.199–3T(i)(7)(ii) provide that a qualifying in-kind partnership includes a partnership engaged solely in the extraction, refining, or processing of oil, natural gas, petrochemicals, or products derived from oil, natural gas, or petrochemicals in whole or in significant part within the United States; or the production or generation of electricity in the United States. Under §§ 1.199–9(i)(2)(iii) and 1.199–3T(i)(7)(ii)(C), a qualifying in-kind partnership may include a partnership engaged solely in an activity or industry designated by the Secretary by publication in the Internal Revenue Bulletin.

By this revenue ruling, the Internal Revenue Service designates the extraction and processing of minerals (as defined in § 1.611–1(d)(5)) as an activity within §§ 1.199–9(i)(2)(iii) and 1.199–3T(i)(7)(ii)(C). Accordingly, a partnership engaged solely in the extraction and processing of minerals within the United States will be a qualifying in-kind partnership under §§ 1.199–9(i)(2) and 1.199–3T(i)(7)(ii).

EFFECTIVE DATE

This revenue ruling is effective for taxable years beginning after December 31, 2004, the effective date of § 199. However, for taxable years beginning before June 1, 2006, a taxpayer may apply this revenue ruling only if the taxpayer applies §§ 1.199–1 through 1.199–8 to that taxable year.

DRAFTING INFORMATION

The principal author of this revenue ruling is David McDonnell of the Office of Associate Chief Counsel (Passthroughs and Special Industries). For further information regarding this revenue ruling, contact Mr. McDonnell at (202) 622–3040 (not a toll-free call).

Section 446.—General Rule for Methods of Accounting

A revenue ruling requiring an accrual method bank with a reasonable expectation of receiving future payments on a loan to include accrued interest (determined under regulations section 1.446–2) in gross income for the taxable year in which the right to receive the interest becomes fixed, notwithstanding bank regulatory rules that prevent accrual of the interest for regulatory purposes. See Rev. Rul. 2007-32, page 1278.

A revenue procedure providing the procedure under which a bank may change its method of accounting for uncollected interest to an elective safe harbor method based on the bank's collection experience. See Rev. Proc. 2007-33, page 1289.

Section 451.—General Rule for Taxable Year of Inclusion

A revenue procedure providing an elective safe harbor method of accounting for a bank's uncollected interest based on the bank's collection experience. See Rev. Proc. 2007-33, page 1289.

---

26 CFR 1.451–1: General rule for taxable year of inclusion.
(Also: Part I, §§ 166, 446; 1.166–2, 1.446–1, 1.446–2.)

Accrual of interest. This ruling requires an accrual method bank with a reasonable expectancy of receiving future payments on a loan to include accrued interest (determined under regulations section 1.446–2(a)(2)) in gross income for the taxable year in which the right to receive the interest becomes fixed, notwithstanding bank regulatory rules that prevent accrual of the interest for regulatory purposes. The ruling also provides guidance as to the period in which a bank that has elected the conformity method of accounting under regulations section 1.166–2(d)(3) can treat uncollected interest as worthless. Rev. Rul. 81–18 distinguished.

Rev. Rul. 2007–32

ISSUES

1. If federal banking rules require a bank to suspend the recognition of certain uncollected "accrued interest" as defined in § 1.446–2 of the Income Tax Regulations as income for regulatory financial statement purposes should the bank also cease recognizing uncollected accrued interest into income for federal income tax purposes?

2. If a bank uses a conformity method of accounting as provided for in § 1.166–2(d) but does not recognize uncollected accrued interest as income for regulatory financial statement purposes, when should the bank recognize a worthless debt with respect to uncollected accrued interest for federal income tax purposes?

3. If a bank receives payments on a loan where the bank for federal income tax purposes either (i) previously recognized the uncollected accrued interest as income and subsequently deducted the accrued interest receivable as a worthless debt under section 166 or (ii) did not recognized the uncollected accrued interest on the loan as income, how should the payments be characterized for federal income tax purposes?

FACTS

X corporation is a bank as defined in § 1.166–2(d)(4)(i). X determines its taxable income using an accrual method of accounting and files its federal income tax returns on a calendar year basis. Loans made by X are subject to § 1.446–2, which determines the amount of "accrued interest" related to each loan for federal income tax purposes.

X is subject to regulatory supervision by federal banking authorities ("supervisory authorities") and is required to prepare regulatory financial statements that comply with federal banking rules. For regulatory financial statement purposes, unless a loan is both well secured and in the process of collection, federal banking rules generally require that X suspend the recognition into income of uncollected accrued interest on a loan and reverse any previously recognized uncollected interest income if:

(i) the loan is maintained on a cash basis because of deterioration in the borrower's financial condition;

(ii) payment in full of principal or interest is not expected; or

(iii) payment of principal or interest has been in default for a period of 90 days or more.

Under federal banking rules, a loan may be considered a bankable asset (*i.e.,* not written off for regulatory financial statement purposes) even if accrued interest on the loan is no longer being recognized as income (or was previously recognized and subsequently charged off) for regulatory financial statement purposes. In this revenue ruling, the loan is referred to as a "non-accrual loan receivable."

In general, federal banking rules require a bank such as X to apply any payment received on a non-accrual loan receivable to reduce its recorded investment in the loan (*i.e.,* treat all monies that come in on the loan as a collection of loan principal) to the extent necessary to eliminate doubt as to collectibility. Therefore, for regulatory financial statement purposes, X characterizes any payment received on a non-accrual loan receivable as a payment of principal rather than a payment of the outstanding accrued interest on the loan until the remaining principal on the non-accrual loan receivable is considered to be fully collectible.

On January 16, 2007, X classifies Loan A as a non-accrual loan receivable for regulatory financial statement purposes because an amount of principal or interest has become 90 days past due. Nonetheless, X reasonably expects the borrower to continue making some but not all payments on the loan.

On January 16, 2007, the uncollected accrued interest on Loan A is $9,000 ($8,000 attributable to the calendar year ending December 31, 2006, and $1,000 attributable to the period January 1, 2007 through January 16, 2007). Prior to January 17, 2007, X recognized the $9,000 as income for regulatory financial statement purposes. During the period January 17, 2007 through December 31, 2007, an additional $23,000 of accrued interest becomes due on Loan A.

Pursuant to federal banking rules, on January 16, 2007, X reverses the $9,000 of uncollected accrued interest that had previously been recognized by making adjustments to appropriate income statement and balance sheet accounts for regulatory financial statement purposes. In addition, federal banking rules do not permit X to recognize as income any of the $23,000 accrued interest attributable to the period January 17, 2007 through December 31, 2007.

On January 1, 2008, X receives a $31,000 payment on Loan A. For regulatory financial statement purposes, X characterizes the $31,000 payment as a recovery of principal rather than a recovery of accrued interest. Therefore, X does not recognize any of the $31,000 payment as interest income for regulatory financial statement purposes.

X's supervisory authorities, in connection with the most recent examination of X's regulatory financial statements and lending practices, have determined that X maintains and applies standards that are consistent with federal banking rules.

LAW AND ANALYSIS

Issue 1.

Section 1.446–2 provides rules for determining the amount of accrued interest (other than interest described in § 1.446–2(a)(2)) that is generated on a loan over time for federal income tax purposes.

Section 1.446–2(a)(1) provides that the period in which a taxpayer recognizes accrued interest (determined under § 1.446–2(b) or § 1.446–2(c)) in gross income is determined under the taxpayer's regular method of accounting.

Section 451(a) provides that the amount of any item of gross income is included in gross income for the taxable year in which received by the taxpayer, unless, under the method of accounting used in computing taxable income, such amount is to be properly accounted for in a different period.

In the case of an accrual method taxpayer, § 1.451–1(a) provides that income is includible in gross income when all the events have occurred which fix the right to receive such income and the amount thereof can be determined with reasonable accuracy. *See also* § 1.446–1(c)(1)(ii).

As an accrual method taxpayer, X generally is required to recognize accrued interest determined under § 1.446–2 into gross income for the taxable year in which all the events have occurred which fix the right to receive such interest and the amount thereof can be determined with reasonable accuracy. *See* § 1.451–1(a). Under the "all events" test, a taxpayer's right to receive income becomes fixed on the earlier of the date that: (1) payment is earned through performance; (2) payment is due; or (3) payment is actually received. Rev. Rul. 84–31, 1984–1 C.B. 127. An amount of accrued interest determined pursuant to § 1.446–2 satisfies the "reasonable accuracy" requirement of § 1.451–1(a).

Although federal banking rules do not permit X to recognize accrued interest related to a non-accrual loan receivable as income for regulatory financial statement purposes, regulatory accounting rules are not controlling for federal income tax purposes. *See Old Colony R. Co. v. Commissioner,* 284 U.S. 552, 562 (1932).

"A fixed right to a determinable amount does not require accrual, however, if the income is uncollectible when the right to receive the income item arises. Accrual of income is not required when a fixed right to receive arises if there is not a reasonable expectancy that the claim will ever be paid." *European Am. Bank & Trust Co. v. United States,* 20 Cl. Ct. 594, 605 (1990) (footnotes omitted), *aff'd per curiam,* 940 F.2d 677 (Fed. Cir. 1991); *see also Jones Lumber Co. v. Commissioner*, 404 F.2d 764, 766 (6th Cir. 1968) (stating that "[t]he right to receive . . . determines the accrual of income unless, at the time the right arises, there exists a reasonable doubt as to its collectibility"); *Koehring Co. v. United States,* 421 F.2d 715, 721 (Ct. Cl. 1970) (stating that "a reasonable doubt as to the collectibility of a debt is a sufficient reason to justify its nonaccrual as income"); Rev. Rul. 80–361, 1980–2 C.B. 164 (citing *Jones Lumber Co., supra.*)

The "no reasonable expectancy of payment" exception to the fundamental rules of income accrual is strictly construed. "For accrual of income to be prevented, uncertainty as to collection must be substantial." *European Am. Bank & Trust Co.,* 20 Cl. Ct. at 605. To treat an item as non-accruable because of doubtful collectibility, the cases generally have required substantial evidence as to the financial instability or insolvency of the debtor. *See Jones Lumber Co.,* 404 F.2d at 766. This substantiation requirement has been applied on a loan by loan basis.

Temporary financial difficulty of a debtor cannot support non-recognition of income absent the existence of real doubt regarding ultimate payment. *Koehring Co.,* 421 F.2d 715, 721–722; *see also Harmont Plaza Inc. v. Commissioner,* 64 T.C. 632, 650 (1975), *aff'd,* 549 F.2d 414 (6th Cir. 1977) (stating that "the fact that a lapse of time is contemplated before actual satisfaction is possible does not constitute the requisite doubtful collectibility"). If there is some doubt regarding receipt of payment but a reasonable person would have an expectancy of payment, then an accrual method taxpayer is required to recognize the income.

When an income item is properly accrued and subsequently becomes uncollectible, a taxpayer's remedy is by way of a bad debt deduction under section 166 rather than through elimination of the accrual. Rev. Rul. 80–361. *See also* § 1.166–1(e) (relating to a bad debt deduction for uncollected income items included as income for the taxable year in which the bad debt deduction is claimed or for a prior taxable year); section 585 (allowing certain banks to deduct additions to a reserve for bad debts in lieu of the bad debt deduction provided by section 166) and § 1.585–2(e)(2) (excluding interest that has not been included in gross income from a loan used to determine additions to the reserve for bad debts). This rule is applicable even when the item is accrued and becomes uncollectible during the same taxable year. *Spring City Foundry Co. v. Commissioner,* 292 U.S. 182 (1934). *See also Atlantic Coast Line Railroad Co. v. Commissioner*, 31 B.T.A. 730, 751 (1934), acq., XIV–2 C.B. (1935).

Rev. Rul. 81–18, 1981–1 C.B. 295, addressed an accrual basis savings and loan association operating on a calendar year for federal income tax purposes. On its 1978 income tax return, the savings and loan recognized into income uncollected accrued interest on a loan. However, no interest payments were ever received on the loan. On January 30, 1979, the savings and loan charged off the previously recognized 1978 accrued interest for regulatory financial accounting purposes and recognized a bad debt deduction for federal income tax purposes. The charge-off was made pursuant to then existing Federal Home Loan Bank Board (FHLBB) regulations. The FHLBB regulations required that interest be treated as uncollectible if any portion of the interest was due but uncollected for a period in excess of 90 days. FHLBB examiners, upon their first audit of the savings and loan after the charge-off, confirmed that the charge-off was properly recognized for regulatory financial statement purposes and made in accordance with established policies of the FHLBB. The ruling considered two issues: (1) whether the savings and loan's claim for the uncollected 1978 interest was worthless for purposes of recognizing a section 166 bad debt deduction; and (2) whether the savings and loan was required under section 451 and § 1.451–1(a) to recognize the uncollected accrued interest on the nonperforming loan for periods after December 31, 1978 under the accrual method of accounting. The ruling concluded that for federal income tax purposes, the savings and loan's claim to the 1978 uncollected accrued interest was a worthless debt for purposes of section 166. The ruling also concluded that the savings and loan was not required to recognize any uncollected accrued interest on the loan after December 31, 1978.

Unlike the situation in Rev. Rul. 81–18, where no payments on the loan were made and there was no reasonable expectation of payment, in this revenue ruling X reasonably expects the borrower to continue making some but not all payments on Loan A. Therefore, the borrower's default on Loan A only demonstrates that timely repayment is not occurring. The late payment of interest by itself is not sufficient to demonstrate that X has no reasonable expectation of payment of the accrued interest related to Loan A. Under these circumstances, the "no reasonable expectancy of payment" exception to the general accrual rule does not apply. *See Koehring Co.*, 421 F.2d at 721–722; *Harmont Plaza Inc.*, 64 T.C. at 650.

As an accrual method taxpayer, X is required to recognize the $8,000 of uncollected 2006 accrued interest as income in X's 2006 taxable year for federal income tax purposes. X is also required to recognize the $24,000 of uncollected 2007 accrued interest in X's 2007 taxable year. The result is the same regardless of whether the bank uses a conformity method of accounting provided for in § 1.166–2(d).

Issue 2.

Section 166(a)(1) provides that a deduction shall be allowed for any debt that becomes worthless during the taxable year. In addition, section 166(a)(2) provides a deduction for "partially worthless debts" not in excess of the part charged off in the taxpayer's books and records within the taxable year to the extent the Commissioner is satisfied that the debt is recoverable only in part. A deduction for a worthless debt arising from an item of taxable income shall be allowed only if the item is recognized as taxable income during the taxable year in which the deduction is claimed or a prior taxable year. *See* § 1.166–1(e).

In general, there is no bright line test for determining the period in which a debt becomes worthless. However, § 1.166–2(d) permits a bank subject to supervision by federal banking authorities to use a conformity method of accounting to determine when a debt becomes worthless. Under a conformity method, debts that are charged off, in whole or in part, for regulatory purposes are conclusively presumed to become worthless for federal income tax purposes at the time of the regulatory charge off. Under a conformity method of accounting, the bank is allowed to recognize a bad debt deduction for the taxable year in which a debt is conclusively presumed to have become worthless. *See* § 1.166–2(d)(3)(ii)(A)(2).

In connection with the most recent examination of X's regulatory financial statements, X's supervisory authorities have determined that X maintains and applies standards that are consistent with federal banking rules. *See* Rev. Proc. 92–84, 1992–2 C.B. 489 (providing the form for the determination). Therefore, X satisfies the express determination requirement of § 1.166–2(d)(3)(iii)(D).

Various procedures can be used by a bank to classify a debt, or portion thereof, as a loss asset described in § 1.166–2(d)(3)(ii)(C). Rev. Rul. 2001–59, 2001–2 C.B. 585. On January 16, 2007, X reverses the recognition of the $9,000 of pre-January 17, 2007 uncollected accrued interest as interest income on Loan A ($8,000 of 2006 interest and $1,000 of interest for the period January 1, 2007 through January 16, 2007) for regulatory financial statement purposes. X's reversal of the accrual of $9,000 of uncollected pre-January 17, 2007 accrued interest, removes the interest receivable from X's books and records for regulatory financial statement purposes. Under federal banking rules, the $9,000 interest receivable is treated as an uncollectible asset of such little value that its inclusion as a bankable asset is not warranted. The reversal of the accrual of the $9,000 of interest receivable constitutes a charge off of the interest receivable as a loss asset for purposes of § 1.166–2(d)(3)(ii)(C).

For regulatory purposes, X does not recognize as income any of the $23,000 of accrued interest attributable to the period January 17, 2007 through December 31, 2007 because X's right to the $23,000 of accrued interest has such little value that recognition of the accrued interest receivable as a bankable asset is not warranted. Under these circumstances, X's failure to recognize the $23,000 of accrued interest for regulatory financial statement purposes is tantamount to recognizing the accrued interest as income and immediately charging off the uncollected accrued interest receivable as a loss asset.

As a result of X's conformity method of accounting under § 1.166–2(d), X will be entitled to claim a worthless debt deduction under section 166 in X's tax year ending December 31, 2007 for the $32,000 of uncollected accrued interest on Loan A ($8,000 of uncollected accrued interest in 2006 and $24,000 of uncollected accrued interest in 2007).

Issue 3.

In general, § 1.446–2(e) provides that each payment made on a loan (other than payments of additional interest or similar charges with regard to amounts that are not paid when due) is treated as a payment of interest to the extent of any accrued interest that is uncollected on the date the payment becomes due. The interest characterization provided for in § 1.446–2(e) applies to all payments made on a loan regardless of the taxpayer's overall method of accounting. For example, the interest characterization provided for in § 1.446–2(e) would apply to a payment on a loan for which the uncollected accrued interest was not previously recognized as income for federal income tax purposes. Similarly, the interest characterization provided for in § 1.446–2(e) would apply to a payment on a loan for which the uncollected accrued interest was previously recognized as income for federal income tax purposes and subsequently deducted as a worthless debt under the taxpayer's method of accounting.

Under § 1.166–1(f), any amount attributable to a recovery of a bad debt, or of a portion of a bad debt, which was allowed as a deduction from gross income in a prior taxable year, is included in gross income for the taxable year of recovery, except to the extent that the recovery is excluded from gross income under the provisions of section 111 and § 1.111–1.

On January 1, 2008, X receives a $31,000 payment on Loan A. For regulatory financial statement purposes, X characterizes the $31,000 as a payment of loan principal. However, under § 1.446–2(e), X is required to characterize any payment received on Loan A (other than payments of additional interest or similar charges with regard to amounts that are not paid when due) as a payment of interest for federal income tax purposes to the extent there is uncollected accrued interest outstanding on Loan A.

Immediately prior to the receipt of the $31,000 payment on January 1, 2008, the uncollected accrued interest on Loan A is $32,000 ($8,000 attributable to 2006 and $24,000 attributable to 2007). Therefore, § 1.446–2(e) requires that X characterize the $31,000 payment on Loan A as a payment of interest for federal income tax purposes. The characterization of the $31,000 payment as interest under § 1.446–2(e) would be the same regardless of whether: (i) X had not yet recognized the $32,000 of uncollected accrued interest on Loan A as income under its method of accounting for federal income tax purposes, (ii) X had recognized the $32,000 of uncollected accrued interest on Loan A as income for federal tax purposes but subsequently deducted the interest receivable as a bad debt under section 166 under its method of accounting, or (iii) X used a conformity method of accounting under § 1.166–2(d).

HOLDINGS

1. X is required to recognize in gross income the uncollected accrued interest on Loan A for federal income tax purposes notwithstanding that federal banking rules required X to suspend the recognition of accrued interest on Loan A into income for regulatory financial statement purposes. For the taxable year ending December 31, 2006, X must recognize in gross income the $8,000 of uncollected accrued interest on Loan A that was generated during 2006. For the taxable year ending December 31, 2007, X must recognize in gross income the $24,000 of uncollected accrued interest on Loan A that was generated during 2007. X must recognize the uncollected accrued interest as gross income in 2006 and 2007 regardless of whether X has elected a conformity method of accounting under § 1.166–2(d)(3) to determine when a debt becomes worthless.

2. As X uses a conformity method of accounting under § 1.166–2(d), X's $32,000 accrued interest receivable related to Loan A ($8,000 of uncollected accrued interest in 2006 and $24,000 of uncollected accrued interest in 2007) is considered worthless for purposes of section 166 in the year the amount is charged off for regulatory financial statement purposes. Therefore, for federal income tax purposes, X is allowed a worthless debt deduction for the $32,000 of uncollected accrued interest written off for regulatory financial statement purposes in the tax year ending December 31, 2007.

3. X is required to characterize the $31,000 payment received on Loan A in 2008 as a payment of interest for federal income tax purposes. The result would be the same whether (i) X had not yet recognized the $32,000 of uncollected accrued interest on Loan A as gross income under its method of accounting for federal income tax purposes, (ii) X had recognized the $32,000 of uncollected accrued interest on Loan A as gross income for federal tax purposes but subsequently deducted the receivable as a bad debt under section 166, or (iii) X used a conformity method of accounting under § 1.166–2(d). If X had previously deducted the $32,000 of uncollected accrued interest as a bad debt for federal income tax purposes then the subsequent $31,000 payment on the loan will be characterized as a partial recovery of that bad debt.

EFFECT ON OTHER RULINGS

Rev. Rul. 81–18 is distinguished with regard to when interest accrues for federal income tax purposes.

DRAFTING INFORMATION

The principal author of this revenue ruling is Timothy Sebastian of the Office of the Associate Chief Counsel (Financial Institutions and Products). For further information regarding this revenue ruling, contact Mr. Sebastian (202) 622–7417.

Section 856.—Definition of Real Estate Investment Trust

A notice provides that if a REIT recognizes currency gain under section 987, the REIT may apply the principles of the proposed regulations under section 987 that were issued on September 7, 2006, to determine whether the currency gain is derived from income described in section 856(c)(2) or (3). See Notice 2007-42, page 1288.

---

26 CFR 1.856–2: Limitations.
(Also § 988; 1.988–2.)

Real estate investment trust (REIT) foreign currency. This ruling provides that section 988 gain that is recognized by a REIT will be qualifying income under section 856(c)(2) or (3) of the Code to the extent that the underlying income so qualifies.

Rev. Rul. 2007–33

ISSUE

If a real estate investment trust (REIT) recognizes foreign currency gain in a section 988 transaction, to what extent is that gain qualifying income for purposes of the REIT income tests under § 856(c) of the Internal Revenue Code?

FACTS

R, a corporation with the U.S. dollar as its functional currency, has elected, and qualifies, to be treated as a REIT under subchapter M of Chapter 1 of the Code. *R* invests both in real property from which *R* derives rental income and in debt instruments that are partially or fully secured by mortgages on real property.

Some of the leases of the real estate that *R* owns provide for rents to be paid in euros. For some of these leases, *R* recognizes rental income for federal income tax purposes before receiving the corresponding rent payments. *R*'s rental income from these euro-denominated leases is described in § 856(c)(2)(C) and in § 856(c)(3)(A).

Some of the mortgage loans that *R* acquires are denominated in euros, and both principal and interest under these loans are payable in euros. *R*'s interest income from these euro-denominated loans is described in § 856(c)(2)(B) and in § 856(c)(3)(B).

R's activities of investing in rent-producing real estate and in mortgage loans are not subject to § 987. Therefore, if the euro changes in value against the dollar, payments of rent under the leases of the real estate and periodic payments made under the mortgage loans may generate foreign currency gain or loss under § 988. *See* § 1.988–2(b).

During its taxable year, *R* recognized rental income on the euro-denominated leases, interest income on the euro-denominated mortgage loans, and section 988 gain on payments received under the leases and the mortgage loans.

LAW AND ANALYSIS

To qualify as a REIT for a taxable year, at least 95 percent of an entity's gross income must be "derived from" the types of income listed in § 856(c)(2), and at least 75 percent of its gross income must be "derived from" the types of income listed in § 856(c)(3). Gains from foreign currency are not specifically enumerated in § 856(c)(2) or (c)(3).

Section 988(c)(1) defines a "section 988 transaction" as any transaction described in § 988(c)(1)(B) if the amount which the taxpayer is entitled to receive (or is required to pay) by reason of such transaction is denominated in terms of a nonfunctional currency or is determined by reference to the value of one or more nonfunctional currencies. Under § 988(c)(1)(B)(i), a section 988 transaction includes the acquisition of a debt instrument or becoming the obligor under a debt instrument. Under § 988(c)(1)(B)(ii), a section 988 transaction also includes accruing (or otherwise taking into account) any item of gross income or receipts which is received after the date on which so accrued or taken into account.

Section 988(b)(1) provides that the term "foreign currency gain" means any gain from a section 988 transaction to the extent that such gain does not exceed gain realized by reason of changes in exchange rates on or after the booking date (as defined in § 988(c)(2)) and before the payment date (as defined in § 988(c)(3)).

Rev. Rul. 74–191, 1974–1 C.B. 170, holds that otherwise-qualifying assets do not fail to satisfy § 856(c)(4) merely because the assets are foreign:

> Neither section 856 of the Code nor the regulations thereunder restrict the term "real estate assets" to those located within the United States. Accordingly, it is held that, for purposes of section 856(c), the term "real property" includes land or improvements thereon located outside the United States and the term "mortgages on real property" includes a security interest which, under the laws of the jurisdiction in which the property is located, is the legal equivalent of a mortgage or deed of trust in the United States.

1974–1 C.B. at 170. It follows from this holding both that rents on foreign real property qualify under § 856(c)(2)–(3) to the same extent that they would qualify if the property were located in the United States and that interest on foreign mortgage loans qualifies under § 856(c)(2)–(3) to the same extent that it would qualify if the loans were governed by United States law and the property were located in the United States. Thus, foreign situs of a REIT's assets does not necessarily prevent the REIT from satisfying the income and asset tests of § 856(c), which must be met in order to qualify as a REIT. Rev. Rul. 74–191, however, does not address the treatment of foreign currency gain that may result from investing in real property or other assets that produce income denominated in a currency other than the taxpayer's functional currency.

The legislative history describing the tax treatment of REITs indicates that the central concern behind the gross income restrictions in § 856(c) is that a REIT's gross income should largely be composed of passive income. For example, H.R. Rep. No. 2020, 86th Cong., 2d Sess. 4 (1960) at 6, 1960–2 C.B. 819, 822–23 states, "One of the principal purposes of your committee in imposing restrictions on types of income of a qualifying real estate investment trust is to be sure the bulk of its income is from passive income sources and not from the active conduct of a trade or business."

Although § 856(c) describes the sources of REIT qualifying income, neither the statute nor its legislative history describes what it means for income to be "derived from" those sources. Because of the close nexus, however, between section 988 gain on payments received by a REIT and the income from which that payment is derived, the section 988 gain qualifies under § 856(c)(2) or (3) to the extent that the underlying income does. Thus, for example, if interest income recognized by *R* qualifies under § 856(c)(2) or (3), then so does the 988 gain from that interest income. Similarly, if an item of income qualifies as rents from real property for purposes of § 856(c)(3)(C), then, for purposes of § 856(c)(3), section 988 gain with respect to that income is derived from a type of income listed in § 856(c)(3)(A)–(H). *Cf.* Rev. Rul. 92–56, 1992–2 C.B. 153 (concluding that a regulated investment company's (RIC's) receipt of a reimbursement of an investment advisory fee was "derived from" the RIC's business of investing in stock, securities, or foreign currencies and was therefore qualifying income under the "other income" provision of § 851(b)(2)).

HOLDING

If section 988 gain is recognized with respect to income recognized by a REIT, the gain qualifies under § 856(c)(2) or (3) to the extent that the underlying income so qualifies.

DRAFTING INFORMATION

The principal author of this revenue ruling is Jonathan D. Silver of the Office of Associate Chief Counsel (Financial Institutions & Products). For further information regarding this revenue ruling, contact Jonathan D. Silver at (202) 622–3930 (not a toll-free call).

Section 987.—Branch Transactions

A notice provides that if a REIT recognizes currency gain under section 987, the REIT may apply the principles of the proposed regulations under section 987 that were issued on September 7, 2006, to determine whether the currency gain is derived from income described in section 856(c)(2) or (3). See Notice 2007-42, page 1288.

Section 988.—Treatment of Certain Foreign Currency Transactions

A revenue ruling holds that if section 988 gain is recognized with respect to income recognized by a REIT, the gain qualifies under section 856(c)(2) or (3) to the extent that the underlying income so qualifies. See Rev. Rul. 2007-33, page 1281.

Section 1035.—Certain Exchanges of Insurance Policies

26 CFR 1.1035–1: Certain exchanges of insurance policies.
(Also § 72.)

Section 1035; certain exchanges of insurance policies. A taxpayer's receipt of a check issued by an insurance company under a non-qualified annuity contract is treated as a taxable distribution, even if the check is endorsed to a second insurance company for the purchase of a second annuity. The transaction is not characterized as a tax-free exchange under section 1035(a)(3) of the Code unless there is a direct exchange or assignment of the original contract.

Rev. Rul. 2007–24

ISSUE

If a Taxpayer receives a check from a life insurance company under a non-qualified annuity contract, does the endorsement of the check to a second company as consideration for a second annuity contract qualify as a tax-free exchange under § 1035(a)(3) of the Internal Revenue Code?

FACTS

A, an individual, owned a non-qualified annuity contract issued by *IC1*, a life insurance company. In 2007, *A* requested that *IC1* issue directly to *IC2*, another life insurance company, a check as consideration for a new annuity contract to be issued by *IC2*. *A* intended the transaction to be treated as a tax-free exchange under § 1035. *IC1* refused to do so and, instead, issued a check to *A*. *A* did not deposit the check, but instead endorsed it to *IC2* as consideration for a new annuity contract.

LAW AND ANALYSIS

Section 72(a) provides that, except as otherwise provided in Chapter 1 of the Internal Revenue Code, gross income includes any amount received as an annuity under an annuity contract. Under § 72(e), amounts received under an annuity contract, but not as an annuity, generally are included in gross income to the extent allocable to income on the contract. That is, they are taxed on an income-first basis. Section 72(e)(5)(E) provides that this rule applies to any amounts received on the complete surrender, redemption, or maturity of an annuity contract.

Section 1035(a)(3) provides that no gain or loss is recognized on the exchange of an annuity contract for another annuity contract. The legislative history of § 1035 explains that § 1035 provides non-recognition treatment for taxpayers who have "merely exchanged an [annuity contract] for another better suited to their needs and who have not actually realized gain." H. Rep. 1337, 83d Cong., 2d Sess. 81 (1954). Under § 1.1035–1, the contracts exchanged must relate to the same insured, and the obligee or obligees under the contract received in the exchange must be the same as those under the original contract.

In Rev. Rul. 72–358, 1972–2 C.B. 473, a taxpayer who owned a life insurance contract issued by one insurance company assigned the contract, prior to its maturity, to a second insurance company in exchange for a variable annuity contract issued by the second company. The ruling concludes that, pursuant to § 1035, no gain or loss is recognized on the exchange. Similarly, Rev. Rul. 2002–75, 2002–2 C.B. 812, concludes that an individual's assignment of an annuity contract issued by one insurance company to a second insurance company, which then deposits the cash surrender value of the assigned contract into a pre-existing annuity contract owned by the same taxpayer, qualifies as a tax-free exchange under § 1035.

In the present case, there was no actual exchange of annuity contracts; nor did *A* assign the *IC1* contract to *IC2*; nor was there a direct transfer from *IC1* to *IC2* of the cash value of the old contract in exchange for the new contract. Instead, *IC1* disbursed a check to *A*, which *A*, in turn, endorsed to *IC2* as consideration for a new contract. Neither § 1035 nor the regulations make any special provision for the purchase of an annuity contract with amounts distributed to the policyholder under another contract. Because the annuity contract was a non-qualified contract, no rollover provision, such as § 403(a)(4), applied to the amount received from *IC1*. Accordingly, the amount that *A* received from *IC1* under the first annuity contract is taxable in 2007 to the extent set forth in § 72(e).

HOLDING

If a Taxpayer receives a check from a life insurance company under a non-qualified annuity contract, the endorsement of the check to a second company as consideration for a second annuity contract does not qualify as a tax-free exchange under § 1035(a)(3). Instead, the amount received is taxable to the extent set forth in § 72(e).

DRAFTING INFORMATION

The principal author of this revenue ruling is Josephine H. Firehock of the Office of Associate Chief Counsel (Financial Institutions & Products). For further information regarding this revenue ruling, contact Josephine H. Firehock at (202) 622–3970 (not a toll-free call).

Part III. Administrative, Procedural, and Miscellaneous

Weighted Average Interest Rates Update

Notice 2007–33

This notice provides guidance as to the corporate bond weighted average interest rate and the permissible range of interest rates specified under § 412(b)(5)(B)(ii)(II) of the Internal Revenue Code. In addition, it provides guidance as to the interest rate on 30-year Treasury securities under § 417(e)(3)(A)(ii)(II).

CORPORATE BOND WEIGHTED AVERAGE INTEREST RATE

Sections 412(b)(5)(B)(ii) and 412(l)(7)(C)(i), as amended by the Pension Funding Equity Act of 2004 and by the Pension Protection Act of 2006, provide that the interest rates used to calculate current liability and to determine the required contribution under § 412(l) for plan years beginning in 2004 through 2007 must be within a permissible range based on the weighted average of the rates of interest on amounts invested conservatively in long term investment grade corporate bonds during the 4-year period ending on the last day before the beginning of the plan year.

Notice 2004–34, 2004–1 C.B. 848, provides guidelines for determining the corporate bond weighted average interest rate and the resulting permissible range of interest rates used to calculate current liability. That notice establishes that the corporate bond weighted average is based on the monthly composite corporate bond rate derived from designated corporate bond indices. The methodology for determining the monthly composite corporate bond rate as set forth in Notice 2004–34 continues to apply in determining that rate. See Notice 2006–75, 2006–36 I.R.B. 366.

The composite corporate bond rate for April 2007 is 5.98 percent. Pursuant to Notice 2004–34, the Service has determined this rate as the average of the monthly yields for the included corporate bond indices for that month.

The following corporate bond weighted average interest rate was determined for plan years beginning in the month shown below.

For Plan Years Beginning in: Month	Year	Corporate Bond Weighted Average	90% to 100% Permissible Range
May	2007	5.80	5.22 to 5.80

30-YEAR TREASURY SECURITIES INTEREST RATE

Section 417(e)(3)(A)(ii)(II) defines the applicable interest rate, which must be used for purposes of determining the minimum present value of a participant's benefit under § 417(e)(1) and (2), as the annual rate of interest on 30-year Treasury securities for the month before the date of distribution or such other time as the Secretary may by regulations prescribe. Section 1.417(e)–1(d)(3) of the Income Tax Regulations provides that the applicable interest rate for a month is the annual interest rate on 30-year Treasury securities as specified by the Commissioner for that month in revenue rulings, notices or other guidance published in the Internal Revenue Bulletin.

The rate of interest on 30-year Treasury securities for April 2007 is 4.87 percent. The Service has determined this rate as the monthly average of the daily determination of yield on the 30-year Treasury bond maturing in February 2037.

Drafting Information

The principal authors of this notice are Paul Stern and Tony Montanaro of the Employee Plans, Tax Exempt and Government Entities Division. For further information regarding this notice, please contact the Employee Plans' taxpayer assistance telephone service at 877–829–5500 (a toll-free number), between the hours of 8:30 a.m. and 4:30 p.m. Eastern time, Monday through Friday. Mr. Stern may be reached at 202–283–9703. Mr. Montanaro may be reached at 202–283–9714. The telephone numbers in the preceding sentences are not toll-free.

Credit for Renewable Electricity Production, Refined Coal Production, and Indian Coal Production, and Publication of Inflation Adjustment Factors and Reference Prices for Calendar Year 2007

Notice 2007–40

This notice publishes the inflation adjustment factors and reference prices for calendar year 2007 for the renewable electricity production credit, the refined coal production credit, and the Indian coal production credit under § 45 of the Internal Revenue Code. The 2007 inflation adjustment factors and reference prices are used in determining the availability of the credits. The 2007 inflation adjustment factors and reference prices apply to calendar year 2007 sales of kilowatt-hours of electricity produced in the United States or a possession thereof from qualified energy resources and to calendar year 2007 sales of refined coal and Indian coal produced in the United States or a possession thereof.

BACKGROUND

Section 45(a) provides that the renewable electricity production credit for any tax year is an amount equal to the product of 1.5 cents multiplied by the kilowatt hours of specified electricity produced by the taxpayer and sold to an unrelated person during the tax year. This electricity must be produced from qualified energy resources and at a qualified facility during the 10-year period beginning on the date the facility was originally placed in service.

Section 45(b)(1) provides that the amount of the credit determined under § 45(a) is reduced by an amount which bears the same ratio to the amount of the credit as (A) the amount by which the reference price for the calendar year in which the sale occurs exceeds 8 cents, bears to (B) 3 cents. Under § 45(b)(2), the 1.5 cent amount in § 45(a), the 8 cent amount in § 45(b)(1), the $4.375 amount in § 45(e)(8)(A), and in § 45(e)(8)(B)(i) the reference price of fuel used as feedstock (within the meaning of § 45(c)(7)(A)) in 2002 are each adjusted by multiplying the amount by the inflation adjustment factor for the calendar year in which the sale occurs. If any amount as increased under the preceding sentence is not a multiple of 0.1 cent, the amount is rounded to the nearest multiple of 0.1 cent.

Section 45(c)(1) defines qualified energy resources as wind, closed-loop biomass, open-loop biomass, geothermal energy, solar energy, small irrigation power, municipal solid waste, and qualified hydropower production.

Section 45(d)(1) defines a qualified facility using wind to produce electricity as any facility owned by the taxpayer that is originally placed in service after December 31, 1993, and before January 1, 2009. See § 45(e)(7) for rules relating to the inapplicability of the credit to electricity sold to utilities under certain contracts.

Section 45(d)(2)(A) defines a qualified facility using closed-loop biomass to produce electricity as any facility (i) owned by the taxpayer that is originally placed in service after December 31, 1992, and before January 1, 2009, or (ii) owned by the taxpayer which before January 1, 2009, is originally placed in service and modified to use closed-loop biomass to co-fire with coal, with other biomass, or with both, but only if the modification is approved under the Biomass Power for Rural Development Programs or is part of a pilot project of the Commodity Credit Corporation as described in 65 Fed. Reg. 63052. Section 45(d)(2)(B) provides that in the case of a qualified facility described in § 45(d)(2)(A)(ii), (i) the 10-year period referred to in § 45(a) is treated as beginning no earlier than the date of enactment of § 45(d)(2)(B)(i); (ii) the amount of the credit determined under § 45(a) with respect to the facility is an amount equal to the amount determined without regard to § 45(d)(2)(B)(ii) multiplied by the ratio of the thermal content of the closed-loop biomass used in the facility to the thermal content of all fuels used in the facility; and (iii) if the owner of the facility is not the producer of the electricity, the person eligible for the credit allowable under § 45(a) is the lessee or the operator of the facility.

Section 45(d)(3)(A) defines a qualified facility using open-loop biomass to produce electricity as any facility owned by the taxpayer which (i) in the case of a facility using agricultural livestock waste nutrients, (I) is originally placed in service after the date of enactment of § 45(d)(3)(A)(i)(I) and before January 1, 2009, and (II) the nameplate capacity rating of which is not less than 150 kilowatts; and (ii) in the case of any other facility, is originally placed in service before January 1, 2009. In the case of any facility described in § 45(d)(3)(A), if the owner of the facility is not the producer of the electricity, § 45(d)(3)(B) provides that the person eligible for the credit allowable under § 45(a) is the lessee or the operator of the facility.

Section 45(d)(4) defines a qualified facility using geothermal or solar energy to produce electricity as any facility owned by the taxpayer which is originally placed in service after the date of enactment of § 45(d)(4) and before January 1, 2009 (January 1, 2006, in the case of a facility using solar energy). A qualified facility using geothermal or solar energy does not include any property described in § 48(a)(3) the basis of which is taken into account by the taxpayer for purposes of determining the energy credit under § 48.

Section 45(d)(5) defines a qualified facility using small irrigation power to produce electricity as any facility owned by the taxpayer which is originally placed in service after the date of enactment of § 45(d)(5) and before January 1, 2009.

Section 45(d)(6) defines a qualified facility using gas derived from the biodegradation of municipal solid waste to produce electricity as any facility owned by the taxpayer which is originally placed in service after the date of enactment of § 45(d)(6) and before January 1, 2009.

Section 45(d)(7) defines a qualified facility that burns municipal solid waste to produce electricity as any facility owned by the taxpayer which is originally placed in service after the date of enactment of § 45(d)(7) and before January 1, 2009. A qualified facility burning municipal solid waste includes a new unit placed in service in connection with a facility placed in service on or before the date of enactment of § 45(d)(7), but only to the extent of the increased amount of electricity produced at the facility by reason of such new unit.

Section 45(d)(8) provides in the case of a facility that produces refined coal, the term "refined coal production facility" means a facility which is placed in service after the date of enactment of § 45(d)(8) and before January 1, 2009.

Section 45(d)(9) defines a qualified facility producing qualified hydroelectric production described in § 45(c)(8) as (A) any facility producing incremental hydropower production, but only to the extent of its incremental hydropower production attributable to efficiency improvements or additions to capacity described in § 45(c)(8)(B) placed in service after the date of enactment of § 45(d)(9) and before January 1, 2009, and (B) any other facility placed in service after the date of enactment of § 45(d)(9) and before January 1, 2009. Section 45(d)(9)(C) provides that in the case of a qualified facility described in § 45(d)(9)(A), the 10-year period referred to in § 45(a) is treated as beginning on the date the efficiency improvements or additions to capacity are placed in service.

Section 45(d)(10) provides in the case of a facility that produces Indian coal, the term "Indian coal production facility" means a facility which is placed in service before January 1, 2009.

Section 45(e)(8)(A) provides that the refined coal production credit is an amount equal to $4.375 per ton of qualified refined coal (i) produced by the taxpayer at a refined coal production facility during the 10-year period beginning on the date the facility was originally placed in service, and (ii) sold by the taxpayer (I) to an unrelated person and (II) during the 10-year period and the tax year. Section 45(e)(8)(B) provides that the amount of credit determined under § 45(e)(8)(A) is reduced by an amount which bears the same ratio to the amount of the increase as (i) the amount by which the reference price of fuel used as feedstock (within the meaning of § 45(c)(7)(A)) for the calendar year in which the sale occurs exceeds an amount equal to 1.7 multiplied by the reference price for such fuel in 2002, bears to (ii) $8.75.

Section 45(e)(10)(A) provides in the case of a producer of Indian coal, the credit determined under section 45 for any taxable year shall be increased by an amount equal to the applicable dollar amount per ton of Indian coal (i) produced by the taxpayer at an Indian coal production facility during the 7-year period beginning on January 1, 2006, and (ii) sold by the taxpayer (I) to an unrelated person, and (II) during such 7-year period and such taxable year.

Section 45(e)(10)(B)(i) defines "applicable dollar amount" for any taxable year as (I) $1.50 in the case of calendar years 2006 through 2009, and (II) $2.00 in the case of calendar years beginning after 2009.

Section 45(e)(2)(A) requires the Secretary to determine and publish in the Federal Register each calendar year the inflation adjustment factor and the reference price for the calendar year. The inflation adjustment factors and the reference prices for the 2007 calendar year were published in the Federal Register on March 29, 2007 (72 Fed. Reg. 14862).

Section 45(e)(2)(B) defines the inflation adjustment factor for a calendar year as the fraction the numerator of which is the GDP implicit price deflator for the preceding calendar year and the denominator of which is the GDP implicit price deflator for the calendar year 1992. The term "GDP implicit price deflator" means the most recent revision of the implicit price deflator for the gross domestic product as computed and published by the Department of Commerce before March 15 of the calendar year.

Section 45(e)(2)(C) provides that the reference price is the Secretary's determination of the annual average contract price per kilowatt hour of electricity generated from the same qualified energy resource and sold in the previous year in the United States. Only contracts entered into after December 31, 1989, are taken into account.

Under § 45(e)(8)(C), the determination of the reference price for fuel used as feedstock within the meaning of § 45(c)(7)(A) is made according to rules similar to the rules under § 45(e)(2)(C).

Under section 45(e)(10)(B)(ii), in the case of any calendar year after 2006, each of the dollar amounts under section 45(e)(10)(B)(i) shall be equal to the product of such dollar amount and the inflation adjustment factor determined under section 45(e)(2)(B) for the calendar year, except that section 45(e)(2)(B) shall be applied by substituting 2005 for 1992.

INFLATION ADJUSTMENT FACTORS AND REFERENCE PRICES

The inflation adjustment factor for calendar year 2007 for qualified energy resources and refined coal is 1.3433. The inflation adjustment factor for Indian coal is 1.0293. The reference price for calendar year 2007 for facilities producing electricity from wind (based upon information provided by the Department of Energy) is 3.29 cents per kilowatt hour. The reference prices for fuel used as feedstock within the meaning of § 45(c)(7)(A), relating to refined coal production (based upon information provided by the Department of Energy) are $31.90 per ton for calendar year 2002 and $48.35 per ton for calendar year 2007. The reference prices for facilities producing electricity from closed-loop biomass, open-loop biomass, geothermal energy, solar energy, small irrigation power, municipal solid waste, and qualified hydropower production have not been determined for calendar year 2007. The IRS is exploring methods of determining those reference prices for calendar year 2008.

PHASE-OUT CALCULATION

Because the 2007 reference price for electricity produced from wind does not exceed 8 cents multiplied by the inflation adjustment factor, the phaseout of the credit provided in § 45(b)(1) does not apply to such electricity sold during calendar year 2007. Because the 2007 reference price of fuel used as feedstock for refined coal does not exceed the $31.90 reference price of such fuel in 2002 multiplied by the inflation adjustment factor and 1.7, the phaseout of credit provided in § 45(e)(8)(B) does not apply to refined coal sold during calendar year 2007. Further, for electricity produced from closed-loop biomass, open-loop biomass, geothermal energy, solar energy, small irrigation power, municipal solid waste, and qualified hydropower production, the phaseout of credit provided in § 45(b)(1) does not apply to such electricity sold during calendar year 2007.

CREDIT AMOUNT BY QUALIFIED ENERGY RESOURCE AND FACILITY, REFINED COAL, AND INDIAN COAL

As required by § 45(b)(2), the 1.5 cent amount in § 45(a)(1), the 8 cent amount in § 45(b)(1), and the $4.375 amount in § 45(e)(8)(A) are each adjusted by multiplying such amount by the inflation adjustment factor for the calendar year in which the sale occurs. If any amount as increased under the preceding sentence is not a multiple of 0.1 cent, such amount is rounded to the nearest multiple of 0.1 cent. In the case of electricity produced in open-loop biomass facilities, small irrigation power facilities, landfill gas facilities, trash combustion facilities, and qualified hydropower facilities, § 45(b)(4)(A) requires the amount in effect under § 45(a)(1) (before rounding to the nearest 0.1 cent) to be reduced by one-half. Under the calculation required by § 45(b)(2), the credit for renewable electricity production for calendar year 2007 under § 45(a) is 2.0 cents per kilowatt hour on the sale of electricity produced from the qualified energy resources of wind, closed-loop biomass, geothermal energy, and solar energy, and 1.0 cent per kilowatt hour on the sale of electricity produced in open-loop biomass facilities, small irrigation power facilities, landfill gas facilities, trash combustion facilities, and qualified hydropower facilities. Under the calculation required by § 45(b)(2), the credit for refined coal production for calendar year 2007 under section 45(e)(8)(A) is $5.877 per ton on the sale of qualified refined coal. The credit for Indian coal production for calendar year 2007 under § 45(e)(10)(B) is $1.544 per ton on the sale of Indian coal.

DRAFTING AND CONTACT INFORMATION

The principal author of this notice is David A. Selig of the Office of Associate Chief Counsel (Passthroughs and Special Industries). For further information regarding this notice, contact Mr. Selig at (202) 622–3040 (not a toll-free call).

Public Comment Invited on Recommendations for 2007–2008 Guidance Priority List

Notice 2007–41

The Department of Treasury and Internal Revenue Service invite public comment on recommendations for items that should be included on the 2007–2008 Guidance Priority List.

Treasury's Office of Tax Policy and the Service use the Guidance Priority List each year to identify and prioritize the tax issues that should be addressed through regulations, revenue rulings, revenue procedures, notices, and other published administrative guidance. The 2007–2008 Guidance Priority List will establish the guidance that the Treasury Department and the Service intend to issue from July 1, 2007, through June 30, 2008. The Treasury Department and the Service recognize the importance of public input to formulate a Guidance Priority List that focuses resources on guidance items that are most important to taxpayers and tax administration. Published guidance plays an important role in increasing voluntary compliance by helping to clarify ambiguous areas of the tax law.

As is the case whenever significant legislation is enacted, the Treasury Department and the Service have continued to dedicate substantial resources during the current plan year to published guidance projects necessary to implement the provisions of the American Jobs Creation Act of 2004, Pub. L. No. 108–357, 118 Stat. 1418, which was enacted on October 22, 2004; the Energy Policy Act of 2005, Pub. L. No. 109–58, 119 Stat. 594, which was enacted on August 8, 2005; the Gulf Opportunity Zone Act of 2005, Pub. L. No. 109–135, 119 Stat. 2577, which was enacted on December 21, 2005; and the Tax Increase Prevention and Reconciliation Act of 2005, Pub. L. No. 109–222, 120 Stat. 345, which was enacted on May 17, 2006. Similarly, the Treasury Department and the Service have devoted substantial resources to published guidance projects necessary to implement the provisions of additional tax legislation that was enacted during the current plan year, such as the Pension Protection Act of 2006, Pub. L. No. 109–280, 120 Stat. 780, which was enacted on August 17, 2006; and the Tax Relief and Health Care Act of 2006, Pub. L. No. 109–432, 120 Stat. 2922, which was enacted on December 20, 2006. The Treasury Department and the Service will continue to evaluate the priority of each guidance project in light of the above-mentioned tax legislation and other developments occurring during the 2007–2008 plan year.

In reviewing recommendations and selecting projects for inclusion on the 2007–2008 Guidance Priority List, the Treasury Department and the Service will consider the following:

1. Whether the recommended guidance resolves significant issues relevant to many taxpayers;

2. Whether the recommended guidance promotes sound tax administration;

3. Whether the recommended guidance can be drafted in a manner that will enable taxpayers to easily understand and apply the guidance;

4. Whether the Service can administer the recommended guidance on a uniform basis; and

5. Whether the recommended guidance reduces controversy and lessens the burden on taxpayers or the Service.

Taxpayers may submit recommendations for guidance at any time during the year. Please submit recommendations by May 31, 2007, for possible inclusion on the original 2007–2008 Guidance Priority List. The Service plans to update the 2007–2008 Guidance Priority List periodically to reflect additional guidance that the Treasury Department and the Service intend to publish during the plan year. The periodic updates allow the Treasury Department and the Service to respond to the need for additional guidance that may arise during the plan year. Recommendations for guidance received after May 31, 2007, will be reviewed for inclusion in the next periodic update.

Taxpayers are not required to submit recommendations for guidance in any particular format. Taxpayers should, however, briefly describe the recommended guidance and explain the need for the guidance. In addition, taxpayers may include an analysis of how the issue should be resolved. It would be helpful if taxpayers suggesting more than one guidance project would prioritize the projects by order of importance. If a large number of projects are being suggested, it also would be helpful if the projects were grouped in terms of high, medium or low priority.

Taxpayers should send written comments to:

Internal Revenue Service
Attn: CC:PA:LPD:PR
(Notice 2007–41)
Room 5203
P.O. Box 7604
Ben Franklin Station
Washington, D.C. 20044

or hand deliver comments Monday through Friday between the hours of 8 a.m. and 4 p.m. to:

Courier's Desk
Internal Revenue Service
Attn: CC:PA:LPD:PR
(Notice 2007–41)
1111 Constitution Avenue, N.W.
Washington, D.C. 20224

Alternatively, taxpayers may submit comments electronically via e-mail to the following address: *Notice.Comments@irscounsel.treas.gov*. Taxpayers should include "Notice 2007–41" in the subject line. All comments will be available for public inspection and copying in their entirety.

For further information regarding this notice, contact Henry Schneiderman of the Office of Associate Chief Counsel (Procedure and Administration) at (202) 622–3400 (not a toll-free call).

Treatment of Currency Gain That a Real Estate Investment Trust (REIT) Recognizes From a Qualified Business Unit (QBU) of the REIT

Notice 2007–42

This notice provides guidance with respect to the circumstances under which § 856(c)(2) or § 856(c)(3) characterizes § 987 gain as qualifying income for purposes of REIT qualification.

BACKGROUND

Under paragraph (3) of § 856(c), at least 75 percent of a REIT's annual gross income must be derived from the types of income listed in that paragraph, often characterized as income from real estate sources. Under paragraph (2) of § 856(c), at least 95 percent of a REIT's annual gross income must be derived from the types of income listed in that paragraph, often characterized as income from "passive" sources, including interest and dividends.

The Service is aware that some REITs have invested in real estate assets outside the United States through entities or partnerships that qualify as QBUs, as defined in § 989(a). The Service has explicitly ruled that otherwise-qualifying assets do not fail to satisfy § 856(c)(4) merely because the assets are foreign:

> Neither section 856 of the Code nor the regulations thereunder restrict the term "real estate assets" to those located within the United States. Accordingly, it is held that, for purposes of section 856(c), the term "real property" includes land or improvements thereon located outside the United States and the term "mortgages on real property" includes a security interest which, under the laws of the jurisdiction in which the property is located, is the legal equivalent of a mortgage or deed of trust in the United States.

Rev. Rul. 74–191, 1974–1 C.B. 170, 170. It follows from this holding both that rents on foreign real property qualify under § 856(c)(2)–(3) to the same extent that they would qualify if the property were located in the United States, and that interest on foreign mortgage loans qualifies under § 856(c)(2)–(3) to the same extent that it would qualify if the loans were governed by United States law and the property were located in the United States. Thus, foreign situs of a REIT's assets does not necessarily prevent the REIT from satisfying the income and asset tests of § 856(c), which must be met in order to qualify as a REIT. Rev. Rul. 74–191, however, does not address the treatment of foreign currency gain that may result from investing in real property or other assets through a QBU with a functional currency other than the dollar.

In general, § 985 provides that all determinations for federal income tax purposes are to be made in the taxpayer's functional currency. Section 985(a). Section 1.985–1(b)(1)(iii) of the Income Tax Regulations provides that, except as otherwise provided by ruling or administrative pronouncement, the U.S. dollar is the functional currency of a QBU that has the United States as its residence, as defined in § 988(a)(3)(B). Section 1.989(a)–1(b)(2)(i) provides that a corporation is a QBU. Section 988(a)(3)(B)(i)(II) provides that the United States is the residence of a corporation that is a United States person. Section 7701(a)(30) provides, in part, that the term "United States person" includes a domestic corporation. Section 7701(a)(4) provides that the term "domestic," as applied to a corporation, means created or organized in the United States or under the law of the United States or any State. Thus, absent a ruling to the contrary, a REIT has the dollar as its functional currency because § 856(a)(3) requires it to be taxable as a domestic corporation.

A REIT may have a QBU that is subject to § 987 and that has a functional currency other than the dollar. *See* § 1.985–1(c). In such a case, a REIT may recognize currency gain under § 987 when the QBU remits property to the REIT. Section 987(3).

Proposed regulations (REG–208270–86, 2006–42 I.R.B. 698 [71 FR 52,876]) under § 987 were issued September 7, 2006. Section 1.987–6(b) of the proposed regulations generally provides that the owner of a § 987 QBU must determine the character of § 987 gain or loss in the year of remittance using the asset method provided in § 1.861–9T(g), as modified by the proposed regulations. The modified gross income method described in § 1.861–9T(j) cannot be used. If finalized as currently proposed, however, the regulations will not apply to REITs. *See* Prop. Treas. Reg. § 1.987–1(b)(1)(iii). Some REITs have requested guidance concerning the status under § 856(c)(2)–(3) of any foreign currency gain that is recognized under § 987 when a QBU remits property to a REIT.

INTERIM GUIDANCE

Because the currency gain from remittances is determined under § 987, the Service believes that it is appropriate for issues that arise in connection with that gain to be addressed under methods similar to those provided in § 987 and the regulations thereunder. The Treasury Department and the Service therefore intend to amend the proposed regulations under § 987 to include guidance concerning the characterization for purposes of § 856(c)(2) and (3) of § 987 gain recognized by a REIT on a remittance from a QBU of the REIT.

Until further guidance is published, if a REIT recognizes § 987 gain, the REIT may apply the principles of the proposed regulations under § 987 issued September 7, 2006 to determine whether that § 987 gain is derived from income that is described in § 856(c)(2)(A) – (H) or § 856(c)(3)(A) – (I).

The principal author of this notice is Jonathan D. Silver of the Office of Associate Chief Counsel (Financial Institutions & Products). For further information regarding this notice, contact Jonathan D. Silver at (202) 622–3930 (not a toll-free call).

26 CFR 601.601: Rules and regulations.
(Also, Part I, §§ 446, 451; 1.446–2, 1.451–1.)

Rev. Proc. 2007–33

TABLE OF CONTENTS

SECTION 1. PURPOSE

This revenue procedure provides the exclusive procedure by which a taxpayer described in SECTION 3 may obtain the Commissioner's consent to change its method of accounting for uncollected interest (other than interest described in § 1.446–2(a)(2) of the Income Tax Regulations) to the safe harbor method provided in SECTION 4 of this revenue procedure.

SECTION 2. BACKGROUND

.01 For certain types of interest, § 1.446–2 provides rules for determining the amount of interest that accrues during an accrual period and the portion of a payment that consists of accrued interest. For descriptions of the types of interest (*e.g.*, original issue discount) to which the § 1.446–2 accrual rules do not apply, see 1.446–2(a)(2).

.02 Section 1.446–2(b) provides that "qualified stated interest" accrues ratably over an accrual period (or periods) to which it is attributable and accrues at the stated rate for the period (or periods). In general, "qualified stated interest" is stated interest that is unconditionally payable in cash or in property (other than debt instruments of the issuer) at least annually at a single fixed rate that appropriately takes into account the length of the interval between payments. *See* 1.1273–1(c).

.03 In the case of interest other than "qualified stated interest," § 1.446–2(c) provides that the amount of interest that accrues for any accrual period is determined under rules similar to those in the regulations under sections 1272 and 1275 of the Internal Revenue Code for the accrual of original issue discount (subject to the modifications set forth in § 1.446–2(d)).

.04 Section 1.446–2(e) provides that each payment on a loan (other than payments of additional interest or similar charges with regard to amounts not paid when due) is treated as a payment of interest to the extent of the accrued but unpaid interest (determined under § 1.446–2(b) and § 1.446–2(c)) as of the date the payment becomes due.

.05 Section 1.446–2(a)(1) provides that a taxpayer determines the taxable year in which to include an amount of accrued interest (determined under § 1.446–2(b) or § 1.446–2(c)) in gross income under the taxpayer's regular method of accounting.

.06 Rev. Rul. 2007–32, page 1278 of this Bulletin, requires an accrual method bank with a reasonable expectancy of receiving future payments on a loan to accrue interest in the taxable year in which the right to receive the interest becomes fixed, notwithstanding bank regulatory rules that prevent accrual of the interest for regulatory purposes. The ruling also provides guidance as to the period in which a taxpayer that has elected the conformity method of accounting under 1.166–2(d)(3) can treat uncollected interest as worthless.

.07 APPENDIX 5A of Rev. Proc. 2002–9, 2002–1 C.B. 327, modified and clarified by Announcement 2002–17, 2002–1 C.B. 561, modified and amplified by Rev. Proc. 2002–19, 2002–1 C.B. 696, amplified, clarified, and modified by Rev. Proc. 2002–54, 2002–2 C.B. 432, states that "for interest to be determined uncollectible, the taxpayer must substantiate, taking into account all the facts and circumstances, that it has no reasonable expectation of payment of the interest." APPENDIX 5A of Rev. Proc. 2002–9 also states that the "substantiation requirement is applied on a loan by loan basis."

.08 Substantiation of uncollectible interest using a loan-by-loan facts and circumstances methodology can be administratively burdensome and impractical, particularly for smaller unsecured loans. For example, a bank may have a significant number of consumer loans. For these loans, the bank's loan files often may not contain updated information regarding the debtors' financial condition or the value of the collateral, if any, securing the loans.

SECTION 3. SCOPE

This revenue procedure applies to a "bank" as defined in 1.166–2(d)(4)(i) that—

(1) uses an accrual method of accounting to determine its taxable income for federal income tax purposes,

(2) is subject to supervision by Federal authorities, or by state authorities maintaining substantially equivalent standards, and

(3) has uncollected interest other than interest described in 1.446–2(a)(2).

SECTION 4. SAFE HARBOR METHOD OF ACCOUNTING FOR UNCOLLECTED INTEREST

.01 *Safe Harbor Method.* Under the safe harbor method of accounting provided by this SECTION 4, a bank determines for each taxable year the amount of uncollected interest (other than interest described in 1.446–2(a)(2)) for which it is considered to have a reasonable expectancy of payment by multiplying: (1) the total accrued (determined under § 1.446–2) but uncollected interest for the year by, (2) the bank's "recovery percentage" (determined under paragraph .02 of this SECTION 4) for that year. Solely for purposes of this safe harbor, the bank is not considered to have a reasonable expectancy of payment for the excess, if any, of the accrued but uncollected interest over the expected collection amount determined using the bank's recovery percentage. The bank includes in gross income the portion of accrued but uncollected interest for which it has a reasonable expectancy of payment. The bank excludes from income the portion of accrued but uncollected interest for which it has no reasonable expectancy of payment.

.02 *Recovery Percentage.* (1) Subject to the limitations and conditions in subparagraphs (2) – (4) of this SECTION 4.02, a bank determines its recovery percentage for each taxable year by dividing—

(a) total payments that the bank received on loans (including principal and interest) during the 5 taxable years immediately preceding the taxable year (or, with the approval of the Commissioner, a shorter period if the bank has less than 6 years of collection experience, *i.e.*, the taxable year and the 5 immediately preceding taxable years), by

(b) total amounts that were due and payable to the bank on loans during the same 5 (or fewer) taxable years.

(2) The recovery percentage cannot exceed 100 percent.

(3) The recovery percentage must be calculated to at least four decimal places.

(4) The data used in the recovery percentage must take into account acquisitions and dispositions as follows:

(a) If a bank acquires the major portion of a trade or business of another person (predecessor) or the major portion of a separate unit of a trade or business of a predecessor, then in applying this revenue procedure for any taxable year ending on or after the acquisition, the data from preceding taxable years of the predecessor attributable to the portion of the trade or business acquired, if available, must be used in determining the bank's recovery percentage.

(b) If a bank disposes of a major portion of a trade or business or the major portion of a separate unit of a trade or business, and the bank furnished the acquiring person the information necessary for the computations required by this revenue procedure, then in applying this revenue procedure for any taxable year ending on or after the disposition, the data from preceding taxable years attributable to the disposed portion of the trade or business may not be used in determining the bank's recovery percentage.

SECTION 5. EXAMPLE

.01 *Facts.* Bank X is a calendar year taxpayer that determines its taxable income using an accrual method of accounting. For 2007, Bank X's accrued but uncollected interest (determined under § 1.446–2) is $51,600. Bank X uses the safe harbor method of accounting described in SECTION 4 of this revenue procedure to determine the amount of uncollected interest for which the Bank has a reasonable expectancy of payment. During the 5 immediately preceding taxable years, Bank X received $73,048,313 of payments on all of its loans. During the same 5-year period, $74,900,705 was due and payable on the loans.

.02 *Analysis.* (1) To determine the portion of the accrued but uncollected interest for which there is a reasonable expectancy of payment, Bank X first calculates its recovery percentage for 2007. Bank X determines its recovery percentage by dividing the $73,048,313 of payments received during the 2002–2006 period by the $74,900,705 that was due and payable during the same period. Bank X's 2007 recovery percentage is 97.5269% [$73,048,313 ÷ $74,900,705 = 97.5269%]. Bank X determines the portion of the uncollected 2007 interest for which it is considered to have a reasonable expectancy of payment by multiplying the $51,600 of accrued but uncollected interest for that year by the 97.5269 recovery percentage. Bank X has a reasonable expectancy of payment for $50,323.88 of the uncollected 2007 interest [$51,600 × 97.5269% = $50,323.88]. Bank X includes the $50,323.88 of uncollected 2007 interest in gross income for 2007.

(2) Bank X is considered not to have a reasonable expectancy of payment for $1,276.12 of the uncollected 2007 interest ($51,600 - $50,323.88 = $1,276.12). Bank X excludes $1,276.12 of the uncollected 2007 interest from its 2007 gross income.

SECTION 6. ADOPTION OF SAFE HARBOR METHOD OF ACCOUNTING

.01 Any change to the safe harbor method provided in SECTION 4 of this revenue procedure is a change in method of accounting to which the provisions of section 446 and section 481, and the regulations thereunder, apply. Under § 1.446–1(e)(2)(i), a taxpayer generally must secure the consent of the Commissioner before changing a method of accounting for federal income tax purposes. Section 1.446–1(e)(3)(ii) authorizes the Commissioner to prescribe administrative procedures setting forth the terms and conditions necessary to obtain consent to change a method of accounting.

.02 If a bank with less than 6 years of collection experience wants to change its method of accounting for uncollected interest to the safe harbor method provided in SECTION 4 of this revenue procedure, the bank is required to follow the provisions of Rev. Proc. 97–27, 1997–1 C.B. 680 (or its successor), as modified and amplified by Rev. Proc. 2002–19, as amplified and clarified by Rev. Proc. 2002–54, except that the scope limitations in section 4.02(2) through (6) of Rev. Proc. 97–27 do not apply to a bank that makes the change for either its first or second taxable year ending on or after December 31, 2006.

.03 If a bank with 6 or more years of collection experience wants to change its method of accounting for uncollected interest to the safe harbor method provided in SECTION 4 of this revenue procedure, the bank is required to follow the automatic change in method of accounting provisions of Rev. Proc. 2002–9 (or its successor), with the following modifications:

(1) the scope limitations in section 4.02 of Rev. Proc. 2002–9 do not apply to a bank that makes the change for either its first or second taxable year ending on or after December 31, 2006; and

(2) the designated automatic accounting change number for changes in method of accounting made pursuant to the revenue procedure is 108.

SECTION 7. REQUEST FOR COMMENTS

The Internal Revenue Service requests comments on this revenue procedure. In particular, comments are requested regarding the appropriate treatment of payments received in future years. For example, comments are requested regarding how to determine the portion, if any, of a payment attributable to amounts that the bank excluded from gross income. All comments should be submitted by August 20, 2007, to:

Internal Revenue Service
P. O. Box 7604
Ben Franklin Station
Washington, DC 20044
Attn: CC:PA:LPD:PRB (FIP)
Room 5529

Alternatively, comments may be submitted electronically directly to the Service via the following e-mail address: *Notice.comments@irscounsel.treas.gov.* Please include "Rev. Proc. 2007–33" in the subject line of any electronic communication. All materials submitted will be available for public inspection and copying.

SECTION 8. EFFECTIVE DATE

This revenue procedure is effective for tax years ending on or after its publication.

SECTION 9. EFFECT ON OTHER DOCUMENTS

Rev. Proc. 2002–9 is modified and amplified to include the accounting method change provided by this revenue procedure.

DRAFTING INFORMATION

The principal author of this revenue procedure is Timothy Sebastian of the Office of the Associate Chief Counsel (Financial Institutions and Products). For further information regarding this revenue procedure, contact Mr. Sebastian (202) 622–7417 (not a toll-free call).

Part IV. Items of General Interest

Notice of Proposed Rulemaking and Notice of Public Hearing

Guidance Under Section 2053 Regarding Post-Death Events

REG–143316–03

AGENCY: Internal Revenue Service (IRS), Treasury.

ACTION: Notice of proposed rulemaking and notice of public hearing.

SUMMARY: This document contains proposed amendments to the regulations relating to the amount deductible from a decedent's gross estate for claims against the estate under section 2053(a)(3) of the Internal Revenue Code (Code). In addition, the proposed regulations update the provisions relating to the deduction for certain state death taxes to reflect the statutory amendments made in 2001 under sections 2053(d) and 2058. The proposed regulations will affect estates of decedents against whom there are claims outstanding at the time of the decedent's death. This document also provides notice of a public hearing on these proposed regulations.

DATES: Written or electronic comments must be received by July 23, 2007. Outlines of topics to be discussed at the public hearing scheduled for August 6, 2007, at 10 a.m., must be received by July 30, 2007.

ADDRESSES: Send submissions to: CC:PA:LPD:PR (REG–143316–03), Room 5203, Internal Revenue Service, PO Box 7604, Ben Franklin Station, Washington, DC 20044. Submissions may be hand delivered Monday through Friday between the hours of 8 a.m. and 4 p.m. to CC:PA:LPD:PR (REG–143316–03), Courier's Desk, Internal Revenue Service, 1111 Constitution Avenue, NW, Washington, DC; or sent electronically via the Federal eRulemaking Portal at *http://www.regulations.gov* (IRS REG–143316–03). The public hearing will be held in the IRS Auditorium, Internal Revenue Building, 1111 Constitution Avenue, NW, Washington, DC.

FOR FURTHER INFORMATION CONTACT: Concerning the proposed regulations, DeAnn K. Malone, at (202) 622–3112; concerning submissions of comments, the hearing, and/or to be placed on the building access list to attend the hearing, Richard Hurst, at (202) 622–2949 (TDD telephone) (not toll-free numbers) or e-mail at *Richard.A.Hurst@irscounsel.treas.gov*.

SUPPLEMENTARY INFORMATION:

Background

Section 2001 of the Code imposes a tax on the transfer of the taxable estate, determined as provided in section 2051, of every decedent, citizen, or resident of the United States. Section 2031(a) generally provides that the value of the decedent's gross estate shall include the value at the time of decedent's death of all property, real or personal, tangible or intangible, wherever situated. Section 2051 provides that the value of the taxable estate is determined by deducting from the value of the gross estate the deductions provided for in sections 2051 through 2058. Pursuant to section 2053(a), "the value of the taxable estate shall be determined by deducting from the value of the gross estate such amounts – (1) for funeral expenses, (2) for administration expenses, (3) for claims against the estate, and (4) for unpaid mortgages on, or any indebtedness in respect of, property where the value of the decedent's interest therein, undiminished by such mortgage or indebtedness, is included in the value of the gross estate, as are allowable by the laws of the jurisdiction, whether within or without the United States, under which the estate is being administered."

The deductions allowable under sections 2051 through 2058 operate to eliminate from estate taxation those portions of the gross estate that are necessarily expended in paying certain claims and expenses of the estate. The rationale for those deductions is that those expended portions of the gross estate are not transferred to the decedent's legatees, beneficiaries, or heirs and, therefore, are not subject to the transfer tax.

The amount an estate may deduct for claims against the estate has been a highly litigious issue. Unlike section 2031, section 2053(a) does not contain a specific directive to value a deductible claim at its date of death value. Section 2053, in fact, specifically contemplates expenses such as funeral and administration expenses, which are only determinable after the decedent's date of death. Although numerous courts have addressed section 2053(a)(3), there is little or no consistency among the conclusions of those courts with regard to the extent (if any) to which post-death events are to be considered in valuing such claims. One line of cases follows the decision in *Ithaca Trust v. Commissioner*, 279 U.S. 151 (1929), holding that the estate tax charitable deduction for a charitable remainder interest was to be determined as of date of death. In Federal judicial circuits where the *Ithaca Trust* date-of-death valuation approach is applied to a claim against a decedent's estate under section 2053(a)(3), courts generally hold that post-death events may not be considered when determining the amount deductible for that claim. At the opposite end of the spectrum, there is a line of cases that follows the Eighth Circuit's opinion in *Jacobs v. Commissioner*, 34 F.2d 233 (8th Cir. 1929), *cert. denied*, 280 U.S. 603 (1929), in which the court considered but rejected the date-of-death valuation approach in determining the deductible amount of a claim against the estate. The court in *Jacobs* distinguished *Ithaca Trust*, stating that, unlike charitable deductions, "...the claims which Congress intended to be deducted were actual claims, not theoretical ones." The court therefore held that only claims presented and determined as valid against the estate and actually paid could be deducted as claims against the estate. *Jacobs*, 34 F.2d at 235. The courts that follow *Jacobs* generally restrict the amount deductible under section 2053(a)(3) to amounts actually paid by the estate in satisfaction of the claim.

Even in the circuits where the date-of-death valuation approach has been applied in determining the amount that may be deducted for a claim against the decedent's estate, courts have recognized exceptions that necessitate taking into account events that occur after the decedent's death. For example, courts have deviated from the date-of-death valuation approach in favor of the actual payment approach when a claim is contested, contingent, unenforceable, becomes unenforceable after the decedent's death, or is not in fact presented for payment. The application and extent of these exceptions are inconsistent from circuit to circuit, however, and cannot be reconciled to form a conclusive rule applicable to all estates.

The result of this lack of consistency in the case law is that similarly situated estates are being treated differently for Federal estate tax purposes, depending only upon the jurisdiction in which the executor resides. The Treasury Department and the IRS believe that similarly situated estates should be treated consistently by having section 2053(a)(3) construed and applied in the same way in all jurisdictions.

One possible approach would be to value claims against a decedent's estate on the basis of the facts existing on the date of the decedent's death. The Treasury Department and the IRS believe, however, that this date-of-death valuation approach, when applied, has required an inefficient use of resources for taxpayers, the IRS, and the courts. Determining a date-of-death value requires the taxpayer and the IRS to retry the substantive issues underlying the claims against the estate in a tax controversy setting. In most cases, the tax controversy is addressed after the issue either has been settled by or has been argued by parties with adverse interests in a court of competent jurisdiction that is more familiar with the nuances of the underlying applicable law. Furthermore, this approach has proven to be expensive, both in terms of appraisal and litigation costs. In addition, this approach generally results in a deduction that is different from the amount actually paid on disputed claims. Finally, the date-of-death valuation approach often forces the taxpayer involved in actively defending against a claim to take contradictory positions on the estate tax return and in the substantive court pleadings, and may actually increase the taxpayer's potential liability.

After carefully considering the numerous judicial decisions and the analysis and conclusion in each, the legislative history of section 2053 and its predecessors, and the various possible alternatives, and in order to further the goal of the effective and fair administration of the tax laws, the proposed regulations adopt rules based on the premise that an estate may deduct under section 2053(a)(3) only amounts actually paid in settlement of claims against the estate. If the resolution of a contested or contingent claim cannot be reached prior to the expiration of the period of limitations for claims for refund, the estate may file a protective claim for refund to preserve its right to claim a deduction under section 2053(a).

Explanation of Provisions

The proposed regulations will amend the regulations under section 2053 to clarify that events occurring after a decedent's death are to be considered when determining the amount deductible under all provisions of section 2053 and that deductions under section 2053 are limited to amounts actually paid by the estate in satisfaction of deductible expenses and claims. Final court decisions as to the amount and enforceability of the claim or expense are accepted in determining the amount deductible if the court passes upon the facts upon which deductibility depends. Settlements are accepted if they are reached in *bona fide* negotiations between adverse parties with valid claims recognizable under applicable law, and if they are not inconsistent with the applicable law. A protective claim for refund may be filed before the expiration of the period of limitations for claims for refund in order to preserve the estate's right to claim a refund if the amount of a liability will not be ascertainable by the time of the expiration of the period of limitations for claims of refund. A deduction is not allowed to the extent the expense or claim is compensated for by insurance or is otherwise reimbursed.

The proposed regulations further provide that no deduction may be taken on an estate tax return for a claim that is potential, unmatured, or contested at the time the return is filed. A protective claim for refund may be filed before the expiration of the period of limitations for claims for refund in order to preserve the estate's right to claim a refund by reason of the deduction of a claim against the estate to the extent that claim is ultimately paid by the estate.

Additional provisions in the proposed regulations provide guidance for other particular circumstances. When a claim against an estate lists multiple defendants, the estate may only deduct the decedent's portion of the liability. Claims by family members or beneficiaries of a decedent's estate will be strictly scrutinized to ensure that they are legitimate claims. If a claim becomes unenforceable after the decedent's death, the estate may not take a section 2053(a)(3) deduction with respect to the claim. If a claim represents a decedent's obligation to make recurring payments that will likely continue for a period extending beyond the final determination of the estate tax liability, a deduction is allowed only as each payment is made, provided the period of limitations for claims for refund has not expired or the estate has properly preserved the claim for refund. Alternatively, a deduction is allowed for the cost of a commercial annuity purchased by the estate from an unrelated dealer in commercial annuities in satisfaction of that obligation.

Finally, the proposed regulations reflect changes made to section 2053(d) and the enactment of section 2058 in 2001 and clarify that the rules in section 20.2053–9 apply only to the estates of decedents dying on or before December 31, 2004.

Proposed Effective Date

The regulations, as proposed, apply to the estate of any decedent dying on or after the date final regulations are published in the **Federal Register**.

Special Analyses

It has been determined that this notice of proposed rulemaking is not a significant regulatory action as defined in Executive Order 12866. Therefore, a regulatory assessment is not required. It has also been determined that section 553(b) of the Administrative Procedure Act (5 U.S.C. chapter 5) does not apply to these regulations, and because these regulations do not impose a collection of information on small entities, the Regulatory Flexibility Act (5 U.S.C. chapter 6) does not apply. Therefore, a Regulatory Flexibility Analysis is not required. Pursuant to section 7805(f) of the Code, this notice of proposed rulemaking will be submitted to the Chief Counsel for Advocacy of the Small Business Administration for comment on its impact on small business.

Comments and Public Hearing

Before these proposed regulations are adopted as final regulations, consideration will be given to any written (a signed original and eight (8) copies) or electronic comments that are submitted timely to the IRS. The IRS and the Treasury Department also request comments on the clarity of the proposed rules and how they can be made easier to understand. All comments will be available for public inspection and copying.

A public hearing has been scheduled for August 6, 2007, at 10 a.m. in the IRS Auditorium, Internal Revenue Service, 1111 Constitution Avenue, NW, Washington, DC. Due to building security procedures, visitors must enter at the Constitution Avenue entrance. In addition, all visitors must present photo identification to enter the building. Because of access restrictions, visitors will not be admitted beyond the immediate entrance area more than 30 minutes before the hearing starts. For information about having your name placed on the building access list to attend the hearing, see the "FOR FURTHER INFORMATION CONTACT" section of this preamble.

The rules of 26 CFR 601.601(a)(3) apply to the hearing. Persons who wish to present oral comments at the hearing must submit electronic or written comments by July 16, 2007, and an outline of the topics to be discussed and the time to be devoted to each topic (signed original and eight (8) copies) by July 30, 2007. A period of 10 minutes will be allotted to each person for making comments. An agenda showing the scheduling of the speakers will be prepared after the deadline for receiving outlines has passed. Copies of the agenda will be available free of charge at the hearing.

Drafting Information

The principal author of these proposed regulations is DeAnn K. Malone, Office of the Chief Counsel, IRS.

* * * * *

Proposed Amendments to the Regulations

Accordingly, 26 CFR part 20 is proposed to be amended as follows:

PART 20—ESTATE TAX; ESTATES OF DECEDENTS DYING AFTER AUGUST 16, 1954

Paragraph 1. The authority citation for part 20 continues to read in part as follows:

Authority: 26 U.S.C. 7805. * * *

Par. 2. Section 20.2051–1 is revised to read as follows:

§20.2051–1 Definition of taxable estate.

(a) The taxable estate of a decedent who was a citizen or resident (see §20.0–1(b)(1)(i)) of the United States at death is determined by subtracting the total amount of the deductions authorized by sections 2052 through 2058 from the total amount which must be included in the gross estate under sections 2031 through 2044. These deductions are in general as follows:

(1) An exemption of $60,000 (section 2052) (applicable only to the estates of decedents dying on or before December 31, 1976).

(2) Funeral and administration expenses and claims against the estate (including certain taxes and charitable pledges) (section 2053).

(3) Losses from casualty or theft during the administration of the estate (section 2054).

(4) Charitable transfers (section 2055).

(5) The marital deduction (section 2056).

(6) Qualified domestic trusts (section 2056A).

(7) Family-owned business interests (section 2057) (applicable only to the estates of decedents dying on or before December 31, 2003).

(8) State death taxes (section 2058) (applicable only to the estates of decedents dying after December 31, 2004).

(b) See section 2106 and these regulations for the computation of the taxable estate of a decedent who was not a citizen or resident of the United States. See also §1.642(g)–1 of this chapter concerning the disallowance for income tax purposes of certain deductions allowed for estate tax purposes.

(c) *Effective date.* The rules of this section apply to the estates of decedents dying on or after the date of publication of the Treasury decision adopting these rules as final regulations in the **Federal Register**.

Par. 3. Section 20.2053–1 is amended by:

1. Revising the introductory text of paragraph (a).

2. Adding two new sentences at the end of paragraph (b)(1).

3. Revising paragraph (b)(2).

4. Redesignating paragraph (b)(3) as (b)(4) and revising the newly-designated paragraph (b)(4).

5. Adding new paragraphs (b)(3), (b)(5), (b)(6), and (e).

The revisions and additions read as follows:

§20.2053–1 Deductions for expenses, indebtedness, and taxes; in general.

(a) *General rule.* In determining the taxable estate of a decedent who was a citizen or resident of the United States at death, there are allowed as deductions under section 2053(a) and (b) amounts falling within the following two categories (subject to the limitations contained in this section and in §§20.2053–2 through 20.2053–10):

* * * * *

(b) * * * (1) * * * In order to properly take into account events occurring after the date of a decedent's death when determining the amount deductible against a decedent's estate, the deduction for any item described in paragraph (a) of this section is limited to the total amount actually paid (subject to any time requirement under paragraph (a) of this section) in settlement or satisfaction of that item. (See however, §20.2053–1(b)(4) for a special rule for deducting certain estimated amounts.)

(2) *Effect of court decree*—(i) *In general.* If the court with appropriate jurisdiction over the administration of the estate reviews and approves expenditures for funeral expenses, administration expenses, claims against the estate, or unpaid mortgages as allowable estate expenditures under local law, the executor may rely on the final judicial decision in that matter to determine the amount deductible for estate tax purposes if the following conditions are satisfied: the expenditures are otherwise deductible under section 2053 and the corresponding regulations; the expenditures have been paid by the estate or meet the requirements for estimated

expenses; the court reviewed the facts relating to the expenditures; and the court's decision is consistent with local law. See §20.2053–2 for additional rules regarding the deductibility of funeral expenses. See §20.2053–3 for additional rules regarding the deductibility of administration expenses. See §20.2053–4 for additional rules regarding the deductibility of claims against the estate. See §20.2053–7 for additional rules regarding the deductibility of unpaid mortgages. If the decision reached by the court is inconsistent with local law, the estate may not rely on the court's decree to establish the amount deductible for estate tax purposes. For example, a local court decree approving an allowance made to an executor in excess of the amount or limit prescribed by statute may not be relied upon to establish the amount deductible under section 2053. An estate will not be denied an otherwise allowable deduction under section 2053 solely because a local court decree has not been entered with respect to that amount if the amount would be allowable under local law and if no court decree is required under applicable law for payment.

(ii) *Consent decree*. An executor may rely on a local court decree rendered by consent to establish the amount deductible under section 2053 for amounts paid (or meeting the requirements for estimated expenses) if the consent was a *bona fide* recognition of the validity of the claim and was accepted by the court as satisfactory evidence upon the merits. Consent given by all parties having interests adverse to that of the claimant will be presumed to be recognition of the claim's validity. See §20.2053–4(b)(4) for special rules to determine the amount deductible for claims by decedent's family members, related entities, or beneficiaries of the decedent's estate or revocable trust.

(3) *Settlements*. An executor may rely on a settlement to establish the amount deductible under section 2053 for amounts paid (or meeting the requirements for estimated expenses) (subject to any applicable time limitation under paragraph (a) of this section) if the following conditions are satisfied: the settlement resolves a *bona fide* issue in an active and genuine contest; the settlement is the product of arm's length negotiations by parties having adverse interests with respect to the claim; and the settlement is within the range of reasonable outcomes under applicable state law governing the issues resolved by the settlement. A settlement that results in a compromise between the positions of such adverse parties and reflects the parties' assessments of the relative strengths of their respective positions is a settlement that is within the range of reasonable outcomes. However, a deduction for amounts paid in settlement of a claim against the decedent's estate will not be allowed if the terms of the settlement are inconsistent with applicable local law. No deduction will be allowed for amounts paid in settlement of an unenforceable claim. See §20.2053–4(b)(4) for special rules to determine the amount deductible for claims by decedent's family members, related entities, or beneficiaries of the decedent's estate or revocable trust. For settlements structured using recurring payments, see §20.2053–4(b)(7).

(4) *Estimated amounts*. A deduction will be allowed for a claim that satisfies all applicable requirements even though its exact amount is not then known, provided that the amount is ascertainable with reasonable certainty, and will be paid. Under this exception to the rule set forth in paragraph (b)(1) of this section, no deduction may be taken upon the basis of a vague or uncertain estimate. If a deduction is allowed in advance of payment and the payment is thereafter waived or otherwise left unpaid, it shall be the duty of the executor to notify the Commissioner and to pay the resulting tax, together with interest. To the extent that the amount of a liability otherwise deductible under section 2053 is not ascertainable with reasonable certainty at the time of examination of the return by the Commissioner, or to the extent that it is not then clear that the amount will be paid, that amount will not be allowed as a deduction by the Commissioner. If the deduction is disallowed in whole or in part on examination of the return and the amount of the liability is subsequently ascertained and paid, relief may be sought by a timely claim for refund as provided by section 6511. A protective claim for refund may be filed before the expiration of the period of limitations for claims for refund in order to preserve the estate's right to claim a refund if the amount of a liability was or will not be paid before the expiration of the period of limitations for claims for refund. Although the protective claim need not state a particular dollar amount or demand an immediate refund, the protective claim must identify the outstanding liability or claim that would have been deductible under section 2053(a) had it already been paid. The protective claim must also describe the reasons and contingencies delaying the determination of the liability or the actual payment of the claim. Action on protective claims will proceed after the executor has notified the Commissioner that the contingency has been resolved.

(5) *Reimbursements*. A deduction is not allowed to the extent that the expense or claim is or could be compensated for by insurance or otherwise reimbursed.

(6) *Examples*. The following examples illustrate the application of this section. Assume that the amounts are payable out of property subject to claims and are allowable by the law of the jurisdiction governing the administration of the estate, whether the applicable jurisdiction is within or without the United States.

Example 1. Estimated amounts, deduction ascertainable. Decedent's (D's) estate was probated in state. State law provides that the personal representative shall receive compensation equal to 2.5 percent of the value of the probate estate. The executor (E) may claim a deduction for estimated fees equal to 2.5 percent of D's probate estate on the estate tax return filed for D's estate as an estimated amount, provided the amount will be paid to E after the estate tax return is filed. To the extent that, at the time of the examination of the return, the amount has not been paid and E cannot satisfy the conditions listed in paragraph (b)(4) of this section and §20.2053–3(b)(1), the deduction will be disallowed, but the executor may file a timely protective claim for refund to protect the estate's right to a refund once the amount has been paid or satisfies the applicable conditions. If the deduction is allowed in advance of payment and the payment is thereafter waived or otherwise left unpaid, it shall be the duty of the executor to notify the Commissioner and to pay the resulting tax, together with interest.

Example 2. Estimated amounts, deduction not ascertainable. Prior to death, Decedent (D) is sued by Claimant (C) for \$100x in a tort proceeding and responds asserting affirmative defenses available to D under applicable local law. C and D are unrelated. D subsequently dies and D's Form 706 is due before a final judgment is entered in the case. The executor (E) of D's estate may not take a deduction for \$100x on D's estate tax return as an estimated amount because the deductible amount cannot be ascertained with reasonable certainty in accordance with §20.2053–4(b)(2). If the amount of the actual liability will not be paid or cannot be ascertained with reasonable certainty before the expiration of the period of limitations for claims for refund, E may file a protective claim before that date in order to preserve the estate's right subsequently to claim a refund.

* * * * *

(e) *Effective date.* The rules of this section apply to the estates of decedents dying on or after the date of publication of the Treasury decision adopting these rules as final regulations in the **Federal Register**.

Par. 4. Section 20.2053–3 is amended by:

1. Redesignating paragraphs (b)(2) and (b)(3) as paragraphs (b)(4) and (b)(5), respectively.

2. Designating the undesignated text following paragraph (b)(1) as new paragraph (b)(3).

3. Revising paragraphs (b)(1) and (c)(1).

4. Adding new paragraphs (b)(2), (d)(3) and (e).

The revisions and additions read as follows:

§20.2053–3 Deductions for expenses of administering estate.

* * * * *

(b) *Executor's commissions.* (1) The executor, in filing the estate tax return, may deduct executor's commissions in such an amount as has actually been paid, or in an amount which at the time of filing the estate tax return may reasonably be expected to be paid, but no deduction may be taken if no commissions are to be collected. If the amount of the commissions has not been fixed by decree of the proper court, the deduction will be allowed on the examination of the return, to the extent that all three of the following conditions are satisfied:

(i) The Commissioner is reasonably satisfied that the commissions claimed will be paid.

(ii) The amount claimed as a deduction is within the amount allowable by the laws of the jurisdiction in which the estate is being administered.

(iii) It is in accordance with the usually accepted practice in the jurisdiction to allow such an amount in estates of similar size and character.

(2) If the conditions described in paragraph (b)(1) of this section are not met, a protective claim for refund may be filed before the expiration of the period of limitations for claims for refund in order to preserve the estate's right to claim a refund for future amounts paid as described in §20.2053–1(b)(4).

(3) If the deduction is disallowed in whole or in part on the examination of the return and a protective claim was timely filed, the disallowance will be subject to modification once the requirements for deductibility are met. If the deduction is allowed in advance of payment and payment is thereafter waived or otherwise left unpaid, it shall be the duty of the executor to notify the Commissioner and to pay the resulting tax, together with interest.

* * * * *

(c) *Attorney's fees.* (1) The executor, in filing the estate tax return, may deduct such an amount of attorney's fees as has actually been paid, or an amount which at the time of filing may reasonably be expected to be paid. If on the examination of the return, the fees claimed have not been awarded by the proper court and paid, the deduction will, nevertheless, be allowed, if the Commissioner is reasonably satisfied that the amount claimed will be paid and that it does not exceed a reasonable remuneration for the services rendered, taking into account the size and character of the estate and the local law and practice. If the amount does not satisfy these requirements, a protective claim for refund may be filed before the expiration of the period of limitations for claims for refund in order to preserve the estate's right to claim a refund for future amounts paid as described in §20.2053–1(b)(4). If the deduction is disallowed in whole or in part on the examination of the return and a protective claim was timely filed, the disallowance will be subject to modification once the requirements for deductibility are met.

* * * * *

(d) * * *

(3) Expenses incurred in defending the estate against claims described in section 2053(a)(3) are deductible as provided in §20.2053–1 if the expenses are incurred incident to the assertion of defenses to the claim available under the applicable law, even if the estate is not ultimately victorious. For purposes of this section, "expenses incurred in defending the estate against claims" include costs relating to the arbitration and mediation of contested issues, costs associated with defending the estate against claims (whether or not enforceable), and costs associated with reaching a negotiated settlement of the issues. Expenses incurred merely for the purpose of unreasonably extending the time for payment, or incurred other than in good faith, are not deductible.

(e) Effective date. The rules of this section apply to the estates of decedents dying on or after the date of publication of the Treasury decision adopting these rules as final regulations in the **Federal Register**.

Par. 5. Section 20.2053–4 is revised to read as follows:

§20.2053–4 Deduction for claims against the estate.

(a) *In general.* (1) For purposes of this section, liabilities imposed by law or arising out of contracts or torts are deductible if they meet the requirements set forth in §20.2053–1 and this section. Except as provided in paragraph (b) of this section, the amounts that may be deducted as claims against a decedent's estate are limited to amounts for legitimate and *bona fide* claims that—

(i) Represent personal obligations of the decedent existing at the time of the decedent's death;

(ii) Are enforceable against the decedent's estate at the time of payment; and

(iii) Are actually paid by the estate in settlement of the claim.

(2) Events occurring after the date of a decedent's death shall be considered when determining the amount deductible against a decedent's estate.

(b) *Special rules*—(1) *Potential and unmatured claims.* Claims that are unmatured on the date of the decedent's death and that later mature and are paid are deductible by the estate. However, no deduction may be taken on an estate tax return for a potential or unmatured claim. If the claim matures and is paid prior to the expiration of the period of limitations for filing a claim for refund, the estate may file a claim for refund as provided by section 6511. A protective claim for refund may be filed before the expiration of the period of limitations for claims for refund in order to preserve the estate's right to claim a refund once the claim against the decedent's estate is matured and is paid or may be estimated as provided in §20.2053–1(b)(4). Although the protective claim need not state a particular dollar amount or demand an immediate refund, the protective claim must identify the outstanding liability or claim that would have been deductible under section 2053(a) had it already been paid, and must describe the reasons and contingencies delaying actual payment of the liability or claim. Action on protective claims will proceed after the executor has notified the Commissioner that the contingency has been resolved.

(2) *Contested claims.* No deduction may be taken on an estate tax return for a claim against the decedent's estate to the extent the estate is contesting the decedent's liability. However, see §20.2053–1(b)(4) relating to estimated amounts.

(3) *Claims against multiple parties.* If the decedent or the decedent's estate is one of two or more parties against whom the claim is being asserted, the estate may only deduct the portion of the total claim due from and paid by the estate, reduced by the total of any reimbursement received from another party, insurance, or otherwise. The estate's deductible portion will also be reduced by the amount or contribution the estate could have collected from another party or an insurer but which the estate declines or fails to attempt to collect. If, however, the estate establishes that the burden of necessary collection efforts would have outweighed the benefit from those efforts, the potential reimbursement will not reduce the estate's deductible portion of the total claim. If the estate establishes that the party from whom a potential reimbursement could be collected could only pay a portion of the potential reimbursement, then only that portion that could reasonably have been expected to be collected will reduce the estate's deductible portion of the total claim.

(4) *Claims by family members, related entities, or beneficiaries.* Relationships with and among a decedent and the decedent's family members, related entities, and beneficiaries may create the potential for collusion in asserting invalid or exaggerated claims in order to reduce the decedent's taxable estate. Thus, notwithstanding §20.2053–1 and paragraph (a) of this section, there will be a rebuttable presumption that claims by a family member of the decedent, a related entity, or a beneficiary of the decedent's estate or revocable trust are not legitimate and *bona fide* and therefore are not deductible. Evidence sufficient to rebut the presumption may include evidence that the claim arises from circumstances that would reasonably support a similar claim by unrelated persons or non-beneficiaries. Similarly, a settlement between a decedent's estate or revocable trust and a family member, a related entity, or a beneficiary of the decedent's estate or revocable trust will be presumed to not be deductible absent evidence of the legitimacy and *bona fide* nature of the claim. For purposes of this section, family members include the spouse of the decedent; the grandparents, parents, siblings, and lineal descendants of the decedent or of the decedent's spouse; and the spouse and lineal descendants of any such grandparent, parent, and sibling. Family members include adopted individuals. For purposes of this section, a related entity is an entity in which the decedent, either directly or indirectly, had a beneficial ownership interest at the time of the decedent's death or at any time during the three-year period ending on the decedent's date of death. Such an entity, however, shall not include a publicly-traded entity nor shall it include a closely-held entity in which the combined beneficial interest, either direct or indirect, of the decedent and the decedent's family members, collectively, is less than thirty percent of the beneficial ownership interests (whether voting or non-voting).

(5) *Unenforceable claims.* Claims that are unenforceable prior to or at the decedent's death are not deductible, even if they are actually paid. Claims that become unenforceable during the administration of the estate are not deductible to the extent that they are paid after they become unenforceable. To the extent that enforceability of a claim is at issue, see paragraph (b)(2) of this section relating to contested claims.

(6) *Claims founded upon a promise.* Except with regard to pledges or subscriptions, (see §20.2053–5), section 2053(c)(1)(A) provides that the deduction for a claim founded upon a promise or agreement is limited to the extent that the promise or agreement was *bona fide* and in exchange for adequate and full consideration in money or money's worth. For this purpose, *bona fide* and for adequate and full consideration in money or money's worth requires that the promise or agreement must have been made in good faith, and that the price must have been an adequate and full equivalent reducible to a money value.

(7) *Recurring payments*—(i) *Non-Contingent obligations.* If a decedent is obligated to make recurring payments on an enforceable and certain claim that are not subject to a contingency and if the payments will continue for a period that will likely extend beyond the final determination of the estate tax liability, the obligation may be deducted as an estimated amount using the rules in §20.2053–1. The amount deductible is the present value of the payments on the decedent's date of death as determined under §20.2031–7(d). See §§20.7520–1 through 20.7520–4. If there is a reasonable likelihood that full satisfaction of the liability will not be made, then the obligation will be deemed to be subject to a contingency for purposes of this section.

(ii) *Contingent obligations.* If a decedent has a recurring obligation to pay an enforceable and certain claim, but the decedent's obligation is subject to a contingency or is otherwise not described in paragraph (b)(7)(i) of this section, the estate's deduction is limited to amounts actually paid by the estate in satisfaction of the claim.

(iii) *Purchase of commercial annuity to satisfy recurring obligation to pay.* If a decedent has a recurring obligation (whether or not contingent) to pay an enforceable and certain claim and the estate purchases a commercial annuity from an unrelated dealer in commercial annuities in an arms-length transaction to satisfy the obligation, the amount deductible by the estate is the sum of—

(A) The amount paid for the commercial annuity; and

(B) Any amount actually paid to the claimant by the estate prior to the purchase of the commercial annuity.

(c) *Interest on claims.* The interest on a deductible claim is itself deductible as a claim under section 2053, but only to the extent of the amount of interest accrued at the date of the decedent's death and actually paid, even if the executor elects the alternate valuation method under section 2032. (Post-death accrued interest may be deductible in appropriate circumstances either as an estate tax administration expense under section 2053 or as an income tax deduction.)

(d) *Examples.* The following examples illustrate the application of paragraphs (a) through (c) of this section. Except as is otherwise provided in the examples, assume that the claimant (C) is not a family member, related entity or beneficiary of the decedent (D) and is not the executor (E). Assume that a claim represents a personal obligation of D existing at the time of D's death and is enforceable against D's estate. Assume that the payment of the claim, where applicable, is made out of property subject to claims (as defined in section 2053(c)(2) and §20.2053–1(c)(2)) and is allowable by the law of the jurisdiction under which the decedent's estate is being administered, or is paid prior to the filing of the estate tax return (including any extension granted under section 6081) from property not subject to claims. Assume that any court decree is based upon the facts upon which deductibility depends and is consistent with applicable local law. Assume that any settlement is reached in *bona fide* negotiations between or among parties having adverse interests with respect to the claim and that the terms of the settlement are not inconsistent with applicable local law.

Example 1. Contested claim, single defendant, no decision. D is sued by C for $100x in a tort proceeding and responds asserting affirmative defenses available to D under applicable local law. D dies and E is substituted as defendant in the suit. D's estate tax return is due before a judgment is reached in the case. D's gross estate includes only property subject to claims and exceeds $100x. E may not take a deduction on the return for the claim under section 2053(a)(3). A deduction may be claimed on the return, however, for expenses incurred prior to the filing of the estate tax return in defending the estate against the claim if the expenses have been paid in accordance with §20.2053–3(c) or (d)(3) or as an estimate under §20.2053–1(b)(4). E may file a protective claim for refund before the expiration of the period of limitations for claims for refund of the estate tax in order to preserve the estate's right to claim a refund if the amount of the liability will not be paid or cannot be ascertained with reasonable certainty by the expiration of that period of limitations. If payment is subsequently made pursuant to a court decision or a settlement, a deduction for the payment, as well as expenses incurred incident to the claim and not previously deducted, may be taken and relief may be sought by supplementing a previously filed protective claim or by filing a claim for refund as provided by section 6511.

Example 2. Contested claim, single defendant, final court decree and payment. The facts are the same as in *Example 1* except that, before the return is timely filed, the court enters a decision in favor of C, no timely appeal is filed, and payment is made. A deduction is allowed for the amount paid in satisfaction of the claim pursuant to the final decision of the local court, including any interest accrued prior to D's death, under section 2053(a)(3). In addition, a deduction may be available under §20.2053–3(d)(3) for expenses incurred prior to the filing of the estate tax return in defending the estate against the claim and in processing payment of the claim.

Example 3. Contested claim, single defendant, settlement and payment. The facts are the same as in *Example 1* except that, before the return is timely filed, a settlement is reached between D's estate and C for $80x and payment is made. A deduction is allowed for the amount of the settlement paid to C ($80x) under section 2053(a)(3). In addition, a deduction may be available under §20.2053–3(d)(3) for expenses incurred prior to the filing of the estate tax return in defending the estate, reaching a settlement, and processing payment of the claim.

Example 4. Contested claim, multiple defendants. The facts are the same as in *Example 1* except that the suit filed by C lists D and K, an unrelated third-party, as defendants. If the claim is not resolved prior to the time the estate tax return is filed, E may not take a deduction for the claim under section 2053(a)(3) on the return. If payment is subsequently made of D's share of the claim pursuant to a court decision or a settlement holding D liable for 40 percent of the amount due and K liable for 60 percent of the amount due, then the estate may take a deduction for the amount paid in satisfaction of the claim representing D's share of the liability as assigned by the court decree ($40x), plus any interest on that share accrued prior to D's death, under section 2053(a)(3). If the court decision finds D and K jointly and severally liable for the entire $100x and D's estate pays the entire $100x but could have reasonably collected $50x from K in reimbursement, the estate may take a deduction under section 2053(a)(3) and paragraph (b)(3) of this section for only $50x and the interest on $50x accrued prior to D's death. In both instances, a deduction may also be available under §20.2053–3(d)(3) for expenses incurred and not previously deducted in defending the estate against the claim and processing payment of the amount due from D.

Example 5. Contested claim, multiple defendants, settlement and payment. The facts are the same as in *Example 1* except that the suit filed by C lists D and K, an unrelated third-party, as defendants. D's estate settles with C for $10x and payment is made before the return is timely filed. E may take a deduction for the amount paid to C in satisfaction of the claim. In addition, a deduction may be available under §20.2053–3(d)(3) for expenses incurred prior to the filing of the estate tax return in defending the estate, reaching a settlement, and processing payment of the claim.

Example 6. Mixed claims. During life, D contracts with C to perform specific work on D's home for $75x. Under the contract, additional work must be approved in advance by D. C performs additional work and sues D for $100x for work completed including the $75x agreed to in the contract. D dies and D's estate tax return is due before a judgment is reached in the case. E contests liability for $25x. E may take a deduction on the return for $75x if it has been paid or if it meets the requirements of an estimated amount. In addition, a deduction may be claimed on the return for expenses incurred in defending the estate against the claim if they have been paid under §20.2053–3(c) or (d)(3) or as an estimate under §20.2053–1(b)(4). E may file a protective claim for refund before the expiration of the period of limitations on claims for refund of the estate tax in order to preserve the estate's right to claim a refund if payment on any amount in excess of $75x is subsequently made in resolution of a claim that would qualify for a deduction under section 2053. To the extent that the expenses incurred in defending the estate against the claim are not deducted as an estimate, they may be included in the protective claim for refund.

Example 7. Unenforceable claims. D is sued by C for $100x in a tort proceeding but the claim is barred by the applicable period of limitations and there is no other recourse available to C. A deduction is not allowed for the claim under section 2053(a)(3) whether or not the estate actually pays money in satisfaction of the claim. A deduction may be available, however, under §20.2053–3(d)(3) for expenses incurred in defending the estate against the claim.

Example 8. Non-contingent and recurring obligation to pay, binding on estate. D's property settlement agreement incident to D's divorce, signed three years prior to D's death, obligates D or D's estate to pay to S, D's former spouse, $20x per year for 10 years. The payments are not conditioned on whether or not S remarries. If S dies prior to the last payment, the terms of the agreement state that the remaining payments are to be made to S's estate or as S may appoint in S's will. Prior to filing D's estate tax return, D's estate pays the first of the 7 payments remaining as of D's death. The estate may take a deduction for the present value of these payments. See §§20.7520–1 through 20.7520–4.

Example 9. Contingent recurring obligation to pay, binding on estate. D's property settlement agreement incident to D's divorce, signed three years prior to D's death, obligates D or D's estate to pay to S, D's former spouse, $20x per year for 10 years. The obligation to make the annual payments ceases upon S's remarriage or S's death prior to the due date of the last payment. Prior to filing D's estate tax return, D's estate pays the first of the 7 payments remaining as of D's death. E may take as a deduction on the return the amount of the 1 payment made prior to the filing of D's estate tax return. Additional payments become deductible as they are paid. E may file a protective claim for refund before the expiration of the period of limitations for claims for refund of the estate tax in order to preserve the estate's right to claim a refund if the amount of the liability will not be paid or is not ascertainable with reasonable certainty by the expiration of the applicable period of limitations. If the total amount to be paid in satisfaction of the liability is not ascertainable with reasonable certainty at the time of examination of the return, relief may be sought by a claim for refund (either actual or protective) as provided by section 6511.

Example 10. Recurring obligation to pay, estate purchases a commercial annuity in satisfaction. D's property settlement agreement incident to D's divorce, signed three years prior to D's death, obligates D or D's estate to pay to S, D's former spouse, $20x per year for 10 years. D's estate purchases a commercial annuity from an unrelated dealer in commercial annuities, XYZ, in a *bona fide* sale to satisfy the obligation to S. E may deduct the entire amount paid to XYZ to obtain the annuity, regardless of whether or not the obligation to S was contingent.

(e) *Effective date.* The rules of this section apply to the estates of decedents dying on or after the date of publication of the Treasury decision adopting these rules as final regulations in the **Federal Register**.

Par. 6. Section 20.2053–6 is amended by revising paragraphs (a) and (c) and adding new paragraphs (g) and (h) to read as follows:

§20.2053–6 Deduction for taxes.

(a) *In general.* Taxes are deductible in computing a decedent's gross estate only as claims against the estate (except to the extent that excise taxes may be allowable as administration expenses), and only to the extent not disallowed by section 2053(c)(1)(B) (see the remaining paragraphs of this section). However, see §§20.2053–9 and 20.2053–10 with respect to the deduction allowed for certain state and foreign death taxes.

* * * * *

(c) *Death taxes.* (1) For the estates of decedents dying on or before December 31, 2004, no estate, succession, legacy or inheritance tax payable by reason of the decedent's death is deductible, except as provided in §20.2053–9 and §20.2053–10 with respect to certain state and foreign death taxes on transfers for charitable, etc., uses. However, see sections 2011 and 2014 and these regulations with respect to credits for death taxes.

(2) For the estates of decedents dying after December 31, 2004, see section 2058 to determine the deductibility of state death taxes.

* * * * *

(g) *Post-death adjustments of deductible tax liability.* Post-death adjustments increasing a tax liability accrued prior to the decedent's death, including increases of taxes deducted under this section, will increase the amount of the deduction taken under section 2053(a)(3) for that tax liability. Similarly, any refund subsequently determined to be due to and received by the estate with respect to taxes deducted by the estate under this section reduces the amount of the deduction taken for that tax liability under section 2053(a)(3). Expenses associated with defending the estate against the increase in tax liability or with obtaining the refund may be deductible under §20.2053–3(d)(3). A protective claim for refund of estate taxes may be filed before the expiration of the period of limitations for claims for refund in order to preserve the estate's right to claim a refund if the amount of a deductible tax liability may be affected by such an adjustment or refund. The application of this section may be illustrated by the following examples:

Example 1. Increase in tax due. After the decedent's death, the Internal Revenue Service examines the gift tax return filed by the decedent in the year before the decedent's death and asserts a deficiency of $100x. The estate spends $30x in a non-frivolous defense against the increased deficiency. The final determination of the deficiency, in the amount of $90x, is paid by the estate. The estate may deduct $90x under section 2053(a)(3) and $30x under §20.2053–3(c)(2) or (d)(3).

Example 2. Refund of taxes paid. Decedent's estate timely files D's individual income tax return for the year in which the decedent died. The estate timely pays the entire amount of the tax due, $50x, as shown on that return. The entire $50x was attributable to income received prior to the decedent's death. Decedent's estate subsequently discovers an error on the income tax return and files a timely claim for refund. Decedent's estate receives a refund of $10x. The estate is only allowed a deduction of $40x under section 2053(a)(3) for the income tax liability accrued prior to the decedent's death. If a deduction for $50x was allowed on the estate tax return prior to the receipt of the refund, it shall be the duty of the executor to notify the Commissioner of the change and to pay the resulting tax, with interest.

(h) *Effective date.* The rules of this section apply to the estates of decedents dying on or after the date of publication of the Treasury decision adopting these rules as final regulations in the **Federal Register**.

Par. 7. Section 20.2053–9 is amended as follows:

1. Revising the heading for paragraph (a) and adding a sentence at the end of paragraph (a).

2. Revising the first and last sentences of paragraph (c).

3. Adding new paragraph (f).

The revisions and addition read as follows:

§20.2053–9 Deduction for certain state death taxes.

(a) *General rules for the estates of decedents dying on or before December 31, 2004.** * * For the estates of decedents dying after December 31, 2004, see section 2058 to determine the deductibility of state death taxes.

* * * * *

(c) *Exercise of election.* The election to take a deduction for a state death tax imposed upon a transfer for charitable, etc., uses shall be exercised by the executor by the filing of a written notification to that effect with the Commissioner. * * * The election may be revoked by the executor by the filing of a written notification to that effect with the Commissioner at any time before the expiration of such period.

* * * * *

(f) *Effective date.* The rules of this section apply to the estates of decedents dying on or before December 31, 2004.

Par. 8. Section 20.2053–10 is amended by revising paragraph (c) and adding a new paragraph (e) to read as follows:

§20.2053–10 Deduction for certain foreign death taxes.

* * * * *

(c) *Exercise of election.* The election to take a deduction for a foreign death tax imposed upon a transfer for charitable, etc., uses shall be exercised by the executor by the filing of a written notification to that effect with the Commissioner. An election to take the deduction for foreign death taxes is deemed to be a waiver of the right to claim a credit under a treaty with any foreign country for any tax or portion thereof claimed as a deduction under this section. The notification shall be filed before the expiration of the period of limitations for assessment provided in section 6501 (usually 3 years from the last day for filing the return). The election may be revoked by the executor by the filing of a written notification to that effect with the Commissioner at any time before the expiration of such period.

* * * * *

(e) *Effective date.* The rules of this section apply to the estates of decedents dying on or after the date of publication of the Treasury decision adopting these rules as final regulations in the **Federal Register**.

Kevin M. Brown,
Deputy Commissioner for Services and Enforcement.

(Filed by the Office of the Federal Register on April 20, 2007, 8:45 a.m., and published in the issue of the Federal Register for April 23, 2007, 72 F.R. 20080)

Dual Consolidated Loss Regulations; Correction

Announcement 2007–49

AGENCY: Internal Revenue Service (IRS), Treasury.

ACTION: Correcting amendments.

SUMMARY: This document contains corrections to final regulations (T.D. 9315, 2007–15 I.R.B. 891) that were published in the **Federal Register** on Monday, March 19, 2007 (72 FR 12902) regarding dual consolidated losses. Section 1503(d) generally provides that a dual consolidated loss of a dual resident corporation cannot reduce the taxable income of any other member of the affiliated group unless, to the extent provided in regulations, the loss does not offset the income of any foreign corporation.

DATES: These correcting amendments are effective April 25, 2007.

FOR FURTHER INFORMATION CONTACT: Jeffrey P. Cowan, (202) 622–3860 (not a toll-free number).

SUPPLEMENTARY INFORMATION:

Background

The final regulations that are the subject of this document are under section 1503(d) of the Internal Revenue Code.

Need for Correction

As published, final regulations (T.D. 9315) contain errors that may prove to be misleading and are in need of clarification.

* * * * *

Correction of Publication

Accordingly, 26 CFR part 1 is corrected by making the following correcting amendments:

PART 1—INCOME TAXES

Paragraph 1. The authority citation for part 1 continues to read as follows:

Authority: 26 U.S.C. 7805 * * *

Par. 2. Section 1.1503(d)–0 is amended by revising the entries (1) and (2) of Section 1.1503(d)–8(b). The revisions read as follows:

§1.1503(d)–0 Table of contents.

* * * * *

§1.1503(d)–8 Effective dates.

* * * * *

(b) * * *

(1) Reduction of term of agreements filed under §§1.1503–2A(c)(3), 1.1503–2A(d)(3), 1.1503–2(g)(2)(i), or 1.1503–2T(g)(2)(i).

(2) Reduction of term of agreements filed under §§1.1503–2(g)(2)(iv)(B)(*2*)(*i*) (1992), 1.1503–2(g)(2)(iv)(B)(*3*)(*i*), or Rev. Proc. 2000–42.

* * * * *

Par. 3. Section 1.1503(d)–5 is amended by revising the last sentence of paragraph (a), the second sentence of paragraph (c)(4)(i)(A), and the only sentence of paragraph (d) to read as follows:

§1.1503(d)–5 Attribution of items and basis adjustments.

(a) * * * The rules in this section apply for purposes of §§1.1503(d)–1 through 1.1503(d)–7.

* * * * *

(c) * * *

(4) * * *

(i) * * *

(A) * * * For purposes of determining items of income, gain, deduction, and loss of the domestic owner that are attributable to the domestic owner's foreign branch separate unit described in the preceding sentence, only items of income, gain, deduction, and loss that are attributable to the domestic owner's interest in the hybrid entity, or transparent entity, as provided in paragraph (c)(3) of this section, shall be taken into account. * * *

* * * * *

(d) * * * The fact that a particular item taken into account in computing the income or dual consolidated loss of a dual resident corporation or a separate unit, or the income or loss of an interest in a transparent entity, is not taken into account in computing income (or loss) subject to a foreign country's income tax shall not cause such item to be excluded from being taken into account under paragraph (b), (c), or (e) of this section.

* * * * *

Par. 4. Section 1.1503(d)–7(c) is amended by revising the last sentence of paragraph (iv) of *Example 5* and the last sentence of paragraph (C) of *Example 40*(ii).

The revisions read as follows:

§1.1503(d)–7 Examples.

* * * * *

(c) * * *

Example 5. * * *

(iv) * * * In addition, pursuant to §1.1503(d)–6(f)(1) and (3) , the deemed transfers pursuant to Rev. Rul. 99–5 as a result of the sale are not treated as triggering events described in §1.1503(d)–6(e)(1)(iv) or (v).

* * * * *

Example 40. * * *

(ii) * * *

(C) * * * Pursuant to §1.1503(d)–6(j)(1)(iii), the domestic use agreement filed by the P consolidated group with respect to the year 1 dual consolidated loss of the Country X separate unit is terminated and has no further effect.

* * * * *

Par. 5. Section 1.1503(d)–8 is amended by revising the heading texts of paragraphs (b)(1) and (2), the only sentence of paragraph (b)(1), the first sentence of paragraph (b)(2) and the last sentence of paragraph (b)(4).

The revisions read as follows:

§1.1503(d)–8 Effective dates.

* * * * *

(b) * * *

(1) *Reduction of term of agreements filed under §§1.1503–2A(c)(3), 1.1503–2A(d)(3), 1.1503–2(g)(2)(i), or 1.1503–2T(g)(i).* If an agreement is filed in accordance with §§1.1503–2A(c)(3), 1.1503–2A(d)(3), 1.1503–2(g)(2)(i), or 1.1503–2T(g)(2)(i) with respect to a dual consolidated loss incurred in a taxable year beginning prior to the application date and an event requiring recapture with respect to the dual consolidated loss subject to the agreement has not occurred as of the application date, then such agreement will be considered by the Internal Revenue Service to apply only for any taxable year up to and including the fifth taxable year following the year in which the dual consolidated loss that is the subject of the agreement was incurred and thereafter will have no effect.

(2) *Reduction of term of agreements filed under §§1.1503–2(g)(2)(iv)(B)(2)(i) (1992), 1.1503–2(g)(2)(iv)(B)(3)(i), or*

Rev. Proc. 2000–42. Taxpayers subject to the terms of a closing agreement entered into with the Internal Revenue Service pursuant to §§1.1503–2(g)(2)(iv)(B)(*2*)(*i*) (1992), 1.1503–2(g)(2)(iv)(B)(*3*)(*i*), or Rev. Proc. 2000–42, 2000–2 C.B. 394, see §601.601(d)(2)(ii)(*b*) of this chapter, will be deemed to have satisfied the closing agreement's fifteen-year certification period requirement if the five-year certification period specified in §1.1503(d)–1(b)(20) has elapsed, provided such closing agreement is still in effect as of the application date, and provided the dual consolidated losses have not been recaptured. * * *

* * * * *

(4) * * * Notwithstanding the general application of this paragraph (b)(4) to events described in §1.1503–2(g)(2)(iv)(B)(*1*)(*i*) through (*iii*) that occur after April 18, 2007, a taxpayer may choose to apply this paragraph (b)(4) to events described in §1.1503–2(g)(2)(iv)(B)(*1*)(*i*) through (*iii*) that occur after March 19, 2007 and on or before April 18, 2007.

* * * * *

LaNita Van Dyke,
Chief, Publications and Regulations Branch, Legal Processing Division, Associate Chief Counsel (Procedure and Administration).

(Filed by the Office of the Federal Register on April 24, 2007, 8:45 a.m., and published in the issue of the Federal Register for April 25, 2007, 72 F.R. 20423)

Part I. Rulings and Decisions Under the Internal Revenue Code of 1986

Section 402A.—Optional Treatment of Elective Deferrals as Roth Contributions

26 CFR 1.402A–1: Designated Roth accounts.

T.D. 9324

DEPARTMENT OF THE TREASURY
Internal Revenue Service
26 CFR Part 1 and 602

Designated Roth Accounts Under Section 402A

AGENCY: Internal Revenue Service (IRS), Treasury.

ACTION: Final Regulations.

SUMMARY: This document contains final regulations under sections 401(k), 402(g), 402A, and 408A of the Internal Revenue Code (Code) relating to designated Roth accounts. These final regulations provide guidance concerning the taxation of distributions from designated Roth accounts under qualified cash or deferred arrangements under section 401(k). These final regulations will affect administrators of, employers maintaining, participants in, and beneficiaries of section 401(k) and section 403(b) plans, as well as owners and beneficiaries of Roth IRAs and trustees of Roth IRAs.

DATES: *Effective Date:* These final regulations are effective *April 30, 2007.*

Applicability Date: These regulations generally apply to taxable years beginning on or after January 1, 2007. For dates of applicability, see §§1.401(k)–1(f)(6), 1.402A–1, A–15, 1.402A–2, A–4 and 1.408A–10, A–6.

FOR FURTHER INFORMATION CONTACT: R. Lisa Mojiri-Azad or William D. Gibbs at 202–622–6060, or Cathy A. Vohs, 202–622–6090 (not toll-free numbers).

SUPPLEMENTARY INFORMATION:

Paperwork Reduction Act

The collection of information contained in these final regulations was reviewed and approved by the Office of Management and Budget (OMB) for review in accordance with the Paperwork Reduction Act of 1995 (44 U.S.C. 3507(d)) under control number OMB–1545–1992.

The collection of information in these final regulations is in 26 CFR §1.402A–2. This information is required to comply with the separate accounting and recordkeeping requirements of section 402A. This information will be used by the IRS and employers maintaining designated Roth accounts to insure compliance with the requirements of section 402A. The collection of information is required to obtain a benefit. The likely recordkeepers are state or local governments, business or other for-profit institutions, nonprofit institutions, and small businesses or organizations.

The estimated annual burden per respondent under control number OMB–1545–1992 is 2.3 hours.

An agency may not conduct or sponsor, and a person is not required to respond to, a collection of information unless it displays a valid control number assigned by the Office of Management and Budget.

Books or records relating to a collection of information must be retained as long as their contents may become material in the administration of any internal revenue law. Generally, tax returns and tax return information are confidential, as required by 26 U.S.C. 6103.

Background

This document contains final regulations under section 402A, and amendments to regulations under sections 401(k), 402(g), and 408A of the Internal Revenue Code. Section 402A, which sets forth rules for designated Roth contributions, was added to the Code by section 617(a) of the Economic Growth and Tax Relief Reconciliation Act of 2001, Public Law 107–16 (115 Stat. 103) (EGTRRA), effective for taxable years beginning after December 31, 2005. These final regulations also reflect certain provisions of the Pension Protection Act of 2006, Public Law 109–280, (120 Stat. 780) (PPA '06), including section 811 of PPA '06, which repealed the sunset provisions of EGTRRA with respect to section 402A.

Section 401(k) sets forth rules for qualified cash or deferred arrangements under which an employee may make an election between cash and an employer contribution to a plan qualified under section 401(a). Section 403(b) permits a similar salary reduction agreement under which payments are made to a section 403(b) plan. Section 402(e)(3) provides that an amount is not includible in an employee's income merely because the employee has an election whether these contributions will be made to the trust or annuity or received by the employee in cash.

Amounts contributed pursuant to these qualified cash or deferred arrangements and salary reduction agreements are defined in section 402(g)(3) as elective deferrals. Section 402(g)(1) provides a limit on the amount of elective deferrals that may be excluded from an employee's income for a taxable year. Section 402(g)(2) provides for the distribution of elective deferrals that exceed the annual limit on elective deferrals (an excess deferral).

A designated Roth contribution is an elective deferral, as described in section 402(g)(3)(A) or (C), that has been designated by an employee, pursuant to section 402A, as not excludable from the employee's gross income. Under section 402A(b)(2), designated Roth contributions must be maintained by the plan in a separate account (a designated Roth account).

Under section 402(a), a distribution from a plan qualified under section 401(a) is taxable under section 72 to the distributee in the taxable year distributed. However, pursuant to section 402A(d)(1), a qualified distribution from a designated Roth account is excludable from gross income. A qualified distribution is defined in section 402A(d)(2) as a distribution that is made after completion of a specified 5-year period and the satisfaction of other specified requirements.

If the distribution is not a qualified distribution, pursuant to section 72, the distribution is included in the distributee's gross income to the extent allocable to income on the contract and excluded from gross income to the extent allocable to investment in the contract (basis). The amount of a distribution allocated to investment in the contract is generally determined by applying to the distribution the ratio of the investment in the contract to the account balance.

Section 402(c) provides rules under which certain distributions from a plan qualified under section 401(a) may be rolled over into another eligible retirement plan. In such a case, the distribution is not currently includible in the distributee's gross income. Under section 402(c)(2), as amended by section 822 of PPA '06, to the extent some or all of the distribution from a plan qualified under section 401(a) would not have been includible in gross income if it were not rolled over, that portion of the distribution can only be rolled over into an individual retirement plan, or through a direct rollover to another qualified plan or section 403(b) plan that agrees to separately account for such rolled over amounts. Section 403(b)(8)(B) provides that the rules of section 402(c)(2) also apply for purposes of the rollover rules under section 403(b)(8).

Under section 402(c)(8) and 402A(c)(3), a distribution from a designated Roth account can be rolled over only to another designated Roth account or to a Roth IRA. Under section 408A, a Roth IRA is a type of individual retirement plan (IRA) under which contributions are never deductible and qualified distributions are excludable from gross income. Section 408A(d)(4) sets forth special ordering rules for the return of basis in the case of a distribution from a Roth IRA. Under the section 408A(d)(4) ordering rules, in a nonqualified distribution from a Roth IRA, basis is recovered before income.

Section 617(d) of EGTRRA amended section 6051(a)(8) to require the reporting of designated Roth contributions on Form W–2, "*Wage and Tax Statement*," and added a new subsection (f) to section 6047 to require plan administrators or other responsible persons of section 401(k) or 403(b) plans to make such returns and reports regarding designated Roth contributions to the Secretary of the Treasury and such other persons the Secretary may prescribe.

Final regulations under section 401(k) were issued on December 29, 2004 (69 FR 78144). Those final regulations reserved §1.401(k)–1(f) for special rules for designated Roth contributions. On January 3, 2006, final regulations were issued that fill in that reserved paragraph and provide additional rules applicable to designated Roth contributions (71 FR 6). The provisions of the final regulations under section 401(k) regarding designated Roth contributions do not address the taxability of distributions from designated Roth accounts or the reporting requirements that apply to contributions of designated Roth contributions or distributions from the accounts.

On January 26, 2006, a notice of proposed rulemaking (REG–146459–05, 2006–8 I.R.B. 504) under section 402A was published in the **Federal Register** (71 FR 4322). The proposed regulations also would have provided guidance with respect to designated Roth contributions under section 403(b) plans by amending the proposed regulations (REG–155608–02, 2004–2 C.B. 924) under section 403(b), published in the **Federal Register** on November 16, 2004 (69 FR 67075). This guidance has not been finalized in this Treasury Decision, but will instead be included in the final regulations under section 403(b). Written comments responding to the notice of proposed rulemaking under section 402A were received. A public hearing was held on July 26, 2006. After consideration of all comments, these final regulations adopt the provisions of the proposed regulations with certain modifications, the most significant of which are highlighted below.

These final regulations under section 402A are intended to provide comprehensive guidance on the taxation of distributions from designated Roth accounts under section 401(k) and section 403(b) plans. These regulations also provide guidance on the reporting requirements with respect to these accounts and include amendments to the provisions of the final section 401(k) regulations relating to designated Roth contributions. In addition, these final regulations include amendments to the regulations under section 402(g) issued in 1991 in order to reflect the enactment of section 402A (as well as other statutory changes since those regulations were issued) and to make changes to conform the regulations under section 402(g) to the final section 401(k) regulations. These final regulations also add a new §1.408A–10 to the existing regulations under section 408A for Roth IRAs (§1.408A–1 through 9) issued in 1999 to reflect the interaction between section 408A and section 402A.

Explanation of Provisions

Overview

These final regulations, like the proposed regulations, provide guidance on the taxation of distributions from designated Roth accounts and other related issues. A designated Roth account is a separate account under a section 401(k) plan or section 403(b) plan to which designated Roth contributions are made, and for which separate accounting of contributions, gains, and losses are maintained. These final regulations retain the rule from the proposed regulations that any transaction or accounting methodology involving an employee's designated Roth account and any other accounts under the plan or plans of an employer that has the effect of directly or indirectly transferring value from another account into the designated Roth account violates the separate accounting requirement under section 402A.

The taxation of a distribution from a designated Roth account depends on whether or not the distribution is a qualified distribution. A qualified distribution from a designated Roth account is not includible in the employee's gross income. A qualified distribution is generally a distribution that is made after a 5-taxable-year period of participation and that either (1) is made on or after the date the employee attains age 59½, (2) is made after the employee's death, or (3) is attributable to the employee's being disabled within the meaning of section 72(m)(7). In response to comments, these final regulations clarify that, in the case of distribution to an alternate payee or beneficiary, the age, death or disability of the participant are used to determine whether the distribution is qualified. The only exception is in the case of a rollover by an alternate payee or surviving spouse to a designated Roth account under a plan of his or her own employer.

Determination of 5-Taxable-Year Period for Qualified Distributions

In order for a distribution from a designated Roth account to be a qualified distribution and thus not includible in gross income, a 5-taxable-year requirement must be satisfied. These final regulations, like the proposed regulations, reflect the rule in section 402A that the 5-taxable-year period during which a distribution is not a qualified distribution begins on the first day of the employee's taxable year for which the employee first had designated Roth contributions made to the plan and ends when 5 consecutive taxable years have been completed. However, if a direct rollover is made from a designated Roth account under another plan, the 5-taxable-year period for the recipient plan begins on the first day of the employee's taxable year for which the employee first had designated Roth contributions made to the other plan, if earlier.

Commentators inquired as to when designated Roth contributions made by a reemployed veteran for a year of qualified military service pursuant to section 414(u), are treated as made for purposes of the 5-taxable-year period of participation. In response to these comments, the final regulations provide that designated Roth contributions made by a reemployed veteran are treated as made in the taxable year with respect to which the contributions relate. Reemployed veterans may identify the year for which a contribution is made for other purposes, such as for entitlement to a match, and the treatment for the five year period of participation rule follows that identification. Absent such an identification, for purposes of determining the first year of the five years of participation under section 402A(d)(2)(B), the contribution is treated as made in the veteran's first taxable year in which the veteran's qualified military service begins, or if later, the first taxable year in which designated Roth contributions could be made under the plan.

Commentators asked how the 5-taxable-year period of participation rule applies to a required minimum distribution made for an earlier year, such as a distribution made on April 1 following the year an employee attains age 70½. They also asked whether, if payments under an annuity stream commence before a qualifying event, the payments after the qualifying event could be qualified distributions (assuming the 5-year period of participation is satisfied). The determination of whether a payment is a qualified distribution is determined based upon the actual year of the payment from the account and does not take into account whether the payment is part of a series of distributions or whether the payment is attributable to a prior calendar year.

In response to comments, these final regulations provide that certain contributions do not start the 5-taxable-year period of participation. For example, a year in which the only contributions consist of excess deferrals will not start the 5-taxable-year period of participation. Further, excess contributions that are distributed to prevent an ADP failure also do not begin the 5-taxable-year period of participation. Finally, contributions returned to the employee pursuant to section 414(w) also do not start the 5-taxable-year period of participation.

Taxation of Nonqualified Distributions

These final regulations retain the rules from the proposed regulations for taxation of nonqualified distributions and provide that a distribution from a designated Roth account that is not a qualified distribution is taxable to the distributee under section 402 (or section 403(b)(1)), treating the designated Roth account as a separate contract under section 72. In applying that treatment, the portion of any distribution that is includible in gross income as an amount allocable to income on the contract and the portion not includible in income as an amount allocable to investment in the contract is generally determined under section 72(e)(8) (or, in the case of an amount received as an annuity, section 72(b) or (d), as applicable).

Some commentators requested that the special ordering rules in section 408A(d), which provide that the first distributions from a Roth IRA are a return of contributions (and thus not includible in gross income) until all contributions have been returned as basis, be applied to distributions from a designated Roth account. They noted that a *pro rata* basis recovery rule in section 72 is difficult to explain to employees receiving a hardship distribution from a designated Roth account because the entire distribution reduces the amount of elective contributions (including designated Roth contributions) available for hardship distribution while, for purposes of determining the amount includible in income under sections 402(a) and 72, only a portion of the distribution is treated as recovery of basis attributable to the designated Roth contributions.

As noted in the preamble to the proposed regulations, because section 402A does not provide that the special ordering rules of section 408A(d) apply to distributions from designated Roth accounts, these final regulations do not apply those special ordering rules. Although designated Roth contributions to a designated Roth account bear some similarity to contributions to a Roth IRA (*e.g.*, contributions to either type of account are after-tax contributions, and qualified distributions from either type of account are excludable from gross income), there are many differences between these types of arrangements. The only special rule under section 402A for nonqualified distributions from a designated Roth account is that the account is treated as a separate contract for purposes of section 72.

Thus, these final regulations do not apply the basis recovery rules in section 408A to distributions from designated Roth accounts. Furthermore, the limit on elective contributions available for hardship distribution is an aggregate limit that takes into account both pre-tax elective contributions and designated Roth contributions. For example, an employee could take all hardship distributions from the pre-tax account, even though part of the amount available for hardship is attributable to designated Roth contributions. Thus, the amount of elective deferrals available for distribution from a designated Roth account on account of hardship generally would be a different amount than the total designated Roth contributions even if the ordering rule in section 408A(d)(4) applied to distributions from designated Roth accounts.

Rollover of Designated Roth Contributions

As described above in the Background section of this preamble, section 402(c)(2), after amendment by section 822 of PPA '06, provides that, if a portion of the distribution from a plan qualified under section 401(a) is not includible in income (determined without regard to the rollover), that portion of the distribution can only be rolled over by a direct rollover of the distribution to another qualified plan, or to a section 403(b) plan, that provides for separate accounting for amounts transferred (and earnings thereon) including separate accounting for the portion of such distribution which is includible in gross income and the portion of such distribution that is not so includible. Alternatively, the distribution can be rolled over to an IRA in either a 60-day rollover or direct rollover.

Section 402A(c)(3) provides that a rollover contribution of a distribution from a designated Roth account may only be made to the extent it is otherwise allowable. Section 402(c)(2) provides rules regarding when a rollover contribution of amounts not includable in gross income are allowable. As noted in the preamble to the proposed regulations, the IRS and Treasury Department believe that the rules in section 402(c)(2) relating to the rollover of a distribution of an amount not includable in gross income apply to a distribution from a designated Roth account.[1] Thus, these regulations retain the rule in the proposed regulations that, in order to roll over any portion of the basis in a designated Roth account into a designated Roth account under another plan, the rollover of the distribution must be accomplished through a direct rollover (*i.e.*, a rollover to another designated Roth account is not available for the portion of the distribution not includible in gross income if the distribution is made directly to the employee). However, for purposes of these regulations, the requirement that the receiving plan separately account for designated Roth contributions that are rolled over has been eliminated because such contributions are independently subject to the separate account requirement of Treas. Reg. §1.401(k)–1(f).[2]

In response to comments, the final regulations clarify that, for purposes of these regulations, if any amount is paid as a direct rollover, that amount is treated as a separate distribution from any amount paid directly to the distributee for purposes of applying section 402(c)(2). Finally, to insure that there is proper accounting in the recipient plan, as described under the heading *Reporting and Recordkeeping*, these final regulations retain the provision in the proposed regulations requiring the distributing plan making the direct rollover is required to report the amount of the investment in the contract and the first year of the 5-year period to the recipient plan so that the recipient plan will not need to rely on information from the distributee.

In response to comments, the definition of designated Roth account has been revised to clarify that the definition only includes accounts under a plan to which designated Roth contributions are made in lieu of elective contributions or deferrals. Thus, the final regulations clarify that a distribution from a designated Roth account may only be rolled over to a section 401(k) plan or section 403(b) plan if that has a designated Roth program.

As in the proposed regulations, the final regulations provide that if the entire amount of a distribution from a designated Roth account is rolled over to another designated Roth account, the amount of the rollover contribution allocated to investment in the contract in the recipient designated Roth account is the amount that would not have been includible in gross income (determined without regard to section 402(e)(4)) if the distribution had not been rolled over. Thus, if an amount that is a qualified distribution is rolled over, the entire amount of the rollover contribution is allocated to investment in the contract. In response to comments, the final regulations clarify that, if the entire account balance of a designated Roth account is rolled over to another designated Roth account, and, at the time of the distribution, the investment in the contract exceeds the balance in the designated Roth account, the investment in the contract in the distributing plan is included in the investment in the contract of the recipient plan.[3]

If a distribution from a designated Roth account is made to an employee, the employee is still able to roll over the entire amount (or any portion thereof) into a Roth IRA within a 60-day period. Under section 402(c)(2), if only a portion of the distribution is rolled over, the portion that is rolled over is treated as consisting first of the amount of the distribution that is includible in gross income. These final regulations, like the proposed regulations, provide that the income limits for contributions for Roth IRAs do not apply for this purpose.

Alternatively, the proposed regulations provided that the employee is permitted to roll over the taxable portion of the distribution to a designated Roth account within a 60-day period. In such a case, additional reporting is required from the recipient plan, as described below under the heading *Reporting and Recordkeeping*. In addition, the employee's period of participation under the distributing plan is not carried over to the recipient plan for purposes of determining whether the employee satisfies the 5-taxable-year requirement under the recipient plan. Commentators objected to this different treatment for indirect rollover contributions claiming that it reduces portability. The IRS and Treasury Department believe that this rule is more consistent with the statutory language and will further encourage direct rollover of distributions from designated Roth accounts which will reduce leakage of these distributions from retirement savings solution. Thus, this rule is retained in the final regulations. However, the final regulations provide that such an indirect rollover contribution starts the 5-taxable-year period of participation under the receiving plan for a participant who has made no prior designated Roth contributions to that plan.

Determination of 5-Taxable-year Period after a Rollover to a Roth IRA

Section 402A and section 408A each provide for a 5-taxable-year period that must be completed in order for a distri-

[1] For distributions from designated Roth accounts, there is the same need for proper accounting of investment in the contract as for distributions from other accounts that include after-tax contributions. In addition, it is necessary to track whether the employee has satisfied the 5-year rule for qualified distributions.

[2] The proposed regulations would have reflected the rule in section 402(c)(2) prior to amendment by PPA '06 that limited rollovers of distributions from qualified plans that are not includible in gross income to direct rollovers to other qualified trusts and not to section 403(b) plans. These final regulations do not retain this restriction on rollovers because of the amendments to section 402(c) made by section 822 of PPA '06.

[3] If the investment in the contract exceeds the account balance and the entire account balance is distributed (and not rolled over), see Rev. Rul. 72–305, 1972–1 C.B. 116, for guidance concerning a deduction for the difference.

bution from a designated Roth account or a Roth IRA to be a qualified distribution. However, each of these sections contains different rules for determining when the 5-taxable-year requirement is satisfied. Generally, under section 402A, satisfaction of the 5-taxable-year requirement with respect to a designated Roth account under a plan is based on the years since a designated Roth contribution was first made by the employee under that plan. In contrast, the 5-year period under section 408A begins with the first taxable year for which a contribution is made to any Roth IRA.

Commentators suggested that, if a distribution from a designated Roth account to an individual is rolled into a Roth IRA, the individual receive credit under the 5-year rule in section 408A for the years since the individual first made a contribution to a designated Roth account. As noted in the preamble to the proposed regulations, the IRS and Treasury Department do not believe that the Code provides for this interaction between the two 5-year rules. Thus, these final regulations retain the rule under the proposed regulations that the 5-taxable-year period described in section 402A and the 5-taxable-year period described in section 408A(d)(2)(B) are determined independently. Thus, in the case of a rollover of a distribution from a designated Roth account maintained under a section 401(k) or 403(b) plan to a Roth IRA, the final regulations, like the proposed regulations, provide that the period that the rolled-over funds were in the designated Roth account does not count towards the 5-taxable-year period for determining qualified distributions from the Roth IRA. However, if an individual had established a Roth IRA in a prior year, the 5-year period for determining qualified distributions from a Roth IRA that began as a result of that earlier Roth IRA contribution applies to any distributions from the Roth IRA (including a distribution of an amount attributable to a rollover contribution from a designated Roth account).

If a nonqualified distribution from a designated Roth account is rolled over into a Roth IRA, the portion of the distribution that constitutes a nontaxable return of investment in the contract is treated as basis in the Roth IRA. However, the final regulations, like the proposed regulations, provide that, if a qualified distribution from a designated Roth account is rolled over into a Roth IRA, the entire amount of the distribution will be treated as basis in the Roth IRA. As a result, a subsequent distribution from the Roth IRA in the amount of the rollover would be treated as a tax-free return of basis regardless of whether the individual had maintained a Roth IRA for 5 years (although the investment return on that amount earned in the Roth IRA would not be excluded from income when distributed unless the distribution satisfied the requirements for a qualified distribution from a Roth IRA). Similar to the case of a rollover to a designated Roth account, if the entire account balance of a designated Roth account is distributed and some or all of the distribution is rolled over to a Roth IRA, and, at the time of the distribution, the investment in the contract exceeds the balance in the designated Roth account, the investment in the contract in the distributing plan is included in the amount treated as a contribution to the Roth IRA.

Certain Amounts not Qualified Distributions

Section 1.402(c)–2, A–4, provides a list of amounts that are not treated as eligible rollover distributions and are instead currently includible in income. These final regulations, like the proposed regulations, provide that these same amounts also cannot be qualified distributions. Distributions described in A–4(a) (distribution of elective deferrals in excess of the section 415 limits), (b) (corrective distribution of excess deferrals), and (c) (corrective distribution of excess contributions or excess aggregate contributions), have statutorily specified tax treatments. In the case of a deemed distribution under section 72(p) or the cost of current life insurance protection, an actual amount has not in fact been distributed. In the case of distributions of dividends deductible under section 404(k), section 72(e)(5)(D) and §1.404(k)–1T provide that these amounts are treated as paid under a separate contract providing only for payment of deductible dividends. However, if a dividend described in section 404(k) has been reinvested in accordance with section 404(k)(2)(iii)(II), then a distribution of the reinvested amount can be a qualified distribution.

In response to comments regarding hardship distributions, the final regulations clarify that an amount is not precluded from being a qualified distribution merely because it is described in section 402(c)(4) as an amount not eligible for rollover. Thus, hardship distributions and required minimum distributions are not precluded from being qualified distributions. Similarly, payments in a stream of periodic payments are not precluded from being qualified distributions merely because they are described in section 402(c)(4)(A).

Distribution of Employer Securities and NUA

The final regulations retain the rules of the proposed regulations relating to the distribution of employer securities and the application of the net unrealized appreciation election of section 402(e)(4). If a qualified distribution includes employer securities, the distribution is not includible in gross income and the basis of each security in the hands of the distributee is the fair market value of the security on the date of the distribution. In such a case, the distributee will receive capital gains treatment at the time of any future disposition of the security, to the extent of any post-distribution appreciation. If a distribution with respect to employer securities is not a qualified distribution, the rules of section 402(e)(4) apply in the same manner as to any other distribution except that the designated Roth account is treated as a separate contract.

Some commentators inquired how these rules apply to the portion of a nonqualified distribution that exceeds the basis of the employer stock at the time of the distribution to the extent not includible in gross income as a return of the employee's designated Roth contributions. As explained in Rev. Rul. 74–398, 1974–2 C.B. 136, the basis of the stock at the time of the disposition will be increased to reflect such amount, so that such amount will not be subsequently taxed as appreciation at the time of a subsequent disposition of the stock.

Annuity contracts

As noted above, in the *Overview* section of this preamble, these final regulations retain the rule from the proposed regulations that any transaction or accounting methodology involving an employee's designated Roth account and any other accounts under the plan or plans of an employer that has the effect of directly or indirectly transferring value from another account into the designated Roth account violates the separate accounting requirement under section 402A. Commentators asked for additional guidance on how this requirement is satisfied for separate accounts maintained within a single annuity contract, in particular how to allocate charges for guarantees under the contract which apply to the total of all accounts under the contract. The IRS and Treasury Department believe that it may be difficult for a single contract to have combined guarantees that apply to both accounts without the potential for a prohibited transfer of value between the accounts, and have not issued guidance on how to account for these guarantees (including related charges). However, this issue will continue to be considered by the IRS and Treasury Department. Therefore, the regulations authorize the Commissioner to provide additional guidance with respect to separate accounting within an annuity contract.

In response to comments, these final regulations clarify that, as previously indicated in §1.402(c)–2, A–10(a), a distribution of an annuity contract from a designated Roth account is not a distribution event for purposes of section 402 or 402A. Thus, in such case, only distributions from the annuity contract are treated as distributions for those purposes. The determination of whether a distribution is a qualified or nonqualified distribution is made at the time of the distribution from the contract.

Reporting and Recordkeeping

These final regulations retain the rule of the proposed regulations that the plan administrator or other responsible party with respect to a plan with a designated Roth account is responsible for keeping track of the 5-taxable-year period for each employee and the amount of designated Roth contributions made on behalf of such employee. In addition, the plan administrator or other responsible party of a plan directly rolling over a distribution is required to provide the plan administrator of the recipient plan (that is, the plan accepting the eligible rollover distribution) with a statement indicating either the first year of the 5-taxable-year period for the employee and the portion of such distribution attributable to basis or that the distribution is a qualified distribution. If the distribution is not a direct rollover to a designated Roth account under another eligible plan, the plan administrator or responsible party must provide to the employee, upon request, this same information, except the statement need not indicate the first year of the 5-taxable-year period. The statement is required to be provided within a reasonable period following the direct rollover (or employee request), but in no event later than 30 days following the direct rollover (or employee request), and the plan administrator or other responsible party for the recipient plan is permitted to rely on these statements. If this information is provided on a statement attached to the check issued to the employee, this requirement would be satisfied.

As noted in the preamble, to the extent that a portion of a distribution is includible in income (determined without regard to the rollover), if any portion of that distribution is rolled over to a designated Roth account by the distributee rather than by direct rollover, the plan administrator of the recipient plan must notify the IRS of its acceptance of the rollover contribution. The final regulations clarify that this reporting is only required to the extent provided in Forms and Instructions. Such Instructions will specify the address to which the notification must be sent and will require the following information: (1) the employee's name and social security number; (2) the amount rolled over; (3) the year in which the rollover contribution was made; and (4) such other information as the Commissioner may prescribe in order to determine that the amount rolled over is a valid rollover contribution. Thus, until relevant Forms and Instructions are released, no reporting is required.

With respect to other reporting, generally, the same reporting requirements apply to plans with designated Roth accounts as apply to other plans. A contribution to and a distribution from a designated Roth account must be reported on Form W–2 and Form 1099–R, "*Distributions From Pensions, Annuities, Retirement or Profit-Sharing Plans, IRAs, Insurance Contracts, etc.*," respectively, in accordance with the instructions thereto. An employee has no reporting obligation with respect to designated Roth contributions under a section 401(k) or 403(b) plan. However, an employee rolling over a distribution from a designated Roth account to a Roth IRA should keep track of the amount rolled over in accordance with the instructions to Form 8606, "*Nondeductible IRAs.*"

Designated Roth Contributions as Excess Deferrals

Even though designated Roth contributions are not excluded from income when contributed, they are treated as elective deferrals for purposes of section 402(g). Thus, to the extent total elective deferrals for the year exceed the section 402(g) limit for the year, the excess amount can be distributed by April 15th of the year following the year of the excess without adverse tax consequences. However, if such excess deferrals are not distributed by April 15th of the year following the year of the excess, these final regulations, like the proposed regulations, provide that any distribution attributable to an excess deferral that is a designated Roth contribution is includible in gross income (with no exclusion from income for amounts attributable to basis under section 72) and is not eligible for rollover. These regulations provide that if there are any excess deferrals that are designated Roth contributions that are not corrected prior to April 15th of the year following the excess, the first amounts distributed from the designated Roth account are treated as distributions of excess deferrals and earnings until the full amount of those excess deferrals (and attributable earnings) are distributed.

Gap Period Income

In addition, these final regulations retain the rule in the proposed regulations which reflected the statutory provisions which require that any distribution of excess deferrals include the applicable earnings from the plan. Unlike the existing final regulations under section 402(g), the earnings include income for the period after the taxable year (gap period income). The calculation of gap period income is comparable to the calculation of the gap period income for excess contributions and excess aggregate contributions under the 2004 final regulations under section 401(k) and 401(m). Thus, gap period income must be included in the distribution of excess deferrals to the extent the employee is or would be credited with allocable gain or loss on those excess deferrals for the gap period if the total account were to be distributed. This gap period income rule applies to both pre-tax excess deferrals and designated Roth contributions and continues to apply even after the 2008 elimination of the rule for excess contributions and excess aggregate contributions under section 902(e)(3) of PPA '06.

Modifications to Final Roth 401(k) Regulations

Some comments received in connection with the proposed regulations raised concerns not about those regulations but rather about the special rules for designated Roth contributions in §1.401(k)–1(f) that were finalized in T.D. 9237, 2006–6 I.R.B. 394, published on January 3, 2006 (71 FR 6). In response to those comments these final regulations make two changes to those special rules. First, these regulations clarify and expand the rule in §1.401(k)–1(f)(3)(ii) to provide that the balance of a participant's designated Roth account and a participant's other accounts under the plan are treated as accounts held under two separate plans (within the meaning of section 414(l)) for purposes of applying not only the special rule in A–11 of §1.401(a)(31)–1 for *de minimis* distributions (reasonably expected to total less than $200) but also both the automatic rollover rules for mandatory distributions under section 401(a)(31)(B) and the rules in A–9 and A–10 of §1.401(a)(31)–1 on the extent to which plans must allow split distributions. Thus, for example, if a participant has less than $1,000 in the participant's designated Roth account and less than $1,000 in the participant's other accounts, the plan will not need to provide the participant with an automatic rollover with respect to the designated Roth account or the other accounts even if the total accrued benefit of the participant under the plan exceeds $1,000.

Second, in response to comments about compensation provided to certain foreign missionaries, the regulations are modified to require that an employer treat designated Roth contribution as not excludible from gross income as elective deferrals rather than treated as includible in gross income. As a result, if section 72(f)(2) applies to a contribution, an employee will have basis as a result of the contribution to the extent that contribution would have been excludible from gross income even if paid directly to the employee and such amount can be treated as a designated Roth contribution even though such amount is income that is not includible in taxable income. Thus, compensation for foreign missionaries is not precluded from being contributed to a designated Roth account merely because the compensation would not have been includible in gross income if paid directly. Finally, the regulations clarify that, for self-employed individuals, the requirement that a designated Roth contribution not be excludible from gross income as an elective deferral for being a designated Roth contribution is only satisfied if the self-employed individual does not claim a deduction for the contribution.

Commentators inquired as to whether catch-up contributions may be designated Roth contributions. Catch-up contributions are treated the same as any other elective deferrals and, thus, a participant's catch-up contributions may either be pre-tax elective deferrals or designated Roth contributions.

Finally, these final regulations revise the special rules for designated Roth contributions in §1.401(k)–1(f) to reflect the repeal in PPA '06 of the sunset of the provisions relating to designated Roth contributions.

Effective Date

Section 402A applies to employees' taxable years beginning on or after January 1, 2006. These final regulations under section 402A are generally applicable for taxable years beginning on or after January 1, 2007. However, certain provisions in these final regulations under section 402A are applicable at the same time as section 402A. These include the clarification that the separate accounting requirement does not permit any transaction or accounting methodology that transfers value between designated Roth accounts and other accounts under a plan and the rules relating to rollovers to designated Roth accounts and Roth IRAs. Similarly, these final regulations under section 408A are applicable at the same time as section 402A. These final regulations also address the treatment of rollover contributions to Roth IRAs and designated Roth accounts.

The final regulations under section 402(g) relating to designated Roth contributions also are applicable at the same time as section 402A. Thus, these final regulations are applicable for excess deferrals for taxable years beginning on or after January 1, 2006. However, unlike the proposed regulations, the rule in these final regulations requiring distribution of gap period income on excess deferrals applies to excess deferrals for taxable years beginning on or after 2007, which are generally distributed on or after January 1, 2008.

Special Analyses

It has been determined that these final regulations are not a significant regulatory action as defined in Executive Order 12866. Therefore, a regulatory assessment is not required. It has also been determined that 5 U.S.C. 553(b) does not apply to these regulations. It is hereby certified that the collection of information in these regulations will not have a significant economic impact on a substantial number of small entities. This certification is based on the fact that most small entities that will maintain a designated Roth account already use a third party provider to administer the plan and the collection of information in these regulations, which is required to comply with the separate accounting and recordkeeping requirements of section 402A(b), will only minimally increase the third party provider's administrative burden with respect to the plan. Therefore, an analysis under the Regulatory Flexibility Act (5 U.S.C. chapter 6) is not required. Pursuant to section 7805(f) of the Code, the proposed regulations preceding these final regulations were submitted to the Chief Counsel for Advocacy of the Small Business Administration for comment on their impact on small business.

Drafting Information

The principal authors of these regulations are R. Lisa Mojiri-Azad, Bill Gibbs and Cathy Vohs, Office of Division Counsel/Associate Chief Counsel (Tax Exempt and Government Entities). However, other personnel from the IRS and Treasury Department participated in the development of these regulations.

* * * * *

Adoption of Amendments to the Regulations

Accordingly, 26 CFR part 1 is amended as follows:

PART 1—INCOME TAXES

Paragraph 1. The authority citation for part 1 is amended by adding an entry in numerical order to read in part as follows:

Authority: 26 U.S.C. 7805 * * *

Section 1.402A–1 is also issued under 26 U.S.C. 402A * * *

Par. 2. Section 1.401(k)–0 is amended as follows:

1. The entry for 1.401(k)–1(f)(2), (3), (4) and (5) are revised.

2. The entry for 1.401(k)–1(f)(6) is added.

§1.401(k)–0 Table of contents.

* * * * *

§1.401(k)–1 Certain cash or deferred arrangements.

* * * * *

(f) * * *

(1) In general.

(2) Inclusion treatment.

(3) Separate accounting required.

(4) Designated Roth contributions must satisfy rules applicable to elective contributions.

(i) In general.

(ii) Special rules for direct rollovers.

(5) Rules regarding designated Roth contribution elections.

(i) Frequency of elections.

(ii) Default elections.

(6) Effective date.

Par. 3. Section 1.401(k)–1(f) is amended as follows:

1. Revise paragraph (f)(1)(ii) and (iii).

2. Redesignate paragraph (f)(2) thru (f)(5) as (f)(3) thru (f)(6).

3. Add a new paragraph (f)(2).

4. Revise the first sentence of designated paragraph (f)(3) and add a sentence at the end.

5. Revise the last sentence of redesignated paragraph (f)(4)(ii).

6. Revise redesignated paragraph (f)(6).

The addition and revision to §1.401(k)–1 read as follows:

§1.401(k)–1 Certain cash or deferred arrangements.

* * * * *

(f) *Special rules for designated Roth contributions.*

(1) * * *

(ii) Treated by the employer as not excludible from the employee's gross income (in accordance with paragraph (f)(2) of this section);

(iii) Maintained by the plan in a separate account (in accordance with paragraph (f)(3) of this section).

(2) *Inclusion treatment.* An elective contribution is generally treated as not excludible from gross income if it is treated as includible in gross income by the employer (*e.g.*, by treating the contribution as wages subject to applicable income tax withholding). However, in the case of a self-employed individual, an elective contribution is treated as not excludible from gross income only if the individual does not claim a deduction for such amount. If an elective contribution would not have been includible in gross income if the amount had been paid directly to the employee (rather than being subject to a cash or deferral election), the elective contribution is nevertheless permitted to be a designated Roth contribution, provided the employee is entitled to treat the amount as an investment in the contract pursuant to section 72(f)(2).

(3) *Separate accounting required.* Under the separate accounting requirement of this paragraph (f)(3), contributions and withdrawals of designated Roth contributions must be credited and debited to a designated Roth account maintained for the employee and the plan must maintain a record of the employee's investment in the contract (that is, designated Roth contributions that have not been distributed) with respect to the employee's designated Roth account. * * * See A–13 of §1.402A–1 for additional requirements for separate accounting.

(4) * * *

(ii) * * * Moreover, a participant's designated Roth account and the participant's other accounts under a plan are treated as accounts held under two separate plans (within the meaning of section 414(l)) for purposes of applying the automatic rollover rules for mandatory distributions under section 401(a)(31)(B)(i)(I) and the special rules in A–9 through A–11 of §1.401(a)(31)–1.

* * * * *

(6) *Effective date.* Section 402A and the provisions of this section 1.401(k)–1(f) apply to taxable years beginning after December 31, 2005.

Par. 4. Section 1.402(g)–1 is amended as follows:

1. Revise the second sentence and add a third sentence to paragraph (a).

2. Add new paragraphs (b)(5) and (b)(6).

3. Revise paragraph (d).

4. Revise paragraph (e)(2) introductory text.

5. Revise paragraph (e)(2)(i).

6. Revise the second sentence and add a new third sentence in paragraph (e)(3)(i)(A).

7. Revise paragraph (e)(5)(i).

8. Add a sentence after the last sentence in paragraph (e)(5)(ii).

9. Revise paragraph (e)(5)(iii).

10. Add paragraph (e)(5)(v).

11. Add paragraph (e)(8)(iv).

The additions and revisions to §1.402(g)–1 read as follows:

§1.402(g)–1 Limitation on exclusion for elective deferrals.

(a) *In general.* * * * Thus, an individual's elective deferrals in excess of the applicable limit for a taxable year (that is, the individual's excess deferrals for the year) must be included in gross income for the year, except to the extent the excess deferrals are comprised of designated Roth contributions, and thus, are already includible in gross income. A designated Roth contribution is treated as an excess deferral only to the extent that the total amount of designated Roth contributions for an individual exceeds the applicable limit for the taxable year or the designated Roth contributions are identified as excess deferrals and the individual receives a distribution of the excess deferrals and allocable income under paragraph (e)(2) or (e)(3) of this section.

(b) * * *

(5) Any designated Roth contributions described in section 402A (before applying the limits of section 402(g) or this section).

(6) Any elective employer contributions to a SIMPLE retirement account, on behalf of an employee pursuant to a qualified salary reduction arrangement as described in section 408(p)(2) (before applying the limits of section 402(g) or this section).

* * * * *

(d) *Applicable limit*—(1) *In general.* Except as provided under paragraph (d)(2) of this section, the applicable limit for an individual's taxable year is the applicable dollar amount set forth in section 402(g)(1)(B). This applicable dollar amount is increased for the taxable year beginning in 2007 and later years in the same manner as the dollar amount under section 415(b)(1)(A) is adjusted pursuant to section 415(d). See §1.402(g)–2 for the treatment of catch-up contributions described in section 414(v).

(2) *Special adjustment for elective deferrals with respect to section 403(b) annuity contracts for certain long-term employees.* The applicable limit for an individual who is a qualified employee (as defined in section 402(g)(7)(C)) and has elective deferrals described in paragraph (b)(3) or (5) of this section for a taxable year is adjusted by increasing the applicable limit otherwise determined under paragraph (d)(1) of this section in accordance with section 402(g)(7).

(e) * * *

(2) *Correction of excess deferrals after the taxable year.* A plan may provide that if any amount is an excess deferral under paragraph (a) of this section:

(i) Not later than the first April 15 (or such earlier date specified in the plan) following the close of the individual's taxable year, the individual may notify each plan under which elective deferrals were made of the amount of the excess deferrals received by the plan. If any designated Roth contributions were made to a plan, the notification must also identify the extent, if any, to which the excess deferrals are comprised of designated Roth contributions. A plan may provide that an individual is deemed to have notified the plan of excess deferrals (including the portion of excess deferrals that are comprised of designated Roth contributions) to the extent the individual has excess deferrals for the taxable year calculated by taking into account only elective deferrals under the plan and other plans of the same employer and the plan may provide the extent to which such excess deferrals are comprised of designated Roth contributions. A plan may instead provide that the employer may notify the plan on behalf of the individual under these circumstances.

* * * * *

(3) * * *

(i) * * *

(A) * * * If any designated Roth contributions were made to a plan, the notification must identify the extent to which, if any, the excess deferrals are comprised of designated Roth contributions. A plan may provide that an individual is deemed to have notified the plan of excess deferrals (including the portion of excess deferrals that are comprised of designated Roth contributions) for the taxable year calculated by taking into account only elective deferrals under the plan and other plans of the same employer and the plan may provide the extent to which such excess deferrals are comprised of designated Roth contributions. * * *

* * * * *

(5) *Income allocable to excess deferrals*—(i) *General rule.* The income allocable to excess deferrals for a taxable year that begins on or after January 1, 2007 is equal to the sum of the allocable gain or loss for the taxable year of the individual and, to the extent the excess deferrals are or will be credited with gain or loss for the period after the close of the taxable year and prior to the distribution (the gap period) if the total account were to be distributed, the allocable gain or loss during that period. The income allocable to excess deferrals for a taxable year that begins before 2007 is determined using the 1.402(g)–1(e)(5) (as it appeared in the April 1, 2006 edition of 26 CFR Part 1).

(ii) *Method of allocating income.* * * * A plan will not fail to use a reasonable method for computing the income allocable to excess deferrals merely because the income allocable to excess deferrals is determined on a date that is no more than 7 days before the distribution.

(iii) *Alternative method of allocating taxable year income.* A plan may determine the income allocable to excess deferrals for the taxable year by multiplying the income for the taxable year allocable to elective deferrals by a fraction. The numerator of the fraction is the excess deferrals by the employee for the taxable year. The denominator of the fraction is equal to the sum of:

(A) The total account balance of the employee attributable to elective deferrals as of the beginning of the taxable year, plus

(B) The employee's elective deferrals for the taxable year.

* * * * *

(v) *Alternative method for allocating taxable year and gap period income.* A plan may determine the allocable gain or loss for the aggregate of the taxable year and the gap period by applying the alternative method provided by paragraph (e)(5)(iii) of this section to this aggregate period. This is accomplished by substituting the income for the taxable year and the gap period for the income for the taxable year and by substituting the elective deferrals for the taxable year and the gap period for the elective deferrals for the taxable year in determining the fraction that is multiplied by that income.

* * * * *

(8) * * *

(iv) *Distributions of excess deferrals from a designated Roth account.* The rules of paragraph (e)(8)(iii) of this section generally apply to distributions of excess deferrals that are designated Roth contributions and the attributable income. Thus, if a designated Roth account described in section 402A includes any excess deferrals, any distribution of amounts attributable to those excess deferrals are includible in gross income (without adjustment for any return of investment in the contract under section 72(e)(8)). In addition, such distributions cannot be qualified distributions described in section 402A(d)(2) and are not eligible rollover distributions within the meaning of section 402(c)(4). For this purpose, if a designated Roth account includes any excess deferrals, any distributions from the account are treated as attributable to those excess deferrals until the total amount distributed from the designated Roth account equals the total of such deferrals and attributable income.

* * * * *

Par. 5. Sections 1.402A–1 and 1.402A–2 are added to read as follows:

§1.402A–1 Designated Roth Accounts

Q–1. What is a designated Roth account?

A–1. A designated Roth account is a separate account under a qualified cash or deferred arrangement under a section 401(a) plan, or under a section 403(b) plan, to which designated Roth contributions are permitted to be made in lieu of elective contributions, that satisfies the requirements of §1.401(k)–1(f) (in the case of a section 401(a) plan).

Q–2. How is a distribution from a designated Roth account taxed?

A–2. (a) The taxation of a distribution from a designated Roth account depends on whether or not the distribution is a qualified distribution. A qualified distribution from a designated Roth account is not includible in the distributee's gross income.

(b) Except as otherwise provided in paragraph (c) of this A–2, a qualified distribution is a distribution that is both—

(1) Made after the 5-taxable-year period of participation defined in A–4 of this section has been completed; and

(2) Made on or after the date the employee attains age 59½, made to a beneficiary or the estate of the employee on or after the employee's death, or attributable to the employee's being disabled within the meaning of section 72(m)(7).

(c) A distribution from a designated Roth account is not a qualified distribution to the extent it consists of a distribution of excess deferrals and attributable income described in §1.402(g)–1(e). See A–11 of this section for other amounts that are not treated as qualified distributions, including excess contributions described in section 401(k)(8), and excess aggregate contributions described in section 401(m)(8), and income, on any of these excess amounts.

Q–3. How is a distribution from a designated Roth account taxed if it is not a qualified distribution?

A–3. Except as provided in A–11 of this section, a distribution from a designated Roth account that is not a qualified distribution is taxable to the distributee under section 402 in the case of a plan qualified under section 401(a) and under section 403(b)(1) in the case of a section 403(b) plan. For this purpose, a designated Roth account is treated as a separate contract under section 72. Thus, except as otherwise provided in A–5 of this section for a rollover, if a distribution is before the annuity starting date, the portion of any distribution that is includible in gross income as an amount allocable to income on the contract and the portion not includible in gross income as an amount allocable to investment in the contract is determined under section 72(e)(8), treating the designated Roth account as a separate contract. Similarly, in the case of any amount received as an annuity, if a distribution is on or after the annuity starting date, the portion of any annuity payment that is includible in gross income as an amount allocable to income on the contract and the portion not includible in gross income as an amount allocable to investment in the contract is determined under section 72(b) or (d), as applicable, treating the designated Roth account as a separate contract. For purposes of section 72, designated Roth contributions are described in section 72(f)(1) or 72(f)(2), to the extent applicable.

Q–4. What is the 5-taxable-year period of participation described in A–2 of this section?

A–4. (a) The 5-taxable-year period of participation described in A–2 of this section for a plan is the period of 5 consecutive taxable years that begins with the first day of the first taxable year in which the employee makes a designated Roth contribution to any designated Roth account established for the employee under the same plan and ends when 5 consecutive taxable years have been completed. For this purpose, the first taxable year in which an employee makes a designated Roth contribution is the year in which the amount is includible in the employee's gross income. Notwithstanding the preceding, however, a contribution that is returned as an excess deferral or excess contribution does not begin the 5-taxable-year period of participation. Similarly, a contribution returned as a permissible withdrawal under section 414(w) does not begin the 5-taxable-year period of participation.

(b) Generally, an employee's 5-taxable-year period of participation is determined separately for each plan (within the meaning of section 414(l)) in which the employee participates. Thus, if an employee has elective deferrals made to designated Roth accounts under two or more plans, the employee may have two or more different 5-taxable-year periods of participation, depending on when the employee first had contributions made to a designated Roth account under each plan. However, if a direct rollover contribution of a distribution from a designated Roth account under another plan is made by the employee to the plan, the 5-taxable-year period of participation begins on the first day of the employee's taxable year in which the employee first had designated Roth contributions made to such other designated Roth account, if earlier than the first taxable year in which a designated Roth contribution is made to the plan. See A–5(c) of this section for additional rules on determining the start of the 5-taxable-year of participation in the case of an indirect rollover.

(c) The beginning of the 5-taxable-year period of participation is not redetermined for any portion of an employee's designated Roth account. This is true even if the entire designated Roth account is distributed during the 5-taxable-year period of participation and the employee subsequently makes additional designated Roth contributions under the plan.

(d) The rule in paragraph (c) of this section applies if the employee dies or the account is divided pursuant to a qualified domestic relations order (QDRO), and thus, a portion of the account is not payable to the employee and is payable to the employee's beneficiary or an alternate payee. In the case of distribution to an alternate payee or beneficiary, generally, the age, death, or disability of the employee is used to determine whether the distribution to an alternate payee or beneficiary is qualified. However, if an alternate payee or a spousal beneficiary rolls the distribution into a designated Roth account in a plan maintained by his or her own employer, such individual's age, disability, or death is used to determine whether a distribution from the recipient plan is qualified. In addition, if the rollover is a direct rollover contribution to the alternate payee's or spousal beneficiary's own designated Roth account, the 5-taxable-year period of participation under the recipient plan begins on the earlier of the date the employee's 5-taxable-year period of participation began under the distributing plan or the date the 5-taxable-year period of participation applicable to the alternate payee's or spousal beneficiary's designated Roth account began under the recipient plan.

(e) If a designated Roth contribution is made by a reemployed veteran for a year of qualified military service pursuant to section 414(u) that is before the year in which the contribution is actually made, the contribution is treated as having been made in the year of qualified military service to which the contribution relates, as designated by the reemployed veteran. Reemployed veterans may identify the year of qualified military service for which a contribution is made for other purposes, such as for entitlement to a match, and the treatment for the 5-taxable-year period of participation rule follows that identification. In the absence of such designation, for purposes of determining the first year of the five years of participation under section 402A(d)(2)(B), the contribution is treated as relating to the first year of qualified military service for which the reemployed veteran could have made designated Roth contributions under the plan, or if later the first taxable year in which designated Roth contributions could be made under the plan.

Q–5. How do the taxation rules apply to a distribution from a designated Roth account that is rolled over?

A–5. (a) An eligible rollover distribution from a designated Roth account is permitted to be rolled over into another designated Roth account or a Roth IRA, and the amount rolled over is not currently includable in gross income. In accordance with section 402(c)(2), to the extent that a portion of a distribution from a designated Roth account is not includible in income (determined without regard to the rollover), if that portion of the distribution is to be rolled over into a designated Roth account, the rollover must be accomplished through a direct rollover (*i.e.*, a 60 day rollover to another designated Roth account is not available for this portion of the distribution). For this purpose, any amount paid in a direct rollover is treated as a separate distribution from any amount paid directly to the employee. If a distribution from a designated Roth account is instead made to the employee, the employee would still be able to roll over the entire amount (or any portion thereof) into a Roth IRA within the 60-day period described in section 402(c)(3).

(b) In the case of an eligible rollover distribution from a designated Roth account that is not a qualified distribution and not paid as a direct rollover contribution, if less than the entire amount of the distribution is rolled over, the part that is rolled over is deemed to consist first of the portion of the distribution that is attributable to income under section 72(e)(8).

(c) If an employee receives a distribution from a designated Roth account, the portion of the distribution that would be includible in gross income is permitted to be rolled over into a designated Roth account under another plan. In such a case, §1.402A–2, A–3, provides for additional reporting by the recipient plan. In addition, the employee's period of participation under the distributing plan is not carried over to the recipient plan for purposes of satisfying the 5-taxable-year period of participation requirement under the recipient plan. Generally, the taxable year in which the recipient plan accepts such rollover contribution is the taxable year that begins the participant's new 5-taxable-year period of participation. However, if the participant is rolling over to a plan in which the participant already has a pre-existing designated Roth account with a longer period of participation, the starting date of the recipient account is used to measure the participant's 5-taxable-year period of participation.

(d) The following example illustrates the application of this A–5:

Example. Employee B receives a $14,000 eligible rollover distribution that is not a qualified distribution from B's designated Roth account, consisting of $11,000 of investment in the contract and $3,000 of income. Within 60 days of receipt, Employee B rolls over $7,000 of the distribution into a Roth IRA. The $7,000 is deemed to consist of $3,000 of income and $4,000 of investment in the contract. Because the only portion of the distribution that could be includible in gross income (the income) is rolled over, none of the distribution is includible in Employee B's gross income.

(e) This A–5 applies for taxable years beginning on or after January 1, 2006.

Q–6. In the case of a rollover contribution to a designated Roth account, how is the amount that is treated as investment in the contract under section 72 determined?

A–6. (a) If a distribution from a designated Roth account is rolled over to another designated Roth account in a direct rollover, the amount of the rollover contribution allocated to investment in the contract in the recipient designated Roth account is the amount that would not have been includible in gross income (determined without regard to section 402(e)(4)) if the distribution had not been rolled over. Thus, if an amount that is a qualified distribution is rolled over, the entire amount of the rollover contribution is allocated to investment in the contract.

(b) If the entire account balance of a designated Roth account is rolled over to another designated Roth account in a direct rollover, and, at the time of the distribution, the investment in the contract exceeds the balance in the designated Roth account, the investment in the contract in the distributing plan is included in the investment in the contract of the recipient plan.

Q–7. After a qualified distribution from a designated Roth account has been made, how is the remaining investment in the contract of the designated Roth account determined under section 72?

A–7. (a) The portion of any qualified distribution that is treated as a recovery of investment in the contract is determined in the same manner as if the distribution were not a qualified distribution. (See A–3 of this section.) Thus, the remaining investment in the contract in a designated Roth account after a qualified distribution is determined in the same manner after a qualified distribution as it would be determined if the distribution were not a qualified distribution.

(b) The following example illustrates the application of this A–7:

Example. Employee C receives a $12,000 distribution, which is a qualified distribution that is attributable to the employee being disabled within the meaning of section 72(m)(7), from C's designated Roth account. Immediately prior to the distribution, the account consisted of $21,850 of investment in the contract (*i.e.*, designated Roth contributions) and $1,150 of income. For purposes of determining recovery of investment in the contract under section 72, the distribution is deemed to consist of $11,400 of investment in the contract [$12,000 x 21,850/(1,150 + 21,850)], and $600 of income [$12,000 x 1,150/(1,150 + 21,850)]. Immediately after the distribution, C's designated Roth account consists of $10,450 of investment in the contract and $550 of income. This determination of the remaining investment in the contract will be needed if C subsequently is no longer disabled and takes a nonqualified distribution from the designated Roth account.

Q–8. What is the relationship between the accounting for designated Roth contributions as investment in the contract for purposes of section 72 and their treatment as elective deferrals available for a hardship distribution under section 401(k)(2)(B)?

A–8. (a) There is no relationship between the accounting for designated Roth contributions as investment in the contract for purposes of section 72 and their treatment as elective deferrals available for a hardship distribution under section 401(k)(2)(B). A plan that makes a hardship distribution under section 401(k)(2)(B) from elective deferrals that includes designated Roth contributions must separately determine the amount of elective deferrals available for hardship and the amount of investment in the contract attributable to designated Roth contributions for purposes of section 72. Thus, the entire amount of a hardship distribution is treated as reducing the otherwise maximum distributable amount for purposes of applying the rule in section 401(k)(2)(B) and §1.401(k)–1(d)(3)(ii) that generally limits hardship distributions to the principal amount of elective deferrals made less the amount of elective deferrals previously distributed from the plan, even if a portion of the distribution is treated as income under section 72(e)(8).

(b) The following example illustrates the application of this A–8:

Example. The facts are the same as in the *Example* in A–7 of this section, except that instead of being disabled, Employee C is receiving a hardship distribution. In addition, Employee C has made elective deferrals that are not designated Roth contributions totaling $20,000 and has received no previous distributions of elective deferrals from the plan. The adjustment to the investment in the contract is the same as in A–7 of this section, but for purposes of determining the amount of elective deferrals available for future hardship distribution, the entire amount of the distribution is subtracted from the maximum distributable amount. Thus, Employee C has only $29,850 ($41,850 - $12,000) available for hardship distribution from C's designated Roth account.

Q–9. Can an employee have more than one separate contract for designated Roth contributions under a plan qualified under section 401(a) or a section 403(b) plan?

A–9. (a) Except as otherwise provided in paragraph (b) of this A–9, for purposes of section 72, there is only one separate contract for an employee with respect to the designated Roth contributions under a plan. Thus, if a plan maintains one separate account for designated Roth contributions made under the plan and another separate account for rollover contributions received from a designated Roth account under another plan (so that the rollover account is not required to be subject to the distribution restrictions otherwise applicable to the account consisting of designated Roth contributions made under the plan), both separate accounts are considered to be one contract for purposes of applying section 72 to the distributions from either account.

(b) If a separate account with respect to an employee's accrued benefit consisting of designated Roth contributions is established and maintained for an alternate payee pursuant to a qualified domestic relations order and another designated Roth account is maintained for the employee, each account is treated as a separate contract for purposes of section 72. The alternate payee's designated Roth account is also a separate contract for purposes of section 72 with respect to any other account maintained for that alternate payee. Similarly, if separate accounts are established and maintained for different beneficiaries after the death of an employee, the separate account for each beneficiary is treated as a separate contract under section 72 and is also a separate contract with respect to any other account maintained for that beneficiary under the plan that is not a designated Roth account. When the separate account is established for an alternate payee or for a beneficiary (after an employee's death), each separate account must receive a proportionate amount attributable to investment in the contract.

Q–10. What is the tax treatment of employer securities distributed from a designated Roth account?

A–10. (a) If a distribution of employer securities from a designated Roth account is not a qualified distribution, section 402(e)(4)(B) applies. Thus, in the case of a lump-sum distribution that includes employer securities, unless the taxpayer elects otherwise, net unrealized appreciation attributable to the employer securities is not includible in gross income; and such net unrealized appreciation is not included in the basis of the distributed securities and is capital gain to the extent such appreciation is realized in a subsequent taxable transaction.

(b) In the case of a qualified distribution of employer securities from a designated Roth account, the distributee's basis in the distributed securities for purposes of subsequent disposition is their fair market value at the time of distribution.

Q–11. Can an amount described in A–4 of §1.402(c)–2 with respect to a designated Roth account be a qualified distribution?

A–11. No. An amount described in A–4 of §1.402(c)–2 with respect to a designated Roth account cannot be a qualified distribution. Such an amount is taxable under the rules of §§1.72–16(b), 1.72(p)–1, A–11 through A–13, 1.402(g)–1(e)(8), 1.401(k)–2(b)(2)(vi), 1.401(m)–2(b)(2)(vi), or 1.404(k)–1T. Thus, for example, loans that are treated as deemed distributions pursuant to section 72(p), or dividends paid on employer securities as described in section 404(k) are not qualified distributions even if the deemed distributions occur or the dividends are paid after the employee attains age 59½ and the 5-taxable-year period of participation defined in A–4 of this section has been satisfied. However, if a dividend is reinvested in accordance with section 404(k)(2)(A)(iii)(II), the amount of such a dividend is not precluded from being a qualified distribution if later distributed. Further, an amount is not precluded from being a qualified distribution merely because it is described in section 402(c)(4) as an amount not eligible for rollover. Thus, a hardship distribution is not precluded from being a qualified distribution.

Q–12. If any amount from a designated Roth account is included in a loan to an employee, do the plan aggregation rules of section 72(p)(2)(D) apply for purposes of determining the total amount an employee is permitted to borrow from the plan, even though the designated Roth account generally is treated as a separate contract under section 72?

A–12. Yes. If any amount from a designated Roth account is included in a loan to an employee, notwithstanding the general rule that the designated Roth account is treated as a separate contract under section 72, the plan aggregation rules of section 72(p)(2)(D) apply for purposes of determining the maximum amount the employee is permitted to borrow from the plan and such amount is based on the total of the designated Roth contribution amounts and the other amounts under the plan. To the extent a loan is from a designated Roth account, the repayment requirement of section 72(p)(2)(C) must be satisfied separately with respect to that portion of the loan and with respect to the portion of the loan from other accounts under the plan.

Q–13. Does a transaction or accounting methodology involving an employee's designated Roth account and any other accounts under the plan or plans of an employer that has the effect of transferring value from the other accounts into the designated Roth account violate the separate accounting requirement of section 402A?

A–13. (a) Yes. Any transaction or accounting methodology involving an employee's designated Roth account and any other accounts under the plan or plans of an employer that has the effect of directly or indirectly transferring value from another account into the designated Roth account violates the separate accounting requirement under section 402A. However, any transaction that merely exchanges investments between accounts at fair market value will not violate the separate accounting requirement.

(b) In the case of an annuity contract which contains both a designated Roth account and any other accounts, the Commissioner may prescribe additional guidance of general applicability, published in the Internal Revenue Bulletin (see 601.601(d)(2) of this chapter), to provide additional rules for allocation of income, expenses, gains and losses among the accounts under the contract.

(c) This A–13 applies to designated Roth accounts for taxable years beginning on or after January 1, 2006.

Q–14. How is an annuity contract that is distributed from a designated Roth account treated for purposes of section 402A?

A–14. A qualified plan distributed annuity contract within the meaning of §1.402(c)–2, A–10(a) that is distributed from a designated Roth account is not treated as a distribution for purposes of section 402 or 402A. Instead, the amounts paid under the annuity contract are treated as distributions for purposes of sections 402 and 402A. Thus, the period after the annuity contract is distributed and before a payment from the annuity contract is made is included in determining whether the five-year period of participation is satisfied. Further, for purposes of determining if a distribution is a qualified distribution, the determination of whether a distribution is made on or after the date the employee attains age 59½, made to a beneficiary or the estate of the employee on or after the employee's death, or attributable to the employee's being disabled within the meaning of section 72(m)(7) is made based on the facts at the time the distribution is made from the annuity contract. Thus for example, if an employee first makes a designated Roth contribution to a designated Roth account in 2006 at age 56, receives a distributed annuity contract within the meaning of §1.402(c)–2, A–10(a) in 2007 purchased only with assets from the designated Roth account, and then receives a distribution from the contract in 2011 at age 60, the distribution is a qualified distribution.

Q–15. When are section 402A and this §1.402A–1 applicable?

A–15. Section 402A is applicable for taxable years beginning on or after January 1, 2006. Except as otherwise provided in A–5 and A–13 of this section, the rules of this §1.402A–1 apply for taxable years beginning on or after January 1, 2007.

§1.402A–2 Reporting and recordkeeping requirements with respect to designated Roth accounts.

Q–1. Who is responsible for keeping track of the 5-taxable-year period of participation and the investment in the contract, *i.e.*, the amount of unrecovered designated Roth contributions for the employee?

A–1. The plan administrator or other responsible party with respect to a plan with a designated Roth account is responsible for keeping track of the 5-taxable-year period of participation for each employee and the amount of investment in the contract (unrecovered designated Roth contributions) on behalf of such employee. For purposes of the preceding sentence, in the absence of actual knowledge to the contrary, the plan administrator or other responsible party is permitted to assume that an employee's taxable year is the calendar year. In the case of a direct rollover from another designated Roth account, the plan administrator or other responsible party of the recipient plan can rely on reasonable representations made by the plan administrator or responsible party with respect to the plan with the other designated Roth account. See A–2 of this section for statements required in the case of rollovers.

Q–2. In the case of an eligible rollover distribution from a designated Roth account, what additional information must be provided with respect to such distribution?

A–2. (a) Pursuant to section 6047(f), if an amount is distributed from a designated Roth account, the plan administrator or other responsible party with respect to the plan must provide a statement as described below in the following situations—

(1) In the case of a direct rollover of a distribution from a designated Roth account under a plan to a designated Roth account under another plan, the plan administrator or other responsible party must provide to the plan administrator or responsible party of the recipient plan either a statement indicating the first year of the 5-taxable-year period described in A–1 of this section and the portion of the distribution that is attributable to investment in the contract under section 72, or a statement that the distribution is a qualified distribution.

(2) If the distribution is not a direct rollover to a designated Roth account under another plan, the plan administrator or responsible party must provide to the employee, upon request, the same information described in paragraph (a)(1) of this A–2, except the statement need not indicate the first year of the 5-taxable-year period described in A–1 of this section.

(b) The statement described in paragraph (a) of this A–2 must be provided within a reasonable period following the direct rollover or distributee request but in no event later than 30 days following the direct rollover or distributee request.

Q–3. If a plan qualified under section 401(a) or a section 403(b) plan accepts a 60-day rollover of earnings from a designated Roth account, what report to the IRS must be provided with respect to such rollover contribution?

A–3. To the extent required in Forms and Instructions, if a plan qualified under section 401(a), or a section 403(b) plan, accepts a rollover contribution (other than a direct rollover contribution) under section 402(c)(2), or section 403(b)(8)(B), of the portion of a distribution from a designated Roth account that would have been includable in gross income, the plan administrator or other responsible party for the recipient plan must notify the Commissioner of its acceptance of the rollover contribution no later than the due date for filing Form 1099–R, "*Distributions From Pensions, Annuities, Retirement or Profit-Sharing Plans, IRAs, Insurance Contracts, etc.*" The Forms and Instructions will specify the address to which the notification is required to be sent and will require inclusion of the employee's name and social security number, the amount rolled over, the year in which the rollover contribution was made, and such other information as the Commissioner may prescribe in order to determine that the amount rolled over is a valid rollover contribution.

Q–4. When is this §1.402A–2 applicable?

A–4. The rules of this §1.402A–2 are applicable for taxable years beginning on or after January 1, 2007.

Par. 6. Section 1.408A–10 is added to read as follows:

§1.408A–10 Coordination between designated Roth accounts and Roth IRAs

Q–1. Can an eligible rollover distribution, within the meaning of section 402(c)(4), from a designated Roth account, as defined in A–1 of §1.402A–1, be rolled over to a Roth IRA?

A–1. Yes. An eligible rollover distribution, within the meaning of section 402(c)(4), from a designated Roth account may be rolled over to a Roth IRA. For purposes of this section, a designated Roth account means a designated Roth account as defined in A–1 of §1.402A–1.

Q–2. Can an eligible rollover distribution from a designated Roth account be rolled over to a Roth IRA even if the distributee is not otherwise eligible to make regular or conversion contributions to a Roth IRA?

A–2. Yes. An individual may establish a Roth IRA and roll over an eligible rollover distribution from a designated Roth account to that Roth IRA even if such individual is not eligible to make regular contributions or conversion contributions (as described in section 408A(c)(2) and (d)(3), respectively) because of the modified adjusted gross income limits in section 408A(b)(3).

Q–3. For purposes of the ordering rules on distributions from Roth IRAs, what portion of a distribution from a rollover contribution from a designated Roth account is treated as contributions?

A–3. (a) Under section 408A(d)(4), distributions from Roth IRAs are deemed to consist first of regular contributions, then of conversion contributions, and finally, of earnings. For purposes of section 408A(d)(4), the amount of a rollover contribution that is treated as a regular contribution is the portion of the distribution that is treated as investment in the contract under A–6 of §1.402A–1, and the remainder of the rollover contribution is treated as earnings. Thus, the entire amount of any qualified distribution from a designated Roth account that is rolled over into a Roth IRA is treated as a regular contribution to the Roth IRA. Accordingly, a subsequent distribution from the Roth IRA in the amount of that rollover contribution is not includible in gross income under the rules of A–8 of §1.408A–6.

(b) If the entire account balance of a designated Roth account is distributed to an employee and only a portion of the distribution is rolled over to a Roth IRA within the 60-day period described in section 402(c)(3), and at the time of the distribution, the investment in the contract exceeds the balance in the designated Roth account, the portion of investment in the contract that exceeds the amount used to determine the taxable amount of the distribution is treated as a regular contribution for purposes of section 408A(d)(4).

Q–4. In the case of a rollover from a designated Roth account to a Roth IRA, when does the 5-taxable-year period (described in section 408A(d)(2)(B) and A–1 of §1.408A–6) for determining qualified distributions from a Roth IRA begin?

A–4. (a) The 5-taxable-year period for determining a qualified distribution from a Roth IRA (described in section 408A(d)(2)(B) and A–1 of §1.408A–6) begins with the earlier of the taxable year described in A–2 of §1.408A–6 or the taxable year in which a rollover contribution from a designated Roth account is made to a Roth IRA. The 5-taxable-year period described in this A–4 and the 5-taxable-year period of participation described in A–4 of §1.402A–1 are determined independently.

(b) The following examples illustrate the application of this A–4:

Example 1. Employee D began making designated Roth contributions under his employer's 401(k) plan in 2006. Employee D, who is over age 59½, takes a distribution from D's designated Roth account in 2008, prior to the end of the 5-taxable-year period of participation used to determine qualified distributions from a designated Roth account. The distribution is an eligible rollover distribution and D rolls it over in accordance with sections 402(c) and 402A(c)(3) to D's Roth IRA, which was established in 2003. Any subsequent distribution from the Roth IRA of the amount rolled in, plus earnings thereon, would not be includible in gross income (because it would be a qualified distribution within the meaning of section 408A(d)(2)).

Example 2. The facts are the same as in *Example 1*, except that the Roth IRA is D's first Roth IRA and is established with the rollover in 2008, which is the only contribution made to the Roth IRA. If a distribution is made from the Roth IRA prior to the end of the 5-taxable-year period used to determine qualified distributions from a Roth IRA (which begins in 2008, the year of the rollover which established the Roth IRA) the distribution would not be a qualified distribution within the meaning of section 408A(d)(2), and any amount of the distribution that exceeded the portion of the rollover contribution that consisted of investment in the contract is includible in D's gross income.

Example 3. The facts are the same as in *Example 2*, except that the distribution from the designated Roth account and the rollover to the Roth IRA occur in 2011 (after the end of the 5-taxable-year period of participation used to determine qualified distributions from a designated Roth account). If a distribution is made from the Roth IRA prior to the expiration of the 5-taxable-year period used to determine qualified distributions from a Roth IRA, the distribution would not be a qualified distribution within the meaning of section 408A(d)(2), and any amount of the distribution that exceeded the amount rolled in is includible in D's gross income.

Q–5. Can amounts distributed from a Roth IRA be rolled over to a designated Roth account as defined in A–1 of §1.402A–1?

A–5. No. Amounts distributed from a Roth IRA may be rolled over or transferred only to another Roth IRA and are not permitted to be rolled over to a designated Roth account under a section 401(a) or section 403(b) plan. The same rule applies even if all the amounts in the Roth IRA are attributable to a rollover distribution from a designated Roth account in a plan.

Q–6. When is this §1.408A–10 applicable?

A–6. The rules of this §1.408A–10 apply for taxable years beginning on or after January 1, 2006.

PART 602—OMB CONTROL NUMBERS UNDER THE PAPERWORK REDUCTION ACT

Par. 7. The authority citation for part 602 continues to read as follows:

Authority: 26 U.S.C. 7805.

Par. 8. In §602.101, paragraph (b) is amended by adding an entry for 1.402A–1 in numerical order to the table to read in part as follows:

§602.101 OMB Control numbers.

* * * * *

(b) * * *

CFR part or section where identified and described	Current OMB control No.
* * * * *	
1.402A–1	1545–1992
* * * * *	

Kevin M. Brown,
Deputy Commissioner for Services and Enforcement.

Approved April 23, 2007.

Eric Solomon,
Assistant Secretary of the Treasury (Tax Policy).

(Filed by the Office of the Federal Register on April 27, 2007, 8:45 a.m., and published in the issue of the Federal Register for April 30, 2007, 72 F.R. 21103)

Section 472.—Last-in, First-out Inventories

26 CFR 1.472–1: Last-in, first-out inventories.

LIFO; price indexes; department stores. The March 2007 Bureau of Labor Statistics price indexes are accepted for use by department stores employing the retail inventory and last-in, first-out inventory methods for valuing inventories for tax years ended on, or with reference to, March 31, 2007.

Rev. Rul. 2007–34

The following Department Store Inventory Price Indexes for March 2007 were issued by the Bureau of Labor Statistics. The indexes are accepted by the Internal Revenue Service, under § 1.472–1(k) of the Income Tax Regulations and Rev. Proc. 86–46, 1986–2 C.B. 739, for appropriate application to inventories of department stores employing the retail inventory and last-in, first-out inventory methods for tax years ended on, or with reference to, March 31, 2007.

In Notice 2007–44, this Bulletin, the Internal Revenue Service announced that it will discontinue publishing the BLS Department Store Inventory Price Indexes in the Internal Revenue Bulletin following the publication of the March 2007 indexes in this revenue ruling.

The Department Store Inventory Price Indexes are prepared on a national basis and include (a) 23 major groups of departments, (b) three special combinations of the major groups — soft goods, durable goods, and miscellaneous goods, and (c) a store total, which covers all departments, including some not listed separately, except for the following: candy, food, liquor, tobacco, and contract departments.

BUREAU OF LABOR STATISTICS, DEPARTMENT STORE INVENTORY PRICE INDEXES BY DEPARTMENT GROUPS
(January 1941 = 100, unless otherwise noted)

	Groups	Mar. 2006	Mar. 2007	Percent Change From Mar. 2006 to Mar. 2007[1]
1.	Piece Goods	442.9	417.0	-5.8
2.	Domestics and Draperies	495.7	473.4	-4.5
3.	Women's and Children's Shoes	703.1	674.1	-4.1
4.	Men's Shoes	875.8	862.7	-1.5
5.	Infants' Wear	569.9	578.9	1.6
6.	Women's Underwear	545.6	563.5	3.3
7.	Women's Hosiery	347.3	340.0	-2.1
8.	Women's and Girls' Accessories	583.1	571.7	-2.0
9.	Women's Outerwear and Girls' Wear	367.6	381.4	3.8
10.	Men's Clothing	542.9	531.7	-2.1
11.	Men's Furnishings	571.3	578.2	1.2
12.	Boys' Clothing and Furnishings	408.0	410.6	0.6
13.	Jewelry	854.9	901.8	5.5
14.	Notions	792.2	793.1	0.1
15.	Toilet Articles and Drugs	1008.3	1014.9	0.7
16.	Furniture and Bedding	603.6	604.7	0.2
17.	Floor Coverings	619.5	609.7	-1.6
18.	Housewares	696.4	694.7	-0.2
19.	Major Appliances	204.2	211.0	3.3

BUREAU OF LABOR STATISTICS, DEPARTMENT STORE
INVENTORY PRICE INDEXES BY DEPARTMENT GROUPS
(January 1941 = 100, unless otherwise noted)

Groups	Mar. 2006	Mar. 2007	Percent Change From Mar. 2006 to Mar. 2007[1]
20. Radio and Television	37.1	33.0	-11.1
21. Recreation and Education[2]	77.2	76.3	-1.2
22. Home Improvements[2]	139.5	141.5	1.4
23. Automotive Accessories[2]	118.4	123.2	4.1
Groups 1–15: Soft Goods	560.6	564.8	0.7
Groups 16–20: Durable Goods	374.7	372.4	-0.6
Groups 21–23: Misc. Goods[2]	93.5	94.2	0.7
Store Total[3]	495.0	497.3	0.5

[1]Absence of a minus sign before the percentage change in this column signifies a price increase.

[2]Indexes on a January 1986 = 100 base.

[3]The store total index covers all departments, including some not listed separately, except for the following: candy, food, liquor, tobacco, and contract departments.

DRAFTING INFORMATION

The principal author of this revenue ruling is John Roman Faron of the Office of Associate Chief Counsel (Income Tax and Accounting). For further information regarding this revenue ruling, contact Mr. Faron at (202) 622-4930 (not a toll-free call).

Section 482.—Allocation of Income and Deductions Among Taxpayers

26 CFR 1.482–1: Allocation of income and deductions among taxpayers.

Revenue rulings obsolete. This ruling obsoletes Rev. Rul. 74–245, 1974–1 C.B. 124, and Rev. Rul. 82–45, 1982–1 C.B. 89, which provide guidance regarding income subject to foreign legal restrictions (also known as blocked income) under section 482. Rev. Ruls. 74–245 and 82–45 obsoleted.

Rev. Rul. 2007–35

Rulings Declared Obsolete

This revenue ruling obsoletes Rev. Rul. 74–245, 1974–1 C.B. 124, and Rev. Rul. 82–45, 1982–1 C.B. 89, which provide guidance regarding income subject to foreign legal restrictions (also known as blocked income). Rev. Ruls. 74–245 and 82–45 are not considered determinative with respect to future transactions. Guidance regarding income subject to foreign legal restrictions for purposes of section 482 is provided in § 1.482–1(h)(2) of the Income Tax Regulations (T.D. 8552, 1994–2 C.B. 93, 125). Therefore, Rev. Rul. 74–351, 1974–2 C.B. 144, does not provide guidance regarding income subject to foreign legal restrictions for purposes of section 482, but may provide guidance regarding income subject to foreign legal restrictions for other purposes.

DRAFTING INFORMATION

The principal author of this revenue ruling is Keith V. Doce of the Office of Associate Chief Counsel (International). For further information regarding this revenue ruling, contact Mr. Doce at (202) 435-5265 (not a toll-free call).

Part III. Administrative, Procedural, and Miscellaneous

Credit for Alternative Fuel Vehicle Refueling Property

Notice 2007–43

SECTION 1. PURPOSE

This notice sets forth interim guidance, pending the issuance of regulations, relating to the new qualified alternative fuel vehicle (QAFV) refueling property credit ("Refueling Property Credit") under § 30C of the Internal Revenue Code. The Internal Revenue Service and the Treasury Department expect that the regulations will incorporate the rules set forth in this notice.

SECTION 2. BACKGROUND

Section 30C provides a credit for QAFV refueling property. Section 30C(c)(1) provides that QAFV refueling property has the same meaning as under § 179A(d) (relating to the deduction allowed for qualified clean-fuel vehicle refueling property placed in service before January 1, 2006) but only with respect to the alternative fuels listed in § 30C(c)(1). The credit is available for property that a taxpayer places in service as QAFV refueling property after December 31, 2005, and on or before December 31, 2009 (December 31, 2014, in the case of property relating to hydrogen).

SECTION 3. SCOPE

This notice provides guidance relating to the computation of the Refueling Property Credit and the treatment for purposes of the credit of converted and dual-use refueling property. This notice does not address: (1) the rule under § 30C(d)(2) preventing the credit from being used to reduce alternative minimum tax liability; or (2) the rule under § 30C(e)(5) requiring recapture of the credit under certain circumstances. The Internal Revenue Service and Treasury Department expect to issue separate guidance relating to these, and other, issues under § 30C.

SECTION 4. DEFINITIONS AND CROSS REFERENCES TO APPLICABLE REGULATIONS

.01 *Definitions*. The following definitions apply for purposes of this notice:

(1) *QAFV refueling property*. QAFV refueling property is any property (other than a building or its structural components) that meets the following requirements:

(i) The property is not used predominantly outside the United States (or, in the case of property described in § 168(g)(4)(G), is property used predominantly in a U.S. possession).

(ii) The property is of a character subject to the allowance for depreciation or is installed on property that is used as the taxpayer's principal residence (within the meaning of § 121)).

(iii) The original use of the property begins with the taxpayer.

(iv) The property is used for—

(a) Storing alternative fuel at the point where the fuel is delivered into the fuel tank of a motor vehicle that is propelled by such fuel; or

(b) Dispensing alternative fuel at such point into the fuel tank of a motor vehicle that is propelled by such fuel.

(2) *Dual-use property*. Dual-use property is refueling property that is used—

(a) To store and/or dispense both alternative fuel and conventional fuel; or

(b) Both to store alternative fuel that is dispensed into the fuel tanks of motor vehicles at the location of the storage facility and to store alternative fuel that is transported to other locations.

(3) *Alternative fuel*. A fuel is an alternative fuel if—

(i) At least 85 percent of its volume consists of one or more of the following: ethanol, natural gas, compressed natural gas, liquefied natural gas, liquefied petroleum gas, or hydrogen; or

(ii) It is a qualifying biodiesel mixture.

(4) *Qualifying biodiesel mixture*. A fuel is a qualifying biodiesel mixture if it is a mixture of biodiesel (as defined in § 40A(d)(1)) and diesel fuel (as defined in § 4083(a)(3)) and the mixture contains at least 20 percent biodiesel. For this purpose, any kerosene in a mixture—

(i) Is disregarded in determining whether the mixture is a mixture of biodiesel and diesel fuel; and

(ii) Is taken into account in determining whether the mixture contains at least 20 percent biodiesel.

(5) *Conventional fuel*. Conventional fuel is any fuel that is not an alternative fuel. Conventional fuel includes diesel fuel that is not in a qualifying biodiesel mixture and gasoline.

(6) *Conventional refueling property*. Conventional refueling property is property that is used to dispense or store only conventional fuel.

(7) *Fuel tank*. The fuel tank of a motor vehicle that is propelled by alternative fuel includes only the tank that supplies fuel to the propulsion engine of the vehicle.

.02 *Cross References to Applicable Regulations*. The following provisions of the Income Tax Regulations (26 CFR Part 1) apply for purposes of this notice:

(1) *Building and structural components*. Whether property is a building or a structural component of a building is determined under the principles of § 1.48–1(e).

(2) *Original use*. Whether the original use of property begins with the taxpayer is determined under the principles of § 1.48–2.

(3) *Placed in service*. The year in which property is placed in service and whether the property is placed in service as QAFV refueling property are determined under the principles of § 1.46–3(d).

(4) *Subject to allowance for depreciation*. Whether property is of a character subject to the allowance for depreciation is determined under the principles of § 1.48–1(b).

(5) *Use outside the United States*. Whether property is used predominantly outside the United States is determined under the principles of § 1.48–1(g).

SECTION 5. COMPUTATION OF CREDIT

.01 *In General*. The Refueling Property Credit is equal to 30 percent of the cost of any property that the taxpayer places in service as QAFV refueling property during the taxable year. The credit is limited to $30,000 per property for property of a character subject to the allowance for depreciation and $1,000 per property for other property. (A proposed technical correction would retroactively change this rule so that a single limitation of $30,000 or $1,000 (depending on whether the property is of a character subject to the allowance for depreciation) applies to all QAFV refueling property placed in service at a location during a taxable year.)

.02 *Cost of QAFV Refueling Property.* The cost of QAFV refueling property is determined under the principles of § 1.46–3(a) and (c) and the following rules:

(1) The cost of QAFV refueling property includes all costs that are required under federal tax principles to be capitalized as a cost of the QAFV refueling property. These costs include the cost of acquiring or constructing the QAFV refueling property or of converting conventional refueling property into QAFV refueling property.

(2) The cost of QAFV refueling property does not include costs that are properly allocable to land or to a building and its structural components. Costs properly allocable to land include, but are not limited to, costs related to the acquisition of land on which the QAFV refueling property is located and expenses for permits, legal fees, project management, or engineering to the extent such expenses are related to the land.

(3) The cost of QAFV refueling property does not include any amount that is taken into account under § 179 (relating to the election to expense certain depreciable business assets).

SECTION 6. CONVERTED AND DUAL-USE PROPERTY

.01 *Converted Refueling Property.*

(1) *In general.* The rules in this section 6.01 apply solely with respect to converted QAFV refueling property. For this purpose, converted QAFV refueling property is QAFV refueling property that was converted from property (including conventional refueling property) that is not QAFV refueling property (non-QAFV property).

(2) *Reconditioned or rebuilt property.* If converted QAFV refueling property is treated under the principles of § 1.48–2 as reconditioned or rebuilt property, the cost of the QAFV refueling property includes the cost of reconditioning or rebuilding the non-QAFV property, but does not include the basis of the non-QAFV property.

(3) *Use as QAFV refueling property treated as original use.* If converted QAFV refueling property, including any parts that were non-QAFV property before the conversion, is treated under the principles of § 1.48–2 as being put to original use when first used as QAFV refueling property, the cost of the QAFV refueling property includes both the adjusted basis of the non-QAFV property immediately before the conversion and the cost of the conversion.

.02 *Dual-Use Property.*

(1) *In general.* In the case of dual-use property that is used to store and/or dispense both alternative fuel and conventional fuel, the cost of the dual-use property is taken into account in computing the Refueling Property Credit only to the extent such cost exceeds the cost of equivalent conventional refueling property. For this purpose, equivalent conventional refueling property is conventional refueling property that is not used to store and/or dispense alternative fuel, but is otherwise comparable to the dual-use property and can store and/or dispense the same amount of conventional fuel as the dual-use property.

(2) *Storage facilities.* In the case of dual-use property that is used both to store alternative fuel that is dispensed into the fuel tanks of motor vehicles at the location of the storage facility and to store fuel that is transported to other locations, the cost of the dual-use property is taken into account in computing the Refueling Property Credit only to the extent such cost exceeds the cost of a storage facility that is equivalent to the dual-use property except that it is used for the sole purpose of storing alternative fuel that is transported to other locations and can store the same amount of alternative fuel as the dual-use property stores for transport to other locations.

SECTION 7. EXAMPLES

.01 *Example 1.* (i) *X* , a fuel wholesaler, acquires an additional storage tank to store alternative fuel at its principal place of business and a fuel tanker truck to transport the alternative fuel from its principal place of business to the retail service stations of *X*'s customers. The fuel tanker truck dispenses alternative fuel into storage tanks at the retail service stations but is not used to dispense the alternative fuel into the fuel tanks of motor vehicles that are propelled by the alternative fuel.

(ii) Neither the storage tank nor the fuel tanker truck is QAFV refueling property within the meaning of section 4.01(1) of this notice. The storage tank is used to store alternative fuel, but it does not store the fuel at the point where the fuel is delivered into the fuel tank of a motor vehicle that is propelled by alternative fuel within the meaning of section 4.01(7) of this notice. Similarly, the fuel tanker truck is used to dispense alternative fuel, but it does not dispense the fuel into the fuel tank of a motor vehicle that is propelled by alternative fuel.

.02 *Example 2.* (i) The facts are the same as in *Example 1*, except that *X* also acquires a pump that is used to dispense alternative fuel from the storage tank into the fuel tanks of *X*'s fuel tanker trucks. The storage tank has the same capacity as the tank that would have been used for the sole purpose of storing the alternative fuel that is supplied to *X*'s customers.

(ii) The pump is QAFV refueling property within the meaning of section 4.01(1) of this notice because it is used to dispense alternative fuel into the fuel tanks of *X*'s fuel tanker trucks. Accordingly, the cost of the pump is taken into account in determining *X*'s Refueling Property Credit.

(iii) The storage tank is also QAFV refueling property because it is used to store alternative fuel at the point where the fuel is delivered into the fuel tanks of the fuel tanker trucks. In addition, however, the storage tank is dual-use property described in section 6.02(2). Under section 6.02, the cost of the storage tank is taken into account in computing the Refueling Property Credit only to the extent that cost exceeds the cost of the storage tank that would have been used for the sole purpose of storing the alternative fuel that is supplied to *X*'s customers. Because no increase in the capacity of the storage tank is needed, none of the storage tank's cost is taken into account in computing the amount of the Refueling Property Credit.

.03 *Example 3.* (i) *Y* is a retail seller of gasoline. In Year 1, *Y* acquires and places in service conventional refueling property consisting of a gasoline storage tank. *Y* claims the allowable depreciation deduction with respect to the gasoline storage tank on its federal income tax return for Year 1. In Year 2, *Y* incurs costs of $10,000 to convert the gasoline storage tank into an alternative fuel storage tank and begins using the converted property as QAFV refueling property.

(ii) If, under the principles of § 1.48–2, the storage tank is treated as reconditioned or rebuilt property, only the $10,000 incurred to convert the gasoline tank into QAFV refueling property is taken into account for purposes of determining *Y*'s Refueling Property Credit for Year 2. If, on the other hand, the converted storage tank is treated, under the principles of § 1.48–2, as being put to original use when first used as QAFV refueling property, the adjusted basis of the storage tank immediately before its conversion into QAFV refueling property also is taken into account for purposes of determining the credit.

SECTION 8. RECORDKEEPING

Section 6001 provides that every person liable for any tax imposed by the Code, or for the collection thereof, must keep such records, render such statements, make such returns, and comply with such rules and regulations as the Secretary may from time to time prescribe. The books and records required by § 6001 must be kept at all times available for inspection by authorized internal revenue officers or employees, and must be retained so long as the contents thereof may become material in the administration of any internal revenue law. Section 1.6001–1(e) of the Procedure and Administration Regulations. In order to satisfy the recordkeeping requirements of § 6001 and the regulations thereunder, a taxpayer that claims the Refueling Property Credit must retain adequate books and records so that, for any taxable year, it can be verified from those books and records that the fuel that is dispensed and/or stored meets the definition of alternative fuel contained in § 30C(c)(1)(A) or (B) and section 4.01(3) of this notice, and that the refueling property otherwise meets the requirements of § 30C and this notice.

SECTION 9. EFFECTIVE DATE

This notice is effective for QAFV refueling property placed in service after December 31, 2005, and on or before December 31, 2009 (December 31, 2014, in the case of property relating to hydrogen).

SECTION 10. DRAFTING INFORMATION

The principal author of this notice is Nicole R. Cimino of the Office of Associate Chief Counsel (Passthroughs and Special Industries). For further information regarding this notice, contact Ms. Cimino at (202) 622–3120 (not a toll-free call).

Department Store Inventory Price Indexes Published by the Bureau of Labor Statistics for Use With the Retail and LIFO Inventory Methods

Notice 2007–44

PURPOSE

This notice informs taxpayers that the Internal Revenue Service will no longer publish the Department Store Inventory Price Indexes prepared by the United States Bureau of Labor Statistics (BLS) in the Internal Revenue Bulletin but will continue to accept the BLS Department Store Inventory Price Indexes for use by department stores employing the last-in, first-out (LIFO) inventory identification method in conjunction with the retail method of valuing inventories.

BACKGROUND

The BLS prepares and publishes monthly Department Store Inventory Price Indexes, designed to measure changes in the retail prices for merchandise carried by department stores. The indexes are determined on a national basis and include 23 major groups of departments, three special combinations of those major groups, and store totals. Each month, the Service reproduces the BLS Department Store Inventory Price Indexes and accepts those indexes in accordance with § 1.472–1(k) of the Income Tax Regulations and Rev. Proc. 86–46, 1986–2 C.B. 739, for use by department stores employing the LIFO inventory identification method in conjunction with the retail method of valuing inventories, in a revenue ruling published in the Internal Revenue Bulletin.

APPLICATION

The Internal Revenue Service will discontinue republishing the BLS Department Store Inventory Price Indexes in the Internal Revenue Bulletin after the publication of the March 2007 indexes in Rev. Rul. 2007–34, this Bulletin. Although the BLS Department Store Inventory Price Indexes will no longer be published in the Internal Revenue Bulletin, the monthly indexes that are applicable to the goods in question will continue to be accepted by the Service under § 1.472–1(k) and Rev. Proc. 86–46, for appropriate application to inventories of department stores employing the retail and LIFO inventory methods in valuing inventories for tax years ended with, or with reference to, the last day of the applicable month.

The most current monthly BLS Department Store Inventory Price Indexes are available on the BLS website at the Consumer Price Indexes (CPI) page at *www.bls.gov/cpi*, in the "Tables Created by BLS" section under "Tables and publications containing Consumer Price Indexes" at "Department Store Inventory Price Indexes *** (PDF)." The BLS Department Store Inventory Price Indexes for prior months are also available on the BLS website at the CPI page (*www.bls.gov/cpi*) in the "Get Detailed CPI Statistics" section under "Create Customized Tables (one screen)" at "Department Store Inventory Price Index." In addition, directions and links to the BLS Department Store Inventory Price Indexes on the BLS website are available on the Internal Revenue Service website at *www.irs.gov*, in the "Tax Professionals" section, under "Resources for Tax Pro" and "Tax Law Issues, Nibbles and Bytes," at "BLS Department Store Inventory Price Indexes."

EFFECT ON OTHER DOCUMENTS

Rev. Proc. 86–46 is modified.

DRAFTING INFORMATION

The principal author of this notice is John Roman Faron of the Office of Assistant Chief Counsel (Income Tax and Accounting). For further information regarding this notice, contact Mr. Faron at (202) 622–4930 (not a toll-free call).

Guidance Regarding Public Inspection of Unrelated Business Income Tax Returns

Notice 2007–45

SECTION 1. PURPOSE

This notice provides interim guidance on section 6104(d)(1)(A)(ii) of the Internal Revenue Code (the Code), which was added by section 1225 of the Pension Protection Act of 2006, Pub. L. No. 109–280, 120 Stat. 780 (2006) (the PPA). This provision imposes a new requirement on all organizations exempt from Federal income tax under section 501(a) of the Code and described in section 501(c)(3) (charities) to make available for public inspection a copy of any annual return filed under section 6011 relating to the tax imposed under section 511. The annual return subject to this public disclosure requirement is filed on Form 990–T, *Exempt Organization Business Income Tax Return*. The requirement applies to any Form 990–T filed by a charity with the IRS after August 17, 2006.

The Internal Revenue Service (IRS) and the Treasury Department expect to revise the regulations under section 6104(d) of the Code to take account of the change to the statute. Until those revised regulations are effective, charities may rely on this notice to comply with section 6104(d)(1)(A)(ii).

SECTION 2. BACKGROUND

Section 6104(d) of the Code requires tax-exempt organizations to make available for public inspection and copying certain annual returns, reports, applications for recognition of exemption, and notices of status. The annual returns must be made available by an organization for inspection during regular business hours by any individual at the principal office of such organization and, if such organization regularly maintains one or more regional or district offices having three or more employees, at each such regional or district office. Also, an organization must provide, upon request of an individual made at such principal office or such a regional or district office, copies of annual returns to such individual without charge other than a reasonable fee for any reproduction and mailing costs.

Prior to the passage of the PPA, annual returns filed under section 6011 relating to the tax imposed under section 511 were not subject to the requirements of section 6104(d). Following enactment of section 6104(d)(1)(A)(ii) in the PPA, the Code requires charities to make available for public inspection and copying by any individual a copy of annual returns the charity files under section 6011 that relate to any tax imposed by section 511. Therefore, except as provided in this notice, the requirements of section 6104(d) apply to any Form 990–T a charity files with the IRS after August 17, 2006.

Section 501(a) of the Code provides for the exemption from Federal income tax for organizations described in section 501(c). Section 501(c)(3) describes organizations that are organized and operated exclusively for religious, charitable, scientific, testing for public safety, literary, or educational purposes, no part of the net earnings of which inures to the benefit of any private shareholder or individual. Section 511(a), in part, imposes a tax for each taxable year on the unrelated business taxable income of any charity, any college or university described in section 511(a)(2)(B), and any corporation wholly owned by one or more such colleges or universities. A college or university is described in section 511(a)(2)(B) if it is an agency or instrumentality of any government or any political subdivision thereof, or is owned or operated by any government or any political subdivision thereof, or by any agency or instrumentality of one or more governments or political subdivisions (state colleges and universities). Section 115(1) of the Code provides that gross income does not include income that is derived from a public utility or from the exercise of any essential governmental function, and accruing to a State or any political subdivision thereof.

Section 301.6104(d)–1 of the Procedure and Administration Regulations sets forth general guidance on making annual returns available for public inspection. Section 301.6104(d)–2 describes how a tax-exempt organization can make its annual return widely available and, therefore, not subject to the requirement to provide copies in response to individual requests, although the regulation stipulates that the organization still must make the annual return available for public inspection. Section 301.6104(d)–3 addresses the standards that apply in determining whether a tax-exempt organization is the subject of a harassment campaign, such that it may, under applicable procedures, obtain relief from the requirement that copies be provided in response to individual requests.

Under section 6652(c)(1)(C) of the Code, a penalty may be imposed on any person for failure to make available for public inspection and copying a copy of Form 990–T. The penalty is payable by the person who fails to comply with the requirements of section 6104(d). The penalty is $20 on each person for each day that the failure continues, not to exceed $10,000 on all persons with respect to any one return. Additionally, a penalty under section 6685 of the Code for willful failure to comply with the requirements of section 6104(d), and a penalty under section 7207 for willfully furnishing fraudulent or false information, may apply.

SECTION 3. INTERIM GUIDANCE

The IRS and the Treasury Department expect to revise regulations under section 6104(d) of the Code to include the new requirements under section 6104(d)(1)(A)(ii). Until the revised regulations are effective, charities may rely on sections 301.6104(d)–1, 301.6104(d)–2, and 301.6104(d)–3 of the regulations, except as otherwise provided in this notice, for guidance on how to comply with section 6104(d)(1)(A)(ii).

Pursuant to this notice, all charities that file Form 990–T are required to make the return public, regardless of whether the charity is otherwise subject to the disclosure requirements of section 6104. For example, although churches are not required to file Form 1023 or Form 990 with the IRS, they are required to file the Form 990–T with the IRS to report unrelated business taxable income. Thus, churches are required, under this notice, to disclose Form 990–T to the public.

In addition, this notice clarifies the application of the statute to state colleges and universities (and their wholly owned corporations). State colleges and universities are generally eligible to exclude their income from gross income under section 115 of the Code. The application of section 115 effectively provides an exemption from income tax. A state college or university may also be exempt from income tax under section 501(a) as an organization described in section 501(c)(3) if it applies for and receives a determination letter in accordance with section 508 of the Code. The exclusion from gross income under section 115 applies regardless of whether the state or college or university elects to apply for a determination letter. Nonetheless, some state colleges and universities may seek exemption under section 501(a) as well in order to be listed in IRS Publication 78, which many donors and grantmakers use to confirm that an organization is eligible to receive deductible contributions under section 170. State colleges and universities (and their wholly-owned corporations) that rely solely on section 115 to relieve them of liability for income tax are nonetheless subject to UBIT under section 511(a)(2)(B). State colleges and universities (and their wholly-owned corporations) that receive determination letters confirming that they are exempt under section 501(a) as organizations described in section 501(c)(3) are subject to UBIT under section 511(a)(2)(A), and possibly also under section 511(a)(2)(B).

Section 6104(d)(1)(A)(ii), as enacted, requires disclosure by all organizations that are exempt from tax under section 501(a) that are described in section 501(c)(3). The statute does not provide an exception for organizations that also benefit from the income exclusion provided by section 115. Thus, the statute requires that state colleges and universities that have been recognized by the IRS as exempt under section 501(a) as organizations described in section 501(c)(3), disclose Form 990–T to the public. However, the statute does not require state colleges and universities that are subject to tax under section 511(a) solely by virtue of section 511(a)(2)(B), and that have not been recognized by the IRS as exempt under section 501(a) as organizations described in section 501(c)(3), to make public their Forms 990–T.

The guidelines on making annual returns available for public inspection set forth in section 301.6104(d)–1 of the regulations generally apply, except that for purposes of section 6104(d)(1)(A)(ii), the definition of "annual information return" in section 301.6104(d)–1(b)(4)(i) includes an exact copy of the Form 990–T filed by a charity with the IRS after August 17, 2006, including all schedules, attachments, and supporting documents, and the exclusion of the Form 990–T from that definition in section 301.6104(d)–1(b)(4)(ii) does not apply.

Charities that make their Form 990–T widely available in accordance with the provisions in section 301.6104(d)–2 of the regulations do not need to comply with an individual request for a copy of such return, though they still must make such return available for public inspection. The widely available exception requires that the Form 990–T be posted in a format that exactly reproduces the image of the return as it was originally filed with the IRS after August 17, 2006, including all schedules, attachments, and supporting documents. For instance, the organization will be treated as having made its Form 990–T for a given year widely available if it posts its Form 990–T as a PDF file on the organization's website.

The provisions of section 301.6104(d)–3 are applicable to a request for a charity's Form 990–T that is part of a harassment campaign. An organization that believes that the requests for Form 990–T are part of a single coordinated effort to disrupt the operations of the tax-exempt organization, rather than to collect information about the organization, may apply for a determination from the IRS that the organization is the subject of a harassment campaign and suspend compliance with the requests for copies of Form 990–T, provided that it files the request for determination with 10 business days of the suspension. The IRS's determination that the organization is the subject of a harassment campaign allows an organization not to comply with any requests for copies of Form 990–T that it reasonably believes are part of the campaign.

SECTION 4. EXCEPTION WHERE FORM 990–T USED SOLELY TO REQUEST TELEPHONE EXCISE TAX REFUND

For 2006, exempt organizations must use Form 990–T if they wish to request a refund of telephone excise tax paid after February 28, 2003, and before August 6, 2006. See Notice 2006–50, 2006–25 I.R.B. 1141, for more information regarding the telephone tax refund.

A charity that files a Form 990–T solely to request a refund of the federal telephone excise tax is not required to make that Form 990–T available for public inspection and copying. However, if a charity files a Form 990–T to request a refund of the federal telephone excise tax and to report unrelated business taxable income under section 511, the charity is required to make that Form 990–T available for public inspection and copying in its entirety.

SECTION 5. REQUEST FOR COMMENTS

The IRS and the Treasury Department invite comments on implementation of the public inspection requirement of section 6104(d)(1)(A)(ii). Comments are requested specifically on the application of the public inspection requirement of section 6104(d)(1)(A)(ii) to organizations that are exempt from Federal income tax under section 501(a) and described in section 501(c)(3), that may also exclude their income from gross income under section 115(1) or other legal principles.

Comments should refer to Notice 2007–45 and be submitted by June 30, 2007, to:

Internal Revenue Service
CC:PA:LPD:PR (Notice 2007–45)
Room 5203
P.O. Box 7604
Ben Franklin Station
Washington, DC 20044

Submissions may be hand delivered Monday through Friday between the hours of 8 a.m. and 4:00 p.m. to:

Courier's Desk
Internal Revenue Service
1111 Constitution Ave., N.W.
Washington, DC 20224
Attn: CC:PA:LPD:PR
(Notice 2007–45)

Alternatively, taxpayers may submit comments electronically to *notice.comments@irscounsel.treas.gov*. Please include "Notice 2007–45" in the subject line of any electronic communications.

All comments will be available for public inspection and copying.

SECTION 6. DRAFTING INFORMATION

The principal author of this notice is Mary Jo Salins of the Exempt Organizations, Tax Exempt and Government Entities Division. For further information regarding this notice, contact Ms. Salins at (202) 283–9453 (not a toll-free call).

Gaming Industry Tip Compliance Agreement Program

Rev. Proc. 2007–32

SECTION 1. PURPOSE

The Gaming Industry Tip Compliance Agreement Program (GITCA Program) is designed to promote compliance by gaming industry employers and employees with the provisions of the Internal Revenue Code relating to tip income and to reduce disputes under section 3121(q).

The GITCA Program was established by Revenue Procedure 2003–35, 2003–1 C.B. 919, in May 2003. This revenue procedure provides an updated model Gaming Industry Tip Compliance Agreement for use by the Internal Revenue Service and gaming industry employers. The new model agreement has been revised to enhance administration of the GITCA Program by both the employers and the Service and to facilitate and promote the use of current financial information technology in the tip reporting process.

SECTION 2. OVERVIEW

Under the GITCA Program, a gaming industry employer and the Internal Revenue Service work together to reach a Gaming Industry Tip Compliance Agreement that establishes minimum tip rates for tipped employees in specified occupational categories, prescribes a threshold level of participation by the employer's employees, and reduces compliance burdens for the employer and enforcement burdens for the Service.

SECTION 3. EMPLOYER PARTICIPATION

.01 With the consent of the Service, all employers operating a gaming establishment may participate in the GITCA Program. Either the Service or an employer may suggest the employer's potential participation in the program.

.02 The Service's decision to refuse participation by any employer in this program is not subject to review.

SECTION 4. GAMING INDUSTRY TIP COMPLIANCE AGREEMENTS

.01 To participate in this program, an employer must execute a Gaming Industry Tip Compliance Agreement. The Gaming Industry Tip Compliance Agreement shall conform to all requirements of this revenue procedure and will use the form appended to this revenue procedure as Exhibit 1.

.02 An executed Gaming Industry Tip Compliance Agreement shall supersede all existing tip compliance agreements between an employer and the Service. A gaming industry employer under any existing tip compliance agreement with the Service, including a Tip Rate Determination Agreement, may request to change to a Gaming Industry Tip Compliance Agreement.

.03 In general, Gaming Industry Tip Compliance Agreements shall be for a term of three years. For new properties and for properties that do not have a prior agreement with the Service, however, the initial term of the Agreement may be for a shorter period.

.04 All Gaming Industry Tip Compliance Agreements may be renewed for additional terms of up to three years, in accordance with Section IX of the model Gaming Industry Tip Compliance Agreement. Beginning not later than six months prior to the termination date of a Gaming Industry Tip Compliance Agreement, the Service and the employer shall commence discussions as to any appropriate revisions to the agreement, including any appropriate revisions to the tip rates described in Section VIII of the model Gaming Industry Tip Compliance Agreement. In the event that the Service and the employer have not reached final agreement on the terms and conditions of a renewal agreement, the parties may, by mutual agreement, extend the existing agreement for an appropriate time to finalize and execute a renewal agreement.

.05 Decisions regarding renewal of a Gaming Industry Tip Compliance Agreement are not subject to review.

SECTION 5. DEEMED COMPLIANCE WITH SECTION 6053

An employer who complies with the reporting requirements of Section V of its Gaming Industry Tip Compliance Agreement, and participating employees of the employer who report in accordance with the agreement, will be deemed to be in compliance with the reporting requirements of section 6053 of the Internal Revenue Code for the taxable periods during which the agreement remains in effect.

SECTION 6. EFFECTIVE DATE

This revenue procedure is effective May 2, 2007.

SECTION 7. EFFECT ON OTHER DOCUMENTS

Revenue Procedure 2003–35 is superseded. All Gaming Industry Tip Compliance Agreements executed pursuant to Revenue Procedure 2003–35 will remain in effect until the expiration date set forth in that Agreement, unless superseded by the execution of a Gaming Industry Tip Compliance Agreement under section 4.02 of this revenue procedure.

SECTION 8. PAPERWORK REDUCTION ACT

The collection of information contained in this revenue procedure has been reviewed and approved by the Office of Management and Budget in accordance with the Paperwork Reduction Act (44 U.S.C. § 3507) under control number 1545–1530. This control number was received under preceding Revenue Procedure 2003–35 and was renewed in June 2006. An agency may not conduct or sponsor, and a person is not required to respond to, a collection of information unless the collection of information displays a valid OMB control number.

The collection of information in this revenue procedure is in the section titled GAMING INDUSTRY TIP COMPLIANCE AGREEMENTS. This information is required to evaluate the suitability of the GITCA Program for the particular taxpayer and to assess the validity of the proposed tip rates. The collection of information is required to obtain the benefits described in this revenue procedure. The likely respondents are businesses or other for-profit institutions.

The estimated total annual reporting burden under this revenue procedure has been reduced from the burden under Revenue Procedure 2003–35. Under this revenue procedure, the estimated total annual reporting burden is 5,000 hours.

The estimated annual burden per respondent is an average of 10 hours, depending on individual circumstances. The estimated number of respondents is 500.

The estimated frequency of responses is 1 time per year per respondent.

Books or records relating to a collection of information must be retained as long as their contents may become material in the administration of any internal revenue law. Generally tax returns and return information are confidential, as required by 26 U.S.C. § 6103.

SECTION 9. DRAFTING AND CONTACT INFORMATION

The principal author of this revenue procedure is Jason Spitzer of the Office of Associate Chief Counsel (Procedure & Administration). For further information about this revenue procedure, contact Jason Spitzer at (202) 622–7950 (not a toll-free number) or by email at *jason.a.spitzer@irscounsel.treas.gov*. For inquiries into participating in the GITCA Program or for questions about the program, contact the office of the Chief, Employment Tax, Specialty Programs, at 202–283–2438 (not a toll-free number).

Exhibit 1

Gaming Industry Tip Compliance Agreement

I. PARTIES

The parties to this Agreement are ______________________________ (hereinafter "Employer") and the Commissioner of the Internal Revenue Service (hereinafter "Service"; collectively "the Parties"). This Agreement will establish tip rates for all Participating Employees of the Employer. This Agreement is pursuant to Revenue Procedure 2007–XX.

II. APPENDICES

The Parties have agreed to:

A. The Occupational Categories, shifts, outlets, and tip rates for all participating employees of the Employer, set forth in Appendix A;

B. A Narrative Summary of Tip Rate Calculation Methodology (specific to the Employer), set forth in Appendix B;

C. The Model Gaming Employee Tip Reporting Agreement, set forth in Appendix C;

D. The Model Extension Agreement set forth in Appendix D;

E. The Employer-Computed Tip Reporting Process Certification Form, set forth in Appendix E (but only if the Employer uses an Employer-Computed Tip Reporting Process to compute and report the tips of Participating Employees as described in Section V.J of this Agreement); and

F. The GITCA Contact Listing for both the Service and the Employer, set forth in Appendix F.

III. INTENDED BENEFICIARIES

The Participating Employees of the Employer are intended beneficiaries of this Agreement.

IV. EMPLOYEE PARTICIPATION

A. For purposes of this Agreement, an "Eligible Employee" means an individual employed by the Employer who:

(1) performs a job function in an Occupational Category described in Appendix A of this Agreement; and

(2) regularly and routinely receives tips, directly or indirectly, of at least $20 per month during the course of the individual's employment.

B. A "Participating Employee" is an Eligible Employee who:

(1) filed, if required to do so by law, federal income tax returns for the three taxable years that precede the Effective Date of this Agreement or, if the employee has not yet filed, files these returns prior to signing the Model Gaming Employee Tip Reporting Agreement provided in Appendix C of this Agreement;

(2) gives to the Employer a signed Model Gaming Employee Tip Reporting Agreement;

(3) either (i) reports and continues to report tips to the Employer at or above the "tip rates" set forth in Section VIII of this Agreement, or (ii) works for an Employer that utilizes an Employer-Computed Tip Reporting Process to compute and report the tips of Participating Employees for the taxable year as described in Section V.J of this Agreement, and

(4) timely files federal income tax returns that report those tips.

C. A Participating Employee who revokes the election under the Model Gaming Employee Tip Reporting Agreement to participate in the tip reporting program under this Agreement must begin reporting tips to the Employer effective on the first day of the next payroll period, as provided by section 6053 of the Internal Revenue Code and shall be treated as a Nonparticipating Employee for the entire taxable year in which the revocation occurred. The Employee may not enter into a new Model Gaming Employee Tip Reporting Agreement with the Employer until January 1 of the following taxable year.

D. If a Participating Employee reports tips to his or her Employer in an amount below the tip rate set forth in Section VIII of this Agreement, the employee will be deemed to have revoked his or her election under the Model Gaming Employee Tip Reporting Agreement and will be treated as specified in paragraph C of this section.

E. An Eligible Employee who has filed federal income tax returns for the three taxable years that precede the Effective Date of this Agreement but has not fully paid the tax liability reported on the returns, or has additional tax liability due to, for example, a completed examination of the returns or the filing of amended returns, may participate in this program. To participate, however, the employee must contact the local office of the Service within the later of 60 days of electing to become a Participating Employee under this Agreement or 60 days of commencing employment to resolve the tax liability.

F. For purposes of this Agreement, a "Nonparticipating Employee" is any Eligible Employee who does not meet the definition of a Participating Employee.

G. An employee may report tips on the employee's federal income tax return below the tip rates if the employee can substantiate, with adequate books and records, that the employee earned less tip income than would be reflected by applying the tip rates. As indicated in Section IV.D., this employee would be considered a Nonparticipating Employee.

V. EMPLOYER PROGRAM

A. The Employer agrees to encourage all of its Eligible Employees to become Participating Employees and to sign the Model Gaming Employee Tip Reporting Agreement, attached as Appendix C. The Employer agrees to keep these agreements for at least the period of limitation on assessment of employment tax for the years in which this Agreement is in effect and to make the agreements available to the Service upon request.

B. The Employer shall withhold and pay tax based upon tips reported, as required by law.

C. The Employer shall include all reported tips on Forms W–2.

D. The Employer acknowledges that the Service has authority, including the issuance and enforcement of summonses pursuant to sections 7602, 7604, and 7609 of the Code, to secure the information necessary for the Service to develop the tip rates of Nonparticipating Employees.

E. The Employer shall maintain the following records, to be made available to the Service upon request:

(1) Employee Records. For each Eligible Employee, the Employer will maintain a record of the employee's name and social security number; the date on which the employee was hired by the Employer; the employee's Occupational Category or Categories, as set forth in Appendix A; the employee's reported tips; the employee's shift(s) and hours; outlet(s) worked; and the employee's wages.

(2) Gaming Establishment Records. For each instance of toke and chip-cashing, where the information is in the possession or control of the Employer, the Employer will maintain a record of the dollar amount of tokes and chips presented to the Employer for cashing by the toke committee (or other representatives of Eligible Employees), a list of the tip splits furnished to the Employer by its Eligible Employees or the toke committee (or other representatives of Eligible Employees), and other separate records of the amounts presented to the Employer for cashing by the toke committee. The Service acknowledges that the records of the toke committee reflecting the actual division of tips may not be in the Employer's possession or control.

(3) Food and Beverage Operations Records. If the Occupational Categories set forth in Appendix A include food or beverage servers, the Employer will maintain gross receipts subject to food or beverage tipping, and aggregate receipts showing charged tips.

(4) Tip Rates Records. The Employer will maintain any other records relevant to determining tip rates, as may be required by other governmental agencies.

The Employer must retain the records listed in this section for at least 4 years after April 15 following the calendar year to which the records relate.

F. The Employer shall furnish to the Service the following documents:

(1) Annual Report. An annual report showing the following information for each Nonparticipating Employee:

a. The employee's name and social security number;

b. Occupational Category or Categories;

c. shift(s) and hours;

d. outlet(s) worked;

e. wages and reported tips; and

f. total hours worked in each applicable Occupational Category, shift, and outlet.

Tips reported to the Employer by a Nonparticipating Employee do not need to be segregated by outlet.

The report is due on or before March 31 of the year after the calendar year, or any portion thereof, during which this Agreement was in effect.

(2) Additional Annual Report. Unless an Employer uses an Employer-Computed Tip Reporting Process (as described in Section V.J and as certified under Appendix E) to compute and report the tips of Participating Employees, the Employer must furnish an additional annual report showing for each Participating Employee the information described in paragraph F(1) of this section. The report is due on or before March 31 of the year after the calendar year, or any portion thereof, during which this Agreement was in effect.

(3) Additional Information — Food & Beverage Establishments. If the Occupational Categories listed in Appendix A include employees of large food and beverage establishments as defined in section 6053(c)(4) of the Code, the Employer shall provide annually to the Service, on or before the Form 8027 filing date, the following information:

a. the gross receipts subject to food and beverage tipping;

b. the aggregate amount of charge receipts attributable to such gross receipts;

c. the aggregate amount of charged tips shown on the charge receipts;

d. the sum of (i) the aggregate amount of tips reported by Nonparticipating Employees to the Employer and (ii) the amount the Employer is required to report under section 6051 of the Code with respect to service charges of less than 10 percent; and

e. the amount allocated to each Nonparticipating Employee under section 6053(c)(3) of the Code.

(4) Allocated Tips Reporting Requirements. The Employer shall report on Forms W–2 issued to Nonparticipating Employees tips allocated pursuant to section 6053 of the Code. The Employer is not required to report allocated tips on Forms W–2 issued to Participating Employees. In addition, the Employer is not required to complete the portion of Form 8027 related to tip allocations to Participating Employees.

(5) Time and Attendance System/Payroll Processing System Report. For each calendar year, the Employer shall provide a report generated from the Employer's time-and-attendance system or payroll processing system that evidences the tip rates utilized by the Employer in the preparation of the Forms W–2 and to implement this Agreement. The report will contain information showing the tip rates for each Occupational Category, shift, and outlet. The report will include the total number of the Employer's Eligible Employees as of December 31. The report is due on or before March 31 of the year after the calendar year, or any portion thereof, during which this Agreement was in effect.

G. If the Employer complies with the terms of this Agreement with respect to its Participating Employees, provides the information described in paragraph F(1) of this section with respect to its Nonparticipating Employees on Forms 8027 (or the equivalent information in an alternate form deemed acceptable by the Service) and Forms W–2, and provides the information specified in Paragraph F (3), the Employer shall be deemed to satisfy the requirement that the Employer prepare and file Forms 8027 with respect to all of its Employees.

H. If the Employer fails to maintain or provide any material information in the manner described in paragraphs E and F of this section, following notice and demand to the Employer for the information, the Service may employ any lawful means, including the issuance and enforcement of summonses pursuant to sections 7602, 7604, and 7609 of the Code, in order to secure that information.

I. In the event of a material breach by the Employer of its obligation to maintain or provide the information described in paragraphs E and F of this section that continues following notice and demand for the information by the Service, the restrictions in Section VII.A on methods of determination of additional liabilities under section 3121(q) of the Code shall be deemed to be waived by the Employer and shall be inapplicable for all taxable periods occurring after the date of the material breach, and the Service shall be permitted to determine employer liability by any lawful means.

J. For purposes of this Agreement, the term "Employer-Computed Tip Reporting Process" means a process established, maintained, and controlled by the Employer under which the time-and-attendance and payroll processing systems used for operation and management of the Employer's business are applied by the Employer during the term of this Agreement to compute, without intervention by the employee, the tips reportable in respect of each Participating Employee by:

(1) tracking and reporting each Participating Employee's Occupational Category or Categories, shift(s), outlet(s), and hours worked at each Occupational Category, shift, and outlet to which the Participating Employee is assigned during a particular workday;

(2) subjecting this information to review and validation by the Employer's management in the ordinary course of business operations for independent business purposes;

(3) recording and preserving this information as part of the Employer's time-and-attendance or payroll processing systems or in other applicable and available business records of the Employer;

(4) applying the tip rates applicable under this Agreement to the Participating Employee's work assignments by multiplying the tip rates by the total hours worked by the Participating Employee at each Occupational Category, shift, and outlet worked during the particular workday or payroll cycle (or in the case of amounts described in Section V.E(2), determining reportable tips utilizing the list of tip splits as determined by the toke committee (or other representatives of Eligible Employees as provided in Section V.E(2) of this Agreement);

(5) treating the tip amounts computed under paragraph (4) as tips reported to the Employer by the Participating Employee and withholding and paying applicable taxes on the computed tips; and

(6) reporting the tips as determined by the Employer to the Participating Employee and the Service on Form W–2 for the taxable year.

K. The Employer's process shall qualify as an Employer-Computed Tip Reporting Process under this Agreement upon the certification of the Employer, with the concurrence of the Service (which shall not be unreasonably withheld), that the process satisfies the requirements of paragraph J of this section. Qualification may be subsequently reviewed by the Service in conjunction with the renewal of this Agreement. Nothing in this section limits the Service's ability to perform a Compliance Review at any time of any underlying data per Section XIII.

VI. TIP EXAMINATIONS OF EMPLOYEES

A. Except as provided in paragraph B. of this section, the Service will not examine a Participating Employee's tip income for any taxable year that ends after the Effective Date of this Agreement to which this Agreement applies, provided that each of the following conditions is met:

(1) The employee is a Participating Employee for the entire taxable year (or such portion thereof during which the employee earns tip income). In the case of a new employee, he or she must become a Participating Employee within 60 days after commencement of employment with the Employer as an Eligible Employee.

(2) The Participating Employee:

a. reports the tips earned during the taxable year to the Employer at or above the tip rates set forth in Section VIII of this Agreement, or

b. works for an Employer that utilizes an Employer-Computed Tip Reporting Process to compute and report the tips of Participating Employees on Forms W–2; and

c. timely files a federal income tax return for the taxable year that reports tips and wages reported on Form W–2.

B. If an employee becomes a Participating Employee more than 60 days after becoming employed as an Eligible Employee, the Service may examine the Participating Employee's tip income received before the employee becomes a Participating Employee, except for the period the employee was a Participating Employee of the Employer or of another Employer under a tip compliance agreement (GITCA, TRDA, TRAC, or similar agreement) during any taxable year. Once the employee becomes a Participating Employee, the Service will not examine the employee's tip income received during the period the employee remains a Participating Employee.

C. The Service will not examine tip income of a Participating Employee for any taxable year that ends on or before the Effective Date of this Agreement, provided that during that prior period the employee was:

(1) a Participating Employee, as defined in Section IV, of the Employer under a predecessor agreement between the Employer and the Service and satisfied the terms and conditions of that agreement in that prior taxable year;

(2) a Participating Employee, as defined in Section IV, of another employer who had a Gaming Industry Tip Compliance Agreement (or other tip compliance agreement, such as a Tip Rate Determination Agreement) with the Service and satisfied the terms and conditions of that agreement in that prior taxable year; or

(3) an employee of (i) an employer that did not have a Gaming Industry Tip Compliance Agreement (or predecessor agreement) with the Service or (ii) the Employer had a Gaming Industry Tip Compliance Agreement (or predecessor agreement), but the employee was not an Eligible Employee within the meaning of that agreement, and the employee filed, if required to do so by law, federal income tax returns for the three taxable years that preceded the year of the Effective Date of this Agreement.

D. In the case of Participating Employees of an Employer that does not have a certified Employer-Computed Tip Reporting Process, if the Service believes on the basis of information provided by the Employer pursuant to Section V.F(2) that the Participating Employee did not report tips on his or her federal income tax return as required by Section VIII of this Agreement, the Service shall confirm with the Employer the accuracy of the Participating Employee data received from the Employer prior to making any determination that tips have not been reported at or above the applicable rates.

E. A Nonparticipating Employee is subject to the full range of compliance and enforcement procedures of the Service, at any time, including during the term of this Agreement. (The treatment of the Employer in the case of Nonparticipating Employees is set forth in Section VII.A(2)).

F. At the Service's discretion, the Service may continue any ongoing examination of any employees of the Employer begun by the Service before the Effective Date of this Agreement.

VII. TIP EXAMINATIONS OF EMPLOYER

A. With respect to any taxable year during which this Agreement is in effect:

(1) the Service may not assert liability against the Employer pursuant to section 3121(q) of the Code with respect to the tip income of Participating Employees (except in the limited case provided in subparagraph (2)(ii) immediately below).

(2) the Service may assert liability against the Employer pursuant to section 3121(q) of the Code based on (i) tips received by a Nonparticipating Employee if the asserted liability is based upon the final results of an audit or agreement of the Nonparticipating Employee or (ii) the reporting of additional tip income by an employee.

B. At the Service's discretion, the Service may continue any ongoing examination of the Employer begun by the Service before the Effective Date of this Agreement.

VIII. TIP RATES

A. This section sets forth the applicable tip rates under this Agreement. The Parties established the applicable tip rates as follows:

(1) Employees Who Pool Tips. In satisfaction of their tip reporting obligations under section 6053(a) of the Code with respect to employees who pool tips, these employees or their employee group representatives (*e.g.*, the toke committee) shall present to the Employer a listing of the actual share of pooled tips received by or given to each employee. This listing must reconcile to the tips presented to the Employer's cage for cashing. The tip rate in the case of these employees is the amount of tips so reported to the Employer with respect to each employee.

(2) Other Tipped Employees — Specified Occupational Categories. Based on information available from the Employer, historical information available to the Service, and generally accepted accounting principles, the Employer and the Service have agreed to separate tip rates for the occupational categories or subcategories of Eligible Employees ("Occupational Category"), shifts, and outlets listed on Appendix A for each of the years during which this Agreement is in effect. These rates specify tips received, by hour, by shift, by drink, by percentage of sales, or other mutually agreed and verifiable bases of measurement depending on the nature of the work performed.

B. Tip Rates and Occupational Categories.

(1) In General. The applicable Tip Rates and Occupational Categories established by this Agreement shall remain in effect for the term of this Agreement, unless modified pursuant to paragraph B(2) or (3) of this section.

(2) Mutual Agreement Process. The Service or the Employer may propose revisions to tip rates or Occupational Categories during the term of the Agreement. The non-proposing party will notify the proposing party in writing of approval or disapproval within 60 calendar days of receipt of the proposed revision. The non-proposing party will not unreasonably withhold approval. If accepted, the revisions will become effective upon the date agreed to by the Parties.

(3) Request for Tip Rate Modification. Upon the occurrence of one of the following specific events:

a. a significant change in the nature of the business (or segment thereof) in which the Participating Employee earns tips (*e.g.*, an Employer converts an upscale restaurant into a coffee shop),

b. a decrease of 20 percent or more in the Employer's gross monthly revenue as compared to the same month of the previous year, or

c. a drop below 50 percent in the participation rate of any Occupational Category as of the participation measurement date,

the Employer may request that the Service agree to a modification in the relevant tip rate of an affected Participating Employee within an Occupational Category (*e.g.*, an outlet or shift) that is appropriate in amount and duration, consent to which shall not be unreasonably withheld.

The process established in paragraph B(3) of this section for the revision of a tip rate upon the occurrence of specific events in no way limits the circumstances that may give rise to a request for revision of a tip rate under the mutual agreement process described in paragraph B(2) of this section.

IX. TERM OF AGREEMENT

A. This Agreement shall commence on the Effective Date and shall terminate on ________________. The "Effective Date" of this Agreement shall be ________________.

B. The Service and the Employer agree that, beginning not later than six months prior to the termination date described in paragraph A., they shall commence discussions as to any appropriate revisions to this Agreement, including any appropriate revisions to the tip rates described in Section VIII. In the event that the Service and the Employer have not reached final agreement on the terms and conditions of a renewal Agreement to become effective beginning on ____________, the Parties may, by mutual agreement, extend this agreement for an appropriate time to finalize and execute a renewal Agreement.

C. Neither the Employer's nor the Service's decisions regarding renewal of agreements are subject to review.

X. TERMINATION OF AGREEMENT; SURVIVAL OF TERMS

A. If employee participation is below 75 percent of the Eligible Employees, the Service and the Employer shall meet to discuss the cause of the decline in the participation rate and appropriate measures to increase the participation rate. At the meetings, the Employer shall provide information with respect to the records necessary for assessing the tip rate and for assessing the procedures used to encourage all of the Employer's Eligible Employees to be Participating Employees.

(1) If the Employer undertakes good faith discussions with the Service on these matters and the Employer is not in breach of its obligations under Section V.A, the Service may not terminate the Agreement.

(2) If the Employer fails to undertake good faith discussions with the Service on these matters or the Employer is in breach of its obligations under Section V.A, the Service may terminate the Agreement.

B. The Service may terminate this Agreement by written notice if participation falls below 50 percent of the Eligible Employees. Termination by the Service shall become effective on the first day of the first payroll period after the 60th day after the date of the written notice.

C. This Agreement may be terminated upon the joint agreement of the Employer and the Service, without the consent of any Participating Employee. The effective date of termination shall be as agreed to by the Employer and the Service.

D. If either party fails to comply with any material provision of this Agreement, the non-defaulting party, at its option, may terminate this Agreement by giving written notice of termination to the other party. Termination of the Agreement shall be effective upon receipt of the notice by the other party.

E. If this Agreement is terminated pursuant to the terms of this agreement, the mutual obligations of the Parties shall remain in effect through the effective date of termination. The agreements set forth in Sections VI and VII shall survive termination with respect to taxable periods (or portion thereof) that occur prior to the effective date of termination.

XI. PRECEDENTIAL VALUE

The contents of this agreement may not be used or cited as precedent by any other Employer or other taxpayer and will not bind, or otherwise control, the Parties for taxable years or issues not covered by this Agreement.

XII. FAILURE TO COMPLY

If the Employer fails or refuses to provide any of the information required by this Agreement, the Service may employ any lawful means, including the issuance and enforcement of summonses pursuant to sections 7602, 7604, and 7609 of the Code, in order to secure the information.

XIII. COMPLIANCE REVIEW

The Employer agrees that a compliance review or other inspection of books and records, as required for compliance with the terms of this Agreement, will not be considered an examination or inspection of books of account for purposes of section 7605(b) of the Code or the Service's policy and procedures for reopening cases closed after examination, or an audit for purposes of section 530 of the Revenue Act of 1978.

XIV. EXCLUSION OF CERTAIN EMPLOYEES

This Agreement does not cover employees of the Employer working in housekeeping and those employees shall not be considered Eligible Employees for purposes of this Agreement.

XV. OTHER AGREEMENTS SUPERSEDED

This Agreement shall supersede all existing tip compliance agreements between the Employer and the Service.

XVI. ENTIRE AGREEMENT

This Agreement contains the final and entire agreement between the Employer and the Service.

By signing this Gaming Industry Tip Compliance Agreement, the Parties certify that they have read and agreed to the terms of this document, including all Appendices.

EMPLOYER:

By ______________________

TITLE ______________________

EIN# ______________________

Address ______________________

____

____

____

Date ______________________

INTERNAL REVENUE SERVICE:

By ______________________

TITLE ______________________

Address ______________________

____

____

____

Date ______________________

APPENDIX A

Occupational Categories, Outlets, Shifts and Tip Rates

Occupational Category	Outlet	Shift	Tip Rate Yr. 1	Tip Rate Yr. 2	Tip Rate Yr. 3

APPENDIX B

Narrative Summary of Tip Rate Calculation Methodology

APPENDIX C

Model Gaming Employee Tip Reporting Agreement

I am an employee of ______________, and by signing this agreement I am choosing to participate in the tip reporting program administered by my employer under the Gaming Industry Tip Compliance Agreement between my employer and the Internal Revenue Service (Service).

I understand that I have responsibilities under this agreement and agree to the following terms and conditions.

A. General Responsibilities.

(1) I will report tips to my employer at or above the tip rate that has been established pursuant to the Gaming Industry Tip Compliance Agreement for my job or have my employer compute my reportable tips for me using the tip rate. [I understand that I may revoke this agreement and report (either to my employer or to the Service) tips below the tip rate if I can substantiate, to the satisfaction of the Service and subject to a possible review by the Service, that I earned less tip income than would be reflected by applying the tip rate].

(2) I will file my Federal income tax returns on a timely basis and report those tips and the rest of my earnings from my job as shown on the Form W–2 that my employer gives me, as well as any other income.

(3) For each of the three years prior to the date of this agreement, if required to do so, I have filed a Federal income tax return on a timely basis. If I have filed all of these tax returns but have not fully paid the tax I owe, I must contact the local office of the Service within 60 days from now to resolve my account.

If I fulfill my responsibilities and continue to participate under this tip reporting program, I will receive important benefits under this agreement.

B. Benefits Under Agreement.

(1) If I report to my employer tips at or above the tip rate that has been established for my job or if my employer computes my reportable tips for me using the tip rate and reports them to me and to the Service on Form W–2, the Service will not audit my tip income received after the date of this agreement during which the Gaming Industry Tip Compliance Agreement between my employer and the Service is in effect.

(2) The Service also will not audit my tip income for any prior tax year during which (i) I was a participant in a prior tip compliance agreement while working for my current employer or a former employer, or (ii) I had no opportunity to participate in a prior tip compliance agreement because I worked in a job that was not covered by a tip compliance agreement or because my employer did not have a tip compliance agreement with the Service.

(3) If I was eligible to participate in an employer's tip compliance agreement in prior tax years but did not do so, I will not be protected from an audit of my tip income for those prior years, but I will receive protection from audit of my tip income received after the date of this agreement during which the Gaming Industry Tip Compliance Agreement between my employer and the Service is in effect.

(4) If I sign this agreement within 60 days after I first became employed with my current employer, I will be protected from an audit of my tip income received after the beginning date of employment during which the Gaming Industry Tip Compliance Agreement between my employer and the Service is in effect. If I sign this agreement more than 60 days after I first became employed with my current employer, I will be protected from an audit of my tip income received after the date of this agreement during which the Gaming Industry Tip Compliance Agreement between my employer and the Service is in effect.

C. Revocation of Agreement. I understand that the following additional terms and conditions apply to this agreement.

(1) I may revoke this agreement in writing to my employer at any time.

(2) If I report tips to my employer or the service below the established tip rate, this agreement will be automatically revoked.

(3) If this agreement is revoked, I must begin reporting my tips to my employer, beginning with the tips I receive on the first day of the next payroll period.

(4) Upon revocation of this agreement, I will no longer be protected from an audit of my tip income for the tax year in which I revoke the agreement.

(5) After revocation of this agreement, I will not be able to sign up again for my employer's tip reporting program until January 1 of the year after I revoke this agreement.

D. Term of Agreement. This agreement shall remain in effect as long as there is a Gaming Industry Tip Compliance Agreement between my employer and the service, and I have not taken any actions to terminate this agreement either by notifying my employer in writing or by reporting tips to my employer or the Service in an amount less than the agreed upon rates.

By signing below, I agree to fulfill my responsibilities under this agreement and to participate in the tip reporting program pursuant to the Gaming Industry Tip Compliance Agreement between my employer and the Service.

____________________	____________________
Signature	Social Security Number
____________________	____________________
Printed Name of Employee	____________________
	____________________
	Address

APPENDIX D

Model Extension Agreement

The Gaming Industry Tip Compliance Agreement (Agreement) signed by the Employer, ____________________ and the Internal Revenue Service (the Parties), effective on ____________, shall expire on, ____________.

The Parties wish to renew the Agreement, but have not reached final agreement on the terms and conditions of the renewal. In order to allow more time to finalize and execute a renewal, the Parties agree to extend the original Agreement until ____________.

EMPLOYER:	**INTERNAL REVENUE SERVICE:**
By ____________________	By ____________________
TITLE ____________________	TITLE ____________________
EIN# ____________________	
Date ____________________	Date ____________________

APPENDIX E

Employer-Computed Tip Reporting Process Certification

____

(name of Employer)

certifies that it utilizes an Employer-Computed Tip Reporting Process within the meaning of Section V.J of the Gaming Industry Tip Compliance Agreement to compute and report tips of Participating Employees on Forms W–2.

____

Employer Representative & Date

****

A representative of the Internal Revenue Service has reviewed the Employer's Certification and

____

(Concurs/Does Not Concur)

If the representative of the IRS does not concur with the Employer's Certification, the representative will provide the Employer with the actions necessary to attain certification.

____

IRS Representative & Date

APPENDIX F

GITCA Contact Listing

IRS Contacts:

IRS Program Manager

Name

____

Address

____

____

____

Telephone

____

E-Mail ________________________

IRS Tax Manager (Local Office)

Name

____

Address

____

____

____

Telephone

____

E-Mail ________________________

IRS Examiner

Name ____________________________

Address ____________________________

____

____

Telephone ____________________________

E-Mail ____________________________

Taxpayer Advocate (Local Office)

Name ____________________________

Address ____________________________

____

____

Telephone ____________________________

E-Mail ____________________________

Employer Contacts:

Name ____________________________

Address ____________________________

____

____

Telephone ____________________________

E-Mail ____________________________

---

26 CFR 601.602: Tax forms and instructions. (Also: Part 1, §§ 1, 223.)

Rev. Proc. 2007–36

SECTION 1. PURPOSE

This revenue procedure modifies and supersedes section 3.24(1) of Rev. Proc. 2006–53, 2006–48 I.R.B. 996, which provides inflation adjusted items for 2007 for Health Savings Accounts (HSAs) under § 223 of the Internal Revenue Code. This revenue procedure also provides inflation adjusted items for HSAs for 2008.

SECTION 2. BACKGROUND

Section 303 of the Health Opportunity Patient Empowerment Act of 2006, Title III of the Tax Relief and Health Care Act of 2006, Pub. L. No. 109–432, 120 Stat. 2922 (2006) (the Act), changes the maximum annual contribution for HSAs. Under prior law, the maximum annual HSA contribution was the lesser of the deductible of the high deductible health plan or the indexed statutory amount. For taxable years beginning after December 31, 2006, § 303 of the Act amends § 223(b) to provide that the maximum annual HSA contribution is the indexed statutory amount, without reference to the deductible of the high deductible health plan.

Section 304 of the Act amends the rules for calculating cost-of-living adjustments for HSA amounts in § 223. Section 304 of the Act amends § 223(g) to provide that, for cost-of-living adjustments made for taxable years beginning after 2007, § 1(f)(4) is applied using March 31 instead of August 31 as the close of the 12-month period described in § 1(f)(4). Section 223(g) also provides that the adjusted amounts under § 223 will be published no later than June 1 of the preceding calendar year.

SECTION 3. MODIFICATION OF SECTION 3.24(1) OF REV. PROC. 2006–53

Section 3.24(1) of Rev. Proc. 2006–53 is modified to read as follows:

(1) *Annual contribution limitation.* For calendar year 2007, the limitation on deductions under § 223(b)(2)(A) for an individual with self-only coverage under a high deductible health plan is $2,850. For calendar year 2007, the limitation on deductions under § 223(b)(2)(B) for an individual with family coverage under a high deductible health plan is $5,650.

SECTION 4. INFLATION ADJUSTED ITEMS FOR HSAs FOR 2008

Annual contribution limitation. For calendar year 2008, the limitation on deductions under § 223(b)(2)(A) for an individual with self-only coverage under a high deductible health plan is $2,900. For calendar year 2008, the limitation on deductions under § 223(b)(2)(B) for an individual with family coverage under a high deductible health plan is $5,800.

High deductible health plan. For calendar year 2008, a "high deductible health plan" is defined under § 223(c)(2)(A) as a health plan with an annual deductible that is not less than $1,100 for self-only coverage or $2,200 for family coverage, and the annual out-of-pocket expenses (deductibles, co-payments, and other amounts, but not premiums) do not exceed $5,600 for self-only coverage or $11,200 for family coverage.

SECTION 5. EFFECT ON OTHER DOCUMENTS

Section 3.24(1) of Rev. Proc. 2006–53 is modified and superseded.

SECTION 6. EFFECTIVE DATES

Section 3 of this revenue procedure is effective for calendar year 2007. Section 4 of this revenue procedure is effective for calendar year 2008.

SECTION 7. DRAFTING INFORMATION

The principal author of this revenue procedure is Marnette M. Myers of the Office of Associate Chief Counsel (Income Tax & Accounting). For further information regarding this revenue procedure, contact Marnette M. Myers at (202) 622–4920 (not a toll-free call).

Part IV. Items of General Interest

Anti-Avoidance and Anti-Loss Reimportation Rules Applicable Following a Loss on Disposition of Stock of Consolidated Subsidiaries; Correction

Announcement 2007–50

AGENCY: Internal Revenue Service (IRS), Treasury.

ACTION: Correction to final and temporary regulations.

SUMMARY: This document contains corrections to final and temporary regulations (T.D. 9322, 2007–18 I.R.B. 1100) that were published in the Federal Register on Tuesday, April 10, 2007 (71 FR 17804) providing guidance to corporations filing consolidated returns and apply an anti-avoidance rule and revising an anti-loss reimportation rule that applies following a disposition of stock of a subsidiary at a loss.

FOR FURTHER INFORMATION CONTACT: Theresa Abell, (202) 622–7700 or Phoebe Bennett, (202) 622–7770 (not toll-free numbers).

SUPPLEMENTARY INFORMATION:

Background

The final and temporary regulations (T.D. 9322) that is the subject of these corrections are under section 1502 of the Internal Revenue Code.

Need for Correction

As published, these final and temporary regulations (T.D. 9322) contain errors that may prove to be misleading and are in need of clarification.

Correction of Publication

Accordingly, these final and temporary regulations (T.D. 9322) that were the subject of FR Doc. E7–6541, are corrected as follows:

1. On page 17805, column 1, in the preamble, under the paragraph heading "*Background and Explanation of Provisions*" paragraph 2, line 6 from the bottom of the column, the language "the loss reimportation rule is also" is corrected to read "the anti-loss reimportation rule is also".

2. On page 17805, column 2, in the preamble, under the paragraph heading "*Special Analyses*", line 5 from the top of the column, the language "U.S.C. 553(b)(B) that prior notice and" is corrected to read "U.S.C. 553(b)(3)(B) that prior notice and".

3. On page 17805, column 2, in the preamble, under the paragraph heading "*Special Analyses*", line 16 from the top of the column, the language "reference notice of the proposed" is corrected to read "reference notice of proposed".

LaNita Van Dyke,
Branch Chief,
Publications and Regulations Branch,
Legal Processing Division,
Office of Associate Chief Counsel
(Procedure and Administration).

(Filed by the Office of the Federal Register on April 30, 2007, 8:45 a.m., and published in the issue of the Federal Register for May 1, 2007, 72 F.R. 23771)

Deletions From Cumulative List of Organizations Contributions to Which are Deductible Under Section 170 of the Code

Announcement 2007–51

The names of organizations that no longer qualify as organizations described in section 170(c)(2) of the Internal Revenue Code of 1986 are listed below.

Generally, the Service will not disallow deductions for contributions made to a listed organization on or before the date of announcement in the Internal Revenue Bulletin that an organization no longer qualifies. However, the Service is not precluded from disallowing a deduction for any contributions made after an organization ceases to qualify under section 170(c)(2) if the organization has not timely filed a suit for declaratory judgment under section 7428 and if the contributor (1) had knowledge of the revocation of the ruling or determination letter, (2) was aware that such revocation was imminent, or (3) was in part responsible for or was aware of the activities or omissions of the organization that brought about this revocation.

If on the other hand a suit for declaratory judgment has been timely filed, contributions from individuals and organizations described in section 170(c)(2) that are otherwise allowable will continue to be deductible. Protection under section 7428(c) would begin on May 29, 2007, and would end on the date the court first determines that the organization is not described in section 170(c)(2) as more particularly set forth in section 7428(c)(1). For individual contributors, the maximum deduction protected is $1,000, with a husband and wife treated as one contributor. This benefit is not extended to any individual, in whole or in part, for the acts or omissions of the organization that were the basis for revocation.

Security Warranty, Inc.
San Antonio, TX
Franklin Foundation, Inc.
Gaithersburg, MD
Howard Family Foundation
Chicago, IL
Center for Electronic Art
Woodacre, CA
Richard & Jane Pater
Charitable Foundation
Salt Lake City, UT

Foundations Status of Certain Organizations

Announcement 2007–52

The following organizations have failed to establish or have been unable to maintain their status as public charities or as operating foundations. Accordingly, grantors and contributors may not, after this date, rely on previous rulings or designations in the Cumulative List of Organizations (Publication 78), or on the presumption arising from the filing of notices under section 508(b) of the Code. This listing does *not* indicate that the organizations have lost their status as organizations described in section 501(c)(3), eligible to receive deductible contributions.

Former Public Charities. The following organizations (which have been treated as organizations that are not private foundations described in section 509(a) of the Code) are now classified as private foundations:

Adoptions Abroad, Houston, TX
American Council for Adjunct Faculty, Inc., Columbia, MD
And Bibles for All, Salem, OR
Ark Adventures, Inc., Weatherford, TX
Batavia Youth Football, Inc., Cincinnati, OH
Bonim Lamokom, Inc., Brooklyn, NY
Butlee's Handicap Outdoor Adventures Corporation, Brockton, MA
Childrens Global Relief Project, Inc., Elmont, NY
Citizens Advisory Panel, Inc., Bridgehampton, NY
Clemente Garcia Jr. Community Learning Center, Corpus Christi, TX
Community Home Services, Inc., Georgetown, TX
Community Vision, Carlsbad, NM
Cornerstone Art Group, Sherman Oaks, CA
Cuerda Floja Arts Troupe, Oak Park, IL
E J Ralph Foundation, Inc., Riverdale, NY
Federal Hill Foundation, Incorporated, Arlington, VA
Friends of Summit Children's Residence Center, Inc., Upper Nyack, NY
Gaelic Language Foundation, New York, NY
Gina Eisenman Foundation, Inc., San Diego, CA
Gods Will for Africa, Columbia, SC
Grassroots Foundation, Inc., Oak Park, IL
Greater Weatherly Ambulance Association, Inc., Weatherly, PA
Hebron House, Inc., North Brunswick, NJ
Hogar Divino Jesus, Inc., Toa Baja, PR
Institut De La Maison De Bourbon, Thomasville, GA
Jesus Cares Ministry, Inc., Irvington, NJ
Kamp Kiwanis Childrens Foundation, Inc., Lexington, NC
Kansas City 4wd Association, Inc., Olathe, KS
Kentucky Blasting Conference, Keene, KY
Kiwanis Club of Flamingo-Hialeah Foundation, Inc., Hialeah, FL
Milwaukee Marauders, Inc., Grafton, WI
Miracle League of Maryland, Baltimore, MD
Musicians Uplifting Services in the Community, Jackson, MI
National Football League Players Association — Tampa Bay Chapter, Tampa, FL
Nepali Tibetan Education Center, South Pasadena, CA
Nevada Medical and Aesthetic Nonprofit Organization, Sacramento, CA
Old West Enrichment Center, Inc., Tallahassee, FL
Possibility Ranch, Lake Arrowhead, CA
Redemption Home of Love, McKinney, TX
Resurrection Group, Ltd., New York, NY
Riley Arts Foundation, Pasadena, CA
Rochester Rowing Club of Minnesota, Rochester, MN
Rock Solid Foundations, Inc., Norcross, GA
Sail Musical on Tour Corp, Readington, NJ
SATEC, Nine Mile Falls, WA
Shoppers Charitable Foundation, Inc., Lanham, MD
Simi Valley Future Stars, Inc., Simi Valley, CA
Skate Park Association International, Inc., Los Angeles, CA
Soma (Strategies for the Organic Management of Agriculture), Inc., New York, NY
Starving Pets & Animals Rescue Effort, Stanwood, WA
Tawana Williams Outreach, Inc., Wilson, NC
Treasured Hearts Ministry, Somerset, MA
United Hispanics Union All, All, Against The Lead, Miami, FL
Vietnamese Physician Foundation of Northern California, San Jose, CA
Watertown Firestation No 2 Foundation, Inc., Watertown, WI
Whoa-Womens Hockey Organization of Arizona, Chandler, AZ
Wilson Midget Football Association, Easton, PA
Womens Eleemosynary Foundation aka District 1 PWA Charitable Education Foundation, Chicago, IL
Worthy Center, Bakersfield, CA

If an organization listed above submits information that warrants the renewal of its classification as a public charity or as a private operating foundation, the Internal Revenue Service will issue a ruling or determination letter with the revised classification as to foundation status. Grantors and contributors may thereafter rely upon such ruling or determination letter as provided in section 1.509(a)–7 of the Income Tax Regulations. It is not the practice of the Service to announce such revised classification of foundation status in the Internal Revenue Bulletin.

Part I. Rulings and Decisions Under the Internal Revenue Code of 1986

Section 42.—Low-Income Housing Credit

The adjusted applicable federal short-term, mid-term, and long-term rates are set forth for the month of June 2007. See Rev. Rul. 2007-36, page 1339.

Section 199.—Income Attributable to Domestic Production Activities

26 CFR 1.199–5T: Application of section 199 to pass-thru entities.

A revenue procedure specifies the conditions under which certain eligible partnerships and S corporations may calculate qualified production activities income (QPAI) and W–2 wages at the entity level, as well as the manner for allocating and reporting these amounts to partners and shareholders for purposes of determining each partner's or shareholder's § 199 deduction for the taxable year. See Rev. Proc. 2007-34, page 1345.

A revenue procedure provides guidance for determining when statistical sampling may be used for purposes of § 199 of the Internal Revenue Code and establishes acceptable statistical sampling methodologies. See Rev. Proc. 2007-35, page 1349.

Section 280G.—Golden Parachute Payments

Federal short-term, mid-term, and long-term rates are set forth for the month of June 2007. See Rev. Rul. 2007-36, page 1339.

Section 382.—Limitation on Net Operating Loss Carryforwards and Certain Built-In Losses Following Ownership Change

The adjusted applicable federal long-term rate is set forth for the month of June 2007. See Rev. Rul. 2007-36, page 1339.

Section 412.—Minimum Funding Standards

The adjusted applicable federal short-term, mid-term, and long-term rates are set forth for the month of June 2007. See Rev. Rul. 2007-36, page 1339.

Section 467.—Certain Payments for the Use of Property or Services

The adjusted applicable federal short-term, mid-term, and long-term rates are set forth for the month of June 2007. See Rev. Rul. 2007-36, page 1339.

Section 468.—Special Rules for Mining and Solid Waste Reclamation and Closing Costs

The adjusted applicable federal short-term, mid-term, and long-term rates are set forth for the month of June 2007. See Rev. Rul. 2007-36, page 1339.

Section 482.—Allocation of Income and Deductions Among Taxpayers

Federal short-term, mid-term, and long-term rates are set forth for the month of June 2007. See Rev. Rul. 2007-36, page 1339.

Section 483.—Interest on Certain Deferred Payments

The adjusted applicable federal short-term, mid-term, and long-term rates are set forth for the month of June 2007. See Rev. Rul. 2007-36, page 1339.

Section 642.—Special Rules for Credits and Deductions

Federal short-term, mid-term, and long-term rates are set forth for the month of June 2007. See Rev. Rul. 2007-36, page 1339.

Section 807.—Rules for Certain Reserves

The adjusted applicable federal short-term, mid-term, and long-term rates are set forth for the month of June 2007. See Rev. Rul. 2007-36, page 1339.

Section 846.—Discounted Unpaid Losses Defined

The adjusted applicable federal short-term, mid-term, and long-term rates are set forth for the month of June 2007. See Rev. Rul. 2007-36, page 1339.

Section 1274.—Determination of Issue Price in the Case of Certain Debt Instruments Issued for Property

(Also Sections 42, 280G, 382, 412, 467, 468, 482, 483, 642, 807, 846, 1288, 7520, 7872.)

Federal rates; adjusted federal rates; adjusted federal long-term rate and the long-term exempt rate. For purposes of sections 382, 642, 1274, 1288, and other sections of the Code, tables set forth the rates for June 2007.

Rev. Rul. 2007–36

This revenue ruling provides various prescribed rates for federal income tax purposes for June 2007 (the current month). Table 1 contains the short-term, mid-term, and long-term applicable federal rates (AFR) for the current month for purposes of section 1274(d) of the Internal Revenue Code. Table 2 contains the short-term, mid-term, and long-term adjusted applicable federal rates (adjusted AFR) for the current month for purposes of section 1288(b). Table 3 sets forth the adjusted federal long-term rate and the long-term tax-exempt rate described in section 382(f). Table 4 contains the appropriate percentages for determining the low-income housing credit described in section 42(b)(2) for buildings placed in service during the current month. Finally, Table 5 contains the federal rate for determining the present value of an annuity, an interest for life or for a term of years, or a remainder or a reversionary interest for purposes of section 7520.

REV. RUL. 2007–36 TABLE 1

Applicable Federal Rates (AFR) for June 2007

Period for Compounding

	Annual	*Semiannual*	*Quarterly*	*Monthly*
Short-term				
AFR	4.84%	4.78%	4.75%	4.73%
110% AFR	5.33%	5.26%	5.23%	5.20%
120% AFR	5.82%	5.74%	5.70%	5.67%
130% AFR	6.31%	6.21%	6.16%	6.13%
Mid-term				
AFR	4.64%	4.59%	4.56%	4.55%
110% AFR	5.11%	5.05%	5.02%	5.00%
120% AFR	5.59%	5.51%	5.47%	5.45%
130% AFR	6.06%	5.97%	5.93%	5.90%
150% AFR	7.01%	6.89%	6.83%	6.79%
175% AFR	8.19%	8.03%	7.95%	7.90%
Long-term				
AFR	4.91%	4.85%	4.82%	4.80%
110% AFR	5.41%	5.34%	5.30%	5.28%
120% AFR	5.90%	5.82%	5.78%	5.75%
130% AFR	6.41%	6.31%	6.26%	6.23%

REV. RUL. 2007–36 TABLE 2

Adjusted AFR for June 2007

Period for Compounding

	Annual	*Semiannual*	*Quarterly*	*Monthly*
Short-term adjusted AFR	3.52%	3.49%	3.47%	3.46%
Mid-term adjusted AFR	3.68%	3.65%	3.63%	3.62%
Long-term adjusted AFR	4.15%	4.11%	4.09%	4.08%

REV. RUL. 2007–36 TABLE 3

Rates Under Section 382 for June 2007

Adjusted federal long-term rate for the current month	4.15%
Long-term tax-exempt rate for ownership changes during the current month (the highest of the adjusted federal long-term rates for the current month and the prior two months.)	4.15%

REV. RUL. 2007–36 TABLE 4

Appropriate Percentages Under Section 42(b)(2) for June 2007

Appropriate percentage for the 70% present value low-income housing credit	8.11%
Appropriate percentage for the 30% present value low-income housing credit	3.48%

REV. RUL. 2007–36 TABLE 5 Rate Under Section 7520 for June 2007	
Applicable federal rate for determining the present value of an annuity, an interest for life or a term of years, or a remainder or reversionary interest	5.6%

Section 1288.—Treatment of Original Issue Discount on Tax-Exempt Obligations

The adjusted applicable federal short-term, mid-term, and long-term rates are set forth for the month of June 2007. See Rev. Rul. 2007-36, page 1339.

Section 7520.—Valuation Tables

The adjusted applicable federal short-term, mid-term, and long-term rates are set forth for the month of June 2007. See Rev. Rul. 2007-36, page 1339.

Section 7872.—Treatment of Loans With Below-Market Interest Rates

The adjusted applicable federal short-term, mid-term, and long-term rates are set forth for the month of June 2007. See Rev. Rul. 2007-36, page 1339.

Part III. Administrative, Procedural, and Miscellaneous

Credit for New Qualified Heavy-Duty Hybrid Motor Vehicles

Notice 2007–46

SECTION 1. PURPOSE.

This notice sets forth interim guidance, pending the issuance of regulations, relating to the new qualified hybrid motor vehicle credit under § 30B(a)(3) and (d) of the Internal Revenue Code. Specifically, this notice provides procedures for a vehicle manufacturer (or, in the case of a foreign vehicle manufacturer, its domestic distributor) to certify to the Internal Revenue Service (Service) both:

(1) that a heavy-duty vehicle of a particular make, model, and model year meets certain requirements that must be satisfied to claim the new qualified hybrid motor vehicle credit under § 30B(a)(3) and (d); and

(2) the amount of the credit allowable with respect to that vehicle. This notice also provides guidance to taxpayers who purchase qualified vehicles regarding the conditions under which they may rely on the vehicle manufacturer's (or, in the case of a foreign vehicle manufacturer, its domestic distributor's) certification in determining whether a credit is allowable with respect to the vehicle and the amount of the credit. The Service and the Treasury Department expect that the regulations will incorporate the rules set forth in this notice.

SECTION 2. BACKGROUND.

Section 30B(a)(3) provides for a credit determined under § 30B(d) for certain new qualified hybrid motor vehicles. The new qualified hybrid motor vehicle credit for a heavy-duty hybrid motor vehicle is determined under § 30B(d)(2)(B) and is an amount equal to the applicable percentage of the qualified incremental hybrid cost of the vehicle. The qualified incremental hybrid cost is the excess of the manufacturer's suggested retail price for the qualified vehicle over the manufacturer's suggested retail price for a comparable vehicle. However, the qualified incremental hybrid cost of a vehicle is limited depending upon the gross vehicle weight rating of the vehicle. The applicable percentage varies depending upon the increase in the city fuel economy of the qualified vehicle relative to a comparable vehicle.

SECTION 3. SCOPE OF NOTICE.

.01 *Vehicles Covered.* This notice applies only to heavy-duty hybrid motor vehicles. Guidance concerning the new qualified hybrid motor vehicle credit for passenger automobiles and light trucks is provided in Notice 2006–9, 2006–6 I.R.B. 413.

.02 *Rules Common to All Qualifying Vehicles.* This notice does not address a number of rules that are common to all motor vehicles that qualify for credits under § 30B, including (1) rules under which lessors may claim the credits allowable under § 30B, (2) the rule preventing the credits from being used to reduce alternative minimum tax liability, and (3) rules relating to recapture of the credit. Certain rules applicable to all motor vehicles that qualify for credits under § 30B are described in Fact Sheet 2007–9 (*http://www.irs.ustreas.gov/newsroom/article/0,,id=165649,00.html*).

SECTION 4. MEANING OF TERMS.

The following definitions apply for purposes of this notice:

(1) *In General.* Terms used in this notice and not defined in this section have the same meaning as when used in § 30B.

(2) *Heavy-Duty Hybrid Motor Vehicle.* The term "heavy-duty hybrid motor vehicle" means any hybrid motor vehicle that is not a passenger automobile or light truck within the meaning of section 4(2) of Notice 2006–9. Thus, a hybrid motor vehicle (including a hybrid motor vehicle that is a medium-duty passenger vehicle, as defined in 40 C.F.R. § 600.002–08) that has a gross vehicle weight rating of more than 8,500 pounds will be treated as a heavy-duty hybrid motor vehicle for purposes of this notice.

(3) *Manufacturer.* (a) *In general.* The "vehicle manufacturer" or "manufacturer" of a heavy-duty hybrid motor vehicle is—

(i) the person engaged in the manufacturing or assembling of the completed heavy-duty hybrid motor vehicle for introduction into commerce; and

(ii) if applicable, any person (other than the person described in section 4(3)(a)(i)) that installs the systems that convert a vehicle powered solely by an internal combustion or heat engine using consumable fuel into the completed heavy-duty hybrid motor vehicle.

(b) For purposes of this section 4(3)—

(i) a "completed heavy-duty hybrid motor vehicle" is a new heavy-duty hybrid motor vehicle that is ready for use and requires no further manufacturing or assembly operations; and

(ii) "introduction into commerce" occurs when a vehicle manufacturer ships a completed motor vehicle from a facility of the manufacturer to a distributor, retailer, or consumer.

(4) *City Fuel Economy.* (a) *In general.* The term "city fuel economy" means the fuel economy measured in a manner that is substantially similar to the manner in which city fuel economy is measured in accordance with procedures under 40 C.F.R. Part 600, as in effect on August 8, 2005. A manufacturer may develop and use for this purpose any procedures that the manufacturer reasonably determines to be substantially similar to the procedures under 40 C.F.R. Part 600, as in effect on August 8, 2005. In addition, the Service will not challenge a manufacturer's determination of city fuel economy using any safe harbor measurement method listed in section 4(4)(c) of this notice if that method is consistently used to determine city fuel economy for both the qualified heavy-duty hybrid motor vehicle and the comparable vehicle to which the qualified vehicle's fuel economy is compared in providing the certification under this notice.

(b) *Carry-over models.* The city fuel economy determined under section 4(4)(a) of this notice for a vehicle of a particular make, model, and model year may be used as the city fuel economy for any carry-over model of that vehicle. For this purpose, a vehicle is a carry-over model with respect to a vehicle produced in an earlier model year if the vehicles are of the same make and model and the design of the model has not changed since such earlier model year.

(c) *Safe harbor measurement methods*. The safe harbor measurement methods listed in this section 4(4)(c) are any of the following:

(i) In the case of heavy-duty hybrid motor vehicles that are medium-duty passenger vehicles, as defined in 40 C.F.R. 600.002–08, measurement in accordance with procedures under 40 C.F.R. Part 600, as in effect on the date the manufacturer's certification is provided.

(ii) In the case of heavy-duty hybrid motor vehicles that are not medium-duty passenger vehicles, as defined in 40 C.F.R. 600.002–08, measurement using the carbon balance method applied to emissions measured using either the procedures in 40 C.F.R. Part 86, Subpart B and 40 C.F.R. § 86.1863–07 or the procedures in the California Interim Certification Procedures for 2004 and Subsequent Model Hybrid-Electric Vehicles in the Urban Bus and Heavy-Duty Vehicle Classes.

(5) *Comparable Vehicle*. (a) *In general*. The term "comparable vehicle" means, for purposes of determining the qualified incremental hybrid cost and the increase in city fuel economy of a qualified heavy-duty hybrid motor vehicle, any vehicle that is powered solely by a gasoline or diesel internal combustion engine and is comparable in weight, size, and use to the qualified vehicle. For this purpose—

(i) a vehicle produced by the same manufacturer as the qualified vehicle is comparable in use only if it is manufactured in the same model year as the qualified vehicle; and

(ii) a vehicle produced by a person other than the manufacturer of the qualified vehicle is comparable in use only if it is manufactured in the same 12-month period as the qualified vehicle.

(b) *Manufacturer to choose among multiple comparable vehicles*. If more than one model of vehicle is comparable in weight, size, and use to the qualified vehicle, the manufacturer of the qualified vehicle may choose a vehicle of any model that is comparable in weight, size, or use and treat that vehicle as the comparable vehicle for purposes of providing a certification under this notice.

(6) *Model Year*. The term "model year" means—

(a) the vehicle manufacturer's annual production period (determined under regulations prescribed by the Administrator of the Environmental Protection Agency for purposes of the administration of title II of the Clean Air Act (42 U.S.C. 7521 *et seq.*)); or

(b) the calendar year in which the vehicle is manufactured, if the vehicle manufacturer has no annual production period for that make and model of vehicle.

(7) *Total Traction Power*. The term "total traction power" means the sum of the peak power from the rechargeable energy storage system and the heat engine peak power of the vehicle, except that if the storage system is the sole means by which the vehicle can be driven, the total traction power is the peak power of the storage system.

SECTION 5. MANUFACTURER'S CERTIFICATION.

.01 *When Certification Permitted*. A vehicle manufacturer (or, in the case of a foreign vehicle manufacturer, its domestic distributor) may certify to purchasers that a heavy-duty hybrid motor vehicle of a particular make, model, and model year meets all requirements (other than those listed in section 5.02 of this notice) that must be satisfied to claim the new qualified hybrid motor vehicle credit, and the amount of the credit allowable under § 30B(a)(3) and (d) with respect to the vehicle, if the following requirements are met:

(1) The manufacturer (or, in the case of a foreign vehicle manufacturer, its domestic distributor) has submitted to the Service, in accordance with section 6 of this notice, a certification with respect to the vehicle and the certification satisfies the requirements of section 5.03 of this notice; and

(2) The manufacturer (or, in the case of a foreign vehicle manufacturer, its domestic distributor) has received an acknowledgment of the certification from the Service.

.02 *Purchaser's Reliance*. Except as provided in section 5.06 of this notice, a purchaser of a heavy-duty hybrid motor vehicle may rely on the manufacturer's (or, in the case of a foreign vehicle manufacturer, its domestic distributor's) certification concerning the vehicle and the amount of the credit allowable with respect to the vehicle (including in cases in which the certification is received after the purchase of the vehicle). The purchaser may claim a credit in the certified amount with respect to the vehicle if the following requirements are satisfied:

(1) The vehicle is placed in service by the taxpayer after December 31, 2005, and is purchased on or before December 31, 2009.

(2) The original use of the vehicle commences with the taxpayer.

(3) The vehicle is acquired for use or lease by the taxpayer, and not for resale.

(4) The vehicle is used predominantly in the United States.

.03 *Content of Certification*. The certification must contain the following information:

(1) The name, address, and taxpayer identification number of the certifying entity;

(2) The make, model, model year, and any other appropriate identifiers of the motor vehicle;

(3) A statement that the vehicle is made by a manufacturer;

(4) The amount of the credit for the vehicle (showing computations);

(5) The manufacturer's suggested retail price for the vehicle;

(6) The manufacturer's suggested retail price for a comparable vehicle;

(7) The make, model, and model year of a comparable vehicle;

(8) The gross vehicle weight rating of the vehicle;

(9) The city fuel economy of the vehicle and evidence that—

(a) the city fuel economy was measured in a manner that is substantially similar to the manner in which city fuel economy is measured in accordance with procedures under 40 C.F.R § 600, as in effect on August 5, 2005 (including a description of the procedures used to measure city fuel economy and a description of the manufacturer's basis for reasonably determining that those procedures are substantially similar to the procedures under 40 C.F.R. § 600, as in effect on August 5, 2005); or

(b) a safe harbor measurement method listed in section 4(4)(c) of this notice was consistently used to determine city fuel economy for both the qualified heavy-duty hybrid motor vehicle and the comparable vehicle to which the qualified vehicle's fuel economy is compared in providing the certification;

(10) A statement that the motor vehicle draws propulsion energy from onboard sources of stored energy that are both an internal combustion or heat engine using consumable fuel, and a rechargeable energy storage system;

(11) Evidence that the maximum power available from the rechargeable energy storage system during a standard 10 second pulse power or equivalent test is—

(a) at least 10 percent of the vehicle's total traction power, in the case of a vehicle that has a gross vehicle weight rating of more than 8,500 pounds and not more than 14,000 pounds, and

(b) at least 15 percent of the vehicle's total traction power, in the case of a vehicle that has a gross vehicle weight rating of more than 14,000 pounds;

(12) The total traction power of the vehicle;

(13) A statement that the vehicle complies with the applicable provisions of the Clean Air Act;

(14) A statement that the vehicle complies with the applicable air quality provisions of state law of each state that has adopted the provisions under a waiver under § 209(b) of the Clean Air Act or a list identifying each state that has adopted applicable air quality provisions with which the vehicle does not comply;

(15) A statement that the vehicle complies with the motor vehicle safety provisions of 49 U.S.C. §§ 30101 through 30169;

(16) A copy of the certificate of conformity under the Clean Air Act certifying the vehicle's internal combustion or heat engine as meeting the emission standards set in the regulations prescribed by the Administrator of the Environmental Protection Agency for 2004 through 2007 model year diesel heavy-duty engines or ottocycle heavy-duty engines, as applicable; and

(17) A declaration, applicable to the certification and any accompanying documents, signed by a person currently authorized to bind the manufacturer (or, in the case of a foreign vehicle manufacturer, its domestic distributor) in these matters, in the following form:

"Under penalties of perjury, I declare that I have examined this certification, including accompanying documents, and to the best of my knowledge and belief, the facts presented in support of this certification are true, correct, and complete."

.04 *Multiple manufacturers.* If more than one person is treated as the manufacturer of a vehicle under section 4(3) of this notice, the requirements of section 5.03 of this notice are treated as satisfied if each item of information described in section 5.03(2) through 5.03(16) is provided by one of the manufacturers and each manufacturer providing such information also provides the identifying information described in section 5.03(1) and the declaration described in section 5.03(17).

.05 *Acknowledgment of Certification.* The Service will review the original signed certification and issue an acknowledgment letter to the vehicle manufacturer (or, in the case of a foreign vehicle manufacturer, its domestic distributor) within 30 days of receipt of the request for certification. This acknowledgment letter will state whether purchasers may rely on the certification.

.06 *Effect of Erroneous Certification.*

(1) *Erroneous Certification.* The acknowledgment that the Service provides for a certification is not a determination that a vehicle qualifies for the credit, or that the amount of the credit is correct. The Service may, upon examination (and after any appropriate consultation with the Department of Transportation or the Environmental Protection Agency), determine that the vehicle is not a new qualified heavy-duty hybrid motor vehicle or that the amount of the credit determined by the manufacturer (or, in the case of a foreign vehicle manufacturer, its domestic distributor) to be allowable with respect to the vehicle is incorrect. In either event, the manufacturer's (or, in the case of a foreign vehicle manufacturer, its domestic distributor's) right to provide a certification to future purchasers of the heavy-duty hybrid motor vehicles will be withdrawn, and purchasers who acquire a vehicle after the date on which the Service publishes an announcement of the withdrawal may not rely on the certification. Purchasers may continue to rely on the certification for vehicles they acquired on or before the date on which the announcement of the withdrawal is published (including in cases in which the vehicle is not placed in service and the credit is not claimed until after that date), and the Service will not attempt to collect any understatement of tax liability attributable to such reliance. Manufacturers (or, in the case of foreign vehicle manufacturers, their domestic distributors) are reminded that an erroneous certification may result in the imposition of penalties:

(a) under § 7206 for fraud and making false statements; and

(b) under § 6701 for aiding and abetting an understatement of tax liability in the amount of $1,000 ($10,000 in the case of understatements by corporations) per return on which a credit is claimed in reliance on the certification).

SECTION 6. TIME AND ADDRESS FOR FILING CERTIFICATION.

.01 *Time for Filing Certification.* In order for a certification under section 5 of this notice to be effective for new qualified heavy-duty hybrid motor vehicles placed in service during a calendar year beginning after December 31, 2006, the certification must be received by the Service not later than December 31st of that calendar year. For new qualified heavy-duty hybrid motor vehicles placed in service during 2006, the certification must be received by the Service not later than December 31, 2007.

.02 *Address for Filing.* Certifications under section 5 of this notice must be sent to:

Internal Revenue Service,
Industry Director, Large and
Mid-Size Business, Heavy
Manufacturing and Transportation,
Metro Park Office Complex — LMSB,
111 Wood Avenue, South,
Iselin, New Jersey 08830.

SECTION 7. PAPERWORK REDUCTION ACT.

The collection of information contained in this notice has been reviewed and approved by the Office of Management and Budget in accordance with the Paperwork Reduction Act (44 U.S.C. 3507) under control number 1545–2060.

An agency may not conduct or sponsor, and a person is not required to respond to, a collection of information unless the collection of information displays a valid OMB control number.

The collections of information in this notice are in section 5. This information is required to be collected and retained in order to ensure that vehicles meet the requirements for the new qualified hybrid motor vehicle credit under § 30B(a)(3) and (d). This information will be used to determine whether the vehicle for which the credit is claimed by a taxpayer is property that qualifies for the credit. The collection of information is required to obtain a benefit. The likely respondents are corporations and partnerships.

The estimated total annual reporting burden is 240 hours.

The estimated annual burden per respondent varies from 35 hours to 45 hours, depending on individual circumstances, with an estimated average burden of 40 hours to complete the certification required under this notice. The estimated number of respondents is 6.

The estimated annual frequency of responses is on occasion.

Books or records relating to a collection of information must be retained as long as their contents may become material in the administration of any internal revenue law. Generally, tax returns and tax return information are confidential, as required by 26 U.S.C. 6103.

SECTION 8. DRAFTING INFORMATION.

The principal author of this notice is Nicole R. Cimino of the Office of Associate Chief Counsel (Passthroughs and Special Industries). For further information regarding this notice, contact Ms. Cimino at (202) 622–3120 (not a toll-free call).

---

26 CFR 601.105: Examination of returns and claims for refund, credit or abatement; determination of correct tax liability.
(Also Part I, §§ 199; 1.199–1 through 1.199–9, 1.199–3T, 1.199–5T, 1.199–7T, 1.199–8T.)

Rev. Proc. 2007–34

SECTION 1. PURPOSE

Section 199 of the Internal Revenue Code provides a deduction for income attributable to domestic production activities. This revenue procedure specifies the conditions under which certain partnerships and S corporations may choose to calculate qualified production activities income (QPAI) and W–2 wages as defined by § 1.199–2T(e)(2) of the temporary Income Tax Regulations (W–2 wages) at the entity level, as well as the manner for allocating and reporting QPAI and W–2 wages to partners or shareholders.

SECTION 2. BACKGROUND

Section 199(a)(1) allows a deduction equal to 9 percent (3 percent for taxable years beginning in 2005 or 2006, and 6 percent for taxable years beginning in 2007, 2008, or 2009) of the lesser of (A) the QPAI of the taxpayer for the taxable year, or (B) taxable income (determined without regard to § 199) for the taxable year (or, for an individual, adjusted gross income).

Section 199(b)(1) limits the deduction for a taxable year to 50 percent of the W–2 wages paid by the taxpayer for the taxable year. For this purpose, § 199(b)(2)(A) defines the term W–2 wages to mean, with respect to any person for any taxable year of such person, the sum of the amounts described in § 6051(a)(3) and (8) paid by such person with respect to employment of employees by such person during the calendar year ending during such taxable year.

Section 199(c)(1) defines QPAI for any taxable year as an amount equal to the excess, if any, of the taxpayer's domestic production gross receipts (DPGR) over the sum of the cost of goods sold (CGS) allocable to DPGR and other expenses, losses, or deductions (other than the deduction allowed by § 199) (deductions) that are properly allocable to such receipts. Section 1.199–4(b) of the Income Tax Regulations provides rules for determining CGS allocable to DPGR. Section 1.199–4(c) provides rules for determining the deductions that are properly allocable to DPGR or to gross income attributable to DPGR. Section 1.199–4(a) and (d) provides that a taxpayer generally must allocate and apportion its deductions using the § 861 method, as determined under the rules of §§ 1.861–8 through 1.861–17 and §§ 1.861–8T through 1.861–14T, subject to the rules in § 1.199–4(d). Section 1.199–4(e) provides that an eligible taxpayer may use the simplified deduction method to apportion deductions between DPGR and non-DPGR. Section 1.199–4(f) provides that a qualifying small taxpayer may use the small business simplified overall method to apportion CGS and deductions between DPGR and non-DPGR.

Section 199(d)(1) provides special rules for applying § 199 to pass-thru entities. Section 199(d)(1)(A) provides that (i) § 199 shall be applied at the partner or shareholder level, (ii) each partner or shareholder shall take into account such person's allocable share of each item described in § 199(c)(1)(A) or (B) (determined without regard to whether the items described in § 199(c)(1)(A) exceed the items described in § 199(c)(1)(B)), and (iii) each partner or shareholder shall be treated for purposes of § 199(b) as having W–2 wages for the taxable year in an amount equal to such person's allocable share of the W–2 wages of the partnership or S corporation for the taxable year (as determined under regulations prescribed by the Secretary).

Section 199(d)(1)(C) provides that the Secretary may prescribe rules requiring or restricting the allocation of items and wages under § 199(d)(1) and may prescribe such reporting requirements as the Secretary determines appropriate.

For taxable years beginning after May 17, 2006, § 1.199–2T(e)(2) provides that the term W–2 wages includes amounts described in § 1.199–2(e)(1) (paragraph (e)(1) wages) that are properly allocable to DPGR for purposes of § 199(c)(1). Under § 1.199–2(e)(1), paragraph (e)(1) wages with respect to any person for any taxable year of such person, means the sum of the amounts described in § 6051(a)(3) and (8) paid by such person with respect to employment of employees by such person during the calendar year ending during such taxable year.

Section 1.199–5T(b)(1)(ii) and (c)(1)(ii) provides that the Secretary may, by publication in the Internal Revenue Bulletin, permit a partnership or S corporation to calculate a partner's or shareholder's share of QPAI and W–2 wages at the entity level, instead of allocating to that partner or shareholder its share of the entity's items and paragraph (e)(1) wages for determining the § 199 deduction at the partner or shareholder level. If a partnership or S corporation does calculate QPAI and W–2 wages at the entity level, such an entity then allocates to each partner or shareholder its share of QPAI (subject to the limitations of § 1.199–5T(b)(2) and (c)(2)) (which may be less than zero) and

W–2 wages from the entity, which then are to be combined with the partner's or shareholder's QPAI and W–2 wages from other sources, if any.

Whether a partnership or S corporation is an eligible entity (as defined in section 3.01 of this revenue procedure), and thus able to calculate QPAI and W–2 wages on behalf of some or all of its partners or shareholders, is determined at the entity level. Similarly, the determination as to what cost allocation method an eligible entity may use (specifically, the § 861 method, the simplified deduction method, or the small business simplified overall method) is determined and applied at the entity level (subject to any additional conditions, rules, and procedures as may be provided by publication in the Internal Revenue Bulletin).

SECTION 3. CALCULATION AND ALLOCATION OF QPAI AND W–2 WAGES AT THE ENTITY LEVEL

.01 *Entities eligible to calculate QPAI and W–2 wages at the entity level.* Pursuant to § 1.199–5T(b)(1)(ii) and (c)(1)(ii), each of the following entities (eligible entity) may calculate QPAI and W–2 wages on behalf of its partners or shareholders:

(a) an eligible § 861 partnership (as defined in section 5.01 of this revenue procedure), but only on behalf of qualifying partners;

(b) an eligible widely-held pass-thru entity (as defined in section 5.02 of this revenue procedure); and

(c) an eligible small pass-thru entity (as defined in section 5.03 of this revenue procedure).

.02 *Ineligible entities.* Qualifying in-kind partnerships (under § 1.199–3T(i)(7)) and EAG partnerships (as described in § 1.199–3T(i)(8)) may not compute a partner's share of QPAI and W–2 wages at the entity level.

.03 *Cost allocation methods for calculating QPAI and W–2 wages at the entity level.* An eligible entity may choose to calculate QPAI and W–2 wages at the entity level (subject to the limitations and requirements set forth in this revenue procedure) for any taxable year in which it qualifies as an eligible entity. The cost allocation methods available to an eligible entity choosing to report under this revenue procedure are as follows.

(a) *Section 861 method.* An eligible § 861 partnership (as defined in section 5.01 of this revenue procedure) choosing to calculate QPAI and W–2 wages at the entity level must use the § 861 method of § 1.199–4(d), subject to section 3.03(d) of this revenue procedure. A partnership using this method may use the wage expense safe harbor under § 1.199–2T(e)(2)(ii), or another reasonable method that is satisfactory to the Secretary based on all of the facts and circumstances, to calculate W–2 wages at the entity level.

(b) *Simplified deduction method.* An eligible widely-held pass-thru entity (as defined in section 5.02 of this revenue procedure) choosing to calculate QPAI and W–2 wages at the entity level must use the simplified deduction method of § 1.199–4(e), subject to section 3.03(d) of this revenue procedure. A partnership or S corporation using this method may use the wage expense safe harbor under § 1.199–2T(e)(2)(ii), or another reasonable method that is satisfactory to the Secretary based on all of the facts and circumstances, to calculate W–2 wages at the entity level.

(c) *Small business simplified overall method.* An eligible small pass-thru entity (as defined in section 5.03 of this revenue procedure) choosing to calculate QPAI and W–2 wages at the entity level must use the small business simplified overall method of § 1.199–4(f), subject to section 3.03(d) of this revenue procedure. A partnership or S corporation using this method also may use the small business simplified overall method safe harbor under § 1.199–2T(e)(2)(iii), or another reasonable method that is satisfactory to the Secretary based on all of the facts and circumstances, to calculate W–2 wages at the entity level.

(d) *Entities eligible to use more than one allocation method.* A partnership or S corporation meeting the qualifications of more than one type of eligible entity may choose to use any one of the methods, as described in section 3.03(a) through (c) of this revenue procedure, for calculating QPAI and W–2 wages at the entity level for which it is eligible for the taxable year. For example, an entity that qualifies as both an eligible widely-held pass-thru entity and an eligible small pass-thru entity for a taxable year may choose to use either the simplified deduction method of § 1.199–4(e) or the small business simplified overall method of § 1.199–4(f) for calculating QPAI. If the entity uses the simplified deduction method, then it may calculate W–2 wages using either the wage expense safe harbor or another reasonable method that is satisfactory to the Secretary based on all of the facts and circumstances. If the entity uses the small business simplified overall method, then it may calculate W–2 wages using either the small business simplified overall method safe harbor or another reasonable method that is satisfactory to the Secretary based on all of the facts and circumstances.

.04 *Changes in method.* For purposes of § 199, the following changes will not constitute changes in method of accounting to which the statutory and regulatory provisions of §§ 446 and 481 apply:

(a) A change in an eligible entity's method for calculating QPAI at the entity level among those methods described in section 3.03 of this revenue procedure; and

(b) A change from calculating QPAI and W–2 wages at the entity level to calculating such amounts at the partner or shareholder level, or vice versa.

.05 *Rules for calculating QPAI at the entity level.* Solely for calculating QPAI and W–2 wages at the entity level in accordance with its applicable cost allocation method for the taxable year, an eligible entity as described in section 3.01 of this revenue procedure must apply the following rules:

(a) A partnership must take into account any separately stated items described in § 702(a)(1) through (7) and any nonseparately stated items described in § 702(a)(8);

(b) An S corporation must take into account any separately stated items described in § 1366(a)(1)(A) and any nonseparately stated items described in § 1366(a)(1)(B);

(c) Income items, the inclusion of which ordinarily is determined at the partner or shareholder level, must be included by the partnership or S corporation;

(d) Expense items, the deduction or capitalization of which is determined at the partner or shareholder level, must be subtracted by the partnership or S corporation;

(e) Any limitation on the deduction of expense items that is ordinarily applied at the partner or shareholder level must be disregarded by the partnership or S corporation;

(f) Any expenditure described in § 59(e)(2), regarding the optional writeoff provided for certain tax preferences, must be taken into account by the partnership or S corporation without regard to any election by the partner or shareholder;

(g) Any expenditure which, at the election of the partner or shareholder, may be taken into account as a deduction or as a credit, must be disregarded by the partnership or S corporation;

(h) Any depletion deduction described in § 613A must be computed and taken into account by the partnership or S corporation without regard to any limitations at the partner or shareholder level;

(i) Any increase or decrease in the bases of partnership assets pursuant to § 743 must be taken into account by the partnership;

(j) Any partnership items allocated by an eligible § 861 partnership to a partner that is not a qualifying partner (including items allocated to such a partner pursuant to § 704(c)) must be excluded by the partnership for purposes of calculating the QPAI and W–2 wages to be allocated to its qualifying partners (see section 4.03 of this revenue procedure); and

(k) The QPAI computed at the entity level (and thus the QPAI allocated to each partner or shareholder) will be less than zero if the entity's DPGR does not exceed the sum of the entity's items to be deducted in computing QPAI.

.06 *Allocation of QPAI and W–2 wages calculated at the entity level.*

(a) *QPAI.* Generally, an eligible entity that calculates QPAI at the entity level for a taxable year must allocate its QPAI for that taxable year among its partners or shareholders in the same proportion as gross income is allocated to its partners or shareholders for that taxable year. However, if such an entity has no gross income for a taxable year, then it must allocate QPAI in that year among its partners or shareholders in proportion to its partners' profits interests or shareholders' ownership interests.

(b) *W–2 wages.* An eligible entity that calculates QPAI at the entity level for the entity's taxable year also must calculate W–2 wages for that taxable year by determining the amount of paragraph (e)(1) wages that is properly allocable to DPGR for purposes of § 199(c)(1). The eligible entity then allocates its W–2 wages among its partners or shareholders in the same manner as it allocates wage expense among its partners or shareholders for that taxable year.

SECTION 4. REPORTING AND EFFECT ON PARTNERS AND SHAREHOLDERS

.01 *In general.* If an eligible entity calculates QPAI and W–2 wages at the entity level, then each partner (except for a partner that is not a qualifying partner with respect to an eligible § 861 partnership) or shareholder is allocated (in accordance with section 3.06 of this revenue procedure) its share of QPAI (which may be less than zero) and W–2 wages from the eligible entity, and the partner or shareholder then must combine those amounts with the partner's or shareholder's QPAI and W–2 wages from other sources, if any. See § 1.199–5T(b)(1)(ii) and (c)(1)(ii). If an eligible entity computes QPAI and W–2 wages at the entity level, no partner or shareholder receiving an allocation of the entity's QPAI and W–2 wages may recalculate its share of QPAI or W–2 wages from the entity using another cost allocation method (although the partner or shareholder must adjust its share of QPAI from the entity to account for certain disallowed losses or deductions, and for the allowance of suspended losses or deductions). In addition, no partner or shareholder of such an eligible entity that receives an allocation of the entity's QPAI and W–2 wages may take into account any of the items from that entity that go into the computation of the partner's or shareholder's share of QPAI and W–2 wages from that entity in calculating its QPAI and W–2 wages from any other source (for example, in allocating and apportioning deductions from another source or in determining whether a threshold or *de minimis* rule applies). If a partnership or S corporation, whether by ineligibility or choice, does not compute QPAI and W–2 wages at the entity level, then each partner or shareholder is allocated (in accordance with §§ 702 and 704, or § 1366, respectively) its share of the entity's items (including items of income, gain, loss, and deduction, CGS allocated to such items of income, gross receipts included in such items of income, and paragraph (e)(1) wages), for purposes of calculating the § 199 deduction at the partner or shareholder level. See § 1.199–5T(b) and (c).

.02 *Reporting exception.* Section 199(d)(5) provides that § 199 is applied by only taking into account items that are attributable to the actual conduct of a trade or business. For example, a securities partnership (as defined in § 1.704–3(e)(3)(iii)) not engaged in a trade or business need not include on its Schedule K–1 (or other relevant form) any items required solely for § 199, unless a partner requests this information.

.03 *Partners in eligible § 861 partnerships.* Pursuant to § 6031(b), an eligible § 861 partnership that chooses to calculate QPAI and W–2 wages at the entity level reports allocable shares of QPAI and W–2 wages directly to those partners that were qualifying partners (as defined in section 5.04 of this revenue procedure) at all times during the partnership's taxable year (or, if such partners were partners for less than the entire taxable year, for the portion of the partnership's taxable year during which they were partners). A qualifying partner must use its share of QPAI and W–2 wages as reported by the partnership in calculating its § 199 deduction. If an eligible § 861 partnership has partners that are not qualifying partners (as defined in section 5.04 of this revenue procedure), it must allocate (in accordance with §§ 702 and 704) and report to each such partner that partner's allocable share of the partnership's items of income, gain, loss, and deduction, CGS allocated to such items of income, gross receipts included in such items of income, and paragraph (e)(1) wages, so that the partner is able to calculate its § 199 deduction. To the extent that any partner that is not a qualifying partner is allocated its share of the partnership's items (rather than a share of the partnership's QPAI and W–2 wages), such items shall not be taken into account for purposes of calculating the QPAI and W–2 wages to be allocated to the qualifying partners.

.04 *Partners or shareholders in eligible widely-held pass-thru entities or eligible small pass-thru entities.* Pursuant to § 6031(b) or § 6037(b), an eligible widely-held pass-thru entity or an eligible small pass-thru entity that chooses to calculate QPAI and W–2 wages at the entity level reports allocable shares of QPAI and W–2 wages directly to its partners or shareholders. Each partner or shareholder must use its reported share of QPAI and W–2 wages (subject to section 4.05 of this revenue procedure) in calculating its § 199 deduction.

.05 *Adjustment for disallowed losses or deductions and for the allowance of suspended losses or deductions.* An eligible entity that calculates QPAI at the entity level also must report to each partner (except for a partner that is not a qualifying partner with respect to an eligible § 861 partnership) or shareholder its allocable share (as determined under §§ 702 and 704, or § 1366, respectively) of the aggregate amount of losses or deductions attributable to the entity's qualified production activities. A partner or shareholder to which an allocation of QPAI and W–2 wages is made must increase its reported share of QPAI by its allocable share of losses or deductions attributable to the entity's qualified production activities that reduced QPAI for the entity level calculation but that are disallowed by the application of § 465, 469, 704(d), or 1366(d) for the taxable year. Such a partner or shareholder also must decrease its reported share of QPAI by its allocable share of any previously suspended losses or deductions attributable to the entity's qualified production activities that are currently allowed by application of § 465, 469, 704(d), or 1366(d) for the taxable year. However, losses or deductions of a partnership or S corporation that are disallowed for taxable years beginning on or before December 31, 2004, are not taken into account in a later taxable year for purposes of computing the partner's or shareholder's QPAI for that later taxable year, whether or not those losses or deductions are allowed for other purposes.

SECTION 5. DEFINITIONS

.01 *Eligible § 861 partnership.* An eligible § 861 partnership is a partnership that, for the current taxable year—

(a) has at least 100 partners on any day during the partnership's taxable year,

(b) is composed at all times during the taxable year of interests, at least 70 percent of which are held by qualifying partners (as defined in section 5.04 of this revenue procedure), and

(c) has DPGR.

.02 *Eligible widely-held pass-thru entity.* An eligible widely-held pass-thru entity is a partnership or S corporation that, for the current taxable year—

(a) satisfies the requirements of § 1.199–4(e)(2) (definition of eligible taxpayer), determined as though the partnership or S corporation were the taxpayer,

(b) has total CGS and deductions, the sum of which is $100 million or less,

(c) has DPGR,

(d) for every day of the current taxable year, is composed entirely of partners, or S corporation shareholders, that are individuals, estates, or trusts described (or treated as described) in § 1361(c)(2), and

(e) for every day of the taxable year, is—

(i) a partnership in which no partner has a profits or capital interest exceeding 10 percent (determined after aggregating the interests of any related persons as defined in section 5.06 of this revenue procedure) of the total profits or capital interests of the partnership, or

(ii) an S corporation with a shareholder described in § 1361(c)(6) in which no shareholder owns shares exceeding 10 percent (determined after aggregating the interests of any related persons as defined in section 5.06 of this revenue procedure) of the total shares of the S corporation.

.03 *Eligible small pass-thru entity.* An eligible small pass-thru entity is a partnership or S corporation that, for the current taxable year—

(a) satisfies the requirements of § 1.199–4(f)(2) (definition of qualifying small taxpayer), determined as though the partnership or S corporation were the taxpayer,

(b) has total costs (as defined in § 1.199–4(f)(3)) of $5 million or less,

(c) has DPGR, and

(d) in the case of a partnership, does not have an ineligible entity (as described in section 3.02 of this revenue procedure) as a partner.

.04 *Qualifying partner.* A qualifying partner is a partner in an eligible § 861 partnership that, on each day during the partnership's taxable year that such person is a partner of the partnership, such person—

(a) is not a general partner or a managing member of a partnership organized as a limited liability company under state law,

(b) does not materially participate in the activities of the partnership as determined in section 5.05 of this revenue procedure,

(c) does not hold a profits or capital interest in the partnership of 5 percent or greater (determined after aggregating the partner's interests with those of any related persons as defined in section 5.06 of this revenue procedure), or

(d) is not an ineligible entity under section 3.02 of this revenue procedure.

.05 *Material participation.* (a) *Individual partners.* For purposes of section 5.04(b) of this revenue procedure, whether an individual partner materially participates in the activities of the partnership (treating all the partnership's activities as a single activity) is determined under § 1.469–5(f)(1); § 1.469–5T(a)(1) through (3) and (7), (b)(2)(ii) and (iii), (f)(2) through (4), and (k) *Examples 1* through *3*, *7* and *8*; and section 5.05(b) of this revenue procedure.

(b) *Partners that are not individuals.* For purposes of section 5.04(b) of this revenue procedure, a partner that is not an individual is treated as materially participating in the activities of the partnership if the partner's owners, directors, officers, employees, or fiduciaries are treated collectively as materially participating in the activities of the partnership under the rules described in section 5.05(a) of this revenue procedure. The activities of the partner's owners, directors, officers, employees, and fiduciaries must be combined and treated as the activities of the partner for this purpose. For example, assume that X, a corporation, is a limited partner in a partnership. A, an employee of X, and B, an officer of X, participate in the activities of the partnership for 300 hours and 201 hours, respectively, during the partnership's taxable year. Under these facts, X is treated as materially participating in the partnership for the taxable year.

.06 *Related persons.* For purposes of this revenue procedure, persons are related if they bear a relationship to each other that is described in § 267(b) or § 707(b), disregarding § 267(e)(1) and (f)(1)(A).

SECTION 6. EXAMPLE

The following example illustrates an application of the rules in this revenue procedure. Assume that each partner has sufficient adjusted gross income or taxable income so that the § 199 deduction is not limited by § 199(a)(1)(B), and that the partnership and each of its partners (whether individual or corporate) are calendar year taxpayers.

Example. Small business simplified overall method. A, an individual, and X, a corporation, are partners in PRS. PRS engages in manufacturing activities that generate both DPGR and non-DPGR. X, but not A, has other manufacturing activities that generate DPGR and W–2 wages. A and X share all items of income, gain, loss, deduction, and credit equally. For the 2010 taxable year, PRS has total costs of no more than $5 million, and it qualifies and chooses to calculate QPAI and W–2 wages at the entity level under section 3.03(c) of this revenue procedure for the 2010 taxable year. For 2010, PRS has total gross receipts of $2,000x ($1,000x of which is DPGR), CGS of $900x (including $400x of wage expenses), and deductions of $700x (including $50x of R&E expenditures under § 174(a) and $100x of § 179 expenses). In this example, the paragraph (e)(1) wages are equal to the $400x of wage expenses. PRS uses the safe harbor under § 1.199–2T(e)(2)(iii) to calculate W–2 wages. Accordingly, PRS's W–2 wages equal $200x ($400x of wages described in § 1.199–2(e)(1) multiplied by ($1,000x DPGR divided by $2,000x total gross receipts)). Pursuant to section 3.05(f) of this revenue procedure, PRS disregards A's election under § 59(e) to write off A's share of R&E expenditures over 10 years. In addition, pursuant to section 3.05(e) of this revenue procedure, PRS disregards any limitation under § 179(b) on A's ability to deduct A's share of the § 179 expenses. Under the small business simplified overall method, PRS's CGS and deductions apportioned to DPGR equal $800x (($900x CGS plus $700x of other deductions) multiplied by ($1,000x DPGR divided by $2,000x total gross receipts)). Accordingly, PRS's QPAI is $200x ($1,000x DPGR minus $800x CGS and other deductions). Under section 3.06(a) of this revenue procedure, PRS's QPAI is allocated $100x to A and $100x to X. Under section 3.06(b) of this revenue procedure, PRS's W–2 wages are allocated $100x to A and $100x to X. Because A engages in no other activities generating DPGR, A's tentative deduction is $9x (its $100x share of QPAI from PRS multiplied by .09), subject to the § 199(b)(1) wage limitation (50% of A's $100x share of W–2 wages from PRS, as defined by § 1.199–2T(e)(2)). Because X does engage in other production activities generating DPGR, X must combine its $100x share of QPAI and its $100x share of W–2 wages from PRS with its QPAI and W–2 wages from all other sources, and X is not permitted to recompute its share of QPAI from PRS using another cost allocation method.

SECTION 7. EFFECTIVE DATE

This revenue procedure is effective for taxable years beginning on or after May 11, 2007. However, taxpayers may apply this revenue procedure to taxable years beginning after May 17, 2006.

SECTION 8. REQUEST FOR COMMENTS

Comments on all aspects of this revenue procedure are welcome. The IRS specifically requests comments on the clarity of these rules and how they can be made easier to understand and to implement. All comments will be available for public inspection and copying. Send comments to: CC:PA:LPD:PR (Rev. Proc. 2007–34), room 5203, Internal Revenue Service, PO Box 7604, Ben Franklin Station, Washington, DC 20044. Submissions may be hand-delivered Monday through Friday between the hours of 8 a.m. and 4 p.m. to CC:PA:LPD:PR (Rev. Proc. 2007–34), Courier's Desk, Internal Revenue Service, 1111 Constitution Avenue, NW, Washington, DC. Submissions may also be sent electronically via the Internet to the following e-mail address: *Notice.comments@irscounsel.treas.gov*. Include the revenue procedure number (Rev. Proc. 2007–34) in the subject line. Comments must be received on or before August 9, 2007.

DRAFTING INFORMATION

The principal author of this revenue procedure is Martin Schäffer, formerly of the Office of Associate Chief Counsel (Passthroughs and Special Industries). For further information regarding this revenue procedure, contact William Kostak at (202) 622–3060 (not a toll-free call).

---

26 CFR 601.105: Examination of returns and claims for refund, credit or abatement; determination of correct tax liability.
(Also Part I, §§ 199; 1.199–1 through 1.199–9, 1.199–3T, 1.199–5T, 1.199–7T, 1.199–8T.)

Rev. Proc. 2007–35

SECTION 1. PURPOSE

This revenue procedure provides guidance for determining when statistical sampling may be used for purposes of § 199 of the Internal Revenue Code and establishes acceptable statistical sampling methodologies.

SECTION 2. BACKGROUND

.01 Section 199(a)(1) allows a deduction equal to 9 percent (3 percent in the case of taxable years beginning in 2005 or 2006, and 6 percent in the case of taxable years beginning in 2007, 2008, or 2009) of the lesser of (A) the qualified production activities income (QPAI) of the taxpayer for the taxable year, or (B) taxable income (determined without regard to § 199) for the taxable year (or, in the case of an individual, adjusted gross income (AGI)). Section 199(b)(1) limits the deduction for a taxable year to 50 percent of the W–2 wages paid by the taxpayer during the calendar year that ends in such taxable year.

.02 Section 199(c)(1) defines QPAI for any taxable year as an amount equal to the excess (if any) of (A) the taxpayer's domestic production gross receipts (DPGR) for such taxable year, over (B) the sum of (i) the cost of goods sold (CGS) that are allocable to such receipts; and (ii) other expenses, losses, or deductions (other than the deduction under § 199) that are properly allocable to such receipts.

.03 Section 199(c)(2) provides that the Secretary shall prescribe rules for the proper allocation of items described in § 199(c)(1) for purposes of determining QPAI. Such rules shall provide for the proper allocation of items whether or not such items are directly allocable to DPGR.

.04 Section 199(c)(4)(A) defines DPGR to mean the taxpayer's gross receipts that are derived from: (i) any lease, rental, license, sale, exchange, or other disposition of (I) qualifying production property (QPP) that was manufactured, produced, grown, or extracted (MPGE) by the taxpayer in whole or in significant part within the United States; (II) any qualified film produced by the taxpayer; or (III) electricity, natural gas, or potable water (collectively, utilities) produced by the taxpayer in the United States; (ii) in the case of a taxpayer engaged in the active conduct of a construction trade or business, construction of real property performed in the United States by the taxpayer in the ordinary course of such trade or business; or (iii) in the case of a taxpayer engaged in the active conduct of an engineering or architectural services trade or business, engineering or architectural services performed in the United States by the taxpayer in the ordinary course of such trade or business with respect to the construction of real property in the United States.

.05 Section 199(c)(4)(B) excepts from DPGR gross receipts of the taxpayer that are derived from: (i) the sale of food and beverages prepared by the taxpayer at a retail establishment; (ii) the transmission or distribution of utilities; or (iii) the lease, rental, license, sale, exchange, or other disposition of land.

.06 Section 199(c)(5) defines QPP to mean: (A) tangible personal property; (B) any computer software; and (C) any property described in § 168(f)(4) (certain sound recordings).

.07 Section 199(c)(6) defines a qualified film to mean any property described in § 168(f)(3) if not less than 50 percent of the total compensation relating to production of the property is compensation for services performed in the United States by actors, production personnel, directors, and producers. The term does not include property with respect to which records are required to be maintained under 18 U.S.C. § 2257 (generally, films, videotapes, or other matter that depict actual sexually explicit conduct and are produced in whole or in part with materials that have been mailed or shipped in interstate or foreign commerce, or are shipped or transported or are intended for shipment or transportation in interstate or foreign commerce).

.08 Section 199 was added to the Code by section 102 of the American Jobs Creation Act of 2004 (Act) (Public Law 108–357), and amended by section 403(a) of the Gulf Opportunity Zone Act of 2005 (GOZA) (Public Law 109–135), section 514 of the Tax Increase Prevention and Reconciliation Act of 2005 (Public Law 109–222), and section 401 of the Tax Relief and Health Care Act of 2006 (Public Law 109–432). Section 102(e)(1) of the Act, as amended by section 403(a)(19) of GOZA, provides that section 199 shall apply to taxable years beginning after December 31, 2004. Section 102(e)(2) of the Act, as amended by section 403(a)(19) of GOZA, provides that, in determining the deduction under § 199, items arising from a taxable year of a partnership, S corporation, estate, or trust beginning before January 1, 2005, shall not be taken into account for purposes of § 199(d)(1).

SECTION 3. SCOPE

This revenue procedure applies to a taxpayer filing an original return, under examination, in litigation, or making a refund claim with respect to § 199.

SECTION 4. APPLICATION

.01 *In general.* For purposes of § 199, the use of statistical sampling will be considered a reasonable method that is satisfactory to the Secretary to the extent the sampling methodology used meets the requirements of section 4.02 of this revenue procedure and follows the procedures provided in Appendix A (Sampling Plan Standards), Appendix B (Sampling Documentation Standards), and Appendix C (Technical Formulas). For example, pursuant to this revenue procedure, statistical sampling may be used to:

(1) allocate gross receipts between DPGR and non-DPGR under § 1.199–1(d)(1) of the Income Tax Regulations;

(2) determine whether gross receipts qualify as DPGR on an item-by-item basis under § 1.199–3(d)(1);

(3) allocate CGS between DPGR and non-DPGR under § 1.199–4(b)(2)(i); and

(4) allocate deductions that are properly allocable to DPGR or gross income attributable to DPGR under § 1.199–4(c)(1).

.02 *When statistical sampling is appropriate.* The appropriateness of using a statistical sample for purposes of § 199 is a facts and circumstances determination. Factors used in determining whether a statistical sample is appropriate include, but are not limited to, the time required to analyze large volumes of data, the cost of analyzing data, the existence of verifiable information relevant to the taxpayer's § 199 calculation, and the availability of more accurate information. For purposes of § 199, statistical sampling will generally be considered appropriate if the taxpayer can demonstrate a compelling reason for its use.

.03 *Examples.*

Example 1. *X* manufactures domestically and sells a variety of mechanical fasteners, including bolts, nuts, and screws. Some of these products are not manufactured by *X* but instead are purchased from non-related entities. In many cases, products that are purchased by *X* are the same type of products manufactured by *X*. In addition, *X* manufactures the same products in Mexico. Because these products come in many different sizes, compounds, and packages, *X* sells over five thousand products, each of which may constitute an item within the meaning of § 1.199–3(d)(1).

X has a separate stock keeping unit (SKU) for each of its products. *X*'s computerized sales journal does not identify whether a product sold was manufactured by *X* in the United States, manufactured by *X* in Mexico, or manufactured by a non-related entity. However, *X*'s sales journal does maintain the SKU number for each product and is capable of determining the gross receipts derived from the sale of each product. *X* has devised a methodology to determine what portion, if any, of the gross receipts derived from the sale of each SKU qualifies as DPGR. *X* estimates it needs one staff-day to make this determination for each SKU. Therefore, *X* would have to spend over five thousand staff-days to make a determination regarding DPGR with respect to all of its sales.

In this case, it would be appropriate for *X* to use statistical sampling to determine DPGR derived from the sale of each product.

Example 2. *Y* domestically manufactures fertilizer. When *Y* sells its fertilizer to a customer, it does so by entering into a contract wherein *Y* agrees to apply its fertilizer to the customer's lawn. The application services provided by *Y* are not an MPGE activity. Each contract contains variables such as the amount of fertilizer to apply, the frequency of the service, the size of lawn, and specific customer discounts. Each of these variables affects the total contract price.

Y's computerized accounting system does not track what portion of its gross receipts is derived from the sale of fertilizer and what portion is derived from services. In 2005, *Y* had 20,000 separate contracts. *Y* has determined that there is sufficient information in each contract to separate the fertilizer application services from the sale of fertilizer. However, the time and expense involved in the manual review of 20,000 contracts make this determination impractical. In this case, it would be reasonable for *Y* to use statistical sampling to determine the DPGR derived from the sale of fertilizer.

Example 3. *PRS* provides a broad range of consulting services for dental practices. In addition to its consulting services, *PRS* develops and licenses specialized software for managing dental records. *PRS*' consulting services are not an MPGE activity, while its development and licensing of software is. In 2005 *PRS* had 50 customers. *PRS* can determine the amount of DPGR generated in a particular tax year through a simple review of its contracts. Given the limited number of contracts to be reviewed, pursuant to section 4.02 of this section, there is no compelling reason for *PRS*'s use of statistical sampling to determine its DPGR.

Example 4. *Z* produces, distributes, and licenses motion pictures and has been doing so since 1930. *Z* has a collection of over 5,000 films some of which *Z* produced within the United States and some of which it produced abroad. *Z* believes that historical records exist with respect to each film in its collection and that by reviewing these records it is possible to determine whether a particular film represents a "qualified film" produced by *Z* within the meaning of § 199(c)(4)(A)(i)(II) and (c)(6). However, the time and costs involved in obtaining and reviewing such records on an individual film basis are significant. In this case, *Z* could use statistical sampling to determine the DPGR derived from the license of its film collection.

Example 5. Assume the same facts as in *Example 4* except that Z develops and executes a proper sampling plan as described in Appendix A. In the process, Z discovers that for some of the sampled films it has no historical records and no reliable data can be obtained from other sources that would help determine whether or not each film represents a "qualified film" produced by Z within the meaning of § 199(c)(4)(A)(i)(II) and (c)(6). In accordance with Paragraph 5 of Appendix A, Z must give a value to any film selected as part of its sample. Therefore, if a film is selected for which no historical records and no reliable data can be obtained, Z will be required to treat the selected film as failing the requirements to be a "qualified film" produced by Z for purposes of § 199(c)(4)(A)(i)(II) and (c)(6).

Example 6. X manufactures and sells a variety of tools. Some tools sold by X are manufactured entirely by X in the United States. Other tools sold by X are purchased for resale from F, an unrelated foreign corporation. X maintains a computerized sales journal which tracks whether a tool sold by X was manufactured by X or F. Assuming the gross receipts derived from the sale of tools manufactured by X qualify as DPGR and gross receipts derived from the sale of tools purchased from F for resale do not qualify as DPGR, the use of statistical sampling by X to compute its DPGR from the sale of tools would not be appropriate because evidence is readily available from another source that can be demonstrated to be a more accurate determination of DPGR.

.04 *Limitations.*

(1) This revenue procedure applies only to § 199.

(2) This revenue procedure does not establish the correctness of a taxpayer's interpretation of § 199.

(3) This revenue procedure does not preclude the Internal Revenue Service from raising or pursuing any income, employment, or other tax issues identified in the review of a statistical sample.

SECTION 5. EFFECTIVE DATE

This revenue procedure is generally effective for taxable years beginning on or after May 11, 2007. However, taxpayers may apply this revenue procedure to taxable years beginning after December 31, 2004, and before May 11, 2007.

SECTION 6. PAPERWORK REDUCTION ACT

The collection of information contained in this revenue procedure has been reviewed and approved by the Office of Management and Budget in accordance with the Paperwork Reduction Act (44 U.S.C. 3507) under control number 1545–2072.

An agency may not conduct or sponsor, and a person is not required to respond to, a collection of information unless the collection of information displays a valid OMB control number.

The collection of information in this revenue procedure is in Appendix B. This information is required to ensure compliance with the statistical sampling methodology contained in this revenue procedure. The information will be used to evaluate compliance with the procedures described in this revenue procedure. The collection of information is mandatory. The likely recordkeepers are businesses or other for-profit institutions.

The estimated total annual recordkeeping burden is 2,400 hours. The estimated annual burden per recordkeeper varies from 6 to 10 hours, depending on individual circumstances, with an estimated average of 8 hours. The estimated number of recordkeepers is 300.

Books or records relating to a collection of information must be retained as long as their contents may become material in the administration of any internal revenue law. Generally tax returns and tax return information are confidential, as required by 26 U.S.C. 6103.

DRAFTING INFORMATION

The authors of this revenue procedure are David McDonnell and Lauren Ross Taylor of the Office of Associate Chief Counsel (Passthroughs and Special Industries). For further information regarding this revenue procedure, contact Mr. McDonnell or Ms. Taylor at (202) 622–3040 (not a toll-free call). For further information regarding Appendices A, B, and C, contact Michael Curley of the Large and Mid-Size Business Division at (630) 699–6020 (not a toll-free call).

APPENDIX A

SAMPLING PLAN STANDARDS

The statistical sampling must be conducted in accordance with the following methodology.

1. The statistical sample must be conducted in an unbiased scientific manner with the goal of achieving the correct answer. Any attempt to manipulate the process to achieve a desired result will invalidate the sample. However, steps designed to improve the precision of the estimate, such as stratification techniques, are acceptable and often preferred.

2. Statistical sampling methodology may not include the use of judgment sampling.

3. Taxpayers may apply the results of a statistical sample only to transactions that both (a) occurred in the taxable year in which the § 199 deduction is recognized and (b) involve items included in the population from which the statistical sample was taken.

4. Any estimated amount must be based on a statistical sample, in which each sampling unit has a known (non-zero) chance of selection, using either a simple random sampling method or stratified random sampling method.

5. A conclusion must be reached as to the treatment of each selected sampling unit. It is never valid to replace a sampling unit that was selected in the random selection process with another sampling unit, merely because documentation is unavailable or difficult to obtain. In evaluating a sampling unit, the decision reached as to the treatment of the sampling unit must be the same as the conclusion which would be reached if that sampling unit was encountered in a 100% analysis. Therefore, a sampling unit with documentation that is unavailable or difficult to obtain must be treated as failing the § 199 requirement(s) being tested.

6. In general, the computation of any estimated amount must be at the least advantageous 95% one-sided confidence limit. The "least advantageous" confidence limit is either the upper or lower limit that results in the least benefit to the taxpayer. However, if the precision of estimated difference divided by the estimated difference does not exceed 10%, the point estimate may be used in place of the least advantageous confidence limit. All strata for which "substantially all" of the population sampling units are sampled will be treated as 100% strata. That is, the overall point estimate and its precision will be estimated by treating all 100% strata appropriately for the sample design used. Also, the calculation of the denominator for the relative precision will exclude all 100% strata. For this revenue procedure, "substantially all" is defined as 80% or more.

7. Recognizing that many methods exist to estimate population values from the sample data, only the following estimators will be considered acceptable by the Service. Variable estimators permitted include the mean (also known as the direct projection method), difference (using "paired variables"), (combined) ratio (using a variable of interest and a "correlated" variable), and (combined) regression (using a variable of interest and a "correlated" variable). The first variable used for the difference, ratio and regression estimators must be the variable used in the mean estimator. The second variable used for the difference, ratio and regression estimators must be a variable that can be paired with the first variable and should be related to the first variable. For example, in a typical audit-sampling situation, the first variable would be the audited value of a transaction and the second variable would be the originally reported value of the same transaction. Because the latter two variable methods are statistically biased, there must be a demonstration that the bias is negligible before the Service will accept the method.

8. Variable sampling plans must use the qualifying final estimate with the smallest overall standard error as an absolute value (for example, the size of the estimate is irrelevant in the determination of the reported value).

9. Variable sampling plans must calculate confidence limits by addition and subtraction of the precision of the estimate from the point estimate in which the determination of precision proceeds by multiplication of the standard error by (i) the 95% one-sided confidence coefficient based on the Student's t-distribution with the appropriate degrees of freedom, or (ii) 1.645 (the normal distribution), assuming the sample size is at least 100 in each non-100% stratum.

10. To demonstrate that little statistical bias exists for either the (combined) ratio or regression method, the following applies after excluding all strata tested on 100% basis (the entire population of a stratum is selected for evaluation).

a. The total sample size of all strata must be at least 100 units.

b. Each stratum for a population estimate should contain at least 30 sample units.

c. The coefficient of variation of the paired variable must be 15% or less. The coefficient of variation of the paired variable (y) is defined as the standard error of the total "y" variables divided by point estimate of the total "y" variables when the "y" variables are commonly the reported values in accounting situations.

d. The coefficient of variation of the primary variable of interest, represented by either the corrected value or the difference between the reported and corrected values in common accounting situations, must be 15% or less. The coefficient of variation for the corrected value (x) is defined as the standard error of the total "x" variables divided by point estimate of the total "x" variables when the "x" variables are commonly the corrected values in accounting situations. The coefficient of variation for the difference (d) between the reported and corrected values (x-y) is defined as the smaller of the standard error of the total "x-y" or total "d" variables divided by the amount equaling total population value represented by "Y" plus point estimate of the total "x-y" or total "d" variables or the standard error of the total "x-y" or total "d" variables divided by the total "x-y" or total "d" variables when the "x-y" variables are commonly the difference (d) between the reported (y) and corrected (x) values in accounting situations.

e. For only the (combined) ratio method, the reported values of units must be of the same sign.

11. A written sampling plan is required prior to the execution of a sample. A plan must include the following:

a. The objective of the plan including a description of the value for estimation and the applicable taxable year;

b. Population definition and reconciliation of the population to the tax return;

c. Definition of the sampling frame;

d. Definition of the sampling unit;

e. Source of the random numbers, the starting point or seed, and the method of selection;

f. Sample size, along with supporting factors in the determination;

g. Method to associate random numbers to the frame;

h. Steps to ensure that the serialization of the frame is independent of the drawing of random numbers;

i. Steps for evaluating the sampling unit; and

j. The estimator that was used for appraising the sample.

APPENDIX B

SAMPLING DOCUMENTATION STANDARDS

The taxpayer must retain adequate documentation to support the statistical application, sample unit findings, and all aspects of the sample plan and execution. The execution of the sample must include information for each of the following items:

1. The seed or starting point of the random numbers;

2. The pairing of random numbers to the frame along with supporting information to retrace the process;

3. List of sampling units selected and the results of the evaluation of each unit;

4. Supporting documentation such as notes, invoices, purchase orders, and project descriptions that support the conclusion reached about each sample item;

5. The calculation of the projected estimate(s) to the population, including computation of the standard error of the estimate(s);

6. A statement describing any slips or blemishes in the execution of the sampling procedure and any pertinent decision rules; and

7. Computation of all associated adjustments.

APPENDIX C

TECHNICAL FORMULAS

The formulas below are included to clarify the statistical sampling terms used and to ensure consistent application of the procedures described in the revenue procedure.

UNSTRATIFIED (SIMPLE RANDOM SAMPLE) MEAN ESTIMATOR	STRATIFIED MEAN ESTIMATOR

Sample Mean of Audited Amounts

$$\overline{x} = \frac{\Sigma x_j}{n}$$

Estimate of Total Audited Amount

$$\hat{X}_M = N\,\overline{x} \qquad\qquad \hat{X}_{Ms} = \Sigma\left(N_i \overline{x}_i\right)$$

Estimated Standard Deviation of the Audited Amount

$$S_x = \sqrt{\frac{\left[\Sigma\left(x_j^2\right)\right] - n\left(\overline{x}^2\right)}{n-1}}$$

Estimated Standard Error of the Total Audited Amount

$$\hat{\sigma}\left(\hat{X}_M\right) = \frac{N S_x \sqrt{1 - n/N}}{\sqrt{n}} \qquad\qquad \hat{\sigma}\left(\hat{X}_{Ms}\right) = \sqrt{\Sigma\left[N_i\left(N_i - n_i\right)\frac{S_{x_i}^{\;2}}{n_i}\right]}$$

Achieved Precision of the Total Audited Amount

$$A'_M = \frac{N U_R S_x \sqrt{1 - n/N}}{\sqrt{n}} \qquad\qquad A'_{Ms} = U_R \sqrt{\Sigma\left[N_i\left(N_i - n_i\right)\frac{S_{x_i}^{\;2}}{n_i}\right]}$$

UNSTRATIFIED (SIMPLE RANDOM SAMPLE) DIFFERENCE ESTIMATOR	STRATIFIED DIFFERENCE ESTIMATOR

Estimate of Total Difference

$$\hat{D} = N\overline{d} \qquad\qquad \hat{D}_S = \Sigma\left(N_i \overline{d_i}\right)$$

Estimate of Total Audited Amount

$$\hat{X}_D = Y + \hat{D} \qquad\qquad \hat{X}_{Ds} = Y + \hat{D}_s$$

Estimated Standard Deviation of the Difference Amount

$$S_D = \sqrt{\frac{\left[\Sigma\left(d_j^2\right)\right] - n\left(\overline{d}^2\right)}{n-1}}$$

UNSTRATIFIED (SIMPLE RANDOM SAMPLE) DIFFERENCE ESTIMATOR	STRATIFIED DIFFERENCE ESTIMATOR

Estimated Standard Error of the Difference Amount

$$\hat{\sigma}\left(\hat{D}\right)=\frac{NS_D\sqrt{1-n/N}}{\sqrt{n}}$$

$$\hat{\sigma}\left(\hat{D}_S\right)=\sqrt{\Sigma\left[N_i\left(N_i-n_i\right)\frac{S_{D_i}^2}{n_i}\right]}$$

Achieved Precision of the Difference Amount

$$A'_D=\frac{NU_RS_D\sqrt{1-n/N}}{\sqrt{n}}$$

$$A'_{Ds}=U_R\sqrt{\Sigma\left[N_i\left(N_i-n_i\right)\frac{S_{D_i}^2}{n_i}\right]}$$

UNSTRATIFIED (SIMPLE RANDOM SAMPLE) RATIO ESTIMATOR	STRATIFIED COMBINED RATIO ESTIMATOR

Estimated Ratio of Audited Amount to Recorded Amount

$$R=\frac{\Sigma x_j}{\Sigma y_j}=1+\frac{\Sigma d_j}{\Sigma y_j}$$

$$\hat{R}_C=\frac{\Sigma\left(N_i\overline{x}_i\right)}{\Sigma\left(N_i\overline{y}_i\right)}=1+\frac{\Sigma\left(N_i\overline{d}_i\right)}{\Sigma\left(N_i\overline{y}_i\right)}$$

Estimate of Total Audited Amount

$$\hat{X}_R=Y\hat{R}$$

$$\hat{X}_{Rc}=Y\hat{R}_C$$

Estimated Standard Deviation of the Ratio

$$S_R=\sqrt{\frac{\Sigma\left(x_j^2\right)+\hat{R}^2\Sigma\left(y_j^2\right)-2\hat{R}\Sigma\left(x_jy_j\right)}{n-1}}$$

Estimated Standard Deviation of the Ratio in i[th] Stratum

$$S_{Rc_i}=\sqrt{\frac{\left[\left(\Sigma x_{ij}^2-\left(\Sigma x_{ij}\right)^2/n_i\right)\right]+\left[\hat{R}_C^2\left(\Sigma y_{ij}^2-\left(\Sigma y_{ij}\right)^2/n_i\right)\right]-\left[2\hat{R}_C\left(\Sigma x_{ij}y_{ij}-n_i\overline{x}_i\overline{y}_i\right)\right]}{n_i-1}}$$

Estimated Standard Error of the Ratio Amounts

$$\hat{\sigma}\left(\hat{X}_R\right)=\frac{NS_R\sqrt{1-n/N}}{\sqrt{n}}$$

$$\hat{\sigma}\left(\hat{X}_{Rc}\right)=\sqrt{\Sigma\left[N_i\left(N_i-n_i\right)\frac{S_{Rc_i}^2}{n_i}\right]}$$

Achieved Precision of the Ratio Amounts

$$A'_R=\frac{NU_RS_R\sqrt{1-n/N}}{\sqrt{n}}$$

$$A'_{Rc}=U_R\sqrt{\Sigma\left[N_i\left(N_i-n_i\right)\frac{S_{Rc_i}^2}{n_i}\right]}$$

UNSTRATIFIED (SIMPLE RANDOM SAMPLE) REGRESSION ESTIMATOR	STRATIFIED COMBINED REGRESSION ESTIMATOR

Estimated Regression Coefficient

$$b = \frac{[\Sigma(x_j y_j)] - n\overline{x}\,\overline{y}}{[\Sigma(y_j^2)] - n(\overline{y}^2)} = 1 + \frac{[\Sigma(d_j y_j)] - n\overline{dy}}{[\Sigma(y_j^2)] - n(\overline{y}^2)}$$

$$b_c = \frac{\Sigma N_i (N_i - n_i) S_{XYi}/n_i}{\Sigma N_i (N_i - n_i) S_{Yi}^2/n_i} = 1 + \frac{\Sigma N_i (N_i - n_i) S_{DYi}/n_i}{\Sigma N_i (N_i - n_i) S_{Yi}^2/n_i}$$

Estimate of Total Audited Amount

$$\hat{X}_G = N\overline{x} + b(Y - N\overline{y})$$

$$\hat{X}_{Gc} = \Sigma(N_i \overline{x}_i) + b_c[Y - \Sigma(N_i \overline{y_i})]$$

Estimated Standard Deviation of the Regression Amounts

$$S_G = \sqrt{\frac{1}{n-2}\left[[\Sigma(x_j^2)] - n(\overline{x}^2) - \frac{(\Sigma(x_j y_j) - n\overline{x}\,\overline{y})^2}{\Sigma(y_j^2) - n(\overline{y}^2)}\right]}$$

Estimated Covariance between the Audited and Recorded Amounts in i^{th} Stratum

$$S_{XY_i} = \frac{[\Sigma(x_{ij} y_{ij})] - n_i \overline{x}_i \overline{y}_i}{n_i - 1}$$

Estimated Standard Deviation between the Audited and Recorded Amounts in i^{th} Stratum

$$S_{GC_i} = \sqrt{S_{Xi}^2 - 2b_C S_{XY_i} + b_C^2 S_{Yi}^2}$$

Estimated Standard Error of the Audited and Recorded Amounts

$$\hat{\sigma}\left(\hat{X}_G\right) = \frac{N S_G \sqrt{1 - n/N}}{\sqrt{n}}$$

$$\hat{\sigma}\left(\hat{X}_{Gc}\right) = \sqrt{\Sigma\left[N_i (N_i - n_i)\frac{S_{Gc_i}^2}{n_i}\right]}$$

Achieved Precision of the Audited and Recorded Amounts

$$A'_G = \frac{N U_R S_G \sqrt{1 - n/N}}{\sqrt{n}}$$

$$A'_{Gc} = U_R \sqrt{\Sigma\left[N_i (N_i - n_i)\frac{S_{Gc_i}^2}{n_i}\right]}$$

Definition of Symbols

TERM	DEFINITION
n	Sample Size
N	Population Size
x	The value of the sampling unit that is being used as the primary variable of interest. In audit sampling, this would be the audited (or revised) value of the transaction.
y	The value of the sampling unit that is being used as the "paired" variable that is related to the variable of interest. In audit sampling, this would be the reported (or original) value of the transaction.
d	The value of the sampling unit that is the difference between "paired" variable (y) and the variable of interest (x). That is, $d = x - y$. In audit sampling, this would be the difference (or the change) of each transaction's value.
X	The total value of the primary variable of interest. In audit sampling, this would be the estimated total audited value of the population. Typically, this value is not known for the entire population and is estimated based on the statistical sample selected.
Y	The total value of the variable that is paired with variable of interest. In audit sampling, this would be the total reported value of the population. Typically, this value is known for the entire population and may be estimated based on the statistical sample selected.
D	The total value of the difference between the "paired" variable and the variable of interest. In audit sampling, this would be the estimated total difference of the population. Typically, this value is not known for the entire population and is estimated based on the statistical sample selected.
U_R	The confidence coefficient which is based on either the Student's t-distribution or the normal distribution. For example, a 95% one-sided confidence coefficient based on the normal distribution is 1.645. This term is often referred to as the t-value and the z-value.

Part IV. Items of General Interest

Notice of Proposed Rulemaking

Guidance Regarding the Active Trade or Business Requirement Under Section 355(b)

REG–123365–03

AGENCY: Internal Revenue Service (IRS), Treasury.

ACTION: Notice of proposed rulemaking.

SUMMARY: This document contains proposed regulations that provide guidance regarding the active trade or business requirement under section 355(b) of the Internal Revenue Code. These proposed regulations provide guidance on issues involving the active trade or business requirement under section 355(b), including guidance resulting from the enactment of section 355(b)(3). These proposed regulations will affect corporations and their shareholders.

DATES: Written or electronic comments and requests for a public hearing must be received by August 6, 2007.

ADDRESSES: Send submissions to: CC:PA:LPD:PR (REG–123365–03), room 5203, Internal Revenue Service, PO Box 7604, Ben Franklin Station, Washington, DC 20044. Submissions may be hand-delivered Monday through Friday between the hours of 8 a.m. and 4 p.m. to CC:PA:LPD:PR (REG–123365–03), Courier's Desk, Internal Revenue Service, 1111 Constitution Avenue, NW, Washington, DC, or sent electronically via the Federal eRulemaking Portal at *www.regulations.gov* (IRS REG–123365–03).

FOR FURTHER INFORMATION CONTACT: Concerning the proposed regulations, Russell P. Subin, (202) 622–7790; concerning submissions and the hearing, Kelly Banks, (202) 622–7180 (not toll-free numbers).

SUPPLEMENTARY INFORMATION:

Background and Explanation of Provisions

A. *Background and Overview of the Key Aspects of the Proposed Regulations*

1. *Background*

Section 355(a) of the Internal Revenue Code (Code) provides that, under certain circumstances, a corporation may distribute stock and securities of a corporation it controls to its shareholders and security holders without causing either the corporation or its shareholders and security holders to recognize income, gain or loss. Sections 355(a)(1)(C) and 355(b)(1) generally require that the distributing corporation (distributing) and controlled corporation (controlled) each be engaged, immediately after the distribution, in the active conduct of a trade or business. Section 355(b)(2)(A) provides that a corporation shall be treated as engaged in the active conduct of a trade or business if and only if it is engaged in the active conduct of a trade or business, or substantially all of its assets consist of stock and securities of a corporation controlled by it (immediately after the distribution) which is so engaged. For this purpose, control is defined under section 368(c). All references to control in this preamble are references to control as defined in section 368(c).

Section 202 of the Tax Increase Prevention and Reconciliation Act of 2005, Public Law 109–222 (120 Stat. 345, 348) (TIPRA) amended section 355(b) by adding section 355(b)(3). Section 355(b)(3)(A), as amended by Division A, Section 410 of the Tax Relief and Health Care Act of 2006, Public Law 109–432 (120 Stat. 2922, 2963), provides that in the case of any distribution made after May 17, 2006, a corporation shall be treated as meeting the requirement of section 355(b)(2)(A) if and only if such corporation is engaged in the active conduct of a trade or business. Section 355(b)(3)(B) provides that for purposes of section 355(b)(3)(A) (and, consequently, section 355(b)(2)(A)), all members of such corporation's separate affiliated group (SAG) shall be treated as one corporation (SAG rule). For purposes of the preceding sentence, a corporation's SAG is the affiliated group which would be determined under section 1504(a) if such corporation were the common parent and section 1504(b) did not apply.

Thus, the separate affiliated group of distributing (DSAG) is the affiliated group that consists of distributing as the common parent and all corporations affiliated with distributing through stock ownership described in section 1504(a)(1)(B) (regardless of whether the corporations are includible corporations under section 1504(b)). The separate affiliated group of controlled (CSAG) is determined in a similar manner (with controlled as the common parent). Accordingly, unlike prior law, a corporation is not treated as engaged in the active conduct of a trade or business solely as a result of substantially all of its assets consisting of stock, or stock and securities, of one or more corporations that are merely controlled by it (immediately after the distribution) each of which is engaged in the active conduct of a trade or business.

Section 355(b)(2)(B) requires that the trade or business have been actively conducted throughout the five-year period ending on the date of the distribution (pre-distribution period). Section 355(b)(2)(C) provides that the trade or business must not have been acquired in a transaction in which gain or loss was recognized, in whole or in part, within the pre-distribution period. Section 355(b)(2)(D), as amended in 1987 and 1988, provides that control of a corporation which (at the time of acquisition of control) was conducting the trade or business must not have been directly or indirectly acquired by any distributee corporation or by distributing during the pre-distribution period in a transaction in which gain or loss was recognized, in whole or in part. See Public Law 100–203 (101 Stat. 1330, 1330–411 (1987)) and Public Law 100–647 (102 Stat. 3342, 3605 (1988)). For purposes of section 355(b)(2)(D), all distributee corporations which are members of the same affiliated group (as defined in section 1504(a) without regard to section 1504(b)) shall be treated as one distributee corporation. The requirements under section 355(b) are collectively referred to in this preamble as either the active trade or business requirement or the requirements of section 355(b).

Accordingly, the requirements of section 355(b) are generally satisfied if distributing and controlled each have engaged in the active conduct of a trade or business throughout the pre-distribution period, are so engaged immediately after the distribution, and there have been no acquisitions of control of distributing or controlled during such period.

The active trade or business requirement is one of several requirements that must be satisfied in order for a distribution to qualify under section 355. For example, section 355(a)(1)(B) states that a transaction must not be used principally as a device for distributing the earnings and profits of distributing, controlled, or both. In addition, §1.355–2(b)(1) provides that section 355 will apply to a transaction only if it is carried out for one or more corporate business purposes.

The active trade or business requirement, in tandem with the device prohibition and business purpose requirement, limits a corporation's ability to convert dividend income into capital gain through the use of a section 355 distribution. See S. Rep. No. 83–1622, at 50–51 (1954) and *Coady v. Commissioner*, 33 TC 771, 777 (1960), *acq.*, 1965–2 C.B. 4, *aff'd*, 289 F.2d 490 (6th Cir. 1961). In *Coady*, the Tax Court stated that one purpose of section 355(b) is "to prevent the tax-free separation of *active* and *inactive* assets into *active* and *inactive* corporate entities." The court also stated that a tax-free separation under section 355 "will involve the separation only of those assets attributable to the carrying on of an active trade or business…." *Coady*, 33 TC at 777.

The IRS and Treasury Department are aware of a number of issues that have arisen regarding the active trade or business requirement, including issues arising as a result of the enactment of section 355(b)(3). The following sections describe the active trade or business requirement and the significant issues that are addressed in these proposed regulations. No inference should be drawn from these proposed regulations regarding the definition of trade or business or active trade or business under any other provision of the Code or Treasury regulations, even if such provision specifically references section 355. Comments are requested as to whether or the extent to which these proposed regulations should apply to other provisions that specifically reference section 355.

2. *Overview of the key aspects of the proposed regulations*

Principally, these proposed regulations provide guidance regarding the application of section 355(b)(3), the application of the acquisition rules in section 355(b)(2)(C) and (D) and the impact thereon of section 355(b)(3), and the determination of whether a corporation is engaged in a trade or business through the attribution of trade or business assets and activities from a partnership.

As discussed in section A.1. of this preamble, section 355(b)(3) treats all SAG members as one corporation. Accordingly, as discussed in detail in section B. of this preamble, these proposed regulations provide that subsidiary SAG members (SAG members that are not the common parent of such SAG) are treated like divisions of distributing or controlled, as the case may be. These proposed regulations also clarify that controlled may be a DSAG member during the pre-distribution period. Most significantly, these provisions treat a stock acquisition that results in a corporation becoming a subsidiary SAG member as an asset acquisition. As a result, the applicability of section 355(b)(2)(D) is substantially reduced. Further, as discussed in section E. of this preamble, this treatment alters the analysis regarding whether an existing business may be expanded as a result of a stock acquisition.

Notwithstanding that these proposed regulations provide that certain stock acquisitions may be treated as asset acquisitions under section 355(b)(3), purchases of stock of controlled during the pre-distribution period may be subject to section 355(a)(3)(B). See section F. of this preamble.

As discussed in detail in section C. and section D. of this preamble, these proposed regulations interpret section 355(b)(2)(C) and (D) to mean that a corporation generally cannot use its assets to acquire a trade or business to be relied on to facilitate a distribution under section 355. Accordingly, these proposed regulations generally prohibit acquisitions made in exchange for distributing's assets even if no gain or loss is recognized in connection with the acquisition. Further, these proposed regulations provide certain exceptions to the literal application of section 355(b)(2)(C) and (D) for acquisitions in which gain or loss is recognized where the purposes of that section are not violated. However, these proposed regulations do not disregard the recognition of gain or loss in transactions between affiliates unless the affiliates are members of the same SAG. See section G. of this preamble.

Section I. of this preamble explains how these proposed regulations clarify a corporation's ability to be attributed the trade or business assets and activities of a partnership. Most significantly, these partnership provisions yield results similar to the rules regarding the satisfaction of the continuity of business enterprise requirement, and thus allow a partner to be attributed the partnership's trade or business assets and activities where the partner owns a significant interest in the partnership.

B. *TIPRA*

Congress enacted section 355(b)(3) because it was concerned that, prior to a distribution under section 355, corporate groups conducting business in separate corporate entities often had to undergo elaborate restructurings to place active businesses in the proper entities to satisfy the active trade or business requirement. See, for example, H.R. Rep. No. 109–304, at 53, 54 (2005). By treating a SAG as one corporation, Congress believed that it would greatly reduce the need for such restructurings. However, the introduction of the affiliation-based SAG rule into the active trade or business requirement significantly impacts the application of section 355(b)(2) in certain situations.

Accordingly, consistent with congressional intent, these proposed regulations provide several rules interpreting section 355(b)(3) in a manner that diminishes the need for pre-distribution restructurings while fully integrating the various provisions in section 355(b). These rules are intended to more closely reflect the way corporate groups structure their businesses while, at the same time, ensuring that the purposes underlying section 355(b)(2)(C) and (D) are not circumvented.

Specifically, to accomplish these objectives the IRS and Treasury Department believe that it is appropriate to apply the SAG rule by disregarding the separate existence of all subsidiary SAG members for purposes of determining whether distributing and controlled satisfy the requirements of section 355(b).

1. *SAG rule applicable during the pre-distribution period*

The IRS and Treasury Department believe that it is appropriate to apply the SAG rule for purposes of determining whether the trade or business was actively conducted throughout the pre-distribution period and whether the requirements of section 355(b)(2)(C) or (D) have been violated.

The SAG rule applies for purposes of determining whether distributing and controlled are engaged in the active conduct of a trade or business immediately after the distribution. Specifically, the legislative history to section 355(b)(3) describes the corporations included in the DSAG and CSAG by reference to post-distribution affiliation. See H.R. Rep. No. 109–455, at 88 (2006) (Conf. Rep.); H.R. Rep. No. 109–304, at 54 (2005). However, there is nothing in the statute or legislative history that precludes the SAG rule from applying throughout the pre-distribution period.

The IRS and Treasury Department believe that applying the SAG rule throughout the pre-distribution period is consistent with the single-entity approach. If the SAG rule is not applied during the pre-distribution period, there may be unintended consequences. For example, assume that an active trade or business is segmented among the SAG members in a manner that precludes any one member from individually being treated as engaged in an active trade or business. Under the SAG rule the segments are aggregated and may be treated as a single active trade or business immediately after the distribution. However, if the SAG rule is not applied throughout the pre-distribution period, there would be no five-year active trade or business because no one member would be engaged in that trade or business. The IRS and Treasury Department do not believe there is any policy reason to apply the SAG rule in such a disparate manner. Accordingly, these proposed regulations apply the SAG rule throughout the pre-distribution period. This approach is consistent with Congressional intent to view SAGs as an aggregate for purposes of the active trade or business requirement.

Because the SAG rule treats all SAG members as one corporation, the separate existence of subsidiary SAG members is disregarded and all assets (and activities) owned (and performed) by SAG members are treated as owned (and performed) by distributing or controlled, as the case may be, for purposes of determining whether distributing or controlled is engaged in a five-year active trade or business. Therefore, where one DSAG or CSAG member satisfies the active trade or business requirement, distributing or controlled, as the case may be, satisfies the active trade or business requirement.

Consistent with the foregoing, these proposed regulations provide that the SAG rule also applies for purposes of determining whether there has been an impermissible acquisition, as discussed in section C. of this preamble, of a trade or business during the pre-distribution period under section 355(b)(2)(C) or (D). Because the SAG rule disregards the separate existence of subsidiary SAG members, these proposed regulations generally treat stock acquisitions that result in a corporation becoming a subsidiary SAG member as a direct acquisition of any assets (or activities) owned (or performed) by the acquired corporation. Further, these proposed regulations generally disregard transfers of assets (or activities) that are owned (or performed) by the SAG immediately before and immediately after the transfer. Such transfers cannot result in an acquisition. Under the SAG rule, such transfers have the effect of a transfer between divisions of a single corporation.

2. *The DSAG may include CSAG members throughout the pre-distribution period*

The IRS and Treasury Department believe that it is appropriate to include the CSAG members in the DSAG during the pre-distribution period if the applicable affiliation requirements are satisfied. The IRS and Treasury Department believe this approach is consistent with the purposes of section 355(b)(3) and the SAG rule's general single-entity approach, and provides flexibility for the division of SAG members between distributing and controlled.

For example, assume that during the pre-distribution period, segments or portions of the business to be conducted by controlled are held by distributing (or other subsidiaries that are not directly or indirectly owned by controlled) and that distributing intends to transfer those portions of the business to controlled immediately prior to the distribution. If the DSAG does not include the CSAG members throughout the pre-distribution period, it is possible that neither SAG would be engaged in the active conduct of that trade or business throughout the pre-distribution period, because neither SAG would have all the appropriate segments of that business to satisfy the active trade or business requirement. The IRS and Treasury Department believe that such a result is inconsistent with the purposes of section 355(b)(3). Accordingly, by including the CSAG members in the DSAG throughout the pre-distribution period if the ownership requirements are satisfied, these proposed regulations give appropriate credit to five-year active trades or businesses regardless of how the assets and activities may be owned (and performed) by the SAG members throughout the pre-distribution period.

3. *Acquisitions of stock in subsidiary SAG members*

Section 355(b)(3) treats SAG members as one corporation for purposes of satisfying the requirements of section 355(b). As a result, the SAG rule alters the application of section 355(b)(2)(C) and (D) with respect to the acquisition of stock of a corporation that is or becomes a subsidiary SAG member. Further, because section 355(b)(3) supplanted the holding company rule in section 355(b)(2)(A), section 355(b)(2)(D) is now only applicable to certain acquisitions of stock of distributing and certain acquisitions of stock of controlled.

The SAG rule alters the application of section 355(b)(2)(C) and (D) with respect to the acquisition of stock of a corporation that is or becomes a subsidiary SAG member. Section 355(b)(3) treats SAG members as one corporation for purposes of satisfying section 355(b). Consequently, a transaction that results in a corporation — including controlled — becoming a subsidiary SAG member is treated as a direct acquisition of all the assets (and activities) owned (and performed) by the acquired corporation at the time of the acquisition. Thus, such an acquisition is tested under section 355(b)(2)(C) rather than section 355(b)(2)(D). Nevertheless, as discussed in sections B.4. and C.3.a.ii. of this preamble, section 355(b)(2)(D) has continuing limited application.

In addition, an acquisition that results in a corporation becoming a subsidiary SAG member in a transaction in which gain or loss is recognized might satisfy the requirements of section 355(b)(2)(C) as an expansion of one of the acquiring SAG's existing businesses, as discussed in section E. of this preamble. Finally, because the SAG rule treats subsidiary SAG members like divisions, the acquisition of additional stock of a current subsidiary SAG member has no effect for purposes of applying section 355(b)(2)(C).

4. *Acquisitions of control of controlled where it is not a DSAG member*

While section 355(b)(2)(D) is not applicable to acquisitions of stock of subsidiary SAG members, the requirements of section 355(b)(2)(D) must be satisfied where the DSAG acquires control of controlled where controlled is not and does not become a DSAG member prior to the distribution. This rule applies where distributing acquires stock constituting control of controlled but not stock meeting the requirements of section 1504(a)(2).

C. *Acquisitions of a Trade or Business*

Section 355(b)(2)(C) and (D) generally provides that a trade or business acquired, directly or indirectly, during the pre-distribution period will not satisfy the active trade or business requirement unless it was acquired in a transaction in which no gain or loss was recognized. The IRS and Treasury Department believe that these provisions have been and should continue to be interpreted and applied in a manner consistent with the overall purposes of section 355. For example, in certain situations, transactions in which gain or loss is recognized have been found not to violate the purposes of section 355(b)(2)(C) and (D). See, for example, *C.I.R. v. Gordon*, 382 F.2d 499 (2d Cir.1967), *rev'd on other grounds*, 391 US 83 (1968) (discussed in section C.2. of this preamble). Additionally, while the enactment of section 355(b)(3) substantially revised how distributing and controlled may satisfy the active trade or business requirement, TIPRA did not contain conforming amendments to section 355(b)(2)(C) and (D). As such, the IRS and Treasury Department also believe that a purpose-based interpretation of section 355(b)(2) is essential to harmonize these provisions. Accordingly, these proposed regulations interpret and apply section 355(b)(2)(C) and (D), and section 355(b)(3), in a manner consistent with their purpose, even if not always consistent with the literal language of the statute.

1. *Purpose of section 355(b)(2)(C) and (D)*

Section 355 "contemplates that a tax-free separation shall involve only the separation of assets attributable to the carrying on of an active business." S. Rep. No. 83–1622, at 50 (1954). The active trade or business requirement is intended to ensure that only these types of separations qualify under section 355. Further, it operates as an additional safeguard to the device prohibition (a prohibition against disguised dividends) in section 355(a)(1)(B).

As discussed in section A. of this preamble, the active trade or business requirement is designed to limit the potential for the conversion of dividend income into capital gain through a section 355 distribution. Specifically, section 355(b)(2)(C) and (D) is intended to prevent dividend avoidance otherwise available through the purchase of a new business in order to facilitate a tax-free distribution under section 355. See *Gordon*, 382 F.2d at 506–507 (stating that "[t]o safeguard against this possibility, subsections (b)(2)(C) and (D) prohibit acquisition of a trade or business, or of a corporation, in a transaction in which gain or loss was recognized."). Thus, the statute prohibits acquisitions of a trade or business in which gain or loss is recognized. Nevertheless, the recognition of gain or loss, in and of itself, does not violate the purposes of section 355. Rather, recognition of gain or loss is generally indicative of the type of consideration used in the transaction. Typically, a transaction in which gain or loss is recognized consists of an acquisition in exchange for assets. On the other hand, a transaction in which no gain or loss is recognized typically consists of an acquisition in exchange for the corporation's equity.

Accordingly, the IRS and Treasury Department believe that the common purpose of section 355(b)(2)(C) and (D) is to prevent distributing from using assets — instead of its stock or stock of a corporation in control of distributing — to acquire a new trade or business in anticipation of distributing that trade or business (or facilitating the distribution of another trade or business) to its shareholders in a tax-free distribution. A distribution of a corporation holding assets that would have been used to effect a purchase generally would be treated as a dividend and section 355 was not intended to allow a tax-free separation of such assets. Acquiring a new trade or business using these assets and distributing it (or an existing trade or business) would effectively accomplish such a separation, and should not qualify under section 355.

Complementing the principle that the common purpose of section 355(b)(2)(C) and (D) is to prevent distributing from using its assets — instead of its stock, or stock of a corporation in control of distributing — to acquire a new trade or business is the notion that section 355 is intended to apply to separations of active trades or businesses with which the participants have a historic relationship. Section 355, like the reorganization provisions, involves the maintenance by the shareholders of a continuing interest in their business or businesses in modified corporate forms. For section 355 to apply to a divisive transaction, it is essential that distributing and its shareholders have a historic relationship with the active trades or businesses in the two resulting corporations. See, for example, §1.355–1(b) ("[section 355] applies only to the separation of existing businesses that have been in active operation for at least five years … and which, in general, have been owned, directly or indirectly, for at least five years by the distributing corporation"). These requirements ensure that the historic owners of the acquired trade or business are participants in the divisive transaction and minimize the potential for transactions that violate the common purpose of section 355(b)(2)(C) and (D).

Where distributing issues its own equity (or uses the equity of a corporation in control of distributing) to acquire an active trade or business in a transaction in which no gain or loss is recognized, distributing is not acquiring the trade or business in exchange for its assets and the historic owners of the trade or business will be participants in the divisive transaction. In such cases, the common purpose of section 355(b)(2)(C) and (D) is carried out.

Finally, an additional purpose of section 355(b)(2)(D) is to prevent a distributee corporation from acquiring control of distributing in anticipation of a distribution to which section 355 would otherwise apply, enabling the disposition of controlled without the proper recognition of corporate level gain. See H.R. Rep. No. 100–391, at 1080, 1082–1083 (1987).

2. *Current law and the §1.355–3(b)(4) regulations*

Under current law, several authorities depart from the literal language of section 355(b)(2)(C) and (D) in order to carry out the common purpose underlying section 355(b)(2)(C) and (D). For example, in *Gordon*, gain was recognized when distributing transferred a trade or business to controlled. The Second Circuit concluded that, even though gain was recognized, section 355(b)(2)(C) was not violated because new assets were not brought within the combined corporate shells of distributing and controlled. Therefore, the common purpose of section 355(b)(2)(C) and (D) was not violated. Furthermore, Rev. Rul. 69–461, 1969–2 C.B. 52, held that a first-tier subsidiary's taxable distribution of stock of a second-tier subsidiary to its parent did not violate section 355(b)(2)(D). The ruling stated that section 355(b)(2)(D) is intended to prevent the acquisition of control of a corporation from a party not within the direct or indirect control of distributing. In addition, Rev. Rul. 78–442, 1978–2 C.B. 143, held that gain under section 357(c) on the transfer from distributing to controlled does not violate section 355(b)(2)(C). Rev. Rul. 78–442 stated that section 355(b)(2)(C) is intended to prevent the acquisition of a trade or business by distributing or controlled from an outside party in a taxable transaction within five years of a distribution.

Similarly, §1.355–3(b)(4) (generally applicable to distributions on or before December 15, 1987, but applied in various situations by the IRS administratively to distributions occurring after that date) provides an exception from the literal language of section 355(b)(2)(C) and (D) for the direct or indirect acquisition of a trade or business by one member of an affiliated group from another member of the group, stating that an acquisition from another member of the affiliated group "is not the type of transaction to which section 355(b)(2)(C) and (D) is intended to apply." See §1.355–3(b)(4)(iii).

Section 1.355–3(b)(4) also departs from the literal language of section 355(b) in providing that a trade or business acquired, directly or indirectly, within the pre-distribution period in a transaction in which the basis of the assets acquired was not determined in whole or in part by reference to the transferor's basis does not qualify under section 355(b)(2), even though no gain or loss was recognized by the transferor. See §1.355–3(b)(4)(i). The reason for this departure is that in some circumstances a transaction in which no gain or loss is recognized may nevertheless constitute a prohibited acquisition of a trade or business in exchange for assets.

3. *The proposed regulations*

Consistent with current law (and §1.355–3(b)(4)), these proposed regulations generally prohibit acquisitions in which gain or loss was recognized but apply section 355(b)(2)(C) and (D) in a manner consistent with their purposes. Accordingly, these proposed regulations provide for certain exceptions for acquisitions in which gain or loss is recognized, and prohibit certain transactions in which no gain or loss is recognized.

a. Certain Transactions in Which Recognized Gain or Loss is Disregarded

Under these proposed regulations, certain acquisitions are excepted from the general rule under section 355(b)(2)(C) and (D) that a trade or business, or control of a corporation engaged in a trade or business, cannot satisfy the active trade or business requirement if it was acquired during the pre-distribution period in a transaction in which gain or loss was recognized. These transactions are so excepted because they do not violate the purposes of section 355(b)(2)(C) and (D).

i. Certain Acquisitions by the DSAG or CSAG

These proposed regulations provide a number of exceptions to the application of section 355(b)(2)(C) and (D) not contained in the current regulations (or §1.355–3(b)(4)). One of these exceptions disregards any gain or loss recognized in connection with an acquisition by the CSAG from the DSAG of a trade or business, an interest in a partnership engaged in a trade or business, or stock of a corporation engaged in a trade or business. This exception is appropriate because it is not a use of distributing's assets to acquire the trade or business.

Another exception disregards gain or loss recognized in an acquisition solely as a result of the payment of cash to shareholders for fractional shares where the cash paid represents a mere rounding off of the fractional shares in the exchange and is not separately bargained for consideration. The IRS and Treasury Department believe that this is not the type of transaction to which section 355(b)(2)(C) or (D) is intended to apply. Although such a transaction involves a small use of assets, these proposed regulations except such acquisitions because the small amount of assets are not separately bargained for and are used merely to simplify the exchange. Other authorities reach similar conclusions in the context of reorganizations. See Rev. Rul. 66–365, 1966–2 C.B. 116, amplified by Rev. Rul. 81–81, 1981–1 C.B. 122, (concluding that cash in lieu of fractional shares does not violate the solely for voting stock requirement of section 368(a)(1)(B) and (C) because it was merely a mathematical rounding off for simplicity, and the transaction "was for all practical purposes 'solely in exchange for voting stock'").

In addition, as discussed in section G. of this preamble, these proposed regulations provide a limited exception for taxable acquisitions from affiliates that are members of the same SAG. Specifically, acquisitions between SAG members (where the assets (or activities) are owned (or performed) by the SAG immediately before and immediately after the transfer) are disregarded whether they are taxable or not.

Like the current regulations, these proposed regulations provide that acquisitions that expand a pre-existing business are generally exempted from the nonrecognition requirement. See §1.355–3(b)(3)(ii). While these transactions may involve the use of the DSAG's or CSAG's assets, they are not acquisitions of a new or different trade or business. Because the DSAG or CSAG, as the case may be, is already in the business, such transactions are not considered acquisitions of a trade or business under section 355(b)(2)(C) and (D).

ii. Certain Acquisitions by a Distributee Corporation

Consistent with the principles of Rev. Rul. 74–5, 1974–1 C.B. 82, obsoleted by Rev. Rul. 89–37, 1989–1 C.B. 107, these proposed regulations disregard the recognition of gain or loss in applying section 355(b)(2)(D) to certain acquisitions of the stock of distributing by a distributee corporation. Prior to the 1987 and 1988 amendments noted in section A.1. of this preamble, section 355(b)(2)(D) was not violated in a case where distributing distributed the stock of controlled even though a purchaser acquired distributing's stock during the pre-distribution period in a transaction in which gain or loss was recognized. See Rev. Rul. 74–5 (reasoning that the purpose of section 355(b)(2)(D) was to prevent distributing, rather than the shareholder of distributing, from accumulating excess funds to purchase the stock of a corporation engaged in an active trade or business). However, Rev. Rul. 74–5 held that the purchaser could not then further distribute the stock of controlled until five years after such purchase, reasoning that the purchaser, the distributing corporation in the second distribution, indirectly acquired the stock of controlled through another corporation, the distributing corporation in the first distribution.

The 1987 and 1988 amendments to section 355(b)(2)(D) prohibited such transactions because of a concern that such acquisitions were similar to transactions that permitted a corporation to dispose of an appreciated subsidiary without the proper recognition of gain contrary to the repeal of the *General Utilities* doctrine. For example, assume P, a corporation, acquired the stock of D in a transaction in which gain or loss was recognized and D immediately distributed the stock of C to P in a section 355 transaction. P would allocate its basis in the newly acquired D stock between the D stock and the C stock received in the distribution. P could then potentially sell the C stock without the appropriate recognition of gain. See H.R. Rep. No. 100–391, at 1080, 1082–1083 (1987).

However, there are transactions that violate the literal requirements of section 355(b)(2)(D) but do not violate the purpose of the 1987 and 1988 amendments. For example, assume that for more than five years, T, a corporation, owned all of the stock of D, which in turn owned all the stock of C. Throughout this period, D and C have each engaged in the active conduct of a trade or business. In year 6, P acquires the stock of T in a transaction in which gain or loss is recognized, and holds the T stock with a cost basis determined under section 1012. In year 7, P liquidates T in a transaction to which section 332 applies and in which no gain or loss is recognized, thereby eliminating its cost basis in the T stock. Thereafter, P holds the D stock with a basis equal to T's basis in the D stock. In year 8, D distributes the C stock to P. Under these facts, P cannot dispose of the D or C stock without recognizing the same amount of gain or loss that T would have recognized.

Similarly, assume the same facts as the previous example, except that in year 6 P acquires all of T's assets, including the D stock, in exchange for P stock and cash in a reorganization described in section 368(a)(1)(A). Because all of the cash is distributed to the T shareholders, T does not recognize any gain, and P's basis in the D stock is equal to T's basis in the D stock. See section 362(b). In year 7, D distributes the C stock to P. Under these facts, P cannot dispose of the D or C stock without recognizing the same amount of gain or loss that T would have recognized.

The IRS and Treasury Department believe that the distributee corporation language in section 355(b)(2)(D)(i) is intended only to prevent transactions that are contrary to the repeal of the *General Utilities* doctrine. In both of the examples just described, neither the D stock nor C stock can be disposed of in a manner that is contrary to the repeal of the *General Utilities* doctrine. Accordingly, these proposed regulations provide that section 355(b)(2)(D) is not violated where there is a direct or indirect acquisition by a distributee corporation of control of distributing in one or more transactions in which gain or loss is recognized where the basis of the acquired distributing stock in the hands of the distributee corporation is determined in whole by reference to the transferor's basis. However, consistent with the principles of Rev. Rul. 74–5, this rule is only applicable with respect to a distribution by the acquired distributing, and does not apply for purposes of any subsequent distribution by any distributee corporation.

b. Certain Nonrecognition Transactions Treated as Recognition Transactions

Because the IRS and Treasury Department believe that acquisitions made in exchange for assets violate the common purpose of section 355(b)(2)(C) and (D) even if no gain or loss is recognized, these proposed regulations provide that such transactions are treated as transactions in which gain or loss is recognized.

i. Acquisitions in Exchange for Assets

As discussed in section C.1. of this preamble, the common purpose underlying section 355(b)(2)(C) and (D) is that distributing generally should not be able to use its assets to acquire a new trade or business in anticipation of distributing that trade or business (or facilitating the distribution of another trade or business) to its shareholders in a tax-free transaction. Similarly, and also discussed in section C.1. of this preamble, section 355(b), by permitting the use of distributing stock to acquire a trade or business, ensures a historic relationship between the distributing shareholders and the trades or businesses relied upon to satisfy the active trade or business requirement.

The following examples illustrate distributing's use of its assets to acquire a new trade or business.

First, assume that D, a corporation that does not directly conduct a five-year active trade or business, owns all of the stock of C, a corporation with a five-year active trade or business. D wishes to spin-off C to its shareholders, but to do so D must satisfy the active trade or business requirement. Accordingly, D contributes assets to an unrelated partnership that is engaged in a five-year active trade or business in a transaction to which section 721 applies in exchange for an interest in the partnership that otherwise satisfies the requirements for D to be attributed the trade or business assets and activities of the partnership, as discussed in section I. of this preamble. Two years after the transfer, when D's only active trade or business is the business conducted by the partnership, D distributes the C stock *pro rata* to the D shareholders.

Alternatively, assume that D, a corporation with a five-year active trade or business, transfers assets to unrelated T, a corporation with a five-year active trade or business, in a transaction to which section 351 applies in exchange for an amount of T stock constituting control. Two years after the transfer, when T's only active trade or business is the business T conducted before D's transfer, D distributes the T stock *pro rata* to the D shareholders.

Similarly, assume that D, a corporation with a five-year active trade or business, owns all of the stock of C, a corporation that does not have a five-year active trade or business but has other assets. To cause C to satisfy the active trade or business requirement, D arranges for C to acquire a five-year active trade or business from T, an unrelated corporation, in a reorganization described in section 368(a)(1)(A). In the reorganization, the shareholders of T receive solely common stock of C representing 20 percent or less of the voting power of all classes of C stock. Two years after the reorganization, D distributes the C stock *pro rata* to the D shareholders.

In each of these examples, D has directly or indirectly acquired a trade or business in exchange for assets. See and compare Situation 2 of Rev. Rul. 2002–49, 2002–2 C.B. 288, (corporation's use of appreciated securities to acquire a trade or business of a partnership in a transaction to which section 721 applies is treated as an acquisition in which gain or loss was recognized); section 4.01(29) of Rev. Proc. 2007–3, 2007–1 I.R.B. 108, (the IRS will not ordinarily rule where distributing acquires control of controlled by transferring inactive assets in a transaction meeting the requirements of section 351(a) or section 368(a)(1)(D) and in which no gain or loss is recognized). While these transactions satisfy the literal requirements of section 355(b)(2)(C) or (D), the underlying common purpose of those provisions has been violated. In each case, distributing has acquired in exchange for distributing's assets, either directly or indirectly through the issuance of controlled stock the trade or business to be relied on by distributing or controlled.

Furthermore, in each of these examples, the historic owners have supplied a trade or business for distributing or controlled, but they are not participants in the divisive transaction. Not being shareholders of D, the position of the historic owners of the acquired business is not altered by the distribution of the controlled stock. Accordingly, neither distributing nor the distributing shareholders have a historic relationship with the separated businesses, and the distribution of the controlled stock is not the type of transaction to which section 355 was intended to apply.

By contrast, had D issued its own stock in the reorganization in the last example, the substance of the transaction would be different. D would not have indirectly acquired a trade or business in exchange for assets but rather for its own equity. Because D would not be purchasing a business for its shareholders, the distribution is not a substitute for a taxable distribution of the consideration that would have been used in the purchase. Furthermore, where D stock is used as the consideration the former T shareholders would have joined D's shareholder base, and become participants in the divisive reorganization.

These proposed regulations prohibit the acquisition of a trade or business directly or indirectly in exchange for assets in order to ensure that the common purpose of section 355(b)(2)(C) and (D) is satisfied. Such an acquisition also would include a swap of an interest in an existing five-year active trade or business for an interest in a new active trade or business. This type of an acquisition could occur through the formation of a joint venture structure.

For example, assume D and X form a partnership joint venture in which D contributes a five-year active trade or business (ATBD) and X contributes a different five-year active trade or business (ATBX). D and X each receive a 50-percent interest in the partnership. D's interest is sufficient to satisfy the requirements for D to be attributed the partnership's trade or business assets and activities (as discussed in section I. of this preamble). Prior to a potential section 355 distribution by D, and within five years of the contribution, the partnership sells ATBD.

D cannot rely on ATBX until five years after the acquisition of its interest in the partnership because, in effect, at the time of the contributions D exchanged a 50-percent undivided interest in ATBD for a 50-percent undivided interest in ATBX. Therefore, D acquired its interest in ATBX in exchange for its assets. While this was a transaction in which no gain or loss was recognized, the exchange of assets violates the common purpose of section 355(b)(2)(C) and (D). Further, the historic owner of ATBX would not participate in any distribution of controlled stock by D. Accordingly, such a distribution would not be the type of transaction to which section 355 was intended to apply.

Similarly, a corporation can effectively swap its assets through the issuance of stock of a subsidiary (including controlled). Accordingly, these proposed regulations provide a specific rule to address tax-free acquisitions involving the issuance of subsidiary stock. These proposed regulations provide that if a SAG directly or indirectly owns stock of a subsidiary (including a subsidiary SAG member) and the subsidiary directly or indirectly acquires a trade or business, an interest in a partnership engaged in a trade or business, or stock of a corporation engaged in a trade or business from a person other than such SAG in exchange for stock of such subsidiary in a transaction in which no gain or loss is recognized (the acquisition), solely for purposes of applying section 355(b)(2)(C) or (D) with respect to the trade or business, partnership interest, or stock acquired by the subsidiary in the acquisition, the subsidiary's stock directly or indirectly owned by the SAG immediately after the acquisition is treated as acquired at the time of the acquisition in a transaction in which gain or loss is recognized.

This rule reflects the fact that although the acquiring subsidiary did not make the acquisition in exchange for its assets (it issued its own stock), the SAG that owns stock of the subsidiary has exchanged an indirect interest in the subsidiary's assets for an indirect interest in the trade or business acquired by the subsidiary in the acquisition. Thus, the SAG has indirectly acquired a portion of the subsidiary's newly acquired trade or business (equal to the shareholder's stock interest in the subsidiary immediately after the acquisition) in exchange for assets. Further, the IRS and Treasury Department believe that it would be inappropriate to allow such acquired trade or business to be relied on to satisfy the active trade or business requirement within five years of its acquisition because the historic owners of that trade or business would not participate in any distribution of controlled stock.

However, because such a transaction does not result in an acquisition of any pre-existing trade or business of the subsidiary, this rule merely treats the SAG's stock in the subsidiary immediately after the acquisition as acquired in a gain or loss transaction for purposes of applying section 355(b)(2)(C) or (D) to the newly acquired trade or business. Further, the impact of such a transaction on the ability to rely on the newly acquired trade or business to satisfy the requirements of section 355(b) depends upon how much subsidiary stock the SAG owns immediately after the transaction.

For example, assume D owns all of the sole class of stock of S, a corporation that does not conduct a five-year active trade or business. T, an unrelated corporation with a five-year active trade or business (ATBT), merges into S in a reorganization described in section 368(a)(1)(A) and (D) solely in exchange for 80 percent of the S stock, and no gain or loss is recognized. Immediately after the merger, D owns only 20 percent of the sole class of S stock. Solely for purposes of determining whether ATBT can be relied on to satisfy the active trade or business requirement, D is treated as having acquired its 20 percent of the S stock at the time of the merger of T into S in a transaction in which gain or loss was recognized. Accordingly, as described in section D.2.a. of this preamble regarding certain multi-step acquisitions of a subsidiary SAG member, if D subsequently acquired the 80 percent of the S stock held by the other shareholders solely in exchange for D voting stock in a reorganization described in section 368(a)(1)(B) in which no gain or loss was recognized, S would become a DSAG member and D could rely on ATBT to satisfy the active trade or business requirement.

Accordingly, in light of all of these concerns, these proposed regulations generally provide that acquisitions paid for in whole or in part, directly or indirectly, with assets of the DSAG will be treated as acquisitions in which gain or loss is recognized. However, if a DSAG member or controlled acquires the trade or business solely in exchange for distributing stock, distributing acquires control of controlled solely in exchange for distributing stock, or controlled acquires the trade or business from distributing solely in exchange for stock of controlled, in a transaction in which no gain or loss is recognized, the requirements of section 355(b)(2)(C) and (D) are satisfied. Such acquisitions are not made in exchange for assets of the DSAG.

An additional question arising under section 355(b)(2)(C) and (D) is whether the assumption of liabilities is treated as a payment of money or other property, and hence the use of assets. See *United States v. Hendler*, 303 US 564, reh'g denied, 304 US 588 (1938) (viewing an assumption of a liability by a transferee as in substance a payment to the transferor). Congress has indicated that the assumption of liabilities is not to be treated as the payment of money or other property in certain transactions in which no gain or loss is recognized. For example, the assumption of liabilities is not treated as the payment of money or other property in certain exchanges to which section 351 or 361 applies. See section 357(a). Further, the assumption of liabilities does not violate the solely for voting stock requirement in a reorganization described in section 368(a)(1)(C) where the acquiring corporation does not otherwise exchange money or other property. See section 368(a)(1)(C) and (a)(2)(B). Because Congress has granted this special treatment for liability assumptions in certain nonrecognition transactions, the IRS and Treasury Department believe that similar treatment is generally appropriate for purposes of section 355(b)(2)(C) and (D). Accordingly, these proposed regulations provide that the assumption by the DSAG or CSAG of liabilities of a transferor shall not, in and of itself, be treated as the payment of assets if such assumption is not treated as the payment of money or other property under any other applicable provision.

Finally, these proposed regulations clarify that an acquisition to which section 304(a)(1) applies does not satisfy the requirements of section 355(b)(2)(C) or (D). The IRS and Treasury Department believe that a stock acquisition to which section 304 applies is a transaction in which gain or loss is recognized for purposes of section 355(b)(2)(C) and (D) even if it merely results in the transferor's receipt of dividend income. These proposed regulations clarify that, regardless of the tax consequences to the transferor, such a transaction is an acquisition made in exchange for assets, and therefore does not satisfy the requirements of section 355(b)(2)(C) and (D).

ii. Partnership Distributions

These proposed regulations provide that an acquisition consisting of a distribution from a partnership is generally treated as a transaction in which gain or loss is recognized because it constitutes an acquisition in exchange for assets. That is, the distributee partner is generally exchanging an indirect interest in all the assets of the partnership for a direct interest in the property distributed. However, these proposed regulations provide that if the corporation is already attributed the trade or business assets and activities of a partnership, the corporation's acquisition of such trade or business assets and activities from the partnership is not, in and of itself, the acquisition of a new trade or business. Further, these proposed regulations provide that an acquisition consisting of a *pro rata* distribution from a partnership of stock or an interest in a lower-tier partnership is not an acquisition in exchange for assets to the extent the distributee partner did not acquire the interest in the distributing partnership during the pre-distribution period in a transaction in which gain or loss was recognized and to the extent the distributing partnership did not acquire the distributed stock or partnership interest within such period. In such a case, the distributee partner has merely exchanged an indirect interest for a direct interest in the distributed stock or partnership interest, and continues to possess the same indirect interest in the remaining assets of the partnership.

iii. Lack of Transferred Basis

Section 1.355–3(b)(4)(i) provides that a trade or business acquired, directly or indirectly, within the pre-distribution period in a transaction in which the basis of the assets acquired was not determined in whole or in part by reference to the transferor's basis does not qualify under section 355(b)(2), even though no gain or loss was recognized by the transferor. These proposed regulations do not include a similar provision. The IRS and Treasury Department believe that the prohibition against acquisitions in exchange for assets fully addresses such acquisitions.

c. Application of Section 355(b)(2)(C) and (D) to Predecessors

Unlike §1.355–3(b)(4)(i), which only took "a predecessor in interest" into account for purposes of applying section 355(b)(2)(D), these proposed regulations provide that any reference to a corporation includes a reference to a predecessor of such corporation in applying both section 355(b)(2)(C) and (D). The IRS and Treasury Department believe that predecessors should be taken into account in applying both section 355(b)(2)(C) and (D) because the same policy concerns exist regardless of whether the transaction involves the acquisition of assets or stock. For this purpose, the proposed regulations define a predecessor of a corporation as a corporation that transfers its assets to such corporation in a transaction to which section 381 applies. The IRS and Treasury Department believe that it is appropriate to take predecessors into account in applying these provisions in order to appropriately minimize the significance of which corporation is the acquiror and which corporation is the target.

Further, because the SAG rule effectively treats SAG members as a single-entity for purposes of section 355(b), these proposed regulations also apply section 355(b)(2)(C) and (D) to acquisitions during the pre-distribution period by corporations that later become DSAG or CSAG members. These types of acquisitions are similar to predecessor asset acquisitions.

4. *Requests for comments regarding exceptions to section 355(b)(2)(C) and (D)*

The IRS and Treasury Department request comments regarding whether any additional exceptions to section 355(b)(2)(C) and (D) are appropriate. In particular, the IRS and Treasury Department request comments regarding whether acquisitions in which gain is recognized solely as a result of the application of section 367 should be treated as violating section 355(b)(2)(C) or (D). The IRS and Treasury Department also request comments regarding whether an exception should exist for taxable acquisitions made by distributing solely in exchange for distributing stock because such acquisitions are not made in exchange for distributing's assets and do not appear to violate the common purpose of section 355(b)(2)(C) and (D).

In addition, the IRS and Treasury Department request comments regarding whether a redemption of stock should be a transaction to which section 355(b)(2)(C) or (D) applies. Under current law, no relief is provided for such transactions. See *McLaulin v. Commissioner*, 276 F.3d 1269 (11th Cir. 2001) (concluding that section 355(b)(2)(D) applies when distributing acquires control of a subsidiary through a redemption of subsidiary stock). Compare Rev. Rul. 57–144, 1957–1 C.B. 123. Specifically, comments are requested on whether all types of redemptions should be subject to the same rule, whether the treatment of redemptions should be determined by the source of payment, whether the redemption constitutes an indirect exchange for assets of distributing or controlled, and the method of making these determinations. Alternatively, the IRS and Treasury Department request comments on whether an exception should be provided for redemptions of shareholders that exercise dissenters' rights. Compare Rev. Rul. 68–285, 1968–1 C.B. 147, (concluding that cash paid to dissenting target corporation shareholders by the target corporation does not violate the solely for voting stock requirement of section 368(a)(1)(B)) with Rev. Rul. 73–102, 1973–1 C.B. 186, (concluding that cash paid to dissenting target corporation shareholders by the acquiring corporation is treated as money or other property paid by the acquiring corporation for the properties of the target corporation in a reorganization under section 368(a)(1)(C)). These proposed regulations do not include an exception for redemptions generally or for those in connection with the exercise of dissenters' rights.

Finally, the IRS and Treasury Department request comments regarding whether a transaction in which a distributee corporation acquires in a transaction in which no gain or loss is recognized newly issued stock of distributing in exchange for money or property previously acquired for cash during the pre-distribution period should be treated as a transaction in which gain or loss is recognized. For example, assume D and C have each engaged in the active conduct of a trade or business for more than five years. During the pre-distribution period, P, an unrelated corporation, purchases trucks and transfers them to D in exchange for D stock meeting the requirements of section 368(c) in a transaction to which section 351 applies. No gain or loss is recognized. D subsequently distributes all the C stock to P in a separate transaction within five years of P's acquisition of the D stock. Notwithstanding that this transaction satisfies the literal requirements of section 355(b)(2)(D), it appears to violate the *General Utilities* doctrine because it permits the distributee corporation, P, to receive a fair market value basis (or close to a fair market value basis) in the distributing stock, enabling the potential sale of controlled stock without the appropriate recognition of gain. Additionally, the IRS and Treasury Department are studying whether the principles of the foregoing rule should be extended to any distributee in regulations under section 355(d), and request comments on this point.

D. *Treatment of Certain Multi-step Acquisitions*

These proposed regulations provide specific rules regarding the application of section 355(b)(2)(C) and (D) to certain multi-step acquisitions. Based on the interpretation of section 355(b)(2)(D), and the enactment of section 355(b)(3), the IRS and Treasury Department believe that it is appropriate to apply section 355(b)(2)(C) and (D) to multi-step acquisitions in a consistent manner. Further, the IRS and Treasury Department believe that it is appropriate to treat certain multi-step acquisitions of target corporation stock as satisfying the requirements of section 355(b)(2)(C) or (D) (as applicable) notwithstanding that some portion of the stock may have been acquired in a separate transaction in which gain or loss was recognized.

1. *Multi-step acquisition of control of distributing or controlled*

a. Direct Acquisitions

Section 355(b)(2)(D) provides that control of distributing or controlled may be acquired within the pre-distribution period provided that "in each case in which such control was so acquired, it was so acquired, only by reason of transactions in which gain or loss was not recognized in whole or in part, or only by reason of such transactions combined with acquisitions before the beginning of such period." The IRS and Treasury Department interpret this language to mean that at the time control is first acquired, the acquiring corporation (or its SAG) is required to own stock meeting the requirements of section 368(c) that was acquired in one or more transactions in which no gain or loss was recognized or by reason of such transactions combined with acquisitions before the beginning of the pre-distribution period. Thus, at the time an acquiring corporation (or its SAG) first satisfies the section 368(c) control requirement, the acquiring corporation (or its SAG) must possess section 368(c) control without relying on any stock acquired in a transaction in which gain or loss was recognized during the pre-distribution period.

For example, assume that C has two classes of stock outstanding. X owns all 95 shares of the class A stock of C representing 95 percent of the voting power and 70 percent of the value and Y owns all of the class B stock of C representing five percent of the voting power and 30 percent of the value. In year 1, unrelated D acquires 10 shares of the class A C stock from X in a transaction in which gain or loss is recognized. In year 2, D acquires an additional 80 shares of class A C stock from X in a separate transaction in which no gain or loss is recognized. In year 3, D acquires the remaining five shares of class A C stock from X in a separate transaction in which gain or loss is recognized. In year 4, D distributes the 95 shares of class A C stock to the D shareholders. Assuming all of the other requirements of section 355(b) are satisfied, the requirements of section 355(b)(2)(D)(ii) are satisfied because at the time D first acquired control of C (immediately after the year 2 acquisition), D owned an amount of C stock constituting control that was acquired in a transaction in which no gain or loss was recognized (the 80 shares of class A C stock acquired in year 2). (However, the 10 shares of class A C stock acquired in year 1 and the five shares of class A C stock acquired in year 3 may be treated as boot under section 355(a)(3)(B).)

On the other hand, assume the same facts as the previous example, except that, in year 2, D acquires only 75 shares of class A C stock from X. The requirements of section 355(b)(2)(D)(ii) are not satisfied because at the time D first acquired control of C (immediately after the year 2 acquisition), D did not own an amount of C stock constituting control that was acquired in one or more transactions in which no gain or loss was recognized or acquired prior to the pre-distribution period. D only owns C voting stock representing 75 percent of the total voting power that was acquired in a transaction in which no gain or loss was recognized. The result would be the same if the year 3 acquisition was also a transaction in which no gain or loss was recognized.

b. Indirect Acquisitions

These proposed regulations also provide that the principles of this rule will be applied with respect to an indirect acquisition of distributing or controlled stock. For example, assume T corporation owns stock of C (an unaffiliated subsidiary) constituting control (and no more). Unrelated D acquires 10 percent of the sole outstanding class of stock of T in a transaction in which gain or loss is recognized. In a separate transaction, T merges into D solely in exchange for D stock in a transaction in which no gain or loss is recognized. In applying this multi-step acquisition rule to D's subsequent acquisition of control of C in the merger, the prior acquisition of T stock in the transaction in which gain or loss was recognized is treated as an acquisition of 10 percent of the C stock owned by T (representing 8 percent of the total combined voting power of the C stock) in a transaction in which gain or loss is recognized. Accordingly, the requirements of section 355(b)(2)(D)(ii) are not satisfied because at the time D first acquires control of C, D does not own an amount of C stock constituting control that was acquired in one or more transactions in which no gain or loss is recognized or acquired prior to the pre-distribution period. At that time, D had only acquired C stock representing 72 percent of the total combined voting power of the C stock in a transaction in which no gain or loss is recognized.

2. *Other multiple-step acquisitions*

As discussed in sections A.1., B.1., and B.3. of this preamble, if D acquires section 1504(a)(2) stock of a corporation, the acquired corporation will become a DSAG member and the corporation will be treated like a division of D for purposes of the active trade or business requirement. As such, D is treated as if it acquired the assets and activities of the new subsidiary SAG member, and the acquisition must satisfy the requirements of section 355(b)(2)(C) rather than section 355(b)(2)(D). If D subsequently acquires the remaining stock of the corporation in a separate transaction, such acquisition is disregarded for purposes of satisfying the active trade or business requirement (regardless of whether gain or loss was recognized in the separate transaction) because the subsidiary is already treated as a division of D for this purpose. The IRS and Treasury Department believe that the order of these acquisitions should not be determinative in applying section 355(b)(2)(C), provided that at the time the corporation first becomes a subsidiary SAG member, the SAG owns section 1504(a)(2) stock in the corporation without relying on any stock acquired in a transaction in which gain or loss was recognized during the pre-distribution period.

a. Direct SAG Acquisitions

Consistent with the treatment of multi-step acquisitions of control of a corporation discussed in section D.1. of this preamble, these proposed regulations provide that multi-step acquisitions of stock resulting in a corporation becoming a subsidiary SAG member will satisfy the requirements of section 355(b)(2)(C), provided that at the time the corporation first becomes a subsidiary SAG member, the SAG owns section 1504(a)(2) stock in the corporation without relying on any stock acquired in a transaction in which gain or loss was recognized during the pre-distribution period.

For example, assume that in year 1, D does not conduct an active trade or business and has owned control of C for more than five years. C and T, an unrelated corporation, have each engaged in the active conduct of a trade or business for more than five years. In year 1, D acquires 10 percent of T's sole outstanding class of stock in a transaction in which gain or loss was recognized. In year 2, D acquires an additional 80 percent of T's stock in a separate transaction in which no gain or loss was recognized. T becomes a DSAG member as a result of the year 2 stock acquisition. In year 3, D distributes the C stock to the D shareholders. Assuming all of the other requirements of section 355(b) are satisfied, the requirements of section 355(b)(2)(C) are satisfied because at the time T first became a DSAG member (immediately after the year 2 acquisition), D owned an amount of T stock meeting the requirements of section 1504(a)(2) that was acquired in a transaction in which no gain or loss was recognized (the T stock acquired in year 2).

On the other hand, assume the same facts as the previous example except that, in year 2, D only acquires an additional 75 percent of T's stock. The requirements of section 355(b)(2)(C) are not satisfied because at the time T first became a DSAG member (immediately after the year 2 acquisition), D did not own an amount of T stock meeting the requirements of section 1504(a)(2) that was acquired in one or more transactions in which no gain or loss was recognized or acquired prior to the pre-distribution period. D owns only 75 percent of T's stock that was acquired in a transaction in which no gain or loss was recognized. The result would be the same even if, in year 3 prior to the distribution of the C stock, D acquired the remaining 15 percent of the T stock in a transaction in which no gain or loss is recognized.

b. Indirect SAG Acquisitions

Similar to the rule regarding multi-step acquisitions of control of distributing or controlled, these proposed regulations also provide that the principles of this rule will be applied with respect to an indirect acquisition by the SAG of stock of a corporation that becomes a SAG member. For example, assume a DSAG member acquires 25 percent of the sole outstanding class of stock of T, a corporation that wholly owns S, in a transaction in which gain or loss is recognized. In a separate transaction, another DSAG member acquires all of the stock of S from T solely in exchange for D voting stock in a reorganization described in section 368(a)(1)(B) in which no gain or loss is recognized. As a result, S becomes a DSAG member. In applying this multi-step acquisition rule to the DSAG's subsequent acquisition of S stock, the acquisition of 25 percent of the T stock in the transaction in which gain or loss was recognized will be treated as an acquisition of 25 percent of the S stock in a transaction in which gain or loss is recognized. Accordingly, the requirements of section 355(b)(2)(C) are not satisfied because at the time S first becomes a DSAG member, the DSAG does not own section 1504(a)(2) stock of S that was acquired in one or more transactions in which no gain or loss is recognized or acquired prior to the pre-distribution period.

c. Multi-step Asset Acquisitions

Because stock acquisitions that result in a corporation becoming a subsidiary SAG member are treated as direct acquisitions of the target corporation's assets for purposes of applying section 355(b), these proposed regulations apply a comparable multi-step acquisition rule to acquisitions of stock in non-SAG members where such non-members' assets are subsequently directly acquired by a SAG member. Specifically, these proposed regulations provide that if immediately before a SAG's direct acquisition of a trade or business (or an interest in a partnership engaged in a trade or business) held by a corporation (owner) in a transaction to which section 381 applies and in which no gain or loss is recognized, the SAG owns an amount of stock of the owner that it acquired in one or more transactions during the pre-distribution period in which gain or loss was recognized such that all of the other stock of the owner does not meet the requirements of section 1504(a)(2), such direct acquisition shall be treated as a transaction in which gain or loss was recognized. Thus, these proposed regulations apply section 355(b)(2)(C) to multi-step acquisitions in the same manner regardless of whether the separate steps result in the target corporation becoming a subsidiary SAG member or result in a direct acquisition of the target corporation's assets.

For example, assume that in year 1, D does not conduct an active trade or business, and has owned control of C for more than five years. C and T, an unrelated corporation, have each engaged in the active conduct of a trade or business for more than five years. In year 1, D acquires 10 percent of T's sole outstanding class of stock in a transaction in which gain or loss was recognized. In year 2, in a separate reorganization described in section 368(a)(1)(A), T merges into D and the T shareholders receive solely D stock in exchange for their T stock. No gain or loss is recognized in the merger. In year 3, D distributes the stock of C to the D shareholders. Assuming all of the other requirements of section 355(b) are satisfied, the requirements of section 355(b)(2)(C) are satisfied because, at the time D acquires T's active trade or business, D did not own an amount of T stock that was acquired in one or more transactions during the pre-distribution period in which gain or loss was recognized such that all of the other T stock does not meet the requirements of section 1504(a)(2).

On the other hand, assume the same facts as the previous example except that in year 1 D acquires 21 percent of T's stock. The requirements of section 355(b)(2)(C) are not satisfied because, at the time D acquires T's active trade or business, D owned an amount of T stock that was acquired in one or more transactions during the pre-distribution period in which gain or loss was recognized such that all of the other T stock does not meet the requirements of section 1504(a)(2).

These proposed regulations also provide that the principles of this rule will be applied with respect to an indirect acquisition of the target corporation's stock by the SAG.

E. *Expansion Acquisitions*

The legislative history, the courts, and the current regulations acknowledge that a trade or business can undergo many changes during the pre-distribution period and still satisfy the requirements of section 355(b). See H.R. No. 83–2543, at 37, 38 (1954) (Conf. Rep.); *Estate of Lockwood v. Commissioner*, 350 F.2d 712 (8th Cir. 1965); and §1.355–3(b)(3)(ii). Furthermore, §1.355–3(b)(3)(ii) provides "if a corporation engaged in the active conduct of one trade or business during that five-year period purchased, created, or otherwise acquired another trade or business in the same line of business, then the acquisition of that other business is ordinarily treated as an expansion of the original business, all of which is treated as having been actively conducted during that five-year period, unless that purchase, creation, or other acquisition effects a change of such a character as to constitute the acquisition of a new or different business." Therefore, an acquired trade or business that is an expansion of the original trade or business inherits the business history of the expanded business.

None of these authorities, however, addresses whether an existing trade or business can be expanded by acquiring the stock of a corporation engaged in a trade or business in the same line of business as the acquiror. Because the SAG rule causes a stock acquisition in which the acquired corporation becomes a subsidiary SAG member to be treated as an asset acquisition, a corporation engaged in a trade or business should be able to expand its existing trade or business by acquiring stock of a corporation (including controlled) engaged in a trade or business in the same line of business provided the acquisition results in the acquired corporation becoming a subsidiary SAG member.

On the other hand, section 355(b)(3) does not allow a corporation to rely on the trade or business of a non-SAG subsidiary — even if the corporation controls the subsidiary — to satisfy the active trade or business requirement. As such, it effectively precludes stock expansions where the acquired corporation does not become a subsidiary SAG member. The IRS and Treasury Department believe that section 355(b)(3) is the exclusive means by which a corporation is attributed the assets (or activities) owned (or conducted) by another corporation. Accordingly, a stock acquisition that does not result in the acquired corporation becoming a subsidiary SAG member should not be an expansion of the SAG's original business.

In addition, these proposed regulations provide certain facts and circumstances to be considered in determining whether one trade or business is in the same line of business as another trade or business. The inclusion of these facts and circumstances in these proposed regulations is not intended to be a substantive change, but merely to clarify and restate the current law regarding expansions. See Rev. Rul. 2003–18, 2003–1 C.B. 467, and Rev. Rul. 2003–38, 2003–1 C.B. 811. Some of the examples from the current regulations have been altered in these proposed regulations to reflect this inclusion (as well as certain stylistic changes).

F. *Rules Related to Hot Stock*

Section 355(a)(3)(B) provides that stock of controlled acquired by distributing during the pre-distribution period in a transaction in which gain or loss is recognized is treated as boot. Section 1.355–2(g) provides guidance regarding the application of section 355(a)(3)(B). The IRS and Treasury Department request comments regarding whether §1.355–2(g) should be amended to adopt rules under section 355(a)(3)(B) similar to those provided in these proposed regulations for determining whether an acquisition is one in which gain or loss is recognized for purposes of section 355(b)(2)(C) or (D).

In particular, the IRS and Treasury Department request comments concerning the application of section 355(a)(3)(B) to acquisitions of stock of controlled in gain or loss transactions that, under these proposed regulations, are not treated as violating the requirements of section 355(b). For example, where distributing acquires stock of controlled in a gain or loss transaction that is treated as an expansion of distributing's existing trade or business (because controlled is in distributing's line of business and becomes a DSAG member), what portion, if any, of the acquired stock should be subject to section 355(a)(3)(B)?

The current authorities may suggest a linkage between the interpretation of sections 355(a)(3)(B) and 355(b). See §1.355–2(g)(1) (not applying section 355(a)(3)(B) to a taxable acquisition from an affiliate); Rev. Rul. 78–442 (stating "[l]ikewise, for the same reasons [that section 355(b)(2)(C) does not apply], section 355(a)(3)[(B)] of the Code is not applicable"). However, section 355(b)(3) by its literal terms does not appear to apply for purposes section 355(a)(3)(B).

The IRS and Treasury Department continue to study how to coordinate the application of these provisions and request comments in this regard. Accordingly, these proposed regulations contain no proposal to change §1.355–2(g) at this time.

G. *Limited Affiliate Exception*

Other than with respect to transfers of assets (or activities) that are owned (or performed) by the SAG immediately before and immediately after the transfer, these proposed regulations do not include the special treatment accorded affiliated group members in §1.355–3(b)(4)(iii). Thus, these proposed regulations treat non-SAG member affiliates of distributing or controlled in the same manner as unrelated persons for purposes of applying section 355(b)(2)(C) and (D). While distributing is the common parent of its SAG, distributing may be a subsidiary member of a larger affiliated group. Therefore, not all members of distributing's affiliated group are DSAG members.

Section 1.355–3(b)(4)(iii) provides that acquisitions by one member of an affiliated group from another member of the group are disregarded in applying section 355(b)(2)(C) and (D), even if gain or loss is recognized. Section 1.355–3(b)(4)(iii) provides for this treatment for affiliates because although "[t]he requirements of section 355(b)(2)(C) and (D) are intended to prevent the direct or indirect acquisition of a trade or business by a corporation in anticipation of a distribution by the corporation of that trade or business in a distribution to which section 355 would otherwise apply[,]" acquisitions from affiliates are not the type of transaction to which these provisions were intended to apply. Section 1.355–3(b)(4)(iv) defines the term "affiliated group" as an affiliated group as defined in section 1504(a) (without regard to section 1504(b)), except that the term "stock" includes nonvoting stock described in section 1504(a)(4).

The IRS and Treasury Department believe that limiting this special treatment to transfers in which the assets (or activities) remain in the SAG (as opposed to the larger affiliated group) is more consistent with the purposes of section 355(b)(3). As discussed in section A.1. of this preamble, section 355(b)(3) states, in effect, that in determining whether distributing or controlled is engaged in a trade or business all DSAG or CSAG members, as the case may be, are treated as one corporation. Therefore, a transfer of trade or business assets (or activities) from one SAG member to another SAG member is disregarded, and is not an acquisition for purposes of section 355(b)(2)(C) (or section 355(b)(2)(D) in the case of stock of controlled that is not a DSAG member). The SAG rule implies a corollary, which is that if the trade or business assets (or activities) are not owned (or performed) by the SAG, such assets (or activities) should generally not be able to be acquired from outside the SAG in a transaction in which gain or loss is recognized. Thus, these proposed regulations generally do not permit taxable acquisitions of an active trade or business from outside the SAG.

The IRS and Treasury Department recognize that not providing this special treatment for non-SAG member affiliates is a change from how the law has been administered in various situations. Further, the IRS and Treasury Department recognize that this change can represent a relaxing or tightening of the law in this area, depending upon the circumstances. For example, under these proposed regulations the requirements of section 355(b)(2)(C) are satisfied where P, a higher-tier affiliate of distributing, purchases a trade or business for cash and contributes it to distributing solely in exchange for distributing stock in a transaction in which no gain or loss is recognized. On the other hand, under these proposed regulations, the requirements of section 355(b)(2)(C) are not satisfied where P has actively conducted a trade or business for more than five years and sells it to D in exchange for cash.

H. *Activities Performed by Certain Related Parties*

Current §1.355–3(b)(2)(iii) provides, in part, that to satisfy the active trade or business requirement, the corporation itself generally is required to perform active and substantial management and operational functions. That regulation further provides that activities performed by the corporation itself generally do not include activities performed by independent contractors. In this regard, "a corporation must engage in entrepreneurial endeavors of such a nature and to such an extent as to qualitatively distinguish its operations from mere investments [, and] ... there should be objective indicia of such corporate operations." *Rafferty v. Commissioner*, 452 F.2d 767, 772 (1st Cir. 1971) *cert. denied* 408 US 922 (1972) (concluding that a corporation that did not pay salaries or rent, did not employ independent contractors, and merely collected rent, paid taxes, and kept separate books, failed to satisfy these requirements). The IRS and Treasury Department believe that a corporation may rely on the activities performed by certain related parties in conducting its "entrepreneurial endeavors," and such activities can constitute "objective indicia" of corporate operations.

While section 355(b)(3) treats all SAG members as one corporation, the IRS and Treasury Department are aware that affiliated groups of corporations that include non-SAG member affiliates might use employees of one member of the group to perform management or operational functions for another member of the group. The IRS and the Treasury Department believe that a corporation can satisfy the active trade or business requirement even if all the management and operational functions are performed by employees of affiliates that are not members of either the DSAG or CSAG. In other words, the DSAG or CSAG can be engaged in "entrepreneurial endeavors" that are distinguishable from mere passive investment even if the management and operational functions are performed for the DSAG or CSAG by employees of non-SAG affiliates. Such individuals bear a close enough relationship to the DSAG or CSAG to be distinguished from mere independent contractors for purposes of the active trade or business requirement. The IRS and Treasury Department believe that this treatment is appropriate and consistent with previously published guidance.

Issued prior to the enactment of section 355(b)(3), Rev. Rul. 79–394, 1979–2 C.B. 141, amplified by Rev. Rul. 80–181, 1980–2 C.B. 121, concludes that controlled satisfies the active trade or business requirement even though all of the operational activities of its business are conducted by an affiliate's employees before the distribution. The IRS and Treasury Department believe that extending the principles of Rev. Rul. 79–394 and Rev. Rul. 80–181 to the performance of management (in addition to operational) functions by employees of an affiliate is consistent with the purposes underlying the active trade or business requirement. Accordingly, these proposed regulations provide that, in determining whether a corporation is engaged in the active conduct of a trade or business, activities (including management and operational functions) performed by employees of the corporation's affiliates (including non-SAG members) are taken into account.

Furthermore, the IRS and Treasury Department believe that a corporation can satisfy the active trade or business requirement even if all the management and operational functions are performed by shareholders of the corporation if it is closely held. The shareholders of closely held corporations possess a close relationship with the corporation, similar to employees of affiliates. Accordingly, these proposed regulations provide that, in determining whether a corporation is engaged in the active conduct of a trade or business, activities (including management and operational functions) performed by shareholders of a closely held corporation are taken into account in certain cases.

The IRS and Treasury Department do not believe that the absence of an exception for acquisitions from non-SAG member affiliates is inconsistent with concluding that a corporation can satisfy the active trade or business requirement by relying on the management and operational functions performed by employees of non-SAG member affiliates. Relying on the activities of such employees does not involve the acquisition of a trade or business. As such, it is not the type of transaction or arrangement section 355(b)(2) was intended to address. Accordingly, the IRS and Treasury Department believe it is appropriate to apply a broader standard with respect to relying on employees of non-SAG member affiliates.

While it is appropriate to consider the management and operational activities of employees of all affiliates in determining whether a corporation satisfies the active trade or business requirement, the IRS and Treasury Department believe that a corporation should satisfy the active trade or business requirement only if it (or another SAG member, or a partnership from which the trade or business assets and activities are attributed) is the principal owner of the goodwill and significant assets of the trade or business for Federal income tax purposes. Accordingly, a corporation will be treated as engaged in the active conduct of a trade or business only if, for Federal income tax purposes, it (or its SAG member, or a partnership from which the trade or business assets and activities are attributed) is the principal owner of the goodwill and significant assets of the trade or business. Accordingly, some of the examples from the current regulations have been altered in these proposed regulations to reflect this goodwill and significant asset standard (as well as certain stylistic changes).

I. *Activities Conducted by a Partnership*

Revenue Ruling 92–17, 1992–1 C.B. 142, and Rev. Rul. 2002–49, 2002–2 C.B. 288, address in a number of fact situations whether a corporation that is a partner in a partnership can satisfy the active trade or business requirement by reason of its ownership of the partnership interest where the partnership conducts a trade or business. Those rulings illustrate that a corporation owning a 20-percent interest in a state law partnership or limited liability company (LLC) that is classified as a partnership for Federal income tax purposes can be treated as engaged in the active conduct of the trade or business of the partnership if the corporation performs active and substantial management functions for the partnership's business. In addition, Rev. Rul. 2002–49 concludes that such a corporation can be treated as engaged in the active conduct of a partnership's trade or business, even if another partner also performs active and substantial management functions for the partnership's trade or business.

Consistent with the principles set forth in Rev. Rul. 92–17 and Rev. Rul. 2002–49 regarding satisfying the active trade or business requirement through an interest in a partnership, these proposed regulations provide that for purposes of section 355(b) a partner will be attributed the trade or business assets and activities of a partnership if the partner (1) performs active and substantial management functions for the partnership with respect to the trade or business assets or activities (for example, makes decisions regarding significant business issues of the partnership and regularly participates in the overall supervision, direction, and control of the employees performing the operational functions for the partnership), and (2) owns a meaningful interest in the partnership. Further, because a partnership might only conduct a portion of a trade or business, the IRS and Treasury Department believe that a partner that satisfies these requirements can be attributed the portions of a trade or business (or assets and activities) that are conducted by a partnership. Under these circumstances the IRS and Treasury Department believe that it is appropriate to aggregate the partnership's trade or business assets and activities with those of the partner for purposes of determining whether the partner satisfies the active trade or business requirement. However, the stock of a corporation held by the partnership is not attributed to a partner.

The IRS and Treasury Department understand that the facts presented in Rev. Rul. 92–17 and Rev. Rul. 2002–49 do not necessarily reflect the exclusive methods by which corporations engage in a trade or business through a partnership. In particular, the IRS and Treasury Department understand that both the management and operational activities of an LLC are often conducted by the LLC itself, rather than by its members, to protect its members from liability for the LLC's activities. In these cases, Rev. Rul. 92–17 and Rev. Rul. 2002–49 do not explicitly support the conclusion that a corporation may rely on the trade or business assets and activities of an LLC to satisfy the active trade or business requirement, since no activities are performed by the corporate partner.

The IRS and Treasury Department believe that, in certain cases, a partner that owns a significant interest in an entity that is treated as a partnership for Federal income tax purposes should be attributed the trade or business assets and activities of a partnership, even if the partner does not directly conduct any activities relating to the business of the partnership. By comparison, the IRS and Treasury Department have promulgated regulations regarding the treatment of acquired assets held by a partnership for purposes of satisfying the continuity of business enterprise requirement applicable to reorganizations. Those regulations provide that a partner will be treated as owning the acquired target business assets used in the business of a partnership in satisfaction of the continuity of business enterprise requirement if the members of the qualified group, in the aggregate, own an interest in the partnership representing a significant interest in that partnership business. See §1.368–1(d)(4)(iii)(B)(*1*). Those regulations include an example concluding that the continuity of business enterprise requirement is satisfied where a partner owns a one-third interest in a partnership that continues the business of the target corporation, even though the partner performs no management or operational functions for that business. See §1.368–1(d)(5) *Example 9*.

These proposed regulations yield results similar to the continuity of business enterprise rule in determining whether the active trade or business requirement is satisfied when a corporation conducts a trade or business or portions of a trade or business through a partnership but does not participate in the partnership's activities. Specifically, these proposed regulations provide that for purposes of section 355(b) a partner will be attributed the trade or business assets and activities of a partnership provided the partner owns a significant interest in the partnership. The IRS and Treasury Department intend that the term "significant interest" requires an ownership interest that is greater than that suggested by the term "meaningful interest," which is the level of ownership required for a partner to be attributed the trade or business assets and activities of a partnership in cases where the partner performs active and substantial management functions for the partnership.

However, a partner will be attributed the trade or business assets and activities of a partnership only during the period it owns a significant interest or alternatively owns a meaningful interest and performs active and substantial management functions.

J. *Additional Requests for Comments*

The IRS and Treasury Department request comments regarding whether the regulations should include a rule that would treat an acquisition in which no gain or loss is recognized as an acquisition in which gain or loss is recognized if that would be the treatment had the transaction been executed in the opposite direction. For example, assume that, in year 1, P, a corporation not engaged in an active trade or business, acquires 50 percent of all of the outstanding stock of D (which is engaged in an active trade or business, and owns control of C, which is also engaged in an active trade or business) in a transaction in which gain or loss is recognized, and then, in a separate transaction in year 3, D merges into P solely in exchange for P stock in a transaction described in section 368(a)(1)(A) in which no gain or loss is recognized. P then distributes the C stock to its shareholders in year 4. Under these proposed regulations, P is treated as having acquired D's trade or business and control of C during the pre-distribution period in a transaction in which gain or loss is recognized because P acquired more than 20 percent of D's stock during the pre-distribution period in a transaction in which gain or loss was recognized (see sections D.1.b. and D.2.c. of this preamble). However, if P merges downstream into D solely in exchange for D stock in a reorganization described in section 368(a)(1)(A) and (D) in which no gain or loss is recognized, there literally is not an acquisition in which gain or loss is recognized under these proposed regulations, because D did not acquire any interest in an active trade or business from P. Comments are requested regarding whether the result should differ depending upon the direction of the merger. See and compare §1.355–3(b)(4)(ii) (predecessor of distributing acquiring control of distributing).

Further, the IRS and Treasury Department request comments regarding the appropriate methods of measuring indirect acquisitions of stock for purposes of the rules regarding multi-step acquisitions, as discussed in section D. of this preamble. Specifically, comments are requested regarding how the indirect acquisition should be measured where the acquired corporation has multiple classes of stock outstanding, or where the acquired entity is a partnership. For example, assume T is a corporation that owns all of the stock of a subsidiary, S, and T has class A common stock, class B common stock, and preferred stock outstanding. If D acquires 10 percent of the T class A common stock, how should one determine what percentage of S stock D has indirectly acquired? Should it be based on the value of the T stock D acquired relative to the value of all of the T stock or other factors? How should the voting power of the acquired T stock be taken into account in applying these rules to potential indirect acquisitions of control?

In addition, the IRS and Treasury Department request comments regarding whether the parameters of the good faith and inadvertence exceptions in Notice 2004–37, 2004–1 C.B. 947, regarding the value requirement in section 1504(a)(2)(B) should apply for purposes of determining whether corporations are SAG members even if they are not members of a consolidated group. That is, the IRS and Treasury Department request comments regarding whether the policies underlying the SAG rule and the reference to section 1504(a) in section 355(b)(3)(B) suggest that the good faith and inadvertence exceptions should apply and be interpreted in the same way for SAG membership as for affiliation for purposes of filing consolidated returns.

The IRS and Treasury Department also request comments regarding whether the regulations should clarify the circumstances under which the separation of a segment of an active trade or business should be treated as a separate active trade or business after it is spun off and, if so, what the governing principle should be. See, for example, §1.355–3(c) *Example 9* (separation of a corporation's research department from the rest of its manufacturing business).

Although these regulations are generally proposed to be applicable to distributions that occur after the date these regulations are published as final regulations in the **Federal Register**, the IRS and Treasury Department invite comments regarding whether it would be appropriate and desirable to allow taxpayers to elect to apply these provisions retroactively (subject to the applicability of section 355(b)(3)).

Proposed Effective Date

These proposed regulations are proposed to apply to distributions that occur after the date these regulations are published as final regulations in the **Federal Register**.

Special Analyses

It has been determined that this notice of proposed rulemaking is not a significant regulatory action as defined in Executive Order 12866. Therefore, a regulatory assessment is not required. It has also been determined that section 553(b) of the Administrative Procedure Act (5 U.S.C. chapter 5) does not apply to these regulations, and, because these regulations do not impose a collection of information on small entities, the Regulatory Flexibility Act (5 U.S.C. chapter 6) does not apply. Pursuant to section 7805(f) of the Code, these regulations have been submitted to the Chief Counsel for Advocacy of the Small Business Administration for comment on its impact on small businesses.

Comments and Requests for Public Hearing

Before these proposed regulations are adopted as final regulations, consideration will be given to any written (a signed original and eight (8) copies) or electronic comments that are submitted timely to the IRS. The IRS and Treasury Department request comments on the clarity of the proposed rules and how they can be made easier to understand. All comments will be available for public inspection and copying. A public hearing will be scheduled if requested in writing by any person that timely submits written comments. If a public hearing is scheduled, notice of the date, time, and place for the public hearing will be published in the **Federal Register**.

Drafting Information

The principal author of these proposed regulations is Russell P. Subin of the Office of Associate Chief Counsel (Corporate). However, other personnel from the IRS and Treasury Department participated in their development.

Availability of IRS Documents

IRS revenue rulings, procedures, and notices cited in this preamble are made available by the Superintendent of Documents, U.S. Government Printing Office, Washington, DC 20402.

* * * * *

Proposed Amendments to the Regulations

Accordingly, 26 CFR part 1 is proposed to be amended as follows:

PART 1—INCOME TAXES

Paragraph 1. The authority citation for part 1 continues to read in part as follows:

Authority: 26 U.S.C. 7805 * * *

Par. 2. Section 1.355–0 is amended by revising the entries under §1.355–3.

The revisions are as follows:

§1.355–0 Outline of sections.

* * * * *

§1.355–3 Active conduct of a trade or business.

(a) General requirements.

(b) Active conduct of a trade or business defined.

(1) In general.

(i) Directly engaged in a trade or business.

(ii) Treatment of a separate affiliated group.

(iii) Separate affiliated group defined.

(2) Active conduct of a trade or business immediately after the distribution.

(i) In general.

(ii) Trade or business.

(iii) Active conduct.

(iv) Limitations.

(v) Partner attributed the trade or business assets and activities of a partnership.

(A) In general.

(B) Significant interest.

(C) Meaningful interest.

(D) Other factors.

(3) Active conduct for the pre-distribution period.

(i) In general.

(ii) Change and expansion.

(iii) Certain transactions with partnerships that do not constitute acquisitions.

(4) Special rules for an acquisition of a trade or business.

(i) In general.

(A) Application of section 355(b)(2)(C).

(B) Application of section 355(b)(2)(D).

(C) Gain or loss recognized.

(ii) Certain transactions treated as transactions in which gain or loss is recognized.

(A) Certain tax-free acquisitions made in exchange for assets.

(B) Distributions from partnerships.

(iii) Certain transactions in which recognized gain or loss is disregarded.

(A) Transfers to controlled.

(B) Cash for fractional shares.

(C) Certain acquisitions of control of distributing.

(iv) Operating rules for acquisitions.

(A) Predecessors.

(B) Certain multi-step acquisitions of control of distributing or controlled.

(C) Certain multi-step acquisitions of a subsidiary SAG member.

(D) Certain multi-step asset acquisitions.

(E) Acquisitions involving the issuance of subsidiary stock.

(F) Acquisitions of controlled stock where controlled is or becomes a DSAG member.

(G) Treatment of stock received in certain tax-free exchanges.

(H) Situations where the separate existence of a subsidiary SAG member is respected.

(c) Definitions.

(1) Affiliate.

(2) Controlled.

(3) Distributing.

(4) Pre-distribution period.

(d) Conventions and examples.

(1) Conventions.

(2) Examples.

* * * * *

Par. 3. Section 1.355–1 is amended by revising paragraph (a) to read as follows:

§1.355–1 Distribution of stock and securities of a controlled corporation.

(a) *Effective date of certain sections.* Except as otherwise provided, §§1.355–1, 1.355–2, and 1.355–4 apply to transactions occurring after February 6, 1989. Section 1.355–3 applies to distributions after the date these regulations are published as final regulations in the **Federal Register**. For transactions occurring on or before that date but after February 6, 1989, see 26 CFR 1.355–3 (revised as of April 1, 2007). For all transactions occurring on or before February 6, 1989, see 26 CFR 1.355–1 through 1.355–4 (revised as of April 1, 1987). Sections 1.355–1, 1.355–2, and 1.355–4 do not reflect the amendments to section 355 made by the Revenue Act of 1987 and the Technical and Miscellaneous Revenue Act of 1988. For the effective date of §§1.355–6 and 1.355–7, see §§1.355–6(g) and 1.355–7(k), respectively.

* * * * *

Par. 4. Section 1.355–3 is revised to read as follows:

§1.355–3 Active conduct of a trade or business.

(a) *General requirements.* Under section 355(b)(1), a distribution of stock, or stock and securities, of controlled (as defined in paragraph (c)(2) of this section) qualifies under section 355 only if—

(1) Distributing (as defined in paragraph (c)(3) of this section) and controlled are each engaged in the active conduct of a trade or business immediately after the distribution (section 355(b)(1)(A)); or

(2) Immediately before the distribution, distributing had no assets other than stock or securities of the controlled corporations (without regard to paragraph (b)(1)(ii) of this section), and each of the controlled corporations is engaged in the active conduct of a trade or business immediately after the distribution (section 355(b)(1)(B)). A *de minimis* amount of assets held by distributing shall be disregarded for purposes of this paragraph (a)(2).

(b) *Active conduct of a trade or business defined*—(1) *In general*—(i) *Directly engaged in a trade or business.* Section 355(b)(2) provides rules for determining whether a corporation is treated as engaged in the active conduct of a trade or business under section 355(b)(1). Section 355(b)(2)(A) and (b)(3)(A) provides that a corporation is treated as engaged in the active conduct of a trade or business if and only if such corporation is engaged in the active conduct of a trade or business. Accordingly, except as provided in paragraph (b)(1)(ii) of this section, a corporation is not treated as engaged in the active conduct of a trade or business under such Internal Revenue Code section solely as a result of substantially all of its assets consisting of stock, or stock and securities, of one or more corporations controlled by it (immediately after the distribution) each of which is engaged in the active conduct of a trade or business.

(ii) *Treatment of a separate affiliated group*. Under section 355(b)(3)(B), solely for purposes of determining whether a corporation is engaged in the active conduct of a trade or business, all members of a corporation's separate affiliated group (SAG) (as defined in paragraph (b)(1)(iii) of this section) shall be treated as one corporation. This treatment applies for all purposes of determining whether a corporation is engaged in the active conduct of a trade or business. Accordingly, for this purpose, transfers of assets (or activities) that are owned (or performed) by the SAG immediately before and immediately after the transfer are disregarded and are not acquisitions under paragraph (b)(4) of this section. Further, a transaction that results in a corporation becoming a subsidiary SAG member (a SAG member that is not the common parent of such SAG) is treated as an acquisition of any assets (or activities) that are owned (or performed) by the acquired corporation at such time. Therefore, the acquisition of additional stock of a current subsidiary SAG member has no effect for purposes of applying paragraph (b)(4)(i)(A) of this section.

(iii) *Separate affiliated group defined*. A corporation's SAG is the affiliated group which would be determined under section 1504(a) if such corporation were the common parent and section 1504(b) did not apply. Thus, the separate affiliated group of distributing (DSAG) is the affiliated group that consists of distributing as the common parent and all corporations affiliated with distributing through stock ownership described in section 1504(a)(1)(B) (regardless of whether the corporations are includible corporations under section 1504(b)). The separate affiliated group of controlled (CSAG) is determined in a similar manner (with controlled as the common parent). Accordingly, prior to a distribution, the DSAG may include CSAG members if the applicable ownership requirements are met. Further, the determination of whether a corporation is a DSAG or CSAG member shall be made separately for each distribution, and without regard to whether such corporation is a SAG member with respect to any other distribution. Any reference to DSAG or CSAG is a reference to distributing or controlled, respectively, if such corporation is not the common parent of a SAG (that is, such corporation does not own stock in any corporation that is a subsidiary member of its SAG). Further, any reference to a SAG is a reference to distributing or controlled, as the context may require, if such corporation is not the common parent of a SAG.

(2) *Active conduct of a trade or business immediately after the distribution*—(i) *In general*. For purposes of section 355(b), a corporation shall be treated as engaged in the active conduct of a trade or business immediately after the distribution if the assets and activities of the corporation satisfy the requirements and limitations described in paragraphs (b)(2)(ii), (b)(2)(iii), and (b)(2)(iv) of this section. See paragraph (b)(2)(v) of this section for additional special rules that apply to determine whether a corporation is attributed the trade or business assets and activities of a partnership.

(ii) *Trade or business*. A corporation shall be treated as engaged in a trade or business immediately after the distribution if a specific group of activities is being carried on by the corporation for the purpose of earning income or profit, and the activities included in such group include every operation that forms a part of, or a step in, the process of earning income or profit. Such group of activities ordinarily must include the collection of income and the payment of expenses.

(iii) *Active conduct*. For purposes of section 355(b), the determination of whether a trade or business is actively conducted will be made from all of the facts and circumstances. Generally, the corporation is required itself to perform active and substantial management and operational functions. Activities performed by a corporation include activities performed by employees of an affiliate (as defined in paragraph (c)(1) of this section), and in certain cases by shareholders of a closely held corporation, if such activities are performed for the corporation. For example, activities performed by a corporation include activities performed for the corporation by its sole shareholder. However, the activities of employees of affiliates (or, in certain cases, shareholders) are only taken into account during the period such corporations are affiliates (or persons are shareholders) of the corporation. A corporation will not be treated as engaged in the active conduct of a trade or business unless it (or its SAG, or a partnership from which the trade or business assets and activities are attributed) is the principal owner of the goodwill and significant assets of the trade or business for Federal income tax purposes. Activities performed by a corporation generally do not include activities performed by persons outside the corporation, including independent contractors, unless those activities are performed by employees of an affiliate (or, in certain cases, by shareholders). However, a corporation may satisfy the requirements of this paragraph (b)(2)(iii) through the activities that it performs itself, even though some of its activities are performed by persons that are not its employees, or employees of an affiliate (or, in certain cases, shareholders). Separations of real property all or substantially all of which is occupied before the distribution by the DSAG or CSAG will be carefully scrutinized in applying the requirements of section 355(b) and this section.

(iv) *Limitations*. The active conduct of a trade or business does not include—

(A) The holding for investment purposes of stock, securities, land, or other property; or

(B) The ownership and operation (including leasing) of real or personal property used in a trade or business, unless the owner performs significant services with respect to the operation and management of the property.

(v) *Partner attributed the trade or business assets and activities of a partnership*—(A) *In general*. For purposes of section 355(b), a partner in a partnership will be attributed the trade or business assets and activities of that partnership during the period that such partner satisfies the requirements of paragraph (b)(2)(v)(B) or (b)(2)(v)(C) of this section. However, for purposes of this paragraph (b)(2)(v), the stock of a corporation owned by the partnership is not attributed to a partner. For purposes of determining the activities that are conducted by the partnership that may be attributed to the partner under this paragraph (b)(2)(v), the activities of independent contractors, and partners that are not affiliates (or, in certain cases, shareholders) of the partner, are not taken into account. For this purpose, the activities of partners that are affiliates (or, in certain cases, shareholders) of the partner are only taken into account during the period that such partners are affiliates (or, in certain cases, shareholders) of the partner.

(B) *Significant interest.* The trade or business assets and activities of a partnership will be attributed to a partner if the partner (or its SAG) directly (or indirectly through one or more other partnerships) owns a significant interest in the partnership.

(C) *Meaningful interest.* The trade or business assets and activities of a partnership will be attributed to a partner if the partner or affiliates (or, in certain cases, shareholders) of the partner performs active and substantial management functions for the partnership with respect to the trade or business assets and activities (for example, makes decisions regarding significant business issues of the partnership and regularly participates in the overall supervision, direction, and control of the employees performing the operational functions for the partnership), and the partner (or its SAG) directly (or indirectly through one or more other partnerships) owns a meaningful interest in the partnership. Whether such active and substantial management functions are performed with respect to the trade or business assets and activities of the partnership will be determined from all of the facts and circumstances. The number of partners providing management functions will not be determinative.

(D) *Other factors.* In deciding whether the requirements of paragraph (b)(2)(v)(B) or (b)(2)(v)(C) of this section are satisfied, the formal description of the partnership interest (for example, general or limited) will not be determinative and the extent to which the partner is responsible for liabilities of the partnership will not be relevant.

(3) *Active conduct for the pre-distribution period*—(i) *In general.* Under section 355(b)(2), a trade or business that is relied upon to meet the requirements of section 355(b) must have been actively conducted throughout the pre-distribution period (as defined in paragraph (c)(4) of this section) by the DSAG or CSAG, or actively conducted throughout the pre-distribution period and acquired during such period by the DSAG or CSAG in a transaction in which no gain or loss is recognized as provided in paragraph (b)(4) of this section. For purposes of section 355(b)(2)(B), activities that constitute a trade or business under paragraph (b)(2) of this section shall be treated as described in the preceding sentence if such activities were actively conducted throughout the pre-distribution period.

(ii) *Change and expansion.* The fact that a trade or business underwent change during the pre-distribution period (for example, by the addition of new or the dropping of old products, changes in production capacity, and the like) shall be disregarded, provided that the changes are not of such a character as to constitute the acquisition of a new or different business. In particular, if a SAG engaged in the active conduct of one trade or business during the pre-distribution period (the original business) purchased, created, or otherwise acquired (either directly, through an interest in a partnership, or as a result of a corporation becoming a subsidiary SAG member) another trade or business (the acquired business) in the same line of business, the acquisition of the acquired business is ordinarily treated as an expansion of the original business, all of which is treated as having been actively conducted by the acquiring SAG during the pre-distribution period, unless the acquired business effects a change of such a character as to constitute the acquisition of a new or different business. For purposes of this paragraph (b)(3)(ii), in determining whether an acquired business is in the same line of business as the original business, all facts and circumstances shall be considered, including the following—

(A) Whether the product of the acquired business is similar to that of the original business;

(B) Whether the business activities associated with the operation of the acquired business are the same as the business activities associated with the operation of the original business; and

(C) Whether the operation of the acquired business involves the use of the experience and know-how that the owner of the original business developed in the operation of the original business or, alternatively, whether the operation of the acquired business draws to a significant extent on the existing experience and know-how of the owner of the original business and the success of the acquired business will depend in large measure on the goodwill associated with the original business and the name of the original business.

(iii) *Certain transactions with partnerships that do not constitute acquisitions.* If a partner is attributed the trade or business assets and activities of a partnership under paragraph (b)(2)(v) of this section, the partner's acquisition of such trade or business assets and activities from the partnership is not, in and of itself, the acquisition of a new or different trade or business. In addition, if a partner transfers to a partnership trade or business assets and activities that the partner actively conducted immediately before the transfer and, immediately after the transfer, the partner is attributed the trade or business assets and activities of the partnership under paragraph (b)(2)(v) of this section, such transfer is not, in and of itself, the acquisition of a new or different trade or business by the transferor partner.

(4) *Special rules for an acquisition of a trade or business*—(i) *In general*—(A) *Application of section 355(b)(2)(C).* Under section 355(b)(2)(C) and (b)(3), a trade or business or an interest in a partnership engaged in a trade or business relied on to meet the requirements of section 355(b) must not have been acquired by either the DSAG or CSAG during the pre-distribution period unless it was acquired in a transaction in which no gain or loss was recognized. Further, a trade or business must not have been acquired by either the DSAG or CSAG during the pre-distribution period as a result of a corporation becoming a subsidiary SAG member unless such corporation became a subsidiary SAG member as a result of one or more transactions in which no gain or loss was recognized or by reason of such transactions combined with acquisitions before the pre-distribution period. This paragraph (b)(4)(i)(A) also applies with respect to any acquisition during the pre-distribution period of a trade or business, an interest in a partnership engaged in a trade or business, or stock of a corporation engaged in a trade or business by a corporation that later becomes a subsidiary SAG member. See paragraphs (b)(4)(iv)(C) and (b)(4)(iv)(D) of this section regarding the application

of this paragraph (b)(4)(i)(A) to certain multi-step acquisitions.

(B) *Application of section 355(b)(2)(D).* Under section 355(b)(2)(D), control of distributing must not have been acquired (at the time it was conducting the trade or business to be relied on) directly or indirectly by any distributee corporation, and control of controlled must not have been acquired (at the time it was conducting the trade or business to be relied on) directly or indirectly by the DSAG, during the pre-distribution period in one or more transactions in which gain or loss was recognized. This paragraph (b)(4)(i)(B) also applies with respect to any acquisition of stock of controlled during the pre-distribution period by a corporation that later becomes a DSAG member. For purposes of this paragraph (b)(4)(i)(B), and paragraphs (b)(4)(iii)(C) and (b)(4)(iv)(B) of this section, all distributee corporations that are affiliates shall be treated as one distributee corporation. This paragraph (b)(4)(i)(B) does not apply with respect to an acquisition of stock of any corporation other than distributing or controlled. See paragraph (b)(4)(iv)(B) of this section regarding the application of this paragraph (b)(4)(i)(B) to certain multi-step acquisitions of control. Further, see paragraph (b)(4)(iv)(F) of this section regarding certain acquisitions of stock in controlled to which paragraph (b)(4)(i)(A) of this section (and not this paragraph (b)(4)(i)(B)) applies.

(C) *Gain or loss recognized.* Any reference to gain or loss recognized includes gain or loss treated as recognized under paragraphs (b)(4)(ii) or (b)(4)(iv) of this section.

(ii) *Certain transactions treated as transactions in which gain or loss is recognized.* The common purpose of section 355(b)(2)(C) and (D) is to prevent the direct or indirect acquisition of the trade or business to be relied on by a corporation in exchange for assets in anticipation of a distribution to which section 355 would otherwise apply. Generally, if a DSAG member or controlled acquires the trade or business solely in exchange for distributing stock, distributing acquires control of controlled solely in exchange for distributing stock, or controlled acquires the trade or business from distributing solely in exchange for stock of controlled, in a transaction in which no gain or loss was recognized, the requirements of section 355(b)(2)(C) and (D) are satisfied. On the other hand, if the trade or business is acquired in exchange for assets of distributing (other than stock of a corporation in control of distributing used in a reorganization) the requirements of section 355(b)(2)(C) and (D) are generally not satisfied. For example, acquisitions by controlled (while controlled by distributing) from an unrelated party made in exchange for controlled stock have the effect of an indirect acquisition by distributing in exchange for distributing's assets. Such acquisitions violate the purpose of section 355(b)(2)(C) even if no gain or loss is recognized. Therefore, as provided in paragraphs (b)(4)(ii)(A) and (b)(4)(ii)(B) of this section, if the DSAG or CSAG acquires a trade or business, an interest in a partnership engaged in a trade or business, or stock of a corporation engaged in a trade or business in exchange for assets of the DSAG in a transaction in which no gain or loss is recognized, for purposes of paragraph (b)(4)(i) of this section such acquisition will be treated as one in which gain or loss is recognized.

(A) *Certain tax-free acquisitions made in exchange for assets.* An acquisition paid for in whole or in part, directly or indirectly, with assets of the DSAG will be treated as an acquisition in which gain or loss is recognized even if no gain or loss is actually recognized. Acquisitions described in this paragraph (b)(4)(ii)(A) include for example, a transaction in which the DSAG or CSAG acquires stock of a corporation engaged in the trade or business to be relied on by transferring assets not constituting the trade or business to be relied on to such corporation in exchange for stock of such corporation, the DSAG or CSAG acquires an interest in a partnership engaged in the trade or business to be relied on by contributing assets not constituting the trade or business to be relied on to the partnership, the DSAG or CSAG acquires stock of a corporation engaged in the trade or business in an exchange to which section 304(a)(1) applies, or distributing acquires a trade or business in exchange for its stock and assets in a transaction in which no loss is recognized by virtue of section 351(b). See also paragraph (b)(4)(iv)(E) of this section regarding the extent to which an acquisition involving the issuance of subsidiary stock constitutes an acquisition paid for with assets. However, the assumption by the DSAG or CSAG of liabilities of a transferor shall not, in and of itself, be treated as the payment of assets if such assumption is not treated as the payment of money or other property under any other applicable provision. In addition, an acquisition in which no gain or loss is recognized consisting of a *pro rata* distribution to which section 355 applies (to the extent the stock with respect to which the distribution is made was not acquired during the pre-distribution period in a transaction in which gain or loss was recognized), a distribution from a partnership that is explicitly excluded from paragraph (b)(4)(ii)(B) of this section, a reorganization described in section 368(a)(1)(E) or (F), and an exchange to which section 1036 applies, are not acquisitions described in this paragraph (b)(4)(ii)(A).

(B) *Distributions from partnerships.* An acquisition consisting of a distribution from a partnership is generally an acquisition paid for with assets of the DSAG, and will be treated as an acquisition in which gain or loss is recognized even if no gain or loss is actually recognized. However, an acquisition consisting of a *pro rata* distribution from a partnership of stock or an interest in lower-tier partnership is not an acquisition described in this paragraph (b)(4)(ii)(B) (and consequently not described in paragraph (b)(4)(ii)(A) of this section) to the extent the distributee partner did not acquire the interest in the distributing partnership during the pre-distribution period in a transaction in which gain or loss was recognized and to the extent the distributing partnership did not acquire the distributed stock or partnership interest within such period. This paragraph (b)(4)(ii)(B) (and consequently paragraph (b)(4)(ii)(A) of this section) does not apply to any partnership distribution to which paragraph (b)(3)(iii) of this section (regarding distributions from partnerships that are not, in and of themselves, the acquisition of a new or different trade or business) applies.

(iii) *Certain transactions in which recognized gain or loss is disregarded.* The common purpose of section 355(b)(2)(C) and (D) is to prevent the direct or indirect acquisition of the trade or business to be relied on by a corporation in exchange for assets in anticipation of a distribution to which section 355 would otherwise apply. An additional purpose of section 355(b)(2)(D) is to prevent a distributee corporation from acquiring control of distributing in anticipation of a distribution to which section 355 would otherwise apply, enabling the disposition of controlled stock without recognizing the appropriate amount of gain. The acquisitions described in paragraphs (b)(4)(iii)(A) through (b)(4)(iii)(C) of this section are not the types of acquisitions to which section 355(b)(2)(C) or (D) is intended to apply. Therefore, for purposes of paragraph (b)(4)(i) of this section, the recognition of gain or loss is disregarded if a trade or business, an interest in a partnership engaged in a trade or business, or stock of a corporation engaged in a trade or business is acquired in a transaction described in any of paragraphs (b)(4)(iii)(A) through (b)(4)(iii)(C) of this section.

(A) *Transfers to controlled.* An acquisition by the CSAG from the DSAG provided the DSAG controls controlled immediately after the acquisition.

(B) *Cash for fractional shares.* An acquisition that would satisfy the requirements of paragraph (b)(4)(i) of this section but for the payment of cash to shareholders for fractional shares in the transaction, provided that the cash paid represents a mere rounding off of the fractional shares in the exchange and is not separately bargained for consideration.

(C) *Certain acquisitions of control of distributing.* A direct or indirect acquisition by a distributee corporation of control of distributing, in one or more transactions, where the basis of the acquired distributing stock in the hands of the distributee corporation is determined in whole by reference to the transferor's basis. This paragraph (b)(4)(iii)(C) is only applicable with respect to a distribution by the acquired distributing, and does not apply for purposes of any subsequent distribution by any distributee corporation.

(iv) *Operating rules for acquisitions*—(A) *Predecessors.* References to a corporation shall include references to a predecessor of such corporation. For this purpose, a predecessor of a corporation is a corporation that transfers its assets to such corporation in a transaction to which section 381 applies.

(B) *Certain multi-step acquisitions of control of distributing or controlled.* A distributee corporation's acquisition of stock in distributing or a DSAG's acquisition of stock in controlled in one or more transactions in which gain or loss was recognized during the pre-distribution period will not prevent a distributee corporation's acquisition of distributing stock or a DSAG's acquisition of controlled stock constituting control of distributing or controlled in one or more separate transactions in which no gain or loss is recognized from satisfying the requirements of paragraph (b)(4)(i)(B) of this section, provided that, at the time control of distributing or controlled is first acquired, the acquiring distributee corporation owns an amount of distributing stock or the acquiring DSAG owns an amount of controlled stock, as the case may be, constituting control that was acquired in one or more transactions in which no gain or loss was recognized or by reason of such transactions combined with acquisitions before the pre-distribution period. The principles of this paragraph (b)(4)(iv)(B) will be applied with respect to an indirect acquisition of distributing or controlled stock.

(C) *Certain multi-step acquisitions of a subsidiary SAG member.* An acquisition of stock in a corporation (target) by a SAG in one or more transactions in which gain or loss was recognized during the pre-distribution period will not prevent a SAG's acquisition of target stock resulting in target becoming a subsidiary SAG member in one or more separate transactions in which no gain or loss is recognized from satisfying the requirements of paragraph (b)(4)(i)(A) of this section, provided that, at the time that target first becomes a subsidiary SAG member, the SAG owns an amount of target stock meeting the requirements of section 1504(a)(2) that was acquired in one or more transactions in which no gain or loss was recognized or by reason of such transactions combined with acquisitions before the pre-distribution period. The principles of this paragraph (b)(4)(iv)(C) will be applied with respect to an indirect acquisition of target stock by the SAG.

(D) *Certain multi-step asset acquisitions.* Notwithstanding paragraph (b)(4)(i)(A) of this section, if immediately before a SAG's direct acquisition of a trade or business (or an interest in a partnership engaged in a trade or business) held by a corporation (owner) in a transaction to which section 381 applies and in which no gain or loss is recognized, the SAG owns an amount of stock of the owner that it acquired in one or more transactions during the pre-distribution period in which gain or loss was recognized such that all of the other stock of the owner does not meet the requirements of section 1504(a)(2), such direct acquisition shall be treated as a transaction in which gain or loss was recognized. The principles of this paragraph (b)(4)(iv)(D) will be applied with respect to an indirect acquisition of the owner stock by the SAG.

(E) *Acquisitions involving the issuance of subsidiary stock.* If a SAG directly or indirectly owns stock of a subsidiary (including a subsidiary SAG member) and the subsidiary directly or indirectly acquires a trade or business, an interest in a partnership engaged in a trade or business, or stock of a corporation engaged in a trade or business from a person other than such SAG in exchange for stock of such subsidiary in a transaction in which no gain or loss is recognized (the acquisition), solely for purposes of applying this paragraph (b)(4) with respect to the trade or business, partnership interest, or stock acquired by the subsidiary in the acquisition, the subsidiary's stock directly or indirectly owned by the SAG immediately after the acquisition is treated as acquired at the time of the acquisition in a transaction in which gain or loss is recognized.

(F) *Acquisitions of controlled stock where controlled is or becomes a DSAG member.* With respect to an acquisition of stock in controlled, if controlled is or becomes a DSAG member, paragraph (b)(4)(i)(A) of this section applies and paragraph (b)(4)(i)(B) of this section does not apply for purposes of determining whether the requirements of section 355(b) are satisfied with respect to controlled.

(G) *Treatment of stock received in certain tax-free exchanges.* Any stock received in a reorganization described in section 368(a)(1)(E) or (F), or in an exchange to which section 1036 applies, in which no gain or loss is recognized is treated as acquired in the same manner as the stock surrendered.

(H) *Situations where the separate existence of a subsidiary SAG member is respected.* The separate existence of a subsidiary SAG member will be respected for purposes of determining whether a transaction qualifies for nonrecognition treatment under other provisions of the Internal Revenue Code. For example, for purposes of determining whether section 351 applies or whether the transaction qualifies as a reorganization described in section 368(a), the separate existence of the subsidiary SAG member is respected.

(c) *Definitions*. For purposes of this section the following definitions apply:

(1) *Affiliate*. An affiliate is any member of an affiliated group as defined in section 1504(a) (without regard to section 1504(b)).

(2) *Controlled*. *Controlled* is the controlled corporation.

(3) *Distributing*. *Distributing* is the distributing corporation.

(4) *Pre-distribution period*. The *pre-distribution period* is the five-year period ending on the date of the distribution.

(d) *Conventions and examples*—(1) *Conventions*. The examples in paragraph (d)(2) of this section illustrate section 355(b) and this section. No inference should be drawn from any of these examples as to whether any requirements of section 355 other than those of section 355(b), as specified, are satisfied. Throughout these examples, C, D, D2, P, S, S1, S2, S3, T, X, Y, and Z are corporations, and Partnership is an entity that is treated as a partnership for Federal income tax purposes under §301.7701–3 of this chapter. Further, assume any transfer described in *Examples 1* through *25* that is not identified as a purchase (defined in paragraph (d)(1)(iii) of this section) satisfies all the requirements of paragraph (b)(4) of this section as a transaction in which no gain or loss is recognized. Except as otherwise provided, for more than five years D has owned section 368(c) stock (as defined in paragraph (d)(1)(iv) of this section) but not section 1504(a)(2) stock (as defined in paragraph (d)(1)(v) of this section) of C. Furthermore, the following definitions apply:

(i) *ATB*. *ATB* is any active trade or business. ATB1 and ATB2 are not in the same line of business under paragraph (b)(3)(ii) of this section.

(ii) *New subsidiary*. A *new subsidiary* is a newly formed wholly owned corporation.

(iii) *Purchase*. A *purchase* is an acquisition for cash.

(iv) *Section 368(c) stock*. *Section 368(c) stock* is stock constituting control within the meaning of section 368(c).

(v) *Section 1504(a)(2) stock*. *Section 1504(a)(2) stock* is stock meeting the requirements of section 1504(a)(2).

(2) *Examples*. Generally, *Examples 1* and *2* illustrate the general requirements in paragraph (a) of this section, *Examples 3* through *9* illustrate the SAG rules in paragraphs (b)(1)(ii) and (b)(1)(iii) of this section, *Examples 10* through *25* illustrate the rules regarding the active trade or business and active conduct for the pre-distribution period in paragraphs (b)(2) and (b)(3) of this section, *Examples 26* through *40* illustrate the acquisition rules in paragraphs (b)(4)(i) through (b)(4)(iii) of this section, and *Examples 41* through *51* illustrate the operating rules for acquisitions in paragraph (b)(4)(iv) of this section. The examples are as follows:

Example 1. Spin-off. For more than five years, D and C have engaged in the active conduct of ATB1 and ATB2, respectively. D distributes the C stock to the D shareholders, and each corporation continues the active conduct of its respective trade or business. Because both D and C are engaged in the active conduct of a trade or business immediately after the distribution and such trades or businesses have been actively conducted by such corporations throughout the pre-distribution period, the requirements of section 355(b) have been satisfied. See paragraphs (a)(1) and (b)(3) of this section.

Example 2. Split-up. The facts are the same as *Example 1* except that D transfers all of its assets (including ATB1) other than the C stock to new subsidiary S, and then distributes the C stock and S stock to the D shareholders. Because C and S are respectively engaged in the active conduct of ATB2 and ATB1 immediately after the distribution, ATB2 has been actively conducted by C throughout the pre-distribution period, and together D (prior to the transfer to S) and S (after the transfer to S) have actively conducted ATB1 throughout the pre-distribution period, the requirements of section 355(b) have been satisfied. See paragraphs (a)(2) and (b)(3) of this section.

Example 3. Subsidiary SAG member's business. For more than five years, D has owned section 1504(a)(2) stock but not section 368(c) stock of S. Throughout this period, C and S have engaged in the active conduct of ATB1 and ATB2, respectively. In year 8, D distributes the C stock to the D shareholders. Because D owns section 1504(a)(2) stock of S, S is a DSAG member. See paragraph (b)(1)(iii) of this section. D and S are treated as one corporation for purposes of determining whether D is engaged in an active trade or business. See paragraph (b)(1)(ii) of this section. Therefore, D is engaged in the active conduct of ATB2 both throughout the pre-distribution period and immediately after the distribution. Accordingly, D and C both satisfy the requirements of section 355(b).

Example 4. Additional subsidiary SAG member shares acquired. The facts are the same as *Example 3* except that in year 6, D acquires the remaining S stock. D's acquisition of the remaining S stock in year 6 has no effect for purposes of determining whether D satisfies the requirements of section 355(b)(2)(C) because the DSAG is already engaged in the active conduct of ATB2. See paragraph (b)(1)(ii) of this section. Section 355(b)(2)(D) does not apply to D's acquisition of S stock. See paragraph (b)(4)(i)(B) of this section. Accordingly, D and C both satisfy the requirements of section 355(b).

Example 5. Segmented CSAG business. For more than five years, C has owned all the stock of S1, S2, and S3. Throughout this period, D has engaged in the active conduct of ATB1. Throughout this same period, S1, S2, and S3 have each engaged in a different essential segment of ATB2. While the three segments of ATB2 would together constitute the active conduct of a trade or business, none of S1, S2, or S3 would be considered engaged in the active conduct of an ATB individually. In year 6, D distributes the C stock to the D shareholders. C owns section 1504(a)(2) stock of S1, S2, and S3, therefore, C, S1, S2, and S3 are CSAG members. See paragraph (b)(1)(iii) of this section. C, S1, S2, and S3 are treated as one corporation for purposes of determining whether C is engaged in the active conduct of a trade or business. See paragraph (b)(1)(ii) of this section. Therefore, C is engaged in the active conduct of ATB2 both throughout the pre-distribution period and immediately after the distribution. Accordingly, D and C both satisfy the requirements of section 355(b).

Example 6. Segmented DSAG business. The facts are the same as *Example 5* except that D owns all of the C stock and all of the S3 stock, and D transfers the S3 stock to C immediately prior to the distribution. Prior to D's transfer of the S3 stock to C, D owns section 1504(a)(2) stock of S3 and C, and C owns section 1504(a)(2) stock of S1 and S2, therefore, D, C, S1, S2, and S3 are DSAG members. See paragraph (b)(1)(iii) of this section. D, C, S1, S2, and S3 are treated as one corporation for purposes of determining whether D and C are engaged in the active conduct of a trade or business, and accordingly the transfer of the S3 stock to C is disregarded. See paragraph (b)(1)(ii) of this section. After the transfer, C owns section 1504(a)(2) stock of S3, and the CSAG includes C, S1, S2, and S3. See paragraph (b)(1)(iii) of this section. C, S1, S2, and S3 are treated as one corporation for purposes of determining whether C is engaged in the active conduct of a trade or business. See paragraph (b)(1)(ii) of this section. Throughout the pre-distribution period, D, C, S1, S2, and S3 are treated as one corporation and both D and C are engaged in the active conduct of ATB1 and ATB2. See paragraphs (b)(1) and (b)(2) of this section. Immediately after the distribution, D is engaged in the active conduct of ATB1 and C is engaged in the active conduct of ATB2. Because D and C were engaged in the active conduct of ATB1 and ATB2 throughout the pre-distribution period and, immediately after the distribution, D is engaged in the active conduct of ATB1 and C is engaged in the active conduct of ATB2, D and C both satisfy the requirements of section 355(b).

Example 7. Failed segmented business. The facts are the same as *Example 6* except that D owns section 368(c) stock but not section 1504(a)(2) stock of C. Prior to D's transfer of the S3 stock, the DSAG includes only D and S3, and the CSAG includes only

C, S1, and S2. See paragraph (b)(1)(iii) of this section. Therefore, prior to the transfer of the S3 stock, ATB2 does not exist because no one SAG conducts all three of the essential segments of the trade or business. Accordingly, C does not satisfy the requirements of section 355(b) because ATB2 was not actively conducted throughout the pre-distribution period. See paragraph (b)(3)(i) of this section.

Example 8. Jointly owned partnership. For more than five years, D has owned all of the stock of C, and D and C each have owned a 17-percent interest in Partnership. Throughout this period, D and Partnership have engaged in the active conduct of ATB1 and ATB2, respectively. In year 6, D transfers its 17-percent interest in Partnership to C and distributes all of the C stock to the D shareholders. Because D owns section 1504(a)(2) stock of C, C is a DSAG member. See paragraph (b)(1)(iii) of this section. D and C are treated as one corporation for purposes of determining whether D and C are engaged in the active conduct of a trade or business. See paragraph (b)(1)(ii) of this section. Accordingly, throughout the pre-distribution period, D and C are each treated as owning a 34-percent interest in Partnership. As such, both D and C are treated as engaged in the active conduct of both ATB1 and ATB2 throughout the pre-distribution period. See paragraphs (b)(2)(v)(A) and (b)(2)(v)(B) of this section. The transfer of the Partnership interest is disregarded because it is between SAG members. See paragraph (b)(1)(ii) of this section. After the distribution, C owns 34 percent of Partnership and is therefore engaged in the active conduct of ATB2. See paragraphs (b)(2)(v)(A) and (b)(2)(v)(B) of this section. Therefore, D and C both satisfy the requirements of section 355(b).

Example 9. Sequential application of the SAG rule—(i) *Facts.* For more than five years, D2 has owned all of the stock of D, and D has owned all of the stock of C. Throughout this period, D2 has engaged in the active conduct of ATB1 and ATB2, and D has engaged in the active conduct of ATB1. C, individually, has not engaged in the active conduct of any ATB. In year 6, D distributes all of the C stock to D2 (first distribution). Immediately thereafter, D2 transfers ATB2 to C and distributes all of the C stock to the D2 shareholders (second distribution).

(ii) *Analysis—first distribution.* Because D owns section 1504(a)(2) stock of C, C is a DSAG member prior to the first distribution. See paragraph (b)(1)(iii) of this section. D and C are treated as one corporation for purposes of determining whether D and C are engaged in the active conduct of a trade or business with respect to the first distribution. See paragraphs (b)(1)(ii) and (b)(1)(iii) of this section. Accordingly, throughout the pre-distribution period, D and C are each treated as engaged in ATB1 with respect to the first distribution. However, for purposes of determining whether D's distribution of the C stock to D2 satisfies the requirements of section 355(b) immediately after the first distribution, C is the only CSAG member (D2 is not a member of any SAG with respect to the first distribution). See paragraph (b)(1)(iii) of this section. Accordingly, C does not satisfy the requirements of section 355(b) with respect to the first distribution because C is not engaged in the active conduct of an ATB immediately after the first distribution.

(iii) *Analysis — second distribution.* Because D2 owns section 1504(a)(2) stock of D and C (and D owned section 1504(a)(2) stock of C before the first distribution), D2, D, and C are D2 SAG members throughout the pre-distribution period with respect to the second distribution. See paragraph (b)(1)(iii) of this section. Further, for purposes of the second distribution D's distribution of the C stock to D2 is disregarded because it is between D2 SAG members. See paragraphs (b)(1)(ii) and (b)(1)(iii) of this section. D2, D, and C are treated as one corporation for purposes of determining whether D2 and C are engaged in the active conduct of a trade or business with respect to the second distribution. See paragraphs (b)(1)(ii) and (b)(1)(iii) of this section. Accordingly, throughout the pre-distribution period, D2 and C are each treated as engaged in the active conduct of ATB1 and ATB2 with respect to the second distribution. The transfer of ATB2 to C is disregarded because it is between D2 SAG members. See paragraph (b)(1)(ii) of this section. Immediately after the second distribution, C is engaged in the active conduct of ATB2. Therefore, D2 and C both satisfy the requirements of section 355(b) with respect to the second distribution.

Example 10. Limitations — securities and vacant land. For more than five years, D has owned investment securities and vacant land. D has conducted no activities with respect to the vacant land, but D will subsequently subdivide the vacant land, install streets and utilities, and sell the developed lots to various homebuilders. D cannot currently satisfy the requirements of section 355(b) because the holding of investment securities does not constitute the active conduct of a trade or business. See paragraph (b)(2)(iv)(A) of this section. Furthermore, no significant development activities have been conducted with respect to the vacant land. See paragraph (b)(3) of this section.

Example 11. Limitations — occupied real estate — active. For more than five years, D, a bank, has owned an eleven-story office building, the ground floor of which D has occupied while engaged in the active conduct of its banking business. The remaining ten floors are rented to various tenants. Throughout this period, the building has been managed, operated, repaired, and maintained by employees of D. D transfers the building along with the significant assets used to operate the building and the goodwill associated with the building to new subsidiary C and distributes the C stock to the D shareholders. Henceforth, C's employees will manage, operate, repair, and maintain the building. D and C both satisfy the requirements of section 355(b). See paragraph (b)(3) of this section.

Example 12. Limitations — occupied real estate — not active. For more than five years, D, a bank, has owned a two-story building, the ground floor and one half of the second floor of which D has occupied while engaged in the active conduct of its banking business. The other half of the second floor has been rented as storage space to a neighboring retail merchant. D transfers the building and the goodwill associated with the building to new subsidiary C and distributes the C stock to the D shareholders. After the distribution, D leases from C the space in the building that it formerly occupied. Under the lease, D will repair and maintain its portion of the building and pay property taxes and insurance. C does not satisfy the requirements of section 355(b) because it is not engaged in the active conduct of a trade or business immediately after the distribution. See paragraph (b)(2)(iv)(A) of this section. This example does not address the question of whether the activities of D with respect to the building prior to the separation would constitute the active conduct of a trade or business.

Example 13. No significant activities. For more than five years, D owned land on which it has engaged in the active conduct of the ranching business. Oil has been discovered in the area, and it is apparent that oil may be found under the land on which the ranching business is conducted. D has engaged in no significant activities in connection with its mineral rights. D transfers its mineral rights to new subsidiary C and distributes the C stock to the D shareholders. C will actively pursue the development of the oil producing potential of the property. C does not satisfy the requirements of section 355(b) after the distribution because D was not engaged in significant exploitation activities with respect to the mineral rights throughout the pre-distribution period. See paragraph (b)(3) of this section.

Example 14. Vertical division — state contracts. For more than five years, D has engaged in the active conduct of a single business of constructing sewage disposal plants and other facilities. D transfers one half of its assets to new subsidiary C. These assets include a contract for the construction of a sewage disposal plant in State M, construction equipment, cash, goodwill, and other tangible and significant assets. D retains a contract for the construction of a sewage disposal plant in State N, construction equipment, cash, goodwill, and other tangible and significant assets. D distributes the C stock to one of D's shareholders in exchange for all of his D stock. D and C both satisfy the requirements of section 355(b). See paragraphs (b)(2) and (b)(3)(i) of this section.

Example 15. Vertical division — location. For more than five years, D has engaged in the active conduct of owning and operating two men's retail clothing stores, one in the downtown area of the City of G and one in a suburban area of G. D transfers the store building, fixtures, inventory, and other significant assets related to the operations of the suburban store and the goodwill attributable to that store to new subsidiary C. D also transfers to C the delivery trucks and delivery personnel that formerly served both stores. Henceforth, D will contract with a local public delivery service to make its deliveries. D retains the warehouses that formerly served both stores. Henceforth, C will lease warehouse space from an unrelated public warehouse company. D then distributes the C stock to the D shareholders. D and C both satisfy the requirements of section 355(b). See paragraphs (b)(2) and (b)(3)(i) of this section.

Example 16. Horizontal division — research. For more than five years, D has engaged in the active conduct of manufacturing and sale of household products. Throughout this period, D has maintained a research department for use in connection with its manufacturing activities. The research department has 30 employees actively engaged in the development of new products. D transfers the research department (which has significant assets and goodwill) to new subsidiary C and distributes the C stock to the D shareholders. After the distribution, C continues its research operations on a contractual basis with several corporations, including D. D and C both satisfy the requirements of section 355(b). See paragraphs (b)(2) and (b)(3)(i) of this section. The result is the same if, after the distribution, C continues its research operations but furnishes its services only to D. See paragraphs (b)(2) and (b)(3)(i) of this section. However, see §1.355–2(d)(2)(iv)(C) (related function device factor) for possible evidence of device.

Example 17. Horizontal division — sales. For more than five years, D has engaged in the active conduct of processing and selling meat products. D derives income from no other source. D separates the sales function from the processing function by transferring the significant business assets related to the sales function, the goodwill associated with the sales function, and cash for working capital to new subsidiary C. D then distributes the C stock to the D shareholders. After the distribution, C purchases for resale the meat products processed by D. D and C both satisfy the requirements of section 355(b). See paragraphs (b)(2) and (b)(3)(i) of this section. However, see §1.355–2(d)(2)(iv)(C) (related function device factor) for possible evidence of device.

Example 18. Expansion and vertical division — location. For more than five years, D has engaged in the active conduct of owning and operating hardware stores in several states. In year 6, D purchased all of the assets of a hardware store in State M, where D had not previously conducted business. In year 8, D transfers the State M hardware store and related significant assets and goodwill to new subsidiary C and distributes the C stock to the D shareholders. After the distribution, the State M hardware store has its own manager and is operated independently of the other stores. Because —

(i) The product of the State M hardware store is similar to the product of D's hardware stores in the other states;

(ii) The business activities associated with the operation of the State M hardware store are the same as the business activities associated with the operation of D's hardware stores in the other states; and

(iii) The operation of a hardware store in State M involves the use of the experience and know-how that D developed in the operation of the hardware stores in the other states, the hardware store in State M is in the same line of business as the hardware stores in the other states. Therefore, the acquisition of the State M hardware store constitutes an expansion of D's existing business and its acquisition does not constitute the acquisition of a new or different business under paragraph (b)(3)(ii) of this section. Accordingly, D and C both satisfy the requirements of section 355(b).

Example 19. Expansion and horizontal division — Internet. For more than five years, D has engaged in the active conduct of operating a retail shoe store business, under the name D. Throughout this period, D's sales are made exclusively to customers who frequent its retail stores in shopping malls and other locations. D's business enjoys favorable name recognition, customer loyalty, and other elements of goodwill in the retail shoe market. D creates an Internet web site and begins selling shoes at retail on the web site. To a significant extent, the operation of the web site draws upon D's existing experience and know-how. The web site is named "D.com" to take advantage of the name recognition, customer loyalty, and other elements of goodwill associated with D and the D name and to enhance the web site's chances for success in its initial stages. Eight months after beginning to sell shoes on the web site, D transfers all of the web site's assets and liabilities (all of which include the significant assets and goodwill associated with the web site's business) to new subsidiary C and distributes the C stock to the D shareholders. The product of the retail shoe store business and the product of the web site are the same (shoes), and the principal business activities of the retail shoe store business are the same as those of the web site (purchasing shoes at wholesale and reselling them at retail). Although selling shoes on a web site requires some know-how not associated with operating a retail store, such as familiarity with different marketing approaches, distribution chains, and technical operations issues, the web site's operation does draw to a significant extent on D's existing experience and know-how, and the web site's success will depend in large measure on the goodwill associated with D and the D name. Therefore, the creation by D of the Internet web site does not constitute the acquisition of a new or different business under paragraph (b)(3)(ii) of this section. Accordingly, it is an expansion of D's retail shoe store business, all of which is treated as having been actively conducted throughout the pre-distribution period. Therefore, D and C both satisfy the requirements of section 355(b).

Example 20. Expansion — acquiring a SAG member. For more than five years, D has owned all of the stock of C. Throughout this period, C and unrelated T have engaged in the active conduct of ATB1. In year 6, D purchases all of the T stock. In year 8, D distributes all of the C stock to the D shareholders. Throughout the period that C is a DSAG member, D is engaged in the active conduct of ATB1. See paragraph (b)(1)(ii) of this section. Moreover, because D acquired section 1504(a)(2) stock of T, D is treated as having acquired T's assets (and activities), and that acquisition constitutes an expansion of ATB1. See paragraphs (b)(1)(ii) and (b)(3)(ii) of this section. Therefore, D and C both satisfy the requirements of section 355(b). The result would be the same if D had owned all of the T stock for more than five years, and purchased all of the C stock in year 6. See paragraphs (b)(1)(ii), (b)(3)(ii), (b)(4)(i), and (b)(4)(iv)(F) of this section.

Example 21. No expansion — acquiring only control of controlled. For more than five years, D and unrelated C have engaged in the active conduct of ATB1. In year 6, D purchases section 368(c) stock but not section 1504(a)(2) stock of C. In year 8, D distributes the C stock to the D shareholders. While D and C are in the same line of business, the acquisition does not result in an expansion of D's business under paragraph (b)(3)(ii) of this section because D is not treated as having acquired C's assets (and activities). Accordingly, D has acquired control of C in violation of section 355(b)(2)(D). See paragraph (b)(4)(i)(B) of this section. However, if D acquires additional C stock thereby causing C to become a DSAG member, D would be treated as having acquired C's assets (and activities) and the acquisition would constitute an expansion of ATB1. See paragraphs (b)(1)(ii), (b)(3)(ii), (b)(4)(i), and (b)(4)(iv)(F) of this section. In such a case, D and C both would satisfy the requirements of section 355(b).

Example 22. Partnership — meaningful but not significant. For more than five years, unrelated X and Y have owned a 20-percent and 33 1/3-percent interest, respectively, in Partnership. The remaining interests in Partnership are owned by unrelated parties. For more than five years, Partnership has manufactured power equipment. But for the performance of all its management functions by employees of X, Partnership would satisfy all the requirements of paragraph (b)(2)(i) of this section. X and/or Y will be attributed the trade or business assets and activities of Partnership only if the corporation satisfies the requirements of paragraph (b)(2)(v)(B) or (b)(2)(v)(C) of this section. See paragraph (b)(2)(v)(A) of this section. While X does not satisfy the requirements of paragraph (b)(2)(v)(B) of this section because X's interest in Partnership is not significant, under paragraph (b)(2)(v)(C) of this section, X owns a meaningful interest in Partnership and performs active and substantial management functions for the trade or business assets and activities of Partnership. Therefore, X is attributed the trade or business assets and activities of Partnership. Accordingly, X is engaged in the active conduct of the business of manufacturing power equipment. See paragraph (b)(2) of this section. In determining whether Y is engaged in the business of manufacturing power equipment, the management functions performed by X for Partnership are not taken into account. See paragraph (b)(2)(v)(A) of this section. Therefore, although Y is attributed Partnership's trade or business assets and activities under paragraph (b)(2)(v)(B) of this section because Y owns a significant interest in Partnership, Y is not engaged in the business of manufacturing power equipment because neither Y nor Partnership perform any management functions for the business. See paragraph (b)(2)(iii) of this section.

Example 23. Partnership — significant but not meaningful. The facts are the same as *Example 22* except that all the management functions related to the business of Partnership are performed by employees of Partnership. Because employees of Partnership perform all of the management functions related to the trade or business assets and activities of manufacturing power equipment, Partnership itself satisfies all the requirements of paragraph (b)(2)(i) of this section. X neither owns a significant interest in Partnership nor performs active and substantial management functions with respect to the trade or business assets and activities of Partnership. Accordingly, X does not satisfy the requirements of paragraph (b)(2)(v)(B) or (b)(2)(v)(C) of this section, X is not attributed the trade or business assets and activities of Partnership's business of manufacturing power equipment, and X is not engaged in the active conduct of the business of manufacturing power equipment. On the other hand, because Y owns a significant interest in Partnership, Y satisfies the requirements of paragraph (b)(2)(v)(B) of this section. Therefore, Y is attributed the trade or business assets and activities of Partnership's business. Accordingly, Y satisfies the requirements of paragraph (b)(2)(i) of this section and is engaged in the active conduct of the business of manufacturing power equipment.

Example 24. Partnership — significant by many. The facts are the same as *Example 23* except that X, Y, and Z each own a 33 1/3-percent interest in Partnership. Because X, Y, and Z each own a significant interest in Partnership, each of X, Y, and Z satisfies the requirements of paragraph (b)(2)(v)(B) of this section. Accordingly, each of X, Y, and Z is attributed the trade or business assets and activities of Partnership, satisfies the requirements of paragraph (b)(2)(i) of this section, and is engaged in the active conduct of the business of manufacturing power equipment.

Example 25. Non-SAG affiliates—(i) *Facts.* For more than five years, X has owned 10 percent of the stock of D2, D2 has owned all the stock of D and S, and D has owned all the stock of C. Throughout this period, D has manufactured furniture that it sells to furniture stores and has been the principal owner of the goodwill and significant assets associated with that business and C has owned and operated a laundry business and has been the principal owner of the goodwill and significant assets associated with that business. Throughout this period, however, employees of S have performed all the active and substantial management and operational functions of the furniture business for D and the laundry business for C. D distributes the C stock to D2 (first distribution) and D2 distributes the C stock to X in exchange for all of X's D2 stock (second distribution). After the distributions, employees of X perform all the active and substantial management and operational functions of the laundry business for C that the employees of S performed before the distributions and the employees of S continue to perform the same activities for D as they did before the distributions.

(ii) *Analysis — first distribution.* In determining whether the furniture manufacturing business and laundry business have been actively conducted throughout the pre-distribution period and immediately after the first distribution, the activities performed for those businesses include activities performed by employees of affiliates of D and C (even if they are not DSAG or CSAG members). Accordingly, such activities include the activities performed by the employees of S for D and C. See paragraph (b)(2)(iii) of this section. D and C own the goodwill and significant assets associated with their respective businesses both throughout the pre-distribution period and immediately after the first distribution, and are treated as performing active and substantial management and operational functions for their respective businesses both throughout the pre-distribution period and immediately after the first distribution. Therefore, D and C both satisfy the requirements of section 355(b) with respect to the first distribution.

(iii) *Analysis — second distribution.* Because D2 owns section 1504(a)(2) stock of D, C, and S (and D owned section 1504(a)(2) stock of C before the first distribution), D2, D, C, and S are D2 SAG members throughout the pre-distribution period with respect to the second distribution. See paragraph (b)(1)(iii) of this section. Accordingly, D2, D, C, and S are treated as one corporation for purposes of determining whether D2 is engaged in an active trade or business with respect to the second distribution. See paragraph (b)(1)(ii) of this section. Accordingly, for purposes of the second distribution, D2 has been engaged in the furniture manufacturing business and the laundry business throughout the pre-distribution period. Further, for purposes of the second distribution D's distribution of the C stock to D2 is disregarded because it is between D2 SAG members. See paragraph (b)(1)(ii) of this section. D and S continue to be D2 SAG members immediately after the second distribution. See paragraph (b)(1)(iii) of this section. Accordingly, D2 is engaged in the furniture manufacturing business immediately after the second distribution. In determining whether C is engaged in the active conduct of a trade or business immediately after the second distribution, the activities performed for the laundry business include activities performed by employees of affiliates of C (even if they are not CSAG members). Accordingly, immediately after the second distribution, such activities include the activities performed for C by the employees of X. See paragraph (b)(2)(iii) of this section. C owns the goodwill and significant assets associated with the laundry business both throughout the pre-distribution period and immediately after the second distribution, and is treated as performing active and substantial management and operational functions both throughout the pre-distribution period and immediately after the second distribution. Therefore, D2 and C both satisfy the requirements of section 355(b) with respect to the second distribution.

Example 26. Purchased ATB and SAG member. For more than five years, P has owned all of the stock of D and S1, and D and S1 have owned all of the stock of S2 and S3, respectively. Throughout this period, S1 and S3 have engaged in the active conduct of ATB1 and ATB2, respectively. In year 6, S2 purchases ATB1 and all of the S3 stock from S1 on the same day. In year 6, the DSAG acquired ATB1 and ATB2 (as a result of S3 becoming a DSAG member) in a transaction in which gain or loss was recognized. Accordingly, if D were to make a distribution, it could not rely on ATB1 or ATB2 to satisfy the requirements of section 355(b) unless the DSAG's year 6 acquisition of ATB1 and ATB2 is not in the pre-distribution period. See paragraph (b)(4)(i)(A) of this section. The fact that S2 acquired ATB1 and the S3 stock from an affiliate is not relevant.

Example 27. Purchased ATB prior to entering. For more than five years, T has engaged in the active conduct of ATB1. In year 6, S purchased ATB1 from T. In year 7, D acquired all of the S stock from the S shareholders solely in exchange for D stock in a transaction to which section 351 applied and in which no gain or loss was recognized. As a result, S became a DSAG member. Although S became a DSAG member in a transaction in which no gain or loss was recognized, S, a corporation that later became a DSAG member, acquired ATB1 in a transaction in which gain or loss was recognized. Accordingly, if D were to make a distribution, it could not rely on ATB1 to satisfy the requirements of section 355(b) unless S's year 6 acquisition of ATB1 is not in the pre-distribution period. See paragraph (b)(4)(i)(A) of this section.

Example 28. ATB (or new SAG member) for stock of distributing or a corporation in control of distributing in a reorganization — transfer of ATB to controlled. For more than five years, unrelated T and Z have owned all of the stock of X and Y, respectively, and X and Y have engaged in the active conduct of ATB1 and ATB2, respectively. Unrelated P owns all of the stock of D. In year 6, D acquires all of X's assets (including ATB1) from X solely in exchange for D stock in a reorganization described in section 368(a)(1)(A), and all of Y's assets (including ATB2) from Y solely in exchange for P stock in a reorganization described in section 368(a)(1)(A) by reason of section 368(a)(2)(D). No gain or loss is recognized on either acquisition. In a separate transaction, D transfers ATB2 to new subsidiary C in exchange for all of the C stock in a transaction that satisfies the requirements of section 351 and in which no gain or loss is recognized. If D were to distribute the C stock in a separate transaction, D and C can rely on ATB1 and ATB2, respectively, to satisfy the requirements of section 355(b). ATB1 and ATB2 were acquired in transactions in which no gain or loss was recognized, and were not acquired in exchange for assets of the DSAG. See paragraph (b)(4)(ii) of this section. The result would be the same if D acquired all of the assets of T (including the X stock) and Z (including the Y stock) in the reorganizations instead of acquiring the assets of X and Y, and then transferred the Y stock to C. See paragraphs (b)(1)(ii) and (b)(4)(ii) of this section.

Example 29. Taxable transfer of ATB by distributing to controlled. The facts are the same as the original facts in *Example 28* except that before and after the transfer to C, D owned section 368(c) stock but not section 1504(a)(2) stock of C, and recognized gain under section 357(c) on the transfer of ATB2 to C. D and C can rely on ATB1 and ATB2, respectively, to satisfy the requirements of section 355(b). See paragraph (b)(4)(iii)(A) of this section. The result would be the same if C purchased ATB2 from D. The result would also be the same if D acquired all of the assets of T (including the X stock) and Z (including the Y stock) in the reorganizations instead of acquiring the assets of X and Y, and then C purchased the Y stock from D. See paragraphs (b)(1)(ii) and (b)(4)(iii)(A) of this section.

Example 30. Assets for controlled stock in a section 351 transaction. For more than five years, unrelated D and C have engaged in the active conduct of ATB1 and ATB2, respectively. In year 6, D transfers trucks to C to be used in ATB2 in exchange for section 368(c) stock of C in a transaction to which section 351 applies and in which no gain or loss is recognized. If D were to distribute the C stock, C could not rely on ATB2 to satisfy the requirements of section 355(b) unless D's year 6 acquisition of the C stock is not in the pre-distribution period because D acquired section 368(c) stock of C, a corporation engaged in ATB2, in exchange for assets not constituting the trade or business. See paragraphs (b)(4)(i)(B) and (b)(4)(ii)(A) of this section. The result would be the same even if C became a DSAG member as a result of the year 6 transfer. See paragraphs (b)(4)(i)(A) and (b)(4)(ii)(A) of this section.

Example 31. ATB for controlled stock in a reorganization. For more than five years, unrelated D and T have engaged in the active conduct of ATB1 and ATB2, respectively. Throughout this period, D has owned all of the sole class of C stock. In year 6, T merges into C solely in exchange for C stock in a reorganization described in section 368(a)(1)(A) and in which no gain or loss is recognized. As a result, the T shareholders receive 20 percent of the sole class of C stock. Because C acquired ATB2 in exchange for C stock, solely for purposes of determining whether ATB2 can be relied on to satisfy the requirements of section 355(b), D is treated as having acquired its 80 percent of the C stock in year 6 in a transaction in which gain or loss was recognized. See paragraph (b)(4)(iv)(E) of this section. Accordingly, if D were to distribute the C stock, C could not rely on ATB2 to satisfy the requirements of section 355(b) unless C's year 6 acquisition of ATB2 is not in the pre-distribution period because ATB2 was in effect indirectly acquired in exchange for D's assets. See paragraphs (b)(4)(i)(A), (b)(4)(ii)(A), and (b)(4)(iv)(E) of this section.

Example 32. ATB and controlled stock for distributing stock in a section 351 transaction. For more than five years, T and unrelated C have engaged in the active conduct of ATB1 and ATB2, respectively. Unrelated P owns all of the stock of D. In year 6, P purchases ATB1 from T, and section 368(c) stock of C from the C shareholders. In year 6, P contributes the C stock and ATB1 to D solely in exchange for additional D stock in a transaction to which section 351 applies and in which no gain or loss is recognized. If D were to subsequently distribute the C stock in a separate transaction, D can rely on ATB1, and C can rely on ATB2 to satisfy the requirements of section 355(b) because neither ATB1 nor control of C was acquired in exchange for assets of the DSAG. See paragraphs (b)(4)(i)(A), (b)(4)(i)(B), and (b)(4)(ii) of this section. The fact that P, an affiliate of D, purchased ATB1 and section 368(c) stock of C in year 6 is not relevant.

Example 33. ATB for distributing stock in a section 351 transaction with section 357(c) gain. The facts are the same as *Example 32* except that D has owned section 368(c) stock of C for more than five years, P only purchases ATB1 from T, and P recognizes under section 357(c) gain on the transfer of ATB1 to D as a result of D assuming liabilities of P. D cannot rely on ATB1 to satisfy the requirements of section 355(b) until D's year 6 acquisition of ATB1 is no longer in the pre-distribution period because D acquired ATB1 in a transaction in which gain or loss was recognized. See paragraph (b)(4)(i)(A) of this section.

Example 34. Partnership distributions. For more than five years, X and Y have engaged in the active conduct of ATB1 and ATB2, respectively. Throughout this period, unrelated D has owned a 90-percent interest in Partnership. D is attributed any trade or business assets and activities of Partnership under paragraph (b)(2)(v) of this section. In year 6, Partnership purchases ATB1 from X and all of the Y stock from its owner. In year 9, Partnership distributes ATB1 and all of the Y stock to D in a non-liquidating distribution. Assume that no gain or loss is recognized by Partnership or any partner on the distribution. As a result of the distribution, Y becomes a DSAG member, and D is treated as having acquired Y's assets (and activities). See paragraphs (b)(1)(ii) and (b)(1)(iii) of this section. If D were to make a distribution, ATB1 could not be relied on to satisfy the requirements of section 355(b) unless Partnership's year 6 acquisition of ATB1 is not in the pre-distribution period. See paragraphs (b)(2)(v), (b)(3)(iii), and (b)(4)(ii)(B) of this section. If D were to make a distribution, ATB2 could not be relied on to satisfy the requirements of section 355(b) unless D's year 9 acquisition of the Y stock is not in the pre-distribution period. See paragraphs (b)(2)(v)(A) and (b)(4)(ii)(B) of this section. Alternatively, if in year 9 Partnership only makes a *pro rata* distribution of all the Y stock to its partners such that D receives 90 percent of the Y stock, ATB2 cannot be relied on until Partnership's year 6 acquisition of all of the Y stock is no longer in the pre-distribution period. See paragraph (b)(4)(ii)(B) of this section.

Example 35. Partnership distribution (new SAG member). For more than five years, D has owned a 50-percent interest in Partnership. The remaining interests in Partnership are owned by unrelated parties. Throughout this period, Partnership has engaged in the active conduct of ATB1, and D has been attributed the trade or business assets and activities of Partnership's ATB1 under paragraph (b)(2)(v) of this section. In year 6, pursuant to an integrated plan, Partnership contributes ATB1 to new subsidiary S, and distributes all of the S stock to D in liquidation of D's 50-percent interest in Partnership. Assume that no gain or loss is recognized by Partnership or any partner on the distribution. As a result, S becomes a DSAG member, and D is treated as having acquired S's assets (and activities). See paragraphs (b)(1)(ii) and (b)(1)(iii) of this section. Because D was attributed ATB1 immediately before the incorporation and distribution by Partnership, and S became a DSAG member as a result of the distribution, Partnership's distribution of the S stock to D is not an acquisition of ATB1. See paragraphs (b)(3)(iii) and (b)(4)(ii)(B) of this section. Accordingly, if D were to make a distribution, it could rely on ATB1 to satisfy the requirements of section 355(b).

Example 36. Transfer of partnership in a reorganization and distribution. For more than five years, T has owned a 40-percent interest in Partnership which has engaged in the active conduct of ATB1. Throughout this period, T has been attributed the trade or business assets and activities of Partnership's ATB1 under paragraph (b)(2)(v) of this section. In year 6, T merges into S, a wholly owned subsidiary of unrelated D, solely in exchange for D stock in a reorganization described in section 368(a)(1)(A) by reason of section 368(a)(2)(D). No gain or loss is recognized. If D were to make a distribution, D can rely on ATB1 because ATB1 has been actively conducted throughout the pre-distribution period, and the interest in Partnership was acquired in a transaction in which no gain or loss was recognized and was not acquired in exchange for assets of the DSAG. See paragraphs (b)(2)(v), (b)(3)(i), and (b)(4)(ii) of this section. The results would be the same if T owned only a 20-percent interest in Partnership, employees of T performed active and substantial management functions for Partnership's trade or business assets and activities prior to the merger, and employees of S (or an affiliate of S) performed active and substantial management functions for Partnership's trade or business assets and activities after the merger. See paragraphs (b)(2)(iii), (b)(2)(v), (b)(3), and (b)(4)(ii) of this section.

Example 37. Transferred ATB sold (SAG member). For more than five years, D and unrelated T have engaged in the active conduct of ATB1 and ATB2, respectively. In year 6, D contributes ATB1 to T in exchange for T stock in a transaction to which section 351 applies. No gain or loss is recognized on the contribution. Immediately after the contribution T is a DSAG member. In year 8, in response to unanticipated market changes, T sells ATB1 to an unrelated third party. Although T became a DSAG member as a result of D acquiring T stock in exchange for ATB1 in a transaction in which no gain or loss was recognized, ATB1 is not the trade or business to be relied upon. Accordingly, D cannot rely on ATB2 until the year 6 transaction is no longer in the pre-distribution period because D acquired ATB2 in exchange for D's assets not constituting the active trade or business to be relied on. See paragraphs (b)(4)(i)(A) and (b)(4)(ii)(A) of this section.

Example 38. Transferred ATB sold (partnership). The facts are the same as *Example 37* except that, in year 6, D and T contribute ATB1 and ATB2, respectively, to Partnership in a transaction to which section 721 applies. In the exchange, D and T each receive a 50-percent interest in Partnership. In year 8, in response to unanticipated market changes, Partnership sells ATB1 to an unrelated third party. If D were to make a distribution, D could not rely on ATB2 under paragraph (b)(2)(v)(B) of this section unless the year 6 transaction is not in the pre-distribution period because D acquired ATB2 in exchange for D's assets not constituting the trade or business to be relied on. See paragraphs (b)(4)(i)(A) and (b)(4)(ii)(A) of this section.

Example 39. Indirect acquisition of control of distributing's ATB. For more than five years, D and T have engaged in the active conduct of ATB1 and ATB2, respectively. All of the T stock is owned by individuals. In year 6, T purchases all the stock of D in a transaction in which gain or loss is recognized. In a separate transaction, T merges downstream into D solely in exchange for D stock in a reorganization described in section 368(a)(1)(A) and (D). No gain or loss is recognized. In year 7, D transfers ATB2 formerly conducted by T to new subsidiary C, and then distributes the C stock to the D shareholders. Although D acquired ATB2 solely in exchange for D stock in a transaction in which no gain or loss was recognized, the requirements of section 355(b) are not satisfied because ATB1, the business of D, was indirectly acquired by T, a predecessor of D, during the pre-distribution period in a transaction in which gain or loss was recognized. See paragraphs (b)(4)(i)(A) and (b)(4)(iv)(A) of this section. The result would be the same if prior to the year 6 acquisition D and wholly owned subsidiary C were engaged in the active conduct of ATB1 and ATB2, respectively, and T had no ATB.

Example 40. Exception for corporate distributee. For more than five years, T has owned all of the stock of D which in turn owned all of the stock of C. Throughout this period, D and C have engaged in the active conduct of ATB1 and ATB2, respectively. In year 6, P purchases all the stock of T. In year 7, P liquidates T in a transaction in which no gain or loss is recognized under section 332. Under section 334(b), P's basis in the D stock is determined in whole by reference to T's basis in the D stock. In year 8, D distributes the C stock to P. While the D stock was indirectly acquired in a taxable transaction, the adjusted basis that P, the distributee corporation, has in the D stock was determined in whole by reference to T's adjusted basis. Accordingly, D and C satisfy the requirements of section 355(b). See paragraph (b)(4)(iii)(C) of this section. If P were to distribute either the D stock or C stock, neither ATB1 nor ATB2 could be relied on unless the year 6 acquisition of the T stock is not in the pre-distribution period. See paragraph (b)(4)(iii)(C) of this section. The results would be the same if P acquired all of T's assets in exchange for P stock and other property in a reorganization described in section 368(a)(1)(A).

Example 41. Acquisition of section 368(c) stock of controlled, DSAG member. For more than five years, D has owned section 1504(a)(2) stock but not section 368(c) stock of C. Throughout this period, C has engaged in the active conduct of ATB1. In year 6, D purchased additional shares of C stock. As a result, D acquired section 368(c) stock of C. If D were to make a distribution of the C stock, C could rely on ATB1 to satisfy the requirement of section 355(b). C was a DSAG member, so D was engaged in ATB1 prior to the year 6 purchase of additional C stock. Accordingly, D's acquisition of additional stock of a DSAG member is disregarded in applying paragraph (b)(4)(i)(A) of this section, and paragraph (b)(4)(i)(B) of this section does not apply to this acquisition of additional C stock. See paragraphs (b)(1)(ii) and (b)(4)(iv)(F) of this section.

Example 42. Controlled becoming a DSAG member. For more than five years, D has owned section 368(c) stock but not section 1504(a)(2) stock of C. Throughout this period, D and C have engaged in the active conduct of ATB1 and ATB2, respectively. In year 6, D purchases the remaining C stock. If D distributes all the C stock, C cannot rely on ATB2 to satisfy the requirements of section 355(b) because C became a DSAG member (and thus D acquired ATB2) in a transaction in which gain or loss was recognized. See paragraphs (b)(1)(ii), (b)(4)(i)(A), and (b)(4)(iv)(F) of this section.

Example 43. Nontaxable multi-step acquisition of control. For more than five years, unrelated D and C have engaged in the active conduct of ATB1 and ATB2, respectively. C has two classes of stock outstanding. X owns all 95 shares of the class A stock of C, representing 95 percent of the voting power and 70 percent of the value, and Y owns all of the class B stock of C, representing five percent of the voting power and 30 percent of the value. In year 6, D acquires 10 shares of class A C stock from X in a transaction in which gain or loss was recognized. In year 7, in a separate transaction, D acquires an additional 80 shares of class A C stock from X solely in exchange for D voting stock in a reorganization described in section 368(a)(1)(B). No gain or loss is recognized. In year 8, in a separate transaction, D acquires the remaining five shares of class A C stock from X in a transaction in which gain or loss was recognized. Because D only acquires 70 percent of the value of C stock, C does not become a DSAG member. In year 9, D distributes the 95 shares of class A C stock to the D shareholders. At the time D first acquired control of C, D owned an amount of C stock constituting control that was acquired in a transaction in which no gain or loss was recognized. Accordingly, D and C both satisfy the requirements of section 355(b). See paragraphs (b)(4)(i)(B) and (b)(4)(iv)(B) of this section.

Example 44. Taxable multi-step acquisition of control. The facts are the same as *Example 43* except that in year 7 D acquires 70 shares of class A C stock solely in exchange for D voting stock in a reorganization described in section 368(a)(1)(B). No gain or loss is recognized. At the time D first acquired control of C, D did not own an amount of C stock constituting control that was acquired in one or more transactions in which no gain or loss was recognized or by reason of such transactions combined with acquisitions before the pre-distribution period. Accordingly, C cannot rely on ATB2 to satisfy the requirements of section 355(b) until D's year 6 acquisition of the 10 shares of class A C stock is no longer in the pre-distribution period. See paragraphs (b)(4)(i)(B) and (b)(4)(iv)(B) of this section.

Example 45. Taxable acquisition of control. For more than five years, unrelated D and C have engaged in the active conduct of ATB1 and ATB2, respectively. In year 6, D acquires section 368(c) stock but not section 1504(a)(2) stock of C from unrelated T in a reorganization described in section 368(a)(1)(A) by reason of section 368(a)(2)(E) through the use of a newly created transitory subsidiary of D. In the reorganization, T receives consideration 95 percent of which is D voting common stock and five percent of which is cash. Because D acquired control of C in a single transaction in which gain or loss was recognized, paragraph (b)(4)(iv)(B) of this section does not apply. Accordingly, C cannot rely on ATB2 to satisfy the requirements of section 355(b) until D's year 6 acquisition of control of C is no longer in the pre-distribution period. See paragraph (b)(4)(i)(B) of this section.

Example 46. Taxable multi-step indirect acquisition of control. For more than five years, C has engaged in the active conduct of ATB1. T owns exactly 80 percent of the total combined voting power of all classes of C stock entitled to vote and 80 percent of the total number of shares of all other classes of C stock, but T owns less than 80 percent of the total value of the C stock. In year 6, unrelated D acquires 10 percent of the sole outstanding class of stock of T in a transaction in which gain or loss is recognized. In year 8, in a separate transaction, T merges into D solely in exchange for D stock in a reorganization described in section 368(a)(1)(A). No gain or loss is recognized. As a result, D owns section 368(c) stock of C. Because D indirectly acquired 10 percent of the C stock owned by T in year 6, at the time D first acquired control of C, D did not own stock constituting control of C that it acquired in one or more transactions in which no gain or loss was recognized or by reason of such transactions combined with acquisitions before the pre-distribution period. Accordingly, C cannot rely on ATB1 to satisfy the requirements of section 355(b) until D's year 6 acquisition of the T stock is no longer in the pre-distribution period. See paragraphs (b)(4)(i)(B) and (b)(4)(iv)(B) of this section.

Example 47. Nontaxable multi-step acquisition of SAG member (or ATB). For more than five years, S has engaged in the active conduct of ATB1. X owns all 100 shares of the sole outstanding class of S stock. In year 6, unrelated D acquires 10 shares of S stock from X in a transaction in which gain or loss was recognized. In year 7, in a separate transaction, D acquires an additional 80 shares of S stock from X solely in exchange for D voting stock in a reorganization described in section 368(a)(1)(B). No gain or loss is recognized. As a result, S becomes a DSAG member. In year 8, in a separate transaction, D acquires another 5 shares of S stock from X in a transaction in which gain or loss was recognized. Because at the time S first became a DSAG member, D owned an amount of S stock meeting the requirements of section 1504(a)(2) that was acquired in a transaction in which no gain or loss was recognized, D can rely on ATB1 to satisfy the requirements of section 355(b) as of the year 7 transaction. See paragraphs (b)(4)(i)(A) and (b)(4)(iv)(C) of this section. The acquisition by D of other S stock in a separate transaction in which gain or loss was recognized during the pre-distribution period is disregarded. See paragraph (b)(1)(ii) of this section. The result would be the same if, in year 7, instead of acquiring S stock in a reorganization described in section 368(a)(1)(B), S merged into D in exchange for D stock in a reorganization described in section 368(a)(1)(A) in which no gain or loss was recognized. See paragraphs (b)(4)(i)(A) and (b)(4)(iv)(D) of this section.

Example 48. Taxable multi-step acquisition of SAG member (or ATB). The facts are the same as *Example 47* except that in year 6 D acquires 21 shares of S stock in a transaction in which gain or loss was recognized, and in year 7, in a separate transaction, D acquires an additional 79 shares of S stock solely in exchange for D voting stock in a reorganization described in section 368(a)(1)(B). No gain or loss is recognized, and S becomes a DSAG member. D cannot rely on ATB1 to satisfy the requirements of section 355(b) until D's year 6 acquisition of the 21 shares of S stock is no longer in the pre-distribution period because at the time S first became a DSAG member D did not own an amount of S stock meeting the requirements of section 1504(a)(2) that was acquired in one or more transactions in which no gain or loss was recognized or by reason of such transactions combined with acquisitions before the pre-distribution period. See paragraphs (b)(4)(i)(A) and (b)(4)(iv)(C) of this section. The result would be the same if, in year 7, in a separate transaction, instead of D's acquiring S stock, S merged into D in exchange for D stock in a reorganization described in section 368(a)(1)(A) in which no gain or loss was recognized. See paragraphs (b)(4)(i)(A) and (b)(4)(iv)(D) of this section. The result would also be the same if in year 6 D acquired 10 shares of S stock in a transaction in which gain or loss was recognized and, in year 7, in a separate transaction, D acquired an additional 70 shares of S stock solely in exchange for D voting stock in a reorganization described in section 368(a)(1)(B). See paragraphs (b)(4)(i)(A) and (b)(4)(iv)(C) of this section.

Example 49. Nontaxable multi-step indirect acquisition using subsidiary stock. For more than five years, X has owned all of the sole outstanding class of S stock. Throughout this period, S and unrelated T have engaged in the active conduct of ATB1 and ATB2, respectively. In year 6, T merges into S solely in exchange for S stock in a reorganization described in section 368(a)(1)(A). No gain or loss is recognized. Immediately after the merger, X and the former T shareholders own 80 percent and 20 percent of the S stock, respectively. In year 8, unrelated D acquires all of the S shares held by X solely in exchange for D voting stock in a reorganization described in section 368(a)(1)(B). No gain or loss is recognized. As a result, S becomes a DSAG member. Because D acquired ATB1 and ATB2 in a transaction in which no gain or loss was recognized, solely in exchange for D stock, D can rely on both ATB1 and ATB2 to satisfy the requirements of section 355(b). Because X is neither a predecessor of D nor a DSAG member, paragraph (b)(4)(iv)(E) of this section is not applicable.

Example 50. Taxable multi-step indirect acquisition using subsidiary stock. The facts are the same as *Example 49* except that, for more than five years, D has owned 50 percent of the sole outstanding class of X stock. In year 8, instead of D acquiring the S stock, S merges into D solely in exchange for D stock in a reorganization described in section 368(a)(1)(A). No gain or loss is recognized. Because D indirectly owned S stock and S acquired ATB2 in exchange for S stock, paragraph (b)(4)(iv)(E) of this section is applicable. Under paragraph (b)(4)(iv)(E) of this section, for purposes of applying paragraph (b)(4) of this section with respect to ATB2, D is treated as having indirectly acquired in year 6 the S stock it indirectly owns immediately after the merger of T into S in a transaction in which gain or loss was recognized. Thus, D is treated as having indirectly acquired 40 percent of the S stock in a transaction in which gain or loss is recognized at the time of the merger of T into S. Further, if the merger of T into S is in the pre-distribution period, under paragraph (b)(4)(iv)(D) of this section, D will be treated as having acquired ATB2 in a transaction in which gain or loss is recognized because, immediately before the merger of S into D, D indirectly owned 40 percent of the S stock that had been acquired in a transaction in which gain or loss was recognized. Accordingly, D cannot rely on ATB2 to satisfy the requirements of section 355(b) until the year 6 merger of T into S is no longer in the pre-distribution period. However, D can rely on ATB1 to satisfy the requirements of section 355(b). Alternatively, if X, instead of S, merged into D, S would become a DSAG member and X would be a predecessor of D. If so, for purposes of applying paragraph (b)(4) of this section with respect to ATB2, D is treated as having acquired 80 percent of the S stock in year 6 in a transaction in which gain or loss was recognized. Accordingly, D cannot rely on ATB2 to satisfy the requirements of section 355(b) until the year 6 merger of T into S is no longer in the pre-distribution period. See paragraphs (b)(1)(iii), (b)(4)(i)(A), (b)(4)(iv)(A), and (b)(4)(iv)(E) of this section. However, D can rely on ATB1 to satisfy the requirements of section 355(b).

Example 51. Taxable multi-step indirect acquisition of SAG member (or ATB). For more than five years, T has engaged in the active conduct of ATB1. Throughout this period, X owned all of the sole outstanding class of T stock, and D owned 50 percent of the sole outstanding stock of S. In year 6, S acquires 50 percent of the sole outstanding class of the X stock in a transaction in which gain or loss is recognized. In year 8, X merges into D solely in exchange for D stock. No gain or loss is recognized. As a result, T becomes a DSAG member. Because D indirectly acquired more than 20 percent of the T stock (D indirectly acquired 25 percent of T) in year 6, at the time T first became a DSAG member D did not own an amount of T stock meeting the requirements of section 1504(a)(2) that it acquired in one or more transactions in which no gain or loss was recognized or by reason of such transactions combined with acquisitions before the pre-distribution period. Accordingly, D cannot rely on ATB1 to satisfy the requirements of section 355(b) until D's year 6 indirect acquisition of the T stock is no longer in the pre-distribution period. See paragraphs (b)(4)(i)(A) and (b)(4)(iv)(C) of this section. The result would be the same if, instead of X, in year 8, T merged into D solely in exchange for D stock. See paragraphs (b)(4)(i)(A) and (b)(4)(iv)(D) of this section.

Kevin M. Brown,
Deputy Commissioner for Services and Enforcement.

(Filed by the Office of the Federal Register on May 4, 2007, 8:45 a.m., and published in the issue of the Federal Register for May 8, 2007, 72 F.R. 20612)

Determining the Amount of Taxes Paid for Purposes of Section 901; Correction

Announcement 2007–53

AGENCY: Internal Revenue Service (IRS), Treasury.

ACTION: Correction to notice of proposed rulemaking.

SUMMARY: This document contains a correction to notice of proposed rulemaking (REG–156779–06, 2007–17 I.R.B. 1015) that was published in the **Federal Register** on Friday, March 30, 2007 (71 FR 15081) providing guidance relating to the determination of the amount of taxes paid for purposes of section 901.

FOR FURTHER INFORMATION CONTACT: Bethany A. Ingwalson, (202) 622–3850 (not a toll-free number).

SUPPLEMENTARY INFORMATION:

Background

The notice of proposed rulemaking (REG–156779–06) that is the subject of this correction is under section 901 of the Internal Revenue Code.

Need for Correction

As published, this notice of proposed rulemaking (REG–156779–06) contains an error that may prove to be misleading and is in need of clarification.

Correction of Publication

Accordingly, the notice of proposed rulemaking (REG–156779–06), that was the subject of FR Doc. E7–5862, is corrected as follows:

On page 15085, column 3, in the preamble, first full paragraph of the column, under the paragraph heading "*3. Comments and Proposed Regulations*", lines 1 and 2, the language "The fifth condition is that the counterparty is a person (other than the" is corrected to read "The fifth condition is that the arrangement involves a counterparty. A counterparty is a person (other than the".

LaNita Van Dyke,
*Branch Chief,
Publications and Regulations Branch,
Legal Processing Division,
Office of Associate Chief Counsel
(Procedure and Administration).*

(Filed by the Office of the Federal Register on May 9, 2007, 8:45 a.m., and published in the issue of the Federal Register for May 10, 2007, 72 F.R. 26576)

Section 1367 Regarding Open Account Debt; Correction

Announcement 2007–54

AGENCY: Internal Revenue Service (IRS), Treasury.

ACTION: Correction to notice of proposed rulemaking.

SUMMARY: This document contains corrections to a notice of proposed rulemaking (REG–144859–04, 2007–20 I.R.B. 1245) that was published in the **Federal Register** on Thursday, April 12, 2007 (72 FR 18417) relating to the treatment of open account debt between S corporations and their shareholders.

FOR FURTHER INFORMATION CONTACT: Stacy L. Short or Deanne M. Burke, (202) 622–3070 (not a toll-free number).

SUPPLEMENTARY INFORMATION:

Background

The correction notice that is the subject of this document is under section 1367 of the Internal Revenue Code.

Need for Correction

As published, the notice of proposed rulemaking (REG–144859–04) contains errors that may prove to be misleading and are in need of clarification.

Correction of Publication

Accordingly, the publication of proposed rulemaking (REG–144859–04), which was the subject of FR Doc. E7–6764, is corrected as follows:

1. On page 18417, column 3, in the preamble, under the caption "DATES:",

first sentence of the paragraph, the language "Written or electronic comments and requests for a public hearing must be received by July 11, 2007." is corrected to read "Written or electronic comments must be received by July 10, 2007.".

2. On page 18418, column 1, in the preamble, under the caption "FOR FURTHER INFORMATION CONTACT:", lines six through eleven, the language "attend the hearing, Richard Hurst at (202) 622–2949 (TDD Telephone) (not toll-free numbers) and his e-mail address is *Richard.A.Hurst@irscounsel.treas.gov*, (202) 622–7180 (not toll-free numbers)." is corrected to read "attend the hearing, Richard Hurst at *Richard.A.Hurst@irscounsel.treas.gov*, (202) 622–7180 (not toll-free numbers).

3. On page 18420, column 2, in the preamble, under the paragraph heading "Comments and Public Hearing", the second paragraph of the column, first line, the language "The rules of 26 CFR 606.601(a)(3)" is corrected to read "The rules of 26 CFR 601.601(a)(3)".

§1.1367–2 [Corrected]

4. On page 18422, column 1, §1.1367–2, first paragraph of the column, third line of the paragraph, the language "1. The section heading is revised." is corrected to read "1. The section heading and paragraph are revised.".

5. On page 18422, column 1, §1.1367–2, first paragraph of the column, lines four through seven are removed.

§1.1367–3 [Corrected]

6. On page 18422, column 1, §1.1367–3, second paragraph of the column, the language of the paragraph heading "§1.1367–3 Effective dates and transitional rules." is corrected to read "§1.1367–3 Effective date.".

LaNita Van Dyke,
Chief, Publications and Regulations Branch, Legal Processing Division, Associate Chief Counsel (Procedure and Administration).

(Filed by the Office of the Federal Register on May 7, 2007, 8:45 a.m., and published in the issue of the Federal Register for May 8, 2007, 72 F.R. 26011)

Rollovers to Prototype Roth IRAs

Announcement 2007–55

This announcement provides that sponsors of prototype Roth IRAs who wish to accept rollover contributions from designated Roth accounts described in § 402A of the Internal Revenue Code must amend their prototype Roth IRA documents to reflect that the Roth IRA permits these rollover contributions.

Internal Revenue Code § 402A, added by section 617 of the Economic Growth and Tax Relief Reconciliation Act of 2001 ("EGTRRA"), Pub. L. 107–16, authorizes employers to offer, beginning in 2006, a qualified Roth contribution program as part of a § 401(k) plan or a § 403(b) plan. An eligible rollover distribution from a designated Roth account established under the program can be rolled over only to another designated Roth account or to a Roth IRA. Rev. Proc. 2002–10, 2002–1 C.B. 401, provided guidance on amending IRAs and IRA-based plans to reflect changes to the Code made by EGTRRA, but the guidance did not address qualified Roth contribution programs. Consequently, currently approved prototype Roth IRAs generally do not contain language permitting the acceptance of rollovers from designated Roth accounts.

Sponsors of prototype Roth IRAs may now wish to amend their documents to provide for the acceptance of rollovers from designated Roth accounts. In order for a Roth IRA that is intended to be a prototype Roth IRA to accept an eligible rollover contribution from a designated Roth account prior to an amendment permitting such rollovers, the prototype Roth IRA document must be amended and adopted no later than December 31, 2007, in accordance with procedures acceptable under Rev. Proc. 2002–10. Thus, if a prototype Roth IRA accepts a rollover from a designated Roth account prior to the date of amendment, the mere acceptance of such rollover contribution will not affect the Roth IRA's prototype status provided the adoption of the amendment is timely. No application to the Service is required for continued reliance on an Opinion Letter. The model Roth IRAs (Forms 5305–R, 5305–RA and 5305–RB) already contain language permitting the acceptance of rollovers from designated Roth accounts, thus, users of such forms do not need to amend their IRA document to permit such rollovers.

The Roth IRA Listing of Required Modifications ("LRMs"), including acceptable designated Roth account rollover language, is available on the Service's Web Site at *www.irs.gov*. (Search for "LRMs".) These LRMs have also been updated to reflect other recent law changes, such as section 833(c) of the Pension Protection Act of 2006, P.L. 109–280, relating to inflation adjustments to the modified adjusted gross income limits that are used to determine the amount of Roth IRA contributions.

Deletions From Cumulative List of Organizations Contributions to Which are Deductible Under Section 170 of the Code

Announcement 2007–56

The names of organizations that no longer qualify as organizations described in section 170(c)(2) of the Internal Revenue Code of 1986 are listed below.

Generally, the Service will not disallow deductions for contributions made to a listed organization on or before the date of announcement in the Internal Revenue Bulletin that an organization no longer qualifies. However, the Service is not precluded from disallowing a deduction for any contributions made after an organization ceases to qualify under section 170(c)(2) if the organization has not timely filed a suit for declaratory judgment under section 7428 and if the contributor (1) had knowledge of the revocation of the ruling or determination letter, (2) was aware that such revocation was imminent, or (3) was in part responsible for or was aware of the activities or omissions of the organization that brought about this revocation.

If on the other hand a suit for declaratory judgment has been timely filed, contributions from individuals and organizations described in section 170(c)(2) that are otherwise allowable will continue to be deductible. Protection under section 7428(c) would begin on June 4, 2007, and would end on the date the court first determines that the organization is not described in section 170(c)(2) as more particularly set forth in section 7428(c)(1). For individual contributors, the maximum deduction protected is $1,000, with a husband and wife treated as one contributor. This benefit is not extended to any individual, in whole or in part, for the acts or omissions of the organization that were the basis for revocation.

Freedom Financial Consultants, Inc.
Lakeland, FL
Vista Vision 2000, Inc.
Norfolk, VA
Safeguarding America for Everyone (SAFE) Foundation, Inc.
Upper Marlboro, MD
Homeownership Foundation of America, Inc.
Baltimore, MD

Part I. Rulings and Decisions Under the Internal Revenue Code of 1986

Section 197.—Amortization of Goodwill and Certain Other Intangibles

Gain to a distributor from the cancellation of an agreement to distribute a manufacturer's products is section 1231 gain and may be treated as capital if the agreement is property of a character subject to the allowance for depreciation under section 167. For this purpose, property is treated as being of such a character if it is amortizable under section 197. See Rev. Rul. 2007-37, page 1390.

Section 401.—Qualified Pension, Profit-Sharing, and Stock Bonus Plans

26 CFR 1.401(a)–1: Post –ERISA qualified plans and qualified trusts; in general.

T.D. 9325

DEPARTMENT OF THE TREASURY
Internal Revenue Service
26 CFR Part 1

Distributions From a Pension Plan Upon Attainment of Normal Retirement Age

AGENCY: Internal Revenue Service (IRS), Treasury.

ACTION: Final regulations.

SUMMARY: This document contains final regulations under sections 401(a) and 411(d)(6) of the Internal Revenue Code. These regulations provide rules permitting distributions to be made from a pension plan upon the attainment of normal retirement age prior to a participant's severance from employment with the employer maintaining the plan. These regulations provide the public with guidance regarding distributions from qualified pension plans and will affect administrators of, and participants in, such plans.

DATES: *Effective Date:* These regulations are effective May 22, 2007.

Applicability Dates: These regulations are generally applicable May 22, 2007. For dates of applicability, see §§1.401(a)–1(b)(4) and 1.411(d)–4, A–12(a).

FOR FURTHER INFORMATION CONTACT: Cathy A. Vohs at (202) 622–6090 or Janet A. Laufer at (202) 622–6080 (not a toll-free number).

SUPPLEMENTARY INFORMATION:

Background

Section 401(a) sets forth the qualification requirements for a trust forming part of a stock bonus, pension, or profit-sharing plan of an employer. Several of these qualification requirements are based on a plan's normal retirement age. Section 411(a)(8) defines the term "normal retirement age" as the earlier of (a) the time a participant attains normal retirement age under the plan or (b) the later of the time a plan participant attains age 65 or the 5th anniversary of the time a plan participant commenced participation in the plan.

The definition of normal retirement age is important in applying the rules under section 411(b) which are designed to preclude avoidance of the minimum vesting standards through the backloading of benefits (for example, a benefit formula under which the rate of benefit accrual is increased disproportionately for employees with longer service) because those rules are based on the benefit payable at normal retirement age. Normal retirement age is also relevant for applying the rules relating to suspension of benefits under section 411(a)(3)(B) and the rules under section 411(b)(1)(H)(iii) that permit a plan to offset accruals after normal retirement age by either the actuarial value of distributions made after normal retirement age or the actuarial value of increases in the benefits due to delay in payment. Normal retirement age is also used in determining the minimum benefit for non-key employees in the case of a top-heavy defined benefit plan. See section 416(c)(1)(A) and (E). Also, the vesting requirements of sections 401(a)(7) and 411 are based upon normal retirement age.

Section 411(d)(6) generally prohibits a qualified plan from being amended to reduce a participant's accrued benefit and, for this purpose, an elimination or reduction of an early retirement benefit or a retirement-type subsidy, or an elimination of an optional form of benefit, is treated as a reduction in the accrued benefit. The Secretary has the authority under section 411(d)(6) to allow amendments that eliminate an optional form of benefit.

Section 401(a) permits three types of plans to qualify under section 401(a): stock bonus, pension, and profit-sharing plans. Section 1.401–1(a)(2)(i) and (b)(1)(i) of the Income Tax Regulations interprets what it means to be a "pension plan," and has done so since the publication of those regulations as T.D. 6203, 1956–2 C.B. 219 (see §601.601(d)(2)(ii)(*b*)). These regulations (the 1956 regulations) provide that a qualified plan under section 401(a) is a program and arrangement which is established and maintained by an employer "in the case of a pension plan, to provide for the livelihood of the employees or their beneficiaries after the retirement of such employees through the payment of benefits determined without regard to profits."[1] The 1956 regulations defining a qualified pension plan further provide that a pension plan must be "a plan established and maintained by an employer primarily to provide systematically for the payment of definitely determinable benefits to his employees over a period of years, usually for life, after retirement."

Following the enactment of the Employee Retirement Income Security Act of 1974 (ERISA), 93 Public Law 406 (88 Stat. 829), the regulations under section 401(a) were modified to provide that the 1956 regulations continued to apply, except as otherwise provided. See §1.401(a)–1(b)(1)(i) and (ii). Accordingly, a pension plan is generally not permitted to pay benefits before retirement. See also Rev. Rul. 56–693, 1956–2 C.B. 282, as modified by Rev.

[1] This rule is limited to a pension plan, which is either a defined benefit plan or a defined contribution plan that is not a stock bonus or profit-sharing plan (generally referred to as a money purchase pension plan). Other rules apply to stock bonus plans and profit-sharing plans.

Rul. 60–323, 1960–2 C.B. 148 (see §601.601(d)(2)(ii)(*b*)).

Rev. Rul. 71–24, 1971–1 C.B. 114, (see §601.601(d)(2)(ii)(*b*)) provides guidance for the treatment of benefits under a pension plan for employees who continue employment after normal retirement age. Rev. Rul. 71–24 includes an example that indicates that benefits are permitted to commence during employment after normal retirement age.

Rev. Rul. 71–147, 1971–1 C.B. 116, (see §601.601(d)(2)(ii)(*b*)) provides that the normal retirement age in a pension or annuity plan is generally the lowest age specified in the plan at which the employee has the right to retire without the consent of the employer and receive retirement benefits based on the amount of the employee's service on the date of retirement at the full rate set forth in the plan (that is, without actuarial or similar reduction because of retirement before some later specified age). While ordinarily the normal retirement age under pension and annuity plans is age 65, Rev. Rul. 71–147 permitted a different age to be specified, but an age lower than 65 was permitted only if the age represented the age at which employees customarily retire in the particular company or industry, and was not a device to accelerate funding.

Following the enactment of section 411(a)(8) (defining normal retirement age as described earlier in this preamble) under ERISA, Rev. Rul. 71–147 was modified by Rev. Rul. 78–120, 1978–1 C.B. 117 (see §601.601(d)(2)(ii)(*b*)). Under Rev. Rul. 78–120, for purposes of section 411, a pension plan is permitted to have a normal retirement age lower than age 65, regardless of the age at which employees customarily retire in the particular company or industry.

Section 401(a)(36), added by section 905(b) of the Pension Protection Act of 2006, Public Law 109–280 (120 Stat. 780) (PPA '06), provides that a trust forming part of a pension plan is not treated as failing to constitute a qualified trust under section 401(a) solely because the plan provides that a distribution may be made from such trust to an employee who has attained age 62 and who is not separated from employment at the time of such distribution. Section 401(a)(36) applies to distributions in plan years beginning after December 31, 2006.

On November 10, 2004, a notice of proposed rulemaking (REG–114726–04, 2004–2 C.B. 857) under section 401 was published in the **Federal Register** (69 FR 65108) (the proposed regulations). The proposed regulations would have allowed in-service distributions after normal retirement age, but would not have permitted a normal retirement age to be set so low as to be a subterfuge to avoid qualification requirements. The proposed regulations would also have permitted in-service distributions before normal retirement age under a *bona fide* phased retirement program.

On March 14, 2005, the IRS held a public hearing on the proposed regulations. Written comments responding to the notice of proposed rulemaking were also received. In light of the enactment of section 401(a)(36) by PPA '06, only portions of the proposed regulations are being finalized at this time. The IRS recently issued a notice requesting comments as to whether the portions of the proposed regulations relating to in-service distributions pursuant to a *bona fide* phased retirement program should be finalized. See Notice 2007–8, 2007–3 I.R.B. 276 (see §601.601(d)(2)(ii)(*b*)). The portions of the proposed regulations relating to normal retirement age and in-service distribution upon attainment of normal retirement age are being finalized by this Treasury Decision. The significant revisions to the proposed regulations are discussed in this preamble.

Explanation of Provisions and Summary of Comments

I. *Overview*

This Treasury Decision modifies existing regulations, including the regulations at §1.401(a)–1 which generally require a pension plan to be maintained primarily to provide systematically for the payment of definitely determinable benefits after retirement. These regulations provide two exceptions to this rule. First, they clarify that a pension plan is permitted to commence payment of retirement benefits to a participant after the participant has attained normal retirement age. The regulations also provide rules on how low a plan's normal retirement age is permitted to be and include a related exception to the anti-cutback rules of section 411(d)(6) to allow conforming amendments during a transitional period. Second, the regulations reflect the provisions of new section 401(a)(36).

II. *Normal Retirement Age*

A. *In General*

These regulations adopt the rule of the proposed regulations under which a pension plan (a defined benefit plan or money purchase pension plan) is permitted to pay benefits upon an employee's attainment of normal retirement age, even if the employee has not yet had a severance from employment with the employer maintaining the plan. Comments generally supported the inclusion of this rule as reflecting existing practice among some pension plans, based on an example in Rev. Rul. 71–24.

These regulations also include rules restricting a plan's normal retirement age. The proposed regulations would have provided that a plan's normal retirement age could not be set so low as to be a subterfuge to avoid the requirements of section 401(a), and, accordingly, normal retirement age could not be earlier than the earliest age that is reasonably representative of a typical retirement age for the covered workforce.[2] Some comments expressed concern about the specifics of this rule, including concern about how it might be applied in various circumstances, and suggested that the regulations contain a safe harbor for which there would be no need for a demonstration of the typical retirement age for the covered workforce.

These final regulations modify the proposed regulations to replace the subterfuge standard with a requirement that the normal retirement age under a plan be an age that is not earlier than the earliest age that is reasonably representative of the typical retirement age for the industry in which the covered workforce is employed. To address comments about the need for a safe harbor age, these regulations provide that

[2] The preamble to the proposed regulations noted that, while a low normal retirement age may have a significant cost effect on a traditional defined benefit plan, this effect is not as significant for defined contribution plans or for certain hybrid defined benefit plans.

a normal retirement age of at least age 62 is deemed to be not earlier than the typical retirement age for the industry in which the covered workforce is employed. Thus, a plan satisfies this safe harbor if its normal retirement age is age 62, or if its normal retirement age is the later of age 62 or another specified date, such as the later of age 62 or the fifth anniversary of plan participation. However, a plan that is subject to section 411 cannot provide for a normal retirement age that is later than the later of the time the participant attains age 65 or the fifth anniversary of the time the participant commenced participation in the plan. See section 411(a)(8)(B).

If a plan's normal retirement age is earlier than age 62, the determination of whether the age is not earlier than the earliest age that is reasonably representative of the typical retirement age for the industry in which the covered workforce is employed is based on all of the relevant facts and circumstances. If the normal retirement age is between ages 55 and 62, then it is generally expected that a good faith determination of the typical retirement age for the industry in which the covered workforce is employed that is made by the employer (or, in the case of a multiemployer plan, made by the trustees) will be given deference, assuming that the determination is reasonable under the facts and circumstances. However, a normal retirement age that is lower than age 55 is presumed to be earlier than the earliest age that is reasonably representative of the typical retirement age for the industry of the relevant covered workforce absent facts and circumstances that demonstrate otherwise to the Commissioner.

In the case of a plan where substantially all of the participants in the plan are qualified public safety employees (within the meaning of section 72(t)(10)(B), as added by section 828 of PPA '06), a normal retirement age of age 50 or later is deemed not to be earlier than the earliest age that is reasonably representative of the typical retirement age for the industry in which the covered workforce is employed. Under section 72(t)(10)(B), a qualified public safety employee means any employee of a State or political subdivision of a State who provides police protection, firefighting services, or emergency medical services for any area within the jurisdiction of such State or political subdivision.

B. *Section 411(d)(6) Relief*

These regulations include an amendment to the existing regulations under section 411(d)(6) to permit a plan to be amended during a transition period to conform to the rules concerning normal retirement age. Thus, a plan amendment that changes the normal retirement age under the plan to a later normal retirement age (pursuant to these regulations) does not violate section 411(d)(6) merely because the amendment eliminates a right to an in-service distribution prior to the amended normal retirement age. However, this rule does not provide any other relief. For example, this rule does not permit the amendment to reduce benefits in some other manner that fails to satisfy section 411(d)(6). Neither does the rule provide relief under section 411(a)(9) (requiring that the normal retirement benefit not be less than the greater of any early retirement benefit payable under the plan or the benefit under the plan commencing at normal retirement age), section 411(a)(10) (if the amendment changes the plan's vesting rules), or section 4980F (or section 204(h), the parallel provision of ERISA) (relating to amendments that reduce the rate of future benefit accrual). See also Rev. Rul. 81–210, 1981–2 C.B. 89 (see §601.601(d)(2)(ii)(*b*)). An example is included to illustrate this rule.

Effective Dates

These regulations are generally applicable May 22, 2007. In the case of a governmental plan (as defined in section 414(d)), these regulations apply with respect to plan years beginning on or after January 1, 2009. In the case of a plan maintained pursuant to one or more collective bargaining agreements that have been ratified and are in effect on May 22, 2007, these regulations do not apply before the first plan year that begins after the last of the agreements terminates determined without regard to any extension thereof (or, if earlier, May 22, 2010).

A provision of a plan that results in the failure of the plan to satisfy §1.401(a)–1(b)(2) or (3) is a disqualifying provision described in §1.401(b)–1(b)(3)(i). Therefore, the remedial amendment period rules of §1.401(b)–1 apply. For example, in the case of a plan with a calendar plan year that is maintained by an employer with a calendar taxable year (and the plan is not a governmental plan and is not maintained pursuant to a collective bargaining agreement), the plan's remedial amendment period with respect to §1.401(a)–1(b)(2) and (3) ends on the date prescribed by law for the filing of the employer's income tax return (including extensions) for the 2007 taxable year.

In the case of a plan amendment that increases the plan's normal retirement age pursuant to this regulation, the amendment may also eliminate a right to an in-service distribution prior to the normal retirement age under the plan as amended without violating section 411(d)(6) if the amendment is adopted after May 22, 2007, and on or before the last day of the applicable remedial amendment period under §1.401(b)–1 with respect to the requirements of §1.401(a)–1(b)(2) and (3). For purposes of section 1107 of PPA '06, such an amendment is not made pursuant to PPA '06 and is not made pursuant to any regulation issued under PPA '06.

Special Analyses

It has been determined that this Treasury Decision is not a significant regulatory action as defined in Executive Order 12866. Therefore, a regulatory assessment is not required. It also has been determined that section 553(b) of the Administrative Procedure Act (5 U.S.C. chapter 5) does not apply to these regulations, and because the regulation does not impose a collection of information requirement upon small entities, the Regulatory Flexibility Act (5 U.S.C. chapter 6) does not apply. Pursuant to section 7805(f) of the Internal Revenue Code, the notice of proposed rulemaking preceding these regulations was submitted to the Small Business Administration for comment on its impact on small business.

Drafting Information

The principal authors of these regulations are Christopher A. Crouch (formerly of the Office of the Division Counsel/Associate Chief Counsel (Tax Exempt and Government Entities)), Cathy A. Vohs and Janet A. Laufer of the Office of the Division Counsel/Associate Chief Counsel (Tax Exempt and Government Entities).

However, other personnel from the IRS and Treasury Department participated in their development.

* * * * *

Adoption of Amendments to the Regulations

Accordingly, 26 CFR part 1 is amended as follows:

PART 1—INCOME TAXES

Paragraph 1. The authority citation for part 1 is amended by adding an entry in numerical order to read in part as follows:

Authority: 26 U.S.C. 7805 * * *

Section 1.401(a)–1 also issued under 26 U.S.C. 401. * * *

Par. 2. Section 1.401(a)–1 is amended by:

1. Revising paragraph (b)(1)(i).
2. Adding paragraphs (b)(2), (b)(3), and (b)(4).

The additions and revision read as follows:

§1.401(a)–1 Post-ERISA qualified plans and qualified trusts; in general.

* * * * *

(b) * * *

(1) * * *

(i) In order for a pension plan to be a qualified plan under section 401(a), the plan must be established and maintained by an employer primarily to provide systematically for the payment of definitely determinable benefits to its employees over a period of years, usually for life, after retirement or attainment of normal retirement age (subject to paragraph (b)(2) of this section). A plan does not fail to satisfy this paragraph (b)(1)(i) merely because the plan provides, in accordance with section 401(a)(36), that a distribution may be made from the plan to an employee who has attained age 62 and who is not separated from employment at the time of such distribution.

* * * * *

(2) *Normal retirement age*—(i) *General rule*. The normal retirement age under a plan must be an age that is not earlier than the earliest age that is reasonably representative of the typical retirement age for the industry in which the covered workforce is employed.

(ii) *Age 62 safe harbor*. A normal retirement age under a plan that is age 62 or later is deemed to be not earlier than the earliest age that is reasonably representative of the typical retirement age for the industry in which the covered workforce is employed.

(iii) *Age 55 to age 62*. In the case of a normal retirement age that is not earlier than age 55 and is earlier than age 62, whether the age is not earlier than the earliest age that is reasonably representative of the typical retirement age for the industry in which the covered workforce is employed is based on all of the relevant facts and circumstances.

(iv) *Under age 55*. A normal retirement age that is lower than age 55 is presumed to be earlier than the earliest age that is reasonably representative of the typical retirement age for the industry in which the covered workforce is employed, unless the Commissioner determines that under the facts and circumstances the normal retirement age is not earlier than the earliest age that is reasonably representative of the typical retirement age for the industry in which the covered workforce is employed.

(v) *Age 50 safe harbor for qualified public safety employees*. A normal retirement age under a plan that is age 50 or later is deemed to be not earlier than the earliest age that is reasonably representative of the typical retirement age for the industry in which the covered workforce is employed if substantially all of the participants in the plan are qualified public safety employees (within the meaning of section 72(t)(10)(B)).

(3) *Benefit distribution prior to retirement*. For purposes of paragraph (b)(1)(i) of this section, retirement does not include a mere reduction in the number of hours that an employee works. Accordingly, benefits may not be distributed prior to normal retirement age solely due to a reduction in the number of hours that an employee works.

(4) *Effective date*. Except as otherwise provided in this paragraph (b)(4), paragraphs (b)(2) and (3) of this section are effective May 22, 2007. In the case of a governmental plan (as defined in section 414(d)), paragraphs (b)(2) and (3) of this section are effective for plan years beginning on or after January 1, 2009. In the case of a plan maintained pursuant to one or more collective bargaining agreements that have been ratified and are in effect on May 22, 2007, paragraphs (b)(2) and (3) of this section do not apply before the first plan year that begins after the last of such agreements terminate determined without regard to any extension thereof (or, if earlier, May 22, 2010). See §1.411(d)–4, A–12, for a special transition rule in the case of a plan amendment that increases a plan's normal retirement age pursuant to paragraph (b)(2) of this section.

Par. 3. Section 1.411(d)–4 is amended by adding Q&A–12 as follows:

§1.411(d)–4 Section 411(d)(6) protected benefits.

* * * * *

Q–12. Is there a transition period during which a plan is permitted to eliminate a right to in-service distributions in connection with an amendment to ensure that the plan's normal retirement age satisfies the requirements of §1.401(a)–1(b)(2)?

A–12. (a) *In general*. A plan amendment that changes the normal retirement age under the plan to a later normal retirement age pursuant to §1.401(a)–1(b)(2) does not violate section 411(d)(6) merely because it eliminates a right to an in-service distribution prior to the amended normal retirement age. However, this paragraph does not provide relief from any other applicable requirements; for example, this relief does not permit the amendment to violate section 411(a)(9) (requiring that the normal retirement benefit not be less than the greater of any early retirement benefit payable under the plan or the benefit under the plan commencing at normal retirement age), section 411(a)(10) (if the amendment changes the plan's vesting rules), section 411(d)(6) (other than elimination of the right to an in-service distribution prior to the amended normal retirement age), or section 4980F (relating to an amendment that reduces the rate of future benefit accrual). This paragraph only applies to a plan amendment that is adopted after May 22, 2007, and on or before the last day of the applicable remedial amendment period under §1.401(b)–1 with respect to the requirements of §1.401(a)–1(b)(2) and (3).

(b) *Example*. The following example illustrates the application of this section:

(i) *Facts*. (A) Plan A is a defined benefit plan intended to be qualified under section 401(a). Plan A is maintained by a calendar year taxpayer and has a normal retirement age that is age 45. For employees who cease employment before normal retirement age with a vested benefit, Plan A permits benefits to commence at any date after the attainment of normal retirement age through attainment of age 70½ and provides for benefits to be actuarially increased to the extent they commence after normal retirement age. For employees who continue employment after attainment of normal retirement age, Plan A provides for benefits to continue to accrue and permits benefits to commence at any time, with an actuarial increase in benefits to apply to the extent benefits do not commence after normal retirement age. Age 45 is an age that is earlier than the earliest age that is reasonably representative of the typical retirement age for the industry in which the covered workforce is employed.

(B) On February 18, 2008, Plan A is amended, effective May 22, 2007, to change its normal retirement age to the later of age 65 or the fifth anniversary of participation in the plan. The amendment provides full vesting for any participating employee who is employed on May 21, 2007, and who terminates employment on or after attaining age 45. The amendment provides employees who cease employment before the revised normal retirement age and who are entitled to a vested benefit with the right to be able to commence benefits at any date from age 45 to age 70½. The plan amendment also revises the plan's benefit accrual formula so that the benefit for prior service (payable commencing at the revised normal retirement age or any other age after age 45) is not less than would have applied under the plan's formula before the amendment (also payable commencing at the corresponding dates), based on the benefit accrued on May 21, 2007, and provides for service thereafter to have the same rate of future benefit accrual. Thus, for any participant employed on May 21, 2007, with respect to benefits accrued for service after May 21, 2007, the amount payable under the plan (as amended) at any benefit commencement date after age 45 is the same amount that would have been payable at that benefit commencement date under the plan prior to amendment. The plan amendment also eliminates the right to an in-service distribution between age 45 and the revised normal retirement age. Plan A has been operated since May 22, 2007, in conformity with the amendment adopted on February 18, 2008.

(ii) *Conclusion.* The plan amendment does not violate section 411(d)(6). Although the amendment eliminates the right to commence benefits in-service between age 45 and the revised normal retirement age, the amendment is made before the last day of the remedial amendment period applicable to the plan under §1.401(b)–1 with respect to the requirements of §1.401(a)–1(b)(2) and (3), and therefore the amendment is permitted under paragraph (a) of this A–12. Further, the amendment does not result in a reduction in any benefit for service after May 22, 2007. Thus, the amendment does not result in a reduction in any benefit for future service, and advance notice of a significant reduction in the rate of future benefit accrual is not required under section 4980F.

Kevin M. Brown,
Deputy Commissioner for Services and Enforcement.

Approved May 9, 2007.

Eric Solomon,
Assistant Secretary of the Treasury (Tax Policy).

(Filed by the Office of the Federal Register on May 21, 2007, 8:45 a.m., and published in the issue of the Federal Register for May 22, 2007, 72 F.R. 28604)

Section 1221.—Capital Asset Defined

26 CFR 1.1221–1: Meaning of terms.
(Also §§ 197, 1231, 1241, 1245, 1253; 1.1241–1.)

Cancellation of distributorship agreement. This ruling holds that the cancellation of an agreement to distribute a manufacturer's products may be a sale or exchange of property. The gain may be capital gain or treated as capital gain and may be subject to recapture.

Rev. Rul. 2007–37

ISSUE

1. Is the cancellation of a distributor agreement between a manufacturer and a distributor of the manufacturer's products a sale or exchange of property?

2. Is any resulting gain to the distributor capital gain or treated as capital gain?

FACTS

X manufactures automobile N. X sells N through a network of automobile distributors with which X enters into distributor agreements. The distributor agreements generally provide that a distributor may sell N within a prescribed geographic area and may renew the agreement as long as the distributor performs according to the agreement.

In 1994, A entered into a distributor agreement with X to sell N. The amount of A's payment to X for the agreement is not contingent on the productivity, use, or disposition of the right to sell N, but rather is a fixed sum. Since then, A has been continuously engaged in the trade or business of selling N. A makes a substantial capital investment in its distributorship as reflected in the cost of its N inventory.

X plans to discontinue production of N in 2007, and offers payments to distributors to cancel their N distributor agreements. In 2007, A accepts X's payment of $40x in cancellation of its N distributor agreement with X. A's basis in the distributor agreement is $10x. A has no section 1231 losses.

LAW

Section 1241 of the Internal Revenue Code provides that amounts received by a distributor of goods for the cancellation of a distributor agreement in which the distributor has a substantial capital investment are amounts received in exchange for the agreement. Section 1.1241–1(b) of the Income Tax Regulations defines "cancellation" of a distributor agreement as a termination of all the contractual rights of a distributor with respect to a particular distributorship, other than by the expiration of the agreement in accordance with its terms.

Section 1.1241–1(c) provides that § 1241 applies to a distributor agreement only if (i) it is for marketing or marketing and servicing of goods, (ii) the distributor has made a substantial capital investment in the distributorship, and (iii) the capital investment is reflected in physical assets such as inventories of tangible goods, equipment, machinery, storage facilities, or similar property.

Section 1221 defines "capital asset" as property held by the taxpayer, whether or not it is connected with the taxpayer's trade or business. However, property used in a taxpayer's trade or business and of a character that is subject to the allowance for depreciation provided in § 167 is not a capital asset. Section 1221(a)(2).

Under § 1231, gain from the sale or exchange of property that is not a capital asset may be treated as capital gain if the property is used in the trade or business, is held for more than one year, and is property of a character subject to the allowance for depreciation under § 167. If a taxpayer has a net gain for a taxable year from sales or exchanges of property used in the trade or business as defined in § 1231(b) (as well as from certain involuntary conversions of property), each gain or loss from such sales or exchanges is treated under § 1231(a)(1) as a long-term capital gain or loss. If a net loss results, each gain or loss is treated under § 1231(a)(2) as not arising from the sale or exchange of a capital asset. Generally, the result of the operation of § 1231 in a taxable year is to give the taxpayer the benefit of long-term capital gains treatment on net gains and ordinary loss treatment on net losses. However, § 1231(c) provides that the net section 1231 gain for any taxable year is treated as ordinary income to the extent of the taxpayer's non-recaptured net section 1231 losses for the five most recent preceding taxable years.

Since section 1231 gain includes gain from the sale or exchange of property of a character subject to an allowance for depreciation under § 167, section 1231 gain may be subject to recapture under § 1245. Section 1245 provides for recapture of depreciation and amortization if the property sold or exchanged is section 1245 property. Section 1245 property includes any personal property, including intangible personal property, of a character subject to the allowance for depreciation under § 167. See § 1245(a)(3)(A) and § 1.1245–3(b)(2).

Franchises subject to § 197

Under § 197(f)(7), property that is an "amortizable section 197 intangible" is treated as property of a character subject to the allowance for depreciation under § 167. An "amortizable section 197 intangible" is any section 197 intangible that is acquired by the taxpayer on or after the effective date of § 197 (in general, August 11, 1993; or July 26, 1991, if there is a valid retroactive election under § 1.197–1T) and is held in connection with the conduct of a trade or business. Section 197(c)(1) and § 13261(g)(2) of Pub. L. No. 103–66. Under § 197(d)(1)(F), a "section 197 intangible" includes any franchise, trademark, or trade name. Section 197(f)(4) defines the term "franchise" by reference to § 1253(b)(1), which provides that a franchise includes an agreement that gives the right to sell goods within a specified area.

Since an amortizable section 197 intangible, including a franchise, is property of a character subject to an allowance for depreciation under § 167, it is not a capital asset for purposes of § 1221. However, if an amortizable section 197 intangible is used in a trade or business and held for more than one year, gain or loss on its sale or exchange generally qualifies as a section 1231 gain or loss. Similarly, an amortizable section 197 intangible is section 1245 property and any section 1231 gain from the sale or exchange of an amortizable section 197 intangible may be subject to recapture under § 1245.

Franchises acquired on or after January 1, 1970, and before the effective date of § 197

Whether a franchise acquired on or after January 1, 1970 (the effective date of § 1253), and before the effective date of § 197, is a capital asset under § 1221 or section 1231(b) property depends on whether the franchise is amortizable under § 1253 and whether, because of such amortization, it is property of a character subject to the allowance for depreciation under § 167. For this purpose, the relevant provisions of § 1253 are those in effect before its amendment in 1993, and references to § 1253 in this section of this revenue ruling are to the provisions in effect before its 1993 amendment.

In general, intangible assets acquired before the effective date of § 197 could be amortized only if they had a limited useful life, the length of which could be estimated with reasonable accuracy. Section 1.167(a)–3. Although franchises in many cases have indefinite useful lives, § 1253 allowed the cost of franchises in which the transferor retained any significant power, right, or continuing interest to be either deducted in the taxable year paid or amortized over a specified period of time. Section 1253(d)(1), which was not affected by the 1993 amendment, provides that a purchaser of a franchise may deduct certain contingent payments under § 162(a). Section 1253(d)(2) provided that payments not deductible under § 1253(d)(1) were recoverable over a period of time that depended on whether the payments were made in a lump sum, in approximately equal installments over a specified period, or under another payment arrangement. For transfers after October 2, 1989, § 1253(d)(2) did not apply if the transfer of the franchise involved principal payments in excess of $100,000, but the taxpayer could elect under § 1253(d)(3) to recover the cost of the franchise ratably over a 25-year period beginning with the taxable year of the transfer. Thus, although § 1253 did not explicitly provide that a franchise was treated as property of a character subject to the allowance for depreciation, it permitted acquisition costs to be amortized as if the franchise had a limited useful life.

Property amortizable under provisions of the Code other than § 167 has been held to be "property of a character which is subject to the allowance for depreciation under § 167" and § 1231(b) property. See *Tom F. Baker v. Commissioner*, 38 T.C. 9 (1962); *McEnery v. Commissioner*, T.C. Memo. 1967–213. "It has long been established that an amortizable item is 'of a character subject to depreciation' as required under § 1231(b)." *Estate of Shea v. Commissioner*, 57 T.C. 15, 23 (1971), *acq.* 1973–2 C.B. 3. Therefore, property that was amortizable under § 1253 is properly treated as property of a character subject to the allowance for depreciation under § 167 and as section 1231(b) property rather than a capital asset.

The amortizable character of franchises transferred during the period between 1969 and the effective date of § 197 also determines their proper treatment for purposes of § 1245. For transfers after October 2, 1989, § 1245(a)(2)(C) provided that deductions allowable under § 1253(d)(2) or (d)(3) were treated as deductions for amortization for purposes of § 1245, and § 1245(a)(3) provided that property subject to the allowance for amortization in § 1253(d)(2) or (d)(3) was section 1245 property. The legislative history relating to the 1989 amendments of section 1245 and 1253 stated that no inference was intended as to the recapture requirements of prior law. As noted above, however, under the prior law the cost of a franchise was amortizable under § 1253(d)(2), including in cases in which the principal payments exceeded $100,000. As is the case for purposes of § 1231, any franchise the cost of which was amortized under § 1245(d)(2) is properly treated for purposes of § 1245 as property of a character subject to the allowance for depreciation under § 167. Accordingly, such a franchise is section 1245 property.

Therefore, a distributor agreement acquired after 1969 and before the effective date of § 197, for a fixed payment, including a fixed sum payable in a series of approximately equal payments, is amortizable under § 1253 and is treated as property of a character subject to the allowance for depreciation in § 167. Because it is property of a character subject to the allowance for depreciation, it is not a capital asset, but gain from the sale or exchange of such property may be treated as capital gain under § 1231 and may be subject to recapture under § 1245.

Franchises acquired before January 1, 1970

A distributor agreement entered into before January 1, 1970 (the effective date of § 1253), is not amortizable, is not property of a character subject to the allowance for depreciation in § 167, and is a capital asset under § 1221. See Rev. Rul. 55–374, 1955–1 C.B. 370; Rev. Rul. 88–24, 1988–1 C.B. 306.

ANALYSIS

In the present case, A's distributor agreement with X is for the marketing of goods, and A has made a substantial investment of capital in the distributorship as reflected in A's inventory value. The cancellation did not occur by reason of the expiration of the agreement in accordance with its terms and the cancellation terminates all of A's rights to sell product N. Therefore, §1241 applies to the cancellation of the agreement and X's payment to A in cancellation of A's distributor agreement is treated as an amount received in exchange for the agreement.

A's distributor agreement gives A the right to sell N within a specific geographic area. Therefore, the agreement is a franchise under § 1253(b)(1). A entered into the distributor agreement after August 10, 1993, and holds it in connection with the conduct of a trade or business. Thus, the distributor agreement is an "amortizable section 197 intangible" and property of a character subject to the allowance for depreciation provided in § 167, and is not a capital asset. A's gain of $30x from the payment for the cancellation of the distributor agreement qualifies under § 1231 as long-term capital gain, subject to recapture under § 1245 and recharacterization under § 1231(c).

If A had entered into the distributor agreement with X after 1969, but before the effective date of § 197, gain from the cancellation of the agreement would similarly qualify for § 1231 treatment. Because A paid X a fixed amount for the distributor agreement, the agreement would be amortizable under § 1253, and as a result would be property of a character that is subject to an allowance for depreciation under § 167. The $30x gain from the cancellation would be treated as long-term capital gain under § 1231, subject to any applicable recapture under § 1245 and recharacterization under § 1231(c).

If A had entered into the distributor agreement with X before 1970, the agreement would be a capital asset and the $30x gain from the cancellation would be capital gain.

HOLDING

1. The cancellation of a distributor agreement between a manufacturer and a distributor of the manufacturer's products is a sale or exchange of property if the distributor has made a substantial capital investment in the distributorship and the investment is reflected in physical assets.

2. Any resulting gain to the distributor is capital gain if the agreement is a capital asset. The gain is section 1231 gain and may be treated as capital if the agreement is property of a character subject to the allowance for depreciation under § 167. For this purpose, property is treated as being of such a character if it is amortizable under § 197 or § 1253. The section 1231 gain may be subject to recapture under § 1245.

DRAFTING INFORMATION

The principal author of this revenue ruling is Maxine Woo-Garcia of the Office of Associate Chief Counsel (Income Tax & Accounting). For further information regarding this revenue ruling, contact Ms. Woo-Garcia at (202) 622–7900 (not a toll-free call).

Section 1231.—Property Used in the Trade or Business and Involuntary Conversions

Gain to a distributor from the cancellation of an agreement to distribute a manufacturer's products is section 1231 gain and may be treated as capital if the agreement is property of a character subject to the allowance for depreciation under section 167. For this purpose, property is treated as being of such a character if it is amortizable under section 197 or section 1253. See Rev. Rul. 2007-37, page 1390.

Section 1241.—Cancellation of Lease or Distributor's Agreement

26 CFR 1.1241–1: Cancellation of lease or distributor's agreement.

The cancellation of a distributor agreement between a manufacturer and a distributor of the manufacturer's products is a sale or exchange of property if the distributor has made a substantial capital investment in the distributorship and the investment is reflected in physical assets. See Rev. Rul. 2007-37, page 1390.

Section 1245.—Gain From Dispositions of Certain Depreciable Property

Gain to a distributor from the cancellation of an agreement to distribute a manufacturer's products is section 1231 gain and may be treated as capital if the agreement is property of a character subject to the allowance for depreciation under section 167. For this purpose, property is treated as being of such a character if it is amortizable under section 197 or section 1253. The section 1231 gain may be subject to recapture under section 1245. See Rev. Rul. 2007-37, page 1390.

Section 1253.—Transfers of Franchises, Trademarks, and Trade Names

Gain to a distributor from the cancellation of an agreement to distribute a manufacturer's products is section 1231 gain and may be treated as capital if the agreement is property of a character subject to the allowance for depreciation under section 167. For this purpose, property is treated as being of such a character if it is amortizable under section 1253. See Rev. Rul. 2007-37, page 1390.

Part III. Administrative, Procedural, and Miscellaneous

Deductibility of Lodging Expenses

Notice 2007–47

PURPOSE

This notice advises taxpayers that the Internal Revenue Service and the Department of the Treasury intend to amend regulations under § 262 of the Internal Revenue Code relating to the deductibility of lodging expenses.

BACKGROUND

Section 162(a) allows as a deduction all the ordinary and necessary business expenses paid or incurred during the taxable year in carrying on any trade or business. Section 162(a)(2) provides that expenses deductible under § 162(a) include traveling expenses (including lodging expenses that are not lavish or extravagant under the circumstances) while away from home in the pursuit of a trade or business.

Section 262(a) provides generally that no deduction is allowed for personal, living, or family expenses.

Section 1.262–1(b)(5) of the Income Tax Regulations provides that the costs of a taxpayer's lodging not incurred in traveling away from home are personal expenses and are not deductible unless they qualify as deductible expenses under § 217.

Under § 1.132–5(a) of the Income Tax Regulations, the value of a working condition fringe is not included in the gross income of an employee. A "working condition fringe" is any property or service provided to an employee of an employer to the extent that, if the employee paid for the property or service, the amount would be allowable as a deduction under § 162 or 167.

INTERIM GUIDANCE

The Service and the Department of the Treasury expect to amend § 1.262–1(b)(5) to provide that the costs of a taxpayer's lodging not incurred in traveling away from home are personal expenses and are not deductible unless they qualify as deductible expenses under § 162 or 217.

Pending the issuance of additional published guidance, the Service will not apply § 1.262–1(b)(5) to expenses for lodging of an employee not incurred while the employee is traveling away from home that an employer provides to the employee, or requires the employee to obtain, under the following conditions:

(1) The lodging is on a temporary basis;

(2) The lodging is necessary for the employee to participate in or be available for a *bona fide* business meeting or function of the employer; and

(3) The expenses are otherwise deductible by the employee, or would be deductible if paid by the employee, under § 162(a).

This issue will not be raised in any taxable year ending on or before publication of the guidance and, if already raised as an issue in examination or before the Office of Appeals or the Tax Court in a taxable year ending on or before May 23, 2007, the issue will not be pursued by the Service.

DRAFTING INFORMATION

The principal author of this notice is R. Matthew Kelley of the Office of the Associate Chief Counsel (Income Tax & Accounting). For further information concerning this notice, contact Mr. Kelley at (202) 622–7900 (not a toll-free call).

Part IV. Items of General Interest

Notice of Proposed Rulemaking

Dependent Child of Divorced or Separated Parents or Parents Who Live Apart

REG–149856–03

AGENCY: Internal Revenue Service (IRS), Treasury.

ACTION: Notice of proposed rulemaking.

SUMMARY: This document contains proposed regulations relating to a claim that a child is a dependent by parents who are divorced, legally separated under a decree of separate maintenance, separated under a written separation agreement, or who live apart at all times during the last 6 months of the calendar year. The proposed regulations reflect amendments under the Working Families Tax Relief Act of 2004 (WFTRA) and the Gulf Opportunity Zone Act of 2005 (GOZA).

DATES: Written or electronic comments or a request for a public hearing must be received by July 31, 2007.

ADDRESSES: Send submissions to CC:PA:LPD:PR (REG–149856–03), room 5203, Internal Revenue Service, POB 7604, Ben Franklin Station, Washington, DC 20044. Submissions may be hand-delivered Monday through Friday between the hours of 8 a.m. and 4 p.m. to CC:PA:LPD:PR (REG–149856–03), Courier's Desk, Internal Revenue Service, 1111 Constitution Avenue, NW, Washington, DC. Alternatively, taxpayers may submit comments electronically via the IRS internet site via the Federal eRulemaking Portal at *www.regulations.gov* (indicate IRS and REG–149856–03).

FOR FURTHER INFORMATION CONTACT: Concerning the proposed regulations, Victoria Driscoll (202) 622–4920; concerning the submission of comments and/or a request for a hearing, Regina Johnson (202) 622–3175 (not toll-free numbers).

SUPPLEMENTARY INFORMATION:

Paperwork Reduction Act

The IRS and the Department of the Treasury, as part of their continuing efforts to reduce paperwork and respondent burden, invite the general public to comment on proposed and/or continuing collections of information in accordance with the Paperwork Reduction Act of 1995 (PRA) (44 U.S.C. 3506(c)(2)(A)). This helps to ensure that requested data are provided in the desired format, reporting burden (time and financial resources) is minimized, collection instruments are clearly understood, and the impact of collection requirements on respondents is properly assessed. The IRS and the Department solicit comments on the information collection request (ICR) included in this proposed regulatory action. A copy of the ICR may be obtained by contacting the OMB Unit, SE:W:CAR:MP:T:T:SP, Internal Revenue Service, Room 6406, 1111 Constitution Ave., NW, Washington, DC 20224.

The collection of information in this proposed rule is being reviewed by the Office of Management and Budget (OMB) in accordance with the Paperwork Reduction Act of 1995 in connection with OMB Control Number 1545–0074. This control number is assigned to all information collections associated with individual tax returns (series 1040 and associated forms and schedules, and related regulatory information collections). Information collections associated with control number 1545–0074 are subject to annual public comment and approval by OMB in accordance with the Paperwork Reduction Act.

The collection of information in these proposed regulations is in §1.152–4(d). The information will help the IRS determine if a taxpayer may claim a child as a dependent when the parents of the child are divorced or separated or lived apart at all times during the last six months of a calendar year. The collection of information is required to obtain a benefit. The information will be reported on IRS Form 8332. The time needed to complete and file this form will vary depending on individual circumstances. The estimated burden for individual taxpayers filing this form is included in the estimates shown in the instructions for their individual income tax return.

The public is invited to provide comments on this information collection, particularly comments that:

Evaluate whether the proposed collection of information is necessary for the proper performance of the functions of the IRS, including whether the information will have practical utility;

Evaluate the burden of the proposed collection of information, including how the burden on those who are to respond may be minimized, including through the use of appropriate automated, electronic, mechanical, or other technological collection techniques or other forms of information technology, such as permitting electronic submission of responses; and

Enhance the quality, utility, and clarity of the information to be collected.

Comments should be sent to the Office of Information and Regulatory Affairs, OMB, Room 10235, New Executive Office Building, Washington, DC 20503; Attention: Desk Officer for the Department of the Treasury. Comments may be submitted through July 2, 2007.

Background

This document contains proposed amendments to 26 CFR part 1 relating to section 152(e) and the entitlement of divorced or separated parents or parents who live apart at all times during the last 6 months of the calendar year to claim a child as a dependent.

Under section 151, a taxpayer may deduct an exemption amount for a dependent. Section 152, as amended by section 201 of WFTRA (Public Law No. 108–311, 118 Stat. 1166), defines *dependent* in general as a qualifying child or a qualifying relative.

Section 152(c), which defines qualifying child, states that the qualifying child must have the same principal place of abode as the taxpayer for more than one-half of the taxable year. Section 152(c)(1)(B). Section 152(c)(4)(B) provides that, if both parents of a child claim the child as a qualifying child and do not file a joint return together, the child is treated as the qualifying child of the parent with whom the child resides for the longer period of time during the taxable year. If the child resides with both parents for an equal amount of time during the taxable year, the child is treated as the qualifying child of the parent with the higher adjusted gross income. As part of the definition of a qualifying relative, section 152(d)(1)(C) requires that the taxpayer provide over one-half of the individual's support for the calendar year. The principal place of abode requirement of section 152(c)(1)(B), the tie-breaking rule of section 152(c)(4)(B), and the support rule of section 152(d)(1)(C), do not apply if section 152(e) applies.

Section 152(e), which was amended by section 404 of GOZA (Public Law No. 109–135, 119 Stat. 2577), provides rules for parents who (1) are divorced or legally separated under a decree of divorce or separate maintenance, (2) are separated under a written separation agreement, or (3) live apart at all times during the last 6 months of the calendar year. Under section 152(e)(1), a child of parents described in section 152(e) is treated as the qualifying child or qualifying relative of the noncustodial parent if the child receives over one-half of the child's support during the calendar year from the child's parents, the child is in the custody of one or both of the child's parents for more than one-half of the calendar year, and the requirements of section 152(e)(2) or section 152(e)(3) are met.

The requirements of section 152(e)(2) are met if the custodial parent signs a written declaration that the custodial parent will not claim a child as a dependent for a taxable year and the noncustodial parent attaches the declaration to the noncustodial parent's tax return. The requirements of section 152(e)(3) are met if a qualified pre-1985 instrument allocates the dependency exemption to the noncustodial parent and the noncustodial parent provides at least $600 for the support of the child during the calendar year.

Section 152(e)(4) defines *custodial parent* as the parent having custody for the greater portion of the calendar year and *noncustodial parent* as the parent who is not the custodial parent.

If a child is treated as the qualifying child or qualifying relative of the noncustodial parent under section 152(e), then that parent may claim the child for purposes of the dependency deduction under section 151 and the child tax credit under section 24, if the other requirements of those provisions are met. Whether a child is a qualifying child for purposes of head of household filing status, the child and dependent care credit, or the earned income credit, is determined without regard to section 152(e). See sections 2(b)(1)(A)(i) (head of household), 21(e)(5) (dependent care credit), and 32(c)(3) (earned income credit).

The special rule of section 152(e)(1) for parents living apart during the last six months of the calendar year was added by section 423(a) of the Deficit Reduction Act of 1984 (Public Law No. 98–369, 98 Stat. 494) (the 1984 Act). The 1984 Act also amended the exceptions in section 152(e)(2). Regulations under section 152(e)(1) and (2) (§1.152–4 of the Income Tax Regulations) were published on March 20, 1971, and amended on October 15, 1971, and August 20, 1979. Temporary regulations reflecting the amendments made by the 1984 Act (§1.152–4T) were published on August 31, 1984.

Explanation of Provisions

These proposed regulations update §1.152–4 by deleting obsolete provisions, revising language to improve clarity, and incorporating the provisions of §1.152–4T. The proposed regulations also provide guidance on issues that have arisen in the administration of section 152(e).

1. *Definition of Custodial Parent*

Under the proposed regulations, the custodial parent is the parent with whom the child resides for the greater number of nights during the calendar year. The noncustodial parent is the parent who is not the custodial parent. The proposed regulations further provide that, if a child is temporarily absent from a parent's home for a night, the child is treated as residing with the parent with whom the child would have resided for the night. However, if the child resides with neither parent for a night, for example because another party is entitled to custody of the child for that night, the child is treated as not residing with either parent for that night. Comments are requested specifically on alternative methods of allocating nights when a child resides with neither parent and whether nights residing with neither parent should not be allocated to either parent. The proposed regulations provide a tie-breaking rule that, if a child resides with each parent for an equal number of nights during the calendar year, the parent with the higher adjusted gross income for the calendar year is treated as the custodial parent. Cf. section 152(c)(4)(B).

Sections 151 and 152, not state law, determine whether a divorced or separated parent may claim an exemption for a child for Federal income tax purposes. A state court order or decree does not operate to allocate the federal exemption between parents.

2. *Requirements for Release of the Right to Claim a Child*

Section 152(e)(2) provides that a custodial parent may release a claim to an exemption for a child by signing a written declaration (in such form and manner as the Secretary may prescribe by regulations) that he or she will not claim the child as a dependent. The noncustodial parent must attach the written declaration to the tax return to claim a dependency exemption for the child. Section 1.152–4T, Q&A–3, states that the written declaration may be made on a form developed by the IRS. Form 8332, *Release of Claim to Exemption for Child of Divorced or Separated Parents*, currently is used for this purpose. The temporary regulations further provide that any declaration not made on that form must conform to the substance of the form. Section 1.152–4T, Q&A–4, states that a claim to an exemption may be released for a single year, for a number of years, or for all future years, as specified in the declaration.

The proposed regulations incorporate these rules and further provide that a written declaration must include an unconditional statement that the custodial parent will not claim the child as a dependent for the specified year or years. A statement is unconditional if it does not expressly condition the custodial parent's waiver of the right to claim the child as a dependent on the noncustodial parent's meeting of an obligation such as the payment of support. The written declaration must specify the year or years for which the release is effective. A written declaration that does not specify a year or years has no effect. A written declaration that specifies all future years is treated as specifying the first taxable year after the taxable year the release is executed and all subsequent taxable years. A court order or decree may not serve as the written declaration required by section 152(e)(2).

3. *Revocation of Release of Claim*

The proposed regulations provide that a custodial parent who released the right to claim a child may revoke the release for future taxable years by providing written notice of the revocation to the other parent. The revocation may be made on a form designated by the IRS, such as Form 8332, which may be revised for this purpose, or by a written declaration that conforms to the substance of that form, whether or not the release was made on the form, and must specify the year or years for which the revocation is effective. A revocation that does not specify a year or years has no effect. A revocation that specifies all future years is treated as specifying the first taxable year after the taxable year the revocation is executed and all subsequent taxable years. The revocation may be effective no earlier than the taxable year that begins in the first calendar year after the calendar year in which the parent revoking the release provides notice of the revocation to the other parent. The parent revoking the release must attach the original or a copy of the revocation to the parent's tax return for any taxable year the parent claims the exemption as a result of the revocation, and keep a copy of the revocation and evidence of delivery of written notice of revocation to the noncustodial parent.

4. *Never Married Parents*

In *King v. Commissioner*, 121 T.C. 24 (2003), the United States Tax Court decided that section 152(e) applies to parents who had never married each other. The parents lived apart for the years at issue, and each had claimed a dependency deduction for the same child. In concluding that the Form 8332 executed by the custodial parent released her claim to the deduction, the court determined that section 152(e)(1)(A)(iii), which refers to parents who "live apart at all times during the last 6 months of the calendar year," encompasses both married parents and parents who never married each other. The proposed regulations follow the decision in *King v. Commissioner*.

5. *Effective Date*

The regulations are proposed to apply to taxable years beginning after the date the regulations are published as final regulations in the **Federal Register**.

Special Analyses

This notice of proposed rulemaking is not a significant regulatory action as defined in Executive Order 12866. Therefore, a regulatory assessment is not required. It has also been determined that section 553(b) of the Administrative Procedure Act (5 U.S.C. chapter 5) does not apply to these regulations and, because the regulations do not impose a collection of information on small entities, the Regulatory Flexibility Act (5 U.S.C. chapter 6) does not apply. Pursuant to section 7805(f) of the Code, this notice of proposed rulemaking will be submitted to the Chief Counsel for Advocacy of the Small Business Administration for comment on its impact on small business.

Comments and Requests for a Public Hearing

Before these proposed regulations are adopted as final regulations, consideration will be given to any written (a signed original and eight (8) copies) or electronic comments that are submitted timely to the IRS. The IRS and Treasury Department request comments on the clarity of the proposed regulations and how they can be made easier to understand. All comments will be available for public inspection and copying. A public hearing may be scheduled if requested in writing by any person who timely submits written comments. If a public hearing is scheduled, notice of the date, time, and place for the public hearing will be published in the **Federal Register**.

Drafting Information

The principal author of these regulations is Victoria J. Driscoll of the Office of Associate Chief Counsel (Income Tax and Accounting). However, other personnel from the IRS and Treasury Department participated in their development.

* * * * *

Proposed Amendment to the Regulations

Accordingly, 26 CFR part 1 is proposed to be amended as follows:

PART 1—INCOME TAXES

Paragraph 1. The authority citation for part 1 is amended by adding an entry to read in part as follows:

Authority: 26 U.S.C. 7805 * * *

§1.152–4 also issued under 26 U.S.C. 152(e).

Par. 2. Section 1.152–4 is revised to read as follows:

§1.152–4 Special rule for a child of divorced or separated parents or parents who live apart.

(a) *In general.* A taxpayer may claim a dependency deduction for a child (as defined in section 152(f)(1)) only if the child is the qualifying child of the taxpayer under section 152(c) or the qualifying relative of the taxpayer under section 152(d). Section 152(c)(4)(B) provides that a child who is claimed as a qualifying child by parents who do not file a joint return together is the qualifying child of the parent with whom the child resided for a longer period of time during the taxable year or, if the child resided with both parents for an equal period of time, of the parent with the higher adjusted gross income. However, a child is treated as the qualifying child or qualifying relative of the noncustodial parent if the custodial parent releases the claim to the exemption under section 152(e) and this section.

(b) *Release of claim by custodial parent*—(1) *In general.* Under section 152(e)(1), notwithstanding section 152(c)(1)(B), (c)(4)(B), and (d)(1)(C), a child is treated as the qualifying child or qualifying relative of the noncustodial parent (as defined in paragraph (c) of this section) if the requirements of paragraphs (b)(2) and (b)(3) of this section are met.

(2) *Support, custody, and parental status.* The requirements of this paragraph (b)(2) are met if the parents of the child

provide over one-half of the child's support for the calendar year, the child is in the custody of one or both parents for more than one-half of the calendar year, and the parents—

(i) Are divorced or legally separated under a decree of divorce or separate maintenance;

(ii) Are separated under a written separation agreement; or

(iii) Live apart at all times during the last 6 months of the calendar year whether or not they are or were married.

(3) *Release of claim to child.* The requirements of this paragraph (b)(3) are met if—

(i) The custodial parent signs a written declaration that the custodial parent will not claim the child as a dependent for the taxable year beginning in that calendar year and the noncustodial parent attaches the declaration to the noncustodial parent's return for the taxable year; or

(ii) A qualified pre-1985 instrument, as defined in section 152(e)(3)(B), effective for the taxable year beginning in that calendar year, provides that the noncustodial parent is entitled to the dependency exemption for the child and the noncustodial parent provides at least $600 for the support of the child during the calendar year.

(c) *Custodial parent*—(1) *In general.* The *custodial parent* is the parent with whom the child resides for a greater number of nights during the calendar year, and the *noncustodial parent* is the parent who is not the custodial parent.

(2) *Absences.* For purposes of this paragraph (c), when a child resides with neither parent for a night, the child is treated as residing with the parent with whom the child would have resided for the night but for the absence. However, if the child would have resided with neither parent for a night during an absence (for example, because a court awarded custody of the child to a third party for the period of absence), the child is treated as residing with neither parent for the night of the absence.

(3) *Special rule for equal number of nights.* If a child is in the custody of one or both parents for more than one-half of the calendar year and the child resides with each parent for an equal number of nights during the calendar year, the parent with the higher adjusted gross income for the calendar year is treated as the custodial parent.

(d) *Written declaration*—(1) *Form of declaration*—(i) *In general.* The written declaration under paragraph (b)(3)(i) of this section must constitute the custodial parent's unconditional release of the parent's claim to the child as a dependent for the year or years for which the declaration is effective. A declaration is unconditional if it does not expressly condition the custodial parent's release of the right to claim the child as a dependent on the noncustodial parent's meeting of an obligation such as the payment of support. A written declaration must name the noncustodial parent to whom the exemption is released. A written declaration must specify the year or years for which it is effective. A written declaration that does not specify a year or years has no effect. A written declaration that specifies all future years is treated as specifying the first taxable year after the taxable year of execution and all subsequent taxable years. A court order or decree may not serve as the written declaration.

(ii) *Form designated by IRS.* A written declaration may be made on a form designated by the IRS (currently Form 8332, *Release of Claim to Exemption for Child of Divorced or Separated Parents*). A written declaration not on the form designated by the IRS must conform to the substance of that form.

(2) *Attachment to return.* A noncustodial parent must attach the original written declaration to the parent's return for the taxable year in which the child is claimed as a dependent. If a release of a claim to a child is for more than one year, the noncustodial parent must attach the original written declaration to the parent's return for the first taxable year for which the release is effective. The noncustodial parent must attach a copy of the written declaration to the parent's return for each subsequent taxable year for which the noncustodial parent claims the child as a dependent.

(3) *Revocation of written declaration*—(i) *In general.* A written declaration described in paragraph (d)(1) of this section may be revoked by providing written notice of the revocation to the other parent. The revocation may be effective no earlier than the taxable year that begins in the first calendar year after the calendar year in which the parent revoking the written declaration provides the written notice.

(ii) *Form of revocation.* The revocation may be made on a form designated by the IRS whether or not the written declaration was made on a form designated by the IRS. A revocation not on that form must conform to the substance of the form. The revocation must specify the year or years for which the revocation is effective. A revocation that does not specify a year or years has no effect. A revocation that specifies all future years is treated as specifying the first taxable year after the taxable year the revocation is executed and all subsequent taxable years.

(iii) *Attachment to return.* The custodial parent must attach the original revocation to the parent's return for the taxable year for which the custodial parent claims a child as a dependent. If a revocation is for more than one year, the custodial parent must attach the original revocation to the parent's return for the first taxable year for which the revocation is effective and a copy of the revocation to the parent's return for each subsequent taxable year for which the custodial parent claims the child as a dependent. The custodial parent must keep a copy of the revocation and evidence of delivery of written notice of the revocation to the noncustodial parent.

(e) *Coordination with other sections.* A child who is treated as the qualifying child or qualifying relative of the noncustodial parent under section 152(e) and this section is treated as a dependent of both parents for purposes of sections 105(b), 132(h)(2)(B), and 213(d)(5).

(f) *Examples.* The provisions of this section are illustrated by the following examples which assume that each taxpayer's taxable year is the calendar year, one or both of the child's parents provide over one-half of the child's support for the calendar year, the child is in the custody of one or both parents for more than one-half of the calendar year, and the child otherwise meets the requirements of a qualifying child under section 152(c). In addition, in each of the examples, there is no qualified pre-1985 instrument in effect. The examples are as follows:

Example 1. (i) B and C, the parents of Child, are divorced. In 2007, Child resides with B for 7 months and with C for 5 months. B signs a Form 8332 for 2007 allowing C to claim Child as a dependent for that year.

(ii) Under paragraph (c) of this section, B is the custodial parent of Child in 2007 because B is the parent with whom Child resides for the greater number of nights in 2007. Because B signs a Form 8332, under paragraph (b) of this section, Child is treated as the qualifying child of C if C attaches the Form 8332 to C's 2007 return.

Example 2. (i) D and E, the parents of Child, are divorced. In 2007, Child resides with D for 7 months and with E for 5 months. D, the custodial parent, does not execute a Form 8332 or similar declaration for 2007.

(ii) Because D does not execute a Form 8332 or similar declaration for 2007, section 152(e) and this section do not apply to determine whether Child is treated as the qualifying child of D or E. Instead, whether Child is the qualifying child of D or E is determined under section 152(c).

Example 3. F and G, who never married, are the parents of Child. In 2007, Child spends alternate weeks residing with F and G. During a week when Child is residing with F, F gives Child permission to spend a night at the home of a friend. Under paragraph (c)(2) of this section, the night Child spends at the friend's home is treated as a night in which Child resides with F for purposes of determining whether Child is residing with F or G for the greater number of nights in the calendar year.

Example 4. J and K are the divorced parents of Child. In 2007, Child spends alternate periods residing with J or K. In August of 2007, J and Child spend 10 nights together in a hotel while on vacation. Under paragraph (c) of this section, the 10 nights when J and Child are on vacation are treated as nights in which Child resides with J for purposes of determining whether Child is residing with J or K for the greater number of nights in the calendar year.

Example 5. (i) In 2006, L and M, the parents of Child, execute a written separation agreement. The agreement provides that Child will live with L and that M will make monthly child support payments to L. The agreement further provides that L will not claim Child as a dependent in 2007 and in subsequent alternate years. The agreement does not expressly condition L's agreement not to claim Child as a dependent on M's payment of child support or any other condition. The agreement contains all the other information requested on Form 8332. M attaches the agreement to M's tax returns for 2007 and 2009.

(ii) In 2008, M fails to provide child support for Child, and L signs a Form 8332 revoking the release of L's right to claim Child as a dependent for 2009 and delivers a copy of the Form 8332 to M. L attaches the Form 8332 revoking the release to L's tax return for 2009 and keeps a copy of the revocation and evidence of delivery of written notice to M.

(iii) M may claim Child as a qualifying child for 2007 because L releases the right to claim Child as a dependent under paragraph (b)(3) of this section by executing the separation agreement, and M attaches the separation agreement to M's tax return in accordance with paragraphs (d)(1) and (d)(2) of this section. The separation agreement qualifies as a written declaration under paragraph (d)(1) of this section because L's agreement not to claim Child as a dependent is not conditioned on M's payment of support or meeting of any other obligation, and the agreement otherwise conforms to the substance of Form 8332. For 2009, only L may claim Child as a qualifying child because in 2008 L revokes the release of the claim in accordance with paragraph (d)(3) of this section, and the revocation takes effect in 2009, the taxable year that begins in the first calendar year after L provides written notice of the revocation to M.

Example 6. The facts are the same as *Example 5*, except that the agreement expressly states that L agrees not to claim Child as a dependent only if M is current in the payment of support for Child at the end of the calendar year. The separation agreement does not qualify as a written declaration under paragraph (d)(1) of this section because L's agreement not to claim Child as a dependent is conditioned on M's payment of support. Therefore, M may not claim Child as a qualifying child in 2007 or 2009.

Example 7. (i) N and P are the divorced parents of Child. Child resides with N for ten months and with P for two months in each year 2007 through 2009. In 2007, N provides a written statement to P that provides that N will not claim Child as a dependent but does not specify a year or years. P attaches the statement to P's returns for 2007 through 2009.

(ii) Because the written statement provided by N does not specify the year or years for which P may claim Child as a qualifying child, under paragraph (d)(1) of this section, the written statement is not a written declaration that conforms to the substance of Form 8332. Therefore, P may not claim Child as a qualifying child in 2007 through 2009.

Example 8. (i) R and S are the divorced parents of Child. Child resides solely with R. The divorce decree requires S to pay child support to R and requires R to execute a Form 8332 to release the right to claim Child as a qualifying child to S. R fails to sign a Form 8332 for 2007, and S attaches an unsigned Form 8332 to S's return for 2007.

(ii) Child is the qualifying child of R for 2007. The order in the divorce decree requiring R to execute a Form 8332 is ineffective to allocate the right to claim Child as a qualifying child to S. Furthermore, under paragraph (d)(1) of this section, the unsigned Form 8332 does not conform to the substance of Form 8332. Therefore, S may not claim Child as a qualifying child in 2007.

(iii) If, however, R executes a Form 8332 for 2007 and S attaches the Form 8332 to S's return, then S may claim Child as a qualifying child for 2007 under paragraph (d)(1) of this section.

(g) *Effective date.* This section applies to taxable years beginning after the date these regulations are published as final regulations in the **Federal Register**.

Kevin M. Brown,
Deputy Commissioner for Services and Enforcement.

(Filed by the Office of the Federal Register on May 1, 2007, 8:45 a.m., and published in the issue of the Federal Register for May 2, 2007, 72 F.R. 24192)

Notice of Proposed Rulemaking

Mortality Tables for Determining Present Value

REG–143601–06

AGENCY: Internal Revenue Service (IRS), Treasury.

ACTION: Notice of proposed rulemaking.

SUMMARY: This document contains proposed regulations providing mortality tables to be used in determining present value or making any computation for purposes of applying certain pension funding requirements. These regulations affect sponsors, administrators, participants, and beneficiaries of certain retirement plans.

DATES: Written or electronic comments and requests for a public hearing must be received by August 27, 2007.

ADDRESSES: Send submissions to: CC:PA:LPD:PR (REG–143601–06), room 5203, Internal Revenue Service, PO Box 7604, Ben Franklin Station, Washington, DC 20044. Submissions may be hand-delivered Monday through Friday between the hours of 8 a.m. and 4 p.m. to CC:PA:LPD:PR (REG–143601–06), Courier's Desk, Internal Revenue Service, 1111 Constitution Avenue, NW, Washington, DC, or sent electronically, via the Federal eRulemaking Portal at *www.regulations.gov* (IRS-REG–143601–06).

FOR FURTHER INFORMATION CONTACT: Concerning the regulations, Bruce Perlin, Lauson C. Green, or Linda S. F. Marshall at (202) 622–6090; concerning submissions and requests for a public hearing, Kelly Banks at (202) 622–7180 (not toll-free numbers).

SUPPLEMENTARY INFORMATION:

Background

Section 412 provides minimum funding requirements for defined benefit pension plans. The Pension Protection Act of 2006 (PPA), Public Law 109–280 (120 Stat. 780), makes extensive changes to those minimum funding requirements that generally apply for plan years beginning on or after January 1, 2008. Section 430, which was added by PPA, specifies the minimum funding requirements that apply to defined benefit plans that are not multiemployer plans pursuant to section 412.[1] Section 430(a) defines the minimum required contribution for a defined benefit plan that is not a multiemployer plan by reference to the plan's funding target for the plan year. Under section 430(d)(1), a plan's funding target for a plan year generally is the present value of all benefits accrued or earned under the plan as of the beginning of the plan year.

Section 430(h)(3) provides rules regarding the mortality tables to be used under section 430. Under section 430(h)(3)(A), except as provided in section 430(h)(3)(C) or (D), the Secretary is to prescribe by regulation mortality tables to be used in determining any present value or making any computation under section 430. Those tables are to be based on the actual experience of pension plans and projected trends in such experience. In prescribing those tables, the Secretary is required to take into account results of available independent studies of mortality of individuals covered by pension plans. This standard for issuing the mortality table under section 430(h)(3)(A) is the same as the standard for issuing updated mortality tables pursuant to the review under section 412(l)(7)(C)(ii)(III) of the mortality table used in determining a plan's current liability pursuant to section 412(l)(7)(C)(ii)(I) for plan years before the effective date of the PPA changes.

Section 430(h)(3)(C) provides rules for a plan sponsor's use of substitute mortality tables. Upon the request of a plan sponsor and approval by the Secretary, mortality tables that meet the requirements for substitute mortality tables are used in determining present value or making any computation under section 430 during the period of consecutive plan years (not to exceed 10) specified in the request. Substitute mortality tables cease to be in effect as of the earliest of the date on which there is a significant change in the participants in the plan by reason of a plan spinoff or merger or otherwise, or the date on which the plan actuary determines that those tables do not meet the requirements for substitute mortality tables. The plan sponsor's request to use substitute mortality tables is to be made at least 7 months before the first day of the first plan year for which substitute mortality tables are to apply. A request to use substitute mortality tables is deemed approved unless the Secretary denies approval for the use of those mortality tables within 180 days of the request (subject to extension of this period by mutual agreement).

Mortality tables meet the requirements for substitute mortality tables if the pension plan has a sufficient number of plan participants and the plan has been maintained for a sufficient period of time in order to have credible mortality experience, and such tables reflect the actual experience of the plan and projected trends in general mortality experience of participants in pension plans. Except as provided by the Secretary, a plan sponsor cannot use substitute mortality tables for any plan unless substitute mortality tables are established and used for each other plan maintained by the plan sponsor and the plan sponsor's controlled group.

Section 430(h)(3)(D) provides for the use of separate mortality tables with respect to certain individuals who are entitled to benefits on account of disability. These separate mortality tables are permitted to be used with respect to disabled individuals in lieu of the generally applicable mortality tables provided pursuant to section 430(h)(3)(A) or the substitute mortality tables under section 430(h)(3)(C). The Secretary is to establish separate tables for individuals with disabilities occurring in plan years beginning before January 1, 1995, and in later plan years, with the mortality tables for individuals with disabilities occurring in those later plan years applying only to individuals who are disabled within the meaning of Title II of the Social Security Act.

Section 431, which was added by PPA, specifies the minimum funding requirements that apply to multiemployer plans. Under section 431(c)(6)(B), a plan's full funding limitation cannot be less than the excess (if any) of 90 percent of the current liability of the plan (including the expected increase in current liability due to benefits accruing during the plan year) over the value of the plan's assets. Section 431(c)(6)(D)(iv)(II) provides that the Secretary may by regulation prescribe mortality tables to be used in determining a plan's current liability for purposes of section 431(c)(6). The standards for these mortality tables are the same as the standards for mortality tables to be prescribed under section 430(h)(3)(A). Section 431(c)(6)(D)(iv)(I) provides that, until mortality tables are prescribed under section 431(c)(6)(D)(iv)(II), the mortality table used in determining a plan's current liability for purposes of section 431(c)(6) is the table prescribed by the Secretary that is based on the prevailing commissioners' standard table (described in section 807(d)(5)(A)) used to determine reserves for group annuity contracts issued on January 1, 1993.

Notice 2003–62, 2003–2 C.B. 576, was issued as part of the periodic review pursuant to section 412(l)(7)(C)(ii)(III) of the mortality tables used in determining current liability pursuant to section 412(l)(7)(C)(ii)(I). At the time Notice 2003–62 was issued, the IRS and the Treasury Department were aware of two reviews of mortality experience for pension plan participants undertaken by the Retirement Plans Experience Committee of the Society of Actuaries (the UP–94 Study and the RP–2000 Mortality Tables Report),[2] and commentators were invited to submit any other independent studies of pension plan mortality experience. Notice 2003–62 also requested the submission of studies regarding projected trends in mortality experience. With respect to projecting mortality improvements, the IRS and the Treasury Department requested comments regarding the advantages and

[1] Section 302 of the Employee Retirement Income Security Act of 1974, as amended (ERISA) sets forth funding rules that are parallel to those in section 412 of the Code, and section 303 of ERISA sets forth additional funding rules for defined benefit plans (other than multiemployer plans) that are parallel to those in section 430 of the Code. Under section 101 of Reorganization Plan No. 4 of 1978 (43 FR 47713) and section 302 of ERISA, the Secretary of the Treasury has interpretive jurisdiction over the subject matter addressed in these proposed regulations for purposes of ERISA, as well as the Code. Thus, these proposed Treasury regulations issued under section 430 of the Code apply as well for purposes of section 303 of ERISA.

[2] The UP–94 Study, prepared by the UP–94 Task Force of the Society of Actuaries, was published in the Transactions of the Society of Actuaries, Vol. XLVII (1995), p. 819. The RP–2000 Mortality Tables Report was released in July, 2000. Society of Actuaries, RP–2000 Mortality Tables Report, at *http://www.soa.org/ccm/content/research-publications/experience-studies-tools/the-rp-2000-mortality-tables/*.

disadvantages of reflecting these trends on an ongoing basis through the use of generational, modified generational or sequentially static mortality tables. See §601.601(d)(2)(ii)(*b*) of this chapter.

On December 2, 2005, the IRS issued proposed regulations under section 412(l)(7) (REG–124988–05, 2005–2 C.B.1186 [70 FR 72260–01]) setting forth mortality tables to be used for nondisabled pension plan participants (the 2005 proposed regulations). Those proposed regulations would have required plans of 500 or more participants (including both active and inactive participants) to use separate mortality tables for nonannuitant and annuitant periods. Those separate tables were derived from the RP–2000 mortality tables, with different projection periods for annuitants and nonannuitants based on an estimate of the duration of the respective liabilities. Small plans, defined as those with fewer than 500 participants, would have been permitted to use a combined table that applied the same mortality rates to both annuitants and nonannuitants under the 2005 proposed regulations. Those proposed regulations provided for updated tables to be issued annually using the current year as the new base year and using a specified set of projection factors to reflect expected improvements in mortality.

The 2005 proposed regulations were finalized in the **Federal Register** on February 2, 2007 (T.D. 9310, 2007–9 I.R.B. 601 [72 FR 4955]). Those final regulations permit all plans to use a blended table for 2007 rather than require that large plans use separate annuitant and nonannuitant tables (as would have been required under the 2005 proposed regulations). The IRS and the Treasury Department believe that using separate annuitant and nonannuitant tables results in a more accurate measure of a plan's current liability. However, in view of the sweeping PPA changes and the resulting need to overhaul actuarial valuation systems, it was determined that all plans (and not just small plans) should be permitted to use the combined mortality tables for the 2007 plan year.

Explanation of Provisions

Generally Applicable Mortality Tables

These proposed regulations set forth the methodology the IRS and the Treasury Department would use to establish mortality tables as provided under section 430(h)(3)(A) to be used for participants and beneficiaries to determine present value or make any computation under section 430. These mortality tables would apply as well for purposes of determining the current liability of a multiemployer plan pursuant to section 431(c)(6)(D)(iv)(II). In addition, pursuant to §1.412(l)(7)–1(a), these proposed regulations would apply for purposes of determining the current liability of a plan for which application of the PPA changes to section 412 is delayed (see sections 104 through 106 of PPA). Under the proposed regulations, mortality tables to be used with respect to disabled individuals would be provided in guidance published in the Internal Revenue Bulletin (IRB).

The new mortality tables under section 430(h)(3)(A) would be based on the tables contained in the RP–2000 Mortality Tables Report. In response to Notice 2003–62, commentators generally recommended that the RP–2000 mortality tables be the basis for the mortality tables used under section 412(l)(7)(C)(ii). The IRS and the Treasury Department reviewed the RP–2000 mortality tables and the accompanying report published by the Society of Actuaries, and determined to use the RP–2000 mortality tables as the basis for final regulations under section 412(l)(7)(C)(ii) because the RP–2000 mortality tables form the best available basis for predicting mortality of pension plan participants and beneficiaries (other than disabled individuals) based on pension plan experience, including expected trends. Because section 430 applies this same standard, the mortality tables set forth in these proposed regulations under section 430 are also based on the RP–2000 mortality tables. Like the mortality tables provided in the final section 412(l) regulations, the mortality tables set forth in these proposed regulations are gender-distinct because of significant differences between expected male mortality and expected female mortality. See §601.601(d)(2)(ii)(*b*) of this chapter.

The mortality tables set forth in these proposed regulations would provide separate mortality rates for annuitants and nonannuitants. This distinction has been made because the RP–2000 Mortality Tables Report indicates that these two groups have significantly different mortality experience. This is particularly true at typical ages for early retirees, where the number of health-induced early retirements results in a population that has higher mortality rates than the population of currently employed individuals. While the use of separate mortality rates for these groups of individuals will likely entail changes in programming of actuarial software, the IRS and the Treasury Department believe that the improvement in accuracy resulting from the use of separate mortality tables for annuitants and nonannuitants more than offsets the added complexity.

Under these proposed regulations, the annuitant mortality tables would be applied to determine the present value of benefits for annuitants. The annuitant mortality tables are also used for nonannuitants (active employees and terminated vested participants) for the periods beginning when the nonannuitants are projected to commence receiving benefits, while the nonannuitant mortality tables are applied for the periods before nonannuitants are projected to commence receiving benefits. For any period in which an annuitant is projected to be receiving benefits, the mortality table applicable to any beneficiary of that annuitant is the annuitant mortality table.

The RP–2000 Mortality Tables Report sets forth mortality tables that reflect expected mortality as of 2000, along with projection factors that are used to reflect the impact of expected improvements in mortality. Similarly, the mortality tables set forth in the proposed regulations are based on expected mortality as of 2000 and reflect the impact of expected improvements in mortality. Commentators to prior guidance generally stated that the projection of mortality improvement is desirable because it reflects expected mortality more accurately than using mortality tables that do not reflect such projection. The IRS and the Treasury Department agree with these comments, and believe that failing to project mortality improvement in determining the funding target would tend to result in underfunding. The proposed regulations permit plan sponsors to apply the projection of mortality improvement in either of two ways: through use of static tables that are updated annually to reflect expected improvements in mortality, or through use of generational tables.

The proposed regulations set forth base tables for annuitants and nonannuitants, as well as a set of projection factors. The base tables set forth in the proposed regulations generally provide the same rates as the RP–2000 mortality tables, except that they have been extended so that the annuitant and nonannuitant tables have mortality rates available at each age. The RP–2000 Mortality Tables Report did not develop annuitant rates before age 50 or nonannuitant rates after age 70. The extended nonannuitant tables in these proposed regulations were created by (1) using nonannuitant rates through age 70, (2) using annuitant rates for ages over 80, and (3) blending the rates to produce a smooth transition between the two tables, using increasing fractions. The total difference between the rates at ages 70 and 80 is divided by 55; the rate at age 71 is set equal to the rate at age 70 plus 1/55 of the total difference, the age 72 rate is equal to the rate at age 71 plus 2/55 of the total difference, etc.

A similar approach was used to develop the base tables for annuitants. For male annuitants, annuitant rates from the RP–2000 Mortality Tables Report were used for ages 50 and over, nonannuitant rates from the RP–2000 Mortality Tables Report were used through age 40, and rates between ages 41 and 49 were smoothed to create a smooth transition using the same methodology as was used for the nonannuitant tables. For female annuitants, annuitant rates from the RP–2000 Mortality Tables Report were used for ages 50 and over. However, to avoid anomalous results, female nonannuitant rates were used through age 46 (rather than age 40) and, accordingly, rates were smoothed between ages 47 and 49. The smoothing methodology for the female annuitant tables was the same as that used for the male tables but, because a shorter transition period was used, the difference between the age 46 and the age 50 mortality rates was smoothed using a denominator of 10 instead of 55.

For a plan sponsor that chooses to use the generational mortality tables, the mortality rate for each particular age would be projected for each individual participant to reflect projected improvement for the period of time until the participant reaches the particular age using the applicable base table along with the projection factors provided under the proposed regulations. These projection factors are from Mortality Projection Scale AA, which was recommended for use in the UP–94 Study and in the RP–2000 Mortality Tables Report. For example, to obtain the age 54 mortality rate for a male annuitant born in 1974 using the generational mortality tables, the age 54 male annuitant table rate is projected 28 years using the age 54 male Projection Scale AA rate set forth in the proposed regulations. The projection period is 28 years because a participant born in 1974 would attain age 54 in 2028, 28 years after the base year of the tables set forth in the proposed regulations. In this instance, because the male age 54 annuitant rate is .005797 under the base table, and the male age 54 Projection Scale AA rate set forth in paragraph (d) of §1.430(h)(3)–1 is .020, the age 54 male annuitant rate for participants born in 1974 is .003293 ($.005797 * (1-.020)^{28}$).

The static mortality tables that would be permitted to be used under the proposed regulations are constructed from the base table used for purposes of the generational mortality tables. The static mortality tables are projected from the base table for the year 2000 through the year of valuation with further projection to reflect the approximate expected duration of liabilities. The static mortality tables for annuitants under the proposed regulations reflect projection through the year of valuation with a further projection period of 7 years, and the static mortality tables for nonannuitants under the proposed regulations reflect projection through the year of valuation with a further projection period of 15 years. These projection periods were selected as the expected average duration of liabilities and are consistent with projection periods suggested by commentators. To be consistent with the original construction of the RP–2000 mortality tables, both the static annuitant and nonannuitant tables use the rates from the projected annuitant table for ages 80 and over and from the projected nonannuitant table for ages 40 and younger (ages 44 and younger for females). For a smooth transition between the different projection periods for annuitants versus nonannuitants, the rates for ages 71 through 79 and for ages 41 through 49 (ages 45 through 49 for females) were smoothed using the same technique as that used in constructing the base tables.

The static mortality tables that would apply with respect to valuation dates occurring during 2008 are set forth in the proposed regulations. The mortality tables to be used for valuation dates in subsequent years would be published in the IRB. Comments are requested regarding whether it would be desirable to publish a series of tables for each of a number of years (such as five years) along with final regulations, with tables for subsequent years to be published in the IRB.

As an example of the use of the static tables for the 2008 calendar plan year, with respect to a 45-year-old active participant who is projected to commence receiving an annuity at age 55, the funding target would be determined using the applicable nonannuitant mortality table for the period before the participant attains age 55 (so that the probability of an active male participant living from age 45 to the age of 55 using the mortality table that would apply in 2008 is 98.61%) and the applicable annuitant mortality table after the participant attains age 55. Similarly, if a 45-year-old terminated vested participant is projected to commence an annuity at age 65, the funding target would be determined using the applicable nonannuitant mortality table for the period before the participant attains age 65 and the applicable annuitant mortality table for ages 65 and above.

These proposed regulations would provide an option for smaller plans (plans where the total of active and inactive participants is less than 500) that choose to use static mortality tables to use a single blended static table for all participants — in lieu of the separate tables for annuitants and nonannuitants — in order to simplify the actuarial valuation for these plans. This blended table would be constructed from the separate nonannuitant and annuitant tables using the nonannuitant/annuitant weighting factors published in the RP–2000 Mortality Tables Report. However, because the RP–2000 Mortality Tables Report does not provide weighting factors before age 51 or after age 69, the IRS and the Treasury Department would extend the table of weighting factors (using straight-line interpolation) for ages 41 through 50 (ages 45–50 for females) and for ages 70 through 79 in order to develop the blended table.

Substitute Mortality Tables

These proposed regulations would set forth the framework for the development and use of substitute mortality tables in connection with present value determinations and other computations under section 430(h)(3)(C). The provision generally provides for the use of substitute mortality tables by a plan that is subject to section 430, in lieu of the mortality tables provided under section 430(h)(3)(A) and §1.430(h)(3)–1, upon written request of the plan sponsor and approval of the Commissioner.

Substitute mortality tables must reflect the actual mortality experience of the pension plan maintained by the plan sponsor for which the tables are to be used and that mortality experience must be credible. Separate mortality tables must be established for each gender under the plan, and a substitute mortality table is permitted to be established for a gender only if the plan has credible mortality experience with respect to that gender. If the mortality experience for one gender is credible but the mortality experience for the other gender is not credible, the substitute mortality tables are used for the gender that has credible mortality experience, and the mortality tables under §1.430(h)(3)–1 are used for the gender that does not have credible mortality experience. If separate mortality tables under section 430(h)(3)(D) are used for certain disabled individuals under a plan, then those individuals are disregarded for all purposes with respect to substitute mortality tables under section 430(h)(3)(C). Thus, if the mortality tables under section 430(h)(3)(D) are used for certain disabled individuals under a plan, mortality experience with respect to those individuals must be excluded in determining mortality rates for substitute mortality tables with respect to a plan.

Under the proposed regulations, a substitute mortality table is based on credible mortality experience for a gender within a plan if and only if the mortality experience is based on at least 1,000 deaths within that gender over the period covered by the experience study. The experience study must be based on mortality experience data over a 2, 3, or 4-consecutive year period, the last day of which must be less than 3 years before the first day of the first plan year for which the substitute mortality tables are to apply. The 1,000 deaths threshold is set at a level so that there is a high degree of confidence that the plan's past mortality experience will be predictive of its future mortality, and is consistent with relevant actuarial literature (see, for example, Thomas N. Herzog, *Introduction to Credibility Theory* (1999); Stuart A. Klugman, *et al.*, *Loss Models: From Data to Decisions* (2004)).

Development of a substitute mortality table under the proposed regulations requires creation of a base table and identification of a base year, which are then used to determine a substitute mortality table. The base table would be developed from a study of the mortality experience of the plan using amounts-weighted data. The proposed regulations set forth rules regarding development of amounts-weighted mortality rates for an age and the determination of the base year. The proposed regulations provide that amounts-weighted mortality rates may be derived from amounts-weighted mortality rates for age groups. Guidance issued by the Commissioner may specify grouping rules (for example, 5-year age groups, except for extreme ages) and methods for developing amounts-weighted mortality rates for individual ages from amounts-weighted mortality rates initially determined for each age group. In addition, the proposed regulations would provide that base tables may be constructed either directly through graduation of amounts-weighted mortality rates or indirectly by applying a level percentage to tables prescribed by section 430(h)(3)(A), provided that the resulting tables sufficiently reflect the plan's mortality experience. The Commissioner may permit the construction of base tables through application of a level percentage to other recognized mortality tables, applying similar standards to ensure that the resulting tables are sufficiently reflective of the plan's mortality experience.

In general, substitute mortality tables are permitted to be used for a plan only if the use of substitute mortality tables is approved for each other pension plan subject to the requirements of section 430 that is maintained by the plan sponsor or by a member of the sponsor's controlled group. However, under the proposed regulations, the use of substitute mortality tables for one plan would not be prohibited merely because another plan subject to section 430 that is maintained by the plan sponsor (or by a member of the plan sponsor's controlled group) cannot use substitute mortality tables because neither the males nor the females under that plan have credible mortality experience for a plan year. Thus, if a sponsor's controlled group contains two pension plans subject to section 430, each of which has credible mortality experience for at least one gender, either both plans must obtain approval from the Commissioner to use substitute mortality tables or neither plan may use substitute mortality tables. By contrast, if for one of those plans neither males nor females have credible mortality experience, then the plan without credible mortality experience will not interfere with the ability of the plan with credible mortality experience to use substitute mortality tables.

Under the proposed regulations, the requirement that the plan sponsor demonstrate the lack of credible mortality experience for both the male and female populations in other plans maintained by the plan sponsor (and by members of the plan sponsor's controlled group) must be satisfied annually. For each plan year in which a plan uses substitute mortality tables, the demonstration that both genders of another plan maintained by the plan sponsor do not have credible mortality experience (that is, there are less than 1,000 deaths within each gender) must be made using a 4-year period for mortality experience that ends less than 3 years before the first day of that plan year.

For example, a plan sponsor that requests to use substitute mortality tables for a plan for the plan year that begins January 1, 2008, would have to show, as part of its submission to the Commissioner, that both the male and female populations in all other defined benefit plans of the plan sponsor (and in the plan sponsor's controlled group) that are subject to section 430 and that do not use substitute mortality tables do not have credible mortality experience using a 4-year period that ends no earlier than January 2, 2005 (that is, each gender in those plans did not experience 1,000 deaths during that 4-year period). If the plan sponsor chooses to use the 4-year period from January 1, 2003, through December 31, 2006, to demonstrate the lack of credible mortality experience for the other plans, then the plan can rely on this same data to demonstrate the lack of credible mortality experience for 2009 as well because the less-than-3-years requirement is still met with respect to the 2009 plan year. However, the plan would not be able to use this same data to demonstrate lack of credibility for the 2010 plan year because the last day of the experience study used for the demonstration (the January 1, 2003 — December 31, 2006 period) is too distant in time (3 or more years) from the first day of the plan year (January 1, 2010).

Although the proposed regulations permit a plan sponsor to use an experience study to demonstrate a lack of credible mortality experience for a plan population for multiple years, plan sponsors are encouraged to update experience studies annually as new mortality data become available for the plan population. In such a case, if an updated test reveals 1,000 or more deaths for the more recent 4-year period, the plan sponsor nonetheless will be able to continue to use substitute mortality tables for one plan year by demonstrating that the other plans in the controlled group do not have credible mortality experience based on the earlier experience study. This will give the plan sponsor sufficient time to develop substitute mortality tables for the plan population with newly credible mortality experience and to obtain the Commissioner's approval to use those tables prior to the first year substitute mortality tables are to be used for that population.

Under the proposed regulations, a plan's substitute mortality tables must be generational mortality tables. Substitute mortality tables are determined using the base mortality tables developed from the experience study and the projection factors provided in Projection Scale AA, as set forth in §1.430(h)(3)–1(d). Under the generational mortality tables, the probability of an individual's death at a particular age is determined as the individual's base mortality rate (that is, the applicable base mortality rate from the base mortality table for the age for which the probability of death is being determined) multiplied by the mortality improvement factor. The mortality improvement factor is equal to (1 - projection factor for that age)^n, where n is equal to the projection period (that is, the number of years between the base year for the base mortality table and the year for which the probability of death is being determined).

The proposed regulations would require separate tables to be established for males and females under a plan. Under the proposed regulations, separate substitute mortality tables would be permitted (but not required) to be established for separate populations within a gender, such as annuitants and nonannuitants or hourly and salaried individuals. The proposed regulations would provide that separate substitute mortality tables are permitted to be used for a separate population within a gender under a plan only if all individuals of that gender in the plan are divided into separate populations, each separate population has credible mortality experience (determined in the same manner as determining whether a gender has credible mortality experience), and the separate substitute mortality table for each separate population is developed using mortality experience data for that population. For example, in the case of a plan that has credible mortality experience data for both its male hourly and male salaried populations, separate substitute mortality tables could be used for those two separate populations. However, if the plan does not have credible mortality experience for its male salaried population, it would not be permissible to use substitute mortality tables for its male hourly population and the standard mortality tables described in §1.430(h)(3)–1 for its male salaried population.

The requirement that each separate population have credible mortality experience does not apply in the case of separate mortality tables that are developed for annuitant and nonannuitant populations within a gender. Thus, the proposed regulations would provide that substitute mortality tables for separate annuitant and nonannuitant populations may be used within a gender even if only one of those separate populations has credible mortality experience. Similarly, if separate populations with credible mortality experience are established within a gender, then any of those populations may be further subdivided into separate annuitant and nonannuitant subpopulations, provided that at least one of the two resulting subpopulations has credible mortality experience. In such a case, the standard mortality tables under §1.430(h)(3)–1 must be used for a resulting subpopulation that does not have credible mortality experience. For example, in the case of a plan that has credible mortality experience for both its male hourly and salaried individuals, if the male salaried annuitant population has credible mortality experience, it may use substitute mortality tables with respect to that population even if the male salaried nonannuitant population uses the standard mortality tables under §1.430(h)(3)–1 (because that nonannuitant population does not have credible mortality experience). For purposes of demonstrating that an annuitant or nonannuitant population within a gender or within a separate population does not have credible mortality experience, the demonstration of lack of credible mortality experience is made on the same basis as for purposes of demonstrating a lack of credible mortality experience for a gender.

The proposed regulations would provide a limited time period during which a newly acquired plan that does not use substitute mortality tables does not prevent another plan from using substitute mortality tables. Under the proposed regulations, the use of substitute mortality tables for a plan is not prohibited merely because a newly acquired plan does not use substitute mortality tables, but only through the last day of the plan year of the plan using substitute mortality tables that contains the end of the period described in section 410(b)(6)(C). For the following plan year, the mortality tables prescribed under §1.430(h)(3)–1 would apply with respect to the plan (and all other plans within the plan sponsor's controlled group, including the acquired plan) unless approval to use substitute mortality tables has been obtained with respect to the acquired plan, or the acquired plan cannot use substitute mortality tables because neither the males nor the females under the plan have credible mortality experience. For example, if the employer acquires a plan in September 2009 that does not use substitute mortality tables and that has a plan year that ends June 30, the acquisition of that plan will not impair the continued use of substitute mortality tables by a pre-existing calendar year plan of the employer through the end of the 2011 calendar year. This is because the section 410(b)(6)(C) transition period for the newly acquired plan will end on June 30, 2011. Under the proposed regulations, a plan is treated as a newly acquired plan if it is acquired or otherwise becomes maintained by the plan sponsor (or by a member of the plan sponsor's controlled group) in connection with a merger, acquisition, or similar transaction described in §1.410(b)–2(f). The proposed regulations would provide that a plan is also treated as a newly acquired plan if it is established in connection with a transfer in accordance with section 414(l) of assets and liabilities from another employer's plan in connection with a merger, acquisition, or similar transaction described in §1.410(b)–2(f).

In the case of a newly acquired plan, the demonstration of whether credible mortality experience exists for the plan may be made by either including or excluding mortality experience data for the period prior to the date the plan becomes maintained by a member of the new plan sponsor's controlled group. If a plan sponsor excludes mortality experience data prior to the date the plan became maintained within the new plan sponsor's controlled group, the exclusion must apply for all populations within the plan. For example, it is impermissible to include the data for hourly individuals for the pre-acquisition period but exclude the data for salaried individuals for that same period.

In order to demonstrate a lack of credible mortality experience with respect to a gender for a plan year, a special rule applies if the plan's mortality experience demonstration for a plan year is made by excluding mortality experience for the period prior to the date the newly acquired plan becomes maintained within the new plan sponsor's controlled group. In such a case, an employer is permitted to demonstrate a plan's lack of credible mortality experience using an experience study period of less than four years, provided that the experience study period begins with the date the plan becomes maintained within the employer's controlled group and ends not more than one year and one day before the first day of the plan year with respect to which the lack of credible mortality experience demonstration is made.

The proposed regulations would provide rules for aggregating plans for purposes of using substitute mortality tables. Under the proposed regulations, in order to use a set of substitute mortality tables for two or more plans, the applicable rules are applied by treating those plans as a single plan. In such a case, the substitute mortality tables must be used for all such plans and must be based on data collected with respect to all such plans. Although plans generally are not required to be aggregated, the proposed regulations would require a plan to be aggregated with any plan that was previously spun off from that plan if one purpose of the spinoff was to avoid the use of substitute mortality tables for any of the plans involved in the spinoff.

Under the proposed regulations, in order to use substitute mortality tables with respect to a plan, a plan sponsor must submit a written request to the Commissioner that demonstrates that those substitute mortality tables comply with applicable requirements. A request to use substitute mortality tables must state the first plan year and the term of years (not more than 10) that the tables are requested to be used. In general, substitute mortality tables cannot be used for a plan year unless the plan sponsor submits the written request to use substitute mortality tables at least 7 months prior to the first day of the first plan year for which the substitute mortality tables are to apply. However, the timing of the written request to use substitute mortality tables does not prevent a plan from using substitute mortality tables for a plan year if the written request is submitted no later than October 1, 2007. This special rule allows plan sponsors sufficient time to review the proposed regulations and other guidance and prepare requests to use substitute mortality tables for use in 2008.

Under the proposed regulations, experience data cannot be used to develop a base table if the number of individuals in the population covered by the table (for example, the male annuitants) as of the last day of the plan year before the year the request to use substitute mortality tables is made (or a reasonable estimate of that number), compared to the average number of individuals in that population over the years covered by the experience study on which the substitute mortality tables are based, reflects a difference of 20 percent or more, unless it is demonstrated to the satisfaction of the Commissioner that the experience data is accurately predictive of future mortality of that plan population (taking into account the effect of the change in individuals) after appropriate adjustments to the data are made (for example, excluding data from individuals with respect to a spun-off portion of the plan).

Under the proposed regulations, the Commissioner may, in revenue rulings and procedures, notices and other guidance published in the IRB (see §601.601(d)(2)(ii)(*b*) of this chapter), provide additional guidance regarding the approval and use of substitute mortality tables under section 430(h)(3)(C) and related matters. The IRS will shortly issue a revenue procedure that will set forth the requirements related to requests to use substitute mortality tables.

In general, the Commissioner has a 180-day period to review a request for the use of substitute mortality tables. If the Commissioner does not issue a denial within this 180-day period, the request is deemed to have been approved unless the Commissioner and the plan sponsor have agreed to extend that period. The Commissioner may request additional information with respect to a submission. Failure to provide that information on a timely basis is grounds for denial of the plan sponsor's request. In addition, the Commissioner will deny a request if the request fails to meet the requirements to use substitute mortality tables or if the Commissioner determines that a substitute mortality table does not sufficiently reflect the mortality experience of the applicable plan population.

The proposed regulations would provide rules regarding the duration of use of substitute mortality tables. Under the proposed regulations, substitute mortality tables generally are used with respect to a plan for the term of consecutive plan years specified in the plan sponsor's written request to use such tables and approved by the Commissioner, or such shorter period prescribed by the Commissioner in the approval to use substitute mortality tables. If the term of use of a substitute mortality table ends for any reason, the mortality tables specified in §1.430(h)(3)–1 will apply with respect to the plan unless the plan sponsor has obtained approval to use substitute mortality tables for a further term. The proposed regulations would provide that a plan's substitute mortality tables cannot be used as of the earliest of the following: the second plan year following the plan year in which there is a significant change in the population covered by the substitute mortality table (generally, a change of at least 20% from the average number of individuals included in the experience study); or the plan year following the plan year in which a substitute mortality table for a plan population is no longer accurately predictive of future mortality of that population, as determined by the Commissioner or as certified by the plan's actuary to the satisfaction of the Commissioner. In addition, the proposed regulations would provide that a plan's substitute mortality tables cannot be used after the date specified in guidance published in the IRB (see §601.601(d)(2)(ii)(*b*) of this chapter) pursuant to a replacement of mortality tables specified under section 430(h)(3)(A) (other than annual updates to the static mortality tables).

Applicability Date

These regulations are proposed to apply to plan years beginning on or after January 1, 2008.

Mortality Tables Used Under Section 417(e)

Section 417(e)(3)(B)(i), as amended by PPA, provides that the applicable mortality table (which is used to determine the minimum present value of certain distributions as required by section 417(e)(3)) is a mortality table, modified as appropriate by the Secretary of the Treasury, based on the mortality table specified for the plan year under section 430(h)(3)(A) (without regard to the option to use substitute mortality tables under section 430(h)(3)(C) or the separate mortality tables for disabled individuals under section 430(h)(3)(D)). This change is effective for plan years beginning after December 31, 2007. Comments are requested regarding how the mortality tables provided under proposed §1.430(h)(3)–1 should be modified for use in applying the minimum present value rules of section 417(e)(3).[3] Issues to be addressed include whether to use annuitant mortality rates or combined mortality rates and whether use of generational mortality tables is appropriate.

Special Analyses

It has been determined that this notice of proposed rulemaking is not a significant regulatory action as defined in Executive Order 12866. Therefore, a regulatory assessment is not required. It also has been determined that section 553(b) of the Administrative Procedure Act (5 U.S.C. chapter 5) does not apply to these regulations, and because the regulation does not impose a collection of information on small entities, the Regulatory Flexibility Act (5 U.S.C. chapter 6) does not apply. Pursuant to section 7805(f) of the Code, this notice of proposed rulemaking will be submitted to the Chief Counsel for Advocacy of the Small Business Administration for comment on its impact on small business.

Comments and Requests for Public Hearing

Before these proposed regulations are adopted as final regulations, consideration will be given to any written (a signed original and eight (8) copies) or electronic comments that are submitted timely to the IRS. The IRS and the Treasury Department specifically request comments on the clarity of the proposed regulations and how they may be made easier to understand. All comments will be available for public inspection and copying. A public hearing will be scheduled if requested in writing by any person that timely submits written comments. If a public hearing is scheduled, notice of the date, time, and place for the public hearing will be published in the **Federal Register**.

Drafting Information

The principal authors of these regulations are Bruce Perlin, Lauson C. Green, and Linda S. F. Marshall, Office of Division Counsel/Associate Chief Counsel (Tax Exempt and Government Entities). However, other personnel from the IRS and the Treasury Department participated in the development of these regulations.

* * * * *

Amendments to the Regulations

Accordingly, 26 CFR part 1 is proposed to be amended as follows:

PART 1—INCOME TAXES

Paragraph 1. The authority citation for part 1 continues to read, in part, as follows:

Authority: 26 U.S.C. 7805 * * *

Par. 2. Section 1.430(h)(3)–1 is added to read as follows:

§1.430(h)(3)–1 Mortality tables used to determine present value.

(a) *Basis for mortality tables*—(1) *In general.* This section sets forth rules for the mortality tables to be used in determining present value or making any computation under section 430. Generally applicable mortality tables for participants and beneficiaries are set forth in this section pursuant to section 430(h)(3)(A). In lieu of using the mortality tables provided under this section with respect to participants and beneficiaries, plan-specific substitute mortality tables are permitted to be used for this purpose pursuant to section 430(h)(3)(C) provided that the requirements of §1.430(h)(3)–2 are satisfied. Mortality tables that may be used with respect to disabled individuals are to be provided in guidance published in the Internal Revenue Bulletin. See §601.601(d)(2)(ii)(*b*) of this chapter.

(2) *Static tables or generational tables permitted.* The generally applicable mortality tables provided under section 430(h)(3)(A) are the static tables described in paragraph (a)(3) of this section and the generational mortality tables described in paragraph (a)(4) of this section. A plan is permitted to use either of those sets of mortality tables with respect to participants and beneficiaries pursuant to this section.

(3) *Static tables.* The static mortality tables that are permitted to be used pursuant to paragraph (a)(2) of this section are updated annually to reflect expected improvements in mortality experience as described in paragraph (c)(2) of this section. Static mortality tables that are to be used with respect to valuation dates occurring during 2008 are provided in paragraph (e) of this section. The mortality tables to be

[3] Substitute mortality tables described in Code section 430(h)(3)(C) and §1.430(h)(3)–2 of these proposed regulations do not apply for purposes of the requirements of section 417(e).

used with respect to valuation dates occurring in later years are to be provided in guidance published in the Internal Revenue Bulletin. See §601.601(d)(2)(ii)(*b*) of this chapter.

(4) *Generational mortality tables*—(i) *In general.* The generational mortality tables that are permitted to be used pursuant to paragraph (a)(2) of this section are determined pursuant to this paragraph (a)(4) using the base mortality tables and projection factors set forth in paragraph (d) of this section. Under the generational mortality tables, the probability of an individual's death at a particular age is determined as the individual's base mortality rate (that is, the applicable mortality rate from the table set forth in paragraph (d) of this section for the age for which the probability of death is being determined) multiplied by the mortality improvement factor. The mortality improvement factor is equal to (1 - projection factor for that age)^n, where n is equal to the projection period. For this purpose, the projection period is the number of years between 2000 and the year for which the probability of death is being determined.

(ii) *Examples of calculation.* As an example of the use of generational mortality tables under paragraph (a)(4)(i) of this section, for purposes of determining the probability of death at age 54 for a male annuitant born in 1974, the base mortality rate is .005797, the projection factor is .020, and the projection period (the period from the year 2000 until the year the participant will attain age 54) is 28 years, so that the mortality improvement factor is .567976, and the probability of death at age 54 is .003293. Similarly, under these generational mortality tables, the probability of death at age 55 for the same male annuitant would be determined by using the base mortality rate and projection factor at age 55, and a projection period of 29 years (the period from the year 2000 until the year the participant will attain age 55). Thus, the base mortality rate is .005905, the projection factor is .019, so that the mortality improvement factor is .573325 ((1-.019)^{29}), and the probability of death at age 55 is .003385 (.573325 times .005905). Because these generational mortality tables reflect expected improvements in mortality experience, no periodic updates are needed.

(b) *Use of the tables*—(1) *Separate tables for annuitants and nonannuitants*—(i) *In general.* Separate tables are provided for use for annuitants and nonannuitants. The nonannuitant mortality table is applied to determine the probability of survival for a nonannuitant for the period before the nonannuitant is projected to commence receiving benefits. The annuitant mortality table is applied to determine the present value of benefits for each annuitant, and for each nonannuitant for the period beginning when the nonannuitant is projected to commence receiving benefits. For purposes of this section, an annuitant means a plan participant who has commenced receiving benefits and a nonannuitant means a plan participant who has not yet commenced receiving benefits (for example, an active employee or a terminated vested participant). A participant whose benefit has partially commenced is treated as an annuitant with respect to the portion of the benefit which has commenced and a nonannuitant with respect to the balance of the benefit. In addition, for any period in which an annuitant is projected to be receiving benefits, any beneficiary with respect to that annuitant is also treated as an annuitant for purposes of this paragraph (b)(1).

(ii) *Examples of calculation.* As an example of the use of separate annuitant and nonannuitant tables under paragraph (b)(1)(i) of this section, with respect to a 45-year-old active participant who is projected to commence receiving an annuity at age 55, the funding target would be determined using the nonannuitant mortality table for the period before the participant attains age 55 (so that, if the static mortality tables are used pursuant to paragraph (a)(3) of this section, the probability of an active male participant living from age 45 to age 55 using the table that applies for a plan year beginning in 2008 is 98.61%) and the annuitant mortality table for the period ages 55 and above. Similarly, if a 45-year-old terminated vested participant is projected to commence an annuity at age 65, the funding target would be determined using the nonannuitant mortality table for the period before the participant attains age 65 and the annuitant mortality table for ages 65 and above.

(2) *Small plan tables.* If static mortality tables are used pursuant to paragraph (a)(3) of this section, as an alternative to the separate static tables specified for annuitants and nonannuitants pursuant to paragraph (b)(1) of this section, a combined static table that applies the same mortality rates to both annuitants and nonannuitants is permitted to be used for a small plan. For this purpose, a small plan is defined as a plan with fewer than 500 participants (including both active and inactive participants).

(c) *Construction of static tables*—(1) *Source of basic rates.* The static mortality tables that are used pursuant to paragraph (a)(3) of this section are based on the base mortality tables set forth in paragraph (d) of this section.

(2) *Projected mortality improvements.* The mortality rates under the base mortality tables are projected to improve using the projection factors provided in Projection Scale AA, as set forth in paragraph (d) of this section. Using these projection factors, the mortality rate for an individual at each age is determined as the individual's base mortality rate (that is, the applicable base mortality rate from the table set forth in paragraph (d) of this section for the individual at that age) multiplied by the mortality improvement factor. The mortality improvement factor is equal to (1 - projection factor for that age)^n, where n is equal to the projection period. The annuitant mortality rates for a plan year are determined using a projection period that runs from the calendar year 2000 until 7 years after the calendar year that contains the valuation date for the plan year. The nonannuitant mortality rates for a plan year are determined using a projection period that runs from the calendar year 2000 until 15 years after the calendar year that contains the valuation date for the plan year. Thus, for example, for a plan year with a January 1, 2012, valuation date, the annuitant mortality rates are determined using a projection period that runs from 2000 until 2019 (19 years) and the nonannuitant mortality rates are determined using a projection period that runs from 2000 until 2027 (27 years).

(3) *Construction of combined tables for small plans.* The combined mortality tables that are permitted to be used for small plans pursuant to paragraph (b)(2) of this section are constructed from the separate nonannuitant and annuitant tables using the weighting factors for small plans that are set forth in paragraph (d) of this sec-

tion. The weighting factors are applied to develop these mortality tables using the following equation: Combined mortality rate = [nonannuitant rate * (1- weighting factor)] + [annuitant rate * weighting factor].

(d) *Base mortality tables and projection factors*. The following base mortality tables and projection factors are used to determine generational mortality tables for purposes of determining present value or making any computation under section 430 as set forth in paragraph (a)(4) of this section. In addition, the following base mortality tables and projection factors are used to determine the static mortality tables that are used for purposes of determining present value or making any computation under section 430 as set forth in paragraphs (a)(3) and (c) of this section. See §1.430(h)(3)–2(c)(3) for rules regarding the required use of the projection factors set forth in this paragraph (d) in connection with a plan-specific substitute mortality table.

Age	MALE	MALE	MALE	MALE	FEMALE	FEMALE	FEMALE	FEMALE
	Base Non-Annuitant Mortality Rates (Year 2000)	Base Annuitant Mortality Rates (Year 2000)	Scale AA Projection Factors	Weighting Factors for Small Plans	Base Non-Annuitant Mortality Rates (Year 2000)	Base Annuitant Mortality Rates (Year 2000)	Scale AA Projection Factors	Weighting Factors for Small Plans
1	0.000637	0.000637	0.020	-	0.000571	0.000571	0.020	-
2	0.000430	0.000430	0.020	-	0.000372	0.000372	0.020	-
3	0.000357	0.000357	0.020	-	0.000278	0.000278	0.020	-
4	0.000278	0.000278	0.020	-	0.000208	0.000208	0.020	-
5	0.000255	0.000255	0.020	-	0.000188	0.000188	0.020	-
6	0.000244	0.000244	0.020	-	0.000176	0.000176	0.020	-
7	0.000234	0.000234	0.020	-	0.000165	0.000165	0.020	-
8	0.000216	0.000216	0.020	-	0.000147	0.000147	0.020	-
9	0.000209	0.000209	0.020	-	0.000140	0.000140	0.020	-
10	0.000212	0.000212	0.020	-	0.000141	0.000141	0.020	-
11	0.000219	0.000219	0.020	-	0.000143	0.000143	0.020	-
12	0.000228	0.000228	0.020	-	0.000148	0.000148	0.020	-
13	0.000240	0.000240	0.020	-	0.000155	0.000155	0.020	-
14	0.000254	0.000254	0.019	-	0.000162	0.000162	0.018	-
15	0.000269	0.000269	0.019	-	0.000170	0.000170	0.016	-
16	0.000284	0.000284	0.019	-	0.000177	0.000177	0.015	-
17	0.000301	0.000301	0.019	-	0.000184	0.000184	0.014	-
18	0.000316	0.000316	0.019	-	0.000188	0.000188	0.014	-
19	0.000331	0.000331	0.019	-	0.000190	0.000190	0.015	-
20	0.000345	0.000345	0.019	-	0.000191	0.000191	0.016	-
21	0.000357	0.000357	0.018	-	0.000192	0.000192	0.017	-
22	0.000366	0.000366	0.017	-	0.000194	0.000194	0.017	-
23	0.000373	0.000373	0.015	-	0.000197	0.000197	0.016	
24	0.000376	0.000376	0.013	-	0.000201	0.000201	0.015	-
25	0.000376	0.000376	0.010	-	0.000207	0.000207	0.014	-
26	0.000378	0.000378	0.006	-	0.000214	0.000214	0.012	-
27	0.000382	0.000382	0.005		0.000223	0.000223	0.012	-
28	0.000393	0.000393	0.005	-	0.000235	0.000235	0.012	-

Age	MALE	MALE	MALE	MALE	FEMALE	FEMALE	FEMALE	FEMALE
	Base Non-Annuitant Mortality Rates (Year 2000)	Base Annuitant Mortality Rates (Year 2000)	Scale AA Projection Factors	Weighting Factors for Small Plans	Base Non-Annuitant Mortality Rates (Year 2000)	Base Annuitant Mortality Rates (Year 2000)	Scale AA Projection Factors	Weighting Factors for Small Plans
29	0.000412	0.000412	0.005	-	0.000248	0.000248	0.012	-
30	0.000444	0.000444	0.005	-	0.000264	0.000264	0.010	-
31	0.000499	0.000499	0.005	-	0.000307	0.000307	0.008	-
32	0.000562	0.000562	0.005	-	0.000350	0.000350	0.008	-
33	0.000631	0.000631	0.005	-	0.000394	0.000394	0.009	-
34	0.000702	0.000702	0.005	-	0.000435	0.000435	0.010	-
35	0.000773	0.000773	0.005	-	0.000475	0.000475	0.011	-
36	0.000841	0.000841	0.005	-	0.000514	0.000514	0.012	-
37	0.000904	0.000904	0.005	-	0.000554	0.000554	0.013	-
38	0.000964	0.000964	0.006	-	0.000598	0.000598	0.014	-
39	0.001021	0.001021	0.007	-	0.000648	0.000648	0.015	-
40	0.001079	0.001079	0.008	-	0.000706	0.000706	0.015	-
41	0.001142	0.001157	0.009	0.0045	0.000774	0.000774	0.015	-
42	0.001215	0.001312	0.010	0.0091	0.000852	0.000852	0.015	-
43	0.001299	0.001545	0.011	0.0136	0.000937	0.000937	0.015	-
44	0.001397	0.001855	0.012	0.0181	0.001029	0.001029	0.015	-
45	0.001508	0.002243	0.013	0.0226	0.001124	0.001124	0.016	0.0084
46	0.001616	0.002709	0.014	0.0272	0.001223	0.001223	0.017	0.0167
47	0.001734	0.003252	0.015	0.0317	0.001326	0.001335	0.018	0.0251
48	0.001860	0.003873	0.016	0.0362	0.001434	0.001559	0.018	0.0335
49	0.001995	0.004571	0.017	0.0407	0.001550	0.001896	0.018	0.0419
50	0.002138	0.005347	0.018	0.0453	0.001676	0.002344	0.017	0.0502
51	0.002288	0.005528	0.019	0.0498	0.001814	0.002459	0.016	0.0586
52	0.002448	0.005644	0.020	0.0686	0.001967	0.002647	0.014	0.0744
53	0.002621	0.005722	0.020	0.0953	0.002135	0.002895	0.012	0.0947
54	0.002812	0.005797	0.020	0.1288	0.002321	0.003190	0.010	0.1189
55	0.003029	0.005905	0.019	0.2066	0.002526	0.003531	0.008	0.1897
56	0.003306	0.006124	0.018	0.3173	0.002756	0.003925	0.006	0.2857
57	0.003628	0.006444	0.017	0.3780	0.003010	0.004385	0.005	0.3403
58	0.003997	0.006895	0.016	0.4401	0.003291	0.004921	0.005	0.3878
59	0.004414	0.007485	0.016	0.4986	0.003599	0.005531	0.005	0.4360
60	0.004878	0.008196	0.016	0.5633	0.003931	0.006200	0.005	0.4954
61	0.005382	0.009001	0.015	0.6338	0.004285	0.006919	0.005	0.5805
62	0.005918	0.009915	0.015	0.7103	0.004656	0.007689	0.005	0.6598
63	0.006472	0.010951	0.014	0.7902	0.005039	0.008509	0.005	0.7520
64	0.007028	0.012117	0.014	0.8355	0.005429	0.009395	0.005	0.8043

Age	MALE Base Non-Annuitant Mortality Rates (Year 2000)	MALE Base Annuitant Mortality Rates (Year 2000)	MALE Scale AA Projection Factors	MALE Weighting Factors for Small Plans	FEMALE Base Non-Annuitant Mortality Rates (Year 2000)	FEMALE Base Annuitant Mortality Rates (Year 2000)	FEMALE Scale AA Projection Factors	FEMALE Weighting Factors for Small Plans
65	0.007573	0.013419	0.014	0.8832	0.005821	0.010364	0.005	0.8552
66	0.008099	0.014868	0.013	0.9321	0.006207	0.011413	0.005	0.9118
67	0.008598	0.016460	0.013	0.9510	0.006583	0.012540	0.005	0.9367
68	0.009069	0.018200	0.014	0.9639	0.006945	0.013771	0.005	0.9523
69	0.009510	0.020105	0.014	0.9714	0.007289	0.015153	0.005	0.9627
70	0.009922	0.022206	0.015	0.9740	0.007613	0.016742	0.005	0.9661
71	0.010912	0.024570	0.015	0.9766	0.008309	0.018579	0.006	0.9695
72	0.012892	0.027281	0.015	0.9792	0.009700	0.020665	0.006	0.9729
73	0.015862	0.030387	0.015	0.9818	0.011787	0.022970	0.007	0.9763
74	0.019821	0.033900	0.015	0.9844	0.014570	0.025458	0.007	0.9797
75	0.024771	0.037834	0.014	0.9870	0.018049	0.028106	0.008	0.9830
76	0.030710	0.042169	0.014	0.9896	0.022224	0.030966	0.008	0.9864
77	0.037640	0.046906	0.013	0.9922	0.027094	0.034105	0.007	0.9898
78	0.045559	0.052123	0.012	0.9948	0.032660	0.037595	0.007	0.9932
79	0.054469	0.057927	0.011	0.9974	0.038922	0.041506	0.007	0.9966
80	0.064368	0.064368	0.010	1.0000	0.045879	0.045879	0.007	1.0000
81	0.072041	0.072041	0.009	1.0000	0.050780	0.050780	0.007	1.0000
82	0.080486	0.080486	0.008	1.0000	0.056294	0.056294	0.007	1.0000
83	0.089718	0.089718	0.008	1.0000	0.062506	0.062506	0.007	1.0000
84	0.099779	0.099779	0.007	1.0000	0.069517	0.069517	0.007	1.0000
85	0.110757	0.110757	0.007	1.0000	0.077446	0.077446	0.006	1.0000
86	0.122797	0.122797	0.007	1.0000	0.086376	0.086376	0.005	1.0000
87	0.136043	0.136043	0.006	1.0000	0.096337	0.096337	0.004	1.0000
88	0.150590	0.150590	0.005	1.0000	0.107303	0.107303	0.004	1.0000
89	0.166420	0.166420	0.005	1.0000	0.119154	0.119154	0.003	1.0000
90	0.183408	0.183408	0.004	1.0000	0.131682	0.131682	0.003	1.0000
91	0.199769	0.199769	0.004	1.0000	0.144604	0.144604	0.003	1.0000
92	0.216605	0.216605	0.003	1.0000	0.157618	0.157618	0.003	1.0000
93	0.233662	0.233662	0.003	1.0000	0.170433	0.170433	0.002	1.0000
94	0.250693	0.250693	0.003	1.0000	0.182799	0.182799	0.002	1.0000
95	0.267491	0.267491	0.002	1.0000	0.194509	0.194509	0.002	1.0000
96	0.283905	0.283905	0.002	1.0000	0.205379	0.205379	0.002	1.0000
97	0.299852	0.299852	0.002	1.0000	0.215240	0.215240	0.001	1.0000
98	0.315296	0.315296	0.001	1.0000	0.223947	0.223947	0.001	1.0000
99	0.330207	0.330207	0.001	1.0000	0.231387	0.231387	0.001	1.0000
100	0.344556	0.344556	0.001	1.0000	0.237467	0.237467	0.001	1.0000

Age	MALE	MALE	MALE	MALE	FEMALE	FEMALE	FEMALE	FEMALE
	Base Non-Annuitant Mortality Rates (Year 2000)	Base Annuitant Mortality Rates (Year 2000)	Scale AA Projection Factors	Weighting Factors for Small Plans	Base Non-Annuitant Mortality Rates (Year 2000)	Base Annuitant Mortality Rates (Year 2000)	Scale AA Projection Factors	Weighting Factors for Small Plans
101	0.358628	0.358628	0.000	1.0000	0.244834	0.244834	0.000	1.0000
102	0.371685	0.371685	0.000	1.0000	0.254498	0.254498	0.000	1.0000
103	0.383040	0.383040	0.000	1.0000	0.266044	0.266044	0.000	1.0000
104	0.392003	0.392003	0.000	1.0000	0.279055	0.279055	0.000	1.0000
105	0.397886	0.397886	0.000	1.0000	0.293116	0.293116	0.000	1.0000
106	0.400000	0.400000	0.000	1.0000	0.307811	0.307811	0.000	1.0000
107	0.400000	0.400000	0.000	1.0000	0.322725	0.322725	0.000	1.0000
108	0.400000	0.400000	0.000	1.0000	0.337441	0.337441	0.000	1.0000
109	0.400000	0.400000	0.000	1.0000	0.351544	0.351544	0.000	1.0000
110	0.400000	0.400000	0.000	1.0000	0.364617	0.364617	0.000	1.0000
111	0.400000	0.400000	0.000	1.0000	0.376246	0.376246	0.000	1.0000
112	0.400000	0.400000	0.000	1.0000	0.386015	0.386015	0.000	1.0000
113	0.400000	0.400000	0.000	1.0000	0.393507	0.393507	0.000	1.0000
114	0.400000	0.400000	0.000	1.0000	0.398308	0.398308	0.000	1.0000
115	0.400000	0.400000	0.000	1.0000	0.400000	0.400000	0.000	1.0000
116	0.400000	0.400000	0.000	1.0000	0.400000	0.400000	0.000	1.0000
117	0.400000	0.400000	0.000	1.0000	0.400000	0.400000	0.000	1.0000
118	0.400000	0.400000	0.000	1.0000	0.400000	0.400000	0.000	1.0000
119	0.400000	0.400000	0.000	1.0000	0.400000	0.400000	0.000	1.0000
120	1.000000	1.000000	0.000	1.0000	1.000000	1.000000	0.000	1.0000

(e) *Static mortality tables with respect to valuation dates occurring during 2008.* The following static mortality tables are used pursuant to paragraph (a)(3) of this section for determining present value or making any computation under section 430 with respect to valuation dates occurring during 2008.

Age	MALE	MALE	MALE	FEMALE	FEMALE	FEMALE
	Non-Annuitant Mortality Rates	Annuitant Mortality Rates	Optional Combined Table for Small Plans	Non-Annuitant Mortality Rates	Annuitant Mortality Rates	Optional Combined Table for Small Plans
1	0.000400	0.000400	0.000400	0.000359	0.000359	0.000359
2	0.000270	0.000270	0.000270	0.000234	0.000234	0.000234
3	0.000224	0.000224	0.000224	0.000175	0.000175	0.000175
4	0.000175	0.000175	0.000175	0.000131	0.000131	0.000131
5	0.000160	0.000160	0.000160	0.000118	0.000118	0.000118
6	0.000153	0.000153	0.000153	0.000111	0.000111	0.000111
7	0.000147	0.000147	0.000147	0.000104	0.000104	0.000104
8	0.000136	0.000136	0.000136	0.000092	0.000092	0.000092

Age	MALE Non-Annuitant Mortality Rates	MALE Annuitant Mortality Rates	MALE Optional Combined Table for Small Plans	FEMALE Non-Annuitant Mortality Rates	FEMALE Annuitant Mortality Rates	FEMALE Optional Combined Table for Small Plans
9	0.000131	0.000131	0.000131	0.000088	0.000088	0.000088
10	0.000133	0.000133	0.000133	0.000089	0.000089	0.000089
11	0.000138	0.000138	0.000138	0.000090	0.000090	0.000090
12	0.000143	0.000143	0.000143	0.000093	0.000093	0.000093
13	0.000151	0.000151	0.000151	0.000097	0.000097	0.000097
14	0.000163	0.000163	0.000163	0.000107	0.000107	0.000107
15	0.000173	0.000173	0.000173	0.000117	0.000117	0.000117
16	0.000183	0.000183	0.000183	0.000125	0.000125	0.000125
17	0.000194	0.000194	0.000194	0.000133	0.000133	0.000133
18	0.000203	0.000203	0.000203	0.000136	0.000136	0.000136
19	0.000213	0.000213	0.000213	0.000134	0.000134	0.000134
20	0.000222	0.000222	0.000222	0.000132	0.000132	0.000132
21	0.000235	0.000235	0.000235	0.000129	0.000129	0.000129
22	0.000247	0.000247	0.000247	0.000131	0.000131	0.000131
23	0.000263	0.000263	0.000263	0.000136	0.000136	0.000136
24	0.000278	0.000278	0.000278	0.000142	0.000142	0.000142
25	0.000298	0.000298	0.000298	0.000150	0.000150	0.000150
26	0.000329	0.000329	0.000329	0.000162	0.000162	0.000162
27	0.000340	0.000340	0.000340	0.000169	0.000169	0.000169
28	0.000350	0.000350	0.000350	0.000178	0.000178	0.000178
29	0.000367	0.000367	0.000367	0.000188	0.000188	0.000188
30	0.000396	0.000396	0.000396	0.000210	0.000210	0.000210
31	0.000445	0.000445	0.000445	0.000255	0.000255	0.000255
32	0.000501	0.000501	0.000501	0.000291	0.000291	0.000291
33	0.000562	0.000562	0.000562	0.000320	0.000320	0.000320
34	0.000626	0.000626	0.000626	0.000345	0.000345	0.000345
35	0.000689	0.000689	0.000689	0.000368	0.000368	0.000368
36	0.000749	0.000749	0.000749	0.000389	0.000389	0.000389
37	0.000806	0.000806	0.000806	0.000410	0.000410	0.000410
38	0.000839	0.000839	0.000839	0.000432	0.000432	0.000432
39	0.000869	0.000869	0.000869	0.000458	0.000458	0.000458
40	0.000897	0.000897	0.000897	0.000499	0.000499	0.000499
41	0.000928	0.000955	0.000928	0.000547	0.000547	0.000547
42	0.000964	0.001070	0.000965	0.000602	0.000602	0.000602
43	0.001007	0.001243	0.001010	0.000662	0.000662	0.000662
44	0.001058	0.001474	0.001066	0.000727	0.000727	0.000727
45	0.001116	0.001763	0.001131	0.000776	0.000779	0.000776

Age	MALE	MALE	MALE	FEMALE	FEMALE	FEMALE
	Non-Annuitant Mortality Rates	Annuitant Mortality Rates	Optional Combined Table for Small Plans	Non-Annuitant Mortality Rates	Annuitant Mortality Rates	Optional Combined Table for Small Plans
46	0.001168	0.002109	0.001194	0.000824	0.000882	0.000825
47	0.001225	0.002513	0.001266	0.000873	0.001037	0.000877
48	0.001284	0.002975	0.001345	0.000944	0.001244	0.000954
49	0.001345	0.003495	0.001433	0.001021	0.001502	0.001041
50	0.001408	0.004072	0.001529	0.001130	0.001812	0.001164
51	0.001472	0.004146	0.001605	0.001252	0.001931	0.001292
52	0.001538	0.004168	0.001718	0.001422	0.002142	0.001476
53	0.001647	0.004226	0.001893	0.001617	0.002415	0.001693
54	0.001767	0.004281	0.002091	0.001842	0.002744	0.001949
55	0.001948	0.004428	0.002460	0.002100	0.003130	0.002295
56	0.002177	0.004663	0.002966	0.002400	0.003586	0.002739
57	0.002446	0.004983	0.003405	0.002682	0.004067	0.003153
58	0.002758	0.005413	0.003926	0.002933	0.004565	0.003566
59	0.003046	0.005876	0.004457	0.003207	0.005130	0.004045
60	0.003366	0.006435	0.005095	0.003503	0.005751	0.004617
61	0.003802	0.007175	0.005940	0.003818	0.006418	0.005327
62	0.004180	0.007904	0.006825	0.004149	0.007132	0.006117
63	0.004680	0.008864	0.007986	0.004490	0.007893	0.007049
64	0.005082	0.009807	0.009030	0.004838	0.008715	0.007956
65	0.005476	0.010861	0.010232	0.005187	0.009613	0.008972
66	0.005994	0.012218	0.011795	0.005531	0.010586	0.010140
67	0.006363	0.013527	0.013176	0.005866	0.011632	0.011267
68	0.006557	0.014731	0.014436	0.006189	0.012774	0.012460
69	0.006876	0.016273	0.016004	0.006495	0.014055	0.013773
70	0.007009	0.017702	0.017424	0.006784	0.015529	0.015233
71	0.007888	0.019586	0.019312	0.007411	0.016975	0.016683
72	0.009646	0.021747	0.021495	0.008666	0.018881	0.018604
73	0.012283	0.024223	0.024006	0.010548	0.020673	0.020433
74	0.015799	0.027024	0.026849	0.013058	0.022912	0.022712
75	0.020195	0.030622	0.030486	0.016195	0.024916	0.024768
76	0.025470	0.034131	0.034041	0.019959	0.027451	0.027349
77	0.031624	0.038547	0.038493	0.024351	0.030694	0.030629
78	0.038657	0.043489	0.043464	0.029370	0.033835	0.033805
79	0.046569	0.049071	0.049064	0.035017	0.037355	0.037347
80	0.055360	0.055360	0.055360	0.041291	0.041291	0.041291
81	0.062905	0.062905	0.062905	0.045702	0.045702	0.045702
82	0.071350	0.071350	0.071350	0.050664	0.050664	0.050664

Age	MALE	MALE	MALE	FEMALE	FEMALE	FEMALE
	Non-Annuitant Mortality Rates	Annuitant Mortality Rates	Optional Combined Table for Small Plans	Non-Annuitant Mortality Rates	Annuitant Mortality Rates	Optional Combined Table for Small Plans
83	0.079534	0.079534	0.079534	0.056255	0.056255	0.056255
84	0.089800	0.089800	0.089800	0.062565	0.062565	0.062565
85	0.099680	0.099680	0.099680	0.070761	0.070761	0.070761
86	0.110516	0.110516	0.110516	0.080120	0.080120	0.080120
87	0.124300	0.124300	0.124300	0.090716	0.090716	0.090716
88	0.139683	0.139683	0.139683	0.101042	0.101042	0.101042
89	0.154366	0.154366	0.154366	0.113903	0.113903	0.113903
90	0.172706	0.172706	0.172706	0.125879	0.125879	0.125879
91	0.188113	0.188113	0.188113	0.138232	0.138232	0.138232
92	0.207060	0.207060	0.207060	0.150672	0.150672	0.150672
93	0.223365	0.223365	0.223365	0.165391	0.165391	0.165391
94	0.239646	0.239646	0.239646	0.177391	0.177391	0.177391
95	0.259578	0.259578	0.259578	0.188755	0.188755	0.188755
96	0.275506	0.275506	0.275506	0.199303	0.199303	0.199303
97	0.290981	0.290981	0.290981	0.212034	0.212034	0.212034
98	0.310600	0.310600	0.310600	0.220611	0.220611	0.220611
99	0.325288	0.325288	0.325288	0.227940	0.227940	0.227940
100	0.339424	0.339424	0.339424	0.233930	0.233930	0.233930
101	0.358628	0.358628	0.358628	0.244834	0.244834	0.244834
102	0.371685	0.371685	0.371685	0.254498	0.254498	0.254498
103	0.383040	0.383040	0.383040	0.266044	0.266044	0.266044
104	0.392003	0.392003	0.392003	0.279055	0.279055	0.279055
105	0.397886	0.397886	0.397886	0.293116	0.293116	0.293116
106	0.400000	0.400000	0.400000	0.307811	0.307811	0.307811
107	0.400000	0.400000	0.400000	0.322725	0.322725	0.322725
108	0.400000	0.400000	0.400000	0.337441	0.337441	0.337441
109	0.400000	0.400000	0.400000	0.351544	0.351544	0.351544
110	0.400000	0.400000	0.400000	0.364617	0.364617	0.364617
111	0.400000	0.400000	0.400000	0.376246	0.376246	0.376246
112	0.400000	0.400000	0.400000	0.386015	0.386015	0.386015
113	0.400000	0.400000	0.400000	0.393507	0.393507	0.393507
114	0.400000	0.400000	0.400000	0.398308	0.398308	0.398308
115	0.400000	0.400000	0.400000	0.400000	0.400000	0.400000
116	0.400000	0.400000	0.400000	0.400000	0.400000	0.400000
117	0.400000	0.400000	0.400000	0.400000	0.400000	0.400000
118	0.400000	0.400000	0.400000	0.400000	0.400000	0.400000

Age	MALE	MALE	MALE	FEMALE	FEMALE	FEMALE
	Non-Annuitant Mortality Rates	Annuitant Mortality Rates	Optional Combined Table for Small Plans	Non-Annuitant Mortality Rates	Annuitant Mortality Rates	Optional Combined Table for Small Plans
119	0.400000	0.400000	0.400000	0.400000	0.400000	0.400000
120	1.000000	1.000000	1.000000	1.000000	1.000000	1.000000

(f) *Applicability date.* This section applies for plan years beginning on or after January 1, 2008.

Par. 3. Section 1.430(h)(3)–2 is added to read as follows:

§1.430(h)(3)–2 Plan-specific substitute mortality tables used to determine present value.

(a) *In general.* This section sets forth rules for the use of substitute mortality tables under section 430(h)(3)(C) in determining any present value or making any computation under section 430 in accordance with §1.430(h)(3)–1(a)(1). In order to use substitute mortality tables, a plan sponsor must obtain approval to use substitute mortality tables for the plan in accordance with the procedures set forth in paragraph (b) of this section. Paragraph (c) of this section sets forth rules for the development of substitute mortality tables, including guidelines for determining whether a plan has sufficient credible mortality experience to use substitute mortality tables. Paragraph (d) of this section sets forth special rules regarding the use of substitute mortality tables. The Commissioner may, in revenue rulings and procedures, notices and other guidance published in the Internal Revenue Bulletin (see §601.601(d)(2)(ii)(*b*) of this chapter), provide additional guidance regarding approval and use of substitute mortality tables under section 430(h)(3)(C) and related matters.

(b) *Procedures for obtaining approval to use substitute mortality tables*—(1) *Written request to use substitute mortality tables*—(i) *General requirements.* In order to use substitute mortality tables, a plan sponsor must submit a written request to the Commissioner that demonstrates that those substitute mortality tables meet the requirements of section 430(h)(3)(C) and this section. This request must state the first plan year and the term of years (not more than 10) that the tables are requested to be used.

(ii) *Time for written request*—(A) *In general.* Except as provided in paragraph (b)(1)(ii)(B) of this section, substitute mortality tables cannot be used for a plan year unless the plan sponsor submits the written request described in paragraph (b)(1)(i) of this section at least 7 months prior to the first day of the first plan year for which the substitute mortality tables are to apply.

(B) *Special rule for requests submitted on or before October 1, 2007.* Notwithstanding the rule of paragraph (b)(1)(ii)(A) of this section, the timing of the written request described in paragraph (b)(1)(i) of this section does not prevent a plan from using substitute mortality tables for a plan year provided that the written request is submitted no later than October 1, 2007.

(2) *Commissioner's review of request*—(i) *In general.* During the 180-day period that begins on the date the plan sponsor submits a request to use substitute mortality tables for a plan pursuant to this section, the Commissioner will determine whether the request to use substitute mortality tables satisfies the requirements of this section (including any published guidance issued pursuant to paragraph (a) of this section), and will either approve or deny the request. The Commissioner will deny a request if the request fails to meet the requirements of this section or if the Commissioner determines that a substitute mortality table does not sufficiently reflect the mortality experience of the applicable plan population.

(ii) *Request for additional information.* The Commissioner may request additional information with respect to the submission. Failure to provide that information on a timely basis constitutes grounds for denial of the request.

(iii) *Deemed approval.* Except as provided in paragraph (b)(2)(iv) of this section, if the Commissioner does not issue a denial within the 180-day review period, the request is deemed to have been approved.

(iv) *Extension of time permitted.* The Commissioner and a plan sponsor may, before the expiration of the 180-day review period, agree in writing to extend that period, provided that any such agreement also specifies any revisions in the plan sponsor's request, including any change in the requested term of use of the substitute mortality tables.

(c) *Development of substitute mortality tables*—(1) *Mortality experience requirements*—(i) *In general.* Substitute mortality tables must reflect the actual mortality experience of the pension plan maintained by the plan sponsor for which the tables are to be used and that mortality experience must be credible mortality experience as described in paragraph (c)(1)(ii) of this section. Separate mortality tables must be established for each gender under the plan, and a substitute mortality table is permitted to be established for a gender only if the plan has credible mortality experience with respect to that gender.

(ii) *Credible mortality experience.* There is credible mortality experience for a gender within a plan if and only if, over the period covered by the experience study described in paragraph (c)(2)(ii) of this section, there are at least 1,000 deaths within that gender.

(iii) *Gender without credible mortality experience*—(A) *In general.* If, for the first year for which a plan uses substitute mortality tables, one gender has credible mortality experience but the other gender does not have credible mortality experience, the substitute mortality tables are used for the gender that does have credible mortality experience and the mortality tables under §1.430(h)(3)–1 are used for the gender that does not have credible mortality experience. For a subsequent plan year, the plan sponsor may continue to use substitute mortality tables for the gender with credible mortality experience without using substitute mortality tables for the other gender only if the other gender continues to lack credible mortality experience for that subsequent plan year.

(B) *Demonstration of lack of credible mortality experience for a gender.* In order to demonstrate that a gender within a plan does not have credible mortality experience for a plan year, the mortality experience of that population must be analyzed using a 4-year experience study that ends less than 3 years before the first day of that plan year. For example, if a plan uses substitute mortality tables based on credible mortality experience for its male population and the standard mortality tables under §1.430(h)(3)–1 for its female population, there must be an experience study which shows that the plan's female population does not have at least 1,000 deaths in a 4-year period that ends less than 3 years before the first day of that plan year.

(iv) *Disabled individuals.* Under section 430(h)(3)(D), separate mortality tables are permitted to be used for certain disabled individuals. If such separate mortality tables are used for those disabled individuals, then those individuals are disregarded for all purposes under this section. Thus, if the mortality tables under section 430(h)(3)(D) are used for disabled individuals under a plan, mortality experience with respect to those individuals must be excluded in developing mortality rates for substitute mortality tables under this section.

(2) *Base table and base year*—(i) *In general.* Development of a substitute mortality table under this section requires creation of a base table and identification of a base year under this paragraph (c)(2). The base table and base year are then used to determine a substitute mortality table under paragraph (c)(3) of this section.

(ii) *Experience study and base table requirements*—(A) *In general.* The base table for a plan population must be developed from an experience study of the mortality experience of that plan population that generates amounts-weighted mortality rates based on experience data for the plan over 2, 3, or 4 consecutive years. The last day of the final year reflected in the experience data must be less than 3 years before the first day of the first plan year for which the substitute mortality tables are to apply. For example, if July 1, 2008, is the first day of the first plan year for which the substitute mortality tables will be used, then an experience study using calendar year data must include data collected for a period that ends no earlier than December 31, 2005.

(B) *Amounts-weighted mortality rates.* The amounts-weighted mortality rate for an age is equal to the quotient determined by dividing the sum of the accrued benefits (or payable benefits, in the case of individuals in pay status) for all individuals at that age at the beginning of the year who died during the year, by the sum of the accrued benefits (or payable benefits, in the case of individuals in pay status) for all individuals at that age at the beginning of the year, with appropriate adjustments for individuals who left the relevant plan population during the year for reasons other than death. Because amounts-weighted mortality rates for a plan cannot be determined without accrued (or payable) benefits, the mortality experience study used to develop a base table cannot include periods before the plan was established.

(C) *Grouping of ages.* Amounts-weighted mortality rates may be derived from amounts-weighted mortality rates for age groups. The Commissioner, in revenue rulings and procedures, notices, and other guidance, may specify grouping rules (for example, 5-year age groups, except for extreme ages such as ages above 100 or below 20) and methods for developing amounts-weighted mortality rates for individual ages from amounts-weighted mortality rates initially determined for each age group.

(D) *Base table construction.* The base tables must be constructed from the amounts-weighted mortality rates determined in paragraph (c)(2)(ii)(B) of this section. The base tables must be constructed either directly through graduation of the amounts-weighted mortality rates or indirectly by applying a level percentage to the applicable mortality table set forth in §1.430(h)(3)–1, provided that the adjusted table sufficiently reflects the mortality experience of the plan. The Commissioner also may permit the use of other recognized mortality tables in the construction of base tables, applying a similar mortality experience standard.

(iii) *Base year requirements.* Where there are 2 years of experience data, the base year is the calendar year in which the first year of the experience data begins. Where there are 3 or 4 years of experience data, the base year is the calendar year in which the second year of the experience data begins. If the base table is constructed by applying a level percentage to a table set forth in §1.430(h)(3)–1, then the percentage must be applied to the table under §1.430(h)(3)–1 after it has been projected to the base year using Projection Scale AA, as set forth in §1.430(h)(3)–1(d). Thus, for example, if the base year of the mortality experience study is 2004, the applicable base (year 2000) mortality rates must be projected four years prior to determining the level percentage to be applied to the applicable projected base (year 2000) mortality rates.

(iv) *Change in number of individuals covered by table.* Experience data cannot be used to develop a base table if the number of individuals in the population covered by the table (for example, the male annuitant population) as of the last day of the plan year before the year the request to use substitute mortality tables is made, compared to the average number of individuals in that population over the years covered by the experience study on which the substitute mortality tables are based, reflects a difference of 20 percent or more, unless it is demonstrated to the satisfaction of the Commissioner that the experience data is accurately predictive of future mortality of that plan population (taking into account the effect of the change in individuals) after appropriate adjustments to the data are made (for example, excluding data from individuals with respect to a spun-off portion of the plan). For this purpose, a reasonable estimate of the number of individuals in the population covered by the table may be used, such as the estimated number of participants and beneficiaries used for purposes of the PBGC Form 1-ES.

(3) *Determination of substitute mortality tables*—(i) *In general.* A plan's substitute mortality tables must be generational mortality tables. Substitute mortality tables are determined using the base mortality tables developed pursuant to paragraph (c)(2) of this section and the projection factors provided in Projection Scale AA, as set forth in §1.430(h)(3)–1(d). Under the generational mortality tables, the probability of an individual's death at a particular age is determined as the individual's base mortality rate (that is, the applicable mortality rate from the base mortality table for the age for which the probability of death is being determined) mul-

tiplied by the mortality improvement factor. The mortality improvement factor is equal to $(1 - \text{projection factor for that age})^n$, where n is equal to the projection period (the number of years between the base year for the base mortality table and the calendar year in which the individual attains the age for which the probability of death is being determined).

(ii) *Example of calculation.* As an example of the use of generational mortality tables under paragraph (c)(3)(i) of this section, if approved substitute mortality tables are based on data collected during 2005 and 2006, the base year would be the first year of experience (2005) because the substitute tables are based on two years of experience data. If the tables show a base mortality rate of .006000 for male annuitants at age 54, the probability of death at age 54 for a male annuitant born in 1974 would be determined using the base mortality rate of .006000, the age–54 projection factor of .020 (pursuant to the Scale AA Projection Factors set forth in §1.430(h)(3)–1(d)) and a projection period of 23 years. The projection period is the number of years between the base year of 2005 and the calendar year in which the individual reaches age 54. Accordingly, the mortality improvement factor would be .628347 and the probability of death at age 54 would be .003770.

(4) *Separate tables for specified populations*—(i) *In general.* Except as provided in this paragraph (c)(4), separate substitute mortality tables are permitted to be used for separate populations within a gender under a plan only if—

(A) All individuals of that gender in the plan are divided into separate populations;

(B) Each separate population has credible mortality experience as provided in paragraph (c)(4)(iii) of this section; and

(C) The separate substitute mortality table for each separate population is developed using mortality experience data for that population.

(ii) *Annuitant and nonannuitant separate populations.* Notwithstanding paragraph (c)(4)(i)(B) of this section, substitute mortality tables for separate populations of annuitants and nonannuitants within a gender may be used even if only one of those separate populations has credible mortality experience. Similarly, if separate populations that satisfy paragraph (c)(4)(i)(B) of this section are established, then any of those populations may be further subdivided into separate annuitant and nonannuitant subpopulations, provided that at least one of the two resulting subpopulations has credible mortality experience. The standard mortality tables under §1.430(h)(3)–1 are used for a resulting subpopulation that does not have credible mortality experience. For example, in the case of a plan that has credible mortality experience for both its male hourly and salaried individuals, if the male salaried annuitant population has credible mortality experience, it may use substitute mortality tables with respect to that population even if the male salaried nonannuitant population uses the standard mortality tables under §1.430(h)(3)–1 (because that nonannuitant population does not have credible mortality experience).

(iii) *Credible mortality experience for separate populations.* In determining whether a separate population within a gender has credible mortality experience, the requirements of paragraph (c)(1)(ii) of this section must be satisfied but, in applying that paragraph, the separate population should be substituted for the particular gender. In demonstrating that an annuitant or nonannuitant population within a gender or within a separate population does not have credible mortality experience, the requirements of paragraph (c)(1)(iii) of this section must be satisfied but, in applying that paragraph, the annuitant (or nonannuitant) population should be substituted for the particular gender.

(d) *Special rules*—(1) *All plans in controlled group must use substitute mortality tables*—(i) *In general.* Except as otherwise provided in this paragraph (d)(1), substitute mortality tables are permitted to be used for a plan only if the use of substitute mortality tables is approved under this section for each other pension plan subject to the requirements of section 430 that is maintained by the sponsor and by each member of the plan sponsor's controlled group. For purposes of this section, the term *controlled group* means any group treated as a single employer under subsection (b), (c), (m), or (o) of section 414.

(ii) *Plans without credible experience*—(A) *In general.* For the first year for which a plan uses substitute mortality tables, the use of substitute mortality tables for the plan is not prohibited merely because another plan described in paragraph (d)(1)(i) of this section cannot use substitute mortality tables because neither the males nor the females under that other plan have credible mortality experience for a plan year. For each subsequent plan year, the plan sponsor may continue to use substitute mortality tables for the plan with credible mortality experience without using substitute mortality tables for the other plan only if neither the males nor the females under that other plan have credible mortality experience for that subsequent plan year.

(B) *Analysis of mortality experience.* For each plan year in which a plan uses substitute mortality tables, in order to demonstrate that the male and female populations of another plan maintained by the plan sponsor (or by a member of the plan sponsor's controlled group) do not have credible mortality experience, the requirements of paragraph (c)(1)(iii)(B) of this section must be satisfied for that plan year. Thus, a plan is not prohibited from using substitute mortality tables for a plan year merely because another plan in the controlled group of the plan sponsor does not have at least 1,000 male deaths and does not have at least 1,000 female deaths in a 4-year period that ends less than 3 years before the first day of that plan year.

(iii) *Newly acquired plans not using substitute mortality tables*—(A) *In general.* The use of substitute mortality tables for a plan is not prohibited merely because a newly acquired plan does not use substitute mortality tables, but only through the last day of the plan year of the plan using substitute mortality tables that contains the end of the period described in section 410(b)(6)(C). Thus, for the following plan year, the mortality tables prescribed under §1.430(h)(3)–1 apply with respect to the plan (and all other plans within the plan sponsor's controlled group, including the acquired plan) unless—

(*1*) Approval to use substitute mortality tables has been obtained with respect to the acquired plan pursuant to paragraph (b)(1) of this section; or

(*2*) The acquired plan cannot use substitute mortality tables because neither the males nor the females under the plan have credible mortality experience as described in paragraph (c)(1)(ii) of this section (as determined in accordance with the rules of paragraph (d)(1)(iv) of this section).

(B) *Definition of newly acquired plan.* For purposes of this section, a plan is treated as a newly acquired plan if it becomes maintained by the plan sponsor (or by a member of the plan sponsor's controlled group) in connection with a merger, acquisition, or similar transaction described in §1.410(b)–2(f). In addition, a plan also is treated as a newly acquired plan for purposes of this section if a plan is established in connection with a transfer in accordance with section 414(l) of assets and liabilities from another employer's plan in connection with a merger, acquisition, or similar transaction described in §1.410(b)–2(f).

(iv) *Demonstration of credible mortality experience for newly acquired plan*—(A) *In general.* In general, in the case of a newly acquired plan described in paragraph (d)(1)(iii) of this section, the demonstration of whether credible mortality experience exists for the plan for a plan year may be made by either including or excluding mortality experience data for the period prior to the date the plan becomes maintained by a member of the new plan sponsor's controlled group. If a plan sponsor excludes mortality experience data for the period prior to the date the plan becomes maintained within the new plan sponsor's controlled group, the exclusion must apply for all populations within the plan.

(B) *Demonstration of credible mortality experience.* Regardless of whether mortality experience data for the period prior to the date a newly acquired plan becomes maintained within the new plan sponsor's controlled group is included or excluded for a plan year, the provisions of this section, including the demonstration of credible mortality experience in accordance with paragraph (c)(1)(ii) of this section, must be satisfied before substitute mortality tables may be used with respect to the plan. Thus, for example, the plan must meet the rule in paragraph (c)(2)(ii)(A) of this section that the base table be based on mortality experience data for the plan over a 2, 3, or 4-consecutive year period that ends less than 3 years before the first day of the plan year for which substitute mortality tables will be used.

(C) *Demonstration of lack of credible mortality experience.* In the case of a newly acquired plan described in paragraph (d)(1)(iii) of this section, in order to demonstrate a lack of credible mortality experience with respect to a gender for a plan year, the rules of paragraph (c)(1)(iii)(B) of this section generally will apply. However, a special rule applies if the plan's mortality experience demonstration for a plan year is made by excluding mortality experience for the period prior to the date the plan becomes maintained by a member of the new plan sponsor's controlled group. In such a case, an employer is permitted to demonstrate a plan's lack of credible mortality experience using an experience study period of less than four years, provided that the experience study period begins with the date the plan becomes maintained within the sponsor's controlled group and ends not more than one year and one day before the first day of the plan year with respect to which the lack of credible mortality experience demonstration is made. Thus, if the transaction occurred on July 1, 2010, in order to demonstrate a lack of credible mortality experience for males and females for the plan year beginning January 1, 2012 (the first day of the plan year following the section 410(b)(6)(C) transition period), there must be an experience study which shows that the plan's male and female populations each do not have 1,000 deaths during the period from July 1, 2010 – December 31, 2010. Similarly, in order to perform the demonstration to show a lack of credible mortality experience for the plan year beginning January 1, 2013, there must be an experience study which shows that the plan's male and female populations each do not have 1,000 deaths during the period from July 1, 2010 – December 31, 2011.

(2) *Duration of use of tables.* Except as provided in paragraph (d)(4) of this section, substitute mortality tables are used with respect to a plan for the term of consecutive plan years specified in the plan sponsor's written request to use such tables under paragraph (b)(1) of this section and approved by the Commissioner, or such shorter period prescribed by the Commissioner in the approval to use substitute mortality tables. Following the end of such term of use, or following any early termination of use described in paragraph (d)(4) of this section, the mortality tables specified in §1.430(h)(3)–1 apply with respect to the plan unless approval under paragraph (b)(1) of this section has been received by the plan sponsor to use substitute mortality tables for a further term.

(3) *Aggregation*—(i) *Permissive aggregation of plans.* In order for a plan sponsor to use a set of substitute mortality tables with respect to two or more plans, the rules of this section are applied by treating those plans as a single plan. In such a case, the substitute mortality tables must be used for the aggregated plans and must be based on data collected with respect to those aggregated plans.

(ii) *Required aggregation of plans.* In general, plans are not required to be aggregated for purposes of applying the rules of this section. However, for purposes of this section, a plan is required to be aggregated with any plan that was previously spun off from that plan for purposes of this section if the Commissioner determines that one purpose of the spinoff is to avoid the use of substitute mortality tables for any of the plans that were involved in the spinoff.

(4) *Early termination of use of tables*—(i) *General rule.* A plan's substitute mortality tables cannot be used as of the earliest of—

(A) The plan year in which the plan fails to satisfy the requirements of paragraph (c)(1) of this section (regarding credible mortality experience requirements and demonstrations);

(B) The plan year in which the plan fails to satisfy the requirements of paragraph (d)(1) of this section (regarding use of substitute mortality tables by controlled group members);

(C) The second plan year following the plan year in which there is a significant change in individuals covered by the plan as described in paragraph (d)(4)(ii) of this section;

(D) The plan year following the plan year in which a substitute mortality table used for a plan population is no longer accurately predictive of future mortality of that population, as determined by the Commissioner or as certified by the plan's actuary to the satisfaction of the Commissioner; or

(E) The date specified in guidance published in the Internal Revenue Bulletin (see §601.601(d)(2)(ii)(*b*) of this chapter) pursuant to a replacement of mortality tables specified under section 430(h)(3)(A) and §1.430(h)(3)–1 (other than annual updates to the static mortality tables issued pursuant to §1.430(h)–1(a)(3)).

(ii) *Significant change in coverage*—(A) *Change in coverage from time of experience study.* For purposes of applying the rules of paragraph (d)(4)(i)(C) of this section, a significant change in the individuals covered by a substitute mortality table occurs if there is an increase or decrease in the number of individuals of at least 20 percent compared to the average number of individuals in that population over the years covered by the experience study on which the substitute mortality tables are based. However, a change in coverage is not treated as significant if the plan's actuary certifies in writing to the satisfaction of the Commissioner that the substitute mortality tables used for the plan population continue to be accurately predictive of future mortality of that population (taking into account the effect of the change in the population).

(B) *Change in coverage from time of certification.* For purposes of applying the rules of paragraph (d)(4)(i)(C) of this section, a significant change in the individuals covered by a substitute mortality table occurs if there is an increase or decrease in the number of individuals covered by a substitute mortality table of at least 20 percent compared to the number of individuals in a plan year for which a certification described in paragraph (d)(4)(ii)(A) of this section was made on account of a prior change in coverage. However, a change in coverage is not treated as significant if the plan's actuary certifies in writing to the satisfaction of the Commissioner that the substitute mortality tables used by the plan with respect to the covered population continue to be accurately predictive of future mortality of that population (taking into account the effect of the change in the plan population).

(e) *Applicability date.* This section applies for plan years beginning on or after January 1, 2008.

Par. 4. Section 1.431(c)(6)–1 is added to read as follows:

§1.431(c)(6)–1 Mortality tables used to determine current liability.

The mortality assumptions that apply to a defined benefit plan for the plan year pursuant to section 430(h)(3)(A) and §1.430(h)(3)–1(a)(2) are used to determine a multiemployer plan's current liability for purposes of applying the rules of section 431(c)(6). A multiemployer plan is permitted to apply either the static mortality tables used pursuant to §1.430(h)(3)–1(a)(3) or generational mortality tables used pursuant to §1.430(h)(3)–1(a)(4) for this purpose. However, for this purpose, a multiemployer plan is not permitted to use substitute mortality tables under §1.430(h)(3) 2.

Kevin M. Brown,
Deputy Commissioner for Services and Enforcement.

(Filed by the Office of the Federal Register on May 23, 2007, 9:35 a.m., and published in the issue of the Federal Register for May 29, 2007, 72 F.R. 29456)

Limitations on Benefits and Contributions Under Qualified Plans; Correction

Announcement 2007–57

AGENCY: Internal Revenue Service (IRS), Treasury.

ACTION: Correcting amendments.

SUMMARY: This document contains corrections to final regulations (T.D. 9319, 2007–18 I.R.B. 1041) that were published in the **Federal Register** on Thursday, April 5, 2007 (72 FR 16878) regarding the limitations of section 415, including updates to the regulations for numerous statutory changes since comprehensive final regulations were last published under section 415.

DATES: These correcting amendments are effective May 23, 2007.

FOR FURTHER INFORMATION CONTACT: Vernon S. Carter at (202) 622–6060 or Linda S. F. Marshall at (202) 622–6090 (not toll-free numbers).

SUPPLEMENTARY INFORMATION:

Background

The final regulations that are the subject of this document are under sections 401(a), 401(a)(4), 401(a)(9), 401(k), 402, 414(s), 415, 416, 457, and 924 of the Internal Revenue Code.

Need for Correction

As published, final regulations (T.D. 9319) contain errors that may prove to be misleading and are in need of clarification.

* * * * *

Correction of Publication

Accordingly, 26 CFR part 1 is corrected by making the following correcting amendments:

PART 1—INCOME TAXES

Paragraph 1. The authority citation for part 1 continues to read as follows:

Authority: 26 U.S.C. 7805 * * *

Par. 2. Section 1.402(c)–2, A–4 is revised by inserting colon to read as follows:

§1.402(c)–2 Eligible rollover distributions; questions and answers.

* * * * *

A–4: * * *

* * * * *

Par. 3. Section 1.415(b)–1 is amended by revising the only sentence of paragraph (c)(5)(i)(A), and the second sentence of *Example 6.* paragraph (iv). The revisions read as follows:

§1.415(b)–1 Limitations for defined benefit plans.

* * * * *

(c) * * *

(5) * * *

(i) * * *

(A) The benefit is paid in a form to which section 417(e)(3) does not apply.

* * * * *

Example 6. * * *

(iv) * * * With respect to the single-sum distribution, the annual amount of the actuarially equivalent straight life annuity commencing at the same age determined using the plan's actuarial factors is equal to $45,000. * * *

* * * * *

Par. 4. Section 1.415(d)–1 is amended by revising the paragraph heading to read as follows:

§1.415(d)–1 Cost-of-living adjustments.

* * * * *

Par. 5. Section 1.415(f)–1 is amended by revising the last sentence of paragraph (d)(1) to read as follows:

§1.415(f)–1 Aggregating plans.

* * * * *

(d) * * *

(1) * * * Instead, the transferee plan takes into account the transferred benefits that are actually provided under the transferee plan (see §1.415(b)–1(b)(3)(i)(C)) and, pursuant to paragraph (c)(1) of this section, any nontransferred benefits provided under plans maintained by the predecessor employer with respect to a participant whose benefits have been transferred to the transferee plan.

* * * * *

Par. 6. Section 1.457–5(d) *Example 2.* paragraphs (ii) and (iii) are amended by revising the third sentence of (ii) and (iii) to read as follows:

§1.457–5 Individual limitation for combined annual deferrals under multiple eligible plans.

* * * * *

(d) * * *

Example 2. * * *

(ii) * * * Alternatively, Participant E could instead elect to defer the following combination of amounts: an aggregate total of $15,000 to Plans X, Y, and Z, if no contribution is made to Plan W; an aggregate total of $20,000 to any of the four plans, assuming at least $5,000 is contributed to Plan W; or $22,000 to Plan W and none to any of the other three plans.

(iii) * * * If the underutilized amount under Plans W, X, and Y for year 2006 were in each case zero (because E had always contributed the maximum amount or E was a new participant) or an amount not in excess of $5,000, the maximum exclusion under this section would be $20,000 for Participant E for year 2006 ($15,000 plus the $5,000 age 50 catch-up amount), which Participant E could contribute to any of the plans assuming at least $5,000 is contributed to Plan W.

* * * * *

LaNita Van Dyke,
Chief, Publications and Regulations Branch,
Legal Processing Division,
Associate Chief Counsel (Procedure and Administration).

(Filed by the Office of the Federal Register on May 22, 2007, 8:45 a.m., and published in the issue of the Federal Register for May 23, 2007, 72 F.R. 28854)

Part I. Rulings and Decisions Under the Internal Revenue Code of 1986

Section 72.—Annuities; Certain Proceeds of Endowment and Life Insurance Contracts

26 CFR 1.72 –1: Introduction.
(Also: § 7702A.)

Insurance companies; aggregation of multiple modified endowment contracts (MECs). This ruling holds that if a taxpayer that owns multiple modified endowment contracts issued by the same insurance company in the same calendar year exchanges some of those MECs for new MECs issued by a second insurance company, the new contracts are not aggregated with the remaining contracts.

Rev. Rul. 2007–38

ISSUE

If a taxpayer that owns multiple modified endowment contracts (MECs) issued by the same insurance company in the same calendar year exchanges some of those MECs for new MECs issued by a second insurance company, are the new contracts required to be aggregated with the remaining original contracts under § 72(e)(12) of the Internal Revenue Code?

FACTS

In Year 1, Original Company, an insurance company subject to tax under Part 1 of subchapter L, issued to Taxpayer multiple life insurance contracts (Original Contracts) that were modified endowment contracts (MECs) within the meaning of § 7702A. The Original Contracts covered the lives of employees, officers and directors who were employed by Taxpayer at the time the contracts were issued. Taxpayer appropriately treated the Original Contracts as a single MEC under the authority of § 72(e)(11) (redesignated as § 72(e)(12) by the Pension Protection Act of 2006, Pub. L. No. 109–280, § 844(a), 120 Stat. 780).

In Year 4, Taxpayer exchanged some of the Original Contracts for new life insurance contracts (New Contracts) issued by an unrelated life insurance company (New Company) in an exchange that qualified for nonrecognition of gain or loss under § 1035. The new contracts were also MECs within the meaning of § 7702A. Taxpayer received no consideration in the exchange.

LAW AND ANALYSIS

Section 1035 provides that no gain or loss is recognized on the exchange of a life insurance contract for another life insurance contract, or for an endowment or annuity contract. Under § 1.1035–1 of the Income Tax Regulations, nonrecognition of gain or loss on the exchange of life insurance contracts is limited to cases where the policies exchanged relate to the same insured.

Section 7702A defines a modified endowment contract (MEC) as a contract that meets the requirement of § 7702 but fails to meet the 7-pay test of § 7702A(b), or that is received in exchange for a contract that is a MEC. Under § 7702A(b), a contract fails to meet the 7-pay test if the accumulated amount paid under the contract at any time during the first seven contract years exceeds the sum of the net level premiums that would have been paid on or before that time if the contract provided for paid-up future benefits after the payment of seven level annual premiums.

Section 72(e)(10) provides that a MEC is subject to the rules of § 72(e)(2)(B) (which taxes non-annuity distributions on an income-out-first basis) and § 72(e)(4)(A) (which generally treats loans, assignments, or pledges of any portion of the value of a MEC as non-annuity distributions). Further, under § 72(v), an amount received under a MEC may be subject to a 10% additional tax.

Section 72(e)(12)(A)(i) provides that, for purposes of determining the amount that is includible in gross income under § 72(e), all MECs issued by the same company to the same policyholder during a calendar year are treated as a single MEC. Section 72(e)(12) was added to the Code by the Technical and Miscellaneous Revenue Act of 1988 (TAMRA), § 5012(d)(2), 1988–3 C.B. 324. The legislative history stated:

> In order to stop the marketing of serial contracts that are designed to avoid the rules applicable to modified endowment contracts, the conference agreement provides that all modified endowment contracts issued by the same insurer (or affiliates) to the same policyholder during any 12-month period are to be aggregated for purposes of determining the amount of any distribution that is includible in gross income. In addition, all annuity contracts issued by the same insurer (or affiliates) to the same policyholder during any 12-month period are to be aggregated for purposes of determining the amount of any distribution that is includible in gross income. Finally, the Treasury Department is provided regulatory authority to prevent the avoidance of the rules contained in section 72(e) through the serial purchase of contacts or otherwise.

H.R. Conf. Rep. No. 1104, 100th Cong., 2d Sess. II–103 (1988), 1988–3 C.B. 593. The provision was subsequently amended by the Omnibus Budget Reconciliation Act of 1989 (OBRA), Pub. L. No. 101–239, § 7815(a)(5), 103 Stat. 2414 (1989), to strike the term "12-month period" and in its place insert "calendar year." The OBRA conference report reiterates that the provision applies to contracts "that are issued by the same insurer (or affiliates.)" H. Conf. Rep. No. 386, 101st Cong., 1st Sess. 665 (1989).

In the present case, the Original Contracts were issued to Taxpayer by the same company in the same calendar year and were, accordingly, aggregated in accordance with § 72(e)(12). After the exchange of some of the Original Contracts for New Contracts, the remaining Original Contracts were still issued to Taxpayer by the same company (Original Company) in the same calendar year (Year 1) and, accordingly, are still treated as a single MEC. Likewise, the New Contracts received in the exchange were issued to Taxpayer by the same company (New Company) in the same calendar year (Year 4) and, accordingly, are also treated as a single MEC. The remaining Original Contracts and the New Contracts are not aggregated with each other, however, because they were not issued to Taxpayer by the same company in the same calendar year. The result in this case would be the same if, instead of individually issued MECs, the Original Contracts and New Contracts were evidenced by certificates that were issued under a group contract or master contract and that were treated as separate contracts for purposes of §§ 817(h), 7702, and 7702A.

HOLDING

If a taxpayer that owns multiple modified endowment contracts (MECs) issued by the same insurance company in the same calendar year exchanges some of those MECs for new MECs issued by a second insurance company, the new contracts are not required to be aggregated with the remaining original contracts under § 72(e)(12).

DRAFTING INFORMATION

The principal author of this revenue ruling is Melissa S. Luxner of the Office of Associate Chief Counsel (Financial Institutions & Products). For further information regarding this revenue ruling, contact Ms. Luxner at (202) 622–3970 (not a toll-free call).

Section 430.—Minimum Funding Standards for Single-Employer Defined Benefit Pension Plans

Procedures with respect to applications for requests for letter rulings on substitute mortality tables under section 430(h)(3)(C) of the Code and section 303(h)(3)(C) of the Employee Retirement Income Security Act of 1974 are set forth. See Rev. Proc. 2007-37, page 1433.

Section 501.—Exemption From Tax on Corporations, Certain Trusts, etc.

26 CFR 1.501(c)(3)–1: Organizations organized and operated for religious, charitable, scientific, testing for public safety, literary or educational purposes, or for the prevention of cruelty to children or animals.

Exempt organizations; political campaigns. This ruling provides 21 examples illustrating the application of the facts and circumstances to be considered to determine whether an organization exempt from income tax under section 501(a) of the Code as an organization described in section 501(c)(3) has participated in, or intervened in (including the publishing or distributing of statements), any political campaign on behalf of (or in opposition to) any candidate for public office.

Rev. Rul. 2007–41

Organizations that are exempt from income tax under section 501(a) of the Internal Revenue Code as organizations described in section 501(c)(3) may not participate in, or intervene in (including the publishing or distributing of statements), any political campaign on behalf of (or in opposition to) any candidate for public office.

ISSUE

In each of the 21 situations described below, has the organization participated or intervened in a political campaign on behalf of (or in opposition to) any candidate for public office within the meaning of section 501(c)(3)?

LAW

Section 501(c)(3) provides for the exemption from federal income tax of organizations organized and operated exclusively for charitable or educational purposes, no substantial part of the activities of which is carrying on propaganda, or otherwise attempting to influence legislation (except as otherwise provided in section 501(h)), and which does not participate in, or intervene in (including the publishing or distributing of statements), any political campaign on behalf of (or in opposition to) any candidate for public office.

Section 1.501(c)(3)–1(c)(3)(i) of the Income Tax Regulations states that an organization is not operated exclusively for one or more exempt purposes if it is an "action" organization.

Section 1.501(c)(3)–1(c)(3)(iii) of the regulations defines an "action" organization as an organization that participates or intervenes, directly or indirectly, in any political campaign on behalf of or in opposition to any candidate for public office. The term "candidate for public office" is defined as an individual who offers himself, or is proposed by others, as a contestant for an elective public office, whether such office be national, State, or local. The regulations further provide that activities that constitute participation or intervention in a political campaign on behalf of or in opposition to a candidate include, but are not limited to, the publication or distribution of written statements or the making of oral statements on behalf of or in opposition to such a candidate.

Whether an organization is participating or intervening, directly or indirectly, in any political campaign on behalf of or in opposition to any candidate for public office depends upon all of the facts and circumstances of each case. For example, certain "voter education" activities, including preparation and distribution of certain voter guides, conducted in a non-partisan manner may not constitute prohibited political activities under section 501(c)(3) of the Code. Other so-called "voter education" activities may be proscribed by the statute. Rev. Rul. 78–248, 1978–1 C.B. 154, contrasts several situations illustrating when an organization that publishes a compilation of candidate positions or voting records has or has not engaged in prohibited political activities based on whether the questionnaire used to solicit candidate positions or the voters guide itself shows a bias or preference in content or structure with respect to the views of a particular candidate. See also Rev. Rul. 80–282, 1980–2 C.B. 178, amplifying Rev. Rul. 78–248 regarding the timing and distribution of voter education materials.

The presentation of public forums or debates is a recognized method of educating the public. See Rev. Rul. 66–256, 1966–2 C.B. 210 (nonprofit organization formed to conduct public forums at which lectures and debates on social, political, and international matters are presented qualifies for exemption from federal income tax under section 501(c)(3)). Providing a forum for candidates is not, in and of itself, prohibited political activity. See Rev. Rul. 74–574, 1974–2 C.B. 160 (organization operating a broadcast station is not participating in political campaigns on behalf of public candidates by providing reasonable amounts of air time equally available to all legally qualified candidates for election to public office in compliance with the reasonable access provisions of the Communications Act of 1934). However, a forum for candidates could be operated in a manner that would show a bias or preference for or against a particular candidate. This could be done, for example, through biased questioning procedures. On the other hand, a forum held for the purpose of educating and informing the voters, which provides fair and impartial treatment of candidates, and which does not promote or advance one candidate over another, would not constitute participation or intervention in any political campaign on behalf of or in opposition to any candidate for public office. See Rev. Rul. 86–95, 1986–2 C.B. 73 (organization that proposes to educate voters by conducting a series of public forums in congressional districts during congressional election campaigns is not participating in a political campaign on behalf of any candidate due to the neutral form and content of its proposed forums).

ANALYSIS OF FACTUAL SITUATIONS

The 21 factual situations appear below under specific subheadings relating to types of activities. In each of the factual situations, all the facts and circumstances are considered in determining whether an organization's activities result in political campaign intervention. Note that each of these situations involves only one type of activity. In the case of an organization that combines one or more types of activity, the interaction among the activities may affect the determination of whether or not the organization is engaged in political campaign intervention.

Voter Education, Voter Registration and Get Out the Vote Drives

Section 501(c)(3) organizations are permitted to conduct certain voter education activities (including the presentation of public forums and the publication of voter education guides) if they are carried out in a non-partisan manner. In addition, section 501(c)(3) organizations may encourage people to participate in the electoral process through voter registration and get-out-the-vote drives, conducted in a non-partisan manner. On the other hand, voter education or registration activities conducted in a biased manner that favors (or opposes) one or more candidates is prohibited.

Situation 1. *B*, a section 501(c)(3) organization that promotes community involvement, sets up a booth at the state fair where citizens can register to vote. The signs and banners in and around the booth give only the name of the organization, the date of the next upcoming statewide election, and notice of the opportunity to register. No reference to any candidate or political party is made by the volunteers staffing the booth or in the materials available at the booth, other than the official voter registration forms which allow registrants to select a party affiliation. *B* is not engaged in political campaign intervention when it operates this voter registration booth.

Situation 2. *C* is a section 501(c)(3) organization that educates the public on environmental issues. Candidate *G* is running for the state legislature and an important element of her platform is challenging the environmental policies of the incumbent. Shortly before the election, *C* sets up a telephone bank to call registered voters in the district in which Candidate *G* is seeking election. In the phone conversations, *C*'s representative tells the voter about the importance of environmental issues and asks questions about the voter's views on these issues. If the voter appears to agree with the incumbent's position, *C*'s representative thanks the voter and ends the call. If the voter appears to agree with Candidate *G*'s position, *C*'s representative reminds the voter about the upcoming election, stresses the importance of voting in the election and offers to provide transportation to the polls. *C* is engaged in political campaign intervention when it conducts this get-out-the-vote drive.

Individual Activity by Organization Leaders

The political campaign intervention prohibition is not intended to restrict free expression on political matters by leaders of organizations speaking for themselves, as individuals. Nor are leaders prohibited from speaking about important issues of public policy. However, for their organizations to remain tax exempt under section 501(c)(3), leaders cannot make partisan comments in official organization publications or at official functions of the organization.

Situation 3. President *A* is the Chief Executive Officer of Hospital *J*, a section 501(c)(3) organization, and is well known in the community. With the permission of five prominent healthcare industry leaders, including President *A*, who have personally endorsed Candidate *T*, Candidate *T* publishes a full page ad in the local newspaper listing the names of the five leaders. President *A* is identified in the ad as the CEO of Hospital *J*. The ad states, "Titles and affiliations of each individual are provided for identification purposes only." The ad is paid for by Candidate *T*'s campaign committee. Because the ad was not paid for by Hospital *J*, the ad is not otherwise in an official publication of Hospital *J*, and the endorsement is made by President *A* in a personal capacity, the ad does not constitute campaign intervention by Hospital *J*.

Situation 4. President *B* is the president of University *K*, a section 501(c)(3) organization. University *K* publishes a monthly alumni newsletter that is distributed to all alumni of the university. In each issue, President *B* has a column titled "My Views." The month before the election, President *B* states in the "My Views" column, "It is my personal opinion that Candidate *U* should be reelected." For that one issue, President *B* pays from his personal funds the portion of the cost of the newsletter attributable to the "My Views" column. Even though he paid part of the cost of the newsletter, the newsletter is an official publication of the university. Because the endorsement appeared in an official publication of University *K*, it constitutes campaign intervention by University *K*.

Situation 5. Minister *C* is the minister of Church *L*, a section 501(c)(3) organization and Minister *C* is well known in the community. Three weeks before the election, he attends a press conference at Candidate *V*'s campaign headquarters and states that Candidate *V* should be reelected. Minister *C* does not say he is speaking on behalf of Church *L*. His endorsement is reported on the front page of the local newspaper and he is identified in the article as the minister of Church *L*. Because Minister *C* did not make the endorsement at an official church function, in an official church publication or otherwise use the church's assets, and did not state that he was speaking as a representative of Church *L*, his actions do not constitute campaign intervention by Church *L*.

Situation 6. Chairman *D* is the chairman of the Board of Directors of *M*, a section 501(c)(3) organization that educates the public on conservation issues. During a regular meeting of *M* shortly before the election, Chairman *D* spoke on a number of issues, including the importance of voting in the upcoming election, and concluded by stating, "It is important that you all do your duty in the election and vote for Candidate *W*." Because Chairman *D*'s remarks indicating support for Candidate *W* were made during an official organization meeting, they constitute political campaign intervention by *M*.

Candidate Appearances

Depending on the facts and circumstances, an organization may invite political candidates to speak at its events without jeopardizing its tax-exempt status. Political candidates may be invited in their capacity as candidates, or in their individual capacity (not as a candidate). Candidates may also appear without an invitation at organization events that are open to the public.

When a candidate is invited to speak at an organization event in his or her capacity as a political candidate, factors in determining whether the organization participated or intervened in a political campaign include the following:

- Whether the organization provides an equal opportunity to participate to political candidates seeking the same office;
- Whether the organization indicates any support for or opposition to the candidate (including candidate introductions and communications concerning the candidate's attendance); and
- Whether any political fundraising occurs.

In determining whether candidates are given an equal opportunity to participate, the nature of the event to which each candidate is invited will be considered, in addition to the manner of presentation. For example, an organization that invites one candidate to speak at its well attended annual banquet, but invites the opposing candidate to speak at a sparsely attended general meeting, will likely have violated the political campaign prohibition, even if the manner of presentation for both speakers is otherwise neutral.

When an organization invites several candidates for the same office to speak at a public forum, factors in determining whether the forum results in political campaign intervention include the following:

- Whether questions for the candidates are prepared and presented by an independent nonpartisan panel,
- Whether the topics discussed by the candidates cover a broad range of issues that the candidates would address if elected to the office sought and are of interest to the public,
- Whether each candidate is given an equal opportunity to present his or her view on each of the issues discussed,
- Whether the candidates are asked to agree or disagree with positions, agendas, platforms or statements of the organization, and
- Whether a moderator comments on the questions or otherwise implies approval or disapproval of the candidates.

Situation 7. President *E* is the president of Society *N*, a historical society that is a section 501(c)(3) organization. In the month prior to the election, President *E* invites the three Congressional candidates for the district in which Society *N* is located to address the members, one each at a regular meeting held on three successive weeks. Each candidate is given an equal opportunity to address and field questions on a wide variety of topics from the members. Society *N*'s publicity announcing the dates for each of the candidate's speeches and President *E*'s introduction of each candidate include no comments on their qualifications or any indication of a preference for any candidate. Society *N*'s actions do not constitute political campaign intervention.

Situation 8. The facts are the same as in *Situation 7* except that there are four candidates in the race rather than three, and one of the candidates declines the invitation to speak. In the publicity announcing the dates for each of the candidate's speeches, Society *N* includes a statement that the order of the speakers was determined at random and the fourth candidate declined the Society's invitation to speak. President *E* makes the same statement in his opening remarks at each of the meetings where one of the candidates is speaking. Society *N*'s actions do not constitute political campaign intervention.

Situation 9. Minister *F* is the minister of Church *O*, a section 501(c)(3) organization. The Sunday before the November election, Minister *F* invites Senate Candidate *X* to preach to her congregation during worship services. During his remarks, Candidate *X* states, "I am asking not only for your votes, but for your enthusiasm and dedication, for your willingness to go the extra mile to get a very large turnout on Tuesday." Minister *F* invites no other candidate to address her congregation during the Senatorial campaign. Because these activities take place during official church services, they are attributed to Church *O*. By selectively providing church facilities to allow Candidate *X* to speak in support of his campaign, Church *O*'s actions constitute political campaign intervention.

Candidate Appearances Where Speaking or Participating as a Non-Candidate

Candidates may also appear or speak at organization events in a non-candidate capacity. For instance, a political candidate may be a public figure who is invited to speak because he or she: (a) currently holds, or formerly held, public office; (b) is considered an expert in a non political field; or (c) is a celebrity or has led a distinguished military, legal, or public service career. A candidate may choose to attend an event that is open to the public, such as a lecture, concert or worship service. The candidate's presence at an organization-sponsored event does not, by itself, cause the organization to be engaged in political campaign intervention. However, if the candidate is publicly recognized by the organization, or if the candidate is invited to speak, factors in determining whether the candidate's appearance results in political campaign intervention include the following:

- Whether the individual is chosen to speak solely for reasons other than candidacy for public office;
- Whether the individual speaks only in a non-candidate capacity;
- Whether either the individual or any representative of the organization

makes any mention of his or her candidacy or the election;
- Whether any campaign activity occurs in connection with the candidate's attendance;
- Whether the organization maintains a nonpartisan atmosphere on the premises or at the event where the candidate is present; and
- Whether the organization clearly indicates the capacity in which the candidate is appearing and does not mention the individual's political candidacy or the upcoming election in the communications announcing the candidate's attendance at the event.

Situation 10. Historical society *P* is a section 501(c)(3) organization. Society *P* is located in the state capital. President *G* is the president of Society *P* and customarily acknowledges the presence of any public officials present during meetings. During the state gubernatorial race, Lieutenant Governor *Y*, a candidate, attends a meeting of the historical society. President *G* acknowledges the Lieutenant Governor's presence in his customary manner, saying, "We are happy to have joining us this evening Lieutenant Governor *Y*." President *G* makes no reference in his welcome to the Lieutenant Governor's candidacy or the election. Society *P* has not engaged in political campaign intervention as a result of President *G*'s actions.

Situation 11. Chairman *H* is the chairman of the Board of Hospital *Q*, a section 501(c)(3) organization. Hospital *Q* is building a new wing. Chairman *H* invites Congressman *Z*, the representative for the district containing Hospital *Q*, to attend the groundbreaking ceremony for the new wing. Congressman *Z* is running for reelection at the time. Chairman *H* makes no reference in her introduction to Congressman *Z*'s candidacy or the election. Congressman *Z* also makes no reference to his candidacy or the election and does not do any political campaign fundraising while at Hospital *Q*. Hospital *Q* has not intervened in a political campaign.

Situation 12. University *X* is a section 501(c)(3) organization. *X* publishes an alumni newsletter on a regular basis. Individual alumni are invited to send in updates about themselves which are printed in each edition of the newsletter. After receiving an update letter from Alumnus *Q*, *X* prints the following: "Alumnus *Q*, class of 'XX is running for mayor of Metropolis." The newsletter does not contain any reference to this election or to Alumnus *Q*'s candidacy other than this statement of fact. University *X* has not intervened in a political campaign.

Situation 13. Mayor *G* attends a concert performed by Symphony *S*, a section 501(c)(3) organization, in City Park. The concert is free and open to the public. Mayor *G* is a candidate for reelection, and the concert takes place after the primary and before the general election. During the concert, the chairman of *S*'s board addresses the crowd and says, "I am pleased to see Mayor *G* here tonight. Without his support, these free concerts in City Park would not be possible. We will need his help if we want these concerts to continue next year so please support Mayor *G* in November as he has supported us." As a result of these remarks, Symphony *S* has engaged in political campaign intervention.

Issue Advocacy vs. Political Campaign Intervention

Section 501(c)(3) organizations may take positions on public policy issues, including issues that divide candidates in an election for public office. However, section 501(c)(3) organizations must avoid any issue advocacy that functions as political campaign intervention. Even if a statement does not expressly tell an audience to vote for or against a specific candidate, an organization delivering the statement is at risk of violating the political campaign intervention prohibition if there is any message favoring or opposing a candidate. A statement can identify a candidate not only by stating the candidate's name but also by other means such as showing a picture of the candidate, referring to political party affiliations, or other distinctive features of a candidate's platform or biography. All the facts and circumstances need to be considered to determine if the advocacy is political campaign intervention.

Key factors in determining whether a communication results in political campaign intervention include the following:

- Whether the statement identifies one or more candidates for a given public office;
- Whether the statement expresses approval or disapproval for one or more candidates' positions and/or actions;
- Whether the statement is delivered close in time to the election;
- Whether the statement makes reference to voting or an election;
- Whether the issue addressed in the communication has been raised as an issue distinguishing candidates for a given office;
- Whether the communication is part of an ongoing series of communications by the organization on the same issue that are made independent of the timing of any election; and
- Whether the timing of the communication and identification of the candidate are related to a non-electoral event such as a scheduled vote on specific legislation by an officeholder who also happens to be a candidate for public office.

A communication is particularly at risk of political campaign intervention when it makes reference to candidates or voting in a specific upcoming election. Nevertheless, the communication must still be considered in context before arriving at any conclusions.

Situation 14. University *O*, a section 501(c)(3) organization, prepares and finances a full page newspaper advertisement that is published in several large circulation newspapers in State *V* shortly before an election in which Senator *C* is a candidate for nomination in a party primary. Senator *C* represents State *V* in the United States Senate. The advertisement states that S. 24, a pending bill in the United States Senate, would provide additional opportunities for State *V* residents to attend college, but Senator *C* has opposed similar measures in the past. The advertisement ends with the statement "Call or write Senator *C* to tell him to vote for S. 24." Educational issues have not been raised as an issue distinguishing Senator *C* from any opponent. S. 24 is scheduled for a vote in the United States Senate before the election, soon after the date that the advertisement is published in the newspapers. Even though the advertisement appears shortly before the election and identifies Senator *C*'s position on the issue as contrary to *O*'s position, University *O* has not violated the political campaign intervention prohibition because the advertisement does not mention the election or the candidacy of Senator *C*, education issues have not been raised as distinguishing Senator *C* from any opponent, and the timing of the advertisement and the identification of Senator *C* are directly related to the specifically identified legislation University *O* is supporting and appears immediately before the United States Senate is scheduled to vote on that particular legislation. The candidate identified, Senator *C*, is an officeholder who is in a position to vote on the legislation.

Situation 15. Organization *R*, a section 501(c)(3) organization that educates the public about the need for improved public education, prepares and finances a radio advertisement urging an increase in state funding for public education in State *X*, which requires a legislative appropriation. Governor *E* is the governor of State *X*. The radio advertisement is first broadcast on several radio stations in State *X* beginning shortly before an election in which Governor *E* is a candidate for re-election. The advertisement is not part of an ongoing series of substantially similar advocacy communications by Organization *R* on the same issue. The advertisement cites numerous statistics indicating that public education in State *X* is under funded. While the advertisement does not say anything about Governor *E*'s position on funding for public education, it ends with "Tell Governor *E* what you think about our under-funded schools." In public appearances and campaign literature, Governor *E*'s opponent has made funding of public education an issue in the campaign by focusing on Governor *E*'s veto of an income tax increase the previous year to increase funding of public education. At the time the advertisement is broadcast, no legislative vote or other major legislative activity is scheduled in the State *X* legislature on state funding of public education. Organization *R* has violated the political campaign prohibition because the advertisement identifies Governor *E*, appears shortly before an election in which Governor *E* is a candidate, is not part of an ongoing series of substantially similar advocacy communications by Organization *R* on the same issue, is not timed to coincide with a non election event such as a legislative vote or other major legislative action on that issue, and takes a position on an issue that the opponent has used to distinguish himself from Governor *E*.

Situation 16. Candidate *A* and Candidate *B* are candidates for the state senate in District *W* of State *X*. The issue of State *X* funding for a new mass transit project in District *W* is a prominent issue in the campaign. Both candidates have spoken out on the issue. Candidate *A* supports funding the new mass transit project. Candidate *B* opposes the project and supports State *X* funding for highway improvements instead. *P* is the executive director of *C*, a section 501(c)(3) organization that promotes community development in District *W*. At *C*'s annual fundraising dinner in District *W*, which takes place in the month before the election in State *X*, *P* gives a lengthy speech about community development issues including the transportation issues. *P* does not mention the name of any candidate or any political party. However, at the conclusion of the speech, *P* makes the following statement, "For those of you who care about quality of life in District *W* and the growing traffic congestion, there is a very important choice coming up next month. We need new mass transit. More highway funding will not make a difference. You have the power to relieve the congestion and improve your quality of life in District *W*. Use that power when you go to the polls and cast your vote in the election for your state senator." *C* has violated the political campaign intervention as a result of *P*'s remarks at *C*'s official function shortly before the election, in which *P* referred to the upcoming election after stating a position on an issue that is a prominent issue in a campaign that distinguishes the candidates.

Business Activity

The question of whether an activity constitutes participation or intervention in a political campaign may also arise in the context of a business activity of the organization, such as selling or renting of mailing lists, the leasing of office space, or the acceptance of paid political advertising. In this context, some of the factors to be considered in determining whether the organization has engaged in political campaign intervention include the following:

- Whether the good, service or facility is available to candidates in the same election on an equal basis,
- Whether the good, service, or facility is available only to candidates and not to the general public,
- Whether the fees charged to candidates are at the organization's customary and usual rates, and
- Whether the activity is an ongoing activity of the organization or whether it is conducted only for a particular candidate.

Situation 17. Museum *K* is a section 501(c)(3) organization. It owns an historic building that has a large hall suitable for hosting dinners and receptions. For several years, Museum *K* has made the hall available for rent to members of the public. Standard fees are set for renting the hall based on the number of people in attendance, and a number of different organizations have rented the hall. Museum *K* rents the hall on a first come, first served basis. Candidate *P* rents Museum *K*'s social hall for a fundraising dinner. Candidate *P*'s campaign pays the standard fee for the dinner. Museum *K* is not involved in political campaign intervention as a result of renting the hall to Candidate *P* for use as the site of a campaign fundraising dinner.

Situation 18. Theater *L* is a section 501(c)(3) organization. It maintains a mailing list of all of its subscribers and contributors. Theater *L* has never rented its mailing list to a third party. Theater *L* is approached by the campaign committee of Candidate *Q*, who supports increased funding for the arts. Candidate *Q*'s campaign committee offers to rent Theater *L*'s mailing list for a fee that is comparable to fees charged by other similar organizations. Theater *L* rents its mailing list to Candidate *Q*'s campaign committee. Theater *L* declines similar requests from campaign committees of other candidates. Theater *L* has intervened in a political campaign.

Web Sites

The Internet has become a widely used communications tool. Section 501(c)(3) organizations use their own web sites to disseminate statements and information. They also routinely link their web sites to web sites maintained by other organizations as a way of providing additional information that the organizations believe is useful or relevant to the public.

A web site is a form of communication. If an organization posts something on its web site that favors or opposes a candidate for public office, the organization will be treated the same as if it distributed printed material, oral statements or broadcasts that favored or opposed a candidate.

An organization has control over whether it establishes a link to another site. When an organization establishes a link to another web site, the organization is responsible for the consequences of establishing and maintaining that link, even if the organization does not have control over the content of the linked site. Because the linked content may change over time, an organization may reduce the risk of political campaign intervention by monitoring the linked content and adjusting the links accordingly.

Links to candidate-related material, by themselves, do not necessarily constitute political campaign intervention. All the facts and circumstances must be taken into account when assessing whether a link produces that result. The facts and circumstances to be considered include, but are not limited to, the context for the link on the organization's web site, whether all candidates are represented, any exempt purpose served by offering the link, and the directness of the links between the organization's web site and the web page that contains material favoring or opposing a candidate for public office.

Situation 19. M, a section 501(c)(3) organization, maintains a web site and posts an unbiased, nonpartisan voter guide that is prepared consistent with the principles discussed in Rev. Rul. 78–248. For each candidate covered in the voter guide, *M* includes a link to that candidate's official campaign web site. The links to the candidate web sites are presented on a consistent neutral basis for each candidate, with text saying "For more information on Candidate *X*, you may consult [URL]." *M* has not intervened in a political campaign because the links are provided for the exempt purpose of educating voters and are presented in a neutral, unbiased manner that includes all candidates for a particular office.

Situation 20. Hospital *N*, a section 501(c)(3) organization, maintains a web site that includes such information as medical staff listings, directions to Hospital *N*, and descriptions of its specialty health programs, major research projects, and other community outreach programs. On one page of the web site, Hospital *N* describes its treatment program for a particular disease. At the end of the page, it includes a section of links to other web sites titled "More Information." These links include links to other hospitals that have treatment programs for this disease, research organizations seeking cures for that disease, and articles about treatment programs. This section includes a link to an article on the web site of *O*, a major national newspaper, praising Hospital *N*'s treatment program for the disease. The page containing the article on *O*'s web site contains no reference to any candidate or election and has no direct links to candidate or election information. Elsewhere on *O*'s web site, there is a page displaying editorials that *O* has published. Several of the editorials endorse candidates in an election that has not yet occurred. Hospital *N* has not intervened in a political campaign by maintaining the link to the article on *O*'s web site because the link is provided for the exempt purpose of educating the public about Hospital *N*'s programs and neither the context for the link, nor the relationship between Hospital *N* and *O* nor the arrangement of the links going from Hospital *N*'s web site to the endorsement on *O*'s web site indicate that Hospital *N* was favoring or opposing any candidate.

Situation 21. Church *P*, a section 501(c)(3) organization, maintains a web site that includes such information as biographies of its ministers, times of services, details of community outreach programs, and activities of members of its congregation. *B*, a member of the congregation of Church *P*, is running for a seat on the town council. Shortly before the election, Church *P* posts the following message on its web site, "Lend your support to *B*, your fellow parishioner, in Tuesday's election for town council." Church *P* has intervened in a political campaign on behalf of B.

HOLDINGS

In situations 2, 4, 6, 9, 13, 15, 16, 18 and 21, the organization intervened in a political campaign within the meaning of section 501(c)(3). In situations 1, 3, 5, 7, 8, 10, 11, 12, 14, 17, 19 and 20, the organization did not intervene in a political campaign within the meaning of section 501(c)(3)

DRAFTING INFORMATION

The principal author of this revenue ruling is Judith Kindell of Exempt Organizations, Tax Exempt and Government Entities Division. For further information regarding this revenue ruling, contact Ms. Kindell at (202) 283–8964 (not a toll-free call).

Section 707.—Transactions Between Partner and Partnership

26 CFR 1.707–1: Transactions between partner and partnership.

Partnership property; transfer. This ruling concludes that a transfer of partnership property to a partner in satisfaction of a guaranteed payment under section 707(c) of the Code is a sale or exchange under section 1001, and not a distribution under section 731.

Rev. Rul. 2007–40

ISSUE

Is a transfer of partnership property to a partner in satisfaction of a guaranteed payment under section 707(c) a sale or exchange under section 1001, or a distribution under section 731?

FACTS

Partnership purchased Blackacre for \$500x. *A*, a partner in *Partnership*, is entitled to a guaranteed payment under section 707(c) of \$800x. Subsequently, when the fair market value of Blackacre is \$800x and *Partnership*'s adjusted basis in Blackacre is \$500x, *Partnership* transfers Blackacre to *A* in satisfaction of the guaranteed payment to *A*.

LAW AND ANALYSIS

Section 731(b) provides that no gain or loss shall be recognized to a partnership on a distribution to a partner of property, including money.

Section 707(c) provides that, to the extent determined without regard to the income of the partnership, payments to a partner for services or for the use of capital are considered as made to one who is not a member of the partnership, but only for the purposes of § 61(a) (relating to gross income) and, subject to § 263, for purposes of § 162(a) (relating to trade or business expenses).

Section 61(a)(3) provides the general rule that gross income includes gains derived from dealings in property. In addition, section 1001(a) provides that the gain from the sale or other disposition of property shall be the excess of the amount realized over the adjusted basis provided in section 1011 for determining gain, and the loss shall be the excess of the adjusted basis over the amount realized.

Section 1001(b) further provides, in part, that the amount realized from the sale or other disposition of property shall be the sum of any money received plus the fair market value of the property (other than money) received.

A taxpayer that conveys appreciated or depreciated property in satisfaction of an obligation, or in exchange for the performance of services, recognizes gain or loss equal to the difference between the basis in the distributed property and the property's fair market value. *See, e.g., International Freighting Corp., Inc. v. Commissioner*, 135 F.2d 310 (2d Cir. 1943), *United States v. General Shoe Corp.*, 282 F.2d 9 (6th Cir. 1960).

A transfer of partnership property in satisfaction of a partnership's obligation to make a guaranteed payment under section 707(c) is a sale or exchange under section 1001. Because the transfer is a sale or exchange under section 1001, it is not a distribution within the meaning of section 731. Accordingly, the nonrecognition rule in section 731(b) does not apply to the transfer.

Partnership realizes a $300x gain when *Partnership* transfers Blackacre in satisfaction of its section 707(c) guaranteed payment to *A*, the difference between the adjusted basis of the property ($500x) to the partnership and the property's fair market value ($800x).

HOLDING

A transfer of partnership property to a partner in satisfaction of a guaranteed payment under section 707(c) is a sale or exchange under section 1001, and not a distribution under section 731.

DRAFTING INFORMATION

The principal author of this revenue ruling is Jason T. Smyczek of the Office of the Associate Chief Counsel (Passthroughs and Special Industries). For further information regarding this revenue ruling, contact Mr. Smyczek at (202) 622–3050 (not a toll-free call).

Part III. Administrative, Procedural, and Miscellaneous

Treatment Under Section 367(b) of Property Used to Purchase Parent Stock From Parent Shareholders in Certain Triangular Reorganizations

Notice 2007–48

SECTION 1. OVERVIEW

On September 22, 2006, the Internal Revenue Service (IRS) and the Treasury Department (Treasury) issued Notice 2006–85, 2006–41 I.R.B. 677, to address certain transactions involving foreign corporations where a subsidiary acquires stock of its parent from its parent for use in a triangular reorganization. Comments were requested in section 7 of that notice regarding similar transactions, including transactions where a subsidiary acquires stock of its parent from a person unrelated to its parent (such as from the public on the open market).

For reasons similar to those discussed in section 2 of Notice 2006–85, the IRS and Treasury believe that taxpayers' characterization of these transactions, as well as other transactions involving acquisitions from related parties, raises significant policy concerns. Accordingly, this notice amplifies Notice 2006–85 by announcing that the IRS and Treasury will issue regulations under section 367(b) of the Internal Revenue Code to address these and similar transactions.

SECTION 2. REGULATIONS TO BE ISSUED UNDER SECTION 367(b)

The definitions provided in section 1 of Notice 2006–85 also apply for purposes of this notice.

The regulations will apply to triangular reorganizations where P or S (or both) is foreign and, pursuant to the reorganization, S acquires from one or more P shareholders, in exchange for property, all or a portion of the P stock that is used to acquire the stock or assets of T (T could be either related or unrelated to P and S before the transaction). In such a case, the regulations under section 367(b) will make adjustments with respect to P and S that will have the effect of a distribution of property from S to P under section 301(c). The amount of the distribution shall equal the amount of money plus the fair market value of other property transferred from S to P's shareholders in exchange for the P stock used to acquire the stock or assets of T. Therefore, the regulations will require, as appropriate, an inclusion in P's gross income as a dividend, a reduction in P's basis in its S stock (or, as appropriate, T stock), and the recognition of gain by P from the sale or exchange of property.

The adjustments also will provide, as appropriate, that the amount of property deemed distributed to P is considered to be contributed by P to S immediately thereafter and therefore increases P's basis in S. See, *e.g.*, Treas. Reg. § 1.367(b)–2(e)(3)(ii).

Finally, the regulations will provide for appropriate corresponding adjustments to be made, such as a reduction of S's earnings and profits as a result of the distribution (consistent with the principles of section 312).

The section 367(b) adjustments described above shall be made prior to the application of other provisions. For example, after giving effect to the 367(b) adjustments, S's purchase and transfer of P stock will then be taken into account under generally applicable rules, including sections 304, 358, and 368.

The regulations will address similar transactions in which S acquires the P stock used in the reorganization from a related party that purchased the P stock in a related transaction. The regulations also will include a rule that takes into account the earnings and profits of other corporations, as appropriate, if one of the principal purposes of creating, organizing, or funding S is to avoid the adjustments described in this notice or Notice 2006–85. See, *e.g.*, Treas. Reg. §§ 1.304–4T and 1.956–1T(b)(4).

SECTION 3. EFFECTIVE DATE

The regulations described in this notice will apply to transactions occurring on or after May 31, 2007. The regulations described in this notice will not, however, apply to a transaction that was completed on or after May 31, 2007, if the reorganization was entered into pursuant to a written agreement that was (subject to customary conditions) binding before May 31, 2007 and all times thereafter, but only to the extent that: (1) S acquired the P stock to be used in the reorganization prior to May 31, 2007, or (2) S had a commitment to acquire the P stock to be used in the reorganization from an unrelated party pursuant to a written agreement that was (subject to customary conditions) binding before May 31, 2007 and at all times thereafter, or pursuant to a tender offer announced prior to May 31, 2007 that is subject to section 14(d) of the Securities and Exchange Act of 1934 [15 U.S.C. 78n(d)(1)] and Regulation 14(D) (17 CFR 240.14d–1 through 240.14d–101) or that is subject to comparable foreign laws.

No inference is intended as to the treatment of transactions described herein under current law.

SECTION 4. COMMENTS

The IRS and Treasury request comments on the regulations to be issued under this notice and continue to request comments on those issues discussed in section 7 of Notice 2006–85, including, for example, any issues regarding the source and timing of the adjustments to be made with respect to P and S.

SECTION 5. EFFECT ON OTHER DOCUMENTS

Notice 2006–85 is amplified.

SECTION 6. DRAFTING INFORMATION

The principal author of this notice is Daniel McCall of the Office of Associate Chief Counsel (International). However, other personnel from the IRS and Treasury participated in its development. For further information regarding this notice, contact Mr. McCall at (202) 622–3860 (not a toll-free call).

Covered Employees Under Section 162(m)(3)

Notice 2007–49

PURPOSE

This notice provides guidance on identifying covered employees for purposes of § 162(m)(3) of the Internal Revenue Code.

BACKGROUND

Section 162(a)(1) allows as a deduction all of the ordinary and necessary expenses paid or incurred during the taxable year in carrying on any trade or business, including a reasonable allowance for salaries or other compensation for personal services actually rendered.

Section 162(m)(1) provides, in general, that in the case of any publicly held corporation, no deduction shall be allowed for applicable employee remuneration with respect to any covered employee to the extent that the amount of such remuneration for the taxable year with respect to such employee exceeds $1,000,000.

Section 162(m)(3) defines a "covered employee" as any employee of the taxpayer if, (A) as of the close of the taxable year, such employee is the chief executive officer of the taxpayer or is an individual acting in such a capacity, or (B) the total compensation of such employee for the taxable year is required to be reported to shareholders under the Securities Exchange Act of 1934 by reason of such employee being among the 4 highest compensated officers for the taxable year (other than the chief executive officer).

Section 1.162–27(c)(2)(ii) of the Income Tax Regulations provides that whether an individual is the chief executive officer or among the four highest compensated officers (other than the chief executive officer) is determined pursuant to the executive compensation disclosure rules under the Exchange Act.

The Securities and Exchange Commission's ("SEC") rules relating to executive compensation disclosure under the Exchange Act are contained in Item 402 of Regulation S-K, 17 CFR 229.402. A final rule amending the SEC executive compensation disclosure rules was published in the Federal Register on September 8, 2006 (71 FR 53158) ("amended disclosure rules"). Among other things, the amended disclosure rules altered the composition of the group of executives that are covered by the disclosure rules. Like the pre-amendment disclosure rules ("old disclosure rules"), the amended disclosure rules refer to these executives as "named executive officers." Companies must comply with the amended disclosure rules for fiscal years ending on or after December 15, 2006.

Under the amended disclosure rules, named executive officers consist of, in relevant part, (i) all individuals serving as the registrant's principal executive officer or acting in a similar capacity during the last completed fiscal year ("PEO"), regardless of compensation level; (ii) all individuals serving as the registrant's principal financial officer or acting in a similar capacity during the last completed fiscal year ("PFO"), regardless of compensation level; and (iii) the registrant's three most highly compensated executive officers other than the PEO and PFO who were serving as executive officers at the end of the last completed fiscal year. Under the old disclosure rules, named executive officers consisted of, in relevant part, (i) all individuals serving as the registrant's chief executive officer or acting in a similar capacity during the last completed fiscal year ("CEO"), regardless of compensation level; and (ii) the registrant's four most highly compensated executive officers other than the CEO who were serving as executive officers at the end of the last completed fiscal year.

The definition of covered employee in § 162(m)(3) mirrored the definition of named executive officers under the old disclosure rules, but it is not the same as that definition under the amended disclosure rules. This is because the amended disclosure rules increase the number of executives who are named executive officers by virtue of their position from one to two, and reduce the number of executives who are named executive officers based on their compensation level from four to three. Thus, while the amended disclosure rules continue to require disclosure for five executive officers, two executives are now covered by the rules based on their positions, and three are covered by the rules based on their level of compensation. In contrast, a covered employee for purposes of § 162(m)(3) consists of only one executive officer based on his or her position and four officers based on their level of compensation.

Under § 162(m)(3) and § 1.162–27(c)(2)(ii), covered employees are determined by looking to the Exchange Act. Thus, guidance clarifying the meaning of covered employees is necessary because the definition in § 162(m)(3) does not track the definition of named executive officers in the amended disclosure rules. In particular, guidance is necessary because the amended disclosure rules (1) require disclosure for the principal executive officer, while the definition of covered employee in § 162(m)(3)(A) uses the term chief executive officer; (2) require disclosure based on compensation level for three executive officers, while the definition of covered employee in § 162(m)(3)(B) applies the deduction limitation by reason of compensation level to four officers; and (3) require disclosure with respect to the principal financial officer by reason of that officer's position (and not by reason of such officer being among the taxpayer's highest compensated officers), while the only officer within the scope of § 162(m) based on a specific position is the chief executive officer.

Accordingly, based upon the statutory language of § 162(m)(3), which has not been amended since the amended disclosure rules were promulgated, the following guidance is provided. The IRS will interpret the term "covered employee" for purposes of § 162(m) to mean any employee of the taxpayer if, as of the close of the taxable year, such employee is the principal executive officer (within the meaning of the amended disclosure rules) of the taxpayer or an individual acting in such a capacity, or if the total compensation of such employee for that taxable year is required to be reported to shareholders under the Exchange Act by reason of such employee being among the 3 highest compensated officers for the taxable year (other than the principal executive officer or the principal financial officer). Accordingly, the term covered employee for purposes of § 162(m) does not include those individuals for whom disclosure is required under the Exchange Act on account of the individual being the taxpayer's principal financial officer (within the meaning of the amended disclosure rules) or an individual acting in such a capacity.

The principal author of this notice is Jean Casey of the Office of Division Counsel/Associate Chief Counsel (Tax Exempt & Government Entities). For further information regarding this notice, contact Jean Casey at (202) 622–6030 (not a toll-free call).

Guidance Regarding Deductions by Individuals for Qualified Conservation Contributions

Notice 2007–50

PURPOSE

This notice provides guidance relating to the percentage limitations imposed by § 170(b)(1)(E) of the Internal Revenue Code (Code) on "qualified conservation contributions" made by individuals. Section 170(b)(1)(E) was added to the Code by section 1206(a)(1) of the Pension Protection Act of 2006, Pub. L. No. 109–280, 120 Stat. 780 (2006) (PPA), and is effective for contributions made in taxable years beginning after December 31, 2005, and before January 1, 2008.

BACKGROUND

A. Percentage limitations and carryover rules under § 170(b)(1) and § 170(d)(1) of the Code: General rules

Section 170(a) of the Code generally allows a deduction, subject to certain limitations, for any charitable contribution (as defined in § 170(c)), payment of which is made during the taxable year. Section 1.170A–1(c)(1) of the Income Tax Regulations provides that the amount of a contribution of property is generally the fair market value of the property at the time of the contribution, subject to certain limitations in § 170(e).

The amount of charitable contributions that an individual may deduct in a taxable year is limited to the applicable percentage of the individual's contribution base, pursuant to § 170(b)(1). Section 170(b)(1)(G) provides that the term "contribution base" means the individual's adjusted gross income, computed without regard to any net operating loss carryback.

The applicable percentage of an individual's contribution base varies, depending on the donee organization and the property contributed. For example, for cash contributions made to organizations described in § 170(b)(1)(A), the applicable percentage is 50 percent. For cash contributions to organizations described in § 170(b)(1)(B), and contributions of capital gain property to organizations described in § 170(b)(1)(A), the applicable percentage is generally 30 percent. The term "capital gain property" is defined in § 170(b)(1)(C)(iv) as any capital asset or property which is property used in the trade or business (as defined in § 1231(b)) the sale of which at its fair market value at the time of the contribution would have resulted in gain which would have been long-term capital gain.

Under § 170(b)(1) and (d)(1), any charitable contribution made during the taxable year in excess of the applicable contribution base generally is carried forward for up to 5 succeeding taxable years (after the contribution year) in order of time.

The total of all charitable contributions deducted in a taxable year may not exceed 50 percent of the individual's contribution base. The contributions that are deducted against the contribution base must follow the order of priority set forth in § 170(b)(1) and (d)(1). For example, if during a taxable year an individual makes a cash contribution and a capital gain property contribution to one or more organizations described in § 170(b)(1)(A), generally the cash contribution is taken into account before the capital gain property contribution in determining the allowable deduction for the year and any carryovers to future years. If the cash contribution equals 50 percent of the contribution base, the entire amount of the capital gain property contribution is carried forward for up to 5 succeeding taxable years (after the contribution year) in order of time. Furthermore, the capital gain property contribution carryover retains its character in the carryover years as a capital gain property contribution to which the 30 percent limitation applies. For additional details about the percentage limitations and carryover rules, see § 1.170A–8 and § 1.170A–10.

Different percentage limitations and carryover rules, which are not relevant here, apply to C corporations. See § 170(b)(2) and (d)(2).

B. Changes to § 170(b)(1) made by § 1206(a)(1) of the PPA, applicable to qualified conservation contributions made in taxable years beginning after December 31, 2005, and before January 1, 2008

I. *General rule: 50 percent limitation*

Section 1206(a)(1) of the PPA added § 170(b)(1)(E) to the Code to increase the percentage limitations and carryover period applicable to qualified conservation contributions made in taxable years beginning after December 31, 2005, and before January 1, 2008. Under § 170(b)(1)(E)(i), an individual may be allowed a deduction for any qualified conservation contribution to an organization described in § 170(b)(1)(A) to the extent the aggregate of such contributions does not exceed the excess of 50 percent of the individual's contribution base over the amount of all other charitable contributions allowed under § 170(b)(1) (the 50 percent limitation). Thus, the 30 percent limitation applicable to contributions of capital gain property under § 170(b)(1)(C) does not apply to qualified conservation contributions. If the aggregate amount of qualified conservation contributions exceeds the 50 percent limitation, § 170(b)(1)(E)(ii) provides that the excess will be treated (consistent with § 170(d)(1)) as a charitable contribution to which § 170(b)(1)(E)(i) applies in each of the 15 succeeding years in order of time.

II. *100 percent limitation applicable to certain qualified conservation contributions taken into account by individuals who are qualified farmers or ranchers*

Section 170(b)(1)(E)(iv) provides a special rule for a qualified conservation contribution taken into account by an individual who in the taxable year of the contribution is a qualified farmer or rancher, defined in § 170(b)(1)(E)(v) as a taxpayer whose gross income from the trade or business of farming (within the meaning of § 2032A(e)(5)) is greater than 50 percent of the taxpayer's gross income for the taxable year. For such an individual, § 170(b)(1)(E)(iv)(I) provides a general rule that the 50 percent limitation described above is increased to 100 percent (the 100 percent limitation).

However, for any contribution of property made after August 17, 2006, that is used or available for use in agriculture or livestock production, the 100 percent limitation applies only if the contribution is subject to a restriction that the property remain available for agriculture or livestock production. If the contribution is not subject to such a restriction, the 50 percent limitation applies.

III. *Effect of qualified conservation contributions on the computation of charitable contribution deductions and carryovers*

i) In general

Qualified conservation contributions are not taken into account in determining the amount of other allowable charitable contributions. Therefore, for purposes of applying § 170(b)(1)(E) and (d)(1), qualified conservation contributions are not treated as described in § 170(b)(1)(A), (B), (C), or (D). Moreover, § 170(b)(1)(A), (B), (C), and (D) apply without regard to contributions described in § 170(b)(1)(E)(i).

ii) Qualified conservation contributions taken into account by qualified farmers and ranchers

Section 170(b)(1)(E)(iv)(II) provides that the percentage limitations applicable to qualified conservation contributions taken into account by a qualified farmer or rancher are applied in the following order: First, contributions of property to which the 50 percent limitation applies are taken into account; then contributions of property to which the 100 percent limitation applies are taken into account.

QUESTIONS AND ANSWERS

Q–1. How do the percentage limitations and the carryover rules apply in a taxable year in which an individual has made a qualified conservation contribution and one or more contributions subject to the limitations in § 170(b)(1)(A), (B), (C), or (D)?

A–1. The qualified conservation contribution may be taken into account only after taking into account contributions subject to the limitations in § 170(b)(1)(A), (B), (C), and (D).

For example, in taxable year 2007 individual *B*, a calendar year taxpayer who is not a qualified farmer or rancher in 2007, has a contribution base of $100. During 2007 *B* makes $60 of cash contributions to organizations described in § 170(b)(1)(A) (that is, contributions to which the 50 percent limitation of § 170(b)(1)(A) applies), and a qualified conservation contribution of capital gain property under § 170(b)(1)(C)(iv) with a fair market value of $80. Assuming all other requirements of § 170 are met, in 2007 *B* may deduct $50 of the cash contributions. The unused $10 of cash contributions is carried forward for up to 5 years. No current deduction is allowed for the qualified conservation contribution, but the entire $80 qualified conservation contribution deduction is carried forward for up to 15 years.

Q–2. How do the percentage limitations and the carryover rules apply if the individual is a qualified farmer or rancher for the taxable year in which the contribution is made?

A–2. Using the example in A–1 of this notice, if in 2007 *B* is a qualified farmer or rancher eligible for the 100 percent limitation in § 170(b)(1)(E)(iv), *B* may deduct $50 for the qualified conservation contribution in addition to the $50 deduction for cash contributions. As in A–1, the unused $10 of cash contributions is carried forward for up to 5 years. The unused $30 of the qualified conservation contribution is carried forward for up to 15 years.

Q–3. Do the 50 percent and 100 percent limitations in § 170(b)(1)(E)(i) and (iv) apply to all contributions of real property interests?

A–3. No. The 50 and 100 percent limitations in § 170(b)(1)(E) apply only to qualified conservation contributions, defined in § 170(h)(1) as a contribution of a qualified real property interest to a qualified organization, exclusively for conservation purposes. A qualified real property interest is defined in § 170(h)(2) as any of the following interests: A) the entire interest of the taxpayer other than a qualified mineral interest; B) a remainder interest; and C) a restriction (granted in perpetuity) on the use which may be made of the real property.

For example, a qualified real property interest, as defined in § 170(h)(2), does not include the taxpayer's entire interest in real property. Consequently, a contribution of the taxpayer's entire interest in real property does not qualify for the 50 and 100 percent limitations under § 170(b)(1)(E). For purposes of determining whether an entire interest in real property has been contributed, the retention of an insubstantial right or interest in the real property is disregarded. *See* § 1.170A–7(b)(1)(i); *see also*, *e.g.*, Rev. Rul. 75–66, 1975–1 C.B. 85.

Q–4. How may an individual determine whether the individual is a qualified farmer or rancher for the taxable year of the contribution (and thus may be eligible for the 100 percent limitation)?

A–4. An individual is a qualified farmer or rancher if the individual's gross income from the trade or business of farming (as defined in § 2032A(e)(5)) in the taxable year of the contribution is greater than 50 percent of the individual's total gross income for the taxable year of the contribution.

Gross income includes all income from whatever source derived, except as otherwise provided. Section 61(a); § 1.61–3. Gross income from the trade or business of farming is the gross income from activities described in § 2032A(e)(5). Such activities include cultivating the soil; raising or harvesting any agricultural or horticultural commodity; raising, shearing, feeding, caring for, training, and management of animals; handling, drying, packing, grading, or storing on a farm any agricultural or horticultural commodity in its unmanufactured state but only if the owner, operator, or tenant of the farm regularly produces more than one-half of the commodity; and the planting, cultivating, caring for, or cutting of trees, or the preparation (other than milling) of trees for market.

Q–5. If a qualified conservation contribution is made by a pass-through entity such as a partnership or S corporation, is the determination made at the entity level as to whether an individual who is a partner or shareholder is a qualified farmer or rancher for the taxable year of the contribution?

A–5. No. Section 170(b)(1)(E)(iv)(I) indicates that a qualified farmer or rancher must be an individual. Therefore, the determination is made at the partner or shareholder level as to whether an individual who is a partner or shareholder is a qualified farmer or rancher for the taxable year of the contribution.

Q–6. Is income from a sale (including a bargain sale) of a conservation easement included in the individual's gross income from the trade or business of farming?

A–6. No. A sale (including a bargain sale) of a conservation easement is not an activity described in § 2032A(e)(5). Therefore, income derived from such a sale is not included in the individual's gross income from the trade or business of farming. However, the income from such a sale is included in the individual's gross income.

Q–7. Is income from the sale of timber included in the individual's gross income from the trade or business of farming?

A–7. Yes. The planting, cultivating, caring for, or cutting of trees, or the preparation (other than milling) of trees for market are activities described in § 2032A(e)(5). Therefore, income from the sale of timber is included in the individual's gross income from the trade or business of farming, and is also included in the individual's gross income.

Q–8. Is income from fees to permit hunting and fishing on the property included in an individual's gross income from the trade or business of farming?

A–8. No. Hunting and fishing activities are not activities described in § 2032A(e)(5). Therefore, income derived from permitting such activities is not included in the individual's gross income from the trade or business of farming. However, the income is included in the individual's gross income.

Q–9. Must a qualified conservation contribution be of property used or available for use in agriculture or livestock production in order for a qualified farmer or rancher to qualify for the 100 percent limitation under § 170(b)(1)(E)(iv)(I)?

A–9. No. Section 170(b)(1)(E)(iv)(I) requires that an individual be a qualified farmer or rancher to qualify for the 100 percent limitation. It does not require that the qualified conservation contribution be of property used or available for use in agriculture or livestock production. However, if the property is used or available for use in agriculture or livestock production, the restriction described in § 170(b)(1)(E)(iv)(II) may apply. See Q–10 and A–10 of this notice. See Q–13 of this notice for an example illustrating the application of § 170(b)(1)(E)(iv).

Q–10. If a qualified farmer or rancher makes a qualified conservation contribution of property used or available for use in agriculture or livestock production, must the contribution be subject to a restriction that the property remain available for such use in order to qualify for the 100 percent limitation?

A–10. The answer depends on the date of the contribution. If the contribution was made after August 17, 2006, the contribution must be subject to such a restriction in order to qualify for the 100 percent limitation. The contribution may qualify for the 50 percent limitation if the contribution lacks such a restriction. If the contribution was made on or before August 17, 2006, no such restriction is required in order to qualify for the 100 percent limitation.

Q–11. Does property used or available for use in agriculture or livestock production include the portions of the property upon which the following types of improvements are located: Dwellings used for family living by the farmer or rancher, a lessee that operates the property, or their employees; other types of buildings used for agriculture or livestock purposes; and roads throughout the property?

A–11. Yes. The portions of the property upon which such improvements are located are treated as property used or available for use in agriculture or livestock production. *See, e.g.*, § 1.170A–14(f), Example 5. To qualify for the 100 percent limitation, a qualified conservation contribution of the property made after August 17, 2006, by a qualified farmer or rancher must include a restriction that the entire property, including the portions upon which the improvements are located, remain available for agriculture or livestock production. If the contribution is not subject to such a restriction over the entire property, the contribution will not qualify for the 100 percent limitation, but may qualify for the 50 percent limitation.

Q–12. How may a qualified farmer or rancher comply with the requirement that a qualified conservation contribution of property used or available for use in agriculture or livestock production be subject to a restriction that the property (including the portions of the property upon which improvements described in Q–11 of this notice are located) remain available for such production?

A–12. The qualified conservation contribution must include a restriction that the property remain available for agriculture or livestock production, and must ensure that the property is protected from any use that would interfere with agriculture or livestock production. For example, a qualified conservation contribution of property used or available for use in agriculture or livestock production might include in the document of conveyance prohibitions against construction or placement of buildings (except those used for agriculture or livestock production purposes, or dwellings used for family living by the qualified farmer or rancher, a lessee that operates the property, or their employees); removal of mineral substances in any manner that adversely affects the property's agriculture or livestock production potential; and other uses detrimental to retention of the property for use in agriculture or livestock production. *See, e.g.*, § 1.170A–14(f), Example 5.

Q–13. Individual *B*, a calendar year taxpayer who is a qualified farmer or rancher for 2007, makes qualified conservation contributions during that year with respect to *B*'s 1,000 acre property. Of *B*'s 1,000 acres, 950 acres are used (or available for use) in agriculture or livestock production, and 50 acres are used as a game preserve that is unavailable for use in agriculture or livestock production. *B* contributes a qualified conservation contribution with respect to the 950 acre property, and a separate qualified conservation contribution with respect to the 50 acre property. The contribution with respect to the 950 acre property includes a restriction that the property remain available for use in agriculture or livestock production. Provided *B* meets all requirements of § 170, do both contributions qualify for the 100 percent limitation under § 170(b)(1)(E)(iv)?

A–13. Yes.

DRAFTING INFORMATION

The principal authors of this notice are Amy S. Wei and Patricia M. Zweibel of the Office of Associate Chief Counsel (Income Tax & Accounting). For further information regarding this notice, contact Ms. Wei or Ms. Zweibel at (202) 622–7900 (not a toll-free call).

---

26 CFR 601.201: Rulings and determination letters. (Also Part I, § 430.)

Rev. Proc. 2007–37

SECTION 1. PURPOSE

The purpose of this revenue procedure is to set forth the procedure by which the sponsor of a defined benefit plan, other than a multiemployer plan, may request and obtain approval for the use of plan-specific substitute mortality tables in accordance with § 430(h)(3)(C) of the Internal Revenue Code (Code) and section 303(h)(3)(C) of the Employee Retirement Income Security Act of 1974, as amended (ERISA).

SECTION 2. BACKGROUND INFORMATION

.01 Section 412 of the Code provides minimum funding requirements for defined benefit pension plans. Section 430, which was added by the Pension Protection Act of 2006, Pub. L. No. 109–280, 120 Stat. 780, specifies the minimum funding requirements for defined benefit plans other than multiemployer plans pursuant to § 412 and is generally effective for plan years beginning on or after January 1, 2008. Section 430(h)(3)(A) sets forth rules regarding the use of generally applicable mortality tables for purposes of § 430. Section 430(h)(3)(C) and section 303(h)(3)(C) of ERISA provide that the Secretary of the Treasury may approve substitute mortality tables to be used in determining any present value or making any computation under those sections for a period not to exceed ten years. Mortality tables meet the requirements for substitute mortality tables if the pension plan has a sufficient number of plan participants and the plan has been maintained for a sufficient period of time in order to have credible mortality experience, and such tables reflect the actual experience of the plan and projected trends in general mortality experience of participants in pension plans. Except as provided by the Secretary, a plan sponsor cannot use substitute mortality tables for any plan unless substitute mortality tables are established and used for each other plan subject to § 430 of the Code that is maintained by the plan sponsor and the plan sponsor's controlled group.

.02 Proposed regulation § 1.430(h)(3)–1, which sets forth proposed rules regarding the use of generally applicable mortality tables for purposes of § 430, and proposed regulation § 1.430(h)(3)–2, which sets forth proposed rules for the use of substitute mortality tables under § 430(h)(3)(C) (referred to elsewhere in this revenue procedure as the "proposed regulations"), were published in the Federal Register on May 29, 2007, at 72 FR 29456. Under the proposed regulations (REG–143601–06, 2007–24 I.R.B. 1398), substitute mortality tables must reflect the actual mortality experience of the pension plan maintained by the plan sponsor for which the tables are to be used and that mortality experience must be credible. Separate mortality tables must be established for each gender under the plan, and a substitute mortality table is permitted to be established for a gender only if the plan has credible mortality experience with respect to that gender. If the mortality experience for one gender is credible but the mortality experience for the other gender is not credible, then the substitute mortality tables are used for the gender that has credible mortality experience, and the mortality tables under proposed regulation § 1.430(h)(3)–1 are used for the gender that does not have credible mortality experience. If separate mortality tables under § 430(h)(3)(D) are used for certain disabled individuals under a plan, then those individuals are disregarded for all purposes with respect to substitute mortality tables under § 430(h)(3)(C). Thus, if the mortality tables under § 430(h)(3)(D) are used for certain disabled individuals under a plan, mortality experience with respect to those individuals must be excluded in determining mortality rates for substitute mortality tables with respect to a plan.

Under the proposed regulations, a substitute mortality table is based on credible mortality experience for a gender within a plan if and only if the mortality experience is based on at least 1,000 deaths within that gender over the period covered by the experience study. The experience study must be based on mortality experience data over a 2, 3, or 4-consecutive year period, the last day of which must be less than 3 years before the first day of the first plan year for which the substitute mortality tables are to apply.

Development of a substitute mortality table under the proposed regulations requires creation of a base table (Base Table) and identification of a base year (Base Year), which are then used to determine generational substitute mortality tables. The Base Table must be developed from a study of the mortality experience of the plan using amounts-weighted data. The proposed regulations also set forth rules regarding development of amounts-weighted mortality rates for an age and the determination of the Base Year. The proposed regulations provide that amounts-weighted mortality rates may be derived from amounts-weighted mortality rates for age groups.

The proposed regulations provide that Base Tables may be constructed either directly through graduation of amounts-weighted mortality rates or indirectly by applying a level percentage to tables prescribed by § 430(h)(3)(A), provided that the resulting tables sufficiently reflect the plan's mortality experience. The Service may permit the construction of Base Tables through application of a level percentage to other recognized mortality tables, applying similar standards to ensure that the resulting tables are sufficiently reflective of the plan's mortality experience.

As noted above, except as provided by the Secretary, a plan sponsor cannot use substitute mortality tables for any plan unless substitute mortality tables are established and used for each other plan subject to § 430 that is maintained by the plan sponsor and the plan sponsor's controlled group. Under the proposed regulations, the use of substitute mortality tables for one plan would not be prohibited merely because another plan maintained by the plan sponsor (or by a member of the plan sponsor's controlled group) cannot use substitute mortality tables because neither the males nor the females under that other plan have credible mortality experience for a plan year. Thus, if a sponsor's controlled group maintains two pension plans subject to § 430, each of which has credible mortality experience for at least one gender, then either both plans must obtain approval from the Service to use substitute mortality tables or neither plan may use substitute mortality tables. By contrast, if, for one of those plans, neither males nor females have credible mortality experience, then the plan without credible mortality experience will not interfere with the ability of the plan with credible mortality experience to use substitute mortality tables.

SECTION 3. GENERAL ADMINISTRATIVE PROCEDURES

.01 *Compliance with Regulations.* Until final regulations under § 430(h)(3)(C) are issued, requests for the use of substitute mortality tables must satisfy the requirements of proposed regulation § 1.430(h)(3)–2. After those final regulations are issued, requests must satisfy the requirements of the final regulations.

.02 *Submission.* Requests for the use of substitute mortality tables must be submitted to:

Internal Revenue Service
Attention: EP Letter Rulings
P.O. Box 27063
McPherson Station
Washington, D.C. 20038

The user fee required by section 6.01(10) (All other letter rulings) of Rev. Proc. 2007–8, 2007–1 I.R.B. 230, or its successors, must be sent with such requests.

.03 *Necessary Procedural Documents.* A request will not be considered unless it complies with (1) through (3) below.

(1) The request (and any subsequently provided additional information) must be signed by the employer maintaining the plan(s) (the "applicant") or an authorized representative of the applicant who must be identified in (a), (b), (c), (d) or (e) of section 9.02(11) of Rev. Proc. 2007–4, 2007–1 I.R.B. 118, or its successors. Where an authorized representative signs the request or will appear before the Service in connection with the request, a properly signed and dated Form 2848, *Power of Attorney and Declaration of Representative*, must be submitted with the request. An individual is not an authorized representative of the applicant merely on account of being the administrator or trustee of the plan.

(2) The request also must contain a declaration in the following form: "Under penalties of perjury, I declare that I have examined this request, or this modification to the request, including accompanying documents, and, to the best of my knowledge and belief, the request or the modification contains all the relevant facts relating to the request, and such facts are true, correct, and complete." This declaration must be signed by the applicant (*e.g.*, an authorized officer of a corporation). The signature of an individual with a power of attorney will not suffice for the declaration. See section 9.02(13) of Rev. Proc. 2007–4.

(3) Because a request for the use of substitute mortality tables constitutes a request for a ruling, compliance with § 6110 of the Code is also required. Section 601.201 of the Statement of Procedural Rules sets forth the requirements applicable to requests for rulings and determination letters which are subject to § 6110. Section 601.201(e) furnishes specific instructions to applicants.

The applicant must provide with the request either a statement of proposed deletions and the statutory basis for each proposed deletion, or a statement that no information other than names, addresses, and taxpayer identifying numbers need be deleted.

.04 *Checklist.* A checklist has been provided in Appendix A for the convenience of the applicant submitting the request. This checklist should be signed, by the applicant or authorized representative, and dated and placed on top of the request.

SECTION 4. DEADLINE FOR REQUESTING THE USE OF SUBSTITUTE MORTALITY TABLES

.01 *In General.* A request for the use of substitute mortality tables generally must be submitted at least 7 months prior to the first day of the first plan year for which the substitute mortality tables are to apply. Thus, for example, if the first plan year to which substitute mortality tables are to apply is the plan year that begins January 1, 2009, then the deadline is June 1, 2008. Notwithstanding the generally applicable deadline, a request to use substitute mortality tables is timely if it is submitted on or before October 1, 2007.

.02 *Incomplete Requests.* Generally, an incomplete request for the use of substitute mortality tables will be summarily denied absent mutual agreement of the Service and the applicant to extend the 180-day period specified under § 430(h)(3)(C)(v)(II). Except as provided in section 5.06 of this revenue procedure, the applicant should not assume that the Service will agree to extend the 180-day period for a request that does not include substantially all of the applicable information specified in sections 5 through 13 of this revenue procedure.

SECTION 5. GENERAL RULES

.01 The Service will deny a request if the request fails to meet the requirements of this revenue procedure or if the Service determines that a substitute mortality table does not sufficiently reflect the mortality experience of the applicable plan population.

.02 If separate mortality tables are used for disabled individuals pursuant to § 430(h)(3)(D), then those individuals are disregarded for all purposes under this revenue procedure.

.03 A separate request must be made with respect to each plan (the "Plan"), or group of plans that are permissively aggregated (the "Permissive Group"), for which the use of a substitute mortality table or tables is requested. The request must include a complete copy of the Base Tables that will form the basis for the substitute mortality tables that will be used. The request must state the first day of the first plan year for which the substitute mortality tables are to be applicable (the "Requested Effective Plan Year") and must state the term of years (not more than 10) that the tables are requested to be used. Each request also must identify the Base Year of the Base Tables.

.04 The request must include a description of the populations within the Plan (or the Permissive Group) for which the use of substitute mortality tables is requested and a description of the populations, if any, for which the use of substitute mortality tables is not requested.

For example, if the use of substitute mortality tables is requested for nondisabled female individuals (but for no other individuals) where separate mortality tables are used for disabled individuals pursuant to § 430(h)(3)(D), then the population for whom the use of substitute mortality tables is requested would be described as "Nondisabled Females" and the population for whom the use of substitute mortality tables is not requested would be described as "Nondisabled Males."

Similarly, if the use of substitute mortality tables is requested for male annuitants (but not male non-annuitants) and for females on a combined annuitant/nonannuitant basis, in each case including disabled individuals, then the populations for whom the use of substitute mortality tables is requested would be described as "Male Annuitants" and "Females", and the population for whom the use of substitute mortality tables is not requested would be described as "Male Nonannuitants."

.05 The request must include the plan identification information described in Section 6, the credible mortality experience demonstrations described in Section 7, the stability demonstrations described in Section 8, the lack of credible mortality experience demonstrations described in Section 9, the unadjusted mortality experience described in Section 10, the Base Table construction methods as set forth in Section 11 or 12, and the demonstrations with respect to the Base Tables described in Section 13.

.06 If there are other plans subject to § 430 maintained by the applicant, or members of the applicant's controlled group, that have credible mortality experience for which the use of substitute mortality tables will be requested in a separate request, then the Service will not summarily deny the request for the use of substitute mortality tables on the grounds that all plans with credible mortality experience maintained by the applicant would not be using substitute mortality tables, but only if the applicant requests that the 180-day review period provided under § 430(h)(3)(C)(v)(II) not begin for the initial request and any such separate request until the date all such separate requests have been received, and only if those separate requests are submitted within 90 days after the receipt of the initial request (and no later than the deadline that applies to each such separate request under section 4 of this revenue procedure). In the absence of such a request for a delay in the start of the 180-day review period, or if all such separate requests are not submitted within 90 days after the receipt of the initial request, the Service will summarily deny the request for the use of substitute mortality tables on the grounds that all plans with credible mortality experience maintained by the applicant would not be using substitute mortality tables.

Example. Employer E maintains Plans A and B, both of which are calendar year plans that have each had over 2,500 deaths in each of the last five years. Employer E submits a request for the use of substitute mortality tables for Plan A for the 2009 plan year that is received on February 15, 2008 (the "A Request"). To avoid denial of the A Request on the grounds that all plans with credible mortality experience maintained by the applicant would not be using substitute mortality tables, Employer E requests that the 180-day review period of the A Request not begin until the receipt of a separate request for the 2009 plan year from Employer E for the use of substitute mortality tables by Plan B. The Service agrees to defer commencement of the 180-day period, but will summarily deny the application unless Employer E submits a separate request for the use of substitute mortality tables for Plan B no later than May 15, 2008.

.07 If two or more plans are permissively aggregated for the purpose of constructing substitute mortality tables, then such plans are treated as a single plan for all purposes of this revenue procedure. Accordingly, if two or more plans are permissively aggregated, then all populations within the plans must be so aggregated.

Example. Employer F maintains Plans C, D, and E, each of which had 500 male deaths and 100 female deaths in each of the last five years. Employer F may request to use one substitute male mortality table and one substitute female mortality table for the aggregation of Plans C, D, and E. However, Employer F may not aggregate Plans C, D, and E and request to use one substitute female mortality table for Plans C, D, and E, and three separate substitute male mortality tables for Plans C, D, and E.

SECTION 6. IDENTIFICATION OF PLANS

.01 The following plan information must be provided for the Plan (or for each plan within the Permissive Group) for which the use of substitute mortality tables is requested:

(1) Plan name;

(2) Plan number;

(3) Plan year (*i.e.*, calendar, or if fiscal, the first and last day);

(4) Employer identification number;

(5) Date of plan establishment; and

(6) Copies of the actuarial valuation reports for each plan year which begins or ends during the Experience Study Period as defined in section 7.01 of this revenue procedure.

.02 The following information must be provided for each plan that is subject to § 430 maintained by the applicant, or members of the applicant's controlled group, for which the use of substitute mortality tables is not requested:

(1) Plan name;

(2) Plan number;

(3) Plan year (*i.e.*, calendar, or if fiscal, the first and last day);

(4) Employer identification number;

(5) Date of plan establishment;

(6) If the plan is newly acquired, the date of the merger, acquisition, or similar transaction described in § 1.410(b)–2(f) of the regulations, and the date described in § 410(b)(6)(C)(ii)(II); and

(7) The Lack of Credible Mortality Experience Demonstration Period, or, if the plan is not required to identify such a period, the applicable exception. (See section 9 of this revenue procedure.)

.03 The following additional information must be provided with respect to each plan that is subject to § 430 that is maintained by the applicant, or member of the applicant's controlled group, that was spun off from another plan that is maintained by the applicant within the five-year period preceding the date of the request:

(1) The plan name and the plan number of the spun off plan, and the plan name and number of the plan from which the spinoff occurred;

(2) The employer identification number of the employer maintaining the spun off plan and the employer identification number of the employer maintaining the plan from which the spinoff occurred;

(3) The date of the spinoff;

(4) The approximate number of individuals covered by the spun off plan as of the date of the spinoff and the approximate number of individuals covered by the plan from which the spinoff occurred, prior to the spinoff; and

(5) The reason for the spinoff.

SECTION 7. DEMONSTRATIONS OF CREDIBLE MORTALITY EXPERIENCE

.01 The applicant's request must identify the period of time covered by the mortality experience study (the "Experience Study Period") used to develop the Base Table(s) and must identify the Base Year. Different Experience Study Periods for different populations within a plan are not permitted. Except as provided in subsection .02 of this section, different Experience Study Periods for different plans within the Permissive Group are not permitted. Thus, a plan that does not have mortality experience for the entire Experience Study Period may not be included in the Permissive Group. Similarly, a plan that was acquired subsequent to the first day of the Experience Study Period may be included in the Permissive Group only if the applicant includes mortality experience for the full Experience Study Period. Thus, in such cases, the mortality experience study must include mortality experience that occurred before the date of acquisition.

.02 A plan that came into existence by reason of a spinoff from the Plan (or from a plan within the Permissive Group) during the Experience Study Period may be included in the Permissive Group. In such a case, the period of time covered by the mortality experience study with respect to the spun off plan will begin as of the date of the spinoff. However, the mortality experience of the individuals covered by the spun off plan from the first day of the Experience Study Period to the date of the spinoff would be included as part of the experience of the single plan that existed before the spinoff.

.03 In order to demonstrate credible mortality experience, the number of deaths during each year of the Experience Study Period (and, in total, for the entire Experience Study Period) within each population for which the use of substitute mortality tables is requested must be provided in tabular form.

SECTION 8. DEMONSTRATION OF STABILITY

.01 The following information must be provided in tabular form for each population within the Plan (or plans within the Permissive Group) for which the use of a substitute mortality table is requested, aggregating all plans that have the same plan year:

(1) The average number of individuals within the population during the Experience Study Period; and

(2) The number of individuals within the population as of the last day of the plan year immediately preceding the plan year during which the use of substitute mortality tables is requested.

A reasonable estimate of the number of plan individuals, such as the estimated number of participants and beneficiaries used for purposes of PBGC Form 1–ES, may be used to provide the information requested in subsection .01(1) of this section.

.02 If the difference between (1) and (2) of subsection .01 of this section within any population, for any plan year, reflects a difference of 20 percent or more, then an analysis that shows that the mortality experience during the Experience Study Period is still accurately predictive of the future mortality of the population must be submitted.

SECTION 9. DEMONSTRATIONS OF LACK OF CREDIBLE MORTALITY EXPERIENCE

.01 *General Rule.* For all plans maintained by the applicant, except as described in subsections .02 and .03 of this section, the 4-year period of time used to demonstrate a lack of credible mortality experience must be identified (the "Lack of Credible Mortality Experience Demonstration Period").

.02 *General Exception.* Plans described in paragraphs (1), (2), or (3) are not required to identify a Lack of Credible Mortality Experience Demonstration Period.

(1) Plans for which the use of substitute mortality tables is requested for all populations (other than disabled populations for whom the tables prescribed under § 430(h)(3)(D) are used);

(2) Plans for which the use of substitute mortality tables has previously been approved by the Service and the term of years of such approval ends subsequent to the last day of the Requested Effective Plan Year; and

(3) Newly acquired plans for which the last day of the period described in § 410(b)(6)(C) is a date on or after the first day of the plan year for which the use of substitute mortality tables is requested.

.03 *Exception for Certain Newly Acquired Plans.* Newly acquired plans (as defined in § 1.430(h)(3)–2) for which the last day of the period described in § 410(b)(6)(C) is a date prior to the first day of the plan year for which the use of substitute mortality tables is requested, and for which the applicant has elected not to include mortality experience prior to the date of the acquisition, may identify a Lack of Credible Mortality Experience Demonstration Period less than 4 years in length. For such plans, the Lack of Credible Mortality Experience Demonstration Period must begin no later than the date of acquisition of the plan and end not more than one year and one day before the first day of the plan year for which the use of substitute mortality tables is requested.

.04 *Demonstrations of Plan-Wide Lack of Credible Mortality Experience.* The following information must be provided in tabular form for each plan that is not within the Permissive Group and which does not fall within one of the exceptions provided in subsection .02 of this section:

(1) The number of male deaths during the Lack of Credible Mortality Experience Demonstration Period; and

(2) The number of female deaths during the Lack of Credible Mortality Experience Demonstration Period.

.05 *Demonstrations of Lack of Credible Mortality Experience for Certain Populations.* The number of deaths for the population during the Lack of Credible Mortality Experience Demonstration Period must be provided in tabular form for each relevant population within the Plan (or plans within the Permissive Group) for which the use of substitute mortality tables is not requested.

The relevant populations for this purpose would, for example, be nondisabled females if the request was to use a substitute mortality table for nondisabled males (but for no other individuals) where separate mortality tables were used for disabled individuals pursuant to § 430(h)(3)(D). Similarly, the relevant populations would be male non-annuitants and females, in each case including disabled individuals, if the request was to use a substitute mortality table for male annuitants (but not for male non-annuitants) where separate mortality tables were not used for disabled individuals pursuant to § 430(h)(3)(D).

SECTION 10. UNADJUSTED MORTALITY EXPERIENCE

.01 *In General.* The following information must be provided in tabular form for all individuals within each population for whom the use of a separate mortality table is requested, for each year of the Experience Study Period, and for the Experience Study Period in its entirety, for all ages between 18 and 100 (except as provided in subsection .03 of this section):

(1) The sum of the accrued benefits (or payable benefits, in the case of individuals in pay status) of all individuals at that age at the beginning of the year, other than individuals who left the population during the year for reasons other than death;

(2) The sum of the accrued (or payable) benefits of all individuals at that age at the beginning of the year who left the population during the year for reasons other than death, adjusted to reflect exposure periods of less than one year;

(3) The sum of the accrued (or payable) benefits of all individuals at that age at the beginning of the year who died during the year;

(4) The quotient determined by dividing the sum of the accrued (or payable) benefits of all individuals at that age who died during the year by the sum of the accrued (or payable) benefits for all individuals at that age adjusted for individuals at that age who left the population for reasons other than death (*i.e.*, the amount determined in paragraph (3), divided by the total of the amounts determined in paragraphs (1) and (2);

(5) The total number of individuals at that age at the beginning of the year;

(6) The total number of individuals at that age at the beginning of the year who left the population for reasons other than death;

(7) The total number of individuals at that age at the beginning of the year who died during the year; and

(8) The average accrued benefit of all individuals at that age at the beginning of the year.

.02 *Adjustment for Exposure Periods of Less than One Year.* The request must include a description of the method(s) used to adjust the accrued benefits of individuals who left for reasons other than death to reflect exposure periods of less than one year.

.03 *Grouping of Ages.* The information requested in subsection .01 of this section may be presented in five-year age groups. In such cases, the groups at the extreme ages may include more than five ages provided such groups either do not include ages greater than age 24 or do not include ages less than age 95. Thus, for example, an age group consisting of all ages 24 and lower would be permissible whereas an age group consisting of all ages 25 and lower would not be permissible.

.04 *Unadjusted Base Tables.* An Unadjusted Base Table for each population for which the use of substitute mortality tables is requested shall, for all ages or all groups of ages, consist of the quotients determined in paragraph (4) of subsection .01 of this section for the Experience Study Period in its entirety. The request must include a complete copy of each such Unadjusted Base Table.

SECTION 11. BASE TABLE CONSTRUCTION – GENERAL METHOD

.01 *In General.* Except as otherwise provided in Section 12 of this revenue procedure, a Base Table for a population must be created from the Unadjusted Base Table for the population through the application of a graduation method generally used by the actuarial profession in the United States (*e.g.*, Whittaker-Henderson Type B, Karup-King). Section 12 of this revenue procedure provides for an alternate method of constructing a Base Table through the application of a fixed percentage to the mortality rates of a Standard Mortality Table, projected to the Base Year.

.02 *Information Regarding Graduation Methods.* The graduation method must be identified and the parameters of the graduation method used must be specified (*e.g.*, for Whittaker-Henderson Type B, the number of differences and the "h" value must be specified). If more than one graduation is performed, then the parameters must be specified for each such graduation.

.03 *Intermediate Values.* If more than one graduation is performed in the process of adjusting an Unadjusted Base Table to a Base Table, then a copy of each intermediate table so created must be provided.

.04 *Rationale.* The rationale for the selection of each particular graduation method used must be provided along with the rationale for the selection of the particular parameters used as part of the method.

.05 *Extension to Extreme Ages.* At extreme ages for which insufficient data exists, the Base Tables must be extended to blend into the applicable Standard Mortality Table, provided in subsection .06 of this section, projected to the Base Year using Projection Scale AA, as set forth in the proposed regulations. In such cases, the method (and the rationale for the method) used for the extension must be described.

.06 *Standard Mortality Tables.* For purposes of this revenue procedure, the following are the Standard Mortality Tables:

(1) The Male Base Non-Annuitant Mortality Table (Year 2000) as set forth in § 1.430(h)(3)–1;

(2) The Male Base Annuitant Mortality Table (Year 2000) as set forth in § 1.430(h)(3)–1;

(3) The Female Base Non-Annuitant Mortality Table (Year 2000) as set forth in § 1.430(h)(3)–1;

(4) The Female Base Annuitant Mortality Table (Year 2000) as set forth in § 1.430(h)(3)–1;

(5) The Male Base Combined Mortality Table (Year 2000) determined in accordance with subsection .07 of this section; and

(6) The Female Base Combined Mortality Table (Year 2000) determined in accordance with subsection .07 of this section.

.07 *Gender-Specific Base (Year 2000) Mortality Combined Tables.* For purposes of this revenue procedure, the Male Base Combined Mortality Table (Year 2000) is the table determined through application of the male Weighting Factors for Small Plans (the "Weights") to the Male Base Non-Annuitant and Annuitant Mortality Tables (Year 2000) as set forth in § 1.430(h)(3)–1. Similarly, the Female Base Combined Mortality Table (Year 2000) is the table determined through application of the female Weights to the Female Base Non-Annuitant and Annuitant Mortality Tables (Year 2000) as set forth in § 1.430(h)(3)–1.

SECTION 12. BASE TABLE CONSTRUCTION – ALTERNATE METHOD

.01 *General Rule.* A Base Table for a population may be created by applying a fixed percentage (the "Fixed Percentage") to the mortality rates in the Projected Applicable Standard Mortality Table, only if the requirements of subsections .02 and .03 of this section are satisfied and the Service determines that the resulting Base Table sufficiently reflects the mortality experience of the applicable plan population.

For this purpose the Projected Applicable Standard Mortality Table is the applicable Standard Mortality Table, projected to the Base Year using Projection Scale AA, as set forth in § 1.430(h)(3)–1. See subsection .05 of this section with regard to the possible use of other mortality tables for this purpose.

Under this section 12, the Unadjusted Base Mortality Tables must be constructed using five-year age groups. For each Base Table constructed using the alternate method described in this section, the Fixed Percentage and the mortality table to which such percentage is to be applied must be identified. In addition, for each so constructed Base Table, the ratios of the mortality rates from the Unadjusted Base Mortality Table for the population to the central age mortality rates (*i.e.*, the mortality rates for the ages that are the midpoints of the age ranges) from the Projected Applicable Standard Mortality Table must be provided, in tabular form, for all five-year age groups for which mortality experience is available.

.02 *Selection of the Fixed Percentage.*

(1) If the applicable Standard Mortality Table for a population is the table provided in either section 11.06(1) or section 11.06(3) of this revenue procedure, then the Fixed Percentage must be within two percentage points of the arithmetic average of the ratios of the mortality rates from the Unadjusted Base Mortality Table for the population to the central age mortality rates from the Projected Applicable Standard Mortality Table of each of the five-year age groups from the 35–39 age group to the 60–64 age group, inclusive, unless the applicant can demonstrate that a different set of five-year age groups (consisting of no less than six such groups) is more appropriate for this purpose.

(2) If the applicable Standard Mortality Table for a population is the table provided in either section 11.06(2) or section 11.06(4) of this revenue procedure, then the Fixed Percentage must be within two percentage points of the arithmetic average of the ratios of the mortality rates from the Unadjusted Base Mortality Table for the population to the central age mortality rates from the Projected Applicable Standard Mortality Table of each of the five-year age groups from the 55–59 age group to the 80–84 age group, inclusive, unless the applicant can demonstrate that a different set of five-year age groups (consisting of no less than six such groups) is more appropriate for this purpose.

(3) If the applicable Standard Mortality Table for a population is the table provided in either section 11.06(5) or section 11.06(6) of this revenue procedure, then the Fixed Percentage must be within two percentage points of the arithmetic average of the ratios of the mortality rates from the Unadjusted Base Mortality Table for the population to the central age mortality rates from the Projected Applicable Standard Mortality Table of each of the five-year age groups from the 45–49 age group to the 80–84 age group, inclusive, unless the applicant can demonstrate that a different set of five-year age groups (consisting of no less than eight such groups) is more appropriate for this purpose.

.03 *Consistency Requirement.* The consistency requirement of this subsection .03 is satisfied only if each of the applicable ratios described in subsection .02 of this section is within 10 percentage points of the Fixed Percentage.

.04 *Terminal Age.* Notwithstanding subsection .01 of this section, the mortality rate for the terminal age in any Base Table created by applying a Level Percentage to a Standard Mortality Table shall be 1.000.

.05 *Other Mortality Tables.* The Service will consider requests for the approval of Base Tables constructed through the application of a fixed percentage to the mortality rates of other published generally accepted mortality tables (*e.g.*, the 1983 Group Annuity Mortality Table) using standards similar to those provided in subsections .01 through .04 of this section.

.06 *Example.* The age group rates from the Male Unadjusted Base Table (determined in accordance with section 10 of this revenue procedure), the central age rates from the Male Base Combined Mortality Table (Year 2000), projected to the Base Year, and the ratios of such rates are as follows:

	A	B	C
Age Group	Mortality Rate from Unadjusted Base Mortality Table	Base Combined Mortality Table (Year 2000), Projected to the Base Year, Age Group Mortality Rate	Ratio of Mortality Rate from Unadjusted Mortality Table to Base Mortality Rate (Year 2000)
45 to 49	0.00163	0.00165	98.79%
50 to 54	0.00211	0.00241	87.55%
55 to 59	0.00376	0.00431	87.24%
60 to 64	0.00765	0.00812	94.21%
65 to 69	0.01569	0.01506	104.18%
70 to 74	0.02439	0.02502	97.48%
75 to 79	0.03768	0.04387	85.89%
80 to 84	0.07948	0.07732	102.79%
Arithmetic Average Percentage			**94.77%**

In accordance with subsection .02 of this section, the Fixed Percentage to be applied to the Male Base Mortality Table (Year 2000), projected to the Base Year, must be between 92.77% and 96.77%. However, a Fixed Percentage that is less than 94.18% would fail to satisfy the requirements of subsection .03 of this section because the ratio for the 65–69 Age Group (*i.e.*, 104.18%) would then not be within 10 percentage points of a Fixed Percentage less than 94.18%. Similarly, a Fixed Percentage that is greater than 95.89% would fail the requirements of subsection .03 because the ratio for the 75–79 Age Group (*i.e.*, 85.89%) would then not be within 10 percentage points of a Fixed Percentage greater than 95.89%. Accordingly, under the facts in this example, if the applicant were to request the use of a Base Table constructed through the application of a percentage to the Male Base Mortality Table (Year 2000) that is a fixed integer, the applicant would be limited to a Fixed Percentage of 95%.

SECTION 13. DEMONSTRATIONS WITH RESPECT TO BASE TABLES

The following information must be provided with respect to each population for which the use of substitute mortality tables is requested:

.01 *Generational Mortality Tables.* Sample generational mortality tables, as of the Requested Effective Plan Year, for individuals whose years of birth are 1940, 1950, and 1960, constructed from the Base Tables using methodology in accordance with § 1.430(h)(3)–1 (except that the projection period used to determine each particular mortality improvement factor is the number of years between the Base Year and the year for which the probability of death is determined).

.02 *Funding Target Comparisons.* The liability of the plan(s) for which the use of substitute mortality tables is requested as of the valuation date for a plan year ending no earlier than one year and one day before the first plan year to which the substitute mortality tables will apply (the "Comparison Year"). The liability is to be measured using generational mortality tables determined in accordance with the methodology described in subsection .01 of this section. The liability is to be provided separately for active participants, terminated vested participants, and retirees and beneficiaries in pay status, and is to be determined as follows:

(1) For Comparison Years beginning in 2006, the liability to be reported is the Current Liability recalculated using the mortality tables published in § 1.412(l)(7)–1 of the regulations, and, for comparison, what the Current Liability would have been if the substitute mortality table(s) had been used to determine Current Liability, in each case holding all other assumptions constant.

(2) For Comparison Years beginning in 2007, the liability to be reported is the Current Liability and, for comparison, what the Current Liability would have been if the substitute mortality table(s) had been used to determine Current Liability, holding all other assumptions constant.

(3) For Comparison Years beginning after 2007, the liability to be reported is the Funding Target, determined without regard to at-risk assumptions under § 430(i), and, for comparison, what the Funding Target would have been if the substitute mortality table(s) had been used to determine the Funding Target, holding all other assumptions constant.

.03 *Annuity Factors.* The following annuity factors based on generational mortality tables for individuals whose year of birth is 1950, determined using interest and mortality assumptions consistent with those used under subsection .02 of this section.

(1) For all Base Tables with the exception of annuitant Base Tables:

(a) Deferred to age 55 factors at quinquennial ages from 20 to 50; and

(b) Deferred to age 65 factors at quinquennial ages from 20 to 60.

(2) For all Base Tables with the exception of nonannuitant Base Tables, immediate annuity factors at quinquennial ages from 50 to 90.

.04 *Graphical Displays.* A comparison in the form of graphs with the X-axis representing age and the Y-axis representing the mortality rate, for each of the following pairs of mortality rates, for each population for which the use of substitute mortality tables is requested:

(1) The mortality rates from the Base Unadjusted Mortality Table and the mortality rates from the proposed Base Table; and

(2) The mortality rates from the proposed Base Table and from the applicable Standard Mortality Table (as described in section 11.06 of this revenue procedure), projected to the Base Year.

SECTION 14. EFFECTIVE DATE

This revenue procedure is effective for all requests for the use of plan-specific substitute mortality tables in accordance with § 430(h)(3)(C) of the Code and section 303(h)(3)(C) of ERISA.

SECTION 15. PAPERWORK REDUCTION ACT

The collection of information contained in this revenue procedure has been reviewed and approved by the Office of Management and Budget in accordance with the Paperwork Reduction Act (44 U.S.C. section 3507) under control number 1545–2073.

An agency may not conduct or sponsor, and a person is not required to respond to, a collection of information unless the collection of information displays a valid OMB control number.

The collection of information in this revenue procedure is in sections 3 through 13. This collection of information is required to evaluate, process and obtain approval of the request for the use of substitute mortality tables. This information will be used to make determinations under § 430(h)(3) of the Code. The likely respondents are businesses or other for-profit institutions and nonprofit institutions.

The estimated total annual reporting/recordkeeping burden is 25,400 hours.

The estimated annual burden per respondent/recordkeeper varies from 335 to 681 hours, depending on individual circumstances, with an estimated average burden of 508 hours. The estimated annual number of respondents/recordkeepers is 50.

The estimated annual frequency of responses is once every 10 years.

Books or records relating to a collection of information must be retained as long as their contents may become material in the administration of any internal revenue law. Generally, tax returns and tax return information are confidential, as required by 26 U.S.C. section 6103.

DRAFTING INFORMATION

The principal author of this revenue procedure is Lawrence E. Isaacs of the

Employee Plans, Tax Exempt and Government Entities Division. For further information regarding how this revenue procedure applies to employee plans matters, contact the Employee Plans Customer Assistance Service between the hours of 9 a.m. and 4:30 p.m. Eastern time, Monday through Friday at 1 877 829 5500 (a toll-free call). Mr. Isaacs may be reached at *retirementplanquestions@irs.gov* and his telephone number is (202) 283–9710 (not a toll-free call).

Appendix A

REQUEST FOR THE USE OF SUBSTITUTE MORTALITY TABLES CHECKLIST
IS YOUR SUBMISSION COMPLETE?

Instructions

The Service will be able to respond more quickly to your request for the use of substitute mortality tables if it is carefully prepared and complete. To ensure your request is in order, use this checklist. Answer each question in the checklist by indicating Y for yes, N for no, or N/A for not applicable. Explanations must be provided for N or N/A responses. **Sign and date the checklist (as taxpayer or authorized representative) and place it on top of your request.**

You must submit a completed copy of this checklist with your request. If a completed checklist is not submitted with your request or if explanations are not provided for N and N/A responses, then your submission will be considered incomplete for purposes of determining the first day of the 180-day period described in § 430(h)(3)(C)(v)(II) of the Code.

1. If you want to designate an authorized representative, have you included a properly executed Form 2848 (*Power of Attorney and Declaration of Representative*)?
2. Have you satisfied all the requirements of Rev. Proc. 2007–4 or its successors (especially concerning signatures and penalties of perjury statement)? (See sections 3.03(1) and (2))
3. Have you included statement of proposed deletions? (See section 3.03(3))
4. Have you included the user fee required under Rev. Proc. 2007–8 or its successors? (See section 3.02)
5. Have you included a copy of the Base Tables which will form the basis for the substitute mortality tables whose use is requested? (See section 5.03)
6. Have you identified the first day of the first plan year for which the use of substitute mortality tables is requested? (See section 5.03)
7. Have you stated the number of years for which the use of substitute mortality tables is requested? (See section 5.03)
8. Have you identified the Base Year of the Base Tables? (See section 5.03)
9. Have you included a description of the populations for which the use of substitute mortality tables is requested? (See section 5.04)
10. Have you included a description of the populations for which the use of substitute mortality tables is not requested? (See section 5.04)
11. Have you requested that the 180-day review period not begin until a separate request is received for another plan(s) maintained by the applicant is received? (See section 5.06)
12. Have you identified all plans subject to § 430 maintained by the applicant, or members of the applicant's controlled group, including the additional information required for spun-off plans under section 6.03? (See section 6)
13. Have you identified the Experience Study Period? (See section 7.01)
14. Have you included a table showing the number of deaths, for each applicable population within the Plan (or within the Permissive Group), for each year (and in total) of the Experience Study Period? (See section 7.03)
15. Have you included a table showing the average number of individuals during the Experience Study Period and the number of individuals within the population as of the last day of the plan year immediately preceding the plan year during which the use of substitute mortality tables is requested for each population within the Plan (or plans within the Permissive Group) for which the use of a substitute mortality table is requested? (See section 8)
16. Have you included a table for each plan that is not within the Permissive Group showing the number of male and female deaths during the plan's Lack of Credible Mortality Experience Demonstration Period, including identification of the Lack of Credible Mortality Experience Demonstration Period? (See sections 9.01 and 9.04)

17. Have you included a table for each population within the Plan (or plans within the Permissive Group) for which the use of substitute mortality tables is not requested, showing the number of deaths within the population? (See section 9.05)

18. Have you included a table showing the accrued benefits, counts of individuals covered under the plan, and other information for all ages (or groups of ages) for each year (and in total) of the Experience Study Period? (See section 10.01)

19. Have you included a description of the method(s) used to adjust the accrued benefits of individuals who left for reasons other than death? (See section 10.02)

20. Have you included complete copies of each Unadjusted Base Table? (See section 10.04)

21. Have you identified the graduation method(s) used to create the Base Table(s) from the Unadjusted Base Table(s), along with any intermediate tables resulting from applying the graduation method(s)? (See sections 11.02 and 11.03)

22. Have you provided the rationale(s) for use of the particular graduation method(s) selected? (See section 11.04)

23. Have you described the method used to extend the Base Tables to extreme ages? (See section 11.05)

24. Have you identified a Fixed Percentage and a mortality table associated with all Base Tables constructed using the alternate method provided in section 12? (See section 12.01)

25. Have you included a table showing the ratios of the mortality rates from the Unadjusted Base Mortality Table to the central age mortality rates from the Projected Applicable Standard Mortality Table for each Base Table constructed using the alternate method of section 12? (See section 12.01)

26. Have you included (three) sample generational mortality tables as of the Requested Effective Plan Year? (See section 13.01)

27. Have you included a comparison of hypothetical funding targets determined using standard mortality tables and generational tables developed from the proposed Base Tables? (See section 13.02)

28. Have you included annuity factors based on generational mortality tables for individuals whose year of birth is 1950 for each population for which the use of substitute mortality factors is requested? (See section 13.03)

29. Have you included graphical displays of the rates from the Base Unadjusted Mortality Tables, the proposed Base Tables, and the applicable Standard Mortality Tables? (See section 13.04)

26 CFR 601.602: *Tax forms and instructions.*
(*Also Part 1, §§ 3504, 6011, 6061, 6302; 31.3504–1, 31.6011(a)–7, 31.6061–1, 31.6302–1.*)

Rev. Proc. 2007–38

TABLE OF CONTENTS

SECTION 1. PURPOSE

.01 This revenue procedure provides the requirements for completing and submitting Form 8655, *Reporting Agent Authorization* (Authorization). An Authorization allows a taxpayer to designate a Reporting Agent to perform the following acts on behalf of a taxpayer:

(1) Sign and electronically file Form 940, *Employer's Annual Federal Unemployment (FUTA) Tax Return*; Form 941, *Employer's QUARTERLY Federal Tax Return*; Form 944, *Employer's ANNUAL Federal Tax Return*; and those forms set forth in section 4.02(1) of this revenue procedure.

(2) Sign and file on paper the tax returns set forth in section 4.02(2) of this revenue procedure.

(3) Make federal tax deposits (FTDs) and other federal tax payments (FTPs) and submit FTD information and FTP information electronically as described in section 4.02(3) of this revenue procedure.

(4) Receive duplicate copies of official notices, correspondence, deposit requirements, transcripts, or other information as described in section 4.02(4) of this revenue procedure.

(5) Receive duplicate copies of official notices, correspondence, deposit requirements, transcripts, or other information with respect to FTDs and FTPs as described in section 4.02(5) of this revenue procedure.

.02 The technical specifications for filing Authorization information are published separately in Publication 1474, *Technical Specifications Guide For Reporting Agent Authorization and Federal Tax Depositors*.

SECTION 2. BACKGROUND

.01 Section 1.6011–1 of the Income Tax Regulations and § 31.6011(a)–7 of the Employment Taxes and Collection of Income Tax at Source Regulations (Employment Tax Regulations) provide that each return required under the regulations, together with any prescribed copies or supporting data, must be filled in and disposed of in accordance with applicable forms, instructions, and regulations. Section 31.6011(a)–7 provides that the return may be made by an agent authorized by the person required to make the return.

.02 Section 31.6061–1 of the Employment Tax Regulations provides that a return may be signed for the taxpayer by an agent duly authorized in accordance with § 31.6011(a)–7 to make the return. Section 1.6061–1 of the Income Tax Regulations provides that a return may be signed by an agent who is duly authorized under § 1.6012–1(a)(5) or (b) to make the return.

.03 Section 31.6302–1 of the Employment Tax Regulations provides the rules for depositing employment taxes. Section 31.6302–1(h) implements section 6302(h) of the Internal Revenue Code, which requires the use of an electronic fund transfer system for the collection of federal depository taxes. The Electronic Federal Tax Payment System (EFTPS) is the electronic fund transfer system developed to collect these taxes. Rev. Proc. 97–33, 1997–2 C.B. 371, provides general information about EFTPS, and Rev. Proc. 98–32, 1998–1 C.B. 935, provides information about EFTPS programs for Reporting Agents making FTDs and FTPs on behalf of multiple taxpayers.

.04 The Service has prescribed Form 8655 as the appropriate authorization form for a taxpayer to use to designate a Reporting Agent to perform the actions set forth in section 4.02 of this revenue procedure.

.05 All references in this revenue procedure to forms and publications include all future revisions and successor forms and publications.

SECTION 3. SIGNIFICANT CHANGES TO REV. PROC. 2003–69

.01 This revenue procedure modifies and supersedes Rev. Proc. 2003–69, 2003–2 C.B. 403, by making the following changes to Rev. Proc. 2003–69.

(1) Form 8655 may now be used to authorize Reporting Agents to:

(a) Sign and file Form 944, *Employer's ANNUAL Federal Tax Return*; Forma 944–PR, *Planilla Para La Declaración ANUAL Del Patrono*; Forma 944(SP), *Declaración Federal ANUAL de Impuestos del Patrono o Empleador*; Form 944–SS, *Employer's Annual Federal Tax Return (American Samoa, Guam, the Commonwealth of the Northern Mariana Islands, and the U.S. Virgin Islands)*; additional forms set forth on Form 8655; and amended forms and any successor forms that replace those listed.

(b) Make FTDs and FTPs and submit FTD and FTP information electronically for the tax deposits and payments reported on Form 944.

(c) Receive confidential taxpayer information from the Service to assist in responding to notices relating to Form W–2 and Form 1099 Series information returns filed by the Reporting Agent on behalf of the taxpayer.

(2) Section 5.09 has been added to provide that a Reporting Agent must provide the taxpayer with a complete copy of any return filed by the Reporting Agent.

(3) Section 6.01 has been revised to provide that an Authorization must be made on a Form 8655 with a revision date of May 2005 or later, or on an approved substitute form.

(4) Section 6.02 has been revised to provide that an Authorization may be signed and submitted electronically under procedures promulgated by the Service.

(5) Sections 8 through 11 set forth reasons for suspending a Reporting Agent from the Reporting Agent program, the administrative review process for proposed suspensions, the effect of a suspension, and the procedures for administratively appealing a suspension.

(6) Section 13 (former section 9) updates the list of other related documents.

SECTION 4. DEFINITIONS

.01 *Reporting Agent.* A Reporting Agent is an accounting service, franchiser, bank, service bureau, or other entity authorized to perform on behalf of a taxpayer one or more of the acts described in this revenue procedure.

.02 *Authorization.* An Authorization allows a taxpayer to designate a Reporting Agent to:

(1) Sign and file electronically Form 940, Form 941, Form 944; and those forms set forth on Form 8655, and amended and any successor forms.

(2) Sign and file on paper Form 944, Forma 940–PR, *Planilla Para La Declaración ANUAL Del Patrono—La Contribución Federal Para El Desempleo (FUTA)*; Forma 941–PR, *Planilla Para La Declaración Federal Trimestral Del Patrono—La Contribución Federal Al Seguro Social Y Al Seguro Medicare*; Form 941–SS, *Employer's QUARTERLY Federal Tax Return*; Form 943, *Employer's Annual Federal Tax Return for Agricultural Employees*; Forma 943–PR, *Planilla Para La Declaración Anual De La Contribución Federal Del Patrono De Empleados Agrícolas*; Forma 944–PR, *Planilla Para La Declaración ANUAL Del Patrono*; Forma 944(SP), *Declaración Federal ANUAL de Impuestos del Patrono o Empleador*; Form 944–SS, *Employer's Annual Federal Tax Return (American Samoa, Guam, the Commonwealth of the Northern Mariana Islands, and the U.S. Virgin Islands)*; Form 945, *Annual Return of Withheld Federal Income Tax*; Form 1042, *Annual Withholding Tax Return for U.S. Source Income of Foreign Persons*; and Form CT–1, *Employer's Annual Railroad Retirement Tax Return*, and any amended and successor forms.

(3) Make FTDs and FTPs and submit FTD information and FTP information electronically for the taxes deposited and payments reported on applicable returns set forth on Form 8655.

(4) Receive duplicate copies of official notices, correspondence, deposit requirements, transcripts, or other information with respect to the tax returns described in section 4.01(1) or (2) of this revenue procedure.

(5) Receive duplicate copies of official notices, correspondence, deposit requirements, transcripts, or other information with respect to FTDs and FTPs.

.03 *Reporting Agent's List.* A Reporting Agent's List (Agent's List) identifies all taxpayers for whom a Reporting Agent will file tax returns, make FTDs and FTPs, or submit FTD information and FTP information electronically. A separate Authorization must be submitted for each taxpayer on the Agent's List.

SECTION 5. SCOPE OF REPORTING AGENT AUTHORIZATION

.01 The scope of an Authorization for the filing of returns listed on Form 8655 is as follows:

(1) A taxpayer may authorize a Reporting Agent to sign and file on the taxpayer's behalf any or all of the returns listed on Form 8655 and any amended and successor forms. A Form 8655 that authorizes a Reporting Agent to sign and file a Form 941, Form 941–SS, Forma 941–PR, Form 944, Form 944–SS, Forma 944(SP), or Forma 944–PR also authorizes the Reporting Agent to sign any other form in the Form 941 or 944 series of returns.

(2) A taxpayer may authorize a Reporting Agent to receive duplicate copies of notices, correspondence, deposit requirements, transcripts, or other information

with respect to the returns filed by the Reporting Agent.

(3) A taxpayer may authorize a Reporting Agent to receive confidential taxpayer information from the Service to assist in responding to notices relating to the Form W–2 or Form 1099 series of information returns.

(4) An Authorization that permits a Reporting Agent to make returns also permits a Reporting Agent to request information from the Service or submit information to the Service about the returns filed by the Reporting Agent. This authority extends to any information concerning penalties that may arise from the returns, including information that may assist the Service in determining whether it would be appropriate to grant relief from any penalties arising from the returns. This authority continues regardless of a change in filing requirements. For instance, if a Reporting Agent, pursuant to an Authorization, made and filed a Form 941 on behalf of a taxpayer prior to the Service notifying the taxpayer that the taxpayer's filing requirements was changed from Form 941 to Form 944, the Reporting Agent has authority to continue to request information from the Service or submit information to the Service about the previously-filed Form 941, assuming the Reporting Agent's authorization remains in effect.

(5) An Authorization, however, does not permit the Reporting Agent to request the abatement of any penalties that may arise from the returns filed by the Reporting Agent or to perform in any other way any acts that constitute representation of the taxpayer within the meaning of § 601.501(b)(13) of the Statement of Procedural Rules.

.02 The scope of an Authorization for making FTDs and FTPs and submitting FTD information and FTP information electronically is as follows:

(1) A taxpayer may authorize a Reporting Agent to make FTDs and FTPs for any taxes reported on any of the returns listed on Form 8655 and to submit FTD information and FTP information electronically on the taxpayer's behalf. A Form 8655 that authorizes a Reporting Agent to prepare and make FTDs and FTPs on Form 990–C, *Farmers' Cooperative Association Income Tax Return*, also authorizes a Reporting Agent to prepare and make FTDs and FTPs on Form 1120–C, *U.S. Income Tax Return for Cooperative Associations*.

(2) A taxpayer may authorize a Reporting Agent to receive duplicate copies of notices and correspondence for FTDs and FTPs made by the Reporting Agent for the taxpayer.

(3) Regardless of the method designated by the taxpayer, a Reporting Agent must make FTDs and submit FTD information through the EFTPS for a taxpayer that is required to make FTDs and submit FTD information through the EFTPS pursuant to section 6302(h).

(4) An Authorization that permits a Reporting Agent to make FTDs and FTPs also permits the Reporting Agent to request information from the Service or submit information to the Service on the FTDs and FTPs submitted by the Reporting Agent. It further permits the Reporting Agent to submit any information concerning penalties that may arise from the returns, including information that may assist the Service in determining whether it would be appropriate to grant relief from penalties. This authority continues regardless of a change in forms. For instance, if a Reporting Agent had authority to make FTDs and FTPs in connection with Form 990–C and did so, and the Service later replaces Form 990–C with Form 1120–C, absent a change to the Authorization, the Reporting Agent has authority to make FTDs and FTPs on behalf of the taxpayer in connection with Form 1120–C. The Reporting Agent also retains authority to request information from the Service or submit information to the Service about the FTDs and FTPs relating to Form 990–C.

(5) An Authorization does not permit the Reporting Agent to request the abatement of any penalties that may arise from the FTDs or FTPs made by the Reporting Agent or to perform in any other way any acts that constitute representation of the taxpayer within the meaning of § 601.501(b)(13) of the Statement of Procedural Rules.

.03 An Authorization becomes effective for the tax period(s) designated by the Reporting Agent and taxpayer and remains in effect for subsequent periods until revoked by the taxpayer or terminated by the Reporting Agent or the Service, subject to the following:

(1) The Service must accept the Authorization and Agent's List before the Reporting Agent may file a return on behalf of a taxpayer.

(2) The Reporting Agent must comply with the requirements of Rev. Proc. 98–32, 1998–1 C.B. 935, before the Reporting Agent may make electronic FTDs or FTPs on behalf of a taxpayer or submit FTD information or FTP information electronically.

(3) See section 13 of this revenue procedure for a list of other applicable guidance.

.04 A new Authorization must be submitted to the Service for any increase or decrease in the scope of the authority of a Reporting Agent to act on behalf of the taxpayer, or if the taxpayer appoints a new Reporting Agent. Receipt by the Service of an Authorization designating a new Reporting Agent terminates the authority of the prior Reporting Agent for all purposes for tax periods beginning on or after the effective date of the new Authorization. An Authorization designating a new Reporting Agent also terminates the authority of the prior Reporting Agent to receive duplicate copies of notices. For the tax periods beginning before the effective date of the new Authorization, the prior Reporting Agent retains the authority specified in the prior Authorization unless the taxpayer explicitly revokes the prior Authorization.

.05 An Authorization does not relieve the taxpayer of the responsibility (or from liability for failing) to ensure that all tax returns are filed timely and that all FTDs and FTPs are made timely.

.06 A Reporting Agent may use an Authorization to file paper returns listed on Form 8655 on behalf of a taxpayer only if:

(1) The late receipt of payroll information from a taxpayer has jeopardized the timely electronic filing of the taxpayer's return;

(2) The paper return amends Form 940 filed under the magnetic tape or electronic filing programs referenced in section 13 of this revenue procedure;

(3) The Service's rejection of an electronic filing has jeopardized the timely filing of the taxpayer's return;

(4) The returns are listed in section 4.02(2) of this revenue procedure; or

(5) The electronic filing coordinator for a Reporting Agent participating in an electronic filing program referenced in section

13 of this revenue procedure has requested paper returns.

.07 A Reporting Agent authorized by Form 8655 may prepare a paper tax return for the taxpayer's signature.

.08 Each paper tax return must be signed by the taxpayer, by the taxpayer's authorized representative, or by a Reporting Agent permitted in section 5.06 of this revenue procedure to file paper returns on behalf of the taxpayer.

.09 The Reporting Agent must provide the taxpayer with a complete copy of any returns filed by the Reporting Agent. This information may be provided on a replica of an official form or in any other format that provides all of the return information and references the line numbers of the official form.

.10 A Reporting Agent must keep a copy of each Authorization designating that Reporting Agent as an agent for a taxpayer at the Reporting Agent's principal place of business and make it available for examination by the Service until the period of limitations for assessment of tax for the last return filed pursuant to the Authorization expires.

SECTION 6. COMPLETING AN AUTHORIZATION

.01 An Authorization must be submitted on Form 8655 with a revision date of May 2005 or later or on an approved substitute form as described in Publication 1167, *General Rules and Specifications for Substitute Forms and Schedules*. When completing Form 8655, a taxpayer may strike out any non-applicable portions of the form. Once completed, a Reporting Agent may fax the Authorization to the Service.

.02 An Authorization must be signed by the taxpayer or an authorized representative holding a power of attorney that specifically authorizes the representative to sign returns on behalf of the taxpayer. If the Authorization provides that the Reporting Agent is authorized to receive tax return notices, correspondence, deposit requirements, and transcripts from the Service, or discuss taxpayer account information with Service representatives and is signed by a person other than the taxpayer, the authorized representative must be authorized both to receive, and to designate others to receive, tax return information (as defined in section 6103(b)(2)) of the taxpayer. The Authorization may be signed and submitted electronically under procedures promulgated by the Service.

.03 Except to the extent provided in section 6.04 of this revenue procedure, an Authorization will remain in effect until the Service receives a revocation of the Authorization or a new Authorization or a Reporting Agent is suspended.

.04 A new Authorization is not required to replace an Authorization made on Form 8655 with a revision date before October 1995 (or made on an equivalent substitute) that was previously submitted to the Service by a Reporting Agent if the Authorization places no restriction on the medium for filing Forms 940 or 941 and the Reporting Agent advises the taxpayer that its Forms 940 and 941 may be filed electronically and that the taxpayer has the option to reject electronic filing. A Reporting Agent may use whatever method the Reporting Agent deems the most efficient and timely method to convey the advice. A taxpayer's rejection of electronic filing of Forms 940 or 941 must be submitted in writing to the Reporting Agent, and upon receipt the Reporting Agent must immediately remove the taxpayer from the Agent's List or database of taxpayers for which the Reporting Agent files returns electronically.

SECTION 7. SUBMITTING A REPORTING AGENT AUTHORIZATION

.01 A Reporting Agent that intends to use an Authorization to electronically file Forms 940, Forms 941, or Forms 944, or make FTDs or FTPs (and submit related information) electronically must formally apply to the Service for these privileges. The application process for permission to electronically file Forms 940, 941, and 944 and for participation in EFTPS is contained in the documents (or their successors) listed in section 13 of this revenue procedure. Applications must be accompanied by individual Authorizations, signed as provided in section 6.02 of this revenue procedure, and an Agent's List (if required by the applicable guidance document).

.02 An Agent's List must contain each taxpayer's employer identification number. Agent's Lists may be filed electronically, as appropriate, but if the number of taxpayers/clients exceeds 100, the Agent's List must be filed electronically. For specific information concerning the requirements for filing and updating Agent's Lists, see Publication 1474 and the documents listed in section 13 of this revenue procedure. The Service contacts listed in section 13 of this revenue procedure may also be contacted for this information.

SECTION 8. SUSPENSION

.01 The Service reserves the right to suspend a Reporting Agent from the Reporting Agent program for the following reasons (this list is not all inclusive):

(1) Failing to perform the acts described in section 4.02 of this revenue procedure or Publication 1474.

(2) Submitting payment information on behalf of taxpayers for which the Reporting Agent did not receive Authorizations.

(3) Failing to comply with the requirements of any regulation, revenue procedure, or other published guidance applicable to Reporting Agents.

(4) Failing to cooperate with the Service's efforts to monitor Reporting Agents and investigate abuse in the Reporting Agent program.

(5) Receiving significant complaints about the Reporting Agent's performance in the Reporting Agent program.

.02 If the Service informs a Reporting Agent that a certain action is a reason for suspension and the action continues, the Service may send the Reporting Agent a notice proposing suspension of the Reporting Agent from the Reporting Agent program. A notice proposing suspension, however, may be sent without a warning if the Reporting Agent's actions indicate an intentional disregard of the rules. A notice proposing suspension will describe the reasons for the proposed suspension, the length of the suspension, and the conditions that need to be met before the suspension will terminate.

SECTION 9. ADMINISTRATIVE REVIEW PROCESS FOR PROPOSED SUSPENSION

.01 A Reporting Agent that receives a notice proposing suspension from the Reporting Agent program, as described in section 8.02 of this revenue procedure, may request an administrative review prior to the suspension taking effect.

.02 The request for an administrative review must be in writing and contain detailed reasons, with supporting documentation, for withdrawal of the proposed suspension.

.03 The written request for an administrative review and a copy of the notice proposing suspension must be delivered to the address designated in the notice within 30 days of the effective date on the notice.

.04 If a written request for administrative review is timely submitted, the Service will, after consideration of the request, either issue a suspension letter or notify the Reporting Agent in writing that the proposed suspension is withdrawn.

.05 Failure to submit a timely written request for an administrative review irrevocably terminates the Reporting Agent's right to an administrative review of the proposed suspension, and the Service will issue a suspension letter.

SECTION 10. EFFECT OF SUSPENSION

.01 The Reporting Agent's suspension will continue for the length of time specified in the suspension letter, or until the conditions for terminating the suspension have been met, whichever is later. If a Reporting Agent is suspended, the Service's subsequent determination of whether a reason for suspension has been corrected is not subject to administrative review or appeal.

.02 After suspension, a Reporting Agent may not perform the acts described in this revenue procedure. As an exception, a Reporting Agent may submit an FTD if the FTD is due not more than 30 days after the effective date on the suspension letter. A Reporting Agent, however, cannot submit FTPs during the suspension period.

.03 A Reporting Agent must provide written notification of a suspension from the Reporting Agent program to each taxpayer in the program within 10 days from the date on the suspension letter. This notification must be provided irrespective of the length of the suspension or how quickly the Reporting Agent believes it may meet the conditions for terminating the suspension.

.04 A Reporting Agent will be able to perform the acts described in section 4.02 of this revenue procedure without re-registering in the Reporting Agent program after the stated suspension period expires; and the reason(s) for suspension are corrected.

SECTION 11. APPEAL OF A SUSPENSION

.01 If a Reporting Agent receives a suspension letter from the Service, the Reporting Agent is entitled to appeal, by written protest, to the Service. The written protest must be delivered to the address designated on the suspension letter. During the appeals process, the suspension remains in effect.

.02 The written protest must be received by the Service within 30 days of the effective date on the suspension letter. The written protest must contain detailed reasons, with supporting documentation, for withdrawal of the suspension.

.03 Failure to appeal within the 30-day period described in section 11.02 of this revenue procedure irrevocably terminates the Reporting Agent's right to appeal the suspension under section 11.01.

SECTION 12. INTERNAL REVENUE SERVICE CONTACTS

Publication 1474 and Publication 1167 may be obtained electronically via the Service's website at *http://www.irs.gov*. In addition, requests for Publication 1474 and questions regarding this revenue procedure may be addressed to the Service at:

Internal Revenue Service
Accounts Management Service Center
MS 6748 RAF Team
1973 N Rulon White Blvd
Ogden, UT 84201

SECTION 13. OTHER RELATED DOCUMENTS

These documents describe programs that require an Authorization as a prerequisite to participation:

(1) For rules regarding Form 944, see §§ 31.6011(a)–1T, 31.6011(a)–4T, and 31.6302–1T of the Employment Tax Regulations.

(2) For electronic filing of Form 940 and 941, see Rev. Proc. 2005–60, 2005–2 C.B. 449.

(3) For participation in EFTPS, see Rev. Proc. 98–32, 1998–1 C.B. 935.

(4) For the Service's e-file program generally, see Publication 3112, *IRS e-file Application and Participation.*

SECTION 14. EFFECT ON OTHER DOCUMENTS

This revenue procedure modifies and supersedes Rev. Proc. 2003–69, 2003–2 C.B. 403.

SECTION 15. EFFECTIVE DATE

This revenue procedure is effective June 18, 2007.

SECTION 16. DRAFTING INFORMATION

The principal author of this revenue procedure is Michael Hara of the Office of Associate Chief Counsel (Procedure and Administration). Mr. Hara may be contacted at (202) 622–4910 (not a toll-free number).

---

26 CFR 601.201: Rulings and determination letters. (Also Part I, § 102.)

Rev. Proc. 2007–39

SECTION 1. PURPOSE

This revenue procedure amplifies Rev. Proc. 2007–3, 2007–1 I.R.B. 108, which sets forth areas of the Internal Revenue Code in which the Internal Revenue Service will not issue letter rulings or determination letters.

SECTION 2. BACKGROUND

Section 3 of Rev. Proc. 2007–3 sets forth a list of those areas of the Internal Revenue Code under the jurisdiction of the Associate Chief Counsel (Corporate), the Associate Chief Counsel (Financial Institutions and Products), the Associate Chief Counsel (Income Tax and Accounting), the Associate Chief Counsel (Passthroughs and Special Industries), the Associate Chief Counsel (Procedure and Administration), and the Division Counsel/Associate Chief Counsel (Tax Exempt and Government Entities) relating to issues on which the Internal Revenue Service will not issue letter rulings or determination letters.

SECTION 3. PROCEDURE

Rev. Proc. 2007–3 is amplified by adding the following to section 3.01: Section 102. Gifts and Inheritances. Whether a transfer is a gift within the meaning of § 102(a).

SECTION 4. EFFECT ON OTHER DOCUMENTS

Rev. Proc. 2007–3 is amplified.

SECTION 5. EFFECTIVE DATE

This revenue procedure applies to all ruling requests pending or received in the National Office on or after June 1, 2007.

SECTION 6. DRAFTING INFORMATION

The principal author of this revenue procedure is Amy Pfalzgraf of the Office of Associate Chief Counsel (Income Tax and Accounting). For further information regarding this revenue procedure, contact Ms. Pfalzgraf at (202) 622–4960 (not a toll-free call).

Part IV. Items of General Interest

Limitations on Benefits and Contributions Under Qualified Plans; Correction

Announcement 2007–58

AGENCY: Internal Revenue Service (IRS), Treasury.

ACTION: Correction to final regulations.

SUMMARY: This document contains a correction to final regulations (T.D. 9319, 2007–18 I.R.B. 1041) that were published in the **Federal Register** on Thursday, April 5, 2007 (72 FR 16878) regarding the limitations of section 415, including updates to the regulations for numerous statutory changes since comprehensive final regulations were last published under section 415.

DATES: This correction is effective May 23, 2007.

FOR FURTHER INFORMATION CONTACT: Vernon S. Carter at (202) 622–6060 or Linda S. F. Marshall at (202) 622–6090 (not toll-free numbers).

SUPPLEMENTARY INFORMATION:

Background

The correction notice that is the subject of this document is under sections 401(a), 401(a)(4), 401(a)(9), 401(k), 402, 414(s), 415, 416, 457, and 924 of the Internal Revenue Code.

Need for Correction

As published, final regulations (T.D. 9319) contain an error that may prove to be misleading and is in need of clarification.

Correction of Publication

Accordingly, the publication of the final regulations (T.D. 9319), which was the subject of FR Doc. E7–5750, is corrected as follows:

On page 16883, column 2, in the preamble, under the paragraph heading "*C. Determination of High-3 Average Compensation*", first line from the bottom of the last paragraph of that heading, the language "participant in rehired." is corrected to read "participant is rehired."

LaNita Van Dyke,
Chief, Publications and Regulations Branch, Legal Processing Division, Associate Chief Counsel (Procedure and Administration).

(Filed by the Office of the Federal Register on May 22, 2007, 8:45 a.m., and published in the issue of the Federal Register for May 23, 2007, 72 F.R. 28854)

Guidance for Employers Concerned About Certain Mid-Year Changes to a Section 401(k) Safe Harbor Plan

Announcement 2007–59

The Internal Revenue Service has learned that some employers have concerns about adding provisions during a plan year to their § 401(k) safe harbor plans (described in § 401(k)(12) of the Internal Revenue Code) in order to take advantage of recently effective changes to the rules for § 401(k) plans, such as a qualified Roth contribution program (as defined in § 402A) or hardship withdrawals described in part III of Notice 2007–7, 2007–5 I.R.B. 395, when the pre-year safe harbor notice required by § 401(k)(12)(D) does not include information about the added provisions.

This announcement provides that a plan will not fail to satisfy the requirements to be a § 401(k) safe harbor plan merely because of mid-year changes to implement a qualified Roth contribution program (as defined in § 402A) or the hardship withdrawals described in part III of Notice 2007–7.

Comments are requested as to whether additional guidance is needed with respect to mid-year changes to a § 401(k) safe harbor plan (other than changes described in this announcement or in § 1.401(k)–3(f) of the Income Tax Regulations (relating to mid-year amendments to become a safe harbor plan using nonelective contributions) and § 1.401(k)–3(g) (relating to mid-year amendments to suspend or reduce safe harbor matching contributions)). Written comments should be submitted by September 17, 2007. Send submissions to CC:PA:LPD:DRU (Announcement 2007–59), Room 5203, Internal Revenue Service, POB 7604, Ben Franklin Station, Washington, D.C. 20044. Comments may be hand delivered to CC:PA:LPD:DRU (Announcement 2007–59), Room 5203, Internal Revenue Service, 1111 Constitution Avenue, NW, Washington, DC. Alternatively, comments may be submitted via the Internet at *notice.comments@irscounsel.treas.gov* (Announcement 2007–59). All comments will be available for public inspection.

Drafting Information

The principal authors of this announcement are Roger Kuehnle of the Employee Plans, Tax Exempt and Government Entities Division and Cathy Vohs and Bill Gibbs of the Office of the Division Counsel/Associate Chief Counsel (Tax Exempt and Government Entities). For further information regarding this announcement, please contact the Employee Plans taxpayer assistance answering service between 8:30 a.m. and 4:30 p.m., Eastern time, Monday through Friday at 1–877–829–5500 (a toll-free call) or Mr. Kuehnle at *retirementplanquestions@irs.gov*.
Ms. Vohs may be reached at 202–622–6090 and Mr. Gibbs may be reached at 202–622–6060 (not toll-free calls).

Part I. Rulings and Decisions Under the Internal Revenue Code of 1986

Section 6621.—Determination of Rate of Interest

26 CFR 301.6621–1: Interest rate.

Interest rates; underpayments and overpayments. The rate of interest determined under section 6621 of the Code for the calendar quarter beginning July 1, 2007, will be 8 percent for overpayments (7 percent in the case of a corporation), 8 percent for underpayments, and 10 percent for large corporate underpayments. The rate of interest paid on the portion of a corporate overpayment exceeding $10,000 will be 5.5 percent.

Rev. Rul. 2007–39

Section 6621 of the Internal Revenue Code establishes the rates for interest on tax overpayments and tax underpayments. Under section 6621(a)(1), the overpayment rate is the sum of the federal short-term rate plus 3 percentage points (2 percentage points in the case of a corporation), except the rate for the portion of a corporate overpayment of tax exceeding $10,000 for a taxable period is the sum of the federal short-term rate plus 0.5 of a percentage point for interest computations made after December 31, 1994. Under section 6621(a)(2), the underpayment rate is the sum of the federal short-term rate plus 3 percentage points.

Section 6621(c) provides that for purposes of interest payable under section 6601 on any large corporate underpayment, the underpayment rate under section 6621(a)(2) is determined by substituting "5 percentage points" for "3 percentage points." See section 6621(c) and section 301.6621–3 of the Regulations on Procedure and Administration for the definition of a large corporate underpayment and for the rules for determining the applicable date. Section 6621(c) and section 301.6621–3 are generally effective for periods after December 31, 1990.

Section 6621(b)(1) provides that the Secretary will determine the federal short-term rate for the first month in each calendar quarter.

Section 6621(b)(2)(A) provides that the federal short-term rate determined under section 6621(b)(1) for any month applies during the first calendar quarter beginning after such month.

Section 6621(b)(3) provides that the federal short-term rate for any month is the federal short-term rate determined during such month by the Secretary in accordance with § 1274(d), rounded to the nearest full percent (or, if a multiple of 1/2 of 1 percent, the rate is increased to the next highest full percent).

Notice 88–59, 1988–1 C.B. 546, announced that, in determining the quarterly interest rates to be used for overpayments and underpayments of tax under section 6621, the Internal Revenue Service will use the federal short-term rate based on daily compounding because that rate is most consistent with section 6621 which, pursuant to section 6622, is subject to daily compounding.

Rounded to the nearest full percent, the federal short-term rate based on daily compounding determined during the month of April 2007 is 5 percent. Accordingly, an overpayment rate of 8 percent (7 percent in the case of a corporation) and an underpayment rate of 8 percent are established for the calendar quarter beginning July 1, 2007. The overpayment rate for the portion of a corporate overpayment exceeding $10,000 for the calendar quarter beginning July 1, 2007, is 5.5 percent. The underpayment rate for large corporate underpayments for the calendar quarter beginning July 1, 2007, is 10 percent. These rates apply to amounts bearing interest during that calendar quarter.

Interest factors for daily compound interest for annual rates of 5.5 percent, 7 percent, 8 percent, and 10 percent are published in Tables 16, 19, 21, and 25 of Rev. Proc. 95–17, 1995–1 C.B. 556, 570, 573, 575, and 579.

Annual interest rates to be compounded daily pursuant to section 6622 that apply for prior periods are set forth in the tables accompanying this revenue ruling.

DRAFTING INFORMATION

The principal author of this revenue ruling is Wendy Kribell of the Office of Associate Chief Counsel (Procedure & Administration). For further information regarding this revenue ruling, contact Ms. Kribell at (202) 622–4570 (not a toll-free call).

TABLE OF INTEREST RATES

PERIODS BEFORE JUL. 1, 1975 — PERIODS ENDING DEC. 31, 1986

OVERPAYMENTS AND UNDERPAYMENTS

PERIOD	RATE	In 1995–1 C.B. DAILY RATE TABLE
Before Jul. 1, 1975	6%	Table 2, pg. 557
Jul. 1, 1975—Jan. 31, 1976	9%	Table 4, pg. 559
Feb. 1, 1976—Jan. 31, 1978	7%	Table 3, pg. 558
Feb. 1, 1978—Jan. 31, 1980	6%	Table 2, pg. 557
Feb. 1, 1980—Jan. 31, 1982	12%	Table 5, pg. 560
Feb. 1, 1982—Dec. 31, 1982	20%	Table 6, pg. 560
Jan. 1, 1983—Jun. 30, 1983	16%	Table 37, pg. 591
Jul. 1, 1983—Dec. 31, 1983	11%	Table 27, pg. 581

TABLE OF INTEREST RATES		
PERIODS BEFORE JUL. 1, 1975 — PERIODS ENDING DEC. 31, 1986 – Continued		
OVERPAYMENTS AND UNDERPAYMENTS		
PERIOD	RATE	In 1995–1 C.B. DAILY RATE TABLE
Jan. 1, 1984—Jun. 30, 1984	11%	Table 75, pg. 629
Jul. 1, 1984—Dec. 31, 1984	11%	Table 75, pg. 629
Jan. 1, 1985—Jun. 30, 1985	13%	Table 31, pg. 585
Jul. 1, 1985—Dec. 31, 1985	11%	Table 27, pg. 581
Jan. 1, 1986—Jun. 30, 1986	10%	Table 25, pg. 579
Jul. 1, 1986—Dec. 31, 1986	9%	Table 23, pg. 577

TABLE OF INTEREST RATES

FROM JAN. 1, 1987 — DEC. 31, 1998

	OVERPAYMENTS			UNDERPAYMENTS		
		1995–1 C.B.			1995–1 C.B.	
	RATE	TABLE	PG	RATE	TABLE	PG
Jan. 1, 1987—Mar. 31, 1987	8%	21	575	9%	23	577
Apr. 1, 1987—Jun. 30, 1987	8%	21	575	9%	23	577
Jul. 1, 1987—Sep. 30, 1987	8%	21	575	9%	23	577
Oct. 1, 1987—Dec. 31, 1987	9%	23	577	10%	25	579
Jan. 1, 1988—Mar. 31, 1988	10%	73	627	11%	75	629
Apr. 1, 1988—Jun. 30, 1988	9%	71	625	10%	73	627
Jul. 1, 1988—Sep. 30, 1988	9%	71	625	10%	73	627
Oct. 1, 1988—Dec. 31, 1988	10%	73	627	11%	75	629
Jan. 1, 1989—Mar. 31, 1989	10%	25	579	11%	27	581
Apr. 1, 1989—Jun. 30, 1989	11%	27	581	12%	29	583
Jul. 1, 1989—Sep. 30, 1989	11%	27	581	12%	29	583
Oct. 1, 1989—Dec. 31, 1989	10%	25	579	11%	27	581
Jan. 1, 1990—Mar. 31, 1990	10%	25	579	11%	27	581
Apr. 1, 1990—Jun. 30, 1990	10%	25	579	11%	27	581
Jul. 1, 1990—Sep. 30, 1990	10%	25	579	11%	27	581
Oct. 1, 1990—Dec. 31, 1990	10%	25	579	11%	27	581
Jan. 1, 1991—Mar. 31, 1991	10%	25	579	11%	27	581
Apr. 1, 1991—Jun. 30, 1991	9%	23	577	10%	25	579
Jul. 1, 1991—Sep. 30, 1991	9%	23	577	10%	25	579
Oct. 1, 1991—Dec. 31, 1991	9%	23	577	10%	25	579
Jan. 1, 1992—Mar. 31, 1992	8%	69	623	9%	71	625
Apr. 1, 1992—Jun. 30, 1992	7%	67	621	8%	69	623
Jul. 1, 1992—Sep. 30, 1992	7%	67	621	8%	69	623
Oct. 1, 1992—Dec. 31, 1992	6%	65	619	7%	67	621
Jan. 1, 1993—Mar. 31, 1993	6%	17	571	7%	19	573
Apr. 1, 1993—Jun. 30, 1993	6%	17	571	7%	19	573
Jul. 1, 1993—Sep. 30, 1993	6%	17	571	7%	19	573
Oct. 1, 1993—Dec. 31, 1993	6%	17	571	7%	19	573
Jan. 1, 1994—Mar. 31, 1994	6%	17	571	7%	19	573
Apr. 1, 1994—Jun. 30, 1994	6%	17	571	7%	19	573
Jul. 1, 1994—Sep. 30, 1994	7%	19	573	8%	21	575
Oct. 1, 1994—Dec. 31, 1994	8%	21	575	9%	23	577
Jan. 1, 1995—Mar. 31, 1995	8%	21	575	9%	23	577
Apr. 1, 1995—Jun. 30, 1995	9%	23	577	10%	25	579
Jul. 1, 1995—Sep. 30, 1995	8%	21	575	9%	23	577
Oct. 1, 1995—Dec. 31, 1995	8%	21	575	9%	23	577
Jan. 1, 1996—Mar. 31, 1996	8%	69	623	9%	71	625
Apr. 1, 1996—Jun. 30, 1996	7%	67	621	8%	69	623
Jul. 1, 1996—Sep. 30, 1996	8%	69	623	9%	71	625
Oct. 1, 1996—Dec. 31, 1996	8%	69	623	9%	71	625

TABLE OF INTEREST RATES

FROM JAN. 1, 1987 — DEC. 31, 1998 – Continued

	OVERPAYMENTS			UNDERPAYMENTS		
		1995–1 C.B.			1995–1 C.B.	
	RATE	TABLE	PG	RATE	TABLE	PG
Jan. 1, 1997—Mar. 31, 1997	8%	21	575	9%	23	577
Apr. 1, 1997—Jun. 30, 1997	8%	21	575	9%	23	577
Jul. 1, 1997—Sep. 30, 1997	8%	21	575	9%	23	577
Oct. 1, 1997—Dec. 31, 1997	8%	21	575	9%	23	577
Jan. 1, 1998—Mar. 31, 1998	8%	21	575	9%	23	577
Apr. 1, 1998—Jun. 30, 1998	7%	19	573	8%	21	575
Jul. 1, 1998—Sep. 30, 1998	7%	19	573	8%	21	575
Oct. 1, 1998—Dec. 31, 1998	7%	19	573	8%	21	575

TABLE OF INTEREST RATES

FROM JANUARY 1, 1999 — PRESENT

NONCORPORATE OVERPAYMENTS AND UNDERPAYMENTS

	RATE	1995–1 C.B. TABLE	PAGE
Jan. 1, 1999—Mar. 31, 1999	7%	19	573
Apr. 1, 1999—Jun. 30, 1999	8%	21	575
Jul. 1, 1999—Sep. 30, 1999	8%	21	575
Oct. 1, 1999—Dec. 31, 1999	8%	21	575
Jan. 1, 2000—Mar. 31, 2000	8%	69	623
Apr. 1, 2000—Jun. 30, 2000	9%	71	625
Jul. 1, 2000—Sep. 30, 2000	9%	71	625
Oct. 1, 2000—Dec. 31, 2000	9%	71	625
Jan. 1, 2001—Mar. 31, 2001	9%	23	577
Apr. 1, 2001—Jun. 30, 2001	8%	21	575
Jul. 1, 2001—Sep. 30, 2001	7%	19	573
Oct. 1, 2001—Dec. 31, 2001	7%	19	573
Jan. 1, 2002—Mar. 31, 2002	6%	17	571
Apr. 1, 2002—Jun. 30, 2002	6%	17	571
Jul. 1, 2002—Sep. 30, 2002	6%	17	571
Oct. 1, 2002—Dec. 31, 2002	6%	17	571
Jan. 1, 2003—Mar. 31, 2003	5%	15	569
Apr. 1, 2003—Jun. 30, 2003	5%	15	569
Jul. 1, 2003—Sep. 30, 2003	5%	15	569
Oct. 1, 2003—Dec. 31, 2003	4%	13	567
Jan. 1, 2004—Mar. 31, 2004	4%	61	615
Apr. 1, 2004—Jun. 30, 2004	5%	63	617
Jul. 1, 2004—Sep. 30, 2004	4%	61	615
Oct. 1, 2004—Dec. 31, 2004	5%	63	617
Jan. 1, 2005—Mar. 31, 2005	5%	15	569
Apr. 1, 2005—Jun. 30, 2005	6%	17	571
Jul. 1, 2005—Sep. 30, 2005	6%	17	571
Oct. 1, 2005—Dec. 31, 2005	7%	19	573
Jan. 1, 2006—Mar. 31, 2006	7%	19	573
Apr. 1, 2006—Jun. 30, 2006	7%	19	573
Jul. 1, 2006—Sep. 30, 2006	8%	21	575
Oct. 1, 2006—Dec. 31, 2006	8%	21	575
Jan. 1, 2007—Mar. 31, 2007	8%	21	575
Apr. 1, 2007—Jun. 30, 2007	8%	21	575
Jul. 1, 2007—Sep. 30, 2007	8%	21	575

TABLE OF INTEREST RATES

FROM JANUARY 1, 1999 — PRESENT

CORPORATE OVERPAYMENTS AND UNDERPAYMENTS

	OVERPAYMENTS			UNDERPAYMENTS		
		1995–1 C.B.			1995–1 C.B.	
	RATE	TABLE	PG	RATE	TABLE	PG
Jan. 1, 1999—Mar. 31, 1999	6%	17	571	7%	19	573
Apr. 1, 1999—Jun. 30, 1999	7%	19	573	8%	21	575
Jul. 1, 1999—Sep. 30, 1999	7%	19	573	8%	21	575
Oct. 1, 1999—Dec. 31, 1999	7%	19	573	8%	21	575
Jan. 1, 2000—Mar. 31, 2000	7%	67	621	8%	69	623
Apr. 1, 2000—Jun. 30, 2000	8%	69	623	9%	71	625
Jul. 1, 2000—Sep. 30, 2000	8%	69	623	9%	71	625
Oct. 1, 2000—Dec. 31, 2000	8%	69	623	9%	71	625
Jan. 1, 2001—Mar. 31, 2001	8%	21	575	9%	23	577
Apr. 1, 2001—Jun. 30, 2001	7%	19	573	8%	21	575
Jul. 1, 2001—Sep. 30, 2001	6%	17	571	7%	19	573
Oct. 1, 2001—Dec. 31, 2001	6%	17	571	7%	19	573
Jan. 1, 2002—Mar. 31, 2002	5%	15	569	6%	17	571
Apr. 1, 2002—Jun. 30, 2002	5%	15	569	6%	17	571
Jul. 1, 2002—Sep. 30, 2002	5%	15	569	6%	17	571
Oct. 1, 2002—Dec. 31, 2002	5%	15	569	6%	17	571
Jan. 1, 2003—Mar. 31, 2003	4%	13	567	5%	15	569
Apr. 1, 2003—Jun. 30, 2003	4%	13	567	5%	15	569
Jul. 1, 2003—Sep. 30, 2003	4%	13	567	5%	15	569
Oct. 1, 2003—Dec. 31, 2003	3%	11	565	4%	13	567
Jan. 1, 2004—Mar. 31, 2004	3%	59	613	4%	61	615
Apr. 1, 2004—Jun. 30, 2004	4%	61	615	5%	63	617
Jul. 1, 2004—Sep. 30, 2004	3%	59	613	4%	61	615
Oct. 1, 2004—Dec. 31, 2004	4%	61	615	5%	63	617
Jan. 1, 2005—Mar. 31, 2005	4%	13	567	5%	15	569
Apr. 1, 2005—Jun. 30, 2005	5%	15	569	6%	17	571
Jul. 1, 2005—Sep. 30, 2005	5%	15	569	6%	17	571
Oct. 1, 2005—Dec. 31, 2005	6%	17	571	7%	19	573
Jan. 1, 2006—Mar. 31, 2006	6%	17	571	7%	19	573
Apr. 1, 2006—Jun. 30, 2006	6%	17	571	7%	19	573
Jul. 1, 2006—Sep. 30, 2006	7%	19	573	8%	21	575
Oct. 1, 2006—Dec. 31, 2006	7%	19	573	8%	21	575
Jan. 1, 2007—Mar. 31, 2007	7%	19	573	8%	21	575
Apr. 1, 2007—Jun. 30, 2007	7%	19	573	8%	21	575
Jul. 1, 2007—Sep. 30, 2007	7%	19	573	8%	21	575

TABLE OF INTEREST RATES FOR
LARGE CORPORATE UNDERPAYMENTS

FROM JANUARY 1, 1991 — PRESENT

	RATE	1995–1 C.B. TABLE	PG
Jan. 1, 1991—Mar. 31, 1991	13%	31	585
Apr. 1, 1991—Jun. 30, 1991	12%	29	583
Jul. 1, 1991—Sep. 30, 1991	12%	29	583
Oct. 1, 1991—Dec. 31, 1991	12%	29	583
Jan. 1, 1992—Mar. 31, 1992	11%	75	629
Apr. 1, 1992—Jun. 30, 1992	10%	73	627
Jul. 1, 1992—Sep. 30, 1992	10%	73	627
Oct. 1, 1992—Dec. 31, 1992	9%	71	625
Jan. 1, 1993—Mar. 31, 1993	9%	23	577

TABLE OF INTEREST RATES FOR
LARGE CORPORATE UNDERPAYMENTS

FROM JANUARY 1, 1991 — PRESENT – Continued

	RATE	1995–1 C.B. TABLE	PG
Apr. 1, 1993—Jun. 30, 1993	9%	23	577
Jul. 1, 1993—Sep. 30, 1993	9%	23	577
Oct. 1, 1993—Dec. 31, 1993	9%	23	577
Jan. 1, 1994—Mar. 31, 1994	9%	23	577
Apr. 1, 1994—Jun. 30, 1994	9%	23	577
Jul. 1, 1994—Sep. 30, 1994	10%	25	579
Oct. 1, 1994—Dec. 31, 1994	11%	27	581
Jan. 1, 1995—Mar. 31, 1995	11%	27	581
Apr. 1, 1995—Jun. 30, 1995	12%	29	583
Jul. 1, 1995—Sep. 30, 1995	11%	27	581
Oct. 1, 1995—Dec. 31, 1995	11%	27	581
Jan. 1, 1996—Mar. 31, 1996	11%	75	629
Apr. 1, 1996—Jun. 30, 1996	10%	73	627
Jul. 1, 1996—Sep. 30, 1996	11%	75	629
Oct. 1, 1996—Dec. 31, 1996	11%	75	629
Jan. 1, 1997—Mar. 31, 1997	11%	27	581
Apr. 1, 1997—Jun. 30, 1997	11%	27	581
Jul. 1, 1997—Sep. 30, 1997	11%	27	581
Oct. 1, 1997—Dec. 31, 1997	11%	27	581
Jan. 1, 1998—Mar. 31, 1998	11%	27	581
Apr. 1, 1998—Jun. 30, 1998	10%	25	579
Jul. 1, 1998—Sep. 30, 1998	10%	25	579
Oct. 1, 1998—Dec. 31, 1998	10%	25	579
Jan. 1, 1999—Mar. 31, 1999	9%	23	577
Apr. 1, 1999—Jun. 30, 1999	10%	25	579
Jul. 1, 1999—Sep. 30, 1999	10%	25	579
Oct. 1, 1999—Dec. 31, 1999	10%	25	579
Jan. 1, 2000—Mar. 31, 2000	10%	73	627
Apr. 1, 2000—Jun. 30, 2000	11%	75	629
Jul. 1, 2000—Sep. 30, 2000	11%	75	629
Oct. 1, 2000—Dec. 31, 2000	11%	75	629
Jan. 1, 2001—Mar. 31, 2001	11%	27	581
Apr. 1, 2001—Jun. 30, 2001	10%	25	579
Jul. 1, 2001—Sep. 30, 2001	9%	23	577
Oct. 1, 2001—Dec. 31, 2001	9%	23	577
Jan. 1, 2002—Mar. 31, 2002	8%	21	575
Apr. 1, 2002—Jun. 30, 2002	8%	21	575
Jul. 1, 2002—Sep. 30, 2002	8%	21	575
Oct. 1, 2002—Dec. 31, 2002	8%	21	575
Jan. 1, 2003—Mar. 31, 2003	7%	19	573
Apr. 1, 2003—Jun. 30, 2003	7%	19	573
Jul. 1, 2003—Sep. 30, 2003	7%	19	573
Oct. 1, 2003—Dec. 31, 2003	6%	17	571
Jan. 1, 2004—Mar. 31, 2004	6%	65	619
Apr. 1, 2004—Jun. 30, 2004	7%	67	621
Jul. 1, 2004—Sep. 30, 2004	6%	65	619
Oct. 1, 2004—Dec. 31, 2004	7%	67	621
Jan. 1, 2005—Mar. 31, 2005	7%	19	573
Apr. 1, 2005—Jun. 30, 2005	8%	21	575
Jul. 1, 2005—Sep. 30, 2005	8%	21	575
Oct. 1, 2005—Dec. 31, 2005	9%	23	577
Jan. 1, 2006—Mar. 31, 2006	9%	23	577
Apr. 1, 2006—Jun. 30, 2006	9%	23	577
Jul. 1, 2006—Sep. 30, 2006	10%	25	579
Oct. 1, 2006—Dec. 31, 2006	10%	25	579
Jan. 1, 2007—Mar. 31, 2007	10%	25	579

TABLE OF INTEREST RATES FOR LARGE CORPORATE UNDERPAYMENTS

FROM JANUARY 1, 1991 — PRESENT – Continued

	RATE	1995–1 C.B. TABLE	PG
Apr. 1, 2007—Jun. 30, 2007	10%	25	579
Jul. 1, 2007—Sep. 30, 2007	10%	25	579

TABLE OF INTEREST RATES FOR CORPORATE OVERPAYMENTS EXCEEDING $10,000

FROM JANUARY 1, 1995 — PRESENT

	RATE	1995–1 C.B. TABLE	PG
Jan. 1, 1995—Mar. 31, 1995	6.5%	18	572
Apr. 1, 1995—Jun. 30, 1995	7.5%	20	574
Jul. 1, 1995—Sep. 30, 1995	6.5%	18	572
Oct. 1, 1995—Dec. 31, 1995	6.5%	18	572
Jan. 1, 1996—Mar. 31, 1996	6.5%	66	620
Apr. 1, 1996—Jun. 30, 1996	5.5%	64	618
Jul. 1, 1996—Sep. 30, 1996	6.5%	66	620
Oct. 1, 1996—Dec. 31, 1996	6.5%	66	620
Jan. 1, 1997—Mar. 31, 1997	6.5%	18	572
Apr. 1, 1997—Jun. 30, 1997	6.5%	18	572
Jul. 1, 1997—Sep. 30, 1997	6.5%	18	572
Oct. 1, 1997—Dec. 31, 1997	6.5%	18	572
Jan. 1, 1998—Mar. 31, 1998	6.5%	18	572
Apr. 1, 1998—Jun. 30, 1998	5.5%	16	570
Jul. 1, 1998—Sep. 30, 1998	5.5%	16	570
Oct. 1, 1998—Dec. 31, 1998	5.5%	16	570
Jan. 1, 1999—Mar. 31, 1999	4.5%	14	568
Apr. 1, 1999—Jun. 30, 1999	5.5%	16	570
Jul. 1, 1999—Sep. 30, 1999	5.5%	16	570
Oct. 1, 1999—Dec. 31, 1999	5.5%	16	570
Jan. 1, 2000—Mar. 31, 2000	5.5%	64	618
Apr. 1, 2000—Jun. 30, 2000	6.5%	66	620
Jul. 1, 2000—Sep. 30, 2000	6.5%	66	620
Oct. 1, 2000—Dec. 31, 2000	6.5%	66	620
Jan. 1, 2001—Mar. 31, 2001	6.5%	18	572
Apr. 1, 2001—Jun. 30, 2001	5.5%	16	570
Jul. 1, 2001—Sep. 30, 2001	4.5%	14	568
Oct. 1, 2001—Dec. 31, 2001	4.5%	14	568
Jan. 1, 2002—Mar. 31, 2002	3.5%	12	566
Apr. 1, 2002—Jun. 30, 2002	3.5%	12	566
Jul. 1, 2002—Sep. 30, 2002	3.5%	12	566
Oct. 1, 2002—Dec. 31, 2002	3.5%	12	566
Jan. 1, 2003—Mar. 31, 2003	2.5%	10	564
Apr. 1, 2003—Jun. 30, 2003	2.5%	10	564
Jul. 1, 2003—Sep. 30, 2003	2.5%	10	564
Oct. 1, 2003—Dec. 31, 2003	1.5%	8	562
Jan. 1, 2004—Mar. 31, 2004	1.5%	56	610
Apr. 1, 2004—Jun. 30, 2004	2.5%	58	612
Jul. 1, 2004—Sep. 30, 2004	1.5%	56	610
Oct. 1, 2004—Dec. 31, 2004	2.5%	58	612
Jan. 1, 2005—Mar. 31, 2005	2.5%	10	564
Apr. 1, 2005—Jun. 30, 2005	3.5%	12	566
Jul. 1, 2005—Sep. 30, 2005	3.5%	12	566
Oct. 1, 2005—Dec. 31, 2005	4.5%	14	568

TABLE OF INTEREST RATES FOR CORPORATE
OVERPAYMENTS EXCEEDING $10,000

FROM JANUARY 1, 1995 — PRESENT – Continued

	RATE	1995–1 C.B. TABLE	PG
Jan. 1, 2006—Mar. 31, 2006	4.5%	14	568
Apr. 1, 2006—Jun. 30, 2006	4.5%	14	568
Jul. 1, 2006—Sep. 30, 2006	5.5%	16	570
Oct. 1, 2006—Dec. 31, 2006	5.5%	16	570
Jan. 1, 2007—Mar. 31, 2007	5.5%	16	570
Apr. 1, 2007—Jun. 30, 2007	5.5%	16	570
Jul. 1, 2007—Sep. 30, 2007	5.5%	16	570

Part III. Administrative, Procedural, and Miscellaneous

Weighted Average Interest Rates Update

Notice 2007–51

This notice provides guidance as to the corporate bond weighted average interest rate and the permissible range of interest rates specified under § 412(b)(5)(B)(ii)(II) of the Internal Revenue Code. In addition, it provides guidance as to the interest rate on 30-year Treasury securities under § 417(e)(3)(A)(ii)(II).

CORPORATE BOND WEIGHTED AVERAGE INTEREST RATE

Sections 412(b)(5)(B)(ii) and 412(l)(7)(C)(i), as amended by the Pension Funding Equity Act of 2004 and by the Pension Protection Act of 2006, provide that the interest rates used to calculate current liability and to determine the required contribution under § 412(l) for plan years beginning in 2004 through 2007 must be within a permissible range based on the weighted average of the rates of interest on amounts invested conservatively in long term investment grade corporate bonds during the 4-year period ending on the last day before the beginning of the plan year.

Notice 2004–34, 2004–1 C.B. 848, provides guidelines for determining the corporate bond weighted average interest rate and the resulting permissible range of interest rates used to calculate current liability. That notice establishes that the corporate bond weighted average is based on the monthly composite corporate bond rate derived from designated corporate bond indices. The methodology for determining the monthly composite corporate bond rate as set forth in Notice 2004–34 continues to apply in determining that rate. See Notice 2006–75, 2006–36 I.R.B. 366.

The composite corporate bond rate for May 2007 is 6.01 percent. Pursuant to Notice 2004–34, the Service has determined this rate as the average of the monthly yields for the included corporate bond indices for that month.

The following corporate bond weighted average interest rate was determined for plan years beginning in the month shown below.

For Plan Years Beginning in: Month	Year	Corporate Bond Weighted Average	90% to 100% Permissible Range
June	2007	5.81	5.23 to 5.81

30-YEAR TREASURY SECURITIES INTEREST RATE

Section 417(e)(3)(A)(ii)(II) defines the applicable interest rate, which must be used for purposes of determining the minimum present value of a participant's benefit under § 417(e)(1) and (2), as the annual rate of interest on 30-year Treasury securities for the month before the date of distribution or such other time as the Secretary may by regulations prescribe. Section 1.417(e)–1(d)(3) of the Income Tax Regulations provides that the applicable interest rate for a month is the annual interest rate on 30-year Treasury securities as specified by the Commissioner for that month in revenue rulings, notices or other guidance published in the Internal Revenue Bulletin.

The rate of interest on 30-year Treasury securities for May 2007 is 4.90 percent. The Service has determined this rate as the monthly average of the daily determination of yield on the 30-year Treasury bond maturing in February 2037.

Drafting Information

The principal authors of this notice are Paul Stern and Tony Montanaro of the Employee Plans, Tax Exempt and Government Entities Division. For further information regarding this notice, please contact the Employee Plans' taxpayer assistance telephone service at 877–829–5500 (a toll-free number), between the hours of 8:30 a.m. and 4:30 p.m. Eastern time, Monday through Friday. Mr. Stern may be reached at 202–283–9703. Mr. Montanaro may be reached at 202–283–9714. The telephone numbers in the preceding sentences are not toll-free.

Qualifying Advanced Coal Project Program

Notice 2007–52

SECTION 1. PURPOSE

This notice updates the procedures for the allocation of credits under the qualifying advanced coal project program of § 48A of the Internal Revenue Code and defines certain terms for purposes of § 48A. The purpose of the qualifying advanced coal project program is the deployment of advanced coal-based generation technologies. To further this purpose, the method of allocation is being modified for allocation rounds after 2006. Under the modified method of allocation, the U.S. Department of Energy ("DOE") will rank a certified project relative to other certified projects in each pool and credits will be allocated to projects based on the DOE ranking. The modified allocation method will substantially favor projects that capture and sequester carbon dioxide emissions and will favor to a lesser extent projects optimized for future carbon dioxide capture.

SECTION 2. BACKGROUND AND CHANGES

.01 Section 46 provides that the amount of the investment credit for any taxable year is the sum of the credits listed in § 46. That list includes the qualifying advanced coal project credit.

.02 The qualifying advanced coal project credit is provided under § 48A. Section 48A(a) provides that the qualifying advanced coal project credit for a taxable year is an amount equal to (1) 20 percent of the qualified investment (as defined in § 48A(b)) for that taxable year in certified qualifying advanced coal projects (as defined in § 48A(c)(1) and (e)) using an integrated gasification combined cycle (IGCC) (as defined in § 48A(c)(7)), and (2) 15 percent of the qualified investment for that taxable year in other certified qualifying advanced coal projects.

.03 Section 48A(d)(3)(A) provides that the aggregate credits allowed under § 48A(a) may not exceed $1.3 billion. Section 48A(d)(3)(B) provides that (i) $800 million of credits are to be allocated to IGCC projects, and (ii) $500 million of credits are to be allocated to projects that use other advanced coal-based generation technologies (as defined in § 48A(c)(2) and (f)).

.04 Section 48A(e)(3)(A) provides that the credits for IGCC projects must be allocated in accordance with the procedures set forth in § 48A(d), and in relatively equal amounts to (i) projects using bituminous coal as a primary feedstock, (ii) projects using subbituminous coal as a primary feedstock, and (iii) projects using lignite as a primary feedstock. Further, § 48A(e)(3)(B) provides that IGCC projects that include (i) greenhouse gas capture capability (as defined in § 48A(c)(5)), (ii) increased by-product utilization, and (iii) other benefits must be given high priority in the allocation of credits for IGCC projects.

.05 Section 48A(f) prescribes the requirements that must be satisfied to qualify as an advanced coal-based generation technology. These include requirements that the unit be designed to attain specified standards for emissions or removal of certain pollutants. As originally enacted, § 48A(f) required that a unit be designed to achieve 99-percent removal of sulfur dioxide. Section 203(a) of the Tax Relief and Health Care Act of 2006, Pub. L. 109–432, 120 Stat. 2922 (December 20, 2006), modified this test for units designed for the use of feedstock substantially all of which is subbituminous coal. Such a unit satisfies the modified test if it achieves either 99-percent removal of sulfur dioxide or an emission level of not more than 0.04 pounds of sulfur dioxide per million Btu, determined on a 30-day average.

.06 The at-risk rules in § 49 and the recapture and other special rules in § 50 apply to the qualifying advanced coal project credit. Further, the qualifying advanced coal project credit generally is allowed in the taxable year in which the eligible property (as defined in § 48A(c)(3)) is placed in service (as defined in section 3.04 of this notice) by the taxpayer. Pursuant to § 48A(d)(2)(E), a taxpayer that receives a certification under § 48A(d)(2)(D) has 5 years from the date of issuance of the certification to place the qualifying advanced coal project in service.

.07 Section 48A(d)(1) provides that the Secretary, in consultation with the Secretary of Energy, shall establish a qualifying advanced coal project program for the deployment of advanced coal-based generation technologies. The Treasury Department and the Internal Revenue Service established this program in Notice 2006–24, 2006–11 I.R.B. 595.

.08 This notice modifies the qualifying advanced coal project program established in Notice 2006–24 in a number of respects. The significant changes made by this notice include the following:

(1) The Large and Mid-Size Business Division (LMSB) of the Service will allocate the advanced coal project credits and issue the certification under § 48A(d)(2). The filing instructions in section 5.04 provide LMSB addresses to reflect this change.

(2) Section 3 defines certain terms for purposes of § 48A.

(3) The method of allocation is modified for allocation rounds after 2006. Under the modified method of allocation, the DOE will rank a certified project relative to other certified projects in each pool and credits will be allocated to projects based on the DOE ranking. The modified allocation method will substantially favor projects that capture and sequester carbon dioxide emissions and will favor to a lesser extent projects optimized for future carbon dioxide capture. Sections 4.02(3) and (4) reflect this change in the method by which credits under § 48A are allocated to projects.

(4) Section 4.02(8) provides that the period for submitting the application for § 48A certification (i) ends on March 3, 2008, for the 2007–08 allocation round and (ii) begins on March 4, 2008, and ends on March 2, 2009, for the 2008–09 allocation round. Changes also are made to the dates in sections 4.02(10) and (11) for accepting or rejecting a taxpayer's application for § 48A certification and for executing closing agreements.

(5) Section 4.02(9) provides that the due date for the application for DOE certification is October 31, that DOE will rank certified projects, and that the due date for the DOE certification and ranking is March 1. Section 4.02(9) also clarifies that the DOE certification and ranking (for projects determined to be feasible) are provided to the Service.

(6) Section 4.02(11) provides that a successor in interest must execute a new closing agreement with the Service no later than the due date (including extensions) of the successor in interest's Federal income tax return for the taxable year in which the transfer occurs.

(7) The information required to be included in the application for DOE certification is modified. Section 5.02 requires submission of additional information regarding the number and types of turbines to be used in the project and with respect to the sulfur dioxide removal. Appendix B provides additional information regarding program policy factors. Applicants will no longer be required to submit independent financial reports.

(8) Section 5.02(13) defines the term "substantially all" for purposes of determining whether a project's subbituminous coal usage qualifies it for the modified sulfur dioxide removal test provided in § 48A(f)(1).

(9) Section 5.03 requests that a taxpayer submit with the application for § 48A certification a declaration consenting to the disclosure by the Service of certain return information if the taxpayer is awarded an allocation of qualifying advanced coal project credits. The form of the declaration is set forth in Appendix C.

(10) Sections 5.03(1) and 5.04 require that a taxpayer submit one paper copy and one electronic version on a floppy disc or a CD of the application for § 48A certification (including the application for DOE certification).

(11) Section 7.02 provides more details on who may sign the penalties of perjury statement.

(12) Section 7.03 provides that the Service and the DOE must be informed if the plans for the project change in any significant respect from the plans set forth in the applications for § 48A and DOE certification, and also provides the consequences of any significant change to the plans set forth in the applications.

(13) Section 7.06 provides that the DOE will offer debriefings to applicants that submitted an application for DOE certification.

(14) Section 10 provides guidance regarding Freedom of Information Act requests for records relating to the qualifying advanced coal project program.

SECTION 3. DEFINITIONS

The following definitions apply for purposes of § 48A and this notice:

.01 *Coal.* Section 48A(c)(4) defines the term "coal" as meaning anthracite, bituminous coal, subbituminous coal, lignite, and peat. Coal includes waste coal (that is, usable material that is a byproduct of the previous processing of anthracite, bituminous coal, subbituminous coal, lignite, or peat). Examples of waste coal include fine coal of any of the listed ranks, coal of any of the listed ranks obtained from a refuse bank or slurry dam, anthracite culm, bituminous gob, and lignite waste.

.02 *Total Nameplate Generating Capacity.*

(1) Except as provided in section 3.02(2) of this notice, the total nameplate generating capacity of a project is the aggregate of the numbers (in megawatts) stamped on the nameplate of each generator to be used in the project.

(2) If the number stamped on the nameplate of a generator is not determined at the International Standard Organization (ISO) optimal conditions of 59 degrees Fahrenheit, 60% relative humidity, and 14.7 psia at sea level, the number stamped on the nameplate is disregarded and the generator's capacity (in megawatts) determined at such optimal conditions is used in its place.

.03 *Fuel Input.*

(1) *In general.* The term "fuel input" means, with respect to any type of fuel, the amount of such fuel used during normal plant operations. The amounts of the fuel used are measured (i) in British thermal units (Btus) on an energy input basis and (ii) pursuant to applicable standards prescribed by the American Society for Testing and Materials (ASTM). For example, § 48A(e)(1)(B) provides that the fuel input for the project, when completed, must be at least 75 percent coal. This requirement is satisfied if, after completion and during normal plant operations, coal provides 75 percent of the project's fuel measured in Btus on an energy input basis and pursuant to applicable ASTM standards.

(2) *Only normal plant operations taken into account.* Only fuel used during normal plant operations is taken into account for purposes of § 48A and sections 5.02(5) and 5.02(13) of this notice. Normal plant operations are operations other than during periods of initial plant certification, plant startup, plant shutdown, integrated gasifier shutdown for gasification system maintenance, or interruption of the coal supply to the project resulting from an event of force majeure (including an act of God, war, strike, or other similar event beyond the control of the taxpayer). For example, the fuel input during the initial plant certification may consist entirely of natural gas or other non-coal fuels because fuel used during initial plant certification is disregarded in determining whether the 75-percent coal usage requirement of § 48A(e)(1)(B) is satisfied.

.04 *Placed In Service.* For purposes of § 48A, property is placed in service in the taxable year in which the property is placed in a condition or state of readiness and availability for a specifically assigned function. *See* § 1.46–3(d)(1)(ii) of the Income Tax Regulations. Thus, a qualifying advanced coal project or eligible property (as defined in § 48A(c)(3)) that is a part of the project is placed in service in the taxable year in which the project is placed in a condition or state of readiness and availability for producing electricity from coal.

SECTION 4. QUALIFYING ADVANCED COAL PROJECT PROGRAM

.01 *In General.* The Service will consider a project under the qualifying advanced coal project program only if the DOE provides a certification ("DOE certification") and ranking (if any) for the project. Accordingly, a taxpayer must submit, for each qualifying advanced coal project: (1) an application for certification by the DOE ("application for DOE certification"), and (2) an application for certification under § 48A(d)(2) by the Service ("application for § 48A certification"). Both applications may be submitted only during the 3-year period beginning on February 21, 2006. Certifications will be issued and credits will be allocated to projects in annual allocation rounds. The initial allocation round was conducted in 2006. Additional allocation rounds will be conducted in 2007–08 and, if necessary, in 2008–09.

.02 *Program Specifications.*

(1) The Service determines the amount of the qualifying advanced coal project credits allocated to a qualifying advanced coal project at the time the Service accepts the application for § 48A certification for that project in accordance with section 4.02(10) of this notice (see section 5 of this notice for the requirements applicable to the application for DOE certification and the application for § 48A certification).

(2) The qualifying advanced coal project credits of $1.3 billion and the applications for certification are separated into the following four pools:

(a) Projects using an advanced coal-based generation technology other than IGCC. The aggregate amount of qualifying advanced coal project credit for this pool is $500 million. The maximum amount of credits that will be allocated to a project is $125 million. In the 2006 allocation round, $250 million of credits was allocated from this pool. Therefore, $250 million of credits is available for allocation from this pool in 2007–08.

(b) IGCC projects using bituminous coal as a primary feedstock. The aggregate amount of qualifying advanced coal project credit for this pool is $267 million. The maximum amount of credits that will be allocated to a project is $133.5 million. In the 2006 allocation round, $267 million of credits (the entire amount available) was allocated from this pool. Accordingly, no allocation round for this pool will be conducted in 2007–08.

(c) IGCC projects using subbituminous coal as a primary feedstock. The aggregate amount of qualifying advanced coal project credit for this pool is $267 million. The maximum amount of credits that will be allocated to a project is $133.5 million. In the 2006 allocation round, no credits were allocated from this pool. Therefore, $267 million of credits is available for allocation from this pool in 2007–08.

(d) IGCC projects using lignite as a primary feedstock. The aggregate amount of qualifying advanced coal project credit for this pool is $266 million. The maximum amount of credits that will be allocated to a project is $133 million. In the 2006 allocation round, $133 million of credits was allocated from this pool. Accordingly, $133 million of credits is available for allocation from this pool in 2007–08.

(3) For projects using an advanced coal-based generation technology other than IGCC, DOE will rank the certified projects in descending order (that is, first, second, third, etc.) and the $250 million available for allocation will be allocated as follows in the allocation round in 2007–08:

(a) If the requested allocation of credits for projects that DOE has certified for this pool does not exceed the amount available for allocation, each certified project will be allocated the full amount of credit requested.

(b) If the requested allocation of credits for projects that DOE has certified for this pool exceeds the amount available for allocation, the amount available for allocation will be allocated as follows:

(i) The project receiving the highest ranking (that is, first) will be allocated the full amount of credit requested (but not exceeding the amount available for allocation) before any credit is allocated to a lower-ranked project. The amount available for allocation is reduced by the amount of credit so allocated and only the remainder is available for allocation to a lower-ranked project.

(ii) Second and lower-ranked projects will be entitled to similar priority in the allocation of credits and allocations to such projects will similarly reduce the remainder of the amount available for allocation until the amount available for allocation from the pool is exhausted.

(4) For each IGCC pool described in section 4.02(2)(c) or (d) of this notice, DOE will rank the certified projects in descending order (that is, first, second, third, etc.) and the amount available for allocation from the pool will be allocated as follows in the allocation round in 2007–08:

(a) If the requested allocation of credits for projects that DOE has certified for an IGCC pool described in section 4.02(2)(c) or (d) of this notice does not exceed the amount available for allocation from that pool, each certified project will be allocated the full amount of credit requested.

(b) If the requested allocation of credits for projects that DOE has certified for an IGCC pool described in section 4.02(2)(c) or (d) of this notice exceeds the amount available for allocation from that pool, the amount available for allocation will be allocated as follows:

(i) The project receiving the highest ranking (that is, first) will be allocated the full amount of credit requested (but not exceeding the amount available for allocation from the pool) before any credit is allocated to a lower-ranked project. The amount available for allocation from the pool is reduced by the amount of credit so allocated and only the remainder is available for allocation to a lower-ranked project.

(ii) Second and lower-ranked projects will be entitled to similar priority in the allocation of credits and allocations to such projects will similarly reduce the remainder of the amount available for allocation from the pool until the amount available for allocation from the pool is exhausted.

(5) If the amount available for allocation from a pool is not fully allocated in the 2007–08 allocation round, a similar allocation round will be conducted in 2008–09. Generally, the results of each year will be announced. See section 5.03(2) of this notice for further information about this announcement.

(6) If the same project would otherwise be allocated credits under both the qualifying advanced coal project program under this notice and the qualifying gasification project program under Notice 2007–53, 2007–26 I.R.B. 1474, the following rules apply:

(a) The qualifying gasification project credit may not be allocated to the project with respect to any qualified investment under § 48B for which a qualifying advanced coal project credit is allowed under § 48A; and

(b) The qualifying gasification project credit may be allocated to the project with respect to the qualified investment under § 48B for which a qualifying advanced coal project credit is not allowed under § 48A.

(7) For each allocation round there will be an annual application period during which a taxpayer may file its application for § 48A certification. The Service will consider a project in an allocation round only if the application for § 48A certification for the project is submitted during the application period for that round and the DOE provides the DOE certification and the DOE ranking (if any) for the project before the end of the application period.

(8) For the allocation round conducted in 2007–08, the application period begins on October 3, 2006, and ends on March 3, 2008, and any completed application for § 48A certification received by the Service after October 2, 2006, and before March 4, 2008, will be deemed to be submitted by the taxpayer on March 3, 2008. For the allocation round to be conducted in 2008–09, the application period begins on March 4, 2008, and ends on March 2, 2009, and any completed application for § 48A certification received by the Service after March 3, 2008, and before March 3, 2009, will be deemed to be submitted by the taxpayer on March 2, 2009. For purposes of this notice, an application that is submitted by U.S. mail will be treated as received by the Service on the date of the postmark and an application submitted by a private delivery service will be treated as received by the Service on the date recorded or the date marked in accordance with § 7502(f)(2)(C).

(9) See section 5.02 of this notice and Appendix B to this notice for the information to be submitted to the DOE in an application for DOE certification. Appendix B to this notice also provides the instructions and address for filing the application for DOE certification. The DOE will determine the feasibility of the project and, if the project is determined to be feasible, will provide a DOE certification for the project to the Service. If the DOE certifies two or more projects in a pool described in section 4.02(2) of this notice, the DOE also will rank each of the projects it certifies (for example, first, second, third, etc.) relative to other certified projects in the same pool. If an application for DOE certification is postmarked on or before October 31 of a calendar year, the DOE will determine the feasibility of the project and (for projects determined to be feasible) provide the DOE certification and the DOE ranking (if any) to the Service by March 1 of the year following that calendar year.

(10) By April 30 of the calendar year in which an application for § 48A certification is deemed to be submitted (as determined under section 4.02(8) of this notice), the Service will accept or reject the taxpayer's application for § 48A certification and will notify the taxpayer, by letter, of its decision.

(11) If the taxpayer's application for § 48A certification is accepted, the acceptance letter will state the amount of the credit allocated to the project. If a credit is allocated to a taxpayer's project, the taxpayer will be required to execute a closing agreement in the form set forth in Appendix A to this notice. By June 30 of the calendar year in which an application for § 48A certification is accepted, the taxpayer must execute and return the closing agreement to the Service at the appropriate address listed in section 5.04 of this notice or listed in later guidance published in the Internal Revenue Bulletin. The Service will execute and return the closing agreement to the taxpayer by August 31 of such calendar year. The executed closing agreement applies only to the accepted taxpayer. Accordingly, any successor in interest must execute a new closing agreement with the Service no later than the due date (including extensions) of the successor in interest's Federal income tax return for the taxable year in which the transfer occurs. If the successor in interest does not execute a new closing agreement, the following rules apply:

(a) In the case of an interest acquired at or before the time the qualifying advanced coal project is placed in service, any credit allocated to the project will be fully forfeited (and rules similar to the recapture rules of § 50(a) apply with respect to qualified progress expenditures); and

(b) In the case of an interest acquired after the qualifying advanced coal project is placed in service, the project ceases to be investment credit property and the recapture rules of § 50(a) (and similar rules with respect to qualified progress expenditures) apply.

SECTION 5. APPLICATIONS FOR CERTIFICATIONS

.01 *In General.* An application for § 48A certification and a separate application for DOE certification must be submitted for each qualifying advanced coal project. If an application for DOE certification does not include all of the information required by section 5.02 of this notice and meet the requirements in sections 7.01 and 7.02 of this notice, the DOE may decline to accept the application. If an application for § 48A certification does not include all of the information listed in section 5.03(1) of this notice and meet the requirements in sections 7.01 and 7.02 of this notice, the application will not be accepted by the Service.

.02 *Information Required in the Application for DOE Certification.* An application for DOE certification must include all of the information requested in Appendix B to this notice and all of the following:

(1) The name, address, and taxpayer identification number of the taxpayer. If the taxpayer is a member of an affiliated group filing consolidated returns, also provide the name, address, and taxpayer identification number of the common parent of the group.

(2) The name and telephone number of a contact person.

(3) The name and address (or other unique identifying designation) of the qualifying advanced coal project.

(4) A statement specifying whether the project is an IGCC project or a qualifying advanced coal project that uses another advanced coal-based technology.

(5) In the case of an IGCC project, a statement specifying the type of coal (bituminous coal, subbituminous coal, or lignite) that will be the primary feedstock. An application for DOE certification with respect to an IGCC project will not be considered unless one of these types of coal is the primary feedstock. For purposes of § 48A(e)(3)(A), a type of coal is the primary feedstock only if at all times more than 50 percent of the cumulative total fuel input (coal and any other fuel input) used in normal plant operations (as defined in section 3.03(2) of this notice) of the project will consist of that type of coal.

(6) The estimated total cost of the project and the estimated total qualified investment in the eligible property that will be part of the project.

(7) The amount of the qualifying advanced coal project credit requested for the project. The amount requested must not exceed the maximum amount provided in section 4.02(2) of this notice.

(8) If the taxpayer is or will be requesting an amount of the qualifying gasification project credit under § 48B for the same project, a statement specifying the amount of credit the taxpayer is or will be requesting under § 48B.

(9) A statement specifying whether the project is a new electric generation unit (as defined in § 48A(c)(6)), a retrofit of an existing electric generation unit, or a repower of an existing electric generation unit.

(10) In the case of an IGCC project, a statement specifying whether the project is entitled to priority for greenhouse gas capture capability (as defined in § 48A(c)(5)) or increased by-product utilization and, if entitled to priority, a statement identifying which of these priorities apply to the IGCC project.

(11) A statement specifying the number and types of generators to be used in the project (for example, two combustion turbine generators and one steam turbine generator).

(12) The exact total nameplate generating capacity (as defined in section 3.02 of this notice) of the project.

(13) In the case of a project that will not achieve 99-percent removal of sulfur dioxide, a statement that the project is designed for the use of a feedstock substantially all of which is subbituminous coal and will achieve an emission level of not more than 0.04 pounds of sulfur dioxide per million Btu, determined on a 30-day average. For this purpose, a project is designed for the use of feedstock substantially all of which is subbituminous coal if at all times 80 percent or more of the cumulative total fuel input (coal and any other fuel input) used in normal plant operations (as defined in section 3.03(2) of this notice) of the project will be subbituminous coal. Such a project meets the requirements in § 48A(f)(1) by achieving either 99-percent removal of sulfur dioxide or an emission level of not more than 0.04 pounds of sulfur dioxide per million Btu, determined on a 30-day average. All other qualifying advanced coal projects must achieve 99-percent removal of sulfur dioxide.

.03 *Information To Be Included in the Application for § 48A Certification.*

(1) *Information required in the application for § 48A certification.* Pursuant to § 48A(d)(2)(B), an application for § 48A

certification must include all of the following:

(a) The name, address, and taxpayer identification number of the taxpayer. If the taxpayer is a member of an affiliated group filing consolidated returns, also provide the name, address, and taxpayer identification number of the common parent of the group.

(b) The name, telephone number, and fax number of a contact person. For such person, attach a properly executed power of attorney, preferably on Form 2848, *Power of Attorney and Declaration of Representative*.

(c) One paper copy and one electronic version on a floppy disc or a CD of the completed application for DOE certification submitted with respect to the project in accordance with section 5.02 of this notice.

(2) *Consent to disclosure of allocation*. In order to provide the public with information on how the qualifying advanced coal project credits authorized by Congress have been allocated and facilitate oversight of the qualifying advanced coal project program, the Service intends to publish the results of the allocation process. The Service expects that a list identifying the taxpayers and projects to which credits are allocated and specifying the amount of credit allocated to each would be of particular interest to the public. Pursuant to § 6103, consent is required in order to disclose any return information with respect to taxpayers awarded an allocation. Therefore, the Service requests that each taxpayer submit with the application for § 48A certification a declaration, consenting to the disclosure by the Service of the following return information in the event a qualifying advanced coal project credit is allocated to the taxpayer's project: (a) the name of the taxpayer; (b) if the taxpayer is a member of an affiliated group filing consolidated returns, the name of the common parent of the group; (c) the type and location of the project to which the application relates; and (d) the amount of the qualifying advanced coal project credit allocated to the project. To provide a valid consent, the declaration must be in the form set forth in Appendix C. A taxpayer is not required to consent to disclosure of this information in order to receive an allocation of the qualifying advanced coal project credit, and neither the presence nor the absence of such a consent will be taken into account in the evaluation of a taxpayer's application. The Service will not publish any return information relating to a taxpayer if the taxpayer does not consent to disclosure of this information or does not receive an allocation of the qualifying advanced coal project credit.

.04 *Instructions and Address for Filing § 48A Application*. One paper copy and one electronic version on a floppy disc or a CD of the application for § 48A certification must be submitted. Applications for § 48A certification should be marked: SECTION 48A APPLICATION FOR CERTIFICATION. There is no user fee for these applications.

(1) Applications submitted by U.S. mail must be sent to:

Internal Revenue Service
Industry Director, Natural Resources and Construction
Attn: Executive Assistant
1919 Smith Street
Stop HOU 1000
Houston, TX 77002

Applications submitted by a private delivery service must be sent to:

Internal Revenue Service
Industry Director, Natural Resources and Construction
Attn: Executive Assistant
1919 Smith Street, Floor P2
Stop HOU 1000
Houston, TX 77002

(2) Applications may also be hand delivered Monday through Friday between the hours of 8 a.m. and 4 p.m. Central time to:

Internal Revenue Service
Industry Director, Natural Resources and Construction
Attn: Executive Assistant
1919 Smith Street, Floor P2
Stop HOU 1000
Houston, TX 77002

SECTION 6. ISSUANCE OF CERTIFICATION

.01 *In General*. Section 48A(d)(2)(D) provides that a taxpayer shall have 2 years from the date of acceptance of the § 48A application during which to provide evidence that the criteria set forth in § 48A(e)(2) have been met. Pursuant to § 48A(e)(2), a project shall be eligible for certification only if (A) the taxpayer has received all federal and state environmental authorizations or reviews necessary to commence construction of the project, and (B) the taxpayer, except in the case of a retrofit or repower of an existing generation unit, has purchased or entered into a binding contract for the purchase of the main steam turbine or turbines for the project, except that this contract may be contingent upon receipt of a certification under § 48A(d)(2). Section 48A(d)(2)(E) provides that a taxpayer that receives a certification has 5 years from the date of issuance of the certification to place the project in service and that the certification is void if the project is not placed in service by the end of that five-year period.

.02 *Requirements for Certification*. Within 2 years from the date that the Service accepts the taxpayer's application for § 48A certification under section 4.02(10) of this notice, the taxpayer must submit to the Service documentation establishing that the requirements of § 48A(e)(2) are satisfied. See also sections 7.01 and 7.02 of this notice for other requirements that must be satisfied. The taxpayer should mark the package "SECTION 48A CERTIFICATION REQUIREMENTS" and send it to the appropriate address listed in section 5.04 of this notice or listed in later guidance published in the Internal Revenue Bulletin.

.03 *Service's Action on Certification*. After receiving the material in section 6.02 of this notice, the Service will decide whether or not to certify the project and will notify the taxpayer, by letter, of that decision. If the Service certifies the project, the date of this letter is the date of issuance of the certification.

SECTION 7. OTHER REQUIREMENTS

.01 *Signature*. Each submission under sections 5 and 6 of this notice must be signed and dated by the taxpayer. A stamped signature or faxed signature is not permitted.

.02 *Penalties of Perjury Statement*.

(1) Each submission under sections 5 and 6 of this notice must be accompanied by the following declaration: "Under

penalties of perjury, I declare that I have examined this submission, including accompanying documents, and, to the best of my knowledge and belief, all of the facts contained herein are true, correct, and complete."

(2) The declaration must be signed and dated by the taxpayer. The person signing for the taxpayer must have personal knowledge of the facts. Further, the declaration must be signed by an officer on behalf of a corporation, a general partner on behalf of a state-law partnership, a member-manager on behalf of a limited liability company, a trustee on behalf of a trust, and the proprietor in the case of a sole proprietorship. If the taxpayer is a member of an affiliated group filing consolidated returns, the declaration also must be signed by a duly authorized officer of the common parent of the group. A stamped signature or faxed signature is not permitted.

.03 *Significant Change in Plans.* The Service and DOE must be informed if the plans for the project change in any significant respect from the plans set forth in the applications for § 48A and DOE certification. Any significant change to the plans set forth in the applications will have the following effects:

(1) The Service will disregard any certification or ranking provided by DOE unless DOE is informed of the change before the date on which DOE provides the certification or ranking (that is, the Service will not consider the project unless DOE provides a new, timely certification and ranking (if any) on or after the date on which DOE is informed of the change); and

(2) Any acceptance provided by the Service and any allocation or certification based on that acceptance will be void unless the Service is informed of the change before the date on which the acceptance is provided under section 4.02(10) of this notice.

.04 *Effect of an Acceptance, Allocation, or Certification.* An acceptance, allocation, or certification by the Service under this notice is not a determination that a project qualifies for the qualifying advanced coal project credit under § 48A. The Service may, upon examination (and after any appropriate consultation with DOE), determine that the project does not qualify for this credit.

.05 *No Right to a Conference or Appeal.* A taxpayer does not have a right to a conference relating to any matters under this notice. Further, a taxpayer does not have a right to appeal the decisions made under this notice (including the acceptance or rejection of the application for DOE or § 48A certification, the amount of credit allocated to the project, or whether or not to certify the project) to an Associate Chief Counsel or any other official of the Service.

.06 *DOE Debriefings.* Although a taxpayer does not have a right to a conference relating to any matters under this notice, the DOE will offer debriefings to all applicants that submitted an application for DOE certification. This debriefing will be held by the DOE after the Service has accepted the applications for § 48A certification (as determined under section 4.02(10) of this notice). The sole purpose of the debriefing is to enable applicants to develop better proposals in future allocation rounds by providing DOE's review of the strengths and weaknesses of their application for DOE certification.

SECTION 8. REVIEW AND REDISTRIBUTION

.01 *In General.* Section 48A(d)(4)(A) provides that the credits allocated under § 48A must be reviewed not later than August 8, 2011. Pursuant to § 48A(d)(4)(B), credits available under § 48A(d)(3)(B)(i) and (ii) may be reallocated if (i) there is an insufficient quantity of qualifying applications for certification pending at the time of the review; or (ii) any certification made pursuant to § 48A(d)(2) has been revoked pursuant to § 48A(d)(2)(D). If credits under § 48A(d)(3)(B)(i) and (ii) are available for reallocation, § 48A(d)(4)(C) authorizes the conduct of an additional program for applications for certification.

.02 *Review and Redistribution of Credits.*

(1) *In general.* If, after the allocation round in 2008–09, the entire credit for a pool is not fully subscribed (that is, the aggregate credit for the pool has not been fully allocated), the remaining credits from that pool will be reallocated to pools that have been fully subscribed. Credits from pools not fully subscribed will be reallocated to fully subscribed pools in proportion to the aggregate amounts of credit specified for the fully subscribed pools in section 4.02(2) of this notice. Future guidance will prescribe the procedures applicable to applications for certification with respect to the reallocated credits.

(2) *Reduction or forfeiture of allocated credits.* Under the closing agreement set forth in Appendix A to this notice, the qualifying advanced coal project credits allocated under section 4 of this notice will be reduced or forfeited in certain situations. A taxpayer must notify the Service of the amount of any reduction or forfeiture required under the closing agreement. This notification must be sent to the appropriate address listed in section 5.04 of this notice or listed in later guidance published in the Internal Revenue Bulletin.

The amount of any reduction or forfeiture of the allocated credits will be returned to the appropriate allocation pool and included in the aggregate credit remaining to be allocated in the allocation round following the reduction or forfeiture. If the reduction or forfeiture occurs after the allocation round in 2008–09, future guidance will prescribe procedures applicable to applications for certification with respect to the returned credits.

SECTION 9. QUALIFIED PROGRESS EXPENDITURES

.01 Section 48A(b)(3) provides that rules similar to the rules of § 46(c)(4) and (d) (as in effect on the day before the enactment of the Revenue Reconciliation Act of 1990) shall apply for purposes of § 48A. Former §§ 46(c)(4) and 46(d) provided the rules for claiming the investment credit on qualified progress expenditures (as defined in former § 46(d)(3)) made by a taxpayer during the taxable year for the construction of progress expenditure property (as defined in former § 46(d)(2)).

.02 In the case of self-constructed property (as defined in former § 46(d)(5)(A)), former § 46(d)(3)(A) defined qualified progress expenditures to mean the amount that is properly chargeable (during the taxable year) to capital account with respect to that property. With respect to a qualifying advanced coal project that is self-constructed property, amounts paid or incurred are chargeable to capital account at the time and to the extent they are properly includible in computing basis under the taxpayer's method of accounting (for example, after applying the requirements of § 461, including the economic performance requirement of § 461(h)).

.03 To claim the qualifying advanced coal project credit on the qualified progress expenditures paid or incurred by a taxpayer during the taxable year for construction of a qualifying advanced coal project, the taxpayer must make an election under the rules set forth in § 1.46–5(o) of the Income Tax Regulations. A taxpayer may not make the qualified progress expenditures election for a qualifying advanced coal project until the taxpayer has received an acceptance letter for the project under section 4.02(10) of this notice.

.04 If a taxpayer makes the qualified progress expenditures election pursuant to section 9.03 of this notice, rules similar to the recapture rules in § 50(a)(2)(A)-(D) apply. In addition to the cessation events listed in § 50(a)(2)(A), examples of other events that will cause the project to cease being a qualifying advanced coal project are:

(1) Failure to satisfy any of the certification requirements in § 48A(e)(2) within 2 years from the date that the Service accepted the taxpayer's application for § 48A certification for the project under section 4.02(10) of this notice;

(2) Failure to receive a certification for the project in accordance with section 6.03 of this notice;

(3) Failure to place the project in service within 5 years from the date of issuance of the certification under section 6.03 of this notice; or

(4) A significant change to the plans for the project as set forth in the applications for § 48A and DOE certification if, under section 7.03 of this notice, the Service's acceptance of the project is void as a result of the change.

SECTION 10. DISCLOSURE OF INFORMATION

.01 *In general.* Any information contained in the application for DOE certification, the application for § 48A certification, or the documentation submitted by the taxpayer pursuant to section 6.02 of this notice is subject to § 6103 and to any other applicable exemption set forth in the Freedom of Information Act (the FOIA). Examples of FOIA exemptions include the FOIA trade secrets and commercial or financial information exemption of 5 U.S.C. 552(b)(4) and the FOIA personal privacy exemption of 5 U.S.C. 552(b)(6)).

.02 *FOIA requests.* Anyone interested in submitting a request for records under the FOIA with respect to the qualifying advanced coal project program under § 48A (including a request for records relating to the application for DOE certification) should direct a request that conforms to the Service's FOIA regulations, found at 26 C.F.R. § 601.702, to the following address:

IRS FOIA Request
Baltimore Disclosure Office
Room 940
31 Hopkins Plaza
Baltimore, MD 21201

SECTION 11. EFFECT ON OTHER DOCUMENTS

Notice 2006–24 is clarified, modified, amplified, and superseded.

SECTION 12. EFFECTIVE DATE

This notice is effective June 7, 2007.

SECTION 13. PAPERWORK REDUCTION ACT

The collection of information contained in this notice has been reviewed and approved by the Office of Management and Budget in accordance with the Paperwork Reduction Act (44 U.S.C. § 3507) under control number 1545–2003.

An agency may not conduct or sponsor, and a person is not required to respond to, a collection of information unless the collection of information displays a valid OMB control number.

The collections of information in this notice are in sections 4, 5, 6, 7, 8, and Appendix B of this notice. This information is required to obtain an allocation of qualifying advanced coal project credits. This information will be used by the Service to verify that the taxpayer is eligible for the qualifying advanced coal project credits. The collection of information is required to obtain a benefit. The likely respondents are business or other for-profit institutions.

The estimated total annual reporting burden is 4,950 hours.

The estimated annual burden per respondent varies from 70 to 150 hours, depending on individual circumstances, with an estimated average of 110 hours. The estimated number of respondents is 45.

The estimated annual frequency of responses is on occasion.

Books or records relating to a collection of information must be retained as long as their contents may become material in the administration of any internal revenue law. Generally, tax returns and tax return information are confidential, as required by 26 U.S.C. § 6103.

SECTION 14. DRAFTING INFORMATION

The principal author of this notice is Ruba Nasrallah of the Office of Associate Chief Counsel (Income Tax & Accounting). For further information regarding this notice, contact Jaime Park of the Office of Associate Chief Counsel (Passthroughs & Special Industries) at (202) 622–3110 (not a toll-free call). For further information regarding the application for § 48A certification, the documentation to be submitted to the Service establishing that the requirements of § 48A(e)(2) are satisfied, and the issuance of the certification that the requirements of § 48A(e)(2) are satisfied, contact Kimberly Edwards, Executive Assistant, Office of the Industry Director, Natural Resources and Construction, at (713) 209–3615 (not a toll-free number).

APPENDIX A

CLOSING AGREEMENT

Under § 7121 of the Internal Revenue Code, [insert taxpayer's name, address, and identifying number] ("Taxpayer") and the Commissioner of Internal Revenue ("Commissioner") make the following closing agreement:

WHEREAS:

1. On or before March [insert date and year], Taxpayer submitted to the Internal Revenue Service ("IRS"), an application for certification under the qualifying advanced coal project program described in Notice 2007–52 ("Application for § 48A Certification");

2. Taxpayer's Application for § 48A Certification is for the qualifying advanced coal project (the "Project") described below—

(1) The Project will use [insert either "an integrated gasification combined cycle (as defined in § 48A(c)(7))" or "an advanced coal-based technology (as defined in § 48A(c)(2) and (f)) other than an integrated gasification combined cycle"];

(2) The Project will be located at [insert address or other identifying designation];

(3) The Project is [insert either: "a new electric generation unit (as defined in § 48A(c)(6))"; "a retrofit of an existing electric generation unit (as defined in § 48A(c)(6))"; or "a repower of an existing electric generation unit (as defined in § 48a(c)(6)");

(4) The Project will have a total nameplate generating capacity (as defined in section 3.02 of Notice 2007–52) of at least [insert number] megawatts;

[If the Project is an integrated gasification combined cycle project, insert:

(5) At all times more than 50 percent of the cumulative total fuel input (as defined in section 3.03(1) of Notice 2007–52 and including coal and any other fuel input) used during normal plant operations (as defined in section 3.03(2) of Notice 2007–52) for the Project will be [insert either: "bituminous coal"; "subbituminous coal"; or "lignite"];] and

3. On [insert date of acceptance letter issued under section 4.02(10) of Notice 2007–52], the IRS accepted Taxpayer's Application for § 48A Certification for the Project and allocated a qualifying advanced coal project credit under § 48A in the amount of $[insert number] to the Project.

NOW IT IS HEREBY DETERMINED AND AGREED FOR FEDERAL INCOME TAX PURPOSES THAT:

1. The total amount of the qualifying advanced coal project credit to be claimed for the Project under § 48A(a) must not exceed $[insert the number in WHEREAS clause #3].

2. If Taxpayer fails to satisfy any of the certification requirements in § 48A(e)(2) within the time specified in § 48A(d)(2)(D) (2 years from [insert the date in WHEREAS clause #3]), or if the IRS does not issue a certification for the Project under Notice 2007–52, the qualifying advanced coal project credit in the amount of $[insert the number in WHEREAS clause #3] allocated to the Project is fully forfeited.

3. If the Project is not placed in service by Taxpayer within 5 years of the date of issuance of the certification as determined under section 6.03 of Notice 2007–52, the qualifying advanced coal project credit in the amount of $[insert the number in WHEREAS clause #3] allocated to the Project is fully forfeited.

4. If the plans for the Project change in any significant respect from the plans set forth in the application for DOE certification (as defined in section 4.01 of Notice 2007–52) and the Application for § 48A Certification (as defined in section 4.01 of Notice 2007–52) and, under section 7.03 of Notice 2007–52, the acceptance of Taxpayer's Application for § 48A Certification on [insert the date in WHEREAS clause #3] is void, the qualifying advanced coal project credit in the amount of $[insert the number in WHEREAS clause #3] allocated to the Project is fully forfeited.

[If the Project is not an integrated gasification combined cycle project, insert:

5. If the Project fails to satisfy any of the requirements in § 48A(e)(1)(A), (C), (D), (E), and (F) for a qualifying advanced coal project or, during normal plant operations (as defined in section 3.03(2) of Notice 2007–52), fails to satisfy the requirement in § 48A(e)(1)(B) for a qualifying advanced coal project—

(1) at the time the Project is placed in service, the qualifying advanced coal project credit in the amount of $[insert the number in WHEREAS clause #3] allocated to the Project is fully forfeited; and

(2) after the Project is placed in service (and after satisfying all such requirements at the time the Project is placed in service), the Project ceases to be investment credit property and the recapture rules of § 50(a) apply.]

[If the Project is an integrated gasification combined cycle project, insert:

5. (1) If the Project fails to satisfy any of the requirements in § 48A(e)(1)(A), (C), (D), (E), and (F) for a qualifying advanced coal project or, during normal plant operations (as defined in section 3.03(2) of Notice 2007–52), fails to satisfy the requirement in § 48A(e)(1)(B) for a qualifying advanced coal project—

(a) at the time the Project is placed in service, the qualifying advanced coal project credit in the amount of $[insert the number in WHEREAS clause #3] allocated to the Project is fully forfeited; and

(b) after the Project is placed in service (and after satisfying all such requirements at the time the Project is placed in service), the Project ceases to be investment credit property and the recapture rules of § 50(a) apply.

(2) If at any time more than 50 percent of the cumulative total fuel input (as defined in section 3.03(1) of Notice 2007–52 and including coal and any other fuel input) used during normal plant operations (as defined in section 3.03(2) of Notice 2007–52) is not [insert the primary feedstock in WHEREAS clause #2(5)], the Project ceases to be investment credit property and the recapture rules of § 50(a) apply.]

6. Taxpayer will not claim the qualifying gasification project credit under § 48B for any qualified investment for which the qualifying advanced coal project credit is allowed under § 48A.

7. If Taxpayer elects to claim the qualifying advanced coal project credit on the qualified progress expenditures paid or incurred by Taxpayer during the taxable year(s) during which the Project is under construction and the Project ceases to be a qualifying advanced coal project (whether before, at the time, or after the Project is placed in service), rules similar to the recapture rules in § 50(a)(2)(A) through (D) apply.

8. This agreement applies only to Taxpayer. Any successor in interest must execute a new closing agreement with the IRS. If the interest is acquired at or before the time the Project is placed in service and the successor in interest fails to execute a new closing agreement, the qualifying advanced coal project credit in the amount of $[insert the number in WHEREAS clause #3] allocated to the Project is fully forfeited. If the interest is acquired after the time the Project is placed in service and the successor in interest fails to execute a new closing agreement, the Project ceases to be investment credit property and the recapture rules of § 50(a) apply.

THIS AGREEMENT IS FINAL AND CONCLUSIVE EXCEPT:

1. The matter it relates to may be reopened in the event of fraud, malfeasance, or misrepresentation of a material fact;

2. It is subject to the Internal Revenue Code sections that expressly provide that effect be given to their provisions (including any stated exception for § 7122) notwithstanding any law or rule of law; and

3. If it relates to a tax period ending after the date of this Closing Agreement, it is subject to any law enacted after such date, which applies to the tax period.

By signing, the parties certify that they have read and agreed to the terms of this Closing Agreement.

Taxpayer: [insert name and identifying number]

By: ________________________________ **Date Signed:** ________________

[insert name]

Title: [insert title]
[insert taxpayer's name]

Commissioner of Internal Revenue

By: ________________________________ **Date Signed:** ________________

[insert name]

Title: [insert title]

I have examined the specific matters involved and recommend the acceptance of the proposed agreement.

(Receiving Officer) ______________________

(Title) ______________________

Date Signed ______________________

I have reviewed the specific matters involved and recommend the acceptance of the proposed agreement.

(Reviewing Officer) ______________________

(Title) ______________________

Date Signed ______________________

APPENDIX B

APPLICATION FOR DOE CERTIFICATION

REQUEST FOR SUPPLEMENTAL APPLICATION INFORMATION FOR DOE

The Internal Revenue Service ("IRS") and the Department of Energy ("DOE") seek to certify applications that demonstrate a high likelihood of being successfully implemented by the applicants. To qualify, projects must be economically feasible and use the appropriate clean coal technology.

This request for submission of supplemental application information:

1. Describes the information to be provided by the applicant seeking a certification of feasibility, and
2. Lists the evaluation criteria and Program Policy Factors to be used by DOE in the evaluation of applications.

In conducting this evaluation, the DOE may utilize assistance and advice from qualified personnel from other Federal agencies and/or non-conflicted contractors. DOE will obtain assurances in advance from all evaluators that application information shall be kept confidential and used only for evaluation purposes. DOE reserves the right to request clarifications and/or supplemental information from some or all applicants through written submissions and/or oral presentations.

Notice is given that DOE may determine whether or not to provide a certification to the IRS at any time after the application has been received, without further exchanges or discussions. Therefore, all applicants are advised to submit their most complete and responsive application.

Applications will not be returned.

SUBMISSION INFORMATION FOR DOE CERTIFICATION APPLICATION

A. General

This request, together with the information in sections 5.02, 7.01, and 7.02 of Notice 2007–52 includes all the information needed to complete an application for DOE certification. All applications shall be prepared in accordance with this request in order to provide a standard basis for evaluation and to ensure that each application will be uniform as to format and sequence.

Each application should clearly demonstrate the applicant's capability, knowledge, and experience in regard to the requirements described herein.

Applicants should fully address the requirements of Notice 2007–52 and this request and **not** rely on the presumed background knowledge of reviewers. DOE may reject an application that does not follow the instructions regarding the organization and content of the application when the nature of the deviation and/or omission precludes meaningful review of the application.

B. Unnecessarily Elaborate Applications

Unnecessarily elaborate brochures or other presentations beyond those sufficient to present a complete and effective application are not desired. Elaborate art work, graphics and pictures are neither required nor encouraged.

C. Application Submission for DOE Certification

The application submission to DOE must include the information and documentation required by sections 5.02, 7.01, and 7.02 of Notice 2007–52.

An application to DOE will not be considered in the allocation round conducted in 2007–08 unless it is postmarked by October 31, 2007, and will not be considered in the allocation round conducted in 2008–09 unless it is postmarked by October 31, 2008. Two paper copies and one electronic version on a floppy disc or a CD of the Application must be submitted to:

Melissa Robe
National Energy Technology Laboratory
3610 Collins Ferry Road
Morgantown, WV 26507

Note that under section 5.03(1) of Notice 2007–52, one paper copy and one electronic version must be sent to the IRS as part of the application for IRS certification. The application for IRS certification will not be considered in the allocation round conducted in 2007–08 unless it is submitted to the IRS by March 3, 2008, and will not be considered in the allocation round conducted in 2008–09 unless it is submitted to the IRS by March 2, 2009.

THE INFORMATION REQUIRED BY THIS REQUEST MUST BE SUBMITTED USING THE FORMAT AND THE HEADINGS OF THE "PROJECT INFORMATION MEMORANDUM" AS DESCRIBED BELOW.

To aid in evaluation, applications shall be clearly and concisely written and logically assembled. All pages of each part shall be appropriately numbered and identified with the name of the applicant and the date.

The application, including the Project Information Memorandum, MUST be formatted in one of the following software applications:

Microsoft Word^{tm} 2002 or later edition
Microsoft Excel^{tm} 2002 or later edition
Adobe Acrobat^{tm} PDF 6.0 or later edition

Financial models should be submitted using the Excel^{tm} spreadsheet and must include calculation formulas and assumptions.

The applicant is responsible for the integrity and structure of the electronic files. The DOE will not be responsible for reformatting, restructuring or converting any files submitted under this announcement.

The Project Information Memorandum, *excluding Appendices*, shall not exceed seventy-five (75) pages. Pages in excess of the page limitation will not be considered for evaluation. All text shall be typed, single spaced, using 12 point font, 1 inch margins, and unreduced 8–1/2-inch by 11-inch pages. Illustrations and charts shall be legible with all text in legible font. Pages shall be sequentially numbered. Except as otherwise noted herein the page guidelines previously set forth constitute a limitation on the total amount of material that may be submitted for evaluation. No material may be incorporated in any application by reference as a means to circumvent the page limitation.

D. Form of Project Information Memorandum

PROJECT INFORMATION MEMORANDUM

I. SUMMARY AND INTRODUCTION

- Description of the Project
- Financing and Ownership Structure
- Describe the main parties to the project, including background, ownership and related experience
- Current Project Status and Schedule to Beginning of Construction

II. TECHNOLOGY AND TECHNICAL INFORMATION

Provide a description of the proposed technology, including sufficient supporting information (such as vendor guarantees, process flow diagrams, equipment descriptions, information on each major process unit and the total plant, compositions of major streams, and the technical plan for achieving the goals proposed for the project) as would be needed to allow DOE to confirm that the technical requirements of § 48A are met. Specifically the applicant should:

- Provide evidence sufficient to demonstrate that the proposed technology meets the definition of "Advanced Coal-Based Generation Technology," either as integrated gasification combined cycle (IGCC) technology, or other advanced coal-based electric generation technology meeting the heat rate requirement of 8530 Btu/kWh. For advanced coal-based electric generation:
  - The applicant must provide evidence sufficient to justify the actual heat rate and heat rate corrected to conditions specified in § 48A(f)(2)
  - For projects including existing units, the applicant must provide evidence sufficient to justify that the proposed technology meets heat rate requirements specified in § 48A(f)(3)
- Provide evidence sufficient to justify that the proposed project is designed to meet the following performance requirements:
  - SO2 (subbituminous coal is 80 percent or more of fuel input)........99 percent removal or emissions not more than 0.04 lbs/MMBTU
  - SO2 (subbituminous coal is not more than 80 percent of fuel input)..........................99 percent removal
  - SO2 (for all projects other than subbituminous coal projects).......................99 percent removal
  - NOx emissions..............0.07 lbs / MMBTU
  - PM emissions.................0.015 lbs / MMBTU
  - Hg percent removal.........90 percent
- Provide evidence sufficient to demonstrate that the project meets the requirements for qualifying advanced coal projects as specified under § 48A(e)(1) including:
  - The project will power a new electric generation unit or retrofit/repower an existing electric generation unit. At least 50% of the useful output of the project is electrical power.
  - The fuel for the project is at least 75% coal (as defined in § 48A(c)(4) and section 3.01 of Notice 2007–52), on an energy input basis.
  - The project is located at one site and has a total nameplate electric power generating capacity (as defined in section 3.02 of Notice 2007–52) of at least 400 MW

III. APPLICANT'S CAPABILITY TO ACCOMPLISH THE TECHNICAL OBJECTIVES

Provide a narrative supporting the Applicant's capability to accomplish the technical objectives of the proposed project, including supporting documentation demonstrating that the applicant has assembled a team that is formally committed to participate in the proposed project.

- Provide information to support that the applicant has assembled a team with the skills and resources needed to implement the project as proposed. Provide signed agreements or letters from team members demonstrating that the proposed team members are fully committed to the project.
- Provide information, including examples of prior similar projects completed by applicant, EPC contractor, and suppliers of major subsystems or equipment, which support the capabilities of the applicant and its team members to design, construct, permit, and operate the facility. The applicant should demonstrate that the team members have a corporate history of successful completion of similar projects.
- Provide information to support that key personnel of the applicant and its team members have knowledge, experience, and adequate degree of involvement to successfully implement the project.
- Include the project status and relevant information from ongoing engineering activities. Also include in an appendix any engineering report or reports used by the applicant to develop the project and to estimate costs and operating performance. Include copies of any signed agreements to support project status claims regarding preliminary design studies, FEED, and EPC-type agreements.

IV. PRIORITY FOR INTEGRATED GASIFICATION COMBINED CYCLE PROJECTS

For IGCC Projects, the applicant must submit information sufficient for categorization and prioritization of projects for certification, including:

- Identification of the primary feedstock (as defined in section 5.02(5) of Notice 2007–52), and all other feedstocks.
- If applicable, evidence demonstrating that the project will be capable of adding components that can capture, separate and permanently sequester greenhouse gases.
- A plan showing how project by-products will be marketed and utilized.
- Other benefits, if any.

V. SITE CONTROL AND OWNERSHIP

Provide evidence that demonstrates the overall feasibility of implementing the project at the proposed site.

- Provide evidence that the applicant owns or controls a site in the United States of sufficient size to allow the proposed project to be constructed and operated on a long-term basis. Documentation such as a deed demonstrating the applicant owns the project site, a signed option to purchase the site from the site owner, or a letter of intent by the site owner to sell the site to the applicant should be provided.
- Describe the current infrastructure at the site available to meet the needs of the project.
- Provide documentation supporting applicant's conclusion that the proposed site can fully meet all environmental, coal supply, water supply, transmission interconnect, and public policy requirements. Such documentation may include signed agreements, letters of intent, or term sheets, such as coal supply, water supply, and product transportation, etc., and regulatory approvals supporting the key claims.
- Provide detailed plans, schedules and status updates, particularly, for sites with pre-existing conditions that could impact the proposed project. Pre-existing conditions may include, but are not limited to, sites with mandated environmental remediation efforts; brown-field sites that will require building demolition; or sites requiring substantial rerouting of existing roads, railroads, transmission lines or pipelines prior to the start of the project.
- Applicants must select one "proposed site." However, projects with key physical or logistical elements that require close integration with another system for the project to succeed should provide information on all integrated systems regardless of where they are located. Example 1: a power plant designed to operate exclusively on coal from a to-be-opened mine should provide supporting documentation for the new mine. Example 2: an oxygen-blown IGCC plant planning to purchase oxygen from a third party who will construct a plant exclusively for this project should provide documentation for the oxygen supplier.

VI. UTILIZATION OF PROJECT OUTPUT

Provide evidence that demonstrates that a majority of the project output is reasonably expected to be acquired or utilized.

- Provide a projection of the anticipated costs of electricity and other marketable by-products produced by the plant.
- Provide documentation establishing that a majority of the output of the plant is reasonably expected to be acquired or utilized. Such documentation should be signed by authorizing officials of both the buyer and seller, and may include: Sales Agreements, Letters of Intent, Memoranda of Understanding, Option Agreements, and Power Purchase Agreements.
- Describe any energy sales arrangements that exist or that may be contemplated (*e.g.*, a Power Purchase Agreement or Energy Sales Agreement) and summarize their key terms and conditions.
- Include as an appendix any independent Energy Price Market Study that has been done in connection with this project, or if no independent market study has been completed, provide a copy of the applicant-prepared market study.
- Identify and describe any firm arrangements to sell non-power output, and provide any evidence of such arrangements. If the project produces a product in addition to power, include as an appendix any related market study of price and volume of sales expected for that product.

VII. PROJECT ECONOMICS

Describe the project economics and provide satisfactory evidence of economic feasibility as demonstrated through the financial forecast and the underlying project assumptions. The project economic and financial assumptions should be clearly stated and explained.

Show calculation of the amount of tax credit applied for based on allowable cost.

VIII. PROJECT DEVELOPMENT AND FINANCIAL PLAN

Provide the total project budget and major plant costs (*e.g.*, development, operating, capital, construction, and financing costs). Provide the estimated annual budget for and source of project development costs from the time of the application until the beginning of construction, including legal, engineering, financial, environmental, overhead, and other development costs. Describe the overall approach to project development and financing sufficient to demonstrate project viability. Provide a complete explanation of the source and amount of project equity. Provide a complete explanation of the source and amount of project debt. Provide the audited financial statements for the most recently ended three fiscal years and quarterly interim financial statements for the current fiscal year for (a) the applicant, (b) for any of the project parties providing funding, and (c) for any third party funding source. If the applicant or another party does not have audited financial statements, the applicant or the party should provide equivalent financial statements prepared by the applicant or the party, in accordance with Generally Accepted Accounting Principles, and certified as to accuracy and completeness by the Chief Financial Officer of the party providing the statements.

For internally financed projects, provide evidence that the applicant has sufficient assets to fund the project with its own resources. Identify any internal approvals required to commit such assets. Include in an appendix copies of any board resolution or other approval authorizing the applicant to commit funds and proceed with the project.

For projects financed through debt instruments either unsecured or secured by assets other than the project, provide evidence that the applicant has sufficient creditworthiness to obtain such financing along with a discussion of the status of such instruments. Identify any internal approvals required to commit the applicant to pursue such financing. Include in an appendix copies of any board resolution or other approval authorizing the applicant to commit to such financing.

For projects financed through investor equity contributions, describe the source and status of each contribution. Discuss each investor's financial capability to meet its commitments. Include in an appendix, copies of any executed investment agreements.

If financing through a public offering or private placement of either debt or equity is planned for the project, provide the expected debt rating for the issue and an explanation of applicant's justification for the rating. Describe the status of any discussions with prospective investment bankers or other financial advisors.

Include as an appendix copies of any existing funding commitments or expressions of interest from funding sources for the project.

For projects employing non-recourse or limited recourse debt financing, provide a complete discussion of the approach to, and status of, such financing. In an appendix, provide an Excel based financial model of the project, with formulas, so that review of the model calculations and assumptions may be facilitated; provide *pro-forma* project financial, economic, capital cost, and operating assumptions, including detail of all project capital costs, development costs, interest during construction, transmission interconnection costs, other operating expenses, and all other costs and expenses.

IX. PROJECT CONTRACT STRUCTURE

Describe the current status of each of the agreements set forth below. Include as an appendix copies of the contracts or summaries of the key provisions of each of the following agreements:

- Power Purchase Agreement (if not fully explained in Section IV).
- Coal Supply: describe the source and price of coal supply for the project. Include as an appendix any studies of coal supply price and amount that have been prepared. Include a summary of the coal supply contract and a signed copy of the contract.
- Coal Transportation: explain the arrangements for transporting coal, including costs.
- Operations & Maintenance Agreement: include a summary of the terms and conditions of the contract and a copy of the contract.
- Shareholders Agreement: summarize key terms and include the agreement as an appendix.
- Engineering, Procurement and Construction Agreement: describe the key terms of the existing or expected EPC contract arrangement, including firm price, liquidated damages, hold-backs, performance guarantees, etc.
- Water Supply Agreement: confirm the amount, source, and cost of water supply.
- Transmission Interconnection Agreement: explain the requirements to connect to the system and the current status of negotiations in this respect.

X. PERMITS INCLUDING ENVIRONMENTAL AUTHORIZATIONS

- Provide a complete list of all federal, state, and local permits, including environmental authorizations or reviews, necessary to commence construction of the project.
- Explain what actions have been taken to date to satisfy the required authorizations and reviews, and the status of each.
- Provide a description of the applicant's plan to obtain and complete all necessary permits, and environmental authorizations and reviews.

XI. STEAM TURBINE PURCHASE

- If applicant plans to purchase a steam turbine or turbines for the project, indicate the prospective vendors for the turbine and explain the current status of purchase negotiations, and provide a timeline for negotiation and purchase with expected purchase date.

XII. PROJECT SCHEDULE

- Provide an overall project schedule which includes technical, business, financial, permitting and other factors to substantiate that the project will meet the 2 year project certification and 5 year placed-in-service requirement.
- The project schedule should be comprehensive and provide sufficient detail to demonstrate how applicant will meet the certification and placed-in-service requirements. The schedule should demonstrate that the applicant understands the required tasks, and has allowed realistic times for accomplishing the technical and financial tasks. The schedule should include the milestone accomplishments needed to obtain the financing for the project.
- Applicants should document their progress toward meeting the 2 year completion of permitting deadline. Existing permits and permit applications must be specific to the project proposed. If existing permits are not specific for the proposed coal-based project (*e.g.*, the permits are for oil-fired or natural gas-based units), specific plans, procedures and schedules for reapplying, modifying and/or renegotiating permits should be provided. Any local, state or federal permitting schedules which may impact the overall project schedule should be included.
- Applicant should document their progress toward obtaining engineering design information (FEED) to initiate permitting activities and to finalize the turbine generator purchase specification within the 2 year window. Most often, this requires final site, technology, process selection. Signed FEED and/or EPC-type agreements, if available, should be provided.

APPENDICES

- Copy of internal or external engineering reports.
- Copy of site plan, together with evidence that applicant owns or controls a site. Examples of evidence would include a deed, or an executed contract to purchase or lease the site.
- Information supporting applicant's conclusion that the site is fully acceptable as the project site with respect to environment, coal supply, water supply, transmission interconnect, and public policy reasons.
- Power Purchase or Energy Sales Agreement.
- Energy Market Study.
- Market Study for non-power output.
- Financial Model of project.
- Financial statements for the applicant and other project funding sources for the most recently ended three fiscal years, and the unaudited quarterly interim financial statements for the current fiscal year.
- Expressions of interest or commitment letters from funding sources.
- For each project contract, if no contract currently exists, provide a summary of the expected terms and conditions.
- List of all federal, state, and local permits, including environmental authorizations or reviews, necessary to commence construction.

E. Evaluation Criteria

Advanced coal projects: will be evaluated on whether they meet all the requirements of § 48A.

Technical: will be evaluated on whether the applicant has demonstrated the capability to accomplish the technical objectives.

Site: will be evaluated on the basis that the site requirement for ownership or control has been met, and that the site is suitable for the proposed project.

Economic: will be evaluated on whether the project has demonstrated economic feasibility, taking into consideration the submitted financial and project development and structural information and financial plan.

Schedule: will be evaluated on the applicant's ability to meet the 2 year project certification and the 5 year placed-in-service requirement.

F. Program Policy Factors to be used by DOE in the evaluation of applications

Section 48A identifies minimum requirements for consideration for the qualifying advanced coal project credit, including the project's technical feasibility, cost, and applicant's ability. In the event that there are more qualified (certifiable) applications than there are available tax credits, the DOE will apply additional factors to rank eligible IGCC and non IGCC projects based on their ability to advance coal technology beyond its current state.

If there are more certified applications than available credits for a pool described in section 4.02(2) of Notice 2007–52, DOE will rank the certified projects in descending order (that is, first, second, third, etc.), based on evaluation of the following Program Policy Factors. Factors 1, 2, and 3 are Primary Ranking Factors. A certified project that satisfies one of these factors will be ranked ahead of each project that satisfies only factors listed below that factor. Specifically, all certified projects satisfying Factor 1 will be selected before any project that does not satisfy Factor 1; all projects satisfying Factor 2 will be ranked ahead of any project that satisfies only Factor 3 and/or one or more Secondary Ranking Factors; and all projects satisfying Factor 3 will be ranked ahead of any project that does not satisfy any Primary Ranking Factors.

Primary Ranking Factors:

1. Capture and sequestration of 50 percent or more carbon dioxide emissions. Only projects capturing and sequestering 50 percent or more of the plant's carbon dioxide emissions will satisfy this factor. Within this factor, higher rankings will be given to those projects capturing and sequestering higher percentages of plant carbon dioxide emissions.

2. Use of advanced technologies that optimize the plant for future carbon dioxide capture (for example, gasifier sizing and pressure, air separation unit sizing, and quench system) as well as systems that are designed to capture and sequester less than 50 percent of the carbon dioxide. Within this factor, higher rankings will be given to those projects capturing and sequestering higher percentages of plant carbon dioxide emissions and/or requiring less retrofitting to implement greater than 50 percent carbon capture and sequestration.

3. Location of the facility within 25 miles of potential carbon sequestration locations and carbon dioxide (CO2) pipelines or pipeline easements. Within this factor, higher rankings will be given to those projects with the facility located closer to potential carbon sequestration locations and carbon dioxide (CO2) pipelines or pipeline easements.

Secondary Ranking Factors:

- Location of the facility relative to potential carbon sequestration locations and carbon dioxide (CO2) pipelines or pipeline easements (for facilities not meeting Factor 3).
- Presentation of other environmental, economic, or performance benefits (including, in the case of an IGCC project, priority factors that are listed in section 5.02(10) of Notice 2007–52 and are not included in the Primary Ranking Factors).
- Higher plant efficiency.
- Geographic distribution of potential markets.
- The ratio of total nameplate generating capacity (as defined in section 3.02 of Notice 2007–52) to requested tax credit.
- Diversity of technology approaches and methods.

G. Supplemental Technical and Financial Guidance for Section D "Project Information Memorandum"

Technology and Technical Information

- It is important that the applicant select a specific gasification system for their project. Without that decision, it is difficult to provide the necessary specific design information needed for DOE to evaluate the project feasibility with respect to performance, emissions, outputs of major streams as well as capital and operating costs.
- The Applicant's capability to meet the legislated heat rate and/or environmental targets should be supported with design information, and or vendor guarantees which are project, site and coal specific.

Project Economics

- Applicants should demonstrate the project's economic feasibility and financial viability by providing a clear statement and explanation of the economic and financial assumptions made by the applicant, and a financial forecast for the project. The financial forecast should flow logically from the applicant's assumptions and be consistent with them. Applicants should include assumptions regarding financial and economic issues that may not be included in the project costs but have a direct impact on the project. The examples given in the "Site Control and Ownership" section are relevant here and their impact on the project economics should be discussed here.

Project Development and Financial Plan

- The information provided by the applicant in this section should demonstrate that the applicant's financial plan for developing the project is feasible and that the applicant will have access to necessary financing. The applicant should explain the source and timing for obtaining all financing, including the project development costs. It is important that the applicant explain and provide evidence that it has the capacity to fund the pre-construction project development costs, together with a budget for and description of those costs. Note that financial information is required for the applicant and for any other funding source.

Project Contract Structure

- This section requires that the applicant demonstrate an understanding of the commercial contracting process and show progress in establishing the framework of contracts and agreements that a project typically requires. Applicants should show that their intended contract structure is reasonable and that their assumptions relative to price, terms, and conditions are consistent with current market conditions. Evidence of final agreements, agreements in principle, or summaries of terms and conditions between the applicant and contract counterparties should be provided if available.

APPENDIX C

CONSENT TO PUBLIC DISCLOSURE OF CERTAIN QUALIFYING ADVANCED COAL PROJECT PROGRAM APPLICATION INFORMATION

In the event that the Application for § 48A Certification of [(*Insert name of applicant-taxpayer here*): ________________] (the Applicant-Taxpayer) for an allocation of qualifying advanced coal project credits under section 48A of the Internal Revenue Code is approved, the undersigned authorized representative of the Applicant-Taxpayer hereby consents to the disclosure by the Internal Revenue Service through publication of a Notice in the Internal Revenue Bulletin or a press release of: (1) the name of the Applicant-Taxpayer; (2) if the Applicant-Taxpayer is a member of an affiliated group filing consolidated returns, the name of the common parent of the group; (3) the type and location of the project that is the subject of the Application for § 48A Certification; and (4) the amount of the allocation, if any, of qualifying advanced coal project credits for such project. The undersigned understands that this information might be published, broadcast, discussed, or otherwise disseminated in the public record.

This authorization shall become effective upon the execution thereof. Except to the extent disclosure is authorized herein, the returns and return information of the undersigned taxpayer are confidential and are protected by law under the Internal Revenue Code.

I certify that I have the authority to execute this consent to disclose on behalf of the taxpayer named below.

Date: ________________

Signature: ________________________

Print name: ________________________

Title: ________________________

Name of Applicant-Taxpayer: ________________________

Taxpayer Identification Number: ________________________

Taxpayer's Address:

____

____

____

Note: Treasury Regulations require that the Internal Revenue Service must receive this consent within 60 days after it is signed and dated.

Qualifying Gasification Project Program

Notice 2007–53

SECTION 1. PURPOSE

This notice updates the procedures for the allocation of credits under the qualifying gasification project program of § 48B of the Internal Revenue Code and defines certain terms for purposes of § 48B. The purpose of the qualifying gasification project program is to consider and award certifications for qualified investment eligible for credits under § 48B to qualifying gasification project sponsors. To further this purpose, the method of allocation is being modified for allocation rounds after 2006. Under the modified method of allocation, the U.S. Department of Energy ("DOE") will rank a certified project relative to other certified projects and credits will be allocated to projects based on the DOE ranking. The modified allocation method will substantially favor projects that capture and sequester carbon dioxide emissions and will favor to a lesser extent projects optimized for future carbon dioxide capture.

SECTION 2. BACKGROUND AND CHANGES

.01 Section 46 provides that the amount of the investment credit for any taxable year is the sum of the credits listed in § 46. That list includes the qualifying gasification project credit.

.02 The qualifying gasification project credit is provided under § 48B. Section 48B(a) provides that the qualifying gasification project credit for a taxable year is an amount equal to 20 percent of the qualified investment (as defined in § 48B(b)) for that taxable year in qualifying gasification projects.

.03 The term "qualifying gasification project" is defined in § 48B(c)(1) as meaning any project that (A) employs gasification technology, (B) will be carried out by an eligible entity (as defined in section 3.02 of this notice), and (C) includes a qualified investment of which an amount not to exceed $650 million is certified under the qualifying gasification program as eligible for credit under § 48B. Pursuant to § 48B(c)(2), gasification technology is any process that converts a solid or liquid product from coal (as defined in section 3.01 of this notice), petroleum residue (as defined in § 48B(c)(8)), biomass (as defined in § 48B(c)(4)), or other materials that are recovered for their energy or feedstock value into a synthesis gas composed primarily of carbon monoxide and hydrogen for direct use or subsequent chemical or physical conversion.

.04 The qualifying gasification project credit generally is allowed in the taxable year in which the eligible property (as defined in § 48B(c)(3)) is placed in service (as defined in section 3.05 of this notice) by the taxpayer. Further, the at-risk rules in § 49 and the recapture and other special rules in § 50 apply to the qualifying gasification project credit.

.05 Section 48B(d)(1) provides that the Secretary, in consultation with the Secretary of Energy, shall establish a qualifying gasification project program to consider and award certifications for qualified investment eligible for credits under § 48B to qualifying gasification project sponsors. The Treasury Department and the Internal Revenue Service established this program in Notice 2006–25, 2006–11 I.R.B. 609. Pursuant to § 48B(d)(2), certificates of eligibility may be issued under the program only during the 10-year period beginning on October 1, 2005.

.06 This notice modifies the qualifying gasification project program established in Notice 2006–25 in a number of respects. The significant changes made by this notice include the following:

(1) Large and Mid-Size Business Division (LMSB) of the Service will allocate the qualifying gasification project credits. The filing instructions in section 5.04 provide LMSB addresses to reflect this change.

(2) Section 3 defines certain terms for purposes of § 48B.

(3) The method of allocation is modified for allocation rounds after 2006. Under the modified method of allocation, the DOE will rank a certified project relative to other certified projects and credits will be allocated to projects based on the DOE ranking. The modified allocation method will substantially favor projects that capture and sequester carbon dioxide emissions and will favor to a lesser extent projects optimized for future carbon dioxide capture. Section 4.02(4) reflects this change in the method by which credits under § 48B are allocated to projects.

(4) Section 4.02(8) provides that the period for submitting the application for § 48B certification (i) ends on March 3, 2008, for the 2007–08 allocation round and (ii) begins on March 4, 2008, and ends on March 2, 2009, for the 2008–09 allocation round. Changes also are made to the dates in sections 4.02(10) and (12) for accepting or rejecting a taxpayer's application for § 48B certification and for executing closing agreements.

(5) Section 4.02(9) provides that the due date for the application for DOE certification is October 31, that DOE will rank certified projects, and that the due date for the DOE certification and ranking is March 1. Section 4.02(8) also clarifies that the DOE certification and ranking (for projects determined to be feasible) are provided to the Service.

(6) Section 4.02(12) provides that a successor in interest must execute a new closing agreement with the Service no later than the due date (including extensions) of the successor in interest's Federal income tax return for the taxable year in which the transfer occurs.

(7) The information required to be included in the application for DOE certification is modified. Section 5.02 requires submission of additional information regarding the priority benefits of the project. Appendix B provides additional information regarding program policy factors. Applicants will no longer be required to submit independent financial reports.

(8) Section 5.03 requests that a taxpayer submit with the application for § 48B certification a declaration consenting to the disclosure by the Service of certain return information if the taxpayer is awarded an allocation of qualifying gasification project credits. The form of the declaration is set forth in Appendix C.

(9) Sections 5.03(1) and 5.04 require that a taxpayer submit one paper copy and one electronic version on a floppy disc or a CD of the application for § 48B certification (including the application for DOE certification).

(10) Section 6.02 provides more details on who may sign the penalties of perjury statement.

(11) Section 6.03 provides that the Service and the DOE must be informed if the plans for the project change in any signifi-

cant respect from the plans set forth in the applications for § 48B and DOE certification, and also provides the consequences of any significant change to the plans set forth in the applications.

(12) Section 6.06 provides that the DOE will offer debriefings to applicants that submitted an application for DOE certification.

(13) Section 9 provides guidance regarding Freedom of Information Act requests for records relating to the qualifying gasification project program.

SECTION 3. DEFINITIONS

The following definitions apply for purposes of § 48B and this notice:

.01 *Coal.* Section 48B(c)(6) defines the term "coal" as meaning anthracite, bituminous coal, subbituminous coal, lignite, and peat. Coal includes waste coal (that is, usable material that is a byproduct of the previous processing of anthracite, bituminous coal, subbituminous coal, lignite, or peat). Examples of waste coal include fine coal of any of the listed ranks, coal of any of the listed ranks obtained from a refuse bank or slurry dam, anthracite culm, bituminous gob, and lignite waste.

.02 *Eligible entity.* Section 48B(c)(7) defines "eligible entity" as meaning any person whose application for certification is principally intended for use in a domestic project that employs domestic gasification applications related to chemicals, fertilizers, glass, steel, petroleum residues, forest products, and agriculture (including feedlots and dairy operations). For purposes of § 48B, a qualifying gasification project is carried out by an eligible entity if the project supplies more than 50 percent of the thermal output in British thermal unit (Btu) from the gasification process in the form of synthesis gas for direct use or subsequent chemical or physical conversion in an application related to one or more of the industries listed in § 48B(c)(7) or if more than 50 percent of the fuel input in Btu to the gasification process is supplied from one or more of the industries listed in § 48B(c)(7).

.03 *Total synthesis gas capacity.* The total synthesis gas capacity of a project is the total MMBtu per hour of the synthesis gas (higher heating value (HHV)) at the gasifier outlet of the project. The synthesis gas must be composed primarily of carbon monoxide and hydrogen for direct use or subsequent chemical or physical conversion.

.04 *Fuel Input.*

(1) *In general.* The term "fuel input" means, with respect to any type of fuel, the amount of such fuel used during normal plant operations. The amounts of the fuel used are measured (i) in British thermal units (Btus) on an energy input basis and (ii) pursuant to applicable standards prescribed by the American Society for Testing and Materials (ASTM). For example, § 48B(d)(3)(D) provides that the fuels identified in § 48B(c)(2) will at all times cumulatively comprise at least 90 percent of the total fuels (fuels identified in § 48B(c)(2) and any other fuel input) required by the project. This requirement is satisfied if, after completion and during normal plant operations, the fuels identified in § 48B(c)(2) will cumulatively comprise at least 90 percent of the project's total fuels measured in Btus on an energy input basis and pursuant to applicable ASTM standards.

(2) *Only normal plant operations taken into account.* Only fuel used during normal plant operations is taken into account for purposes of § 48B. Normal plant operations are operations other than during periods of initial plant certification, plant startup, plant shutdown, interconnected gasifier(s) shutdown for gasification system maintenance, or interruptions of the supply of fuels identified in § 48B(c)(2) to the project resulting from an event of force majeure (including an act of God, war, strike, or other similar event beyond the control of the taxpayer). For example, the fuel input during the initial plant certification may consist entirely of natural gas or other fuels not identified in § 48B(c)(2) because fuel used during initial plant certification is disregarded in determining whether the requirement of § 48B(d)(3)(D) to use 90 percent of the fuels identified in § 48B(c)(2) is satisfied.

.05 *Placed In Service.* For purposes of § 48B, property is placed in service in the taxable year in which the property is placed in a condition or state of readiness and availability for a specifically assigned function. *See* § 1.46–3(d)(1)(ii) of the Income Tax Regulations. Thus, a qualifying gasification project or eligible property (as defined in § 48B(c)(3)) that is a part of the project is placed in service in the taxable year in which the project is placed in a condition or state of readiness and availability for producing synthesis gas from the feedstocks identified in § 48B(c)(2).

SECTION 4. QUALIFYING GASIFICATION PROJECT PROGRAM

.01 *In General.* The Service will consider a project under the qualifying gasification project program only if the DOE provides a certification ("DOE certification") and ranking (if any) for the project. Accordingly, for each qualifying gasification project, a taxpayer must submit: (1) an application for certification by the DOE ("application for DOE certification"), and (2) an application for certification under § 48B by the Service ("application for § 48B certification"). Both applications may be submitted only during the 3-year period beginning on February 21, 2006. Certifications will be issued and credits will be allocated to projects in annual allocation rounds. The initial allocation round was conducted in 2006. Additional allocation rounds will be conducted in 2007–08 and, if necessary, in 2008–09.

.02 *Program Specifications.*

(1) The Service determines the amount of the qualifying gasification project credits allocated to a qualifying gasification project at the time the Service accepts the application for § 48B certification for that project in accordance with section 4.02(9) of this notice. The qualified investment in the project will be certified as eligible for the credit to the extent such investment does not exceed the amount of the credit allocated to the project multiplied by five. See section 5 of this notice for the requirements applicable to the application for DOE certification and the application for § 48B certification.

(2) The certification for a project cannot apply to more than $650 million of the qualified investment in the project. Thus, the maximum amount of qualifying gasification project credits that will be allocated to a project is $130 million.

(3) Pursuant to § 48B(d)(1), the aggregate amount of credits allocated to all qualifying gasification projects may not exceed $350 million. In the 2006 allocation round, $349,663,000 of credits was allocated. Therefore, $337,000 of credits is available for allocation in 2007–08.

(4) DOE will rank the certified projects in descending order (that is, first, second, third, etc.) and the $337,000 available for allocation will be allocated as follows in the allocation round in 2007–08:

(a) If the requested allocation of credits for projects that DOE has certified does not exceed the amount available for allocation, each certified project will be allocated the full amount of credit requested.

(b) If the requested allocation of credits for projects that DOE has certified exceeds the amount available for allocation, the amount available for allocation will be allocated as follows:

(i) The project receiving the highest ranking (that is, first) will be allocated the full amount of credit requested (but not exceeding the amount available for allocation) before any credit is allocated to a lower-ranked project. The amount available for allocation is reduced by the amount of credit so allocated and only the remainder is available for allocation to a lower-ranked project.

(ii) Second and lower-ranked projects will be entitled to similar priority in the allocation of credits and allocations to such projects will similarly reduce the remainder of the amount available for allocation until the amount available for allocation is exhausted.

(5) If the amount available for allocation is not fully allocated in the 2007–08 allocation round, a similar allocation round will be conducted in 2008–09. Generally, the results of each year will be announced. See section 5.03(2) of this notice for further information about this announcement.

(6) If the same project would otherwise be allocated credits under both the qualifying gasification project program under this notice and the qualifying advanced coal project program under Notice 2007–52, 2007–26 I.R.B. 1456, the following rules apply:

(a) The qualifying gasification project credit may not be allocated to the project with respect to any qualified investment under § 48B for which a qualifying advanced coal project credit is allowed under § 48A; and

(b) The qualifying gasification project credit may be allocated to the project with respect to the qualified investment under § 48B for which a qualifying advanced coal project credit is not allowed under § 48A.

(7) For each allocation round, there will be an annual application period during which a taxpayer may file its application for § 48B certification. The Service will consider a project in an allocation round only if the application for § 48B certification for the project is submitted during the application period for that round and the DOE provides the DOE certification and the DOE ranking (if any) for the project before the end of that application period.

(8) For the allocation round conducted in 2007–08, the application period begins on October 3, 2006, and ends on March 3, 2008, and any completed application for § 48B certification received by the Service after October 2, 2006, and before March 4, 2008, will be deemed to be submitted by the taxpayer on March 3, 2008. For the allocation round to be conducted in 2008–09, the application period begins on March 4, 2008, and ends on March 2, 2009, and any completed application for § 48B certification received by the Service after March 3, 2008, and before March 3, 2009, will be deemed to be submitted by the taxpayer on March 2, 2009. For purposes of this notice, an application that is submitted by U.S. mail will be treated as received by the Service on the date of the postmark and an application submitted by a private delivery service will be treated as received by the Service on the date recorded or the date marked in accordance with § 7502(f)(2)(C).

(9) See section 5.02 of this notice and Appendix B to this notice for the information to be submitted to the DOE in an application for DOE certification. Appendix B to this notice also provides the instructions and address for filing the application for DOE certification. The DOE will determine the feasibility of the project and, if the project is determined to be feasible, will provide a DOE certification for the project to the Service. If the DOE certifies two or more projects, the DOE also will rank each of the projects it certifies (for example, first, second, third, etc.) relative to other certified projects. If an application for DOE certification is postmarked on or before October 31 of a calendar year, the DOE will determine the feasibility of the project and (for projects determined to be feasible) provide the DOE certification and the DOE ranking (if any) to the Service by March 1 of the year following that calendar year.

(10) By April 30 of the calendar year in which an application for § 48B certification is deemed to be submitted (as determined under section 4.02(8) of this notice), the Service will accept or reject the taxpayer's application for § 48B certification and will notify the taxpayer, by letter, of its decision.

(11) A taxpayer that receives an acceptance letter under section 4.02(10) of this notice has 7 years from the date of the acceptance letter to place the project in service and if the project is not placed in service by the end of that period then the acceptance letter is void.

(12) If the taxpayer's application for § 48B certification is accepted, the acceptance letter will state the amount of the credit allocated to the project and the amount of qualified investment that is certified as eligible for the credit. If a credit is allocated to a taxpayer's project, the taxpayer will be required to execute a closing agreement in the form set forth in Appendix A to this notice. By June 30 of the calendar year in which an application for § 48B certification is accepted, the taxpayer must execute and return the closing agreement to the Service at the appropriate address listed in section 5.04 of this notice or listed in later guidance published in the Internal Revenue Bulletin. The Service will execute and return the closing agreement to the taxpayer by August 31 of such calendar year. The executed closing agreement applies only to the accepted taxpayer. Accordingly, any successor in interest must execute a new closing agreement with the Service no later than the due date (including extensions) of the successor in interest's Federal income tax return for the taxable year in which the transfer occurs. If the successor in interest does not execute a new closing agreement, the following rules apply:

(a) In the case of an interest acquired at or before the time the qualifying gasification project is placed in service, any credit allocated to the project will be fully forfeited (and rules similar to the recapture rules of § 50(a) apply with respect to qualified progress expenditures); and

(b) In the case of an interest acquired after the qualifying gasification project is placed in service, the project ceases to be investment credit property and the recapture rules of § 50(a) (and similar rules with respect to qualified progress expenditures) apply.

SECTION 5. APPLICATIONS FOR CERTIFICATIONS

.01 *In General.* An application for § 48B certification and a separate application for DOE certification must be submitted for each qualifying gasification project. If an application for DOE certification does not include all of the information required by section 5.02 of this notice and meet the requirements in sections 6.01 and 6.02 of this notice, the DOE may decline to accept the application. If an application for § 48B certification does not include all of the information listed in section 5.03 of this notice and meet the requirements in sections 6.01 and 6.02 of this notice, the application will not be accepted by the Service.

.02 *Information Required in the Application for DOE Certification.* An application for DOE certification must include all of the information requested in Appendix B to this notice and all of the following:

(1) The name, address, and taxpayer identification number of the taxpayer. If the taxpayer is a member of an affiliated group filing consolidated returns, also provide the name, address, and taxpayer identification number of the common parent of the group.

(2) The name and telephone number of a contact person.

(3) The name and address (or other unique identifying designation) of the qualifying gasification project.

(4) A statement specifying the projected placed-in-service date of the qualifying gasification project.

(5) The estimated total cost of the project and the estimated total qualified investment in the eligible property that will be part of the project.

(6) The amount of the qualifying gasification project credit requested for the project. The amount requested must not exceed $130 million (the maximum amount permitted under § 48B(a) and (c)(1)(C)).

(7) If the taxpayer is or will be requesting an amount of the qualifying advanced coal project credit under § 48A for the same project, a statement specifying the amount of credit the taxpayer is or will be requesting under § 48A.

(8) The exact total synthesis gas capacity (as defined in section 3.03 of this notice) of the project.

(9) A statement specifying whether the project is entitled to priority for carbon capture capability (as defined in § 48B(c)(5)), for using renewable fuel, or for having project teams with experience that demonstrates successful and reliable operations of the gasification technology on the domestic fuels identified in § 48B(c)(2), and, if entitled to priority, a statement identifying which of these priorities apply to the project.

(10) Documentation or other evidence establishing that the taxpayer is financially viable without the receipt of additional federal funding associated with the qualifying gasification project.

.03 *Information To Be Included in the Application for § 48B Certification.*

(1) *Information required in the application for § 48B certification.* An application for § 48B certification must include all of the following:

(a) The name, address, and taxpayer identification number of the taxpayer. If the taxpayer is a member of an affiliated group filing consolidated returns, also provide the name, address, and taxpayer identification number of the common parent of the group.

(b) The name, telephone number, and fax number of a contact person. For such person, attach a properly executed power of attorney, preferably on Form 2848, *Power of Attorney and Declaration of Representative*.

(c) One paper copy and one electronic version on a floppy disc or a CD of the completed application for DOE certification submitted with respect to the project in accordance with section 5.02 of this notice.

(2) *Consent to disclosure of allocation.* In order to provide the public with information on how the qualifying gasification project credits authorized by Congress have been allocated and facilitate oversight of the qualifying gasification project program, the Service intends to publish the results of the allocation process. The Service expects that a list identifying the taxpayers and projects to which credits are allocated and specifying the amount of credit allocated to each would be of particular interest to the public. Pursuant to § 6103, consent is required in order to disclose any return information with respect to taxpayers awarded an allocation. Therefore, the Service requests that each taxpayer submit with the application for § 48B certification a declaration, consenting to the disclosure by the Service of the following return information in the event a qualifying gasification project credit is allocated to the taxpayer's project: (a) the name of the taxpayer; (b) if the taxpayer is a member of an affiliated group filing consolidated returns, the name of the common parent of the group; (c) the type and location of the project to which the application relates; and (d) the amount of the qualifying gasification project credit allocated to the project. To provide a valid consent, the declaration must be in the form set forth in Appendix C. A taxpayer is not required to consent to disclosure of this information in order to receive an allocation of the qualifying gasification project credit, and neither the presence nor the absence of such a consent will be taken into account in the evaluation of a taxpayer's application. The Service will not publish any return information relating to a taxpayer if the taxpayer does not consent to disclosure of this information or does not receive an allocation of the qualifying gasification project credit.

.04 *Instructions and Address for Filing § 48B Application.* One paper copy and one electronic version on a floppy disc or a CD of the application for § 48B certification must be submitted. Applications for § 48B certification should be marked: SECTION 48B APPLICATION FOR CERTIFICATION. There is no user fee for these applications.

(1) Applications submitted by U.S. mail must be sent to:

Internal Revenue Service
Industry Director, Natural Resources
and Construction
Attn: Executive Assistant
1919 Smith Street
Stop HOU 1000
Houston, TX 77002

Applications submitted by a private delivery service must be sent to:

Internal Revenue Service
Industry Director, Natural Resources and Construction
Attn: Executive Assistant
1919 Smith Street, Floor P2
Stop HOU 1000
Houston, TX 77002

(2) Applications may also be hand delivered Monday through Friday between the hours of 8 a.m. and 4 p.m. Central time to:

Internal Revenue Service
Industry Director, Natural Resources and Construction
Attn: Executive Assistant
1919 Smith Street, Floor P2
Stop HOU 1000
Houston, TX 77002

SECTION 6. OTHER REQUIREMENTS

.01 *Signature.* Each submission under section 5 of this notice must be signed and dated by the taxpayer. A stamped signature or faxed signature is not permitted.

.02 *Penalties of Perjury Statement.*

(1) Each submission under section 5 of this notice must be accompanied by the following declaration: "Under penalties of perjury, I declare that I have examined this submission, including accompanying documents, and, to the best of my knowledge and belief, all of the facts contained herein are true, correct, and complete."

(2) The declaration must be signed and dated by the taxpayer. The person signing for the taxpayer must have personal knowledge of the facts. Further, the declaration must be signed by an officer on behalf of a corporation, a general partner on behalf of a state-law partnership, a member-manager on behalf of a limited liability company, a trustee on behalf of a trust, and the proprietor in the case a sole proprietorship. If the taxpayer is a member of an affiliated group filing consolidated returns, the declaration also must be signed by a duly authorized officer of the common parent of the group. A stamped signature or faxed signature is not permitted.

.03 *Significant Change in Plans.* The Service and DOE must be informed if the plans for the project change in any significant respect from the plans set forth in the applications for § 48B and DOE certification. Any significant change to the plans set forth in the applications will have the following effects:

(1) The Service will disregard any certification or ranking provided by DOE unless DOE is informed of the change before the date on which DOE provides the certification or ranking (that is, the Service will not consider the project unless DOE provides a new, timely certification and ranking (if any) on or after the date on which DOE is informed of the change); and

(2) Any acceptance provided by the Service and any allocation or certification based on that acceptance will be void unless the Service is informed of the change before the date on which the acceptance is provided under section 4.02(10) of this notice.

.04 *Effect of an Acceptance or Allocation.* An acceptance or allocation by the Service under this notice is not a determination that a project qualifies for the qualifying gasification project credit under § 48B. The Service may, upon examination (and after any appropriate consultation with DOE), determine that the project does not qualify for this credit.

.05 *No Right to a Conference or Appeal.* A taxpayer does not have a right to a conference relating to any matters under this notice. Further, a taxpayer does not have a right to appeal the decisions made under this notice (including the acceptance or rejection of the application for DOE or § 48B certification or the amount of credit allocated to the project) to an Associate Chief Counsel or any other official of the Service.

.06 *DOE Debriefings.* Although a taxpayer does not have a right to a conference relating to any matters under this notice, the DOE will offer debriefings to all applicants that submitted an application for DOE certification. This debriefing will be held by the DOE after the Service has accepted the applications for § 48B certification (as determined under section 4.02(10) of this notice). The sole purpose of the debriefing is to enable applicants to develop better proposals in future allocation rounds by providing DOE's review of the strengths and weaknesses of their application for DOE certification.

SECTION 7. REVIEW AND REDISTRIBUTION

.01 *In General.* Section 48B(d)(1) provides for the review and redistribution of credits allocated under the qualifying gasification project program under rules similar to the rules of § 48A(d)(4).

.02 *Review and Redistribution of Credits.*

(1) *In general.* If, after the allocation round in 2008–09, the aggregate credit of $350 million is not fully subscribed (that is, the aggregate credit is not fully allocated), an additional program for applications for certification to allocate the remaining credits will be conducted. Future guidance will prescribe the procedures applicable to applications for certification with respect to the remaining credits.

(2) *Reduction or forfeiture of allocated credits.* Under the closing agreement set forth in Appendix A to this notice, the qualifying gasification project credits allocated under section 4 of this notice will be reduced or forfeited in certain situations. A taxpayer must notify the Service of the amount of any reduction or forfeiture required under the closing agreement. This notification must be sent to the appropriate address listed in section 5.04 of this notice or listed in later guidance published in the Internal Revenue Bulletin.

The amount of any reduction or forfeiture of the allocated credits will be returned and included in the aggregate credit remaining to be allocated in the allocation round following the reduction or forfeiture. If the reduction or forfeiture occurs after the allocation round in 2008–09, future guidance will prescribe procedures applicable to applications for certification with respect to the returned credits.

SECTION 8. QUALIFIED PROGRESS EXPENDITURES

.01 Section 48B(b)(3) provides that rules similar to the rules of § 46(c)(4) and (d) (as in effect on the day before the enactment of the Revenue Reconciliation Act of 1990) shall apply for purposes of § 48B. Former §§ 46(c)(4) and 46(d) provided the rules for claiming the investment credit on qualified progress expenditures (as defined in former § 46(d)(3)) made by a taxpayer during the taxable year for the construction of progress expenditure property (as defined in former § 46(d)(2)).

.02 In the case of self-constructed property (as defined in former § 46(d)(5)(A)), former § 46(d)(3)(A) defined qualified progress expenditures to mean the amount that is properly chargeable (during the taxable year) to capital account with respect to that property. With respect to a qualifying gasification project that is self-constructed property, amounts paid or incurred are chargeable to capital account at the time and to the extent they are properly includible in computing basis under the taxpayer's method of accounting (for example, after applying the requirements of § 461, including the economic performance requirement of § 461(h)).

.03 To claim the qualifying gasification project credit on the qualified progress expenditures paid or incurred by a taxpayer during the taxable year for construction of a qualifying gasification project, the taxpayer must make an election under the rules set forth in § 1.46–5(o) of the Income Tax Regulations. The taxpayer may not make the qualified progress expenditures election for a qualifying gasification project until the taxpayer has received an acceptance letter for the project under section 4.02(10) of this notice.

.04 If a taxpayer makes the qualified progress expenditures election pursuant to section 8.03 of this notice, rules similar to the recapture rules in § 50(a)(2)(A)-(D) apply. In addition to the cessation events listed in § 50(a)(2)(A), examples of other events that will cause the project to cease being a qualifying gasification project are:

(1) Failure to place the project in service within 7 years from the date of the acceptance letter under section 4.02(10) of this notice; or

(2) A significant change to the plans for the project as set forth in the applications for § 48B and DOE certification and, under section 6.03 of this notice, the Service's acceptance of the project is void as a result of the change.

SECTION 9. DISCLOSURE OF INFORMATION

.01 *In general.* Any information contained in the application for DOE certification or the application for § 48B certification is subject to § 6103 and to any other applicable exemption set forth in the Freedom of Information Act (the FOIA). Examples of FOIA exemptions include FOIA trade secrets and commercial or financial information exemption of 5 U.S.C. 552(b)(4) and the FOIA personal privacy exemption of 5 U.S.C. 552(b)(6)).

.02 *FOIA requests.* Anyone interested in submitting a request for records under the FOIA with respect to the qualifying gasification project program under § 48B (including a request for records relating to the application for DOE certification) should direct a request that conforms to the Service's FOIA regulations, found at 26 C.F.R. § 601.702, to the following address:

IRS FOIA Request
Baltimore Disclosure Office
Room 940
31 Hopkins Plaza
Baltimore, MD 21201

SECTION 10. EFFECT ON OTHER DOCUMENTS

Notice 2006–25 is clarified, modified, amplified, and superseded.

SECTION 11. EFFECTIVE DATE

This notice is effective June 7, 2007.

SECTION 12. PAPERWORK REDUCTION ACT

The collection of information contained in this notice has been reviewed and approved by the Office of Management and Budget in accordance with the Paperwork Reduction Act (44 U.S.C. § 3507) under control number 1545–2002.

An agency may not conduct or sponsor, and a person is not required to respond to, a collection of information unless the collection of information displays a valid OMB control number.

The collections of information in this notice are in sections 4, 5, 6, 7, and Appendix B of this notice. This information is required to obtain an allocation of qualifying gasification project credits. This information will be used by the Service to verify that the taxpayer is eligible for the qualifying gasification project credits. The collection of information is required to obtain a benefit. The likely respondents are business or other for-profit institutions.

The estimated total annual reporting burden is 1,700 hours.

The estimated annual burden per respondent varies from 50 to 125 hours, depending on individual circumstances, with an estimated average of 85 hours. The estimated number of respondents is 20.

The estimated annual frequency of responses is on occasion.

Books or records relating to a collection of information must be retained as long as their contents may become material in the administration of any internal revenue law. Generally, tax returns and tax return information are confidential, as required by 26 U.S.C. § 6103.

SECTION 13. DRAFTING INFORMATION

The principal author of this notice is Ruba Nasrallah of the Office of Associate Chief Counsel (Income Tax & Accounting). For further information regarding this notice, contact Jaime Park of the Office of Associate Chief Counsel (Passthroughs & Special Industries) at (202) 622–3110 (not a toll-free call). For further information regarding the application for § 48B certification, contact Kimberly Edwards, Executive Assistant, Office of the Industry Director, Natural Resources and Construction, at (713) 209–3615 (not a toll-free number).

APPENDIX A

CLOSING AGREEMENT

Under § 7121 of the Internal Revenue Code, [insert taxpayer's name, address, and identifying number] ("Taxpayer") and the Commissioner of Internal Revenue ("Commissioner") make the following closing agreement:

WHEREAS:

1. On or before March [insert date and year], Taxpayer submitted to the Internal Revenue Service ("IRS"), an application for certification under the qualifying gasification project program described in Notice 2007–53 ("Application for § 48B Certification");

2. Taxpayer's Application for § 48B Certification is for the qualifying gasification project (the "Project") described below—

(1) The Project will be located at [insert address or other identifying designation];

(2) The Project will have a total synthesis gas capacity (as defined in section 3.03 of Notice 2007–53) of at least [insert number] total MMBtu per hour of synthesis gas. The synthesis gas is composed primarily of carbon monoxide and hydrogen for direct use or subsequent chemical or physical conversion;

(3) The fuels identified in § 48B(c)(2) will at all times cumulatively comprise at least 90 percent of the total fuel input (as defined in section 3.04(1) of Notice 2007–53 and including fuels identified in § 48B(c)(2) and any other fuel input) required by the Project for normal plant operations (as defined in section 3.04(2) of Notice 2007–53) for the production of chemical feedstocks, liquid transportation fuels, or co-production of electricity; and

3. On [insert date of acceptance letter issued under section 4.02(9) of Notice 2007–53], the IRS accepted Taxpayer's Application for § 48B Certification for the Project and allocated a qualifying gasification project credit under § 48B in the amount of $[insert number] to the Project.

NOW IT IS HEREBY DETERMINED AND AGREED FOR FEDERAL INCOME TAX PURPOSES THAT:

1. The total amount of the qualifying gasification project credit to be claimed for the Project under § 48B(a) must not exceed $[insert the number in WHEREAS clause #3].

2. If the Project is not placed in service by Taxpayer within 7 years of [insert the date in WHEREAS clause #3], the qualifying gasification project credit in the amount of $[insert the number in WHEREAS clause #3] allocated to the Project is fully forfeited.

3. If the plans for the Project change in any significant respect from the plans set forth in the application for DOE certification (as defined in section 4.01 of Notice 2007–53) and the Application for § 48B Certification (as defined in section 4.01 of Notice 2007–53) and, under section 6.03 of Notice 2007–53, the acceptance of Taxpayer's Application for § 48B Certification on [insert the date in WHEREAS clause #3] is void, the qualifying advanced coal project credit in the amount of $[insert the number in WHEREAS clause #3] allocated to the Project is fully forfeited.

4. (1) If the Project fails to use gasification technology as defined in § 48B(c)(2) or is not carried out by an eligible entity (as defined in section 3.02 of Notice 2007–53), the qualifying gasification project credit in the amount of $[insert the number in WHEREAS clause #3] allocated to the Project is fully forfeited.

(2) If, at any time, the fuels identified in § 48B(c)(2) with respect to the gasification technology for the Project do not cumulatively comprise at least 90 percent of the total fuel input (as defined in section 3.04(1) of Notice 2007–53 and including fuels identified in § 48B(c)(2) and any other fuel input) required by the Project for normal plant operations (as defined in section 3.04(2) of Notice 2007–53) for the production of chemical feedstocks, liquid transportation fuels, or co-production of electricity, the Project ceases to be investment credit property and the recapture rules of § 50(a) apply.

5. Taxpayer will not claim the qualifying advanced coal project credit under § 48A for any qualified investment for which the qualifying gasification project credit is allowed under § 48B.

6. If Taxpayer elects to claim the qualifying gasification project credit on the qualified progress expenditures paid or incurred by Taxpayer during the taxable year(s) during which the Project is under construction and if the Project ceases to be a qualifying gasification project (whether before, at the time, or after the Project is placed in service), rules similar to the recapture rules in § 50(a)(2)(A) through (D) apply.

7. This agreement applies only to Taxpayer. Any successor in interest must execute a new closing agreement with the IRS. If the interest is acquired at or before the time the Project is placed in service and the successor in interest fails to execute a new closing agreement, the qualifying gasification project credit in the amount of $[insert the number in WHEREAS clause #3] allocated to the Project is fully forfeited. If the interest is acquired after the time the Project is placed in service and the successor in interest fails to execute a new closing agreement, the Project ceases to be investment credit property and the recapture rules of § 50(a) apply.

THIS AGREEMENT IS FINAL AND CONCLUSIVE EXCEPT:

1. The matter it relates to may be reopened in the event of fraud, malfeasance, or misrepresentation of a material fact;

2. It is subject to the Internal Revenue Code sections that expressly provide that effect be given to their provisions (including any stated exception for § 7122) notwithstanding any law or rule of law; and

3. If it relates to a tax period ending after the date of this Closing Agreement, it is subject to any law enacted after such date, which applies to the tax period.

By signing, the parties certify that they have read and agreed to the terms of this Closing Agreement.

Taxpayer: [insert name and identifying number]

By: ______________________________ **Date Signed:** ____________________

[insert name]

Title: [insert title]

[insert taxpayer's name]

Commissioner of Internal Revenue

By: ______________________________ **Date Signed:** ____________________

[insert name]

Title: [insert title]

I have examined the specific matters involved and recommend the acceptance of the proposed agreement.

(Receiving Officer) ____________________

(Title) ____________________

Date Signed ____________________

I have reviewed the specific matters involved and recommend the acceptance of the proposed agreement.

(Reviewing Officer) ____________________

(Title) ____________________

Date Signed ____________________

APPENDIX B

APPLICATION FOR DOE CERTIFICATION

REQUEST FOR SUPPLEMENTAL APPLICATION INFORMATION FOR DOE

The Internal Revenue Service ("IRS") and the Department of Energy ("DOE") seek to certify applications that demonstrate a high likelihood of being successfully implemented by the applicants. To qualify, projects must be economically feasible and use the appropriate gasification technology.

This request for submission of supplemental application information:

1. Describes the information to be provided by the applicant seeking a certification of feasibility, and
2. Lists the evaluation criteria and Program Policy Factors to be used by DOE in the evaluation of applications.

In conducting this evaluation, the DOE may utilize assistance and advice from qualified personnel from other Federal agencies and/or non-conflicted contractors. DOE will obtain assurances in advance from all evaluators that application information shall be kept confidential and used only for evaluation purposes. DOE reserves the right to request clarifications and/or supplemental information from some or all applicants through written submissions and/or oral presentations.

Notice is given that DOE may determine whether or not to provide a certification to the IRS at any time after the application has been received, without further exchanges or discussions. Therefore, all applicants are advised to submit their most complete and responsive application.

Applications will not be returned.

SUBMISSION INFORMATION FOR DOE CERTIFICATION APPLICATION

A. General

This request, together with the information in sections 5.02, 6.01, and 6.02 of Notice 2007–53 includes all the information needed to complete an application for DOE certification. All applications shall be prepared in accordance with this request in order to provide a standard basis for evaluation and to ensure that each application will be uniform as to format and sequence.

Each application should clearly demonstrate the applicant's capability, knowledge, and experience in regard to the requirements described herein.

Applicants should fully address the requirements of Notice 2007–53 and this request and **not** rely on the presumed background knowledge of reviewers. DOE may reject an application that does not follow the instructions regarding the organization and content of the application when the nature of the deviation and/or omission precludes meaningful review of the application.

B. Unnecessarily Elaborate Applications

Unnecessarily elaborate brochures or other presentations beyond those sufficient to present a complete and effective application are not desired. Elaborate art work, graphics and pictures are neither required nor encouraged.

C. Application Submission for DOE Certification

The application submission to DOE must include the information and documentation required by sections 5.02, 6.01, and 6.02 of Notice 2007–53.

An application will not be considered in the allocation round conducted in 2007–08 unless it is postmarked by October 31, 2007, and will not be considered in the allocation round conducted in 2008–09 unless it is postmarked by October 31, 2008. Two paper copies and one electronic version on a floppy disc or a CD of the Application must be submitted to:

Melissa Robe
National Energy Technology Laboratory
3610 Collins Ferry Road
Morgantown, WV 26507

Note that under section 5.03(1) of Notice 2007–53, one paper copy and one electronic version must be sent to the IRS as part of the application for IRS certification. The application for IRS certification will not be considered in the allocation round conducted in 2007–08 unless it is submitted to the IRS by March 3, 2008, and will not be considered in the allocation round conducted in 2008–09 unless it is submitted to the IRS by March 2, 2009.

THE INFORMATION REQUIRED BY THIS REQUEST MUST BE SUBMITTED USING THE FORMAT AND THE HEADINGS OF THE PROJECT INFORMATION MEMORANDUM AS DESCRIBED BELOW.

To aid in evaluation, applications shall be clearly and concisely written and logically assembled. All pages of each part shall be appropriately numbered and identified with the name of the applicant and the date.

The application, including the Project Information Memorandum, MUST be formatted in one of the following software applications:

Microsoft Word[tm] 2002 or later edition
Microsoft Excel[tm] 2002 or later edition
Adobe Acrobat[tm] PDF 6.0 or later edition

Financial models should be submitted using the Excel[tm] spreadsheet and must include calculation formulas and assumptions.

The applicant is responsible for the integrity and structure of the electronic files. The DOE will not be responsible for reformatting, restructuring or converting any files submitted under this announcement.

The Project Information Memorandum, *excluding Appendices*, shall not exceed seventy-five (75) pages. Pages in excess of the page limitation will not be considered for evaluation. All text shall be typed, single spaced, using 12 point font, 1 inch margins, and unreduced 8–1/2-inch by 11-inch pages. Illustrations and charts shall be legible with all text in legible font. Pages shall be sequentially numbered. Except as otherwise noted herein the page guidelines previously set forth constitute a limitation on the total amount of material that may be submitted for evaluation. No material may be incorporated in any application by reference as a means to circumvent the page limitation.

D. Form of Project Information Memorandum

PROJECT INFORMATION MEMORANDUM

I. SUMMARY AND INTRODUCTION

- Description of the Project
- Financing and Ownership Structure
- Describe the main parties to the project, including background, ownership and related experience
- Current Project Status and Schedule to Beginning of Construction

II. TECHNOLOGY AND TECHNICAL INFORMATION

Provide a description of the proposed technology, including sufficient supporting information (such as vendor guarantees, process flow diagrams, equipment descriptions, information on each major process unit and the total plant, compositions of major streams, and the technical plan for achieving the goals proposed for the project) as would be needed to allow DOE to confirm that the technical requirements of § 48B are met. Specifically, the applicant should:

- Provide evidence sufficient to demonstrate that the proposed technology will employ gasification technology as defined in § 48B(c)(2).
- Present information sufficient to justify the total amount of synthesis gas (as defined in § 48B(c)(2)) to be produced by the project (synthesis gas capacity). Provide the total MMBtu/hr of the syngas (HHV) at the gasifier outlet.
- Provide evidence sufficient to ensure that fuels defined in § 48B(c)(2) will comprise 90 percent of the total fuel input (fuels defined in § 48B(c)(2) and any other fuel input) for the project. Provide the total quantities of CO, H2, CH4, CO2, and water in the syngas.
- Identify the domestic industry for which the proposed project is intended to be used.
- Identify the specific products and quantities produced by the proposed project, providing sufficient evidence to support claims.
- Provide evidence that indicates, for projects using non renewable fuels, the gasification technology design reflects reasonable consideration for, and is capable of, accommodating equipment necessary to capture carbon dioxide for later use or sequestration. Include the project status and relevant information from ongoing engineering activities. Also include in an appendix any engineering report or reports used by the applicant to develop the project and to estimate costs and operating performance.

III. APPLICANT'S CAPABILITY TO ACCOMPLISH THE TECHNICAL OBJECTIVES

Provide a narrative supporting the applicant's capability to accomplish the technical objectives of the proposed project, including supporting documentation demonstrating that the applicant has assembled a team that is formally committed to participate in the proposed project.

- Provide information to support that the applicant has assembled a team with the skills and resources needed to implement the project as proposed. Provide signed agreements or letters from team members demonstrating that the proposed team members are fully committed to the project.
- Provide information, including examples of prior similar projects completed by applicant, EPC contractor, and suppliers of major subsystems or equipment, which support the capabilities of the applicant and its team members to design, construct, permit, and operate the facility. The applicant should demonstrate that the team members have a corporate history of successful completion of similar projects.
- Provide information to support that key personnel of the applicant and its team members have knowledge, experience, and adequate degree of involvement to successfully implement the project.
- Include the project status and relevant information from ongoing engineering activities. Also include in an appendix any engineering report or reports used by the applicant to develop the project and to estimate costs and operating performance. Included copies of any signed agreements to support project status claims regarding preliminary design studies, FEED, and EPC-type agreements.

IV. SITE CONTROL AND OWNERSHIP

- Provide evidence that the applicant owns or controls a site in the United States of sufficient size to allow the proposed project to be constructed and operated on a long-term basis. Documentation such as a deed demonstrating the applicant owns the project site, a signed option to purchase the site from the site owner, or a letter of intent by the site owner to sell the site to the applicant should be provided.
- Describe the current infrastructure at the site available to meet the needs of the project.
- Provide documentation supporting applicant's conclusion that the proposed site can fully meet all environmental, feedstock supply, water supply, transportation and public policy requirements. Such documentation may include signed agreements, letters of intent, or term sheets, such as coal supply, water supply, and product transportation, etc., and regulatory approvals supporting the key claims.
- Provide detailed plans, schedules and status updates, particularly, for sites with pre-existing conditions that could impact the proposed project. Pre-existing conditions may include, but are not limited to, sites with mandated environmental remediation efforts; brown-field sites that will require building demolition; or sites requiring substantial rerouting of existing roads, railroads, or pipelines prior to the start of the project.
- Applicants must select one "proposed site." However, projects with key physical or logistical elements that require close integration with another system for the project to succeed should provide information on all integrated systems regardless of where they are located. Example 1: a gasification plant designed to operate exclusively on coals from a to-be-opened mine should provide supporting documentation for the new mine. Example 2: an oxygen-blown gasification plant planning to purchase oxygen from a third party who will construct a plant exclusively for this project should provide documentation for the oxygen supplier.

V. UTILIZATION OF PROJECT OUTPUT

- Provide evidence that a market exists for the products of the proposed project as evidenced by contracts or written statements of intent from potential customers. Such documentation should be signed by authorizing officials by both the buyer and seller, and may include: Sales Agreements, Letters of Intent, Memoranda of Understanding, and Option Agreements.
- Describe any sales arrangements that exist or that may be contemplated and summaries of their key terms and conditions.
- Include as an appendix any independent Market Study that has been done in connection with this project, or if no independent market study has been completed, provide a copy of the applicant-prepared market study.

VI. PROJECT ECONOMICS

Describe the project economics and provide satisfactory evidence of economic feasibility as demonstrated through the financial forecast and the underlying project assumptions. The project economic and financial assumptions should be clearly stated and explained.

Discuss the market potential for the proposed technology beyond the project proposed by the applicant.

Show calculation for the amount of tax credit applied for based on allowable cost.

VII. PROJECT DEVELOPMENT AND FINANCIAL PLAN

Provide the total project budget and major plant costs (*e.g.*, development, operating, capital, construction, and financing costs). Provide the estimated annual budget for and source of project development costs from the time of the application until the beginning of construction, including legal, engineering, financial, environmental, overhead, and other development costs. Describe the overall approach to project development and financing sufficient to demonstrate project viability. Provide a complete explanation of the source and amount of project equity. Provide a complete explanation of the source and amount of project debt. Provide the audited financial statements for the applicant for the most recently ended three fiscal years, and the unaudited quarterly interim financial statements for the current fiscal year for (a) the applicant, (b) for any of the project parties providing funding, and (c) for any third party funding source. If the applicant or another party does not have audited financial statements, the applicant or the party should provide equivalent financial statements prepared by the applicant or the party, in accordance with Generally Accepted Accounting Principles, and certified as to accuracy and completeness by the Chief Financial Officer of the party providing the statements. Applicant should demonstrate that the award recipient is financially viable without the receipt of additional federal funding associated with the proposed project.

For internally financed projects, provide evidence that the applicant has sufficient assets to fund the project with its own resources. Identify any internal approvals required to commit such assets. Include in an appendix copies of any board resolution or other approval authorizing the applicant to commit funds and proceed with the project.

For projects financed through debt instruments either unsecured or secured by assets other than the project, provide evidence that the applicant has sufficient creditworthiness to obtain such financing along with a discussion of the status of such instruments. Identify any internal approvals required to commit the applicant to pursue such financing. Include in an appendix, copies of any board resolution or other approval authorizing the applicant to commit to such financing.

For projects financed through investor equity contributions, discuss the source and status of each contribution. Discuss each investor's financial capability to meet its commitments. Include in an appendix, copies of any executed investment agreements.

If financing through a public offering or private placement of either debt or equity is planned for the project, provide the expected debt rating for the issue and an explanation of applicant's justification for the rating. Describe the status of any discussions with prospective investment bankers or other financial advisors.

For projects employing nonrecourse debt financing, provide a complete discussion of the approach to, and status of, such financing. In an appendix, provide (1) an Excel based financial model of the project, with formulas, so that review of the model calculations and assumptions may be facilitated; provide *pro-forma* project financial, economic, capital cost, and operating assumptions, including detail of all project capital costs, development costs, interest during construction, other operating expenses, and all other costs and expenses.

VIII. PROJECT CONTRACT STRUCTURE

Describe the current status of each of the agreements set forth below. Include as an appendix copies of the contracts or summaries of the key provisions of each of the following agreements:

- Raw Material Input Supply: describe the source and price of raw material inputs for the project. Include as an appendix any studies of price and amount of raw materials that have been prepared. Include a summary of any supply contracts and a signed copy of the contracts.
- Transportation: explain the arrangements for transporting project inputs and outputs, including costs.
- Operations & Maintenance Agreement: include a summary of the terms and conditions of the contract and a copy of the contract.
- Shareholders Agreement: summarize key terms and include the agreement as an appendix.
- Engineering, Procurement and Construction Agreement: describe the key terms of the existing or expected EPC contract arrangement, including firm price, liquidated damages, hold-backs, performance guarantees, etc.
- Water Supply Agreement: confirm the amount, source, and cost of water supply.

IX. PERMITS INCLUDING ENVIRONMENTAL AUTHORIZATIONS

- Provide a complete list of all federal, state, and local permits, including environmental authorizations or reviews, necessary to commence construction of the project.
- Explain what actions have been taken to date to satisfy the required authorizations and reviews, and the status of each.
- Provide a description of the applicant's plan to obtain and complete all necessary permits, and environmental authorizations and reviews.
- Existing permits and permit applications must be specific to the project proposed. If existing permits are not specific for the proposed project (*i.e.*, permits for oil-fired or natural gas-based systems), specific plans, procedures and schedules for reapplying, modifying and/or renegotiating permits should be provided.

X. PROJECT SCHEDULE

- Provide an overall project schedule which includes technical, business, financial, permitting and other factors to substantiate that the project will meet the 7 year requirement for placing the plant in service.
- The project schedule should be comprehensive and provide sufficient detail to demonstrate how applicant will meet the placed-in-service requirement. The schedule should demonstrate that the applicant understands the required tasks, and has allowed realistic times for accomplishing the technical and financial tasks. The schedule should include the milestone accomplishments needed to obtain the financing for the project.

APPENDICES

- Copy of internal or external engineering reports.
- Copy of site plan, together with evidence that applicant owns or controls a site. Examples of evidence would include a deed, or an executed contract to purchase or lease the site.
- Information supporting applicant's conclusion that the site is fully acceptable as the project site with respect to environment, raw material supply, water supply, and public policy reasons.
- Project Market Study.
- Financial Model of project.
- Financial statements for the applicant and other project funding sources for the most recently ended three fiscal years, and the unaudited quarterly interim financial statements for the current fiscal year.
- Expressions of interest or commitment letters from funding sources.
- For each project contract, if no contract currently exists, provide a summary of the expected terms and conditions.
- List of all federal, state, and local permits, including environmental authorizations or reviews, necessary to commence construction.
- Copies of any contract or written statements from customers of intent to purchase project products.

E. Evaluation Criteria:

Industrial Gasification Projects: will be evaluated on whether they meet all the requirements of § 48B.

Technical: will be evaluated on whether the applicant has demonstrated the capability to accomplish the technical objectives.

Site: will be evaluated on the basis that the site requirement for ownership or control has been met, and that the site is suitable for the proposed project.

Economic: will be evaluated on whether the project has demonstrated economic feasibility, taking into consideration the submitted financial and project development and structural information and financial plan.

Schedule: will be evaluated on the applicant's ability to meet the 7 year placed-in-service requirement.

F. Program Policy Factors to be used by DOE in the evaluation of applications

Section 48B identifies minimum requirements for consideration for the qualifying gasification project credit, including the project's technical feasibility, cost, and applicant's ability. In the event that there are more qualified (certifiable) applications than there are available tax credits, the DOE will apply additional factors to rank eligible projects based on their ability to advance the deployment of industrial gasification technology beyond its current state.

If there are two or more certified applications than available credits, DOE will rank the certified projects in descending order (that is, first, second, third, etc.), based on evaluation of the following Program Policy Factors. Factors 1, 2, and 3 are Primary Ranking Factors. A certified project that satisfies one of these factors will be ranked ahead of each project that satisfies only factors listed below that factor. Specifically, all certified projects satisfying Factor 1 will be selected before any project that does not satisfy Factor 1; all projects satisfying Factor 2 will be ranked ahead of any project that satisfies only Factor 3 and/or one or more Secondary Ranking Factors; and all projects satisfying Factor 3 will be ranked ahead of any project that does not satisfy any Primary Ranking Factors.

Primary Ranking Factors:

1. Capture and sequestration of 50 percent or more of carbon dioxide emissions. Only projects capturing and sequestering 50 percent or more of the plant's carbon dioxide emissions will satisfy this factor. Within this factor, higher rankings will be given to those projects capturing and sequestering higher percentages of plant carbon dioxide emissions.

2. Use of advanced technologies that optimize the plant for future carbon dioxide capture (for example, gasifier sizing and pressure, air separation unit sizing, and quench system) as well as systems that are designed to capture and sequester less than 50 percent of the carbon dioxide. Within this factor, higher rankings will be given to those projects capturing and sequestering higher percentages of plant carbon dioxide emissions and/or requiring less retrofitting to implement greater than 50 percent carbon capture and sequestration.

3. Location of the facility within 25 miles of potential carbon sequestration locations and carbon dioxide (CO2) pipelines or pipeline easements. Within this factor, higher rankings will be given to those projects with the facility located closer to potential carbon sequestration locations and carbon dioxide (CO2) pipelines or pipeline easements.

Secondary Ranking Factors:

- Location of the facility relative to potential carbon sequestration locations and carbon dioxide (CO2) pipelines or pipeline easements (for facilities not meeting Factor 3).
- Presentation of other environmental, economic, or performance benefits (including priority factors that are listed in section 5.02(9) of Notice 2007–53 and are not included in the Primary Ranking Factors).
- Higher plant efficiency.
- Geographic distribution of potential markets.
- The ratio of total synthesis gas capacity (as defined in section 3.03 of Notice 2007–53) to requested tax credit.
- Diversity of technology approaches and methods.

G. Supplemental Technical and Financial Guidance for Section D "Project Information Memorandum"

Technology and Technical Information

- It is important that the applicant select a specific gasification system for their project. Without that decision, it is difficult to provide the necessary specific design information needed for DOE to evaluate the project feasibility with respect to performance, emissions, outputs of major streams as well as capital and operating costs.

Project Economics

- Applicants should demonstrate the project's economic feasibility and financial viability by providing a clear statement and explanation of the economic and financial assumptions made by the applicant, and a financial forecast for the project. The financial forecast should flow logically from the applicant's assumptions and be consistent with them. Applicants should include assumptions regarding financial and economic issues that may not be included in the project costs but have a direct impact on the project. The examples given in the "Site Control and Ownership" section are relevant here and their impact on the project economics should be discussed here.

Project Development and Financial Plan

- The information provided by the applicant in this section should demonstrate that the applicant's financial plan for developing the project is feasible and that the applicant will have access to necessary financing. The applicant should explain the source and timing for obtaining all financing, including the project development costs. It is important that the applicant explain and provide evidence that it has the capacity to fund the pre-construction project development costs, together with a budget for and description of those costs. Note that financial information is required for the applicant and for any other funding source.

Project Contract Structure

- This section requires that the applicant demonstrate an understanding of the commercial contracting process and show progress in establishing the framework of contracts and agreements that a project typically requires. Applicants should show that their intended contract structure is reasonable and that their assumptions relative to price, terms, and conditions are consistent with current market conditions. Evidence of final agreements, agreements in principle, or summaries of terms and conditions between the applicant and contract counterparties should be provided, if available.

APPENDIX C

CONSENT TO PUBLIC DISCLOSURE OF CERTAIN QUALIFYING GASIFICATION PROJECT PROGRAM APPLICATION INFORMATION

In the event that the Application for § 48B Certification of [(*Insert name of applicant-taxpayer here*): ________________] (the Applicant-Taxpayer) for an allocation of qualifying gasification project credits under section 48B of the Internal Revenue Code is approved, the undersigned authorized representative of the Applicant-Taxpayer hereby consents to the disclosure by the Internal Revenue Service through publication of a Notice in the Internal Revenue Bulletin or a press release of: (1) the name of the Applicant-Taxpayer; (2) if the Applicant-Taxpayer is a member of an affiliated group filing consolidated returns, the name of the common parent of the group; (3) the type and location of the project that is the subject of the Application for § 48B Certification; and (4) the amount of the allocation, if any, of qualifying gasification project credits for such project. The undersigned understands that this information might be published, broadcast, discussed, or otherwise disseminated in the public record.

This authorization shall become effective upon the execution thereof. Except to the extent disclosure is authorized herein, the returns and return information of the undersigned taxpayer are confidential and are protected by law under the Internal Revenue Code.

I certify that I have the authority to execute this consent to disclose on behalf of the taxpayer named below.

Date: ____________________

Signature: ______________________________

Print name: ______________________________

Title: ______________________________

Name of Applicant-Taxpayer: ______________________________

Taxpayer Identification Number: ______________________________

Taxpayer's Address:

____
____
____

Note: Treasury Regulations require that the Internal Revenue Service must receive this consent within 60 days after it is signed and dated.

---

26 CFR 601.602: Tax forms and instructions.
(Also: Part 1, 6011, 6012, 6033, 6037, 6061, 1.6011–1(a), 1.6012–5, 301.6061–1(b).)

Rev. Proc. 2007–40

TABLE OF CONTENTS

SECTION 1. PURPOSE

This revenue procedure informs Authorized IRS *e-file* Providers of their obligations to the Internal Revenue Service (the Service), taxpayers, and other participants in the IRS *e-file* Program, and combines the rules governing IRS *e-file*.

SECTION 2. BACKGROUND AND CHANGES

.01 Section 1.6011–1(a) of the Income Tax Regulations provides that every person subject to income tax must make a return or statement as required by the regulations. The return or statement must include the information required by the applicable regulations or forms.

.02 Section 301.6061–1(b) of the Regulations on Procedure and Administration authorizes the Secretary to prescribe in forms, instructions, or other appropriate guidance the method of signing any return, statement, or other document required to be made under any provision of the internal revenue laws or regulations.

.03 Section 1.6012–5 of the Income Tax Regulations provide that the Commissioner may authorize the use, at the option of a person required to make a return, of a composite return in lieu of any form specified in 26 CFR Part 1 (Income Tax), subject to such conditions, limitations, and special rules governing the preparation, execution, filing, and correction thereof as the Commissioner may deem appropriate.

.04 Section 6011(e)(1) of the Internal Revenue Code (the Code) gives specific authority for the Service and the Treasury Department to "prescribe regulations providing standards for determining which returns must be filed on magnetic media or in other machine-readable form." On January 12, 2005, the Service and the Treasury Department published in the Federal Register (T.D. 9175, 2005–1 C.B. 665 [70 FR 2012–01]) temporary regulations mandating the electronic filing of certain Forms 1120, 1120S, 990 and 990–PF under sections 301.6011–5T, 301.6037–2T, and 301.6033–4T. On November 12, 1999, the Service and the Treasury Department also published in the Federal Register (T.D. 8843, 1999–2 C.B. 590 [64 FR 61502]) final regulations mandating the electronic filing of certain Forms 1065 under section 301.6011–3.

.05 This revenue procedure combines the rules governing IRS *e-file* including the rules governing electronic filing of:

(1) Form 56, *Notice Concerning Fiduciary Relationship*;

(2) Form 720, *Quarterly Federal Excise Tax Return*;

(3) Form 940, *Employer's Annual Federal Unemployment (FUTA) Tax Return*;

(4) Form 941, *Employer's QUARTERLY Federal Tax Return*;

(5) Form 944, *Employer's ANNUAL Federal Tax Return*;

(6) Form 990, *Return of Organization Exempt From Income Tax*;

(7) Form 990–EZ, *Short Form Return of Organization Exempt From Income Tax*;

(8) Form 990–PF, *Return of Private Foundation or Section 4947(a)(1) Nonexempt Charitable Trust Treated as a Private Foundation*;

(9) Form 1040 and 1040A, *U.S. Individual Income Tax Return*, and Form 1040EZ, *Income Tax Return for Single and Joint Filers With No Dependents*;

(10) Form 1041, *U.S. Income Tax Return for Estates and Trusts*;

(11) Form 1065, *U.S. Return of Partnership Income*;

(12) Form 1120, *U.S. Corporation Income Tax Return*;

(13) Form 1120–POL, *U.S. Income Tax Return for Certain Political Organizations*; and

(14) Form 1120S, *U.S. Income Tax Return for an S Corporation*;

(15) Form 2290, *Heavy Highway Vehicle Use Tax Return*;

(16) Form 2350, *Application for Extension of Time To File U.S. Income Tax Return*;

(17) Form 2688, *Application for Additional Extension of Time To File U.S. Individual Income Tax Return*;

(18) Form 4868, *Application for Automatic Extension of Time To File U.S. Individual Income Tax Return*;

(19) Form 7004, *Application for Automatic 6-Month Extension of Time To File Certain Business Income Tax, Information, and Other Returns*;

(20) Form 8849, *Claim for Refund of Excise Taxes*;

(21) Form 8868, *Application for Extension of Time To File an Exempt Organization Return*;

(22) Form 9465, *Installment Agreement Request*; and

(23) Any successor forms to the forms listed above, and any future forms or returns that may be filed by Authorized IRS *e-file* Providers.

.06 This revenue procedure does not cover procedures governing electronic filing of Form 1040NR, *U.S. Nonresident Alien Income Tax Return*. For procedures governing the electronic filing of Form 1040NR, see Rev. Proc. 2000–24, 2000–1 C.B. 1133.

.07 This revenue procedure also does not cover providers of information returns that are filed under the FIRE (Filing Information Returns Electronically) Program.

See Publication 1220, *Specifications for Filing Forms 1098, 1099, 5498 and W2-G Electronically or Magnetically*. The information returns not covered by this revenue procedure include:

(1) Form 1042–S, *Foreign Person's U.S. Source Income Subject to Withholding*;

(2) Form 1098 series;

(3) Form 1099 series;

(4) Form 5498, *IRA Contribution Information*;

(5) Form 8027, *Employer's Annual Information Return of Tip Income and Allocated Tips*; and

(6) Form W–2G, *Certain Gambling Winnings*.

.08 Many of the rules governing participation in IRS *e-file* are now set forth in IRS Publications. See section 5.01 of this revenue procedure.

.09 Rev. Proc. 2005–60, 2005–2 C.B. 449, is revised by adding a new section 9 that provides that the IRS may deny an application to participate in IRS *e-file* or revoke an Authorized IRS *e-file* Provider's participation in IRS *e-file* if the firm, a Principal, or Responsible Official has been enjoined from filing returns because of a Federal or State court order or injunction or other legal action that would prevent participation in the program. In such cases the denied applicant or *e-file* provider will not be entitled to seek administrative review of the denial under the procedures set out in this revenue procedure.

SECTION 3. DEFINITIONS

.01 Authorized IRS *e-file* Provider. A participant in IRS *e-file* is referred to as an "Authorized IRS *e-file* Provider." The five categories of Authorized IRS *e-file* Providers are:

(1) Electronic Return Originator. An Electronic Return Originator (ERO) originates the electronic submission of returns.

(2) Intermediate Service Provider. An Intermediate Service Provider receives tax return information from an ERO (or from a taxpayer or tax-exempt organization that files electronically using a personal computer, modem or the Internet, and commercial tax preparation software), processes the return information, and either forwards the information to a Transmitter, or sends the information back to the ERO (or taxpayer or tax-exempt organization).

(3) Software Developer. A Software Developer develops software for the purposes of (a) formatting electronic return information according to publications issued by the Service that set forth electronic return file specifications and record layouts for tax returns; and/or (b) transmitting electronic tax return information directly to the Service.

(4) Transmitter. A Transmitter transmits electronic return information directly to the Service.

(5) Reporting Agent. A Reporting Agent is an accounting service, franchiser, bank, service bureau, or other entity that complies with Rev. Proc. 2007–38, 2007–25 I.R.B. 1442, and is authorized to perform one or more of the acts listed in Rev. Proc. 2007–38 on behalf of a taxpayer.

The five categories of Authorized IRS *e-file* Providers are not mutually exclusive. For example, an ERO can, at the same time, be a Transmitter, Software Developer, or Intermediate Service Provider depending on the function(s) performed.

.02 Responsible Official. A Responsible Official is an individual with authority over the IRS *e-file* operation of the office(s) of the Authorized IRS *e-file* Provider, is the first point of contact with the Service, and has authority to sign revised IRS *e-file* applications. A Responsible Official is responsible for ensuring that the Authorized IRS *e-file* Provider adheres to the provisions of this revenue procedure and the publications and notices governing the IRS *e-file* Program.

.03 Principal. The Principal for a business or organization includes the following:

(1) Sole Proprietorship. The sole proprietor is the Principal for a sole proprietorship.

(2) Partnership. Each partner who has a 5 percent or more interest in a partnership is a Principal. If no partner has at least a 5 percent or more interest in the partnership, the Principal is an individual authorized to act for the partnership in legal and/or tax matters.

(3) Corporation. The President, Vice–President, Secretary, and Treasurer are each a Principal of the corporation.

(4) Other. The Principal for an entity that is not a sole proprietorship, partnership, or corporation is an individual authorized to act for the entity in legal and/or tax matters.

SECTION 4. ACCEPTANCE TO PARTICIPATE IN THE IRS *e-file* PROGRAM

.01 Sole proprietors, businesses, and organizations that wish to become an Authorized IRS *e-file* Provider must apply for participation and must be accepted by the Service.

.02 The procedures governing application to the IRS *e-file* Program are included in Publication 3112, *IRS e-file Application and Participation*.

.03 The circumstances under which the Service may deny participation in the IRS *e-file* Program are also included in Publication 3112. An applicant who is denied participation may seek administrative review of the denial except as provided for in section 8 of this revenue procedure.

.04 To continue participation in the IRS *e-file* Program, an Authorized IRS *e-file* Provider must adhere to all requirements of this revenue procedure and the publications and notices governing IRS *e-file*.

SECTION 5. RESPONSIBILITIES OF AN AUTHORIZED IRS *e-file* PROVIDER

.01 To ensure that returns are accurately and efficiently filed, an Authorized IRS *e-file* Provider must comply with the provisions of this revenue procedure and all publications and notices governing IRS *e-file*. The Service will from time to time update such publications and notices to reflect changes to the program. It is the responsibility of the Authorized IRS *e-file* Provider to ensure that it complies with the latest version of all publications and notices. The publications and notices governing the IRS *e-file* Program include:

(1) Publication 1345, *Handbook for Authorized IRS e-file Providers of Individual Income Tax Returns*;

(2) Publication 1345A, *Filing Season Supplement for Authorized IRS e-file Providers of Individual Income Tax Returns*;

(3) Publication 1346, *Electronic Return File Specifications and Record Layouts for Individual Income Tax Returns*;

(4) Publication 1436, *Test Package for Electronic Filers of Individual Income Tax Returns*;

(5) Publication 1437, *Procedures for the 1041 e-file Program, U.S. Income Tax Return for Estates and Trusts*;

(6) Publication 1438, *File Specifications, Validation Criteria and Record Layouts for the Form 1041 e-file Program, U.S. Income Tax Return for Estates and Trusts*;

(7) Publication 1438–A, *(Supplement) for the 1041 e-file Program, U.S. Income Tax Return for Estates and Trusts*;

(8) Publication 1474, *Technical Specifications Guide For Reporting Agent Authorization and Federal Tax Depositors*;

(9) Publication 1524, *Procedures for 1065 e-file Program, U.S. Return of Partnership Income*;

(10) Publication 1525, *File Specifications, Validation Criteria and Record Layouts for the 1065 e-file Program, U.S. Return of Partnership Income*;

(11) Publication 1855, *Technical Specifications Guide for the Electronic Filing of Form 941, Employer's Quarterly Federal Tax Return*;

(12) Publication 3112, *IRS e-file Application and Participation*;

(13) Publication 3416, *1065 e-file Program, U.S. Return of Partnership Income (Publication 1525 Supplement)*;

(14) Publication 3715, *Technical Specifications Guide for the Electronic Filing of Form 940, Employer's Federal Unemployment (FUTA) Tax Return*;

(15) Publication 3823, *Employment Tax e-file System Implementation and User Guide*;

(16) Publication 4162, *Modernized e-file Test Package for Forms 1120/1120S*;

(17) Publication 4163, *Modernized e-file (MeF) Information for Authorized IRS e-file Providers of Forms 1120/1120S*;

(18) Publication 4164, *Modernized e-file (MeF) Guide for Software Developers and Transmitters*;

(19) Publication 4206, *Information for Authorized IRS e-file Providers of Exempt Organization Filings*; and

(20) Postings to the IRS web site at: *http://www.irs.gov* on the Internet, and published and future guidance in the Internal Revenue Bulletin and the Federal Register.

.02 The publications and notices listed in section 5.01 supplement this revenue procedure. A violation of any provision of these publications and notices is considered a violation of this revenue procedure and may subject an Authorized IRS *e-file* Provider to the sanctions provided in section 7 of this revenue procedure.

.03 The security of taxpayer accounts and personal information is a top priority for the Service. It is the responsibility of each Authorized IRS *e-file* Provider to have security systems in place to prevent unauthorized access to taxpayer accounts and personal information by third parties. The Gramm-Leach-Bliley Act, codified at 15 U.S.C. §§ 6801–6827, includes rules applicable to Authorized IRS *e-file* Providers that are designed to ensure the security and privacy of taxpayer information. Violation of the provisions of the Gramm-Leach-Bliley Act and the implementing rules and regulations promulgated by the Federal Trade Commission, or violations of the non-disclosure rules contained in sections 6713 or 7216 or the regulations promulgated thereunder, are considered violations of this revenue procedure and may subject an Authorized IRS *e-file* Provider to penalties as set forth in section 6 of this revenue procedure or sanctions provided in section 7 of this revenue procedure.

.04 In addition to the responsibilities defined in 5.01, 5.02, and 5.03 above, additional Authorized IRS *e-file* Providers responsibilities may be defined in statutes and regulations, revenue procedures, publications, postings to the IRS web site at: *http://www.irs.gov* on the Internet, and published and future guidance in the Internal Revenue Bulletin and the Federal Register.

SECTION 6. PENALTIES

.01 Penalties for Disclosure or Use of Information.

(1) An Authorized IRS *e-file* Provider is a tax return preparer under the definition of section 7216(a) of the Code. Tax return preparers are subject to criminal penalties for unauthorized disclosure or use of tax return information. See section 7216 (a). In addition, section 6713 establishes civil penalties for unauthorized disclosure or use of income tax return information by tax return preparers.

(2) In certain situations, under section 7216(b)(2), disclosure of tax return information among Authorized IRS *e-file* Providers for the purpose of electronically filing a return is permissible. For example, an ERO may pass on tax return information to an Intermediate Service Provider and/or a Transmitter for the purpose of having an electronic return formatted and transmitted to the Service.

.02 Other Preparer Penalties.

(1) Preparer penalties may be imposed against an individual or firm meeting the definition of a tax return preparer under section 7701(a)(36) and section 301.7701–15. Preparer penalties that may be imposed under appropriate circumstances include, but are not limited to, those set forth in sections 6694, 6695, and 6713. **Caution: The regulations cited in this section 6.02 do not reflect amendments to the definition of tax return preparer made by the Small Business and Work Opportunity Act of 2007.**

(2) Under section 301.7701–15(d)(1), Authorized IRS *e-file* Providers are not tax return preparers for the purpose of assessing most preparer penalties as long as their services are limited to "typing, reproduction, or other mechanical assistance in the preparation of a return or claim for refund."

(3) If an ERO, Intermediate Service Provider, Transmitter, or the product of a Software Developer alters the tax return information in a nonsubstantive way, this alteration will be considered to come under the "mechanical assistance" exception described in section 301.7701–15(d)(1), and will not cause an Authorized IRS *e-file* Provider to become a tax return preparer. A nonsubstantive change is a correction or change limited to a transposition error, misplaced entry, spelling error, or arithmetic correction.

(4) If an ERO, Intermediate Service Provider, Transmitter, or the product of a Software Developer alters tax return information in a way that does not come under the "mechanical assistance" exception, such Authorized IRS *e-file* Provider may be held liable for tax return preparer penalties.

.03 Other Penalties. In addition to the above specified provisions, the Service may impose all appropriate preparer, non-preparer, and disclosure penalties against an Authorized IRS *e-file* Provider as warranted under the circumstances.

SECTION 7. MONITORING AND SANCTIONING AN AUTHORIZED IRS *e-file* PROVIDER

.01 The Service will monitor Authorized IRS *e-file* Providers for compliance with the rules governing IRS *e-file*. The Service may sanction an Authorized IRS *e-file* Provider for violating any provision of this revenue procedure or the publications and notices governing IRS *e-file*.

.02 Sanctions that the Service may impose upon an Authorized IRS *e-file* Provider for violations described in section 7.01 of this revenue procedure include a written reprimand, suspension or expulsion from the program, and other sanctions, depending on the severity of the infraction. Publication 3112 describes the infraction categories and the rules governing the imposition of sanctions.

SECTION 8. ADMINISTRATIVE REVIEW PROCESS

.01 An applicant that has been denied participation in IRS *e-file* (see section 4.03 of this revenue procedure) has the right to an administrative review (except as provided in Section 9, below). During the administrative review process, the denial of participation remains in effect.

.02 An Authorized IRS *e-file* Provider may seek administrative review for any sanction the Service may impose under section 7 of this revenue procedure.

.03 Publication 3112 describes the procedures regarding administrative review of a denial of participation in IRS *e-file* and any sanction imposed by the Service.

SECTION 9. DENIAL OF APPLICATION OR REVOCATION OF AN AUTHORIZED IRS *e-file* PROVIDER'S PARTICIPATION IN IRS *e-file* DUE TO COURT INJUNCTION OR OTHER LEGAL ACTION

.01 The Service may deny an Application to participate in IRS *e-file* or revoke an Authorized IRS *e-file* Provider's participation in IRS *e-file* if the Provider, a Principal, or Responsible Official is enjoined from filing returns because of a Federal or State court injunction.

.02 The Service may deny an application or revoke an Authorized IRS *e-file* Provider's participation in IRS *e-file* if the Provider, Principal, or Responsible Official is prohibited from filing returns by any Federal or State legal action that would prohibit them from participation. A type of such legal action would be a Federal Executive Order such as Executive Order 13224 (September 23, 2001), which involves prohibitions directed at terrorist individuals or organizations. An organization described in this Executive Order would not be given IRS *e-file* privileges.

.03 If an Authorized IRS *e-file* Provider's participation in IRS *e-file* is revoked under this section, the Authorized IRS *e-file* Provider is not entitled to the Administrative Review Process set forth in Section 8 and cannot administratively appeal a revocation of its participation in IRS *e-file*. Nor can an applicant appeal its denial to participate in the program. If, however, the injunction or other legal action expires or a reviewing court reverses it, the enjoined Authorized IRS *e-file* Provider or denied applicant may reapply to participate in IRS *e-file* after the injunction or other legal action expires or the appellate decision reversing the injunction becomes final.

SECTION 10. PILOT PROGRAMS

.01 The Service regularly conducts pilot programs to introduce new technology into the IRS *e-file* Program. These pilot programs are usually conducted within a limited geographic area or within a limited taxpayer or practitioner community. The Service establishes rules for participating in these pilot programs and embodies these rules in an implementing document typically referred to as a "Memorandum of Understanding" or "Memorandum of Agreement." Pilot participants must agree to the provisions of the implementing document in order to participate in the pilot program.

.02 An implementing document supplements this revenue procedure, but does not supersede it.

.03 A violation of a provision of an implementing document is considered a violation of this revenue procedure and may subject the participant to sanctions (see section 7 of this revenue procedure).

SECTION 11. EFFECT ON OTHER DOCUMENTS

Rev. Proc. 2005–60, 2005–2 C.B. 449, is superseded.

SECTION 12. EFFECTIVE DATE

This revenue procedure is effective June 25, 2007.

SECTION 13. INTERNAL REVENUE SERVICE OFFICE CONTACT

All questions regarding this revenue procedure should be directed to the Service. The telephone number for this purpose is (202) 283–0261 (not a toll-free number).

SECTION 14. DRAFTING INFORMATION

The principal author of this revenue procedure is Michael E. Hara of the Office of Associate Chief Counsel (Procedure & Administration). For further information regarding this revenue procedure, contact Michael E. Hara at (202) 622–4910 (not a toll-free call).

---

26 CFR 1.601.204: Changes in accounting periods and in methods of accounting.
(Also Part 1: §§ 446, 475; 1.475(a)–4.)

Rev. Proc. 2007–41

SECTION 1. PURPOSE

Section 1.475(a)–4 of the Income Tax Regulations (the safe harbor valuation regulations) permits dealers in securities and dealers in commodities to elect to use the values of eligible positions reported on certain financial statements as the fair market values of those positions for purposes of section 475 of the Internal Revenue Code (Code). This revenue procedure designates the securities and commodities that are eligible positions for purposes of the safe harbor valuation regulations. This revenue procedure also illustrates the application of the safe harbor to taxpayers who are both dealers and traders.

SECTION 2. BACKGROUND

.01 Section 475(a) of the Internal Revenue Code requires dealers in securities to value their securities at fair market value as of the last business day of the year. Section 475(e) allows dealers in commodities to elect this same mark-to-market treatment for their commodities. Section 475(f) allows traders in securities (and traders in commodities) to elect mark-to-market treatment for positions held in connection with the taxpayer's securities trading business (or commodities trading business, as the case may be).

.02 Section 475(c)(2) defines security as any—

(A) share of stock in a corporation;

(B) partnership or beneficial ownership interest in a widely held or publicly traded partnership or trust;

(C) note, bond, debenture, or other evidence of indebtedness;

(D) interest rate, currency, or equity notional principal contract;

(E) evidence of interest in, or a derivative financial instrument in, any security described in subparagraph (A), (B), (C), or (D) [of section 475(c)(2)], or any currency, including any option, forward contract, short position, and any similar financial instrument in such a security or currency; and

(F) position which –

(i) is not a security described in subparagraph (A), (B), (C), (D), or (E) [of section 475(c)(2)];

(ii) is a hedge with respect to such a security, and;

(iii) is clearly identified in the dealer's records as being described in [subparagraph (F) of section 475(c)(2)] before the close of the day on which it was acquired or entered into (or such other time as the Secretary may by regulations prescribe).

Subparagraph (E) [of section 475(c)(2)] shall not include any contract to which section 1256(a) applies.

.03 Section 475(e)(2) defines commodity as:

(A) any commodity which is actively traded (within the meaning of section 1092(d)(1));

(B) any notional principal contract with respect to any commodity described in subparagraph (A) [of section 475(e)(2)];

(C) any evidence of an interest in, or a derivative instrument in, any commodity described in subparagraph (A) or (B) [of section 475(e)(2)], including any option, forward contract, futures contract, short position, and any similar instrument in such a commodity; and

(D) any position which —

(i) is not a commodity described in subparagraph (A), (B), or (C) [of section 475(e)(2)],

(ii) is a hedge with respect to such a commodity, and

(iii) is clearly identified in the taxpayer's records as being described in [subparagraph (D) of section 475(2)(2)] before the close of the day on which it was acquired or entered into (or such other time as the Secretary may by regulations prescribe).

.04 Section 475(g) provides that the Secretary shall prescribe regulations as may be necessary or appropriate to carry out the purposes of § 475. The legislative history of § 475 indicates that, under this regulatory authority, the Secretary may issue regulations to permit the use of valuation methodologies that reduce the administrative burden of compliance on taxpayers but that nevertheless clearly reflect income for federal income tax purposes. H.R. Rep. No. 213, 103d Cong., 1st Sess. 616 (1993), 1993–3 C.B. 494.

.05 On June 12, 2007, the Internal Revenue Service and the Treasury Department published the safe harbor valuation regulations in the **Federal Register** (T.D. 9328). These regulations provide an elective safe harbor method for valuation under § 475 for dealers in securities and dealers in commodities. Under the safe harbor in § 1.475(a)–4, an eligible taxpayer (as defined in § 1.475(a)–4) may elect that, if certain conditions and limitations are met, the values reported for certain eligible positions for financial reporting purposes are treated as those positions' fair market values for purposes of § 475.

.06 Section 1.475(a)–4(c) defines an eligible taxpayer as "(1) a dealer in securities, as defined in section 475(c)(1) and the regulations thereunder; or (2) a dealer in commodities, as defined in section 475(e) and any regulations thereunder, that is subject to an election under section 475(e)."

.07 Section 1.475(a)–4(g) states, "For any taxpayer, an eligible position is any security or commodity that the Commissioner in a revenue procedure or other published guidance designates with respect to that taxpayer as an eligible position for purposes of this safe harbor."

SECTION 3. SCOPE

This revenue procedure designates eligible positions under § 1.475(a)–4(g) for electing eligible taxpayers under § 1.475(a)–4(c).

SECTION 4. ELIGIBLE POSITIONS FOR SAFE HARBOR

Pursuant to § 1.475(a)–4(g), the following are designated as eligible positions for purposes of the safe harbor valuation regulations:

.01 With respect to an eligible taxpayer described in § 1.475(a)–4(c)(1), any security within the meaning of § 475(c)(2) and the regulations thereunder.

.02 With respect to an eligible taxpayer described in § 1.475(a)–4(c)(2), any commodity within the meaning of § 475(e)(2) and any regulations thereunder.

SECTION 5. EXAMPLES

The following examples illustrate the application of this revenue procedure:

.01 *Example 1.*

X is both a dealer in securities and a dealer in physical commodities. In a business unrelated to its commodities dealing business, *X* is a trader in commodity derivatives. With respect to the commodity trading business, *X* has made a mark-to-market election under § 475(f)(2) but has not made the commodity dealer election under § 475(e). *X* makes the valuation safe harbor election under § 1.475(a)–4.

Because *X* is a dealer in securities, *X* is an eligible taxpayer within the meaning of § 1.475(a)–4(c)(1). Accordingly, *X*'s securities are eligible positions with respect to *X*, and, if all other requirements are met, may be covered by the valuation safe harbor. Because *X* has not made the election under § 475(e), however, *X* is not described in § 1.475(a)–4(c)(2). For that reason, *X*'s commodity positions are not eligible positions with respect to *X*, and the positions in the commodity trading business (which are marked to market pursuant to § 475(f)) are not covered by the valuation safe harbor.

.02 *Example 2.*

Y is a dealer in commodities and is a trader in securities but is not a dealer in securities. *Y* makes the elections under § 475(e) (the commodity dealer election), under § 475(f) (the election to apply § 475 to its securities trading business), and under § 1.475(a)–4 (the valuation safe harbor election).

Because *Y* is an eligible taxpayer described in § 1.475(a)–4(c)(2), *Y*'s commodity positions are eligible positions with respect to *Y*. Although *Y* also marks to market the securities held in connection with *Y*'s securities trading business, those securities are not eligible positions with respect to *Y* because *Y* is not an eligible taxpayer described in § 1.475(a)–4(c)(1).

SECTION 6. EFFECTIVE DATES

This revenue procedure is effective on June 12, 2007.

SECTION 7. DRAFTING INFORMATION

The principal author of this revenue procedure is Marsha Ann Sabin or John W. Rogers III of the Office of Associate Chief Counsel (Financial Institutions & Products). For further information regarding this revenue procedure, contact Marsha Ann Sabin or John W. Rogers III at (202) 622–3950 (not a toll-free call).

Part IV. Items of General Interest

Notice of Proposed Rulemaking and Notice of Public Hearing

Employer Comparable Contributions to Health Savings Accounts Under Section 4980G

REG–143797–06

AGENCY: Internal Revenue Service (IRS), Treasury.

ACTION: Notice of proposed rulemaking and notice of public hearing.

SUMMARY: This document contains proposed regulations providing guidance on employer comparable contributions to Health Savings Accounts (HSAs) under section 4980G in instances where an employee has not established an HSA by December 31st and in instances where an employer accelerates contributions for the calendar year for employees who have incurred qualified medical expenses. In general, these proposed regulations affect employers that contribute to employees' HSAs. This document also provides notice of a public hearing on these proposed regulations.

DATES: Written or electronic comments must be received by August 29, 2007. Outlines of topics to be discussed at the public hearing scheduled for September 27, 2007, at 10:00 am, must be received by August 28, 2007.

ADDRESSES: Send submissions to: CC:PA:LPD:PR (REG–143797–06), Internal Revenue Service, POB 7604, Ben Franklin Station, Washington, DC 20044. Submissions may be hand delivered to CC:PA:LPD:PR (REG–143797–06), Courier's Desk, Internal Revenue Service, 1111 Constitution Avenue, NW, Washington, DC. Alternatively, taxpayers may submit comments electronically via the Federal eRulemaking Portal at *www.regulations.gov* (IRS - REG 143797 06). The public hearing will be held in the IRS Auditorium, Internal Revenue Service, 1111 Constitution Avenue, NW, Washington, DC.

FOR FURTHER INFORMATION CONTACT: Concerning the proposed regulations, Mireille Khoury at (202) 622–6080; concerning submissions of comments, the hearing, and/or to be placed on the building access list to attend the hearing, Kelly Banks at (202) 622–7180 (not toll-free numbers).

SUPPLEMENTARY INFORMATION:

Paperwork Reduction Act

The collections of information contained in this notice of proposed rulemaking have been submitted to the Office of Management and Budget for review in accordance with the Paperwork Reduction Act of 1995 (44 U.S.C. 3507(d)). Comments on the collections of information should be sent to the **Office of Management and Budget**, Attn: Desk Officer for the Department of the Treasury, **Office of Information and Regulatory Affairs**, Washington, DC 20503, with copies to the Internal Revenue Service, Attn: IRS Reports Clearance Officer, SE:W:CAR:MP:T:T:SP, Washington, DC 20224. Comments on the collection of information should be received by July 31, 2007.

Comments are specifically requested concerning:

Whether the proposed collections of information are necessary for the proper performance of the functions of the IRS, including whether the information will have practical utility;

The accuracy of the estimated burden associated with the proposed collection of information;

How the quality, utility, and clarity of the information to be collected may be enhanced;

How the burden of complying with the proposed collection of information may be minimized, including through the application of automated collection techniques or other forms of information technology; and

Estimates of capital or start-up costs and costs of operation, maintenance, and purchase of services to provide information.

The collection of information in these proposed regulations is in Q & A–14. This information is needed for purposes of making HSA contributions to employees who establish an HSA after the end of the calendar year but before the last day of February. The likely respondents are employers that contribute to employees' HSAs.

Estimated total annual reporting burden: 1,250,000 hours.

The estimated annual burden per respondent is .25 hour.

Estimated number of respondents: 5,000,000.

The estimated annual frequency of responses: 1.

An agency may not conduct or sponsor, and a person is not required to respond to, a collection of information unless it displays a valid control number assigned by the Office of Management and Budget.

Books or records relating to a collection of information must be retained as long as their contents may become material in the administration of any internal revenue law. Generally, tax returns and tax return information are confidential, as required by 26 U.S.C. 6103.

Background

This document contains proposed Pension Excise Tax Regulations (26 CFR part 54) under section 4980G of the Internal Revenue Code (Code). Under section 4980G, an excise tax is imposed on an employer that fails to make comparable contributions to the HSAs of its employees.

Section 1201 of the Medicare Prescription Drug, Improvement, and Modernization Act of 2003 (Act), Public Law 108–173, (117 Stat. 2066, 2003) added section 223 to the Code to permit eligible individuals to establish HSAs for taxable years beginning after December 31, 2003. Section 4980G was also added to the Code by the Act. Section 4980G(a) imposes an excise tax on the failure of an employer to make comparable contributions to the HSAs of its employees for a calendar year. Section 4980G(b) provides that rules and requirements similar to section 4980E (the comparability rules for Archer Medical Savings Accounts (Archer MSAs)) apply for purposes of section 4980G. Section 4980E(b) imposes an excise tax equal to 35% of the aggregate amount contributed by the employer to the Archer MSAs of employees during the calendar year if an employer fails to make comparable contributions to the Archer MSAs of its employees in a calendar year. Accordingly, if an employer fails to make comparable contributions to the HSAs of its employees during a calendar year, an excise tax equal to 35% of the aggregate amount contributed by the employer to the HSAs of its employees during that calendar year is imposed on the employer. See sections 4980G(a) and (b) and 4980E(b). See also Notice 2004–2, 2004–1 C.B. 269, Q & A–32.

On August 26, 2005, proposed regulations (REG–138647–04, 2005–2 C.B. 697) on the comparability rules of section 4980G were published in the **Federal Register** (70 FR 50233). On July 31, 2006, final regulations (REG–138647–04, 2006–3 I.R.B. 328) on the comparability rules were published in the **Federal Register** (71 FR 43056). The final regulations clarified and expanded upon the guidance regarding the comparability rules published in Notice 2004–2 and in Notice 2004–50, 2004–2 C.B. 196, Q & A–46 through Q & A–54. See §601.601(d)(2) of this chapter. Q & A–6(b) of the final regulations reserved the issue dealing with an employee who has not established an HSA by the end of the calendar year. These proposed regulations address that reserved issue and one additional issue concerning the acceleration of employer contributions.

Section 4980G was amended by section 306 of the Tax Relief and Health Care Act of 2006, Public Law 109–432 (120 Stat. 2922), effective for taxable years beginning after December 31, 2006. Treasury and IRS expect to publish guidance on the amendment to section 4980G.

Explanation of Provisions

Employee Has Not Established HSA by December 31

The proposed regulations provide a means for employers to comply with the comparability requirements with respect to employees who have not established an HSA by December 31, as well as with respect to employees who may have established an HSA but not notified the employer of that fact. The proposed regulations provide that, in order to comply with the comparability rules for a calendar year with respect to such employees, the employer must comply with a notice requirement and a contribution requirement. In order to comply with the notice requirement, the employer must provide all such employees, by January 15 of the following calendar year, written notice that each eligible employee who, by the last day of February, both establishes an HSA and notifies the employer that he or she has established the HSA will receive a comparable contribution to the HSA. For each such eligible employee who establishes an HSA and so notifies the employer by the end of February, the employer must contribute to the HSA by April 15 comparable amounts (taking into account each month that the employee was a comparable participating employee) plus reasonable interest. The notice may be delivered electronically. The proposed regulations provide sample language that employers may use as a basis in preparing their own notices.

Acceleration of Employer Contributions

The proposed regulations also address a second issue relating to acceleration of contributions. They provide that, for any calendar year, an employer may accelerate part or all of its contributions for the entire year to the HSAs of employees who have incurred during the calendar year qualified medical expenses exceeding the employer's cumulative HSA contributions at that time. If an employer accelerates contributions for this reason, these contributions must be available on an equal and uniform basis to all eligible employees throughout the calendar year and employers must establish reasonable uniform methods and requirements for acceleration of contributions and the determination of medical expenses. An employer is not required to contribute reasonable interest on either accelerated or non-accelerated HSA contributions. But see Q & A–6 and Q & A–12 in §54.4980G–4 for when reasonable interest must be paid.

Other issues

These proposed regulations concern only section 4980G. Other statutes may impose additional requirements (for example, the Health Insurance Portability and Accountability Act of 1996 (HIPAA) (sections 9801–9803)).

Proposed Effective Date

It is proposed that these regulations apply to employer contributions made on or after the date the final regulations are published in the **Federal Register**. However, taxpayers may rely on these regulations for guidance pending the issuance of final regulations. Alternatively, until the publication of final regulations, an employer may continue to rely on the last sentence of Q & A–6(a) of section 54.4980G–4 of the proposed regulations published in the **Federal Register** on August 26, 2005, which provides that, an employer is not required to make comparable contributions for a calendar year to an employee's HSA if the employee has not established an HSA by December 31st of the calendar year.

Special Analyses

It has been determined that this notice of proposed rulemaking is not a significant regulatory action as defined in Executive Order 12866. Therefore, a regulatory assessment is not required. It also has been determined that section 553(b) of the Administrative Procedure Act (5 U.S.C. chapter 5) does not apply to these regulations. It is hereby certified that the collection of information in these regulations will not have a significant economic impact on a substantial number of small entities. This certification is based on the fact the estimated burden associated with the information collection averages 15 minutes per respondent. Moreover, a model notice has been provided for employers who are subject to this collection of information and any burden imposed on employees due to the collection of information in these regulations will be outweighed by the benefit of receiving HSA contributions. Therefore, a Regulatory Flexibility Analysis under the Regulatory Flexibility Act (5 U.S.C. Chapter 6) is not required. Pursuant to section 7805(f) of the Internal Revenue Code, this regulation will be submitted to the Chief Counsel for Advocacy of the Small Business Administration for comment on its impact on small business.

Comments and Public Hearing

Before these proposed regulations are adopted as final regulations, consideration will be given to any written comments (a signed original and eight (8) copies) or electronic comments that are submitted timely to the IRS. The IRS and Treasury Department request comments on the clarity of the proposed regulations and how they can be made easier to understand. All comments will be available for public inspection and copying.

A public hearing has been scheduled for September 27, 2007, beginning at 10 a.m. in the Auditorium, Internal Revenue Service, 1111 Constitution Avenue, NW, Washington, DC. Due to building security procedures, visitors must enter at the Constitution Avenue entrance. In addition, all visitors must present photo identification to enter the building. Because of access restrictions, visitors will not be admitted beyond the immediate entrance area more than 30 minutes before the hearing starts. For information about having your name placed on the building access list to attend the hearing, see the "FOR FURTHER INFORMATION CONTACT" section of this preamble.

The rules of 26 CFR 601.601(a)(3) apply to the hearing. Persons who wish to present oral comments at the hearing must submit written or electronic comments by August 30, 2007, and an outline of the topics to be discussed and the amount of time to be devoted to each topic (a signed original and eight (8) copies) August 28, 2007. A period of 10 minutes will be allotted to each person for making comments. An agenda showing the scheduling of the speakers will be prepared after the deadline for receiving outlines has passed. Copies of the agenda will be available free of charge at the hearing.

Drafting Information

The principal author of these proposed regulations is Mireille Khoury, Office of Division Counsel/Associate Chief Counsel (Tax Exempt and Government Entities), Internal Revenue Service. However, personnel from other offices of the IRS and Treasury Department participated in their development.

* * * * *

Proposed Amendment to the Regulations

Accordingly, 26 CFR part 54 is proposed to be amended as follows:

PART 54—PENSION EXCISE TAXES

Paragraph 1. The authority citation for part 54 continues to read in part as follows:

Authority: 26 U.S.C. 7805 * * *

Par. 2. Section 54.4980G–0 is amended by adding entries for Q & A–14, Q & A–15 and Q & A–16 to read as follows:

§54.4980G–0 Table of contents.

* * * * *

§54.4980G–4 Calculating comparable contributions.

* * * * *

Q–14: How does an employer comply with the comparability rules if an employee has not established an HSA by December 31st?

Q–15: For any calendar year, may an employer accelerate part or all of its contributions for the entire year to the HSAs of employees who have incurred, during the calendar year, qualified medical expenses (as defined in section 223(d)(2)) exceeding the employer's cumulative HSA contributions at that time?

Q–16: What is the effective date for the rules in Q & A–14 and 15 of this section?

Par. 3. Section 54.4980G–4 is amended by:

1. Removing paragraph (b) and redesignating paragraph (c) as paragraph (b) in Q & A–6.

2. Adding Q & A–14, Q & A–15 and Q & A–16.

The additions read as follows:

§54.4980G–4 Calculating comparable contributions.

* * * * *

Q–14: Does an employer fail to satisfy the comparability rules for a calendar year if the employer fails to make contributions with respect to eligible employees because the employee has not established an HSA or because the employer does not know that the employee has established an HSA?

A–14: (a) *In general.* An employer will not fail to satisfy the comparability rules for a calendar year merely because the employer fails to make contributions with respect to an eligible employee because the employee has not established an HSA or because the employer does not know that the employee has established an HSA, if—

(1) The employer provides timely written notice to all such eligible employees that it will make comparable contributions for eligible employees who, by the last day of February of the following calendar year, both establish an HSA and notify the employer (in accordance with a procedure specified in the notice) that they have established an HSA; and

(2) For each such eligible employee who establishes an HSA and so notifies the employer on or before the last day of February of such following calendar year, the employer contributes to the HSA comparable amounts (taking into account each month that the employee was a comparable participating employee) plus reasonable interest by April 15th of such following calendar year.

(b) *Notice.* The notice described in paragraph (a) of this Q & A–14 must be provided to each eligible employee who has not established an HSA by December 31 or if the employer does not know if the employee established an HSA. The employer may provide the notice to other employees as well. However, if the employee has earlier notified the employer that he or she has established an HSA, or if the employer has previously made contributions to that employee's HSA, the employer may not condition making comparable contributions on receipt of any additional notice from that employee. For each calendar year, a notice is deemed to be timely if the employer provides the notice no earlier than 90 days before the first HSA employer contribution for that calendar year and no later than January 15 of the following calendar year.

(c) *Model notice.* Employers may use the following sample language as a basis in preparing their own notices.

Notice to Employees Regarding Employer Contributions to HSAs:

This notice explains how you may be eligible to receive contributions from [employer] if you are covered by a High Deductible Health Plan (HDHP). [Employer] provides contributions to the

Health Savings Account (HSA) of each employee who is [insert employer's eligibility requirements for HSA contributions] ("eligible employee"). If you are an eligible employee, you must do the following in order to receive an employer contribution:

(1) establish an HSA on or before the last day in February of [insert year after the year for which the contribution is being made] and;

(2) notify [insert name and contact information for appropriate person to be contacted] of your HSA account information on or before the last day in February of [insert year after year for which the contribution is being made]. [Specify the HSA account information that the employee must provide (*e.g.*, account number, name and address of trustee or custodian, etc.) and the method by which the employee must provide this account information (*e.g.*, in writing, on a certain form, etc.)].

If you establish your HSA on or before the last day of February in [insert year after year for which the contribution is being made] and notify [employer] of your HSA account information, you will receive your HSA contributions, plus reasonable interest, for [insert year for which contribution is being made] by April 15 of [insert year after year for which contribution is being made]. If, however, you do not establish your HSA or you do not notify us of your HSA account information by the deadline, then we are not required to make any contributions to your HSA for [insert applicable year]. You may notify us that you have established an HSA by sending an [e-mail or] a written notice to [insert name, title and, if applicable, e-mail address]. If you have any questions about this notice, you can contact [insert name and title] at [insert telephone number or other contact information].

(e) *Electronic delivery*. An employer may furnish the notice required under this section electronically. See §1.401(a)–21 of this chapter.

(f) *Examples*. The following examples illustrate the rules in this Q & A–14:

Example 1. In a calendar year, Employer Q contributes to the HSAs of current employees who are eligible individuals covered under any HDHP. For the 2009 calendar year, Employer Q contributes $50 per month on the first day of each month, beginning January 1st, to the HSA of each employee who is an eligible employee on that date. For the 2009 calendar year, Employer Q provides written notice satisfying the content requirements on October 16, 2008 to all employees regarding the availability of HSA contributions for eligible employees. For eligible employees who are hired after October 16, 2008, Employer Q provides such a notice no later than January 15, 2010. Employer Q's notice satisfies the notice requirements in paragraph (a)(1) of this Q & A–14.

Example 2. Employer R's written cafeteria plan permits employees to elect to make pre-tax salary reduction contributions to their HSAs. Employees making this election have the right to receive cash or other taxable benefits in lieu of their HSA pre-tax contribution. Employer R automatically contributes a non-elective matching contribution to the HSA of each employee who makes a pre-tax HSA contribution. Because Employer R's HSA contributions are made through the cafeteria plan, the comparability requirements do not apply to the HSA contributions made by Employer R. Consequently, Employer R is not required to provide written notice to its employees regarding the availability of this matching HSA contribution. See Q & A–1 in §54.4980G–5 for treatment of HSA contributions made through a cafeteria plan.

Example 3. In a calendar year, Employer S maintains an HDHP and only contributes to the HSAs of eligible employees who elect coverage under its HDHP. For the 2009 calendar year, Employer S employs ten eligible employees. For the 2009 calendar year, all ten employees have elected coverage under Employer S's HDHP and have established HSAs. For the 2009 calendar year, Employer S makes comparable contributions to the HSAs of all ten employees. Employer S satisfies the comparability rules. Thus, Employer S is not required to provide written notice to its employees regarding the availability of HSA contributions for eligible employees.

Example 4. In a calendar year, Employer T contributes to the HSAs of current full-time employees with family coverage under any HDHP. For the 2009 calendar year, Employer T provides timely written notice satisfying the content requirements to all employees regardless of HDHP coverage. Employer T makes identical monthly contributions to all eligible employees (meaning full time employees with family HDHP coverage) that establish HSAs. Employer T contributes comparable amounts (taking into account each month that the employee was a comparable participating employee) plus reasonable interest to the HSAs of the eligible employees that establish HSAs and provide the necessary information after the end of the year but on or before the last day of February, 2010. Employer T makes no contribution to the HSAs of employees that do not establish an HSA and provide the necessary information on or before the last day of February, 2010. Employer T satisfies the comparability requirements.

Example 5. For 2007, Employer V contributes to the HSAs of current full time employees with family coverage under any HDHP. Employer V has 500 current full time employees. As of the date for Employer V's first HSA contribution for the 2007 calendar year, 450 employees have established HSAs. Employer V provides timely written notice satisfying the content requirements only to those 50 current full time employees who have not established HSAs. Employer V makes identical quarterly contributions to the 450 employees who established HSAs. Employer V contributes comparable amounts to the eligible employees who establish HSAs and provide the necessary information after the end of the year but on or before the last day of February, 2008. Employer V makes no contribution to the HSAs of employees that do not establish an HSA and provide the necessary information on or before the last day of February, 2008. Employer V satisfies the comparability rules.

Q–15: For any calendar year, may an employer accelerate part or all of its contributions for the entire year to the HSAs of employees who have incurred, during the calendar year, qualified medical expenses (as defined in section 223(d)(2)) exceeding the employer's cumulative HSA contributions at that time?

A–15: (a) *In general*. Yes. For any calendar year, an employer may accelerate part or all of its contributions for the entire year to the HSAs of employees who have incurred, during the calendar year, qualified medical expenses exceeding the employer's cumulative HSA contributions at that time. If an employer accelerates contributions to employees' HSAs, all accelerated contributions must be available throughout the calendar year on an equal and uniform basis to all eligible employees. Employers must establish reasonable uniform methods and requirements for accelerated contributions and the determination of medical expenses.

(b) *Satisfying comparability*. An employer that accelerates contributions to the HSAs of its employees will not fail to satisfy the comparability rules because employees who incur qualifying medical expenses exceeding the employer's cumulative HSA contributions at that time have received more contributions in a given period than comparable employees who do not incur such expenses, provided that all comparable employees receive the same amount or the same percentage for the calendar year. Also, an employer that accelerates contributions to the HSAs of its employees will not fail to satisfy the comparability rules because an employee who terminates employment prior to the end of the calendar year has received more contributions on a monthly basis than employees who work the entire calendar year. An employer is not required to contribute reasonable interest on either accelerated or non-accelerated HSA contributions. But see Q & A–6 and Q & A–12 of this section for when reasonable interest must be paid.

Q–16: What is the effective date for the rules in Q & A–14 and 15 of this section?

A–16: It is proposed that these regulations apply to employer contributions made on or after the date the final regulations are published in the **Federal Register**. However, taxpayers may rely on these regulations for guidance pending the issuance of final regulations. Alternatively, until the publication of final regulations, an employer may continue to rely on the last sentence of Q & A–6(a) of section 54.4980G–4 of the proposed regulations published in the **Federal Register** on August 26, 2005, which provides that, an employer is not required to make comparable contributions for a calendar year to an employee's HSA if the employee has not established an HSA by December 31st of the calendar year.

Kevin M. Brown,
Deputy Commissioner for Services and Enforcement.

(Filed by the Office of the Federal Register on May 31, 2007, 8:45 a.m., and published in the issue of the Federal Register for June 1, 2007, 72 F.R. 30501)

Foundations Status of Certain Organizations

Announcement 2007–60

The following organizations have failed to establish or have been unable to maintain their status as public charities or as operating foundations. Accordingly, grantors and contributors may not, after this date, rely on previous rulings or designations in the Cumulative List of Organizations (Publication 78), or on the presumption arising from the filing of notices under section 508(b) of the Code. This listing does *not* indicate that the organizations have lost their status as organizations described in section 501(c)(3), eligible to receive deductible contributions.

Former Public Charities. The following organizations (which have been treated as organizations that are not private foundations described in section 509(a) of the Code) are now classified as private foundations:

A Reel Chance, Clayton, NJ
About Planning Parties, Inc., Loganville, GA
Abundant Grace Gospel Ministry, Inc., Webster, NY
Acacia Charities, Inc., Glens Falls, NY
African American Women Against Aids, Dallas, TX
Agape Diversified Care-Givers, Incorporated, Detroit, MI
A. J. Hoffman Foundation, Inc., Florham Park, NJ
Al Sami Charity Foundation, Dove Canyon, CA
American Home Dream Foundation, Arlington, TX
Appeal of the Nobel Peace Laureates Foundation, Inc., Washington, DC
Asian Transplantation Awareness in Southern California, Orange, CA
A.S.S.K., Honolulu, HI
Baby Sudz, Inc., Houston, TX
Benefits USA Foundation, Columbia, SC
Bluecollar.org, Mobile, AL
Bronzeville Community Development Association, Chicago, IL
Burnham Educational Center, Seattle, WA
Carlas Lil Angels Learning Center, Cedar Hill, TX
Carol Morgan School Foundation, Inc., Miami, FL
Center for International Relations Corp., Arlington, VA
Central Florida Cancer Institute Foundation, Davenport, FL
Chee Murray Charitable Foundation, Sugar Land, TX
Childrens Bridge, Inc., Wayne, NJ
Christian Transdenominational Spiritual Group & Enlightenment, Tallahassee, FL
Christian W. Konstanzer Fund of the Kiwanis Club of Mt. Clemens, Inc., Mt. Clemens, MI
Citadel of Hope Community Development Corp., Hillside, NJ
Color Country Chapter of Candlelighters Childhood Cancer, St. George, UT
Community Health Resource, Inc., Hogansville, GA
Computer Literate Learning Center, Inc., Clarkston, GA
Computer Repair & Networking Organization, New York, NY
Crane Area Schools Education Foundation, Inc., Crane, OR
Curtis L. Backmon Sr. Foundation, Baltimore, MD
Daomi Foundation, Phoenixville, PA
Don Seibel Memorial Scholarship Foundation, Finksburg, MD
Educating Little People, York, PA
Edwards Foundation, Beaverton, OR
Enrique E. Pina Sr. Ministry, Millington, TN
Enterprise Unlimited, Los Angeles, CA
Ethiopian Humanitarian Foundation, San Diego, CA
FAC Services, Inc., East Point, GA
Fathersday DC, Inc., St. Petersburg, FL
First Creative Research Consultants, Inc., Beaumont, TX
FMC Foundation, Inc., New York, NY
Focused Kids, Inc., Memphis, TN
Foreign Trade Institute, Denver, CO
Forensic Institute of Auto Theft Analysis, Big Bend, WI
Fresh Anointing Deliverance Center, Inc., Boston, GA
Fulton County Child Abuse Prevention Council, Rochester, IN
Global Health Vision A NJ Nonprofit Corporation, Plainfield, NJ
Good Samaritan Development Corporation, Wilson, NC
Heartbridge, Inc., Kailua Kona, HI
Heartland Womens Foundation, Inc., Tribune, KS
Heavenly Cradle Day Care Center, St. Louis, MO
Helen Residence, Inc., Roselle, NJ
Help for Children of America, Inc., Hartsdale, NY
Help Mom Work at Home Christian Child Care Guild, Seattle, WA
Her Place, Inc., Baltimore, MD
Hope Housing Redevelopment Corporation, San Antonio, TX
Humanitarian Action Network for Democratization and Security, Galveston, TX
Hunting Park Development, Inc., Philadelphia, PA
Impowerment Group, Providence, RI
Innercourt Ministries, Inc., Hinesville, GA
International Diversity Education Center, Ridgewood, NJ
International Institute of Success Dynamics, Boston, MA
International Midwives Exchange, Inc., High Falls, NY
Italian American Cultural Arts Corp., Yonkers, NY
J & J Youth Home & Health Care Services, Inc., Carson, CA
J Live N Me Workplace Ministries, Incorporated, Temple, TX
Jawad Omair Yasin Foundation, Oklahoma City, OK

John Lee Comer Center, Montgomery, AL
Julius Deloatche Basketball Camp, Peoria, IL
Kansas Dental Association Relief Fund, Incorporated, Topeka, KS
Kidney Research Fund USA, Bryn Mawr, PA
Kids RULE, Inc., Boca Raton, FL
Lab Consulting, Inc., Tulsa, OK
Lambert Friends Ministries, Inc., Portland, OR
Life Trades Center, Verona, WI
Lineam, Inc., Norco, LA
Loganworks, Port Angeles, WA
Love Arms for Boys, Inc., El Cerrito, CA
Maui Jazz Project, Inc., Kahului, HI
McTaggert Court 2, Inc., Akron, OH
Mission Now, Inc., St. Louis, MO
My Sisters & Me Ministries, Inc., Gary, IN
National Educational Diversity Students of America Organization, Van Buren, ME
New Lifestyle Living, Inc., Linden, NJ
Northeast Conservatory of Music, Delmar, NY
Oaktree Assisted Living, Inc., Yardley, PA
Oasis Veritas, St. Louis Park, MN
On Common Ground, Quincy, CA
PACES – Performing Arts and Cultural Exchange Studios, Kealakekua, HI
Palee Walton Ministries, Inc., Oakland, CA
Parkford Apartments Tenants Association, Library, PA
Pasco Community Development Foundation, Inc., Brooklyn, MD
Peanut Butter Project, Alameda, CA
Phase I & Phase II Sober Living, Bakersfield, CA
Phoenix Outreach Community Development Corporation, Houston, TX
Piller Family Foundation in Memory of Raizy Rivky and Eli Piller, Brooklyn, NY
Place of Grace Ministries, Carlisle, PA
Project USA Corp., Cranston, RI
Pucho, Inc., Buffalo, NY
Pueri Sancti Spiriti, Albuquerque, NM
Rainbow Ministry, Everett, MA
Raptor Rehabilitation Project, Inc., Catalina, AZ
Ritu Sinha Charitable Foundation, Staten Island, NY
Roc-Link, Inc., Irvine, CA
Rolando McClain Crisis Center, Inc., Isola, MS
Saint George Foundation for Social Sciences, Houston, TX
San Francisco Revival Ministry, San Leandro, CA
Save Our Sons, Inc., Atlanta, GA
Seva Fund Foundation, Inc., Morro Bay, CA
Shelbina Community Advancement Corporation, Shelbina, MO
So Be It Entertainment, Harrisburg, PA
Sons of Abraham, Philadelphia, PA
Southeastern Bat Diversity Network, Muncie, IN
Southern Foundation for the Advancement of Arts and Education, Cumming, GA
Spinnaker Cove Nature Preserve and Conservation Area, Inc., Indianapolis, IN
Squeaky Wheel Foundation, Surrey, ME
STI Empowerment Fund, Inc., Hempstead, NY
Switchback Association, Renton, WA
T L Foundation, Chicago, IL
Take Time Out, Inc., Farmington Hills, MI
Taxpayer Assistance Center, Inc., Philadelphia, PA
Tierra Institute International, Huntington Beach, CA
Tom Weyers Memorial Scholarship Trust, Appleton, WI
True Love Ministries, Lancaster, CA
Unaffiliated Baptist Churches of America, Sioux Falls, SD
United Missios Christian Awareness Ministry, Marietta, GA
United States Airpower Museum, Fresno, CA
Unity of the Faith Ministries, Inc., Mt. Vernon, NY
Up the Unity, Inc., Washington, DC
Upromise Education Foundation, Needham, MA
Waterfront Housing GP Corp., Pittsburgh, PA
West Los Angeles Christian Outreach, Inc., Los Angeles, CA
Young Aesthetics Society, Hodgdon, ME
Youth Excelling Socially, Inc., Little Rock, AR

If an organization listed above submits information that warrants the renewal of its classification as a public charity or as a private operating foundation, the Internal Revenue Service will issue a ruling or determination letter with the revised classification as to foundation status. Grantors and contributors may thereafter rely upon such ruling or determination letter as provided in section 1.509(a)–7 of the Income Tax Regulations. It is not the practice of the Service to announce such revised classification of foundation status in the Internal Revenue Bulletin.

INDEX

The abbreviation and number in parenthesis following the index entry refer to the specific item; the number in italic type following the parenthesis refers to the page number on which the item appears.

Key to Abbreviations:

Ann	Announcement
CD	Court Decision
DO	Delegation Order
EO	Executive Order
PL	Public Law
PTE	Prohibited Transaction Exemption
RP	Revenue Procedure
RR	Revenue Ruling
SPR	Statement of Procedural Rules
TC	Tax Convention
TD	Treasury Decision
TDO	Treasury Department Order

EMPLOYEE PLANS

EMPLOYEE PLANS—Cont.

EMPLOYEE PLANS—Cont.

EMPLOYMENT TAX

ESTATE TAX

ESTATE TAX—Cont.

EXCISE TAX

EXEMPT ORGANIZATIONS

GIFT TAX

INCOME TAX

INCOME TAX—Cont.

INCOME TAX—Cont.

INCOME TAX—Cont.

INCOME TAX—Cont.

SELF-EMPLOYMENT TAX

U.S. GPO: 2008—349–524/80010